KU-724-118

The Virgin Illustrated
ENCYCLOPEDIA of ROCK

ART DIRECTION/ADAPTATION/DESIGN: Nick Wells.
With grateful thanks to Helen Courtney, Sue Evans, Dave Jones, Colin Rudderham, also to Patrick McCreeth and Jacqui Caulton.

EDITORIAL DIRECTION: Lucinda Hawksley.
With special thanks to Sonya Newland, Claire Dashwood and Polly Willis, also to Kirsten Bradbury, Jane Chalker, Penny Clarke, Harry Doherty, Dawn Eden, Tony Hall, Michael Heatley (and all at Northdown Publishing), Lesley Malkin, Damien Moore, Johnny Rogan, Sharon Rose, Helen Tovey, Amanda Tomlins and Jason Wallace for their invaluable assistance. Particular thanks also to Colin Larkin and Sue Pipe at Muze UK, Rob Shreeve and KT Forster at Virgin Publishing and Bob Nirkind at Billboard Books.

PICTURE RESEARCH: Frances Banfield.
With thanks to Steve Gillett, John Halsall, Angela Lubrano, Gary Stickland and John Stickland.

The typography used in this book is based on classic versions of Baskerville, Futura and Trajan. The images were scanned and manipulated at The Foundry.

First published in 1998 by
VIRGIN PUBLISHING LTD
Thames Wharf Studios
Rainville Road
Hammersmith
London W6 9HT

Published in the USA by Billboard Books, an imprint of Watson-Guptill Publications

Adapted and produced by
FLAME TREE PUBLISHING,
a part of The Foundry Creative Media Company Ltd
Crabtree Hall, Crabtree Lane, London SW6 6TY

ISBN 1-85227-786-6

A catalogue record for this book is available from the British Library

Printed and bound in Italy by LEM

The Virgin Illustrated ENCYCLOPEDIA of ROCK

Virgin

HOW TO USE THIS BOOK

THE 1800 ENTRIES IN THIS BOOK ARE ARRANGED IN alphabetical order to cover the best of rock and pop music from the 1920s onwards. Specific genres like R&B, blues, country, hip hop and techno artists are included, but only where they directly impact on the broader music scene, e.g. bluesman John Lee Hooker is included whereas blues roots artist Lead Belly is not.

The entries are an edited down, updated version of the already published *Virgin Concise Encyclopedia of Popular Music* by Colin Larkin. We have tried to retain the flavour and comprehensiveness of this original book, but the creation of an illustrated version out of a much bigger, words-only reference work has necessitated some, not always desirable, shortcuts.

The selection of the 1800 names out of the many thousands of possibilities does represent our own, much argued-over view of what's happening and what happened. Inevitably, during the making of the book some artists didn't make the final selection: next time we'll look at them all again.

MAIN ENTRIES

- There is no simple solution to the surprisingly complex issue of alphabetical order: individuals are listed by surname i.e. Lennon, John, but Alice Cooper on the other hand can be found under 'A' because it is used both by the band and the individual; however Iggy Pop is categorised under Pop, Iggy because this is his own, adopted, name. There are some historical curiosities like Puff Daddy being found under Combs, Sean 'Puffy', because this is how he started, with only recent releases as Puff Daddy.
- Bands such as A Tribe Called Quest are in section A because the 'A' is a vital part of their name. Bands like the Kinks, whose names start with 'the', are found under the main part of their name because 'the' is simply a prefix.
- The names of artists or bands appearing in bold means that they have their own entry elsewhere in the Encyclopedia.
- The names of albums, EPs, books, newspapers, magazines, television and radio programmes, stage plays, musicals and films are all in italics. Major works of classical music are also in italics.
- Individual song titles appear in single quotation marks.
- An artist's year of birth is given wherever possible. In spite of exhaustive research we cannot find everyone's details for a number of reasons: birth certificates for the the 20s, 30s and 40s are difficult to come by; many artists, particularly post-punk, seem prone to giving false names and dates of birth as a matter of fashion.

SIDE BARS

- These provide a snapshot of each artist or band. They provide a quick way of sampling their tastes and influences and refer you ➧ to other entries in the Encyclopedia. They also include main albums and further details of collaborators, connections, influences and further references where space permits. The full listing of albums, books, videos and films appears in the final 34 pages of the book in comprehensive and, necessarily, microscopic detail.
- An entry with no side bar information means that a band/artist has released no albums, or only compilations.

Albums – up to three of the artist's best albums. (N.B. compilations are not included in the side bars, only in the end matter at the back of the Encyclopedia.)

Collaborators – those people who have worked with the artist, i.e. producers, prominent session players, duet partners etc.

Connections – significant bands to which the artist previously belonged, actors they have worked with, bands who share the same label, associations/movements the artist has been involved with etc.

Influences – some of the people who have affected the artist either personally or musically. These influences sometimes include poets, authors or events.

Further References – usually one film, video or book. These often include films or videos the artist has starred in, composed for, or which have been made about their life and books either written by or about the artist. The complete list appears in the end matter.

END MATTER

- We have tried to provide a complete listings of albums, compilations, films, videos and books. Due to limitations of space, compilations by major record companies have been included at the expense of budget versions.
- Albums, videos and films with alternative names in different parts of the world appear with both titles; for instance the 1964 Ray Charles film *Blues For Lovers* was also known as *Ballad In Blue*.

ALBUM RATINGS

The star-rating system used in this book has been retained from the original Encyclopedia, which combined author Colin Larkin's experienced ear with that of many critics, reviewers and fans.

★★★★★ An outstanding classic in the true sense of the word; an album that no comprehensive record collection should be without.
★★★★ Excellent, highly recommended. One of the artist's best.
★★★ Good by the artist's usual standards. Recommended.
★★ Disappointing in comparison to the artist's usual work or the expected level for a first album.
★ Poor and to be avoided unless you fervently want a full collection. Some albums of course, have no stars ....

Nick Wells, ADAPTER/ART DIRECTOR

A NOTE ON RECORD SALES

Originally an album could attain gold status only by the amount of money it made; fluctuating prices created a need for a new system and, from 1974 onwards albums and singles started to be judged by how many copies were sold as follows:

US SINGLES

Gold Singles – sales of 1,000,000 copies pre-1989; 500,000 copies post-1989.
Platinum Singles – sales of 2,000,000 copies pre-1989; 1,000,000 copies post-1989.

US ALBUMS

1958–74:
Gold Albums – sales of $1,000,000.
Post-1974:
Gold Albums – sales of 500,000 copies.
Platinum Albums – sales of 1,000,000 copies.

UK SINGLES

Silver Singles – sales of 200,000 copies.
Gold Singles – sales of 400,000 copies.
Platinum Singles – sales of 600,000 copies.

UK ALBUMS

Silver Albums – sales of 60,000 copies.
Gold Albums – sales of 100,000 copies.
Platinum Albums – sales of 300,000 copies.

PICTURE ACKNOWLEDGEMENTS

London Features International: 6(br), 9(l), 9(r), 10(tl), 12(t), 16, 18(r), 19, 24, 29(b), 30, 34, 35(b), 36(b), 38(r), 39(b), 42(l), 43(l), 43(r), 44(r), 47, 49(b), 53(r), 54(r), 55, 59(l), 59(r), 65(t), 68 (l), 68(r), 70(t), 82(b), 84(b), 90(r), 99, 100(l), 102, 104(c), 106(br), 108(l), 109, 110(tl), 111, 115, 116(r), 118, 125(r), 130(r), 132(bl), 136(r), 139(l), 141, 145(l), 148, 151, 154(b), 156, 159(l), 160(r), 163(t), 163(b), 166, 168(l), 168(r), 175, 188(r), 191(l), 191(br), 194(l), 196(l), 204(l), 204(br), 207(l), 209(l), 211(l), 214(r), 225, 226, 228, 229, 230(tr), 232(l), 234(l), 236(r), 237, 241, 242, 247, 250(br), 251(l), 252(r), 254, 255(l), 259, 263(tr), 265(br), 266, 270(r), 271(br), 272, 282, 285(l), 286, 288, 293(t), 295, 296, 298(b), 299(r), 300(l), 300(r), 301(l), 302(r), 304(r), 320(l), 320(r), 310(tl), 312(l), 315, 323(l), 323(r), 324(c), 324(tr), 325, 331, 334(tl), 334(r), 337(l), 340(b), 343, 346(r), 347(l), R.E. Aaron 289, E. Adebari 22(tl), M. Alan 345(l), Archive 128(tl), L. Anderson 18(l), M. Anker 248, R. Baras 224(r), 257(c), C. Barritt 155(l), 197, 321(t), A. Boot 7(l), 164, A. Butt 276(l), K. Callahan 13(r), 37(b), 220(l), 231, 299(l), R. J. Capak 291(br), A. Catlin 58(r), 89(r), 246(l), J.M. Cole 136(l), P. Conty 90(l), P. Cox 81(r), 179, 188(bl), 260(r), 304(l), 311(r), 327, K. Cummins 57(r), 73(l), 103(c), 135(l), 149(l), 191(c), 192(r), 202(r), 238(c), 262(r), 313(l), 336(r), 349(l), D. Dale 110(bl), J. Davy 98(tl), S. DeBatselier 269, G. De Guire 94(r), G. De Roos 127(l), G. De Sota 88(bl), Mike Diver 279, A. Dixon 67, DuBose 204(tr), N. Elgar 233(r), Fienstein 316(r), D. Fisher 49(tl), 119(l), 221(l), 223(r), 238(r), 307, F. Forcino 20, 292(r), S. Fowler 110(br), 131(l), 174(t), 306(r), 321(b), 348, Goedefroit Music 106(br), J. Goedefroit 96(r), 258, F. R Griffin 137, 185(l), 334(bl), Griffin 107(c), 177(l), 199(b), 215, 273, 308, C. Gunther 77(t), 129(br), 176, 278(l), M. Hadley 293(b), Hein/Topline 27, 244, J. Hicks 29(tl), J. Hughes 230(l), W. Idele 48(b), A. Keidis 274(r), G. Knaeps 75(l), 122(r), 133, 150(r), 194(r), 262(l), 305, D. Koppel 70, K. Kulish 69, 72, L. Lawry 311(l), P. Loftus 32, 46(r), 146(r), J. Macoska 284, R. Marino 10(r), 11, 12(b), 108(r), 328, 337(r), C. Mason 53(l), 212(r), 290, 340(t), P. Mazel 283(l), 322, K. Mazur 21(r), 81(l), 171, 173, 192(l), 245, 275(b), 338(r), 342(tr), L. McAffee 303, Mountain 143(r), P. Mountain 249, I. Musto 44(l), 66(r), 209(r), 213(t), 221(r), 277, P. Nicholls 288(l), T. Paton 103(l), A. Phillips 232(r), D. Picerno 140, Prior 199(t), N. Preston 240(r), N. Preston & A. Kent 291(tl), M. Putland 220(r), S. Rapport 45, 120(r), 227(l), 285(r), 310(r), 342(l), K. Regan 51, 123(b), 230(br), D. Ridgers 40(bc), 85, 100(r), 101(l), 155(r), 211(r), 268(b), 329(l), J. Roca 222(tr), W. Roelen 31, T. Sheehan 14, 61(l), 78, 89(l), 217(l), 267(tl), 302(l), 309(l), 312(r), H. Snitzer 297(c), G. Swaine 112, 275(t), 287, 306(bl), 318(r), 326(r), G. Swenie 195, S. Thomann, 319, G. Tucker 252(l), K. Weingart 235, J. Whatling 255(r), R. Wolfson 7(r), 174(bl), 219, 224(l), M. Yates 46(l). **Steve Gillett, London:** 15, 50(c), 64(r), 65(b), 92(r), 138, 182(r), 205, 264(c), 267(cb), 281(bl), 349. **Angela Lubrano, London:** 17(r), 22(r), 26(r), 42(r), 48(t), 77(br), 92(l), 98(r), 122(l), 126, 134(tl), 178, 196(r), 208(l), 227(tr), 234(r), 250(t), 264(r), 271(l), 330. **Jeff Tamarkin, New Jersey:** 79, 86(l). **Star File Photo Agency, New York:** 33(r), 76(r), 216, B. Gruen 200, 212(l), J. Mayer 157(l), 203, C. Pulin 125(l), 292(l), J.J. Sia 189(l), L. Seifert 121, B. Wentzell 180, V. Zuffante 63, 113(l). **Ebet Roberts, New York:** 25(tr), 33(l), 105(l), 146(l), 160(l), 181, 190, 218, 263(l), 326(bl), 341(l). **Redferns, London:** 80, 91, 104(r), G.A. Baker Archives 57(l), 74, F. Costello 35(tl), 35(tr), 187, I. Dickson 276(r), Gems 114(tr), 115(tl), M. Hatchett 236(l), M. Hutson 261(l), M. Ochs Archives 256(r), D. Redfern 144(b), 154(t), 177(r), 186(b), 213(b), 333(l). **Fender Musical Instruments Corporation** (Stratocaster): 144(c). **Gibson** (Les Paul Standard): 257.

All Album images courtesy of Foundry Arts and Foundry Arts/John Stickland, with thanks to all the record companies and publicity/management agencies who supplied and gave their permission to use promotional photographs and record and CD sleeves in the book.

Every effort has been made to contact copyright holders. If any omissions do occur the publisher would be delighted to give full credit in subsequent reprints and editions.

Key to picture locations
l - Left, r - Right, c - Centre, t - Top, b - Bottom, tr - Top right, tl - Top left, tc - Top centre, br - Bottom right, bl - Bottom left, bc - Bottom centre

A FLOCK OF SEAGULLS
Albums
A Flock Of Seagulls (Jive 1982)★★★
Listen (Jive 1983)★★★
➧ p.350 for full listings
Further References
Video: *A Flock of Seagulls* (Sony Video 45 1983)

A TRIBE CALLED QUEST
Albums
Beats, Rhymes And Life (Jive 1996)★★★★
➧ p.350 for full listings
Collaborators
Queen Latifah ➧ p.270
Jungle Brothers
Connections
De La Soul
Janet Jackson ➧ p.195
Influences
Lou Reed ➧ p.274
Stevie Wonder ➧ p.342
Earth, Wind And Fire ➧ p.130

A-Ha
Albums
Stay On These Roads (Warners 1988)★★★
East Of The Sun, West Of The Moon (Warners 1990)★★★
➧ p.350 for full listings
Influences
Everly Brothers ➧ p.139
Further References
Book: *Aha: The Story So Far*, Marcussen

Abba
Albums
Arrival (Epic 1976)★★★
The Album (Epic 1977)★★★
Super Trouper (Epic 1980)★★★
➧ p.350 for full listings
Connections
Hootenanny Singers
Tim Rice
Influences
Eurovision Song Contest
Beatles ➧ p.38
Further References
Film: *Abba -The Movie*
Videos: *Abba: The Video Hits* (Screen Legends 1988)

A FLOCK OF SEAGULLS

NEW WAVE ELECTRO-POP GROUP FROM LIVERPOOL, ENGLAND. THE BAND – MIKE SCORE (b. 1957; KEYBOARDS/vocals), Ali Score (drum machine/vocals), Paul Reynolds (b. 1962; guitar) and Frank Maudsley (b. 1959; bass) – followed an adventurous EP with *A Flock Of Seagulls*, a splendid example of futurist pop that included 'I Ran (So Far Away)' (US Top 10, 1982). *Listen* was another infectious collection of songs, but 'Wishing (I Had A Photograph Of You)' was their only UK success. Reynolds departed after *The Story Of A Young Heart*; that and *Dream Come True* were way below par and the band disintegrated. Score organized a new version of the band in 1989, which toured the USA and issued 'Magic' before splitting up.

A TRIBE CALLED QUEST

THREE-PIECE US MALE RAP GROUP: Q-TIP (b. JONATHAN DAVIS, 1970), ALI SHAHEED MUHAMMED (b. 1970) AND Phife (b. Malik Taylor, 1970). Their 1989 debut, 'Description Of A Fool', was followed by the hit 'Bonita Applebum'. Their biggest success was with 'Can I Kick It?', typically a refined jazz/hip hop cross. As members of the Native Tongues Posse (with **Queen Latifah** and the Jungle Brothers) they were promoters of the Africentricity movement which aimed to make US Africans aware of their heritage, a theme emphasized in their music. *People's Instinctive Travels And The Paths Of Rhythm* was more eclectic, whereas *Low End Theory* saw them return to their roots with a more bracing, harder funk sound, aided by jazz bassist Ron Carter. Tracks like 'The Infamous Date Rape' stoked controversy, while samples from **Lou Reed**, **Stevie Wonder** and **Earth, Wind And Fire** were used in a frugal and intelligent manner. By *Midnight Marauders* there were allusions to the rise of gangsta rap, although they maintained the optimism predominant on their debut.

After three years, *Beats, Rhymes And Life* was released – the album debuted at US number 1.

A-HA

FORMED IN 1982, THIS NORWEGIAN POP GROUP FEATURED MORTEN HARKET (b. 1959; LEAD VOCALS), MAGNE Furuholmen (b. 1962; keyboards/vocals) and Pal Waaktaar (b. 1961; guitar/vocals). 'Take on Me' (US number 1/UK number 2) was followed by 'The Sun Always Shines On TV' (UK number 1/US Top 20). A world tour and a further series of hits ensued including 'Train Of Thought' and 'Hunting High And Low'.

In 1987, Waaktaar composed the theme for the James Bond film *The Living Daylights* with John Barry and, in 1988, after two pop albums, the group attempted a more serious work with *Stay On These Roads*. In 1989, Harket starred in the film *Kamilla And The Thief* and recorded a one-off single with Bjorn Eidsvag. A-Ha found further UK chart success in 1990 with a revival of the **Everly Brothers**' 'Crying In The Rain' and 'Angel' in 1993. *Memorial Beach* however was critically ignored.

ABBA

THE ACRONYM ABBA, COINED IN 1973, REPRESENTED THE COMING TOGETHER OF FOUR LEADING FIGURES IN Scandinavian pop. Agnetha Faltskog (b. 1950) had achieved pop success in the group's native Sweden with 'I Was So In Love' (1968). Faltskog teamed up with Björn Ulvaeus (b. 1945; ex-Hootenanny Singers) and released a few records overseas as Northern Lights, before joining Benny Andersson (b. 1946; ex-Hep Stars) and Norwegian solo singer Anni-Frid ('Frida') Lyngstad (b. 1945).

Under the guidance of Scandinavian svengali Stig Anderson (d. 1997), Björn and Benny joined forces for one album, *Lycka*. Meanwhile Ulvaeus continued to work with the Hootenanny Singers in the studio. The marriage of Björn and Agnetha, followed by that of Benny and Anni-Frid, laid the romantic and musical foundations of Abba. In 1973, the quartet (now known as Björn & Benny, Agnetha & Anni-Frid) represented their country in the Eurovision Song Contest with the infectious 'Ring Ring'. They succeeded the following year as Abba, with the more polished 'Waterloo', which not only won the contest, but topped the UK charts and infiltrated the US Top 10.

The middling success of the re-released 'Ring Ring' and singalong 'I Do I Do I Do I Do I Do' provided little indication of the chart domination that was to follow. In 1975, Abba returned with the worldwide hit 'SOS', a powerhouse pop production highlighted by immaculately executed counter harmonies and an infectiously melodic arrangement. This classic Abba sound was evident on their first trilogy of consecutive UK chart-toppers, 'Mamma Mia', 'Fernando' and 'Dancing Queen'. The last also brought them their only US number 1 and precipitated their rise to pop superstardom with sales unmatched since the golden age of the **Beatles**.

In 1977, they celebrated a second trilogy of UK chart-toppers ('Knowing Me Knowing You', 'The Name Of The Game' and 'Take A

Chance On Me'), enhanced by some of the finest promotional videos of the period. They began the 80s with two more UK number 1s, 'The Winner Takes It All' and 'Super Trouper', taking their UK chart-topping tally to nine in just over six years. Depite the dissolution of both marriages in the group, they maintained a high profile for a while – eclipsing the car manufacturers Volvo as Sweden's largest earners of foreign currency. However, in 1982 they elected to rest the group. Agnetha and Anni-Frid subsequently went solo, unsuccessfully, while Björn and Benny enjoyed a productive relationship with Tim Rice, culminating in London's West End musical *Chess*.

ABC

UK BAND ABC WERE DOMINATED BY THE STUNNING VOCAL RANGE AND SONGWRITING SKILLS OF LEAD singer Martin Fry (b. 1958). The band was formed after Fry interviewed electronic musicians Mark White (b. 1961; guitar) and Stephen Singleton (b. 1959; saxophone) for his fanzine *Modern Drugs*. Fry took artistic control of their group, Vice Versa, changing the name to ABC and steering the music towards a more 'poppy' course. The group was completed by bassist Mark Lickley and drummer David Robinson – later replaced by David Palmer (b. 1961).

Their 1981 debut, 'Tears Are Not Enough', made the UK Top 20, followed by three Top 10 hits with 'Poison Arrow', 'The Look Of Love' and 'All Of My Heart'. Their pristine pop songs were displayed on the superb *Lexicon Of Love*. This Trevor Horn-produced UK number 1 was a formidable collection of melodramatic pop love songs. However, the failure of *Beauty Stab* to emulate the debut's success, resulted in a personnel upheaval, which by 1984 left only Fry and White. They continued as ABC using session musicians and changing their image for *How To Be A Zillionaire*. 'Be Near Me' reached the US Top 10 and '(How To Be A) Millionaire' the Top 20.

Fry became seriously ill and was absent for great lengths of time owing to treatment for Hodgkin's Disease, but they returned with the memorable UK Top 20/US Top 5 hit 'When Smokey Sings' in 1987. However, the success of their debut album has so far not been matched and, by the mid-90s, only Fry remained from the original band. *Skyscraping* was a good attempt at recreating the band's peak, but sounded dated.

ABDUL, PAULA

ABDUL (b. 1963), THE CHOREOGRAPHER OF THE LA LAKERS BASKETBALL cheerleaders team, was spotted by the **Jacksons** and employed to assist the group on dance routines for their live tour dates. Later she choreographed **Janet Jackson**'s videos, their immediate success focused attention on Abdul's dance talents and she quickly found herself in demand from a string of other artists looking for a high MTV profile. Her first single, 'Straight Up' (1988), hit US number 1, and was followed by three other chart-toppers: 'Forever Your Girl', 'Cold Hearted' and 'Opposites Attract'. *Forever Your Girl* (US number 1/UK number 6) was followed by a collection of remixes, *Shut Up And Dance* (1990). In 1991, *Spellbound* reached US number 1, spawning two number 1 singles, 'Rush Rush' and 'The Promise Of A New Day'.

Her popularity in Europe although substantial, is nonetheless no match for her image in the USA. She returned in 1995 (after a long absence due to a lawsuit) with the number 1 'My Love Is For Real', which preceded *Head Over Heels*.

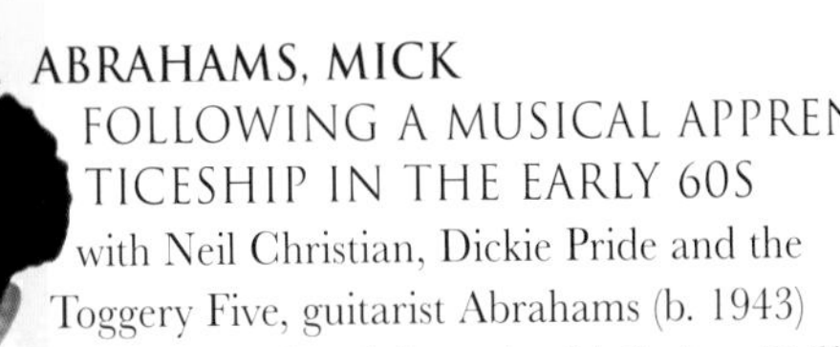

ABRAHAMS, MICK

FOLLOWING A MUSICAL APPRENTICESHIP IN THE EARLY 60S with Neil Christian, Dickie Pride and the Toggery Five, guitarist Abrahams (b. 1943) made a career breakthrough with **Jethro Tull** and **Blodwyn Pig**. He embarked on a largely unsuccessful solo career in 1971. His *Mick Abrahams* and *At Last*, as the Mick Abrahams Band, featured Walt Monahan (bass), Bob Sergeant (keyboards/vocals) and Ritchie Dharma (drums). Abrahams subsequently made a guitar tuition album that eventually outsold his previous catalogue, although he left the music business in 1975.

Returning in 1991, *All Said And Done* demonstrated a mature musician playing anglo-blues music. He resurrected Blodwyn Pig in 1993 and released *Lies*. *One* was a stripped-down blues guitar record, on which Abrahams was able to shine in the musical territory with which he is most comfortable and he continued with more unadulturated blues on *Mick's Back* (1996).

ABC

Albums

The Lexicon Of Love (Neutron 1982)★★★★★

Up (Neutron 1989)★★★

➽ p.350 for full listings

Connections

Trevor Horn ➽ p.74

Influences

Vice Versa

Modern Drugs

Further References

Videos: *Mantrap* (1989)

Absolutely (1991)

ABDUL, PAULA

Albums

Forever Your Girl (Virgin 1989)★★★

Spellbound (Virgin 1991)★★★

➽ p.350 for full listings

Connections

Jacksons ➽ p.196

Janet Jackson ➽ p.195

Influences

MTV

Further References

Skat Strut/Opposites Attract (Virgin 1991)

ABRAHAMS, MICK

Albums

Have Fun Learning The Guitar (SRT 1975)★★★

Mick's Back (Indigo 1996)★★★

➽ p.350 for full listings

Influences

Neil Christian

Jethro Tull ➽ p.199

Blodwyn Pig ➽ p.53

AC/DC
Albums
Let There Be Rock (Atlantic 1977)★★★★
Highway To Hell (Atlantic 1979)★★★★
For Those About To Rock We Salute You (Atlantic 1981)★★★★
➽ p.350 for full listings
Influences
George Young
Harry Vanda
Matt Lange
Easybeats ➽ p.131
Valentines
Rockers Fraternity
The Spectators
Manfred Mann's Earth Band ➽ p.223
Firm
Gary Moore ➽ p.238
Further References
Video: *No Bull: Live At The Plaza Del Toros* (Warner Vision 1996)
Books: *The AC/DC Story*, Paul Ezra
The World's Most Electrifying Rock 'n' Roll Band, Malcolm Dome (ed.)

ACE
Albums
Five-A-Side (Anchor 1974)★★★
Time For Another (Anchor 1975)★★
No Strings (Anchor 1977)★★
➽ p.350 for full listings
Influences
Bees Make Honey
Frankie Miller ➽ p.233
Eric Clapton ➽ p.92
Squeeze ➽ p.306
Mike And The Mechanics ➽ p.233

ACKLES, DAVID
Albums
David Ackles aka The Road To Cairo (Elektra 1968)★★★
American Gothic (Elektra 1972)★★★★
Five And Dime (Columbia 1973)★★★
➽ p.350 for full listings
Influences
Bernie Taupin ➽ p.200
Elton John ➽ p.200
Spooky Tooth ➽ p.306

ACTION
Albums
The Ultimate Action (1980)★★
Action Speaks Louder Than (1985)★★
Brain — The Lost Recordings 1967/8 (Autumn Stone Archives 1995)★★
➽ p.350 for full listings
Influences
Sandra Barry
Beatles ➽ p.38
George Martin ➽ p.226

AC/DC

THIS THEATRICAL AUSTRALIAN HARD ROCK BAND WAS FORMED IN 1973 BY SCOTTISH-BORN MALCOLM YOUNG (b. 1953; rhythm guitar). Young – whose elder brother George had already achieved Australian stardom in **Easybeats** – enlisted his younger brother

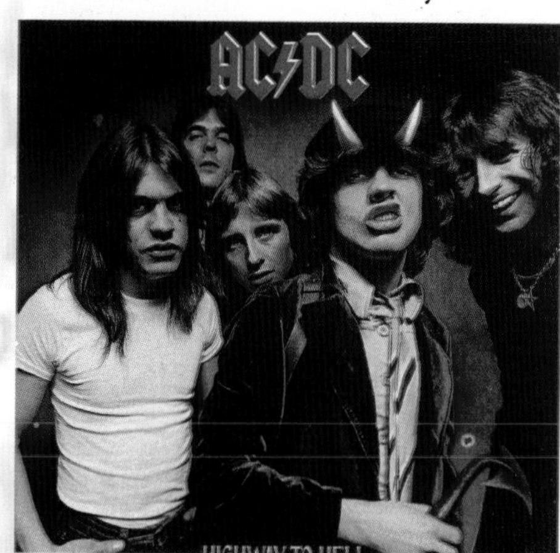
AC/DC

Angus (b. 1959; guitar). Their sister later suggested that Angus wear his school uniform on stage, a gimmick that became their trademark. In 1974, the Youngs and vocalist Dave Evans moved to Melbourne, where Mark Evans (b. 1956; bass) and Phil Rudd (b. 1954; drums) joined. Another Scotsman, Bon Scott (b. Ronald Scott, 1946, d. 1980; ex-Valentines, Fraternity and Spectors), graduated from being the band's chauffeur to vocalist, when Dave Evans refused to go on stage in 1974. The AC/DC line-up which welcomed him had already recorded a single, 'Can I Sit Next To You?', but it was his voice that graced their first two albums, *High Voltage* and *T.N.T.* Both sets were produced by George Young and his writing partner, Harry Vanda (ex-Easybeats). Neither album was issued outside Australia, though Britain's Atlantic Records did offer a selection of material from both as *High Voltage* in 1976. These albums brought them to the attention of Atlantic, who relocated the band to London in 1976. Bassist Mark Evans, tired of touring, was replaced by English bassist Cliff Williams (b. 1949; ex-Home) in 1977.

Once AC/DC began to tour outside Australia, the band quickly amassed a cult following, as much for the unashamed gimmickry of their live show as for their furious, frequently risqué brand of hard rock. *Let There Be Rock* broke them as a UK chart act, with its contents including the perennial crowd-pleaser, 'Whole Lotta Rosie'. However, it was *Highway To Hell* which established them as international stars. This, the band's first album with producer Mutt Lange, also proved to be their last with Bon Scott. On 20 February 1980, after a night of heavy drinking, he was left unconscious in a friend's car, and was later found dead, having choked on his own vomit.

...THEIR FURIOUS, FREQUENTLY RISQUE BRAND OF HARD ROCK

Scott's death threatened the band's future, but his replacement, former Geordie lead singer Brian Johnson (b. 1947), proved more than equal to the task. His first album with the band, *Back In Black*, reached number 1 in the UK and Australia, and spawned the hit 'Rock 'n' Roll Ain't Noise Pollution'. In 1981 *For Those About To Rock We Salute You* was released, the band topped the bill at the Castle Donington festival and achieved two Top 20 UK singles. After *Flick Of The Switch* (1983), drummer Phil Rudd left to become a helicopter pilot, replaced by Simon Wright (b. 1963; ex-A II Z and Tytan) – who in turn departed to join Dio in 1990. His replacement was Chris Slade (b. 1946; ex-**Manfred Mann's Earth Band**, Firm and **Gary Moore**).

AC/DC maintained an increasingly relaxed schedule through the 80s, touring to support each album release. When Malcolm Young was unfit to tour in 1988 his cousin, Stevie Young (ex-Starfighters), temporarily deputized. Paul Greg also stepped in for Cliff Williams on the US leg of their 1991 tour. A year earlier *The Razor's Edge* had been one of the more successful albums of their later career, producing a Top 20 UK hit, 'Thunderstruck'. In 1992, they issued a live album, whose attendant single, 'Highway To Hell', made the UK Top 20. With Brian Johnson long having buried the ghost of Bon Scott, the band shows no signs of varying its winning musical formula. *Ballbreaker* was a near-return to form.

ACE

FORMED IN THE UK IN 1972 AND ORIGINALLY CALLED ACE FLASH AND THE DYNAMOS. ACE WAS FORMED BY **Paul Carrack** (b. 1951; keyboards/vocals), Alan 'Bam' King (b. 1946; guitar/vocals), Phil Harris (b. 1948; guitar/vocals), Terry 'Tex' Comer (b. 1949; bass) and Steve Witherington (b. 1953; drums). All members were assembled from known bands and all were solid musicians. Before they recorded their debut, *Five-A-Side*, Witherington was replaced by drummer Fran Byrne (b. 1948; ex-Bees Make Honey).

Ace became one of the darlings of the UK pub rock circuit with their polished funky pop music; 'How Long', a perfectly crafted song, became a UK Top 20 hit and reached the US Top 3. The band eventually moved to America but disbanded in 1977 when most of the remaining members joined **Frankie Miller**'s band. Paul Carrack has played in **Eric Clapton**'s band, joined **Squeeze** and is now part of **Mike And The Mechanics**. He re-recorded 'How Long' which became a hit again in 1996.

ACKLES, DAVID

PART OF A SHOWBUSINESS FAMILY, US-BORN ACKLES (b. 1937) WAS A CHILD ACTOR, TURNED SONGWRITER. David Ackles aka The Road To Cairo, showcased a mature talent, whose deep, sonorous delivery matched an often desolate lyricism (such as 'The Candy Man' from *Subway To The Country*). Both releases garnered considerable acclaim. Bernie Taupin, lyricist for **Elton John**, produced Ackles' third selection, *American Gothic*, which included the melancholic 'Montana Song', and **Spooky Tooth** recorded a sensitive version of his 'Down River'.

Although *Five And Dime* maintained his outstanding qualities, due to commercial indifference, no further records followed. This considerable talent still commands cultish respect.

ACTION

FORMED IN KENTISH TOWN, LONDON, IN 1965, THE GROUP CONSISTED OF REGGIE KING (VOCALS), ALAN 'Bam' King (guitar), Pete Watson (guitar), Mike Evans (bass) and Roger Powell (drums). As the Boys, they recorded one single, 'It Ain't Fair', and served as a backing group for up-and-coming singer Sandra Barry. Rechristened the Action, they established a reputation as one of the best Mod groups and became the subject of a BBC2 television documentary. The **Beatles**' producer **George Martin** supervised their recordings for his newly established independent company, AIR, bestowing a crystal-clear sound on 'Land Of 1000 Dances', 'I'll Keep On Holding On', 'Baby You've Got It', 'Never Ever' and 'Shadows And Reflections'. Watson left in 1966, but the group persevered; the following year Ian Whiteman joined. He, in turn, was replaced by ex-Savoy Brown guitarist, Martin Stone.

The Action failed to secure a hit but several completed masters appeared belatedly on *The Ultimate Action* CD. During their final months the group took a new name, Azoth, before reverting to the Action, but the departure of Reggie King brought this period of indecision to a permanent close. King later recorded a solo album while his former colleagues, with Whiteman back in the fold, embraced progressive rock as Mighty Baby. Although credited to the Action, *Action Speaks Louder Than* consists of Mighty Baby demo recordings.

ADAM AND THE ANTS

FORMED IN 1977, THE BAND COMPRISED **ADAM ANT** (b. STUART LESLIE GODDARD, 1954; GUITAR/VOCALS), backed by Lester Square (guitar), Andy Warren (bass/vocals) and Paul Flanagan (drums). Heavily influenced by the **Sex Pistols**, they used bondage gear and sado-masochistic imagery in their live act and repertoire. The line-up was relatively *ad hoc* between 1977 and 1979 with Mark Gaumont replacing Lester Square (who joined the **Monochrome Set** – as Andy Warren would later do) and colourful manager Jordan occasionally taking vocals.

The Ants released one studio album, *Dirk Wears White Sox*, but it was poorly received. At the end of the decade, Adam sought the advice of Pistols manager Malcolm McLaren. He suggested a radical shift in musical policy and a daring new look. In 1980, the Ants abandoned their leader to form McLaren's newsworthy **Bow Wow Wow**, but with a fresh set of Ants – Marco Pirroni (b. 1959; guitar/vocals), Kevin Mooney (bass/vocals) and two drummers, Terry Lee Miall (b. 1958) and Merrick (b. Chris Hughes, 1954) – Adam reinvented himself. Out went the punk riffs and bondage, replaced by a sound heavily influenced by the Burundi Black drummers. With Adam's Apache war paint and colourful, piratical costume, the new Ants enjoyed three UK hits in 1980, culminating in the number 2 'Ant Music'. With his striking looks and clever use of costume, Adam Ant was a natural pin-up. His portrayal of a highwayman ('Stand And Deliver') and pantomime hero ('Prince Charming') brought two UK number 1s and ushered in an era of 'New Pop', where fancy dressing-up and catchy, melodic songs without a message became the norm. In 1981, Mooney was replaced by Gary Tibbs (b. 1958; ex-**Roxy Music**). Having dominated his group since 1977, it came as little surprise when Adam announced that he was dissolving the unit in 1982 to go solo.

ADAM ANT

THE MULTI-TALENTED ADAM ANT (b. STUART LESLIE GODDARD, 1954) BEGAN HIS CAREER LEADING ADAM And The Ants. He also starred in Derek Jarman's film *Jubilee*, with vocalist/actress Toyah. Adam went solo in early 1982, retaining his old musical partner Marco Pirroni, and relaunched himself with 'Goody Two Shoes', which hit UK number 1 in June. 'Friend Or Foe' followed, hitting UK number 5; thereafter the spell was broken. **Phil Collins** was recruited as producer to halt Adam's sudden decline and the pantomime-influenced 'Puss In Boots' duly made the UK Top 5. However, the revival was only temporary, and by the end of 1983 Adam's chart career was practically non-existent. The original god of the New Pop seemed commercially bankrupt, his place taken by new idols. Even an appearance at Live Aid in 1985 with 'Vive Le Rock' only produced a number 50 UK chart entry and Adam returned adroitly to acting and his previous career, graphic design.

A surprise chart comeback in 1990 with 'Room At The Top' appeared a lucky strike which did not seriously distract the singer from his thespian pursuits. A new album in 1995, promoted by concert appearances in London, provoked further media saturation and good reviews, but little in terms of sales.

ADAMS, BRYAN

CANADIAN BRYAN ADAMS' (B. 1959) SOLO CAREER COMMENCED IN 1978 WHEN HE BEGAN WRITING SONGS with Jim Vallance (ex-Prism). Some of these early collaborations were recorded by **Loverboy**, **Bachman-Turner Overdrive** and **Bonnie Tyler** among others. In 1979, Adams signed a contract with A&M, putting together a band which included Vallance on drums, with Ken Scott (lead guitar) and Dave Taylor (bass). Their debut, 'Let Me Take You Dancing', was followed by a self-titled album (featuring Jeff 'Skunk' Baxter of **Steely Dan**). *You Want It, You Got It* scraped into the US charts.

Cuts Like A Knife (1983) was Adams's breakthrough, reaching US number 8 and going platinum – it did not chart in the UK until three years later. It saw Vallance replaced by Mickey Curry – though he maintained his songwriting partnership with Adams. The first single from the album, 'Straight From The Heart', also made the US Top 10, and two follow-up singles, 'Cuts Like A Knife' and 'This Time', reached the Top 20 and Top 30, respectively. *Reckless*, returned the singer to the Top 10 and reached UK number 7. 'Run To You' fared well on both sides of the Atlantic, as did 'Somebody'. He scored a US number 1 in 1985 with 'Heaven', the b-side of which was 'Diana'.

Adams appeared at Live Aid and co-wrote (with Vallance) the Canadian benefit record for Ethiopia, 'Tears Are Not Enough'. The defiant and celebratory 'Summer Of '69' returned him to the US Top 10 and he ended a successful year duetting with **Tina Turner** on 'It's Only Love'.

Into The Fire became a US/UK Top 10 hit, boasting songs of a more political bent, informed by Adams's charity work and tours for Amnesty International. It also saw the last Adams/Vallance songwriting collaboration, and the end of a five-album tenure with producer Bob Clearmountain. 'Heat Of The Night' provided Adams with his fifth US Top 10 hit, although subsequent single releases fared less well. He contributed to records by **Mötley Crüe**, **Belinda Carlisle**, Charlie Sexton and others.

In 1988, Adams guested at the Nelson Mandela birthday party concert at Wembley Stadium, and in 1990 appeared at the special Berlin performance of *The Wall*. All was eclipsed, however, by his contribution to the 1991 film, *Robin Hood, Prince Of Thieves*. The soundtrack single, '(Everything I Do) I Do It For You', was a phenomenal chart success, staying at UK number 1 for 16 weeks – the longest run since 1953. It also hit US number 1. The follow-up, 'Can't Stop This Thing We Started', and another strong ballad, 'Thought I'd Died And Gone To Heaven', charted strongly, as did 'All For Love', a collaboration with **Sting** and **Rod Stewart**. 'Have You Ever Really Loved A Woman' topped a number of worldwide charts in 1995. The acclaimed *18 'Til I Die* (1996) was followed by *Bryan Adams Unplugged* (1997).

ADAM AND THE ANTS

Albums
Kings Of The Wild Frontier (Columbia 1980)★★★
➧ p.350 for full listings

Influences
Sex Pistols ➧ p.292
Monochrome Set ➧ p.236
Bow Wow Wow ➧ p.63
Roxy Music ➧ p.283

Further References
Book: *Adam And The Ants*, Fred and Judy Vermorel

ADAM ANT

Albums
Strip (Columbia 1983)★★★
➧ p.350 for full listings

Collaborators
Toyah

Influences
Phil Collins ➧ p.98

Further References
Book: *Adam Ant Tribal Rock Special*, Martha Rodriguez

ADAMS, BRYAN

Albums
Waking Up The Neighbours (A&M 1992)★★★
Bryan Adams Unplugged (A&M 1997)★★★
➧ p.350 for full listings

Collaborators
Bachman-Turner Overdrive ➧ p.28
Bonnie Tyler ➧ p.325
Tina Turner ➧ p.324
Sting ➧ p.324
Rod Stewart ➧ p.310

Connections
Mötley Crüe ➧ p.240
Belinda Carlisle ➧ p.81

Influences
Steely Dan ➧ p.308

Further References
Video: *Reckless* (1984)
Book: *Bryan Adams: A Fretted Biography*, Mark Duffett (1995)

ADAMS, OLETA
Albums
Circle Of One (Fontana 1990)★★★
Movin' On (Fontana 1995)★★★
Come Walk With Me (Harmony 1997)★★★
➽ p.350 for full listings
Collaborators
Tears for Fears ➽ p.317
Influences
Gospel
Brenda Russell
Elton John ➽ p.200

ADAMSON, BARRY
Albums
Soul Murder (Mute 1992)★★★★
Oedipus Schmoedipus (Mute 1996)★★★★
➽ p.350 for full listings
Influences
Magazine ➽ p.222
Visage ➽ p.331
Nick Cave ➽ p.85
Bad Seeds ➽ p.85

ADVERTS
Albums
Crossing The Red Sea With The Adverts (Bright 1978)★★★
The Wonders Don't Care: The Complete Radio Recordings (Pilot 3 1997)★★★
➽ p.350 for full listings
Collaborators
Damned ➽ p.110
Influences
Chelsea ➽ p.88
Generation X ➽ p.161
Doctors Of Madness ➽ p.121

AEROSMITH
Albums
Toys In The Attic (Columbia 1975)★★★★
Pump (Geffen 1989)★★★★
Nine Lives (Columbia 1997)★★★★
➽ p.350 for full listings
Collaborators
Run DMC ➽ p.284
Connections
Ted Nugent ➽ p.249
Guns N' Roses ➽ p.170
Influences
Cream ➽ p.103
Jam ➽ p.196
Rolling Stones ➽ p.281
Further References
Videos: *Live Texas Jam '78* (CMV Enterprises 1989)

ADAMS, OLETA

THIS FINE SOUL SINGER HAD A GOSPEL UPBRINGING IN THE USA. ADAMS FORMED HER OWN TRIO IN THE 80S and recorded two self-funded albums that sold poorly. She was singing cabaret in a hotel bar in Kansas when she was discovered by Roland Orzabel and Curt Smith of **Tears For Fears** in 1985. In 1987, they invited her to sing on 'Woman In Chains' and 'Badman's Song', from *The Seeds Of Love*. She went on to join the band as a semi-permanent third member, both live and in the studio. This led to her own contract with Phonogram. Orzabel produced her *Circle Of One* (UK number 1/US Top 20) and wrote her first single, 'Rhythm Of Life'. Her biggest hit to date came with Brenda Russell's 'Get Here' in 1991.

Oleta's second album was less successful and her third, *Movin' On*, reversed the trend of smooth balladry to funky up-tempo dance-orientated numbers, including a powerful cover of **Elton John**'s 'Don't Let The Sun Go Down On Me'. She moved into the Gospel market with *Come Walk With Me.*

ADAMSON, BARRY

THE ORIGINAL **MAGAZINE** BASSIST, AND ALSO A MEMBER OF **VISAGE** AND **NICK CAVE**'S BAD SEEDS, Adamson's (b. 1959) solo output has largely been in the field of instrumental music intended for films. His debut EP, *The Man With The Golden Arm* (1988), included the first of his spectacular cover versions of *James Bond* film themes. The title track was also included on *Moss Side Story*, the soundtrack to a non-existent *film noir* about the Manchester suburb, which presaged his later scores.

Delusion allowed Adamson to garnish a real film with his music; since then he has been in constant demand by a variety of directors. His seductive mood pieces and instrumentals stand by themselves without any visual, situation-specific stimuli. The excellent *Soul Murder*, dominated by Adamson's trademark keyboard surges, earned him a Mercury Prize nomination in 1992, a feat he also repeated in 1994 with *The Negro Inside Me. Oedipus Schmoedipus* was another strong album.

ADVERTS

THE ADVERTS WERE FRONTED BY VOCALIST TIM 'TV' SMITH AND GAYE ADVERT (BASS/VOCALS), with Howard Pickup (b. 1951, d. 1997; guitar) and Laurie Driver (drums). **Damned** guitarist Brian James was so impressed by their performance that he offered them a support slot, and introduced them to Stiff Records. Their debut, 'One Chord Wonders', was well received and its follow-up, 'Gary Gilmore's Eyes', was a macabre but euphoric slice of punk/pop that catapulted the Adverts into the UK Top 20. One of the first punk groups to enjoy commercial success, the quartet also boasted the first female punk star in Gaye Advert.

Despite tabloid newspaper publicity, 'Safety In Numbers', failed to chart, although its successor, 'No Time To Be 21', reached number 38. Their debut album, *Crossing The Red Sea With The Adverts*, was barely recorded before Driver was ousted and replaced by former **Chelsea/Generation X** drummer John Towe, who left shortly afterwards, succeeded by Rod Latter. Changing record labels, personnel problems and unsuitable production dogged their progress, while *Cast Of Thousands* went largely ignored.

On 27 October 1979, with a line-up comprising Smith, Dave Sinclair (drums), Mel Weston (keyboards), Eric Russell (guitar) and bassist Colin Stoner (ex-**Doctors Of Madness**), the Adverts gave their last performance, at Slough College of Art.

AEROSMITH

ONE OF AMERICA'S MOST POPULAR HARD-ROCK ACTS, AEROSMITH FORMED IN 1970 WHEN VOCALIST STEVEN Tyler (b. Steven Victor Tallarico, 1948; vocals) joined Joe Perry (b. Anthony Joseph Perry, 1950; guitar) in a **Cream**-styled rock combo. Together with Tom Hamilton (b. 1951; bass), Joey Kramer (b. 1950; drums) and Ray Tabano (guitar), the group's original line-up was complete. Tabano was quickly replaced by Brad Whitford (b. 1952). After their first gig, at the Nipmuc Regional High School, the band took the name Aerosmith. Their popularity grew, and a triumphant gig at Max's Kansas City, led to a recording deal.

In 1973, Aerosmith secured a minor chart-placing with their self-titled debut album. Its attendant single, 'Dream On', initially peaked at number 59 and became a Top 10 hit in 1976. *Get Your Wings* introduced a fruitful working relationship with producer Jack Douglas, culminating in the highly successful *Toys In The Attic*, which sold in excess of six million copies worldwide. *Rocks* achieved platinum status and Aerosmith maintained their pre-eminent position with *Draw The Line* and the powerful *Live! Bootleg*.

In 1978, Aerosmith appeared in the ill-fated *Sgt. Pepper's Lonely Hearts Club Band* film, and although their version of 'Come Together' reached the US Top 30, tension between Tyler and Perry proved irreconcilable. The guitarist left the group following *Night In The Ruts* and subsequently founded the Joe Perry Project. Jimmy Crespo joined Aerosmith in 1980, but the following year Brad Whitford left to pursue a new musical career. Rick Dufay debuted on *Rock In A Hard Place*, but this set failed to capture the fire of the group's classic recordings.

Contact between the group and Perry and Whitford was re-established during a 1984 tour. Antagonisms were set aside, and the following year, the quintet's most enduring line-up was performing together again. *Done With Mirrors* was a tentative first step, after which Tyler and Perry rid themselves of drug and alcohol dependencies. In 1986, they accompanied **Run DMC** on 'Walk This Way', an Aerosmith song from *Toys In The Attic* and a former US Top 10 entry. The collaboration rekindled interest in Aerosmith's career. *Permanent Vacation* became one of their best-selling albums, and the first to make an impression in the UK, while the highly-acclaimed *Pump* and *Get A Grip* emphasized their revitalization.

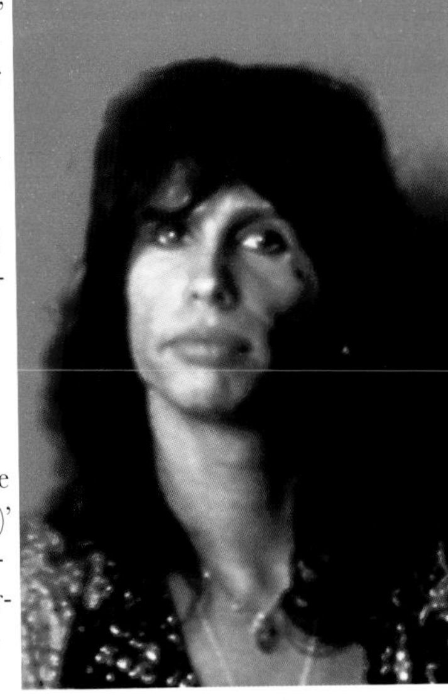

In the mid-90s, the band spent an age recording *Nine Lives*. The hit single 'Falling In Love (Is Hard On The Knees)' preceded its release in 1997. Those wishing to immerse themselves in this extraordinary band should invest in the impressive 13-CD box set *Box Of Fire*.

AFGHAN WHIGS

FROM CINCINNATI, OHIO, AND ORIGINAL STALWARTS OF THE SUB POP RECORDS EMPIRE, AFGHAN WHIGS were widely classified as favoured proponents of grunge. The band comprised Rick McCollum (b. 1965; guitar), Steve Earle (b. 1966; drums), John Curley (b. 1965; bass) and Greg Dulli (b. 1965; guitar/vocals). Dulli first met Curley in jail, where they were being held overnight for, respectively, urinating in front of a police officer and drug-dealing. When Afghan Whigs provoked the interest of the major labels, Dulli insisted that he produce their records and direct their videos. Their major label debut was *Gentlemen*.

In 1994, Dulli was part of the group who recorded a soundtrack for the Stuart Sutcliffe (**Beatles**) biopic, singing as **John Lennon**. Other band members were Mike Mills (**R.E.M.**), Don Fleming (Gumball), Dave Grohl (**Nirvana** and **Foo Fighters**) and Thurston Moore (**Sonic Youth**). Dulli also covered **Barry White**'s 'Can't Get Enough Of Your Love' for the soundtrack to *Beautiful Girls*. *Black Love* confirmed the soul influence, and featured cover versions of **Marvin Gaye**'s 'Let's Get It On' and the **Who**'s 'Quadrophenia'.

AFRIKA BAMBAATAA

BAMBAATAA'S (b. AFRIKA BAMBAATAA AASIM, 1960) INFLUENCE ON RAP'S DEVELOPMENT IS PIVOTAL. HE WAS THE founding father of his native New York's Zulu Nation, whose name was inspired by the film *Zulu*, and the code of honour and bravery of its black participants. Zulu Nation (and its head) helped transform the gangs of the late 70s into the hip hop crews of the early 80s. By 1980, he was the pre-eminent hip hop DJ in New York. He made his recording debut the same year, producing two versions of 'Zulu Nation Throwdown' for Cosmic Force and Soul Sonic Force. Signing to the independent label Tommy Boy Records, he made his first own-name release in 1982, as Afrika Bambaataa And The Jazzy Five, with 'Jazzy Sensation' (based on Gwen Guthrie's 'Funky Sensation'). It was followed by 'Planet Rock', a wholly synthesized record, this time based on **Kraftwerk**'s 'Trans-Europe Express'. It took hip hop music far beyond its existing street rhyme and percussion break format. The contribution of Arthur Baker and John Robie is also highly significant, for in turn they gave birth to the 'electro' rap movement which dominated the mid-80s. 'Planet Rock' also gave its name to the record label Bambaataa established.

'Looking For The Perfect Beat' continued the marriage of raw lyrics and synthesized electro-boogie, and was another major milestone for the genre. The follow-up album, *Beware (The Funk Is Everywhere)* included a take on the **MC5**'s 'Kick Out The Jams' (produced by **Bill Laswell**). Bambaataa also recorded an album as part of Shango, backed by Material members Laswell and Michael Beinhorn.

Bambaataa went on to record two vastly different and unexpected singles – 'World Destruction' with ex-**Sex Pistols**' vocalist John Lydon, and 'Unity' with **James Brown**. *The Light* included an enterprising cast: **UB40**, Nona Hendryx, **Boy George**, **Bootsy Collins**, Yellowman and **George Clinton**. *The Decade Of Darkness (1990-2000)* included an update of James Brown's 'Say It Loud (I'm Black And I'm Proud)'.

AIR SUPPLY

FORMED AROUND RUSSELL HITCHCOCK (b. 1949; VOCALS) AND GRAHAM RUSSELL (b. 1950; GUITAR/ vocals), Air Supply turned out a solid string of seven US Top 5 singles between 1980-82. The duo first came together in Sydney, Australia, during 1976 whilst performing in a production of *Jesus Christ Superstar*. Forming a sextet with Frank Esler-Smith (b. 1948; keyboards), Ralph Cooper (b. 1951; drums), David Green (b. 1949; bass) and David Moyse (b. 1957; lead guitar), they were only successful locally. By 1977, the group was augmented by Singaporean guitarist, Rex Goh (b. 1951).

Signing with Arista in 1980, the group's first album included the hit title track 'Lost In Love' and successful singles 'All Out Of Love' and 'Every Woman In The World'. The Top 10 *The One That You Love* yielded three more hits, including the number 1 title track. In 1983, they achieved their second US number 2 with 'Making Love Out Of Nothing At All'. Towards the end of the decade the popularity of Air Supply declined, although they continued to tour regularly. They disbanded in 1988 but reformed in 1991.

AKKERMAN, JAN

AKKERMAN (b. 1946) BEGAN HIS CAREER IN HIS NATIVE AMSTERDAM IN 1958, AS ONE OF JOHNNY AND THE Cellar Rockers. Their drummer, Pierre Van Der Linden, later played with Akkerman in the Hunters, during the guitarist's five years of study at the city's Music Lyceum. With Van Der Linden, Bert Ruiter (bass) and Kaz Lux (vocals), Akkerman formed Brainbox, a hard rock outfit whose only album was issued in 1969. For Akkerman's keen participation in rehearsals with the nascent **Focus**, Brainbox dismissed him.

In 1971, after the release of *In And Out Of Focus*, Akkerman asked Van Der Linden to join him in a new group for which it made sense to retain the name Focus, having recruited Thijs Van Leer and Cyril Havermans from that band. Among the major factors in the band's success were Akkerman's powers of improvisation on his trademark **Les Paul** guitar (he was named Best Guitarist in a *Melody Maker* poll in 1973) and his skill as an arranger. His solo albums were widely acclaimed although the first, *Profile*, was simply an accumulation of tracks taped during the interval between Brainbox and Focus. *Tabernakel* was a more ambitious affair, containing Jan's developing dexterity on the lute, and guest appearances by Tim Bogert and Carmine Appice.

Akkerman left Focus in 1976 to begin sessions with Lux for what became *Eli*. Several more jazz fusion collections followed including the lushly orchestrated *Arunjuez* and a 1979 live set. Although his periodic reunions with Focus have attracted most attention, he also recorded *The Talisman* (1988) and *To Oz And Back* (1989) as part of Forcefield with Ray Fenwick (ex-**Spencer Davis Group**) and Cozy Powell before retracing a solo path with *The Noise Of Art*.

AFGHAN WHIGS

Albums

Big Top Halloween (Ultrasuede 1988)★★★
Congregation (Sub Pop 1992)★★★
➧ p.350 for full listings

Collaborators

Stuart Sutcliffe

Connections

R.E.M. ➧ p.275
Nirvana ➧ p.248
Foo Fighters ➧ p.149
Sonic Youth ➧ p.302

Influences

Beatles ➧ p.38
John Lennon ➧ p.214
Barry White ➧ p.337
Marvin Gaye ➧ p.159
Who ➧ p.338

AFRIKA BAMBAATAA

Albums

Planet Rock — The Album (Tommy Boy 1986)★★★★
The Decade Of Darkness (1990-2000) (EMI 1991)★★★
➧ p.350 for full listings

Collaborators

Arthur Baker
John Robbie
Shango
John Lydon ➧ p.293
James Brown ➧ p.70
UB40 ➧ p.326
Nona Hendryx
Boy George ➧ p.65
Bootsy Collins ➧ p.98
Yellowman
George Clinton ➧ p.94

Influences

Zulu Nation
Kraftwerk ➧ p.210
MC5 ➧ p.228
Bill Laswell ➧ p.212
Michael Beinhorn
Sex Pistols ➧ p.293

AIR SUPPLY

Albums

The One That You Love (Arista 1981)★★★
Air Supply (Arista 1985)★★
The Earth Is ... (1991)★★
➧ p.350 for full listings

AKKERMAN, JAN

Albums

Talent For Sale (Imperial 1968)★★★
Tabernakel (Atlantic 1974)★★★★
Arunjuez (Columbia 1978)★★★
➧ p.350 for full listings

Collaborators

Tim Bogert
Carmine Appice
Forcefield

Connections

Brainbox
Focus ➧ p.148

Influences

Melody Maker
Shadows ➧ p.293

ALABAMA
Albums
Wild Country (LSI 1977)★★★
Feels So Right (RCA 1981)★★★
Southern Star (RCA 1989)★★★
➧ p.350 for full listings
Collaborators
Lionel Richie ➧ p.293

ALABAMA

ONE OF THE BIGGEST US COUNTRY ROCK ACTS OF THE 80S, ALABAMA WERE ORIGINALLY FORMED IN 1969 AS Wild Country by cousins Jeff Cook (b. 1949; guitar/vocals), Randy Owen (b. 1949; guitar/vocals) and Teddy Gentry (b. 1952; bass/vocals). They recorded for several small labels in the 70s before changing their name to Alabama in 1977. A sequence of hits followed the success of 'I Want To Be With You', at which point they recruited drummer Mark Herndon (b. 1955). After 'My Home's In Alabama' reached the US Top 20 they signed to RCA Records. Country hits followed with 'Tennessee River' and 'Feels So Right'; later singles, such as 'Love In The First Degree', acquired crossover pop success. Of their five platinum albums during the 80s, the most successful was *40 Hour Week*.

In 1986, they worked with **Lionel Richie**, but their recent work has seen them return almost exclusively to the C&W charts. Their environmental anthem, 'Pass It On Down' was released in 1990 and in 1995, the group celebrated its 15th anniversary with sales of over 50 million albums, and the Academy Of Country Music's Artist Of The Decade Award for their work in the 80s. By 1995, they had amassed 40 number 1s.

ALARM
Albums
Declaration (IRS 1984)★★★
Strength (IRS 1985)★★★
Eye Of The Hurricane (IRS 1987)★★★
➧ p.350 for full listings
Connections
Clash ➧ p.93
Influences
U2 ➧ p.326
Pete Seeger ➧ p.291
Tony Visconti
Further References
Videos: *Spirit Of '86* (Hendring Video 1986)
Change (PMI 1990)
Book: *The Alarm*, Rick Taylor

ALARM

FORMED IN RHYL, WALES, DURING 1981, THIS ENERGETIC POP GROUP COMPRISED MIKE PETERS (b. 1959; GUITAR/vocals), David Sharp (b. 1959; guitar/vocals), Eddie MacDonald (b. 1959; bass) and Nigel Twist (b. 1958; drums). Originally known as Seventeen, they changed their name after recording 'Alarm Alarm'. Peters was anxious to steer the group in the direction of **U2** however, by the time of the Alarm's first UK hit, '68 Guns', their style and imagery most closely resembled the **Clash**. The declamatory verve continued on 'Where Were You Hiding When The Storm Broke' and their traditional rock influence was emphasized in their ostentatious image. Behind the high energy there was a lighter touch eloquently evinced on their reading of **Pete Seeger**'s 'The Bells Of Rhymney', which they performed in aid of the coal miners' strike in 1984.

Change (produced by Tony Visconti) was also released in a Welsh-language version (*Newid*). Mike Peters embarked on a solo career in the 90s following the dissolution of the band.

ALBION COUNTRY BAND
Albums
Albion River Hymn March (1979)★★★
Give Me A Saddle And I'll Trade You A Car (Topic 1989)★★★
Albion Heart (HTD 1995)★★★★
➧ p.350 for full listings
Collaborators
Shirley Collins
Richard Thompson ➧ p.320
Martin Carthy ➧ p.83
John Kirkpatrick
Influences
Steeleye Span ➧ p.308
Fairport Convention ➧ p.141

ALBION COUNTRY BAND

THIS TRADITIONAL UK FOLK ENSEMBLE WAS FOUNDED IN 1972 BY DEFECTING **STEELEYE SPAN** BASSIST ASHLEY Hutchings (b. 1945). Royston Wood (b. 1935; vocals), American Sue Draheim (b. 1949; fiddle) and Steve Ashley (guitar) completed the new venture alongside Simon Nicol (b. 1950; guitar) and Dave Mattacks (b. 1948; drums), two of Hutchings' former colleagues from **Fairport Convention**. The early line-up disintegrated six months after its inception and a caretaker unit, which included **Richard Thompson**, fulfilled outstanding obligations. Hutchings, Nicol and new drummer Roger Swallow then pieced together a second Country Band with folk acolytes, **Martin Carthy**, Sue Harris and John Kirkpatrick. Their lone album, *Battle Of The Field*, recorded in 1973, was withheld until 1976, and only issued following public demand. Hutchings, Nicol and Mattacks were reunited in the Etchingham Steam Band, a part-time group formed to support Shirley Collins. The group subsequently evolved into the Albion Dance Band. *Lark Rise To Candleford* was a typical project, an adaptation of Flora Thompson's novel set to music.

The group entered the 80s as the Albion Band, retaining a mixture of traditional and original material. Musicians continued to arrive and depart with alarming regularity, and by the end of the 80s the personnel tally easily exceeded one hundred. On one occasion in 1980, the entire band quit *en masse*, forming the critically acclaimed Home Service. Throughout, Ashley Hutchings has remained at the helm. He has also released over a dozen solo albums. The line-up for *Acousticity* comprised Hutchings, Nicol, vocalist Christine White and violinist Ashley Reed.

ALEXANDER, ARTHUR
Albums
You Better Move On (Dot 1962)★★★
Alexander The Great (Dot 1964)★★★
Lonely Just Like Me (Elektra 1993)★★★
➧ p.350 for full listings
Connections
Beatles ➧ p.38
Rolling Stones ➧ p.281
Johnny Kidd ➧ p.204

ALEXANDER, ARTHUR

US-BORN ALEXANDER'S (b. 1940, d. 1993) RECORDINGS WERE ALSO COVERED EXTENSIVELY. 'ANNA (GO TO HIM)', a US R&B Top 10 hit, and 'You Better Move On' were covered, respectively, by the **Beatles** and the **Rolling Stones**, while 'A Shot Of Rhythm And Blues' became an essential British beat staple (notably by Johnny Kidd). Alexander's subsequent work was produced in Nashville, where his poppier perceptions undermined the edge of his earlier work. Later singles included 'Go Home Girl' and the haunting 'Soldier Of Love'. A pop hit was secured with 'Every Day I Have To Cry Some' (1975), but success remained short-lived.

For many years Alexander worked as a bus driver, but began to perform again in 1993 – *Lonely Just Like Me* was his first album in 21 years. He signed a new recording and publishing contract in May 1993, suffering the cruellest fate when he collapsed and died the following month, three days after performing in Nashville with his new band.

ALICE COOPER

US STAR ALICE COOPER (b. VINCENT DAMON FURNIER, 1948) BECAME KNOWN AS THE 'master of shock rock' during the 70s and remained a popular hard-rock artist into the 90s. Furnier invented an androgynous, outrageously attired character to attract attention and the band played deliberately abrasive rock music with the intention of shocking and even alienating those attending its concerts. In 1969, the Alice Cooper band found a kindred spirit in **Frank Zappa**, who signed them to his new Straight Records label. The group recorded two albums, *Pretties For You* and *Easy Action*, before switching to Straight's parent label, Warner Brothers Records, in 1970. By that time Cooper had taken on more extreme tactics in his live performances, using a guillotine and electric chair as stage props and a live snake as part of his wardrobe. In 1971 'Eighteen' reached US number 21; in 1972, the rebellious 'School's Out' single and album made the US Top 10 and UK number 1. A streak of best-selling albums followed: the number 1 *Billion Dollar Babies* and *Muscle Of Love*, *Alice Cooper's Greatest Hits* and *Welcome To My Nightmare*, all of which reached the US Top 10. The last was his first true solo album as the band fractured and Cooper officially adopted the Alice Cooper name for his own.

The late 70s saw him appearing in films such as *Sextette* and *Sgt. Pepper's Lonely Hearts Club Band*. In 1978, Cooper admitted chronic alcoholism and underwent treatment; *From The Inside*, with songs co-written by Bernie Taupin, reflected on the experience. His band continued touring, and between 1979 and 1982 featured ex-**Iron Butterfly** lead guitarist Mike Pinera. Cooper continued recording into the early 80s with diminishing results. In 1986, after a four-year recording absence, he signed to MCA Records, but none of his albums for that label reached the US charts. In 1989, *Trash*, his first for Epic Records, returned him to the Top 40 and yielded a Top 10 single, 'Poison', his first in 12 years. *Hey Stoopid* found him accompanied by **Joe Satriani**, Steve Vai and Slash and Axl from **Guns N'Roses**, while his 90s tours saw Cooper drawing a new, younger audience who considered him a heavy metal pioneer. This impression was immortalized by Cooper's appearance in *Wayne's World*.

ALICE IN CHAINS

FORMED IN 1987 IN SEATTLE, USA, BY LAYNE STALEY (b. 1967; VOCALS) AND JERRY CANTRELL (b. 1966; GUITAR/vocals) with Mike Starr (bass) and Sean Kinney (b. 1966; drums). They developed a sound which mixed **Black Sabbath**-style riffing with Staley and Cantrell's unconventional vocal arrangements and strong songwriting. After dispensing with their early moniker, Fuck, the group became Alice In Chains, a name coined by Staley for 'a parody heavy metal band that dressed in drag'. *Facelift* received excellent reviews, but took off slowly. Boosted by US touring, 'Man In The Box' became an MTV favourite, and the album went gold in 1991.

The band then released the gentler *Sap*, featuring guests from **Heart**, **Soundgarden** and **Mudhoney**. *Dirt* was a dark, cathartic work with many personal lyrics, including 'Rooster' (about Cantrell's father's Vietnam War experience), which became a live centrepiece, but critical attention focused on a sequence of songs referring to Staley's past heroin problems. Despite the controversy, *Dirt* was the critics' album of the year in many metal magazines, entering the US charts at number 6. 'Would?' became a hit, boosted by the band's appearance playing the song in the film *Singles*. Bassist Michael Inez (b. 1966; ex-**Ozzy Osbourne**) replaced Starr, and the band embarked on a sell-out tour of Europe and the USA. Alice In Chains contributed to *The Last Action Hero* soundtrack and the third Lollapalooza tour.

In 1994, *Jar Of Flies* became the first EP to top the US album charts, entering at number 1. Staley put together a side-project, Mad Season, with **Pearl Jam**'s Mike McCready and **Screaming Trees**' Barrett Martin, amid rumours that Alice In Chains had split. In 1994, gigs, including **Woodstock** II, were cancelled, due to Staley's 'health problems', however, the band managed a further album in 1995.

ALIEN SEX FIEND

ESSENTIALLY AN ALIAS FOR THE ECCENTRIC NICK WADE, ALIEN SEX FIEND EMERGED AS PART OF THE EARLY 80S UK gothic punk movement. Wade had previously released two singles as Demon Preacher – shortened to the Demons for a third single. He formed Alien Sex Fiend in 1982, aided by David James (guitar), partner Christine Wade (synthesizer) and Johnny 'Ha Ha' Freshwater (drums). The group released the cassette-only *The Lewd, The Mad, The Ugly And Old Nick*, before signing with Anagram. Wade, whose stage image of ghoulish, thick, white, pancake make-up revealed his strongest influence, **Alice Cooper**, emphasized that debt with 'Ignore The Machine' (1983). *Who's Been Sleeping In My Brain* was followed by 'Lips Can't Go' and in 1984 by 'R.I.P.'/'New Christian Music', 'Dead And Buried' and 'E.S.T. (Trip To The Moon)', to coincide with *Acid Bath*. *Liquid Head In Tokyo* celebrated a Japanese tour, but was the last output for Johnny Ha Ha. As a three-piece, the band released 'I'm Doin' Time In A Maximum Security Twilight Home' (1985), accompanied by *Maximum Security*.

IT – The Album arrived in time for a tour supporting Alice Cooper and a cover of Red Crayola's late-60s classic, 'Hurricane Fighter Plane', surfaced in 1987, followed by 'The Impossible Mission'. A retrospective, *All Our Yesterdays*, coincided with Yaxi Highriser's departure. Under the guise of the Dynamic Duo, Wade then issued 'Where Are Batman And Robin?'. 'Bun Ho' continued a more open-minded musical policy, confirmed on *Another Planet*, while 'Haunted House' saw the adoption of dance techniques. After the live double album *Too Much Acid?*, the band returned with 'Now I'm Being Zombified' and the experimental *Curse*. They re-emerged in 1993 with *The Altered States Of America*. The group provided the music to the CD-ROM game *Inferno*, before establishing their own 13th Moon Records label and releasing the *Evolution* EP and *Nocturnal Emissions*.

ALICE COOPER

Albums
Love It To Death (Warners 1971)★★★★
School's Out (Warners 1972)★★★★
Billion Dollar Babies (Warners 1973)★★★★
➽ p.350 for full listings

Collaborators
Bernie Taupin
Joe Satriani ➽ p.288
Steve Vai
Slash ➽ p.170
Axl Rose ➽ p.170

Connections
Frank Zappa ➽ p.348

Influences
Iron Butterfly ➽ p.193
Guns N' Roses ➽ p.170

Further References
Videos: *The Nightmare Returns* (Hendring Video 1987)
Alice Cooper Trashes The World (CMV Enterprises 1990)
Book: *Me: Alice: The Autobiography Of Alice Cooper*, Alice Cooper with Steven Gaines

ALICE IN CHAINS

Albums
Dirt (Columbia 1992)★★★★
Jar Of Flies mini-album (Columbia 1994)★★★★
➽ p.350 for full listings

Collaborators
Heart ➽ p.178
Soundgarden ➽ p.303
Mudhoney ➽ p.242

Connections
Black Sabbath ➽ p.51
Staley and Cantrell
Ozzy Osbourne ➽ p.253
Pearl Jam ➽ p.257
Screaming Trees ➽ p.290

Influences
Nirvana ➽ p.248

Further References
Videos: *Live Facelift* (1994)
MTV Unplugged (SMV 1996)

ALIEN SEX FIEND

Albums
Acid Bath (Anagram 1984)★★★
Here Cum Germs mini-album (Plague-Anagram 1987)★★★
Nocturnal Emissions (13th Moon 1997)★★★
➽ p.350 for full listings

Influences
Alice Cooper ➽ p.12

Further References
Videos: *A Purple Glistener* (Jettisoundz 1984)
Overdose (Jettisoundz 1988)
Liquid Head In Tokyo (ReVision 1991)

ALISHA'S ATTIC
Albums
Alisha Rules The World (Mercury 1996)★★★
➧ p.350 for full listings
Connections
Brian Poole And The Tremeloes ➧ p.263

ALL ABOUT EVE
Albums
All About Eve (Mercury 1987)★★★
Scarlet And Other Stories (Mercury 1989)★★★
Ultraviolet (MCA 1992)★★
➧ p.350 for full listings
Connections
Sisters of Mercy
Mice
Influences
The Mission ➧ p.234
Church ➧ p.92
Further References
Videos: *Martha's Harbour* (Polygram Music Video 1988)
Kind Of Fool (Polygram Music Video 1989)

ALLIN, G. G.
Albums
As G. G. Allin And The Jabbers *Always Was, Is, And Always Shall Be* (Orange 1980)★★
as G. G. Allin And The Holy Men *You Give Love A Bad Name* (Homestead 1987)★★
as G. G. Allin *Doctrine Of Mayhem* (Black And Blue 1990)★★
➧ p.350 for full listings
Collaborators
MC5 ➧ p.228
Dinosaur Jr ➧ p.118
Influences
Stooges ➧ p.311

ALLISON, LUTHER
Albums
Reckless (Ruf 1997)★★★★
Live In Montreux 1976-1994 (Ruf 1997)★★★★
➧ p.350 for full listings
Connections
Jimmy Dawkins
Magic Slim
Magic Sam
Muddy Waters ➧ p.242
Little Richard ➧ p.217
Freddie King ➧ p.206
Bill Lindemann
Influences
Jimi Hendrix ➧ p.180
Rolling Stones ➧ p.281

ALISHA'S ATTIC

ALISHA'S ATTIC COMPRISES SISTERS SHELLIE (b. *c.* 1971) AND KAREN POOLE (b. *c.* 1972), THE DAUGHTERS OF BRIAN POOLE, leader of **Brian Poole And The Tremeloes**. The UK duo were signed to Mercury Records in 1995 after their demo tape was passed to Howard Berman. In 1996, the sisters entered the studio with producer David A. Stewart, to work on sessions for their debut, 'I Am, I Feel'. To promote it they set out on their first national tour, with a full supporting band. Despite their instant breakthrough in the UK chart, however, the sisters had spent over eight years writing songs together, ensuring a large stockpile of material for their credible debut album, *Alisha Rules The World*.

ALL ABOUT EVE

ORIGINALLY CALLED THE SWARM, ALL ABOUT EVE EMERGED ON THE LATE 80S UK 'GOTHIC' SCENE. BASSIST Julianne Regan (b. 1964; vocals; ex-Gene Loves Jezebel) and Tim Bricheno (guitar; ex-Aemotti Crii), provided much of the band's material. After various early personnel changes, the rhythm section was stabilized with Andy Cousin (bass; ex-Aemotti Crii) and Mark Price (drums). Given encouragement by rising stars the **Mission** (for whom Regan had sung backing vocals), All About Eve developed a solid following. Regan's predilection for white-witchcraft, mysticism and tarot cards, provided a taste of the exotic with a mixture of goth rock and 70s folk. Early singles 'Our Summer' and 'Flowers In Our Hair' achieved great success in the UK independent charts. After signing to Mercury Records, they secured a Top 10 hit with 'Martha's Harbour' (1988).

Both their albums reached the UK Top 10, but in 1990, a rift between the group and Bricheno resulted in his departure to join Sisters Of Mercy. The recruitment of **Church** guitarist Marty Willson-Piper on a part-time basis revitalized the group's drive, although the subsequent album, *Touched By Jesus*, was only a middling success. A stormy dispute with Phonogram Records, saw All About Eve leave the label in 1991 and sign to MCA. After releasing *Ultraviolet*, the group split, with Cousin joining the Mission. Regan formed Mice in 1995, recruiting Cousin and Price along with ex-Cardiacs guitarist Bic. They released a debut album in 1996.

ALLIN, G. G.

A CULT ICON IN SOME CIRCLES, ALLIN (b. KEVIN ALLIN, d. 1993) SPECIALIZED IN CLUMSY **STOOGES**-DERIVED garage punk and lyrical vulgarity. The rock world had become accustomed to foul language, but on *Always Was, Is, And Always Shall Be*, it was applied with ferocity and regularity to all manner of bodily functions – 'Pussy Summit Meeting' was a typical title. Allin's first band, the Jabbers, defected after recording the *No Rules* EP in 1983, but their leader regrouped with the Scumfucs after briefly fronting the Cedar Street Sluts. After the Scumfucs split, interest was reactivated by the compilation *Hated In The Nation*, which included his 1981 single with members of **MC5**, 'Gimme Some Head', and a collaboration with J. Mascis of **Dinosaur Jr**.

Allin moved to Homestead Records, recording solo and with Homestead's boss, Gerard Cosloy, as the Holy Men. In the early 90s, Allin served a four-year jail sentence for aggravated assault with intent to mutilate. Throughout his imprisonment, he claimed that he would commit suicide on stage on his return, but was denied the opportunity when he died of a drugs overdose in 1993. His last recordings were attributed to the Murder Junkies.

ALLISON, LUTHER

THE 14TH OF 15 CHILDREN, US GUITARIST ALLISON (b. 1939, d. 1997) SPENT HIS YOUTH WORKING WITH HIS siblings in the local cotton fields. He also sang with a family gospel group, before moving to Chicago in 1951. Around 1957, he formed his own band with his brother Grant. They gigged occasionally under the name of the Rolling Stones and later the Four Jivers. After a year, the group disbanded and Allison went on to work with Jimmy Dawkins, Magic Slim, Magic Sam, **Muddy Waters**, **Little Richard**, **Freddie King** and others until the mid-60s.

In 1967, he recorded a session for Bill Lindemann, later issued by the collector label Delmark. He toured California, recording as accompanist to Sunnyland Slim and Shakey Jake Harris. He made his first album under his own name in 1969. In the early 70s, he recorded for **Motown Records**' subsidiary label, Gordy, and since the late 70s has spent much of his time in France.

He has since recorded for many labels, usually funk or **Jimi Hendrix**- and **Rolling Stones**-influenced rock. In the late 80s, he recorded two well-received albums, *Serious* and *Soul Fixin' Man*. By the mid-90s, he was reaching a peak, winning W.C. Handy awards and experiencing financial success with *Blue Streak*. This Indian summer of his career was cruelly cut short when, in July 1997, he was diagnosed as having lung cancer; just over a month later, he died.

ALLMAN BROTHERS BAND

FORMED IN GEORGIA, USA, IN 1969 BY GUITARIST DUANE ALLMAN (B. 1946, D. 1971), THE BAND INCLUDED HIS brother Gregg (b. 1947; keyboards/vocals), Forrest Richard 'Dickie' Betts (b. 1943; guitar), Raymond Berry Oakley (b. 1948, d. 1972; bass), Butch Trucks (b. Claude Hudson Trucks Jnr; drums) and Jai 'Jaimoe' Johanny Johanson (b. John Lee Johnson, 1944; drums). Duane and Gregg Allman were members of pop/soul ensemble Hour Glass, which broke up when demo tapes for a projected third album were rejected by their record company. Duane then found employment at the Fame studio where he participated in several sessions, for **Aretha Franklin**, **Wilson Pickett** and **King Curtis**, prior to instigating this new sextet. The band were a popular live attraction and their first two albums, *The Allman Brothers Band* and *Idlewild South*, were marked by strong blues-based roots, while the two-album set, *Live At The Fillmore East*, showcased the group's emotional fire. The set brought the band to the brink of stardom, while Duane's reputation as an outstanding slide guitarist was enhanced by his contribution to **Derek And The Dominos**' *Layla*.

Tragedy struck on 29 October 1971, when this gifted musician was killed in a motorcycle accident. The remaining members completed *Eat A Peach*, which consisted of live and studio material, before embarking on a mellower direction with *Brothers And Sisters*. A second pianist, Chuck Leavell, was added to the line-up, but just as the group recovered its momentum, Berry Oakley was killed in an accident, on 11 November 1972. Gregg Allman (who later married **Cher**, twice) and Dickie Betts embarked on solo careers while Leavell, Johanson and new bassist Lamar Williams (b. 1947, d. 1983) formed Sea Level. After a notorious drugs trial in 1976, in which Gregg testified against a former road manager, the other members vowed never to work with the vocalist again, but a reconstituted 1978 line-up included Allman, Betts and Trucks. *Enlightened Rogues* was a commercial success, but subsequent albums fared less well and in 1982 the Allman Brothers Band split for a second time.

In 1989, a new line-up – Gregg Allman (organ/vocals), Betts (lead guitar/vocals), Warren Haynes (slide/lead guitar/vocals), Allen Woody (bass), Johnny Neel (keyboards), Trucks (drums) and Mark Quinones (percussion) – spawned the credible *Seven Turns*. Neel left the band and the remaining sextet made *Shades Of Two Worlds*. Quinones (congas and percussion) joined for *An Evening With The Allman Brothers Band* in 1992.

Their 1994 album, *Where It All Begins*, was recorded live in the studio, with production by Allman Brothers veteran Tom Dowd.

ALMIGHTY

THIS SCOTTISH HARD ROCK QUARTET WAS FORMED IN 1988 BY GUITARIST/VOCALIST RICKY WARWICK, GUITARIST Pete Friesen, bassist Floyd London and drummer Stumpy Munroe. Along with Little Angels, Quireboys and the Dogs D'Amour, the Almighty spearheaded a revival in British heavy rock during the late 80s. Signing to Polydor in 1989, they released *Blood, Fire And Love* to critical acclaim followed by a perfunctory live mini-album, which included a cover of **Bachman-Turner Overdrive**'s, 'You Ain't Seen Nothin' Yet'. *Soul Destruction* included the UK Top 20 hit, 'Free 'n' Easy'.

Internal tensions led to personnel changes and the arrival of Canadian Peter Friesen. Mark Dodson's production gave the band a heavier sound, yet retaining the Almighty's characteristic aggressive delivery. Success with 'Addiction' was followed by heavy touring. After a UK Top 5 placing for *Powertrippin'*, Almighty signed to Chrysalis Records. *Just Add Life* included two co-writing ventures between Warwick and former members of the Ruts, 'Independent Deterrent' and 'All Sussed Out' (urging fans not to vote Conservative at the next UK general election). Warwick left in 1996 and the band folded soon after.

ALMOND, MARC

FOLLOWING THE DEMISE OF **SOFT CELL** AND THEIR ADVENTUROUS OFFSHOOTS **MARC AND THE MAMBAS** and Marc And The Willing Sinners, Almond (b. Peter Marc Almond, 1956) embarked on a solo career with *Vermin In Ermine*. *Stories Of Johnny*, released the following year, was superior and displayed Almond's undoubted power as a torch singer. Prior to the album's release, he charted in a disco-inspired duet with **Bronski Beat** titled 'I Feel Love (Medley)'. The single combined two **Donna Summer** hits ('I Feel Love' and 'Love To Love You Baby') with snatches of John Leyton's 'Johnny Remember Me', all sung in high register by fellow vocalist Jimmy Somerville. The controversial *Mother Fist And Her Five Daughters* did little to enhance his career which seemed commercially in the descendent by the time of the *Singles* compilation.

Almond's old commercial sense was emphasized by the opportune revival of 'Something's Gotten Hold Of My Heart' with **Gene Pitney**. This melodramatic single was sufficient to provide both artists with their first number 1s as soloists. Almond returned in 1990 with a cover album of **Jacques Brel** songs and *Enchanted* which featured the singer's usual flamboyant style complemented by flourishes of flamenco guitar and violin. In 1992, Almond revived David McWilliams' 'The Days Of Pearly Spencer'. He returned to the cold electronic sounds of the 80s with *Fantastic Star* in early 1996. That year he ended a fifteen-year contract with his manager, 'Stevo'.

ALLMAN BROTHERS BAND

Albums
The Allman Brothers Band (Capricorn 1969)★★★★
Idlewild South (Capricorn 1970)★★★★
Live At The Fillmore East (Capricorn 1971)★★★★
➧ p.350 for full listings

Connections
Aretha Franklin ➧ p.153
Wilson Pickett ➧ p.260
King Curtis ➧ p.206
Derek And The Dominos ➧ p.116
Cher ➧ p.89

Further References
Videos: *Brothers Of The Road* (RCA/Columbia 1988)
Live At Great Woods (1993)
Book: *Midnight Riders: The Story Of The Allman Brothers Band*, Scott Freeman

ALMIGHTY

Albums
Blood, Fire And Love (Polydor 1989)★★★
Powerstrippin' (Polydor 1993)★★★
Crank (Chrysalis 1994)★★★
➧ p.350 for full listings

Connections
Little Angels
Quireboys ➧ p.270
Dogs D'Amour
Bachman-Turner Overdrive ➧ p.28

Influences
Metallica ➧ p.232
Soundgarden ➧ p.303
Therapy? ➧ p.319

Further References
Soul Destruction Live (Polygram Music Video 1991)

ALMOND, MARC

Albums
Stories Of Johnny (Some Bizarre 1985)★★★
Marc Sings Jacques (Some Bizarre 1989)★★★
Absinthe: The French Album (Some Bizarre 1994)★★★
➧ p.350 for full listings

Collaborators
Bronski Beat ➧ p.68
Gene Pitney ➧ p.261

Connections
Soft Cell ➧ p.302
Marc And The Mambas ➧ p.224
Donna Summer ➧ p.313
Jacques Brel ➧ p.67
David McWilliams

Influences
Jimmy Somerville ➧ p.68

Further Reference:
Videos: *1984 – 1987* (1987)
Live In Concert (Windsong 1993)
Book: *The Last Star: A Biography Of Marc Almond*, Jeremy Reed

ALTAMONT FESTIVAL
Influences
Woodstock Festival ➽ p.343
Rolling Stones ➽ p.281
Jefferson Airplane ➽ p.198
Crosby, Stills, Nash And Young ➽ p.106
Grateful Dead ➽ p.167

ALTERED IMAGES
Albums
Happy Birthday (Epic 1981)★★★
➽ p.350 for full listings
Collaborators
Siouxsie And The Banshees
Connections
Hipsway
Texas
Influences
John Peel ➽ p.258

ALTERNATIVE TV
Albums
The Image Has Cracked (Deptford Fun City 1978)★★
➽ p.350 for full listings
Connections
Sniffin' Glue
Generation X ➽ p.161

AMBOY DUKES
Albums
Journey To The Center Of Your Mind (Mainstream 1968)★★★
➽ p.350 for full listings
Connections
Them ➽ p.319

AMEN CORNER
Albums
National Welsh Coast Live Explosive Company (Immediate 1969)★★★
➽ p.350 for full listings
Connections
Fairweather
Strawbs ➽ p.312
Influences
Beatles ➽ p.38

AMERICA
Albums
America (Warners 1972)★★★
➽ p.350 for full listings
Connections
Neil Young ➽ p.346
David Geffen ➽ p. 155
Influences
Crosby, Stills And Nash ➽ p.106
Beatles ➽ p.38
George Martin ➽ p.
Further References
Video: *Live In Central Park* (PMI 1986)

AMERICAN MUSIC CLUB
Albums
Mercury (Warners/Reprise 1993)★★★★
➽ p.350 for full listings
Influences
Iggy Pop ➽ p.264
Rolling Stone ➽ p.280

ALTAMONT FESTIVAL

THE FREE FESTIVAL AT THE ALTAMONT RACEWAY, CALIFORNIA, WAS HELD ON 6 DECEMBER 1969. ALTAMONT was the first major musical event since the peaceful 'happening' at the **Woodstock Festival** earlier in the year and it tarnished the reputation of the new music revolution. The festival spirit died when Meredith Hunter, an 18-year-old black spectator, was beaten and stabbed to death by a group of Hell's Angels, while the **Rolling Stones** were onstage. Mick Jagger, only yards away, was oblivious to what was happening at his feet.

The Angels had been recruited by the organizers to keep the peace as security guards: their fee was as much alcohol and drugs as they could consume. Tempers had earlier become frayed when **Santana**'s performance had been interrupted by a scuffle and **Jefferson Airplane**, who followed, had singer **Marty Balin** knocked unconscious by a blow from one of the Angels.

Other artists appearing in front of the 300,000-strong crowd included **Crosby, Stills, Nash And Young** and the **Flying Burrito Brothers**. Although the **Grateful Dead** were members of the organizing committee, they ended up not performing. The film *Gimme Shelter* ends with the Altamont tragedy and is an interesting, if gory, piece of celluloid rock history. **David Crosby** controversially defended the Angels' actions in a lengthy **Rolling Stone** interview, deeming them victims of appalling organization.

ALTERED IMAGES

FORMED IN 1979, THIS GLASWEGIAN POP ENSEMBLE FEATURED CLARE GROGAN (VOCALS), JOHNNY MCELHONE (guitar; later of Hipsway and Texas), Tony McDaid (bass) and Michael 'Tich' Anderson (drums). Before their recorded debut, Grogan starred in the film, *Gregory's Girl*. In 1980, Altered Images toured with **Siouxsie And The Banshees** and subsequently employed bassist Steve Severin as producer. Another champion of their work was influential UK disc jockey **John Peel**. Their BBC radio sessions secured a contract with Epic Records, and two unsuccessful singles followed – the early 80s indie classic 'Dead Pop Stars' and 'A Day's Wait'. With the addition of guitarist Jim McInven, the group completed their debut, *Happy Birthday*, in 1981. The infectious title track, produced by Martin Rushent, soared to UK number 2, establishing the elfin Grogan as a punkish Shirley Temple. 'I Could Be Happy' and 'See Those Eyes' were also hits, but the group's second album, *Pinky Blue*, was badly received.

With 1983's *Bite*, Grogan took on a more sophisticated, adult image, lost Tich and McInven, gained Stephen Lironi (guitar/drums) and found new producers Tony Visconti and Mike Chapman. The experiment brought another Top 10 hit, 'Don't Talk To Me About Love'. Following a brief tour, featuring David Wilde (drums) and Jim Prime (keyboards), the group disbanded. Grogan pursued an acting career (notably on television in *Red Dwarf* and *Eastenders*), recorded a solo album, *Love Bomb*, and reappeared fronting new group, Universal Love School.

ALTERNATIVE TV

FORMED IN 1977, ATV WAS THE BRAINCHILD OF MARK PERRY (b. *c.* 1957), THE EDITOR OF BRITAIN'S seminal punk fanzine *Sniffin' Glue*. The original line-up featured Perry (vocals), Scottish guitarist Alex Fergusson (b. 1952), Micky Smith (bass) and John Towe (drums, ex-**Generation X**), but later underwent several changes. ATV are best remembered for a series of uncompromising singles, including their self-effacing debut, 'Love Lies Limp', and the declamatory 'How Much Longer?'. A disillusioned Perry abandoned the group in 1979 in favour of the Good Missionaries and subsequent projects: the Door And The Window and the Reflections. He returned to recording under the ATV banner in 1981 and continued to do so throughout the 80s. Fergusson went on to join Psychic TV, before turning his hand to producing **Gaye Bykers On Acid** and the Popguns. Perry was stated to be working with Fergusson once more in 1995.

AMBOY DUKES

ORIGINALLY FROM MICHIGAN, USA, THE AMBOY DUKES – JOHN DRAKE (VOCALS), **TED NUGENT** (b. 1949; LEAD guitar), Steve Farmer (rhythm guitar), Rick Lorber (keyboards), Bill White (bass) and Dave Palmer (drums) – achieved notoriety for their rendition of 'Journey To The Center Of Your Mind', which reached the US Top 20. The brash version of **Them**'s 'Baby Please Don't Go' set the tone for the group's subsequent albums on which Farmer's rather pretentious lyrics often undermined the music. The band were highly competent on instrumentals, such as the evocative 'Scottish Tea'. Frequent changes in personnel (Drake, Lorber and White were replaced by Rusty Day, Andy Solomon and Greg Arama), made little difference to the Amboy Dukes' development, as the group increasingly became an outlet for Nugent. He unveiled a new line-up in 1974 with *Call Of The Wild*, then abandoned the band's name and embarked on a solo career.

AMEN CORNER

FORMED IN CARDIFF, WALES, THIS R&B-STYLED SEPTET CONSISTED OF **ANDY FAIRWEATHER-LOW** (b. 1950; VOCALS), Derek 'Blue Weaver' (b. 1949; organ), Neil Jones (b. 1949; guitar), Clive Taylor (b. 1949; bass), Allen Jones (b. 1948; baritone sax), Mike Smith (b. 1947; tenor sax) and Dennis Byron (b. 1949; drums). After charting with 'Gin House Blues' (1967), the group swiftly ploughed more commercial ground with 'World Of Broken Hearts', 'Bend Me, Shape Me' and 'High In The Sky'. They subsequently moved from Decca to Andrew Oldham's Immediate record label and enjoyed their only UK number 1 with '(If Paradise Is) Half As Nice' in 1969. Following one final UK Top 10 hit, 'Hello Suzie', they split. Andy Fairweather-Low subsequently formed Fairweather and then went solo while Blue Weaver joined the **Strawbs**. The brass section became Judas Jump.

AMERICA

FORMED IN THE LATE 60S, AMERICA COMPRISED ENGLISHMAN DEWEY BUNNELL (b. 1951) AND TWO Americans, Dan Peek (b. 1950) and Gerry Beckley (b. 1952). Heavily influenced by **Crosby, Stills & Nash**, they employed similarly strong counter-harmonies backed by acoustic guitar. Their first single, 'A Horse With No Name', proved a massive UK hit and, with backing by Warner Brothers Records and management by former UK 'underground' disc jockey Jeff Dexter, the single topped the US charts. The debut album, *America*, fitted perfectly into the soft rock style of the period and paved the way for a series of further hits including 'I Need You', 'Ventura Highway',

'Tin Man' and 'Lonely People'. **David Geffen** eventually took over the running of their affairs. With former **Beatles** producer **George Martin**, the trio returned to US number 1 with the melodic 'Sister Golden Hair'.

In 1977, Dan Peek left to concentrate on more spiritual material, in the wake of his conversion to Christianity. America continued as a duo, and returned to form in 1982 with the **Russ Ballard**-produced *View From The Ground*, which included the hit 'You Can Do Magic'; in 1994 they released *Hourglass*.

AMERICAN MUSIC CLUB

SAN FRANCISCO'S AMERICAN MUSIC CLUB WAS FORMED BY **MARK EITZEL** (b. 1959; GUITAR/VOCALS); WITH DANNY Pearson (b. 1959; bass), Tim Mooney (b. 1958; drums), Vudi (b. Mark Pankler, 1952; guitar) and occasionally Bruce Kaphan (b. 1955; steel guitar). From his earliest appearances, Eitzel's onstage demeanour rivalled the extravagances of **Iggy Pop**. In the early days he was also a fractious heavy drinker, until the day AMC signed to a major label after several acclaimed independent albums. Before this, he had left the band twice, once after the tour to support *Engine*, and once after *Everclear*. He also temporarily fronted Toiling Midgets. Following *Everclear*, in 1991, **Rolling Stone** elected Eitzel their Songwriter Of The Year.

Mercury was the band's debut for a major record label – song titles such as 'What Godzilla Said To God When His Name Wasn't Found In The Book Of Life' illustrated that Eitzel's peculiar lyrical scenarios were still intact. 1994's *San Francisco*, brought further acclaim. Eitzel went solo in 1995.

AMERICAN SPRING

SISTERS MARILYN AND DIANE ROVELL FIRST ATTRACTED ATTENTION DURING THE EARLY 60S. AS MEMBERS OF the Honeys they enjoyed a fruitful association with **Beach Boys** leader **Brian Wilson**, who produced them and employed them backing voices for his own group's releases. The Rovell sisters were initially known as Spring, and recorded two low-key singles before completing their self-titled album, which included John Guerin (drums) and **Larry Carlton** (guitar). This evocative set balanced crafted rearrangements of established material – 'Tennessee Waltz', and 'Everybody' – with several exquisite originals from the Beach Boys family.

American Spring was dissolved following the release of 'Shyin' Away', but their legacy was rekindled during the 80s, when Marilyn and Diane joined Ginger Blake in a revamped Honeys.

AMON DUUL II

THIS INVENTIVE ACT EVOLVED OUT OF A COMMUNE BASED IN MUNICH, GERMANY. THE COLLECTIVE SPLIT INTO TWO factions in 1968, following an appearance at the Essen Song Days Festival where they supported the **Mothers Of Invention** and the **Fugs**. The political wing, known as Amon Duul, did record four albums, but Amon Duul II was recognized as the musical faction. Renate Knaup-Krotenschwanz (percussion/vocals), John Weinzierl (guitar/bass), Falk Rogner (organ), Dave Anderson (bass), Dieter Serfas (drums), Peter Leopold (drums) and Shrat (percussion) completed *Phallus Dei* in 1969 with the aid of Christian Burchard (vibes) and Holger Trulzsh (percussion). A double set, *Yeti*, proved more popular, combining space-rock with free-form styles. Serfas, Shrat and Anderson quit (the latter joined **Hawkwind** before forming Amon Din); Lothar Meid from jazz-rock collective Utopia, left and rejoined Amon Duul II on several occasions, while producer Olaf Kubler often augmented live performances on saxophone.

Chris Karrer (guitar/violin) joined Weinzierl and Renate on another two-album package, *Dance Of The Lemmings*, which featured shorter pieces linked together into suites. The melodic *Carnival In Babylon* was succeeded by *Wolf City*. By that point they were at the vanguard of German rock, alongside **Can**, **Faust** and **Tangerine Dream**. *Vive La Trance* was a marked disappointment and the group's tenure at United Artists ended with the budget-priced *Live In London*, recorded during their 1972 tour. *Lemmingmania* compiled various singles recorded between 1970 and 1975.

Hijack and *Made In Germany* showed a group of dwindling power and four members, including Renate and Falk, left on the latter's release. Weinzierl quit the line-up following *Almost Alive*, leaving Karrer to lead the ensemble through *Only Human*. Amon Duul II was officially dissolved in 1980 although within a year several founding musicians regrouped for the disappointing *Vortex*. Weinzierl kept the name upon moving to Wales where, with Dave Anderson, he completed *Hawk Meets Penguin* and *Meetings With Menmachines Unremarkable Heroes Of The Past* which were credited to Amon Duul (UK). Karrer, Renate, Weinzierl and Leopold reunited in 1989 to play at Robert Calvert's memorial concert in London, and again, in 1992, in order to protect the rights to the Amon Duul II name. They recommenced recording with Lothar Meid.

AMOS, TORI

AMOS (b. MYRA ELLEN AMOS, 1963) WAS ENROLLED IN BALTIMORE'S PEABODY INSTITUTE AS A FIVE-YEAR-OLD prodigy. In 1980, aged 17, she released (as Ellen Amos) 'Baltimore'/ 'Walking With You' on the MEA label (named after her own initials). She favoured cover versions such as **Joni Mitchell**'s 'A Case Of You', Billie Holiday's 'Strange Fruit' and **Bill Withers**' 'Ain't No Sunshine', later staples of her live set. Amos then adopted the first name Tori, after a remark that she didn't 'look much like an Ellen, more like a Tori'.

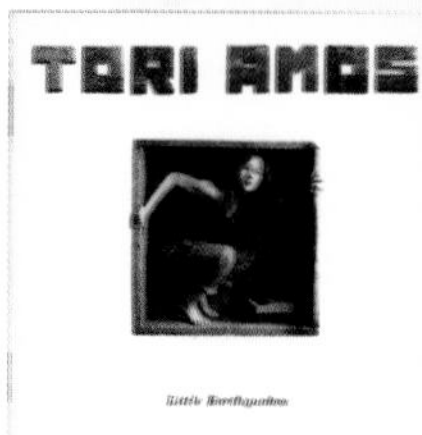

Amos then moved to front pop-rock band Y Kant Tori Read, the band included guitarist Steve Farris (ex-Mr. Mister), drummer Matt Sorum (future **Cult** and **Guns N'Roses**), Vinny Coliauta (**Frank Zappa**), Peter White (co-writer to **Al Stewart**) and Kim Bullard (ex-**Poco**), but the production and material did her few favours. Tori lowered her profile for a while after this undignified release, though she did appear on albums by Al Stewart and Stan Ridgway. She also persevered in writing her own songs, and eventually a tape reached Atlantic Records' co-chairman, Doug Morris. Deciding that her sound would not be to the taste of the average American FM-listener, he sent Amos to the UK, and East West Records.

Amos moved to London in 1991 and played small-scale gigs around the capital. Her 'debut' EP, *Me And A Gun* (1991), tackled the emotive topic of her rape by an armed 'fan' as she drove him home after a gig. An acclaimed debut album, *Little Earthquakes*, followed in 1992. Much of the following year was spent writing and recording a second album with co-producer and partner Eric Rosse. The result, *Under The Pink*, included a guest appearance from Trent Reznor (**Nine Inch Nails**). 'Cornflake Girl' reached UK number 4, and Amos was heralded in the press, alongside Polly Harvey (**PJ Harvey**) and **Björk**, as part of a new wave of intelligent, literate female songwriters. This was cemented with the release of the sexually charged *Boys For Pele*. In 1998, she released *From the Choirgirl Hotel*.

AMERICAN SPRING

Albums
Spring UK title *American Spring* (1972)★★★
➽ p.350 for full listings

Connections
Beach Boys ➽ p.36
Larry Carlton ➽ p.81

Influences
Brian Wilson ➽ p.340

AMON DUUL II

Albums
Yeti (Liberty 1970)★★★★

Collaborators
Mothers Of Invention ➽ p.239
The Fugs ➽ p.155
➽ p.350 for full listings

Connections
Hawkwind ➽ p.177
Can ➽ p.79
Faust ➽ p.144
Tangerine Dream ➽ p.316

AMOS, TORI

Albums
Little Earthquakes (East West 1992)★★★★
➽ p.350 for full listings

Collaborators
Al Stewart ➽ p.309
Nine Inch Nails ➽ p.248

Connections
Cult ➽ p.107
Guns N'Roses ➽ p.170
Frank Zappa ➽ p.348
PJ Harvey ➽ p.262
Björk ➽ p.48

Influences
Joni Mitchell ➽ p.235

Further References
Book: *All These Years*, Kalen Rogers

ANDERSON, JON
Albums
as Jon And Vangelis *Friends Of Mr. Cairo* (Polydor 1981)★★★★
➽ p.350 for full listings
Collaborators
Vangelis ➽ p.329
Connections
Association ➽ p.23
Yes ➽ p.346

ANDERSON, JON

DURING HIS FORMATIVE YEARS ANDERSON (b. 1944) FRONTED THE WARRIORS, AN ASPIRING BEAT GROUP. Despite the single 'You Came Along' (1964), the quartet failed to make much headway and in 1967 the singer went solo as Hans Christian Anderson. His releases included a version of 'Never My Love', a US hit for the **Association**, but this temporary phase ended on joining Mabel Greer's Toyshop, which in turn evolved into **Yes**.

A solo recording, *Olias Of Sunhillow*, was welcomed by Yes aficionados during a hiatus in the parent group's career, but it was *Short Stories*, a collaboration with **Vangelis**, that emphasized Anderson's new-found liberty. He left Yes in 1980 as his attendant single, 'I Hear You Now', soared into the UK Top 10; the following year 'I'll Find My Way Home' reached number 6. The singer continued his solo work with *Song Of Seven* and *Animation*, but found greater commercial success in two further albums with Vangelis, *Friends Of Mr. Cairo* and *Private Collection*.

In 1983, Anderson rejoined Yes. Internal ructions led to his departure again but, having completed *3 Ships* and *In The City Of Angels*, he became involved in protracted legal arguments over the rights to the group's name. He then toured with disaffected ex-members, initially as the Affirmative, latterly as Anderson, Wakeman, Bruford And Howe, but the dispute was settled in 1991; the group retained their original name and embarked on a major tour. In the mid-90s, Anderson's long-held fascination with music from Latin America resulted in the excellent *Deseo*.

ANDERSON, LAURIE
Albums
Big Science (Warners1982)★★★★
➽ p.350 for full listings
Collaborators
Peter Gabriel ➽ p.157
Lou Reed ➽ p.274
Connections
Chic ➽ p.89
Further References
Video: *Home Of The Brave* (Warners 1991)

ANDERSON, LAURIE

A PRODUCT OF NEW YORK'S AVANT-GARDE ART SCENE, ANDERSON (b. LAURA Phillips Anderson, 1950) eschewed her initial work as a sculptor in favour of performing. *The Life And Times Of Josef Stalin*, which premiered in 1973, was a 12-hour epic containing many of the audio-visual elements the artist brought to her music. *Big Science* included the eight-minute vocoder-laden 'O Superman' (1981), a cult hit in Europe that reached UK number 2. *Mr. Heartbreak* featured contributions from **Peter Gabriel** and writer William Burroughs, while her sprawling five-album set, *United States*, chronicled an ambitious, seven-hour show. *Home Of The Brave* resumed the less radical path of her second album and was co-produced by former **Chic** guitarist Nile Rodgers. The guests on *Bright Red* included **Lou Reed**, Adrian Belew and ex-Fixx guitarist Jamie West-Oram, with production by Gabriel.

ANDREWS, CHRIS
Albums
Yesterday Man (Decca 1965)★★
➽ p.350 for full listings
Connections
Adam Faith ➽ p.142

ANDREWS, CHRIS

ORIGINALLY LEAD SINGER IN CHRIS RAVEL AND THE RAVERS, ANDREWS (b. 1938) FOUND greater success as a songwriter. Signed by manager Eve Taylor, he composed hits for her artists **Adam Faith** (including 'The First Time', 'I Love Being In Love With You' and 'Someone's Taken Maria Away') and **Sandie Shaw** ('Girl Don't Come', 'Long Live Love' and 'Message Understood'). He enjoyed chart success during 1965-66 with two catchy, upbeat numbers, 'Yesterday Man' and 'To Whom It Concerns'. Although he occasionally recorded additional solo singles, no further hits were forthcoming. He subsequently continued his career as a songwriter.

ANGELIC UPSTARTS
Albums
Teenage Warning (Warners 1979)★★★
➽ p.350 for full listings
Influences
Clash ➽ p.93
Damned ➽ p.110
Sex Pistols ➽ p.292

ANGELIC UPSTARTS

THIS POLITICALLY MOTIVATED, HARDLINE PUNK QUARTET FORMED IN 1977, IN SOUTH SHIELDS, ENGLAND. They were the brainchild of Mensi (vocals), with Cowie, Warrington and Taylor completing the line-up. Strongly influenced by the **Clash**, **Damned** and **Sex Pistols**, they released 'Murder Of Liddle Towers' in 1979. The song condemned police brutality and identified strongly with the youth culture of the day. After signing to Warner Brothers Records, they released the provocative *Teenage Warning* (1979) and *We Gotta Get Out Of This Place* (1980).

The band suffered regular outbreaks of violence at their live shows from National Front supporters, who sought to counter the group's left-wing politics. As the 80s progressed, the band gradually saw their fan base dwindle, and they ground to a halt in 1986. They re-formed for a brief period in 1988 and then once again in 1992, releasing *Bombed Out*.

ANIMALS
Albums
The Animals (Columbia 1964)★★★★
Most Of The Animals (Columbia 1966)★★★★
➽ p.350 for full listings

ANIMALS

FORMED IN NEWCASTLE-UPON-TYNE, ENGLAND, IN 1963, WHEN VOCALIST **ERIC BURDON** (b. 1941), JOINED LOCAL R&B band the Alan Price Combo. The Animals comprised **Alan Price** (b. 1942; piano), Hilton Valentine (b. 1943; guitar), John Steel (b. 1941; drums) and Chas Chandler (b. Bryan James Chandler, 1938; bass). By 1963, their raucous and exciting stage act, had created them an integral part of the fast-burgeoning, London club scene. Produced by **Mickie Most**, they debuted with 'Baby Let Me Take You Home', followed by their version of Josh White's 'House Of The Rising Sun' – a pop song about a New Orleans brothel, lasting four-and-a-half minutes. Despite Columbia's fears it was too long, it leapt to the top of the worldwide charts. The combination of Valentine's simplistic guitar introduction and Price's shrill organ complemented Burdon's remarkably mature and bloodcurdling vocal. Over the next two years the Animals had seven further transatlantic hits. Their choice of material was exemplary and many of their hits contained thought-provoking lyrics, from the angst-ridden 'I'm Crying' to the frustration and urban despair of Cynthia Weil and Barry Mann's 'We Gotta Get Out Of This Place'. During this time Price departed (reportedly suffering from aerophobia), and was replaced by Dave Rowberry from the Mike Cotton Sound; Steel left in 1966, replaced by Nashville Teens drummer Barry Jenkins. The new band scored with 'Its My Life' and 'Inside Looking Out'.

By 1967, Burdon and Valentine had become totally immersed in psychedelia, musically and chemically. This alienated them from the rest of the group, leading to its disintegration. Chandler went on to discover and manage the **Jimi Hendrix** Experience. Burdon, however, retained the name and reappeared as Eric Burdon And The New Animals. Having moved to the USA, they courted the west coast sound, 'San Franciscan Nights' perfectly echoed the moment, while 'Monterey' eulogized the **Monterey Pop Festival** of 1967. A number of musicians passed through the New Animals, notably John Weider, Vic Briggs (formerly of Steampacket), Danny McCulloch, **Zoot Money** and Andy Summers.

ANKA, PAUL

A PROLIFIC SONGWRITER AND CHILD PRODIGY, CANADIAN ANKA (b. 1941) BECAME A 50S TEEN-IDOL. HE hit the scene in 1957 with the self-written 'Diana', which reached UK and US number 1, selling a reported 10 million copies worldwide. This was followed by a series of hits such as 'You Are My Destiny', 'Lonely Boy', 'Put Your Head On My Shoulder' and 'Puppy Love'. Pubescent worries and condescending parents were familiar themes and contributed to his success.

As the 50s wound to a close, he moved away from teen ballads and planned for a long-term future as a songwriter. His 'It Doesn't Matter Anymore' was a posthumous UK number 1 for **Buddy Holly** in 1959, the same year that Anka starred in the film *Girls' Town*. In 1962, he starred in the more serious *The Longest Day*. During the 60s, the former teen star was in demand on the night-club circuit and a regular at New York's Copacabana and Los Angeles' Coconut Grove. The success of **Donny Osmond**, who took 'Puppy Love' to the top in Britain, kept Anka's early material alive for a new generation. Songwriting success continued, most notably with Frank Sinatra's reading of his lyric to 'My Way' and **Tom Jones**'s million-selling 'She's A Lady'. In the 70s, Anka returned to US number 1 with '(You're) Having My Baby', a risqué duet with his protégée Odia Coates. A spree of hits followed and, in 1983, Anka was back in the charts with 'Hold Me Till The Mornin' Comes'. He continued to play lucrative seasons in Las Vegas and Atlantic City, and toured Europe in 1992 for the first time in 25 years. In 1996 he released his first album aimed at the Latin market with some of his greatest hits sung in Spanish and duetting with artists such as **Celine Dion**, Julio Iglesias and Jose Luis Rodriguez.

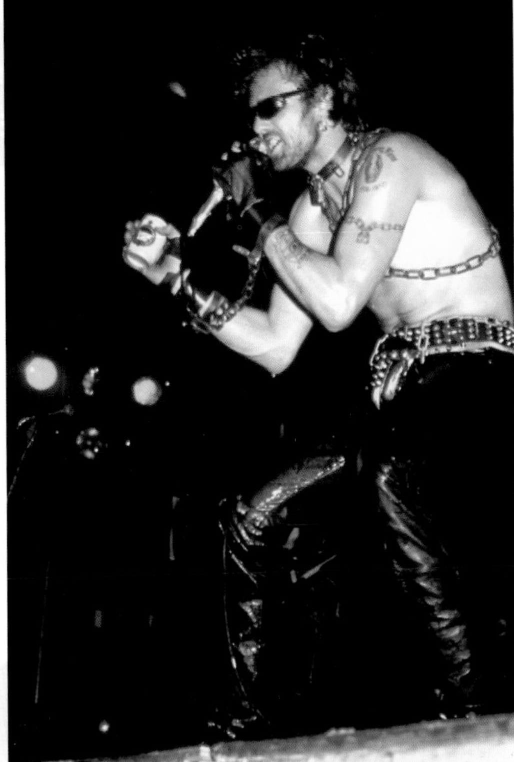

ANTHRAX

NEW YORK-BASED THRASH METAL OUTFIT COMPRISING SCOTT 'NOT' Ian (b. Scott Rosenfeld, 1963; rhythm guitar), Neil Turbin (vocals), Dan Spitz (b. 1963; lead guitar), Dan Lilker (bass; replaced by Frank Bello (b. 1965) in 1983) and Charlie Benante (b. 1962; drums). Managed by Johnny Z, head of the independent Megaforce Records, the quintet released *Fistful Of Metal* (1984), which garnered fair reviews and was a steady seller. For a time Ian, Lilker and Benante were also part of Stormtroopers Of Death, a hard core band with a satirical outlook. Lilker left, followed by Turbin, whose initial replacement, Matt Fallon, was quickly succeeded by Joey Belladonna (b. 1960). This line-up released the *Armed And Dangerous* EP in 1985, and signed to Island Records. *Spreading The Disease* was well received, and the band's European profile was raised considerably by their support slot on **Metallica**'s Damage Inc tour. *Among The Living* established Anthrax in the speed-metal scene, producing UK hits in 'I Am The Law' and 'Indians'. A humorous rap song, 'I'm The Man', became both a hit and a favourite encore. However, *State Of Euphoria* was a patchy affair, with the group suffering a media backlash over their image, until live work restored their reputation. *Persistence Of Time*, a dark and relentless work, produced another hit – **Joe Jackson**'s 'Got The Time' – and *Attack Of The Killer B's*, which was essentially a collection of b-sides, became one of Anthrax's most popular albums. This was followed by a hit collaboration with **Public Enemy**, 'Bring The Noise', which led to the bands touring together.

After Anthrax signed a new contract with Elektra Records, Belladonna was fired, replaced by ex-Armored Saint frontman John Bush (b. 1963; vocals). 1994 saw Bush start his own R&B offshoot, Ho Cake, which included former Armored Saint personnel Joey Vera (bass) and Jeff Duncan (guitar), as well as Shawn Duncan (drums), Tony Silbert (keyboards) and Bruce Fernandez. In 1995, Anthrax began work on *Stomp 442*, an unremittingly brutal collection of hardcore and metal produced by the Butcher Brothers. Spitz was ejected from the band just prior to recording and his guitar parts were played by his former guitar technician, Paul Cook, **Pantera**'s Dimebag Darrell, and the group's drummer, Charlie Benante.

ANTI-NOWHERE LEAGUE

LEADING LIGHTS IN THE EARLY 80S UK PUNK SCENE, ALONG WITH CONTEMPORARIES GBH and the Exploited, this quartet from Kent, England, betrayed their talent in biker leather, chains and hardcore obscenity. Led by Animal (b. Nick Karmer; vocals) and Magoo (guitar), their catalogue of sexual outrage veered from the satirical to the genuinely offensive, with a string of four-letter words, lyrics of rabid misogyny and the glorification of bestiality. Their most memorable moment was a thrashy cover version of **Ralph McTell**'s 'Streets Of London', which replaced the song's folksy sentiments with the barbed, snarling rhetoric of the gutter. Thousands of copies of the single were seized and destroyed by the police as the b-side, 'So What', was deemed obscene.

The group reached number 1 in the UK Independent charts, a feat accomplished a further three times in 1982 with 'I Hate People', 'Woman' and 'For You'. As their punkish appeal receded, the group abbreviated their name to the League and turned to a punk/metal hybrid, with *The Perfect Crime* boasting several fine songs. They disbanded in 1988 but there have been several revivals, including the 1989 reunion that resulted in *Live And Loud*.

APHEX TWIN

THE APHEX TWIN (b. RICHARD JAMES, *c.* 1972) BEGAN MAKING MUSIC IN HIS EARLY TEENS, BEFORE SIGNING to R&S Records. His breakthrough release came with the techno/ambient 'Didgeridoo' in 1992. The Aphex Twin is not his only pseudonym, he has worked as: Polygon Window on Warp Records (*Surfing On Sine Waves*), Caustic Window ('Joyrex J5', 'Joyrex J4') on Rephlex Records – a label he co-owns – and sundry other releases by Blue Calx and PCP all bear his mark.

James became highly sought after for his remixing skills, particularly by 'progressive' indie bands like Meat Beat Manifesto, **Curve**, **Jesus Jones**, **Saint Etienne**, Seefeel and the **Cure**. The *On* EP (1993) followed his signing to Warp Records on a permanent basis, under a contract which licenses material to Sire Records in the US. *Selected Ambient Works Vol 2* prompted a world tour. *Ventolin & Remixes*, effectively two 12-inch EPs which build into a single album, introduced trip hop and industrial flavours alongside the trademark lo-fi electro stance, while *I Care Because You Do* was a little more conservative, with tracks such as 'Start As You Mean To Go On' bearing an uncanny similarity to the much earlier '73 Yips' composition.

Connections
Mickie Most ➧ p.239
Jimi Hendrix ➧ p.180
Beatles ➧ p.38
Rolling Stones ➧ p.281
Influences
Monterey Pop Festival ➧ p.237
Further References
Video: *Animalistic* (The Gold Standard 1995)
Films: *Get Yourself A College Girl* (1964)
It's A Bikini World (1967)

ANKA, PAUL
Albums
Paul Anka Swings For Young Lovers (ABC 1960)★★★★
➧ p.350 for full listings
Collaborators
Celine Dion ➧ p.119
Julio Iglesias
Jose Luis Rodriguez
Connections
Buddy Holly ➧ p.184
Donny Osmond ➧ p.254
Frank Sinatra
Tom Jones ➧ p.201
Further References
Films: *Girl's Town aka The Innocent And The Damned* (1959)
Lonely Boy (1962)
The Longest Day (1962)

ANTHRAX
Albums
Sound Of White Noise (Elektra 1993)★★★★
➧ p.350 for full listings
Collaborators
Metallica ➧ p.232
Public Enemy ➧ p.269
Connections
Joe Jackson ➧ p.195
Urge Overkill ➧ p.327
Pantera ➧ p.255
Further References
Videos: *Oidivnikufesin N.F.V.* (1988)
Videos P.O.V. (1990)
N.F.V. (1991)

ANTI-NOWHERE LEAGUE
Albums
as The League *The Perfect Crime* (GWR 1987)★★★
➧ p.351 for full listings
Connections
GBH
The Exploited ➧ p.140
Ralph McTell ➧ p.230

APHEX TWIN
Albums
Selected Ambient Works '85-'92 (R&S 1992) ★★★★
➧ p.351 for full listings
Connections
Meat Beat Manifesto
Curve ➧ p.108
Jesus Jones ➧ p.199
Saint Etienne ➧ p.287
Seefeel
Cure ➧ p.108

APHRODITE'S CHILD
Albums
666 — The Apocalypse Of St. John (Vertigo 1972)★★★
➽ p.351 for full listings
Connections
Vangelis ➽ p.329

APPLE, FIONA
Albums
Tidal (Columbia 1996)
➽ p.351 for full listings
Connections
Alanis Morissette ➽ p.238
Beatles ➽ p.38
Influences
Maya Angelou

APPLEJACKS (UK)
Albums
The Applejacks (Decca 1964)★★
➽ p.351 for full listings
Connections
John Lennon ➽ p.214
Paul McCartney ➽ p.229
Kinks ➽ p.207

APRIL WINE
Albums
The Nature Of The Beast (Capitol 1981)★★★
➽ p.351 for full listings
Connections
Dino Dinelli
Gene Cornish
Further References
Video: *Live In London* (PMI 1986)

ARCHER, TASMIN
Albums
Great Expectations (EMI 1993)★★★
➽ p.351 for full listings
Collaborators
Elvis Costello's Attractions ➽ p.101
Connections
Bonnie Tyler ➽ p.325
Further References
Video: *When It Comes Down To It* (1993)

ARGENT
Albums
All Together Now (Epic 1972)★★★
➽ p.351 for full listings
Connections
Zombies ➽ p.349
Russ Ballard ➽ p.31
Three Dog Night ➽ p.321
Kiss ➽ p.208
Kinks ➽ p.207

ARKARNA
Albums
Fresh Meat (WEA 1997)
➽ p.351 for full listings
Connections
Dread Zone ➽ p.125
Leftfield ➽ p.213
Deep Forest ➽ p.113
Godley And Creme ➽ p.164

APHRODITE'S CHILD

FORMED IN GREECE DURING THE MID-60S, APHRODITE'S CHILD CONSISTED OF EGYPTIAN-BORN DEMIS ROUSSOS (b. 1947; vocals), alongside Greek musicians **Vangelis** Papathanassiou (b. Evangalos Odyssey Papathanassiou, 1943; keyboards) and Lucas Sideras (b. 1944; drums). In 1968, the trio enjoyed a massive European hit with the haunting ballad 'Rain And Tears'. The group enjoyed cultish popularity, particularly after a second album, *It's Five O'Clock*. The conceptual *666* marked an artistic peak with its 'Break' almost becoming a hit. Roussos subsequently found international fame as a purveyor of MOR material while Papathanassiou achieved notable solo success as Vangelis.

APPLE, FIONA

GROWING UP IN A DYSFUNCTIONAL NEW YORK FAMILY, FIONA APPLE (b. 1977) SOON DISCOVERED THE impetus to articulate frustrations, which would eventually result in widespread comparisons to **Alanis Morissette** for her 1996 debut, *Tidal*. As a child she was introduced to the **Beatles** by her step-father, while her mother educated her in jazz standards. By the age of 11 she was writing her own songs, as a means of coping with shyness, a lack of confidence about her appearance and her rape ordeal at the age of 12. She found solace in the poetry of Maya Angelou, which she maintains was her biggest influence. Her debut album was the result of songs recorded on a cheap tape recorder in her bedroom, which a friend played to a Columbia Records' executive.

APPLEJACKS (UK)

THIS EARLY 60S UK POP GROUP COMPRISED MARTIN BAGGOTT (B. 1947; GUITAR), PHILIP CASH (b. 1947; GUITAR), Megan Davies (b. 1944; bass), Don Gould (b. 1947; organ), Al Jackson (b. 1945; vocals) and Gerry Freeman (b. 1947; drums). Signed by Decca A&R representative Mike Smith, the Applejacks found UK Top 10 chart success in 1964 with the memorable 'Tell Me When'. The follow-up, 'Like Dreamers Do' (taken from the famous **Lennon** and **McCartney** Decca audition tape) reached the UK Top 20, but the next single, 'Three Little Words', failed to chart. The group turned next to the **Kinks**'s catalogue for Ray Davies's moody 'I Go To Sleep'. Its failure effectively signalled the Applejacks' doom and they returned to the northern club scene.

APRIL WINE

FORMED IN 1969 IN MONTREAL, QUEBEC, THIS HARD ROCK GROUP BECAME AN IMMEDIATE SUCCESS. THROUGH fluctuating line-ups they arrived at steady membership by the late 70s, including original lead singer Myles Goodwyn (b. 1948; vocals/guitar), Brian Greenway (b. 1951; guitar), Gary Moffet (b. 1949; guitar), Steve Lang (b. 1949; bass) and Jerry Mercer (b. 1939; drums). Among their first admirers were former Rascals members Dino Dinelli and Gene Cornish, who produced early material for the group. Their first album featured David Henman (guitar), Jim Clench (bass) and Richie Henman (drums). *Electric Jewels* saw the line-up switch with Gary Moffet and Jerry Mercer replacing the Henman brothers. Clench was replaced by Steve Lang on *The Whole World's Going' Crazy* with Greenaway added as third guitarist in time for *First Glance*.

April Wine enjoyed three Top 40 singles and five albums in the US charts; *Harder... Faster* went gold and *The Nature Of The Beast* went platinum. The group broke up in the mid-80s but re-formed in the 90s.

ARCHER, TASMIN

SINGER-SONGWRITER ARCHER (b. *c.* 1964) MET FUTURE SONGWRITING PARTNERS JOHN HUGHES (GUITAR), AND John Beck (keyboards) at a studio in Bradford, England. Over five years they worked together (originally as the Archers) until they had built up a strong song catalogue which would allow Tasmin to capitalize on the success of 'Sleeping Satellite' (UK number 1, 1993). The follow-up single, 'In Your Care', was about the evils of child abuse, and her debut album covered topics such as urban decay. Despite the support of **Elvis Costello**'s Attractions, her second album sold poorly.

ARGENT

WHEN 60S POP GROUP THE **ZOMBIES** DISINTEGRATED, KEYBOARDIST ROD ARGENT (b. 1945) WASTED NO TIME in forming a band that would enable his dexterity as pianist and songwriter to flourish. The unit included Russ Ballard (b. 1947; guitar/vocals), Bob Henrit (b. 1944; drums) and Jim Rodford (b. 1941; bass). Their critically acclaimed debut contained Ballard's 'Liar', a song that became one of their concert regulars. *All Together Now* contained the exhilarating 'Hold Your Head Up' which became a transatlantic Top 5 hit, and *In Deep* produced another memorable hit with 'God Gave Rock 'N' Roll To You' (a 1992 hit for **Kiss**). Ballard left in 1974 to pursue a solo career and his place was taken by two new members, John Verity (b. 1949; guitar/bass/vocals) and John Grimaldi (b. 1955; cello/mandolin/violin). Argent disbanded in 1976 and Rodford joined the **Kinks**.

ARKARNA

FORMED IN ENGLAND IN THE MID-90S, 'FUTURE-DANCE TRIO' ARKARNA COMPRISE OLLIE JACOBS (b. *c.* 1975; MIXER/vocals), James Barnett (b. *c.* 1974; guitar) and Lalo Creme (b. *c.* 1974; guitar). Jacobs, the group's programmer and vocalist, had worked as an engineer and producer in his father's London studios from the age of 14, mixing for artists ranging from **Dread Zone** and **Leftfield** to **Deep Forest**. Acoustic guitarist and backing vocalist Barnett was formerly a member of Lunarci, who recorded for Big Life Records and regularly appeared on the Megadog club scene. Lalo Creme is the son of Lol Creme, of **Godley And Creme**. The trio were signed to WEA Records in 1995, but had to wait over a year before the release of their debut single, 'House On Fire', followed by 1997's *Fresh Meat*.

ARMATRADING, JOAN

THE ARMATRADING FAMILY MOVED FROM THE WEST INDIES TO BIRMINGHAM, ENGLAND, IN 1958, AND JOAN (b. 1950) taught herself to play piano and guitar. She met Pam Nestor (b. 1948) when they were working in a touring cast of the hippie musical, *Hair*. Armatrading and Nestor worked as a songwriting team, before Armatrading released her debut, *Whatever's For Us*; the album was a greater critical than commercial success. Armatrading and Nestor dissolved their partnership after the album; Nestor made an excellent one-off single for Chrysalis in the late 70s, but seems not to have recorded since.

By 1975, Armatrading was signed to A&M worldwide, however *Back To The Night* was unsuccessful and it was not until 1976 and *Joan Armatrading* that she hit the limelight. It made the UK Top 20, and includes her only UK Top 10 hit 'Love And Affection'. *Show Some Emotion* became her first album to reach the UK Top 10 and *To The Limit* made the UK Top 20, although neither

album included a hit single. In 1979, her partnership with Johns ended with *Steppin' Out*, a live album recorded in the USA, which did not chart on either side of the Atlantic.

Me Myself I was Armatrading's first album to reach the US Top 40. It also returned her to the UK Top 10, and included two minor UK hit singles: the title track and 'All The Way From America'. *Walk Under Ladders* featured the celebrated Jamaican rhythm section of **Sly Dunbar** and Robbie Shakespeare and reached the UK Top 10; charting somewhat lower in the US. *The Key* included 'Drop The Pilot' (her second biggest UK hit single) and largely restored Armatrading to international commercial prominence, peaking just outside the US Top 30 and reaching the UK Top 10. Later that year, a 'Best Of' album, *Track Record*, made the UK Top 20. 1985's *Secret Secrets* featured bass player Pino Palladino and **Joe Jackson**. While the album once again made the UK Top 20, it was not a major US success, despite a sleeve shot taken by celebrated photographer Robert Mapplethorpe. *Sleight Of Hand*, Armatrading's first self-produced album, was her least successful album in commercial terms since her debut, stalling outside the UK Top 30 and considerably lower in the USA.

The Shouting Stage was her most impressive album in some time but was relatively unsuccessful, despite featuring **Mark Knopfler** of **Dire Straits** and Mark Brzezicks of **Big Country**. *Hearts And Flowers* again demonstrated that even though the quality of Armatrading's output was seldom less than exemplary, it rarely achieved its commercial desserts. 1991 brought a further compilation album, *The Very Best Of Joan Armatrading*. In 1994 she released *What's Inside*.

ARNOLD, P. P.

ARNOLD (b. PATRICIA ARNOLD, 1946) FIRST CAME TO PROMINENCE IN 1966 AS A MEMBER OF **IKE AND TINA Turner**'s backing group, the Ikettes. Relocating to England from America, she was signed to Andrew Loog Oldham's Immediate label, and was backed on tour by **Nice**. Her exceptional version of **Cat Stevens**' 'The First Cut Is The Deepest', was a UK Top 20 hit in 1967 and she enjoyed a second major hit in 1968 with Chip Taylor's 'Angel Of The Morning', arranged by future **Led Zeppelin** bassist John Paul Jones. Highly regarded among her musical peers for the power and clarity of her voice, her first two albums were produced by Mick Jagger (the second in conjunction with **Steve Marriott**). Arnold repaid Marriott's production work by contributing powerful vocals to the **Small Faces**' hit 'Tin Soldier'. Never quite hitting the big time, Arnold began increasingly to concentrate on acting, appearing in such musicals as *Catch My Soul*, *Jesus Christ Superstar* and *Starlight Express*. She remains a session singer for many artists ranging from **Dr John** to **Nils Lofgren**, **Freddie King** and many more.

ARRESTED DEVELOPMENT

THIS RAP COLLECTIVE FROM ATLANTA, GEORGIA, ARE HEADED BY SPEECH (b. TODD THOMAS, 1968; VOCALS). He met DJ Headliner (b. Timothy Barnwell, 1967) while they were students in Atlanta. Speech, then known as DJ Peech, had already formed Disciples Of Lyrical Rebellion, a proto-gangsta outfit, which evolved into Secret Society. They changed the name to Arrested Development and found new members, including Aerle Taree (b. Taree Jones, 1972; clothes design/vocals), Montsho Eshe (b. Temelca Garther, 1974; dancer), and Rasa Don (b. Donald Jones, 1968; drums). Spritualist Baba Oje, whom Speech had known as a child, was added as the group's symbolic head man. The band drew on a black country narrative as well as more universal themes. Speech writes a regular column for the *20th Century African* newspaper and takes his views on race issues on lecture tours. Cited by many critics as the most significant breakthrough of 1992, 'People Everyday' and 'Mr Wendal' confirmed their commercial status. Their debut album embraced a number of issue-based narratives, 'Mama's Always On The Stage' a feminist treatise, and 'Children Play With Earth', an exhortation for children to get back in touch with the natural world. They released the live album, *Unplugged*, with a 17-person line-up. Speech's first production project, with fellow Southern funk-rappers Gumbo, also met with critical approval. A second album *Zingalamaduni*, Swahili for 'beehive of culture', emerged in 1994, once again extending their audience beyond the hip hop congnoscenti. As well as introducing new vocalist Nadirah Shakoor, plus DJ Kwesi Asuo (alias DJ Kermit; DJ/Vocals) and dancer Ajile, it saw the departure of Taree who had gone back to college. The band split in 1995.

ARRIVAL

THIS LATE-60S LIVERPOOL GROUP CAME TOGETHER WHEN DYAN BIRCH (b. 1949), TEAMED UP WITH PADDIE McHugh (b. 1946) and Frank Collins (b. 1947) of local group the Excels. A second Merseyside vocalist Carroll Carter (b. 1948) was added, along with Lloyd Courtney (b. 1947), Don Hume (b. 1950) and Tony O'Malley (b. 1948). The septet sent a tape to Decca Records' A&R representative Tony Hall, who was so impressed by the group's sound that he decided to record and manage them. Their early 70s Top 20 UK hits, 'Friends' and 'I Will Survive' were urgent performances with excellent vocals, however the seven-piece band proved unwieldy and eventually split. Birch, Collins, O'Malley and McHugh re-emerged in **Kokomo**.

ARMATRADING, JOAN

Albums

Me Myself I (A&M 1980)★★★★

➧ p.351 for full listings

Collaborators

Sly Dunbar and Robbie Shakespeare ➧ p.325

Joe Jackson ➧ p.195

Mark Knopfler ➧ p.209

Connections

Pam Nestor

Influences

Hair

Richard Gottehrer

ARNOLD, P. P.

Albums

First Lady Of Immediate (Immediate 1967)★★

➧ p.351 for full listings

Collaborators

Nice ➧ p.247

Small Faces ➧ p.300

Dr John ➧ p.125

Nils Lofgren ➧ p.217

Freddie King ➧ p.206

Connections

Ike and Tina Turner ➧ p.324

Led Zeppelin ➧ p.213

Mick Jagger ➧ p.281

Steve Marriott ➧ p.225

Andrew Lloyd Webber

Influences

Cat Stevens ➧ p.309

ARRESTED DEVELOPMENT

Albums

Three Years, Five Months, And Two Days In The Life Of ... (Chrysalis 1992)★★★★

➧ p.351 for full listings

Connections

Gumbo

Further References

Videos: *Unplugged: Video* (Chrysalis 1993)

ARRIVAL

Albums

Arrival I (Decca 1970)★★★

➧ p.351 for full listings

Connections

Kokomo ➧ p.209

ARROWS
Albums
First Hit (Rak 1976)★★
➽ p.351 for full listings

ARROWS

FORMED IN 1973, THE ARROWS – JAKE HOOKER (b. 1952; GUITAR/SAXOPHONE), ALAN MERRILL (b. 1951; BASS/ piano/harmonica) and Paul Varley (b. 1952; drums/piano) – were one of several US groups associated with the glam-rock/bubblegum team of songwriters Chinn and Chapman. Their debut, 'A Touch Too Much', reached the UK Top 10 in 1974, but despite securing their own television series, the group's only other success was 'My Last Night With You', which peaked at number 25. This 50s-styled performance contrasted with the perky pop of its predecessors, but the Arrows were unable to shake off the teenybop tag. The trio broke up, but Hooker and Merrill's song, 'I Love Rock 'N' Roll' provided **Joan Jett And The Blackhearts** with a US number 1 in 1982.

ART OF NOISE
Albums
Who's Afraid Of The Art Of Noise (ZTT 1984)★★★
➽ p.351 for full listings
Connections
Trevor Horn ➽ p.74
Prince ➽ p.267

ART OF NOISE

FORMED IN 1983, UK-BASED ART OF NOISE WERE THE FIRST ARTISTS TO BE signed to Trevor Horn's ZTT Records. The nucleus of the group was Anne Dudley (b. 1956; keyboards/ arrangements), J. J. Jeczalik (b. 1955; keyboards/production) and Gary Langan (various instruments, production). At the end of 1984, the ensemble reached the UK Top 10 with 'Close (To The Edit)'. In 1985, the group left ZTT, from then on their career consisted chiefly of working with other artists. A revival of 'Peter Gunn' with **Duane Eddy** hit the UK Top 10, followed by a collaboration with the television cartoon-animated character Max Headroom on 'Paranoimia'. Their finest and most bizarre backing role, however, was reserved for **Tom Jones** who made a Top 10 comeback with a version of **Prince**'s 'Kiss'. Having enjoyed several years of quirky chart success, Art Of Noise split in 1990.

ASH
Albums
1977 (Infectious 1996)★★★★
➽ p.351 for full listings
Connections
Owen Morris
Influences
Oasis ➽ p.250
Phil Spector ➽ p.304
Beach Boys ➽ p.36

ASH

FORMED IN COUNTY DOWN, NORTHERN IRELAND, ASH BEGAN TO MAKE HEADWAY IN 1994, PLAYING sprightly, youthful punk-pop. Rick 'Rock' McMurray (b. 1975; drums), Tim Wheeler (b. 1977; guitar/vocals) and Mark Hamilton (b. 1977; bass) were still at school when their single, 'Jack Named The Planets', was released in a limited edition of 1,000 copies. Their appeal easily translated to an American alternative climate and they signed to Warner/ Reprise Records; in the UK they signed to Infectious Records.

A seven-song mini-album was recorded in Wales, in 1994, with **Oasis** producer Owen Morris. 'Girl From Mars' reached UK number 11, followed by 'Angel Interceptor', 'Goldfinger' and their chart-topping debut album *1977*, its title inspired by the release date of the film *Star Wars*. It rose straight to UK number 1.

The group were inspired by **Phil Spector** and the **Beach Boys** as well as science-fiction – 'Darkside Lightside' was another tribute to *Star Wars*. They added a new member in 1997 when guitarist Charlotte Hatherley joined from Nightnurse; the band returned to the UK Top 10 with the title song of the film *A Life Less Ordinary* (1997).

ASHER, PETER
Connections
James Taylor ➽ p.317
Linda Ronstadt ➽ p.282
John Stewart
Joni Mitchell ➽ p.235
10,000 Maniacs ➽ p.318

ASHER, PETER

FOLLOWING THE DEMISE OF **PETER AND GORDON** IN 1968, ASHER (b. 1944) CONTINUED HIS GROWING INTEREST in record production. His first outside work was with ex-**Manfred Mann** lead singer **Paul Jones.** After being appointed head of A&R at UK's Apple Records, Asher signed **James Taylor** and produced his first album. After resigning, Asher took Taylor and moved to the USA where he has lived ever since. His involvement with Taylor has lasted for over 20 years as both manager and producer. Additionally, he has overseen the careers of artists including **Linda Ronstadt**, **Bonnie Raitt**, J.D. Souther, **Andrew Gold**, John Stewart, **10,000 Maniacs** and **Joni Mitchell**. Asher won Grammies in 1978 and 1990 for Producer of the Year.

ASHFORD AND SIMPSON
Albums
A Musical Affair (Warners 1980)★★★
➽ p.351 for full listings

ASHFORD AND SIMPSON

NICKOLAS 'NICK' ASHFORD (b. 1942) AND VALERIE SIMPSON (b. 1946) MET IN THE CHOIR OF HARLEM'S WHITE ROCK Baptist Church. Having recorded, unsuccessfully, as a duo, they joined Jo 'Joshie' Armstead, at the Scepter/Wand label where their compositions were recorded by Ronnie Milsap ('Never Had It So Good'), Maxine Brown ('One Step At A Time'), the **Shirelles** and Chuck Jackson. Their 'Let's Go Get Stoned' gave **Ray Charles** a number 1 US R&B hit in 1966. Ashford and Simpson then joined **Holland/ Dozier/Holland** at **Motown Records** where their best-known songs included 'Ain't No Mountain High Enough', 'You're All I Need To Get By', 'Reach Out And Touch Somebody's Hand' and 'Remember Me'. Simpson also began 'ghosting' for Tammi Terrell when the latter became too ill to continue her partnership with **Marvin Gaye**, and she sang on part of the duo's *Easy* album.

In 1971, Simpson embarked on a solo career, but two years later she and Ashford were recording together for Warner Brothers Records; they married in 1974. By the end of the decade, the couple enjoyed success with 'It Seems To Hang On' (1978) and 'Found A Cure' (1979) alongside production for **Diana Ross** (*The Boss*) and **Gladys Knight** (*The Touch*). In 1984 'Solid' became an international hit.

ASIA

A SUPERGROUP CONSISTING OF WELL-KNOWN MUSICIANS FROM BRITISH ART-ROCK BANDS. ASIA WAS FORMED IN 1981 by John Wetton (b. 1949; vocals), Geoff Downes (keyboards), Steve Howe (b. 1947; guitar) and Carl Palmer (b. 1950; drums/percussion). Wetton had recently left the progressive band UK; Howe and Downes had just left **Yes** and Palmer had left **Emerson, Lake And Palmer**. The group's debut album stayed at US number 1 for nine weeks, 'Heat Of The Moment' reached the US Top 5 and 'Only Time Will Tell' was moderately successful.

The group released *Alpha*, it reached the US Top 10, as did 'Don't Cry', but its sales failed to match those of the debut. Wetton left the group, replaced by Greg Lake (b. 1948), another ELP alumnus; in 1985, he rejoined the band for *Astra*, however, its comparatively low chart position precipitated the band's dissolution. By early 1990, Howe had left to join a regenerated Yes, with Pat Thrall, an ex-**Pat Travers Band** member, moving in to take his place. *Then And Now* was a mixture of six earlier recordings and four new songs.

ASLEEP AT THE WHEEL

RAY BENSON (b. 1951; GUITAR/VOCALS), CHRISTINE O'CONNELL (b. 1953; VOCALS), LUCKY OCEANS (b. REUBEN Gosfield, 1951; steel guitar), Floyd Domino (piano) and Leroy Preston (rhythm guitar, drums) made up this protean western swing-styled unit. Initially based in West Virginia, they moved to Texas, and a more receptive audience, in the wake of their debut album. They had a US Top 10 single with 'The Letter That Johnny Walker Read' (1973) and won a Grammy for their version of Count Basie's 'One O'Clock Jump'. Despite undoubted live appeal and an appearance in the rock film *Roadie*, more widespread success eluded them. The Bob Wills tribute album featured several guest artists, including **Willie Nelson**, Chet Atkins, Merle Haggard and **Dolly Parton**.

ASSOCIATES

SCOTTISH VOCALIST BILLY MACKENZIE (b. 1957, d. 1997) AND ALAN RANKINE FORMED THE ASSOCIATES IN 1979. AFTER A minor label recording of **David Bowie**'s 'Boys Keep Swinging', they were signed to Fiction Records where they released the critically acclaimed *The Affectionate Punch*. They formed their own Associates label (distributed by Sore/WEA) and enjoyed a Top 10 chart breakthrough with 'Party Fears Two'. Further Top 30 hits followed with 'Club Country' and '18 Carat Love Affair'/'Love Hangover', but MacKenzie became involved in other projects and split with Rankine in 1983.

In 1984, MacKenzie reconvened the Associates, releasing several very low chart entries, *Perhaps*, a relatively poor-selling album and *The Glamour Chase* (unreleased) –MacKenzie was dropped from WEA in 1988. In 1990, he returned with *Wild And Lonely*, which was stylistically similar to the earlier

work. The disappointing follow-up, *Outernational*, was released under MacKenzie's own name, after which he retired from the music business for several years. In 1996, he signed to Nude and demoed new material written in collaboration with Steve Aungle. Following a bout of depression after his mother's death, MacKenzie was found dead at his parents' home in January 1997. The posthumously released *Beyond The Sun* contained the new recordings he was working on at the time of his death.

ASSOCIATION

POP/PSYCHEDELIC HARMONY GROUP OF THE MID-60S, COMPRISING GARY ALEXANDER (LEAD VOCALS), RUSS Giguere (guitar/vocals), Brian Coles (d. 1972; bass/vocals), Jim Yester (guitar/vocals), Ted Bluechel (drums) and Terry Kirkham (keyboards). After 'Babe I'm Gonna Leave You' and a folk rock version of **Bob Dylan**'s 'One Two Many Mornings', they found success with Tandyn Almer's 'Along Comes Mary' (US Top 10). The Association's image was ambiguous: genuinely psychedelic in spirit, they also sang ballads, appeared in smart suits and largely wrote their own material. Terry Kirkham gave them their first number 1 with 'Cherish', while their debut album, *And Then ... Along Comes*, displayed their harmonic talent. Another US chart-topper, 'Windy', was followed by a number 2 with 'Never My Love'. Their smooth balladeering was consistently balanced by aberrations such as the genuinely weird track 'Pandora's Golden Heebie Jeebies' on *Renaissance*.

However the group failed to attract a devoted following and by the late 70s their sales were dwindling. Gary Alexander left briefly for a trip to India and returned with a new name, 'Jules', while their long-standing producer Jerry Yester, replaced Zal Yanovsky in the **Lovin' Spoonful**. The Association continued to release accomplished singles such as 'Time For Living', but soon lost ground. A soundtrack for the movie *Goodbye Columbus* (1969) and a reasonable 'comeback' album, *Waterbeds In Trinidad* (1972), brought new hope, but the death of founder-member Brian Coles from drug abuse accelerated their eventual move on to the revivalist circuit.

ASTLEY, RICK

IN 1987, ASTLEY (b. 1966) RECORDED 'LEARNING TO LIVE' WITH OCHI BROWN AND WAS PART OF RICK AND LISA who released 'When You Gonna'. He also sang on the UK number 1 'Let It Be' by Ferry Aid.

His solo 'Never Gonna Give You Up' became the biggest UK single of 1987 and his debut album, *Whenever You Need Somebody*, also reached UK number 1, selling over a million copies. When Astley was launched in the USA in 1988, he was an instant success, topping the US charts with his first two singles. Under the wing of **Stock, Aitken And Waterman**, Astley achieved seven UK and four US Top 10 singles.

Astley eventually left the winning production and writing team. After a lengthy break, he resurfaced in 1991 with *Free* which included guest appearances from **Elton John** and Mark King (**Level 42**). 'Cry For Help', which he had co-written and produced, put him back into the Top 10 on both sides of the Atlantic.

ASWAD

REGGAE GROUP FORMED IN LONDON, ENGLAND, IN 1975, FEATURING GUYANAN-BORN BRINSLEY FORDE (b. 1952; guitar/vocals), George Oban (bass), Angus Gaye (b. 1959; drums) and Jamaican-born Donald Griffiths (b. 1954; vocals). Additional musicians included Vin Gordon, Courtney Hemmings, Bongo Levi, Karl Pitterson and Mike Rose. Taking their name from the Arabic word for black, they attempted a fusion of Rastafari with social issues more pertinent to London. *Aswad*, which highlighted the plight of the immigrant Jamaican, was well received. A more ethnic approach was evident on the superior follow-up, *Hulet*. The departure of Oban, who was replaced by Tony 'Gad' Robinson did little to diminish their fortunes. Forde appeared in the film *Babylon*, with Aswad's 'Warrior Charge' on its soundtrack.

Live And Direct (1982) was recorded at London's Notting Hill Carnival. In 1984, they charted with 'Chasing The Breeze' and a cover of Toots Hibbert's '54-46 (Was My Number)'. *Distant Thunder* was the launching pad for a significant stylistic overhaul and the shift to lightweight funk and soul made them national chart stars. The album bore a 1988 UK number 1 in 'Don't Turn Around' which, coupled with their riveting live act, made them major stars; **Shabba Ranks** appeared on *Too Wicked* (1990). *Big Up* (1997) received a more muted reception.

ASYLUM CHOIR

US DUO FEATURING **LEON RUSSELL** (b. 1942; PIANO/VOCALS) AND MARC BENNO (b. 1947; GUITAR). ALTHOUGH Benno was relatively unknown, Russell was an established session figure in Los Angeles. *Look Inside The Asylum Choir* received enthusiastic reviews, but its marriage of psychedelia and white R&B was not a commercial success and their label refused the duo's follow-up album. Russell later purchased the master tape and released the set on his own label, Shelter Records, in the wake of his fame as a solo act. Benno also embarked on an independent career and played on the **Doors**' *LA Woman*.

Collaborators
Holland/Dozier/Holland ➧ p.183
Marvin Gaye ➧ p.159
Diana Ross ➧ p.283
Gladys Knight ➧ p.209
Connections
Shirelles ➧ p.295
Ray Charles ➧ p.88
Influences
Motown ➧ p.240
Further References
Film: *Body Rock* (1984)

ASIA
Albums
Asia (Geffen 1982)★★★
➧ p.351 for full listings
Connections
Yes ➧ p.346
Emerson, Lake and Palmer ➧ p.135

ASLEEP AT THE WHEEL
Albums
Texas Gold (Capitol 1975)★★★★
➧ p.351 for full listings
Collaborators
Willie Nelson ➧ p.245

ASSOCIATES
Albums
Sulk (Sire 1982)★★★
➧ p.351 for full listings
Connections
David Bowie ➧ p.64

ASSOCIATION
Albums
And Then ... Along Comes (Valiant 1966)★★★★
➧ p.351 for full listings
Connections
Bob Dylan ➧ p.128
Lovin' Spoonful ➧ p.219

ASTLEY, RICK
Albums
Free (RCA 1991)★★★
➧ p.351 for full listings
Collaborators
Elton John ➧ p.200
Level 42 ➧ p.215

ASWAD
Albums
Live And Direct (Mango/Island 1983)★★★
➧ p.351 for full listings
Collaborators
Shabba Ranks ➧ p.273

ASYLUM CHOIR
Albums
Asylum Choir II (1971)★★
➧ p.351 for full listings
Collaborators
Doors ➧ p.123

ATLANTA RHYTHM SECTION
Albums
A Rock And Roll Alternative (Polydor 1977)★★★★
p.351 for full listings
Connections
Roy Orbison p.252
Classics IV p.93

ATOMIC ROOSTER
Albums
In Hearing Of (Pegasus 1971)★★★
p.351 for full listings

Collaborators
Pink Floyd p.261
Connections
Emerson, Lake and Palmer p.135
Chris Farlowe p.143
Dexys Midnight Runners p.117

AU PAIRS
Albums
Playing With A Different Sex (Human 1981)★★★
p.351 for full listings

AUDIENCE
Albums
Friends Friends Friends (Charisma 1970)★★★
p.351 for full listings
Collaborators
Faces p.141

AUSTIN, PATTI
Albums
Every Home Should Have One (Qwest 1981)★★★★
p.351 for full listings
Collaborators
Paul Simon p.296
Billy Joel p.199
Joe Cocker p.95
Roberta Flack p.146
Steely Dan p.308
Blues Brothers p.57
Connections
Quincy Jones p.201
Harry Belafonte
Further References
Film: *Tucker* (1988)

AUTEURS
Albums
New Wave (Hut 1993)★★★★
p.351 for full listings
Connections
Pixies p.261
Nirvana p.248

AVERAGE WHITE BAND
Albums
AWB (Atlantic 1974)★★★★
p.351 for full listings

ATLANTA RHYTHM SECTION

THE CREAM OF THE STUDIO MUSICIANS FROM GEORGIA, USA, THE ATLANTA RHYTHM SECTION CAME TOGETHER in 1970 after working at a **Roy Orbison** recording session. The group – Dean Daughtry (b. 1946; keyboards; ex-**Classics IV**), Robert Nix (drums), J.R. Cobb (b. 1944; guitar; ex-), vocalist Rodney Justo (replaced after the first album by Ronnie Hammond), Barry Bailey (b. 1948; guitar) and Paul Goddard (b. 1945; bass) – recorded two albums for Decca in 1972, neither of which made an impact, before signing to Polydor in 1974.

Their first Polydor album, *Third Annual Pipe Dream*, only reached US number 74 and the next two albums fared worse, but in 1977, 'So Into You' reached the US Top 10, as did its album, *A Rock And Roll Alternative*. Their follow-up, *Champagne Jam*, went to the Top 10 in 1978, together with 'Imaginary Lover', after which Nix left, replaced by Roy Yeager (b. 1946). The group's last hit on Polydor was a 1979 remake of 'Spooky'. A switch to Columbia in 1981 gave the group one last chart album, *Quinella*, and a US Top 30 single, 'Alien', after which they faded from the national scene, although continuing to record.

ATOMIC ROOSTER

FORMED IN 1969 AT THE HEIGHT OF THE UK PROGRESSIVE ROCK BOOM, THE ORIGINAL ROOSTER LINE-UP comprised Vincent Crane (b. 1945, d. 1989; organ; ex-Crazy World Of Arthur Brown), Nick Graham (bass) and Carl Palmer (b. 1950; drums; ex-Crazy World Of Arthur Brown). After only one album, however, the unit fragmented with Graham joining Skin Alley and Palmer founding **Emerson, Lake And Palmer**. Crane and new members John Cann (guitar/vocals) and Paul Hammond (drums) – both ex-Andromeda – released *Death Walks Behind You*, followed in 1971 by 'Tomorrow Night' and 'The Devil's Answer'. With Pete French (from Cactus) the trio recorded *In Hearing Of*, then split. Cann and Hammond joined Bullet, then Hardstuff; French formed Leafhound. Crane recruited new members, guitarist Steve Bolton, bassist Bill Smith, drummer Rick Parnell and **Chris Farlowe**. A shift towards blue-eyed soul won few new fans, and Crane finally dissolved the band in 1974.

The final Atomic Rooster studio album included guest stints from Dave Gilmour (**Pink Floyd**), Bernie Torme (Gillan) and John Mazarolli (guitars) in place of Cann. In 1983, Crane accepted an invitation to record and tour with **Dexys Midnight Runners** appearing on their *Don't Stand Me Down*. Tragically he committed suicide in 1989.

AU PAIRS

UK BAND THE AU PAIRS CONSISTED OF LESLEY WOODS (GUITAR/LEAD VOCALS), PAUL FOAD (LEAD GUITAR), JANE Munro (bass) and Pete Hammond (drums). They began their career in 1980 with the *You* EP followed by *Playing With A Different Sex* (1981). Their singles covered a variety of subjects, from the controversial (such as 'Armagh') to the frankly personal (such as 'Sex Without Stress'). They continued to record until 1983 when they split after Woods failed to show for a concert in Belgium.

Munro had left six months prior to the band's eventual dissolution. Woods settled in Europe before returning to London to form all-female band the Darlings. Foad formed End Of Chat with Hammond and trumpeter Graham Hamilton.

AUDIENCE

THIS LONDON-BASED ACT – HOWARD WERTH (GUITAR/VOCALS), KEITH GEMMELL (SAXOPHONE), TREVOR Williams (bass/vocals) and Tony Connor (drums) – made its recording debut in 1969 with art-rock Audience. The quartet was then signed by the fledgling Charisma Records, where *Friends Friends Friends* and *House On The Hill* confirmed their quirky, quintessentially English style of rock. A US tour supporting the **Faces** followed, but internal friction resulted in Gemmell's departure. Patrick Neubergh (saxophone) and Nick Judd (keyboards) joined for *Lunch*, but the group was dissolved following its release.

AUSTIN, PATTI

AT THE AGE OF NINE, AUSTIN (b. 1948) TRAVELLED TO EUROPE WITH **QUINCY JONES**; AT 16, SHE TOURED WITH Harry Belafonte and, at 17, she began recording. In 1969, 'Family Tree' was an R&B hit. She worked on television jingles and during the 70s she was one of New York's busiest session singers, working with **Paul Simon**, **Billy Joel**, **Frankie Valli**, **Joe Cocker**, **George Benson** and **Roberta Flack** among others. Her solo albums included self-penned, jazz-influenced material. Her long-standing association with Quincy Jones continued and his composition 'The Dude' featured her lead vocal, winning a Grammy in 1982. Austin had another hit with the title track of *Every Home Should Have One*, while 'Razzamatazz' (with Quincy Jones) was a UK Top 20 hit in 1981. Her duet with **James Ingram**, 'Baby Come To Me', became the theme music for the television soap opera *General Hospital* and reached US number 1 and UK number 11 in 1983. Another Austin/Ingram duet, 'How Do You Keep The Music Playing?', from the film *Best Friends*, was nominated for an Oscar. She also sang themes for the films *Two Of A Kind* (1984) and *Shirley Valentine* (1988), and had an R&B hit with 'Gimme Gimme'. In 1992, Austin was a guest vocalist on an album of George Gershwin songs by the Hollywood Bowl Orchestra.

AUTEURS

TRUCULENT UK INDIE STARS THE AUTEURS WERE SPEARHEADED BY LUKE HAINES (b. 1967; VOCALS/GUITAR; ex-Servants), alongside Glenn Collins (b. 1968; drums; ex-Dog Unit and Vort Pylon) and Alice Readman (b. 1967; bass; ex-Servants). Cellist James Banbury joined in 1993.

In 1982, they released 'Showgirl' notable for Haines's impressive use of language. Their debut album was lavishly praised and they missed out on the 1993 Mercury Prize award by just one vote. *Now I'm A Cowboy* continued the pattern of press eulogy and public indecisiveness, on a set soaked with Haines's class obsessions. *After Murder Park* was produced by Steve Albini, whose previous credits included **Nirvana**'s *In Utero* and the **Pixies**' *Surfer Rosa*. Haines then dissolved the Auteurs and released an uneven album as Baader-Meinhof.

AVERAGE WHITE BAND

THIS SCOTTISH BEAT GROUP FEATURED ALAN GORRIE (b. 1946; BASS/VOCALS), MIKE ROSEN (TRUMPET/GUITAR; EX-Eclection), replaced by Hamish Stuart (b. 1949; guitar/vocals), Owen 'Onnie' McIntyre (b. 1945; guitar), Malcolm 'Mollie' Duncan (b. 1945; saxophone), Roger Ball (b. 1944; saxophone/keyboards) and Robbie McIntosh (b. 1950, d. 1974; drums). Although their 1973 debut, *Show Your Hand*, showed promise, it was not until the band was signed to Atlantic that its true potential blossomed. *AWB* was a superb collection, the highlights included a spellbinding version of the **Isley Brothers**' 'Work To Do', and the rhythmic original instrumental 'Pick Up The Pieces' (US number 1/UK Top 10). AWB topped the US album charts but this euphoric period was halted abruptly in 1974 by the tragic death of Robbie McIntosh following an accidental heroin overdose. He was replaced by Steve Ferrone (b. 1950; ex-Bloodstone).

The group secured further success with 'Cut The Cake', but subsequent releases proved more formulaic. A pairing with singer **Ben E. King** (*Benny And Us*), 'Walk On By' and 'Let's Go Round Again', were more inventive. The Average White Band retired during much of the 80s as the members pursued individual projects. Hamish Stuart later surfaced in **Paul McCartney**'s *Flowers In The Dirt* touring group, and was unavailable when the band re-formed in 1989. The resulting *After Shock* featured Gorrie, Ball and McIntyre alongside Alex Ligertwood (ex-**Santana**). In 1997, Gorrie wrote for and performed with **Hall and Oates**.

AVONS

SISTERS-IN-LAW ENGLISH-BORN VALERIE (b. 1936) AND EIRE-BORN ELAINE MURTAGH (b. 1940) ORIGINALLY PERFORMED as the Avon Sisters. Producer Norrie Paramor signed them after hearing them at the 1958 BBC Radio Exhibition. They released 'Which Witch Doctor' with the Mudlarks followed by their debut solo release, a cover version of 'Jerri O' – both failed to chart. Jersey-born Ray Adams (b. 1938) was recruited and they changed their name to the Avons. The trio's first single was a cover version of Paul Evans's 'Seven Little Girls Sitting In The Back Seat' (1959), it was their only UK Top 20 chart entry. After three minor hits, they last charted with a cover version of 'Rubber Ball' in 1961. In 1962, a song they had written, 'Dance On', became an instrumental UK number 1 for the **Shadows** and reached the UK Top 20 in 1963 courtesy of Kathy Kirby. Despite further recordings, the Avons had no other hits.

AYERS, KEVIN

A FOUNDER MEMBER OF **SOFT MACHINE**, THIS TALENTED SINGER-SONGWRITER ABANDONED THE GROUP IN 1968. Ayers' (b. 1945) debut album, *Joy Of A Toy*, nonetheless bore a debt to his former colleagues, all of whom contributed to this innovative collection. In 1970, Ayers formed the Whole World, featuring saxophonist Lol Coxhill, guitarist **Mike Oldfield** and pianist/arranger David Bedford. *Shooting At The Moon*, a radical, experimental release, was a landmark in British progressive rock. Coxhill left the Whole World shortly afterwards and his departure precipitated their demise. Oldfield and Bedford contributed to *Whatevershebringswesing*, but Ayers never quite fulfilled his undoubted potential, despite moments of inspiration on *Bananamour*.

A high profile appearance at London's Rainbow Theatre resulted in *June 1 1974*, on which Ayers was joined by **John Cale**, **Nico** and **Brian Eno**. Unfortunately, later albums such as, *Sweet Deceiver*, *Yes We Have No Mañanas* and *Rainbow Takeaway* were lower profile. Despite this, Kevin Ayers retains a committed cult following.

AYNSLEY DUNBAR RETALIATION

FORMED IN 1967 BY EX-**JOHN MAYALL** DRUMMER AYNSLEY DUNBAR. Having recorded an informal version of **Buddy Guy**'s 'Stone Crazy' with an embryonic line-up of **Rod Stewart** (vocals), **Peter Green** (guitar) and Jack Bruce (bass), Dunbar created a permanent Retaliation around Jon Morshead (guitar; ex-**Johnny Kidd And The Pirates** and Shotgun Express), Keith Tillman (bass) and ex-**Alexis Korner** vocalist, Victor Brox. After 'Warning'/'Cobwebs', Tillman was replaced by Alex Dmochowski. *The Aynsley Dunbar Retaliation* had one side devoted to concise performances and the other to freer, instrumentally based workouts. *Dr. Dunbar's Prescription* offered strong original songs and several judicious cover versions. The group is best recalled for *Retaliation* aka *To Mum From Aynsley And The Boys*, produced by John Mayall and featuring Tommy Eyre (keyboards; ex-Grease Band). In 1969, Dunbar and Eyre left to form Aynsley Dunbar's Blue Whale. *Remains To Be Heard* was culled from remaining masters and newer recordings by the extant trio with singer Annette Brox; the Retaliation broke up soon after its completion.

AZTEC CAMERA

BRITISH POP OUTFIT FORMED IN 1980 BY SONGWRITER RODDY FRAME (b. 1964; VOCALS), WITH CAMPBELL OWENS (bass) and Dave Mulholland (drums). A regular turnover of band members ensued while Frame put together the songs that made up High Land, Hard Rain. Three singles in the UK independent charts had already made the band a critics' favourite, but this album of light acoustic songs was a memorable work, with 'Oblivious' reaching UK number 18. The **Mark Knopfler**-produced *Knife* broke no new ground, but, now signed to WEA, the band was pushed on to the world stage. Frame retreated back to Scotland following the tour, until *Love* (1987). This introverted yet over-produced album showed Frame's continuing development, with **Elvis Costello**-influenced song structures. Its comparative failure was rectified the following year with two further hits, 'How Men Are' and 'Somewhere In My Heart'. As a result, *Love* belatedly became a substantial success.

The band returned in 1990 with the acclaimed *Stray*. Frame then delivered *Dreamland* and *Frestonia*, strong collections of emotionally direct, honest songs that rivalled Aztec Camera's debut of a decade earlier. Aztec Camera disintegrated in 1996, as Frame became embroiled in his own writing for a solo project.

AZTEC TWO-STEP

FOLK-INFLUENCED US DUO, COMPRISING NEAL SHULMAN (GUITAR/VOCALS) AND REX FOWLER (GUITAR/ VOCALS) who debuted in 1972. Aztec Two-Step showcased their informal style and featured admirable support from several exemplary associates with Jerry Yester producing the set. Subsequent releases, while accomplished, featured a less interesting supporting cast and lacked the charm of that first set.

Collaborators
Ben E. King ➧ p.205
Connections
Duran Duran ➧ p.127
Paul McCartney ➧ p.229
Santana ➧ p.288
Hall and Oates ➧ p.172
Influences
Isley Brothers ➧ p.194

AVONS
Albums
The Avons (Columbia/Hull 1960)★★
➧ p.351 for full listings

AYERS, KEVIN
Albums
Shooting At The Moon (Harvest 1970)★★★★
➧ p.351 for full listings
Collaborators
John Cale ➧ p.78
Nico ➧ p.247
Brian Eno ➧ p.136

AYNSLEY DUNBAR RETALIATION
Albums
Dr. Dunbar's Prescription (Liberty 1968)★★★
➧ p.351 for full listings

AZTEC CAMERA
Albums
Frestonia (Warners 1995)★★★★
➧ p.351 for full listings

AZTEC TWO-STEP
Albums
See It Was Like This... (Flying Fish 1989)★★★
➧ p.351 for full listings

B. DEREK
Albums
Bullet From A Gun (Tuff Audio 1988)★★★
➜ p.351 for full listings
Connections
Overlord X
MC Duke
PoW

B-52'S
Albums
B-52's (Warners 1979)★★★★
Cosmic Thing (Reprise 1989)★★★
➜ p.351 for full listings
Collaborators
Julee Cruise ➜ p.107
Connections
John Lennon ➜ p.214
Chic ➜ p.89

B. BUMBLE AND THE STINGERS
➜ p.351 for full listings
Influences
Kim Fowley
Rimsky-Korsakov
Tchaikovsky

BABES IN TOYLAND
Albums
Fontanelle (Reprise/WEA 1992)★★★★
Painkillers (Reprise/WEA 1994)★★★
Nemesisters (Reprise/WEA 1995)★★★★
➜ p.351 for full listings
Connections
Courtney Love ➜ p.182
Jennifer Finch ➜ p.211
Spanish Fly
Influences
Sister Sledge ➜ p.298
Eric Carmen ➜ p.82
Further References
Book: *Babes In Toyland: The Making And Selling Of A Rock And Roll Band*, Neal Karlen

BABYBIRD
Albums
Ugly Beautiful (Echo 1996)★★★
Dying Happy (Baby Bird 1997)★★
➜ p.351 for full listings

BABYFACE
Albums
For The Cool In You (Epic 1993)★★★
➜ p.351 for full listings

B., DEREK

AGED 15, DEREK BOWLAND (b. 1966) STARTED WORKING AS A DJ, TRAVELLING AROUND LONDON CLUBS. HE THEN worked for pirate radio stations before beginning his own WBLS station. In 1987 he became an A&R man for Music Of Life. Alongside Simon Harris he signed several of the most notable early UK hip hop groups, including Overlord X, MC Duke and Demon Boyz. He subsequently started to record his own material for the label. In New York, Derek met the DJ Mr Magic, who set him up with a licensing deal in the USA. His debut single, 'Rock The Beat', and the following, 'Get Down' made an early impact. He hit the UK charts in 1988 with 'Goodgroove' and was the only rapper on the Free Mandela bill at Wembley Stadium. Further minor hits came with 'Bad Young Brother' and 'We've Got The Juice'. He is currently a member of PoW.

B-52'S

THE QUIRKY B-52'S SONGS SHOW MANY INFLUENCES, INCLUDING 50S' ROCK 'N' roll, punk and commercial dance music. Formed in Georgia, USA, in 1976, the group took their name from the bouffant hairstyle worn by Kate Pierson (b. 1948; organ/vocals) and Cindy Wilson (b. 1957; guitar/vocals). The line-up was completed by Cindy's brother Ricky (b. 1953, d. 1985; guitar), Fred Schneider (b. 1951; keyboards/vocals) and Keith Strickland (b. 1953; drums). The lyrically bizarre but musically thunderous 'Rock Lobster' led to them being signed to Island Records in the UK. Their debut, *B-52's*, became a strong seller and established the band on the American campus circuit during the early 80s. 'Rock Lobster' was a belated US hit in 1980. Subsequent albums continued to defy categorization, their love of melodrama and pop culture running side by side. Tragically Ricky Wilson died of AIDS, but the band continued, reaching a commercial peak in 1989 with the powerful 'Love Shack', and its accompanying video. In 1992 the group parted company with Cindy Wilson and recorded *Good Stuff* with producer Don Was (Was (Not Was)) and Nile Rodgers (**Chic**). During a 1992 concert, actress Kim Basinger stood in for Wilson, as did **Julee Cruise** in 1993. The group achieved huge commercial success in 1994 with the theme song to *The Flintstones*.

B. BUMBLE AND THE STINGERS

US GROUP FORMED BY POP SVENGALI KIM FOWLEY AT RENDEZVOUS RECORDS. THEIR 'BUMBLE BOOGIE' (1961), an adaptation of Rimsky-Korsakov's *Flight Of The Bumble Bee*, reached US number 21. 1962's 'Nut Rocker' only reached US number 23, but this propulsive instrumental, an irreverent reading of Tchaikovsky's *Nutcracker Suite*, soared to UK number 1 and, 10 years later, again reached the Top 20. The group – R.C. Gamble (b. 1940), Terry Anderson (b. 1941; guitar), Jimmy King (b. 1938; rhythm guitar) and Don Orr (b. 1939; drums) – completed a UK tour in 1962.

BABES IN TOYLAND

US HARDCORE ROCK TRIO FORMED IN 1987, COMPRISING KAT BJELLAND (b. KATHERINE BJELLAND, 1963; VOCALS/ guitar; ex-Sugar Baby Doll), Michelle Leon (bass) and Lori Barbero (b. 1960; drums/vocals). A debut album, produced by Jack Endino, was recorded live with overdubbed vocals. After signing to WEA, they recorded the mini-album *To Mother*. In 1992 Leon was replaced by Maureen Herman (b. 1966) and their next album *Fontanelle* received favourable reviews. When the group took a break in 1993, Lori Barbero formed her own label, Spanish Fly, while Kat worked with her husband Stuart Grey (of Lubricated Goat) on two projects, Crunt and KatSu. Babes In Toyland reconvened in time for the Lollapalooza tour; *Nemesisters* included memorable cover versions of **Sister Sledge**'s 'We Are Family' and **Eric Carmen**'s 'All By Myself' alongside original compositions such as 'Memory' and 'Scherezadian 22'. Herman was replaced by Danna Cochran in 1996.

BABYBIRD

BABYBIRD HAS BEEN BOTH MAN AND BAND. IN THE FIRST INCARNATION, STEPHEN JONES (b. 1962) recorded over 400 songs as four-track demos, going on to release several dozen of them across his self-released albums, between July 1995 and August 1996. The albums quickly acquired a cult following. In 1996, Jones signed to Chrysalis offshoot label Echo and assembled a live band for the first time, comprising Huw Chadbourne (b. 1963; keyboards), Robert Gregory (b. 1967; drums), John Pedder (b. 1962; bass) and Luke Scott (b. 1969; guitar), with whom he recorded *Ugly Beautiful*, a 'debut' received with mixed emotions by critics but lapped up by the public on the back of 'You're Gorgeous'. Jones proved himself an able performer and the band have retained their cult status as well as more commercial adulation.

BABYFACE

BABYFACE (b. KENNETH EDMONDS, 1959) HAS BEEN PERFORMING SINCE THE MID-70S, IN THE FUNK OUTFIT Manchild, although his achievements as a songwriter and producer throughout the late 80s and 90s, especially with L.A. Reid, sometimes overshadowed his solo efforts. However it was not until 1995, when his 'When Can I See You' won a Grammy, that he could claim the commercial success already heaped on his own protégés, such as **Boyz II Men**, **Bobby Brown** and **Toni Braxton**. Since the split with Reid, Babyface's main success has been as a producer and writer of film soundtracks, with *The Bodyguard* and *Waiting To Exhale* both going multi-platinum. In 1996 his solo album, *The Day*, included guest spots from **Stevie Wonder**, **Eric Clapton**, **LL Cool J**, **Mariah Carey** and Shalamar.

BABYLON ZOO

FORMED IN ENGLAND, 90S POP GROUP BABYLON ZOO WERE THE CREATION OF SINGER, WRITER AND PRODUCER JAS Mann (b. Jaswinder Mann, 1971). His first band, the Sandkings, enjoyed minor success in UK indie circles in the early 90s. Clive Black of Phonogram Records signed Babylon Zoo, then moved – with the band – to Warner Brothers Records in 1993. An album had been prepared and sleeves for 'Fire Guided Light' were printed, but Babylon Zoo's debut was put on hold again when Black moved to EMI Records in 1995. However, promotional copies of 'Spaceman' had already been distributed, and it was chosen to tie in with a new Levi's jean commercial. When released as a single in 1996, it entered the UK chart at number 1 – becoming the fastest-selling debut record in UK chart history. *The Boy With The X-Ray Eyes*, produced at Mann's New Atlantis Productions music/artwork/video centre, included new age tracts such as 'Is Your Soul For Sale?'.

BABYS

BRITISH ROCK GROUP COMPRISING JOHN WAITE (b. 1955; VOCALS/BASS), MIKE CORBY (b. 1955; GUITAR/ keyboards), Walter 'Wally' Stocker (b. 1954; guitar) and Tony Brock (b. 1954; drums; ex-Combustion and Strider). They were promoted as the most promising newcomers of 1976, but while *The Babys* offered a competent blend of pop and rock, it lacked an identifiable sound and image. Jonathan Cain replaced Corby following the release of *Head First* and the Babys achieved US success, including two Top 20 singles with 'Isn't It Time' and 'Every Time I Think Of You'. Ricky Phillips joined as bass player for their final two albums.

BACCARA

SPANISH GIRL DUO WHO HAD A UK NUMBER 1 IN 1977 WITH THE DISCO-ORIENTATED 'YES SIR, I CAN BOOGIE'. Sung by Maria Mendiola and Mayte Mateus, it was written and produced by the German team of Frank Dostal (ex-Rattles) and Rolf Soja, backed by studio musicians. There was a UK Top 10 follow-up 'Sorry I'm A Lady', after which the group faded from view.

BACHARACH, BURT

COMPOSER AND ARRANGER BACHARACH (b. 1928) WAS RAISED IN NEW YORK. A JAZZ AFICIONADO, HE PLAYED in various ensembles during the 40s. After his discharge from the army, he worked as a pianist, arranger and conductor for a number of artists including Vic Damone, Steve Lawrence, Polly Bergen and the Ames Brothers. From 1956-58, Bacharach worked as musical director for Marlene Dietrich, and registered his first hit as a composer with the Five Blobs' 'The Blob' (written for a horror b-movie) with co-composer Mack David. A more fruitful partnership followed when Burt was introduced to Mack's brother, Hal David. In 1958, Bacharach/David's 'The Story Of My Life', was a US Top 20 hit for Marty Robbins. Greater success followed with Perry Como's 'Magic Moments' (UK number 1/US number 4). However, Bacharach and David did not work together exclusively until 1962. In the meantime, Bacharach found a new songwriting partner, Bob Hilliard, with whom he composed several recordings for the **Drifters**. During the early 60s, Bacharach and David wrote for many successful US and UK artists. Frankie Vaughan's 'Tower Of Strength' gave them their third UK number 1, as well as another US Top 10 hit, in a version by Gene McDaniels. **Gene Pitney** achieved two of his early hits with the duo's 'The Man Who Shot Liberty Valence' and 'Twenty Four Hours From Tulsa'.

From 1962 onwards, the formidable writing team steered **Dionne Warwick**'s career with an array of hit songs including 'Anyone Who Had A Heart', 'Walk On By', and 'Do You Know The Way To San Jose?'. They also maintained a quotient of UK number 1s, thanks to first-class cover versions by **Cilla Black** ('Anyone Who Had A Heart'), **Sandie Shaw** ('There's Always Something There To Remind Me'), the **Walker Brothers** ('Make It Easy On Yourself') and Herb Alpert ('This Guy's In Love With You'). Bacharach's melodies and the deftness of touch neatly complemented David's soul-tortured, romantic lyrics.

The duo were also popular as composers of film scores. *What's New Pussycat?* brought them an Oscar nomination and another hit when **Tom Jones** recorded the title song. Further hits and Academy Award nominations followed for the films *Alfie* and *Casino Royale* (which featured 'The Look Of Love'). Finally, in 1969, a double Oscar celebration was achieved with the score from *Butch Cassidy And The Sundance Kid* and its award-winning 'Raindrops Keep Falling On My Head'. The duo then completed their own musical, *Promises, Promises*, the enormously successful show enjoyed a lengthy Broadway run.

In 1970, Bacharach wrote the **Carpenters**' hit 'Close To You' yet, remarkably, he did not enjoy another chart success for over 10 years. An acrimonious split from Hal David, the break-up of Bacharach's marriage and the loss of his most consistent hitmaker, Dionne Warwick were all factors. Worse followed when his musical *Lost Horizon* was a commercial disaster.

It was not until 1981 that Bacharach's dry run ended, when he met a lyricist of genuine commercial fire – future wife Carole Bayer Sager. Their Oscar-winning 'Arthur's Theme' (co-written with Peter Allen and **Christopher Cross**) made the charts. The couple provided hits for **Roberta Flack** ('Making Love') and Neil Diamond ('Heartlight'). In 1986, Bacharach enjoyed two US number 1s, 'That's What Friends Are For' (an AIDS charity record by Warwick and 'Friends' – **Elton John**, **Gladys Knight** and **Stevie Wonder**) and 'On My Own' (**Patti Labelle** and **Michael McDonald**).

In the late 80s, Bacharach and Sager wrote film songs such as 'They Don't Make Them Like They Use To' (*Tough Guys*), 'Everchanging Time' (*Baby Boom*), and 'Love Is My Decision' (*Arthur 2: On The Rocks*), for which he also wrote the score. In 1989, US vocalist Sybil revived 'Don't Make Me Over', and a year later **Deacon Blue** went to number 2 with their *Four Bacharach And David Songs* EP. In 1992, when Bacharach and Sager separated, he and David finally reunited. Their songs included 'Sunny Weather Lover' for Dionne Warwick's new album. In 1994, a musical revue, *Back To Bacharach And David*, opened in New York, and in 1995, BBC Television transmitted a major film profile, *Burt Bacharach: ... This Is Now*, which was narrated by Dusty Springfield. Of late, leading figures in contemporary popular music – such as Jarvis Cocker of **Pulp**, Michael Stipe of **R.E.M.**, and **Paul Weller** – have all covered his songs.

BACHELORS

FORMED IN 1958 AS THE HARMONY CHORDS THEN AS THE HARMONICHORDS, THE GROUP FEATURED brothers Conleth (b. 1941) and Declan Cluskey (b. 1942) and John Stokes (b. Sean James Stokes, 1940). The Dublin-born trio initially worked as a mainstream folk act, all three playing harmonicas. In 1961, Decca's A&R head Dick Rowe signed them and suggested their new name. With the assistance of producer Shel Talmy, the group scored a UK Top 10 hit with a revival of the Lew Pollack/Erno Rapee song 'Charmaine' (1963). After three unsuccessful follow-ups they struck again with a string of easy listening pop hits including several revivals. In 1966, they revealed their former folk roots and surprisingly completely outmanoeuvred **Simon And Garfunkel** by taking 'The Sound Of Silence' to UK number 3.

In later years, the Bachelors achieved success on the cabaret circuit with a line-up that remained unchanged for 25 years, however, in 1984, John Stokes left after a dispute. After taking legal action he received compensation. His replacement was Peter Phipps.

Collaborators
L.A Reid
Stevie Wonder ➽ p.342
Eric Clapton ➽ p.92
Connections
Manchild
Further References
Video: Tender Lover (CBS 1990)

BABYLON ZOO
Albums
The Boy With The X-Ray Eyes (EMI 1996)★★
➽ p.351 for full listings

BABYS
Albums
The Babys (Chrysalis 1976)★★★
Head First (Chrysalis 1978)★★★
➽ p.351 for full listings
Connections
Spontaneous Combustion

BACCARA
Albums
Baccara (RCA 1978)★
➽ p.351 for full listings
Connections
Rattles

BACHARACH, BURT
Albums
Hit Maker — Burt Bacharach (London 1965)★★★
Casino Royale soundtrack (RCA 1967)★★★
Butch Cassidy And The Sundance Kid soundtrack (A&M 1970)★★★
➽ p.351 for full listings
Collaborators
Vic Damone
Steve Lawrence
Carpenters ➽ p. 82
Christopher Cross ➽ p.106
Deacon Blue ➽ p.112
Connections
Drifters ➽ p.126
Gene Pitney ➽ p.261
Dionne Warwick ➽ p. 334
Cilla Black ➽ p. 49
Walker Brothers ➽ p. 332
Tom Jones ➽ p. 201
Dusty Springfield ➽ p. 305
Pulp ➽ p. 269
Influences
Perry Como
Frankie Vaughan
Carole Bayer Sager

BACHELORS
Albums
The Bachelors (1963)★★★
Bachelors' Girls (Decca 1966)★★★
➽ p.351 for full listings
Connections
Harmony Chords
Influences
Lew Pollack
Dorothy Solomon
Further References
Film: *It's All Over Town* (1964)

BACHMAN-TURNER OVERDRIVE
Albums
Not Fragile (Mercury 1974)★★★★
➽ p.351 for full listings
Connections
Guess Who ➽ p.168
Further References
Book: *This Is My Song: The Authorized Biography*, Martin Melhuish

BAD BRAINS
Albums
I Against I (SST 1986)★★★
➽ p.351 for full listings
Collaborators
Madonna ➽ p.222
Connections
Faith No More ➽ p.142
Cars ➽ p.83

BAD COMPANY
Albums
Bad Company (Island 1974)★★★★
➽ p.351 for full listings
Connections
Free ➽ p.154
Mott The Hoople ➽ p. 241
Ted Nugent ➽ p. 249

BAD MANNERS
Albums
Gosh, It's Bad Manners (Magnet 1981)★★★★
➽ p.351 for full listings

BAD RELIGION
Albums
Suffer (Epitaph 1988)★★★★
➽ p.351 for full listings
Connections
Offspring ➽ p.251
Further References
Video: *Along the Way* (Epitaph 1993)

BADFINGER
Albums
No Dice (Apple 1970)★★★★
Straight Up (Apple 1972)★★★★
➽ p.351 for full listings
Collaborators
Nilsson ➽ p.247
Connections
Beatles ➽ p.38
Influences
Paul McCartney ➽ p.229
Further References
Book: *Without You: The Tragic Story of Badfinger*, Dan Matovina

BADOWSKI, HENRY
Albums
Life Is A Grand (A&M 1981)★★★
➽ p.351 for full listings
Connections
Chelsea ➽ p.88
Captain Sensible ➽ p.81
Damned ➽ p.110

BACHMAN-TURNER OVERDRIVE

CANADIAN HARD-ROCK GROUP FORMED BY RANDY BACHMAN (b. 1943; GUITAR/LEAD VOCALS; EX **GUESS Who**). In 1970, Bachman had recorded a solo album before forming Brave Belt with his brother Robbie (b. 1943; drums), C. F. 'Fred' Turner (b. 1943; bass/vocals) and Chad Allan. Brave Belt recorded two unsuccessful albums in 1971-72, after which Allan was replaced by another Bachman brother, Tim. In 1972 the new band took its new name and, in 1973, signed to Mercury. They released a self-titled debut album which made a minor impact in the USA and Canada; Tim Bachman then departed, replaced by Blair Thornton (b. 1950). After constant US touring, *Bachman-Turner Overdrive II* provided their breakthrough, reaching US number 4 and yielding the number 12 'Takin' Care Of Business'. *Not Fragile* (1974) topped the US album charts and provided the US number 1/UK number 2 'You Ain't Seen Nothing Yet'. *Four Wheel Drive* (1975) was the group's last Top 10 recording, although they continued to release singles and albums until the end of the 70s. Randy Bachman departed in 1977, replaced by Jim Clench, who appeared on Freeways. In 1978, the band officially changed its name to BTO but could not revive its earlier fortunes. In 1984, Randy Bachman, Tim Bachman and C. F. Turner regrouped and released a second self-titled album. The group continued touring into the 90s.

BAD BRAINS

BLACK AMERICAN HARDCORE PUNK AND DUB REGGAE OUTFIT FORMED IN 1978. THE LINE-UP FEATURED H. R. (b. Paul Hudson; vocals), his brother Earl Hudson (drums), Dr. Know (guitar) and Darryl Jennifer (bass). Little studio material remains from the band's early period, though 'Pay To Cum' and 'Big Takeover' are regarded as punk classics. They continued through the 80s, until H. R. went solo. In 1988, he was temporarily replaced by ex-**Faith No More** vocalist Chuck Moseley, while Mackie took over on drums – an unsuccessful move. In 1994, **Madonna** offered them a place on her Maverick label, with H. R. returning to the fold. *God Of Love*, produced by Ric Ocasek (ex-**Cars**), concentrated more on dub and rasta messages than hardcore. In 1995, H. R. left the band after assaulting fellow members; he was subsequently arrested and charged with a drugs offence.

BAD COMPANY

HEAVY ROCK GROUP FORMED IN THE UK IN 1973, COMPRISING PAUL Rodgers (b. 1949; vocals; ex-Free), Simon Kirke (b. 1949; vocals/drums; ex-**Free**), Mick Ralphs (b. 1944; vocals/guitar; ex-**Mott The Hoople**) and Boz Burrell (b. Raymond Burrell, 1946; bass guitar). Bad Company were akin to a blues-based supergroup; with strong vocals placed beside tough melody lines and hard riffing. Their debut album was well-received and a string of albums through the 70s brought them chart success in both their homeland and in the US. They achieved singles success with several powerful songs, notably 'Can't Get Enough Of Your Love' and 'Feel Like Makin' Love'.

Following almost a decade of extensive gigging and regular albums, the group split up in 1983. A new version of the group, with former **Ted Nugent** vocalist Brian Howe replacing Rodgers, came together for *Fame And Fortune*. The band's subsequent releases have been a pale shadow of their first two, with the late 80s/early 90s Bad Company revolving around Mick Ralphs and Simon Kirke. In 1994, Bad Company's legacy was remastered by G. M. and re-released.

BAD MANNERS

FORMED IN 1979 WHEN THE UK 2-TONE SKA REVIVAL WAS AT ITS PEAK, THE GROUP FEATURED BUSTER Bloodvessel (b. Douglas Trendle, 1958; lead vocals), Gus 'Hot Lips' Herman (trumpet), Chris Kane (saxophone), Andrew 'Marcus Absent' Marson (saxophone), Winston Bazoomies (harmonica), Brian 'Chew-it' Tuitti (drums), David Farren (bass), Martin Stewart (keyboards) and Louis 'Alphonzo' Cook (guitar). The group enjoyed a string of UK hits, commencing with the catchy 'Ne-Ne Na-Na Na-Na Nu-Nu' followed by 11 UK chart entries, including four Top 10 hits, 'Special Brew', 'Can Can', 'Walking In The Sunshine' and 'My Girl Lollipop'. The band dissolved in 1990, re-forming sporadically.

BAD RELIGION

HARDCORE BAND FORMED IN CALIFORNIA IN 1980. THE LINE-UP – GREG GRAFFIN (VOCALS), BRETT GUREWITZ (guitar), Jay Lishrout (drums) and Jay Bentley (bass) – debuted with the poorly produced *Bad Religion*, on Epitaph records (formed by Gurewitz). Pete Finestone took over as drummer in 1982. *How Could Hell Be Any Worse* created local and national interest, but *Into The Unknown* disillusioned fans when the emphasis shifted to slick keyboard textures. In 1984, Greg Hetson and Tim Gallegos took over guitar and bass, while Gurewitz took time out due to drink and drug problems. A comeback, *Back To The Known*, was better received and, in 1987, Gurewitz rejoined for a show while Hetson worked with former band Circle Jerks. Gurewitz retired in 1994 to look after the Epitaph label, which was enjoying success with **Offspring** and others. The line-up of the band in 1996 was Graffin, Hetson, Brian Baker (guitar), Bentley and Bobby Schayer (drums). *The Gray Race* was their major label debut.

BADFINGER

ORIGINALLY AN ALL-WELSH GROUP COMPRISING PETE HAM (b. 1947, d. 1975; VOCALS), MIKE GIBBINS (b. 1949; drums), David Jenkins (guitar) and Ron Griffiths (bass), using the name the Iveys. Influenced by the **Hollies**, they were vocally tight and very melodic. During 1967, they backed operatic pop singer David Garrick before trying their luck on the **Beatles**' label Apple. By this time, Jenkins had been replaced by Liverpudlian Tom Evans (b. 1947, d. 1983), who wrote their label debut, 'Maybe Tomorrow', produced by Tony Visconti. The single passed unnoticed, as did the UK follow-up, 'Walls Ice Cream', so the group reinvented themselves as Badfinger. Shortly afterwards, Griffiths was replaced by Joey Molland (b. 1948). The new line-up enjoyed an immediate transatlantic hit with **Paul McCartney**'s 'Come And Get It' and contributed to the film soundtrack of *The Magic Christian*. 'No Matter What' was a transatlantic Top 10 hit and by the beginning of the 70s, Badfinger were something of an Apple house band. They appeared on three solo Beatles recordings (*All Things Must Pass*, 'It Don't Come Easy' and *Imagine*) as well as appearing at **George Harrison**'s Bangladesh benefit concert.

In 1972, **Nilsson** enjoyed a transatlantic chart topper with the Ham/Evans ballad 'Without You', but subsequently the group failed to exploit their full potential. By the time of their final Apple recording, *Ass*, Molland was writing over half their songs, but he left soon after. Tragically, a year later, Pete Ham hanged himself, after a long period of personal and professional worries. Consequently, the band split. Nearly four years later, Molland and Evans re-formed the group, but still commercial success proved elusive and in 1983 Tom Evans committed suicide. Following the discovery of some home recorded tapes a final album was put together; it was issued in 1997.

BADOWSKI, HENRY

BADOWSKI JOINED PUNK BAND **CHELSEA** ON BASS, BUT IN EARLY 1978, AFTER ONLY A FEW MONTHS, HE ENLISTED as drummer for Wreckless Eric. He also sang and played keyboards with the short-lived King (a punk/psychedelic group that included **Captain Sensible**), played bass with the Doomed and played drums with Good Missionaries (created by Mark Perry from **Alternative TV**). In 1979, he started his solo career with 'Making Love With My Wife'. The b-side, 'Baby Sign Here With Me', was originally part of the King live set and utilized the talents of James Stevenson (bass, guitar; ex-Chelsea), and Alex Kolkowski (violin) and Dave Berk (drums) from the Johnny Moped Band. Badowski released two more singles, 'My Face' and 'Henry's In Love' followed by *Life Is A Grand*, a slice of psychedelia that signalled the end of his solo career.

BADU, ERYKAH

BADU (b. 1971) IS AN UNCOMPROMISING R&B PERFORMER. HER DEBUT ALBUM WAS largely self-written, and was co-produced with the Roots D'Angelo collaborator Bob Power and friends and colleagues from her days on the Memphis music scene. Before turning solo, Badu performed alongside **Free** in the group Erykah Free. The album, which fluctuated between warm jazz textures and hip-hop and soul rhythms, won critical praise.

BAEZ, JOAN

US BORN BAEZ'S (b. 1941) APPEARANCE AT THE 1959 NEWPORT FOLK FESTIVAL ESTABLISHED HER AS A VIBRANT interpreter of traditional material. Her first four albums featured American and British ballads, but as the civil rights campaign intensified, she became increasingly identified with the protest movement. Her reading of 'We Shall Overcome', first released on *Joan Baez In Concert/Part 2*, achieved anthem status; the album also featured **Bob Dylan**'s 'Don't Think Twice, It's All Right'. The duo subsequently toured together, becoming romantically involved, and over the years Baez interpreted many of Dylan's songs. Baez also covered work by contemporary writers including **Phil Ochs**, brother-in-law Richard Farina, **Tim Hardin** and **Donovan**, as well as composing her own material.

In the 60s, Baez founded the Institute for the Study Of Nonviolence; her commitment to peace resulted in jail on two occasions for participation in anti-war rallies. In 1968, Baez married David Harris, a peace activist who was later imprisoned for draft resistance. They divorced in 1972.

Although her version of the **Band**'s 'The Night They Drove Old Dixie Down' was a hit in 1971, Baez found it hard to maintain a consistent commercial profile. Her devotion to politics continued and *Where Are You Now My Son*, included recordings made in North Vietnam. In 1979, she founded Humanitas International, a rapid-response human rights group that was instrumental in rescuing the Boat People. She has received numerous awards and honorary doctorates for her work.

Diamonds And Rust, brought further musical success and the title track, the story of her relationship with Dylan, presaged their reunion, in the legendary Rolling Thunder Revue. That, in turn, inspired her one entirely self-penned album, *Gulf Winds*. On *Speaking Of Dreams*, which celebrated 30 years of performing, she duetted with **Paul Simon**, **Jackson Browne** and the **Gipsy Kings**.

BAKER, ANITA

US SOUL SINGER ANITA BAKER (b. 1957) WAS THE GRAND-DAUGHTER OF A MINISTER WHO GREW UP WITH church and gospel music. After vocal duties with local bands she joined the semi-professional Chapter 8 in 1979 and sang on 'I Just Wanna Be Your Girl'. *The Songstress* brought her to wider notice, after which she signed to Elektra Records. Baker, with Chapter 8 colleague Michael Powell, partly funded and executively produced her second album, *Rapture*. A mature and emotional album, it won R&B awards for 'Sweet Love', 'Caught Up In The Rapture' and 'Giving You The Best That I Got'. In 1987, Baker appeared on the Winans' 'Ain't No Need To Worry' and in 1990 duetted with Howard Hewlett (ex-Shalamar). She wrote nearly all of *Compositions* which featured Greg Phillinganes (keyboards), Steve Ferrone (drums; ex-**Average White Band**), Ricky Lawson (drums) and Nathan East (bass). 1994 heralded the disappointing *Rhythm Of Love*.

BAKER, GINGER

THIS BRILLIANTLY ERRATIC UK DRUMMER WAS ALREADY AN EXPERIENCED MUSICIAN WHEN HE FORMED **CREAM** WITH **Eric Clapton** and **Jack Bruce** in 1967. Baker (b. Peter Baker, 1939) had drummed with trad-jazz bands, working with Terry Lightfoot, Acker Bilk, **Alexis Korner**'s Blues Incorporated and the Graham Bond Organization. After Cream, Baker joined **Steve Winwood**, Rick Grech and Clapton in **Blind Faith**, followed by the ambitious Airforce. Baker then left Britain to live in Nigeria, where he cultivated an interest in African music and built his own recording studio (**Paul McCartney**'s *Band On The Run* was recorded there). He formed Nigerian band, Salt, and recorded with Fela Ransome-Kuti.

In 1973, Baker returned to Britain and formed the Baker Gurvitz Army. His solo album *11 Sides Of Baker* was justifiably panned in 1977, but he returned with Energy in 1979, briefly joined **Atomic Rooster**, **Hawkwind** and later formed Ginger Baker's Nutters. In 1986, he played on PiL's UK Top 20 hit 'Rise'. In 1994, he joined Jack Bruce and **Gary Moore** and, as **BBM**, they released an accomplished and satisfying album. Baker has since returned to jazz, recording with Bill Frisell and Charlie Haden.

BADU, ERYKAH

Albums
Baduizm (Kedar/Universal 1997)★★★★
➧ p.351 for full listings

Connections
Roots
Free ➧ p. 154

BAEZ, JOAN

Albums
Farewell Angelina (Vanguard 1965)★★★★
The Night They Drove Old Dixie Down (Vanguard 1979)★★★★
➧ p.351 for full listings

Collaborators
Bob Dylan ➧ p.128
Phil Ochs ➧ p.251
Tim Hardin ➧ p.174
Donovan ➧ p.123
Band ➧p.31
Paul Simon ➧ p.296
Jackson Browne ➧ p.71
Gipsy Kings ➧ p.159

Connections
Institute for the Study Of Nonviolence
Humanitas International

Influences
1959 Newport Folk Festival

Further References
Book: *Daybreak: An Intimate Journey*, Joan Baez

BAKER, ANITA

Albums
Rapture (Elektra 1986)★★★★
➧ p.351 for full listings

Collaborators
Shalamar
Average White Band ➧ p.25

Further References
Book: *Rapture*, Anita Baker (Columbia Pictures 1987)
Video: *Sweet Love* (WEA Music Video 1989)

BAKER, GINGER

Albums
Falling Off The Roof (Atlantic 1996)★★★★
➧ p.351 for full listings

Collaborators
Acker Bilk

Connections
Cream ➧ p.103
Blues Incorporated
Graham Bond Organisation
Blind Faith ➧ p.53
Atomic Rooster ➧ p. 24
Hawkwind ➧ p. 177
BBM ➧ p.35

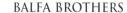

BAKER, LAVERN
Albums
LaVern Baker (Atlantic 1957)★★★★
Rock And Roll With LaVern (Atlantic 1957)★★★★
Blues Ballads (Atlantic 1959)★★★★
➽ p.351 for full listings
Collaborators
Jackie Wilson ➽ p.340

BALAAM AND THE ANGEL
Albums
The Greatest Story Ever Told (Virgin 1986)★★★
Days of Madness (Virgin 1989)★★★
➽ p.351 for full listings
Collaborators
Cult ➽ p.107
Influences
Doors ➽ p.123

BALDRY, LONG JOHN
Albums
Long John's Blues (United Artists 1965)★★★
Lookin' At Long John (United Artists 1965)★★★
Right To Sing The Blues (Stony Plain 1997)★★★
➽ p.351 for full listings
Collaborators
Elton John ➽ p.200
Connections
Hoochie Coochie Men

BALFA BROTHERS
Albums
Balfa Brothers Play Traditional Cajun Music (Swallow 1965)★★★★
The Cajuns (Sonet 1972)★★★
➽ p.351 for full listings
Connections
Balfa Toujours

BAKER, LAVERN

US SINGER BAKER (b. DELORES WILLIAMS, 1929, d. 1997) WAS DISCOVERED IN 1947 IN A CHICAGO NIGHTCLUB, by bandleader Fletcher Henderson. Although still a teenager she won a contract with the influential OKeh Records, later securing a contract with Atlantic. 'Tweedle Dee' reached both the US R&B and pop charts in 1955. It sold in excess of one million copies, as did 'Jim Dandy' in 1957. In 1959, she enjoyed a number 6 pop hit with 'I Cried A Tear' and throughout the decade remained one of black music's leading performers. Although eclipsed by newer acts during the 60s, she enjoyed success with 'Saved' (**Leiber And Stoller**), and 'See See Rider'. Baker's final chart entry came with 'Think Twice', a 1966 duet with **Jackie Wilson**.

While entertaining US troops in Vietnam, she became ill, and went to the Philippines to recuperate. She stayed there for 22 years, reviving her career at New York's Village Gate club in 1991. She was elected to the US Rock And Roll Hall Of Fame and starred in the Broadway musical *Black And Blue* in the early 90s. Sadly ill health made her final years miserable.

BALAAM AND THE ANGEL

THIS UK ROCK BAND INCLUDED BOTH POST-PUNK GOTHIC AND 60S ELEMENTS. ORIGINALLY FEATURING THE Morris brothers, Jim (b. 1960; guitar/recorder/keyboards), Mark (b. 1963; lead vocals/bass) and Des (b.1964; drums), they began their career playing working men's clubs as a children's cabaret act.

Balaam And The Angel supported the **Cult** on three successive tours before founding Chapter 22 Records, along with manager Craig Jennings. Their Chapter 22 debut, 'World Of Light', appeared in 1984, although 'Day And Night' was their most impressive release from this period. Their debut album *The Greatest Story Ever Told* was apparently inspired by the **Doors**. A new guitarist, Ian McKean, entered for *Live Free Or Die*. In 1991, they became Balaam, and released the mini-album, *No More Innocence*.

BALDRY, LONG JOHN

BEGINNING HIS CAREER PLAYING FOLK AND JAZZ IN THE LATE 50S, BALDRY (b.1941) TOURED WITH **Ramblin' Jack Elliott** before moving into R&B. After a spell with the Blues Incorporated, he joined Cyril Davies' R&B All Stars, then fronted the Hoochie Coochie Men, which also included **Rod Stewart**. Baldry and Stewart also joined forces in Steam Packet, featuring Brian Auger and Julie Driscoll. After a brief period with Bluesology (including a young **Elton John**), Baldry went solo to record pop taking 'Let The Heartaches Begin', a despairing ballad, to UK number 1 in 1967. His chart career continued with the Olympic Games theme, 'Mexico', which also made the Top 20. By the end of the 60s, the hits ceased and another change of direction was ahead: furs and a beard replaced suits and neat haircuts, as Baldry attempted to establish himself with a new audience. With production assistance from Rod Stewart and Elton John, he recorded *It Ain't Easy*, but it failed to sell. After a troubled few years in the USA he emigrated to Canada, where he performed on the club circuit. A new album was released in 1993 titled *It Still Ain't Easy*.

BALFA BROTHERS

THE BALFA BROTHERS GREW UP IN ABJECT POVERTY IN LOUISIANA, USA. THEIR DISTINCTIVE CAJUN-STYLE music offered a means of escape and relief and in the mid-40s, Will (b. *c*. 1920, d. 1979; fiddle), Harry (b. 1931; accordion) and Dewey (b. 1927, d. 1992; fiddle/harmonica/accordion/guitar) began to play locally. During the 50s Dewey frequently played and recorded with Nathan Abshire. He also appeared at the Newport Folk Festival in 1964, playing with Gladius Thibodeaux (accordion) and Louis Lejeune (fiddle). In 1967, Dewey was joined by Will, Rodney (b. 1934, d. 1979; guitar/harmonica/vocals), daughter Nelda and local farmer Hadley Fontenot (accordion) and the unit toured the USA and Europe as the Balfa Brothers. Their recording of 'Drunkard's Sorrow Waltz' was a bestselling Cajun single. They played for, and appeared in, the 1972 film *Spend It All*. Dewey also formed his nightclub orchestra. In the mid-70s, they recorded with Nathan Abshire and appeared in a documentary on Cajuns. In 1979, Will and Rodney were tragically killed in a car accident. Dewey continued to perform and record as the Balfa Brothers with, among others, Tony, his daughter Christine, Ally Young (accordion), Dick Richard, Mark Savoy (b. 1940; accordion), Robert Jardell (accordion) and Peter Schwartz (bass/fiddle/piano). Dewey remained active in music until his death. Christine and Nelda, continued the family tradition by playing and recording with other Cajun musicians – including Mike Chapman, Dick Powell and Kevin Wimmer – as Balfa Toujours.

BALIN, MARTY

A PAINTER, SCULPTOR AND DANCER, BALIN (b. MARTYN JEREL BUCHWALD, 1943) BEGAN HIS RECORDING CAREER in the early 60s. Two Balin singles recorded for the Challenge label invoked the saccharine pop of the era, whereas work with the Town Criers and the Gateway Singers was reminiscent of the New Christy Minstrels. Inspired by the **Byrds**' 'Mr. Tambourine Man', Balin founded **Jefferson Airplane** in 1965. Their first three albums owed much to his romanticism, compositions and voice but by the time of *Volunteers* Balin's role had been greatly reduced and he left in 1971.

Balin then produced for Grootna, several members of which joined him for *Bodacious D. F.*. Balin rejoined his former colleagues (now **Jefferson Starship**) in 1975. His return coincided with Starship's most successful period, which included a US number 1, the Balin-penned 'Miracles'. In 1979, he left again and, having completed the soundtrack to *Rock Justice*, went solo. 'Hearts' reached the US Top 10 and 'Atlanta Lady (Something About Your Love)' reached the Top 30. In 1986, he joined Airplane's Paul Kantner and Jack Casady in the KBC Band. The original Airplane reformed in 1989, and again, with Kantner and Casady, in 1994.

BALLARD, RUSS

BALLARD (b. 1945) STARTED HIS CAREER WITH THE DAYBREAKERS, THE BACKING GROUP TO BUSTER MEAKLE, future mainstay of Unit Four Plus Two. Daybreaker drummer Robert Henrit and Ballard joined **Adam Faith**'s Roulettes; Ballard played keyboards before transferring to guitar. The Roulettes recorded a handful of Ballard numbers, including 'Help Me Help Myself' (1967). While part of Unit Four Plus Two, Ballard co-wrote their final single, '3.30' (1969), before he and Henrit joined **Argent**. Ballard's compositions complemented those of Rod Argent and his 'God Gave Rock And Roll To You' was a hit. **Three Dog Night** reached the US Top 10 with a version of Ballard's 'Liar' in 1972.

Ballard remained with Argent for a further two years before going solo. Neither *Russ Ballard* nor *Winning* attracted sufficient attention, so he concentrated on session work and writing material for acts including

America, **Hot Chocolate** and **Rainbow**. **Ringo Starr** featured the Ballard composition 'As Far As You Go' on *Old Wave*.

In 1979, Ballard recorded *At The Third Stroke* (with its 'You Can Do Voodoo' single) which, like *Barnet Dogs* and *Into The Fire*, was a likeable collection. In recent times the Little Angels and **Magnum** have recorded his songs and **Kiss** had a hit in 1992 with 'God Gave Rock 'N' Roll To You', after Ballard composed the soundtrack to the 1991 film, *Bill And Ted's Bogus Journey*.

BALLS

ALTHOUGH THIS UK ROCK GROUP BARELY MANAGED A YEAR OF EXISTENCE, THEY WERE ONE OF THE FIRST true 'supergroups'. The line-up of Denny Laine (vocals/guitar; ex-**Moody Blues**) and ex-**Move** Trevor Burton and **Steve Gibbons** (vocals), was augmented sporadically by Alan White (drums; ex-Plastic Ono Band), Jackie Lomax, Richard Tandy (**ELO**), Mike Kelly (**Spooky Tooth**), Keith Smart (drums) and Dave Morgan (bass). They released one single in 1971, financially backed by their creator/manager Tony Secunda. 'Fight For My Country' failed, despite being heavily plugged by the UK pirate radio station, Geronimo.

BANANARAMA

KEREN WOODWARD (b. 1961), SARAH DALLIN (b. 1961) AND SIOBHAN FAHEY (b. 1958) FORMED BANANARAMA IN 1980. After singing at parties and pubs in their native London, the group were recorded by former **Sex Pistols**' drummer Paul Cook on the Swahili Black Blood cover 'Ai A Mwana'. The single caught the attention of **Fun Boy Three** vocalist Terry Hall and the group backed his trio on their revival of 'It Ain't What You Do, It's The Way That You Do It'. The Fun Boy Three subsequently backed Bananarama on their Velvelettes' cover 'Really Saying Something' (1982) which reached the UK Top 10.

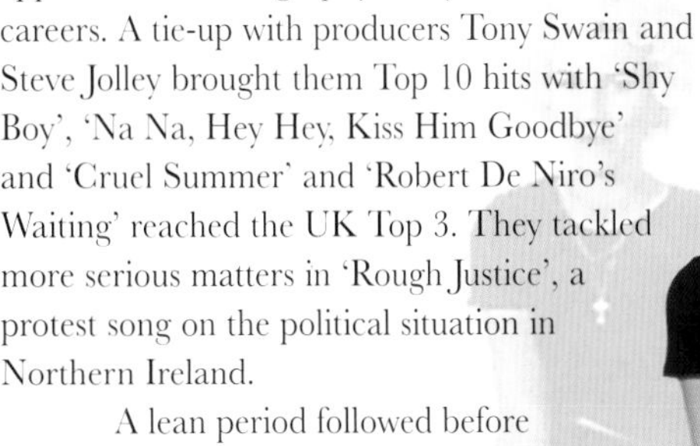

Bananarama had a strong visual image and a refreshingly unaffected approach to choreography. They also retained considerable control over their careers. A tie-up with producers Tony Swain and Steve Jolley brought them Top 10 hits with 'Shy Boy', 'Na Na, Hey Hey, Kiss Him Goodbye' and 'Cruel Summer' and 'Robert De Niro's Waiting' reached the UK Top 3. They tackled more serious matters in 'Rough Justice', a protest song on the political situation in Northern Ireland.

A lean period followed before Bananarama joined **Stock, Aitken And Waterman** for a remake of **Shocking Blue**'s 'Venus', a US number 1. 'I Heard A Rumour' boasted some excellent harmonies and strong arrangement and their biggest UK hit followed with 'Love In The First Degree'. In 1987 Siobhan Fahey left, married **Eurythmics**' David A. Stewart and formed **Shakespears Sister**. Her replacement, Jacqui Sullivan, went solo in 1991 and Sarah and Keren continued as a duo. The last chart entry before the band disolved in 1993 was 'Last Thing On My Mind'.

BAND

WHEN THE BAND EMERGED IN 1968 WITH MUSIC FROM BIG PINK, THEY WERE ALREADY A SEASONED AND COHESIVE unit. Four of the group, Canadians **Robbie Robertson** (b. Jaime Robbie Robertson, 1943; guitar/vocals), Richard Manuel (b. 1943, d. 1986; piano/drums/vocals) and Rick Danko (b. 1943; bass/vocals), and English organist Garth Hudson (b. Eric Hudson, 1937), had embraced rock 'n' roll during its first flush of success. One by one they joined the Hawks, a backing group formed by **Ronnie Hawkins**, which included American Levon Helm (b. Mark Levon Helm, 1942; drums/vocals). 'Bo Diddley' (1963) was a major Canadian hit and the following *Mojo Man* featured Helm on vocals for 'She's 19' and 'Farther Up The Road'. The quintet then left Hawkins and toured America's small-town bars, before settling in New York.

Robertson, Helm and Hudson supported blues singer John Hammond Jnr on his debut single, 'I Wish You Would' (1964), before supporting **Bob Dylan** on his 'electric' 1966 world tour. They later recorded the famous *Basement Tapes* in Dylan's Woodstock retreat. *Music From Big Pink* placed traditional American music in an environment of acid-rock and psychedelia, its woven, wailing harmonies suggested the fervour of sanctified soul, while the instrumental pulse drew inspiration from carnivals, country and R&B.

The Band confirmed the quintet's unique qualities, with Robertson emerging as principal songwriter. It contained several classics – 'Across The Great Divide', 'The Unfaithful Servant' and 'The Night They Drove Old Dixie Down' – as well as 'Rag Mama Rag', an ebullient UK Top 20 hit. The Band then resumed touring, the perils of which were chronicled on *Stage Fright*. In 'The Rumour' they created one of the era's most telling portraits, yet the group's once seamless sound had grown increasingly formal, a dilemma that increased on *Cahoots*. It was followed by a warm in-concert set, *Rock Of Ages*, arranged by **Allan Toussaint**, and *Moondog Matinee*, a selection of favourite cover versions.

In 1974, the Band backed Dylan on *Planet Waves* and undertook the extensive tour documented on *Before The Flood*. The experience renewed their creativity and *Northern Lights Southern Cross*, their strongest set since *The Band*, included 'Acadian Driftwood', one of Robertson's most evocative compositions. However, the band split the following year with a gala performance (*The Last Waltz*) in San Francisco. The many guests included Dylan, **Eric Clapton**, **Muddy Waters**, **Van Morrison**, **Neil Young**, **Joni Mitchell** and **Paul Butterfield**.

The Band completed contractual obligations with *Islands*, a somewhat tepid set. Helm then pursued a career as a performer and actor, Danko recorded a solo album, while Hudson played session appearances. Robertson scored soundtracks to several Scorsese films, but refused to join the Band reunions of 1984 and 1985. A third tour ended in tragedy when Manuel hanged himself in a motel room. His death inspired 'Fallen Angel' on Robertson's outstanding 'comeback' album, but he still refused to join his colleagues when they regrouped again in 1991.

BALIN, MARTY

Albums

Rock Justice (1980)★★

Lucky (Emi America 1983)★★

➧ p.351 for full listings

Connections

Jefferson Airplane ➧ p.198

Jefferson Starship ➧ p.198

Influences

Byrds ➧ p. 77

BALLARD, RUSS

Albums

Russ Ballard (Epic 1975)★★★

At The Third Stroke (Epic 1979)★★★

Fire Still Burns (EMI 1986)★★★

➧ p.351 for full listings

Collaborators

Roulettes

Rod Argent

Connections

Three Dog Night ➧ p.321

Hot Chocolate ➧ p.187

Rainbow ➧ p.272

Ringo Starr ➧ p.307

Kiss ➧ p.208

BANANARAMA

Albums

Deep Sea Skiving (London 1983)★★★

Bananarama (London 1984)★★★

True Confessions (London 1986)★★★

➧ p.351 for full listings

Collaborators

Fun Boy Three ➧ p.155

Connections

Sex Pistols ➧ p.292

Shakespears Sister ➧ p.293

Further References

Videos: *Bananarama* (1984)

Bananarama: Video Singles (1987)

BAND

Albums

Music From Big Pink (Capitol 1968)★★★★

The Band (Capitol 1969)★★★★

Stage Fright (Capitol 1970)★★★★

➧ p.351 for full listings

Collaborators

Ronnie Hawkins ➧ p.177

Bob Dylan ➧ p.128

Eric Clapton ➧ p.92

Van Morrison ➧ p.238

Neil Young ➧ p. 346

Joni Mitchell ➧ p. 235

Paul Butterfield ➧ p.76

Connections

Allan Toussaint ➧ p.323

Further References

Video: *The Last Waltz* (Warner Home Video 1988)

Books: *This Wheel's On Fire: Levon Helm And The Story Of The Band*, Levon Helm with Stephen Davis

BANGLES
Albums
All Over The Place (Columbia 1985)★★★
Different Light (Columbia 1986)★★★★
➽ p.351 for full listings
Collaborators
Prince ➽ p.267
Connections
Runaways ➽ p.284
Influences
Soft Boys ➽ p.302
Katrina and the Waves ➽ p.203
Mamas and the Papas ➽ p.223
Simon and Garfunkel ➽ p. 297
Further References
Videos: *Bangles Greatest Hits* (SMV 1990)
Babe-Osity Live (Turtle 1992)

BANKS, DARRELL
Albums
Darrell Banks Is Here (Atco 1967)★★★
➽ p.351 for full listings

BANTON, BUJU
Albums
Stamina Daddy (Techniques 1991)★★★
Mr. Mention (Penthouse 1991)★★★★
Inna Heights (VP 1997)★★★
➽ p.351 for full listings

BARBARIANS
Albums
Are You A Boy Or Are You A Girl (Laurie 1966)★★
➽ p.351 for full listings

BAR-KAYS
Albums
Soul Finger (Stax 1967)★★★★
Do You See What I See (Polydor 1972)★★★
Contagious (Mercury 1987)★★★
➽ p.352 for full listings
Collaborators
Otis Redding ➽ p.274
Isaac Hayes ➽ p.178
Albert King ➽ p.205
Connections
River Arrows
Further References
Film: *Breakdance – The Movie* (1984)

BARCLAY JAMES HARVEST
Albums
Short Stories (Harvest 1971)★★★
Everyone Is Everybody Else (Polydor 1974)★★★★
Octoberon (Polydor 1976)★★★
➽ p.352 for full listings
Further References
Videos: *Berlin A Concert For The People* (Channel 5 1982)
Glasnost (Channel 5 1988)

BANGLES

KNOWN AS THE COLOURS, THE BANGS AND FINALLY THE BANGLES, THIS LOS ANGELES QUARTET MASTERED THE art of melodic, west-coast, guitar-based pop. The band (formed in 1981) comprised Susanna Hoffs (b. 1962; guitar/vocals), Debbi Peterson (b. 1961; drums/vocals), Vicki Peterson (b. 1958; guitar/vocals) and Annette Zilinkas (bass/vocals). The Bangles' first recordings were made on their own Downkiddie label and then for Miles Copeland's Faulty Products, which resulted in the eponymous mini-album. On signing to CBS in 1983, Zilinkas departed and was replaced by former **Runaways** member Michael Steele (b. 1954; bass/vocals). 'Hero Takes A Fall' failed to chart, but their interpretation of 'Going Down To Liverpool' reached UK number 56 and their debut album, *All Over The Place*, scraped into the US chart. However it was the US/UK number 2 'Manic Monday' (written by **Prince**) and the success of *Different Light* that really won an audience. Their interpretation of Jules Shear's 'If She Knew What She Wants' showed touches of mid-60s **Mamas And The Papas**, while 'Walk Like An Egyptian' gave the group a US number 1/UK number 3. Their version of **Simon And Garfunkel**'s 'Hazy Shade Of Winter', which was featured in the film *Less Than Zero*, reached US number 2/ UK number 11 in 1988. *Everything* generated the hit singles 'In Your Room' (1988) and 'Eternal Flame' (1989, UK/US number 1). 'Be With You' and 'I'll Set You Free' were less successful, and by the end of the year the group dissolved. Susanna Hoffs went solo.

BANKS, DARRELL

BANKS (b. DARRELL EUBANKS, 1938, d. 1970) SPRANG TO FAME IN 1966 WITH HIS DEBUT, 'OPEN THE DOOR TO Your Heart'. A second hit, 'Somebody (Somewhere) Needs You' (1966), followed, but the singer's progress was undermined by an inability to remain with one label for any length of time. By 1967, he had signed to Atlantic (Atco) and in 1969 to Stax (Volt). Banks' later work included 'I'm The One Who Loves You' and 'No One Blinder (Than A Man Who Won't See)'. He was shot dead in March 1970 during a gun duel with a policeman who had been having an affair with his girlfriend.

BANKS, HOMER

US-BORN BANKS (b. 1941) WORKED FOR EMERGING STAX RECORDS, THOUGH AT FIRST HIS TALENTS WENT LARGELY unnoticed. **Isaac Hayes** and David Porter helped set up Banks' solo recording debut for the Genie label in 1964, and in 1966 they wrote '60 Minutes Of Your Love' for the Minit label. Banks recorded five singles between 1966 and 1968, including 'A Lot Of Love', and maintained connections with Stax. By the 70s, he was writing many hits with regular collaborators such as Raymond Jackson, Carl Hampton and Bettye Crutcher, including 'Who's Making Love' (**Johnnie Taylor**) and 'If Loving You Is Wrong (I Don't Want To Be Right)' (Luther Ingram). Banks also co-wrote Shirley Brown's 1974 hit, 'Woman To Woman'. After the demise of Stax, Banks wrote and/or produced for various artists.

BANTON, BUJU

RAISED IN JAMAICA, BANTON (b. MARK MYRIE, 1973) BEGAN his DJ apprenticeship aged 13, with the Rambo Mango and Sweet Love sound systems. Fellow DJ Clement Irie took him to producer Robert French for his debut release, 'The Ruler', in 1986. By 1990 his deep voice drew comparisons with **Shabba Ranks**. Together with Dave Kelly (an engineer at Donovan Germain's Penthouse Studio) he wrote many of his hits, including 'Love Mi Browning', 'Women Nuh Fret' and 'Big It Up'.

Penthouse released *Mr. Mention* and Banton's records began to dominate the reggae charts and led to a signing with Mercury. By 1993, his lyrics dealt increasingly with cultural issues. 'Tribal War', featuring an all-star ensemble, was voiced in response to Jamaica's warring political factions, 'Operation Ardent' railed against Kingston's curfew laws, and 'Murderer' was provoked by the shooting of his friend, fellow DJ, Pan Head.

BARBARIANS

FORMED IN 1964 IN MASSACHUSETTS, USA, THE BARBARIANS – JEFF MORRIS, JERRY CAUSI, BRUCE Benson and 'Moulty' Molten – debuted with 'Hey Little Bird', prior to signing a contract with Laurie Records. In 1965 they enjoyed a minor US hit with 'Are You A Boy Or Are You A Girl?', succeeded by 'Moulty', a monologue from the group's one-armed drummer about his disability. Molten left the Barbarians in 1967. The remaining trio moved to San Francisco, where they formed Black Pearl.

BAR-KAYS

JIMMY KING (b. 1949; GUITAR), RONNIE CALDWELL (b. 1948; ORGAN), Phalin Jones (b. 1949; saxophone), Ben Cauley (b. 1947; trumpet), James Alexander (bass) and Carl Cunningham (b. 1949; drums) were originally known as the River Arrows. Signed to Stax, the Bar-Kays were groomed as that label's second-string house band by Al Jackson (**Booker T. And The MGs**). They were **Otis Redding**'s touring backing group, and the tragic plane crash that took Redding's life in 1967 also claimed King, Caldwell, Jones and Cunningham. Alexander, who missed the flight, put together a new line-up with Ben Cauley, the sole survivor of the accident. Cauley soon dropped out, leaving the bassist at the helm of a frequently changing line-up. The Bar-Kays provided backing for artists including **Isaac Hayes** and **Albert King** and pursued a funk-based direction on their own releases. With vocalist Larry Dodson, 'Son Of Shaft' (1972) reached the US R&B Top 10, whereas 'Shake Your Rump To The Funk', 'Move Your Boogie Body' and 'Freakshow On The Dancefloor' were aimed at the disco market. Since 1987 the group has featured Dodson, Harvey Henderson (tenor saxophone) and Stewart (keyboards).

BARCLAY JAMES HARVEST

FORMED IN ENGLAND, THE BAND COMPRISED STEWART 'WOOLLY' WOLSTENHOLME (b. 1947; KEYBOARDS /VOCALS), John Lees (b. 1947; guitar/vocals), Les Holroyd (b. 1948; bass/vocals) and Mel Pritchard (b. 1948; drums). Following their inauspicious debut on Parlophone, the band became one of Harvest's first signings. Their blend of melodic 'underground' music was initially acclaimed, although commercial success eluded them for years. Their early albums featured the mellotron and they were able to combine earthy guitar with harmony vocals. Fortunes changed when they signed with Polydor, releasing *Everyone Is Everybody Else* and in 1976 they reached the charts with *Octoberon*, which contained 'Rock 'n' Roll Star' and 'Suicide'. After *XII* Wolstenholme left and released a solo album *Maestoso*. Barclay James Harvest's live *Concert For The People*, recorded in Berlin (where the band are major stars), became their most commercially successful record in the UK.

BARDENS, PETER

AN ACCOMPLISHED ORGANIST, BARDENS (b. 1945) WAS A FOUNDER-MEMBER OF THE CHEYNES, BEFORE A BRIEF spell in **Them**. By 1966 he was fronting the club-based Peter B's, which included drummer Mick Fleetwood and guitarist **Peter Green**. They recorded 'If You Wanna Be Happy', before being absorbed into Shotgun Express, a soul-inspired revue featuring **Rod Stewart**. Bardens later formed the short-lived Village, before releasing his first solo album, *The Answer* (1970). This informal selection featured Peter Green, under the pseudonym 'Andy Gee'. *Peter Bardens* was more focused and showcased the artist's touring group, which included Victor Brox (ex-**Aynsley Dunbar Retaliation**). In 1972 Bardens formed **Camel**; remaining with them for six years before going solo again with *Heart To Heart*. He has since divided his time between session work and crafted 80s rock, exemplified on *Seen One Earth*.

BARENAKED LADIES

CANADIAN GROUP FORMED IN 1988 BY SONGWRITERS STEVEN PAGE (b. 1970; GUITAR/VOCALS) AND ED ROBERTSON (b. 1970; guitar/vocals). Brothers Jim (b. 1970; bass/keyboards) and Andrew Creeggan (b. 1971; congas) and Tyler Stewart (b. 1967; drums) were soon added. The group had an intensive series of club dates and issued a five-song EP. Their debut album, *Gordon*, sold half a million copies in Canada. Their melodic pop with its strong harmonies and string-driven acoustics were evident on songs such as 'Be My Yoko Ono' and 'If I Had A Million Dollars'.

BARLOW, GARY

EX-LEAD SINGER WITH **TAKE THAT**, BARLOW (b. 1971) BEGAN HIS MUSICAL APPRENTICESHIP AGED 12, AS pianist in a social club. By age 14 he had moved on to cabaret, supporting artists such as Ken Dodd. His first attempt at a solo career came two years later, but his compositions (which already included 'A Million Love Songs') aroused little interest.

Nigel Martin-Smith, who was piecing together a UK version of **New Kids On The Block**, contacted him for Take That; the group scored a series of number 1 singles and albums, with Barlow as chief songwriter. He went solo again in 1996, at the same time as fellow Take That members, Robbie Williams and Mark Owen: Barlow reached UK number 1 first, with 'Forever Love'.

Gary then split from his manager and re-recorded almost all of his first album. A year later, with six new tracks, *Open Road* was finally released.

BARRETT, SYD

UK-BORN BARRETT (b. ROGER KEITH BARRETT, 1946) EMBRACED MUSIC IN THE EARLY 60S AS A MEMBER of Geoff Mutt and the Mottoes, a group modelled on **Cliff Richard** And The **Shadows**. He acquired his 'Syd' sobriquet at school, where his friends included **Roger Waters** and Dave Gilmour. Later, while an art student in London, Barratt played in the aspiring R&B act, the Hollering Blues. Meanwhile Waters had formed his own group and invited Barrett to join. They took the name the '**Pink Floyd** Sound' from an album featuring blues musicians Pink Anderson and Floyd Council.

Having dropped their suffix, Pink Floyd became part of London's nascent 'underground' scene. Barrett was their principal songwriter, composing the hits 'Arnold Layne' and 'See Emily Play', as well as the bulk of *The Piper At The Gates Of Dawn*. Barratt's child-like, often *naïve* compositional style was offset by his highly original playing. An impulsive, impressionistic guitarist, his unconventional use of feedback, slide and echo did much to transfer the mystery and imagery of Pink Floyd's live sound into a studio equivalent.

Sadly an indulgence in hallucinogenic drugs led to a disintegration in Barrett's mental health (reflected on 'Apples And Oranges'). Dave Gilmour joined in 1968, prompting suggestions that Barrett would retire from live work and concentrate solely on songwriting. Instead he departed the following April.

Within a month Barrett began a solo album. Several tracks were completed with the aid of Willie Wilson (ex-Joker's Wild), and **Humble Pie** drummer, Jerry Shirley. On 'No Use Trying', Barrett was supported by the **Soft Machine**.

Gilmour took a keen interest in the sessions. In June he suggested that he and Waters should produce some tracks, and the rest of the album was completed in three days. *The Madcap Laughs* is an artistic triumph on which Syd's fragile vocals and delicate melodies create a hypnotic, ethereal atmosphere. It contains some of his finest performances, notably 'Octopus', which was issued as a single, and 'Golden Hair', a poem from James Joyce's *Chamber Music*. In 1970 Barratt began recording a second album with Gilmour as producer. *Barrett* was more assertive, but less poignant, than its predecessor, it included the chilling 'Rats', one of the singer's most vitriolic performances.

Barrett completed a session for BBC Radio 1's 'Sounds Of The Seventies', but despite declaring himself 'totally together', he was becoming a recluse. The following year he put together a group with bassist Jack Monck (ex-Delivery) and former Pink Fairies/**Pretty Things** drummer Twink. They supported Eddie 'Guitar' Burns in Cambridge and later, now dubbed Stars, shared a bill with the **MC5**. Syd failed to surface for their next date and shows were cancelled.

Pink Floyd included a tribute to Barrett, 'Shine On You Crazy Diamond', on the best-selling *Wish You Were Here*, but, regrettably, Barrett's precarious mental state precluded any further involvement in music. *Opel* comprised unissued masters and alternate takes, enhancing his reputation for startling, original work as evinced by the affecting title track, bafflingly omitted from *The Madcap Laughs*. Barrett is rumoured to have returned to painting.

BARDENS, PETER
Albums
Peter Bardens (Transatlantic 19712)★★★
Seen One Earth (Capitol 1987)★★★
Big Sky (HTD 1994)★★★
➽ p.352 for full listings
Collaborators
Rod Stewart ➽ p.310
Connections
Them ➽ p.319
Aynsley Dunbar Retaliation ➽ p.25
Camel ➽ p.78
Further References
Video: *Water Colours: Video* (1992)

BARENAKED LADIES
Albums
Gordon (Sire 1992)★★★★
Maybe You Should Drive (Sire 1994)★★★
Born On A Pirate Ship (Reprise 1996)★★★★
➽ p.352 for full listings

BARLOW, GARY
Albums
Open Road (RCA 1997)★★★
➽ p.324 for full listings
Connections
Take That ➽ p.316
Influences
New Kids on the Block ➽ p.245

BARRETT, SYD
Albums
The Madcap Laughs (Harvest 1970)★★★
Barrett (Harvest 1970)★★★
The Peel Sessions (Strange Fruit 1995)★★★
➽ p.352 for full listings
Collaborators
Humble Pie ➽ p.190
Soft Machine ➽ p.302
Robert Wyatt ➽ p.344
MC5 ➽ p.228
Connections
Pink Floyd ➽ p.261
Pretty Things ➽ p.266
Influences
Cliff Richard and the Shadows ➽ p.277
Further References
Video: *Syd Barrett's First Trip* (Vex 1993)
Book: *Syd Barrett: The Madcap Laughs*, Pete Anderson and Mick Rock

BARRON KNIGHTS
Albums
Call Up The Groups (Columbia 1964)★★★
Scribed (Columbia 1967)★★★
Twisting The Knights Away (1981)★★★
➧ p.352 for full listings
Connections
Rolling Stones ➧ p.281
Searchers ➧ p.290
Dave Clark Five ➧ p.111
Influences
Beatles ➧ p.38
Further References
Book: *Once A Knight: History Of The Barron Knights*, Pete Langford

BARRY, LEN
Albums
with the Dovells *Len Barry Sings With The Dovells* (Cameo 1964)★★★
➧ p.352 for full listings
Connections
Bosstones

BARTHOLOMEW, DAVE
Albums
Fats Domino Presents Dave Bartholomew (Imperial 1961)★★★
New Orleans House Party (Imperial 1963)★★★
The Spirit Of New Orleans (1993)★★★
➧ p.352 for full listings
Collaborators
Fats Domino ➧ p.122
Little Richard ➧ p.217
Frankie Ford ➧ p.149
Connections
Chuck Berry ➧ p.45
Influences
Smiley Lewis
Lloyd Price ➧ p.266

BASSEY, SHIRLEY
Albums
The Bewitching Miss Bassey (1959)★★★
Big Spender (1971)★★★
Let Me Sing And I'm Happy (1988)★★★
➧ p.352 for full listings
Collaborators
Yello ➧ p.345
Influences
George Harrison ➧ p.176
Further References
Video: *Shirley* (EMI 1997)

BATT, MIKE
Albums
The Hunting Of The Snark (1986)★★★
➧ p.352 for full listings
Collaborators
Rolling Stones ➧ p.281
Bob Dylan ➧ p.128
Simon and Garfunkel ➧ p.297
Elton John ➧ p. 200
Cliff Richard ➧ p.277

BARRON KNIGHTS

FORMED IN ENGLAND, THE BARRON KNIGHTS ROSE FROM OBSCURITY AFTER THEIR APPEARANCE ON THE **Beatles**' 1963 Christmas Show. Duke D'mond (b. Richard Palmer, 1945; vocals/rhythm guitar), Butch Baker (b. Leslie John Baker, 1941; guitar/banjo/vocals), 'P'nut' Langford (b. Peter Langford, 1943; guitar/vocals), Barron Antony (b. Antony Michael John Osmond, 1940; bass/vocals) and Dave Ballinger (b. 1941; drums) scored a UK Top 3 hit the following year with 'Call Up The Groups', a parodic medley of contemporary releases. Two similar singles, 'Pop! Go The Workers' (number 5) and 'Merrie Gentle Pops' (number 9) were followed by unsuccessful attempts at conventional releases. The Barron Knights pursued a lucrative cabaret circuit career throughout the late 60s and early 70s, before two further Top 10 hits, 'Live In Trouble' and 'A Taste Of Aggro'.

BARRY, JEFF

BARRY (b. 1938) BEGAN HIS CAREER AS A SINGER, RECORDING FOR RCA AND Decca (1959-62), alongside concurrent success as a songwriter, most notably with 'Tell Laura I Love Her' – a US Top 10 hit for Ray Peterson and a UK number 1 for Ricky Valance.

In 1961, Barry was contracted to Trinity Music for whom he completed over 100 compositions and gained experience in arranging, producing and recording demos. Ellie Greenwich, who he later married, proved to be the most enduring of his many collaborators. Together they wrote 'Maybe I Know' (Leslie Gore) and 'Do Wah Diddy' (Exciters/**Manfred Mann**) and, as the Raindrops, recorded 'The Kind Of Boy You Can't Forget' (US Top 20). However, they are best known for their work with **Phil Spector** including 'Da Doo Ron Ron' and 'Then He Kissed Me' (the **Crystals**), 'Be My Baby' and 'Baby, I Love You' (the **Ronettes**) and 'River Deep, Mountain High' (**Ike And Tina Turner**). The duo wrote and co-produced releases for the **Dixie Cups**, **Shangri-Las** and Neil Diamond. When their marriage ended in 1965, Barry resumed his recording career but achieved greater success in partnership with singer Andy Kim, writing, producing and performing for the Archies' cartoon series.

BARRY, LEN

BARRY (b. LEONARD BORRISOFF, 1942) BEGAN HIS CAREER AS VOCALIST ON THE BOSSTONES' 1958 SINGLE 'MOPE-Itty Mope' before joining the Dovells (1961-63). As a soloist, his white soul vocals were best exemplified on the chart-topper '1-2-3' and 'Like A Baby'. He also enjoyed a minor US hit with 'Somewhere' (a song that P. J. Proby had already taken to the charts in the UK). By the 70s, Barry had moved into production.

BARTHOLOMEW, DAVE

A PRODUCER, ARRANGER, SONGWRITER, BANDLEADER AND ARTIST, BARTHOLOMEW (b. 1920) PRODUCED AND co-wrote most of **Fats Domino**'s hits for Imperial Records. Bartholomew performed in marching bands, formed his first band in New Orleans in the late 40s and backed **Little Richard** on early recordings. In 1948, Bartholomew discovered Domino in New Orleans and introduced him to Imperial. They collaborated on 'The Fat Man' (1950), which became the first of over a dozen hits co-authored by the pair and produced by Bartholomew. Bartholomew's other credits included Smiley Lewis's 'I Hear You Knocking' and 'One Night' (later a, toned-down, hit for **Elvis Presley**), **Lloyd Price**'s 'Lawdy Miss Clawdy', and records for Earl King, Roy Brown, Huey 'Piano' Smith, Robert Parker, **Frankie Ford** and Snooks Eaglin. In 1963, Imperial was sold to Liberty Records at which point Bartholomew left.

In 1972, **Chuck Berry** reworked Bartholomew's 'My Ding-A-Ling', and achieved his only US number 1. In 1981, Bartholomew recorded a Dixieland album and in the 90s was involved with occasional special events such as the New Orleans Jazz & Heritage Festival.

BASSEY, SHIRLEY

AFTER TOURING THE UK IN REVUES AND VARIETY SHOWS, BASSEY (b. 1937) had her first hit with 'Banana Boat Song' (1957), followed by 'Kiss Me Honey Honey, Kiss Me'. The unique Bassey phrasing started to emerge in 1959 with 'As I Love You' (UK number 1), and continued through to the mid-70s in songs including 'As Long As He Needs Me', 'You'll Never Know' and 'For All We Know'. In 1962 she was accompanied on *Let's Face The Music* by top US arranger/conductor Nelson Riddle. The Welsh singer's rise to the top was swift and by the early 60s she was headlining in New York and Las Vegas. In 1964, she had a US hit with 'Goldfinger' – she also sang the James Bond themes for 'Diamonds Are Forever' and 'Moonraker'. In 1969, she moved to Switzerland.

In 1976, the American Guild Of Variety Artists voted her 'Best Female Entertainer', that year she also celebrated 20 years of recording with a British tour. In 1977 she received a Britannia Award for the 'Best Female Solo Singer In The Last 50 Years'.

In 1981, Bassey announced her semi-retirement, but continued to appear occasionally throughout the 80s and recorded a few albums. In one of pop's more unlikely collaborations, she was teamed with **Yello** in 1987 for 'The Rhythm Divine'. In the 90s Bassey has shown herself to be an enduring, powerful and exciting performer with hits such as 'Big Spender', 'Nobody Does It Like Me' and 'Tigress Of Tiger Bay'. In 1993, she received the CBE. Her 40th Anniversary UK concert tour attracted favourable reviews.

BATT, MIKE

BEGINNING HIS CAREER AS AN IN-HOUSE MUSIC PUBLISHER /SONGWRITER, BATT (b. 1950) MOVED INTO PRODUCTION, working on albums by Hapshash And The Coloured Coat and the **Groundhogs**. By 1973 he discovered a hit-making machine: the Wombles, a children's television programme that spawned a number of hit singles. He continued to produce for other artists, including the **Kursaal Flyers**, **Steeleye Span** and Linda Lewis. He released eponymous orchestral albums, including portraits of the **Rolling Stones**, **Bob Dylan**, **Simon And Garfunkel**, **George Harrison**, **Elton John** and **Cat Stevens**. As a soloist, Batt hit number 4 with 'Summertime City' in 1975, and Art Garfunkel took his 'Bright Eyes' to number 1 in 1979. Since then, Batt has continued to write for films and musicals, including **David Essex**'s 'A Winter's Tale' (lyrics by Tim Rice). His 1986 concept album featured Sir John Gielgud, Roger Daltrey, **Julian Lennon**, and **Cliff Richard**, accompanied by the London Symphony Orchestra.His stage musical, *The Hunting Of The Snark*, opened in London in 1991 but closed seven weeks later. In the late 90s, the Wombles reclaimed their former popularity.

BAUHAUS

ORIGINALLY KNOWN AS BAUHAUS 1919, THIS UK QUARTET FEATURED PETER MURPHY (VOCALS), **Daniel Ash** (vocals/guitar), David Jay aka David J. (vocals/bass) and Kevin Haskins (drums). Within months of forming they recorded their debut, 'Bela Lugosi's Dead'. They recorded for various independent labels – Small Wonder, Axix, 4AD and Beggars Banquet – and recorded four albums in as many years, of which *Mask* proved the most accessible. They had a cameo appearance in the film *The Hunger*, starring **David Bowie**, and later took advantage of the Bowie connection to record a copy of 'Ziggy Stardust', their only UK Top 20 hit. The group disbanded in 1983. Murphy briefly joined **Japan**'s Mick Karn in Dali's Car, the remaining three members soldiered on as Love And Rockets.

BAY CITY ROLLERS

FORMED DURING 1967 IN EDINBURGH, THE ROLLERS WERE A **BEATLES** COVER GROUP based around brothers Derek (b. 1955; drums) and Alan Longmuir (b. 1953; bass). After meeting entrepreneur Tam Paton, they played on the Scottish circuit until their big break in 1971; within months the group were in the UK Top 10. 'Keep On Dancing', produced by **Jonathan King**, proved a one-off and for the next couple of years the group struggled. After various personnel shuffles, the group added another three Edinburgh musicians: Les McKeown (b. 1955; vocals), Stuart 'Woody' Wood (b. 1957; guitar) and Eric Faulkner (b. 1955; guitar). With the songwriting assistance of Phil Coulter and Bill Martin, they enjoyed a run of hits, including 'Remember (Sha La La)', 'Shang-A-Lang', 'Summerlove Sensation' and 'All Of Me Loves All Of You'. In 1975, they enjoyed two consecutive UK number 1s, 'Bye Bye Baby' and 'Give A Little Love' and topped the US charts with 'Saturday Night'.

Line-up changes followed with the arrival of Ian Mitchell and Billy Lyall, but during the next three years, disaster struck. McKeown was charged with reckless driving after hitting and killing a 75-year-old widow, Eric Faulkner and Alan Longmuir attempted suicide, Paton was jailed for committing indecent acts with underage teenagers, Ian Mitchell starred in a pornographic movie and Billy Lyall died from an AIDS-related illness. A tawdry conclusion to one of the most famous teenybop acts in British pop history.

BBM

THE 'SUPERGROUP' OF **GARY MOORE** (b. 1952; VOCALS/GUITAR), **JACK BRUCE** (b. JOHN SYMON ASHER BRUCE, 1943; bass/vocals) and **Ginger Baker** (b. Peter Baker, 1939; drums) was formed in 1993. Their album was highly derivative of some of the songs on **Cream**'s *Disraeli Gears* and *Wheels Of Fire*. 'Waiting In The Wings' was indebted to 'White Room', 'City Of Gold' was similar to 'Crossroads' and 'Why Does Love (Have To Go Wrong)?' recalled 'We're Going Wrong'. Those that had pined for a Cream reunion were placated by this album's fusion of heavy metal and blues, but the group fell out at the end of a media-only performance at London's Marquee Club. The band effectively folded, bequeathing only one good album.

BE-BOP DELUXE

BILL NELSON (b. 1948), NICK CHATTERTON-DEW (DRUMS), ROBERT BRYAN (BASS) AND IAN PARKIN (GUITAR) RECORDED *Axe Victim* as Be-Bop Deluxe. Nelson soon disbanded the group and formed a new band, taking members from that fragmented unit. This short-lived combo also broke up. With the addition of New Zealander Charlie Tumahai (d. 1995) and Simon Fox, Nelson released *Futurama* and *Sunburst Finish* (including the hit 'Ships In The Night'). Nelson's talent began to dominate the band but as his guitar virtuosity grew, the songs became weaker. He left in 1978 to form Red Noise, retaining Andrew Clarke from the old band.

Connections
Groundhogs ➽ p.168
Kursaal Flyers ➽ p.211
Steeleye Span ➽ p.308

BAUHAUS
Albums
Mask (Beggars Banquet 1981)★★★
The Sky's Gone Out (Beggars Banquet 1982)★★★
Burning From The Inside (Beggars Banquet 1983)★★
➽ p.352 for full listings

Collaborators
David Bowie ➽ p.64
Further References
Video: *Shadow Of Light* (Kace International Products 1984).
Book: *Dark Entries: Bauhaus And Beyond*, Ian Shirley.

BAY CITY ROLLERS
Albums
Rollin' (Bell 1974)★★★
Once Upon A Star (Bell 1975)★★★
Wouldn't You Like It (Bell 1975)★★★
➽ p.352 for full listings
Collaborators
Jonathan King ➽ p.206
Connections
Four Seasons ➽ p.151
Influences
Beatles ➽ p.38
Further References
Video: *Shang-A-Lang: The Very Best Of...* (1993)
Books: *The Bay City Rollers Scrapbook*, David Golumb

BBM
Albums
Around The Next Dream (Virgin 1994)★★★.
➽ p.352 for full listings
Influences
Cream ➽ p.103

BE-BOP DELUXE
Albums
Sunburst Finish (Harvest 1976)★★★
Modern Music (Harvest 1976)★★★
Live! In The Air Age (Harvest 1977)★★★
➽ p.352 for full listings
Connections
Red Noise
John Peel ➽ p.258

BEACH BOYS
Albums
Pet Sounds (Capitol 1966)★★★★★
Sunflower (Brother 1970)★★★★★
Surf's Up (Brother 1971)★★★★★
➧ p.352 for full listings

BEACH BOYS

FORMED IN CALIFORNIA IN 1961 BY BROTHERS BRIAN (b. 1942), CARL (b. 1946, d. 1998) AND DENNIS WILSON

(b. 1944, d. 1983), Al Jardine (b. 1942) and Mike Love (b. 1941). Brian's songwriting ability and Dennis's fondness for surfing culminated in 'Surfin'' – the track brought them a recording contract with Capitol. Over the next 18 months the Beach Boys had 10 US hits and released four albums of surfing and hot-rod songs (David Marks, temporarily replaced Al Jardine). However their punishing workload began to affect Brian, who was additionally writing material for **Jan And Dean**.

In 1963, the Beach Boys hit the UK via 'Surfin' USA', which mildly interrupted the Merseybeat domination. The predominantly working-class image of the British beat-group scene was at odds with the clean and wholesome west-coast lifestyle. During 1964, a further four albums were released, culminating in the *Christmas Album* – eight albums in just over two years, six of which were arranged and produced by Brian, in addition to his having written 63 out of the 84 songs. However, the **Beatles** had begun to dominate the US charts, and in their wake the British invasion took place. This drove Brian to compete against the Beatles, gaining some pyrrhic revenge, when in 1966 the Beach Boys were voted number 1 group worldwide by the UK music press (the Beatles came second).

Wilson's maturity as a composer was developing with classics like 'I Get Around', 'California Girls' and 'God Only Knows' and the quality of albums such as *Summer Days And Summer Nights!!* and *Today* was extremely high. Many of Wilson's songs portrayed his own insecurity as an adolescent and songs such as 'In My Room', 'Wouldn't It Be Nice' and 'Girl Don't Tell Me' found a receptive audience who could relate to the lyrics. While their instrumentals were average, the vocal combination was immaculate: both Carl and Brian had perfect pitch, even though Brian was deaf in one ear (reputedly from his father's beatings).

In private the 'musical genius' was working on his self-intended masterpiece, *Pet Sounds*. It was released in 1966 to outstanding reviews but, for an inexplicable reason, poor sales. Brian was devastated when it only reached US number 10, and was mortified when the Beatles' *Sgt Peppers Lonely Hearts Club Band* was released a year later. He had already experienced two nervous breakdowns and retired from performing with the group, turning instead to barbiturates. Publicly he was briefly replaced by **Glen Campbell**, then by Bruce Johnston. Yet through this turmoil the Beach Boys rose to their peak at the end of 1966 with 'Good Vibrations'. They then embarked on a major European tour, releasing 'Heroes And Villains' (lyrics by **Van Dyke Parks**). Brian meanwhile attempted a counter attack on the Beatles, with a project to be known as 'Smile'. This became the band's albatross, although it was never officially released. The painstaking hours spent on this project is now one of pop's legendary tales. Parts of the material surfaced on their next three albums, and further tracks appeared on other collections up until 1971.

Conflict between Brian and the rest of the band was also surfacing. Love in particular wanted to continue with their immaculate pop music, and argued that Brian was getting too 'far out'. Indeed, Brian's reclusive nature, fast-increasing weight and growing dependence on drugs added fuel to Love's argument. *Smiley Smile* in 1967 and *Wild Honey* the following year were comparative failures. Their music had lost its cohesiveness and their mentor and guiding light had by now retreated to his bed. In Europe the group were still having hits, and even had a surprise UK chart topper in 1968 with 'Do It Again'; with Mike Love's nasal vocals taking the lead on a song harping back to better times.

In 1969, the Beach Boys left Capitol in a blaze of litigation. *Sunflower* was an artistic triumph but a commercial disaster, on which Dennis contributed four songs including 'Forever'. Over the next year they set about rebuilding their US credibility, having lost ground to the new wave bands from San Francisco. They toured constantly, and the arrival of *Surf's Up* in 1971 completed their remarkable renaissance. The record's ecological stance was years ahead of its time, and critics were unanimous in praise.

As Dennis co-starred with **James Taylor** in the cult road movie *Two-Lane Blacktop*, Brian's life was deteriorating into mental instability. Miraculously the band were able to maintain their career despite shifting personnel. The addition of Ricky Fataar, Blondie Chaplin and Daryl Dragon gave the band a fuller sound, culminating in *Holland* – for which the entire Beach Boys organization (including wives and children) moved to Holland for eight months. A year later, *Endless Summer*, a compilation, unexpectedly rocketed to the top of the US charts, reinforcing Love and Jardine's theory that all anybody wanted of the Beach Boys was surfing and car songs. With the addition of James William Guercio (ex-**Chicago**), the band enjoyed major concert tour success, and ended 1974 as **Rolling Stone**'s 'Band of the Year'. *Spirit Of America*, another compilation of earlier tracks, stayed on the American charts for almost a year. Meanwhile, Brian had deteriorated further and was undergoing therapy. However in 1976, *15 Big Ones* scored a hit with **Chuck Berry**'s 'Rock And Roll Music'. The publicity centred on a tasteless 'Brian Is Back' campaign, with the now obese Wilson being unwillingly pushed into the spotlight.

In 1977 the band signed a recording contract with CBS (reputedly worth $8,000,000) on the terms that Brian contributed at least four new songs and a total of 70 per cent of the material for each album. The first album was the patchy *LA* (*Light Album*); it produced a sizeable hit with Al Jardine's 'Lady Lynda'.

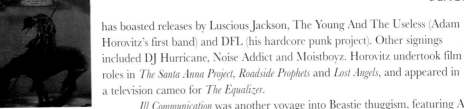

The next official Beach Boys work was *Keeping The Summer Alive*, a poor album, made without Dennis (by now he had a serious cocaine habit which hampered the recording of his solo album *Pacific Ocean Blue*); during 1980 only Love and Jardine survived from the original group. Carl delivered his first solo album, a beautifully sung, well-produced record that flopped. One track, 'Heaven', later became a regular part of the Beach Boys' repertoire and was later dedicated to Dennis.

In 1982, Brian Wilson was officially dismissed, and was admitted to hospital, weighing a massive 320 pounds. A year later, Dennis was tragically drowned while diving from his boat. His death snapped his brother out of his stupor, and Brian gradually re-emerged to participate onstage. A clean and healthy-looking band graced the back of *The Beach Boys*. Following this collection, and without a recording contract, they decided to concentrate on touring the world. In 1987, they teamed up with rap act the **Fat Boys** for a remake of the **Surfaris**' 'Wipe Out'.

In 1988, Brian returned with the solo album for which his fans had waited over 20 years. The critics and fans loved it, but sadly the album sold only moderately well. At the same time the Beach Boys released 'Kokomo', included in the film *Cocktail*; unexpectedly it went to US number 1. In 1990, the Beach Boys took Brian to court in an alleged attempt to wrest his $80 million fortune from him: maintaining he was insane and unable to look after himself. He defended the case but eventually reluctantly accepted a settlement. He was then officially sacked/resigned and proceeded to get back monies which had been pouring in from his back catalogue. However Mike Love then issued a writ to Brian claiming he co-wrote 79 songs with him, including 'California Girls', 'I Get Around' and 'Surfin' USA'. In 1993 the band continued to tour, and during 1994 mutterings were heard that the pending lawsuit would be settled, as Love and Brian were at least speaking to each other. Late that year it was announced that a substantial settlement had been made to Love. In 1995 a thin, handsome, recently remarried Wilson met with Love – not only had they mended the rift but were writing songs together.

Carl Wilson underwent treatment for cancer in 1997, tragically losing his battle in 1998.

BEASTIE BOYS

FORMED IN NEW YORK AROUND ADAM 'MCA' YAUCH (b. 1967; VOCALS), MIKE 'D' DIAMOND (b. 1965; VOCALS), John Berry and Kate Shellenbach (who both departed after 'Pollywog Stew') and Adam 'Ad Rock' Horovitz (b. 1966; vocals/guitar). *Cookie Puss* offered the first evidence of rap and friend and sometime band member, Rick Rubin, signed them to his fledgling Def Jam label. Their debut revealed a collision of bad attitudes, spearheaded by the raucous single, 'Fight For Your Right To Party'. There was nothing self-conscious or sophisticated about the lyrics, just complaints about their parents confiscating their pornography or telling them to turn the stereo down. However *Licensed To Ill* became the first rap album to top the US charts and by the time 'No Sleep Till Brooklyn' and 'She's On It' charted, the band had become a *cause célèbre*. Their stage shows regularly featured caged, half-naked females, while their Volkswagen pendants resulted in a crime wave with fans stealing from vehicles throughout the UK.

After a break for solo projects, the band re-assembled in 1989, but the public had forgotten them. *Paul's Boutique* (co-produced by the Dust Brothers) remains one of rap's most overlooked pieces, a complex reflection of pop culture which is infinitely subtler than their debut. *Check Your Head* saw them returning to their thrash roots and in the meantime the Beasties had invested wisely, setting up their own magazine, studio and label, Grandy Royal. This has boasted releases by Luscious Jackson, The Young And The Useless (Adam Horovitz's first band) and DFL (his hardcore punk project). Other signings included DJ Hurricane, Noise Addict and Moistboyz. Horovitz undertook film roles in *The Santa Anna Project*, *Roadside Prophets* and *Lost Angels*, and appeared in a television cameo for *The Equalizer*.

Ill Communication was another voyage into Beastie thuggism, featuring A Tribe Called Quest's 'Q Tip', and a second appearance from Biz Markie, following his debut on *Check Your Head*. *The In Sound From Way Out* was merely b-sides and instrumental takes. Yauch became a Buddhist, speaking out publicly against US trade links with China, because of China's annexation of Tibet.

BEAT (UK)

FOUNDED IN ENGLAND IN 1978, THE ORIGINAL BEAT COMPRISED DAVE WAKELING (b. 1956; VOCALS/GUITAR), ANDY Cox (b. 1956; guitar), David Steele (b. 1960; bass) and Everett Morton (b. 1951; drums). Local pub-circuit success led to them being signed to the Two-Tone label and the Beat expanded to include punk rapper Ranking Roger (b. Roger Charlery, 1961) and Jamaican saxophonist Saxa (who also played with **Prince Buster**). Their ska/pop fusion led to their debut single, a cover of **Smokey Robinson**'s 'Tears Of A Clown', reaching the UK Top 10. They then formed their own label, Go Feet, and had several 1980s hits, displaying sharp-witted lyrics. 'Mirror In The Bathroom' and 'Best Friend' worked both as observations on personal relationships and more generalized putdowns of the 'Me' generation; their political awareness led to 'Stand Down Margaret' (about British Prime Minister Margaret Thatcher). Their debut album, *I Just Can't Stop It*, included several hit singles. Within a year, however, their pop-based style was replaced by a stronger reggae influence. *Wha'ppen* and *Special Beat Service* were well received, but the run of hits temporarily evaporated. By 1982, Saxa had retired, replaced by Wesley Magoogan. The Beat continued to tour extensively, but their dissolution was imminent. Ironically, their career ended as it had begun – with a cover of Andy Williams' 60s hit, 'Can't Get Used To Losing You' – their biggest UK hit.

Ranking Roger and Dave Wakeling went on to form **General Public** while Andy Cox and David Steele recruited Roland Gift to launch the **Fine Young Cannibals**.

Collaborators
Jan and Dean ➽ p.197
Van Dyke Parks
James Taylor ➽ p.317
Chuck Berry ➽ p. 45
Connections
Beatles ➽ p.38
Chicago ➽ p. 90
Fat Boys ➽ p. 143
Glen Campbell ➽ p.79
Rolling Stone ➽ p.280

Influences
Surfaris ➽ p.314

Further References
Video: *Beach Boys: An American Band* (Vestron Music Video 1988)
Film: *Girls On The Beach* (1965)
Book: *The Beach Boys And The California Myth*, David Leaf

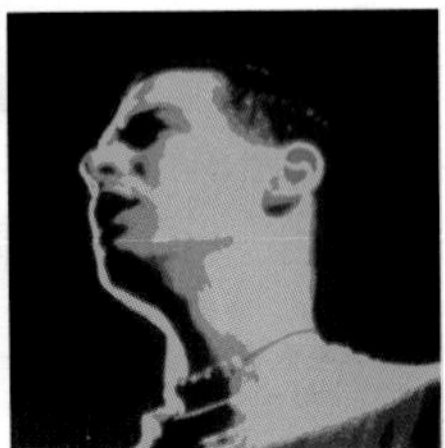

BEASTIE BOYS
Albums
Paul's Boutique (Capitol 1989)★★★★
Check Your Head (Capitol 1992)★★★★
Ill Communication (Capitol 1994)★★★★
➽ p.352 for full listings
Collaborators
A Tribe Called Quest ➽ p.6
Connections
Rick Rubin ➽ p.284
Dust Brothers
The Young and the Useless
DFL
Noise Addict
Influences
Led Zeppelin ➽ p.213
Further References
Videos: *Sabotage* (1994)
The Skills To Pay The Bills (1994)

BEAT (UK)
Albums
I Just Can't Stop It (Go-Feet 1980)★★★★
Wha'ppen (Go-Feet 1981)★★★
Special Beat Service (Go-Feet 1982)★★★
➽ p.352 for full listings
Connections
Prince Buster ➽ p.267
General Public ➽ p.156
Fine Young Cannibals ➽ p.145
Influences
Smokey Robinson ➽ p.279
Further References
Book: *The Beat: Twist And Crawl*, Malu Halasha.

BEAT FARMERS
Albums
Tales Of The New West (Rhino 1985)★★★
Van Go (Curb 1986)★★★
The Pursuit Of Happiness (Curb 1987)★★★
➔ p.352 for full listings
Connections
Long Ryders ➔ p.218
Influences
Johnny Cash ➔ p.84
Tom Waits ➔ p. 332
Kinks ➔ p.207

BEATLES
Albums
Rubber Soul (Parlophone 1965)★★★★★
Sgt. Pepper's Lonely Hearts Club Band (Parlophone 1967)★★★★★
Abbey Road (Apple 1969)★★★★★
➔ p.352 for full listings
Collaborators
Tony Sheridan ➔ p.295
Billy Preston ➔ p.266
Connections
Byrds ➔ p.77
Quarrymen

George Harrison ➔ p.176
Hollies ➔ p.183
Johyn Lennon ➔ p.214
George Martin ➔ p.226
Paul McCartney ➔ p.229
Oasis ➔ p.250
Brian Poole and the Tremeloes ➔ p.263
Rolling Stones ➔ p.281
Phil Spector ➔ p.304
Ringo Starr ➔ p.307
Wings ➔ p.340
The Wilburys

BEAT FARMERS

THE BEAT FARMERS WAS FORMED IN 1983 IN SAN DIEGO, USA, BY DRUMMER/VOCALIST 'COUNTRY' DICK MONTANA (b. Dan McLain 1955, d. 1995). Their intelligent hybrid of punk, pop and country was showcased on the group's debut, *Tales Of The New West* (featuring Peter Case, Chip and Tony Kinman (Rank And File) and Sid Griffin (**Long Ryders**)). Prior to the *Pursuit Of Happiness* Montana's partner was guitarist Buddy Blue, who was replaced by Joey Harris. They covered **Johnny Cash** and **Tom Waits** songs alongside their own material, including the rustic 'Texas' and the sceptical 'God Is Here Tonight'. Harris emerged as a songwriter on *Poor & Famous*, alongside vocalist/guitarist Jerry Raney, with Montana taking a back seat. Although *Loud And Plowed* included covers of the **Kinks** and George Jones, the highlight of the live album was its documentation of Montana's idiosyncratic stage presence.

In the 90s Montana suffered from thyroid cancer which limited the Beat Farmers' activities, however they signed to independent label Sector 2 and completed two albums. Montana was also a member of the Pleasure Barons, an *ad hoc* roots band that included Dave Alvin (**Blasters**), John Doe (**X**), Mojo Nixon and Harris.

Montana died while on stage with the Beat Farmers at the Longhorn Saloon in British Columbia, promoting the release of *Manifold*. A posthumous solo collection was released in 1996.

BEATLES

THE LIVERPOOL PHENOMENON THAT BECAME THE BEATLES BEGAN IN 1957 WHEN TEENAGER **PAUL MCCARTNEY** (b. 1942) auditioned as guitarist for the Quarrymen, a skiffle group led by **John Lennon** (b. 1940, d. 1980). Within a year, a 15-year-old **George Harrison** (b. 1943; guitar) was recruited, alongside Stuart Sutcliffe (b. 1940, d. 1962). After a brief spell as Johnny And The Moondogs, the band rechristened themselves the Silver Beetles. In 1960, they played before impresario Larry Parnes, winning the dubious distinction of a support slot on a tour of Scotland with autumnal idol Johnny Gentle.

Later that year the group were renamed the Beatles. A full-time drummer, Pete Best (b. 1941) was recruited and they secured a residency at Bruno Koschminder's Indra Club in Hamburg, honing their repertoire of R&B and rock 'n' roll favourites during six-hour-sets. Already, the musical/lyrical partnership of Lennon/McCartney was bearing fruit, anticipating a body of work unparalleled in modern popular music. The image of the group was also changing, most noticeably with their fringed haircuts or, as they were later known, the 'mop-tops', the creation of Sutcliffe's German fiancée Astrid Kirchherr. The first German trip ended when the under-age Harrison was deported in 1960 and the others lost their work permits. Afterwards the group reassembled for regular performances at Liverpool's Cavern Club and briefly returned to Germany where they performed at the Top Ten club and backed **Tony Sheridan** on 'My Bonnie'. Meanwhile, Sutcliffe decided to leave, staying in Germany to paint. McCartney then took up the bass guitar.

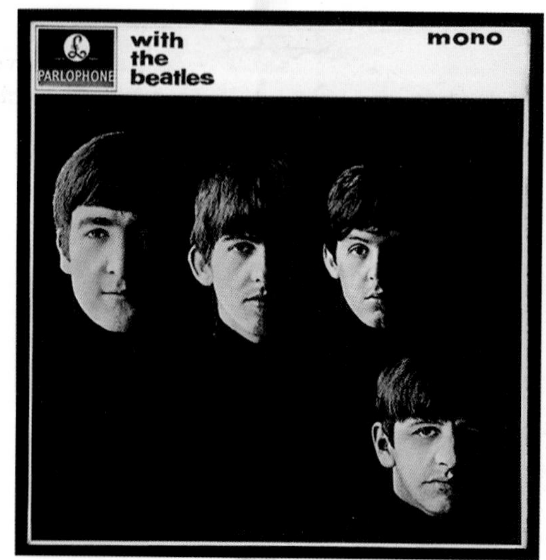

In 1961, **Brian Epstein** became their manager. Despite his enthusiasm, several major record companies passed up the Beatles, although they were granted an audition with Decca in 1962. After some prevarication, the label rejected the group in favour of **Brian Poole And The Tremeloes**.

The tragic news that Stuart Sutcliffe had died in Hamburg of a brain haemorrhage, took the Beatles back to Germany. While there, they began playing at Hamburg's Star Club. Shortly afterwards Epstein found a Beatles convert in EMI producer **George Martin**, who signed the group to Parlo-phone; three months later, Best was sacked – he looked the part, but his drumming was poor. His replacement was **Ringo Starr** (b. Richard Starkey, 1940), the extrovert and locally popular drummer from Rory Storm And The Hurricanes.

At the end of 1962, the Beatles reached the UK charts with their debut, 'Love Me Do'. The single was far removed from the traditional 'beat combo' sound, and the use of Lennon's harmonica made the song stand out. On 13 February 1963 the Beatles appeared on UK television's *Thank Your Lucky Stars* to promote 'Please Please Me'; they were seen by six million viewers. The single, with its distinctive harmonies and infectious group beat, soon topped the UK charts and signalled the imminent overthrow of the solo singer in favour of an irresistible wave of Mersey talent. From this point, the Beatles progressed artistically and commercially with each successive record. After seven weeks at the top with 'From Me To You', they released 'She Loves You' – the catchphrase 'Yeah, Yeah, Yeah' was echoed in frequent newspaper headlines. The single hit number 1, retreated, then returned to the top seven weeks later as Beatlemania gripped the nation. The Beatles became a household name. 'She Loves You' was replaced by 'I Want To Hold Your Hand', which had UK advance sales of over one million and entered the charts at number 1.

Until 1964, America had proven a barren ground for British pop artists. The Beatles changed that. 'I Want To Hold Your Hand' was helped by the band's television appearance on the *Ed Sullivan Show* and soon surpassed UK sales. By April, they held the first five places in the *Billboard* Hot 100, while in Canada they boasted nine records in the Top 10.

By 1965, Lennon and McCartney's writing had matured to a startling degree and their albums were relying less on other material. Their first two films, *A Hard Day's Night* and *Help!*, were not the usual pop celluloid cash-ins but were witty and inventive; they achieved critical acclaim as well as box office success. 1965 also saw the Beatles awarded MBEs for services to British industry and the release of their first double-sided number 1, 'We Can Work It Out'/'Day Tripper'.

At Christmas 1965, the Beatles released *Rubber Soul*, an album that was not a collection of would-be hits or favourite cover versions, as the previous releases had been, but a startingly diverse collection, ranging from the pointed satire of 'Nowhere Man' to the reflective 'In My Life'. Pointers to their future styles, included Harrison's use of sitar on 'Norwegian Wood' – that same year, the **Byrds**, **Yardbirds** and **Rolling Stones** also incorporated Eastern-influenced sounds into their work. Significantly George Harrison also wrote two songs for *Rubber Soul*, 'Think For Yourself' and 'If I Needed Someone' (later a hit for the **Hollies**).

During 1966, the Beatles continued performing their increasingly complex arrangements before scarcely controllable fans, but the novelty of fandom was wearing frustratingly thin. By the summer, the group were exhausted and defeated. They played their last official performance at Candlestick Park, San Francisco, on 29 August.

The gloriously elaborate harmonies and charmingly prosaic theme of 'Paperback Writer' were another step forward, followed by a double-sided chart topper, 'Yellow Submarine'/'Eleanor Rigby'. The attendant album *Revolver* was equally varied, with Harrison's caustic 'Taxman', McCartney's plaintive 'For No One' and Lennon's drug-influenced 'I'm Only Sleeping' and the mantric and then-scary 'Tomorrow Never Knows'. The latter is seen as the most effective evocation of a LSD experience ever recorded.

After 1966, the Beatles retreated into the studio. 'Penny Lane'/'Strawberry Fields Forever', their first release for over six months, broke their long run of consecutive UK number 1s – it was kept off the top by Engelbert Humperdinck's 'Release Me' – nevertheless, this landmark single brilliantly captured the talents of Lennon and McCartney. It was intended to be the jewel in the crown of their next album, but by the summer of 1967 they had sufficient material to release 13 new tracks on *Sgt. Pepper's Lonely Hearts Club Band*. This turned out to be no mere pop album but a cultural icon embracing pop art, garish fashion, drugs, instant mysticism and freedom from parental control. Although the Beatles had previously experimented with collages on *Beatles For Sale* and *Revolver*, they took the idea further on the sleeve of *Sgt. Pepper* which included photos of every influence on their lives that they could remember. The album had a gatefold sleeve, cardboard cut-out figurines, and, for the first time on a pop record, printed lyrics. The music had evolved too: instead of the traditional breaks between songs, one track merged into the next, linked by studio talk, laughter, electronic noises and animal sounds. The album closed with the epic 'Day In The Life', the Beatles' most ambitious work to date, featuring what Lennon described as 'a sound building up from nothing to the end of the world'.

While *Sgt. Pepper's Lonely Hearts Club Band* topped the album charts, the group appeared on a live television broadcast playing 'All You Need Is Love'. The following week it entered many of the world's charts at number 1; but there was sadness, too – on 21 August 1967, Brian Epstein was found dead, from a cumulative overdose of the drug Carbitrol. With spiritual guidance from the Maharishi Mahesh Yogi, the Beatles took Epstein's death calmly and decided to proceed without a manager. The first fruits of their post-Epstein labour was the film *Magical Mystery Tour*, screened on UK television on Boxing Day 1967. The phantasmogorical movie received mixed reviews, but nobody could complain about the music.

In 1968, the Beatles became increasingly involved with running their company, Apple Corps (alongside a mismanaged boutique that came and went). The first Apple single, 'Hey Jude', was a warm-hearted ballad that progressed over its seven-minute duration into a rousing singalong finale. Their third film, *Yellow Submarine*, was a cartoon, and the graphics were acclaimed as a landmark in animation. The soundtrack album was half instrumental, with George Martin responsible for some interesting orchestral work. Only four new proper Beatle tracks were included, among them Lennon's 'Hey Bulldog', Harrison's 'Only A Northern Song' and 'It's All Too Much'. With their prolific output, the group crammed the remainder of their most recent material on to a double album, *The Beatles* (now known as *The White Album*), released in a stark white cover.

Despite continued commercial success, the Beatles' inability as business executives was becoming apparent from the parlous state of Apple, to which Allen Klein attempted to restore some order. At the end of the decade, they released the number 1 'Get Back', a return-to-roots venture which featured **Billy Preston** on organ. Cameras were present at their next recording sessions, as they ran through dozens of songs, many of which they had not played since Hamburg. A select few also witnessed the band's last 'public' performance on the rooftop of the Apple headquarters in Savile Row, London. Amid the uncertainty of 1969, the Beatles enjoyed their final UK number 1 with 'Ballad Of John And Yoko', on which only Lennon and McCartney performed.

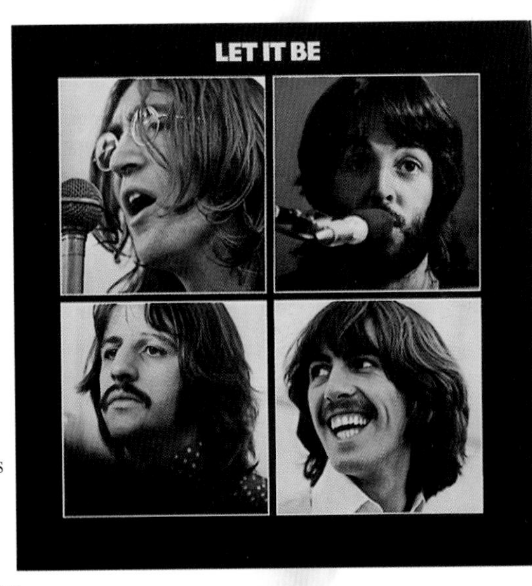

In a sustained attempt to cover the increasing cracks, they reconvened for *Abbey Road*. The accompanying single coupled Lennon's 'Come Together' with Harrison's 'Something'. The latter gave Harrison the kudos he deserved; it has become the second most covered Beatle song (the most popular is 'Yesterday'). The album reached only UK number 4, the group's lowest chart position since 1962.

With various solo projects coming up, the Beatles stumbled through 1970, their disunity emphasized in the depressing film *Let It Be*, which shows Harrison and Lennon clearly unhappy about McCartney's attitude towards the band. The subsequent album, finally pieced together by producer **Phil Spector**, was a controversial and bitty affair. It included an orchestrated 'Long And Winding Road' which provided their final US number 1, and there was their last official single, 'Let It Be', which entered the UK charts at number 2, only to drop to number 3 the following week; the final sad anti-climax before the inevitable split. The acrimonious dissolution of the Beatles, like that of no other group before or since, symbolized the end of an era that they had dominated and helped create.

John Lennon's tragic murder put an end to speculation of any reunions, but in 1995, the first volume of *Anthology* was released – a collection of 52 previously unreleased out-takes and demo versions recorded between 1958 and 1964, plus eight spoken tracks taken from interviews. The album was accompanied by an excellent six-part television series, made with the help of Harrison, McCartney and Starr, and by the release of 'Free As A Bird', the first song recorded by the Beatles since their break-up. The reaction to *Anthology 2* was ecstatic. *Anthology 3* could not improve upon the previous collection but there were gems to be found. Countless groups are loved, but the Beatles are universally and unconditionally adored.Thirty years on, and such is the quality of the songs that none have dated either lyrically or musically.

Influences
Chuck Berry ➡ p.45
Johnny Gentle
Little Richard ➡ p.217

Further References
Videos: *On The Road* (1990),
Books: *Shout! The True Story Of The Beatles* by Philip Norman
The Beatles Book, Norman Parkinson and Maureen Cleave.

BEAU BRUMMELS
Albums
Introducing The Beau Brummels (Autumn/Pye International 1965)★★★
Beau Brummels 66 (Warners 1966)★★★
Triangle (Warners 1967)★★★
➽ p.352 for full listings
Collaborators
Randy Newman ➽ p.246
Everly Brothers ➽ p.139
Connections
Sparklers
Harpers Bizarre ➽ p. 175
Influences
Beatles ➽ p.38
Searchers ➽ p.290

BEAUTIFUL SOUTH
Albums
Welcome To The Beautiful South (Go! Discs 1989)★★★
Choke (Go! Discs 1990)★★★
0898 (Go! Discs 1992)★★★
➽ p.352 for full listings

Connections
Housemartins ➽ p.188
Anthill Runaways
Soul II Soul ➽ p.303
Beats International
Further References
Videos: *The Pumpkin* (Polygram Music Video 1992)
Carry On Up The Charts (1995).

BEAVER AND KRAUSE
Albums
Ragnarock (Limelight 1969)★★★
Gandharva (Warners 1971)★★★
A Guide To Electronic Music (Nonesuch 1975)★★★
➽ p.352 for full listings
Collaborators
Beatles ➽ p.38
Beach Boys ➽ p.36
Rolling Stones ➽ p.281
Mike Bloomfield ➽ p.54

BECK
Albums
Mellow Gold (Geffen 1994)★★★★
Odelay (Geffen 1996)★★★★
Where It's At/Lloyd Price Express (Geffen 1996)★★★.
➽ p.352 for full listings
Collaborators
Calvin Johnson

BEAU BRUMMELS

FORMED IN SAN FRANCISCO IN 1964 BY VOCALIST SAL VALENTINO WITH RON ELLIOTT (b. 1943; GUITAR/VOCALS), Ron Meagher (b. 1941; bass) and John Petersen (b. 1942; drums). Playing a staple diet of current hits and material by the **Beatles** and **Searchers**, the Beau Brummels enjoyed a committed local following. Declan Mulligan (guitar) subsequently joined.

Local entrepreneurs Tom Donahue and Bob Mitchell signed the group to their label, Autumn. 'Laugh Laugh' (1964) broached the US Top 20; 'Just A Little' (1965), reached number 8 and the hits continued. The group's first two albums fused folk, country and R&B; they proved Elliott a distinctive songwriter, while Valentino's deep, tremulous delivery provided an unmistakable lead. Mulligan left in 1965, but the group continued to make progress.

In 1966, they moved to Warner Brothers Records. New member, Don Irving, was featured on their disappointing next collection, *Beau Brummels 66*; Irving and Petersen both left (the latter later joined **Harpers Bizarre**) and the remaining trio completed the exquisite *Triangle*. Meagher left in 1967 and undertook several projects: songwriting and arranging albums for **Randy Newman**, the **Everly Brothers** and Harpers Bizarre. Elliott and Valenremained to complete *Bradley's Barn*, an early excursion into country - rock, before separating. Valentino issued three solo singles before founding Stoneground. Elliott completed *The Candlestickmaker*, formed the disappointing Pan, then undertook session work.

The original Beau Brummels regrouped in 1974, although Meagher was replaced by Dan Levitt. *Beau Brummels* was an engaging collection, but progress halted in 1975 when Petersen left for a Harpers Bizarre reunion. Peter Tepp provided a temporary replacement, but the project was abandoned.

The Beau Brummels have since enjoyed several short-lived resurrections. Archive recordings have kept the group's name and music alive.

BEAUTIFUL SOUTH

THIS HIGHLY LITERATE UK POP GROUP GREW FROM THE ASHES OF THE **HOUSEMARTINS**. THE LINE-UP featured vocalists Paul Heaton (b. 1962) and David Hemmingway (b. 1960) who recruited Sean Welch (bass), Briana Corrigan (vocals), former Housemartins roadie David Stead (drums) and Heaton's new co-writer, David Rotheray (guitar). Continuing an association with Go! Discs, their first single was 'Song For Whoever' which reached UK number 2 in 1989. *Welcome To The Beautiful South* (1989) was critically praised and 'A Little Time' (1990) became their first number 1.

'My Book' provided one of Heaton's most cutting lyrics and also saw Jazzie B. of **Soul II Soul** sue for the slight use of the 'Back To Reality' refrain. A writer able to deal with emotive subjects in an intelligent and forthright manner, Heaton's next topic was alcoholism in 'Old Red Eyes Is Back'. However, Corrigan objected to the lyrics of '36D' (a song about topless models) and left the band after *0898*. Her replacement, Jacqui Abbot, was introduced on 'Everybody's Talkin'', and more fully on *Miaow*. The singles collection, *Carry On Up The Charts* dominated the listings in late 1994 and early 1995. 'Rotterdam' and 'Don't Marry Her', from *Blue Is The Colour*, continued their run of hit singles.

BEAVER AND KRAUSE

PAUL BEAVER (b. 1925, d. 1975) AND BERNIE KRAUSE WERE EARLY EXPONENTS OF ELECTRONIC MUSIC. BEAVER played in several jazz groups before exploring synthesized instrumentation, later contributing sound effects to various film soundtracks (*Catch 22* and *Performance*). Krause came from the folk group the Weavers before working at **Motown Records**; moving on to Elektra Records, he met Beaver. Their use of tape loops and improvisation pushed back the boundaries of rock and their session work graced albums by the **Beatles**, **Beach Boys**, **Rolling Stones**, **Simon And Garfunkel** and **Neil Young** among others. *Gandharva*, recorded in San Francisco's Grace Cathedral, proved their most popular release, featuring contributions from **Mike Bloomfield** and saxophonist Gerry Mulligan. Beaver completed a solo album, *Perchance To Dream*, prior to his death and Krause has pursued a career in electronic music.

BECK

BECK HANSEN (b. 1970) ROSE SWIFTLY TO PROMINENCE IN 1994 WITH HIS COMBINATION OF FOLK AND GUITAR sounds. His guitar-playing was inspired by the blues of Mississippi John Hurt, which he would deliver with improvised lyrics while busking. After dropping out of school at 16, he played his first gigs in-between sets at LA clubs. His music was now a *pot pourri* of diverse influences – street hip-hop, Delta blues, Presbyterian hymns, punk with scat lyrics – and the whole was beginning to take shape as he released his first single, 'MTV Makes Me Want To Smoke Crack'.

'Loser', produced with hip-hop technician Karl Stephenson, was finally released after a year's delay. Critics called it an anthem for doomed youth. The major labels swooped for his signature which Geffen Records won, although Beck had already set in motion two independent records – 'Steve Threw Up' for Bong Load and A *Western Harvest Field By Moonlight*, on Fingerpaint Records. Geffen's contract allowed Beck to continue recording material for other companies. *Mellow Gold*, the debut album for Geffen was one of three albums released in 1994, alongside *Stereo Pathetic Soul Manure* on LA's Flipside independent, and a collaboration with Calvin Johnson of Beat Happening, emerged on K Records. *Odelay* (1996) was his next major release and reaped numerous Album Of The Year awards in the music press. It spawned several successful singles, including 'Where It's At' and a Noel Gallagher (**Oasis**) remix of 'Devil's Haircut'.

BECK, JEFF

UK-BORN BECK (b. 1944) WAS A COMPETENT PIANIST AND GUITARIST BY THE AGE OF 11. His first band was the locally acclaimed Tridents, before he replaced guitarist **Eric Clapton** in the **Yardbirds**, silencing sceptical fans by his guitar pyrotechnics utilizing feedback and distortion. The tension between Beck and joint lead guitarist **Jimmy Page** was finally resolved during a US tour in 1966: Beck walked out and never returned. His solo career was launched in 1967 with 'Hi-Ho Silver Lining', featuring his trademark guitar solo. The record was a hit and has re-entered the charts on several occasions. The follow-up, 'Tallyman', was also a minor hit, but Beck's ambitions lay in other directions. The Jeff Beck Group, formed in 1968, consisted of Beck, **Rod Stewart** (vocals), Ron Wood (bass), **Nicky Hopkins** (piano) and Mickey Waller (drums); they released *Truth*. It was a major US success, resulting in the band undertaking a number of arduous tours. *Cosa Nostra Beck-Ola*, were similarly successful, although Stewart and Wood had by now departed for the **Faces**. Beck contributed some sparkling guitar and received equal billing with **Donovan** on the hit single 'Goo Goo Barabajagal (Love Is Hot)'. Beck formed another group with Cozy Powell, Max Middleton and Bob Tench, and recorded two further albums, *Rough And Ready* and *Jeff Beck Group*.

In 1973, Beck formed the trio Beck, Bogert And Appice with two former members of **Vanilla Fudge**. Soon afterwards, he introduced yet another musical dimension, this time forming an instrumental band. The result was the excellent *Blow By Blow*, a million-seller as was its follow-up, *Wired*, on which he combined rock, jazz and blues. Beck teamed up with Jan Hammer for a live album, after which he effectively retired for three years. He returned in 1980 with *There And Back* and found himself riding the album charts once more. During the 80s, Beck's appearances were sporadic, though he did work with **Tina Turner**, **Robert Plant** and **Jimmy Page**. In the mid-80s he toured with Rod Stewart and was present on his version of 'People Get Ready'.

Flash proved his least successful album to date, but the release of a box set in 1992, chronicling his career, was a fitting tribute. Following an award in 1993 for his theme music (with Jed Stoller) for TV's *Frankie's House*, he released *Crazy Legs*, a tribute to the music of **Gene Vincent.** For this, Beck stuck to a clean, low-volume rock 'n' roll sound. He made his acting debut, playing Brad the serial killer in *The Comic Strip Presents ... Gregory: Diary Of A Nutcase.*

BEE GEES

HUGELY SUCCESSFUL TRIO COMPRISING TWINS MAURICE AND ROBIN GIBB (b. 1949) AND THEIR ELDER BROTHER

Barry (b. 1946). As children, they performed regularly in Manchester, England, before the family emigrated to Australia in 1958. The boys began performing as a harmony trio and, christened the Bee Gees, an abbreviation of Brothers Gibb, they signed to the Australian label Festival Records, releasing a series of singles written by Barry. While 'Spicks And Specks' was topping the Australian charts, the brothers were on their way to London to audition for Robert Stigwood. This led to a record contract with Polydor and the swift release of 'New York Mining Disaster, 1941'. The single with its evocative, intriguing lyrics and striking harmony provoked premature comparison with the Beatles and gained the group a UK hit. During this period, Australians Colin Peterson (drums) and Vince Melouney (guitar) joined. The second UK single, 'To Love Somebody', departed from the narrative power of their previous offering towards a more straightforward ballad style. Although it failed to reach the Top 40, the song was covered on many occasions, most notably by **Nina Simone**, **Eric Burdon** And The **Animals** and **Janis Joplin**.

By 1967, the group had their first UK number 1 with 'Massachusetts'. They experimented with different musical styles and briefly followed the **Beatles** and the **Rolling Stones** along the psychedelic road, but their progressive forays confused their audience, and the double album *Odessa* failed to match the work of their major rivals. Their singles remained adventurous, with the unusual tempo of 'World' followed by the neurotic romanticism of 'Words'. Both singles hit the UK Top 10 but signs of commercial fallibility followed with the relatively unsuccessful double a-side 'Jumbo'/'The Singer Not The Song'. The group next turned to the heart-rending 'I've Gotta Get A Message To You' – their second UK number 1 and sixth consecutive US Top 20 hit. The group then showed their talent as composers, penning the Marbles' Top 10 UK hit 'Only One Woman'.

Internal bickering led to a year of chaos, but after reuniting in 1970 they went on to have two major US hits with 'Lonely Days' and the chart-topping 'How Can You Mend A Broken Heart'. Yet, despite transatlantic hits in 1972 with 'My World' and 'Run To Me', the group's appeal diminished to an all-time low and three hitless years.

Eventually they teamed up with famed producer Arif Mardin, resulting in *Mr. Natural.* The album indicated a noticeable R&B/soul influence which was extended on *Main Course*. Now living in Miami, the group gathered together a formidable backing unit: Alan Kendall (guitar), Dennis Bryon (drums) and Blue Weaver (keyboards). 'Jive Talkin'', a pilot single from the album, zoomed to US number 1 and brought them back to the UK Top 10. The group were perfectly placed to promote and take advantage of the underground dance scene in the USA, and their next album, *Children Of The World*, went platinum; 'You Should Be Dancing' reached US number 1 and 'Love So Right', hit number 3. The trio's soundtrack contributions also provided massive hits for Yvonne Elliman ('If I Can't Have You') and Tavares ('More Than A Woman'). The Bee Gees' reputation as the new gods of the discotheque was consummated on the movie soundtrack *Saturday Night Fever*, which sold in excess of 30 million copies. The group achieved a staggering run of six consecutive chart toppers, including 'How Deep Is Your Love', 'Stayin' Alive' and 'Night Fever'. Their grand flurry continued with the movie *Grease*, for which they produced the chart-topping title track by **Frankie Valli**. Ill-advisedly the group then took the starring role in the movie *Sgt. Pepper's Lonely Hearts Club Band*. The film proved an embarrassing detour for both the brothers and their co-star **Peter Frampton**.

As the 70s ended the Bee Gees increasingly switched towards production. Although they released *Spirits Having Flown* (1979) and *Living Eyes* (1981), greater attention was being focused on their chart-topping younger brother Andy. With the group's activities on hold, Barry emerged as the most prolific producer and songwriter. He duetted with Barbra Streisand on 'Guilty' and composed and sang on **Dionne Warwick**'s 'Heartbreaker'. The brothers also wrote 'Islands In The Stream' (**Kenny Rogers/Dolly Parton**) and **Diana Ross**'s 'Chain Reaction'.

The group reunited in 1987 for the hugely successful *ESP*. Their 'comeback' single 'You Win Again' was warmly received by usually hostile critics and gave the group their fifth UK number 1. Sadly, the death of Andy in 1988 added a tragic note to the proceedings.

At the 1997 BRIT Awards, the ineffable institution that is the Bee Gees was given true recognition, this was followed by a glut of press and television promotion for *Still Waters*, – a sizeable hit.

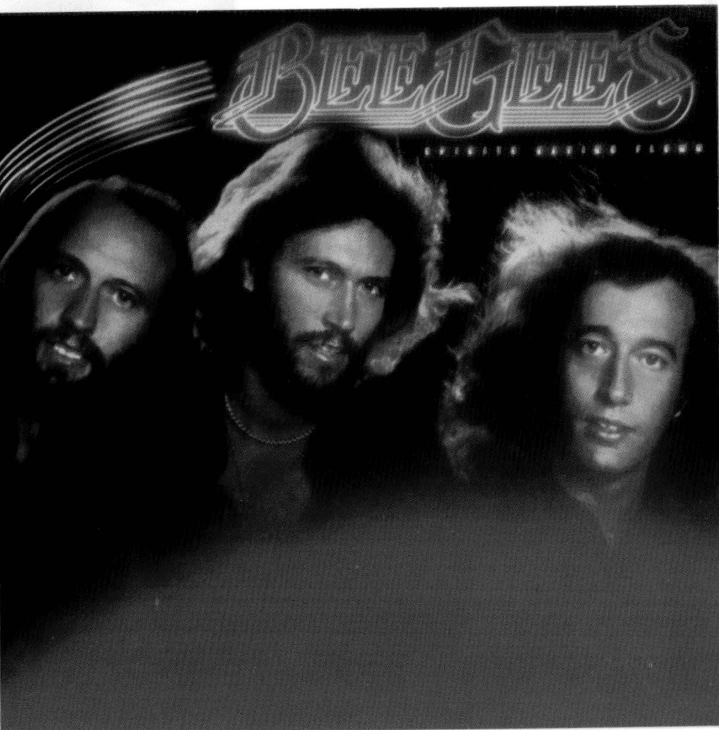

Connections
Oasis ➧ p.250
Influences
Leadbelly
Woody Guthrie ➧ p.170

BECK, JEFF
Albums
Truth (EMI 1968)★★★
Blow By Blow (Epic 1975)★★★★
Crazy Legs (Epic 1993)★★★
➧ p.352 for full listings
Collaborators
Donovan ➧ p.123
Tina Turner ➧ p.324
Robert Plant ➧ p.262
Rod Stewart ➧ p.310
Connections
Yardbirds ➧ p.345
Jeff Beck Group ➧ p.41
Faces ➧ p.141
Vanilla Fudge ➧ p.329
Influences
Gene Vincent ➧ p. 330
Further References
Book: *Rock Fun 3 Photo Gallery: Jeff Beck* (Japan)

BEE GEES
Albums
The Bee Gees First (Polydor 1967)★★★★
Horizontal (Polydor 1968)★★★★
Main Course (RSO 1975)★★★★
➧ p.352 for full listings
Collaborators
Peter Frampton ➧ p.152
Barbra Streisand
Dionne Warwick ➧ p.334
Dolly Parton ➧ p.256
Kenny Rogers ➧ p.280
Diana Ross ➧ p.283
Influences
Beatles ➧ p.38
Rolling Stones ➧ p.281
Further References
Video: *Bee Gees: Video Biography* (Virgin Vision 1988)
Books: *The Official Sgt. Pepper's Lonely Hearts Club Band Scrapbook*, Robert Stigwood and Dee Anthony
Bee Gees: The Authorized Biography, Barry, Robin and Maurice Gibb as told to David Leaf

BELL, ARCHIE, AND THE DRELLS
Albums
Tighten Up (Atlantic 1968)★★★★
Dance Your Troubles Away (TSOP 1976)★★★
➧ p.352 for full listings

BELL, FREDDIE, AND THE BELLBOYS
Albums
Rock 'n' Roll All Flavours (Mercury 1958)★★★
Bells Are Swinging (20th Century 1964)★★
Rockin' is Our Business (Bear Family 1996)★★★
➧ p.352 for full listings
Collaborators
Tommy Steele
Roberta Linn
Connections
Elvis Presley ➧ p.265

BELL, MAGGIE
Albums
Queen Of The Night (Super 1974)★★★
Suicide Sal (Polydor 1975)★★★
➧ p.352 for full listings
Collaborators
B.A. Robertson ➧ p.278
Connections
Frankie and Johnny
Stone the Crows
Midnight Flyer
Rod Stewart

BELLAMY BROTHERS
Albums
Let Your Love Flow (Warners 1976)★★★★
The Two And Only (Warners 1979)★★★,
Over The Line (Bellamy Brothers 1997)★★★
➧ p.352 for full listings
Connections
Jericho
Further References
Video: *Best Of The Best* (Start Video 1994)

BELLY
Albums
Star (Sire/4AD 1993)★★★
King (Sire/4AD 1995)★★
➧ p.352 for full listings
Connections
Throwing Muses ➧ p.321
Breeders ➧ p.67
L7 ➧ p.211

BELOVED
Albums
Happiness (Atlantic 1990)★★★
Conscience (East West 1993)★★★
Single File (East West 1997)★★★
➧ p.352 for full listings
Connections
Steve Hillage ➧ p.182

BELL, ARCHIE, AND THE DRELLS

THIS AMERICAN VOCAL SOUL GROUP WAS FORMED BY ARCHIE BELL (b. 1944), WITH JAMES WISE (b. 1948) AND Willie Parnell (b. 1945). By their first record in 1967, the group comprised Bell, Wise, Huey 'Billy' Butler and Joe Cross. 'Tighten Up' sold in excess of three million copies and reached US number 1, whilst Bell, who had been drafted into the army, was recuperating from a wound received in Vietnam. The Drells continued recording with producers **Gamble And Huff**; for live performances, fake 'Archie Bells' were enlisted and whenever possible, the real Bell would join them in the studio. These sessions produced three more hits: 'I Can't Stop Dancing', 'Doin' The Choo-Choo' (both 1968) and '(There's Gonna Be A) Showdown' (1969). Paradoxically, the singles were less successful once Bell left the forces. 'Here I Go Again' was a UK hit in 1972.

In 1975, they enjoyed several R&B successes on their TSOP/ Philadelphia International label, including 'Let's Groove (Part 1)' (1976) and 'Soul City Walk' (1975) which entered the UK Top 20 in 1976. Archie Bell recorded a solo album in 1981 and charted with 'Any Time Is Right'. He still actively pursues a singing career.

BELL, FREDDIE, AND THE BELLBOYS

THIS US ROCK 'N' ROLL SIX-PIECE OUTFIT WAS LED BY FREDDIE BELL (b. 1931; VOCALS). THEIR REPERTOIRE included a version of Willie Mae Thornton's 'Hound Dog' in 1955, which **Elvis Presley** saw them performing live in 1956 – he recorded his own version. In 1956, the Bellboys appeared in the first rock 'n' roll movie, *Rock Around The Clock*, and were the first US rock act to tour the UK, supporting Tommy Steele.

'Giddy Up A Ding Dong' reached UK number 4; other singles included 'The Hucklebuck', 'Teach You To Rock' and 'Rockin' Is My Business'. They appeared in another film, *The Swingin' Set* (*Get Yourself A College Girl* in the US) (1964), singing with Roberta Linn. Bell now lives in Las Vegas for most of the year and tours the world in the remaining weeks.

BELL, MAGGIE

SCOTTISH SINGER BELL (b. 1945) BEGAN HER CAREER IN THE MID-60S AS THE FEATURED SINGER IN SEVERAL resident dancehall bands. She made her recording debut in 1966, completing two singles with Bobby Kerr as Frankie And Johnny, before joining guitarist Leslie Harvey in Power, a hard-rock group that evolved into Stone The Crows. This earthy, soul-based band became a popular live attraction.

After Harvey's tragic death in 1972, the band disintegrated. Bell embarked on a solo career with *Queen Of The Night*, produced by Jerry Wexler and featuring the cream of New York's session musicians. The anticipated success did not materialize and further releases also flopped. 'Hazell' (1978), the theme tune to a popular television series, was a minor UK hit but 'Hold Me', a tongue-in-cheek duet with **B.A. Robertson**, remains her only other chart entry. Bell subsequently fronted Midnight Flyer and can be seen on the blues club circuit.

BELL, THOM

BELL (b. 1941) STUDIED CLASSICAL PIANO AS A CHILD. IN 1959 HE TEAMED UP WITH KENNY GAMBLE IN A VOCAL duo before joining Gamble's harmony group, the Romeos. At 19 Bell was working with **Chubby Checker**, conducting and arranging the singer's material. Bell contributed original songs and later joined Checker's production company. As a session musician he met the **Delfonics**, and when their manager, Stan Watson, formed his Philly Groove outlet in 1968, Bell's shimmering production work was evident on 'La La Means I Love You' (1968) and 'Didn't I Blow Your Mind This Time' (1970). Bell then resumed work with Kenny Gamble who, with Leon Huff, was forging the classic Philadelphia sound.

Bell also worked with the **O'Jays**, Jerry Butler and the **Stylistics**. Between 1971 and 1974, he fashioned the latter's finest releases – 'You Are Everything' (1971), 'Betcha By Golly Wow' and 'I'm Stone In Love With You' (both 1972). He went on to enjoy success with the **(Detroit) Spinners**, the **Bee Gees** and Johnny Mathis, and continued his career as a producer, arranger and songwriter.

BELLAMY BROTHERS

AMERICAN BROTHERS HOWARD (b. 1946) AND DAVID BELLAMY (B. 1950) BEGAN THEIR CAREER IN POP AND soul. They formed Jericho in 1968, but disbanded three years later, to begin writing songs for other artists (David's 'Spiders And Snakes' was a Top 3 hit for Jim Stafford). In 1976, the Bellamy Brothers reached US number 1 and the UK Top 10 with 'Let Your Love Flow'. In 1979 'If I Said You Had A Beautiful Body (Would You Hold It Against Me)?' became the first of 10 country chart singles for the group and reached the UK Top 3. By the late 80s, the brothers were recording country hits on a regular basis. In 1995 they updated 'Old Hippie' with 'Old Hippie (The Sequel)'.

BELLY

BASED IN RHODE ISLAND, USA, BELLY CONSIST OF TANYA DONELLY (b. 1966; VOCALS/GUITAR), THOMAS GORMAN (b.1966; lead guitar), Chris Gorman (b. 1967; drums) and Gail Greenwood (b. 1960; bass). Donelly, along with half-sister Kristin Hersh, was a founding member of **Throwing Muses**. She had also worked with the **Breeders** before moving on to Belly. They formed in 1991, originally including Fred Abong (ex-Throwing Muses; bass), soon replaced by Leslie Langston (ex-Throwing Muses), who was replaced by Greenwood.

Belly debuted with the EPs *Slow Dust* and *Gepetto*, followed by *Star*. *Feed The Tree* gave them a chart hit and reached UK number 2. Included on it was a version of 'Trust In Me' (from Disney's *The Jungle Book*). *King* was recorded with producer Glyn Johns, and featured writing contributions from Tom Gorman and Greenwood for the first time. The band split in 1996 and Donnelly went solo. Greenwood joined **L7**.

BELOVED

FORMED IN THE UK IN 1983 AS THE JOURNEY THROUGH – COMPRISING JON MARSH (b. *c.* 1964), GUY GOUSDEN and Tim Havard. The Beloved fell into place a year later when Steve Waddington (b. *c.* 1959; guitar) joined. Tentative stabs at heavy psychedelia evolved into a more pop-orientated formula by the mid-80s. In 1988 Waddington and Marsh, influenced by the nascent 'rave' scene, split from Gousden and Harvard and started forging their own path. The revitalized duo dived into the deep end of the exploding dance movement, attaining commerciality with the ambient 'Sun Rising'. *Happiness* perfectly embodied the vibe of the times, but by 1993's *Conscience*, Marsh had left former partner Waddington), with his wife Helena as his new creative foil. The resultant album was more whimsical and understated than previous affairs, with a pop feel. Their third album relied heavily on electronic gimmickry, detracting attention from individual songs. Returning in 1996 with *X*, the group's sound showed no signs of progression.

BEN FOLDS FIVE

FORMED IN NORTH CAROLINA, USA, BEN FOLDS FIVE COMPRISE BEN FOLDS (PIANO/VOCALS), ROBERT SLEDGE (BASS) and Darren Jessee (drums). Their eponymous debut album (1996) displayed the group's offbeat, ever-inventive style. Their live shows were also breathtaking. *Whatever And Ever Amen* combined humour with the sadness of broken relationships. A rock group without a lead guitar, Ben Folds Five are unusual and distinctive. In 1998, they were back in the UK charts and touring.

BENATAR, PAT

AFTER TRAINING AS AN OPERA SINGER BENATAR (b. PAT ANDRZEJEWSKI, 1953) BECAME A MAJOR hitmaker in the early 80s, adept at both mainstream rock and powerful ballads. Her hit debut album *In The Heat Of The Night*, produced by **Mike Chapman**, spawned three US chart singles. Benatar released her second album, *Crimes Of Passion*, in 1980. This collection, which later won a Grammy for Best Female Rock Vocal Performance, rose to US number 2, while the hard-rocking 'Hit Me With Your Best Shot', became her first *Billboard* Top 10 single. *Precious Time* (1981) reached US number 1 and, although no Top 10 singles resulted, Benatar won another Grammy for 'Fire And Ice'. In 1982 Benatar married producer Neil Geraldo, who played guitar in her band and wrote most of her material. She released *Get Nervous*, which reached US number 4. In 1983, 'Love Is A Battlefield' reached US number 5, as did 'We Belong' (1984) from *Tropico*. The former single reached the UK Top 20 hit in 1985. That same year, 'Invincible', from the film *Legend Of Billie Jean*, reached the US Top 10, but *Seven The Hard Way* (1985) indicated a decline in popularity. A compilation album, *Best Shots*, was released in 1987. Since then Benatar has reportedly gone into acting.

BENNETT, CLIFF

CLIFF BENNETT (b. 1940) FORMED THE REBEL ROUSERS IN EARLY 1961. TAKING THEIR NAME FROM A **DUANE EDDY** hit, the group comprised Mick King (lead guitar), Frank Allen (bass), Sid Phillips (piano/saxophone) and Ricky Winters (drums). With a repertoire of rock 'n' roll, blue-eyed soul and R&B, the group recorded several unsuccessful singles. A succession of R&B covers brought no further success and, early in 1964, Allen departed to replace Tony Jackson in the **Searchers**. The Rebel Rousers finally had a Top 10 hit, 'One Way Love', in November 1964. This brassy, upbeat cover version of the **Drifters**' original augured well, but the follow-up, 'I'll Take You Home', stalled at number 43. A move to **Brian Epstein**'s NEMs management secured them the invaluable patronage of the **Beatles**, and **Paul McCartney** produced 'Got To Get You Into My Life' from the recently released *Revolver*. Peaking at number 6, the single was their second and last Top 10 hit.

In 1969, Bennett dissolved the group to reinvent himself for the progressive market. The result was Toe Fat. In 1972, he tried again with Rebellion, and, three years later, Shanghai, but without success. He still plays semi-professionally.

BENNETT, TONY

THE SON OF AN ITALIAN FATHER AND AMERICAN MOTHER, BENNETT (b. ANTHONY DOMINICK Benedetto, 1926) became a talented artist, exhibiting in New York, Paris and London. His tenor voice (which deepened over the years) led Bennett to sing during service with the US Army's entertainment unit, in World War II. After the army, he worked in clubs as Joe Bari; he was spotted by Bob Hope who changed his name to Tony Bennett. In 1950, he was signed to Columbia and, a year later, topped the US chart with 'Because Of You' and 'Cold, Cold Heart'. Other 50s hits, mostly backed by the Percy Faith Orchestra, included 'Rags To Riches', 'Stranger In Paradise' (from *Kismet*) and 'In The Middle Of An Island'. In 1958, *Basie Swings – Bennett Sings* was a precursor to later jazz-based work. That same year 'Firefly', by Cy Coleman and Carolyn Leigh, hit the US Top 40.

In 1962, he cameback with 'I Left My Heart In San Francisco' (which won a Grammy Award) and a sell-out Carnegie Hall concert, which was released as a double-album set. He continued his long association with pianist/arranger Ralph Sharon, and frequently featured cornet soloist Bobby Hackett. Bennett made the 60s singles charts with contemporary songs such as 'I Wanna Be Around', 'The Good Life' and 'If I Ruled The World' plus US Top 40 albums. In the 70s, Bennett made albums with jazz musicians Ruby Braff and Bill Evans. Returning to Columbia in the 80s, he released *The Art Of Excellence*, which included a duet with **Ray Charles**, and *Bennett/Berlin*, a celebration of Irving Berlin.

In 1991, he celebrated 40 years in the business with a concert in London. In 1993 and 1994 he was awarded Grammys for 'Best Traditional Pop Performance' for *Perfectly Frank* and *Steppin' Out*. He also appeared on the *David Letterman Show* and performed an *Unplugged* session on MTV. The latter teamed him with **k.d. lang** and **Elvis Costello**. The 90s are proving to be his most critically acclaimed decade.

Further References
Video: *Happiness: Video 1990* Atlantic.

BEN FOLDS FIVE
Albums
Ben Folds Five (Caroline 1996)★★★
Whatever And Ever Amen (Epic 1997)★★★★
➧ p.352 for full listings

BENATAR, PAT
Albums
In The Heat Of The Night (Chrysalis 1979)★★★
Seven The Hard Way (Chrysalis 1985)★★★
Innamorata (CMC 1997)★★★
➧ p.352 for full listings
Further References
Book: *Benatar*, Doug Magee
Film: *American Pop* (1981)

BENNETT, CLIFF
Albums
Cliff Bennett And The Rebel Rousers (Parlophone 1965)★★★
Drivin' You Wild (MFP 1966)★★★
Got To Get You Into Our Lives (Parlophone 1967)★★★
➧ p.352 for full listings
Connections
Rebel Rousers
Searchers ➧ p.290
Paul McCartney ➧ p.229
Influences
Duane Eddy ➧ p.132
Drifters ➧ p.126

BENNETT, TONY
Albums
If I Ruled The World (Columbia 1959)★★★★
with Bill Evans *The Bennett Evans Album* (Mobile Fidelity 1975)★★★★
MTV Unplugged (Columbia 1994)★★★★
➧ p.352 for full listings
Collaborators
Ray Charles ➧ p.88
k.d Lang ➧ p.212
Elvis Costello ➧ p.101
Connections
Billie Holiday
Further References
Videos: *Tony Bennett Live: Watch What Happens* (Sony 1991)
The Art Of The Singer (SMV 1996)
Book: *What My Heart Has Seen*, Tony Bennett

BENSON, GEORGE
Albums
It's Uptown (Columbia 1966)★★★★
Breezin' (Warners 1976)★★★★
Give Me The Night (Warners 1980)★★★★
➽ p.352 for full listings
Collaborators
Herbie Hancock ➽ p.174
Wes Montgomery
Earl Klugh
Miles Davis
Joe Farrell
Aretha Franklin ➽ p.153
Influences
Jefferson Airplane ➽ p.198
Bobby Darin ➽ p.111
Nat King Cole

BENTON, BROOK
Albums
It's Just A Matter Of Time (Mercury 1959)★★★
with Dinah Washington *The Two Of Us — With Dinah Washington* (Mercury 1960)★★★★
Born To Sing The Blues (Mercury 1964)★★★
➽ p.352 for full listings
Collaborators
Dinah Washington
Connections
Clyde McPhatter
Roy Hamilton

BERLIN
Albums
Pleasure Victim (Geffen 1983)★★
Love Life (Geffen 1984)★★
➽ p.352 for full listings

BERRY, CHUCK
Albums
One Dozen Berrys (Chess 1958)★★★★★
St. Louis To Liverpool (Chess 1964)★★★★★
➽ p.352 for full listings
Connections
Chuck Berry Combo
Muddy Waters ➽ p.242
Beach Boys ➽ p.36
Influences
Nat King Cole
Dave Bartholomew ➽ p.34
Further References
Book: *Chuck Berry: The Autobiography*, Chuck Berry.
Films: *Go Johnny Go* (1958)
American Hot Wax (1976)

BENSON, GEORGE

THIS AMERICAN GUITARIST AND SINGER (b. 1943) PLAYED IN VARIOUS R&B OUTFITS IN THE 50S, AND RECORDED 'It Should Have Been Me' in 1954. By 1965 he was an established jazz guitarist, having worked with Brother Jack McDuff, **Herbie Hancock** and, crucially, Wes Montgomery (whose repertoire was drawn from pop, light classical and other non-jazz sources). Further testament to Benson's prestige was the presence of Hancock, Earl Klugh, Miles Davis, Joe Farrell and other jazz musicians on his early albums.

From *Beyond The Blue Horizon*, an arrangement of **Jefferson Airplane**'s 'White Rabbit' was a turntable hit and, after *Bad Benson* reached the US album lists, the title song of *Supership* cracked European charts. Benson signed to Warner Brothers Records, winning Grammy awards with 1976's *Breezin'* and its memorable 'This Masquerade'. Reissues of his earlier work included *The Other Side Of Abbey Road*, a track-for-track interpretation of the entire **Beatles** album. Profit from film themes such as 'The Greatest Love Of All' (from the *The Greatest*) and the million-selling *Give Me The Night* have allowed him to revisit his jazz roots via 1987's excellent *Collaboration* with Earl Klugh, and a merger with **Aretha Franklin** on 'Love All The Hurt Away'. Revivals of 'On Broadway' – a US Top 10 single from 1978's *Weekend In LA* – and **Bobby Darin**'s 'Beyond The Sea (La Mer)' proved marketable. Benson also found success with Nat 'King' Cole's 'Nature Boy' – and a lesser hit with Cole's 'Tenderly' in 1989. In 1990, he staged a collaboration with the Count Basie Orchestra, accompanied by a sell-out UK tour. He continued to release albums through the 90s.

BENTON, BROOK

A STYLISH, MELLIFLUENT SINGER, BENTON (b. BENJAMIN FRANKLIN PEAY, 1931, d. 1988) BEGAN RECORDING IN 1953, but his first major hit came in 1959, after forging a songwriting partnership with Clyde Otis and Belford Hendricks. 'It's Just A Matter Of Time' reached the US Top 3, followed by 'So Many Ways' (1959), 'The Boll Weevil Song' (1961) and 'Hotel Happiness' (1962). Duets with Dinah Washington, 'Baby (You've Got What It Takes)', a million-seller, and 'A Rockin' Good Way (To Mess Around And Fall In Love)', topped the R&B listings in 1960. His releases encompassed standards, blues and spirituals, while his compositions were recorded by Nat 'King' Cole, Clyde McPhatter and Roy Hamilton.

Later releases failed to recapture his previous success, but by the end of the decade, he rose to the challenge of younger acts with a series of excellent recordings for Atlantic Records' Cotillion subsidiary. His languid, atmospheric version of 'Rainy Night In Georgia' (1970) was an international hit. Benton continued to record for a myriad of outlets during the 70s, including Brut, Stax and MGM. Sadly he died of pneumonia while weakened by spinal meningitis, aged 56.

BERLIN

LOS ANGELES ELECTRO-POP GROUP FORMED IN 1979. JOHN CRAWFORD (BASS/SYNTHESIZER, EX-Videos), Terri Nunn (b. 1961; vocals), Virginia McCalino (vocals), Jo Julian (synthesizer), Chris Velasco (guitar) and Dan Van Patten (drums, ex-Barbies) signed to IRS in the USA, but managed only one single before breaking up in 1981. Crawford and Nunn formed a new band with David Diamond (guitars), Rick Olsen (guitar), Matt Reid (keyboards) and Rod Learned (drums). The 1983 mini-album *Pleasure Victim* (not released in the UK) was followed by *Love Life* in 1984. They gained a US Top 30 hit with 'No More Words' (1984), before the line-up changed to Crawford, Nunn and Rob Brill (drums) in 1985. By 1986, they had a transatlantic number 1 with 'Take My Breath Away', the theme song to the movie *Top Gun*; it re-entered the charts in 1988 and reached the UK Top 3 on reissue in 1990. Follow-up singles have fared less well.

BERNS, BERT

THIS SONGWRITER-PRODUCER (b. 1929, d. 1967) BEGAN COMPOSING UNDER THE PSEUDONYMS 'BERT RUSSELL' and 'Russell Byrd', and in 1960 formed a partnership with Phil Medley. Their first major success came with 'Twist And Shout', transformed into an anthem by the **Isley Brothers** and regularly performed as a show-stopper by the **Beatles**. Berns subsequently replaced **Leiber And Stoller** as the **Drifters**' writer/producer. He also worked with artists including **Ben E. King** and Barbara Lewis, although his finest work was saved for **Solomon Burke** on 'Goodbye Baby', 'Everybody Needs Somebody To Love' and 'The Price'. Berns forged a partnership with Jerry Ragovoy which included work for Garnet Mimms and Lorraine Ellison, plus 'Piece Of My Heart' which was recorded by Erma Franklin and later **Janis Joplin**. A spell in Britain resulted in sessions with **Them** and **Lulu**, before returning home to inaugurate the Bang and Shout labels. The former included the **McCoys**, the Strangeloves and **Van Morrison**, while Shout was responsible for several soul releases by Roy C, Bobby Harris, Erma Franklin and Freddy Scott. Berns died of a heart attack in a New York hotel.

BERRY, CHUCK

CHUCK BERRY (b. CHARLES BERRY, 1926) LEARNED GUITAR WHILE IN HIS TEENS – A PERIOD BLIGHTED BY A THREE-year spell in Algoa Reformatory for armed robbery. On his release, Berry undertook several jobs while pursuing part-time spots in St. Louis bar bands. In 1951, he purchased a tape recorder to capture ideas for compositions and, in 1952, joined Johnnie Johnson (piano) and Ebby Hardy (drums) in the house-band at the Cosmopolitan Club. The trio became a popular attraction, playing a mixture of R&B, country and standards. The guitarist also fronted his own group, the Chuck Berry Combo.

In 1955, **Muddy Waters** advised Berry to approach Chess, resulting in a recording deal and 'Maybellene'. It topped the R&B chart and reached US number 5.

Berry enjoyed further US R&B hits with 'Thirty Days' and 'No Money Down', before producing a stream of classics: 'Roll Over Beethoven', 'Too Much Monkey Business' and 'Brown-Eyed Handsome Man'. His subsequent releases include such titles as 'Rock And Roll Music' (1957), 'Sweet Little Sixteen', 'Johnny B. Goode' (both 1958) and 'Let It Rock' (1960). Berry drew from both country and R&B and based his vocal style on Nat 'King' Cole. Both the **Beatles** and **Rolling Stones** acknowledged their debt to Berry and the **Beach Boys** rewrote 'Sweet Little Sixteen' as 'Surfin' USA'.

Between 1955 and 1960, Berry enjoyed 17 R&B Top 20 entries and appeared in the films *Go Johnny Go*, *Rock, Rock, Rock* and *Jazz On A Summer's Day*. However, on 28 October 1961, he was convicted of 'transporting an under-age girl across state lines for immoral purposes' and served 20 months. He emerged just as 'Memphis Tennessee' (1963), recorded in 1958, reached the UK Top 10. He wrote several compositions during his incarceration, including 'Nadine', 'No Particular Place To Go', 'You Never Can Tell' and 'Promised Land', each of which reached the UK Top 30.

Inevitably his chart success waned and, in 1966, he sought vainly to regenerate his career by moving from Chess to Mercury Records. He returned to Chess in 1969, with 'Tulane'. *Back Home* and *San Francisco Dues* were cohesive selections and in-concert appearances showed a renewed purpose. 'My Ding-A-Ling' topped both the US and UK charts and was his biggest – and his last major – hit. Despite new recordings, Berry became confined to the revival circuit.

Berry's legal entanglements resurfaced in 1979 when he was imprisoned for income tax evasion. Upon release he embarked on a punishing world tour, but with little result. In 1986, the artist celebrated his 60th birthday with gala performances in St. Louis and New York, and a documentary, *Hail! Hail! Rock 'N' Roll*.

BERRY, DAVE

WITH BACKING GROUP, THE CRUISERS, UK-BORN BERRY (b. DAVID HOLGATE GRUNDY, 1941) EVENTUALLY SIGNED TO Decca. There he found success with a version of **Chuck Berry**'s 'Memphis Tennessee' in 1963. Covers of Arthur Crudup's 'My Baby Left Me' and **Burt Bacharach**'s 'Baby It's You' were minor hits, but the band's breakthrough came with Geoff Stevens's 'The Crying Game', which reached the UK Top 5 in 1964. **Bobby Goldsboro**'s 'Little Things' and Ray Davies's 'This Strange Effect' provided further chart success, which concluded with the B.J. Thomas opus, 'Mama', in 1966. Berry continues to tour abroad.

BERRY, RICHARD

BERRY (b. 1935, d. 1997) BEGAN RECORDING IN 1953 UNDER VARIOUS NAMES (THE HOLLYWOOD BLUE JAYS, THE FLAIRS, the Crowns, the Dreamers, the Pharaohs). His most famous moments on record are his bass vocal contributions to the Robins' 'Riot In Cell Block No. 9' and as 'Henry', **Etta James**'s boyfriend, on 'Roll With Me Henry (The Wallflower)'. His claim to fame is composing rock 'n' roll's 'Louie Louie', which he recorded in 1956, but he had to wait seven years for its success with the **Kingsmen**. The song spawned over 300 cover versions, including those by the **Kinks**, the **Beach Boys** and **Paul Revere And The Raiders**. During the 60s and 70s, Berry became a soul singer. He recorded for west coast labels and continued performing until his death.

BETTER THAN EZRA

BETTER THAN EZRA WERE FORMED IN NEW ORLEANS, USA, IN 1988, COMPRISING Kevin Griffin (vocals/ guitar), Cary Bonnecaze (drums) and Tom Drummond (bass). Better Than Ezra's cassette-only release, *Surprise*, featured spikey guitar pop in the tradition of the **Replacements**. *Delux* sold over 25,000 copies and was reissued on Elektra; 'Good' helped to push the album into the US Top 50. Bonnecaze was replaced by Travis McNabb for *Friction Baby*.

BETTIE SERVEERT

FORMED IN AMSTERDAM, THE NETHERLANDS, BETTIE SERVEERT COMPRISED CAROL VAN DIJK (VOCALS), PETER Visser (guitar), Herman Bunskoeke (bass) and Berend Dubbe (drums). They named the band after Dutch tennis player Bettie Stove (the literal translation for their name is 'Bettie serves'). Their debut was a buoyant record with a sound reminiscent of **Belly** at their most jovial; it sold well in the USA. *Lamprey* indicated a more introspective, blues-based approach. They were warmly received on dates with **Jeff Buckley** in 1995, while 'Crutches', released as a single, impressed UK critics. *Dust Bunnies* was another well-received collection.

BEVIS FROND

BEVIS FROND IS JUST ONE PERSON: GUITARIST NICK SALOMAN. INFLUENCED BY **JIMI HENDRIX** AND **CREAM**, Saloman formed the Bevis Frond Museum while at school. After the group disbanded, he formed the Von Trap Family (later Room 13). Later Saloman recorded *Miasma*, it became a collector's item. He then released *Inner Marshland* and *Triptych* on his own Woronzow Records. London's Reckless Records released *Bevis Through The Looking Glass* and *The Auntie Winnie Album*. Saloman's brand of raw, imaginative blues guitar drew many converts and *Any Gas Faster* was widely lauded. *Magic Eye* was an inconsistent collaboration with ex-Pink Fairy drummer Twink.

Saloman then released the double set *New River Head*, (1991), *It Just Is*, (1992) and *Beatroots*, recorded as the Fred Bison Five. He set up underground magazine *Ptolemaic Terrascope* in the late 80s; it is a loyal correspondent of the UK psychedelic scene. *Superseeder* was an appealing blend of Saloman's electric and acoustic styles.

BHUNDU BOYS

THE BHUNDU BOYS WERE FORMED IN HARARE, ZIMBABWE, IN 1980 BY BIGGIE TEMBO (b. RODWELL Marasha, 1958, d. 1995; guitar/vocals), Rise Kagona (guitar), David Mankaba (d. 1991; bass), Shakie Kangwena (b. 1956, d. 1993; keyboards) and Kenny Chitsvatsa (drums). The Boys achieved fame in Zimbabwe and in Britain with their idiosyncratic jit style of dance music. Their rise owed much to the pioneering work of bandleader and vocalist Thomas Mapfumo. The band itself was a product of Zimbabwe's late 70s war of liberation, the name Bhundu ('bush') being chosen to commemorate the freedom fighters. Beginning with traditional Zimbabwean folk music, they replaced any lingering vestiges of rock and soul for a wholly Zimbabwean approach. But while Mapfumo's style was based on traditional, rural Shona mbira ('thumb piano') music, the Bhundu's, although occasionally embracing the mbira, were altogether more eclectic and urban, drawing on the traditions of tribal people in Zimbabwe. Jit found almost immediate acceptance amongst the youth of post-independence Zimbabwe and between 1981 and 1984 the band had four number 1s – 'Baba Munini Francis', 'Wenhamo Haaneti', 'Hatisitose' and 'Ndimboze'. *The Bhundu Boys*, *Hupenyu Hwenasi* and *Shabini*, proved equally popular. In 1986, they moved to Britain, establishing a reputation as one of the most exciting bands in the country, helped by their incessant touring. In 1987, the band signed to WEA, released *Tsvimbodzemoto* and supported **Madonna** at London's Wembley Stadium. However, while the sales of *Shabini* had made the Bhundus stars of the independent scene, they failed to achieve mainstream success and were dropped from WEA in 1990. Shortly afterwards, Biggie Tembo left and several members succumbed to AIDS. The Bhundu Boys re-emerged in 1991 with the live set, *Absolute Jit*, on the Discafrique label. Tragically Tembo hanged himself in 1995, a chilling epitaph to a once pioneering group.

BERRY, DAVE
Albums
Dave Berry (Decca 1964)★★★
The Special Sound Of Dave Berry (Decca 1966)★★★
One Dozen Berrys (Ace Of Clubs 1966)★★★
➧ p.353 for full listings
Connections
Cruisers
Influences
Chuck Berry ➧ p.45
Burt Bacharach ➧ p.27
Bobby Goldsboro ➧ p.162

BERRY, RICHARD
Albums
Richard Berry And The Dreamers (Crown 1963)★★★
Great Rhythm & Blues Oldies (1977)★★★
➧ p.353 for full listings
Collaborators
Etta James ➧ p.196
Connections
Kingsmen ➧ p.207
Kinks ➧ p.207
Beach Boys ➧ p.36

BETTER THAN EZRA
Albums
Deluxe (SWELL 1993/Elektra 1995)★★★
Friction Baby (Elektra 1996)★★★
➧ p.353 for full listings
Connections
Vigilantes of Love
Influences
Replacements ➧ p.276

BETTIE SERVEERT
Albums
Palomine (Beggars Banquet 1993)★★★
Dust Bunnies (Beggars Banquet 1997)★★★
➧ p.353 for full listings

BEVIS FROND
Albums
Miasma (Woronzow 1987)★★★
New River Head (Woronzow 1991)★★★★
➧ p.353 for full listings
Connections
Pink Fairy
Influences
Jimi Hendrix ➧ p.180
Cream ➧ p.103

BHUNDU BOYS
Albums
Shabini (Discafrique 1985)★★★★
Tsvimbodzemoto (Discafrique 1987)★★★★
True Jit (WEA 1988)★★★★
➧ p.353 for full listings
Collaborators
Madonna ➧ p.222
Connections
Wild Dragons

BIG AUDIO DYNAMITE
Albums
No. 10 Upping Street (Columbia 1986)★★★★
➽ p.353 for full listings
Connections
Clash ➽ p.93
Aztec Camera ➽ p.25

BIG BLACK
Albums
Atomizer (Homestead/Blast First 1986)★★★
➽ p.353 for full listings
Connections
Pixies ➽ p.261
Breeders ➽ p.67
PJ Harvey ➽ p.262
Nirvana ➽ p.248

BIG AUDIO DYNAMITE

GUITARIST MICK JONES (b. 1955; EX-**CLASH**) FORMED BIG AUDIO DYNAMITE (B.A.D.) WITH DJ AND FILM-maker Don Letts (keyboards/effects). They recruited Dan Donovan (keyboards) Leo Williams (bass) and Greg Roberts (drums). *This Is Big Audio Dynamite* featured cut-up funk spiced with sampled sounds; it's follow-up included writing contributions from former Clash vocalist Joe Strummer. In 1988, Jones came close to death from pneumonia, which caused a delay in the release of *Megatop Phoenix*. This led to the break-up of the band and by 1990 and *Kool-Aid*, Jones had assembled a completely new line-up (B.A.D. II) featuring Nick Hawkins (guitar), Gary Stonedage (bass) and Chris Kavanagh (drums, ex-Sigue Sigue Sputnik). DJ Zonka was drafted in to provide live 'scratching' and mixing.

Jones contributed to the *Flashback* soundtrack and **Aztec Camera**'s 'Good Morning Britain'. Donovan married and separated from Patsy Kensit (**Eighth Wonder**) and joined the re-formed Sigue Sigue Sputnik. Jones regrouped in 1995 for the accomplished *P-Funk*, which mixed imported west coast hip-hop beats with jungle textures and rock 'n' roll.

BIG BLACK

FROM ILLINOIS, USA, BIG BLACK DEBUTED IN 1983 WITH THE SIX-TRACK EP LUNGS. FRONTED BY guitarist/vocalist Steve Albini, the group underwent several changes before completing *Bulldozer*. A more settled line-up was formed around Albini, Santiago Durango (guitar) and Dave Riley aka David Lovering (bass). *Atomizer* (1986) established the trio as one of America's leading independent acts with their blend of post-hardcore, post-industrial styles. Melvin Belli replaced Durango for *Songs About Fucking*, their best-known album. However Albini tired of his creation and dissolved the group before the record's release. He became a producer, working with the **Pixies** (*Surfer Rosa*), the **Breeders** (*Pod*) and Tad (Salt Lick), before forming the short-lived Rapeman. He subsequently produced **PJ Harvey**'s *Rid Of Me* and **Nirvana**'s *In Utero*. Afterwards he returned to a group format with Shellac. Durango recorded two EPs as Arsenal.

BIG BOPPER
Albums
Chantilly Lace (Mercury 1959)★★★
➽ p.353 for full listings
Collaborators
Buddy Holly ➽ p.184
Ritchie Valens ➽ p.328

BIG BOPPER

AFTER A SPELL AS A DJ, THE BIG BOPPER (B. JILES PERRY RICHARDSON, 1930, D. 1959) WON A CONTRACT WITH Mercury, releasing two unsuccessful singles in 1957. The following year, he recorded 'Chantilly Lace', a rock 'n' roll classic. The follow up, 'Big Bopper's Wedding' proved popular enough to win him a place on a tour with **Buddy Holly** and **Ritchie Valens**. On 3 February 1959, a plane carrying the three stars crashed, leaving no survivors. Few of Richardson's recordings were left for posterity, though there was a posthumous album, *Chantilly Lace*, which included the rocking 'White Lightning'. In 1960, Johnny Preston took the Big Bopper's composition 'Running Bear' to US/UK number 1.

BIG COUNTRY
Albums
The Crossing (Mercury 1983)★★★★
➽ p.353 for full listings
Further References
Book: *Big Country: A Certain Chemistry*, John May

BIG COUNTRY

STUART ADAMSON (b. 1958; GUITAR/VOCALS; EX-SKIDS) FORMED SCOTTISH BAND BIG COUNTRY IN 1982. HE recruited Bruce Watson (b. 1961; guitar) and, after an initial rhythm section proved incompatible, Mark Brzezicki (b. 1957; drums) and Tony Butler (b. 1957; bass). Both guitarists wove a ringing, 'bagpipe' sound from their instruments and the group's debut album included the hits, 'Fields Of Fire (400 Miles)' and 'In A Big Country'. 'Chance', 'Wonderland' and 'Look Away' all reached the UK Top 10, while a second collection, *Steeltown*, was also a commercial success. Their fourth album offered little new, although its leading single, 'King Of Emotion', broached the UK Top 20.

Live – Without The Aid Of A Safety Net was a lacklustre album and *Eclectic* (1996), their stab at an unplugged album, was unsatisfying on CD; however the band's accompanying tour was well-received. Surprisingly, the band split up in 1997.

BIG DISH

FORMED IN SCOTLAND IN 1983, THE BIG DISH – STEVEN LINDSAY (VOCALS/GUITAR/KEYBOARDS), BRIAN MCFIE (guitar), Raymond Docherty (bass) and Ian Ritchie (saxophone/programming) – rose to prominence in 1986 with *Swimmer*. Compared with **Prefab Sprout**, **Aztec Camera** and **Danny Wilson**, their singles (including 'Prospect Street' and 'Big New Beginning') nevertheless failed to chart. Lindsay, McFie and Docherty then completed the American-influenced *Creeping Up On Jesus*. In 1991, the Big Dish re-emerged with a new contract, an official line-up of Lindsay and McFie and a minor hit single in 'Miss America'; however *Satellites* lacked the depth of their initial work.

BIG HEAD TODD AND THE MONSTERS

FORMED IN COLORADO, USA, IN 1986, THE BAND PUT TOGETHER TWO ALBUMS AND SEVERAL SINGLE RELEASES to little initial interest. Songwriter Todd Park Mohr (vocals/guitar), Rob Squires (bass) and Brian Nevin (drums) finally broke through with *Midnight Radio*, released on their own label. Finally signing to Giant Records in 1993, they made *Sister Sweetly*, produced with David Z (**Prince**, **Fine Young Cannibals**, BoDeans) at Paisley Park studios. Guitarist **Leo Kottke** contributed to 'Soul For Every Cowboy'. *Strategem* unveiled further gritty displays of rural blues rock.

BIG STAR

FORMED IN MEMPHIS, USA, IN 1971, BIG STAR EVOLVED WHEN EX-**BOX TOPS** SINGER ALEX CHILTON JOINED local group, Ice Water – Chris Bell (d. 1978; guitar/vocals), Andy Hummel (bass) and Jody Stephens (drums). The quartet made an impressive debut with *#1 Record*, which skilfully synthesized British pop and 60s-styled Los Angeles harmonies, however its commercial potential was marred by poor distribution and internal friction led to Bell's departure in 1972.

The group reconvened later in the year, releasing *Radio City* (1974) which lacked the polish of its predecessor. Corporate apathy doomed the project and an embittered Big Star retreated following a brief, ill-starred tour on which John Lightman replaced a disaffected Hummel. Chilton and Stephens worked on a projected third album with the assistance of **Steve Cropper** (guitar), Jim Dickinson (piano) and Tommy McLure (bass), but the group broke up without officially completing the set. *3rd* has subsequently appeared in various mixes.

In 1993, Chilton and Stephens re-formed the band (with two of the **Posies**) for a one-off gig; it was so successful that they briefly toured the UK.

BIG THREE

FORMED IN LIVERPOOL, IN 1961, AS AN OFFSHOOT FROM CASS AND THE CASSANOVAS, THE BIG THREE comprised Johnny Gustafson (vocals/bass), Johnny Hutchinson (vocals/drums) and Adrian Barber (guitar). In 1962, Barber relocated to Germany and was replaced by Brian Griffiths, who debuted at the Star Club, Hamburg. After signing with the **Beatles**' manager **Brian Epstein**, success seemed assured, but characteristic unruliness proved their undoing. They achieved only two minor hits, a cover version of 'Some Other Guy' and 'By The Way'. A live EP *At The Cavern* was followed by an acrimonious split with Epstein only months into their relationship. By 1963, Griffiths and Gustafson found alternative employment with the Seniors and Hutchinson recruited Paddy Chambers and Faron as replacements; however less than a year later, the Big Three disbanded. Gustafson later joined the **Merseybeats**, and, in the 70s, **Roxy Music**.

BIKINI KILL

PIONEERS OF THE 90S RADICAL FEMINIST MUSICAL MOVEMENT NAMED RIOT GRRRL, USA'S BIKINI KILL WERE PERCEIVED TO be the transatlantic cousins of UK band Huggy Bear – they made a shared album in 1993. Hailing from Washington, and led by the haranguing voice of Kathleen Hanna, Bikini Kill believed that indie rock was just as sexist as mainstream rock. Also in the group were Billy Karren (guitar), Tobi Vail (drums) and Kathi Wilcox (bass). *Pussy Whipped* included direct takes on sexual politics. 'Rebel Girl', the group's anthem which had already been recorded twice (once in single form with **Joan Jett** as producer), made a third appearance. When the initial spark of Riot Grrrl died down, Bikini Kill remained its most vibrant legacy until disbanding.

BIOHAZARD

FORMED IN NEW YORK, IN 1988, BIOHAZARD COMPRISED EVAN SEINFELD (BASS/VOCALS), BILLY GRAZIEDI (guitar/vocals), Bobby Hambel (guitar) and Danny Schuler (drums). An independent debut, *Biohazard* led to a major contract with Warner Brothers Records in 1992. *Urban Discipline* was recorded in under two weeks on a tiny budget, but proved to be the band's breakthrough album. Blisteringly heavy with lyrics to match, it drew massive praise, as did live shows. The band recorded a well-received track with rappers Onyx for the *Judgement Night* soundtrack and *State Of The World Address* was recorded in seven weeks. Hambel was sacked from the band in 1995 prior to the recording of *Mata Leao*. His replacement was Rob Echeverria (ex-**Helmet**).

BIRDS

FORMED IN ENGLAND, IN 1964, ALI MCKENZIE (VOCALS), TONY MUNROE (GUITAR/VOCALS), RON WOOD (guitar/vocals), Kim Gardner (bass/vocals) and Pete McDaniels (drums) were originally known as the Thunderbirds. They truncated their name to avoid confusion with **Chris Farlowe**'s backing group. One of the era's most powerful R&B groups, the Birds' legacy is confined to just four singles, but 'Leaving Here' and 'No Good Without You Baby' (both 1965), show their reputation is deserved. Alas, the group is better known for a scurrilous publicity stunt, wherein seven writs were served on the American **Byrds**, demanding they change their name and claiming loss of income. The US group ignored the charges. The Birds broke up in 1966 when Gardner joined **Creation**, then Ashton, Gardner And Dyke and Badger. Wood also joined Creation, then the **Jeff Beck** Group, the **Faces**, and the **Rolling Stones**.

BIRKIN, JANE

ENGLISH ACTRESS JANE BIRKIN (b. 1946) TURNED SINGER AS A RESULT OF HER ASSOCIATION with French composer Serge Gainsbourg. He had originally recorded a track with Brigette Bardot entitled 'Je T'Aime ... Moi Non Plus' but 'She thought it was too erotic and she was married'. Birkin had no such reservations and expertly simulated the sensual heavy breathing that gave the disc its notoriety. Originally released in the UK by Philips/Fontana, the company dissociated itself from the disc's controversial matter by ceasing production while the record was number 2 in the charts. The ever-opportunistic entrepreneur Phil Solomon accepted the banned composition which was reissued on his Major Minor label and reached number 1 in 1969. 'Je T'Aime ...' re-entered the UK charts in 1974. In 1996, Birkin released an album of songs written by her ex-partner.

BIRTHDAY PARTY

THIS AUSTRALIAN OUTFIT BEGAN AS NEW WAVE BAND BOYS NEXT DOOR. AFTER ONE album, the band relocated to London and switched names. Birthday Party – **Nick Cave** (b. 1957; vocals), Roland S. Howard (guitar, ex-Obsessions; Young Charlatans), Mick Harvey (b. 1958; guitar/drums/organ/piano), Tracy Pew (d. 1986; bass) and Phil Calvert (drums) – debuted with 'Fiend Catcher'. In Australia they recorded their first album and the single, 'Release The Bats', was **John Peel**'s favourite record of 1981. **Barry Adamson** (ex-**Magazine**), Roland Howard's brother Harry and Chris Walsh helped out on the recording of the follow-up at live shows. After collaborating with the **Go-Betweens** on 'After The Fireworks' (as the Tuf Monks), they moved to Berlin. Calvert was dropped (moving on to **Psychedelic Furs**), while the four remaining members worked on projects with Lydia Lunch and **Einsturzende Neubaten**, among others. Harvey left in 1983, temporarily replaced on drums by Des Heffner. After a final gig in Melbourne, the band split. Howard joined Crime And The City Solution alongside Harry and Harvey, who also continued in Cave's solo band the Bad Seeds.

BIG DISH
Albums
Swimmer (Virgin 1986)★★★
➽ p.353 for full listings

BIG HEAD TODD AND THE MONSTERS
Albums
Midnight Radio (Big Records 1990)★★★
➽ p.353 for full listings
Collaborators
Prince ➽ p.267
Fine Young Cannibals p.145

BIG STAR
Albums
3rd (PVC 1978)★★★★
➽ p.353 for full listings
Collaborators
Steve Cropper ➽ p.105
Connections
Box Tops ➽ p.65
Posies ➽ p.264

BIG THREE
Albums
Cavern Stomp (1982)★★★
➽ p.353 for full listings
Connections
Flamingos ➽ p.147
Merseybeats ➽ p.232
Roxy Music ➽ p.283

BIKINI KILL
Albums
Bikini Kill (K Records 1992)★★★
➽ p.353 for full listings
Connections
Joan Jett p.199

BIOHAZARD
Albums
State Of The World Address (Warners 1994)★★★.
➽ p.353 for full listings
Connections
Helmet ➽ p.179

BIRDS
Albums
These Birds Are Dangerous (1965)★★
➽ p.353 for full listings
Connections
Creation ➽ p.104
Jeff Beck ➽ p.41
Faces ➽ p.141
Rolling Stones ➽ p.281

BIRKIN, JANE
Albums
Jane Birkin And Serge Gainsbourg (Fontana 1969)★★★
➽ p.353 for full listings

BIRTHDAY PARTY
Albums
Prayers On Fire (Thermidor 1981)★★★
➽ p.353 for full listings
Connections
Magazine ➽ p. 222
Go-Betweens ➽ p.160
Psychedelic Furs ➽ p.268

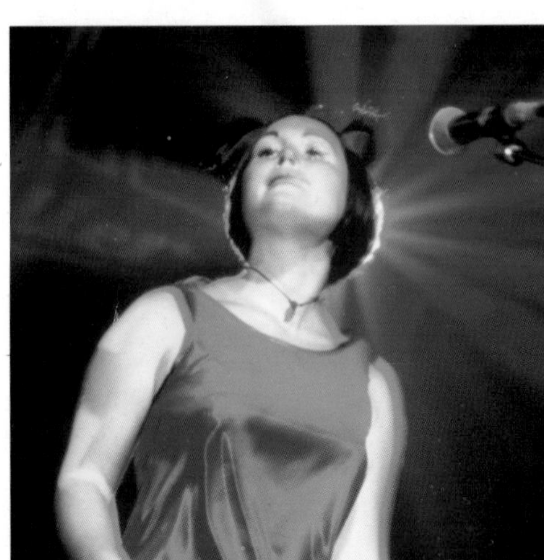

BIS
Albums
The New Transistor Heroes (Wiiija 1997)★★★
➧ p.353 for full listings
Influences
Bikini Kill ➧ p.47

BISHOP, ELVIN
Albums
Let It Flow (Capricorn 1974)★★★
Struttin' My Stuff (Capricorn 1975)★★★★
Ace In The Hole (Alligator 1995)★★★
➧ p.353 for full listings
Connections
Paul Butterfield Blues Band ➧ p.76
Allman Brothers Band ➧ p.14
Jefferson Starship ➧ p.198
Dr. John ➧ p.125

BISHOP, STEPHEN
Albums
Careless (ABC 1976)★★★
Bish (ABC 1978)★★★
Bowling In Paris (Atlantic 1989)★★★
➧ p.353 for full listings
Connections
Art Garfunkel ➧ p.154
Four Tops ➧ p.152
Chaka Khan ➧ p.204
Barbra Streisand
Phil Collins ➧ p.98
Steve Cropper ➧ p.105
Eric Clapton ➧ p.92
Sting ➧ p.310
Randy Crawford ➧ p.103
Influences
Beatles ➧ p.38

BJÖRK
Albums
Debut (One Little Indian 1993)★★★★
Post (One Little Indian 1995)★★★★
Homogenic (One Little Indian 1997)★★★
➧ p.353 for full listings

BIS

FORMED IN EDINBURGH, SCOTLAND, BIS COMPRISED MANDA RIN (VOCALS/ keyboards/bass) and brothers Steve Sci-Fi (vocals/ guitar) and John Disco (guitar). The brothers started a band at school and enlisted Rin in 1994. They made a commercial breakthrough in 1996 when they became the first unsigned band to appear on *Top Of The Pops*. They appeared again a week later as 'Kandy Pop' entered the UK Top 30. They had previously released a limited edition of the *Transmissions On The Teen-C Tip!*, featuring the **Bikini Kill**-inspired 'Kill Yr Boyfriend'. They signed to Wiiija Records in 1996 and their album debut came the following year, by which time the group were facing increasingly hostile criticism from the music press.

BISHOP, ELVIN

AS AN ASPIRING GUITARIST, BISHOP (b. 1942) FREQUENTED CHICAGO'S BLUES CLUBS AND IN 1965 HE JOINED A CLUB'S house band. This group became the **Paul Butterfield Blues Band**. Bishop was featured on four Butterfield albums, but left in 1968 following the release of *In My Own Dream*. He was initially signed to **Bill Graham**'s Fillmore label, but these and other early recordings achieved only local success. In 1974, he signed to Capricorn Records which favoured the hippie/hillbilly image Bishop had nurtured. Six albums followed, including *Let It Flow, Juke Joint Jump* and a live set, *Live! Raisin' Hell*, but it was a 1975 release, *Struttin' My Stuff*, which proved most popular. It included 'Fooled Around And Fell In Love' which reached US number 3. The featured voice was Mickey Thomas (later of **Jefferson Starship**). After Thomas's departure, Bishop's career suffered a further setback in 1979 when Capricorn filed for bankruptcy. The guitarist's recorded output has been thin on the ground since, although he recorded on the Alligator label with **Dr. John** on *Big Fun* and *Ace In The Hole*.

BISHOP, STEPHEN

BISHOP (b. 1951) FORMED HIS FIRST GROUP, THE WEEDS, IN 1967. THEY RECORDED SOME **BEATLES**-INSPIRED DEMOS IN Los Angeles before disbanding. In 1976, Bishop landed a contract with ABC via the patronage of **Art Garfunkel**. His debut, *Careless*, was much in the style of Garfunkel and featured top Los Angeles session players. It was nominated for a Grammy and, like the succeeding Bish, hovered in the lower reaches of the national Top 40. The accompanying singles (particularly 'On And On' from *Careless*) also fared well. The **Four Tops**, **Chaka Khan** and Barbra Streisand covered his compositions and Bishop gained studio assistance from Khan, Garfunkel, Gary Brooker, **Steve Cropper**, **Phil Collins** and others. He contributed to Collins's *Face Value* (1981), and composed 'Separate Lives', the theme from the movie *White Nights*.

Bishop also wrote the theme songs to *National Lampoon's Animal House* ('Dream Girl'), *Roadie* ('Your Precious Love' with Yvonne Elliman), and *Tootsie* ('It Might Be You', a non-original). He also tried his hand at acting. *Red Cab To Manhattan*, embraced a stab at big band jazz and included 'Don't You Worry', a tribute to the Beatles. *Bowling In Paris* featured contributions from **Eric Clapton**, Phil Collins, **Sting** and **Randy Crawford**.

BJÖRK

FORMER **SUGARCUBES** VOCALIST, BJÖRK (b. BJÖRK GUDMUNDSDÓTTIR, 1965), made her 'debut' in 1977, as an 11-year old prodigy, with an album of cover versions recorded in her native Iceland. Her next recording outfit was Tappi Takarrass (which apparently translates as 'cork that bitch's arse'), who recorded two albums between 1981 and 1983. A higher profile role was afforded via work with KUKL, who introduced her to future Sugarcubes Einar Örn and Siggi.

Björk returned to Iceland after the Sugarcubes' six-year career, recording a solo album in 1990 backed by a local be-bop group. She re-emerged in 1993 with *Debut* and appeared at the 1993 BRIT Awards duetting with **PJ Harvey**. *Debut* also won awards, for Best International Newcomer and Best International Artist, at the 1994 BRIT Awards and included four hit singles. Also in 1994, Björk co-wrote the title track to **Madonna**'s *Bedtime Stories*.

Post was a more eclectic album, ranging from the hard techno beats of 'Army Of Me' to the shimmering 'Hyper-ballad'. Following a desultory remix album (*Telegram*), Björk released her third solo set, *Homogenic*. The album was notable for lyrics revealing a more personal side to the singer as well as the fact that Björk produced it.

US hit, reaching number 9. Black retired from touring in 1962, and the group continued performing, under the same name without him. They continued playing even after Black died of a brain tumour in October 1965. The Bill Black Combo achieved a total of 19 US chart singles and was still working under the leadership of bassist Bob Tucker in the late 80s.

BLACK, CILLA

BLACK (b. PRISCILLA WHITE, 1943) APPEARED AS GUEST SINGER WITH various groups at Liverpool's Cavern club, and was brought to the attention of **Brian Epstein**. He changed her name and exploited her girl-next-door appeal. Her first single was a brassy powerhouse reworking of the **Beatles**' unreleased 'Love Of The Loved', which reached the UK Top 40 in 1963. She changed her style with **Burt Bacharach**'s 'Anyone Who Had A Heart' and emerged a ballad singer of immense power. 'You're My World' was another brilliantly orchestrated, impassioned ballad, which reached UK number 1. By this time, Black was outselling all her Merseyside rivals except the Beatles. By the end of 1964, she was one of the most successful female singers of her era and continued to release cover versions of superb quality, including the **Righteous Brothers**' 'You've Lost That Lovin' Feelin'' and **Randy Newman**'s 'I've Been Wrong Before'. In 1965, she ceased recording and worked on her only film, *Work Is A Four Letter Word*, but returned the following year with 'Love's Just A Broken Heart' and 'Alfie'.

In 1968, Black moved into television work. Throughout the late 60s, she continued to register Top 10 hits, including 'Surround Yourself With Sorrow', 'Conversations' and 'Something Tells Me'. She wound down her recording career in the 70s and concentrated on live work and television commitments. Black entered the 90s as one of the highest paid family entertainers in the British music business, with two major UK television shows, *Blind Date* and *Surprise Surprise*. In 1993, she celebrated 30 years in show business with an album, video, book, and television special, all entitled *Through The Years*.

BJORN AGAIN

AUSTRALIAN **ABBA** IMPRESSIONISTS (BJORN VOLOVEUS, AGNETHA FALSTART, BENNY ANDERWEAR AND FRIDA) who feature near note-perfect renditions of 'Fernando', 'Dancing Queen', 'Name Of The Game' et al. The group was formed in 1989 and their cult status was enhanced by an appearance at England's Reading Festival, where **Nirvana**'s Kurt Cobain was among their admirers. They responded with a live jam of 'Smells Like Swede Spirit'. Proof of their impact, and the rediscovered pop magic of Abba, came with **Erasure**'s number 1 *Abbaesque*. Bjorn Again replied with the EP *Erasuresque*.

BLACK

POP BAND FROM LIVERPOOL, ENGLAND, ORIGINALLY FEATURING COLIN VEARNCOMBE (VOCALS; EX-EPILEPTIC TITS), Dave Dickie (keyboards) and Jimmy Sangster (bass). Black signed to the Liverpool independent record label Eternal, sponsored by Pete Wylie and **Wah!**. Vearncombe's distinctive voice soon led to a signing with WEA Records, but, after the failure of two singles, 'Hey Presto' and 'More Than The Sun', they were dropped. Despite this setback, Black soon found themselves with an unexpected hit, 'Wonderful Life', this time attracting the attention of A&M; their second single for the label, 'Sweetest Smile', reached the UK Top 10. Their debut album followed, though 1988's *Comedy* was more impressive. A hiatus followed before a third album, *Black*, featuring guest vocalists **Robert Palmer** and Sam Brown. *Are We Having Fun Yet?* continued in a similar vein.

BLACK, BILL

BLACK (b. WILLIAM PATTON BLACK, 1926, d. 1965) WAS THE BASS-PLAYING HALF OF THE SCOTTY AND BILL TEAM THAT backed **Elvis Presley** on his earliest live performances. He played on Presley's earliest Sun tracks, including 'That's All Right', and toured with Presley alongside guitarist Scotty Moore; later, drummer D.J. Fontana was added to the group.

In 1959, after leaving Presley, the Bill Black Combo was formed, with Reggie Young (guitar), Martin Wills (saxophone), Carl McAvoy (piano) and Jerry Arnold (drums). The group favoured an instrumental R&B-based sound tempered with jazz. Their first chart success was 'Smokie Part 2' (1959), but it was the follow-up, 'White Silver Sands' (1960), that gave the group its biggest

Collaborators
PJ Harvey ➽ p.262
Connections
Sugarcubes ➽ p.313
Madonna ➽ p.222
Influences
Beatles ➽ p.38
Further References
Videos: *Björk* (Propaganda 1994)
Joga (One Little Indian 1997)
Book: *Post: The Official Björk Book*, Penny Phillips

BJORN AGAIN
Album
Flashback (1993)★★★
➽ p.353 for full listings
Influences
Abba ➽ p.6
Erasure ➽ p.138

BLACK
Albums
Wonderful Life (A&M 1987)★★★
Comedy (A&M 1988)★★★★
Are We Having Fun Yet? (A&M 1993)★★★
➽ p.353 for full listings
Collaborators
Robert Palmer ➽ p.255
Sam Brown
Connections
Last Chant

BLACK, BILL
Albums
Smokie (Hi 1960)★★★
Solid And Raunchy (Hi 1960)★★★★,
Let's Twist Her (Hi 1962)★★★★
➽ p.353 for full listings
Collaborators
Elvis Presley ➽ p.265
Connections
Bill Black Combo ➽ p.48

BLACK, CILLA
Albums
Cilla (Parlophone 1965)★★★
Sher-oo (Parlophone 1968)★★★
Modern Priscilla (EMI 1978)★★★
➽ p.353 for full listings
Influences
Beatles ➽ p.38
Burt Bacharach ➽ p. 27
Righteous Brothers ➽ p.278
Randy Newman ➽ p. 246
Further References
Film: *Ferry Cross The Mersey* (1964)
Video: *Throughout The Years* (1993)

BLACK, FRANK
Albums
Teenager Of The Year (4AD 1994)★★★★
The Cult Of Ray (Epic 1996)★★★
➤ p.353 for full listings
Connections
Pixies ➤ p.261
Captain Beefheart ➤ p.80

BLACK, MARY
Albums
By The Time It Gets Dark (Dara 1987)★★★
Babes In The Wood (Grapevine 1991)★★★★
➤ p.353 for full listings
Collaborators
Declan Sinnott
Connections
De Dannan

BLACK BOX
Albums
Dreamland (RCA 1990)★★★
Remixed Reboxed Black Box/Mixed Up (RCA 1991)★★★
➤ p.353 for full listings
Collaborators
Loleatta Holloway
Influences
Earth, Wind and Fire ➤ p.130
ABC ➤ p.7
Further References
Video: *Video Dreams* (1990)

BLACK CROWES
Albums
Shake Your Money Maker (Def American 1990)★★★
The Southern Harmony And Musical Companion (Def American 1992)★★★★
Three Snakes And One Charm (American 1996)★★★
➤ p.353 for full listings
Collaborators
Aerosmith ➤ p.10
ZZ Top ➤ p.349
Connections
Green on Red ➤ p.166
Influences
Otis Redding ➤ p.274
Rolling Stones ➤ p.281
Further References
Videos: *Who Killed That Bird On Your Windowsill ... The Movie* (1993)
Sometimes Salvation (Def American 1993)
Book: *The Black Crowes*, Martin Black

BLACK, FRANK

THIS US VOCALIST/GUITARIST LED THE PIXIES UNDER THE NAME BLACK FRANCIS. FRANCIS (b. CHARLES FRANCIS Kitteridge III, 1965) embarked on a solo career as Frank Black in 1993. His self-titled debut featured Nick Vincent (drums) and Eric Drew Feldman (guitar/saxophone; ex-**Captain Beefheart**'s Magic Band). Feldman produced the set which featured fellow Beefheart acolyte Jeff Morris Tepper and ex-Pixies guitarist Joey Santiago. *Frank Black* showed its creator's quirky grasp of pop, but after *Teenager Of The Year*, Black was dropped by 4AD Records. A new release on the Epic label (preceded by the single 'Men In Black') failed to improve his solo standing.

BLACK, MARY

BLACK (b. 1955) BEGAN SINGING IN DUBLIN'S FOLK CLUBS AND MARY BLACK REACHED NUMBER 4 IN THE IRISH CHARTS in 1983. Mary also provided backing vocals and production work for *The Black Family Favourites* in 1984 and joined De Dannan, recording *Song For Ireland* and *Anthem*. She left in 1986, teaming up with producer Declan Sinnott for *Without The Fanfare*, which went gold.

In 1991, Black returned from an American tour in order to finish *Babes In The Wood*, released the same year. The album was number 1 in the Irish charts. Her 1991 tours in England/Japan were efforts to reach a wider audience. Until *Babes In The Wood*, her albums had not had a full distribution in Britain.

BLACK BOX

LEADING EXPONENTS OF ITALIAN HOUSE MUSIC, BLACK BOX WAS FORMED IN THE 80S, MADE UP OF THREE STUDIO musicians – Daniele Davoli, Mirko Limoni and Valerio Simplici – collectively known as Groove Groove Melody; singer Katrine (b. Catherine Quinol) frequently sang for them. Simplici, a clarinet teacher, played in La Scala Classical Music Orchestra; Davoli was a club DJ (DJ Lelewel) and Limoni was the computer and keyboard whizz-kid for Italian pop stars, Spagna. Katrine featured as vocalist on 'Ride On Time' (UK number 1 for six weeks in 1989), but controversy reigned after the realization that the voice of **Loleatta Holloway** was also sampled, from her late-70s single, 'Love Sensations'. A deal was eventually worked out with Salsoul (who owned the rights) as both companies benefited from 800,000 UK sales.

Under seven or more pseudonyms, Groove Groove Melody turned out numerous records. As Black Box their hits included 'I Don't Know Anybody Else', 'Everybody Everybody' and a cover of 'Fantasy'. They were also responsible for **ABC**'s 1991 comeback single, 'Say It'. In 1995 they released 'Not Anyone'.

BLACK CROWES

BROTHERS CHRIS (b. 1966; VOCALS) AND RICH ROBINSON (b. 1969; GUITAR) FORMED THE BAND UNDER THE NAME Mr. Crowe's Garden in 1984. Six bassists and three drummers passed through before the band stabilized with Johnny Colt (b. 1966; bass) and Steve Gorman (b. 1965; drums; ex-Mary My Hope). His predecessor, Jeff Sullivan, went on to join Drivin' N' Cryin'. Jeff Cease joined the group as second guitarist in 1988. As the Black Crowes, they were signed to the Def American label by George Drakoulias, who produced the debut, *Shake Your Money Maker*, an album blending soul and uncomplicated R&B. Influenced by **Otis Redding**, they covered his 'Hard to Handle', but the record's highlight was 'She Talks To Angels', an emotive ballad about a drug addict. Their live performances drew **Rolling Stones** comparisons, the band's image being very much rooted in the 70s, with Chris Robinson's thin frame dominating the stage. The first single 'Jealous Again' was a US hit, and the band supported on **Aerosmith**'s *Pump* tour. Canadian keyboard player Ed Hawrysch, who had played on the album, joined in 1991 and the band were invited to support **ZZ Top**.

They were asked to join the European Monsters of Rock tour, opening at the Donington festival in England and culminating in a massive free show in Moscow. Prior to these dates, Robinson collapsed suffering from exhaustion following an acoustic showcase at Ronnie Scott's in London; he recovered to undertake the tour. Cease was replaced with Marc Ford (guitar/vocals; ex-Burning Tree) and they began their second album. *The Southern Harmony And Musical Companion* (1992) received positive reviews. The permanent addition of Hawrysch and the use of female backing singers had allowed the band to develop and Robinson had advanced lyrically. With both the album and single, 'Remedy', a success, the Black Crowes returned to the road for the hugely popular High As The Moon tour. 1994 saw the release of *Amorica* – a previously completed album (Tall) had been scrapped, with only five songs retained. Live shows saw the debut of percussionist Chris Trujillo and the now seven-piece band produced some tight-but-loose performances. *Three Snakes And One Charm* was felt by many to be their last album. Ford and Colt both left the band in 1997.

BLACK FLAG

FORMED IN 1977 IN LOS ANGELES, BLACK FLAG ROSE TO BECOME ONE OF AMERICA'S LEADING HARDCORE groups. The initial line-up – Keith Morris (vocals), Greg Ginn (guitar), Chuck Dukowski (bass) and Brian Migdol (drums) – completed *Nervous Breakdown* (1978), but in 1979 Morris left to form the Circle Jerks. Several members joined and left before **Henry Rollins** (b. 1961; vocals), Dez Cadenza (guitar) and Robo (drums) joined Ginn and Dukowski for *Damaged*, the group's first full-length album. Originally scheduled for release by MCA, the company withdrew support, citing outrageous content, and the set appeared on the quintet's own label, SST Records. Ginn continued to lead Black Flag in tandem with Rollins and the music's power remained undiminished. Pivotal albums included *My War* and *In My Head* while their diversity was showcased on *Family Man*. The group split in 1986 following the release of *Who's Got The 10 1/2?*, following which Ginn switched his attentions to labelmates Gone. Rollins went on to a successful solo career.

BLACK GRAPE

THERE WAS IMMENSE MEDIA INTEREST IN THE POST-**HAPPY MONDAYS** PURSUITS OF SINGER SHAUN RYDER (b. 1962) and 'dancer' Bez (b. Mark Berry). The debut album, *It's Great When You're Straight...Yeah*, received ecstatic reviews. The germination of Black Grape had occurred only weeks after the dissolution of the Happy Mondays. The band

Ryder put together was initially named the Mondays, and included Kermit (b. Paul Leveridge), ex-Paris Angels guitarist 'Wags' (b. Paul Wagstaff), second guitarist Craig Gannon (ex-**Smiths**) and Martin Smith (Intastella). By the time Black Grape had taken their new name and were recording their debut album, both Smith and Gannon had departed, replaced by Danny Saber (co-writer; ex-**Cypress Hill**), Ged Lynch (drums) and Stephen Lironi (ex-**Altered Images**). The title of the album partly expressed Ryder's decision to turn away from hard drug abuse. His much-publicized 'cut-up' lyrics were present, along with his trademark scat coupling of meaningless phrases used primarily for their phonetic value. Kermit's growling raps balanced the slurring Ryder delivery perfectly and the group were rewarded with a UK number 1 album. During an eventful 1996, the band toured regularly but lost the services of Bez, while Kermit announced his own side-project Man Made in 1997. With new vocalist Psycho on board, the long-awaited *Stupid, Stupid, Stupid* was released to mixed reviews.

BLACK OAK ARKANSAS

FORMED IN THE LATE 60S, BLACK OAK ARKANSAS TOOK ITS NAME FROM THE US TOWN AND STATE WHERE SINGER Jim 'Dandy' Mangrum (b. 1948) was born. The other members were: Ricky Reynolds (b. 1948; guitar), Stanley Knight (b. 1949; guitar), Harvey Jett (guitar), Pat Daugherty (b. 1947; bass) and drummer Wayne Evans, replaced on the third album by Thomas Aldrich (b. 1950). As Knowbody Else, they recorded an unsuccessful album for Stax Records in 1969. In 1971, they changed their name, signed with Atco Records and recorded a self-titled album that introduced them to the US charts. Touring steadily, this hard rock/southern boogie band built a core following. Of their 10 US-charting albums between 1971 and 1976, *High On The Hog* proved the most commercially successful, peaking at number 52. It featured the best-selling 1974 Top 30 single, 'Jim Dandy' (sung by female vocalist Ruby Starr, who reappeared on the 1976 *Live! Mutha* album).

In 1975, Jett was replaced by James Henderson (b. 1954) and in 1976, Black Oak Arkansas had their final chart single, 'Strong Enough To Be Gentle'. By 1977 only Mangrum remained from the original band and there was no further record success. Mangrum kept variations of the group on the road during the 80s and recorded a solo album in 1984.

BLACK SABBATH

TERRY 'GEEZER' BUTLER (b. 1949; BASS), TONY IOMMI (b. 1948; GUITAR), BILL WARD (b. 1948; DRUMS) AND 'OZZY' **Osbourne** (b. 1948; vocals) grew up together in England. They were originally known as Earth, which they changed to Black Sabbath in 1969. Their name comes from the title of a cult horror film. The line-up remained unchanged until 1973 when **Rick Wakeman**, keyboard player for **Yes**, was drafted in to play on *Sabbath Bloody Sabbath*. By 1977 personnel difficulties were beginning to take their toll, and the music was losing some of its earlier orchestral, bombastic sheen; Ozzy Osbourne went solo the following year. He was replaced by Dave Walker (ex-Savoy Brown), then by Ronnie James Dio, who left in 1982, replaced by **Ian Gillan**. *Born Again* failed to capture the original vitality of the group and by 1986, Iommi was the only original band member, alongside Geoff Nichols (keyboards) Glenn Hughes (vocals; ex-**Deep Purple**), Dave Spitz (bass), and Eric Singer (drums). In 1986, the surprisingly blues-sounding *Seventh Star* was released, with lyrics and music by Iommi. Hughes left, replaced by Ray Gillen, an American singer who failed to record anything with them. Tony Martin was the vocalist on 1987's *The Eternal Idol* and 1988's *Headless Cross*. Martin has remained with them intermittently since that time and has been replaced at various times by Rob Halford (Judas Priest), Osbourne and Dio. By 1991, the band was suffering from flagging record sales and declining credibility, so Iommi recruited original bassist, Butler. Cozy Powell was recuperating after being crushed by his horse, and so Vinnie Appice became Sabbath's new drummer. Ronnie Dio completed the 1982–83 line-up. Ozzy's attempts to re-form the original group for a 1992 tour faltered when the others demanded an equal share in the spoils. In 1994 a tribute album, *Nativity In Black*, was released, which featured appearances from all four original members. Spurred by the new interest in the group, the Powell, Iommi and Nichols line-up, with Tony Martin returning as singer and Neil Murray on bass, completed *Forbidden* (1995), featuring **Ice-T** on 'Illusion Of Power'. In 1996, the line-up was Iommi, Martin, Murray and Bobby Rondinelli (drums).

BLACK UHURU

FORMED IN JAMAICA BY GARTH DENNIS, DERRICK 'DUCKY' SIMPSON AND DON MCCARLOS IN THE EARLY 70S, BLACK Uhuru first recorded a version of **Curtis Mayfield**'s 'Romancing To The Folk Song' as Uhuru (Swahili for 'Freedom'). Dennis and McCarlos both left and 'Ducky' enlisted Michael Rose as lead singer; Errol Nelson sang harmonies. This line-up sang for Prince Jammy on 1977's *Love Crisis*, later reissued and retitled *Black Sounds Of Freedom*. Nelson left soon afterwards and Puma Jones (b. Sandra Jones, 1953, d. 1990) took over. This combination began work for **Sly Dunbar** and Robbie Shakespeare's Taxi label in 1980, and Black Uhuru mania gripped the Jamaican reggae audience. The solid bedrock of **Sly And Robbie**'s rhythms with Puma and Duckie's eerie harmonies provided a perfect counterpoint to Rose's tortured vocals as his songs wove tales of the hardships of Jamaican life. *Showcase*, later reissued as *Vital Selection*, gave equal prominence to the vocal and instrumental versions of songs such as 'General Penitentiary', 'Shine Eye Gal' and 'Abortion'; it was a massive seller.

Their albums for Mango/Island continued in the same militant vein, and *Anthem* was remixed for the American market and earned a Grammy. Michael Rose left in the mid-80s for a solo career and Junior Reid took over lead vocals, however, after a couple of moderately well-received albums, he went solo. For *Now* Don Carlos returned to his former position as lead singer, reuniting the original triumvirate of Carlos, Duckie Simpson and Garth Dennis. Puma Jones died of cancer in 1990. She had left the band after *Brutal*, replaced by Olafunke.

BLACK FLAG
Albums
Damaged (SST 1981)★★★★
In My Head (SST 1985)★★★
Annihilate this week (live) (SST 1990)★★★
➽ p.353 for full listings
Further References
Video: *Black Flag Live* (Jettisoundz 1984)

BLACK GRAPE
Albums
It's Great When You're Straight ... Yeah (Radioactive 1995)★★★★
Stupid, Stupid, Stupid (Radioactive 1997)★★★
➽ p.353 for full listings
Connections
Happy Mondays ➽ p.174
Smiths ➽ p.301
Cypress Hill ➽ p.108
Altered Images ➽ p.16
Further References
Videos: *The Grape Tapes* (Radioactive 1997)
Book: *Shaun Ryder: Happy Mondays, Black Grape And Other Traumas*, Mick Middles

BLACK OAK ARKANSAS
Albums
Street Party (Atco 1974)★★
➽ p.353 for full listings
Collaborators
Ruby Starr

BLACK SABBATH
Albums
Paranoid (Vertigo 1970)★★★★
Sabbath Bloody Sabbath (World Wide Artists 1974)★★★
Heaven And Hell (Vertigo 1980)★★★
➽ p.353 for full listings
Collaborators
Ice-T ➽ p.191
Connections
Yes ➽ p.346
Savoy Brown
Deep Purple ➽ p.113
Judas Priest ➽ p.202
Clash ➽ p.93
Influences
Polka Tulk
Further References
Videos: *Never Say Die* (VCL 1986)
Book: *Black Sabbath*, Chris Welch.

BLACK UHURU
Albums
Red (Mango/Island 1981)★★★★
Brutal (RAS 1986)★★★★
➽ p.353 for full listings
Collaborators
Sly Dunbar ➽ p.126
Influences
Curtis Mayfield ➽ p.228
Further References
Videos: *Tear It Up* (1989)

BLACK WIDOW
Albums
Sacrifice (Columbia 1970)★★★
Black Widow (Columbia 1971)★★
Three (Columbia 1971)★★
➽ p.353 for full listings
Connections
Showaddywaddy ➽ p.296

BLACKMORE, RITCHIE
Connections
Deep Purple ➽ p.113
Rainbow ➽ p.272

BLACKWELL, OTIS
Albums
Singin' The Blues (Davis 1956)★★
These Are My Songs (Inner City 1978)★★
➽ p.353 for full listings
Collaborators
Elvis Presley ➽ p.265
Jerry Lee Lewis ➽ p.215
Jimmy Jones ➽ p.201
Cliff Richard ➽ p.277

BLAINE, HAL
Albums
Deuces, T's, Roadsters & Drums (RCA Victor 1963)★★
Drums! Drums! A Go Go (Dunhill 1966)★★
Have Fun!!! Play Drums!!! (Dunhill 1969)★★
➽ p.353 for full listings
Collaborators
Sam Cooke ➽ p.100
Crystals ➽ p.107
Ronettes ➽ p.282
Righteous Brothers ➽ p.278
Beach Boys ➽ p.36
Elvis Presley ➽ p.265
John Denver ➽ p.115
Connections
Phil Spector ➽ p.304
Influences
Jan and Dean ➽ p.197

BLASTERS
Albums
American Music (Rollin' Rock 1980)★★★
The Blasters (Slash 1981)★★★
Non Fiction (Slash 1983)★★★
➽ p.353 for full listings
Collaborators
Jordanaires ➽ p.201
Connections
Los Lobos ➽ p.218
Further References
Book: *Any Rough Times Are Now Behind You*, Dave Alvin

BLIGE, MARY J.
Albums
What's The 411? (Uptown 1992)★★★
What's The 411? — Remix Album (Uptown 1993)★★★
Share My World (MCA 1997)★★★★
➽ p.353 for full listings

BLACK WIDOW

A PROGRESSIVE ROCK BAND FROM LEICESTER, ENGLAND, THE GROUP WAS FORMED AS SOUL BAND PESKY GEE IN 1966 by Jim Gannon (vocals/guitar/vibraphone) with Kay Garrett (vocals), Kip Trevor (vocals/guitar/harmonica), Zoot Taylor (keyboards), Clive Jones (woodwind), Bob Bond (bass) and Clive Box (drums). Pesky Gee made one album before re-forming, without Garrett, as Black Widow. The band's first album and its elaborate stage act were based by Gannon on research into black magic rituals.

The group toured throughout Europe and appeared at the **Isle of Wight Festival**s of 1969 and 1970. A debut album reached the UK Top 40 and after its release Romeo Challenger and Geoff Griffiths replaced Box and Bond. Later albums abandoned the witchcraft theme. On *Three*, John Culley replaced Gannon who later worked with Trevor on an abortive project to turn the *Black Widow* stage show into a Broadway musical. Gannon went on to play with songwriter Kenny Young in Fox and Yellow Dog before joining Sherbet and moving to Australia. Trevor worked as a session singer and is now a music publisher while Challenger plays drums for **Showaddywaddy**.

BLACKMORE, RITCHIE

BRITISH GUITARIST, BLACKMORE (b.1945), SPENT HIS EARLY CAREER IN MIKE DEE AND THE JAYWALKERS before joining Screaming Lord Sutch And His Savages in 1962. Within months he had switched to the Outlaws, a principally instrumental group which served as the studio houseband for producer Joe Meek. Blackmore briefly joined the group, the Wild Boys, in 1964, and completed an idiosyncratic solo single, 'Little Brown Jug'/'Getaway', before jumping between Neil Christian's Crusaders, the Savages and the Roman Empire. When a short-lived act, Mandrake Root, broke up in 1967, Ritchie opted to live in Hamburg, but was invited back to London in 1968 to join organist Jon Lord in **Deep Purple**. Blackmore's powerful, urgent runs became an integral part of their attraction. He left in 1975 and joined forces with the USA-based Elf to form Ritchie Blackmore's **Rainbow**. He was also involved in the Deep Purple reunion, undertaken in 1984, although animosity between the guitarist and vocalist **Ian Gillan** resulted in the latter's departure.

BLACKWELL, OTIS

BLACKWELL (b. 1931) WAS ONE OF THE GREATEST US SONGWRITERS OF THE ROCK 'N' ROLL ERA. HIS FIRST release was his 'Daddy Rolling Stone', a Jamaican favourite, where it was recorded by Derek Martin. During the mid-50s, Blackwell also recorded for RCA and Groove before turning to writing songs for other artists. In 1956, his 'Fever' was a huge success for Peggy Lee; soon 'All Shook Up' began a highly profitable association with co-writer **Elvis Presley**. The rhythmic tension of the song perfectly fitted Elvis's stage persona and was his first UK number 1. 'Don't Be Cruel' (1956), 'Paralysed' (1957), 'Return To Sender' (1962) and 'One Broken Heart For Sale' followed. There was a distinct similarity between Blackwell's vocal style and Presley's, which has led to speculation that Elvis adopted some of Blackwell's mannerisms. Blackwell also provided hits for **Jerry Lee Lewis** ('Breathless' and 'Great Balls Of Fire', 1958), Dee Clark ('Hey Little Girl' and 'Just Keep It Up', 1959), **Jimmy Jones** ('Handy Man', 1960) and **Cliff Richard** ('Nine Times Out Of Ten', 1960). Blackwell also recorded R&B material for numerous labels, and makes occasional live appearances.

BLACKWELL, ROBERT 'BUMPS'

ARRANGER AND STUDIO BANDLEADER WITH SPECIALTY RECORDS, BLACKWELL (b. 1918, d. 1985) LED A BAND IN Seattle. He arranged and produced gospel and R&B singles for **Lloyd Price** and Guitar Slim and wrote a series of stage revues – *Blackwell Portraits* – much in the same vein as the *Ziegfeld Follies*. His Bumps Blackwell Jnr Orchestra featured, at various times, **Ray Charles** and **Quincy Jones**. He also worked with Lou Adler and Herb Alpert before taking over the A&R department at Specialty. In 1955, he recorded **Little Richard**'s 'Tutti Frutti' and was a key producer and songwriter in the early days of rock 'n' roll. Along with John Marascalco he wrote 'Ready Teddy', 'Rip It Up', and, with Enotris Johnson and Little Richard, 'Long Tall Sally'. Blackwell helped launch the careers of former gospel singers **Sam Cooke** and Wynona Carr and, after leaving Specialty, was involved in setting up Keen Records. In 1981 he co-produced the title track of **Bob Dylan**'s *Shot Of Love*, before his death from pneumonia.

BLAINE, HAL

DRUMMER BLAINE (b. HAROLD SIMON BELSKY, 1929) CLAIMS TO BE THE MOST-RECORDED MUSICIAN IN history. The Los Angeles-based session musician says he has performed on over 35,000 recordings – 350 reached the US Top 10. After a stint in the army, he became a professional drummer, first with the Novelteers (also known as the Stan Moore Trio) and then with singer Vicki Young (later his first wife). At the end of the 50s he worked with Tommy Sands, then singer Patti Page and took on session work in the late 50s, beginning on a **Sam Cooke** record. His first Top 10 single was **Jan And Dean**'s 'Baby Talk' in 1960. His huge discography includes drumming for **Phil Spector**'s sessions, including hits by the **Crystals**, **Ronettes** and **Righteous Brothers**. He played on many of the **Beach Boys**' greatest hits and on sessions for **Elvis Presley**, the **Association**, **Gary Lewis And The Playboys**, the **Mamas And The Papas**, **Johnny Rivers**, the **Byrds**, **Simon And Garfunkel**, the **Monkees**, the **Carpenters**, **John Lennon**, **Ringo Starr**, **George Harrison**, the **Supremes**, **John Denver**, the **Fifth Dimension**, **Captain And Tennille**, **Cher** and hundreds of others. In the late 70s, Blaine's schedule slowed and by the 80s his involvement in the LA studio scene virtually drew to a halt. In 1990 he wrote a book about his experiences, *Hal Blaine And The Wrecking Crew*.

BLASTERS

FORMED IN LOS ANGELES IN 1979, THE BLASTERS WERE ONE OF THE LEADING PROPONENTS OF THE US 'ROOTS-rock' 80s revival. The group – Phil Alvin (vocals), his songwriter brother Dave (guitar), John Bazz (bass) and Bill Bateman (drums) – debuted with *American Music* (1980), a critically applauded fusion of rockabilly, R&B, country and blues. In 1981, the group released the Top 40 *Blasters*, for which pianist Gene Taylor joined and saxophonist Lee Allen guested. A live EP recorded in London followed in 1982 but it was *Non Fiction* which earned the band its greatest acclaim. Saxophonist Steve Berlin joined then moved to **Los Lobos** when *Hard Line* was issued. The album included backing vocals by the **Jordanaires**. Dave Alvin left to join **X**, and was replaced by Hollywood Fats, who died of a heart attack at the age of 32. Phil Alvin and Berlin kept a version of the group together until 1987. Both Alvin brothers have recorded solo albums and worked on other projects.

BLIGE, MARY J.

BLIGE'S (b. 1971) DEBUT ALBUM SOLD OVER TWO MILLION COPIES; MANY OF THE BEST SONGS WERE WRITTEN FOR her by POV. The hip-hop quotient was represented by bass-driven rhythms, the soul stylings including her affecting voice. Guest appearances from rappers Grand Puba and Busta Rhymes were a bonus. According to her publicity handout, *Share My World* marked 'her personal and musical rebirth'.

BLIND FAITH

FORMED IN 1969, BLIND FAITH WERE ONE OF THE EARLIEST 'SUPERGROUP'S. **ERIC CLAPTON** (b. 1945; GUITAR/vocals), **Ginger Baker** (b. 1939; drums), **Steve Winwood** (b. 1948; keyboards/vocals) and Rick Grech (b. 1945, d. 1990; bass/violin) stayed together for one highly publicized, million-selling album and a lucrative major US tour. Their debut was a free concert in front of an estimated 100,000 at London's Hyde Park, in 1969. The controversial album cover depicted a topless pre-pubescent girl holding a phallic chrome model aeroplane and included only one future classic, Clapton's 'Presence Of The Lord'. Live Blind Faith tracks can be heard on the Winwood box set, *The Finer Things*.

BLIND MELON

US POP-ROCK BAND BLIND MELON – GLEN GRAHAM (DRUMS), SHANNON HOON (d. 21 OCTOBER 1995; vocals), Rogers Stevens (guitar), Christopher Thorn (guitar) and Brad Smith (bass) – entered the US mainstream in 1993. Graham's sister, Georgia, portrayed as an awkward, publicity-shy youngster adorned in a bee-suit, featured on their debut album, in the video for their second single, 'No Rain' she became a cult icon. Their album reached US number 3. Two years of touring followed, including dates at **Woodstock** II in America and **Glastonbury Festival** in England.

Soup was less accessible than many expected, recorded in New Orleans during bouts of drug-related non-activity (Hoon confessed that he could not actually remember making the record). It was generally known that Hoon had unsuccessfully fought heroin addiction for some time, sadly he died from a heroin overdose. *Nico* (named after Hoon's stepdaughter), was released in 1997. It was a sad, patched-together affair that the remaining members felt morally obliged to release.

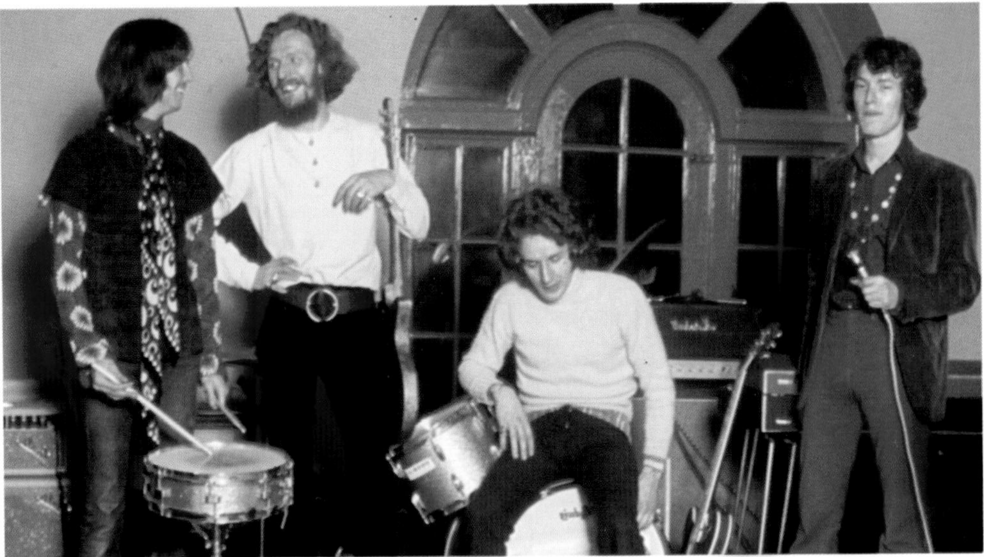

BLODWYN PIG

BRITISH BAND FORMED WHEN **MICK ABRAHAMS** (b. 1943; GUITAR) LEFT **JETHRO TULL**. ABRAHAMS FLUID PLAYING blended well with the rest of the band, Jack Lancaster (saxophone), Andy Pyle (bass) and Ron Berg (drums). *Ahead Rings Out*, a critical success, contained a mixture of various styles of progressive blues. The band were a prolific live attraction. The second album showed great moments, notably Abrahams' punchy 'See My Way' and Lancaster's long pieces such as 'San Francisco Sketches'. However Abrahams departed, replaced by Pete Banks (ex-**Yes**) and Larry Wallis. Lancaster led and they became Lancaster's Bomber, and finally, Lancaster. Four years later, Abrahams and Lancaster re-formed Blodwyn Pig with Pyle and ex-Tull drummer Clive Bunker, but it became evident that their day was long-past.

Lancaster became a producer, Abrahams set up a financial consultancy business and Pyle briefly joined the **Kinks**. Abrahams resurrected the group in the 90s to play club dates, performing new material, with Dick Heckstall-Smith, Clive Bunker and Andy Pyle. *Lies* appeared on Abrahams's own label with a line-up including David Lennox (keyboards) Mike Summerland (bass) Jackie Challoner (vocals) and Graham Walker (drums).

BLOOD, SWEAT AND TEARS

THE JAZZ/ROCK EXCURSIONS MADE BY BLOOD, SWEAT AND TEARS OFFERED A REFRESHING CHANGE TO 60S guitar-dominated rock. The band was conceived by **Al Kooper** (b. 1944; keyboards/vocals), together with Steve Katz (b. 1945; guitar; **Blues Project**), Randy Brecker (b. 1945; saxophone) and Jerry Weiss. Kooper departed soon after their debut album and Brecker and Weiss were replaced by Chuck Winfield (b. 1943; trumpet), Lew Soloff (b. 1944; trumpet) and David Clayton-Thomas (b. David Thomsett, 1941; vocals). The latter took over as vocalist to record *Blood Sweat And Tears*. The album topped the US album charts, sold millions of copies, won a Grammy award and spawned three major worldwide hits: 'You've Made Me So Very Happy', 'Spinning Wheel' and 'And When I Die'. The following two albums were both considerable successes, with their gutsy brass arrangements, occasional biting guitar solos and Clayton-Thomas's growling vocal delivery. Following *BS&T4*, Clayton-Thomas departed for a solo career, resulting in a succession of lead vocalists, including Jerry LaCroix (b. 1943). The band never regained their former glory, even following the return of Clayton-Thomas, although *New City* reached the US album charts. The band re-formed briefly in 1988 to play their back catalogue.

Collaborators
Grand Puba
Busta Rhymes

BLIND FAITH
Albums
Blind Faith (Polydor 1969)★★★
➽ p.353 for full listings

BLIND MELON
Albums
Blind Melon (Capitol 1993)★★★★
Soup (Capitol 1995)★★
Nico (Capitol 1997)★★
➽ p.353 for full listings
Connections
Rolling Stone ➽ p.280
Woodstock II ➽ p.343
Glastonbury Festival ➽ p.160
Further References
Videos: *Letters From A Porcupine* (Capitol 1996)

BLODWYN PIG
Albums
Ahead Rings Out (Chrysalis 1969)★★★★
Getting To This (Chrysalis 1970)★★★
Modern Alchemist (Indigo 1997)★★
➽ p.353 for full listings
Connections
Jethro Tull ➽ p.199
Yes ➽ p.346
Kinks ➽ p.207

BLOOD, SWEAT AND TEARS
Albums
Child Is Father To The Man (Columbia 1968)★★★
Blood, Sweat And Tears (Columbia 1969)★★★★
Blood, Sweat And Tears 3 (Columbia 1970)★★★
➽ p.353 for full listings
Connections
Blues Project ➽ p.57
Further References
Book: *Blood, Sweat And Tears*, Lorraine Alterman

BLONDIE
Albums
Blondie (Private Stock 1976)★★★
Plastic Letters (Chrysalis 1978)★★★
Parallel Lines (Chrysalis 1978)★★★★
➤ p.353 for full listings

Connections
Television ➤ p.317
Eurythmics ➤ p.139
Sex Pistols ➤ p.292
Further References
Video: *Eat To The Beat* (Chrysalis Music Video 1988)
Books: *Rip Her To Shreds: A Look At Blondie*, Paul Sinclair
Making Tracks: The Rise Of Blondie, Debbie Harry, Chris Stein and Victor Bockris

BLOOM, BOBBY
Albums
The Bobby Bloom Album (1970)★★★
➤ p.353 for full listings
Collaborators
Monkees ➤ p.236

BLOOMFIELD, MIKE
Albums
with Al Kooper and Stephen Stills *Super Session* (Columbia 1968)★★★
Retrospective (1984)★★★
➤ p.353 for full listings
Collaborators
Bob Dylan ➤ p.128
Stephen Stills ➤ p.310
Al Kooper ➤ p.210
Connections
Paul Butterfield ➤ p.76
Electric Flag ➤ p.134
Further References
Book: *The Rise And Fall Of An American Guitar Hero*, Ed Ward

BLOSSOM TOES
Albums
We Are Ever So Clean (Marmalade 1967)★★★★
➤ p.353 for full listings
Connections
Family ➤ p.143
Cockney Rebel ➤ p. ➤ p.96
Rod Stewart ➤ p.310

BLOW, KURTIS
Albums
Ego Trip (Mercury 1984)★★★
America (Mercury 1985)★★★
➤ p.353 for full listings

BLONDIE

BLONDIE WAS FORMED IN NEW YORK CITY IN 1974 WHEN **DEBORAH HARRY** (b. 1945; VOCALS), CHRIS Stein (b.1950; guitar), Fred Smith (bass) and Bill O'Connor (drums) abandoned the revivalist Stilettos for an independent musical direction. Backing vocalists Julie and Jackie, then Tish and Snookie, augmented the early line-up, but progress was undermined by the departure of Smith for **Television** and the loss of O'Connor. James Destri (b. 1954; keyboards), Gary Valentine (bass) and Clement Burke (b. 1955; drums) joined Harry and Stein and secured a recording contract through producer Richard Gottehrer; *Blondie* adeptly combined melody with purpose.

After internal disputes, Valentine left and the arrival of Frank Infante (guitar) and Nigel Harrison (bass) triggered the group's most consistent period. *Plastic Letters* contained two UK Top 10 hits: 'Denis' and '(I'm Always Touched By Your) Presence Dear', while *Parallel Lines*, produced by **Mike Chapman**, included the UK chart-topping 'Heart Of Glass' and 'Sunday Girl' (both 1979). *Eat To The Beat* spawned the successful 'Union City Blue' and 'Atomic'. 'Call Me', produced by Giorgio Moroder, was taken from the film soundtrack of *American Gigolo* and reached UK/US number 1. *Autoamerican* provided two further US chart toppers in 'The Tide Is High' and 'Rapture' – the former, originally recorded by reggae group the Paragons, reached UK number 1. Despite commercial ascendancy, Blondie was beset by internal difficulties, as the media increasingly focused on Harry and the distinction between the group's name and her persona became increasingly blurred. After the release of her solo album, *Koo Koo, The Hunter*, became Blondie's final recording – Stein's ill health (a genetic disease, pemphigus) brought an attendant tour to a premature end. Both Stein and Harry absented themselves from full-time performing.

Harry later resumed her solo career, while Burke briefly joined the **Eurythmics** for *Revenge*, and then Chequered Past. In 1997, Harry re-formed Blondie to record new material and tour.

BLOOM, BOBBY

NEW YORK-BASED BLOOM (d.1971) BEGAN HIS CAREER DURING THE 60S AS ONE OF SEVERAL ENTREPRENEURS central to the Kama Sutra/Buddah group of labels. He made several solo recordings, including 'Love Don't Let Me Down' and 'Count On Me', and formed a partnership with composer/producer **Jeff Barry**. They contributed material for the **Monkees**, notably 'Ticket On A Ferry Ride' and 'You're So Good To Me'. Bloom's effervescent 'Montego Bay' reached the US Top 10 and UK Top 3 in 1970. This adept combination of calypso and rock was maintained on 'Heavy Makes You Happy' and *The Bobby Bloom Album*, which Barry produced. Bloom was accidentally shot in 1971.

BLOOMFIELD, MIKE

FOR MANY, BLOOMFIELD (b. 1944, d. 1981) WAS THE FINEST WHITE BLUES GUITARIST AMERICA HAS SO FAR PRODUCED. Although signed to Columbia Records in 1964 as the Group (with Charlie Musslewhite and Nick Gravenites), it was his emergence in 1965 as the guitarist in the **Paul Butterfield** Blues Band that brought him to public attention. Bloomfield was **Bob Dylan**'s lead electric guitarist at Newport, and again on *Highway 61 Revisited*. On leaving Butterfield in 1967, he formed **Electric Flag**, although he left shortly afterwards. *Super Session*, with **Stephen Stills** and **Al Kooper**, became his biggest-seller and led to a short but lucrative career with Kooper. 'Stop' epitomized Bloomfield's style: clean, crisp, sparse and emotional, but it was five years before his next satisfying work appeared, *Triumvirate*, with John Paul Hammond and **Dr. John**. Plagued with a long-standing drug habit he occasionally supplemented his income by scoring music for pornographic movies. He wrote soundtracks for *The Trip* (1967), *Medium Cool* (1969) and *Steelyard Blues* (1973). In 1975, he was cajoled into forming KGB with Ric Grech, Barry Goldberg and Carmine Appice. The album was a disaster and Bloomfield resorted to playing mostly acoustic music. He had a prolific year in 1977, releasing five albums, the most notable being the critically acclaimed *If You Love These Blues, Play 'Em As You Please*. Another burst of activity occurred shortly before his death (from a suspected drug overdose), when three albums' worth of material was recorded.

BLOSSOM TOES

BRIAN GODDING (GUITAR/VOCALS/KEYBOARDS), JIM CREGAN (GUITAR/VOCALS), BRIAN BELSHAW (BASS/vocals) and Kevin Westlake (drums) initially known as the Ingoes, became Blossom Toes in 1967 upon the launch of manager Giorgio Gomelsky's Marmalade label. *We Are Ever So Clean* was an enthralling selection, astutely combining English pop with a quirky sense of humour. *If Only For A Moment* marked Westlake's departure, he was replaced by John 'Poli' Palmer, then Barry Reeves. A heavier sound was shown to great effect on 'Peace Lovin' Man', but the set was less distinctive. The quartet dissolved in 1970. Cregan later found fame with **Cockney Rebel** and **Rod Stewart**.

BLOW MONKEYS

LED BY DR ROBERT (b. BRUCE ROBERT HOWARD, 1961; GUITAR), THE BLOW MONKEYS TOOK THEIR NAME FROM AUSTRALIAN slang for Aboriginal didgeridoo players. The band were Tony Kiley (b. 1962; drums), Neville Henry (saxophone) and Mick Anker (b. 1957; bass). They recorded for RCA in 1984 but made no headway in the charts until 1986 with 'Digging Your Scene', one of the earliest songs about AIDS. The following January they had their biggest hit with 'It Doesn't Have To Be This Way'. '(Celebrate) The Day After You', banned by the BBC featured the voice of **Curtis Mayfield**. 'You Don't Own Me' appeared on the successful *Dirty Dancing* soundtrack and minor hits followed. In 1989, Dr Robert recorded a

duet (under his own name) with soul singer Kym Mazelle. 'Wait' went into the UK Top 10, and the year ended with 'Slaves No More' with the Blow Monkeys, featuring Sylvia Tella. Their last minor hit was 1990's 'Springtime For The World'. Following the break-up of the band Dr. Robert worked with **Paul Weller** and started a solo career. His debut album was released in 1996.

BLOW, KURTIS

THIS NEW YORK PRODUCER AND RAP PIONEER HAD ONE OF THE GENRE'S EARLIEST HITS WITH 'CHRISTMAS RAPPIN' (1979), written by J.B. Ford and *Billboard* journalist Robert Ford Jnr Blow (b. Kurt Walker, 1959) began work as a DJ, playing in small clubs alongside other early innovators like **Grandmaster Flash**. Signing to Mercury Records, Blow became the first rap artist to cut albums for a major label. His 1979 hit, 'The Breaks', for which his partner Davy D (b. David Reeves Jnr) provided the backing tracks, was a massive influence on the whole hip hop movement. After a quiet period, he re-emerged in 1983 with *Party Time* and an appearance in the movie, *Krush Groove*. *Ego Trip* was an impressive selection bolstered by the presence of **Run DMC** on the minor hit '8 Million Stories'. He rapped on Rene And Angela's hit 'Save Your Love (For Number One)' and produced for the Fearless Four and Dr Jeckyll And Mr Hyde among others.

Blow organized the all-star King Dream Chorus and Holiday Crew who recorded the Martin Luther King tribute, 'King Holiday'. Kingdom Blow featured appearances from **Bob Dylan**, and **George Clinton** on an amazing interpretation of 'Zip-A-Dee-Doo-Dah'. Blow was overtaken by the young guns of the genre he helped to create, a fact underlined by the miserable reception offered *Back By Popular Demand*; he hasn't scored a chart hit since 'I'm Chillin" (1986).

BLOWZABELLA

ESSENTIALLY A UK FOLK DANCE BAND, FORMED IN 1978, THE GROUP WERE WELL KNOWN FOR THEIR FREQUENT changes of personnel. In 1987, sole remaining founder member John Swayne (b. 1940; alto and soprano saxophones/bagpipes) left and Jo Fraser (b. 1960; saxophone/vocals/whistles) joined. The rest of the group were Paul James (b. 1957; bagpipes/soprano saxophone/percussion), Nigel Eaton (b. 1966; hurdy gurdy), Ian Luff (b. 1956; cittern/bass guitar), Dave Roberts (d. 1996; melodeon/darabuka) and Dave Shepherd (fiddle).

Blowzabella toured Brazil in 1987 and *Pingha Frenzy* emerged from over 50 hours of taped sessions. *A Richer Dust* came from music written for the 500th Anniversary of the Battle of Stoke Field. Shepherd left and Andy Cutting (b. 1969; melodeon) joined in 1989. Later that year, Swayne rejoined. The group's repertoire included a wealth of dance material from northern Europe and France. They played a 'farewell tour' in 1990.

BLUE, DAVID

HAVING LEFT THE US ARMY, BLUE (b. STUART DAVID COHEN, 1941, d. 1982) WAS DRAWN INTO THE NASCENT folk circle. He joined a generation of younger performers who rose to prominence in **Bob Dylan**'s wake. Blue signed to Elektra in 1965 and released *Singer/Songwriter Project* – a collaboration with Richard Farina, Bruce Murdoch and Patrick Sky. Although his first full-scale collection in 1966 bore an obvious debt to the folk rock style of *Highway 61 Revisited*, a rudimentary charm was evident. Several acts recorded his compositions, but subsequent recordings with American Patrol were never issued and it was two years before a second album appeared. *These 23 Days In December* showcased a mellow performer, before the release of *Me, S. David Cohen*, which embraced country styles.

In 1972, Blue signed to the Asylum label. *Stories*, was the artist's bleakest, most introspective selection. Subsequent releases included the Graham Nash-produced *Nice Baby And The Angel* and *Com'n Back For More*, but although his 'Outlaw Man', was covered by the **Eagles**, Blue was unable to make a significant commercial breakthrough. During this period, he appeared alongside, Dylan, in the Rolling Thunder Revue. Switching to acting, he appeared in **Neil Young**'s *Human Highway* and Wim Wenders' *An American Friend*. His acerbic wit was one of the highlights of Dylan's *Renaldo And Clara* movie. This underrated artist died while jogging in Washington Square Park.

BLUE AEROPLANES

SINCE FORMING IN BRISTOL, ENGLAND, IN THE EARLY 80S, THE BLUE AEROPLANES HAVE HAD ENDLESS LINE-UP changes, but maintained their original aim to involve a large number of musicians in an almost communal manner. The nucleus of the band has revolved around vocalist Gerard Langley, his brother John (drums/percussion), Nick Jacobs (guitar), Dave Chapman (multi-instrumentalist) and dancer Wojtek Dmochowski. Individuals such as Angelo Bruschini (guitar/bass/organ), John Stapleton (tapes), Ruth Coltrane (bass/mandolin), Ian Kearey (guitar/banjimer/harmonium), Rodney Allen (guitar), Simon Heathfield (bass) and Caroline Halcrow (guitar) have all contributed. After *Bop Art* (1984), the band recorded several well-received EPs succeeded by their second album, *Tolerance*; their third set, *Spitting Out Miracles*, surfaced in 1987. All were characterized by Langley's monotone verse and a deluge of instruments and sounds hinged around the guitar. A double album, *Friendloverplane*, was followed by *Swagger*. Both suggested a more direct, straightforward approach, and this was confirmed on the EP *And Stones*. In 1991, the line-up – Langley, Bruschini, Dmochowski, Allen, Paul Mulreany (drums; ex-**Jazz Butcher**), Andy McCreeth, Hazel Winter and Robin Key – released *Beatsongs*, co-produced by **Elvis Costello** and Larry Hirsch. The fresh-sounding *Life Model* featured Marcus Williams (bass, ex-Mighty Lemon Drops) and Susie Hugg (vocals, ex-Katydids). Following a 10th anniversary tour, *Rough Music* proved to be their best album since *Beatsongs*, but commercial success was elusive.

BLUE CHEER

SAN FRANCISCO'S BLUE CHEER, CONSISTING OF DICKIE PETERSON (b. 1948; VOCALS/BASS), LEIGH STEPHENS (guitar) and Paul Whaley (drums), were inspired by **Jimi Hendrix**. Taking their name from a brand of LSD, they made an immediate impact with *Vincebus Eruptum*, which featured cacophonous interpretations of **Eddie Cochran**'s 'Summertime Blues' (US number 14) and Mose Allison's 'Parchman(t) Farm'. *Outsideinside* was completed in the open air when high volume levels destroyed their studio monitors. Stephens left during the sessions for *New! Improved*, replaced by guitarist Randy Holden; they added Bruce Stephens (bass) when Holden left during the recording sessions. *Blue Cheer* unveiled a reconstituted line-up of Petersen, Burns Kellogg (keyboards), and Norman Mayell (drums/guitar), who replaced Whaley. Stephens was replaced by Gary Yoder for *The Original Human Being*. It featured the atmospheric, raga-influenced 'Babaji (Twilight Raga)', the group's most cohesive work. The band was dissolved in 1971 but re-formed in 1979 with *The Beast Is Back* ... and added guitarist Tony Rainer. *Highlights And Lowlives*, coupled the group with **Anthrax** producer Jack Endino.

Collaborators
Run DMC ➽ p.284
Bob Dylan ➽ p.128
George Clinton ➽ p.94
Connections
Fearless Four ➽ p.
Dr. Jeckyll and Dr. Hyde

BLOW MONKEYS
Albums
Limping For A Generation (RCA 1984)★★★
She Was Only A Grocer's Daughter (RCA 1987)★★★
➽ p.353 for full listings
Collaborators
Curtis Mayfield ➽ p.228
Kym Mazelle
Connections
Paul Weller ➽ p.336
Further References
Videos: *Video Magic* (1988)
Digging Your Scene (1988)
Choices (1989)

BLOWZABELLA
Albums
Blowzabella (Plant Life 1982)★★★
Bobbityshooty (Plant Life 1984)★★★
The Blowzabella Wall Of Sound (Plant Life 1986)★★★
➽ p.353 for full listings

BLUE, DAVID
Albums
with Richard Farina *Singer/Songwriter Project* (1965)★★★
Stories (Line 1971)★★★
Com'n Back For More (Asylum 1975)★★★
➽ p.353 for full listings
Collaborators
Bob Dylan ➽ p.128
Connections
Eagles ➽ p.130

BLUE AEROPLANES
Albums
Bop Art (Abstract 1984)★★★
Beatsongs (Ensign 1991)★★★★
➽ p.353 for full listings
Collaborators
Elvis Costello ➽ p.101
Connections
Jazz Butcher
Mighty Lemon Drops
Katydids

BLUE CHEER
Albums
Vincebus Eruptum (Philips 1968)★★★
Outsideinside (Philips 1968)★★★
➽ p.353 for full listings
Connections
Other Half
Influences
Jimi Hendrix ➽ p.180
Eddie Cochran ➽ p.95

BLUE MINK
Albums
Blue Mink (Regal 1969)★★★
A Time Of Change (Regal 1972)★★★
➽ p.353 for full listings

BLUE NILE
Albums
A Walk Across The Rooftops (Linn/Virgin 1984)★★★★
Hats (Linn/Virgin 1989)★★★
➽ p.353 for full listings

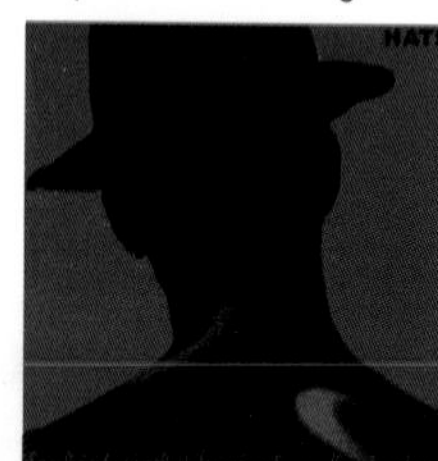

Collaborators
Julian Lennon ➽ p.214
Robbie Robertson ➽ p.279

BLUE ORCHIDS
Albums
The Greatest Hit (Money Mountain) (Rough Trade 1982)★★★
➽ p.353 for full listings
Connections
Fall ➽ p.142
Bluebells ➽ p.56

BLUE ÖYSTER CULT
Albums
Agents Of Fortune (Columbia 1976)★★★★
➽ p.353 for full listings
Collaborators
Patti Smith ➽ p.301
Connections
Alice Cooper ➽ p.12
Influences
Black Sabbath ➽ p.51
Byrds ➽ p.77
Further References
Video: *Live 1976* (Castle Music Pictures 1991)

BLUEBELLS
Albums
Sisters (London 1984)★★★
➽ p.353 for full listings
Connections
Siobhan Fahey ➽ p.31
Smiths ➽ p.301

BLUES BAND
Albums
The Official Blues Band Bootleg Album (Blues Band 1980)★★★★
➽ p.353 for full listings
Connections
Manfred Mann ➽ p.223
John Dummer Blues Band
Family ➽ p.143
Further References
Book: *Talk To Me Baby: The Story Of The Blues Band*, Roy Bainton

BLUE MINK

FORMED IN 1969 BY MADELINE BELL (VOCALS), ROGER COOK (VOCALS), ALAN PARKER (GUITAR), ROGER COULAM (ORGAN), Herbie Flowers (bass) and Barry Morgan (drums). With Cook And (Roger) Greenaway (alias David And Jonathan) providing the material, the group enjoyed a run of hits from 1969-73 including the catchy anti-racist plea 'Melting Pot', 'Good Morning Freedom', and 'Our World'. When the hits stopped they enjoyed continued success as session musicians, writers and soloists.

BLUE NILE

FORMED IN GLASGOW, SCOTLAND, IN 1981, FEATURING PAUL BUCHANAN (VOCALS/GUITAR/SYNTHESIZERS), Robert Bell (synthesizers) and Paul Joseph Moore (piano/synthesizers). Their debut, 'I Love This Life', was followed by 1984's highly praised *A Walk Across The Rooftops*. It was five years before the follow up, *Hats*, continued the shimmering legacy of its predecessor. In the 90s the band journeyed to California to record backing vocals for **Julian Lennon**, eventually working with **Robbie Robertson** and several others. They signed a contract with Warner Brothers Records in 1993. The greatly anticipated *Peace At Last* was highly praised but only a modest success.

BLUE ORCHIDS

BRITISH EXPERIMENTAL POP GROUP FORMED FROM THE **FALL**. UNA BAINES (KEYBOARDS/VOCALS), MARTIN Bramah (guitar/vocals), Rick Goldstar (guitar), Steve Toyne (bass), and Joe Kin (drums) produced a sound that echoed the less esoteric moments of Fall. After their debut, 'The Flood', Ian Rogers became the first in a succession of drummers. After 'Work', the band embarked on a debut album. Toyne left and their third drummer 'Toby' (ex-Ed Banger And The Nosebleeds) came into the line-up. *The Greatest Hit (Money Mountain)* was ambitious and slightly flawed. Mark Hellyer filled the vacant bass position and Goldstraw departed, leaving Bramah to handle guitar duties. 'Agents Of Chance' was followed by 'Sleepy Town' (1985). Nick Marshall (drums) was the back-up to Baines and Bramah this time. Bramah then worked with Karl Burns (ex-Fall).

The Blue Orchids re-formed again in 1991 with 'Diamond Age' and the retrospective *A View From The City*. The new line-up featured Bramah, Craig Gannon (guitar, ex-**Bluebells**, **Smiths**), Martin Hennin (bass) and Dick Harrison (drums). Baines, now Bramah's ex-wife, had departed.

BLUE ÖYSTER CULT

BLUE ÖYSTER CULT SPRANG FROM THE MUSICAL AMBITIONS OF ROCK WRITERS SANDY PEARLMAN AND Richard Meltzer. Based in New York, they put together a group – known variously as the Soft White Underbelly and Oaxaca – to perform their songs. By 1969 the unit, now dubbed the Stalk-Forrest Group, established around Eric Bloom (b. 1944; guitar/vocals), Donald 'Buck Dharma' Roeser (b. 1947; guitar/vocals), Allen Lanier (b. 1986; keyboards/guitar), Joe Bouchard (b. 1948; bass/vocals) and Albert Bouchard (drums). They completed a single, 'What Is Quicksand', before becoming the Blue Öyster Cult. Early releases combined **Black Sabbath**-styled riffs with

obscure lyricism, which engendered an 'intelligent heavy metal' tag. 'Career Of Evil' from *Secret Treaties* – co-written by **Patti Smith** – showed an increasing grasp of commercial hooklines, which flourished on the international **Byrds**-sounding hit, '(Don't Fear) The Reaper'. Smith continued her association with the band on *Agents Of Fortune* and added 'Shooting Shark' to the band's repertoire for *Revolution By Night*. Fantasy writer Michael Moorcock contributed to *Mirrors* and *Cultosaurus Erectus*.

The release of the live *Some Enchanted Evening* brought the group's most innovative era to an end, despite the hit 'Joan Crawford Has Risen From The Grave', drawn from *Fire Of Unknown Origin*. Former road crew boss Rick Downey replaced Al Bouchard in 1981; in 1982, Roeser completed a solo album, *Flat Out*. Joe Bouchard left later, to form Deadringer. 1992 saw the group write and perform the majority of the soundtrack album to the *Bad Channels* horror film.

BLUEBELLS

SCOTTISH QUINTET FORMED IN 1982, COMPRISING BROTHERS DAVID (b. 1964; DRUMS) AND KEN MCCLUSKEY (b. 1962; vocals/harmonica), alongside Robert 'Bobby Bluebell' Hodgens (b. 1959; vocals/guitar), Russell Irvine (guitar) and Lawrence Donegan (bass). The latter two were later replaced by Craig Gannon (b. 1966) and Neal Baldwin. After a couple of pop singles, the Bluebells gained success with 'I'm Falling' (1984), and 'Young At Heart' (UK Top 10), their solitary album achieved Top 30 status. The reissued 'Cath'/'She Will Always Be Waiting' belatedly hit the Top 40. After splitting, Ken and David formed the McCluskey Brothers, releasing, *Aware Of All*, Hodgens formed Up and Craig Gannon joined the **Smiths**. In 1993 Volkswagen used 'Young At Heart' in one of their television advertisements. The song re-entered the UK charts, reaching number 1. The McCluskey brothers returned to folk-singing, releasing *Favourite Colours*.

BLUES BAND

BRITISH BLUES-ROCK OUTFIT PUT TOGETHER BY FORMER MANFRED MANN BAND COLLEAGUES **PAUL JONES** (b. Paul Pond, 1942; vocals, harmonica) and Tom McGuinness (b. 1941; guitar) in 1979. They brought in slide guitarist and singer Dave Kelly (b. 1948) and Gary Fletcher (bass). On drums was McGuinness's hit-making partner from the early 70s, Hughie Flint (b. 1942). They had immediate success on the pub/club/college circuit. *The Official Blues Band Bootleg Album* was literally just that: inability to pay studio bills had forced them to press copies privately from a second copy tape. Arista Records stepped in, releasing the master recording and issuing four further albums by 1983. The band split in 1982, but re-formed three years later. Ex-**Family** drummer Rob Townsend (b. 1947) replaced Flint in 1981. The band performed regularly in the 90s.

BLUES BROTHERS

FORMED IN 1978, THIS US GROUP WAS CENTRED ON COMEDIANS JOHN BELUSHI (b. 1949, d. 1982) AND DAN Aykroyd (b. 1952). Renowned for contributions to the satirical *National Lampoon* team and television's *Saturday Night Live*, the duo formed this 60s-soul-styled revue as a riposte to disco. Assuming the epithets Joliet 'Jake' Blues (Belushi) and Elwood Blues (Aykroyd), they embarked on live appearances with the assistance of a backing group – **Steve Cropper** (guitar), Donald 'Duck' Dunn (bass) and Tom Scott (saxophone). *Briefcase Full Of Blues* topped the US charts, a success that in turn inspired the film **The Blues Brothers** (1980). An affectionate, if anarchic, tribute to soul and R&B, it featured cameo appearances by **Aretha Franklin**, **Ray Charles**, **John Lee Hooker** and **James Brown**. Belushi's death from a drug overdose in 1982 brought the original concept to a premature end, since which time Aykroyd has continued a successful acting career. Several

of the musicians, including Cropper and Dunn, later toured and recorded as the Blues Brothers Band. The original Blues Brothers have also inspired numerous copy-cat/tribute groups. In 1991, interest in the concept was again boosted with a revival theatre production in London's West End. A new film was released in 1998, with Belushi's role taken by John Goodman.

BLUES MAGOOS

FORMED IN NEW YORK IN 1964 AND INITIALLY KNOWN AS THE BLOOS MAGOOS. THE FOUNDING LINE-UP WAS EMIL 'Peppy' Thielhelm (b. 1949; vocals/guitar), Dennis LaPore (lead guitar), Ralph Scala (b. 1947; organ/vocals), Ronnie Gilbert (b. 1946; bass) and John Finnegan (drums); by the end of the year LaPore and Finnegan had been replaced by Mike Esposito (b. 1943) and Geoff Daking (b. 1947). The group quickly became an important part of the emergent Greenwich Village rock scene enjoying one notable hit, '(We Ain't Got) Nothin' Yet' (1966), which reached US number 5. Its garage-band snarl set the tone for *Psychedelic Lollipop*, which contained several equally virulent selections. After *Basic Blues Magoos* (1968), they broke up.

Thielhelm then fronted a revamped line-up: John Leillo (vibes/percussion), Eric Kaz (keyboards), Roger Eaton (bass) and Richie Dickon (percussion). They completed *Never Goin' Back To Georgia* and, with session musicians and no Eaton, the disappointing *Gulf Coast Bound*.

BLUES PROJECT

THE BLUES PROJECT WAS FORMED IN NEW YORK IN THE MID-60S BY GUITARIST DANNY KALB, WITH TOMMY Flanders (vocals), Steve Katz (b. 1945; guitar), Andy Kulberg (b. 1944; bass/flute), Roy Blumenfeld (drums) and **Al Kooper** (b. 1944; vocals/keyboards). They established themselves as the city's leading electric blues band, a prowess demonstrated on their debut, *Live At the Cafe Au Go Go*. Flanders went solo and the resultant five-piece embarked on *Projections*. Before *Live At The Town Hall* was issued, Kooper left to form **Blood, Sweat And Tears**, where he was subsequently joined by Katz. Kalb also quit, but Kulberg and Blumenfeld added Richard Greene (violin), John Gregory (guitar/vocals) and Don Kretmar (bass/saxophone) for a fourth collection, *Planned Obsolescence*. The line-up changed their name to Seatrain.

In 1971, Kalb reclaimed the erstwhile moniker and recorded two further albums with Flanders, Blumenfeld and Kretmar. This version of the band was supplanted by a reunion of the *Projections* line-up for a show in Central Park, after which the Blues Project name was abandoned.

BLUES TRAVELER

NEW YORK BLUES-ROCK QUARTET LED BY SINGER/ HARMONICA PLAYER JOHN POPPER (b. 1967) WITH Brendan Hill (drums), Chan Kinchla (guitar), Bobby Sheehan (bass), they recorded their debut at the end of 1989. The band was befriended at an early stage by Paul Shaffer, band leader and arranger for the David Letterman television show. Letterman's sponsorship of the band stretched to over a dozen appearances in their first four years of existence.

In 1992, Popper was involved in a motorcycle accident which left him injured. *Save His Soul*'s release was consequently delayed, but Popper took the stage again in 1993, in a wheelchair. He continued in this vein for a Horizons of Rock Developing Everywhere tour – an alternative to the Lollapalooza events. A third stint was later undertaken with the Allman Brothers Band, whose Chuck Leavell joined Paul Shaffer in contributing to *Four*, which sold 4 million copies. *Straight On Till Morning* managed to get the balance right between rock and blues.

BLUETONES

FORMED IN LONDON, ENGLAND, IN 1990, THIS MELODIC GUITAR POP BAND CONSISTS OF SCOTT MORRISS (BASS), Eds Chesters (drums), Adam Devlin (guitar) and Mark Morriss (vocals; elder brother of Scott). Their debut single 'Are You Blue Or Are You Blind?' entered the UK Top 40 in 1995. It was followed by 'Bluetonic' (on the Fierce Panda EP as 'No. 11'). The third single, 'Slight Return', was their biggest hit, while *Expecting To Fly*, produced by Hugh Jones, reached UK number 1 in 1996. In 1998, they were back in the charts.

BLUNSTONE, COLIN

BLUNSTONE, (b. 1945), FORMER LEAD VOCALIST OF THE ZOMBIES, POSSESSED A UNIQUE VOICE. TWO OF HIS performances, 'She's Not There' and 'Time Of The Season', have become pop classics.

He started a promising solo career as Neil MacArthur and then reverted to his own name with *One Year* in 1971. *Ennismore* was his finest work, and included two UK chart hits, 'How Could We Dare To Be Wrong' and 'I Don't Believe In Miracles'. After two further albums Blunstone kept a low profile, although he appeared on four **Alan Parsons** Project albums. He resurfaced in 1981 with Dave Stewart's hit remake of **Jimmy Ruffin**'s 'What Becomes Of The Broken Hearted', and the following year had a minor hit with **Smokey Robinson**'s 'Tracks Of My Tears'. During the 80s he attempted further commercial success with Keats, but the group folded shortly after their debut album. His 1991 album, *Sings His Greatest Hits*, featured **Rod Argent** and **Russ Ballard**.

Blunstone sang again on the charity EP *Every Living Moment*. In 1995, his various live BBC recordings were issued, a compilation put together by Legacy/Epic records and finally a new studio album was recorded, *Echo Bridge*.

BLUES BROTHERS
Albums
The Blues Brothers film soundtrack (Atlantic 1980)★★★
➽ p.353 for full listings
Collaborators
Aretha Franklin ➽ p.153
Ray Charles ➽ p.88
John Lee Hooker ➽ p.185
James Brown ➽ p.70
Connections
Saturday Night Live
National Lampoon
John Goodman
Further References
Film: *The Blues Brothers* (1980)

BLUES MAGOOS
Albums
Psychedelic Lollipop (Mercury 1966)★★★
➽ p.353 for full listings

BLUES PROJECT
Albums
Projections (Verve/Forecast 1967)★★★
➽ p.353 for full listings
Connections
Blood, Sweat and Tears ➽ p.53

BLUES TRAVELER
Albums
Four (A&M 1994)★★★★
➽ p.353 for full listings
Collaborators
Allman Brothers Band ➽ p.14

BLUETONES
Albums
Expecting To Fly (Superior Quality 1996)★★★★
➽ p.353 for full listings

BLUNSTONE, COLIN
Albums
One Year (Epic 1971)★★★★
Ennismore (Epic 1972)★★★★
➽ p.353 for full listings
Collaborators
Alan Parsons Project ➽ p.256
Rod Argent ➽ p.20
Russ Ballard ➽ p.31
Connections
Zombies ➽ p.349
Influences
Jimmy Ruffin ➽ p.284

BLUR
Albums
Parklife (Food 1994)★★★★
The Great Escape (Food 1995)★★★★
Blur (Food 1997)★★★★
➽ p.353 for full listings

Collaborators
David Balfe
Andy Ross
Connections
Teardrop Explodes ➽ p.317
Oasis ➽ p.250
Influences
Beatles ➽ p.38
Soft Machine ➽ p.302
Cat Stevens ➽ p.309
Byrds ➽ p.77
Small Faces ➽ p.300
Kinks ➽ p.207
Jam ➽ p.196
Madness ➽ p.221
Further References
Video: *Star Shaped* (1993)
Books: *Blurbook*, Paul Postle
Blur In Their Own Words, Mick St Michael

BLYTH POWER
Albums
A Little Touch Of Harry In The Middle Of The Night cassette only (96 Tapes 1984)★★★
Wicked Women, Wicked Men And Wicket Keepers (Midnight 1986)★★★
The Barman And Other Stories (Midnight 1988)★★★
➽ p.353 for full listings

BMX BANDITS
Albums
Life Goes On (Creation 1994)★★★★
Gettin' Dirty (Creation 1995)★★★★
Theme Park (Creation 1996)★★★★
➽ p.354 for full listings
Connections
Soup Dragons
Faith Healers
Teenage Fanclub ➽ p.317

BOB AND EARL
Albums
Harlem Shuffle (Tip/Sue 1966)★★★
Bob And Earl (Crestview/B&C 1969)★★
Together (Joy 1969)★★
➽ p.354 for full listings
Influences
Barry White ➽ p.337

BLUR

BLUR WERE FORMED IN LONDON WHILE DAMON ALBARN (b. 1968; VOCALS), ALEX JAMES (b. 1968; BASS) AND GRAHAM Coxon (b. 1969; guitar) were students; drummer Dave Rowntree (b. 1964) joined later. The band was initially called Seymour; they started playing bottom of the bill at gigs. One year and a dozen gigs later, the quartet had signed to Food Records, run by ex-**Teardrop Explodes** keyboard player David Balfe and *Sounds* journalist Andy Ross, who suggested the name Blur.

Playing vibrant 90s-friendly pop with a sharp cutting edge, Blur's debut release, 'She's So High' sneaked into the UK Top 50. With the band displaying a breezy confidence in their abilities, 'There's No Other Way' reached UK number 8 in 1991. This success continued when *Leisure* entered

the UK charts at number 2. A relatively fallow period followed when 'Popscene' failed to rise above UK number 34 and Blur seemed set to disappear with the same alacrity with which they had established themselves. *Modern Life Is Rubbish* was presented to their record company but rejected, Balfe insisting that Albarn should write at least two more tracks. The resultant songs, 'For Tomorrow' and 'Chemical World', were the album's singles. When it finally emerged in 1993, its sales profile of 50,000 copies failed to match that of its predecessor or expectations, but touring rebuilt confidence. The 'new' model Blur saw fruition in 1994 with 'Girls & Boys', the first single from what was to prove the epoch-making *Parklife*. This set borrowed liberally from the **Beatles**, the **Small Faces**, the **Kinks**, the **Jam** and **Madness**, topped off by Albarn's knowing, Cockney delivery. Finally there seemed to be substance to the band's more excessive claims. The album gained a Mercury Music Prize nomination, and Blur went on to secure four trophies, including Best Band and Album, at the 1995 BRIT Awards.

The UK press attempted to concoct an Oasis versus Blur campaign when both bands released singles on the same day. In the event, Blur won the chart battle (with 'Country House'); although Oasis took over the headlines on a daily basis. Following the lukewarm reception given to *The Great Escape*, Blur quietly retreated to Iceland to work on new material. The result of their labour was 'Beetlebum' and *Blur*, both UK number 1's. The harder sound (evident on the thrashy 'Song 2') and more downbeat subject matter ('Death Of A Party') recalled their earlier singles.

BLYTH POWER

DRUMMER, SINGER AND SONGWRITER JOSEF PORTA (b. JOSEPH PORTER, 1962) WORKED WITH A VARIETY OF bands. He formed Blyth Power in 1983 with Curtis Youé. Porta's eloquent lyrics, coupled with a punk-influenced mixture of folk and rock drew analogies from England's history: from Watt Tyler and Oliver Cromwell, to the state of present day politics. Though many of Blyth Power's albums have been blighted by inadequate production, they achieved consistent quality, highlighting Porta's mocking social analysis.

Their sixth studio album was released in 1995, this time without long-serving member 'Wob', who went solo. *Paradise Razed*, completed in 10 days with Whisky Priests collaborator Fred Purser, was an accessible introduction to the band with Porta (now called Porter) offering further entertaining insights into British history.

BMX BANDITS

FORMED IN SCOTLAND, IN 1985, THIS IDIOSYNCRATIC GROUP REVOLVES AROUND Douglas Stewart (vocals); despite an early, naïve image, he has proved himself a wry lyricist. Sean Dickson (keyboards), Jim McCulloch (guitar), Billy Wood (vocals) and Willie McArdle (drums) joined Stewart for 'E102', although within months, the first of a host of line-up changes was underway. Dickson formed the Soup Dragons, which McCulloch later joined and the Bandits were buoyed by the arrival of Joe McAlinden (vocals/guitar/saxophone) and Norman Blake (guitar/vocals), Gordon Keen (guitar) and Francis MacDonald (drums). Eugene Kelly (ex-Vaselines) joined the quintet for *Star Wars*, issued by a Japenese label where the Bandits enjoyed a cult following. Blake found success with **Teenage Fanclub**, McAlinden formed Superstar while Kelly and Keen forged Captain America, later known as Eugenius.

The Bandits joined Creation Records in 1993. *Life Goes On*, buoyed by the inclusion of 'Serious Drugs', and *Gettin' Dirty*, a new line-up of Stewart, Francis MacDonald, Finlay MacDonald, John Hogarty and Sishil K. Dade (ex-Soup Dragons) emerged. The results were their finest album to date. *Theme Park* was an equally strong follow-up.

BO STREET RUNNERS

FORMED IN 1964 IN ENGLAND, THE BO STREET RUNNERS COMPRISED JOHN DOMINIC (VOCALS), GARY THOMAS (lead guitar), Royston Fry (keyboards), Dave Cameron (bass) and Nigel Hutchinson (drums). After recording a self-financed EP, they were accepted to appear on the television show *Ready, Steady, Go!*, in the show's talent contest. They won, securing a deal with Decca. 'Bo Street Runner' became their debut single, but despite the publicity, it failed to chart. Glyn Thomas and Tim Hinkley replaced Hutchinson and Fry, while Dave Quincy joined as saxophonist. 'Tell Me What You're Gonna Do' and 'Baby Never Say Goodbye' (for Columbia) ensued. Thomas was then replaced by Mick Fleetwood, and Quincy departed for **Chris Farlowe**. The reshaped Bo Street Runners released a version of the **Beatles**' 'Drive My Car' in 1966. Fleetwood was replaced by Alan Turner and then by Barrie Wilson; when Dominic opted to manage the group, Mike Patto joined as vocalist.

The group disbanded late in 1966, after which Patto recorded a solo single, 'Can't Stop Talkin' 'Bout My Baby' – the b-side, 'Love', was the final Bo Street Runners' recording.

BOB AND EARL

BOBBY DAY (b. BOBBY BYRD, 1932) FORMED THE HOLLYWOOD FLAMES (THEY RELEASED 'BUZZ-BUZZ-BUZZ', 1957), WHICH featured Earl Lee Nelson. Day then secured a solo hit with 'Rockin' Robin' before briefly joining Nelson in the original Bob And Earl. Bob Relf replaced Day when the latter resumed his own career. The **Barry White**-produced 'Harlem Shuffle', their best-known song, was released in 1963. A minor hit in the USA, upon reissue it reached UK number 7 in 1969. Bob And Earl had one more hit: 'Baby It's Over' (1966). Nelson recorded under the name of Jay Dee for Warner Brothers Records in 1973, and also as Jackie Lee, charting in the USA with 'The Duck' (1965), 'African Boo-Ga-Loo' (1968) and 'The Chicken' (1970). Relf wrote Love Unlimited's 1974 hit 'Walking In The Rain'. A new duo, Earl and Bobby Garrett, recorded together, and individually, during the 70s.

BOB AND MARCIA

BOB ANDY AND MARCIA GRIFFITHS HAD TWO UK CHART ENTRIES AT THE TURN OF THE 70S – THE FIRST, A VERSION of **Nina Simone**'s 'Young, Gifted And Black', was a UK Top 5 hit in 1970 and the follow-up, 'Pied Piper', reached number 11. Both Andy and Griffiths were popular artists in Jamaica in their own right before and after their pop crossover success. 'Always Together', which they recorded for **Coxsone Dodd**, failed outside Jamaica.

BOB B. SOXX AND THE BLUE JEANS

ONE OF SEVERAL GROUPS CREATED BY PRODUCER PHIL SPECTOR, THIS SHORT-LIVED TRIO CONSISTED of Darlene Love, Fanita James and Bobby Sheen. The group scored a US Top 10 hit in 1962 with a radical reading of 'Zip-A-Dee-Do-Dah'. Its success spawned an album which mixed restructured standards ('The White Cliffs Of Dover', 'This Land Is Your Land') with original songs. 'Why Do Lovers Break Each Other's Heart?' and 'Not Too Young To Get Married' were issued as singles. The group contributed to Spector's legendary *Christmas Album*.

BOLAN, MARC

BOLAN (b. MARK FELD, 1947, d. 1977) BEGAN SINGING DURING THE MID-60S FOLK BOOM. AS 'TOBY TYLER', he completed several unsuccessful demos before reportedly creating his new surname from (**Bo**)**b Dy**(**lan**). 'The Wizard' (1965), revealed an early penchant for pop mysticism whereas 'The Third Degree', was indebted to R&B. B-side, 'San Francisco Poet', gave the first airing to Bolan's distinctive, tremulous warble, evinced on his third single, 'Hippy Gumbo'. A series of demos was undertaken at this point, several of which surfaced on *The Beginning Of Doves* (1974) and, with overdubs, on *You Scare Me To Death* (1981), but plans for a fourth single were postponed. Frustrated at his commercial impasse, the artist joined John's Children in 1967. He composed their best-known single, 'Desdemona', but left after a matter of months to form **Tyrannosaurus Rex**. Here Bolan gave full range to the 'underground' poetic folk mysticism, redolent of author J.R.R. Tolkien. The unit evolved into **T. Rex** three years later. Between 1970 and 1973 this highly popular attraction enjoyed a run of 10 consecutive Top 5 singles.

After a lean period, a contemporary television series, *Marc*, revived a flagging public profile. This ascendancy ended abruptly when Bolan was killed in a crash in 1977.

BOLTON, MICHAEL

BOLTON (b. MICHAEL BOLOTIN, 1953) BECAME ONE OF AMERICA'S MOST SUCCESSFUL ROCK BALLADEERS OF THE late 80s. He recorded his first single in 1968 and a couple of solo albums. In the late 70s, he became lead singer with hard rock band Blackjack, but their two albums sold poorly.

Turning to songwriting and a solo career, Bolton had greater success as a composer, providing Laura Branigan with the 1983 hit 'How Am I Supposed To Live Without You', co-written with Doug James. He changed his name to Bolton in 1983 and, as a solo performer, persevered with a heavy rock approach; it was not until he shifted to a soul-ballad style on *The Hunger* that he had his own first Top 20 single, 'That's What Love Is All About' (1987). From that point Bolton had a series of blue-eyed soul hits that included a chart-topping version of 'How Am I Supposed To Live Without You' in 1990, as well as 'How Can We Be Lovers' and the 1991 successes 'Love Is A Wonderful Thing' and 'Time, Love And Tenderness'. He also enjoyed a brief, and unexpected, songwriting collaboration with **Bob Dylan.** In 1995 he resurfaced with a hit single 'Can I Touch You ... There?' and a greatest hits package.

BOB AND MARCIA
Albums
Young, Gifted And Black (Harry J 1970)★★★
Pied Piper (Harry J 1971)★★★
Really Together (I-Anka 1987)★★★
➽ p.354 for full listings
Collaborators
Coxsone Dodd ➽ p.121
Influences
Nina Simone ➽ p.297

BOB B. SOXX AND THE BLUE JEANS
Albums
Zip-A-Dee-Doo-Dah (Philles 1963)★★★
➽ p.354 for full listings
Connections
Phil Spector ➽ p.304
Blossoms

BOLAN, MARC
Albums
The Beginning Of Doves (Track 1974)★★
You Scare Me To Death (Cherry Red 1981)★★
The Marc Shows television recordings (Marc On Wax 1989)★★★
➽ p.354 for full listings
Connections
Tyrannosaurus Rex ➽ p.316
Influences
Bob Dylan ➽ p.128
Further References
Video: *Marc* (Channel 5 1989)
Books: *The Warlock Of Love*, Marc Bolan
Marc Bolan: Born To Boogie, Chris Welch and Simon Napier-Bell

BOLTON, MICHAEL
Albums
The Hunger (Columbia 1987)★★★
Soul Provider (Columbia 1989)★★★
The One Thing (Columbia 1993)★★
➽ p.354 for full listings
Collaborators
David Sanborn ➽ p.288
Bob Dylan ➽ p.128
Connections
Laura Branigan
Further References
Videos: *Soul Provider; The Videos* (1990)
This Is Michael Bolton (1992)
Soul & Passion (Sony Music Videos 1992)

BON JOVI
Albums
Slippery When Wet (Vertigo 1986)★★★★
New Jersey (Vertigo 1988)★★★
Keep The Faith (Phonogram 1992)★★★★
➽ p.354 for full listings
Connections
Message
Influences
Bruce Springsteen ➽ p.306
Further References
Book: *Bon Jovi: An Illustrated Biography*, Eddy McSquare
Video: *Access All Areas* (1991)

BONDS, GARY 'U.S.'
Albums
Dance 'Til Quarter To Three (Legrand/Top Rank 1961)★★★
Twist Up Calypso (Legrand/Stateside 1962)★★★
Dedication (EMI America 1981)★★★
➽ p.354 for full listings
Collaborators
Bruce Springsteen ➽ p.306
Connections
Steve Van Zandt ➽ p.329
Further References
Film: *It's Trad, Dad* aka *Ring-A-Ding Rhythm* (1962)

BONE THUGS-N-HARMONY
Albums
E.1999 Eternal (Ruthless/Relativity 1995)★★★★
The Art Of War (Ruthless 1997)★★★★
➽ p.354 for full listings
Connections
Eazy E ➽ p.131
Influences
Stevie Wonder ➽ p.342

BONEY M
Albums
Night Flight To Venus (Atlantic 1978)★★
➽ p.354 for full listings

Influences
Creation ➽ p.104
Further References
Video: *Gold* (1993)
Book: *Boney M*, John Shearlaw

BON JOVI

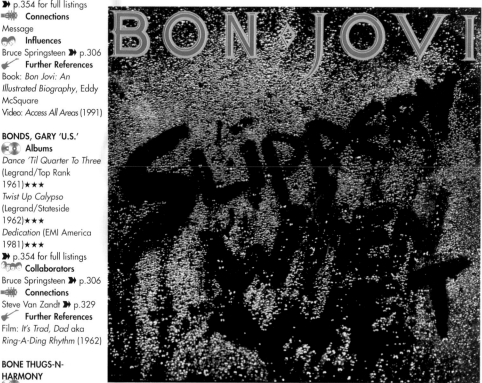

COMMERCIAL HARD ROCK BAND FORMED IN NEW JERSEY, USA AND FRONTED BY **JON BON JOVI** (b. JOHN FRANCIS Bongiovi Jnr, 1962; vocals) with Richie Sambora (b. 1959; guitar, ex-Message), David Bryan (b. David Rashbaum, 1962; keyboards), Tico Torres (b. 1953; drums, ex-Franke And The Knockouts) and Alec John Such (b. 1956; bass,

ex-Message). By 1983, a recording contract with Polygram resulted in *7800 Degrees Fahrenheit*; their debut was greeted with cynicism by the media, which was already reticent at the prospect of the band's manicured image and formularized heavy rock. However *Slippery When Wet* was the biggest-selling rock album of 1987 and 'Wanted Dead Or Alive', 'You Give Love A Bad Name' and 'Livin' On A Prayer', were US hits. *New Jersey* contained 'Living In Sin', a Bon Jovi composition which owed a debt to his hero **Bruce Springsteen**. 1989 was spent touring extensively, before the band temporarily retired. Bon Jovi subsequently went solo and appeared in his first movie, *Young Guns II*.

The commercial incentive to return to Bon Jovi was hard to resist: *Keep The Faith*, with their sound stripped down, satisfied critics and the slick ballad, 'Always', was a chart fixture in 1994. Bryan, meanwhile, released his first solo album. The group's *These Days* included the hit single 'This Ain't A Love Song'. Bon Jovi began to nurture an acting career in the 90s with roles in *Moonlight And Valentino* and *The Leading Man*.

BONDS, GARY 'U.S.'

HAVING INITIALLY SUNG IN VARIOUS GOSPEL GROUPS, BONDS (b. GARY ANDERSON, 1939) EMBRACED SECULAR music upon moving to Norfolk, Virginia. A successful spell in the region's R&B clubs resulted in a contract with local entrepreneur Frank Guida, whose production gave Bonds' releases their distinctive sound. 'New Orleans' set the pattern for the artist's recordings and 'party' atmosphere reached an apogee on 'Quarter To Three', a US chart-topper and the singer's sole million-seller. Bonds enjoyed similar-sounding hits in 1961-62, but his career then declined. He toured the revival circuit until 1978 when long-time devotee **Bruce Springsteen** joined the singer on-stage during a live engagement. Their friendship resulted in *Dedication*, produced by Springsteen and **Steve Van Zandt**. The former contributed three original songs to the set, one of which, 'This Little Girl', reached the US Top 10 in 1981. Their collaboration was maintained with *On The Line*, followed by Bonds' self-produced *Standing In The Line Of Fire*.

BONE THUGS-N-HARMONY

RAP GROUP FORMED IN OHIO, USA, IN 1993. THE BAND FEATURES LAYZIE BONE, BIZZY BONE, KRAYZIE BONE, Wish Bone and Flesh-N-Bone, and were 'discovered and nurtured' by the founder of Ruthless Records, the late **Eazy E**. Their 1994 debut EP, *Creeping On Ah Come Up*, spent over 70 weeks in *Billboard*'s Top 200 album chart, with sales of over four million. *E. 1999 Eternal* went to number 1 in the same album chart, selling over 330,000 copies in its first week of release. The group's popularity is due to their appealing combination of R&B harmonies and rapping, as featured on the single '1st Of Tha Month'. Even if the constantly repeated gangsta vocabulary becomes tiresome, this unit manages somehow to put it into the background.

BONEY M

IN 1976, GERMAN-BASED PRODUCER/COMPOSER FRANK FARIAN INVENTED A GROUP TO FRONT A SINGLE HE HAD already recorded, 'Baby Do You Wanna Bump?', which sold well in Belgium and Holland. The Carribean line-up was Marcia Barrett (b. 1948; vocals), Bobby Farrell (b. 1949, Aruba; vocals), Liz Mitchell (b. 1952; vocals) and Maizie Williams (b. 1951; vocals). In 1976-77, the group enjoyed four UK Top 10 hits with 'Daddy Cool', 'Sunny', 'Ma Baker' and 'Belfast'. Their peak period was 1978, when the chart-topping 'Rivers Of Babylon'/'Brown Girl In The Ring' spent 40 weeks on the UK chart. Its follow-up, 'Rasputin', climbed to number 2 and Boney M ended 1978 with the festive chart-topper 'Mary Boy's Child – Oh My Lord'. They experienced phenomenal success in Europe (over 50 million total sales).

In 1979, they revived **Creation**'s 'Painter Man', which reached the Top 10. The singalong 'Hooray Hooray It's A Holi-Holiday' and 'Gotta Go Home'/'El Lute' were their last Top 20 hits. The commercial power of their catalogue is emphasized by their third number 1 album, *The Magic Of Boney M* (1980).

BONGWATER

BONGWATER EVOLVED IN NEW YORK IN 1987 WHEN MARK KRAMER (GUITAR, EX-**BUTTHOLE SURFERS**) JOINED vocalist/performance artist Ann Magnuson. They completed their debut EP, *Breaking No New Ground*, with the help of guitarist Fred Frith. *Double Bummer* introduced Dave Rick (guitar) and David Licht (drums) to a unit that would remain largely informal. The new set included 'Dazed And Chinese', a version of **Led Zeppelin**'s 'Dazed And Confused' sung in Chinese. Self-penned compositions embraced psychedelia, taped documentaries, pop culture and the *avant garde*. *Too Much Sleep* was more conventional. Magnuson's semi-narrative intonation flourished freely on *The Power Of Pussy*. Rick was replaced by Randolph A. Hudson III in 1991, but following the release of *The Big Sell Out* the group split due to clashes between Kramer and Magnuson.

BONO, SONNY

BONO (b. SALVATORE BONO, 1935, d. 1998) STARTED OUT AS DIRECTOR OF A&R AT SPECIALTY RECORDS. HE CO-wrote 'She Said Yeah' for Larry Williams, later covered by the **Rolling Stones**, and pursued a recording career under numerous aliases, including Don Christy, Sonny Christy and Ronny Sommers. **Phil Spector** inspired

Bono to found the Rush label, but he achieved fame when 'Needles And Pins', a collaboration with Jack Nitzsche, was recorded by **Jackie DeShannon** and the **Searchers**. In 1963 Bono married, Cherilyn La Pierre (**Cher**) and they worked as a duo, first as Caesar And Cleo, then **Sonny And Cher**. In 1965 they enjoyed an international smash with 'I Got You Babe', written, arranged and produced by Bono. Solo projects included, 'Laugh At Me' (US/UK Top 10) 'The Revolution Kind', Bono's disavowal of the counter-culture, did less well.

Inner Views, was a commercial failure and Bono subsequently abandoned solo recordings. Although Sonny and Cher ended the personal partnership in 1974, they continued to host a television show. Bono later concentrated on an acting career, on television and in films, notably *Hairspray* (1988). He was voted mayor of Palm Springs in 1988 and in 1991 announced his intention to run for the senate. Sadly he died in 1998, the victim of a skiing accident.

BONZO DOG DOO-DAH BAND

FORMED IN 1965 BY ART STUDENTS VIVIAN STANSHALL (b. 1943, d. 1995; VOCALS/TRUMPET/DEVICES) AND RODNEY Slater (b. 1941; saxophone), the group also included Neil Innes (b. 1944; vocals/piano/guitar), Roger Ruskin Spear (b. 1943; props/devices/saxophone) and 'Legs' Larry Smith (b. 1944; drums). Various auxiliary members, including Sam Spoons (b. Martin Stafford Ash, 1942), Bob Kerr and Vernon Dudley Bohey-Nowell (b. 1932), augmented the line-up. In 1966, two singles, 'My Brother Makes The Noises For The Talkies' and 'Alley Oop', reflected their transition from trad jazz to pop and in 1967 they released their debut, *Gorilla*. Kerr and others had left for New Vaudeville Band, but the Bonzos secured a residency on the British television children's show, *Do Not Adjust Your Set* – the songs were compiled on *Tadpoles*.

The band featured in the **Beatles**' film *Magical Mystery Tour*, performing the memorable 'Death Cab For Cutie', and in 1968 secured a UK Top 5 hit with 'I'm The Urban Spaceman' (produced by **Paul McCartney** under the pseudonym Apollo C. Vermouth). Further albums, *The Doughnut In Granny's Greenhouse* and *Keynsham*, displayed an endearing eclecticism while displaying a rock-based bent. Newcomers Dennis Cowan (b. 1947), Dave Clague and Joel Druckman toughened the group's live sound. They disbanded in 1970, but a reconvened line-up completed *Let's Make Up And Be Friendly* in 1972.

BOO RADLEYS

FORMED IN 1988 IN LIVERPOOL BY SICE (b. SIMON ROWBOTTOM, 1969; GUITAR, VOCALS), MARTIN CARR (b. 1968; guitar), Timothy Brown (b. 1969; bass) and Steve Drewitt (drums), they took their name from a character in the novel *To Kill A Mockingbird*. *Ichabod And I* showcased the band's talent for guitar-blasted melodies, where timeless tunes were bolstered with up-to-date effects pedals.

In 1990, Drewitt left for Breed and was replaced by Robert Cieka (b. 1968), just as the Boo Radleys signed to Rough Trade Records for the EP *Every Heaven*. A move to Creation Records was rewarded with *Everything's Alright Forever*, which broke them out of the indie ghetto. *Giant Steps* saw the band producing a set that retraced the grandeur of Merseybeat, bringing them several Album Of The Year awards in the UK. An evident attempt to wrest chart domination away from **Oasis** or **Blur**, *Wake Up* lacked the ususal chaotic experimentalism, replaced instead by sweeping vistas of orchestrated pop. The spirit of the Boo Radleys was captured in the follow-up, *C'Mon Kids*, their most challenging album to date, but it was a commercial failure. Sice also released a solo album as Eggman, revealing a hidden melodic talent.

BONGWATER
Albums
Breaking No New Ground mini-album (Shimmy-Disc 1987)★★★
The Power Of Pussy (Shimmy-Disc 1991)★★★★
The Peel Sessions (Strange Fruit 1991)★★★
➧ p.354 for full listings
Connections
Butthole Surfers ➧ p.76
Influences
Moody Blues ➧ p.237
Led Zeppelin ➧ p.213

BONO, SONNY
Albums
Inner Views (1967)★
➧ p.354 for full listings
Collaborators
Cher ➧ p.89
Connections
Jackie DeShannon ➧ p.116
Searchers ➧ p.290
Sonny and Cher ➧ p.302
Influences
Phil Spector ➧ p.304
Further References
Book: *And The Beat Goes On*, Sonny Bono.

BONZO DOG DOO-DAH BAND
Albums
Gorilla (Liberty 1967)★★★
The Doughnut In Granny's Greenhouse (Liberty 1968)★★★
Tadpoles (Liberty 1969)★★★
➧ p.354 for full listings
Collaborators
Beatles ➧ p.38
Further References
Film: *Adventures Of The Son Of Exploding Sausage* (1969)

BOO RADLEYS
Albums
Everything's Alright Forever (Creation 1992)★★★
Wake Up (Creation 1995)★★★★
C'mon Kids (Creation 1996)★★★★
➧ p.354 for full listings

Connections
Eggman
Influences
John Peel ➧ p.258

BOO-YAA T.R.I.B.E.
Albums
New Funky Nation (4th & Broadway 1990)★★★
Doomsday (Bulletproof 1994)★★★
Angry Samoans (Bulletproof 1997)
➔ p.354 for full listings
Connections
Michael Jackson ➔ p.195

BOOKER T. AND THE MGS
Albums
Green Onions (Stax 1962)★★★★
Mo' Onions (1963)★★★★
Soul Dressing (Stax 1965)★★★★
➔ p.354 for full listings
Collaborators
Wilson Pickett ➔ p.260
Sam And Dave ➔ p.288
Al Green ➔ p.166
Neil Young ➔ p.346
Connections
Mar-Keys ➔ p.224
Bar-Kays ➔ p.32

BOOMTOWN RATS
Albums
The Boomtown Rats (Ensign 1977)★★★
A Tonic For The Troops (Ensign 1978)★★★
The Fine Art Of Surfacing (Ensign 1979)★★★
➔ p.354 for full listings
Influences
Bob Geldof ➔ p.156
Further References
Videos: *A Tonic For The Troops* (VCL 1986)
Books: *The Boomtown Rats: Having Their Picture Taken*, Peter Stone
Is That It? Bob Geldof

BOSTON
Albums
Boston (Epic 1976)★★★★
Don't Look Back (Epic 1978)★★★
Third Stage (MCA 1986)★★★
➔ p.354 for full listings

BOTHY BAND
Albums
Old Hag You Have Killed Me (1976)★★★★
The Bothy Band (1976)★★★★
Live In Concert (Windsong 1994)★★★
➔ p.354 for full listings
Connections
Planxty ➔ p.262
Chieftains ➔ p.90

BOW WOW
Albums
Bow Wow (Invitation 1976)★★★
Telephone (SMS 1980)★★★
Helter Skelter (Arista 1989)★★★
➔ p.354 for full listings

BOO-YAA T.R.I.B.E.

OF SAMOAN DESCENT, BOO-YAA T.R.I.B.E. WERE BORN IN LOS ANGELES, WHERE THEIR FATHER WAS A BAPTIST minister. Their name was slang for a shotgun being discharged. As members of the Bloods gang, every member had endured a stretch in prison, and one of their brothers, Robert 'Youngman' Devoux, was shot dead. The brothers freely admit to having had involvement with drug production and brokering, as well as gun running. Ultimately the group headed for Japan to escape the gang warfare, staying with their Sumo wrestler cousin. There they subsisted by working as a rap/dance outfit in Tokyo.

Island Records were the first to see a potential market for a sound which fused gangster imagery with hardcore hip hop. They appeared in **Michael Jackson**'s Walt Disney film *Captain EO* as breakdancers, as well as television shows *Fame* and *The A-Team*. The line-up boasts lead rapper Ganxsta Ridd (aka Paul Devoux), EKA, Rosco, Ganxsta OMB, The Godfather (aka Ted Devoux), and Don-L. Powerful singles like 'Psyko Funk' represented a genuine, bullying rap presence. They returned in 1994 with a second album, featuring further gangland narratives.

BOOKER T. AND THE MGS

FORMED IN MEMPHIS, USA, IN 1962 AS A SPIN-OFF FROM THE MAR-KEYS, THE GROUP COMPRISED BOOKER T. JONES (b. 1944; organ), **Steve Cropper** (b. 1941; guitar), Lewis Steinberg (bass) and Al Jackson Jnr (b. 1934, d. 1975; drums). 'Green Onions', the MGs' first hit, evolved out of a blues riff. Its simple, smoky atmosphere, punctuated by Cropper's cutting guitar, provided the blueprint for a series of excellent records.

Steinberg was replaced on bass by Donald 'Duck' Dunn (b. 1941) and their intuitive interplay became the bedrock of classic Stax, the foundation on which the label and studio sound was built. The quartet appeared on all the company's notable releases, including 'In The Midnight Hour' (**Wilson Pickett**), 'Hold On I'm Comin'' (**Sam And Dave**) and 'Walkin' The Dog' (Rufus Thomas). Although Jones divided his time between recording and studying, the MGs charted consistently in their own right. 'Hang 'Em High' (1968) and 'Time Is Tight' (1969) were both US Top 10 singles and 'Melting Pot' (1971) reached the Top 50. The group split in 1971, but in 1973 Jackson and Dunn put together a reconstituted group with Bobby Manuel and Carson Whitsett; the resultant *The MGs*, was a disappointment.

Jackson worked for **Al Green** and Syl Johnson, but was shot dead in his Memphis home in 1975. Cropper, who had released a solo album, *With A Little Help From My Friends* (1971), set up his TMI studio/label. He latterly rejoined Dunn, ex-**Bar-Kay** drummer Willie Hall and the returning Jones for *Universal Language*. Cropper and Dunn also played in the film *The Blues Brothers* in 1980. 'Green Onions' was reissued and became a Top 10 hit in 1979. Jones's 1981 album, *I Want You*, reached the R&B charts. They were inducted into the Rock And Roll Hall Of Fame in 1992. The group backed **Neil Young** in 1993, but a projected joint album was cancelled following the announcement that Dunn had cancer.

BOOMTOWN RATS

FORMED IN 1975, THIS IRISH GROUP COMPRISED **BOB GELDOF** (b. ROBERT Frederick Zenon Geldof, 1954; vocals), Gerry Roberts (vocals/guitar), Johnnie Fingers (keyboards), Pete Briquette (bass) and Simon Crowe (drums). Before moving to London, they signed to the recently established Ensign Records. Their self-titled debut, a UK chart success, included 'Looking After No. 1' and 'Mary Of The Fourth Form', which both reached the UK Top 20. The following *A Tonic For The Troops* featured the biting 'She's So Modern' and quirky 'Like Clockwork'. A third hit from the album, the acerbic urban protest 'Rat Trap', secured them their first UK number 1. In spite of their R&B leanings, the group were initially considered in some quarters as part of the punk upsurge and were banned in their home country.

The Fine Art Of Surfacing coincided with their finest moment, 'I Don't Like Mondays', the harrowing true-life story of an American teenage girl who went to school with a shotgun. The single proved almost impossible to match, despite the energetic follow-up, 'Someone's Looking At You'. The Rats were still hitting the UK Top 5 and released an understated comment on Northern Ireland in 'Banana Republic'. By 1982, the group had fallen from critical and commercial grace and their subsequent recordings seemed *passé*. For Geldof, more important work lay ahead with the founding of Band Aid. The Rats performed at the Live Aid concert (1985) before bowing out the following year at Dublin's Self Aid benefit.

BOSTON

HOME-MADE DEMOS RECORDED BY THE ENTERPRISING TOM SCHOLZ (b. 1947) EARNED INTEREST FROM EPIC Records. Fran Sheehan (b. 1949; bass), Brad Delp (b. 1951; guitar/vocals), Barry Goudreau (b. 1951; guitar) and Sib Hashian (b. 1949; drums) joined Scholz and the name Boston was adopted. Their first release was a US Top 3 album which sold 16 million copies in the USA alone and spent two years in the US charts. 'More Than A Feeling' contained all the ingredients of adult-orientated rock; upfront guitar, powerful lead vocal and heavy bass and drums. Two years later they repeated the formula with *Don't Look Back* which also topped the US charts. Goudreau released a solo album before quitting to form Orion.

Boston, in the guise of Scholz and Delp, returned seven years later with *Third Stage* which spawned two further US hit singles, 'Amanda' (number 1) and 'We're Ready'. *Walk On* was a disappointing fourth album.

BOTHY BAND

FORMED IN 1975, THIS IRISH FOLK-ROCK GROUP FEATURED DONAL LUNNY (SYNTHESIZER/DULCIMER; ex-**Planxty**), Michael O'Domhnaill (guitar/vocals), Triona Ni Domhnaill (clarinet/harpsichord), Paddyn Glackin (fiddle), and Matt Molloy (flute/ whistle). Tommy Peoples (fiddle) and Paddy Keenan (pipes), also played in the group before it folded in 1979. Despite their traditional background and tunes, the group pursued a rock-orientated style. After five albums, Triona Ni Domhnaill moved to the USA, forming Touchstone, while her brother Michael, along with fiddle player Kevin Burke, based themselves in Portland, Oregon, where they released albums from their own studio. After the break up of the Bothy Band, Planxty reformed.

BOW WOW

FORMED IN 1976 THIS HEAVY METAL JAPANESE GROUP COMPRISED KYOJI YAMAMOTO (VOCALS/GUITAR), MITSUHIRO Saito (vocals/guitar), Kenji Sano (bass) and Toshiri Niimi (drums). They incorporated classical Japanese music within a framework of westernized rock, influenced by **Kiss**, **Led Zeppelin** and **Aerosmith.** On *Asian Volcano*, their eleventh album, the vocals were sung in English for the first time, but the band sounded uncomfortable with the transition. Two shows at London's Marquee Club were recorded for the live album, *Holy Expedition*. In 1983 they became Vow Wow, adding an extra vocalist and keyboard player to pursue a more melodic direction.

Yamamoto has also released two solo albums: *Horizons* (1980) and *Electric Cinema* (1982). **Whitesnake**'s Neil Murray joined for a short time in 1987.

BOW WOW WOW

FORMED IN LONDON IN 1980 BY FORMER **SEX PISTOLS** MANAGER MALCOLM MCLAREN, BOW WOW WOW consisted of former **Adam And The Ants** members: David Barbe (b. David Barbarossa, 1961; drums), Matthew Ashman (b. 1962, d. 1995) and Leigh Gorman (b. 1961; bass). This trio was called upon to back McLaren's latest protégée, 14-year-old Annabella Lu Win (b. Myant Myant Aye, 1966). Bow Wow Wow debuted with 'C30, C60, C90, Go'. Its follow-up, the cassette-only *Your Cassette Pet*, featured eight tracks in an EP format. Although innovative and exciting, the group received limited chart rewards with EMI.

After signing with RCA, McLaren promoted the group with a series of publicity stunts, amid outrageous talk of paedophiliac pop as jailbait Annabella had her head shaven into a Mohican and appeared in tribal clothes. Further controversy ensued when she was photographed semi-nude on an album sleeve pastiche. A UK Top 10 hit followed with 'Go Wild In The Country', a frenzied, almost animalistic display of sensuous exuberance. An average cover version of 'I Want Candy' also clipped the Top 10, but by then McLaren was losing control of his concept. Singer Lieutenant Lush was briefly recruited and threatened to steal the limelight from McLaren's *Ingénue* so was subsequently ousted, only to reappear in **Culture Club** as **Boy George**. By 1983, amid uncertainty and disillusionment, Bow Wow Wow folded. The backing group briefly soldiered on as the Chiefs Of Relief, while Annabella took a sabbatical, reappearing in 1985 for an unsuccessful solo career. In 1998, a new version of the band, including Annabella, went on tour.

Connections
Whitesnake ➽ p.337

Influences
Kiss ➽ p.208
Led Zeppelin ➽ p.213
Aerosmith ➽ p.10

BOW WOW WOW

Albums
Your Cassette Pet mini-album (EMI 1980)★★★★
See Jungle! See Jungle! Go Join Your Gang, Yeah, City All Over! Go Ape Crazy! (RCA 1981)★★★
I Want Candy (RCA 1982)★★
➽ p.354 for full listings

Connections
Sex Pistols ➽ p.292
Adam and the Ants ➽ p.9
Culture Club ➽ p.108

Influences
Brian Poole and the Tremeloes ➽ p.263

BOWIE, DAVID
Albums
Hunky Dory (RCA Victor 1972)★★★★★
The Rise And Fall Of Ziggy Stardust And The Spiders From Mars (RCA Victor 1972)★★★★★
Low (RCA Victor 1977)★★★★
➽ p.354 for full listings
Collaborators
Mick Ronson ➽ p.282
Mott the Hoople ➽ p.241
Lulu ➽ p.219
John Lennon ➽ p.214
Brian Eno ➽ p.136
Robert Fripp ➽ p.154
Queen ➽ p.270
Bing Crosby
Pat Metheny ➽ p.233
Mick Jagger ➽ p.281
Peter Frampton ➽ p.152
Connections

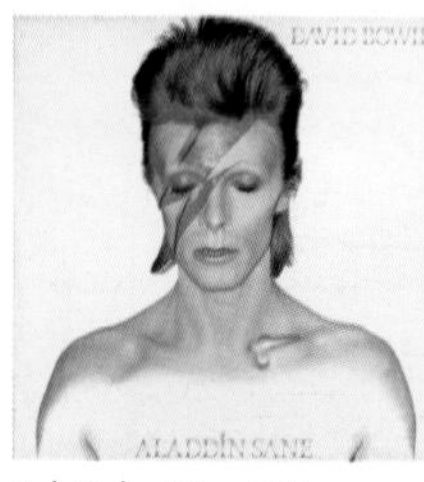

Bob Dylan ➽ p.128
Velvet Underground ➽ p.329
Iggy Pop ➽ p.264
Influences
Lou Reed ➽ p.274
Martha and the Vandellas ➽ p.226
Further References
Films: *The Man Who Fell To Earth* (1976)
Merry Christmas Mr Lawrence (1983)
Book: *Free Spirit*, Angie Bowie

BOX OF FROG
Albums
Box Of Frogs (Epic 1984)★★★
Interchords (Epic 1984)★★★
Strange Land (Epic 1986)★★★
➽ p.354 for full listings
Collaborators
Jeff Beck ➽ p.41
Rory Gallagher ➽ p.152
Jimmy Page ➽ p.255
Connections
Yardbirds ➽ p.345
Medecine Head ➽ p.231

BOX TOPS
Albums
The Letter/Neon Rainbow (Bell 1967)★★★
Cry Like A Baby (Bell 1968)★★★
Non Stop (Bell 1968)★★★
➽ p.354 for full listings
Connections
Big Star ➽ p.46

BOWIE, DAVID

THE MERCURIAL, BOWIE (b. DAVID ROBERT JONES, 1947) UNDERWENT A VERITABLE ODYSSEY OF CAREER MOVES and minor crises before establishing himself as a major performer. He began playing saxophone during his teens, initially with school groups. In the early 60s, his style was decidedly orthodox, all mod clothes and R&B riffs. Over the next few years, he went through a succession of backing groups including the King Bees, the Manish Boys, the Lower Third and the Buzz. In 1966, he changed his surname due to the emergence of Davy Jones of the **Monkees**. He also came under the wing of manager Kenneth Pitt, who nurtured his career for the remainder of the decade. A contract with the fashionable Decca subsidiary, Deram, saw Bowie achieve high-profile publicity but subsequent singles and a well-promoted debut album failed to sell. Bowie even attempted a cash-in novelty number, 'The Laughing Gnome'. In 1969, he finally broke through with the UK Top 10 hit 'Space Oddity', released to coincide with the American moon launch. Unfortunately, Bowie seemed unable to follow up the single with anything similarly clever.

A remarkable series of changes in Bowie's life, both personal and professional, occurred in 1970, culminating in him swapping Kenneth Pitt for the more strident Tony De Fries. Amid this period of flux, Bowie completed his first major work, an extraordinary album entitled *The Man Who Sold The World*. With musical assistance from **Mick Ronson**, drummer Mick Woodmansey and producer Tony Visconti on bass, Bowie employed an arrestingly heavy sound, aided by the eerie synthesizer work of Ralph Mace to embellish his chillingly dramatic vocals. The package was completed with a striking cover revealing Bowie lounging seductively in a flowing dress.

With the svengali-like De Fries aggressively promoting his career, Bowie signed to RCA and completed *Hunky Dory* in 1971. The album was lighter in tone than its predecessor with Bowie reverting to acoustic guitar on some tracks and exploring a more commercial, yet still intriguing, direction with tributes to **Bob Dylan** and the **Velvet Underground**. Up until this point, Bowie had experimented with diverse ideas, themes and images that coalesced effectively, though not necessarily coherently. The complete fusion was revealed in 1972 on *The Rise And Fall Of Ziggy Stardust And The Spiders From Mars*.

Bowie seemed to have the Midas touch and his production talents brought rewards for his old hero **Lou Reed** (*Transformer* and 'Walk On The Wild Side') and a resurrected **Mott The Hoople** who had their first hit with 'All The Young Dudes'. The track 'Oh You Pretty Things' (from *Hunky Dory*) had already provided a hit for Peter Noone and an equally unlikely artist, **Lulu**, enjoyed a Top 10 smash courtesy of 'The Man Who Sold The World'. Meanwhile, Bowie had undertaken a world tour and achieved a UK number 1 with *Aladdin Sane*, another concept work which centred on global destruction. While still at his peak, Bowie shocked the rock world on 4 July 1974 by announcing his retirement. It later transpired that it was not Bowie who was retiring, but Ziggy Stardust.

After recording a US broadcast television special entitled 'The 1980 Floor Show', Bowie produced *Diamond Dogs*. Having failed to receive permission to use the title *1984*, he nevertheless adapted George Orwell's famous novel, but without the familiar sound of the Spiders From Mars and the cutting guitar work of Mick Ronson. A massive tour of USA and Canada saw the 'Diamond Dogs' spectacle at its most excessive and expansive. Beneath the spectacle, the music tended to be somewhat forgotten.

Bowie's popularity was as great as ever in the mid-70s when he effectively righted the wrongs of history by taking 'Space Oddity' to number 1, six years after its initial UK chart entry. He also enjoyed his first US number 1, 'Fame', which featured the voice and co-composing skills of **John Lennon**. The song appeared on *Young Americans*, which saw the emergence of a new Bowie, successfully tackling Philadelphia soul. Bowie also worked on Nicholas Roeg's film *The Man Who Fell To Earth*, in which he was given the leading role of the displaced alien – the movie received mixed reviews. Bowie's next persona was the Thin White Duke, the icy character who came to life on *Station To Station*, with **Brian Eno**.

The duo relocated to Berlin for a cycle of albums which displayed Bowie at his least commercial and most ambitious. *Low* and *Heroes* (both 1977), were predominantly instrumental works whose mood was strongly influenced by Eno's minimalist electronics. Surprisingly, segments from each album found their way on to a live album *Stage*. Following a best-forgotten appearance in the movie *Just A Gigolo*, Bowie concluded his collaborative work with Eno on 1979's *Lodger*. Generally regarded as the least impressive of the Eno triology, it nevertheless contained some strong songs.

Bowie's thespian pursuits continued with a critically acclaimed starring role in the Broadway production of *The Elephant Man*. He also released a new album which leaned closer to the rock mainstream. *Scary Monsters (And Super Creeps)* was adventurous, with its modern electro-pop and distorted electric guitar, provided by former **King Crimson** helmsman **Robert Fripp**. The album contained the reflective 'Ashes To Ashes', which included references to one of Bowie's earlier creations, Major Tom. It was his first UK number 1 since 'Space Oddity'.

The early 80s saw Bowie taking on a series of diverse projects including an appearance in Bertolt Brecht's *Baal*, surprise chart collaborations with

Queen ('Under Pressure') and Bing Crosby ('Peace On Earth/Little Drummer Boy') and two more starring roles in the films *The Hunger* and *Merry Christmas Mr Lawrence*. A switch from RCA to EMI saw Bowie release his most commercial work since the early 70s with *Let's Dance* (1983), produced by Nile Rodgers of **Chic**. The title track gave Bowie his third solo UK number 1 and effectively revitalized his recording career. He had two further hits that year, both narrowly missing UK number 1, 'China Girl' and 'Modern Love'.

Let's Dance was quickly followed by the anti-climactic *Tonight*, which attracted universally bad reviews but managed to spawn a hit single with 'Blue Jean'. During 1985, Bowie was chiefly in demand as a collaborator, first with the **Pat Metheny** Group on 'This Is Not America' (from the film *The Falcon And The Snowman*) and next with Mick Jagger on a reworking of **Martha And The Vandellas**' 'Dancing In The Street' for Live Aid.

His next venture, the much-publicized movie *Absolute Beginners*, divided the critics, but its strong title track provided Bowie with a major hit. He also starred in the fantasy film *Labyrinth* and sang the theme of the anti-nuclear war cartoon film *When The Wind Blows*. In 1987, Bowie teamed up with former classmate **Peter Frampton** for the 'Glass Spider' tour. The attendant album, *Never Let Me Down*, was poorly received. Never predictable, Bowie decided to put a group together in 1989 and called upon the services of Reeves Gabrels (guitar), Tony Sales (bass) and Hunt Sales (drums) – the two brothers had worked with **Iggy Pop** and **Todd Rundgren**. The unit took their name from the title song of their new album, *Tin Machine*, a set that displayed some good, old-fashioned guitar work, occasionally bordering on heavy metal. Ironically, it was the re-release of his back catalogue on CD that brought a more positive response from his followers and in order to promote the campaign Bowie set out on an acoustic 'greatest hits' tour. *Black Tie White Noise* was his strongest album in years and entered the UK charts at number 1.

In 1995, Bowie signed a major recording contract with Virgin Records America. His first release was *Outside*, a collaboration with Brian Eno that received mixed reviews and disappointing sales. In his 50th year the dance/techno-inspired *Earthling* was issued. For once, the cracks were beginning to show.

BOX OF FROGS

BOX OF FROGS WERE WELCOMED WITH WIDESPREAD EXCITEMENT IN THE UK PRESS ON THEIR ARRIVAL IN the early 80s by dint of their collective heritage. Jim McCarty (b. 1943; drums), Paul Samwell-Smith (b. 1943; bass) and Chris Dreja (b. 1945; guitar) were founding members of the **Yardbirds**. Vocalist John Fiddler was from **Medicine Head**. 1984's *Box Of Frogs* saw them reprise the spirit of energized R&B. It included a cameo appearance from **Jeff Beck**, while both **Rory Gallagher** and **Jimmy Page** contributed to the follow-up collection, *Strange Land*. Box Of Frogs dispersed shortly after its release. McCarty subsequently joined the British Invasion All-Stars.

BOX TOPS

FORMED IN 1965, THIS MEMPHIS-BASED QUINTET – ALEX CHILTON (b. 1950; GUITAR/HARMONICA/VOCALS), GARY Talley (b. 1947; lead guitar), Billy Cunningham (b. 1950; rhythm guitar), John Evans (b. 1949; bass) and Danny Smythe (b. 1949; drums) – sprang to fame when their debut single, 'The Letter', became an international hit. Their appeal lay in Chilton's raspy delivery and Dan Penn's complementary production, a combination repeated on further successes, 'Neon Rainbow', 'Cry Like A Baby', 'Soul Deep' and 'Choo-Choo Train'. Rick Allen (b. 1946) replaced Evans in 1968, but the group's gifted singer remained its focal point. The band broke up in 1969, but Chilton reappeared in the critically acclaimed **Big Star**. A one-off reunion took place in Los Angeles in 1997.

BOY GEORGE

DURING THE EARLY 80S BOY GEORGE (b. George O'Dowd, 1961) became a regular on the London 'New Romantic' club scene. He appeared, briefly, in Malcolm McLaren's **Bow Wow Wow**, pushing George's name into the spotlight. A meeting with former disc jockey Mikey Craig (b. 1960; bass) resulted in the forming of In Praise Of Lemmings. After the addition of former **Adam And The Ants** drummer Jon Moss (b. 1957) and Roy Hay (b. 1961; guitar/keyboards), the group was renamed **Culture Club**. Boy George's appetite for publicity and media manipulation seemed endless, but it was his involvement with drugs that brought his downfall when a visiting New York keyboard player, Michael Rudetski, died of a heroin overdose while staying at George's London home.

George's public renouncement of drugs coincided with the dissolution of Culture Club and the launch of a solo career. His debut, a cover of the **Bread**/Ken Boothe hit, 'Everything I Own', (1987), gave him his first UK number 1 since 'Karma Chameleon' (1983). He formed his own record label, More Protein, in 1989, and fronted a band, Jesus Loves You, reflecting his new-found spiritual awareness and love of reggae and soul. *Cheapness And Beauty* was a blend of punky glam pop, at odds with his perceived 90s image of fading superstar. The album was preceded by an unlikely cover of **Iggy Pop**'s 'Funtime' and its release coincided with the publication of the artist's autobiography (1995).

BOY GEORGE

Albums
Sold (Virgin 1987)★★★
Tense Nervous Headache (Virgin 1988)★★
Cheapness And Beauty (Virgin 1995)★★★
➧ p.354 for full listings

Connections
Bow Wow Wow ➧ p.63
Adam and the Ants ➧ p.9
Culture Club ➧ p.108

Influences
Bread ➧ p.67
Iggy Pop ➧ p.264

Further References
Book: *Take It Like A Man*, Boy George

BOYZ II MEN

THIS US CLOSE-HARMONY TEENAGE SOUL GROUP DEBUTED WITH A TOP 3 SINGLE, 'Motownphilly'. Wanya 'Squirt' Morris (b. 1973), Michael 'Bass' McCary (b. 1972), Shawn 'Slim' Stockman (b. 1972) and Nathan 'Alex-Vanderpool' Morris (b. 1971) formed the band in 1988. Michael Bivins of Bell Biv Devoe took the group under his wing and brought them to **Motown Records**. Their debut album – one side dance, one side ballad – sold over seven million copies. The formula was repeated with *II* which sold eight million copies in the USA. It spawned the number 1 singles, 'I'll Make Love To You', 'On Bended Knee' and 'One Sweet Day' (with **Mariah Carey**).

BOYZ II MEN

Albums
Cooleyhighharmony (Motown 1991)★★★
II (Motown 1994)★★★★
Remix, Remake, Remember (Motown 1996)★★★★
➧ p.354 for full listings

Collaborators
Mariah Carey ➧ p.81

Further References
Video: *Then II Now* (Motown Video 1994)

BOYZONE
Albums
A Different Beat (Polydor 1996)★★★
➧ p.354 for full listings
Connections
Take That ➧ p.316
Influences
The Osmonds ➧ p.254
Cat Stevens ➧ p.309
Further References
Videos: *Said And Done* (VVL 1995)

BRADY, PAUL
Albums
Full Moon (Demon 1984)★★★★
Primitive Dance (Mercury 1987)★★★★
Spirits Colliding (Fontana 1995)★★★★
➧ p.354 for full listings
Collaborators
Dire Straits ➧ p.120
Eric Clapton ➧ p.92
Mark Knopfler ➧ p.209
Connections
Planxty ➧ p.262
Roger Chapman ➧ p.87
Dave Edmunds ➧ p.132
Santana ➧ p.288

BRAGG, BILLY
Albums
Brewing Up With Billy Bragg (Go! Discs 1984)★★★★
Talking With The Taxman About Poetry (Go! Discs 1986)★★★★
William Bloke (Cooking Vinyl 1996)★★★★.
➧ p.354 for full listings

Collaborators
Wet Wet Wet ➧ p.337
Connections
Kirsty MacColl ➧ p.221
Paul Weller ➧ p.336
Jimmy Somerville ➧ p.68
Influences
Beatles ➧ p.38
Further References
Book: *Midnight In Moscow*, Chris Salewicz.

BRAND NEW HEAVIES
Albums
Brand New Heavies (Acid Jazz 1990)★★★
Heavy Rhyme Experience: Vol. 1 (ffrr 1992)★★★
Shelter (London 1997)★★★
➧ p.354 for full listings
Influences
James Taylor ➧ p.317

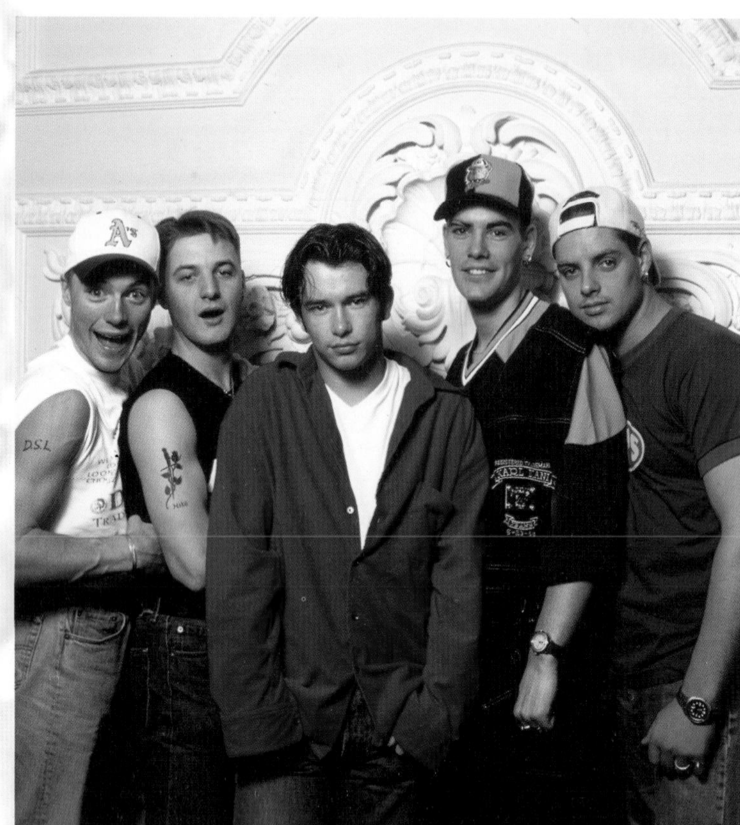

BOYZONE

CONSIDERED BY MANY TO BE THE INHERITORS OF TAKE THAT'S BOY BAND THRONE, BOYZONE ARE A QUINTET of unaffected young Irish men tailored for mainstream success by Polydor Records and manager/promoter Louis Walsh. Mikey Graham and Keith Duffy were recruited from their jobs as mechanics, Shane Lynch from an architecture course, while Ronan Keating and Stephen Gately were enlisted directly from school.

Their first single, a cover of the **Osmonds**' 'Love Me For A Reason', was produced by Take That collaborator Mike Hedges. It became an instant success in 1994, peaking at UK number 2 and selling 700,000 copies. *All Said And Done* (1995) sold over one million copies worldwide. Alongside 'Love Me For A Reason', it included hit singles, 'Key To My Life', 'So Good' and a cover of **Cat Stevens**' 'Father And Son'.

BRADY, PAUL

A MEMBER OF DUBLIN R&B GROUP THE KULT, BRADY (b. 1947), LATER EMBRACED FOLK MUSIC WITH THE Johnstons. He subsequently joined **Planxty**, where he met Andy Irvine. *Andy Irvine/Paul Brady* prefaced Brady's solo career which began with the much-lauded *Welcome Here Kind Stranger* (1978). The singer abandoned folk in 1981 with *Hard Station*, which included the Irish chart-topping single, 'Crazy Dreams' (later covered by **Roger Chapman** and **Dave Edmunds**) also included was 'Night Hunting Time', later recorded by **Santana**.

True For You followed a prolific period where Brady toured supporting **Dire Straits** and **Eric Clapton**. **Tina Turner**'s versions of 'Steel Claw' and 'Paradise Is Here' cemented Brady's reputation as a songwriter. He collaborated with **Mark Knopfler** on the soundtrack to *Cal*, before completing a strong live album, *Full Moon*. *Trick Or Treat* was recorded under the aegis of former **Steely Dan** producer, Gary Katz. **Bonnie Raitt**, an admirer of Brady's work, gave his career a significant boost by including two of his songs on her 1991 album *Luck Of The Draw*.

BRAGG, BILLY

BRAGG (b. STEVEN WILLIAM BRAGG, 1957) IS REGARDED AS ONE OF THE MOST COMMITTED LEFT-WING POLITICAL performers in UK pop/rock. After forming the ill-fated punk group Riff Raff, Bragg briefly joined the British Army (Tank Corp), before buying his way out for a solo musical career. Bragg undertook a maverick tour of the concert halls of Britain, ready at a moment's notice to fill in as support for almost any act. His lyrics, full of passion, anger and wit, made him a truly original character on the UK music scene. Managed by Peter Jenner, his *Life's A Riot With Spy Vs Spy* reached the UK Top 30. *Brewing Up With Billy Bragg*, reached number 16. At Bragg's insistence, the albums were kept at a below-average selling price. In 1985, **Kirsty MacColl** reached UK number 7 with his 'New England'.

Omnipresent at political rallies, and benefits, particularly during the 1984 Miners' Strike, Bragg produced powerful pro-Union songs and the EP title track, 'Between The Wars'. He was instrumental in creating the socialist musicians collective 'Red Wedge', including pop luminaries **Paul Weller**, Junior Giscombe and Jimmy Somerville. Despite the politicizing, Bragg was still writing love songs such as 'Levi Stubbs' Tears', which appeared on the UK Top 10 album *Talking To The Taxman About Poetry*. In 1988, a cover of the **Beatles**' 'She's Leaving Home', shared a double a-side single release with **Wet Wet Wet**'s 'With A Little Help From My Friends', which resulted in a UK number 1. In 1991, Bragg issued *Don't Try This At Home*, arguably his most commercial work. The album featured a shift towards personal politics, most noticeably on 'Sexuality'. *William Bloke* was less angry and more ironic.

BRAND NEW HEAVIES

SIMON BARTHOLOMEW AND ANDY LEVY FORMED THE BRAND NEW HEAVIES, ALONGSIDE DRUMMER JAN Kincaid and keyboardist Ceri Evans. They had one failed contract with Acid Jazz, who tried to launch them as a 'rare groove' outfit, before they joined with US label Delicious Vinyl. The latter's management put them in touch with N'Dea Davenport who had provided backing vocals for **George Clinton** and Bruce Willis. Word spread throughout the USA and they were sampled heavily on a number of early 90s rap records; in return many rap artists guested on their second album, *Heavy Rhyme Experience: Vol. 1*. Ceri Evans left in 1992 to undertake production work for Alison Limerick and Galliano, recording solo as Sunship ('Muthafuckin''/'The 13th Key').

In the UK, 'Dream On Dreamer' and 'Midnight At The Oasis' reached the Top 20 in 1994. Soul singer Siedah Garrett replaced Davenport in 1997, and they enjoying further chart success with their cover version of **James Taylor**'s 'You've Got A Friend'.

BRAND X

ONE OF THE MOST COMMERCIALLY SUCCESSFUL OF THE BRITISH JAZZ/ROCK GROUPS OF THE 70S AND 80S. *Moroccan Roll* (1977) reached number UK 37, while *Is There Anything About* crept in at number 93. The original line-up featured John Goodsall (guitar), Robin Lumley (keyboards), Percy Jones (bass, ex-Liverpool Scene), **Phil Collins** (drums) and Maurice Pert (percussion). They produced sharp arrangements of appealing melodies, often with a gangling counterpoint provided by Jones's slurred fretless bass lines. All the musicians also undertook studio work and Collins expanded his role with **Genesis** after **Peter Gabriel**'s departure. As his solo career took off, he left Brand X, to be replaced by Chuck Burgi, and then by Mike Clarke. A little later Percy Jones left and was replaced by John Gilbin.

BRAXTON, TONI

BRAXTON (b. 1968) WAS SIGNED TO ARISTA RECORDS IN 1990, WITH HER FOUR SISTERS, as the Braxtons. 'The Good Life' brought them to the attention of producers L.A. and **Babyface**, who provided Toni with solo successes such as 'Another Sad Love Song' and 'You Mean The World To Me'. Though described as the 'new **Whitney Houston**', her vocal talent has found an audience in garage and house circles, and her debut album sold more than two million copies. She won a Grammy for Best New Artist in 1993. *Secrets* repeated the success of her debut, particularly in her homeland.

BREAD

BREAD WAS FORMED IN 1969 WHEN DAVID GATES (b. 1940), A LEADING LOS ANGELES session musician, produced an album for the Pleasure Faire, a group which included vocalist/guitarist Rob Royer. Songwriter James Griffin contributed several compositions to the set and the three aspirants then decided to pool resources. All were assured multi-instrumentalists, and although not a commercial success, their debut album established a penchant for melodious soft-rock. Mike Botts augmented the group for *On The Water*, which included the million-selling 'Make It With You', while *Manna* spawned a further gold disc with 'If', later successfully revived by actor/singer Telly Savalas. Royer was replaced by keyboard veteran Larry Knechtel but Bread's smooth approach was left unruffled as they achieved further international success with , 'Baby I'm-A Want You' (1971), 'Everything I Own' and 'Guitar Man' (both 1972). Increasing friction between Gates and Griffin led to the group's collapse. The combatants embarked on solo careers while Botts joined the **Linda Ronstadt** Band, but they reconvened in 1976 for *Lost Without Your Love*, the title track of which reached the US Top 10. Guitarist Dean Parks joined when Griffin resumed his independent direction, but *The Goodbye Girl* failed to emulate its predecessors and Bread again disbanded, only to reunite in 1997.

BREEDERS

RESTLESS WITH HER SUBORDINATE ROLE IN THE **PIXIES**, BASSIST KIM DEAL (b. 1961; GUITAR/VOCALS/SYNTHESIZERS) forged this spin-off project with **Throwing Muses** guitarist Tanya Donelly (b. 1966). Breeders was originally the name of a group Deal fronted prior to the Pixies, with her twin sister Kelley. Deal and Donelly initially undertook sessions with Muses drummer David Narcizo. Joined by bassist Josephine Wiggs (b. 1965) from British act the Perfect Disaster, the Breeders recorded *Pod* during a Pixies tour of Britain. Britt Walford from Kentucky hardcore group Slint, drummed on the record under the pseudonym Shannon Doughton. A four-track EP, *Safari*, followed. The group was augmented by Kelley Deal (guitar/vocals), but despite critical and commercial acclaim, the Breeders remained a sideline.

Deal rekindled the group in 1993 but Donelly had left to form **Belly**. Wiggs abandoned Honey Tongue, a group she had formed with Jon Mattock from Spiritualized, to rejoin the Deal twins. Jim MacPherson (b. 1966; drums; ex- Raging Mantras), completed the line-up featured on *Last Splash*. Less abrasive than its predecessor, this revealed Deal's encompassing mock C&W ('Driving All Night'), grunge-styled instrumentals ('Roi') and ballads ('Do You Love Me Now?'). In 1996, Kim Deal underwent drug rehabilitation and Kelley left for The Last Hard Men. A new line convened in 1997 featuring Michelle O'Dean (guitar), Carrie Bradley (violin), Louis Lerma (bass) and Nate Farley (guitar), together with Deal and MacPherson.

BREL, JACQUES

BREL (b. 1929, d. 1978) BEGAN A CAREER IN PARIS AS A SINGING COMPOSER. IMPRESARIO JACQUES Canetti presented him regularly at Pigalle's Theatre Des Trois Baudets, where he was accompanied by his guitar and a small backing band. His performances, embracing fierce anger, romanticism and world-weariness, captivated the audiences and his popularity increased after 'Quand On N'A Que L'Amour'. Other domestic hits included 'Le Valse De Mille Temps', 'Les Bourgeois', 'Les Dames Patronesses' and 'Les Flamands'. His lyricism remained intrinsically Gallic until 1957's *American Debut*, from which a substantial English-speaking following grew. Brel strongly influenced the output of such diverse wordsmiths as **Leonard Cohen**, **David Bowie** and **Scott Walker**. Brel reached a global market by proxy when his material was translated, as instanced by the **Kingston Trio**'s 1964 rendition of 'Le Moribund' as 'Seasons In The Sun' (a UK number 1 for Terry Jacks a decade later). He played two sell-out Carnegie Hall shows but was keener on developing his movies career with *Les Risques Du Metier* and *La Bande A Bonnet*.

Brel eventually withdrew to Polynesia, returning only fleetingly to Paris for one-take recording sessions, but his work remained in the public eye through a three-year Broadway run of the musical *Jacques Brel Is Alive And Well And Living In Paris* (later a film). Brel's death from cancer was marked by a million-selling compilation album.

BRETT MARVIN AND THE THUNDERBOLTS

UK SKIFFLE-CUM-BLUES JUG BAND ACT, FEATURING GRAHAM HINE (GUITAR/VOCALS), JIM PITTS (GUITAR/vocals/harmonica), Jona Lewie (b. John Lewis; keyboards/vocals), Pete Gibson (trombone/vocals/percussion), Dave Arnott (drums) and percussionists Keith Trussell and Big John Randall. Their debut album aroused novelty-based interest, but the unit only enjoyed commercial success after adopting the pseudonym Terry Dactyl And The Dinosaurs. 'Seaside Shuffle', reached number 2 in 1972, but the Thunderbolts soon reverted to their original name. Lewie embarked on a solo career following the group's first break-up. Various permutations of this band continued to perform. In 1993 *Boogie Street* saw the addition of Taffy Davies (vocals/piano/clarinet/mandolin) and Pete Swan (bass).

BRICKELL, EDIE

US VOCALIST BRICKELL'S FIRST BREAK AS A VOCALIST CAME IN 1985, WHEN SHE WAS ASKED TO FRONT LOCAL JAZZ-influenced band the New Bohemians, as their popularity grew they signed to Geffen Records as Edie Brickell And The New Bohemians. *Shooting Rubber Bands At The Moon* went platinum in the USA, where it reached number 4 (UK number 25). 'What I Am?', the attendant single reached US number 7/UK number 31.

Brickell's singing echoes **Rickie Lee Jones**, **Joni Mitchell** and **Kate Bush**. Her picturesque lyrics often dwell on the minutiae of life, with amusing twists and phraseology. The band's second album *Ghost Of A Dog* was not as successful as their debut, and little was heard of Brickell until her solo *Picture Perfect Morning* (1994). 'Solo' is something of a misnomer; featuring jazz-fusion player Michael Brecker, the **Dixie Cups**, **Dr. John**, Steve Gadd, Cyril and Art Neville, and **Barry White**. The ensemble was produced by Roy Halee and **Paul Simon** (her husband since June 1992).

BRAND X
Albums
Unorthodox Behaviour (Charisma 1976)★★★
Is There Anything About (Columbia 1982)★★★
➧ p.354 for full listings
Connections
Phil Collins ➧ p.98

BRAXTON, TONI
Albums
Toni Braxton (Arista 1994)★★★
Secrets (Arista 1996)★★★
➧ p.354 for full listings
Connections
Babyface ➧ p.26
Whitney Houston ➧ p.188
Further References
Video: *The Home Video* (1994)

BREAD
Albums
Manna (Elektra 1971)★★★
Baby I'm-A Want You (Elektra 1972)★★★
Lost Without Your Love (Elektra 1977)★★★
➧ p.354 for full listings
Connections
Linda Ronstadt ➧ p.282

BREEDERS
Albums
Pod (4AD 1990)★★★
Last Splash (4AD 1993)★★★
➧ p.354 for full listings
Connections
Pixies ➧ p.261
Throwing Muses ➧ p.321
Belly ➧ p.42

BREL, JACQUES
Albums
Les Flamandes (Polydor 1998)★★★
Jef (Polydor 1998)★★★
➧ p.354 for full listings
Connections
Kingston Trio ➧ p.207

BRETT MARVIN AND THE THUNDERBOLTS
Albums
Brett Marvin And The Thunderbolts (Sonet 1970)★★★
➧ p.354 for full listings

BRICKELL, EDIE
Albums
Shooting Rubberbands at the Stars (Geffen 1989)★★★
Ghost of a Dog (Geffen 1990)★★★
➧ p.354 for full listings
Collaborators
Dixie Cups ➧ p.120
Dr. John ➧ p.125
Barry White ➧ p.337
Connections
Rickie Lee Jones ➧ p.201
Joni Mitchell ➧ p.235
Paul Simon ➧ p.296

BRINSLEY SCHWARZ
Albums
Silver Pistol (United Artists 1972)★★★★
» p.354 for full listings
Connections
Elvis Costello » p.101
Graham Parker » p.256

BRISTOL, JOHNNY
Albums
Hang On In There Baby (MGM 1974)★★★
» p.354 for full listings
Connections
Supremes » p.314
Edwin Starr » p.307
Detroit Spinners » p.116
Stevie Wonder » p.342

BROMBERG, DAVID
Albums
How Late'll Ya Play 'Til? (Fantasy 1976)★★★
Sideman Serenade (Rounder 1990)★★★
» p.354 for full listings
Collaborators
Jay and the Americans » p.198
Blood, Sweat and Tears » p.53
Chubby Checker » p.88
Bob Dylan » p.128
Grateful Dead » p.165
Emmylou Harris » p.175
Linda Ronstadt » p.282
Dr John » p.125

BRONSKI BEAT
Albums
The Age Of Consent (Forbidden Fruit 1984)★★★
» p.354 for full listings
Collaborators
Marc Almond » p.15
Connections
Erasure » p.138
Communards » p.99

BROOK BROTHERS
Albums
Brook Brothers (Pye 1961)★★★
» p.354 for full listings
Further References
Film: *It's Trad, Dad aka Ring-A-Ding Rhythm* (1962)

BRINSLEY SCHWARZ

FORMED FROM KIPPINGTON LODGE, THE INITIAL LINE-UP – BRINSLEY SCHWARZ (GUITAR/VOCALS), BARRY Landerman (organ/vocals), **Nick Lowe** (b. 1949; bass/vocals) and Pete Whale (drums) – remained intact until 1968 when Bob Andrews replaced Landerman. In 1969, they recruited drummer, Billy Rankin, and renamed themselves in deference to their lead guitarist.

Their debut, *Brinsley Schwarz*, was pleasant but undemanding, although *Despite It All* showed more promise. A second guitarist, Ian Gomm (b. 1947), was added prior to *Silver Pistol*, arguably the group's most unified and satisfying release. *Nervous On The Road* featured 'Don't Lose Your Grip On Love', while '(What's So Funny 'Bout) Peace, Love and Understanding', later revived by **Elvis Costello**, made its debut on *The New Favourites Of Brinsley Schwarz*. The group broke up in 1975. Schwarz and Andrews later joined **Graham Parker** And The Rumour while Gomm and Lowe went solo.

BRISTOL, JOHNNY

BRISTOL (b. 1939) STARTED OUT WITHIN THE NASCENT TAMLA/**MOTOWN** CIRCLE. HE FIRST RECORDED IN 1960 as part of Johnny And Jackie (Jackie Beavers). They recorded the original version of 'Someday We'll Be Together' (1961), which was a hit for the **Supremes** in 1969. Bristol forged a successful career as a producer and songwriter with **Edwin Starr**, **Detroit Spinners**, **Stevie Wonder** and **Junior Walker**. He relaunched his performing career with 'Hang On In There Baby' (1974), but was unable to repeat that early hit, except for a UK Top 40 hit in 1980, duetting with Ami Stewart on 'My Guy – My Girl'. He continued to release singles throughout the 80s.

BROMBERG, DAVID

BROMBERG (b. 1945) WAS PROFICIENT ON GUITAR (PRIMARILY ACOUSTIC), VIOLIN, MANDOLIN AND BANJO, his music took in elements of folk, blues, bluegrass and rock, combined with comedy and narrative stories. He started out in New York in the 60s, where he performed on sessions for artists such as **Jay And The Americans**, **Blood, Sweat And Tears**, **Chubby Checker** and **Bob Dylan**. He then signed a recording contract with Columbia and released a self-titled album in 1971. His next two albums, *Demons In Disguise* and *Wanted Dead Or Alive*, included guest appearances by members of the **Grateful Dead**. *Midnight On The Water* featured appearances including **Emmylou Harris**, **Linda Ronstadt**, **Dr. John** and **Bonnie Raitt**. In 1976, Bromberg signed to Fantasy Records, released albums including the live *How Late'll Ya Play 'Til*. In 1977, he appeared with acoustic musicians, including Vassar Clements and D.J. Fontana, on *Hillbilly Jazz*.

Bromberg occasionally performed one-off gigs throughout the 80s, including an annual appearance at New York club the Bottom Line. In 1990, Bromberg resurfaced on Rounder Records with a new album, *Sideman Serenade*. Bromberg retained a devoted following into the 90s, despite his relaxed work schedule.

BRONSKI BEAT

FORMED IN 1983, THIS ANGLO-SCOTTISH GROUP COMPRISED JIMMY SOMERVILLE (b. 1961; VOCALS), STEVE Bronski/Forrest (keyboards) and Larry Steinbachek (keyboards). After establishing themselves in London's gay community, the trio were signed to London Records. 'Smalltown Boy' drew attention to Somerville's falsetto vocal, which became their hallmark. The single climbed to UK number 3 and the follow-up, 'Why?', another Top 10 single, emphasized their debut to producer Giorgio Moroder.

By the end of 1984, Somerville was well-known as a tireless homosexual rights campaigner. *The Age Of Consent* met a mixed reaction in the music press, but a sprightly cover of George Gershwin's 'It Ain't Necessarily So' scaled the charts. In 1985, the Bronskis teamed up with **Marc Almond** for an extraordinary version of **Donna Summer**'s 'I Feel Love' interwoven with the refrains of 'Love To Love You Baby' and 'Johnny Remember Me'. The single reached the UK Top 3 in April 1985, but at the end of the month Somerville left the group. He resurfaced in the **Communards**, before relocating to San Francisco. Bronski Beat found a replacement in John Foster and initially enjoyed some success. The catchy 'Hit That Perfect Beat' returned them to the Top 3 and two further albums followed. Foster was replaced in 1988 by Jonathan Hellyer.

BROOK BROTHERS

GEOFFREY (b. 1943) AND RICKY BROOK (b. 1940) A POP DUO FROM HAMPSHIRE, ENGLAND, WERE OFTEN called the British **Everly Brothers**. They first recorded in 1960 for Top Rank Records and their first single was a cover of the Brothers Four's US hit 'Greenfields', followed by a double-sided cover 'Please Help Me I'm Falling'/'When Will I Be Loved'. With producer Tony Hatch, their second release, 'Warpaint', entered the UK Top 20, as did 'Ain't Gonna Wash For A Week'. They had three smaller UK hits in 1962-63, appeared in the film *It's Trad Dad* and recorded on **Decca** as the Brooks before fading from the scene.

BROOKE, JONATHA

INITIALLY RECORDING WITH THE STORY, SINGER-SONGWRITER BROOKE EARNED COMPARISONS IN THE 90S WITH **RICKIE LEE Jones**. The Story were effectively a duo of Brooke with Jennifer Kimball, a creative partnership which spanned 12 years. After two albums with the Story, Kimball departed, in the same week that the group were dropped by Elektra despite sales of over 100,000 for *The Angel In The House*. Brooke relegated the Story's name to that of support billing for 1996's *Plumb*, produced by husband, the jazz pianist Alain Mallet. The backing band featured Michael Rivard (bass), Duke Levine (guitar) and drummer Abe Laboriel. A wide-ranging collection, *Plumb* included such diverse selections as the Irish jig 'Charming' (with uillean piper Jerry O'Sullivan) and the despondent 'The War' (with **Bruce Cockburn**).

BROOKS, ELKIE

BROOKS (b. ELAINE BOOKBINDER, 1946) BEGAN HER CAREER TOURING THE UK DURING THE EARLY 60S with the **Eric Delaney** Band. Her early records included versions of 'Hello Stranger' and 'The Way You Do The Things You Do'. In 1970, she joined Dada, a 12-piece jazz-rock act featuring **Robert Palmer** (vocals) and Pete Gage (guitar). These three artists subsequently formed the core of Vinegar Joe, a popular soul/rock act. That group dissolved in 1974, and Elkie embarked on a solo career. She enjoyed two UK Top 10 hits with 'Pearl's A Singer' and 'Sunshine After The Rain' (both 1977), but her once raucous approach, became increasingly tempered by MOR trappings. 'Fool If You Think It's Over' and 'Nights In White Satin' (both 1982) enhanced the singer's reputation for dramatic cover versions, but 'No More The Fool', composed by **Russ Ballard**, revived her contemporary standing, reaching the UK Top 5 in 1986. An attendant album achieved double-gold status, while *Bookbinder's Kid* emphasized this revitalization with further songs by Ballard and material by **Bryan Adams**.

BROOKS, GARTH

BROOKS (b. TROYAL GARTH BROOKS, 1962) STARTED OUT IN OKLAHOMA NIGHT CLUBS BEFORE SIGNING TO CAPITOL Records with producer Allen Reynolds. His first album, *Garth Brooks* had a western swing and country feel and included a revival of a **Jim Reeves**' 'I Know One', a western saga ('Cowboy Bill') and several new love songs ('The Dance', 'If Tomorrow Never Comes' and his own 'Not Counting You'). *No Fences*, was even better, including his concert-stopping 'Friends In Low Places', and a revival of the **Fleetwoods**' 'Mr. Blue', both written by Dwayne Blackwell. The album sold ten million copies in the USA. *Ropin' The Wind* sold four million copies in its first month of release and topped both the US pop and country charts. His version of **Billy Joel**'s 'Shameless' was a US country number 1, as were 'The Thunder Rolls', 'Two Of A Kind' and 'Working On A Full House'.

After a brief break for fatherhood, Brooks re-emerged with a Christmas record, *Beyond The Season*, and another album, *The Chase* (selling five million copies in four months); moving away from the honky-tonk style of his debut towards a 70s-orientated soft-rock sound. Brooks reached the UK charts in 1994 with 'The Red Strokes'. *Fresh Horses* was his first album to have simultaneous world-wide release, and a further international hit came with 'She's Every Woman'. In 1995, he took over his own business affairs with the help of his wife Sandy. His worldwide album sales reached 60 million in 1996, making him the all-time biggest-selling solo artist in the world.
Brooks was named Entertainer Of The Year at the 1997 Country Music Awards. At the end of the year he released *Sevens*, which debuted at number 1 in the *Billboard* pop and country charts with pre-orders of more than five million.

BROOKS, HARVEY

ELECTRIC BASSIST BROOKS (b. HARVEY GOLDSTEIN) WAS ONE OF NEW YORK'S LEADING SESSION MUSICIANS DURING the 60s. He contributed to **Bob Dylan**'s *Highway 61 Revisited* and recorded with several electric folk acts, including **Richie Havens**, **Tom Rush** and Eric Anderson. In 1967, he joined the **Electric Flag** at the behest of guitarist **Mike Bloomfield**, but both musicians left following the release of the group's debut album. They then joined **Al Kooper** and **Stephen Stills** for the highly-successful *Super Session* (1968). Although Brooks joined the short-lived Thundermug, he continued a lucrative studio career with the **Doors** (*The Soft Parade*), Paul Kantner (*Blows Against The Empire*), **John Martyn** (*Stormbringer*) and Seals And Crofts (*Summer Breeze*). He was also reunited with Al Kooper on Dylan's *New Morning* (1970).

BROS

TWINS MATTHEW AND LUKE GOSS (VOCALS) WERE BORN IN LONDON, ENGLAND IN 1968. ALONG WITH SCHOOL friend Craig Logan (b. 1969; guitar) they formed a group named Cavier before changing the name to Bros. Securing the services of **Pet Shop Boys** manager Tom Watkins and producer Nicky Graham, they scraped into the UK charts with 'I Owe You Nothing'. Well groomed and ambitious, the group soon attracted a fanatical teenage fan following. Their second single, 'When Will I Be Famous' was promoted aggressively and climbed to number 2. 'Drop The Boy' soon followed, again just missing the number 1 spot. By now established as *the* teen idols of 1988, the group's first single 'I Owe You Nothing' was re-promoted and reached number 1. A string of Top 10 singles followed, including 'I Quit', 'Cat Among The Pigeons', 'Too Much', 'Chocolate Box' and 'Sister'. Fortunes gradually took a downward turn: in 1989 Logan was ousted and Bros became embroiled in an acrimonious legal battle with their manager. Written off as mere teenybop fodder, they actively pursued a more serious direction and returned to the UK Top 10 with 'Are You Mine?' and the album *Changing Faces* in 1991. By 1993 the phenomenon had passed; both twins have now gone into acting, appearing in stage musicals throughout the UK.

BROTHERHOOD OF MAN

POP VOCAL GROUP FORMED IN LONDON IN 1969 BY SONGWRITER TONY HILLER. THE LEAD singer was Tony Burrows (ex-Ivy League, **Flowerpot Men**, **Edison Lighthouse**) and the group's first success was Hiller's 'United We Stand' (1970), a UK Top 10 hit. With changing personnel, the group continued to record, unsuccessfully, for Deram and Dawn in the early 70s until, in 1976, they represented the UK in the Eurovision Song Contest. Appearing as an **Abba**-inspired male/female quartet led by Martin Lee and Lee Sheridan, Brotherhood Of Man's breezy rendition of 'Save Your Kisses For Me' won the competition and became an international hit. The group followed with a series of UK successes including the number 1s, 'Angelo' and 'Figaro'. Thereafter, their popularity dwindled although 'Lightning Flash' (1982) was a minor hit.

BROUDIE, IAN

AS WELL AS PILOTING THE **LIGHTNING SEEDS**, BROUDIE (b.1958) HAS ESTABLISHED HIMSELF AS A POP PRODUCER. He started out in the O'Boogie Brothers (with future **Culture Club** drummer Jon Moss) and subsequently joined Big In Japan, Merseyside's primal punk band. Broudie then moved on to the Opium Eaters, with Pete Wylie, Budgie and Paul Rutherford (future star of **Frankie Goes To Hollywood**). They never recorded. His next group was the Original Mirrors, formed with Steve Allen (of Deaf School), who secured a contract with Mercury Records. Despite two albums, the group had collapsed by the beginning of the 80s and Broudie moved into production. The first record he produced, **Echo And The Bunnymen**'s 'Rescue', was their first UK Top 20 single. In 1983, he formed Care, with ex-Wild Swans singer Paul Simpson. Broudie returned to production in 1986 for the **Icicle Works**' *If You Want To Defeat Your Enemy Sing His Song*. He inaugurated the Lightning Seeds in 1989 to record their UK Top 20 debut single, 'Pure' – they also enjoyed success with 'The Life Of Riley', 'Perfect' and 'Lucky You' (co-written with Terry Hall, who Broudie had previously worked with in **Colour Field**).

BROOKE, JONATHA
Albums
Plumb (Blue Thumb 1996)★★★
➧ p.354 for full listings
Collaborators
Bruce Cockburn ➧ p.95
Influences
Rickie Lee Jones ➧ p.201

BROOKS, ELKIE
Albums
Shooting Star (A&M 1978)★★★
➧ p.354 for full listings
Collaborators
Eric Delaney Band ➧ p.114
Robert Palmer ➧ p.255
Bryan Adams ➧ p.9
Connections
Brenda Lee ➧ p.213
Temptations ➧ p.318
Russ Ballard ➧ p.31

BROOKS, GARTH
Albums
No Fences (Liberty 1990)★★★★
➧ p.354 for full listings
Connections
Fleetwoods ➧ p.148
Influences
Jim Reeves ➧ p.275
Billy Joel ➧ p.199
Further References
Books: *One Of A Kind, Workin' On A Full House*, Rick Mitchell

BROOKS, HARVEY
Albums
How To Play Electric Bass (1966)★
➧ p.354 for full listings
Collaborators
Bob Dylan ➧ p.128
Richie Havens ➧ p.177
Tom Rush ➧ p.285
Al Kooper ➧ p.210
Stephen Stills ➧ p.310
Doors ➧ p.123
John Martyn ➧ p.226
Connections
Electric Flag ➧ p.134

BROS
Albums
Push (Columbia 1988)★★★
➧ p.354 for full listings

BROTHERHOOD OF MAN
Albums
B For Brotherhood (Pye 1978)★★
➧ p.354 for full listings
Connections
Edison Lighthouse ➧ p.132
Influences
Abba ➧ p.6

BROUDIE, IAN
Collaborators
Lightning Seeds ➧ p.216
Echo And The Bunnymen ➧ p.131
Icicle Works ➧ p.192
Terry Hall ➧ p.98
Connections
Culture Club ➧ p.108
Frankie Goes To Hollywood ➧ p.153

BROWN, ARTHUR
Albums
The Crazy World Of Arthur Brown (Track 1968)★★★
Requiem (1982)★★
Order From Chaos — Live 1993 (Voiceprint 1994)★★★
➽ p.354 for full listings
Connections
Chris Farlowe ➽ p.143
Atomic Rooster ➽ p.24
Mothers of Invention ➽ p.239

BROWN, BOBBY
Albums
Don't Be Cruel (MCA 1988)★★★★
Dance! ... Ya Know It! (MCA 1989)★★★★
Forever (MCA 1997)★★★
➽ p.354 for full listings
Connections
Babyface ➽ p.26
Whitney Houston ➽ p.188
Further References
Video: *His Prerogative* (MCA 1989)

BROWN, JAMES
Albums
Live At The Apollo (King 1963)★★★★★
Live At The Apollo, Volume 2 (King 1968)★★★★
Soul Syndrome (TK 1980)★★★★
➽ p.354 for full listings

Further References
Film: *The Blues Brothers* (1980)
Video: *James Brown And Friends* (Video Collection 1988)
Book: *Living In America: The Soul Saga Of James Brown*, Cynthia Rose

BROWN, ARTHUR

UK VOCALIST BROWN (b. 1942) FORMED AN R&B GROUP – BLUES AND BROWN – WHILE A STUDENT. HE FRONTED A succession of bands, then moved to Paris in 1966 where he honed a theatrical and visual image. He contributed two songs to *La Curee*, a Roger Vadim film starring Jane Fonda.

In 1967, he formed the first Crazy World Of Arthur Brown with Vincent Crane (b. 1943, d. 1989; organ), Drachen Theaker (drums) and, later, Nick Greenwood (bass). They were quickly adopted by the 'underground' audience, where Brown's facial make-up, dervish dancing and fiery helmet earned them immediate notoriety. The group scored a UK number 1 with the compulsive 'Fire'. The attendant album, *The Crazy World Of Arthur Brown*, contained many stage favourites, including 'Spontaneous Apple Creation' and 'Come And Buy'. Theaker and Crane left the band and although Crane later returned, Carl Palmer, formerly of **Chris Farlowe**'s Thunderbirds, joined as drummer. Brown's most successful group ended in 1969 when the newcomer and Crane formed **Atomic Rooster**.

Brown moved to Dorset, where a music commune had been established. Reunited with Theaker, he completed *Strangelands*, before embarking on a new direction with Kingdom Come. Brown resumed a solo career in 1974, but despite a memorable cameo as the Priest in Ken Russell's film, *Tommy*, subsequent recordings proved disappointing. His voice was muted on *Dance*, and a reconciliation with Crane for *Chisholm In My Bosom* was little better. Brown went into semi-retirement and pursued a career as a carpenter and decorator in Texas, with former **Mothers Of Invention** drummer, Jimmy Carl Black.

BROWN, BOBBY

A FORMER MEMBER OF NEW EDITION, BROWN (b. 1969) EMERGED IN THE LATE 80S AS THE KING OF NEW JACK

Swing. On his debut album he was joined by Larry Blackmon and John Luongo, but it was the follow-up set, and the seamless production technique of Teddy Riley and L.A. and **Babyface**, that pushed him up the charts. Cuts such as the US number 1 'My Prerogative' were infectious dance workouts. He married **Whitney Houston** in 1992, and has appeared in film roles, including a cameo in *Ghostbusters II*. In 1995, 'Two Can Play That Game' reached the UK Top 10, following which he began working with New Edition. A new album appeared at the end of 1997 amid rumours of marital strife and bad behaviour.

BROWN, JAMES

AFTER A CHEQUERED ADOLESCENCE, INCLUDING A CONVICTION FOR THEFT AT THE AGE OF 16, THE legendary James Brown (b. 1928) joined the Gospel Starlighters, who evolved into the Flames after embracing R&B. In 1955 their demo of 'Please Please Please' saw them signed to the King/Federal company. A re-recorded version of the song was issued in 1956. Credited to 'James Brown And The Famous Flames', it reached number 5 in the US R&B list. Further releases fared poorly until 1958, when 'Try Me' rose to US R&B number 1. However, it was *Live At The Apollo*, that established the singer; raw, alive and uninhibited, it confirmed Brown as *the* voice of black America. His energetic songs, such as 'Night Train' and 'Shout And Shimmy', contrasted with slower sermons such as 'I Don't Mind' and 'Bewildered', but it was the orchestrated weepie, 'Prisoner Of Love'

(1963), that gave Brown his first US Top 20 pop single.

Throughout the 60s, Brown recorded increasingly unconventional songs, including 'Papa's Got A Brand New Bag', 'I Got You (I Feel Good)', 'It's A Man's Man's Man's World' and 'Money Won't Change You'. In 1967, Alfred Ellis replaced Nat Jones as Brown's musical director and 'Cold Sweat' introduced further radical refinements to the group's presentation, followed by a string of hits, including 'Say It Loud – I'm Black And I'm Proud' (1968), 'Mother Popcorn' (1969), and 'Get Up (I Feel Like Being A) Sex Machine' (1970). In 1971, Brown moved to Polydor and unveiled a new backing band, the JBs. Led by Fred Wesley, it featured such seasoned players as Maceo Parker and St. Clair Pinckney. However, as the decade progressed, his work became less compulsive and the advent of disco saw a drop in Brown's popularity.

He returned with a vengeance in 1986 with 'Livin' In America'. An international hit, it was followed by two R&B Top 10 entries, 'How Do You Stop' (1987) and 'I'm Real' (1988). However, the resurrection was abruptly curtailed in 1988 when the singer was imprisoned for illegal possession of drugs and firearms, aggravated assault and failure to stop for the police.

During the 90s, he has continued to have further problems with the law and a continuing battle to quit drugs. However, he remains one of the most dynamic performers of the century.

BROWN, JOE

BROWN (b. 1941) HAS SUSTAINED A CAREER FOR OVER 30 YEARS AS A CHEERFUL 'COCKNEY' ROCK 'N' ROLL SINGER and guitarist. In 1956, he formed the Spacemen skiffle group, which became the backing group on Jack Good's television series *Boy Meets Girls* in 1959. Brown was regarded as one of the finest guitarists in the UK and his services were frequently in demand. Rechristened Joe Brown And The Bruvvers, the group joined Larry Parnes's successful stable of artists and signed to Decca. He first charted with 'Darktown Strutters Ball' in 1960 and UK Top 10 hits on the Pye Piccadilly label in 1962-63 with 'A Picture Of You', 'It Only Took A Minute' and 'That's What Love Will Do'. He appeared in the film *What A Crazy World* and in the mid-60s starred in the hit musical *Charlie Girl*.

In the early 70s, Brown put together country-rock band Home Brew, which featured his wife Vicki (vocals), Ray Glynn (guitar), Pete Oakman (bass/violin), Jeff Peters (bass), Dave Hynes (drums) and Kirk Duncan (piano). Tragically, Vicki died from cancer in 1991.

Brown has occasionally appeared for other artists; in 1982 he appeared on **George Harrison**'s *Gone Troppo*. His daughter Sam Brown forged her own career as a notable rock singer and Joe released a well-received album in 1997.

BROWNE, JACKSON

BROWNE (b. 1948) BEGAN WRITING SONGS AT THE INSTIGATION OF TWO HIGH SCHOOL FRIENDS. IN 1966, HE JOINED the **Nitty Gritty Dirt Band**, only to leave within six months. An ensuing deal with Nina Music, the publishing arm of Elektra Records, resulted in several of Browne's songs being recorded by the label's acts, including **Tom Rush**. Browne had meanwhile ventured to New York, where he accompanied singer **Nico** during her engagement at Andy Warhol's Dom club.

A demo tape resulted in a recording deal with the newly established Asylum Records. *Jackson Browne/Saturate Before Using* showed increased potential, with **David Crosby** adding sterling support, including his own readings of 'Jamaica Say You Will', 'Rock Me On The Water' and 'Doctor My Eyes' (US Top 10). Browne also drew plaudits for 'Take It Easy', which he wrote with Glenn Frey (**Eagles**). Jackson's own version of 'Take It Easy' appeared on *For Everyman*, which also featured 'These Days', one of the singer's most popular early songs. The album introduced a long-standing relationship with multi-instrumentalist David Lindley, but although the punchy 'Redneck Friend' became a regional hit, the set was not a commercial success.

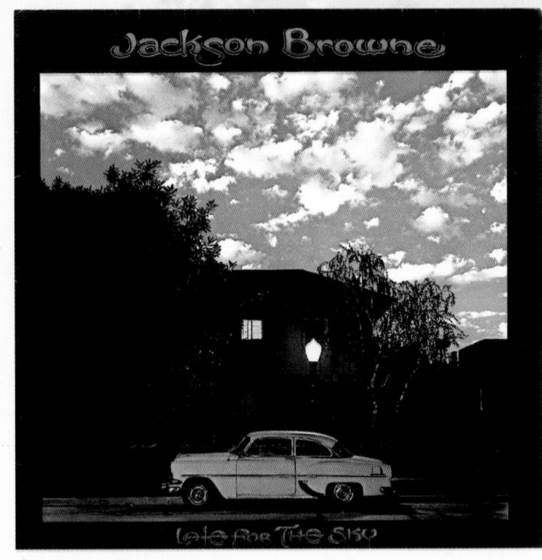

Late For The Sky was a stronger collection, on which Browne offered a more contemporary perspective. *The Pretender*, produced by Jon Landau, included 'Here Come Those Tears Again' and the anthemic title track, the poignancy of which was enhanced by the suicide of Jackson's wife, Phyllis, in 1976. *The Pretender* earned a gold disc and the singer's newfound commercial appeal was emphasized with *Running On Empty*, from which 'Stay' reached US number 20 and UK number 12 – his only British hit to date.

During the 70s, Jackson pursued a heightened political profile through his efforts on behalf of the anti-nuclear lobby, for whom he organized benefit concerts. It was 1980 before he completed a new studio album, but although *Hold On* was undeniably well-crafted, it lacked the depth of earlier work. Commitments to social causes and his personal life only increased Browne's artistic impasse and *Lawyers In Love* was a major disappointment. *Lives In The Balance*, which addressed the Reagan presidential era, showed a greater sense of accomplishment, a feature continued on *World In Motion*. *I'm Alive* clearly demonstrated that after more than twenty years of writing songs, it is possible to remain as sharp and fresh as ever, whereas *Looking East* was limp and lifeless.

BRUCE, JACK

BRUCE (b. JOHN SYMON ASHER, 1943) HAS UTILIZED HIS BASS PLAYING TO BRIDGE FREE JAZZ AND HEAVY ROCK. He started out with **Alexis Korner**'s band and then as a key member of the pioneering Graham Bond Organisation. Following brief stints with **John Mayall**'s Bluesbreakers and **Manfred Mann**, Bruce joined former colleague, **Ginger Baker**, who, together with **Eric Clapton**, formed **Cream**. He popularized the bass, an instrument that had previously not featured prominently in rock music. Upon the break-up of Cream, Bruce released an exemplary solo album, *Songs For A Tailor*. Pete Brown's imaginative and surreal lyrics were the perfect foil to Bruce's furious and complex bass patterns. Evocative songs such as 'Theme For An Imaginary Western' and 'The Weird Of Hermiston' enabled Bruce's vocal ability to shine, with piercing clarity.

Throughout the early 70s, a series of excellent albums and constantly changing line-ups gave him a high profile. His involvement with Tony Williams' Lifetime and his own West, Bruce And Laing, enhanced his position in the jazz and rock world. A further aggregation, Jack Bruce And Friends, included jazz guitarist **Larry Coryell** and former **Jimi Hendrix** drummer Mitch Mitchell. Bruce added vocals to Carla Bley's *Escalator Over The Hill*, and Bley was a member of the 1975 version of the Jack Bruce Band. In 1979, he toured as a member of John McLaughlin's **Mahavishnu Orchestra**. The 80s started with a new Jack Bruce Band which featured guitarist Dave 'Clem' Clempson and David Sancious. The ill-fated heavy rock trio BLT formed in 1981 with guitarist **Robin Trower** and drummer Bill Lordan but disintegrated after two albums; their debut, *BLT*, reached the US Top 40. After a period of retirement, *Automatic* (1987) was followed by the impressive *A Question Of Time*. In 1994, he formed **BBM**, with **Gary Moore** and Baker.

BRUFORD, BILL

A FOUNDER MEMBER OF **YES** IN 1968, BRUFORD (b. 1949) LEFT THE GROUP AT THE HEIGHT OF ITS POPULARITY. AN accomplished drummer, he joined **King Crimson**, remaining there until **Robert Fripp** dissolved the band in 1974. Bruford subsequently worked with Pavlov's Dog, before forming the jazz-rock ensemble, UK. The initial line-up featured guitarist Allan Holdsworth, who joined the drummer for his solo debut *Feels Good To Me*. The two musicians then broke away to found Bruford, with Dave Stewart (keyboards) and Jeff Berlin (bass). Bill's independent career was sidelined in 1981 when Fripp invited him to join the reconstituted King Crimson, but it collapsed again; he toured with Al DiMeola and David Torn, subsequently forming his own jazz-based group, Bill Bruford's Earthworks, which included keyboardist Django Bates and saxophonist Iain Ballamy.

He became involved with the re-union of Yes in the late 80s, touring and recording under the banner of **Anderson, Bruford, Wakeman** And Howe. He was also part of the reformed King Crimson for *Thrak*.

BRYANT, BOUDLEAUX

BOUDLEAUX (b. DIADORIUS BOUDLEAUX BRYANT, 1920, d. 1987) STARTED PERFORMING IN A FAMILY BAND WITH his four sisters and brothers, playing at county fairs in the Midwest USA. In 1937, Boudleaux began playing with the Atlanta Symphony Orchestra as well as with jazz and country music groups. For several years he went on the road, playing in radio station bands in Detroit and Memphis before joining Hank Penny's Radio Cowboys.

In 1945, he married **Felice** Scaduto (b. 1925) and they began composing together, including 'Country Boy' which became a hit for Jimmy Dickens. The duo moved to Nashville as staff writers for Acuff-Rose; among their numerous successes in the 50s were 'Have A Good Time' (**Tony Bennett**), 'Hey Joe' Frankie Laine and the Eddy Arnold hits 'I've Been Thinking' and 'The Richest Man'. In 1957, the Bryants switched to material for the **Everly Brothers**. Beginning with 'Bye Bye Love', they supplied a stream of songs that were melodramatic vignettes of teen life. Several of them were composed by Boudleaux alone, including the wistful 'All I Have To Do Is Dream', the tough and vengeful 'Bird Dog', 'Devoted To You' and 'Like Strangers'. At this time he wrote what has become his most recorded song, 'Love Hurts'. This sorrowful, almost self-pitying ballad is a favourite with the country rock fraternity. From the early 60s, the Bryants returned to the country sphere, composing the standard 'Rocky Top' as well as providing hits for artists such as Sonny James ('Baltimore') and Roy Clark ('Come Live With Me'). Shortly before Boudleaux's death in 1987, the Bryants were inducted into the Songwriters' Hall Of Fame.

BROWN, JOE
Albums
A Picture Of Joe Brown (Ace Of Clubs 1962)★★★
Live (Piccadilly 1963)★★★
Fifty Six And Taller Than You Think (Demon 1997)★★★
➽ p.354 for full listings
Collaborators
George Harrison ➽ p.176

BROWNE, JACKSON
Albums
Jackson Browne aka Saturate Before Using (Asylum 1972)★★★★
For Everyman (Asylum 1973)★★★★
I'm Alive (Elektra 1994)★★★★
➽ p.354 for full listings
Collaborators
Tom Rush ➽ p.285
Nico ➽ p.247
David Crosby ➽ p.105
Connections
Nitty Gritty Dirt Band ➽ p.249
Eagles ➽ p.130

BRUCE, JACK
Albums
Songs For A Tailor (Polydor 1969)★★★★
Cities Of the Heart (CMP 1994)★★★★
with Paul Jones *Alexis Korner Memorial Concert Vol. 1* (Indigo 1995)★★★
➽ p.354 for full listings
Collaborators
Mahavishnu Orchestra ➽ p.222
Connections
Alexis Korner ➽ p.210
John Mayall ➽ p.228
Manfred Mann ➽ p.223
Ginger Baker ➽ p.29
Eric Clapton ➽ p.92
Robin Trower ➽ p.324
BBM ➽ p.35

BRUFORD, BILL
Albums
The Bruford Tapes (Editions EG 1980)★★★★
Earthworks (Editions EG 1987)★★★★
Dig (Editions EG 1989)★★★
➽ p.354 for full listings
Connections
Yes ➽ p.346
King Crimson ➽ p.206
Robert Fripp ➽ p.154
Anderson, Bruford, Wakeman And Howe

BRYANT, BOUDLEAUX
Albums
Boudleaux Bryant's Best Sellers (Monument 1963)★★★
➽ p.354 for full listings
Connections
Tony Bennett ➽ p.43
Everly Brothers ➽ p.139
Influences
Felice Bryant ➽ p.72

BRYANT, FELICE
Albums
A Touch Of Bryant (CMH 1979)★★
Surfin' On A New Wave (1979)★★
➽ p.354 for full listings
Connections
Everly Brothers ➽ p.139
Bob Dylan ➽ p.128
Buddy Holly ➽ p.184
Influences
Boudleaux Bryant ➽ p.71

BRYSON, PEABO
Albums
Reaching For The Sky (Capitol 1978)★★★
I Am Love (Capitol 1981)★★★
Positive (Elektra 1988)★★★
➽ p.354 for full listings
Collaborators
Natalie Cole ➽ p.97
Melissa Manchester ➽ p.223
Roberta Flack ➽ p.146
Celine Dion ➽ p.119

BUCKINGHAM, LINDSEY
Albums
Law And Order (Asylum 1981)★★★
Go Insane (Elektra 1984)★★
Out Of The Cradle (Reprise 1992)★★
➽ p.354 for full listings
Connections
Stevie Nicks ➽ p.247
Fleetwood Mac ➽ p.147

BRYANT, FELICE

THE LYRICIST OF SOME OF THE **EVERLY BROTHERS**' BIGGEST HITS, FELICE BRYANT (b. FELICE SCADUTO, 1925) WAS A member of one of the most famous husband-and-wife songwriting teams in pop and country music. Recordings of their 750 published songs have sold over 300 million copies in versions by over 400 artists as diverse as **Bob Dylan** and Lawrence Welk. Of Italian extraction, Felice was already writing lyrics when she met **Boudleaux Bryant**. After their marriage in 1945 the duo wrote together. The success of 'Country Boy' for Jimmy Dickens led them to Nashville where they were the first full-time songwriters and pluggers. During the 50s, the Bryants' country hits were often covered by pop artists such as Al Martino, Frankie Laine and **Tony Bennett**.

In 1957, they switched to composing teenage pop material for the Everly Brothers. Among the hits they supplied were 'Bye Bye Love', 'Wake Up Little Susie', 'Problems', 'Poor Jenny' and 'Take A Message To Mary'. They also composed 'Raining In My Heart' (**Buddy Holly**) and the witty 'Let's Think About Livin'' (Bob Luman). After the rock 'n' roll era had subsided, the Bryants returned to the country scene, composing prolifically throughout the 60s and 70s in bluegrass and American Indian folk material. Their most enduring song being 'Rocky Top', first recorded by the Osborne Brothers in 1969. In the late 70s, Felice and Boudleaux recorded their own compositions for the first time.

BRYSON, PEABO

THIS TALENTED SOUL SINGER AND PRODUCER WAS A MEMBER OF MOSES DILLARD AND THE TEX-TOWN Display and Michael Zager's Moon Band. Between 1976 and 1978, Bryson (b. Robert Peabo Bryson, 1951) had hits with 'Reaching For The Sky' and 'I'm So Into You'. His numerous appearances in *Billboard*'s R&B chart include 'Underground Music', 'Feel The Fire', 'Crosswinds', 'She's A Woman' and 'Minute By Minute'. 'Gimme Some Time', a 1979 duet with Natalie Cole, was the first of several successful partnerships. Despite hits with **Melissa Manchester** and Regina Belle, the singer is best known for his work with **Roberta Flack**, and in particular the ballad 'Tonight, I Celebrate My Love' (1983), which reached number 5 on the US R&B chart and UK number 2. Such releases have obscured Bryson's own career, which included the 1984 US Top 10 hit 'If Ever You're In My Arms Again'. Soundtrack duets with **Celine Dion** ('Beauty And The Beast') and Regina Belle ('A Whole New World (Aladdin's Theme)') in 1992 provided Bryson with further chart success.

BUCKINGHAM, LINDSEY

BUCKINGHAM (b. 1947) BEGAN HIS CAREER AS A FOLK-SINGER BEFORE JOINING FRITZ, AN ASPIRING BAY AREA rock band featuring vocalist **Stevie Nicks**. When Fritz folded in 1971, the couple formed Buckingham Nicks. The 1973 self-titled album made little commercial impression and Buckingham undertook session work.

When Bob Welch left **Fleetwood Mac** in 1974, Mick Fleetwood invited the pair to join as replacements. *Fleetwood Mac* and the multi-million selling *Rumours* established them as one of the world's top-selling acts; Buckingham's skills as a singer, composer, guitarist and producer were crucial to this success. However, following the release of *Tusk*, both he and Nicks went solo. Buckingham's debut, *Law And Order*, continued the craftsmanship displayed on earlier work, but although one of the tracks, 'Trouble', reached the US Top 10, it failed to match the profile Nicks had achieved with her first release. Both artists resumed their roles with Fleetwood Mac for Mirage (1982), but subsequently pursued individual paths. The title song from a second collection, *Go Insane*, provided another hit, and although he returned to the parent group's fold for the excellent *Tango In The Night* (1987), Buckingham officially parted from the unit the following year.

BUCKINGHAMS

FORMED IN CHICAGO, USA, IN 1966, THE BUCKINGHAMS ORIGINALLY FEATURED DENNIS TUFANO (b. 1946; VOCALS), Carl Giammarese (b. 1947; lead guitar), Dennis Miccoli (organ), Nick Fortune (b. 1946; bass) and Jon Jon Poulos (b. 1947, d. 1980; drums). Although their first hit, 'Kind Of A Drag' was their only gold disc, the group enjoyed a consistent run of US chart successes throughout 1967, achieving two further Top 10 entries with 'Don't You Care' and 'Mercy Mercy Mercy'. Miccoli was later replaced by Marty Grebb (b. 1946) Despite slick, commercial singles, their albums showed a desire to experiment and, unable to reconcile their image and ambitions, they split in 1970. Poulos later managed several local acts, but died of drug-related causes in 1980. Tufano and Giammarese continued working as a duo, while Grebb later worked with **Chicago**.

BUCKLEY, JEFF

THE SON OF RESPECTED SINGER-SONGWRITER **TIM BUCKLEY**, JEFF BUCKLEY (b. 1966, d. 1997) FIRST GARNERED ATTENTION at a Tim Buckley tribute, performing 'Once I Was'. He made appearances at several of New York's clubs, recording his debut mini-album at the Sin-é coffee-house. This tentative four-song set included two original compositions, alongside versions of **Van Morrison**'s 'The Way Young Lovers Do' and Edith Piaf's 'Je N'En Connais Pas La Fin'. Having secured a contract with Sony Records, Buckley completed the critically acclaimed *Grace* with Michael Tighe (guitar), Mick Grondhal (bass) and Matt Johnson (drums). An expressive singer, Buckley soared and swept across this collection, which included cover versions alongside breathtaking original songs. His live appearances blended expressive readings of material from *Grace* with an array of interpretations ranging from **Big Star** ('Kanga Roo') to the **MC5** ('Kick Out The Jams').

Buckley, a gifted, melodic composer, was about to resume work on his second album when he drowned in a hazardous stretch of the Mississippi.

BUCKLEY, TIM

A RADIANT TALENT, BUCKLEY (b. 1947, d. 1975) BEGAN HIS SOLO CAREER IN THE FOLK CLUBS OF LOS ANGELES. HE WAS discovered by manager Herb Cohen who secured Buckley's recording deal with Elektra. *Tim Buckley* introduced the artist's skills, but his vision flourished more fully on a second selection, *Goodbye And Hello*. Although underscored by arrangements now deemed over-elaborate, the set featured 'Morning Glory', one of Buckley's most evocative compositions. With *Happy Sad* he forsook the services of long-time lyricist Larry Beckett, employing Lee Underwood (guitar) and David Friedman (vibes). This expansive style was maintained on *Blue Afternoon* and *Lorca*, but while the former largely consisted of haunting, melodious folk-jazz performances, the latter offered a more radical, experimental direction. Its emphasis on improvisation inspired *Starsailor*, which included the delicate 'Song To The Siren' (revived by This Mortal Coil in 1983). *Greetings From LA* marked a newfound fascination with contemporary black music. Buckley's influence has increased with time.

BUCKS FIZZ

BUCKS FIZZ WAS ORIGINALLY CONCEIVED AS A VEHICLE FOR SINGER/PRODUCER/MANAGER NICHOLA MARTIN to appear in the Eurovision Song Contest. With her partner, later husband, Andy Hill producing and composing material, Martin auditioned hundreds of applicants before deciding on Mike Nolan (b. 1954), Bobby G (b. Robert Gubby, 1957), Jay Aston (b. 1961) and Cheryl Baker (b. Rita Crudgington, 1954). Baker had previously appeared as a Eurovision entrant with Coco. So impressed was Martin with her discoveries that she suppressed her singing ambitions. With 'Making Your Mind Up', the manufactured Bucks Fizz duly won the 1981 Contest and scored a UK number 1. Within 12 months they had two UK number 1s, 'The Land Of Make Believe' and 'My Camera Never Lies'. After 'When We Were Young', their chart performance declined.

In 1984, the group was involved in a coach crash and Nolan was incapacitated for a considerable period. Matters worsened when Aston became involved in an affair with Hill, thereby straining the relationship with Martin. Martin subsequently conducted another mass audition and chose the totally unknown 21-year-old Shelley Preston (b. 1964). Although the new line-up was not able to match the success of its predecessor, 'New Beginning' returned them to the Top 10.

BUDGIE

HARD ROCK GROUP FORMED IN CARDIFF, WALES, BY JOHN BURKE SHELLEY (b. 1947; BASS/ACOUSTIC GUITAR/LEAD vocals) and Ray Phillips (b. 1949; drums) in 1968. Joined by Tony Bourge (b. 1948; lead guitar/vocals) the trio were signed to MCA Records. Phillips quit in 1974, before their fourth album, and was replaced by Pete Boot (b. 1950), who was replaced in turn by Steve Williams.

With the success of *In For The Kill*, Budgie won over a wider audience. Their sixth album, *If I Was Brittania I'd Waive The Rules*, was their first on A&M Records and *Impeckable* was the last to feature Bourge, who left in 1978, joining Phillips in Tredegar. He was replaced by John Thomas. The group's popularity grew in the USA, with Rob Kendrick (ex-Trapeze) standing in for Thomas. Returning to Britain, Budgie's reputation and influence on a younger generation of musicians brought them consistent work until Shelley wound up the group in 1988. Phillips used the name Six Ton Budgie for a new line-up featuring his son, Justin, on guitar.

BUCKINGHAMS
Albums
Kind Of A Drag (USA 1967)★★★
Time And Changes (Columbia 1967)★★★
Portraits (Columbia 1968)★★★
➽ p.354 for full listings
Connections
Chicago ➽ p.90
Further References
Video: *Made in the USA* (Hollywood 1992)

BUCKLEY, JEFF
Albums
Live At Sin-é mini-album (Big Cat 1992)★★★
Grace (Sony 1994)★★★★
Live From The Bataclan mini-album (Columbia 1996)★★
➽ p.354 for full listings

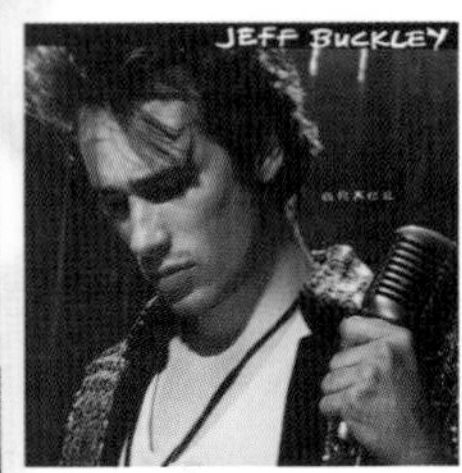

Connections
Van Morrison ➽ p.238
Influences
Tim Buckley ➽ p.73
Edith Piaf
Elkie Brooks ➽ p.69
Leonard Cohen ➽ p.96

BUCKLEY, TIM
Albums
Happy Sad (Elektra 1968)★★★★
Blue Afternoon (Straight 1969)★★★★
Dream Letter-Live In London 1968 (Demon 1990)★★★★
➽ p.355 for full listings

BUCKS FIZZ
Albums
Bucks Fizz (RCA 1981)★★
Are You Ready? (RCA 1982)★★
Hand Cut (RCA 1983)★★
➽ p.355 for full listings
Connections
Abba ➽ p.6
Coco
Further References
Video: *Greatest Hits: Bucks Fizz* (1986)

BUDGIE
Albums
Squawk (MCA 1972)★★
If I Was Brittania I'd Waive The Rules (A&M 1976)★★
Deliver Us From Evil (RCA 1982)★★
➽ p.355 for full listings
Connections
George Hatcher Band
Trapeze
Six Ton Budgie

BUFFALO SPRINGFIELD
Albums
Buffalo Springfield Again (Atco 1967)★★★★★
➧ p.355 for full listings
Collaborators
David Crosby ➧ p.105
Connections
Mothers of Invention ➧ p.239
Poco ➧ p.262
Loggins And Messina ➧ p.218
Blood, Sweat and Tears ➧ p.53
Rhinoceros ➧ p.277
Crosby, Stills, Nash and Young ➧ p.106

BUFFALO TOM
Albums
Let Me Come Over (Situation 2 1992)★★★★
➧ p.355 for full listings
Connections
Dinosaur Jr ➧ p.118
Influences
Hüsker Dü ➧ p.190
Soul Asylum ➧ p.302

BUFFETT, JIMMY
Albums
Barometer Soup (Margaritaville 1995)★★★★
➧ p.355 for full listings
Collaborators
Rita Coolidge ➧ p.100
James Taylor ➧ p.317
Steve Winwood ➧ p.341
Connections
Coral Reefer Band

BUGGLES
Albums
The Age Of Plastic (Island 1980)★★
➧ p.355 for full listings
Collaborators
Yes ➧ p.346
Connections
Asia ➧ p.22

BURDON, ERIC
Albums
Ring Of Fire (Capitol 1974)★★★
➧ p.355 for full listings
Connections
Animals ➧ p.18
War ➧ p.333
Influences
Jimi Hendrix ➧ p.180
Further References
Books: *Wild Animals*, Andy Blackford

BURKE, SOLOMON
Albums
The Bishop Rides South (Charly 1988)★★★★
➧ p.355 for full listings

BURNETT, T-BONE
Albums
The Criminal Under My Own Hat (Columbia 1992)★★★
➧ p.355 for full listings
Collaborators
Bob Dylan ➧ p.128
Delaney and Bonnie ➧ p.114
B- 52's ➧ p.26

BUFFALO SPRINGFIELD

THROUGHOUT A CONSTANTLY CHANGING LINE-UP, BUFFALO SPRINGFIELD'S MAIN MEMBERS COMPRISED: **Stephen Stills** (b. 1945; guitar/vocals), **Neil Young** (b. 1945; guitar/vocals), Richie Furay (b. 1944; guitar/vocals), Dewey Martin (b. 1942; drums), Bruce Palmer (b. 1947) and Jim Messina (b. 1947; bass). Furay and Stills worked together in the Au Go-Go Singers in the mid-60s, where they met Young, at the time a solo singer, having previously worked with Palmer in the Mynah Birds. In 1966, the quartet started a band in Los Angeles; following a series of successful gigs at the prestigious *Whiskey A Go-Go*, they were signed to Atco. Ego problems were compounded by Palmer's drug problems. Eventually, Young's former associate Ken Koblun was recruited as a replacement, in turn replaced by Jim Fielder (b. 1947). Their only major hit was 'For What Its Worth (Hey Whats That Sound)' (1967).

Young's unpredictability meant that he would sometimes not show up at gigs, or leave the group for long periods. His main replacement was ex-Daily Flash guitarist Doug Hastings (b. 1946), although **David Crosby** deputized at the **Monterey Pop Festival**. The album *Last Time Around* was patched together by producer and Messina, after the band had broken up for the final time. *Buffalo Springfield Again* remains their finest work.

Furay later formed **Poco** and continued his country-rock leanings. Messina joined with Furay and later with **Kenny Loggins** as **Loggins and Messina**. Fielder joined **Blood Sweat And Tears**. Hastings joined **Rhinoceros**. Dewey Martin formed New Buffalo Springfield, later New Buffalo. Young and Stills went on to mega-stardom as members of **Crosby, Stills, Nash and Young** and high-profile soloists.

BUFFALO TOM

MELODIC HARDCORE TRIO FEATURING BILL JANOWITZ (VOCALS/GUITAR), TOM MAGINNIS (DRUMS) AND CHRIS Colbourn (bass), formed in 1986. Their first album was produced by **Dinosaur Jr**'s J. Mascis. By *Let Me Come Over* (1992), the band had established a promising reputation. *Big Red Letter Day* showed a more polished, orchestrated approach to songwriting, which contrasted with the three-week sessions for 1995's *Sleepy Eyed*. Janowitz released a country-styled solo debut in 1996, backed by Joey Burns and John Convertino.

BUFFETT, JIMMY

AFTER POORLY PRODUCED SOLO ALBUMS, BUFFET (b.1946) WROTE THE POIGNANT 'RAILROAD LADY' WITH JERRY Jeff Walker; it was recorded by Lefty Frizzell and Merle Haggard. Buffet's *A White Sport Coat And A Pink Crustacean* included several story-songs ('The Great Filling Station Holdup', 'Peanut Butter Conspiracy'), together with the lazy feel of 'He Went To Paris', recorded by Waylon Jennings. *Living And Dying In 3/4 Time* included his US Top 30 hit 'Come Monday'. Buffett also wrote the music for the film *Rancho Deluxe*.

In 1975, he formed the Coral Reefer Band. Arguably his best album, *Changes In Latitudes, Changes In Attitudes*, included the million-selling 'Margaritaville'. He continued to record prolifically, including contemporary rock, but his songs began to lack sparkle. His best album tracks were remakes of standards, 'Stars Fell On Alabama' and 'On A Slow Boat To China'. *Hot Water* included guest appearances by **Rita Coolidge**, **James Taylor** and **Steve Winwood**, but failed to restore him to the charts.

BUGGLES

TREVOR HORN AND GEOFF DOWNES MET AS SESSION MUSICIANS IN 1977; POOLING THEIR RESOURCES, they formed Buggles. Their debut, 'Video Killed The Radio Star' became Island Records' first number 1 single (1979). Its innovative video was later used to launch MTV in the USA. The duo enjoyed three further chart entries with 'The Plastic Age', 'Clean Clean' and 'Elstree', but remained a studio group. They were invited to replace **Jon Anderson** and **Rick Wakeman** in **Yes** in 1980; the liaison lasted a few months when Downes departed to form **Asia**; Horn became a record producer and founded ZTT Records.

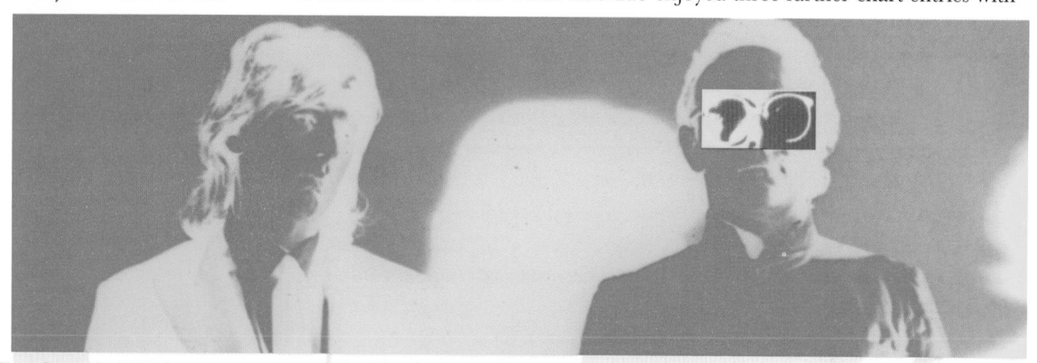

BURDON, ERIC

THIS ENGLISH SINGER (b. 1941), ORIGINALLY CAME TO PROMINENCE AS LEAD SINGER OF THE **ANIMALS** IN 1963. Following the demise of Eric Burdon And The New Animals, he linked up with the black jazz/rock band Nite Shift, and, together with his friend Lee Oskar, they became Eric Burdon And **War**. 'Spill The Wine' preceded the well-received *Eric Burdon Declares War*. Both this and the follow-up, *Black Man's Burdon*, combined ambitious arrangements mixing flute with Oskar's harmonica. In the early 70s, after parting company, War went on to become hugely successful, while Burdon's career stalled. He teamed up with Jimmy Witherspoon on *Guilty* and attempted a heavier rock approach with *Sun Secrets* and *Stop*.

In 1980, Burdon formed Fire Dept in Germany, making *Last Drive*. He finally fulfilled long-standing big-screen ambitions by appearing in the film *Comeback* – as a fading rock star. Throughout the 80s Burdon continued to perform, with little recorded output, while experiencing drug and alcohol problems. His 1977 and 1983 reunion albums with the Animals were poorly received. Burdon's popularity in Germany continued, though his profile in the UK and USA decreased.

BURKE, SOLOMON

FROM 1955-59, BURKE (b. 1936) ATTEMPTED VARIOUS STYLES UNTIL 'BE BOP GRANDMA', ATTRACTED THE attention of Atlantic Records. An eclectic performer, his 'Just Out Of Reach' (1961) was a US Top 30 hit, before he began asserting a soul direction with 'Cry To Me' (1962). His sonorous voice was then heard on a succession of singles, including 'If You Need Me' (1963) and 'Everybody Needs Somebody To Love' (1964). This exceptional period culminated with 'The Price'. 'Take Me (Just As I Am)' reached the US Top 50, but Burke left Atlantic for Bell Records shortly afterwards. *Proud Mary* was a soul classic; its title track (written by John Fogerty) charted in the USA. The 70s saw a move to MGM, but his work there was marred by inconsistency. The same was true of his spells at Dunhill and Chess, although his collaborations with Swamp Dogg collected on *From The Heart* recalled his old power. On *Soul Alive*, he sounded inspired, infusing his 'greatest hits' with a new-found passion. A strong studio collection, *A Change Is Gonna Come*, followed a 1987 European tour. Burke continued recording into the 90s.

BURNETT, T-BONE

TEXAN-BORN BURNETT (b. JOHN HENRY BURNETT, 1945) STARTED OUT PRODUCING DELBERT AND GLEN AND recorded a solo album for Uni. After touring with **Delaney And Bonnie** and the **B-52's** he joined **Bob Dylan**'s Rolling Thunder Revue. He then founded the Alpha Band, who made three albums between 1976 and 1979. After the demise of the Alpha Band, Burnett made a solo album for Takoma, aided by **Ry Cooder** and **Richard Thompson**. He later toured with Thompson and **Elvis Costello**, releasing a 1985 single with the latter as the Coward Brothers. Burnett has produced artists including **Leo Kottke**, **Los Lobos** and **Bruce Cockburn** and has co-written with Bono of **U2**.

BURNETTE, DORSEY

DORSEY (b. 1932, d. 1979) FORMED THE **JOHNNY BURNETTE** TRIO WITH YOUNGER BROTHER JOHNNY in 1953. After appearing in the film *Rock, Rock, Rock* in 1956, Dorsey left. He recorded with Johnny, as The Texans, and wrote major hits for **Ricky Nelson**, including 'It's Late' and 'Waitin' In School'. 'Tall Oak Tree' and 'Hey Little One', (1960), were both big hits showcasing his country-style voice. In the 70s he had 15 Top 100 country hits. His son Billy Burnette is also a recording artist.

BURNETTE, JOHNNY

HAVING ATTENDED THE SAME HIGH SCHOOL AS **ELVIS PRESLEY**, BURNETTE (b. 1934, d. 1964) FORMED A TRIO with his brother **Dorsey Burnette** (string bass) and Paul Burlison (guitar). The group recorded 'Go Mule Go' for Von Records and were subsequently signed to Coral, where they enjoyed a minor hit with 'Tear It Up'. After touring with **Carl Perkins** and **Gene Vincent** in 1956, they changed personnel, recruiting drummer Tony Austin. That year, the trio featured in **Alan Freed**'s movie *Rock, Rock, Rock* and issued a number of singles, including 'Honey Hush', 'The Train Kept A-Rollin'', 'Eager Beaver Baby', 'Drinkin' Wine', 'Spo-Dee-O-Dee' and 'If You Want It Enough'. The trio broke up in 1957 and the Burnette brothers moved on to enjoy success as songwriters. They provided **Ricky Nelson** with many of his hits.

Their own releases, 'Dreamin'' and 'You're Sixteen', were transatlantic Top 10 hits, perfectly suited to Burnette's light but expressive vocal, but a series of lesser successes followed with 'Little Boy Sad', 'Big Big World', 'Girls' and 'God, Country And My Baby'. Burnette formed his own label Magic Lamp in 1964. In August that year, he fell from his boat in California and drowned. His son Rocky subsequently achieved recording success in the 70s.

BURNING SPEAR

JAMAICAN BURNING SPEAR (b. WINSTON RODNEY, 1948) APPROPRIATED THE NAME FROM FORMER MAU MAU leader Jomo Kenyatta, then president of Kenya. He entered the music business in 1969 after **Bob Marley** organized an audition for him with **Coxsone Dodd**. Spear continued to make records for Dodd until 1974 and 'Joe Frazier' (aka 'He Prayed') made the Jamaican Top 5 in 1972. In 1975, Ocho Rios sound system owner Jack Ruby (Laurence Lindo), Burning Spear, Rupert Wellington and Delroy Hines, began working on the material for *Marcus Garvey* (1975). Its popularity caused Island to release a companion set, *Garvey's Ghost* (1976). Rodney began to release music on his Spear label at the end of 1975, he also produced 'On That Day' by Burning Junior, and 'Love Everyone' by Phillip Fullwood (both 1976). In 1976, Jack Ruby released a solo single and album, which marked the end of their collaboration. Spear also dropped Willington and Hines. 1977 saw the release of *Dry & Heavy*, which reworked many of his Studio One classics, and a live album recorded at London's Rainbow Theatre, backed by trumpeter Bobby Ellis and **Aswad**.

In 1978, Spear parted with Island and issued *Marcus Children*. In 1980, he signed to EMI issuing the stunning *Hail H.I.M.*. Two excellent dubs of *Social Living* and *Hail H.I.M.* also appeared as *Living Dub Vols. 1* and *2*, mixed by engineer Sylvan Morris.

Spear released albums regularly, and toured widely. *Resistance*, nominated for a Grammy in 1984, was a particularly strong set highlighting his impressive, soulful patois. *People Of The World* encompassed an all-female horn section, *Mistress Music* added rock musicians (including former members of **Jefferson Airplane**) and *Mek We Dweet* was a return to his unique, intense style.

BURTON, JAMES

ONE OF THE MOST DISTINGUISHED OF ROCK AND COUNTRY ROCK GUITAR PLAYERS, BURTON (b. 1939) toured and recorded with **Ricky Nelson** and **Elvis Presley** amongst others. His first recording was 'Suzie Q', sung by Dale Hawkins (1957). Burton performed with country singer Bob Luman, before spending six years touring and recording with Nelson, perfecting a guitar sound known as 'chicken pickin''. Among the best examples of this style are 'Hello Mary Lou', 'Never Be Anyone Else But You' and the rockabilly-flavoured 'Believe What You Say'. During the 60s and 70s, Burton worked as a session guitarist with artists including **Buffalo Springfield**, **Judy Collins**, **Joni Mitchell** and **Michael Nesmith**. He also made two albums of his own, one in collaboration with steel guitarist Ralph Mooney.

During the 70s, Burton's work took him in contrasting directions. With pianist Glen D. Hardin (ex-**Crickets**) he was a mainstay of Elvis Presley's touring and recording band from 1969-77, but he also played a leading role in the growing trend towards country/rock fusion. Burton's most significant performances in this respect came on the albums of **Gram Parsons**. He has also worked with **Emmylou Harris**, **Jesse Winchester**, **Ronnie Hawkins**, **Rodney Crowell**, Phil Everly, **J.J. Cale** and Nicolette Larson and toured with **Jerry Lee Lewis**. As a result of an accident in 1995, Burton lost the use of his hands and has been receiving treatment to enable him to play the guitar again. He faced bankruptcy after financing his own treatment. A fund has been set up to help him and benefit concerts were held.

BUSH

THIS CONTEMPORARY ROCK BAND, FORMED IN LONDON, ENGLAND, FOUND THEIR INITIAL SUCCESS IN THE USA. By 1995, their debut album had become a million-seller, while highly promoted UK artists such as **Blur** and **Oasis** were still struggling to achieve one tenth of those sales. Bush had previously spent two years toiling around small London venues.

Sixteen Stone was principally written by Gavin Rossdale (b. 1967; vocals/guitar), who had previously recorded two singles with his first band, Midnight. The songs on *Sixteen Stone* dealt with issues including an IRA bomb ('Bomb'), death ('Little Things'), religious cults ('Monkey') and sex ('Testosterone'). The rest of the band comprises Dave Parsons (b. 1965; bass; ex-Transvision Vamp), Robin Goodridge (b. 1966; drums; ex-Beautiful People) and Nigel Pulsford (b. 1964; guitar; ex-King Blank). After gaining airplay on Los Angeles' KROQ station in 1994, particularly for the single 'Everything Zen', interest in the band snowballed and their debut sold three million. Steve Albini was chosen to produce their second set. Their third album, *Razorblade Suitcase*, entered the US album chart at number 1.

Ry Cooder ➧ p.100
Elvis Costello ➧ p.101
Connections
Alpha Band
Bono ➧ p.326
Leo Kottke ➧ p.210
Los Lobos ➧ p.218

BURNETTE, DORSEY
Albums
Dorsey Burnette's Greatest Hits (Era 1969)★★★
➧ p.355 for full listings
Connections
Johnny Burnette Trio ➧ p.75
Ricky Nelson ➧ p.244

BURNETTE, JOHNNY
Albums
as the Johnny Burnette Trio *Rock 'N' Roll Trio* (Coral 1957)★★★★
➧ p.355 for full listings
Collaborators
Carl Perkins ➧ p.258
Gene Vincent ➧ p.330
Connections
Dorsey Burnette ➧ p.75
Alan Freed ➧ p.154
Ricky Nelson ➧ p.244

BURNING SPEAR
Albums
Marcus Garvey (Mango/Island 1975)★★★★★
➧ p.355 for full listings
Collaborators
Aswad ➧ p.23
Connections
Coxsone Dodd ➧ p.121
Jefferson Airplane ➧ p.198
Influences
Bob Marley ➧ p.225

BURTON, JAMES
Albums
The Guitar Sounds Of James Burton (A&M 1971)★★
➧ p.355 for full listings
Collaborators
Ricky Nelson ➧ p.244
Elvis Presley ➧ p.265
Buffalo Springfield ➧ p.74
Joni Mitchell ➧ p.235
Michael Nesmith ➧ p.245
Gram Parsons ➧ p.256
Emmylou Harris ➧ p.175
Jerry Lee Lewis ➧ p.215
Connections
Crickets ➧ p.105

BUSH
Albums
Razorblade Suitcase (Trauma 1996)★★★★
➧ p.355 for full listings
Collaborators
Steve Albini

BUSH, KATE
Albums
The Kick Inside (EMI 1978)★★★★
The Dreaming (EMI 1982)★★★★
Hounds Of Love (EMI 1985)★★★★
➽ p.355 for full listings

Collaborators
Peter Gabriel ➽ p.151
Connections
Dave Gilmour
Donald Sutherland
Influences
Emily Brontë
Pink Floyd ➽ p.261
Jung
James Joyce
Further References
Video: *Hair Of The Hound* (1986)
Books: *Kate Bush: Princess of Suburbia*, Fred and Judy Vermorel, Target Books

BUTTERFIELD, PAUL
Albums
Paul Butterfield Blues Band (Elektra 1966)★★★★
East-West (Elektra 1966)★★★★
The Legendary Paul Butterfield Rides Again (1986)★★★
➽ p.355 for full listings
Collaborators
Bob Dylan ➽ p.128
Connections
Mike Bloomfield ➽ p.54
Elvin Bishop ➽ p.48
David Sanborn ➽ p.288
Influences
John Mayall ➽ p.228

BUTTHOLE SURFERS
Albums
Butthole Surfers (Alternative Tentacles 1983)★★★
Electriclarryland (Capitol 1996)★★★★
➽ p.355 for full listings
Further References
Video: *Blind Eye Sees All* (Touch And Go)

BUZZCOCKS
Albums
Another Music In A Different Kitchen (United Artists 1978)★★★★
Love Bites (United Artists 1978)★★★
Trade Test Transmissions (Castle 1993)★★★
➽ p.355 for full listings

BUSH, KATE

WHILE STILL AT SCHOOL, BUSH (b. 1958) WAS DISCOVERED BY **PINK FLOYD**'S DAVE GILMOUR, WHO WAS SO IMPRESSED by the imaginative quality of her songwriting that he financed demo recordings. EMI Records encouraged her to develop her writing, dancing and singing in preparation for a long-term career. The apprenticeship ended in 1978 with the release of 'Wuthering Heights', inspired by Emily Bronte's novel. It reached UK number 1. An attendant album, *The Kick Inside*, was a further example of her diversity as a songwriter. 'The Man With The Child In His Eyes' was typical of her romantic, sensual style of writing, and provided her with another Top 10 success. Bush consolidated her position with *Lionheart* and during 1979 undertook her first major tour. The live shows were most notable for her mime work and elaborate stage sets. *Kate Bush On Stage* also reachd the Top 10. After guesting on **Peter Gabriel**'s 'Games Without Frontiers', Bush was back in the charts with 'Breathing' and 'Babooshka'. The latter was her most accomplished work since 'Wuthering Heights', with a clever story line and strong vocal. *Never For Ever* entered the UK album charts at number 1 and further hits followed with 'Army Dreamers' and 'December Will Be Magic'. At this point, Bush was still regarded as a mainstream pop artist, although *The Dreaming* suggested a new direction.

A two-year hiatus followed during which Bush perfected work which would elevate her to new heights in the pop pantheon. The pilot single, 'Running Up That Hill' was a dense and intriguing composition. *Hounds Of Love* revealed Bush at the zenith of her powers. Songs such as the eerily moving 'Mother Stands For Comfort' and the dramatic 'Cloudbusting' underlined her strengths, not only as a writer and singer, but as a producer. 'The Ninth Wave', fused Arthurian legend and Jungian psychology in a musical framework, part orchestral and part folk. After a hit duet with Peter Gabriel, 'Don't Give Up', Bush took an extended sabbatical to plot a follow-up album. In 1989, she returned with *The Sensual World*, in which she experimented with various musical forms, including a Bulgarian folk troupe. The instrumentation included uiliean pipes, whips, valiha, celtic harp, tupan and viola. There was even a literary adaptation, with Bush adapting Molly Bloom's soliloquy from James Joyce's *Ulysses* for the enticing 'The Sensual World'. The album attracted the keen attention of the high-brow rock press and Bush found herself celebrated as one of the most adventurous and distinctively original artists of her era. A variety of artists contributed to the enigmatic *The Red Shoes*.

BUTTERFIELD, PAUL

US ARTIST BUTTERFIELD (b. 1942, d. 1987) HELPED SHAPE THE DEVELOPMENT OF BLUES MUSIC PLAYED BY WHITE musicians in the same way that **John Mayall** and Cyril Davies were doing in the UK. He sang, composed and led a series of seminal bands throughout the 60s, but it was his earthy Chicago-style harmonica-playing that gained him attention. **Mike Bloomfield**, Mark Naftalin, **Elvin Bishop**, **David Sanborn** and Nick Gravenites were some of the outstanding musicians that passed through his bands. His performance at the 1965 Newport Folk Festival gave him the distinction of being the man who supported **Bob Dylan**'s musical heresy by going electric. *Better Days* went on the road to a lukewarm response, and during subsequent years he struggled to find success, plagued by ill health. *East-West* remains his best-selling and most acclaimed work, although the rawness of the debut album attracts many critical admirers.

BUTTHOLE SURFERS

FORMERLY KNOWN AS THE ASHTRAY BABY HEADS, THIS MAVERICK QUARTET FROM TEXAS, USA, MADE ITS RECORDING debut in 1983 with a self-titled mini-album. Gibson 'Gibby' Haynes (vocals), Paul Sneef (b. Paul Leary Walthall, guitar) and King Koffey (drums) were initially indebted to the punk/hardcore scene and employed explicit lyrics. Having endured a succession of bass players, including Kramer from Shockabilly and Bongwater, the Buttholes secured the permanent services of Jeff Pinker, alias Tooter, alias Pinkus, in 1985. The Surfers' strongest work appears on *Locust Abortion Technician* and *Hairway To Steven*. *Digital Dump*, a house-music project undertaken by Haynes and Tooter (as 'Jack Officers'), was followed by *pioughd*, which showed their continued ability to enrage and Paul Leary's solo, *The History Of Dogs*. The delay of *Electriclarryland* was as a result of objections received from the estate of Rodgers And Hammerstein when the band wanted to call the album *Oklahoma!*. Tagged as the sickest band in the world, they thrive on their own on-stage obscenities.

BUZZCOCKS

FORMED IN ENGLAND IN 1976, THE GROUP FEATURED PETE SHELLEY (b. PETER MCNEISH, 1955; VOCALS/GUITAR), HOWARD Devoto (b. Howard Trafford; vocals), Steve Diggle (bass) and John Maher (drums). A support spot on the **Sex Pistols**' infamous 'Anarchy' tour prefaced the Buzzcocks' debut recording, *Spiral Scratch*. Devoto left in February 1977, only to resurface later that year with **Magazine**. A reshuffled Buzzcocks, with Shelley taking lead vocal and Garth Davies (later replaced by Steve Garvey) on bass, won a contract with United Artists. They recorded some of the finest pop-punk singles of their era, including 'Orgasm Addict', 'What Do I Get?', 'Love You More' and 'Ever Fallen In Love (With Someone You Shouldn't've)'. After three albums Shelley quit for a solo career. Steve Diggle re-emerged

with Flag Of Convenience. The group re-formed in 1989, then again in 1990 with former **Smiths** drummer Mike Joyce. For their first major tour since the break-up, Shelley and Diggle were joined by Tony Arber (bass) and Phil Barker (drums). A comeback album (*Trade Test Transmissions*) added to their legacy, although a disappointing live album failed to convince.

BYRDS

ORIGINALLY A TRIO, THE JET SET, THIS US GROUP FEATURED JIM (**ROGER**) **MCGUINN** (b. JAMES JOSEPH McGuinn, 1942; vocals/lead guitar), **Gene Clark** (b. Harold Eugene Clark, 1941, d. 1991; vocals/tambourine/rhythm guitar) and **David Crosby** (b. David Van Cortlandt, 1941; vocals/rhythm guitar). Essentially ex-folkies caught up in the **Beatles** craze, they were signed to a one-off singles contract with Elektra which resulted in the commercially unsuccessful 'Please Let Me Love You' (released as the Beefeaters). By late 1964, the band included bassist Chris Hillman (b. 1942) and drummer Michael Clarke (b. Michael Dick, 1944, d. 1993). Under the supervision of manager/producer Jim Dickson, they recorded, slowly and painfully perfecting their unique brand of folk rock.

In 1964, they signed to CBS Records as the Byrds, assigned to producer Terry Melcher (b. 1942, d. 1991). Their debut, 'Mr Tambourine Man', was a glorious creation, fusing the lyrical genius of **Bob Dylan** with the harmonic and melodious ingenuity of the Beatles. The opening guitar sound, of a Rickenbacker 12-string, has been linked to the Byrds and McGuinn ever since. By 1965, the single had reached US and UK number 1. Their debut album, *Mr Tambourine Man*, was a surprisingly solid work that included four Dylan covers and some exceptionally strong torch songs from Clark. The Byrds then spent months in the studio before releasing their third single, 'Turn! Turn! Turn!' (US number 1). The album of the same name again showed Clark in the ascendant with 'The World Turns All Around Her' and 'Set You Free This Time'. McGuinn's presence was also felt on 'It Won't Be Wrong' and 'He Was A Friend Of Mine' (lyrics pertaining to the Kennedy assassination).

In 1966, the group had parted from Melcher and branched out to embrace raga and jazz. The awesome 'Eight Miles High' effectively elevated them to the artistic level of the Beatles and the **Rolling Stones**, but their commercial standing was blasted by a radio ban alleging that their latest hit was a 'drugs song'. The setback was worsened by Clark's abrupt departure. Continuing as a quartet, the Byrds recorded *Fifth Dimension*, a clever amalgam of hard, psychedelic-tinged pop and rich folk rock orchestration. Their chart fortunes were already waning by this time and neither the quizzically philosophical '5-D (Fifth Dimension)' nor the catchy 'Mr Spaceman' made much impression.

1967 proved the pivotal year in their career, commencing with 'So You Want To Be A Rock 'N' Roll Star', complete with taped screams from their ill-fated UK tour, and a guest appearance from **Hugh Masekela**. *Younger Than Yesterday* proved their best album yet, ably capturing the diverse songwriting skills of Crosby, McGuinn and Hillman and ranging in material from the raga-tinged 'Mind Gardens' to the country-influenced 'Time Between' and all styles in between. Their creative ascendancy coincided with intense inter-group rivalry, culminating in the dismissal of David Crosby (later of **Crosby, Stills And Nash**). The remaining Byrds recruited former colleague Gene Clark, who lasted a mere three weeks. Drummer Michael Clarke was dismissed soon afterwards, leaving McGuinn and Hillman to assemble the stupendous *The Notorious Byrd Brothers*. For this album, the Byrds used recording studio facilities to remarkable effect, employing phasing, close microphone technique and various sonic experiments to achieve the sound they desired. Producer Gary Usher who worked on this and their previous album contributed significantly towards their ascension as one of rock's most adventurous and innovative bands. Successful readings of **Gerry Goffin** and **Carole King**'s 'Goin' Back' and 'Wasn't Born To Follow' were placed alongside Byrds originals such as 'Dolphin's Smile', 'Tribal Gathering' and 'Draft Morning'.

In 1968, Hillman's cousin Kevin Kelley took over on drums and **Gram Parsons** added musical weight as singer/composer/guitarist. Under Parsons' guidance, the group plunged headlong into country, recording the much-acclaimed *Sweetheart Of The Rodeo*. A perfectly timed reaction to the psychedelic excesses of 1967, the album pre-dated Dylan's *Nashville Skyline* by a year and is generally accepted as the harbinger of country rock. However, sales were poor and further conflict ensued when Parsons dramatically resigned on the eve of their ill-advised South Africa tour in 1968.

Late 1968 saw the group at their lowest ebb, with Hillman quitting after a dispute with new manager Larry Spector. The embittered bassist soon reunited with Parsons in the **Flying Burrito Brothers**. McGuinn, meanwhile, assumed total control of the Byrds and assembled an entirely new line-up: Clarence White (vocals/guitar), John York (vocals/bass) and Gene Parsons (vocals/drums). This new phase began promisingly with 'Bad Night At The Whiskey', backed by the McGuinn/Gram Parsons song 'Drug Store Truck Driving Man'. York contributed to two albums, *Dr Byrds & Mr Hyde* and *Ballad Of Easy Rider*, before being replaced by Skip Battin. This unlikely but stable line-up lasted from 1969-72 and re-established the Byrds' reputation with the hit 'Chestnut Mare' and the bestselling (*Untitled*). After three successive albums with their first producer Melcher, they again severed their connections with him and hurriedly attempted to record a compensatory work, *Farther Along* – it only served to emphasize their disunity. McGuinn eventually dissolved the group after agreeing to participate in a recorded reunion of the original Byrds for Asylum Records. Released in 1973, *Byrds*, on which they attempted **Neil Young**'s 'Cowgirl In The Sand' and **Joni Mitchell**'s 'For Free',

received mixed reviews and the group re-splintered. That same year tragedy struck when Clarence White was killed by a drunken driver and, less than three months later, Gram Parsons died from a drug overdose.

By the 80s, the individual members were either recording for small labels or touring without a record contract. Crosby, meanwhile, had plummeted into a narcotic netherworld and into prison. He emerged re-formed and enthusiastic, and set about resurrecting the Byrds with McGuinn and Hillman. A five-way reunion of the Byrds, for a live album and world tour, was proposed, but the old conflicts frustrated it. However, McGuinn, Crosby and Hillman completed four songs in 1990, which were subsequently included on a boxed set featuring 90 songs. The group were each inducted into the rock 'n' roll Hall of Fame in 1991. The chance of playing together again finally elapsed with the deaths of Gene Clark later that year and Michael Clarke in 1993.

BYRNE, DAVID

BYRNE (b. 1952) WAS BORN IN SCOTLAND BUT RAISED IN THE US. HE FORMED **TALKING HEADS** WITH TWO FELLOW students; they evolved from New York's punk milieu into one of America's leading attractions. *My Life In The Bush Of Ghosts*, a collaboration with **Brian Eno**, was widely praised by critics for its adventurous blend of sound collages, ethnic influences and vibrant percussion, which contrasted with Byrne's ensuing solo album, *The Catherine Wheel*. The soundtrack to Twyla Tharp's modern ballet, this set was the prelude to an intensive period in the parent group's career, following which Byrne began composing and scripting a feature film. *True Stories*, which Byrne directed and starred in, was the subject of an attendant Talking Heads album.

The Knee Plays, on which David worked with playwright Robert Wilson, confirmed interests emphasized in 1987 by his collaboration with Ryuichi Sakamoto and Cong Su on the soundtrack for Bertolucci's *The Last Emperor*. Byrne continued recording with his group, but by the end of the 80s intimated a reluctance to appear live with them. Instead he assembled a 14-strong Latin-American ensemble which toured the USA, Canada, Europe and Japan to promote *Rei Momo*. *The Forest* included European orchestral music, while his Luaka Bop label served as an outlet for a series of world music albums with a pop edge, including several devoted to Brazilian recordings.

Collaborators
Sex Pistols » p.292
Connections
Magazine » p.222
Smiths » p.301
Further References
Videos: *Auf Wiedersehen* (Ikon Video 1989)
Playback (IRS 1992)
Book: *Buzzcocks: The Complete History*, Tony McGartland

BYRDS
Albums
Mr Tambourine Man (Columbia 1965)★★★★
Younger Than Yesterday (Columbia 1967)★★★★★
The Notorious Byrd Brothers (Columbia 1968)★★★★★
» p.355 for full listings

Collaborators
Hugh Masekela » p.227
Gram Parsons » p.256
Connections
Beatles » p.38
Rolling Stones » p.281
Crosby, Stills And Nash » p.106
Gerry Goffin » p.161
Flying Burrito Brothers » p.148
Influences
Bob Dylan » p.128
Neil Young » p.346
Joni Mitchell » p.235
Further References
Books: *Timeless Flight: The Definitive Biography Of The Byrds*, Johnny Rogan
The Byrds, Bud Scoppa
Timeless Flight Revisited, Johnny Rogan

BYRNE, DAVID
Albums
with Brian Eno *My Life In The Bush Of Ghosts* (Polydor 1981)★★★★
The Complete Score From The Broadway Production Of The Catherine Wheel soundtrack (Sire 1981)★★★★
Feelings (Warners 1997)★★★
» p.355 for full listings
Collaborators
Brian Eno » p.136
Connections
Talking Heads » p.316
Further References
Video: *True Stories* (1986)
Books: *American Originals: David Byrne*, John Howell
Strange Ritual: Pictures And Words, David Byrne

CABARET VOLTAIRE
Albums
Red Mecca (Rough Trade 1981)★★★
➽ p.358 for full listings
Connections
Soft Cell ➽ p.302
Influences
Can ➽ p.79
Brian Eno ➽ p.136
Further References
Video: *TV Wipeout* (1984)

CAGE, JOHN
Albums
Sonata And Interlude For Prepared Piano (1976)★★★★
➽ p.358 for full listings
Influences
Edgar Varese
Further References
Book: *For The Birds*, John Cage and Daniel Charles

CALE, J. J.
Albums
Naturally (Shelter 1971)★★★
➽ p.358 for full listings
Collaborators
Roger Tillison
Connections
Area Code 615
Little Feat ➽ p.216
Influences
Eric Clapton ➽ p.92

CALE, JOHN
Albums
Paris 1919 (Reprise 1973)★★★★
➽ p.358 for full listings
Collaborators
Nick Drake ➽ p.125
Brian Eno ➽ p.136
Kevin Ayers ➽ p.25
Connections
Leonard Bernstein
Dream Syndicate ➽ p.125
Velvet Underground ➽ p.329
Nico ➽ p.247
Stooges ➽ p.311
Little Feat ➽ p.216
Patti Smith ➽ p.301
Influences
Lou Reed ➽ p.274
Andy Warhol ➽ p.329
Further References
Video: *Songs For Drella* (Warner Music Video 1991)

CAMEL
Albums
The Snow Goose (Decca 1975)★★★
➽ p.358 for full listings
Connections
Them ➽ p.319
Caravan ➽ p.81
Influences
Peter Frampton ➽ p.152
Further References
Video: *Pressure Points (Camel Live)* (Polygram Music Video 1984).

CABARET VOLTAIRE

EXPERIMENTAL, INNOVATIVE, ELECTRONIC-DANCE GROUP FORMED IN SHEFFIELD, ENGLAND, IN 1974. STEPHEN Mallinder (bass/vocals), Richard H. Kirk (guitar/wind instruments) and Chris Watson (electronics/tapes) strove to avoid the confines of traditional pop music and their early appearances veered towards performance art. They contributed two tracks to Factory Records' 1978 double EP, *A Factory Sample* before signing to Rough Trade Records for the *Extended Play* EP. 'Nag, Nag, Nag' (1979) was a head-on rush of distorted guitar with a driving beat and the trio started to use sampled 'noise', cut-up techniques and tape loops.

Watson left in 1981 and, in 1982, Eric Random (guitar) was recruited for a Solidarity benefit concert, performing as the Pressure Company. The resulting album was *Live In Sheffield 19 January 1982*. 1982 also saw the release of *2 x 45*, 'Temperature Drop', the Japanese live album *Hai!* and Mallinder's solo set, *Pow Wow*. After leaving Rough Trade in 1983, while also releasing 'Fools Game' on Les Disques du Crépescule and 'Yashar' on Factory, the group signed a joint contract with Some Bizzare/Virgin Records. 'Just Fascination' and 'The Crackdown' featured Dave Ball (keyboards; **Soft Cell**). In 1984, 'Sensoria' ripped the dance charts apart, setting the tone for much of Caberet Voltaire's subsequent work.

By 1987, they had transferred to EMI/Parlophone Records, releasing 'Don't Argue', 'Here To Go' and 'Code' – introducing a more commercial dance slant, lacking the earlier, experimental approach. In 1988, Mallinder collaborated with Ball and Mark Brydon, in Love Street, releasing 'Galaxy'. Leaving EMI, Cabaret Voltaire returned to Les Disques du Crépescule for 'What Is Real' (1991) and the well-received *Body And Soul*. *International Language* and *The Conversation* were more minimalist.

CAGE, JOHN

US-BORN CAGE (b. 1912, d. 1992) WAS AN *AVANT-GARDE* COMPOSER AND EXPERIMENTAL MUSICIAN, AS WELL AS A POET, teacher, writer, commercial artist and lecturer. After studying with Arnold Schoenberg and Adolph Weiss in the 30s, he moved on to his own compositions, heavily influenced by the work of Edgar Varese. By his twenties he was a leading exponent of the *musique concrete* movement that combined electronics with traditional sounds and led to the development of the synthesizer. His 'utilized sounds' included doors slamming, pouring water and radio static. His most famous piece of music is '4 minutes 33 seconds', which consists entirely of silence (barring natural environmental sounds), to this Cage encouraged performers to add their own artistic input.

CALE, J. J.

US ARTIST CALE (b. JEAN JACQUES CALE, 1938) BEGAN PLAYING GUITAR professionally in a 50s western swing group. With the advent of rock 'n' roll, he led Johnnie Cale And The Valentines, before attempting a career in country music. Cale then played in a variety of bar bands, worked as a studio engineer and recorded several singles before collaborating with songwriter Roger Tillison on a psychedelic album, *A Trip Down Sunset Strip*.

In 1967, **Eric Clapton** recorded Cale's 'After Midnight', this led to Cale being signed to record *Naturally*, including 'Crazy Mama' (US Top 30). His laconic, almost lachrymose, delivery became a trademark, alongside sympathetic support from David Briggs (keyboards), Norbert Putnam (bass) and Tim Drummond (drums). *Really* confirmed the high quality of the artist's compositions, but *Okie* and *Troubadour* lacked *Really*'s immediacy. *Troubadour* contained Cale's own version of 'Cocaine', another song popularized by Clapton. Despite the inclusion of the popular 'Money Talks', his two Phonogram albums, *Grasshopper* and *8*, were unsuccessful.

Cale re-emerged in 1989 with *Travel Log*; on it his guitar style retained its rhythmic, yet relaxed pulse. *Closer To You* (featuring ex-**Little Feat** keyboardist Bill Payne) and *Guitar Man* were more of the same with faultless musical support.

CALE, JOHN

WELSH-BORN CALE (b. 1940) WAS A STUDENT OF VIOLA AND KEYBOARDS WHEN HE WAS INTRODUCED TO ELECTRONIC music. After moving to New York, he joined the Dream Syndicate, an *avant-garde* ensemble. Cale also began playing rock and met **Lou Reed**; the group they formed together became the **Velvet Underground**. Cale remained with them until 1968.

Cale produced albums for **Nico** and for the **Stooges**, before embarking on a solo career with *Vintage Violence*. Those anticipating a radical set were pleasantly surprised by its melodic flair. *Church Of Anthrax*, a pairing with Terry Riley, and the imaginative *The Academy In Peril*, reaffirmed his experimental reputation. He assembled a backing band that included **Little Feat** members Lowell George and Richard Hayward; they recorded *Paris 1919*. Cameos on albums by **Nick Drake** and Mike Heron preceded *Fear*, which featured **Brian Eno**, the latter also contributed to *Slow Dazzle* and appeared with Cale, Nico and **Kevin Ayers** on *June 1 1974*.

The disappointing *Helen Of Troy* was balanced by Cale's strong production on **Patti Smith**'s *Horses*. *Music For A New Society* marked a renewed sense of adventure, adeptly combining the popular and cerebral. Cale continued to offer innovative music and *Words For The Dying* matched his initial work for purpose and imagination. *Songs For Drella*, a 1990 collaboration with Lou Reed as a tribute to Andy Warhol, was lauded by critics and audiences alike. Cale was part of the Velvet Underground reunion in 1993 but old wounds between himself and Reed re-opened, and Cale was soon back to recording idiosyncratic solo albums. During the 90s he continued touring with excellent backing musicians.

CAMEL

FORMED IN THE UK IN 1972, CAMEL FEATURED DOUG FERGUSON (b. 1947; BASS), ANDY WARD (b. 1952; DRUMS), Andy Latimer (b. 1947; guitar/flute/vocals) and **Peter Bardens** (b. 1945; keyboards; ex-**Them**). Bardens dominated the group's sound to the extent that it came to be known as Peter Bardens' Camel. An adaptation of *The Snow Goose* reached the UK Top 30, however after *Moonmadness* Ferguson departed, replaced by Richard Sinclair (ex-**Caravan**). They consolidated their position with the Top 30 *Rain Dances* and *Breathless* before Bardens' replacement, Jan Schelhaas (ex-Caravan), left room for lighter song structures typified on *The Single Factor*. The group continued to record and perform into the 80s when the final line-up – Latimer, Ton Scherpenzeel (keyboards), Christopher Rainbow (vocals), Paul Burgess (drums) and Colin Bass (bass) – closed proceedings with the live set, *Pressure Points*. *Never Let Go* was recorded during their 20th anniversary tour.

CAMEO

US SOUL/FUNK GROUP (ORIGINALLY THE NEW YORK CITY PLAYERS) FORMED IN 1974. LARRY 'MR. B' BLACKMON (drums/vocals/production) and vocalists Thomas Jenkins and Nathan Leftenant recorded their debut, *Cardiac Arrest* with various backing musicians. Subsequent albums gained modest positions in the US pop chart. In 1984, 'She's Strange' gave Cameo their first UK Top 40 pop single. After the success of 1985's 'Single Life' (UK Top 20), 'She's Strange' was remixed and peaked at number 22. In 1986, 'Word Up' reached UK number 3 and US number 6.

By the 90s, their commercial success had dramatically waned and Jenkins left in 1992.

CAMPBELL, GLEN

US-BORN CAMPBELL (b. 1936) FORMED GLEN CAMPBELL AND THE WESTERN WRANGLERS IN 1958. AFTER BRIEFLY joining the **Champs**, he released a solo single, 'Too Late To Worry – Too Blue To Cry', which crept into the US charts. He then took on the arduous – and brief – task of replacing **Brian Wilson** on touring commitments with the **Beach Boys**, but he soon returned to session work and recording, enjoying a minor hit with **Buffy Sainte-Marie**'s 'The Universal Soldier'.

By 1967, his solo career was taking off and his version of 'Gentle On My Mind' won a Grammy for Best Country 'n' Western Recording of 1967. Campbell's finest work was recorded during the late 60s, most notably a superb trilogy of hits written by **Jim Webb**: 'By The Time I Get To Phoenix', 'Wichita Lineman' and 'Galveston'. Campbell also began acting, starring with John Wayne in the film *True Grit* (1969). He recorded duets with country singer Bobbie Gentry, including a hit revival of the **Everly Brothers**' 'All I Have To Do Is Dream'. Further hits included 'Honey Come Back', 'It's Only Make Believe' and 'Dream Baby', followed by a film appearance in *Norwood* (1970) and a duet album with Anne Murray. His first US number 1 was 'Rhinestone Cowboy'; the second was with a version of **Allan Toussaint**'s 'Southern Nights'. Numerous hit compilations followed and Campbell duetted with **Rita Coolidge** and Tanya Tucker. In 1988, Campbell returned to Jim Webb for the title track to *Still Within The Sound Of My Voice*.

CAMPER VAN BEETHOVEN

WITTY GARAGE ROCK BAND FORMED IN CALIFORNIA, USA, IN 1983. BY 1987 THE LINE-UP FEATURED DAVID LOWERY (b. 1960; vocals/guitar), Greg Lisher (guitar), Chris Pederson (drums), Jonathan Segal (violin) and Victor Krummenacher (bass). *Telephone Free Landslide Victory* contained the single 'Take The Skinheads Bowling'. The anagrammatic *Vampire Can Mating Oven* signalled their last Rough Trade release before a move to Virgin. *Our Beloved Revolutionary Sweetheart* was produced by Dennis Herring.

When the group folded, Lisher, Krummenacher, Pederson and guitarist David Immerglück formed Monks Of Doom, Jonathan Segal released a solo album and David Lowery formed **Cracker**.

CAN

EXPERIMENTAL GERMAN UNIT FOUNDED BY TWO CLASSICAL MUSIC STUDENTS, IRMIN SCHMIDT (b. 1937; KEYBOARDS) and Holger Czukay (b. 1938; bass). Michael Karoli (b. 1948; guitar), Jaki Liebezeit (b. 1938; drums) and David Johnson (flute; departed in 1968) joined later, as did American vocalist Malcolm Mooney. *Monster Movie* introduced many of Can's subsequent trademarks: Schmidt's choppy, percussive keyboard style, Karoli's incisive guitar and the relentless, hypnotic pulse of its rhythm section. The group completed several other masters, later to appear on *Can Soundtracks* and *Delay 1968*, prior to the departure of Mooney. He was replaced by Japanese vocalist Kenji 'Damo' Suzuki (b. 1950). *Tago Mago*, a sprawling, experimental double set, followed. Can also began exploring a more precise, even ambient direction on *Ege Bamyasi* and *Future Days*. Suzuki left in 1973.

In 1976, the group hit the UK Top 30 with 'I Want More'. Can was later augmented by Rosko Gee (bass; ex-**Traffic**) and Reebop Kwaku Baah (percussion; ex-Traffic), but the departure of Czukay signalled their demise. The group completed *Out Of Reach* without him, but the bassist returned to edit their next release, *Can*. The unit dissolved in 1978. A re-formed Can, complete with Mooney, returned in 1987 with *Rite Time*.

CANDLEBOX

CALIFORNIAN BAND CANDLEBOX – KEVIN MARTIN (VOCALS), PETER KLETT (GUITAR), BARDI MARTIN (BASS) AND SCOTT Mercado (drums) – signed to **Madonna**'s Maverick label. 'Far Behind' and 'You' were hits and *Candlebox* sold three million copies in the USA alone. The album was a mixture of traditional pop-metal and Seattle-styled grunge. *Lucy* was a major disappointment.

CANNED HEAT

BLUES/ROCK GROUP FORMED IN LOS ANGELES IN 1965 BY ALAN WILSON (b. 1943, d. 1970; VOCALS/HARMONICA/ guitar) and Bob 'The Bear' Hite (b. 1943, d. 1981; vocals). They were joined by Frank Cook (drums), Henry Vestine (b. 1944, d. 1997; guitar; ex-**Mothers Of Invention**) and Larry Taylor (bass; ex-**Jerry Lee Lewis**, **Monkees**). Canned Heat's debut album was promising rather than inspired, but the arrival of Mexican drummer Alfredo Fito (b. Adolfo De La Parra, 1946) brought a new-found confidence, displayed on *Boogie With Canned Heat*; the set included a remake of Jim Oden's 'On The Road Again' (UK Top 10/US Top 20, 1968). A double album, *Livin' The Blues*, included a version of Charley Patton's 'Pony Blues' and a 19-minute *tour de force*, 'Parthenogenesis', which charted in the US and UK.

In 1969 and 1970, Canned Heat recorded four more albums, including a collaboration with **John Lee Hooker**, and released a documentary of their 1970 European tour. Vestine left, replaced by Harvey Mandel and the reshaped band enjoyed UK hits with a cover of **Wilbert Harrison**'s 'Let's Work Together' (number 2) and the cajun-inspired 'Sugar Bee'; tragically they were shattered by the suicide of Wilson in 1970.

Taylor and Mandel left to join **John Mayall**; Vestine returned and Antonio De La Barreda became their new bassist. They completed *Historical Figures And Ancient Heads* before Hite's brother Richard replaced Barreda for the *The New Age*. The changes continued throughout the decade, undermining their strength of purpose, although spirits lifted with the release of *Human Condition*. Sadly, in April 1981, following a gig, the gargantuan Hite died of a heart attack. Despite the loss of many key members, the Canned Heat name has survived. Larry Taylor and Fito De La Parra now pursue the nostalgia circuit with various former members.

CAMEO
Albums
Single Life (Atlanta Artists 1985)★★★★
➧ p.355 for full listings
Connections
New York City Players

CAMPBELL, GLEN
Albums
It's The World Gone Crazy (Capitol 1981)★★★★
➧ p.355 for full listings
Collaborators
Beach Boys ➧ p.36
Bobbie Gentry
Rita Coolidge ➧ p.100
Tanya Tucker
Connections
Glen Campbell And The Western Wranglers ➧ p.79
Champs ➧ p.86
Brian Wilson ➧ p.340
Buffy Sainte-Marie ➧ p.288
Jim Webb ➧ p.335
John Wayne
Influences
Everly Brothers ➧ p.139
Allan Toussaint ➧ p.323
Further References
Video: *Glen Campbell* (Castle Music Pictures 1991)
Book: *Rhinestone Cowboy: An Autobiography*, Glen Campbell with Tom Carter

CAMPER VAN BEETHOVEN
Albums
Our Beloved Revolutionary Sweetheart (Virgin 1988)★★★★
➧ p.355 for full listings
Connections
Cracker ➧ p.102

CAN
Albums
Monster Movie (United Artists 1969)★★★★
➧ p.355 for full listings
Collaborators
Peter Gilmore
Connections
Traffic ➧ p.323
David Sylvian ➧ p.197
Eurythmics ➧ p.139

CANDLEBOX
Albums
Candlebox (Maverick/ Warners 1994)★★★★
➧ p.355 for full listings
Connections
Madonna ➧ p.222

CANNED HEAT
Albums
Hallelujah (Liberty 1969)★★★★
➧ p.355 for full listings
Collaborators
John Lee Hooker ➧ p.185
Connections
Mothers Of Invention ➧ p.239
Jerry Lee Lewis ➧ p.215
Monkees ➧ p.236
John Mayall ➧ p.228

CANNON, FREDDY
Albums
The Explosive! Freddy Cannon (Swan/Top Rank 1960)★★★★
➽ p.355 for full listings
Collaborators
G-Clefs ➽ p.151
Connections
Dion ➽ p.119
Belmonts ➽ p.119

CAPALDI, JIM
Albums
Short Cut Draw Blood (Island 1975)★★★★
➽ p.355 for full listings
Connections
Dave Mason ➽ p.227
Traffic ➽ p.323
Space Cadets
Influences
Steve Winwood ➽ p.341
Boudleaux Bryant ➽ p.71
Eagles ➽ p.130
Further References
Book: *Keep On Running: The Steve Winwood Story*, Chris Welch

CAPITOLS
Albums
We Got A Thing That's In The Groove (Atco 1966)★★
➽ p.355 for full listings

CAPLETON
Albums
Gold (Charm 1991)★★★★
➽ p.355 for full listings
Connections
Pan Head

CAPRIS (60S)
Albums
There's A Moon Out Again (Ambient Sound 1982) re-released as *Morse Code Of Love* (Collectables 1992)★★
➽ p.355 for full listings

CAPTAIN AND TENNILLE
Albums
Love Will Keep Us Together (A&M 1975)★★★
➽ p.355 for full listings
Collaborators
Beach Boys ➽ p.36
Influences
Neil Sedaka ➽ p.291
Further References
Book: *Captain And Tennille*, James Spada

CAPTAIN BEEFHEART
Albums
Trout Mask Replica (1969)★★★★★
➽ p.355 for full listings
Connections
Mothers Of Invention ➽ p.239
Influences
Frank Zappa ➽ p.348
Further References
Book: *Captain Beefheart: The Man And His Music*, Colin David Webb

CANNON, FREDDY

US-BORN CANNON (b. FREDDY PICARIELLO, 1940) FRONTED FREDDY KARMON AND THE HURRICANES AND PLAYED guitar on sessions for the **G-Clefs**. 'Tallahassee Lassie' (1959) was released on Swan, a label part-owned by Dick Clark, who often featured Cannon on his US *Bandstand* television programme and road shows. The single was the first of Cannon's 21 US hits over seven years; these included 'Way Down Yonder In New Orleans' (1959) and 'Palisades Park' (1962). *The Explosive! Freddy Cannon* (1960) was the first rock album to top the UK charts.

He returned briefly to the charts in 1981 in the company of the **Belmonts**, with 'Let's Put The Fun Back Into Rock 'N' Roll'.

CAPALDI, JIM

ENGLISH MUSICIAN CAPALDI (b. 1944; VOCALS/PIANO/ DRUMS) WAS PART OF **TRAFFIC** BEFORE RELEASING A US-charting solo album, *Oh How We Danced*. He continued to record albums at regular intervals. *Short Cut Draw Blood* proved his finest work, containing two hits: 'It's All Up To You' and **Boudleaux Bryant**'s 'Love Hurts'. He toured with his band, the Space Cadets, in 1976.

In 1989, he returned with *Some Came Running*, contributed to **Steve Winwood**'s multi-million selling *Roll With It* and *Refugees Of The Heart*, and co-wrote the US hit 'One And Only Man'. In 1994, Traffic re-formed for a major world tour and album *Far From Home* and in 1996, Capaldi won a BMI Award for 'Love Will Keep Us Alive', co-written with Peter Vale and recorded by the **Eagles**. He also contributed to Winwood's *Junction 7*.

CAPITOLS

US R&B TRIO ORIGINALLY KNOWN AS THE THREE CAPS, FORMED AROUND 1962. DONALD STORBALL (GUITAR/VOCALS) and Samuel George (d. 1982; drums/lead vocals) were discovered by record producer Ollie McLaughlin, but their first single, 'Dog And Cat', failed to have any impact. Four years later, Storball and George recruited Richard McDougall (vocals/piano) and recorded the soulful dance number 'Cool Jerk', which reached the US Top 10. Unable to produce a successful follow-up, the group disbanded in 1969. George was fatally stabbed in 1982.

CAPLETON

JAMIACAN-BORN REGGAE ARTIST CAPLETON (b. CLIFTON BAILEY) HAD HIS FIRST BIG HIT WITH 'NUMBER ONE (ON THE Good Look Chart)' (1990). In 1991, many of his recordings were compiled on *Capleton Gold*, he voiced half an album for Gussie P, joined Johnny Osbourne on 'Special Guest' and duetted with Bobby Zarro on 'Young, Fresh And Green'. In December he visited the UK with the late Pan Head, courting controversy over a shooting incident at one London venue, and recording 'Dance Can't Done'.

1992's 'Armshouse' was a stirring call for unification within music. The singles 'F.C.T.', 'Matey A Dead', 'Make Hay' and 'Unno Hear' were followed by 'Everybody Needs Somebody' and 'Mankind' among others, maintaining his growing reputation. In 1994, he recorded with Brian and Tony Gold and Nadine Sutherland, and worked with Gussie Clarke.

CAPRIS (60S)

FORMED IN NEW YORK IN 1958, THE CAPRIS FEATURED NICK SANTAMARIA (LEAD VOCALS), MIKE MINCELLI (FIRST TENOR), Vinny Nacardo (second tenor), Frank Reins (baritone) and John Apostol (bass). They were best known for the doo-wop ballad 'There's A Moon Out Tonight' (1961, US number 3). The group never had another hit, but have stayed together. In 1982, they recorded an album that included an update of their hit.

CAPTAIN AND TENNILLE

US-BORN TONI TENNILLE (b. 1943) CO-WROTE THE 1972 rock musical Mother Earth. When it was staged in Los Angeles, the house band included Daryl Dragon (b. 1942; keyboards). Tennille and Dragon then toured with the **Beach Boys**' backing group before writing and producing 'The Way I Want To Touch You'. Their first hit was 'Love Will Keep Us Together' (1975), a **Neil Sedaka** composition which established them as a close harmony favourite. It sold a million copies, as did 'Lonely Night (Angel Face)'and 'Muskrat Love'. 'You Never Done It Like That' (1978) reached the Top 10 before 'Do That To Me One More Time' reached US number 1. Tennille later made solo albums of standard ballads. A reunited pair issued *Twenty Years Of Romance* in 1995.

CAPTAIN BEEFHEART

CALIFORNIAN CAPTAIN BEEFHEART (b. DON VAN VLIET, 1941) SHARED AN INTEREST IN R&B WITH **FRANK ZAPPA**. An attempt to form a band together failed, but Zappa (and members of the **Mothers Of Invention**) reappeared frequently during Beefheart's career. The first Magic Band was formed in 1964, featuring Beefheart, Alex St. Clair Snouffer (guitar), Doug Moon (guitar), Paul Blakely (drums) and Jerry Handley (bass), unfortunately ensuing singles failed.

Beefheart reappeared with *Safe As Milk*, *Strictly Personal* and *Trout Mask Replica*, with which he reached his peak. Crudely recorded by Zappa, it contained a wealth of bizarre pieces, with Beefheart using his octave range to great effect. The definitive Magic Band were present on this record: Mascara Snake (unidentified, reputedly Beefheart's cousin), Antennae Jimmy Semens (Jeff Cotton), Drumbo (John French), Zoot Horn Rollo (Bill Harkelroad) and Rockette Morton (Mark Boston). Reportedly the band recorded and played most of the tracks in one studio, while Beefheart added his lyrics in another. A similar theme was adopted for *Lick My Decals Off, Baby* and *Spotlight Kid*, although the latter had a more structured musical format.

Beefheart also contributed vocals to 'Willie The Pimp' on Zappa's *Hot Rats*. Following *Clear Spot* and a heavy touring schedule, the Magic Band split from Beefheart to form Mallard. Beefheart signed to the UK's Virgin Records, releasing two albums, including the critically acclaimed *Unconditionally Guaranteed*. In 1975, Beefheart and Zappa released *Bongo Fury*, a live set recorded in Texas.

In latter years, Beefheart has toured and recorded only occasionally and since 1982, there have been no new recordings. Don Van Vliet is now a respected artist and sculptor. In 1993, it was alleged that he was suffering from multiple sclerosis.

CAPTAIN SENSIBLE

TOGETHER WITH DAVE VANIAN, BRIAN JAMES AND CHRIS MILLER (RAT SCABIES), CAPTAIN SENSIBLE (b. RAYMOND Burns, 1954) formed the **Damned**. A riotous character with an unnerving sense of charm, Sensible performed at gigs dressed in various guises. The Damned were frequently inactive and Sensible formed King with ex-**Chelsea** bassist Henry Badowski – the group lasted three months. He then recorded 'Jet Boy Jet Girl' with the Softies and performed on Johnny Moped's *Cycledelic*, followed by *This Is Your Captain Speaking*. With fellow Damned member Paul Gray, he produced the Dolly Mixtures' 'Been Teen' and 'Everything And More'.

Signed by A&M as a solo act, he recorded a cover version of Rodgers and Hammerstein's 'Happy Talk' (1982) – the single shot to UK number 1. He subsequently released two albums in close collaboration with lyricist **Robyn Hitchcock**, and had further hits with 'Wot' and 'Glad It's All Over'. He left the Damned in 1984. 'Wot, No Meat?' (1985), with girlfriend Rachel Bor, emphasized his commitment to vegetarianism.

Revolution Now was critically panned, but *Live At The Milky Way* was better received. Sensible also played bass in the psychedelically inclined The Space Toad Experience, who released *Time Machine* (1996). He re-formed the Damned in 1996.

CARAVAN

FORMED IN CANTERBURY, ENGLAND, IN 1968. PYE HASTINGS (b. 1947; GUITAR/VOCALS), DAVID SINCLAIR (b. 1947; KEYboards), Richard Sinclair (b. 1948; bass/vocals) and Richard Coughlan (b. 1947; drums) debuted with *If I Could Do It All Over Again, I'd Do It All Over You*, but it was not until *In The Land Of Grey And Pink* that they achieved commercial plaudits. Dave Sinclair then joined **Matching Mole**, replaced by Steve Miller for *Waterloo Lily*. Richard Sinclair left for **Hatfield And The North**, before David returned to a line-up of Hastings, Coughlan, John Perry (b. 1947; guitar) and Geoff Richardson (b. 1950; viola/violin). A rigorous touring schedule was punctuated by *For Girls Who Go Plump In The Night* and *Symphonia*, but further personnel changes undermined the group's early charm. Although *Cunning Stunts* provided a surprise US chart entry, Caravan were increasingly confined to a rock backwater. Hastings continued to lead the group into the 80s and the original quartet reunited for *Back To Front*. A new album was issued in 1995; it was particularly successful in Japan.

CARDIGANS

SWEDISH BAND FEATURING BENGT LAGERBERG (DRUMS), PETER SVENSSON (guitar), Lars Olof Johansson (keyboards), Nina Persson (vocals) and Magnus Sveningsson (bass). *Emmerdale* featured delicate, intricate melodies; *Life* included a cover of 'Sabbath Bloody Sabbath'. Strong media coverage prompted healthy sales in Sweden, the UK and Japan. On *First Band On The Moon*, the strongest material was the straightforward pop of such tracks as 'Been It' and 'Never Recover'. The band enjoyed a huge UK hit in 1997 with the re-released 'Lovefool', featured on the soundtrack to *William Shakespeare's Romeo And Juliet*.

CAREY, MARIAH

US-SINGER CAREY (b. 1970) MET BEN MARGULIES (b. *c.* 1963; KEYBOARDS) while working as an R&B session singer; they became songwriting partners. With Carey writing the melodies and most of the lyrics, and Margulies arranging the songs, they developed a simple blend of soul, gospel and pop. Sony Music's US president Tommy Mottola signed Carey after hearing their demo. Her first single, 'Visions Of Love', was a smash hit and her debut album stayed at US number 1 for 22 weeks.

Carey won 1991 Grammies for Best Female Vocalist and Best New Artist. In five years her albums sold over 30 million copies. *Daydream* sold over 6 million in the USA, within three months of release.

CARLISLE, BELINDA

WHEN THE **GO-GO'S** BROKE UP IN 1985, CARLISLE (b. 1958) WENT SOLO. AFTER THE EXCESSES OF HER FORMER GROUP, she underwent a period of physical recuperation and image remodelling – emerging as the quintessential young Californian. With artistic assistance from Charlotte Caffey (Go-Go's), Carlisle hit the US Top 3 with 'Mad About You' (1986) and her first album reached US number 13. She achieved international acclaim with the infectious 'Heaven Is A Place On Earth'. This winning formula was subsequently used for a string of albums and other chart singles such as 'Circle In The Sand' and 'We Want The Same Thing'. *A Woman And A Man* featured Nick Beggs (ex-**Kajagoogoo**), Susannah Hoffs (ex-**Bangles**) and **Brian Wilson** (ex-**Beach Boys**).

CARLTON, LARRY

US GUITARIST CARLTON (b. 1948) HAS COURTED ROCK, JAZZ AND ACOUSTIC 'NEW AGE'. HE SPENT THE 70S WORKING AS a session musician, he played for **Steely Dan** and on numerous **Joni Mitchell** albums. Moving away from session work, his solo debut appeared in 1978, but it was not until *Sleepwalk* that Carlton was fully accepted as a solo artist. *Alone But Never Alone* proved a critical and commercial success, *Discovery* broadened Carlton's following, while the live *Last Night* saw a return to his jazz roots. With *On Solid Ground*, Carlton demonstrated a stronger rock influence and produced a credible cover of **Eric Clapton**'s 'Layla' and **Steely Dan**'s 'Josie'. He was awarded Grammies in 1981 and 1987 for his version of 'Minute By Minute'. In 1988, Carlton was shot in the neck by an intruder at his studio; luckily he made a full recovery.

CARMEL

UK GROUP FORMED IN 1981 BY CARMEL MCCOURT (b. 1958; VOCALS), JIM PARIS (b. 1957; double bass) and Gerry Darby (b. 1959; drums/percussion). The release of 'Storm' and a mini-album in 1982, drew praise, alternating between soulful ballads, gospel, blues and stomping jazz. Carmel tasted success with the gospel-tinged 'Bad Day', featuring the Attractions' Steve Nieve and the backing vocals of Helen Watson and Rush Winters but *The Drum Is Everything* failed to capture the vitality of the singles.

While the jazz fashion faded in the UK, Carmel found a more appreciative audience in Europe, particularly France. *The Falling* was their most successful studio performance, aided by several producers including **Brian Eno** and Hugh Johns. The group's earlier talent for producing imaginative covers has seen them tackling **Randy Newman**'s 'Mama Told Me Not To Come', Tommy Edwards's 'It's All In The Game' and Duke Ellington's 'Azure'.

CAPTAIN SENSIBLE
Albums
Live At The Milky Way (Humbug 1994)★★★★
➧ p.355 for full listings

Collaborators
Robyn Hitchcock ➧ p.182
Connections
Damned ➧ p.110
Chelsea ➧ p.88

CARAVAN
Albums
Waterloo Lily (Deram 1972)★★★★
➧ p.355 for full listings
Connections
Soft Machine ➧ p.302
Matching Mole ➧ p.227
Hatfield And The North ➧ p.177

CARDIGANS
Albums
First Band On The Moon (Mercury 1996)★★★★
➧ p.355 for full listings

CAREY, MARIAH
Albums
Mariah Carey (1990)★★★
Music Box (Columbia 1993)★★★
➧ p.355 for full listings
Further References
Video: *Mariah Carey* (1994)

CARLISLE, BELINDA
Albums
Heaven On Earth (Virgin 1987)★★★
➧ p.355 for full listings
Connections
Go-Go's ➧ p.160
Kajagoogoo ➧ p.203
Bangles ➧ p.32
Beach Boys ➧ p.36
Further References
Video: *Belinda Live* (1988)

CARLTON, LARRY
Albums
Alone But Never Alone (MCA 1986)★★★★
➧ p.355 for full listings
Collaborators
Steely Dan ➧ p.308
Joni Mitchell ➧ p.235
Influences
Eric Clapton ➧ p.92

CARMEL
Albums
Everybody's Got A Little ... Soul (London 1987)★★★
➧ p.356 for full listings
Influences
Brian Eno ➧ p.136
Randy Newman ➧ p.246
Duke Ellington

CARMEN, ERIC
Albums
Eric Carmen (Arista 1975)★★★
» p.356 for full listings
Connections
Raspberries » p.273

CARNES, KIM
Albums
Mistaken Identity (EMI America 1981)★★★★
» p.356 for full listings
Collaborators
James Ingram » p.192
Lyle Lovett » p.219
Connections
Frank Sinatra
Barbara Streisand
Kenny Rogers » p.280
Influences
Jackie DeShannon » p.116

CARPENTER, MARY-CHAPIN
Albums
Come On, Come On (Columbia 1992)★★★★
Stones In The Road (Columbia 1994)★★★★
» p.356 for full listings
Connections
Joan Baez » p.29
Tom Waits » p.332
Bread » p.67
Influences
John Stewart
Gene Vincent » p.330
Further References
Video: *Shut Up And Kiss Me* (1994), *5* (1994)

CARPENTERS
Albums
Close To You (A&M 1970)★★★★
» p.356 for full listings
Connections
John Bettis
Influences
Herb Alpert
Beatles » p.38
Burt Bacharach » p.27
Hal David » p.27
Marvelettes » p.226
Further References
Video: *Only Yesterday (Richard & Karen Carpenter's Greatest Hits)* (Channel 5 1990)
Book: *The Carpenters: The Untold Story*, Ray Coleman

CARR, JAMES
Albums
You Got My Mind Messed Up (Goldwax 1966)★★★★
» p.356 for full listings
Collaborators
Quinton Claunch
Connections
Sunset Travellers

CARR, VIKKI
Albums
Color Her Great (1963)★★★
The First Time Ever (I Saw Your Face) (1972)★★★
» p.356 for full listings

CARMEN, ERIC

US-BORN CARMEN (b. 1949) FIRST ACHIEVED SUCCESS WITH THE **RASPBERRIES**. HE WROTE AND SANG LEAD ON ALL their US successes: 'Go All The Way', 'I Wanna Be With You' and 'Let's Pretend', and was the sole member to prosper commercially when the group split in 1975.

In 1976, he scored an international hit with 'All By Myself', enjoyed two further US Top 20 entries with 'Never Gonna Fall In Love Again' (1976) and 'Change Of Heart' (1978), and returned to the US Top 10 in 1987 with 'Hungry Eyes' (from the film *Dirty Dancing*). In 1988, 'Make Me Lose Control' reached number 3. Carmen's recent work lacks the panache of his early releases.

CARNES, KIM

GRAVELLY-VOICED, US SINGER CARNES (b. 1945) STARTED OUT WITH THE NEW CHRISTY MINSTRELS IN THE 60S, BEFORE *Kim Carnes* (1975) brought her critical favour. She was also reaping great success as a songwriter with husband Dave Ellington: Frank Sinatra, Barbra Streisand and **Kenny Rogers** all recorded her songs. In 1979, Carnes/Ellington wrote all the material for Rogers' best selling *Gideon*; Rogers also duetted with Carnes on the hit 'Don't Fall In Love With A Dreamer' (1980).

In 1981, Carnes topped the US charts for nine weeks with 'Bette Davis Eyes', winning a Grammy; *Mistaken Identity* also reached US number 1. Subsequent albums have made a respectable showing. During 1984, she had two major hits: 'What About Me' (with Kenny Rogers and **James Ingram**) and 'Make No Mistake, He's Mine' (with Barbra Streisand). *View From The House* included the country hit 'Speed Of The Sound Of Loneliness', featuring **Lyle Lovett**.

CARPENTER, MARY-CHAPIN

BY 1986, CARPENTER (b. 1958) WAS A NEW JERSEY STAR, WINNING FIVE WASHINGTON AREA MUSIC AWARDS WITHOUT having made a record. After signing to a major Nashville label, she attracted cover versions of her songs by artists such as Tony Rice and **Joan Baez**. Carpenter has also recorded cover versions, including 'Downtown Train' (**Tom Waits**) and 'Quittin' Time'(**Bread**) from *State Of The Heart*. In 1991, she made the US country charts with a revival of **Gene Vincent**'s 'Right Now'. Her 1992 hit, 'I Feel Lucky', preceded the release of *Come On, Come On*.

Carpenter's acceptance by a country audience was sealed when she was voted the CMA's Female Vocalist. *Stones In The Road* brought fresh melody to an old and sometimes predictable genre and *A Place In The World* maintained her reputation in the country field, as well as gaining her a mainstream rock audience.

CARPENTERS

AMERICAN BROTHER-AND-SISTER DUO: RICHARD (b. 1946; PIANO) AND KAREN CARPENTER (b. 1950, d. 1983; VOCALS/drums). Richard originally backed Karen, who was signed to the small Magic Lamp label in 1965. After winning a battle of the bands contest at the Hollywood Bowl they signed to RCA, but no material was issued. In 1967, the siblings teamed up with John Bettis in the short-lived Spectrum. A&M president Herb Alpert heard some demos and signed them. In 1969, their debut, *Offering*, was issued, but failed to chart – it took a version of the **Beatles**' 'Ticket To Ride' to set their hit career in motion. A wonderful reading of **Burt Bacharach** and Hal David's 'Close To You', complete with superbly understated piano arrangement, took them to US number 1 and was a worldwide hit. In 1970, they were back at US number 2 with 'We've Only Just Begun'. Throughout 1971, the duo continued with such hits as 'For All We Know', 'Rainy Days And Mondays' and 'Superstar'/'Bless The Beasts And Children'. They also received Grammy Awards for Best New Artist and Best Vocal Performance and launched their own television series.

In 1972-73, 'Goodbye To Love', 'Sing' and 'Yesterday Once More' all reached the US Top 10 and 'Top Of The World' reached number 1. A cover of the **Marvelettes**/Beatles 'Please Mr Postman' brought them back to number 1 in 1974, the same year they played at the White House. There was a noticeable decline in their Top 40 performance during the second half of the 70s, with personal and health problems taking their toll. Richard became addicted to prescription drugs, entering a clinic in 1978 to overcome his addiction. Karen, meanwhile, was suffering from anorexia nervosa.

Karen completed a solo album during 1979 but it was destined to remain unreleased for many years. Thereafter, she reunited with Richard for *Made In America*, and for their final US Top 20 hit with 'Touch Me When We're Dancing'. Tragically, on 4 February 1983, Karen died from anorexia.

CARR, JAMES

MISSISSIPPI-BORN CARR (b. 1942) SANG GOSPEL IN THE SUNSET TRAVELLERS AND THE Harmony Echoes before going solo. It took four singles to define his style, but 'You've Got My Mind Messed Up' burned with an intensity few contemporaries could match. It was followed by 'Love Attack' (1966), 'Pouring Water On A Drowning Man' (1966), 'Dark End Of The Street' (1967) and 'Hold On' (1971). In 1977, he teamed up with former mentor Roosevelt Jamison.

In 1979, Carr toured Japan; unfortunately the first concert was a disaster when he 'froze' on stage. He relaxed on subsequent dates. In 1991, he released an album of new material, *Take Me To The Limit*, with Quinton Claunch and Jamison and, in 1993, he recorded *Soul Survivor*.

CARR, VIKKI

TEXAN-BORN CARR (b. FLORENCIA BISENTA DE CASILLAS MARTINEZ CARDONA, 1941) STARTED SINGING WITH THE 'Irish Mexican' Pepe Callahan Orchestra, teamed up with the Chuck Leonard Quartette and eventually went solo. She was regularly featured as vocalist on the *Ray Anthony Show* in 1962, and enjoyed a much publicized friendship with **Elvis Presley**. Her biggest hit, 'It Must Be Him (Seul Sur Son Etoile)' (1967), sold over a million copies. Follow-up hits in the UK included 'There I Go' and 'With Pen In Hand'. She became a popular MOR concert performer, as demonstrated on the 1969 live album *For Once In My Life*. She also performed live in the White House for Presidents Nixon (1970) and Ford (1974).

Later, she became very involved in charity work, setting up a scholarship fund for Chicano children. Her popularity in the 90s centred on the Latin market, singing in her native language.

CARRACK, PAUL

AFTER **ACE** SPLIT IN 1977, CARRACK (b. 1951; VOCALS/KEYBOARDS) JOINED **FRANKIE MILLER'S** BAND; IN 1978, HE MOVED on to **Roxy Music**, appearing on *Manifesto* and *Flesh And Blood*. After recording *Nightbird*, Carrack joined **Squeeze** as **Jools Holland**'s replacement, appearing on *East Side Story*. He then teamed up with **Nick Lowe**, and released his second solo album, *Suburban Voodoo*, reaching the US Top 40 with 'I Need You'. A regular member of **Eric Clapton**'s band in the mid-80s, he was enlisted as lead singer of **Mike And The Mechanics** in 1985; his distinctive voice was heard on 'Silent Running (On Dangerous Ground)' and 'All I Need Is A Miracle'. In 1987, he had a minor UK hit with 'When You Walk In The Room', followed by 'Don't Shed A Tear' (US Top 10). *Groove Approved* was highly successful in America and, in 1995, *Blue Views* gave him the solo recognition he has long deserved.

CARS

FORMERLY KNOWN AS CAP'N SWING, THIS US GROUP'S STABLE LINE-UP COMPRISED RIC Ocasek (b. Richard Otcasek, 1949; guitar/vocals), Benjamin Orr (b. Benjamin Orzechowski; bass/vocals), Greg Hawkes (keyboards), Elliot Easton (b. Elliot Shapiro, 1953; guitar) and David Robinson (drums). Since their excellent pop/new wave debut, *The Cars*, they have never deviated from writing catchy, well-crafted songs. In 1984, they enjoyed worldwide success with 'Drive'; a year later the song was featured in the Live Aid concert. The band broke up at the end of the 80s in favour of solo work, and Ocasek became busy as a record producer, notably with **Weezer** in 1994.

CARTER, CARLENE

CARLENE CARTER (b. REBECCA CARLENE SMITH, 1955) IS THE DAUGHTER OF COUNTRY SINGERS CARL SMITH AND JUNE Carter. After her parents divorced, Carlene's mother married **Johnny Cash**. Carlene later joined her mother and stepfather on the road and was featured on Cash's *The Junkie And The Juicehead Minus Me*. In 1978, she made an appealing, upbeat rock album with **Graham Parker** And The Rumour, including 'Easy From Now On', recorded by **Emmylou Harris**. Carter struggled with the dance tracks on her second album, *Two Sides To Every Woman*, before releasing *Musical Shapes* – produced by new husband **Nick Lowe**. Her 1981 album, *Blue Nun*, featured members of **Rockpile** and **Squeeze**.

After *C'est Bon* (originally called *Gold Miner's Daughter*) and her marriage break-up, Carter was featured in *Too Drunk To Remember*, a short film shown at the London Film Festival, based on one of her songs. In 1985, she appeared in *Pump Boys And Dinettes*. In 1995, she released *Little Acts Of Treason*, which was comparatively bland.

CARTER USM

FORMED FROM UK GROUP JAMIE WEDNESDAY, JIMBOB (b. JAMES MORRISON, 1960) AND FRUITBAT (b. LESLIE CARTER, 1958) acquired a drum machine and – taking their name from a newspaper cutting – created Carter The Unstoppable Sex Machine. The dance single 'Sheltered Life' made little impression, but the following 'Sheriff Fatman' (1989) was an exciting amalgam of a great riff and strident lyrics. *101 Damnations* was an innovative melting pot of samples, ideas and tunes, shot through with a punk-inspired ethos; 'Rubbish' and 'Anytime, Anyplace, Anywhere' were followed by the controversial 'Bloodsports For All'. *30 Something* reached the UK Top 10, but the Top 20 'After The Watershed' experienced copyright problems relating to the **Rolling Stones**'s 'Ruby Tuesday'.

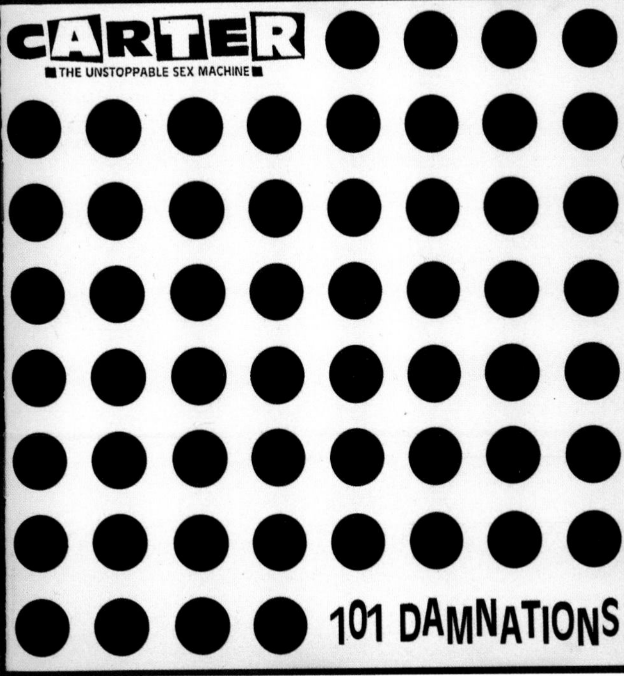

Carter's albums displayed a gradually more sophisticated approach, though the cornerstone of their appeal remained their incisive lyrics and propulsive live shows. They released *Starry Eyed And Bollock Naked*, a collection of b-sides, recruited a full-time drummer, Wez, and played a historic gig in Zagreb, Croatia – the first band to play there since the start of the civil war. Early copies of *Worry Bomb*, included a live recording of the concert. In 1996, Carter recruited Salv (bass; ex-**S*M*A*S*H**), guitarist Steve B. (brother of Wez) and Simon Painter (keyboards; later replaced by Ben). A mini-album was released in 1997.

CARTHY, MARTIN

ENGLISH-BORN CARTHY (b. 1940) STARTED OUT AS AN ACTOR BEFORE BECOMING A SKIFFLE GUITARIST AND SINGER, WITH the Thameside Four, in 1959. Carthy's first solo recording was *Hootenanny In London*, which included 'Your Baby 'As Gone Down The Plug Hole', later revived by **Cream**.

Carthy became resident guitarist at London's top folk club, the Troubadour; where he taught songs to visiting Americans including **Bob Dylan** and **Paul Simon** – they later adapted his 'Lord Franklin' and 'Scarborough Fair'. Carthy and **Leon Rosselson**, recorded as the Three City Four before Martin went solo; *Byker Hill* featured violinist Dave Swarbrick.

From 1969-72, he was a member of **Steeleye Span**, with whom he first played electric guitar, later he joined more traditional vocal group the Watersons, which included his wife Norma Waterson. In the 80s, he toured and recorded with Brass Monkey, took part in concept albums by the **Albion Country Band** and worked in *Transports*, Peter Bellamy's 'folk opera'. In the 90s, he worked with his daughters Eliza and Norma Waterson.

Connections
Pepe Callahan Orchestra
Chuck Leonard Quartette
Ray Anthony Show
Elvis Presley ➧ p.265

CARRACK, PAUL
Albums
Blue Views (IRS 1995)★★★★
➧ p.356 for full listings
Collaborators
Nick Lowe ➧ p.219
Eric Clapton ➧ p.92
Connections
Ace ➧ p.8
Frankie Miller's Band ➧ p.233
Roxy Music ➧ p.283
Squeeze ➧ p.306
Mike and the Mechanics ➧ p.233

CARS
Albums
Heartbeat City (Elektra 1984)★★★★
➧ p.356 for full listings
Connections
Cap'n Swing
Weezer ➧ p.336
Further References
Video: *Heartbeat City* (Warner Music Video 1984)
Book: *The Cars*, Philip Kamin

CARTER, CARLENE
Albums
Little Love Letters (Giant 1993)★★★
➧ p.356 for full listings
Collaborators
Graham Parker And The Rumour ➧ p.256
Connections
Emmylou Harris ➧ p.175
Rockpile ➧ p.280
Squeeze ➧ p.306
Influences
Johnny Cash ➧ p.84
Nick Lowe ➧ p.219
Further References
Video: *Open Fire* (Hendring Video 1990)

CARTER USM
Albums
101 Damnations (Big Cat 1990)★★★★
➧ p.356 for full listings
Connections
S*M*A*S*H ➧ p.300
Further References
Video: *In Bed With Carter* (PMI 1991)

CARTHY, MARTIN
Albums
Landfall (Philips 1971)★★★★
➧ p.356 for full listings
Collaborators
Albion Country Band ➧ p.12
Connections
Cream ➧ p.103
Bob Dylan ➧ p.128
Paul Simon ➧ p.296
Steeleye Span ➧ p.308

CASCADES
Albums
Rhythm Of The Rain (Valiant 1963)★★★
➽ p.356 for full listings
Further References
Film: Catalina Caper (1967)

CASH, JOHNNY
Albums
I Walk The Line (Columbia 1964)★★★★
Johnny Cash At San Quentin (Columbia 1969)★★★★
➽ p.356 for full listings

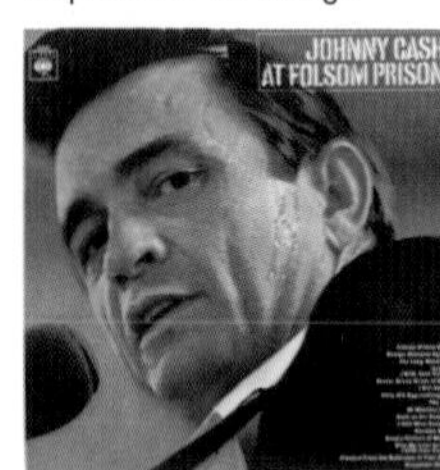

Collaborators
Carl Perkins ➽ p.258
Carter Family ➽ p.83
Emmylou Harris ➽ p.175
Everly Brothers ➽ p.139
Paul McCartney ➽ p.229
Connections
Sam Phillips ➽ p.260
Bob Dylan ➽ p.128
The Evangel Temple Choir
Further References
Video: *Riding The Rails* (Hendring Video 1990)
Book: *A Boy Named Cash*, Albert Govoni

CASH, ROSANNE
Albums
Interiors (Columbia 1990)★★★★
10 Song Demo (Capitol 1996)★★★★
➽ p.356 for full listings
Collaborators
Bobby Bare
Connections
Rodney Crowell ➽ p.107
Emmylou Harris ➽ p.175
Tom Petty ➽ p.260
David Malloy
Influences
Johnny Cash ➽ p.84
Further References
Video: *Live – The Interiors Tour* (1994)
Book: *Bodies Of Water*, Rosanne Cash

CASSIDY, DAVID
Albums
Cherish (Bell 1972)★★
➽ p.356 for full listings
Collaborators
Tim Rice
Andrew Lloyd Webber
George Michael ➽ p.233
Petula Clark ➽ p.93
Connections
Rolling Stone ➽ p.280
Cliff Richard ➽ p.277
Dave Clark ➽ p.111
Willy Russell

CASCADES

FORMED IN THE LATE 50S IN CALIFORNIA, THE CASCADES WERE BEST KNOWN FOR THEIR US NUMBER 3 'RHYTHM OF The Rain' (1963). The group featured John Gummoe (vocals/guitar), Eddy Snyder (piano), Dave Stevens (bass), Dave Wilson (saxophone) and Dave Zabo (drums). Their first single, 'Second Chance', failed but 'Rhythm Of The Rain' became a soft-rock classic. Two more albums recorded in the late 60s failed to revive the group's fortunes and they disbanded in 1969.

CASH, JOHNNY

AFTER A SPELL IN THE US ARMY, CASH (b. 1932) DEVELOPED HIS 'BOOM CHICKA BOOM' SOUND WITH TWO FRIENDS: Luther Perkins (lead guitar) and Marshall Grant (bass). Their first record, 'Hey Porter'/'Cry, Cry, Cry', credited to Johnny Cash And The Tennessee Two, was released in 1955 and reached number 14 on the US country charts. It was followed by 'Folsom Prison Blues'.

Carl Perkins's drummer, W. S. Holland, joined Cash in 1958, resulting in the Tennessee Three. 'I Walk The Line' reached US number 17 and they achieved further pop hits with the 'Ballad Of A Teenage Queen', 'Guess Things Happen That Way' and 'The Ways Of A Woman In Love'. Sun Records launched their first album, *Johnny Cash With His Hot And Blue Guitar*. Cash recalled his Mississippi childhood in songs such as 'Five Foot High And Risin'', 'Pickin' Time' and 'Cisco Clifton's Filling Station'; his cautionary tale, 'Don't Take Your Guns To Town', sold half a million copies. However, Cash's work began to suffer when he started taking hard drugs.

In 1963, Mexican brass was added to the ominous 'Ring Of Fire', the single was another pop hit. Cash's roadshow in the 60s featured Carl Perkins (who played guitar for Cash after Luther Perkins's death), the Statler Brothers and the Carter Family. One night Cash proposed to June Carter on stage; they were married in 1968. Their successful duets include 'Jackson' and 'If I Were A Carpenter'.

In 1968, Columbia released *Johnny Cash At Folsom Prison*, one of the most atmospheric of all live albums. The Folsom Prison concert was followed by one at San Quentin, which was filmed for a television documentary. Shortly afterwards, the humourous 'A Boy Named Sue' gave Cash his only US Top 10 pop hit and reached UK number 4. This popularity brought him his own television series (1969-71), but, despite notable guests such as Bob Dylan, the show was not a great success. Cash has often found strength and comfort in religion and he has recorded many spiritual albums. He justified himself commercially when 'A Thing Called Love', written by Jerry Reed, made with the Evangel Temple Choir, reached UK number 4 in 1972.

Cash made his acting debut in *Five Minutes To Live* (1960) and starred opposite Kirk Douglas in *A Gunfight* (1972). In 1986, he released the whimsical 'The Night Hank Williams Came To Town'. In 1988, he made *Water From The Wells Of Home*, with **Emmylou Harris**, the **Everly Brothers** and **Paul McCartney** among others; his 60s composition 'Tennessee Flat-Top Box' became a US country number 1 for daughter **Rosanne**; and various UK modern folk artists recorded an album of his songs *'Til Things Are Brighter*, with proceeds going to an AIDS charity.

Cash has found it difficult to obtain record contracts of late, but released the low-key *American Recordings*, produced by Rick Rubin in 1994. Cash announced he was suffering from Parkinson's disease in 1997, and was hospitalized with double pneumonia soon afterwards.

CASH, ROSANNE

THE DAUGHTER OF **JOHNNY CASH** AND VIVIAN LIBERTO. IN THE LATE 70S, CASH (b. 1955) SPENT A YEAR IN ENGLAND working for CBS Records (her father's label) and signed a recording contract in Germany with Ariola. Cash was influenced by British punk, but on her return to Nashville, began recording with CBS as a neo-country act. She married producer **Rodney Crowell** in 1979, the year of her first CBS album, *Right Or Wrong*; many of her backing musicians were members of **Emmylou Harris**'s Hot Band. The album included three US country hits including 'No Memories Hangin' Round' (with Bobby Bare). *Seven Year Ache* went gold, reaching the Top 30 of the US pop chart and including three US country number 1s. *Somewhere In The Stars* also reached the pop Top 100 and included three country chart singles, and *Rhythm And Romance* included four US country hits.

King's Record Shop yielded four US country number 1s including Rosanne's revival of her father's 1962 hit, 'Tennessee Flat Top Box'. On her fifth US country number 1, 'It's A Small World', Cash duetted with Crowell. She won a Grammy in 1985 for Best Country Vocal Performance Female, and in 1988 won *Billboard*'s Top Single Artist Award.

Interiors, a hauntingly introspective album, was released after her marriage breakdown. The emotional fall-out was subsequently explored by Cash on her bleak and compelling *The Wheel*. In 1996, she demoed new material for Capitol who persuaded her to release the songs in their unadorned state, feeling the sparse arrangements complemented the introspective nature of the material. Cash also published a collection of short stories, *Bodies Of Water*.

CASSIDY, DAVID

CASSIDY (b. 1950) RECEIVED HIS BIG BREAK AFTER BEING CAST IN TELEVISION'S **THE PARTRIDGE FAMILY**. BEFORE LONG, THE Partridge Family were registering pop hits, with Cassidy taking lead vocals on their 1970 US chart-topper, 'I Think I Love You'. Further hits followed and, in 1971, he was launched as a solo artist – within a month he reached US number 1 with a revival of the **Association**'s 'Cherish'. In 1972, he hit UK number 2 with 'Could It Be Forever' and enjoyed a chart-topper with a revival of the **Young Rascals**' 'How Can I Be Sure?'. 'Rock Me Baby' just failed to reach the UK Top 10 and peaked at US number 38; it was his last American hit.

By 1973, Cassidy was concentrating on the UK, this was rewarded with 'I Am A Clown' (Top 3) and 'Daydreamer'/'The Puppy Song' (number 1). He recycled several well-known songs, including the **Beatles**' 'Please Please Me' and the **Beach Boys**' 'Darlin''. By the mid-70s, his teen-idol days were drawing in, so he returned to acting, appearing in *Joseph And The Amazing Technicolor Dreamcoat*. In 1985, he made a surprise return to the UK Top 10 with the self-penned 'The Last Kiss', featuring backing vocals from **George Michael**. Two years later, he took over the lead role of **Dave Clark**'s musical, *Time*. In 1993, he appeared with his teen-idol younger brother Shaun and singer **Petula Clark**, in the Broadway production of *Blood Brothers*.

CAST

MUCH OF THE ATTENTION SURROUNDING CAST – JOHN POWER (VOCALS/GUITAR), PETER WILKINSON (BASS; EX-**Chuck Berry**), Keith O'Neill (drums) and Skin (b. Liam Nyson; guitar) – arose from Power having played bass in the **La's**. Cast debuted with 'Fine Time' (UK Top 20) and their first album, *All Change*, introduced them as one of the UK's brightest prospects. It was therefore a surprise that their second album, *Mother Nature Calls*, did not create the same ripples of excitement, despite well-received concerts and appearances at UK festivals.

CASTAWAYS

FORMED IN MINNESOTA IN 1962, THE CASTAWAYS MADE ONE APPEARANCE ON THE US CHARTS IN 1965 WITH 'Liar, Liar', a garage-rock gem marked by organ and heavily echoed vocals. Roy Hensley (guitar), Denny Craswell (drums) and Dick Roby (bass) originated the group, recruiting Bob Folschow (guitar) and Jim Donna (keyboards). They recorded several other singles but none charted. Craswell left to join Crow in 1970, but the remaining four still performed together in the late 80s. 'Liar, Liar' reappeared in 1987, used in the film *Good Morning Vietnam*.

CATE BROTHERS

US SOUTHERN-SOUL DUO COMPRISING TWINS ERNIE AND EARL CATE (b. 1942). ERNIE (PIANO/VOCALS) AND EARL (guitar/vocals) signed to Asylum in 1975 and released their first album with assistance from, among others, **Steve Cropper**, Donald 'Duck' Dunn, Timothy B. Schmit (ex-**Poco**, **Eagles**), Nigel Olsson (**Elton John**), Klaus Voormann (**Band**) and Levon Helm (Band). 'Union Man', *In One Eye And Out The Other* and 'Can't Change My Heart' all charted, but there were no further commercial successes, although two albums were recorded in the 70s. In the early 80s, the brothers and current band members joined Helm and others in a re-formation of the Band, the entire quartet replacing guitarist **Robbie Robertson**. No recordings have emerged since the 70s.

CAVE, NICK

AFTER THE **BIRTHDAY PARTY** DISBANDED, AUSTRALIAN VOCALIST NICK CAVE (b. 1957) TEAMED UP WITH GERMAN guitarist Blixa Bargeld (b. 1959; ex-**Einsturzende Neubauten**), **Barry Adamson** (bass/other instruments; ex-**Magazine**) and fellow Australian and multi-instrumentalist Mick Harvey (b. 1958). They became the Bad Seeds. *From Here To Eternity* was accompanied by a startling rendition of

Elvis Presley's 'In the Ghetto'. *The First Born Is Dead* followed, but the Bad Seeds made their mark with *Kicking Against The Pricks*, bolstered by 'The Singer'. Cave had always drawn from a variety of sources, from **Captain Beefheart** to delta blues. The subsequent *Your Funeral, My Trial* emphasized the power of his self-penned compositions. The taut 'The Mercy Seat' was followed by the milder, though still menacing, 'Oh Deanna'. These elements were present on *Tender Prey* and *The Good Son*.

In 1989, Cave's first novel, *And The Ass Saw The Angel*, was published. His film appearances include Wim Wenders' *Wings Of Desire* (1987) and a powerful performance as a prison inmate in the Australian production *Ghosts Of The Civil Dead* (1989). An unexpected duet with **Kylie Minogue** on 'Where The Wild Roses Grow' was a major hit; this spawned *Murder Ballads*, a dark concept album. *The Boatman's Call* was one of his best.

CCS

CCS – COLLECTIVE CONSCIOUSNESS SOCIETY – WAS A COLLABORATION BETWEEN FRENCH BLUES TRADITIONALIST **Alexis Korner** (b. 1928, d. 1984; vocals/guitar), producer **Mickie Most** and arranger John Cameron. Formed in 1970, the group featured Peter Thorup (vocals), plus several of Britain's leading jazz musicians, including Harry Beckett, Les Condon (trumpets), **Johnnie Watson** (trombone), **Don Lusher** (trombone), Ronnie Ross (flute), Ray Warleigh (flute), Herbie Flowers (bass), Spike Heatley (bass), Tony Carr (drums) and Bill Le Sage (percussion). The unit's commercial, brass-laden sound remained consistent over three albums. Their version of **Led Zeppelin**'s 'Whole Lotta Love', which became the theme to BBC television's *Top Of The Pops*, reached number 13 in 1970, followed by 'Walkin'' and 'Tap Turns On The Water'. CCS was dissolved in 1973 when Korner and Thorup formed Snape.

Influences
Jack Cassidy
Cowsills
Partridge Family
Association ➽ p.23
Young Rascals ➽ p.347
Beatles ➽ p.38
Beach Boys ➽ p.36
Further References
Book: *Meet David Cassidy*, James A. Hudson

CAST
Albums
Mother Nature Calls (Polydor 1997)★★★
➽ p.356 for full listings
Collaborators
John Leckie
Connections
Chuck Berry ➽ p.45
La's ➽ p.212

CASTAWAYS
Connections
Crow
Further References
Film: *It's A Bikini World* (1967)

CATE BROTHERS
Albums
The Cate Brothers (Asylum 1975)★★★
In One Eye And Out The Other (Asylum 1976)★★★
➽ p.356 for full listings
Collaborators
Steve Cropper ➽ p.105
Donald Dunn
Timothy Schmit
Nigel Olsson
Klaus Voorman
Levon Helm

CAVE, NICK
Albums
Murder Ballads (Mute/Reprise 1996)★★★★
The Boatman's Call (Mute 1997)★★★★
➽ p.356 for full listings
Collaborators
Kylie Minogue ➽ p.234
Connections
Wim Wenders
Influences
The Birthday Party ➽ p.47
Elvis Presley ➽ p.265
Captain Beefheart ➽ p.80
Further References
Video: *Road To God Knows Where* (BMG Video 1990)
Book: *And The Ass Saw The Angel*, Nick Cave

CCS
Albums
CCS aka *Whole Lotta Love* (RAK 1970)★★★
CCS (2) (RAK 1972)★★★
The Best Band In The Land (RAK 1973)★★★
➽ p.356 for full listings
Connections
King Crimson ➽ p.206
Influences
Led Zeppelin ➽ p.213

CHAD AND JEREMY
Albums
Yesterday's Gone (1964)★★★
➽ p.356 for full listings
Influences
Peter And Gordon ➽ p.259

CHAIRMEN OF THE BOARD
Albums
Skin I'm In (Invictus 1974)★★★
➽ p.356 for full listings
Connections
The Showmen
100 Proof

CHAKA DEMUS AND PLIERS
Albums
For Every Kinda People (Island 1996)★★★★
➽ p.356 for full listings
Collaborators
Jack Radics
Connections
Nicodemus Jr Chaka
Influences
Sly Dunbar ➽ p.126/p.300
Robbie Shakespeare ➽ p.300
Further References
Video: *Tease Me* (Island Video 1994)

CHAMELEONS
Albums
Strange Times (Geffen 1987)★★★★
➽ p.356 for full listings
Connections
The Sons Of God
Further References
Video: *Live At The Hacienda* (1994)

CHAMPS
Albums
Go Champs Go (Challenge 1958)★★★
➽ p.356 for full listings

CHANDLER, GENE
Albums
The Duke Of Earl (Vee Jay 1962)★★★★
➽ p.356 for full listings
Collaborators
Barbara Acklin
Connections
Dukays

CHAD AND JEREMY

CHAD STEWART (b. 1943; VOCALS/GUITAR/BANJO/KEYBOARDS/SITAR) AND JEREMY CLYDE (b. 1944; VOCALS/guitar) started out with Stewart providing the musical accompaniment to Clyde's lyrics. Their early brand of folk-influenced pop, similar to **Peter And Gordon**, was commercially unsuccessful in their native UK. However they had four US Top 30 hits, including 'Yesterday's Gone' and 'A Summer Song'. A concept album, *Of Cabbages And Kings*, signalled a switch to progressive styles, but this ambitious and sadly neglected work was unsuccessful and the pair broke up in 1969. Clyde later pursued an acting career, while Stewart began writing musicals.

CHAIRMEN OF THE BOARD

BRIEFLY KNOWN AS THE GENTLEMEN, THIS DETROIT-BASED QUARTET WAS INSTIGATED BY GENERAL NORMAN JOHNSON (b. 1944), with Danny Woods (b. 1944), Eddie Curtis and Canadian Harrison Kennedy. The group secured an international hit with their debut, 'Give Me Just A Little More Time', followed by the vibrant '(You've Got Me) Dangling On A String'. The group ceased recording in 1971, but singles continued to appear until 1976.

Johnson also worked with the Honey Cone and 100 Proof, while he and Woods kept the Chairmen name afloat with live performances. Johnson subsequently enjoyed a series of late 70s R&B hits before reuniting with Woods. 'Loverboy' (1984) reflected their enduring popularity on the American 'beach'/vintage soul music scene, and was a minor UK hit.

CHAKA DEMUS AND PLIERS

CHAKA DEMUS (b. JOHN TAYLOR, 1965), THE RAPPING HALF OF THIS JAMAICAN PAIRING, BEGAN HIS CAREER chatting on a variety of sound systems, the most famous of these being Supreme and Jammy's (as Nicodemus Jr Chaka). He cut his first single, 'Increase Your Knowledge', soon after and a sporadic string of 45s bearing his name followed. A move to Penthouse Studio for 'Chaka On The Move' (1987) led to his friendship with Pliers.

Pliers (b. Everton Banner, 1965) first found fame cutting sides with Black Scorpio (Maurice Johnson). While playing shows in Miami in 1991, Chaka and Pliers decided to team up. 'Gal Wine' for Ossie Hibbert led to a slew of reggae chart successes: 'Rough This Year', 'Love Up The Gal', 'Without Love' and 'Worl' A Girls' among them. A teaming with producers **Sly Dunbar** and Robbie Shakespeare created a new model of 'Murder She Wrote'. 'Tease Me' was a bright ragga-pop record and 'She Don't Let Nobody' and 'Twist & Shout' (featuring **Jack Radics**) were also successes.

CHAMELEONS

FORMED IN MANCHESTER, ENGLAND, IN 1981, FEATURING Mark Burgess (vocals/bass), Reg Smithies (guitar), Dave Fielding (guitar) and Brian Schofield (drums). Early singles included 'In Shreds', 'As High As You Can Go' and 'A Person Isn't Safe Anywhere These Days'. Their *Script Of The Bridge* and *What Does Anything Mean Basically?* revealed them as a promising guitar-based group with a strong melodic sense. *Strange Times* was very well received by the critics. However, just as a breakthrough beckoned, their manager Tony Fletcher died, and amid the ensuing chaos, the group folded. Two spin-off groups, the Sun And The Moon and the Reegs lacked the charm of their powerful but unrealized mother group. Burgess also released a solo album.

CHAMPS

FORMED IN LOS ANGELES IN 1957, INITIALLY COMPRISING DAVE BURGESS (RHYTHM GUITAR), DANNY FLORES (saxophone/piano), Cliff Hills (bass), Buddy Bruce (lead guitar) and Gene Alden (drums). Flores taught the others 'Tequila' from a riff he had worked on to play at Los Angeles clubs. Issued in 1958 as the b-side to 'Train To Nowhere', radio stations preferred it to the a-side and the track made number 1. A new line-up, formed for touring purposes, included Flores, Burgess, Alden, Dale Norris (guitar) and Joe Burnas (bass). Flores and Alden left in 1958 and were replaced by Jim Seals (saxophone), Dash Crofts (drums) and Dean Beard (piano). Seals and Crofts remained with the group until its termination. The Champs had a further seven chart singles in 1962, but none came close to matching their debut's success. Burgess was replaced by guitarist **Glen Campbell** in 1960. The Champs disbanded in 1964.

CHANDLER, GENE

CHICAGO-BORN CHANDLER (b. EUGENE DIXON, 1937) IS BEST REMEMBERED FOR HIS US NUMBER 1, 'DUKE OF EARL' (1962). The million-selling single featured the Dukays, a doo-wop quintet featuring Shirley Jones, James Lowe, Earl Edwards and Ben Broyles. After a brief hiatus Chandler returned with some **Curtis Mayfield**-penned hits, including 'Rainbow' (1963). The relationship blossomed with 'Just Be True' (1964) and 'Nothing Can Stop Me' (1965). Other successes included 'There Goes The Lover', 'From The Teacher To The Preacher' (with Barbara Acklin) and 'Groovy Situation'.

During the disco boom a revitalized Chandler released 'Get Down', 'When You're Number 1' and 'Does She Have A Friend'. Recordings with Jaime Lynn and Fastfire continued his career into the 80s.

CHANNEL LIGHT VESSEL

UK ROCK POP BAND FORMED IN 1993 WHEN ROGER ENO MET KATE ST. JOHN (OBOE/SAXOPHONE; EX-**VAN MORRISON**). Eno is best known for his solo work and television and film scores, which include *Mr Wroe's Virgins*. They began writing what would become *The Familiar* together, before meeting **Bill Nelson**. The trio toured Japan in 1994 and were joined by US instrumentalist Laraaji and cellist Mayumi Tachibana. *Automatic* was a sumptuous interchange of musical ideas, after which each member returned to solo careers. Tachibana was unable to join the reconstituted group in 1996, where other musicians such as Ian Freese joined the line-up. *Excellent Spirits* was more upbeat and rhythmic.

CHANTAYS

US-BASED GROUP FEATURING BOB SPICKARD (LEAD GUITAR), BRIAN Carman (guitar/saxophone), Bob Marshall (piano), Warren Waters (bass) and Bob Welsh (drums; later replaced by Steve Kahn). They formed the Chantays in 1962, and secured success with 'Pipeline' the following year; this atmos-pheric surfing instrumental brought a new level of sophistication to an often one-dimensional genre. The group broke up following a handful of unsuccessful releases, but a re-formed line-up emerged during the 80s in the wake of a surfing resurgence.

CHAPIN, HARRY

CHAPIN (b. 1942, d. 1980) DIRECTED THE OSCAR-NOMINATED FILM *LEGENDARY CHAMPIONS* IN 1968, BEFORE TURNING to music. In 1971, he began playing clubs in his native New York with John Wallace (bass), Ron Palmer (guitar) and Tim Scott (cello). In 1972, his debut *Heads And Tales* and the six-minute single 'Taxi' enjoyed minor success. Chapin's writing strength emerged through fascinating narrative songs, often with a twist in the tale; 'W-O-L-D', about the life of a local disc jockey, went on to become an FM radio classic. At Christmas 1974, Chapin reached US number 1 with the evocative 'Cat's In The Cradle'. After a series of albums, he wrote the Broadway musical revue, *The Night That Made America Famous*, in the same year that he won an Emmy for his musical work on the children's television series, *Make A Wish*. His double album *Greatest Stories – Live* received a gold record award.

During the late 70s, he became increasingly involved in politics and was a delegate at the 1976 Democratic Convention. The title track to his album *Sequel* (a story sequel to 'Taxi') gave him his final US Top 30 entry. On 16 July, while travelling to a benefit concert, he was killed when his car was hit by a truck. A Harry Chapin Memorial Fund was subsequently launched.

CHAPMAN, MICHAEL

CHAPMAN (b. 1941) EMERGED FROM BRITAIN'S FOLK CLUB CIRCUIT WITH 1968'S RAINMAKER. FULLY QUALIFIED SURVIVOR reached the UK Top 50 in 1970, and included the emotional 'Postcards Of Scarborough'. His solo work from the 70s and 80s was captured on *Almost Alone* and a brief collaboration with former colleague, Rick Kemp, resulted in 'All Day, All Night'/'Geordie's Down The Road' (1983). After recovering from a heart attack in 1991, and playing alongside Kemp in his band Savage Amusement, Chapman recorded *Still Making Rain* and hit a late peak with *Navigation*. *Dreaming Out Loud* was another good album.

CHAPMAN, ROGER

CHAPMAN (b. 1942) PROGRESSED FROM LOCAL UK GROUPS TO A BEATLES-ESQUE SOJOURN IN Germany with the (UK) Exciters. When Ric Grech left the Exciters to join the Farinas, Chapman followed. Changing their name to **Family** they returned to London in 1966. When Family broke up in 1973 the Chapman/Whitney songwriting partnership continued in Streetwalkers; they produced a couple of excellent hard rock albums but split up after three years. Chapman's first solo output, *Chappo*, was well received. The mid-80s saw some less successful albums, but *Walking The Cat* demonstrated his resilience. *Kiss My Soul* (1996) was his best work for many years.

CHAPMAN, TRACY

US SINGER-SONGWRITER-GUITARIST CHAPMAN (b. 1964) GOT HER BIG BREAK DURING NELSON MANDELA'S 70th birthday concert at Wembley Stadium, London, in 1988. Owing to headliner **Stevie Wonder**'s enforced walk-out, her spot was extended. Her debut album, *Tracy Chapman*, climbed to US number 1 within days, and became an international success selling over 3 million copies. 'Fast Car' reached the UK Top 5 and 'Talkin' 'Bout A Revolution' was a concert favourite. She appeared with **Peter Gabriel**, **Sting** and other artists for a worldwide tour in aid of Amnesty International. Afterwards, she lost momentum with *Crossroads*, but *New Beginning* found a much wider audience in the USA.

CHARLATANS (UK)

TIM BURGESS (b. 1968; LEAD VOCALS), MARTIN BLUNT (b. 1965; BASS), JON BAKER (b. 1969; GUITAR), JON BROOKES (b. 1969; drums) and Rob Collins (b. 1963, d. 1996; keyboards) fused 60s melodies, Hammond organ riffs and a generally loose feel so that 1990's 'Indian Rope' sold well enough to secure a contract with Beggars Banquet Records/Situation 2. 'The Only One I Know', borrowed from the **Byrds** and **Booker T. And The MGs**, provided a UK Top 10 hit, followed by the popular 'Then' and the band's debut album, *Some Friendly*. A fourth single, 'Over Rising', steered away from the previous organ-based approach.

1992 brought major problems: *Between 10th And 11th* disappointed, Blunt suffered a nervous breakdown, Baker departed (replaced by Mark Collins) and Rob Collins was jailed as an accessory to armed robbery. *Up To Our Hips*, produced by **Steve Hillage**, repaired some of the damage. Their revival in both the singles and albums charts continued, until tragedy struck in July 1996 when Collins was killed in a car crash. Martin Duffy (**Primal Scream**) was drafted in temporarily and, in 1997, keyboard player Tony Rogers was recruited for touring purposes. In 1997, the swirling and glorious *Tellin' Stories* was released.

CHARLATANS (USA)

'UNDERGROUND' SAN FRANCISCAN ROCK GROUP, FORMED IN 1964 BY GEORGE HUNTER (AUTOHARP/TAMBOURINE), Mike Wilhelm (guitar/vocals) and Richard Olsen (bass/clarinet/vocals). They recruited pianist Michael Ferguson and drummer Sam Linde, who was later replaced by **Dan Hicks**. By this time, the group had honed their *mélange* of blues, folk and R&B, but 'The Shadow Knows' was the sole release by this line-up. Disillusioned, Hicks, Ferguson and Hunter left; Olsen and Wilhelm persevered. In 1969, they completed *The Charlatans* with Darrell De Vore (piano) and Terry Wilson (drums); the band then dissolved. Hicks formed Dan Hicks And His Hot Licks; Wilhelm fronted Loose Gravel; Ferguson joined Tongue And Groove; Olsen became a producer at Pacific High Studios and

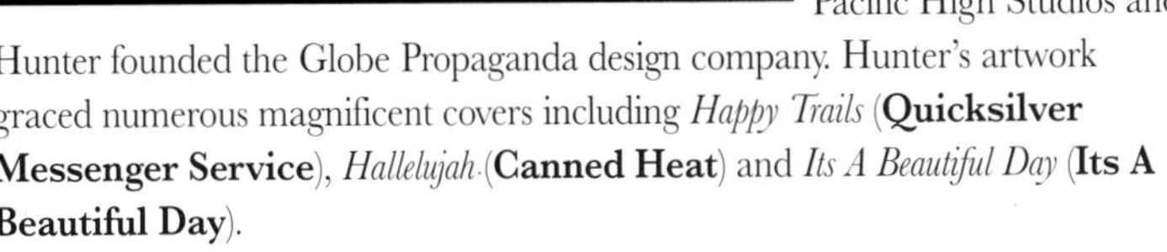

Hunter founded the Globe Propaganda design company. Hunter's artwork graced numerous magnificent covers including *Happy Trails* (**Quicksilver Messenger Service**), *Hallelujah* (**Canned Heat**) and *Its A Beautiful Day* (**Its A Beautiful Day**).

Influences
Curtis Mayfield ➧ p.228
Further References
Film: *Don't Knock The Twist* (1962)

CHANNEL LIGHT VESSEL
Albums
Excellent Spirits (All Saints 1996)★★★★
➧ p.356 for full listings
Connections
Van Morrison ➧ p.238
Bill Nelson ➧ p.244

CHANTAYS
Albums
Pipeline (Downey 1963)★★★
Two Sides Of The Chantays (Dot 1964)★★★
➧ p.356 for full listings

CHAPIN, HARRY
Albums
Verities And Balderdash (Elektra 1974)★★★★
➧ p.356 for full listings
Further References
Book: *Taxi: The Harry Chaplin Story*, Peter M. Coan

CHAPMAN, MICHAEL
Albums
Fully Qualified Survivor (Harvest 1970)★★★★
➧ p.356 for full listings

CHAPMAN, ROGER
Albums
Walking The Cat (1989)★★★
➧ p.356 for full listings
Connections
Family ➧ p.143
Influences
Beatles ➧ p.38

CHAPMAN, TRACY
Albums
Tracy Chapman (Elektra 1988)★★★★
➧ p.356 for full listings
Collaborators
Peter Gabriel ➧ p.151
Sting ➧ p.310

CHARLATANS (UK)
Albums
Tellin' Stories (Beggars Banquet 1997)★★★★
➧ p.356 for full listings
Connections
Primal Scream ➧ p.267
Influences
Stone Roses ➧ p.311
Happy Mondays ➧ p.174
Byrds ➧ p.77
Booker T. And The MGs ➧ p.62

CHARLATANS (USA)
Albums
The Charlatans (Philips 1969)★★★
➧ p.356 for full listings
Connections
Dan Hicks And His Hot Licks ➧ p.181

CHARLES, RAY
Albums
Modern Sounds In Country And Western (ABC 1962)★★★★★
➧ p.356 for full listings
Influences
Guitar Slim
Further References
Book: *Brother Ray, Ray Charles' Own Story*, Ray Charles and David Ritz

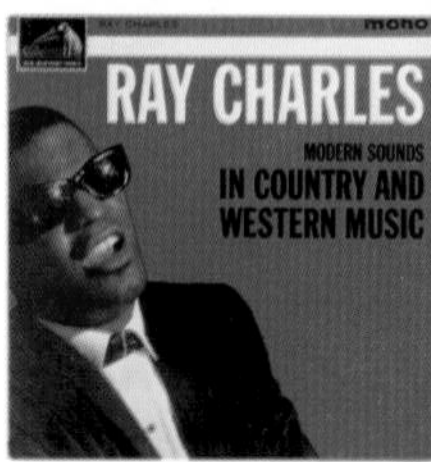

CHARLES AND EDDIE
Albums
Duophonic (Stateside/Capitol 1992)★★★
➧ p.356 for full listings
Connections
Dust Brothers

CHEAP TRICK
Albums
Heaven Tonight (Epic 1978)★★★★
➧ p.356 for full listings
Connections
Ruffians
Further References
Video: *Every Trick In The Book* (CMV Enterprises 1990)

CHECKER, CHUBBY
Albums
Let's Twist Again (Parkway 1961)★★★★
➧ p.356 for full listings
Collaborators
Bobby Rydell ➧ p.286
Connections
Fat Boys ➧ p.143

CHARLES, RAY

AS A RESULT OF GLAUCOMA, CHARLES (b. RAY CHARLES ROBINSON, 1930) WAS COMPLETELY BLIND BY THE AGE of seven. He learned to read and write music in braille and was proficient on several instruments by the time he left school. He began recording in 1949 and this early, imitative approach was captured on several sessions. Three years later, Atlantic Records acquired his contract, but his early work revealed only an occasional hint of the passions later unleashed. Charles's individual style emerged as a result of his work with Guitar Slim, whose gospel-based fervour greatly influenced Charles's thinking. This effect was fully realized in the successful 'I Got A Woman' (1954) followed by 'This Little Girl Of Mine' (1955), 'Talkin' 'Bout You' (1957) and 'Don't Let The Sun Catch You Crying' (1959) among others. However, Charles was equally adept at slow ballads, as his 'Drown In My Own Tears' and 'I Believe To My Soul' (both 1959) clearly show.

In 1959, Charles left Atlantic for ABC, where he secured both musical and financial freedom. 'Georgia On My Mind' (1960) and 'Hit The Road Jack' (1961) established the artist as an international name and in 1962, *Modern Sounds In Country And Western*, a best-selling landmark collection, produced the million-selling single 'I Can't Stop Loving You'. Its success defined the pattern for Charles's later career; the edges were blunted, the vibrancy was stilled as Charles's repertoire grew increasingly inoffensive. Charles's 80s work included more country-flavoured collections and a cameo appearance in the film *The Blues Brothers*, but the period is better marked by his powerful appearance on the USA For Africa release, 'We Are The World' (1985).

CHARLES AND EDDIE

CALIFORNIAN-BORN EDDIE CHACON BEGAN IN A LOCAL SOUL BAND; HIS RECORDING CAREER CONTINUED ON PROJECTS with the Dust Brothers and Daddy-O. Charles Pettigrew grew up in Philadelphia and sang with pop band Down Avenue. The duo debuted with the worldwide hit 'Would I Lie To You?', followed by 'NYC (Can You Believe This City)' in 1993. Both tracks were on their debut, *Duophonic*, which consisted mainly of original material, notably 'December 2' (about Chacon's brother's death). Their second album proved disappointing.

CHEAP TRICK

RICK NIELSEN (b. 1946; GUITAR/VOCALS) AND Tom Petersson (b. 1950; bass/vocals) first recorded as members of US group Fuse. The duo then joined Thom Mooney and Robert 'Stewkey' Antoni (both ex-Nazz), before Mooney was replaced by drummer Brad Carlson (aka Bun E. Carlos, b. 1951). In 1973, 'Stewkey' left and vocalist Randy 'Xeno' Hogan joined – soon replaced by Robin Zander (b. 1952; guitar/vocals). *Cheap Trick* introduced the group's inventive flair and striking visual image: Zander and Petersson's good looks with Carlos's seedy garb and Nielsen's baseball cap, bow-tie and monogrammed sweater. The band completed *In Color* within months of their debut, offering a smoother sound with a grasp of melody.

At Budokan followed a highly successful tour of Japan and became the quartet's first platinum disc. *Dream Police* added little to the sound and producer **George Martin** barely deflected this sterility on *All Shook Up*. A disaffected Petersson left in 1982, replaced briefly by Pete Comita, then by Jon Brant. Neither *One On One* nor the **Todd Rundgren**-produced *Next Position Please* halted Cheap Trick's commercial slide, but *Standing On The Edge* offered hopes of a renaissance. In 1986, 'Mighty Wings' appeared in the smash-hit film *Top Gun* and Petersson returned. *Lap Of Luxury* went multi-platinum when its single, 'The Flame', reached US number 1 in 1988. *Busted* scaled similar heights. In 1998, they toured the US.

CHECKER, CHUBBY

CHECKER'S (b. ERNEST EVANS, 1941) MUSICAL CAREER BEGAN IN 1959, WHEN HE MET KAL MANN; THE SONGWRITER penned Checker's debut, 'The Class'. Checker became one of several artists to enjoy the patronage of Dick Clark's influential *American Bandstand* television show and the successful Cameo-Parkway label. He achieved national fame in

1960 with 'The Twist', a compulsive dance-based performance which became an institution. The single topped the US chart in 1960 and again in 1961, and twice entered the UK charts, reaching number 14 in 1962. 'Pony Time' (1961) became Checker's second gold disc and second US number 1, before 'Let's Twist Again' established him as an international attraction. It inspired competitive releases by the **Isley Brothers** ('Twist And Shout'), **Joey Dee** ('Peppermint Twist') and **Sam Cooke** ('Twisting The Night Away') while Checker mined its appeal on a surprisingly soulful 'Slow Twistin'' (with Dee Dee Sharp) and 'Teach Me To Twist' (with **Bobby Rydell**).

Checker recorded a slew of opportunistic singles including 'The Fly' (1961) and 'Limbo Rock' (1962), both of which sold over one million copies. However, dance-inspired records devoted to the Jet, the Swim and the Freddie were less successful. Even so, Checker had a remarkable run of 32 US chart hits up to 1966.

Latterly, Checker was confined to the revival circuit, reappearing in 1975 when 'Let's Twist Again' re-entered the UK Top 5. The **Fat Boys**' 'The Twist (Yo Twist)', with Chubby guesting on vocals, climbed to UK number 2 in 1988.

CHEECH AND CHONG

AMERICAN RICHARD 'CHEECH' MARIN (b. 1946) BECAME ACQUAINTED WITH CANADIAN TOMMY CHONG (b. 1940) while escaping induction into the US Army. Chong performed in Bobby Taylor And The Vancouvers, but the duo's plans for a rock group were sidelined on discovering comedy. Cheech And Chong pursued subjects apposite to hippie culture – long hair, drugs, sex and police harassment – and won a Best Comedy Album Grammy for *Los Cochinos*. This spawned three US hits, including 'Basketball Jones Featuring Tyrone Shoelaces'. In 1979, they began a film career with *Up In Smoke*. *Get Out Of My Room* included the hit 'Born In East LA' – a satire on **Bruce Springsteen**'s 'Born In The USA'. Following their break-up in the late 80s, Marin went on to great success as a comedy actor, including being a hyena voice in *The Lion King*.

CHELSEA

UK PUNK BAND FORMED IN 1977, FEATURING GENE OCTOBER (VOCALS), BRIAN JAMES (GUITAR), GEOFF MYLES (BASS) AND Chris Bashford (drums). Specializing in sub-three-minute vitriolic outbursts on unemployment, inner-city decay and the destruction of British society, their lyrics were always more interesting than their music. The songs formed a pattern of up-tempo numbers, marred by basic studio techniques. As a body of work, the songs become jarring, but individually, their music is exciting and energetic. The band continued to record throughout the 80s.

CHEMICAL BROTHERS

UK DUO TOM ROWLANDS (b. 1970) AND EDWARD SIMONS (b. 1971) MET IN 1989 AT UNIVERSITY. INSPIRED BY Manchester's Hacienda Club, they launched their own, Naked Under The Leather. As the Dust Brothers, they released 'Song To The Siren'; Rowlands was currently a member of indie-dance band Ariel ('Let It Slide', 1993) but left in favour of the Dust Brothers. They were invited to remix for local act Lionrock, as well as the **Leftfield**/Lydon opus 'Open Up' and **Saint Etienne**. Their own recordings included the *14th Century Sky* EP and 'Kling To Me And I'll Klong To You'. Both revealed hip hop beats with elements of the late-80s rave/acid scene. The *My Mercury Mouth* EP secured Single Of The Week Awards and further remixes for the **Charlatans** and **Prodigy** followed.

Due to the US Dust Brothers, they changed their name to the Chemical Brothers. *Exit Planet Dust*, followed, a hard-hitting mix of house beats and rock 'n' roll with psychedelic trimmings; Tim Burgess (**Charlatans**) guested. 'Setting Sun' (1996), a collaboration with Noel Gallagher (**Oasis**), was a hit as was *Dig Your Own Hole*.

CHER

CHER (b. CHERILYN SARKARSIAN LA PIER, 1946) STARTED OUT AS A SESSION SINGER, DURING WHICH TIME SHE MET future husband **Sonny Bono**. After two singles (as Caeser And Cleo), the duo achieved international acclaim as **Sonny And Cher**. Cher also sustained a solo career, securing several hits, including a cover of the **Byrds**' 'All I Really Want To Do'. 'Bang Bang', with its gypsy beat and maudlin violins was a worldwide smash in 1966, followed by 'I Feel Something In The Air' and 'You Better Sit Down Kids'. She also appeared in two minor 60s' films, *Good Times* (1967; with Sonny) and *Chastity* (1969).

In 1971, the zestful, 'Gypsies, Tramps And Thieves' and its attendant album saw her back in the ascendent. Two further US number 1s ('Half Breed' and 'Dark Lady') preceded her divorce from Sonny. In 1975, she released the **Jimmy Webb**-produced *Stars* and one album with Gregg Allman, *Allman And Woman: Two The Hard Way*. By the late 70s, she became a regular media fixture, amid speculation over her relationships with Allman, Gene Simmons (**Kiss**) and Les Dudek.

In 1981, Cher appeared on **Meat Loaf**'s 'Dead Ringer For Love' but recording took a back seat to acting. A leading role in *Come Back To The Five And Dime, Jimmy Dean, Jimmy Dean* (1982) was followed by an Oscar nomination in *Silkwood* (1983). Appearances in *Mask* (1985), *The Witches Of Eastwick* (1987), *Suspect* (1987) and *Moonstruck* (1987) followed. The album *Cher* and its concomitant Top 10 single 'I Found Someone', preceded her 1991 number 1, 'The Shoop Shoop Song (It's In His Kiss)', the theme song to her film *Mermaids*. In 1995, she released a credible cover of Marc Cohn's 'Walking In Memphis' which preceded *It's A Man's World*.

CHERRY, NENEH

SWEDISH-BORN CHERRY (b. 1964) IS THE STEP-DAUGHTER OF JAZZ TRUMPETER DON CHERRY. She joined English post-punk band Rip, Rig And Panic in 1981 as a vocalist, later performing with several ex-members as Float Up CP. In the mid-80s she sang backing vocals for the **Slits** and **The The**. In 1989, Cherry recorded a series of dance hits including 'Buffalo Stance', 'Manchild' and 'Kisses On The Wind'. Her main co-writer was Cameron McVey, whom she married. Cherry contributed to the AIDS-charity collection, *Red Hot And Blue*, singing Cole Porter's 'I've Got You Under My Skin'.

CHI-LITES

FORMED IN 1960 AS THE HI-LITES, EUGENE RECORD (b. 1940), ROBERT LESTER (b. 1942), CREADEL JONES (b. 1939) AND Marshall Thompson (b. 1941) mixed doo-wop and street-corner harmony. A series of releases followed before 'I'm So Jealous' (1964) introduced their new name, Marshall And The Chi-Lites – the 'Chi' celebrating their origins in Chicago. Johnson left later that year and, with the release of 'You Did That To Me', they became the Chi-Lites.

Record formed a songwriting partnership with Barbara Acklin, and together they created many of his group's finest moments. 'Give It Away' (1969) became their first US hit, followed by the wistful 'Have You Seen Her' (1971), the US number 1 'Oh Girl' (1972) and 'You Don't Have To Go' (1976) among others. Jones left in 1973, replaced by Stanley Anderson, then by Willie Kensey. In 1976, Record left for a short-lived solo career. David Scott and Danny Johnson replaced him but the original quartet of Record, Jones, Lester and Thompson re-formed in 1980. The title track of *Bottoms Up* (1983) became a Top 10 soul single but further releases failed to sustain that success. Creadel Jones retired and Record left again, leaving Thompson with the Chi-Lites' name. They continued touring into the 90s.

Influences
Isley Brothers » p.194
Joey Dee » p.113
Sam Cooke » p.100
Further References
Film: *Don't Knock The Twist* (1962)

CHEECH AND CHONG
Albums
Los Cochinos (Ode 1973)★★
» p.356 for full listings
Collaborators
Bobby Taylor And The Vancouvers
Influences
Bruce Springsteen » p.306

CHELSEA
Albums
Chelsea (Step Forward 1979)★★★
» p.356 for full listings

CHEMICAL BROTHERS
Albums
Dig Your Own Hole (Freestyle Dust 1997)★★★★
» p.356 for full listings
Collaborators
Leftfield » p.213
Saint Etienne » p.287
Charlatans » p.87
Prodigy » p.268
Noel Gallagher » p.250
Connections
Dust Brothers
Influences
Hacienda Club

CHER
Albums
Love Hurts (Geffen 1991)★★★
» p.356 for full listings
Collaborators
Phil Spector » p.304
Gregg Allman » p.14
Meatloaf » p.230
Connections
Caeser And Cleo » p.60
Sonny And Cher » p.60
Influences
Sonny Bono » p.60
Byrds » p.77

CHERRY, NENEH
Albums
Man (Hut 1996)★★★
» p.356 for full listings
Collaborators
Slits » p.300
The The » p.319
Connections
Rip, Rig and Panic
Influences
Don Cherry
Cole Porter

CHI-LITES
Albums
(For God's Sake) Give More Power To The People (Brunswick 1971)★★★★
» p.356 for full listings
Collaborators
Barbara Acklin
Connections
Chanteurs
Marshall And The Chi-Lites

CHIC
Albums
Take It Off (Atlantic 1981)★★★★
➧ p.356 for full listings
Collaborators
New York City
Sister Sledge ➧ p.298
Diana Ross ➧ p.283
David Bowie ➧ p.64
Madonna ➧ p.222
Robert Palmer ➧ p.255
Connections
Big Apple Band
LaBelle ➧ p.212
Duran Duran ➧ p.127

CHICAGO
Albums
Chicago Transit Authority (Columbia 1969)★★★★
➧ p.356 for full listings
Collaborators
Beach Boys ➧ p.36
Connections
Chicago Transit Authority
Stephen Stills ➧ p.310
Further References
Video: *In Concert At The Greek Theatre* (Warner Music Vision 1994)

CHICKEN SHACK
Albums
Forty Blue Fingers Freshly Packed And Ready To Serve (Blue Horizon 1968)★★★★
➧ p.356 for full listings
Connections
Traffic ➧ p.323
Jethro Tull ➧ p.199
Influences
John Lee Hooker ➧ p.185
Freddie King ➧ p.206

CHICORY TIP
Albums
Son Of My Father (Columbia 1972)★★
➧ p.356 for full listings

CHIEFTAINS
Albums
with Van Morrison *Irish Heartbeat* (Mercury 1988)★★★★
➧ p.356 for full listings

CHIC

US GROUP CHIC WAS BUILT AROUND NILE RODGERS (b. 1952; GUITAR) AND BERNARD EDWARDS (b. 1952, d. 1996; BASS). THEY joined the Big Apple Band in 1971, backing hit group New York City on tour. Two female singers, Norma Jean Wright and Luci Martin, and drummer Tony Thompson were recruited. Wright later went solo, replaced by Alfa Anderson. They scored an immediate hit with 'Dance Dance Dance (Yowsah, Yowsah, Yowsah)' (1977), which introduced wit and sparkling instrumentation to the maligned disco genre. In 1978, 'Le Freak' sold over four million copies and 'Good Times' (US number 1) went gold.

Edwards and Rodgers also guested for **Sister Sledge**, **Diana Ross** and Sheila B. Devotion, but Chic's later work was treated with indifference. Edwards's solo album, *Glad To Be Here*, was a disappointment, and Rodgers', *Adventures In The Land Of Groove*, fared little better.

Rodgers' then worked on **David Bowie**'s 'Let's Dance' and produced **Madonna**'s, 'Like A Virgin', while Edwards took control of recording the Power Station, the **Duran Duran** offshoot. Edwards also provided the backbone to **Robert Palmer**'s 1986 hit, 'Addicted To Love'. In 1992 the duo re-formed Chic, releasing 'Chic Mystique' and an album.

CHICAGO

FORMED IN 1966 IN CHICAGO, THE BAND FEATURED TERRY KATH (b. 1946, d. 1978; GUITAR/VOCALS), PETER CETERA (b. 1944; bass/vocals), Robert Lamm (b. 1944; keyboards/vocals), Walt Perry (b. Walter Parazaider, 1945; saxophone), Danny Seraphine (b. 1948; drums), James Pankow (b. 1947; trombone) and Lee Loughnane (b. 1941; trumpet). The horn section set the group apart from other mid-60s rock bands and, in 1969, manager Jim Guercio landed the group a contract with Columbia. With jazz influences the group released its self-titled album in 1969. Although it missed the Top 10, the album stayed on the US charts for 171 weeks. The group also enjoyed hits with 'Does Anybody Really Know What Time It Is' and 'Beginnings'.

In 1970, still working in the jazz-rock idiom, they released *Chicago II*. By the early 70s they began breaking away from jazz toward more mainstream pop, resulting in such light-rock staples as 'Colour My World', the 1976 transatlantic number 1 'If You Leave Me Now' and the 1982 number 1 'Hard To Say I'm Sorry'. Five consecutive Chicago albums topped the charts between 1972 and 1975.

In 1974, Lamm recorded a poor-selling solo album and the group recruited Brazilian percussionist Laudir de Oliveira. The following year they toured with the **Beach Boys**. In 1977, after *Chicago X* was awarded a Best Album Grammy, Guercio and the group parted ways. On 23 January 1978, Kath accidentally shot himself, fatally; the group continued, with Donnie Dacus (ex-**Stephen Stills**) joining on guitar. Duce was soon replaced, briefly, by Chris Pinnick.

In 1981, Bill Champlin (keyboards) joined, Chicago signed to Full Moon Records and Cetera released a mildly successful solo album. After leaving the group in 1985 (replaced by Jason Scheff), he released two further solo albums. Chicago continued to record into the 90s.

CHICKEN SHACK

CHICKEN SHACK WAS THE PRODUCT OF GUITARIST STAN WEBB AND ANDY SYLVESTER (BASS). THE BAND ENJOYED A long residency at Hamburg's Star Club before returning to England in 1967. Christine Perfect (b. 1943; piano/vocals) then joined the line-up as did drummer Dave Bidwell. *Forty Blue Fingers Freshly Packed And Ready To Serve* was a fine balance between original songs and material by **John Lee Hooker** and **Freddie King**, to whom Webb was stylistically indebted. The quartet enjoyed two minor hits with 'I'd Rather Go Blind' and 'Tears In The Wind'.

Perfect, who left for a solo career (as Christine McVie), was replaced by Paul Raymond, until Raymond and Bidwell departed for Savoy Brown, a group Sylvester later joined. Webb reassembled Chicken Shack with John Glassock (bass; ex-**Jethro Tull**) and Paul Hancox (drums). They completed the disappointing *Imagination Lady* before Bob Daisley replaced Glassock, but the trio broke up in 1973, after *Unlucky Boy*. The guitarist established a completely new line-up for *Goodbye Chicken Shack*, before dissolving the band to join Savoy Brown. Chicken Shack were resurrected on several occasions.

CHICORY TIP

POP QUARTET FORMED IN KENT, ENGLAND, IN 1968 BY SINGER PETER HEWSON (b. 1950). HE RECRUITED BARRY MAYGER (b. 1950; bass), Brian Shearer (b. 1951; drums) and Dick Foster (guitar). Foster was replaced in 1972 by Rod Cloutt (b. 1949; lead guitar/synthesizer/organ). 'Son Of My Father' topped the UK charts in 1972 and Chicory Tip rode the glam rock wagon long enough to enjoy two further UK Top 20 hits with 'What's Your Name?' (1972) and 'Good Grief Christina' (1973). In the USA, the band were marketed as Chicory.

CHIEFTAINS

THE ORIGINAL CHIEFTAINS LINE-UP – PADDY MOLONEY (b. 1938; UILLEANN PIPES/TIN WHISTLE), SEAN POTTS (b. 1930; tin whistle/bodhran), Michael Tubridy (b. 1935; flute/concertina/whistle) and Martin Fay (b. 1936; fiddle) – met in Eire in the late 50s as members of Ceolteoiri Chaulann, a folk orchestra led by Sean O'Raida. After *Chieftains 1* (1964), the group chose to remain semi-professional and further recordings were sporadic. Sean Keane (b. 1946; fiddle/whistle), Peadar Mercier (b. 1914; bodhran/bones) and Derek Bell (b. 1935; harp/dulcimer/oboe) joined the line-up which then became a full-time venture. *Chieftains 5* marked their debut with Island Records; they featured on **Mike Oldfield**'s *Ommadawn* and contributed to the soundtrack of Stanley Kubrick's film, *Barry Lyndon* (1975). In 1976, Mercier was replaced by Kevin Conneff; in 1979 Matt Molloy (flute; ex-**Planxty**) joined. Moloney's skilled arrangements allowed the group to retain its freshness despite the many changes in personnel.

During the 80s, the group provided two film soundtracks plus collaborations with flute player, James Galway. They also released *Irish Heartbeat*, a collaboration with **Van Morrison**. In the 90s, the band found favour in the USA with *The Long Black Veil*. *The Bells Of Dublin* featured participation from **Rickie Lee Jones**, **Elvis Costello**, **Nanci Griffith**, **Jackson Browne** and **Marianne Faithfull**.

CHIFFONS

FORMED IN THEIR NATIVE NEW YORK, ERSTWHILE BACKING SINGERS JUDY CRAIG (b. 1946), BARBARA LEE JONES (b. 1947, d. 1992), Patricia Bennett (b. 1947) and Sylvia Peterson (b. 1946) are best recalled for their international hit 'He's So Fine' (1963). The song later acquired a dubious infamy when its melody appeared on **George Harrison**'s million-selling 'My Sweet Lord'. The group charted with 'One Fine Day' (1963) and 'Sweet Talkin' Guy' (1966). Later they recorded their own version of 'My Sweet Lord'.

CHILDS, TONI

US-BORN CHILDS FIRST WORKED WITH DAVID RICKETTS, COLLABORATING ON THE SOUNDTRACK TO ECHO PARK. Union featured Zimbabwean music, as well as more conventional singer-songwriter touches, and earned her a Grammy nomination for Best Female Rock Vocal, while 'Don't Walk Away' blended dense, dreamlike imagery with Childs's rugged alto delivery. *House Of Hope*, although a commercial disappointment, boasted fine songwriting and *The Woman's Boat* featured **Robert Fripp** and Kurt Wallinger (**World Party**).

CHILLI WILLI AND THE RED HOT PEPPERS

UK BAND CHILLI WILLI BEGAN LIFE AS A FOLKSY-CUM-COUNTRY DUO: MARTIN STONE (b. 1946; GUITAR/ MANdolin/vocals) and Phil 'Snakefinger' Lithman (b. 1949, d. 1987; guitar/lap-steel/fiddle/ piano/ vocals). Both were former members of an aspiring early 60s blues group before Lithman moved to the States and Stone joined the Savoy Brown Blues Band and Mighty Baby. They were reunited on *Kings Of The Robot Rhythm*, an informal collection which featured blues singer Jo-Ann Kelly and several members of **Brinsley Schwarz**.

In 1972, the duo recruited Paul 'Dice Man' Bailey (b. 1947; guitar/ saxophone/banjo), Paul Riley (b. 1951; bass) and Pete Thomas (b. 1954; drums) and gradually became one of Britain's most compulsive live attractions, however *Bongos Over Balham* failed to capture the group's in-concert passion and they disbanded in 1975. Thomas joined the Attractions, Riley played with **Graham Parker**'s band, Bailey helped form Bontemps Roulez, Stone joined the Pink Fairies and Lithman returned to San Francisco where, as Snakefinger, he re-joined the **Residents**.

CHINA CRISIS

FORMED IN LIVERPOOL, ENGLAND, IN 1979 BY GARY DALY (b. 1962; VOCALS) AND EDDIE LUNDON (b. 1962; GUITAR). In 1982, 'African And White' made a critical impact, despite only just breaking into the UK Top 50. The duo then recruited Gazza Johnson (bass) and Kevin Wilkinson (drums) and 'Christian', taken from *Difficult Shapes And Passive Rhythms*, reached UK number 12. With the follow-up to their second album, they had two further Top 50 hits: 'Tragedy And Mystery' and 'Working With Fire And Steel'. Later hits included 'Wishful Thinking' and 'King In A Catholic Style (Wake Up)'.

Flaunt The Imperfection reached the UK Top 10, but the follow-up, the uneven *What Price Paradise?*, saw a drop in China Crisis's fortunes. A two-year hiatus saw a reunion with Becker which resulted in the critically acclaimed *Diary Of A Hollow Horse*.

CHOCOLATE WATCH BAND

US POP GROUP WHOSE ORIGINAL LINE-UP – NED TORNEY (GUITAR), Mark Loomis (guitar/vocals), Jo Kleming (organ), Richard Young (bass), Danny Phay (lead vocals) and Pete Curry (drums) – was assembled in California in 1964. Gary Andrijasevich replaced Curry within weeks. In 1965, Torney, Kleming and Phay defected to local outfit, the Topsiders – the latter's guitarist, Sean Tolby, joined Loomis and Andrijasevich. Dave Aguilar (vocals) and Bill Flores (bass) soon joined.

Their best work includes 'Don't Need No Lovin'', 'No Way Out' and 'Are You Gonna Be There (At The Love In)'. Several Chocolate Watch Band masters featured studio musicians, while a substitute vocalist, Don Bennett, was employed on certain sessions. A disillusioned Aguilar quit the line-up prior to the release of *The Inner Mystique*. Phay resumed his place on the disappointing *One Step Beyond*. The group dissolved in 1970.

CHRISTIANS

FORMED IN LIVERPOOL, ENGLAND, IN 1984, FEATURING HENRY PRIESTMAN (b. 1955; KEYBOARDS) AND THE CHRISTIAN brothers Roger (b. 1950), Garry (b. 1955) and Russell (b. 1956). Until then, the brothers had performed as a soul a cappella trio, under a variety of names (most notably as Natural High). Priestman became the group's main songwriter and their combination of pop and soul earned them a string of UK hits including 'Forgotten Town', 'Hooverville (They Promised Us The World)' and 'Ideal World'.

In 1987, Roger left, but 1988 brought further hits with 'Born Again' and a Top 10 cover of the **Isley Brothers**' 'Harvest For The World'. They also participated on the charity single 'Ferry Across The Mersey'. In 1989, Roger released a solo single 'Take It From Me' and *Roger Christian*. The group's *Colours* hit UK number 1 on its first week in the chart.

CHRISTIE, LOU

CHRISTIE (b. LUGEE ALFREDO GIOVANNI SACCO, 1943) STARTED OUT AS A SESSION SINGER IN NEW YORK. HE recorded unsuccessfully with the Classics and Lugee and the Lions; however his high falsetto ensured his solo 'The Gypsy Cried' (1963) achieved sales in excess of one million, 1964's 'Two Faces Have I' proved equally successful. After US military service, Christie achieved a third golden disc with 'Lightnin' Strikes' (1966), his vocal histrionics set against a Tamla/**Motown**-styled backbeat. 'Rhapsody In The Rain' (1966), was another Top 20 entry, despite a ban for 'suggestive lyric'.

In 1969, Christie had his final Top 10 hit with 'I'm Gonna Make You Mine'; despite numerous singles in the 80s, Christie was unable to regain commercial ground. He still performs on the US rock 'n' roll revival circuit.

CHRISTIE, TONY

UK-BORN CHRISTIE (b. ANTHONY FITZGERALD, 1944) WAS A SELF-TAUGHT GUITARIST WHO BECAME A PROFESSIONAL SINGER. His vocal mannerisms, similar to **Tom Jones**, were demonstrated on the 1970 hit 'Las Vegas'. *I Did What I Did For Maria* (UK number 2) was followed by the million-selling 'Is This The Way To Amarillo' and 'Avenues And Alleyways' sparked off robust sales for *With Loving Feeling*. A 'best of' selection rounded off his career as a serious chart contender – though he was heard on the *Evita* studio cast album in 1978.

CHROME

NEW WAVE/PUNK/INDUSTRIAL BAND FORMED IN SAN FRANCISCO IN 1976. Their first recording line-up – John L. Cyborg (b. John Lambdin; vocals/guitar/bass), Gary Spain (vocals/guitar/bass), Mike Low (guitar/synthesizer/bass) and Damon Edge (guitar/synthesizer/drums) – recorded 1977's *The Visitation*. Low then departed, replaced by Helios Creed.

In the early 80s, the band fractured and Edge and Creed recruited John and Hilary Stench. After *Third From The Sun*, the band ground to a halt in 1983. Edge resurrected the name for several unsatisfactory albums.

Collaborators
Mike Oldfield ➧ p.251
Van Morrison ➧ p.238
Connections
Ceolteoiri Chaulann
Planxty ➧ p.262
Further References
Video: *Live In China* (1991)

CHIFFONS
Albums
One Fine Day (Laurie 1963)★★
➧ p.357 for full listings
Connections
Gerorge Harrison ➧ p.176

CHILDS, TONI
Albums
Union (A&M 1988)★★★★
➧ p.357 for full listings
Collaborators
Robert Fripp ➧ p.154

CHILLI WILLI AND THE RED HOT PEPPERS
Albums
Kings Of The Robot Rhythm (Revelation 1972)★★★
➧ p.357 for full listings
Connections
Brinsley Schwarz ➧ p.68
Graham Parker's Band ➧ p.256

CHINA CRISIS
Albums
Difficult Shapes And Passive Rhythms (Virgin 1983)★★★
➧ p.357 for full listings

CHOCOLATE WATCH BAND
Albums
The Inner Mystique (Tower 1968)★★★
➧ p.357 for full listings

CHRISTIANS
Albums
The Christians (Island 1987)★★★★
➧ p.357 for full listings
Connections
Natural High
Influences
Isley Brothers ➧ p.194

CHRISTIE, LOU
Album
Lightnin' Strikes (MGM 1966)★★★
➧ p.357 for full listings

CHRISTIE, TONY
Albums
I Did What I Did For Maria (MCA 1971)★★★
➧ p.357 for full listings
Influences
Tom Jones ➧ p.201

CHROME
Albums
Blood On The Moon (Siren 1981)★★★
➧ p.357 for full listings
Connections
Pearl Harbour And The Explosions

CHUCK D.
Album
Autobiography Of Mistachuck (Mercury 1996) ★★★★
p.357 for full listings
Collaborators
Isaac Hayes p.178
Connections
Public Enemy p.269

CHUCK D.

AFTER **PUBLIC ENEMY** SPLIT IN THE MID-90S, A CHUCK D. (b. CARLTON DOUGLAS RIDENHOUR, 1960) SOLO ALBUM, *Autobiography Of Mistachuck*, reinforced his credentials as rap's most eloquent commentator. One of the most effective tracks was 'But Can You Killer The Nigga In You?', a collaboration with **Isaac Hayes**.

CHUMBAWAMBA
Albums
Tubthumper (EMI 1997)★★★★
p.357 for full listings
Connections
John Lennon p.214

CHUMBAWAMBA

AN ANARCHIST GROUP FORMED IN LEEDS, ENGLAND WHO FIRST PLAYED LIVE IN 1983, THE band alternated between instruments and theatricals on stage and record. The current line-up is Harry Hamer, Alice Nutter, Boff, Mavis Dillon, Louise Mary Watts, Danbert Nobacon, Paul Greco and Dunstan Bruce. Their first single, 'Revolution', opened with the sound of **John Lennon**'s 'Imagine', before having it removed from the stereo and smashed. The follow-up, 'We Are The World' was banned from airplay and *Pictures Of Starving Children Sell Records* used polemic to denounce Band Aid. Other targets included multinationals, apartheid and imperialism. Their discourse was made all the more articulate by the surprising diversity of musics employed, from polka to ballad to thrash. *English Rebel Songs* acknowledged their place in the folk protest movement, and *Slap!* saw hope in rebellious dance music.

Somewhat abandoning their previous austerity, 'Tubthumping', their ode to alcohol, narrowly missed UK number 1 in 1997. The following album was much slicker than past efforts, particularly noteworthy were 'The Good Ship Lifestyle', 'Drip Drip Drip' and 'Mary Mary'.

CHURCH
Albums
Gold Afternoon Fix (Arista 1990)★★★★
p.357 for full listings
Collaborators
All About Eve p.14
Go-Betweens p.160
Connections
Television p.317
Influences
Byrds p.77

CHURCH

FORMED IN AUSTRALIA IN 1980, THE CHURCH COMPRISED ENGLISH BASSIST-VOCALIST STEVEN KILBEY (b. *c.* 1960), with Australian Peter Koppes (guitar/vocals), English guitarist-vocalist Marty Willson-Piper and Nick Ward (drums). Australian Richard Ploog replaced Ward after their debut, *Of Skin And Heart*. *Starfish* gained them college radio airplay in the USA, earning a Top 30 hit with 'Under The Milky Way'. Ploog left in 1991, replaced by Jay Dee Daugherty (ex-**Patti Smith**, **Television**).

After various solo and session ventures, Kilbey and McLennan made a second album, *Snow Job*, in 1996.

CITY BOY
Albums
Young Men Gone West (Vertigo 1977)★★★
p.357 for full listings
Connections
Cyndi Lauper p.213

CITY BOY

POP-ROCK GROUP FORMED IN BIRMINGHAM, ENGLAND, IN THE early 70s. The original line-up – 'Lol' Lawrence Mason (vocals), Steve Broughton (guitar), Mike Slamer (guitar) and Max Thomas (guitar/keyboards) – turned professional in 1975. Chris Dunn (bass) joined and Roger Kent (drums), soon replaced by Roy Ward (drums/vocals). After several unsuccessful albums, '5-7-0-5' made the UK Top 10, this was followed by two more hits. Dunn and Broughton left at this point, Dunn managed Tight Fit while Broughton went on to write for **Cyndi Lauper** and others. Mason formed the Maisonettes and wrote songs for Samantha Fox. Slamer formed Streets with Steve Walsh and went into session and production work. Ward sang backing vocals and drummed for Tokyo Charm.

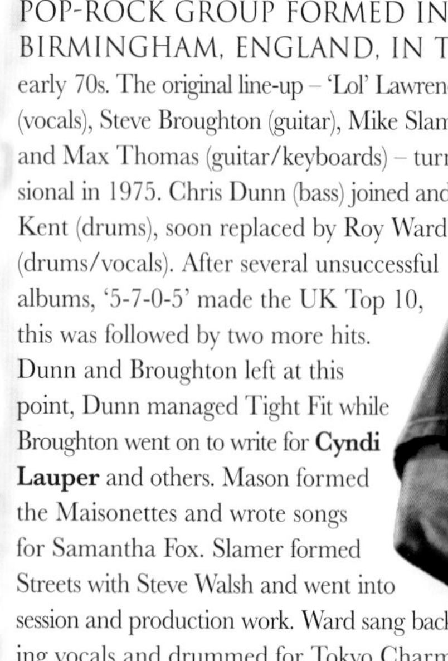

CLAIL, GARY, AND THE ON U SOUND SYSTEM
Albums
Emotional Hooligan (On-U-Sound 1991)★★★
p.357 for full listings
Connections
Slits p.300
Aswad p.23
Simply Red p.298

CLAIL, GARY, AND THE ON U SOUND SYSTEM

THE ON U SOUND SYSTEM GREW FROM TACKHEAD, ROOTS RADICS, AKABU, DUB SYNDICATE AND OTHERS. It was officially launched in 1980 by Adrian Sherwood for a one-off album by the New Age Steppers (including members of **Slits** and **Aswad**). The second album was by the Mothmen (now the rhythm section for **Simply Red**). An impressive roster of collaborative productions ensued. When Clail joined Tackhead, he became involved with On U Sound; 'Human Nature' was a hit in 1991. Clail works mainly as a producer and mixer.

CLANNAD
Albums
Macalla (RCA 1985)★★★
p.357 for full listings
Collaborators
Bono p.326
Enya p.137
Further References
Video: *Past Present* (1989)

CLANNAD

HAILING FROM EIRE, CLANNAD HAVE SUCCESSFULLY BRIDGED FOLK AND ROCK. 'CLANNAD' ('FAMILY' IN GAELIC) FORMED IN 1970, initially to play folk festivals in Ireland.The line-up comprises Maire Brennan (b. Marie Ni Bhroanain, 1952; harp/vocals), Pol Brennan (guitar/vocals/percussion/flute), Ciaran Brennan (guitar/bass/vocals/keyboards), Padraig Duggan (guitar/vocals/mandolin) and Noel Duggan (guitar/vocals). Clannad initially caught wide UK attention when they recorded the theme tune for television's *Harry's Game* in 1982, it reached number 5. In 1984, they recorded the soundtrack to television's *Robin Of Sherwood*; in 1985, the song received a British Academy Award. Further chart success followed with the UK Top 20 hit 'In A Lifetime' (1986), on which Maire duetted with Bono from **U2**. Maire's sister, **Enya** (b. 1961) went solo after three years with the band. Clannad continue to perform.

CLAPTON, ERIC

THE YOUNG ERIC (b. ERIC PATRICK CLAPP, 1945) LEARNT GUITAR BY COPYING THE GREAT BLUES GUITARISTS NOTE FOR NOTE. His first band was the Roosters, a local R&B group that included Tom McGuinness, later of **Manfred Mann.** In 1963, Clapton was recruited by the **Yardbirds**, to replace Tony Topham. Clapton stayed for 18 months; leaving when the Yardbirds took a more pop-orientated direction. Next, he joined **John Mayall**'s Bluesbreakers, with whom he made one album, the classic *Bluesbreakers*.

The formation of **Cream** in 1966, saw Clapton join **Jack Bruce** and **Ginger Baker**. Cream lasted just over two years, after which Clapton joined Baker, **Steve Winwood** and Rick Grech as **Blind Faith**. This 'supergroup' recorded one self-titled album and made a lucrative American tour. During the tour, Clapton befriended **Delaney And Bonnie**, who he later joined. He played on one album, *Delaney And Bonnie On Tour*, and three months later, absconded with three band members to make the disappointing *Eric Clapton*. The band became **Derek And The Dominos**. As Clapton struggled to overcome an engulfing heroin habit, the **Who**'s **Pete Townshend** organized the famous Eric Clapton At The Rainbow concert as part of his rehabilitation crusade, along with Steve Winwood, Rick Grech, Ron Wood and **Jim Capaldi**. Clapton's appearance broke two years of silence, and he played a majestic and emotional set. Although still addicted, this represented a turning point, and he underwent treatment in London's Harley Street.

A rejuvenated Clapton released the buoyant *461 Ocean Boulevard* in 1974; gone were the long guitar solos, replaced by relaxed vocals over shorter, more compact songs. It hit US number 1 and UK number 3 and its singles were also hits, notably **Bob Marley**'s 'I Shot The Sheriff' (US number 1). Also included was the autobiographical 'Give Me Strength' and the mantric 'Let It Flow'. *There's One In Every Crowd* and the live *E. C. Was Here* maintained his reputation and were followed by two more major albums, *Slowhand* and *Backless*. Further singles success came with 'Lay Down Sally' and 'Promises'.

All Clapton's 80s albums sold massively and were critically well received; **Ry Cooder**, **Phil Collins** and **Tina Turner** guested. 1989's *Journeyman* went one better; not only were his voice and songs creditable but 'Slowhand' had rediscovered the guitar.

Clapton has appeared at Live Aid and on television documentaries, released two biographies, and performs an annual season of concerts at London's Royal Albert Hall – in 1991, he played 24 nights. Although the tragic death of his son Conor in 1991 halted his career for some months (resulting in the poignant hit 'Tears In Heaven'), *Unplugged* (1992) became one of his most successful albums. On it he demonstrated his blues roots, playing acoustically with his band (including **Andy Fairweather-Low**). *From The Cradle*, an electric blues album, was a worthy release.

CLARK, GENE

CLARK (b. 1944, d. 1991) JOINED THE NEW CHRISTY MINSTRELS IN 1963. AFTERWARDS HE TEAMED UP WITH JIM (**ROGER**) **McGuinn** and **David Crosby** in the Jet Set. This trio evolved into the **Byrds**. Clark contributed significantly to their first two albums; classics from this period include 'Feel A Whole Lot Better', 'Here Without You' and 'Set You Free This Time'. Following the release of 'Eight Miles High' (1966), he dramatically left the group.

With producer Jim Dickson, Clark recorded a solo album with the Gosdin Brothers, followed by two albums with Doug Dillard as **Dillard And Clark**. In 1968, Crosby left the Byrds and Clark re-joined, he left within weeks. He revitalized his career with *White Light* (1971), but a lack of touring forestalled his progress. After a recorded reunion with the original Byrds in 1973, he recorded a solo album for Asylum Records. *No Other* was highly acclaimed, but sales again proved disappointing, as with his next venture. The original Byrds re-formed in the late 70s and enjoyed brief success, but during the recording of *City* (1980), Clark left amid some acrimony. Afterwards he mainly recorded for small labels, occasionally touring solo or with other ex-Byrds. Clark died from heart failure.

CLARK, GUY

TEXAN-BORN CLARK (b. 1941) WORKED IN TELEVISION AND AS A PHOTOGRAPHER. HE BRIEFLY PERFORMED IN A FOLK trio with Kay K. T. Oslin, before moving to Los Angeles. Clark then wrote songs such as 'LA Freeway', 'Desperados Waiting For A Train' and 'Texas 1947' (by **Johnny Cash**). *Old No. 1* was critically acclaimed but failed to chart on either side of the Atlantic and *Texas Cooking*, was no more successful. *Better Days* included a US country chart single, 'Homegrown Tomatoes'.

CLARK, PETULA

WELSH-BORN PETULA (b. 1932) WAS A CHILD PERFORMER. BY 1943, SHE HAD HER OWN PROGRAMME WITH THE ACCENT on wartime, morale-building songs. She made her first film, *Medal For The General*, in 1944 and went on to appear in over 20 feature films. By 1949 she was recording, and throughout the 50s had several hits.

Her international breakthrough began in 1964 with Tony Hatch's 'Downtown'. It became a big hit in western Europe and reached US number 1. Clark's subsequent recordings of Hatch songs, including 'Don't Sleep In The Subway', 'My Love' and 'I Know A Place', all made the US Top 10. Her recording of 'This Is My Song', written by Charles Chaplin for the film, *A Countess From Hong Kong* (1967), reached UK number 1. In 1968, Clark revived her film career in *Finian's Rainbow* followed by a part in MGM's 1969 remake of *Goodbye, Mr. Chips*.

Between 1981 and 1982, she played the part of Maria in the London revival of *The Sound Of Music*. In 1989, PYS Records issued a version of her 'Downtown', with the original vocal accompanied by 'acid house' backing. It went to UK number 10.

Clark has also written songs, sometimes they are penned under the pseudonym of Al Grant; she wrote the music and appeared in the West End musical, *Someone Like You*. In 1992, toured the UK and in 1993 joined the cast of *Blood Brothers* on Broadway.

CLASH

UK BAND THE CLASH STARTED OUT SUPPORTING THE **SEX PISTOLS** ON THEIR 'ANARCHY TOUR'. GUITARIST MICK JONES (b. 1955) had formed London SS in 1975, whose members had included bassist Paul Simonon (b. 1956) and drummer Nicky 'Topper' Headon (b. 1955). The early Clash line-up had included Joe Strummer (b. John Graham Mellor, 1952), guitarist Keith Levene and drummer Terry Chimes, the latter two left in 1976. The band signed to CBS, recording *The Clash* (UK number 12) in just three weeks; a brilliant evocation of mid-70s England.

Blue Öyster Cult's Sandy Pearlman produced *Give 'Em Enough Rope* (UK number 2). They increasingly embraced reggae elements, seemingly a natural progression from their anti-racist stance, and had a minor UK hit with '(White Man) In Hammersmith Palais' in 1978, followed by the frothy punk-pop of 'Tommy Gun' – their first Top 20 hit.

London Calling marked a return to almost top form, but the triple set, *Sandinista!*, was too sprawling. The experienced producer Glyn Johns was brought in for the snappy *Combat Rock*, recorded with Chimes after Headon abruptly left the group. 'Rock The Casbah' became a US Top 10 hit and reached UK number 30. During 1982 they toured the USA supporting the **Who**.

Jones left in 1983 and the Clash struggled, despite *Cut The Crap* making it to UK number 16. Strummer finally disbanded the Clash in 1986 and turned to acting and production; he supervised the soundtrack to the film *Sid And Nancy*. Mick Jones formed **Big Audio Dynamite**. In 1991, they made a dramatic return to the charts when 'Should I Stay Or Should I Go?' (UK number 17, in 1982) was used in a Levi's jeans advertisement. The re-release reached number 1.

CLASSICS IV

FORMED IN FLORIDA, USA, THE CLASSICS IV FEATURED DENNIS YOST (VOCALS), JAMES COBB (LEAD GUITAR), Wally Eaton (rhythm guitar), Joe Wilson (bass) and Kim Venable (drums). Seasoned session musicians, they had already worked on records by **Tommy Roe**, Billy Joe Royal and the Tams. Between 1968 and 1969, they enjoyed three soft-rock US hits with 'Spooky', 'Stormy' and 'Traces'. Cobb left and, despite the recruitment of guitarist Dean Daughtry, the loss of his songwriting proved insurmountable. Classics IV enjoyed only one more minor hit, 'What Am I Crying For' (1972). Cobb and Daughtry later formed the **Atlanta Rhythm Section**.

CLAPTON, ERIC
Albums
Slowhand (RSO 1977)★★★★
Journeyman (Duck 1989)★★★★
➽ p.357 for full listings

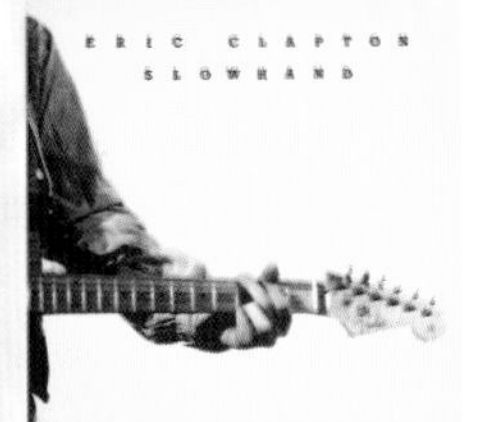

Collaborators
Ry Cooder ➽ p.100
Phil Collins ➽ p.98
Tina Turner ➽ p.324
Andy Fairweather-Low ➽ p.142
Connections
Yardbirds ➽ p.345
John Mayall ➽ p.228
Cream ➽ p.103
Blind Faith ➽ p.53
Delaney And Bonnie ➽ p.114
Derek And The Dominoes ➽ p.116
Pete Townshend ➽ p.323
Influences
Bob Marley ➽ p.225
Further References
Book: *Eric Clapton: Lost In The Blues*, Harry Shapiro

CLARK, GENE
Albums
No Other (Asylum 1974)★★★★
➽ p.357 for full listings
Connections
Byrds ➽ p.77

CLARK, GUY
Albums
Old No. 1 (RCA 1975)★★★★
➽ p.357 for full listings
Collaborators
Johnny Cash ➽ p.84
Rodney Crowell ➽ p.107

CLARK, PETULA
Albums
Downtown (Pye 1964)★★★★
➽ p.357 for full listings

CLASH
Albums
London Calling double album (Columbia 1979)★★★★
➽ p.357 for full listings
Collaborators
Sex Pistols ➽ p.292
Who ➽ p.338
Connections
Big Audio Dynamite ➽ p.46
Influences
Rolling Stone ➽ p.280
Blue Öyster Cult ➽ p.56
Further References
Book: *Last Gang In Town: Story Of The Clash*, Marcus Gray

CLASSICS IV
Albums
Spooky (Liberty 1968)★★★
➽ p.357 for full listings
Connections
Atlanta Rhythm Section ➽ p.24

CLIFF, JIMMY
Albums
The Harder They Come film soundtrack (Mango/Island 1972)★★★★★
➽ p.357 for full listings
Collaborators
Procol Harum ➽ p.268
UB40 ➽ p.326
Connections
Paul Simon ➽ p.296
Cat Stevens ➽ p.309
Further References
Film: *The Harder They Come* (1972)

CLIMAX BLUES BAND
Albums
Blues From The Attic (HTD 1994)★★★
➽ p.357 for full listings
Connections
John Mayall ➽ p.228

CLINE, PATSY
Albums
Sentimentally Yours (Decca 1962)★★★★
➽ p.357 for full listings
Collaborators
Jerry Lee Lewis ➽ p.215
Influences
Shirley Temple
Further References
Book: *Patsy Cline: Sweet Dreams*, Ellis Nassour

CLINT EASTWOOD AND GENERAL SAINT
Albums
Jah Lights Shining (Vista Sounds 1984)★★★.
➽ p.357 for full listings
Connections
General Saint
Influences
General Echo

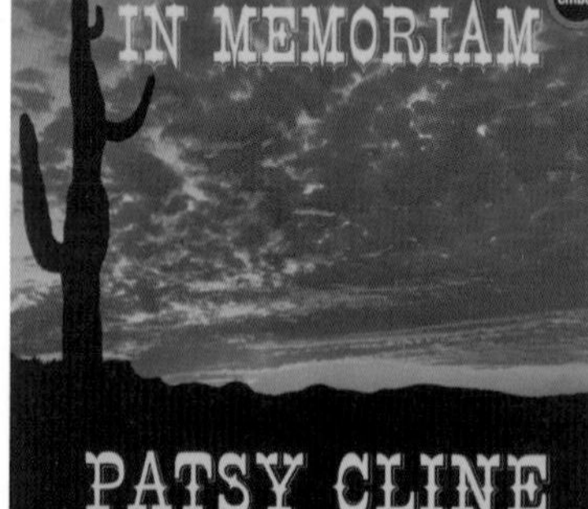

CLINTON, GEORGE
Albums
You Shouldn't-Nuf Bit Fish (Capitol 1984)★★★★
➽ p.357 for full listings
Collaborators
Bootsy Collins ➽ p.98
Dr. Dre ➽ p.124
Connections
Parliament ➽ p.256
Funkadelic ➽ p.156
Further References
Video: *Mothership Connection* (Virgin Vision 1987)

CLIFF, JIMMY

ONE OF THE GREAT POPULARIZERS OF REGGAE MUSIC, JAMAICAN JIMMY CLIFF'S (b. JAMES CHAMBERS, 1948) EARLY singles, 'Daisy Got Me Crazy' (with Count Boysie) and 'I'm Sorry', were followed by the local hit 'Hurricane Hattie'. Cliff joined producer Leslie Kong in 1963, singing 'King Of Kings' and 'Dearest Beverly' in a hoarse, raucous voice. Afterwards, Cliff moved to London and, by 1968, was being groomed as a solo star to the underground rock market. The shift away from conventional reggae was made by a cover of **Procul Harum**'s 'Whiter Shade of Pale'.

In 1968, Cliff represented Jamaica in the International Song Festival with 'Waterfall'. He finally broke through in 1969 with 'Wonderful World, Beautiful People'. 'Vietnam' was a small hit the following year, and was described by **Bob Dylan** as the best protest song he had heard. **Paul Simon** booked the same rhythm section, studio and engineer to record 'Mother And Child Reunion'. In local terms, however, its success was outstripped by a cover of **Cat Stevens**'s 'Wild World'. Cliff's role in the film *The Harder They Come* (1972) made him Jamaica's most marketable property.

Outside the reggae world, Cliff remains best known for writing 'Many Rivers To Cross', a massive hit for **UB40**, however, his popularity in Africa and South America is enormous.

CLIMAX BLUES BAND

ORIGINALLY THE CLIMAX CHICAGO BLUES BAND, THIS ENDURING BRITISH GROUP FEATURED COLIN COOPER (b. 1939; vocals/saxophone), Peter Haycock (b. 1952; vocals/guitar), Richard Jones (keyboards), Arthur Wood (keyboards), Derek Holt (b. 1949; bass) and George Newsome (b. 1947; drums). 1969's *The Climax Chicago Blues Band* evoked early **John Mayall** and Savoy Brown but *Plays On* (minus Jones) displayed a new-found maturity. A freer, flowing pulse and rock-based elements were reflected on *A Lot Of Bottle* and *Tightly Knit*.

Jones rejoined in 1975 and they enjoyed a surprise UK number 10 with 'Couldn't Get It Right' (1976); the success proved temporary. In 1994, the only original member was Cooper, who recruited George Glover (keyboards/vocals), Lester Hunt (guitar/vocals), Roy Adams (drums) and Roger Inniss (bass). Their live album, *Blues From The Attic* sounded remarkably fresh.

CLINE, PATSY

US-BORN PATSY (b. VIRGINIA PATTERSON HENSLEY, 1932, d. 1963) BEGAN HER CAREER when she approached Wally Fowler, a noted *Opry* artist. Taken aback by her overt approach, he let her sing for him and included her in that night's show. In 1952, she met Bill Peer, a disc jockey and musician, who was touring with his band, the Melody Boys And Girls. He hired Patsy as lead vocalist. In 1953, Patsy married Gerald Cline. In 1954, she signed a two-year contract with Four-Star, a Pasadena-based independent company. She made her first four recordings in 1955, under the production of pianist, guitarist and arranger Owen Bradley. 'A Church, A Courtroom And Then Goodbye' was the chosen song, but it failed to reach the country charts, nor did further recordings including 'I Love You Honey' and the rockabilly 'Stop, Look And Listen'.

In an effort to secure a country hit, she recorded 'Walking After Midnight', in a session that also included 'A Poor Man's Roses (Or A Rich Man's Gold)' and 'The Heart You Break May Be Your Own'. The record reached country number 2 and pop number 12; 'A Poor Man's Roses' also reached country number 14.

Her next single, 'I Fall To Pieces', quickly became a country number 1 and peaked at pop number 12. In 1961, she completed a four-day recording session that included 'True Love', 'The Wayward Wind', 'San Antonio Rose' and her now legendary 'Crazy' (country number 2/pop number 9). In 1962, 'She's Got You' reached country number 1 and pop number 14. It also became her first entry in the UK Top 50. Her last recording session took place on 7 February 1963. On 5 March, Cline, together with country singers Cowboy Copas and Hawkshaw Hawkins, set off on a five-hundred-mile flight to Nashville, in a small aircraft piloted by Randy Hughes. Patsy died when the aircraft crashed in Tennessee. At the time of her death, Cline's recording of 'Leaving On Your Mind' was in both country and pop charts; before the year was over, 'Sweet Dreams' and 'Faded Love' were Top 10 country and minor pop hits.

CLINT EASTWOOD AND GENERAL SAINT

JAMAICAN-BORN EASTWOOD CAME TO PROMINENCE IN BRITAIN IN THE LATE 70S WITH HIT REGGAE SINGLES AND albums such as *African Youth*, *Death In The Arena* and *Sex Education*. In the early 80s, he teamed up with General Saint. Their first release, a tribute to the late General Echo, topped the reggae charts as did the follow-up, 'Another One Bites The Dust' (1981). They were instrumental in the Jamaican DJ style crossing over to the early 80s pop audience.

CLINTON, GEORGE

THE MASTERMIND BEHIND THE HIGHLY SUCCESSFUL **PARLIAMENT** AND **FUNKADELIC**, GEORGE 'DR FUNKENSTEIN' Clinton's (b. 1940) empire crumbled at the beginning of the 80s. Restrained from recording by a breach-of-contract lawsuit and unable to meet the running expenses of his considerable organization, he found himself personally and professionally destitute. After finally settling most of his debts and overcoming a cocaine addiction, he resumed recording. With the P-Funk All Stars, he secured two minor hits, 'Hydrolic Pump' and 'One Of Those Summers' (both 1982), before the solo 'Loopzilla'. *Computer Games* featured several ex-Funkadelic/Parliament cohorts, including Bernie Worrell and **Bootsy Collins**, while 'Atomic Dog' (1983), was a US R&B number 1. Clinton continued as a soloist and with the P-Funk All Stars, pursuing his eclectic, eccentric vision on *Some Of My Best Jokes Are Friends* and *The Cinderella Theory*. *Hey Man ... Smell My Finger* featured a cameo by **Dr. Dre**.

CLOCK DVA

FORMED IN SHEFFIELD, ENGLAND, IN THE EARLY 80S. *WHITE SOULS IN BLACK SUITS* FEATURED Adi Newton (vocals), Steven James Taylor (bass/vocals/guitar), Paul Widger (guitar), Roger Quail (drums) and Charlie Collins (saxophone). There had already been three previous line-ups, including guitarist Dave Hammond, and synthesizer players Joseph Hurst and Simon Elliot-Kemp.

John Valentine Carruthers (guitar), Paul Browse (saxophone), Dean Dennis (bass) and Nick Sanderson (drums) joined, although Carruthers and Sanderson departed after *Advantage*, and Clock DVA continued as a trio. They re-emerged with *Buried Dreams*. By *Transitional Voices*, Browse had been replaced by Robert Baker.

CLOVER

FORMED IN CALIFORNIA FROM THE TINY HEARING AID COMPANY: BASSIST JOHNNY CIAMBOTTI, JOHN MCFEE (b. 1953; guitar/pedal steel guitar/vocals), Alex Call (guitar/vocals) and Mitch Howie (drums). They became Clover in 1967. *Clover* proved their reputation as a feisty bar band, but suffered from primitive production. *Forty-Niner* was a marked improvement. Unable to break out of their stifling good-time niche, a dispirited Howie left, replaced by Huey (Louis) Lewis (vocals/harmonica), Sean Hopper (keyboards/vocals) and Mickey Shine (drums). In 1976, the group went to Britain and accompanied **Elvis Costello** on *My Aim Is True*.

Despite two promising albums, Clover were unable to make a significant breakthrough and returned to the USA in 1978, where they folded. McFee joined the **Doobie Brothers**; Lewis and Hooper formed **Huey Lewis And The News**.

CLOVERS

US R&B VOCAL ENSEMBLE FORMED IN WASHINGTON, DC, IN 1946. IN 1950, the Clovers featured John 'Buddy' Bailey (b. 1930; lead), Matthew McQuater (tenor), Harold Lucas (baritone) and Harold Winley (bass) and Bill Harris (b. 1925, d. 1988; guitar). In 1952, Charles White (b. 1930) became the Clovers' new lead, when Buddy Bailey was drafted into the Army. In 1953, Billy Mitchell took over from White. Bailey rejoined in 1954 but Mitchell remained and the two alternated the leads. The Clovers had three US R&B number 1s with 'Don't You Know I Love You', 'Fool, Fool, Fool' (both 1951) and 'Ting-A-Ling' (1952), plus four number 2 R&B hits. They only made the US pop charts twice: 'Love Love Love' (number 30, 1956) and 'Love Potion No. 9' (number 23, 1959). In 1961, the Clovers split into rival groups and the hits dried up.

COASTERS

VOCAL GROUP FROM LOS ANGELES, PRODUCED BY **LEIBER AND STOLLER**. THE group formed in 1955, featuring Carl Gardner (b. 1928; lead) and Bobby Nunn (b. 1925, d. 1986; bass), Leon Hughes (b. 1938; tenor), Billy Guy (b. 1936; lead/baritone) and Adolph Jacobs (guitar). Hughes was replaced in 1956 by Young Jessie, who was replaced by Cornell Gunther (b. 1936, d. 1990). In 1958, Nunn was replaced by Will 'Dub' Jones (b. 1939). Earl Carroll (b. Gregory Carroll, 1937) replaced Gunther in 1961.

The Coasters first charted with 'Down In Mexico' (US R&B Top 10) in 1956 and 1957's 'Searchin''/'Young Blood' established them as major rock 'n' roll stars. Three more giant hits sustained their career: 'Yakety Yak', 'Charlie Brown' and 'Poison Ivy'. In the early 60s, the group fractured. They were inducted into the Rock And Roll Hall Of Fame in 1987.

COCHRAN, EDDIE

EDDIE COCHRAN (b. EDWARD COCHRANE, 1938, d. 1960) BEGAN AS A COUNTRY SINGER; SOON BECOMING AN outstanding rockabilly guitarist with his trademark Gretsch guitar. In 1956, after his cameo performance of 'Twenty Flight Rock' in the film *The Girl Can't Help It*, he was signed by Liberty Records. 'Sittin' In The Balcony' reached the US Top 20 ; the following 'Summertime Blues' (1957) and 'C'mon Everybody' (1958) have become timeless classics. Tragically, while holidaying in Britain, Cochran was killed in a car crash; **Gene Vincent** and Sharon Sheeley (co-writer of 'Something Else') were badly injured.

'Three Steps To Heaven', his biggest hit, topped the UK chart shortly after his untimely death. 'Weekend' was the last of his classics, another tale of simple youthful enthusiasm for life.

COCKBURN, BRUCE

CANADIAN SINGER-SONGWRITER WHO RECORDED MANY EARLY ALBUMS INSPIRED BY HIS CHRISTIANITY. AFTER Cockburn's (b. 1945) breakthrough single 'Wondering Where The Lions Are' (from *Dancing In The Dragon's Jaws*), his lyrical gaze turned to more secular matter on *World Of Wonders*. More recent work has embraced environmental concerns, such as 'If A Tree Falls'and 'Radium Rain'. Bruce Cockburn is enormously popular in his homeland, yet his brand of folk rock remains only a cult item elsewhere. Despite being created in conjunction with producer **T-Bone Burnett**, mixer Glyn Johns and Columbia Records, *Dart To The Heart* was only a commercial success in Canada.

COCKER, JOE

UK-BORN COCKER (b. JOHN ROBERT COCKER, 1944) STARTED out in 1961 with Sheffield band the Cavaliers (later Vance Arnold And The Avengers). He formed the first Grease Band in 1966, with Chris Stainton (bass). After two years of solid club gigs, they were rewarded with a recording session. The single 'Marjorine' was a minor hit and Cocker and Stainton assembled a new Grease Band with Mickey Gee (guitar), Tommy Reilly (drums) and Tommy Eyre (keyboards). The resulting single was recorded with session musicians including **Jimmy Page** and B. J. Wilson. The single, **Lennon** and **McCartney's** 'With A Little Help From My Friends', went to UK number 1 in 1968.

Their debut album failed to chart in the UK but was a US hit. Cocker and his band started touring America in 1969, and became huge stars through exposure on the *Ed Sullivan Show* and constant performing. By the end of 1969 Cocker had a further two hits with **Dave Mason**'s 'Feelin' Alright' and **Leon Russell**'s 'Delta Lady', together with another solid and successful album *Joe Cocker!*

The 70s began with the famous Mad Dogs And Englishmen tour – over 60 dates were played in as many days. A subsequent film and double album were released, although it was reported that Cocker was bankrupted by the whole charade. He then slid into a drink-and-drug stupor that lasted through most of the decade. Despite this he still managed to produce hits, including 'Midnight Rider', 'You Are So Beautiful' and 'Put Out The Light'. His albums were patchy, except for *I Can Stand A Little Rain*. Apart from a minor hit guesting with the Crusaders on 'I'm So Glad I'm Standing Here Today', little was heard from him until 1982, when he returned to US number 1 with **Jennifer Warnes** on the soundtrack to *An Officer And A Gentlemen*. The song 'Up Where We Belong' also reached the UK singles chart in 1983.

His anniversary tour in 1994 was accompanied by his best album in years, *Have A Little Faith*. He paid tribute to himself in 1996 with *Organic*, containing many remakes from his catalogue.

CLOCK DVA
Albums
Thirst (Fetish 1981)★★★
➧ p.357 for full listings

CLOVER
Albums
Love On The Wire (Vertigo 1977)★★★
➧ p.357 for full listings
Collaborators
Elvis Costello ➧ p.101
Connections
Doobie Brothers ➧ p.123
Huey Lewis and the News ➧ p.215
Influences
Nick Lowe ➧ p.219

CLOVERS
Albums
Dance Party (Atlantic 1959)★★★★
➧ p.357 for full listings
Connections
Dominoes

COASTERS
Albums
The Coasters (Atco 1958)★★★★
➧ p.357 for full listings
Connections
Cadillacs
Further References
Book: *The Coasters*, Bill Millar

COCHRAN, EDDIE
Albums
Cherished Memories (Liberty 1962)★★★★
➧ p.357 for full listings
Connections
Cochran Brothers
Further References
Film: *Go Johnny Go* (1958)

COCKBURN, BRUCE
Albums
Nothing But A Burning Light (Columbia 1992)★★★★
➧ p.357 for full listings

COCKER, JOE
Albums
With A Little Help From My Friends (Regal Zonophone 1969)★★★★
➧ p.351 for full listings
Collaborators
Jimmy Page ➧ p.255
Influences
John Lennon ➧ p.214
Paul McCartney ➧ p.229
Dave Mason ➧ p.227
Leon Russell ➧ p.286
Further References
Book: *Joe Cocker: With A Little Help From My Friends*, J. P. Bean

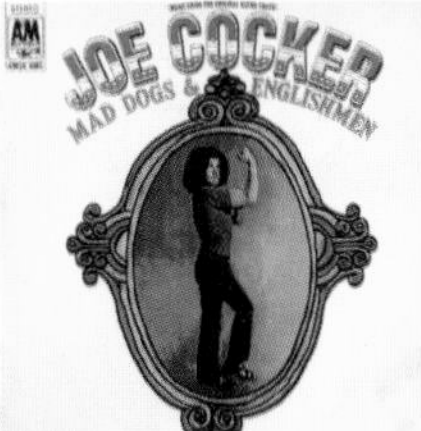

COCKNEY REBEL
Albums
The Human Menagerie (EMI 1973)★★★
Psychomodo (EMI 1974)★★★
➧ p.357 for full listings
Collaborators
Sarah Brightman
Connections
Family ➧ p.143
Influences
Roxy Music ➧ p.283
David Bowie ➧ p.64
George Harrison ➧ p.176

COCTEAU TWINS
Albums
Heaven Or Las Vegas (4AD 1990)★★★★
➧ p.357 for full listings

Influences
Ivo Watts-Russell
John Peel ➧ p.258

COGAN, ALMA
Albums
How About Love (Columbia 1962)★★★
➧ p.357 for full listings
Collaborators
Frankie Vaughan
Further References
Book: *Alma Cogan*, Sandra Caron

COHEN, LEONARD
Albums
The Songs Of Leonard Cohen (Columbia 1968)★★★★
I'm Your Man (Columbia 1988)★★★★
The Future (Columbia 1992)★★★★
➧ p.357 for full listings
Collaborators
Phil Spector ➧ p.304
Connections
Judy Collins ➧ p.98
Further References
Film: *Bird On A Wire* (1972)
Video: *Songs From The Life Of Leonard Cohen* (CMV Enterprises 1989)
Book: *Flowers For Hitler*, Leonard Cohen

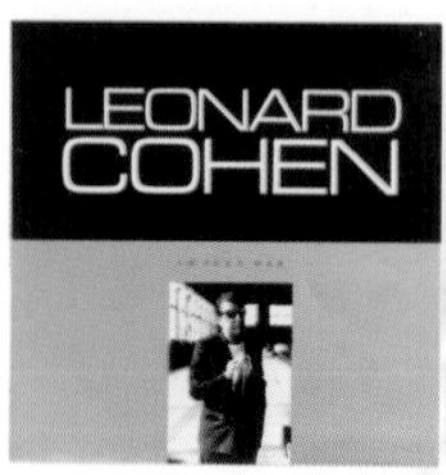

COCKNEY REBEL

FORMED IN ENGLAND IN 1973 BY STEVE HARLEY (b. STEVEN NICE, 1951) WITH JEAN-PAUL CROCKER, PAUL AVRON Jeffreys (b. 1952, d. 1988 in the Lockerbie air disaster), Milton Reame-James and Stuart Elliott. Their debut hit 'Judy Teen' was a confident start after which the group was reconstructed. The most stable line-up featured Jim Cregan (guitar; ex-**Family**), George Ford (keyboards), Lindsay Elliott (percussion), Duncan McKay (keyboards) and Stuart Elliott, the band's original drummer. Their first two albums remain their best works and they reached UK number 1 with 'Make Me Smile (Come Up And See Me)'. Harley's limited but interesting vocal range was put to the test on **George Harrison**'s 'Here Comes the Sun' (1976), which made the UK Top 10.

Harley returned to the best-sellers in 1986, duetting with Sarah Brightman in the title song from *The Phantom Of The Opera*. In 1992, Harley returned to the UK Top 50 with the re-released 'Make Me Smile (Come Up And See Me)' and embarked on a major tour.

COCTEAU TWINS

FORMED IN SCOTLAND, IN 1982, THE COCTEAU TWINS ORIGINALLY FEATURED ELIZABETH FRASER (b. 1958), ROBIN Guthrie and Will Heggie (bass; departed in 1983). Their first album, *Garlands*, was given extensive airplay by BBC Radio 1 DJ **John Peel**. *Head Over Heels* smoothed over the rougher edges of its predecessor with Guthrie adding layers of echo and phased drum effects. The group was also involved in This Mortal Coil. Simon Raymonde joined on bass and two superb EPs, *Sunburst And Snowblind* and *Pearly-Dewdrops' Drops*, dominated the independent charts.

1984's *Treasure* saw the group scaling new heights, and was followed by several EPs, *Aikea-Guinea*, *Tiny Dynamine* and *Echoes In A Shallow Bay*. *Victorialand*, recorded without Raymonde, had a lighter, acoustic sound. Raymonde returned for the *Love's Easy Tears* EP.

On *Blue Bell Knoll* it seemed they had lost their touch, but the stunning *Heaven Or Las Vegas* redeemed their reputation. 'Iceblink Luck' reached the UK Top 40 and the band resumed touring. They signed a new contract with Fontana Records in 1992 and completed *Four-Calendar Café*, for the first time Fraser's lyrics were audible. The band then released a Christmas single, 'Frosty The Snowman'. *Milk And Kisses* was preceded by two EPs, *Otherness* and *Twinlights*.

COGAN, ALMA

UK-BORN COGAN (b. 1932, d. 1966) FIRST FOUND SUCCESS WITH THE NOVELTY HIT 'BELL BOTTOM BLUES' (UK TOP 5, 1954). A cover of Kitty Kallen's 'Little Things Mean A Lot' followed as did duets with Frankie Vaughan on a couple of unsuccessful singles. Her lone UK number 1 was 'Dreamboat' (1955) before another novelty song 'Never Do A Tango With An Eskimo'. By the end of the 50s, Cogan had notched up 18 UK chart entries, more than any female singer of her era.

Cogan was diagnosed as suffering from cancer; during convalescence she wrote a number of songs and continued recording. In 1966, she collapsed while working in Sweden and was flown back to London. On 26 October, she lost her fight.

COHEN, LEONARD

CANADIAN-BORN COHEN (b. 1934) STARTED OUT AS A NOVELIST, *THE FAVOURITE GAME* AND *BEAUTIFUL LOSERS* offered the mixture of sexual and spiritual longing, despair and black humour, prevalent in his lyrics. Two early songs, 'Suzanne' and 'Priests', were recorded by **Judy Collins**; the former was also included on *The Songs Of Leonard Cohen*. The weary loneliness portrayed by his intonation was enhanced by the barest of accompaniment. *Songs From A Room* maintained a similar pattern, but despite the inclusion of 'Story Of Isaac' and 'Bird On A Wire', lacked the commercial impact of its predecessor. Although Cohen's lugubrious delivery had slackened by *Songs Of Love And Hate*, it contained two of his finest compositions: 'Joan Of Arc' and 'Famous Blue Raincoat'.

New Skin For The Old Ceremony showed his talent was undiminished and included the disconsolate track 'Chelsea Hotel', an account of Cohen's sexual encounter with **Janis Joplin**. A second impasse in his career ended in 1977 with *Death Of A Ladies' Man*, an unlikely collaboration with **Phil Spector**. A grandiose backing proved ill-fitting and Cohen later disowned the project. *Recent Songs* and *Various Positions* were underrated collections and the singer's career seemed destined to remain confined to a small, committed audience until **Jennifer Warnes** released *Famous Blue Raincoat* (1987), a commercially successful album consisting solely of Cohen's songs. His own next set, *I'm Your Man*, was afforded widespread attention and attendant live performances formed the core of a BBC television documentary. His talent was confirmed by the excellent *The Future*.

COLD BLOOD

A POPULAR LIVE ATTRACTION IN THEIR NATIVE SAN FRANCISCO, COLD BLOOD WERE FORMED IN 1968. The band – Lydia Pense (vocals), Larry Field (guitar), Paul Matute (keyboards), Danny Hull (saxophone), Jerry Jonutz (saxophone), David Padron (trumpet), Larry Jonutz (trumpet), Paul Ellicot (bass) and Frank J. David (drums) – were signed to **Bill Graham**'s Fillmore label in 1969. Later releases failed to recapture the gritty quality of their early records, despite their final album being produced by **Steve Cropper**.

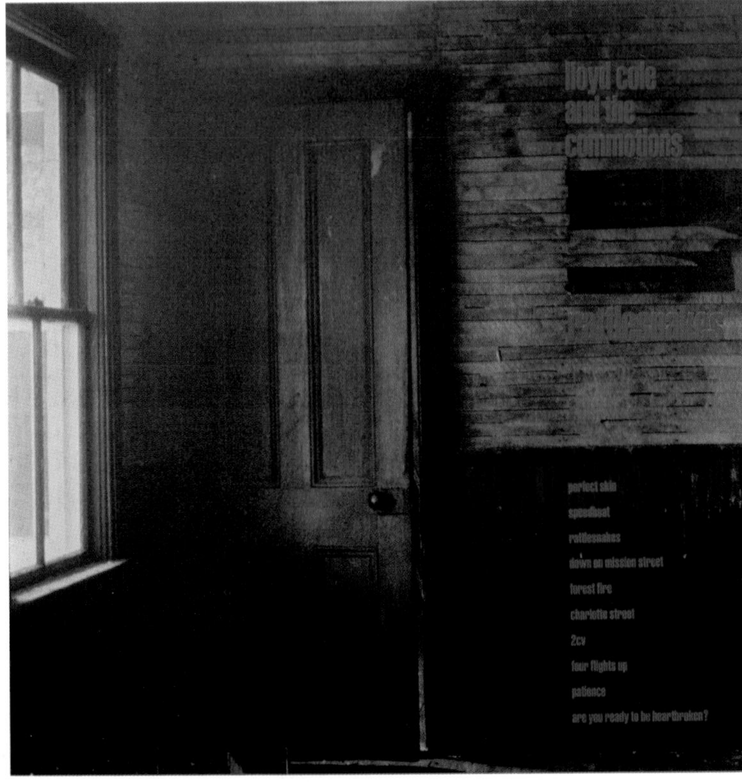

COLE, LLOYD

ENGLISH SINGER-SONGWRITER LLOYD COLE (b. 1961) EMERGED FROM THE POST-PUNK RENAISSANCE. THE Commotions – Neil Clark (b. 1955; guitar), Blair Cowan (keyboards), Lawrence Donegan (b. 1961; bass) and Stephen Irvine (b. 1959; drums) – completed the line-up responsible for *Rattlesnakes*, a critically lauded set that merged **Byrds**-like guitar to Cole's **Lou Reed**-inspired intonation. The attendant 'Perfect Skin' reached the UK Top 30, while the follow-up album, *Easy Pieces*, spawned two Top 20 entries in 'Brand New Friend' and 'Lost Weekend'. Unfortunately, their style seemed laboured on *Mainstream* and Cole disbanded his group.

The solo *Lloyd Cole* showed signs of an artistic rejuvenation, but *Don't Get Weird On Me, Babe* and *Bad Vibes*, although good in parts, failed to lift the atmosphere of bookish lyrics rendered without true depth.

COLE, NATALIE

THE DAUGHTER OF NAT 'KING' COLE, NATALIE (b. 1950) SURVIVED EARLY PRESSURES TO EMULATE HER FATHER'S laid-back style. Signed to Capitol in 1975, her debut, 'This Will Be', reached the US Top 10 and was the first of three consecutive number 1s. Natalie maintained her popularity into the 80s but drug dependency took a professional and personal toll.

In 1984, she emerged from a rehabilitation centre and began recording *Everlasting*. From this came three hits, 'Jump Start', 'I Live For Your Love' and 'Pink Cadillac'. In 1991, she recorded a unique tribute to her late father – a 'duet' with him on his original recording of 'Unforgettable'. The accompanying album won seven Grammy Awards, including best album and song. Two years later she released *Take A Look*, which included a version of 'Cry Me A River'.

COLE, PAULA

US POP-ROCK SINGER-SONGWRITER PAULA COLE (b. *c.* 1968) LAUNCHED HER CAREER WITH THE SPIRITED, PERSUASIVE *Harbinger*. Among several notable tracks was the high-impact single, 'I Am So Ordinary'. Cole toured as a member of **Peter Gabriel**'s Secret World Live band, and he repaid the compliment by contributing backing vocals to the ballad, 'Hush Hush Hush', on *This Fire*. In 1998, 'Where Have All The Cowboys Gone' achieved widespread fame.

COLLECTIVE SOUL

FORMED IN GEORGIA, USA, IN THE EARLY 80S, COLLECTIVE SOUL HONED STRONG, HOOK-LADEN POP-ROCK SONGS, including 'Shine' (1994). Brothers Ed (vocals/guitar) and Dean Roland (guitars) recruited Ross Childress (lead guitar), Will Turpin (bass) and Shane Evans (drums). After years of rejection from major labels, Ed disbanded the group in 1992 – a year later, they were signed to Atlantic Records. 'Breathe' failed to replicate the success of 'Shine', but the group's debut album became a million-seller. 'Gel' was the first single from their second album and was featured on the soundtrack to the cult film *Jerky Boys*. They returned with *Disciplined Breakdown*.

COLLINS, ALBERT

NEVADA-BORN COLLINS (b. 1932, d. 1993) WAS A MASTER GUITARIST: USING NON-STANDARD TUNING AND SLASHING out blocked chords and sharp flurries of treble notes on his Fender Telecaster. His first singles, released from 1958 onwards, were shuffle instrumentals including 'The Freeze' and 'Frosty', but it was not until the late 60s that he began singing too. A series of splendid studio and live albums over the following years extended his basic Texas style across the boundaries of jazz and funk, establishing him as a major international blues attraction.

A lull in his career was broken by 1978's *Ice Pickin'*. On this, he was supported by the Icebreakers – Larry Burton (guitar), Chuck Smith (saxophone), Casey Jones (drums), A. C. Reed (saxophone) and Alan Batts (keyboards). Two live albums, *Frozen Alive* and *Live In Japan*, emphasized Collins's charismatic stage presence. This talented man endured a terminal disease with great humility; his death at 61 was a cruel shock.

COLD BLOOD
Albums
Cold Blood (San Francisco 1969)★★★
Sisyphus (San Francisco 1971)★★★
➽ p.351 for full listings
Connections
Santana ➽ p.288
Pointer Sisters ➽ p.263
Influences
Tower of Power ➽ p.323

COLE, LLOYD
Albums
with the Commotions *Rattlesnakes* (Polydor 1984)★★★★
with the Commotions *Easy Pieces* (Polydor 1985)★★★
Don't Get Weird On Me, Babe (Polydor 1991)★★★
➽ p.357 for full listings
Connections
Commotions
Influences
Byrds ➽ p.77
Lou Reed ➽ p.274
Further References
Videos: *From The Hip* (Polygram Music Video 1988)
1984 – 1989 (Lloyd Cole & The Commotions) (Channel 5 1989)

COLE, NATALIE
Albums
Inseparable (Capitol 1975)★★★★
Natalie ... Live! (Capitol 1978)★★★★
Unforgettable ... With Love (Elektra 1991)★★★★
➽ p.357 for full listings
Further References
Video: *Holly & Ivy* (Warner Music Vision 1995)

COLE, PAULA
Albums
Harbinger (Imago 1994)★★★
➽ p.357 for full listings
Collaborators
Peter Gabriel ➽ p.151

COLLECTIVE SOUL
Albums
Hints, Allegations & Things Left Unsaid (Atlantic 1993)★★★
Collective Soul (Atlantic 1995)★★★★
➽ p.357 for full listings

COLLINS, ALBERT
Albums
Ice Pickin' (Alligator 1978)★★★★
Frostbite (Alligator 1980)★★★★
The Ice Man (Charisma/Point Blank 1991)★★★★
➽ p.358 for full listings
Connections
Icebreakers
Influences
Clarence 'Gatemouth' Brown
Frankie Lee Sims

COLLINS, BOOTSY
Albums
Bootsy? Player Of The Year (Warners 1978)★★★
➽ p.358 for full listings
Connections
James Brown ➽ p.70
George Clinton ➽ p.94

COLLINS, EDWYN
Albums
Gorgeous George (Setanta 1994)★★★★
➽ p.358 for full listings
Collaborators
Roddy Frame ➽ p.25
Connections
Orange Juice ➽ p.252
Further References
Video: *Phantasmagoria* (Alternative Image 1992)

COLLINS, JUDY
Albums
In My Life (1966)★★★★
➽ p.358 for full listings
Collaborators
Jacques Brel
Bertolt Brecht
Leonard Cohen ➽ p.96
Joni Mitchell ➽ p.235
Stephen Stills ➽ p.310
Connections
Byrds ➽ p.77
Influences
Bob Dylan ➽ p.128
Further References
Book: *Trust Your Heart: An Autobiography*, Judy Collins

COLLINS, PHIL
Albums
Hello, I Must Be Going (Virgin 1982)★★★★
➽ p.358 for full listings

Collaborators
John Martyn ➽ p.226
Robert Plant ➽ p.262
Eric Clapton ➽ p.92
Connections
Genesis ➽ p.156
Influences
Supremes ➽ p.314
Further References
Video: *Live At Perkin's Palace* (1986)
Book: *Phil Collins*, Johnny Waller

COLOUR FIELD
Albums
Deception (Chrysalis 1987)★★★
➽ p.358 for full listings
Connections
Specials ➽ p.304
Fun Boy Three ➽ p.155
Influences
Sly And The Family Stone ➽ p.300

COLLINS, BOOTSY

BOOTSY COLLINS (b. WILLIAM COLLINS, 1951) WAS AN INTEGRAL PART OF THE JBS, **JAMES BROWN**'S BACKING GROUP who replaced the Famous Flames. Between 1969 and 1971, Collins's distinctive basswork propelled some of the era's definitive funk anthems. Later, Collins and several others switched to **George Clinton**'s **Parliament/ Funkadelic** organization. The bassist's popularity inspired the formation of Bootsy's Rubber Band. Collins's outrageous image emphasized a mix of funk and fun exemplified by 'Psychotic-bumpschool' (1976), 'The Pinocchio Theory' (1977) and 'Bootzilla' (1978). Collins and the Bootzilla Orchestra were employed for the production of Malcolm McLaren's 1989 album *Waltz Darling* and by the early 90s the Rubber Band had started touring again. *Fresh Outta "P" University* was his best work since his 70s' peak.

COLLINS, EDWYN

FOLLOWING THE COLLAPSE OF **ORANGE JUICE**, SCOTTISH SINGER EDWYN COLLINS (b. 1959) WENT SOLO. BOTH THE Orange Juice producer, Dennis Bovell, and drummer Zeke Manyika were present on Collins's solo debut, *Hope And Despair*, as was **Aztec Camera**'s Roddy Frame. The single 'Don't Shilly Shally' was produced by Robin Guthrie (**Cocteau Twins**). *Hellbent On Compromise* was a more intimate and atmospheric recording.

Collins produced for other artists and worked with the Setanta Records roster before 'A Girl Like You' became the most successful instalment in his 15-year recording career, entering the Top 10 in Australia, France and the UK. Three years later Collins returned with *I'm Not Following You*.

COLLINS, JUDY

JUDY COLLINS (b. 1939) WAS ORIGINALLY TRAINED AS A CLASSICAL PIANIST. SIGNED TO ELEKTRA IN 1961, HER EARLY releases emphasized her traditional repertoire, however, by the release of *Judy Collins #3*, her clear soprano was tackling more contemporary material. This pivotal selection, included **Bob Dylan**'s 'Farewell'; it was arranged by Jim (**Roger**) **McGuinn**.

Judy Collins' Fifth Album was the artist's last purely folk collection, including compositions by Dylan, Richard Farina, Eric Andersen and **Gordon Lightfoot** alongside songs culled from theatre's bohemian fringes. *In My Life* embraced **Jacques Brel**, Bertolt Brecht, Kurt Weill and the then-unknown **Leonard Cohen**; on *Wildflowers* she introduced **Joni Mitchell** and in the process enjoyed a popular hit with 'Both Sides Now'. These releases were marked by Joshua Rifkin's string arrangements, which became a feature of her work.

Who Knows Where The Time Goes featured **Stephen Stills** and Van Dyke Parks. *Whales And Nightingales* was equally impressive, and included the million-seller 'Amazing Grace'. Soon Collins, never a prolific writer, began to rely on outside material and, shortly, to look for outside interests. She remained committed to the political causes born from the 60s protest movement and fashioned a new career by co-producing a film documentary which was nominated for an Academy Award. Collins secured another international hit in 1975 with a version of 'Send In The Clowns'. In recent years, she has shown a gift for writing novels.

COLLINS, PHIL

AFTER A WHILE WORKING WITH **GENESIS**, AS DRUMMER AND VOCALIST, COLLINS (b. 1951) PRODUCED THE SOLO album *Face Value*; it immediately confirmed him as a songwriter of note. Recorded during the collapse of his first marriage, it rawly conveyed all his most intense emotions. The stand-out track 'In The Air Tonight', reached UK number 2. Over the next decade Collins made a further five albums with Genesis, in addition to his solo work. *Hello, I Must Be Going* was similarly successful and his excellent cover of the **Supremes'** 'You Can't Hurry Love' was a worldwide hit in 1982. He became a highly successful record producer and session drummer, working with such artists as **John Martyn**, **Robert Plant**, **Adam And The Ants**, Frida, **Eric Clapton**, **Brand X** and **Howard Jones**. Additionally, his specially commissioned film-soundtrack song for *Against All Odds* reached US number 1 and UK number 2. He played drums on Band Aid's 'Do They Know Its Christmas' and, a few weeks later, was again near the top of the US charts duetting with Philip Bailey on the infectious 'Easy Lover'. Barely pausing for breath, he released *No Jacket Required* which topped charts worldwide.

Collins made musical history on 13 July 1985 by appearing at both Live Aid concerts – in London, and, courtesy of Concorde, in Philadelphia. A second duet and film soundtrack, this time with Marilyn Martin for *White Nights* made 'Separate Lives' his fourth US chart-topper. In 1986, Collins toured the world with Eric Clapton's band. 1987 was spent filming for his starring role in *Buster* and 1989 saw the release of his fourth solo album; it immediately topped the charts, spawning further hit singles. In the 90s, in addition to continuing with Genesis, he contributed to **David Crosby's** *Thousand Roads*, co-writing the hit 'Hero', and starred in the film *Frauds*. *Both Sides* in 1993 was a return to the stark emotion of *Face Value*. Collins later left Genesis.

COLOUR FIELD

AFTER APPEARING WITH ENGLISH BANDS **THE SPECIALS** AND **THE FUN BOY THREE**, TERRY HALL (b. 1959; GUITAR/ vocals) formed Colour Field with Karl Sharle (bass) and Toby Lyons (guitar/keyboards) in 1983. He was aided by friends and produced strong pop songs featuring his rather flat vocals; 'Thinking Of You' (1985) reached the UK Top 20. Their debut album reached UK number 12, but the failure of subsequent singles reduced them to a duo of Hall and Lyons. They reappeared in 1987 with a cover of **Sly And The Family Stone**'s 'Running Away' and a second album that gave a poor showing on the UK chart; the group split up shortly afterwards.

COLVIN, SHAWN

US SINGER COLVIN (b. 1956) STARTED OUT IN A HARD ROCK GROUP, THEN A COUNTRY SWING BAND. AFTER A BRIEF sojourn playing solo acoustic sessions, she appeared in off-Broadway productions such as *Pump Boys And Dinettes*, *Diamond Studs* and *Lie Of The Mind*. Her debut, on which she was backed by fellow guitarist and songwriting partner John Leventhal, pulled together arresting material with an understated approach and was awarded a 1989 Grammy for Best Folk Album. It was co-produced by **Suzanne Vega**'s producer Steve Addaboo and Leventhal, with Vega guesting.

Colvin recorded a second album with **Joni Mitchell**'s husband, Larry Klein; he also joined her on tour. After two strong collections, Colvin returned in 1994 with an album of cover versions. *A Few Small Repairs* was more rock-orientated and lyrically strong.

COMBS, SEAN 'PUFFY'

NEW YORKER SEAN 'PUFFY' COMBS AKA PUFF DADDY IS A SUCCESSFUL HIP-HOP ARTIST AND PRODUCER FOR ARTISTS including **TLC**. He began his career dancing in a **Fine Young Cannibals** video, before finding a job at Uptown Records, run by **Motown Records** boss Andre Harrell. By the age of 18, he was Uptown's head of A&R; he launched his own company, Bad Boy Entertainment, in 1993. Quickly assembling a pool of talented R&B and hip-hop artists, Bad Boy enjoyed huge success, with artists such as controversial rapper Notorious B.I.G. It was the latter's untimely death that led to Combs's 1997 album *Life After Death ... Till Death Us Do Part*, which reached US number 1. It also inspired his international number 1, 'I'll Be Missing You', a version of the **Police**'s 'Every Breath You Take', with new lyrics.

COMMANDER CODY AND HIS LOST PLANET AIRMEN

COUNTRY ROCK BAND FORMED IN AMERICA IN 1967. ORIGINALLY FEATURING COMMANDER CODY (b. GEORGE Frayne IV, 1944; piano), John Tichy (lead guitar), Steve Schwartz (guitar), Don Bolton aka the West Virginia Creeper (pedal steel), Stephen Davis (bass) and Ralph Mallory (drums), though only Frayne, Tichy and Bolton remained, by 1968. On the Airmen's debut, *Lost In The Ozone*, Billy C. Farlowe (vocals/harp), Andy Stein (b. 1948; fiddle/saxophone), Billy Kirchen (b. 1948; lead guitar), 'Buffalo' Bruce Barlow (b. 1948; bass) and Lance Dickerson (b. 1948; drums) had joined. This earthy collection covered rockabilly, western swing, country and jump R&B. Despite the US Top 10 single, 'Hot Rod Lincoln' (1972), the group's allure began to fade. *Live From Deep In The Heart Of Texas* and *We've Got A Live One Here* redressed the balance, but individual members grew disillusioned. Tichy's departure preceded an almost total desertion in 1976. The following year Cody released his first solo album, *Midnight Man*, before convening the New Commander Cody Band. Cody And Farlowe re-formed the Lost Planet Airmen in the 90s.

COMMODORES

FORMED IN ALABAMA, USA, IN 1967. **LIONEL RICHIE** (b. 1949; KEYBOARDS/SAXOPHONE/VOCALS), THOMAS McCLARY (b. 1950; guitar) and William King (b. 1949; trumpet) were joined by Andre Callahan (drums), Michael Gilbert (bass) and Milan Williams (b. 1949; keyboards). By 1969, Callahan and Gilbert were replaced by Walter 'Clyde' Orange (b. 1947) and Ronald LaPread (b. 1950). In 1970, they recorded an album for Atlantic, subsequently released as *Rise Up*; it included instrumental covers alongside original material. In 1972, they secured a support slot on an American tour with the **Jackson Five**, and were signed to **Motown Records**. They continued to tour with the Jackson Five for three years, after which they supported the **Rolling Stones**. The instrumental 'Machine Gun' gave them their first US hit, followed by, among others, 'Slippery When Wet', 'Easy' and 'Too Hot To Trot'. Richie's love song 'Three Times A Lady', became a transatlantic number 1. The follow-up, 'Sail On', introduced a country flavour and Richie began receiving commissions from artists such as **Kenny Rogers**. After 'Still' (1979) gave the Commodores another US pop and soul number 1, they attempted to move into a more experimental blend of funk and rock on *Heroes* – a commercial failure. This, and Richie's successful duet with **Diana Ross** on 'Endless Love', persuaded him to go solo.

In 1984, McClary also launched a solo career with an album for Motown. He was replaced by English vocalist J. D. Nicholas (b. 1952; ex-**Heatwave**), who was featured on the group's 1985 hit single 'Nightshift'. After a major US soul chart hit, 'Goin' To The Bank' (1986), subsequent releases were disappointing.

COMMUNARDS

AFTER LEAVING **BRONSKI BEAT** IN 1985, SCOTTISH VOCALIST JIMMY SOMERVILLE (b. 1961) TEAMED UP WITH classically-trained, English pianist Richard Coles (b. 1962) to form the Committee, this was changed to the Communards (borrowed from a 19th-century group of French Republicans). Their disco-styled debut 'You Are My World' reached the UK Top 30, its follow-up, 'Disenchanted', was another minor hit and, in 1986, the group reached number 1 with a revival of 'Don't Leave Me This Way', featuring vocalist Sarah Jane Morris. After 'So Cold The Night' (UK Top 10), the group blazed back into the Top 5 with their version of 'Never Can Say Goodbye'.

When Somerville wound down the group's activities, he went solo scoring hits with a cover of 'You Make Me Feel (Mighty Real)' and 'Read My Lips'.

COMSAT ANGELS

FORMED, AS RADIO EARTH, IN SHEFFIELD, ENGLAND, AT THE END OF THE 70S, STEPHEN FELLOWS (GUITAR/VOCALS), Mik Glaisher (drums), Kevin Bacon (bass) and Andy Peake (keyboards) merged the zest of punk with mature songwriting, using a strong keyboard element on their promising debut, *Waiting For A Miracle*. After becoming Comsat Angels, they shortened their name to CS Angels in the US when communications giant Comsat threatened legal action. *Sleep No More* reached UK number 51 but *Fiction* only skimmed the Top 100. *Land* spawned a near-hit single with 'Independence Day' (also on their first album).

In 1990, the band became Dream Command and released *Fire On The Moon*. Bacon quit only to re-join when they reverted to their original name for *My Mind's Eye*. *The Glamour* featured bassist Terry Todd and guitarist Simon Anderson.

CONCRETE BLONDE

HOLLYWOOD ROCK BAND CONCRETE BLONDE WAS FORMED IN 1986 OUT OF DREAM 6. EARLE (PRODUCTION; ex-**Sparks**) and Jim Mankey (guitars), Johnette Napolitano (bass/vocals) and Harry Rushakoff (drums) recorded *Concrete Blonde* before *Free*, when Alan Bloch (bass) joined, allowing Napolitano to concentrate on singing. *Bloodletting* was the band's strongest album and saw the introduction of percussionist Paul Thompson (ex-**Roxy Music**). *Mexican Moon* included Hispanic influences. When Napolitano left, the others disbanded.

COLVIN, SHAWN
Albums
A Few Small Repairs (Columbia 1996)★★★★
➧ p.358 for full listings
Collaborators
Suzanne Vega ➧ p.329
Influences
Joni Mitchell ➧ p.235

COMBS, SEAN 'PUFFY'
Albums
as Puff Daddy And The Family *Hell Up In Harlem* (Bad Boy 1996)★★★★
➧ p.358 for full listings
Connections
TLC ➧ p.322
Fine Young Cannibals ➧ p.145
Influences
Police ➧ p.263

COMMANDER CODY AND HIS LOST PLANET AIRMEN
Albums
Hot Licks, Cold Steel And Truckers' Favourites (Paramount 1972)★★★
➧ p.358 for full listings

COMMODORES
Albums
Machine Gun (Motown 1974)★★★★
➧ p.358 for full listings
Collaborators
Jackson Five ➧ p.195
Rolling Stones ➧ p.281
Diana Ross ➧ p.283
Connections
Mystics
Kenny Rogers ➧ p.280
Heatwave ➧ p.178
Further References
Video: *Cover Story* (Stylus Video 1990)

COMMUNARDS
Albums
Red (London 1987)★★★.
➧ p.358 for full listings
Collaborators
Sarah Jane Morris
Connections
Bronski Beat ➧ p.68
Influences
Harold Melvin ➧ p.231
Gloria Gaynor ➧ p.155
Further References
Video: *Communards: The Video Singles* (1987)

COMSAT ANGELS
Albums
Seven Day Weekend (Jive 1985)★★★
➧ p.358 for full listings

CONCRETE BLONDE
Albums
Bloodletting (IRS 1990)★★★
➧ p.358 for full listings
Connections
Sparks ➧ p.303
Roxy Music ➧ p.283

CONLEY, ARTHUR
Albums
Sweet Soul Music (Atco 1967)★★★★
p.358 for full listings
Influences
Sam Cooke p.100

CONTOURS
Albums
Do You Love Me (Gordy 1962)★★★
p.358 for full listings
Influences
Jackie Wilson p.340

COODER, RY
Albums
Paradise And Lunch (Reprise 1974)★★★★
p.358 for full listings
Collaborators
Jackie DeShannon p.116
Randy Newman p.246
Little Feat p.216
Rolling Stones p.281
Connections
Capitain Beefheart p.80
Nick Lowe p.219
John Hiatt p.181

COOKE, SAM
Albums
Mr. Soul (RCA 1963)★★★★
p.358 for full listings

COOKIES
p.358 for full listings
Collaborators
Ray Charles p.88

COOLIDGE, RITA
Albums
Anytime Anywhere (A&M 1977)★★★★
p.358 for full listings
Collaborators
Eric Clapton p.92
Stephen Stills p.310
Leon Russell p.286
Booker T. Jones p.62

CONLEY, ARTHUR

US-BORN ARTHUR CONLEY (b. 1946) FIRST RECORDED AS ARTHUR AND THE CORVETS. HE SIGNED TO HIS MENTOR **Otis Redding**'s Jotis label and released singles on Volt and Stax Records before his 'Sweet Soul Music' (1967) hit the charts. A thin reworking of **Sam Cooke**'s 'Yeah Man' was released before 'Funky Street' (US Top 20), but Redding's tragic death also forestalled Conley's progress. *Sweet Soul Music* was a strong collection.

CONTOURS

FORMED AS AN R&B VOCAL GROUP IN DETROIT IN 1959: BILLY GORDON (LEAD VOCALS), BILLY HOGGS, JOE BILLINGSLEA and Sylvester Potts. Hubert Johnson (d. 1981) joined in 1960, and it was his cousin, **Jackie Wilson**, who secured the group a contract with **Motown Records**. In 1962, 'Do You Love Me' reached US number 3, its frantic blend of R&B and the twist dance craze also powered the following 'Shake Sherry'. 'Do You Love Me' was covered by **Brian Poole And The Tremeloes**, Faron's **Flamingos** and the **Dave Clark Five**. As the Contours' line-up went through several changes, they had occasional R&B successes with 'Can You Jerk Like Me', **Smokey Robinson**'s 'First I Look At The Purse', and the dance number 'Just A Little Misunderstanding'.

Despite Johnson's suicide in 1981, a trio consisting of Billingslea, Potts and Jerry Green were still performing into the 80s. Billingslea, Potts, Arthur Hinson, Charles Davis and Darrel Nunlee issued *Running In Circles*; former lead vocalist Joe Stubbs recorded *Round And Round* and former lead vocalist Dennis Edwards later enjoyed success with the **Temptations**, and as a soloist.

COODER, RY

BY AGE 17, US-BORN COODER (b. RYLAND COODER, 1947) WAS PART OF A BLUES ACT WITH SINGER **JACKIE DESHANNON**. In 1965, he formed the Rising Sons with drummer Ed Cassidy (ex-**Taj Mahal**, **Spirit**); he also played on sessions, notably with **Paul Revere And The Raiders**, **Captain Beefheart**, **Randy Newman**, **Little Feat** and Van Dyke Parks, as well as guesting on the soundtracks of *Candy* and *Performance* and the **Rolling Stones**' *Let It Bleed*.

Cooder's debut album included material by **Lead Belly**, Sleepy John Estes and Blind Willie Johnson, and offered a patchwork of Americana that became his trademark. The rather desolate *Boomer's Story* completed Cooder's early trilogy and, in 1974, he released the buoyant *Paradise And Lunch*. *Chicken Skin Music* featured Flaco Jiminez and Gabby Pahuini.

Cooder later embraced a more mainstream approach with *Bop Till You Drop*, an ebullient, rhythmic, yet rock-based collection, which featured several R&B standards, including 'Little Sister' and 'Don't Mess Up A Good Thing'. *Borderline* and *The Slide Area* offered similar fare. Soundtracks *The Long Riders*, *Paris, Texas* and *Crossroads*, owed much to the spirit of adventure prevalent in his early work. In 1992, Cooder joined up with **Nick Lowe**, Jim Keltner and **John Hiatt** for Little Village. He was acclaimed for his successful collaborations with V. M. Bhatt on *A Meeting By the River* and with **Ali Farka Toure** on *Talking Timbuktu*.

COOKE, SAM

BETWEEN 1951 AND 1956, US-BORN COOKE (b. SAM COOK, 1931, d. 1964) SANG LEAD WITH THE **SOUL STIRRERS**. 'Loveable'/'Forever' was issued as a single – disguised under the pseudonym 'Dale Cook' to avoid offending the gospel audience – before 'You Send Me' sold in excess of two million copies. Further hits, including 'Only Sixteen' and 'Wonderful World', followed and hits like 'Chain Gang' (1960), 'Cupid' (1961) and 'Twistin' The Night Away' (1962), displayed a pop craft later offset by such grittier offerings as 'Bring It On Home To Me', 'Little Red Rooster' and '(Ain't That) Good News'. On 11 December 1964, following an altercation with a girl he had picked up, the singer was fatally shot by the manageress of a Los Angeles motel. The ebullient 'Shake' became a posthumous hit, but its serene coupling, 'A Change Is Gonna Come', was a more melancholic epitaph.

COOKIES

US VOCAL TRIO FORMED IN THE EARLY 50S BY DORETTA (DOROTHY) JONES. EARLY MEMBERS, INCLUDING PAT LYLES, Ethel 'Dolly' McCrae and Margorie Hendrickse, recorded seven singles, of which 'In Paradise' reached the R&B Top 10. However, the group was better known for session work, and can be heard on releases by Joe Turner ('Lipstick, Powder And Paint') and Chuck Willis ('It's Too Late'). The Cookies also backed **Ray Charles** on several occasions. They enjoyed two US Top 20 hits with 'Chains' (later covered by the **Beatles**) and 'Don't Say Nothin' Bad (About My Baby)' and also appeared on various releases by **Little Eva**, herself an auxiliary member of the group.

COOLIDGE, RITA

PART-WHITE, PART-CHEROKEE INDIAN, COOLIDGE (b. 1944) RECORDED BRIEFLY BEFORE BECOMING A SESSION SINGER for **Eric Clapton** and **Stephen Stills** among others. Stills wrote a number of songs about her including 'Cherokee', 'The Raven' and 'Sugar Babe'. In 1969-70, Coolidge toured with **Delaney And Bonnie** and **Leon Russell** (whose'Delta Lady' was inspired by Coolidge), after which she was signed to A&M. Her debut album included the cream of LA session musicians, and was followed by almost annual releases during the 70s. Coolidge also made several albums with **Kris Kristofferson**, to whom she was married between 1973 and 1979. Her first hit singles were a cover of 'Higher And Higher' and 'We're All Alone'. The following year, her version of the **Temptations**' 'The Way You Do The Things You Do' reached the Top 20. Coolidge was less active as a recording star in the 80s, although in 1983 she recorded 'All Time High' the theme to the James Bond movie *Octopussy*.

COOLIO

US HIP HOP RAPPER COOLIO (b. ARTIS IVEY, 1964) started out with the World-Class Wreckin' Crew. His debut solo release was 'Whatcha Gonna Do', one of the first Los Angeles rap records, followed by 'You're Gonna Miss Me'. *It Takes A Thief* went platinum. 'Gangsta's Paradise' was a resigned lament performed with the gospel singer 'LV' and a full choir. Featured in the film *Dangerous Minds*, it went to US and UK number 1 and won a Grammy, in 1996, for Best Rap Solo Performance.

COPE, JULIAN

WELSH-BORN COPE (b. 1957) STARTED OUT IN THE CRUCIAL THREE WITH IAN McCULLOCH **(ECHO AND THE BUNNYMEN)** and Pete Wylie. Cope then founded the **Teardrop Explodes**; in 1984, he went solo with *World Shut Your Mouth*. A third album, *Skellington*, was rejected by his label, which resulted in Cope switching to Island Records. *Saint*

Julian became his best-selling album to date, but a tour to promote *My Nation Underground*, was abandoned when he became too ill to continue. In 1991, *Peggy Suicide* garnered considerable praise but he was dropped from Island after *Jehovakill*. Later albums were issued on small labels.

COPELAND, STEWART

COPELAND (b. 1952) BEGAN HIS CAREER IN THE UK BAND **CURVED AIR** BEFORE ASSUMING THE IDENTITY OF 'WELSH' artist Klark Kent and releasing an album. He then joined the **Police**, before immersing himself in television and film projects. He wrote, produced and played music for Francis Ford Coppola's *Rumble Fish*, before releasing *The Rhythmatist*, which offered a cultural survey of the sounds of Africa within a rock idiom. Copeland's next soundtrack work was the US television serial *The Equalizer* before starting work with Stanley Clarke and Deborah Holland in Animal Logic.

CORROSION OF CONFORMITY

MID-80S AMERICAN HARDCORE CROSSOVER BAND, ORIGINALLY KNOWN AS NO LABELS, FORMED IN NORTH CAROLINA by Reed Mullin (drums), Woody Weatherman (guitar) and Mike Dean (bass/vocals) in 1982. *Eye For An Eye* mixed hardcore speed power-riffing, and a metallic crossover was evident with *Animosity*. Following the blistering *Technocracy*, with Simon Bob on vocals, Bob and Dean left, replaced by Karl Agell (vocals), Pepper Keenan (guitar/vocals) and Phil Swisher (bass). *Blind* saw a slower, more melodic, but still fiercely heavy style. The departure of Agell and Swisher slowed their momentum. *Deliverance*, with Keenan taking lead vocals and Dean back in place, was a considerable departure from their hardcore musical roots.

CORYELL, LARRY

US-BORN CORYELL (b. 1943) FIRST WORKED AS A GUITARIST IN 1958 IN A ROCK 'N' ROLL BAND WITH MICHAEL MANDEL (keyboards). In 1965, he joined Chico Hamilton's band, overlapping with legendary guitarist Gabor Szabo, whom he eventually replaced. In 1966, Coryell formed Free Spirits with American Indian tenor player Jim Pepper. He toured with Gary Burton (1967-68), played on Herbie Mann's *Memphis Underground* (1968) and performed on Michael Mantler's *Jazz Composers Orchestra*.

Fairyland, recorded live with soul veterans Chuck Rainey (bass) and Bernard 'Pretty' Purdie (drums), was packed with sublime solos. *Barefoot Boy* featured jazz drummer Roy Haynes and electric feedback and distortion. Coryell then formed Eleventh House with Mandel, disbanding it shortly afterwards. He began playing with other guitarists – Philip Catherine, McLaughlin, Paco De Lucia and John Scofield – and played on Charles Mingus's *Three Or Four Shades Of Blue* and recorded arrangements of Stravinsky . In the mid-80s, Coryell started playing electric again and, in 1990, recorded easy, unassuming acoustic jazz with Don Lanphere.

COSTELLO, ELVIS

ENGLISH VOCALIST COSTELLO (b. DECLAN McMANUS, 1954) CAME TO PROMINENCE DURING the UK punk era and was signed to Stiff Records. His **Nick Lowe**-produced debut, *My Aim Is True*, featured members of **Clover**. His new band, the Attractions, gave Costello a solid base: bassist Bruce Thomas, drummer Pete Thomas (ex-**Chilli Willi And The Red Hot Peppers**) and keyboardist Steve Nieve. *This Year's Model* and singles ensued, prior to the release of the vitriolic *Armed Forces*. During 1981, he spent time in Nashville recording a country album, *Almost Blue*. His eighth album was the strong *Imperial Bedroom*.

As the Imposter he released 'Pills And Soap', an attack on Thatcherism. In 1986, he released the rock 'n' roll-influenced *King Of America* and the introspective *Blood And Chocolate*. Later, he collaborated with **Paul McCartney**, co-writing a number of songs for *Flowers In The Dirt*, and released *Spike*. His collaboration with the Brodsky Quartet in 1993 was commercially ignored, but *Brutal Youth* renewed critical approbation.

COUGARS

FORMED IN 1961 IN BRISTOL, ENGLAND. KEITH 'ROD' OWEN (GUITAR/ARRANGER), DAVE TANNER (RHYTHM GUITAR), Adrian Morgan (bass) and Dave Hack (drums) were signed to EMI by A&R manager Norrie Paramor. Their debut, 'Saturday Night At The Duck Pond', a frenetic reworking of Tchaikovsky's 'Swan Lake', incurred a BBC ban on the grounds that it 'defaced a classical melody', but nonetheless reached number 33. Tchaikovsky was also the inspiration for several ensuing releases, including 'Red Square' and 'Caviare And Chips', but the group was unable to repeat its initial success.

COUNTING CROWS

CALIFORNIA-BASED FOLK ROCK BAND FEATURING ADAM DURITZ (b. *c.* 1964; VOCALS), DAVID BRYSON (GUITAR), MAT Malley (bass), Steve Bowman (drums), Charlie Gillingham (Hammond organ/keyboards) and Dan Vickrey (lead guitar/mandolin). Their well-received debut, produced by **T-Bone Burnett**, mixed traditional R&B with a raw, rocky delivery. The MTV rotation of 'Mr Jones' undoubtedly augmented sales, as did critical reaction. By mid-1995 their debut had sold over 5 million copies in the US. *Recovering The Satellites* debuted at US number 1 in 1996.

COUNTRY JOE AND THE FISH

FORMED IN 1965, IN CALIFORNIA, AS THE INSTANT ACTION JUG BAND. FORMER FOLK SINGER **COUNTRY JOE McDONALD** (b. 1942) established the group with guitarist Barry Melton (b. 1947), the only musicians to remain in the line-up throughout its history. The group's earliest recording, 'I Feel Like I'm Fixin' To Die Rag' (1965), was a virulent attack on the Vietnam war. In 1966, the expanded line-up – McDonald, Melton, David Cohen (guitar/keyboards), Paul Armstrong (bass) and John Francis Gunning (drums) – pressed an EP; Armstrong and Gunning were soon replaced by Bruce Barthol and Gary 'Chicken' Hirsh. This reshaped quintet recorded *Electric Music For The Mind And Body*, followed by *I Feel Like I'm Fixin' To Die* (including a tribute to **Janis Joplin**).

Here We Are Again was completed by various musicians, including Peter Albin and Dave Getz, and included the country-tinged 'Here I Go Again'. Mark Kapner (keyboards), Doug Metzner (bass) and Greg Dewey (drums), joined McDonald and Melton in 1969. The new line-up was responsible for the fiery final album, *C.J. Fish*. *Reunion* was a disappointment.

COOLIO
Albums
Gangsta's Paradise (Tommy Boy 1995)★★★★
➧ p.358 for full listings
Collaborators
Dr. Dre ➧ p.124

COPE, JULIAN
Albums
Peggy Suicide (Island 1991)★★★★
➧ p.358 for full listings
Connections
Echo and the Bunnymen ➧ p.131
Teardrop Explodes ➧ p.317

COPELAND, STEWART
Albums
The Leopard Son (Ark 21 1996)★★★
➧ p.358 for full listings
Connections
Curved Air ➧ p.108
Police ➧ p.263

CORROSION OF CONFORMITY
Albums
Animosity (Death/Metal Blade 1985)★★★
➧ p.358 for full listings

CORYELL, LARRY
Albums
Spaces (Vanguard 1970)★★★★
➧ p.358 for full listings

COSTELLO, ELVIS
Albums
This Year's Model (Radar 1978)★★★★★
➧ p.358 for full listings

Collaborators
Paul McCartney ➧ p.229
Connections
Nick Lowe ➧ p.219
Clover ➧ p.95

COUNTING CROWS
Albums
August And Everything After (Geffen 1993)★★★★
➧ p.358 for full listings
Collaborators
T-Bone Burnett ➧ p.75

COUNTRY JOE AND THE FISH
Albums
Electric Music For The Mind And Body (Vanguard 1967)★★★
➧ p.358 for full listings
Connections
Janis Joplin ➧ p.201

COVAY, DON
Albums
See Saw (Atlantic 1966)★★★★
➽ p.358 for full listings
Collaborators
Marvin Gaye ➽ p.154
Little Richard ➽ p.217
Connections
Gladys Knight and the Pips ➽ p.209
Steve Cropper ➽ p.105

COWBOY JUNKIES
Albums
The Trinity Session (RCA 1988)★★★★
➽ p.358 for full listings

COYNE, KEVIN
Albums
Blame It On The Night (Virgin 1974)★★★★
➽ p.358 for full listings
Collaborators
Dagmar Krause
Connections
Zoot Money ➽ p.236
Further References
Book: *Show Business*, Kevin Coyne

CRACKER
Albums
Cracker (Virgin 1992)★★★
➽ p.358 for full listings
Connections
Camper Van Beethoven ➽ p.79

CRADLE OF FILTH
Albums
Supreme Vampiric Evil (Cacophonous 1994)★★★
➽ p.358 for full listings
Connections
Brutality

CRAMER, FLOYD
Albums
Last Date (RCA 1961)★★★★
➽ p.358 for full listings
Collaborators
Jim Reeves ➽ p.275
Elvis Presley ➽ p.265
Patsy Cline ➽ p.94
Roy Orbison ➽ p.252

CRAMPS
Albums
Flamejob (Medicine 1994)★★★
➽ p.358 for full listings
Connections
Gun Club ➽ p.170
Ricky Nelson ➽ p.244

CRANBERRIES
Albums
No Need To Argue (Island 1994)★★★★
➽ p.358 for full listings
Connections
Public Image Limited ➽ p.269
Further References
CD-ROM: *Doors And Windows* (Philips 1995)★★
Book: *The Cranberries*, Stuart Bailey

COVAY, DON

US-BORN COVAY (b. 1938) STARTED OUT IN HIS FAMILY'S GOSPEL QUARTET. HE CROSSED TO SECULAR MUSIC WITH THE Rainbows, a group that included **Marvin Gaye**, and his solo career began in 1957 as part of the **Little Richard** revue. On 'Bip Bop Bip' Covay was billed as 'Pretty Boy'. His original version of 'Pony Time' lost out to **Chubby Checker**'s version, but a further dance-oriented offering, 'Popeye Waddle' (1962), was a hit. **Solomon Burke** recorded Covay's 'I'm Hanging Up My Heart For You' and **Gladys Knight And The Pips** reached the US Top 20 with 'Letter Full Of Tears'. 'See-Saw', co-written with **Steve Cropper**, paved the way for other exceptional singles, including 'Sookie Sookie' and 'Iron Out The Rough Spots' (both 1966). Covay's ill-fated Soul Clan (with Solomon Burke, **Wilson Pickett**, **Joe Tex** and **Ben E. King**) ended after one single, but his songs remained successful – **Aretha Franklin** won a Grammy for her performance of 'Chain Of Fools'. In 1993, the Rhythm & Blues Foundation honoured Covey with a Pioneer Awards.

COWBOY JUNKIES

CANADIANS MICHAEL TIMMINS (b. 1959; GUITAR) AND ALAN ANTON (b. ALAN ALIZOJVODIC, 1959; BASS) FORMED an unsuccessful UK-based group, Hunger Project, in 1979; followed by an experimental instrumental group, Germinal. Returning to Toronto, they joined forces with Timmins's sister Margo (b. 1961; vocals) and brother Peter (b. 1965; drums). As the Cowboy Junkies they recorded *Whites Off Earth Now!!*.

The Trinity Session was recorded with one microphone in the Church of Holy Trinity, Toronto, costing $250. It sold 250,000 copies in North America. The *Caution Horses* included several vintage country songs and, by the release of *Lay It Down* the band was recorded to the highest standards. Timmins's understated guitar alongside Margo's eerie vocals have found favour with a rock audience.

COYNE, KEVIN

A FORMER ART STUDENT, PSYCHIATRIC THERAPIST AND SOCIAL WORKER, COYNE (b. 1944) PURSUED A SINGING career in English pubs and clubs, later joining London-based Siren. Coyne left the band in 1972, to complete the promising *Case History*. *Marjory Razor Blade* emphasized his idiosyncratic talent, with guttural delivery highlighting his lyrically raw compositions.

Inspired by country blues, Coyne constructed the self-effacing *Blame It On The Night* before forming a group around **Zoot Money** (keyboards), Andy Summers (guitar), Steve Thompson (bass) and Peter Wolf (drums) to promote *Matching Head And Feet*; this line-up also recorded *Heartburn*. His work was not out of place in the punk era, while *Babble*, a collaboration with vocalist Dagmar Krause was a triumph. 80s recordings, including *Pointing The Finger* and *Politicz*, showed an undiminished fire. *Peel Sessions* (featuring radio broadcasts, 1974-90) is a testament to the artist's divergent style.

CRACKER

A ROWDY UPDATE OF THE 70S CALIFORNIAN FOLK ROCK FRATERNITY, CRACKER ARE FRONTED BY DAVID LOWERY (b. 1960; EX-**Camper Van Beethoven**) and guitarist Johnny Hickman (b. *c.* 1959). Cracker recorded a self-titled debut album, which melded influences as diverse as psychedelia, country rock and delta blues. *Kerosene Hot* saw a more permanent rhythm aggregation in David Lowering and Bruce Hughes. *The Golden Age*'s move towards country rock indicated their future direction.

CRADLE OF FILTH

AN OUTLANDISH UK BAND OF THE EARLY 90S SATANIC BLACK METAL REVIVAL. VISUALLY, CRADLE OF FILTH WERE influenced by the Scandinavian bands who led the movement: adopting black and white make-up ('corpse-paint') and funereal garb, while incorporating fire-breathing and drenching themselves in blood on stage. After the successful *Supreme Vampiric Evil*, the group underwent personnel changes, before the mini-album *Vempire, Or, Dark Phaerytales In Phallustein*. By now the group incorporated singer Dani, Irish keyboard player Damien and guitarists Stuart and Jared. *Dusk* explored their fascination with vampire mythology and Victorian and Medieval romanticism. Bassist Jeff Acres joined in 1995 and guitarist Bryan Hipp departed in 1996.

CRAMER, FLOYD

CRAMER (b. 1933, d. 1997), A VASTLY EXPERIENCED NASHVILLE SESSION PLAYER, WORKED WITH **JIM REEVES**, **ELVIS Presley**, Chet Atkins, **Patsy Cline**, **Roy Orbison** and Kitty Lester. His delicate rock 'n' roll sound was highlighted in his first major hit, 'Last Date' (1960); two of his notable hits were 'On The Rebound' and 'San Antonio Rose'. In 1980, he had a major hit with the theme from TV soap *Dallas*. Sadly, Cramer died from cancer in December 1997.

CRAMPS

FORMED IN OHIO, USA, IN 1976, THE ORIGINAL CRAMPS – LUX INTERIOR (b. ERICK LEE PURKHISER; VOCALS), 'Poison' Ivy Rorschach (b. Kirsty Marlana Wallace; guitar), Bryan Gregory (guitar) and his sister, Pam Balam (drums) – moved to New York and the emergent punk scene. Miriam Linna briefly replaced Balam, before Nick Knox (b. Nick Stephanoff) became their permanent drummer. Their first singles and debut album blended the frantic rush of rockabilly with 60s garage-band panache.

Bryan Gregory departed suddenly after 'Drug Train' and Kid Congo (Powers) (b. Brian Tristan; ex-**Gun Club**) appeared on *Psychedelic Jungle*, but later rejoined his former band; replacements have included Fur and Candy Del Mar. In 1991, Interior and Rorschach fronted a rejuvenated line-up with Slim Chance (bass) and Jim Sclavunos (drums). *Flamejob* showed that the group had become virtually a pantomine act.

CRANBERRIES

DOLORES O'RIORDAN (b. DOLORES MARY EILEEN O'RIORDAN, 1971; VOCALS), NOEL HOGAN (b. 1971; GUITAR/main songwriter), his brother Mike (b. 1973; bass) and Feargal Lawler (b. 1971; drums) emanate from Limerick, Eire. They were originally named The Cranberry Saw Us. After their debut EP, *Uncertain*, the band's manage-

ment was taken over by Rough Trade Records supremo Geoff Travis and Jeanette Lee (ex-**Public Image Limited**). *Everybody Else Is Doing It, So Why Can't We?* was issued following 'Dreams' and 'Linger', sold well in the UK and US and the band became a hot radio and concert prospect. *No Need To Argue* followed, including the strong single 'Zombie', and *To The Faithful Departed* was equally well-received.

CRASH TEST DUMMIES

CANADIAN GROUP FEATURING BRAD ROBERTS (VOCALS/ GUITAR), HIS YOUNGER BROTHER DAN (BASS), BENJAMIN Darvill (mandolin/harmonica) and Ellen Reid (piano/accordion/backing vocals). Their debut, *The Ghosts That Haunt Me* (a blend of blues-based rock 'n' roll and folk pop), rose to Canadian number 1, on the back of the hit single 'Superman's Song'. *God Shuffled His Feet* introduced drummer Michel Dorge and was co-produced by **Talking Heads**' Jerry Harrison. Their breakthrough arrived with the distinctive '*Mmmm Mmmm Mmmm*' which reached US number 12 in 1994. Indifferent songs blighted *A Worm's Life*, lost the momentum gained by '*Mmmm Mmmm Mmmm*' and failed to sell.

CRAWFORD, RANDY

US VOCALIST RANDY CRAWFORD (b. VERONICA CRAWFORD, 1952) WAS A REGULAR PERFORMER AT CINCINNATI'S nightclubs. After moving to New York, she began singing with jazz musicians, including **George Benson** and Cannonball Adderley. She was signed to Warner Brothers Records as a solo act, but achieved fame as the (uncredited) voice on 'Street Life', a major hit for the Crusaders. Crawford toured extensively with the group, whose pianist, Joe Sample, provided her with 'Now We May Begin'.

As a soloist, Crawford enjoyed further successes with 'One Day I'll Fly Away' (UK number 2), 'You Might Need Somebody', 'Rainy Night in Georgia' (both UK Top 20) and her 1981 album *Secret Combination* (UK number 2). After a five-year respite, she returned in 1986 with the haunting 'Almaz'. Curiously, this soulful, passionate singer has found greater success in the UK than in her homeland and she recorded *Rich And Poor* in London.

CRAY, ROBERT

CRAY (b. 1953) PLAYS A MIXTURE OF PURE BLUES, SOUL AND ROCK. ALTHOUGH HE FORMED HIS FIRST BAND IN 1974, it was not until *Bad Influence* that his name became widely known (his debut, *Who's Been Talking*, failed when the record label folded). The Robert Cray Band featured Richard Cousins (bass), Dave Olson (drums) and Peter Boe (keyboards) and their *Strong Persuader* became the most successful blues album for over two decades. **Eric Clapton** recorded Cray's 'Bad Influence' and invited him to record with him and play at his 1989 concerts in London.

Midnight Stroll featured a new line-up that gave Cray a tougher-sounding unit and moved him out of mainstream blues towards R&B and soul. His quartet in the mid-90s featured Kevin Hayes (drums), Karl Sevareid (bass) and Jim Pugh (keyboards). *Some Rainy Morning* was Cray's vocal album and *Sweet Potato Pie* featured the **Memphis Horns** on a cover of 'Trick Or Treat'.

CRAZY HORSE

CRAZY HORSE EVOLVED IN 1969 WHEN **NEIL YOUNG** INVITED DANNY WHITTEN (d. 1972; GUITAR), AMERICAN BILLY Talbot (bass) and Puerto Rican Ralph Molina (drums) to accompany him on his album, *Everybody Knows This Is Nowhere*. The impressive results inspired a tour, but although the group also contributed to Young's *After The Goldrush*, their relationship was sundered in the light of Whitten's growing drug dependency. *Crazy Horse*, completed with the assistance of Jack Nitzsche and **Nils Lofgren**, featured several notable performances, including the emotional 'I Don't Want To Talk About It', later revived by **Rod Stewart** and **Everything But The Girl**.

After Whitten died from a heroin overdose, Talbot and Molina kept the group afloat with various members, but neither *Loose* or *At Crooked Lake* compared with their excellent debut. Reunited with Young for *Tonight's The Night* and *Zuma*, and buoyed by the arrival of American guitarist Frank Stampedro, the group released *Crazy Moon*, followed by *Ragged Glory* and *Sleeps With Angels*. They also worked with **Ian McNabb** on his excellent 1994 album *Head Like A Rock*.

CREAM

BRITISH BAND FEATURING **JACK BRUCE** (b. JOHN SYMON ASHER, 1943; BASS/VOCALS), **ERIC CLAPTON** (b. ERIC PATRICK Clapp, 1945; guitar) and **Ginger Baker** (b. Peter Baker, 1939; drums). Cream's debut single, 'Wrapping Paper' made the lower reaches of the charts and was followed by 'I Feel Free', which unleashed such energy that it could only be matched by **Jimi Hendrix**. The excellent *Fresh Cream* preceeded *Disraeli Gears*, which firmly established Cream in the USA. Landmark songs such as 'Sunshine Of Your Love' and 'Strange Brew' were performed with precision.

One disc of the two-record set, *Wheels Of Fire*, captured Cream live, at their inventive and exploratory best. While it sat on top of the US charts, they announced they would disband at the end of the year, after two final concerts. The famous Royal Albert Hall farewell concerts were captured on film; the posthumous *Goodbye* repeated the success of its predecessors.

The three members reformed in 1993 for a one-off performance at the Rock 'n' Roll Hall Of Fame awards in New York.

CRASH TEST DUMMIES
Albums
God Shuffled His Feet (RCA 1994)★★★★
➧ p.358 for full listings
Further References
Video: *Symptomology Of A Rock Band* (1994)

CRAWFORD, RANDY
Albums
Everything Must Change (Warners 1980)★★★
➧ p.358 for full listings
Collaborators
George Benson ➧ p.44
Connections
Crusaders

CRAY, ROBERT
Albums
with Albert Collins, Johnny Copeland *Showdown!* (Alligator 1985)★★★★
Don't Be Afraid Of The Dark (Mercury 1988)★★★★
➧ p.358 for full listings
Collaborators
Eric Clapton ➧ p.92
Connections
Robert Cray Band ➧ p.103
Influences
Isaac Hayes ➧ p.178
Further References
Video: *Smoking Gun* (Polygram Music Video 1989)

CRAZY HORSE
Albums
Crazy Horse (Reprise 1970)★★★★
➧ p.358 for full listings

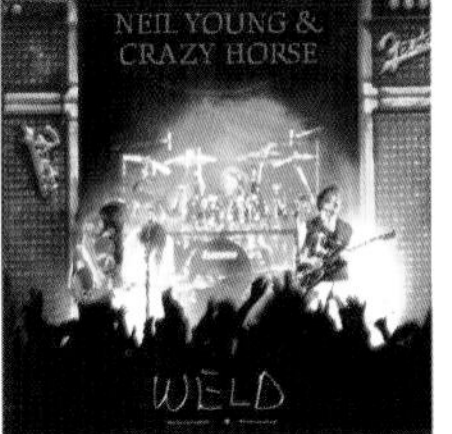

Collaborators
Ian McNabb ➧ p.230
Neil Young ➧ p.346
Connections
Rockets
Rod Stewart ➧ p.310
Everything But the Girl ➧ p.140

CREAM
Albums
Disraeli Gears (Polydor 1967)★★★★★
➧ p.358 for full listings
Connections
Bluesbreakers ➧ p.228
Graham Bond
Eric Clapton ➧ p.92
Ginger Baker ➧ p.29
Further References
Video: *Strange Brew* (Warner Music Video 1992)
Book: *Strange Brew*, Chris Welch

CREATION
Albums
We Are Paintermen (Hi-Ton 1967)★★★
➽ p.358 for full listings
Connections
Mark Four
Kinks ➽ p.207
Merseybeats ➽ p.232
Byrds ➽ p.77

CREDIT TO THE NATION
Albums
Take Dis (One Little Indian 1993)★★★
➽ p.358 for full listings
Connections
Nirvana ➽ p.248
Influences
Chumbawamba ➽ p.92

CREEDENCE CLEARWATER REVIVAL
Albums
Bayou Country (Fantasy 1969)★★★★
Green River (Fantasy 1969)★★★★
Willie And The Poor Boys (Fantasy 1969)★★★★
➽ p.358 for full listings

Connections
Golliwogs
Further References
Book: *Inside Creedence*, John Hallowell

CRENSHAW, MARSHALL
Albums
Marshall Crenshaw (Warners 1982)★★★★
➽ p.358 for full listings
Collaborators
Nilsson ➽ p.247
Arthur Alexander ➽ p.12
Merle Haggard
Gin Blossoms ➽ p.159
Influences
John Lennon ➽ p.214

CREW-CUTS
Albums
Rock And Roll Bash (Mercury 1957)★★★
➽ p.358 for full listings

CRICKETS
Albums
In Style With The Crickets (Coral1960)★★★★
➽ p.358 for full listings
Connections
Buddy Holly ➽ p.184
Bobby Vee ➽ p.329
Paul McCartney ➽ p.229

CREATION

BRITISH MOD/POP-ART ACT, WHICH GREW FROM BEAT GROUP, THE MARK FOUR. KENNY PICKETT (b. 1942, d. 1997; vocals), Eddie Phillips (lead guitar), Mick Thompson (rhythm guitar), John Dalton (bass) and Jack Jones (drums) completed four singles under this appellation before Dalton left (for the **Kinks**) and Thompson abandoned music. Bob Garner (ex-**Merseybeats**) and **Tony Sheridan** joined and the band became Creation. Their early singles, 'Making Time' and 'Painter Man', offered the same propulsive power as the **Who**, while Phillips's distinctive bowed-guitar sound was later popularized by **Jimmy Page**. Unfortunately, clashes between Pickett and Garner caused the singer's departure in 1967 and, although several strong records followed, they lacked the impact of earlier recordings.

The group split in February 1968, but re-formed in March around Pickett, Jones, Kim Gardner (bass) and Ron Wood (guitar; ex-**Birds**). This realignment proved temporary and, impromptu reunions apart, Creation broke up in June 1968. After 25 years, the band re-formed and made a live album, *Lay The Ghost*, followed by an all-new album (issued on Creation) in 1996.

CREDIT TO THE NATION

UK HIP HOP GROUP FEATURING MC FUSION (b. MATTY HANSON, 1971), WITH DANCERS TYRONE AND KELVIN (aka T-Swing and Mista-G). Credit To The Nation broke through in 1993 after several months of sponsorship by **Chumbawamba**, with whom they recorded their first single. They also shared a lyrical platform which attacked racism, sexism and homophobia.

'Call It What You Want' sampled the guitar motif used by **Nirvana** on 'Smells Like Teen Spirit'. This found them an audience in hip indie kids outside the hardcore rap fraternity. A backlash ensued causing Hanson to move out of his home, after threats on his life. However, the band continued with 'Teenage Sensation' (UK Top 30) and 'Hear No Bullshit, See No Bullshit, Say No Bullshit'.

CREEDENCE CLEARWATER REVIVAL

SAN FRANCISCAN GROUP FORMED IN 1959, FEATURING JOHN FOGERTY (b. 1945; LEAD GUITAR/VOCALS), TOM FOGERTY (b. 1941, d. 1990; rhythm guitar/vocals), Stu Cook (b. 1945; bass) and Doug Clifford (b. 1945; drums). Initially known as the Blue Velvets, the quartet auditioned for the Fantasy label, who renamed them the Golliwogs to capitalize on the current 'British Invasion'. The quartet turned fully professional in 1967 and became Creedence Clearwater Revival.

Their debut album reflected a musical crossroads. Revamped Golliwogs tracks and new John Fogerty originals slotted alongside several rock 'n' roll standards, including 'Suzie Q' (US number 11) and 'I Put A Spell On You'. *Bayou Country* was a more substantial affair and 'Proud Mary' reached UK/US Top 10 and went gold. More importantly, it introduced the mixture of Southern creole styles, R&B and rockabilly through which the best of the group's work was filtered. *Green River* contained two highly successful singles, 'Green River' and 'Bad Moon Rising' (UK number 1).

They reached a peak with *Cosmo's Factory*, which included three gold singles – 'Travellin' Band', 'Up Around The Bend' and 'Looking Out My Back Door' – as well as an elongated reading of 'I Heard It Through The Grapevine'. The album deservedly became 1970's best-selling set, however, relationships between the Fogerty brothers grew increasingly strained, reflected in the disappointing *Pendulum*.

Although it featured their eighth gold single in 'Have You Ever Seen The Rain', the set lacked the intensity of its predecessors. Tom Fogerty went solo in 1971 and, although the remaining members continued to work as a trio, the band had lost much of its impetus. Creedence Clearwater Revival was officially disbanded in 1972.

CRENSHAW, MARSHALL

AFTER PORTRAYING **JOHN LENNON** IN THE STAGE SHOW BEATLEMANIA, CRENSHAW (b. 1954) FORGED A SOLO CAREER as a performer of the classic urban-American pop song. With an echo-laden guitar sound that harked back to the 60s, Crenshaw performed alongside his brother Robert (drums/vocals) and Chris Donato (bass/vocals); their debut album contained Crenshaw's US hit, 'Someday, Someway'. A lean period was relieved by the success of Owen Paul's cover of his 'My Favourite Waste Of Time' (UK Top 3, 1986).

Crenshaw made film appearances in *Peggy Sue Got Married* and *La Bamba* (portraying Buddy Holly). Further album releases were acclaimed and, in the 90s, Crenshaw guested on albums for **Nilsson**, **Arthur Alexander** and Merle Haggard, and contributed to the Gin Blossoms' 'Til I Hear It From You'. He broke a five-year silence with a new album in 1996.

CREW-CUTS

FORMED IN TORONTO, CANADA, IN 1952, THE CREW-CUTS WERE A WHITE VOCAL QUARTET THAT ACHIEVED 50S SUCCESS by covering black R&B songs; their version of 'Sh-Boom' was at number 1 for nine weeks. The group featured Rudi Maugeri (b. 1931; baritone), Pat Barrett (b. 1931; tenor), John Perkins (b. 1931; lead) and his brother Ray (b. 1932; bass).

Initially called the Canadaires, the group received its first break in the USA, where they appeared on Gene Carroll's TV programme. Their first recording, an original composition 'Crazy 'Bout Ya Baby', made the US Top 10. In addition to 'Sh-Boom', other Top 10 placings were 'Earth Angel' (1955), 'Ko Ko Mo (I Love You So)' (1955) and 'Gum Drop' (1955). The Crew-Cuts had 14 chart singles in 1957; they disbanded in 1963.

CRICKETS

US GROUP WHO BACKED **BUDDY HOLLY** AND CONTINUED TO RECORD AND TOUR AFTER HIS death. In addition to Holly, the original members were Jerry Allison (b. 1939; drums), Joe B. Mauldin (bass) and Nicky Sullivan (guitar). When Holly was signed to Decca in 1957, it was decided that their Nashville-produced tracks should be released under two names, as Holly solo items (on Coral) and as the Crickets (on Brunswick). 'That'll Be The Day', credited to the Crickets, was their first number 1. Other Crickets' successes, with Holly on lead vocals, included 'Oh Boy', 'Maybe Baby' and 'Think It Over'. When Holly went fully solo in 1958, the Crickets did not accompany him on his final tour. Allison and Norman Petty had already begun recording independently, issuing 'Love's Made A Fool Of You' with Earl Sinks on lead vocals. On the later singles 'Peggy Sue Got Married' and 'More Than I Can Say' Sinks was replaced by Sonny Curtis (b. 1937; guitar/vocals). 'More Than I Can Say' was a hit for **Bobby Vee**, and in 1961 the Crickets moved to Vee's label, Liberty Records, recording an album with him the following year; Glen D. Hardin (b. 1939; piano) joined at this point. The group also released a series of singles between 1962 and 1965. These made little impact in the USA but 'Please Don't Ever Change' (a **Carole King/Gerry Goffin** number) and 'My Little Girl' were UK Top 20 hits.

There followed a five-year hiatus as Curtis and Allison worked as songwriters and session musicians. The most recent phase of the Crickets' career was stimulated by the purchase, from **Paul McCartney**'s publishing company, of much of the group's song catalogue. During the 80s, Allison took the band on revival tours and returned to recording in 1987 with original bassist Mauldin and newcomer Gordon Payne (guitar/vocals). They released *Three-Piece* on Allison's Rollercoaster label.

CROCE, JIM

US MUSICIAN CROCE (b. 1943, d. 1973) PLAYED IN VARIOUS ROCK BANDS BEFORE MOVING INTO THE NEW YORK folk circuit in 1967. By 1969, he and his wife Ingrid (b. 1947) were signed to Capitol Records for *Approaching Day*. Meanwhile, he continued with songwriting and secured a new contract with ABC. The title track to *You Don't Mess Around With Jim* was a US Top 10 hit; along with 'Operator (That's Not The Way It Feels)', it established him as a songwriter.

In July 1973, he topped the US charts with 'Bad Boy Leroy Brown'. Two months later, he died in a plane crash at Natchitoches, Louisiana, along with guitarist Maury Mulheisen. Posthumously, he reached the Top 10 with 'I Got A Name', featured in the film *The Last American Hero*. The contemplative 'Time In A Bottle' was released in late 1973 and reached US number 1. It was a fitting valediction. During 1974, further releases kept Croce's name in the US charts, including 'I'll Have To Say I Love You In A Song' and 'Workin' At The Car Wash Blues'.

CROPPER, STEVE

A FOUNDER-MEMBER OF **THE MAR-KEYS**, GUITARIST CROPPER (b. 1942) WORKED WITH SEVERAL GROUPS, THE MOST successful of which was **Booker T. And The MGs**. Cropper's songwriting and arranging skills were prevalent on many of these performances, including 'Knock On Wood' (**Eddie Floyd**), 'In The Midnight Hour' (**Wilson Pickett**) and '(Sittin' On) The Dock Of The Bay' (**Otis Redding**). Cropper recorded a solo album, *With A Little Help From My Friends*, and featured prominently on the **Rod Stewart** UK number 1, *Atlantic Crossing*.

Cropper was also a member of the **Blues Brothers**. They recorded three albums, following which Cropper released his second solo collection, *Playing My Thang*. Since then, Cropper's clipped, high treble sound with his Fender Telecaster has been heard on countless records.

CROSBY, DAVID

HAILING FROM A HIGH-SOCIETY HOLLYWOOD FAMILY, CROSBY (b. 1941) DROPPED OUT OF ACTING SCHOOL IN THE EARLY 60S to concentrate on singing. Along the way he played informally with a number of influential musicians including Travis Edmunson, Fred Neil, Dino Valenti, Paul Kantner and David Freiberg. Towards the end of 1963, Crosby demoed several songs, including covers of **Ray Charles**'s 'Come Back Baby' and Hoyt Axton's 'Willie Gene' (these surfaced on the archive compilation *Early LA*).

Failing to secure a record deal, Crosby met two like-minded rock 'n' roll enthusiasts: Jim McGuinn and **Gene Clark**. After forming the Jet Set, they systematically refined their unusual style for mass consumption. With the arrival of bassist Chris Hillman and drummer Michael Clarke, the Jet Set became the **Byrds**. Crosby remained with them for three years, and his rhythm guitar work, arranging skills and superb harmonic ability greatly contributed to their international success. By 1966, he was emerging as their spokesman on-stage and during the succeeding two years contributed a significant number of songs to their repertoire including 'What's Happening?!?!', 'Why' and 'Everybody's Been Burned'. However, his outspokenness and domineering tendencies resulted in his dismissal in 1967.

After a sabbatical in which he produced **Joni Mitchell**'s debut album, Crosby resurfaced as part of **Crosby, Stills And Nash**. Crosby wrote some of their most enduring songs including 'Guinevere', 'Long Time Gone' and 'Déja Vu'. During their peak period he finally recorded his solo album, *If I Could Only Remember My Name*. An extraordinary work, it was essentially a mood piece with Crosby using guitar and vocal lines to superb effect. On 'Music Is Love' and 'What Are Their Names?' the songs were built from single riffs and developed towards a startling crescendo of instrumentation and vocal interplay. Crosby's lyrical skill was in evidence on the electric 'Cowboy Movie' (with Rita Coolidge), the moving 'Traction In The Rain' (with Joni Mitchell on dulcimer) and the poignant 'Laughing'. There were also a number of choral experiments, culminating in the eerie Gregorian chanting of 'I'd Swear There Was Somebody Here'.

Crosby continued to work with Graham Nash, **Stephen Stills** and **Neil Young** in various permutations but by the end of the decade he was alone, playing before small audiences and dependent upon heroin. In 1980, a completed album was rejected by Capitol and Crosby began to rely even more severely on drugs. A series of arrests for firearm offences and cocaine possession forced him into a drug rehabilitation centre but he absconded, only to be arrested again. He was imprisoned in 1985. A year later, he emerged corpulent and clean and engaged in a flurry of recording activity with former colleagues. The decade ended with the release of a second solo album, *Oh Yes I Can*, and a strong-selling autobiography, *Long Time Gone*.

90s work with Stills and Nash was followed by work with **Phil Collins**, after they met on the set of the movie *Hook*, in which they both appeared. The resulting *Thousand Roads*, an accessible if overtly slick album, produced a Crosby/Collins minor UK hit with 'Hero'. Since then, Crosby has acted more, including a television appearance in *Roseanne*. In the mid-90s, Crosby underwent major surgery for a liver transplant. A worthy live album was issued during his convalescence in 1995.

Influences
Gerry Goffin ➧ p.161
Further References
Film: *Girls On The Beach* (1965)
Video: *My Love Is Bigger Than A Cadillac* (Hendring 1990)

CROCE, JIM
Albums
You Don't Mess Around With Jim (ABC 1972)★★★
I Got A Name (ABC 1973)★★★
➧ p.358 for full listings
Further References
Book: *The Faces I've Been*, Jim Croce

CROPPER, STEVE
Albums
with Albert King, 'Pops' Staples *Jammed Together* (Stax 1969)★★★
➧ p.358 for full listings
Collaborators
Eddie Floyd ➧ p.148
Wilson Pickett ➧ p.260
Otis Redding ➧ p.274
Rod Stewart ➧ p.310
Connections
Mar-Keys ➧ p.224
Booker T. And The MGs ➧ p.62
Blues Brothers ➧ p.57
Further References
Film: *The Blues Brothers* (1980)

CROSBY, DAVID
Albums
If I Could Only Remember My Name (Atlantic 1971)★★★★★
Thousand Roads (Atlantic 1993)★★★
King Biscuit Flower Hour Presents: David Crosby (BMG 1996)★★★
➧ p.358 for full listings
Collaborators
Ray Charles ➧ p.88
Joni Mitchell ➧ p.235
Phil Collins ➧ p.98
Connections
Jim McGuinn
Gene Clark ➧ p.93
Jet Set
Byrds ➧ p.77
Crosby, Stills and Nash ➧ p.106

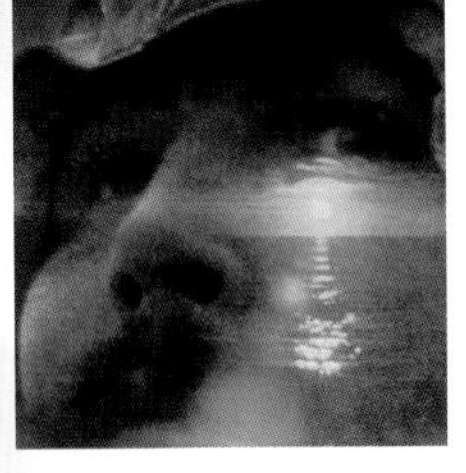

Influences
Beatles ➧ p.68
Further References
Book: *Timeless Flight*, Johnny Rogan

CROSBY, STILLS AND NASH
Albums
Crosby, Stills And Nash (Atlantic 1969)★★★★
CSN (Atlantic 1977)★★★★
Crosby Stills And Nash 4-CD box set (Atlantic 1991)★★★★★
➤ p.358 for full listings
Connections
Buffalo Springfield ➤ p.74
Hollies ➤ p.183
Further References
Book: *Prisoner Of Woodstock*, Dallas Taylor

CROSBY, STILLS, NASH AND YOUNG
Albums
Deja Vu (Atlantic 1970)★★★★
➤ p.358 for full listings

Connections
Joni Mitchell ➤ p.235
Influences
Woodstock Festival ➤ p.343
Further References
Book: *Prisoner Of Woodstock*, Dallas Taylor

CROSS, CHRISTOPHER
Albums
Christopher Cross (Warners 1980)★★★
Another Page (Warners 1983)★★★
➤ p.358 for full listings
Collaborators
Michael McDonald ➤ p.229
Burt Bacharach ➤ p.27
Connections
Flash

CROW, SHERYL
Albums
Tuesday Night Music Club (A&M 1993)★★★★
➤ p.358 for full listings

Collaborators
Michael Jackson ➤ p.195
Eric Clapton ➤ p.92
Bob Dylan ➤ p.128
Stevie Wonder ➤ p.342
Mick Jagger ➤ p.281

CROSBY, STILLS AND NASH

DAVID CROSBY (b. 1941; EX-**BYRDS**) AND STEPHEN STILLS (b. 1945; EX-**BUFFALO SPRINGFIELD**) JOINED ENGLISHMAN Graham Nash (b. 1942; ex-**Hollies**) in 1969. Their eponymous debut album was a superlative achievement containing several of their finest-ever songs: 'Long Time Gone', 'Suite: Judy Blue Eyes', 'Lady Of The Island' and 'Wooden Ships'. Strong lyrics, solid acoustic musicianship and staggeringly faultless three-part harmonies were the mixture that they concocted and it influenced a generation of American performers. The need to perform live convinced them to extend their ranks and, with **Neil Young**, they reached an even bigger international audience as **Crosby, Stills, Nash And Young**.

Internal bickering and policy differences split the group at its peak and although **Crosby And Nash** proved a successful offshoot, the power of the original trio was never forgotten. It was not until 1977 that the original trio reunited for *CSN*, a strong comeback with highlights including 'Shadow Captain', 'Dark Star' and 'Cathedral'. They toured the USA and seemed totally united, but subsequent recording sessions proved unsatisfactory and they drifted apart once more. Five years passed, during which Crosby's drug abuse alienated him from his colleagues. Stills and Nash set about recording an album, but were eventually persuaded by Atlantic Records' founder Ahmet Ertegun to bring back Crosby. He returned late in the sessions and although his contribution was not major, he did proffer one of the strongest tracks, 'Delta'. The resulting *Daylight Again* was disproportionately balanced, but the songs were nevertheless good. Stills's title track was one of his best and Nash's offerings included 'Wasted On The Way' (US Top 10). It re-established CS&N as one of the major concert attractions of the day.

Following a European tour, the trio splintered again, with Crosby incapacitated by cocaine addiction. Upon his release from prison, he reunited CSN&Y for an album and took CS&N on the road; unfortunately, *Live It Up*, their first recording as a trio in 10 years, was disappointing. A magnificent CD box set was put together by Nash in 1991; this included unreleased tracks and alternative versions and led to a critical reappraisal. Live concerts in 1994 and *After The Storm* underlined their continued strength.

CROSBY, STILLS, NASH AND YOUNG

DAVID CROSBY (b. 1941), STEPHEN STILLS (b. 1945) AND ENGLISHMAN GRAHAM NASH (b. 1942) FIRST CAME together in **Crosby, Stills And Nash** before recruiting **Neil Young** (b. 1945). The quartet appeared at **Woodstock** and established a format of playing two sets, one acoustic and one electric. Instant superstars, their *Deja Vu*, was one of the biggest sellers of 1970 and included some of their finest material from a time when they were at their most inventive. There was even a US Top 10 single with their reading of **Joni Mitchell**'s 'Woodstock'.

In 1970, four demonstrators at Kent State University were shot and killed. Young wrote the protest song 'Ohio' as a result. Recorded within 24 hours of its composition, the song captured the foursome at their most musically aggressive and politically relevant. A series of concerts produced the double set *Four Way Street*, however, by the time of its release in 1971, the group had scattered to pursue solo projects.

Their cultural and commercial clout deemed it inconceivable that the quartet would not reconvene and, during 1974, they undertook a stupendous stadium tour. A second studio album, *Human Highway*, produced some exceptionally strong material but was shelved prior to completion. Two years later, the Stills/Young Band appeared – a short-lived venture which floundered in acrimony and misunderstanding. By the late 70s, the CSN&Y concept had lost its appeal to punk-influenced music critics who regarded their political idealism as naïve and their technical perfection as elitist and clinical.

In 1988, the quartet reunited for *American Dream*, a superlative work, almost one hour long and containing some exceptionally strong material including the sardonic title track, the brooding 'Night Song', Crosby's 'Compass' and Nash's 'Soldiers Of Peace'.

CROSS, CHRISTOPHER

CROSS (b. CHRISTOPHER GEPPERT, 1951) WAS SIGNED TO WARNER BROTHERS RECORDS ON THE STRENGTH OF HIS songwriting talents. His debut album spawned hits in 'Ride Like The Wind' (featuring **Michael McDonald**), 'Sailing', 'Never Be The Same' and 'Say You'll Be Mine'. Cross was awarded 5 Grammy Awards in 1981, including Best Album of the Year. He also sang and co-wrote, with Carole Bayer Sager, **Burt Bacharach** and Peter Allen, the theme song, 'Best That You Can Do' (US number 1/UK Top 10) for the hit film *Arthur* (1981). *Another Page* featured the popular 'Think Of Laura' (1983, US Top 10), but later years have seen a decline in Cross's sales.

CROW, SHERYL

CROW (b. 1962) STARTED OUT ON THE LA SESSION SCENE, PLAYING FOR NAMES INCLUDING **ERIC CLAPTON**, **BOB Dylan**, **Stevie Wonder**, **Rod Stewart**, **George Harrison**, **Don Henley**, **John Hiatt**, **Joe Cocker** and **Sinead O'Connor**; Bette Midler and Wynona Judd also recorded her songs. Crow then spent eighteen months backing **Michael Jackson** on his *Bad* world tour (the experience is chronicled in her 'What Can I Do For You').

In 1994, she sang with **Mick Jagger** in front of 65,000 in Miami and was one of only two female acts to appear at **Woodstock** II, in front of 300,000. In 1995, she opened for the **Eagles** at their comeback concerts, and toured extensively – solo and with Cocker.

Tuesday Night Music Club took almost a year to make an impact, despite the marginal success of 'Run Baby Run' and 'Leaving Las Vegas', finally 'All I Want To Do' charted (US number 2/UK number 4). By 1997, the album had sold over 7 million copies in the USA alone. *Sheryl Crow* retained some of the spontaneity, courage and flair of its predecessor and won a Grammy for Best Rock Album in 1997.

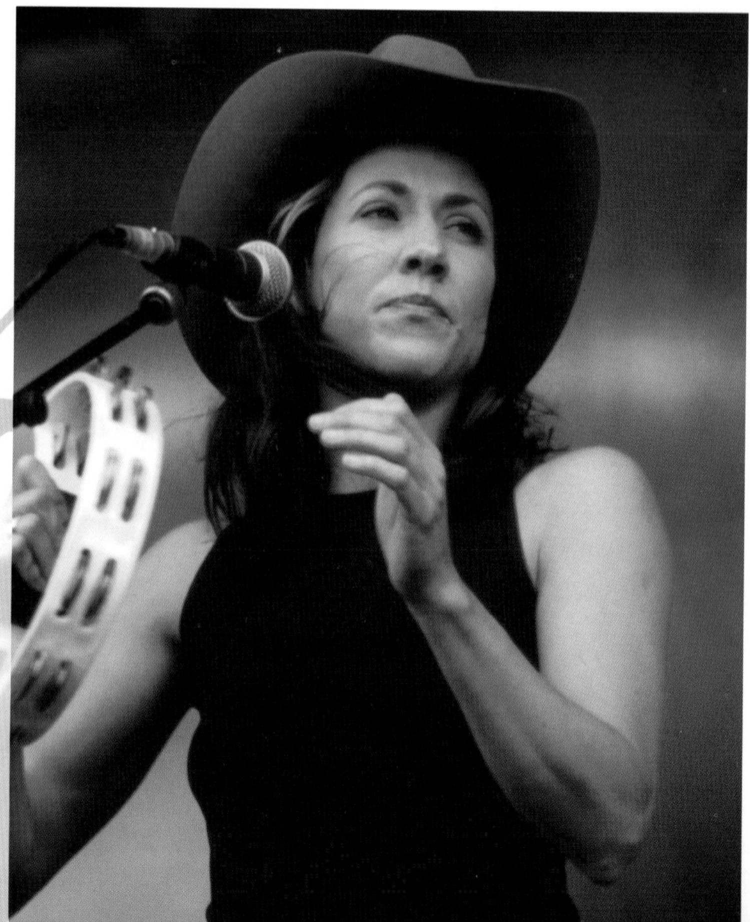

CROWDED HOUSE

AFTER THE BREAK-UP OF **SPLIT ENZ**, NEIL FINN (b. 1958; GUITAR/SONGWRITING) AND PAUL HESTER (DRUMS) RECRUITED Craig Hooper (guitar) and Nick Seymour (bass) to form the Mullanes in 1986. Moving to Los Angeles, they signed to Capitol, changed their name to Crowded House, and worked with producer Mitchell Froom. Hooper left and the trio's debut album was released to little fanfare, but two singles became US chart hits – 'Don't Dream It's Over' (number 2) and 'Something So Strong' (number 7) – in 1987. A subdued reaction to the second album failed to consolidate the group's reputation in the singles chart despite reaching the US Top 40.

Paul Young gave the group some welcome publicity in the UK by singing 'Don't Dream It's Over' at the Nelson Mandela concert at Wembley Stadium in 1988. Neil's brother Tim Finn joined the band in early 1991 and they reached the UK Top 20 with 'Fall At Your Feet' (1991) and the Top 10 'Weather With You' (1992). *Woodface* also reached the UK Top 10.

In November 1991, Tim Finn decided to leave and continue with his solo career. Both brothers were awarded the OBE in 1993 for their contribution to New Zealand music. In 1996, they announced their farewell, bowing out with an excellent compilation package, including 3 new songs. Their final performance was in Sydney on 24 November 1996.

CROWELL, RODNEY

TEXAN-BORN CROWELL (b. 1950) STARTED OUT AS A SONG-WRITER AT JERRY REED'S PUBLISHING COMPANY AND worked with **Emmylou Harris**'s Hot Band. Crowell's 'Bluebird Wine' appeared on Harris's *Pieces of the Sky*; his 'Till I Gain Control Again' was on *Elite Hotel*, and her *Quarter Moon In A Ten Cent Town* featured his 'I Ain't Living Long Like This' and 'Leaving Louisiana In The Broad Daylight'. In 1978, he recorded *Ain't Living Long Like This*, using an all-star line-up including the Hot Band, **Ry Cooder**, Jim Keltner and **Willie Nelson**.

In 1979, Crowell married **Rosanne Cash**, and has subsequently produced most of her albums. In 1980 his *But What Will The Neighbors Think* included a US Top 40 single, 'Ashes By Now'; the subsequent, self-produced *Rodney Crowell* did less well. *Street Language* included three US country chart singles, and established him as a country artist. *Diamonds And Dirt* spawned five US country number 1s and *Keys To The Highway* was largely recorded with country band, the Dixie Pearls.

Crowell's songs have been covered by **Bob Seger**, Waylon Jennings and George Jones among others, and he has produced for Sissy Spacek, **Guy Clark** and Bobby Bare. *Life Is Messy* followed shortly after his marriage break-up and subsequent albums, such as *Let The Picture Paint Itself* and *Jewel Of The South*, have also chronicled his personal problems.

CRUISE, JULEE

CRUISE FIRST ROSE TO FAME AS THE MUSICAL STAR OF DAVID LYNCH'S CULT TELEVISION SERIES, *TWIN PEAKS*, ON THE SHOW'S memorable theme tune, 'Falling'. Her critically-acclaimed debut, *Floating Into The Night*, mixed the sense of small-town melodrama and macabre with her own, measured vocal. She then appeared in another Lynch/Badalamenti production, *Industrial Symphony No. 1*, in which she was suspended above an industrial landscape by a web of wires.

CRYSTALS

60S US VOCAL GROUP PRODUCED BY **PHIL SPECTOR**. THE GROUP FEATURED DEE DEE KENNIBREW (b. DOLORES Henry, 1945), La La Brooks (b. 1946), Pat Wright (b. 1945), Mary Thomas (b. 1946) and Barbara Alston. Their 1961 debut was 'There's No Other (Like My Baby)', followed by 'Uptown' and **Gene Pitney**'s 'He's A Rebel'. The latter featured the lead vocals of Darlene Wright. It became a US number 1 and UK number 19. La La Brooks returned to lead vocals on two further hits 'Da Doo Ron Ron (When He Walked Me Home)' and 'Then He Kissed Me'.

The Crystals were overlooked when Spector devoted more time to the **Ronettes**, and consequently their career faltered. New members passed through, including Frances Collins, but the band were prematurely banished to the nostalgia circuit.

CULT

FORMED IN THE UK AS SOUTHERN DEATH CULT IN 1981. IAN ASTBURY (b. 1962; VOCALS), HAQ QURESHI DAVID 'Buzz' Burrows (guitar) and Barry Jepson (bass) debuted in 1982 with the double a-side 'Moya'/'Fatman', and released a self-titled album. Astbury then formed Death Cult with Ray 'The Reverend' Mondo (drums) and Jamie Stewart (bass), plus guitarist Billy Duffy (b. 1959). They debuted in 1983 with an eponymous four-track 12-inch. Mondo swapped drumming positions with Sex Gang Children's Nigel Preston (d. 1992).

1984 saw them change their name to the Cult. *Dreamtime* was boosted by the anthemic 'Spiritwalker', after which Les Warner (b. 1961; ex-**Johnny Thunders**, **Julian Lennon**) replaced Preston. *Love* spawned two UK Top 20 hit singles, 'She Sells Sanctuary' and 'Rain'. *Electric* saw their transition to heavy rock completed; it was a transatlantic success. The group added bass player Kid 'Haggis' Chaos (b. Mark Manning; ex-Zodiac Mindwarp And The Love Reaction), with Stewart switching to rhythm guitar. Both he and Warner left in 1988 and *Sonic Temple* saw them temporarily recruit drummer Mickey Curry. *Ceremony*, a retrogressive collection of songs, featured Charley Drayton (bass) and Curry. *The Cult* included the Kurt Cobain tribute 'Sacred Life'. By this time, however, Astbury had departed for the Holy Barbarians.

CROWDED HOUSE

Albums
Woodface (Capitol 1991)★★★★
➧ p.358 for full listings

Collaborators
Mitchell Froom

Connections
Paul Young ➧ p.347
Split Enz ➧ p.305

Further References
Video: *Farewell To The World: Live At The Sydney Opera House* (Polygram Video 1997)
Book: *Private Universe: The Illustrated Biography*, Chris Twomey and Kerry Doole

CROWELL, RODNEY

Albums
Ain't Living Long Like This (Warners 1978)★★★★
Street Language (Columbia 1986)★★★★
Diamonds And Dirt (Columbia 1988)★★★★
➧ p.358 for full listings

Collaborators
Emmylou Harris ➧ p.175
Ry Cooder ➧ p.100
Willie Nelson ➧ p.245
Rosanne Cash ➧ p.84
Bob Seger ➧ p.292

Connections
Guy Clark ➧ p.93

CRUISE, JULEE

Albums
Floating Into The Night (Warners 1990)★★★
➧ p.358 for full listings

Collaborators
Angelo Badalamenti

Influences
David Lynch

CRYSTALS

Albums
He's A Rebel (Philles 1963)★★★
➧ p.358 for full listings

Collaborators
Darlene Wright

Connections
Phil Spector ➧ p.304

Influences
Gene Pitney ➧ p.261

CULT

Albums
Sonic Temple (Beggars Banquet 1989)★★★
➧ p.358 for full listings

Connections
Julian Lennon ➧ p.214

Further References
Videos: *Pure Cult* (1993)

CULTURE BEAT
Albums
Horizon (Epic 1991)★★★
p.358 for full listings
Collaborators
Shamen p.294

CULTURE CLUB
Albums
Colour By Numbers (Virgin 1983)★★★★
p.358 for full listings
Connections
Bow Wow Wow p.63
Damned p.110
Influences
MTV
Further References
Book: *Culture Club: When Cameras Go Crazy*, Kasper de Graaf and Malcolm Garrett

CURE
Albums
Faith (Fiction 1981)★★★★
p.351 for full listings
Collaborators
Siouxsie And The Banshees p.298
Influences
Glastonbury Festival p.160
Further References
Book: *Ten Imaginary Years*, Lydia Barbarian, Steve Sutherland and Robert Smith

CURVE
Albums
Doppelganger (AnXious 1992)★★★
p.358 for full listings
Collaborators
David A. Stewart p.139
Connections
Eurythmics p.139
Leftfield p.213
Echobelly p.131

CURVED AIR
Albums
Air Conditioning (Warners 1970)★★★
p.358 for full listings
Connections
Roxy Music p.283
Police p.263
Influences
Sisyphus

CYPRESS HILL
Albums
Cypress Hill (Ruffhouse 1991)★★★★
p.358 for full listings
Collaborators
Pearl Jam p.257

CYRKLE
Albums
Neon (Columbia 1967)★★
p.358 for full listings
Collaborators
Simon and Garfunkel p.297
Connections
Harpers Bizarre p.175
Influences
Beatles p.38
Seekers p.291

CULTURE BEAT

EURO-DANCE GROUP CREATED IN 1989 BY GERMAN DJ TORSTEN FENSLAU (b. *c.* 1964, d. 1993) WITH THE MORE visual duo, Jay Supreme and Tania Evans. After a few years DJ-ing Fenslau moved into production, scoring a solo hit as Out Of The Ordinary with 'Los Ninos Mix'. Culture Beat racked up dance-floor hits with 'No Deeper Meaning', 'Mr Vain' and 'Got To Get It'. In its wake Fenslau remixed for the **Shamen** ('Coming On Strong') and released 'Come Into My Heart' (as Abfahrt) and was behind Cheery Lips' 'Das Erdbbermund'. Sadly, Fenslau was killed in a car crash in November 1993. The Culture Beat members carried on his work, scoring another Top 10 hit with 'Anything' in 1994. Alex Abraham became Fenslau's replacement, alongside long-term collaborators Peter Zweier and Nosie Katzman.

CULTURE CLUB

UK BAND CULTURE CLUB, FORMED IN 1981, FEATURED **BOY GEORGE** (b. GEORGE O'DOWD, 1961; VOCALS; EX-**BOW WOW Wow**), Roy Hay (b. 1961; guitar/keyboards), Mikey Craig (b. 1960; bass) and Jon Moss (b. 1957; drums; ex-**Damned**, **Adam Ant**). Culture Club were signed to Virgin Records in 1982 and released a couple of non-chart singles, 'White Boy' and 'I'm Afraid Of Me' before reaching UK number 1 with the melodic 'Do You Really Want To Hurt Me?' and the Top 3 'Time (Clock Of The Heart)'. *Kissing To Be Clever* lacked the consistent excellence of their singles, but was still a fine pop record.

In 1983, *Kissing To Be Clever* climbed into the US Top 20, while their two UK singles both reached number 2. 'Church Of The Poison Mind', with guest vocalist Helen Terry, gave them another UK number 2, followed by the infectious 'Karma Chameleon' (UK/US number 1). *Colour By Numbers* reached UK number 1 and US number 2. The momentum was maintained through 1983-84 with strong singles such as 'Victims', 'It's A Miracle' and 'Miss You Blind', which all reached either the US or UK Top 10. In 1984, 'The War Song' hit UK number 2, but thereafter, chart performances took an increasing back seat. 1986's 'Move Away' was their only other Top 10 hit.

After much media attention over his self-confessed heroin addiction, Boy George announced Culture Club's demise in 1987. He has since enjoyed solo chart success. The band re-formed in the late 90s and toured in 1998.

CURE

UK GROUP FORMED IN 1976 AS THE EASY CURE. ROBERT SMITH (b. 1959; GUITAR/VOCALS), MICHAEL DEMPSEY (bass) and Laurence 'Lol' Tolhurst (b. 1959) issued the Albert Camus-inspired 'Killing An Arab' (1978) on the independent Small Wonder Records. By 1979, the group were attracting glowing reviews, particularly in the wake of 'Boys

Don't Cry'. *Three Imaginary Boys* was also well received, and was followed by a support spot with **Siouxsie And The Banshees**. Dempsey left, replaced by Simon Gallup and Mathieu Hartley (keyboards) joined.

By 1980, the Cure were developing less as a pop group than a guitar-laden rock group. The atmospheric 12-inch 'A Forest' gave them their first UK Top 40 hit, while the strong *17 Seconds* reached the Top 20. In 1981, they released 'Primary', 'Charlotte Sometimes' and 'Faith' and the well-received *Pornography*, but there were internal problems. Hartley had lasted only a few months and, in 1982, Gallup, was replaced by Steve Goulding. However they continued with 'The Walk, 'The Love Cats' and 'The Caterpillar'.

In 1985, they released their most commercially successful album yet, *The Head On The Door*. The following year, they re-recorded their second single, 'Boys Don't Cry', which became a minor UK hit. By now, the group was effectively Smith and Tolhurst, with others flitting through. With the retrospective *Standing On A Beach* singles collection the Cure underlined their longevity during an otherwise quiet year. During 1987 they undertook a tour of South America and enjoyed several more minor UK hits with 'Why Can't I Be You?', 'Catch' and 'Just Like Heaven'.

A two-year hiatus followed before the release of *Disintegration* (UK Top 3). Their run of line-up changes culminated in the departure of Tolhurst (to form Presence), leaving Smith as the sole original member; he announced that he would not be undertaking any further tours. 1990 ended with the release of *Mixed Up*, a double album compiling re-recordings and remixes. By 1992, the line-up featured Smith, a reinstated Gallup, Perry Bamonte (keyboards/guitar), Porl Thompson (guitar) and Boris Williams (drums). In 1993, Thompson left and former member Tolhurst unsuccessfully sued Smith, the band and its record label, for alleged unpaid royalties. Following a successful bill-topping gig at the 1995 **Glastonbury Festival** the band started work on *Wild Mood Swings* (1996). The line-up on this album was Smith, Bamonte, Gallup, Jason Cooper (drums) and Roger O'Donnell (keyboards).

CURVE

CHART-TOPPING INDIE ACT FEATURING TONI HALLIDAY (b. *c.* 1965; VOCALS) AND DEAN GARCIA (GUITAR). THEY began as State Of Play and released two singles and an album, *Balancing The Scales*. As Curve, three EPs, *Blindfold*, *Frozen* and *Cherry*, were well received by the UK indie rock press. They recruited Debbie Smith (guitar), Alex Mitchell (guitar) and Monti (drums), but two albums and a series of singles failed to build on the press profile and the band eventually sundered in 1994. They reformed in 1997 for live gigs and the album *Come Clean*.

CURVED AIR

UK BAND FORMED IN EARLY 1970. SONJA KRISTINA (b. 1949; VOCALS), DARRYL WAY (b. 1948; VIOLIN), FLORIAN Pilkington Miksa (b. 1950), Francis Monkman (b. 1949; keyboards) and Ian Eyre (bass) were signed by Warner Brothers Records for £100,000.

Air Conditioning was heavily promoted and enjoyed a particular curiosity value as one of rock's first picture disc albums. In 1971, the group enjoyed their sole UK Top 5 hit with 'Back Street Luv', while *Second Album* won favour with the progressive music audience. By *Phantasmagoria*, Eyre had left, replaced by Mike Wedgewood (b. 1956). Monkman and Way also left in 1972. With Kristina as the sole original member, the line-up consistently changed thereafter and included Eddie Jobson (b. 1955; later of **Roxy Music**) and **Stewart Copeland** (b. 1952; later of **Police**). Following a two-year hiatus during which Kristina sang in the musical *Hair*, the group re-united, with Way returning for touring purposes. After two further albums, they split in 1977.

CYPRESS HILL

LOS ANGELES RAP GROUP WHO RELEASED SONGS SUCH AS 'I WANNA GET HIGH', 'LEGALISE IT' AND 'INSANE IN The Brain' – they are champions of NORML (National Organization For The Reform Of Marijuana Laws). Their music blends full and funky R&B, with tales of dope and guns. The band features DJ Muggs (b. Lawrence Muggerud, *c.* 1969), Cuban vocalists B-Real (b. Louis Freeze, *c.* 1970) and Sen Dog (b. Sen Reyes, *c.* 1965) and Eric Bobo (percussion). As a teenager, Sen Dog, with his younger brother Mellow Man Ace, formed the prototype rap outfit, DVX, and claims to have invented the Spanglish 'lingo' style.

Cypress Hill's debut set went platinum and *Black Sunday*, debuted at Number 1 in the US R&B and pop charts; the gun-touting 'Cock The Hammer' turned up on the soundtrack to Schwarzenegger's *Last Action Hero*. Their reputation for violent lyrics was underscored when they appeared on the soundtrack for *Mad Dog And Glory*, in a scene which accompanies a drug killing. Their most recent soundtrack appearance occurred when they recorded a track with **Pearl Jam**, 'The Real Thing', for *Judgement Night*. Sen Dog left in 1996 and was replaced by DJ Scandalous.

CYRKLE

US HARMONY POP ACT FOUNDED – AS THE RHONDELLS – BY DON DANNEMANN (GUITAR/ VOCALS) AND TOM Dawes (guitar/vocals), with Earl Pickens (keyboards) and Marty Fried (drums). After an introduction to **Brian Epstein**, the Rhondells were signed to his NEMS roster; **John Lennon** reputedly suggested the name the Cyrkle. The incipient act then broke up temporarily, leaving Dawes free to tour with **Simon And Garfunkel**. **Paul Simon** offered him 'Red Rubber Ball', a song he co-wrote with Bruce Woodley of the **Seekers**; it gave the reconvened Cyrkle a US number 2 in 1966.

Cyrkle supported the **Beatles** on the latter's final tour but, having passed on another Simon composition, '59th Street Bridge Song (Feeling Groovy)', the Cyrkle enjoyed their final Top 20 entry with 'Turn Down Day', which featured Dawes on sitar. Pickens was replaced by Mike Losecamp for *Neon*, but the death of Epstein in 1967 virtually ended the Cyrkle's career. and they broke up in 1968.

D'ARBY, TERENCE TRENT
Albums
Introducing The Hardline According To Terence Trent D'Arby (Columbia 1987)★★★★
➽ p.359 for full listings
Collaborators
Luke Goss
Further References
Book: *Neither Fish Nor Flesh: Inspiration For An Album*, Paolo Hewitt

DA LENCH MOB
Albums
Guerillas In The Mist (Street Knowledge 1992)★★★★
➽ p.359 for full listings
Connections
T-Bone
Influences
Ice Cube ➽ p.191

DALE, DICK
Albums
King Of The Surf Guitar (Capitol 1963)★★★
➽ p.359 for full listings
Connections
Beach Boys ➽ p.36
Leo Fender ➽ p.144
Stevie Ray Vaughan

DALEK I LOVE YOU
Albums
Compass Kum'pass (Backdoor 1980)★★★
➽ p.359 for full listings
Connections
OMD ➽ p.252

DAMNED
Albums
Damned Damned Damned (Stiff 1977)★★★★
➽ p.359 for full listings

Collaborators
Sex Pistols ➽ p.292
Connections
Captain Sensible ➽ p.81
Nick Lowe ➽ p.219
Pink Floyd ➽ p.261
Nick Mason
Eddie and the Hot Rods ➽ p.132
Influences
Beatles ➽ p.38
Further References
Book: *The Damned: The Light At The End Of The Tunnel*, Carol Clerk

DANNY AND THE JUNIORS
➽ p.359 for full listings
Connections
Lesley Gore
Len Barry ➽ p.34
Fabian ➽ p. 141

D'ARBY, TERENCE TRENT

US-BORN D'ARBY (b. 1962) STARTED OUT WITH LOCAL FUNK BAND, TOUCH, IN 1983. HIS FIRST SOLO SINGLE, 'IF YOU Let Me Stay', reached the UK Top 10 and *Introducing The Hardline According To Terence Trent D'Arby* was one of the most successful debut albums of its time. *Neither Fish Nor Flesh* was a commercial and artistic failure, but the more rock-orientated *Symphony Or Damn* was better received. *Vibrator* continued the transition from smooth soul to a harder-edged sound. It was preceded by 'Holding On To You', and 'Supermodel Sandwich', which appeared on the soundtrack of the film *Pret-A-Porter*. The album featured a new recording line-up of Luke Goss (drums; ex-**Bros**), Branford Marsalis (saxophone), Patrice Rushen (piano) and Charlie Sepulveda (trumpet).

DA LENCH MOB

HARDCORE GANGSTA RAPPERS AND PROTÉGÉS OF **ICE CUBE**; DA LENCH MOB WERE SIGNED TO HIS STREET Knowledge label. Before *Guerillas In The Mist*, they backed their benefactor on his first three solo recordings. The group features J-Dee and the backing duo of T-Bone and Jerome Washington (aka Shorty). J-Dee was dropped after his arrest for attempted murder and subsequent imprisonment. His replacement was Maulkley whose vocals were dubbed over the previously completed *Planet Of Da Apes*. T-Bone was also charged with murder, and East West dropped the band in 1994.

DALE, DICK

US-BORN DALE (b. RICHARD MONSOUR, 1937) FIRST GAINED POPULARITY AS A LOCAL COUNTRY SINGER. HIS FIRST RECORD was 'Ooh-Whee-Marie' on Del-Tone, his father's label for whom he recorded nine singles between 1959 and 1962; 'Let's Go Trippin'' (1961) is considered to be the first instrumental surf record. He then formed the Del-Tones and sparked the surf music craze on the US west coast in the early 60s. Dale played left-handed without reversing the strings and started to fine-tune the surf guitar style. He met **Leo Fender**, the inventor of the Fender guitar and amplifier line, and together they worked on designing equipment more suitable for surf guitar.

Surfer's Choice made the national album charts and Capitol signed Dale in 1963; 'The Scavenger' and *Checkered Flag* made the US charts. Dale continued to record throughout the 60s and 70s but a cancer scare, which he overcame, sidelined his career. His music was rediscovered in the 80s, and in 1987 he recorded a version, with Stevie Ray Vaughan, of the **Chantays**' 'Pipeline' for the film *Back To The Beach*. *Tribal Thunder* and *Unknown Territory*, showed that Dale's influence remained strong. 'Misirlou' was featured in the film *Pulp Fiction*, bringing Dale new recognition with a younger audience.

DALEK I LOVE YOU

FORMED IN 1977 BY ALAN GILL (GUITAR/VOCALS) AND DAVID BALFE (BASS/VOCALS/SYNTHESIZER). DISAGREEMENT OVER the band's name – Balfe wanted the Daleks, Gill preferred Darling I Love You – saw the compromised title. Dave Hughes (keyboards), Chris 'Teepee' Shaw (synthesizer), plus a drum machine completed the first of many line-ups. In 1978, Balfe left to join Big In Japan. *Compass Kum'pass* was released in 1980 in the wake of groups such as **OMD** and **Tubeway Army** who had brought electronics into the mainstream. 'Holiday In Disneyland', 'Ambition' and *Dalek I Love You* meshed layered synth and psychedelic fragments. A re-formed Dalek I Love You recorded *Naive* in 1985.

DAMNED

UK PUNK GROUP FORMED IN 1976. **CAPTAIN SENSIBLE**, RAT SCABIES (b. CHRIS MILLER, 1957; DRUMS; EX-LONDON SS), Brian James (b. Brian Robertson; guitar; ex-London SS) and Dave Vanian (b. David Letts; vocals) supported the **Sex Pistols** at the 100 Club just two months after forming. They were then signed to Stiff Records. In 1976, they released 'New Rose' – generally regarded as the first UK punk single – *Damned Damned Damned* was produced by **Nick Lowe**. Lu Edmunds joined as a second guitarist; soon afterwards Scabies quit, replaced by percussionist Jon Moss. *Music For Pleasure*, produced by **Pink Floyd**'s Nick Mason, was mauled by the critics; the Damned were dropped from Stiff and split in 1978.

Sensible, Vanian and Scabies formed the Doomed before becoming legally entitled to use the name Damned. Joined by Algy Ward (bass), they had their first Top 20 single, 'Love Song'. Minor hits followed. Ward was replaced by Paul Gray (ex-**Eddie And The Hot Rods**), Sensible went solo in 1984 and Roman Jugg (guitar/keyboards) and Bryn Merrick (bass) joined Scabies and Vanian. In 1986, the group reached UK number 3 with a cover of Barry Ryan's 'Eloise'. They continued to record and tour into the 90s, sometimes with Sensible and lately without Scabies.

DANNY AND THE JUNIORS

PHILADELPHIA-BASED, ITALIAN-AMERICAN VOCAL QUARTET – DANNY RAPP (b. 1941, d. 1983; LEAD VOCALS), DAVE WHITE (first tenor), Frank Mattei (second tenor) and Joe Terranova (baritone). Formed in 1955 as the Juvenairs, their song 'Do The Bop' came to the attention of Dick Clark who suggested changing it to 'At The Hop'. The re-named song was released in 1957 and shot to the top of the US chart; it also reached the UK Top 3. Their only other US Top 20 hit was the similar sounding 'Rock 'n' Roll Is Here To Stay'. They recorded songs about such dance crazes as the Twist, Mashed Potato, Pony, Cha Cha, Fish, Continental Walk and Limbo, but could not repeat their earlier success. White left the group in the early 60s and composed a number of hits for singers such as Lesley Gore and **Len Barry**, recording a solo album in 1971. In the 70s, they played the 'oldies' circuit with a line-up that included **Fabian**'s ex-backing singer Jimmy Testa. In 1976, a re-issue of 'At The Hop' returned them to the UK Top 40. Rapp was found dead in 1983 having apparently committed suicide.

DANNY WILSON

SCOTTISH POP ACT WHO HAD THEIR FIRST HIT IN 1985 WITH A BLEND OF **Steely Dan** and soul harmonics. *Meet Danny Wilson* boasted the hits 'Mary's Prayer' and 'Davy'; the subsequent album provided another hit in 'Second Summer Of Love'. After they split, vocalist Gary Clark released his debut solo album, *Ten Short Songs About Love* (1993).

DANSE SOCIETY

UK GOTHIC ROCK GROUP ORIGINALLY TITLED DANSE CRAZY. THE LINE-UP – STEVE RAWLINGS (VOCALS), PAUL Gilmartin (drums), Lyndon Scarfe (keyboards), Paul Nash (guitar) and Tim Wright (bass) – released 'Clock', followed by the EP *No Shame In Death*. After *Seduction* they signed to Arista Records. 'Wake Up' pre-dated the 'gothic' scene by at least a year, followed by *Heaven Is Waiting*. Internal rifts saw Scarfe leave, replaced by David Whitaker. When they returned with 'Say It Again' (produced by **Stock, Aitken And Waterman**), it was to a bemused audience who had not anticipated such a sudden shift in style. They split in 1986.

DANTALIAN'S CHARIOT

FORMED IN LONDON IN 1967, **ZOOT MONEY** (VOCALS/ KEYBOARDS), ANDY SOMERS (GUITAR), PAT DONALDSON (bass) and Colin Allen (drums) released only one single 'The Madman Running Through The Fields'. Money and Somers subsequently joined **Eric Burdon** And The New **Animals**, Donaldson joined Fotheringay and Allen played with **John Mayall** and Stone The Crows. Money has remained a popular singer and actor, while Somers, as Andy Summers, found fame in the **Police**.

DARIN, BOBBY

DARIN (b. WALDEN ROBERT CASSOTTO, 1936, d. 1973) ENTERED THE MUSIC BUSINESS IN THE MID-50S. LINKING UP WITH Don Kirshner, they produced the single, 'My First Love'; leading to a contract with Decca. Darin's next single 'Splish Splosh' was a worldwide hit. He also recorded in the Ding Dongs, from which sprang the Rinky Dinks, the backing artists on 'Early In The Morning'. Darin's solo release, 'Queen Of The Hop', sold a million copies, followed by 'Plain Jane' and 'Dream Lover' (UK number 1/US number 2).

Darin then became master of the supper club circuit – a dramatic change of direction. 'Mack The Knife', composed by Bertolt Brecht and Kurt Weill for the musical *The Threepenny Opera*, proved a million-seller and effectively raised Darin to new status as a 'serious singer'. His hit treatments of 'La Mer (Beyond The Sea)', 'Clementine', 'Won't You Come Home Bill Bailey?' and 'You Must Have Been A Beautiful Baby' revealed his ability to tackle variety material and transform it to his own ends.

In 1960, Darin moved into films, appearing in *Come September*, *State Fair*, *Hell Is For Heroes* and *Captain Newman MD*. He returned to pop with 'Multiplication' and 'Things' and recorded an album of **Ray Charles**'s songs. During the beat boom era, Darin reverted to show tunes such as 'Baby Face' and 'Hello Dolly', before a 1965 folk rock hit, 'We Didn't Ask To Be Brought Here'. Successful readings of **Tim Hardin** and **John Sebastian** songs, demonstrated his potential as a cover artist. A more political direction was evident on *Born Walden Robert Cassotto* and *Commitment* and the late 60s saw Darin involved in related interests. Darin suffered from a weak heart, which finally proved fatal.

DARKMAN

RAPPER DARKMAN (b. BRIAN MITCHELL, *c.* 1970) GREW UP IN LONDON. IT WAS with the Sound Systems that he first learnt his craft as an entertainer, setting up his own system, Platinum. He began his own label, Powercut, in 1987. One of its earliest releases, *One Love Sound*, was widely appraised as the first to combine reggae and hip hop. His first release as Darkman, 'What's Not Yours', was included on the *Jus The Way* compilation. 'Yabba Dabba Doo' and 'She Used To Call Me' maintained his commitment to the rap/reggae interface.

DARTS

UK BAND FORMED BY IAIN THOMPSON (BASS), JOHN DUMMER (DRUMS), HAMMY HOWELL (KEYBOARDS), HORATIO Hornblower (b. Nigel Trubridge; saxophone) and singers Rita Ray, Griff Fender (b. Ian Collier), bassist Den Hegarty and Bob Fish. Their debut single – a medley of 'Daddy Cool' and **Little Richard**'s 'The Girl Can't Help It' – ascended the UK Top 10 in 1977, kicking off three years of entries in both the singles and albums lists that mixed stylized self-compositions ('It's Raining', 'Don't Let It Fade Away') with predominant revamps of such US hits as 'Come Back My Love', 'Boy From New York City', 'Get It' and 'Duke Of Earl'. When Hegarty left in 1979, replaced by Kenny Edwards, their records were less successful. With the exit of Howell and Dummer, Darts were no longer chart contenders.

DAVE CLARK FIVE

ONE OF THE MOST POPULAR BRITISH BEAT GROUPS OF THE MID-60S. ORIGINALLY A BACKING GROUP FOR SINGER Stan Saxon the line-up featured Dave Clark (b. 1942; drums/vocals), Mike Smith (b. 1943; organ/vocals), Rick Huxley (b. 1942; bass guitar), Lenny Davidson (b. 1944; lead guitar) and Denis Payton (b. 1943; saxophone).

Failing to find success with cover versions, the group elected to record their own material. 'Glad All Over' reached UK number 1 in 1964, removing the **Beatles**' 'I Want To Hold Your Hand' from the top spot. The Five swiftly released the less memorable, but even more boot-thumping, 'Bits And Pieces', which made number 2. Their UK chart career was erratic over the next two years, although they enjoyed a Top 10 hit with 'Catch Us If You Can' (1965) from the eponymous film, in which they starred.

17 *Billboard* Top 40 hits included 'Because', 'I Like It Like That' and their sole US number 1 'Over And Over'. Back in the UK, they enjoyed a belated and highly successful shift of style with the Barry Mason/Les Reed ballad 'Everybody Knows'. Slipping into the rock 'n' roll revivalist trend of the early 70s, they charted with 'Good Old Rock 'N' Roll' and 'More Good Old Rock 'N' Roll', before bowing out in 1971. Clark became a successful entrepreneur, purchasing the rights to the pop show *Ready Steady Go!*, and financing his musical *Time*.

DAVE DEE, DOZY, BEAKY, MICK AND TICH

FORMED IN 1961 AS DAVE DEE AND THE BOSTON. DAVE DEE (b. DAVID HARMAN, 1943; VOCALS), DOZY (b. TREVOR DAVIES, 1944; bass), Beaky (b. John Dymond, 1944; guitar), Mick (b. Michael Wilson, 1944; lead guitar) and Tich (Ian Amey, 1944) performed rock 'n' roll spiced with comedy routines and risqué patter. After supporting the **Honeycombs** on a 1964 UK tour, they were signed to Fontana and released two unsuccessful singles, 'No Time' and 'All I Want', then came the UK chart hit, 'You Make It Move'. The diversity of their hits maintained the group's appeal but they lost ground at the end of the 60s. Dave Dee left for an unsuccessful solo career before venturing into A&R. The remaining quartet split after one minor hit, 'Mr President', and an album, *Fresh Ear*.

DANNY WILSON
Albums
Be Bop Mop Top (Virgin 1989)★★★
p.359 for full listings
Connections
Steely Dan p.308

DANSE SOCIETY
Albums
Heaven Is Waiting (Arista 1984)★★★
p.359 for full listings
Connections
Stock, Aitken And Waterman p.310

DANTALIAN'S CHARIOT
Albums
Chariot Rising (Wooden Hill 1997)★★★
p.359 for full listings
Connections
John Mayall p.228
Police p.263

DARIN, BOBBY
Albums
If I Were A Carpenter (Atlantic 1966)★★★★
p.359 for full listings
Connections
Connie Francis p.152
Influences
Ray Charles p.88
John Sebastian p. 291
Further References
Book: *Dream Lovers*, Dodd Darin

DARKMAN
Albums
Worldwide (Wild Card 1995)★★★
p.359 for full listings

DARTS
Albums
Darts (Magnet 1977)★★
p.359 for full listings
Influences
Little Richard p.217
Gene Vincent p. 330
Gene Chandler p. 86

DAVE CLARK FIVE
Albums
A Session With The Dave Clark Five (Columbia 1964)★★★★
p.359 for full listings
Connections
Brian Poole and the Tremeloes p.263
Contours p.100
Beatles p.38
Further References
Films: *Get Yourself A College Girl* (1964),

DAVE DEE, DOZY, BEAKY, MICK AND TICH
Albums
If Music Be The Food Of Love (Fontana 1967)★★★
p.359 for full listings
Collaborators
Honeycombs p.185

DAWN
Albums
Tuneweaving (Bell1973)★★★
» p.359 for full listings
Collaborators
Motown » p.240
Del Shannon » p.294

DAZZ BAND
Albums
Joystick (Motown 1983)★★★
» p.359 for full listings

DB'S
Albums
Stands For Decibels (Albion 1981)★★★★
» p.359 for full listings

DE BURGH, CHRIS
Albums
Into The Light (A&M 1986)★★★
» p.359 for full listings
Influences
Moody Blues » p.237

DE LA SOUL
Albums
3 Feet High And Rising (Tommy Boy 1989)★★★
» p.359 for full listings
Collaborators
Queen Latifah » p.270
Influences
Curiosity Killed The Cat
Steely Dan » p. 308
Further References
Video: *3 Feet High And Rising* (1989)

DEACON BLUE
Albums
Raintown (CBS 1987)★★★★
» p.359 for full listings
Influences
Steely Dan » p. 308
Further References
Video: *The Big Picture Live* (1990)

DEAD BOYS
Albums
Young, Loud And Snotty (Sire 1977)★★★
» p.359 for full listings
Connections
Lords of the New Church » p.218

DEAD CAN DANCE
Albums
Spiritchaser (4AD 1995)★★★★
» p.359 for full listings

DEAD KENNEDYS
Albums
Fresh Fruit For Rotting Vegetables (IRS/Cherry Red 1980)★★★
» p.359 for full listings
Further References
Video: *Live In San Francisco* (Hendring Video 1987)

DEAD OR ALIVE
Albums
Youthquake (Epic 1985)★★★
» p.359 for full listings

DAWN

FORMED IN 1970 BY US SINGER TONY ORLANDO (b. 1945). AFTER HEARING A DEMO OF 'CANDIDA', ORLANDO RECORDED it himself with session vocalists Telma Hopkins and Joyce Vincent and hired instrumentalists. This single was attributed to Dawn. After 'Candida' and 'Knock Three Times' topped international charts, the troupe were billed as 'Tony Orlando and Dawn'. Though the impetus slackened with 'What Are You Doing Sunday' and a 'Happy Together'/'Runaway' medley (with **Del Shannon**), 'Tie A Yellow Ribbon Round The Old Oak Tree' proved *the* hit song of 1973. 'Say Has Anybody Seen My Sweet Gypsy Rose' exuded a ragtime mood that prevailed throughout the associated album. The group had their last US number 1 with 'He Don't Love You', a rewrite of a **Jerry Butler** single.

DAZZ BAND

A COMBINATION OF TWO CLEVELAND FUNK OUTFITS FORMED IN THE 70S BY BOBBY HARRIS. THE RESULT WAS THE vocalists and hornplayers Harris, Pierre DeMudd and Skip Martin III, and Eric Fearman (guitar), Kevin Frederick (keyboards), Kenny Pettus (percussion), Michael Wiley (bass) and Isaac Wiley (drums).

Coining the word 'Dazz' – 'danceable jazz' – Harris initially named the band Kinsman Dazz and had two minor US hits in 1978 and 1979. They graduated towards a less melodic funk sound, enjoying a US Top 10 hit with 'Let It Whip' (1982), which won a Grammy. British success followed with 'Let It All Blow'. *Jukebox* marked a transition towards a more rock-oriented sound which brought them continued success in the specialist black music charts. In 1985, Marlon McClain and Keith Harrison replaced Fearman and Frederick.

DB'S

FOUNDERS OF THE DB'S, CHRIS STAMEY (GUITARS/VOCALS), GENE HOLDER (BASS) AND WILL RIGBY (DRUMS) MADE their names locally with the Sneakers, alongside Mitch Easter (guitar/vocals). After two EPs, Easter departed and the remaining three joined keyboardist Peter Holsapple to create the dB's. 'I Thought (You Wanted To Know)' was released in 1978, followed by two albums which failed to make any significant commercial impact. Stamey went solo, replaced by Jeff Beninato. In the 1990s, Stamey and Holsapple reconvened to record *Mavericks*.

DE BURGH, CHRIS

DE BURGH (b. CHRISTOPHER DAVIDSON, 1948) BEGAN WRITING POP SONGS WHILST A STUDENT. HE WAS HIGHLY successful in Canada, South Africa, Europe and South America, finally having a UK hit in 1982 with *The Getaway*, which featured 'Don't Pay The Ferryman'. After 11 years of touring and two dozen singles, De Burgh finally reached UK number 1 with 'Lady In Red' (1986) which 'Missing You' (1988) narrowly missed. *Into The Light* continued his run of chart successes and *Flying Colours* became his biggest selling album to date, reaching UK number 1. In 1991, following the Gulf War, De Burgh donated all proceeds from his song 'The Simple Truth' to the Kurdish refugees. His 1992 release *Power Of Ten* maintained his standards. After the death of Princess Diana, he released a tribute single.

DE LA SOUL

DE LA SOUL CONSISTED OF POSDNOUS (b. KELVIN MERCER, 1969), TRUGOY THE DOVE (b. DAVID JUDE JOLICEUR, 1968), and Pasemaster Mace (b. Vincent Lamont Mason Jnr, 1970). Less harsh than many of their fellow rappers, De La Soul's pleasantly lilting rhythms included the hit singles with 'Me Myself And I', and 'The Magic Number', as well as 'Mama Gave Birth To The Soul Children' (with **Queen Latifah**).

De La Soul Is Dead returned to tougher rhythms with a mellow approach that belied difficult subject matter. Infectious songs like 'Ring Ring Ring (Ha Ha Hey)' kept them in the singles chart and *Buhloone Mindstate* saw them move towards the stylings of their debut.

DEACON BLUE

FORMED IN GLASGOW IN 1985 WHEN SINGER-SONG-WRITER RICKY ROSS (b. 1957) WAS ADVISED BY HIS SONG publishers to find a group to perform his compositions. Deacon Blue's name came from **Steely Dan**'s 'Aja' and consisted of James Prine (b. 1960; keyboards), Graeme Kelling (b. 1957; guitar), Ewan Vernal (b. 1964; bass) and Dougie Vipond (b. 1960; drums). Vocalist Lorraine McIntosh (b. 1964) joined after *Raintown*. 'Dignity' was the group's first hit, followed by 'Chocolate Girl' and 'Real Gone Kid'. *When The World Knows Your Name* topped the UK album charts in 1989. They released two more albums and split in 1995.

DEAD BOYS

ONE OF THE FIRST WAVE PUNK/NO WAVE BANDS IN THE USA. THE BAND – STIV BATORS (d. 1990; VOCALS), JIMMY Zero (rhythm guitar), Cheetah Chrome (b. Gene Connor; lead guitar), Jeff Magnum (bass) and Johnny Blitz (drums) – debuted with one of the earliest US punk records, *Young, Loud And Snotty*. They split in 1980 with Bators recording two solo albums before forming **Lords Of The New Church**. Bators was killed in an automobile accident in France.

DEAD CAN DANCE

UK GROUP WHO MINGLED THEIR TRADEMARK MALE/FEMALE VOCALS WITH CHANTS AND DRAWLING GUITAR. THE CORE duo of Brendan Perry and Lisa Gerrard released *Spleen And Ideal*, featuring cello, trombones and tympani. Within *The Realm Of A Dying Sun* was uneven in tone, *The Serpent's Egg* was inspired by Middle-East music while *Aion* used Gregorian chants. *Into The Labyrinth* confirmed Perry's greater awareness of electronics and samplers; *Spiritchaser* owed debts to African and South American music.

DEAD KENNEDYS

SAN FRANCISCAN PUNK BAND: JELLO BIAFRA (b. ERIC BOUCHER, 1958; VOCALS), KLAUS FLOURIDE (BASS), EAST Bay Ray Glasser (guitar) and Ted (b. Bruce Slesinger; drums; later replaced by Darren H. Peligro). Their debut single, 'California Uber Alles', attacked the policies of Californian governor Jerry Brown. 'Too Drunk To Fuck' made the UK Top 40. *Fresh Fruit For Rotting Vegetables* followed a broadly traditional musical format, whereas *In God We Trust Inc.* was full blown thrash. *Plastic Surgery Disasters* saw the band branch out again. *Frankenchrist* was more considered, with songs such as 'Soup Is Good Food'. *Bedtime For Democracy* was the band's final studio recording, returning to the aggressive speed of the previous mini-album. The group split soon after.

DEAD OR ALIVE

UK BAND FORMED BY PETE BURNS (b. 1959; VOCALS) AND MARTIN HEALY (KEYBOARDS) WITH SUE JAMES (BASS), JOE Musker (drums) and numerous guitarists. The band's television plugs sent a revival of **KC And The Sunshine Band**'s 'That's The Way I Like It' into the UK Top 30 in 1984. 'You Spin Me Round (Like A Record)', from *Youthquake*, reached number 1 in 1985 and was **Stock, Aitken And Waterman**'s first UK hit. Soundalike follow-ups fared less well. Later backing musicians included Timothy Lever (keyboards), Mike Percy (bass), Steve McCoy (drums), Russ Bell (guitar) and Chris Page (keyboards). In the 90s they found greater success abroad – *Nukleopatra* was a major hit in Japan.

DEBARGE

US GROUP FORMED IN 1978 BY BUNNY DEBARGE AND HER FOUR BROTHERS, MARK, JAMES, RANDY AND ELDRA. SIGNED to **Motown Records** in 1979, they were marketed as successors to the **Jackson Five**. The group (known as the DeBarges) were launched with *The DeBarges* and gained their first soul hit 18 months later. 'I Like It' was a success

in the pop charts as were 'All This Love' and 'Time Will Reveal'. In 1985 they had their biggest hit – 'Rhythm Of The Night' (US number 3) from the soundtrack to Motown's film *The Last Dragon*. The follow-up, 'Who's Holding Donna Now?', was almost as successful. El DeBarge went solo in 1985; Bunny departed in 1987. Only Mark and James appeared on *Bad Boys*, by which time their commercial impetus had been lost. The group's wholesome image was ruined by the 1988 arrest and conviction of their brothers Bobby and Chico on drug charges.

DEE, JOEY, AND THE STARLITERS

US GROUP FORMED IN 1958. JOEY DEE (b. JOSEPH DINICOLA, 1940; VOCALS), CARLTON LATIMER (KEYBOARDS), WILLIE Davis (drums), Larry Vernieri (backing vocals) and David Brigati (backing vocals) took up residency at New York's Peppermint Lounge in 1960. In 1961, a year after **Chubby Checker**'s 'The Twist' topped the US chart, Dee's 'Peppermint Twist' shot to number 1 and *Doin' The Twist At The Peppermint Lounge* reached number 2. In 1962 the group starred in *Hey Let's Twist* and *Vive Le Twist*. Their version of the **Isley Brothers**' 'Shout', reached number 6. Dee appeared in the film *Two Tickets To Paris* and his solo version of **Johnny Nash**'s 'What Kind Of Love is This?' (1962) became his final Top 20 entry.

DEE, KIKI

VOCALIST WHO MADE HER RECORDING DEBUT WITH MITCH MURRAY'S 'EARLY NIGHT' (1963). AFTER A SERIES OF **Phil Spector**-inspired releases, Kiki (b. Pauline Matthews, 1947) began covering contemporary soul hits, leading to a recording deal with Tamla/**Motown Records** – the first white British act to be so honoured. Artistically lauded, Kiki only found commercial success after signing with **Elton John**'s Rocket label in 1973. He produced *Loving And Free*, spawning 'Amoureuse' (UK Top 20). She had further chart success with 'I Got The Music In Me' (1974) and 'How Glad I Am' (1975), fronting the Kiki Dee Band – Jo Partridge (guitar), Bias Boshell (piano), Phil Curtis (bass) and Roger Pope (drums). A Dee-John duet, 'Don't Go Breaking My Heart', topped the UK and US charts in 1976. In 1984, she appeared in the musical, *Pump Boys And Dinettes* and, three years later, released *Angel Eyes*, co-produced by David Stewart (**Eurythmics**).

She was nominated for a Laurence Olivier Award in 1989 after appearing in the musical *Blood Brothers*. Her next duet with Elton John, 'True Love' (1993), reached number 2. In 1995 she released *Almost Naked*.

DEEP FOREST

AMBIENT TECHNO/NEW AGE GROUP (ERIC MOUQUET AND FILM COMPOSER MICHEL SANCHEZ) BASED IN FRANCE. 'Sweet Lullaby' (1993) was based on the sampled voices of Pygmies drawn directly from the African rain forest. Remixes of 'Sweet Lullaby' were made by both Apollo 440 and Jam And Spoon. (Deep Forest in turn remixed Apollo 440's 1994 single, 'Liquid Cool'.) *Deep Forest* went platinum in Australia and they won a Best World Music Album Grammy for *Boheme* in 1996. *Boheme* continued previous themes, visiting new areas of the world including Mongolia, Taiwan, India and Hungary.

DEEP PURPLE

UK BAND FORMED IN 1968 AROUND CHRIS CURTIS (b. 1942; DRUMS; EX-**SEARCHERS**), JON LORD (b. 1941; KEYBOARDS), Nick Simper (b. 1945; bass; ex-**Johnny Kidd And The Pirates**) and **Ritchie Blackmore** (b. 1945; guitar). Curtis dropped out within days, and Rod Evans (b. 1947; vocals) and Ian Paice (b. 1948; drums) joined. *Shades Of Deep Purple* included rearrangements of 'Hey Joe' and 'Hush' (US Top 5); *The Book Of Taliesyn* and *Deep Purple* also featured several reworkings, notably 'River Deep Mountain High' (**Ike And Tina Turner**), alongside original material. In 1969, Evans and Simper were replaced by **Ian Gillan** (b. 1945; vocals) and Roger Glover (b. 1945; bass). Often acknowledged as the 'classic' Deep Purple line-up, the quintet made its album debut on *Concerto For Group And Orchestra*, recorded with the London Philharmonic Orchestra. Its successor, *Deep Purple In Rock*, established the group as a leading heavy metal attraction and 'Black Night' reached UK number 2.

'Strange Kind Of Woman' entered the Top 10, while *Fireball* and *Machine Head* topped the album chart, the latter including 'Smoke On The Water'. Platinum-selling *Made In Japan* captured their live prowess, but *Who Do We Think We Are?* marked the end of the line-up. Gillan and Glover's departures robbed Deep Purple of an expressive frontman and imaginative arranger, although David Coverdale (b. 1951; vocals) and Glenn Hughes (b. 1952; bass, ex-Trapeze) brought a new impetus. *Burn* and *Stormbringer* reached the Top 10, but in 1975 Blackmore left to form **Rainbow**. Tommy Bolin (b. 1951, d. 1976; ex-**James Gang**) joined for *Come Taste The Band*, but his jazz/soul style was incompatible with the group's sound; they folded in 1976 following a farewell UK tour. Coverdale then formed **Whitesnake**, Paice and Lord joined Tony Ashton in Paice, Ashton And Lord, and Bolin died of a heroin overdose. In 1984, Gillan, Lord, Blackmore, Glover and Paice completed *Perfect Strangers* and vocalist Joe Lynn Turner was brought in for *Slaves And Masters*. Gillan rejoined in 1993 only to quit and Blackmore left in 1994, briefly replaced by **Joe Satriani**. Steve Morse (guitar), Lord, Gillan, Glover and Paice recorded the credible *Purpendicular* in 1996.

DEBARGE
Albums
All This Love (Gordy 1982)★★★
➧ p.359 for full listings
Connections
Jackson Five ➧ p.195
Michael Jackson ➧ p.195
Influences
Mowtown Records ➧ p.240

DEE, JOEY, AND THE STARLITERS
Albums
Back At The Peppermint Lounge-Twistin (Roulette 1961)★★★
➧ p.359 for full listings
Influences
Chubby Checker ➧ p.88
Isley Brothers ➧ p.194
Johnny Nash ➧ p.244

DEE, KIKI
Albums
I've Got The Music In Me (Rocket 1974)★★★
➧ p.359 for full listings
Collaborators
Elton John ➧ p.200
Connections
Motown ➧ p.240
Eurythmics ➧ p.139
Influences
Phil Spector ➧ p.304
Aretha Franklin ➧ p.153

DEEP FOREST
Albums
Boheme (Columbia 1995)★★★★
➧ p.359 for full listings

DEEP PURPLE
Albums
Machine Head (Purple 1972)★★★★
➧ p.359 for full listings
Connections
Searchers ➧ p.290
Ritchie Blackmore ➧ p.52
Ike and Turner ➧ p. 324
Ian Gillan ➧ p.158
Rainbow ➧ p. 272
James Gang ➧ p. 197
Whitesnake ➧ p.337
Joe Satriani ➧ p.288
Further References
Video: *California Jam* (1984)

DEF LEPPARD
Albums
Pyromania (Mercury 1983)★★★★
Hysteria (Mercury 1987)★★★★
➽ p.359 for full listings

Connections
Whitesnake ➽ p.337
Further References
Videos: *Historia* (1988)
Visualise (1993)
Book: *Biographize: The Def Leppard Story*, Dave Dickson

DEKKER, DESMOND
Albums
The Israelites (Beverley's 1969)★★★★
➽ p.359 for full listings
Collaborators
Specials ➽ p.304
Connections
Jimmy Cliff ➽ p.94
Graham Parker ➽ p.256

DEL AMITRI
Albums
Change Everything (A&M 1992)★★★★
Some Other Sucker's Parade (A&M 1997)★★★★
➽ p.359 for full listings

Further References
Video: *Let's Go Home* (WL1996)

DEL-VIKINGS
Albums
They Sing – They Swing (Mercury 1957)★★★
➽ p.114 for full listings

DELANEY, ERIC
Albums
Swingin' Thro' The Shows (1960)★★★
➽ p.359 for full listings
Connections
George Martin ➽ p.226

DELANEY AND BONNIE
Albums
Accept No Substitute – The Original Delaney & Bonnie (Elektra 1969)★★★

DEF LEPPARD

UK HARD ROCK BAND FORMED BY PETE WILLIS (b. 1960; GUITAR), RICK SAVAGE (b. 1960; BASS) AND TONY KENNING (drums). Originally called Atomic Mass, they became Def Leppard when Joe Elliott (b. 1959; vocals) joined. In 1978, Steve Clark (b. 1960, d. 1991; guitar) was recruited. After several gigs, the band replaced Kenning with Frank Noon; in 1979 they recorded a debut EP after which Noon left. Rick Allen (b. 1963) became their permanent drummer.

Pyromania saw another change in the band's line-up – Willis was sacked and replaced by Phil Collen (b. 1957). On New Year's Eve 1984, drummer Rick Allen lost his left arm in a car crash; he resumed work after he had perfected a specially designed kit which he could play with his feet. This severely delayed the recording of *Hysteria*, which eventually sold 15 million copies worldwide producing two Top 5 US singles, 'Armageddon It' and 'Pour Some Sugar On Me'.

As work began on their next album, Clark was found dead in his London flat from a mixture of drugs and alcohol; Def Leppard soldiered through the recording sessions for *Adrenalize* (US number 1). Their replacement guitarist, Vivian Campbell (b. 1962; ex-**Whitesnake**), made his debut at a Dublin gig and appeared on the 1996 collection *Slang*.

DEKKER, DESMOND

JAMAICAN-BORN DEKKER (b. DESMOND DACRES, 1942) BEGAN WORK AS A WELDER BEFORE FINDING A MUSIC MENTOR in Leslie Kong. In 1963, he released his first single, 'Honour Your Father And Mother', before teaming up with backing group, the Aces. Together they enjoyed 20 Jamaican number 1s, during the mid-late 60s. Dekker's *James Bond* inspired '007 (Shanty Town)' went into the UK charts in 1967, and he came second in the Jamaican Song Festival with 'Unity' in the same year, continuing his chart-topping run in his home country with such titles as 'Hey Grandma', 'Rude Boy Train' and 'Sabotage'.

In 1969, 'Israelites' became the first reggae song to top the UK charts and reached the US Top 10. The follow up, 'It Mek', reached the UK Top 10. Dekker's British success, buoyed by consistent touring, spearheaded the arrival of a number of Jamaican chart acts; Dekker moved to the UK in 1969. A version of **Jimmy Cliff**'s 'You Can Get It If You Really Want', from the film *The Harder They Come*, reached UK number 2 and in 1975, 'Sing A Little Song' reached number 16.

During the 2-Tone ska/mod revival in 1980, Dekker recorded *Black And Dekker* with **Graham Parker**'s Rumour, but the experiment was not commercially successful. *Compass Point* was his last attempt at chart action. In 1993, Dekker released *King Of Kings* with four original members of the **Specials**. His unmistakable falsetto vocal remains one of reggae's most memorable.

DEL AMITRI

GLASWEGIAN SEMI-ACOUSTIC ROCK BAND FORMED BY JUSTIN CURRIE (b. 1964; VOCALS/PIANO/BASS) AND IAIN Harvie (b. 1962; guitar). They were joined for *Sense Sickness* by Bryan Tolland (guitar) and Paul Tyagi (drums). Del Amitri released their debut album in 1985, a few years before they made the UK singles chart with 'Kiss This Thing Goodbye', 'Nothing Ever Happens' and 'Spit In The Rain'. The reissue of 'Kiss This Thing Goodbye' reached the US charts. Despite faltering singles success, 1992's *Change Everything* went platinum. Touring continued throughout that year while most of 1993 was spent working on *Twisted*. The album further refined their AOR formula, with lyrics mainly concerned with loneliness and relationships. *Some Other Sucker's Parade* was an energetic set of ironic electric 12-string soundalikes.

DEL-VIKINGS

THE FIRST SUCCESSFUL MULTIRACIAL ROCK 'N' ROLL BAND. FORMED IN 1956 BY MEMBERS OF THE US AIR FORCE, THE BAND featured Clarence Quick (bass), Corinthian 'Kripp' Johnson (b. 1933, d. 1990; lead/tenor), Samuel Patterson (lead/tenor), Don Jackson (baritone) and Bernard Robertson (second tenor). When Air Force assignments dragged away Patterson and Robertson they were replaced by Norman Wright and Dave Lerchey (the first white member). 'Come Go With Me' (1957) reached US number 4.

When Jackson was transferred by the Air Force, he was replaced by second white member, Donald 'Gus' Backus. 'Down In Bermuda' was ignored, but 'Whispering Bells' made US number 9. Johnson left, replaced by William Blakely, and the new line-up debuted with 'Cool Shake' (1957). Johnson then formed his own Del-Vikings with Arthur Budd, Eddie Everette, Chuck Jackson and original member Don Jackson. They released 'Willette' and 'I Want To Marry You' to little commercial recognition. Their next release was credited to the Del-Vikings And Kripp Johnson, but this did not prevent Mercury Records suing to ensure ownership; the confusion abated when Johnson rejoined the Del-Vikings in 1958. He sang lead on 'You Cheated' and 'How Could You'. Several excellent releases followed, but none revisited the chart action of old.

DELANEY, ERIC

AFTER PLAYING IN SEVERAL BANDS, UK-BORN DELANEY (b. 1924) FORMED HIS OWN UNIT IN 1954, AROUND HIS 'Siamese twin drum kit', revolving stage and a distinctive percussion sound. Delaney's recording of 'Oranges And Lemons' helped the band take off, they toured the UK Variety circuit in 1955, and visited the USA. Typical of their repertoire were 'Roamin' In The Gloamin'', 'Hornpipe Boogie', 'Cockles And Muscles', 'Say Si Si', 'Fanfare Jump' and *Cha-Cha-Cha Delaney*.

In 1960, Delaney made *Swingin' Thro' The Shows*, produced by **George Martin**. In the 80s he was still touring with a small group. In 1991, Delaney was ill with a condition he described as 'Lumbar Sacral Spondylosis'.

DELANEY AND BONNIE

DELANEY BRAMLETT (b. 1939) STARTED OUT IN THE SHINDIGS, THE HOUSE BAND ON US TELEVISION'S SHINDIG. HE ALSO made several unsuccessful solo singles prior to meeting Bonnie Lynn (b. 1944); she had already sung with names including **Ike And Tina Turner**. The couple's first album, *Home*, was released in the wake of *Accept No Substitute* – this exemplary white-soul collection featured several excellent Delaney compositions, including 'Get Ourselves Together' and 'Love Me A Little Bit Longer'.

An expanded ensemble, featuring Bobby Keys (saxophone), Jim Price (trumpet), Bobby Whitlock (guitar), Carl Radle (bass) and Jim Keltner (drums), toured America with **Blind Faith**. This period was documented on *On Tour* and a powerful single, 'Comin' Home'. Despite lavish praise by the media and from **George Harrison** and **Dave Mason**, the backing group left for **Joe Cocker**'s *Mad Dogs And Englishmen* escapade. *To Bonnie From Delaney*, recorded with the Dixie Flyers and **Memphis Horns**, lacked the purpose of previous albums. After two more albums, the couple's marriage soured and they broke up in 1972.

DELFONICS

FORMED IN PHILADELPHIA, USA, IN 1965, ORIGINALLY AS THE FOUR GENTS, THE DELFONICS FEATURED WILLIAM Hart (b. 1945; tenor), Wilbert Hart (b. 1947), Randy Cain (b. 1945) and Ritchie Daniels. Their early releases appeared on local independent labels until their manager, Stan Watson, founded Philly Groove. After Daniels' military conscription, the remaining trio recorded their debut, 'La La Means I Love You'. The hit prepared the way for several symphonic creations, including 'I'm Sorry' (1968) and 'Didn't I (Blow Your Mind This Time)' (1970). Much of their sumptuous atmosphere was due to producer **Thom Bell**'s remarkable use of brass and orchestration, but 'Trying To Make A Fool Out Of Me' (1970), the group's tenth consecutive R&B chart entry, marked the end of this relationship. In 1971, Cain was replaced by Major Harris, whose departure three years later coincided with the Delfonics' downhill slide.

DELLS

SOUL VOCAL AND CLOSE HARMONY GROUP FORMED IN 1953 AS THE EL-RAYS. JOHNNY FUNCHES (LEAD), MARVIN Junior (b. 1936; tenor), Verne Allison (b. 1936; tenor), Lucius McGill (b. 1935; tenor), Mickey McGill (b. 1937; baritone) and Chuck Barksdale (b. 1935; bass) released one record, 'Darling Dear I Know' (1953). After a name change they recorded 'Tell The World' (1955), followed by 'Oh What A Night' (R&B number 4). In 1965 they returned to the R&B chart with 'Stay In My Corner' – a later version reached the US Top 10. However their sole UK hit was a medley of 'Love Is Blue' and 'I Can Sing A Rainbow' (1969).

The Dells continued to prosper through the 70s and 80s, and in the 90s contributed music to the film *The Five Heartbeats*. Their only line-up changes occurred when Lucius McGill left the El-Rays and, in 1958, when Funches was replaced by Johnny Carter (b. 1934; ex-**Flamingos**).

DENNY, SANDY

DENNY (b. ALEXANDRA ELENE MACLEAN DENNY, 1947, d. 1978) began singing in folk clubs around her native London, featuring material by **Tom Paxton** and Jackson C. Frank alongside traditional English songs. Work from this early period was captured on *Sandy And Johnny* (with Johnny Silvo) and *Alex Campbell & His Friends*. The following year, Denny spent six months as a member of the **Strawbs**. Their lone album together was not released until 1973, but this melodic work included the original version of her famed composition, 'Who Knows Where The Time Goes'. In 1968, Sandy joined **Fairport Convention**, leaving shortly afterwards to form Fotheringay.

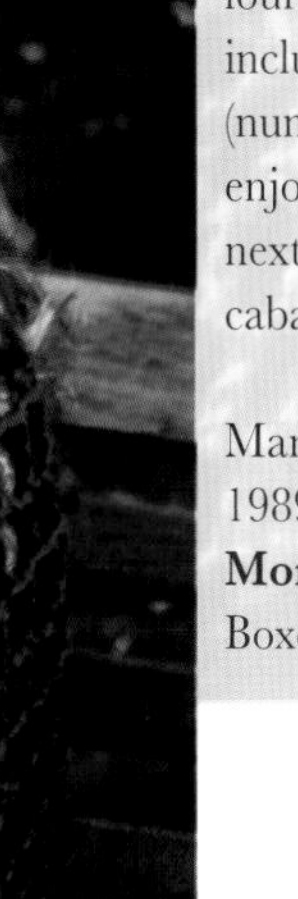

Denny's debut solo album, *North Star Grassman And The Ravens*, included contributions from **Richard Thompson**. *Sandy* was another memorable collection, but *Like An Old Fashioned Waltz* closed this particular period and Denny rejoined Fairpoint Convention in 1974. A live set and *Rising For The Moon* followed. After completing *Rendezvous*, plans were afoot to record a new set in America; tragically, after falling down a staircase, Denny died from a cerebral haemorrhage.

DENVER, JOHN

DENVER (b. HENRY JOHN DEUTSCHENDORF JNR, 1943, d. 1997) WAS 'DISCOVERED' IN A LOS ANGELES nightclub. He initially joined the Back Porch Majority, a nursery group for the **New Christy Minstrels**, but soon left for the Chad Mitchell Trio, where he forged a reputation as a talented songwriter. The Mitchell Trio became known as Denver, Boise and Johnson before Denver went solo in 1969. One of his evocative compositions, 'Leaving On A Jet Plane', provided an international hit for **Peter, Paul And Mary**, and was the highlight of Denver's debut album, *Rhymes And Reasons*. Subsequent releases, *Take Me To Tomorrow* and *Whose Garden Was This*, garnered some attention, but it was not until the release of *Poems, Prayers And Promises* that the singer enjoyed popular acclaim – 'Take Me Home, Country Roads', broached the US Top 3 and became a UK Top 20 hit for **Olivia Newton-John** in 1973. The song's light style was consolidated on the albums *Aerie* and *Rocky Mountain High*. 'I'd Rather Be A Cowboy' (1973) and 'Sunshine On My Shoulders' (1974) were both gold singles, while 'Annie's Song' secured Denver's international status when it topped the UK charts. Subsequently it took classical flautist James Galway to UK number 3 in 1978. Denver had two US number 1s in 1975 with 'Thank God I'm A Country Boy' and 'I'm Sorry'and his status as an all-round entertainer was enhanced by many television spectaculars, including *Rocky Mountain Christmas*, and further gold-record awards for *An Evening With John Denver* and *Windsong*. He continued to enjoy a high profile and forged a concurrent acting career with his role in the film comedy *Oh, God*. In 1981 opera singer Placido Domingo duetted with Denver on 'Perhaps Love'. Later in the decade Denver increasingly devoted time to charitable work and ecological interests. Tragically he died in 1997 when his private plane crashed into the Pacific Ocean.

DENVER, KARL

SCOTTISH SINGER DENVER (b. ANGUS McKENZIE, 1934) developed a love of contrasting folk forms while travelling and his repertoire consisted of traditional material from the Middle East, Africa and China. His flexible voice and unusual inflections brought much contemporary comment. The artist enjoyed four UK Top 10 hits during 1961-62, including 'Marcheta' and 'Wimoweh' (number 4). Denver continued to enjoy minor chart success over the next two years, before turning to cabaret work.

Denver has been based in Manchester for many years, and in 1989 collaborated with the **Happy Mondays** on 'Lazyitis (One Armed Boxer)'.

Delaney & Bonnie & Friends On Tour With Eric Clapton (Atco 1970)★★★★
➧ p.359 for full listings
Collaborators
Blind Faith ➧ p.53
Dixie Flyers And The Memphis Horns
Connections
Ike And Tina Turner ➧ p.324
George Harrison ➧ p.176
Dave Mason ➧ p.227
Joe Cocker ➧ p.95
Further References
Film: *Catch My Soul* (1974)

DELFONICS
Albums
La La Means I Love You (Philly Groove 1968)★★★
➧ p.359 for full listings
Connections
Thom Bell ➧ p.42

DELLS
Albums
There Is (Cadet 1968)★★★★
➧ p.359 for full listings
Influences
Dionne Warwick ➧ p.334

DENNY, SANDY
Albums
Sandy (Island 1972)★★★★
The BBC Sessions 1971-1973 (Strange Fruit 1997)★★★★
➧ p.359 for full listings
Collaborators
Johnny Silvo
Strawbs ➧ p.312
Fairport Convention ➧ p.141
Richard Thompson ➧ p.320
Connections
Tom Paxton ➧ p.257
Further References
Book: *Meet On The Ledge*, Patrick Humphries

DENVER, JOHN
Albums
Spirit (RCA 1976)★★★★
➧ p.359 for full listings
Collaborators
Placido Domingo
The Muppets
Connections
Paul Peter And Mary ➧ p.260
Olivia Newton-John ➧ p.247
Influences
New Christy Minstrels
the Chad Mitchell Trio
Further References
Video: *The Wildlife Concert* (Sony 1995)
Book: *John Denver*, Leonore Fleischer

DENVER, KARL
Albums
Wimoweh (Decca 1961)★★★
➧ p.359 for full listings
Collaborators
Happy Mondays ➧ p.174

DEPECHE MODE
Albums
Violator (Mute 1991)★★★★
Songs Of Faith & Devotion (Mute 1993)★★★★
➽ p.359 for full listings

Connections
Yazoo ➽ p.345
Further References
Videos: *Some Great Videos* (Virgin Vision 1986)
Strange Too – Another Violation (BMG Video 1990)
Book: *Depeche Mode: Strangers – The Photographs*, Anton Corbijn

DEREK AND THE DOMINOS
Albums
Layla And Other Assorted Love Songs (Polydor 1970)★★★★
➽ p.359 for full listings
Connections
Eric Clapton ➽ p.92
Blind Faith ➽ p.53
Delaney And Bonnie ➽ p.114
Influences
Jimi Hendrix ➽ p.180

DESCENDENTS
Albums
I Don't Want To Grow Up (New Alliance 1985)★★★
Enjoy (New Alliance 1986)★★★
➽ p.359 for full listings
Connections
Black Flag ➽ p.50

DESERT ROSE BAND
Albums
Running (MCA 1988)★★★★
Pages Of Life (MCA 1989)★★★★
➽ p.359 for full listings
Connections
Byrds ➽ p.77
Flying Burrito Brothers ➽ p.148
Dillards ➽ p.118
Gram Parsons ➽ p.256
Dwight Yoakam ➽ p.346

DESHANNON, JACKIE
Albums
Don't Turn Your Back On Me (1964)★★★
This Is Jackie DeShannon (Imperial 1965)★★★
Your Baby Is A Lady (1974)★★★
➽ p.359 for full listings
Collaborators
Sharon Sheeley

DEPECHE MODE

UK 'ELECTRO-SYNTH' GROUP WHO MADE THEIR DEBUT AS A GUITAR-PLAYING TRIO: VINCE CLARKE (b. 1960), ANDY Fletcher (b. 1960) and Martin Gore (b. 1961). Following a series of concerts, they were spotted by Daniel Miller, who signed them to his independent Mute Records. They had previously issued one track on Stevo's *Some Bizzare* compilation in 1981, recorded with Clarke on vocals; later they recruited Dave Gahan (b. 1962) as permanent lead vocalist. 'Dreaming Of Me' (1981) started a run of hits which totalled 23 chart entries throughout the 80s. Principal songwriter Clarke left after *Speak And Spell* to form **Yazoo**. The writing was taken over by Martin Gore and Alan Wilder (b. 1959; synthesizer/vocals) joined. The gentle, hypnotic ambience of 'See You' was an early demonstration of Gore's sense of melody and his lyrics tended to tackle subversive subjects (for instance, sado-masochism in 'Master and Servant').

During the early 90s, their albums continued to reach the UK Top 10, and they began to sell in Europe and America, particularly after *The Violator* tour. The album presented a harder sound, informed by Gahan's patronage of the American rock scene; this was continued on *Songs Of Faith & Devotion*. In 1996, Wilder departed and Gahan was hospitalized by a suspected overdose. He recovered determined to stay clean and pursue a future with the band. *Ultra* was a surprisingly good album.

DEREK AND THE DOMINOS

FORMED BY **ERIC CLAPTON** (b. 1945) IN 1970 FOLLOWING HIS DEPARTURE FROM **BLIND FAITH** and A brief involvement with **Delaney And Bonnie**. Together with Carl Radle (d. 1980; bass), Bobby Whitlock (keyboards/vocals), Jim Gordon (drums) and Duane Allman (guitar), the band recorded *Layla And Other Assorted Love Songs*. The band were only together for a year, during which time they toured small clubs in the UK and USA. In addition to the classic 'Layla', the album contained Clapton's co-written compositions mixed with blues classics such as 'Key To The Highway' and a sympathetic reading of **Jimi Hendrix**'s 'Little Wing'. The subsequent live album, recorded on their US tour, demonstrated their considerable potential.

DESCENDENTS

US PUNK BAND FEATURING FRANK NAVETTA (VOCALS/GUITAR), TONY Lombardo (vocals/bass) and Bill Stevenson (drums). They recorded 'Ride The Wild' and collaborated with singer Cecilia for six months before Milo Auckerman became their first regular vocalist. They recorded their debut, *Milo Goes To College*, with Auckerman. Ray Cooper replaced Navetta on guitar in 1985, Doug Carrion (bass) joined around 1986 and Stevenson left for **Black Flag**. The band reconvened three years later with *I Don't Want To Grow Up*. Auckerman's eventual replacement in the band was Dave Smalley. After the Descendents disbanded, several members formed All.

DESERT ROSE BAND

COUNTRY ROCK BAND FORMED IN THE MID-80S. CHRIS HILLMAN (LEAD VOCALS/GUITAR; EX-**BYRDS**, **FLYING Burrito Brothers**), Herb Pedersen (vocals/guitar; ex-**Dillards**), Bill Bryson (vocals/bass), Jay Dee Maness (pedal-steel guitar; ex-**Gram Parsons**' International Submarine Band, Byrds), John Jorgenson (guitar/mandolin/six-string bass) and Steve Duncan (drums; ex-**Dwight Yoakam**) were signed to the independent Curb Records by Dick Whitehouse. Their highly accomplished self-titled first album included a reworking of 'Time Between', previously recorded by Hillman on the Byrds' *Younger Than Yesterday*. The follow-up, *Running*, was another strong work, particularly the title track, which dealt with Hillman's father's suicide and *Pages Of Life* featured the memorable anti-drugs song, 'Darkness On The Playground'. In 1991, Maness was replaced by Tom Brumley; later Jorgenson's decision to go solo threatened the group's momentum, and they split up.

DESHANNON, JACKIE

HIGHLY TALENTED SINGER-SONGWRITER INFLUENCED BY GOSPEL, COUNTRY AND BLUES. DESHANNON (b. 1944) commenced recording in 1960 with a series of minor-label releases. Her collaborations with Sharon Sheeley resulted in several pop songs including 'Dum Dum' and 'Heart In Hand' (**Brenda Lee**), and 'Trouble' (the Kalin Twins). DeShannon then forged partnerships with Jack Nitzsche ('When You Walk In The Room', the **Searchers**, 1964) and **Randy Newman**. Despite some excellent singles, Jackie's own recording career failed to achieve the heights attained with her compositions, by **Helen Shapiro**, **Marianne Faithfull**, the **Byrds** and the Critters. However she reached the Top 10 with the **Burt Bacharach**/Hal David-penned 'What The World Needs Now Is Love' (1965) and 'Put A Little Love In Your Heart' (1969) reached number 4.

Although she continued to write and record, DeShannon was unable to sustain the same profile during the 70s and 80s; yet her songs continued to provide hits for others, notably 'Bette Davis Eyes' (**Kim Carnes** 1981), 'Breakaway' (Tracey Ullman, 1983) and 'Put A Little Love In Your Heart' (**Annie Lennox** and **Al Green**, 1988).

DETROIT SPINNERS

FORMED IN DETROIT, USA, AS THE DOMINGOES. HENRY FAMBROUGH (b. 1935), Robert 'Bobby' Smith (b. 1937), Billy Henderson (b. 1939), Pervis Jackson and George Dixon (vocals; replaced by Edgar 'Chico' Edwards) became the Spinners in 1961 (the prefix '**Motown**' and/or 'Detroit' was added in the UK to avoid confusion with the Spinners folk group). Producer and songwriter Harvey Fuqua sang lead on the group's debut single, 'That's What Girls Are Made For', which broached the US Top 30. 'I'll Always Love You' (1965) was a minor US hit, but it was not until 1970 that the Spinners achieved a major success with a version of **Stevie Wonder**'s 'It's A Shame' (US/UK Top 20).

Edwards was replaced by G. C. Cameron, who was replaced by Philippe Wynne (b. Philip Walker, 1941, d. 1984). With producer **Thom Bell**, the Spinners completed a series of singles including 'I'll Be Around', 'Could It Be I'm Falling In Love' and 'Then Came You', (with **Dionne Warwick**). 'Ghetto Child' and 'The Rubberband Man' brought international success. John Edwards replaced Wynne in 1977, but the Spinners continued to enjoy hits, notably with 'Working My Way Back To You/Forgive Me Girl' (UK number 1/US number 2). However line-up instability began to take its toll.

DEUS

FORMED IN BELGIUM, IN THE EARLY 90S, TOM BARMAN (VOCALS/GUITAR) AND STEFF KAMIL CARLENS (BASS) BEGAN as a songwriting duo. They recruited Julle De Borgher (drums), Klaas Janzoons (violin) and Rudy Trouvé (guitar) and the group gave their earliest performances at Antwerp's bohemian Music Box. Sharing a mutual affection for the works of **Captain Beefheart** and **Tom Waits**, the group set about writing a wide-ranging set of songs that zig-zagged between a number of musical traditions. Their first successful single was 'Suds And Soda', followed by the similarly bracing 'Via'.

With Island Records, the group embarked on their debut, the well-received *Worst Case Scenario*. Group members then concentrated on their array of solo and collaborative projects. In the interim dEUS issued a mail-order-only album, *My Sister Is A Clock*. *In A Bar, Under The Sea* offers shades of **Beach Boys**, yet these influences do not detract from the startling originality of their sound.

DEVO

US NEW WAVE BAND FORMED IN 1972, FEATURING GERALD CASALE (BASS/VOCALS), ALAN MYERS (DRUMS), MARK Mothersbaugh (vocals/keyboards/guitar), Bob Mothersbaugh (guitar/vocals), and Bob Casale (guitar/vocals). Their name comes from the theory of devolution; they presented this with electronic music, using strong robotic and mechanical overtones. The visual representation and marketing exaggerated modern life and their debut album was a synthesis of pop and sarcastic social commentary. It produced their biggest UK hit – a savage take on the **Rolling Stones**'s '(I Can't Get No) Satisfaction'. *Freedom Of Choice* included 'Girl You Want' and 'Whip It', the latter giving them a million-selling single.

At their peak, Devo inspired and informed, but eventually began to lose momentum; *New Traditionalists* signalled a creative descent and successive albums were released to diminishing returns. *Total Devo* saw Myers replaced by David Kendrick, but the band had lost its status as innovators. Despite falling out of fashion, Devo attracted interest from certain groups in the new decade: **Nirvana** covered Devo's 'Turnaround', and both **Soundgarden** and Superchunk offered remakes of 'Girl You Want'.

DEXYS MIDNIGHT RUNNERS

SOUL-INSPIRED UK GROUP FORMED IN 1978 BY KEVIN ROWLAND (b. 1953) AND AL ARCHER (GUITAR) OF PUNK group, the Killjoys. They recruited Pete Williams (piano/organ), J. B. (tenor saxophone), Steve Spooner (alto saxophone), Pete Saunders (piano/organ), Big Jim Patterson (trombone) and Bobby Junior (drums). Rowland brilliantly fashioned the group's image, using Robert De Niro's film *Mean Streets* as an inspiration for their New York Italian docker chic. Their debut 'Dance Stance' crept into the UK Top 40, but the follow-up 'Geno' (a tribute to 60's soul singer Geno Washington) reached number 1 in 1980.

The pop-soul masterpiece *Searching For The Young Soul Rebels* was released to critical acclaim and commercial success. Its single, 'There There My Dear', reached UK Top 10, but the band started to fragment. Rowland and Patterson were then joined by Secret Affair drummer Seb Shelton, Micky Billingham (keyboards), Paul Speare (tenor saxophone), Brian Maurice (alto saxophone), Steve Wynne (bass) and Billy Adams (guitar).

Early 1982 saw Dexys augmented by a fiddle section, the Emerald Express, featuring Helen O'Hara; Rowland's latest experiment was to fuse Northern soul with Irish traditional music. This shift was reflected in their new image of hoedown gypsy chic – neckerchiefs, earrings, stubble and leather jerkins. The new group's first release, 'The Celtic Soul Brothers' failed to chart, but its successor 'Come On Eileen' (1982) reached number 1. *Too-Rye-Ay* (UK number 2) was another startling work and the group undertook an extensive – and theatrical – tour. Further line-up changes included the departure of Patterson, but the group went on to reap considerable American success – 'Come On Eileen' reached US number 1 in 1983.

Further hits included a cover of **Van Morrison**'s 'Jackie Wilson Said' and 'Let's Get This Straight From The Start' before Dexys underwent a long hibernation. They returned as a quartet: Rowland, Adams, O'Hara and Nicky Gatefield, with a new image of chic shirts and ties and neatly-cut hair. *Don't Stand Me Down* received favourable reviews but sold poorly. Although Dexys charted again with 'Because Of You', the commercial failure led to the group dissolving in 1987. Rowland returned the following year as a soloist with the light-pop album, *The Wanderer*. Creation Records signed him for an album in 1996.

DIAMOND HEAD

PART OF THE NEW WAVE OF BRITISH HEAVY METAL. FORMED IN 1979, THE ORIGINAL LINE-UP – SEAN HARRIS (vocals), Brian Tatler (guitar), Colin Kimberley (bass) and Duncan Scott (drums) – debuted with the blues-infuenced 'Sweet And Innocent'; 'Play It Loud' and 'Shoot Out The Lights' (both 1981) received minor acclaim. *Lightning To The Nation* was hard rock with soaring vocals, followed by two EPs, *Diamond Lights* and *Four Cuts*. *Borrowed Time* offered Led Zeppelin-style hard rock.

During sessions for *Canterbury*, both Kimberley and Scott left, replaced by bassist Merv Goldsworthy and drummer Robbie France. Unfortunately, the album was poorly received and the group split in 1985. In 1991, Harris and Tatler re-formed Diamond Head with newcomers Eddie Nooham (bass) and Karl Wilcox (drums). The band undertook a short, low-key UK club tour using the name Dead Reckoning, then declared officially that they had re-formed. 'Wild On The Streets' rediscovered the spirit lost in 1985. The band finally broke up after a tour to support the release of their final album in 1993.

Connections
Brenda Lee ➽ p.213
Searchers ➽ p.290
Randy Newman ➽ p.246
Helen Shapiro ➽ p.294
Marianne Faithfull ➽ p.142
Byrds ➽ p.77
Critters
Burt Bacharach ➽ p.27
Kim Carnes ➽ p.82
Tracey Ullman
Annie Lennox ➽ p.214
Al Green ➽ p.166

DETROIT SPINNERS
Albums
The (Detroit) Spinners (Atlantic 1973)★★★★
Mighty Love (Atlantic 1974)★★★★
Pick Of The Litter (Atlantic 1975)★★★★
➽ p.359 for full listings
Collaborators
Dionne Warwick ➽ p.334
Connections
Harvey Fuqua
Stevie Wonder ➽ p.342
Thom Bell ➽ p.42

DEUS
Albums
In A Bar, Under The Sea (Island 1996)★★★★
➽ p.359 for full listings
Influences
Captain Beefheart ➽ p.80
Tom Waits ➽ p.332
Beach Boys ➽ p.36

DEVO
Albums
Q: Are We Not Men? A: We Are Devo! (Warners 1978)★★★★
➽ p.359 for full listings
Connections
Rolling Stones ➽ p.281
Nirvana ➽ p.248
Soundgarden ➽ p.303

DEXYS MIDNIGHT RUNNERS
Albums
Soul Rebels (EMI 1980)★★★★
Too-Rye-Ay (Mercury 1982)★★★★
➽ p.359 for full listings
Connections
Van Morrison ➽ p.238

DIAMOND HEAD
Albums
Lightning To The Nations (Woolfe 1981)★★★
Borrowed Time (MCA 1982)★★★
Death & Progress (Bronze 1993)★★★
➽ p.359 for full listings
Influences
Led Zeppelin ➽ p.213
Further References
Video: *Diamond Head* (1981)

DIDDLEY, BO

AN EARLY BOXING CAREER SPAWNED THE SOBRIQUET 'BO DIDDLEY' (b. OTHA ELLAS BATES (LATER KNOWN AS ELLAS McDaniel), 1928); after which the singer worked the blues clubs of Chicago. In 1954, he teamed up with Billy Boy Arnold and recorded demos of 'I'm A Man' and 'Bo Diddley'; their backing ensemble featured Otis Spann (piano), Lester Davenport (harmonica), Frank Kirkland (drums) and Jerome Green (maracas). Diddley's distorted, amplified, custom-made guitar, with its rectangular shape and pumping rhythm style, became a familiar, much-imitated trademark. His jive-talking routine with 'Say Man' (US Top 20, 1959) continued on 'Pretty Thing' and 'Hey Good Lookin'' (1963), which just reached the UK charts. Diddley had become an R&B legend: the **Pretty Things** named themselves after one of his songs, while his work was covered by artists including the **Rolling Stones**, **Animals**, **Manfred Mann**, **Kinks** and **Yardbirds**. Diddley subsequently jammed on albums by **Chuck Berry** and **Muddy Waters**, and appeared at rock festivals. His classic version of 'Who Do You Love' became a staple cover for a new generation of US acts, most notably **Quicksilver Messenger Service**, while **Juicy Lucy** took the song into the UK Top 20.

In an attempt to update his image, Diddley released *The Black Gladiator*, but *Where It All Begins*, produced by Johnny Otis, was the most interesting of his post-60s albums. In 1979, Diddley toured with the **Clash** and in 1984 took a cameo role in the film *Trading Places*. *A Man Amongst Men* featured Richie Sambora, Jimmie Vaughan, Ronnie Wood, Keith Richards, Billy Boy Arnold, **Johnny 'Guitar' Watson** and the **Shirelles**.

DIDDLEY, BO
Albums
Superblues (Checker 1968)★★★
➽ p.359 for full listings
Collaborators
Chuck Berry ➽ p.45
Muddy Waters ➽ p.242
Clash ➽ p.93
Richie Sambora
Jimmie Vaughan
Johnny 'Guitar' Watson ➽ p.334
Shirelles ➽ p.295
Connections
Pretty Things ➽ p.266
Rolling Stones ➽ p.281
Animals ➽ p.18
Manfred Mann ➽ p.223
Kinks ➽ p.207
Yardbirds ➽ p.345
Influences
John Lee Hooker ➽ p.185
Muddy Waters ➽ p.242
Juicy Lucy ➽ p.202
Further References
Book: *Where Are You Now Bo Diddley?*, Edward Kiersh

DIFRANCO, ANI
Albums
Not A Pretty Girl (Righteous Babe 1995)★★★★
➽ p.359 for full listings

DIFRANCO, ANI

PROLIFIC 90S FEMINIST SINGER-SONGWRITER ANI DIFRANCO (b. 1971) EMERGED AS A LITERATE, EBULLIENT AND NATURAL live performer, who won converts from both folk and rock audiences. Her promising debut album contained lyrics informed by feminist theory but never subsumed by rhetoric or preciousness and her versatile guitar playing was displayed on *Not So Soft*. *Imperfectly* included more complex musical arrangements, incorporating viola, trumpet and mandolin, and *Puddle Dive* refined her approach. The self-produced *Dilate* was more rock-orientated and, at times, came across as self-parodic. DiFranco's sympathetic collaboration with Utah Phillips was well received, as was *Living In Clip*, her double live album.

DIGITAL UNDERGROUND

P-FUNK ADVOCATES DIGITAL UNDERGROUND WERE FORMED IN CALIFORNIA, IN THE MID-80S. SHOCK-G (b. GREGORY E. Jacobs; keyboards/vocals) and Chopmaster J (samples/percussion) recruited DJ Fuze (b. David Elliot, 1970) among others. Shock-G subsequently introduced his alter-ego, Eddie 'Humpty Hump' Humphrey, and Money B. They mixed P-Funk with **Funkadelic** samples, evident on most of their recordings, including a concept debut album. *This Is An EP* included two tracks from the dreadful *Nothing But Trouble* film in which Digital Underground appeared; *The Body Hat Syndrome* sounded highly derivative. 2Pac, formerly a full-time member, joined for a few verses on 'Wussup Wit The Luv', complaining about drug dealers selling to children, a rare outbreak of moral responsibility. There were three newcomers for *Body Hat*: DJ Jay Z, Clee and Saafir (aka the Saucy Nomad). *Future Rhythm* appeared after a three-year gap.

DILLARD AND CLARK

DOUG DILLARD (b. 1937; EX-**DILLARDS**) AND **GENE CLARK** (b. HAROLD EUGENE CLARK, 1944, d. 1991; EX-**BYRDS**) JOINED forces in 1968 to form one of the first country rock groups. Backed by the Expedition – Bernie Leadon (banjo/guitar), Don Beck (dobro/mandolin) and David Jackson (string bass) – they recorded two albums. *The Fantastic Expedition Of Dillard And Clark* featured several strong compositions by Clark and Leadon including 'The Radio Song' and 'Train Leaves Here This Mornin'' (which Leadon took to his next group, the **Eagles**). By their second album, Dillard and Clark displayed a stronger country influence with the induction of Jon Corneal (drums; ex-**Flying Burrito Brothers**), Byron Berline (fiddle) and Donna Washburn (vocals). *Through The Morning, Through The Night* combined country standards with Clark originals and featured sumptuous duets between Clark and Washburn that pre-empted the work of **Gram Parsons** and **Emmylou Harris**. The group scattered in various directions at the end of the 60s.

DILLARDS

US BLUEGRASS GROUP FORMED BY BROTHERS RODNEY (b. 1942; GUITAR/VOCALS) AND DOUG DILLARD (b. 1937; BANJO/vocals). Roy Dean Webb (b. 1937; mandolin/vocals) and Mitch Jayne (b. 1930; bass) completed the original line-up; they began recording for Elektra in 1962. *Back Porch Bluegrass* and *The Dillards Live! Almost!* established them as one of America's leading traditional acts. *Pickin' & Fiddlin'* was recorded with violinist Byron Berline; Dewey Martin (b. 1942; drums) also joined and Doug Dillard left to work with **Gene Clark** (ex-**Byrds**). Herb Pedersen joined in 1968 and the reshaped quartet completed *Wheatstraw Suite* and *Copperfields*. Pedersen was replaced by Billy Rae Latham for *Roots And Branches*, on which the unit's transformation to full-scale electric instruments was complete. Drummer Paul York, was now featured in the line-up, but further changes were wrought when Jayne dropped out following *Tribute To The American Duck*.

Rodney Dillard has since remained at the helm of a capricious act; he was also reunited with his prodigal brother in Dillard-Hartford-Dillard, which included multi-instrumentalist John Hartford.

DINOSAUR JR

ALTERNATIVE ROCK BAND FROM MASSACHUSETTS, ORIGINALLY CALLED DINOSAUR. J. MASCIS (b. 1965; VOCALS/GUITAR). LOU Barlow (bass) and Murphy (b. Patrick Murphy) evolved from hardcore band Deep Wound. During Dinosaur Jr's career, internal rifts never seemed far from the surface, while their leader's monosyllabic press interviews and general disinterest in rock 'n' roll machinations gave the impression of 'genius anchored by lethargy'. *You're Living All Over Me* featured backing vocals from **Sonic Youth**'s Lee Ranaldo – it also brought them to the attention of hippie group Dinosaur, who insisted the band change their name.

Real recognition came with the release of the huge underground anthem 'Freak Scene', but its parent album, *Bug*, and attendant tour saw Barlow depart. He was temporarily replaced by Donna on 'The Wagon'; subsequent members included Don Fleming, Jay Spiegel and Van Connor (**Screaming Trees**). By *Green Mind*, Dinosaur Jr had effectively become the J. Mascis show, with him playing almost all the instruments. Murphy left and *Where You Been* did not build on the commercial inroads previously forecasted. *Without A Sound* included 'Feel The Pain' and 'On The Brink', featuring Mike Johnson (b. 1965; bass).

Mascis produced other artists, including the **Breeders**, wrote the soundtrack for and appeared in Allison Anders' film *Gas, Food, Lodging* and recorded solo. *Hand It Over* saw a return to Mascis's melodic grunge sound.

DION AND THE BELMONTS

BETWEEN 1958 AND 1960 DION (b. DION DIMUCCI, 1939) AND THE BELMONTS WERE ONE OF THE LEADING DOO-WOP groups: they had nine hits in two years, including a classic reading of the Doc Pomus and Mort Shuman song 'Teenager in Love'. Dion went solo in 1960 and had immediate US success with 'Lonely Teenager'. The following year he had two consecutive hits with 'Runaround Sue' and 'The Wanderer' and sustained an incredible output of hits – he was in the US charts for the whole of 1963. In 1964, he disappeared from the scene to fight a serious heroin addiction. Although he and the Belmonts reunited briefly in 1967, little was heard of him until 1968. He returned during a turbulent year in American history; his emotional 'Abraham, Martin And John' was perfectly timed and climbed to US number 4.

In 1969, *Dion* was released, including sensitive covers of songs by **Bob Dylan**, **Joni Mitchell**, **Leonard Cohen**, and **Jimi Hendrix**. He reunited with the Belmonts in 1973, and in 1975 **Phil Spector** produced 'Born To Be With You'. An album of the same name failed, and an underrated *The Return Of The Wanderer* appeared in 1978. For the next few years Dion recorded sporadically, releasing Christian albums including *Inside Job* and *Kingdom Of The Street*. He returned to rock 'n' roll in 1988 playing with **Bruce Springsteen**, and released *To Frankie*. He was elected to the Rock And Roll Hall Of Fame in 1989.

DION, CELINE

CANADIAN CHANTEUSE CELINE DION (b. 1968), YOUNGEST IN A FAMILY OF 12, BEGAN SINGING in her family's touring folk group. Dion's mother wrote her first song for her, which she recorded with her brother at the age of 12; René Angélil, a local rock manager, took over the young star's guidance. Following a series of French Canadian albums, she made her English language debut with *Unison*. Despite four hit singles, true international recognition proved elusive until her US number 1 soundtrack from Disney's *Beauty And The Beast*, which won an Academy Award and a Grammy. Following a tribute collection comprising Dion's interpretations of the songs of Canadian writer Luc Lamondon, she concentrated on developing an international audience. 'Beauty And The Beast' formed the centrepiece of her second English language album, which also produced the hit singles 'Love Can Move Mountains', 'Water From The Moon', 'If You Asked Me To' and 'Did You Give Enough Love'.

Dion's 'When I Fall In Love', the theme tune to the hit movie *Sleepless In Seattle*, was included on *The Colour Of My Love* alongside a cover of Jennifer Rush's classic, 'The Power Of Love'. It saw her work with songwriters including David Foster, Dianne Warren, Phil Goldstone, **Albert Hammond**, Charlie Dore and Ric Wake alongside producers including Guy Roche and Aldo Nova. 'Think Twice' (1995) spent several weeks at UK number 1 and charted strongly in the US. The album, and its follow-up *Falling Into You*, simultaneously topped both UK and US charts and, in 1996, Dion was chosen to sing at the opening of the Olympic Games in Atlanta, USA. In 1997, she was back at number 1 with 'My Heart Will Go On', the theme song from the hit film *Titanic*.

DIGITAL UNDERGROUND
Albums
Sons Of The P (Tommy Boy 1991)★★★
➧ p.360 for full listings

DILLARD AND CLARK
Albums
Through The Morning, Through The Night (A&M 1969)★★★★
➧ p.360 for full listings
Connections
Dillards ➧ p.118
Byrds ➧ p.77
Gene Clark ➧ p.93
Eagles ➧ p.130
Flying Burrito Brothers ➧ p.148
Gram Parsons ➧ p.256
Emmylou Harris ➧ p.175

DILLARDS
Albums
Wheatstraw Suite (Elektra 1968)★★★★
➧ p.360 for full listings
Connections
Gene Clark ➧ p.93
Further References
Book: *Everybody On The Truck*, Lee Grant

DINOSAUR JR
Albums
Bug (SST 1988)★★★★
➧ p.360 for full listings
Connections
Sonic Youth ➧ p.302
Screaming Trees ➧ p.290
Breeders ➧ p.67

DION AND THE BELMONTS
Albums
Together (Laurie 1963)★★★
➧ p.360 for full listings
Collaborators
Bruce Springsteen ➧ p.306
Connections
Bob Dylan ➧ p.128
Joni Mitchell ➧ p.235
Leonard Cohen ➧ p.96
Jimi Hendrix ➧ p.180
Phil Spector ➧ p.304
Dave Edmunds ➧ p.132
Further References
Book: *The Wanderer*, Dion DiMucci with Davin Seay

DION, CELINE
Albums
The Colour Of My Love (Epic 1994)★★★★
➧ p.360 for full listings
Collaborators
Albert Hammond ➧ p.173
Influences
Jennifer Rush
Further References
Video: *The Colour Of My Love Concert* (Epic Music Video 1995)

DIRE STRAITS
Albums
Dire Straits (Vertigo 1978)★★★★
Making Movies (Vertigo 1980)★★★★
Brothers In Arms (Vertigo 1985)★★★
➧ p.360 for full listings

Connections
Mark Knopfler ➧ p.209
Bob Dylan ➧ p.128
Tina Turner ➧ p.324
Man ➧ p.223
Further References
Video: *Alchemy Live* (1988)
Books: *Dire Straits*, Michael Oldfield
Mark Knopfler: The Unauthorised Biography, Myles Palmer

DISPOSABLE HEROES OF HIPHOPRISY
Albums
Hiphoprisy Is The Greatest Luxury (4th & Broadway 1992)★★★★
with William Burroughs: *Spare Ass Annie & Other Tales* (4th & Broadway 1993)★★★
➧ p.360 for full listings
Collaborators
William Burroughs

DIVINE COMEDY
Albums
Promenade (Setanta 1994)★★★
Casanova (Setanta 1996)★★★★
A Short Album About Love mini-album (Setanta 1997)★★★★
➧ p.360 for full listings
Connections
Sean Hughes
Influences
Scott Walker ➧ p.333

DIXIE CUPS
Albums
Chapel Of Love (Red Bird 1964)★★★
Iko Iko reissue of first album (Red Bird 1965)★★★
➧ p.360 for full listings
Connections
Jerry Leiber
Mike Stoller
Jeff Barry ➧ p.34
Ronettes ➧ p.282
Crystals ➧ p.107

DIRE STRAITS

SCOTTISH BROTHERS **MARK KNOPFLER** (b. 1949) AND DAVID (b. 1951) JOINED UP WITH BASSIST JOHN ILLSLEY (b. 1949) and drummer Pick Withers in London, in the 70s. Their repertoire included a basic blues progression called 'Sultans Of Swing'. It was picked up by Radio London DJ Charlie Gillett, and by the end of 1977 the group were recording their debut, *Dire Straits*, with producer Muff Winwood. The album reached US number 2.

Communique, produced by Jerry Wexler and Barry Beckett, sold three million copies worldwide. It missed the commercial edge of the debut but developed Knopfler's trademark of incisive, cynical lyricism. Before the recording of *Making Movies*, David Knopfler went solo, he was replaced by Hal Lindes and Alan Clark (keyboards). Mark was criticized for not varying his songwriting formula but the album still spawned a UK Top 10 single with 'Romeo And Juliet'. *Love Over Gold* fared better in the USA and its single, 'Private Investigations' (1982), reached UK number 2. Knopfler then produced **Bob Dylan**'s *Infidels* (1983) and wrote 'Private Dancer' (a hit for **Tina Turner** in 1984).

In 1983, Withers left Dire Straits, replaced by ex-**Man** drummer Terry Williams, the group then completed an arduous world tour. A live double set, *Alchemy*, filled the gap before *Brothers In Arms* (1985). The latter was US number 1 for nine weeks and spent three years in the UK chart. Dire Straits' appearance at Live Aid boosted sales, as did their 200-date tour. 'Money For Nothing' – Knopfler's wry comment about rock stars – reached US number 1.

Having already written two film scores, for *Local Hero* (1983) and *Cal* (1984), Knopfler wrote the music for the fantasy comedy *The Princess Bride* in 1987. In 1990, he formed an *ad hoc* group, the Notting Hillbillies. Their self-titled debut album was disappointing and the group disbanded after one UK tour. John Illsley has also released two poorly received albums, *Never Told A Soul* (1984) and *Glass* (1988). In 1991, Dire Straits announced a 'comeback' tour and the release of a new album, *On Every Street*.

DISPOSABLE HEROES OF HIPHOPRISY

SAN FRANCISCAN HIP HOP DUO: RONO TSE (PERCUSSION) AND MICHAEL FRANTI (VOCALS). THEY WORKED TOGETHER for several years, most notably in *avant-garde* industrial jazz band the Beatnigs. Franti's raps were articulate and challenging, breaking down his subject matter beyond the black/white rhetoric of much urban rap. 'Language Of Violence' took to task rap's penchant for homophobia, forging a link between a wider circle of prejudice. In 1993, they recorded an album with author William Burroughs, but, as the year closed, they split. Franti has recorded as Spearhead, with producer Joe 'The Butcher' Nicolo. There were also liaisons with the Disposables' live guitarist Charlie Hunter, and a projected dub album with Adrian Sherwood. Rono worked with rappers Mystic Journeymen.

DIVINE COMEDY

THESE DAYS THE DIVINE COMEDY IS JUST ONE MAN, NEIL HANNON (b. 1970). INFLUENCED AS MUCH BY CLASSICAL AS popular music, his debut *Fanfare For The Comic Muse*, was filled with elegant, resourceful observations on the perversities of Irish and British life. The prevailing influences on *Liberation* and *Promenade* included Michael Nyman, European art and **Scott Walker**. Critics praised both albums. *Promenade* included 'The Booklovers', in which Hannon recounted the names of some 60 authors, leaving a gap for them to answer (many of the replying voices were provided by the Irish comedian Sean Hughes). A breakthrough beyond critical success came in 1996 with the highly accessible, yet bleak, *Casanova*. He followed this with a wondrous mini-album, *A Short Album About Love*, featuring seven heavily orchestrated new songs. Along the way he provided theme music for television programmes, most notably *Father Ted*.

DIXIE CUPS

FORMED IN NEW ORLEANS IN 1963, THE DIXIE CUPS FEATURED SISTERS BARBARA ANN (b. 1943) AND ROSA LEE Hawkins (b. 1944) and their cousin Joan Marie Johnson (b. 1945). The girls formed the Meltones for a high school talent contest in 1963 and were subsequently signed to **Leiber And Stoller**, who were then starting their own record label, Red Bird. The Dixie Cups recorded 'Chapel Of Love' (1964); the song had failed for the **Ronettes** and the **Crystals**, but this time reached US number 1. The Dixie Cups then toured the USA and released a number of follow-up singles, four of which charted, including 'People Say' (number 12) and 'Iko Iko' (number 20). The Dixie Cups have had no further hits but continue to perform, minus Johnson.

DIXON, WILLIE

MISSISSIPPI-BORN DIXON (b. 1915, d. 1992) FORMED THE FIVE BREEZES WITH BABY DOO CASTON. THEIR 1940 RECORDINGS blended blues, jazz, pop and vocal group harmonies. After 10 months in prison for resisting the draft, Dixon formed the Four Jumps Of Jive before reuniting with Caston in the Big Three Trio. The trio featured vocal harmonies and the jazz-influenced guitar work of Ollie Crawford.

By 1951, Dixon was working at Chess Records as producer, A&R representative, session musician, talent scout, songwriter and, occasionally, name artist. He was largely responsible for the sound of Chicago blues on Chess and Cobra, and of the music of **Chuck Berry** and **Bo Diddley**. He was used on gospel sessions by Duke/Peacock, and to play bass behind Rev. Robert Ballinger. Dixon's productions of his own songs included **Muddy Waters**' 'I'm Your Hoochie Coochie Man', **Howlin' Wolf**'s 'Spoonful', Diddley's 'You Can't Judge A Book By Its Cover'and **Otis Rush**'s 'I Can't Quit You Baby'.

In the 60s, Dixon teamed up with Memphis Slim to play the folk revival's notion of blues. Many British R&B bands recorded his songs, including the **Rolling Stones** and **Led Zeppelin**. After leaving Chess, Dixon went into independent production with his own labels, Yambo and Spoonful, and resumed a recording and performing career.

DJ JAZZY JEFF AND THE FRESH PRINCE

JAZZY JEFF (b. JEFFREY TOWNES, 1965) STARTED DJ-ING IN THE MID-70S; HE MET THE FRESH PRINCE (b. WILL SMITH, 1968) and the two secured a recording deal. Their early records included **James Brown** lifts placed next to steals from cartoon characters. In the late 80s they released million-selling teen anthems like 'Girls Ain't Nothing But Trouble', which sampled the *I Dream Of Jeannie* theme. They became the first rap act to receive a Grammy Award (for 'Parents Just Don't Understand'). *He's The DJ, I'm The Rapper* contained more accessible pop fare, the sample of *Nightmare On Elm Street* being the closest they come to street-level hip hop. Television's *The Fresh Prince Of Bel Air* augmented the Prince's profile (he also moved on to major film roles, beginning with *Six Degrees Of Separation* and continuing on to the mega-hit *Men in Black*, for which he also sang the title track). Jeff, meanwhile, has formed A Touch Of Jazz Inc, a stable of producers working on rap/R&B projects. The duo picked up a second Grammy for 'Summertime' (1991), before scoring a UK number 1 with 'Boom! Shake The Room' (1993).

DJ SHADOW

DJ SHADOW (b. G. JOSH DAVIS, *c.* 1972) BEGAN TO PUT TOGETHER BEATS AND SAMPLES ON PRIMITIVE EQUIPMENT at an early age. His 1993 debut for Mo Wax Records, the atmospheric 'Influx', stands as a benchmark in *avant-garde* hip hop circles. A diverse source of inspirations are apparent on further recordings 'Lost And Found' (1994) and 'What Does Your Soul Look Like' (1995). Shadow has also collaborated with Blackalicious, has remixed several DJ Krush singles and runs his own Soulsides label. He remains resolutely underground.

DOCTORS OF MADNESS

UK POST-PUNK GROUP FEATURING RICHARD 'KID' STRANGE (VOCALS/GUITAR/KEYBOARDS/PERCUSSION), STONER (bass/vocals/percussion), Peter (drums/percussion/vocals) and Urban (guitar/violin). The Doctors had issued two rock albums verging on the theatrical by late 1976: *Late Night Movies, All Night Brainstorms* and *Figments Of Emancipation*. Much of their momentum was lost, however, when they issued only one single in 1977, 'Bulletin'. By *Sons Of Survival*, the post-punk era had arrived and the Doctors Of Madness seemed acutely anachronistic. They broke up soon afterwards, their career later summarized on a compilation, *Revisionism*.

Strange went solo, his releases included 'International Language' (1980) and *The Phenomenal Rise Of Richard Strange*.

DODD, COXSONE

DODD (B. CLEMENT SEYMOUR DODD) WAS AMONGST THE FIRST IN JAMAICA to run his own sound system – Sir Coxsone The Down Beat – a forerunner to the mobile discos of the 60s. The music favoured was hard R&B, with Shirley And Lee, Amos Milburn and Lyn Hope being particular favourites. Titles were scratched out on the records and songs were renamed to prevent rival sounds unearthing their identity.

In the mid-50s, the supply of hard R&B records dried up as smoother productions began to find favour in America. These were not popular in Jamaica, so the sound system operators started to make their own music. At the end of the 50s, Coxsone's Worldisc label included local artists such as Jackie Estick, Lascelles Perkins, Clue J And His Blues Blasters and Theophilius Beckford. Other artists recorded later included the Jiving Juniors, featuring a young Derrick Harriott, Clancy Eccles, the Charmers (featuring Lloyd Tyrell aka Lloyd Charmers), Cornell Campbell and Owen Gray. Some of these early recordings can be found on *All Star Top Hits* and *Oldies But Goodies Vol. 1 & 2*.

Dodd's productions caught the mood of the times and, from R&B to ska, he was always at the forefront. Throughout the ska era he ruled with records like 'Spit In The Sky' (Delroy Wilson), 'Hallelujah' (Maytals), 'Rude Boy Gone A Jail' (Clarendonians), 'I've Got To Go Back Home' (Bob Andy), **Wailers** songs, **Lee Perry** tunes and dozens of fiery instrumentals by the Skatalites (the Coxsone backing group).

Dodd opened his own studio, Studio One, in the early 60s; it became the generic title for all Coxsone productions thereafter. During 1967-70, the hits flowed in a veritable deluge: by late 1966, ska's furious pace had begun to give way to the slower rocksteady beat and Dodd's raw, almost organic productions from this period formed what amounts to the foundation of reggae music in the following decades. Much of this incredible output appeared on several UK labels, featuring such artists as Ken Boothe, Alton Ellis, the Heptones, Marcia Griffiths, John Holt, Slim Smith, Delroy Wilson and the in-house session band the Soul Vendors/Sound Dimension.

Younger producers, some of whom had learnt their trade while with Coxsone, began to take over in the early 70s, leaving Coxsone a less prominent role. Nonetheless, he still produced a great deal of fine 70s music including some of the earliest material from Horace Andy, Dennis Brown, the Wailing Souls, **Burning Spear**, Dennis Alcapone, Dillinger and Freddie McKay. As the dancehall style began to take hold, he was once more in full swing with recording artists such as Freddie McGregor, Sugar Minott, Willie Williams and DJs Michigan And Smiley and the Lone Ranger. This proved to be the final golden period for Studio One, however, and in the mid-80s Dodd closed his Brentford Road studio and relocated to New York.

In 1991, Dodd celebrated 35 years in the business with two huge shows in Jamaica, featuring many of the people he had worked with over the years.

DIXON, WILLIE
Albums
Willie's Blues (Bluesville 1959)★★★
Mighty Earthquake And Hurricane (1983)★★★
Across The Borderline (1993)★★★
➧ p.360 for full listings
Connections
Chuck Berry ➧ p.45
Bo Diddley ➧ p.118
Muddy Waters ➧ p.242
Howlin' Wolf ➧ p.189
Otis Rush ➧ p.285
Rolling Stones ➧ p.281
Led Zeppelin ➧ p.213
Influences
Baby Doo Caston
Further References
Book: *I Am The Blues*, Willie Dixon

DJ JAZZY JEFF AND THE FRESH PRINCE
Albums
He's The DJ, I'm The Rapper (Jive 1988)★★★
➧ p.360 for full listings
Influences
James Brown ➧ p.70

DJ SHADOW
Albums
Midnight In A Perfect World (Mo Wax 1996)★★★
Endtroducing (Mo Wax 1996)★★★★
➧ p.360 for full listings
Influences
Grandmaster Flash ➧ p.164

DOCTORS OF MADNESS
Albums
Late Night Movies, All Night Brainstorms (Polydor 1976)★★★
Solo: Richard Strange *The Live Rise Of Richard Strange* (Ze/PVC 1980)★★★
➧ p.360 for full listings

DODD, COXSONE
Albums
Various: *AllStar Top Hits* (Studio One 1961)★★★★
Oldies But Goodies (Vols 1 & 2) (Studio One 1968)★★★★
Best Of Studio One (Vols. 1, 2, & 3) (Heartbeat 1983-87)★★★★
➧ p.360 for full listings
Connections
Burning Spear ➧ p.75
Clue J And His Blues Blasters
Theophilius Beckford
Monty Alexander & The Cyclones
Jiving Juniors
Marcia Griffiths
John Holt
Slim Smith
Delroy Wilson
Influences
Bob Marley And The Wailers ➧ p.225
Lee Perry ➧ p.259

DODGY

IN THE MID-80S, NIGEL CLARKE (VOCALS/BASS) AND drummer Matthew Priest left Birmingham, England – and local goth band Three Cheers For Tokyo – to move to London. They recruited Andy Miller (guitar) and spent a year practising the three-part harmonies that would become their trademark. By taking over a wine bar, the group created their own weekly hangout: DJs mixed up indie and dance cuts, with the band playing as the finale. *The Dodgy Album*, filled with buoyant 60s-styled pop tunes, failed to sell, but 1994's *Homegrown* produced two memorable singles in 'Staying Out For The Summer' and 'So Let Me Go Far'. *Free Peace Sweet* was a solid album containing some good songs, yet, overall, it fell short of the quality that many had expected.

DODGY
Albums
The Dodgy Album (A&M 1993)★★★★
➽ p.360 for full listings

DOLBY, THOMAS

DOLBY (b. THOMAS MORGAN ROBERTSON, 1958), A SELF-taught musician/vocalist/ songwriter, and computer programmer, started building his own synthesizers at the age of 18. With his own hand-built PA system he acted as sound engineer on tours by the Members, **Fall** and the Passions.

He co-founded Camera Cub with Bruce Wooley in 1979, before joining the Lene Lovich backing group in 1980, for whom he wrote 'New Toy'. His first solo output was 'Urges' (1981) followed by 'Europa' and 'The Pirate Twins' (both 1982). For a series of 1982 concerts at the Marquee he recruited Matthew Seligman (ex-**Soft Boys**) and Kevin Armstrong (**Thompson Twins**); he also contributed to albums by M, **Joan Armatrading** and **Foreigner**. Other collaborations included **Stevie Wonder**, **Herbie Hancock**, **Dusty Springfield**, **Howard Jones** and Grace Jones and he backed **David Bowie** at Live Aid. His best known singles, 'She Blinded Me With Science' and 'Hyperactive' made the UK Top 40 and the latter reached the US Top 5; it also charted in the UK again when re-released in 1996. Dolby has produced for **Prefab Sprout** and **Joni Mitchell**, and has scored music for several films.

DOLBY, THOMAS
Albums
The Golden Age Of Wireless (Venice In Peril 1982)★★★★
➽ p.360 for full listings
Collaborators
Soft Boys ➽ p.302
Thompson Twins ➽ p.320
Joan Armatrading ➽ p.20
Foreigner ➽ p.150
Stevie Wonder ➽ p.342
Herbie Hancock ➽ p.174
Dusty Springfield ➽ p.305
Howard Jones ➽ p.201
Grace Jones
David Bowie ➽ p.64
Connections
Fall ➽ p.142
Prefab Sprout ➽ p.264
Joni Mitchell ➽ p.235
Further References
Video: *The Gate To The Mind's Eye* (Miramar Images 1994)

DOLLAR

UK SINGING DUO PRODUCED BY TREVOR HORN. THEREZE BAZAAR AND DAVID VAN DAY (b. 1957) MADE A PROMISING start with 1978's 'Shooting Star' (UK number 14). For the next four years, it was unusual for the latest Dollar single to miss the Top 20. The team's biggest work included: 'Love's Gotta Hold On Me', a revival of the **Beatles**' 'I Want to Hold Your Hand', 'Mirror Mirror (Mon Amour)', 'Give Me Back My Heart' and the futuristic 'Videotheque'. By 1982, Dollar signed off with a 'best of' compilation. While Van Day managed a small hit with 'Young Americans Talking' (1983), overall lack of solo record success prompted a reunion in 1986, but with only minor impact. Van Day subsequently joined **Bucks Fizz**, Bazaar moved to Australia and out of the music business.

DOLLAR
Albums
Shooting Stars (Carrere 1979)★★
➽ p.360 for full listings
Connections
Trevor Horn
Bucks Fizz ➽ p.73
Influences
Beatles ➽ p.38

DOMINO, FATS

WHILE WORKING IN A FACTORY, DOMINO (b. ANTOINE DOMINO, 1928) PLAYED IN LOCAL US CLUBS; IN 1949, HE WAS discovered by bandleader **Dave Bartholomew** and Imperial Records' Lew Chudd. His first recording, 'The Fat Man' (1950), hit the R&B Top 10 and launched his unique partnership with Bartholomew who co-wrote and arranged dozens of Domino tracks over the next two decades. Domino's playing was derived from the rich mixture of musical styles found in New Orleans, including traditional jazz, Latin rhythms, boogie-woogie, Cajun and blues. Among his musicians were Lee Allen (saxophone), Frank Field (bass) and Walter 'Papoose' Nelson (guitar).

By 1955, rock 'n' roll had arrived and young white audiences were ready for Domino's music. His first pop success came with 'Ain't That A Shame' (1955), followed by 'Bo Weevil' and the catchy 'I'm In Love Again' (US Top 10). Domino's next big success came with a pre-rock 'n' roll song, 'Blueberry Hill'; inspired by Louis Armstrong's 1949 version, Domino used his creole drawl to perfection. Fats had nearly 20 US Top 20 singles between 1955 and 1960, among them was the majestic 'Walking To New Orleans', a Bobby Charles composition that became a string-laden tribute to the sources of his musical inspiration. He continued to record prolifically, maintaining a consistently high level of performance. In the mid-60s, Domino recorded several albums with producers Felton Jarvis and Bill Justis; he also toured North America and Europe. He continued this pattern of work into the 70s.

In 1986, Domino was inducted into the Rock And Roll Hall Of Fame, and won Hall Of Fame and Lifetime Achievement awards at the 1987 Grammies. In 1993, Domino was back in the studio recording his first sessions proper for 25 years, resulting in *Christmas Is A Special Day*.

DONEGAN, LONNIE

SCOTTISH-BORN DONEGAN (b. ANTHONY DONEGAN, 1931) WAS A GUITARIST IN A SKIFFLE BAND BEFORE A SPELL IN THE army found him drumming in the Wolverines Jazz Band. After his discharge, he played banjo with Ken Colyer and then Chris Barber; with both outfits Donegan sang a couple of blues-tinged American folk tunes as a 'skiffle' break. His 1954 version of Lead Belly's 'Rock Island Line' (from Barber's *New Orleans Joys*) was a US hit.

Donegan possessed an energetic whine far removed from the gentle plumminess of other UK pop vocalists. His string of familiar songs include: 'Don't You Rock Me Daddy-O', 'Grand Coulee Dam', 'Does Your Chewing Gum Lose Its Flavour On The Bedpost Over Night' and 'Jimmy Brown The Newsboy'. He experimented with bluegrass, spirituals, Cajun and Appalachian music and when the skiffle boom diminished, he broadened his appeal with olde-tyme music hall/pub singalong favourites, and a more pronounced comedy element – his 'My Old Man's A Dustman' (1960), sensationally entered the UK charts at number 1. Two years later, Donegan's Top 20 run ended as it had started, with a Lead Belly number ('Pick A Bale Of Cotton'); between 1956 and 1962 he had produced 34 hits.

On *Putting On The Style* (produced by **Adam Faith**), Donegan re-made old smashes backed by a wealth of artists who were lifelong fans; the idea was **Paul McCartney**'s. 'Spread A Little Happiness' (1982) was also a minor success. Donegan continues to entertain and in the early 90s, toured occasionally with Chris Barber. In 1995 he was presented with an Ivor Novello Award for Outstanding Contribution To British Music. In 1997, he was working on his long-awaited autobiography.

DONOVAN

ADOPTED BY THE PIONEERING UK TELEVISION SHOW *READY STEADY GO!*, DONOVAN (b. DONOVAN LEITCH, 1946) launched his career with 'Catch The Wind', followed by 'Colours' and 'Turquoise'. Donovan's finest work, however, was as ambassador of 'flower power' with singles like 'Sunshine Superman' and 'Mellow Yellow'; his subtle drug references endeared him to the hippie movement. He enjoyed several hits with light material such as the calypso-influenced 'There Is A Mountain' and 'Jennifer Juniper' (written during a much-publicized sojourn with Maharishi Mahesh Yogi). Donovan's drug/fairy tale imagery reached its apotheosis on the Lewis Carroll-influenced 'Hurdy Gurdy Man' and as the 60s closed he fell from commercial grace. His collaboration with **Jeff Beck** on 'Goo Goo Barabajagal (Love Is Hot)' showed a more gutsy approach, while a number of the tracks on the boxed set *A Gift From A Flower To A Garden* displayed a jazzier feel. *Cosmic Wheels* was an artistic, and commercial, success and *Essence To Essence* was a bitter disappointment.

In 1991, the **Happy Mondays** invited him to tour with them. Their irreverent tribute 'Donovan' underlined this new-found favouritism. A new album was released, a flood of reissues arrived and *Troubadour*, a CD box set, covered the vital material from his career. He undertook a major UK tour in 1992 and played **Glastonbury Festival** in 1993. *Sutras*, released to a considerable amount of press coverage, achieved little in terms of sales.

DOOBIE BROTHERS

FORMED IN SAN JOSE IN 1970 BY TOM JOHNSON (GUITAR) AND JOHN HARTMAN (b. 1950; DRUMS). ORIGINAL BASSIST Greg Murphy was quickly replaced by Dave Shogren; Patrick Simmons (b. 1950; guitar) then joined. Within six months the group had become the Doobie Brothers, taken from a slang term for a marijuana cigarette. Their debut album, although promising, was commercially unsuccessful and contrasted with their tougher live sound. A new bassist, Tiran Porter and second drummer, Michael Hossack (b. 1950), joined for the excellent *Toulouse Street*, which spawned the anthem-like 'Listen To The Music'. *The Captain And Me* contained two US hits, 'Long Train Running' and 'China Grove', while *What Were Vices...*, a largely disappointing album, featured the Doobies' first US chart-topper, 'Black Water'.

Michael Hossack was replaced by Keith Knudsen (b. 1952) for Stampede, which also introduced guitarist, Jeff 'Skunk' Baxter (b. 1948; ex-**Steely Dan**). In 1975, **Michael McDonald** (b. 1952; keyboards/vocals) joined, when Johnson succumbed to a recurrent ulcer problem. Although the guitarist rejoined in 1976, he left again in 1977. McDonald gradually assumed control of the group's sound, instilling the soul-based perspective on *Minute By Minute* and its US number 1, 'What A Fool Believes'. Hartman and Baxter left and *One Step Closer* featured newcomers John McFee (b. 1953; guitar), Cornelius Bumpus (b. 1952; saxophone/keyboards) and Chet McCracken (b. 1952; drums). Willie Weeks subsequently replaced Porter, but by 1981 the Doobies' impetus was waning; they split in 1982. McDonald and Simmons went solo and Johnson released two albums, *Everything You've Heard Is True* (1979) and *Still Feels Good To Me* (1981). A re-formed unit, comprising the *Toulouse Street* line-up plus Bobby Lakind (congas), completed *Cycles* – 'The Doctor' reached the US Top 10.

DOORS

JIM MORRISON (b. JAMES DOUGLAS MORRISON, 1943, d. 1971) WAS INSPIRED BY THE POETRY OF WILLIAM BLAKE. In 1965, fellow student Ray Manzarek (b. 1935; keyboards) asked Morrison to join his R&B band, Rick And The Ravens; the band also included the Manzarek's two brothers and drummer John Densmore (b. 1945) was recruited. The group recorded six Morrison songs. Manzarek's brothers were replaced by Robbie Krieger (b. 1946; guitar) and Morrison was established as the vocalist. Elektra's managing director, Jac Holzman, signed the group in 1966.

The Doors (1967) unveiled a group of contrasting influences: Manzarek's thin sounding organ recalled garage-band style, but Krieger's liquid guitar playing and Densmore's imaginative drumming were already clearly evident. Morrison's striking, dramatic voice added power to the exceptional compositions, which included the pulsating 'Break On Through'. Cover versions, including Bertolt Brecht/Kurt Weill's 'Alabama Song (Whisky Bar)', exemplified the group's disparate influences and the single 'Light My Fire' reached US number 1.

Strange Days showcased the exceptional 'When The Music's Over' and the quartet enjoyed further chart success with 'People Are Strange' (US Top 20), but it was 1968 before they secured another number 1 with 'Hello I Love You'; it was also the group's first major UK hit. The Doors' first European tour showcased several tracks from *Waiting For The Sun*, including the declamatory 'Five To One', and a fierce protest song, 'The Unknown Soldier'. The following *The Soft Parade* was a major disappointment, although 'Touch Me' reached the US Top 3.

However, commercial success exacted pressure on Morrison, whose frustration with his role as a pop idol grew more pronounced. In 1969, following a concert in Miami, the singer was indicted for indecent exposure, public intoxication and profane, lewd and lascivious conduct. He was acquitted of all but the minor charges. Paradoxically, this furore re-awoke the Doors' creativity. *Morrison Hotel*, a tough R&B-based collection, matched the best of their early releases and featured seminal performances in 'Roadhouse Blues' and 'You Make Me Real'. Two volumes of Morrison's poetry, *The Lords* and *The New Creatures*, had been published and, having completed sessions for a new album, he left for Paris where he hoped to follow a literary career. Tragically, on 3 July 1971, Jim Morrison was found dead in his bathtub.

LA Woman, his final recording, is one of the Doors' finest achievements, including the superb 'Riders On The Storm'. The others continued to work as the Doors, but while *Other Voices* showed some promise, *Full Circle* was severely flawed and the group soon dissolved. In 1978, they supplied music to a series of poetry recitations, which Morrison had taped during the *LA Woman* sessions; the resulting *An American Prayer* was a major success. In 1991, director Oliver Stone released the cult film *The Doors.*

DOMINO, FATS
Albums
Rock And Rollin' (Imperial 1956)★★★★
p.360 for full listings
Connections
Dave Bartholomew p.34
Beatles p.38

DONEGAN, LONNIE
Albums
Tops With Lonnie (Pye 1958)★★★★
p.360 for full listings
Connections
Elvis Presley p.265
Adam Faith p.142
Paul McCartney p.229

DONOVAN
Albums
Mellow Yellow (Epic 1967)★★★★
p.360 for full listings
Collaborators
Jeff Beck p.41
Influences
Bob Dylan p.128

DOOBIE BROTHERS
Albums
Takin' It To The Streets (Warners 1976)★★★★
p.360 for full listings
Collaborators
Michael McDonald p.229
Influences
Allman Brothers Band p.14

DOORS
Albums
LA Woman (Elektra 1971)★★★★
p.360 for full listings
Further References
Book: *Burn Down The Night*, Craig Kee Strete

DOUG E. FRESH

SELF-PROCLAIMED AS THE ORIGINAL HUMAN BEATBOX – ABLE TO IMITATE THE SOUND OF A RHYTHM MACHINE – Caribbean-born Fresh (b. Douglas E. Davis) broke through in 1985 with the release of 'The Show'. Joined by MC Ricky D (aka Slick Rick), the single matched rhymes with a bizarre array of human sound effects, courtesy of Fresh. A debut album included live contributions from Bernard Wright (synthesizer) and Jimmy Owens (trumpet), as well as a spirited anti-abortion cut. The follow-up saw him allied to **Public Enemy**'s Bomb Squad production team. He was the first genuine rapper to appear at Jamaica's Reggae Sunsplash festival, followed by a spell recording alongside Papa San and Cocoa Tea.

In 1993, after reuniting with Slick Rick, he released 'I-Right (Alright)'. *Play* featured Luther Campbell of **2 Live Crew**.

DOUG E. FRESH
Albums
Oh, My God! (Reality 1985)★★★
» p.360 for full listings
Collaborators
2 Live Crew » p.325
Connections
Public Enemy » p.269

DOUGLAS, CARL

JAMAICAN-BORN DOUGLAS WAS WORKING WITH PRODUCER BIDDU DURING 1974 WHEN THE NECESSITY TO RECORD A b-side to 'I Want To Give You My Everything' resulted in 'Kung Fu Fighting' – apparently recorded in 10 minutes. Pye elevated the song to an a-side and, capturing the contemporary cult interest in Kung Fu, the song topped the US and UK charts. Douglas kept up the novelty long enough to chart again with 'Dance The Kung Fu'. Three years later, he returned to the UK Top 30 with 'Run Back', since which little has been heard of him.

DOUGLAS, CARL
Albums
Kung Fu Fighter (Pye 1976)★★
» p.360 for full listings

DOWNING, WILL

DURING THE LATE 70S, DOWNING APPEARING ON RECORDINGS BY ARTISTS INCLUDING **ROSE ROYCE**, **BILLY OCEAN**, Jennifer Holliday and Nona Hendryx. His own career was launched in the mid-80s, when he joined Arthur Baker's group Wally Jump Jnr And The Criminal Element – Wally Jump, Craig Derry, Donny Calvin, Dwight Hawkes, Rick Sher, Jeff Smith and Michigan And Smiley. Downing later went solo, recording his debut album in 1988. 'A Love Supreme' reached UK number 1 and he had further hits with 'In My Dreams', and a remake of the **Roberta Flack** and Donny Hathaway duet 'Where Is The Love', on which he partnered **Mica Paris**. His later albums did not approach the popularity of his debut.

DOWNING, WILL
Albums
Will Downing (4th & Broadway 1988)★★★★
Moods (4th & Broadway 1995)★★★
» p.360 for full listings
Collaborators
Billy Ocean » p.251
Mica Paris » p.256
Connections
Roberta Flack » p.146

DOWNLINERS SECT

FORMED IN 1962 AS THE DOWNLINERS. AFTER THE ORIGINAL LINE-UP FELL APART, FOUNDER MEMBERS DON CRAINE (vocals/rhythm guitar) and Johnny Sutton (drums) recruited Keith Grant (bass) and Terry Gibson (lead guitar). Having added the 'Sect' suffix, they recorded a privately pressed EP, *A Nite In Great Newport Street*. A version of **Jimmy Reed**'s 'Baby What's Wrong' (1964) was their first single, by which time Ray Sone (harmonica) had joined. Their musical approach was showcased on their debut album, but in 1965, they confused any prospective audience with *The Country Sect*, an album of folk and country material, and *The Sect Sing Sick Songs* EP. Sone left the group prior to recording *The Rock Sect's In*.

When two pop-oriented singles, 'Glendora' and 'Cost Of Living', failed to chart, Gibson and Sutton left, replaced by Bob Taylor and Kevin Flanagan; pianist Matthew Fisher (later of **Procol Harum**) also joined briefly. Craine left after 'I Can't Get Away From You', after which Grant and Sutton took the group to Sweden, where they recorded a handful of tracks before disbanding. Craine and Grant revived Sect in 1976 in the wake of the pub rock/R&B phenomenon, and continued to lead the group throughout the 80s.

DOWNLINERS SECT
Albums
Showbiz (1979)★★★
» p.360 for full listings
Connections
Jimmy Reed » p.274
Procol Harum » p.268
Influences
Pretty Things » p.266

DOZIER, LAMONT

DOZIER (b. 1941) SANG ALONGSIDE SEVERAL **MOTOWN** NOTABLES IN THE ROMEOS AND THE VOICE MASTERS during 1957-58. He befriended local songwriter and producer Berry Gordy and was one of Gordy's first signings. Dozier issued 'Let's Talk It Over' (as 'Lamont Anthony') in 1960, followed by two further singles. In 1963, he recorded with **Eddie Holland** before becoming part of the writing and production team with Eddie and his brother Brian. **Holland/Dozier/Holland** graced the majority of Motown's hits for the next five years, most notably with the **Supremes** and the **Four Tops**. Dozier contributed lyrics and music to the partnership's creations.

Dozier and the Hollands left Motown in 1967 to set up rival companies, Invictus and Hot Wax Records. Dozier resumed his own recording career in 1972, registering a US hit with 'Why Can't We Be Lovers', and receiving critical acclaim for a series of duets with Brian Holland. In 1973-74, Dozier issued *Out Here On My Own* and *Black Bach*, and he enjoyed major US hits with 'Trying To Hold Onto My Woman', 'Fish Ain't Bitin'', and 'Let Me Start Tonite'. *Peddlin' Music On The Side* included the classic 'Goin' Back To My Roots' – a big hit for **Odyssey** in the early 80s. Dozier continued production work, overseeing **Aretha Franklin** amongst others. In the late 70s and early 80s, Dozier's soul music lost ground to the burgeoning disco scene. He re-emerged in 1983 with *Bigger Than Life*.

DOZIER, LAMONT
Albums
Peddlin' Music On The Side (Warners 1977)★★★
» p.360 for full listings
Collaborators
Eddie Holland » p.182
Supremes » p.314
Four Tops » p.152
Connections
Mowtown Records » p.240
Holland/Dozier/Holland » p.183
Martha And The Vandellas » p.226
Odyssey » p.251
Aretha Franklin » p.153

DR DRE

GANGSTA RAPPER DRE (b. ANDRE YOUNG) STARTED OUT AS A DJ IN LOS ANGELES. AT AGE 17, HE FORMED THE WORLD Class Wreckin' Cru; *The Chronic* confirmed rap's commercial breakthrough. Dre's work with **Eazy E**, D.O.C., Above The Law and **Snoop Doggy Dogg** broke new ground. Snoop had already rapped with Dre on the hits, 'Deep Cover' and 'Nuthin' But A 'G' Thang'. After joining **NWA**, Dre became house producer for Eazy E's Ruthless Records – seven out of eight albums he produced for them went platinum. Dre has also produced an album for Michel'le. His production skills clearly outshine his limited rapping ability.

DR DRE
Albums
The Chronic (Death Row 1993)★★★
Ist Round Knockout (Triple X 1996)★★★
» p.360 for full listings
Collaborators
Eazy E » p.131
Snoop Doggy Dogg » p.302
Connections
NWA » p.249
Wreckin' Cru

DR. FEELGOOD

PUB ROCK BAND FORMED IN 1971. DR. FEELGOOD – LEE BRILLEAUX (b. 1953, d. 1994; VOCALS/HARMONICA), WILKO Johnson (b. John Wilkinson, 1947; guitar), John B. Sparks (b. 1953; bass), John Potter (piano) and 'Bandsman' Howarth (drums) – broke into the London scene in 1974. When Potter and Howarth dropped out, the remaining trio recruited John 'The Big Figure' Martin (drums). *Down By The Jetty* received critical approbation, but the quartet only secured commercial success with *Stupidity*. Johnson left; his replacement, John 'Gypie' Mayo, was an accomplished guitarist, but lacked his predecessor's striking visual image. Dr. Feelgood then embarked on a more mainstream direction, which was only intermittently successful. 'Milk And Alcohol' (1978) was their sole UK Top 10 hit. In 1981, Johnny Guitar replaced Mayo; in 1982 Sparks and the Big Figure left the band. In 1993, Brilleaux was diagnosed as having lymphoma and had to break the band's often-inexorable touring schedule for the first time in over 20 years. He died the following year.

DR. FEELGOOD
Albums
Down By The Jetty (United Artists 1975)★★★★
» p.360 for full listings

DR. HOOK

DR. HOOK AND THE MEDICINE SHOW BEGAN AS A NEW JERSEY BAR BAND WITH ONE-EYED DR. HOOK (b. RAY Sawyer, 1937; vocals), Denis Locorriere (b. 1949; guitar/vocals), George Cummings (b. 1938; lead/slide guitar), William Francis (b. 1942; keyboards) and Jay David (b. 1942; drums). They were chosen to record the film score to *Playboy* cartoonist Shel Silverstein's *Who's Harry Kellerman And Why Is He Saying*

These Terrible Things About Me? (1970), and later backed Silverstein's singing on record. The band were signed to CBS and success followed with 'Sylvia's Mother', 'Sloppy Seconds' and 'The Cover Of The **Rolling Stone**' (banned by the BBC in the UK).

With Rik Elswit (b. 1945; guitar) and Jance Garfat (b. 1944; bass), they completed *Belly Up*. They were then joined by drummer John Wolters (b. John Christian Wolters, 1945, d. 1997); by then, they were billed as Dr. Hook. A revival of **Sam Cooke**'s 'Only 16' was followed by the title track of *A Little Bit More*. Next came a UK number 1 with 'When You're In Love With A Beautiful Woman' from the million-selling *Pleasure And Pain*. *Sometimes You Win* was the wellspring of more smashes.

Throughout the 80s, Dr. Hook's chart strikes were mainly in North America, becoming more sporadic as the decade wore on. Sawyer's solo career and Locorriere's efforts as a Nashville-based songwriter had all but dissolved the group by 1990.

DR. JOHN

DR. JOHN (b. MALCOLM JOHN REBENNACK, 1940) IS A CONSUMMATE NEW ORLEANS MUSICIAN, WHO BLENDS FUNK, rock 'n' roll, jazz and R&B. He started out as a session musician, playing guitar, keyboards and other instruments. His first recording under his own name was 'Storm Warning' (1957) followed by an album (1958); others followed with little success. In 1958 he co-wrote 'Lights Out', recorded by Jerry Byrne, and toured with **Frankie Ford**. By 1962, Rebennack had played on countless sessions for such renowned producers as **Phil Spector**, Harold Battiste, H. B. Barnum and **Sonny Bono**. He also formed his own bands during the early 60s but with no success. By the mid-60s he had moved to Los Angeles, where he fused his New Orleans roots with the psychedelic sound, and developed the persona Dr John Creux, The Night Tripper. He used an intoxicating brew of voodoo incantations and New Orleans heritage, but *Zu Zu Man* did not catch on; however *Gris Gris* received critical acclaim. This exceptional collection included 'Walk On Gilded Splinters' and inspired several similarly styled successors. The same musical formula and exotic image were pursued on *Babylon* and *Remedies*. In 1971, Dr. John charted for the first time with *Dr. John, The Night Tripper (The Sun, Moon And Herbs)*, followed by *Gumbo* and 'Iko Iko'. His biggest US hit came in 1973 with 'Right Place, Wrong Time'; the accompanying album, *In The Right Place*, was also his best-seller. 'Such A Night' (1973) also charted.

He toured with New Orleans band the Meters, recorded *Triumvirate* with Michael Bloomfield and John Hammond, recorded *Bluesiana Triangle* with jazz musicians Art Blakey and David 'Fathead' Newman and released *In A Sentimental Mood*, which included a duet with Rickie Lee Jones. In 1997 he recorded tracks with Spiritualized, **Supergrass**, **Paul Weller** and **Primal Scream**.

DRAKE, NICK

DRAKE (b. 1948, d. 1974) BEGAN RECORDING IN 1967; HE SUBSEQUENTLY WORKED WITH PRODUCER JOE BOYD. A SERIES of demos were then completed (part of which surfaced on the posthumous release *Time Of No Reply*) before Drake began work on his debut album.

Five Leaves Left was a mature, melodic collection featuring Robert Kirby (strings), **Richard Thompson** (guitar) and Danny Thompson (bass). Drake's languid, almost unemotional intonation contrasted with the warmth of his musical accompaniment. *Bryter Layter* was more worldly and jazz-based, featuring Lyn Dobson (flute) and Ray Warleigh (saxophone). In 1971, Nick resumed recording with *Pink Moon*. Completed in two days, its stark, desolate atmosphere made for uncomfortable listening. It was 1974 before he re-entered a studio. On 25 November 1974, Nick Drake was found dead. The coroner's verdict was suicide.

DREAD ZONE

UK TRANCE-DUB CLUB TRIO: GREG ROBERTS, LEO WILLIAMS AND TIM BRAN. ROBERTS IS RESPONSIBLE FOR RHYTHMS and sampling, Bran for programming. Part of Dread Zone's distinctive charm is drawn from Roberts's appetite for cult films – many of his samples are taken from this field, dialogue from b-movies being a particular favourite. 'House Of Dread' came with a 'Howard Marks' remix (Marks is among the world's most famous cannabis traffikers). 'Zion Youth' broached the UK Top 40 in 1995 and was followed by *Second Light*.

DREAM SYNDICATE

SONGWRITER STEVE WYNN (GUITAR/VOCALS), KARL PRECODA (GUITAR), KENDRA SMITH (BASS) AND DENNIS DUCK (DRUMS) released their finest song, 'Tell Me When It's Over' (1983), as their first UK single; *Medicine Show* appeared in 1984. *This Is Not The New Dream Syndicate Album* recycled their early live recordings and by *Out Of The Grey* the band's approach was gradually shifting to the mainstream. *Ghost Stories* was followed by 'I Have Faith', and then came a live swan-song offering, *Live At Raji's*, in 1989.

Wynn eventually left for a similarly acclaimed but commercially unsuccessful solo career.

DR. HOOK

Albums
Sloppy Seconds (Columbia 1972)★★★
Pleasure And Pain (Capitol1978)★★★
Sometimes You Win (Capitol 1979)★★★
➽ p.360 for full listings

Connections
Rolling Stones ➽ p.281
Sam Cooke ➽ p.100

Further References
Video: *Completely Hooked* (PMI 1992)

DR. JOHN

Albums
Gris Gris (Atco 1968)★★★★
Dr. John's Gumbo (Atco 1972)★★★★
➽ p.360 for full listings

Collaborators
Frankie Ford
Supergrass ➽ p.313
Paul Weller ➽ p.336
Primal Scream ➽ p.267

Connections
Phil Spector ➽ p.304
Sonny Bono ➽ p.60

Further References
Videos: *Doctor John And Chris Barber, Live At The Marquee Club* (Jettisoundz 1986)
Live At The Marquee (Hendring Video 1990)
Book: *Dr. John: Under A Hoodoo Moon*, Mac Rebennack with Jack Rummel

DRAKE, NICK

Albums
Five Leaves Left (Island 1969)★★★★
Bryter Layter (Island 1970)★★★★
➽ p.360 for full listings

Collaborators
Richard Thompson ➽ p.320

Influences
Bert Jansch
John Renbourn

Further References
Books: *Nick Drake*, David Housden
Nick Drake: A Biography, Patrick Humphries

DREAD ZONE

Albums
Second Light (Virgin 1995)★★★★
➽ p.360 for full listings

DREAM SYNDICATE

Albums
The Days Of Wine And Roses (Ruby 1982)★★★★
Medicine Show (A&M 1984)★★★
Out Of The Grey (Big Time 1986)★★★
➽ p.360 for full listings

Influences
Lou Reed ➽ p.274
Neil Young ➽ p.346

DRIFTERS
Albums
Save The Last Dance For Me (Atlantic 1961)★★★★
The Good Life With The Drifters (Atlantic 1964)★★★★
There Goes My First Love (Bell1975)★★★
➽ p.360 for full listings
Connections
Ben E. King ➽ p.205
Searchers ➽ p.290
Bert Berns ➽ p.44
Further references
Books: *The Drifters: The Rise And Fall Of The Black Vocal Group*, Bill Millar
Save The Last Dance For Me: The Musical Legacy 1953-92, Tony Allan and Faye Treadwell

DUB WAR
Albums
Dub Warning mini-album (Words Of Warning 1994)★★★
Words Of Dubwarning (Words Of Warning 1996)★★★
Wrong Side Of Beautiful (Earache 1996)★★★★
➽ p.360 for full listings
Influences
Brand New Heavies ➽ p.66
Jamiroquai ➽ p.197

DUBLINERS
Albums
Finnegan Wakes (Transatlantic 1966)★★★★
A Drop Of The Hard Stuff (1967)★★★★
The Dubliners (Major Minor 1968)★★★★
➽ p.360 for full listings
Collaborators
Pogues ➽ p.263
Further References
Book: *The Dubliners Scrapbook*, Mary Hardy

DUBSTAR
Albums
Disgraceful (Food 1995)★★★★
Goodbye (Food 1997)★★★★
➽ p.360 for full listings
Influences
Saint Etienne ➽ p.287

DUNBAR, SLY
Albums
Go Deh Wid Riddim (Crystal 1977)★★★
Sly-Go-Ville (Mango/Island 1982)★★★
➽ p.360 for full listings
Collaborators
Lee Perry ➽ p.259
Connections
Sly and Robbie ➽ p.300
Al Green ➽ p.166
Black Uhuru ➽ p. 51

DRIFTERS

R&B VOCAL GROUP FORMED IN 1953 IN NEW YORK. CLYDE McPHATTER (TENOR), GERHART THRASHER, ANDREW Thrasher and Bill Pinkney achieved a number 1 R&B hit with their debut, 'Money Honey', as Clyde McPhatter and the Drifters. Follow-up releases, including 'Such A Night', 'Lucille' and 'Honey Love', also proved highly successful, mixing gospel and rock 'n' roll styles. McPhatter's was drafted into the armed forces in 1954; on his release he went solo. His former group enjoyed late-50s success with 'Adorable', 'Steamboat', 'Ruby Baby' and 'Fools Fall In Love', featuring a variety of lead singers. A greater emphasis on pop material ensued, but tension between the group and manager, George Treadwell, resulted in an irrevocable split. Having fired the line-up in 1958, Treadwell, who owned the copyright to the name took on **Ben E. King** (tenor), Charlie Thomas (tenor), Doc Green Jnr (baritone), Elsbearry Hobbes (b. *c.* 1936, d. 1996; bass) and guitarist Reggie Kimber. They declared their new-found role with 'There Goes My Baby'.

Further excellent releases followed, notably 'Dance With Me' (1959), 'This Magic Moment' (1960) and 'Save The Last Dance For Me' (US number 1/UK number 2). King went solo in 1960, replaced by Rudy Lewis (d. 1964). The Drifters continued to enjoy hits and songs such as 'Sweets For My Sweet', 'Up On The Roof' and 'On Broadway'. Johnny Moore, who had returned to the line-up in 1963, took over the lead vocal slot after Lewis's death. 'Under The Boardwalk', recorded the day after the latter's passing, was the Drifters' last US Top 10 pop hit.

Bert Berns joined, bringing a soul-based urgency to their work ('One Way Love' and 'Saturday Night At The Movies') and their career was revitalized in 1972 when the re-releases, 'At The Club' and 'Come On Over To My Place', reached the UK Top 10. British songwriters/producers Tony Macauley, Roger Cook and Roger Greenaway fashioned a series of singles redolent of the Drifters' 'classic' era. Between 1973 and 1975, the group, still led by Moore, enjoyed six UK Top 10 hits, including 'Kissin' In The Back Row Of The Movies' and 'There Goes My First Love'. In 1982, Moore was replaced by Ben E. King. They were inducted into the Rock And Roll Hall Of Fame in 1988.

DUB WAR

DUB WAR (A COLLISION OF RAGGA AND PUNK, SHOT THROUGH WITH STEELY METALLIC GUITAR) EMERGED IN 1994. Formed in Wales in 1993, Jeff Rose (guitar), Richie Glover (bass), Martin Ford (drums) and Benji (vocals) all came from diverse musical backgrounds, including punk and dancehall reggae. The EP *Mental* featured remixes from Senser, **Brand New Heavies** and **Jamiroquai**, and was followed by a further EP, *Gorrit*. By their first album, *Pain*, the band had established a strong live following. *Wrong Side Of Beautiful* was their finest album to date.

DUBLINERS

FORMED IN 1962 AS THE RONNIE DREW GROUP. BARNEY MACKENNA (b. 1939), LUKE KELLY (b. 1940), CIARAN BOURKE (b. 1936) and Ronnie Drew (b. 1935) were known faces in Dublin's post-skiffle folk haunts. In 1964, Kelly left for England's folk scene; Bob Lynch and John Shehan (b. 1939) joined. After *Dubliners In Concert*, the band played theatre bars, made several albums for Transatlantic and gained a strong following on the Irish folk circuit.

In 1965, the group turned professional, and Kelly returned, replacing Lynch who wished to stay semi-professional. Major UK hits followed with 1967's censored 'Seven Drunken Nights' and 'Black Velvet Band'. 'Never Wed An Old Man' was only a minor hit, but *A Drop Of The Hard Stuff* and three of its successors charted well. A brain haemorrhage forced Bourke's retirement in 1974, and Drew's return to the ranks was delayed by injuries sustained in a road accident. Nevertheless, Drew's trademark vocal was heard on the group's 25th anniversary single, 'The Irish Rover', a merger with the **Pogues** that reached the UK Top 10.

DUBSTAR

FORMED IN 1994 WHEN DJ STEVE HILLIER (SONGWRITING/PROGRAMMING) MET CHRIS WILKIE (GUITAR); THEY recruited student Sarah Blackwood (b. *c.* 1972; vocals). Their debut, *Disgraceful*, mixed club-orientated dance beats in addition to strong hooks and pop dynamics. It failed to produce a breakthrough, despite critical acclaim and the Top 40 single 'Stars'; that changed with the UK Top 20 single 'Not So Manic Now'. *Goodbye*, contained more bittersweet songs and spawned two hit singles; 'Cathedral Park' and 'No More Talk'.

DUNBAR, SLY

IN 1969, JAMAICAN-BORN DUNBAR (b. LOWELL DUNBAR, 1952) BEGAN RECORDING WITH **LEE PERRY**. HE PLAYED drums on 'Night Doctor' by the Upsetters, then on Dave Barker and Ansell Collins's 'Double Barrel' before beginning a working friendship with Robbie Shakespeare (b. 1953; bass) as **Sly And Robbie**. In 1972-73, Sly joined Skin Flesh And Bones; the same year, Sly and Robbie became founder members of the Revolutionaries, Channel One studio's houseband. Sly's technical proficiency drove him to develop original drum patterns, his inventive and entertaining playing can be heard on dub and instrumental albums such as *Vital Dub*, *Satta Dub* and *Revolutionary Sounds*, as well as supporting the Mighty Diamonds on their classic *Right Time*. He then released two disappointing solo albums, *Simple Sly Man* (1978) and *Sly Wicked And Slick* (1979). Around this time, Sly was the first drummer to integrate synthesized drums into his playing.

In 1979, Sly And Robbie moved into record production with their own Taxi label, scoring with **Black Uhuru**'s best-selling *Showcase*. In 1984, they became official members of Black Uhuru, but left later that year after the departure of Michael Rose. At the same time, they established Ini Kamoze, released Dennis Brown's *Brown Sugar* and Sugar Minott's *Sugar And Spice*, plus three ground-breaking albums with Grace Jones. They have recorded widely with many artists and changed the musical world; their restless creativity ensures that they will continue to do so.

DUNN, HOLLY

DUNN (b. 1957; VOCALS/GUITAR) STARTED OUT WITH THE FREEDOM FOLK SINGERS, REPRESENTING TEXAS IN THE White House bicentennial celebrations. Later, she joined her brother, Chris Waters, who had moved to Nashville as a songwriter; together they wrote 'Out Of Sight, Not Out Of Mind' for Cristy Lane. Among her other songs are 'An Old Friend' (Terri Gibbs), 'Love Someone Like Me' (New Grass Revival), 'Mixed Emotions' (Bruce Murray) and 'That Old Devil Moon' (Marie Osmond). *Across The Rio Grande* was a traditional yet contemporary country album which won much acclaim, her 'You Really Had Me Going' was a country number 1 and other country hits included 'Strangers Again' and 'That's What Your Love Does To Me'. *Getting It Dunn* was her last album for Warner Brothers, and she is now signed to the independent label River North. *Life And Love And All The Stages* was undistinguished, and she may find it difficult returning to the mainstream.

DURAN DURAN

UK NEW ROMANTIC POP GROUP, WHO TOOK THEIR NAME FROM A CHARACTER IN THE MOVIE *BARBARELLA*. VOCALIST Simon Le Bon (b. 1958), pianist Nick Rhodes (b. Nicholas Bates, 1962), guitarist Andy Taylor (b. 1961), bassist John Taylor (b. 1960) and drummer Roger Taylor (b. 1960) charted with their debut, 'Planet Earth'. The follow-up, 'Careless Memories', barely scraped into the UK Top 40, but 'Girls On Film', accompanied by a risqué **Godley And Creme** video featuring nude models, took them to the UK Top 10. Two albums quickly followed as did hits like 'Hungry Like A Wolf' and 'Say A Prayer'. Soon they had broken into the US Top 10 twice and 'Is There Something I Should Know?', a gloriously catchy pop song, entered the UK charts at number 1. An impressive run of UK Top 10 hits followed over the next three years, including 'New Moon On Monday', 'The Reflex' (UK/US number 1), 'Wild Boys' and 'A View To A Kill' (a James Bond movie theme). At the peak of their success, they decided to venture into other projects, such as the Power Station and Arcadia. By the late 80s they had lost many original fans, and even such interesting songs as 'The Skin Trade' only scraped the Top 20.

Le Bon, Rhodes and John Taylor continued recording, with Warren Cuccurullo and Sterling Campbell joining in 1989; Campbell left in 1991. 'Ordinary World' became a major transatlantic hit in 1993, followed by 'Come Undone', both taken from *Duran Duran*.

DUROCS

SAN FRANCISCAN DUO FORMED IN 1979. RON NAGLE (VOCALS/KEYBOARDS) FOUNDED THE PIONEERING MYSTERY Trend, composed incidental music to several horror films (notably *The Exorcist*) and co-wrote the best-seller 'Don't Touch Me There' (the **Tubes**); Scott Mathews (guitar/drums) had played in several groups, including the **Elvin Bishop** Band.

Duroc's songs were recorded by Michelle Phillips and Barbra Streisand. *The Durocs* was a strong effort but sold poorly, and the project was abandoned when Capitol refused to release a second set. The duo continued to compose and record together, and later released a single under the name the Profits. Nagle is now a renowned ceramic artist.

DURUTTI COLUMN

UK-BORN VINI REILLY (b. VINCENT GERARD REILLY, 1953) AND HIS DURUTTI COLUMN COMBINED ELEMENTS OF jazz, electronic and folk music. Reilly played guitar in 1977 hopefuls Ed Banger And The Nosebleeds, before television presenter and Factory Records founder Tony Wilson invited him to join Dave Rowbotham (d. 1991; guitar) and Chris Joyce (drums) in 1978. They became the Durutti Column and recruited vocalist Phil Rainford and bass player Tony Bowers. They recorded on *A Factory Sampler EP*.

Eventually Reilly was the only original member left, although *The Return Of The Durutti Column* also featured Hannett, Pete Crooks (bass), and Toby (drums). Durutti Column soon established a solid cult following, particularly abroad, but live appearances were sporadic, as Reilly suffered from an eating disorder and was frequently too ill to play.

In 1980, Reilly and Hannett helped out on Pauline Murray's first solo album. The Durutti Column's own recordings over the next few years were a mixed batch recorded by Reilly with assistance from (to name just a few) drummers Donald Johnson and Bruce Mitchell; Maunagh Flemin and Simon Topping on horns; further brass players Richard Henry, Tim Kellett, and Mervyn Fletcher; violinist Blaine Reininger and cellist Caroline Lavelle. A striking example of late period Durutti Column was captured on *Vini Reilly*, released in 1989. Reilly has also played guitar for artists including Anne Clarke, Richard Jobson and **Morrissey**.

In 1991, Dave Rowbotham was discovered axed to death at his home, leading to a murder hunt. Following Factory's bankruptcy in 1992, Reilly released *Sex And Death*. On *Fidelity* the Durutti sound remained the same.

DURY, IAN

THE ZENITH OF DURY'S (b. 1942) MUSICAL CAREER, *NEW BOOTS AND PANTIES*, CAME IN 1977, WHEN youth was being celebrated amid power chords and bondage trousers – he was 35. Dury was stricken by polio at the age of seven. Initially he taught art before joining **Kilburn And The High Roads**, reinterpreting R&B numbers and later adding his own wry lyrics in a semi-spoken cockney slang. The Blockheads' debut spent more than a year in the UK albums chart.

Dury lampooned the excesses of the music business on 'Sex And Drugs And Rock And Roll' and secured a UK number 1 with 'Hit Me With Your Rhythm Stick' (1979). *Do It Yourself* and *Laughter* lacked the impact of his debut, but he continued to make records in the 80s as well as film and television acting. In 1989, he co-wrote the musical *Apples*. *The Bus Driver's Prayer* was a welcome return to recording.

DUNN, HOLLY

Albums
Holly Dunn (MTM 1986)★★★
The Blue Rose Of Texas (Warners 1989)★★★
Getting It Dunn (Warners 1992)★★★
➽ p.360 for full listings
Further References
Video: *Cowboys Are My Weakness* (1995)

DURAN DURAN

Albums
Duran Duran (EMI 1981)★★★
Rio (EMI 1982)★★★
Notorious (EMI 1986)★★★
Thank You (Capitol 1995)★★★
➽ p.360 for full listings
Connections
Godley and Creme ➽ p.161
Further References
Videos: *Sing Blue Silver* (1984)
Three To Get Ready (1990)
Book: *Duran Duran: Their Story*, Kasper De Graff and Malcolm Garrett

DUROCS

Albums
The Durocs (Capitol1979)★★★
➽ p.127 for full listings
Collaborators
Tubes ➽ p.324
Connections
Elvin Bishop ➽ p.48
Michelle Phillips
Barbra Streisand

DURUTTI COLUMN

Albums
The Return Of The Durutti Column (Factory 1980)★★★
Vini Reilly (Factory 1989)★★★★
Fidelity (Crépescule 1996)★★★
➽ p.360 for full listings
Connections
Morrissey ➽ p.239

DURY, IAN

Albums
New Boots And Panties (Stiff 1977)★★★★
Do It Yourself (Stiff 1979)★★★
The Bus Driver's Prayer And Other Stories (Demon 1992)★★★
➽ p.360 for full listings
Collaborators
Kilburn and the High Roads ➽ p.205

DYLAN, BOB
Albums
Highway 61 Revisited (Columbia 1965)★★★★★
Blonde On Blonde (Columbia 1966)★★★★★,
Blood On The Tracks (Columbia 1975)★★★★★
➽ p.360 for full listings

DYLAN, BOB

AS A TEENAGER, DYLAN (b. ROBERT ALLEN ZIMMERMAN, 1941) LISTENED TO R&B, **HANK WILLIAMS** AND EARLY rock 'n' roll. After he began spending time with local musicians in the beatnik coffeehouses of Dinkytown, he began to include blues tunes into the folk repertoire he played at local clubs. In 1960, Dylan adopted a persona based upon the **Woody Guthrie** romantic hobo figure of the film *Bound For Glory*; he also assumed a new voice, speaking with an Okie twang, and adopted a 'hard travellin'' appearance. Having met Jesse Fuller, a blues performer who played guitar and harmonica simultaneously by using a harp rack, Dylan began to teach himself to do the same. Determined to be a professional musician, he set out for New York; arriving in January 1961.

Dylan's impact on Greenwich Village was immediate and enormous. He captivated anyone who saw him with his energy, charisma and rough-edged authenticity. He was paid for playing harmonica on records by Harry Belafonte and Carolyn Hester, and came to the attention of producer John Hammond – Columbia signed Dylan in Autumn 1961.

Bob Dylan was a collection of folk and blues standards, often about death, sorrows and the trials of life – songs that had been in Dylan's repertoire over the past year – but it was the inclusion of two of his own compositions, notably the tribute, 'Song To Woody', that pointed the way forward. Over the next few months, Dylan wrote dozens of songs, many of them topical, and became interested in the Civil Rights movement. 'Blowin' In The Wind' (1962), was the most famous of his protest songs and was included on *The Freewheelin' Bob Dylan*. In the meantime, Dylan had written and recorded several other political songs, including 'Masters Of War' and 'A Hard Rain's A-Gonna Fall', and one of his greatest love songs, 'Don't Think Twice, It's All Right'. 'Blowin' In The Wind' recorded by **Peter, Paul And Mary** became a huge US hit, bringing Dylan's name to international attention. **Joan Baez**, already a successful folk singer, began covering Dylan songs. Soon she was introducing him to her audience and the two became lovers.

Dylan's songwriting became more astute and wordy: biblical and other literary imagery showed in songs like 'When The Ship Comes In' and 'Times They Are A-Changin''. At the March On Washington, 28 August 1963, Dylan sang 'Only A Pawn In Their Game' in front of 400,000 people; the next day, he read of the murder of black waitress Hattie Carroll, this inspired 'The Lonesome Death Of Hattie Carroll' (included on *The Times They Are A-Changin'*).

In 1964, becoming increasingly frustrated with the 'spokesman of a generation' tag, Dylan wrote *Another Side Of Bob Dylan*. This included the disavowal of his past, 'My Back Pages' alongside newer songs such as 'Mr Tambourine Man', 'Gates Of Eden' and 'It's Alright Ma, I'm Only Bleeding'. The years 1964-66 were Dylan's greatest as a writer and as a performer; they were also his most influential years producing *Bringing It All Back Home*, *Highway 61 Revisited* and the double album *Blonde On Blonde*.

Another Side Of Bob Dylan was his last solo acoustic album for almost 30 years. Intrigued by the **Beatles** – he had visited London to play one concert in 1964 – and excited by the **Animals**' 'House Of The Rising Sun', he and producer Tom Wilson fleshed out some of the *Bringing It All Back Home* songs with rock 'n' roll backings, such as 'Subterranean Homesick Blues' and 'Maggie's Farm'. 'Like A Rolling Stone', was written after his final series of UK acoustic concerts in 1965, and was commemorated in D.A. Pennebaker's documentary film, *Don't Look Back*. Dylan said that he began to write 'Like A Rolling Stone' having decided to 'quit' singing and playing. The sound came from blues guitarist **Michael Bloomfield**, **Harvey Brooks** (bass) and **Al Kooper** (organ). It was producer Tom Wilson's last, and greatest, Dylan track and at six minutes, destroyed the formula of the sub-three-minute single forever. It was a huge hit, alongside the **Byrds**' version of 'Mr Tambourine Man' (1965).

It should have come as no surprise to those who went to see Dylan at the Newport Folk Festival on 25 July that he was now a fully fledged folk rocker; but, backed by the **Paul Butterfield** Blues Band, Dylan's 'new sound' was met with bewilderment and hostility – Dylan seemed to find the experience exhilarating and liberating. He had felt ready to quit, now he was ready to start again, to tour the world with a band. Dylan discovered the Hawks (later to become the **Band**) and they took to the road in the autumn of 1965: USA, Hawaii, Australia, Scandinavia and Britain, with a hop over to Paris in 1966. Dylan was deranged and dynamic, the group wild and mercurial.

Back in America in 1966, Dylan was physically exhausted, but had to complete a film and finish *Tarantula*, an overdue book for Macmillan. He owed Columbia two more albums, and was booked to play a series of concerts right up to the end of the year. On 29 July 1966, Dylan was injured in a motorcycle accident near his home in up-State New York. He was nursed through his convalescence by his wife, Sara – they had married in 1965 – and was visited only rarely. After several months, Dylan was joined by the Hawks, who rented a house nearby. Every day they met and played music – the final therapy that Dylan needed. A huge amount of material was recorded in the basement and, eventually, came a clutch of new compositions, the *Basement Tapes*. Some of the songs were surreally comic: 'Please Mrs Henry', 'Quinn The Eskimo', 'Million Dollar Bash'; others were soul-searchingly introspective: 'Tears Of Rage', 'Too Much Of Nothing', 'I Shall Be Released'. Many were covered by, and became hits for, other artists and groups. Dylan's own recordings of some of the songs were not issued until 1975.

In 1968, Dylan appeared with the Band, at the Woody Guthrie Memorial Concert at Carnegie Hall, New York. The following month *John Wesley Harding* was released, featuring songs such as 'All Along The Watchtower', 'The Ballad Of Frankie Lee & Judas Priest', 'Dear Landlord' and 'Drifter's Escape'. The record's final song, 'I'll Be Your Baby Tonight', was unambivalently simple and presaged the warmer love songs of *Nashville Skyline*.

Dylan chose to avoid **Woodstock**, but he did play at the **Isle Of Wight Festival** in 1970. In a baggy Hank Williams-style white suit, he was a completely different Bob Dylan from the rabbit-suited marionette who had howled and screamed in the teeth of audience hostility three years earlier. He crooned his new, if unexciting, set of songs and in doing so left the audience just as bewildered as those who had booed back in 1966 – that was nothing compared with the puzzlement which greeted *Self Portrait*. It most closely resembled the preceding bootleg collection *Great White Wonder*. Both were double albums; both offered mish-mash mix-ups of undistinguished live tracks, alternate takes, odd cover versions, botched beginnings and

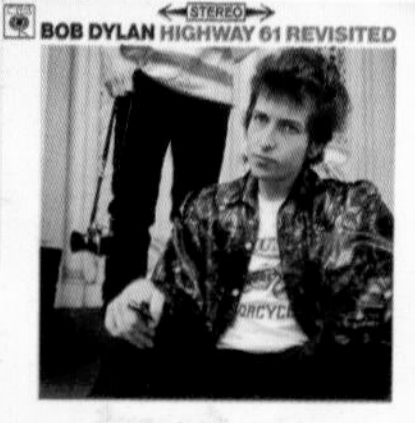

Collaborators
Harry Belafonte
Paul Butterfield ➽ p.76
Blues Band ➽ p.56
Band ➽ p.31
Roger McGuinn ➽ p.229
Ramblin' Jack Elliott ➽ p.135
Allen Ginsberg

Mick Ronson ➽ p.282
Bobby Neuwirth
Ronee Blakley
Mark Knopfler ➽ p.209
Pick Withers ➽ p.341
Ron Wood ➽ p.343
Keith Richards
Tom Petty And The Heartbreakers ➽ p.260
George Harrison ➽ p.176
Jeff Lynne ➽ p.220
Tom Petty ➽ p.260
Roy Orbison ➽ p.252

endings. **Rolling Stone** was vicious: 'What is this shit?' the review began.

'We've Got Dylan Back Again' reported the same magazine just four months later, heralding the hastily released *New Morning* as a 'return to form'. However, Dylan was restless and his appearance at the Concert For Bangladesh benefit was his only live performance between 1970 and 1974, although he cropped up frequently as a guest on other people's albums. He began to explore his Jewishness.

In 1973, Dylan played the enigmatic Alias in Sam Peckinpah's *Pat Garrett & Billy The Kid*, for which he also supplied the soundtrack music (including 'Knocking On Heaven's Door'); he also left CBS, having been persuaded by **David Geffen** to sign to Asylum. Columbia released *Dylan*, an album of out-takes and warm-ups, presumably intending to embarrass Dylan or to steal some of the thunder from his first Asylum album, *Planet Waves* (recorded with the Band). In terms of merit, there was no contest, although a few of the *Dylan* tracks were interesting.

'LIKE A ROLLING STONE', WAS WRITTEN AFTER HIS FINAL SERIES OF UK ACOUSTIC CONCERTS IN 1965

A US tour followed. Tickets were sold by post and attracted six million applications. The recorded evidence, *Before The Flood*, certainly oozed energy, but lacked subtlety: Dylan seemed to be trying too hard, pushing everything too fast. *Blood On The Tracks*, originally recorded in 1974, was a marked improvement. Dylan substituted some of the songs with reworked versions: 'Tangled Up In Blue', 'Idiot Wind', 'If You See Her Say Hello', 'Shelter From The Storm', 'Simple Twist Of Fate', 'You're A Big Girl Now' . . . one masterpiece followed another. Dylan had separated from Sara and this was a diary of despair.

If Dylan the writer was reborn with *Blood On The Tracks*, Dylan the performer re-emerged on the Rolling Thunder Revue. Moving from small town to small town with a variable line-up, basically consisting of Dylan, Joan Baez, **Roger McGuinn**, **Ramblin' Jack Elliott**, Allen Ginsberg, **Mick Ronson**, Bobby Neuwirth and **Ronee Blakley**. The Revue was conceived in Greenwich Village in the summer of 1975 and hit the road in New England on 31 October. Dylan – face painted white, hat festooned with flowers – was inspired, delirious, imbued with a new vitality and singing like a demon. A focal point of the Revue had been the case of wrongly imprisoned boxer Hurricane Carter and Dylan's song 'Hurricane' was included just about every night. It was also on his next album *Desire*.

In 1979, Dylan became a born-again Christian, releasing an album of evangelical songs, *Slow Train Coming*, recorded with Jerry Wexler and Barry Beckett, and featuring **Dire Straits**' **Mark Knopfler** and Pick Withers. He played a series of powerful concerts featuring nothing but his new Christian material. The second Christian album, *Saved*, was less impressive, however, and his fervour became more muted. Gradually, old songs began to be reworked into the live set and by *Shot Of Love* it was no longer clear whether or not Dylan's faith remained firm.

Dylan dropped from sight for most of 1982, but the following year he was back in the studio, again with Knopfler, for *Infidels*. Some songs were strong – 'I&I' and 'Jokerman' among them – others relatively unimpressive. 1985 opened with Dylan contributing to the 'We Are The World', USA For Africa single, and after the release of *Empire Burlesque*, a patchy record but boasting the beautiful 'Dark Eyes', he played at Live Aid. Dylan recruited **Rolling Stones** Ron Wood and Keith Richards to help him out – the results were disastrous. Matters were redeemed a little at the Farm Aid concert in September. Backed by **Tom Petty And The Heartbreakers**, it was immediately apparent that Dylan had found his most sympathetic and adaptable backing band since the Hawks. The year ended positively, with the release of the five album (3-CD) retrospective, *Biograph*.

Between two tours, Dylan appeared in his second feature film, *Hearts Of Fire*, co-starring Rupert Everett and Fiona Flanagan. The poor movie was preceded by a poor album, *Knocked Out Loaded*, which only had the epic 'Brownsville Girl' (co-written with playwright Sam Shepard) to recommend it.

Down In The Groove, an album of mostly cover versions, was released in June 1988, the same month as Dylan played the first shows of what was to become known as the Never-Ending Tour. Backed by a three-piece band, Dylan had stripped down his sound and his songs and seemed re-energized. This same year he found himself one of the **Traveling Wilburys** with **George Harrison**, **Jeff Lynne**, Tom Petty and **Roy Orbison** – a jokey band assembled on a whim. Their album, *Volume One*, was a huge commercial success. Dylan's next album emerged as his best of the 80s: *Oh Mercy*, recorded informally in New Orleans and produced by **Daniel Lanois**, sounded fresh and good, and the songs were strong.

Not without its merits, *Under The Red Sky* was for most a relative disappointment, as was the Roy-Orbison-bereft Wilburys follow-up, *Volume Three*. However, the touring continued, with Dylan's performances becoming increasingly erratic – sometimes splendid, often shambolic. The three-volume collection of out-takes and rarities, *The Bootleg Series, Volumes 1-3 (Rare And Unreleased) 1961-1991*, redeemed him somewhat, as did the 30th Anniversary Celebration concert in Madison Square Garden in 1992, in which some of rock music's greats and not-so-greats paid tribute to Dylan.

Both *Good As I Been To You* and *World Gone Wrong* , were collections of old folk and blues material, performed, for the first time since 1964, solo and acoustically. *Greatest Hits Volume 3* threw together a clump of old non-hits and *Unplugged* saw Dylan revisiting a set of predominantly 60s songs in desultory fashion. In 1997, Dylan suffered a serious inflammation of the heart muscles. He was discharged from hospital after a short time, eliciting his priceless quote to the press: 'I really thought I'd be seeing Elvis soon'.

Connections
Peter, Paul and Mary ➽ p.260
Joan Baez ➽ p.29
Michael Bloomfield ➽ p.54
Harvey Brooks ➽ p.69
Al Kooper ➽ p.210
Byrds ➽ p.77
David Geffen ➽ p.155
Traveling Wilburys ➽ p.323
Daniel Lanois ➽ p.212

Influences
Hank Williams ➽ p.339
Woody Guthrie ➽ p.170
Beatles ➽ p.38
Animals ➽ p.18

Further References
Video: *MTV Unplugged* (1995)
Books: *Bob Dylan In His Own Write*, Bob Dylan
On The Road With Bob Dylan: Rolling With The Thunder, Larry Sloman

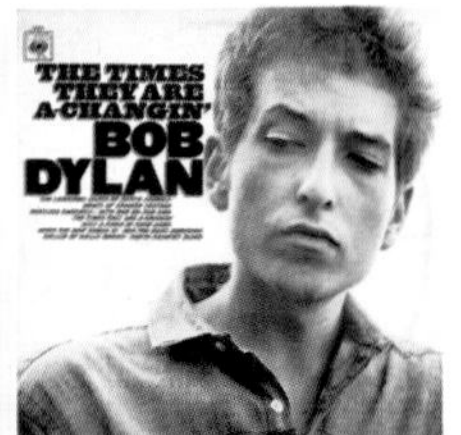

EAGLES
Albums
On The Border (Asylum 1974)★★★★
Hotel California (Asylum 1976)★★★★★
➽ p.361 for full listings

Connections
David Geffen ➽ p.155
Joe Walsh ➽ p.333
James Gang ➽ p.197
Rolling Stones ➽ p.281
Further References
Books: *The Eagles*, John Swenson
The Long Run: The Story Of The Eagles, Marc Shapiro

EARLE, STEVE
Albums
Copperhead Road (MCA 1988)★★★★
El Corazón (Warner Bros 1997)★★★★.
➽ p.361 for full listings
Collaborators
Pogues ➽ p.263
Emmylou Harris ➽ p.175
Influences
Bruce Springsteen ➽ p.306

EARLS
Albums
Remember Me Baby (Old Town 1963)★★★
➽ p.361 for full listings
Collaborators
ABC ➽ p.7

EARTH, WIND AND FIRE
Albums
Open Our Eyes (Columbia 1974)★★★★
That's The Way Of The World (Columbia 1975)★★★★
➽ p.361 for full listings
Collaborators
MC Hammer ➽ p.173
Sly Stone ➽ p.300

EAST 17
Albums
Walthamstow (London 1993)★★★★
Stay Another Night (London 1995)★★★
➽ p.361 for full listings
Connections
Bros ➽ p.69
Pet Shop Boys ➽ p.259
Influences
Take That ➽ p.316
Further References
Book: *East 17: Talk Back*, Carl Jenkins

EAGLES

FORMED IN LOS ANGELES IN 1971, BERNIE LEADON (b. 1947; GUITAR/VOCALS), RANDY MEISNER (b. 1947; BASS/VOCALS), Glenn Frey (b. 1948; guitar/vocals) and Don Henley (b. 1947; drums/vocals) were signed to Asylum. *The Eagles* contained 'Take It Easy' and 'Witchy Woman', both of which reached the US Top 20 and established their country rock sound. *Desperado* contained several of their most enduring compositions, including the emotional title track; the follow-up, *On The Border*, reasserted their commerciality. 'Best Of My Love' was their first US number 1.

After 1974, a reshaped quintet attained superstar status with the platinum-selling *One Of These Nights*. This included 'Lyin' Eyes', 'Take It To The Limit' and the title track which topped the US charts. Leadon left in 1975, replaced by **Joe Walsh** (b. 1947; ex-**James Gang**). *Hotel California* topped the US album charts for eight weeks and spawned two number 1s: the title track and 'New Kid In Town'. The set sold nine million copies in its year of release. 'Please Come Home For Christmas' was their sole recorded offering for 1978. In 1979, Meisner was replaced by Timothy B. Schmit (b. 1947), but the Eagles' impetus was waning. *The Long Run* was disappointing, despite containing the US number 1 'Heartache Tonight', and the group split up in 1982.

They eventually re-formed and the resulting album proved they were still one of the world's most popular acts. Their 1994-95 US tour was one of the largest-grossing on record.

EARLE, STEVE

US-BORN EARLE (b. 1955) PLAYED ACOUSTIC GUITAR FROM AGE 11 AND BEGAN SINGING IN BARS AND COFFEE HOUSES. He formed a back-up band, the Dukes, and was signed to CBS, who subsequently released *Early Tracks*. Recognition came when he and the Dukes signed to MCA and made a 'New Country' album, *Guitar Town*. The title track was a potent blend of country and rock 'n' roll. Earle's songs often told of the restlessness of blue-collar workers; he wrote 'The Rain Came Down' for the Farm Aid II benefit, and 'Nothing But A Child' was for an organization to help homeless children. In 1988, he released an album with a heavy-metal feel, *Copperhead Road*, which included the Vietnam saga 'Johnny Come Lately', recorded with the **Pogues**.

After a lengthy break, allegedly to detox, Earle returned with *Train A Comin'*, featuring Peter Rowan and **Emmylou Harris**. In the mid-90s, a cleaned-up Earle started his own label, E-Squared. He also contributed to the film soundtrack of *Dead Man Walking*.

EARLS

THE EARLS WERE ONE OF THE MOST ACCOMPLISHED WHITE DOO-WOP GROUPS OF THE EARLY 60S. LARRY CHANCE (b. Larry Figueiredo, 1940; vocals) formed the group in the late 50s with first tenor Robert Del Din (b. 1942), second tenor Eddie Harder (b. 1942), baritone Larry Palumbo (b. 1941) and bass John Wray (b. 1939). For their first single, the group revived the Harptones's 1954 R&B hit 'Life Is But A Dream' (1961). In 1962, the group released 'Remember Then', which reached the Top 30. The Earls continued to release singles until 1965, but the only one to make an impact was a maudlin version of 'I Believe'. With various personnel changes, Chance continued to lead the group on occasional records for Mr G and **ABC**.

EARTH, WIND AND FIRE

FORMED IN THE 60S FROM CHICAGO'S BLACK MUSIC SESSION CIRCLE. IN 1969, DRUMMER MAURICE WHITE (b. 1941) formed the Salty Peppers. The group – Verdine White (b. 1951; bass), Michael Beale (guitar), Wade Flemmons (vocals), Sherry Scott (vocals), Alex Thomas (trombone), Chet Washington (tenor saxophone), Don Whitehead (keyboards) and Yackov Ben Israel (percussion) – embraced jazz, R&B, funk and elements of Latin and ballad styles. After a couple of albums, White pieced together a second group, Earth, Wind and Fire, around Ronnie Laws (b. 1950; saxophone/guitar), Philip Bailey (b. 1951; vocals), Larry Dunn (b. Lawrence Dunhill, 1953; keyboards), Roland Battista (guitar) and Jessica Cleaves (b. 1948; vocals). Two 1974 releases, *Head To The Sky* and *Open Our Eyes*, established the group as an album act, while the following year 'Shining Star' reached number 1 in the US R&B and pop charts.

By the end of the decade they had regular successes with such singles as 'After The Love Has Gone' and 'Boogie Wonderland'. The line-up remained unstable, with new musicians joining periodically. Following 11 gold albums, 1983's *Electric Universe* was an unexpected commercial flop, and prompted a four-year break. A core quintet recorded *Touch The World* (1987) but they failed to reclaim their former standing. *Heritage* (1990) featured cameos from **MC Hammer** and Sly Stone. 1997's *In The Name Of Love* was a back-to-basics album.

EAST 17

EAST 17 FEATURED TONY MORTIMER (b. 1970), BRIAN HARVEY (b. 1974), JOHN HENDY (b. 1971) AND TERRY COLDWELL (b. 1974), who met at school. The band was named after their London postal code and their debut, *Walthamstow*, after their home area. With former **Bros** svengali, Tom Watkins, as manager they cultivated an image of youthful arrogance and 'street style' in obvious opposition to **Take That**. Their debut, 'House Of Love', became a major hit in 1992, peaking at UK number 10. 'Deep' reached the Top 5 and both 'Slow It Down' and a lacklustre cover of the **Pet Shop Boys**' 'West End Girls' made the UK Top 20.

1993's 'It's Alright' reached UK number 3 and their first two 1994 singles, 'Around The World' and 'Steam', continued their commercial ascendancy. They finally hit UK number 1 in 1994 with 'Stay Another Day'. Harvey was sacked by the band in 1997 after some ill-chosen comments about the drug Ecstasy.

EAST OF EDEN

FORMED IN 1968, THIS VERSATILE UK GROUP ORIGINALLY FEATURED DAVE ARBUS (VIOLIN), RON GAINES (ALTO saxophone), Geoff Nicholson (lead guitar), Andy Sneddon (bass) and Geoff Britton (drums). Their debut, *Mercator Projected*, offered a combination of progressive rock, jazz and neo-eastern predilections, but this direction contrasted with the novelty tag placed on the group in the wake of their surprise hit, 'Jig A Jig'. This lightweight, fiddle-based instrumental reached UK number 7 in 1971.

By 1972, East of Eden had shed every original member. Joe O'Donnell (violin), Garth Watt-Roy (guitar, ex-Greatest Show On Earth), Martin Fisher (bass) and Jeff Allen (drums, ex-Beatstalkers) then maintained the group's name before their demise later in the decade.

EASTON, SHEENA

SCOTTISH SINGER EASTON (b. SHEENA SHIRLEY ORR, 1959) DEBUTED WITH 'MODERN GIRL' (1979), FOLLOWED BY 'Nine To Five' which sold over a million copies in the USA (as 'Morning Train'). American success followed and Easton was given the theme to the 1981 James Bond film, *For Your Eyes Only*. Hits from her second album included 'When He Shines' and the title track, 'You Could Have Been With Me'. In 1983, Easton recorded 'We've Got Tonight' with **Kenny Rogers** before 'Sugar Walls' (1984) – which provoked attacks by moralists on its sexual implications. Her recent couple of albums have lacked the charm of her earlier work.

EASYBEATS

FORMED IN SYDNEY, AUSTRALIA, IN 1964, THIS BEAT GROUP COMPRISED DUTCH GUITARISTS Harry Vanda (b. Harold Wandon, 1947), Dick Diamonde (b. 1947), English vocalist Steve Wright (b. 1948), Scottish guitarist George Young (b. 1947) and English drummer Gordon 'Snowy' Fleet (b. 1946). After a series of Australian hits, including six number 1s, the group relocated to England in 1966. There they worked with top producer Shel Talmy, resulting in one of the all-time great beat singles, 'Friday On My Mind' (UK number 6). Unable to follow up their hit, the group split with Talmy during the recording of their first UK-released album. They returned to the UK charts in 1968 with 'Hello How Are You'. Vanda and Young began writing material for other artists, and in 1969, the Easybeats split up. Ironically, they enjoyed a US hit some months later with 'St Louis'.

EAZY E

THERE ARE THOSE CRITICS WHO DID NOT TAKE WELL TO CALIFORNIAN EAZY E's (b. Eric Wright, 1963, d. 1995) 'whine' and, as intended, his debut managed to offend just about every imaginable faction. His work as part of **NWA**, and head of Ruthless Records, (founded in 1985, allegedly with drug money) had already made him a household name. His debut solo album contained a clean and a dirty side. The first was accomplished with very little merit, cuts such as 'We Want Eazy' being self-centred and pointless. The 'street' side, however, was more provocative. His ongoing bitter rivalry against former NWA member **Dr Dre** provided much of his lyrical subject matter, including 'Real Muhaphukkin' G's'. Once a pivotal figure of gangsta rap, he died having succumbed to AIDS.

ECHO AND THE BUNNYMEN

THIS RENOWNED LIVERPOOL GROUP FORMED IN 1978, FEATURING IAN McCULLOCH (b. 1959), WILL SERGEANT (b. 1958; guitar), Les Patterson (b. 1958; bass) and a drum machine they christened 'Echo'. They made their vinyl debut in 1979 with 'Read It In Books', produced by whizz-kid entrepreneurs Bill Drummond and Dave Balfe. McCulloch's brooding live performance and vocal inflections drew comparisons with Jim Morrison.

After signing to Korova Records (distributed by Warner Brothers), they replaced 'Echo' with West Indian-born Pete De Freitas (b. 1961, d. 1989). Their second single, 'Rescue', had a confident, driving sound, and *Crocodiles* proved impressive with a wealth of strong arrangements and compulsive guitarwork. After the less melodic 'The Puppet', the group toured extensively and issued an EP, *Shine So Hard*, which crept into the UK Top 40. *Heaven Up Here* and *Porcupine* were critically acclaimed and 'The Cutter' gave them their biggest hit so far. In 1984, they charted with 'The Killing Moon' and the accompanying *Ocean Rain* reached the US Top 100. In 1986, De Freitas was replaced by Mark Fox (ex-**Haircut 100**), but he returned within months. However, with *Echo And The Bunnymen* they began to lose their appeal, while a version of the **Doors**' 'People Are Strange' left fans and critics perplexed. In 1988, McCulloch went solo; the Bunnymen carried on with Noel Burke succeeding McCulloch. Tragically, just as they were beginning rehearsals, De Freitas was killed in a road accident. The group struggled on, recruiting new drummer Damon Reece and adding road manager Jake Brockman on guitar/synthesizer. In 1992, they released *Reverberation*, but to little effect. The group split in the summer of the same year.

McCulloch and Sergeant reunited in 1993 as **Electrafixion**, with Reece. In 1996, an announcement was made that the three remaining original members would go out as Echo And The Bunnymen once again. McCulloch, Pattinson and Sergeant released the well-received *Evergreen* in 1997. In 1998, they appeared on England's World Cup football theme song.

ECHOBELLY

UK INDIE POP BAND LED BY THE ANGLO-ASIAN SINGER SONYA AURORA MADAN, with Swedish guitarist Glenn Johansson, Debbie Smith (guitar, ex-**Curve**), Andy Henderson (drums) and Alex Keyser (bass). After breaking the UK Top 40 with 'I Can't Imagine The World Without Me', the group became the darlings of the British music press. The original, rejected title of their debut album was taken from a Suffragette's reply when asked when women would obtain the vote: 'Today, Tomorrow, Sometime, Never'. The group began to win US support, leading to an American contract with Sony. *On* advanced their strengths, with notable songs including the hit 'Great Things'. Smith left in 1997, replaced by Julian Cooper. *Lustra* was a poorly received album that saw the band struggling to establish their musical direction.

EAST OF EDEN
Albums
Snafu (Deram 1970)★★★
East Of Eden (Harvest 1971)★★★
➧ p.361 for full listings

EASTON, SHEENA
Albums
A Private Heaven (EMI 1984)★★★★
What Comes Naturally (MCA 1991)★★★
➧ p.361 for full listings
Collaborators
Kenny Rogers ➧ p.280

EASYBEATS
Albums
Volume 3 (1966)★★★
Good Friday (United Artists 1967)★★★
➧ p.361 for full listings

EAZY E
Albums
Eazy-Duz-It (Ruthless/Priority 1988)★★★
Str.8 Off The Streetz Of Muthaphukkin' Compton (Ruthless 1995)★★★
➧ p.361 for full listings
Collaborators
NWA ➧ p.249
Connections
Dr Dre ➧ p.124

ECHO AND THE BUNNYMEN
Albums
Crocodiles (Korova 1980)★★★★
Porcupine (Korova 1983)★★★★
➧ p.361 for full listings

Connections
Haircut 100 ➧ p.172
Electrafixation ➧ p.134
Influences
Doors ➧ p.123
Further References
Book: *Never Stop: The Echo & The Bunnymen Story*, Tony Fletcher

ECHOBELLY
Albums
Everyone's Got One (Rhythm King 1994)★★★
On (Rhythm King 1995)★★★★
➧ p.361 for full listings
Connections
Curve ➧ p.108

EDDIE AND THE HOT RODS
Albums
Teenage Depression (Island 1976)★★★★
➽ p.361 for full listings
Connections
Sam The Sham And The Pharoahs ➽ p.288
Kursaal Flyers ➽ p.211
Damned ➽ p.110

EDDY, DUANE
Albums
Twangy Guitar-Silky Strings (RCA Victor 1962)★★★★
➽ p.361 for full listings

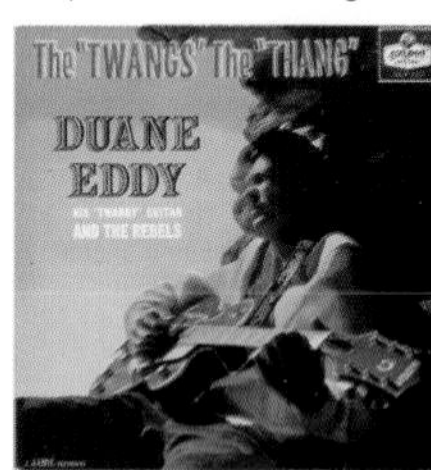

Connections
Art of Noise ➽ p.22
Jeff Lynne ➽ p.220
Paul McCartney ➽ p.229
George Harrison ➽ p.176
Ry Cooder ➽ p.100
Influences
Beatles ➽ p.38
Further References
Film: *Because They're Young* (1960)

EDGAR BROUGHTON BAND
Albums
Wasa Wasa (Harvest 1969)★★★★
➽ p.361 for full listings
Collaborators
Blind Faith ➽ p.53

EDDIE AND THE HOT RODS

FORMED IN 1975, THIS ENGLISH QUINTET ORIGINALLY COMPRISED BARRIE MASTERS (VOCALS), LEW LEWIS (harmonica), Paul Gray (bass), Dave Higgs (guitar) and Steve Nicol (drums). After one classic single, 'Writing On The Wall', Lewis left, though he appeared on the high-energy 'Horseplay', the flipside of their cover of **Sam The Sham And The Pharoahs**' 'Wooly Bully'.

The Rods pursued a tricky route between pub rock and punk. During 1976, the group broke house records at the Marquee Club and captured their power on a live EP. The arrival of guitarist Graeme Douglas (ex-**Kursaal Flyers**) gave the group a more commercial edge and a distinctive jingle-jangle sound. 'Do Anything You Want To Do' reached the UK Top 10 and *Life On The Line* was well received. However, Douglas left, followed by Gray (who joined the **Damned**) and Masters disbanded the group for a spell; they re-formed for pub gigs and small label appearances. *Gasoline Days* was depressingly retro.

EDDY, DUANE

THE SIMPLE 'TWANGY' GUITAR SOUND OF NEW YORKER DUANE EDDY (b. 1938) IS LEGENDARY. TOGETHER WITH producer Lee Hazelwood, Eddy co-wrote a deluge of hits mixed with versions of standards, using the bass strings of his Grestch guitar recorded through an echo chamber. The debut 'Movin' 'N' Groovin'' made the lower end of the US chart, and for the next six years Eddy repeated this formula with greater success. His backing group, the Rebel Rousers was a tight, experienced band featuring saxophonists Jim Horn and Steve Douglas and pianist Larry Knechtel. Among their greatest hits were 'Rebel-Rouser', 'Peter Gunn' and 'Theme From Dixie'. One of Eddy's most memorable hits was the superlative theme music for the film *Because They're Young*. Sadly, the hits dried up in 1964.

Tony Macauley wrote 'Play Me Like You Play Your Guitar' for him in 1975, and after more than a decade he was back in the UK Top 10. He returned to the charts in 1986, playing his 'Peter Gunn' with **Art Of Noise**. The following year, **Jeff Lynne** produced Eddy's first album for many years, joined by **Paul McCartney**, George Harrison and **Ry Cooder**.

EDGAR BROUGHTON BAND

POPULAR ON LONDON'S 'UNDERGROUND' SCENE, THE BAND COMPRISED EDGAR BROUGHTON (b. 1947; GUITAR/ vocals), Steve Broughton (b. 1950; drums/vocals) and Arthur Grant (bass/ guitar/vocals). Edgar's growling voice was often compared to that of **Captain Beefheart**. During the **Blind Faith** free concert in Hyde Park, the Broughtons incited the crowd to a frenzy with 'Out Demons, Out'. Despite airplay from **John Peel**, the political and sexual themes of their songs had dated by the early 70s. Broughton was still performing on London's pub circuit in the 90s.

EDISON LIGHTHOUSE

UK CONGLOMERATION BASED AROUND SINGER TONY BURROWS; THE BACKING MUSICIANS WERE ORIGINALLY part of Greenfield Hammer. The Tony Macauley/Barry Mason composition 'Love Grows (Where My Rosemary Goes)' was their breakthrough, zooming to UK number 1 and the US Top 5.

When Burrows moved on, his backing musicians continued under the name Edison. Macauley, meanwhile, owned the name Edison Lighthouse and conjured up another group for recording and touring purposes. The manufactured spin-off band failed to exploit their chart-topping name, although they did scrape into the lower rungs of the Top 50 with 'It's Up To You, Petula'.

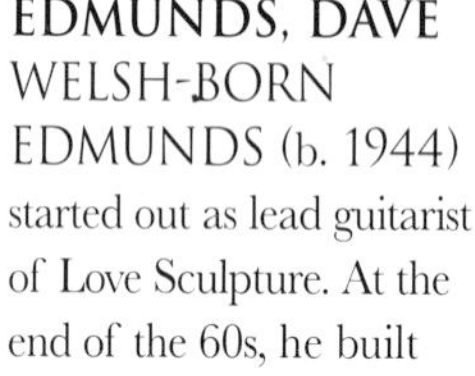

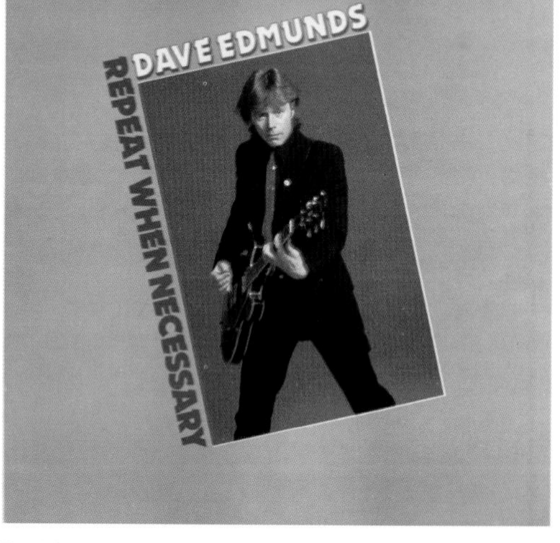

EDMUNDS, DAVE

WELSH-BORN EDMUNDS (b. 1944) started out as lead guitarist of Love Sculpture. At the end of the 60s, he built his own recording studio, Rockfield, where he worked with Shakin' Stevens, the **Flamin' Groovies** and **Brinsley Schwarz** among others. Edmunds and Schwarz's bass player, **Nick Lowe**, formed a musical partnership that lasted many years.

Dave had hits with Smiley Lewis's 'I Hear You Knocking', the **Ronettes**' 'Baby, I Love You' and the Chordettes' 'Born To Be With You'. In 1975, his debut *Subtle As A Flying Mallet* was eclipsed by his credible performance in the film *Stardust*. *Get It* (1977) featured the fast-paced Nick Lowe composition, 'I Knew the Bride', which gave Edmunds another hit. Lowe wrote many of the songs on *Tracks On Wax* (1978), during a hectic stage in Edmunds' career when he played with **Emmylou Harris**, **Carl Perkins** and his own band **Rockpile**, and appeared at the Knebworth Festival and the Rock For Kampuchea concert. He interpreted **Elvis Costello**'s 'Girls Talk', 'Crawling From The Wreckage' (written by **Graham Parker**), 'Queen Of Hearts' and 'Sweet Little Lisa'.

The regular band of Edmunds, Lowe, Billy Bremner and Terry Williams became a favourite on the pub-rock circuit, but, although successful, *Seconds Of Pleasure* was unable to do justice to the atmosphere created at live shows. In 1981, Edmunds charted with the Stray Cats; they recorded George Jones's 'The Race Is On'. Edmunds' style changed for the **Jeff Lynne**-produced *Information* (1983). During the mid-80s he worked with the **Fabulous Thunderbirds**, **Jeff Beck**, **Dr. Feelgood**, **k.d. lang** and **Status Quo**, followed by a tour and his live album, *I Hear You Rockin'*.

EELS

LOS ANGELES-BASED EELS WERE FORMED IN 1995, THE BRAIN-CHILD OF THE MYSTERIOUS E (b. MARK EVERETT; VOCALS, guitar, keyboards) and drummer Butch. They recruited bassist Tommy and released 'Novocaine For The Soul', a big college/alternative hit in 1996. However, despite their apparently conventional power-trio line-up, Eels are fascinated by sonic experimentation. Co-producer Simpson's dance background and experience of sampling expanded *Beautiful Freak*'s overall sound with hip hop rhythm loops, earning them success in the UK as well as the US.

EGG

EGG WAS FORMED IN 1968 BY DAVE STEWART (KEYBOARDS), HUGH MONTGOMERY 'MONT' CAMPBELL (BASS/VOCALS) and Clive Brooks (drums). They recorded two albums, *Egg* and *The Polite Force*, between 1970 and 1972. When Brooks left for the more orthodox, blues-based **Groundhogs**; Egg dissolved. The three original members were later reunited for *The Civil Surface*.

Stewart and Campbell worked together in National Health, but then embarked on separate paths. The former has latterly enjoyed several hit singles by rearranging well-known 60s songs. 'It's My Party', a collaboration with Barbara Gaskin, topped the UK charts in 1981.

808 STATE

UK BAND FEATURING MARTIN PRICE (b. 1955), GRAHAM MASSEY (b. 1960), DARREN PARTINGTON (b. 1969) AND Andy Barker (b. 1969). Together with Gerald Simpson, they began recording as a loose electro house collective, and rose to prominence at the end of 1989 with 'Pacific State'. *Newbuild* and *Quadrastate* helped to establish them as premier exponents of UK techno dance. *Ex:El* featured the vocals of **New Order**'s Bernard Sumner on 'Spanish Heart', and **Björk** on 'Oops' (also a single) and 'Qmart'. They also worked with Mancunian rapper MC Tunes on *North At Its Heights* and several singles.

In 1991, Price missed their US tour, electing to work on solo projects instead. 808 State persevered with another fine album in 1993, which saw a new rash of collaborations. Massey occupied himself co-writing Björk's 'Army Of Me' and other material on *Post*. Martin Price departed, but *Don Solaris* finally arrived after a gap of four years.

EIGHTH WONDER

UK BAND BUILT AROUND SINGER/ACTRESS PATSY KENSIT (b. 1968). EIGHTH WONDER COMPRISED GEOFF BEAUCHAMP (guitar), Alex Godson (keyboards) and Jamie Kensit (guitar). The group gained a minor UK hit with 'Stay With Me' in 1985. Kensit later landed the role of Crêpe Suzette in the 1986 film *Absolute Beginners* – a critical and commercial flop. Kensit and Eighth Wonder found greater success in 1988 with 'I'm Not Scared', 'Cross My Heart' and a Top 50 album *Fearless*. Kensit later restored her acting credibility *Lethal Weapon* (1991), although she is most famous for her marriages: to **Simple Minds**' Jim Kerr in 1992 and **Oasis**'s Liam Gallagher in 1997.

EINSTURZENDE NEUBATEN

GERMAN BAND EINSTURZENDE NEUBATEN MADE THEIR LIVE DEBUT IN 1980. THE LINE-UP COMPRISED BLIXA BARGELD (b. 1959; guitar/vocals), N.U. Unruh (percussion), Beate Bartel and Gudrun Gut. Alexander Van Borsig (sound technician), an occasional contributor, joined for their first single, 'Fur Den Untergang'. When Bartel and Gut left to form Mania D and Matador they were replaced by F. M. (Mufti) and Einheit (percussion).

Their first official album was *Kollaps*, a collage of sounds created by unusual rhythmic instruments ranging from steel girders to pipes and canisters. Bassist Marc Chung joined for their 1982 12-inch, 'Durstiges Tier'; 1984's *Strategien Gegen Architekturen* was compiled with Jim Thirlwell (**Foetus**), while the band performed an ill-fated gig at London's ICA. Bargeld spent the rest of the year touring as bass player for **Nick Cave**, going on to record several studio albums as a Bad Seed.

Funf Auf Der Nach Oben Offenen Richterskala was followed by *Haus Der Luege*, which included the sounds of riots around the Berlin Wall. *Tabula Rasa* was also politically inclined.

Connections
John Peel ➽ p.258
Influences
Captain Beefheart ➽ p.80

EDMUNDS, DAVE
Albums
Repeat When Necessary (Swansong 1979)★★★★
➽ p.361 for full listings
Collaborators
Shakin' Stevens ➽ p.309
Flamin' Groovies ➽ p.147
Brinsley Schwarz ➽ p.68
Nick Lowe ➽ p.219
Emmylou Harris ➽ p.175
Carl Perkins ➽ p.258
Stray Cats
Fabulous Thunderbirds ➽ p.141
Jeff Beck ➽ p.41
Dr. Feelgood ➽ p.125
k.d. lang ➽ p.212
Status Quo ➽ p.308
Connections
Graham Parker ➽ p.256
Jeff Lynne ➽ p.220
Influences
Ronettes ➽ p.282
Elvis Costello ➽ p.101
Further References
Film: *Give My Regards To Broad Street* (1985)

EELS
Albums
Beautiful Freak (DreamWorks 1996/MCA 1997)★★★★
➽ p.361 for full listings

EGG
Albums
Egg (Nova 1970)★★★
➽ p.361 for full listings
Collaborators
Barbara Gaskin
Connections
Groundhogs ➽ p.168

808 STATE
Albums
808:90 (Creed 1989)★★★★
➽ p.361 for full listings
Collaborators
Bernard Sumner
Björk ➽ p.48
Connections
New Order ➽ p.246
Sugarcubes ➽ p.313

EIGHTH WONDER
Albums
Fearless (Columbia 1988)★★
➽ p.361 for full listings
Connections
Jim Kerr ➽ p.297
Liam Gallagher ➽ p.250

EINSTURZENDE NEUBATEN
Albums
Ende Neu (Mute 1996)★★★
➽ p.361 for full listings
Collaborators
Nick Cave ➽ p.85
Connections
Foetus ➽ p.149
Further References
Video: *Liebeslieder* (Studio 1993)

EITZEL, MARK
Albums
West (Warners 1997)★★★★
➽ p.361 for full listings
Connections
Disposable Heroes Of Hiphoprisy ➽ p.120

EITZEL, MARK

CALIFORNIAN SONGWRITER MARK EITZEL (b. 1959, EX-AMERICAN MUSIC CLUB) RECORDED HIS FIRST SOLO ALBUM in 1996. *60 Watt Silver Lining* departed a little from Eitzel's reputation as a despondent writer. It featured long-standing American Music Club contributor Bruce Kaplan (pedal-steel guitar/piano), drummer Simone White (**Disposable Heroes Of Hiphoprisy**) and **Mark Isham** (trumpet). Alongside a cover version of **Carole King**'s 'There Is No Easy Way Down' were typically detailed narratives such as 'Some Bartenders Have The Gift Of Pardon' and 'Southend On Sea'. *West* was a startling departure with Eitzel sounding positively upbeat.

ELASTICA
Albums
Elastica (Deceptive 1995)★★★★
➽ p.361 for full listings
Connections
Suede ➽ p.312
Stranglers ➽ p.311

ELASTICA

UK INDIE BAND FEATURING JUSTINE FRISCHMANN (b. *c.* 1970; VOCALS/GUITAR; ex-**Suede**), Donna Matthews (bass), Justin Welch (drums) and Annie Holland (guitar). Elastica soon proved themselves with a series of stunning singles including 'See That Animal' (co-written with Suede's Brett Anderson) and 'Waking Up', one of the most exciting singles to hit the charts in 1995. The group's debut album included four hit singles. Frischmann's lyrics fitted the post-feminist 90s perfectly.

Holland departed in 1996, replaced by Sheila Chipperfield, and Dave Bush (keyboards) became the fifth member.

ELECTRAFIXION
Albums
Burned (Sire/Warners 1995)★★★
➽ p.361 for full listings
Connections
Johnny Marr ➽ p.301
Influences
Echo And The Bunnymen ➽ p.131

ELECTRAFIXION

ELECTRAFIXION WERE FORMED IN LIVERPOOL, ENGLAND, IN 1994, BY TWO former members of **Echo And The Bunnymen**, Will Sergeant (b. 1958; guitar) and Ian McCulloch (b. 1959; vocals/guitar). The demise of Echo And The Bunnymen had been followed by a period of bitterness between the two, but with McCulloch's solo career stalling after a good start, they started working together again. Tony McGuigan (drums) and Leon DeSilva (bass) were also in the band. Their first low-key concerts in 1994, were followed by the EP *Zephyr. Burned* featured 11 McCulloch/Sergeant originals, plus two co-compositions with Johnny Marr (ex-**Smiths**). Electrafixion joined the **Boo Radleys** on tour in 1995. Their future was curtailed by the re-formation of Echo And The Bunnymen in 1997.

ELECTRIBE 101
Albums
Electribal Memories (Mercury 1990)★★★
➽ p.361 for full listings

ELECTRIBE 101

ELECTRO-DANCE BAND CENTRED AROUND GERMAN SINGER BILLIE RAY MARTIN. IN 1985, MARTIN LEFT FOR ENGLAND, in search of a sympathetic hearing. An advert ('Soul Rebel seeks genius') brought her to Electribe 101: Joe Stevens, Les Fleming, Rob Cimarosti and Brian Nordhoff. 'Talking With Myself' and 'Tell Me When The Fever Ended' were instant hits with the acid generation. In particular, they welcomed the arrival of a voice which drew comparisons to Marlene Dietrich and **Aretha Franklin**. Despite the acclaim, Electribe 101 broke up shortly afterwards, with Martin going solo. The others formed Groove Corporation.

ELECTRIC FLAG
Albums
A Long Time Comin' (Columbia 1968)★★★★
➽ p.361 for full listings
Connections
Buddy Miles ➽ p.233

ELECTRIC FLAG

ELECTRIC FLAG WAS FORMED IN 1967 BY THE LATE **MIKE BLOOMFIELD** (b. 1944, d. 1981; GUITAR). THE BAND FEATURED **Buddy Miles** (drums/vocals), Nick Gravenites (vocals), Barry Goldberg (keyboards), Harvey Brooks (bass), Peter Strazza (tenor saxophone), Marcus Doubleday (trumpet) and Herbie Rich (baritone saxophone). Their debut at the **Monterey Pop Festival** was a noble start, followed by the hit album, *A Long Time Comin'*, with additional members Stemziel (Stemsy) Hunter and Mike Fonfara. The band was unable to follow this release, and immediately began to dissolve.

The second album was a pale shadow of their debut, with only 'See To Your Neighbour' showing signs of a unified performance. Miles then left to form the Buddy Miles Express, while Gravenites became a songwriting legend in San Francisco. Following years of session work, Brooks reappeared in Sky. An abortive Flag reunion produced the lacklustre *The Band Kept Playing*.

ELECTRIC LIGHT ORCHESTRA

ELO ORIGINALLY FEATURED **ROY WOOD** (b. 1946; VOCALS/CELLO/WOODWIND/GUITARS), **JEFF LYNNE** (b. 1947; VOCALS/piano/guitar) and Bev Bevan (b. 1945; drums). They completed an experimental debut set with the aid of Bill Hunt (french horn) and Steve Woolam (violin), and reached the UK Top 10 with '10538 Overture' (1972). When Woolam departed, Hugh McDowell (b. 1953), Andy Craig (cellos), Richard Tandy (b. 1948; keyboards/bass/piano/guitar) and Wilf Gibson (b. 1945; violin) were recruited. They played a series of indifferent live appearances, following which Wood took Hunt and McDowell to form **Wizzard**.

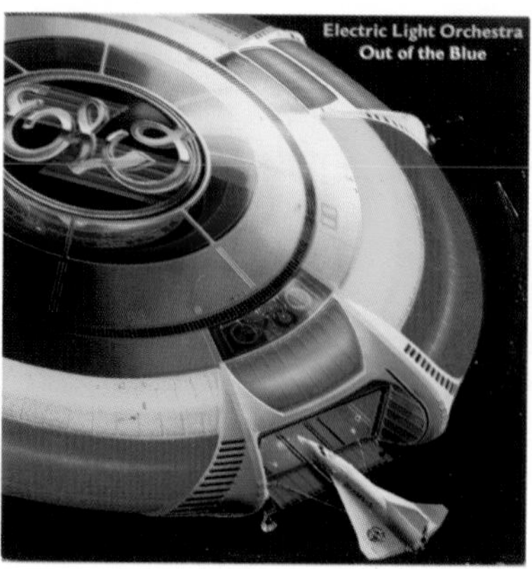

A reshaped line-up completed *ELO II* and scored a Top 10 single with a version of 'Roll Over Beethoven'. They enjoyed a third hit with 'Showdown', but the ensuing 'Ma Ma Ma Ma Belle' and 'Can't Get It Out Of My Head' (US Top 10) failed to chart in the UK. However the attendant album, *Eldorado*, went gold. By this point the group's line-up had stabilized around Lynne, Bevan, Tandy, McDowell, Kelly Grouchett (bass), Mik Kaminski (violin) and Melvyn Gale (cello). They achieved considerable commercial success with *A New World Record*, *Out Of The Blue* and *Discovery*.

Between 1976 and 1981, ELO scored an unbroken run of 15 UK Top 20 singles, including 'Telephone Line', 'Mr. Blue Sky' and 'Don't Bring Me Down'; the line-up now featured Lynne, Bevan, Tandy and Grouchett. Recurrent legal and distribution problems undermined ELO's momentum: *Time* and *Secret Messages* lacked the verve of earlier work. Few releases and Lynne's growing disenchantment led to him going solo and the group splitting up. In 1991, Bevan emerged with ELO 2.

ELECTRIC PRUNES

FORMED IN LOS ANGELES IN 1965, THE ELECTRIC PRUNES FEATURED JIM LOWE (VOCALS/GUITAR/AUTOHARP), Ken Williams (lead guitar), James 'Weasel' Spagnola (guitar), Mark Tulin (bass) and Quint (b. Michael Weakley; drums – quickly replaced by Preston Ritter). The quintet debuted with the low-key 'Ain't It Hard' before the US Top 20 hits 'I Had Too Much To Dream (Last Night)' and 'Get Me To The World On Time'. These blended the drive of garage/punk rock, the rhythmic pulse of the **Rolling Stones** and the experimentalism of the emerging psychedelic movement. The Prunes' debut album was hampered by indifferent material, but the excellent *Underground* featured some of their finest achievements. Sadly, the Prunes were unable to sustain their hit profile. Ritter was replaced by the prodigal Quint before the remaining original members dropped out during sessions for *Mass In F Minor*. An entirely new line-up completed the lacklustre *Just Good Old Rock 'N' Roll*.

ELECTRONIC

FORMED IN ENGLAND IN 1989, ELECTRONIC FEATURED JOHNNY MARR (b. JOHN MAHER, 1963; GUITAR; EX-**SMITHS**) AND Bernard Sumner (b. 1956; songwriter; ex-**New Order**). Electronic marked Marr's move into more commercial territory; their first single, 'Getting Away With It' (1989), featuring Neil Tennant (**Pet Shop Boys**), reached UK number 12.

Electronic capitalized on the new credibility that dance music had acquired, using 'electronic' dance rhythms and indie guitar pop. In 1991, a self-titled debut album followed two more UK Top 20 singles, 'Get The Message' and 'Feel Every Beat'. The album was also very well received, reaching UK number 2 (number 1 the indie chart). In 1992, 'Disappointed' reached UK number 6, however *Raise The Pressure* –a blend of Pet Shop Boys harmony with the occasional hint of wah-wah pedal from Marr – was uninspiring.

ELGINS

US-BORN JOHNNY DAWSON, CLEO MILLER AND ROBERT FLEMING (LATER REPLACED BY NORBERT McCLEAN) performed as the Downbeats in the late 50s, recording two singles for **Motown**. In 1962, Saundra Mallett (who issued 'Camel Walk' for Tamla) joined them, the group became the Elgins. 'Darling Baby' – written and produced by **Holland/Dozier/Holland** – reached the US R&B Top 10 in 1966. 'Heaven Must Have Sent You' matched that success, but after one further hit, the group broke up. In 1971, they enjoyed two unexpected UK Top 20 hits when Motown reissued 'Heaven Must Have Sent You' and the former b-side 'Put Yourself In My Place'. The band re-formed to tour Britain but recording plans foundered.

In 1989, Dawson, Yvonne Allen, Mclean and Jimmy Charles recorded a new arrangement of 'Heaven Must Have Sent You'. In the 90s, they released *Take The Train* and *Sensational*.

ELLIOTT, RAMBLIN' JACK

NEW YORKER ELLIOTT (b. ELLIOTT CHARLES ADNOPOZ, 1931) MET **WOODY GUTHRIE** IN 1949. THE PAIR TRAVELLED AND sang together before Elliot emerged as a talent in his own right. *Jack Elliott Sings The Songs Of Woody Guthrie* was the artist's first American album. Further releases included *Jack Elliott*, which featured **Bob Dylan** (harmonica, as 'Tedham Porterhouse'), and *Young Brigham* (with songs by **Tim Hardin** and the **Rolling Stones**). In 1975, Elliott was joined by Dylan during an appearance at a Greenwich Village club; he then became a natural choice for Bob's Rolling Thunder Revue. Elliot continued his erratic, but intriguing, path with the excellent *Kerouac's Last Dream*.

ELY, JOE

TEXAN-BORN ELY (b. 1948) FORMED HIS FIRST BAND AT THE AGE OF 13, PLAYING A FUSION OF COUNTRY AND R&B. He later joined singer-songwriters Jimmie Gilmore and George 'Butch' Hancock in the Flatlanders. When Ely was signed to MCA in the late 70s, recordings by the Flatlanders were anthologized on *One Road More*.

In 1976, Ely's own band – Jesse Taylor (guitar), Lloyd Maines (steel drum), Gregg Wright (bass), Steve Keeton (drums) and Ponty Bone (accordion) – recorded three unsuccessful albums, *Joe Ely*, *Honky Tonk Masquerade*, and *Down On The Drag*, before Keeton was replaced by Robert Marquam and Wright by Michael Robertson for *Musta Notta Gotta Lotta*.

In 1980, the Ely Band toured extensively with the **Clash**, and released *Live Shots*. The album featured Taylor, Marquam, Wright, Bone and Maines; it was no more successful than the previous three. In 1984, Ely recorded *Hi-Res*, with a completely new band of little-known musicians.

By 1987, Ely assembled a new band: David Grissom (lead guitar), Jimmy Pettit (bass) and Davis McLarty (drums). They recorded two artistically stunning albums, *Lord Of The Highway* and *Dig All Night*; the ensuing interest resulted in two albums of Ely's early material being released. In 1990, the band recorded a powerhouse live album in Austin, *Live At Liberty Lunch*. His 1995 *Letter To Laredo* was a return to his earlier sound.

EMERSON, LAKE AND PALMER

ELP COMPRISED KEITH EMERSON (b. 1944; KEYBOARDS), GREG LAKE (b. 1948; VOCALS/BASS) AND CARL PALMER (b. 1951; drums/percussion). They appeared at the much-publicized 1970 **Isle of Wight Festival** and were signed to Island Records, completing their self-titled debut album, the same year.

In 1971, they introduced their arrangement of Mussorgsky's *Pictures At An Exhibition*, then the concept album *Tarkus*. Extensive tours and albums followed over the next three years including *Trilogy*, *Brain Salad Surgery* and an extravagant triple-live album. With solo outings becoming increasingly distracting, the group released one final studio album, *Love Beach*, before embarking on a farewell world tour.

In 1986, a serious re-formation was attempted. Palmer declined, so Emerson and Lake teamed up with hit drummer Cozy Powell to produce *Emerson, Lake And Powell*. When Powell quit, Palmer re-joined for a projected album in 1987, but the sessions proved fruitless. Instead, Emerson recruited Hush drummer Robert Berry for the poor-selling *To The Power Of Three*. In the early 90s, the original trio re-formed.

EMF

FORMED IN ENGLAND, IN 1989, EMF FEATURED JAMES ATKIN (b. 1969; VOCALS), IAN DENCH (b. 1964; GUITAR/ keyboards), Derry Brownson (b. 1970; keyboards/samples), Zak Foley (b. 1970; bass), Mark Decloedt (b. 1969; drums) and Milf (DJ). The band claimed EMF stood for Epsom Mad Funkers (or Ecstasy Mother Fuckers) – Parlophone Records claimed it stood for Every Mother's Favourites. They were signed to Parlophone after just four gigs and without a demo – an opportunism that was rewarded when their debut, 'Unbelievable', reached the UK Top 5 and debut album sales exceeded two million. 1992's *Stigma* disappointed, however, with sales less than one-fifth of the debut.

Their label encouraged a three-year gap between 1992's *Unexplained* EP and 1995's *Cha Cha Cha*. Producer Johnny Dollar walked out of the sessions and the resulting album failed to sell. Having been dropped by Parlophone, the band split up.

ELECTRIC LIGHT ORCHESTRA
Albums
Out Of The Blue (Jet 1977)★★★★
➧ p.361 for full listings
Connections
Roy Wood ➧ p.343
Jeff Lynne ➧ p.220
Wizzard ➧ p.342
Further References
Book: *The Electric Light Orchestra Story*, Bev Bevan

ELECTRIC PRUNES
Albums
The Electric Prunes (Reprise 1967)★★★
➧ p.361 for full listings
Influences
Rolling Stones ➧ p.281

ELECTRONIC
Albums
Electronic (Factory 1991)★★★★
➧ p.361 for full listings
Collaborators
Neil Tennant ➧ p.259
Connections
Smiths ➧ p.301
New Order ➧ p.246
The The ➧ p.319

ELGINS
Albums
Darling Baby (VIP 1966)★★★
➧ p.361 for full listings
Connections
Holland/Dozier/Holland ➧ p.183

ELLIOTT, RAMBLIN' JACK
Albums
Jack Elliott Sings The Songs Of Woody Guthrie (1960)★★★
➧ p.361 for full listings
Collaborators
Woody Guthrie ➧ p.170
Bob Dylan ➧ p.128

ELY, JOE
Albums
Dig All Night (HighTone 1988)★★★★
➧ p.361 for full listings
Collaborators
Clash ➧ p.93

EMERSON, LAKE AND PALMER
Albums
Pictures At An Exhibition (Island 1971)★★★★
➧ p.361 for full listings

EMF
Albums
Schubert Dip (Parlophone 1991)★★★★
➧ p.361 for full listings

EMOTIONS
Albums
So I Can Love You (Stax 1970)★★★
Come Into Our World (ARC 1979)★★★
➽ p.361 for full listings
Connections
Earth, Wind And Fire ➽ p.130

EN VOGUE
Albums
Funky Divas (East West 1992)★★★★
➽ p.361 for full listings
Collaborators
MC Hammer ➽ p.173
Influences
Curtis Mayfield ➽ p.228
Further References
Video: *Funky Divas* (1992)

ENGLAND DAN AND JOHN FORD COLEY
Albums
England Dan And John Ford Coley (A&M 1971)★★★
Dowdy Ferry Road (Big Tree 1977)★★★
➽ p.361 for full listings

ENID
Albums
Something Wicked This Way Comes (Enid 1983)★★★
Tripping The Light Fantastic (Mantella 1995)★★★
➽ p.361 for full listings
Influences
Barclay James Harvest
➽ p.32
Further References
Video: *Stonehenge Free Festival 1984* (Visionary 1995)

ENIGMA
Albums
MCMXC AD (Virgin 1990)★★★★
The Cross Of Changes (Virgin 1993)★★★★
Le Roi Est Mort, Vive Le Roi! (Virgin 1996)★★★★
➽ p.361 for full listings

EMOTIONS

THE HUTCHINSON SISTERS, WANDA (b. 1951; LEAD VOCAL), SHEILA AND JEANETTE, RECORDED FOR SEVERAL LOCAL companies before reaching Stax. Their debut, 'So I Can Love You' (1969), reached the US Top 40, and introduced a series of excellent singles, including 'Show Me How' (1971) and 'I Could Never Be Happy' (1972). A fourth sister, Pamela, eventually joined the group. The Emotions moved to Columbia in 1976, working under Maurice White of **Earth, Wind And Fire**. 'Best Of My Love' (1977) was a US number 1 and the sisters sang on 'Boogie Wonderland' (1979), an energetic collaboration with White's group.

EN VOGUE

VOCAL DANCE/R&B OUTFIT – DAWN ROBINSON (b. *c.* 1965), TERRY ELLIS (b. *c.* 1966), CINDY HERRON (b. *c.* 1963) AND Maxine Jones (b. *c.* 1962) – formed in Oakland, California in 1988, after producers Denzil 'Denny' Foster and Thomas McElroy decided to establish their own 'girl group'.

The group joined **MC Hammer**'s 1990 tour, and Freddie Jackson's a year later. They went on to enjoy singles success with 'Hold On' and 'Lies' (1990) – the latter introduced female rapper Debbie T, and added a new, post-feminist outlook to traditional R&B. Their second album featured two **Curtis Mayfield** cover versions, and produced further hits in 'Free Your Mind' and 'Give It Up, Turn It Loose'. Following a lengthy break from recording, during which Robinson left to pursue a solo career, they returned to a competitive market with *EV3*.

ENGLAND DAN AND JOHN FORD COLEY

DAN SEALS (b. 1950) FORMED A PARTNERSHIP WITH JOHN FORD COLEY (b. 1951) AND THEY FIRST WORKED AS SOUTHWEST F.O.B. – 'Freight On Board'. The name did not last, but not wanting to be called Seals And Coley, they settled on England Dan And John Ford Coley. Their first albums for A&M Records sold moderately well, but they struck gold in 1976 with a move to Big Tree Records. The single 'I'd Really Love To See You Tonight' went to number 2 in the US charts, and also reached the UK Top 30. The resulting album, *Nights Are Forever*, was a big seller and the title track, 'Nights Are Forever Without You', was another Top 10 single. They had further US hits with 'It's Sad To Belong' and 'Love Is The Answer'. When the duo split, Seals, after a few setbacks, became a country star. Coley found a new partner, but their 1981 album, *Kelly Leslie And John Ford Coley*, was not a success.

ENID

INFLUENTIAL ART-ROCKERS, FORMED IN 1974 BY ROBERT JOHN GODFREY (b. 1947; KEYBOARDS) WITH GUITARISTS Stephen Stewart and Francis Lickerish. Godfrey had joined **Barclay James Harvest** as musical director in 1969, but left in 1972 and recorded a solo album, *The Fall Of Hyperion* (1973).

Enid's debut, *In The Region of the Summer Stars*, appeared in 1976. Despite an ever-changing line-up, subsequent concept albums, rock operas and tours saw them increasing their cult audience and playing large venues. A move to Pye Records just as the label went bankrupt in 1980 broke up the band. Godfrey formed his own label, distribution and studio with Stewart, but re-formed Enid in 1983. Operating as independents, their following continued to grow, and the fifth album, *Something Wicked This Way Comes*, was their biggest success yet. In 1986, the group presented *Salome*, as a ballet at London's Hammersmith Odeon. In 1988, Godfrey dissolved the band, re-emerging in 1990 as manager of Come September, for whom he writes, but does not perform.

ENIGMA

AMBIENT POP SCULPTORS ENIGMA ARE THE BRAINCHILD OF PIANIST MICHAEL CRETU (b. 1957). AFTER WORKING AS A studio musician and arranger, he released his debut solo album, *Legionare* (1983). He then worked with the 1985 number 1 European success, Moti Special, as writer, producer and keyboard player. He put together his most commercially successful project, Enigma, two years later. 'Sadeness Part 1' hit UK number 1 in 1990. The accompanying *MCMXC AD* also topped the charts and spent 57 weeks on the UK list. Gold or platinum status was attained in 25 countries. Film director Robert Evans then invited Cretu to compose the title song to the film *Sliver*, resulting in the release of 'Carly's Song' and 'Carly's Loneliness'.

After three years, he produced a follow-up. It was hardly the expected blockbuster, but 'Return To Innocence' (1994) reached UK number 9 and demonstrated his enduring appeal to the record-buying public.

ENO, BRIAN

WHILE STUDYING AT ART SCHOOLS IN HIS NATIVE ENGLAND, ENO (b. BRIAN PETER GEORGE ST. BAPTISTE DE LA SALLE ENO, 1948) fell under the influence of *avant-garde* composers Cornelius Cardew and **John Cage**. Although he could not play an instrument, Eno liked tinkering with multi-track tape recorders and in 1968 wrote the limited edition theoretical handbook, *Music For Non Musicians*.

Eno joined **Roxy Music** in 1971 as a 'technical adviser', but before long his powerful visual image began to rival that of **Bryan Ferry**. He left on 21 June 1973 – the same day, he began his solo career in earnest, writing 'Baby's On Fire'. Shortly afterwards, he formed a temporary partnership with **Robert Fripp**. In 1973, their esoteric *No Pussyfooting* was released; a tour followed and, with the entire Roxy line-up (bar Ferry) Eno completed *Here Come The Warm Jets*.

A one-off punk single 'Seven Deadly Finns' prompted a tour with the Winkies, during which Eno's right lung collapsed. Convalescing, he visited America, recorded demos with **Television** and worked with **John Cale**. In 1974, he played alongside Cale, **Kevin Ayers** and **Nico** in London.

Taking Tiger Mountain (By Strategy) was followed by production credits on albums by **Robert Wyatt**, Robert Calvert and Phil Manzanera. This led to Eno's experiments with environment-conscious music. He formed the Obscure Records label whose third release was his own *Discreet Music*. He also completed *Another Green World*, a meticulously crafted work. After performing in Phil Manzanera's 801, he began a fruitful alliance with **David Bowie** on *Low*, *Heroes* and *Lodger*. Despite that workload, he managed to complete his next solo work, *Before And After Science*. Eno then turned his attention to soundtracks before returning to ambient music. *Music For Films* was a pot-pourri of material suitable for playing while watching movies, then came *Music For Airports*. Eno also remained in demand by **Ultravox**, Cluster, Harold Budd, **Devo** and **Talking Heads**; in 1981 he produced a Top 30 album for the Heads, *My Life In The Bush Of Ghosts* – a collaboration with **David Byrne**, that fused 'found voices' with African rhythms.

In 1980, Eno worked with Canadian producer/engineer **Daniel Lanois**. Between them they produced *Voices*, by Eno's brother Roger, and a collaboration with Harold Budd, *The Plateaux Of Mirror*. This association with Lanois culminated in **U2**'s *The Unforgettable Fire*, *The Joshua Tree*, *Achtung Baby* and *Zooropa*. In 1990, Eno completed a collaborative album with John Cale, *Wrong Way Up*. The following year Eno released *My Squelchy Life*, which was withdrawn, revised, and re-released in 1992 as *Nerve Net*. It fused 'electronically-treated dance music, eccentric English pop, cranky funk, space jazz, and a myriad of other, often dazzling sounds'. In 1995, he worked with David Bowie on *Outside*, **Jah Wobble** on *Spanner* and shared composing credits with Bono, Adam Clayton and Larry Mullen Jr on *Passengers: Original Soundtracks 1*.

ENYA

ENYA (b. EITHNE NI BHRAONAIN, 1961; EX-**CLANNAD**) WAS A CLASSICALLY TRAINED PIANIST. ENYA'S KEYBOARD-PLAYING days for Clannad lasted for three years after which she was asked to record the music for the BBC television series *The Celts*. This was subsequently released as her debut album in 1987. The album was largely ignored, however, the following year Enya released *Watermark* in much the same vein and had a surprise UK number 1 with 'Orinoco Flow'. Working with her long-time collaborators, Roma Ryan (lyricist) and Nicky Ryan (producer), Enya followed the chart-topper with two smaller hits – 'Evening Falls' and 'Storms In Africa Part II'. She returned in the early 90s with *Shepherd Moons*, which, by the mid-90s, had reached world sales of 10 million. *The Memory Of Trees* was more of the same.

EPSTEIN, BRIAN

EPSTEIN (b. 1934, d. 1967) BEGAN HIS WORKING LIFE OVERSEEING THE NORTH END ROAD MUSIC STORES (NEMS) in Liverpool, England. In 1961, a customer requested 'My Bonnie' by a group called the **Beatles**; Epstein subsequently attended one of their gigs at the Cavern club and, against the advice of his friends, became a pop manager.

He transformed the Beatles: banned them from swearing or eating on stage, encouraged the establishment of a rehearsed repertoire and persuaded them to wear smart, grey lounge suits. In early 1962, Epstein won a record deal, thanks to the producer **George Martin**. During October 1962, a management contract was belatedly finalized with the Beatles – Epstein received 25 per cent of their earnings, a figure he maintained for all future signings. Weeks later, he struck a deal with music publisher Dick James, which culminated in the formation of Northern Songs, a company dealing exclusively with compositions by **John Lennon** and **Paul McCartney**. The powers agreed on a 50/50 split: half to Dick James and his partner; 20 per cent each to Lennon and McCartney, and 10 per cent to Epstein.

Long before the Beatles became the most successful entertainers in British music history, Epstein had signed his second group **Gerry And The Pacemakers**. Scouring the Cavern for further talent he soon added Tommy Quickly, the **Fourmost**, **Billy J. Kramer And The Dakotas**, the **Big Three** and **Cilla Black**. His artists dominated the UK charts throughout the year – nine number 1 hits spanning 32 weeks. One area where Epstein was deemed fallible was in the merchandising agreements that he concluded on behalf of the Beatles; lost revenue that Brian had allowed to slip through his fingers was revealed in the *Wall Street Journal*: Americans had spent approximately $50 million on Beatles goods by the end of 1964, while the world market was estimated at roughly £40 million. Epstein attempted to rectify this through litigation, and even contributed massive legal expenses himself, but the stigma of the unfortunate deal remained.

Epstein engineered the Beatles' Hollywood Bowl concert, an event which indelibly changed rock performances. While the Beatles were conquering the New World, Epstein was expanding his empire, notably with the career of Cilla Black; he immediately recognized her lasting charm as the gauche, unpretentious girl-next-door.

When the Beatles ceased touring, Epstein's role in their day-to-day lives was minimal. He turned to other areas, purchasing London's Savile Theatre and alternating serious drama with Sunday pop shows. NEMS, meanwhile, ceased to inspire him and was offered to Robert Stigwood.

By 1967, Epstein was losing control. Drug dependence, homosexual guilt and tabloid harrassment brought him to the verge of a nervous breakdown and attempted suicide. In August 1967, the Beatles were attending a course in Transcendental Meditation with the Maharishi Mahesh Yogi. Brian, meanwhile, was lying dead at his London home. The inquest subsequently established death from a cumulative overdose of the sleep-inducing drug Carbitrol. Although suicide was suspected, the coroner concluded a verdict of accidental death from 'incautious self-overdoses'.

Epstein is rightly regarded as a great manager who valued the Beatles' reputation above all else. He insulated them from corporate avarice and prevented EMI from marketing cheap reissues or unauthorized compilations. For Epstein, honour meant more than profit and he brought an integrity to pop management that few of his successors have matched.

EQUALS

TWINS DERV (b. 1948; VOCALS) AND LINCOLN GORDON (b. 1948; RHYTHM GUITAR), **EDDY GRANT** (b. 1948; LEAD GUITAR), Patrick Lloyd (b. 1948; rhythm guitar) and John Hall (b. 1947; drums) began playing together in 1965. Their best-remembered single, 'Baby Come Back', was originally recorded as a b-side (1966). The quintet's early releases made little impression until 'Baby Come Back' became a major hit in Germany (1967), and later topped the Dutch and Belgian charts. This propulsive, infectious song was then reissued in Britain where it eventually reached number 1. Although the Equals enjoyed other hits, only 'Viva Bobby Joe' (1969) and 'Black Skinned Blue-Eyed Boys' (1970) reached the Top 10. Chief songwriter Grant went solo in 1971, after which the group underwent several personnel changes before finding security on the cabaret circuit. Their career was resurrected in 1978 when Grant signed them to his Ice label for *Mystic Synster*.

ENO, BRIAN

Albums

Here Come The Warm Jets (Island 1974)★★★★

Ambient 1: Music For Airports (Polydor/EG 1979)★★★★

➧ p.361 for full listings

Collaborators

Daniel Lanois ➧ p.212
John Cale ➧ p.78
Robert Fripp ➧ p.154
Television ➧ p.317
Kevin Ayers ➧ p.25
Nico ➧ p.247
David Bowie ➧ p.64
Ultravox ➧ p.327
Devo ➧ p.117
Talking Heads ➧ p.316
David Byrne ➧ p.77
Jah Wobble ➧ p.196

Connections

Roxy Music ➧ p.283
Bryan Ferry ➧ p.144
U2 ➧ p.326

Influences

Cornelius Cardew
John Cage ➧ p.78

Further References

Video: *Mistaken Memories Of Medieval Manhattan* (Hendring)

Book: *The Vertical Colour Of Sound*, Eric Tamm

ENYA

Albums

Watermark (Warners 1988)★★★★

➧ p.361 for full listings

Connections

Clannad ➧ p.92

EPSTEIN, BRIAN

Connections

Beatles ➧ p.38
George Martin ➧ p.226
Gerry And The Pacemakers ➧ p.158
Fourmost ➧ p.152
Billy J. Kramer And The Dakotas ➧ p.211
Big Three ➧ p.47
Cilla Black ➧ p.49

Further References

Book: *Brian Epstein: The Man Who Made The Beatles*, Ray Coleman

➧ p.361 for full listings

EQUALS

Albums

Unequalled Equals (President 1967)★★★

➧ p.361 for full listings

Connections

Eddy Grant ➧ p.164

ERASURE
Albums
Wonderland (Mute 1986)★★★
Erasure (Mute 1995)★★★
➧ p.361 for full listings
Connections
Depeche Mode ➧ p.116
Yazoo ➧ p.345
Influences
Pet Shop Boys ➧ p.259
Further References
Video: *Live Wild* (Warner Brothers 1994)

ERICKSON, ROKY
Albums
Roky Erickson And The Aliens (Columbia 1980)★★★
All That May Do My Rhyme (Trance Syndicate 1995)★★★
➧ p.361 for full listings
Connections
Thirteenth Floor Elevators ➧ p.320

ESCORTS (UK)
Albums
3 Down 4 To Go (1973)★★
➧ p.361 for full listings
Connections
Moody Blues ➧ p.237
Swinging Blue Jeans ➧ p.315
Hollies ➧ p.183

ESSEX, DAVID
Albums
Rock On (Columbia 1973)★★★
David Essex (Columbia 1974)★★★
➧ p.361 for full listings
Connections
Jeff Wayne ➧ p.335
Further References
Book: *The David Essex Story*, George Tremlett

ESTEFAN, GLORIA
Albums
Into The Light (Epic 1991)★★★★
Abriendo Puertas (Epic 1995)★★★★
➧ p.361 for full listings
Collaborators
Miami Sound Machine ➧ p.138
Further References
Video: *The Evolution Tour: Live In Miami* (Epic Music Video 1996)

ESTEFAN, GLORIA, AND MIAMI SOUND MACHINE
Albums
Anything For You (UK) (Epic 1988)★★★★
➧ p.361 for full listings
Further References
Book: *Gloria Estefan*, Grace Catalano

ERASURE

KEYBOARD PLAYER AND ARRANGER VINCE CLARKE (b. 1961; EX-**DEPECHE MODE**, **YAZOO**, THE ASSEMBLY) DECIDED TO undertake a new project in 1985. The plan was to record an album with 10 different singers, but after auditioning vocalist Andy Bell, Erasure was formed. Erasure hit the UK chart with 'Sometimes' (1986), which reached number 2, and was followed by 'It Doesn't Have To Be Me' (1987). The following month their second album, *Circus*, reached the UK Top 10, and since then their popularity has grown rapidly. Their many memorable hits such as 'Victim Of Love', 'The Circus' and 'A Little Respect' have established them as serious rivals to the **Pet Shop Boys** as the world's leading vocal/synthesizer duo. Their singles and album sales continue to increase with successive releases, and *The Innocents*, *Wild!*, *Chorus* and the *Abba-Esque* EP have all reached UK number 1.

ERICKSON, ROKY

ERICKSON (b. ROGER ERKYNARD ERICKSON, 1947) CAME TO THE FORE IN **THIRTEENTH FLOOR ELEVATORS**. HE COMPOSED 'You're Gonna Miss Me', the group's most popular single, before the unit broke up in 1968. Arrested on a drugs charge, Erickson faked visions to avoid imprisonment, but was instead committed to Rusk State Hospital for the Criminally Insane. On his release in 1971, he began a low-key solo career, recording several singles with new backing group, Bleib Alien. In 1980, the guitarist secured a deal with CBS but the resulting *Roky Erickson And The Aliens*, was a disappointment.

Erickson was imprisoned in 1990 for stealing mail, but his plight inspired Sire Records' *Where The Pyramid Meets The Eye*, wherein 19 acts interpreted many of his best-known songs. Following his release from a mental institution, a grizzled Erickson recorded *All That May Do My Rhyme*, one of his better efforts.

ESCORTS (UK)

TERRY SYLVESTER (VOCALS/GUITAR), JOHN KINRADE (LEAD GUITAR) AND MIKE GREGORY (b. 1947; VOCALS/BASS) formed the Escorts in Liverpool, England, in 1962. Original drummer John Foster, aka Johnny Sticks, was replaced by Pete Clark (b. 1947) in 1963. They debuted in 1964 with an interpretation of 'Dizzie Miss Lizzie', two months later they scored a minor hit with 'The One To Cry'. Their next release, 'I Don't Want To Go On Without You', was also recorded by the **Moody Blues** – and charted. Subsequent releases proved unsuccessful.

Sylvester left for the **Swinging Blue Jeans**, then replaced Graham Nash in the **Hollies**; by mid-1966, Kinrade and Gregory had recruited Paddy Chambers (guitar) and Paul Comerford (drums) to release 'From Head To Toe', the Escorts' final single.

ESSEX, DAVID

ESSEX (b. DAVID COOK, 1947) BEGAN SINGING IN THE MID-60S, RECORDING A SERIES OF UNSUCCESSFUL SINGLES FOR A variety of labels. On the advice of manager Derek Bowman, he switched to acting, receiving his big break with the lead in the stage musical *Godspell*. His role in the 50s-inspired film *That'll Be The Day* reactivated Essex's recording career and the song he composed for the film, 'Rock On', was a transatlantic Top 10 hit. During the mid-70s, he registered two UK number 1s, 'Gonna Make You A Star' and 'Hold Me Close', plus three Top 10 hits. After parting with producer **Jeff Wayne**, Essex continued to chart, though less successfully.

As his teen appeal waned, Essex's serious acting commitments increased, most notably with the role of Che Guevara in the stage musical *Evita*. His lead part in the film *Silver Dream Machine* resulted in a hit of the same title. The Christmas hit, 'A Winter's Tale', kept his chart career alive, as did the equally successful 'Tahiti' – which anticipated one of his biggest projects to date, the elaborate musical *Mutiny*. In 1993, Essex embarked on a UK concert tour, and issued *Cover Shot*, a collection of mostly 60s songs. He toured in 1994 and released a new album, produced by Wayne.

ESTEFAN, GLORIA

CUBAN-BORN ESTEFAN (b. GLORIA FAJARDO, 1957) ORIGINALLY ROSE TO PROMINENCE IN THE 70S BY JOINING Emilio Estefan in Miami Sound Machine (later **Gloria Estefan, And Miami Sound Machine**). She married Emilio in 1978 and Miami Sound Machine recorded a sequence of Spanish-language albums during the late 70s and early 80s, becoming massively successful in the USA, Europe and Latin America. She then launched her solo career with *Cuts Both Ways* (1989); three singles from which reached the US Top 10, including the number 1, 'I Don't Wanna Lose You'.

In 1990, her impetus was halted by a serious road accident. She returned in 1991 with *Into The Light* and an eight-month world tour.

Mi Tierra and *Abriendo Puertas* were Spanish-language albums that distanced her somewhat from the American pop mainstream, but proved hugely popular in South America. *Destiny* was her first English-language collection for over five years – excepting the lacklustre collection of pop covers, *Hold Me, Thrill Me, Kiss Me*.

ESTEFAN, GLORIA, AND MIAMI SOUND MACHINE

FORMED IN MIAMI, USA IN 1973, THIS LATIN/FUNK/POP GROUP WAS ORIGINALLY A TRIO CALLED THE MIAMI LATIN BOYS, comprising Emilio Estefan (keyboards), Juan Avila (bass) and Enrique 'Kiki' Garcia (drums). Joined by Gloria Fajardo in 1975, the quartet changed its name to Miami Sound Machine. They recorded their first single, 'Renecer' (1975), for a local Hispanic company.

In 1979, the group recorded its first album, sung entirely in Spanish; it was distributed by CBS Records International. They recorded seven Spanish-language records during the next six years, becoming successful in predominantly US Hispanic areas, Central and South America and in Europe. Meanwhile, the group's membership grew to nine musicians. Their first English-language single, 'Dr. Beat', was released in 1984 and became a club/Top 10 hit in the UK. Signed to Epic Records, their first US chart single was 'Conga' (1985), followed by 1986's US Top 10 singles, 'Bad Boy' and 'Words Get In The Way'. Their first English-language album, *Primitive Love*, reached number 23 that same year. The group officially changed its name to **Gloria Estefan** And Miami Sound Machine in 1987, followed by 'Rhythm Is

Gonna Get You' (1987) and *Let it Loose*, 'Can't Stay Away From You', 'Anything For You' (number 1) and '1-2-3' (all 1988).

After a near-fatal road accident in their tour bus in 1990, the group were incapacitated for almost a year. Gloria left in 1991 to pursue her solo career.

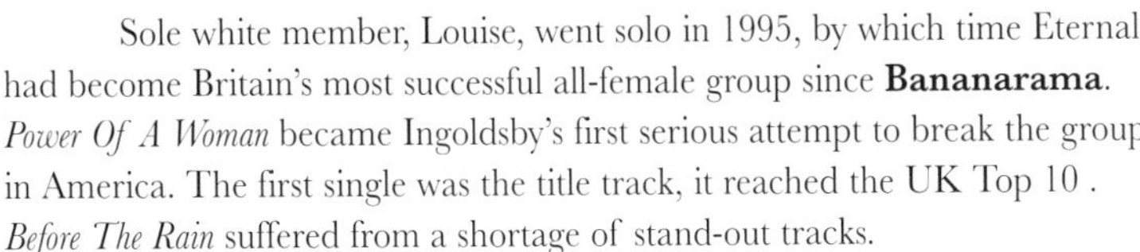

ETERNAL

THIS UK POP DANCE QUARTET ORIGINALLY COMPRISED LEAD singer Easther Bennett, her sister Vernie, Louise Nurding and Kelle Bryan; they were taken on by manager Dennis Ingoldsby. Their first two singles, 'Stay' and 'Save Our Love', made an immediate impact on the UK charts, launching the group as *the* teen phenomena of 1993. These were followed by the more strident 'Just A Step From Heaven' and *Always And Forever*, which spawned six Top 15 UK hits.

Sole white member, Louise, went solo in 1995, by which time Eternal had become Britain's most successful all-female group since **Bananarama**. *Power Of A Woman* became Ingoldsby's first serious attempt to break the group in America. The first single was the title track, it reached the UK Top 10 . *Before The Rain* suffered from a shortage of stand-out tracks.

ETHERIDGE, MELISSA

ETHERIDGE (b. 1961) WAS STILL A TEENAGER WHEN SHE BEGAN PLAYING PIANO AND GUITAR IN VARIOUS COVERS bands around Kansas. Relocating to Los Angeles, she was spotted by Island Records chief Chris Blackwell and signed in 1986. Her first break was writing the music for the film *Weeds*; when the band she had recruited failed, she settled for Kevin McCormick on bass and Craig Kampf on drums (later replaced by Maurigio Fritz Lewak). The first album was recorded live in the studio and spawned 'Bring Me Some Water', an eventual Grammy nominee. Former **Iggy Pop** sideman Scott Thurston had made a guest appearance on the first album and he returned for the second, alongside various other artists. In the early 90s, the excellent *Never Enough* won a Grammy. *Yes I Am* was a similar mix of up-tempo 'love crazy' material. The Hugh Padgham-produced *Your Little Secret* was further confirmation of her writing talents. She won the 1996 ASCAP songwriter of the year award.

EURYTHMICS

DAVID A. STEWART (b. 1952) AND **ANNIE LENNOX** (b. 1954) MET IN LONDON AND FORMED THE **TOURISTS**, A BAND able to fuse new wave energy with well-crafted pop songs. Following the Tourists' split, Lennox and Stewart formed the Eurythmics in 1980. Their debut *In The Garden*, a rigidly electronic-sounding album, failed to sell, but the duo persevered and glimpsed the charts with the synthesizer-based 'Love Is A Stranger'. The subsequent *Sweet Dreams* spawned a number of hits, all accompanied by an imaginative series of self-produced videos. The title track made US number 1, and was followed in quick succession by a reissued 'Love Is A Stranger', 'Who's That Girl', and the celebratory 'Right By Your Side'. *Touch* (1984) became a huge success.

The soundtrack to the film *1984* was poorly received, but this was remedied by the excellent *Be Yourself Tonight*, which contained less synthesized pop and more rock music, including a glorious soul duet with **Aretha Franklin** on 'Sisters (Are Doin' It For Themselves)'. During 1985, Lennox experienced serious throat problems, which forced the band to cancel their appearance at Live Aid. That same month, however, they enjoyed their sole UK chart topper, 'There Must Be An Angel'. Lennox made her big-screen debut in *Revolution*, with Donald Sutherland and Al Pacino. Stewart, meanwhile, became a highly sought-after record producer.

In 1986, *Revenge* was released, including 'Missionary Man', 'Thorn In My Side' and the comparatively lightweight 'The Miracle Of Love'. *Savage* maintained the standard and *We Too Are One* became their most successful album to date, staying at number 1 into 1990.

In addition to his production work, Stewart made his own solo albums. In 1992, Lennox issued her solo debut, *Diva*, followed by the well-received *Medusa* (1995).

EVERCLEAR

COMPRISING ART ALEXAKIS (VOCALS/GUITAR), CRAIG MONTOYA (BASS/VOCALS) AND GREG EKLUND (DRUMS). Everclear were formed in Oregon, USA, in 1991. Alexakis had previously worked as a roadie for a succession of punk bands, but decided to start his own group after a near-fatal cocaine overdose. They debuted in 1994 with *World Of Noise*, which included the intriguing 'Sparkle'. It was followed by the mini-album, *White Trash Hell*, bringing in a recording contract with Capitol. In 1995, they released the critically lauded *Sparkle And Fade*.

EVERLY BROTHERS

DON (b. 1937) AND PHIL EVERLY (b. 1939) WERE CHILD PERFORMERS, APPEARING ON THEIR PARENTS' (COUNTRY ARTISTS Ike and Margaret) radio shows throughout the 40s.

In 1957 they took **Felice** and **Boudleaux Bryants**' 'Bye Bye Love', to US number 2 and UK number 6. This was quickly followed by more irresistible Bryant songs, 'Wake Up Little Susie', 'All I Have To Do Is Dream', 'Bird Dog', 'Problems', 'So Sad' and 'Devoted To You'. By the end of the 50s they were the world's number 1 vocal group.

After signing with the newly formed Warner Brothers Records for $1 million, they delivered the superlative 'Cathy's Clown' (written by Don). No Everly record had sounded like this before and the echo-laden production and treble-loaded harmonies took it to US/UK number 1. The brothers continued to release Top 10 records, surprisingly proving more popular in Britain than their homeland. However, the advent of the beat boom pushed them out of the spotlight and while they continued to make hit records, none came near to their previous achievements. After a few years of declining fortunes, the brothers parted acrimoniously – the only time they met over the next 10 years was at their father's funeral.

Both went solo, with varying degrees of success. While Don maintained a steady career, playing with **Albert Lee**, Phil concentrated on songwriting. 'She Means Nothing To Me' was a striking duet with **Cliff Richard** which put the Everly name back in the UK Top 10. In 1983 they hugged and made up and their emotional reunion was made to an ecstatic audience at London's Royal Albert Hall. The following year *EB84* was released and gave them another major hit with **Paul McCartney**'s 'Wings Of A Nightingale'. In 1986 they joined the Rock 'n' Roll Hall Of Fame.

ETERNAL

Albums
Power Of A Woman (First Avenue/EMI 1995)★★★
➽ p.361 for full listings
Influences
Bananarama ➽ p.31
Further References
Video: *Always And Forever* (1994)

ETHERIDGE, MELISSA

Albums
Never Enough (Island 1991)★★★★
➽ p.361 for full listings
Collaborators
Scott Thurston
Connections
Iggy Pop ➽ p.264

EURYTHMICS

Albums
Sweet Dreams (Are Made Of This) (RCA 1983)★★★★
Be Yourself Tonight (RCA 1985)★★★★
➽ p.361 for full listings

Collaborators
Aretha Franklin ➽ p.153
Connections
Annie Lennox ➽ p.214
Tourists ➽ p.322
Further References
Book: *Eurythmics: Sweet Dreams: The Definitive Biography*, Johnny Waller

EVERCLEAR

Albums
Sparkle And Fade (Capitol 1995)★★★★
➽ p.361 for full listings

EVERLY BROTHERS

Albums
A Date With The Everly Brothers (Warners 1960)★★★★
Gone Gone Gone (Warners 1965)★★★★
➽ p.361 for full listings
Collaborators
Cliff Richard ➽ p.277
Connections
Felice Bryant ➽ p.72
Boudleaux Bryant ➽ p.71
Elvis Presley ➽ p.265
Albert Lee ➽ p.213
Influences
Paul McCartney ➽ p.229
Further References
Books: *The Everly Brothers: Walk Right Back*, Roger White
Ike's Boys, Phyllis Karpp

EVERYTHING BUT THE GIRL
Albums
Eden (Blanco y Negro 1984)★★★★
The Language of Life (Blanco y Negro 1990)★★★★
Walking Wounded (Atlantic 1996)★★★★
➽ p.361 for full listings
Collaborators
Massive Attack ➽ p.227
Influences
Cole Porter
Further References
Book: *Patient: The History Of A Rare Illness*, Ben Watt

EXILE
Albums
Exile (Wooden Nickel 1973)★★★★
Still Standing (Arista 1990)★★★★
➽ p.361 for full listings

EXPLOITED
Albums
Punk's Not Dead (Secret 1981)★★★
Troops Of Tomorrow (Secret 1982)★★★
➽ p.361 for full listings
Further References
Video: *Rock & Roll Outlaws* (Visionary 1995)

EXTREME
Albums
Pornograffitti (A&M 1990)★★★
III Sides To Every Story (A&M 1992)★★★★
➽ p.361 for full listings
Connections
Van Halen ➽ p.328

EXTREME NOISE TERROR
Albums
The Peel Sessions (Strange Fruit 1990)★★★
Retro-bution (Earache 1995)★★★
➽ p.361 for full listings
Collaborators
Chaos UK
Connections
John Peel ➽ p.258
KLF ➽ p.208
Influences
ENT
Napalm Death ➽ p.243
Further References
Video: *From One Extreme To The Other* (Jettisoundz 1989)

EYC
Albums
Express Yourself Clearly (Gasoline Alley 1994)★★★
➽ p.361 for full listings
Collaborators
East 17 ➽ p.130
Connections
Boo-Yaa T.R.I.B.E. ➽ p.62

EVERYTHING BUT THE GIRL

UK DUO TRACEY THORN (b. 1962) AND BEN WATT (b. 1962) MET WHILE students. They performed together in, and released a produced version of, Cole Porter's 'Night And Day' (1982). Thorn made a solo mini-album, *A Distant Shore* (1982), which was a strong seller in the UK independent charts; Watt released the critically acclaimed *North Marine Drive* (1983).

In 1984, they reached the UK chart with 'Each And Everyone', which preceded their superb *Eden*. Their biggest single breakthrough came with a version of Danny Whitten's 'I Don't Want To Talk About It' (1988), which reached the UK Top 3. *The Language Of Life*, a more jazzy collection, found further critical acclaim, however, the more pop-orientated follow-up, *World-wide* (1991), was released to mediocre reviews. *Amplified Heart* repaired the damage somewhat. Following Thorn's vocal contributions to **Massive Attack**'s *Protection*, a drum and bass remix of 'Missing' from 1996's *Walking Wounded* became a big club hit, and put Everything But The Girl back in the charts.

EXILE

FORMED IN KENTUCKY, USA, IN 1963 AS THE EXILES – THEY BECAME EXILE IN 1973. IN 1978, THEY REACHED US NUMBER 1 with 'Kiss You All Over', followed by two more pop-chart singles before switching to country in 1983. At the time, the group featured J. P. Pennington (vocals/guitar), Buzz Cornelison (keyboards), Les Taylor (vocals/guitar), Marlon Hargis (vocals/keyboards), Sonny LeMaire (vocals/bass) and drummer Steve Goetzman. Their country career was more lucrative with their first country chart single, 'High Cost Of Leaving', reaching number 27; it was followed by four successive number 1s in 1984, including 'Woke Up In Love' and 'Crazy For Your Love', and six further number 1s by 1987.

Hargis was replaced by Lee Carroll in 1985 and Pennington was replaced by Paul Martin in 1989. The group signed to Arista in 1989 with a noticeable decline in its level of commercial success. They were dropped by the label in 1993 and broke up soon afterwards. A new version with Pennington and Taylor was on the road in 1996.

EXPLOITED

SCOTTISH PUNK QUARTET FORMED IN 1980 BY VOCALIST WATTIE BUCHAN AND GUITARIST 'BIG JOHN' DUNCAN. Recruiting Dru Stix (b. Drew Campbell; drums) and Gary McCormick (bass), they signed to Secret Records in 1981 and released *Punk's Not Dead*. The band quickly earned themselves a certain low-life notoriety – songs such as 'Fuck A Mod', for example, set youth tribe against youth tribe without any true rationale – yet they were the only member of the third generation punk set to make it on to BBC Television's *Top Of The Pops*, with 1981's 'Dead Cities'. They continue to release material on a regular basis.

EXTREME

BOSTON QUARTET FEATURING GARY CHERONE (b. 1961; VOCALS), PORTUGUESE GUITARIST NUNO BETTENCOURT (b. 1966), Pat Badger (b. 1967; bass) and Paul Geary (b. 1961; drums). An original Extreme line-up found themselves on television in 1985, via an MTV competition, but it was the arrival of Bettencourt in 1986 and Badger in 1987 that gave them lift-off. Following a recording contract with A&M, the group made their vinyl debut with 'Play With Me' (from the soundtrack to *Bill And Ted's Excellent Adventure*). A self-titled debut album followed and met with widespread critical indifference. *Pornograffitti* was a stunning second release and the big breakthrough came when the simple acoustic ballad, 'More Than Words', reached US number 1/UK number 2. Their appearance at the Freddie Mercury concert, during sessions for *III Sides To Every Story*, gave them considerable exposure beyond the heavy metal fraternity. Cherone toured and recorded with **Van Halen** in 1998.

EXTREME NOISE TERROR

EXTREME NOISE TERROR FORMED IN 1985 AND WERE SIGNED BY MANIC EARS RECORDS AFTER THEIR FIRST GIG. Their debut was a split album with Chaos UK, and showed ENT in the process of twisting traditional punk influences. Along with the **Napalm Death**, they attracted the interest of **John Peel** in 1987, recording a session that was later released. Drummer Mick Harris, who had left Napalm Death to replace ENT's original drummer, in turn departed. His replacement was Stick (Tony Dickens), who joined existing members Dean Jones (vocals), Phil Vane (vocals) and Pete Hurley (guitar). Mark Bailey replaced Mark Gardiner, who himself had replaced Jerry Clay, on bass. After a tour of Japan, they released *Phonophobia*; this was followed by a version of **KLF**'s '3am Eternal'.

In 1993, ENT toured widely, signing to Earache Records the following year. By this time the line-up included Lee Barrett (bass) replacing Bailey, Ali Firouzbakht (lead guitar) and Pig Killer (drums). Together they released *Retro-bution*.

EYC

US POP BAND EYC (AN ACRONYM FOR EXPRESS YOURSELF CLEARLY) FEATURED DAMON BUTLER, DAVE LOEFFLER AND Trey Parker. Butler and Parker met while working as back-up dancers, after meeting Loeffler they began to record demos together and a video clip that could show off their dance moves. After being signed by Gasoline Alley Records, their first single, 'Feelin' Alright' (1993) reached UK number 16 and they won the 1993 *Smash Hits* 'Best Newcomer' award. Their 10-track debut album was released in 1994, and included the club hit, 'Get Some'. The album rose to UK number 14 in the week of its release, before the band set out on a European tour with **East 17**. EYC scored further success with 1994's 'One More Chance'.

FABIAN

US-BORN FABIAN (b. FABIANO FORTE BONAPARTE, 1943) WAS 'DISCOVERED' BY TALENT SCOUTS, PETER DE ANGELIS AND Bob Marucci, in 1957. They contracted him to their Chancellor Records as a tamed **Elvis Presley**. Accompanied by the Four Dates, Fabian's first two singles – 'I'm In Love' and 'Lilly Lou' – were only regional hits, but after a string of television performances and a coast-to-coast tour, he found himself in *Billboard*'s Top 40 with 'I'm A Man'.

Fabian's recording career peaked with 1959's million-selling 'Tiger' and *Hold That Tiger*, but his decline was as rapid as his launch. His first serious miss came with 'About This Thing Called Love' (1960), thereafter he traded his doomed musical career for one in films, such as the 1962 war epic *The Longest Day*.

FABULOUS THUNDERBIRDS

FORMED IN TEXAS, USA, IN 1977. JIMMY VAUGHAN (b. 1951; GUITAR), KIM WILSON (b. 1951; VOCALS/HARMONICA), Keith Ferguson (b. 1946, d. 1997; bass) and Mike Buck (b. 1952; drums) debuted with *The Fabulous Thunderbirds* aka *Girls Go Wild*, containing powerful original songs as well as sympathetic cover versions. Fran Christiana (b. 1951; drums; ex-**Roomful Of Blues**) replaced Mike Buck in 1980, and Preston Hubbard (b. 1953) joined after Ferguson departed. Wilson and Vaughan remained at the helm until Vaughan jumped ship in 1995. The Danny Korchmar-produced *Roll Of The Dice* was the first album with Wilson leading the band and showed the new lead guitarist, Kid Ramos, having a difficult job to fill.

FACES

FORMED FROM UK MOD GROUP THE **SMALL FACES**. RONNIE LANE (b. 1946; BASS), KENNY JONES (b. 1948; DRUMS), IAN McLagan (b. 1945; organ), **Rod Stewart** (b. 1945; vocals) and Ron Wood (b. 1947; guitar) debuted with *First Step*, reflecting their boozy, live appeal; the excellent follow-up, *Long Player*, enhanced this with its strong mix of staunch rock songs. After Stewart's solo career took off in 1971 the Faces effectively became his backing group. Although they enjoyed increasingly commercial appeal with *A Nod's As Good As A Wink ... To A Blind Horse* and a string of memorable good-time singles, there was no doubt that the focus on Stewart unbalanced the unit. Despite further hits with 'Pool Hall Richard', 'You Can Make Me Dance, Sing, Or Anything' and a live album, the band clearly lacked unity. In 1975, Stewart separated from the group. The band unexpectedly reunited for a one-off appearance at the BRIT Awards in 1993.

FAGEN, DONALD

NEW YORKER FAGEN (b. 1948) JOINED WALTER BECKER IN SEVERAL GROUPS. THE DUO THEN FORGED A CAREER AS songwriters and spent several years backing **Jay And The Americans** before forming **Steely Dan**. Steely Dan's music brilliantly combined the thrill of rock with the astuteness of jazz, but their partnership was sundered in 1981.

Fagen re-emerged with *The Nightfly*, which included a version of the **Drifters**' 'Ruby Baby', and the close harmony styled 'Maxine'. In 1990, Fagen was reunited with Becker at New York's Hit Factory studios, signalling the revival of Steely Dan. In 1993, *Kamakiriad* was released, to critical acclaim.

FAIRGROUND ATTRACTION

JAZZ-TINGED ANGLO/SCOTTISH POP BAND: **EDDI READER** (b. 1959; VOCALS), MARK NEVIN (GUITAR), SIMON EDWARDS (guitaron) and Roy Dodds (drums). Reader first linked with Nevin for the Compact Organisation sampler *The Compact Composers*, singing on two of his songs. In 1985, they built Fairground Attraction around his songs, recruiting Edwards and Dodds.

Signed to RCA Records, they set about recording a debut album, as the gentle skiffle of 'Perfect' topped the UK charts in 1988. They subsequently won Best Single and Best Album categories at the BRIT Awards. The group's promise was cut short when the band split, and Reader went on to acting and a solo career, releasing her debut album, *Mir Mama*, in 1992.

FAIRPORT CONVENTION

UK BAND FORMED IN 1967 AROUND IAIN MATTHEWS (b. IAN MATTHEWS MACDONALD, 1946; VOCALS), JUDY DYBLE (b. 1949; vocals), Ashley Hutchings (b. 1945; bass), **Richard Thompson** (b. 1949; guitar/vocals), Simon Nicol (b. 1950; guitar/vocals) and Martin Lamble (b. 1949, d. 1969; drums). Their self-titled debut album was a cult favourite, but sold poorly. When Dyble departed, **Sandy Denny** (b. Alexandra Denny, 1948, d. 1978) joined, bringing a traditional folk-feel to their work which began to appear on the superlative *What We Did On Our Holidays*. This contained some of their finest songs, but Matthews left soon after its release, unhappy with the direction. Tragedy struck a few months later when Lamble and their friend Jeannie Franklyn were killed in a road accident.

Unhalfbricking, although not as strong as the former, contained two excellent readings of **Bob Dylan**'s 'Percy's Song' and 'Si Tu Dois Partir' (If You Gotta Go, Go Now). The album charted, as did the latter Dylan number. The next album was astonishing – they played jigs and reels, and completed all 27 verses of the traditional 'Tam Lin', featuring new members Dave Swarbrick (b. 1947; violin), and Dave Mattacks (b. 1948; drums). The subsequent *Liege And Lief* was a milestone; they had created British folk rock in spectacular style. This change created internal problems and Hutchings left to form **Steeleye Span** and Denny departed to form Fotheringay. Dave Pegg (bass) joined and Swarbrick became lead vocalist. They wrote much of the next two albums' material before Thompson left. *Full House*, the first all-male Fairport album, was instrumentally strong with extended tracks like 'Sloth'. The concept album, *Babbacombe Lee*, although critically welcomed, failed to sell and Simon Nicol left to form the **Albion Country Band** with Hutchings.

Sandy Denny rejoined, as did Dave Mattacks (twice), but by the end of the 70s the name was put to rest. Since their swansong in 1979, an annual reunion has taken place and is now a major event on the folk calendar. The band have no idea which ex-members will turn up! They have also continued to release albums. Ric Sanders took over from Swarbrick in 1985 and *Gladys Leap* featured Simon Nicol back on lead vocals.

FABIAN
Albums
Hold That Tiger (Chancellor 1959)★★
➧ p.361 for full listings
Influences
Elvis Presley ➧ p.265
Further References
Films: *Hound Dog Man* (1959)
Dr Goldfoot And The Girl Bomb (1966)
American Pop (1981)

FABULOUS THUNDERBIRDS
Albums
The Fabulous Thunderbirds aka *Girls Go Wild* (Chrysalis 1979)★★★★
➧ p.361 for full listings
Connections
Roomful Of Blues ➧ p.282
Further References
Video: *Tuff Enuff* (Hendring Video 1990)

FACES
Albums
Long Player (Warners 1971)★★★★
➧ p.361 for full listings
Connections
Small Faces ➧ p.300
Rod Stewart ➧ p.310

FAGEN, DONALD
Albums
Kamakiriad (Reprise 1993)★★★★
➧ p.362 for full listings
Connections
Jay And The Americans ➧ p.198
Steely Dan ➧ p.308
Four Freshman ➧ p.150
Influences
Drifters ➧ p.126

FAIRGROUND ATTRACTION
Albums
First Of A Million Kisses (RCA 1988)★★★
➧ p.362 for full listings

FAIRPORT CONVENTION
Albums
What We Did On Our Holidays (Island 1969)★★★★★
Jewel In The Crown (Woodworm 1995)★★★★
➧ p.362 for full listings
Connections
Strawbs ➧ p.312
Steeleye Span ➧ p.308
Albion Country Band ➧p.12
Influences
Jefferson Airplane ➧ p.198
Byrds ➧ p.77
Bob Dylan ➧ p.128
Further References
Books: *Meet On The Ledge*, Patrick Humphries
The Woodworm Era: The Story Of Today's Fairport Convention, Fred Redwood and Martin Woodward

FAIRWEATHER-LOW, ANDY
Albums
Spider Jivin' (A&M 1974)★★★
➧ p.362 for full listings
Collaborators
Chris Rea ➧ p.273
George Harrison ➧ p.176
Eric Clapton ➧ p.92
Connections
Amen Corner ➧ p.16
Fairweather ➧ p.142

FAITH, ADAM
Albums
From Adam With Love (Parlophone 1962)★★★
➧ p.362 for full listings
Collaborators
Lonnie Donegan ➧ p.122
Leo Sayer ➧ p.289
Connections
Chris Andrews ➧ p.18
Further References
Films: *Beat Girl* (1960)
What A Whopper (1961)
Book: *Acts Of Faith*, Adam Faith

FAITH NO MORE
Albums
Introduce Yourself (Slash 1987)★★★★
The Real Thing (London 1989)★★★
➧ p.362 for full listings
Connections
Bad Brains ➧ p.28
Further References
Book: *Faith No More: The Real Story*, Steffan Chirazi

FAITHFULL, MARIANNE
Albums
Broken English (Island 1979)★★★★
➧ p.362 for full listings
Influences
Rolling Stones ➧ p.281
Further References
Book: *Faithfull*, Marianne Faithfull and David Dalton

FALL
Albums
Live At The Witch Trials (Step Forward 1979)★★★★
This Nation's Saving Grace (Beggars Banquet 1985)★★★★
➧ p.362 for full listings

Influences
Kinks ➧ p.207
Further References
Book: *Paintwork: A Portrait Of The Fall*, Brian Edge

FAIRWEATHER-LOW, ANDY

WELSH GUITARIST AND SINGER WHO FORMED POP/SOUL BAND **AMEN CORNER**. IT WAS FAIRWEATHER-LOW'S (b. 1950) intention to play guitar but as they had too many guitarists and no vocalists, he took on singing duties. The band enjoyed a run of hit singles and when they split, Fairweather-Low and the brass section formed **Fairweather**. They signed to RCA Records' new progressive label Neon and immediately blew their underground 'cool' by having a hit with 'Natural Sinner', however after a couple of less successful singles they too broke up.

Fairweather-Low returned in 1975 with an album and hit single 'Reggae Tune'. Another memorable big hit, 'Wide Eyed And Legless', highlighted his characteristic voice. Subsequent releases failed to chart and he spent more time playing on sessions and live gigs. In 1990, Fairweather-Low toured with **Chris Rea** and in 1991 with **George Harrison** and **Eric Clapton**.

FAITH, ADAM

LONDON-BORN **ADAM FAITH** (b. TERENCE NELHAMS, 1940) REACHED THE UK CHART 24 TIMES IN SEVEN years. His career opened with two chart toppers, 'What Do You Want' and 'Poor Me'. In a short period of time he appeared in three films and was interviewed on the BBC's *Face To Face*. The following year, still enjoying chart hits, he appeared in the film *Mix Me A Person*.

In the beat era, Faith was assigned the Roulettes (featuring **Russ Ballard**) and songwriter **Chris Andrews** fed him a brief second wave of infectious beat-group hits most notably 'The First Time'. In the mid-60s, he gave up singing and went into repertory theatre acting. Faith has produced records for Roger Daltrey and **Lonnie Donegan** and managed **Leo Sayer**; he still works on the perimeter of the music world, and released an album in 1993.

FAITH NO MORE

FORMED IN SAN FRANCISCO IN 1980, FAITH NO MORE WERE AMONG THE FIRST TO EXPERIMENT WITH THE fusion of funk, thrash and hardcore styles. The band – Jim Martin (b. 1961; guitar), Roddy Böttum (b. 1963; keyboards), Bill Gould (b. 1963; bass), Mike Bordin (b. 1962; drums) and Chuck Moseley (vocals) – recorded a low-budget, self-titled debut on the independent Mordam label, followed by the groundbreaking *Introduce Yourself* on Slash. It encompassed a variety of styles and was well received by the critics; however, internal disputes led to the firing of Moseley on the eve of widespread press coverage. Moseley went on to gig temporarily with **Bad Brains**, before putting his own band, Cement, together. His replacement, Mike Patton (b. 1968), was even more flamboyant and an accomplished singer. *The Real Thing* was a runaway success, with the single 'Epic' denting the UK Top 20. *Live At The Brixton Academy* was released as a stopgap, while the band toured for nearly three years.

Patton temporarily defected, but the group returned with *Angel Dust* (US Top 10). However, in 1994, the ever-volatile line-up changed again as Jim Martin was ousted in favour of Trey Spruance. *Album Of The Year* received a mixed reaction, including one or two scathing reviews. They disbanded in 1998.

FAITHFULL, MARIANNE

LONDON-BORN FAITHFULL (b. 1946) BEGAN HER SINGING CAREER AFTER BEING INTRODUCED INTO THE **ROLLING Stones**' circle; a plaintive Jagger/Richard song, 'As Tears Go By' (1964), became her debut single. It was the first of four UK Top 10 hits. Her albums reflected an impressive balance between folk and rock, but her doomed relationship with Mick Jagger undermined her ambitions as a performer. Faithfull also pursued thespian aspirations, but withdrew from the public eye following a failed suicide attempt. She re-emerged in 1976 with *Dreamin' My Dreams*, but a further period of seclusion followed; she rekindled her career three years later with the impressive *Broken English*. Faithfull's later releases followed a similar pattern, but nowhere was the trauma of her personal life more evident than on *Blazing Away*, a live album on which the singer reclaimed songs from her past. *A Secret Life* was a return to the brooding atmosphere of *Broken English*, but, although her voice was still captivating, the songs were generally uninspiring.

FALL

UK BAND FORMED BY THE MERCURIAL MARK E. SMITH (b. 1957) IN 1977. THE FIRST LINE-UP – UNA BAINES (ELECTRIC piano), Martin Bramah (guitar), Karl Burns (drums) and Tony Friel (bass) – debuted with 'Bingo Master's Breakout', a good example of Smith's surreal vision. With the independent label Step Forward, they recorded three singles, including the savage 'Fiery Jack', plus *Live At The Witch Trials*. In 1980, they signed to Rough Trade Records and released 'How I Wrote Elastic Man' and 'Totally Wired'. A series of line-up changes saw the arrival and subsequent departures of Marc Riley, Mike Leigh, Martin Bramah, Yvonne Pawlett and Craig Scanlon.

The Fall's convoluted career produced a series of discordant, yet frequently fascinating albums, from the early menace of *Dragnet* to the chaotic *Hex Enduction Hour*. An apparent change in the group's image and philosophy occurred during 1983 with the arrival of Smith's future wife Brix. She first appeared on *Perverted By Language*, but her presence was felt more keenly when the group unexpectedly emerged as a potential chart act with 'There's A Ghost In My House' and later the **Kinks**' 'Victoria'. On later albums such as *This Nation's Saving Grace* and *The Frenz Experiment*, they lost none of their earlier charm, but the work seemed more focused and accessible. Drummer Simon Wolstenscroft and Marcia Schofield joined, Brix left as did Schofield.

The band's 90s output continued successfully, helped by their hugely committed following. Brix returned to guest on *Cerebral Caustic*; meanwhile Smith had recorded four consistently strong albums. *In The City* (a live set) was followed by Smith's thirtieth album, *Levitate*, which experimented with jungle and hip hop.

FAME, GEORGIE

IT TOOK A NUMBER OF YEARS BEFORE FAME (b. CLIVE POWELL, 1943) AND HIS BAND THE BLUE FLAMES HAD commercial success, although he was a major force in the popularizing of early R&B, bluebeat and ska at London's Flamingo club. *Rhythm And Blues At The Flamingo* was released in 1963, followed by the UK number 1, 'Yeh Yeh'. He continued with another eleven hits, including the UK chart toppers, 'Get Away' and 'The Ballad Of Bonnie And Clyde' (his only US Top 10 single). After 'Sunny' and 'Sitting In The Park' he veered towards straight pop. While his albums showed a more progressive style his singles became lightweight and he teamed up with **Alan Price** to produce some catchy pop songs.

In recent times, Fame has toured with **Van Morrison** as keyboard player. In the early 90s, Fame had recorded a new album *Cool Cat Blues*; favourable reviews and regular concert appearances indicated a new phase. A reggae reworking of 'Yeh Yeh' and a graceful version of Carmichael's 'Georgia' are but two outstanding tracks. Fame followed this with *The Blues And Me*, an album of a similarly high standard.

FAMILY

ONE OF BRITAIN'S LEADING PROGRESSIVE ROCK BANDS OF THE LATE 60S AND EARLY 70S, LED BY THE VOCALLY demonic **Roger Chapman** (b. 1942) with Rick Grech (b. 1946, d. 1990; violin/bass), Charlie Whitney (b. 1944; guitar), Rob Townsend (b. 1947; drums)

and Jim King (flute/saxophone). Their first album was given extensive exposure on **John Peel**'s BBC radio programme and became a cult record.

Following the release of their most successful album, *Family Entertainment*, Family experienced an ever-changing line-up: Grech departed, replaced by John Weider, before John Wetton in 1971 and Jim Cregan in 1972. Poli Palmer (b. John Palmer, 1943) superseded Jim King in 1969 who was ultimately replaced by Tony Ashton in 1972. Throughout this turmoil they had singles success with 'No Mules Fool', 'Strange Band', 'In My Own Time' and the infectious 'Burlesque'. Family disintegrated after their disappointing swansong *It's Only A Movie*.

FANNY

US BAND FORMED IN 1970 AND TOUTED AS THE 'FIRST ALL-FEMALE ROCK GROUP'. JEAN MILLINGTON (b. 1950; BASS/vocals), June Millington (b. 1949; guitar/vocals), Alice de Buhr (b. 1950; drums) and Nickey Barclay (b. 1951; keyboards) blended driving hard rock and rock 'n' roll. In 1974, June Millington and de Buhr were replaced by Patti Quatro (sister of **Suzi Quatro**) and Brie Brandt. None of their albums charted in the UK and their US sales were minimal.

Charity Ball was their best work and the title song reached the US Top 40. Ironically it was as the band were fragmenting in 1975 that they scored their biggest hit, 'Butter Boy'.

FARM

FORMED IN ENGLAND IN 1983 BY PETER HOOTON (b. 1962; VOCALS), STEVE GRIMES (b. 1962; GUITAR), PHILLIP Strongman (bass) and Andy McVann (drums). By 1984 John Melvin, George Maher, Steve Levy and Anthony Evans had joined, bringing with them a brass section and adding a northern soul influence to the Farm's pop sound. Two years on, Roy Boulter (b. 1964), Keith Mullen (guitar) and Carl Hunter (b. 1965; bass) joined; the horn section departed and Ben Leach (b. 1969; keyboards) joined. After the flop of their fourth independent release, 'Body And Soul', the Farm started their own Produce label and had a fortuitous meeting with dance producer Terry Farley. Consequently, a cover version of the **Monkees**' 'Stepping Stone' was augmented with club beats and samples. 'Groovy Train' and 'All Together Now' swept the band into the UK Top 10, followed in 1991 by their debut album, *Spartacus*, which entered the UK charts at number 1.

Unfortunately, *Love See No Colour* was bland and colourless and failed to break the UK Top 75. In 1994, they retreated to a more orthodox guitar/bass/drums approach for *Hullabaloo*.

FARLOWE, CHRIS

FARLOWE (b. JOHN HENRY DEIGHTON, 1940) STARTED OUT DURING THE 50S SKIFFLE BOOM WHEN HIS JOHN HENRY Skiffle Group won the all-England championship. He then formed the original Thunderbirds, which remained semi-professional until 1962. He made his recording debut that year with the pop-oriented 'Air Travel', but failed to secure commercial success until 1966 when his version of the **Rolling Stones**' 'Out Of Time' (produced by Mick Jagger) reached UK number 1. Several minor hits followed, as well as a brace of pop/soul albums.

Farlowe and the Thunderbirds remained one of the country's most impressive R&B acts, although session musicians were increasingly employed for recording purposes. In 1970, the singer founded a new group, the Hill. Their sole album, *From Here To Mama Rosa*, was not a commercial success and Farlowe joined ex-colleague Dave Greenslade in Colosseum. This powerful group disbanded in 1971, and Farlowe retired from rock. He re-emerged in 1975 with *The Chris Farlowe Band, Live*, but failed to find a satisfactory niche for his powerful, gritty voice.

FAT BOYS

NEW YORK TRIO ORIGINALLY KNOWN AS THE DISCO 3. DARREN 'THE HUMAN BEATBOX/BUFF LOVE' ROBINSON

(b. 1968, d. 1995), Mark 'Prince Markie Dee' Morales, and Damon 'Kool Rockski' Wimbley were discovered by Charlie Stetler (later manager of **Dr. Dre** and Ed Lover).

Crushin' is arguably their best album, yielding a major hit with the **Beach Boys** on 'Wipe Out' (1987). One year and one album later they scored with another collaboration, this time with **Chubby Checker** on 'The Twist (Yo' Twist)'. It peaked at UK number 2, the highest position at the time for a rap record. The track 'Are You Ready For Freddy', on *Coming Back Hard Again*, was used as a *Nightmare On Elm Street* theme tune. They also starred in the movie *Disorderlies*.

They were the only rappers at Live Aid and appeared with Checker at Nelson Mandela's 70th Birthday Party. The decade closed with the release of the disappointing *On And On*, overshadowed by its 'concept' of being a 'rap-pera', and offering a lukewarm adaptation of gangsta concerns. Prince Markie Dee went solo, he also produced and wrote for **Mary J. Blige** and El **DeBarge** amongst others.

FATIMA MANSIONS

FORMED IN 1989 BY SINGER-SONGWRITER CATHAL COUGHLAN FROM CORK, EIRE. FATIMA MANSIONS WERE taken on by Kitchenware Records to record *Against Nature*, it achieved almost universal critical acclaim. Andreas O'Gruama's guitar contributed richly to the final results, although the band was primarily a vehicle for Coughlan.

Bugs Fucking Bunny was dropped as the title of the second album, in favour of *Viva Dead Ponies*. This time Coughlan's lyrics were totally submerged in vitriolic observations on the absurdities of living in the UK. Further paranoia, bile and doses of his full-bodied vocals were poured into the mini-album *Bertie's Brochures* (1991). After a short break, Coughlan returned with the release of *Lost In The Former West*; he also recorded two self-indulgent albums under the banner of Bubonique, before releasing a solo album in 1996.

FAME, GEORGIE
Album
Rhythm And Blues At The Flamingo (Columbia 1963)★★★★
Cool Cat Blues (Go Jazz 1991)★★★★
➽ p.362 for full listings
Collaborators
Alan Price ➽ p.266
Van Morrison ➽ p.238

FAMILY
Albums
Music In A Doll's House (Reprise 1968)★★★★
Bandstand (Reprise 1972)★★★★
➽ p.362 for full listings
Influences
John Peel ➽ p.258

FANNY
Albums
Fanny (Reprise 1970)★★★
➽ p.362 for full listings
Connections
Pleasure Seekers

FARM
Albums
Spartacus (Produce 1991)★★★★
➽ p.362 for full listings
Influences
Monkees ➽ p.236
Further References
Video: *Groovy Times* (Produce 1991)

FARLOWE, CHRIS
Albums
Chris Farlowe And The Thunderbirds aka Stormy Monday (Columbia 1966)★★★
Lonesome Road (Indigo 1995)★★★
➽ p.362 for full listings
Connections
Thunderbirds
Influences
Rolling Stones ➽ p.281

FAT BOYS
Albums
The Fat Boys Are Back! (Sutra 1985)★★★
Coming Back Hard Again (Tin Pan Apple/Polydor 1988)★★★
➽ p.362 for full listings
Collaborators
Chubby Checker ➽ p.88
Connections
Mary J. Blige ➽ p.53
Influences
Beach Boys ➽ p.36

FATIMA MANSIONS
Albums
Viva Dead Ponies (Kitchenware 1990)★★★★
➽ p.362 for full listings
Further References
Video: *Y'Knaa* (1994)

FAUST
Albums
So Far (Polydor 1972)★★★
The Faust Tapes (Virgin 1973)★★★
➽ p.362 for full listings

FELICIANO, JOSÉ
Albums
Feliciano! (RCA 1968)★★★★
El Americano (Polygram 1996)★★★
➽ p.362 for full listings
Connections
Steve Cropper ➽ p.105
Influences
Doors ➽ p.123
Bee Gees ➽ p.41

FELT
Albums
Forever Breathes The Lonely Word (Creation 1986)★★★★
➽ p.362 for full listings

FENDER, LEO
Further References
Books: *The Fender Book: A Complete History Of Fender Electric Guitars*, Tony Bacon and Paul Day
Fender Custom Shop Guitar Gallery, Richard Smith
➽ p.362 for full listings

FERRY, BRYAN
Albums
The Bride Stripped Bare (Polydor 1978)★★★★
➽ p.362 for full listings

FAUST

FORMED IN GERMANY IN 1971. WERNER DIERMAIER, JEAN HERVE PERON, RUDOLF SOSNA, HANS JOACHIM IRMLER, Gunther Wusthoff and Armulf Meifert released *Faust*, a conscious attempt to forge a new western 'rock' music wherein fragments of sound were spliced together to create a radical collage. Released in a clear sleeve and clear vinyl, the album was viewed as an experimental masterpiece. *So Far* proved less obtuse, and the group secured a high-profile recording deal with Virgin. *The Faust Tapes* retailed at the price of a single (then 49p); this inspired marketing ploy generated considerable interest, but Faust's music remained non-mainstream. Despite line-up changes, Faust remained active throughout the 70s and 80s. *Rien* was a return to ambient noise.

FELICIANO, JOSÉ

FELICIANO (b. 1945; GUITAR/ACCORDION) WAS BORN BLIND. HE STARTED OUT IN 1962, PERFORMING A MIXTURE of Spanish and American material in the folk clubs and coffee houses of Greenwich Village. Signed to RCA, he released 'Everybody Do The Click' before recording an impressive debut album in 1964. Its impassioned arrangements of recent hits were continued on *Feliciano!*. His first hit was a Latin treatment of the **Doors**' 'Light My Fire'.

Feliciano's version of the **Bee Gees**' 'The Sun Will Shine' was a minor UK hit, but the 1970s saw RCA concentrating on Feliciano's Spanish-language material, promoted throughout Latin America. Feliciano continued to record English-language songs, notably on *Compartments*.

When **Motown** set up its own Latin music label in 1981 Feliciano headed the roster, recording *Romance In The Night* as well as Grammy-winning Latin albums. In 1987, he signed a three-pronged deal with EMI to record classical guitar music and English pop as well as further Spanish-language recordings. He also pursued his jazz interests. After joining Polygram Latino records, he released *El Americano*.

FELT

ENGLISH POP OUTFIT FORMED IN 1980 BY LAWRENCE HAYWARD (VOCALS/GUITAR). EARLY COLLABORATORS included Maurice Deebank (guitar), Nick Gilbert (bass) and Tony Race (drums). Gary Ainge replaced Race and Gilbert left, replaced by Mick Lloyd. Martin Duffy (organ) joined for *Ignite The Seven Cannons*.

Cult status arrived with 'Penelope Tree' and they were afforded critical respect, though little in the way of commercial recognition. The nearest they came was 1985's 'Primitive Painters', and later that year they signed to Creation Records. Their stay at Creation saw high points in *Forever Breathes The Lonely Word* and *Poem Of The River*. Felt bowed out with *Me And A Monkey On The Moon*, having achieved their stated task of surviving 10 years, 10 singles and 10 albums.

FENDER, LEO

IN THE MID-40S, CALIFORNIAN-BORN FENDER (b. 1909, d. 1991) BEGAN WORK WITH 'DOC' KAUFFMAN, PRODUCING guitar amplifiers. He developed a new smaller pick-up and designed a solid-body guitar based on the Hawaiian steel, with which to demonstrate it. Local musicians were most intrigued with the guitar, and Fender decided to concentrate his efforts in that direction. In 1946, he left Kauffman and formed the Fender Electrical Instrument Company. In 1948, Fender launched the Broadcaster (later called the Telecaster) which remained virtually unchanged for the next 30 years, although there were a few variations such as the Esquire (1954), the Thinkline (1969), the Deluxe (1972) and the Custom (1972). Fender's next major instrument was the Stratocaster, developed in 1953. Like the Telecaster, the Stratocaster was virtually untouched in design over the next few decades.

In 1955, Fender became ill and in 1965, convinced that he had little time to live, The Fender Electrical Instrument Company was sold to CBS for $13 million – shortly afterwards Fender made a complete recovery. Later he formed the CLF Research Company before returning to consultancy for Music Man guitars. In the 80s, he formed G&L (George and Leo) Guitars with long-time associate George Fullerton. They continued to make popular instruments, although names like the F100-1 series were less appealing than their forebears.

Leo Fender died in 1991 aged 82. The Fender name is also attached to the Musicmaster (1956), the Jazzmaster (1958), the Jaguar (1961), and the Starcaster (1975). He also moved into electric basses in 1951 with the Precision and then the Jazz Bass (1960), Bass VI (1962) and the Telecaster Bass (1968).

FERRY, BRYAN

UK VOCALIST FERRY (b. 1945) APPEARED WITH A NUMBER OF LOCAL GROUPS BEFORE FORMING **ROXY Music.** During their rise to fame, he plotted a parallel solo career, beginning in 1973 with *These Foolish Things*, an album of favourite cover versions. It received mixed reviews but paved the way for similar works including **David Bowie**'s *Pin Ups* and **John Lennon**'s *Rock 'N' Roll*. Ferry continued the cover game with the less-impressive *Another Time Another Place*. A gutsy revival of Dobie Gray's 'The In Crowd' brought him a UK Top 20 hit.

By 1976, Ferry had switched to R&B covers on *Let's Stick Together*. It was not until 1977 that he finally wrote an album's worth of songs for a solo work. *In Your Mind* spawned a couple of minor hits with 'This Is Tomorrow' and 'Tokyo Joe'. This was followed by the highly accomplished *The Bride Stripped Bare*. It was another seven years before Ferry recorded solo again. The comeback, *Boys And Girls*, was stylistically similar to his work with Roxy Music and included the hits 'Slave To Love' and 'Don't Stop The Dance'. The album *Bête Noire* was a notable hit indicating that Ferry's muse was still very much alive.

FIELDS OF THE NEPHILIM

UK ROCK GROUP FORMED IN 1983. CARL MCCOY (VOCALS), TONY PETTITT (BASS), PETER YATES (GUITAR) and the Wright brothers, Nod (b. Alexander; drums) and Paul (guitar) had two major UK independent hit singles with 'Preacher Man' and 'Blue Water' and *Dawn Razor* skimmed the UK album chart. *The Nephilim* (UK number 14) announced the group's arrival as one of the principal rock acts of the day. They also broached the national singles chart with 'Moonchild' (independent chart number 1), 'Psychonaut' and 'Summerland (Dreamed)'. In 1991, McCoy left taking the 'Fields Of The Nephilim' name with him.

FIFTH DIMENSION

ORIGINALLY KNOWN AS THE VERSATILES AND LATER AS THE VOCALS, MARILYN McCOO (b. 1943), FLORENCE LaRue (b. 1944), Billy Davis Jnr (b. 1940), Lamont McLemore (b. 1940) and Ron Townsend (b. 1941) were a soul-influenced harmony group, based in Los Angeles. Ebullient pop singles, including 'Go Where You Wanna', 'Up Up And Away' and 'Carpet Man', established their fresh voices. After two albums, they turned to **Laura Nyro**, whose beautiful soul-styled songs continued their success and introduced the group to the R&B charts. In 1971, they reached US number 2 with the haunting 'One Less Bell To Answer'.

In 1976, McCoo and Davis left for a successful career both as a duo and as solo artists. They had a US number 1 duet in 1976 with 'You Don't Have To Be A Star', followed in 1977 by their last Top 20 hit, 'Your Love'.

FINE YOUNG CANNIBALS

ENGLISH POP TRIO FORMED IN 1983. EX-**BEAT** MEMBERS ANDY COX (b. 1960; GUITAR) AND DAVID STEELE (b. 1960; bass/keyboards) recruited Roland Gift (b. 1961; vocals) and were quickly picked up by London Records after a video screening on the UK music television show *The Tube*. 'Johnny Come Home', dominated by Gift's sparse and yearning vocals, reached the UK Top 10 and defined the band's sound. The following 'Blue' set out an early political agenda, attacking the Conservative Government.

After their debut album reached UK number 11, the first of a series of distinctive cover versions emerged with 'Suspicious Minds', then a radical rendition of 'Ever Fallen In Love'. The band's biggest hit to date was the rock/dance fusion of 'She Drives Me Crazy'. Their second album topped the US and UK charts and spawned five singles; 'Good Thing' was the most successful, reaching US number 1. In 1990, they won Best British Group and Best Album categories at the BRIT Awards, but felt compelled to return them for political reasons. The band's 1996 compilation album was well received.

FIREBALLS

FORMED IN 1957 IN NEW MEXICO, USA. GEORGE TOMSCO (b. 1940; GUITAR), CHUCK THARP (b. 1941; VOCALS), DANNY Trammell (b. 1940; rhythm guitar), Stan Lark (b. 1940; bass) and Eric Budd (b. 1938; drums) placed 11 singles in the US charts between 1959 and 1969, beginning with the instrumental 'Torquay'. After two other minor chart singles, Tharp left; he was replaced by Jimmy Gilmer (b. 1940). In 1962, the Fireballs recorded *Torquay*, after which Budd was replaced by Doug Roberts. In early 1963, now billed as Jimmy Gilmer And The Fireballs, they recorded 'Sugar Shack', using an unusual keyboard called a Solovox to give the record a distinctive sound. The result was one of the best-selling hits of 1963; an album of the same title also charted. Despite subsequent singles and albums, the group was unable to capitalize on that success. Their version of **Tom Paxton**'s 'Bottle Of Wine' (1968) reached US number 9 and was followed by three minor chart singles, but the Fireballs' time had clearly expired, and they disbanded.

FIREFALL

SECOND-GENERATION US COUNTRY ROCK BAND. THE INITIAL LINE-UP – EX-**FLYING BURRITO BROTHERS** RICK Roberts (b. 1950; guitar/vocals) and Michael Clarke (b. Michael Dick, 1943; drums), Mark Andes (b. 1948; bass), Jock Bartley (guitar/vocals), David Muse (keyboards/saxophone/flute) and Larry Burnett (guitar/vocals) – produced three strong-selling albums. *Luna Sea* contained a further major US hit with the memorable 'Just Remember I Love You'. *Elan* featured the sparkling hit 'Strange Way' which featured a breathy jazz-influenced flute solo. They continued to produce sharply engineered albums with Muse adding other instruments, giving a new flavour to a guitar-dominated style.

Connections
Roxy Music ➽ p.283
David Bowie ➽ p.64
John Lennon ➽ p.214
Further References
Book: *Roxy Music: Style With Substance – Roxy's First Ten Years*, Johnny Rogan

FIELDS OF THE NEPHILIM
Albums
The Nephilim (Situation 2 1988)★★★
➽ p.362 for full listings
Further References
Videos: *Morphic Fields* (Situation 2 1989)
Revelations (Beggars Banquet 1993)

FIFTH DIMENSION
Albums
Love's Lines, Angles And Rhymes (Bell 1971)★★★
➽ p.362 for full listings
Collaborators
Laura Nyro ➽ p.249

FINE YOUNG CANNIBALS
Albums
Fine Young Cannibals (London 1985)★★★
The Raw And The Cooked (London 1989)★★★★
➽ p.362 for full listings

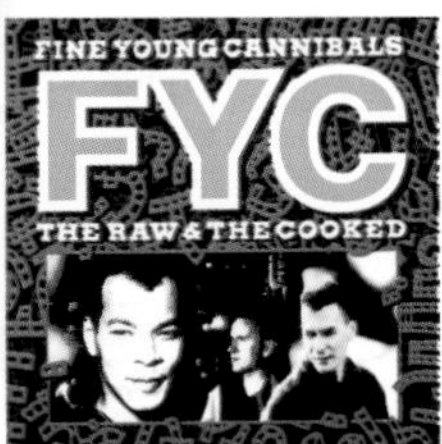

Connections
Beat ➽ p.37
Influences
Buzzcocks ➽ p.76
Further References
Video: *The Finest* (London 1996)
Book: *The Sweet And The Sour: The Fine Young Cannibals' Story*, Brian Edge

FIREBALLS
Albums
The Fireballs (Top Rank 1960)★★★
Sensational (1963)★★★
➽ p.362 for full listings
Connections
Jimmy Gilmer And The Fireballs
Influences
Tom Paxton ➽ p.257

FIREFALL
Albums
Firefall (Atlantic 1976)★★★
Elan (Atlantic 1978)★★★
➽ p.362 for full listings
Connections
Flying Burrito Brothers ➽ p.148

FIREHOSE
Albums
Ragin', Full-On (SST 1987)★★★
Flyin' The Flannel (Columbia 1991)★★★
➽ p.362 for full listings
Connections
Minutemen

FIRESIGN THEATRE
Albums
How Can You Be In Two Places At Once When You're Not Anywhere At All (Columbia 1969)★★★★
Don't Crush That Dwarf, Hand Me The Pliers (Columbia 1970)★★★★
➽ p.362 for full listings
Influences
Byrds ➽ p.77

FISCHER, LARRY 'WILD MAN'
Albums
Larry Fischer Sings Popular Songs (Birdman 1997)★★★
➽ p.362 for full listings
Connections
Frank Zappa ➽ p.348
Mothers of Invention ➽ p.239

FISH
Albums
Acoustic Session (Dick Bros 1994)★★★
Sunsets On Empire (Dick Bros 1997)★★★★
➽ p.362 for full listings
Collaborators
Peter Hammill ➽ p.173
Connections
Marillion ➽ p.224
Influences
Kinks ➽ p.207
Moody Blues ➽ p.237

FISHBONE
Albums
Truth And Soul (Columbia 1988)★★★★
The Reality Of My Surroundings (Columbia 1991)★★★
➽ p.362 for full listings
Connections
Jungle Brothers

FIVE STAR
Albums
Silk And Steel (Tent 1986)★★★
➽ p.362 for full listings

FLACK, ROBERTA
Albums
First Take (Atlantic 1970)★★★★
Roberta (Atlantic/East West 1995)★★★
➽ p.362 for full listings
Collaborators
Donny Hathaway
Further References
Book: *Roberta Flack: Sound Of Velvet Melting*, Linda Jacobs

FIREHOSE

PROPULSIVE US HARDCORE TRIO FORMED IN 1985.

Mike Watt (vocals/bass) and George Hurley (drums) recruited eD fROMOHIO (b. Ed Crawford), and debuted with the impressive *Ragin', Full-On*. *If'n* and *FROMOHIO* revealed a group that, although bedevilled by inconsistency, was nonetheless capable of inventive, exciting music. The group's variety argued against commercial fortune, but the band were still signed by Columbia Records in 1991; they released the slightly more disciplined *Flyin' The Flannel* that year. Following disappointing critical and commercial response to *Mr Machinery Operator*, the group split in 1995.

FIRESIGN THEATRE

SATIRICAL/COMEDY GROUP FORMED IN LOS ANGELES, USA IN 1967. THE SURREAL HUMOUR OF PHILIP PROCTOR,

Peter Bergman, David Ossman and Phil Austin found favour with the late 60s 'underground' audience. Produced by Gary Usher, they were also used to provide the spectacular gunshot effects on 'Draft Morning' on the **Byrds**' *Notorious Byrd Brothers*. A series of adventurous albums, included *How Can You Be In Two Places At Once When You're Not Anywhere At All*, *Don't Crush That Dwarf, Hand Me The Pliers* and *I Think We're All Bozos On This Bus*, while *Dear Friends* included several highlights from their radio shows. Their prolific output slackened towards the end of the decade, but the Firesign Theatre subsequently found a sympathetic haven at Rhino Records. Another series of excellent albums ensued, before the group began transferring their routines to video.

FISCHER, LARRY 'WILD MAN'

FISCHER (b. 1945) WAS A PROMINENT FIXTURE ON LOS ANGELES' SUNSET STRIP DURING THE LATE 60S. HE BECAME

associated with **Frank Zappa** who produced his debut, *An Evening With Wild Man Fischer*. Some critics deemed it voyeuristic, while others proclaimed it a work of art and a valid documentary. Fischer made several live appearances with the **Mothers Of Invention**, but it was seven years before he recorded again. After completing a single advertising the Rhino Records store, he was signed to their fledgling label. Three further albums continued the disquieting atmosphere of that first release.

FISH

SCOTTISH-BORN FISH (b. DEREK WILLIAM DICK, 1958) SANG FOR THE STONE DOME BEFORE AUDITIONING FOR

Marillion by writing lyrics for their instrumental 'The Web'. Marillion went from strength to strength, with Fish structuring a series of elaborately linked concept albums, which were still capable of yielding hit singles.

After the hugely successful *Clutching At Straws*, Fish began to disagree with the band about their musical direction and in 1988 he went solo. His debut album utilized stylistically diverse elements such as folk tunes and brass arrangements, but he also retained a mixture of hard rockers and ballads. In 1989, he worked with **Peter Hammill** on his opera, *The Fall Of The House Of Usher*, but they clashed and Fish was replaced on the project by Andy Bell. His 1993 release was a desultory album of cover versions, including the **Kinks**' 'Apeman' and the **Moody Blues**' 'Question'. His 1997 album put him back in favour.

FISHBONE

FUNK METAL HYBRID FROM LOS ANGELES, USA. CHRIS 'MAVERICK MEAT' DOWD (b. 1965; TROMBONE/KEYBOARDS),

'Dirty' Walter Kibby (b. 1964; trumpet/horn/vocals), 'Big' John Bigham (b. 1969), Kendall Jones (b. guitar), Philip 'Fish' Fisher (b. 1967; drums), John Fisher (b. 1965; bass) and Angelo Moore (b. 1965; lead vocals) debuted with a conventional metal mini-album before the more adventurous *Truth And Soul*.

Subsequent recordings saw Fishbone working with rap artists, although *The Reality Of My Own Surroundings* had more in common with the hard-spined funk of Sly Stone. 'Fight The Youth' and 'Sunless Saturday' demonstrated a serious angle with socio-political, anti-racist and anti-drug lyrics, alongside their lighter more humorous songs.

Transatlantic commercial breakthrough offered itself with *Monkey*, but media coverage about Jones, who had left to join a religious cult, was damaging. Appearing on 1993's Lollapalooza tour failed to restore the group's diminishing reputation, as did a lacklustre 1996 album.

FIVE STAR

BRITISH POP ACT FORMED BY THE FIVE SIBLINGS OF THE PEARSON FAMILY: DENIECE (b. 1968), DORIS (b. 1966),

Lorraine (b. 1967), Stedman (b. 1964) and Delroy (b. 1970). 'Problematic' failed to chart as did 'Hide And Seek' and 'Crazy', however, when producer Nick Martinelli took over, 'All Fall Down' (1985) charted, followed by 'Let Me Be The One'. By the time the band's debut album was released, they had worked through six different producers and countless studios. 'System Addict', the seventh single from *Luxury Of Life*, became the first to break the Top 10. 'Can't Wait Another Minute' and 'Find The Time' repeated the feat.

Silk And Steel climbed slowly to the top of the UK charts, eventually going triple platinum and spawning several singles, including 'Rain And Shine' (UK number 2). Continued success was followed by bad investments, financial instability and alleged bankruptcy. Attempts to resurrect their career in America on Epic failed.

FLACK, ROBERTA

FLACK (b. 1937) WAS DISCOVERED SINGING AND PLAYING JAZZ IN A WASHINGTON NIGHTCLUB. *FIRST TAKE* AND

Chapter Two garnered considerable acclaim and Flack achieved huge success with a poignant version of 'First Time Ever I Saw Your Face'. Further hits came with 'Where Is The Love?' (1972), a duet with Donny Hathaway, and 'Killing Me Softly With His Song' (1973). Her cool, almost unemotional style benefited from a measured use of slow material, although she seemed less comfortable on up-tempo songs. After wavering in the mid-70s, further duets with Hathaway, 'The Closer I Get To You' (1978) and 'You Are My Heaven' (1980), showed a return to form. In the 80s, Flack enjoyed a fruitful partnership with **Peabo Bryson**, notably the hit 'Tonight I Celebrate My Love' (1983).

FLAMIN' GROOVIES

FORMED IN 1966 IN SAN FRANCISCO. ROY LONEY (b. 1946; VOCALS), TIM LYNCH (b. 1946; GUITAR), CYRIL JORDAN (b. 1948; guitar) and George Alexander (b. 1946; bass) recruited Danny Mihm (drums) and embarked on a direction markedly different from the city's prevalent love of extended improvisation. Their official debut, *Supersnazz*, revealed a strong debt to traditional rock 'n' roll, although subsequent albums, *Flamingo* and *Teenage Head*, offered a more contemporary perspective.

After *Teenage Head*, Loney and Lynch were replaced by Chris Wilson and James Farrell. The Groovies enjoyed a cult popularity in Europe and a series of superb recordings were made during a brief spell in Britain; several of these formed the basis of *Shake Some Action*, the Groovies' majestic homage to 60s pop. Subsequent releases relied on a tried formula where a series of cover versions disguised a lack of original songs. A reconstituted Groovies toured Europe, Australia and New Zealand and completed a handful of new recordings, including *One Night Stand*.

FLAMINGOS

US BAND FORMED IN 1951. ZEKE CAREY (b. 1933), JAKE CAREY (b. 1926), PAUL WILSON (b. 1935, d. 1988) AND JOHNNY Carter (b. 1934) originally performed with lead singer Sollie McElroy (b. 1933, d. 1995), who brought the group regional fame on 'Golden Teardrops' in 1954. He was replaced by Nate Nelson (b. 1932, d. 1984) who appeared on the magnificent ballad 'I'll Be Home' (1956, R&B number 5). When Carter and Zeke Carey received military drafts, Tommy Hunt (b. 1933) and Terry Johnson (b. 1935) joined. The band signed with End Records in 1958. Their biggest US hits followed, including 'I Only Have Eyes For You' and 'Nobody Loves Me Like You'.

During the early 60s the Flamingos lost the rest of their original members, except for Jake and Zeke Carey. The cousins managed to achieve some minor hits during the soul era, notably 'Boogaloo Party' (1969, UK number 26). The Flamingos' last US chart record was the 1970 'Buffalo Soldier'.

FLASH CADILLAC AND THE CONTINENTAL KIDS

FORMED IN COLORADO, USA IN 1969, ONE OF SEVERAL GROUPS TO PARODY 50S ROCK IN THE WAKE OF **Sha Na Na**. Flash Cadillac (b. Kenny Moe; vocals), Sam McFadin (guitar/vocals), Linn Phillips (guitar/vocals), George Robinson (saxophone), Kris Angelo (keyboards/vocals), Warren 'Butch' Knight (bass/vocals) and Ricco Masino (drums) released a promising debut album. The following, *There's No Face Like Chrome*, contained material indebted to 50s, 60s and 70s styles. Although they enjoyed two minor US hits with 'Dancin' On A Saturday Night' and 'Good Times Rock 'n' Roll', Flash Cadillac were unable to escape a revivalist tag and broke up.

FLEETWOOD MAC

FORMED IN ENGLAND IN 1967 BY EX-**JOHN MAYALL'S BLUESBREAKERS PETER GREEN** (b. PETER GREENBAUM, 1946; guitar) and Mick Fleetwood (b. 1947; drums). They secured a recording contract with Blue Horizon Records on the strength of Green's reputation as a blues guitarist. Second guitarist Jeremy Spencer (b. 1948) was recruited until another ex-Bluesbreaker, John McVie (b. 1945; bass), joined. Peter Green's Fleetwood Mac, as the group was initially billed, made its debut on 12 August 1967 at Windsor's National Jazz And Blues Festival. Their debut, *Fleetwood Mac*, reached the UK Top 5 and established a distinctive balance between Green and Spencer. The group also enjoyed two minor hits with 'Black Magic Woman' and 'Need Your Love So Bad'.

Mr. Wonderful was another triumph, but while Spencer was content with his established style, Green extended his compositional boundaries with several haunting contributions. *Mr. Wonderful* also featured contributions from Christine Perfect (b. 1943; piano; **Chicken Shack**) and a four-piece horn section. Guitarist, Danny Kirwan (b. 1950) joined in 1968 and they had an immediate UK number 1 with 'Albatross' a moody instrumental. It reached UK number 2 when it was reissued in 1973 and was the group's first million-seller.

After a couple of label changes, the group released the superb *Then Play On*. This unveiled Kirwan's songwriting talents; Spencer was notably absent from most of the sessions. Fleetwood Mac now enjoyed an international reputation, but Peter Green left the band in 1970 as his parting single, the awesome 'The Green Manalishi', became another Top 10 hit. He was replaced by Christine Perfect on *Kiln House*. In 1971 the group was rocked for a second time when Spencer disappeared midway through an American tour – he had joined a religious sect, the Children Of God. Green deputized for the remainder of the tour, before Californian musician Bob Welch (b. 1946) was recruited. The new line-up was consolidated on *Future Games* and *Bare Trees*. Neither made much impression with UK audiences but in America the group found a strong following.

Kirwan's chronic stage-fright led to his dismissal, replaced by Bob Weston (ex-**Long John Baldry**), vocalist Dave Walker also joined but left after eight months, having barely completed work on *Penguin*. The remaining quintet completed *Mystery To Me* before Weston, who had been having an affair with Fleetwood's wife, was fired midway through a US tour and the remaining dates were cancelled. Welch left in 1974.

Fleetwood employed **Stevie Nicks** and **Lindsey Buckingham**, who had already released a self-named album. This became Fleetwood Mac's most successful line-up and *Fleetwood Mac* was a promise fulfilled. The newcomers provided easy, yet memorable compositions with smooth harmonies, while the British contingent gave the group its edge and power. The dramatic 'Rhiannon' gave them their first in a long line of US Top 20 singles. *Rumours* proved more remarkable still. Despite the McVies' divorce and Buckingham and Nicks splitting up, the group completed a stunning collection of exquisite songs: 'Go Your Own Way', 'Don't Stop', 'Second Hand News' and 'Dreams', with both melody and purpose. *Rumours* has sold upwards of 25 million copies and is the second best-selling album of all time.

Tusk, an ambitious double set, showed a group unafraid to experiment. An in-concert selection, *Fleetwood Mac: Live*, was released as a stopgap in 1980 and it was a further two years before a new collection, *Mirage*, appeared. Five years then passed before *Tango In The Night*, a dramatic return to form. The collection was, however, Buckingham's swansong, although his departure was not officially confirmed until 1988. By that point two replacement singer/guitarists, Rick Vito (b. 1950) and Billy Burnette (b. 1953), had joined and the new line-up debuted with the successful *Behind The Mask*. However, despite the addition of ex-**Traffic** guitarist **Dave Mason** and Bekka Bramlett (b. 1970; daughter of **Delaney And Bonnie**), *Time* failed to ignite any spark. In 1997, the famous *Rumours* line-up reunited, releasing a live album on the album's 20th anniversary. In 1998, Fleetwood Mac won a BRIT Award for Lifetime Achievement.

FLEETWOOD MAC

FLAMIN' GROOVIES

Albums

Shake Some Action (Sire 1976)★★★★

➽ p.362 for full listings

Further References

Book: *Bucketfull Of Groovies*, Jon Storey

FLAMINGOS

Albums

Flamingos Serenade (End 1959)★★★

➽ p.362 for full listings

Further References

Film: *Go Johnny Go* (1958)

FLASH CADILLAC AND THE CONTINENTAL KIDS

Albums

There's No Face Like Chrome (Epic 1974)★★★

➽ p.362 for full listings

Connections

Sha Na Na ➽ p.293

FLEETWOOD MAC

Albums

Then Play On (Reprise 1969)★★★★

Rumours (Warners 1977)★★★★

➽ p.362 for full listings

Connections

Chicken Shack ➽ p.90
Long John Baldry ➽ p.30
Traffic ➽ p.323
Delaney And Bonnie ➽ p.114

Influences

Elmore James ➽ p.196

Further References

Video: *In Concert – Mirage Tour* (Spectrum 1983)

Book: *Fleetwood Mac: The Authorized History*, Samuel Graham

FLEETWOODS
Albums
Mr. Blue (Dolton 1959)★★★★
➽ p.362 for full listings

FLO AND EDDIE
Albums
Immoral, Illegal & Fattening (Columbia 1974)★★★
➽ p.362 for full listings
Collaborators
Frank Zappa ➽ p.348
Marc Bolan ➽ p.59
Connections
Turtles ➽ p.325

FLOATERS
Albums
Floaters (ABC 1977)★★★
➽ p.362 for full listings

FLOWERPOT MEN
Albums
Let's Go To San Francisco (1988)★★★
➽ p.362 for full listings
Connections
Deep Purple ➽ p.113

FLOYD, EDDIE
Albums
Knock On Wood (Stax 1967)★★★
➽ p.362 for full listings
Collaborators
Booker T. And The MGs ➽ p.62
Mar-Keys ➽ p.224

FLYING BURRITO BROTHERS
Albums
The Gilded Palace Of Sin (A&M 1969)★★★★★
The Last Of The Red Hot Burritos (A&M 1972)★★★★
➽ p.362 for full listings
Influences
Gram Parsons ➽ p.256

FOCUS
Albums
Moving Waves (Blue Horizon 1971)★★★★
➽ p.362 for full listings
Connections
Jan Akkerman ➽ p.11

FOETUS
Albums
Deaf (Self Immolation 1981)★★★
➽ p.362 for full listings
Collaborators
Marc Almond ➽ p.15
Nick Cave ➽ p.85

FOGELBERG, DAN
Albums
The Innocent Age (Full Moon 1981)★★★★
➽ p.362 for full listings
Collaborators
Roger McGuinn ➽ p.229
Jackson Browne ➽ p.71
Joe Walsh ➽ p.333
Buffy Sainte-Marie ➽ p.288
Eagles ➽ p.130

FLEETWOODS

US DOO-WOP GROUP FORMED IN THE LATE 50S. GARY TROXELL (b. 1939), GRETCHEN CHRISTOPHER (b. 1940) AND Barbara Ellis (b. 1940) composed 'Come Softly To Me'. The haunting and catchy song shot to US number 1 and the UK Top 10. Their third release, 'Mr. Blue', was also a US number 1 and made Troxell one of the leaders in the teen idol stakes. In the midst of their success he was drafted into the navy, his place being taken when necessary by Vic Dana. Despite Troxell's absence, the US hits continued and they totalled nine Top 40 hits between 1959 and 1963 which included the number 10 hit 'Tragedy'.

The trio resurfaced in 1973 when they signed with producer Jerry Dennon; no hits came from this collaboration.

FLO AND EDDIE

LEAD SINGERS (AND SONGWRITERS) OF THE **TURTLES**, MARC VOLMAN AND HOWARD KAYLAN TOOK THEIR name – the Phlorescent Leech and Eddie – from two of their roadies. They then joined **Frank Zappa** for tours and recordings. Zappa wrote suitably operatic lines for their strong voices and the results are undeniably effective. The sleeve of *Just Another Band From LA* – with Zappa reduced to a puppet in Kaylan's hand – seems to imply they had taken control of the group. They certainly split amidst much animosity.

The comedy albums they released subsequently lacked the punch of their work with Zappa, however, they did enliven the rock scene with an animated satirical film, *Cheap*, and a weekly radio show, *Flo & Eddie By The Fireside*. They also supplied their powerful falsettos to give **Marc Bolan**'s voice a lift on many **T. Rex** hits.

FLOATERS

US GROUP – CHARLES CLARK (LIBRA), LARRY CUNNINGHAM (CANCER), PAUL MITCHELL (LEO), RALPH MITCHELL (Aquarius) and latterly, Jonathan 'Mighty Midget' Murray – who were responsible for one of soul's more aberrant moments. 'Float On', with its astrological connotations was saved from utter ignominy by a light, almost ethereal melody line that was effective enough to provide the group with a US number 2 and a UK number 1 in 1977.

FLOWERPOT MEN

UK GROUP FORMED IN 1967 TO EXPLOIT THE FLOWER-power boom. Their 'Let's Go To San Francisco' reached the Top 5 and a quartet of session vocalists – Tony Burrows, Robin Shaw, Pete Nelson and Neil Landon – then assumed the name. The group completed several well-sculpted releases, notably 'A Walk In The Sky'. An instrumental section, comprising Ged Peck (guitar), Jon Lord (organ), Nick Simper (bass) and Carlo Little (drums), accompanied the singers on tour, but this line-up was dissolved when Lord and Simper founded **Deep Purple**.

FLOYD, EDDIE

FLOYD (b. 1935) WAS A FOUNDER-MEMBER OF THE DETROIT-BASED FALCONS, PRESENT ON THEIR 'YOU'RE SO FINE' (1959) and 'I Found A Love' (1962). He joined the Stax organization in 1965, making his mark as a composer. He employed the session bands **Booker T. And The MGs** and the **Mar-Keys** and recorded 'Things Get Better' (1965), followed by the anthem-like 'Knock On Wood' (1966). Although subsequent releases were less successful, a series of powerful singles, including 'Love Is A Doggone Good Thing' (1967) and 'Big Bird' (1968), confirmed Floyd's stature both as a performer and songwriter.

When Stax went bankrupt in 1975, Floyd moved to Malaco Records; he left for Mercury in 1977. In 1988, he linked up with William Bell's Wilbe venture and issued his *Flashback* album. In 1990, Floyd appeared live with a re-formed Booker T. And The MGs.

FLYING BURRITO BROTHERS

LOS ANGELES BAND FORMED IN 1968. **GRAM PARSONS** (b. 1946, d. 1973; GUITAR/VOCALS) AND CHRIS HILLMAN (b. 1942; guitar/vocals) recruited 'Sneaky' Pete Kleinow (pedal steel), Chris Ethridge (bass) and various drummers. *The Gilded Palace Of Sin* allowed the founding duo's vision of a pan-American music to flourish freely; this artistic triumph was never repeated. *Burrito Deluxe*, on which Bernie Leadon replaced Ethridge and Michael Clarke (b. Michael Dick, 1944) became the permanent drummer, showed a group unsure of direction. Parsons went solo in 1970 and with the arrival of songwriter Rick Roberts, the Burritos again asserted their high quality. The underrated *The Flying Burrito Brothers* was a cohesive, purposeful set, but unfortunately, the group was again bedevilled by defections. In 1971 Leadon and Kleinow left; Al Perkins (pedal steel), Kenny Wertz (guitar), Roger Bush (bass) and Byron Berline (fiddle) joined.

The Last Of The Red Hot Burritos captured the excitement and power of the group live. The band split in 1971, but much to the consternation of Hillman, 'Sneaky' Pete Kleinow later commandeered the Burritos' name and in 1975 completed *Flying Again* with Chris Ethridge, Gene Parsons (guitar/vocals) and Gib Guilbeau (fiddle). The arrival of country veteran John Beland provided the group with a proven songwriter worthy of the earlier pioneering line-up. The 1997 line-up was Beland, Guilbeau, Kleinow, Larry Patton (bass) and Gary Kubal (drums).

FOCUS

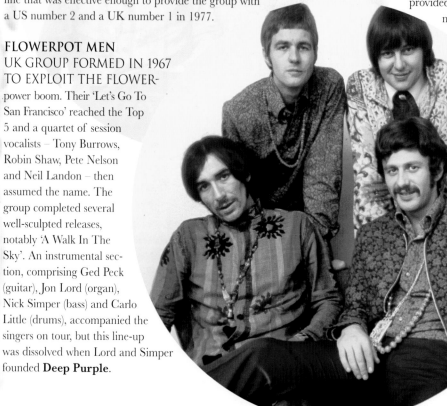

THIJS VAN LEER (KEYBOARDS/FLUTE/VOCALS), MARTIN DRESDEN (BASS) and Hans Cleuver (drums) backed several Dutch singers before 1969's catalytic enlistment of guitarist **Jan Akkerman**. The new quartet's first collective essay as recording artists was humble, but heartened by audience response Focus released a *bona fide* album debut with a spin-off single, 'House Of The King'; it sold well in continental Europe. The Mike Vernon-produced *Moving Waves* embraced vocal items (in English), melodic instrumentals and the startling 'Hocus Pocus' (UK Top 20). After reshuffles in which only Van Leer and Akkerman surfaced from the original personnel, 'Sylvia', shot into the UK Top 5; *Focus III* also reached the upper echelons of the charts. An in-concert album from London and *Hamburger Concerto*

both marked time artistically and, following 1975's *Mother Focus*, Akkerman left to concentrate on his parallel solo career. Van Leer elected to stick with a latter-day Focus. The 1972 line-up re-formed solely for a Dutch television special in 1990.

FOETUS

AFTER FOUNDING HIS OWN RECORD COMPANY, SELF IMMOLATION, IN 1980, AUSTRALIAN *EMIGRÉ* JIM FOETUS (b. Jim Thirlwell) set about 'recording works of aggression, insight and inspiration'. Foetus released a series of albums, such as *Deaf*, *Ache*, *Hole* and *Nail;* Thirlwell presented a harrowing aural netherworld of death, lust, disease and spiritual decay. In 1983, Foetus undertook a rare tour, performing with **Marc Almond**, **Nick Cave** and Lydia Lunch.

Thirlwell's first studio album in seven years was *Gash*, an album that led to a reappraisal of his work as one of the key figures in the development of the 'industrial' music movement.

FOGELBERG, DAN

FOGELBERG (b. 1951; SONGWRITING/GUITAR/PIANO) WAS DISCOVERED BY NASHVILLE PRODUCER NORBERT PUTNAM, resulting in *Home Free* for Columbia. This highly relaxed album was notable for the backing musicians involved, including **Roger McGuinn**, **Jackson Browne**, **Joe Walsh** and **Buffy Sainte-Marie**. Despite these, the album was unsuccessful and Fogelberg was dropped by Columbia. He returned to session work, moved to Colorado, and later released *Souvenirs*. In 1975, he supported the **Eagles**.

Netherlands, achieved some recognition, but generally Fogelberg has enjoyed better chart success in the USA than in the UK: 'Longer' (1980) reached US number 2, but missed the UK Top 50. 'Same Auld Lang Syne' and 'Leader Of The Band' (both from *The Innocent Age*) reached the US Top 10. The excellent *High Country Snows* saw a return to his bluegrass influences and was in marked contrast to the harder-edged *Exiles*.

FONTANA, WAYNE

AFTER CHANGING HIS NAME IN HONOUR OF **ELVIS PRESLEY'S** DRUMMER D.J. FONTANA, WAYNE (b. GLYN ELLIS, 1945) was signed to the appropriately named Fontana Records. His backing group, the Mindbenders, provided a gritty accompaniment. Their first minor hit was the unremarkable 'Hello Josephine' (1963). The group finally broke through with their fifth release, 'Um, Um, Um, Um, Um' (UK number 5). The 1965 follow-up, 'The Game Of Love', hit number 2. Thereafter the group struggled, with 'Just A Little Bit Too Late' and 'She Needs Love' being their only further hits. In 1965, Wayne went solo with 'It Was Easier To Hurt Her' before finding success with the catchy 'Come On Home'.

FOO FIGHTERS

US BAND FORMED IN 1994 BY DAVE GROHL (b. 1969; VOCALS/GUITAR; EX-**NIRVANA** drummer) who recruited Pat Smear (guitar), Nate Mendel (b. 1968; bass) and William Goldsmith (b. 1972; drums). Their debut, 'This Is A Call' (1995), was released on Roswell/Capitol Records. Media analysis of the group's debut album focused on tracks such as 'I'll Stick Around', which some alleged was an attack on Kurt Cobain's widow, Courtney Love. Detractors pointed at the similarity to Nirvana in the construction of several tracks, and Grohl's inability to match Cobain's evocation of mood. Goldsmith left during the recording of their second album, replaced by Taylor Hawkins. *The Colour And The Shape* was another hard and tough album of blisteringly paced songs, lightened by the band's great grasp of melody. Pat Smear left in 1998; he was replaced by Franz Stahl.

FORBERT, STEVE

US-BORN FORBERT (b. 1955) FIRST RECORDED IN 1977 FOR NEMPEROR; HE WAS BRIEFLY HERALDED AS 'THE NEW **Dylan**' because of his lyrics. Forbert's biggest commercial success came with 'Romeo's Tune' (1979, US Top 20) but after four albums his contract was terminated.

His 1988 album for Geffen Records was produced by Garry Tallent from **Bruce Springsteen**'s E Street Band. After a four-year gap, Forbert returned with the highly praised *The American In Me*, produced by Pete Anderson.

FORD, FRANKIE

NEW ORLEANS ROCKER FRANKIE FORD (b. FRANCIS GUZZO, 1939) FIRST APPEARED ON TED MACK'S AMATEUR HOUR *Talent Show*, where he sang with Carmen Miranda and Sophie Tucker. In 1958 he was asked to audition for Ace Records. Subsequently, he released his first single, 'Cheatin' Woman'. Fellow musician Huey 'Piano' Smith (b. 1934) had previously recorded a self-penned song, 'Sea Cruise'; Ford recorded a new vocal and it was released under the title Frankie Ford with Huey 'Piano' Smith and his Clowns. It sold over a million copies and reached the US Top 20.

Ford left Ace in 1960 to form his own Spinet Records and signed to Liberty in 1960; he never repeated the success of 'Sea Cruise'. Ford continued to record for obscure labels throughout the 70s. In 1971, he opened a club in New Orleans' French Quarter where he became a cabaret fixture and tourist attraction. His four recordings of 'Sea Cruise' have now sold over 30 million copies worldwide.

FORDHAM, JULIA

FORMERLY ONE OF **MARI WILSON'S** BACKING VOCALISTS, ENGLISH-BORN FORDHAM (b. 1962) WENT SOLO IN 1986 achieving an initial UK chart hit with the Top 30 'Happy Ever After' (number 1 in Japan) in 1988; a self-titled debut album and the follow-up both reached the UK Top 20. Her biggest success came with '(Love Moves In) Mysterious Ways', which reached number 19 in 1992.

FONTANA, WAYNE
Albums
The Game Of Love (Fontana 1965)★★★
➧ p.362 for full listings
Collaborators
Bert Berns ➧ p.44

FOO FIGHTERS
Albums
Foo Fighters (Roswell/Capitol 1995)★★★★
The Colour And The Shape (Roswell/Capitol 1997)★★★★
➧ p.362 for full listings

Connections
Nirvana ➧ p.248
Alanis Morissette ➧ p.238

FORBERT, STEVE
Albums
Rocking Horse Head (Revolution 1996)★★★
➧ p.362 for full listings
Connections
E Street Band
Influences
Bob Dylan ➧ p.128

FORD, FRANKIE
Albums
Frankie Ford (1976)★★
➧ p.362 for full listings

FORDHAM, JULIA
Albums
Swept (Circa 1991)★★★
➧ p.362 for full listings
Collaborators
Mari Wilson ➧ p.340
Further References
Video: *Porcelain* (Virgin 1990)

FOREIGNER
Albums
4 (Atlantic 1981)★★★★
Agent Provocateur (Atlantic 1985)★★★
➽ p.362 for full listings

Collaborators
Junior Walker ➽ p.332
Further References
Film: *Footloose – (Soundtrack Song)* (1984)

FORTUNES
Albums
The Fortunes I (Decca 1965)★★★
➽ p.362 for full listings

FOUNDATIONS
Albums
Digging The Foundations (Pye 1969)★★
➽ p.362 for full listings
Further References
Film: *The Cool Ones* (1967)

FOUNTAINS OF WAYNE
Album
Fountains Of Wayne (Scratchie/Atlantic 1997)★★★★
➽ p.362 for full listings
Connections
Smashing Pumpkins ➽ p.301
Posies ➽ p.264
Belltower

4 NON BLONDES
Album
Bigger, Better, Faster, More! (Interscope 1993)★★★
➽ p.362 for full listings
Collaborators
Prince ➽ p.267
Neil Young ➽ p.346

FOUR FRESHMEN
Albums
Voices In Modern (Capitol 1955)★★★
4 Freshmen And 5 Trumpets (Capitol 1957)★★★
Freshmen Favorites Volume 2 (Capitol 1959)★★★
➽ p.362 for full listings

FOUR MEN AND A DOG
Album
Barking Mad (Topic 1991)★★★★
Shifting Gravel (Topic 1993)★★★★
➽ p.362 for full listings
Collaborators
Planxty ➽ p.262

FOREIGNER

TRANSATLANTIC BAND FORMED IN 1976. MICK JONES (b. 1944; GUITAR/VOCALS) RECRUITED IAN McDonald (b. 1946; guitar/keyboards/horns/ vocals), Lou Gramm (b. Lou Grammatico, 1950; vocals), Dennis Elliott (b. 1950; drums), Al Greenwood (keyboards) and Edward Gagliardi (b. 1952; bass) and the band released *Foreigner*. Jones and Gramm wrote most of their material, including classics such as 'Feels Like The First Time' and 'Cold As Ice'. In 1979, Rick Wills (bass) replaced Gagliardi.

1980 saw the departure of McDonald and Greenwood which led to the guest appearances of Thomas Dolby and **Junior Walker** on *4*, the hit 'Waiting For A Girl Like You' was lifted from the album. The following 'I Want To Know What Love Is' proved to be Foreigner's greatest commercial success, topping the charts on both sides of the Atlantic.

In the mid-80s the members of Foreigner were engaged in solo projects, including Gramm's successful *Ready Or Not* (1987). The band then released *Inside Information*, in many respects it was a poor record and a portent of things to come. In 1990, Gramm left the band and Jones recruited Johnny Edwards to provide vocals for *Unusual Heat;* however in 1994, Jones and Gramm launched a reunited Foreigner. The band were back on the road in 1995 to promote *Mr Moonlight*. The album was only a moderate success, even though it was a typical Foreigner record.

FORTUNES

UK BEAT GROUP FORMED IN 1963: GLEN DALE (b. 1943; VOCALS/GUITAR); ROD ALLEN (b. RODNEY BAINBRIDGE, 1944; bass) and Barry Pritchard (b. 1944; guitar). After perfecting their harmonic blend, the group recruited David Carr (b. 1943; keyboards) and Andy Brown (b. 1946; drums). Their debut, 'Summertime Summertime' passed without notice, but the following 'Caroline' was taken up as the theme song for the pirate station Radio Caroline. In 1965 the group reached the UK and US Top 10 with 'You've Got Your Troubles'. 'Here It Comes Again' and 'This Golden Ring' displayed their easy listening appeal, but unexpectedly Dale left. The group continued and scored an unexpected US hit with 'Here Comes That Rainy Day Feeling Again' (1971). Back in the UK, they also enjoyed their first hits in over five years with 'Freedom Come Freedom Go' and 'Storm In A Teacup'.

FOUNDATIONS

UK GROUP FORMED IN 1967. LONDON RECORD DEALER BARRY CLASS INTRODUCED THE FOUNDATIONS TO songwriters Tony Macauley and John MacLeod, whose composition 'Baby, Now That I've Found You' became the group's debut release. The single reached UK number 1 and, eventually, US number 9; global sales exceeded three million. The group's multiracial line-up included West Indians Clem Curtis (b. 1940; vocals), Pat Burke (b. 1937; tenor saxophone/flute), Mike Elliot (b. 1929; tenor saxophone) and Eric Allan Dale (b. 1936; trombone), Londoners Alan Warner (b. 1947; guitar), Peter Macbeth (b. 1943; bass) and Tim Harris (b. 1948; drums) and Sri Lankan Tony Gomez (b. 1948; organ). They scored a second multi-million-seller in 1968 with 'Build Me Up, Buttercup' and enjoyed further success with similarly styled releases, including 'Back On My Feet Again' and 'Any Old Time' (both 1968). Curtis was replaced by Colin Young (b. 1944), and the departure of Elliot signalled internal dissatisfaction. 'In The Bad Bad Old Days' (1969) returned the group to the UK Top 10, but the minor hit, 'Born To Live And Born To Die' (1969), was their last chart entry.

FOUNTAINS OF WAYNE

IDIOSYNCRATIC US POP DUO: ADAM SCHLESINGER AND CHRIS COLLINGWOOD (b. *c.* 1967). THEY ORIGINALLY signed a recording contract as the Wallflowers, but abandoned their claim to the name and the proposed record never appeared. Despite problems over freedom of contract that dogged them for three years, they continued to play the occasional gig as Pinwheel, then as Ivy. By the time they finally recorded, Schlesinger had become co-owner of Scratchie Records (with D'Arcy Wretzky and James Iha of **Smashing Pumpkins**). The result was a self-titled collection of 12 brittle songs. The first single from the album, 'Radiation Vibe', reached UK number 32. The band also achieved a flurry of publicity when their song 'That Thing You Do!' was included in the Tom Hanks film of the same name. By the time Fountains Of Wayne began their European tour of 1997 they had recruited Brian Young (**Posies**) on drums and guitarist Jody Porter.

4 NON BLONDES

SAN FRANCISCAN QUARTET: LINDA PERRY (b. *c.* 1965; GUITAR/ VOCALS) ALONGSIDE CHRISTA HILLHOUSE (b. 1962; BASS), Roger Rocha (guitar) and Dawn Richardson (drums). Hillhouse and Perry, who began the band, had to cancel their first-ever rehearsal on 7 October 1989 when an earthquake hit the Bay Area. 'What's Up' (1993, UK number 2) was followed by a Top 10 debut album, *Bigger, Better, Faster, More!*. Selling half a million copies in the USA, it also topped charts in Germany and Sweden. Perry's songs quickly became the dominant force within 4 Non Blondes, many of the band's songs were lifted from her solo repertoire, including 'Spaceman', the follow-up to 'What's Up'. The band later supported **Prince** and **Neil Young**.

FOUR FRESHMEN

FORMED IN INDIANA, USA, IN 1948. LEAD VOCALIST BOB FLANIGAN (b. 1926), HIS COUSINS ROSS BARBOUR (b. 1928) and Don Barbour (b. 1929, d. 1961), and Hal Kratzsch (d. 1970) were signed to Capitol Records. Their first hit, 'It's A Blue World' (1952) reached US number 30.

1953 saw Kratzsch leave, replaced by Ken Errair (b. 1930, d. 1968). Errair departed in 1955, replaced by Ken Albers. By that time the group had logged two more Top 40 hits, 'It Happened Once Before' and 'Mood Indigo'.

Three final chart singles were issued in 1955-56. Don Barbour left in 1960, replaced by Bill Comstock (who left in 1972). Ross Barbour stayed on until 1977 and Ken Albers until 1982. Flanigan remained with the group into the early 90s. Don Barbour was killed in a car crash, Kratzsch died of cancer and Errair died in a plane crash.

FOUR MEN AND A DOG

FOUR MEN AND A DOG'S DEBUT ALBUM, BARKING MAD, WAS A SPECTACULAR DISTILLATION OF THE NEW AND THE old. Including everything from jigs and reels to probably the first-ever Irish folk rap song. It featured three musicians who have subsequently left the band, Donal Murphy, Brian McGrath and singer Mick Daly. By 1993 the line-up was: Gino Lupari (bodhran), Cathal Hayden (fiddle), Conor Keane (accordion) and Gerry O'Connor (banjo); guitarist Artie McGlynn (ex-**Planxty**) joined later. They classify their sound as 'traditional music with balls'.

Shifting Gravel was not so well received, with critical complaints about the central presence of newly acquired pop/rock singer-songwriter Kevin Doherty, whose stylistic departures overshadowed some of the original Celtic gusto of the debut. His input was more restrained on *Doctor A's Secret Remedies*, however, and his songwriting much improved.

FOUR PENNIES

BEAT GROUP FROM BLACKBURN, ENGLAND. LIONEL MORTON (B. 1942; VOCALS/RHYTHM GUITAR), FRITZ Fryer (b. David Roderick Carnie Fryer, 1944; lead guitar), Mike Wilsh (b. 1945; bass) and Alan Buck (b. 1943; drums) scored a UK number 1 in 1964 with 'Juliet'. They enjoyed three further Top 20 entries with 'I Found Out The Hard Way', 'Black Girl' (both 1964) and 'Until It's Time For You To Go' (1965), but were unable to sustain a long career.

FOUR PREPS

US VOCAL GROUP FORMED IN THE EARLY 1950S. BRUCE BELLAND, GLEN LARSON, MARVIN INABNETT AND ED COBB began singing together as teenagers. They were signed by Capitol and their first session yielded 'Dreamy Eyes' (1956), which was a minor hit. The follow-up, '26 Miles (Santa Catalina)', reached number 2 and 'Big Man' made number 3. Despite their prolific output, chart success largely eluded them. Subsequent singles failed to make the US Top 10 although the group did score a Top 10 album, *Four Preps On Campus*. Their final charting single, 1964's 'A Letter To The **Beatles**', parodied Beatlemania but was allegedly withdrawn from distribution upon request by the Beatles' management. The group continued until 1967.

FOUR SEASONS

US VOCAL GROUP FORMED IN 1956. VOCALISTS **FRANKIE VALLI** (B. FRANCIS Castelluccio, 1937), brothers Nick and Tommy DeVito (b. 1936) and Hank Majewski were initially known as the Variatones, then the Four Lovers (they enjoyed a minor US hit with 'You're The Apple Of My Eye', composed by **Otis Blackwell**). After being dropped by RCA Records, they recorded a single for Epic, following which Valli departed – he rejoined later. Meanwhile, the Four Lovers released several records under pseudonymous names, during which Nick DeVito and Majewski departed, replaced by Nick Massi (b. 1935) and Bob Gaudio (b. 1942). The group became the Four Seasons, signed to Vee Jay Records and released 'Sherry' followed by 'Big Girls Don't Cry', 'Walk Like A Man' and 'Rag Doll', which were also US number 1s.

In 1965, Massi left, replaced by Joe Long. Valli, meanwhile, was continuing to enjoy solo hits. At the end of the decade, the group attempted to establish themselves as a more serious act with the poorly received *Genuine Imitation Life Gazette*. When Tommy DeVito left in 1970, the lucrative Four Seasons back catalogue and rights to the group name rested with Valli and Gaudio. A brief tie-up with **Motown** saw the release of *Chameleon* which despite favourable reviews sold poorly. Meanwhile, Valli was receiving unexpected UK success.

While Valli was back at number 1 with 'My Eyes Adored You' (1975), the latest group line-up charted with 'Who Loves You'. Immense success followed as the group became part of the disco boom sweeping America. The nostalgic 'December 1963 (Oh What A Night)' was a transatlantic number 1 in 1976, but the following year, Valli left the group again to concentrate on his solo career. He had a US number 1 with the Barry Gibb film theme, *Grease*, while the Four Seasons continued with drummer Gerry Polci on lead vocals. Valli returned to the group for a double album recorded live at Madison Square Garden.

4 SKINS

LONDON, ENGLAND BAND OF FOUR SKINHEADS, WHO SPECIALIZED IN VITRIOLIC THREE-CHORD 'YOB-ROCK'. Their membership was fluid, including no less than four lead singers, with only Hoxton Tom (bass) still resident between their first and second albums. With a blatantly patriotic image, the band attracted National Front supporters to their live shows, which occasionally erupted into full-scale riots. Lyrically they expounded on racism, police brutality and corrupt governments. From a creative standpoint, the band had ground to a halt by 1983.

FOUR PENNIES
Albums
Two Sides Of The Four Pennies (Philips 1964)★★★
Mixed Bag (Philips 1966)★★★
➧ p.362 for full listings

FOUR PREPS
Albums
Four Preps (Capitol 1958)★★★★
The Things We Did Last Summer (Capitol 1958)★★★★
Campus Encore (Capitol 1962)★★★
➧ p.362 for full listings
Connections
Beatles ➧ p.38

FOUR SEASONS
Albums
Sherry And 11 Others (Vee Jay 1962)★★★
Edizione D'Oro (Philips 1969)★★★
➧ p.363 for full listings
Collaborators
Otis Blackwell ➧ p.52
Connections
Four Lovers
Further References
Film: *Beach Ball* (1964)

4 SKINS
Albums
The Good, The Bad And The 4 Skins (Secret 1982)★★
➧ p.363 for full listings

FOUR TOPS
Albums
Four Tops On Top (Motown 1966)★★★★
with the Supremes *The Magnificent Seven* (Motown 1970)★★★★
➧ p.363 for full listings
Collaborators
Holland/Dozier/Holland ➧ p.183
Marvin Gaye ➧ p.159
Moody Blues ➧ p.237
Temptations ➧ p.318
Influences
Left Banke ➧ p.213
Tim Hardin ➧ p.174
Influences
Brian Epstein ➧ p.137
Further References
Film: *Ferry Cross The Mersey* (1964)

FOUR TOPS

LEVI STUBBS (b. *c.* 1938), RENALDO 'OBIE' BENSON (b. 1937), LAWRENCE PEYTON (b. *c.* 1938, d. 1997) AND ABDUL 'DUKE' Fakir (b. c. 1938), first sang together at a party in Detroit in 1954 as the Four Aims. In 1956, they changed their name to the Four Tops and recorded a one-off single. After teaming up with **Holland/Dozier/Holland**, they released 'Baby I Need Your Loving', which showcased the group's strong harmonies and the gruff, soulful lead vocals of Levi Stubbs; it reached the US Top 20. The following year, 'I Can't Help Myself', topped the charts. Holland/Dozier/Holland continued to write and produce for the Four Tops until 1967. The pinnacle of this collaboration was 'Reach Out I'll Be There', a transatlantic hit in 1966. In 1967, the Four Tops began to widen their appeal with soul-tinged versions of pop hits, such as the **Left Banke**'s 'Walk Away Renee' and **Tim Hardin**'s 'If I Were A Carpenter'. The departure of Holland, Dozier and Holland from **Motown** brought a temporary halt to the group's progress, and it was 1970 before they regained their hit status with a revival of Tommy Edwards' 'It's All In The Game'. Another revival, Richard Harris's 'MacArthur Park', brought success in 1971, while Benson also co-wrote **Marvin Gaye**'s hit 'What's Going On'.

After working with the **Moody Blues** on 'A Simple Game' (1972), the Four Tops elected to leave Motown, who were relocating to California. They signed with Dunhill, and restored their chart success with the theme to the movie *Shaft In Africa*, 'Are You Man Enough'. At the end of the decade, they joined Casablanca Records, and secured a soul number 1 with 'When She Was My Girl'. Subsequent releases also charted in Britain and America.

In 1983, the group performed a storming medley of their 60s hits with the **Temptations** during the Motown 25th Anniversary television special. They re-signed to the label for *Back Where I Belong*, one side of which was produced by Holland/Dozier/Holland. However, disappointing sales and disputes about the group's musical direction led them to leave Motown once again. With Arista, they found immediate success with the singles 'Indestructible' and 'Loco In Acapulco' (both 1988), the latter taken from the soundtrack to the film *Buster*. The Four Tops retained a constant line-up from their inception up until Peyton's death in 1997.

FOURMOST
Albums
First And Fourmost (Parlophone 1965)★★★
➧ p.363 for full listings
Collaborators
John Lennon ➧ p.214
Paul McCartney ➧ p.229

FOURMOST

UK BAND ORIGINALLY KNOWN AS THE BLUE JAYS, THEN THE FOUR JAYS, THEN THE FOUR MOSTS. BRIAN O'HARA (b. 1942; lead guitar/vocals), Mike Millward (b. 1942, d. 1966; rhythm guitar/vocals), Billy Hatton (b. 1941; bass) and Dave Lovelady (b. 1942; drums) achieved momentary fame under the management wing of **Brian Epstein**. Two commercial **Lennon** and **McCartney** songs, 'Hello Little Girl' and 'I'm In Love', served as their initial a-sides, but 'A Little Lovin'' became the quartet's biggest hit (1964, UK number 6). The Fourmost's later releases veered from **Motown** ('Baby I Need Your Lovin'') to George Formby ('Aunt Maggie's Remedy'), however they faltered in the wake of the R&B boom.

FOURPLAY
Albums
Fourplay (Warners 1991)★★★★
➧ p.363 for full listings
Influences
Roberta Flack ➧ p.146
Donny Hathaway

FOURPLAY

US GROUP WHO BLENDED POP AND CONTEMPORARY JAZZ. THE BAND – BOB JAMES (KEYBOARDS), LEE RITENOUR (guitar), Nathan East (bass) and Harvey Mason (drums) – saw their debut spend 31 weeks at number 1 on *Billboard*'s Contemporary Jazz Albums chart. *Between The Sheets* also reached number 1 in the chart. *Elixir* featured a succession of typically smooth instrumentals and sung numbers. The first single from the album, 'The Closer I Get To You', was an update of the **Roberta Flack** and Donny Hathaway duet.

FRAMPTON, PETER
Albums
Frampton Comes Alive! (A&M 1976)★★★★
Peter Frampton (Relativity 1994)★★★
➧ p.363 for full listings
Connections
Frampton's Camel

FRAMPTON, PETER

UK-BORN FRAMPTON'S (b. 1950) SOLO CAREER DEBUTED WITH 'WIND OF CHANGE' IN 1971, ALTHOUGH HE immediately set about forming a band, Frampton's Camel, to carry out US concert dates. The group featured Mike Kellie (drums), Mickey Gallagher (keyboards) and Rick Wills (bass). *Frampton* was a great success in the USA, while in the UK he was commercially ignored. The following year a double set, *Frampton Comes Alive!*, reached US number 1 and stayed in the charts for two years. It became the biggest-selling live album in history and has sold over 12 million copies. The follow-up *I'm In You*, sold in vast quantities, though not to the same scale. In 1978, Frampton suffered a near fatal car crash and when he returned in 1979 with *Where I Should Be*, his star was dwindling. The album garnered favourable reviews, but was his last successful record.

Following *The Art Of Control* Frampton 'disappeared' until 1986, when he was signed to Virgin Records and released the synthesizer-laced *Premonition*. He returned to session work thereafter.

FRANCIS, CONNIE

US-BORN FRANCIS (b. CONCETTA ROSA MARIA FRANCONERO, 1938) BEGAN PERFORMING PROFESSIONALLY AGED 11. After winning an *Arthur Godfrey Talent Show*, she changed her name and signed to MGM Records in 1955. 'Majesty Of Love', her 10th release, a duet with Marvin Rainwater, was her first US chart entry. In 1957, she was persuaded to record the 1923 song 'Who's Sorry Now'; it reached US number 4 and UK number 1. Her other hits included 'My Happiness', 'Among My Souvenirs' and 'Stupid Cupid' (UK number 1), 'Where The Boys Are' (by **Neil Sedaka** and Howard Greenfield), 'Lipstick On Your Collar', 'Everybody's Somebody's Fool' (her first US number 1) and 'Don't Break The Heart That Loves You' (US number 1).

Francis made her film debut in 1960 with *Where The Boys Are*, and followed it with similar comedy musicals such as *Follow The Boys* (1963), *Looking For Love* (1964) and *When The Boys Meet The Girls* (1965). Outdated by the 60s beat boom, she worked in nightclubs in the late 60s, and did much charity work for UNICEF and similar organizations, besides entertaining US troops in Vietnam.

In 1974, she was the victim of a rape in her motel room after a performance. She later sued the motel for negligence, reputedly receiving damages of over three million dollars. For several years afterwards she did not perform publically, and underwent psychiatric treatment. She resumed performing in 1981, returning to the same motel and an enthusiastic reception. In 1992, she was diagnosed as suffering from 'a complex illness', however, in 1993 she signed a new recording contract with Sony, buoyed by the fact that her 1959 hit, 'Lipstick On Your Collar', was climbing high in the UK charts, after appearing as the title of a Dennis Potter television drama.

FRANK AND WALTERS

THREE-PIECE BAND FROM CORK, EIRE. PAUL LINEHAN (VOCALS/BASS), NIALL LINEHAN (GUITAR) AND ASHLEY Keating (drums) attracted immediate press attention through a debut EP on the Setanta label. Two Single of The Week awards later, 'Fashion Crisis Hits

New York' proved another instant favourite. They were signed to Go! Discs and a third EP, led off by the infectious 'Happy Busman', was piloted by **Edwyn Collins**. However, the resulting debut album failed to fulfil critical expectations. 'This Is Not A Song' and a reissued 'Fashion Crisis Hits New York' offered chart hits via bigger promotion and production. By the time of the more earnest *The Grand Parade* the fickle world of pop had moved on.

FRANKIE GOES TO HOLLYWOOD

UK BAND FORMED IN 1980. HOLLY JOHNSON (b. WILLIAM JOHNSON, 1960; VOCALS) RECRUITED PAUL RUTHERFORD (b. 1959; vocals), Nasher Nash (b. Brian Nash, 1963; guitar), Mark O'Toole (b. 1964; bass) and Peter Gill (b. 1964; drums) and released their debut single, 'Relax', produced by Trevor Horn. A superb dance track with a suggestive lyric, the single was banned on BBC radio and television in Britain – this proved the single's best marketing ploy and it topped the UK charts for five weeks, selling almost two million copies. The group's image of Liverpool laddishness coupled with the overt homosexuality of Johnson and Rutherford merely added to their sensationalism.

The follow up, 'Two Tribes', was an awesome production built round a throbbing, infectious riff. The topical lyric dealt with the escalation of nuclear arms and the prospect of global annihilation; it included a chilling voice-over from actor Patrick Allen taken from government papers on the information to be given to the public in the event of nuclear war. It entered the chart at number 1, where it stayed for nine weeks while the revitalized 'Relax' sat at number 2.

Welcome To The Pleasure Dome contained a number of covers, including **Bruce Springsteen**'s 'Born To Run', **Dionne Warwick**'s 'Do You Know The Way To San Jose?' and **Gerry And The Pacemakers**' 'Ferry Across The Mersey'. The sound was epic, glorious and critically acclaimed. 1984 ended with a change of style as Frankie enjoyed their third number 1 with the moving festive ballad 'The Power Of Love'. They became the second act in UK pop history to see their first three singles reach the top. The following year, their fourth single ('Welcome To The Pleasure Dome') stalled at number 2. They were never again to attain their previous ascendancy.

'Rage Hard', their 1986 comeback, reached UK number 4, but seemed decidedly anti-climactic. *Liverpool* cost a small fortune but lacked the charm and vibrancy of its predecessor. Within a year, Frankie broke up.

FRANKLIN, ARETHA

US VOCALIST ARETHA (b. 1942) KNEW THE MAJOR GOSPEL STARS MAHALIA JACKSON AND CLARA WARD, WHO GAVE her valuable tutelage. Aged 12, she left her choir to become a featured soloist; two years later she began recording for JVB and Checker. Between 1956 and 1960, her output was devotional, but the secular success of **Sam Cooke** encouraged a change of emphasis. After a dozen patchy albums with Columbia, a disillusioned Franklin joined Atlantic resulting in 'I Never Loved A Man (The Way I Loved You)' (1966). The single soared into the US Top 10. The following releases, including 'Do Right Woman – Do Right Man', 'Respect', 'Baby I Love You' and '(You Make Me Feel Like) A Natural Woman', proclaimed her 'Queen Of Soul'.

Despite Franklin's professional success, her relationship with husband and manager Ted White disintegrated, and while excellent singles such as 'Think' and 'I Say A Little Prayer' were released, others betrayed a discernible lethargy.

In 1970 she was back on form with 'Call Me', 'Spirit In The Dark' and 'Don't Play That Song'. *Aretha Live At Fillmore West* restated her in-concert power and in 1972, another live appearance resulted in *Amazing Grace*, a double gospel set. Throughout the early 70s, Aretha enjoyed three R&B chart-toppers, 'Angel', 'Until You Come Back To Me (That's What I'm Gonna Do)' and 'I'm In Love'. Sadly, the rest of the decade was marred by recordings that were at best predictable, at worst dull. However a cameo role in the film *The Blues Brothers*, rekindled her flagging career and saw a move to Arista. In the mid-80s, she charted with **Annie Lennox** ('Sisters Are Doin' It For Themselves') and **George Michael** ('I Knew You Were Waiting (For Me)'); the latter went to US and UK number 1 in 1987. Franklin's *Through The Storm* contained more powerful duets: with **Elton John** on the title track, **James Brown** ('Gimme Some Lovin'', remixed by Prince for 12-inch), and **Whitney Houston** ('It Isn't, It Wasn't, It Ain't Never Gonna Be'). As her 'return to gospel' *One Lord One Faith One Baptism* proved, she is still a commanding singer.

Further References
Book: *Frampton!: An Unauthorized Biography*, Susan Katz

FRANCIS, CONNIE
Albums
Who's Sorry Now? (MGM 1958)★★★★
My Thanks To You (MGM 1959)★★★★
➧ p.363 for full listings
Further References
Films: *Jamboree aka Disc Jockey Jamboree* (1957)
Follow The Boys (1962)
Book: *Who's Sorry Now?*, Connie Francis

FRANK AND WALTERS
Albums
Trains, Boats And Planes (Go! Discs 1992)★★★
➧ p.363 for full listings
Connections
Edwyn Collins ➧ p.98

FRANKIE GOES TO HOLLYWOOD
Albums
Welcome To The Pleasure Dome (ZTT 1984)★★★
➧ p.363 for full listings

Connections
Godley And Creme ➧ p.164
Influences
Bruce Springsteen ➧ p.306
Dione Warwick ➧ p.334
Gerry And The Pacemakers ➧ p.162
Further References
Book: *Frankie Say: The Rise Of Frankie Goes To Hollywood*, Danny Jackson

FRANKLIN, ARETHA
Albums
I Never Loved A Man The Way That I Love You (Atlantic 1967)★★★★★
Aretha: Lady Soul (Atlantic 1968)★★★★★
➧ p.363 for full listings
Collaborators
Annie Lennox ➧ p.214
George Michael ➧ p.233
Elton John ➧ p.200
James Brown ➧ p.70
Whitney Houston ➧ p.188
Influences
Sam Cooke ➧ p.100
Further References
Film: *The Blues Brothers* (1980)
Book: *Aretha Franklin*, Mark Bego

FRED, JOHN, AND HIS PLAYBOY BAND
Albums
John Fred And His Playboys (Paula 1966)★★★
p.363 for full listings

FREDDIE AND THE DREAMERS
Albums
Freddie And The Dreamers (Columbia 1963)★★★
Freddie And The Dreamers (Mercury 1965)★★★
p.363 for full listings
Further References
Film: *Every Day's A Holiday* aka *Seaside Swingers* (1965)

FREE
Albums
Tons Of Sobs (Island 1968)★★★
Fire And Water (Island 1970)★★★★
p.363 for full listings
Influences
Alexis Korner p.210
Further References
Video: *Free* (1989)

FREED, ALAN
Connections
Chuck Berry p.45
Fats Domino p.122
Bill Haley p.172
Elvis Presley p.265
p.363 for full listings
Further References
Films: *Don't Knock The Rock* (1956)
Go Johnny Go (1958)
Book: *Big Beat Heat: Alan Freed And The Early Years Of Rock 'n' Roll*, John A. Jackson

FRED, JOHN, AND HIS PLAYBOY BAND

DURING THE EARLY 60S, VARIOUS VERSIONS OF THE PLAYBOY BAND RECORDED FOR SMALL INDEPENDENT record labels but it was not until the end of 1967 that success finally came with the international hit, 'Judy In Disguise (With Glasses)'. Although the US group were generally perceived as a novelty group, they were tight and well organized. Fred's (b. John Fred Gourrier, 1941) blue-eyed soul vocals were evident on *Agnes English*, which included a rasping version of 'She Shot A Hole In My Soul'. The group split at the end of the 60s.

FREDDIE AND THE DREAMERS

UK GROUP FEATURING FREDDIE GARRITY (b. 1940; VOCALS), ROY CREWSDON (b. 1941; GUITAR), DEREK QUINN (b. 1942; guitar), Pete Birrell (b. 1941; bass) and Bernie Dwyer (b. 1940; drums). Their debut, 'If You Gotta Make A Fool Of Somebody', was an R&B favourite, followed by the lighter 'I'm Telling You Now' and 'You Were Made For Me'. Further hits followed in 1964 with 'Over You', 'I Love You Baby', 'Just For You', and 'I Understand'. The group's appeal declined in the UK but early in 1965, they made a startling breakthrough in America where 'I'm Telling You Now' topped the charts. A US Top 20 hit rapidly followed with 'Do The Freddie'.

The band split at the end of the decade. In the mid-70s, Freddie revived the group, with new personnel, for revival concerts.

FREE

BRITISH BLUES BAND FORMED IN 1968. **PAUL RODGERS** (b. 1949; VOCALS), **PAUL KOSSOFF** (b. 1950, d. 1976; GUITAR), Andy Fraser (b. 1952; bass) and Simon Kirke (b. 1949; drums) gained early encouragement from **Alexis Korner**, but having completed an excellent, earthy debut album, *Tons Of Sobs*, began honing a more individual style with their second set. The powerful original songs, including 'I'll Be Creeping', showed a maturing talent. Their stylish blues rock reached its commercial peak on *Fire And Water*, containing 'All Right Now' (1970, UK number 2/US number 4).

Highway revealed a more mellow perspective highlighted by an increased use of piano at the expense of Kossoff's guitar. This was due, in part, to friction within the group and Free broke up in 1971, paradoxically in the wake of another hit, 'My Brother Jake'. They regrouped the following year when spin-off projects faltered.

Free At Last offered some of the unit's erstwhile fire and included another UK Top 20 hit, 'Little Bit Of Love'. However, Kossoff's increasing ill health and Fraser's departure for the Sharks undermined any new-found confidence; although the guitarist rejoined the quartet for several British dates his contribution to Free's final album, *Heartbreaker*, was muted.

FREED, ALAN

AS AN INFLUENTIAL DISC JOCKEY, FREED (b. 1926, d. 1965) MADE ENEMIES AMONG THE MUSIC BUSINESS ESTABLISHment by championing black artists. His first radio job was in 1946, playing classical records; he moved on to Ohio to play current pop material and in 1951 joined WJW Cleveland. There, Freed hosted a show consisting of R&B originals rather than white pop cover versions. Entitled *Moondog's Rock 'N' Roll Party*, the show attracted large audiences of white teenagers. His local success led him to New York and WINS in 1953. Still a champion of black artists, such as **Chuck Berry** and **Fats Domino**, Freed hosted major live shows at the Paramount Theater; however, with the rise of **Bill Haley**, **Elvis Presley** and Pat Boone, Freed's power as a disc jockey was weakened. In particular, he became a target of opponents of rock 'n' roll such as Columbia's A&R chief Mitch Miller; when Freed refused to play Columbia releases he was fired by WINS. Freed's arrest on a charge of inciting a riot at a Boston concert left him ill-prepared to deal with the accusations laid by a Congressional investigation in 1959. It emerged that independent labels had provided cash or publishing rights to Freed in return for the airplay they were denied by the prejudices of other radio stations. In 1962, Freed was found guilty of bribery, this was followed by charges of tax evasion.

FRIJID PINK

KELLY GREEN (VOCALS/HARMONICA), GARY RAY THOMPSON (GUITAR), THOMAS BEAUDRY (BASS), LARRY Zelanka (keyboards) and Rick Stevens (drums) emerged from the hard rock circuit in Detroit, USA. In 1970, they scored a surprise transatlantic hit with their interpretation of 'The House Of The Rising Sun' (US number 7/UK number 4). Subsequent chart entries, 'Sing A Song For Freedom' and 'Heartbreak Hotel' (both 1971), were confined to the lower regions of the US chart, confirming a suspicion that the song, rather than the group, was responsible for their early success.

FRIPP, ROBERT

UK-BORN GUITARIST, COMPOSER AND PRODUCER, FRIPP (b. 1946) JOINED THE LEAGUE OF GENTLEMEN AND LATER founded Giles Giles And Fripp with brothers Pete and Mike Giles. This eccentric trio completed one album before evolving into **King Crimson**. Between 1969 and 1974, Fripp led several contrasting versions of this constantly challenging group, during which time he also enjoyed an artistically fruitful collaboration with **Brian Eno**. *No Pussyfooting* and *Evening Star* were among the era's leading *avant-garde* recordings.

Having disbanded King Crimson, Fripp retired from music altogether. He re-emerged in 1977, contributing to **David Bowie**'s *Heroes*, before producing and playing on **Peter Gabriel**'s second album. Fripp reconstituted King

Crimson in 1981. Three well-received albums followed, during which time the guitarist pursued a parallel path leading a new League Of Gentlemen. Both units disbanded later in the decade and Fripp subsequently performed and gave tutorials under the 'League Of Crafty Guitarists' banner.

FUGAZI

US UNDERGROUND BAND FEATURING IAN MACKAYE (VOCALS/GUITAR), HIS CO-LYRICIST GUY PICCIOTTO, Brendan Canty (drums) and Joe Lally (bass). Fugazi ensure that door prices are kept down, mainstream press interviews are shunned and they maintain a commitment to all-age shows that shames many bands. The band have forged a consistent and challenging discography. Although they have concentrated primarily on touring rather than studio efforts, each of their albums has sold over 100,000 copies, produced entirely independently within their own Dischord Records framework.

FUGEES

NEW YORK CREW WHOSE NAME IS SHORTENED from Refugees (two of the three are expatriate Haitians). Their style is that of dry, cushioning beats, matched by the clever wordplay of rappers Wyclef 'Jef' Jean (b. 1970), Lauryn 'L' Hill (b. 1975) and Prakazrel 'Pras' Michel (b. 1972). Their lyrical concerns are somewhat different, some of their targets include America's perception of Haitians as 'Boat People' and their own mixed-gender status. 'Our music is a paradoxical thing. We blend soft and hardcore elements into it': musically this includes rapping over acoustic guitars, as well as more upbeat numbers, both modes in which Fugees excel.

FUGS

NEW YORK BAND FORMED IN 1965. THE FUGS COMBINED BOHEMIAN POETRY WITH AN ENGAGING MUSICAL naïvety and the shock tactic of outrage. Writers Ed Sanders, Tuli Kupferberg and Ken Weaver made their recording debut on the Broadside label, which viewed the group's work as 'ballads of contemporary protest'. The set included poetry by William Blake alongside such tracks as 'I Couldn't Get High' and 'Slum Goddess'; the trio was supported by several musicians from the Holy Modal Rounders. The Fugs' album was subsequently issued by ESP, a notorious outlet for the *avant-garde*. In 1967, the group switched to Reprise. Although *Tenderness Junction* featured a more proficient backing group the subject matter remained as before. *It Crawled Into My Hand, Honest*, released the following year, was another idiomatic record.

They disbanded to avoid the dangers of self-parody. *Fugs 4 Rounders Score* contained unreleased Holy Modal Rounders material. Sanders and Kupferberg resumed work as the Fugs during the 80s. During the 90s, Sanders and Kupferberg retrieved the rights to their ESP recordings. Subsequent repackages have been augmented by archive photographs and previously unissued recordings.

FULLER, BOBBY

US-BORN BOBBY FULLER (b. 1943, d. 1966) MADE HIS RECORDING DEBUT IN 1961 WITH 'YOU'RE IN LOVE'. FULLER LATER moved to Los Angeles where his group, the Bobby Fuller Four, became a leading attraction. In 1966, the group reached the US Top 10 with an ebullient reading of the **Crickets**' 'I Fought The Law'. This was followed up by a Top 30 hit, 'Love's Made A Fool Of You'. The singer's stature seemed assured, but on 18 July 1966, Fuller's body was discovered in a parked car in Los Angeles. His death was attributed to asphyxia through the forced inhalation of gasoline, but further investigations as to the perpetrators remain unresolved.

FUN BOY THREE

(VOCALS/DRUMS) AND LYNVAL GOLDING (GUITAR) LAUNCHED THE FUN BOY THREE. THEIR UK TOP 20 debut was the extraordinary 'The Lunatics Have Taken Over The Asylum'. The single effectively established the trio as both original and innovative commentators. For their follow-up, they teamed up with the then-unknown **Bananarama** for a hit revival of 'It Ain't What You Do It's The Way That You Do It'. The Bananarama connection continued when the Fun Boy Three appeared on their hit 'Really Saying Something'.

By 1982, the band were proving themselves adept at writing political songs and reviving, and remoulding, classic songs. The wonderfully cynical comment on teenage love and pregnancy, 'Tunnel Of Love', proved the trio's last major statement.

FUN LOVIN' CRIMINALS

HIP-HOP/ALTERNATIVE ROCK CROSSOVER GROUP FORMED IN NEW YORK IN THE EARLY 1990S. BY 1994, HUEY (VOCALS/ guitar), Steve (drums/programming) and Fast (bass/keyboards/harmonica) had begun releasing their first independent singles. With samples drawn from films such as *Pulp Fiction*, obscure cover versions and lyrical narratives describing New York's criminal underclass, they soon drew comparisons to the **Beastie Boys**, among others. The excellent *Come Find Yourself* and a string of single releases (including 'Fun Lovin' Criminal', 'Scooby Snacks' and 'King Of New York') secured strong airplay, alongside a series of rave reviews for their concert appearances.

FRIJID PINK
Albums
Defrosted (Parrot 1970)★★
➧ p.363 for full listings

FRIPP, ROBERT
Albums
Exposure (Polydor 1979)★★★★
with Andy Summers *I Advance Masked* (A&M 1982)★★★★
➧ p.363 for full listings
Collaborators
Brian Eno ➧ p.136
David Bowie ➧ p.64
Peter Gabriel ➧ p.157
Connections
King Crimson ➧ p.206
Further References
Book: *Robert Fripp: From King Crimson To Guitar Craft*, Eric Tamm

FUGAZI
Albums
Repeater (Dischord 1990)★★★★
➧ p.363 for full listings

FUGEES
Albums
The Score (Ruffhouse 1996)★★★★
➧ p.363 for full listings
Further References
Video: *The Score* (SMV 1996)
Book: *Fugees: The Unofficial Book*, Chris Roberts

FUGS
Albums
The Village Fugs aka *The Fugs First Album* (ESP 1965)★★★★
Virgin Fugs (ESP 1966)★★★★
➧ p.363 for full listings
Collaborators
Ed Sanders
Tuli Kupferberg

FULLER, BOBBY
Albums
I Fought The Law aka *Memorial Album* (Mustang 1966)★★★★
➧ p.363 for full listings
Influences
Crickets ➧ p.105

FUN BOY THREE
Albums
Waiting (Chrysalis 1983)★★★
➧ p.363 for full listings
Collaborators
Bananarama ➧ p.31

FUN LOVIN' CRIMINALS
Album
Come Find Yourself (EMI/Chrysalis 1996)★★★★
➧ p.363 for full listings
Connections
Beastie Boys ➧ p.37

FUNKADELIC

Albums

Maggot Brain (Westbound 1971)★★★★

Let's Take It To The Stage (Westbound 1975)★★★★

The Electric Spanking Of War Babies (Warners 1981)★★★★

➧ p.363 for full listings

Connections

Parliament ➧ p.256

FUNKADELIC

GEORGE CLINTON (b. 1940) ESTABLISHED THIS INVENTIVE, EXPERIMENTAL US GROUP FROM THE 1969 LINE-UP OF **Parliament**: Raymond Davis (b. 1940), Grady Thomas (b. 1941), Calvin Simon (b. 1942) and Clarence 'Fuzzy' Haskins (b. 1941), plus the backing group: Bernard Worrell (b. 1944; keyboards), William Nelson Jnr (b. 1951; bass), Eddie Hazel (b. 1950, d. 1992; lead guitar), Lucius Ross (b. 1948; rhythm guitar) and Ramon 'Tiki' Fulwood (b. 1944; drums). The new band laced hard funk with a heady dose of psychedelia. Although few of their singles entered the R&B Top 30, Funkadelic consistently reached the chart's lower placings.

In 1977, Clinton moved from the Westbound label to Warner Brothers Records and in 1978 the compulsive 'One Nation Under A Groove' was a million-seller. By this point the distinctions between Funkadelic and Parliament were becoming increasingly blurred. Funkadelic secured another major hit in 1979 with '(Not Just) Knee Deep'; three long-time associates, Clarence Haskins, Calvin Simon and Grady Thomas, then broke away, taking the Funkadelic name with them. Despite an early R&B hit, 'Connections And Disconnections', they were unable to maintain their own direction and the group later dissolved. Now recording as the P-Funk All Stars, Clinton's 1996 album *The Awesome Power Of A Fully Operational Mothership* was a superb blend of Funkadelic and Parliament.

FUNKDOOBIEST

Albums

Which Doobie U B (Immortal 1993)★★★

Wopbabuloop (Immortal 1993)★★★

Brothas Doobie (Epic 1995)★★★

➧ p.363 for full listings

FUNKDOOBIEST

FUNKDOOBIEST – SON DOOBIE, DJ RALPH M THE MEXICAN AND TOMAHAWK FUNK (AKA T-BONE) – DEBUTED WITH the incessant 'Bow Wow Wow', which instantly launched them into the hearts of a nation of B-boys. Their debut album was a reinstatement of old school principles, as Son Doobie eulogized in interviews: 'I'm an old skool supremacist. I'm a hip hop inspector, I'm a fundamentalist, to me hip hop is a religion. You know it can't be trivialized'. Funkdoobiest are certainly not the most politically correct of rappers – many of their lyrics are vividly pro-pornography. At least their commitment to rap's history is as staunch as their fondness for exposed flesh.

FUNKMASTERS

A COLLECTION OF UK FUNK MUSICIANS, VOCALISTS AND RAPPER BO KOOL, MASTERMINDED BY REGGAE RADIO disc jockey Tony Williams. Williams produced several records under this name, including 'Love Money' (1982), one of the earliest UK rap tracks. The act's only chart success came in 1984 with 'It's Over', a Tony Williams song that made the UK Top 10 on his Master Funk label. The hit introduced the public to the voice of Julie Roberts (b. 1962), who was working in the USA when the record charted and had to be substituted for all promotion work.

FURY, BILLY

Albums

The Sound Of Fury (Decca 1960)★★★★

➧ p.363 for full listings

Connections

Tornados ➧ p.322

Further References

Film: *I've Gotta Horse* (1965)

FURY, BILLY

UK SINGER FURY (b. RONALD WYCHERLEY, 1940, d. 1983) JOINED LARRY PARNES'S MANAGEMENT STABLE. HIS debut single, 'Maybe Tomorrow' (1959) reached the UK Top 20; in 1960, he released *The Sound Of Fury*, which consisted entirely of his own songs. Fury found his greatest success with a series of dramatic ballads which, in suggesting a vulnerability, enhanced the singer's undoubted sex appeal. His stylish good looks complimented a vocal prowess, blossoming in 1961 with a cover version of Tony Orlando's 'Halfway To Paradise'. This superior single, arranged and scored by Ivor Raymonde, established a pattern that provided Fury with 16 further UK Top 30 hits. Supported initially by the **Tornados**, then the Gamblers, the singer showed a wider repertoire live than his label would allow on record.

Bedevilled by ill health and overtaken by changing musical fashions, Fury's final hit came in 1965 with 'Give Me Your Word'. The following year he left Decca for Parlophone, debuting with 'Hurtin' Is Lovin'', but he was unable to regain his erstwhile success. In 1971, he underwent open-heart surgery, but recovered to record 'Will The Real Man Stand Up' on his own Fury label. A second major operation in 1976 forced Billy to retire again, but he re-emerged at the end of the decade with new recordings of his best-known songs, and several live and television appearances. In 1981, Fury struck a new deal with Polydor, but his health was rapidly deteriorating and on 28 January 1983 he succumbed to a fatal heart attack.

FUTURE SOUND OF LONDON

FUTURE SOUND OF LONDON EMERGED IN THE 90S, THE BRAINCHILD OF BRITISH STUDENTS GARY COBAIN AND Dougans. The duo recorded discordant electronic pieces together, but it was not until the house explosion of 1988 that they discovered like minds and a new musical structure. Their projects spawned Semi Real ('People Livin' Today'), Yage, Metropolis (*Metropolis* EP), Art Science Technology, Mental Cube ('So This Is Love' on Debut), Candese, Intelligent Communication and Smart Systems. However, under the title Future Sound Of London they scored a major crossover success with 'Papua New Guinea'. Still under the FSOL banner they released the single 'Cascade' (1993), which clocked in at an amazing 30 minutes and 50 seconds. Originally recorded in five separate segments, it was pieced together specially for the release. Taken from their second album, 'Cascade' combined breakbeats with rumbling bass and heavy atmospherics. Utilizing their Amorphous Androgynous *nom de plume* they also recorded the *Tales Of Ephidrina* long player, one of many concurrent pseudonymous excursions. They have also earned their way as a remix team, rejigging Inner City's 'Praise' among others. Rather than tour in a conventional manner, they have organized 'radio tours', intermittently broadcasted on various BBC stations, and produced their own film/music collage in a series of American planetariums.

G-CLEFS

US DOO-WOP-STYLED VOCAL GROUP. BROTHERS TEDDY, CHRIS, TIMMY AND ARNOLD SCOTT AND RAY GIBSON started out singing gospel, were spotted by Pilgrim Records' Jack Gould and debuted in 1956 with 'Ka Ding Dong' (R&B Juke Box Top 10/US Top 40). Following another three releases, they took a break. When Arnold, the youngest member, left school in 1960 they re-formed and joined Terrace Records. Their version of 'I Understand' and 'Auld Lang Syne' were their only US Top 10 and UK Top 20 entries, although the follow-up, 'A Girl Has To Know', charted.

G., KENNY

US SAXOPHONIST KENNY GORELICK (b. 1959) PLAYED WITH **BARRY WHITE**'S LOVE UNLIMITED ORCHESTRA BEFORE recording with local funk band Cold, Bold & Together and backing many leading artists on local shows. He then joined the Jeff Lorber Fusion, recording on Arista Records; in 1981 Arista signed him to a solo contract. Produced by Preston Glass and Narada Michael Walden, *Duotones* was a major success, spawning 'Songbird' (1987, US Top 10). Kenny G. was also in demand to play solos on albums by **Whitney Houston**, **Natalie Cole** and **Aretha Franklin** among others.

Silhouette featured guest artists including **Smokey Robinson**; the album sold over three million copies worldwide. Kenny's success continued with the multi-platinum *Breathless*, followed by *Miracles: The Holiday Album* (US number 1). *Breathless* sold over 11 million copies in the USA alone and remained at the top of the *Billboard* jazz chart for over 18 months. It was toppled in 1996 by *The Moment*, the new album from . . . Kenny G.

G., WARREN

DESPITE AFFILIATIONS TO GANGSTA RAP, WARREN G. (b. WARREN GRIFFIN III, *c.* 1971; HALF-BROTHER TO **DR DRE**) dedicated his debut album to 'Jesus' and departed from rap norms with his employment of live musicians. Warren began rapping and producing while working at a record store; he helped form Dre's *Dogg Pound* collective, with Nate Dogg and **Snoop Doggy Dogg**. He produced a track for MC Breed ('Gotta Get Mine') and appeared on *The Chronic* and *Doggy Style*; he also wrote, produced and guested on Mista Grimm's 'Indo Smoke' and 2Pac's 'Definition Of A Thug'.

Warren G.'s debut, 'Regulate', was built around a sample of **Michael McDonald**'s 'I Keep Forgettin''. *Regulate* achieved double-platinum status. Following a US tour with **R. Kelly** and **Heavy D**, he concentrated on producing the debut of Da Twinz, part of the collective involved with *Regulate*. In 1996, 'What's Love Got To Do With It' (from the film *Super Cop*) reached German number 1 and UK Top 5.

GABRIEL, PETER

AFTER SEVEN YEARS FRONTING **GENESIS**, GABRIEL (b. 1950) WENT SOLO IN 1975. HIS FIRST ALBUM INCLUDED 'Solsbury Hill', which made the UK Top 20. The album charted in the UK and the USA, and Gabriel began a US tour, nervous of facing UK audiences. The second album made the UK Top 10 and just missed the *Billboard* Top 20. It contained chiefly introspective, experimental music, but sales figures were healthy. However, Atlantic Records refused to distribute his third album in the USA, finding it too maudlin. Mercury Records stepped in and with Steve Lillywhite's production the collection was far from Atlantic's feared 'commercial suicide'. 'Games Without Frontiers' was a UK Top 5 hit, and 'Biko' (about Stephen Biko) became an anti-racist anthem. *Peter Gabriel (Security)* appeared more accessible; a German-language edition was also released. After *Peter Gabriel Plays Live*, Gabriel composed the haunting film soundtrack to *Birdy*.

So brought commercial acceptance, containing the US number 1 'Sledgehammer'. His duet with **Kate Bush**, 'Don't Give Up', reached the UK Top 10. Throughout the 80s, Gabriel dedicated time to world music and sponsored the 1982 WOMAD (World Music And Dance) Festival. He became heavily involved in Amnesty International and recorded with **Youssou N'Dour**. They toured the USA under the banner of 'Conspiracy Of Hope', raising money for Amnesty. In 1989, Gabriel wrote the score for *The Last Temptation Of Christ*. *Shaking The Tree* was a greatest hits collection. Although *Us* fell short of the high standard of *So*, it put Gabriel back in the public eye.

FUTURE SOUND OF LONDON

Albums

as Amorphous Androgynous *Tales Of Ephidrina* (Virgin 1993)★★★★
Lifeforms (Virgin 1994)★★★★
p.363 for full listings

G., KENNY

Albums

G Force (Arista 1983)★★★
Breathless (Arista 1992)★★★★
The Moment (Arista 1996)★★★
p.363 for full listings

Collaborators

Barry White p.337
Whitney Houston p.188
Natalie Cole p.97
Aretha Franklin p.153
Smokey Robinson p.279

G., WARREN

Albums

Regulate ... G Funk Era (Violator/RAL1994)★★★
Take A Look Over Your Shoulder (Reality) (G Funk Music/Def Jam 1997)★★★★
p.363 for full listings

Collaborators

Nate Dogg
Snoop Doggy Dogg
p.302

Connections

Dr Dre p.124
Michael McDonald p.229
R. Kelly p.204
Heavy D p.179

GABRIEL, PETER

Albums

Peter Gabriel (Charisma 1977)★★★
Peter Gabriel (Security) (Charisma 1982)★★★★
So (Virgin 1986)★★★★
p.363 for full listings

Collaborators

Robert Fripp p.154
Kate Bush p.76
Youssou N'Dour p.243

Connections

Genesis p.161

Further References

Videos: *Point Of View (Live In Athens)* (1989)
Computer Animation: Vol. 2 (1994)
Book: *Peter Gabriel: An Authorized Biography*, Spenser Bright

GALLAGHER AND LYLE
Albums
The Last Cowboy (A&M 1974)★★★
➽ p.363 for full listings
Collaborators
Terry Britten
Connections
Art Garfunkel ➽ p.159
Tina Turner ➽ p.324
Michael Jackson ➽ p.195

GALLAGHER, RORY
Albums
Blueprint (Polydor 1973)★★★★
Tattoo (Polydor 1973)★★★★
➽ p.363 for full listings

Collaborators
Jerry Lee Lewis ➽ p.215
Albert King ➽ p.205
Connections
Taste ➽ p.317
Sensational Alex Harvey Band ➽ p.292
Nine Below Zero ➽ p.248
Influences
Lonnie Donegan ➽ p.122
Woody Guthrie ➽ p.171
Chuck Berry ➽ p.45
Muddy Waters ➽ p.242
Further References
Video: *Live In Cork* (Castle Hendring Video 1989)

GANG OF FOUR
Albums
Entertainment! (Warners 1979)★★★★
Shrinkwrapped (Castle 1995)★★★
➽ p.363 for full listings
Connections
Shriekback ➽ p.296
Curve ➽ p.108

GAP BAND
Albums
The Gap Band II (Mercury 1979)★★★★
➽ p.363 for full listings

GARBAGE
Albums
Garbage (Mushroom 1995)★★★★
➽ p.363 for full listings
Collaborators
Tricky ➽ p.324
Connections
Smashing Pumpkins ➽ p.301
U2 ➽ p.326
Nirvana ➽ p.248
Further References
Video: *Garbage Video* (Mushroom 1996)

GALLAGHER AND LYLE

SCOTTISH SONGWRITERS BENNY GALLAGHER (VOCALS/GUITAR) AND GRAHAM LYLE (VOCALS/GUITAR) began their career with 'Mr. Heartbreak's Here Instead', a 1964 single for Dean Ford And The Gaylords. They later moved to London as in-house composers for Apple. Their 'International', was recorded by Mary Hopkin.

In 1969, they joined McGuinness Flint, for whom they wrote 'When I'm Dead And Gone' (1970) and 'Malt And Barley Blues' (1971), before leaving for an independent career. Several well-crafted albums followed, showing their flair for folk-styled melody. *Breakaway* was a commerical breakthrough, spawning 'I Wanna Stay With You' and 'Heart On My Sleeve' (both UK number 6); **Art Garfunkel** took a version of the title track into the US Top 40.

Gallagher and Lyle parted following the release of *Lonesome No More*; both have continued as successful songwriters. Lyle later found a new partner, Terry Britten, with whom he composed 'What's Love Got To Do With It' (**Tina Turner**) and 'Just Good Friends' (**Michael Jackson**).

GALLAGHER, RORY

IRISH-BORN GALLAGHER (b. 1949, d. 1995) PUT TOGETHER THE BLUES-BASED ROCK TRIO **TASTE** IN 1965. WHEN THEY split in 1970, Gallagher went solo, supported by Gerry McAvoy (bass) and Wilgar Campbell (drums). Gallagher's bottleneck guitar playing made him a major live attraction. Campbell was replaced by Rod De'ath following the release of *Live In Europe* (with Lou Martin on keyboards). This line-up was responsible for Gallagher's major commercial triumphs, *Blueprint* and *Irish Tour '74*. De'ath and Martin left in 1978. Drummer Ted McKenna (ex-**Sensational Alex Harvey Band**) joined the ever-present McAvoy but was later replaced by Brendan O'Neill. Blues harmonica virtuoso Mark Feltham (ex-**Nine Below Zero**) became a full-time 'guest'. Gallagher toured America over 30 times and the world twice. His records sold millions. He recorded with his heroes, such as **Jerry Lee Lewis** and **Albert King**, and contributed to the work of the Fureys, Davy Spillane and Joe O'Donnell. Gallagher died following complications after a liver transplant.

GAMBLE AND HUFF

LEON HUFF (b. 1942) WAS AN ESTABLISHED SESSION MUSICIAN; SONGWRITER KENNY GAMBLE (b. 1943) WAS A member of the Romeos, a Philadelphia group Huff joined later. The duo produced the Soul Survivors' 'Expressway To Your Heart' (1967, US Top 10), followed by the Intruders' 'Love Is Like A Baseball Game'. Gamble and Huff also provided hits for **Archie Bell And The Drells** ('I Can't Stop Dancing'), Jerry Butler ('Only The Strong Survive') and **Wilson Pickett** ('Don't Let The Green Grass Fool You').

The duo formed the Neptune label, accumulating an impressive roster of acts, many of whom were retained when its successor, Philadelphia International, was founded in 1971. Philadelphia was responsible for many of the decade's finest soul singles, including 'If You Don't Know Me By Now' (**Harold Melvin And The Blue Notes**) and 'Me And Mrs Jones' (Billy Paul). Their music formed a natural stepping stone between Tamla/**Motown** and disco, but this pre-eminent position was undermined by a 1975 bribes-for-airplay scandal. Gamble was fined $2,500 and the pair's work suffered. Their last consistent commercial success came with **Teddy Pendergrass**; the Philly-soul sound was unable to adapt to the new decade.

GANG OF FOUR

UK BAND FORMED IN 1977. JON KING (VOCALS/MELODICA), ANDY GILL (GUITAR), DAVE ALLEN (DRUMS) AND HUGO Burnham (drums) debuted in 1978 with a three-track EP, *Damaged Goods*. Burnham's pounding, compulsive drumming and Gill's staccato, stuttering guitar work, framed their overtly political lyrics. They maintained this direction on *Entertainment!*, while introducing the interest in dance music that marked future recordings. 'At Home He's A Tourist' was issued, but encountered censorship problems over its pre-AIDS reference to 'rubbers'. Allen departed (for **Shriekback**), replaced by Sara Lee. *Songs Of The Free* featured the tongue-in-cheek 'I Love A Man In Uniform', which seemed destined for chart success until disappearing from radio playlists in the wake of the Falklands conflict. Burnham was fired in 1983 and a three-piece line-up completed *Hard* with session musicians. The group dissolved the following year.

King and Gill exhumed the Gang Of Four name in 1990 and released *Mall*; it did little commercially. *Shrinkwrapped* was better, with the addition of drummer Steve Monti (ex-**Curve**).

GAP BAND

US FUNK SEPTET LED BY THREE BROTHERS, CHARLES, RONNIE AND ROBERT WILSON. AFTER TWO MINOR US HITS in 1977, they hit the R&B Top 10 with 'Shake', 'Steppin' (Out)' and 'I Don't Believe You Want To Get Up And Dance' – better known by its subtitle, 'Oops, Up Side Your Head' (1980, UK Top 10). 'Burn Rubber (Why Do You Wanna Hurt Me)' (1980), 'You Dropped A Bomb On Me' and 'Party Train' (both 1982) all topped the UK chart, while 'Big Fun' (1986) reached the UK Top 5. Three years later they recorded the theme song to *I'm Gonna Git You Sucka*.

GARBAGE

US GROUP FOUNDED IN 1994. BUTCH VIG (PRODUCER FOR **SMASHING Pumpkins**, **U2** and **Nirvana**), Steve Marker and Duke Erikson recruited Scottish singer Shirley Manson. Garbage's debut 'Vow' was widely acclaimed, as was 'Subhuman'; both borrowed from various traditions, notably punk, glam rock and art rock. This eclecticism was further explored on their self-titled debut album, a dark collection of songs mainly about fear, lust and envy. 'Only Happy When It Rains' charted as did a remix of 'Milk' (featuring **Tricky**). Further chart success came with 'Stupid Girl' (1997).

GARCIA, JERRY

MERCURIAL **GRATEFUL DEAD** GUITARIST JERRY GARCIA (b. 1942, d. 1995) WAS A LEADING LIGHT ON THE WEST COAST musical scene – credited on **Jefferson Airplane**'s *Surrealistic Pillow* as 'musical and spiritual adviser' and known locally as 'Captain Trips'. In addition to session work with the Airplane, he worked with **David Crosby**, Paul Kantner, **Jefferson Starship**, **New Riders Of The Purple Sage** and **Crosby, Stills, Nash And Young**, as well as various spin-offs involving David Nelson, John Kahn (b. 1948, d. 1996), Merl Saunders and Howard Wales. Garcia played banjo and pedal-steel guitar, mastering rock 'n' roll/blues and country/bluegrass, without a hint of musical overlap – despite having lost the third finger of his left hand. Following his heroin addiction and much publicized near-death in 1986, Garcia continued touring and recording, with the Dead and on his own. He died from a heart attack.

GARFUNKEL, ART

THE POSSESSOR OF ONE OF THE MOST PITCH-PERFECT VOICES IN POPULAR MUSIC HAS HAD A SPARSE RECORDING career since the demise of **Simon And Garfunkel**. Art's solo recording career actually started while he was singing with Simon as the duo Tom And Jerry, with two singles released under the name Artie Garr, 'Dream Alone' (1959) and 'Private World' (1960). Garfunkel also acted, appearing in *Catch 22*, *Carnal Knowledge*, *Bad Timing* and *Good To Go*.

Art's debut album, *Angel Clare*, contained 'All I Know' (US Top 10); in the UK two of his records made number 1, 'I Only Have Eyes For You' and 'Bright Eyes'. In 1978 '(What A) Wonderful World' featured **James Taylor** and **Paul Simon**. Simon and Garfunkel appeared together occasionally on television and on record, and in 1981 performed at the historic Central Park concert. They struggled through a world tour, opening up old wounds; until once again parting company. Since then Garfunkel has released occasional albums, largely attributable to the songwriting of **Jim Webb**.

GAYE, MARVIN

THE SON OF A MINISTER, GAYE (b. MARVIN PENTZ GAY JNR, 1939, d. 1984) LEFT HIS FATHER'S CHURCH CHOIR TO TEAM up with **Don Covay** and Billy Stewart in the R&B vocal group the Rainbows. In 1957, he joined the Marquees; the following year the group was taken under the wing of producer/singer Harvey Fuqua. When Fuqua moved to Detroit in 1960, Marvin went with him, becoming a session singer and vocalist for **Motown**. In 1961, Marvin married Gordy's sister, Anna, and was offered a solo recording contract. Renamed Marvin Gaye, he began his career as a jazz balladeer, but in 1962, was persuaded to record R&B, obtaining his first hit with 'Stubborn Kind Of Fellow' (R&B Top 10). In 1965, Gaye began to record in a more sophisticated style. 'How Sweet It Is (To Be Loved By You)' epitomized his new direction; it was followed by two R&B number 1s, 'I'll Be Doggone' and 'Ain't That Peculiar'.

Motown teamed Gaye with their leading female vocalist, **Mary Wells**, for some romantic duets. When Wells left Motown in 1964, Gaye recorded with Kim Weston until 1967; she was succeeded by Tammi Terrell. The Gaye/Terrell partnership represented the apogee of the soul duet. In 1968 he issued the epochal 'I Heard It Through The Grapevine' – the label's biggest-selling record to date – but his career was derailed by the death of Terrell in 1970.

In 1971, Gaye emerged with a set of recordings which eventually formed his most successful solo album. He combined his spiritual beliefs with increasing concern about poverty, discrimination and political corruption in America, creating a fluid instrumental backdrop for *What's Going On*. After the soundtrack to the 'blaxploitation' thriller *Trouble Man*, Gaye shifted his attention from the spiritual to the sexual with *Let's Get It On*. He also collaborated with **Diana Ross** on a sensuous album of duets in 1973. The break-up of his marriage to Anna Gordy in 1975 delayed work on his next album. *I Want You* was merely a pleasant reworking of *Let's Get It On*, albeit slightly more contemporary. The title track was a number 1 soul hit however, as was his 1977 disco extravaganza, 'Got To Give It Up'.

In 1980, Gaye moved to Europe where he began work on an ambitious concept album *In Our Lifetime*. When it emerged, Gaye and Motown entered into a huge dispute that led to Gaye leaving for Columbia in 1982. He re-emerged with 'Sexual Healing', which combined his passionate soul vocals with a contemporary electro-disco backing. *Midnight Love* offered no equal surprises, but the success of the single seemed to herald a new era in Gaye's music. The intensity of his cocaine addiction made it impossible for him to work on another album, and he fell into a prolonged bout of depression. On 1 April 1984, a violent disagreement led to Marvin Gay Snr shooting his son dead.

GAYE BYKERS ON ACID

UK ROCK GROUP WHO COMBINED BIKER ATTIRE WITH PSYCHEDELIA AND HIPPIE CAMP. LED BY MARY MILLINGton, aka Mary Mary (b. Ian Garfield Hoxley; vocals) alongside Kevin Hyde (drums), Robber (b. Ian Michael Reynolds; bass) and Tony (b. Richard Anthony Horsfall; guitar) – later complemented by DJ William Samuel Ronald Monroe ('Rocket Ronnie'). Their debut album, *Drill Your Own Hole*, required purchasers to do just that – the record was initially issued without a hole in its centre. After leaving Virgin Records, they set up their own label, Naked Brain.

When the band dissolved, Hyde formed GROWTH, Tony formed Camp Collision, and Mary Mary joined Pigface. In the 90s, he formed Hyperhead, with Karl Leiker.

GARCIA, JERRY

Albums

Garcia (Warners 1972)★★★

How Sweet It Is (Grateful Dead Records 1997)★★★

➽ p.363 for full listings

Collaborators

Jefferson Airplane ➽ p.198
David Crosby ➽ p.105
Paul Kantner
Starship
New Riders Of The Purple Sage ➽ p.246
Crosby, Stills, Nash And Young ➽ p.106

Connections

Grateful Dead ➽ p.167

Further References

Books: *Garcia – A Signpost To A New Space*, Charles Reich and Jann Wenner
Grateful Dead – The Music Never Stopped, Blair Jackson

GARFUNKEL, ART

Albums

Angel Clare (Columbia 1973)★★★

The Very Best Of – Across America (Virgin 1996)★★★

➽ p.363 for full listings

Collaborators

Paul Simon ➽ p.296
James Taylor ➽ p.317
Jimmy Webb ➽ p.335

Connections

Simon And Garfunkel ➽ p.297

GAYE, MARVIN

Albums

What's Going On (Tamla 1971)★★★★★

Let's Get It On (Tamla 1973)★★★★★

➽ p.363 for full listings

Collaborators

Don Covay ➽ p.102
Mary Wells ➽ p.336
Tammi Terrell
Diana Ross ➽ p.283

Connections

Moonglows ➽ p.237
Berry Gordy
Motown ➽ p.240

Further References

Books: *Divided Soul: The Life Of Marvin Gaye*, David Ritz
I Heard It Through The Grapevine: Marvin Gaye, The Biography, Sharon Davis

GAYE BYKERS ON ACID

Albums

GrooveDiveSoapDish (Bleed 1989)★★★

➽ p.363 for full listings

Connections

Killing Joke ➽ p.205
Ministry ➽ p.234
Public Image Ltd ➽ p.269

Further References

Book: *Drill Your Own Hole* (Virgin Vision 1987)

GAYLE, CRYSTAL
Albums
When I Dream (United Artists 1978)★★★★
Miss The Mississippi (Columbia 1979)★★★★
➤ p.363 for full listings
Collaborators
Allen Reynold
Tom Waits ➤ p.332
Connections
Neil Sedaka ➤ p.291
Johnnie Ray ➤ p.273
Influences
Beatles ➤ p.38
Peter, Paul And Mary ➤ p.260

GAYNOR, GLORIA
Albums
Experience Gloria Gaynor (MGM 1975)★★★
➤ p.363 for full listings
Collaborators
Johnny Nash ➤ p.244
Connections
Jay Ellis

GEFFEN, DAVID
➤ p.363 for full listings
Collaborators
Laura Nyro ➤ p.249
Crosby, Stills And Nash ➤ p.106
Joni Mitchell ➤ p.235
Jackson Browne ➤ p.71
Linda Ronstadt ➤ p.282
Connections
Asylum Records
Elektra Records
Warner Brothers Pictures
Geffen Records
John Lennon ➤ p.214
George Michael ➤ p.233
Further References
Book: *The Hit Men*, Frederick Dannen

GEILS, J., BAND
Albums
Showtime! (EMI 1982)★★★
➤ p.363 for full listings
Connections
Albert Collins ➤ p.97
Otis Rush ➤ p.285
John Lee Hooker ➤ p.185

GELDOF, BOB
Albums
The Vegetarians Of Love (Mercury 1990)★★★
➤ p.363 for full listings
Collaborators
Boomtown Rats ➤ p.62
Midge Ure ➤ p.327
Connections
Pink Floyd ➤ p.261
Band Aid
Further References
Book: *Is That It?*, Bob Geldof

GENE
Albums
Olympian (Costermonger 1995)★★★★
➤ p.363 for full listings

GAYLE, CRYSTAL

US-BORN GAYLE (b. BRENDA GAIL WEBB, 1951) WAS THE SISTER OF LORETTA LYNN. IN THE LATE 60S, GAYLE SIGNED with her sister's recording label USA Decca and chose her performing name. Lynn wrote some of Gayle's first records ('Sparklin' Look Of Love', 'Mama, It's Different This Time') and therein lay the problem – Crystal Gayle sounded like Loretta Lynn. Gayle first entered the US country charts in 1970 with 'I've Cried (The Blue Right Out Of My Eyes)', which was followed by 'Everybody Oughta Cry' and 'I Hope You're Having Better Luck Than Me'. There was nothing original about the records so Gayle left the label.

After joining United Artists, she was teamed with producer-songwriter Allen Reynolds and recorded his US country hit, 'Wrong Road Again' (1974). Several other songwriters also supplied Gayle with excellent songs, and she had a country hit with 'Beyond You', written by herself and her lawyer/manager/husband Vassilios 'Bill' Gatzimos. Gayle entered the US country Top 10 with the title song from *Somebody Loves You*, and followed it with her first country number 1, 'I'll Get Over You'. In 1976, Gayle was voted Female Vocalist of the Year by the Academy of Country Music, but Reynolds knew there was a bigger market than country for her records. He seized the opportunity when Leigh wrote the jazz-tinged ballad 'Don't It Make My Brown Eyes Blue'. The single won Grammy Awards for Best Female Country Vocal Performance and Best Country Song. Its attendant album, *We Must Believe In Magic*, became the first million-selling album by a female country artist. In 1979, Gayle became the first US country artist to perform in China.

When I Dream was a lavish production crediting 50 musicians. British writer Roger Cook gave her a soulful ballad, 'Talking In Your Sleep' (UK number 11/US number 18). In 1979, Gayle signed with Columbia and quickly had a US pop hit with 'Half The Way'. She had three country number 1s among her 10 hits for the label, recorded an excellent version of **Neil Sedaka**'s 'The Other Side Of Me' and revived an early country record, Jimmie Rodgers' 'Miss The Mississippi And You'.

In 1982, Gayle moved to Elektra and worked on the soundtrack of the film *One From The Heart* with **Tom Waits**. In recent years, Gayle joined Capitol and her *Ain't Gonna Worry* reunited her with Reynolds. Buzz Stone produced *Three Good Reasons*, which was a heartening return to her country roots.

GAYNOR, GLORIA

GAYNOR (b. 1947) WAS DISCOVERED SINGING IN A MANHATTAN NIGHTclub by future manager, Jay Ellis. Together with producers Tony Bongiovia and Meco Monardo, he created an unswerving disco backbeat propelling such exemplary Gaynor performances as 'Never Can Say Goodbye' (1974) and 'Reach Out I'll Be There' (1975).

In 1979, 'I Will Survive' topped the UK and US charts and 'I Am What I Am' was a UK hit in 1983. 'I Will Survive' has been re-released successfully several times.

GEFFEN, DAVID

GEFFEN (b. 1941) BECAME **LAURA NYRO**'S MANAGER IN 1968, SIGNING HER TO COLUMBIA RECORDS; HE THEN FORMED a company with Elliott Roberts to manage **Crosby, Stills And Nash**, **Joni Mitchell**, **Jackson Browne**, **Linda Ronstadt** and others. He started Asylum Records in 1970; in 1971 it was sold to WEA Records for $7,000,000 with Geffen as chairman. He became chief of Elektra/Asylum in 1973 (briefly signing **Bob Dylan**), then vice-chairman of Warner Brothers Pictures two years later. In 1976, ill-health forced Geffen to leave the business but he returned in 1980 with Geffen Records, whose roster included **John Lennon**. He also started Geffen Films. Among his movie productions was *Little Shop Of Horrors*, while on Broadway he produced *Cats* and *Dreamgirls*. In 1989, Geffen sold his label to MCA for over $500 million in stock, taking further profits when MCA was bought by Matsushita. He remained chairman of Geffen Records and introduced a new label, DGC, followed by Dreamworks, who negotiated to buy out **George Michael** from Sony.

GEILS, J., BAND

US GROUP FORMED IN 1969. J. GEILS (b. JEROME GEILS, 1946; GUITAR), PETER WOLF (b. 1947; VOCALS), MAGIC DICK (b. Richard Salwitz, 1945; harmonica), Seth Justman (b. 1951; keyboards), Danny Klein (b. 1946; bass) and Stephan Jo Bladd (b. 1942; drums) were originally known as the J. Geils Blues Band. Their first two albums were tough, raw R&B. The following *Bloodshot* went gold in the US and *Monkey Island* reclaimed the fire and excitement of the first two albums. The group moved from Atlantic to EMI at the end of the 70s, achieving an international hit with 'Centrefold' (1982). Now divorced from its blues roots, the J. Geils Band was unsure of its direction; in 1984 Wolf went solo – midway through a recording session. The group completed a final album, *You're Gettin' Even, While I'm Gettin' Old*, without him.

GELDOF, BOB

IRISH-BORN GELDOF (b. 1954) STARTED OUT AS A ROCK JOURNALIST in Canada. Back in Dublin, he formed Nitelife Thugs, which evolved into the **Boomtown Rats**. After a series of hits, including two UK number 1s, the group fell from favour.

After appearing in the film of **Pink Floyd**'s *The Wall*, Geldof turned his attention to the dreadful famine that was plaguing Ethiopia in 1984. Shocked by horrific television pictures, Geldof organized Band Aid and wrote 'Do They Know It's Christmas?'. The charity single sold in excess of three million copies and inspired Live Aid, in which rock's elite played before a worldwide television audience of over 1,000,000,000. Geldof continued to help administer Band Aid, putting his singing career on hold for a couple of years.

After publishing his autobiography, he recorded the solo album, *Deep In The Heart Of Nowhere*, including the minor hit 'This Is The World Calling'. *The Vegetarians Of Love* included folk and cajun flavourings and was a hit.

Due to the acrimonious break-up of his marriage to Paula Yates, Geldof has remained in the newspaper headlines since 1994. Throughout he has retained his dignity.

GENE

FOPPISH AESTHETIC UK BAND FORMED IN 1993. STEVE MASON (b. 1971; GUITAR), MARTIN ROSSITER (b. 1971; vocals), Kevin Miles (b. 1967; bass) and Matt James (b. 1966; drums) wrote songs together and debuted with the double a-side 'For The Dead'/'Child's Body'. Single Of The Week and Month awards followed from UK magazines. Excellent support performances to **Pulp** followed, where Rossiter's stage presence illuminated Gene's performance. Their second single was a triple a-side: 'Be My Light, Be My Guide', 'This Is Not My Crime' and 'I Can't Help Myself'. A third single, 'Sleep Well Tonight', followed an appearance at the Reading Festival, and a tour of mainland Europe with **Elastica** and **Oasis**. It saw them break the Top 40 and the release of 'Haunted By You' (1995) prefigured a debut album proper. *To See The Lights* collected together b-sides and live recordings, acting as a stopgap for *Drawn To The Deep End*.

GENERAL PUBLIC

WHEN UK BAND THE **BEAT** DISBANDED, VOCALISTS DAVE WAKELING AND RANKING ROGER FORMED GENERAL Public with Horace Panter (bass; ex-**Specials**), Stoker (drums), Micky Billingham (keyboards), Kevin White (guitar) and a saxophonist. A self-titled debut single combined pop with an underlying dance feel and brushed the UK charts. Their fine debut album, *All The Rage*, was largely ignored in the UK. They tried again with *Hand To Mouth*, but despite the single 'Faults And All', the world seemed oblivious and General Public disappeared.

A new album appeared in 1995 featuring Wakeling, Ranking Roger, Michael Railton (vocals/keyboards), Norman Jones (vocals/percussion), Wayne Lothian (bass) and Dan Chase (drums). The album sounded fresh and energetic with invigorating originals such as 'It Must Be Tough' and 'Rainy Days' alongside a ska/reggae version of **Van Morrison**'s 'Warm Love'.

GENERATION X

UK PUNK GROUP FORMED IN LONDON IN 1976. **BILLY IDOL** (b. WILLIAM BROAD, 1955; VOCALS; EX-**CHELSEA**), TONY James (bass/vocals; ex-Chelsea), Bob Andrews (guitar/vocals) and John Towe (drums; replaced by Mark Laff in 1977) were signed to Chrysalis Records. They scraped the UK chart with 'Your Generation' and 'Ready Steady Go'. Following 'Friday's Angels' (1979), Terry Chimes (ex-**Clash**) replaced Laff. Their biggest commercial success was with 'King Rocker' (1979, UK number 11). The group lasted until 1981.

Idol went on to solo stardom, John Towe joined the **Adverts**, Terry Chimes rejoined the Clash, while Tony James reinvented himself in Sigue Sigue Sputnik.

GENESIS

UK BAND FORMED AT CHARTERHOUSE SCHOOL. **PETER GABRIEL** (b. 1950; VOCALS), TONY BANKS (b. 1951; KEYBOARDS) and Chris Stewart (drums) joined forces with Anthony Philips (guitar/vocals) and Mike Rutherford (b. 1950; bass/guitar/vocals) from a rival group. In 1967, they sent a demo to another Charterhouse alumnus, **Jonathan King** at Decca Records; he christened the band Genesis. They recorded 'The Silent Sun' in 1968 and issued their unsuccessful debut album *From Genesis To Revelation* in 1969. After joining Tony Stratton-Smith's Charisma Records in 1970, the group recruited drummer **Phil Collins** (b. 1951).

Trespass sold poorly and, despite the addition of guitarist Steve Hackett (b. 1950), *Nursery Cryme* also failed commercially. Success on the Continent brought renewed faith and eventually, with *Foxtrot*, they reached the UK Top 20. Their profile heightened with the best-selling *Selling England By The Pound* and *The Lamb Lies Down On Broadway*, but they were under-

mined by the shock departure of Gabriel in 1975.

Phil Collins took over as vocalist and *A Trick Of The Tail* and *Wind And Wuthering* were well received. In 1977, Hackett went solo and Genesis carried on as a trio. *And Then There Were Three* went gold and *Duke* reached UK number 1. *Abacab* reached the US Top 10 and, helped by Collins's high solo profile, they enjoyed their biggest UK hit singles with 'Mama', 'Thats All' and 'Illegal Alien'. Both *Genesis* and *Invisible Touch* topped the UK charts, the latter also reached US number 1.

In the mid-80s, Collins went fully solo while Rutherford formed **Mike And The Mechanics**. Genesis soldiered on with 'Invisible Touch' (1986, US number 1) and four US Top 5 singles. In 1991, the group reconvened to record and issue *We Can't Dance*; it immediately topped the charts. Collins decided to remain solo, however, and a replacement was found in Ray Wilson. He was heard on 1997's *Calling All Stations*.

GENTLE GIANT

BRITISH BAND FORMED IN 1969 BY THE SHULMAN BROTHERS: DEREK (b. 1947; VOCALS/GUITAR/BASS), RAY (b. 1949; vocals/bass/violin) and Phil (b. 1937; saxophone) with Kerry Minnear (b. 1948; keyboards/vocals), Gary Green (b. 1950; guitar/vocals) and Martin Smith (drums). They signed to Vertigo in 1970 and, with producer Tony Visconti, completed an ambitious debut album.

Smith left after *Acquiring The Taste*. His replacement, Malcolm Mortimore, appeared on *Three Friends*, but a motorcycle accident forced his departure. John 'Pugwash' Weathers (b. 1947) joined for *Octopus*, but an attendant tour ended with Phil's retirement from music. The group then encountered problems in America when *In A Glass House* was deemed too uncommercial for release.

Free Hand became their best-selling UK album; an ascendancy that faltered when *Interview* invoked the experimental style of earlier releases. *Playing The Fool* confirmed their in-concert dexterity, but subsequent albums unsuccessfully courted an AOR audience. *Civilian* was an attempt at regaining glory, but Minnear's departure signalled their demise. Gentle Giant split in 1980.

Connections
Pulp ➽ p.269
Elastica ➽ p.134
Oasis ➽ p.250
Influences
Paul Weller ➽ p.336
Small Faces ➽ p.300
Smiths ➽ p.301

GENERAL PUBLIC
Albums
Hand To Mouth (Virgin 1986)★★★
➽ p.363 for full listings
Connections
Beat ➽ p.37
Specials ➽ p.304
Van Morrison ➽ p.238

GENERATION X
Albums
Generation X (Chrysalis 1978)★★★
➽ p.363 for full listings
Collaborators
Billy Idol ➽ p.192
Connections
Chelsea ➽ p.88
Clash ➽ p.93
Adverts ➽ p.10

GENESIS
Albums
The Lamb Lies Down On Broadway (Charisma 1974)★★★★
Duke (Charisma 1980)★★★★
➽ p.363 for full listings

Collaborators
Peter Gabriel ➽ p.157
Phil Collins ➽ p.98
Connections
Jonathan King ➽ p.206
Mike And The Mechanics ➽ p.233
Further References
Book: *Genesis: A Biography*, Dave Bowler and Brian Dray

GENTLE GIANT
Albums
Free Hand (Chrysalis 1975)★★★
The Official 'Live' Gentle
➽ p.363 for full listings
Collaborators
Tony Visconti
Connections
Sugarcubes ➽ p.313
Polygram
Influences
Yes ➽ p.346
King Crimson ➽ p.206

GEORGE BAKER SELECTION
Albums
Paloma Blanca (Warners 1975)★★
p.363 for full listings
Connections
Johnathan King p.206

GERMS
Albums
GI (Slash 1979)★★★
p.363 for full listings
Collaborators
White Zombie p.337
Courtney Love p.182
Melvins p.231
Mudhoney p.242
Connections
Belinda Carlisle p.81
Black Flag p.50
Dead Kennedys p.112

GERRY AND THE PACEMAKERS
Albums
How Do You Like It? (Columbia 1963)★★★★
p.363 for full listings
Connections
Brian Epstein p.137
Influences
Beatles p.38
Further References
Book: *I'll Never Walk Alone*, Gerry Marsden with Ray Coleman

GIBBONS, STEVE
Albums
Down In The Bunker (Polydor 1978)★★★★
p.363 for full listings
Collaborators
Albert Lee p.213
Connections
Fairport Convention p.141
Moody Blues p.237
Move p.241
Idle Race p.192
UB40 p.326

GILL, VINCE
Albums
When Love Finds You (MCA 1994)★★★★
p.363 for full listings
Collaborators
Rosanne Cash p.84
Dire Straits p.120
Gladys Knight p.209
Dolly Parton p.256
Connections
Pure Prairie League p.269
Rodney Crowell p.107

GEORGE BAKER SELECTION

LED BY BAKER (b. GEORGE BOUENS; VOCALS) THIS MOR DUTCH QUINTET SCALED EUROPEAN AND NORTH American charts in 1970 with their debut 'Little Green Bag' – composed by Bouens and group member, Jan Visser. Bouens wrote their next major hit, 'Una Paloma Blanca', which caught a holiday mood during 1975. It reached the UK and Australasian Top 10 and sold a million copies in Germany. There were no further international hits but, despite many personnel changes, the band continued as domestic chart contenders until the 80s.

GERMS

CALIFORNIAN PUNK BAND FORMED IN 1977, COMPRISING DARBY CRASH (b. PAUL BEAHM; VOCALS), PAT SMEAR (guitar), Lorna Doom (bass) and **Belinda Carlisle** (drums). Carlisle left and was replaced by a succession of percussionists, including future **X** drummer D.J. Bonebrake. The first single, 'Forming' (1977) is considered by some to be the first example of post-punk 'hardcore'. After their only album, *GI*, the group disbanded in early 1980 but re-formed later that year. A week after their first reunion concert, Crash died of a heroin overdose. A Germs tribute album was issued in 1996 featuring **White Zombie**, Courtney Love, the **Melvins**, **Mudhoney** and others.

GERRY AND THE PACEMAKERS

GERRY MARSDEN (b. 1942; GUITAR/VOCALS), FREDDIE MARSDEN (b. 1940; DRUMS) AND JOHN 'LES' CHADWICK (b. 1943; bass) formed the Pacemakers in 1959; Les Maguire (b. 1941; piano) joined in 1961. After successful spells in German beat clubs, they became the second group signed to **Brian Epstein**. 'How Do You Do It', rejected as unsuitable by the **Beatles**, gave the Pacemakers a number 1 hit. Further chart-toppers 'I Like It' and 'You'll Never Walk Alone' (both 1963), followed – the group became the first act to have their first three releases reach number 1. Their lone album revealed a penchant for R&B, alongside 'Ferry Cross The Mersey' (1965) the theme song to the Pacemakers' starring film *I'll Be There*. It was their final Top 20 entry.

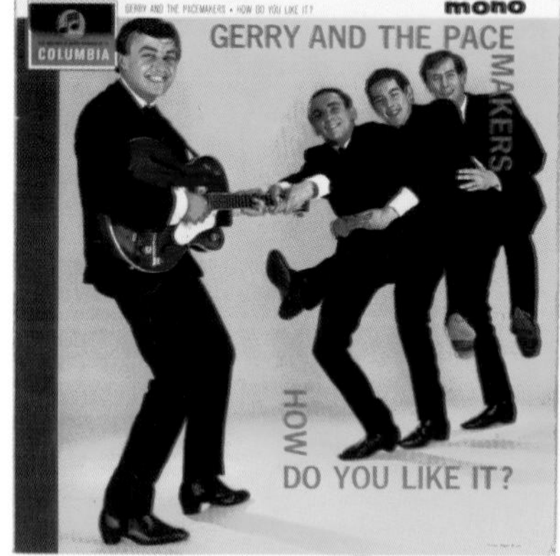

In 1967, Gerry went solo. He remained a popular figure in television and on cabaret and in 1985, following the Bradford City Football Club fire tragedy, an all-star charity recording of 'You'll Never Walk Alone' reached UK number 1. The charity re-recording of 'Ferry Cross The Mersey', for the victims of the Hillsborough crowd disaster in 1989, also reached number 1.

GIBBONS, STEVE

GIBBONS (b. *c.* 1942) STARTED OUT IN 1958 AS VOCALIST WITH UK BAND THE DOMINETTES; THEY BECAME THE Uglys in 1962 (the bassist was Dave Pegg, later of **Fairport Convention**). In 1969, the Uglys split and Gibbons joined Denny Laine (ex-**Moody Blues**), Trevor Burton (ex-**Move**) and session guitarists **Albert Lee** and **Chris Spedding** in **Balls**. They released *Short Stories* before disbanding in 1971.

Gibbons briefly joined the **Idle Race**, which became the Steve Gibbons Band. The early line-up included Burton (bass), Dave Carroll and Bob Wilson on guitars, and Bob Lamb (drums). Their debut album was followed by Gibbons's Top 20 hit with **Chuck Berry**'s 'Tulane' (1977), from *Caught In The Act*. Soon afterwards Lamb quit, later he produced the early work of **UB40**.

In the early 80s, the Steve Gibbons Band recorded two albums. Burton left the band but Gibbons continued to be a popular live performer.

GILL, VINCE

US-BORN GILL (b. VINCENT GRANT GILL, 1957) STARTED OUT WITH BLUEGRASS GROUP MOUNTAIN SMOKE; IN 1975 HE joined Bluegrass Alliance with Sam Bush and Dan Crary. In 1979, he demonstrated his vocal, guitar, banjo and fiddle talents with **Pure Prairie League**, appearing on their albums *Can't Hold Back*, *Firin' Up* and *Something In The Night*. Gill then joined **Rodney Crowell**'s backing group, the Cherry Bombs. He began his solo recording career with a six-track mini-album, *Turn Me Loose* and a duet with **Rosanne Cash**, 'If It Weren't For Him'. He was among the musicians on Patty Loveless's albums, and she duetted with him on 'When I Call Your Name' (Country Music Association's Single Of The Year).

Gill added vocal harmonies to **Dire Straits**' *On Every Street*. In 1991, he reached the US country Top 10 with 'Pocket Full Of Gold', 'Liza Jane' and 'Look At Us', and was voted the Male Vocalist Of The Year at the 1991 Country Music Association's Annual Awards Show. In 1992, he won Male Vocalist Of The Year and Song Of The Year with 'Look At Us'. Patty Loveless and Ricky Skaggs guested on the excellent *When Love Finds You*; Gill has also duetted with **Gladys Knight** and **Dolly Parton**. *High Lonesome Sound* explored several styles of American music.

GILLAN, IAN

UK VOCALIST GILLAN (b. 1945) FORMED HIS FIRST BAND AGED 16. LATER, HE JOINED **DEEP PURPLE**, ALONG WITH Welsh bass guitarist Roger Glover (b. 1945). They formed the legendary 'Mk II' line-up with **Ritchie Blackmore**, Jon Lors and Ian Paice. Gillan left in 1973, having purchased a recording studio in London, Kingsway Studios. He recorded a solo album, *Child In Time* with Ray Fenwick (guitar), Mike Moran (keyboards), Mark Nauseef (drums) and John Gustafson (bass). His next two albums featured Colin Towns (keyboards) and demonstrated a jazz-rock influence. None were particularly successful, however, and Gillan disbanded the Ian Gillan Band in 1978.

Within a few months, he was back in the studio with Leon Genocky (drums), Steve Byrd (guitar) and John McCoy (bass) and Towns to record *Gillan* (1978). This excellent album was never released in the UK, although several of the tracks appeared on the next album, *Mr. Universe*, recorded with Pete Barnacle (drums). The album was instrumental in developing the New Wave Of British Heavy Metal, as was *Glory Road*. Now with Bernie Torme on guitar and drummer Mick Underwood, Gillan produced one of his finest albums, *For Gillan Fans Only*.

After the slightly disappointing *Future Shock*, Torme left, replaced by Janick Gers, who featured on *Double Trouble* (one studio and one live album). 1982 saw the release of *Magic*, sadly the group's last recording. Gillan then joined **Black Sabbath**.

After one album and a tour with Sabbath, Deep Purple reunited, but Gillan left in 1989. He performed a short tour as his alter ego, Garth Rockett, before recording vocals for the Rock Aid Armenia version of 'Smoke On The Water'. By the end of 1989, Gillan had assembled a band to record a solo album, *Naked Thunder*, labelled middle-of-the-road by some critics, Gillan described it as 'hard rock with a funky blues feel'. *Toolbox* was released to critical acclaim. Gillan rejoined Deep Purple in 1992, recorded and toured, before quitting once more. Shortly afterwards he rejoined again.

GIN BLOSSOMS

US COUNTRY ROCK BAND FORMED IN 1987. ROBIN WILSON (VOCALS/ACOUSTIC GUITAR), JESSE VALENZUELA (GUITAR/mandolin), Phillip Rhodes (drums), Bill Leen (bass) and Doug Hopkins (d. 1993; guitar) featured regularly on MTV. Their 'Hey Jealousy' was a hit and *New Miserable Experience* sold over 4 million copies in the USA. However, after struggling for years against depression and alcoholism, chief songwriter Hopkins became so unstable that he was fired in 1992. A bitter wrangle ensued.

His 'Hey Jealousy' and 'Found Out About You' became major hits and on 3 December 1993, Hopkins left a detox unit and shot himself. Scott Johnson took over on guitar, but Hopkins's songwriting was more difficult to replace. **Marshall Crenshaw** co-wrote the hit ''Til I Hear It From You', but *Congratulations I'm Sorry* was predictably weaker.

GIPSY KINGS

FLAMENCO BAND FORMED FROM FAMILY GROUP LOS REYES (THE KINGS). IN 1982, NICOLAS AND ANDRE REYES teamed up with family member Chico Bouchikhi and three cousins: Diego, Tonino and Paci Baliardó. Each member sang and played guitar with Nicolas as lead vocalist. Their worldwide debut was their self-titled album, by which time several collections had already been released in Spain and mainland Europe. The music blended Nueva Andalucia flamenco with percussive foot stamps, handclaps and vocals drawn from Arabic music. To their multi-guitar sound, they added other components, including drums, bass, percussion and synthesizers. *Gipsy Kings* reached Canadian/Australian number 1 and UK number 16. The ensuing *Mosaique* incorporated elements of jazz (featuring jazz/salsa artist Ruben Blades) and 50s/60s pop. In the early 90s, the personnel shuffled, releasing a less successful live album.

GIRLSCHOOL

ALL-FEMALE HEAVY METAL BAND FOUNDED BY TEENAGERS ENID WILLIAMS (BASS/VOCALS) AND KIM McAuliffe (b. 1959; guitar/vocals). Kelly Johnson (guitar/vocals) and Denise Dufort (drums) joined in 1978. Their independently produced single, 'Take It All Away', led to a tour with **Motörhead**. Under Lemmy's sponsorship, Vic Maile produced the band's first two albums. After a minor hit with 'Race With The Devil', the group combined with Motörhead as Headgirl. They reached the UK Top 10 with the EP *St Valentine's Day Massacre*. Williams was replaced by bass player Gill Weston; Williams subsequently formed Framed, before joining Moho Pack. Later, she sang country and opera.

Girlschool persevered with the glam-influenced *Play Dirty*. In 1984, Johnson went solo (unsuccessfully) and Girlschool added guitarist Chris Bonacci and lead singer Jacqui Bodimead; turning more towards glam rock they recorded with **Gary Glitter** in 1986. After the departure of Weston in 1987, Tracey Lamb (bass) was brought in, while McAuliffe left to work with punk singer Beki Bondage and present the cable show *Raw Power*. Later she formed Strange Girls with Toyah, Dufort and Williams. Following a Russian tour supporting **Black Sabbath**, Girlschool split up. In the 90s, McAuliffe brought the group back together with Jackie Carrera (bass).

GLASTONBURY FESTIVAL

FARMER MICHAEL EAVIS (b. 1935), INSPIRED BY THE 1970 BATH BLUES FESTIVAL, PRESENTED THE FIRST GLASTONBURY Festival (or Fayre) a few weeks later on his land at Worthy Farm in the West of England. **T. Rex** headlined before an audience of 1500. After 1971's event, featuring **David Bowie** and **Fairport Convention**, the festival was not held again until 1979's Year Of The Child Benefit Concert. Since then it has grown in size and prestige.

Ten per cent of Glastonbury's gross receipts are always passed on to charity. Each year there are displays of cabaret, film, theatre and environmental activism, as well as a musical doctrine which encompasses folk, jazz, classical and world music alongside headlining rock bands. Continuing to grow in popularity, the 1995 festival sold its entire 80,000 allocation within one week of tickets going on sale. Eavis decided not to hold a 1996 festival, and the 1997 event came close to being a disaster amidst a deluge of mud and rain. Nevertheless, the festival atmosphere continued and the event sold out in 1998.

GLITTER, GARY

UK GLAM ROCK STAR GLITTER (b. PAUL GADD, 1940) STARTED OUT IN SKIFFLE GROUP, PAUL RUSSELL AND THE REBELS. Then known as Paul Raven, he recorded an unsuccessful debut, 'Alone In The Night'. His cover of 'Tower Of Strength' lost out to **Frankie Vaughan**'s UK chart-topper. After unsuccessful attempts to revitalize his career, he relaunched as Gary Glitter, complete with thigh-high boots and silver costume. His debut, 'Rock 'N' Roll Part 2', unexpectedly reached UK number 2 and the US Top 10. Although he failed to establish himself in America, his UK career traversed the early 70s, until the punk explosion of 1977. Among his many UK Top 10 hits were three number 1s: 'I'm The Leader Of The Gang (I Am)', 'I Love You Love Me Love' and 'Always Yours'.

An accidental drug overdose and bankruptcy each threatened to end his career, but he survived and continues to play regular UK concerts. In recent years, Glitter has experienced damaging media exposure over allegations of child abuse and pornography.

GILLAN, IAN
Albums
Glory Road (Virgin 1980)★★★★
➽ p.364 for full listings
Collaborators
Ritchie Blackmore ➽ p.52
Mick Fleetwood ➽ p.147
Connections
Deep Purple ➽ p.113
Black Sabbath ➽ p.51
Further References
Book: *Child In Time: The Life Story Of The Singer From Deep Purple*, Ian Gillan with David Cohen

GIN BLOSSOMS
Albums
New Miserable Experience (A&M 1993)★★★★
➽ p.364 for full listings
Collaborators
Marshall Crenshaw ➽ p.104
Influences
R.E.M. ➽ p.275
Birds ➽ p.47

GIPSY KINGS
Albums
Mosaique (Elektra 1989)★★★
➽ p.364 for full listings
Collaborators
Ruben Blades

GIRLSCHOOL
Albums
Play Dirty (Bronze 1983)★★★
➽ p.364 for full listings
Collaborators
Gary Glitter ➽ p.163
Connections
Motorhead ➽ p.240
Johnny Kidd ➽ p.204
Black Sabbath ➽ p.51
Further References
Video: *Bronze Rocks* (1985)

GLASTONBURY FESTIVAL
Albums
Various *Glastonbury 25th Anniversary – A Celebration* (Chrysalis 1995)★★★
➽ p.364 for full listings
Connections
Michael Eavis
T. Rex ➽ p.316
David Bowie ➽ p.64
Fairport Convention ➽ p.141
Influences
Frank Zappa ➽ p.348
Led Zeppelin ➽ p.213

GLITTER, GARY
Albums
Remember Me This Way (Bell1974)★★
➽ p.364 for full listings
Connections
Frankie Vaughan
Further References
Book: *Leader: The Autobiography Of Gary Glitter*, Gary Glitter with Lloyd Bradley

GO WEST
Albums
Indian Summer (Chrysalis 1992)★★★
➽ p.364 for full listings
Collaborators
Peter Frampton ➽ p.152
Further References
Video: *Aces And Kings: The Best Of The Videos* (Chrysalis 1993)

GO-BETWEENS
Albums
Springhill Fair (Sire 1984)★★★★
16 Lovers Lane (Beggars Banquet 1988)★★★★
➽ p.364 for full listings
Connections
Church ➽ p.92
Lloyd Cole ➽ p.96
Influences
Bob Dylan ➽ p.128
Velvet Underground ➽ p.329
Monkees ➽ p.236
Television ➽ p.317
Talking Heads ➽ p.316
Patti Smith ➽ p.301
Further References
Video: *That Way* (1993)

GO-GO'S
Albums
Beauty And The Beat (IRS 1981)★★★
➽ p.364 for full listings
Connections
Belinda Carlisle ➽ p.81
Influences
Blondie ➽ p.54

GODLEY AND CREME
Albums
The History Mix Volume 1 (Polydor 1985)★★★
➽ p.364 for full listings
Connections
10cc ➽ p.318
Visage ➽ p.331
Duran Duran ➽ p.127
Police ➽ p.263
Herbie Hancock ➽ p.174
Frankie Goes To Hollywood ➽ p.153
Further References
Videos: *Cry* (Polygram 1988), *Mondo Video* (Virgin 1989)

GOFFIN, GERRY
Albums
It Ain't Exactly Entertainment (1973)★★★
➽ p.364 for full listings
Collaborators
Carole King ➽ p.205
Connections
Neil Sedaka ➽ p.291
Shirelles ➽ p.295
Bobby Vee ➽ p.329
Little Eva ➽ p.216
Herman's Hermits ➽ p.180
Righteous Brothers ➽ p.278
Aretha Franklin ➽ p.153
Manfred Mann ➽ p.223
Diana Ross ➽ p.283

GO WEST

UK SONGWRITERS, PETER COX (b. 1955; VOCALS) AND RICHARD DRUMMIE (GUITAR/KEYBOARD/VOCALS), formed Go West in 1982. They had a string of pop-rock hits in 1985 with, 'We Close Our Eyes', 'Call Me' and 'Don't Look Down', and a successful debut album. 'One Way Street' was written for the *Rocky IV* soundtrack and 'King Of Wishful Thinking' appeared in the film *Pretty Woman*.

Indian Summer came after a lengthy gap, demonstrating that the group had developed and matured.

GO-BETWEENS

FORMED IN BRISBANE, AUSTRALIA, BY SONGWRITERS ROBERT FORSTER (b. 1957; GUITAR/VOCALS) AND GRANT McLennan (b. 1958; bass/guitar/vocals). They first recorded as a trio with drummer Dennis Cantwell: 'Lee Remick'/'Karen' (1978) and 'People Say'/'Don't Let Him Come Back' (1979). By 1979, they had recruited Tim Mustafa (drums), Malcolm Kelly (organ), Candice (tambourine/vocals) and Jacqueline (tambourine/vocals). They later reverted to the trio format: Forster, McLennan and Lindy Morrison (b. 1951). The band briefly visited Britain to record, 'I Need Two Heads', returning to Australia to record *Send Me A Lullaby*. *Before Hollywood* garnered favourable reviews, the highlight being McLennan's evocative 'Cattle And Cane'. They later recruited Robert Vickers (b. 1959; bass).

Despite moving to a major label and *Springhill Fair* receiving critical acclaim, success still eluded them. *Liberty Belle And The Black Diamond Express* was by far their best album to date and the introduction of Amanda Brown (b. 1965; violin/oboe/guitar/keyboards) added an extra dimension and smoother texture to their sound. *Tallulah* reached UK number 91, after which Robert Vickers left, replaced by John Willsteed (b. 1957). Prior to the release of *16 Lovers Lane*, 'Streets Of Your Town' was given generous airplay, yet failed to make any chart impact. The album only reached number 81. Forster and McLennan dissolved the group in 1989 and both released solo albums. McLennan also released an album with fellow Antipodean Steve Kilbey (**Church**). McLennan joined Forster on-stage in 1991, and they supported **Lloyd Cole** that same year. Both artists continued to release solo records at regular intervals throughout the 90s, and in 1997 the group re-formed for special live dates.

GO-GO'S

ALL-FEMALE GROUP FORMED IN CALIFORNIA IN 1978. **BELINDA CARLISLE** (b. 1958; LEAD VOCALS), JANE WIEDLIN (b. 1958; rhythm guitar/vocals), Charlotte Caffey (b. 1953; lead guitar/keyboards), Elissa Bello (drums) and Margot Olaverra (bass) performed bright, infectious harmony pop songs; they were signed to UK and US labels, but were mostly successful in America. By their debut, *Beauty And The Beat* (US number 1), Olaverra was replaced by Kathy Valentine and Bello by Gina Schock. 'Our Lips Are Sealed' went to the US Top 20, and 'We Got The Beat' reached US number 2. *Vacation* provided a further US Top 10 hit with the title track; *Talk Show* and 'Head Over Heels' (1984) reached the US Top 20, but the over-indulgent group were starting to burn out.

The group dissolved in 1985, Carlisle subsequently pursued a successful solo career; Caffey formed the Graces with Meredith Brooks and Gia Campbell; Schock formed House of Schock, and Wiedlin had a few minor film roles. The Go-Go's re-formed briefly in 1990 for a benefit for the anti-fur trade organization PETA. A fuller reunion took place in 1994, after which Valentine and Schock formed The Delphines.

GODLEY AND CREME

UK DUO FORMED IN 1976. KEVIN GODLEY (b. 1945; VOCALS/DRUMS) AND LOL CREME (b. 1947; VOCALS/GUITAR) HAD previously been involved with the Mockingbirds, Hotlegs and **10cc**. They intended to abandon mainstream pop in favour of a more elaborate project, resulting in the triple album *Consequences*. The work was lampooned in the music press, as was the duo's invention of a new musical instrument, the 'Gizmo' gadget. An edited version of the work was later issued but also failed to sell.

Finally they had a UK Top 10 hit with 'Under My Thumb', followed by 'Wedding Bells' and 'Cry', but they found their greatest success as video makers for such artists as **Visage**, **Duran Duran**, Toyah, the **Police**, **Herbie Hancock** and **Frankie Goes To Hollywood**.

GOFFIN, GERRY

GOFFIN (b. 1939) MARRIED FELLOW SONGWRITER **CAROLE KING**. IN 1960, THEY MET PUBLISHER DON KIRSHNER following the release of 'Oh! Neil', King's answer to **Neil Sedaka**'s 'Oh! Carol'. They joined the staff of Kirshner's company, where their early compositions included 'Will You Still Love Me Tomorrow?' (the **Shirelles**), 'Take Good Care Of My Baby' (**Bobby Vee**) and 'Up On The Roof' (the **Drifters**). Goffin also enjoyed success with Jack Keller and **Barry Mann**, but his compositions with King proved the most memorable. Together they wrote 'The Loco-Motion' (**Little Eva**), 'One Fine Day' (the **Chiffons**), 'I'm Into Something Good' (Earl-Jean/**Herman's Hermits**) and **Aretha Franklin**'s 'A Natural Woman', among others. However, professional and personal pressure led to their marriage ending in 1967. Goffin enjoyed a less public profile than his successful ex-wife, however **Blood, Sweat And Tears** recorded 'Hi De Hi', **Grand Funk Railroad** covered 'The Loco-Motion' and Carole later paid tribute to their partnership with *Pearls*, a selection of their 60s collaborations.

During the 70s, Goffin worked as a producer for artists including **Diana Ross**. He recorded a solo album, *It Ain't Exactly Entertainment*, but failed to emulate King's popularity. He recorded again in 1996.

GOLD, ANDREW

US GUITARIST/VOCALIST/KEYBOARD PLAYER GOLD (b. 1951) MET GUITARIST KENNY EDWARDS IN BRYNDLE AND THE Rangers. The pair subsequently pursued their careers as part of **Linda Ronstadt**'s backing group. Gold also contributed to sessions for **Carly Simon**, **Art Garfunkel** and **Loudon Wainwright**. He completed his solo debut in 1975 and enjoyed a transatlantic hit with 'Lonely Boy' (1976) and a UK number 5 with 'Never Let Her Slip Away'. In the wake of the disappointing *Whirlwind*, Gold toured with Ronstadt before forming Wax with Graham Gouldman in 1986. In 1992, Undercover had a major UK hit with a dance version of 'Never Let Her Slip Away'.

GOLDEN EARRING

FORMED IN 1961 IN THE HAGUE, NETHERLANDS, BY GEORGE KOOYMANS (b. 1948; GUITAR/VOCALS) AND RINUS Gerritsen (b. 1946; bass/vocals), along with Hans Van Herwerden (guitar) and Fred Van Der Hilst (drums). In 1965, they reached the Dutch Top 10 with their debut, 'Please Go'. By now, Kooymans and Gerritsen had been joined by Frans Krassenburg (vocals), Peter De Ronde (guitar) and Jaap Eggermont (drums); they became one of the most popular 'nederbeat' attractions. Barry Hay (b. 1948; lead vocals/flute/saxophone/guitar) replaced Krassenburg in 1966; De Ronde also left. Their first Dutch number 1, 'Dong-Dong-Di-Ki-Di-Gi-Dong' (1968), saw them branching out into Europe and the USA. Eggermont left, replaced by Cesar Zuiderwijk (b. 1948) in 1969. Their compulsive *Eight Miles High* found an international audience.

In 1972, they were invited to support the **Who** on a European tour. In 1973, they had a Dutch number 1/UK Top 10 hit with 'Radar Love' which, in 1974, reached the US Top 20. However, long term overseas success was elusive. Robert Jan Stips joined between 1974 and 1976, followed by Eelco Gelling (guitar), but by 1980 the group had reverted to Kooymans, Gerritsen, Hay and Zuiderwijk. Their reputation as a top European live act was reinforced by *Second Live*. *Cut* spawned 'Twilight Zone' (US Top 10), followed by a tour of the United States and Canada.

GOLDEN PALOMINOS

UNORTHODOX ROCK GROUP FORMED IN 1981 BY DRUMMER ANTON FIER (EX-**PERE UBU**). THEIR ALBUMS HAVE featured guests such as John Lydon (**Sex Pistols**, PiL), Michael Stipe (**R.E.M.**), **Bob Mould**, **T-Bone Burnett** and **Jack Bruce**. Other band members have included **Bill Laswell** (bass). *Drunk With Passion* featured 'Alive And Living Now', and the excellent 'Dying From The Inside Out'. *Visions of success* and the maverick talents employed on *Blast Of Silence* failed to match the impact of the debut. For *This Is How It Feels*, Fier recruited singer Lori Carson, who added both warmth and sexuality to that and the subsequent *Pure*. **Bootsy Collins** (guitar) also joined. In recent years, remixes of Golden Palominos work have been appearing in UK clubs.

GOLDSBORO, BOBBY

GOLDSBORO (b. 1941) FIRST CAME TO PROMINENCE AS A GUITARIST IN **ROY ORBISON**'S TOURING BAND IN 1960. IN 1964, he reached the US Top 10 with the self-penned 'See The Funny Little Clown', followed by minor US hits. International status came in 1968 with 'Honey'. The song stayed at US number 1 for five weeks and was number 2 twice: in 1968 and 1975. Goldsboro had 70s hits with 'Watching Scotty Grow' and 'Summer (The First Time)' among others. He subsequently turned to country music, finding considerable success in the 80s.

GONG

ANARCHIC, EXPERIMENTAL ENSEMBLE FORMED BY GUITARIST DAEVID ALLEN (EX-**SOFT MACHINE**). GILLI SMYTH aka Shanti Yoni (vocals), Didier Malherbe aka Bloomdido Bad De Grasse (saxophone/flute), Christian Tritsch aka The Submarine Captain (bass) and Pip Pyle (drums) had assisted Allen on his solo collection *Banana Moon*; Gong was formed when the musicians moved to a communal farmhouse in France, in 1971. Lauri Allen replaced Pyle as the group completed *Continental Circus* and *Camembert Electrique*: quirky, *avant-garde* music mixed with hippie-based surrealism. Subsequent releases included an ambitious 'Radio Gnome Invisible' trilogy; *Flying Teapot*, *Angel's Egg* and *You*. This saw the band reach their peak of commercial success with colourful live performances, and the addition of **Steve Hillage** (guitar), Mike Howlett (bass) and Tim Blake (synthesizer).

Allen left in 1975 and the band abandoned his original, experimental vision for a tamer style. Within months, Hillage also left, leaving Pierre Moerlen, drummer since 1973, in tenuous control. Mike Howlett left soon after and was replaced by Hanny Rowe; Allan Holdsworth joined on guitar. After inaction in the early 80s, the Gong name was used in performances alongside anarcho space/jazz rock group Here And Now, before being absorbed by the latter. By the late 80s and 90s, Gong was under the control of its original leader.

GOO GOO DOLLS

US ROCK TRIO, FORMED IN 1986. ROBBY TAKAC (VOCALS/BASS), JOHNNY RZEZNIK (VOCALS/GUITAR) AND GEORGE (drums) began with unlikely cover versions on *Jed*, such as a version of **Creedence Clearwater Revival**'s 'Down On The Corner' and **Prince**'s 'I Could Never Take The Place Of Your Man' on *Hold Me Up*. Both albums featured unpretentious pop-punk songwriting, and the band received strong media coverage. *A Boy Named Goo* was produced by **Pere Ubu**, **Hüsker Dü** and **Sugar** accomplice Lou Giordano. Their career showed signs of stalling in 1997 following litigation with Warner Bros.

GOLD, ANDREW
Albums
Andrew Gold (Asylum 1976)★★★
➧ p.364 for full listings
Collaborators
Graham Gouldman
Connections
Linda Ronstadt ➧ p.282
Carly Simon ➧ p.296
Art Garfunkel ➧ p.159
Loudon Wainwright ➧ p.331

GOLDEN EARRING
Albums
The Naked Truth (Columbia 1992)★★★
➧ p.364 for full listings
Connections
Who ➧ p.338

GOLDEN PALOMINOS
Albums
The Golden Palominos (OAO/Celluloid 1983)★★★★
➧ p.364 for full listings
Collaborators
Bob Mould ➧ p.241
T-Bone Burnett ➧ p.75
Jack Bruce ➧ p.71
Bill Laswell ➧ p.212
Connections
Pere Ubu ➧ p.258

GOLDSBORO, BOBBY
Albums
Today (United Artists 1969)★★★
➧ p.364 for full listings
Connections
Roy Orbison ➧ p.252

GONG
Albums
Radio Gnome Invisible Part 1–The Flying Teapot (Virgin 1973)★★★★
➧ p.364 for full listings
Collaborators
Steve Hillage ➧ p.182
Connections
Soft Machine ➧ p.302
Further References
Video: *Gong Maison* (1993)

GOO GOO DOLLS
Albums
A Boy Named Goo (Warners 1995)★★★★
➧ p.364 for full listings
Collaborators
Pere Ubu ➧ p.258
Hüsker Dü ➧ p.190
Sugar ➧ p.313
Connections
Replacements ➧ p.276
Creedence Clearwater Revival ➧ p.104
Prince ➧ p.267

GRAHAM, BILL
Connections
Jefferson Airplane ➽ p.198
Quicksilver Messenger Service ➽ p.270
Grateful Dead ➽ p.167
B.B. King ➽ p.205
Muddy Waters ➽ p.242
Miles Davis ➽ p.167
Bob Dylan ➽ p.128
Crosby, Stills, Nash And Young ➽ p.106
Huey Lewis And The News ➽ p.215
Santana ➽ p.288
Further References
Book: *Bill Graham Presents*, Bill Graham and Robert Greenfield
➽ p.364 for full listings

GRAHAM, LARRY
Albums
One In A Million You (Warners 1980)★★★
Just Be My Lady (Warners 1981)★★★
Fired Up (1985)★★★
➽ p.364 for full listings
Collaborators
Aretha Franklin ➽ p.153
Connections
Sly And The Family Stone ➽ p.300

GRAND FUNK RAILROAD
Albums
On Time (Capitol 1969)★★★
We're An American Band (Capitol 1973)★★★
Good Singin', Good Playin' (MCA 1976)★★★
➽ p.364 for full listings
Connections
? And The Mysterians ➽ p.270

GRANDMASTER FLASH
Albums
As Grandmaster Flash And The Furious Five *The Message* (Sugarhill 1982)★★★
Greatest Messages (Sugarhill 1984)★★★
Ba-Dop-Boom-Bang (Elektra 1987)★★★
➽ p.364 for full listings
Collaborators
Kurtis Blow ➽ p.55
Kid Creole ➽ p.204

GRANT, EDDY
Albums
Message Man (Ice 1977)★★★
Paintings Of The Soul (Ice 1982)★★★
Can't Get Enough (Ice/RCA 1983)★★★
➽ p.364 for full listings
Connections
Equals ➽ p.137

GRAHAM, BILL

A RUSSIAN-JEW, GRAHAM (b. WOLFGANG WOLODIA GRAJONCA, 1931, d. 1991) ESCAPED TO NEW YORK DURING 1941. By 1965 he was managing the San Francisco Mime Troupe and organizing benefit gigs. This brought contact with the rock fraternity and he began promoting concerts at the city's Fillmore Auditorium – it became the showcase for the 'San Francisco Sound', exemplified by **Jefferson Airplane**, **Quicksilver Messenger Service**, the **Grateful Dead** and Big Brother And The Holding Company. By 1968, Graham had bought the Carousel Ballroom, renaming it the Fillmore West, followed by Fillmore East on New York's Second Avenue.

A hard-headed entrepreneur, Graham nevertheless contributed regularly to local organizations in the form of benefits. He was also instrumental in introducing black artists on billings to a predominantly white audience, such as **B.B. King**, Leon Thomas, Raahsan Roland Kirk, Miles Davis, **Muddy Waters** and Ravi Shankar. By the end of 1971, Graham had closed down both halls, but his sabbatical was brief and during the next decade he was involved in national tours by **Bob Dylan** and **Crosby, Stills, Nash And Young**, as well as major one-off events. On 13 July 1985, Graham organized the American Live Aid concert for famine relief.

Graham died in a helicopter crash, returning from a **Huey Lewis And The News** concert he had promoted in California. His funeral service was attended by members of the Grateful Dead, **Santana** and Quicksilver Messenger Service, who offered musical tributes.

GRAHAM, LARRY

US-BORN GRAHAM (b. 1946) WAS PROFICIENT ON SEVERAL INSTRUMENTS. A MEMBER OF **SLY AND THE FAMILY STONE** between 1967 and 1972, he left to form the funk band, Graham Central Station. In 1980, he went solo, beginning successfully with 'One In A Million You' (US Top 10). The singer enjoyed R&B hits with 'When We Get Married' (1980) and 'Just Be My Lady' (1981). In 1987, he charted with 'If You Need My Love Tonight', a duet with **Aretha Franklin**.

GRAND FUNK RAILROAD

HEAVY ROCK GROUP – MARK FARNER (b. 1948; GUITAR), MEL SCHACHER (b. 1951; BASS; EX-**? AND THE MYSTERIANS**) and Don Brewer (1948; drums) – formed in 1968. Farner and Brewer had released 'I (Who Have Nothin)' (US number 46) before Schacher joined. The trio's singles made the charts but Grand Funk proved its real strength in the album market. *On Time* reached number 27, followed by the number 11 *Grand Funk*. In 1970, they became a major concert attraction, and their albums routinely reached the Top 10 for the next four years. Of those, *We're An American Band* was the biggest seller, reaching number 2. In 1971, Grand Funk became only the second group (after the **Beatles**) to sell out New York's Shea Stadium.

Live Album reached number 5, and 1971 saw the release of *Survival* and *E Pluribus Funk*. In 1972, the group fired their manager, resulting in a series of million-dollar lawsuits. John Eastman, father of Linda McCartney, became their new manager. In 1973, the group shortened its name to Grand Funk, and added a fourth member, keyboardist Craig Frost (b. 1948). They cracked the singles market with 'We're An American Band', but in 1975, with their popularity considerably diminished, the group reverted to its original name. The following year, after *Good Singin', Good Playin'* failed to reach the Top 50, Farner went solo. The others stayed together, adding guitarist Billy Elworthy and changing their name to Flint – commercial success eluded them. Grand Funk (Farner, Brewer and bassist Dennis Bellinger) re-formed for 1981-83 and recorded *Grand Funk Lives* and *What's Funk?*. Failing to recapture former glories, they split again. The band reunited for a benefit concert for Bosnian orphans in 1997.

GRANDMASTER FLASH

GRANDMASTER FLASH (b. JOSEPH SADDLER, 1958) WAS A PIVOTAL FORCE IN EARLY RAP MUSIC. PETER 'DJ' JONES TOOK him under his wing, and Flash set about combining Jones's timing on the decks with the sort of records that Kool Herc was spinning. In the early 70s, he discovered the way to 'segue' records smoothly together without missing a beat, highlighting the 'break' – the point in a record where the drum rhythm is isolated or accentuated – and repeating it. The complexity and speed of his method earned him the nickname Flash. He then invited a vocalist to share the stage with him, working first with Lovebug Starski, then Keith Wiggins (Cowboy of the Furious Five). Eventually, Ray Chandler saw commercial potential in Flash's abilities.

Flash put together a strong line-up of local talent: Grandmaster Melle Mel (b. Melvin Glover) and his brother Kid Creole (b. Nathaniel Glover), joining Cowboy. Duke Bootee (b. Ed Fletcher) and **Kurtis Blow** subsequently joined, but were eventually replaced by Rahiem (b. Guy Todd Williams) and Scorpio (b. Eddie Morris, aka Mr Ness). The Zulu Tribe was also inaugurated to act as security at live events: rival MCs had sprung up; Flash, Kook Herc and Afrika Bambaataa would hide their records from prying eyes to stop their 'sound' being pirated, and record labels were removed to avoid identifying marks.

The Furious Five debuted on 2 September 1976. Shortly afterwards they released their first record, 'Super Rappin'. Although hugely popular within the hip hop fraternity, it failed to make commercial inroads; Flash tried again with 'We Rap Mellow' and 'Flash To The Beat'. Joe Robinson Jnr of Sugarhill Records stepped in. His wife, Sylvia, wrote and produced their subsequent record, 'Freedom'. On the back of a major tour, the first in rap's embryonic history, the single went gold. The follow-up, 'Birthday Party', was totally eclipsed by 'Grandmaster Flash On The Wheels Of Steel', a musical *tour de force*, showcasing the Flash quickmixing and scratching skills. It, too, was overshadowed when the band recorded one of Robinson's most memorable compositions: 'The Message'. In just over a month the record went platinum, yet despite the record's success Flash was receiving little money from Sugarhill, so he left for Elektra Records, taking Kid Creole and Rahiem with him. The others continued as Melle Mel and the Furious Five, scoring nearly instantly with 'White Lines (Don't Do It)'.

In the 80s, Flash was largely absent until he was reunited with his Furious Five in 1987 for a **Paul Simon**-hosted charity concert in New York and again when he hosted New York's WQHT Hot 97 show. Unfortunately, the reunion did not include Cowboy, who died in 1989 after a slow descent into crack addiction. Flash also helped out on Terminator X's *Super Bad*, which brought together many of the old-school legends.

GRANT, EDDY

WEST INDIAN-BORN GRANT (b. EDMOND MONTAGUE GRANT, 1948) WAS 24 YEARS OLD, WITH SEVERAL HITS TO his credit, when he left the **Equals** to form his own production company in England. After producing other acts, he debuted with *Message Man*. Grant sang and played every note, recorded it in his own studio, and released it on his own label, Ice Records. He had developed his own sound – part reggae, part funk – pop with credibility. 'Living On The Front Line' (1979) reached UK number 11, and Grant found himself a new audience. 'Do You Feel My Love' and 'Can't Get Enough Of You' kept him in the UK Top 20. In 1982, he moved to Barbados, signed Ice Records to RCA, and reached UK number 1 with 'I Don't Wanna Dance'. 'Electric Avenue' (1983) was a transatlantic number 2, and its album *Killer On The Rampage* proved his biggest seller. The huge hits eluded him until 1988, with the anti-apartheid song 'Gimme Hope Jo'anna'.

GRANT LEE BUFFALO

LOS ANGELES BAND FORMED IN 1989. GRANT LEE PHILLIPS (b. 1963; VOCALS/12-STRING GUITAR), PAUL KIMBLE (b. 1960; bass/keyboards) and Joey Peters (b. 1965; drums) were influenced by American music 'that's based on story-telling and improvization, blues, jazz or country'. By 1991, they had recorded 11 songs, a tape of which was passed to **Bob Mould**, who released 'Fuzzy' on his Singles Only Label (SOL). A month later, they had a contract with Slash Records. A debut album was recorded with Kimble producing. The songs attacked modern America's complacency and pursuit of material wealth, harking back to a golden age of American optimism. 'America Snoring' was written in response to the Los Angeles riots, and 'Stars N' Stripes' was Phillips' evocative homage to **Elvis Presley**'s Vegas period.

Mighty Joe Moon proved more restrained, but the keynote spirituality implicit in earlier recordings was maintained by 'Rock Of Ages'. The more vocally orientated *Copperopolis* broke away from the traditional rock band format by introducing pedal-steel guitar (Greg Leisz), bass clarinet (Ralph Carney) and violin (Bob Fergo).

GRATEFUL DEAD

THE ENIGMATIC AND MERCURIAL GRATEFUL DEAD EVOLVED IN 1965. Their name was chosen from a randomly opened copy of the *Oxford English Dictionary* – the band were somewhat chemically stimulated at the time. The original line-up – **Jerry Garcia** (b. Jerome John Garcia, 1942, d. 1995; lead guitar), Bob Weir (b. Robert Hall, 1947; rhythm guitar), Phil Lesh (b. Philip Chapman, 1940; bass), Ron 'Pigpen' McKernan (b. 1945, d. 1973; keyboards) and Bill Kreutzmann (b. 1946; drums) – were synonymous with the San Francisco/Acid Rock scene. In 1965, they took part in Ken Kesey's Acid Tests: Stanley Owsley manufactured the then-legal LSD and plied the band with copious amounts. This hallucinogenic opus was recorded on to tape over a six-month period, and documented in Tom Wolfe's book *The Electric Kool-Aid Acid Test*.

By the time their first album was released in 1967 they were already a huge cult band. *Grateful Dead* sounds raw today, but it was a brave, early attempt to capture a live concert sound on a studio album. *Anthem Of The Sun* was much more satisfying. The non-stop suite of ambitious segments with tantalizing titles such as 'The Faster We Go The Rounder We Get' and 'Quadlibet For Tenderfeet' was an artistic success and their innovative and colourful album covers were among the finest examples of San Franciscan art (Kelley Mouse Studios). *Aoxomoxoa* contained structured songs and hints of mellowing surfaced on 'China Cat Sunflower' and the sublime 'Mountains Of The Moon'. In concert, the band were playing longer and longer sets, sometimes lasting six hours with only as many songs.

The band now added a second drummer, Micky Hart, and a second keyboard player, Tom Constanten; it was this line-up that produced *Live Dead*. Their peak of improvisation is best demonstrated on 'Dark Star': during its 23 minutes, the music simmers, builds and explodes four times. On *Workingman's Dead* and *American Beauty*, a strong **Crosby, Stills And Nash** harmony influence prevailed. The Dead then reverted to releasing live sets, issuing a second double album closely followed by the triple, *Europe '72*. Sadly, after years of alcohol abuse, McKernan died in 1973. He was replaced by Keith Godcheaux and his vocalist wife Donna. The jazz-influenced *Wake Of The Flood* was their most commercially successful album to date; with this and subsequent studio albums the band produced a more mellow sound.

As a touring band the Dead continued to prosper, but their studio albums began to lose direction. The Godcheauxs left in 1979; sadly on 21 July 1980, Keith was killed in a car crash. *Go To Heaven*, with new keyboard player Brent Mydland, betrayed a hint of disco-pop and the album sleeve showed the band posing in white suits. Ironically, it was this disappointing record that spawned their first, albeit minor, success in the US singles chart with 'Alabama Getaway'. After years of drug experimentation, Garcia succumbed to heroin addiction and came close to death when he went into a diabetic coma in 1986.

The joy of his survival showed in their first studio album in seven years, *In The Dark*. A stunning return to form, it resulted in a worldwide hit 'Touch Of Grey'; MTV exposure introduced them to a whole new generation of fans. *Built To Last* was dull, but they continued to play to vast audiences.

In 1990, Mydland died from a lethal combination of cocaine and morphine. His temporary replacement was **Bruce Hornsby** until Vince Welnick was recruited full-time. Garcia then became seriously ill with a lung infection. After a long spell in hospital he returned, but, on 9 August 1995, suffered a fatal heart attack. In the USA the reaction was comparable to the death of Kennedy, Luther King, **Presley** and **Lennon**. At a press conference in December the band announced that they would bury the band name along with him. All the members, except Kreutzmann, have continued with solo careers.

Further References
Videos: *Live In London* (PMI 1986)
Walking On Sunshine (PMI 1989)

GRANT LEE BUFFALO
Albums
Fuzzy (Slash 1993)★★★
Mighty Joe Moon (Slash 1994)★★★
Copperopolis (Slash 1996)★★★
➧ p.364 for full listings
Connections
Bob Mould ➧ p.241
Elvis Presley ➧ p.265

GRATEFUL DEAD
Albums
Live/Dead (Warners 1970)★★★★
Workingman's Dead (Warners 1970)★★★★★
American Beauty (Warners 1970)★★★★★
➧ p.364 for full listings

Collaborators
Jerry Garcia ➧ p.158
Bruce Hornsby ➧ p.186
Influences
Crosby, Stills And Nash ➧ p.106

Further References
Video: *Grateful Dead In Concert* (RCA Video 1984)
Books: *Drumming At The Edge Of Magic*, Mickey Hart
Conversations With The Grateful Dead, David Gans

GREAT SOCIETY
Albums
Conspicuous Only In Its Absence (Columbia 1968)★★★
» p.364 for full listings
Connections
Jefferson Airplane » p.198
Further References
Books: *The Jefferson Airplane And The San Francisco Sound*, Ralph J. Gleeson
Grace Slick – The Biography, Barbara Rowe
Don't You Want Somebody To Love, Darby Slick

GREEN, AL
Albums
Al Green Gets Next To You (Hi 1971)★★★★
Let's Stay Together (Hi 1972)★★★★
» p.364 for full listings
Connections
Temptations » p.318
Further References
Video: *Gospel According To Al Green* (Hendring Video 1990)

GREEN, PETER
Albums
Little Dreamer (PVK 1980)★★★
tribute album *Rattlesnake Guitar: The Music Of Peter Green* (Coast To Coast 1995)★★★
» p.364 for full listings
Collaborators
John Mayall » p.228
Peter Bardens » p.33
Mick Fleetwood » p.147
Fleetwood Mac » p.147
Rod Stewart » p.310
Connections
Eric Clapton » p.92
Gary Moore » p.238
Further References
Book: *Peter Green: The Biography*, Martin Celmins

GREEN DAY
Albums
39/Smooth (Lookout 1990)★★★
Dookie (Reprise 1994)★★★★
» p.364 for full listings
Connections
Woodstock Festival » p.343

GREEN ON RED
Albums
The Killer Inside Me (Mercury 1987)★★★★
Here Come The Snakes (Red Rhino 1989)★★★★
» p.364 for full listings
Collaborators
Al Kooper » p.210
Influences
Neil Young » p.346

GREAT SOCIETY

FORMED IN 1965 BY GRACE SLICK (b. GRACE BARNETT WING, 1939; VOCALS/PIANO/RECORDER/GUITAR), HER HUSBAND Jerry (drums) and his brother Darby Slick (lead guitar). David Minor (rhythm guitar) and Bard DuPont (bass) completed the original line-up – DuPont was replaced by Peter Vandergelder (bass/saxophone). One of the first San Franciscan rock groups, they were active for 13 months and issued one single, 'Someone To Love' (later known as 'Somebody To Love'). This intriguing Darby Slick composition was adopted by **Jefferson Airplane**, the group Grace joined in 1966. The Great Society split on her departure, but two live collections, released after her fame, show rare imagination. The first album features 'White Rabbit', a composition Grace introduced to her new companions, which is preceded by a lengthy instrumental passage in a raga style that typified the Great Society's approach.

GREEN, AL

AFTER A SPELL IN THE GREENE BROTHERS, A GOSPEL QUARTET, URBANE SINGER AL GREEN (b. AL GREENE, 1946) MADE his first recordings in 1960. In 1964, he helped form the Creations with Curtis Rogers and Palmer Jones. These two wrote and produced 'Back Up Train', and a 1967 R&B hit for his new group, Al Greene And The Soul Mates. Similar releases fared less well, prompting Green's decision to work solo. In 1969, he met Willie Mitchell, who took the singer to Hi Records. 'I Can't Get Next To You' (1970) was their first best-seller, previously a hit for the **Temptations**. 'Tired Of Being Alone' (1971, US number 11/UK number 4) introduced a smoother perspective. It was followed by 'Let's Stay Together' (1971), 'I'm Still In Love With You' (1972) and 'Call Me (Come Back Home)' (1973). However, following an argument, his girlfriend, Mary Woodson shot herself dead in 1974. Scarred and shaken, Green's work grew increasingly predictable. The partnership with Mitchell was dissolved and Green opened his own recording studio, American Music. The first single, 'Belle', reached the US R&B Top 10; the accompanying album was a 'critics favourite', as were the later Hi collections, however further singles failed. In 1979, Green fell from a stage – he took this as a religious sign and released *The Lord Will Make A Way* (a gospel-only recording) followed by *He Is The Light*. A practising minister, he nonetheless reached the UK singles chart with the secular 'Put A Little Love In Your Heart' (1989). *Don't Look Back* was a sparkling return after many years away from recording new material.

GREEN, PETER

UK-BORN PETER GREEN (b. PETER GREENBAUM, 1946) BECAME ONE OF SEVERAL TEMPORARY GUITARISTS IN **John Mayall**'s Bluesbreakers during **Eric Clapton's** 1965 sabbatical. When Clapton returned, Green joined **Peter Bardens** (organ), Dave Ambrose (bass) and Mick Fleetwood (drums) in a short-lived club band, the Peter B's. They completed one single, 'If You Wanna Be Happy'/'Jodrell Blues' (1966); the instrumental b-side showcased Green's already distinctive style. They subsequently played for Shotgun Express, backing **Rod Stewart** and Beryl Marsden, but Green left after a few weeks. He rejoined Mayall in 1966 when Clapton left to form **Cream**. Green made several contributions to the Bluesbreakers' work, most notably on *A Hard Road*. In 1967, Green left to form **Fleetwood Mac** with Mick Fleetwood. They became one of the most popular groups of the era, developing blues-based origins into an exciting, experimental unit. However, Green grew increasingly unstable and he left in 1970; he has followed an erratic course since.

His solo debut, *The End Of The Game*, was perplexing. He made sporadic session appearances, but, following a cameo role on Fleetwood Mac's *Penguin*, dropped out of music altogether. In the mid-70s, he was committed to two mental institutions. Green returned with *In The Skies*, a light but optimistic collection. *Little Dreamer* offered a more blues-based perspective. In 1982, Green (now Greenbaum) toured unsatisfactorily with Kolors. A hastily concocted album of out-takes and unfinished demos was issued. In 1995, **Gary Moore** recorded an album of Peter Green tracks, *Blues For Greeny*. In 1996, Green showed up on-stage at a Gary Moore gig; he later played a live gig. In August, he played with the Splinter Group, Cozy Powell (drums), Nigel Watson (guitar) and Neil Murray (bass), at the Guildford Blues Festival; they issued an album in 1997. Green remains Britain's finest-ever white blues guitarist.

GREEN DAY

ALTERNATIVE CALIFORNIAN ROCK ACT – BILLY JOE ARMSTRONG (b. 1972; VOCALS/GUITAR), MIKE DIRNT (b. 1972; bass/vocals) and Tre Cool (b. Frank Edwin Wright III, 1972; drums/vocals) – formed after all three members had played in various local bands. Green Day (the name inspired by their propensity for marijuana) debuted with the *1000 Hours* EP. Their debut album, *39/Smooth*, was recorded in one day. Previous drummer Kiffmeyer booked their first national tour, but then left the band to concentrate on college. Cool was asked to fill in. He wrote the comedic 'Dominated Love Song' for *Kerplunk!*, which sold over 50,000 records. Afterwards, they signed to Warner Brothers' subsidiary Reprise Records. A&R man Rob Cavallo produced *Dookie* which sold over 9 million copies in the USA. Their arduous touring schedule was the chief reason for their rise, with appearances on the 1994 Lollapalooza package and the revived **Woodstock** event. The band were nominated in no less than four Grammy categories, and by 1995 had sold over 10 million albums worldwide, a stunning achievement for a punk-pop band. *Insomniac* had a hard act to follow and was disappointing.

GREEN ON RED

US BAND FORMED IN 1981. DAN STUART (GUITAR/VOCALS), JACK WATERSON (BASS) AND VAN CHRISTIAN (DRUMS) started out as the Serfers. Christian was replaced by Alex MacNicol, and Chris Cacavas added on keyboards for the first EP, *Two Bibles*, released under their new name. They attracted attention as part of the 60s-influenced 'paisley underground'; however, Green On Red's sound owed more to **Neil Young** and country/blues traditions. In 1984, Chuck Prophet IV joined on lead guitar. Sophisticated arrangements on *The Killer Inside Me* saw the group pushing for mainstream recognition, but shortly afterwards Waterson and Cacavas left to go solo. Prophet and Stuart forged ahead, using session musicians for *Here Come The Snakes*. Both have operated outside the group, most notably Stuart's involvement on *Danny And Dusty*. In 1991, Green On Red re-emerged with *Scapegoats*, recorded with **Al Kooper** on keyboards. Prophet's solo career took off in 1993 with *Balinese Dancer*. The group have been inactive since *Too Much Fun*.

GREENBAUM, NORMAN

GREENBAUM (b. 1942) FOUNDED LOS ANGELES JUG BAND DR. WEST'S MEDICINE SHOW AND JUNK BAND, WHO achieved a minor hit with the novelty 'The Eggplant That Ate Chicago'. The group split in 1967 and Greenbaum retired from music to run a farm in California. In 1970, however, one of his recordings, 'Spirit In The Sky', unexpectedly scaled the US charts, reaching number 3 and later making UK number 1. Greenbaum was teased out of retirement to record a couple of albums. In 1986, the British group Doctor And The Medics revived 'Spirit In The Sky', reaching UK number 1. The song was also prominently used in the film *Apollo 13*, leading to the release of a new compilation album. Despite poor health, Greenbaum has started to write new material.

GREGSON AND COLLISTER

UK FOLK MUSIC DUO: CLIVE GREGSON (b. 1955; GUITAR/KEYBOARDS/VOCALS) AND CHRISTINE COLLISTER (b. 1961; guitar/percussion/vocals). Gregson was already known as the writer and prominent frontman of Any Trouble, with whom he recorded five albums before turning solo. After *Strange Persuasions* in 1985, he became a member of the **Richard Thompson** Band. In addition, he produced albums by such artists as the **Oyster Band**, Stephen Fearing and Keith Hancock. Another solo album, *Welcome To The Workhouse*, comprised hitherto unreleased material. Collister was discovered in a local club by Gregson and joined the Richard Thompson Band. Gregson's lyrical ability and harmonies, together with Collister's warm, sensuous vocals produced a number of critically acclaimed albums.

In 1992, they played a farewell tour, following which Collister worked with Barb Jungr and Heather Joyce in the Jailbirds. Both Gregson and Collister continue to work and perform but separately. Collister toured with Richard Thompson in the mid-90s, and Gregson worked with Boo Hewerdine as well as releasing solo records.

GRIFFITH, NANCI

US-BORN GRIFFITH (b. 1953) GREW UP IN A THEATRICAL FAMILY. IN 1978 HER FIRST ALBUM, *THERE'S A LIGHT Beyond These Woods*, was released by a local company. In 1982, *Poet In My Window* was released by another local label; like its predecessor, it was re-released in 1986 by the nationally distributed Philo/Rounder label. The only song not written by Griffith herself was 'Tonight I Think I'm Gonna Go Downtown', penned by Jimmie Gilmore and John Reed. Her father, Marlin Griffith, provided harmony vocals on 'Wheels'.

By 1984 she had met Jim Rooney, who produced *Once In A Very Blue Moon*. Following on the heels of this artistic triumph came *Last Of The True Believers*. The album became Griffith's first to be released in the UK. Signed by MCA, her debut album for the label was *Lone Star State Of Mind*. Attracting most attention was Julie Gold's 'From A Distance', a song that became a standard by the 90s as covered by Bette Midler, **Cliff Richard** and many others. *Little Love Affairs* was supposedly a concept album, but major songs included 'Outbound Plane', '(My Best Pal's In Nashville) Never Mind' and 'Sweet Dreams Will Come'. Griffith later recorded and released a live album, *One Fair Summer Evening*.

Storms, produced by the legendary Glyn Johns (who geared the album's sound towards American radio), became Griffith's biggest seller. Although it was a sales breakthrough for Griffiths, it failed to attract country audiences. Her major European market was Ireland, where she was accorded near-superstar status. *Late Night Grande Hotel* was produced by the British team of Rod Argent and Peter Van Hook, and included a duet with Phil Everly, 'It's Just Another Morning Here'. *Other Voices Other Rooms* was a wholehearted success artistically and commercially. Griffith interpreted some outstanding songs by artists such as **Bob Dylan** ('Boots Of Spanish Leather'), **John Prine** ('Speed Of The Sound Of Loneliness') and **Ralph McTell** ('From Clare To Here'). The exquisite *Flyer* maintained her popularity with some excellent new material.

GROUNDHOGS

FORMED IN 1963 FROM STRUGGLING UK BEAT GROUP THE DOLLARBILLS. TONY 'T.S.' MCPHEE (b. 1944; GUITAR), JOHN Cruickshank (vocals/harp), Bob Hall (piano), Pete Cruickshank (b. 1945; bass) and Dave Boorman (drums) also adopted a 'John Lee' prefix in honour of **John Lee Hooker**, whom they subsequently backed. John Lee's Groundhogs recorded two singles before breaking up in 1966.

In 1968, they re-formed Groundhogs alongside Steve Rye (vocals/harmonica) and Ken Pustelnik (drums). They debuted with the rudimentary *Scratching The Surface*, after which Rye left. *Blues Obituary* contained 'Mistreated' and 'Express Man', which became in-concert favourites. *Thank Christ For The Bomb* cemented a growing popularity, Pustelnik left following *Who Will Save The World?* in 1972. Former **Egg** drummer Clive Brooks (b. 1949) was an able replacement but, despite continued popularity, subsequent recordings lacked the fire of early releases. They broke up in 1975, although McPhee maintained the name for *Crosscut Saw* and *Black Diamond*.

McPhee resurrected the Groundhogs in 1984 after interest in an archive release, *Hoggin' The Stage*. Pustelnik was one of several musicians McPhee used for touring, the most effective line-up completed by Dave Anderson (bass), and Mike Jones (drums).

GTOS

AN ACRONYM FOR GIRLS TOGETHER OUTRAGEOUSLY. THIS ALL-FEMALE GROUP WAS LAUDED IN 1969 AS PART OF **FRANK Zappa**'s Straight label roster. Initially known as the Laurel Canyon Ballet Company, they were among the best-known members of the 60s groupie sub-culture. After meeting the overtly polite Tiny Tim, the members abandoned surnames to became Miss Lucy, Miss Pamela, Miss Christine (d. 1972), Miss Sparky, Miss Mercy, Miss Sandra and Miss Cynderella. Miss Christine became governess to Zappa's daughter, and they occasionally performed live with the **Mothers Of Invention**. Zappa and guitarist Lowell George produced the GTOs' *Permanent Damage*, but the album's release was almost cancelled when Mercy, Cynderella and Sparky were arrested on drugs charges. The GTOs split into two with final recordings made solely by Pamela and Sparky. The group fragmented, but retained contact with the rock élite. Christine was pictured on the cover of Zappa's *Hot Rats*, on **Todd Rundgren**'s *Runt*, and was the subject of the **Flying Burrito Brothers**' 'Christine's Tune' (amended to 'She's The Devil In Disguise' following her death).

GREENBAUM, NORMAN
Albums
Petaluma (Reprise 1972)★★
➧ p.364 for full listings

GREGSON AND COLLISTER
Albums
A Change In The Weather (Special Delivery 1989)★★★★
The Last Word (Special Delivery 1992)★★★★
➧ p.364 for full listings
Connections
Any Trouble
Richard Thompson ➧ p.320
Oyster Band

GRIFFITH, NANCI
Albums
Last Of The True Believers (Philo 1986)★★★★
Lone Star State Of Mind (MCA 1987)★★★★
Blue Roses From The Moon (East West 1997)★★★★
➧ p.364 for full listings
Connections
Lyle Lovett ➧ p.219
Cliff Richard ➧ p.277
Bob Dylan ➧ p.128
John Prine ➧ p.268
Ralph McTell ➧ p.230

GROUNDHOGS
Albums
Blues Obituary (Liberty 1969)★★★
Hogwash (United Artists 1972)★★★
➧ p.364 for full listings
Connections
Egg ➧ p.132
Influences
John Lee Hooker ➧ p.185

GTOs
Albums
Permanent Damage (Straight 1969)★★
➧ p.364 for full listings
Connections
Frank Zappa ➧ p.348
Mothers Of Invention ➧ p.239
Flying Burrito Brothers ➧ p.148
Further References
Book: *I'm With The Band*, Pamela Des Barres

GUESS WHO
Albums
Canned Wheat Packed By The Guess Who (RCA 1969)★★★
➽ p.364 for full listings
Connections
Johnny Kidd And The Pirates ➽ p.204
Bachman Turner Overdrive ➽ p.28
James Gang ➽ p.197
Influences
Buddy Holly ➽ p.184

GUIDED BY VOICES
Albums
Bee Thousand (Scat/Matador 1994)★★★★
Mag Earwhig! (Matador 1997)★★★★
➽ p.364 for full listings

GUN (90S)
Albums
Gallus (A&M 1992)★★★
Swagger (A&M 1994)★★★★
➽ p.364 for full listings
Connections
Simple Minds ➽ p.297
Rolling Stones ➽ p.281

GUN CLUB
Albums
Fire Of Love (Ruby 1981)★★★
Mother Juno (Fundamental1987)★★★
Lucky Jim (New Rose 1993)★★★
➽ p.364 for full listings
Influences
Cramps ➽ p.102
Futher References
Video: *Live At The Hacienda, 1983* (1994)

GUNS N'ROSES
Albums
Appetite For Destruction (Geffen 1987)★★★★
G N' R Lies (Geffen 1989)★★★
Use Your Illusion I (Geffen 1991)★★★
➽ p.364 for full listings

Collaborators
Michael Jackson ➽ p.195
Connections
Cult ➽ p.107
Bob Dylan ➽ p.128
Ozzy Osbourne ➽ p.253
Nine Inch Nails ➽ p.248
Further References
Book: *World's Most Outrageous Hard Rock Band*, Paul Elliot

GUESS WHO

CANADA'S MOST POPULAR ROCK BAND OF THE 60S AND EARLY 70S HAD ITS ROOTS IN CHAD ALLAN AND THE Reflections, formed in 1962. The original line-up consisted of Allan (b. Allan Kobel; guitar/vocals), Jim Kale (bass), Randy Bachman (guitar), Bob Ashley (piano) and Garry Peterson (drums). Their debut, 'Tribute To **Buddy Holly**', was released in 1962. Further singles followed, and by 1965 the group had become Chad Allan and the Expressions, with their cover of **Johnny Kidd And The Pirates**' 'Shakin' All Over', which hit Canadian number 1 and US number 22. Ashley left and was replaced by Burton Cummings, who shared lead vocal duties with Allan for a year. In 1966, the group released, *Shakin' All Over*. The words 'Guess Who?' were printed on the cover, prompting their new name. That year Allan left, replaced briefly by Bruce Decker; when he left, Cummings became chief vocalist.

In 1967, Guess Who had their first UK chart single with 'His Girl'. A brief, disorganized UK tour left the group in debt, and they returned to Canada, recording Coca-Cola commercials and appearing on television. In 1968, with financial backing from producer Jack Richardson, Guess Who recorded *Wheatfield Soul*. 'These Eyes' reached Canadian number 1 and earned the group a US contract, reaching US number 6 in 1969. That year *Canned Wheat Packed By The Guess Who* also charted, as did 'Laughing', the b-side of 'These Eyes', and 'Undun' (US number 22). The year was wrapped up with a number 5 single, 'No Time'.

In 1970, 'American Woman' became the Guess Who's only US number 1, and *American Woman* went to the US Top 10. In July, Bachman left the group and resurfaced with Chad Allan in Brave Belt, and again with **Bachman Turner Overdrive**. A Guess Who album recorded while Bachman was still in the group was cancelled, and he was replaced by guitarists Kurt Winter and Greg Leskiw. In 1971, *Greatest Hits* reached number 12. Leskiw and Kale left in 1972, replaced by Don McDougall and Bill Wallace. In 1974, Winter and McDougall left, replaced by Domenic Troiano (ex-**James Gang**). That year, 'Clap For The Wolfman' reached US number 6. It proved to be the group's final hit – in 1975 Cummings disbanded Guess Who to go solo.

In 1979, a new Guess Who, featuring Allan, Kale, McDougall and three new members, recorded and toured, without success. Similar regroupings (minus Cummings) also failed. A 1983 Guess Who reunion aroused some interest followed by a Bachman and Cummings tour in 1987.

GUIDED BY VOICES

US ALTERNATIVE ROCK BAND LED BY ROBERT POLLARD ALONGSIDE TOBIN SPROUT. THE GROUP DEBUTED WITH the *Forever Since Breakfast* EP – progressive rock lacking in technical ability. Their first four albums similarly failed, but *Propeller* was an improvement. 'Exit Flagger' became their first bona fide 'classic'; the accompanying *The Grand Hour* EP also featured 'Shocker In Gloomtown'. *Vampire On Titus* finally brought the group out of obscurity and into the 'lo-fi' movement. 'Static Airplane Jive' and 'Fast Japanese Spin Cycle' preceded *Bee Thousand*, arguably their best album. *Crying Your Knife Away*, followed by *Box*, built on their new-found popularity, as Jim Greer (bass) joined. *Under The Bushes, Under The Stars*, a 24-track collection of minimal pop songs, pulled away from lo-fi, building on their singles' success. 'My Valuable Hunting Knife', was voted one of the 50 best singles of 1995 by UK rock magazine *Select*. *Mag Earwhig!* proved to be as worthy as any previous recordings.

GUN (90S)

SCOTTISH ROCK BAND WHO EMERGED IN 1989 WITH *TAKING ON THE WORLD*. BACKED BY A SPECTACULAR LIVE show, Gun – Mark Rankin (vocals), Scott Shields (drums), 'Baby' Stafford (guitar) and the Gizzi brothers, Giuliano 'Joolz' (guitar) and Dante (bass) – reached the UK charts with singles like 'Better Days', 'Money (Everybody Loves Her)' and 'Inside Out'. After supporting **Simple Minds**, they were chosen to support the **Rolling Stones** on their 1990 *Urban Jungle* UK tour. Afterwards Stafford went solo, replaced by Alex Dixon, and Gun pressed on with *Gallus*. In 'Steal Your Fire', 'Higher Ground' and 'Welcome To The Real World', Gun boasted a tougher, more muscular songwriting approach. By the time of *Swagger*, Mark Kerr had replaced Shields. Recorded in two weeks, *Swagger* continued its predecessor's back-to-basics approach with its rock foundation shot through with punk. Arguably the worst item contained on it, a rock version of **Cameo**'s funk classic 'Word Up', was the first single and their biggest single success (UK Top 10), winning them a new legion of fans. Kerr departed in 1996.

GUN CLUB

FORMED IN LOS ANGELES, IN 1980. LED BY VOCALIST JEFFREY LEE PIERCE (b. 1958, d. 1996), THE GROUP WAS initially completed by Kid Congo Powers (b. Brian Tristan; guitar) who later defected to the **Cramps**, Rob Ritter (bass) and Terry Graham (drums). *Fire Of Love*, was inspired by delta blues and psychobilly. Pierce's compositions were sometimes clumsily deep south but were generally non-specific in their hate-mongering. *Miami* established the group as one of America's leading 'alternative' acts. Further changes in personnel, including Congo's prodigal return, ultimately blunted Pierce's confidence and he disbanded the group for a solo career in 1985. *Two Sides Of The Beast* was issued in commemoration.

In 1987, Gun Club re-formed to record *Mother Juno*, but subsequent albums were disappointing. Pierce battled with alcoholism while the group's ranks fluctuated. In the 90s, he reconstituted the Gun Club with Congo, Nick Sanderson (drums) and his Japanese wife Romi Mori (bass); sadly he died from a brain haemorrhage, compounded by years of alcoholism and drug problems.

GUNS N'ROSES

US HEAVY ROCK BAND OF THE LATE 80S. AXL ROSE (AN ANAGRAM OF ORAL SEX) (b. WILLIAM BAILEY, 1962) AND IZZY Stradlin (b. Jeffrey Isbell, 1962) met in 1984. With Tracii Guns (guitar) and Rob Gardner (drums), they formed a rock band called in turn Rose, Hollywood Rose and **L.A. Guns**. Soon afterwards, Guns and Gardner left, replaced by drummer Steven Adler (b. 1965) and English guitarist Slash (b. Saul Hudson, 1965). With bass player Duff McKagan (b. Michael McKagan, 1964), the band was renamed Guns N'Roses. Following a disastrous US Hell Tour '85, Guns N'Roses released an EP, *Live?!*@ Like A Suicide*, winning interest from critics and record companies. In 1986, the group signed to Geffen Records, who reissued the EP. During 1987 they toured extensively. In 1988, Rose was kicked out, then reinstated – within three days.

Appetite For Destruction sold 20 million copies worldwide and reached US number 1 within a year. 'Welcome To The Jungle' was used on

the soundtrack of the Clint Eastwood film, *Dead Pool*, and reached the UK Top 30. The group toured regularly – and controversially – in the US and Europe, and, in 1989, *G N' R Lies* became a transatlantic hit. This was followed by 'Sweet Child O' Mine', 'Paradise City' and 'Patience'. However, Rose's lyrics for 'One In A Million' were widely criticized as homophobic. Guns N'Roses' career was littered with incidents involving drugs, drunkenness and public disturbance offences in 1989-90. In 1990, Adler was replaced by Matt Sorum (b. 1960; ex-**Cult**), followed by Dizzy Reed (b. Darren Reed; keyboards) for a 1991 world tour. The group then released *Use Your Illusion I* and *II* – reaching US numbers 1 and 2 – preceded by a version of **Bob Dylan**'s 'Knockin' On Heaven's Door' from the soundtrack of *Days Of Thunder*. Further hits, 'You Could Be Mine' (featured in the film *Terminator II*) and 'Don't Cry', followed. Stradlin found the pressure too much and left late in 1991, to form the Ju Ju Hounds. He was replaced by Gilby Clarke. Slash's growing reputation led to guest appearances for Dylan and **Michael Jackson**.

At the end of 1993, *The Spaghetti Incident* was issued. Duff McKagan released his debut solo album and in 1994, Gilby Clarke left. His replacement, Paul Huge, was in turn replaced by Zakk Wylde (ex-**Ozzy Osbourne**), who fell out irreconcilably with Rose before recording a note. In 1995, Stradlin was reinstated but by the end of the year Rose and Slash were again at loggerheads, and no new album was imminent. Slash confirmed Rose's departure in November 1996 – reversed in February 1997 when Rose allegedly purchased the rights to the Guns N'Roses name. Later in the year Robin Finck (ex-**Nine Inch Nails**) was recruited to replace Slash.

GUTHRIE, ARLO

ARLO (b. 1947) WAS THE ELDEST SON OF FOLKSINGER **WOODY GUTHRIE**. HIS LENGTHY BALLAD, 'ALICE'S Restaurant Massacre', part humorous song, part narrative, achieved popularity following Arlo's appearance at the 1967 Newport Folk Festival. It became the cornerstone of his debut album and inspired a feature film. An early song, 'Highway In The Wind', was successfully covered by Hearts And Flowers as Arlo emerged from the shadow of his father. *Running Down The Road* indicated a new-found maturity, but his talent truly flourished on a series of 70s recordings, notably *Hobo's Lullaby*, *Last Of The Brooklyn Cowboys* and *Amigo*. 'Presidential Rag' was a vitriolic commentary on Watergate, and 'Children Of Abraham' addressed the Arab/Israeli conflict. In 1972, Guthrie enjoyed a US Top 20 hit with 'City Of New Orleans'; today he remains a popular figure on the folk circuit. He returned to his most famous song in 1995 with a reworked 'The Massacre Revisited'.

GUTHRIE, WOODY

A MAJOR FIGURE OF AMERICA'S FOLK HERITAGE. GUTHRIE (b. WOODROW WILSON GUTHRIE, 1912, d. 1967) MOVED TO California in 1935, working on Los Angeles' KFVD radio station. Having befriended singer Cisco Houston and actor Will Geer, he established his left-wing credentials with joint appearances at union meetings and migrant labour camps. His reactions to the poverty he witnessed inspired his finest compositions, notably 'Pastures Of Plenty', 'Dust Bowl Refugees', 'Vigilante Man' and 'This Land Is Your Land'. At the end of the 30s, Guthrie travelled to New York, where he undertook a series of recordings for the folk-song archive at the Library Of Congress. The 12 discs he completed were later released commercially by Elektra.

Guthrie continued to traverse the country and in 1940 met **Pete Seeger** at a folk-song rally. Together they formed the Almanac Singers with Lee Hayes and Millard Lampell, which in turn inspired the Almanac House, a co-operative apartment in New York's Greenwich Village which became the focus of the east coast folk movement. In 1942, Guthrie joined the Headline Singers with Lead Belly, Sonny Terry and Brownie McGhee. He and Houston then enlisted in the merchant marines, until the end of World War II, after which Guthrie began recording again for various labels. Guthrie retained his commitment to the union movement and his prolific output continued unabated until the end of the 40s, when he succumbed to Huntington's Chorea. He was hospitalized by this lingering illness for fifteen years, until his death.

GUY, BUDDY

LOUISIANA-BORN BUDDY GUY (b. GEORGE GUY, 1936) TAUGHT HIMSELF TO PLAY THE BLUES ON A HOME-MADE guitar. By the mid-50s, he was playing with leading performers, including Slim Harpo and Lightnin' Slim. In 1957, Guy moved to Chicago, joined the Rufus Foreman Band and became established as an artist in his own right. His first single was released the following year. Shortly afterwards he met **Willie Dixon**, who took him to Chess Records. As part of the company's house band he appeared on sessions by **Muddy Waters** and **Howlin' Wolf**, as well as his own recordings, most notably 'First Time I Met The Blues' and 'Stone Crazy'. Guy also established a fruitful partnership with Junior Wells featuring on the harpist's early releases, *Hoodoo Man Blues* and *It's My Life Baby*. Guy's following albums combined classic 'Chicago' blues with contemporary soul styles, winning him attention from the rock audience. He appeared at the Fillmore auditorium and supported the **Rolling Stones** on their 1970 tour.

In 1990, he guested at **Eric Clapton**'s blues night at London's Royal Albert Hall. Guy's *Damn Right I Got The Blues* was recorded with the assistance of Clapton, **Jeff Beck** and **Mark Knopfler**, and the critical acclaim was further enhanced by *Feels Like Rain*. The trilogy of recent albums was completed with *Slippin' In* and *Live! The Real Deal*, recorded with G.E. Smith and the Saturday Night Live Band.

GWAR

THEATRICAL SHOCK-ROCK HEAVY METAL QUINTET FROM VIRGINIA, USA. ODERUS URUNGUS (VOCALS), BALSAC, THE Jaws Of Death (guitar), Flattus Maximus (guitar), Beefcake The Mighty (bass) and Nippleus Erectus (drums) are primarily renowned for an outrageous live show involving papier mâché masks, blood-splattered torture implements and buggery with a crucifix – their UK tour was stopped after just three dates. GWAR (apparently God What A Racket) were also taken to court in the US over allegedly displaying a penis as a stage-prop (the band suggested, bizarrely, that it was some form of fish). The rudimentary thrash music takes second place to the visuals, without which, their albums are anti-climactic.

GUTHRIE, ARLO

Albums

Alice's Restaurant (Reprise 1967)★★★★

Amigo (Reprise 1976)★★★★

➽ p.364 for full listings

Connections

Woody Guthrie ➽ p.171

Further References

Film: *Alice's Restaurant* (1969)

GUTHRIE, WOODY

Albums

Dust Bowl Ballads 1940 recordings (Folkways 1950)★★★★

Dust Bowl Ballads 1940 recordings (Rounder 1964)★★★★

This Land Is Your Land (Smithsonian/Folkways 1967)★★★★

➽ p.364 for full listings

Collaborators

Pete Seeger ➽ p.291

Connections

Arlo Guthrie ➽ p.171

Further References

Video: *Vision Shared: A Tribute To Woody Guthrie* (CMV Enterprises 1989)

Book: *Seeds Of Man: An Experience Lived And Dreamed*, Woody Guthrie

GUY, BUDDY

Albums

Buddy Guy And Junior Wells Play The Blues (Atlantic 1972)★★★★

Feels Like Rain (Silvertone 1993)★★★★

➽ p.364 for full listings

Collaborators

Jeff Beck ➽ p.41

Mark Knopfler ➽ p.209

Eric Clapton ➽ p.92

Connections

Willie Dixon ➽ p.120

Muddy Waters ➽ p.242

Howlin' Wolf ➽ p.189

Further References

Video: *Messin' With The Blues* (BMG Video 1991)

Book: *Damn Right I Got The Blues: Blues Roots Of Rock 'N' Roll*, Donald E. Wilcock and Buddy Guy

GWAR

Albums

Hell-O (Shimmy Disc 1988)

Carnival Of Chaos (Metal Blade 1997)

➽ p.364 for full listings

Further References

Videos: *The Movie* (1990)

Phallus In Wonderland (1992)

Tour De Scum (1994)

H.P. LOVECRAFT
Albums
H.P. Lovecraft (Philips 1967)★★★
H.P. Lovecraft II (Philips 1968)★★★
as H.P. Lovecraft *Live – May 11, 1968* (Sundazed 1992)★★
➽ p.364 for full listings
Connections
Shadows of Knight ➽ p.293

HAIRCUT 100
Albums
Pelican West (Arista 1982)★★★★
Paint On Paint (Arista 1984)★★
➽ p.364 for full listings
Connections
Nick Heywood
Further References
Books: *The Haircut 100 Catalogue*, Sally Payne
Haircut 100: Not A Trace Of Brylcreem, no editor listed

HALEY, BILL, AND HIS COMETS
Albums
Rock Around The Clock (Decca 1956)★★★★
Rock And Roll Stage Show (Decca 1956)★★★★
Just Rock And Roll Music (1973)★★★
➽ p.364 for full listings

Connections
Alan Freed ➽ p.154
Further References
Film: *Don't Knock The Rock* (1956)

HALF MAN HALF BISCUIT
Albums
Back In The DHSS (Probe Plus 1986)★★★
Some Call It Godcore (Probe Plus 1995)★★★
Voyage To The Bottom Of The Road (Probe 1997)★★★
➽ p.364 for full listings
Connections
John Peel ➽ p.258
Further References
Video: *Live* (Alternative Image 1993)

HALL AND OATES
Albums
Abandoned Luncheonette (Atlantic 1973)★★★
Private Eyes (RCA 1981)★★★★
H_2O (RCA 1982)★★★★
➽ p.364 for full listings

H.P. LOVECRAFT

CHICAGO BAND FORMED BY GEORGE EDWARDS (GUITAR/VOCALS) AND DAVID MICHAELS (KEYBOARDS/WOODWIND/vocals), who debuted in 1967 with a folk rock reading of 'Anyway That You Want Me'. Initially backed by local outfit, The Rovin' Kind, until Tony Cavallari (lead guitar), Jerry McGeorge (bass) and Michael Tegza (drums) joined. *H.P. Lovecraft* fused haunting folk-based material with graphic contemporary compositions: 'Wayfaring Stranger', 'Let's Get Together' and 'The White Ship' were highlights. McGeorge was replaced by Jeffrey Boylan for *H.P. Lovecraft II* before the group disintegrated.

In 1971, Tegza formed Lovecraft with Jim Dolinger (guitar), Michael Been (bass) and Marty Grebb (keyboards). They completed *Valley Of The Moon* – a set that bore little resemblance to its predecessors. In 1975, Tegza employed a new line-up for *We Love You Whoever You Are*.

HAIRCUT 100

UK BAND – **NICK HEYWARD** (b. 1961; VOCALS), LES NEMES (BASS) AND GRAHAM JONES (GUITAR) – FORMED IN 1980. Memphis Blair Cunningham (drums), Phil Smith (saxophone) and Mark Fox (percussion) joined in 1981. They secured a deal with Arista where, produced by Bob Sargeant, their teen appeal and smooth punk-pop sound became a winning combination. Their debut 'Favourite Shirts (Boy Meets Girl)' reached UK number 4 and 'Love Plus One' fared even better. When Heyward left, he was replaced by Mark Fox. Subsequent singles sold poorly and, after *Paint On Paint*, they disbanded.

HALEY, BILL, AND HIS COMETS

HALEY (b. 1925, d. 1981) STARTED OUT IN COUNTRY MUSIC WITH THE FOUR ACES OF WESTERN SWING. HIS NEXT group, the Saddlemen, played western swing mixed with polka. Haley's fusion of country, R&B and a steady beat was to provide the backbone of rock 'n' roll.

In 1953, Haley formed Bill Haley And His Comets. Their first single 'Crazy Man Crazy' became the first rock 'n' roll Top 20 US hit. After signing to Decca in 1954, Haley recorded several important songs, including 'Rock Around The Clock' – its spine-tingling guitar breaks and inspired drumming were unlike any previous recording. Initially it was only a minor hit. Haley then recorded 'Shake Rattle And Roll' whose jive-style lyrics, brilliant saxophone and upright bass brought a new sound into the US Top 20. Less important hits followed until, in 1955, 'Rock Around The Clock' was included in the controversial film *The Blackboard Jungle*. Suddenly, it became rock 'n' roll's anthem, soaring to US/UK number 1. Haley dominated the US/UK charts throughout 1955-56 with such songs as 'Rock-A-Beatin' Boogie', 'See You Later Alligator', and 'Rudy's Rock'. In 1957, he became the first rock 'n' roll star to tour abroad; he was mobbed on arrival in London.

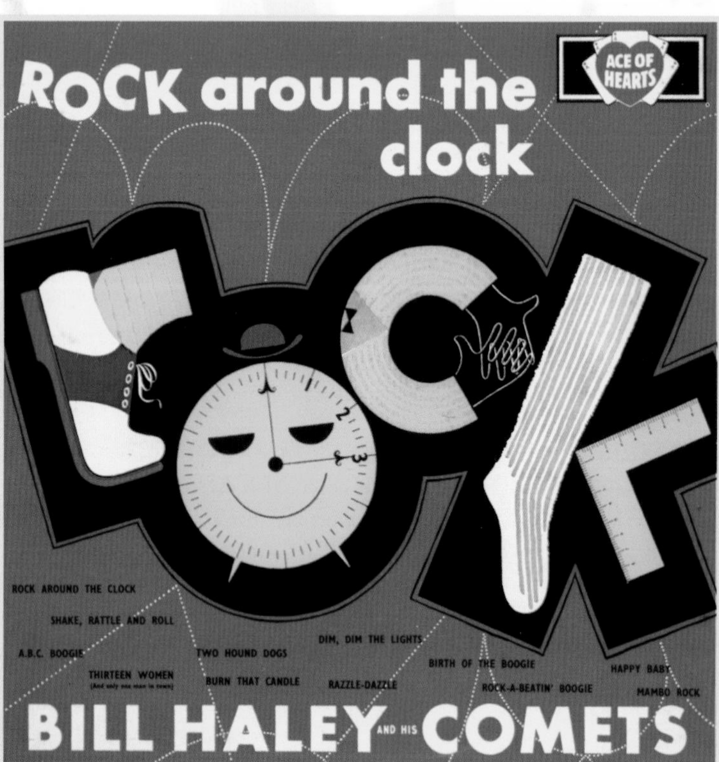

Haley's star burned brightly for a couple of years, but once **Elvis Presley** exploded on to the scene, Haley swiftly lost his standing among his young audience. 'Rock Around The Clock' returned to the UK Top 20 in 1968 and 1974.

HALF MAN HALF BISCUIT

BRITISH BAND FROM THE MID-80S. NEIL CROSSLEY (VOCALS/BASS), SI BLACKWELL (GUITAR), NIGEL BLACKWELL (vocals/guitar), David Lloyd (keyboards) and Paul Wright (drums) were signed to Probe Plus in 1985. Thanks to disc jockey **John Peel**, *The Trumpton Riots* 12-inch EP (1986) stayed in the indie charts for weeks. Inspired by cult television celebrities, their unforgettable song titles include '99% Of Gargoyles Look Like Bob Todd' and 'I Love You Because (You Like Jim Reeves)'. Displaying a disinterest in ambition, they turned down television appearances that clashed with their football club's home matches. They split at the peak of their success but re-formed mid-1990 for a version of 'No Regrets'. The subsequent *McIntyre, Treadmore And Davitt* and *This Leaden Pall* continued to mine the band's parochial good humour, and with *Voyage To The Bottom Of The Road* the group had become a British institution.

HALL AND OATES

AMERICAN DUO DARYL HALL (b. DARYL FRANKLIN HOHL, 1949; FALSETTO) AND JOHN OATES (b. 1949; BARITONE) met in 1969. They were discovered by Tommy Mottola of Chappell Music and signed to Atlantic. Their three albums for the label sold few copies, before the million-selling 'Sara Smile', on RCA, followed by 'Rich Girl' (1977, US number 1). After the unimpressive *X-Static* the self-produced *Voices* spawned four hit singles, notably a remake of the **Righteous Brothers**' 'You've Lost That Lovin' Feelin'' and the haunting 'Every Time You Go Away'. For the next five years hit followed hit, including 'Maneater', 'I Can't Go For That (No Can Do)', 'Out Of Touch' and 'Family Man' (a **Mike Oldfield** composition).

During a three-year hiatus in the partnership, Hall recorded his second solo album, produced by Dave Stewart. Reunited in 1988, Hall And Oates had a big US hit with 'Everything Your Heart Desires', followed by the 1990 hit 'So Close' (producers **Jon Bon Jovi** and Danny Kortchmar added a strong rock flavour). The duo did not record together again until *Marigold Sky*.

HALLYDAY, JOHNNY

BY THE LATE 50S, PARISIAN JOHNNY HALLYDAY (b. JEAN-PHILIPPE SMET, 1943) HAD BECOME A ROCK 'N' ROLLER. An apprenticeship of singing to a jukebox of US discs made him sound like an American. A 1960 radio debut led to Vogue contracting him for 'T'Ai Mer Follement'. After a million-selling bilingual cover of **Chubby Checker**'s 'Let's Twist Again' (1961) and a film appearance, this svelte blond was to France what **Elvis Presley** was to the USA.

Johnny Hallyday Sings America's Rockin' Hits indicated his future direction and his interpretations of songs such as 'The House Of The Rising Sun',

'Black Is Black', and 'Hey Joe' followed. After little success in the UK or USA, Johnny commanded audiences of 25,000 in Africa and South America. Hallyday continued to thrive on a certain hip sensibility, manifested in his block-bookings of fashionable studios in Britain and the USA, and employment of top session musicians – all prominent on 1975's *Flagrant Delit* which, like most of his albums, contained a few Hallyday originals. Hallyday remains one of the few Europeans to be regarded with remotely strong interest outside his own country.

HAMMER, M.C.

AFTER FAILING TO MAKE IT IN PROFESSIONAL BASEBALL, HAMMER (b. STANLEY KIRK BURRELL, 1962) RELEASED THE single 'Ring 'Em'. Backed by two DJs and three singers, he cut *Feel My Power*. Capitol Records paid a reported advance of $750,000 and reissued the album as *Let's Get It Started*. The following *Please Hammer Don't Hurt 'Em* stayed at US number 1 for 21 weeks. 'U Can't Touch This' achieved near constant rotation on MTV, with dance routines to equal **Michael Jackson**. The single sampled **Rick James**'s 'Super Freak', creating a precedent for follow-ups 'Have You Seen Her' (the **Chi-Lites**) and 'Pray' (**Prince**; 'When Doves Cry'). Despite an on-going duel with white rapper **Vanilla Ice** and media allegations of both artists' plagiarism, Hammer's album achieved a multitude of awards, including Grammys, Bammys and International Album Of The Year at the Canadian Juno awards, reflecting its global success. Its long-awaited successor, *Too Legit To Quit*, featured a direct challenge to Michael Jackson. Sleeve notes expounded his desire for black youth to rid themselves of drugs and resurrect Christian morality through self-education. A sustained challenge would inevitably be limited by his own admission that: 'I'm not a singer. I'm a rapper'. Despite a soundtrack hit with 'The Addams Family', heavily promoted in the film of the same title, Hammer's fortunes declined.

HAMMILL, PETER

IN 1967 PETER HAMMILL (b. 1948; VOCALS/PIANO/GUITAR) FORMED UK BAND **VAN DER GRAAF GENERATOR** WITH Hugh Banton (keyboards/bass) and Guy Evans (drums). David Jackson (saxophone) joined in 1968. Hammill had intended to release a solo album, but the band used his material, resulting in *Aerosol Grey Machine*. They enjoyed greater success in Europe than in the UK and broke up in 1972.

Hammill continued solo with limited success, and has maintained a prolific output ever since. The quality of his work keeps mainstream artists turning to him for inspiration. He has achieved autonomy in his work – owning his studio and label – but, despite writing for ballets and an opera version of Edgar Allan Poe's *The Fall Of The House Of Usher*, he has never fully escaped the legacy of Van Der Graaf Generator.

HAMMOND, ALBERT

BRITISH-BORN HAMMOND (b. *c.* 1943) BEGAN A SONGWRITING PARTNERSHIP WITH MIKE HAZELWOOD, A RADIO Luxembourg presenter in 1966. After international success in 1968 with 'Little Arrows' for Leapy Lee, they hit in the UK with the Pipkins' 'Gimme Dat Ding'. They reached the UK Top 10 in 1969 with 'Way of Life' before moving to Los Angeles. In 1971, Hammond became the first artist contracted to the Mums label. His second single, 'It Never Rains In Southern California', sold a million in the USA. Hammond's initial triumphs have not been matched since, although subsequent songwriting hits include 'The Air That I Breathe' (with Hazelwood) for the **Hollies**, '99 Miles From LA' for **Art Garfunkel**, and 'When I Need You' (with Carole Bayer Sager) for **Leo Sayer**.

Collaborators
Mike Oldfield ➧ p.251
Jon Bon Jovi ➧ p.60
Connections
Dave Stewart
Influences
Righteous Brothers ➧ p.278
Paul Young ➧ p.347

HALLYDAY, JOHNNY
Albums
Johnny Hallyday Sings America's Rockin' Hits (Philips 1961)★★★
Les Grands Success De Johnny Hallyday (1988)★★★
La Nuit Johnny 42-CD box set (1993)★★★
➧ p.365 for full listings
Influences
Chubby Checker ➧ p.88

HAMMER, M.C.
Albums
Feel My Power (Bustin' 1987)★★★
Let's Get It Started (Capitol 1988)★★★
Please Hammer Don't Hurt 'Em (Capitol 1990)★★★
➧ p.365 for full listings
Influences
Rick James ➧ p.197
Chi-Lites ➧ p.89
Prince ➧ p.267
Further References
Book: *M.C. Hammer: U Can't Touch This*, Bruce Dessau

HAMMILL, PETER
Albums
Over (Charisma 1977)★★★
And Close As This (Virgin 1986)★★★★
X My Heart (Fie! 1996)★★★
➧ p.365 for full listings
Connections
Van Der Graaf Generator ➧ p.328
Further References
Video: *In The Passionskirche, Berlin MCMXCII* (Studio 1993)
Books: *The Lemming Chronicles*, David Shaw-Parker
Killers, Angels, Refugees, Peter Hammill

HAMMOND, ALBERT
Albums
It Never Rains In Southern California (Mum 1973)★★
Free Electric Band (Mum 1973)★★★
Albert Hammond (Mum 1974)★★
➧ p.365 for full listings
Collaborators
Hollies ➧ p.183
Art Garfunkel ➧ p.159
Leo Sayer ➧ p.289
Connections
Diamond Boys

HANCOCK, HERBIE
Albums
Headhunters (Columbia 1974)★★★★★
➽ p.365 for full listings
Further References
Video: *Herbie Hancock And The Rockit Band* (Columbia 1984)

HANOI ROCKS
Albums
Bangkok Shocks, Saigon Shakes, Hanoi Rocks (Johanna 1981)★★★
➽ p.365 for full listings
Connections
Clash ➽ p.93
Influences
Creedence Clearwater Revival ➽ p.104
Further References
Video: *All Those Wasted Years* (1988)

HANSON
Albums
Middle Of Nowhere (Mercury 1997)★★★
➽ p.365 for full listings
Connections
Black Grape ➽ p.51

HAPPY MONDAYS
Albums
Pills 'N' Thrills And Bellyaches (Factory 1990)★★★★
➽ p.365 for full listings

Connections
John Cale ➽ p.78
Talking Heads ➽ p.316
Influences
Donovan ➽ p.123

HANCOCK, HERBIE

HANCOCK (b. 1940) FIRST ENJOYED MINOR FAME WHEN A VERSION OF HIS 'WATERMELON Man', by Mongo Santamaría, reached the US Top 10. Until the mid-60s Hancock led bands for club engagements and record dates before joining Miles Davis's quintet, with whom he stayed for more than five years. In 1968, Hancock formed a sextet with musicians including Julian Priester, Buster Williams and Eddie Henderson. Playing much Hancock material, they became one of the most popular and influential jazz-rock bands in the early 70s. From 1969, Hancock extensively used electronic keyboard instruments, including synthesizers. In 1973, the group dwindled to a quartet whose music leaned towards jazz-funk and the first album, *Headhunters*, sold well into the burgeoning disco scene. By the end of the decade, Hancock cut down on straight jazz performances. His numerous disco successes included 'You Bet Your Love' (1979, UK Top 20) and *Future Shock* (with the group Material), which spawned 'Rockit' (UK Top 10/US number 1). In 1986, Hancock wrote and played the score, and acted in the film *'Round Midnight*, winning an Academy Award.

HANOI ROCKS

FINNISH HEAVY ROCK BAND FORMED IN 1980. MICHAEL MONROE (b. MATTI FAGERHOLM; vocals), Nasty Suicide (b. Jan Stenfors; guitar), Andy McCoy (b. Antti Hulkko; guitar), Sam Yaffa (b. Sami Takamaki; bass) and Gyp Casino (b. Jesper Sporre; drums) debuted with 'I Want You' (1980), followed by *Bangkok Shocks, Saigon Shakes, Hanoi Rocks*. They then recorded *Oriental Beat* in London. In 1983 they were signed to CBS, and hit the UK charts for the first and only time in 1984 with a cover version of **Creedence Clearwater Revival**'s 'Up Around The Bend'. The year ended in tragedy when Casino's replacement, Razzle (b. Nicholas Dingley), was killed in a car crash in the US. Terry Chimes (ex-**Clash**) replaced Razzle. In 1985 Monroe left to go solo.

HANSON

PRECOCIOUS GROUP OF TEENAGE BROTHERS FROM OKLAHOMA, USA, WHO PLAY AN ENERGETIC BLEND OF **Jackson 5**-styled harmonies and crafted pop/soul melodies. Isaac (b. 1981; guitar/piano/vocals), Taylor (b. 1983; keyboards/vocals) and Zac Hanson (b. 1986, Tulsa, Oklahoma; drums, vocals) began writing and performing in 1992. Two self-distributed CDs and extensive live performances followed. Playing at the South by Southwest Music Convention for unsigned bands, they linked with manager Chris Sabec, landing a deal with Mercury Records. Their self-penned 'MMMBop' reached US/UK number 1. *Middle Of Nowhere* followed, recorded with 'name' producers Steve Lironi (**Black Grape**, **Space**) and the Dust Brothers (**Beck**), featuring four of their own songs alongside collaborations with established songwriters, including Barry Mann and Cynthia Weill.

HAPPY MONDAYS

UK URBAN FOLK BAND WHO DEBUTED WITH *HAPPY MONDAYS' SQUIRREL AND G-MAN TWENTY FOUR HOUR PARTY PEOPLE Plastic Face Carnt Smile (White Out)*, produced by **John Cale**. From the group's formation in the early 80s the line-up remained virtually unchanged: Shaun Ryder (b. 1962; vocals), his brother Paul Ryder (b. 1964; bass), Mark Day (guitar), Gary Whelan (drums), Paul Davis (keyboards) and 'Bez' (b. Mark Berry; percussion). *Bummed*, produced by Martin Hannett, was layered with diverse dance rhythms, and followed by 'Step On' (1990, UK Top 10). *Pills 'N' Thrills And Bellyaches* reached UK number 1. In tribute to 60s singer **Donovan**, they recorded 'Donovan'. Strong support from Factory Records and strong media coverage led to impressive sales. Success was tempered with unpleasant publicity, which came to a head when Shaun Ryder announced he was a heroin addict undergoing detoxification. A highly publicized strife-torn recording session in the Caribbean resulted in *Yes Please!*, but media interest was waning and the group split up.

HARDCASTLE, PAUL

HARDCASTLE (b. 1957) IS A PRODUCER, MIXER, COMPOSER AND KEYBOARD WIZARD. HIS FIRST GROUP WAS FIRST Light. After four minor solo hits, '19' (1985), a song about the Vietnam conflict utilizing spoken news reports, reached UK number 1. The follow up, 'Just For The Money', was based on the Great Train Robbery and boasted the voices of Bob Hoskins and Sir Laurence Olivier. His next success was 'Papa's Got A Brand New Pigbag' under the pseudonym Silent Underdog. In 1986, he wrote the *Top Of The Pops* theme, 'The Wizard', before switching to production for young funk band LW5 and providing remixes for various artists.

HARDIN, TIM

BY 1964, HARDIN (b. 1941, d. 1980) WAS A REGULAR IN NEW YORK'S GREENWICH VILLAGE CAFÉS, PLAYING A UNIQUE blend of poetic folk/blues. His poignant *Tim Hardin 1* included 'Misty Roses' (covered by **Colin Blunstone**). *Tim Hardin 2* featured his original version of 'If I Were A Carpenter', an international hit for **Bobby Darin** and the **Four Tops**. However, Hardin was disappointed with these releases, and his career faltered. A conceptual work, *Suite For Susan Moore And Damion* rekindled his former fire but his gifts then seemed to desert him. Hardin's work has been interpreted by many artists, including Wilson Phillips and **Rod Stewart** ('Reason to Believe') and **Scott Walker** ('Lady Came From Baltimore'). He interpreted the work of other songwriters, including **Leonard Cohen**, but his resigned delivery seemed maudlin. Tim Hardin died, almost forgotten and totally underrated, of a heroin overdose.

HARPER, BEN

US-BORN ACOUSTIC FOLK-ROCKER HARPER (b. 1969) SOAKED UP A VARIETY OF MUSICAL INFLUENCES, FROM SON HOUSE and Skip James to **Bob Marley** and **Bob Dylan** and gave his first performance at the age of 12. His acoustic guitar style came from the great folk and blues artists practised on his distinctive 'Weissenborn' – a hollow-neck lap-slide guitar. In 1992, Harper played with **Taj Mahal** and performed alongside bluesman Brownie McGhee. His debut for Virgin Records earned good reviews in 1994. Afterwards Harper contributed the music to Morgan Freeman's narration on the film *Follow The Drinking Gourd*. *Fight For Your Mind* continued to explore lyrical themes of freedom and the restraint of self-expression, alongside the deeply personal 'By My Side'.

HARPER, ROY

HARPER (b. 1941) BEGAN PLAYING IN HIS BROTHER'S SKIFFLE GROUP, BEFORE BUSKING around Europe. On returning to England, he became resident at London's Les Cousins club. *The Sophisticated Beggar* was recorded in primitive conditions, but contained the rudiments of his highly personal style. *Come Out Fighting Genghis Smith* attracted an underground audience, but he was unhappy with producer Shel Talmy's arrangements and with the cover. *Folkjokeopus* (which contained 'McGoohan's Blues') was considered patchy. *Flat, Baroque And Berserk* was released on Harvest, who allowed him considerable artistic licence. *Stormcock* featured contributions from **Jimmy Page** who appeared on several succeeding releases including *Lifemask*, another remarkable, if self-indulgent set and *Valentine*. *HQ* introduced Trigger, Harper's short-lived backing group: Chris Spedding (guitar), Dave Cochran (bass) and **Bill Bruford** (drums).

Harper appeared memorably on **Pink Floyd**'s *Wish You Were Here*, taking lead vocals on 'Have A Cigar', but his subsequent work lacked passion and *The Unknown Soldier* was a bleak, depressing set. *Once* was critically acclaimed as a return to form. Commercial success has eluded Harper, but he retains a committed following.

HARPERS BIZARRE

TED TEMPLEMAN (LEAD VOCALS/GUITAR), DICK SCOPPETTONE (VOCALS/GUITAR), DICK YOUNG (VOCALS/BASS), Eddie James (vocals/guitar) and John Peterson (drums/vocals; ex-**Beau Brummels**) formed Harpers Bizarre in 1966. A cover of **Simon And Garfunkel**'s '59th Street Bridge Song (Feelin' Groovy)' reached the US Top 20. Their first album, arranged by **Leon Russell**, with compositions by **Randy Newman**, proved an enticing debut. After covering Van Dyke Parks' 'Come To The Sunshine', they worked with him on a revival of Cole Porter's 'Anything Goes'. The group split in 1969. Templeman became a producer for Warner Brothers Records and three of the original line-up reunited six years later for *As Time Goes By*.

HARRIS, EMMYLOU

US SINGER HARRIS (b. 1947) FIRST RECORDED IN 1970. SHE THEN MET **GRAM PARSONS**, WHO NEEDED A FEMALE partner. She appeared on his two studio albums, *GP* and *Grievous Angel*. The latter was released after Parsons' drug-related death.

Parsons' manager encouraged Harris to make a solo album using the same musicians, the Hot Band: **James Burton** (guitar), Glen D. Hardin (piano), Hank DeVito (steel guitar), Emory Gordy Jnr (bass), John Ware and the virtually unknown **Rodney Crowell**. Harris released a series of excellent and often successful albums: *Pieces Of The Sky*, *Elite Hotel*, *Luxury Liner* and *Quarter Moon In A Ten Cent Town*. *Blue Kentucky Girl* was closer to pure country music than the country rock that had become her trademark, and *Roses In The Snow* was her fourth US Top 40 album. *Evangeline* and *Cimmaron* were better sellers, but a live album, *Last Date*, was largely ignored. Harris had also appeared on **Bob Dylan**'s *Desire* and the **Band**'s *The Last Waltz*.

Harris was invited by producer Glyn Johns and British singer-songwriter Paul Kennerley to participate in a concept album written by Kennerley, *The Legend Of Jesse James*. Harris and Kennerley later married, and together wrote and produced *The Ballad Of Sally Rose* and the similarly excellent *13*. Neither recaptured Harris's previous chart heights.

In 1987, Harris worked on *Trio* – a Grammy-winning collaboration with **Linda Ronstadt** and **Dolly Parton** – and her own *Angel Band*, a low-key acoustic collection. *Bluebird* was a return to form, but commercially limp. *Brand New Dance* was relatively unsuccessful, and the Hot Band was dropped in favour of bluegrass-based acoustic quintet the Nash Ramblers. In 1991, Harris and the Nash Ramblers were permitted to record a live album in Nashville. The record was poorly received, and in 1992, she was dropped by Warner Brothers Records, after 20 years.

In her 1995 album, she boldly stepped away from country-sounding arrangements and recorded the stunning **Daniel Lanois-**produced *Wrecking Ball*. Songwriters included **Neil Young**, Lanois, **Steve Earle** and **Anna McGarrigle**. Harris described this album as her 'weird' record; the album won a Grammy in 1996 for Best Contemporary Folk Album.

HARRIS, JET, AND TONY MEEHAN

TERENCE 'JET' HARRIS (b. 1939; GUITAR) AND DANIEL JOSEPH ANTHONY MEEHAN (b. 1943; DRUMS) BEGAN THEIR PARTnership in 1959 in the **Shadows**. Meehan left in 1961 to work in Decca's A&R department; in 1962 Harris went solo with 'Besame Mucho'. 'The Man With The Golden Arm' gave him a UK Top 20 hit prior to reuniting with Meehan in 1963. The duo's debut, 'Diamonds', reached UK number 1, while 'Scarlett O'Hara' and 'Applejack', reached the Top 5. All featured Harris's low-tuned Fender Jaguar guitar with Meehan's punchy drum interjections. A bright future was predicted, but a serious car crash undermined Harris's confidence and the pair split up.

HARDCASTLE, PAUL
Albums
Paul Hardcastle (Chrysalis 1985)★★★
p.365 for full listings
Collaborators
Bob Hoskins
Sir Laurence Olivier

HARDIN, TIM
Albums
Tim Hardin 1 (Verve Forecast 1966)★★★
p.365 for full listings
Collaborators
Rod Stewart p.310
Scott Walker p.333
Connections
Colin Blunstone p.57
Bobby Darin p.111
Four Tops p.152

HARPER, BEN
Albums
Fight For Your Mind (Virgin 1995)★★★
p.365 for full listings
Collaborators
Taj Mahal p.316
Influences
Bob Marley p.225
Bob Dylan p.128

HARPER, ROY
Albums
Lifemask (Harvest 1973)★★★★
p.365 for full listings
Collaborators
Jimmy Page p.255
Pink Floyd p.261

HARPERS BIZARRE
Albums
Feelin' Groovy (Warners 1967)★★★
p.365 for full listings
Collaborators
Leon Russell p.286
Randy Newman p.246
Connections
Beau Brummels p.40
Influences
Simon And Garfunkel p.297

HARRIS, EMMYLOU
Albums
Pieces Of The Sky (Reprise 1975)★★★★
p.365 for full listings
Collaborators
Gram Parsons p.256
Linda Ronstadt p.282
Dolly Parton p.256
Neil Young p.346
Connections
Rodney Crowell p.107
Bob Dylan p.128
Band p.31
Further References
Video: *Thanks To You* (1990)

HARRIS, JET, AND TONY MEEHAN
Connections
Shadows p.293
p.365 for full listings

HARRISON, GEORGE
Albums
All Things Must Pass (Apple 1970)★★★★
Cloud Nine (Dark Horse 1987)★★★
➽ p.365 for full listings
Collaborators
Bob Dylan ➽ p.128
Eric Clapton ➽ p.92
Leon Russell ➽ p.286
Derek And The Dominos ➽ p.116
Badfinger ➽ p.28
Tom Petty ➽ p.260
Roy Orbison ➽ p.252
Connections
Beatles ➽ p.38
Traveling Wilburys ➽ p.323
Influences
Carl Perkins ➽ p.258
Further References
Book: *I Me Mine*, George Harrison

HARRISON, WILBERT
Albums
Kansas City (Sphere Sound 1965)★★★
➽ p.365 for full listings
Connections
Bryan Ferry ➽ p.144
Canned Heat ➽ p.79

HARRY, DEBORAH
Albums
Def, Dumb And Blonde (Chrysalis 1989)★★★
➽ p.365 for full listings
Connections
Shangri-Las ➽ p.294
Blondie ➽ p.54
Chic ➽ p.90

HARTMAN, DAN
Albums
Instant Replay (Blue Sky 1978)★★★
➽ p.365 for full listings

HARRISON, GEORGE

AS THE YOUNGEST MEMBER OF THE **BEATLES**, HARRISON (b. 1943) WAS CONSTANTLY OVERSHADOWED BY **JOHN Lennon** and **Paul McCartney**. Although 'Don't Bother Me' (*With The Beatles*), 'I Need You' (*Help!*) and 'If I Needed Someone' (*Rubber Soul*) revealed considerable compositional talent, they were swamped by his colleagues' prodigious output. Instead, Harrison honed a distinctive guitar style and was responsible for adding the sitar into the pop lexicon. He flexed solo ambitions with the would-be film soundtrack, *Wonderwall*, and the trite *Electronic Sounds*, before commencing work on *All Things Must Pass*, which boasted support from **Derek And The Dominos**, **Badfinger** and **Phil Spector**, and included 'I'd Have You Anytime', (co-written with **Bob Dylan**). 'My Sweet Lord' deftly combined melody with mantra and soared to the top of the US and UK charts. His next project was 'Bangla Desh', a single inspired by a plea to aid famine relief. Charity concerts featuring Harrison, Dylan, **Eric Clapton** and **Leon Russell**, were held at New York's Madison Square Gardens in 1971.

Living In The Material World reached US number 1, as did 'Give Me Love (Give Me Peace On Earth)'. A disastrous US tour was the unfortunate prelude to *Dark Horse* and, his marriage to Patti Boyd now over, the set reflected its creator's depression. Subsequent releases fell short of his initial recordings, but during this period George became involved with his heroes, the Monty Python comedy team, in the successful film *Life Of Brian*. In 1980, his parent label, Warner Brothers Records, rejected the first version of *Somewhere In England*, deeming its content below standard. The reshaped collection included 'All Those Years Ago', George's homage to the murdered John Lennon, which featured contributions from Paul McCartney and **Ringo Starr**. The song reached the UK Top 3 when issued as a single. He then pursued other interests, notably with his company Handmade Films, until 1986 when he commenced work on a projected new album. Production was shared with **Jeff Lynne**, and Harrison's version of Rudy Clark's 'Got My Mind Set On You' reached UK number 2 and US number 1. The intentionally Beatles-influenced 'When We Was Fab' was another major success, while *Cloud Nine* proved equally popular. Harrison also played a pivotal role within the **Traveling Wilburys**.

In 1992, he made his first tour for many years in Japan with long-time friend Eric Clapton giving him support, and reappeared on stage in England at a one-off benefit concert in 1992.

HARRISON, WILBERT

HARRISON (b. 1929, d. 1994) FIRST FOUND SUCCESS IN THE LATE 50S WITH 'KANSAS CITY' (US NUMBER 1/US R&B number 1). A later series of releases included 'Let's Stick Together', revived many years later by **Bryan Ferry**. Harrison continued to record, rather unsuccessfully, throughout the 60s, until 'Let's Work Together' returned him to the public eye. The song ultimately became better known with **Canned Heat**'s hit version (UK number 2/US number 17). Its originator, meanwhile, made several excellent albums in the wake of his new-found popularity.

HARRY, DEBORAH

SPELLS IN A SUCCESSION OF *AVANT-GARDE* GROUPS IN THE MID-60S PRECEDED HARRY'S (b. 1945) TENURE IN THE WIND In The Willows, a baroque folk/rock act. In 1973, she joined the Stilettos. The following year she formed **Blondie**. They became one of the leading pop groups of the late 70s and Harry became the leading female rock sex-symbol. In 1981, she released her solo debut *Koo Koo*, produced by **Chic** mainstays Nile Rodgers and Bernard Edwards. The set failed to capture Blondie's style and the singer resumed her commitment to the group until Stein's recurrent ill-heath brought the act to an end.

Harry pursued an acting career, including a comic role in the 1987 film, *Hairspray*. In 1986 she released *Rockbird* featuring 'French Kissing In The USA' (UK Top 10). Three years later Debbie returned to the UK Top 20, with the Tom Bailey and Alannah Currie composition, 'I Want That Man'. The accompanying album, *Def, Dumb And Blonde* achieved a similar chart position. In the 90s, Harry toured with the Jazz Passengers before Blondie re-formed in 1998.

HARTMAN, DAN

HARTMAN'S (b. 1951, d. 1994) MULTI-INSTRUMENTAL TALENTS AND LIGHT TENOR WERE FIRST HEARD IN BANDS LED BY **Johnny Winter** and Edgar Winter. Hartman co-wrote *They Only Come Out At Night*, which contained the million-selling single, 'Frankenstein'. *Instant Replay* was internationally successful. but after the relative failure of *Relight My Fire*, he concentrated on production. Among his production and songwriting clients were the **Average White Band**, **Neil Sedaka**, **James Brown**, **Muddy Waters**, **Diana Ross**, and **Chaka Khan**. In 1985, he returned to the US Top 10 with 'I Can Dream About You' (for the *Streets Of Fire* soundtrack). His last major production projects included tracks for Holly Johnson and **Tina Turner**. He died from AIDS-related complications in 1994. Posthumously **Black Box** sampled his material on 'Ride On Time', while **Take That** took 'Relight My Fire' to UK number 1.

HARVEY, ALEX

IN 1955, GLASGOW-BORN HARVEY (b. 1935, d. 1982) JOINED SAXOPHONIST BILL PATRICK IN A JAZZ-SKIFFLE BAND. The unit became the Kansas City Counts, and joined the Ricky Barnes All-Stars as pioneers of Scottish rock 'n' roll. By the end of the decade, the group was known as Alex Harvey's (Big) Soul Band. Having cemented popularity in Scotland and the north of England, Harvey moved to Hamburg where he recorded *Alex Harvey And His Soul Band*, returning to the UK a year later. *The Blues* included idiosyncratic readings of 'Danger Zone', 'Waltzing Matilda' and 'The Big Rock Candy Mountain'. Harvey dissolved the Soul Band in 1965, looking to pursue a folk-based direction. In 1967 in London, he formed Giant Moth. Mox (flute), Jim Condron (guitar/bass) and George Butler (drums) supported the singer on 'Someday Song' and 'Maybe Someday', but the venture was a failure. Harvey took a job in the pit band for the musical *Hair*, which in turn inspired *Hair Rave Up Live From The Shaftesbury Theatre*. In 1969, he released *Roman Wall Blues* including 'Midnight Moses', a composition Harvey took to the **Sensational Alex Harvey Band**.

HATFIELD, JULIANA

AMERICAN SINGER-SONGWRITER HATFIELD (b. 1967; GUITAR) BECAME A FAVOURITE OF THE EARLY 90S INDIE media. She fronted Blake Babies before releasing a solo album – which she has since denounced, finding its revelations embarrassing. Her second collection was more strident and self-assured, and featured Dean Fisher (bass) and Todd Philips (drums) in the Juliana Hatfield Three. Hatfield's breathless vocals were still apparent on *Only Everything* (her retreat to solo billing); it included 'Dumb Fun', the compulsory allusion to Kurt Cobain's suicide.

HATFIELD AND THE NORTH

UK BAND FORMED IN 1972: DAVID SINCLAIR (KEYBOARDS), PHIL MILLER (GUITAR), RICHARD SINCLAIR (BASS/VOCALS) and Pip Pyle (drums). Within months Sinclair left, replaced by Dave Stewart (ex-**Egg**). The group completed two albums, combining skilled musicianship with quirky melodies. Obtuse song titles like 'Gigantic Land Crabs In Earth Takeover Bid' emphasized an air of detached intellectualism. Their chosen genre was losing its tenuous appeal, however, and they split in 1975.

HAVENS, RICHIE

US SINGER HAVENS (b. RICHARD PIERCE HAVENS, 1941) STARTED OUT IN GOSPEL MUSIC, BUT BY 1962 HE WAS A popular Greenwich Village folk artist. A black singer in a predominantly white idiom, Havens' early work combined folk material with New York-pop inspired compositions. His soft, gritty voice and distinctive guitar playing revealed a burgeoning talent on *Mixed Bag* and *Something Else Again*. However, he established his reputation by his interpretations of songs by other acts, including the **Beatles** and **Bob Dylan**.

Havens opened **Woodstock Festival** with a memorable appearance. *Richard P. Havens 1983*, was arguably his artistic apogee, offering several empathic cover versions and some of the singer's finest compositions. He later established an independent label, Stormy Forest, and enjoyed a US Top 20 hit with 'Here Comes The Sun'.

HAWKES, CHESNEY

THE SON OF FORMER **TREMELOES** WRITER and vocalist Chip Hawkes, Chesney (b. 1971) shot to UK number 1 with 'The One And Only', written by **Nik Kershaw**. The subsequent 'I'm A Man Not A Boy' was critically derided. In 1998, he toured with Kershaw.

HAWKINS, RONNIE

US-BORN HAWKINS (b. 1935) FIRST RECORDED IN CANADA, RECORDING 'RRRRACKET TIME' WITH THE RON HAWKINS Quartet. In 1959, he reached US number 45 with 'Forty Days' (a version of **Chuck Berry**'s 'Thirty Days'). His version of Young Jessie's 'Mary Lou' then reached US number 26. He became known as Mr. Dynamo and pioneered a dance called the Camel Walk. In 1960, Hawkins became the first rock 'n' roller to involve himself in politics with a plea for a murderer on Death Row, 'The Ballad Of Caryl Chessman' (to no avail). He later formed the Hawks, comprising Levon Helm, **Robbie Robertson**, Garth Hudson, Richard Manuel and Rick Danko. Their 1963 single of two **Bo Diddley** songs, 'Bo Diddley' and 'Who Do You Love', was psychedelia before its time. 'Bo Diddley' was a Canadian hit and Hawkins later made the country his home. The Hawks recorded for Atlantic Records, as Levon and the Hawks, before being recruited by **Bob Dylan**, as the **Band**.

Hawkins had Canadian Top 10 hits with 'Home From The Forest', 'Bluebirds Over The Mountain' and 'Talkin' Silver Cloud Blues'. In 1970, he befriended **John Lennon** and **Yoko Ono**, and the promotional single on which Lennon praises Hawkins' 'Down In The Alley' is a collector's item. Hawkins tried acting, with a role in the disastrous film *Heaven's Gate*, and his better-known performance in *The Last Waltz*. He also appeared in Bob Dylan's Rolling Thunder Revue and played 'Bob Dylan' in the film *Renaldo And Clara*. In 1985, Hawkins joined **Joni Mitchell**, **Neil Young** and others for the Canadian Band Aid record, 'Tears Are Not Enough', by Northern Lights.

HAWKINS, 'SCREAMIN' JAY'

REPORTEDLY RAISED BY BLACKFOOT INDIANS, HAWKINS (b. JALACY HAWKINS, 1929) BECAME A PROFESSIONAL PIANIST, playing with artists such as James Moody, Lynn Hope and Count Basie. In 1950, he began developing an act based on his almost operatic bass-baritone voice, and in 1956, Screamin' Jay signed with Columbia's reactivated OKeh subsidiary, enjoying enormous success with his manic rendition of 'I Put A Spell On You', which he had recorded earlier as a ballad. The record sold over a million, becoming a rock classic and invoking hundreds of cover versions. Remaining with OKeh until 1958, Hawkins ran the gamut of his weird-but-wonderful repertoire with recordings of straight R&B songs and the bizarre 'Hong Kong', 'Alligator Wine' and 'There's Something Wrong With You'. Hawkins spent most of the 60s playing one-nighters and making occasional one-off recordings with independent labels. A brace of late-60s albums extended his idiosyncratic reputation. *Black Music For White People* included a rap interpretation of 'I Put A Spell On You', and revealed a largely undiminished power.

Collaborators
Todd Rundgren ➽ p.284
Ian Hunter ➽ p.190
Stevie Wonder ➽ p.342
Average White Band ➽ p.25
Neil Sedaka ➽ p.291
James Brown ➽ p.70
Diana Ross ➽ p.283
Tina Turner ➽ p.324

HARVEY, ALEX
Albums
Alex Harvey And His Soul Band (Polydor 1964)★★★
➽ p.365 for full listings
Connections
Sensational Alex Harvey Band ➽ p.292
Influences
Woody Guthrie ➽ p.171
Cisco Houston ➽ p.188

HATFIELD, JULIANA
Albums
Only Everything (Mammoth 1995)★★★
➽ p.365 for full listings

HATFIELD AND THE NORTH
Albums
The Rotters' Club (Virgin 1975)★★★
➽ p.365 for full listings
Connections
Egg ➽ p.132

HAVENS, RICHIE
Albums
Richard P. Havens 1983 (Forecast 1969)★★★★
➽ p.365 for full listings
Influences
Beatles ➽ p.38
Bob Dylan ➽ p.128
Further References
Films: *Catch My Soul* (1974)
Hearts of Fire (1989)

HAWKES, CHESNEY
Albums
Buddy's Song soundtrack (Chrysalis 1991)★★
➽ p.365 for full listings
Connections
Nik Kershaw ➽ p.204

HAWKINS, RONNIE
Albums
Arkansas Rock Pile (Roulette 1970)★★
➽ p.365 for full listings
Collaborators
John Lennon ➽ p.214
Yoko Ono ➽ p.252
Joni Mitchell ➽ p.235
Connections
Bob Dylan ➽ p.128
Band ➽ p.31
Influences
Chuck Berry ➽ p.45
Bo Diddley ➽ p.118

HAWKINS, 'SCREAMIN' JAY'
Albums
I Put A Spell On You (Epic 1959)★★★★
➽ p.365 for full listings
Further References
Film: *Mystery Train* (1989)

HAWKWIND
Albums
In Search Of Space (United Artists 1971)★★★
It Is The Business Of The Future To Be Dangerous (Essential 1993)★★★
➽ p.365 for full listings
Connections
Pretty Things ➽ p.266
Motörhead ➽ p.240
David Bowie ➽ p.64
Further References
Book: *This Is Hawkwind, Do Not Panic*, Kris Tate

HAWKWIND

FOUNDED IN A LONDON HIPPIE ENCLAVE IN THE LATE 60S. HAWKWIND – DAVE BROCK (GUITAR/VOCALS), NIK TURNER (saxophone/vocals), Mick Slattery (guitar), Dik Mik (electronics), John Harrison (bass) and Terry Ollis (drums) – debuted with *Hawkwind*, produced by Dick Taylor (ex-**Pretty Things**). By 1972, the group consisted of Brock, Turner, Del Dettmar (synthesizer), Lemmy (b. Ian Kilmister; bass), Simon King (drums), Stacia (dancer) and poet/writer Robert Calvert (vocals). Science-fiction writer Michael Moorcock deputized part-time for Calvert. The group's science-fiction image was apparent in titles like *In Search Of Space* and *Space Ritual*. They enjoyed a freak UK number 3 with 'Silver Machine', but

this flirtation with a wider audience ended prematurely – 'Urban Guerilla' was hastily withdrawn after terrorist bombs exploded in London.

The group lost impetus in 1975 when Lemmy was fired after an arrest on drugs charges during a US tour – he subsequently formed **Motörhead**. Following the release of *Astounding Sounds, Amazing Music*, Turner was fired. Later additions Paul Rudolph, Alan Powell and Simon House also left. House joined **David Bowie**'s band and Brock, Calvert and King became the Hawklords. In 1979, they had reverted to Hawkwind and Calvert had gone solo. Dave Brock remained at the helm and new players included Huw Lloyd Langton (a guitarist on the group's debut album), Tim Blake (synthesizer) and **Ginger Baker** (drums). Nik Turner also reappeared. In 1990, their popularity resurged with the rave culture; *Space Bandits* reflected this new interest. It also saw the return of Simon House and the inclusion of their first female vocalist, Bridgett Wishart. However, *Palace Springs* showed that inspiration was lacking – it contained five new versions of early tracks. 1992 saw a successful US tour, but the group fell apart on their return. The remaining trio became totally dance/rave-orientated.

HAYES, Isaac
Albums
Hot Buttered Soul (Enterprise 1969)★★★★
➽ p.365 for full listings
Collaborators
Johnnie Taylor ➽ p.317
Connections
Mar-Keys ➽ p.224

HAYES, ISAAC

HAYES (b. 1942) PLAYED PIANO AND ORGAN FOR SEVERAL MEMPHIS GROUPS AND RECORDED A FEW SINGLES. IN 1964, he attracted the attention of Stax Records. After session work with **Mar-Keys** saxophonist Floyd Newman, Hayes remained as a stand-in for Booker T. Jones. He then began songwriting with David Porter, enjoying success with **Sam And Dave**'s 'Hold On I'm Comin'' and writing for Carla Thomas and **Johnnie Taylor**. *Hot Buttered Soul* established Hayes' reputation, however, *The Isaac Hayes Movement*, *To Be Continued* and *Black Moses* were less satisfying. *Shaft* was a highly successful film soundtrack; the theme was covered later by Eddy And The Soul Band, reaching UK number 13. Hayes left Stax in 1975 following a row over royalties, setting up his Hot Buttered Soul label. Declared bankrupt in 1976, he moved to Polydor and Spring.

In 1981, he retired for five years before re-emerging with 'Ike's Rap', (US R&B Top 10). Although trumpeted as a return to form, Hayes' mid-90s albums for Pointblank indicated little progress.

HEALEY, JEFF
Albums
See The Light (Arista 1989)★★★★
➽ p.365 for full listings
Collaborators
Albert Collins ➽ p.97
B.B. King ➽ p.205
Mark Knopfler ➽ p.209
George Harrison ➽ p.176
Jeff Lynne ➽ p.220
Connections
Jeff Healey Band ➽ p.178
Further References
Film: *Roadhouse* (1989)

HEALEY, JEFF

BLIND SINCE HE WAS A YEAR OLD, CANADIAN-BORN HEALEY (b. 1966) IS A PROFICIENT MULTI-INSTRUMENTALIST, WHITE blues-rock guitarist and singer. In 1985, he played with Texas bluesman **Albert Collins** who introduced him to Stevie Ray Vaughan. The Jeff Healey Band – Joe Rockman (bass/vocals) and Tom Stephen (drums) – was formed the same year. They released singles and videos on their own Forte label, before signing to Arista in 1988. *See The Light* sold nearly two million copies; a world tour followed. *Hell To Pay* tended towards hard rock and **Mark Knopfler**, **George Harrison**, **Jeff Lynne** and Bobby Whitlock guested; over 2 million copies were sold. *Feel This* was a strong and energetic rock/blues album, and *Cover To Cover* was a collection of favourite songs by some of Healey's mentors.

HEART
Albums
Dreamboat Annie (Mushroom 1976)★★★★
➽ p.365 for full listings
Connections
Spirit ➽ p.305
Further References
Video: *If Looks Could Kill* (1988)

HEART

US ROCK BAND FEATURING SISTERS ANN (b. 1951) AND NANCY WILSON (b. 1954). ANN RELEASED TWO SINGLES ON a local label in 1967. After a series of unreleased demos she and Nancy left for Canada, to find a backing band – Steve Fossen (bass) and Roger Fisher (guitar). Michael Derosier (drums) joined later. After *Dreamboat Annie* on Mushroom Records, their second single, 'Crazy On You', brought public attention. Shortly afterwards *Little Queen* and 'Barracuda' charted in the US. By *Dog And Butterfly*, Nancy was dating Fisher, while Ann was involved with his brother, Mike (now their unofficial manager). When the relationships soured, Roger Fisher left the band. The guitar parts were covered on tour by Nancy and multi-instrumentalist Howard Leese, who became permanent. By *Private Audition*, Fossen and Derosier were also on the verge of departure, replaced by Mark Andes (ex-**Spirit**) and Denny Carmassi. Heart was waning, although temporarily bolstered by 'Almost Paradise...Love Theme From Footloose' (US number 7).

In 1985, Heart joined Capitol, resulting in an image transformation. *Heart* reached US number 1, including 'What About Love', 'Never' and 'These Dreams' (US number 1). *Bad Animals* reached US number 2. *Brigade* included 'All I Wanna Do Is Make Love To You' (UK Top 10/US number 1). Both sisters then became involved in solo projects, while former companions Fossen, Roger Fisher and Derosier embarked on a new dual career with Alias. The sisters returned as Heart in 1993, backed by Schuyler Deale (bass), John Purdell (keyboards), Denny Carmassi (drums) and Lease (guitar). The hit 'Will You Be There (In The Morning)' preceded *Desire Walks On*. *The Road Home*, an acoustic live album produced by John Paul Jones, marked their 20th anniversary.

HEARTBREAKERS

FORMED IN NEW YORK IN 1975. **RICHARD HELL** (BASS; EX-**TELEVISION**) JOINED DISAFFECTED **NEW YORK DOLLS** **Johnny Thunders** (guitar/vocals) and Jerry Nolan (drums); Walter Lure (guitar/vocals) joined later. They enjoyed cult popularity and, when Hell left (replaced by Billy Rath), they moved to London and punk. They supported the **Sex Pistols** on the 1976 Anarchy tour, signed to Track Records and released 'Chinese Rocks', a paean to heroin co-written by Dee Dee Ramone. *L.A.M.F.* indicated the group's strengths, but was marred by unfocused production; Nolan left.

The Heartbreakers split in 1977, re-forming in 1978 with drummer Ty Styx. The name was dropped and resurrected several times, until Thunders was found dead in April 1991.

HEATWAVE

ALTHOUGH BASED IN BRITAIN, HEATWAVE WAS FORMED BY JOHNNIE AND KEITH WILDER AFTER THEY LEFT THE US Army. They recruited songwriter Rod Temperton, Eric Johns, Jessie Whitten, Ernest Berger and Mario Mantese. Between 1977 and 1981 they enjoyed a series of transatlantic hits, including 'Boogie Nights', 'Always And Forever' and 'Mind Blowing Decisions'. Temperton left in 1977 to concentrate on songwriting. His clients include **George Benson**, **Herbie Hancock** and **Michael Jackson**.

Heatwave's progress was marred by a series of tragedies: Whitten was stabbed to death; Mantese left after a severe car crash and Johnnie Wilder was paralyzed as a result of another road accident. Courageously, he remained at the helm, producing and singing in the studio; vocalist J. D. Nicholas, took his place on stage. However, Heatwave were unable to endure and in 1984 Nicholas left for the **Commodores**.

HEAVEN 17

UK SYNTHESIZER TRIO FORMED BY IAN CRAIG MARSH (b. 1956), MARTYN WARE (b. 1956) AND VOCALIST GLENN Gregory (b. 1958). '(We Don't Need This) Fascist Groove Thang' reached UK number 45 and *Penthouse And Pavement* was a best-seller; the following 'Temptation' (1983, UK Top 10) featured guest vocalist Carol Kenyon. Predominantly a studio group, a series of albums followed. Meanwhile, the group's production services were still in demand and Ware co-produced **Terence Trent D'Arby**'s best-selling *The Hardline According To Terence Trent D'Arby*. *Bigger Than America* was a welcome belated surprise.

HEAVY D AND THE BOYZ

JAMAICAN-BORN HEAVY D (b. DWIGHT MYERS, 1967) FRONTED A MAINSTREAM RAP OUTFIT ALTHOUGH HIS RHYMES are imbued with warmth rather than breast-beating machismo. His debut album, helmed by Teddy Riley, comprised funk alongside hints of the New Jack Swing sound. Riley also produced the follow-up, with fellow rap production legend Marley Marl. Q-Tip (**A Tribe Called Quest**), Big Daddy Kane and Pete Rock And CL Smooth all featured on 'Don't Curse', from *Peaceful Journey*. The album also included a tribute to former backing vocalist T-Roy (b. Troy Dixon, *c.* 1968, d. 1990), who was killed in an accident while on tour. The other 'Boyz' are G. Whiz (b. Glen Parrish) and DJ Eddie F (b. Edward Ferrell).

'Now That We've Found Love' (1991) reached UK number 2, and Heavy D made a high-profile guest appearance on **Michael Jackson**'s 'Jam' and sister **Janet**'s 'Alright With Me'. *Blue Funk* saw Heavy return to hardcore territory with guest production from Pete Rock and DJ Premier, and his 1994 set *Nuttin' But Love* saw him reunite with rap's top rank of producers.

HELL, RICHARD

HELL (b. RICHARD MYERS, 1949) EMBODIED THE NEW YORK PUNK GENRE. IN 1971, HE FOUNDED THE NEON BOYS WITH guitarist **Tom Verlaine**, and first performed several of his best-known songs, including 'Love Comes In Spurts', in this group. The group subsequently became **Television** – Hell's torn clothing inspired Malcolm McLaren's ideas for the **Sex Pistols**. Hell left in 1975 and formed the **Heartbreakers** with **Johnny Thunders** and drummer Jerry Nolan. He reappeared in 1976 fronting Richard Hell And The Voidoids, with guitarists Bob Quine and Ivan Julian and drummer Marc Bell. Their debut EP appeared later that year giving the group underground popularity. 'Blank Generation' achieved anthem-like proportions as an apposite description of punk. A version of the song became the title track of the Voidoids' dazzling debut album, which also featured 'Another World', and a fiery interpretation of John Fogerty's 'Walk Upon The Water'. *Blank Generation* is one of punk's definitive statements. Bell left for the **Ramones** in 1978; Quine subsequently left to become a session musician and sometime **Lou Reed** sideman.

Hell later issued the **Nick Lowe**-produced 'The Kid With The Replaceable Head', followed by an EP and then *Destiny Street*. Quine returned, joined by **Material** drummer Fred Maher. Once again Hell withdrew from recording, opting for film work, notably Susan Seidelman's *Smithereens*. Sporadic live appearances continued, followed by *Funhunt*, a composite of three Voidoid line-ups. In 1991, Hell resumed recording in the Dim Stars: Thurston Moore and Steve Shelley (**Sonic Youth**) and Don Fleming (Gumball). A live three-single set was succeeded by *3 New Songs*, an EP credited to Hell, but comprising Dim Stars' recordings. *Dim Stars* showed Hell's powers undiminished.

HELLOWEEN

FORMED IN 1984 IN HAMBURG, AND COMPRISING KAI HANSEN (GUITAR/VOCALS), MICHAEL WEIKATH (GUITAR), Markus Grosskopf (bass) and Ingo Schwichenburg (drums). *Death Metal* was followed by *Helloween*, *Walls Of Jericho* and an EP, *Judas*. The band gained a strong following with their unique blend of high-speed power metal. After *Judas*, vocalist/frontman Michael Kiske joined. *Keeper Of The Seven Keys Part I* took a much more melodic approach.

Helloween toured Europe, building a sizeable following. *Keeper Of The Seven Keys Part II* preceded a successful appearance at the Donington Monsters Of Rock Festival. Then came the EP *Dr. Stein*. However, the band were looking for a new label; as a stopgap they released *Live In The UK*, recorded at the Hammersmith Odeon. Hansen then left (Roland Grapow replaced him). A protracted legal battle with their record company kept them out of action until 1990. They finally signed to EMI where *Pink Bubbles Go Ape* showed up the loss of Hansen. Kiske was dismissed, as was Ingo Schwichenberg. Andi Deris (vocals) and Ulli Kusch (drums) replaced them in time for their Castle/Raw Power debut, *Master Of The Rings* (Japanese number 1).

HELMET

FORMED BY PAGE HAMILTON (b. 1960) WITH HENRY BOGDAN (BASS), PETER MENGEDE (GUITAR) AND JOHN Stanier (drums). The band's clean-cut image contrasts with their brutally heavy music. Hamilton's lyrics draw from his life in New York and Oregon roots. *Strap It On* sold modestly but created considerable interest, and *Meantime* showed smoother rhythmic songs without compromising their sound. They toured widely, with **Faith No More** in the USA and **Ministry** in Europe, before undertaking headline dates of their own. In 1993, Mengede was replaced by Rob Echeverria. Before a third album, the group recorded 'Just Another Victim' with House Of Pain for the *Judgement Night* soundtrack. *Betty* featured co-production from Todd Ray, plus one track concocted with Butch Vig, 'Milquetoast', which featured on the soundtrack for *The Crow*. *Aftertaste* is their finest release to date.

HEARTBREAKERS
Albums
L.A.M.F. Revisited remixed version of their debut (Jungle 1984)★★★
➧ p.365 for full listings
Collaborators
Sex Pistols ➧ p.292
Connections
Television ➧ p.317
New York Dolls ➧ p.246

HEATWAVE
Albums
Too Hot To Handle (Epic 1977)★★★★
➧ p.365 for full listings
Connections
George Benson ➧ p.44
Herbie Hancock ➧ p.174
Michael Jackson ➧ p.195
Commodores ➧ p.99

HEAVEN 17
Albums
Penthouse And Pavement (Virgin 1981)★★★
➧ p.365 for full listings
Connections
Terence Trent D'Arby ➧ p.110

HEAVY D AND THE BOYZ
Albums
Nuttin' But Love (Uptown 1994)★★★★
➧ p.365 for full listings
Collaborators
Michael Jackson ➧ p.195
Janet Jackson ➧ p.195
Connections
A Tribe Called Quest ➧ p.6

HELL, RICHARD
Albums
as Richard Hell & The Voidoids *Blank Generation* (Sire 1977)★★★★
➧ p.365 for full listings
Collaborators
Lou Reed ➧ p.274
Connections
Tom Verlaine ➧ p.330
Television ➧ p.317
Heartbreakers ➧ p.178
New York Dolls ➧ p.246
Ramones ➧ p.272
Sonic Youth ➧ p.302

HELLOWEEN
Albums
Keeper Of The Seven Keys Part I (Noise 1987)★★★
➧ p.365 for full listings

HELMET
Albums
Aftertaste (Interscope 1997)★★★★
➧ p.365 for full listings
Collaborators
Faith No More ➧ p.142
Ministry ➧ p.234

HENDRIX, JIMI
Albums
Are You Experienced? (Track 1967)★★★★★
Axis: Bold As Love (Track 1967)★★★★★
➽ p.365 for full listings

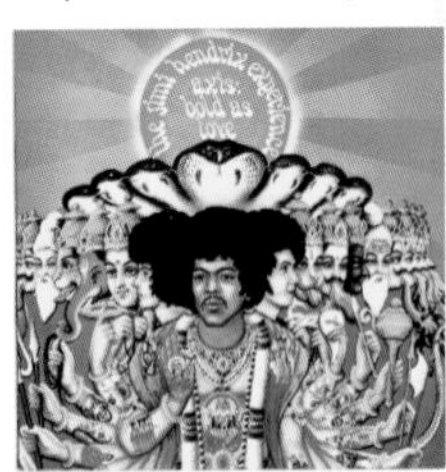

Collaborators
Sam Cooke ➽ p.100
Valentinos ➽ p.328
Traffic ➽ p.323
Steve Winwood ➽ p.341
Jefferson Airplane ➽ p.198
Connections
Spirit ➽ p.305
Jimi Hendrix Experience ➽ p.180
Influences
Bob Dylan ➽ p.128
Further References
Video: *Jimi Hendrix Plays Berkeley* (Palace Video 1986)
Book: *Jimi: An Intimate Biography Of Jimi Hendrix*, Curtis Knight

HENLEY, DON
Albums
Building The Perfect Beast (Geffen 1984)★★★★
➽ p.365 for full listings
Collaborators
Linda Ronstadt ➽ p.282
Stevie Nicks ➽ p.247
Connections
Eagles ➽ p.130

HERD
Albums
Paradise Lost (1968)★★★
Nostalgia (Bumble 1973)★★★
➽ p.365 for full listings
Collaborators
Andy Fairweather-Low ➽ p.142
Status Quo ➽ p.308
Connections
Peter Frampton ➽ p.152
Humble Pie ➽ p.190

HERMAN'S HERMITS
Albums
Herman's Hermits (Columbia 1965)★★★
Mrs Brown You've Got A Lovely Daughter (Columbia 1968)★★★
➽ p.365 for full listings
Collaborators
Connie Francis ➽ p.152
Influences
Sam Cooke ➽ p.100
Further References
Film: *Hold On* (1965)

HENDRIX, JIMI

SELF-TAUGHT (LEFT-HANDED WITH A RIGHT-HANDED GUITAR), HENDRIX (b. JOHNNY ALLEN HENDRIX, 1942, d. 1970) joined several Seattle R&B bands while still at school, before enlisting as a paratrooper. He began working with various touring revues backing, among others, **Sam Cooke** and the **Valentinos**.

In 1965, Hendrix joined struggling soul singer Curtis Knight in New York, signing a punitive contract with Knight's manager, Ed Chalpin. In 1966, Hendrix, now calling himself Jimmy James, formed a quartet, which featured future **Spirit** member Randy California. They were appearing at the Cafe Wha? in Greenwich Village when Chas Chandler recognized Hendrix's extraordinary talent. Chandler persuaded Hendrix to go to London, and became his co-manager in partnership with Mike Jeffries (aka Jeffreys). Auditions for a suitable backing group yielded Noel Redding (b. 1945; bass) and John 'Mitch' Mitchell (b. 1947; drums). The Jimi Hendrix Experience debuted in France in October 1966. Back in England they released their first single, 'Hey Joe' (UK Top 10), in December. The dynamic follow-up was 'Purple Haze'. Exceptional live appearances characterized by distortion, feedback, sheer volume and Hendrix's flamboyant stage persona enhanced the group's reputation. The Experience completed an astonishing debut album. *Axis: Bold As Love* revealed a new lyrical capability, notably in the title track and the jazz-influenced 'Up From The Skies'. It completed an artistically and commercially triumphant year. Hendrix grew tired of the wild man image however, and the last official Experience album, *Electric Ladyland*, was released in October. This extravagant double set featured contributions from Chris Wood and **Steve Winwood** (both **Traffic**) and Jack Casady (**Jefferson Airplane**) and included two UK hits, 'The Burning Of The Midnight Lamp' and 'All Along The Watchtower' – amazingly **Bob Dylan** later adopted Hendrix's interpretation.

Hendrix's life was becoming problematic – he was arrested in Toronto for possessing heroin; Chas Chandler had withdrawn from the managerial partnership and Redding and Hendrix now had irreconcilable differences. The Experience played its final concert on 29 June 1969; Hendrix subsequently formed Gypsies Sons And Rainbows with Mitchell, Billy Cox (bass), Larry Lee (rhythm guitar), Juma Sultan and Jerry Velez (both percussion). This short-lived unit closed the **Woodstock Festival**, during which Hendrix performed his famed rendition of the 'Star Spangled Banner'. In October he formed an all-black group, Band Of Gypsies, with Cox and drummer **Buddy Miles**, intending to accentuate the African-American dimension in his music. The trio's potential was marred by pedestrian drumming and unimaginative compositions, and they split after a mere three concerts. Hendrix started work on *First Rays Of The New Rising Sun* (finally released in 1997), and later resumed performing with Cox and Mitchell.

On 18 September 1970, his girlfriend, Monika Danneman, was unable to wake Hendrix. An ambulance was called, but he was pronounced dead on arrival at a nearby hospital. The inquest recorded an open verdict, with death caused by suffocation due to inhalation of vomit. Two posthumous releases, *Cry Of Love* and *Rainbow Bridge*, mixed portions of the artist's final recordings with masters from earlier sources. Many guitarists have imitated his technique; few have mastered it and none have matched his skill. Litigation regarding ownership of his recordings was finally resolved in 1997, when the Hendrix family won back the rights from Alan Douglas.

HENLEY, DON

DRUMMER AND VOCALIST HENLEY (b. 1947) STARTED OUT WITH COUNTRY ROCK UNIT FOUR SPEEDS AND FELICITY. They completed an album under producer **Kenny Rogers**, but split up when Henley joined **Linda Ronstadt**'s touring band. This group formed the basis for the **Eagles**. Henley's distinctive voice took lead on most of their songs, many of which he co-composed. When the Eagles broke up, Henley brought out *I Can't Stand Still*. 'Leather And Lace', a duet with **Stevie Nicks**, reached the US Top 10.

A songwriting partnership with guitarist Danny Kortchmar resulted in several compositions, including 'Dirty Laundry' (1982, US number 3). *Building The Perfect Beast* proved highly popular, attaining platinum status in 1985 and spawning two US Top 10 singles in 'The Boys Of Summer' and 'All She Wants To Do Is Dance'. His songwriting skills were demonstrated by *The End Of The Innocence* and, in 1994, Henley was back with the Eagles.

HERD

UK GROUP FORMED IN 1965. TERRY CLARK (VOCALS), ANDY BOWN (BASS/VOCALS/ORGAN), GARY TAYLOR (GUITAR) AND Tony Chapman (drums) were later joined by guitarist **Peter Frampton**. In 1967, new songwriting managers Ken Howard and Alan Blaikley promoted the reluctant Frampton to centre stage. The psychedelic 'I Can Fly' was followed by *Orpheus In The Underworld* – a UK Top 10 hit. After Virgil, Howard And Blaikley tackled Milton with 'Paradise Lost'. The Herd were marketed for teenzine consumption, with Frampton voted the 'Face of '68' by *Rave* magazine. A more straightforward hit followed with 'I Don't Want Our Loving To Die', and Howard and Blaikley were dropped in favour of Andrew Loog Oldham; their next single, 'Sunshine Cottage', missed by a mile. Yet another manager, Harvey Lisberg, came to nothing and Frampton left to form **Humble Pie**. For a brief period, the remaining members struggled on, but to no avail. Bown later teamed up with **Andy Fairweather-Low** and appeared on the road with **Status Quo**.

HERMAN'S HERMITS

UK GROUP HERMAN'S HERMITS WERE DISCOVERED IN 1963 BY MANAGER HARVEY LISBERG AND HIS PARTNER CHARLIE Silverman. The line-up emerged as Peter Noone (vocals), Karl Green (bass), Keith Hopwood (rhythm guitar), Lek Leckenby (lead guitar) and Barry Whitwam (drums). A link with producer **Mickie Most** and an infectious cover of Earl Jean's 'I'm Into Something Good' brought a UK number 1 in 1964. By early 1965, the group had settled into covering 50s songs such as the **Rays**' 'Silhouettes' and **Sam Cooke**'s 'Wonderful World', when an extraordinary invasion of America saw them challenge the **Beatles**, selling over 10 million records in under 12 months. A non-stop stream of hits over the next two years transformed them into teen idols. Director Sam Katzman even cast them in the films *When The Boys Meet The Girls* (co-starring **Connie Francis**) and *Hold On!*

The hits continued until as late as 1970 when Noone finally decided to pursue a solo career.

HEYWARD, NICK

HEYWARD (b. 1961) LEFT UK GROUP **HAIRCUT 100**, IN 1982, TO GO SOLO. 'WHISTLE DOWN THE WIND' AND 'TAKE THAT Situation' (both 1983) were similar to the style of his former group. His debut album, *North Of A Miracle*, (including 'Blue Hat For A Blue Day') won critical approval and sold well. He completed a move away from his teenage audience with the funk-influenced 'Warning Sign' but commercial success was limited. In 1988 'You're My World' and *I Love You Avenue* (both Warner Brothers Records) failed to reach the mainstream and Heyward concentrated on his second career, graphic art. In 1992, he returned with a new album, *From Monday To Sunday*, and tour dates alongside **Squeeze**. Over the next two years he toured regularly, particularly in the USA, supporting **Belly**, **Lemonheads**, **Mazzy Star** and **Therapy?**. Much effort went into *Tangled* but it did not find commercial favour. He worked on Edward Ball's 1996 solo album, and signed to Creation Records in 1997. *The Apple Bed* was perplexing; all the regular Heyward trademarks were up to standard yet overall it was disappointing.

HIATT, JOHN

AMERICAN SINGER, GUITARIST AND SONGWRITER, JOHN HIATT'S (b. 1952) MATERIAL HAS BEEN RECORDED BY various acts, including **Dr. Feelgood**, **Searchers**, **Iggy Pop**, **Bob Dylan**, **Nick Lowe**, and **Rick Nelson**. Hiatt started out in local R&B bands. In 1970 he signed to Epic, recording two albums. He left and toured solo before signing to MCA for two further albums. In 1980, **Ry Cooder** took him on as guitarist in his band. He played on *Borderline* and several subsequent albums and tours. Hiatt's solo album *All Of A Sudden* was followed by another almost every year, all produced by Tony Visconti and **Nick Lowe**. Lowe played regularly with Hiatt's band, and the duo became half of a new 'supergroup' with Cooder and Jim Keltner (veteran journeyman drummer) in Little Village. A disappointing self-titled album was released in 1992. Hiatt's songwriting reputation has since grown and his own recent recorded output has included two of his best albums, *Perfectly Good Guitar* and *Walk On*.

HICKS, DAN

AMERICAN-BORN FORMER FOLK MUSICIAN, HICKS (b. 1941) JOINED THE **CHARLATANS** IN 1965, REPLACING ORIGINAL drummer Sam Linde. This trailblazing group is credited with pioneering the 60s San Francisco sound. Hicks swapped the drumkit for guitar, vocals and composing before establishing a new group, Dan Hicks And His Hot Licks, with David LaFlamme (violin) and Bill Douglas (bass). Within months, the group had reshaped around Sid Page (violin), Jaime Leopold (bass) John Webber (guitar) and singers Tina Gancher and Sherri Snow. *Original Recordings* drew on country, 30s vocal jazz and quirky, deadpan humour and included 'I Scare Myself', later revived by **Thomas Dolby**. Webber, Gancher and Snow dropped out, replaced by Maryanne Price and Naomi Ruth Eisenberg. *Where's The Money*, recorded live at the Los Angeles Troubadour, *Striking It Rich*, with John Girton on guitar and *Last Train To Hicksville* completed their catalogue before Hicks went solo. Page, Girton and Price played on *It Happened One Bite*. During the 80s Hicks formed the Acoustic Warriors with James 'Fingers' Shupe (fiddle, mandolin) and Alex Baum (bass).

HIGH LLAMAS

FORMED IN LONDON, ENGLAND BY FORMER **MICRODISNEY** SEAN O'HAGAN. O'HAGAN SPENT THREE YEARS incubating the High Llamas' debut album; though a low-profile release, it received several encouraging reviews. A second High Llamas album, *Gideon Gaye*, was produced on a budget of just £4,000 and released on the independent label Target Records. Again, the critical response was encouraging, enticing Sony Records to offer O'Hagan a contract. *Gideon Gaye* was subsequently re-released via the group's own Alpaca Park label, handled internationally by Sony/Epic Records. A single taken from it, 'Checking In, Checking Out', made the German charts. *Hawaii* is a reincarnation of the **Beach Boys**' *Friends*, *Smiley Smile*, *Sunflower* and *Pet Sounds* combined, and is melodic, winsome and fresh-sounding.

HIGH TIDE

HEAVY/PSYCHEDELIC PROGRESSIVE BRITISH BAND FORMED IN 1969 BY TONY HILL (EX-**MISUNDERSTOOD**; GUITAR/ vocals/keyboards), Simon House (violin/piano), Roger Hadden (drums/organ) and Peter Pavli (ex-White Rabbit; bass). They signed to Liberty Records who were eager to join the progressive-rock bandwagon; *High Tide* was a more than credible debut. Their second album sold badly, however, and Liberty dropped them. After numerous tours they became involved with **Arthur Brown**, Magic Muscle and Rustic Hinge.

HIGHWAY 101

THIS MANUFACTURED US GROUP COMPRISED BASSIST CURTIS STONE, SESSION GUITARIST JACK DANIELS AND singer Paulette Carlson and was formed by Chuck Morris, manager of the **Nitty Gritty Dirt Band** and **Lyle Lovett**, and Scott 'Cactus' Moser. In 1987, they had their first US country hits with 'The Bed You Made For Me' (number 4) and 'Whiskey, If You Were A Woman' (number 2). They topped the US country charts with 'Somewhere Tonight'. Carlson left in 1990, and Nikki Nelson was recruited for *Bing Bang Boom*. The title track was a successful single, but the album failed to sell in the same quantities. Daniels quit in 1992 and the group made a final album, *The New Frontier*, before disbanding.

HEYWARD, NICK

Albums
Tangled (Epic 1995)★★★★
➧ p.365 for full listings
Collaborators
Squeeze ➧ p.306
Belly ➧ p.42
Lemonheads ➧ p.214
Mazzy Star ➧ p.228
Connections
Haircut 100 ➧ p.172
Further References
Book: *The Haircut 100 Catalogue*, Sally Payne

HIATT, JOHN

Albums
Bring The Family (A&M 1987)★★★★
Perfectly Good Guitar (A&M 1993)★★★★
➧ p.365 for full listings
Collaborators
Ry Cooder ➧ p.100
Connections
Dr. Feelgood ➧ p.125
Iggy Pop ➧ p.264
Bob Dylan ➧ p.128
Nick Lowe ➧ p.219

HICKS, DAN

Albums
with the Hot Licks *The Original Recordings* (Epic 1969)★★★
Where's The Money? (Blue Thumb/MCA 1971)★★★
➧ p.365 for full listings
Connections
Charlatans ➧ p.87
Dan Hicks And His Hot Licks ➧ p.181

HIGH LLAMAS

Albums
Santa Barbara (Vogue/Mute 1994)★★★
Hawaii (Alpaca Park 1996)★★★
➧ p.365 for full listings
Connections
Microdisney ➧ p.233

HIGH TIDE

Albums
Sea Shanties (Liberty 1969)★★★★
➧ p.365 for full listings
Connections
Misunderstood ➧ p.235
Arthur Brown ➧ p.70

HIGHWAY 101

Albums
The New Frontier (Liberty 1993)★★★
Reunited (Willow Tree 1996)★★★
➧ p.365 for full listings
Connections
Nitty Gritty Dirt Band ➧ p.249
Lyle Lovett ➧ p.219

HILLAGE, STEVE

GUITARIST HILLAGE (b. 1951) PLAYED WITH URIEL IN 1967 ALONGSIDE MONT CAMPBELL (BASS), CLIVE BROOKS (drums) and Dave Stewart (organ) (the latter trio carried on as **Egg**). In 1971, Hillage formed Khan with Nick Greenwood (bass), Eric Peachey (drums) and Dick Henningham; Dave Stewart joined later. The band split in 1972. Hillage released his first solo album *Fish Rising* in 1975, and began his writing partnership with long-time girlfriend Miquette Giraudy.

In the 80s, Hillage moved into production, including albums by **Robin Hitchcock** and **Simple Minds**. In 1991 he returned to recording and live performance as leader of System 7, including disc jockey **Paul Oakenfold**, Alex Paterson of the **Orb** and Mick MacNeil of Simple Minds. System 7 produce ambient dance music, combining house beats with progressive guitar riffs and healthy bursts of soul and disco.

HILLAGE, STEVE
Albums
Fish Rising (Virgin 1975)★★★
Rainbow Dome Musick (Virgin 1979)★★★
System 7 (Ten 1991)★★★★
➧ p.365 for full listings
Collaborators
Simple Minds ➧ p.297
Connections
Egg ➧ p.132
Khan
Robin Hitchcock
Orb ➧ p.252

HIS NAME IS ALIVE

FORMED IN 1987 IN LIVONIA, MICHIGAN, USA, HIS NAME IS ALIVE (AN OBSCURE REFERENCE TO ABRAHAM LINCOLN) was established by Warren Defever (b. 1969; guitar/bass/vocals/samples) with Angela Carozzo (vocals) and Karin Oliver (guitar/vocals). Their first single was 'Riotousness And Postrophe' (1987), followed by 'His Name Is Alive' (1987), 'I Had Sex With God' (1988) and 'Eutectic' (1988). After the release of *Livonia*, Carozzo departed, while Denise James (vocals), Melissa Elliott (guitar), Jymn Auge (guitar) and Damian Lang (drums) joined. A cover version of **Ritchie Blackmore**'s 'Man On The Silver Mountain', was included on the 1992 EP *Dirt Eaters*.

HIS NAME IS ALIVE
Albums
Livonia (4AD 1990)★★★
Home Is In Your Head (4AD 1991)★★★
Stars On E.S.P. (4AD 1996)★★★★
➧ p.365 for full listings
Influences
Ritchie Blackmore ➧ p.52

HITCHCOCK, ROBYN

UK-BORN HITCHCOCK MADE HIS EARLY REPUTATION WITH THE POST-PUNK PSYCHEDELIC GROUP THE **SOFT BOYS**. After they split in 1981 he wrote for **Captain Sensible**, before forming the Egyptians, around erstwhile colleagues Andy Metcalfe (bass), Morris Windsor (drums) and Roger Jackson (keyboards). Hitchcock's predilection for the bizarre revealed itself in titles such as 'Man With The Light Bulb Head (. . . I Turn Myself On In The Dark)', 'My Wife And My Dead Wife', and 'Uncorrected Personality Traits'. A move to A&M Records saw the release of *Globe Of Frogs*, which included 'Ballroom Man', a US college-radio favourite. Despite a devoted UK cult following, Hitchcock spent the early 90s concentrating on the United States (occasionally guesting with **R.E.M.**). He has also re-formed the Soft Boys and continues to release albums, including reissues.

HITCHCOCK, ROBYN
Albums
with the Egyptians *Fegmania!* (Slash 1985)★★★★
with the Egyptians *Gotta Let This Hen Out!* (Relativity 1985)★★★★
with the Egyptians *Element Of Light* (Glass Fish 1986)★★★★
➧ p.365 for full listings
Collaborators
R.E.M ➧ p.275
Connections
Soft Boys ➧ p.302
Captain Sensible ➧ p.81

HOLE

EX-STRIPPER AND ACTRESS COURTNEY LOVE (b. 1965; VOCALS/GUITAR) FRONTS THIS US HARDCORE GUITAR band. She joined an ill-fated Sugar Baby Doll (with **L7**'s Jenifer Finch and Kat Bjelland), then a formative line-up of Bjelland's **Babes In Toyland**. In Los Angeles, she formed Hole with Caroline Rue (drums), Jill Emery (bass) and Eric Erlandson (guitar). The band's singles 'Retard Girl', 'Dicknail', and 'Teenage Whore', and favourable UK press coverage, helped make Hole one of the most promising new groups of 1991. Their debut album, produced by Don Fleming (Gumball, B.A.L.L.) and Kim Gordon (**Sonic Youth**), was followed by massive exposure supporting **Mudhoney** throughout Europe – with Love achieving notoriety as the first woman musician to 'trash' her guitar on stage in the UK. In 1992, Emery and Rue left the group; the same year that Love married **Nirvana** singer/guitarist Kurt Cobain. Cobain's suicide on the eve of the release of *Live Through This* practically obliterated the impact of Hole's new set, despite another startling collection of songs written with intellect as well as invective. Replacements for Emery and Rue had been found in Kristen Pfaff (bass) and Patty Schemel (drums), though Pfaff was found dead from a heroin overdose, shortly after the album's release, and just two months after Cobain's death. She was replaced by Melissa Auf Der Maur for Hole's 1994-95 tour, including dates in Australasia and Europe. Again Love dominated headlines with her stage behaviour. In 1997 she moved back into acting with a starring role in *The People Vs Larry Flynt*. *My Body, The Hand Grenade* was a compilation of rare and unreleased material from the group's early days, compiled by Erlandson.

HOLE
Albums
Pretty On The Inside (City Slang 1991)★★★
Live Through This (Geffen 1994)★★★★
➧ p.365 for full listings

Collaborators
Mudhoney ➧ p.242
Connections
Babes In Toyland ➧ p.26
Faith No More ➧ p.142
Sonic Youth ➧ p.302
Further References
Books: *Courtney Love*, Nick Wise
Look Through This, Susan Wilson

HOLLAND, EDDIE

EDDIE (b. 1939), BROTHER OF BRIAN HOLLAND, WAS ACTIVE IN THE MUSIC SCENE FROM THE MID-50S ONWARDS, leading the Fideltones vocal group, and producing demo recordings for **Jackie Wilson**. In 1961, he was signed to Berry Gordy's fledgling **Motown Records**; his 'Jamie' becoming a US Top 30 hit. In 1964, further chart successes included 'Leaving Here'. That year he also helped to inaugurate the **Holland/Dozier/Holland** partnership, Motown's all-time most successful writing and production team. Working mostly as the lyricist, Holland was involved in hits for artists such as the **Supremes** and the **Four Tops**. He also collaborated with other writers/producers, notably on the **Temptations**' 'I'm Losing You' and 'Beauty Is Only Skin Deep'; the Velvelettes' 'He Was Really Saying Something' and 'Needle In A Haystack' and Shorty Long's dancefloor classic 'Function At The Junction'.

HOLLAND, JOOLS

LONDONER HOLLAND (b. JULIAN HOLLAND, 1958; KEYBOARDS) JOINED LOCAL BAND **SQUEEZE** IN 1974, ALONGside Glen Tilbrook and Chris Difford. Squeeze hit the pop charts at the same time as their pianist enjoyed his first solo release, the *Boogie Woogie* EP. In 1980, Holland played a farewell gig with Squeeze, before being replaced by **Paul Carrack**. He then formed the Millionaires with Mike Paice (saxophone), Pino Palladino (bass) and Martin T. Deegan (drums). Their debut 'Bumble Boogie' was released in 1981 and, after a few more Millionaires singles, Holland went solo in 1983 with 'Crazy Over You'. Despite further singles, Holland became best known for his presentation of the UK television pop show *The Tube*. In 1985, he rejoined Squeeze, playing sporadically with them until 1990. Further television appearances included presenting the resurrected *Juke Box Jury* and the 1992 BBC 2 series, *Later*, as well as playing piano on *Don't Forget Your Toothbrush*. In 1994 he undertook a tour with the ambitious, yet excellent, Jools Holland Rhythm And Blues Orchestra, in support of the album of the same name.

HOLLAND/DOZIER/HOLLAND

BROTHERS **EDDIE HOLLAND** (b. 1939) AND BRIAN HOLLAND (b. 1941), WITH **LAMONT DOZIER** (b. 1941) FORMED ONE OF the most successful composing and production teams in popular music history. All three were prominent in the Detroit R&B scene from the mid-50s, Brian Holland as lead singer with the Satintones, Eddie with the Fideltones, and Dozier with the Romeos. By the early 60s, they had all become part of Berry Gordy's **Motown** concern, working as performers and as writers/arrangers. After masterminding the **Marvelettes**' 1961 smash 'Please Mr Postman', Brian and Eddie formed a production team with Freddy Gorman. In 1963, Gorman was replaced by Dozier. Over the next five years, they wrote and produced records by almost all the major Motown artists, among them a dozen US number 1s. Their earliest successes came with **Marvin Gaye**, for whom they wrote 'Can I Get A Witness?', 'Little Darling', 'How Sweet It Is (To Be Loved By You)' and 'You're A Wonderful One', and **Martha And The Vandellas**, who had hits with 'Heatwave', 'Quicksand', 'Nowhere To Run' and 'Jimmy Mack'.

These achievements, however, paled alongside the team's run of success with the **Supremes**. Ordered by Berry Gordy to construct vehicles for the wispy vocal talents of **Diana Ross**, they produced 'Where Did Our Love Go?', a simplistic but irresistible slice of lightweight pop-soul. The record reached US number 1, as did its successors, 'Baby Love', 'Come See About Me', 'Stop! In The Name Of Love' and 'Back In My Arms Again'. Holland/Dozier/Holland produced and wrote a concurrent series of hits for the **Four Tops**. 'Baby I Need Your Loving' and 'I Can't Help Myself' illustrated their stylish way with up-tempo material; '(It's The) Same Old Song' was a self-mocking riposte to critics of their sound, while 'Reach Out I'll Be There', a worldwide number 1, pioneered what came to be known as 'symphonic soul'. The trio also found success with the **Miracles**, Kim Weston, and the **Isley Brothers**.

In 1967 they split from Berry Gordy and Motown. Legal disputes officially kept them out of the studio for several years, but they launched their own Invictus and Hot Wax labels in 1968. Hits by artists such as the **Chairmen Of The Board** and Freda Payne successfully mined the familiar vein of the trio's Motown hits, but business difficulties and personal conflicts gradually wore down the partnership in the early 70s, and in 1973 Dozier left to forge a solo career. Invictus and Hot Wax were dissolved a couple of years later. Occasional reunions by the trio since have failed to rekindle their former artistic fires.

HOLLIES

FRIENDS ALLAN CLARKE (b. 1942; VOCALS), AND GRAHAM NASH (b. 1942; VOCALS/GUITAR) HAD BEEN SINGING together for a number of years in Manchester, England, when they added Eric Haydock (b. 1943; bass) and Don Rathbone (drums), to become the Fourtones and then the Deltas in 1962. With local guitar hero Tony Hicks (b. 1943) they became the Hollies, and were signed to the **Beatles**' label, Parlophone. Their first two singles, covers of the **Coasters**, both made the UK charts. Rathbone was replaced by Bobby Elliott (b. 1942) on their first album. This and their second album contained most of their live act and stayed in the UK charts, while a train of hit singles continued from 1963-74. Infectious, well-produced hits such as Doris Troy's 'Just One Look', 'Here I Go Again' and the sublime 'Yes I Will' all contained their trademark soaring harmonies.

As their career progressed, Clarke, Hicks and Nash developed into a strong songwriting team, and wrote most of their own b-sides (under the pseudonym 'L. Ransford'). On their superb third collection, *Hollies* (1965), their talents blossomed with 'Too Many People'. Their first UK number 1 was 'I'm Alive' (1965), followed within weeks by Graham Gouldman's 'Look Through Any Window'. Early in 1966, the group enjoyed their second number 1, 'I Can't Let Go', which topped the *New Musical Express* chart jointly with the **Walker Brothers**' 'The Sun Ain't Gonna Shine Anymore'.

Haydock was sacked in 1966 and replaced by Bernie Calvert (b. 1942; ex-Dolphins). The Hollies success continued unabated with Graham Gouldman's 'Bus Stop', the exotic 'Stop! Stop! Stop!' and the poppier 'On A Carousel', all UK Top 5 hits, and, finally, major hits in the USA. The Hollies embraced 'flower power' with *For Certain Because* and *Evolution*. Inexplicably, the excellent *Butterfly* (1967) failed to make either the US or UK charts. The following year during the proposals to make *Hollies Sing Dylan*, Nash announced his departure for **Crosby, Stills And Nash**. His replacement was Terry Sylvester of the **Escorts**. Clarke, devastated by Nash's departure, went solo after seven further hits, including 'He Ain't Heavy He's My Brother'. The band soldiered on with the strange induction of Mickael Rickfors from Sweden.

Clarke returned to celebrate the worldwide hit, 'The Air That I Breathe', composed by **Albert Hammond**. In 1981, Sylvester and Calvert left the group, but a Stars On 45-type segued single, 'Holliedaze', was a hit, and Graham Nash was flown over for the television promotion. This reunion prompted *What Goes Around*, which made the US charts.

In 1988, when a television commercial used 'He Ain't Heavy', they topped the charts again. In 1993, the Hollies were given an Ivor Novello award to honour their contribution to British music.

HOLLAND, EDDIE

Albums
Eddie Holland (Motown 1962)★★★
➽ p.365 for full listings

Collaborators
Jackie Wilson ➽ p.340

Connections
Holland/Dozier/Holland ➽ p.183
Supremes ➽ p.314
Temptations ➽ p.318

HOLLAND, JOOLS

Albums
Jools Holland And His Millionaires (A&M 1981)★★★
Jools Holland Meets Rock 'A' Boogie Billy (1984)★★★
Sex And Jazz And Rock And Roll (Coluseum 1996)★★★
➽ p.365 for full listings

Connections
Squeeze ➽ p.306
Millionaires

HOLLAND/DOZIER/HOLLAND

Collaborators
Marvin Gaye ➽ p.159
Martha And The Vandellas ➽ p.226
Supremes ➽ p.314
Diana Ross ➽ p.283
Four Tops ➽ p.152
Isley Brothers ➽ p.194
➽ p.365 for full listings

Connections
Marvelettes ➽ p.226

HOLLIES

Albums
In The Hollies' Style (Parlophone 1964)★★★★
The Hollies (Parlophone 1965)★★★★
Would You Believe (Parlophone 1966)★★★★
➽ p.365 for full listings

Collaborators
Albert Hammond ➽ p.173

Connections
Dolphins
Crosby, Stills And Nash ➽ p.106
Escorts ➽ p.138

Influences
Coasters ➽ p.95

Further References
Film: *It's All Over Town* (1964)

HOLLOWAY, BRENDA
Albums
Every Little Bit Hurts (Tamla 1964)★★★
The Artistry Of Brenda Holloway (Motown 1968)★★★
All It Takes (1991)★★★
➧ p.365 for full listings
Collaborators
Beatles ➧ p.38
Jimmy Ruffin ➧ p.284
Connections
Spencer Davis Group ➧ p.304

HOLLY, BUDDY
Albums
The Buddy Holly Story (Coral 1959)★★★★★
The Buddy Holly Story, Vol. 2 (Coral 1959)★★★★★
From The Original Master Tapes (MCA 1985)★★★★★
➧ p.366 for full listings
Collaborators
Bill Haley And His Comets ➧ p.172
Elvis Presley ➧ p.265
Jerry Lee Lewis ➧ p.215
Chuck Berry ➧ p.45
Ritchie Valens ➧ p.328
Big Bopper ➧ p.46
Connections
Crickets ➧ p.105
Fireballs ➧ p.145
Influences
Hank Williams ➧ p.339
Further References
Books: *Buddy Holly: A Biography In Words, Photographs And Music*, Elizabeth & Ralph Peer
The Buddy Holly Story, John Goldrosen
Remembering Buddy, John Goldrosen & John Beecher

HOLLOWAY, BRENDA

BRENDA HOLLOWAY (b. 1946) BEGAN HER RECORDING CAREER IN THE EARLY 60S, WITH PRODUCER HAL DAVIS. In 1964 she was spotted by a **Motown Records** talent scout and signed to the label later that year. Her debut, 'Every Little Bit Hurts', established her bluesy soul style, and was covered by the **Spencer Davis Group** in Britain. She enjoyed further success with 'I'll Always Love You' (1964), 'When I'm Gone' and 'Operator' (both 1965), and played on the **Beatles**' 1965 US tour. After subsequent singles, Holloway began to devote more time to songwriting with her sister Patrice, and Motown staff producer Frank Wilson – producing her 1968 single 'You've Made Me So Very Happy'. In 1968, Holloway's contract with Motown was terminated. She released a gospel album in 1983 and, in 1989, teamed with **Jimmy Ruffin** for a duet, 'On The Rebound'.

HOLLY, BUDDY

HOLLY (b. CHARLES HARDIN HOLLEY, 1936, d. 1959) WAS ONE OF THE FIRST MAJOR ROCK 'N' ROLL GROUNDBREAKERS, and one of its most influential artists. Holly's musical influences included both C&W music and 'race' music, or R&B. He made his first stage appearance aged five in a talent contest with his brothers; he won $5. During his Texan childhood, Holly learned to play guitar, violin and piano; in 1949 formed a bluegrass duo, Buddy And Bob, with friend Bob Montgomery.

In 1952, Buddy And Bob added Larry Welborn (bass) and were given their own radio programme, *The Buddy And Bob Show*, performing country material with occasional R&B songs. KDAV disc jockey Hipockets Duncan became the trio's manager. Further recording took place at KDAV but no material was released. In 1954 the trio added fiddler Sonny Curtis and steel guitarist Don Guess to the group and made more recordings. That year the group, now including drummer Jerry Allison, opened concerts for **Bill Haley And His Comets** and **Elvis Presley** in Texas.

After a false start with Decca Records, Holly formed the **Crickets** with Allison and Niki Sullivan on rhythm guitar. On 25 February 1957, a rock 'n' roll version of Holly's 'That'll Be The Day' was recorded. The song was a revelation, containing one of the most gripping vocals and distinctive galloping riffs of any 50s record. Joe B. Mauldin joined as the Crickets' bassist following those sessions. The song was issued by Brunswick Records and with Norman Petty now as manager, the single underwent heavy promotion and reached US and UK number 1 in 1957. As the record was released, the Crickets performed at such venues as New York's Apollo Theatre and the Howard Theater in Washington, D.C., winning mostly-black audiences.

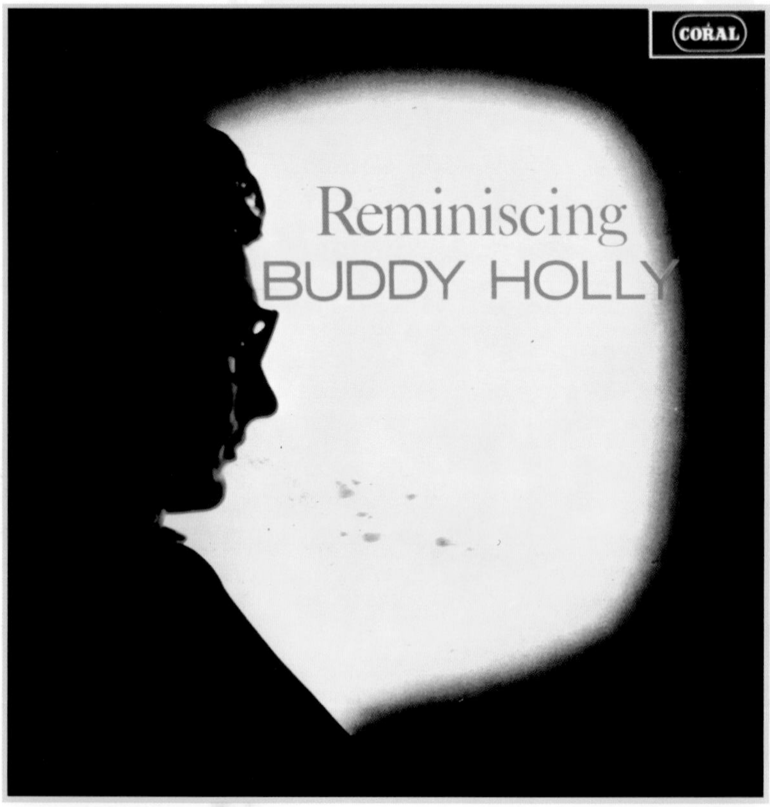

The group recorded prolifically in 1957, including classics like 'Words Of Love', 'Maybe Baby', 'Not Fade Away', 'Everyday', 'Peggy Sue' and 'Oh Boy'. Holly was innovative in the studio, making much use of new production techniques. Brunswick continued to issue recordings under the Crickets' name while Holly signed on as a solo artist to Coral Records, although most releases featured the entire group, often with other musicians and vocal group, the Picks. Holly and the Crickets only charted 11 times in the USA during their brief career and no albums charted during Holly's lifetime.

In early 1957, the Crickets recorded, then toured Australia for six days; followed by a UK tour. 'Maybe Baby' became the fourth Holly/Crickets single to chart in the USA, reaching number 17 (and UK number 4). The group returned to the USA and immediately headed out on a US tour assembled by disc jockey **Alan Freed**, also featuring such popular artists as **Jerry Lee Lewis** and **Chuck Berry**. Coral released the frantic 'Rave On' in May and although it reached only number 37 in the USA, it made number 5 in the UK. Following the tour, Holly recorded two songs written by **Bobby Darin** without the Crickets; they remained unreleased but signalled an impending split between Holly and the group. While in New York Holly met Maria Elena Santiago, whom he married two months later. During that summer Holly recorded 'Heartbeat', 'Love's Made A Fool Of You' and 'Wishing'. Guitarist Tommy Allsup played on the latter two and was subsequently asked to join the Crickets.

Holly and the Crickets toured the US and Canada during October, by which time there was apparently friction between the Hollys and the Pettys. Buddy and Maria Holly travelled apart from the group between dates. After the trip, Holly announced to manager/producer Petty that he was leaving him. To Holly's surprise the other Crickets chose to leave Holly and stay with Petty; Holly allowed them use of the group's name and they continued to record without him. Meanwhile, Holly, producer Dick Jacobs and studio musicians (including a string section) recorded 'True Love Ways', 'It Doesn't Matter Anymore' (written by **Paul Anka**), 'Raining In My Heart' and 'Moondreams'. They were held for later release while 'It's So Easy' was released; it failed to chart in the US. 'Heartbeat' was issued in December and became the last Holly single to chart in the US during his lifetime. The superb 'It Doesn't Matter Anymore' was released posthumously and provided Holly with his only UK number 1.

In January 1959, he began assembling a band to take on the 'Winter Dance Party' tour of the US Midwest. Allsup was hired on guitar, Waylon Jennings on bass and Carl Bunch on drums. They were billed as the Crickets despite the agreement to give Holly's former band mates that name. Also starring **Ritchie Valens**, the **Big Bopper**, **Dion And The Belmonts** and unknown Frankie Sardo, the tour began 23 January 1959 in Milwaukee, Wisconsin. Following a 2 February date in Clear Lake, Iowa, Holly, Valens and the Big Bopper chartered a small plane to take them to the next date in Moorhead, Minnesota. The plane crashed minutes after take-off, killing all three stars and the pilot.

Holly's popularity increased after his death, even as late as the 80s unreleased material was still being released. In 1962, Norman Petty took some demos Holly had recorded at home in 1958 and had the instrumental group the **Fireballs** along play to them, creating new Buddy Holly records from the unfinished tapes. In 1965, *Holly In The Hills*, comprising the early Buddy and Bob radio station recordings, was released and charted in the UK. Compilation albums also charted in both the USA and the UK, as late as the 70s. During the 70s the publishing rights to Holly's song catalogue were purchased by **Paul McCartney**, who began sponsoring annual Buddy Holly Week celebrations. A Buddy Holly Memorial Society was formed in the USA; a 1978 film, *The Buddy Holly Story*; and a musical play *Buddy*, also commemorated his life.

HOLLYWOOD ARGYLES

IN 1960 THE SINGLE 'ALLEY OOP' HIT US NUMBER 1. IT WAS WRITTEN BY DALLAS FRAZIER, PRODUCED BY BOBBY REY and featured Gary S. Paxton on vocals. At the time Paxton, part of Skip And Flip, was contracted to Brent Records, while his single was issued on Lute Records – Hollywood Argyles was created, including Paxton, Rey, Ted Marsh, Gary Webb, Deary Weaver and Ted Winters. Further singles by the Hollywood Argyles, on such labels as Paxley (co-owned by Paxton and producer Kim Fowley), failed to reach the charts. Paxton later started the Garpax label, which released the number 1 'Monster Mash' by **Bobby 'Boris' Pickett**.

HONEYCOMBS

FORMED IN LONDON IN 1963, THE GROUP WAS ORIGINALLY KNOWN AS THE SHERABONS AND COMPRISED DENIS D'ell (b. Denis Dalziel; vocals), Anne 'Honey' Lantree (drums), John Lantree (bass), Alan Ward (lead guitar) and Martin Murray (rhythm guitar), later replaced by Peter Pye. Pye Records released their debut, 'Have I The Right' – although the group were obliged to change their name. When 'Have I The Right' hit UK number 1 in 1964, the group's pop star future seemed assured. However, a dramatic flop with the follow-up 'Is It Because' caused concern, barely saved by 'That's The Way'. The group faltered amid line-up changes and poor morale, before moving inexorably towards cabaret and the revivalist circuit.

HONEYDRIPPERS

FORMED IN 1984, THE HONEYDRIPPERS INCLUDED **LED ZEPPELIN** ALUMNI **ROBERT PLANT** (VOCALS) AND **JIMMY Page** (guitar), former **Chic** bassist Nile Rodgers and guitarist **Jeff Beck**. *Honeydrippers Volume 1*, a mini-album, featured an interpretation of **Ray Charles**'s 'I Got A Woman'. Phil Phillips's 'Sea Of Love' gave the group a surprise US Top 10 hit single, but despite this success, the concept has not been followed up, partly because of the individuals' commitment to their separate careers.

HOODOO GURUS

SINGER-SONGWRITER DAVE FAULKNER, PREVIOUSLY PLAYED IN THE GURUS, BEFORE JOINING SCIENTISTS' GUITARIST Rod Radalj in an untitled band. With the arrival of another ex-Scientist, drummer Jim Baker, the band was named Le Hoodoo Gurus. The Sydney-based trio eventually evolved into the tight, hypnotic garage-rock machine which became venerated in underground circles, especially on the US west coast. The power-pop playing of Brad Sheperd (guitar, harmonica) with the rhythm section of Baker and Clyde Bramley (bass) led to their influential *Stoneage Romeos* debut of 1983. Dedicated to US television sitcom legends Arnold Ziffel and Larry Storch, it included the stage favourite '(Let's All) Turn On' and the nonsensical 'I Was A Kamikaze Pilot'. *Mars Needs Guitars!*, with Mark Kingsmill taking over on drums, was slightly hampered by inferior production, but the tunes were still memorable. A rarer outbreak of melodicism was introduced on *Blow Your Cool!*, with the band joined by the **Bangles** on several selections. In 1988, Bramley was replaced by Rick Grossman, followed by the band's finest album to date, *Magnum Cum Louder*. *Kinky* drew lyrical targets from US and Australian pop culture, though there was little stylistic variation to the band's themes. *Crank* brought in **Ramones**' producer Ed Stasium, but, like follow-up *Blue Cave*, was a weaker effort. The Hoodoo Gurus seem set to remain a cult band.

HOOKER, JOHN LEE

HOOKER (b. 1917) PLAYED GUITAR WITH HIS STEPFATHER WILLIAM MOORE AT DANCES, BEFORE RUNNING AWAY TO Memphis, Tennessee, aged 14, where he met and played with Robert Lockwood. He moved to Cincinnatti, where he sang with gospel quartets before moving to Detroit in 1943. There he played in the blues clubs and bars at the heart of the black section, developing his unique guitar style. In 1948 he was finally given the chance to record. Accompanied only by his own electric guitar and constantly tapping foot, 'Boogie Chillen', was a surprise commercial success for Modern Records.

From the late 40s to the early 50s, Hooker recorded prolifically. His successful run with Modern produced such classics as 'Crawling King Snake', 'In The Mood', 'Rock House Boogie' and 'Shake Holler & Run'. Under a deliberately bewildering array of pseudonyms, he also released on a variety of labels. He played the R&B circuit across the country, further developing his popularity with the black-American public. In 1955, he severed his connection with Modern and began a long association with Vee Jay Records of Chicago.

By now, the solo format was deemed old-fashioned, so all of these recordings used a tight little band, often including Eddie Taylor on guitar, as well as piano and various combinations of horns. The association with Vee Jay proved very satisfactory, promoting further extensive tours. In the late 50s, Hooker appeared regularly at folk clubs and folk festivals. He was lionized by a new audience mainly of young, white listeners. In the early 60s his reputation grew as he was often cited by younger pop and rock musicians as a major influence. The connection with a new generation of musicians led to various 'super sessions', and bore fruit most successfully in the early 70s with the release of *Hooker 'N' Heat*, in which he played with the American rock blues band **Canned Heat**. Although enthusiasm for blues waned in the late 70s and early 80s, Hooker's standing has rarely faltered and he has continued to tour, latterly with the Coast To Coast Blues Band. A remarkable transformation came in 1989 when he recorded *The Healer*. This superb album featured guests on most tracks including **Bonnie Raitt**, **Los Lobos** and Carlos **Santana** on the title track. *Mr Lucky* reached number 3 in the UK album charts, setting a record for Hooker, at 74, as the oldest artist to achieve that position. In his old age, Hooker has begun to fulfil the role of elder statesman of the blues, but this has not prevented him from touring and he continues to perform and record.

HOLLYWOOD ARGYLES
Album
The Hollywood Argyles (Lute 1960)★★★
➽ p.366 for full listings
Connections
Bobby 'Boris' Pickett ➽ p.260

HONEYCOMBS
Albums
The Honeycombs (Pye 1964)★★★
All Systems Go (Pye 1965)★★★
Here Are The Honeycombs (Vee Jay 1964)★★★
➽ p.366 for full listings

HONEYDRIPPERS
Albums
Honeydrippers Volume 1 (Es Paranza 1984)★★★
12 Days Of Christmas (Shattered 1997)★★★
➽ p.366 for full listings
Influences
Ray Charles ➽ p.88

HOODOO GURUS
Albums
Stoneage Romeos (Big Time/A&M 1983)★★★
Mars Need Guitars! (Big Time/Elektra 1985)★★★
Magnum Cum Louder (RCA 1989)★★★★
➽ p.366 for full listings
Collaborators
Bangles ➽ p.32
Connections
Scientists

HOOKER, JOHN LEE
Albums
I'm John Lee Hooker (Vee Jay 1959)★★★★
Hooker 'N' Heat (Specialty 1971)★★★★
The Healer (Chameleon 1989)★★★★★
➽ p.366 for full listings

Collaborators
Canned Heat ➽ p.79
Coast To Coast Blues Band
Bonnie Raitt ➽ p.272
Los Lobos ➽ p.218
Further References
Film: *The Blues Brothers* (1980)
Video: *Survivors – The Blues Today* (Hendring Video 1989)
Book: *Boogie Chillen: A Guide To John Lee Hooker*

HOOTERS
Albums
Out Of Body (1993)★★★
➽ p.366 for full listings
Connections
Donald Fagan ➽ p.141

HOOTIE AND THE BLOWFISH
Albums
Fairweather Johnson (Atlantic 1996)★★★
➽ p.366 for full listings

Collaborators
David Crosby ➽ p.105
Connections
R.E.M. ➽ p.275

HOPKINS, LIGHTNIN'
Albums
Blues In My Bottle (Bluesville 1962)★★★★
➽ p.366 for full listings
Further References
Book: *Lightnin' Hopkins: Blues'*, M. McCormick

HOPKINS, NICKY
Albums
No More Changes (1976)★★
➽ p.366 for full listings
Collaborators
Cliff Bennett ➽ p.43
Rolling Stones ➽ p.281
George Harrison ➽ p.176
John Lennon ➽ p.214

HOOTERS

THE AMERICAN HOOTERS (FORMED IN 1978) FUSED FOLK, ROCK AND SKA. THEY WERE LED BY ROB HYMAN AND ERIC Brazilian, and had several mid-80s hits, as MTV exposure took 'All You Zombies', 'And We Danced', 'Day By Day' and 'Where Do The Children Go' into the *Billboard* charts. All four were included on their debut album, which received universally strong reviews. On *Zig Zag* they pursued a more sober direction, with songs such as 'Give The Music Back' and 'Don't Knock It 'Til You Try It', but moderate sales led to a dramatic self-appraisal. *Out Of Body* revealed the Hooters' customary catchy rock verve, but with a new focus on folk-rock, and the addition of multi-instrumentalist Mindy Jostyn (ex-**Donald Fagen**'s New Rock 'N' Soul Revue). Despite a revitalized sound, the Hooters failed to regain lost commercial ground, and returned to session playing.

HOOTIE AND THE BLOWFISH

THIS SOUTH CAROLINA QUARTET FORMED IN THE EARLY 90S. IT COMPRISES: DARIUS RUCKER (HOOTIE; VOCALS), Mark Bryan (guitar), Dean Felber (bass) and Jim 'Soni' Sonefield (drums). They produced a self-financed EP, containing 'Hold My Hand', and sold over 50,000 copies at gigs. Their debut album, *Cracked Rear View* followed and eventually made the US Top 10. It took its title from a **John Hiatt** lyric and was produced by **R.E.M./John Cougar Mellencamp** associate Don Gehman. 'Hold My Hand' was included on the set and featured guest vocals from **David Crosby**. The album became one of the most successful rock debuts of all time. A critically acclaimed tour in 1994 encompassed more than 300 dates and, at the 1995 Grammy Awards, they picked up Best New Artist and Best Pop Performance By A Group. Any follow-up album was bound to be anti-climatic and although *Fairweather Johnson* debuted in the US chart at number 1, by the band's previous standards the album was seen as something of a flop – by anybody else's standards it was a massive success.

HOPKINS, LIGHTNIN'

ONE OF THE LAST GREAT COUNTRY BLUES SINGERS, HOPKINS' (b. SAM HOPKINS, 1912, d. 1982) LENGTHY CAREER began in the Texas bars and juke joints of the 20s.

His work first came to prominence when, after being discovered by Sam Charters at the age of 47, *The Roots Of Lightnin' Hopkins* was released in 1959. His sparse acoustic guitar, narrated prose and harsh, emotive voice appealed to the American folk boom of the early 60s. By that time, Hopkins was re-established as a major force on the college and concert-hall circuit. In 1967 he was the subject of an autobiographical film, *The Blues Of Lightnin' Hopkins*, which won the Gold Hugo award at the Chicago Film Festival. He experimented with a 'progressive' electric album: *The Great Electric Show And Dance*. During the 70s, he toured compulsively in the USA, Canada and, in 1977, Europe, until ill health forced him to slow down. When Hopkins died, his status as one of the major voices of the blues was assured.

HOPKINS, NICKY

A CLASSICALLY TRAINED PIANIST, HOPKINS (b. 1944, d. 1994) EMBRACED ROCK 'N' ROLL IN 1960 WHEN, INSPIRED BY **Chuck Berry**, he joined the Savages, a seminal pre-**Beatles** group led by Screaming Lord Sutch. In 1962 Hopkins accompanied **Cliff Bennett** and his Rebel Rousers at Hamburg's *Star Club*, before becoming a founder-member of Cyril Davies' R&B All Stars. Hopkins' distinctive fills were prevalent on releases by the **Who**, **Dusty Springfield**, **Tom Jones** and the **Kinks**, the latter of whom paid tribute with 'Session Man' from *Face To Face*. Hopkins later released a version of the Kinks' 'Mr. Pleasant', before completing the novelty-bound *Revolutionary Piano Of Nicky Hopkins*. He contributed to the **Rolling Stones**'s *Their Satanic Majesties Request*, establishing a rapport continued over several successive releases – it is his distinctive piano playing that opens the Stones's 'We Love You'.

In 1968, the pianist joined the **Jeff Beck** Group, leaving in 1969 for the **Steve Miller** Band. After moving to California, Hopkins switched to the **Quicksilver Messenger Service** with whom he completed two albums, including *Shady Grove* (which featured his lengthy solo 'Edward, The Mad Shirt Grinder'). Hopkins was also a member of Sweet Thursday, a studio-based group that included guitarist Jon Mark. A second solo album, *The Tin Man Was A Dreamer* featured **George Harrison**, Mick Taylor and Klaus Voorman. Hopkins worked on countless sessions, including **John Lennon**'s *Imagine* and **Jefferson Airplane**'s *Volunteers*. In 1979 he joined Night, alongside vocalist Chris Thompson (ex-**Manfred Mann's Earth Band**) and guitarist Robbie McIntosh (future **Pretenders**). However, Hopkins left the line-up following the release of their debut album, and returned to session playing, contributing to Ron Wood's *1,2,3,4*. Hopkins was dogged by ill health; his death in 1994 followed complications after stomach surgery.

HORNSBY, BRUCE, AND THE RANGE

PIANIST AND CONTRACT SONGWRITER, HORNSBY (b. 1954) BURST ON TO THE MARKET IN 1986 WITH A TRANSATLANTIC hit single 'The Way It Is'. His first album, part produced by **Huey Lewis**, featured David Mansfield (violin/mandolin/guitar), Joe Puerta (bass), John Molo (drums) and George Marinelli (guitar). Hornsby followed the first album with *Scenes From The South Side*, an even stronger collection including the powerful 'The Valley Road' – the single won him a composer's Grammy for the best bluegrass recording, as performed by the **Nitty Gritty Dirt Band**. The third collection *Night On The Town* featured **Jerry Garcia** on guitar; following the death of the **Grateful Dead**'s Brent Mydland (26 July 1990), Hornsby joined as a temporary replacement. In addition to many session/guest appearances during the early 90s, Hornsby found time to record *Harbour Lights*, a satisfying and more acoustic-sounding record. A new album in 1995 resorted back to the commercial-sounding formula of his debut.

HORSLIPS

IRISH FOLK-ROCK BAND FORMED IN 1970, COMPRISING BARRY DEVLIN (BASS/VOCALS), DECLAN SINNOTT (LEAD guitar/vocals), Eamonn Carr (drums/vocals), Charles O'Connor (violin), and Jim Lockhart (flute/violin/keyboards). Sinnott later joined Moving Hearts, and was replaced by Gus Gueist and John Fean in turn. The group supported **Steeleye Span**. Irish legends were the theme for many of their songs. They maintained a strong cult following, but only *The Book Of Invasions – A Celtic Symphony*, reached the UK Top 40. *The Man Who Built America* received a great deal of airplay when released, but wider acceptance evaded them, and the group split. Fean, O'Connor and Carr later formed Host, with Chris Page (bass), and Peter Keen (keyboards).

HOT CHOCOLATE

HIGHLY COMMERCIAL UK POP GROUP, COMPRISING PATRICK OLIVE (PERCUSSION), FRANKLYN DE ALLIE (GUITAR) – he left shortly afterwards – and Ian King (drums); Errol Brown (vocals/songwriting), Tony Wilson (bass/songwriting) and Larry Ferguson (piano) joined later. Apple signed them for a reggae version of the Plastic Ono Band's 'Give Peace A Chance', and the group also provided the hit 'Think About Your Children' for Mary Hopkin. A year later, Hot Chocolate signed to RAK and composed **Herman's Hermits** hit 'Bet Yer Life I Do'. In 1970, Hot Chocolate enjoyed their own first hit with 'Love Is Life'. Over the next year, Harvey Hinsley (guitar) and Tony Connor (drums) joined the group.

Hot Chocolate's formidable run of UK Top 10 hits include 'I Believe (In Love)', 'Brother Louie', 'Emma', 'You Sexy Thing', 'No Doubt About It', 'Girl Crazy' and 'It Started With A Kiss'. In 1987, they reached UK number 1 with the **Russ Ballard** song 'So You Win Again'. Wilson departed in 1976, but the group split when Errol Brown left in 1987. Brown had a hit with 'Personal Touch', and completed two albums. In 1997, the group sprung back into the limelight when 'You Sexy Thing' featured in the smash hit British film *The Full Monty*.

HOT GOSSIP

OSTENSIBLY A RISQUE DANCE TROUPE, HOT GOSSIP ALSO MADE IT TO NUMBER 6 IN THE UK CHARTS WITH, 'I LOST My Heart To A Starship Trooper' (1978). The follow-up single was credited to Sarah Brightman And The Starship Troopers. Hot Gossip were formed by dance teacher Arlene Phillips, and appeared regularly at Maunkbury's night-club in London before being spotted by the director of the *Kenny Everett Television Show*.

HOT TUNA

US GROUP COMPRISING TWO MEMBERS OF **JEFFERSON AIRPLANE**, JACK CASADY (BASS) AND JORMA KAUKONEN (guitar/vocals); often using colleagues Paul Kantner (guitar) and Spencer Dryden (drums) alongside guests. Stage appearances were initially integrated within the Airplane's performances, but during one of the Airplane's rest periods, the duo began to appear in their own right, often with drummer Joey Covington. Hot Tuna released a self-titled debut (with harmonica player Will Scarlet guesting). By their second album, with violinist Papa John Creach and drummer Sammy Piazza, the line-up displayed the combination of electric and acoustic rock/blues for which Casady and Kaukonen had been looking. Creach departed before *The Phosphorescent Rat*, and Piazza left; he was replaced by Bob Steeler. By their sixth album they sounded like a rumbling heavy rock traditional-ragtime blues band. The group maintained a hardcore following, but in the late 70s Casady embarked on an ill-advised excursion into 'punk' with SVT. In the 90s, Hot Tuna were still performing.

HOTHOUSE FLOWERS

BUSKING IN DUBLIN AS THE INCOMPARABLE BENZINI BROTHERS, LIAM O'MAONLAI (FORMERLY OF CONGRESS, who became **My Bloody Valentine**; vocals) and Fiachna O'Broainain (guitar) won the Street Entertainers Of The Year Award in 1985. Recruiting Maria Doyle, they became the folk-inspired Hothouse Flowers, taking their name from a Wynton Marsalis album. Highly praised in **Rolling Stone** magazine before they had even secured a recording contract, an appearance on RTE's Saturday-night chat programme *The Late Show* led to the issue of a single on **U2**'s Mother label, 'Love Don't Work That Way' (1987). Although commercially unsuccessful, PolyGram Records signed them. Their debut single, 'Don't Go', reached UK number 11, followed by further hits, including a cover version of **Johnny Nash**'s 'I Can See Clearly Now', 'Give It Up', and 'Movies'. Their debut album, *People*, reached UK number 2, but further albums showed little musical progression, and by 1995 O'Maonlai had formed Alt with Andy White and Tim Finn.

Connections
Who ➧ p.338
Tom Jones ➧ p.201
Kinks ➧ p.207
Jeff Beck Group ➧ p.41
Steve Miller Band ➧ p.234
Influences
Chuck Berry ➧ p.45

HORNSBY, BRUCE, AND THE RANGE
Albums
Scenes From The South Side (RCA 1988)★★★★
➧ p.366 for full listings
Collaborators
Huey Lewis ➧ p.215
Jerry Garcia ➧ p.158
Connections
Grateful Dead ➧ p.167

HORSLIPS
Albums
The Man Who Built America (1979)★★★
➧ p.366 for full listings
Collaborators
Steeleye Span ➧ p.308

HOT CHOCOLATE
Albums
Every 1's A Winner (RAK 1978)★★★
➧ p.366 for full listings
Collaborators
Herman's Hermits ➧ p.180

HOT TUNA
Albums
Burgers (Grunt 1972)★★★★
➧ p.366 for full listings
Connections
Jefferson Airplane ➧ p.198

HOTHOUSE FLOWERS
Albums
People (London 1988)★★★
➧ p.366 for full listings
Connections
My Bloody Valentine ➧ p.242

HOUSE OF LOVE
Albums
House Of Love (Creation 1988)★★★
Babe Rainbow (Fontana 1992)★★★
➧ p.366 for full listings

HOUSEMARTINS
Albums
London 0 Hull 4 (Go! Discs 1986)★★★★
➧ p.366 for full listings

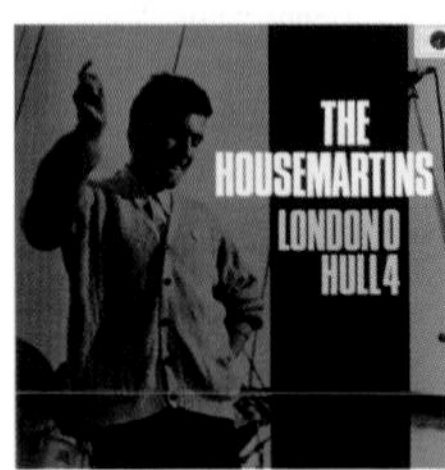

Connections
Beautiful South ➧ p.40
Further References
Book: *The Housemartins, Tales From Humberside*, Nick Swift

HOUSTON, CISSY
Albums
Presenting Cissy Houston (Major Minor 1970)★★★
Cissy Houston (Private Stock 1977)★★★
Face To Face (House Of Blues 1996)★★★
➧ p.366 for full listings
Collaborators
Solomon Burke ➧ p.74
Wilson Pickett ➧ p.260
Sweet Inspirations ➧ p.315
Connections
Dionne Warwick ➧ p.334
Whitney Houston ➧ p.188

HOUSTON, THELMA
Albums
Qualifying Heats (MCA 1987)★★★
Throw You Down (Reprise 1990)★★★
➧ p.366 for full listings
Influences
Jimmy Webb ➧ p.335

HOUSTON, WHITNEY
Albums
Whitney Houston (Arista 1985)★★★★
Whitney (Arista 1987)★★★★
➧ p.366 for full listings
Collaborators
Chaka Khan ➧ p.204
Teddy Pendergrass ➧ p.258
Influences
Cissy Houston ➧ p.188
Dionne Warwick ➧ p.334
Dolly Parton ➧ p.256

HOUSE OF LOVE

UK-BORN GUY CHADWICK (VOCALS/GUITAR) TEAMED UP WITH PETE EVANS (DRUMS), TERRY BICKERS (GUITAR), Chris Groothuizen (bass) and Andrea Heukamp (vocals/guitar) to form the House Of Love. Their debut single, 'Shine On', was released in 1987 after which Heukamp left the group. 'Christine' on their debut album was rightly acclaimed, and the album was nominated the best record of 1988. Tipped as the group most likely to succeed in 1989, reinforced by the release of 'Destroy The Heart', they were signed to PhonoGram. The first two singles for the label, 'Never' and 'I Don't Know Why I Love You', stalled at number 41, while the album suffered huge delays. By Christmas 1989, Bickers had quit, immediately replaced by Simon Walker, and early in 1990 the long-awaited *Fontana* appeared – to mixed reviews. Extensive touring followed, ending with the departure of Walker, tentatively replaced by original member Andrea Heukamp. The House Of Love re-emerged in 1991 with an acclaimed EP featuring the excellent 'The Girl With The Loneliest Eyes' and in 1992 *Babe Rainbow* was released to some critical acclaim. Following *Audience Of The Mind* the band collapsed, Chadwick re-emerging a year later with the Madonnas.

HOUSEMARTINS

THE HOUSEMARTINS, PAUL HEATON (VOCALS, GUITAR), STAN COLLIMORE (BASS), TED KEY (GUITAR) and Hugh Whitaker (drums) signed to Go! Discs, and their songwriting talent quickly emerged. In 1985, Key departed, replaced by Norman Cook. Their first UK hit, 'Happy Hour' in 1986, reached number 3. Their UK Top 10 debut album *London 0 Hull 4* further established them and their cappella version of 'Caravan Of Love' gave them a UK number 1.

Early in 1987 the Housemartins won the BPI award for Best Newcomers of the year. In the summer, David Hemmingway replaced Whitaker. An acclaimed EP, *Five Get Over Excited* followed, after which the group displayed their left-wing politics by performing at the 'Red Wedge' concerts. 'Me And The Farmer' was another Top 20 hit. The group issued their final studio album, the self-mocking *The People Who Grinned Themselves To Death*. Announcing that they had only intended the Housemartins to last for three years, they split in 1988. The original line-up grew into such groups as the **Beautiful South** and Beats International.

HOUSTON, CISSY

HOUSTON'S (b. EMILY DRINKARD, 1933, USA) BEGAN SINGING IN THE FAMILY GOSPEL GROUP, the Drinkard Singers, alongside nieces Dee Dee and **Dionne Warwick**. They backed artists including **Solomon Burke** and **Wilson Pickett**. Between 1967 and 1970 Houston was lead vocalist with the quartet **Sweet Inspirations**. Her subsequent solo releases included 'I'll Be There' (1970), 'Be My Baby' (1971) and 'Think It Over' (1978), but her career was later eclipsed by her daughter **Whitney Houston**. Cissy has now returned to the gospel fold.

HOUSTON, THELMA

THELMA HOUSTON SPENT THE LATE 60S TOURING WITH THE GOSPEL GROUP THE ART REYNOLDS SINGERS. IN 1969, writer/arranger **Jimmy Webb** composed and produced *Sunshower*. The album mixed the fluency of jazz with the passion of soul, and offered Houston sophisticated, witty lyrics. *Sunshower* won great critical acclaim and a contract with **Motown Records**. In 1976 Houston reworked 'Don't Leave Me This Way'. Her disco interpretation achieved impressive sales on both sides of the Atlantic. She then issued a series of albums in the late 70s, and also collaborated with Jerry Butler; the results were consistent sellers among the black audience. Houston enjoyed wider exposure in the late 70s with film roles in *Death Scream*, *Norman ... Is That You?* and *The Seventh Dwarf*. She re-emerged in 1987 and 1990 with critically acclaimed but commercially disappointing albums. Houston's inconsistent chart record belies the calibre of her vocal talents.

HOUSTON, WHITNEY

WHITNEY HOUSTON (b. 1963, USA) FOLLOWED HER MOTHER **CISSY** AND COUSIN **DIONNE WARWICK** BY BEGINNING her career in gospel. Early performances include backing **Chaka Khan**, and lead vocals on the Michael Zager Band's single 'Life's A Party'. By 1983 she had signed to Arista Records; in 1984 'Hold Me', a duet with **Teddy Pendergrass**, crept into the US Top 50. *Whitney Houston* was released in 1984, creeping up the charts before topping them in early 1985. The singles 'You Give Good Love' and 'Saving All My Love For You' made US numbers 3 and 1 respectively; the latter also topped the charts in the UK and much of the rest of the world. 'How Will I Know' and 'Greatest Love Of All' both topped the US charts in rapid succession and Houston won a series of prestigious awards.

'I Want To Dance With Somebody (Who Loves Me)', released in 1987, was a transatlantic number 1, creating *Whitney* the first album by a female artist to debut at number 1 on the US album charts, a feat it also achieved in the UK. The album included a version of 'I Know Him So Well' (sung with Cissy) and 'Didn't We Almost Have It All' – her fifth successive US number 1. 'So Emotional' and 'Where Do Broken Hearts Go' continued the sequence, breaking a record previously shared by the **Beatles** and the **Bee Gees**. Another series of awards followed, including Pop Female Vocal and Soul/R&B Female Vocal categories in the American Music Awards. She recorded the title track to the 1988 Olympics tribute *One Moment In Time*, while 'I'm Your Baby Tonight' put her back at number 1. Despite the relatively modest success of the album of the same name (US number 3), 'All The Man That I Need' compensated by becoming her ninth number 1. Her version of 'The Star Spangled Banner' was released, and she performed it to returning Gulf War troops. In 1992, Houston married singer **Bobby Brown**, a short-lived, tempestuous affair. The same year she made her acting debut in the film *The Bodyguard*. She lifted two songs recorded on the phenomenally successful soundtrack album.

HOWLIN' WOLF

HOWLIN' WOLF (b. CHESTER ARTHUR BURNETT, 1910, d. 1976) WAS ONE OF THE MOST important post-war blues players. Throughout his Mississippi youth he sang at local parties and juke joints. He emulated performers like Charley Patton and Tommy Johnson, although his hoarse, powerful voice and eerie 'howling' were peculiarly his own.

Wolf met people such as Shines, **Robert Johnson**, and Sonny Boy 'Rice Miller' Williamson. Williamson and Wolf's half-sister Mary, taught him to play harmonica, and he also experimented with the guitar. He then formed his own group and was approached by a west Memphis radio station which brought him to the attention of **Sam Phillips** who asked him to record, making separate agreements with the Bihari Brothers in California and the Chess Brothers of Chicago. Successful early recordings led to competition between these two camps, but eventually he went to Chicago where he built a powerful reputation on the club circuit, with such classics as 'Smokestack Lightning' and 'Killing Floor'. Wolf's music was a significant influence on rock and many of his best-known songs – 'Sitting On Top Of The World', 'I Ain't Superstitious', 'Killin' Floor', 'Back Door Man' and 'Little Red Rooster' – were recorded by acts as diverse as the **Doors**, **Cream**, the **Rolling Stones**, the **Yardbirds** and **Manfred Mann**. Few, however, rivalled the originals. *The London Howlin' Wolf Sessions* saw Wolf and long-serving guitarist Hubert Sumlin joined by an array of guests, including **Eric Clapton**, **Steve Winwood**, and Rolling Stones Bill Wyman and Charlie Watts.

Wolf continued to tour until his death in 1976.

HUE AND CRY

BROTHERS PATRICK (VOCALS/LYRICS) AND GREGORY KANE (PIANO/KEYBOARDS/MUSIC) STARTED AS A BAND IN 1986. Although they use session players, some of their most powerful work has been just voice and piano – including the 1989 *Bitter Suite*. Their first single, 'I Refuse' (1986) flopped, but the soul-fired 'Labour Of Love' (1987) gave them a UK hit. They received much attention for the memorable 'Looking For Linda', but since then only their work as a duo has attracted any attention. The *Violently* EP in 1989 contained a cover of **Kate Bush**'s 'The Man With The Child In His Eyes'. In 1991, they left long-term label Circa. Patrick remained prominent outside of music; he has worked as a television presenter and music journalist and is the Rector of Glasgow University. *Stars Crash Down*, the band's most recent album, features contributions from fellow Scots **Eddi Reader** and Vernal and Prime from **Deacon Blue**. *Piano & Vocal* was a bold project that worked because of the strength of Pat Kane's voice.

HUES CORPORATION

FORMED IN 1969 IN LOS ANGELES, THE VOCAL TRIO COMPRISED HUBERT ANN KELLY (SOPRANO), ST. CLAIR LEE (baritone) and Fleming Williams (tenor). Their first record, 'Goodfootin'' (1970), failed to chart. They signed with RCA Records in 1973, charting with 'Freedom For The Stallion'. 'Rock The Boat' was released in 1974 and reached number 1 in the US pop charts and number 6 in the UK. Tommy Brown replaced Williams after the single hit. The group continued to record into the late 70s, but were unable to repeat their earlier success. In 1983 'Rock The Boat' made another chart appearance when Forrest took it to the UK Top 5.

HUMAN LEAGUE

FORMED IN 1978, THE LINE-UP COMPRISED IAN CRAIG MARSH (SYNTHESIZER), MARTYN WARE (SYNTHESIZER), Philip Oakey (vocals) and Addy Newton (visual director), later replaced by Adrian Wright. In 1978, the group signed to independent label Fast Product. Their first single, 'Being Boiled', secured a tie-in deal with Virgin Records. Their debut, *Reproduction*, sold steadily, while the EP *Holiday, '80*, won them an appearance on *Top Of The Pops*. Oakey became the focal point of the group, leading to internal friction which the chart success of *Travelogue* was unable to stem and in late 1980, Marsh and Ware left. They went on to found BEF and **Heaven 17**. Oakey chose two teenagers with no knowledge of the music business, Susanne Sulley and Joanne Catherall, and the new line-up was completed by bassist Ian Burden and ex-**Rezillos** guitarist Jo Callis. They contrasted radically with the original Human League, producing a series of pure pop UK hits in 1981. *Dare* sold over five million copies and Christmas chart-topper, 'Don't You Want Me', became the biggest-selling UK single of 1981, and became a US number 1, spearheading a British invasion of 'new pop' artists.

The group took a long sabbatical, releasing only a couple of hits – 'Mirror Man' and '(Keep Feeling) Fascination' – and a mini-album of dance remixes, before *Hysteria* (1984), which met a mixed response. The attendant singles, 'The Lebanon', 'Life On Your Own' and 'Louise', all reached the UK Top 20 and Oakey ended 1984 by teaming up with Giorgio Moroder for a successful single and album. Two years passed – and Wright and Callis departed – before *Crash*. In 1990, the group returned with a new album, which found a cool response. *Octopus* and a series of hit singles appeared five years later; much of the freshness and simplicity of *Dare* was in the new collection. The Human League have shown a remarkable ability to triumph.

HOWLIN' WOLF

Albums

Moaning In The Moonlight (Chess 1959)★★★★
More Real Folk Blues (Chess 1967)★★★★
The Back Door Wolf (Chess 1973)★★★★
➽ p.366 for full listings

Collaborators

Eric Clapton ➽ p.92
Steve Winwood ➽ p.341
Bill Wyman

Connections

Doors ➽ p.123
Cream ➽ p.103
Manfred Mann ➽ p.223

HUE AND CRY

Albums

Seduced And Abandoned (Circa 1987)★★★
Remote/The Bitter Suite (Circa 1989)★★★
Piano & Voice (Permanent 1995)★★★
➽ p.366 for full listings

Influences

Kate Bush ➽ p.76

HUES CORPORATION

Albums

Freedom For The Stallion (RCA 1974)★★
Your Place Or Mine (Warners 1978)★★
➽ p.366 for full listings

HUMAN LEAGUE

Albums

Dare (Virgin 1981)★★★★
Love And Dancing (Virgin 1982)★★★
Octopus (East West 1995)★★★
➽ p.366 for full listings

Connections

Heaven 17 ➽ p.178
Rezillos ➽ p.276

Further References

Video: *Greatest Video Hits* (Warners 1995)
Books: *The Story Of A Band Called The Human League*, Alaska Ross and Jill Furmanovsky
The Human League: Perfect Pop, Peter Nash

HUMBLE PIE
Albums
As Safe As Yesterday Is (Immediate 1969)★★★
Humble Pie (A&M 1970)★★★
Rock On (A&M 1971)★★★
➽ p.366 for full listings
Connections
Herd ➽ p.180
Small Faces ➽ p.300
Spooky Tooth ➽ p.306

HUMBLEBUMS
Albums
First Collection Of Merrie Melodies (1968)★★★
The New Humblebums (1969)★★★
Open Up The Door (1970)★★★
➽ p.366 for full listings
Connections
Gerry Rafferty ➽ p.271
Stealers Wheel ➽ p.308

HUNTER, IAN
Albums
You're Never Alone With A Schizophrenic (Chrysalis 1979)★★★
Short Back And Sides (Chrysalis 1981)★★★
as Ian Hunter's Dirty Laundry *Ian Hunter's Dirty Laundry* (Norsk 1995)★★★
➽ p.366 for full listings
Collaborators
Aynsley Dunbar ➽ p.25
David Sanborn ➽ p.288
Queen ➽ p.270
Connections
Mott The Hoople ➽ p.241
Generation X ➽ p.161
Doctor And The Medics
Sex Pistols ➽ p.292
Further References
Book: *Diary Of A Rock 'N' Roll Star*, Ian Hunter

HÜSKER DÜ
Albums
Zen Arcade (SST 1984)★★★★
Flip Your Wig (SST 1985)★★★★
Warehouse: Songs And Stories (Warners 1987)★★★★
➽ p.366 for full listings
Connections
Sugar ➽ p.313
Influences
Byrds ➽ p.77

HYLAND, BRIAN
Albums
Sealed With A Kiss (ABC 1962)★★★
Here's To Our Love (Philips 1964)★★
Brian Hyland (1970)★★
➽ p.366 for full listings

HUMBLE PIE

FORMED IN 1969, COMPRISING **PETER FRAMPTON** (GUITAR/VOCALS, EX-**HERD**), **STEVE MARRIOTT** (GUITAR/VOCALS, ex-**Small Faces**), Greg Ridley (bass, ex-**Spooky Tooth**) and Jerry Shirley (drums). The line-up had a UK Top 5 hit with its debut, 'Natural Born Bugie'. Their first two albums blended hard-rock with several acoustic tracks. Frampton departed for a solo career when they abandoned acoustic tracks. Humble Pie added former Colosseum guitarist Dave Clempson; *Smokin'* from this period was their highest ranking UK chart album. Humble Pie split in 1975.

HUMBLEBUMS

SCOTTISH FOLK-SINGING DUO COMPRISING TAM HARVEY (GUITAR/MANDOLIN) AND BILLY CONNOLLY (GUITAR/banjo). Their *First Collection of Merrie Melodies* showcased a quirky sense of humour, enhanced when Harvey was replaced by **Gerry Rafferty** who introduced a gift for melody. *The New Humblebums*, featured several excellent compositions, including 'Please Sing A Song For Us' and 'Her Father Didn't Like Me Anyway'. *Open Up The Door* confirmed Rafferty's skills but the contrast between his compositions and his partner's more whimsical offerings became too great. Connolly returned to the folk circuit before becoming a successful comedian. Rafferty began his solo career in 1971 before forming **Stealers Wheel**.

HUNTER, IAN

HUNTER'S (b. 1946) GRAVELLY VOCALS AND IMAGE-CONSCIOUS LOOKS ESTABLISHED HIM AS **MOTT THE HOOPLE**'S focal point. He remained their driving force until 1974 when he began a solo career. Mott guitarist **Mick Ronson** quit at the same time and Ronson produced and played on *Ian Hunter*, which contained the Hunter's sole UK hit, 'Once Bitten Twice Shy'. After a tour as Hunter/Ronson with Peter Arnesen (keyboards), Jeff Appleby (bass) and Dennis Elliott (drums), they parted ways. *All American Alien Boy* featured **Aynsley Dunbar**, **David Sanborn** and several members of **Queen**, but the set lacked passion. *Overnight Angels* continued this trend towards musical conservatism, although Hunter aligned himself with punk by producing *Beyond The Valley Of The Dolls* for **Generation X**. *You're Never Alone With A Schizophrenic* marked his reunion with Ronson and subsequent live dates were commemorated on *Ian Hunter Live/Welcome To The Club*. 1990 saw *YUI Otra* with Ronson. He appeared at the 1992 Freddy Mercury AIDS benefit and in 1995 fronted an all-star band, Ian Hunter's Dirty Laundry.

HÜSKER DÜ

HÜSKER DÜ (THEIR NAME MEANS 'DO YOU REMEMBER?') WERE A US PUNK TRIO FORMED IN 1979. THE MUSIC OF **Bob Mould** (guitar/vocals), Greg Norton (bass) and Grant Hart (drums) has inspired thousands of bands. They began as an aggressive hardcore thrash band before expanding to other musical formats. Their first single, 'Statues', was released on the small Reflex label in 1981. In 1982, a debut album, *Land Speed Record*, arrived on New Alliance Records, but the EP, *In A Free Land Everything Falls Apart* (1983) saw them back on Reflex. By their second EP, *Metal Circus*, Hüsker Dü had become a critics' favourite. *Zen Arcade* (1984) brought about a stylistic turning point and was followed by a non-album version of the **Byrds**' 'Eight Miles High'. A 1985 album, *New Day Rising*, maintained their reputation as a favourite of critics and college radio stations. After *Flip Your Wig* the band signed with Warner Brothers Records, and issued *Candy Apple Grey* (1986) and *Warehouse: Songs And Stories* (1987). In 1988 Hart was sacked, and the group soon disbanded. Mould and Hart continued as solo artists, before Mould formed the **Sugar** in 1991.

HYLAND, BRIAN

A DEMONSTRATION DISC, RECORDED WITH HYLAND'S (b. 1943) HIGH SCHOOL GROUP THE DELPHIS, ALERTED KAPP Records to his vocal talent. In 1960 his 'Itsy Bitsy Teenie Weenie Yellow Polkadot Bikini', topped the US charts. Having switched to ABC Paramount, the singer enjoyed further success with 'Let Me Belong To You' (1961; US Top 20) and 'Ginny Come Lately' (1962; UK Top 10), before securing a second gold award for 'Sealed With A Kiss'. Hyland continued to enjoy US chart entries, notably with 'The Joker Went Wild' and 'Run, Run, Look And See' (both 1966), and reasserted his career in 1970 with a version of the Impressions' 'Gypsy Woman'; his third million-seller. This rekindled success proved shortlived and the artist later ceased recording.

IAN, JANIS

IAN (b. JANIS EDDY FINK, 1951) STARTED OUT with the controversial 'Society's Child (Baby I've Been Thinking)'. Her dissonant, almost detached delivery, enhanced the lyricism of superior folk-rock albums, notably *For All The Seasons Of Your Mind*. *Between The Lines* contained 'At Seventeen', Ian's sole US chart topper. *Revenge* (1995) moved firmly into smooth pop.

ICE CUBE

AT 16, ICE CUBE (b. O'SHEA JACKSON, 1969) PENNED 'BOYZ 'N THE HOOD'. HIS DEBUT ALBUM DREW immediate mainstream attention with its controversial lyrical platform and was attacked for its homophobia, violence and sexism. Conversely, Ice Cube overlooks a production empire (Street Knowledge) run by a woman, and he fostered the career of female rapper Yo Yo. His defence is 'I put a mirror to black America'.

Cube produced two excellent sets, *The Predator* and *Lethal Injection*; the former included reflections on the Los Angeles riots. He starred in John Singleton's 1991 hit film, *Boyz 'N The Hood*, and later appeared in Singleton's *Higher Learning* as well as in the 1992 film *Trespassers*. Having completed four million-selling albums, Ice Cube has attracted the attention of those outside the hip hop fraternity.

ICE-T

ONE OF THE MOST OUTSPOKEN WEST COAST RAPPERS, ICE-T (b. TRACY MARROW, *c.* 1958) TAKES his name from black exploitation author Iceberg Slim. 'The Coldest Rapper' (1983), made him the first Los Angeles hip hop artist and he was subsequently held under contract by Willie Strong for several years. Disillusioned, he made his money from crime before appearing in the film *Breakin'*, which included his 'Reckless' cut on the soundtrack. He followed it with 'Killers', but the breakthrough came with 'Ya Don't Know', credited with being the first West Coast hip hop artefact. Ice-T's debut, *Rhyme Pays*, served as a mission statement: hardcore raps on street violence and survival the order of the day. His four LPs in three years, based on his experiences as an LA gang member, created a stir in the US. In 1989, he reached the UK charts with 'High Rollers', followed by a teaming with **Curtis Mayfield** on 'Superfly' (1990), before starting his own record company, Rhyme Syndicate.

In the 90s, Ice-T contributed the title track to the gangster movie *Colors*, and starred as a cop in *New Jack City*; he also appeared in the film *Trespassers*. *Home Invasion* contained 'Ice Muthafuckin' T' with the lyric, 'Every fucking thing I write, Is going to be analysed by somebody white'.

IAN, JANIS

Albums
For All The Seasons Of Your Mind (Verve 1967)★★★
Between The Lines (Columbia 1975)★★★★
Hunger (Windham Hill 1997)★★★
➧ p.366 for full listings

Further References
Book: *Who Really Cares?*, Janis Ian

ICE CUBE

Albums
AmeriKKKa's Most Wanted (Priority 1990)★★★★
Death Certificate (Priority 1991)★★★
Featuring Ice Cube (Priority 1997)★★★
➧ p.366 for full listings

Collaborators
Yo Yo
Ice-T ➧ p.191

Connections
NWA ➧ p.249
Street Knowledge
John Singleton

Further References
Films: *Boyz 'N The Hood* (1991)
Higher Learning
Trespass (1992)

ICE-T

Albums
Rhyme Pays (Sire 1987)★★★
OG: Original Gangster (Syndicate/Sire 1991)★★★★
The Ice Opinion (Ichiban 1997)★★★
➧ p.366 for full listings

Collaborators
Curtis Mayfield ➧ p.228
Ice Cube ➧ p.191
Body Count

Connections
Willie Strong
Rhyme Syndicate
Walter Hill

Influences
Iceberg Slim

Further References
Video: *OG – The Original Gangster Video* (1991)
Book: *The Ice Opinion*, Ice-T and Heidi Seigmund
Film: *Breakdance*

ICICLE WORKS
Albums
The Icicle Works (Beggars Banquet 1984)★★★
p.366 for full listings
Collaborators
Ian Broudie p.69
Connections
Black p.48
Ringo Starr p.307

IDLE RACE
Albums
The Birthday Party (Liberty 1968)★★★
p.366 for full listings
Connections
Move p.241
Steve Gibbons Band p.162

IDOL, BILLY
Albums
Rebel Yell (Chrysalis 1984)★★★★
p.366 for full listings
Collaborators
Neil Young p.346
Who p.338
Connections
Chelsea p.88
Generation X p.161

IFIELD, FRANK
Albums
I'll Remember You (1963)★★★
p.366 for full listings
Further References
Film: *Up Jumped A Swagman* (1965)

ICICLE WORKS

THE ICICLE WORKS WERE FORMED BY **IAN McNABB** (b. 1962; VOCALS/GUITAR; EX-CITY LIMITS), CHRIS LAYHE (BASS) AND Chris Sharrock (drums; ex-Cherry Boys). They made their recording debut in 1981 with a mini-LP, *Ascending*, before founding their Troll Kitchen label and releasing 'Nirvana'. They came to the attention of Beggars Banquet Records and 'Birds Fly (Whisper To A Scream)' was an indie hit. The following 'Love Is A Wonderful Colour' reached the UK Top 20. With producer **Ian Broudie**, their sound gradually shifted from subtle pop to harder rock. Layhe was replaced by Roy Corkhill (ex-**Black**), and Sharrock by Zak Starkey, son of **Ringo Starr**. This line-up prospered for a while but in 1989 McNabb assembled a new band. They signed a new contract with Epic and released an album before McNabb went solo.

IDLE RACE

DAVE PRITCHARD (GUITAR), GREG MASTERS (BASS) AND ROGER SPENCER (DRUMS) STARTED AS THE NIGHTRIDERS in 1966, but when guitarist/composer **Jeff Lynne** (b. 1947) joined, the group took the name Idle Race.

By 1967, Lynne was contributing the bulk of their original material; he also produced their second album, *Idle Race*; however, public indifference led to Lynne's departure (for the **Move**). Pritchard, Masters and Spencer recruited Mike Hopkins and Roy Collum, the latter was then replaced by Dave Walker. This reshaped quintet was responsible for *Time Is*. When Walker left, his place was taken by Birmingham veteran **Steve Gibbons**. Pritchard and Spencer left, replaced by Bob Lamb and Bob Wilson, and Dave Carroll replaced Hopkins. When Masters left in 1971, the group became the Steve Gibbons Band.

IDOL, BILLY

WHILE AT UNIVERSITY, UK-BORN IDOL (b. WILLIAM MICHAEL ALBERT BROAD, 1955) FORMED **CHELSEA**. He then founded **Generation X** in 1976. Idol subsequently launched his solo career in New York and recorded *Don't Stop*, featuring a revival of **Tommy James And The Shondells**' 'Mony Mony'. In 1987, he took 'Mony Mony' to US number 1, as well as reaping hits with 'White Wedding' and 'Rebel Yell'. In 1988, he performed in **Neil Young**'s Bridge School Benefit concert and, in 1989, guested in the charity performance of the **Who**'s *Tommy* in London. Idol's brand of heavy punk was perfectly honed and showcased on *Cyberpunk*.

IFIELD, FRANK

UK-BORN IFIELD (b. 1937) EMIGRATED TO AUSTRALIA AS A CHILD. IN 1957, HE came to prominence with 'Whiplash', a song about the 1851 Australian goldrush. Shortly afterwards, he reached UK number 1 with 'I Remember You', the first million-selling record in England. In 1962, Ifield was back at number 1 with 'Lovesick Blues' and then with Gogi Grant's 'The Wayward Wind'. 'Confessin'' was his fourth UK chart-topper – but the beat boom put an end to his success. He continued his career, playing in pantomime and stage productions, before reverting to cabaret work. In the 90s, Ifield was residing in Australia.

IMAGINATION

BRITISH FUNK BAND IMAGINATION WERE FORMED BY LEE JOHN (b. JOHN LESLEY McGREGOR, 1957; VOCALS), ASHLEY Ingram (b. 1960; guitar) and Errol Kennedy. They made an immediate impact with 'Body Talk', and enjoyed further UK Top 5 entries with 'Just An Illusion' and 'Music And Lights'. However, the run of hits dried up by 1984, when John left. Having switched to RCA in 1986, Imagination made a minor comeback in 1988 with 'Instinctual'.

INCREDIBLE STRING BAND

SCOTTISH FOLK GROUP FORMED IN 1965, FEATURING MIKE HERON (b. 1942), ROBIN WILLIAMSON (b. 1943) AND CLIVE Palmer. In 1966, they completed *The Incredible String Band*, a unique blend of traditional and original material, but broke up upon its completion. Heron and Williamson reunited in 1967 to record *5000 Spirits Or The Layers Of The Onion*.

Changing Horses and *I Looked Up* demonstrated a transformation to a rock-based perspective although *U* reflected something of their earlier charm. Malcolm Le Maistre joined for *Liquid Acrobat As Regards The Air* and Gerald Dott (woodwinds/keyboard) joined for *No Ruinous Feud*. By this point, the two founding members were becoming estranged, musically and socially. In 1974, they ended their partnership.

INDIGO GIRLS

AMY RAY (b. 1964; VOCALS/GUITAR) AND EMILY SALIERS (b. 1963; VOCALS/GUITAR) MET WHILE AT SCHOOL IN Georgia, USA. They started to perform together, initially as the B Band, then as Saliers And Ray. As Indigo Girls, they released *Strange Fire* before signing to Epic in 1988. *Indigo Girls* featured Michael Stipe (**R.E.M.**) and **Hothouse Flowers**, included 'Closer To Fine', went gold and won a Grammy. *Rites Of Passage* featured traditional songs such as 'The Water Is Wide' alongside a cover of **Dire Straits**' 'Romeo And Juliet', making it the Indigo Girls' broadest set to date. *Swamp Ophelia* (1993) saw the duo swap acoustic for electric guitars. *Shaming Of The Sun* broke no new ground.

INGRAM, JAMES

US-BORN INGRAM (b. 1956) FORMED REVELATION FUNK IN THE 70S; HE ALSO WORKED AS A DEMO SINGER AND IS featured on **Quincy Jones**'s *The Dude* (1981). Signed to Jones's Qwest label, Ingram had a US number 1 duetting with **Patti Austin** on 'Baby, Come To Me' in 1981. In 1984, he released *It's Your Night*, which spawned the hit 'Ya Mo B There'. Ingram's subsequent albums, *Never Felt So Good* and *It's Real*, failed to live up to the promise of his earlier work, however his compositions include 'P.Y.T. (Pretty Young Thing)' (written with Jones), for **Michael Jackson**'s hit *Thriller*.

INSPIRAL CARPETS

UK BAND INSPIRAL CARPETS WAS FORMED BY GRAHAM LAMBERT (guitar) and Stephen Holt (vocals); they recruited drummer Craig Gill, organist Clint Boon and bassist David Swift. Boon's **Doors**-influenced playing later became the group's trademark. After their debut EP, *Planecrash*, the group were asked to record a **John Peel** session for BBC Radio 1. In 1988, the band left their label acrimoniously; Holt and Swift were replaced by Tom Hingley and Martyn Walsh and the band signed with Mute Records. 'This Is How It Feels' was a hit and *Life* was critically acclaimed, although further singles had less impact. The band were released from Mute in 1995 with their former company issuing an epitaph, *The Singles*.

INTELLIGENT HOODLUM

THE HOODLUM (b. PERCY CHAPMAN, *c.* 1968) FIRST RELEASED 'COKE IS IT', LATER RE-TITLED 'TRAGEDY', at the age of 14. His next move was to Rikers Island prison, on a drug-related sentence, where he spent his time reading. The Intelligent Hoodlum moniker indicated he'd renounced his illegal moves while acknowledging the part his criminal past had played in his development. Now a practising Muslim, and affiliated to the Nation of Islam, Hoodlum also set up his own organization, MAAPS – Movement Against the American Power Structure.

INXS

FORMED IN SYDNEY, AUSTRALIA IN 1977. INITIALLY NAMED THE FARRISS BROTHERS, INXS COMPRISED TIM (b. 1957; guitar), Jon (b. 1961; drums) and Andrew Farriss (b. 1959; keyboards), Michael Hutchence (b. 1960, d. 1997; lead vocals), Kirk Pengilly (b. 1958; guitar/saxophone/vocals) and Garry Beers (b. 1957; bass/vocals). Their recording career began in 1980 with 'Simple Simon'. Their second album, *Underneath The Colours*, sold well, and the following *Shabooh Shoobah* reached the Top 5.

'Original Sin' (1985) and the accompanying *The Swing*, reached Australian number 1 and *Listen Like Thieves* consolidated their worldwide success, although the UK proved a problematic market. They toured the States and Europe constantly, and the overwhelming success of *Kick* brought a transatlantic hit with 'Need You Tonight' in 1988. Before the release of *X*, all members had a 12-month break. Their 1993 set, *Full Moon, Dirty Hearts*, included the single 'The Gift' and a Hutchence/Chrissie Hynde (**Pretenders**) duet, 'Kill The Pain'. The video of 'The Gift' was banned by MTV, due to its use of Holocaust and Gulf War footage. Tragically, in November 1997, Michael Hutchence was found hanged in his hotel room.

IRON BUTTERFLY

IRON BUTTERFLY WAS FORMED IN THE USA BY DOUG INGLE (b. 1946; ORGAN/VOCALS) WHO ADDED RON BUSHY (b. 1941; drums), Eric Brann (b. 1950; guitar), Lee Dorman (b. 1945; bass/vocals) and, briefly, Danny Weiss. *In-A-Gadda-Da-Vida* (*In The Garden Of Eden*) became a multi-million seller and the record industry's first platinum disc. The follow-up, *Ball*, was a lesser success. Brann was later replaced by two guitarists, Larry 'Rhino' Rheinhart (b. 1948) and Mike Pinera (b. 1948), and *Metamorphosis* was a confused collection.

By 1993, their second album had sold 25 million copies. In 1995, the band re-formed for an anniversary tour.

IRON MAIDEN

FORMED IN LONDON, ENGLAND, IN 1976, BY STEVE HARRIS (b. 1957; BASS). IRON MAIDEN WERE THE FOREMOST BAND in the new wave of British heavy metal. After several personnel changes, their debut EP featured Harris, Dave Murray (b. 1958; guitar), Paul Di'anno (b. 1959; vocals) and Doug Sampson (drums). The group made its live debut in 1977 and released *The Soundhouse Tapes*.

In 1979, guitarist Tony Parsons joined for *Metal For Muthas*, however he was replaced shortly by Dennis Stratton (b. 1954); Sampson was replaced by Clive Burr (b. 1957). **Iron Maiden**, a roughly produced album, reached UK number 4 after a tour with **Judas Priest**. The superior *Killers* saw Stratton replaced by Adrian Smith (b. 1957). The release of *Number Of The Beast* was crucial to the band's development; it was also the debut of Di'anno's replacement Bruce Dickinson (b. Paul Bruce Dickinson, 1958). *Piece Of Mind* continued their success, reaching US number 14. *Powerslave* was heavily criticized, but their reputation was saved by *Live After Death*, a double album package of their best-loved material recorded live on their 11-month world tour. *Somewhere In Time* was a slight departure, featuring more melody than before, and heralding the use of guitar synthesizers. After a slight hiatus, the concept album, *Seventh Son Of A Seventh Son* was released.

After another world trek, the band announced a year's break, during which Dickinson released the solo *Tattooed Millionaire* and a book, *The Adventures Of Lord Iffy Boatrace*. The group planned a return to the old style (which saw Adrian Smith leave, replaced by Janick Gers) and the live show was to be scaled down in a return to much smaller venues. *No Prayer For The Dying* was reminiscent of mid-period Iron Maiden, and was well-received, bringing enormous UK hits with 'Holy Smoke' and 'Bring Your Daughter To The Slaughter' (their first UK number 1). Another world tour followed and, despite being denounced 'satanists' in Chile, 1992 saw the band debut at UK number 1 with *Fear Of The Dark*. Despite this, Dickinson left shortly afterwards. His replacement was Blaze Bayley (b. 1963) who debuted on *X-Factor* – easily proving his worth. Smith resurfaced in Psycho Motel, in 1996.

ISAACS, GREGORY

JAMAICAN SUPERSTAR ISAACS (b. 1951) BEGAN WITH RUPIE EDWARDS' SUCCESS RECORDS IN THE EARLY 70S. HE SET up his own African Museum shop and label in 1973 and, by 1980, had signed to Front Line, becoming the number one star in the reggae world.

A new contract with Charisma Records' Pre label set up the UK release of two further classic albums. He was, however, beset by personal and legal problems in the mid-80s and was even jailed in Kingston's notorious General Penitentiary – his release was celebrated with *Out Deh*. Rumours abound about Gregory's rude-boy lifestyle, but he would claim he has to be tough to maintain his position within Kingston's notorious musical industry.

ISAAK, CHRIS

CALIFORNIAN ISAAK (b. 1956) STARTED OUT IN ROCKABILLY BAND SILVERTONE, WITH JAMES CALVIN WILSEY (guitar), Rowland Salley (bass) and Kenney Dale Johnson (drums). All remained with Isaak as his permanent backing band. His debut *Silvertone* was raw and diverse, while the self-titled follow-up saw him hone his style to sophisticated R&B; he finally achieved a major hit with 'Wicked Game'. His acting career has ploughed a parallel path with cameo roles in *Married To The Mob*, *Silence Of The Lambs* and the hit TV show *Friends*.

IMAGINATION
Albums
Body Talk (R&B 1981)★★
➽ p.366 for full listings

INCREDIBLE STRING BAND
Albums
5000 Spirits Or The Layers Of The Onion (Elektra 1967)★★★★
➽ p.366 for full listings

INDIGO GIRLS
Albums
Indigo Girls (Epic 1989)★★★
➽ p.366 for full listings
Collaborators
R.E.M. ➽ p.275
Hothouse Flowers ➽ p.187
Connections
Wonder Stuff ➽ p.343

INGRAM, JAMES
Albums
It's Your Night (Qwest 1983)★★
➽ p.366 for full listings
Collaborators
Quincy Jones ➽ p.201
Michael Jackson ➽ p.195

INSPIRAL CARPETS
Albums
Life (Mute 1990)★★★
➽ p.366 for full listings
Influences
Doors ➽ p.123

INTELLIGENT HOODLUM
Albums
Saga Of A Hoodlum (A&M 1993)★★★★
➽ p.366 for full listings
Influences
Chuck D ➽ p.91

INXS
Albums
Kick (Mercury 1987)★★★
➽ p.366 for full listings
Connections
Chrissie Hynde ➽ p.266
Kylie Minogue ➽ p.234

IRON BUTTERFLY
Albums
In-A-Gadda-Da-Vida (Atco 1968)★★★★
➽ p.366 for full listings

IRON MAIDEN
Albums
Seventh Son Of A Seventh Son (EMI 1988)★★★★
➽ p.366 for full listings
Collaborators
Judas Priest ➽ p.202

ISAACS, GREGORY
Albums
Out Deh! (Mango/Island 1983)★★★★
➽ p.366 for full listings

ISAAK, CHRIS
Albums
Chris Isaak (Warners 1987)★★★
➽ p.366 for full listings

ISHAM, MARK
Albums
Vapour Drawings (Windham Hill 1983)★★★★
➧ p.366 for full listings
Collaborators
Van Morrison ➧ p.238
Suzanne Vega ➧ p.329

ISLE OF WIGHT FESTIVAL
Connections
Bob Dylan ➧ p.128
Who ➧ p.338
Joe Cocker ➧ p.95
Band ➧ p.31
Jimi Hendrix ➧ p.180
Taste ➧ p.317
Family ➧ p.143
Doors ➧ p.123
Ten Years After ➧ p.318
Sly And The Family Stone ➧ p.300
Leonard Cohen ➧ p.96
Jethro Tull ➧ p.199

ISLEY BROTHERS
Albums
Twist And Shout (Wand 1962)★★★★
➧ p.366 for full listings
Collaborators
Jimi Hendrix ➧ p.180
Connections
Beatles ➧ p.38
Holland/Dozier/Holland ➧ p.183
Four Tops ➧ p.152
Influences
Motown ➧ p.240
Jimi Hendrix ➧ p.180
James Brown ➧ p.70
Bob Dylan ➧ p.128
Stephen Stills ➧ p.310
Carole King ➧ p.205

IT'S A BEAUTIFUL DAY
Albums
It's A Beautiful Day (Columbia 1969)★★★
➧ p.366 for full listings
Collaborators
Cream ➧ p.103

JACKSON, JANET
Albums
Janet (Virgin 1993)★★★★
➧ p.367 for full listings
Collaborators
Paula Abdul ➧ p.7

JACKSON, JERMAINE
Albums
Let's Get Serious (Motown 1980)★★★
➧ p.367 for full listings
Collaborators
Devo ➧ p.117
Stevie Wonder ➧ p.342
Connections
Motown ➧ p.240

JACKSON, JOE
Albums
Night And Day (A&M 1982)★★★★
➧ p.367 for full listings

ISHAM, MARK

MARK ISHAM (b. *c.* 50S) BEGAN STUDYING THE JAZZ TRUMPET WHILE AT SCHOOL AND EXPLORED ELECTRONIC in his early 20s. For a time he pursued parallel careers as a classical, jazz and rock musician, but by the early 70s, he concentrated on jazz. As co-leader of pianist Art Lande's Rubisa Patrol, he recorded two albums in the late 70s. Together with Peter Mannu (guitar), Patrick O'Hearn (synthesizer) and Terry Bozzio (drums), he set up Group 87 in 1979, releasing a self-titled debut album in 1981.

Isham then recorded and toured as part of **Van Morrison**'s band and, during the 80s, developed his compositional skills, to produce a very visual, narrative form of music. He has taken that thread into film music, scoring the award-winning documentary *The Life And Times Of Harvey Milk*, the film *Mrs Soffel*, and writing music to accompany children's fairy tales. Throughout his career, Isham has remained a prolific session man, whose work encompasses recordings with artists as varied as saxophonist David Liebman, and **Suzanne Vega**.

ISLE OF WIGHT FESTIVAL

THE UK'S ANSWER TO **WOODSTOCK**. THE FIRST, LOW-PROFILE, ISLE OF WIGHT EVENT PRECEDED ITS COUNTER-part by a year. However, it was the publicity explosion resulting from Woodstock, together with the stimulus of a summer of free Hyde Park festivals, which fuelled the success of the 1969 IOW Festival. **Bob Dylan** headlined alongside acts including the **Who**, **Joe Cocker** and the **Band**. The 1969 festival was marred by poor organization but that did not stop the event being repeated the following August Bank Holiday. The 1970 line-up included **Jimi Hendrix**, **Taste**, **Family**, the **Doors**, **Ten Years After**, **Sly And The Family Stone**, **Leonard Cohen** and **Jethro Tull**. The organizers (the Foulk brothers) were less than pleased as their losses mounted, and declared that there would be no more Isle Of Wight Festivals.

ISLEY BROTHERS

THREE BROTHERS, O'KELLY (b. 1937, d. 1986), RUDOLPH (b. 1939) AND RONALD ISLEY (b. 1941), BEGAN SINGING GOSPEL in their home town of Cincinnati, USA, in the early 50s, accompanied by their brother Vernon, who died in a car crash around 1957. Moving to New York, the trio issued one-off singles before being signed by RCA. The Isleys had already developed a tight vocal unit, with Rudolph and O'Kelly supporting Ronald's strident tenor leads. The self-composed 'Shout' epitomized this approach. The group switched labels to Wand in 1962, where they enjoyed a major hit with a cover version of the Top Notes' 'Twist And Shout', an arrangement that was subsequently copied by the **Beatles**.

A brief spell with Atlantic Records in 1964 produced a classic R&B record, 'Who's That Lady?', but with little success. Tired of the lack of control over their recordings, the Isleys formed their own company, T-Neck Records, in 1964 – an unprecedented step for black performers. The label's first release, 'Testify', showcased their young lead guitarist, **Jimi Hendrix**, and allowed him free rein to display his virtuosity and range of sonic effects. However, the record's experimental sound went unnoticed at the time, and the Isleys were forced to abandon both T-Neck and Hendrix, and sign a contract with **Motown**. They were allowed little involvement in the production of their records and the group were teamed with the **Holland/Dozier/Holland** partnership, who effectively treated them as an extension of the **Four Tops**, fashioning songs for them accordingly.

Tired of the formula and company power games, the Isleys reactivated T-Neck in 1969, along with a change of image from the regulation mohair suits to a freer, funkier 'west coast' image, reflected in their choice of repertoire. At this point they recruited their two younger brothers, Ernie (b. 1952; guitar) and Marvin (bass), as well as a cousin, Chris Jasper (keyboards). While their mid-60s recordings were enjoying overdue success in Britain, the Isleys were scoring enormous US hits with their new funk-influenced releases, notably 'It's Your Thing' and 'I Turned You On'. They issued a succession of ambitious albums in this vein between 1969 and 1972, among them a live double set that featured extended versions of their recent hits, and *In The Beginning*, a collection of their 1964 recordings with Jimi Hendrix.

In the early 70s, the Isleys incorporated into their repertoire a variety of rock material by composers such as **Bob Dylan**, **Stephen Stills** and **Carole King**. Their dual role as composers and interpreters reached a peak in 1973 on *3+3*, the first album issued via a distribution agreement with CBS Records. Ernie's powerful, sustained guitar-work, strongly influenced by Hendrix, became a vital ingredient in the Isleys' sound, and was featured heavily on the album's 'That Lady'. Throughout the rest of the 70s, the Isleys issued a succession of slick, impressive soul albums, divided between startlingly tough funk numbers and subdued ballads. *The Heat Is On* (1975) represented the pinnacle of both genres and 'Harvest For The World' (1976) proved to be one of their most popular recordings in Britain. 'It's A Disco Night', a UK hit in 1980, demonstrated their command of the idiom, but a growing sense of self-parody infected the Isleys' music in the early 80s.

Ernie and Marvin Isley and Chris Jasper left in 1984 to form the successful Isley, Jasper, Isley combination. The original trio soldiered on, but the sudden death of O'Kelly from a heart attack on 31 March 1986 brought their 30-year partnership to an end. Ronald and Rudolph dedicated *Smooth Sailin'* to him.

IT'S A BEAUTIFUL DAY

THIS SAN FRANCISCO-BASED UNIT CENTERED ON THE VIRTUOSO SKILLS OF VIOLINIST DAVID LaFLAMME. PATTI Santos (b. 1949, d. 1989; vocals), Hal Wagenet (guitar), Linda LaFlamme (b. 1941; keyboards), Mitchell Holman (bass) and Val Fluentes (drums) completed the line-up which won a major recording contract in the wake of its appearance on **Cream**'s farewell concert bill. *It's A Beautiful Day* was marked by 'White Bird' with which the group is inexorably linked. Subsequent releases, *Marrying Maiden*, *Choice Quality Stuff* and *Live At Carnegie Hall* showed a pot-pourri of musical influences. LaFlamme later abandoned his creation after a protracted lawsuit. Late period members Bud Cockrell (bass) and David Jenkins (guitar) resurfaced in Pablo Cruise, while Linda and Santos enjoyed low-key solo careers. The violinist briefly resuscitated the band in 1978 as It Was A Beautiful Day.

JACKSON, JANET

JANET (b. 1966) IS THE YOUNGEST OF THE FAMILY THAT PRODUCED THE **Jackson Five**. She signed to A&M Records in 1982, recording her self-titled debut album, followed by *Dream Street*. Both albums sold only moderately. Jackson's breakthrough came with *Control*, which reached number 1 and ultimately sold over

four million copies in the USA. *Janet Jackson's Rhythm Nation 1814* was followed by a concert tour in 1990. By the end of the year she had scooped eight *Billboard* awards. *Janet* entered the US album chart at number 1. The compilation album *Design Of A Decade* was another huge seller, and her first studio set in four years, *The Velvet Rope*, was a deeply personal album which dealt frankly with her much self-publicized emotional breakdown.

JACKSON, JERMAINE

JERMAINE (b. 1954) WAS A MEMBER OF THE **JACKSON FIVE**. BESIDES PLAYING BASS, HE ACTED AS VOCAL COUNTER-point to his younger brother **Michael Jackson**. Like his brothers Michael and Jackie, Jermaine was singled out by Motown for a solo career, and had an immediate US Top 10 hit with 'Daddy's Home', in 1972. When the other members of the Jackson Five decided to leave Motown in 1975, he elected to remain. **Stevie Wonder** wrote and produced 'Let's Get Serious' in 1979. 'You Like Me Don't You' brought him another hit as did 'Let Me Tickle Your Fancy', an unlikely collaboration with **Devo**. In 1984, he joined the Jacksons on the *Victory* album and tour, and his own *Jermaine Jackson* featured a sparkling duet with Michael on 'Tell Me We're Not Dreaming'.

JACKSON, JOE

UK-BORN JACKSON (b. 1955) WAS SIGNED BY A&M RECORDS IN 1978. HIS DEBUT, 'IS SHE REALLY GOING OUT WITH HIM?' was not an immediate hit, but by the time *Look Sharp* was released, the song had become one of the stand-out numbers of his live shows. The reggaefied *Beat Crazy* began a trend of changing musical direction. *Jumpin' Jive* was a throwback to the music of the 40s. One of his most satisfying works came in 1982 with *Night And Day*. *Body And Soul* was also critically acclaimed, but after this Jackson's fortunes began to decline and *Blaze Of Glory* was a commercial failure. In 1991 he signed to Virgin Records, releasing *Laughter And Lust*.

JACKSON, LaTOYA

LaTOYA (b. 1956) SERVED AS A BACKING VOCALIST TO THE **JACKSONS** BEFORE EMBARKING ON A SOLO CAREER WITH Polydor in 1980. But she couldn't emulate the success of her younger sister Janet; her highest single chart position was with the US number 56, 'Hearts Don't Lie' (1984).

JACKSON, MICHAEL

JACKSON (b. 1958) WAS A FOUNDER-MEMBER OF THE **JACKSON FIVE** AT THE AGE OF FOUR AND SOON BECAME the group's lead vocalist. The Jackson Five were signed to **Motown Records** at the end of 1968; their early releases, including chart-toppers 'I Want You Back' and 'I'll Be There', illustrated his remarkable maturity.

Michael Jackson's first solo release was 'Got To Be There', a major US and UK hit. His revival of 'Rockin' Robin' (1972) reached US number 1, as did the sentimental film theme 'Ben'. As the Jackson Five's sales slipped in the mid-70s, Michael's solo career was put on hold. He continued to reserve his talents for the group after they were reborn as the **Jacksons** in 1976. He re-entered the public eye with a starring role in the film musical *The Wiz*, collaborating on the soundtrack album with **Quincy Jones**. Their partnership was renewed in 1979 when Jones produced *Off The Wall*, which topped the charts in the UK and USA, and contained two number 1s, 'Don't Stop Till You Get Enough' and 'Rock With You'.

Jackson continued to tour and record with the Jacksons after this solo success, while media speculation grew about his private life; he was increasingly portrayed as a figure trapped in eternal childhood. In 1982 *Thriller*, Jackson's second album with Quincy Jones, was released, and has become one of the most commercially successful albums of all time. It produced a run of successful hit singles, each accompanied by a ground-breaking promotional video.

Amidst this run of hits, he slotted in 'Say Say Say', his second chart-topping duet, with **Paul McCartney**. Jackson had by now become an almost mythical figure: a group of Jehovah's Witnesses announced that he was the Messiah; he was said to be taking drugs to change his skin colour to white; it was claimed that he had undergone extensive plastic surgery to alter his appearance; and photographs were published that suggested he slept in a special chamber to prevent himself ageing. More prosaically, Jackson began 1985 by co-writing and performing on the international number 1 USA For Africa benefit single 'We Are The World'. *Bad*, again with Quincy Jones, sold in multi-millions, but in comparison with *Thriller*, it was deemed disappointing. Unabashed, Jackson undertook a lengthy world concert tour to promote the album, and published his autobiography, *Moonwalker*. The long-awaited *Dangerous* justifiably scaled the charts.

In 1993, the world was shocked by allegations of child sexual abuse directed at Jackson. No charges were made, but Jackson left the USA and went into hiding. In 1994, Jackson married Lisa Marie Presley ; the marriage collapsed 19 months later, giving further rise to media allegations that it was merely a set-up to improve his soiled image. He did, however, enhance his reputation with *HIStory Past, Present And Future, Book 1*. One half of the double set chronicled his past hits, but there was the equivalent of a new album forming the second half. *Blood On The Dancefloor – HIStory In The Mix* was a collection of remixes and new material that spawned further hit singles.

JACKSON, MILLIE

US-BORN MILLIE JACKSON'S (b. 1944) CONTROVERSIAL SINGING CAREER BEGAN PROFESSIONALLY IN 1964. 'HURTS So Good' was a big hit and her subsequent direction was shaped in 1974 with the release of *Caught Up*. The sexual element in her work embraced either the pose of adultress or of wronged wife. *Still Caught Up* continued the saga, but Jackson's style later verged on self-parody. *Feelin' Bitchy* and *Live And Uncensored* required warning stickers.

JACKSON FIVE

THE JACKSON FIVE – BROTHERS JACKIE (b. SIGMUND ESCO Jackson, 1951), Tito (b. Toriano Adaryll Jackson, 1953), **Jermaine** (b. 1954), Marlon (b. 1957) and **Michael Jackson** (b. 1958) – began playing local Indiana clubs in 1962, with Michael as lead vocalist. They signed to **Motown Records** in 1968. Their debut single, 'I Want You Back', became the fastest-selling record in the company's history and three of their next five singles also reached US number 1. By 1973, they had dropped the teenage stylings of their early hits, and perfected a harder brand of funk. In 1975 they signed to Epic, leading Motown boss Berry Gordy to sue them for alleged breach of contract. The case was settled in 1980, with the brothers paying Gordy $600,000, and allowing Motown all rights to the 'Jackson Five' name.

JACKSON, LATOYA
Albums
Hearts Don't Lie (Private Stock 1984)★★
➽ p.367 for full listings

JACKSON, MICHAEL
Albums
Thriller (Epic 1982)★★★★★
HIStory Past, Present And Future, Book 1 (Epic 1995)★★★★
➽ p.367 for full listings
Collaborators
Paul McCartney ➽ p.229
Quincy Jones ➽ p.201
Connections
John Lennon ➽ p.214
Influences
Motown ➽ p.240
Further References
Video: *Michael Jackson: The Magic And The Madness*
Book: *Moonwalker*, Michael Jackson

JACKSON, MILLIE
Albums
Caught Up (Spring 1974)★★★★
➽ p.367 for full listings
Collaborators
Elton John ➽ p.200

JACKSON FIVE
Albums
ABC (Motown 1970)★★★★
➽ p.367 for full listings
Influences
Motown ➽ p.240
Further References
Book: *Jackson Five*, Charles Morse

JACKSONS
Albums
Destiny (Epic 1978)★★★★
➽ p.367 for full listings
Collaborators
Michael Jackson ➽ p.195

JAH WOBBLE
Albums
Take Me To God (Island 1994)★★★★
➽ p.367 for full listings
Collaborators
Edge ➽ p.326
Sinead O'Connor ➽ p.250
Primal Scream ➽ p.267
Brian Eno ➽ p.136
Connections
Public Image Limited ➽ p.269

JAM
Albums
All Mod Cons (Polydor 1978)★★★★
➽ p.367 for full listings
Connections
Paul Weller ➽ p.336
Kinks ➽ p.207
Stiff Little Fingers ➽ p.310
Style Council ➽ p.312
Influences
Who ➽ p.338
Kinks ➽ p.207
Further References
Book: *The Jam: A Beat Concerto, The Authorized Biography*, Paolo Hewitt

JAMES
Albums
Gold Mother (Fontana 1990)★★★★
➽ p.367 for full listings
Collaborators
Brian Eno ➽ p.136
Further References
Video: *Come Home Live* (Polygram 1991)

JAMES, ELMORE
Connections
Jimi Hendrix ➽ p.180
Fleetwood Mac ➽ p.147
John Mayall ➽ p.228
➽ p.367 for full listings

JAMES, ETTA
Albums
Tell Mama (Cadet 1968)★★★★
➽ p.367 for full listings
Influences
Muddy Waters ➽ p.242
Further References
Book: *Rage To Survive*, Etta James with David Ritz

JAMES, RICK
Albums
Street Songs (Gordy 1981)★★★★
➽ p.367 for full listings
Collaborators
Neil Young ➽ p.346
Smokey Robinson ➽ p.279
Connections
Temptations ➽ p.318
Motown ➽ p.240

JACKSONS

JACKIE (b. SIGMUND ESCO JACKSON, 1951), TITO (b. TORIANO ADARYLL JACKSON, 1953), MARLON (b. 1957), **MICHAEL** (b. 1958) and Randy Jackson (b. Steven Randall Jackson, 1962) changed from the **Jackson Five** to the Jacksons in 1976, following their departure from **Motown Records**. At the same time, Randy replaced his brother **Jermaine**. They had difficulty continuing their former incarnation's success, although 'Blame It On The Boogie' caught the mood of the burgeoning disco market. The Jacksons' 1981 US tour emphasized Michael's dominance over the group, and the resulting *Live* included many of his solo hits. Between 1981 and the release of *Victory* in 1984, Michael issued *Thriller*. By now media and public attention was focused firmly on Michael and after internal arguments he eventually left the group. It was five years before the Jacksons' next project was complete. *2300 Jackson Street* highlighted their dilemma: once the media realized that Michael was not involved, they lost interest.

JAH WOBBLE

AN INNOVATIVE BASS PLAYER, LONDON-BORN WOBBLE (b. JOHN WARDLE) BEGAN HIS CAREER WITH **PUBLIC IMAGE Limited.** By 1980, Wobble had gone solo. 1983 saw him joining with his hero Holger Czukay and **U2**'s The Edge for *Snake Charmer*. In 1987, he met guitarist Justin Adams and they put together Invaders Of The Heart and unexpectedly achieved a return to the mainstream. Wobble was in demand again, notably as collaborator with **Sinead O'Connor** and **Primal Scream**. This was quickly followed by Invaders Of The Heart's *Rising Above Bedlam*. Wobble's creative renaissance has continued into the 90s, and, in 1995, he collaborated with **Brian Eno** on *Spanner*.

JAM

UK GROUP – **PAUL WELLER** (b. 1958; VOCALS/GUITAR), BRUCE FOXTON (b. 1955; BASS/VOCALS) AND RICK BUCKLER (b. Paul Richard Buckler, 1955; drums) – who were signed to Polydor Records in 1977. Although emerging at the peak of punk, the Jam seemed divorced from the movement, with their musical influences firmly entrenched in the mod style. Their debut, 'In The City', was a high-energy outing and the follow-up, 'All Around The World', infiltrated the UK Top 20. For the next year, they registered only minor hits.

A turning point in the group's fortunes occurred with the release of 'Down In The Tube Station At Midnight' (1978). This song saw them emerge as social commentators *par excellence*. *All Mod Cons* was widely acclaimed and thereafter the group rose to extraordinary heights. With *Setting Sons*, Weller fused visions of British colonialism with urban decay. Its superbly constructed 'Eton Rifles' (1979) gave the Jam their first UK Top 10 single. In 1980, they secured their first UK number 1 with 'Going Underground'. While they continued to log number 1s with 'Start' and 'A Town Called Malice', the US market remained untapped.

In 1982, the group's run of UK chart-toppers was interrupted by 'The Bitterest Pill (I Ever Had To Swallow)' which peaked at number 2. Weller then announced that they were disbanding. Their final single, 'Beat Surrender', entered the UK chart at number 1, an extraordinary conclusion to a remarkable but brief career.

JAMES

TIMOTHY BOOTH (b. 1960; VOCALS), JAMES GLENNIE (b. 1963; BASS), JAMES GOTT (GUITAR) AND GAVAN WHELAN (drums) signed with Manchester's Factory Records in 1983. They signed to Sire Records in 1985 and released *Stutter*. Dave Baynton-Power later replaced Whelan and the group was augmented by Saul Davies (guitar/violin), Mark Hunter (keyboards) and Andy Diagram (trumpet). Fontana Records re-released an earlier track, 'Sit Down' which reached UK number 2. *Seven* marked a change of direction and an emphasis on unconventional song structures. The upshot was a fall-off in commercial viability. *Laid* and its hit single was the first to make an impression in the USA. The move into ambient electronics had been signposted by the 1993 Sabres Of Paradise remix of 'Jam J'. In 1997, the group released *Whiplash* and the hit single 'She's A Star'.

JAMES, ELMORE

MISSISSIPPI LEGEND ELMORE JAMES (b. 1918, d. 1963) IS CHIEFLY recalled for his debut release, 'Dust My Broom', which was marked by James's unfettered vocals and searing electric slide guitar. James moved to Chicago where he formed the Broomdusters. Subsequent recordings, including 'Bleeding Heart' and 'Shake Your Moneymaker', were later adopted by **Jimi Hendrix** and **Fleetwood Mac** and James's distinctive 'bottleneck' style resurfaced in countless British blues bands. **John Mayall**'s 'Mr. James' was a thoughtful tribute to this significant performer who suffered a fatal heart attack in May 1963.

JAMES, ETTA

JAMES'S (b. JAMESETTA HAWKINS, 1938) 'ROLL WITH ME HENRY', LATER RETITLED 'THE WALLFLOWER' IN AN EFFORT to disguise its risqué lyric, became an R&B number 1. Having secured a contract with Chess, Californian James unleashed a series of powerful songs, including 'All I Could Do Was Cry' (1960) and 'Pushover' (1963). In 1967 Chess took her to the Fame studios and the resultant *Tell Mama* was a triumph. *Etta James* earned her a US Grammy nomination.

Etta Is Betta Than Evah completed her Chess contract, and she moved to Warner Brothers. The live *Late Show* albums were followed by *Seven Year Itch*, her first album for Island. This, and the subsequent *Stickin' To My Guns*, found her back on form. Following the use in a television advertisement of her version of **Muddy Waters**' 'I Just Want To Make Love To You', she found herself near the top of the UK charts in 1996, followed by *Love's Been Rough On Me*.

JAMES, RICK

THE NEPHEW OF **TEMPTATIONS** VOCALIST MELVIN FRANKLIN, JAMES (b. JAMES JOHNSON, 1948) PIONEERED A CROSS-over style between R&B and rock in the mid-60s. In 1965, he formed the Mynah Birds with **Neil Young** and **Motown Records** signed the band. In the early 70s, James formed the funk combo Main Line and he rapidly evolved a more individual style, which he labelled 'punk funk'. *Street Songs* was a Grammy-nominated record that catapulted James into the superstar bracket. His drift towards a more conservative image was heightened when he duetted with **Smokey Robinson** on 'Ebony Eyes'. He was angered by constant media comparisons of his work with that of **Prince**, and cancelled plans to star in an autobiographical film in the wake of his rival's *Purple Rain*. After releasing *The Flag* in 1986, he signed to Reprise Records, where he immediately achieved a soul number 1 with 'Loosey's Rap'. Impeded by drug problems, James was jailed in 1991 for various offences. He was released in 1996.

JAMES, TOMMY, AND THE SHONDELLS

THE SHONDELLS, COMPRISING TOMMY JAMES, LARRY COVERDALE (GUITAR), CRAIG VILLENEUVE (KEYBOARDS), Larry Wright (bass) and Jim Payne (drums), secured a deal with the local Snap label in 1962. Their first release, 'Hanky Panky' eventually sold in excess of one million copies. Signing to Roulette, James assembled a new Shondells which settled around a nucleus of Eddie Gray (guitar), Ronnie Rossman (keyboards), Mike Vale (b. 1949; bass) and Pete Lucia (drums). The addition of production/songwriting team Ritchie Cordell and Bo Gentry resulted in a string of hits, including 'I Think We're Alone Now' and 'Out Of The Blue' (1968). 'Mony Mony' (1968) was a UK number 1. James then wrote, arranged and produced 'Crimson And Clover', which topped the US chart and garnered sales of over five million copies. This desire to experiment continued with the album *Cellophane Symphony*. In 1970, the group and singer parted on amicable terms. In 1980, the singer had another million-seller with 'Three Times In Love'.

JAMES GANG

FORMED IN 1967 IN CLEVELAND, OHIO, USA, THE EMBRYONIC JAMES GANG COMPRISED GLENN SCHWARTZ (GUITAR/vocals), Tom Kriss (bass/vocals) and Jim Fox (drums/vocals). Schwartz left in 1969 but **Joe Walsh** proved a competent replacement on *Yer Album*. Kriss was replaced by Dale Peters for *The James Gang Rides Again*. *Thirds* was another highlight, but Walsh quit to pursue solo ambitions. Roy Kenner (vocals) and Dom Troiano (guitar) joined Fox and Peters for *Straight Shooter* and *Passin' Thru*. Troiano was then replaced by Tommy Bolin who provided new bite and purpose, and *Bang* was a marked improvement. *Miami* coincided with Bolin's departure to **Deep Purple**, following which the James Gang was dissolved. Fox and Peters resurrected the name the following year, adding Bubba Keith (vocals) and Richard Shack (guitar) for the undistinguished *Jesse Come Home*.

JAMIROQUAI

JASON 'JAY' KAY'S UK FUNK GROUP JAMIROQUAI SIGNED TO SONY Records after the single 'When You Gonna Learn?'. Inspired by 60s funksters **Sly Stone** and **Gil Scott-Heron**, Kay (b. *c*. 1969) integrated those influences into a 90s pop format that also combined 'new age' mysticism. His first major label album entered the chart at number 1. The second album was a considerable creative improvement. Songs such as 'Kids', and 'Morning Glory' gave his obvious vocal talents better service. *Travelling Without Moving* confirmed Jamiroquai as a highly commercial act, selling to date over five and a half million copies worldwide.

JAN AND DEAN

STUDENTS AT EMERSON JUNIOR HIGH SCHOOL, LOS ANGELES, JAN BERRY (b. 1941) AND DEAN TORRANCE (b. 1940) formed the Barons but its members gradually drifted away, leaving Berry, Torrance and singer Arnie Ginsburg. In 1958, the trio recorded 'Jennie Lee' which became a surprise hit, although Torrance was drafted prior to its success. The duo went on to enjoy a Top 10 entry with 'Baby Talk'. In 1963 they released, 'Linda',which was redolent of the **Beach Boys** linking the futures of the two groups. **Brian Wilson** co-wrote 'Surf City', Jan And Dean's first number 1 hit. In 1996, Berry crashed his sports car incurring severe brain damage and ending the duo's association.

JANE'S ADDICTION

FORMED IN LOS ANGELES, USA, IN 1986, BY VOCALIST PERRY FARRELL (b. 1959). WITH THE ADDITION OF GUITARIST DAVE Navarro, bassist Eric A. and drummer Stephen Perkins, Jane's Addiction incorporated elements of punk, rock, folk and funk. They debuted with a live album which received widespread acclaim. In the USA, because of censorship, *Ritual De Lo Habitual* was released in a plain envelope with the text of the First Amendment written on it. Farrell split the band in 1992 and formed **Porno For Pyros**. In the summer of 1997, the original band reunited and two new tracks appeared on a compilation of live material, demos and out-takes.

JAPAN

FORMED IN LONDON IN EARLY 1974, THIS GROUP COMPRISED DAVID SYLVIAN (b. DAVID BATT, 1958; VOCALS), HIS brother Steve Jansen (b. Steven Batt, 1959; drums), Richard Barbieri (b. 1958; keyboards) and Mick Karn (b. Anthony Michaelides, 1958; saxophone). A second guitarist, Rob Dean, joined later. Joining Virgin Records in 1980, their fortunes improved thanks to the emergence of the New Romantic movement and they registered three UK Top 20 hits. Disagreements between Karn and Sylvian undermined the group's progress and they split in late 1982.

JARRE, JEAN-MICHEL

FRENCH-BORN JARRE'S (b. 1948) FIRST FULL-SCALE ELECTRONIC OPUS, *OXYGENE*, REACHED NUMBER 2 IN THE UK charts, signalling his arrival as a commercial force. The subsequent *Equinoxe* explored the emotive power of orchestrated electronic rhythms and melody. With *Magnetic Fields* Jarre undertook his first tour to China. 1983's *Music For Supermarkets* proved his most elusive release; just one copy was pressed and auctioned for charity before the masters were destroyed. *Zoolook* was unfavourably received and prompted a two year absence from recording. *Revolutions* appeared in the shops shortly after a London Docklands concert in 1988. *Waiting For Cousteau* earned a world record for attendance at a music concert when two million people crammed in to Paris on Bastille Day to witness 'La Defence'.

JAMES, TOMMY, AND THE SHONDELLS
Albums
I Think We're Alone Now (Roulette 1967)★★★
➽ p.367 for full listings
Connections
Billy Joel ➽ p.199

JAMES GANG
Albums
The James Gang Rides Again (ABC 1970)★★★★
➽ p.367 for full listings
Connections
Joe Walsh ➽ p.333
Deep Purple ➽ p.113

JAMIROQUAI
Albums
Travelling Without Moving (Sony 1996)★★★★
➽ p.367 for full listings
Influences
Sly Stone ➽ p.300
Gil Scott-Heron ➽ p.290

JAN AND DEAN
Albums
Ride The Wild Surf (Liberty 1964)★★★
➽ p.367 for full listings
Collaborators
Brian Wilson ➽ p.36
Beach Boys ➽ p.36
Influences
Beach Boys ➽ p.36
Further References
Book: *Jan And Dean*, Allan Clark

JANE'S ADDICTION
Albums
Nothing's Shocking (Warners 1988)★★★★
➽ p.367 for full listings
Connections
Lollapalooza concerts
Porno For Pyros ➽ p.264

JAPAN
Albums
Gentlemen Take Polaroids (Virgin 1980)★★★
➽ p.367 for full listings
Connections
Ryuichi Sakamoto ➽ p.345
Influences
Smokey Robinson And The Miracles ➽ p.279
Further References
Book: *A Tourist's Guide To Japan*, Arthur A. Pitt

JARRE, JEAN-MICHEL
Albums
Oxygene (Polydor 1977)★★★★
➽ p.367 for full listings
Influences
Pierre Schaeffer
Further References
Book: *The Unofficial Jean-Michel Jarre Biography*, Graham Needham

JARREAU, AL
Albums
Spirits And Feelings (Happy Bird 1984)★★★
➤ p.367 for full listings
Influences
Jon Hendricks ➤ p.180

JASON AND THE SCORCHERS
Albums
Thunder And Fire (A&M 1989)★★★
➤ p.367 for full listings
Influences
Hank Williams ➤ p.339

JAY AND THE AMERICANS
Albums
Come A Little Bit Closer (United Artists 1964)★★★
➤ p.367 for full listings
Collaborators
Leiber And Stoller ➤ p.214

JAYHAWKS
Albums
Tomorrow The Green Grass (American 1995)★★★★
➤ p.367 for full listings
Influences
Flying Burrito Brothers ➤ p.148

JAZZ BUTCHER
Albums
Fishcotheque (Creation 1988)★★★
➤ p.367 for full listings
Connections
Bauhaus ➤ p.35

JEFFERSON AIRPLANE
Albums
Surrealistic Pillow (RCA 1967)★★★★
Crown Of Creation (RCA 1968)★★★★
➤ p.367 for full listings
Connections
Marty Balin ➤ p.30
Monterey Pop Festival ➤ p.237
Woodstock ➤ p.343
Hot Tuna ➤ p.187
Jefferson Starship ➤ p.198

JEFFERSON STARSHIP
Albums
Red Octopus (Grunt 1975)★★★★
➤ p.367 for full listings
Collaborators
Bernie Taupin ➤ p.200
Connections
Quicksilver Messenger Service ➤ p.270
Turtles ➤ p.325
Marty Balin ➤ p.30
Aynsley Dunbar ➤ p.25
Influences
Jefferson Airplane ➤ p.198

JELLYFISH
Albums
Bellybutton (Virgin 1991)★★★★
➤ p.367 for full listings
Influences
10cc ➤ p.318
Queen ➤ p.270
Badfinger ➤ p.28

JARREAU, AL

JARREAU'S (b. 1940) STYLE DISPLAYS MANY INFLUENCES, INCLUDING JAZZ, THE WORK OF **JON HENDRICKS** AND African and Oriental music. More commercially successful than most jazz singers, Jarreau's work in the 70s and 80s consistently appealed to young audiences attuned to fusions in popular music. He has continued into the 90s.

JASON AND THE SCORCHERS

THIS COUNTRY ROCK 'N' ROLL-STYLED US BAND COMPRISED JASON RINGENBERG (b. 1959; VOCALS, GUITAR, harmonica), Warner Hodges (b. 1959; guitar), Jeff Johnson (bass) and Perry Bags (b. 1962; drums). After four albums the Scorchers split up. Jason Ringenberg's solo debut was *One Foot In The Honky Tonk*. The band re-formed and released *A Blazing Grace*, and under their original name, Jason And The Nashville Scorchers, they released *Reckless Country Soul*, a collection of their old material.

JAY AND THE AMERICANS

THIS NEW YORK-BASED ACT WAS FORMED IN 1961 WHEN FORMER MYSTICS VOCALIST JOHN 'JAY' TRAYNOR (b. 1938) joined ex-Harbor Lites duo Kenny Vance and Sandy Deane. Howie Kane (b. Howard Kerschenbaum) completed the line-up. Jay And The Americans scored a US Top 5 hit with their second single 'She Cried', but in 1962 Traynor left. The remaining trio recruited David 'Jay' Black (b. 1941) who introduced fifth member Marty Saunders (guitar) to the band, and the following year established his new role with the powerful 'Only In America'. 'Come A Little Bit Closer' became a US Top 3 entry and 'Livin' Above Your Head' is now recognized as one of the group's finest recordings.

JAYHAWKS

THIS BAND FROM MINNEAPOLIS, MINNESOTA, USA, BOASTED A CORE LINE-UP OF MARK OLSEN (VOCALS/GUITAR) AND Gary Louris (vocals/guitar), joined by Ken Callahan (bass), and subsequently Karen Grotberg (keyboards) and Marc Perlman, who replaced Callahan. They combine rugged country imagery with harsh, rough-hewn bar blues. Olson left the band in 1996 leaving Louris as the main songwriter. *Sound Of Lies* related to the break-up of his marriage.

JAZZ BUTCHER

FROM NORTHAMPTON AND FORMED IN 1982, JAZZ BUTCHER SERVED AS A VEHICLE FOR THE SONGWRITING talents of Pat Fish (b. Patrick Huntrods; guitar, vocals). Although early group line-ups were erratic – including Rolo McGinty, Alice Thompson and ex-**Bauhaus** bassist David J – the one constant member during the early years was lead guitarist Max Eider. The classic Jazz Butcher line-up, including Felix Ray (bass) and 'Mr' O. P. Jones (drums), disintegrated with the departure of Eider in 1987. By the time of *Fishcotheque*, Fish was working virtually alone, but for guitarist Kizzy O'Callaghan. The Jazz Butcher (Conspiracy) comprising Fish, O'Callaghan, Laurence O'Keefe (bass), Paul Mulreany (drums) and Alex Green (saxophone) signed to Creation Records. Fish quit at the end of 1995.

JEFFERSON AIRPLANE

THIS US GROUP WAS FORMED IN 1965 BY **MARTY BALIN** (b. MARTYN JEREL BUCHWALD, 1942; VOCALS/GUITAR) WITH Paul Kantner (b. 1941; guitar/vocals) and Jorma Kaukonen (b. 1940; guitar/vocals). Bob Harvey and Jerry Peloquin gave way to Alexander 'Skip' Spence and Signe Anderson (b. Signe Toly Anderson, 1941), later replaced by Spencer Dryden (b. 1938; drums) and Jack Casady (b. 1944). Anderson departed shortly after the release of their debut *Jefferson Airplane Takes Off* and was

replaced by Grace Slick (b. Grace Barnett Wing, 1939; vocals). Slick was already well known with her former band, the **Great Society**, and donated two of their songs, 'White Rabbit' and 'Somebody To Love', to the Airplane. Both titles became US Top 10 hits. This national success continued with *After Bathing At Baxter's* and *Crown Of Creation*. They maintained a busy schedule and released a live album, *Bless Its Pointed Little Head* in 1969.

Volunteers was an excellent album, but it marked the decline of Balin's role in the band. Additionally, Dryden departed and the offshoot **Hot Tuna** began to take up more of Casady and Kaukonen's time. Kantner released a concept album, *Blows Against The Empire*, bearing the name Paul Kantner And The **Jefferson Starship**.

Following a greatest-hits selection, *Worst Of*, and the departure of Balin, the band released the cleverly packaged *Bark* on their own Grunt label. The disappointing *Long John Silver* was followed by a gutsy live outing, *30 Seconds Over Winterland*. This was the last album to bear their name. The Airplane title was resurrected in 1989 when Slick, Kaukonen, Casady, Balin and Kantner re-formed and released *Jefferson Airplane* to an indifferent audience.

JEFFERSON STARSHIP

THIS BAND EVOLVED FROM **JEFFERSON AIRPLANE** AFTER PAUL KANTNER (b. 1941; GUITAR/VOCALS) HAD PREVIOUSLY released *Blows Against The Empire* in 1970, billed as Paul Kantner And The Jefferson Starship. The official debut was *Dragonfly* (1974) which was an immediate success. Joining Kantner on this album were Grace Slick (b. Grace Barnett Wing, 1939; vocals), Papa John Creach (b. 1917, d. 1994; violin), former **Quicksilver Messenger Service** bassist David Freiberg (b. 1938; vocals/keyboards), Craig Chaquico (b. 1954; lead guitar), ex-**Turtle** John Barbata (drums) and Pete Sears (bass/keyboards). **Marty Balin** joined in 1975 and the ensuing *Red Octopus* became their most successful album.

Spitfire and *Earth* continued their success, although the band had now become a hard rock outfit. Balin's lighter 'Count On Me' was a US Top 10 hit in 1978. Slick and Balin both left the band, the latter replaced by Mickey Thomas. Drummer **Aynsley Dunbar** (b. 1946) also joined.

The tension broke in 1985 when, following much acrimony over ownership of the band's name, Kantner was paid off and took with him half the group's moniker. His former band became Starship. Both Thomas and Freiberg left during these antagonistic times.

Knee Deep In The Hoopla in 1985 became their most successful album since *Red Octopus*. Two singles from the album, 'We Built This City' (written by Bernie Taupin) and 'Jane', both reached US number 1 and, the following year, they reached the top spot on both sides of the Atlantic with the theme from the film *Mannequin*, 'Nothing's Gonna Stop Us Now'.

JELLYFISH

THIS US POP BAND WAS COMPOSED OF ANDY STURMER (DRUMS, VOCALS), JASON FALKNER (GUITAR), CHRIS Manning (bass) and Roger Manning (keyboards). *Bellybutton* remains one of the most exciting debuts of the 90s and was followed in 1993 by the similarly crafted *Spilt Milk*. The line-up in 1993 included Eric Dover (guitar), who replaced Falkner, and Tim Smith (bass), who took over from Chris Manning, but the band collapsed shortly afterwards.

JESUS AND MARY CHAIN

FORMED IN EAST KILBRIDE, SCOTLAND, THIS QUARTET, COMPRISING WILLIAM REID (VOCALS, GUITAR), JIM REID (vocals, guitar), Douglas Hart (bass) and Murray Dalglish (drums), moved to London in 1984 and signed to Creation Records where their debut, 'Upside Down' became a hit. Soon afterwards, Dalglish was replaced on drums by **Primal Scream** vocalist Bobby Gillespie, who returned to his former group the following year. The group then signed to Blanco y Negro. The Reid Brothers issued their highly acclaimed debut, *Psychocandy*. Their second album *Darklands* was followed by a tempestuous tour of Canada and America. By the arrival of *Automatic*, the band was effectively just a duo using programmed synth drums. *Honey's Dead* housed a powerful lead single in 'Reverence', which brought the band back to the charts. For the self-produced *Stoned & Dethroned*, the brothers swapped feedback for an acoustic, singer-songwriter approach.

JESUS JONES

JESUS JONES WAS FORMED IN LONDON IN 1988 BY SINGER/SONGWRITER MIKE EDWARDS (b. 1964), SUPPORTED by Gen (b. Simon Matthews, 1964; drums), Al Jaworski (b. 1966; bass), Jerry De Borg (b. 1963; guitar) and Barry D (b. Iain Richard Foxwell Baker, 1965; keyboards). *Liquidizer* was an energetic debut album. *Doubt* spent six weeks at the top of the US alternative chart and in the UK it reached number 1. 'Right Here, Right Now' was a major success in the USA, but *Perverse* marked a fall-off in their domestic popularity.

JETHRO TULL

JETHRO TULL WAS FORMED IN LUTON, ENGLAND, IN 1967 WHEN IAN ANDERSON (b. 1947; VOCALS/FLUTE) AND GLENN Cornick (b. 1947; bass), joined up with **Mick Abrahams** (b. 1943; guitar/vocals) and Clive Bunker (b. 1946; drums). A residency at London's Marquee club and a sensational appearance at the 1968 Sunbury Blues Festival confirmed a growing reputation. Their debut LP, *This Was*, reached the UK Top 10, largely on the strength of Tull's live reputation. For many spectators, Jethro Tull was the name of the extrovert frontman Anderson – the other musicians were merely his underlings. This impression gained credence through the group's internal ructions. Mick Abrahams left in 1968 and Martin Barre (b. 1946) joined Tull for *Stand Up*. The group was then augmented by John Evan (b. 1948; keyboards). *Benefit* duly followed and with it three UK Top 10 singles, 'Living In The Past', 'Sweet Dream' (both 1969) and 'The Witch's Promise' (1970). Cornick then quit and Jeffrey Hammond-Hammond (b. 1946), was brought in for *Aqualung*.

Clive Bunker left in 1971, replaced by Barriemore Barlow (b. 1949). *Thick As A Brick* topped the US chart and reached UK number 5, but critics began questioning Anderson's reliance on obtuse concepts and *A Passion Play* was labelled pretentious. *War Child*, a US number 2, failed to chart in the UK, although *Minstrel In The Gallery* proved more popular. *Too Old To Rock 'N' Roll, Too Young To Die* marked the departure of Hammond-Hammond in favour of John Glascock (b. 1953, d. 1979), and David Palmer was added as a second keyboards player. From here the group embarked on another successful phase which lasted until Glascock's death. In 1980, Anderson began a projected solo album, retaining Barre and new bassist Dave Pegg (ex-**Fairport Convention**). The finished product, *A*, was ultimately issued under the Jethro Tull banner, and was followed by two more group selections. Since then Jethro Tull has continued to record and perform live, using a nucleus of Anderson, Barre and Pegg.

JETT, JOAN, AND THE BLACKHEARTS

PRODUCER KIM FOWLEY TOOK US-BORN JETT (b. JOAN LARKIN, 1960) AND HER GROUP UNDER HIS WING AND named it the **Runaways**. They recorded three punk-tinged hard rock albums which were successful in Japan and England where they recorded their swan-song, *And Now ... The Runaways*. After the group split, Jett moved to New York where her first solo album became a best-selling US independent record. With her group the Blackhearts (guitarist Ricky Byrd, bassist Gary Ryan and drummer Lee Crystal), Jett recorded *I Love Rock 'N' Roll*. The title track spent seven weeks at US number 1 in 1982. *Glorious Results Of A Misspent Youth* again retreated to Jett's past with the Runaways. After *Good Music* Crystal and Ryan left. *Up Your Alley* brought another hit with 'I Hate Myself For Loving You', before 1990's *The Hit List*. *Notorious* saw her hook up with Paul Westerberg of the **Replacements** while *Pure And Simple* featured a guest appearance from **L7**, emphasizing Jett's influence on a new generation of female rockers.

JEWEL

SINGER-SONGWRITER JEWEL (b. JEWEL KILCHER, 1974) LEFT HER HOME IN ALASKA AT THE AGE OF 16 TO STUDY OPERA in Michigan, Illinois. Regular concerts at the Innerchange coffee shop quickly attracted several major label A&R staff. Warners won her signature and released her debut album, *Pieces Of You* in 1995 – it achieved gold status.

JIVE BUNNY AND THE MASTERMIXERS

JIVE BUNNY, A UK MALE PRODUCTION/MIXING GROUP COMPRISING JOHN PICKLES AND DISC JOCKEY IAN Morgan, became UK chart-toppers with their first three singles equalling the record held by **Gerry And The Pacemakers** (1963) and **Frankie Goes To Hollywood** (1984).

JOEL, BILLY

JOEL (b. 1949), A CLASSICALLY TRAINED PIANIST FROM HICKSVILLE, USA, JOINED HIS FIRST GROUP, THE ECHOES, IN 1964. A demo of Joel's original compositions led to the release of his debut album, *Cold Spring Harbor*. Columbia Records signed Joel to a long-term contract. The title track to *Piano Man* became a US Top 30 single in 1973. After *Street Life Serenade* and *Turnstiles*, his fortunes flourished with the release of *The Stranger*. *52nd Street* spawned another smash single, 'My Life', while the singer's first US number 1, 'It's Still Rock 'N' Roll To Me', came from a subsequent release, *Glass Houses*. *The Nylon Curtain* featured two notable 'protest' compositions, 'Allentown' and 'Goodnight Saigon'. However, he returned to simpler matters with *An Innocent Man* which included the effervescent best-seller 'Uptown Girl'. He returned to live work in 1998 with a stadium tour in Europe with **Elton John**.

JESUS AND MARY CHAIN
Albums
Psychocandy (Blanco y Negro 1985)★★★★
➧ p.367 for full listings
Connections
Primal Scream ➧ p.267
Influences
Syd Barrett ➧ p.261

JESUS JONES
Albums
Liquidizer (Food 1989)★★★
➧ p.367 for full listings
Further References
Video: *Big In Alaska* (PMI 1991)

JETHRO TULL
Albums
This Was (Chrysalis 1968)★★★★
Stand Up (Chrysalis 1969)★★★★
➧ p.367 for full listings
Collaborators
Mick Abrahams ➧ p.7
Connections
Fairport Convention ➧ p.141
Further References
Video: *Slipstream* (Chrysalis 1981)

JETT, JOAN, AND THE BLACKHEARTS
Albums
I Love Rock 'N' Roll (Boardwalk 1981)★★★★
➧ p.367 for full listings
Collaborators
Grandmaster Flash And The Furious Five ➧ p.166
L7 ➧ p.211
Connections
Runaways ➧ p.284
Replacements ➧ p.276
Influences
Arrows ➧ p.22

JEWEL
Albums
Pieces Of You (Atlantic 1995)★★★★
➧ p.367 for full listings

JIVE BUNNY AND THE MASTERMIXERS
Albums
Jive Bunny – The Album (1989)★★★
➧ p.367 for full listings
Collaborators
Gerry And The Pacemakers ➧ p.162
Frankie Goes To Hollywood ➧ p.153

JOEL, BILLY
Albums
The Stranger (Columbia 1977)★★★★
River Of Dreams (Columbia 1993)★★★★
➧ p.367 for full listings
Collaborators
Elton John ➧ p.200
Connections
Barry White ➧ p.337
Further References
Book: *Billy Joel: A Personal File*, Peter Gambaccini

JOHN, ELTON
Albums
Goodbye Yellow Brick Road (DJM 1973)★★★★
Made In England (Mercury/Rocket 1995)★★★★
➧ p.367 for full listings
Collaborators
Long John Baldry ➧ p.30
Hollies ➧ p.183
Kiki Dee ➧ p.113
Wham! ➧ p.337
Bonnie Raitt ➧ p.272
Paul Young ➧ p.347
k.d. lang ➧ p.212
Little Richard ➧ p.217
George Michael ➧ p.223
Billy Joel ➧ p.199
Influences
Beatles ➧ p.28
Rolling Stones ➧ p.281
Further References
Book: *A Conversation With Elton John And Bernie Taupin*, Paul Gambaccini

JOHNNY AND THE HURRICANES
Albums
Stormsville (1960)★★★
➧ p.367 for full listings

JOHNSON, LINTON KWESI
Albums
Making History (Island 1984)★★★★
➧ p.367 for full listings
Connections
Poet And The Roots
LKJ Records

JOHNSON, ROBERT
Albums
Robert Johnson Delta Blues Legend (Charly 1992)★★★★★
➧ p.367 for full listings
Further References
Book: *Searching For Robert Johnson*, Peter Guralnick

JON SPENCER BLUES EXPLOSION
Albums
Now I Got Worry (Mute 1996)★★★★
➧ p.367 for full listings
Collaborators
Beck ➧ p.40
Connections
Pussy Galore
Beastie Boys ➧ p.37
Wu-Tang Clan ➧ p.344
Moby ➧ p.235
Influences
Isaac Hayes ➧ p.178

JONES, HOWARD
Albums
Human's Lib (WEA 1984)★★★★
➧ p.367 for full listings
Collaborations
OMD ➧ p.252
China Crisis ➧ p.91

JOHANSEN, DAVID

JOHANSEN (b. 1950) GAINED RECOGNITION IN THE EARLY 70S AS LEAD SINGER OF THE **NEW YORK DOLLS**. THE DOLLS came together in late 1971 and recorded two albums before Johansen launched a solo career in 1978, signing for Blue Sky. He released four rock/R&B-oriented solo albums. In 1983, under the name Buster Poindexter, Johansen began performing a set of vintage R&B numbers, show tunes, and jump blues. He recorded albums including *Buster Poindexter* and *Buster Goes Berserk*. He was still popular as Poindexter in the early 90s.

JOHN, ELTON

JOHN (b. REGINALD KENNETH DWIGHT, 1947) FORMED HIS FIRST BAND, BLUESOLOGY, IN THE EARLY 60S AND TURNED professional in 1965. In 1966, **Long John Baldry** joined the band, which included Elton Dean (saxophone) and Caleb Quaye (guitar). John eventually began to explore the possibilities of a music publishing contract. The shy John soon met Bernie Taupin and, realizing they had similar musical tastes, they began to write together.

In 1968, John, adopting a new name taken from the first names of his former colleagues Dean and Baldry, and Taupin were signed by Dick James as staff writers for his new company DJM. In 1969, *Empty Sky* was released; over the next few months, John played on sessions with the **Hollies** and made budget recordings for cover versions released in supermarkets.

His long wait for recognition ended the following year when Gus Dudgeon produced the outstanding *Elton John*, which included 'Border Song' (UK number 2) and 'Your Song'. The momentum was maintained with *Tumbleweed Connection* and over the next few years Elton John became a superstar. Between 1972 and 1975 he had seven consecutive number 1 albums, variously spawning memorable hits including 'Rocket Man', 'Daniel', 'Saturday Night's Alright For Fighting', 'Goodbye Yellow Brick Road', 'Candle In The Wind' and 'Someone Saved My Life Tonight'.

In 1976, he topped the UK charts with 'Don't Go Breaking My Heart' (a duet with **Kiki Dee**), and released a further two million-selling albums, *Here And There* and *Blue Moves*. By 1979 the John/Taupin partnership went into abeyance as Taupin moved to Los Angeles and John started writing with Gary Osborne. The partnership produced few outstanding songs other than the solo 'Song For Guy'.

Elton's albums during the early 80s were patchy, and only when he started working exclusively with Taupin again did his record sales pick up. The first renaissance album was *Too Low For Zero*, which scaled the charts. During 1985 he appeared at **Wham!**'s farewell concert, and at Live Aid. He completed the year with another massive album, *Ice On Fire*.

In 1986, he and Taupin contested a lengthy and expensive court case for back royalties against DJM. In 1988, he released *Reg Strikes Back* and the fast-tempo 'I Don't Want To Go On With You Like That'. At the end of the decade, he released two more outstanding albums *Sleeping With The Past* and *The One*.

In 1991, the *Sunday Times* announced that John had entered the list of the top 200 wealthiest people in Britain. In 1993, an array of guest musicians appeared on John's *Duets*, including **Bonnie Raitt**, **Paul Young**, **k.d. lang**, **Little Richard** and **George Michael**. Five new songs by the artist graced the soundtrack to 1994's Disney blockbuster, *The Lion King*. In 1995 John produced one of his best albums, *Made In England*, which scaled the charts worldwide.

Together with the **Beatles** and **Rolling Stones**, Elton John is Britain's most successful artist of all time. In 1997 he sang at the funeral of Diana, Princess Of Wales, where his performance of 'Candle In The Wind 97' was seen by an estimated 2 billion people.

JOHNNY AND THE HURRICANES

FORMED BY AMERICAN TENOR SAXOPHONIST JOHNNY PARIS (b. 1940) WITH BASSIST LIONEL 'BUTCH' MATTICE AND drummer Tony Kaye, Johnny And The Hurricanes released 'Red River Rock', which featured the trademark sound of rasping saxophone and the organ of Paul Tesluk. The group continued the hit run in the USA and UK with such instrumentals as 'Rocking Goose'. In 1963, an entirely new group of Johnny Paris-led Hurricanes toured the UK. By this time, however, their instrumental sound was becoming anachronistic and they were consumed by the beat boom.

JOHNSON, LINTON KWESI

JAMAICAN-BORN JOHNSON'S (b. 1952) FAMILY EMIGRATED TO LONDON IN 1963. AFTER TAKING A DEGREE IN sociology in 1973 he published two books, *Voices Of The Living And The Dead* (1974) and *Dread Beat And Blood* (1975). Johnson also wrote about reggae for *Black Music*, and experiments with reggae bands culminated in 1977's *Dread Beat An' Blood* recorded as Poet And The Roots. In 1978, Johnson issued *Forces Of Victory*, this time under his own name, followed by *Bass Culture*. *LKJ In Dub* was released in the same year as *Inglan Is A Bitch*, his third book. He finally returned to the studio in 1990 to record *Tings An' Times*, a more reflective set.

JOHNSON, ROBERT

JOHNSON (b. ROBERT LEROY JOHNSON, *c.* 1911, d. 1938) WAS ONE OF THE FIRST TO MAKE CREATIVE USE OF OTHERS' recorded efforts, adapting and augmenting their ideas to bring originality to the compositions they inspired. Johnson recorded 29 compositions between November 1936 and June 1937 and the power and precision of his guitar playing are evident from the first. Eight titles were recorded over two days, including 'Walkin' Blues' and 'Cross Road Blues', the song an echo of the legend that Johnson had sold his soul to the Devil to achieve his musical skill. He was poisoned by a jealous husband while performing in a jook joint in Mississippi. His name was kept alive in the 80s by a comprehensive reissue project.

JON SPENCER BLUES EXPLOSION

WHEN PUSSY GALORE DISBANDED, SINGER/GUITARIST JON SPENCER FORMED THE NEW GROUP WITH RUSSELL SIMINS (drums) and Judah Bauer (guitar). On early recordings the group's sound resembled little more than a trimmed-down variant on Spencer's earlier group, but successive albums added new elements of blues, soul and rockabilly. *Orange* blended a string section reminiscent of **Isaac Hayes** with hip-hop touches. *Now I Got Worry* featured 'Chicken Dog', a collaboration with Rufus Thomas.

JONES, HOWARD

JONES (b. JOHN HOWARD JONES, 1955) WAS OFFERED A SESSION BY BBC DISC JOCKEY **JOHN PEEL** WHICH LED TO tours with **OMD** and **China Crisis**. He charted in the UK with his first single 'New Song'. His debut *Human's Lib* topped the UK charts. In 1985, he formed a touring band with brother Martin on bass, and Trevor Morais on drums. He continues to record sporadically and even joined the unplugged with *Live Acoustic America* in 1996.

JONES, JIMMY

JONES (b. 1937) WHO HAD SPENT A LONG APPRENTICESHIP SINGING IN R&B DOO-WOP GROUPS, BECAME A ROCK 'N' roll star in the early 60s. In 1956, Jones formed the Savoys, later renamed the **Pretenders**. Success finally came when Jones launched a solo career, hitting with his debut, 'Handy Man' and following up with 'Good Timin''. In 1960 'Handy Man' reached number 3, 'Good Timin'' number 1.

JONES, PAUL

JONES (b. 1942) BEGAN HIS SINGING CAREER WHILE STUDYING AT OXFORD UNIVERSITY. STARTING WITH THE trailblazing Blues Incorporated, he subsequently joined the Mann Hugg Blues Brothers, which evolved into **Manfred Mann** in 1963. He left the line-up in 1966, enjoying two UK Top 5 hits with 'High Time' (1966) and 'I've Been A Bad, Bad Boy' (1967). In 1979, he rekindled his first musical love with the formation of the **Blues Band**. He has continued to lead this popular unit whenever acting commitments allow.

JONES, QUINCY

JONES (b. QUINCY DELIGHT JONES JNR, 1933) BEGAN PLAYING THE TRUMPET AS A CHILD. WHEN HE JOINED LIONEL Hampton in 1951 it was as both performer and writer. Leaving Hampton in 1953, Jones wrote arrangements for many musicians, including, Count Basie and Tommy Dorsey. He worked with Frank Sinatra, Johnny Mathis and **Ray Charles**. As a record producer, Jones became the first black vice-president of Mercury's New York division. Later, he spent 12 years with A&M Records before starting up his own label, Qwest. In the 70s and 80s, in addition to many film soundtracks, he produced successful albums for **George Benson** (*Give Me The Night*), while for **Michael Jackson** he helped to create *Off The Wall* and *Thriller*. A major film documentary, *Listen Up: The Lives Of Quincy Jones*, was released in 1990. *Q's Jook Joint* was a retrospective of his 50 years in the music business.

JONES, RICKIE LEE

JONES (b. 1954) EMERGED IN 1979 WITH A BUOYANT DEBUT ALBUM LYRICALLY INDEBTED TO BEAT AND JAZZ STYLES, including 'Chuck E.'s In Love', a US Top 5 single. Although *Rickie Lee Jones* garnered popular success, the singer refused to be rushed into a follow-up. Two years later, *Pirates* revealed a hitherto hidden emotional depth. *Girl At Her Volcano*, marked time until the release of *The Magazine* in 1984, which confirmed the artist's imagination. However, it was six years before a further album, *Flying Cowboys*, was issued. The set marked a fruitful collaboration with Glasgow group, the **Blue Nile**. *Naked Songs* featured her 'unplugged' while *Ghostyhead* embraced dance/techno rhythm.

JONES, TOM

JONES (b. THOMAS JONES WOODWARD, 1940) BEGAN HIS MUSICAL CAREER IN 1963 AS VOCALIST IN THE WELSH group Tommy Scott And The Senators. After signing with former **Viscounts** vocalist Gordon Mills he changed his name to Tom Jones. His first single, 'Chills And Fever', failed to chart but, early in 1965, Jones's second release 'It's Not Unusual', composed by Mills and Les Reed, reached UK number 1. Jones enjoyed lesser hits that year with the ballads 'Once Upon A Time' and 'With These Hands'. Meanwhile, Mills astutely ensured that his star was given first choice for film theme songs, and 'What's New Pussycat?' became a major US/UK hit. By 1966, however, Jones's chart fortunes were in decline. Mills took drastic action by regrooming his protégé for an older market. By Christmas 1966, Jones was effectively relaunched owing to the enormous success of 'Green Green Grass Of Home', which topped the charts for seven weeks. In 1967, he enjoyed one of his biggest UK hits with the intense 'I'll Never Fall In Love Again', which climbed to number 2. The hit run continued with 'I'm Coming Home' and 'Delilah'.

As the 60s reached their close, Mills took his star to America where he hosted the highly successful television show, *This Is Tom Jones*. Although Jones logged a handful of hits in the UK during the early 70s, his future lay in the lucrative Las Vegas circuit. It was not until after the death of Mills, when his son Mark Woodward took over his management, that the star elected to return to recording. Jones's continued credibility was emphasized when he was invited to record songs written by the mercurial **Van Morrison**.

JOPLIN, JANIS

JOPLIN (b. 1943, d. 1970) DEVELOPED A BRASH, UNCOMPROMISING VOCAL STYLE. IN 1962, SHE JOINED THE WALLER Creek Boys, and her reputation blossomed following the **Monterey Pop Festival**. *Cheap Thrills* contained two Joplin 'standards', 'Piece Of My Heart' and 'Ball And Chain'. **Mike Bloomfield** helped assemble a new act, Janis And The Joplinaires, later known as the Kozmic Blues Band. Sam Andrew (guitar, vocals), Terry Clements (saxophone), Marcus Doubleday (trumpet), Bill King (organ), Brad Campbell (bass) and Roy Markowitz (drums) made up the initial line-up. *I Got Dem Ol' Kozmic Blues Again Mama!* was coolly received, but contained several excellent Joplin vocals. Live shows grew increasingly erratic as her addiction to drugs and alcohol deepened. A slimmed-down group, the Full Tilt Boogie Band, was unveiled in 1970. The debut album sessions were all but complete when Joplin died of a heroin overdose at her Hollywood hotel. *Pearl* remains her most consistent work.

JORDANAIRES

A RENOWNED HARMONY-VOCAL QUARTET BEST-KNOWN FOR ITS LENGTHY WORKING RELATIONSHIP WITH **ELVIS Presley**. Lead vocalist Gordon Stoker was subsequently featured on Presley's first recordings for RCA Victor while the remaining trio – Neal Matthews (tenor), Hoyt Hawkins (baritone) and Hugh Jarrett (bass) – joined him on the session producing 'Hound Dog' and 'Don't Be Cruel'. The quartet continued to accompany him throughout the 50s and 60s, although they were absent from the 'comeback' NBC-TV spectacular, *Elvis* (1968). The recordings in Nashville during June and September 1970, marked the end of the Jordanaires' relationship with Presley. In 1972 they contributed to *Guitar That Shook The World*, the solo debut by Elvis's long-time guitarist Scotty Moore. The Jordanaires – by this point comprising of Stoker, Hawkins, Matthews and new bass player, Lovis Nunley – also released several albums in their own right. In 1996, they added harmonies to alternative US rock band Ween's album, *12 Golden Country Greats*.

JONES, JIMMY
Albums
Good Timin' (MGM 1960)★★★
➧ p.367 for full listings

JONES, PAUL
Albums
Mule (Fat Possum 1995)★★★
➧ p.367 for full listings
Collaborators
Manfred Mann ➧ p.223
Blues Band ➧ p.56

JONES, QUINCY
Albums
Live At Montreux recorded 1991 (Reprise 1993)★★★★
➧ p.367 for full listings
Collaborators
Tommy Dorsey ➧ p.75
Ray Charles ➧ p.88
George Benson ➧ p.44
Michael Jackson ➧ p.195
Further References
Book: *Quincy Jones*, Raymond Horricks

JONES, RICKIE LEE
Albums
Pirates (Warners 1981)★★★★
➧ p.367 for full listings
Collaborators
Blue Nile ➧ p.56
Connections
Tom Waits ➧ p.332
Influences
Laura Nyro ➧ p.249

JONES, TOM
Albums
Green Green Grass Of Home (Decca 1967)★★★★
➧ p.368 for full listings
Collaborators
Les Reed ➧ p.274
Art Of Noise ➧ p.22
Van Morrison ➧ p.238
Connections
Prince ➧ p.267
Further References
Book: *Tom Jones: Biography Of A Great Star*, Tom Jones

JOPLIN, JANIS
Albums
I Got Dem Ol' Kozmic Blues Again Mama! (Columbia 1969)★★★
➧ p.368 for full listings
Connections
Electric Flag ➧ p.134
Mike Bloomfield ➧ p.54
Influences
Kris Kristofferson ➧ p.211
Further References
Book: *Janis Joplin: Her Life And Times*, Deborah Landau

JORDANAIRES
Albums
Land Of Jordan (Capitol 1960)★★★★
➧ p.368 for full listings

JOURNEY
Albums
Escape (Columbia 1981)★★★★
➧ p.368 for full listings
Collaborators
John Waite ➧ p.331
Connections
Santana ➧ p.288
Steve Miller Band ➧ p.234
Tubes ➧ p.324
Aynsley Dunbar ➧ p.25
Jeff Beck ➧ p.41
Jefferson Starship ➧ p.198

JOY DIVISION
Albums
Closer (Factory 1980)★★★★
➧ p.368 for full listings

Connections
New Order ➧ p.246
Paul Young ➧ p.347
Further References
Book: *An Ideal For Living: An History Of Joy Division*, Mark Johnson

JUDAS PRIEST
Albums
British Steel (Columbia 1980)★★★★
➧ p.368 for full listings
Further References
Video: *Painkiller* (1990)
Book: *Heavy Duty*, Steve Gett

JUDDS
Albums
Give A Little Love (Curb/RCA 1986)★★★
➧ p.368 for full listings
Collaborators
Jerry Lee Lewis ➧ p.215
Roy Orbison ➧ p.252
Johnny Cash ➧ p.84
Carl Perkins ➧ p.258
Jordanaires ➧ p.201
Emmylou Harris ➧ p.175
Mark Knopfler ➧ p.120
Bonnie Raitt ➧ p.272
Connections
Wynonna ➧ p.344
Further References
Book: *Love Can Build A Bridge*, Naomi Judd

JUICY LUCY
Albums
Juicy Lucy (Vertigo 1969)★★★
➧ p.368 for full listings
Connections
Zoot Money ➧ p.236
Blodwyn Pig ➧ p.53
Influences
Bo Diddley ➧ p.118

JOURNEY

THIS US ROCK GROUP WAS FORMED IN 1973 BY EX-**SANTANA** MEMBERS NEIL SCHON (b. 1954; GUITAR) AND Gregg Rolie (b. 1948; keyboards), with Ross Valory (b. 1949; bass, ex-**Steve Miller** band) and Prairie Prince (b. 1950; drums, ex-**Tubes**). George Tickner was added later as rhythm guitarist and lead vocalist. In 1974, Prince was replaced by **Aynsley Dunbar** (b. 1946; ex-**Jeff Beck**). Tickner was replaced by vocalist Steve Perry (b. 1953). The switch to highly sophisticated pump rock occurred with the recording of *Infinity.* Dunbar quit and was replaced by Steve Smith (b. 1954). *Evolution* followed and brought the band their first Top 20 hit, 'Lovin', Touchin', Squeezin'', followed by a live double album, *Captured.* Rolie departed after its release, replaced by Jonathan Cain (b. 1950). *Escape* reached number 1 and stayed in the chart for over a year. The follow-up, *Frontiers*, was also successful, and 'Separate Ways' climbed to number 8 in the singles chart. The band reduced to a three-man nucleus of Schon, Cain and Perry to record *Raised On Radio*. This was Journey's last album before Schon and Cain joined forces with **John Waite**'s Bad English in 1988. A *Greatest Hits* compilation was released in 1988 and there were new albums in 1996 and 1997.

JOY DIVISION

ORIGINALLY KNOWN AS WARSAW, THIS MANCHESTER OUTFIT COMPRISED IAN CURTIS (b. 1956, d. 1980; VOCALS), Bernard Dicken/Albrecht (b. 1956; guitar, vocals), Peter Hook (b. 1956; bass) and Steven Morris (b. 1957; drums). Joy Division's debut for Factory Records, *Unknown Pleasures*, was a raw, intense affair, with Curtis at his most manically arresting in 'She's Lost Control'. The charismatic Curtis was renowned for his

neurotic choreography, but by the autumn of 1979, he was suffering epileptic seizures and blackouts on stage. The 1980 single, 'Love Will Tear Us Apart', released the same year that Curtis died, was a haunting account of a fragmented relationship. *Closer* displayed the group at the zenith of their powers. The following year, a double album, *Still*, collected the remainder of the group's material, most of it in primitive form. Within months of Curtis's death, the remaining members sought a fresh start as **New Order**.

JUDAS PRIEST

FORMED IN BIRMINGHAM, ENGLAND, IN 1969, BY GUITARIST K. K. DOWNING (b. KENNETH DOWNING) and bassist Ian Hill. They played their first gig in Essington in 1971, with Alan Atkins (vocals) and John Ellis (drums). Vocalist Rob Halford (b. 1951) and drummer John Hinch joined the unit along with second guitarist Glenn Tipton (b. 1948). In 1974, the band made their debut with *Rocka Rolla*. *Sin After Sin* was a strong collection, with Simon Philips on drums. The band then visited America for the first time with drummer Les Binks, who appeared on *Stained Class*. *Killing Machine* featured shorter, punchier, but still familiar rock songs. *Unleashed In The East* was recorded on the 1979 Japanese tour, and in that year, Binks was replaced on drums by Dave Holland of Trapeze. *British Steel* smashed into the UK album charts at number 3 and *Point Of Entry* was followed by sell-out UK and US tours. The period surrounding *Screaming For Vengeance* and *Defenders Of The Faith* offered a potent brand of headstrong metal. *Turbo*, though, was poorly received. *Ram It Down* saw a return to pure heavy metal, but by this time their popularity was waning. Dave Holland was replaced by Scott Travis for the return to form that was *Painkiller*. The band were taken to court in 1990 following the suicide attempts of two fans in 1985. Both CBS Records and Judas Priest were accused of inciting suicide through their 'backwards messages', but were found not guilty. Soon after, Halford became disheartened with the band and left to form his own outfit, Fight.

JUDDS

NAOMI JUDD (b. DIANA ELLEN JUDD, 1946) MOVED WITH HER DAUGHTERS WYNONNA (b. CHRISTINA CIMINELLA, 1964) and Ashley (b. 1968) from California back to Morrill, Kentucky, where she and the children would sing anything from bluegrass to showbiz standards for their own amusement. When Wynonna nurtured aspirations to be a professional entertainer, her mother moved the family to Nashville in 1979. An exploratory mini-album, which contained the show-stopping 'John Deere Tractor', peaked at number 17, and 1984's 'Mama He's Crazy', became the first of many country chart-toppers for the duo. The Judds' had a second million-selling album with *Rockin' With The Rhythm Of The Rain*. Most Judds records had an acoustic bias – particularly on the sultry ballads selected for *Give A Little Love*. In 1990, a chronic liver disorder forced Naomi to retire from the concert stage leaving Wynonna to begin her long-rumoured solo career. This she did in style, with a remarkable album that touched on gospel, soul and R&B.

JUICY LUCY

JUICY LUCY WAS FORMED IN 1969 BY RAY OWEN (VOCALS), GLEN 'ROSS' CAMPBELL (STEEL GUITAR) AND CHRIS MERCER (tenor saxophone) and were augmented by Neil Hubbard (guitar), Keith Ellis (bass) and Pete Dobson (bass). The sextet enjoyed a surprise hit single with 'Who Do You Love'. Owen was later replaced by former **Zoot Money** singer Paul Williams. A fourth album, *Pieces*, was completed by a reshaped unit of Williams, Mick Moody (guitar), Jean Roussal (keyboards) and ex-**Blodwyn Pig** members Andy Pyle (bass) and Ron Berg (drums). They broke up soon afterwards.

KAJAGOOGOO

NICK BEGGS (b. 1961; VOCALS/BASS), STEVE ASKEW (GUITAR), STUART CRAWFORD (VOCALS/SYNTHESIZER) AND LEAD singer 'Limahl' (b. Chris Hamill, 1958) debuted with 'Too Shy' (1983, UK number 1), co-produced by Nick Rhodes (**Duran Duran**). After 'Ooh To Be Ah', 'Hang On Now' and *White Feathers*, Limahl went solo. Beggs took lead vocals on the hits 'Big Apple' and 'The Lion's Mouth', but they split in 1986.

KALEIDOSCOPE (UK)

FORMED IN LONDON IN 1964, AS THE SIDE KICKS. EDDIE PUMER (GUITAR), PETER DALTREY (VOCALS/KEYBOARDS), Dan Bridgeman (percussion) and Steve Clarke (bass) started as an R&B cover band. *Tangerine Dream* became a cult success; 'A Dream For Julie', 'Jenny Artichoke' and *Faintly Blowing*, failed to chart. A third album was 'lost' when Fontana dropped the band – it was issued in 1991 on the group's self-titled label.

KALEIDOSCOPE (USA)

FORMED IN 1966 BY GUITARISTS DAVID LINDLEY AND CHRIS DARROW. SOLOMON FELDTHOUSE (VOCALS/OUD/caz), John Vidican (drums) and Charles Chester Crill (violin/organ/harmonica/vocals). *Side Trips* combined blues, jazz, folk and ethnic tastes. After *A Beacon From Mars*, Darrow left for the **Nitty Gritty Dirt Band**. Newcomers Stuart Brotman (bass) and Paul Lagos (drums) were featured on *Incredible Kaleidoscope*. Brotman then left, replaced by Ron Johnson, who introduced a funk element; newcomer Jeff Kaplan took on lead vocals. After the disappointing *Bernice*, Feldthouse and Crill left. Richard Aplan joined, but Kaleidoscope dissolved in 1970, after Kaplan's death from a drugs overdose.

KANSAS

US BAND FORMED IN 1972. DAVID HOPE (b. *c.* 1951; BASS), PHIL EHART, (b. 1951; DRUMS/PERCUSSION), KERRY LIVGREN (b. 1949; guitar/vocals), Robert Steinhardt (b. *c.* 1951; violin/strings/vocals), Steve Walsh (b. *c.* 1951; keyboards/vocals) and Richard Williams (b. *c.* 1951; guitars) debuted in 1974. The following two albums went gold, guaranteeing them a high US profile (no Kansas albums made the UK charts). Walsh went solo in the 80s, resulting in *Schemer Dreamer*. His replacement, John Elefante (b. *c.* 1958; keyboards/vocals) wrote four of the songs on *Vinyl Confessions*. They split in 1983 following two unsuccessful albums.

In 1986, Walsh, Ehart and Williams recruited Steve Morse (guitar) and Billy Greer (bass) and released *Power*, followed by three subsequent albums.

KATRINA AND THE WAVES

ANGLO-AMERICAN POP GROUP – KATRINA LESKANICH (b. 1960; VOCALS), KIMBERLEY REW (GUITAR; EX-**SOFT BOYS**), Vince De La Cruz (bass) and Alex Cooper (drums) – who had a major hit with 'Walking On Sunshine' (1985). Rew had previously recorded solo and much of his material was used by Katrina And The Waves. 'Sun Street' followed 'Walking On Sunshine'.

1993 brought a series of reunion gigs, and the band sang for the UK in the 1997 Eurovision Song Contest – they won with 'Love Shine A Light'.

KC AND THE SUNSHINE BAND

FORMED IN FLORIDA, 1973, BY HARRY WAYNE 'KC' CASEY (b. 1951; VOCALS/KEYBOARDS) AND RICHARD FINCH (b. 1954; bass), with Jerome Smith (b. 1953; guitar) and Robert Johnson (b. 1953; drums). Wayne and Finch wrote, arranged and produced their own material. Their hits included 'Queen Of Clubs' (1974, UK Top 10) and three consecutive US number 1s with 'Get Down Tonight', 'That's The Way (I Like It)' (both 1975) and '(Shake, Shake, Shake), Shake Your Body' (1976). 'Give It Up' (1983) reached UK number 1; charting in the US in 1984.

KAJAGOOGOO
Albums
Islands (EMI 1984)★★
» p.368 for full listings
Connections
Nick Rhodes

KALEIDOSCOPE (UK)
Albums
Tangerine Dream (Fontana 1967)★★★
Faintly Blowing (Fontana 1969)★★
White-Faced Lady (Kaleidoscope 1991)★★
» p.368 for full listings
Connections
Fairfield Parlour

KALEIDOSCOPE (USA)
Albums
Side Trips (Epic 1967)★★★
Incredible Kaleidoscope (Epic 1969)★★★
When Scopes Collide (Island 1976)★★★★★
» p.368 for full listings
Connections
Nitty Gritty Dirt Band
» p.249

KANSAS
Albums
Song For America (Kirshner 1975)★★★
Leftoverture (Kirshner 1977)★★★
Point Of Know Return (Kirshner 1977)★★★★
» p.368 for full listings
Connections
White Clover
Influences
Yes » p.346
Genesis » p.161

KATRINA AND THE WAVES
Albums
Walking On Sunshine (Canada 1983)★★★,
» p.368 for full listings
Connections
Bangles » p.32
Soft Boys » p.302
Influences
Eurovision Song Contest

KC AND THE SUNSHINE BAND
Albums
Do It Good (TK 1974)★★★
Part 3 (TK 1976)★★★★
I Like To Do It (Jay Boy 1977)★★★
» p.368 for full listings
Collaborators
George McCrae » p.229

KEITA, SALIF
Albums
Folon (Mango 1995)★★★★
➽ p.368 for full listings
Collaborators
Wally Badarou

KELLY, R.
Albums
12 Play (Jive 1994)★★★★
➽ p.368 for full listings
Collaborators
Gladys Knight ➽ p.209
Connections
Natalie Cole ➽ p.97

KENICKIE
Albums
Kenickie At The Club (EMI 1997)★★★
➽ p.368 for full listings
Connections
Saint Etienne ➽ p.287

KERSHAW, NIK
Albums
The Riddle (MCA 1984)★★★
➽ p.368 for full listings
Collaborators
Chesney Hawkes ➽ p.177

KHAN, CHAKA
Albums
What Cha' Gonna Do For Me (Warners 1981)★★★
➽ p.368 for full listings
Collaborators
Prince ➽ p.267
Stevie Wonder ➽ p.342
Gladys Knight ➽ p.209
Connections
Queen Latifah ➽ p.270

KID CREOLE AND THE COCONUTS
Albums
Fresh Fruit In Foreign Places (Ze 1981)★★★
➽ p.368 for full listings
Collaborators
Haitia Fuller

KIDD, JOHNNY, AND THE PIRATES
Influences
Beatles ➽ p.38
➽ p.368 for full listings

KIHN, GREG
Albums
Kihnspiracy (Beserkley 1983)★★★★
➽ p.368 for full listings
Collaborators
Johnathon Richman ➽ p.277
Connections
Steve Miller Band ➽ p.234
Influences
Bruce Springsteen ➽ p.306
Buddy Holly ➽ p.184

KILBURN AND THE HIGH ROADS
Albums
Wotabunch (Warners 1978)★★
➽ p.368 for full listings
Connections
Ian Dury ➽ p.127

KEITA, SALIF

ALBINO VOCALIST/COMPOSER KEITA (b. 1949) WAS FROM ONE OF MALI'S MOST DISTINGUISHED FAMILIES. HE formed a trio before joining the Rail Band in 1970. In 1973, he switched to main rivals, Les Ambassadeurs. With guitarist Kante Manfila, he extended the band's range, incorporating traditional Malian rhythms and melodies into their Afro-Cuban repertoire. *Les Ambassadeurs Du Motel*, *Les Ambassadeurs De Bamako Vol. 1* and *Les Ambassadeurs De Bamako Vol. 2* followed and in 1980, Keita recorded *Wassolon-Foli*, blending electric reggae with acoustic Malian folksong. He went solo in 1987, debuting with *Soro*.

KELLY, R.

DANCER-SINGER ROBERT KELLY (b. *c.* 1969) FORMED R&B GROUP MGM, AND WON A US TALENT CONTEST ON THE *Big Break* television show. Kelly then worked as musical co-ordinator/producer for acts including **Gladys Knight**.

His second album reached US R&B number 1, spawning the hits 'She's Got That Vibe' and 'Bump 'N Grind'. The following 'I Believe I Can Fly' was featured as the theme for the 1997 movie *Space Jam*.

KENICKIE

UK INDIE GROUP FORMED IN 1994 BY LAUREN LE LAVERNE (VOCALS), MARIE DU SANTIAGO (GUITAR) AND EMMY-KATE Montrose (bass) with Le Laverne's brother Johnny (drums). They signed to the Emidisc label in 1996. *Kenickie At The Club* was a confident and punchy debut.

KERSHAW, NIK

SINGER, GUITARIST, SONGWRITER KERSHAW (b. 1958) PERFORMED IN THE JAZZ-FUNK OUTFIT FUSION; THEY released '*Til I Hear From You*. When Fusion folded, Kershaw signed to MCA Records. His debut, 'I Won't Let The Sun Go Down On Me' (UK number 47) was followed by 'Wouldn't It Be Good' (UK Top 5). A reissue of his debut went to number 2 in 1983. Kershaw was backed by the Krew – Dennis Smith, Keiffer Airey, Tim Moore, Mark Price and Kershaw's wife, Sheri. The first two albums were successful, but the third was a relative failure.

In recent years he has written several hits, notably **Chesney Hawkes**' 'The One And Only'. In 1998, he began a comeback tour, supported by Hawkes.

KHAN, CHAKA

CHAKA KHAN (b. YVETTE MARIE STEVENS, 1953) SANG IN CHICAGO CLUB BANDS BEFORE RELEASING THE SOLO

'I'm Every Woman' (1978); it topped the US R&B chart followed by, 'What Cha' Gonna Do For Me' (1981) and 'Got To Be There' (1982). 'I Feel For You' (1994, US number 2 /UK number 1) established her internationally. Written by **Prince** and featuring **Stevie Wonder** and Melle Mel, it led to a platinum-selling album and won a Grammy for Best R&B Female Performance. 'This Is My Night' and 'Eye To Eye' (1985) reached the UK Top 20, followed by 'I'm Every Woman' (1989, UK Top 10). She collaborated with **Gladys Knight**, Brandy and Tamia on 'Missing You' (1996), from the **Queen Latifah** film *Set It Off*.

KID CREOLE AND THE COCONUTS

THE COCONUTS – KID CREOLE (b. AUGUST DARNELL, 1951), HIS BROTHER STONEY DARNELL, 'SUGAR COATED' ANDY Hernandez (aka Coati Mundi) and several multi-instrumentalists – debuted with the salsa-disco fusion *Off The Coast Of Me*. They found commercial success with *Tropical Gangsters* (*Wise Guy* outside the UK). Three UK Top 10 hits from the album followed: 'I'm A Wonderful Thing, Baby', 'Stool Pigeon' and 'Annie, I'm Not Your Daddy'.

After a second Coconuts album, Hernandez released a solo album and Kid Creole released the solo album *In Praise Of Older Women* (featuring female vocalist Haitia Fuller). More promising was *Private Waters*.

KIDD, JOHNNY, AND THE PIRATES

FORMED IN 1959. KIDD (b. FREDERICK HEATH, 1939, d. 1966; LEAD VOCALS), ALAN CADDY (b. 1940; LEAD GUITAR), Tony Docherty (rhythm guitar), Johnny Gordon (bass) and Ken McKay (drums), plus backing singers Mike West and Tom Brown, debuted with 'Please Don't Touch'. By 1960, Kidd and Caddy were fronting a new rhythm section featuring Brian Gregg (bass) and Clem Cattini (drums). Their first single, 'Shakin' All Over' reached UK number 1. Mick Green then joined on guitar. Under increasing competition from the emergent Liverpool sound, two 1963 hits, 'I'll Never Get Over You' and 'Hungry For Love', owed much to Merseybeat at the expense of the unit's own identity. In 1964, a depressed Kidd talked of retirement. He re-emerged in 1966, fronting the New Pirates, but tragically, on 7 October, he was killed in a car crash.

KIHN, GREG

IN 1975, US SONGWRITER KIHN (b. 1952; VOCALS/GUITAR) PROVIDED TWO SOLO SONGS FOR A COMPILATION ALBUM on Beserkley Records and signed to the label, adding backing vocals on **Jonathan Richman**'s 'Road Runner'.

With Robbie Dunbar (lead guitar), Steve Wright (bass) and Larry Lynch (drums), Kihn played around the San Francisco Bay area and recorded a first album. Dunbar left, replaced by Dave Carpender. When guitarist Gary Phillips joined in 1981, he brought about a more commercial direction which found quick reward. 'The Breakup Song (They Don't Write 'Em)' reached the US Top 20 and *Kihntinued* made US number 4. Carpender left, replaced by Greg Douglas. They managed a US number 2 with the disco-styled 'Jeopardy' (1983), before Kihn went solo. He has since written a novel and still records.

KILBURN AND THE HIGH ROADS

AN IMPORTANT LINK BETWEEN 'PUB ROCK' AND PUNK, KILBURN AND THE HIGH ROADS WERE FORMED IN 1970 BY **Ian Dury** (b. 1942; vocals) and Russell Hardy (b. 1941; piano). The line-up included Ted Speight (guitar), Terry Day (drums), George Khan (saxophone) and Charlie Hart (bass); by 1973, it had changed to Dury, Russell, Keith Lucas

(b. 1950; guitar), Davey Payne (b. 1944; saxophone), David Newton-Rohoman (b. 1948; drums) and Humphrey Ocean (bass; replaced in 1974 by Charlie Sinclair). They completed an album for the Raft label, unfortunately cancelled after the label went bankrupt. Warner Brothers Records, the parent company, chose to drop the group from its roster (later releasing the sessions as *Wotabunch* in the wake of Dury's solo success).

In 1974, they signed to Dawn, and released the superb 'Rough Kids'/'Billy Bentley (Promenades Himself In London)' and 'Crippled With Nerves'/ 'Huffety Puff', but the subsequent *Handsome* captured little of the excitement of a Kilburns' gig. The group then disintegrated.

KILLING JOKE

POWERFUL POST-PUNK UK BAND. JAZ COLEMAN (b. JEREMY COLEMAN; VOCALS/KEYBOARDS), PAUL FERGUSON (DRUMS), 'Geordie' (b. K. Walker; guitar) and Youth (b. Martin Glover Youth, 1960; bass) recorded and released the *Turn To Red* EP. Picked up by UK disc jockey **John Peel**, the band provided a hugely popular session. Via Island Records, the band set up their own Malicious Damage label and a succession of singles followed. They recorded three albums with EG; after which the band disintegrated when Coleman, believing that the apocalypse was imminent, fled to Iceland. He was followed by Youth.

Youth returned to begin work with Ferguson on a new project, Brilliant, until Ferguson himself left for Iceland, taking bassist Paul Raven with him. Brilliant continued with Youth as the only original member. Subsequent Killing Joke output included *Night Time* (including 'Love Like Blood'), *Outside The Gate* (basically a Coleman solo album) and their best album for years, *Extremities, Dirt And Various Repressed Emotions*, with drummer Martin Atkins (ex-**Public Image Limited**). However, the band broke up again, acrimoniously.

Coleman continued with the name. A collaborative project with Anne Dudley resulted in *Songs From The Victorious City. Pandemonium* saw Youth return to join Geordie and Coleman, with the addition of new drummer Geoff Dugmore. *Pandemonium* yielded two UK Top 20 singles, 'Millennium' and 'Pandemonium'. In 1996, they released *Democracy*.

KING, ALBERT

MISSISSIPPI-BORN KING (b. ALBERT NELSON, 1923, d. 1992) RELEASED THE SOLO RECORDING, 'BAD LUCK BLUES' (1953), but it was not until the end of the decade that he embarked on a full-time career. His early work fused his distinctive fretwork to big band-influenced arrangements and included his first successful single, 'Don't Throw Your Love On Me Too Strong'. In 1966, he signed to Stax and began working with **Booker T. And The MGs**. He released 'Born Under A Bad Sign' (1967) and 'The Hunter' (1968). His classic album, *Live Wire/Blues Power*, introduced his music to the white-rock audience.

In 1983, he recommenced recording and an astute programme of new material and careful reissues kept his catalogue alive. In 1990, he guested on guitarist **Gary Moore**'s *Still Got The Blues*.

KING, B.B.

GUITARIST KING (b. RILEY B. KING, 1925) SANG IN GOSPEL GROUPS FROM CHILDHOOD; HE BEGAN ADULT LIFE working on a Mississippi plantation. Aged 20, he went to Memphis, where he busked, and lived with his cousin, Bukka White. He eventually secured work with radio station KWEM, and then with WDIA; this led to DJ-ing on the *Sepia Swing Show*. Here he was billed as 'The Beale Street Blues Boy', later amended to 'Blues Boy King', and then 'B.B. King'. In 1948, he paid off his debts to his former plantation boss.

Radio exposure promoted King's live career, performing with a band whose personnel varied according to availability. At this stage, he was still musically untutored, but after recording for Bullet Records in 1949, he was signed to Modern Records, with whom he recorded for 10 years. In 1952, he reached *Billboard* R&B number 1 with 'Three O'Clock Blues'. Through the 50s, King embarked on his gruelling trail of one-nighters, touring with a 13-piece band. His sound consisted chiefly of a synthesis of the bottleneck styles of the delta blues with the jazzy electric guitar of **T-Bone Walker**. To Walker's flowing, crackling music, King added finger vibrato, his own substitute for the slide. The result was a fluid guitar sound, in which almost every note was bent and/or sustained. He named his beautiful black, gold plated, pearl inlaid Gibson 335 (or 355) guitar 'Lucille'.

In 1960, King moved to ABC, however by the mid-60s, his career seemed in decline. Revitalization came with the discovery of the blues by young whites and, in 1968, King played the Fillmore West with **Johnny Winter** and **Mike Bloomfield**. His revival of **Roy Hawkins**' 'The Thrill Is Gone', which made innovatory use of strings, provided the crucial pop crossover and, in 1970, he recorded his first collaboration with rock musicians, produced by **Leon Russell**. King's career has been smooth sailing ever since: in demand for commercials, movie soundtracks, television theme tunes, and guest appearances. Despite a workaholic schedule, he worked unobtrusively to provide entertainment for prisoners (co-founding the Foundation for the Advancement of Inmate Rehabilitation and Recreation in 1972).

In 1995, King announced that, as he had turned 70, he would be drastically reducing his performing schedule: instead of a regular 300 or more gigs a year, he would be winding down to 200!

B.B. King has made the blues mainstream. The teenager playing in the 40s streets became a man with whom the chairman of the Republican Party in the 80s considered it an honour to play guitar.

KING, BEN E.

US SINGER BEN E. KING (b. BENJAMIN EARL NELSON, 1938) STARTED OUT IN DOO-WOP GROUP, THE FOUR B'S, BEFORE joining the Five Crowns, who became the **Drifters**. King was the lead vocalist and occasional composer on several of their recordings including 'There Goes My Baby' and 'Save The Last Dance For Me'. Going solo in 1960, he recorded 'Spanish Harlem' (1961, US Top 10). 'Stand By Me' (1961) was even more successful and was followed by hits including 'Amor' (1961) and 'Don't Play That Song (You Lied)' (1962).

In 1975, 'Supernatural Thing Part 1' hit the US Top 5. In 1977, a collaboration with the **Average White Band** resulted in two R&B chart entries and *Benny And Us*. In 1986, 'Stand By Me' (US Top 10/UK number 1) was included in a film of the same name.

KILLING JOKE
Albums
Fire Dances (EG 1983)★★★★
➽ p.368 for full listings
Collaborators
Bananarama ➽ p.31
Crowded House ➽ p.107
Connections
Public Image Limited ➽ p.269
Influences
John Peel ➽ p.258

KING, ALBERT
Albums
Live Wire/Blues Power (King 1968)★★★★
➽ p.368 for full listings
Collaborators
Booker T. And The MGs ➽ p.62
Gary Moore ➽ p.238

KING, B. B.
Albums
Rock Me Baby (1964)★★★★
Blues Is King (Bluesway 1967)★★★★
➽ p.368 for full listings
Collaborators
T-Bone Walker ➽ p.333
Johnny Winter ➽ p.341
Mike Bloomfield ➽ p.54
Leon Russell ➽ p.286
U2 ➽ p.326
Further References
CD-ROM: *On The Road With B.B. King* (MCA 1996)★★★★

KING, BEN E.
Albums
Rough Edges (1970)★★★
➽ p.368 for full listings
Collaborators
Average White Band ➽ p.25
Connections
Drifters ➽ p.126

KING, CAROLE
Albums
Tapestry (Ode 1971)★★★★
Fantasy (Ode 1973)★★★★
➽ p.368 for full listings
Collaborators
Gerry Goffin ➽ p.164
Little Eva ➽ p.216
Cookies ➽ p.100
Connections
Shirelles ➽ p.295
Bobby Vee ➽ p.329
Drifters ➽ p.126
Aretha Franklin ➽ p.153
Byrds ➽ p.77
Dusty Springfield ➽ p.305
Monkees ➽ p.236
James Taylor ➽ p.317
Further References
Books: *Carole King*, Paula Taylor
Carole King: A Biography In Words & Pictures, Mitchell S. Cohen

KING, EVELYN 'CHAMPAGNE'
Albums
I'm In Love (RCA 1981)★★★
➽ p.368 for full listings
Connections
Gamble and Huff ➽ p.158

KING, FREDDIE
Albums
Getting Ready (Shelter 1971)★★★★
➽ p.368 for full listings
Collaborators
Leon Russell ➽ p.286
Eric Clapton ➽ p.92
Further References
Video: *Freddie King: Beat 1966* (Vestapol 1995)

KING, JONATHAN
Albums
Try Something Different (Decca 1972)★★
➽ p.368 for full listings
Connections
Genesis ➽ p.161
10cc ➽ p.318

KING CRIMSON
Albums
In Court Of Crimson King (Island 1969)★★★★
Larks Tongues In Aspic (Island 1973)★★★★
➽ p.368 for full listings
Connections
Emerson, Lake And Palmer ➽ p.135
Yes ➽ p.346

KING CURTIS
Albums
It's Party Time (Tru-Sound 1962)★★★★
➽ p.368 for full listings
Collaborators
Aretha Franklin ➽ p.153
John Lennon ➽ p.214
Billy Preston ➽ p.266

KING, CAROLE

KING (b. CAROLE KLEIN, 1942) WAS A PROLIFIC SONGWRITER BY HER EARLY TEENS. SHE LATER MARRIED FELLOW LYRICIST **Gerry Goffin**. She completed a handful of singles, including 'The Right Girl' (1958) and 'Queen Of The Beach' (1959), prior to recording 'Oh Neil' (1960), a riposte to **Sedaka**'s 'Oh Carol'. King and Goffin scored success with the **Shirelles** ('Will You Still Love Me Tomorrow'), **Bobby Vee** ('Take Good Care Of My Baby') and the **Drifters** ('Up On The Roof') and were responsible for much of the early output on the Dimension label. They wrote, arranged and produced hits for **Little Eva** ('The Loco-Motion') and the **Cookies** ('Chains' and 'Don't Say Nothin' Bad About My Baby'); 'It Might As Well Rain Until September' (1962), provided King with a solo hit. Their later compositions included 'A Natural Woman' (**Aretha Franklin**), 'Goin' Back' (**Dusty Springfield** and the **Byrds**) and 'Pleasant Valley Sunday' (the **Monkees**). Their disintegrating marriage was chronicled on King's 'The Road To Nowhere' (1967).

King moved to Los Angeles, and went solo in 1970 with *Writer*, then *Tapestry*, which contained 'You've Got A Friend' (US number 1 for **James Taylor**). *Music* and *Rhymes And Reasons* went gold, as did *Fantasy*, *Wrap Around Joy* (including US number 1, 'Jazzman') and *Thoroughbred*.

Pearls comprised 'classic' Goffin/King songs. In the early 90s, King relocated to Ireland. On *Speeding Time* and *City Streets*, her songwriting skills were still in evidence.

KING, EVELYN 'CHAMPAGNE'

NEW YORKER KING (b. 1960) WAS COACHED BY T. LIFE, WHO WAS A MEMBER OF GAMBLE AND HUFF'S WRITING AND production staff. Her debut, 'Shame' (1977) earned considerable success on the dance/club circuit and made the international pop charts. Her second hit, 'I Don't Know If It's Right', became her second gold disc and she later enjoyed international hits with 'I'm In Love' (1981) and 'Love Come Down' (1982, UK Top 10). *Flirt* was generally considered a return to form.

KING, FREDDIE

60S BLUES SINGER-GUITARIST FREDDIE (AKA FREDDY) (b. BILLY MYLES, 1934, d. 1976) STARTED OUT IN SEVERAL BLUES bands. In 1960, King recorded six titles under his own name, all on the same day, including the instrumental hit 'Hideaway'. He left his current label, King Federal, for the Atlantic subsidiary, Cotillion, but the following albums failed to capture him at his best; nor did his work with **Leon Russell** on his Shelter label. However, King also made many outstanding recordings during this period: *Getting Ready* included the original version of 'Going Down'; *Burglar* featured a duet with **Eric Clapton** on 'Sugar Sweet'. Tragically, this new relationship was cut short when King died of heart failure aged 43. His last stage appearance had taken place three days earlier in his home-town of Dallas.

KING, JONATHAN

BRITISH SONGWRITER KING (b. 1944) HIT THE CHARTS WITH HIS PLAINTIVE PROTEST SONG 'EVERYONE'S GONE TO The Moon' (1965). Hedgehopper's Anonymous gave him his second protest hit with 'It's Good News Week'. As Decca Records' talent-spotter, King discovered **Genesis**, producing their first album; he was also heavily involved in studio novelty numbers such as the Piglets' 'Johnny Reggae', Sakkarin's 'Sugar Sugar' and St. Cecilia's 'Leap Up And Down (Wave Your Knickers In The Air)'.

In 1972, King launched UK Records, best remembered for **10cc**. He also had a hit in his own name during 1975 with 'Una Paloma Blanca'. King has maintained a high-media profile via newspaper columns, radio appearances and his BBC television programme, *Entertainment USA*.

KING CRIMSON

ENGLISH PROGRESSIVE ROCK BAND FORMED IN 1969. **ROBERT FRIPP** (b. 1946; GUITAR) AND MIKE GILES (b. 1942; drums) were joined by Ian McDonald (b. 1946; keyboards) and Greg Lake (b. 1948; vocals/bass). Pete Sinfield supplied lyrics to Fripp's compositions. *In The Court Of The Crimson King* drew ecstatic praise.

Critical popularity ended with *In The Wake Of Poseidon*. The album masked internal strife which saw McDonald and Giles depart to work as a duo and Lake leave to found **Emerson, Lake And Palmer**. Fripp completed the album with various musicians including Gordon Haskell (b. 1946; bass/vocals) and Mel Collins (saxophone), both of whom remained for *Lizard*, and drummer Andy McCullough. Boz Burrell (bass/vocals) and Ian Wallace (drums) replaced Haskell and McCullough. One studio album, *Islands*, and a live selection, *Earthbound*, were released before this line-up collapsed in 1972. Fripp recruited a more radical line-up with John Wetton (b. 1950; bass/vocals), **Bill Bruford** (drums; ex-**Yes**), percussionist Jamie Muir and violinist David Cross (b. 1949). *Larks Tongues In Aspic* resulted; followed by a Fripp, Wetton and Bruford release, *Red*.

In 1974, Fripp went solo, but in 1981, resurrected the group's name for himself, Bruford, Tony Levin (bass) and Adrian Belew (guitar). *Discipline*, *Beat* and *Three Of A Perfect Pair* were just a temporary interlude, and Fripp subsequently resumed his solo career and established a new unit, the League Of Gentlemen.

Fripp reconvened King Crimson in 1994: Belew, Trey Gunn (stick/backing vocals), Levin, Bruford and Pat Mastelotto (acoustic/electric percussion) released *Thrak*.

KING CURTIS

AMERICAN SAXOPHONIST AND SESSION MUSICIAN CURTIS (b. CURTIS OUSLEY, 1934, d. 1971) APPEARED ON COUNTLESS releases, particularly on the Atlantic label. A former member of Lionel Hampton's band, Curtis scored a US R&B number 1 with 'Soul Twist', billed as King Curtis And The Noble Knights. The same group released 'The Monkey' (1963) and 'Soul Serenade' (1964), but the singer took solo credit. Curtis continued his session work alongside establishing his own career; his strongest release was 'Memphis Soul Stew' (1967). He also put together a superb studio group: Richard Tee, Cornell Dupree, Jerry Jemmott and Bernard 'Pretty' Purdie, all of whom contributed to several **Aretha Franklin** records. Curtis guested on **John Lennon**'s *Imagine* and attracted the best session musicians to work on his own albums, including guitarist Duane Allman on *Instant Groove* and **Billy Preston** on *Live At Fillmore West*. This illustrious career was tragically ended when Curtis was stabbed to death outside his New York apartment.

KINGSMEN

US MUSICIANS JACK ELY (VOCALS/GUITAR), MIKE MITCHELL (GUITAR) BOB NORDBY (BASS) AND LYNN EASTON (DRUMS) began working as the Kingsmen in 1958; Don Galluci (keyboards) joined in 1962. The group's debut, 'Louie Louie' (1963) reached US number 2, however internal ructions led to Ely and Norby walking out. Norm Sundholm (bass) and Gary Abbot (drums) joined, but the group soon split.

KINGSTON TRIO

US FOLK REVIVALIST GROUP FORMED IN 1957. BOB SHANE (b. 1934), NICK REYNOLDS (b. 1933) AND DAVE GUARD (b. 1934, d. 1991) had limited singles success; they are most remembered for 'Tom Dooley' (1958, UK number 5/US number 1). *The Kingston Trio* also reached US number 1 and in 1959, *From The Hungry i*, a live recording, reached number 2. *The Kingston Trio At Large* and *Here We Go Again* both reached number 1, as did *Sold Out* and *String Along*. Guard went solo, replaced by John Stewart (b. 1939) in 1961. *Close-Up* (US number 3) was the first release featuring Stewart. The line-up continued until 1967.

Shane later re-formed the group, as the New Kingston Trio, with Roger Gamble and George Grove. Their output was prolific, but marginally successful; they disbanded in 1968. Stewart went solo and continues to record and perform. In 1987, the Trio was on the road again, with Shane, Grove, and newcomer, Bob Haworth.

KINKS

UK BAND FORMED IN 1963, AS THE RAVENS, BY SONGWRITER RAY DAVIES (b. 1944; VOCALS/GUITAR/PIANO).

Ray, his brother Dave (b. 1947; guitar/vocals), Peter Quaife (b. 1943; bass) and latecomer Mick Avory (b. 1944; drums) debuted with 'Long Tall Sally'. It failed to sell, but their third single, 'You Really Got Me', reached UK number 1, boosted by a performance on the UK television show *Ready Steady Go*. This and its successor, 'All Day And All Of The Night', provided a blueprint for hard rock guitar. Over the next two years Ray Davies emerged as a songwriter of startling originality and his band were rarely out of the best-sellers list. The group returned to number 1 with 'Tired Of Waiting For You' (1965).

'Dedicated Follower Of Fashion' brilliantly satirized Carnaby Street narcissism; 'Sunny Afternoon' (UK number 1) dealt with capitalism and class and 'Dead End Street' (1966) was about poverty. Their early albums had contained a staple diet of R&B standards and harmless Davies originals. With *Face To Face* and *Something Else*, however, he set about redefining the English character, with sparkling wit and steely nerve. One of his greatest songs was *Something Else*'s final track, 'Waterloo Sunset', a simple but emotional *tour de force*. It narrowly missed the top of the charts, as did the following 'Autumn Almanac', with its gentle chorus.

By 1968, the Kinks had fallen from UK popularity, despite remaining critically well respected. Two superb concept albums, *The Kinks Are The Village Green Preservation Society* and *Arthur Or The Decline And Fall Of The British Empire*, inexplicably failed to sell, despite containing some of Davies' finest songs.

Quaife left in 1969, replaced by John Dalton, followed by a return to the UK best-sellers lists with 'Lola' (1970), an irresistible fable of transvestism; this marked the beginning of their US breakthrough, reaching the Top 10. The resulting *Lola Versus Powerman And The Moneygoround, Part One* was also a US success. The group now embarked on a series of huge American tours and rarely performed in Britain, although their business operation centre and recording studio, Konk, was based in London. Having signed a new contract with RCA in 1971, the band had now enlarged to incorporate a brass section. Following the country-influenced *Muswell Hillbillies*, however, they suffered a barren period. Ray experienced drug and marital problems, and their live performances revealed a man bereft of his driving, creative enthusiasm.

Throughout the early 70s a series of average, over-ambitious concept albums appeared as Davies' main outlet. In 1976, Dalton departed, as their unhappy and comparatively unsuccessful years with RCA ended. A new contract with Arista engendered a remarkable change in fortunes; both *Sleepwalker* and *Misfits* were excellent, successful albums.

Although still spending most of their time playing to vast US audiences, the Kinks were adopted by the British new wave, and were cited by many punk bands as a major influence. Both the **Jam** ('David Watts') and the **Pretenders** ('Stop Your Sobbing') provided reminders of Davies' 60s songwriting skill, while in 1983 they unexpectedly appeared in the UK singles chart with 'Come Dancing'.

In 1990, they were inducted into the Rock 'n' Roll Hall of Fame, at the time only the fourth UK group to take the honour behind the **Beatles**, the **Rolling Stones** and the **Who**. Quaife and Avory were present at the ceremony. After the comparative failure of *UK Jive* the band left London Records, and after some time without a recording contract, signed with Sony in 1991. *Phobia* was a commercial failure and the band were dropped; they released *To The Bone* on their own Konk label. Ray Davies has made his mark under the Kinks' banner as one of the most perceptive and prolific popular songwriters of our time.

Connections
Lionel Hampton
Noble Knights

KINGSMEN
Albums
Kingsmen On Campus (Wand 1965)★★
➽ p.368 for full listings
Further References
Film: *How To Stuff A Wild Bikini* (1965)

KINGSTON TRIO
Albums
Kingston Trio At Large (Capitol 1959)★★★★
➽ p.368 for full listings
Connections
Whiskeyhill Singers
New Kingston Trio
Further References
Book: *Kingston Trio On Record*, Kingston Korner

KINKS
Albums
Something Else (Pye 1967)★★★★★
The Kinks Are Village Green Preservation Society (Pye 1968)★★★★★
➽ p.368 for full listings
Collaborators
Robert Wace
Grenville Collins
Larry Page
Connections
Ready Steady Go
Jam ➽ p.196
Pretenders ➽ p.266
Beatles ➽ p.38
Rolling Stones ➽ p.281
Who ➽ p.338
Further References
Books: *Kinks: Official Biography*, Jon Savage
Kink: An Autobiography, Dave Davies

KISS
Albums
Destroyer (Casablanca 1976)★★★★
➧ p.368 for full listings
Connections
Black Sabbath ➧ p.51
Influences
Argent ➧ p.20
Further References
Video: *Animalize* (Embassy Home Video 1986)

KISS

FORMED IN 1972 BY PAUL STANLEY (b. PAUL EISEN, 1950; RHYTHM GUITAR/VOCALS) AND GENE SIMMONS (b. CHAIM Witz, 1949; bass/vocals); they recruited Peter Criss (b. Peter Crisscoula, 1947; drums/vocals) and Ace Frehley (b. Paul Frehley, 1951; lead guitar/vocals). Bill Aucoin offered the band a management contract, and within two weeks they were signed to Neil Bogart's recently established Casablanca Records. In just over a year, Kiss had released their first three albums with a modicum of success. In 1975, their fortunes changed with the release of *Alive*, which spawned their first US hit single, 'Rock 'N' Roll All Nite'. The appeal of Kiss has always been based on their live shows: the garish greasepaint make-up, outrageous costumes and pyrotechnic stage effects.

Alive became their first certified platinum album in the USA. *Destroyer* proved just as successful, and gave them their first US Top 10 single, 'Beth'. *Rock And Roll Over*, *Love Gun* and *Alive II* confirmed Kiss as major recording artists. After the release of *Dynasty*, which featured the worldwide hit, 'I Was Made For Lovin' You', cracks appeared in the ranks. Criss left, replaced by session player Anton Fig. Fig played drums on *Unmasked* until a permanent replacement was found, New Yorker Eric Carr (b. 1950, d. 1991).

Music From The Elder represented a radical departure from traditional Kiss music and included several ballads, an orchestra and a choir. Frehley, increasingly disenchanted with the musical direction of the band, left in 1983. By this time the popularity of the band was waning and drastic measures were called for. The legendary make-up which had concealed their true identities for almost 10 years was removed on MTV in the USA.

Vinnie Vincent made his first official appearance on *Lick It Up*, which provided Kiss with their first UK Top 10 hit. The resurgence of the band continued with *Animalize*. Vincent had been replaced by Mark St. John (b. Mark Norton). His association with the band was short-lived, however, as he was struck down by Reiters Syndrome. Bruce Kulick, the brother of long-time Kiss cohort Bob, was drafted in and subsequently became a permanent member. Further commercial success was achieved with *Asylum* and *Crazy Nights*, the latter featuring their biggest UK hit, 'Crazy, Crazy Nights' (1987, number 4). It was followed by a further two Top 40 hit singles, 'Reason To Live' and 'Turn On The Night'. *Hot In The Shade* succeeded their third compilation album, *Smashes, Thrashes And Hits*, and included their highest-charting hit single in the USA, 'Forever' (1990, number 4).

Kiss contributed a cover of **Argent**'s classic, 'God Gave Rock 'N' Roll To You', to the film soundtrack of *Bill And Ted's Bogus Journey*, and brought in replacement drummer Eric Singer (ex-**Black Sabbath**). A stable unit with Bruce Kulick (guitar) and Eric Singer (drums) together with Simmons and Stanley appeared to be on the cards but Frehley and Criss stepped back in for a reunion tour.

KITT, EARTHA
Albums
That Bad Eartha (RCA Victor 1953)★★★★
➧ p.368 for full listings
Further References
Book: *Alone With Me: A New Biography*, Eartha Kitt

KITT, EARTHA

NEW YORKER KITT (b. 1928) STARTED OUT IN KATHARINE DUNHAM'S FAMED DANCING TROUPE. SHE APPEARED ON Broadway in *New Faces Of 1952* introducing 'Monotonous', and later appeared in the film version of the show. Her other Broadway shows included *Mrs. Patterson* (1954) and *Shinbone Alley* (1957). She continued to work in cabaret, theatre, television and films, playing leading roles in *St Louis Blues* (1958), with Nat 'King' Cole, and an all-black version of *Anna Lucasta* (1959), opposite Sammy Davis Jnr.

Kitt's solo songs include 'I Want To Be Evil', 'An Englishman Needs Time', 'Santa Baby', and 'I'm Just An Old-Fashioned Girl'. In 1978, she appeared on Broadway in an all-black version of *Kismet* entitled *Timbuktu*. In 1988, she played Carlotta Campion in the London production of *Follies* and sang Stephen Sondheim's, 'I'm Still Here' – also the title of her autobiography. In the early 90s she appeared in the comedy/horror movie *Ernest Scared Stupid*. She also toured Britain with the Ink Spots in *A Night At The Cotton Club*.

KLAATU
Albums
Klaatu (Capitol 1976)★★★
➧ p.368 for full listings
Connections
Carpenters ➧ p.82
Rolling Stone ➧ p.280
Influences
Beatles ➧ p.38

KLAATU

CANADIAN ROCK TRIO FORMED *c.* 1975 BY VOCALIST, SONG-WRITER AND DRUMMER TERRY DRAPER, ALONG WITH John Woloschuk and Dee Long. Their first single was 'Doctor Marvello/California Jam', a minor Canadian hit. In 1976, they released 'Calling Occupants Of Interplanetary Craft', with its b-side 'Sub Rosa Subway', along with the accompanying album, *Klaatu* (titled *3:47 E.S.T.* in Canada). The band's sound closely resembled that of the latter-day **Beatles** and a US journalist surmised that it might very well *be* the Beatles. The group did nothing to stem the rumours and **Rolling Stone** named Klaatu 'hype of the year' for 1977.

'Calling Occupants...' attained chart status in 1977, when the **Carpenters** took it to US Top 40/UK Top 10. In 1981, after releasing four further albums, the group disbanded.

KLF
Albums
Towards Trance (KLF Communications 1988)★★★★
➧ p.368 for full listings
Connections
Echo And The Bunnymen ➧ p.131
Teardrop Explodes ➧ p.317

KLF

SINCE 1987, THE KLF HAVE OPERATED UNDER A SERIES OF GUISES, ONLY GRADUALLY REVEALING THEIR TRUE NATURE to the public at large. The band's principal spokesman is Bill Drummond (b. William Butterworth, 1953). As co-founder of the Zoo label in the late 70s, he introduced and later managed **Echo And The Bunnymen** and the **Teardrop Explodes**. Later he joined forces with Jimmy Cauty (b. 1954). Their first project was under the title JAMS (Justified Ancients Of Mu Mu – a title lifted from Robert Shea and Robert Anton Wilson's conspiracy novels). The provocatively titled LP *1987 – What The Fuck Is Going On?* was released as KLF (Kopyright Liberation Front). In the wake of the emerging house scene, they compromised the theme tune to British television show *Dr Who*, adding a strong disco beat and **Gary Glitter** yelps – 'Doctorin' The Tardis' was an instant number 1, under the title Timelords. The originators also wrote a book – *How To Have A Number One The Easy Way*. Returning as the KLF, they enjoyed a hit with 'What Time Is Love'. This was followed by the soulful techno hit '3 A.M. Eternal'.

The KLF's 'Justified And Ancient' featured the unmistakable voice of Tammy Wynette and sold millions of records worldwide. They were voted Top British Group by the BPI, and, typically, at the awards party announced that the KLF were no more. Their only 'release' in 1992 came with a version of 'Que Sera Sera'. Since that time, Drummond and Cauty have made several pseudonymous returns to the singles charts, including the 1996 tribute to footballer Eric Cantona, 'Ooh! Aah! Cantona', as 1300 Drums Featuring The Unjustified Ancients Of Mu.

KNACK

FORMED IN LOS ANGELES IN 1978. DOUG FIEGER (VOCALS/GUITAR), PRESCOTT NILES (BASS), BERTON AVERRE (GUITAR) and Bruce Gary (drums) attempted to revive the spirit of the beat boom with matching suits, and short songs boasting solid, easily memorable riffs. They recruited producer **Mike Chapman**, who had previously worked with **Blondie,** and during 1979, the Knack's million-selling debut single 'My Sharona' reached US number 1/UK Top 10.

The Knack proved an instant hit, selling five million copies. At the height of a critical backlash, they issued *But The Little Girls Understand*, but both the sales and the songs were less impressive and by the time of *Round Trip*, their power-pop style seemed decidedly outmoded. In 1981, they disbanded, although a reunion in 1991 resulted in the forgettable *Serious Fun*.

KNACK
Albums
Knack (Capitol 1979)★★★
» p.368 for full listings

KNICKERBOCKERS

US GROUP FORMED IN 1964 BY BUDDY RANDELL (SAXOPHONE) AND JIMMY WALKER (DRUMS/VOCALS), WITH THE Charles brothers, John (bass) and Beau (lead guitar). In 1965, they reached the US Top 20 with 'Lies', a ferocious rocker which many listeners assumed was the **Beatles** in disguise. They broke up in 1968. Randell and Walker both attempted solo careers; for a short time Walker replaced Bill Medley in the **Righteous Brothers**.

KNICKERBOCKERS
Albums
Lies (Challenge 1966)★★★
» p.368 for full listings
Connections
Beatles » p.38
Righteous Brothers » p.278

KNIGHT, GLADYS, AND THE PIPS

GLADYS KNIGHT (b. 1944), HER BROTHER MERALD 'BUBBA' (b. 1942), SISTER BRENDA AND COUSINS ELENOR AND WILLIAM Guest (b. 1941) formed their first vocal group, the Pips, in their native Atlanta in 1952. They recorded for Brunswick in 1958, with another cousin, Edward Patten (b. 1939); Langston George joined in 1959 when Brenda and Elenor left. Three years elapsed before a version of Johnny Otis's 'Every Beat Of My Heart' was leased to Vee Jay Records and went on to top the US R&B charts. George retired in the early 60s, leaving the quartet line-up that survived into the 80s.

In 1966, Gladys Knight and The Pips were signed to **Motown**'s Soul subsidiary and teamed with producer/songwriter Norman Whitfield. In 1967, they had a major hit with the original release of 'I Heard It Through The Grapevine'. In the early 70s, the group slowly moved away from their original blues-influenced sound towards a more MOR harmony blend. Their new approach brought them success with 'Neither One Of Us (Wants To Say Goodbye)' (1972).

Knight and The Pips left Motown when the label moved to Hollywood. At Buddah, they found immediate success with the US chart-topper 'Midnight Train To Georgia', an arresting soul ballad, followed by major hits such as 'I've Got To Use My Imagination' and 'The Best Thing That Ever Happened To Me'. In 1974, they performed **Curtis Mayfield**'s soundtrack songs for the film *Claudine*; the following year, the title track of *I Feel A Song* gave them another soul number 1. In 1975, they released 'The Way We Were/Try To Remember', the centrepiece of *Second Anniversary*, and they began hosting their own US television series.

Gladys made her acting debut in *Pipedream* (1976), for which the group recorded a soundtrack album. Legal problems then forced Knight and The Pips to record separately until 1980. Subsequent releases alternated between the group's R&B and MOR modes. 'Love Overboard' (1988) earned them a Grammy for the Best R&B performance, after which Knight and The Pips split. Merald remained with Gladys when she achieved a UK Top 10 that year with the James Bond movie song 'Licence To Kill', and released *A Good Woman* the following year. She collaborated with **Chaka Khan**, Brandy and Tamia on the minor hit single 'Missing You' in 1996, from the **Queen Latifah** film *Set It Off*.

KNIGHT, GLADYS, AND THE PIPS
Albums
Neither One Of Us (Soul 1973)★★★★
» p.368 for full listings
Collaborators
Chaka Khan » p.204
Connections
Marvin Gaye » p.159
Queen Latifah » p.270
Influences
Curtis Mayfield » p.228

KNOPFLER, MARK

KNOPFLER (b. 1949; **DIRE STRAITS**) IS A COMPOSER AND VOCALIST WITH A TERSE, RESONANT FRETBOARD DEXterity. He was employed by fellow-Brit **Eric Clapton** and Chet Atkins in the 80s; inaugurating a parallel solo career in 1983 with the film score for *Local Hero*. Further soundtracks included *Cal*, *Comfort And Joy* and (with Dire Straits' Guy Fletcher) *The Princess Bride*. After playing with Pick Withers on **Bob Dylan**'s *Slow Train Coming*, Knopfler produced Dylan's *Infidels* (1983). He was also in demand as a session guitarist, working for **Steely Dan** (*Gaucho*), **Phil Lynott** (*Solo In Soho*), **Van Morrison** (*Beautiful Vision*) and **Bryan Ferry** (*Boys And Girls*). In 1989, he and old friends Brendan Croker and Steve Phillips formed the Notting Hillbillies for an album and tour, and, in 1990, he backed Clapton during an Albert Hall season. The 'official' debut album, *Golden Heart*, featured support from slide-blues guitarist Sonny Landreth, singer-songwriter **Paul Brady**, the **Chieftains** and **Vince Gill**.

KNOPFLER, MARK
Albums
Golden Heart (Mercury 1996)★★★
» p.369 for full listings
Collaborators
Bob Dylan » p.128
Steely Dan » p.308
Phil Lynott » p.220
Van Morrison » p.238
Bryan Ferry » p.144
Paul Brady » p.66
Chieftains » p.90
Vince Gill » p.162
Connections
Dire Straits » p.120
Eric Clapton » p.92
Further References
Book: *Mark Knopfler: An Unauthorised Biography*, Myles Palmer

KOKOMO (UK)

SOUL BAND FORMED IN 1973: VOCALISTS DYAN BIRCH, PADDIE MCHUGH AND FRANK COLLINS (EX-ARRIVAL), NEIL Hubbard (guitar), Alan Spenner (bass), Tony O'Malley (piano), Jim Mullen (guitar), Terry Stannard (drums), Joan Linscott (congas) and journeyman saxophonist Mel Collins. Kokomo's debut album was acclaimed but they failed to sustain its promise. This line-up split in 1977, but a reconstituted version of the band appeared on the London gig circuit in the early 80s and recorded one album. Another reunion took place in the late 80s, but faltered when Alan Spenner died in 1991.

KOKOMO (UK)
Albums
Kokomo (Columbia 1975)★★★
» p.369 for full listings

KOOL AND THE GANG

ORIGINALLY FORMED AS A QUARTET (THE JAZZIACS) BY ROBERT 'KOOL' BELL (b. 1950; BASS), ROBERT 'SPIKE' MICKENS (trumpet), Robert 'The Captain' Bell, later known by his Muslim name Amir Bayyan (b. 1951; saxophone/keyboards) and Dennis 'D.T.' Thomas (b. 1951; saxophone). This aspiring US group opened for acts such as Pharaoh Sanders and Leone Thomas. They were later joined by Charles 'Claydes' Smith (b. 1948; guitar) and 'Funky' George Brown (b. 1949; drums), and known as the Soul Town Band. In 1969, they settled on the name Kool And The Gang. The group had 19 US Top 40 hits on their De-Lite label, including 'Funky Stuff'. In 1974, 'Jungle Boogie' and 'Hollywood Swinging' made the Top 10. In 1979, the Gang added vocalists James 'J.T.' Taylor (b. 1953) and Earl Toon Jnr, leading to a new era of success for the group.

'Celebration' was a 1980 platinum disc and US pop number 1. They proved similarly popular worldwide and in the UK, 'Get Down On It' (1981), 'Joanna' (1984) and 'Cherish' (1985) all reached the Top 5. *Celebrate!* reached the Top 10 in 1980.

The original six members remained into the 80s and although newcomer Toon left, Taylor blossomed into an ideal frontman. Taylor departed in 1988, replaced by three singers, Skip Martin (ex-**Dazz Band**), Odeen Mays and Gary Brown. In 1989, Taylor released a solo album, *Sister Rosa*, while the group produced *Sweat*. The new line-up continues to record.

KOOL AND THE GANG
Albums
In Heart (De-Lite 1983)★★★★
» p.369 for full listings
Connections
Dazz Band » p.112

KOOPER, AL
Albums
Easy Does It (Columbia 1970)★★★★
➽ p.369 for full listings
Collaborators
Mike Bloomfield ➽ p.54
Stephen Stills ➽ p.310
Jimi Hendrix ➽ p.180
Rolling Stones ➽ p.281
Nils Lofgren ➽ p.217
Tubes ➽ p.324
Connections
Steely Dan ➽ p.308
Doobie Brothers ➽ p.123
Influences
Bob Dylan ➽ p.128

KORN
Albums
Korn (Immortal 1995)★★★
➽ p.369 for full listings

KORNER, ALEXIS
Albums
Red Hot From Alex aka Alexis Korner's All Star Blues Incorporated (Transatlantic 1964)★★★★
➽ p.369 for full listings
Collaborators
Long John Baldry ➽ p.30
Jack Bruce ➽ p.71
Ginger Baker ➽ p.29
Robert Plant ➽ p.262
Influences
Eric Clapton ➽ p.92
Chris Farlowe ➽ p.143
Zoot Money ➽ p.236

KOSSOFF, PAUL
Albums
Back Street Crawler (Island 1973)★★★
➽ p.369 for full listings
Collaborators
John Martyn ➽ p.226
Connections
Free ➽ p.154

KOTTKE, LEO
Albums
My Feet Are Smiling (Capitol 1973)★★★★
➽ p.369 for full listings
Influences
Byrds ➽ p.77

KRAFTWERK
Albums
Autobahn (Vertigo 1974)★★★★
➽ p.369 for full listings
Connections
Afrika Bambaataa ➽ p.11
Influences
Tangerine Dream ➽ p.316

KRAMER, BILLY J., AND THE DAKOTAS
Albums
Little Children (Imperial 1964)★★★
➽ p.369 for full listings
Collaborators
Brian Epstein ➽ p.137
Influences
Beatles ➽ p.38
Burt Bacharach ➽ p.27

KOOPER, AL

KOOPER (b. 1944) STARTED OUT IN 1959 AS GUITARIST IN THE ROYAL TEENS. HE BECAME A NOTED NEW YORK session musician and later forged a successful songwriting partnership with Bobby Brass and Irwin Levine. In 1965, Kooper attended a **Bob Dylan** session on organ, an instrument with which he was barely conversant. Dylan nonetheless loved his instinctive touch which breathed fire into 'Like A Rolling Stone' and the album *Highway 61 Revisited*. Kooper also guested on Dylan's *Blonde On Blonde*, *New Morning* and *Under The Red Sky*.

The organist then joined the **Blues Project**, but left in 1967 to found **Blood, Sweat And Tears**. He stayed with them for just one album. He accepted a production post at Columbia Records, before recording *Super Session* with **Mike Bloomfield** and **Stephen Stills**. This successful informal jam inspired several inferior imitations, not the least of which was the indulgent *Live Adventures Of Al Kooper And Mike Bloomfield*. Kooper's solo career was effectively relaunched with *I Stand Alone*, a promising but inconsistent set. *You Never Know Who Your Friends Are* and *New York City (You're A Woman)* were among his most popular releases.

Kooper appeared on *Electric Ladyland* (**Jimi Hendrix**) and *Let It Bleed* (**Rolling Stones**) and produced the debut albums by **Nils Lofgren** and the **Tubes**. He established his own label, Sounds Of The South, in Atlanta, Georgia, and signed **Lynyrd Skynyrd**. In 1982, he completed the solo album *Championship Wrestling*, featuring contributions from guitarist Jeff 'Skunk' Baxter (**Steely Dan** and **Doobie Brothers**). Kooper has since been active in recording computerized soundtrack music, and produced *Scapegoats* for **Green On Red**.

KORN

HARDCORE US ROCK BAND FORMED IN THE EARLY 90S. THEY TOURED WIDELY BEFORE RELEASING THEIR SELF-titled debut album. Jonathan Davis (vocals), Reggie Fieldy Arvizu (bass), James Munky Shaffer (guitar), Brian Welch (guitar/vocals) and David Silveria (drums) released their first single, 'Blind', which received major MTV coverage. The album brought commercial breakthrough. The Ross Robinson-produced *Life Is Peachy* had limited commercial success due to explicit lyrics.

KORNER, ALEXIS

AN INSPIRATIONAL FIGURE IN BRITISH MUSIC CIRCLES, KORNER (b. 1928, d. 1984) WAS ALREADY VERSED IN BLACK music when he met Cyril Davies at the London Skiffle Club. Together they transformed the venue into the London Blues And Barrelhouse Club, where they performed together and showcased visiting US bluesmen. When jazz trombonist Chris Barber introduced R&B into his live repertoire, he employed Korner (guitar) and Davies (harmonica). Inspired, the pair formed Blues Incorporated in 1961, establishing the Ealing Rhythm And Blues Club in 1962. Blues Incorporated included Charlie Watts (drums), Art Wood (vocals) and Keith Scott (piano), later featuring **Long John Baldry**, **Jack Bruce**, Graham Bond and **Ginger Baker**. The name 'Blues Incorporated' was dropped when Korner went solo, punctuated by the formation of several temporary groups, including Free At Last (1967), New Church (1969) and Snape (1972). While the supporting cast on such ventures remained fluid, including for a short time **Robert Plant**, the last two units featured Peter Thorup who also collaborated with Korner on **CCS**; they scored notable hits with 'Whole Lotta Love' (1970), 'Walkin'' and 'Tap Turns On The Water' (both 1971).

Korner also began broadcasting for BBC radio, but continued to perform live. He joined Charlie Watts, Ian Stewart, Jack Bruce and Dick Heckstall-Smith in Rocket 88, and Korner's 50th birthday party featured appearances by **Eric Clapton**, **Chris Farlowe** and **Zoot Money**. In 1981, Korner began a 13-part television documentary on the history of rock, but his premature death from cancer left this, and many other projects, unfulfilled.

KOSSOFF, PAUL

BRITISH GUITARIST KOSSOFF (b. 1950, d. 1976) WAS INITIALLY A MEMBER OF BLUES BAND BLACK CAT BONES, WITH drummer Simon Kirke. In 1968, the duo founded **Free** and later worked together in **Kossoff**, Kirke, Tetsu And Rabbit, a spin-off project which completed a lone album in 1971. From 1972, Kossoff was beset by recurring drug and related health problems. Often absent on tour, Kossoff finally went solo. *Back Street Crawler* was excellent, including 'Molten Gold', but it was two years before he was well enough play live. He toured with **John Martyn** in 1975, then assembled a new group, Back Street Crawler. The quintet completed one album before Kossoff suffered a near-fatal heart attack. Specialists forbade an immediate return, but a series of concerts was planned for 1976. However, in March, Paul Kossoff died in his sleep on a flight from Los Angeles to New York.

KOTTKE, LEO

AMERICAN GUITARIST (b. 1945) WHOSE CIRCLE ROUND THE SUN RECEIVED LIMITED EXPOSURE, ALTHOUGH HIS CAREER did not fully flourish until *Six And Twelve String Guitar*. Kottke's desire to expand his repertoire led to *Mudlark* which included instrumental and vocal tracks, notably a version of the **Byrds**' 'Eight Miles High'. Prodigious touring enhanced Kottke's reputation as one of America's finest acoustic 12-string guitarists, although commercial success still eluded him.

KRAFTWERK

GERMAN MUSIC STUDENTS RALF HUTTER (b. 1946; ORGAN) AND FLORIAN SCHNEIDER-ESLEBEN (b. 1947; WOODWIND) drew on the influence of experimental electronic forces such as composer Karlheinz Stockhausen and **Tangerine Dream** to create minimalist music on synthesizers, drum machines and tape recorders. After a debut album, *Tone Float*, the duo formed Kraftwerk with Klaus Dinger and Thomas Homann. After releasing Highrail, Dinger and Homann left to form Neu. Wolfgang Flur (electronic drums) and Klaus Roeder (guitar/violin/keyboards) joined after the duo's *Ralf And Florian*; *Autobahn* established them as purveyors of hi-tech, computerized music. An edited version of the title track (the original was over 22 minutes long) reached the US/UK Top 10. In 1975, Roeder was replaced by Karl Bartos.

Trans-Europe Express and *The Man-Machine* were strong influences on new-wave techno groups; the latter's single 'The Model' (1982) gave them a surprise hit when it reached UK number 1. *Electric Café* was seen as a pioneering dance record and cited as a major influence on a host of dance artists from **Afrika Bambaataa** to the producer Arthur Baker. In 1990, Flur departed, replaced by Fritz Hijbert, and the group achieved further UK chart success with 'The Robots'.

KRAMER, BILLY J., AND THE DAKOTAS

UK SINGER KRAMER (b. WILLIAM HOWARD ASHTON, 1943) ORIGINALLY FRONTED MERSEYBEAT COMBO THE COASTERS, before signing to **Brian Epstein**'s management agency and being teamed with the Dakotas – Mike Maxfield (b. 1944; lead guitar), Robin McDonald (b. 1943; rhythm guitar), Ray Jones (bass) and Tony Mansfield (b. 1943; drums). A UK number 1 with the **Beatles**' 'Do You Want To Know A Secret' (1963), was followed by a run of **John Lennon/Paul McCartney** songs, including the chart-topping 'Bad To Me', 'I'll Keep You Satisfied' (number 4) and 'From A Window' (number 10). 'Little Children' (1964), by US writers Mort Shuman and John McFarland, was their third UK number 1 and reached US number 7, quickly followed by the reissued 'Bad To Me' (Top 10). Their chart reign ended with **Burt Bacharach**'s 'Trains And Boats And Planes' (UK number 12). Kramer went solo in 1967, working the cabaret and nostalgia circuit.

KRAVITZ, LENNY

LENNY KRAVITZ (b. 1964) ATTENDED BEVERLY HILLS HIGH SCHOOL ALONG WITH SLASH (**GUNS N' ROSES**), AND MARIA McKee (**Lone Justice**). In 1987, his demo, containing 'Let Love Rule', led to a contract with Virgin America. The following album, *Let Love Rule* proved highly popular and Kravitz went on to even greater success when **Madonna** recorded his 'Justify My Love'.

Mama Said spawned the hit 'It Ain't Over 'Til It's Over' and won him a bigger fan base in the UK; this was highlighted with the reception of *Are You Gonna Go My Way* and his headlining at the UK's Glastonbury Festival in 1993. *Circus* was a stripped down version of his overall sound and one that displayed his talent as a writer of more contemporary songs. In 1998, he returned to the charts with 'If You Can't Say No' from his heavily promoted new album *5*.

KRISTOFFERSON, KRIS

TEXAN SINGER KRISTOFFERSON (b. 1936) BEGAN HIS CAREER IN EUROPE, BEFORE CONCENTRATING ON SONGWRITING – **Jerry Lee Lewis** became the first to record one of his songs, 'Once More With Feeling'. **Johnny Cash**, a fan of Kristofferson's work, persuaded Roger Miller to record 'Me And Bobby McGee' (co-written with Fred Foster) in 1969. Sammi Smith (and later **Gladys Knight**) scored with 'Help Me Make It Through The Night'.

Kristofferson's own hits began with 'Loving Her Was Easier (Than Anything I'll Ever Do Again)' and 'Why Me'. In 1973, Kristofferson married **Rita Coolidge**, they recorded three albums before divorcing in 1979. Kristofferson also acted, appearing in *Cisco Pike* (1971), *Pat Garrett And Billy The Kid*, and opposite Barbra Streisand in *A Star Is Born* (1976), among others. He returned to country music with *The Winning Hand*, featuring duets with **Brenda Lee**, **Dolly Parton** and **Willie Nelson**. *Highwaymen* headed the country chart in 1985 and Kristofferson toured with Nelson, Cash and Waylon Jennings (as the Highwaymen) issuing two albums. He rejuvenated his career with the release of *A Moment Of Forever*.

KROKUS

SYMPHONIC ROCK GROUP FORMED IN SWITZERLAND, IN 1974. AFTER FOUR YEARS AND TWO RATHER LACKLUSTRE albums, they switched to a hard rock style. The group originally featured Chris Von Rohr (vocals), Fernando Von Arb (guitar), Jurg Naegeli (bass/keyboards), Tommy Kiefer (guitar) and Freddy Steady (drums). Singer 'Maltezer' Marc (b. Marc Storace) joined later. *Metal Rendez-vous* coincided with the resurgence of heavy metal in Britain and they played the 1980 Reading Festival. Their next two albums continued with an aggressive – although radio-friendly – approach, and made the UK album charts. Kiefer left, replaced by ex-roadie Mark Kohler (guitar), while Steve Pace stepped in on drums. Kiefer subsequently returned to replace Rohr. *Headhunter* reached number 25 in the *Billboard* album charts. *The Blitz* (US number 31) was an erratic album and since 1985 there has been a downward trend in the band's fortunes. Tragically, Kesier committed suicide in 1986.

In 1995, the band were touring with a line-up of Storace (vocals), Fernando Von Arb (bass), Maurer (guitar), Kohler (guitar) and Steady (drums); recording sessions followed.

KULA SHAKER

FORMED IN LONDON IN 1994 – ORIGINALLY KNOWN AS THE Kays and then the Lovely Lads. Crispian Mills (b. 1963; vocals), Jay Darlington (keyboards), Paul Winter-Hart (drums) and Alonzo Bevin (bass) embarked on a support tour with **Reef** that resulted in a contract with Columbia Records. Their debut, 'Grateful When You're Dead', immediately entered the UK Top 40. Their debut album entered the UK chart at number 1. The band crowned an extraordinary first year by winning a BRIT Award in 1997 and released a frenetic cover version of Joe South's 'Hush', previously a hit for **Deep Purple**. In 1998, they were back with 'The Sound Of Drums', a UK tour and an album due for release in July.

KURSAAL FLYERS

UK BAND – MADE UP OF PAUL SHUTTLEWORTH (VOCALS), Graeme Douglas (guitar), Vic Collins (guitar/steel guitar/ vocals), Richie Bull (bass/vocals), and Will Birch (drums) – who were signed to **Jonathan King**'s label, UK. *Chocs Away* and *The Great Artiste* were praised, and the group became a popular live attraction. The Kursaals attained commercial success after joining CBS. After 'Little Does She Know' (1975, UK Top 20), the group struggled to find a suitable follow-up. Barry Martin replaced Douglas when the latter joined **Eddie And The Hot Rods**, but the unit disintegrated following *Five Live Kursaals*. Having compiled the commemorative *In For A Spin*, Will Birch reunited the Flyers for *Former Tour De Force Is Forced To Tour*.

L7

FORMED IN THE MID-80S BY GUITARIST/VOCALISTS DONITA SPARKS (b. 1963) AND SUZI GARDNER (b. 1960), with Jennifer Finch (b. 1966; bass/vocals) and Dee Plakas (b. 1960; drums). Sup Pop Records released *Smell The Magic*, a raucous, grunge-flavoured album. *Bricks Are Heavy* brought major success, with the surprisingly poppy 'Pretend We're Dead' (a transatlantic hit). L7 appeared as the band Camel Lips in the film, *Serial Mom*, before the successful *Hungry For Stink*. Jennifer Finch departed in 1996, replaced by Gail Greenwood (**Belly**) for *The Beauty Process*.

KRAVITZ, LENNY
Albums
Are You Gonna Go My Way? (Virgin 1993)★★★
» p.369 for full listings
Influences
Jimi Hendrix » p.180

KRISTOFFERSON, KRIS
Albums
Highwayman (Columbia 1985)★★★★
» p.369 for full listings
Collaborators
Rita Coolidge » p.100
Dolly Parton » p.256
Willie Nelson » p.245
Johnny Cash » p.84
Connections
Gladys Knight » p.209

KROKUS
Albums
Metal Rendez-vous (Ariola 1980)★★★
» p.369 for full listings

KULA SHAKER
Albums
K (Columbia 1996)★★★★
» p.369 for full listings

KURSAAL FLYERS
Albums
Chocs Away (UK 1975)★★★
» p.369 for full listings
Connections
Jonathan King » p.206
Eddie And The Hot Rods » p.132

L7
Albums
Bricks Are Heavy (Slash/London 1992)★★★★
» p.369 for full listings

L.A. GUNS
Albums
Cocked And Loaded (Polygram 1989)★★★
p.369 for full listings
Connections
Guns N' Roses p.170

LA'S
Albums
The La's (Go! Discs 1990)★★★★
p.369 for full listings
Connections
Cast p.84

LaBELLE, PATTI
Albums
The Winner In You (MCA 1986)★★★
p.369 for full listings
Collaborators
Bobby Womack p.342
Michael McDonald p.229

LADYSMITH BLACK MAMBAZO
Albums
Two Worlds One Heart (Warners 1990)★★★★
p.369 for full listings
Connections
Paul Simon p.296

LANE, RONNIE
Albums
One For The Road (GM 1975)★★★★
p.369 for full listings
Connections
Small Faces p.300
Faces p.141
Gallagher and Lyle p.158

LANG, JONNY
Albums
Lie To Me (A&M 1997)★★★
p.369 for full listings
Collaborators
Buddy Guy p.171

LANG, K.D.
Albums
Ingenue (Sire/Warners 1992)★★★★
p.369 for full listings
Collaborators
Roy Orbison p.252
Jordanaires p.201
Influences
Steve Miller p.234

LANOIS, DANIEL
Albums
Acadie (Opal 1989)★★★★
p.369 for full listings

L.A. GUNS

US GROUP FORMED IN 1987 BY GUITARIST TRACII GUNS (EX-**GUNS N'ROSES**) AND PAUL BLACK (LATER REPLACED BY English vocalist Phil Lewis). Mick Cripps (guitar), Kelly Nickels (bass) and Steve Riley (drums) were recruited. *Cocked And Loaded* presented the band as mature songwriters; *Hollywood Vampires* saw them diversifying musically. Despite a successful European tour supporting Skid Row, the group disintegrated.

Guns put together a new outfit, Killing Machine and Lewis formed Filthy Lucre; L.A. Guns was re-formed when both bands failed. *Vicious Circle* was arguably their best recorded work yet.

LA'S

FORMED IN 1986 IN LIVERPOOL, ENGLAND. LEE MAVERS (b. 1962; GUITAR/VOCALS), JOHN POWER (b. 1967; BASS), PAUL Hemmings (guitar) and John Timson (drums) signed with Go! Discs in 1987. Lee's brother, Neil (b. 1971; drums), and guitarist Cammy (b. Peter James Camell, 1967) joined for 'There She Goes', a massive underground hit. In 1990, the reissue reached the UK Top 20. The acclaimed *The La's* followed.

Power departed to set up **Cast** in 1995. Sessions for a second La's album were undertaken, with Mavers playing all the instruments.

LaBELLE, PATTI

THE FORMER LEADER OF **LaBELLE**, PATTI (b. PATRICIA HOLTE, 1944) WENT SOLO IN 1976. After her film debut in *A Soldier's Story* (1984), she resumed recording with 'Love Has Finally Come At Last', a duet with **Bobby Womack**. Two tracks from 1984's hit film *Beverly Hills Cop*, 'New Attitude' (US Top 20) and 'Stir It Up', followed by 'On My Own' (1986) with **Michael McDonald**, all hit the charts. Patti returned to the US stage in 1989, with the 'lost' Duke Ellington musical *Queenie Pie*, and has continued to release strong albums throughout the 90s.

LADYSMITH BLACK MAMBAZO

THE SUCCESS OF **PAUL SIMON'S** *GRACELAND* GAVE A HIGH PROFILE TO THIS SOUTH AFRICAN CHORAL group, founded by Joseph Shabalala in 1960. Until 1975, most of Mambazo's album output concentrated on traditional folk songs, some of them with new lyrics which offered necessarily coded, metaphorical criticisms of the apartheid regime. After 1975, and Shabalala's conversion to Christianity, religious songs were included. In 1987, after *Graceland*, the group released *Shaka Zulu* (produced by Paul Simon). In 1990, *Two Worlds One Heart* marked a radical stylistic departure for the group. On 10 December 1991, Shabalala was shot dead at the roadside.

LANE, RONNIE

A FOUNDER-MEMBER OF THE **SMALL FACES** AND **FACES**, LANE (b. 1946, d. 1997) WENT SOLO IN 1973. HE FORMED A backing group, Slim Chance, which included **Gallagher And Lyle**, and had a UK Top 20 hit with 'How Come?', followed by 'The Poacher' (UK Top 40). Ronnie's debut was *Anymore For Anymore*.

A new line-up of Slim Chance was later convened around Brian Belshaw (bass), Steve Simpson (guitar/mandolin), Ruan O'Lochlainn (keyboards/saxophone), Charlie Hart (keyboards/accordion) and Colin Davey (drums), resulting in *Ronnie Lane's Slim Chance* and *One For The Road*. They disbanded in 1977, although several ex-members appeared on *Rough Mix* (Ronnie's collaboration with **Pete Townshend**) followed by *Mahoney's Last Stand*, with Ron Wood (ex-Faces). Although Lane completed *See Me*, his progress was blighted by multiple sclerosis. His condition deteriorated considerably and money was raised for him through rock benefits. Despite his illness, he still managed to tour the USA and embarked on a Japanese tour during 1990. He finally lost his battle against the disease in 1997.

LANG, JONNY

BLUES GUITARIST/SINGER JONNY LANG (b. 1981) WAS SIGNED TO A&M BEFORE HIS SIXTEENTH BIRTHDAY. HE became leader of Kid Jonny Lang And The Big Bang. *Smokin'* sold 25,000 copies, despite being indepently produced. By the time A&M stepped in, Lang had played alongside such blues greats as **Luther Allison**, Lonnie Brooks and **Buddy Guy**. *Lie To Me* was an impressive major label debut.

LANG, K.D.

A SKILLED PIANIST AND GUITARIST, K.D. LANG (b. KATHRYN DAWN LANG, 1961) scratched a living in the performing arts, classical and *avant-garde* music, before choosing to sing country. After *A Truly Western Experience*, she signed to Sire Records. *Angel With A Lariat* was favoured by influential rock journals, but many country radio stations refused to play it, prejudiced by lang's spiky haircut, vegetarianism and ambiguous sexuality. Nevertheless, she charted via 'Cryin'', a duet with **Roy Orbison** for 1987's *Hiding Out* film soundtrack. In 1988, *Shadowland* was rendered agreeable to country consumers through a Nashville production by Owen Bradley with the **Jordanaires**, **Brenda Lee**, Loretta Lynn, Kitty Wells and other credible guest stars.

In 1992, lang 'came out', the acclaimed *Ingénue* was released and she debuted as an actress in *Salmonberries*. *Drag* featured cover versions including a highly original interpretation of **Steve Miller**'s 'The Joker'.

LANOIS, DANIEL

THIS ESTEEMED CANADIAN PRODUCER (b. 1951) ROSE TO FAME DURING THE LATE 80S, CONTRIBUTING TO MAJOR releases by **Peter Gabriel** (*So*) and **U2** (*The Unforgettable Fire* and *The Joshua Tree*, both with **Brian Eno**). He subsequently produced *Robbie Robertson*, the widely-acclaimed 'comeback' album by the former leader of the **Band**, and in 1989 undertook **Bob Dylan**'s *Oh Mercy*. Lanois also released his own album, *Acadie*, using both English and French. Lanois was also instrumental in redirecting **Emmylou Harris**'s career with *Wrecking Ball*; he also toured with her.

LASWELL, BILL

BASS GUITARIST LASWELL (b. 1950) ESTABLISHED OAO AND CELLULOID, TWO ADVENTUROUS RECORD LABELS, ALONGside his many musical collaborations. He worked on Material's *Third Power*, assembling a band including **Shabba Ranks**, the Jungle Brothers, **Herbie Hancock**, **Sly And Robbie** and Fred Wesley. Laswell and Hancock had already worked together, in Last Exit (on *The Noise Of Trouble*) and on two Hancock albums which he produced. In addition to the albums Laswell has made under his own name, he has produced for a wide range of people, including **Iggy Pop**, **Motörhead**, **Gil Scott-Heron**, **Afrika Bambaataa**, **Yoko Ono**, **Public Image Limited**, **Mick Jagger**, and Manu Dibango.

LAUPER, CYNDI

LAUPER (b. CYNTHIA LAUPER 1953) MET PIANIST JOHN TURI IN 1977; THEY FORMED BLUE ANGEL, RELEASING A SELF-titled album. After splitting with Turi in 1983, she began working on her solo debut, *She's So Unusual* (US number 4). It provided four hit singles, including 'Girls Just Want To Have Fun' and 'Time After Time' (US number 1). She was awarded a Grammy as Best New Artist.

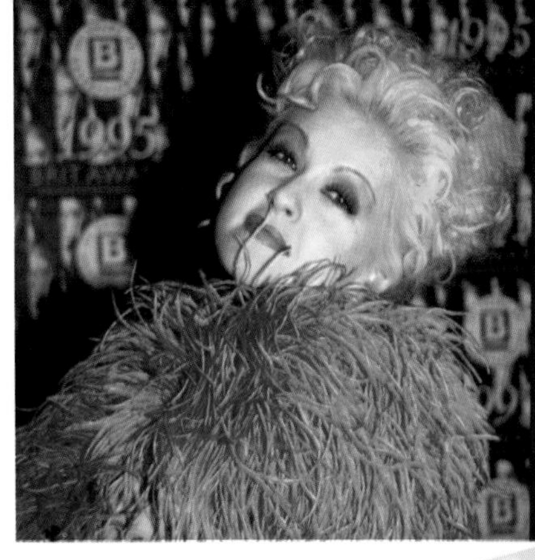

True Colors did not have the same commercial edge as its predecessor, yet the title track reached US number 1/UK Top 20. In 1987, she acted in the poorly-received film *Vibes*. In 1990, she made a brief return to the charts with 'I Drove All Night' from *A Night To Remember* before making another lacklustre film appearance in *Off And Running*. *Hat Full Of Stars* was a successful mix of soul/pop/hip hop, with a smattering of ethnic folk.

LED ZEPPELIN

FORMED IN 1968 BY BRITISH GUITARIST **JIMMY PAGE** (b. 1944) FOLLOWING THE DEMISE OF THE **YARDBIRDS**. John Paul Jones (b. John Baldwin, 1946; bass/keyboards) was recruited, but intended vocalist **Terry Reid** was unable to join, so **Robert Plant** (b. 1948) was chosen, alongside drummer John Bonham (b. 1948, d. 1980). The quartet completed outstanding commitments under the name 'New Yardbirds', before becoming Led Zeppelin.

Signed to Atlantic, the group toured the USA supporting **Vanilla Fudge** before releasing *Led Zeppelin*. The group was already a headline act, drawing sell-out crowds across the USA, when *Led Zeppelin II* confirmed an almost peerless position. The introductory track, 'Whole Lotta Love', has since become a classic. A greater subtlety was revealed on *Led Zeppelin III* and a pastoral atmosphere permeated the set.

Led Zeppelin IV included the anthemic 'Stairway To Heaven' and had sold 16 million copies in the USA by 1996. The praise was more muted for *Houses Of The Holy*, critically queried for its musically diverse selection, yet the effect was inspiring. A US tour broke all previous attendance records, and helped finance an in-concert film, *The Song Remains The Same* (1976), and the formation of their own record label, Swan Song. *Physical Graffiti*, a double set, included material ranging from compulsive hard-rock ('Custard Pie' and 'Sick Again') to pseudo-mystical experimentation ('Kashmir'). Sell-out appearances in the UK followed the release, but rehearsals for a projected world tour had to be abandoned in August 1975 when Plant sustained multiple injuries in a car accident. After his recovery, *Presence* was recorded – advance orders alone assured platinum status, yet it was regarded as a disappointment and UK sales were noticeably weaker.

After a year of inactivity, *In Through The Out Door* was a strong collection on which John Paul Jones emerged as the unifying factor. Rehearsals were then undertaken for another US tour, but in September 1980, Bonham was found dead following a lengthy drinking bout. On 4 December, Swan Song announced that the group had officially retired, although a collection of archive material, *Coda*, was subsequently issued. In 1994, Page and Plant (minus John Paul Jones) released *Unledded*.

LEE, ALBERT

ENGLISH-BORN COUNTRY ROCK GUITARIST LEE (b. 1943) JOINED THE R&B-INFLUENCED **CHRIS FARLOWE** AND THE Thunderbirds. He departed in 1967 for session work. He joined honky-tonk band Country Fever, before recording as Poet And The One Man Band with Chas Hodges (later of Chas And Dave). They became the country-rock band Heads Hands And Feet. In 1975, he joined **Emmylou Harris**'s Hot Band, replacing **James Burton**.

Lee also performed with **Eric Clapton**, **Jackson Browne**, **Jerry Lee Lewis** and **Dave Edmunds**. He played a major part in the historic reunion of the **Everly Brothers** at London's Royal Albert Hall in 1983, and continues to be a member of their regular touring band.

LEE, BRENDA

EVEN IN ADOLESCENCE, LEE'S (b. BRENDA MAE TARPLEY, 1944) VOICE COULD SLIP FROM ANGUISHED INTIMACY through sleepy insinuation to raucous lust. 'Let's Jump The Broomstick' and other jaunty classics kept her in the charts for a decade. By 1956, she was ensured enough airplay for her first single, a revival of **Hank Williams**' 'Jambalaya', to crack the US country chart; her *Billboard* Hot 100 debut came with 1957's 'One Step At A Time'. The next decade brought a greater proportion of heartbreak ballads, such as 'I'm Sorry' and 'Too Many Rivers' – plus a role in the movie *The Two Little Bears*. Lee cut back on touring and recording only intermittently after *Bye Bye Blues*. In 1971, she resurfaced with a huge country hit in **Kris Kristofferson**'s 'Nobody Wins'; and in 1988 guested with Loretta Lynn and Kitty Wells on **k.d. lang**'s *Shadowland*.

LEFT BANKE

FORMED IN 1966 BY PIANIST/COMPOSER MICHAEL BROWN (b. MICHAEL LOOKOFSKY, 1949). PRIOR TO LEFT BANKE, Brown appeared on releases by Reparata And The Delrons and Christopher And The Chaps. Left Banke – Steve Martin (vocals), Jeff Winfield (guitar), Tom Finn (bass) and George Cameron (drums) – reached the US Top 5 with 'Walk Away Renee'. Internal ructions led to Brown completing a third release, 'Ivy Ivy', with session musicians, but the band was reunited for 'Desiree', their final chart entry.

LEFTFIELD

LEFTFIELD WAS ORIGINALLY JUST NEIL BARNES. HE RELEASED A SOLO TRACK, 'NOT FORGOTTEN', BEFORE recruiting Paul Daley. However, as 'Not Forgotten' charted, disputes with label Outer Rhythm followed. Unable to record due to contractual restraints, Leftfield embarked on a career as remixers, for stars including Ultra Nate and Inner City. Later remixes for **David Bowie**, Renegade Soundwave and Yothu Yindi would follow, but by now the duo had already established their Hard Hands imprint. This debuted with the reggae-tinted 'Release The Pressure' (featuring Earl Sixteen), then the more trance-based chart entry 'Song Of Life' (1992). They subsequently teamed up with John Lydon (**Sex Pistols**/PiL) for 'Open Up'. They also produced a soundtrack for the film *Shallow Grave* and recorded (as Herbal Infusion) 'The Hunter'.

LASWELL, BILL
Albums
Hear No Evil (Venture 1988)★★★
➧ p.369 for full listings
Collaborators
Shabba Ranks ➧ p.273
Sly And Robbie ➧ p.300
Iggy Pop ➧ p.264
Afrika Bambaataa ➧ p.11
Yoko Ono ➧ p.252
Mick Jagger ➧ p.281

LAUPER, CYNDI
Albums
She's So Unusual (Portrait 1984)★★★★
➧ p.369 for full listings
Connections
Roy Orbison ➧ p.252

LED ZEPPELIN
Albums
Led Zeppelin (Atlantic 1969)★★★★
➧ p.369 for full listings

Connections
Yardbirds ➧ p.345
Eric Clapton ➧ p.92
Jimmy Page ➧ p.255
Robert Plant ➧ p.262
Influences
Willie Dixon ➧ p.120
Further References
Video: *The Song Remains The Same* (1986)

LEE, ALBERT
Albums
Hiding (A&M 1979)★★★★
➧ p.369 for full listings
Collaborators
Chris Farlowe ➧ p.143
Eric Clapton ➧ p.92
Jackson Browne ➧ p.71
Jerry Lee Lewis ➧ p.215
Dave Edmunds ➧ p.132
Connections
James Burton ➧ p.75
Everly Brothers ➧ p.139

LEE, BRENDA
Albums
Miss Dynamite (Brunswick 1961)★★★★
➧ p.369 for full listings
Collaborators
k.d. lang ➧ p.212

LEFT BANKE
Albums
Walk Away Reneé/Pretty Ballerina (Smash 1967)★★★
➧ p.369 for full listings

LEFTFIELD
Albums
Leftism (Hard Hands/Columbia 1995)★★★★
➧ p.369 for full listings

LEIBER AND STOLLER
Connections
Coasters ➧ p.95
Elvis Presley ➧ p.265
LaVern Baker ➧ p.30
Drifters ➧ p.126
Ben E. King ➧ p.205
Stealer's Wheel ➧ p.308
Elkie Brooks ➧ p.69
Further References
Book: *Baby, That Was Rock & Roll: The Legendary Leiber And Stoller*, Robert Palmer
➧ p.369 for full listings

LEMONHEADS
Albums
Come On Feel The Lemonheads (Atlantic 1993)★★★★
➧ p.369 for full listings
Influences
Simon And Garfunkel
➧ p.297
Further References
Book: *The Lemonheads*, Mick St. Michael

LENNON, JOHN
Albums
John Lennon – Plastic Ono Band (Apple 1971)★★★★★
Imagine (Apple 1971)★★★★
➧ p.369 for full listings
Collaborators
Yoko Ono ➧ p.252
Paul McCartney ➧ p.229
Ringo Starr ➧ p.307
George Harrison ➧ p.176
Eric Clapton ➧ p.92
Elton John ➧ p.200
Connections
Beatles ➧ p.38
Julian Lennon ➧ p.214
Further References
Film: *Let It Be* (1971)
Video: *The Bed-In* (PMI 1991)
Book: *A Twist Of Lennon*, Cynthia Lennon

LENNON, JULIAN
Albums
Valotte (Virgin 1984)★★★
➧ p.369 for full listings
Connections
John Lennon ➧ p.214

LENNOX, ANNIE
Albums
Diva (RCA 1992)★★★★
➧ p.369 for full listings
Collaborators
Blue Nile ➧ p.56
Jeff Lynne ➧ p.220

LEIBER AND STOLLER

JERRY LEIBER (b. 1933) AND MIKE STOLLER (b. 1933) BEGAN THEIR SONGWRITING AND PRODUCTION PARTNERSHIP AT the age of 17. They provided songs for Los Angeles' R&B artists during the early 50s. 'Hard Times' (Charles Brown) was the first Leiber and Stoller hit, but their biggest songs were 'Hound Dog' and 'K.C. Lovin''. In 1954, the duo set up their Spark label to release material by the Robins (soon to become the **Coasters**). Songs like 'Smokey Joe's Cafe', 'Searchin'', 'Yakety Yak' and 'Charlie Brown' bridged the gap between R&B and rock 'n' roll, selling millions in the 50s, while Leiber And Stoller's innovative production techniques widened the scope of the R&B record. They wrote 'Lucky Lips' for Ruth Brown and 'Saved' for **LaVern Baker**, but their most notable productions were for the **Drifters** and **Ben E. King**. Among these were 'On Broadway', 'Spanish Harlem', 'There Goes My Baby', 'I (Who Have Nothing)' and 'Stand By Me'. Leiber and Stoller also supplied **Elvis Presley** with songs like 'Jailhouse Rock', 'Baby I Don't Care', 'Loving You', 'Treat Me Nice' and 'His Latest Flame' and wrote hits for Perry Como, Peggy Lee and **Dion**.

In 1972, they produced albums for UK acts including **Stealer's Wheel** and **Elkie Brooks**. They went into semi-retirement, developing stage shows and their work inspired the hit musical *Smokey Joe's Café*.

LEMONHEADS

HARDCORE BAND FORMED IN BOSTON, USA IN 1985. EVAN DANDO (b. 1967; VOCALS/GUITAR) WAS ORIGINALLY THE drummer-guitarist alongside Jesse Peretz (bass) and Ben Deily (guitar/drums). Their debut EP, *Laughing All The Way To The Cleaners*, was released on Taang!. By 1987, Dando had recruited drummer Doug Trachten, but he stayed permanent only for their debut album, *Hate Your Friends*. After *Lick*, Deily – Dando's long-time co-writer – left and the band split immediately after their acclaimed major label debut, *Lovey*. Dando later re-formed the group with David Ryan (b. 1964), Byron Hoagland (drums) and Peretz. Their cover of **Simon And Garfunkel**'s 'Mrs Robinson' charted. In 1992, Nic Dalton (b. 1966; bass) joined.

The success of *It's A Shame About Ray* placed increased pressure on Evan to write another hit album, and he turned to hard drugs. Sessions were delayed as he took time out to repair a badly damaged voice, allegedly caused by smoking crack. *Come On Feel The Lemonheads* showed his songwriting continuing in its purple patch. The less successful *Car Button Cloth* came in the wake of Dando cleaning himself up and contained some of his most mellow songs to date.

LENNON, JOHN

FOLLOWING THE COLLAPSE OF THE **BEATLES**, LIVERPOOL-BORN JOHN WINSTON ONO LENNON (b. 1940, d. 1980) AND his wife **Yoko Ono**, attempted to transform the world through non-musical means. Their bed-ins in Amsterdam and Montreal, black bag appearances on stage, flirting with political activists and radicals; all received massive media attention, and succeeded in educating people in the idea of world peace.

Lennon's solo career began with *Unfinished Music No 1 – Two Virgins*. Three months later came the equally bizarre *Unfinished Music No 2 – Life With The Lions*; one side consisted of John and Yoko calling out to each other during her stay in a London hospital while pregnant. 'Give Peace a Chance' was followed by 'Cold Turkey' (1969) courtesy of the Plastic Ono Band – Lennon, Ono, **Eric Clapton**, Klaus Voorman and drummer Alan White. This raw rock song about heroin withdrawal was also a hit, although it failed to make the Top 10. The release of *John Lennon – Plastic Ono Band* was a shock to the system for most Beatles' fans. Following psychotherapy, Lennon poured out much of his bitterness from his childhood and adolescence, neat and undiluted. More than any other work in the Lennon canon, this brilliant album was a farewell to the past.

After the strong 'Power To The People', he moved to New York and released the patchy *Imagine* – it immediately went to number 1 internationally. A Christmas single, 'Happy Christmas (War Is Over)', was another song destined for immortality. *Sometime In New York City* was a double set containing a number of political songs; it was written during the peak of Lennon's involvement with hippie-radical, Jerry Rubin. The album's strongest track is yet another song with one of Lennon's statement-like titles: 'Woman Is The Nigger Of The World'. The following year he embarked on his struggle against deportation and the fight for his famous 'green card'.

At the end of 1973, he released *Mind Games*, an album that highlighted problems between him and Yoko and *Walls And Bridges* contained more marital material and a surprise US number 1, 'Whatever Gets You Through The Night'. In November 1974, he made his last ever concert appearance at Madison Square Garden with **Elton John**.

The following year's *Rock 'N' Roll* (UK/US number 6) was a tight and energetic celebration of many of his favourite songs, including a superb version of 'Stand By Me'. In 1980, *Double Fantasy* was released and went straight to number 1 virtually worldwide. Tragically, the following month, while walking home with Yoko after a recording session, John Lennon was murdered by a gunman outside his Manhattan apartment building. The whole world reacted in unprecedented mourning. His work continues worldwide and the superb songwriting team of Lennon and McCartney has still never been bettered.

LENNON, JULIAN

AT TIMES, JULIAN LENNON'S (b. JOHN CHARLES JULIAN LENNON, 1963) VOICE UNCANNILY MIRRORS THAT OF HIS father, **John**. His debut, *Valotte* (produced by Phil Ramone) led to Julian being nominated for a Best New Act Grammy in 1985, however, *The Secret Value Of Daydreaming* was critically ignored. Lennon licked his wounds and returned in 1989 with *Mr. Jordan* and a change of style. Following his previous poor sales, Virgin had released Lennon from his contract, and he had joined a theatrical touring company's production of the play *Mr Holland's Opus* for which he sang the title song. His best-known single is the environmental ballad 'Salt Water'.

LENNOX, ANNIE

LENNOX'S (EX-**EURYTHMICS**) FIRST TWO SOLO EFFORTS REACHED UK NUMBER 1. IN 1990, SHE WON HER FOURTH Best British Female Artist award at the BRITs ceremony, before announcing she was taking a two year sabbatical to concentrate on her family. Her debut solo album was produced with Steve Lipson (**Simple Minds**), and co-written with the **Blue Nile** and **Jeff Lynne**.

Diva shot to UK number 1; *Medusa* offered a wide-ranging selection of covers, mainly of songs previously aired by male vocalists including 'Whiter Shade Of Pale', 'Lover Speaks', 'No More I Love You's' and 'Downtown Lights'. In 1996, Lennox released the limited edition *Live In Central Park*.

LETTERMEN

US CLOSE-HARMONY POP TRIO: BOB ENGEMANN (b. 1936), TONY BUTALA (b. 1940), AND JIM PIKE (b. 1938). AFTER TWO unsuccessful singles, they joined Capitol Records and charted with 'The Way You Look Tonight'. During the 60s, they had 24 US chart albums, 10 of which reached the Top 40. They also had another 19 chart singles including the Top 10 hits 'When I Fall In Love' (1961) and 'Goin' Out Of My Head/Can't Take My Eyes Off You' (1967). Despite nine gold albums and over $25 million in record sales, they have never charted in the UK.

LEVEL 42

INSTRUMENTAL JAZZ/FUNK BAND, FORMED IN 1980. MARK KING (b. 1958; BASS/VOCALS), PHIL GOULD (b. 1957; DRUMS), Boon Gould (b. 1955; guitar) and Mark Lindup (b. 1959; keyboards) debuted with 'Love Meeting Love'. Their Mike Vernon-produced album, an exciting collection of dance and modern soul orientated numbers, made the UK Top 20. Most of their early singles were minor hits until 'The Sun Goes Down (Living It Up)' (1984, UK Top 10). Their worldwide breakthrough came with *World Machine*. Both *Running In The Family* and *Staring At The Sun* were major successes, although the latter had no significant singles. By 1987, the line-up had changed drastically with King and Lindup the only original members.

LEVELLERS

FORMED IN BRIGHTON, ENGLAND. MARK CHADWICK (LEAD VOCALS/GUITAR/BANJO/SONGWRITING), JONATHAN Sevink (fiddle), Alan Miles (vocals/guitars/mandolin/harmonica), Jeremy Cunningham (bass/bouzouki) and Charlie Heather (drums) combined folk instrumentation with rock and punk ethics, releasing the *Carry Me* EP in 1989. After their debut album, they recruited Simon Friend (guitar/vocals/songwriting). They then set off on an extensive UK tour.

Levelling The Land (UK Top 20) was a mixture of English and Celtic folk with powerful guitar-driven rock. The *Fifteen Years* EP (UK number 11) was followed by a compilation of singles and live tracks, *See Nothing, Hear Nothing, Do Something*. The band were disappointed with the lack of progress *The Levellers* demonstrated, and it was two years before the next studio album was released. It sold well and ensured underground popularity. By 1994, they had purchased a disused factory, the Metway, as a base for running the fan club and pressure groups, as well as a studio complex. *Zeitgeist* was recorded there. The group's popularity was confirmed when 'What A Beautiful Day' (1997) reached the UK charts; *Mouth To Mouth* recorded impressive sales.

LEWIS, GARY, AND THE PLAYBOYS

60S US POP GROUP. GARY LEWIS (b. GARY LEVITAL, 1946; VOCALS/DRUMS), ALAN RAMSEY (b. 1943; guitar), John West (b. 1939; guitar), David Costell (b. 1944; bass) and David Walker (b. 1943; keyboards) were signed by Liberty Records and producer **Leon Russell**. Their debut, 'This Diamond Ring', reached US number 1 in 1965, followed by a run of Top 10 hits. Their popularity dwindled when Lewis joined the US military in 1967. After his release in 1968, he returned to the charts with a remake of **Brian Hyland**'s 'Sealed With A Kiss', followed by the **Cascades**' 'Rhythm Of The Rain'. The group disbanded at the end of the 60s.

LEWIS, HUEY, AND THE NEWS

FORMED IN CALIFORNIA, USA IN 1980, BY EX-**CLOVER** MEMBERS HUEY LEWIS (b. HUGH ANTHONY CREGG III, 1951; vocals/ harmonica) and Sean Hopper (keyboards). They recruited Johnny Colla (guitar/saxophone), Mario Cipollina (bass), Bill Gibson (drums) and Chris Hayes (lead guitar). A debut album included 'Do You Believe In Love' (US Top 10). The band's easy-going rock/soul fusion reached its peak with *Sports*, which provided five US Top 20 hits including 'Heart & Soul', 'If This Is It' and 'I Want A New Drug'. Lewis sued Ray Parker Jnr over the latter, claiming it had been plagiarized for the *Ghostbusters* theme. From 1985-86, three Lewis singles headed the US charts: 'The Power Of Love' (theme tune to the film *Back To The Future*), 'Stuck With You' and 'Jacob's Ladder'. 'Perfect World' (1988) was also a success, although *Hard At Play* did less well. Lewis returned with *Four Chords And Several Years Ago*.

LEWIS, JERRY LEE

LEWIS (b. 1935) FIRST RECORDED ON THE LOUISIANA HAYRIDE IN 1954 AND SIGNED TO SUN RECORDS. HIS version of 'Crazy Arms' was his Sun debut, but it was his second single, a revival of Roy Hall's 'Whole Lotta Shakin' Goin' On' (1957) that brought him international fame. The record, which was initially banned as obscene, narrowly missed the top of the US chart and went on to hit number 1 on the R&B and country charts. He stole the show from many other stars in the film *Jamboree* in which he sang 'Great Balls Of Fire' (UK number 1/US number 2).

When he arrived in Britain for a tour in 1958, accompanied by his third wife, Myra, who was also his 13-year-old second cousin, the UK media went crazy – the tour was cancelled after only three concerts. When his version of **Ray Charles**'s 'What'd I Say' hit the UK Top 10 in 1960 (US number 30) it looked like a revival was on the way, but it was not to be.

In 1968, Lewis decided to concentrate on country. This changeover was an instant success and over the next 13 years Lewis was one of country's top-selling artists, topping the chart with records such as 'There Must Be More To Love Than This' (1970), 'Would You Take Another Chance On Me?' (1971) and a revival of 'Chantilly Lace' (1972).

Lewis's behaviour became increasingly erratic. He accidentally shot his bass player in the chest – the musician survived and sued him– and, in 1976, was arrested for waving a gun outside **Elvis Presley**'s Gracelands home. Two years later, Lewis signed to Elektra; unfortunately, his association with the company ended with much-publicized lawsuits. In 1981, Lewis was hospitalized by a haemorrhaged ulcer; he survived and was soon back on the road. In 1982, his fourth wife drowned in a swimming pool. The following year, his fifth wife was found dead at his home following a methodone overdose. A sixth marriage followed, along with more bleeding ulcers and a period in the Betty Ford Clinic.

In 1990, a much-awaited UK tour had to be cancelled when Lewis failed to show. He moved to Dublin, Eire, to avoid the US taxman, but eventually returned to Memphis.

LEWIS, RAMSEY

PIANIST LEWIS (b. 1935) BEGAN HIS CAREER AS A CHURCH ACCOMPANIST. BEFORE JOINING THE CLEFS, A SEVEN-piece dance band. In 1956, he formed a jazz trio with the Clefs' rhythm section Eldee Young (bass) and Isaac 'Red' Holt (drums). 'The In Crowd', an instrumental cover version, reached US number 5, selling over a million copies. 'Hang On Sloopy' reached number 11 and sold another million and the classic 'Wade In The Water' (1966) was a major hit. Lewis never recaptured this commercial peak; although he continued securing *Billboard* Top 100 hits well into the 70s, with over 30 of his albums making the *Billboard* Top 200.

Connections
Eurythmics ➽ p.139
Clash ➽ p.93
Further References
Book: *Annie Lennox*, Lucy O'Brien

LETTERMEN
Albums
Goin' Out Of My Head (1968)★★★
➽ p.369 for full listings

LEVEL 42
Albums
World Machine (Polydor 1985)★★★★
➽ p.369 for full listings
Further References
Book: *Level 42: The Definitive Biography*, Michael Cowton

LEVELLERS
Albums
The Levellers (China 1993)★★★★
➽ p.369 for full listings
Further References
Video: *The Great Video Swindle (Live At Glasgow Barrowlands)* (1992)

LEWIS, GARY, AND THE PLAYBOYS
Albums
She's Just My Style (1966)★★★★
➽ p.369 for full listings
Connections
Leon Russell ➽ p.286
Brian Hyland ➽ p.190
Cascades ➽ p.83

LEWIS, HUEY, AND THE NEWS
Albums
Picture This (Chrysalis 1982)★★★
➽ p.369 for full listings
Connections
Clover ➽ p.95

LEWIS, JERRY LEE
Albums
Jerry Lee Lewis (Sun 1957)★★★★
Jerry Lee's Greatest (Sun 1961)★★★★
➽ p.369 for full listings
Connections
Elvis Presley ➽ p.265
Ray Charles ➽ p.88
Further References
Film: *Beach Ball* (1964)
Book: *Hellfire: The Jerry Lee Lewis Story*, Nick Tosches

LEWIS, RAMSEY
Albums
The In Crowd (Argo 1965)★★★★
➽ p.369 for full listings
Further References
Film: *Gonks Go Beat* (1965)

LIGHTFOOT, GORDON
Albums
Sit Down Young Stranger aka *If You Could Read My Mind* (Reprise 1970)★★★★
➧ p.369 for full listings
Connections
Peter, Paul and Mary ➧ p.260
Bob Dylan ➧ p.128
Johnny Cash ➧ p.84
Elvis Presley ➧ p.265
Jerry Lee Lewis ➧ p.215
Further References
Book: *If You Could Read My Mind*, Maynard Collins

LIGHTHOUSE
Albums
Suite Feeling (RCA 1970)★★★
➧ p.370 for full listings
Collaborators
Al Kooper ➧ p.210
Mike Bloomfield ➧ p.54

LIGHTNING SEEDS
Albums
Dizzy Heights (Epic 1996)★★★★
➧ p.370 for full listings
Connections
Fall ➧ p.142
Wah! ➧ p.331
Icicle Works ➧ p.192
La's ➧ p.212

LINDISFARNE
Albums
Fog On The Tyne (Charisma 1971)★★★★
➧ p.370 for full listings

LITTLE ANTHONY AND THE IMPERIALS
Albums
Goin' Out Of My Head (DCP 1965)★★★
➧ p.370 for full listings
Connections
Delfonics ➧ p.115
Stylistics ➧ p.312
O'Jays ➧ p.250

LITTLE EVA
Album
L-L-L-Loco-Motion (Dimension 1962)★★
➧ p.370 for full listings
Connections
Gerry Goffin ➧ p.164
Kylie Minogue ➧ p.234

LITTLE FEAT
Albums
Feats Don't Fail Me Now (Warners 1974)★★★★
➧ p.370 for full listings
Connections
Standells ➧ p.306
Mothers Of Invention ➧ p.239
Pure Prairie League ➧ p.269

LITTLE RICHARD
Albums
Here's Little Richard (Specialty 1957)★★★★★
➧ p.370 for full listings

LIGHTFOOT, GORDON

CANADIAN SINGER-SONGWRITER LIGHTFOOT (b. 1938) PROVIDED SONGS FOR SEVERAL ACTS, NOTABLY IAN AND Sylvia, **Peter, Paul And Mary**, Marty Robbins, **Bob Dylan**, **Johnny Cash**, **Elvis Presley** and **Jerry Lee Lewis**. As a singer, he debuted in 1966 with *Lightfoot*, followed by *The Way I Feel* and *Did She Mention My Name*, but it was not until 1970 that he made a significant commercial breakthrough with *Sit Down Young Stranger*. The album brought a US Top 5 hit with 'If You Could Read My Mind'; it also included the first recording of **Kris Kristofferson**'s 'Me And Bobbie McGee'. In 1974, Lightfoot reached US number 1 with 'Sundown'; two years later 'The Wreck Of The Edmund Fitzgerald' peaked at number 2.

LIGHTHOUSE

FORMED IN THE USA BY DRUMMER SKIP PROKOP (WHO ALSO APPEARED IN THE **AL KOOPER/MIKE BLOOMFIELD** project *Super Session*), alongside guitarist Ralph Cole and an ambitious string and horn section. A series of personnel changes undermined what potential Lighthouse offered and consequently later albums lacked direction. Al Wilmot (bass) joined, but the group folded at the end of the 70s.

LIGHTNING SEEDS

FORMED BY MUSICIAN **IAN BROUDIE** (b. 1958), WHO HAD PRODUCED SUCH ACTS AS THE **BUNNYMEN**, THE **FALL**, **Wah!** and the **Icicle Works**. Lightning Seeds was an opportunity for Broudie to expand his songwriting. His first single, 'Pure', reached UK number 16. *Cloudcuckooland* followed, encapsulating Broudie's notion of the perfect, sweet pop song. *Sense* and *Jollification* were commercial successes and Broudie put together a full touring band. The line-up was Martin Campbell (bass), Chris Sharrock (drums; ex-**La's**) and Paul Hemmings (guitar, ex-La's).

In 1996, Broudie composed England's football anthem, 'Three Lions' (UK number 1), recorded with comedians David Baddiel and Frank Skinner. Later in the year he reached a creative peak with the gloriously melodic *Dizzy Heights*. The compilation *Like You Do* included two new tracks.

LINDISFARNE

FORMED IN NEWCASTLE, ENGLAND. ALAN HULL (b. 1945, d. 1995; VOCALS/GUITAR/PIANO), SIMON COWE (b. 1948; guitar), Ray Jackson (b. 1948; harmonica/mandolin), Rod Clements (b. 1947; bass/violin) and Ray Laidlaw (b. 1948; drums) were originally known as the Downtown Faction, becoming Lindisfarne in 1968. Their folk-rock debut, *Nicely Out Of Tune*, was followed by the popular *Fog On The Tyne* (UK number 1); its attendant single, 'Meet Me On The Corner' (1972) reached the UK Top 5. *Dingly Dell* was disappointing, and, in 1973, Laidlaw, Cowe and Clements left to form Jack The Lad. Kenny Craddock (keyboards), Charlie Harcourt (guitar), Tommy Duffy (bass) and Paul Nichols (drums) were recruited but this line-up lacked its predecessor's charm and was overshadowed by Hull's concurrent solo career. *Happy Daze* offered some promise, but Lindisfarne disbanded in 1975.

The original quintet later resumed working together, reaching the UK Top 10 with 'Run For Home' (1978). They were unable to repeat this success, but the group's following remains strong.

LITTLE ANTHONY AND THE IMPERIALS

FORMED IN NEW YORK IN 1957. 'LITTLE' ANTHONY GOURDINE (b. 1940), ERNEST WRIGHT JNR (b. 1941), Clarence Collins (b. 1941), Tracy Lord and Glouster Rogers (b. 1940) had their first hit with 'Tears On My Pillow' (1958), followed by 'So Much' (1959) and 'Shimmy Shimmy Ko-Ko-Bop' (1960). In 1964, Gourdine formed a 'new' Imperials around Wright, Collins and Sammy Strain (b. 1940). Their first hit, 'I'm On The Outside (Looking In)', showcased Gourdine's dazzling falsetto. The line-up later drifted apart. Three years later, Collins formed his own 'Imperials', reissuing 'Better Use Your Head', alongside a new recording, 'Who's Gonna Love Me'. In the 80s, Gourdine released *Daylight*.

LITTLE EVA

DISCOVERED BY SONGWRITERS **CAROLE KING** AND **GERRY GOFFIN**, LITTLE EVA (b. EVA NARCISSUS BOYD, 1943) SHOT to fame in 1962 with the international hit 'The Loco-Motion'. She continued to record until 1965, but her only other substantial hit was 'Swinging On A Star', a duet with Big Dee Irwin. She made a UK chart comeback in 1972 with a reissue of 'The Loco-Motion', which peaked at number 11.

LITTLE FEAT

LITTLE FEAT COMBINED ELEMENTS OF COUNTRY, FOLK, BLUES, SOUL AND BOOGIE TO CREATE THEIR SOUND. Lowell George (b. 1945, d. 1979; vocals; ex-**Standells**, **Mothers Of Invention**), Roy Estrada (bass), Bill Payne (b. 1949; keyboards) and Richie Haywood (drums) were later joined by Paul Barrere (b. 1948; guitar), Kenny Gradney (bass) and Sam Clayton (percussion). Their fourth album finally charted in the USA.

However, George was over-indulging with drugs, and his contribution to *Time Loves A Hero* was minimal, although they delivered a great album. Following *Waiting For Columbus*, the band disintegrated and George started work on his solo album, *Thanks, I'll Eat It Here*. During a solo tour, George died from a heart attack. The remaining band re-formed for a benefit concert for his widow and released *Down On The Farm*; it became a considerable success, as did *Hoy-Hoy*.

In 1988, the band re-formed for the successful *Let It Roll*. Craig Fuller (ex-**Pure Prairie League**) took Lowell's place, and the musical direction was guided by the faultless keyboard playing of Bill Payne. *Shake Me Up* was critically acclaimed. Fuller was not present on *Ain't Had Enough Fun*; the band recruited a female lead singer, Shaun Murphy, instead.

LITTLE RICHARD

LITTLE RICHARD (b. RICHARD WAYNE PENNIMAN, 1935) FIRST RECORDED IN 1951, CUTTING EIGHT URBAN BLUES tracks with his mentor Billy Wright's Orchestra. In 1955, after unsuccessful recordings, he recorded a dozen tracks with producer **Robert 'Bumps' Blackwell**. The classic 'Tutti Frutti' was among them and gave him his first R&B and pop hit in the USA. The following 'Long Tall Sally', topped the R&B chart and was the first of three US Top 10 hits. Richard's string of Top 20 hits continued with the double-sider 'Rip It Up'/'Ready Teddy',

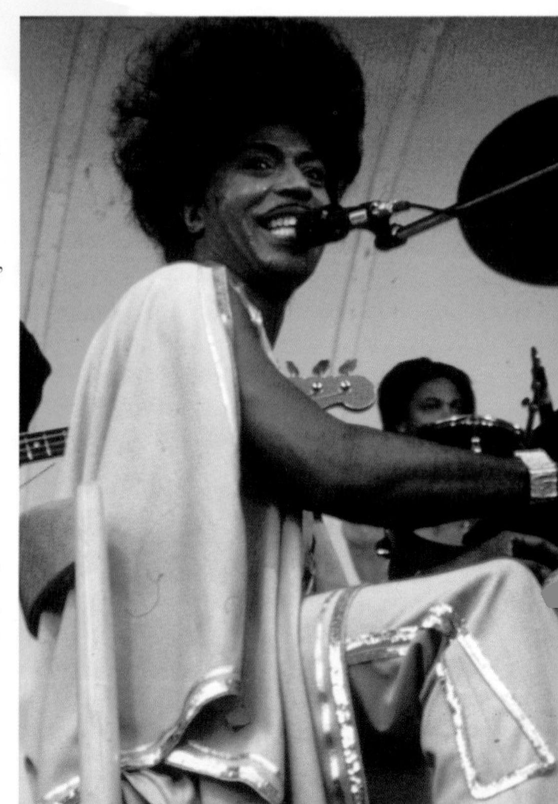

while his frantic, performance of 'Long Tall Sally' and 'Tutti Frutti' in the film *Don't Knock The Rock* helped push his UK single into the Top 3.

His next film and single was *The Girl Can't Help It*, while the remainder of 1957 saw him notch up trans-atlantic hits with the rock 'n' roll classics 'Lucille', 'Keep A Knockin'' and 'Jenny Jenny', and a Top 20 album, *Here's Little Richard*. In 1962, Richard toured the UK for the first time – 'Bama Lama Bama Loo' reached the UK Top 20. In 1964, he signed with Vee Jay where he re-recorded all his hits, revived a few oldies and cut some new rockers – but sales were unimpressive. In the mid-60s, Richard's soulful Vee Jay tracks, 'I Don't Know What You've Got But It's Got Me' and 'Without Love', were among the best recordings of the genre.

The 70s was spent jumping from label to label, recording and touring. In 1986, Richard was one of the first artists inducted into the Rock 'n' Roll Hall of Fame and he acted in the film *Down And Out In Beverly Hills*. Renewed interest spurred WEA to sign him and release *Lifetime Friend*, which included the chart record 'Operator'.

LITTLE RIVER BAND

AUSTRALIANS BEEB BIRTLES (b. GERARD BIRTLEKAMP, 1948; GUITAR), GRAHAM Goble (b. 1947; guitar), Derek Pellicci (drums) and Glen Shorrock (b. 1944; vocals) met in 1975. Rick Formosa (guitar) and Roger McLachlan (bass) joined later. They had immediate Australian success with their first single and album and began aiming overseas; by 1976 they had enjoyed their first appearance in the US charts. Formosa and McLachlan were replaced by David Briggs (b. 1951) and George McArdle (b. 1954). *Diamantina Cocktail* went gold in the USA in 1977, the first time for an Australian act. *Sleeper Catcher* was also hugely successful, selling in Latin-America and Europe.

In 1983, Shorrock went solo, replaced by John Farnham, one of Australia's most popular singers. By 1986, Farnham went solo; in 1988, Shorrock returned. The group later released *Get Lucky*.

LIVE

US ALTERNATIVE ROCK BAND: ED KOWALCYZK (VOCALS), PATRICK DAHLHEIMER, CHAD TAYLOR AND CHAD GRACEY. Their debut, *Mental Jewelery*, had spiritual overtones as did *Throwing Copper*, although Kowalcyzk's lyrics had developed a less literal level. By 1996, *Throwing Copper* had sold six million copies in the USA alone. *Secret Samadhi* looked set to follow the same pattern.

LIVING COLOUR

US ROCK BAND FORMED BY VERNON REID (b. 1958; GUITAR), MUZZ SKILLINGS (BASS) AND WILLIAM CALHOUN (b. 1964; drums) in 1984. Vocalist Corey Glover (b. 1964) joined later. Fusing jazz, blues and soul, alongside commercial hard rock, *Vivid* reached US number 6. In 1985, Reid formed the *Black Rock Coalition* pressure movement alongside Greg Tate.

After working with **Mick Jagger**, the ties with the **Rolling Stones** remained strong, with Reid collaborating on Keith Richards' solo album. They also joined the Stones on their *Steel Wheels* tour.

Time's Up won a Grammy, but Skilling left, replaced by bassist Doug Wimbish (b. 1956) on *Stain*. The band split in 1995. An excellent retrospective, *Pride*, was released following their demise. Reid released a solo album in 1996.

L L COOL J

L L COOL J (b. JAMES TODD SMITH, 1969), STARTED RAPPING at the age of nine; from the age of 13 he was processing his first demos and Rick Rubin of Def Jam Records signed him. The first sighting of L L Cool J ('Ladies Love Cool James') came in 1984 on 'I Need A Beat', however, it was 'I Just Can't Live Without My Radio' which established him. The song was featured in the *Krush Groove* film, in which he also performed. 'I Need Love' reached the UK Top 10.

Musically, Cool is probably best sampled on *Mama Said Knock You Out* (triple platinum), though the follow-up, *14 Shots To The Dome*, was less effective. He has also appeared in the films *The Hard Way* and *Toys*. *Phenomenon* featured guest appearances from Keith Sweat and Ralph Tresvant.

LOEB, LISA

SINGER-SONGWRITER LOEB SPRANG TO FAME IN 1994 WHEN 'Stay (I Missed You)' was used as the theme of the film *Reality Bites*. It reached US number 1 despite Loeb not yet having a recording contract. Geffen Records are alleged to have offered over $1 million for her signature and Loeb set about crafting her debut album, including 'Do You Sleep' in 1995. The album was co-produced with Juan Patino and her band, Nine Stories.

LOFGREN, NILS

IN THE LATE 60S, CHICAGO-BORN LOFGREN (b. 1951) RECORDED AS PAUL DOWELL AND THE DOLPHIN BEFORE forming Grin. He also briefly teamed up with **Neil Young**'s backing group **Crazy Horse** for their debut album, an association that continued. It was widely speculated that Lofgren might replace Mick Taylor in the **Rolling Stones**; instead, he signed to A&M and recorded a self-titled album.

Cry Tough displayed his power as a writer, arranger and musician and was a transatlantic best-seller. When Lofgren's reputation as a solo artist had declined, he embarked on Neil Young's *Trans* tour (1983), followed by a stint with **Bruce Springsteen**'s E Street Band. Later he recorded the solo *Silver Lining*.

LOGGINS, KENNY

LOGGINS (B. 1948) STARTED OUT IN LOGGINS AND MESSINA. AFTER GOING SOLO, HE SPECIALIZED IN ROCK ballads such as 'Whenever I Call You Friend' (1978, US Top 10); the **Nitty Gritty Dirt Band** took his 'House At Pooh Corner' into the US charts. Subsequent success came with 'This Is It' and 'What A Fool Believes', (co-written with **Michael McDonald**), a million-seller and US number 1 for the **Doobie Brothers**. During the 80s, Loggins came to prominence as a writer and performer of theme songs: 'I'm Alright' (*Caddyshack*, 1980), 'Footloose' (*Footloose*, 1984) and the soundtrack of *Top Gun* (1986). This was followed by music for *Caddyshack II*, including another hit, 'Nobody's Fool'. He had a minor hit with 'Convictions Of The Heart' (1991).

Collaborators
Robert 'Bumps' Blackwell ➧ p.52

LITTLE RIVER BAND
Albums
Diamantina Cocktail (Harvest 1977)★★★
➧ p.370 for full listings

LIVE
Albums
Throwing Copper (Radioactive 1994)★★★★
➧ p.370 for full listings

LIVING COLOUR
Albums
Time's Up (Epic 1990)★★★★
➧ p.370 for full listings
Collaborators
Rolling Stones ➧ p.281
Connections
Cheap Trick ➧ p.88
Robert Palmer ➧ p.255
Billy Bragg ➧ p.66

L L COOL J
Albums
Phenomenon (Def Jam 1997)★★★
➧ p.370 for full listings
Collaborators
Rick Rubin ➧ p.284

LOEB, LISA
Albums
Firecracker (Geffen 1997)★★★
➧ p.370 for full listings
Influences
Jimi Hendrix ➧ p.180
Led Zeppelin ➧ p.213
Fugazi ➧ p.154

LOFGREN, NILS
Albums
Nils Lofgren (A&M 1975)★★★★
➧ p.370 for full listings
Collaborators
Crazy Horse ➧ p.103
Neil Young ➧ p.346
Bruce Springsteen ➧ p.306
Connections
Rolling Stones ➧ p.281

LOGGINS, KENNY
Albums
The Unimaginable Fire (Columbia 1997)★★★
➧ p.370 for full listings
Collaborators
Doobie Brothers ➧ p.123
Nitty Gritty Dirt Band ➧ p.249
Connections
Loggins And Messina ➧ p.218
Further References
Film: *Footloose* (1984)

LOGGINS AND MESSINA
Albums
Loggins And Messina (Columbia 1972)★★★★
p.370 for full listings
Connections
Kenny Loggins p.217

LONE JUSTICE
Albums
Lone Justice (Geffen 1985)★★★
p.370 for full listings
Connections
Maria McKee p.230

LONE STAR
Albums
Firing On All Six (CBS 1977)★★★★
p.370 for full listings

LONG RYDERS
Albums
Native Sons (Frontier/Zippo 1984)★★★★
p.370 for full listings
Connections
Dream Syndicate p.125

LONGPIGS
Albums
The Sun Is Often Out (Mother 1996)★★★
p.370 for full listings
Influences
Beatles p.38
Nirvana p.248

LOOP GURU
Albums
Duniya (Nation 1994)★★★
p.370 for full listings

LORDS OF THE NEW CHURCH
Albums
Is Nothing Sacred? (IRS 1983)★★★
p.370 for full listings
Connections
Damned p.110
Sham 69 p.294

LOS LOBOS
Albums
The Neighbourhood (Slash 1990)★★★★
p.370 for full listings
Influences
Richie Valens p.328

LOVE
Albums
Forever Changes (Elektra 1967)★★★★★
p.370 for full listings
Collaborators
Jimi Hendrix p.180
Influences
Burt Bacharach p.27

LOVE AFFAIR
Albums
The Everlasting Love Affair (CBS 1968)★★★
p.370 for full listings

LOGGINS AND MESSINA

KENNY LOGGINS AND **JIM MESSINA** (b. 1947; EX-**POCO**). THEY COMBINED COUNTRY ROCK WITH HINTS OF LATIN, Mexican and R&B. All nine albums reached high US chart positions and spawned several hit singles including 'Your Mama Don't Dance' and 'My Music'. Following an amicable split after 6 years, Loggins went solo. Messina, following three albums, instigated the reformation of Poco in 1989 and a successful album, *Legacy*.

LONE JUSTICE

US COUNTRY-ROCKERS FRONTED BY **MARIA McKEE** (b. 1964). MARIA AND HALF-BROTHER BRYAN MacLEAN FORMED THE Maria McKee Band, later the Bryan MacLean Band. McKee then formed Lone Justice with Ryan Hedgecock (guitar), Don Heffington (drums), Marvin Etzioni (bass) and Benmont Tench (keyboards). They were signed to Geffen. The band's more established line-up included Bruce Brody (keyboards), Greg Sutton (bass) and Rudy Richardson (drums). In 1985, Feargal Sharkey had a UK number 1 with McKee's 'A Good Heart'. Lone Justice split in 1987 with McKee going solo.

LONE STAR

UK HARD ROCK QUINTET FORMED IN 1975 BY KENNY DRISCOLL (LEAD VOCALS), TONY SMITH (GUITAR), PAUL 'Tonka' Chapman (guitar), Pete Hurley (bass) and Dixie Lee (drums). Driscoll was replaced by John Sloman in 1977, before the release of *Firing On All Six*. This album pushed the dual guitars of Chapman and Smith to the forefront and concentrated on heavier material than their debut. Shortly after its release the band disintegrated.

LONG RYDERS

FORMED IN 1981, LONG RYDERS WERE PART OF LOS ANGELES' 'PAISLEY UNDERGROUND' MOVEMENT. SID Griffin Barry Shank (bass/vocals) and Matt Roberts (drums) were joined by Steve Wynn (later of **Dream Syndicate**). Wynn was replaced by Stephen McCarthy. A mini-album, *The Long Ryders*, was completed with Des Brewer (bass) and Greg Sowders (drums), before Tom Stevens replaced Brewer. *Native Sons* suggested a promising future, but, unable to repeat the balance of melody and purpose, they broke up in 1987.

LONGPIGS

FORMED IN SHEFFIELD, ENGLAND, IN 1993. CRISPIN HUNT (VOCALS/GUITAR), RICHARD HAWLEY (GUITAR), SIMON Stafford (bass) and Dee Boyle (bass), released a debut album composed of Hunt's material. After major problems with their first record company, the Longpigs signed a new contract with **U2**'s Mother Records and re-recorded their debut album. *The Sun Is Often Out* was finally released. Songs such as 'She Said' (a chart hit), 'Lost Myself' and 'Sally Dances' confirmed the promise of the earlier singles.

LOOP GURU

JAL MUU'S MIX OF SOUTH AMERICAN PIPE MUSIC AND MORROCAN INDIGENOUS SOUNDS CREATED THE SOUND of Loop Guru. He and Salman Gita form the core of the band, aided by up to 10 guest musicians. The duo have been involved in music since 1980 when they were members of the Megadog enclave. *Duniya* (Urdu for 'The World') placed them at the forefront of the 'world dance' movement. Their magnificent single, 'Paradigm Shuffle', included Martin Luther King's 'I Have A Dream' speech.

LORDS OF THE NEW CHURCH

ROCK BAND FEATURING BRIAN JAMES (b. 1961; GUITAR, EX-**DAMNED**), STIV BATORS (b. 1956; VOCALS; EX-**DEAD BOYS**), Dave Treganna (b. 1954; bass, ex-**Sham 69**) and drummer Nicky Turner (b. 1959). They made their live debut in Paris in 1981. Their debut vinyl, 'New Church', garnered criticism for apparent blasphemy. The single, 'Dance With Me', from *Is Nothing Sacred?*, gained several MTV plays with a video directed by Derek Jarman. Their final studio album, *Method To Our Madness*, revealed a band treading water with stifled heavy rock routines. They disbanded in 1989.

LOS LOBOS

FORMED IN 1974 IN LOS ANGELES BY CESAR ROSAS (b. 1954; VOCALS/GUITAR/MANDOLIN), DAVID HIDALGO (b. *c.* 1954; vocals/guitar/accordion), Luis (Louie) Perez (b. *c.* 1953; drums/guitar/quinto), Conrad Lozano (b. *c.* 1952; vocals/bass/guitarron) and Steve Berlin (b. *c.* 1957). Leaders of the Tex-Mex brand of rock 'n' roll, *Just Another Band From East LA* was a critical success, as was *How Will The Wolf Survive?*, however it only made moderate sales.

In 1987, their title single to the film *La Bamba* became an international number 1 and the first song in Spanish to top the pop charts. *La Pistola Y El Corazon* was an attempt to go back to their roots. *Kiko* moved back to a varied rock approach with hints of cajun, straight rock and soul.

LOVE

FORMED IN 1965 BY BRYAN MacLEAN (b. 1947; GUITAR/ VOCALS), ARTHUR LEE (b. 1945; GUITAR/VOCALS) AND JOHN Echols (b. 1945; lead guitar). Don Conka (d. 1973; drums) and Johnny Fleckenstein were replaced by Alban 'Snoopy' Pfisterer (b. 1947) and Ken Forssi (b. 1943). Their debut single was a version of **Bacharach** and David's 'My Little Red Book'. Love were an instant sensation on the LA club scene and the furiously energetic '7 And 7 Is' (1966) became their second hit. Although 'The Castle' (*Da Capo*) pointed to a new direction, it was *Forever Changes* that put them in the history books. It was Lee's finest work and marked the end of the partnership with Maclean.

A new Love – Lee, Frank Fayad (bass), Jay Donnellan (guitar) and George Suranovitch (drums) – lasted for two albums. Both records contained rare glimpses of *Forever Changes*. *False Start* featured a few memorable moments, including a guitar solo from **Jimi Hendrix**. *Reel To Real* is a truly wretched affair. Lee was diagnosed with Parkinson's disease in 1996.

LOVE AFFAIR

FORMED IN 1966 IN LONDON. STEVE ELLIS (VOCALS), MORGAN FISHER (KEYBOARDS), REX BRAYLEY (GUITAR), Mick Jackson (bass) and Maurice Bacon (drums) performed frequently in clubs on a semi-professional basis. Fisher was briefly replaced by Lynton Guest and the following year Ellis, backed by session musicians, recorded a cover of Robert Knight's 'Everlasting Love'. In 1968, the single hit UK number 1 and Love Affair became instant pop stars. Four more hits followed, 'Rainbow Valley', 'A Day Without Love', 'One Road' and 'Bringing On Back The Good Times', but by the end of the 60s, Steve Ellis left to form the group Ellis.

LOVERBOY

FORMED IN TORONTO, CANADA, IN 1980. MIKE RENO (VOCALS), PAUL DEAN (GUITAR), DOUG JOHNSTON (keyboards), Scott Smith (bass) and Matthew Frenette (drums) were signed by CBS straight away. Their self-titled debut was an American-styled melodic hard rock collection that dipped into reggae and jazz moods. With the hits 'Turn Me Loose' and 'The Kid Is Hot Tonite', *Loverboy* went platinum. The following *Get Lucky*, sold over two million copies. After touring they released the multi-platinum *Keep It Up* from which 'Hot Girls In Love' charted. *Lovin' Every Minute Of It* proved their least successful album, though it still sold over a million copies. *Wildside* featured **Bryan Adams**, Richie Sambora and **Jon Bon Jovi**. 'Notorious' proved the band's most successful single, going platinum three times.

After two years of touring they supported **Def Leppard** on their 1988 European tour. Dean and Reno left to record solo. In 1989, *Big Ones*, a compilation album, was released.

LOVETT, LYLE

TEXAN SINGER-SONGWRITER LYLE LOVETT (b. 1957) BEGAN WRITING SONGS IN THE LATE 70S. HE SANG ON TWO OF **Nanci Griffith**'s early albums, *Once In A Very Blue Moon* (1984) and *Last Of The True Believers* (1985). By 1986, Lovett had signed to MCA/Curb. His self-titled debut album was idiosyncratic, and his acceptance was slow in US country music circles, although it fared better in Europe. *Pontiac* made it clear that Lovett was rather more than a folk or country artist, with guests on the album including **Emmylou Harris**. *Lyle And His Large Band* included an insidiously straight version of the Tammy Wynette standard 'Stand By Your Man', and a version of the R&B oldie 'The Glory Of Love'.

In 1992, Lovett supported **Dire Straits** on their world tour, but it did little to extend his cult following. He acted in the film *The Player* and performed 'You've Got A Friend In Me' with **Randy Newman** for the soundtrack of the movie *Toy Story*. *The Road To Ensenada* mixed Lovett's razor wit with pathos.

LOVIN' SPOONFUL

FORMED IN 1965 BY **JOHN SEBASTIAN** (b. 1944; VOCAL/GUITAR/HARMONICA/AUTOHARP) AND Zalman Yanovsky (b. 1944; guitar/vocals). They recruited Steve Boone (b. 1943; bass) and Joe Butler (b. 1943; drums/vocals). Their unique blend of jug-band, folk, blues and rock 'n' roll, was termed 'electric good-time music' and in two years they notched up 10 US Top 20 hits, all composed by Sebastian. Sebastian also wrote the music for two films, Woody Allen's *What's Up Tiger Lily* and Francis Ford Coppola's *You're A Big Boy Now*. They split, but in 1991, Boone and Butler, together with Jerry and Jim Yester, re-formed the band to tour.

LOWE, NICK

LOWE (b. 1949) BEGAN AS BASS PLAYER/VOCALIST WITH BRITISH BAND KIPPINGTON LODGE, WHICH EVOLVED into **Brinsley Schwarz**. He then went into producing the **Kursaal Flyers**' *Chocs Away* and **Dr. Feelgood**'s *Malpractice*. His own singles were unsuccessful, but he was critically applauded for the catchy 'So It Goes', backed with the prototype punk song, 'Heart Of The City'. He produced **Elvis Costello**'s first five albums as well as albums for the **Damned**, **Clover** and **Dave Edmunds**.

In 1977, Lowe co-founded **Rockpile** and joined the legendary 'Live Stiffs' tour. His own debut, *Jesus Of Cool* (US title: *Pure Pop For Now People*), was a critics' favourite. In 1979, he produced the **Pretenders**' 'Stop Your Sobbing', and released his own *Labour Of Lust*. He married Carlene Carter and in the early 80s, as well as continuing his work with Costello, produced albums with **John Hiatt**, **Paul Carrack**, Carlene Carter and the **Fabulous Thunderbirds**. In 1992, Lowe formed Little Village with **Ry Cooder**, Jim Keltner and John Hiatt; their debut album received a lukewarm response. Much better was *The Impossible Bird* with some of his best lyrics in years; this was followed by the equally strong *Dig My Mood*, a dark and forboding lyrical odyssey of infidelity and sadness.

LUDUS

FOUNDED IN 1978, IN MANCHESTER, ENGLAND. FRONTED BY LYRICIST/VOCALIST LINDER (b. LINDA MULVEY, 1954) with Arthur Cadmon (b. Peter Sadler; guitar/songwriting), Willie Trotter (b. 1959; bass) and drummer Phil 'Toby' Tolman. Their music was jazz-influenced and Linder's lyrics were strongly feminist lyrics.

When Cadmon and Trotter left, replaced by Ian Devine (b. Ian Pincombe), the group saw a slight change in direction in spite of some inspired moments. Ian Devine teamed up in 1989 with singer Alison Statton to form Devine And Statton.

LULU

LULU (b. MARIE MacDONALD McLAUGHLIN LAWRIE, 1948) WAS A BEAT GROUP VOCALIST WITH HER OWN BACKING group, the Luvvers: Ross Nelson (guitar), Jim Dewar (rhythm guitar), Alec Bell (keyboards), Jimmy Smith (saxophone), Tony Tierney (bass) and David Miller (drums). She came to prominence, aged 15, with a version of the **Isley Brothers**' 'Shout' (1964), but over the next two years only two of her eight singles charted. Abandoning the Luvvers, a cover of Neil Diamond's 'The Boat That I Row' (1967) saw an upsurge in her career and an acting part in the film *To Sir With Love*. The theme tune gave her a million-selling US number 1/UK number 6.

Lulu represented Britain in the Eurovision Song Contest: 'Boom-Bang-A-Bang' tied for first place and provided her highest UK chart placing, number 2. After two albums and several flop singles, **David Bowie** intervened to produce and arrange her hit version of 'The Man Who Sold The World'. She later developed her career as an all-round entertainer. Appearances in *Guys And Dolls*, *Song And Dance* and the television programme *The Secret Diary Of Adrian Mole* was followed by a re-recording of 'Shout' (1986). *Independence* was an album of 'modern disco-pop with a flavour of classic soul and R&B'.

LOVERBOY
Albums
Loverboy (Columbia 1980)★★★
➧ p.370 for full listings
Collaborators
Bryan Adams ➧ p.9
Jon Bon Jovi ➧ p.60
Def Leppard ➧ p.114

LOVETT, LYLE
Albums
Pontiac (MCA/Curb 1987)★★★★
➧ p.370 for full listings
Collaborators
Emmylou Harris ➧ p.175
Dire Straits ➧ p.120
Randy Newman ➧ p.246
Nanci Griffith ➧ p.169
Influences
Guy Clark ➧ p.93

LOVIN' SPOONFUL
Albums
Do You Believe In Magic (Kama Sutra 1965)★★★★
➧ p.370 for full listings
Collaborators
John Sebastian ➧ p.291
Connections
Mamas And The Papa ➧ p.223

LOWE, NICK
Albums
The Impossible Bird (Demon 1994)★★★★
➧ p.370 for full listings
Collaborators
Ry Cooder ➧ p.100
Carlene Carter ➧ p.83
John Hiatt ➧ p.181
Paul Carrack ➧ p.83
Fabulous Thunderbirds ➧ p.141
Elvis Costello ➧ p.101
Damned ➧ p.110
Clover ➧ p.95
Dave Edmunds ➧ p.132
Pretenders ➧ p.266
Connections
Brinsley Schwarz ➧ p.68
Kursaal Flyers ➧ p.211
Dr. Feelgood ➧ p.125
Rockpile ➧ p.280
Further References
Film: *Americation* (1979)

LUDUS
Album
Pickpocket (New Hormones 1981)★★★
➧ p.370 for full listings

LULU
Albums
Something To Shout About (Decca 1965)★★★★
➧ p.370 for full listings
Collaborators
David Bowie ➧ p.64
Influences
Isley Brothers ➧ p.194
Further References
Film: *Gonks Go Beat* (1965)

LUSH

MIKI BERENYI (b. 1967; VOCALS/GUITAR), EMMA ANDERSON (b. 1964; GUITAR/BACKING VOCALS), STEVE RIPPON (BASS guitar) and Christopher Acland (b. 1966, d. 1996; drums) debuted in London on 6 March 1988, followed by their mini-album *Scar.* It was critically acclaimed and topped the independent charts. The EP *Mad Love* was less raw but more popular.

Much of 1991 was spent recording their debut album, during which time they also issued an EP, *Black Spring.* When *Spooky* was finally released, many were disappointed, nevertheless, the album reached the national Top 20 and number 1 in the UK independent chart. In 1992, Rippon left, replaced by Phil King (b. 1960). The critical reception that awaited *Split* was fervent. Although *Lovelife* failed to a certain degree in putting Lush in the premier league of pop bands, it did contain 'Single Girl', an effortless classic pop song, and '500'. Tragically, Acland committed suicide in October 1996.

LUSH
Albums
Lovelife (4AD 1996)★★★
➽ p.370 for full listings

LYMON, FRANKIE, AND THE TEENAGERS

US SINGER LYMON (b. 1942, d. 1968) JOINED ALL-VOCAL QUARTET, THE PREMIERS – JIMMY MERCHANT (b. 1940), Sherman Garnes (b. 1940, d. 1977), Herman Santiago (b. 1941) and Joe Negroni (b. 1940, d. 1978) – in 1954; they became the Teenagers. Their debut, 'Why Do Fools Fall In Love?' (US Top 10/UK number 1) sold two million copies. In 1957, Lymon split from the Teenagers, and his career prospects plummeted. Despite recording a strong album, his novelty appeal waned when his voice broke.

By 1961, the teenager was a heroin addict on a drug rehabilitation programme. Although he tried to reconstruct his career, his drug habit remained. In 1964, he was convicted of possessing narcotics. In February 1968, at the age of 25, he was discovered dead on the bathroom floor of his grandmother's New York apartment with a syringe by his side.

LYMON, FRANKIE, AND THE TEENAGERS
Albums
Rock 'N' Roll Party With Frankie Lymon (Guest 1959)★★★
➽ p.370 for full listings

LYNNE, JEFF

LYNNE (b. 1947) JOINED THE NIGHTRIDERS IN 1966. THEY CHANGED THEIR NAME TO **IDLE Race** and, under Lynne's guidance, became a leading exponent of classic late 60s pop. He joined the **Move** in 1970. Together with guitarist Roy Wood, Lynne attempted to form a more experimental outlet for their talents. This resulted in the launch of the **Electric Light Orchestra**, or ELO, of which Lynne took full control upon Wood's departure. Lynne abandoned his creation in 1986 moving into production and winning praise for his work with **George Harrison** (*Cloud Nine*), **Randy Newman** (*Land Of Dreams*), **Roy Orbison** (*Mystery Girl*) and much of **Tom Petty**'s recent output. Lynne also joined the **Traveling Wilburys**.

In 1990, Lynne unveiled his solo debut, *Armchair Theatre.* He produced the **Beatles**' lost tapes, notably 'Free As A Bird' and 'Real Love', and co-produced **Paul McCartney**'s *Flaming Pie* in 1997.

LYNNE, JEFF
Albums
Armchair Theatre (Reprise 1990)★★
➽ p.370 for full listings
Collaborators
George Harrison ➽ p.176
Randy Newman ➽ p.246
Roy Orbison ➽ p.252
Tom Petty ➽ p.260
Beatles ➽ p.38
Paul McCartney ➽ p.229
Connections
Idle Race ➽ p.192
Move ➽ p.241
Electric Light Orchestra ➽ p.134
Traveling Wilburys ➽ p.323
Bob Dylan ➽ p.128

LYNOTT, PHIL

HAVING ENJOYED CONSIDERABLE SUCCESS IN **THIN LIZZY**, LYNOTT (b. 1951, d. 1986) FIRST RECORDED SOLO IN 1980. His first single, 'Dear Miss Lonely Hearts', reached UK number 32 and was followed by *Solo In Soho.* A tribute to **Elvis Presley**, 'King's Call', reached number 35. In 1982, 'Yellow Pearl' (UK Top 20) was used as the theme tune to television show *Top Of The Pops.* In 1983, Thin Lizzy broke up and Lynott joined Grand Slam. In 1985, he partnered **Gary Moore** on the number 5 hit, 'Out In The Fields'. He played his last gig with Grand Slam at the Marquee in London on 3 December 1985. Shortly afterwards he died of heart failure, exacerbated by pneumonia.

LYNOTT, PHIL
Albums
Solo In Soho (Vertigo 1981)★★★
➽ p.370 for full listings
Collaborators
Gary Moore ➽ p.238
Connections
Thin Lizzy ➽ p.320
Influences
Elvis Presley ➽ p.265
Further References
Book: *Songs For While I'm Away*, Phillip Lynott

LYNYRD SKYNYRD

BOOGIE/HARD ROCK BAND FORMED IN FLORIDA IN 1964. RONNIE VAN ZANT (b. 1948, d. 1977; VOCALS), ALLEN COLLINS (b. 1952, d. 1990; guitar), Gary Rossington (b. 1951; guitar), Larry Jungstrom (bass) and Bob Burns (drum) played under various names and released one single, 'Need All My Friends' (1968), before changing their name to Lynyrd Skynyrd. Leon Wilkeson (b. 1952; bass) replaced Jungstrom and **Al Kooper** produced the group's debut album, *Pronounced Leh-Nerd Skin-Nerd*, which also featured guitarist Ed King and Billy Powell (b. 1952; keyboards). Support slots with the **Who** were followed by their momentous anthem, 'Free Bird'. In 1974, the group enjoyed their biggest US hit with 'Sweet Home Alabama', an amusing and heartfelt response to **Neil Young**'s critical 'Southern Man' and 'Alabama'. After the release of *Second Helping*, Burns was replaced by Artimus Pyle (b. 1948) and King retired. *Gimme Back My Bullets* was produced by Tom Dowd. In 1976 Rossington was injured in a car crash, and Steve Gaines (b. 1949, d. 1977; guitar) became King's replacement. Tragedy struck in October 1977: Van Zant, Gaines, his sister Cassie (one of three backing singers) and manager Dean Kilpatrick were killed in a plane crash. Rossington, Collins, Powell and Wilkeson were all seriously injured, but recovered. The new album, *Street Survivors*, was withdrawn as the sleeve featured an unintentionally macabre design of the band surrounded by flames.

In 1987, Lynyrd Skynyrd was revived for a 'reunion' tour featuring Rossington, Powell, Pyle, Wilkeson and King, with Ronnie's brother Johnny Van Zant (vocals) and Randell Hall (guitar). Collins had been paralyzed, and his girlfriend killed, during an automobile accident in 1986 and he died in 1990 from pneumonia. A 20th anniversary performance in 1993, included Rossington, Powell, Wilkeson, King and Johnny Van Zant joined by guests, including **Peter Frampton**, Brett Michaels (**Poison**), Charlie Daniels and Tom Kiefer.

LYNYRD SKYNYRD
Albums
One More From The Road (MCA 1976)★★★★
Street Survivors (MCA 1977)★★★★
➽ p.370 for full listings
Collaborators
Al Kooper ➽ p.210
Who ➽ p.338
Peter Frampton ➽ p.152
Connections
Neil Young ➽ p.346

M PEOPLE

FOUNDED BY SONGWRITER MIKE PICKERING (b. 1958; KEYBOARDS/PROGRAMMING), WITH VOCALIST HEATHER SMALL (b. 1965) and Paul Heard (b. 1960; keyboards/programming). They debuted in 1991 with 'Colour My Life', achieving major success with 'How Can I Love You More'. These singles promoted a debut album, *Northern Soul*. In 1993 on the back of colossal UK hits such as 'Movin' On Up', they were awarded a BRIT Award for Best UK Dance Act. The album *Elegant Slumming* which contained the hits, won them the Mercury Prize for best UK act in any category. *Bizarre Fruit* and its single, 'Search For The Hero', were greeted with mild disappointment. With the addition of bongo/percussion player 'Shovel', the group embarked on a world tour. *Bizarre Fruit II* compiled several remixes and edits as a prelude to *Fresco*, featuring the standout single 'Just For You'.

MacCOLL, KIRSTY

A CHANGE OF LABEL FROM STIFF RECORDS TO POLYDOR BROUGHT MacCOLL (b. 1959) UK TOP 20 SUCCESS IN 1981 with 'There's A Guy Works Down The Chip Shop Swears He's Elvis'. Her country and pop influences was discernible on her strong debut, *Desperate Characters*. In 1984, MacColl returned to the charts with a stirring version of **Billy Bragg**'s 'A New England'. In 1987, she reached number 2 with Shane MacGowan on the **Pogues**' 'Fairytale Of New York'. In 1989, she returned to recording solo with *Kite*. The album included the powerful 'Free World' and a version of the **Kinks**' 'Days', which brought her back to the UK Top 20. *Electric Landlady*, a pun on the **Jimi Hendrix** Experience's *Electric Ladyland*, was another strong album that demonstrated MacColl's diversity and songwriting talent.

MADNESS

THE LINE-UP COMPRISED SUGGS McPHERSON (b. GRAHAM McPHERSON, 1961; VOCALS), MARK BEDFORD (b. 1961; BASS), Mike Barson (b. 1958; keyboards), Chris Foreman (b. 1958; guitar), Lee Thompson (b. 1957; saxophone), Chas Smash (b. Cathal Smythe, 1959; vocals/trumpet) and Dan Woodgate (b. 1960; drums). With 2-Tone, they issued 'The Prince', which reached the UK Top 20. The follow-up, 'One Step Beyond' (a Buster composition) did even better, peaking at number 7. Over the next two years, the group enjoyed an uninterrupted run of UK Top 10 hits, including 'My Girl', 'Baggy Trousers' and 'It Must Be Love'. In 1982, they finally topped the charts with their twelfth chart entry, 'House Of Fun'. More UK hits followed, including 'Wings Of A Dove' and 'The Sun And The Rain', but in late 1983 the group suffered a setback when Barson quit. They continued to release exceptional work in 1984 including 'Michael Caine' and 'One Better Day'. They formed the label, Zarjazz, that year. Its first release was Feargal Sharkey's 'Listen To Your Father' (written by the group), which reached the UK Top 30. In the autumn of 1986, the group announced that they were splitting. Seventeen months later, they reunited as a four-piece under the name The Madness, but failed to find success. In 1992, the original Madness re-formed for two open-air gigs in Finsbury Park, London, which resulted in *Madstock*, a 'live' document of the event. Four chart entries followed; three reissues, 'It Must Be Love', 'House Of Fun' and 'My Girl'; along with 'The Harder They Come'.

M PEOPLE

Albums
Northern Soul (DeConstruction 1992)★★★
Bizarre Fruit (DeConstruction 1994)★★★★
Love Rendezvous (DeConstruction 1995)★★★
➽ p.370 for full listings

Connections
Hothouse Flowers ➽ p.187

Further References
Videos: *Elegant TV* (1994)
Live At G-Mex (BMG 1995)

MacCOLL, KIRSTY

Albums
Desperate Characters (Polydor 1981)★★★
Kite (Virgin 1989)★★★★
Electric Landlady (Virgin 1991)★★★
➽ p.370 for full listings

Collaborators
Pogues ➽ p.263

Connections
Steve Lillywhite

Influences
Billy Bragg ➽ p.66
Kinks ➽ p.207
Jimi Hendrix ➽ p.180

MADNESS

Albums
One Step Beyond (Stiff 1979)★★★★
The Rise And Fall (Stiff 1982)★★★★
Madstock (Go! Discs 1992)★★★
➽ p.370 for full listings

Collaborators
2-Tone

Connections
Feargal Sharkey
Buster

Further References
Videos: *Complete Madness* (Stiff 1984)
Divine Madness (Virgin Vision 1992)
Book: *A Brief Case Of Madness*, Mark Williams

MADONNA
Albums
True Blue (Sire 1986)★★★★
➽ p.370 for full listings

Collaborators
Billy Steinberg
Connections
Carpenters ➽ p.82
Further References
Book: *Madonna: Her Story*, Michael McKenzie
Film: *Evita* (1996)

MAGAZINE
Albums
Real Life (Virgin 1978)★★★
➽ p.370 for full listings
Connections
Buzzcocks ➽ p.76
Barry Adamson ➽ p.10
Siouxsie and the Banshees ➽ p.298

MAGNUM
Albums
Wings Of Heaven (Polydor 1988)★★★★
➽ p.370 for full listings

MAHAVISHNU ORCHESTRA
Albums
The Inner Mounting Flame (Columbia 1972)★★★★
➽ p.370 for full listings
Collaborators
George Martin ➽ p.226

MAHOGANY RUSH
Albums
What's Next (Columbia 1980)★★★
➽ p.370 for full listings
Influences
Jimi Hendrix ➽ p.180

MALMSTEEN, YNGWIE
Albums
Yngwie Malmsteen's Rising Force (Polydor 1984)★★★
➽ p.370 for full listings
Influences
Jimi Hendrix ➽ p.180
Ritchie Blackmore ➽ p.52
Eddie Van Halen ➽ p.328

MAMAS AND THE PAPAS
Albums
If You Can Believe Your Eyes And Ears (Dunhill/RCA Victor 1966)★★★★
➽ p.370 for full listings
Influences
Shirelles ➽ p.295
Further References
Book: *California Dreamin' – The True Story Of The Mamas And Papas*, Michelle Phillips

MADONNA

MADONNA (b. MADONNA LOUISE VERONICA CICCONE, 1958) set up Emmy in 1980 with Steve Bray. Together, Madonna and Bray created dance tracks which led to a recording deal with Sire. Madonna broke out from the dance scene into mainstream pop with 'Holiday'. It reached the US Top 20 and was a Top 10 hit across Europe in 1984. The first of her ten US number 1 hits came with Tom Kelly and Billy Steinberg's catchy 'Like A Virgin' in 1984.

From 1985-87, she turned out a string of hit singles. 'Crazy For You' was co-written by ex-**Carpenters**' collaborator John Bettis, while she and Steve Bray wrote 'Into The Groove'. These were followed by 'Dress You Up', 'Papa Don't Preach', 'True Blue', 'Open Your Heart' and 'La Isla Bonita'. Madonna continued to attract controversy when in 1989 the video for 'Like A Prayer', made links between religion and eroticism. The adverse publicity helped the album of the same title become a global best-seller. In 1990 the extravagant staging of the Blond Ambition world tour were the apotheosis of Madonna's *mélange* of sexuality, song, dance and religiosity. Among the hits of the early 90s were 'Vogue', 'Justify My Love' and 'Rescue Me'. In 1996, she starred in the film musical *Evita*. In 1998, she released the acclaimed *Ray Of Light*.

MAGAZINE

EX-**BUZZCOCKS**' VOCALIST HOWARD DEVOTO BEGAN WRITING SONGS WITH JOHN MCGEOGH IN 1977. THEY FORMED Magazine that year with Devoto (vocals), McGeogh (guitar), **Barry Adamson** (bass), Bob Dickinson (keyboards), and Martin Jackson (drums). Their moody, cold keyboards and harsh rhythms were in contrast to the mood of the day. They were signed to Virgin Records but Dickinson left in November, and their debut, 'Shot By Both Sides', was recorded by the remaining members. Dave Formula was recruited in time to play on *Real Life*. Next to leave was Jackson, replaced by John Doyle in 1978. Only their first single and 1980's 'Sweetheart Contract' charted. As the latter was released, McGeogh left to join **Siouxsie and the Banshees** and Robin Simon was brought in. A tour of the USA and Australia led to Simon's departure and Ben Mandelson came in for the band's last months. The departure of Devoto in 1981 signalled the band's end.

MAGNUM

FORMED IN 1972 BY TONY CLARKIN (GUITAR), BOB CATLEY (VOCALS), KEX GORIN (DRUMS) AND DAVE MORGAN (BASS). In 1978 they won a contract with Jet Records. Between 1978–80, the band released three albums to moderate success. *Chase The Dragon*, (1982) with Mark Stanway (keyboards), gave them their first Top 20 album. Following the release of *Eleventh Hour*, problems began: Clarkin became ill, and a dispute with Jet ensued. FM Revolver signed the band for *On A StoryTeller's Night*. Its Top 40 success prompted Polydor to offer a long-term contract. A Top 30 album and a sell-out UK tour followed. *Wings Of Heaven* (1988) gave them their first gold album and UK Top 10 hit. Top 40 single success came with 'Days Of No Trust', 'Start Talkin' Love' and 'It Must Have Been Love'. The Keith Olsen-produced *Goodnight L.A.* enjoyed Top 10 status and another Top 40 success was achieved with, 'Rocking Chair'. Extensive touring promoted *Goodnight L.A.* and several shows were recorded for a double live set, *The Spirit*. A new contract with EMI began with *Rock Art*.

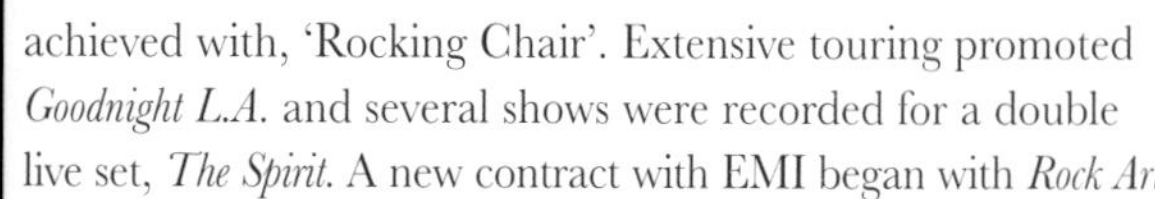

MAHAVISHNU ORCHESTRA

LED BY GUITARIST JOHN McLAUGHLIN, (b. 1942), BETWEEN 1972-76, THE MAHAVISHNU Orchestra played a leading part in jazz/rock fusion. The first line-up included musicians who had played on McLaughlin's solo album, *Inner Mounting Flame*. The high-energy music created by Jan Hammer (keyboards), Jerry Goodman (violin), Rick Laird (bass) and Billy Cobham (drums) made *Birds Of Fire* a US Top 20 hit. After releasing *Between Nothingness And Eternity*, McLaughlin split the group. A year later he re-formed it with new personnel. Jean-Luc Ponty replaced Goodman, Narada Michael Walden replaced Cobham, Gayle Moran took keyboards/vocals and there was a four-piece string section. This group made *Apocalypse* with producer **George Martin**. In 1975, Ponty left and Stu Goldberg (keyboards) played on the final albums.

MAHOGANY RUSH

IN 1970, GUITARIST FRANK MARINO RECRUITED PAUL HARWOOD (BASS) AND JIM AYOUB (DRUMS) AND FORMED Mahogany Rush. Their first three albums were derivative of **Jimi Hendrix**. By 1976, Marino had started to develop his own style and eventually outgrew the Hendrix comparisons. The name was amended to Frank Marino and Mahogany Rush, then to Frank Marino, following the release of *What's Next* and the departure of Ayoub.

MALMSTEEN, YNGWIE

INFLUENCED BY **JIMI HENDRIX**, **RITCHIE BLACKMORE** AND **EDDIE VAN HALEN**, SWEDISH-BORN MALMSTEEN (b. 1963) recorded a series of demos at the age of 14, one of which was picked up by producer and guitarist Mike Varney. Malmsteen joined Steeler and Alcatrazz before being offered a solo deal by Polydor. He released the self-produced *Rising Force*. He then formed Rising Force as a band and recorded two albums. Following an 18-month break Rising Force was resurrected and *Odyssey* was released in 1988. The album reached number 40 on the US *Billboard* album chart. *Eclipse* emerged in 1990 with weak vocals and a restrained Malmsteen on guitar. He switched back to his old style on *No Mercy*, however, which featured classical material and a string orchestra.

MAMAS AND THE PAPAS

FORMED IN LOS ANGELES IN 1965, THIS GROUP CONSISTED OF JOHN PHILLIPS (b. 1935), HIS WIFE MICHELLE (b. Holly Michelle Gilliam, 1944), and former Mugwumps' members Denny Doherty (b. 1941) and Cass Elliot (b. Ellen Naimoi Cohen, 1943, d. 1974). Their debut single, 'California Dreamin', was originally recorded by **Barry McGuire**, whose voice was erased and replaced by Doherty's. The song reached the US Top 5. The richly harmonic follow-up, 'Monday Monday' (US number 1) also established the group in the UK. Further hit singles followed, including 'I Saw Her Again' and a revival of the **Shirelles**' 'Dedicated To The One I Love'.

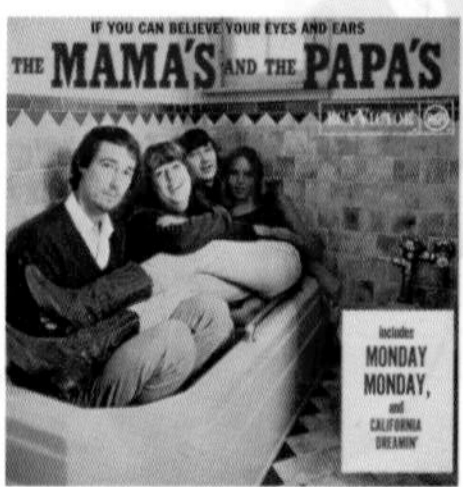

The group's albums went gold. However, marital problems between John and Michelle eroded the stability of the group and she was fired in 1966

and was replaced by Jill Gibson. The group reconvened for *Deliver*, another strong album, which was followed by the autobiographical 'Creeque Alley'. In the winter of 1967, UK concerts at London's Royal Albert Hall were cancelled, amid rumours of a split. The group managed to complete one last album, *The Papas And The Mamas*.

Three years later, the group briefly re-formed for *People Like Us*, but their individual contributions were taped separately and the results were disappointing. In 1982 Phillips and Doherty re-formed the group. The new line-up featured Phillips' actress daughter Laura McKenzie (McKenzie Phillips) and Elaine 'Spanky' McFarlane of Spanky And Our Gang.

MAN

MAN EVOLVED FROM THE BYSTANDERS, A SWANSEA-BASED GROUP SPECIALIZING IN CLOSE-HARMONY POP. MICKY Jones (b. 1946; lead guitar/vocals), Deke Leonard (b. Roger Leonard; guitar), Clive John (guitar/keyboards), Ray Williams (bass) and Jeff Jones (drums) completed Man's debut, *Revelation*, a concept album based on evolution. Man abandoned much of *Revelation*'s gimmicky frills for *2ozs Of Plastic With A Hole In The Middle*. The first in a flurry of line-up changes began when Martin Ace (bass) and Terry Williams (drums) joined the group, but the band only prospered with *Live At the Padgett Rooms, Penarth*. On the departure of Deke Leonard, Micky Jones and Clive John and new members released what is generally considered to be Man's most popular album, the live set, *Be Good To Yourself...At Least Once A Day*. The next album, *Back To The Future* gave Man their highest UK album position, matched the following year with *Rhinos, Winos And Lunatics*, which also saw the return of Leonard. Following the group's success in the USA promoting their album, *Slow Motion*, an ill-fated project with **Quicksilver**'s John Cippolina resulted in the unsatisfactory *Maximum Darkness*. The group's demise came in 1976 after the release of the *Welsh Connection*. During the late 80s, Jones, Leonard, Ace and drummer John 'Pugwash' Weathers (ex-**Gentle Giant**), resuscitated the Man name. In 1993 the group released their first studio album in 16 years, *The Twang Dynasty Road Goes On Forever*.

MANCHESTER, MELISSA

MANCHESTER (b. 1951) LAUNCHED HER CAREER IN 1973 WITH HOME TO MYSELF. HER INTIMATE STYLE SHOWED A debt to New York singer-songwriters, but her self-titled third album was more direct. This collection yielded her first major hit, 'Midnight Blue' (US Top 10), and set her subsequent direction. 'Whenever I Call You Friend', co-written with **Kenny Loggins**, was a best-selling single for him in 1978, while in 1979 Melissa's second US Top 10 was achieved with 'Don't Cry Out Loud'. Three years later she had another hit with 'You Should Hear How She Talks About You'.

MANFRED MANN

THE BAND WAS FORMED AS THE MANN-HUGG BLUES BROTHERS BY MANFRED MANN (b. MANFRED LUBOWITZ, 1940; keyboards) and Mike Hugg (b. 1942; drums/vibraphone). They became Manfred Mann shortly after adding **Paul Jones** (b. Paul Pond, 1942; harmonica/vocals). The line-up was completed by Mike Vickers (b. 1941; flute/guitar/saxophone) and Tom McGuinness (b. 1941; bass). '5-4-3-2-1' provided the first Top 10 hit in early 1964. By the summer, the group had their first UK number 1 with the catchy 'Do Wah Diddy Diddy'. Over the next two years, they charted regularly with hits such as 'Sha La La', and **Bob Dylan**'s 'If You Got To Go, Go Now'. In 1966, they returned to number 1 with 'Pretty Flamingo'. It was the last major hit on which Jones appeared. He was replaced by Michael D'Abo. D'Abo's debut with the group was another hit rendering of a Dylan song, 'Just Like A Woman'; their first for Fontana. Along with the **Byrds**, the group were generally regarded as the best interpreters of Dylan. This was emphasized in 1968 when they registered their third number 1 with Dylan's 'Mighty Quinn'. They ended the 60s with a final flurry of Top 10 hits.

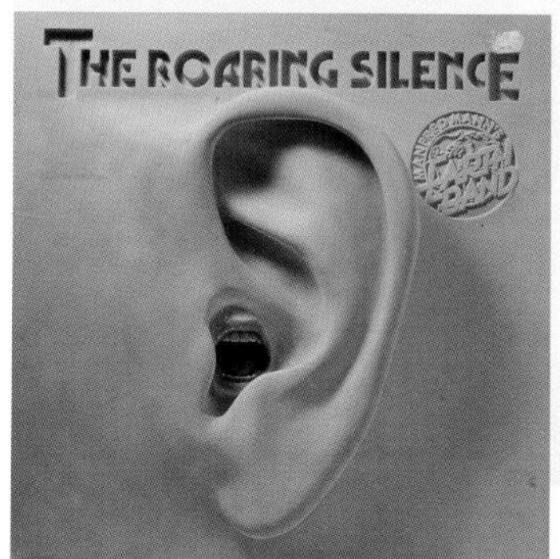

MANFRED MANN'S EARTH BAND

THE FOURTH INCARNATION OF MANFRED MANN HAS SURVIVED FOR ALMOST 20 YEARS. THE BAND COMPRISED Manfred (b. Manfred Lubowitz, 1940; keyboards), Mick Rogers (vocals/guitar), Colin Pattenden (bass) and Chris Slade (drums). Their debut was with the **Bob Dylan** song 'Please Mrs Henry'. It was not until their third offering, *Messin'*, that both success and acclaim arrived. The band hit the mark with a superb interpretation of Holst's *Jupiter*, entitled 'Joybringer'. It became a UK hit in 1973. *Solar Fire* featured another Dylan song, 'Father Of Day'. Rogers departed in 1976. They had a transatlantic hit (US number 1) and worldwide sales of over two million with a version of **Bruce Springsteen**'s 'Blinded By The Light' with vocals from Chris Thompson.

The Roaring Silence became the band's biggest album. After a lengthy absence, they made the US chart in 1984 with 'Runner', featuring the vocals of Mick Rogers. Nine years elapsed before the release of *Soft Vengeance* in 1996.

MANHATTAN TRANSFER

FORMED IN 1969, BY 1972 THE ONLY SURVIVING MEMBER WAS TIM HAUSER (b. 1940; VOCALS), ACCOMPANIED BY Laurel Masse (b. 1954; vocals) Alan Paul (b. 1949; vocals) and Janis Siegel (b. 1953; vocals). Although they covered a variety of vocal styles, their trademark was exquisite harmony. They charted on both sides of the Atlantic. In 1979, Cheryl Bentyne replaced Masse. Their version of **Weather Report**'s 'Birdland' remains a classic.

MANIC STREET PREACHERS

THIS GROUP OF PUNK REVIVALISTS ORIGINALLY COMPRISED JAMES DEAN BRADFIELD (b. 1969; VOCALS/GUITAR), RICHEY Edwards (b. 1966; rhythm guitar), Nicky Wire (b. Nick Jones, 1969; bass) and Sean Moore (b. 1970; drums). The polished, less caustic approach of *Gold Against The Soul* saw moments of sublime lyricism. *The Holy Bible* returned the group to their bleak world-view. Success seemed somehow irrelevant following Edwards' disappearance on 1 February 1995. However, the following year *Everything Must Go*, their first album in Edwards' absence was an outstanding record; although highly commercial. They culminated their finest year by winning three BRIT Awards, for Best Live Act, Best Single ('A Design For Life') and Best Album.

MAN
Albums
Revelation (Pye 1969)★★★
➽ p.370 for full listings
Connections
Gentle Giant ➽ p.157

MANCHESTER, MELISSA
Albums
Bright Eyes (Bell 1974)★★★
➽ p.370 for full listings
Collaborators
Kenny Loggins ➽ p.217

MANFRED MANN
Albums
Mann Made (HMV 1965)★★★★
➽ p.370 for full listings
Connections
Byrds ➽ p.77
Influences
Bob Dylan ➽ p.128
Further References
Book: *Mannerisms: The Five Phases Of Manfred Mann*, Greg Russo

MANFRED MANN'S EARTH BAND
Albums
The Roaring Silence (Bronze 1976)★★★★
➽ p.370 for full listings
Connections
Paul Jones ➽ p.201
Influences
Bob Dylan ➽ p.128
Bruce Sprinsteen ➽ p.306

MANHATTAN TRANSFER
Albums
Manhattan Transfer (Atlantic 1975)★★★★
➽ p.370 for full listings
Influences
Weather Report ➽ p.335

MANIC STREET PREACHERS
Albums
Everything Must Go (Epic 1996)★★★★★
➽ p.370 for full listings
Further References
Book: *Design For Living*, Paula Shutkever

MANILOW, BARRY

AFTER AN UNSUCCESSFUL DEBUT ALBUM, MANILOW (b. Barry Alan Pincus, 1946) took the powerful ballad 'Mandy' to US number 1. This was the prelude to 10 years of remarkable success. Among the biggest hits were 'Could It Be Magic' (1975), 'I Write The Songs' (1976), 'Tryin' to Get The Feeling Again' (1976), 'Looks Like We Made It' (1977), 'Can't Smile Without You' (1978), the upbeat 'Copacabana (At The Copa)' (1978), 'Somewhere In The Night' (1979), 'Ships' (1979) and 'I Made It Through The Rain' (1980). Two albums, *2am Paradise Cafe* and *Swing Street*, marked a change of direction as Manilow emphasized his jazz credentials in collaborations with Gerry Mulligan and Sarah Vaughan. He also appeared on Broadway in two one-man shows including *Showstoppers* (1991). In 1994, the stage musical *Copacabana*, for which Manilow composed the music, opened in London. In the same year, he was the supervising composer and collaborated on several of the songs for the animated feature *Thumbelina*.

MANILOW, BARRY
Albums
2am Paradise Cafe (Arista 1985)★★★
➽ p.370 for full listings
Further References
Video: *The Greatest Hits...And Then Some* (1994)
Book: *Barry Manilow: An Autobiography*, Barry Manilow with Mark Bego

MANN, AIMEE

AIMEE MANN ACHIEVED RECOGNITION AS THE LEAD VOCALIST OF THE CRITICALLY ACCLAIMED 'TIL TUESDAY BUT left to go solo in 1990. *Whatever* was a remarkable set. Mann attacked the corporate music business on 'I've Had It' and detailed estrangement and heartbreak on 'I Should've Known' and 'I Know There's A Word'. Former **Byrds** guitarist **Roger McGuinn** was persuaded to contribute 12-string backing.

MANN, AIMEE
Albums
Whatever (Imago 1993)★★★★
➽ p.370 for full listings
Collaborators
Roger McGuinn ➽ p.229
Connections
Byrds ➽ p.77

MANSUN

MANSUN CONFIRMED THE VALIDITY OF A GOOD PRESS WHEN THEIR 1996 SINGLE, 'STRIPPER VICAR', ENTERED THE UK Top 20. By the advent of *Attack Of The Grey Lantern* early in 1997, the group had become regulars on BBC Television's *Top Of The Pops*. They demanded from Parlophone the freedom to release EPs and the right to self-produce their debut album. The only outside influence on *Attack Of The Grey Lantern* came with remixing by Cliff Norrell and Mike 'Spike' Stent. In 1997, the band released an EP, *Closed For Business*, and continued their endless touring schedule.

MANSUN
Albums
Attack Of The Grey Lantern (Parlophone 1997)★★★★
➽ p.370 for full listings

MAR-KEYS

FORMED IN MEMPHIS, TENNESSEE, USA, THE LINE-UP COMPRISED **STEVE CROPPER** (b. 1941; GUITAR), DONALD 'DUCK' Dunn (b. 1941; bass), Charles 'Packy' Axton (tenor saxophone), Don Nix (b. 1941; baritone saxophone), Wayne Jackson (trumpet), Charlie Freeman (guitar), Jerry Lee 'Smoochy' Smith (organ) and Terry Johnson (drums). In the summer of 1961, their debut hit, 'Last Night', (US *Billboard* number 3) established Satellite, its label. Within months, Satellite had changed its name to Stax and the Mar-Keys became the label's house band. The Mar-Keys underwent changes. Freeman, Nix and Axton left, while Joe Arnold and Bob Snyder joined on tenor and baritone saxophones. They, in turn, were replaced by Andrew Love and Floyd Newman, respectively. Although commercial success under their own name was limited, the group provided the backbone to sessions by **Otis Redding**, **Sam And Dave**, **Wilson Pickett**, Carla Thomas and many others.

MAR-KEYS
Albums
The Great Memphis Sound (Atlantic 1966)★★★
➽ p.370 for full listings
Collaborators
Otis Redding ➽ p.274
Sam And Dave ➽ p.288
Wilson Pickett ➽ p.260
Booker T. And The MGs ➽ p.62
Connections
Steve Cropper ➽ p.105

MARC AND THE MAMBAS

FORMED BY **MARC ALMOND** (b. PETER MARC ALMOND, 1956), MARC AND THE MAMBAS WAS A PSEUDONYM THAT THE singer employed for his more adventurous work. *Untitled* unveiled revivals of material by artists such as **Lou Reed** and **Jacques Brel**. A double album, *Torment And Toreros*, received such poor reviews that Almond announced his retirement. That meant the imminent dissolution of Marc And The Mambas and a return to **Soft Cell**. When that too collapsed at the end of 1983, Almond embarked on a solo career.

MARC AND THE MAMBAS
Albums
Untitled (Some Bizzare 1982)★★
➽ p.370 for full listings
Connections
Marc Almond ➽ p.15
Soft Cell ➽ p.302
Influences
Lou Reed ➽ p.274
Jacques Brel ➽ p.67

MARILLION

THE GROUP FEATURED DOUG IRVINE (BASS), MICK POINTER (b. 1956; DRUMS), STEVE ROTHERY (b. 1959; GUITAR) AND Brian Jelliman (keyboards). After recording the instrumental demo, 'The Web', the band recruited **Fish** (b. Derek William Dick, 1958; vocals) and Diz Minnett (bass) and began building a following through continuous gigging. Before recording their debut, 'Market Square Heroes', Jelliman and Minnitt were replaced by Mark Kelly (b. 1961) and Pete Trewavas (b. 1959). Fish wrote all the lyrics for *Script For A Jester's Tear* and became the group's focal point. Marillion's second album embraced a hard-rock sound and yielded two hits, 'Assassin' and 'Punch And Judy'. In 1985 *Misplaced Childhood* saw the band create an elaborate concept album. 'Kayleigh', a romantic ballad, reached number 2 in the UK. In 1988, Fish left to go solo. Marillion acquired Steve Hogarth who made his debut on *Seasons End*.

MARILLION
Albums
Seasons End (EMI 1989)★★★
➽ p.370 for full listings

MARILYN MANSON

FLORIDA GROUP MARILYN MANSON WERE formed in 1990. They were the first band to be signed to Trent Reznor and John A. Malm Jr's Nothing label. Reznor was also guest musician and executive producer on their 1994 debut album. The group comprises Mr Manson (b. Brian Warner; vocals/tape loops), Daisy Berkowitz (guitar), Twiggy Ramirez (bass), Madonna Wayne Gacy (Hammond organ/samples) and Sara Lee Lucas (drums). Berkowitz left in 1996 and was replaced by Zim Zum. *Antichrist Superstar* (US *Billboard* album chart number 3) contained the American hit single, 'The Beautiful People'.

MARLEY, BOB, AND THE WAILERS

THIS LEGENDARY VOCAL GROUP, FORMED IN 1963, ORIGINALLY COMPRISED SIX MEMBERS: ROBERT NESTA MARLEY (b. 1945, d. 1981), Bunny Wailer (b. Neville O'Riley Livingston, 1947), **Peter Tosh** (b. Winston Hubert McIntosh, 1944, d. 1987), Junior Braithwaite, Beverley Kelso, and Cherry Smith. Bob Marley And The Wailers are the sole Jamaican group to have achieved global-superstar status.

After tuition with vocalist Joe Higgs, they began their recording career in 1963 for **Coxsone Dodd**; in 1962 Marley had also made two singles for producer Leslie Kong – 'Judge Not' and 'One Cup Of Coffee'. During 1963-66, the Wailers made over 70 tracks for Dodd (over 20 of which were local hits) covering a wide stylistic base; from covers of US soul to the newer, 'rude-boy' sounds. In late 1965 Braithwaite left for America; Kelso and Smith also departed.

On 10 February 1966, Marley married the vocalist Rita Anderson. The next day he left for America, returning to Jamaica that October; the Wailers were now a vocal trio. By the end of that year they were making demos for Danny Sims, the manager of **Johnny Nash**. They also began recording for Leslie Kong. By the end of 1969, wider commercial success still eluded them, but the trio began a collaboration with **Lee Perry** that proved crucial to their future. They worked with fellow Jamaicans, the Barrett brothers: Aston 'Family Man' (b. 1946) and Carlton (b. 1950, d. 1987), who became an integral part of the Wailers' sound.

The music made with Perry during 1969-71 stands as a zenith in Jamaican music. It was also the blueprint for Marley's international success. The group continued to record for their own Tuff Gong label after the Perry sessions and came to the attention of Chris Blackwell, then owner of Island Records. Their first album for the company, *Catch A Fire*, sold well enough to warrant issue of *Burnin'* (adding Earl 'Wire' Lindo to the group).

Just as the band was poised on the brink of wider success, internal differences caused Tosh and Livingston to depart. The new Wailers, formed mid-1974, included Marley, the Barrett brothers and Bernard 'Touter' Harvey on keyboards, with vocal harmonies by the I-Threes: Marcia Griffiths, Rita Marley and Judy Mowatt. In 1975 the release of the massively successful *Natty Dread* also saw rapturously received concerts at the London Lyceum. These concerts attracted both black and white; the crossover had begun. At the end of the year Marley achieved his first UK chart hit with 'No Woman No Cry', he also released his first live album, taken from the Lyceum concerts.

Marley survived an assassination attempt on 3 December 1976, leaving Jamaica for 18 months in early 1977. In July he had an operation in Miami to remove cancer cells from his right toe.

His next albums *Exodus* and *Kaya* enjoyed massive international sales. In 1978, he played the One Love Peace Concert in Kingston. The album *Survival* was released to critical acclaim, being particularly successful in Africa. Tragically, his cancer began to spread and he collapsed at Madison Square Garden during a concert in 1980. Marley died on 11 May 1981 in Miami, Florida.

MARMALADE

ORIGINALLY KNOWN AS DEAN FORD AND THE GAYLORDS, THIS GLASGOW-BASED QUINTET ENJOYED success on the Scottish club circuit during 1961-67. Eventually, they changed their name to Marmalade. The line-up then comprised: Dean Ford (b. Thomas McAleese, 1946; lead singer), Graham Knight (b. 1946; vocals/bass), Pat Fairley (b. 1946; rhythm guitar), Willie Junior Campbell (b. 1947; vocals) and Alan Whitehead (b. 1946; drums). The group reached the UK charts in 1968 with 'Lovin' Things' and enjoyed a number 1 with 'Ob-La-Di, Ob-La-Da'. Marmalade became the first *New Musical Express* UK chart-toppers of the 70s with 'Reflections Of My Life'. In 1971, the group suffered a setback when Campbell, their producer and main songwriter, quit. With replacement Hugh Nicolson, they enjoyed several more hits, including 'Cousin Norman', 'Radancer' and 'Falling Apart At The Seams'.

MARRIOTT, STEVE

IN 1961, DECCA ENGAGED MARRIOTT (b. 1947, d. 1991) AS AN **ADAM FAITH** SOUNDALIKE FOR TWO UNSUCCESSFUL singles. He then had another miss in the USA with a cover of the **Kinks**' 'You Really Got Me'. In 1964, he met fellow mod **Ronnie Lane** (bass) with whom he formed the **Small Faces** after recruiting Kenny Jones (drums) and Jimmy Winston (keyboards). Steve (guitar) emerged as the outfit's public face, attacking the early hits such as 'Sha-La-La-La-Lee' and 'My Mind's Eye' with a strangled passion.

On leaving the Small Faces in 1969, Marriott, as mainstay of **Humble Pie**, acquired a solitary UK Top 20 entry. By 1975 when Humble Pie disbanded, he had, however, earned hard-rock stardom accrued over 22 USA tours. He eventually re-formed the Small Faces, but poor sales of two 'comeback' albums blighted their progress. A link-up with Leslie West was mooted and a new Humble Pie released two albums but, from the early 80s, Marriott was heard mostly on the European club circuit. Shortly before he perished in a fire in April 1991, Marriot had been attempting to reconstitute Humble Pie with **Peter Frampton**.

MARSHALL TUCKER BAND

FORMED IN 1971 IN SOUTH CAROLINA, USA, THE MARSHALL TUCKER BAND CONSISTED OF TOY CALDWELL (b. 1948, d. 1993; lead guitarist), his brother, Tommy Caldwell, (b. 1950; bass), Doug Gray (vocals/keyboards), George McCorkle (rhythm guitar), Jerry Eubanks (saxophonist/flautist) and Paul Riddle (drums). The band signed with Capricorn Records and established the southern-rock style. The group's first album reached number 29 in the USA in 1973. Their highest-charting album, *Searchin' For A Rainbow*, came in 1975.

Most of the group's albums were gold or platinum-sellers through 1978, and the 1977 single 'Heard It In A Love Song' was their best-selling, reaching number 14. Following their 1978 *Greatest Hits* album, the band switched to Warner Brothers and released three chart albums through 1981. The group continued to perform after the death of Tommy Caldwell, but never recaptured their 70s success.

MARTHA AND THE MUFFINS

IN 1977, MARTHA JOHNSON JOINED UP WITH MARK GANE (GUITAR), CARL FINKLE (BASS), ANDY HAAS (saxophone) and Tim Gane (drums) to form Martha And The Muffins. They were later joined by Martha Ladly (guitar, then keyboards/trombone). The group signed with DinDisc Records. This led to the release of their debut single, 'Insect Love'. Success followed in 1980 with 'Echo Beach' (UK number 10). Follow-ups fared less well. In 1981, Ladly left to work with the **Associates** and Jocelyn Lanois then replaced Finkle. Following Haas's departure the band released *Dansepare*, before wife and husband team Johnson and Mark Gane formed M+M, who enjoyed a major US hit with 'Black Stations White Stations'. They later released two albums as a duo, *Mystery Walk*, and *The World Is A Ball*. *Modern Lullaby* was released in 1992, but their label went bankrupt shortly after its release.

Connections
Fish ➽ p.146
Further References
Video: *1982-1986 The Videos* (1986)
Book: *Market Square Heroes*, Mick Wall

MARILYN MANSON
Albums
Antichrist Superstar (Nothing/Interscope 1996)★★★
➽ p.370 for full listings
Collaborators
Trent Reznor

MARLEY, BOB, AND THE WAILERS
Albums
Natty Dread (Island 1975)★★★★★
Uprising (Tuff Gong/Island 1980)★★★★
➽ p.370 for full listings
Collaborators
Coxsone Dodd ➽ p.121
Jimmy Cliff ➽ p.94
Lee Perry ➽ p.259
Connections
Peter Tosh ➽ p.322
Johnny Nash ➽ p.244
Desmond Dekker ➽ p.114
Eric Clapton ➽ p.92
Further References
Book: *Bob Marley: The Roots Of Reggae*, McKnight and Tobler

MARMALADE
Albums
Reflections Of My Life (1970)★★★
➽ p.371 for full listings

MARRIOTT, STEVE
Albums
30 Seconds To Midnite (Trax 1989)★★
➽ p.371 for full listings
Collaborators
Ronnie Lane ➽ p.212
Connections
Small Faces ➽ p.300
Humble Pie ➽ p.190
Peter Frampton ➽ p.152
Influences
Adam Faith ➽ p.142
Kinks ➽ p.207
Further References
Films: *Heavens Above* (1962)
Be My Guest (1963)

MARSHALL TUCKER BAND
Albums
The Marshall Tucker Band (Capricorn 1973)★★★★
➽ p.371 for full listings
Further References
Video: *This Country's Rockin'* (1993)

MARTHA AND THE MUFFINS
Albums
This Is The Ice Age (DinDisc 1981)★★★
➽ p.371 for full listings
Connections
Associates ➽ p.23

MARTHA AND THE VANDELLAS
Albums
Come And Get These Memories (Gordy 1963)★★★
Dance Party (Gordy 1965)★★★
➽ p.371 for full listings
Collaborators
Marvin Gaye ➽ p.159
Connections
Martha Reeves ➽ p.275
Influences
Motown ➽ p.240

MARTIN, GEORGE
Albums
Off The Beatle Track (Parlophone 1964)★★★
➽ p. 371 for full listings
Collaborators
Beatles ➽ p.38
America ➽ p.16
Paul McCartney ➽ p.229
Dire Straits ➽ p.120
Rolling Stones ➽ p.281
Connections
Hollies ➽ p.183
Manfred Mann ➽ p.223
Further References
Book: *Summer Of Love: The Making Of Sgt Pepper*, George Martin
Film: *Give My Regards To Broad Street* (1985)

MARTYN, JOHN
Albums
Solid Air (Island 1973)★★★★
Piece By Piece (Island 1986)★★★★
➽ p.371 for full listings

MARVELETTES
Albums
Please Mr Postman (Tamla 1961)★★★★
➽ p. 371 for full listings
Collaborators
Smokey Robinson ➽ p.279
Influences
Motown ➽ p.240

MARVIN, HANK B.
Albums
Hank Plays Holly (Polygram 1996)★★★
➽ p.371 for full listings
Collaborators
Cliff Richard ➽ p.277
Connections
Drifters ➽ p.126
Shadows ➽ p.293

MASEKELA, HUGH
Albums
Trumpet Afnca (1962)★★★★
with Dudu Pukwana *Home Is Where The Music Is* (1972)★★★★
➽ p.371 for full listings

MARTHA AND THE VANDELLAS

MARTHA REEVES (b. 1941), WITH ANNETTE STERLING BEARD, GLORIA WILLIAMS AND ROSALIND ASHFORD, FORMED THE Del-Phis in 1960, and were offered a one-off single release on **Motown**'s Melody subsidiary. Gloria Williams left the group when the single flopped. Renamed Martha And The Vandellas, the group had a US Top 30 success with, 'Come And Get These Memories'. It was 'Dancing In The Street' (US number 2) that represented the pinnacle of their sound. The song, co-written by **Marvin Gaye** and Mickey Stevenson, was the most exciting record Motown had yet made.

'Nowhere To Run' in 1965 was an irresistible dance hit, introducing a new member, Betty Kelly, who replaced Annette Sterling Beard. This line-up scored further Top 10 hits with 'I'm Ready For Love' and the infectious 'Jimmy Mack'. Reeves was taken seriously ill in 1968, resulting in the group disbanding. By 1970, she was able to resume her career, recruiting her sister Lois and Sandra Tilley, to form a new line-up. No major US hits were forthcoming, but in the UK they were able to capitalize on the belated 1969 success of 'Dancing In The Street', and had several Top 30 entries in the early 70s.

MARTIN, GEORGE

MARTIN (b. 1926) BECAME THE WORLD'S MOST FAMOUS RECORD PRODUCER THROUGH HIS WORK WITH THE **Beatles**. He was put in charge of the Parlophone label in 1955, and signed the Beatles in the early 60s, beginning a relationship which lasted until their demise in 1970. Martin's main contribution to the group's music lay in his ability to put their more adventurous ideas into practice.

In 1965, he left EMI and set up his own studios, AIR London, with fellow producers Ron Richards (**Hollies**) and John Burgess (**Manfred Mann**). In the 70s he produced a series of hit albums by **America**. He also maintained the Beatles connection and prepared the 1977 release of the live recording *At The Hollywood Bowl* and produced two of **Paul McCartney**'s solo efforts, *Tug Of War* (1981) and *Pipes Of Peace* (1983). He opened a second studio on the island of Montserrat, which drew such artists as McCartney, **Dire Straits** and the **Rolling Stones**. During the late 80s, he was less prolific as a producer, but his work in remastering the Beatles' for compact disc created remarkable results. In the mid-90s he was a major part of the Beatles' *Anthology* series. He received the Grammy Trustees Award in 1995 and was awarded a knighthood in 1996.

MARTYN, JOHN

AFTER ARRIVING IN LONDON, MARTYN (b. IAIN McGEACHY, 1948) WAS SIGNED INSTANTLY BY CHRIS BLACKWELL, WHOSE Island Records was just finding major success. His first album was the jazz/blues-tinged *London Conversation* (1968). The jazz influence was confirmed when, only nine months later, *The Tumbler* was released. It broke many conventions of folk music, featuring the flute and saxophone of jazz artist Harold MacNair. Soon afterwards, Martyn married singer Beverly Kutner, and as John and Beverly Martyn they produced two well-received albums, *Stormbringer* and *Road To Ruin*. It was the release of *Bless The Weather* and *Solid Air* that established him as a concert hall attraction. *Inside Out* and the mellow *Sunday's Child* both confirmed his standing, although commercial success still eluded him. Frustrated by the music business, Martyn's alcohol and drug intake began taking their toll. *One World*, in 1977, has subtle references to this, but Martyn was going through serious problems and would not produce new work until three years later when, following the end of his marriage, he delivered the stunning *Grace And Danger*, a painfully emotional work. Following this collection, Martyn changed labels to WEA and delivered *Glorious Fool* and *Well Kept Secret*, which moved him firmly into the rock category.

Following the live album *Philenthropy*, Martyn returned to Island Records. The world's first commercially released CD single was Martyn's 'Angeline', a superbly crafted love song to his new wife, which preceded the album *Piece By Piece* in 1986. Enjoying cult status but little commercial success, Martyn slid into another alcoholic trough, returning in 1990 with *The Apprentice*. *Cooltide*, *Couldn't Love You More* and *No Little Boy* preceded a move to Go! Discs, and in 1996 he recorded *And*, an album of new songs which features the cryptical 'Downward Pull Of Human Nature'.

MARVELETTES

DESPITE ENJOYING SEVERAL MAJOR US HITS, THE MARVELETTES WERE UNABLE TO SUSTAIN A CONSISTENT LINE-UP, WHICH made it difficult to overcome their anonymous image. The group was formed in the late 50s in Michigan, USA: Gladys Horton, Georgeanna Marie Tillman (d. 1980), Wanda Young, Katherine Anderson and Juanita Grant. They were spotted at a school talent show by Robert Bateman who co-produced their early releases with Brian Holland. This led to success with 'Please Mr Postman' – a US number 1 in 1961, and Motown's biggest-selling record up to that point.

Smokey Robinson produced a series of hit singles for the group, the most successful being 'Don't Mess With Bill' in 1966. Gladys Horton, the Marvelettes' lead singer, left in 1967, to be replaced by Anne Bogan. They continued to achieve minor soul hits for the remainder of the decade, most notably 'When You're Young And In Love', before splitting up in 1970. In 1989, original members Wanda Rogers and Gladys Horton, plus Echo Johnson and Jean McLain, recorded for Ian Levine's Motor City label, issuing the disco-sounding 'Holding On With Both Hands' and *Now*.

MARVIN, HANK B.

MARVIN (b. BRIAN RANKIN, 1941) WAS ORIGINALLY ASKED TO JOIN BRUCE WELCH'S RAILROADERS, AND MARVIN AND Welch operated briefly as the Geordie Boys before enlisting in an outfit called the **Drifters**, which evolved into the **Shadows**.

After their first disbandment in 1968, Marvin's solo career commenced with 'Goodnight Dick', and 1969's *Hank Marvin* reached 14 in the UK album chart. Marvin's affinity with **Cliff Richard** continued via their hit duets with 'Throw Down A Line' and 'Joy Of Living'. In the early 70s, Marvin amalgamated with Welch and John Farrar for two albums (*Marvin, Welch And Farrar* and *Second Opinion*) dominated by vocals, and another (*Marvin And Farrar*) with Farrar alone.

MASEKELA, HUGH

SOUTH AFRICA'S LEADING TRUMPETER AND BANDLEADER, MASEKELA (b. HUGH RAMPOLO MASEKELA, 1939) WAS FIRST influenced by Duke Ellington, Count Basie, Cab Calloway and Glenn Miller. With trombonist Jonas Gwangwa, Masekela dropped out of school in 1955 to form his first group, the Merry Makers.

By 1958, it was very difficult in South Africa for black bands to make a living. Masekela was obliged to leave the Merry Makers and join the African Jazz and Variety package tour. In 1959, with fellow musician Makeba, Masekela left to join the cast of the 'township musical', *King Kong*. The same year, he formed the pioneering band, the Jazz Epistles, with Gwangwa and Dollar Brand (now Abdullah Ibrahim, piano).

In 1960, Masekela decided to emigrate to the USA. Initially aspiring to become a sideman with Art Blakey, Masekela was instead persuaded by the drummer to form his own band, and put together a quartet which debuted at the Village Gate club in 1961. A year later, he recorded his first album, *Trumpet Africa*, a considerable critical success.

In 1967, Masekela appeared at the legendary **Monterey** Jazz Festival and released two more albums, *Promise Of A Future* and *Coincidence*. Masekela became drawn into the lucrative area of light-weight jazz/pop. His first chart success in the genre was an instrumental version of 'Up Up And Away' in 1967 (US number 71). In 1968, 'Grazin' In The Grass' (US number 1) sold four million copies. The follow-up, 'Puffin' On Down The Track' though was disappointing (US number 71).

In 1970, Masekela formed the Union of South Africa Band with fellow *émigrés* Gwangwa and Caiphus Semenya, but it proved short-lived. Frustrated, Masekela visited London to record *Home Is Where The Music Is* with exiled South African saxonophist Dudu Pukwana. Deciding to find his African roots, Masekela set off in late 1972 on a 'pilgrimage' to west Africa. He finally ended up in Ghana, where he joined the young high-life-meets-funk band Hedzolleh Soundz.

In 1980, with Makeba, Masekela headlined an outdoor concert in Lesotho. In 1982, in a similar venture, they appeared in neighbouring Botswana. Masekela decided to settle in Botswana, 20 miles from the South African border, and signed to the UK label Jive, who flew over to him in a state-of-the-art mobile studio. The sessions resulted in *Technobush* and *Waiting For The Rain*. In 1983, he made his first live appearance in London for over 20 years, at the African Sounds for Mandela concert at Alexandra Palace. In 1986, Masekela severed his links with Jive and returned to the USA, where he signed with Warner Brothers, releasing *Tomorrow*, and joining label-mate **Paul Simon**'s Graceland world tour. In 1989, he co-wrote the music for the Broadway show *Sarafina*, set in a Soweto school and released the album *Up Township*.

Connections
Paul Simon ➧ p.296
Further References
Video: *Vukani* (BMG 1990)

MASON, DAVE

MASON (b. 1944) MET **STEVE WINWOOD** WHEN HE WAS EMPLOYED AS A ROAD MANAGER FOR THE **SPENCER DAVIS Group**. In 1967 Winwood, together with Mason, left to form **Traffic**. Mason joined and left the band on numerous occasions throughout the 60s. He subsequently settled in America in 1969 and enjoyed success as a solo artist. His excellent debut album, *Alone Together*, proved to be his most acclaimed work. By 1973, Mason had settled permanently in America and signed a contract with CBS, the first album being *It's Like You Never Left*. Following a surprise US hit single with 'We Just Disagree', Mason's albums became dull and *Old Crest On A New Wave* was the nadir. Mason kept a relatively low profile during the 80s making one poor album in 1987 and another forgettable release on MCA in 1988. In 1993, after having lived on Mick Fleetwood's estate in California, he joined **Fleetwood Mac**. He left in 1995 and continues to tour.

MASON, DAVE
Albums
Alone Together (Blue Thumb 1970)★★★★
➧ p.371 for full listings
Collaborators
Steve Winwood ➧ p.341
Connections
Spencer Davis Group ➧ p.304
Traffic ➧ p.323
Fleetwood Mac ➧ p.147

MASSIVE ATTACK

THIS LOOSE BRISTOL DANCE/RAP COLLECTIVE FEATURES THE TALENTS OF RAPPER '3D' DEL NAJO (b. *c.* 1966), AND

Daddy G (b. *c.* 1959) and Mushroom (b. *c.* 1968). They started in 1988 having previously released records under the Wild Bunch moniker. Contacts with **Neneh Cherry** led to a meeting with Cameron McVey, who produced Massive Attack's debut album. The resultant *Blue Lines* boasted three hit singles: 'Daydreaming', 'Unfinished Sympathy' and 'Safe From Harm'. 'Unfinished Sympathy' was particularly well received. *Melody Maker* ranked it as the best single of 1991, and it remains a club favourite. Despite *Blue Lines* being widely acclaimed, the band disappeared shortly afterwards. A second album, *Protection*, finally arrived in 1994, with former collaborator Nellee Hooper as producer.

MASSIVE ATTACK
Albums
Blue Lines (Wild Bunch/EMI 1991)★★★★
➧ p.371 for full listings

Collaborators
U2 ➧ p.326
Connections
Neneh Cherry ➧ p.89

MATCHING MOLE

MATCHING MOLE WERE FORMED BY **ROBERT WYATT** AFTER HE LEFT **SOFT MACHINE** IN 1971. HE RECRUITED DAVID Sinclair (keyboards, ex-**Caravan**), Phil Miller (guitar) and Bill McCormick (bass). They secured a contract with CBS, and the group began work on an album. Sinclair left, however, but was replaced by Dave Macrae. After the release of the debut *Matching Mole's Little Red Record*, the group began falling apart, and when Wyatt returned from a disabling accident, he elected to pursue a solo career.

MATCHING MOLE
Albums
Matching Mole's Little Red Record (Columbia 1973)★★★
➧ p.371 for full listings
Connections
Robert Wyatt ➧ p.344
Soft Machine ➧ p.138
Caravan ➧ p.81

MATTHEWS SOUTHERN COMFORT

FORMED IN 1969 BY FORMER **FAIRPORT CONVENTION** SINGER/GUITARIST IAIN MATTHEWS, THE GROUP comprised Mark Griffiths (guitar), Carl Barnwell (guitar), Gordon Huntley (pedal-steel guitar), Andy Leigh (bass) and Ray Duffy (drums). After signing to EMI, they recorded their self-titled debut album in late 1969. In 1970, their next album, *Second Spring* reached the UK Top 40 and was followed by the hit, 'Woodstock'. Success was followed by friction and Matthews decided to go solo. The group disbanded in summer 1972.

MATTHEWS SOUTHERN COMFORT
Albums
Matthews Southern Comfort (EMI 1969)★★★
➧ p.371 for full listings
Connections
Fairport Convention ➧ p.141

MAYALL, JOHN
Albums
Bare Wires (Decca 1968)★★★★★
➽ p.371 for full listings
Collaborators
Eric Clapton ➽ p.92
Jack Bruce ➽ p.71
Aynsley Dunbar ➽ p.25
Peter Green ➽ p.168
Connections
Rolling Stones ➽ p.281
Fleetwood Mac ➽ p.147
Further References
Book: *John Mayall: Blues Breaker*, Richard Newman

MAYFIELD, CURTIS
Albums
Superfly soundtrack (Buddah 1972)★★★★★
➽ p.371 for full listings
Connections
Lenny Kravitz ➽ p.211
Whitney Houston ➽ p.188
Bruce Springsteen ➽ p.306
Rod Stewart ➽ p.310
Elton John ➽ p.200
Steve Winwood ➽ p.341
Further References
Film: *Superfly* (1973)

MAZE (FEATURING FRANKIE BEVERLY)
Albums
Live In Los Angeles (Capitol 1986)★★★★
➽ p.371 for full listings
Connections
Marvin Gaye ➽ p.159

MAZZY STAR
Albums
So Tonight That I Might See (Capitol 1993)★★★
➽ p.371 for full listings

MC5
Albums
Kick Out The Jams (Elektra 1969)★★★★
➽ p.371 for full listings

McBRIDE, MARTINA
Albums
Wild Angels (RCA 1995)★★★★
➽ p.371 for full listings

McCARTNEY, PAUL
Albums
Flaming Pie (Parlophone 1997)★★★★
➽ p.371 for full listings
Collaborators
Bonzo Dog Doo-Dah Band ➽ p.61
Donovan ➽ p.123
Paul Jones ➽ p.201
Steve Miller ➽ p.234
Elvis Costello ➽ p.101
Connections
Beatles ➽ p.38
Moody Blues ➽ p.237
Wings ➽ p.340
Thunderclap Newman ➽ p.321
Further References
Book: *The Paul McCartney Story*, George Tremlett

MAYALL, JOHN

MAYALL (b. 1933) FORMED HIS FIRST BAND, THE POWERHOUSE FOUR, IN 1955. HE THEN MOVED TO LONDON to form his Blues Syndicate, the forerunner to his legendary Bluesbreakers. The astonishing number of musicians who have passed through his bands includes John McVie, **Eric Clapton**, **Jack Bruce**, **Aynsley Dunbar**, **Peter Green** and Mick Taylor.

His 1965 debut, *John Mayall Plays John Mayall*, was a live album. *Bluesbreakers With Eric Clapton* is now a classic. *A Hard Road* featured guitar from Peter Green, while *Crusade* offers a brassier, fuller sound. *The Blues Alone* showed a more relaxed style. *Bare Wires*, arguably Mayall's finest work, was an introspective journey. The similarly packaged *Blues From Laurel Canyon* marked the end of the Bluesbreakers name and, following the departure of Mick Taylor to the **Rolling Stones**, Mayall pioneered a drumless acoustic band featuring Jon Mark (acoustic guitar), Johnny Almond (tenor saxophone/flute), and Stephen Thompson (string bass). The subsequent live album, *The Turning Point*, proved to be his biggest-selling album. Following the double reunion *Back To The Roots*, Mayall's work lost its bite. His last album to chart was *New Year, New Band, New Company* in 1975, featuring, Dee McKinnie (vocals), and future **Fleetwood Mac** guitarist Rick Vito. In 1990 renewed activity and interest followed the release of *A Sense Of Place*. *Wake Up Call* (1993), proved one of his finest albums ever, and became his biggest-selling for over two decades.

MAYFIELD, CURTIS

AS SONGWRITER AND VOCALIST WITH THE IMPRESSIONS, MAYFIELD (b. 1942) HE PENNED A SUCCESSION OF EXEMplary singles between 1961-71, including 'Gypsy Woman' (1961), 'It's All Right' (1963), 'People Get Ready' (1965), 'We're A Winner' (1968) and 'Choice Of Colours' (1969). In 1970, the singer began his solo career with '(Don't Worry) If There's A Hell Below We're All Going To Go'. The following year Mayfield enjoyed his biggest UK success with 'Move On Up' (number 12). His ascendancy was maintained with 'Freddie's Dead' (US R&B number 2/number 4 pop hit) and the theme from 'Superfly' (1972). In 1981, he recorded *Honesty*, his strongest album since the early 70s. In 1990, a freak accident left Mayfield permanently paralyzed from the neck down. In 1993 Warner Brothers released *A Tribute To Curtis Mayfield* featuring various artists, including **Lenny Kravitz**, **Whitney Houston**, **Aretha Franklin**, **Bruce Springsteen**, **Rod Stewart**, **Elton John** and **Steve Winwood**. At the end of 1996, a new album, *New World Order*, was released to excellent reviews.

MAZE (FEATURING FRANKIE BEVERLY)

FRANKIE BEVERLY (b. 1946) FORMED RAW SOUL IN THE EARLY 1970S. THEY MOVED TO SAN FRANCISCO WHERE THEY became the house band at a local club. Discovered by a girlfriend of **Marvin Gaye**, it was he who suggested the name change. So the septet, which featured Wayne aka Wuane Thomas, Sam Porter, Robin Duke, Roame Lowery, McKinley Williams, Joe Provost plus Beverly, became Maze. Their debut album was issued in 1977.

MAZZY STAR

HIGHLY REGARDED DUO FEATURING HOPE SANDOVAL (VOCALS) AND DAVID ROBACK (GUITAR). ROBACK AND Sandoval adopted the name Mazzy Star for their sessions together, which eventually resulted in a critically lauded debut album. They released a comeback album on Capitol in 1993.

MC5

FORMED IN 1964 IN DETROIT, MICHIGAN, USA, AND ORIGINALLY KNOWN AS THE MOTOR CITY FIVE, THE GROUP SPLIT the following year when its rhythm section left over a new song, 'Back To Comm'. Michael Davis (bass) and Dennis Thompson (drums) joined founder-members Rob Tyner (b. Robert Derminer, 1944, d. 1991; vocals), Wayne Kramer (guitar) and Fred 'Sonic' Smith (b. 1949, d. 1994; guitar). A recording contract with the Elektra label resulted in the seminal *Kick Out The Jams*. MC5 later emerged anew on Atlantic Records with a third collection, *High Time*. The departure of Davis, then Tyner, in 1972, brought the MC5 to an end. Their reputation flourished during the punk phenomenon.

McBRIDE, MARTINA

ONE OF THE LEADERS IN CONTEMPORARY COUNTRY MUSIC, *THE TIME HAS COME*, McBRIDE'S (b. MARTINA MARIEA Schiff, 1966) debut album impressed with its treatment of material such as 'Cheap Whiskey' and 'That's Me'. Her breakthrough came after two singles in 1993, 'My Baby Loves Me The Way That I Am' and 'Independence Day'. Sales of her second album, *The Way That I Am*, climbed to the half million mark. In 1995 RCA Records launched her third album, *Wild Angels*. 'Safe In The Eyes Of Love' was a hit although for many, her revival of Delbert McClinton's 'Two More Bottles Of Wine' was a stronger track.

McCARTNEY, PAUL

ALTHOUGH COMMITMENTS TO THE **BEATLES** TOOK PRECEDENCE IN THE 60S, LIVERPOOL-BORN McCARTNEY (b. 1942) pursued several outside projects, ranging from production work for **Cliff Bennett**, Paddy, Klaus And Gibson and the **Bonzo Dog Doo-Dah Band** to appearances on sessions by **Donovan**, **Paul Jones** and **Steve Miller**. However, despite this well-documented independence, the artist ensured a critical backlash by timing the release of *McCartney* to coincide with that of the Beatles' *Let It Be* and his announced departure from the group. *Ram*, credited to McCartney and his wife Linda (b. Linda Eastman, 1942, d. 1998), was also maligned, but nonetheless spawned 'Uncle Albert/Admiral Halsey' (US number 1), and an attendant single, 'Another Day', (UK number 2). Denny Seiwell (drums), was invited to join a group later enhanced by former **Moody Blues**' member Denny Laine. The quartet, dubbed **Wings**, then completed *Wildlife*. Having brought in Henry McCullough (guitar), they released several singles and *Red Rose Speedway*. McCullough and Seiwell left shortly afterwards, but the remaining trio emerged triumphant.

Band On The Run was a major achievement, and restored McCartney's reputation. 'Junior's Farm' provided another hit single before a reconstituted Wings, which now included Jimmy McCulloch (d. 1979; guitar; ex-**Thunderclap Newman**) and Joe English (drums), completed *Venus And Mars*, *Wings At The Speed Of Sound* and the on-tour collection, *Wings Over America*. Although McCulloch and English left, Wings enjoyed its greatest success with 'Mull Of Kintyre' (1977), which sold over 2.5 million copies in the UK alone. Although regarded as disappointing, *London Town* nevertheless included 'With A Little Luck' (US number 1), but although Wings' newcomers Laurence Juber (guitar) and Steve Holly (drums) added weight to *Back To The Egg*, it too was regarded as inferior. McCartney's solo recordings, 'Wonderful Christmastime' (1979), 'Coming Up' (1980) and *McCartney II*, already heralded a new phase. McCartney's feature film, *Give My Regards To Broad Street*, was maligned, although 'No More Lonely Nights', reached UK number 2. *Choba B CCCP, The Russian Album*, provided a respite, before a collaboration with **Elvis Costello** produced material for *Flowers In The Dirt*. *Off The Ground* received lukewarm reviews, but the accompanying tour was one of the highest grossing in the USA that year. The success in 1994-95 of the *Beatles At The BBC* and the magnificent *Anthology* series in 1996, resulted in McCartney's knighthood. *Flaming Pie* was a magnificent return to form.

McCOYS

FORMED IN UNION CITY, INDIANA, USA, IN 1962, THIS BEAT GROUP INITIALLY COMPRISED RICK ZEHRINGER (b. 1947; guitar), his brother Randy (b. 1951; drums), Dennis Kelly (bass) and later Ronnie Brandon (organ). They became the McCoys soon after Randy Hobbs replaced Kelly. The group's debut was 'Hang On Sloopy' (1965), (US number 1/UK Top 5). The group discarded its bubblegum image with the progressive *Infinite McCoys*. When the group disbanded Zehringer joined Edgar Winter before going solo.

McCRAE, GEORGE

McCRAE (b. 1944) JOINED THE JIVIN' JETS, WHO BROKE UP DURING HIS US NAVY SERVICE, BUT RE-FORMED ON HIS return in 1967. McCrae's wife, Gwen McCrae, joined the line-up, but after six months the couple began work together. They recorded two singles, the second of which, 'Lead Me On', won Gwen a solo contract with Columbia. McCrae then began managing his wife's career, but following an R&B Top 20 hit with 'For Your Love' (1973), the pair returned as a duo. 'Rock Your Baby' topped the US and UK charts, while 'I Can't Leave You Alone' (1974) and 'It's Been So Long' (1975) reached the UK Top 10. In 1984, George McCrae enjoyed a final UK chart entry with 'One Step Closer (To Love)'.

McDONALD, COUNTRY JOE

IN 1964, McDONALD (b. 1942) MADE A LOW-KEY ALBUM WITH FELLOW PERFORMER BLAIR HARDMAN, AND LATER FOUNDED the radical pamphlet, **Rag Baby**. An early copy included a four-track record featuring the original version of the singer's anti-Vietnam War song, 'I Feel Like I'm Fixin' To Die Rag'. In 1965, he formed the Instant Action Jug Band, which later evolved into **Country Joe And The Fish**, but by 1969, McDonald had resumed his solo career. Two tribute albums, *Thinking Of Woody Guthrie* and *Tonight I'm Singing Just For You* presaged his first original set, *Hold On, It's Coming*. This was followed by *Quiet Days In Clichy* (film soundtrack) and *War, War, War*. The acclaimed *Paris Sessions* was a critical success, but subsequent releases lacked the artist's early purpose.

McDONALD, MICHAEL

FOLLOWING HIS DEPARTURE FROM THE **DOOBIE BROTHERS** IN 1982, McDONALD (b. 1952) WENT SOLO. DURING THE 80S, his compositions were recorded by numerous artists, including **Aretha Franklin**, **Millie Jackson** and **Carly Simon**. His 'Yah Mo B There', recorded with **James Ingram** in 1984, is a modern-soul classic. The 1985 album *No Lookin' Back* was followed by his number 1 hit with **Patti LaBelle**, 'On My Own'. During that year, he enjoyed international success with 'Sweet Freedom'.

McGARRIGLE, KATE AND ANNA

KATE (b. 1944; KEYBOARDS/GUITAR/VOCALS), AND HER SISTER ANNA (b. 1946; KEYBOARDS/ banjo/vocals), were brought up in Quebec, Canada, learning to sing and perform in both French and English. The sisters became members of the Mountain City Four, before they went their separate ways: **Linda Ronstadt** and Maria Muldaur were two of the artists who recorded their songs. Muldaur's label, Warner Brothers, asked the sisters to record an album. *Kate And Anna McGarrigle* was their debut. *Dancer With Bruised Knees* made the Top 40 in the UK. They took a long break after *Love Over And Over.*

McGRAW, TIM

McGRAW (b. 1967) SIGNED TO CURB RECORDS IN 1990 BUT CHARTED FIRST IN 1992 WITH 'WELCOME TO THE CLUB'. In 1994 his career took off with the single 'Indian Outlaw' (country number 1). The album, *Not A Moment Too Soon*, entered the *Billboard* country chart at number 1. The album sales topped four million and it remained in the Top 5 for over a year. The following album, *All I Want*, also amassed huge sales. His run of success continued with *Everywhere* in 1997.

McGRIFF, JIMMY

McGRIFF (b. JAMES HERRELL, 1936) WAS A MULTI-INSTRUMENTALIST WHO PLAYED PIANO, BASS, VIBES, DRUMS AND saxophone. After military service he began moonlighting as a bassist, backing blues stars such as Big Maybelle. His musical career took off with the single 'I Got A Woman' in 1962, and he had a string of hits released through the Sue label. His memorable 'All About My Girl' remains one of his finest compositions. He helped to popularize a jazz-flavoured style of R&B that is still influential in London clubland's 'acid jazz' circles.

McGUINN, ROGER

AFTER PLAYING AT FOLK CLUBS IN CHICAGO, JIM McGUINN (b. 1942; LEAD GUITAR) BRIEFLY JOINED THE LIMELITERS before becoming accompanist in the Chad Mitchell Trio in 1960. He played on two of their albums, *Mighty Day On Campus* and *Live At The Bitter End*, before leaving. At the Troubadour in Hollywood he formed the Jet Set with **Gene Clark** and **David Crosby**. Following the recruitment of Chris Hillman (bass) and Michael Clarke (drums), the quintet emerged as the **Byrds**. McGuinn became the focal point thanks largely to his 12-string Rickenbacker guitar playing and **Dylan**esque vocal style. He changed his name to Roger before recording the celebrated *The Notorious Byrd Brothers.*

By 1968, he was the last original group member left but he kept the Byrds going until 1973. He went solo that same year, launching his solo career with a self-titled album. The second album, *Peace On You* (1974) was typical in style, but the third album *Thunderbyrd* (1977) was patchy. It did, however, coincide with a UK tour which brought together three ex-Byrds in different groups. Within a year, the trio united as McGuinn, Clark And Hillman. For virtually the whole of the 80s McGuinn performed solo without recording. Later, he won a contract with Arista and set about recording his first album in over a decade. In 1990, he released *Back From Rio*. The album charted on both sides of the Atlantic. His first live album was issued in 1996.

McCOYS
Albums
Hang On Sloopy: The Best Of The McCoys (Legacy 1995)★★★★ (Compilation)
➧ p.371 for full listings

McCRAE, GEORGE
Albums
Rock Your Baby (TK 1974)★★★
➧ p.371 for full listings

McDONALD, COUNTRY JOE
Albums
Thinking Of Woody Guthrie (Vanguard 1970)★★★
➧ p.371 for full listings
Connections
Country Joe And The Fish ➧ p.101

McDONALD, MICHAEL
Albums
If That's What It Takes (Warners 1982)★★★★
➧ p.371 for full listings
Collaborators
James Ingram ➧ p.192
Patti LaBelle ➧ p.212
Connections
Doobie Brothers ➧ p.123
Aretha Franklin ➧ p.153
Millie Jackson ➧ p.195
Carly Simon ➧ p.296

McGARRIGLE, KATE AND ANNA
Albums
Kate And Anna McGarrigle (Warners 1975)★★★★
➧ p.371 for full listings
Connections
Linda Ronstadt ➧ p.282

McGRAW, TIM
Albums
Not A Moment Too Soon (Curb 1994)★★★★
➧ p.371 for full listings

McGRIFF, JIMMY
Albums
Soul Survivors (Milestone 1986)★★★★
➧ p.371 for full listings

McGUINN, ROGER
Albums
Cardiff Rose (Columbia 1976)★★★★
➧ p.371 for full listings
Collaborators
Gene Clark ➧ p.93
David Crosby ➧ p.105
Connections
Byrds ➧ p.77
Influences
Bob Dylan ➧ p.128
Further References
Book: *Timeless Flight: The Definitive Biography of the Byrds*, Johnny Rogan

McGUIRE, BARRY
Albums
Eve Of Destruction (1965)★★★
➜ p.371 for full listings
Connections
Mamas And The Papas ➜ p.223

McKEE, MARIA
Albums
Life Is Sweet (Geffen 1996)★★★★
➜ p.371 for full listings
Connections
Lone Justice ➜ p.218

McKENZIE, SCOTT
Albums
The Voice Of Scott McKenzie (Ode/CBS 1967)★★
➜ p.371 for full listings

McLACHLAN, SARAH
Albums
Fumbling Towards Ecstasy (Arista 1994)★★★★
➜ p.371 for full listings

McLEAN, DON
Albums
American Pie (United Artists 1971)★★★★
➜ p.371 for full listings
Influences
Buddy Holly ➜ p.184
Elvis Presley ➜ p.265
Bob Dylan ➜ p.128
Roy Orbison ➜ p.252

McNABB, IAN
Albums
Head Like A Rock (This Way Up 1994)★★★★
➜ p.371 for full listings
Connections
Icicle Works ➜ p.192

McTELL, RALPH
Albums
Not Until Tomorrow (Reprise 1972)★★★★
➜ p.371 for full listings

MEAT LOAF
Albums
Bat Out Of Hell (Epic 1978)★★★★
➜ p.371 for full listings
Collaborators
Todd Rundgren ➜ p.284
Further References
Book: *Meatloaf: Jim Steinman And The Phenomenology Of Excess*, Sandy Robertson

MEAT PUPPETS
Albums
Mirage (SST 1987)★★★★
➜ p.371 for full listings
Connections
Nirvana ➜ p.248

McGUIRE, BARRY

AFTER LEAVING THE NEW CHRISTY MINSTRELS, McGUIRE (b. 1935) SIGNED TO DUNHILL RECORDS AND WAS ASSIGNED to staff writers P.F. Sloan and Steve Barri. At the peak of the folk-rock boom, they wrote the rabble-rousing protest 'Eve Of Destruction' (US number 1).

McGuire continued to pursue the protest route on the albums *Eve Of Destruction* and *This Precious Time*, but by 1967 he was branching out into acting. After the meagre sales of *The World's Last Private Citizen*, McGuire ceased recording. In 1971 he returned with former **Mamas And The Papas** sideman Eric Hord on *Barry McGuire And The Doctor*. Soon afterwards, McGuire became a Christian evangelist and thereafter specialized in gospel albums.

McKEE, MARIA

BEFORE HER SOLO CAREER McKEE (b. 1964) WAS THE SINGER WITH **LONE JUSTICE**. AFTER IT BROKE UP McKEE RELEASED a solo album which included, 'Show Me Heaven' (UK number 1). McKee moved to Ireland and recorded the UK club hit 'Sweetest Child'. She returned to Los Angeles in 1992, the result being *You Gotta Sin To Get Saved* which reunited three-quarters of the original line-up of Lone Justice: Marvin Etzioni (bass), Don Heffington (drums) and Bruce Brody (keyboards), alongside Gary Louris and Mark Olsen (guitar/vocals) of the **Jayhawks**. McKee seemed more comfortable with the return to rootsy material as highlighted on *Life Is Sweet*.

McKENZIE, SCOTT

McKENZIE (b. PHILIP BLONDHEIM, 1944) BEGAN HIS CAREER IN THE JOURNEYMEN. THE SINGER WAS LATER INVITED BY fellow ex-member John Phillips to join him in Los Angeles. The pairing flourished on the success of 'San Francisco (Be Sure To Wear Some Flowers In Your Hair)' (UK and Europe number 1/US number 4).

McLACHLAN, SARAH

SINGER-SONGWRITER SARAH McLACHLAN (b. 1968) HAS featured on the Canadian folk scene since she was 20. *Fumbling Towards Ecstasy* blends her pastoral and reflective mood with a high-tech production by Pierre Marchand. She has found great success since founding the Lillith Faith tour.

McLEAN, DON

McLEAN (b. 1945) BEGAN HIS RECORDING CAREER IN NEW YORK IN THE EARLY 60S. HIS DEBUT TAPESTRY WAS ISSUED by Mediarts but failed to sell. United Artists issued 'American Pie' (US number 1/UK number 2). The album of the same name was also an enormous success. 'Vincent' fared even better (UK number 1). In 1973 McLean successfully covered **Buddy Holly**'s 'Everyday'. In 1980, he returned to the charts, covering **Roy Orbison**'s 'Crying' (UK number 1/US number 2). In 1991, his original version of 'American Pie' returned to the UK Top 20.

McNABB, IAN

GUITARIST, SINGER AND SONGWRITER McNABB (b. 1960) FAILED TO EARN THE COMMERCIAL REWARDS HE DESERVED with the **Icicle Works**, but his debut solo album, *Truth And Beauty*, was eventually released in 1993. His breakthrough, *Head Like A Rock*, was recorded over three weeks in Los Angeles. The follow-up *Merseybeast* did not build on the critical success of *Head Like A Rock*.

McTELL, RALPH

McTELL (b. 1944) EMERGED IN THE LATE 60S AS ONE OF BRITAIN'S LEADING FOLK singers with his first two albums, *Eight Frames A Second* and *Spiral Staircase*. The latter was notable for 'Streets Of London' (UK number 2). He developed into a singer-songwriter, exemplified on *You Well-Meaning Brought Me Here*. Subsequent releases included the excellent *Not Until Tomorrow* and *Easy*.

MEAT LOAF

MEAT LOAF (b. MARVIN LEE ADAY, 1951) BEGAN HIS CAREER IN 1969 WITH A ROLE IN *HAIR*, WHERE HE MET SOUL VOCALIST

Stoney. Stoney and Meat Loaf recorded a self-titled album in 1971, which spawned the minor *Billboard* hit, 'What You See Is What You Get'. *Hair* closed in 1974, and Meat Loaf joined *More Than You Deserve*, a musical by Jim Steinman. Meat Loaf and Steinman started composing a rock opera. Epic Records and producer **Todd Rundgren** were sympathetic to the demos and they recorded *Bat Out Of Hell* in 1978. After a six-month wait *Bat Out Of Hell* rocketed to the top. It stayed in the UK and US album charts for 395 and 88 weeks respectively, and sold over thirty million copies worldwide, the third biggest-selling album release of all time. However, Meat Loaf had lost his songwriter, as Steinman split to release a follow-up to *Bat Out Of Hell – Bad For Good*. After a three-year gap Meat Loaf's *Dead Ringer* was released (UK album number 1). The title song made the Top 5 in the UK but the album only reached the bottom of the *Billboard* Top 50. Concentrating on European tours helped both *Midnight At The Lost And Found* and *Bad Attitude* into the UK album Top 10. However, Meat Loaf signed a new deal with Virgin Records in 1990, and the Steinman-written and produced *Bat Out Of Hell II – Back Into Hell* (US/UK number 1 album), was a stylistic cloning of its precursor. The public loved it and the lead single 'I'd Do Anything For Love (But I Won't Do That)' reached US/UK number 1.

MEAT PUPPETS

FORMED IN TEMPE, ARIZONA, USA, CURT KIRKWOOD (b. 1959; GUITAR/VOCALS), CRIS KIRKWOOD (b. 1960; BASS/VOCALS) and Derrick Bostrom (b. 1960; drums) made their debut in 1981 with a five-track EP, *In A Car*. *Meat Puppets* on the influential label SST Records offered a mix of thrash punk with hints of country. *Meat Puppets II* was marked by shifts in mood and Kirkwood's vocals. *Up On The Sun* showed the trio moving towards neo-psychedelic melodies. *Mirage* was another critically acclaimed set and *Monster* proved the heaviest set to date. The group then disbanded, reforming in 1991 with a contract with London Records. In 1993, the Kirkwood brothers joined **Nirvana** on their *Unplugged* appearance. *No Joke!* proved to be their most commercial and successful album to date.

MEDICINE HEAD

THE GROUP COMPRISED JOHN FIDDLER (b. 1947; GUITAR/ VOCALS) AND PETER HOPE-EVANS (b. 1947; HARMONICA/ Jew's harp). Their debut album, *Old Bottles New Medicine*, offered atmospheric songs and rumbustious R&B, as did a second set, *Heavy On The Drum*. '(And The) Pictures In The Sky' reached number 22 in 1971, but Hope-Evans then left. Ex-**Yardbird** Keith Relf joined Fiddler and John Davies (drums) for the group's third album, *Dark Side Of The Moon*. Hope-Evans and Fiddler teamed up again in 1972 on *One And One Is One*. The title track reached UK number 3 in 1973, while a second single, 'Rising Sun', reached number 11; as a result, the line-up was expanded with Roger Saunders (b. 1947; guitar), Ian Sainty (bass) and Rob Townsend (b. 1947; drums). Further ructions followed the release of *Thru' A Five* and by 1976 Medicine Head was again reduced to the original duo. *Two Man Band* (1976) marked the end of their collaboration.

MEGA CITY FOUR

THEY STARTED OUT IN 1982 AS CAPRICORN. CHRIS JONES (DRUMS) JOINED WIZ (b. DARREN BROWN; VOCALS/ guitar), Danny (b. Daniel Brown, brother of Wiz; rhythm guitar/ backing vocals) and Gerry (b. Gerald Bryant; bass). A 300-gig touring schedule in 1989 resulted in the title of their debut album, *Tranzophobia*. *Who Cares Wins* was neutered by flat production. A live album preceded 1993's *Magic Bullets*. Sales proved disappointing. They signed to Fire Records in 1995, and released *Soulscraper* in 1996.

MEGADETH

FOUNDED IN SAN FRANCISCO, CALIFORNIA, USA, BY GUITARIST DAVE MUSTAINE (b. 1961) AFTER LEAVING **Metallica** in 1983. Recruiting Dave Ellefson (bass), Chris Poland (guitar) and Gars Samuelson (drums), Mustaine signed to the Combat label. They produced *Killing Is My Business...And Business Is Good* in 1985. Capitol Records then signed them. *Peace Sells...But Who's Buying?* proved a marked improvement. In 1988, Mustaine fired Poland and Samuelson, bringing in Jeff Young and Chuck Behler as replacements before the recording of *So Far, So Good...So What!*, which included a cover of 'Anarchy In The UK', with the **Sex Pistols**' guitarist Steve Jones. *Rust In Peace* featuring the guitar of Marty Friedman was released to critical acclaim. *Countdown To Extinction*, in 1990 dealt with ecological disaster. Reports of Mustaine's drug problems overshadowed sessions for their sixth album, *Youthanasia*.

MEKONS

THE MEKONS MADE THEIR RECORDING DEBUT FOR THE FAST PRODUCT LABEL IN 1978. AFTER TWO SINGLES, THE Mekons were signed to Virgin Records where a line-up of Andy Carrigan (vocals), Mark White (vocals), Kevin Lycett (guitar), Tom Greenhalgh (guitar), Ross Allen (bass) and Jon Langford (drums, later guitar/vocals) completed *The Quality Of Mercy Is Not Strnen*. Despite personnel changes, they have kept their adventurism, embracing world music, folk and roots. In the 90s, three of the core members, Greenhaigh, Langford and Sara Corina (violin), who joined in 1991, relocated to Chicago, Illinois, USA, where the group signed to Quarterstick Records. The band's first release for over three years, *Pussy, King Of The Pirates*, was a collaboration with American writer Kathy Acker.

MELANIE

MELANIE (b. MELANIE SAFKA, 1947) EMERGED DURING THE SINGER-SONGWRITER BOOM OF THE EARLY 70S. HER FIRST US hit, the powerful 'Lay Down' (1970), featured backing by the Edwin Hawkins Singers. In Britain, she broke through with an original version of the **Rolling Stones**' 'Ruby Tuesday'. *Candles In The Rain* was a transatlantic best-seller and 'What Have They Done To My Song, Ma?' gave her another minor hit, outselling a rival version from the **New Seekers**. Her last major success came in 1971 with 'Brand New Key' (US number 1) and proved her biggest hit in Britain. In 1972, Melanie founded Neighbourhood Records.

MELLENCAMP, JOHN

MELLENCAMP (b. 1951) SURVIVED A PHASE AS A GLAM-ROCKER TO BECOME ONE OF AMERICA'S MOST SUCCESSFUL mainstream rock singers. In 1976, his name was changed to Johnny Cougar, and he released *Chestnut Street Incident*. His first charting album was *John Cougar*, which included the US Top 30 single 'I Need A Lover' in 1979. In 1982 *American Fool* headed the US album chart. The following year he became John Cougar Mellencamp. He dropped 'Cougar' in 1989. *Lonesome Jubilee* used fiddles and accordions to illustrate America in recession, while 'Pop Singer' from *Big Daddy* expressed Mellencamp's disillusionment with the music business. He has continued to hit the US charts with amazing rapidity and, up until early 1991, he had charted 21 singles in the US Hot 100 of which nine were Top 10, with one number 1, 'Jack And Diane' in 1982.

MELVIN, HAROLD, AND THE BLUE NOTES

FORMED IN PHILADELPHIA IN 1954, THE BLUE NOTES – HAROLD MELVIN (b. 1939, d. 1997), BERNARD WILSON, JESSE Gillis Jnr., Franklin Peaker and Roosevelt Brodie – began as a doo-wop group. Despite several excellent singles, they failed to make a breakthrough. By the end of the 1960s only Melvin and Wilson remained. Then Theodore '**Teddy' Pendergrass** (b. 1950), drummer in the Blue Notes' backing band, was brought out as the featured vocalist. Lloyd Parkes also joined the group, which was then signed by producers **Gamble And Huff**. Pendergrass was best heard on 'If You Don't Know Me By Now' (1972). 'The Love I Lost' (1973) and 'Where Are All My Friends' (1974) enhanced Pendergrass's reputation and led to his demand for equal billing. Melvin's refusal resulted in the singer's departure, and Melvin And The Blue Notes, with new singer David Ebo, moved to ABC Records. Despite securing a UK Top 5 hit with 'Don't Leave Me This Way' and a US R&B Top 10 hit with 'Reaching For The World'. in 1977, the group failed to recapture its earlier success. They signed to Philly World in 1984, achieving minor UK hit singles the same year with 'Don't Give Me Up' and 'Today's Your Lucky Day'.

MELVINS

DALE CROVER (DRUMS) PLAYED WITH **NIRVANA** FOR A SPELL, WHILE KURT COBAIN OF NIRVANA GUESTED AND CO-produced *Houdini*. The other members of the Melvins, formed in 1984, numbered Buzz Osbourne (vocals/guitar) and Lori Beck (bass). A cover version of Flipper's 'Way Of The World' and 'Sacrifice' sat alongside **Alice Cooper**'s 'Ballad Of Dwight Fry' on the cover album *Lysol*. *Stoner Witch*, saw Crover and Osbourne joined by Mark Deutrom (bass), who had produced the band's first two albums. This time they were working with Garth Richardson of **Red Hot Chili Peppers** and **L7**. Two albums with Atlantic failed to bring commercial success, and the band moved to a subsidiary for *Stag*.

MEDICINE HEAD
Albums
One And One Is One (Polydor 1973)★★★
➽ p.371 for full listings
Connections
Yardbirds ➽ p.345

MEGA CITY FOUR
Albums
Sebastapol Road (Big Life 1991)★★★★
➽ p.371 for full listings
Further References
Book: *Mega City Four: Tall Stories And Creepy Crawlies*, Martin Roach

MEGADETH
Albums
Rust In Peace (Capitol 1990)★★★★
➽ p.371 for full listings
Connections
Metallica ➽ p.232
Sex Pistols ➽ p.292
Further References
Video: *Exposure Of A Dream* (PMI 1993)

MEKONS
Albums
The Curse Of The Mekons (Blast First 1991)★★★
➽ p.371 for full listings

MELANIE
Albums
Candles In The Rain (Buddah 1970)★★★
➽ p.371 for full listings
Connections
New Seekers ➽ p.246

MELLENCAMP, JOHN
Albums
Whenever We Wanted (Mercury 1991)★★★
➽ p.371 for full listings
Further References
Book: *American Fool: The Roots And Improbable Rise Of John Cougar Mellencamp*, Torgoff

MELVIN, HAROLD, AND THE BLUE NOTES
Albums
Wake Up Everybody (Philadelphia International 1975)★★★★
➽ p.371 for full listings
Collaborators
Teddy Pendergrass
➽ p.258
Gamble And Huff ➽ p.158

MELVINS
Albums
Gluey Porch Treatments (Alchemy 1987)★★★
➽ p.371 for full listings
Collaborators
Kurt Cobain ➽ p.248
Connections
Nirvana ➽ p.248
Red Hot Chili Peppers
➽ p.274
L7 ➽ p.211

MEMPHIS HORNS
Albums
Flame Out (Lucky 7 1992)★★★
p.371 for full listings
Collaborators
Al Green p.168
Ann Peebles p.257

MEN THEY COULDN'T HANG
Albums
Waiting For Bonaparte (Magnet 1987)★★★★
p.371 for full listings
Connections
Pogues p.263
Elvis Costello p.101

MENSWEAR
Albums
Nuisance (Laurel 1995)★★★
p.371 for full listings

MERCHANT, NATALIE
Albums
Tigerlily (Elektra 1995)★★★
p.371 for full listings
Connections
10,000 Maniacs p.318

MERCURY REV
Albums
See You On The Other Side (Beggars Banquet/Work 1995)★★★
p.371 for full listings
Influences
Wire p.341
Pere Ubu p.258

MERSEYBEATS
Albums
The Merseybeats (Fontana 1964)★★★★
p.371 for full listings
Collaborators
Brian Epstein p.137
Connections
Big Three p.47

METALLICA
Albums
Metallica (Elektra 1991)★★★★
p.371 for full listings
Influences
Budgie p.73
Diamond Head p.117
Killing Joke p.295
Misfits p.234
Further References
Book: *A Visual Documentary*, Mark Putterford

METHENY, PAT
Albums
Travels (ECM 1983)★★★★
p.371 for full listings
Collaborators
David Bowie p.64

MFSB
Albums
Philadelphia Freedom! (Philadelphia International 1975)★★★
p.371 for full listings
Collaborators
Gamble And Huff p.158

MEMPHIS HORNS

THE MEMPHIS HORNS ALWAYS HAD A FLUID LINE-UP. THE MAINSTAYS, WAYNE JACKSON (TRUMPET) AND ANDREW Love (tenor saxophone), guided the group during their time at Stax and Hi studios. Augmented by James Mitchell (baritone saxophone), Jack Hale (trombone) and either Ed Logan or Lewis Collins (tenor saxophone), the Horns appeared on releases by **Al Green**, **Ann Peebles**, and Syl Johnson. During the mid-70s, the Horns secured four R&B hits including 'Get Up And Dance' and 'Just For Your Love'.

MEN THEY COULDN'T HANG

BUSKING IN SHEPHERDS BUSH, LONDON IN EARLY 1984, LONDON WELSH SINGER CUSH MET BASSIST SHANNE, songwriter and guitarist Paul Simmonds, Ricky Maguire (bass), Scottish guitarist and singer Phil ('Swill') Odgers and his brother John (drums), in time for a ramshackle folk performance at London's alternative country-music festival. The band were quickly signed to **Elvis Costello**'s Demon label, Imp. They released an assured debut, *The Night Of A Thousand Candles*. 'Greenback' was less immediate, but its success led MCA to sign them, resulting in 'Gold Rush' in 1986. A move to Magnet Records led to their finest work, with *Waiting For Bonaparte*. 'The Colours' received airplay, but only skirted the charts. Fledgling label Silvertone's Andrew Lauder signed them next and released *Silvertown*. In 1990, they recorded their final studio album, which saw the addition of Nick Muir. Shortly afterwards they disbanded, following a farewell tour and a live album, *Alive, Alive – O*. The band returned in 1996 to Demon Records for *Never Born To Follow*.

MENSWEAR

THE RISE OF MENSWEAR WAS ONE OF 1995'S BIGGEST UK MEDIA EVENTS AND BEGAN WITH 'DAYDREAMER' (UK number 14). The group was founded by Johnny Dean (b. John Hutchinson Dean, 1971; vocals), Chris Gentry (b. 1977; guitar) and Stuart Black (b. Stuart Lee Black, 1974; bass). The line-up was completed with the addition of Matt Everett (b. Matthew Stephen Everett, 1972; drums) and Simon White (b. Simon Ian White, 1977; guitar). While *Nuisance* possessed a few reasonable tunes, nothing about them justified the initial press interest.

MERCHANT, NATALIE

MERCHANT (b. 1963) JOINED THE HIGHLY REGARDED **10,000 MANIACS** IN 1981. SHE LEFT THE GROUP IN 1992, THREE years before she made her solo bow. Merchant wrote the lyrics and music and produced her debut album, *Tigerlily*. She signed to Elektra Records, after which they promptly dropped 10,000 Maniacs.

MERCURY REV

MERCURY REV ARRIVED IN 1991. HOWEVER, THE SOUNDS PRODUCED BY JONATHAN DONAHUE (VOCALS/GUITAR), David Fridmann (bass), Jimmy Chambers (drums), Sean 'Grasshopper' Mackowiak (guitar), Suzanne Thorpe (flute) and David Baker (vocals, guitar) remain difficult to classify. Their album, *Yerself Is Steam*, although ignored in their native US, created press acclaim in the UK. Their second album, *Boces*, followed the traditions of left-field art rockers such as **Wire** and **Pere Ubu**. Baker was fired in 1994, but *See You On The Other Side* showed no reduction in the band's talents. The band were further reduced to Mackowiak and Donahue in 1997, following their signing to V2 records.

MERSEYBEATS

ORIGINALLY CALLED THE MAVERICKS, THIS LIVERPUDLIAN QUARTET COMPRISED TONY CRANE (VOCALS/LEAD GUITAR), Billy Kinsley (vocals/bass), David Ellis (rhythm guitar) and Frank Sloan (drums). In 1962, they became the Merseybeats. In early line-up changes Ellis and Sloan were replaced by Aaron Williams and John Banks. The Merseybeats were spotted by Fontana and initially signed by **Brian Epstein**. Their biggest hit was 'I Think Of You'. Kinsley left but returned in time for their third major hit, 'Wishin' And Hopin''. Other members included Bob Garner, who was replaced by Johnny Gustafson from the **Big Three**.

There were two more minor hits, 'I Love You, Yes I Do' and 'I Stand Accused'. In 1966, the group split, paving the way for hit duo the Merseys.

METALLICA

THE MOST INNOVATIVE METAL BAND OF THE LATE 80S AND EARLY 90S WERE FORMED IN 1981 BY LARS ULRICH (b. 1963; drums) and James Alan Hetfield (b. 1963; guitar/vocals). They recorded their first demo, *No Life Til' Leather*, with Lloyd Grand (guitar), who was replaced in 1982 by David Mustaine, Jef Warner (guitar) and Ron McGovney (bass). Each joined for a brief spell, and, at the end of 1982, Clifford Lee Burton (b. 1962, d. 1986; bass) arrived, and Mustaine was replaced by Kirk Hammett (b. 1962; guitar). The Ulrich, Hetfield, Burton and Hammett line-up endured until a tour bus accident killed Cliff Burton. The group put thrash metal on the map with their debut, *Kill 'Em All*. Although *Ride The Lightning* was not without distinction, *Master Of Puppets* revealed an appetite for the epic. The remaining three members recruited Jason Newsted (b. 1963; bass). The new line-up's first recording was *The $5.98 EP – Garage Days Revisited* – a collection of covers including material from **Budgie**, **Diamond Head**, **Killing Joke** and the **Misfits**. The 1988 opus, *... And Justice For All*, included a spectacular moment in 'One', also released as a single. 'Enter Sandman' broke the band on a stadium level. *Metallica* had sold 9 million copies in the USA by June 1996, and one month later *Load* became the US number 1.

METHENY, PAT

METHENY (b. 1954), TOGETHER WITH HIS MUSICAL PARTNER LYLE MAYS (KEYBOARDS), INITIATED A ROCK-GROUP FORMAT that produced albums of melodious jazz/rock. Following a major tour, Metheny released *New Chautauqua* and made the US Top 50. He returned to an electric format for *American Garage*. The double set *80/81* featured Michael Brecker, Jack DeJohnette, Charlie Haden and Dewey Redman and was more of a typical jazz album. Metheny had by now become fascinated by the guitar synthesizer or 'synclavier'. He used this to startling effect on *Offramp*. The double set *Travels* showed a band at the peak of its powers, while *Rejoicing* was a modern jazz album. In 1985, Metheny composed the score for *The Falcon And The Snowman* which led to 'This Is Not America' with **David Bowie**, (UK number 12/US Top 40 hit). Ironically, at the same time, Metheny produced *Song X*, with free-jazz exponent Ornette Coleman. He returned to more familiar ground with *Still Life (Talking)* and *Letter From Home*. In 1990, *Reunion* was released and a few months later, together with Dave Holland and Roy Haynes, he made *Question And Answer*. He continued into the 90s with *Secret Story*. After a second live album, *The Road To You*, he released *Zero Tolerence For Silence* with jazz guitarist John Scofield.

MFSB

'MOTHER, FATHER, SISTER, BROTHER', OR MFSB, WAS THE HOUSE BAND EMPLOYED BY PRODUCERS **GAMBLE AND Huff**. Jesse James, Bobby Martin, Norman Harris, Ronnie Baker, Earl Young, Roland Chambers and Karl Chambers came to prominence as performers on 'The Horse', a hit for Cliff Nobles And Co. in 1968. As the James Boys, they replicated that hit with, 'The Mule'. 'TSOP (The Sound Of Philadelphia)', was a million-selling single in 1974.

MICHAEL, GEORGE

MICHAEL (b. GEORGIOS (YORGOS) KYRIACOS PANAYIOTOU, 1963) SERVED HIS POP APPRENTICESHIP IN THE MILLION-selling duo **Wham!** When Wham! split in 1986, Michael went solo. He cut the chart-topping 'A Different Corner', revealing his talent as a singer-songwriter. He also teamed up with **Aretha Franklin** for the uplifting 'I Knew You Were Waiting'. Michael's re-emergence came in 1988. *Faith* followed, and sold in excess of 10 million copies. The album spawned a plethora of hit singles in the USA, including the title track, 'Father Figure', 'One More Try' and 'Monkey'. In 1990, he released his second album, *Listen Without Prejudice, Vol.1*. The first single from the album was 'Praying For Time' (US number 1). In the UK the comeback single was merely a Top 10 hit. He sought to free himself from record label Sony during 1993-94. By mid-1995, Michael had managed to free himself, the buy-out being financed by **David Geffen**'s media empire, Dreamworks, and Virgin Records. Michael announced the formation of his own label, Aegean, in 1997.

MICRODISNEY

THIS POP/FOLK GROUP WAS FORMED IN CORK, EIRE, IN 1980 AND BEGAN RELEASING SINGLES WHICH WERE COLLECTED on *We Hate You White South African Bastards*. It was followed by their first album, *Everybody Is Fantastic*. Their Virgin debut, 'Town To Town', reached the charts and was quickly followed by *Crooked Mile*. Their near-hit 'Singer's Hampstead Home', was an attack on Virgin's fallen idol, **Boy George**. They bowed out with *39 Minutes*, by which time the vitriol was really flowing.

MIDNIGHT OIL

FORMED IN SYDNEY, NEW SOUTH WALES, AUSTRALIA, in 1975, and then known as **Farm**, the nucleus of the band comprised Martin Rotsey (guitar), Rob Hirst (drums) and Jim Moginie (guitar). They were later joined by Peter Garrett (lead vocals). Having signed a contract with CBS/Columbia, it was *10,9,8,7,6,5,4,3,2,1* that gained radio airplay. *Red Sails In The Sunset* is looked on as their best work. The group's peak album chart positions in the UK and USA were achieved with *Diesel And Dust* (US number 21/UK Top 20), while in the US the follow-up, *Blue Sky Mining*, emulated that position.

MIKE AND THE MECHANICS

MIKE RUTHERFORD (b. 1950; BASS) OF **GENESIS** FORMED THE MECHANICS IN 1985. THE LINE-UP COMPRISED **PAUL Carrack** (b. 1951; vocals/keyboards), **Paul Young** (vocals), Peter Van Hooke and Adrian Lee. The group's first hit was 'Silent Running (On Dangerous Ground)' in 1986, followed in 1988 by their first big hit with 'The Living Years'. *Beggar On A Beach Of Gold* was preceded by 'Over My Shoulder'; unfortunately this proved to be the album's only ingot.

MILES, BUDDY

IN 1967, DRUMMER MILES (b. GEORGE MILES, 1945) WAS ASKED TO JOIN **ELECTRIC FLAG** BY guitarist **Mike Bloomfield,** whose departure left Miles in control. Miles retained its horn section for his next venture, the Buddy Miles Express. Their first album, *Expressway To Your Skull*, found a fan in **Jimi Hendrix**. In 1969, Miles joined Hendrix in the ill-fated Band Of Gypsies. The drummer formed the Buddy Miles Band and released *Them Changes*. In 1972 Miles recorded live with **Carlos Santana**. In the mid-90s, Miles reappeared with *Hell And Back*; this included his interpretations of 'All Along The Watchtower' and 'Born Under A Bad Sign'.

MILES, ROBERT

MILES'S (b. ROBERTO CONCINA (AKA ROBERTO MILANI)) 'CHILDREN', A TRANCE HOUSE TRACK with an obvious debt to the ambient tradition, became a surprise UK number 2 hit in 1996. Similar success occurred all over Europe. Originally released on Italian producer Joe T. Vannelli's DBX label, it was released in the mainstream by DeConstruction.

MILLER, FRANKIE (UK)

WITH **BRINSLEY SCHWARZ** AS HIS BACKING GROUP, MILLER (b. 1950) RECORDED HIS FIRST SOLO ALBUM, *ONCE IN A BLUE Moon*, in 1972; by 1975, Miller had formed a band featuring Henry McCullough, Mick Weaver, Chrissie Stewart and Stu Perry. Their album, *The Rock*, met with middling sales. With a new band comprising Ray Minhinnit (guitar), Charlie Harrison (bass), James Hall (keyboards) and Graham Deacon (drums), Miller next recorded *Full House*. Miller went solo for *Perfect Fit* and provided a Top 10 UK hit with 'Darlin''.

MICHAEL, GEORGE
Albums
Faith (Epic 1987)★★★★
➽ p.371 for full listings
Collaborators
Aretha Franklin ➽ p.153
Connections
Wham! ➽ p.337
David Geffen ➽ p.160
Further References
Book: *Wham! (Confidential) The Death Of A Supergroup*, Johnny Rogan

MICRODISNEY
Albums
Love Your Enemies (Creation Rev-Ola 1996)★★★
➽ p.372 for full listings
Connections
Boy George ➽ p.65

MIDNIGHT OIL
Albums
Red Sails In The Sunset (Columbia 1985)★★★★
➽ p.372 for full listings
Connections
Farm ➽ p.143

MIKE AND THE MECHANICS
Albums
Beggar On A Beach Of Gold (Virgin 1995)★★★
➽ p.372 for full listings
Connections
Paul Carrack ➽ p.83
Genesis ➽ p.161

MILES, BUDDY
Albums
Expressway To Your Skull (Mercury 1968)★★★★
➽ p.372 for full listings
Connections
Electric Flag ➽ p.134
Mike Bloomfield ➽ p.54
Jimi Hendrix ➽ p.180

MILES, ROBERT
Albums
23 AM (Arista 1997)★★★
➽ p.372 for full listings

MILLER, FRANKIE (UK)
Albums
Dancing In The Rain (Vertigo 1986)★★★
➽ p.372 for full listings
Collaborators
Brinsley Schwarz ➽ p.68

MILLER, STEVE
Albums
Sailor (Capitol 1968)★★★★★
Book Of Dreams (Capitol 1977)★★★★
➽ p.372 for full listings
Collaborators
Nicky Hopkins ➽ p.186
Paul McCartney ➽ p.229
Connections
Goldberg Miller Blues Band
Steve Miller Band

MINISTRY
Albums
With Sympathy aka *Work For Love* (Arista 1983)★★★
Filth Pig (Warners 1996)★★★
➽ p.372 for full listings
Influences
Bob Dylan ➽ p.128

MINOGUE, KYLIE
Albums
Rhythm Of Love (PWL 1990)★★★
Kylie Minogue (DeConstruction 1997)★★★
➽ p.372 for full listings
Collaborators
Stock, Aitken And Waterman ➽ p.310
Nick Cave ➽ p.85
Manic Street Preachers ➽ p.223
Further References
Book: *The Superstar Next Door*, Sasha Stone

MIRACLES
Albums
Cookin' With The Miracles (Tamla 1962)★★★★
Going To A Go-Go (Tamla 1965)★★★★
➽ p.372 for full listings
Collaborators
Berry Gordy
Holland/Dozier/Holland ➽ p.183
Connections
Smokey Robinson ➽ p.279
Motown ➽ p.240
Further References
Book: *Smokey: Inside My Life*, Robinson and Ritz

MISFITS
Albums
Beware EP (Cherry Red 1979)★★★, *Walk Among Us* (Ruby 1982)★★★
American Psycho (Geffen 1997)★★★
➽ p.372 for full listings
Connections
Damned ➽ p.110

MISSION
Albums
Children (Mercury 1988)★★★
Carved In Sand (Mercury 1990)★★★
➽ p.372 for full listings

MILLER, STEVE

MILLER (b. 1943) MOVED TO CHICAGO IN 1964. INVOLVEMENT IN THE BLUES SCENE WITH BARRY GOLDBERG, resulted in the Goldberg Miller Blues Band. By 1967, after a move to San Francisco, he signed with Capitol as the Steve Miller Band following his appearance at the 1967 **Monterey Pop Festival**. The band at that time included **Boz Scaggs**, Lonnie Turner, Jim Peterman and Tim Davis, and it was this line-up that recorded *Children Of The Future*. The album was a success but it was *Sailor* later that year that became his *pièce de résistance*. Scaggs and Peterman departed after this album, and Miller added **Nicky Hopkins** (keyboards) for *Brave New World*.

He decided to change the format for *Rock Love*, by having half of the album live. Following a European tour, he released *Recall The Beginning ... A Journey From Eden*.

After a gap of 18 months, Miller returned with the US chart-topping single 'The Joker'. The accompanying album was a similar success, (US number 2).

When he reappeared on record three years later, the stunning *Fly Like An Eagle* became his best-selling album and was a major breakthrough in the UK. Almost as successful was the sister album *Book Of Dreams* (1977). A new album, however, was not released for almost four years. The return this time was less spectacular with *Circle Of Love*. Six months later, the catchy 'Abracadabra' (US number 1), followed, but momentum was lost, as a live album and *Italian X-Rays* were failures. He opted out of the mainstream with the excellent *Born 2B Blue* in 1989. *Wide River* in 1993 was a return to his basic rock efforts. Miller's collaboration with **Paul McCartney** on *Flaming Pie* was highly publicized.

MINISTRY

AL JOURGENSON BEGAN PRODUCING MUSIC UNDER THE MINISTRY NAME IN CHICAGO IN THE EARLY 80S, BUT WAS unhappy with the Euro-pop direction of *With Sympathy*. He was happier with *Twitch*, which featured his own guitar, vocals and keyboards as well as Paul Barker (bass and keyboards) and Bill Rieflin (drums). The band evolved a brand of guitar-based industrial metal: *The Land Of Rape And Honey* and *In Case You Didn't Feel Like Showing Up (Live)*. Ministry achieved major success with *Psalm 69* (subtitled *The Way To Succeed And The Way To Suck Eggs*). In 1994, Rieflin was replaced by Ray Washam. *Filth Pig* contained, in true Ministry fashion, a distorted and raucous version of **Bob Dylan**'s 'Lay Lady Lay'.

MINOGUE, KYLIE

MINOGUE'S (b. 1968) WORK WITH HIT PRODUCERS **STOCK, AITKEN AND WATERMAN** moulded her wholesome image to their brand of radio-centred pop. The first UK single 'I Should Be So Lucky', reached number 1. In 1996, she recorded with **Nick Cave** and in 1997 was in the studio with the **Manic Street Preachers**. Her 1997 album title was changed from *Princess* to *Kylie Minogue*.

MIRACLES

THE MIRACLES WERE FOUNDED IN MICHIGAN IN 1955 BY **SMOKEY ROBINSON** (b. WILLIAM ROBINSON, 1940), Emerson Rogers, Bobby Rogers (b. 1940), Ronnie White (b. 1939, d. 1995) and Warren 'Pete' Moore (b. 1939). Emerson Rogers left in 1956, and was replaced by his sister Claudette. After recordings with producer Berry Gordy, the Miracles signed to Gordy's **Motown** label in 1960. Recognizing Robinson's talent, Gordy allowed the group freedom in the studio, resulting in 'Way Over There'. 'Shop Around', then broke both the Miracles and Motown to a national audience. Robinson later scaled down his writing for the group, when they briefly worked with **Holland/Dozier/Holland**. Robinson wrote their most ambitious and enduring songs including 'The Tears Of A Clown' in 1966 (a belated hit in the UK and USA in 1970), 'The Love I Saw In You Was Just A Mirage' and 'I Second That Emotion' in 1967.

In 1971, Robinson announced his intention of leaving the Miracles and launched a solo career to great success in 1973. His replacement was William 'Bill' Griffin (b. 1950). The group responded with *Renaissance*, and the following year, they re-established their position with 'Do It Baby' and 'Don'tcha Love It'. In 1975, 'Love Machine' became the Miracles' first US number 1, while the concept album *City Of Angels* was acclaimed. This twin success proved to be the Miracles' last gasp. In 1977, they lost Billy Griffin, and after a spell as a touring band, the Miracles disbanded in 1980.

MISFITS

A US CULT PUNK BAND, THE MISFITS WERE FORMED IN NEW JERSEY IN 1977 BY GERRY ONLY (BASS) AND GLENN DANZIG (b. 1959; vocals), later adding Bobby Steele (guitar) and Joey Image (drums). Later that year their first single, 'Cough Cool', appeared on their own Plan 9 label. A four-track EP, *Bullet*, was recorded before their debut album, and was followed by 'Horror Business'. A third single, 'Night Of The Living Dead', surfaced in 1979. Steele left, replaced by Jerry's brother Doyle, Googy (aka Eerie Von) played drums during a European tour with the **Damned**. In 1981 the Misfits recorded the seven-track mini-album *Evilive*. The band's only original UK release was a 12-inch EP, *Beware*. In 1997, the band re-formed, minus Danzig, releasing an album for Geffen Records.

MISSION

EVOLVED FROM THE SISTERS OF MERCY, WHEN WAYNE HUSSEY (b. 1959) AND CRAIG Adams split from Andrew Eldritch, Mick Brown (drums) and Simon Hinkler (guitar) came in. After two successful independent singles on *Chapter 22*, they signed to Mercury in 1986. Their major label debut, 'Stay With Me', entered the UK singles charts. *God's Own Medicine* was the first album, followed by *Children* (UK number 2). In 1990 'Butterfly On A Wheel' was released. In February, the third album, *Carved In Sand*, revealed a more sophisticated songwriting approach. In 1992 Craig Adams left, while Hussey brought in Andy Hobson (bass), Rik Carter (keyboards) and Mark Gemini Thwaite (guitar). The *Sum And Substance* compilation was released.

MISUNDERSTOOD

ONE OF PSYCHEDELIA'S FINEST GROUPS, THE MISUNDERSTOOD ORIGINATED IN RIVERSIDE, California, USA. Their first line-up of Greg Treadway (guitar), George Phelps (guitar) and Rick Moe (drums) also included Rick Brown (vocals) and Steve Whiting (bass). Phelps was replaced by Glenn Ross 'Fernando' Campbell (steel guitar). The quintet completed, 'You Don't Have To Go'/'Who's Been Talking?', before leaving for the UK. Tredway was later drafted and replaced by Tony Hill. The group completed six masters in London. 'I Can Take You To The Sun' was their only contemporary release, although 'Children Of The Sun' was issued after their break-up, in 1968. Campbell later re-established the name with several British musicians.

MITCHELL, JONI

AFTER ART COLLEGE, CANADIAN SINGER-SONGWRITER JONI (b. ROBERTA JOAN ANDERSON, 1943) MOVED TO TORONTO, where she married Chuck Mitchell. The two performed together, playing several Mitchell originals including 'The Circle Game'. Later in Detroit, the Mitchells met folk singer **Tom Rush**, who later covered Joni's 'Urge For Going', as well as making 'The Circle Game' an album title track. **Judy Collins** also covered Mitchell's 'Michael From Mountains' and 'Both Sides Now' on her 1967 album *Wildflowers*.

Following her divorce in 1967, Mitchell moved to New York. She was first discovered by manager Elliot Roberts at New York's Cafe Au Go-Go, and shortly afterwards in Coconut Grove, Florida, by former the **Byrds**', **David Crosby**. She and Crosby became lovers, and he went on to produce her debut album *Joni Mitchell* aka *Songs To A Seagull*. Divided into two sections, 'I Came To The City' and 'Out Of The City And Down To The Seaside'. With her next release *Clouds*, Mitchell paused for reflection.

There were signs of important songwriting developments on her third album, *Ladies Of The Canyon*. The extent of Mitchell's commercial acceptance was demonstrated on the humorous 'Big Yellow Taxi' (UK number 11).

Following a sabbatical, Mitchell returned with her most introspective work to-date, *Blue*. 'You Turn Me On, I'm A Radio' gave Mitchell a US Top 30 entry, but a fifteen-month gap ensued before *Court And Spark* appeared. The sweeping 'Help Me' (US number 7) in 1974, brought huge commercial success. The quality of Mitchell's live performances was captured on the live album *Miles Of Aisles*.

In 1975, Mitchell produced the startling *The Hissing Of Summer Lawns*, which not only displayed her increasing interest in jazz, but also world music. Although *Hejira* was equally adventurous, it was noticeably less ornate. The move into jazz territory through 1978-79, first with the double album, *Don Juan's Reckless Daughter*, culminated in her collaboration with Charlie Mingus.

A live double album, *Shadows And Light* followed before Mitchell signed a long-term contract with Geffen Records. The first fruits of this deal were revealed on *Wild Things Run Fast* in 1982. The opening song, 'Chinese Cafe', remains one of her finest compositions. The **Thomas Dolby**-produced *Dog Eat Dog* was critically underrated and represented the best of her 80s work. *Chalk Mark In A Rain Storm* continued in a similar vein, but there was a change of perspective on *Night Ride Home*, issued in 1991 following a three-year gap. After contributing a track, 'If I Could', to **Seal**'s 1994 album, she embarked on her first live dates in 12 years on a tour of Canada, before settling in to the studio to record *Turbulent Indigo*.

MOBY

NEW YORK DJ MOBY (b. RICHARD MELVILLE HALL, *c.* 1966) TOOK THE *TWIN PEAKS* TV THEME, 'UNDER THE GUISE OF Go', into the Top 10 in 1991. The release of 'I Feel It'/'Thousand' in 1993 was even more bizarre. He signed to Mute in 1993. *Ambient* was a collection of unissued cuts from 1988-91. *Story So Far* gathered together a series of tracks he cut for Instinct. The following year Moby released 'Hymn', a track distinguished by a 35-minute ambient mix and a Laurent Garner remix. His own remix catalogue includes **Brian Eno**, LFO ('Tan Ta Ra'), **Pet Shop Boys**, **Erasure** ('Chorus'), **Orbital** ('Speed Freak'), **Depeche Mode** and even **Michael Jackson**.

MOBY GRAPE

THIS ICONOCLASTIC BAND WAS FORMED IN 1966, WITH THE SEMINAL LINE-UP OF ALEXANDER 'SKIP' SPENCE (b. 1946; guitar/vocals), Jerry Miller (b. 1943; guitar/vocals), Bob Mosley (b. 1942; bass/vocals), Don Stevenson (b. 1942; drums) and Peter Lewis (b. 1945; guitar/vocals). With CBS, they became the centre of a huge marketing campaign, whereupon 10 tracks (five singles plus b-sides) were released simultaneously. Only 'Omaha' reached a dismal number 88. The resulting debut, *Moby Grape*, contained all these 10 tracks plus an additional three, and it reached the US Top 30 album charts. Their follow-up, *Wow*, made the US Top 20 chart and came with a free album, *Grape Jam*.

Spence left with drug and mental problems by the release of *Moby Grape '69*. Mosley left after a European tour. The fourth album, *Truly Fine Citizen* was badly received. The band disintegrated, unable to use the name which was, and still is, owned by manager, Matthew Katz. The remaining members have appeared as Maby Grope, Mosley Grape, Grape Escape, Fine Wine, the Melvills, the Grape, the Hermans and the Legendary Grape. The original five reunited for one more undistinguished album in 1971, *20 Granite Creek*.

MOCK TURTLES

THE BAND'S LYNCHPIN WAS SINGER, GUITARIST AND SONGWRITER MARTIN COOGAN, WHO HAD PREVIOUSLY ISSUED A single, 'Hey Judge', on the Mynah label in 1985. As the Mock Turtles, Coogan was joined by Steve Green (bass), Krzysztof Korab (keyboards) and Steve Cowen (drums). The band's first 12-inch EP, *Pomona*, was issued in 1987 after which Martin Glyn Murray (guitar) joined. In 1990 'Lay Me Down' arrived and hot on its heels came a well-received debut, *Turtle Soup*, in June. This lured Siren Records, and their first major label single was a rework of the b-side of 'Lay Me Down', 'Can You Dig It?'. The single was a hit and was followed by 'And Then She Smiles' which failed. Subsequently the highly commercial *Two Sides* suffered from a low profile. The band dissolved when Coogan formed a new band, Ugli, with Korab and Green after Murray left.

Connections
Sisters Of Mercy
Andrew Eldritch
Further References
Video: *From Dusk To Dawn* (Polygram Music Video 1988)
Book: *The Mission – Names Are Tombstones Baby*, Martin Roach with Neil Perry

MISUNDERSTOOD
Albums
Before The Dream Faded (1982)★★ (Compilation)
➧ p.372 for full listings
Collaborators
Rick Brown
Steve Whiting

MITCHELL, JONI
Albums
Blue (Reprise 1971)★★★★★
Court And Spark (Asylum 1974)★★★★★
Shadows And Light (Asylum 1980)★★★★
➧ p.372 for full listings
Collaborators
David Crosby ➧ p.105
Thomas Dolby ➧ p.122
Connections
Tom Rush ➧ p.285
Judy Collins ➧ p.98
Byrds ➧ p.77
Seal ➧ p.290
Further References
Books: *Joni Mitchell*, Leonore Fleischer
Complete Poems And Lyrics, Joni Mitchell

MOBY
Albums
Animal Rights (Mute 1996)★★★★
➧ p.372 for full listings
Collaborators
Brian Eno ➧ p.136
Pet Shop Boys ➧ p.259
Erasure ➧ p.138
Orbital ➧ p.252
Depeche Mode ➧ p.116
Michael Jackson ➧ p.195
Connections
Twin Peaks

MOBY GRAPE
Albums
Moby Grape (CBS 1967)★★★★★
Moby Grape '69 (CBS 1969)★★★★
➧ p.372 for full listings

MOCK TURTLES
Albums
Two Sides (Two Sides 1991)★★★★
➧ p.372 for full listings
Connections
Ugli

MODERN LOVERS
Albums
The Modern Lovers (Beserkley 1976)★★★★
➧ p.372 for full listings
Collaborators
John Cale ➧ p.78
Connections
Jonathan Richman ➧ p.277

MOIST
Albums
Silver (EMI 1994)★★★
➧ p.372 for full listings

MOLLY HATCHET
Albums
Molly Hatchet (Epic 1978)★★★
No Guts ... No Glory (Epic 1983)★★★
➧ p.372 for full listings
Collaborators
Tom Werman

MONEY, ZOOT
Albums
It Should've Been Me (Columbia 1965)★★★
Alexis Korner Memorial Concert Volume 2 (Indigo 1995)★★★
➧ p.372 for full listings
Collaborators
Eric Burdon ➧ p.74
Kevin Coyne ➧ p.102
Kevin Ayers ➧ p.25
Connections
Big Roll Band
Grimms and Ellis

MONKEES
Albums
More Of The Monkees (Colgems 1967)★★★★
Changes (Colgems 1970)★★★
➧ p.372 for full listings
Collaborators
Bob Rafelson
Bert Schneider
Connections
Michael Nesmith ➧ p.245
Tommy Boyce And Bobby Hart
Further References
Film: *Head* (1968)
Video: *The Monkees Collection* (Rhino 1995)
Book: *Monkeemania*, Baker

MONOCHROME SET
Albums
Eligible Bachelors (Cherry Red 1982)★★★
Trinity Road (Cherry Red 1995)★★★
➧ p. 372 for full listings
Connections
Adam And The Ants ➧ p.9

MONTEREY POP FESTIVAL
Albums
Monterey International Pop Festival 4-CD box set (Castle 1992)★★★
➧ p.372 for full listings

MODERN LOVERS

FORMED IN BOSTON, MASSACHUSETTS, USA, THE MODERN LOVERS REVOLVED AROUND SINGER-SONGWRITER **Jonathan Richman** (b. 1951). The group, also included Jerry Harrison (b. 1949; guitar), Ernie Brooks (bass) and David Robinson (drums). Their individual style attracted the interest of **John Cale**, then a staff producer at Warner Brothers. Having completed a series of demos, a disillusioned Richman disbanded the line-up. In 1976, the unfinished tracks were purchased by Beserkley Records which released them as *The Modern Lovers*. The company also signed Richman, whose new album, *Jonathan Richman And The Modern Lovers*, was issued within months. The Modern Lovers enjoyed two surprise UK hits in 1977 with 'Roadrunner' and 'Egyptian Reggae' (numbers 11 and 5 respectively). The Modern Lovers name was dropped the following year when the singer began a solo tour.

MOIST

A CANADIAN VANCOUVER-BASED BAND, FEATURING DAVID USHER (VOCALS), MARK MAKOWY (GUITAR) AND KEVIN Young (keyboards). Makowy brought in Jeff Pearce (bass) and Paul Wilcox (drums). The band released a debut album on their own label in 1994. Picked up by EMI Music Canada just one month later the record went platinum in Canada.

MOLLY HATCHET

THE INITIAL LINE-UP COMPRISED GUITARISTS DAVE HLUBEK, STEVE HOLLAND AND DUANE ROLAND PLUS BONNER Thomas (bass), Danny Joe Brown (vocals) and Bruce Crump (drums). Their debut album, produced by Tom Werman, was an instant success. Brown was replaced by Jimmy Farrar in 1980, before the recording of *Beatin' The Odds*. *Beatin' The Odds* and *Take No Prisoners* peaked on the *Billboard* chart at number 25 and 36, respectively. In 1982, Danny Joe Brown rejoined the band, while Thomas was replaced by Riff West. *No Guts ... No Glory* marked a return to their roots, but flopped. Steve Holden quit and keyboardist John Galvin was recruited for *The Deed Is Done*, a lightweight pop-rock album. In 1985, *Double Trouble Live* saw a return to former styles. In 1989 Hlubek departed, to be replaced by Bobby Ingram. They signed a new deal with Capitol and released *Lightning Strikes Twice*.

MONEY, ZOOT

MONEY (b. GEORGE BRUNO MONEY, 1942) PLAYED IN SEVERAL ROCK 'N' ROLL GROUPS BEFORE FORMING THE Big Roll Band in 1961. By 1963, the line-up had changed to comprise Andy Somers aka Andy Summers (guitar), Nick Newall (saxophone) and Colin Allen (drums). The Big Roll Band secured a residency at London's Flamingo Club, and added Paul Williams (bass/vocals) and Clive Burrows (saxophone), before recording the single, 'The Uncle Willie'. In 1965, the group released its first album, *It Should've Been Me*. A second album, *Zoot!*, recorded live at Klook's Kleek, introduced newcomer Johnny Almond, who replaced Burrows. Only one of their singles, 'Big Time Operator' (1966), broached the UK Top 30.

In 1968, both Money and Somers joined **Eric Burdon** in the New Animals. When the group failed Money completed *Welcome To My Head* and returned to London for *Zoot Money*. He continued with Centipede, and Grimms and Ellis, before joining Somers in the **Kevin Coyne** and **Kevin Ayers** bands. In the early 90s, he was music controller for Melody Radio, but went back on the road by 1995.

MONKEES

IN 1965 US TELEVISION PRODUCERS BOB RAFELSON AND BERT SCHNEIDER BEGAN AUDITIONS FOR A SHOW ABOUT A pop group. The final choice paired two musicians – **Michael Nesmith** (b. Robert Michael Nesmith, 1942; guitar/vocals) and folk singer Peter Tork (b. Peter Halsten Thorkelson, 1944; bass/vocals) – with two budding actors and former child stars – Davy Jones (b. 1945; vocals) and ex-*Circus Boy* star Mickey Dolenz (b. George Michael Dolenz, 1945; drums/vocals). On 12 September 1966, the first episode of *The Monkees* was aired. Attendant singles 'Last Train To Clarksville' (US number 1) and 'I'm A Believer' (US and UK number 1), and a million-selling debut album confirmed the group's position. However, news that the quartet did not play on their records but simply overdubbed vocals fuelled controversy. TV executive Don Kirshner also later called in staff songwriters, infuriating the Monkees' two musicians, in particular Nesmith, who described *More Of The Monkees* as 'the worst album in the history of the world'.

Sales in excess of five million copies exacerbated tension, but after 'A Little Bit Me, A Little Bit You' was issued, without group approval, Kirshner was ousted. Two further 1967 singles, 'Pleasant Valley Sunday' and 'Daydream Believer', achieved gold record status. *Headquarters*, the first Monkees album on which the group played, was a commercial and artistic success, as was *Pisces, Aquarius, Capricorn And Jones Ltd.* It was followed by the disappointing *The Birds, The Bees And The Monkees* and its accompanying single, 'Valleri'. The appeal of their series had waned, and the final episode was screened in 1968. Peter Tork left following the release of their feature film *Head*, but although the remaining trio continued their commercial decline was as spectacular as its ascendancy. Nesmith left for a solo career in 1969.

MONOCHROME SET

DURING LATE 1976, ANDY WARREN (BASS), LESTER SQUARE (GUITAR) AND BID (GUITAR/ VOCALS) WERE PLAYING IN THE B-Sides with **Adam Ant**. When the B-Sides became **Adam And The Ants**, Bid and Lester Square left. They formed the Monochrome Set in 1978. With Jeremy Harrington (bass) and J.D. Haney (drums), the band issued singles during 1979-80 for Rough Trade, including 'He's Frank', 'Eine Symphonie Des Graeuns', 'The Monochrome Set' and 'He's Frank (Slight Return)'. Their debut, *The Strange Boutique*, skirted the UK charts. A second album, *Love Zombies*, followed. Morris Windsor joined for the release of the 'The Mating Game', in 1982, followed by 'Cast A Long Shadow' and the memorable *Eligible Bachelors*. *Volume, Brilliance, Contrast* compiled their Rough Trade recordings and selected BBC Radio 1 sessions, and coincided with another indie hit, 'Jet Set Junta'. The band split in 1985 and Cherry Red Records' El subsidiary issued a retrospective, *Fin! Live*, a year later. In 1989 the band re-formed with *Dante's Casino*.

MONTEREY POP FESTIVAL

THE WEST COAST AMERICAN MUSIC SCENE WAS EFFECTIVELY LAUNCHED AT MONTEREY, CALIFORNIA, USA, ON 16-18 June 1967. The festival was the brainchild of John Phillips, Alan Pariser, **Paul Simon** and Lou Adler.

The three-day festival was a forerunner to **Woodstock**, and history has subsequently shown that Monterey was more 'musically' important, although it was a comparatively small affair with only 35,000 people present at any one time. It was at Monterey that **Jimi Hendrix** first attracted mass attention by burning his guitar; **Janis Joplin** grabbed the audience's imagination with her orgasmic and electrifying performance; **Otis Redding**'s accomplishment was memorable in bringing together black soul and white rock.

Among other the artists who appeared were the **Grateful Dead**, **Electric Flag**, **Canned Heat**, **Buffalo Springfield**, the **Byrds**, the **Mamas And The Papas**, **Eric Burdon And The Animals**, **Hugh Masekela**, **Jefferson Airplane**, Ravi Shankar, **Booker T. And The MGs**, the **Who**, **Moby Grape**, the **Steve Miller Band**, **Country Joe And The Fish**, **Simon And Garfunkel**, Beverly (Martyn), the Paupers, Lou Rawls, the **Association**, **Johnny Rivers**, **Quicksilver Messenger Service**, **Laura Nyro** and the **Blues Project**.

MONTEZ, CHRIS

MONTEZ (b. CHRISTOPHER MONTANEZ, 1943) WAS DISCOVERED BY IMPRESARIO JIM LEE IN 1961, AND ENJOYED AN international hit the following year with 'Let's Dance' (UK number 2), which sold over one million copies. A follow-up, 'Some Kinda Fun', reached the UK Top 10 in 1963. 'The More I See You' gave Montez a second UK Top 3 entry, while minor US successes followed with 'There Will Never Be Another You' and 'Time After Time'.

MOODY BLUES

FORMED IN 1964 BY DENNY LAINE (b. BRIAN HINES, 1944; VOCALS/HARMONICA/GUITAR), MIKE PINDER (b. 1942; piano/keyboards), Ray Thomas (b. 1942; flute/vocals/harmonica), Graeme Edge (b. 1941; drums) and Clint Warwick (b. 1940; bass). They established a strong London following, and soon received their big break performing live on the influential UK television show *Ready Steady Go*. A few months later their Bessie Banks cover, 'Go Now' topped the UK charts and made the US Top 10.

Their excellent debut *The Magnificent Moodies* combined traditional white R&B standards with originals. Warwick and Laine departed in 1966 to be replaced by Justin Hayward (b. 1946) and John Lodge (b. 1945). This period debuted with Hayward's classic, 'Nights In White Satin' (reissues of this in 1973 and 1979 both charted). The accompanying album was a huge success and started a run that continued through a further five albums. During this period they founded Threshold Records.

The band split in 1974 to follow spin-off projects but reunited for the hugely successful *Octave*, although shortly after its release Pinder left. Patrick Moraz joined the band as Hayward's 'Forever Autumn' hit the charts.

MOOG, ROBERT A.

MOOG (b. 1934) WAS RESPONSIBLE FOR DESIGNING THE FIRST COMMERCIALLY VIABLE KEYBOARD SYNTHESIZER. HE began research at New York University in the early 60s and by 1967, the Moog synthesizer was fully developed. It came to public attention in the 1968 recording, *Switched On Bach* by Walter Carlos. Although other firms like ARP and Buchla produced their own versions, Moog stuck as the generic name. Moog's most commercially successful product was the mini-Moog launched in 1971. In the early 70s, the Moog company was acquired by Norlin, owners of the Gibson guitar operation.

MOONGLOWS

THIS R&B VOCAL GROUP WAS FORMED IN CLEVELAND, OHIO, USA, IN 1952. THE GROUP'S CAREER PARALLELED THAT of their mentor disc jockey **Alan Freed**. The group comprised lead singer Bobby Lester (b. 1930, d. 1980), Harvey Fuqua (b. 1929), Alexander 'Pete' Graves (b. 1930) and Prentiss Barnes (b. 1925). The group signed with Chicago-based Chance. Freed used his connections to sign the Moonglows to the fast-rising Chess Records, and the group enjoyed a major hit with 'Sincerely' in 1954.

Other moderate hit singles followed. The original Moonglows disbanded in 1958, and Fuqua carved out a successful career as a producer and record executive, working with **Motown** artists in the 60s and a stable of RCA/Louisville artists in the 70s.

MOORE, CHRISTY

MOORE (b. 1945) BEGAN PLAYING THE CLUB CIRCUIT IN EIRE AND ENGLAND IN THE 60S. IT WAS IN ENGLAND, IN 1969, that he recorded his first album, a collaboration with Dominic Behan, *Paddy On The Road*. His first solo album led to the forming of **Planxty**, where he stayed until 1975. Having once again embarked on a solo career, he became involved in the mid-70s with the Anti-Nuclear Roadshow.

After a brief reunion with Planxty in the late 70s, Moore and fellow Planxty member Donal Lunny split in 1981 to form Moving Hearts. This progression from the former group fused folk with rock. He returned to solo work in 1982.

Connections
Paul Simon ➡ p.296
Woodstock Festival ➡ p.343
Jimi Hendrix ➡ p.180
Janis Joplin ➡ p.201
Otis Redding ➡ p.274
Grateful Dead ➡ p.167
Mamas And The Papas ➡ p.223
Who ➡ p.338
Simon And Garfunkel ➡ p.297

MONTEZ, CHRIS
Albums
Let's Dance And Have Some Kinda Fun!!! (Monogram 1963)★★★
Time After Time (Pye 1966)★★★
➡ p.372 for full listings

MOODY BLUES
Albums
The Magnificent Moodies (Decca 1965)★★★★
Long Distance Voyager (Threshold 1981)★★★★
➡ p.372 for full listings
Further References
Videos: *Cover Story* (Stylus 1990)
Live At Red Rocks (1993)

MOONGLOWS
Albums
Look! It's The Moonglows (Chess 1959)★★★
The Return Of The Moonglows (RCA Victor 1972)★★★
➡ p.372 for full listings
Collaborators
Alan Freed ➡ p.154

MOORE, CHRISTY
Albums
Graffiti Tongue (Grapevine 1996)★★★★
➡ p.372 for full listings
Collaborators
Dominic Behan
Connections
Planxty ➡ p.262

MOORE, GARY
Albums
Still Got The Blues (Virgin 1990)★★★★
Blues For Greeny (Virgin 1995)★★★★
➧ p.372 for full listings
Collaborators
Phil Lynott ➧ p.220
Connections
Skid Row ➧ p.299
Thin Lizzy ➧ p.320
Further References
Video: *Emerald Aisles* (Virgin Vision 1986)

MORISSETTE, ALANIS
Albums
Jagged Little Pill (Maverick/Reprise 1995)★★★★
➧ p.372 for full listings
Connections
Madonna ➧ p.222

MORPHINE
Albums
Yes (Rykodisc 1995)★★★★
Like Swimming (Rykodisc 1997)★★★★
➧ p.372 for full listings

MORRICONE, ENNIO
Albums
The Mission film soundtrack (Virgin 1986)★★★★
➧ p.372 for full listings
Collaborators
Paul Anka ➧ p.19

MORRISON, VAN
Albums
Astral Weeks (Warners 1968)★★★★★
No Guru, No Method, No Teacher (Mercury 1986)★★★★
➧ p.372 for full listings

Collaborators
Bert Berns ➧ p.44
Dr John ➧ p.125
Chieftains ➧ p.90
Georgie Fame ➧ p.142
Cliff Richard ➧ p.277
Tom Jones ➧ p.201
John Lee Hooker ➧ p.185
Connections
Them ➧ p.319
Influences
Wordsworth
Coleridge
T. S. Eliot

MOORE, GARY

A TALENTED, BLUES-INFLUENCED SINGER AND GUITARIST. MOORE (b. 1952) FORMED HIS FIRST MAJOR BAND, **SKID Row**, at age 16 – initially with **Phil Lynott**, who left after a few months to form **Thin Lizzy**. Skid Row continued with Brendan 'Brush' Shields (bass) and Noel Bridgeman (drums), but after just two albums they disbanded, leaving Moore to form the Gary Moore Band. Their debut, *Grinding Stone*, appeared in 1973, but progress stopped in 1974 while Moore assisted Thin Lizzy. Moore subsequently moved into session work before joining Colosseum II in 1976. He made three albums with them but finally became a full-time member of Thin Lizzy. Moore later resumed his solo career, cutting a series of commercially ignored albums until he scored hit singles in 1985 with 'Empty Rooms' and 'Out In The Fields' with Phil Lynott. His breakthrough to mainstream acceptance came in 1990 with *Still Got The Blues*. After these three albums, however, Moore switched tactics. *Dark Days In Paradise* had little blues on offer; instead he attempted rock, AOR and pop.

MORISSETTE, ALANIS

MORISSETTE (b. NADINE MORISSETTE, 1974) ENJOYED CONSIDERABLE critical and public acclaim in her native Canada before achieving international success. Worldwide recognition followed her move to **Madonna**'s Maverick Records in 1994. Her third album, *Jagged Little Pill*, reached *Billboard*'s number 1.

MORPHINE

US TRIO AND PURVEYORS OF LOW-END ALTERNATIVE ROCK/JAZZ. VOCALIST MARK SANDMAN (BASS) IS JOINED BY Dana Colley (baritone saxophone) and Jerome Deupree (drums). The group played a few tentative gigs then released their debut album, *Good*. They picked up Indie Debut Album Of The Year at the Boston Music Awards. They came of age with *Yes* in 1995, having never compromised their line-up. The 1997 compilation *B-Sides And Otherwise* is culled from past singles.

MORRICONE, ENNIO

HIS SCORES FOR 'SPAGHETTI WESTERNS' HAVE MADE MORRICONE (b. 1928) ONE OF THE MOST INFLUENTIAL figures in the film-music world. During the 50s, he wrote songs and arrangements for popular vocalist Gianni Morandi and he later arranged **Paul Anka**'s Italian hit 'Ogni Volta' (1964). Morricone's first film score was for the comedy *Il Federale* in 1961. Three years later he was hired by Sergio Leone to compose music for *A Fistful Of Dollars*. His work on Leone's trilogy of westerns led to collaboration with such European directors as Pontecorvo (*Battle Of Algiers*, 1966), Pasolini (*Big Birds, Little Birds*, 1966) and Bertolucci (*1900*, 1976). In the 70s, he began to compose for US films, such as *Exorcist II* (1977), *Days Of Heaven* (1978), *The Untouchables* (1987) and *Frantic* (1988). Morricone won an Oscar for Roland Joffe's *The Mission* (1986). In 1992, Morricone's score for *Bugsy* received an Oscar nomination. Morricone has recorded several albums of his own music and in 1981 he had a hit with 'Chi Mai'. A double album for Virgin Records in 1988 included Morricone's own selection of his film scores, while in the same year Virgin Venture issued a recording of his classical compositions.

MORRISON, VAN

AT THE AGE OF 12, IRISH-BORN MORRISON (b. GEORGE IVAN MORRISON, 1945) JOINED DEANNIE SANDS AND THE Javelins, a skiffle group, but within two years was an integral part of the Monarchs, a showband which, by 1963, was embracing R&B and soul. The experience Morrison garnered – he took up vocals, saxophone and harmonica – proved invaluable when he returned to Belfast to become one of the founder members of **Them**. This group scored two notable hit singles with 'Baby Please Don't Go' and 'Here Comes The Night' (both 1965), while the former's b-side 'Gloria', is revered as a classic of the garage-band genre. The group dissolved in 1966 following an arduous US tour, but within months the singer had returned to New York at the prompting of producer **Bert Berns**. Their partnership resulted in 'Brown-Eyed Girl'. The single deservedly reached the US Top 10, in turn inspiring the hurriedly issued *Blowin' Your Mind*. Berns' premature death brought this period to a sudden end, and for the ensuing 12 months Morrison punctuated live performances by preparing his next release *Astral Weeks*.

On the following album *Moondance*, tighter, punchier, jazzier arrangements formed the platform for the singer's still-soaring inflections. Both *Van Morrison, His Band And The Street Choir* and *Tupelo Honey* suggested a newfound peace of mind. 'Domino' and 'Wild Night' were the album's respective US hit singles.

Hard Nose The Highway proved disappointing, but Morrison reclaimed his position with the enthralling *It's Too Late To Stop Now*, an in-concert selection on which he was backed by the Caledonia Soul Orchestra. It was succeeded by the pastoral *Veedon Fleece*, a set inspired by a sabbatical in Ireland during 1973. A three-year hiatus ended with the release of *A Period Of Transition*, an undistinguished set on which the singer collaborated with **Dr John**. *Wavelength*, which featured former Them organist **Peter Bardens**, offered a mature musical consistency. Similar qualities abounded on *Into The Music* which included the noticeably buoyant 'Bright Side Of The Road', Van's first solo, albeit minor, UK chart entry. It also featured 'And The Healing Has Begun'. On *Common One* Morrison resumed his introspective path. A greater sense of discipline was seen on *Beautiful Vision*, and *Inarticulate Speech Of The Heart* and *A Sense Of Wonder* continued in a similar vein, but Morrison confirmed his artistic rebirth with *No Guru, No Method, No Teacher*. 'Tir Na Nog' and 'One Irish Rover' continued his long-running affair with Celtic themes, a feature equally relevant on *Poetic Champions Compose*.

Irish Heartbeat, a festive collaboration with traditional act the **Chieftains**, offered a more joyous perspective. By this time (1988) Morrison was resettled in London and had invited R&B vocalist/organist **Georgie Fame** to join his touring revue. *Avalon Sunset* enhanced the singer's commercial ascendancy when 'Whenever God Shines His Light On Me', a duet with **Cliff Richard**, became a UK Top 20 single. In 1991 there was another unlikely collaboration when Morrison recorded several songs with **Tom Jones**. *Too Long In Exile* visited his R&B roots and included a reworked 'Gloria', featuring a duet with **John Lee Hooker**. *Days Like This* was highly accessible, and probably the most 'contented' album he has made since *Tupelo Honey*. Van Morrison With Georgie Fame And Friends *How Long Has This Been Going On* in 1995 was a comfortable jazz album. He continued in this vein with Fame, Ben Sidran and one of his idols, Mose Allison, with a tribute album to the latter in 1996. His 1997 offering was *The Healing Game*, more original songs which the converted loved, but is unlikely to break any new ground.

MORRISSEY

MORRISSEY (b. STEVEN PATRICK MORRISSEY, 1959) BEGAN HIS CAREER AS A MUSIC REVIEWER WITH *RECORD MIRROR*. In 1982 he was approached by guitarist Johnny Maher (later Marr) with the idea of forming a songwriting team – they developed into the **Smiths**, the most important and critically acclaimed UK group of the 80s. In 1987, the Smiths disbanded and Morrissey went solo.

In 1988, he issued his solo debut, 'Suedehead' (UK Top 5). The subsequent *Viva Hate* hit UK number 1 soon after. A further UK Top 10 single came with 'Everyday Is Like Sunday'. A projected 1989 album, *Bona Drag*, was delayed then cancelled, although the title served for a formidable hits and b-side compilation. In 1991, Morrissey issued the long-awaited *Kill Uncle*, and embarked on a world tour, backed by a rockabilly group. The fruits of this collaboration were revealed on *Your Arsenal*, a neat fusion of 50s rockabilly influences and 70s glam rock. *Beethoven Was Deaf*, a live album, was a dismal failure. Morrissey, however, began to cultivate a US following.

Vauxhall And I (UK number 1) proved Morrissey's most outstanding release to date. The compilation, *The World Of Morrissey*, was his last album with EMI/HMV Records, before moving to RCA Victor for 1995's *Southpaw Grammar*. This set opened with 'The Teachers Are Afraid Of The Pupils'. Morrissey released the delayed *Maladjusted* for new label Island.

MOST, MICKIE

IN THE LATE 50S, MOST (b. MICHAEL PETER HAYES, 1938) TOURED AND RECORDED FOR DECCA AS THE MOST Brothers with Alex Wharton. From 1959-63, he worked in South Africa, producing his own hit versions of **Chuck Berry**'s 'Johnny B. Goode' and Ray Peterson's 'Corrina Corrina'. He returned to Britain and became producer of the Newcastle R&B group the **Animals**. Beginning with 'Baby Let Me Take You Home' in 1964, Most supervised seven hit singles by the group and was now in demand as a producer. After his earliest UK successes, Most was given a five-year retainer production deal by CBS in America, under which he produced records by **Lulu**, **Terry Reid**, **Jeff Beck** and **Donovan**. After 1969, he concentrated on running the RAK label. For over a decade, RAK singles were regularly to be found in the UK Top 10.

MOTELS

FORMED IN BERKELEY, CALIFORNIA, IN THE EARLY 70S, THE MOTELS COMPRISED MARTHA DAVIS (VOCALS), JEFF Jourard (guitar), his brother Martin (keyboards/saxophone), former jazzer Michael Goodroe (bass) and UK session drummer Brian Glascock. In 1979, their debut album was issued by Capitol. Like its remaining tracks, the hit ballad 'Total Control' was composed by central figure Davis. Her boyfriend, Tim McGovern, replaced Jeff Jourard during sessions for *Careful*. *All Four One*, at number 16, marked the Motels' UK commercial zenith. In their homeland they enjoyed two US Top 10 hits with 'Only The Lonely' and 'Suddenly Last Summer', but split in 1987.

MOTHERS OF INVENTION

THIS CELEBRATED GROUP WAS FORMED IN 1965 WHEN GUITARIST **FRANK ZAPPA** (b. 1940, d. 1993) REPLACED RAY Hunt in the Soul Giants, a struggling R&B-based bar band. Ray Collins (vocals), Dave Coronado (saxophone), Roy Estrada (bass) and Jimmy Carl Black (drums) completed their early line-up, but Coronado abandoned the group when the newcomer unveiled his musical strategy. Now renamed the Mothers, they embarked on a *mélange* of 50s pop, Chicago R&B and *avant-garde* music, and an appearance at the famed Whiskey A Go-Go resulted in a recording deal through producer Tom Wilson.

Now dubbed the Mothers Of Invention, the group added Elliott Ingber (guitar) before commencing *Freak Out*, rock's first double album. *Absolutely Free*, featured a radically reshaped line-up. Ingber was fired at the end of 1966 while Zappa added a second drummer, Billy Mundi, plus Don Preston (b. 1932; keyboards), Bunk Gardner (horns) and Jim 'Motorhead' Sherwood (saxophone). *We're Only In It For The Money*, featured several barbed attacks on the trappings of 'flower-power'. The album also introduced new member Ian Underwood (saxophone/keyboards). *Cruising With Ruben And The Jets* however, was the last wholly new set committed by the 'original' line-up. Later releases, *Uncle Meat*, *Burnt Weeny Sandwich* and *Weasels Ripped My Flesh*, were all compiled from existing live and studio tapes as tension grew within the group.

A new Mothers was formed in 1970 from the musicians contributing to Zappa's third solo album, *Chunga's Revenge*, and the scatalogical 'on the road' documentary, *200 Motels*. Mark Volman, Howard Kaylan (both vocals) and Jim Pons (bass) joined **Aynsley Dunbar** (drums) and long-standing affiliates Ian Underwood and Don Preston in the group responsible for *Fillmore East – June 1971*. This period was brought to a sudden end at London's Rainbow Theatre, where Zappa sustained multiple back injuries and a compound leg fracture when attacked by a 'fan'. Confined to the studio, Zappa compiled *Just Another Band From L.A.* and used the Mothers epithet for the jazz big band on *The Grand Wazoo*, before the Mothers' name was re-established with a new, tighter line-up in 1973. However, subsequent albums, *Over-Nite Sensation*, *Roxy And Elsewhere* and *One Size Fits All*, are indistinguishable from projects bearing Zappa's name and this now superfluous title was abandoned in 1975, following the release *Bongo Fury*.

Further References
Video: *The Concert* (Channel 5 1990)
Books: *Van Morrison: Into The Music*, Ritchie Yorke
Van Morrison: The Mystic's Music, Howard A. DeWitt

MORRISSEY
Albums
Viva Hate (HMV 1988)★★★★
Your Arsenal (HMV 1992)★★★★
Vauxhall And I (HMV 1994)★★★★
➧ p.372 for full listings

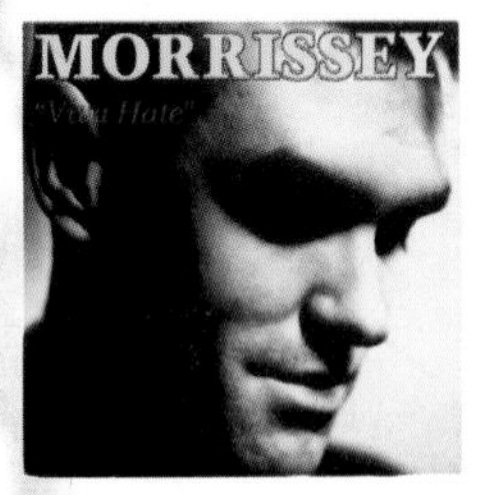

Collaborators
Johnny Maher
Connections
Smiths ➧ p.301
Influences
John Betjemen
Further References
Video: *Introducing Morrissey* (Warner Music Video 1996)
Book: *Morrissey In His Own Words*, John Robertson

MOST, MICKIE
Collaborators
Chuck Berry ➧ p.45
Animals ➧ p.18
Lulu ➧ p.219
Terry Reid ➧ p.275
Jeff Beck ➧ p.40
Donovan ➧ p.123

MOTELS
Albums
The Motels (Capitol 1979)★★★★
➧ p.372 for full listings
Collaborators
Tim McGovern
Influences
Stravinsky

MOTHERS OF INVENTION
Albums
Freak Out (Verve 1966)★★★★★
Absolutely Free (Verve 1967)★★★★★
➧ p.372 for full listings
Collaborators
Tom Wilson
Connections
Frank Zappa ➧ p.348
Aynsley Dunbar ➧ p.25
Further References
Film: *200 Motels* (1970)
Book: *Electric Don Quixote: The Story Of Frank Zappa*, Neil Slaven

MÖTLEY CRÜE
Albums
Girls, Girls, Girls (Elektra 1987)★★★
p.372 for full listings
Collaborators
Tom Werman
Further References
Video: *Decade Of Decadence* (1991)
Book: *Lüde, Crüde And Rüde*, Sylvie and Dome

MOTÖRHEAD
Albums
Ace Of Spades (Bronze 1980)★★★★
No Sleep 'til Hammersmith (Bronze 1981)★★★★
p.372 for full listings

Collaborators
Ozzy Osbourne p.253
Slash p.170
Connections
Operator
Saxon p.289
Guns N'Roses p.170
Wvkeaf
Further References
Video: *Everything Louder Than Everything Else* (1991)
Book: *Motorhead*, Giovanni Dadomo

MOTORS
Albums
Approved By The Motors (Virgin 1978)★★★★
p.372 for full listings
Collaborators
Kursaal Flyers p.211
Connections
Ducks Deluxe

MOTOWN RECORDS
Albums
Hitsville USA: The Motown Singles Collection 1959 — 1971 4-CD box set (Motown 1993)★★★★H
p.372 for full listings
Connections
Eddie Holland p.182
Temptations p.318
Marvelettes p.226
Isley Brothers p.194
Gladys Knight And The Pips p.209
Jackson Five p.195
Commodores p.99
Marvin Gaye p.159
Diana Ross p.282
Lionel Richie p.277
Further References
Video: *Motown 25th: Yesterday, Today, Forever* (MGM/UA 1988)

MÖTLEY CRÜE

THIS HEAVY ROCK BAND WAS FORMED IN 1980 BY NIKKI SIXX (b. FRANK FARANNO, 1958; BASS) AND CONSISTED OF Tommy Lee (b. 1962; drums) and Vince Neil (b. Vince Neil Wharton, 1961; vocals). Mick Mars (b. Bob Deal, 1956; guitar) was later added to the line-up. Their first single, 'Stick To Your Guns'/'Toast Of The Town', was issued in 1981 on their own Leathür label, followed by their self-produced debut, *Too Fast For Love*. The band signed to Elektra in 1982, and the album was remixed and reissued that August. The following year they recorded a new set, *Shout At The Devil*, with producer Tom Werman. He stayed at the helm for the two albums which broke them to a much wider audience in the USA, *Theatre Of Pain* (which sold more than two million copies) and *Girls, Girls, Girls*. The band released *Dr. Feelgood in 1991* (US number 1). Vince Neil was sacked in 1992. His replacement for 1994's self-titled album was John Corabi, although the band's problems continued with a record label/management split and disastrous North American tour. Neil was working with the band again in autumn 1996, after Corabi was also sacked.

MOTÖRHEAD

LEMMY (b. IAN FRAISER KILMISTER, 1945; VOCALS/BASS) FORMED MOTÖRHEAD WITH LARRY WALLIS (GUITAR) AND Lucas Fox (drums). They made their debut supporting Greenslade at the Roundhouse, London, in 1975. Fox then left and was replaced by 'Philthy' Phil Taylor (b. 1954, Chesterfield, England; drums). Motörhead was a four-piece band for less than a month, with Taylor's friend 'Fast' Eddie Clarke (b. 1950; guitar), until Wallis also left. The band made their debut with the eponymous 'Motörhead'/'City Kids'. A similarly-titled debut album charted, before the group moved over to Bronze Records. *Overkill* and *Bomber* firmly established the group's style: a fearsome barrage of instruments topped off by Lemmy's hoarse vocals. Their reputation as a great live band was enhanced by the release of *No Sleep 'Til Hammersmith* (UK number 1). In 1982, Clarke left, citing musical differences, and was replaced by Brian Robertson (b. 1956). This combination released *Another Perfect Day*, but Robertson was replaced in 1983 by Wurzel (b. Michael Burston, 1949; guitar) and Philip Campbell (b. 1961; guitar). Two months later Taylor left and was replaced by ex-**Saxon** Pete Gill. Gill remained with the band until 1987 and played on several fine albums including *Orgasmatron*. By 1987 Phil Taylor had rejoined Motörhead, and the line-up remained unchanged for five years. In 1992, the group released *March Or Die*, which featured guest appearances by **Ozzy Osbourne** and Slash (**Guns N'Roses**). Wurzel left the band in 1996.

MOTORS

THE MOTORS WERE BASED AROUND THE PARTNERSHIP OF NICK GARVEY (b. 1951) AND ANDY McMASTER (B. 1947). IN 1977, they recorded demos together. Soon after they recruited Ricky Wernham (aka Ricky Slaughter; drums). Rob Hendry (guitar) was quickly replaced by Bram Tchaikovsky and the Motors were up and running.

A tour with the **Kursaal Flyers** led to the release of their debut single, 'Dancing The Night Away', and first album, produced by Mutt Lange. However, it was their second single, 'Airport', which became a huge UK hit. After performing at Reading in August the Motors decided to concentrate on new material. Wernham left, while Tchaikovsky formed his own band with the intention of returning to the Motors, though he never did. Garvey and McMaster eventually re-emerged with some new material for *Tenement Steps*. After this the Motors seized up, but both Garvey and McMaster have since released solo singles.

MOTOWN RECORDS

THE CORPORATION WAS FORMED IN 1959 BY BERRY GORDY, A SUCCESSFUL R&B songwriter. He used an $800 loan to finance the release of singles by Marv Johnson and **Eddie Holland** on his Tamla label. Enjoying limited local success, Gordy widened his roster, signing acts including The **Temptations** and **Marvelettes** in 1960. That year, the **Miracles**' 'Shop Around' gave the company its first major US hit, followed in 1961 by their first number 1, the Marvelettes' 'Please Mr Postman'. By 1964, Motown was enjoying regular hits with the **Supremes** and the **Four Tops**, while **Mary Wells**' 'My Guy' helped the label become established internationally.

In 1966, Motown took three steps to widen its empire, snapping up groups such as the **Isley Brothers** and **Gladys Knight And The Pips** from rival labels, opening a Hollywood office to double its promotional capabilities, and snuffing out its strongest opposition in Detroit by buying the Golden World and Ric-Tic group of R&B companies. Two years of comparative failure followed before Motown regained its supremacy in the pop market by launching the career of the phenomenally successful **Jackson Five** in 1969. The early 70s were a period of some uncertainty for the company; several major acts either split up or chose to seek artistic freedom elsewhere, and the decision to concentrate the company's activities in its California office in 1973 represented a dramatic break from its roots. The mid-70s proved to be Motown's least successful period for over a decade; only the emergence of the **Commodores** maintained the label as a contemporary musical force. The departure of **Marvin Gaye** and **Diana Ross** in the early 80s proved a massive blow and, despite the prominence of Commodores' leader **Lionel Richie**, the company failed to keep pace with the fast-moving developments in black music. From 1986, there were increasing rumours that Berry Gordy was ready to sell the label; these were confirmed in 1988, when Motown was bought by MCA.

MOTT THE HOOPLE

THE FOUNDING MEMBERS WERE OVEREND WATTS (b. PETER WATTS, 1947; vocals/bass), Mick Ralphs (b. 1944; vocals/guitar), Verden Allen (b. 1944; organ) and Dale Griffin (b. 1948; vocals/ drums). They were on the point of dissolving when Ralphs sent a demo tape to Island Records's producer Guy Stevens. He responded enthusiastically and, after placing an advertisement in *Melody Maker*, auditioned a promising singer named **Ian Hunter** (b. 1946; vocals/keyboards/ guitar). Their self-titled debut album revealed a very strong **Bob Dylan** influence, most notably in Hunter's nasal vocal inflexions and visual image. Their first album included interpretations of the **Kinks**' 'You Really Got Me' and **Sonny Bono**'s 'Laugh At Me'. Their next three albums were disappointing, however. On 26 March 1972, following the departure of Allen, they quit in disillusionment. **David Bowie** convinced them to carry on and presented them with a stylish UK hit, 'All The Young Dudes'. The catchy 'Honaloochie Boogie' maintained the momentum but then Ralphs quit. With new members Morgan Fisher and Ariel Bender (Luther Grosvenor), Mott enjoyed a run of further UK hits including 'All The Way From Memphis' and 'Roll Away The Stone'. When rumours circulated that Hunter had signed a deal instigating a solo career, with **Mick Ronson** working alongside, the upheaval led to an irrevocable rift within the group resulting in a stormy demise.

MOULD, BOB

THE FORMER GUITARIST, VOCALIST AND CO-COMPOSER IN **HÜSKER DÜ**, MOULD (b. 1960) SURPRISED MANY WITH HIS reflective solo debut, *Workbook*. Jane Scarpantoni (cello) contributed to its air of melancholy, while two members of **Pere Ubu**, Tony Maimone (bass) and Anton Fier (drums; also **Golden Palominos**), added sympathetic support. Maimone and Fier also provided notable support on *Black Sheets Of Rain*, which marked a return to the uncompromising power of the guitarist's erstwhile unit. The artist abandoned his solo career in 1993, reverting to the melodic hardcore trio format with **Sugar**. By 1995 he had reverted once again to his solo career. *Bob Mould* was an excellent album, even though he refused to promote it.

MOUNTAIN

MOUNTAIN WERE FORMED BY GUITARIST LESLIE WEST (b. LESLIE WEINSTEIN, 1945) AND BASSIST FELIX PAPPALARDI (b. 1939, d. 1983) in New York in 1968. Augmented by drummer Corky Laing and Steve Knight on keyboards, they played **Woodstock** in 1970, releasing *Mountain Climbing* (US *Billboard* number 17) shortly afterwards. Their next two albums built on this foundation, as the band refined their style. *Nantucket Sleighride* and *Flowers Of Evil* made the *Billboard* charts at numbers 16 and 35, respectively. A live album followed, but was poorly received. The group temporarily disbanded to follow separate projects. In 1974, Mountain rose again with Alan Schwartzberg and Bob Mann replacing Laing and Knight to record *Twin Peaks*, live in Japan. This line-up was short-lived as Laing rejoined for the recording of the disappointing studio album, *Avalanche*. The band collapsed once more and West concentrated on his solo career. West and Laing resurrected the band with Mark Clarke and released *Go For Your Life*. They toured with **Deep Purple** throughout Europe in 1985, but split up again soon afterwards.

MOVE

FORMED IN LATE 1965 THE ORIGINAL MOVE COMPRISED **ROY WOOD** (VOCALS/GUITAR), CARL WAYNE (VOCALS), Chris 'Ace' Kefford (bass), Trevor Burton (guitar) and Bev Bevan (drums). Under the guidance of Tony Secunda, they signed to Decca's hit subsidiary Deram. Their first two hit singles were the classically inspired 'Night Of Fear' and the upbeat psychedelic 'I Can Hear The Grass Grow'. In 1967, they signed to the reactivated Regal Zonophone label which was launched with the fashionably titled 'Flowers In The Rain'.

In 1968, the group returned with the high energy, 'Fire Brigade'. Soon afterwards, Ace Kefford left the group which continued as a quartet, with Burton switching to bass. Management switches brought further complications. Increasing friction within their ranks culminated in Wayne's departure for a solo career, leaving the Move to carry on as a trio. The heavy-rock sound of 'Brontosaurus' and 'When Alice Comes Down To The Farm' broadened their diverse hit repertoire. The final flurry of Move hits ('Tonight', 'Chinatown' and 'California Man') were bereft of the old invention.

MOYET, ALISON

THE FORMER SINGER OF THE SYNTHESIZER DUO **YAZOO**, MOYET (b. 1961) EMBARKED ON A SOLO CAREER IN 1983. THE debut *Alf* (UK number 1) was a superb recording and 'Invisible', 'Love Resurrection' and 'All Cried Out' were all UK hits, while the album was in the charts for nearly two years. In 1985, she toured with a jazz band, performing standards which included a version of Billie Holiday's 'That Ole Devil Called Love', which became her biggest hit to date. The tour was not well received and following this little was seen or heard of her, apart from a major UK hit with 'Is This Love?' in 1986. *Raindancing* appeared in 1987 and narrowly missed the UK's number 1 position. Two single successes were the driving 'Weak In The Presence Of Beauty' and a sensitive cover of Ketty Lester's 'Love Letters'. Once again Alison disappeared and resurfaced in 1991. She embarked on a UK tour and released *Hoodoo*. *Essex* featured material that was nowhere near as strong as her outstanding voice deserves.

MUD

ORIGINALLY FORMED IN 1966, COMPRISED LES GRAY (b. 1946; VOCALS), DAVE MOUNT (b. 1947; DRUMS/VOCALS), RAY STILES (b. 1946; bass guitar/vocals) and Rob Davis (b. 1947; lead guitar/vocals). In early 1973, they broke through in the UK with 'Crazy' and 'Hypnosis'. There followed an impressive run of twelve more Top 20 hits during the next three years, including three UK number 1 hits: 'Tiger Feet', 'Lonely This Christmas' and 'Oh Boy'.

MOTT THE HOOPLE
Albums
Mott (Columbia 1973)★★★★
The Hoople (Columbia 1974)★★★★
➽ p.372 for full listings
Collaborators
Guy Stevens
Tony De Fries
Connections
Melody Maker
David Bowie ➽ p.64
Influences
Bob Dylan ➽ p.128
Kinks ➽ p.207
Sonny Bono ➽ p.60
Further References
Book: *The Diary Of A Rock 'N' Roll Star*, Ian Hunter

MOULD, BOB
Albums
Bob Mould (Creation/Rykodisk 1996)★★★★
➽ p.372 for full listings
Connections
Hüsker Dü ➽ p.190
Pere Ubu ➽ p.258
Golden Palominos ➽ p.165
Sugar ➽ p.313

MOUNTAIN
Albums
Mountain Climbing (Bell 1970)★★★
Avalanche (Epic 1974)★★★
➽ p.372 for full listings
Collaborators
Deep Purple ➽ p.113
Connections
Woodstock Festival ➽ p.343

MOVE
Albums
The Move (Regal Zonophone 1968)★★★
California Man (Harvest 1974)★★★
➽ p.372 for full listings
Connections
Roy Wood ➽ p.343

MOYET, ALISON
Albums
Alf (Columbia 1984)★★★★
Hoodoo (Columbia 1991)★★★
➽ p.372 for full listings
Connections
Yazoo ➽ p.345
Influences
Billie Holiday

MUD
Albums
Mud Rock (RAK 1974)★★★
➽ p.372 for full listings

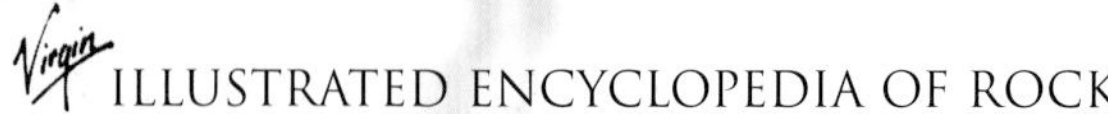

MUDDY WATERS

Albums

Muddy Waters At Newport, 1960 (Chess 1963)★★★★

Muddy Waters, Folk Singer (Chess 1964)★★★★

➽ p.372 for full listings

Collaborators

Big Crawford Band ➽ p.31

Johnny Winter ➽ p.341

Connections

Muddy Waters Band

Further References

Video: *Messin' With The Blues* (BMG 1991)

Book: *Muddy Waters: Mojo Man*, Tooze

MUDHONEY

Albums

Piece Of Cake (Warners 1992)★★★

➽ p.372 for full listings

MUDDY WATERS

ONE OF THE DOMINANT FIGURES OF POST-WAR BLUES, MUDDY WATERS (b. MCKINLEY MORGANFIELD, 1915, d. 1983) was raised in a rural Mississippi town and began performing and touring the south. In 1943, Waters moved to Chicago and by 1948 had signed a contract with the newly founded Aristocrat label, (later Chess Records). Waters' second release, 'I Feel Like Goin' Home'/'I Can't Be Satisfied', was a minor R&B hit and its understated accompaniment from bassist Big Crawford set a pattern for several further singles. By 1951 the guitarist was using a full backing band and the talent he used here ensured that the Muddy Waters Band was Chicago's most influential unit, with a score of seminal recordings, including 'Hoochie Coochie Man', 'I've Got My Mojo Working', 'Mannish Boy', 'You Need Love' and 'I'm Ready'. Although criticized for his use of amplification, Waters' effect on a new generation of white enthusiasts was incalculable. Paradoxically, while these new groups enjoyed commercial success, Waters struggled against indifference. Deemed 'old-fashioned' in the wake of soul music, he was obliged to update his sound and repertoire, resulting in such misjudged releases as *Electric Mud*. The artist did complete a more sympathetic project in *Fathers And Sons* but his work during the 60s was generally disappointing. *The London Sessions* kept Waters in the public eye, as did his appearance in the **Band**'s *The Last Waltz*, but it was a series of collaborations with guitarist **Johnny Winter** that signalled a dramatic rebirth. This pupil produced and arranged four albums that bestowed a sense of dignity to this musical giant's legacy. Waters died of heart failure in 1983.

MUDHONEY

THE BAND COMPRISES BROTHERS MARK ARM (b. 1962; VOCALS) AND STEVE TURNER (b. 1965; GUITAR), PLUS MATT Lukin (b. 1964; bass) and Dan Peters (b. 1967; drums). Mudhoney were the band that first imported the sound of Sub Pop Records to wider shores. In 1988, they released 'Touch Me I'm Sick', one of the defining moments in 'grunge', followed shortly by their debut mini-album; their first album proper (*Mudhoney*) was greeted as a disappointment by many. The EP *Boiled Beef And Rotting Teeth* contained a cover version of the Dicks' 'Hate The Police'. *Every Good Boy Deserves Fudge* was a departure, with Hammond organ intruding into the band's rock formula. After much speculation, Mudhoney moved to Warner Brothers, though many would argue that none of their efforts thus far have managed to reproduce the glory of 'Touch Me I'm Sick'. *My Brother The Cow*, however, revealed a band nearly back at its best.

MUNGO JERRY

MUNGO JERRY – RAY DORSET (VOCALS/ GUITAR), COLIN EARL (PIANO/ VOCALS), PAUL King (banjo/jug/guitar/vocals) and Mike Cole (bass) – achieved fame following an appearance at 1970's Hollywood Pop Festival, in Staffordshire, England. The group's performance coincided with the release of their debut single, 'In The Summertime', which topped the UK chart and, by the end of that year alone, had global sales of six million. Despite an eight-month gap between releases, Mungo Jerry's second single, 'Baby Jump', also reached number 1. By this time, Mike Cole had been replaced by John Godfrey but a third hit, in 1971, 'Lady Rose', showed a continued grasp of melody. The year concluded with another Top 20 release, 'You Don't Have To Be In The Army To Fight In The War'. Dorset released a solo album, prior to convening a new line-up with John Godfrey, Jon Pope (piano) and Tim Reeves (drums). They had another Top 3 hit in 1973 with 'Alright Alright Alright'. 'Longlegged Woman Dressed In Black' became the group's final chart entry. Dorset continued to work with various versions of his creation into the 80s, but was never able to regain the group's early profile.

MY BLOODY VALENTINE

MY BLOODY VALENTINE'S ROOTS LAY IN DUBLIN, WHERE SINGER/GUITARIST KEVIN Shields joined drummer Colm O'Ciosoig in the short-lived Complex. Forming My Bloody Valentine in 1984, the pair were joined by vocalist Dave Conway (vocals) and Tina (keyboards). A mini-album, *This Is Your Bloody Valentine*, made little impression so the band moved to London and recruited Debbie Googe (bass). The 12-inch EP *Geek!* (and the accompanying, 'No Place To Go') emerged on Fever in mid-1986. Later that year, the band signed with Kaleidoscope Sound label for *The New Record By My Bloody Valentine* EP. A switch to the Primitives' label Lazy, produced 'Sunny Sundae Smile' (1987), which meshed bubblegum pop with buzzsaw guitars, a formula that dominated both the mini-album, *Ecstasy*, and 'Strawberry Wine', later that year. The departure of Conway signalled a change in musical direction, reinforced by the arrival of vocalist Belinda Butcher. A further move to Creation Records resulted in the *You Made Me Realise* EP in 1988. *Loveless* reinforced their reputation as one of the prime influences on the late-80s UK independent scene. However, massive studio bills led My Bloody Valentine to leave Creation, moving instead to Island Records.

N'DOUR, YOUSSOU

N'DOUR (b. 1959) IS ONE OF SENEGAL'S GREATEST MUSICAL PIONEERS. ALONG WITH HIS BAND, THE STAR BAND, N'Dour began the fusion of western electric instrumentation and traditional Wolof rhythms and lyrics that became known as mbalax. In 1979 N'Dour left the Star Band, setting up Etoile De Dakar, which he re-formed in 1982 as Super Etoile De Dakar. Ten cassette releases, starting with *Tabaski* in 1981, displayed an increasing fullness and power of arrangement. Outside Senegal his music received wider attention with the western release of two classic albums, *Immigrés* and *Nelson Mandela*. In 1987 N'Dour supported **Peter Gabriel** on a US tour, returning to Dakar to record and explore the traditional sounds of Senegal. *The Lion* and its 1990 follow-up *Set* were the results. For purists in the west, the albums showed rather too much western influence, however, his Senegalese audience received them enthusiastically. *Eyes Open* led some to believe N'Dour had lost his edge. *The Guide* pronounced his talent undiminished and was the first album to be conceived, recorded and produced in Senegal. '7 Seconds', a duet with **Neneh Cherry**, reached number 3 in the UK charts in 1994, only furthering N'Dour's status as a genuine crossover artist.

NAKED CITY

FORMED IN 1990, THIS ACT REVOLVES AROUND ALTO SAXOPHONIST/COMPOSER **JOHN ZORN** (b. 1953). HIS ALBUM *Spy Vs Spy* set the tone for Naked City. Fred Frith (bass); ex-Henry Cow), Bill Frisell (guitar), Wayne Horvitz (keyboards) and Joey Baron (drums) joined Zorn for their debut, *Naked City*. Jazz, surf and noise gelled on this impressive collection. The sense of adventure was maintained on *Torture Garden*. A film soundtrack, *Heretic Jeux Des Dames Cruelles*, maintained Naked City's uncompromising stance. *Grand Guignol* proved even more challenging, combining Debussy's *La Cathedrale Engloutie* and Charles Ives' 'The Cage' with blasts of freeform noise.

NAPALM DEATH

THIS BIRMINGHAM QUINTET FORMED IN 1981. SIDE ONE OF THEIR DEBUT, *SCUM*, FEATURED JUSTIN BROADRICK (guitar), Mick Harris (drums) and Nick Bullen (bass, vocals); side two consisted of Bill Steer (guitar), Jim Whitely (bass) and Lee Dorrian (vocals), later replaced by Barney Greenway – with Harris the only survivor from that first inception. *From Enslavement To Obliteration* bypassed previous extremes in music. Dorrian and Steer left in 1989, being replaced by vocalist Mark 'Barny' Greenway and US guitarist Jesse Pintado. They embarked on the European *Grindcrusher* tour before playing US dates. A second guitarist, Mitch Harris, was added for *Harmony Corruption* and 'Suffer The Children' saw Napalm Death retreat to a purer death-metal sound. In 1992 Danny Herrara replaced Mick Harris on drums. *Utopia Banished* celebrated their survival and a cover version of the **Dead Kennedys**' 'Nazi Punks Fuck Off' reinstated their political motives. *Fear, Emptiness, Despair* confirmed they remain the antithesis of style, melody and taste.

Influences
Dicks

Further References
Video: *No 1 Video In America This Week* (Warner Video 1995)

MUNGO JERRY

Albums
Mungo Jerry (Dawn 1970)★★★
Baby Jump (Pye 1971)★★★
Trouble At Mill (Dawn 1972)★★★
➧ p.372 for full listings

Connections
Hollywood Pop Festival

MY BLOODY VALENTINE

Albums
Isn't Anything (Creation 1988)★★★★
➧ p.372 for full listings

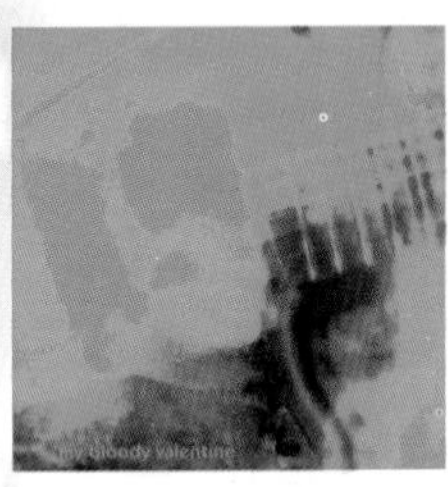

Connections
Complex
Primitives

N'DOUR, YOUSSOU

Albums
Immigres (Celluloid/Earthworks 1984)★★★★
Nelson Mandela (ERT 1985)★★★★
Wommat: The Guide (Columbia 1994)★★★★
➧ p.372 for full listings

Collaborators
Jacob Desvarieux
Branford Marsalis
Neneh Cherry ➧ p.89

Connections
Peter Gabriel ➧ p.157

NAKED CITY

Albums
Black Box (Tzadik 1997)
➧ p.373 for full listings

Connections
John Zorn ➧ p.349

NAPALM DEATH

Albums
From Enslavement To Obliteration (Earache 1988)★★★
The Peel Sessions (Strange Fruit 1989)★★★
➧ p.373 for full listings

Connections
Dead Kennedys ➧ p.112

Further References
Video: *Live Corruption* (Fotodisk 1990)

NASH, JOHNNY
Albums
A Teenager Sings The Blues (ABC 1957)★★★
I Can See Clearly Now (Columbia 1972)★★★
➧ p.373 for full listings
Connections
Bob Marley ➧ p.225

NAZARETH
Albums
Razamanaz (Mooncrest 1973)★★★★
Hair Of The Dog (Mooncrest 1975)★★★★
➧ p.373 for full listings
Connections
Joni Mitchell ➧ p.235
Sensational Alex Harvey Band ➧ p.292
Spirit ➧ p.305
Further References
Video: *Razamanaz* (Hendring 1990)

NELSON, BILL
Albums
Quit Dreaming And Get On The Beam (Mercury 1981)★★★★
➧ p.373 for full listings
Connections
Be-Bop Deluxe ➧ p.35

NELSON, RICKY
Albums
Million Sellers By Rick Nelson (Imperial 1963)★★★★
Garden Party (Decca 1972)★★★★
➧ p.373 for full listings
Connections
James Burton ➧ p.75
Poco ➧ p.262
Bob Dylan ➧ p.128
Further References
Book: *Ricky Nelson: Idol For A Generation*, Joel Selvin

NELSON, SANDY
Albums
Teen Beat (Imperial 1960)★★★
Drums Are My Beat! (Imperial 1962)★★★
Compelling Percussion aka *And Then There Were Drums* (Imperial/London 1962)★★★
➧ p.373 for full listings

NELSON, WILLIE
Albums
Red Headed Stranger (Columbia 1975)★★★★★
The Electric Horseman (Columbia 1979)★★★★ with Waylon Jennings, Jessi Colter, Tompall Glaser
Wanted! The Outlaws (1976-1996, 20th Anniversary) (RCA 1996)★★★★
➧ p.373 for full listings

NASH, JOHNNY

NASH'S (b. 1940) FIRST US CHART ENTRY WAS IN 1957 WITH A COVER OF DORIS DAY'S, 'A VERY SPECIAL LOVE'. HE HAD A Top 5 hit in 1965 with 'Lets Move And Groove Together'. Nash went to Jamaica to promote this hit, and was exposed to ska. Sessions with Byron Lee And The Dragonaires resulted in 'Cupid', 'Hold Me Tight' and 'You Got Soul'. **Bob Marley** wrote 'Stir It Up', which peaked at UK number 13 in 1972. 'I Can See Clearly Now' was a UK Top 5. Other hits included 'Ooh What A Feeling' and 'There Are More Questions Than Answers', but the further he drifted from reggae the less successful the single. His career was again revived when he recorded 'Tears On My Pillow' in Jamaica, reaching UK number 1 in 1975. He also reached the UK chart with 'Let's Be Friends' and '(What) A Wonderful World' before choosing to devote more energy to films and his West Indian recording complex.

NAZARETH

FORMED IN 1968 IN SCOTLAND, NAZARETH ORIGINALLY COMPRISED DAN McCAFFERTY (VOCALS), MANNY Charlton (guitar), Pete Agnew (bass) and Darrell Sweet (drums). *Nazareth* and *Exercises* showed promise, and *Razamanaz*, spawned two UK Top 10 singles – 'Broken Down Angel' and 'Bad Bad Boy' (both 1973). A cover of **Joni Mitchell**'s 'This Flight Tonight' gave the group another hit, while *Hair Of The Dog* established Nazareth internationally. They remained popular throughout the 70s, and added guitarist Zal Cleminson, formerly of the **Sensational Alex Harvey Band**, for *No Mean City*. Cleminson left after *Malice In Wonderland* and was replaced by former **Spirit** keyboard player, John Locke. Guitarist Billy Rankin later joined the group, but dissatisfaction with touring led to Locke's departure following *2XS*. Although Nazareth remained popular in the US and Europe, their stature in the UK was receding. Bereft of a major recording deal, Nazareth suspended their career during the late 80s, and McCafferty pursued solo ambitions. Their impressive 1993 album was *No Jive*, yet their recent low profile in the UK will demand further live work to capitalize on this success.

NELSON, BILL

ALTHOUGH NOTED FOR HIS GUITARWORK WITH **BE-BOP DELUXE**, NELSON'S (b. WILLIAM NELSON, 1948) SOLO RE-leases form more than four-fifths of his total output. He fronted Be-Bop Deluxe for most of the 70s before assembling Bill Nelson's Red Noise. *Sound On Sound* (1979) was an agitated and confused debut, and Nelson returned to solo work. 'Do You Dream In Colour?' provided his highest UK solo chart placing at number 52. After Be-Bop Deluxe split he preferred to experiment with keyboards and sampled sounds, composing pieces that have been used in films and plays. In 1991 he moved towards a stronger and more defined melodic style with *Luminous*. His 1996 release, *After The Satellite Sings*, received excellent reviews.

NELSON, RICKY

IN 1957 NEW JERSEY-BORN NELSON (b. ERIC HILLIARD NELSON, 1940, d. 1985) EMBARKED ON A RECORDING career, with the million-selling 'I'm Walkin''/'A Teenager's Romance' and 'You're My One And Only Love'. He had further success with 'Be-Bop Baby' on the Imperial label. In 1958 Nelson formed a full-time group for live work and recordings, which included **James Burton** (guitar). Early that year Nelson enjoyed his first transatlantic hit with 'Stood Up' and his first US chart-topper with 'Poor Little Fool'. Songs such as 'Believe What You Say', 'Never Be Anyone Else But You', 'Sweeter Than You' and 'I Wanna Be Loved' showed Nelson's ability at singing both ballads and up-tempo material. His issue of the million-selling 'Travelin' Man' (1961) was one of his greatest moments as a pop singer. Pop became less popular with the emergence of the beat boom and in 1966 he switched to country music. In 1969 Nelson formed the Stone Canyon Band, featuring former **Poco** member Randy Meisner (bass), Allen Kemp (guitar), Tom Brumley (steel guitar) and Pat Shanahan (drums). A version of **Bob Dylan**'s 'She Belongs To Me' brought Nelson back into the US charts, and a series of strong albums followed. His sarcastic 'Garden Party' showed his determination to go his own way, as his audiences at the time were more interested in hearing his early material. This was his last hit, selling a million copies. After parting with the Stone Canyon Band in 1974, Nelson's recorded output declined, but he continued to tour. On 31 December 1985, he died in a plane crash near De Kalb, Texas.

NELSON, SANDY

NELSON (b. SANDER L. NELSON, 1938; DRUMS) BEGAN HIS CAREER AS A MEMBER OF THE KIP TYLER BAND. HE BECAME an in-demand session musician, and played on the Teddy Bears' million-selling 'To Know Him Is To Love Him'. He and Bruce Johnston reached the US and UK Top 10 in 1959 with an early demo of 'Teen Beat'. He released a bevvy of singles, echoing the concurrent surf craze, but the appeal quickly waned and 'Teen Beat '65' (1964) was his last chart entry. During the 70s Nelson was featured in one of impresario Richard Nader's *Rock 'N' Roll Revival* shows, but he retired following disco-influenced *Bang Bang Rhythm*.

NELSON, WILLIE

NELSON (b. 1933) WAS WRITING CHEATING-HEART-STYLE SONGS BY THE AGE OF SEVEN. HIS FIRST RECORD, 'LUMBER-jack', written by Leon Payne, was recorded in Vancouver, Washington in 1956. His song, 'Family Bible', which he sold to a guitar scholar for $50, was a country hit for Claude Gray in 1960. 'Night Life' was sold for $150; Ray Price made it a country hit and there have now been over 70 other recordings. Nelson moved to Nashville, where his offbeat, nasal phrasing and dislike of rhinestone trimmings made him radically different from other country musicians.

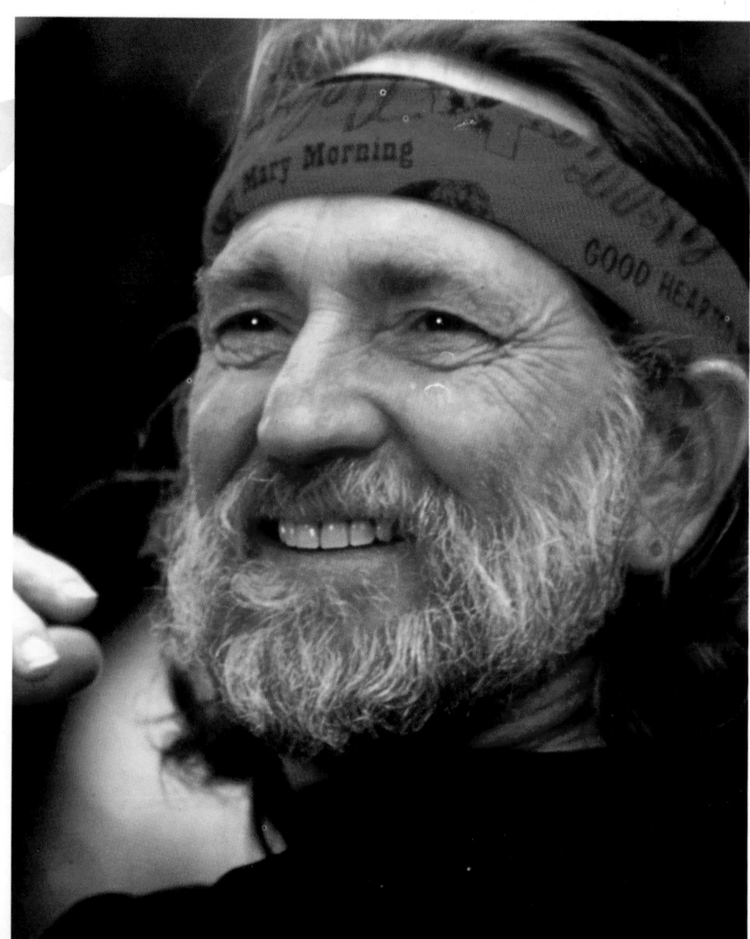

In 1961, three of Nelson's country songs crossed over to the US pop charts: **Patsy Cline**'s 'Crazy', Faron Young's 'Hello Walls' and Jimmy Elledge's 'Funny How Time Slips Away'. Ray Price employed Nelson to play bass with the Cherokee Cowboys, not knowing that he had never played the instrument. In 1963, Nelson had his first country hits as a performer, first in a duet with Shirley Collie, 'Willingly', and then on his own with 'Touch Me'. Among his tracks for Liberty Records were 'Half A Man' and 'River Boy'. When Liberty dropped their country performers, Nelson moved to Monument. He gave **Roy Orbison** 'Pretty Paper', making UK Top 10 in 1964, Nelson's most successful composition in the UK. He and Ray Price joined forces for an album, and Chet Atkins also produced some fine albums for Nelson, including *Texas In My Soul*.

During the 1970s, Nelson toured extensively and his bookings at a rock venue in Austin showed the possibility of a new audience. Waylon Jennings' hit with 'Ladies Love Outlaws' indicated a market for 'outlaw country' music. The term separated them from more conventional country artists, and, with his pigtail and straggly beard, Nelson no longer looked like a country performer. In 1975, Nelson signed with Columbia and in 1975 recorded *Red Headed Stranger*, an album based around an old ballad, 'Red Headed Stranger', which has since become a country classic. 'Blue Eyes Crying In The Rain' was a number 1 country hit and also made number 21 on the US pop charts in 1975. With brilliant marketing, RCA compiled *Wanted! The Outlaws* with Jennings, Nelson, Jessi Colter and Tompall Glaser – the first country album to go platinum, containing the hit single, 'Good Hearted Woman'. The first *Waylon And Willie* (1978) album included 'Mammas, Don't Let Your Babies Grow Up To Be Cowboys', and two beautiful Nelson performances, 'If You Can Touch Her At All' and 'A Couple More Years'. Their two subsequent albums were not successful, although the humorous *Clean Shirt* (1991) was a welcome return to form. **Johnny Cash** and **Kris Kristofferson** joined them for tours and albums as the Highwaymen.

Nelson has recorded numerous country songs, but more significant is his love of standards. *Stardust* (1978; produced by **Booker T. Jones**) took country fans by surprise, with contents resembling a Bing Crosby album. Nelson sang ten standards with devastating effect to a small rhythm section and strings, breathing new life into 'Georgia On My Mind' and 'Someone To Watch Over Me'. The album remained on the US country charts for nearly 10 years. Robert Redford met Nelson at a party in 1982 and invited him to join the cast of *The Electric Horseman*. Willie was cast as Redford's manager, and made a major contribution to the soundtrack with 'My Heroes Have Always Been Cowboys'. Redford wanted to star in the film of *Red Headed Stranger* (1987) but Nelson was eventually cast in the title role. His other films include *Barbarosa*, a remake of *Stagecoach* and the cliché-ridden *Songwriter* with Kris Kristofferson.

Nelson's record label, Lone Star, founded in 1978 with Steven Fromholz and the Geezinslaw Brothers, was not a commercial success, but he later developed a recording studio and golf course at Pedernales, Texas; he produced *Timi Yuro – Today* (1982). He has organized several Farm Aid benefits, and he and **Kenny Rogers** represented country music on the number 1 USA For Africa single, 'We Are The World'.

He rarely writes new compositions, although he wrote 'On The Road Again' for the film *Honeysuckle Rose* (in which he starred), and he also wrote *Tougher Than Leather*, while in hospital with a collapsed lung. Nelson's touring band, **Family**, is a very tight unit featuring musicians who have been with him for many years.

Albums have flowed fast and furiously and *Just One Love* was the high point of his prolific 90s period.

Connections
Patsy Cline ➽ p.94
Roy Orbison ➽ p.252
Johnny Cash ➽ p.84
Kris Kristofferson ➽ p.211
Booker T. Jones ➽ p.62
Kenny Rogers ➽ p.280

Further References
Video: *Nashville Superstar* (Magnum Music 1997)
Book: *Willie: An Autobiography*, Willie Nelson and Bud Shrake

NESMITH, MICHAEL

BEST-KNOWN AS A MEMBER OF THE **MONKEES**, NESMITH (b. ROBERT MICHAEL NESMITH, 1942) ENJOYED A PROLIFIC career in music prior to this group's inception. Two singles were completed with support from the New Christy Minstrels, while Nesmith's compositions, 'Different Drum' and 'Mary Mary', were recorded by the Stone Poneys and **Paul Butterfield**. He formed the First National Band in 1970, joined by former colleagues London, Orville 'Red' Rhodes (pedal steel) and John Ware (drums), completing three albums. The Second National Band, in which Nesmith and Rhodes were accompanied by Johnny Meeks (bass) and Jack Panelli (drums), completed *Tantamount To Treason*. This was followed by *And the Hits Just Keep On Comin'*. *Pretty Much Your Standard Ranch Stash* ended his tenure with RCA, and he founded Pacific Arts. His first release for the label was *The Prison*. His commercial status was reasserted with 'Rio' (1977), from *From A Radio Engine To The Photon Wing*. The attendant video signalled a growing interest in the visual arts, which flourished following *Infinite Rider On The Big Dogma*, his biggest-selling US release. He refused to join the Monkees' 20th Anniversary Tour, and continues to pursue his diverse interests including highly successful video production company Pacific Arts.

NESMITH, MICHAEL
Albums
Loose Salute (RCA 1971)★★★★
Nevada Fighter (RCA 1971)★★★★
➽ p.373 for full listings
Connections
Monkees ➽ p.236
Paul Butterfield ➽ p.76
Further References
Film: *Head* (1968)
Video: *Elephant Parts* (Awareness 1992)

NEW KIDS ON THE BLOCK

FORMED IN 1985, THIS GROUP FROM BOSTON, USA, FEATURED JOE MCINTYRE (b. 1972), JORDAN KNIGHT (b. 1970),

Jonathan Knight (b. 1968), Daniel Wood (b. 1969) and Donald Wahlberg (b. 1969). Their self-titled album fused rap and pop, bringing them popularity among a predominately white teenage audience. They broke into the US charts in 1988 with 'Please Don't Go Girl' and in 1989 became the biggest-selling group in America. A reissue of 'You Got It (The Right Stuff)' reached number 1 in the UK.

NEW KIDS ON THE BLOCK
Albums
New Kids On The Block (Columbia 1986)★★
➽ p.373 for full listings
Further References
Book: *New Kids On The Block*, Lynn Goldsmith

NEW MODEL ARMY

FORMED IN BRADFORD IN 1980, THE GROUP WAS LED BY JUSTIN 'SLADE THE LEVELLER' SULLIVAN (b. 1956; GUITAR, vocals) with Jason 'Moose' Harris (b. 1968; bass, guitar) and Robb Heaton (b. 1962; drums, guitar). Their brand of punk folk/rock attracted a loyal cult following. Their debut album contained militant themes – 'Spirit Of The Falklands' and 'Vengeance'. 'No Rest' peaked at number 28, and *Here Comes The War* revealed few concessions to the mainstream. In 1994, a dance remix of 'Vengeance' was released as a protest against the Criminal Justice Bill.

NEW MODEL ARMY
Albums
Vengeance (Abstract 1984)★★★
Thunder And Consolation (EMI 1989)★★★
➽ p.373 for full listings
Further References
Video: *History: The Videos 85-90* (PMI 1993)

NEW ORDER
Albums
Low Life (Factory 1985)★★★★
Brotherhood (Factory 1986)★★★★
➧ p.373 for full listings
Connections
Joy Division ➧ p.202
Quincy Jones ➧ p.201
Smiths ➧ p.301
Further References
Book: *New Order & Joy Division: Dreams Never End*, Claude Flowers

NEW RIDERS OF THE PURPLE SAGE
Albums
New Riders Of The Purple Sage (Columbia 1971)★★★★
➧ p.373 for full listings
Connections
Grateful Dead ➧ p.167
Jerry Garcia ➧ p.158

NEW SEEKERS
Albums
The New Seekers (Phillips 1969)★★★
➧ p.373 for full listings
Connections
Melanie ➧ p.231

NEW YORK DOLLS
Albums
New York Dolls (Mercury 1973)★★★★
➧ p.373 for full listings
Connections
David Johansen ➧ p.200
Johnny Thunders ➧ p.321
Further References
Book: *New York Dolls*, Steven Morrissey

NEWMAN, RANDY
Albums
Good Old Boys (Reprise 1974)★★★★
➧ p.373 for full listings
Collaborators
Elton John ➧ p.200
James Taylor ➧ p.317
Bonnie Raitt ➧ p.272
Don Henley ➧ p.180
Connections
Gene Pitney ➧ p.261
Dusty Springfield ➧ p.305
Judy Collins ➧ p.98
UB40 ➧ p.326
Cilla Black ➧ p.49
Harry Nilsson ➧ p.247

NEWTON-JOHN, OLIVIA
Albums
with various artists *Grease* film soundtrack (1978)★★★★
➧ p.373 for full listings
Collaborators
Electric Light Orchestra ➧ p.134
Connections
Jackie DeShannon ➧ p.116
Bob Dylan ➧ p.128
John Denver ➧ p.115
Shadows ➧ p.293

NEW ORDER

WHEN **JOY DIVISION'S** IAN CURTIS COMMITTED SUICIDE IN 1980 THE THREE REMAINING MEMBERS, BERNARD

Sumner (b. Bernard Dicken, 1956; guitar, vocals), Peter Hook (b. 1956; bass) and Stephen Morris (b. 1957; drums) continued under the name New Order. Later that year they recruited Morris's girlfriend, Gillian Gilbert (b. 1961; keyboards, guitar) and wrote their debut, *Movement*, released in 1981. Their first single, 'Ceremony' was a UK Top 40 hit. *Power, Corruption And Lies* contained many surprises and memorable songs. 'Blue Monday', released at this time in 12-inch format only, went on to become the biggest-selling 12-inch single of all time in the UK. Their subsequent collaboration with New York producer Arthur Baker spawned 'Confusion' (1983) and 'Thieves Like Us' (1984). Both singles continued their preference for the 12-inch format, stretching in excess of six minutes, and stressing their lack of concern for mainstream radio. *Low Life* appeared in 1985 – their most consistently appealing album to date. Their next album, 1986's *Brotherhood*, containing strong tracks such as 'Bizarre Love Triangle', offered nothing unexpected. It was not until the UK Top 5 single 'True Faith' (1987), that New Order satisfied long-term fans and general public alike. **Quincy Jones**'s remix of 'Blue Monday' provided them with another Top 5 hit. *Technique*, recorded in Ibiza, contained upbeat bass- and drums-dominated tracks that characterized the best of their early output. While playing live, they had a reputation for inconsistency and apathy, as well as refusing to play encores. This was replaced with confident, crowd-pleasing sets. In summer 1990 they reached the UK number 1 with 'World In Motion', accompanied by the England World Cup Squad. Rather than exploiting their recent successes with endless tours, the group branched out into various spin-off ventures. Hook formed the hard-rocking Revenge, Sumner joined former **Smiths** guitarist Johnny Marr in **Electronic** and Morris/Gilbert recorded an album together. In 1991 they reconvened for an album which was eventually released in 1993. *Republic* met with mixed reviews and arrived too late to help the doomed Factory label. The band's members have returned to solo projects.

NEW RIDERS OF THE PURPLE SAGE

FORMED IN 1969, NEW RIDERS WAS A SPIN-OFF FROM THE **GRATEFUL DEAD**. GROUP MEMBERS **JERRY GARCIA** (PEDAL-steel guitar), Phil Lesh (bass) and Mickey Hart (drums) joined John Dawson (b. 1945; guitar, vocals) and David Nelson (guitar). They secured a recording contract in 1971. Dave Torbert replaced Lesh and Spencer Dryden (b. 1938; drums) was installed. They released *New Riders Of The Purple Sage*. The final link with the Dead was severed when Garcia made way for Buddy Cage. *Powerglide* introduced the group's punchier sound and *The Adventures Of Panama Red* brought commercial rewards. Torbert left following *Home, Home On The Road* and was replaced by Skip Battin. In 1978 Dryden took over as manager; Dawson and Nelson remained at the helm until 1981. The New Riders dissolved following *Feelin' Alright*, although Nelson subsequently resurrected the name with Gary Vogenson (guitar) and Rusty Gautier (bass).

NEW SEEKERS

THIS BAND ORIGINALLY COMPRISED EVE GRAHAM (b. 1943; VOCALS), SALLY GRAHAM (VOCALS), CHRIS BARRINGTON (bass/vocals), Laurie Heath (guitar/vocals) and Marty Kristian (b.1947; guitar/vocals). They recorded *The New Seekers* before Heath, Barrington and Sally Graham left, being replaced by Lyn Paul (b. 1949), Peter Doyle (b. 1949) and Paul Layton (b.1947). Covers of **Melanie**'s 'Look What They've Done To My Song, Ma' and 'Beautiful People' rose high up the *Billboard* Hot 100. The chart-topping 'I'd Like To Teach The World To Sing' was their greatest success. Their Eurovision Song Contest entry, 'Beg Steal Or Borrow' and the title track of 1972's *Circles* were also hits. 'You Won't Find Another Fool Like Me' was UK number 1 in 1973.

Doyle was replaced by Peter Oliver (b. 1952; guitar/vocals) in 1974 and 'I Get A Little Sentimental Over You' hurtled up the charts, but they disbanded with a farewell tour of Britain. Two years later, they re-formed before disbanding for the last time in 1978.

NEW YORK DOLLS

FORMED IN 1972, THE LINE-UP CONSISTED OF **DAVID JOHANSEN** (b. 1950; VOCALS), **JOHNNY THUNDERS** (b. JOHN

Anthony Genzale Jnr, 1952, d. 1991; guitar), Arthur Harold Kane (bass), Sylvain Sylvain (guitar/piano) and Jerry Nolan (d. 1992; drums). The band had an outrageous glam-rock image but underneath were a first-rate rock 'n' roll band. Their self-titled debut received critical acclaim, but this never transferred to commercial success. *Too Much Too Soon* indicated that alcohol and drugs were beginning to take their toll and they split after bad reviews. *Red Patent Leather* was a posthumously released live recording from 1975 – *Rock 'N' Roll* offered a more representative collection.

NEWMAN, RANDY

NEWMAN'S (b. 1943) EARLY HIT SONGS INCLUDED 'NOBODY NEEDS YOUR LOVE' AND 'JUST ONE SMILE' BY **GENE PITNEY**, 'I Don't Want To Hear It Anymore' recorded by **Dusty Springfield** and P. J. Proby, 'I Think It's Going To Rain Today', by **Judy Collins**, and **UB40**'s superb 'I've Been Wrong Before', which was a hit for **Cilla Black**. Newman's debut album came in 1968 which, despite heavy marketing in 1969, failed to sell. In 1970 he contributed to the *Performance* soundtrack and that year **Harry Nilsson** recorded an album of his songs. One of the first examples of his film music came in 1971, with *Cold Turkey*, and his score for *Ragtime* earned him an Oscar nomination (1982), and again in 1984 for *The Natural*. 'I Love Love L.A.' was used to promote the Los Angeles 1984 Olympic Games. In 1986 he wrote 'Blue Shadows', the theme for *The Three Amigos!*. More film scores followed, such as *Awakenings*, *Parenthood*, *The Paper*, and *Maverick*. *Faust* featured **Elton John**, **James Taylor**, **Bonnie Raitt** and **Don Henley**, among other superstars. He scored the music for the Disney film *Toy Story* in 1995.

NEWTON-JOHN, OLIVIA

NEWTON-JOHN, (b. 1948) WENT TO LONDON AFTER WINNING A TELEVISION TALENT SHOW, AND RECORDED HER debut single, **Jackie DeShannon**'s 'Till You Say You'll Be Mine'. Olivia became part of a group called Toomorrow. Her debut album (1971) included a Top 10 arrangement of **Bob Dylan**'s 'If Not For You'. Her more typical singles included 'Take Me Home Country Roads', by **John Denver** and, from John Rostill of the **Shadows**, 'Let Me Be There', winning her a Grammy for

Best Female Country Vocal. She performed in 1974's Eurovision Song Contest, and moved to North America and her standing in pop improved considerably with the chart-topper 'I Honestly Love You'.

She became renowned for her duets with other artists, notably in *Grease* in which she and John Travolta sang 'You're The One That I Want' – one of the most successful singles in UK pop history, topping the charts for nine weeks. 'Summer Nights' was also a UK number 1 in 1978. 'Xanadu', the film's title opus with the **Electric Light Orchestra**, was another global number 1. With singles like 'Physical' (1981) and the 1986 album *Soul Kiss*, she adopted a more raunchy image.

Following *The Rumour*, Olivia signed to Geffen for the release of a collection of children's songs and rhymes, *Warm And Tender*. In 1994 she released an album written, produced and paid for herself. It was estimated that she has sold more than 50 million records worldwide.

NICE

THE NICE, ORIGINALLY **P. P. ARNOLD'S** BACK-UP BAND, STARTED WHAT HAS BEEN DESCRIBED AS POMP-ROCK, art-rock and classical-rock. They comprised Keith Emerson (b. 1944; keyboards), Brian 'Blinky' Davison (b. 1942; drums), Lee Jackson (b. 1943; bass/vocals) and David O'List (b. 1948; guitar). After leaving Arnold in October 1967, they quickly built a reputation as a visually exciting band. Their debut, *The Thoughts Of Emerlist Davjack*, came nowhere near reproducing their live sound. *Ars Longa Vita Brevis*, containing 'America' from *West Side Story*, was released before O'List departed and they continued as a trio. They did not break into the US charts, despite UK chart success with *Nice* and *Five Bridges Suite*. *Nice* contained an excellent reading of **Tim Hardin**'s 'Hang On To A Dream'; the latter was a semi-orchestral suite about working-class life in Newcastle-upon-Tyne and also contained versions of 'Intermezzo From The Karelia Suite' by Sibelius, and Tchaikovsky's 'Pathetique'. The band's attempt at fusing classical music and rock together with the Sinfonia of London was admirable.

NICKS, STEVIE

NICKS (b. STEPHANIE NICKS, 1948) MOVED TO LA AND RECORDED *BUCKINGHAM-NICKS* WITH HER BOYFRIEND **Lindsey Buckingham**. This was subsequently used to demonstrate the studio facilities to Mick Fleetwood, and within weeks the duo were invited to join **Fleetwood Mac**. Stevie provided many of the group's best-known and successful songs, including 'Rhiannon' and 'Dreams'. Stevie's solo album, *Bella Donna*, released in 1981, achieved platinum sales. It spawned two US Top 10 singles – 'Stop Dragging My Heart Around', a duet with **Tom Petty** and 'Leather And Lace'. *The Wild Heart* produced the hits 'Stand Back' and 'Nightbird'. *Rock A Little*, was less successful, artistically and commercially. She rejoined Fleetwood Mac for *Tango In The Night*. Nicks continued her solo activities, releasing *The Other Side Of The Mirror* (1989). She rejoined Buckingham in Fleetwood Mac when the *Rumours* line-up reconvened in 1997.

NICO

NICO (b. CHRISTA PAFFGEN (PAVOLSKY), 1938, d. 1988) MET **Rolling Stones**' guitarist Brian Jones during a visit to London, making her recording debut with 'I'm Not Saying'. Nico was introduced to Andy Warhol in New York and starred in *Chelsea Girls*, before joining his protégés, the **Velvet Underground**. Nico contributed to their debut album, but resumed a solo career in 1967 with *Chelsea Girl* which included three compositions by a young **Jackson Browne**. **Lou Reed** and **John Cale** also provided memorable contributions, and Cale produced her subsequent three albums. In 1974 she appeared in a brief tour of the UK with ACNE (**Kevin Ayers**, John Cale and **Brian Eno**). After *The End*, she ceased recording, re-emerging in the post-punk era. Signs of an artistic revival followed treatment for drug addiction, but she died in Ibiza in July 1988, after suffering a cerebral haemorrhage while cycling in intense heat.

NIGHTINGALES

FOLLOWING THE SPLIT IN 1979 OF ROBERT LLOYD'S (b. 1959) BAND, THE PREFECTS, HE ASSEMBLED THE NIGHTINGALES. The line-up included Alan and Paul Apperley, Joe Crow and Eamonn Duffy. 'Idiot Strength' was released in 1981 on the band's own Vindaloo label, with Rough Trade Records. Joe Crow left and his replacements, Nick Beales and Andy Lloyd were two of 15 who would pass through the ranks. Lloyd established himself as one of the more interesting lyricists of the independent chart. After dissolving the group, he concentrated on a solo career.

NILSSON

WHILE WORKING IN BANKING IN LA, NILSSON (b. HARRY EDWARD NELSON III, 1941, d. 1994) TOUTED DEMOS OF HIS early compositions around the city's publishing houses. Producer **Phil Spector** drew on this material, recording 'Paradise' and 'Here I Sit' with the **Ronettes**. None of these were released contemporaneously, but such interest inspired the artist's own releases for the Tower label. Singles included 'You Can't Take Your Love Away From Me' and 'Good Times' (both 1966). In 1967 the **Yardbirds** recorded his 'Ten Little Indians', and he gave up his banking upon hearing the **Monkees**' version of 'Cuddly Toy'. He secured a contract with RCA and made his album debut with *Pandemonium Shadow Show*. His compositions were still popular with other acts; the **Turtles** recorded 'The Story Of Rock 'N' Roll', while **Three Dog Night** enjoyed a US chart-topper and gold disc with 'One'. Nilsson's version of 'One' appeared on *Ariel Ballet*. Nilsson's first US Top 10 hit came after he covered Fred Neil's 'Everybody's Talking', the theme to the film *Midnight Cowboy*. *Harry* included 'The Puppy Song', later a smash for **David Cassidy**, while *Nilsson Sings Newman* comprised solely **Randy Newman** material. *The Point* followed, but Nilsson's greatest success came with *Nilsson Schmilsson* and its attendant single, 'Without You', which sold in excess of one million copies, topping both the US and UK charts and winning a Grammy in 1972. After *Son Of Schmilsson*, Nilsson confounded expectations with *A Little Touch Of Schmilsson In The Night*, containing standards including 'Makin' Whoopee' and 'As Time Goes By'. **John Lennon** produced *Pussy Cats* (1974), comprised largely of pop classics. By the 80s Nilsson had retired from music altogether to pursue business interests. RCA released *A Touch More Schmilsson In The Night* in 1988 offering the singer's renditions of popular favourites. The paradox of Nilsson's career is that despite achieving recognition as a superior songwriter, his best-known and most successful records were penned by other acts.

Further References
Film: *Grease* (1978)
Book: *Olivia Newton-John: Sunshine Supergirl*, Linda Jacobs

NICE
Albums
Five Bridges (Charisma 1970)★★★★
➧ p.373 for full listings
Connections
P. P. Arnold ➧ p.21
Tim Hardin ➧ p.174

NICKS, STEVIE
Albums
The Other Side Of The Mirror (EMI 1989)★★★
➧ p.373 for full listings
Collaborators
Tom Petty ➧ p.260
Connections
Lindsey Buckingham ➧ p.72
Fleetwood Mac ➧ p.147

NICO
Albums
The Marble Index (Elektra 1969)★★★
➧ p.373 for full listings
Connections
Rolling Stones ➧ p.281
Velvet Underground ➧ p.329
Jackson Browne ➧ p.71
Lou Reed ➧ p.274
John Cale ➧ p.78
Kevin Ayers ➧ p.25
Brian Eno ➧ p.136
Further References
Book: *Songs They Never Play On The Radio: Nico, The Last Bohemian*, James Young

NIGHTINGALES
Albums
In The Good Old Country Ways (Vindaloo 1986)★★★
➧ p.373 for full listings

NILSSON
Albums
Nilsson Schmilsson (RCA 1971)★★★★
A Little Touch Of Schmilsson In The Night (RCA 1973)★★★★
➧ p.373 for full listings
Collaborators
Randy Newman ➧ p.246
John Lennon ➧ p.214
Connections
Phil Spector ➧ p.304
Ronettes ➧ p.282
Yardbirds ➧ p.345
Monkees ➧ p.236
Turtles ➧ p.325
Blood, Sweat And Tears ➧ p.53
Three Dog Night ➧ p.321
David Cassidy ➧ p.84

NINE BELOW ZERO
Albums
Third Degree (A&M 1982)★★★★
➽ p.373 for full listings

NINE INCH NAILS
Albums
The Downward Spiral (Nothing 1994)★★★★
➽ p.373 for full listings
Connections
Oliver Stone
David Lynch

1910 FRUITGUM COMPANY
Albums
(1969)★★★
➽ p.373 for full listings

NIRVANA (UK)
Albums
Local Anaesthetic (Vertigo 1971)★★★
➽ p.373 for full listings
Connections
Traffic ➽ p.323
Spooky Tooth ➽ p.306

NIRVANA (USA)
Albums
Nevermind (Geffen 1991)★★★★★
In Utero (Geffen 1993)★★★★
➽ p.373 for full listings
Collaborators
Big Black ➽ p.46
Connections
Mudhoney ➽ p.242
Hole ➽ p.182
Further References
Book: *Route 666: On The Road To Nirvana*, Gina Arnold

NITTY GRITTY DIRT BAND
Albums
The Nitty Gritty Dirt Band (Liberty 1967)★★★
Will The Circle Be Unbroken triple album (United Artists 1972)★★★★
➽ p.373 for full listings
Connections
Jackson Browne ➽ p.71
Kaleidoscope ➽ p.203

NO DOUBT
Albums
Tragic Kingdom (Interscope 1995)★★★★
➽ p.373 for full listings

NUCLEUS
Albums
Elastic Rock (Vertigo 1970)★★★★
➽ p.373 for full listings
Connections
Soft Machine ➽ p.302

NUGENT, TED
Albums
Cat Scratch Fever (Epic 1977)★★★★
➽ p.373 for full listings

NINE BELOW ZERO

AN EXCITING UK R&B BAND OF THE LATE 70S, THE GROUP WAS LED BY GUITARIST/SINGER DENNIS GREAVES AND virtuoso harmonica player Mark Feltham. With Peter Clark (bass, vocals) and Kenny Bradley (drums), Feltham recorded the EP *Packed Fair And Square* (1979), leading to a contract with A&M Records. Stix Burkey replaced Bradley and *Third Degree* was a minor UK hit. They dissolved in the mid-80s but Feltham revived Nine Below Zero at the end of the decade, signing a new recording contract. By the mid-90s they were recording again with A&M.

NINE INCH NAILS

TRENT REZNOR (b. 1965) BEGAN RECORDING AS NINE INCH NAILS IN 1988. PRETTY HATE MACHINE, WRITTEN, PLAYED and co-produced by Reznor, was largely synthesizer-based, but was transformed onstage by a ferocious wall of guitars. Together with the US hit 'Head Like A Hole', it brought platinum status. Reznor's guitar barrage on *Broken* hit the US Top 10, winning a Grammy for 'Wish'. *The Downward Spiral*'s blend of synthesizer textures and guitar fury provided a soundscape for Reznor's exploration of sex, drugs, violence, depression and suicide. The album debuted at US number 2, and a return to live work with Robin Finck (guitar), Danny Lohneer (bass, guitar), James Woolley (keyboards) and Reznor's long-time friend and drummer Chris Vrenna drew praise. The band constructed an acclaimed soundtrack for Oliver Stone's film *Natural Born Killers*. In late 1996 Reznor was working with film director David Lynch on the music score for *Lost Highway*.

1910 FRUITGUM COMPANY

FRUITGUM COMPANY WERE AT THE FOREFRONT OF A BRIEF WAVE OF BUBBLEGUM-POP IN THE LATE 60S. JEFF KATZ AND Jerry Kasenetz, the producers, specialized in studio in-house creations. Writer Joey Levine was the voice behind the hits such as the 1968 nursery game anthem 'Simon Says', '1, 2, 3, Red Light', 'Goody Goody Gumdrops' and 'Special Delivery'. Levine hastily assembled a touring troupe and kept this manufactured group alive until the end of the decade.

NIRVANA (UK)

SONGWRITERS PATRICK CAMPBELL-LYONS AND GEORGE ALEX SPYROPOULUS MET IN LONDON. THEY ESTABLISHED instant rapport and formed a group, adding Ray Singer (guitar), Brian Henderson (bass), Michael Coe (viola/french horn) and Sylvia Schuster (cello). The quintet, dubbed Nirvana, secured a recording deal with Island Records, making their debut in 1967, supporting **Traffic**, Jackie Edwards and **Spooky Tooth**. Their debut, *The Story Of Simon Simopath*, featuring 'Pentecost Hotel', was an episodic fairy tale. The mock libretto told of the hero's journey from a six-dimensional city to a nirvana filled with sirens.

The Alan Bown Set covered 'We Can Help You', receiving considerable airplay, but narrowly failed to chart. Despite their innovative singles, they fell tantalizingly short of a major breakthrough. Campbell-Lyons and Spyropoulus then disbanded the group format and completed a second set as a duo. This featured several of Nirvana's finest songs, including 'Tiny Goddess' and 'Rainbow Chaser', the latter becoming a minor UK hit in 1968. A strong album followed with *All Of Us*, but their following albums, *Black Flower* and *To Markos III* were considerably more low-key. Nirvana's career had already begun to falter when their label rejected *To Markos III*. Having completed a fourth album, *Local Anaesthetic*, Campbell-Lyons became a producer with the Vertigo label, while recording *Songs Of Love And Praise*, a compendium of new songs and re-recorded Nirvana favourites. This release was the last to bear the group's name. In the 90s the band are very much a cult item.

NIRVANA (USA)

FORMED IN WASHINGTON, USA, IN 1988, NIRVANA COMPRISED KURT COBAIN (b. KURT DONALD COBAIN, 1967, d. 1994; guitar/vocals), Krist Novoselic (b. 1965; bass) and Dave Grohl (b. 1969; drums). Having signed to Sub Pop Records, they completed their debut single, 'Love Buzz'/'Big Cheese'. Second guitarist Jason Everman was added prior to *Bleach*. The set quickly attracted Nirvana a cult following. Channing left the group following a European tour, and Dan Peters from **Mudhoney** stepped in temporarily. He was featured on 'Sliver', Nirvana's sole 1990 release. Drummer David Grohl reaffirmed a sense of stability. The trio secured a contract with Geffen Records, and they released *Nevermind*, which broke the band worldwide. It topped the US charts early in 1992 as well as many Album Of

The Year polls. The opening track, 'Smells Like Teen Spirit', reached the UK Top 10, confirming that Nirvana now combined critical and popular acclaim. In early 1992 Cobain and Courtney Love of **Hole** married. It was obvious that Cobain was struggling with his new role as 'spokesman for a generation'. Press interviews ruminated on the difficulties of recording a follow-up album, also of Cobain's using drugs to stem the pain from a stomach complaint. The recording of *In Utero* was produced by **Big Black**/Rapeman alumni Steve Albini. When the record was finally released the effect was not as immediate as *Nevermind*, although Cobain's songwriting remained inspired on 'Penny Royal Tea', 'All Apologies' and 'Rape Me'. His descent into self-destruction accelerated in 1994 as he went into a coma during dates in Italy, before returning to Seattle to shoot himself on 5 April 1994. *Unplugged In New York* offered some small comfort for Cobain's fans, with the singer's understated delivery on various cover versions and Nirvana standards.

NITTY GRITTY DIRT BAND

FORMED IN CALIFORNIA, 1965, THIS BAND COMPRISED JEFF HANNA (b. 1947; GUITAR/VOCALS), BRUCE KUNKEL (GUITAR/vocals), Glen Grosclose (drums), Dave Hanna (guitar/vocals), Ralph Barr (guitar) and Les Thompson (bass/vocals). Grosclose and Dave Hanna quickly made way for Jimmie Fadden (drums/guitar) and **Jackson Browne** (guitar/vocals). Although Browne only remained for a matter of months – he was replaced by John McEuen – his songs remained in the group's repertoire throughout their early career. *Nitty Gritty Dirt Band* comprised jug-band, vaudeville and pop material, ranging from 'Candy Man' to 'Buy For Me The Rain', a minor US hit. *Ricochet* maintained this balance, following which Chris

Darrow, formerly of **Kaleidoscope** (US), replaced Kunkel. The Dirt Band completed two further albums before disbanding in 1969. They reconvened the following year around Jeff Hanna, John McEuen, Jimmie Fadden, Les Thompson and newcomer Jim Ibbotson. The acclaimed *Uncle Charlie And His Dog Teddy* included Jerry Jeff Walker's 'Mr. Bojangles', a US Top 10 hit in 1970. Les Thompson left following *Will The Circle Be Unbroken*, but the remaining quartet continued with *Stars And Stripes Forever* and *Dreams*. In 1976 the group dropped its 'Nitty Gritty' prefix and undertook a pioneering USSR tour the following year. By 1982 the Dirt Band were an American institution with an enduring international popularity. 'Long Hard Road (Sharecropper Dreams)' and 'Modern Day Romance' topped the country charts in 1984 and 1985, respectively, but the following year McEuen retired from the line-up. Bernie Leadon augmented the group for *Working Band*, but left again upon its completion. He was featured on *Will The Circle Be Unbroken Volume Two*. The set deservedly drew plaudits for a group about to enter the 90s with its enthusiasm still intact. *Acoustic*, released in 1994, was a well-produced set.

NO DOUBT

LED BY GWEN STEFANI, THIS QUINTET FROM ORANGE COUNTY, CALIFORNIA, TOOK AMERICA BY STORM IN 1996 following the release of *Tragic Kingdom*. While earlier releases enjoyed critical acclaim, none had sold anything near the six million copies achieved by the chart-topping *Tragic Kingdom*. The group's new-found popularity owed much to the success of 'Just A Girl'. In 1997 'Don't Speak' entered the UK chart at number 1.

NUCLEUS

THE DOYEN OF BRITISH JAZZ-ROCK GROUPS, NUCLEUS WAS FORMED IN 1969 BY TRUMPETER IAN CARR. HE WAS JOINED by Chris Spedding (guitar), John Marshall (drums) and Karl Jenkins (keyboards). They signed to Vertigo and their debut, *Elastic Rock*, was arguably their exemplary work. The same line-up completed *We'll Talk About It Later*, but Spedding's subsequent departure heralded a bewildering succession of changes, undermining their potential. In 1972 Jenkins and Marshall left to join fellow fusion act, **Soft Machine**, and Nucleus became an inadvertent nursery for this 'rival' ensemble. Subsequent albums lacked the innovation of those first releases and Nucleus dissolved during the early 80s.

NUGENT, TED

NUGENT (b. 1949), ASSEMBLED THE **AMBOY DUKES** IN 1964, ASSUMING INCREASING CONTROL AS ORIGINAL MEMBERS dropped out. In 1974 a revitalized unit – dubbed Ted Nugent And The Amboy Dukes – completed the first of two albums, but in 1976 the guitarist embarked on a solo career. Derek St. Holmes (guitar), Rob Grange (bass) and Cliff Davies (drums) joined him for *Ted Nugent* and *Free For All*, both maintaining the high-energy rock of previous incarnations. It was as a live attraction that Nugent made his mark. Ear-piercing guitar and vocals were accompanied by a 'wild man' image. The aggression of a Nugent concert was captured on the platinum-selling *Double Live Gonzo*, featuring many of his best-loved stage numbers: 'Cat Scratch Fever', 'Motor City Madness' and 'Baby Please Don't Go'. Charlie Huhn (guitar) and John Sauter (bass) replaced St. Holmes and Grange for *Weekend Warriors*, with the same line-up remaining for *State Of Shock* and *Scream Dream*. In 1982 Nugent established a new unit which included Derek St. Holmes (vocals) and Carmine Appice (drums; ex-**Vanilla Fudge**) but successive solo releases offered little new material. In 1989 Nugent teamed up with Tommy Shaw (vocals/guitar; ex-**Styx**), Jack Blades (bass; ex-Night Ranger) and Michael Cartellone (drums) to form the successful 'supergroup', Damn Yankees. In 1994, Nugent resumed his solo career with *Spirit Of The Wild*.

Connections
Amboy Dukes ➧ p.16
Vanilla Fudge ➧ p.329
Styx ➧ p.312

Further References
Book: *The Legendary Ted Nugent*, Robert Holland

NUMAN, GARY

LONDON-BORN NUMAN (b. GARY ANTHONY JAMES WEBB, 1958) ENJOYED ENORMOUS SUCCESS AS TUBEWAY ARMY IN the UK in the late 70s. They topped the UK charts in 1979 with 'Are Friends Electric?'. Numan abandoned the group pseudonym for 'Cars' which also topped the UK charts and reached the US Top 10. *The Pleasure Principle* and *Telekon* entered the charts at number 1. His science-fiction orientated lyrics and synthesizer-based rhythms brought further Top 10 successes with 'We Are Glass', 'I Die: You Die' and 'She's Got Claws'. As the decade progressed his record sales declined and his glum-robotic persona was replaced by that of a debonair man-about-town. Despite an atrophied reputation amongst music critics, his fan base remained solid and his recordings continue to reach the lower placings in the UK charts.

NUMAN, GARY
Albums
Telekon (Beggars Banquet 1980)★★★
➧ p.373 for full listings

Further References
Book: *Gary Numan: The Authorized Biography*, Ray Coleman

NWA

LA'S NIGGERS WITH ATTITUDE COMPRISED **DR. DRE** (b. ANDRE YOUNG), DJ YELLA (b. ANTOINE CARRABY), MC REN (b. Lorenzo Patterson) and **Eazy E** (b. Eric Wright, 1973, d. 1995). Founder member **Ice Cube** (b. Oshea Jackson, *c.* 1970) departed for a solo career. Other early members included D.O.C. and Arabian Prince. NWA's first single was 'Boyz N' The Hood', marking out their lyrical territory as guns, violence and 'bitches'. They only performed four raps on their debut, *N.W.A. And The Posse*, so *Straight Outta Compton* was their first major release. In its aftermath rap became polarized into traditional liberal (reflecting the ideas of Martin Luther King) and a black militancy redolent of Malcolm X. In 1989 the FBI investigation into *Straight Outta Compton*'s infamous 'Fuck Tha Police' set a precedent for numerous actions against NWA. *Efil4zaggin* (Niggaz4life spelt backwards), which made US number 1, contained furious blasts of raggamuffin and 70s funk. The UK government used the Obscene Publications Act to seize copies but were forced to return them following legal action. As the decade progressed the remaining members of NWA spent more time on their solo projects, Dr. Dre enjoying huge success as an artist and producer while Ren released a disappointing solo album and EP.

NWA
Albums
Straight Outta Compton (Ruthless 1989)★★★★
➧ p.373 for full listings
Connections
Dr. Dre ➧ p.124
Eazy E ➧ p.131
Ice Cube ➧ p.191

NYRO, LAURA

NYRO'S (b. LAURA NIGRO, 1947, d. 1997) MAIN INFLUENCES RANGED FROM **BOB DYLAN** TO JOHN COLTRANE, BUT HER debut *More Than A New Discovery* (aka *The First Songs*) revealed a talent akin to **Carole King** and Ellie Greenwich. Empathy with soul and R&B enhanced her individuality, although she disowned the set, claiming its arrangements were completed against her wishes. *Eli And The Thirteenth Confession* (containing 'Stone Soul Picnic') complied more closely to Nyro's wishes; showing the growing sense of introspection apparent on *New York Tendaberry* (1969). This set revealed her dramatic intonation. *Christmas And The Beads Of Sweat*, including 'Christmas Is My Soul', offered similar passion while *Gonna Take A Miracle*, a collaboration with producers **Kenny Gamble** and **Leon Huff**, acknowledged the music which provided much of the artist's inspiration. She retired, re-emerging in 1975. *Smile* included 'I Am The Blues'; the attendant promotional tour spawned *Season Of Lights*. She embarked on her first concert tour in over a decade. *Stoned Soul Picnic* was a fitting retrospective, but only weeks after its release Nyro succumbed to cancer.

NYRO, LAURA
Albums
Eli And The Thirteenth Confession (Columbia 1968)★★★★
New York Tendaberry (Columbia 1969)★★★★
➧ p.373 for full listings
Collaborators
Kenny Gamble ➧ p.158
Leon Huff ➧ p.158
Connections
Carole King ➧ p.205
Influences
Bob Dylan ➧ p.128

O'CONNOR, SINEAD
Albums
I Do Not Want What I Haven't Got (Ensign 1990)★★★★
➧ p.373 for full listings
Collaborators
The Edge ➧ p.326
Willie Nelson ➧ p.245
Peter Gabriel ➧ p.157
Connections
Prince ➧ p.267
Bob Dylan ➧ p.128
Kate Bush ➧ p.76
Further References
Book: *Sinead O'Connor: So Different*, Dermott Hayes

O'JAYS
Albums
Love You To Tears (Global Soul/BMG 1997)★★★★
➧ p.373 for full listings
Connections
Gamble And Huff ➧ p.158

O'SULLIVAN, GILBERT
Albums
Back To Front (MAM 1973)★★★★
➧ p.373 for full listings
Connections
Tom Jones ➧ p.201

OAKENFOLD, PAUL
Albums
JD15 – Paul Oakenfold In The Mix (Music Unites 1994)★★★
➧ p.373 for full listings
Collaborators
Andy Weatherall ➧ p.335
Happy Mondays ➧ p.174
Shamen ➧ p.294
Massive Attack ➧ p.227
M People ➧ p.221
New Order ➧ p.246
U2 ➧ p.326
Connections
Deacon Blue ➧ p.112
Stone Roses ➧ p.311
Snoop Doggy Dogg ➧ p.302

OASIS
Albums
(What's The Story) Morning Glory (Creation 1995)★★★★★
➧ p.373 for full listings

Connections
Inspiral Carpets ➧ p.193
Influences
Beatles ➧ p.38
Kinks ➧ p.207
Smiths ➧ p.301
Further References
Book: *Brothers: From Childhood To Oasis: The Real Story*, Paul Gallagher and Terry Christian

O'CONNOR, SINEAD

O'CONNOR (b. 1966) SIGNED WITH ENSIGN RECORDS IN 1985. SHE PROVIDED THE VOCALS TO THE **U2** GUITARIST The Edge's film soundtrack for *The Captive* and debuted with 'Troy' (1987). *The Lion And The Cobra* sold well on the strength of her Top 20 hit 'Mandinka'. She later made her acting debut in *Hush-A-Bye Baby.* To promote her second solo album, O'Connor chose **Prince**'s 'Nothing Compares 2 U'. It demonstrated her strength and vulnerability and was a worldwide hit. *I Do Not Want What I Haven't Got* saw similar global success.

Her 1990 tour of the USA prompted the first stirrings of a backlash: in New Jersey she refused to go onstage after 'The Star Spangled Banner' was played. In 1992, she tore up a photograph of the Pope on US television – her appearance at the **Bob Dylan** celebration concert shortly afterwards was highly charged. In 1993, she guested on **Willie Nelson**'s *Across The Borderline*, duetting as a substitute **Kate Bush** on **Peter Gabriel**'s 'Don't Give Up'. *Universal Mother* found only marginal success.

O'JAYS

EDDIE LEVERT (b. 1942) AND WALTER WILLIAMS (b. 1942) SANG TOGETHER AS A GOSPEL DUO BEFORE FORMING THE doo-wop-influenced Triumphs in 1958. They recruited William Powell, Bill Isles and Bobby Massey and recorded as the Mascots before becoming the O'Jays. Signing to Imperial in 1963, they secured their first hit with 'Lonely Drifter' followed by 'I'll Be Sweeter Tomorrow (Than I Was Today)' (1967, R&B Top 10). Isles then left, followed in 1972 by Massey.

After **Gamble And Huff** signed them to Philadelphia International Records, 'Back Stabbers' (US Top 3) established the group's style; 'Love Train' introduced the protest lyrics that would feature on their later releases. In 1975, Sammy Strain joined when ill health forced William Powell to retire from live performances. Powell continued to record until his death in 1976. 'Message In Our Music' (1976) was a hit and *So Full Of Love* went platinum. The early 80s were commercially fallow, until *Love Fever* with its blend of funk and rap. 'Lovin' You' was a soul number 1. *Love You To Tears* was their best album in many years, echoing the sound of their heyday.

O'SULLIVAN, GILBERT

IRISH SINGER-SONGWRITER O'SULLIVAN (b. RAYMOND O'SULLIVAN, 1946) SIGNED TO CBS, BEFORE BEING launched by Gordon Mills on his new MAM label. He debuted with 'Nothing Rhymed' (1970, UK Top 10). Early UK successes included 'Alone Again (Naturally)' (US number 1), which sold over a million copies. *Himself* included the radio favourite 'Matrimony' (not released as a single). He also enjoyed two consecutive UK number 1s with 'Clair' and 'Get Down'. His most famous single was 'What's In A Kiss?'.

Back To Front reached UK number 1 but, despite further hits, his appeal declined. After a spectacular falling out with Mills, he left MAM and returned to CBS. He became embroiled in a High Court battle against Mills and MAM in 1982. The judge not only awarded O'Sullivan substantial damages and had all agreements with MAM set aside, but decreed that all the singer's master tapes and copyrights should be returned. The case made legal history and had enormous repercussions for the British music publishing world. Nevertheless, O'Sullivan has failed to re-establish his career as a major artist.

OAKENFOLD, PAUL

UK DJ AND REMIXER WHO WAS ACTIVE DURING DANCE MUSIC'S UNDERGROUND DAYS. HE WORKED IN NEW YORK for Arista, then DJ-ed at the Ibiza club. He staged the 'Ibiza Reunion Party' at his Project Club in Streatham, London. He was famed for his sets at the UK's Future Club, Spectrum, Theatre Of Madness, Land Of Oz, Shoom (alongside **Andy Weatherall**) and Hacienda. Oakenfold became synonymous with the Ministry Of Sound and, with Steve Osborne, gave the **Happy Mondays**' 'Wrote For Luck' a new club edge in 1989. Other remix clients included the **Shamen**, **Massive Attack**, **M People**, **New Order**, **Arrested Development** and **U2**. Oakenfold later toured with U2.

He made the transition to full-blown producer for the Happy Mondays, Solid Gold Easy Action and **Deacon Blue**. In 1991, he was nominated for a BRIT Award for Best Producer. He has also worked with the **Stone Roses** and **Snoopy Doggy Dogg**.

OASIS

ENGLISH GROUP WHOSE CREATIVE AXIS IS THE GALLAGHER BROTHERS, LIAM (b. 1972; VOCALS) AND NOEL (b. 1967; guitar/vocals). Noel worked as a guitar technician for the **Inspiral Carpets** on worldwide tours. Meanwhile Liam joined the band Rain, with Paul 'Bonehead' Arthurs (guitar), Tony McCarroll (drums) and Paul 'Guigsy' McGuigan; they became Oasis. When Noel returned, he joined as lead guitarist and insisted they only perform his songs.

In 1993, Oasis supported 18 Wheeler in Glasgow. Their five songs were enough to hypnotize Creation boss Alan McGee, who offered them a contract there and then. Their 'debut' was a one-sided 12-inch promo of 'Columbia'.

1994 began with a torrent of press coverage, much of it focusing on the group's errant behaviour – punch-ups and violent bickering between the Gallaghers guaranteed full media coverage. High-profile dates ensured that expectations for their debut album were phenomenal. The tracks were completed with mixing by Owen Morris and *Definitely Maybe* entered the UK charts at number 1; 'Cigarettes And Alcohol', a stage favourite, reached number 7. 'Whatever', a lush pop song with full orchestration, followed.

In 1995, they finally cracked the US charts. That year, McCarroll left and Alan White sessioned on their second album. The eagerly anticipated *(What's The Story) Morning Glory* was rich and assured. Gallagher's **Beatles**-esque melodies were spectacular, from the acoustic simplicity of 'Wonderwall' to the raucous and dense harmony of 'Don't Look Back In Anger'. Rumours of the band splitting came to a head on their ninth attempt to break America in 1996: following one of their many fights, Noel returned to the UK. By that time, *(What's The Story) Morning Glory* had sold over seven million copies and was on the way to becoming the biggest-selling UK album of all time.

The greatly anticipated third album was introduced with 'D'You Know What I Mean?'. *Be Here Now* sold 800,000 copies in the UK within 24 hours. It received mixed reviews, however, although still drawing heavily on the Beatles, there are some outstanding songs.

OCEAN, BILLY

RAISED IN ENGLAND, OCEAN (b. LESLIE SEBASTIAN CHARLES, 1950) WORKED AS A SESSION SINGER, BEFORE GOING SOLO. His early hits included 'Love Really Hurts Without You' and 'Red Light Spells Danger'. Subsequent releases fared less well. He then began to win a US audience, moving there shortly afterwards. After several R&B successes, 'Caribbean Queen (No More Love On The Run)' was his first US pop number 1, selling over a million copies. A following run of hits included two more number 1s, 'There'll Be Sad Songs (To Make You Cry)' (1986) and 'Get Outta My Dreams, Get Into My Car' (1988). Despite a UK number 1 with 'When The Going Gets Tough, The Tough Get Going' (from the film *The Jewel Of The Nile*), Ocean's luck in Britain constantly fluctuated. However, he has had three UK Top 5 albums, including the *Greatest Hits* collection.

OCEAN COLOUR SCENE

SIMON FOWLER (b. 1966; VOCALS), STEVE CRADDOCK (b. 1961; GUITAR), DAMON MINCHELA (BASS) AND OSCAR HARRISON (drums) peddled a generic indie-guitar sound from 1989. After their debut, 'Sway', Phonogram Records signed the band to Fontana Records. The debut album finally emerged in 1992, but the momentum had been lost; Ocean Colour Scene subsequently walked out on the contract.

Craddock and Minchela worked in **Paul Weller**'s backing band, before Ocean Colour Scene's 'The Riverboat Song' (1996), was heavily promoted on radio , reaching the UK Top 20. The group secured a new contract with MCA and *Moseley Shoals* spawned 'The Day We Caught The Train' (UK Top 10). *Marchin' Already* was released to unexpected critical disapproval, but spawned the excellent 'It's A Beautiful Thing'. In 1998, they sang on England's World Cup football single.

OCHS, PHIL

PHIL OCHS (b. 1940, d. 1976) STARTED OUT WITH THE SUNDOWNERS, BEFORE MOVING TO GREENWICH VILLAGE. His early work led to his involvement with the *Broadside* magazine movement.

After signing to Elektra, he achieved popular acclaim when **Joan Baez** took 'There But For Fortune' into the charts. *Phil Ochs In Concert* featured the wry 'Love Me I'm A Liberal'. Ochs moved to A&M in 1967 and *Pleasures Of The Harbour* emphasized a greater use of orchestration, as well as an increasingly rock-based perspective. Although *Rehearsals For Retirement* documented the political travails of 1968, *Phil Ochs' Greatest Hits* showed an imaginative performer bereft of focus. This period is documented on the controversial *Gunfight At Carnegie Hall*. Ochs' later years were marked by tragedy. An attempted strangulation attack permanently impaired his singing voice and, beset by chronic writers block, Ochs sought solace in alcohol, before succumbing to schizophrenia. He was found hanged at his sister's home.

ODYSSEY

FORMED IN NEW YORK CITY BY VOCALISTS LILLIAN, LOUISE AND CARMEN LOPEZ (ORIGINALLY known as the Lopez Sisters). Carmen left in 1968, was replaced by Tony Reynolds who was then replaced by Bill McEachern. 'Native New Yorker' (1977) reached the US Top 20 and UK number 5. In 1980, Odyssey re-appeared in the UK chart with 'Use It Up And Wear It Out' (number 1). Two more effortless pop/soul offerings reached the Top 5.

OFFSPRING

BRYAN 'DEXTER' HOLLAND (b. 1966; VOCALS/GUITAR) AND GREG KRIESEL (b. 1965; BASS) JOINED MANIC SUBSIDAL, with Doug Thompson (vocals) and Jim Benton (drums). When Thompson left, Holland took over vocals, while Benton was replaced by James Lilja; Kevin 'Noodles' Wasserman (b. 1963; guitar) joined later. Manic Subsidal was rechristened the Offspring in 1985 and released 'I'll Be Waiting'. By 1987, Lilja was replaced by Ron Welty (b. 1971).

A demo was recorded in 1988, but to little avail. Finally, their debut studio album was released; a blend of hardcore with Middle Eastern guitar. *Ignition* was more relaxed and *Smash* combined punk with ska and hard rock. By 1995, *Smash* had reached quadruple platinum sales. Much of 1995 was spent in dispute with their record company. *Ixnay On The Hombre* was well received.

OHIO EXPRESS

US BUBBLEGUM OUTFIT FORMED IN 1967. JOEY LEVINE (LEAD VOCALS), DALE POWERS (LEAD GUITAR), DOUG Grassel (rhythm guitar), Jim Pflayer (keyboards), Dean Krastan (bass) and Tim Corwin (drums) debuted with 'Beg, Borrow And Steal' (1966); it was reissued in 1967 by Cameo Records. In 1968, Ohio Express joined Buddah and released 'Yummy Yummy Yummy' (US/UK Top 5).

The band released six albums, of which only *Ohio Express* and *Chewy Chewy* made any real impact. They split in 1972.

OLDFIELD, MIKE

BRITISH BORN MULTI-INSTRUMENTALIST OLDFIELD (b. 1953) WILL FOREVER BE REMEMBERED FOR *TUBULAR BELLS* which sold 12 million copies worldwide, topped the US and UK charts and stayed in both for more than five years. He began his career providing acoustic-guitar accompaniment to folk songs sung by his older sister, Sally, but left to join **Kevin Ayers** And The Whole World.

Hergest Ridge reached UK number 1, but did not chart in the USA. *Ommadawn* featured **Chieftains**' Paddy Moloney playing uillean pipes, and a team of African drummers. It sold well but the critical response was unfavourable. Virgin saw the records as complementary works and packaged them together in 1976 as *Boxed*. Oldfield had two consecutive Christmas hits with 'In Dulci Jubilo' (1975) and 'Portsmouth' (1976).

Around 1977-78, Oldfield underwent a programme of self-assertiveness. *Incantations* drew strongly on disco influences and *Exposed* was recorded at various concerts where Oldfield played with up to 50 other musicians. *Platinum*, *QE2* and *Five Miles Out* caught Oldfield slightly out of step with his contemporaries as he tried to hone his songwriting. **Hall And Oates** recorded a version of his 'Family Man' (1983, UK Top 20) and Oldfield began working with soprano Maggie Reilly; she sang on the hit 'Moonlight Shadow' (from *Crises*). After *Discovery*, Oldfield wrote the film soundtrack for *The Killing Fields*. On *Islands*, he was joined by vocalists **Bonnie Tyler** and Kevin Ayers. *Earth Moving* failed to challenge the prevailing view of his work as anachronistic.

1992 found him working with Trevor Horn on *Tubular Bells II*; its success resulted in increased sales for *Tubular Bells* and led to a spectacular live concert.

OCEAN, BILLY

Albums
Suddenly (Jive 1984)★★★
➧ p.373 for full listings

OCEAN COLOUR SCENE

Albums
Moseley Shoals (MCA 1996)★★★★
➧ p.373 for full listings

Collaborators
Space ➧ p.303
Echo And The Bunnymen ➧ p.131
Spice Girls ➧ p.304

Connections
Paul Weller ➧ p.336
Noel Gallagher ➧ p.250

OCHS, PHIL

Albums
All The News That's Fit To Sing (Elektra 1964)★★★★
➧ p.373 for full listings

Connections
Joan Baez ➧ p.29

Influences
Woody Guthrie ➧ p.171

Further References
Book: *Phil Ochs: Death Of A Rebel*, Marc Eliott

ODYSSEY

Albums
Hollywood Party Tonight (RCA 1978)★★★
➧ p.373 for full listings

OFFSPRING

Albums
Smash (Epitaph 1994)★★★
➧ p.374 for full listings

Connections
Dead Kennedys ➧ p.112

OHIO EXPRESS

Albums
Ohio Express (Pye 1968)★★★
➧ p.374 for full listings

OLDFIELD, MIKE

Albums
Tubular Bells (Virgin 1973)★★★★
Tubular Bells II (Warners 1992)★★★
➧ p.374 for full listings

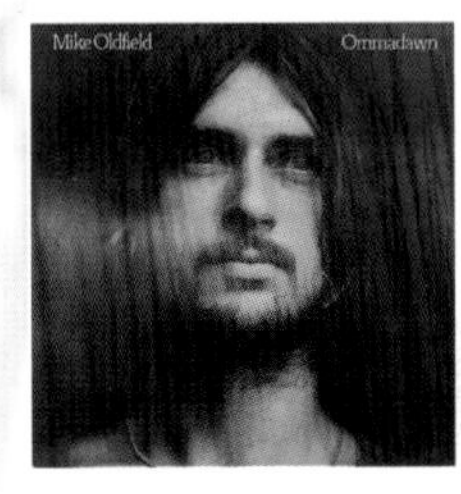

Collaborators
Kevin Ayers ➧ p.25
Bonnie Tyler ➧ p.325

Connections
Chieftains ➧ p.90
Hall And Oates ➧ p.172

Further References
Book: *Mike Oldfield: A Man And His Music*, Sean Moraghan

OMD
Albums
Orchestral Manoeuvres In The Dark (DinDisc 1980)★★★
Universal (Virgin 1996)★★★
» p.374 for full listings
Further References
Book: *Orchestral Manoeuvres In The Dark*, Mike West

ONO, YOKO
Albums
Rising (Geffen 1996)★★★
» p.374 for full listings
Collaborators
John Lennon » p.214
Connections
Beatles » p.38
Plastic Ono Band
Further References
Video: *The Bed-In* (PMI 1991)
Book: *Yoko Ono: A Biography*, Jerry Hopkins

ORANGE JUICE
Albums
Rip It Up (Polydor 1982)★★★★
» p.374 for full listings
Connections
Edwyn Collins » p.98
Aztec Camera » p.25
Further References
Video: *Dada With Juice* (Hendring Video 1989)

ORB
Albums
Orbvs Terrarvm (Island 1995)★★★★
Orblivion (Island 1997)★★★
» p.374 for full listings
Collaborators
Yellow Magic Orchestra » p.346
Connections
Killing Joke » p.205
KLF » p.208
Rickie Lee Jones » p.201
Jean Michel Jarre » p.197

ORBISON, ROY
Albums
Oh Pretty Woman (1964)★★★★
King Of Hearts (Virgin 1992)★★★★
» p.374 for full listings
Collaborators
Emmylou Harris » p.175
Bruce Springsteen » p.306
George Harrison » p.176
Bob Dylan » p.128
Tom Petty » p.260
Jeff Lynne » p.220
Connections
Everly Brothers » p.139
Elvis Presley » p.265
Beatles » p.38
Traveling Wilburys » p.323
Cyndi Lauper » p.213

OMD

UK SYNTHESIZER POP DUO: PAUL HUMPHREYS (b. 1960) AND ANDY McCLUSKEY (b. 1959). IN 1978, THEY PERFORMED with Paul Collister, under their full title Orchestral Manoeuvres In The Dark. Tony Wilson of Factory Records released their debut 'Electricity'; it was re-released when Virgin Records subsidiary, DinDisc, signed them.

Their breakthrough came with the UK Top 10 'Enola Gay'. *Organisation* followed quickly and the more sophisticated *Architecture And Morality* showed a new romanticism. *Dazzle Ships* was a flawed attempt at progression, while *Junk Culture* faced similar critical disdain, but *Crush* was a less orchestrated affair, featuring newcomers Graham and Neil Weir. By *The Pacific Age*, it was obvious that their domestic popularity was slipping. McCluskey retained the name and resurfaced in 1991 with 'Sailing On The Seven Seas'. The resultant album harkened back to *Architecture And Morality*.

ONO, YOKO

JAPANESE-BORN YOKO ONO (b. 1933) MOVED TO THE USA, BECOMING IMMERSED IN THE NEW YORK *AVANT-GARDE* milieu. A reputation as a film-maker and conceptual artist preceded her marriage to **John Lennon** in 1969. Their early collaborations, *Two Virgins*, *Life With The Lions* and *Wedding Album*, were self-indulgent and wilfully obscure, but with the formation of the Plastic Ono Band they forged an exciting musical direction. Unfairly blamed for the **Beatles**' demise, Yoko emerged with a series of excellent compositions, including 'Don't Worry Kyoto'. *Yoko Ono/The Plastic Ono Band* was equally compulsive listening and a talent to captivate or confront was also prevalent on *Fly*, *Approximately Infinite Universe* and *Feeling The Space*. The couple's relationship continued to undergo public scrutiny, and the birth of their son Sean resulted in a prolonged retirement.

The Lennons re-emerged in 1980 with *Double Fantasy*; they were returning home from completing a new Yoko single on the night John was shot dead. The resultant track, 'Walking On Thin Ice', was thus imbued with a certain poignancy, but Ono's ensuing albums have failed to match its intensity. Yoko returned to music in 1995, together with Sean and his band Ima. *Rising* came as a surprise as Ima added great texture to Yoko's strong yet bizarre lyrics.

ORANGE JUICE

SCOTTISH POP GROUP, FORMED IN THE LATE-70S. **EDWYN COLLINS** (b. 1959; VOCALS/LEAD GUITAR), JAMES KIRK (vocals/rhythm guitar), David McClymont (bass) and Steven Daly (drums) began their career on Postcard Records; their singles included 'Falling And Laughing'. After signing to Polydor they issued *You Can't Hide Your Love Forever*. Kirk and Daly were then replaced by Malcolm Ross and Zeke Manyika. *Rip It Up* was another strong work (UK Top 10). The group, reduced to Collins and Manyika, completed the energetic *Texas Fever*, and an eponymous third album, which included 'What Presence?'. Collins subsequently went solo as did Manyika; Ross joined **Aztec Camera**.

ORB

THE ORB IS REALLY ONE MAN, ALEX PATERSON (b. DUNCAN ROBERT ALEX PATERSON); HIS SPECIALIST FIELD IS THE creation of ambient house music. He formed the Orb in 1988 with Jimmy Cauty. The band first appeared on WAU! Mr Modo's showcase set *Eternity Project One* with 'Tripping On Sunshine'. Their first release proper came with 1989's *Kiss* EP; this was followed by their successful subsequent release, 'A Huge Ever-Growing Pulsating Brain Which Rules From The Centre Of The Ultraworld', a marriage of progressive-rock trippiness and a centrepoint sample of Minnie Riperton's 'Loving You'. The group signed with Big Life, but Cauty left to form **KLF** in 1990. He subsequently re-recorded *Space*, the album that was to have been the Orb's debut.

'Little Fluffy Clouds' was the next Orb release, though that ran into difficulties when **Rickie Lee Jones** objected to the sample of her voice. Paterson met future co-conspirator Thrash (b. Kristian Weston) in 1991. Their debut album reached UK number 1, and led to a plunge of remixes for other artists. Further Paterson projects included a remix album for **Yellow Magic Orchestra**. *Pomme Fritz* saw them witness the first signs of a critical backlash, however their progress continued with *Orblivion*.

ORBISON, ROY

ORBISON (b. 1936, d. 1988), A STAFF WRITER FOR ACUFF-ROSE MUSIC, EARNED ROYALTIES FROM THE SUCCESS OF 'Claudette' (the **Everly Brothers**). He later signed with the Monument label and, shortly afterwards, charted in the US with 'Up Town' (1960). A few months later, his 'Only The Lonely' was rejected by **Elvis Presley** and the Everly Brothers, and Orbison decided to record it himself: the song topped the UK charts and narrowly missed US number 1.

The shy and quiet-spoken Orbison donned a pair of dark-tinted glasses to cover up his chronic astigmatism. Over the next five years he enjoyed unprecedented transatlantic success, repeating his formula with further stylish but melancholy ballads, including 'Blue Angel', 'Running Scared', 'Crying', 'Dream Baby', 'Blue Bayou' and 'In Dreams'. He had two UK number 1 singles, 'It's Over' and 'Oh Pretty Woman'.

Tragically, in 1966, his wife Claudette was killed falling from the back of his motorcycle, and in 1968, a fire destroyed his home, taking the lives of his two sons. Orbison's musical direction understandably faltered.

He bounced back in 1980, winning a Grammy for his duet with **Emmylou Harris** on 'That Lovin' You Feelin' Again' from the film *Roadie*. In 1987, he was inducted into the Rock 'N' Roll Hall Of Fame; at the ceremony he sang 'Oh Pretty Woman' with **Bruce Springsteen**. The song had gained huge popularity through being

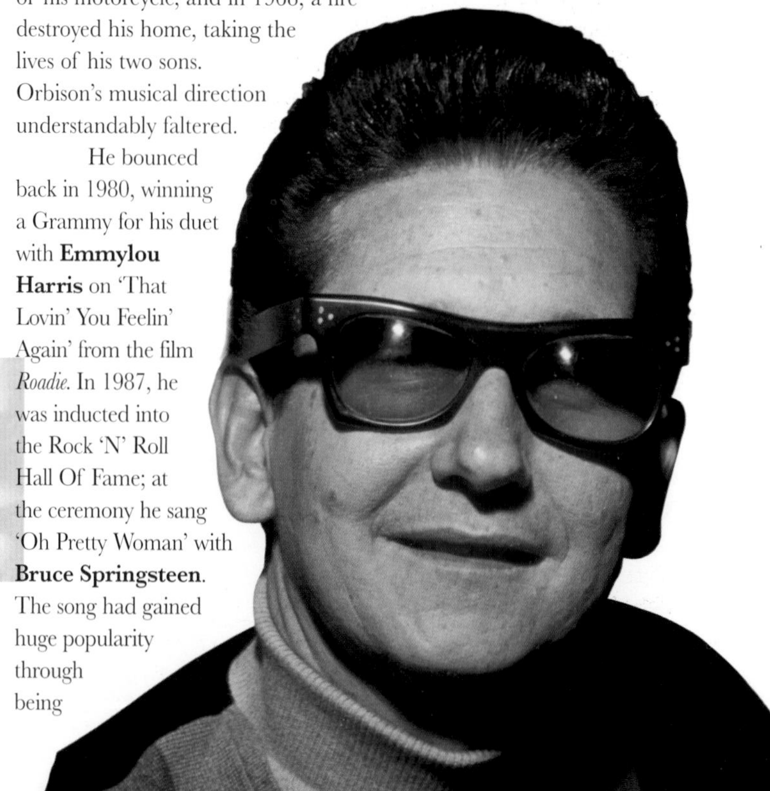

used in the hit film *Pretty Woman*. He then joined the **Traveling Wilburys**; their splendid debut album owed much to Orbison's major input. Less than a month after its critically acclaimed release, Orbison suffered a fatal heart attack. The posthumously released *Mystery Girl* was his most successful album.

ORBITAL

AMBIENT-TECHNO OUTFIT FORMED BY BROTHERS PAUL (b. 1968) AND PHILLIP HARTNOLL (b. 1964). THEY DEBUTED with 'Chime' (1990, UK Top 20); 'Raddiccio' followed in 1992. They also worked on releases by artists such as the **Shamen** and **EMF**. Their debut, *Untitled*, was subsequently referred to as *Untitled 1*. *Snivilisation* was a largely instrumental political concept album. 'The Box' was a fully-fledged film soundtrack – comprising four distinct movements with vocal versions by lyricist Grant Fulton and **Tricky** singer Alison Goldfrapp. The exquisitely dense rhythms on *In Sides* emphasized the group's ability to blend the experimental with the accessible. It included tracks such as 'The Girl With The Sun In Her Hair', recorded using solar power.

OSBORNE, JEFFREY

OSBORNE (b. 1948) SANG WITH LTD (LOVE, TOGETHERNESS AND DEVOTION) FROM 1970 UNTIL ITS DISBANDMENT 12 years later. Under George Duke's supervision, their first album featured the single 'I Really Don't Need No Light' (US Top 40). *Stay With Me Tonight* made slight headway in the UK, but in 1984 'Don't Stop' became his last UK chart entry.

Emotional was a strong album, as were the subsequent singles, one of which, 'You Should Be Mine (The Woo Woo Song)', reached US number 13. He returned with *One Love One Dream* (co-written with Bruce Roberts) and, just prior to a transfer to Arista, he teamed up with **Dionne Warwick** for 1990's 'Love Power'.

OSBORNE, JOAN

JOAN OSBORNE (b. 1963) BEGAN HER SINGING CAREER AT THE ABILENE BLUES BAR IN NEW YORK, USA – PROMPTED by several drinks, she took the stage and sang Billie Holiday's 'God Bless The Child'. Her voice soon gained a solid reputation. *Soul Show* was released on her own Womanly Hips Records in 1991 and in 1993 she became the first signing to Blue Gorilla, a new label set up by Rick Chertoff of PolyGram. Osborne's backing group on *Relish* featured Rob Hyman (keyboards), Eric Brazilian (guitar), Charlie Quintana (drums; also of **Cracker**) and Rainy Orteca (bass). Brazilian wrote the infectious single 'One Of Us'. *Relish* received strong reviews. In 1996, 'One Of Us' was a major UK hit.

OSBOURNE, OZZY

IN 1979, SINGER-SONGWRITER OSBOURNE (b. JOHN OSBOURNE, 1948) LEFT **BLACK SABBATH**. HIS OWN BAND was set up with Lee Kerslake (drums; ex-**Uriah Heep**), **Rainbow**'s Bob Daisley (bass) and Randy Rhoads (guitar); their debut was *Blizzard Of Oz*. By their second album, Daisley and Kerslake had been replaced by drummer Tommy Aldridge and bassist Rudy Sarzo. Osbourne constantly courted publicity, famously having to undergo treatment for rabies after biting the head off a bat. In 1982, Rhoads was killed in an air crash; his replacement was Brad Gillis.

Following a tour which saw Sarzo and Gillis walk out, Osbourne was forced to re-think the line-up; Daisley rejoined, along with guitarist Jake E. Lee. Aldridge left following *Bark At The Moon* and was replaced by Carmine Appice. This combination was short-lived, however, with Randy Castillo replacing Appice, and Phil Soussan joining on bass.

In the late 80s, Osbourne went on trial in America for allegedly using his lyrics to incite youngsters to commit suicide; he was eventually cleared. His lyrics, though, continue to deal with the grimmest of subjects like the agony of insanity, and *The Ultimate Sin* is concerned almost exclusively with nuclear destruction. He embarked on a farewell tour in 1992, but broke four bones in his foot which inhibited his performances greatly. By 1994, he was announcing the imminent release of a new solo album, recorded in conjunction with Steve Vai. *Ozzmosis* is arguably his best album, and was a major success; the line-up was: Geezer Butler (bass), Rick Wakeman (keyboards), Zakk Wylde (guitar/co-songwriting) and Deen Castronovo (drums).

OSIBISA

FORMED IN LONDON, ENGLAND IN 1969, BY THREE GHANAIAN AND THREE CARIBBEAN MUSICIANS, OSIBISA

played a central role in developing an awareness of African music in the 70s. The Ghanaian members – Teddy Osei (saxophone), Sol Amarfio (drums) and Mac Tontoh (trumpet, Osei's brother) – were seasoned members of the Accra highlife scene. Osei and Amafio had played in the Star Gazers, a top Ghanaian highlife band, before setting up the Comets, who scored a large West African hit with 'Pete Pete' (1958). Tontoh was also a member of the Comets, before joining the Uhuru Dance Band. The other founder members of Osibisa were Spartacus R, a Grenadian bass player, Robert Bailey (keyboards) and Wendel Richardson (lead guitar). Ghanaian percussionist Darko Adams 'Potato' (b. 1932, d. 1995) joined soon after. In 1964, Osei formed Cat's Paw, an early blueprint for Osibisa which blended highlife, rock and soul.

Osibisa proved to be an immediate success, with the single 'Music For Gong Gong' a substantial hit in 1970 (three other singles later made the British Top 10: 'Sunshine Day', 'Dance The Body Music' and 'Coffee Song'). Their debut album displayed music whose rock references, especially in the guitar solos, combined with vibrant African cross rhythms. *Woyaya* reached UK number 11; its title track was later covered by **Art Garfunkel**. During the late 70s they spent much of their time on world tours, playing to particularly large audiences in Japan, India, Australia and Africa. In 1980, they performed a special concert at the Zimbabwean independence celebrations. By this time, however, Osibisa's star was in decline in Europe and America. The band continued touring and releasing records, but to steadily diminishing audiences. Osibisa occasionally stage reunion concerts.

Further References
Film: *The Fastest Guitar Alive* (1966)
Book: *Dark Star*, Ellis Amburn

ORBITAL
Albums
Snivilisation (Internal 1994)★★★★
In Sides (Internal 1996)★★★★
➽ p.374 for full listings
Connections
Shamen ➽ p.294
EMF ➽ p.135
Tricky ➽ p.324

OSBORNE, JEFFREY
Albums
Jeffrey Osborne (A&M 1982)★★★
Only Human (Arista 1991)★★★
➽ p.374 for full listings
Collaborators
Dionne Warwick ➽ p.334

OSBORNE, JOAN
Albums
Relish (Blue Gorilla/Mercury 1995)★★★★
➽ p.374 for full listings
Connections
Cracker ➽ p.102

OSBOURNE, OZZY
Albums
Blizzard Of Oz (Jet 1980)★★★
Ozzmosis (Epic 1995)★★★★
➽ p.374 for full listings
Collaborators
Madonna ➽ p.222
Connections
Black Sabbath ➽ p.51
Uriah Heep ➽ p.327
Rainbow ➽ p.272
Further References
Video: *Bark At The Moon* (1990)
Books: *Diary Of A Madman*, Mick Wall
Ozzy Osbourne, Garry Johnson

OSIBISA
Albums
Osibisa (MCA 1971)★★★
Osibirock (Warners 1974)★★★
Ojah Awake (1976)★★★
➽ p.374 for full listings
Connections
Cat's Paw
Art Garfunkel ➽ p.159
Further References
Video: *Warrior* (Hendring 1990)

OSMOND, DONNY
Albums
The Donny Osmond Album (MGM 1971)★★
Make The World Go Away (MGM 1975)★★
➽ p.374 for full listings
Connections
Osmonds ➽ p.254
Donny And Marie
Paul Anka ➽ p.19
Joseph And The Amazing Technicolor Dreamcoat

OSMONDS
Albums
Osmonds (MGM 1971)★★
Our Best To You (MGM 1974)★★
Today (1985)★★
➽ p.374 for full listings
Collaborators
Johnny Bristol ➽ p.68
Connections
Donny Osmond ➽ p.254
Donny And Marie
Further References
Video: *Very Best Of* (Wienerworld 1996)
Books: *At Last ... Donny!*, James Gregory
The Osmond Story, George Tremlett

OTWAY, JOHN
Albums
with Wild Willy Barrett *John Otway & Wild Willie Barrett* (Polydor 1977)★★★
Where Did I Go Right? (Polydor 1979)★★★
Premature Adulation (Amazing Feet 1995)★★★
➽ p.374 for full listings
Collaborators
Wild Willie Barrett
Further References
Video: *John Otway And Wild Willie Barrett* (ReVision 1990)
Book: *Cor Baby That's Really Me*, John Otway

OUTLAWS (USA)
Albums
The Outlaws (Arista 1975)★★★★
Lady In Waiting (Arista 1976)★★★
Bring It Back Alive (Arista 1978)★★★
➽ p.374 for full listings

OZRIC TENTACLES
Albums
Live Ethereal Cereal cassette only (Dovetail 1986)★★★
Pungent Effulgent (Dovetail 1989)★★★
Curious Corn (Snapper 1997)★★★
➽ p.374 for full listings
Connections
Ullulators
Eat Static
music festivals

OSMOND, DONNY

THE MOST SUCCESSFUL SOLO ARTIST TO EMERGE FROM THE FAMILY GROUP, THE **OSMONDS**, DONNY'S (b. DONALD Clark Osmond, 1957) first solo success came in 1971 with a version of Billy Sherrill's 'Sweet And Innocent', which reached the US Top 10. In 1972, Osmondmania reached Britain, and a revival of **Paul Anka**'s 'Puppy Love' gave Donny his first UK number 1. The American singer's clean-cut good looks and perpetual smile brought him massive coverage in the pop press. His material appeared to concentrate on the pangs of adolescent love, which made him the perfect teenage idol for the period. In 1974, Donny began a series of duets with his sister Marie, which included more UK Top 10 hits. After the break-up of the group in 1980, Donny went on to star in the 1982 revival of the musical *Little Johnny Jones*. A decade later, a rugged Osmond returned with 'I'm In It For Love' and the more successful 'Soldier Of Love' which reached the US Top 30. Osmond later played the lead in productions of *Joseph And The Amazing Technicolor Dreamcoat.*

OSMONDS

THIS FAMOUS FAMILY ALL-VOCAL GROUP FROM AMERICA COMPRISED ALAN OSMOND (b. 1949), WAYNE OSMOND (b. 1951), Merrill Osmond (b. 1953), Jay Osmond (b. 1955) and **Donny Osmond** (b. 1957). The group first appeared on the top-rated *Andy Williams Show*. Initially known as the Osmond Brothers they recorded for Andy Williams' record label Barnaby. In 1971, they recorded 'One Bad Apple', which topped the US charts for five weeks. As a group, they enjoyed a string of hits, including 'Down By The Lazy River'. By the time Osmondmania hit the UK in 1972, the group peaked with their ecologically conscious 'Crazy Horses', complete with intriguing electric organ effects. Probably their most ambitious moment came with *The Plan*, in which they attempted to express their Mormon beliefs. Released at the height of their success, the album reached number 6 in the UK. Their sole UK number 1 as a group was 'Love Me For A Reason', composed by **Johnny Bristol**. The family group disbanded in 1980, but two years later, the older members of the group re-formed without Donny and moved into Country & Western.

OTWAY, JOHN

THE ENIGMATIC, MADCAP JOHN OTWAY (b. 1952) FIRST CAME TO PROMINENCE IN THE EARLY 70S WITH HIS guitar/fiddle-playing partner Wild Willie Barrett. Extensive gigging, highlighted by crazy stage antics, won Otway and Barrett a loyal collegiate following and finally a minor hit with 'Really Free' in 1977. Although Otway (with and without Barrett) soldiered on with syllable-stretching workouts such as 'Headbutts', he remains a 70s curio. *Premature Adulation* was Otway's first original album in 12 years.

OUTLAWS (USA)

FORMED IN FLORIDA, USA IN 1974. BILLY JONES (GUITAR), HENRY PAUL (GUITAR), HUGH THOMASSON (GUITAR/ songwriting), Monty Yoho (drums) and Frank O'Keefe (bass; replaced by Harvey Arnold in 1977) earned respect for their unreconstructed country rock. First signing to Arista, their 1975 debut album reached US number 13. The set included the riveting lengthy guitar battle 'Green Grass And High Tides', the highlight of their live act. A coast-to-coast tour in 1976 saw the arrival of second drummer, David Dix. *Bring It Back Alive* was the first album without Paul; his resignation was followed by those of Yoho and Arnold. In 1981, the band was on the edge of the US Top 20 with the title track of *Ghost Riders*. They disbanded shortly after *Los Hombres Malo*. Paul later rejoined Thomasson in a re-formed Outlaws who issued *Soldiers Of Fortune*.

OZRIC TENTACLES

PREDOMINANTLY A FESTIVAL BAND, OZRIC TENTACLES WAS ORIGINALLY A NAME CONJURED UP FOR A PSYCHEDELIC breakfast cereal. Ed Wynne (guitar), his brother Roly (bass), Nick 'Tig' Van Gelder (drums), Gavin Griffiths (guitar) and Joie 'Ozrooniculator' Hinton (keyboards) met at Stonehenge in 1982. By 1983, second synthesizer player, Tom Brookes, had joined; second percussionist Paul Hankin joined later. They became regulars at the psychedelic Club Dog in north London.

In 1984, Griffiths left; Brookes left in 1985 and in 1987 Merv Pepler replaced Van Gelder. Steve Everett later joined on synthesizers, while Marcus Carcus and John Egan added extra percussion and flute. Much of their work from the mid-80s onwards was made available on six cassette-only albums. The early 90s, British neo-hippy, new-age travellers explosion led to bands such as the Ozric Tentacles widening their audience. Hinton and Pepler left in 1994. New members Rad and Seaweed featured on *Become The Other* and *Curious Corn*.

PAGE, JIMMY

A GIFTED ROCK GUITARIST, PAGE (b. JAMES PATRICK PAGE, 1944) BEGAN HIS CAREER DURING THE EARLY 60S.

A member of several groups, he became a respected session musician, playing on releases by **Lulu** and **Them**, and on sessions for the **Kinks** and the **Who**. After releasing 'She Just Satisfies' (1965), he produced singles for **Nico** and **John Mayall**. Page joined the **Yardbirds** in 1966, staying with them until they split in 1968. He formed **Led Zeppelin**, for whom his riffs established the framework on tracks including 'Whole Lotta Love', 'When The Levee Breaks' and 'Achilles Last Stand'. His acoustic technique is featured on 'Black Mountain Side' and 'Tangerine'. His post-Led Zeppelin recordings have been ill-focused. He contributed to the soundtrack of *Death Wish II*, and collaborated with **Paul Rodgers** (ex-**Free**) in Firm. *Outrider* (1988) did much to re-establish his reputation with contributions from **Robert Plant** and Jason Bonham. *Coverdale/Page* (1993) was a successful but fleeting partnership with the former **Whitesnake** singer, but his reunion with Robert Plant for the ironically titled *Unledded* really captured the public's imagination. With **Sean 'Puffy' Combs**, Page provided music for the 1998 film *Godzilla*.

PALMER, ROBERT

PALMER (b. ALAN PALMER, 1949) JOINED THE MANDRAKE PADDLE STEAMER IN THE LATE 60S, THEN THE ALAN BOWN Set, followed by Dada, a jazz/rock unit featuring **Elkie Brooks**. Out of Dada came Vinegar Joe, with which he made three albums. He worked on *Sneakin' Sally Through The Alley* (1974), backed by the Meters and Lowell George.

Little Feat appeared on *Pressure Drop* after Palmer had relocated to the USA. He released *Some People Can Do What They Like* (1976) and then collaborated with **Gary Numan** on *Clues*. 'Johnny And Mary' sneaked into the UK charts and two years later 'Some Guys Have All The Luck' made the Top 20. He joined **Duran Duran**-based Power Station in 1985, but *Riptide* gave him his biggest solo success, making the UK Top 5 followed by US number 1 'Addicted To Love' (1986). *Heavy Nova* was accompanied by the hit 'She Makes My Day' in 1988. *Honey* was another credible release with tracks including 'Know By Now' and the title song.

PANTERA

TEXAN HEAVY-METAL QUARTET FORMED IN 1981. THEY COMPRISED TERRY GLAZE (GUITAR/VOCALS), DARRELL ABBOTT (guitar), Vince Abbott (drums) and Rex Rocker (bass). Drawing inspiration from **Kiss**, **Aerosmith** and **Deep Purple**, they debuted with *Metal Magic* (1983).

Projects In The Jungle indicated that they were building their own sound. *Power Metal* was the first album with Phil Anselmo on lead vocals, but lacked the depth and polish of previous efforts. However, a return to form was made with *Cowboys From Hell* and the following *Vulgar Display Of Power* and *Far Beyond Driven* were both major hits.

PARADISE LOST

FORMED IN YORKSHIRE IN 1981, THIS METAL QUINTET TOOK THEIR NAME FROM JOHN MILTON'S POEM. THEY COMPRISED Nick Holmes (b. 1970), Gregor Mackintosh (b. 1970; guitar), Aaron Aedy (b. 1969; guitar), Stephen Edmondson (b. 1969; bass) and Matthew Archer (b. 1970; drums). *Lost Paradise* was influenced by **Napalm Death** and *Gothic* saw a major innovation in the 'grindcore' genre. They found a wider audience with *Shades Of God* and gained a strong foothold on MTV before the release of *Icon* (1993). Before sessions for a fifth album began, Archer left, being replaced by Lee Morris, who joined in time for *Draconian Times*.

PARIS, MICA

HAVING WORKED WITH HEAVYWEIGHTS INCLUDING **PRINCE**, PARIS (b. MICHELLE WALLEN, 1969) REMAINS AN underrated UK talent. Her potential, however, has not yet been maximized. There are glimpses on her debut album when she matches the dexterity of **Courtney Pine**'s tenor sax on 'Like Dreamers Do'. Her second album used new producers as a remedy but a sense of frustration still pervades her career.

PAGE, JIMMY

Albums
Whatever Happened To Jugula (Beggars Banquet 1985)★★★
with Robert Plant
Unledded/No Quarter (Fontana 1994)★★★
➽ p.374 for full listings

Collaborators
Lulu ➽ p.219
Them ➽ p.319
Kinks ➽ p.207
Who ➽ p.338
Paul Rodgers ➽ p.280

Connections
Nico ➽ p.247
John Mayall ➽ p.228
Yardbirds ➽ p.345
Led Zeppelin ➽ p.213
Free ➽ p.154
Robert Plant ➽ p.262
Whitesnake ➽ p.337

Further References
Book: *Mangled Mind Archive: Jimmy Page*, Adrian T'Vell

PALMER, ROBERT

Albums
Riptide (Island 1985)★★★
Honey (EMI 1994)★★★
➽ p.374 for full listings

Collaborators
Elkie Brooks ➽ p.69
Little Feat ➽ p.216
Gary Numan ➽ p.249
Duran Duran ➽ p.127

Further References
Video: *Some Guys Have All The Luck* (Palace Video 1984)

PANTERA

Albums
Cowboys From Hell (Atco 1990)★★★★
Far Beyond Driven (East West 1994)★★★★
➽ p.374 for full listings

Influences
Kiss ➽ p.208
Aerosmith ➽ p.10
Deep Purple ➽ p.113

PARADISE LOST

Albums
Icon (Music For Nations 1993)★★★★
Draconian Times (Music For Nations 1995)★★★★
➽ p.374 for full listings

Influences
Napalm Death ➽ p.243

Further References
Video: *Harmony Breaks* (1994)

PARIS, MICA

Albums
So Good (4th & Broadway 1989)★★★
➽ p.374 for full listings

Collaborators
Courtney Pine ➽ p.261

Connections
Prince ➽ p.267

PARKER, GRAHAM
Albums
Mona Lisa's Sister (Demon 1988)★★★★
➽ p.374 for full listings
Collaborators
Brinsley Schwarz ➽ p.68

PARLIAMENT
Albums
The Clones Of Doctor Funkenstein (Casablanca 1976)★★★★
Motor-Booty Affair (Casablanca 1978)★★★★
➽ p.374 for full listings
Connections
George Clinton ➽ p.94
Frankie Lymon And The Teenagers ➽ p.220
Funkadelic ➽ p.156
Bootsy Collins ➽ p.98

PARSONS, ALAN
Albums
Tales Of Mystery And Imagination (Charisma 1975)★★★
➽ p.374 for full listings
Connections
Beatles ➽ p.38
Pink Floyd ➽ p.261

PARSONS, GRAM
Albums
G.P. (Reprise 1972)★★★★
Grievous Angel (Reprise 1973)★★★★
➽ p.374 for full listings
Collaborators
Emmylou Harris ➽ p.175
Connections
Byrds ➽ p.77
Flying Burrito Brothers ➽ p.148
Eagles ➽ p.130
Elvis Costello ➽ p.101
Further References
Books: *Gram Parsons: A Music Biography*, Sid Griffin (ed.).

PARTON, DOLLY
Albums
Jolene (RCA 1974)★★★★
Honky Tonk Angels (Columbia 1993)★★★★
➽ p.374 for full listings
Collaborators
Kenny Rogers ➽ p.280
Vince Gill ➽ p.162
Connections
Bee Gees ➽ p.41
Whitney Houston ➽ p.188
Further References
Book: *My Story*, Dolly Parton

PARKER, GRAHAM

R&B VOCALIST PARKER (b. 1950) MADE SEVERAL DEMOS OF HIS ORIGINAL SONGS, AND ONE CAME TO PRODUCER David Robinson's attention. A backing group, (the Rumour), was formed comprising **Brinsley Schwarz** (guitar/vocals), Bob Andrews (keyboards/vocals), Martin Belmont (guitar/vocals, ex-Ducks Deluxe), Andrew Bodnar (bass) and Steve Goulding (drums). Radio London DJ Charlie Gillett helped engender a recording deal and *Howlin' Wind* and *Heat Treatment* received great acclaim. Despite enjoying success with 'Hold Back The Night' (1978), his momentum stalled after divided critical opinion of *Stick To Me* and *The Parkerilla*, despite both reaching the UK Top 20. *Squeezing Out Sparks*, however, reclaimed former glories. *The Up Escalator* marked the end of Parker's partnership with the Rumour. *Mona Lisa's Sister* proved a dramatic return-to-form (1988). Ex-Rumour bassist Andrew Bodnar joined Steve Nieve (keyboards) and Pete Thomas (drums) for *Human Soul*, an ambitious album, indicating Parker's desire to expand the perimeters of his style. In early 1992 he signed to Capitol Records in the USA.

PARLIAMENT

THIS US VOCAL QUINTET FORMED IN 1955 BY **GEORGE CLINTON** (b. 1940), RAYMOND DAVIS (b. 1940), CALVIN Simon (b. 1942), Clarence 'Fuzzy' Haskins (b. 1941) and Grady Thomas (b. 1941). Clinton fashioned his first group, the Parliaments, after the influential **Frankie Lymon And The Teenagers**. The existing line-up first recorded as **Funkadelic** on Westbound Records, changing to Parliament after signing to the Invictus label. They released the eclectic *Osmium*, before their R&B hit, 'Breakdown'. The group's first single, 'Up For The Down Stroke', was more mainstream than Clinton's existing, more radical material. Parliament's success continued with 'Give Up The Funk (Tear The Roof Off The Sucker)' and 'Aqua Boogie (A Psychoalphadiscobetabioaquadoloop)', their hard-kicking funk being matched by a superlative horn section. Their last chart entry was 'Agony Of Defeet' in 1980, but the group continue to tour and record.

PARSONS, ALAN

RECORDING ENGINEER PARSONS (b. 1949) ATTRACTED ATTENTION FOR HIS WORK ON THE **BEATLES**' ALBUM, *Abbey Road*. His artist's reputation was established after contributions to **Pink Floyd**'s *Dark Side Of The Moon*. Parsons forged a partnership with songwriter Eric Woolfson, creating the Alan Parsons Project. *Tales Of Mystery And Imagination*, inspired by Edgar Allen Poe, set the pattern for future releases examining specific themes: science fiction (*I Robot*) and mysticism (*Pyramid*). Parsons and Woolfson created crafted, if sterile, work, calling on session men and guest performers.

PARSONS, GRAM

PARSONS' (b. CECIL INGRAM CONNOR, 1946, d. 1973) BRIEF BUT INFLUENTIAL CAREER BEGAN IN HIGH SCHOOL BAND, the Pacers. He joined the Shilos, modelled on the Journeymen, in 1963. The quartet moved to New York's Greenwich Village, but Parsons left in 1965. Inspired by the folk-rock boom, he founded the International Submarine Band with John Nuese (guitar), Ian Dunlop (bass) and Mickey Gauvin (drums). After two singles and a relocation to LA, Parsons was signed by producer Lee Hazelwood, but with Dunlop and Gauvin now absent from the line-up, Bob Buchanan (guitar) and Jon Corneal (drums) joined for *Safe At Home*. This is viewed as a landmark of country rock's development, blending standards with Parsons originals. By the time it was released, Gram accepted an offer to join the **Byrds**.

Sweetheart Of The Rodeo resulted, blending country and traditional styles – following *Safe At Home*'s mould – but buoyed by excellent harmony work. He then formed the **Flying Burrito Brothers** with ex-Byrd, Chris Hillman, 'Sneaky' Pete Kleinow (pedal-steel guitar) and bassist Chris Ethridge (bass). *The Gilded Palace Of Sin* drew inspiration from southern soul and urban-country music. *Burrito Deluxe* failed to scale the same heights and Parsons was fired in 1970 due to a growing drug dependency. In 1972 Parsons was introduced to **Emmylou Harris** and they completed *G.P.* A tour leading the Fallen Angels followed, but Parsons' self-destructive appetite remained. The set, *Grievous Angel*, blended favourites with original songs. Parsons' death in 1973 as a result of 'drug toxicity' and his desert cremation added to his legend. Parsons' influence on a generation of performers, from the **Eagles** to **Elvis Costello**, is a fitting testament to his talent.

PARTON, DOLLY

AFTER CHILDHOOD APPEARANCES AS A SINGING GUITARIST ON LOCAL RADIO, PARTON, (b. 1946) LEFT SCHOOL IN 1964. She signed to Monument in 1966, yielding a C&W hit, 'Dumb Blonde', as well as enlistment in the *Porter Wagoner Show*. Her country smashes included autobiographical 'Coat Of Many Colours'. She resigned from the show after success with solo 'Jolene'. Her post-1974 repertoire was less overtly country – 1979's 'Baby I'm Burning' was a lucrative stab at disco. In 1977 'Here You Come Again' crossed into the US pop Hot 100. She ventured into film acting, starring in 1981's *9 To 5 Rhinestone* and 1990's *Steel Magnolias*. She teamed up with **Kenny Rogers** in 1993 on 'Islands in the Stream', a **Bee Gees** composition, reaching the US number 1 and Top 10 in the UK. *Trio*, with **Ronstadt** and **Harris**, won a Grammy for best country album (1987). Her CBS debut, *Rainbow*, was poppy though 1989's *White Limozeen* retained the loyalty of her grass-roots following. 'Eagle When She Flies' confirmed her return to country in 1991. In 1992, **Whitney Houston** had a hit with Parton's composition 'I Will Always Love You'. Her 1995 album reprised the latter song as a duet with **Vince Gill**. *Treasures* paid tribute to singer-songwriters of the 60s and 70s.

PAT TRAVERS BAND

CANADIAN GUITARIST PAT TRAVERS MOVED TO LONDON, SETTING UP A GROUP CONSISTING OF PETER 'MARS' Cowling (bass) and drummer Roy Dyke. In 1977, Nicko McBrain, who subsequently joined **Iron Maiden**, replaced Dyke. Travers turned his talents to songwriting. Clive Edwards replaced McBrain, Michael Dycke adding another guitar. Guitarist Pat Thrall and Tommy Aldridge (drums), formerly of **Black Oak Arkansas**, joined to work on *Heat In The Street*. After the *Crash And Burn* tour, subsequent recordings featured Sandy Gennaro (drums) and Michael Shrieve (ex-**Santana**). In 1984, the line-up of Pat Marchino (drums), Barry Dunaway (bass), Jerry Riggs (guitar) and Travers released *Hot Shot*. In 1990, he released *School Of Hard Knocks*. A series of blues-orientated albums, including *Blues Tracks* and *Blues Magnet*, have been released in recent years.

PAUL, LES

PAUL (b. 1915) BEGAN BROADCASTING ON THE RADIO IN THE EARLY 30S AND IN 1936 WAS LEADING HIS own trio. Although his work had a strong country leaning, Paul was highly adaptable, frequently sitting in with jazz musicians. Dissatisfied with the sound of the guitars he played, he developed and designed a solid-bodied instrument at his own expense. Paul's dissatisfaction extended beyond the instrument and into the recording studios. Eager to experiment with a multi-tracking concept, he played multi-track guitar on a succession of recordings, among them 'Brazil' and 'Whispering'. During the 50s Paul continued with similar recordings, while his wife, Mary Ford (b. 1928, d. 1977), sang multiple vocal lines. 'Vaya Con Dios', gave them a US number 1 hit. Paul retired in the early 1960s, returning in the late 70s for two successful albums of duets with Chet Atkins, but by the end of the decade he had retired again. In 1984 he made a comeback to performing and continued to make sporadic appearances throughout the rest of the decade.

PAVEMENT

FORMED IN CALIFORNIA IN 1989, PAVEMENT WERE ORIGINALLY A DUO WITH STEVE MALKMUS (b. 1967; VOCALS, guitar) and Scott 'Spiral Stairs' Kannberg (b. 1967; guitar). They extended to a five-piece, adding Gary Young (b. *c.* 1954; percussion), Bob Nastanovich (b. 1968; drums) and Mark Ibold (b. 1967; bass). The attraction on their debut, *Slay Tracks (1933-1969)*, was Malkmus's observational lyrics. Steve West replaced Young, but they continued rising to the top of the US alternative scene. *Wowee Zowee!* was less accessible. By the time of *Brighten The Corners*, they were identified as an important influence on **Blur**.

PAXTON, TOM

PAXTON (b. 1937) MOVED TO NEW YORK IN THE 60S, BECOMING AN ASPIRING PERFORMER ON GREENWICH VILLAGE'S coffee-house circuit. Two topical song publications, *Sing Out!* and *Broadside*, published his compositions which bore a debt to **Pete Seeger** and Bob Gibson. Paxton signed to Elektra and he recorded his best-known work, *Ramblin' Boy*. Subsequent releases continued this mixture of romanticism, protest and children's songs. *Ain't That News* and *Morning Again* revealed a talent for satire and social comment. *The Things I Notice Now* and *Tom Paxton 6* enhanced Paxton's reputation. Paxton left Elektra during the early 70s, sustaining a loyal following. *How Come The Sun* showed Paxton was still capable of incisive songwriting – 'The Hostage' chronicled the massacre at Attica State Prison.

PEARL JAM

JEFF AMENT (b. 1963; BASS) AND STONE GOSSARD (b. 1966; RHYTHM GUITAR) FORMED THIS ROCK QUINTET IN Seattle in the early 90s. Gossard and Ament played with Mother Love Bone, fronted by Andrew Wood who later died from a heroin overdose. Mike McCready (b. 1965; guitar) and vocalist Eddie Vedder (b. 1966) hooked up with Ament and Gossard to become Pearl Jam, with the addition of drummer Dave Krusen. They signed to Epic in 1991, debuting with *Ten*, which remained in the US Top 20 a year and a half after its release. The following touring commitments brought Vedder to the verge of nervous collapse. Vedder would front a reunited **Doors** on their induction into the Rock 'N' Roll Hall Of Fame in Los Angeles. The eagerly awaited *Vitalogy*, a transatlantic chart-topper seemed overtly concerned with re-establishing the group's grass-roots credibility. There were also numerous references to the death of **Nirvana**'s Kurt Cobain. Drummer Dave Abbruzzese left the band in 1994. *No Code* featured more melody with grunge guitar replaced by steely acoustics. In 1998, they set out on a world tour.

PEEBLES, ANN

AN IMPROMPTU APPEARANCE AT THE ROSEWOOD CLUB, MEMPHIS, LED TO PEEBLES (b. 1947) SECURING A RECORDING contract. Producer Willie Mitchell fashioned an impressive debut single, 'Walk Away' (1969). Her work matured with 'I Can't Stand The Rain', written by Don Bryant, Peebles' husband and a songwriter of ability. 'If You Got The Time (I've Got The Love)' (1979) was her last R&B hit, but her work nonetheless remains amongst the finest in 70s soul. She returned to gospel in the mid-80s, bouncing back with *Call Me* (1990). In 1992 the back-to-the-Memphis-sound *Full Time Love* was issued.

PAT TRAVERS BAND

Albums
Radio Active (Polydor 1981)★★★
➧ p.374 for full listings

Connections
Iron Maiden ➧ p.193
Black Oak Arkansas ➧ p.51
Santana ➧ p.288

PAUL, LES

Albums
Bye, Bye Blues (Capitol 1952)★★★★
➧ p.374 for full listings

Further References
Book: *Les Paul: An American Original*, Mary Alice Shaughnessy

PAVEMENT

Albums
Perfect Sound Forever (Drag City 1991)★★★
Crooked Rain, Crooked Rain (Big Cat 1994)★★★
➧ p.374 for full listings

Connections
Blur ➧ p.58

PAXTON, TOM

Albums
The Things I Notice Now (Elektra 1969)★★★★
➧ p.374 for full listings

Influences
Pete Seeger ➧ p.291

Further References
Book: *Englebert The Elephant*, Tom Paxton and Steven Kellogg.

PEARL JAM

Albums
Ten (Epic 1991)★★★★
No Code (Epic 1996)★★★★
➧ p.374 for full listings

Connections
Kurt Cobain ➧ p.248

Influences
Nirvana ➧ p.248

Further References
Book: *Pearl Jam: The Illustrated Biography*, Brad Morrell

PEEBLES, ANN

Albums
The Handwriting On The Wall (Hi 1979)★★★
➧ p.374 for full listings

PEEL, JOHN
Connections
Velvet Underground ➽ p.329
Captain Beefheart And His Magic Band ➽ p.80
Pink Floyd ➽ p.261
Fleetwood Mac ➽ p.147
Marc Bolan ➽ p.59
Tyrannosaurus Rex ➽ p.316
Joy Division ➽ p.202
Fall ➽ p.142

PENDERGRASS, TEDDY
Albums
Teddy (Philadelphia International 1979)★★★★
T.P. (Philadelphia International 1980)★★★★
➽ p.374 for full listings
Connections
Harold Melvin And The Blue Notes ➽ p.231
Further References
Video: *Teddy Pendergrass Live* (Columbia-Fox 1988).

PENTANGLE
Albums
The Pentangle (Transatlantic 1968)★★★★
Basket Of Light (Transatlantic 1969)★★★★
➽ p.374 for full listings
Collaborators
John Martyn ➽ p.226
Connections
Alexis Korner ➽ p.210
Lindisfarne ➽ p.216
Cat Stevens ➽ p.309

PERE UBU
Albums
The Modern Dance (Blank 1977)★★★★
Dub Housing (Chrysalis 1978)★★★★
➽ p.374 for full listings
Influences
Captain Beefheart ➽ p.80

PERKINS, CARL
Albums
The Dance Album Of Carl Perkins (Sun 1957)★★★★
Hound Dog (Muskateer 1995)★★★
➽ p.374 for full listings
Collaborators
Roy Orbison ➽ p.252
Paul McCartney ➽ p.229
Ringo Starr ➽ p.307
Rosanne Cash ➽ p.84
Eric Clapton ➽ p.92
Connections
Sam Phillips ➽ p.260
Beatles ➽ p.38
Influences
Elvis Presley ➽ p.265
Further References
Film: *Jamboree a.k.a. Disc Jockey Jamboree* (1957)
Video: *This Country's Rockin'* (1993)
Book: *Discipline In Blue Suede Shoes*, Carl Perkins

PEEL, JOHN

PEEL (b. JOHN ROBERT PARKER RAVENSCROFT, 1939) MOVED TO THE USA DURING THE EARLY 60S, AND HIS MUSICAL knowledge resulted in a DJ's job on Oklahoma's KOMA station. In 1967, Peel returned to his native Britain, joining pirate-radio ship Radio London. His late-night *Perfumed Garden* programme on which he introduced the **Velvet Underground** and **Captain Beefheart** And His Magic Band brought him almost instant fame. Peel moved to Radio 1, taking control of *Top Gear* where he continued promoting 'new' music, including **Pink Floyd** and **Fleetwood Mac**. He established the Dandelion label, his closest ties remaining with **Marc Bolan** and **Tyrannosaurus Rex**. He promoted reggae and soul, before finding renewed enthusiasm with punk, broadcasting material by **Joy Division** and the **Fall**. The sole survivor of Radio 1's initial intake in 1967, Peel's shows still gnaw at the barriers of popular music.

PENDERGRASS, TEDDY

PENDERGRASS (b. THEODORE PENDERGRASS, 1950) JOINED **HAROLD MELVIN AND THE Blue Notes** in 1969 as drummer, becoming feature vocalist within a year. His passionate interpretations brought distinction to their material. Clashes with Melvin led to a split and in 1976 Pendergrass embarked on a solo career. 'The Whole Town's Laughing At Me' (1977) and 'Turn Off The Lights' (1979) stand among the best of his early work. A near-fatal car accident in 1982 left him confined to a wheelchair, although his voice was intact. 'It Should've Been You' (1991) reinstated him in people's minds as a major artist.

PENTANGLE

FORMED IN 1967, PENTANGLE WAS INSPIRED BY FOLK ALBUM *BERT AND JOHN*. VOCALIST JACQUI McShee (b. *c.* 1946) joined Danny Thompson (b. 1939; bass) and Terry Cox (drums), both of **Alexis Korner**'s Blues Incorporated, in a quintet which also embraced blues and jazz. *The Pentangle* captured their talents, where the acoustic interplay between Jansch and Renbourn was underscored by Thompson's sympathetic support and McShee's soaring intonation. Their eclectism was expanded on *Sweet Child*, while they enjoyed commercial success with *Basket Of Light*, which included 'Light Flight'. Pentangle disbanded in 1972, following which Thompson began a partnership with **John Martyn**. The original Pentangle reconvened the following year for a European tour and *Open The Door*. McShee, Cox and Jansch were joined by Nigel Portman-Smith (bass) and Mike Piggott for 1986's *In The Round*. Gerry Conway and Rod Clemens (ex-**Lindisfarne**) replaced Cox and Piggott for *So Early In The Spring* (1988). *Think Of Tomorrow*, saw Clements make way for guitarist Peter Kirtley. This line-up completed *One More Road* and *Live*. Jansch became distracted by solo projects and in later shows was replaced by Alun Davies (former **Cat Stevens**' guitarist). Renbourne and McShee celebrated 30 years of playing together with concerts in spring 1996.

PERE UBU

FORMED CLEVELAND, OHIO IN 1975, PERE UBU'S INITIAL LINE-UP COMPRISED DAVID THOMAS (VOCALS), PETER Laughner (d. 1977; guitar), Tom Herman (guitar, bass, organ), Tim Wright (guitar, bass), Allen Ravenstine (synthesizer, saxophone) and Scott Krauss (drums), who completed '30 Seconds Over Tokyo'. Ravenstine, Wright and Laughner left, but bassist Tony Maimone joined Thomas, Herman and Krauss before Ravenstine returned to complete the most innovative version of the group: *The Modern Dance* was exceptional. Rhythmically, the group was reminiscent of **Captain Beefheart**'s Magic Band with Thomas' compelling vocals. *Dub Housing* and *New Picnic Time* maintained this sense of adventure. Guitarist Mayo Thompson replaced Herman in 1979. *The Age Of Walking* was deemed obtuse, and Krauss left. Anton Fier (ex-Feelies) joined Pere Ubu for the *Song Of The Bailing Man*, following the release of *The Sound Of The Sand*, Thomas's first solo album. Thomas released five further solo albums and by 1985 Maimone and Raventine were working with his new group, the Wooden Birds. Krauss sparked a Pere Ubu reunion, appearing for an encore during a Cleveland concert, and by late 1987 the Ubu name was reinstated. Jim Jones (guitar) and Chris Cutler (drums) completed the new line-up for *The Tenement Year*. Cutler and Ravenstine left after *Cloudland*, the latter being replaced by Eric Drew Feldman. *Ray Gun Suitcase* was the first album Thomas produced.

PERKINS, CARL

AMERICAN CARL PERKINS (b. CARL LEE Perkins, 1932, d. 1998) was author of 'Blue Suede Shoes' and one of the most renowned rock-abilly artists recording for Sun in the 50s. In 1953 Carl, brothers Jay and Clayton and drummer W.S. 'Fluke' Holland formed a hillbilly band, playing in Tennessee bars. His technique, borrowed from black musicians, set Perkins apart from many contemporary country guitarists.

After hearing an **Elvis Presley** record in 1954, Perkins decided to pursue a musical career and the Perkins brothers travelled to Memphis to audition for **Sam Phillips** at Sun. Although not initially impressed, he saw their potential. After Phillips sold Presley's Sun contract to RCA, he decided to push Perkins' single, 'Blue Suede Shoes'. It entered the US chart on 3 March 1956 (the day Presley's first single entered the chart), by which time several cover versions had been recorded by various artists. Perkins' version became a huge hit, being the first country record to appear on both R&B and pop charts, in addition to the country chart.

As Perkins began enjoying the fruits of his labour, he and his band were involved in a severe road accident. 'Blue Suede Shoes' became number 2 in the pop chart, a number 1 country hit and an R&B number 2 but, as Perkins was unable to promote the record, the momentum was lost – none of his four future chart singles climbed as high. 'Blue Suede Shoes' was Perkins' only chart single in the UK, being upstaged commercially by Presley's cover. Perkins continued recording for Sun until mid-1958, but 'Boppin' The Blues' only reached number 70, and 'Your True Love', number 67. While at Sun, Perkins recorded numerous rockabilly tracks: 'Everybody's Trying To Be My Baby' and 'Matchbox', both covered by the **Beatles**. In December 1956, Perkins, **Jerry Lee Lewis** and Presley joined in an impromptu jam session at Sun, released two decades later as 'The Million Dollar Quartet'.

In 1958, Perkins signed with Columbia with whom he recorded some good songs, although only 'Pink Pedal Pushers' and 'Pointed Toe Shoes' had any chart success. Later that year Jay Perkins died of a brain tumour and Carl became an alcoholic.

Perkins signed with Decca (1963), touring outside of the USA 1963-64 and met the Beatles while in Britain, watching as they recorded his songs. In 1967, he joined **Johnny Cash**'s band as guitarist and was allotted a guest singing spot during all Cash's concerts and television shows. By 1970, Perkins was back on Columbia, signing with Mercury in 1974. Late that year, Clayton committed suicide and their father died. Perkins left Cash in 1976, going on tour with a band consisting of his two sons, with whom he was still performing in the 90s. In the 80s, Perkins recorded *The Survivors* with Cash and Lewis, and another with Cash, Lewis and **Roy Orbison** in 1986. Much of the 80s he spent working with younger musicians, namely **Paul McCartney** and the Stray Cats. In 1985, he starred in a television-special marking the 30th anniversary of 'Blue Suede Shoes', with **Harrison**, **Ringo Starr**, **Dave Edmunds**, two members of the Stray Cats, **Rosanne Cash** and **Eric Clapton**. In 1987, Perkins was elected to the Rock 'N' Roll Hall Of Fame. He died of a heart attack in January 1998.

PERRY, LEE

'LITTLE' LEE PERRY (b. RAINFORD HUGH PERRY, 1936, AKA SCRATCH AND THE UPSETTER) BEGAN HIS CAREER working for producer **Coxsone Dodd** during the late 50s and early 60s, organizing recording sessions and supervising auditions at Dodd's record shop in Kingston, Jamaica. By 1963 Perry had released his own vocal record – a bluesy, declamatory vocal style over superb backing from the Skatalites, setting a pattern from which Perry rarely deviated.

In 1966 Perry fell out with Dodd and began working with other producers including JJ Johnson, Clancy Eccles and Joe Gibbs, for whom he wrote songs and produced artists such as Errol Dunkley, and the Pioneers. On parting with Gibbs, Perry recorded several titles, including 'People Funny Boy' (1968). In 1968 he set up his own Upsetter label in Jamaica, and had hits with David Isaacs ('Place In The Sun') and the Untouchables ('Tighten Up').

Perry's first UK success was with tenor saxophonist Val Bennett's 'Return Of Django', which spent three weeks at number 5 in the charts during 1969. He also began producing the **Wailers** on records including 'Small Axe', 'Duppy Conqueror' and 'Soul Rebel'.

From 1972-74 Perry consolidated his position as one of Jamaica's leading musical innovators, releasing instrumentals like 'French Connection', 'Black Ipa', and DJ tracks by artists including U-Roy, Dillinger, Dr. Alimantado, I Roy and Charlie Ace.

In 1974 Perry opened a studio (the Black Ark) in Jamaica, scoring a hit with Junior Byles' 'Curly Locks'. His production of Susan Cadogan's 'Hurt So Good' reached number 4 in the UK charts (1975). From 1975 he began to employ studio technology – phase shifters and rudimentary drum machines, producing an instantly recognizable style. By 1976, Island began to release the fruits of this phase, including the Heptones' (*Party Time*), **Bob Marley** And The Wailers ('Jah Live', 'Punky Reggae Party'), George Faith (*To Be A Lover*), Junior Murvin (*Police & Thieves*) and the Upsetters (*Super Ape*).

Perry's behaviour became increasingly strange and bewildering due to infrequent commercial success, and in 1980 he destroyed his studio and left for Britain. Since then he has made a long series of eccentric solo albums, with his earlier work receiving critical and cult attention at the same time. Whatever the future holds, he has made one of the most individual contributions to the development of Jamaican music, both as producer/arranger/writer, and simply as a singularly powerful guiding force during several crucial phases.

PET SHOP BOYS

FORMED IN 1981, THIS UK POP DUO FEATURED NEIL TENNANT (b. 1954; VOCALS) AND CHRIS LOWE (b. 1959; keyboards). Lowe had previously played in a cabaret group, One Under The Eight, while Tennant was employed as a journalist on UK pop magazine *Smash Hits*. In 1984, they issued the Bobby 'O' Orlando-produced 'West End Girls', which passed unnoticed. After being dropped from Epic Records, they were picked up by EMI/Parlophone. In 1986, the re-released 'West End Girls' topped the UK and US charts. *Please* consolidated their position in 1986 and, in 1987, the duo returned to number 1 with 'It's A Sin'. The quality of their melodies was evident in the successful collaboration with **Dusty Springfield** on 'What Have I Done To Deserve This?' which reached number 2. After another well-received album, *Actually*, the group featured in a disappointing film, *It Couldn't Happen Here*. *Introspective* spawned further hits including 'Left To My Own Devices'. A surprise collaboration with Liza Minnelli gave her a hit with 'Results'. In 1991, the group issued the compilation *Discography*. *Alternative* was a double CD of b-sides which demonstrated their pioneering sound in 'leftfield dance pop'.

PERRY, LEE

Albums
Scratch The Upsetter Again (1970)★★★★
Revolution Dub (Cactus 1975)★★★★
➧ p.374 for full listings

Connections
Coxsone Dodd ➧ p.121
Bob Marley and the Wailers ➧ p.225

Further References
Video: *The Ultimate Destruction* (1992)

PET SHOP BOYS

Albums
Actually (Parlophone 1987)★★★★
Behaviour (Parlophone 1990)★★★★
➧ p.374 for full listings

Collaborators
Dusty Springfield ➧ p.305

PETER AND GORDON

PETER ASHER (b. 1944) AND GORDON WALLER (b. 1945) HAD A CRUCIAL ADVANTAGE OVER THEIR CONTEMPORARIES – **Paul McCartney**'s patronage; McCartney was then dating Peter's sister, Jane. 'A World Without Love' quickly became a transatlantic chart-topper. The **Beatle**-connection was evident on 'Woman', which McCartney composed under the pseudonym Bernard Webb. The duo covered **Buddy Holly**'s 'True Love Ways' and the Teddy Bears' retitled 'To Know You Is To Love You'. The partnership was strained by late 1966, but 'Lady Godiva' provided new direction. One year later, they split. Waller pursued an unsuccessful solo career while Asher became a formidable producer and manager.

Further References
Books: *Pet Shop Boys: Introspective*, Michael Crowton

PETER AND GORDON

Albums
Somewhere (Columbia 1966)★★★
➧ p.375 for full listings

Connections
Peter Asher ➧ p.22
Paul McCartney ➧ p.229
Buddy Holly ➧ p.184

Influences
Beatles ➧ p.38

PETER, PAUL AND MARY
Albums
Peter, Paul And Mary (Warners 1962)★★★★
In The Wind (Warners 1963)★★★★
➡ p.375 for full listings
Collaborators
Laura Nyro ➡ p.249
Paul Butterfield ➡ p.76
Mike Bloomfield ➡ p.54
Al Kooper ➡ p.210
Connections
Bob Dylan ➡ p.128
Further References
Video: *Lifelines* (Warner Reprise 1996)

PETTY, TOM, AND THE HEARTBREAKERS
Albums
You're Gonna Get It (Shelter 1978)★★★★
Southern Accents (MCA 1985)★★★★
➡ p.375 for full listings

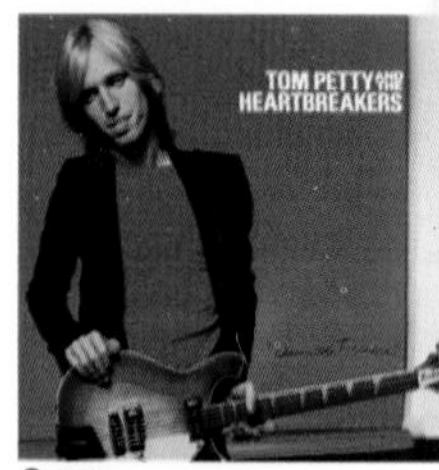

Collaborators
Jeff Lynne ➡ p.220
George Harrison ➡ p.176
Roy Orbison ➡ p.252
Connections
Roger McGuinn ➡ p.229
Del Shannon ➡ p.294
Traveling Wilburys ➡ p.323
Influences
Byrds ➡ p.77

PHAIR, LIZ
Albums
Whip-Smart (Matador 1994)★★★★
➡ p.375 for full listings

PhD
Albums
Is It Safe ? (Warners 1983)★★
➡ p.375 for full listings

PHILLIPS, SAM
Collaborators
Howlin' Wolf ➡ p.189
B.B. King ➡ p.205
Elvis Presley ➡ p.265
Carl Perkins ➡ p.258
Jerry Lee Lewis ➡ p.215

PHISH
Albums
A Live One (Elektra 1995)★★★★
Billy Breathes (Elektra 1996)★★★★
➡ p.375 for full listings
Influences
Grateful Dead ➡ p.167

PETER, PAUL AND MARY

PETER YARROW (b. 1938), NOEL PAUL STOOKEY (b. 1937) AND MARY ALLIN TRAVERS (b. 1937) BEGAN PERFORMING together in 1961. The group's versions of **Bob Dylan**'s 'Blowin' In The Wind' and 'Don't Think Twice, It's Alright' both made the Top 10. They were also renowned for singing children's songs, 'Puff The Magic Dragon' being the most memorable. Their greatest success was 'Leaving On A Jet Plane' (1969) which reached number 1 in the US and number 2 in the UK, but by then the individual members were going in different directions. Yarrow was the primary force behind *You Are What You Eat*, an eccentric hippie film and in 1970 he, Travers and Stookey embarked on solo careers. They reunited briefly in 1972 for a George McGovern Democratic Party rally, and again in 1978. They have since continued to perform material reminiscent of their golden era.

PETTY, TOM, AND THE HEARTBREAKERS

THE HEARTBREAKERS FORMED IN 1971 AND COMPRISED TOM PETTY (b. 1953; GUITAR), MIKE CAMPBELL (b. 1954; guitar), Benmont Tench (b. 1954; keyboards), Stan Lynch (b. 1955; drums) and Ron Blair (b. 1952; bass). With a Rickenbacker guitar and a **Roger McGuinn** voice, Petty's eponymous debut was accepted more in England where anything **Byrds**-like would find an audience. He released *You're Gonna Get It* and *Damn The Torpedoes* followed, during which time he filed for bankruptcy. His cash-flow soon improved as the album went platinum. During the recording of

Southern Accents Petty smashed his hand on the recording console and had to have a metal splint permanently fixed as the bones were too badly broken. The album became another million-seller. The live *Pack Up The Plantation* delighted old fans, but failed to break any new ground. In 1988 **Jeff Lynne** and Petty together with **George Harrison**, **Roy Orbison** and Dylan, formed the **Traveling Wilburys**. Lynne's over-crisp production was evident on *Full Moon Fever* (a solo project) and *Into The Great Wide Open*. A greatest hits album was released in 1993 and became a huge hit in his homeland. This new wave of success inspired *Wildflowers*. Drummer Steve Ferrone replaced Stan Lynch and together with Howie Epstein (bass) they bolstered the permanent band members of Petty, Tench and Campbell into a strong live band.

PHAIR, LIZ

PHAIR (b. 1967) WAS BROUGHT UP IN CHICAGO, ILLINOIS. AT COLLEGE IN OHIO SHE BECAME INVOLVED IN THE LOCAL music scene, soon moving to San Francisco with guitarist friend Chris Brokaw. Phair signed with Matador in the summer of 1992. Ignoring traditional song structures, her approach allowed her to empower her confessional, and occasionally abusive, lyrics. With Casey Rice (guitar) and LeRoy Bach (bass) complementing her playing, Phair produced *Exile In Guyville*, which was widely acclaimed. *Whip-Smart* was a more polished set. The same reception was not given to *Juvenilia*, a stopgap collection of her early recordings.

PHD

THIS UK POP DUO COMPRISED JIM DIAMOND (VOCALS) AND TONY HYMAS (KEYBOARDS). THEIR DEBUT ALBUM included 'I Won't Let You Down', which initially failed to chart. An extra push from WEA paid off when it reached number 3 in the UK charts, with repeated success in Europe. Their second and final album was not successful, and they went their separate ways. Diamond signed a solo deal with A&M, finding further chart success.

PHILLIPS, SAM

PHILLIPS (b. 1923) WAS A RADIO DJ BEFORE OPENING SAM'S MEMPHIS RECORDING STUDIO IN 1950. PHILLIPS' MAIN ambition was to record local blues acts and license the resultant masters. **Howlin' Wolf** and **B.B. King** were among the many acts Phillips produced. Phillips founded Sun Records in 1952, which flourished when Rufus Thomas scored a hit with 'Bear Cat'. Phillips looked to expand the label's horizons by recording country acts, and his wish to find a white singer comfortable with R&B was answered with **Elvis Presley**'s arrival in 1954. The singer's five Sun singles rank among pop's greatest achievements, and helped Phillips further the careers of **Carl Perkins** and **Jerry Lee Lewis**. Phillips' simple recording technique defined classic rockabilly. By the beginning of the 60s new Memphis-based studios, Stax and Hi Records, challenged Sun's pre-eminent position. In 1969 he sold the entire Sun empire to country entrepreneur Shelby Singleton, thus effectively ending an era.

PHISH

COMPRISING TREY ANASTASIO (VOCALS/GUITAR), PAGE McCONNELL (KEYBOARDS/VOCALS), MIKE GORDON (bass/vocals) and Jon Fishman (drums/vocals), Phish were founded in 1983 in New England, USA. They took shape after McConnell's recruitment in 1985 and drawing from jazz, funk, bluegrass, country, punk and pop, and their music soon attracted a following. *Junta* captured their free-flowing improvisations, while *Lawn Boy* was a structured approach to their cross-genre experiments. After *A Picture Of Nectar*, several critics drew comparisons with the **Grateful Dead**. *Hoist* doubled the sales achieved by the enjoyable *Rift*. *Billy Breathes* was assured and relaxed.

PICKETT, BOBBY 'BORIS'

PICKETT (b. 1940) MOVED TO LA IN 1961 AND JOINED A SINGING GROUP CALLED THE CORDIALS. PICKETT AND THE Cordials' Leonard Capizzi wrote 'Monster Mash' to cash in on the dance craze that Dee Dee Sharp's 'Mashed Potato Time' launched in 1962. 'Monster Mash' reached the top of the US charts in time for Halloween 1962, but did not reach the UK charts until 1973, when it reached number 3. It was also successfully covered by the UK group the **Bonzo Bog Doo-Dah Band**.

PICKETT, WILSON

PICKETT (b. 1941) SANG IN SEVERAL DETROIT R&B GROUPS BEFORE JOINING THE FALCONS (ALREADY ESTABLISHED BY the million-selling 'You're So Fine'). Pickett wrote and sang lead on their 1962 hit 'I Found A Love', after which he launched his solo career. In 1964 Pickett signed to Atlantic, forming a partnership with guitarist **Steve Cropper** on 'In The Midnight Hour', 'Mustang Sally' (both 1966) and 'Funky Broadway' (1967). Other collaborators included former **Valentino**, **Bobby Womack**. *The Midnight Mover* contained six songs featuring Womack's involvement. A version of 'Hey Jude', with Duane Allman on guitar, was the highlight of recording sessions at Fame's Muscle Shoals studio. The hits, 'Engine Number 9' (1970) and 'Don't Let The Green Grass Fool You' (1971), resulted from working with producers **Gamble And Huff**. Wilson switched to RCA in 1972, but his previous success was hard to regain. He has worked alongside **Joe Tex**, **Don Covay**, **Ben E. King** and **Solomon Burke** in a revamped Soul Clan.

PINE, COURTNEY

BRITISH PERFORMER, PINE (b. 1964), WAS WITH DWARF STEPS, BEFORE JOINING REGGAE STARS CLINT EASTWOOD AND General Saint. In 1986 he was involved in setting up the Jazz Warriors and came to wider public notice after playing with Charlie Watts's Orchestra, and with Art Blakey at the Camden Jazz Festival. After appearing in the Nelson Mandela 70th Birthday Concert he become much in demand for film and television, and appeared on the soundtrack of *Angel Heart*. His quartet comprised of Kenny Kirkland (piano), Charnett Moffett (bass) and Marvin 'Smitty' Smith (drums). He has also continued to play in reggae and other pop contexts (*Closer To Home*), and frequently collaborates with **Mica Paris**. *Modern Day Jazz Stories* showed a strong rap/hip-hop influence and featured a funky support trio of Ronnie Burrage (drums), Charnett Moffett (bass) and Geri Allen (piano).

PINK FLOYD

PINK FLOYD DEVELOPED AT CAMBRIDGE HIGH SCHOOL, WHERE ROGER KEITH **'SYD' BARRETT** (b. 1946; GUITAR/vocals), **Roger Waters** (b. 1944; bass/vocals) and Dave Gilmour (b. 1944; guitar/vocals) were pupils and friends. On leaving, Waters formed R&B-based Sigma 6 with Nick Mason (b. 1945; drums) and Rick Wright (b. 1945; keyboards). The early line-up included bassist Clive Metcalfe, who was replaced by Bob Close (lead guitar). They fell apart at the end of 1965. Barrett, Waters, Mason and Wright reconvened as Pink Floyd, a name inspired by Georgia blues musicians Pink Anderson and Floyd Council.

By December 1966 the group was appearing regularly at the UFO Club, spearheading Britain's psychedelic movement with improvised sets and a highly visual lightshow. A recording deal was struck with EMI. Their singles were surprisingly different to their live sound, featuring Barrett's quirky melodies and lyrics. 'See Emily Play' reached number 6 in 1967. It was succeeded by *The Piper At The Gates Of Dawn*, encapsulating Britain's 'Summer of Love'. A disastrous US tour wrought unbearable pressure on Barrett's fragile psyche. His indulgence in hallucinogenic drugs exacerbated such problems and his colleagues brought Dave Gilmour into the line-up in 1968. Plans for Syd to maintain a backroom role failed and he left the following April.

The realigned Pink Floyd completed *A Saucerful Of Secrets*. It featured 'Jugband Blues', as well as two songs which became an integral part of their live concerts, the title track and 'Set The Controls For The Heart Of The Sun'. Film soundtrack, *More*, allowed Waters to flex compositional muscles.

Atom Heart Mother was an experiment, partially written with composer Ron Geesin. It featured the first in a series of impressive album covers, designed by the Hipgnosis studio. The seemingly abstract image of *Meddle* is a macro lens shot of an ear. The album contained some classics: 'One Of These Days' and 'Echoes'. Pink Floyd's talent finally exploded in 1973 with *Dark Side Of The Moon*. It became one of the biggest-selling records of all time, currently in excess of 25 million copies. Its run on the *Billboard* chart spanned over a decade, ridding the group of the spectre of Barrett's era. The moving eulogy to Barrett, 'Shine On You Crazy Diamond', was one of the high points of *Wish You Were Here*. *Animals* featured a scathing attack on the 'clean-up television' campaigner, Mary Whitehouse, while the cover photograph of an inflatable pig over Battersea power station, has passed into Pink Floyd folklore. Wright and Gilmour both released solo albums in 1978 amidst rumours of a break-up. They released *The Wall* (1979), a Waters-dominated epic, second only to *Dark Side Of The Moon* in terms of sales. It contained 'Another Brick In The Wall', which restored them to the British singles' chart, and provided them with their sole number 1 hit.

This did not stop Pink Floyd's internal hostility, and Wright left in 1979. Waters totally dominated *The Final Cut*, which comprised songs written for *The Wall*, which the group rejected. Mason's contributions were negligible, Gilmour showed little interest and Pink Floyd's fragmentation was evident to all.

In 1987 Mason and Gilmour decided to work together under the Pink Floyd banner and Rick Wright returned. *A Momentary Lapse Of Reason* sounded more like a Pink Floyd album than its sombre 'predecessor'. A live set, *Delicate Sound Of Thunder* followed, and touring rekindled Wright and Mason's confidence. Waters led an all-star cast for an adaptation of *The Wall*, performed live on the remains of the Berlin Wall in 1990. In 1994 his former colleagues released the accomplished *The Division Bell*. Critical praise confirmed they had survived the loss of yet another 'crucial' member. The legacy of those 'faceless' record sleeves is irrefutable; Pink Floyd's music is somehow greater than the individuals creating it.

PITNEY, GENE

AMERICAN-BORN PITNEY (b. 1941) BEGAN RECORDING IN 1959, FINDING SUCCESS AS A SONGWRITER, PROVIDING **Roy Orbison** with 'Today's Teardrops' and **Bobby Vee** with 'Rubber Ball'. His solo recording career took off in 1961 with 'Town Without Pity' and 'The Man Who Shot Liberty Valance'. In 1963, Pitney toured Britain, and '24 Hours From Tulsa' reached the Top 5. Despite the onslaught of the beat groups, Pitney's big ballads remained popular. Hits from this era included 'I'm Gonna Be Strong' and 'Something's Gotten Hold Of My Heart', which he and **Marc Almond** had success with in 1988, when it topped the UK charts.

PIXIES

THIS GROUP FORMED IN BOSTON, MASSACHUSETTS, BY CHARLES MICHAEL Kittridge Thompson IV aka Black Francis (vocals/guitar) and Joey Santiago (guitar). Kim Deal joined as bassist, introducing drummer David Lovering. Originally known as Pixies In Panoply, they secured a recording contract with 4AD Records. *Come On Pilgrim* introduced an abrasive sound and Francis's oblique lyrics. *Surfer Rosa* exaggerated its predecessor's fury, and *Doolittle* scaled the national Top 10. *Bossanova* blended pure pop and sheer ferocity. *Trompe Le Monde* was even harsher than preceding albums. Following the rechristened **Frank Black**'s departure in early 1993 the band folded. The CD compilation, *Death To The Pixies*, confirmed their lasting influence.

PICKETT, BOBBY 'BORIS'
Albums
The Original Monster Mash (Garpax 1962)★★
➧ p.375 for full listings
Connections
Bonzo Bog Doo-Dah Band ➧ p.61

PICKETT, WILSON
Albums
The Exciting Wilson Pickett (Atlantic 1966)★★★★ *The The Sound Of Wilson Pickett* (Atlantic 1967)★★★★
➧ p.375 for full listings

Collaborators
Steve Cropper ➧ p.105
Bobby Womack ➧ p.342
Connections
Valentinos ➧ p.328
Gamble And Huff ➧ p.158
Joe Tex ➧ p.319
Don Covay ➧ p.102
Ben E. King ➧ p.205

PINE, COURTNEY
Albums
To The Eyes Of Creation (Island 1992)★★★★
➧ p.375 for full listings
Collaborators
Mica Paris ➧ p.256

PINK FLOYD
Albums
Dark Side Of The Moon (Harvest 1973)★★★★★
The Wall (Harvest 1979)★★★★
➧ p.375 for full listings
Connections
Syd Barrett ➧ p.33
Roger Waters ➧ p.334
Further References
Video: *Delicate Sound Of Thunder* (Columbia 1994)
Book: *Pink Floyd: Bricks In The Wall*, Karl Dallas.

PITNEY, GENE
Albums
Just One Smile (Musicor 1967)★★★★
➧ p.375 for full listings
Collaborators
Marc Almond ➧ p.15
Connections
Roy Orbison ➧ p.252
Bobby Vee ➧ p.329

PIXIES
Albums
Doolittle (4AD 1989)★★★★
➧ p.375 for full listings
Connections
Breeders ➧ p.67
Frank Black ➧ p.50

PIZZICATO FIVE
Albums
Made In USA (Matador 1995)★★★★
➧ p.375 for full listings

PJ HARVEY
Albums
To Bring You My Love (Island 1995)★★★★
➧ p.375 for full listings
Connections
Captain Beefheart ➧ p.80
Tom Waits ➧ p.332

PLANT, ROBERT
Albums
with Jimmy Page *No Quarter* (Fontana 1994)★★★★
➧ p.375 for full listings
Collaborators
Led Zeppelin ➧ p.213
Connections
Jimmy Page ➧ p.255
Honeydrippers ➧ p.185
Jeff Beck ➧ p.40
Influences
Motown ➧ p.240

PLANXTY
Albums
The Well Below The Valley (Polydor 1973)★★★★
➧ p.375 for full listings
Connections
Christy Moore ➧ p.237
Paul Brady ➧ p.66
Bob Dylan ➧ p.128

PLATTERS
Albums
The Platters (Federal 1955)★★★★
➧ p.375 for full listings
Further References
Film: *Carnival Rock* (1957)

PM DAWN
Albums
The Bliss Album ...? (Vibrations Of Love & Anger & The Ponderance Of Life & Existence) (Island 1993)★★★★
➧ p.375 for full listings
Collaborators
Boy George ➧ p.65
Connections
Kool And The Gang ➧ p.209

POCO
Albums
Head Over Heels (ABC 1975)★★★★
➧ p.375 for full listings
Connections
Buffalo Springfield ➧ p.305
Eagles ➧ p.130

POGUES
Albums
Rum, Sodomy And The Lash (Stiff 1985)★★★★
➧ p.375 for full listings
Collaborators
Clash ➧ p.93
Elvis Costello ➧ p.101
Kirsty MacColl ➧ p.221
Connections
Steeleye Span ➧ p.308

PIZZICATO FIVE

PIZZICATO FIVE, A UNION OF JAPANESE FASHION MODELS AND SATIRISTS, WERE STARTED BY YASUHARU KONISHI (b. 1959, Japan) in 1984. He was joined by vocalist Maki Nomiya (b. *c.* 1965; vocals) in 1990. Song titles like 'Audrey Hepburn Complex' indicated fascination with retro-chic, leading to 'Twiggy Twiggy''s inclusion on the soundtrack of *Pret-A-Porter*. A compilation album, *Made In USA*, followed. A second album compiled from previous Japanese material, *The Sound Of Music By Pizzicato Five*, included 'Happy Sad'. The band was reduced to the nucleus of Maki and Konishi in mid-1996.

HARVEY, PJ

HARVEY (b. POLLY JEAN HARVEY, 1970) PLAYED SAXOPHONE WITH BOULOGNE BEFORE WRITING HER FIRST SONGS AS part of the Polekats. She joined Automatic Dlamini, contributing saxophone, guitar and vocals, before moving to London, where she worked with bass player Ian Olliver and drummer and backing vocalist Rob Ellis (b. 1962). They first played live in 1991, using the name PJ Harvey. Too Pure Records financed the debut 'Dress'; Olliver was replaced by Stephen Vaughan (b. 1962) on 'five-string fretless bass', after the record's release. 'Dress' and *Dry* caught Island Records' attention. *Rid Of Me* was a vicious stew of rural blues. Its follow-up was forced to lower the extremity threshold. For *To Bring You My Love*, Harvey introduced a haunting ambience. Her band now consisted of guitarist John Parrish (another former colleague from Automatic Dlamini), Jean-Marc Butty (drums), Nick Bagnall (keyboards/bass), Joe Gore (guitar, ex-**Tom Waits**' band) and Eric Feldman (keyboards). She then collaborated with Parish on 1996's theatrical *Dance Hall At Louse Point*.

PLANT, ROBERT

PLANT'S (b. 1948) EARLY CAREER WAS SPENT IN SEVERAL MIDLANDS-BASED R&B BANDS. IN 1965 PLANT JOINED Listen, a **Motown**-influenced act, and signed to CBS. He started his solo career with 'Laughing, Crying, Laughing' and 'Long Time Coming' (both 1967). After Page's Band of Joy split in 1968, **Jimmy Page** invited him to join **Led Zeppelin**. Plant's reputation was forged during this time, but he renewed his solo career following John Bonham's death in 1980. *Pictures At Eleven* unveiled a new partnership with Robbie Blunt (guitar), Paul Martinez (bass) and Jezz Woodruffe (keyboards). *The Principle Of Moments* contained the UK/US Top 20 hit, 'Big Log' (1983). Plant featured in the **Honeydrippers**, which included Page, **Jeff Beck** and Nile Rodgers. Robert fashioned the less conventional *Shaken 'N' Stirred*, and resumed recording in 1987. *Now And Zen* was hailed as a dramatic return to form. His artistic rejuvenation continued on *Manic Nirvana* and *Fate Of Nations*, after which he joined Jimmy Page for the *Unledded/No Quarter* project.

PLANXTY

THIS IRISH GROUP FEATURED **CHRISTY MOORE** (b. 1945; GUITAR/VOCALS), DONAL LUNNY (GUITAR/BOUZOUKI/ synthesizer), Liam O'Flynn (uillean pipes) and Andy Irvine (guitar/ mandolin/bouzouki/vocals). Lunny was replaced by Johnny Moynihan (bouzouki) and **Paul Brady** (b. 1947; vocals/guitar) replaced Moore in 1974. After splitting up, the original group re-formed, this time with Matt Molloy (flute). *Words And Music* featured **Bob Dylan**'s 'I Pity The Poor Immigrant'. When *The Best Of Planxty Live* emerged, they were all pursuing solo projects.

PLATTERS

THE PLATTERS, FOR A SHORT TIME, WERE THE MOST SUCCESSFUL AMERICAN VOCAL GROUP IN THE WORLD. BUCK Ram (b. 1907, d. 1991) formed them in 1953, his talent for composing and arranging enabling them to make a lasting impression upon popular music. Their original line-up, Tony Williams (b. 1928, d. 1992; lead tenor), David Lynch (b. 1929, d. 1981; tenor), Alex Hodge (baritone) and Herb Reed (b. 1931; bass), recorded unsuccessfully in 1954. Paul Robi (b. 1931, d. 1989) replaced Hodge, and Zola Taylor (b. 1934; contralto) joined. Signed to Mercury, their first hit was 1955's 'Only You', reaching the US Top 5. 'Smoke Gets In Your Eyes' was an international number 1 hit single in 1958-59. Lead singer Williams left for a solo career in 1961. Sandra Dawn and Nate Nelson replaced Taylor and Robi. During the late 60s, personnel changes brought confusion as to who were the legitimate Platters. Their legacy has been undermined by the myriad of line-ups performing under that name, some with no links to the group. The group were inducted into the Rock 'N' Roll Hall Of Fame in 1990.

PM DAWN

PM DAWN COMPRISE BROTHERS PRINCE BE (ATTRELL CORDES) AND DJ MINUTE MIX (JARRETT CORDES). AFTER signing to Gee St, they took the name PM Dawn, indicating 'the transition from dark to light'. 'Ode To A Forgetful Mind' was released in 1991. Its follow-up, 'A Watcher's Point Of View', broke the UK charts. Their debut album (1991) confirmed they were one of the most creative forces in rap/dance. 1992 saw two minor UK hits, 'Reality Used To Be A Friend Of Mine' and 'I'd Die Without You', which featured on the soundtrack of *Boomerang*. While writing tracks for *The Bliss*, Prince Be dueted with **Boy George** on 'More Than Likely'. Minute Mix changed his name to J.C. The Eternal, Prince Be becoming The Nocturnal.

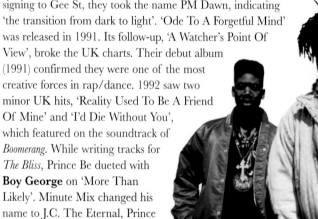

POCO

THIS US COUNTRY-ROCK GROUP FORMED FROM **BUFFALO SPRINGFIELD** AS POGO IN 1968. THEY COMPRISED RICHIE Furay (b. 1944; vocals/guitar), Randy Meisner (b. 1946; vocal/bass), George Grantham (b. 1947; drums/vocals), Jim Messina (b. 1947; vocals/guitar) and Rusty Young (b. 1946; vocals/pedal-steel guitar). They became Poco after complaints from the copyright owner of the Pogo cartoon character. *Pickin' Up The Pieces* was more country than rock and made Poco leaders of the genre. Meisner departed (later co-founding the **Eagles**) and *Poco* was released to critical applause. *Deliverin'* made the US Top 30, the band having added the vocal talent of Timothy B. Schmit (b. 1947; bass/vocals) and Paul Cotton (b. 1943;

vocals/guitar). *From The Inside*, was followed by *A Good Feelin' To Know*, their most critically acclaimed work. Richie left after *Crazy Eyes*.

During the mid-70s the line-up of Cotton, Schmit, Grantham and Young released three albums, *Head Over Heels*, *Rose Of Cimarron* and *Indian Summer*. Schmit and Grantham then left. Charlie Harrison (bass/vocals), Steve Chapman (drums/vocals) and Kim Bullard on keyboards preceded the million-selling *Legend*. This line-up made a further four albums with gradually declining success. In 1990 Furay, Messina, Meisner, Grantham and Young returned with *Legacy*.

POGUES

THE POGUES (ORIGINALLY POGUE MAHONE) WERE FRONTED BY SINGER SHANE MacGOWAN (b. 1957) AND INCLUDED Peter 'Spider' Stacy (tin whistle), Jem Finer (banjo/mandolin), James Fearnley (guitar/piano/accordion), Cait O'Riordan (bass) and Andrew Ranken (drums). After complaints they changed their name (Pogue Mahone is 'kiss my arse' in Gaelic) and attracted **Clash**'s attention, who asked them to be their opening act. In 1984 they signed to Stiff and recorded *Red Roses For Me*. **Elvis Costello** produced *Rum, Sodomy And The Lash*, Philip Chevron replacing Finer. Multi-instrumentalist Terry Woods (a co-founder of **Steeleye Span**) joined and Cait O'Riordan was replaced by Darryl Hunt. *If I Should Fall From Grace With God* sold more than 200,000 copies in the USA and 'Fairytale Of New York' (1987), a duet by MacGowan and **Kirsty MacColl**, was a Christmas UK number 2 hit in the UK. *Peace And Love* featured songs written by nearly every member of the group and its eclectic nature saw them picking up the hurdy-gurdy, the cittern and the mandola. While the rest of the group were strong players, it was widely accepted that MacGowan was the most talented songwriter. In 1991 MacGowan left the band and was replaced by the former Clash singer Joe Strummer. This relationship lasted until June 1992 when Spider Stacy replaced Strummer as lead vocalist. McGowan later re-emerged with his new band, the Popes.

POINTER SISTERS

SISTERS, ANITA (b. 1948), BONNIE (b. 1951), RUTH (b. 1946) AND JUNE (b. 1954), FIRST SANG TOGETHER IN THE WEST Oakland Church of God, California, where their parents were ministers. Bonnie, June and Anita worked as backing singers with several of the region's acts before Ruth joined them in 1972, a year before their debut album was released. Their varied repertoire included a version of **Allen Toussaint**'s 'Yes We Can Can'. They broke up briefly in 1977, but while Bonnie left the remaining trio regrouped and **Bruce Springsteen** crafted million-selling 'Fire'(1979). 'Slow Hand' continued their progress. Although 'Dare Me' was another major hit in 1985, their subsequent work lacked the sparkle of earlier achievements.

POISON

THIS HEAVY-METAL BAND FORMED IN PENNSYLVANIA, USA, IN 1983 BY BRET MICHAELS (b. BRET SYCHALK, 1962; VOCALS) and Rikki Rockett (b. Richard Ream, 1959; drums), joined by Bobby Dall (b. Kuy Kendall, 1958; bass) and Matt Smith (guitar). They worked as Paris, before moving to LA and changing their name. Smith left the band, being replaced by C.C. Deville (b. 1963; guitar). Their first album went double platinum in America. *Open Up And Say...Ahh!* produced their first US number 1, 'Every Rose Has Its Thorn'. *Flesh And Blood*, preceded their official UK debut. Richie Kotzen replaced Deville in 1991. *Native Tongue* established them as purveyors of image-conscious hard-melodic rock. Blues Saraceno replaced Smith in 1995.

POINTER SISTERS
Albums
Special Things (Planet 1980)★★★
➧ p.375 for full listings
Connections
Allen Toussaint ➧ p.323
Bruce Springsteen ➧ p.306

POISON
Albums
Flesh And Blood (Capitol 1990)★★★★
➧ p.375 for full listings
Further References
Video: *7 Days Live* (1994)

POLICE

THIS UK TRIO COMPRISED **STEWART COPELAND** (b. 1952; DRUMS/PERCUSSION/VOCALS), ANDY SUMMERS (b. ANDREW Somers 1942; guitar) and **Sting** (b. Gordon Sumner, 1951; bass/vocals). Ex-**Curved Air**-member Stewart, Sting and Summers came together, leaving original member Henry Padovani no alternative but to leave. Summers' guitar technique blended with Copeland's back-to-front drum technique and Sting's unusual voice.

'Roxanne' failed to chart but was a later success after 'Can't Stand Losing You'. *Outlandos D'Amour* and *Regatta De Blanc* dominated the UK charts for most of 1979, with *Zenyatta Mondatta* their big breakthrough in America. Their third number 1, 'Don't Stand So Close To Me', followed. *Ghost In The Machine* spawned the hits 'Invisible Sun' and 'Every Little Thing She Does Is Magic' their fourth UK number 1.

The band concentrated on solo projects in 1982. Copeland released *Klark Kent*, and wrote the music for the film *Rumblefish*. Summers made an album with **Robert Fripp**. Sting appeared in the film *Brimstone And Treacle*. The Police reconvened in 1983 and released *Synchronicity* which stayed at the top for 17 weeks. Several greatest hits-packages and a live album periodically rekindled interest in the band.

POLICE
Albums
Synchronicity (A&M 1983)★★★★
➧ p.375 for full listings

Collaborators
Robert Fripp ➧ p.154
Connections
Stewart Copeland ➧ p.101
Sting ➧ p.310
Curved Air ➧ p.108
Further References
Book: *The Police*, Lynn Goldsmith

POOLE, BRIAN, AND THE TREMELOES

FORMED BY VOCALIST BRIAN POOLE IN THE LATE 50S (b. 1941), THIS UK POP GROUP DEBUTED IN 1960. THEY SIGNED to Decca in 1962 in favour of the **Beatles**. A cover of the **Isley Brothers**' 'Twist And Shout' brought them a UK Top 10 hit in 1963. The follow-up, 'Do You Love Me?', was number 1 in the UK and 15 other countries. After 'Candy Man' and 'Someone, Someone', their popularity waned, and Poole branched out of writing big ballads. He moved into cabaret, retired to the family butcher business, later resurfacing with a record and publishing company. The Tremeloes went on to achieve enormous chart success under their own name.

POOLE, BRIAN, AND THE TREMELOES
Albums
Twist And Shout With Brian Poole And The Tremeloes (Decca 1963)★★★★
➧ p.375 for full listings
Connections
Beatles ➧ p.38
Isley Brothers ➧ p.194

POP, IGGY
Albums
The Idiot (RCA 1977)★★★★
Lust For Life (RCA 1977)★★★★
➽ p.375 for full listings
Collaborators
Sex Pistols ➽ p.292
Connections
Nico ➽ p.247
John Cale ➽ p.78
Television ➽ p.317
Influences
Doors ➽ p.123
David Bowie ➽ p.64
Further References
Book: *The Lives And Crimes Of Iggy Pop*, Mike West

POP WILL EAT ITSELF
Albums
The Looks Or The Lifestyle (RCA 1992)★★★
➽ p.375 for full listings
Connections
General Public ➽ p.161

PORNO FOR PYROS
Albums
Good God's Urge (Warners 1996)★★★
➽ p.375 for full listings
Connections
Janes Addiction ➽ p.197
Further References
Book: *Perry Farrell: Saga Of A Hypster*, Dave Thompson

PORTISHEAD
Albums
Dummy (Go! Beat 1994)★★★★
Portishead (Go! Beat 1997)★★★★
➽ p.375 for full listings

Collaborators
Massive Attack ➽ p.227
Neneh Cherry ➽ p.89

POSIES
Albums
Frosting On The Beater (Geffen 1993)★★★★
➽ p.375 for full listings
Collaborators
Big Star ➽ p.46
Influences
Hüsker Dü ➽ p.190
Squeeze ➽ p.306

PREFAB SPROUT
Albums
Steve McQueen (Kitchenware 1985)★★★★
➽ p.375 for full listings

POP, IGGY

'GODFATHER OF PUNK', IGGY POP (b. JAMES JEWEL OSTERBURG, 1947) FIRST JOINED BANDS AS DRUMMER. HE picked up the nickname Iggy while with the Iguanas (1964). In 1965 he joined Prime Movers, changing his name to Iggy Stooge. Inspired by seeing the **Doors**, he formed the Psychedelic Stooges with Ron Asheton. Iggy was vocalist and guitarist, Asheton played bass with Asheton's brother Scott later joining on drums. They debuted in Michigan, October 1967. The same year Iggy made his acting debut in a Françoise De Monierre film, also featuring **Nico**. Dave Alexander joined on bass, and 'Psychedelic' was dropped from their name. Ron switched to guitar, leaving Iggy free to concentrate on singing and showmanship.

The Stooges signed to Elektra in 1968 for two albums (the first produced by **John Cale**) *The Stooges* and *Fun House*. Stooge fan **David Bowie** helped Iggy record *Raw Power* in 1972. When no suitable British musicians could be found, Williamson, Scott Thurston and the Ashetons were flown in. The resultant album included 'Search And Destroy'. Bowie's involvement continued as Iggy sailed through stormy seas (including self-admission to an asylum). His live performances are legendary: self-mutilation, sex acts and an invitation to a local gang to kill him on-stage.

After *Raw Power* there were sessions for *Kill City*, which was not released until 1978. The arrival of punk stirred Iggy's interest. (**Television** recorded the tribute 'Little Johnny Jewel'). In 1977 Bowie produced two Iggy albums – *The Idiot* and *Lust For Life*. Key tracks from these included 'Night Clubbin'', 'The Passenger' and 'China Girl'. Iggy guested on backing vocals for Bowie's album *Low*. In the late 70s, Iggy signed to Arista, releasing rather average albums with occasional assistance from Glen Matlock (ex-**Sex Pistols**) and Ivan Kral. He went into vinyl exile after 1982's autobiography and the Chris Stein-produced *Zombie Birdhouse*. During his time out of the studio he cleaned up his drug problems and married. He also developed his acting career, appearing in *Sid And Nancy*, *The Color Of Money*, *Hardware*, and on television in *Miami Vice*. His big return came in 1986 with the Bowie-produced *Blah Blah Blah* and his first-ever UK hit single, a cover of Johnny O'Keefe's 'Real Wild Child'. *American Caesar* from its jokily self-aggrandizing title onwards, revealed continued creative growth.

POP WILL EAT ITSELF

THE GROUP EMERGED AS POP WILL EAT ITSELF IN 1986 WITH A LINE-UP COMPRISING CLINT MANSELL (b. 1963; VOCALS/ guitar), Adam Mole (b. 1962; keyboards), Graham Cobb (b. 1964; drums, later vocals) and Richard Marsh (b. 1965; bass). Their first recording was *The Poppies Say Grr.* Their debut, *Box Frenzy*, displayed their mix of guitar pop with sampling. In 1988 they played in the USSR, signing to RCA soon afterwards. Their second album was a minor hit and during 1990 they achieved mainstream acclaim with 'Touched By The Hand Of Cicciolina'. The group recruited a full-time drummer in 1992 when Fuzz (b. Robert Townshend, 1964; ex-**General Public**) joined, but following *Weird's Bar & Grill* RCA dropped the band. The remix collection *Two Fingers My Friends* did at least underline their tenacity and self-sufficiency.

PORNO FOR PYROS

THIS THEATRICAL ROCK ACT WAS FORMED BY PERRY FARRELL (b. 1959, EX-**JANE'S ADDICTION**) IN 1992. FOLLOWING the demise of his previous act he enlisted former bandmate Stephen Perkins (b. 1967; drums), Martyn Le Noble (b. 1969; bass) and Peter DiStefano (b. 1965; guitar). With Farrell's input and Perkins' talents, similarities between the two bands were inevitable, although Porno For Pyros' shows were more a carnival than traditional rock shows. They headlined at the 1993 UK Reading Festival. Farrell had become a star by the time *Good Gods Urge* was issued.

PORTISHEAD

PORTISHEAD WERE NAMED AFTER THE PORT IN SOUTH-WEST ENGLAND WHERE GEOFF BARROW (b. *c.* 1971) SPENT his teens. Barrow started out as a tape operator, working with **Massive Attack** and **Neneh Cherry**. He recruited jazz guitarist and musical director Adrian Utley (b. *c.* 1957), drummer/programmer Dave and vocalist Beth Gibbons (b. *c.* 1965). They recorded a soundtrack and film, *To Kill A Dead Man*. 'Numb' and 'Sour Times' received good press reaction, but Barrow and Gibbons were reluctant interviewees with no initial interest in playing live. 'Glory Box' entered the UK charts at number 13 in 1995, after several 'album of the year' awards for *Dummy*. Their sound, a mixture of blues, jazz and hip-hop, became known as 'trip hop'. They won the Mercury Music Prize for best album of 1995. The follow-up was delayed when Barrow reached a creative impasse that almost destroyed the band. His perseverance paid off – *Portishead* was released in 1997 to excellent reviews.

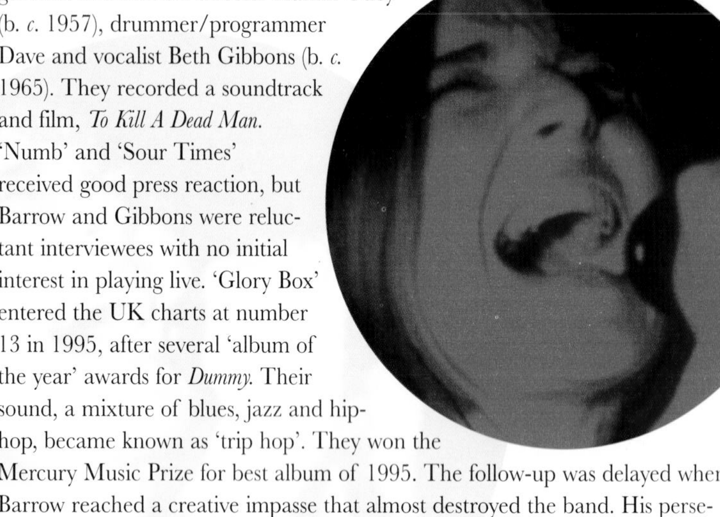

POSIES

JONATHON AUER (VOCALS/GUITAR) AND KEN STRINGFELLOW (VOCALS/GUITAR) WERE BOTH IN BANDS IN THEIR early teens. The Posies are influenced by both **Hüsker Dü** and **Squeeze**, with both members being part of 'industrial-noise' Sky Cries Mary. *Failure* marked them out as lacking in ambition. Signing to Geffen, they enlisted a rhythm section (Dave Fox and Mike Musburger). Their third album, *Frosting On The Beater*, attracted wide acclaim. The group supported **Big Star** on European tours, with Auer and Stringfellow taking part in their re-formation.

PREFAB SPROUT

THEY FORMED IN 1982 AND COMPRISED PADDY McALOON (b. 1957; GUITAR/VOCALS), MARTIN McALOON (b. 1962; BASS), Wendy Smith (b. 1963; vocals/guitar) and Neil Conti (b. 1959). Following 'Lions In My Own Garden', Paddy attracted the attention of the Kitchenware label. *Swoon* made the national chart. *Steve McQueen* (1985) made a respectable showing in the charts, and 'When Love Breaks Down' became a hit. In the USA, *Steve McQueen* was forcibly retitled *Two Wheels Good*. *From Langley Park To Memphis* was a major success worldwide. 'The King Of Rock 'N' Roll' became their biggest hit to date. *Protest Songs*'s success was muted by the continuing sales of *Steve McQueen* and *From Langley Park To Memphis*. McAloon unleashed *Jordan: The Comeback* in 1990, and for many it was the album of the year. McAloon spent the next few years writing songs for Jimmy Nail. *Andromeda Heights* met with a polite response.

PRESIDENTS OF THE UNITED STATES OF AMERICA

FORMED IN SEATTLE, USA, THIS ALTERNATIVE-ROCK BAND BROKE INTO THE US AND UK CHARTS IN 1995. CHRIS Ballew (vocals/two-string bass) and Mark Sandman (**Morphine**) formed Supergroup in 1992. Ballew was also part of **Beck**'s backing band. In 1994 he recruited Dave Dederer (three-string guitar) and drummer Jason Finn, forming Presidents Of The United States Of America. After their eponymous debut, they signed to Columbia and MTV gave 'Lump' rotation play. By 1996 the album had sold over one and a half million copies in the USA, and become a UK Top 20 single. A second album (1996) capitalized on this momentum, but their brand of jokey alternative rock was beginning to wear thin and they disbanded in 1998.

PRESLEY, ELVIS

ELVIS AARON PRESLEY (b. 1935, d. 1977) IS A ROCK LEGEND. HIS EARLIEST MUSICAL INFLUENCE CAME FROM PSALMS AND gospel songs; with a strong grounding in country and blues. These styles combined to provide his unique musical identity.

While a truck driver, Elvis visited Sun Records to record a version of the **Ink Spots**' 'My Happiness' as a birthday present for his mother. The studio manager, Marion Keisker, informed Sun's owner/producer **Sam Phillips** of his potential. Phillips nurtured him before pairing him with country guitarist Scotty Moore and bassist **Bill Black**. Early sessions showed considerable promise, with Presley beginning to alternate his low-key delivery with a high-pitched whine. Phillips saw Presley as a white boy who sang like he was black.

Presley's debut with Sun was 'That's All Right (Mama)', showing his vocal dexterity. The b-side, 'Blue Moon Of Kentucky', was a country song but the arrangement showed that Presley was threatening to slip closer to R&B. Response to these performances was encouraging, with 20,000 copies sold. Presley recorded Roy Brown's 'Good Rockin' Tonight' backed by 'I Don't Care If The Sun Don't Shine' and performed on the *Grand Old Opry* and *Louisiana Hayride* radio programmes. A series of live dates commenced in 1955 with drummer D.J. Fontana added to the ranks. Presley toured clubs in Arkansas, Louisiana and Texas, billed as 'The King Of Western Bop' and 'The Hillbilly Cat'. Audience reaction verged on the fanatical – a result of Presley's semi-erotic performances. The final Sun single was a cover of Junior Parker's 'Mystery Train'.

Colonel Tom Parker, who managed several country artists, persuaded Sam Phillips to release Elvis – RCA paid Sun $35,000. Two days after his 21st birthday, Elvis recorded his first major label tracks, including 'Heartbreak Hotel'. This stayed at US number 1 for eight weeks and reached UK number 2. Presley also made his national television debut – his sexually enticing gyrations subsequently persuading producers to film him exclusively from the waist upwards. Having outsold former Sun colleague **Carl Perkins** with 'Blue Suede Shoes', Presley released a debut album containing several songs he had previously recorded with Phillips.

After his number 1, 'I Want You, I Need You, I Love You', Presley released the most commercially successful double-sided single in pop history, 'Hound Dog'/'Don't Be Cruel'. The former, composed by **Leiber And Stoller**, featured his backing group the **Jordanaires**. It remained at US number 1 for 11 weeks and both sides of the record were massive hits in the UK.

Celluloid fame beckoned next, with *Love Me Tender*, produced by David Weisbert (*Rebel Without A Cause*). Presley's movie debut received mixed reviews but was a box office smash, while the title track topped the US charts for five weeks. After rumours that Presley would be drafted into the US Army, RCA, Twentieth Century Fox and the Colonel stepped up the work-rate and release

schedules. Three major films were completed in the next two-and-a-half years, including *Jailhouse Rock*. The Leiber And Stoller title track was an instant classic which topped the US charts for seven weeks and entered the UK listings at number 1.

By the time *King Creole* was released in 1958, Elvis had joined the US Forces and flown to Germany. In America, the Colonel kept his reputation intact via a series of films, record releases and merchandising. Hits including 'Wear My Ring Around Your Neck', 'Hard Headed Woman' and 'A Big Hunk O' Love' filled the two-year gap and when Elvis reappeared he assumed the mantle of an all-round entertainer. 'It's Now Or Never' revealed the King as an operatic crooner; 'Are You Lonesome Tonight?' allowed Elvis to spout Shakespeare; on celluloid, *GI Blues* played upon his recent Army exploits and showed off his knowledge of German in 'Wooden Heart'. 'Surrender' completed this phase of big ballads in the old-fashioned style. After the 1963 number 1 'Devil In Disguise', a bleak period followed in which songs such as 'Bossa Nova Baby', 'Kiss Me Quick' and 'Blue Christmas' became the rule rather than the exception. Significantly, his biggest success of the mid-60s, 'Crying In The Chapel', had been recorded five years before.

In the wake of the **Beatles**' rise to fame and the beat-boom explosion Presley seemed a figure out of time, and he continued to grind out pointless movies such as *Double Trouble*, *Speedway* and *Live A Little, Love A Little*.

'Guitar Man' and 'US Male' (both 1968) proved a spectacular return to form, he also appeared in the one-hour Christmas *Elvis TV Special*, designed to capture Elvis at his rock 'n' rollin' best, becoming one of the most celebrated moments in pop broadcasting history.

The critical acclaim for his television special prompted Elvis to undertake his most significant recordings in years and he released *From Elvis In Memphis* and *From Memphis To Vegas/From Vegas To Memphis*. On the singles front, Presley was also back on top, most notably on 'In The Ghetto' which hit UK number 2 and US number 3.

'Suspicious Minds' was his first US chart-topper since 1962. Hits such as 'Don't Cry Daddy' dealing with the death of a marriage demonstrated Elvis's ability to read a song. Even his final few films seemed less disastrous than expected and Presley returned as a live performer with a strong backing group including guitarist **James Burton**. His comeback was well-received and one of the live songs, 'The Wonder Of You' (1970), stayed at UK number 1 for six weeks.

During the early 70s, Presley continued his live performances, but suffered the same atrophy that had bedevilled his celluloid career. He relied on some rather patchy albums rather than record any fresh material. The backdrop to Presley's final years was a sordid slump into drug dependency, reinforced by the unreality of a pampered lifestyle in his fantasy home, Gracelands. The dissolution of his marriage to Priscilla in 1973 coincided with further decline and a tendency to gain weight. He collapsed on-stage on a couple of occasions and, on 16 August 1977, his burnt-out body expired. The official cause of death was a heart attack, no doubt brought on by long-term barbiturate usage. In the weeks after his death, his record sales rocketed and 'Way Down' proved his final UK number 1.

The contrasting images of Elvis have come to represent everything positive and everything destructive about the music industry.

PRESIDENTS OF THE UNITED STATES OF AMERICA

Albums

Presidents Of The United States Of America (PopLlama 1995)★★★★

➽ p.375 for full listings

Connections

Morphine ➽ p.238
Beck ➽ p.40

PRESLEY, ELVIS

Albums

Elvis (RCA Victor 1956)★★★★★
Elvis' Golden Records (RCA Victor 1958)★★★★★
The Elvis Presley Sun Collection (RCA 1975)★★★★★
Elvis From Nashville To Memphis: The Essential '60s Masters 5-CD box set (RCA 1993)★★★★★

➽ p.375 for full listings

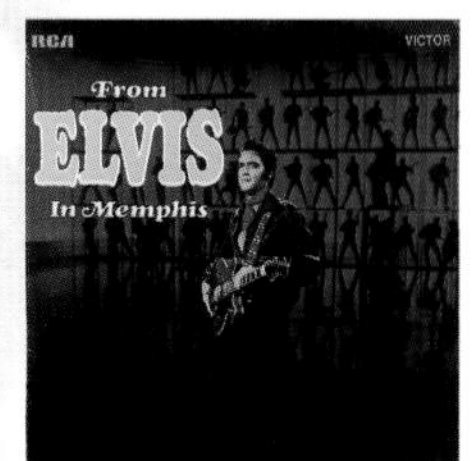

Collaborators

Bill Black ➽ p.48
Jordanaires ➽ p.201
James Burton ➽ p.75

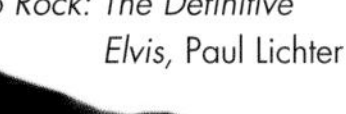

Connections

Sam Phillips ➽ p.260
Carl Perkins ➽ p.258
Leiber And Stoller ➽ p.214
Beatles ➽ p.38

Further References

Film: *Blue Hawaii* (1961)
Video: *68 Comeback Special* (1986)
Book: *The Boy Who Dared To Rock: The Definitive Elvis*, Paul Lichter

PRESTON, BILLY
Albums
The Wildest Organ In Town! (Vee Jay 1966)★★★
The Kids & Me (A&M 1974)★★★
Late At Night (Motown 1980)★★★
➧ p.375 for full listings
Collaborators
Little Richard ➧ p.217
Beatles ➧ p.38
Connections
Ray Charles ➧ p.88
George Harrison ➧ p.176
Joe Cocker ➧ p.95

PRETENDERS
Albums
Pretenders (Warners 1980)★★★★
Pretenders II (Warners 1981)★★★★
Learning To Crawl (Warners 1984)★★★★
➧ p.375 for full listings
Connections
Kinks ➧ p.207
Average White Band ➧ p.25
Simple Minds ➧ p.297
UB40 ➧ p.326
Sonny And Cher ➧ p.302
Further References
Video: *The Isle Of View* (Warner Music Vision 1995)
Books: *Pretenders*, Miles
The Pretenders, Chris Salewicz
The Pretenders: With Hyndesight, Mike Wrenn

PRETTY THINGS
Albums
The Pretty Things (Fontana 1965)★★★★
Get The Picture (Fontana 1965)★★★★
Parachute (Harvest 1970)★★★★
➧ p.375 for full listings
Connections
Rolling Stones ➧ p.281
Who ➧ p.338
Rolling Stone ➧ p.280
Further References
Book: *The Pretty Things: Their Own Story And The Downliners Sect Story*, Mike Stax

PRICE, ALAN
Albums
The Price To Play (Decca 1966)★★★
Between Today And Yesterday (Warners 1974)★★★★
Travellin' Man (Trojan 1986)★★★
➧ p.375 for full listings
Collaborators
Bob Dylan ➧ p.128
Georgie Fame ➧ p.142

PRESTON, BILLY

PRESTON BEGAN HIS MUSICAL CAREER PLAYING ORGAN WITH GOSPEL SINGER MAHALIA JACKSON. PRESTON (b. 1946) worked with **Little Richard** and met the **Beatles** during his 1962 European tour. After relocating to Britain as part of the **Ray Charles** revue, he signed to Apple in 1969. **George Harrison** produced 'That's The Way God Planned It', with Preston contributing keyboards to the Beatles' *Let It Be*. He moved to A&M Records, and had a run of hits, including 'Outa-Space' and 'Nothing From Nothing'. His compositional talents were evident on 'You Are So Beautiful', a US Top 10 hit for **Joe Cocker**. A duet with Syreeta, 'With You I'm Born Again', was an international hit in 1980. He was arrested on a morals charge in the USA during 1991 and he was sentenced to three years for a drugs possession offence in 1997.

PRETENDERS

CHRISSIE HYNDE (b. 1951) CAME TO ENGLAND DURING THE EARLY 70S. AFTER MEETING WITH *NEW MUSICAL EXPRESS* writer Nick Kent she joined the paper, gaining entry into the world of rock. By the time she assembled the Pretenders in 1978, Hynde had gained a great deal of experience. The classic Pretenders line-up comprised: Pete Farndon (b. 1952, d. 1983; bass), James Honeyman-Scott (b. 1956, d. 1982; guitar) and Martin Chambers (b. 1951; drums). Their debut was a version of the **Kinks**' 'Stop Your Sobbing' in 1978. 'Kid' and 'Brass In Pocket' followed (the latter reaching number 1 in the UK). Their debut album was a *tour de force* and remains their finest work.

Throughout 1980 they toured America, and *Pretenders II* came in 1982. In June of that year, Pete Farndon was fired as a result of his drug problem. Two days later Honeyman-Scott was found dead from a concoction of heroin and cocaine. Nine months later Hynde gave birth to a daughter; the father was Kinks' Ray Davies. Two months later Pete Farndon died from a drug overdose.

The new full-time Pretenders were Robbie McIntosh (ex-**Average White Band**) on lead guitar, and bassist Malcolm Foster. *Learning To Crawl* included 'Back On The Chain Gang'. In 1984, Hynde married Jim Kerr of **Simple Minds** and dueted with **UB40** on the remake of **Sonny And Cher**'s 'I Got You Babe'. Following the birth of another daughter, Hynde dismantled the band. *Get Close*, released at the end of 1987, was well received. In 1990 she returned with *Packed!*, still as the Pretenders. *Last Of The Independents* was released in 1994, with Martin Chambers (drums), Adam Seymour (guitar) and Andy Hobson (bass). *Isle Of View* was Hynde performing an acoustic set of Pretenders material, backed by a string quartet.

PRETTY THINGS

THIS ENGLISH R&B BAND FORMED IN 1963. THE ORIGINAL LINE-UP FEATURED A FOUNDER-MEMBER OF THE **ROLLING Stones**, Dick Taylor (b. 1943; guitar), plus Phil May (b. 1944; vocals), Brian Pendleton (b. 1944; rhythm guitar), John Stax (b. 1944; bass) and Peter Kitley (drums), who was quickly replaced by Viv Andrews. Andrews was replaced by Viv Prince. Their brash approach to R&B flourished with 'Don't Bring Me Down' and 'Honey I Need'. Their first album offered much of the same. Skip Alan (b. Alan Skipper, 1948) replaced Prince in 1965. Although the Pretty Things' commercial standing had declined, 'Come See Me', was arguably their finest work. Pendleton and Stax left and *Emotions* was completed with Wally Allen (bass/vocals) and John Povey (b. 1944; keyboards/vocals).

In 1968 they released *S.F. Sorrow*. Dick Taylor's departure in 1969 was highly damaging, although *Parachute* was lauded in **Rolling Stone**. The Pretty Things collapsed in 1971, but May, Povey and Skip Alan re-formed for *Freeway Madness*. May left in 1976. Two years later the *Emotions* line-up plus guitarist Peter Tolson (b. 1951) completed *Cross Talk*. In 1996 the line-up was May, Taylor, Alan, Allen and Povey.

PRICE, ALAN

PRICE'S (b. 1941) FIRST MAJOR BAND, THE ALAN PRICE RHYTHM AND BLUES COMBO, BECAME THE **ANIMALS**. Price found the pressure of touring too much and left the band in 1965. That year he appeared in the movie *Don't Look Back* as one of **Bob Dylan**'s entourage. The Alan Price Set debuted in 1965 with 'Any Day Now'. In 1967 he had two major hits written by **Randy Newman**; 'Simon Smith And His Amazing Dancing Bear' and 'The House That Jack Built'. In 1970 he and **Georgie Fame** had a hit with 'Rosetta'. Price was commissioned to write the music for *O Lucky Man!* in 1973, for which he won a BAFTA. In 1974 Price hit the charts with 'Jarrow Song', and he produced the autobiographical album *Between Today And Yesterday*.

Price starred in *Alfie Darling* in 1975, winning the Most Promising New British Actor award. In addition to writing stage musicals like *Andy Capp* and *Who's A Lucky Boy?* Price took part in two abortive Animals reunions in 1977 and 1983. He recorded a new album in 1996 with his Electric Blues Company, a return to his R&B club days.

PRICE, LLOYD

PRICE (b. 1933) FORMED HIS OWN BAND IN NEW ORLEANS IN 1949 AND IN 1952 SIGNED WITH SPECIALTY. 'LAWDY MISS Clawdy', established his career in the R&B field and he followed with four more Top 10 hits. In 1956 he settled in Washington, DC, setting up a record company with Harold Logan. Price had a hit in 1957 with 'Just Because'. He and Logan revamped 'Stack-O-Lee', a hit for Ma Rainey in the 20s, and made it one of his biggest successes (US R&B and pop number 1, 1959, UK Top 10). Price's chart career peaked in 1959, with hits including 'Where Were You (On Our Wedding Day)' and 'I'm Gonna Get Married'. The hits continued with 'Lady Luck' and 'Question'. Three years later Price resurfaced, making an impact on the emerging soul market with his reworked jazz standards. Price's last chart record was in 1976 on his LPG label.

PRIEST, MAXI

PRIEST (b. MAX ELLIOT, 1962) TOOK HIS NEW NAME UPON CONVERSION TO RASTAFARIANISM. HE WENT ON TOUR with Saxon International, the UK's premier reggae assembly, rubbing shoulders with Smiley Culture. He made his name and reputation as a 'singing' DJ, soon progressing to a more soulful style captured on *You're Safe*. He had a run of hits in 1986, including 'Strollin' On' and scored minor hits with covers of

Robert Palmer's 'Some Guys Have All The Luck' and **Cat Stevens**' 'Wild World'. *Bona Fide* included contributions from **Soul II Soul**.

PRIMAL SCREAM

THE SUCCESSFUL 1991 LINE-UP COMPRISED BOBBY GILLESPIE (b. 1964), ANDREW INNES, ROBERT YOUNG, HENRY OLSEN, Philip 'Toby' Tomanov, Martin Duffy and Denise Johnson. Gillespie formed the band after a stint as drummer in the **Jesus And Mary Chain**. Primal Scream achieved immediate popularity with 'Velocity Girl'. After an album of similarly melodic material they veered towards rock. The early 90s saw Primal Scream reinvented, with the aid of remixers such as **Andy Weatherall**. 'Loaded' invaded Britain's dancefloors to become a Top 10 hit. *Screamadelica* reaped critical acclaim and massive sales, before they relocated to Tennessee to work on the follow-up. This finally emerged in 1994, revealing a stylistic debt to the **Rolling Stones**. In 1996 former **Stone Roses** bassist Gary 'Mani' Mounfield joined the band. *Vanishing Point* was a timely return to the rhythm of *Screamadelica*. Drummer Paul Mulreany left the band in 1997.

PRINCE

PRINCE (b. PRINCE ROGERS NELSON, 1958) WAS NAMED AFTER THE PRINCE ROGER TRIO, OF WHOM HIS FATHER, John Nelson, was a member. He was adopted by the Andersons, and became a close friend of Andre Anderson (later Andre Cymone). He and Anderson joined junior high school band Grand Central, which later became Champagne. He introduced original material into his sets for the first time. His musical development continued with 'Uptown', a musical underground scene that included Flyte Time.

Prince sent shock waves through his new sponsors by spending double his advance on the production of his debut, *Prince – For You*. By 1979 he had put a band together. This featured Cymone (bass), Gayle Chapman and Matt Fink (both keyboards), Bobby Z (drummer) and Dez Dickerson (guitar). Despite spending considerably less time and money on it than its predecessor, *Prince* charted (US number 22) and boasted two successful singles, 'Why You Wanna Treat Me So Bad?' and 'I Wanna Be Your Lover'. A succession of live dates promoting *Dirty Mind* saw Lisa Coleman replacing Chapman. Prince was prolific, and *Controversy* and *1999* followed within 12 months. 'Little Red Corvette' was lifted from the album, gaining significant airplay on MTV. After internal disputes with the Time, Prince began work on the *Purple Rain* film, a glamourized autobiographical piece in which he would star. 'When Doves Cry', from the soundtrack, became the first Prince song to grace the top of the US charts. 'Let's Go Crazy' and 'Purple Rain' (numbers 1 and 2, respectively) further established him as an 80s figurehead. After the end of a huge and successful tour, Prince returned to the studio for a duet with Apollonia. *Around The World In A Day* emerged in 1985 and topped the US charts for three weeks, preceding which Prince announced his retirement from live appearances. Instead, he founded the Minneapolis-based studio/label complex Paisley Park. As work began on a second movie, *Under The Cherry Moon*, 'Kiss' was released, becoming his third US number 1.

He quickly overturned his decision not to perform live, and set out on the *Parade* tour to promote the number 1 album of the same name. Unfortunately, although 'Kiss' and 'Girls And Boys' represented classic Prince innuendo, the rest of the album lacked focus. The shows were spectacular even by Prince standards, but his backing band the Revolution were disbanded at the end of the tour. After *Sign 'O' The Times* came *Lovesexy*. The following year the soundtrack album for *Batman* topped the US charts for six weeks. In 1990 he released *Graffiti Bridge*, accompanying a film of the same title, an album made up entirely of Prince compositions on which he sang just over half. *Graffiti Bridge* was his first commercial let-down for some time, peaking at number 6 in the USA (although it made number 1 in the UK). Prince, as usual, was busy putting together new projects. These included his latest backing outfit, the New Power Generation. They were in place in time for the sessions for *Diamonds And Pearls*, released in 1991. Greeted by critics as a return to form, the New Power Generation were considered his most able and vibrant collaborators since the mid-80s. Taken from it, 'Cream' became a US number 1. Both 'Sexy MF' and 'My Name Is Prince' were included on *Symbol* – which introduced the cryptic 'symbol' that he would legally adopt as his name in 1993. Much of the attention subsequently surrounding the artist concerned his protracted battle against his record company, Warner Brothers. In October he abandoned the symbol moniker, becoming instead 'The Artist Formerly Known As Prince'. He released *The Gold Experience* (1995), a return to the raunchy funk of his 80s prime. 'The Most Beautiful Girl In The World' was his best-selling single for many years. Following the 1996 release of *Chaos And Disorder*, he sacked the New Power Generation and announced he would not be touring, preferring to spend more time with his wife and new baby (who tragically died months after birth). He celebrated his release from the Warner Brothers contract with *Emancipation*, and continues to tour and record.

PRINCE BUSTER

JAMICAN-BORN BUSTER (b. CECIL BUSTAMANTE CAMPBELL, 1938) BEGAN HIS CAREER AS A BOXER, BUT SOON FOUND himself being put to use as a minder for **Coxsone Dodd**'s Down Beat sound system. He claims, like many others, to have invented the ska sound. His first recording session produced one of the all-time classics of Jamaican music, 'Oh Carolina'. Buster released countless records both by himself and other top acts which were subsequently released in the UK on the Blue Beat imprint. He toured the UK in the mid-60s, appeared on *Ready Steady Go* and enjoyed chart success with 'Al Capone'.

Prince Buster taught **Georgie Fame** to do the ska and he influenced other white pop acts – **Madness** named themselves after his song. He invested money in record shops and juke box operations throughout the Caribbean and, in the early 70s, recorded many of the current top names including Big Youth and Dennis Brown. Buster also took to re-pressing his back catalogue on single and releasing old albums both in Jamaica and the UK.

He returned to live work in the latter half of the 80s, and started to record new music again. It is unlikely that any other Jamaican artist (apart from **Bob Marley**) is so regularly played throughout the world.

Connections
Screamin' Jay Hawkins ➧ p.177
Randy Newman ➧ p.246
Further References
Book: *Wild Animals*, Andy Blackford

PRICE, LLOYD
Albums
The Exciting Lloyd Price (ABC 1959)★★★★
Mr. Personality (ABC 1959)★★★★
Mr. Personality Sings The Blues (ABC 1960)★★★★
➧ p.376 for full listings

PRIEST, MAXI
Albums
You're Safe (Virgin 1985)★★
Bona Fide (Ten 1990)★★★
➧ p.376 for full listings
Collaborators
Jesus and Mary Chain ➧ p.199
Connections
Andy Weatherall ➧ p.335
Stone Roses ➧ p.311
Influences
Rolling Stones ➧ p.281

PRINCE
Albums
1999 (Warners 1982)★★★★
Purple Rain film soundtrack (Warners 1984)★★★★
Sign 'O' The Times (Paisley Park 1987)★★★★
➧ p.376 for full listings

Collaborators
Revolution
New Power Generation
Further References
Videos: *Lovesexy Part 1* (Palace Video 1989)
Get Off (Warner Music Video 1991)
Book: *Prince: Imp Of The Perverse*, Barney Hoskyns

PRINCE BUSTER
Albums
Judge Dread Rock Steady (Blue Beat 1967)★★★
Wreck A Pum Pum (Blue Beat 1968)★★★★
On Tour (1966)★★★
➧ p.376 for full listings
Connections
Coxsone Dodd ➧ p.121
Georgie Fame ➧ p.142
Madness ➧ p.221
Bob Marley ➧ p.225

PRINE, JOHN

Albums
John Prine (Atlantic 1972)★★★★
The Missing Years (Oh Boy 1992)★★★★
➽ p.376 for full listings
Connections
Steve Cropper ➽ p.105

PROCLAIMERS
Albums
Sunshine On Leith (Chrysalis 1988)★★★★
➽ p.376 for full listings

PROCOL HARUM
Albums
A Salty Dog (Regal Zonophone 1969)★★★★
Live In Concert With The Edmonton Symphony Orchestra (Chrysalis 1972)★★★★
➽ p.376 for full listings

Connections
Robin Trower ➽ p.324
Influences
Jimi Hendrix ➽ p.180

PRODIGY
Albums
Music For The Jilted Generation (XL 1994)★★★★
The Fat Of The Land (XL 1997)★★★★
➽ p.376 for full listings
Connections
Jesus Jones ➽ p.199
Further References
Video: *Electronic Punks* (XL Recordings 1995)

PRINE, JOHN

PRINE (b. 1946) BEGAN HIS CAREER SINGING IN CHICAGO CLUBS, SIGNING TO ATLANTIC IN 1971. HIS DEBUT ALBUM contained the excellent 'Sam Stone'. Prine has gradually achieved cult status, his songs being increasingly covered by other artists. *Common Sense* (produced by **Steve Cropper**) was his first US Top 100 album. *Bruised Orange* was well received, but the follow-up, *Pink Cadillac*, was not. *The Missing Years* had massive sales and a Grammy award for Best Contemporary Folk Album. His career has taken on a new lease of life in the 90s; Prine presented music programme *Town And Country* for Channel 4 Television in the UK in 1992. *Lost Dogs & Mixed Blessings* was another strong work. In January 1998 he was reported to be seriously ill.

PROCLAIMERS

THIS SCOTTISH FOLK DUO CONSISTED OF IDENTICAL TWINS CRAIG AND CHARLIE REID. THEY HAD A HIT WITH 'LETTER From America' (1987). Pete Wingfield was brought in to produce *Sunshine On Leith*. They reappeared with the *King Of The Road* EP. The title track was taken from the film *The Crossing*. *Hit The Highway* became a major-selling record in the USA during 1994.

PROCOL HARUM

THIS UK GROUP FORMED IN ESSEX, ENGLAND, COMPRISING GARY BROOKER (b. 1945; PIANO/VOCALS), MATTHEW FISHER (b. 1946; organ), Bobby Harrison (b. 1943; drums), Ray Royer (b. 1945; guitar) and Dave Knights (b. 1945; bass). Their debut 'A Whiter Shade Of Pale' made them one of the biggest successes of 1967. It was followed by Top 10 hit 'Homburg'. By the time of the hastily thrown-together album, the band were falling apart. Harrison and Royer departed to be replaced with Barrie 'B.J.' Wilson (b. 1947) and **Robin Trower** (b. 1945), respectively. The other unofficial member of the band was lyricist Keith Reid (b. 1946). *A Salty Dog* was released to critical acclaim.

Fisher and Knights departed and the circle was completed when Chris Copping (b. 1945; organ/bass) joined the group. Trower's **Jimi Hendrix**-influenced guitar patterns on *Broken Barricades* began to give the band a heavier image, not compatible with Reid's fantasy sagas. This was resolved by Trower's departure, the recruitment of Dave Ball (b. 1950) and Alan Cartwright's (bass) addition. The band pursued a more symphonic direction. The success of *Live In Concert With The Edmonton Symphony Orchestra* was unexpected. Further line-up changes ensued with Ball departing and Mick Grabham (ex-Plastic Penny, Cochise) joining in 1972. This line-up became their most stable and they enjoyed four successful and busy years during which they released three albums. 'Nothing But The Truth' and 'The Idol' were high points of *Exotic Birds And Fruit*. 'Pandora's Box' was the jewel in *Procol's Ninth*, giving them another surprise hit single. By the time their final album was released in 1977 the musical climate had dramatically changed and Procol Harum were one of the first casualties of punk. During 1991 they re-formed, and have continued to tour sporadically ever since – the most recent line-up being Brooker, Fisher, Matt Pegg (bass), Geoff Whitehorn (guitar) and Graham Broad (drums).

PRODIGY

THIS BAND, BASED IN BRAINTREE, ESSEX, COMPRISE MC MAXIM, DANCERS KEITH AND LEEROY, PLUS LIAM Howlett (b. *c.* 1971). Howlett, a former break-dancer and DJ, handles most of the compositions and governs the band's style. They began their career with *The Android* EP. The big time beckoned when 'Charly', a children's public information film sample overlaying a pulsating backbeat, reached UK number 3. It signified the crossover of rave music from the clubs to the chart. The Prodigy have been derided by the underground as the group that killed rave. They followed up with the equally impressive *G-Force* EP. By 1993 Howlett was using MC Keith to cover the hip-hop angle, and built his own home studio. He also occupied himself with remixes for Front 242 and **Jesus Jones**. *Music For The Jilted Generation* (1994), confirmed the group's ability. 'Their Law' maintained links to the rave scene that broke the Prodigy by attacking the Criminal Justice Bill, which sought to legislate against such events. Their UK number 1 hit 'Firestarter', prompted complaints that the song incited young people to commit arson. The follow-up 'Beatle' provided a second UK chart-topper. *The Fat Of The Land* was released to ecstatic reviews, becoming a monster hit. More media outrage ensued with the release of 'Smack My Bitch Up' and its 'pornographic' promo.

PSYCHEDELIC FURS

UNTIL THEY RECRUITED DRUMMER VINCE ELY IN 1979, RICHARD BUTLER (b. 1956; VOCALS), ROGER MORRIS (GUITAR), ex-Photon John Ashton (b. 1957; guitar), Duncan Kilburn (woodwinds) and Tim Butler (b. 1958; bass) had difficulty finding work. A Radio 1 session for **John Peel** convinced CBS to sign them. Their debut album was followed by a chart entry with 'Dumb Waiter' from *Talk Talk Talk*. 'Love My Way', from *Forever Now*, nearly reached the UK Top 40. Philip Calvert (ex-**Birthday Party**) replaced Ely in 1982, and they released *Mirror Moves* which included UK Top 30 hit, 'Heaven'. 'Pretty In Pink' featured in the 1986 film of the same title. By 1990, Ashton and the Butler brothers were all that remained of the band. Three years later Richard Butler moved on to Love Spit Love.

PUBLIC ENEMY

PUBLIC ENEMY WERE VIEWED EITHER AS RADICAL AND POSITIVE, OR AS A DISTURBING MANIFESTATION OF A SECTION of the black American ghetto underclass. Their origins can be traced to the college radio station at Adelphi University, New York in 1982. DJ **Chuck D** (b. Carlton Douglas Ridenhour, 1960) and Hank Shocklee were given the chance to mix tracks for the college station, WBAU. They were eventually joined by Flavor Flav (b. William Drayton, 1959). 1984 saw Shocklee and Chuck D mixing basement hip-hop tapes, primarily for broadcast on WBAU. By 1987 they had signed to Rick Rubin's Def Jam label and increased their line-up for musical and visual purposes – Professor Griff 'Minister Of Information' (b. Richard Griffin), DJ Terminator X (b. Norman Rogers) and a four-piece words/dance/martial arts back-up section (Security Of The First World). *Yo! Bum Rush The Show* was characteristically hard. *It Takes A Nation Of Millions To Hold Us Back* signified a clear division between them and the gangsta rappers. Public Enemy were beginning to ask questions. They proved responsive to criticism, evident in Professor Griff's ousting in 1989 following an anti-Semitic statement made in the US press. He was replaced by James Norman. *Fear Of A Black Planet* enhanced the bunker mentality which pervades the project. *Apocalypse 91* was almost as effective. There is a large reservoir of antipathy directed towards them, despite their popularity. 'Don't Believe The Hype' became a powerful a slogan in the late 80s/early 90s. Recently, several members have embarked on solo careers. Their first album in three years was 1994's *Muse Sick N Hour Message* (Music And Our Message). After a break, Public Enemy re-formed in 1998 and are touring and recording again.

PUBLIC IMAGE LIMITED

PUBLIC IMAGE LTD (PIL) WAS THE 'COMPANY' FORMED BY JOHN LYDON (b. 1956) AFTER LEAVING THE **SEX PISTOLS** IN 1978. With Keith Levene (early **Clash** guitarist), bass player **Jah Wobble** (b. John Wardle) and Canadian drummer Jim Walker, they released their debut single in 1978. In 1979 ex-**Raincoats** drummer Richard Dudanski replaced Walker. *Metal Box* came out later that year. One of the era's most radical albums, it blended Lydon's antagonism and Levene's guitar. Dudanski left and **Fall** drummer Karl Burns was enlisted until Martin Atkins (b. 1959) joined in time to tour the USA in 1980. *Paris Au Printemps* was recorded after which Wobble and Atkins left. After *Flowers Of Romance* Pete Jones (b. 1957) became bass player, and Atkins returned on drums. In 1983 Jones and Levene left as 'This Is Not A Love Song' became a Top 5 hit. *This Is What You Want, This Is What You Get*, preceded Lydon's collaboration with **Afrika Bambaataa**. *Album* featured **Ginger Baker**'s drumming talents. Lydon assembled a permanent band the following year, drawing on guitarists John McGeogh (ex-**Magazine**), Lu Edmunds (ex-**Damned**), bass player Allan Dias and drummer Bruce Smith. Lu Edmunds left in 1989 and Smith left in 1990, and the band fell into inactivity again. PiL recruited drummer Mike Joyce (ex-**Smiths**, -**Buzzcocks**), but Lydon concentrated more on his autobiography and other musical projects than PiL in the 90s.

PULP

BASED IN SHEFFIELD, JARVIS COCKER PUT THE FIRST VERSION OF PULP TOGETHER WHILST AT SCHOOL, RECORDING A **John Peel** radio session in 1981. That line-up boasted Cocker (vocals/guitar), Peter Dalton (keyboards), Jamie Pinchbeck (bass) and Wayne Furniss (drums). *After It*, the first evidence of Cocker's lyrical abilities arrived with 'Little Girl (With Blue Eyes)'. By 1992 the group's steady line-up comprised Russell Senior (b. 1962; guitar/violin), Candida Doyle (b. 1964; keyboards), Stephen Mackay (b. 1967; bass) and Nicholas Banks (b. 1966; drums). Their 1994 single, 'Do You Remember The First Time?', was accompanied by a short film in which famous celebrities were quizzed on the loss of their virginity. *His 'N' Hers*, was nominated for the 1994 Mercury Music Prize. *Different Class* was their debut for Island. Russell Senior left the band in 1997.

PURE PRAIRIE LEAGUE

FORMED IN 1971, THIS US COUNTRY ROCK GROUP COMPRISED CRAIG LEE FULLER (VOCALS/GUITAR), GEORGE Powell (vocals, guitar), John Call (pedal steel guitar), Jim Lanham (bass) and Jim Caughlin (drums). Their debut album included 'Tears', and featured a portrait of an ageing cowboy, symbolizing the Old West. The cowboy would be featured on successive album covers. *Bustin' Out* proved their masterwork, one of the most underrated country rock records. In 1975 Fuller left to form American Flyer and Powell continued with bassist Mike Reilly, lead guitarist Larry Goshorn and pianist Michael Connor. Several minor albums followed.

Q

Q HAS CHANGED THE NATURE OF ROCK JOURNALISM SINCE ITS APPEARANCE IN 1986. FOUNDING EDITORS DAVID Hepworth and Mark Ellen and designer Andy Cowles ensured it rapidly established a strong identity at a time when established journals were losing theirs. Fortuitously, they secured an interview with **Paul McCartney** for the first issue, after which UK circulation grew steadily from an initial 41,000 to 173,000 by the end of 1990. By mid-1996, *Q* had reached worldwide sales of over 215,000. The founders went on to establish *Mojo* in 1993. From 1992-95, *Q* was edited by Danny Kelly; Andrew Collins replaced him. Dave Davies took over as editor in 1997.

Q-TIPS

FORMED IN 1979 BY **PAUL YOUNG** (b. 1956), JOHN GIFFORD (GUITAR/VOCALS) AND MICK PEARL (BASS/VOCALS). After releasing a frantic version of **Joe Tex**'s 'SYSLJFM (The Letter Song)' on the independent Shotgun label, the group signed to Chrysalis, but were dropped when their debut album sold poorly. The group then signed to Rewind Records. CBS signed Young as a solo artist at the start of 1982. Q-Tips disbanded after a farewell tour and *Live At Last*.

PSYCHEDELIC FURS
Albums
Psychedelic Furs (Columbia 1980)★★★
➽ p.376 for full listings
Connections
John Peel ➽ p.258
Birthday Party ➽ p.47

PUBLIC ENEMY
Albums
Yo! Bum Rush The Show (Def Jam 1987)★★★★
Fear Of A Black Planet (Def Jam 1990)★★★
➽ p.376 for full listings
Connections
Chuck D ➽ p.92

PUBLIC IMAGE LIMITED
Albums
This Is What You Want, This Is What You Get (Virgin 1984)★★★
Happy? (Virgin 1987)★★★
➽ p.376 for full listings
Collaborators
Afrika Bambaataa ➽ p.11
Ginger Baker ➽ p.29
Leftfield ➽ p.213
Connections
Sex Pistols ➽ p.292
Clash ➽ p.93
Jah Wobble ➽ p.196
Raincoats ➽ p.272
Fall ➽ p.142
Magazine ➽ p.222
Damned ➽ p.110
Smiths ➽ p.301
Buzzcocks ➽ p.76
Further References
Book: *Public Image Limited: Rise Fall*, Clinton Heylin

PULP
Albums
Different Class (Island 1995)★★★★
This Is Hardcore (Island 1998)★★★.
➽ p.376 for full listings
Connections
John Peel ➽ p.258
Michael Jackson ➽ p.195
Further References
Video: *Pulp – A Feeling Called Love* (VVL 1996)
Book: *Pulp*, Martin Aston

PURE PRAIRIE LEAGUE
Albums
Bustin' Out (RCA 1975)★★★★
Two Lane Highway (RCA 1975)★★★★
➽ p.376 for full listings

Q-TIPS
Albums
Q-Tips (Chrysalis 1980)★★★
➽ p.376 for full listings
Connections
Paul Young ➽ p.347
Joe Tex ➽ p.319

QUATRO, SUZI
Albums
Suzi Quatro (RAK 1973)★★★
see p.376 for full listings
Connections
Fanny p.143
Mickie Most p.239
Troggs p.324

QUEEN
Albums
A Night At The Opera (EMI 1975)★★★
see p.376 for full listings

Collaborators
David Bowie p.64
Connections
Annie Lennox p.214
Eurythmics p.139

QUEEN LATIFAH
Albums
All Hail The Queen (Tommy Boy 1989)★★★★
see p.376 for full listings
Collaborators
De La Soul p.112
Shabba Ranks p.273
Connections
Motown Records p.240

QUEENSRŸCHE
Albums
Hear In The New Frontier (EMI 1997)★★★
see p.376 for full listings

? AND THE MYSTERIANS
Albums
96 Tears (Cameo 1966)★★★
see p.376 for full listings
Connections
Cameo p.79
Eddie And The Hotrods p.132
Stranglers p.331

QUICKSILVER MESSENGER SERVICE
Albums
Happy Trails (Capitol 1969)★★★★★
see p.376 for full listings
Connections
Monterey Pop Festival p.237
Nicky Hopkins p.186

QUIREBOYS
Albums
A Bit Of What You Fancy (Parlophone 1989)★★★
see p.376 for full listings
Connections
UFO p.326
Guns N'Roses p.170
Influences
Faces p.141
Mott The Hoople p.241

QUATRO, SUZI

WITH OLDER SISTER, PATTI (LATER OF **FANNY**), SUZI (b. 1950) FORMED THE ALL-FEMALE SUZI SOUL AND THE PLEASURE Seekers in 1964 and toured army bases in Vietnam. In 1971, **Mickie Most** persuaded her to record for his RAK label in England. Backed by UK musicians Alastair McKenzie (keyboards), Dave Neal (drums) and her future husband, Len Tuckey (guitar), a second RAK single, 1973's 'Can The Can', topped worldwide charts at the zenith of the glam-rock craze. The Chinnichap-Quatro run faltered when 'Your Mama Won't Like Me' stuck outside the Top 30.

By the late 80s, Suzi was working with Reg Presley of the **Troggs** on a disco revival of 'Wild Thing'. She went on to sing in the 1986 London production of Irving Berlin's *Annie Get Your Gun*.

QUEEN

FORMED AS A GLAM-ROCK UNIT IN 1972 BY BRIAN MAY (b. 1947; GUITAR) AND ROGER TAYLOR (b. ROGER MEDDOWS-TAYLOR, 1949; drums). When bassist Tim Staffell left, they recruited vocalist Freddie Mercury (b. Frederick Bulsara, 1946, d. 1991) and bassist John Deacon (b. 1951).

Queen were signed to EMI in 1972. Their self-titled album was an interesting fusion of 70s British glam and late 60s heavy rock. A second album fulfilled their early promise by reaching the UK Top 5. Soon after, 'Seven Seas Of Rhye' gave them their first hit single, while *Sheer Heart Attack* consolidated their commercial standing. In 1975, after touring the Far East, they completed the epic 'Bohemian Rhapsody' – it remained at number 1 for nine weeks. *A Night At The Opera* reached UK number 1/US Top 5; *A Day At The Races* continued the bombast. 'Crazy Little Thing Called Love' and 'Another One Bites The Dust' both reached US number 1 and their soundtrack for the film *Flash Gordon* was another success. In 1981, Queen were back at UK number 1 with 'Under Pressure' (a collaboration with **David Bowie**). After a flurry of solo ventures, they returned in fine form with the satirical 'Radio Gaga' (1984). A performance at 1985's Live Aid displayed the group at their most professional and many acclaimed them the stars of the day (though there were others who accused them of hypocrisy for breaking the boycott of apartheid-locked South Africa). In 1991, *Innuendo* entered the UK chart at number 1.

Tragically, the band's ascendancy was stopped by the AIDS-related death of Freddie Mercury, on 24 November 1991. A memorial concert took place at London's Wembley Stadium in 1992, featuring an array of stars. A new Queen album was welcomed in 1995: the Mercury vocals were recorded during his last year of life.

QUEEN LATIFAH

RAP'S FIRST LADY, QUEEN LATIFAH (b. DANA OWENS, 1970) BEGAN WORKING AS THE HUMAN BEATBOX ALONGSIDE female rapping crew Ladies Fresh, before releasing her debut single, 'Wrath Of My Madness' (1988). Her debut album enjoyed favourable reviews. By her third album, she had moved from Tommy Boy to **Motown Records**, and revealed a shift from soul and ragga tones to sophisticated, sassy hip hop. She has also acted in the films *Juice*, *Jungle Fever* and *House Party 2*.

In 1998, Latifah set up her own Flavor Unit record label and management company; she also worked with **De La Soul**, Monie Love and **Shabba Ranks**. Though she is a forthright advocate of black rights, she is also the daughter of and sister to policemen. *Black Reign* is dedicated to the memory of that same brother.

QUEENSRŸCHE

FORMED IN SEATTLE, USA, BY GEOFF TATE (VOCALS), CHRIS DEGARMO (GUITAR), MICHAEL WILTON (GUITAR), EDDIE Jackson (bass) and Scott Rockenfield (drums). In 1983, the band launched their own 206 Records label to house the songs on a self-titled 12-inch EP. EMI Records then offered them a seven-album deal; their debut, *The Warning*, was comparatively disappointing. *Rage For Order* saw the band creating a more distinctive style, making full use of modern technology and *Operation Mindcrime*, a George Orwell-inspired concept album, was greeted with acclaim. Managed by Q-Prime, worldwide sales of over one million lifted the band into rock's first division. *Empire* boasted a stripped-down but still dream-like rock aesthetic, best sampled on 'Silent Lucidity' (US Top 5), which was nominated for a Grammy. *Promised Land* continued the band's tradition of dramatic song structures.

? AND THE MYSTERIANS

FORMED IN 1963 IN TEXAS, USA. ? AND THE MYSTERIANS ENTERED ROCK 'N' ROLL IMMORTALITY AS THE BAND THAT popularized the classic '96 Tears' in 1966 (US number 1/UK number 37). ? (Question Mark) was Mexican vocalist Rudy Martinez (b. 1945) and the Mysterians were Frankie Rodriguez Jnr (b. 1951; keyboards), Robert Lee 'Bobby' Balderrama (b. 1950; lead guitar), Francisco Hernandez 'Frank' Lugo (b. 1947; bass) and Eduardo Delgardo 'Eddie' Serrato (b. 1947; drums). '96 Tears' was initially intended as the b-side of their debut single, but after being popularized by Michigan DJs, Cameo records took it to number 1. Another b-side, '8-Teen' was later a hit as 'Eighteen', for **Alice Cooper** (1971). '96 Tears' was later revived by artists including **Eddie And The Hot Rods** (1976), Garland Jeffreys (1981) and the **Stranglers** (1990).

QUICKSILVER MESSENGER SERVICE

US BAND FORMED IN 1964: DINO VALENTI (VOCALS), JOHN CIPOLLINA (GUITAR), DAVID FREIBERG (b. 1938; BASS/vocals), Jim Murray (vocals/harmonica), Casey Sonoban (drums) and, very briefly, Alexander 'Skip' Spence (b. 1946; guitar/vocals). Their first two albums were hugely influential in the development of the San Francisco scene. Valenti was jailed for a drugs offence and did not rejoin the band until 1969. In 1965, Sonoban left and Gary Duncan (b. Gary Grubb, 1946; guitar) and Greg Elmore (b. 1946) joined. Murray departed after the band's appearance at the **Monterey Pop Festival** in 1967. Duncan left and was replaced by UK session pianist **Nicky Hopkins**. His contributions breathed some life into the disappointing *Shady Grove*. *Just For Love* showed a further decline. In 1987, Gary Duncan recorded an ill-received album carrying the Quicksilver name.

QUIREBOYS

SPIKE (VOCALS), NIGEL MOGG (BASS), CHRIS JOHNSTONE (KEYBOARDS), GUY BAILEY (GUITAR), GINGER (GUITAR) AND COZE (drums) signed to EMI, Coze and Ginger were replaced by Ian Wallace and Guy Griffin. They recorded *A Bit Of What You Fancy*; it was an immediate success, entering the UK charts at number 2. However, after a three year gap, *Bitter Sweet & Twisted* failed to ignite and Spike left. The Quireboys had come to a natural conclusion.

RADIOHEAD

UK ROCK GROUP FORMED IN 1991. THOM YORKE (b. 1968; VOCALS/GUITAR), ED O'BRIEN (b. EDWARD JOHN O'BRIEN, 1968; guitar), Colin Greenwood (b. Colin Charles Greenwood, 1969; bass), Phil Selway (b. Philip James Selway, 1967; drums) and Colin's brother Jonny (b. 1971; guitar/keyboards) were at school together; they became Radiohead in 1991. Their first commercial broadcast followed when 'Prove Yourself' was voted Gary Davies' 'Happening Track Of The Week' on BBC Radio 1. 'Creep' then became *the* alternative rock song in the UK in 1993. Ignored when first released in 1992, its re-release sparked enormous interest as the group toured with Kingmaker and **James**, and reached the UK Top 10. *Pablo Honey* (Top 30) was followed by *The Bends* in 1995. By the end of the year *The Bends* had been universally acclaimed, winning Radiohead a BRIT Awards nomination as the best band of the year. Two years later, the band unveiled its follow-up, *OK Computer*, which received spectacular reviews. In 1998, they embarked on a world tour, including playing the Tibetan Freedom Concert 98.

RAFFERTY, GERRY

GERRY RAFFERTY (b. 1947) BEGAN HIS CAREER WITH THE **HUMBLEBUMS** IN 1968. AFTER ITS DEMISE, TRANSATLANTIC offered him a solo contract. *Can I Have My Money Back?* blended folk and gentle pop music, but it was a commercial failure. After four years with the **Stealers Wheel**, he went solo again with *City To City* in 1978. 'Baker Street' became a hit single and a multi-million seller. The follow-up, *Night Owl*, also featured strong songs with haunting melodies. Since then Rafferty's output has been sparse. He made a single contribution to the film *Local Hero* and his 'Letter From America' was a Top 3 hit for the **Proclaimers** in 1987. *North And South* continued the themes of his previous albums, while *On A Wing And A Prayer* made little impression on the charts. *Over My Head* (1995) was lacklustre and *One More Dream* had a good selection of songs but was marred by having some tracks re-recorded.

RAGE AGAINST THE MACHINE

RAGE AGAINST THE MACHINE'S MUSIC IS AN AGGRESSIVE BLEND OF METAL GUITAR AND HIP-HOP RHYTHMS THAT address the band's concerns about inner-city deprivation, racism, censorship, propaganda and similar issues. Formed in Los Angeles in 1991 by former Lock Up guitarist Tom Morello and ex-Inside Out vocalist Zack de la Rocha, with Timmy C (bass) and Brad Wilk (drums), Rage Against The Machine's self-titled debut was a hit on both sides of the Atlantic, scoring single success with 'Killing In The Name'. *Evil Empire* was more successful (US number 1). Tracks such as the highly political 'Vietnow' and 'Down Rodeo' showed the band at their most angry. In 1998, they were rumoured to be recording a new album.

RADIOHEAD

Albums
OK Computer (Parlophone 1997)★★★★
➽ p.376 for full listings

Connections
James ➽ p.196

Influences
Joy Division ➽ p.202
Smiths ➽ p.301
Talking Heads ➽ p.316

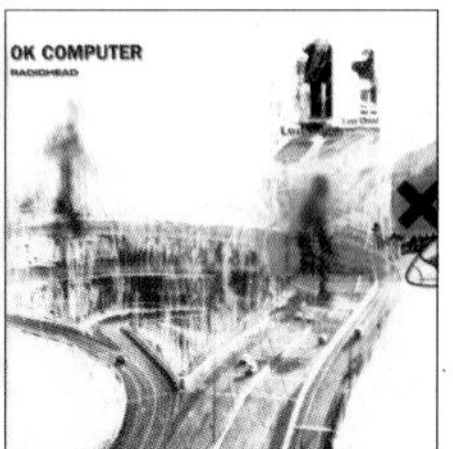

RAFFERTY, GERRY

Albums
City To City (United Artists 1978)★★★★
➽ p.376 for full listings

Connections
Humblebums ➽ p.190
Stealers Wheel ➽ p.308
Proclaimers ➽ p.268

RAGE AGAINST THE MACHINE

Albums
Evil Empire (Epic 1996)★★★★
➽ p.376 for full listings

RAIN PARADE
Albums
Beyond The Sunset (Restless 1985)★★★
➧ p.376 for full listings

RAINBOW
Albums
Rainbow Rising (Polydor 1976)★★★★
➧ p.376 for full listings
Connections
Deep Purple ➧ p.113
Russ Ballard ➧ p.31
Further References
Book: *Rainbow*, Peter Makowski

RAINCOATS
Albums
Looking In The Shadows (Geffen 1996)★★★
➧ p.376 for full listings
Connections
Slits ➧ p.300
Nirvana ➧ p.248
Sonic Youth ➧ p.302

RAITT, BONNIE
Albums
Nick Of Time (Capitol 1989)★★★★
Luck Of The Draw (Capitol 1991)★★★★
➧ p.376 for full listings
Collaborators
Bruce Hornsby ➧ p.186
Jackson Browne ➧ p.71
Bryan Adams ➧ p.9
Connections
Little Feat ➧ p.216
Paul Brady ➧ p.66
Further References
Book: *Just In The Nick Of Time*, Mark Bego

RAMONES
Albums
Ramones (Sire 1976)★★★★
The Ramones Leave Home (Sire 1977)★★★★
➧ p.376 for full listings
Collaborators
Phil Spector ➧ p.304
Connections
Richard Hell ➧ p.179
Ronettes ➧ p.282
Further References
Book: *Ramones: An American Band*, Jim Bessman

RANKS, SHABBA
Albums
Rough & Ready Vol. 1 (Epic 1992)★★★★
➧ p.376 for full listings
Collaborators
Chaka Demus ➧ p.86
Maxi Priest ➧ p.267
Connections
Motown Records ➧ p.240
Temptations ➧ p.318
Further References
Video: *Fresh And Wild X Rated* (1992)

RARE EARTH
Albums
Back To Earth (Rare Earth 1975)★★★
➧ p.376 for full listings

RAIN PARADE

PART OF LOS ANGELES' ROCK RENAISSANCE OF THE EARLY 80S, THE RAIN PARADE DREW FROM LATE 60S INFLUENCES to forge a new brand of psychedelia-tinged rock. After a promising debut single, 'What She's Done To Your Mind', the band – David Roback (vocals/guitar/percussion), brother Steve (vocals/bass), Matthew Piucci (vocals/guitar/sitar), Will Glenn (keyboards/violin) and Eddie Kalwa (drums) – issued *Emergency Third Rail Power Trip* (1983) to critical acclaim and a contract with Island, despite the loss of David Roback (who then formed Opal with Kendra Smith, eventually re-emerging in **Mazzy Star**). His replacement, John Thoman, arrived alongside new drummer Mark Marcum for *Beyond The Sunset*, drawn from live performances in Japan. *Crashing Dream* emerged later in the year, but some of Rain Parade's otherworldly, evocative nature had been lost. Piucci went on to form Gone Fishin' and also recorded an album with Crazy Horse.

RAINBOW

IN 1975 **RITCHIE BLACKMORE** (b. 1945; GUITAR) FORMED RAINBOW WITH RONNIE JAMES DIO (VOCALS), MICKEY Lee Soule (keyboards), Craig Gruber (bass) and Gary Driscoll (drums). Their debut, *Ritchie Blackmore's Rainbow*, was released in 1975. The constant turnover of personnel reflected Blackmore's quest for the ultimate line-up and sound. Jimmy Bain took over from Gruber, and Cozy Powell replaced Driscoll. With Tony Carey on keyboards, *Rainbow Rising* was released. Shortly after, Bob Daisley and David Stone replaced Bain and Carey. After difficulties with Blackmore, Dio departed in 1978. His replacement was Graham Bonnet,who Blackmore had forced out of **Deep Purple** in 1973. *Down To Earth*, which saw the return of Roger Glover on bass, was a marked departure from the Dio days, but has the enduring single, 'Since You've Been Gone', written and originally recorded by **Russ Ballard**. Bonnet and Powell soon became victims of another reorganization of Rainbow's line-up. Bobby Rondinelli (drums) and Joe Lynn Turner (vocals) brought an American feel to the band; a commercial sound was introduced on *Difficult To Cure*, the album which produced 'I Surrender', their biggest hit. Thereafter the group went into decline and, in 1984, the popular Deep Purple reunion marked its end. The group played its last gig on 14 March 1984 in Japan, accompanied by a symphony orchestra, as Blackmore adapted Beethoven's 'Ninth Symphony'. Since then, the name has been resurrected in a number of line-ups. A new studio recording was issued in 1995. The present vocalist is Dougie White.

RAINCOATS

FORMED IN LONDON IN 1976 BY GINA BIRCH AND ANA Da SILVA, RAINCOATS WAS AUGMENTED BY VICKY ASPINALL, manager Shirley O'Loughlin and Palmolive. The Raincoats' debut, 'Fairytale In The Supermarket', appeared on Rough Trade in 1979. A self-titled album the same year boasted a similarly distinctive sound. *Odyshape* followed in 1981, with two further singles, a cover version of Sly Stone's 'Running Away' in 1982, 'Animal Rhapsody' and *The Kitchen Tapes* a year later. The Raincoats delivered their swansong in 1984 with *Moving*. Kurt Cobain of **Nirvana** asked the Raincoats to support Nirvana on upcoming UK dates (he would also write sleeve-notes for the CD reissues of their albums); thus the 1994 model Raincoats featured Da Silva with Birch, joined by violinist Anne Wood (violin) and Steve Shelley (drums). Palmolive was said to be leading a life of religious evangelicism in Texas, while Aspinall was running a dance label. The band re-formed in 1995 and issued *Looking In The Shadows* in 1996. Da Silva and Birch were augmented by Heather Dunn (drums) and Anne Wood.

RAITT, BONNIE

RAITT (b. 1949) ESTABLISHED HER REPUTATION WITH LIVE APPEARANCES THROUGHOUT THE EAST COAST CIRCUIT. The somewhat reverential *Bonnie Raitt* was replaced by the contemporary perspective of *Give It Up*. *Taking My Time*, with assistance from Lowell George and Bill Payne from **Little Feat**, demonstrated greater diversity. Subsequent releases followed a similar pattern, and although *Streetlights* was a disappointment, *Home Plate*, reasserted her talent. The success of *Sweet Forgiveness* was a natural progression on which its follow-up, *The Glow*, failed to capitalize. After *Green Light* and *Nine Lives*, Raitt was dropped by Warner Brothers after 15 years. In 1989 *Nick Of Time* won a Grammy. *Luck Of The Draw* had strong material from **Paul Brady**, **Hiatt** and Raitt herself. It was another multi-million-seller. *Longing In Their Hearts*, spawned further US hits and achieved two million sales. On her first live album, *Road Tested*, Raitt was joined by **Bruce Hornsby**, **Jackson Browne**, Kim Wilson, Ruth Brown, Charles Brown and **Bryan Adams**.

RAMONES

THE RAMONES, JOHNNY RAMONE (b. JOHN CUMMINGS, 1951; GUITAR), DEE DEE RAMONE (b. DOUGLAS COLVIN, 1952; bass) and Joey Ramone (b. Jeffrey Hyman, 1952; drums), made their debut at New York's Performance Studio on 30 March 1974. Two months later, manager Tommy Ramone (b. Tommy Erdelyi, 1952) replaced Joey who switched to vocals. With a residency at the renowned CBGB's club, they were leading proponents of punk rock. *Ramones* was a startling first album. Its high-octane assault drew from 50s kitsch and 60s garage bands, while leather jackets, ripped jeans and an affected dumbness enhanced the music's cartoon quality. The group's debut in London in 1976 influenced a generation of British punk musicians.

The Ramones Leave Home, which included 'Suzie Is A Headbanger' and 'Gimme Gimme Shock Treatment', confirmed the sonic attack of its predecessor. *Rocket To Russia* produced 'Sheena Is A Punk Rocker', their first UK Top 30 hit in 1977. In 1978 Tommy Ramone left for a career in production and Marky Ramone (b. Marc Bell; drums) replaced him for *Road To Ruin*. The band took a starring role in the trivial film *Rock 'N' Roll High School*, which led to collaboration with **Phil Spector**. The resultant release, *End Of The Century*, was a curious hybrid, but contained a sympathetic version of the **Ronettes**' 'Baby I Love You', which became the group's biggest UK hit single when it reached the Top 10. The Ramones entered the 80s looking increasingly anachronistic, and *Pleasant Dreams*, produced by Graham Gouldman, revealed a group outshone by the acts they had inspired. However, *Subterranean Jungle* showed a renewed purpose that was maintained sporadically on *Animal Boy* and *Halfway To Sanity*. Subsequent albums proved anti-climactic. They announced their final gig on 6 August 1996 at The Palace club in Hollywood (captured on the 1997 live album).

RANKS, SHABBA

SHABBA RANKS (b. REXTON GORDON, 1965) RECORDED 'HEAT UNDER SUFFERERS FEET' IN 1985. DESPITE AN ALBUM shared with **Chaka Demus** (*Rough And Rugged*), he could not establish himself and, in 1988, left King Jammys for Bobby Digital's new label and Heatwave sound system, scoring immediately with 'Mama Man', 'Peanie Peanie' and then 'Wicked In Bed', which proved highly successful in 1989.

Mike 'Home T' Bennett teamed Shabba with Cocoa Tea and his vocal group, Home T4, for 'Who She Love' then 'Stop Spreading Rumours'. They took the formula to Gussie Clarke who produced *Holding On* and big hits including 'Pirate's Anthem', 'Twice My Age' (with Krystal) and 'Mr Loverman'. The song was re-voiced with Chevelle Franklin and became an international success in 1993. Shabba dominated reggae music, although recording for few producers apart from Bobby Digital and Gussie Clarke. In 1990 his duet with **Maxi Priest** on 'Housecall' became a major crossover hit. *Raw As Ever* won Shabba a Grammy in 1991, as did *X-tra Naked* in 1992 – the first DJ to win two consecutive Grammy Awards. In 1995, he released 'Let's Get It On' as a trailer for *A Mi Shabba*.

RARE EARTH

SAXOPHONIST GIL BRIDGES AND DRUMMER PETE RIVERA (HOORELBEKE) FORMED THEIR FIRST R&B BAND, THE Sunliners, in Detroit in 1961. John Parrish (bass) joined in 1962; Rod Richards (guitar) and Kenny James (keyboard) followed in 1966. Other members included Ralph Terrana (keyboards), Russ Terrana (guitar) and Fred Saxon (saxophone). After years of unspectacular records the group signed to Verve and released *Dreams And Answers*. They signed to **Motown** in 1969, where a progressive-rock label was named after them. It had an immediate success with a rock-flavoured version of the **Temptations**' hit 'Get Ready', which reached the US Top 10. Another Temptations' classic, '(I Know) I'm Losing You', brought them success in 1970, as did original material such as 'Born To Wander' and 'I Just Want To Celebrate'. Despite personnel changes, the band continued to record and tour into the 80s. At the end of the decade the line-up comprised Gil Bridges, Ray Monette, Edward Guzman, Wayne Baraks, Rick Warner, Dean Boucher and Randy Burghdoff. The band continues to be successful in Germany.

RASPBERRIES

FORMED IN 1970, THE ORIGINAL LINE-UP WAS **ERIC CARMEN** (b. 1949; VOCALS/GUITAR/KEYBOARDS) AND MARTY MURPHY (guitar), as well as Jim Bonfanti (b. 1948; drums). Murphy was quickly replaced by Wally Bryson (b. 1949), who introduced John Alleksic. The latter was relaced by Dave Smalley (b. 1949; guitar/bass). The Raspberries' love of the **Beatles** was apparent on their debut 'Don't Wanna Say Goodbye'. Its melodic flair set the tone of 'Go All The Way', which rose to number 5 in the US chart. The group's talents really blossomed on *Fresh*. *Side 3* reflected a growing split between Carmen and the Bonfanti/Smalley team who were fired in 1973. Scott McCarl (guitar) and Michael McBride (drums) completed the new line-up which debuted the following year with the gloriously ambitious 'Overnight Sensation (Hit Record)'. The attendant album, *Starting Over*, contained several memorable songs, but Carmen clearly required a broader canvas for his work. He disbanded the group in 1975 and embarked on a solo career, while Bryson resurfaced in two disappointing pop/rock bands, Tattoo and Fotomaker.

RAY, JOHNNIE

RAY (b. 1927, d. 1990) WAS ALSO KNOWN AS THE PRINCE OF WAILS, THE NABOB OF SOB AND THE HOWLING SUCCESS because of his highly emotional singing and apparent ability to cry at will. Of North American Indian origin, he was signed by Columbia in 1951. His first record, 'Whiskey And Gin', was followed by 'Cry'.

Always acknowledging his gospel roots, Ray recorded several tracks associated with black artists, including the **Drifters**' R&B hit 'Such a Night' (1954) and 'Just Walkin' In the Rain' (1956), which climbed to US number 2. Three of his US hits reached UK number 1, including 'Yes Tonight Josephine' (1957). His last performance is said to have been on 7 October 1989; he died of liver failure a few months later in Los Angeles.

REA, CHRIS

REA'S (b. 1951) FIRST GROUP WAS MAGDALENE. HIS FIRST SOLO ALBUM INCLUDED THE IMPASSIONED 'FOOL (IF YOU Think It's Over)' which reached the Top 20 in the US and later had success in Britain with **Elkie Brooks**. Throughout the early 80s, he gained in popularity across the Continent, notably with 'Deltics'. Rea's most successful record at this time was 'I Can Hear Your Heartbeat' from *Water Sign*. In Britain, the breakthrough was *Shamrock Diaries*. *Dancing With Strangers* included 'Joys Of Christmas'. In 1989, *The Road To Hell* reached number 1. *Auberge* also topped the UK chart, while its title track reached the UK Top 20. 'Julia' a track from *Espresso Logic* became his 27th UK hit in 1993.

RASPBERRIES
Albums
Starting Over (Capitol 1974)★★★
➽ p.376 for full listings
Connections
Eric Carmen ➽ p.82
Influences
Beatles ➽ p.38

RAY, JOHNNIE
Albums
Johnnie Ray Sings The Big Beat (Columbia 1957)★★★★
➽ p.376 for full listings
Connections
Drifters ➽ p.126
Further References
Book: *The Johnnie Ray Story*, Ray Sonin

REA, CHRIS
Albums
The Road To Hell (Warners 1989)★★★★
➽ p.376 for full listings

Connections
Deep Purple ➽ p.113
Elkie Brooks ➽ p.69

READER, EDDI

AFTER EIGHT YEARS AS A SESSION SINGER, SCOTTISH-BORN READER (b. SADENIA READER, *c.* 1959) REACHED UK NUMBER 1 with **Fairground Attraction**'s 'Perfect' (1988). After their disbandment, Reader embarked on a solo career. Her album, *Mirmama*, included songs of **Loudon Wainwright III**, Fred Neil and **John Prine**, but failed to match RCA's expectations. A second album followed in 1994 which included the Top 40 hit 'Patience Of Angels'. In 1996 a change of image revealed a 50s glamour queen.

REBEL MC

AFTER LEAVING HIS DOUBLE TROUBLE PARTNERS (MICHAEL MENSON AND LEIGH GUEST), REBEL MC (b. MICHAEL ALEC Anthony West, 1965) earned greater plaudits as a solo artist. The single 'Rich An' Getting Richer' was an excellent social commentary rant with dub-synchronized, orchestral mixes. On *Black Meaning Good*, he was joined by Tenor Fly, Barrington Levy, **P. P. Arnold** and Dennis Brown. 'Rebel Music', meanwhile, was remixed by Pasemaster Mase of De La Soul.

READER, EDDI
Albums
Eddi Reader (Blanco y Negro 1994)★★★★
➽ p.376 for full listings
Connections
Fairground Attraction ➽ p.141
Loudon Wainwright III ➽ p.331
John Prine ➽ p.268

REBEL MC
Albums
Word, Sound And Prayer (Desire 1992)★★★
➽ p.376 for full listings
Collaborators
P. P. Arnold ➽ p.21
Connections
De La Soul ➽ p.112

RED HOT CHILI PEPPERS
Albums
Blood, Sugar, Sex, Magik (Warners 1991)★★★★
➽ p.376 for full listings
Connections
Gang Of Four ➽ p.158
George Clinton ➽ p.94
Beatles ➽ p.38
Rick Rubin ➽ p.284
Jane's Addiction ➽ p.197
Further References
Book: *True Men Don't Kill Coyotes*, Dave Thompson

REDBONE
Albums
Cycles (RCA 1978)★★
➽ p.376 for full listings

REDDING, OTIS
Albums
Pain In My Heart (Atco 1964)★★★★
➽ p.376 for full listings
Collaborators
Steve Cropper ➽ p.105
Connections
Rolling Stones ➽ p.281
Sam Cooke ➽ p.100
Temptations ➽ p.318
Monterey Pop Festival ➽ p.237
Bar-Kays ➽ p.32
Further References
Book: *The Otis Redding Story*, Jane Schiesel

REDDY, HELEN
Albums
Ear Candy (Capitol 1977)★★★
➽ p.376 for full listings
Connections
Carole King ➽ p.205
Gerry Goffin ➽ p.164
Cilla Black ➽ p.49

REED, JIMMY
Albums
Rockin' With Reed (Vee Jay 1959)★★★★
➽ p.376 for full listings
Connections
Rolling Stones ➽ p.281
Grateful Dead ➽ p.167

REED, LOU
Albums
Transformer (RCA 1972)★★★★
➽ p.376 for full listings

Connections
John Cale ➽ p.78
Velvet Underground ➽ p.329
David Bowie ➽ p.64
Laurie Anderson ➽ p.18
Further References
Book: *Lou Reed & The Velvets*, Nigel Trevena

RED HOT CHILI PEPPERS

LED BY 'ANTWAN THE SWAN' (b. ANTHONY KIEDIS, 1962; VOCALS), THE BAND'S ORIGINAL LINE-UP ALSO FEATURED 'Flea' (b. Michael Balzary, 1962; bass), Hillel Slovak (b. 1962, d. 1988; guitar) and Jack Irons (drums). The band acquired a contract with EMI America and the **Gang Of Four**'s Andy Gill produced their first album. They then set about building their reputation as a live outfit. Slovak returned to guitar for the second album, this time produced by **George Clinton**. Their third album shifted back to rock from the soul infatuation of its predecessors. The *Abbey Road* EP (1988) featured a pastiche of the famous **Beatles** album pose on the cover (the band were totally naked save for socks covering their genitalia). Slovak took an accidental heroin overdose and died in June. Deeply upset, Irons left, and the band recruited John Frusciante (guitar) and Chad Smith (b. 1962; drums). After the release of *Mother's Milk*, 'Knock Me Down' was issued as a tribute to Slovak. *Blood, Sugar, Sex, Magik*, produced by **Rick Rubin**, was their most commercial excursion. Frusciante was replaced in 1992 by Arik Marshall, who was sacked in 1993; Frusciante returned in 1998. In 1994, Dave Navarro (b. 1967; ex-**Jane's Addiction**) joined to participate in recording *One Hot Minute*; he left in 1998.

REDBONE

REDBONE (FROM AN ANGLICIZED CAJUN EPITHET FOR HALF-BREED) WAS FORMED IN 1968. THE BROTHERS PAT and Lolly Vegas were joined by Tony Bellamy (rhythm guitar/vocals) and Peter DePoe (drums). The quartet scored an international hit with 'Witch Queen Of New Orleans'. In 1974, they enjoyed their sole million-seller, 'Come And Get Your Love', but Redbone could not transform their taut, rhythmic, style into consistent success.

REDDING, OTIS

REDDING (b. 1941, d. 1967) BEGAN RECORDING FOR LOCAL INDEPENDENTS AND 'SHE'S ALRIGHT', CREDITED TO OTIS And The Shooters, was quickly followed by 'Shout Ba Malama'. 'These Arms Of Mine' crept into the American Hot 100 in 1963. He remained a cult figure until 1965 and the release of *Otis Blue*, in which original material nestled beside the **Rolling Stones**' 'Satisfaction' and two songs by **Sam Cooke**. Redding's version of the **Temptations**' 'My Girl' became a UK hit and 'Tramp', a duet with Carla Thomas, also provided success. A triumphant appearance at the **Monterey Pop Festival** suggested that Redding was about to attract a wider following, but tragedy struck on 10 December 1967. The light aircraft in which he was travelling plunged into Lake Monona, Madison, Wisconsin, killing Redding and four members of the **Bar-Kays**. The wistful '(Sittin' On) The Dock Of The Bay', which he had recorded three days earlier, became his only million-seller and US pop number 1. Redding's emotional drive remains compelling, and the songs he wrote, often with guitarist **Steve Cropper**, remain some of soul's most enduring moments.

REDDY, HELEN

A BIG-VOICED INTERPRETER OF ROCK BALLADS, HELEN REDDY (b. 1942) HAD ALREADY STARRED IN HER OWN TELEVISION show before winning a trip to New York in an Australian talent contest in 1966. There, an appearance on the *Tonight Show* led to a contract with Capitol and the 1971 hit single 'I Don't Know How To Love Him' from *Jesus Christ Superstar*. The following year, 'I Am Woman', co-written with Peter Allen, went to number 1 in the US and sold over a million copies. A dozen more hit singles followed. Her 1976 hit, 'I Can't Hear You No More', was composed by **Carole King** and **Gerry Goffin**, while Reddy's final Top 20 record (to date) was a revival of **Cilla Black**'s 1964 chart-topper, 'You're My World', co-produced by Kim Fowley. During the 80s she performed infrequently, but made her first major showcase in years at the Westwood Playhouse, Los Angeles, in 1986. In 1995 she was performing at London's Café Royal in the evenings, while rehearsing by day for a lead in the hit musical *Blood Brothers* on Broadway.

REED, JIMMY

REED (b. MATHIS JAMES REED, 1925, d. 1976) WAS THE MOST SUCCESSFUL BLUES SINGER OF THE 1950S. CONTRACTED by Vee Jay in 1953, his 'You Don't Have To Go' of 1955 was followed by a string of hits such as 'Ain't That Lovin' You Baby', 'You've Got Me Dizzy', 'Bright Lights Big City', 'I'm Gonna Get My Baby' and 'Honest I Do'. Much of this success must be attributed to his friend Eddie Taylor, who played on most of Reed's sessions, and his wife, Mama Reed, who wrote many of his songs. Reed's later years were marred by his unreliability, illness (he was an epileptic) and the bottle. On his visit to Europe in the early 60s it was obvious all was not well. He gained control over his drink problem, but died of respiratory failure. Reed's songs have influenced countless artists. The **Rolling Stones**, **Pretty Things** and the **Grateful Dead** acknowledge a considerable debt to him.

REED, LOU

REED (b. LEWIS ALLEN REED, 1942) MADE HIS US RECORDING DEBUT WITH THE SHADES IN 1957, LATER BECOMING A contract songwriter with Pickwick. His many compositions from this era include 'The Ostrich' (1965), which so impressed the label hierarchy that Reed formed the Primitives to promote it as a single. The group also included **John Cale**, thus sowing the seeds of the **Velvet Underground**. Reed left the group to go solo, releasing *Lou Reed* in 1972. Recorded in London with British musicians, the set had some excellent songs but was marred by indistinct production.

David Bowie, a long-time Velvets aficionado, oversaw *Transformer*. Although uneven, it included the classic 'Walk On The Wild Side', but with *Berlin* Reed returned to the dark side of his talents. A back-up band, built around guitarists Dick Wagner and Steve Hunter, provided muscle on the live *Rock 'N' Roll Animal*, but the subsequent *Sally Can't Dance* showed an artist bereft of direction. *Metal Machine Music* was followed by the sedate *Coney Island Baby*, the inherent charm of which was diluted on the inconsequential *Rock 'N' Roll Heart*. However, its successor, *Street Hassle*, displayed a rejuvenated power, and although *The Bells* and *Growing Up In Public* failed to scale similar heights, they showed new maturity. Reed entered the 80s a stronger, more incisive performer. However, despite the promise of selections such as *The Blue Mask*, few were prepared for *New York*. This splendid return to form created considerable interest in Reed's back-catalogue.

In 1993, Reed joined his legendary colleagues for a high-profile Velvet Underground reunion. *Set The Twilight Reeling* saw Reed in light-hearted mood, perhaps inspired by a romantic partnership with **Laurie Anderson**, one of the guest singers on a cover version of Reed's 'Perfect Day', released in 1997 as a charity single.

REEF

REEF COMPRISED KENWYN HOUSE (b. 1970; GUITAR), GARY STRINGER (b. 1973; VOCALS), DOMINIC GREENSMITH (b. 1970; drums) and Jack Bessant (b. 1971; bass). They rose to fame via an advert for the Sony Mini-Disc portable stereo system. Their first release was 'Good Feeling' in late 1994. *Replenish* (1995) was well received, although comparisons to **Pearl Jam** were widespread. *Glow* put them in the spotlight as a potentially major act, helped by the chart success of 'Place Your Hands'.

REEF
Albums
Glow (Additive 1996)★★★★
➽ p.376 for full listings
Influences
Pearl Jam ➽ p.257

REEVES, JIM

REEVES'S (b. JAMES TRAVIS REEVES, 1923, d. 1964) FIRST SINGING WORK WAS WITH MOON MULLICAN'S BAND in his native Texas. In 1952, Reeves moved to KWKH in Shreveport, where his duties included hosting the *Louisiana Hayride*. He stood in as a performer for **Hank Williams** and was signed immediately to Abbott. In 1953, Reeves received gold discs for 'Mexican Joe' and 'Bimbo'. In 1955, he joined the *Grand Ole Opry* and began recording for RCA, his first hit being 'Yonder Comes A Sucker'. 'Four Walls' (1957) became an enormous US hit, crossing over to the pop market and becoming a template for his future work.

Reeves swapped his western outfit for a suit and tie, and, following his hit 'Blue Boy', his group, the Wagonmasters, became the Blue Boys. Having established a commercial format, 'Gentleman Jim' had success with 'You're The Only Good Thing', 'Adios Amigo', 'Welcome To My World' (UK number 6) and 'Guilty'. Reeves disliked flying and to avoid commercial airlines obtained his own daytime pilot's licence. On 31 July 1964, Reeves and his pianist/manager, Dean Manuel, died when their single-engine plane crashed outside Nashville during a storm. Posthumously, Reeves became a best-selling artist with *40 Golden Greats* topping the album charts in 1975.

REEVES, JIM
Albums
Moonlight And Roses (RCA Victor 1964)★★★★
➽ p.376 for full listings
Connections
Hank Williams ➽ p.339

REEVES, MARTHA

REEVES (b. 1941) WAS SCHOOLED IN BOTH GOSPEL AND CLASSICAL MUSIC, BUT IT WAS VOCAL GROUP R&B THAT caught her imagination. Performing as Martha Lavaille, she joined the fledgling **Motown** in 1961. Berry Gordy offered her the chance to record as **Martha And The Vandellas**. From 1963 they were one of Motown's most successful recording outfits and from 1967 Reeves was given individual credit in front of the group before ill health forced her to retire. She signed a solo contract with MCA in 1973. *Martha Reeves* (1974) earned critical acclaim but was disappointing commercially. Moving to Arista in 1977, she was submerged by the late 70s disco boom on a series of albums that allowed her little room to display her talents. Her subsequent recording contracts have proved unproductive, and, since the early 80s, she has found consistent work on package tours.

REEVES, MARTHA
Albums
Martha Reeves (MCA 1974)★★★
➽ p.376 for full listings
Connections
Motown Records ➽ p.240
Martha And The Vandellas ➽ p.226

REID, TERRY

REID'S (b. 1949) DEBUT SINGLE, 'THE HAND DON'T FIT THE GLOVE', WAS ISSUED IN 1967, BUT GREATER RECOGNITION came in a trio with Pete Solley (keyboards) and Keith Webb (drums). Reid became a popular figure in the USA following a tour supporting **Cream**. His debut *Bang Bang You're Terry Reid*, produced by **Mickie Most**, emphasized the artist's vocal talent and impassioned guitar style. Reid's own compositions included 'Friends', which became a hit for **Arrival**. He re-established his recording career with *The Driver*, which featured able support from **Joe Walsh**, Tim Schmidt and **Howard Jones**.

REID, TERRY
Albums
Bang Bang You're Terry Reid (Epic 1968)★★★★
➽ p.376 for full listings
Collaborators
Joe Walsh ➽ p.333
Howard Jones ➽ p.201
Connections
Cream ➽ p.103

R.E.M.

R.E.M. PLAYED THEIR FIRST CONCERT IN ATHENS, GEORGIA, USA, ON 19 APRIL 1980. THE LINE-UP WAS MICHAEL STIPE (b. 1960; vocals), Peter Buck (b. 1956; guitar), Mike Mills (b. 1958; bass) and

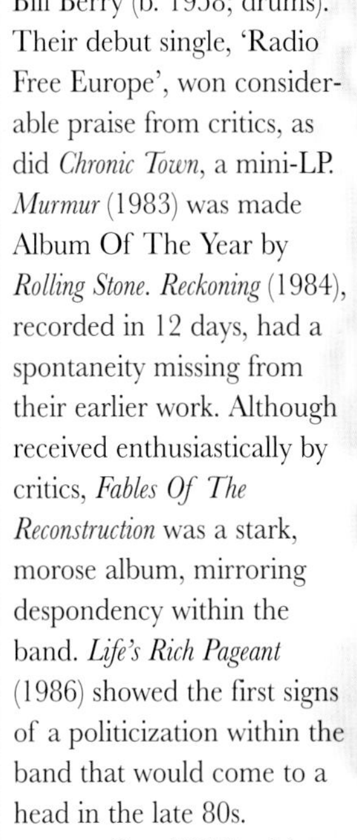

Bill Berry (b. 1958; drums). Their debut single, 'Radio Free Europe', won considerable praise from critics, as did *Chronic Town*, a mini-LP. *Murmur* (1983) was made Album Of The Year by *Rolling Stone*. *Reckoning* (1984), recorded in 12 days, had a spontaneity missing from their earlier work. Although received enthusiastically by critics, *Fables Of The Reconstruction* was a stark, morose album, mirroring despondency within the band. *Life's Rich Pageant* (1986) showed the first signs of a politicization within the band that would come to a head in the late 80s.

Green (1988) sold slowly but steadily in the USA, the attendant single 'Stand' reaching number 6 there, while 'Orange Crush' entered the UK Top 30. The band re-emerged in 1991 with *Out Of Time*. Ostensibly their first album to contain 'love' songs, it was unanimously hailed as a masterpiece and entered the UK Top 5 on its release, topping both US and UK album charts soon after. The accompanying singles, 'Losing My Religion', 'Shiny Happy People', 'Near Wild Heaven' and 'Radio Song', gave them further hits. After picking up countless awards during the early 90s the band has maintained the high standard set by *Out Of Time*. *Automatic For The People* was released in 1992 to universal favour, reaching the top of the charts in the UK and USA. *Monster* showed the band in grunge-like mode, showing fans and critics alike that they had not gone soft. In 1996 the band re-signed with Warner Brothers for the largest recording contract advance in history: $80 million was guaranteed for a five-album contract. *New Adventures In Hi-Fi* was released in September. In 1997 Bill Berry announced he would be leaving R.E.M. after 17 years; the remaining members quickly confirmed that they would be continuing without him.

R.E.M.
Albums
Automatic For The People (Warners 1992)★★★★
➽ p.376 for full listings

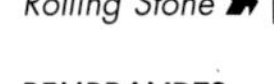

R.E.M.
OUT OF TIME

Connections
Rolling Stone ➽ p.281

REMBRANDTS

THE REMBRANDTS, DANNY WILDE AND PHIL SOLEM, ROSE TO PROMINENCE IN 1995 WITH 'I'LL BE THERE FOR YOU', their theme song to the hit series *Friends*. Their 1991 self-titled debut, included a Top 15 *Billboard* hit, 'Just The Way It Is Baby'. The album peaked at number 88 in the US charts. A full-length version of 'I'll Be There For You' was added during recording sessions for *L.P.* (some copies were shipped without the song being mentioned on the track-listing).

REMBRANDTS
Albums
Rembrandts (East West 1991)★★★
➽ p.376 for full listings
Connections
Friends

REO SPEEDWAGON
Albums
REO Two (Epic 1972)★★★
➧ p.376 for full listings
Connections
Ted Nugent ➧ p.249
Further References
Video: *Wheels Are Turnin'* (Virgin Vision 1987)

REPLACEMENTS
Albums
Pleased To Meet Me (Sire 1987)★★★★
➧ p.377 for full listings

REPUBLICA
Albums
Republica (DeConstruction 1997)★★★
➧ p.377 for full listings
Connections
Björk ➧ p.48
Prefab Sprout ➧ p.264
Prodigy ➧ p.268 ➧ p.
Bow Wow Wow ➧ p.63

RESIDENTS
Albums
Meet The Residents (Ralph 1974)★★★★
➧ p.377 for full listings
Connections
James Brown ➧ p.70
Hank Williams ➧ p.339
Elvis Presley ➧ p.265

RETURN TO FOREVER
Albums
Return To Forever (ECM 1973)★★★★
➧ p.377 for full listings
Connections
Chick Corea

REO SPEEDWAGON

THE GROUP WAS FORMED IN 1970 WHEN NEAL DOUGHTY (b. 1946; PIANO) AND ALAN GRATZER (b. 1948; DRUMS) were joined by Gary Richrath (b. 1949; guitar/songwriter). Barry Luttnell (vocals) and Greg Philbin (bass) completed the line-up for *REO Speedwagon*, but the former was quickly replaced by Kevin Cronin (b. 1951). Although *REO Two* and *Ridin' The Storm Out* eventually achieved gold status, disputes about direction culminated in the departure of their second vocalist. Michael Murphy replaced him in 1974, but when ensuing albums failed to generate interest, Cronin rejoined his former colleagues. Bruce Hall (b. 1953; bass) was also brought in. The live summary, *You Get What You Play For*, became the group's first platinum disc, a distinction shared by its successor, *You Can Tune A Piano, But You Can't Tuna Fish*. *Nine Lives* gave the impression that the band had peaked – a view banished by *Hi Infidelity* (1980), a self-confident collection which topped the US album charts and spawned a series of successful singles. *Wheels Are Turning* recaptured the zest of *Hi Infidelity* and brought a second US number 1 with 'Can't Fight This Feeling'. *Life As We Know It* and its successor, *The Earth, A Small Man, His Dog And A Chicken*, emphasized the group's professionalism with a line-up of Cronin, Doughty, Hall, Dave Amato (b. 1953; lead guitar; ex-**Ted Nugent**), Bryan Hitt (b. 1954; drums) and Jesse Harms (b. 1952; keyboards).

REPLACEMENTS

US POP-PUNK GROUP FORMED IN 1979 WITH PAUL WESTERBERG (b. 1960; GUITAR/VOCALS), TOMMY STINSON (b. 1966; bass), Bob Stinson (b. 1959, d. 1995; guitar) and Chris Mars (b. 1961; drums). Their debut album showcased their power-trash style. Beloved by critics, the group appeared on the verge of mainstream success in America with the release of *Pleased To Meet Me*. However All *Shook Down* was rather subdued and the group disbanded in 1990. Mars was the first to record solo. Later, Westerberg signed under his own name, while Tommy Stinson formed his own bands. Dunlap reappeared on Dan Baird's debut solo album. Bob Stinson died in 1995 of a suspected drug overdose.

REPUBLICA

REPUBLICA FORMED IN LONDON IN 1994 WHEN TIM DORNEY (KEYBOARDS), TEAMED UP WITH Andy Todd (keyboards/bass) who had engineered for artists such as **Björk**, **Prefab Sprout** and Barbra Streisand. They found Saffron (b. 1968; vocals) performing as part of the **Prodigy**'s stage act and began creating a sound which gave club rhythms a radio-friendly, adult-pop sheen. They added David Barbarossa (drums; ex-**Bow Wow Wow**) and Johnny Male (guitar). The US market pounced upon the 1996 single 'Ready To Go', which was followed by the equally impressive 'Drop Dead Gorgeous' and a solid debut album.

RESIDENTS

IN 1972 THE GROUP LAUNCHED RALPH RECORDS AS AN OUTLET FOR THEIR WORK. *MEET THE Residents* established their unconventional style, matching bizarre reconstructions of 60s pop favourites with original material. *Third Reich Rock 'N' Roll* contained two suites devoted to their twisted cover versions, whereas *Not Available* comprised material the group did not wish to release. *The Commercial Album* consisted of 40 tracks lasting exactly 1 minute. *American Composers Series* included *George And James*, a homage to George Gershwin and **James Brown**, *Stars And Hank Forever*, a celebration of **Hank Williams** and John Phillip Sousa, and *The King And Eye*, an album of **Elvis Presley** hits.

RETURN TO FOREVER

US LATIN-INFLUENCED JAZZ GROUP: CHICK COREA (b. 1941; KEYBOARDS), JOE FARRELL (b. 1937, d. 1986; SOPRANO saxophone/flute), Flora Purim (b. 1942; vocals), Stanley Clarke (b. 1951; bass/electric bass) and Airto Moreira (b. 1941; percussion). The group toured and made two commercially successful albums before disbanding in 1973. Keeping Clarke, Corea immediately put together the second of his three successive Return To Forever bands. Hiring Bill Connors to play electric guitar (soon replaced by Earl Klugh and then Al DiMeola), and Lenny White (drums), the second band was more rock oriented. Producing a harder overall sound, it achieved massive popularity, and its 1976 *Romantic Warrior* quickly became its best-selling album. The third, and final, Return To Forever produced soft, unchallenging music and refined itself out of existence in 1980. Corea, Clarke, DiMeola and White joined up for a single tour in 1983.

REVERE, PAUL, AND THE RAIDERS

FORMED IN 1961, THE GROUP COMPRISED PAUL REVERE (PIANO), MARK LINDSAY (b. 1942; VOCALS/SAXOPHONE), Drake Levin (guitar), Mike Holliday (bass) and Michael Smith (drums). Their version of 'Louie Louie' was issued in 1963, but it was local rivals the **Kingsmen** who secured the national hit. In 1965 the Raiders hit their commercial stride with 'Steppin' Out', followed by a series of US hits including 'Just Like Me'. Later members Freddie Weller (guitar), Keith Allison (bass) and Joe (Correro) Jnr. (drums) appeared on *Hard & Heavy (With Marshmallow)* and *Collage*. In 1969, Lindsay embarked on a concurrent solo career, but although 'Arizona' sold over one million copies, later releases were less successful. Two years later, the Raiders had a US chart-topper with 'Indian Reservation', previously a UK hit for Don Fardon, but it proved their final Top 20 hit.

REZILLOS

FORMED IN SCOTLAND IN 1976, THE REZILLOS WERE EUGENE REYNOLDS (b. ALAN FORBES; VOCALS), FAY FIFE (b. Sheila Hynde; vocals), Luke Warm aka Jo Callis (lead guitar), Hi Fi Harris (b. Mark Harris; guitar), Dr. D.K. Smythe (bass), Angel Patterson (b. Alan Patterson; drums) and Gale Warning (backing vocals). Their irreverent repertoire consisted of pre-beat favourites and glam-rock staples. Harris, Smythe and Warning left, while auxiliary member William Mysterious (b. William Donaldson; bass/saxophone) joined on a permanent basis. Signed to Sire, the quintet enjoyed a UK Top 20 hit with the satirical 'Top Of The Pops'. *Can't Stand The Rezillos* also charted, before internal pressures pulled them apart in 1978. Fife and Reynolds formed the Revillos, while the rest of the band became Shake. Callis later found fame in the **Human League**. In the 90s the Revillos/Rezillos re-formed for tours in Japan, and a live album bookmarked their 15-year career.

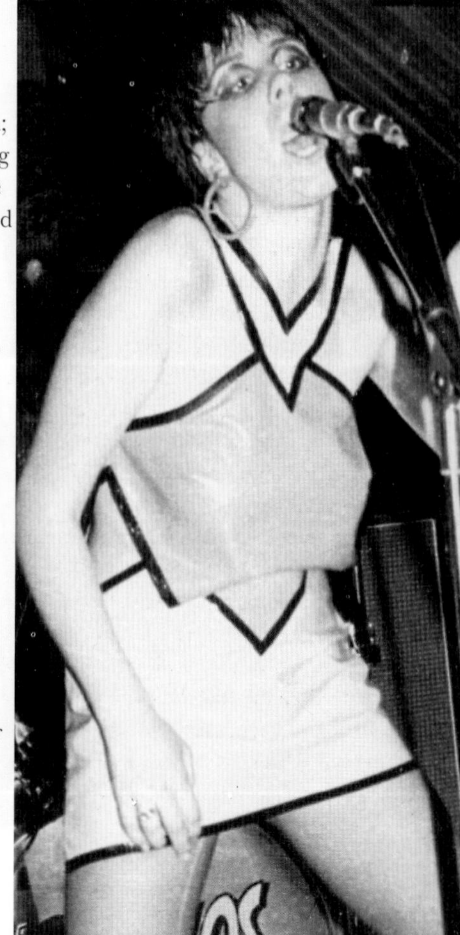

REVERE, PAUL, AND THE RAIDERS
Albums
Goin' To Memphis (1968)★★★
➧ p.377 for full listings
Connections
Kingsmen ➧ p.207

RHINOCEROS

ROCK BAND RHINOCEROS WAS AN ELEKTRA SIGNING OF THE LATE 60S. THE GROUP FEATURED MICHAEL FONFARA (keyboards; ex-**Electric Flag**), Billy Mundi (drums; ex-**Mothers Of Invention**), Doug Hastings (guitar; ex-**Buffalo Springfield**), Danny Weis (guitar; ex-**Iron Butterfly**) and John Finlay (vocals). Unfortunately the music was disappointing. On the self-titled debut album only the **Buddy Miles**-influenced 'You're My Girl (I Don't Want To Discuss It)' and the instrumental 'Apricot Brandy' stood out. Two more disappointing albums followed.

RICH, TONY, PROJECT

RICH'S BIG BREAK FOLLOWED A MEETING WITH **BABYFACE**. RICH THEN CONTRIBUTED SEVERAL SONGS TO AN ALBUM BY **Ann Peebles**, which led to a meeting with her husband L.A. Reid. After hearing his four-track demos, Reid offered him a contract with LaFace. Rich moved to Atlanta in 1993. He produced a session with **Elton John** and the Sounds Of Blackness on a tribute record to **Curtis Mayfield**, plus half an album for 4.0 and 'I Sit Away' for **Boyz II Men**. He also produced for Johnny Gill and conducted remixes on material by **Toni Braxton** and **TLC**. In 1994 he began work on his own debut, *Words*, a blend of R&B and soul.

RICHARD, CLIFF

RICHARD (b. HARRY ROGER WEBB, 1940) BEGAN HIS CAREER AS A ROCK 'N' ROLL PERFORMER IN 1957. Fascinated by **Elvis Presley**, he joined a skiffle group before teaming up with Terry Smart (drums) and Ken Payne (guitar) in the **Drifters**; Ian Samwell (lead guitar) joined later. In 1958, they were seen by theatrical agent George Ganyou who financed a demo tape. EMI producer Norrie Paramor auditioned the quartet and, with a couple of session musicians, they recorded 'Schoolboy Crush'; however the b-side, 'Move It', proved more popular, reaching UK number 2. Meanwhile Richard made his debut on television's *Oh Boy!*, and rapidly replaced **Marty Wilde** as Britain's premier rock 'n' roll talent. Samwell left the Drifters to become a professional songwriter, and by the end of 1958 the line-up was **Hank B. Marvin** and Bruce Welch. The group also changed its name to the **Shadows**, to prevent confusion with the American Drifters.

In 1959, Richard's recording of Lionel Bart's 'Living Doll' gave him a UK number 1; three months later he returned to the top with 'Travellin' Light'. He also starred in two films within 12 months. *Serious Charge*, a non-musical drama, caused controversy because it dealt with homosexual blackmail. *Expresso Bongo* was a cinematic pop landmark.

From 1960 Richard's career progressed well. Hits such as 'Please Don't Tease' (number 1), 'Nine Times Out Of Ten' and 'Theme For A Dream' demonstrated his range, and in 1962 came 'The Young Ones'. A pop anthem to youth, with striking guitar work from Hank Marvin, the song proved one of his most memorable hits. The film of the same name broke box office records and spawned a series of similar movies from its star. His run of UK Top 10 hits continued until 1965, including 'Bachelor Boy', 'Summer Holiday', 'On The Beach' and 'I Could Easily Fall'.

In 1966 he almost retired after converting to fundamentalist Christianity, but chose to use his career as an expression of his faith. In the swiftly changing cultural climate of the late 60s, Richard's hold on the pop charts could not be guaranteed. In the 1968 Eurovision Song Contest the jury placed him a close second with 'Congratulations', which proved one of the biggest UK number 1s of the year. Immediately thereafter, Cliff's chart progress declined until a second shot at the Eurovision Song Contest with 'Power To All Our Friends' brought his only other Top 10 success of the period. In 1976 Bruce Welch of the Shadows was assigned to produce Richard, resulting in the best-selling *I'm Nearly Famous*, which included two major hits, 'Miss You Nights' and 'Devil Woman'. The latter gave Richard a rare US chart success.

Richard adopted a more contemporary sound on *Rock 'N' Roll Juvenile*, but the most startling breakthrough was the attendant single 'We Don't Talk Anymore'; it gave Richard his first UK number 1 in over a decade and reached the US Top 10. The 'new' Richard sound brought further well-arranged hits, such as 'Carrie' and 'Wired For Sound', and ensured he was a chart regular throughout the 80s.

Cliff has displayed a valiant longevity. He parodied one of his earliest hits with comedy quartet the Young Ones, registering another number 1; and he celebrated his 50th birthday with the anti-war hit 'From A Distance'; appeared at the VE Day celebrations in 1995 with Vera Lynn and received a knighthood.

His starring role in the John Farrar and Tim Rice musical, *Heathcliff*, resulted in *Songs From Heathcliff*.

RICHIE, LIONEL

RICHIE (b. 1949) FORMED A SUCCESSION OF R&B GROUPS in the mid-60s. In 1968 he became the lead singer and saxophonist with the **Commodores** – America's most popular 70s soul group – and in 1981, he duetted with **Diana Ross** on the theme song for the film *Endless Love*. Issued as a single, the track topped the UK and US charts, and became one of **Motown**'s biggest hits to date. Its success encouraged Richie to follow a solo career in 1982. His debut, *Lionel Richie*, produced the chart-topping 'Truly', which continued the style of his ballads with the Commodores. In 1983 he released *Can't Slow Down*, which eventually sold more than 15 million copies worldwide. Several Top 10 hits followed, the most successful of which was 'Hello', a sentimental love song far from his R&B roots. In 1986 came *Dancing On The Ceiling*, another phenomenally popular album that produced a run of US and UK hits. Since then, he has kept recording and live work to a minimum. He broke the silence in 1996 with *Louder Than Words*, notable for its well-crafted soul music, which has become known as 'Urban R&B'.

RICHMAN, JONATHAN

RICHMAN (b. 1951) BECAME PROMINENT IN THE EARLY 70S AS LEADER OF THE **MODERN LOVERS**. DRAWING INSPIRATION from 50s pop and the **Velvet Underground**, the group offered a garage-band sound, as evinced on their UK hit 'Roadrunner' and the infectious instrumental 'Egyptian Reggae' in 1977. However, Richman increasingly distanced himself from electric music and disbanded the group in 1978 to pursue a solo career. He exhumed the Modern Lovers name in the 80s without any alteration to his style and continues to enjoy considerable cult popularity. In the 90s he made a cameo appearance in the movie *Kingpin*. In 1996, he signed to **Neil Young**'s label Vapor and released *Surrender To Jonathan*.

REZILLOS
Albums
Can't Stand The Rezillos (Sire 1978)★★★
➽ p.377 for full listings
Connections
Human League ➽ p.189

RHINOCEROS
Albums
Rhinoceros (Elektra 1968)★★★
➽ p.377 for full listings
Connections
Electric Flag ➽ p.134
Mothers Of Invention ➽ p.239
Buffalo Springfield ➽ p.74
Iron Butterfly ➽ p.193
Influences
Buddy Miles ➽ p.233

RICH, TONY, PROJECT
Albums
Words (LaFace/Arista 1996)★★★★
➽ p.377 for full listings
Connections
Babyface ➽ p.26
Elton John ➽ p.200
Curtis Mayfield ➽ p.228
Boyz II Men ➽ p.65
Toni Braxton ➽ p.66
TLC ➽ p.322

RICHARD, CLIFF
Albums
Cliff's Hit Album (Columbia 1963)★★★★
➽ p.377 for full listings
Collaborators
Hank B. Marvin ➽ p.226
Shadows ➽ p.293
Connections
Marty Wilde ➽ p.338
Influences
Elvis Presley ➽ p.265
Further References
Book: *Cliff Richard: The Autobiography*, Steve Turner
Film: *Summer Holiday* (1962)

RICHIE, LIONEL
Albums
Can't Slow Down (Motown 1983)★★★★
Dancing On The Ceiling (Motown 1986)★★★
➽ p.377 for full listings
Collaborators
Diana Ross ➽ p.283
Connections
Commodores ➽ p.99
Motown Records ➽ p.240
Further References
Book: *Lionel Richie: An Illustrated Biography*, David Nathan

RICHMAN, JONATHAN
Albums
as The Modern Lovers *The Modern Lovers* (Beserkley 1976)★★★★
➽ p.377 for full listings
Connections
Modern Lovers ➽ p.236
Neil Young ➽ p.346

RIDE
Albums
Going Blank Again (Creation 1992)★★★★
➧ p.377 for full listings
Connections
Bob Marley ➧ p.225
Free ➧ p.154

RIGHT SAID FRED
Albums
Up (Tug 1992)★★★
➧ p.377 for full listings
Connections
Bob Dylan ➧ p.128
Boy George ➧ p.65

RIGHTEOUS BROTHERS
Albums
You've Lost That Lovin' Feelin' (Philles 1965)★★★★
➧ p.377 for full listings
Connections
Phil Spector ➧ p.304
Knickerbocker ➧ p.209
Further References
Film: *Beach Ball* (1964)

RIMES, LEANN
Albums
Blue (Curb 1996)★★★★
➧ p.377 for full listings
Connections
Patsy Cline ➧ p.94

RIVERS, JOHNNY
Albums
Johnny Rivers At The Whisky A Go Go (Imperial 1964)★★★★
➧ p.377 for full listings
Connections
Elvis Presley ➧ p.265
Johnny Cash ➧ p.84
Ricky Nelson ➧ p.244
Chuck Berry ➧ p.45
Willie Dixon ➧ p.120
Pete Seeger ➧ p.291
Motown Records ➧ p.240
Beach Boys ➧ p.36

ROACHFORD
Albums
Roachford (Columbia 1988)★★★
➧ p.377 for full listings
Collaborators
Terence Trent D'Arby ➧ p.110
Christians ➧ p.91
Connections
Prince ➧ p.267

ROBERTSON, B.A.
Albums
Initial Success (Asylum 1980)★★
➧ p.377 for full listings
Collaborators
Maggie Bell ➧ p.42
Connections
Abba ➧ p.6

ROBERTSON, ROBBIE
Albums
Robbie Robertson (Geffen 1987)★★★★
➧ p.377 for full listings

RIDE

FORMED IN 1988 BY MARK GARDENER (VOCALS/GUITAR), ANDY BELL (GUITAR/VOCALS), STEPHAN QUERALT (BASS) AND Laurence Colbert (drums), their 1990 debut EP reached number 71 in the UK charts. A Top 40 placing followed with the *Play* EP. *Nowhere* reached number 14 and a third EP went into the Top 20. More success followed with *Going Blank Again*, *Carnival Of Light* and *Tarantula*, recorded in London with producer Richard 'Digby' Smith, who worked with **Bob Marley** and **Free**. However following its release Ride split up. In 1997 Bell announced a new band, Hurricane #1.

RIGHT SAID FRED

CAMP UK POP TRIO: BROTHERS RICHARD PETER JOHN FAIRBRASS (b. 1953; VOCALS) AND FRED (b. CHRISTOPHER Abbott Bernard Fairbrass, 1956), plus Rob Manzoli (b. 1954). Fred had toured with **Bob Dylan** and played with Then Jerico in 1989. Richard, originally a bass player, had worked with several prominent artists, including **Boy George**. The band is called after the novelty 1962 Bernard Cribbins' hit. Their initial success was embedded in the kitsch classic 'I'm Too Sexy', with similar follow-ups 'Deeply Dippy' and 'Don't Talk Just Kiss'. In 1991, they sold more singles than any other artist in the UK, excluding **Bryan Adams**, but their second album sold disappointingly.

RIGHTEOUS BROTHERS

DESPITE THE NAME, BILL MEDLEY (b. 1940) AND BOBBY HATFIELD (b. 1940) WERE NOT RELATED. MEDLEY'S SONOROUS baritone blending with Hatfield's soaring high tenor is redolent of classic R&B. A series of excellent singles, notably 'Little Latin Lupe Lu', was the result. **Phil Spector** signed the act to his Philles label. 'You've Lost That Lovin' Feelin'' topped the US and UK charts, but the relationship between performers and mentor rapidly soured. The Righteous Brothers moved outlets in 1966, but despite a gold disc for '(You're My) Soul And Inspiration', they could not sustain their success. They split in 1968, with Medley going solo and Hatfield retaining the name with new partner Jimmy Walker (ex-**Knickerbockers**). The collaboration was short-lived. The original pair were reunited in 1974 for an appearance on *The Sonny And Cher Comedy Hour*. They scored a US Top 3 hit that year with 'Rock 'n' Roll Heaven', but could not regain former glories. A reissue of 'Unchained Melody', a hit for the Righteous Brothers in 1965, topped the UK chart in 1990 after it featured in the film *Ghost*.

RIMES, LEANN

RIMES (b. 1982) RECORDED *ALL THAT*, AGED 11. ONE TRACK, AN ACHING BALLAD, 'BLUE', HAD BEEN WRITTEN BY BILL Mack for **Patsy Cline**, who died before recording it. It was an instant US hit. Her second country number 1 came with the up-tempo 'One Way Ticket (Because I Can)'. *Blue* also topped the country albums chart. At the 1997 Grammy Awards, Rimes won Best New Artist, Best Female Country and Best Country Song for 'Blue', and at the same year's *Billboard* Awards, she won another six honours, including Artist Of The Year. In 1998, she re-established herself in the Top 20 with 'How Do I Live'.

RIVERS, JOHNNY

RIVERS (b. JOHN RAMISTELLA, 1942) ENJOYED A SUCCESSION OF HITS IN THE 60S AND 70S, INITIALLY BY COVERING R&B songs and eventually with his own compositions. In 1958 top disc jockey **Alan Freed** gave the singer his new name, Johnny Rivers. His first single, 'Baby Come Back', was issued that year. At 17, Rivers moved to Nashville, where he wrote songs with Roger Miller, and recorded demo records for **Elvis Presley**, **Johnny Cash** and **Ricky Nelson**, who recorded Rivers' 'Make Believe' in 1960.

His first album for Imperial, *Johnny Rivers At The Whisky A Go Go* (where he was performing), was released in 1964 and yielded his first hit, **Chuck Berry**'s 'Memphis', which reached number 2. Other hits during 1964-65 included Berry's 'Maybelline', Harold Dorman's 'Mountain Of Love', the traditional folk song 'Midnight Special', **Willie Dixon**'s 'Seventh Son' and **Pete Seeger**'s 'Where Have All The Flowers Gone'. Rivers also launched his own Soul City label in 1966, signing the popular **Fifth Dimension**, who went on to have four Top 10 singles on the label. Rivers had hits in 1967 with two **Motown** cover versions, 'Baby I Need Your Lovin'' and 'The Tracks Of My Tears'. Following an appearance at the **Monterey Pop Festival**, the James Hendricks-penned 'Summer Rain', became Rivers' last major hit of the 60s. Early 70s albums such as *Slim Slo Slider*, *Home Grown* and *LA Reggae* were critically lauded but not commercially successful, although the latter gave Rivers a Top 10 single with Huey 'Piano' Smith's 'Rockin' Pneumonia – Boogie Woogie Flu'. A version of the **Beach Boys**' 'Help Me Rhonda' was a minor success in 1975, and two years later Rivers landed his final Top 10 single, 'Swayin' To The Music (Slow Dancin')'. Rivers recorded a handful of albums in the 80s, including a live one featuring the old hits, but none reached the charts.

ROACHFORD

UK ROCK BAND: ANDREW ROACHFORD (VOCALS/KEYBOARDS/PERCUSSION), CHRIS TAYLOR (DRUMS), HAWI Gondwe (guitars) and Derrick Taylor (bass). In early 1988 the band was touring with **Terence Trent D'Arby** and the **Christians**. CBS beat many other labels to them. Two singles and an album came out in late 1988, but it was not until early 1989 that 'Cuddly Toy' was re-released to become a massive hit, closely followed by 'Family Man'. The self-titled album was also rediscovered and the band started to make in-roads into the American market.

ROBERTSON, B.A.

ROBERTSON (b. BRIAN ROBERTSON) HAD THREE UK TOP 10 SINGLES WITH 'BANG BANG', 'KNOCKED IT OFF' AND 'TO BE Or Not To Be'. This Scottish vocalist's tongue-in-cheek delivery was also apparent on 'Hold Me', a duet with **Maggie Bell**, and 'We Have A Dream', on which he fronted the 1982 Scotland World Cup Squad. The following year Robertson scored a minor hit with 'Time', a collaboration with former **Abba** member Frida, and although chart success has since proved elusive, the artist has had a successful career as a songwriter.

ROBERTSON, ROBBIE

ROBERTSON'S (b. JAIME ROBBIE ROBERTSON, 1943) PROFESSIONAL career began in 1960 when he replaced guitarist James Evans in **Ronnie Hawkins**' backing group, the Hawks. The group left Hawkins and first as the Canadian Squires, then as Levon And The Hawks, recorded some singles, including Robertson's 'The Stones I Throw'. The Hawks'

backing sessions for blues singer John Hammond led to their association with **Bob Dylan**. Robertson's raging guitar work helped complete the one-time folksinger's transformation from acoustic sage to electric guru. At the same time Robertson's lyrics assumed a greater depth, while the music of the group, now dubbed the **Band**, drew its inspiration from rural styles and soul music peers. The Band broke up in 1976 following a farewell concert which was captured in the celebratory film *The Last Waltz*, directed by Martin Scorsese, which in turn inspired Roberston's cinematic ambitions. *Carny*, which he also produced, has provided his sole starring role to date, although he maintained a working relationship with Scorsese, scoring several of his films, including *Raging Bull* and *The Color Of Money*.

A 1983 collaboration, *King Of Comedy*, was notable for Robertson's solo track, 'Between Trains'. *Robbie Robertson* (1987) was an exceptional collection and offered state-of-the-art production and notable guest contributions by **U2**, **Peter Gabriel**, **Daniel Lanois** and Gil Evans. It included exceptional compositions in 'Fallen Angel' and 'Broken Arrow'. *Storyville*, however, was a disappointment. He was not part of the re-formed Band in 1993. His most interesting project to date was with the Red Road Ensemble, a group of native Americans. In 1995 he collaborated with Scorsese again, writing the soundtrack for *Casino*.

ROBINSON, SMOKEY

A FOUNDING MEMBER OF THE **MIRACLES** IN 1955, ROBINSON'S (b. WILLIAM ROBINSON, 1940) FLEXIBLE TENOR VOICE MADE him the group's lead vocalist. In 1957 he met Berry Gordy, who produced a series of Miracles singles in 1958 and 1959, all of which featured Robinson as composer and lead singer. In 1960 he signed the Miracles to **Motown** and began grooming Robinson as his second-in-command. Soon, he was charged with developing the talents of **Mary Wells** and the **Supremes**. Between 1962 and 1964 Robinson wrote and produced a series of hit singles for Wells.

Robinson could not turn the Supremes into a hit-making act, but had no such problem with the **Temptations**. Between 1964 and 1965, Robinson was responsible for the records that established their reputation. Throughout the 60s, he combined this production and A&R work with his own career as leader of the Miracles, turning out a succession of high-quality songs. From 1967, Robinson was given individual credit on the Miracles' releases. Two years of commercial decline were righted when their 1965 recording of 'The Tracks Of My Tears' became a major hit in the UK, and the four-year-old 'The Tears Of A Clown' achieved similar success on both sides of the Atlantic in 1970. In 1971 Robinson announced that he would leave the Miracles the following year to concentrate on his role as vice-president of Motown. A year later, Robinson launched his solo career with *Smokey*. He maintained a regular release schedule through the mid-70s, with one new album each year. They made little impact, although Robinson's songwriting was as consistent as ever. His first film soundtrack, *Big Time*, in 1977, won little praise, and it appeared as if his creative peak was past. Instead, in 1979 with 'Cruisin'', he had his biggest chart success since 'The Tears Of A Clown'. Two years later, he gained his first UK number 1 with 'Being With You', a love song that was almost as successful in the US. Throughout the 80s Robinson followed a relaxed release schedule with regular small hits and consistent album sales.

ROBINSON, TOM

ROBINSON (b. 1950) FORMED HIS FIRST GROUP, DAVANQ, WITH DANNY KURSTOW, IN ENGLAND IN 1971. TWO YEARS later, Robinson formed Café Society, which evolved into the Tom Robinson Band with Mark Ambler (keyboard), 'Dolphin' Taylor (drums). TRB's *Power In The Darkness* included the UK Top 40 hit '2468 Motorway'. The quartet's *Rising Free* EP, which followed the disappointing *TRB2*, contained the sing-along 'Glad To Be Gay'. While Kurstow joined ex-**Sex Pistol** Glen Matlock in the Spectres, Robinson led the short-lived Section 27 and began songwriting collaborations with **Elton John** and **Peter Gabriel**. By 1981, he was in Berlin to record *North By Northwest* and work in alternative cabaret and fringe theatre. This period produced 1982's strident 'War Baby' and evocative 'Atmospherics', both in the UK Top 40, and a revival of **Steely Dan**'s 'Rikki Don't Lose That Number', from *Hope And Glory*. *Still Loving You* produced no equivalent, so Robinson regrouped his original band. Robinson developed a successful career as a radio presenter for the BBC. 'The Artist Formerly Known As Gay' on 1996's *Having It Both Ways* hit back at media intrusion.

ROCHES

SISTERS MAGGIE (b. 1951) AND TERRE ROCHE (b. 1953) BEGAN SINGING A MIXTURE OF TRADITIONAL, DOO-WOP AND barbershop quartet songs in New York clubs in the late 60s. Their first recording was as backing singers on **Paul Simon**'s, *There Goes Rhymin' Simon*. Through Simon, the duo recorded an unsuccessful album for CBS in 1975. The following year, younger sister Suzzy joined and the Roches became a trio. With Maggie's whimsical and waspish compositions they became favourites in New York's folk clubs. **Robert Fripp** produced their second album. *Nurds* and *Keep On Doing* maintained a high standard. *Another World* featured a full rock-based sound. Throughout the 80s the Roches continued to perform in New York and appear occasionally at European folk festivals. *Speak* went largely unnoticed in 1989, but *Three Kings* was more memorable. *A Dove* in 1992 featured the 'Ing' Song' a lyrical exercise with every word ending with 'ing'. *Can We Go Home Now?* featured several songs informed by the death of the sisters' father from Alzheimer's disease.

ROCKET FROM THE CRYPT

THE ROCK GROUP ROCKET FROM THE CRYPT FORMED IN 1990. LED BY JOHN 'SPEEDO' REIS (VOCALS/GUITAR), THE other members are N.D. (guitar), Petey X (bass), Atom (drums), Apollo 9 (saxophone) and JC 2000 (trumpet). After a series of low-key recordings they took a break to concentrate on their alter-ego band, Drive Like Jehu, just as they were being tipped as one of the bands 'most likely to' follow **Nirvana**'s international breakthrough. In 1995, they released *The State Of Art Is On Fire*, a six-song vinyl-only 10-inch record and *Hot Charity*, a nine-song vinyl-only album with a pressing of 2,000 copies. By 1996, the group had completed the recording of *Scream, Dracula, Scream!*, their most consistent work to date.

Collaborators
Bob Dylan ➤ p.128
U2 ➤ p.326
Peter Gabriel ➤ p.157
Daniel Lanois ➤ p.212
Connections
Ronnie Hawkins ➤ p.177
Band ➤ p.31

ROBINSON, SMOKEY
Albums
Being With You (Tamla 1981)★★★★
➤ p.377 for full listings
Connections
Miracles ➤ p.234
Motown Records ➤ p.240
Mary Wells ➤ p.336
Supremes ➤ p.314
Temptations ➤ p.318
Further References
Book: *Smokey: Inside My Life*, Smokey Robinson and David Ritz

ROBINSON, TOM
Albums
Power In The Darkness (Harvest 1978)★★★★
➤ p.377 for full listings
Collaborators
Elton John ➤ p.200
Peter Gabriel ➤ p.157
Steely Dan ➤ p.308
Connections
Todd Rundgren ➤ p.284
Sex Pistols ➤ p.292

ROCHES
Albums
The Roches (Warners 1979)★★★★
➤ p.377 for full listings
Connections
Paul Simon ➤ p.296
Robert Fripp ➤ p.154

ROCKET FROM THE CRYPT
Albums
Scream, Dracula, Scream! (Elemental 1996)★★★★
➤ p.377 for full listings
Connections
Nirvana ➤ p.248

ROCKPILE
Albums
Seconds Of Pleasure (F-Beat 1980)★★★
➧ p.377 for full listings
Connections
Dave Edmunds ➧ p.132
Brinsley Schwarz ➧ p.68
Nick Lowe ➧ p.219
Lulu ➧ p.219
Man ➧ p.223
Dire Straits ➧ p.120

RODGERS, PAUL
Albums
Muddy Waters Blues (London 1993)★★★★
➧ p.377 for full listings
Connections
Bad Company ➧ p.28
Free ➧ p.154

ROE, TOMMY
Albums
Sheila (ABC 1962)★★★
Sweet Pea (ABC 1966)★★★
➧ p.377 for full listings
Connections
Wonder Stuff ➧ p.343
Influences
Buddy Holly ➧ p.184

ROGERS, KENNY
Albums
Something's Burning (Reprise 1970)★★★★
The Gambler (United Artists 1978)★★★★
Eyes That See In The Dark (RCA 1983)★★★★
➧ p.377 for full listings
Collaborators
Crystal Gayle ➧ p.160
Bee Gees ➧ p.41
Connections
George Martin ➧ p.226
Further References
Video: with Dolly Parton *Real Love* (RCA/Columbia 1988)
Book: *Making It In Music*, Kenny Rogers and Len Epand

ROLLING STONE
Books: *The Rolling Stone Story*, Robert Draper
Best Of Rolling Stone: Classic Writing From The World's Most Influential Music Magazine, Robert Love
Rolling Stone: The Photographs, Laurie Kratochvil (ed.)
➧ p.377 for full listings
Connections
John Lennon ➧ p.214
Beatles ➧ p.38
Dr. Hook ➧ p.125

ROCKPILE

IN 1979 VOCALIST/GUITARIST **DAVE EDMUNDS** SUSPENDED HIS SOLO CAREER AND JOINED FORCES WITH **NICK LOWE** (ex-**Brinsley Schwarz**), Billy Bremner (bass; ex-**Lulu** And The Luvvers) and Terry Williams (drums; ex-Love Sculpture, with Edmunds, and **Man**). *Seconds Of Pleasure* fused Edmunds' love of classic rock 'n' roll with Lowe's grasp of quirky pop. The quartet split up after internal disputes, although Rockpile members guest on the pair's solo albums (*Twangin'*/Edmunds; *Nick The Knife*/Lowe). The two vocalists subsequently pursued independent paths, while Williams eventually joined **Dire Straits**.

RODGERS, PAUL

RODGERS (b. 1949) BEGAN HIS CAREER IN **FREE**, AFTER WHICH HE BECAME A FOUNDER MEMBER OF **BAD COMPANY**. LATER he was co-founder of the Firm (with **Jimmy Page**), but his solo career had never risen above cult status. *Muddy Waters Blues*, a tribute album, demonstrated Rodgers' natural feeling for the blues. *Now*, released in 1996 and co-produced by Eddie Kramer, saw excellent reviews and healthy sales.

ROE, TOMMY

VOCALIST ROE (b. 1942) BEGAN HIS CAREER WITH HIGH SCHOOL ACT, THE SATINS. THE GROUP PERFORMED SEVERAL of his compositions, notably 'Sheila', which they recorded in 1960. Though unsuccessful, Roe revived the song two years later upon securing a solo deal. This **Buddy Holly**-influenced rocker topped the US chart and reached the Top 3 in Britain. Roe scored two Top 10 hits in 1963 with 'The Folk Singer' and 'Everybody' and, although not a major chart entry, 'Sweet Pea' garnered considerable airplay thanks to pirate radio. The song reached the US Top 10, as did its follow-up, 'Hooray For Hazel', but Roe's biggest hit came in 1969 when 'Dizzy' topped the charts on both sides of the Atlantic. It returned to the top of the UK charts in 1992 in a version by the **Wonder Stuff** and Vic Reeves.

KENNY ROGERS ROLLING STONES

ROGERS, KENNY

BY 1955, US-BORN ROGERS (b. 1938) WAS PART OF A DOO-WOP GROUP, THE SCHOLARS, AND IN 1957 HE RECORDED 'That Crazy Feeling' (as Kenneth Rogers) for a small Houston label. He also recorded 'For You Alone' for the Carlton label as Kenny Rogers The First. After recording solo for Mercury, Rogers joined the New Christy Minstrels while forming a splinter group, The First Edition, with other Minstrels – Mike Settle, Thelma Camacho and Terry Williams. They signed with Reprise and Rogers sang lead on their first major hit, 'Just Dropped In (To See What Condition My Condition Was In)'. The First Edition enhanced Roger Miller's low-key arrangement of 'Ruby, Don't Take Your Love To Town' with an urgent drumbeat. The record, credited to Kenny Rogers And The First Edition, reached US number 6 and UK number 2. The group had further US success with 'Tell It All Brother' and 'Heed The Call'. *The Ballad Of Calico* (1972), written by Michael Murphey, dealt with life in a silver-mining town. The group broke up in 1974 and in 1975 Rogers signed with United Artists. Impotence was an extraordinary subject for a hit record, but 'Lucille' (US number 5, UK number 1) established Rogers as a country star. Rogers toured the UK with **Crystal Gayle**, and formed a successful partnership with Dottie West. 'You Decorated My Life' was another US hit and then came 'Coward Of The County' (US number 3, UK number 1), which became a successful television movie, and the album *Kenny* sold five million copies. Having sold 35 million albums for United Artists, Rogers moved to RCA; *Eyes That See In The Dark* was produced by Barry Gibb and featured the **Bee Gees**. It included 'Islands In The Stream' (US number 1, UK number 7) with **Dolly Parton**. Rogers was also featured on USA For Africa's highly successful 'We Are The World'.

George Martin produced *The Heart Of The Matter*, which led to chart-topping country singles, 'Morning Desire' and 'Tomb Of The Unknown Love'. The title track from *They Don't Make Them Like They Used To* was the theme song for the Kirk Douglas and Burt Lancaster film *Tough Guys*, but overall, Rogers' services on RCA may have disappointed its management, who had spent $20 million to secure his success. He now records for Magnatone.

ROLLING STONE

JANN WENNER FOUNDED *ROLLING STONE* WITH RALPH J. GLEASON, A SEASONED JAZZ AND ROCK COLUMNIST. FIRST published in San Francisco in 1967, the magazine drew its inspiration from the city's underground movement which encompassed both musical and visual arts. *Rolling Stone* was expertly designed and its conventional layout, mirroring that of the 'establishment' press, gave it an air of authority. The magazine exploited a gap in the US market for while the UK boasted *New Musical Express* and *Melody Maker*, the US had no comparable outlet for pop and rock journalism. *Rolling Stone* was uniquely informative, its record reviews were studious and well-argued, while the *Rolling Stone* Interview became a byword for lengthy, detailed examinations of musicians, their work and philosophies. Two interviews with **John Lennon**, wherein he demolished the sanctity surrounding the **Beatles**, established the magazine as a vehicle for controversial subjects, at the same time marking the end of its wholehearted interest in music. Being featured on the cover became as important as being on the front of *Time* or *Newsweek* and **Dr. Hook** brilliantly capitalized on this with the amusing 'Cover Of The *Rolling Stone*' which reached the US Top 3.

Critics bemoaned an increasingly perfunctory coverage of rock – film stars and media figures began attracting a greater percentage of covers. *Rolling Stone*'s relocation to New York in 1977 provided the final break with the past. By the 80s its most popular issues were devoted to single topics, fashion and live concerts and in the 90s it took a more 'alternative rock' direction so that it could not be usurped by the more youthful *Spin*.

ROLLING STONES

ORIGINALLY BILLED AS THE ROLLIN' STONES, THE FIRST LINE-UP OF THIS IMMEMORIAL 60S ENGLISH GROUP WAS Mick Jagger (b. Michael Philip Jagger, 1943; vocals), Keith Richard (b. Keith Richards, 1943; guitar), Brian Jones (b. Lewis Brian Hopkin-Jones, 1942, d. 1969; rhythm guitar) and Ian Stewart (b. 1938, d. 1985; piano). Their patron, **Alexis Korner**, arranged their debut gig at London's Marquee club on 21 July 1962.

In 1962, Bill Wyman (b. William Perks, 1936; bass) joined, as did Charlie Watts (b. 1941; drums) in 1963. Andrew Loog Oldham became their manager, and within weeks Decca's Dick Rowe signed the group. Oldham selected **Chuck Berry**'s 'Come On' as their debut and fired Ian Stewart as not sufficiently pop star-like. After supporting the **Everly Brothers**, **Little Richard**, **Gene Vincent** and Bo Diddley on a UK package tour, the Stones released 'I Wanna Be Your Man', which entered the Top 10 in 1964.

A flurry of recording activity saw the release of an EP and an album both titled *The Rolling Stones*. The third single, 'Not Fade Away', fused **Buddy Holly**'s quaint original with a chunky **Bo Diddley** beat that highlighted Jagger's vocal. With the momentum increasing, Oldham over-reached himself by organizing a US tour which proved premature and disappointing. After returning to the UK, the Stones released a decisive cover of the **Valentinos**' 'It's All Over Now', which gave them their first number 1.

In 1964, 'Little Red Rooster' was released and entered the *New Musical Express* chart at number 1. Their international breakthrough came in 1965. 'The Last Time' saw them emerge with their own distinctive rhythmic style and America finally succumbed to their spell with '(I Can't Get No) Satisfaction'. 'Get Off Of My Cloud' completed their trilogy of 1965 hits.

Allen Klein replaced Eric Easton as Oldham's co-manager and the Stones consolidated their success by renegotiating their Decca contract. 'Mother's Little Helper' and the Elizabethan-style 'Lady Jane', released as US-only singles, effectively displayed their contrasting styles. Both songs were included on *Aftermath*. The recording revealed the Stones as accomplished rockers and balladeers, while their writing potential was emphasized by **Chris Farlowe**'s chart-topping cover of 'Out Of Time'. Back in the singles chart, the group's success continued with '19th Nervous Breakdown' and 'Paint It Black'.

In 1967 the Stones confronted an establishment crackdown. The year began with an accomplished double a-sided single, 'Let's Spend The Night Together'/'Ruby Tuesday' which narrowly failed to reach UK number 1. The accompanying album, *Between The Buttons*, trod water and was also Oldham's final production. On 12 February, Jagger and Richard were arrested at Richard's home and charged with drugs offences. Three months later, Brian Jones was raided and charged with similar offences. The Jagger/Richard trial in June culminated in the duo receiving heavy fines and a salutary prison sentence, although the sentences were quashed on appeal. Three months later, Brian Jones faced a nine-month sentence and suffered a nervous breakdown before having his imprisonment rescinded at the end of the year.

The year ended with *Their Satanic Majesties Request* – the Stones' apparent answer to *Sgt Pepper's Lonely Hearts Club Band*. The album of psychedelic/cosmic experimentation was bereft of the R&B grit that had previously characterized the Stones' sound. The revitalization of the Stones was demonstrated in 1968 with 'Jumpin' Jack Flash', a single that rivalled the best of their previous output. The succeeding album, *Beggars Banquet*, included the socio-political 'Street Fighting Man' and the brilliantly macabre 'Sympathy For The Devil'.

While the Stones were re-establishing themselves, Brian Jones was falling deeper into drug abuse. A conviction in late 1968 prompted doubts about his availability for US tours and he became increasingly jealous of Jagger's leading role in the group. The crisis came in June 1969 when Jones officially left the group. The following month he was found dead in the swimming pool of his home.

The group played out the last months of the 60s with a mixture of vinyl triumph and further tragedy. The sublime 'Honky Tonk Women' was their last UK chart-topper. The new album, *Let It Bleed*, was an exceptional work and a promising debut from Mick Taylor (b. 1948), **John Mayall**'s former guitarist who had replaced Jones weeks before his death.

After concluding their Decca contract with a bootleg-deterring live album, *Get Yer Ya-Ya's Out*, the Stones established their own self-titled label. The first release was a three-track single, 'Brown Sugar'/'Bitch'/'Let It Rock', which contained some of their best work, but narrowly failed to reach UK number 1. The new album, *Sticky Fingers*, was as consistent as it was accomplished, and within a year the group returned with a double album, *Exile On Main Street*.

The Stones' slide into the 70s mainstream began with the patchy *Goat's Head Soup*, while 1974's 'It's Only Rock 'N' Roll' proved a better song title than a single, and the album of the same name was undistinguished.

Mick Taylor departed at the end of 1974, to be replaced by Ron Wood (b. 1947; ex-**Faces**) who appeared on their next release, *Black And Blue*. However, by 1977, the British music press had taken punk to its heart and the Stones were dismissed as champagne-swilling old men, out of touch with their audience.

The Stones responded to the challenge of their younger critics with a comeback album of remarkable power. *Some Girls* was their most consistent work in years. Later that year Keith Richard escaped a jail sentence in Toronto for drugs offences, being fined and ordered to play a couple of charity concerts. As if to celebrate his release and reconciliation with his father, he reverted to Richards, his original family name. The Stones reconvened in 1980 for *Emotional Rescue*, a lightweight album dominated by Jagger's falsetto and over-use of disco rhythms. Nevertheless, the album gave them their first UK number 1 since 1973 and the title track was a Top 10 hit on both sides of the Atlantic. 1981's *Tattoo You* was surprisingly strong and the concomitant single 'Start Me Up' was a reminder of earlier classic singles.

A three-year silence on record was broken by *Dirty Work* in 1986, which saw the Stones sign to CBS and team up with producer Steve Lillywhite, but increasingly they were concentrating on individual projects. Wyman had tasted solo chart success in 1983 with 'Je Suis Un Rock Star', and it came as little surprise when Jagger issued his own solo album, *She's The Boss*, in 1985, and a second album, *Primitive Cool*, in 1987. When Richards released the first solo work of his career in 1988, the Stones' obituary had virtually been written. However, the group reconvened in 1989 and announced that they would be working on a new album and commencing a world tour. Later that year the hastily recorded *Steel Wheels* appeared to generally good critical reception. After nearly 30 years, the Rolling Stones began the 90s with the biggest grossing international tour of all time, and reiterated their intention of playing on indefinitely. *Voodoo Lounge* (1994) was one of their finest recordings, lyrically daring and musically fresh. Riding a crest after an extraordinarily active 1995, *Stripped* dynamically emphasized just how great the Jagger/Richards songwriting team is. The band embarked on a world tour in 1998 – changing their UK dates to 1999 after a change in British tax law.

ROLLING STONES

Albums

Beggars Banquet (London 1968)★★★★★
Let It Bleed (London/Decca 1969)★★★★★
Exile On Main Street (Rolling Stones 1972)★★★★★
➧ p.377 for full listings

Collaborators

Everly Brothers ➧ p.139
Little Richard ➧ p.217
Gene Vincent ➧ p.330

Connections

Alexis Korner ➧ p.210
Buddy Holly ➧ p.184
Valentinos ➧ p.328
Chris Farlowe ➧ p.143
John Mayall ➧ p.228

Further References

CD Rom: *Voodoo Lounge* (Virgin 1995)
Video: *The Stones In The Park* (BMG 1993)
Books: *Satisfaction: The Rolling Stones*, Gered Mankowitz
Golden Stone: The Untold Life And Mysterious Death Of Brian Jones, Laura Jackson

ROLLINS, HENRY

VOCALIST HENRY ROLLINS (b. HENRY GARFIELD, 1961) QUICKLY RETURNED TO ACTION AFTER THE BREAK-UP OF **Black Flag**, releasing *Hot Animal Machine*, followed by the *Drive-By Shooting* EP (under the pseudonym Henrietta Collins And The Wifebeating Childhaters). He formed the Rollins Band in 1987 with Chris Haskett (guitar), Andrew Weiss (bass) and Sim Cain (drums). The group developed their own brand of hard rock, with blues and jazz influences. Rollins' lyrics dealt with social and political themes. *The End Of Silence* contained some of his most introspective lyrics. Rollins owns his publishing company, 2.13.61 (his birthdate), which publishes a wide range of authors. He also has a music publishing enterprise, Human Pitbull, and co-owns a record label with **Rick Rubin**, dedicated to classic punk reissues. He has appeared in the films *The Chase* and *Johnny Mnemonic*. Back with the Rollins Band, *Weight*, saw the band's first personnel change, with Melvin Gibbs replacing Weiss, and adding a funkier spine to the band's still intense core. Rollins' most recent album, 1997's *Come In And Burn*, was uninspiring.

ROLLINS, HENRY

Albums

As the Rollins Band *Live* (Eksakt 1987)★★★
The End Of Silence (Imago 1992)★★★★
Get In The Van (Imago 1994)★★★
➧ p.377 for full listings

Connections

Black Flag ➧ p.50
Rick Rubin ➧ p.284

Further References

Books: *Letters To Rollins*, R.K. Overton
Pissing In The Gene Pool
Get In The Van: On The Road With Black Flag, all titles by Henry Rollins

RONETTES
Albums
Presenting The Fabulous Ronettes Featuring Veronica (Philes 1964)★★★
➽ p.377 for full listings
Connections
Phil Spector ➽ p.304

RONSON, MICK
Albums
Slaughter On Tenth Avenue (RCA 1974)★★★
Play Don't Worry (RCA 1975)★★★
Heaven And Hull (Epic 1994)★★
➽ p.377 for full listings
Collaborators
David Bowie ➽ p.64
John Mellencamp ➽ p.231
Chrissie Hynde ➽ p.266
Connections
Mott The Hoople ➽ p.241
Ian Hunter ➽ p.190
Bob Dylan ➽ p.128
Further References
Book: *Mick Ronson Discography*, Sven Gusevik

RONSTADT, LINDA
Albums
Heart Like A Wheel (Capitol 1974)★★★★
with Emmylou Harris and Dolly Parton *Trio* (Warners 1987)★★★★
Winter Light (Elektra 1993)★★★★
➽ p.377 for full listings
Collaborators
James Ingram ➽ p.192
Dolly Parton ➽ p.256
Emmylou Harris ➽ p.175
Connections
Eagles ➽ p.130
Hank Williams ➽ p.339
Further References
Book: *The Linda Ronstadt Scrapbook*, Mary Ellen Moore
Linda Ronstadt: It's So Easy, Mark Bego

ROOMFUL OF BLUES
Albums
Hot Little Mama (Blue Flame 1981)★★★
Turn It On, Turn It Up (Bullseye Blues 1995)★★★★ *Under One Roof* (Bullseye Blues 1997)★★★
➽ p.377 for full listings

ROSE, TIM
Albums
Tim Rose (Columbia 1967)★★★★
Through Rose Coloured Glasses (Columbia 1969)★★★
➽ p.377 for full listings

RONETTES

VERONICA 'RONNIE' BENNETT (b. 1943), HER SISTER ESTELLE (b. 1944) AND COUSIN NEDRA TALLEY (b. 1946) BEGAN THEIR career as a dance act, the Dolly Sisters. In 1961, having learnt harmony singing, they secured a recording contract. The trio's first single, 'I Want A Boy', was credited to Ronnie And The Relatives, but when 'Silhouettes' followed in 1962, the Ronettes name was in place. They recorded four singles before signing with **Phil Spector**. Their first collaboration, 'Be My Baby', defined the girl-group sound as Spector constructed a cavernous accompaniment around Ronnie's plaintive, nasal voice. The single reached the Top 5 in the USA and UK, succeeded by the equally worthwhile 'Baby I Love You'. The producer's infatuation with Ronnie – the couple later married – resulted in some of his finest work being reserved for her, including 'The Best Part of Breaking Up', 'Walking In The Rain' and 'Is This What I Get For Loving You'. She separated from Spector in 1973, founding a new group with vocalists Denise Edwards and Chip Fields. Ronnie And The Ronettes made their debut that year with 'Lover Lover', before changing their name to Ronnie Spector and the Ronettes for 'I Wish I Never Saw The Sunshine', an impassioned remake of a song recorded by the original line-up, but which remained unissued until 1976. The group's name was then dropped as its lead singer pursued her solo ambitions.

RONSON, MICK

UK GUITARIST RONSON (b. 1945, d. 1993) WAS A MEMBER OF **DAVID BOWIE**'S BACKING GROUP, HYPE, (LATER RENAMED the Spiders From Mars) in 1970. Ronson played lead on Bowie's pivotal albums, *The Man Who Sold The World*, *Hunky Dory*, *The Rise And Fall Of Ziggy Stardust And The Spiders From Mars* and *Aladdin Sane*. After a brief and unsuccessful solo career, Ronson joined **Mott The Hoople** in 1974 and when lead vocalist **Ian Hunter** departed for a solo career, Ronson followed. He subsequently appeared with **Bob Dylan** in the Rolling Thunder Revue. The Hunter-Ronson partnership lasted over 15 years, but it was only on *YUIORTA* that Ronson received equal billing on the sleeve. In 1991 Ronson was treated for cancer, and the following year he appeared with Bowie at the Freddy Mercury AIDS Benefit concert. Just before his death in 1993, Ronson was working on his third album with contributions from artists such as Chrissie Hynde, **John Mellencamp**, Joe Elliott and David Bowie.

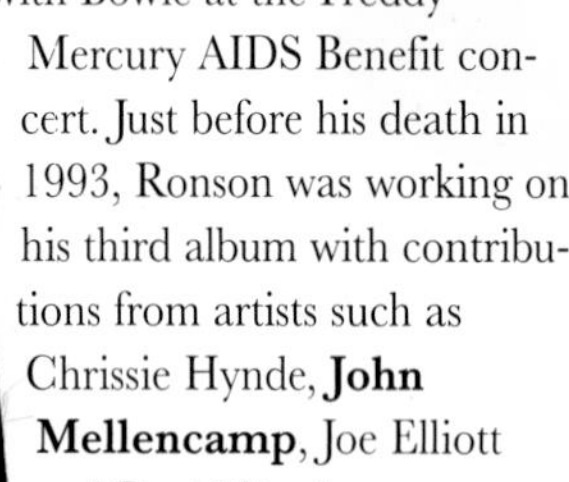

RONSTADT, LINDA

RONSTADT (b. 1946) FIRST SANG IN THE THREE RONSTADTS WITH HER SISTERS. SHE AND GUITARIST BOB KIMMEL moved to Los Angeles, where they were joined by songwriter Kenny Edwards. As the Stone Poneys the trio had a US Top 20 hit with 'Different Drum'. Ronstadt embarked on a solo career in 1968. Her early solo albums, *Hand Sown, Home Grown* and *Silk Purse*, signalled a move towards country-flavoured material. Her third album featured a core of musicians who subsequently formed the **Eagles**. *Don't Cry Now* was undistinguished, while *Heart Like A Wheel* was excellent. This platinum-selling set included 'You're No Good', a US number 1 pop hit, and a dramatic version of **Hank Williams**' 'I Can't Help It', which won Ronstadt a Grammy.

In the 80s her performance in *The Pirates Of Penzance* drew favourable reviews, although her role in the more demanding *La Boheme* was less impressive. Ronstadt also undertook a series of releases with Nelson Riddle, which resulted in three albums of popular standards. In 1987, a duet with **James Ingram** produced 'Somewhere Out There', the theme to the film *An American Tail*. This gave her a number 2 US (UK Top 10) hit, while that same year her collaboration with **Dolly Parton** and **Emmylou Harris**, *Trio*, and a selection of mariachi songs, *Canciones De Mi Padre*, showed an artist determined to challenge preconceptions. Her 1989 set, *Cry Like A Rainstorm*, included the number 2 hit 'Don't Know Much', a haunting duet with Aaron Neville. Her 1996 album, *Dedicated To The One I Love*, was firmly in the middle of the road.

ROOMFUL OF BLUES

FORMED AS A SEVEN-PIECE BAND IN THE LATE 70S, ROOMFUL OF BLUES QUICKLY ESTABLISHED A NATIONAL REPUTATION in the USA with their big band R&B, before breaking into the international scene in the 80s, recording behind 'Big' Joe Turner, Eddie 'Cleanhead' Vinson and Earl King. The group included guitarists Duke Robillard (b. Michael Robillard, 1948) and Ronnie Earl (b. Ronald Earl Horvath, 1953), Curtis Salgado (vocals), Al Copley (piano) and Greg Piccolo (saxophone). Despite personnel changes, the group continues to work regularly, although many similar groups have followed in their wake. When *Turn It On, Turn It Up* was release on 13 October 1995, the Governor of Rhode Island announced an annual Roomful Of Blues day for the state. The present band comprises Carl Querfurth (b. 1956; trombone), John 'JR' Rossi (b. 1942; drums), Doug James (b. Douglas James Schlecht, 1953; saxophone), Matt McCabe (b. 1955; keyboards), Chris Vachon (b. 1957; guitar), Sugar Ray Norcia (b. 1954; vocals/harmonica), Kenny 'Doc' Grace (b. 1951; bass), Bob Enos (b. 1947; trumpet) and Rich Lataille (b. 1952; saxophone).

ROSE, TIM

ROSE (b. 1940) BEGAN HIS PROFESSIONAL CAREER PLAYING GUITAR WITH THE JOURNEYMEN. HE JOINED CASS ELLIOT and James Hendricks in the **Big Three**, before going solo in 1964. A series of singles, including 'Hey Joe' (1966) and 'Morning Dew' (1967), followed.

Tim Rose was assembled from different sessions, but the presence of session musicians – Felix Pappalardi (bass/piano), Bernard Purdie (drums) and Hugh McCracken (guitar) – provided continuity. The set included a dramatic reading of 'I'm Gonna Be Strong', previously associated with **Gene Pitney**, and the haunting anti-war anthem 'Come Away Melinda'. *Through Rose Coloured Glasses* was disappointing. After *Love, A Kind Of Hate Story*, another album, also entitled *Tim Rose*, proved commercially unsuccessful. Resident in London, Rose undertook a short series of live concerts with fellow exile **Tim Hardin**. The *Musician*, released in 1975, revealed a voice which retained its distinctive power, but an artist without direction. In 1976, Rose was recording a country-tinged album which was finally released in 1991 as *The Gambler*. He returned to New York in the late 70s, but little has been heard from him for several years.

ROSE ROYCE

FORMED IN THE USA AS A MULTI-PURPOSE BACKING GROUP, THE ORIGINAL NINE-PIECE WORKED UNDER A VARIETY OF names. In 1973, Kenji Brown (guitar), Victor Nix (keyboards), Kenny Copeland, Freddie Dunn (trumpets), Michael Moore (saxophone), Lequient 'Duke' Jobe (bass), Henry Garner and Terrai Santiel (drums) backed **Edwin Starr** as Total Concept Limited, before supporting Yvonne Fair as Magic Wand. This line-up became the regular studio band behind the Undisputed

Truth and **Temptations**, before embarking on their own recording career with Gwen Dickey. The group took the name Rose Royce in 1976 when they recorded the successful soundtrack to *Car Wash*, the title song of which was a platinum-selling single. Two further songs from the film reached the R&B Top 10 before the band joined producer Norman Whitfield's label. 'Wishing On A Star' and 'Love Don't Live Here Anymore', reached the Top 3 in the UK. In 1977 'Is It Love You're After' was another UK Top 20 record. Since then the group has had little success.

ROSS, DIANA

ROSS (b. 1944) WAS THE FOURTH AND FINAL MEMBER OF THE PRIMETTES. THEY SIGNED TO **MOTOWN** IN 1961, changing their name to the **Supremes**. She was a backing vocalist on their early releases until Berry Gordy insisted she become the lead singer. In 1970 Ross began a long series of successful solo releases with the chart-topping 'Ain't No Mountain High Enough'.

In 1972, she starred in Motown's film biography of Billie Holiday, *Lady Sings The Blues*, winning an Oscar nomination. Subsequent starring roles in *Mahogany* (1975) and *The Wiz* (1978) drew a mixed critical response. In 1973, Ross released an album of duets with **Marvin Gaye**. She enjoyed another US number 1 with 'Touch Me In The Morning', and repeated that success with the theme song from *Mahogany* in 1975. 'Love Hangover' (1976) was a move into the disco field, a shift of direction consolidated on the 1980 album *Diana*, produced by Nile Rodgers and Bernard Edwards of **Chic**. A collaboration with **Lionel Richie** in 1981 produced the chart-topping title track to the film *Endless Love*.

Ross formed her own production company in 1981 and further hits included reworkings of **Frankie Lymon**'s 'Why Do Fools Fall In Love' and **Michael Jackson**'s 'Muscles'. 'Missing You', a tribute to Marvin Gaye, was also successful. In Britain, 'Chain Reaction', an affectionate recreation of her days with the Supremes, written and produced by the **Bee Gees,** was a number 1 hit in 1986. In 1986, Ross married a Norwegian shipping magnate.

ROXY MUSIC

FORMED IN 1971 WITH **BRYAN FERRY** (b. 1945; VOCALS/KEYBOARDS), **BRIAN ENO** (b. BRIAN PETER GEORGE ST. BAPTISTE de la Salle Eno, 1948; electronics/keyboards), Graham Simpson (bass) and Andy Mackay (b. 1946), by early 1972 Paul Thompson (b. 1951; drums) and Phil Manzanera (b. Philip Targett Adams; b. 1951; guitar) had joined. Roxy's self-titled 1972 album for Island had Ferry's 50s-tinged vocals alongside distinctive 60s rhythms and 70s electronics. The follow-up, 'Virginia Plain', combined Ferry's cinematic interests and love of surrealistic art.

The group scored a second UK Top 10 hit with 'Pyjamarama' and released *For Your Pleasure*. Another arresting work, the album featured 'Do The Strand', arguably the group's most effective rock workout. On 1973, Eno left and was replaced by Eddie Jobson (ex-**Curved Air**). After a break to record a solo album, Ferry took Roxy on tour to promote the excellent *Stranded*. 'Street Life', the first album track to be issued as a single, proved another Top 10 hit.

Following his second solo album, Ferry completed work on Roxy's *Country Life*, which ranged from the uptempo single 'All I Want Is You' to the aggressive 'The Thrill Of It All' and the musically exotic 'Triptych'. In spite of a challenging pilot single, 'Love Is The Drug', *Siren* was a disappointment. The 1979 comeback, *Manifesto*, included two hit singles, 'Angel Eyes' and the fatalistic 'Dance Away'. The succeeding *Flesh And Blood* included two UK hit singles, 'Over You' and 'Oh Yeah (On The Radio)'. In 1981 Roxy achieved their first number 1 single with 'Jealous Guy', an elegiac tribute to **John Lennon**. The following year, they released their final album *Avalon*, which topped the album charts and won much praise.

Collaborators
Tim Hardin ➧ p.174
Connections
Big Three ➧ p.47
Gene Pitney ➧ p.261

ROSE ROYCE
Albums
Car Wash (MCA 1976)★★★★
Rose Royce II/In Full Bloom (Whitfield 1977)★★★★
➧ p.377 for full listings
Connections
Edwin Starr ➧ p.307
Temptations ➧ p.318

ROSS, DIANA
Albums
Lady Sings The Blues (Motown 1972)★★★★
Touch Me In The Morning (Motown 1973)★★★
Red Hot Rhythm 'N' Blues (RCA 1987)★★★
➧ p.377 for full listings
Collaborators
Marvin Gaye ➧ p.159
Lionel Richie ➧ p.277
Bee Gees ➧ p.41
Connections
Motown Records ➧ p.240
Supremes ➧ p.314
Chic ➧ p.90
Frankie Lymon ➧ p.220
Further References
Video: *One Woman – The Video Collection* (1993)
Books: *Diana Ross: An Illustrated Biography*, Geoff Brown
Secrets Of The Sparrow, Diana Ross

ROXY MUSIC
Albums
Roxy Music (Island 1972)★★★★
Stranded (Island 1973)★★★★
Avalon (EG 1981)★★★★
➧ p.377 for full listings

Connections
Bryan Ferry ➧ p.144
Brian Eno ➧ p.136
Curved Air ➧ p.108
John Lennon ➧ p.214
Further References
Video: *Total Recall* (Virgin 1990)
Books: *Roxy Music: Style With Substance – Roxy's First Ten Years*, Johnny Rogan
Bryan Ferry & Roxy Music, Barry Lazell and Dafydd Rees

RUBETTES
Albums
We Can Do It, (State 1975)★★★
➽ p.377 for full listings
Further References
Book: *The Rubettes Story*, Alan Rowett

RICK RUBIN
Collaborators
Henry Rollins ➽ p.282
Connections
Beastie Boys ➽ p.37
Run DMC ➽ p.284
Aerosmith ➽ p.10
L L Cool J ➽ p.217
Public Enemy ➽ p.269
Slayer ➽ p.299
Devo ➽ p.117
Gang Of Four ➽ p.158
Tom Verlaine ➽ p.330

RUFFIN, JIMMY
Albums
Top Ten (Soul 1967)★★★
Sunrise (RSO 1980)★★★
➽ p.377 for full listings
Collaborators
Brenda Holloway ➽ p.184
Connections
Temptations ➽ p.318
Motown Records ➽ p.240
Bee Gees ➽ p.41

RUN DMC
Albums
Run DMC (Profile 1984)★★★★
King Of Rock (Profile 1985)★★★★
Raising Hell (Profile 1986)★★★★
➽ p.377 for full listings
Collaborators
Neneh Cherry ➽ p.89
Connections
Rick Rubin ➽ p.284
Aerosmith ➽ p.10
Stone Roses ➽ p.311
Further References
Book: *Run DMC*, B. Adler

RUNAWAYS
Albums
The Runaways (Mercury 1976)★★★
➽ p.377 for full listings
Connections
Joan Jett ➽ p.199
Bangles ➽ p.32
Sweet ➽ p.315
Suzi Quatro ➽ p.269

RUNDGREN, TODD
Albums
The Ballad Of Todd Rundgren (Bearsville 1971)★★★★
Something/Anything? (Bearsville 1972)★★★★
Hermit Of Mink Hollow (Bearsville 1978)★★★★
➽ p.377 for full listings

RUBETTES

FORMER SONGWRITERS OF THE PETE BEST FOUR, WAYNE BICKERTON AND TONY WADDINGTON CREATED THE Rubettes from session musicians after their composition, 'Sugar Baby Love', was rejected by existing acts. A fusion of 50s revivalism and glam rock, it topped the UK charts and entered the US Top 40 in 1974. The song was promoted in concert by Alan Williams (b. 1948; vocals/guitar), Tony Thorpe (b. 1947; guitar), Bill Hurd (b. 1948; keyboards), Mick Clarke (b. 1946; bass) and John Richardson (b. 1948). The five stayed together for another three years.

RUBIN, RICK

RUBIN'S (b. FREDERICK RUBIN) FIRST PRODUCTION WAS 'IT'S YOURS' BY T. La ROCK (1984), BUT IT WAS THE formation of Def Jam with Russell Simmons that enabled him to create the rap/metal, black/white synthesis he wanted; the **Beastie Boys**' experiment with rap was shrewd. However, uniting Simmons' brother's act, **Run DMC**, with Rubin's adolescent heroes, **Aerosmith**, really put Def Jam on the map. 'Walk This Way' and its parent album, *Raising Hell*, was pivotal in introducing black rap to white audiences. The label ranged from the rap of **L L Cool J** and **Public Enemy**, the soul of Oran 'Juice' Jones to the speed metal of **Slayer**. At the end of the 80s Rubin left to form Def American (later American Recordings) and a successful production career, though nothing was as groundbreaking as early Def Jam material. His delight in frill-free intensity is shown in the Infinite Zero collaboration with **Henry Rollins**, re-releasing long-lost obscurities by **Devo**, **Gang Of Four**, **Tom Verlaine** and Suicide's Alan Vega.

RUFFIN, JIMMY

ORIGINALLY A GOSPEL SINGER, RUFFIN (b. 1939) BECAME A SESSION SINGER IN THE EARLY 60S, JOINING **MOTOWN** IN 1961. In 1966 his 'What Becomes Of The Broken-Hearted' was a major US and UK hit. Success in the USA was hard to sustain, so Ruffin concentrated on the British market. In 1980 'Hold On To My Love', written and produced by Robin Gibb of the **Bee Gees**, brought him his first US Top 30 hit for 14 years. A duet with Maxine Nightingale, 'Turn To Me', sold well in 1982, while Ruffin's only other success in the 80s was 'There Will Never Be Another You' (1985). He subsequently recorded two singles with **Brenda Holloway**.

RUN DMC

NEW YORK RAPPERS JOE SIMMONS (b. 1966; BROTHER OF RUSSELL SIMMONS), DARRYL 'DMC' McDANIELS (b. 1964) and DJ 'Jam Master Jay' (b. Jason Mizell, 1965) were originally Orange Crush, becoming Run DMC in 1982. They had a US underground hit with 'It's Like That'. However, it was the single's b-side, 'Sucker MCs', which created the stir. Many critics signpost the single as the birth of modern hip hop, with its stripped down sound and fashion image. Their debut album went gold in 1984, a first for a rap act. They cemented their position with appearances in *Krush Groove*, a fictionalized film biography of Russell Simmons, joint-head of Def Jam with **Rick Rubin**. They broke into the mainstream with the heavy metal/rap collision 'Walk This Way' (featuring Steve Tyler and Joe Perry of **Aerosmith**). By 1987, *Raisin' Hell* had sold three million copies in the US. In the 90s Daniels and Simmons experienced religious conversion, after the former succumbed to alcoholism and the latter was accused of rape. Singles emerged sporadically, notably 'What's It All About', which sampled the **Stone Roses**. Despite making a comeback with *Down With The King*, Run DMC seemed a spent force. However, they hit number 1 in the UK in 1998 with 'It's Like That', a collaboration with Jason Nevins.

RUNAWAYS

FORMED IN 1975, THE RUNAWAYS WERE INITIALLY THE PRODUCT OF PRODUCER/SVENGALI KIM FOWLEY AND TEENAGE lyricist Kari Krome. The original line-up was **Joan Jett** (b. Joan Larkin, 1960; guitar/vocals), Micki Steele (bass) and Sandy West (drums), but was quickly bolstered by Lita Ford (b. 1959; guitar/vocals) and Cherie Currie (vocals). Steele's departure brought several replacements, the last being Jackie Fox (b. Jacqueline Fuchs). Although originally viewed as a vehicle for compositions by Fowley and Mars Bonfire (b. Dennis Edmonton), material by Jett and Krome helped assert the quintet's independence. *The Runaways* showed a group indebted to the 'glam-rock' of the **Sweet** and punchy pop of **Suzi Quatro**, and included the salutary 'Cherry Bomb'. *Queens Of Noise* repeated the pattern, but the strain of touring caused Fox to leave, as it did Currie. Subsequent releases lacked the appeal of the group's early work. The Runaways split in 1980. In 1985, Fowley resurrected the group's name with new personnel. This opportunistic concoction split up on completing *Young And Fast*.

RUNDGREN, TODD

ONE OF ROCK'S ECCENTRIC TALENTS, RUNDGREN (b. 1948) BEGAN HIS CAREER IN LOCAL BAR-BAND WOODY'S TRUCK Stop, before forming the Nazz in 1967. This US quartet completed three albums of anglophile pop/rock before disintegrating in 1970. Rundgren became an engineer – his credits included *Stage Fright* by the **Band** – before recording *Runt*. This exceptionally accomplished album spawned a US Top 20 hit in 'We Got To Get You A Woman' and led to the equally charming *The Ballad Of Todd Rundgren*. *Something/Anything?* contained some of Rundgren's most popular songs, including 'I Saw The Light' and 'It Wouldn't Have Made Any Difference'. *A Wizard, A True Star* offered a similarly dazzling array of styles. *Todd*, a second double-set, was equally ambitious, although less accessible. He formed Utopia, a progressive rock ensemble initially with three musicians on keyboards/synthesizers: Moogy Klingman, M. Frog Labat and Ralph Shuckett, John Segler (then Kasim Sulton) (bass) and John Wilcox (drums). Later Roger Powell assumed all keyboard duties, but the group's penchant for lengthy instrumental interludes remained.

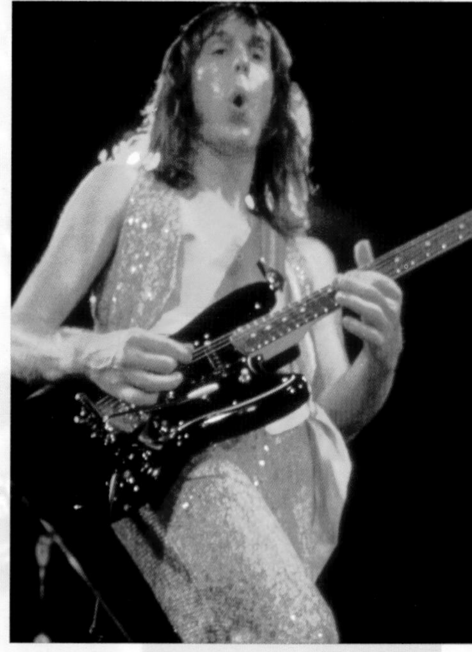

A popular live attraction, Rundgren aficionados regretted Utopia's unrepentant self-indulgence when it encroached into the artist's 'solo' work, notably on *Initiation*. *Faithful* reflected a return to pop with 'Love Of The Common Man' and 'The Verb To Love'. In 1977, Utopia released *Ra* and *Oops! Wrong Planet*. Having already established himself as a producer with the **New York Dolls**, **Grand Funk Railroad** and **Hall And Oates**, Rundgren commenced work on **Meat Loaf**'s *Bat Out Of Hell*. Utopia's *Deface The Music* (1980) was a dazzling pastiche of **Beatles**' music while another 'solo' set, *Healing*, flirted with ambient styles, followed by the inventive *Acappella*. In 1994, Rundgren scored the music for the movie *Dumb And Dumber*. He is still at the forefront of computer technology with 'Interactive' releases.

RUNRIG

SCOTTISH GROUP WITH A FOLK BACKGROUND FORMED IN 1973. INITIALLY A TRIO: BROTHERS RORY MacDONALD (b. 1949; guitar/bass/vocals), Calum MacDonald (b. 1953; drums/percussion/vocals) and Blair Douglas (accordion), the group was joined by Donnie Munroe (b. 1953; vocals/guitar) in 1974. *Play Gaelic* introduced Robert MacDonald who replaced Blair Douglas. Malcolm Jones (b. 1958; guitar/mandolin/accordion) replaced Robert MacDonald (who died of cancer in 1986). *Highland Connection* emphasized electric styles and, in 1980, Iain Bayne (b. 1960) became drummer. The music still retained its rural traditions, but the sound took Runrig beyond the traditional arena. Richard Cherns (keyboard) joined the group for its first European tour, but following the release of *Heartland* he was replaced by Peter Wishart (b. 1962). After the release of *The Cutter And The Clan*, *Searchlight* brought chart success in 1989. *The Big Wheel* reached number 4 in the UK charts and EP *Hearthammer* entered the UK Top 30. Donnie Munro stood as a Labour candidate at the 1997 General Election, and left the band for a political career.

RUSH

CANADIAN HEAVY ROCK BAND: GEDDY LEE (b. GARY LEE WEINRIB, 1953; KEYBOARDS/BASS/VOCALS), ALEX LIFESON (b. Alex Zivojinovich, 1953; guitar) and John Rutsey (drums). In 1973, they recorded a version of **Buddy Holly**'s 'Not Fade Away' as their debut release. Neil Peart (b. 1952; drums), who became the band's main songwriter, replaced Rutsey. *2112* (1976) was based on the work of novelist/philosopher Ayn Rand. Their most popular offering, *A Farewell To Kings*, followed by *Hemispheres* in 1978, was the last of Peart's 'epic' songwriting style. In 1980 their hit single 'Spirit Of Radio' took them beyond their loyal following, and in live shows Lifeson and Lee added keyboards for a fuller sound. *Moving Pictures* was a fusion of technological rock and musical craft, but subsequently inspiration waned. With *Hold Your Fire* (1987) they proved they could still scale their former heights. This was repeated in 1996 with *Test For Echo*.

RUSH, OTIS

RUSH'S (b. 1934) IMPASSIONED SINGING AND PLAYING ON 'I CAN'T QUIT YOU BABY' BROUGHT A TOP 10 R&B HIT IN 1956. He influenced British guitarists such as **Peter Green**, **Eric Clapton** and Mick Taylor. **John Mayall** opened the pivotal *Bluesbreakers* with 'All Your Love' and continued by making Rush better known in the UK with recordings of 'So Many Roads', 'I Can't Quit You Baby' and 'Double Trouble'. *Right Place Wrong Time* (1969) was issued on the independent Bullfrog label. Rush is a guitarist's guitarist – his influence greater than his commercial standing. On *Ain't Enough Comin' In*, his best work in many years, Rush demonstrated total confidence, ably supported by Mick Weaver (organ), Bill Payne (piano) and Greg Rzab (bass).

RUSH, TOM

RUSH (b. 1941) BEGAN PERFORMING IN 1961. *LIVE AT THE UNICORN*, CULLED FROM TWO SETS RECORDED AT ONE OF the region's fabled coffee houses, caught the interest of the renowned Prestige label. *Got A Mind To Ramble* and *Blues Songs And Ballads*, showcased an intuitive interpreter. *Tom Rush*, his first release for Elektra, was one of the era's finest folk/blues sets. 'Panama Limited' demonstrated the artist's accomplished bottleneck guitar style. *Take A Little Walk With Me* contained 'Galveston Flood', but its high points were six electric selections drawn from songs by **Bo Diddley**, **Chuck Berry** and **Buddy Holly**. *The Circle Game* contained material by **Joni Mitchell**, **James Taylor** and **Jackson Browne**, each of whom had yet to record in their own right. The recording also included the singer's own poignant 'No Regrets', later recorded by the **Walker Brothers** and **Midge Ure**.

Tom Rush, the artist's first release for Columbia/CBS, introduced his long-standing partnership with guitarist Trevor Veitch. *Wrong End Of The Rainbow* and *Merrimack County* had much material written by Rush alone or with Veitch. By contrast, a new version of 'No Regrets' was the sole original on *Ladies Love Outlaws* (1974). It was 1982 before a new set, *New Year*, was released. Recorded live, it celebrated the artist's 20th anniversary, while a second live album, *Late Night Radio*, featured cameos from Steve Goodman and Mimi Farina. Little has been heard of Rush in the 90s, and it is many years since he released an album.

Connections
Band ➤ p.31
New York Dolls ➤ p.246
Grand Funk Railroad ➤ p.166
Hall And Oates ➤ p.172
Meat Loaf ➤ p.230

RUNRIG
Albums
Play Gaelic (Lismor 1978)★★★
The Big Wheel (Chrysalis 1991)★★★★
Amazing Things (Chrysalis 1993)★★★
➤ p.378 for full listings
Connections
Big Country ➤ p.46
Further References
Book: *Going Home: The Runrig Story*, Tom Morton

RUSH
Albums
Permanent Waves (Mercury 1980)★★★
Moving Pictures (Mercury 1981)★★★
Signals (Mercury 1982)★★★
➤ p.378 for full listings
Connections
Buddy Holly ➤ p.184
Further References
Videos: *Grace Under Pressure* (1986)
A Show Of Hands (1989)
Book: *Rush Visions: The Official Biography*, Bill Banasiewicz

RUSH, OTIS
Albums:
Chicago – The Blues – Today! (Chess 1964)★★★
Ain't Enough Comin' In (This Way Up 1994)★★★★
Blues Interaction Live In Japan 1986 (Sequel 1996)★★★★
➤ p.378 for full listings
Connections
Peter Green ➤ p.168
Eric Clapton ➤ p.92
John Mayall ➤ p.228

RUSH, TOM
Albums
Tom Rush (Elektra 1965)★★★★
Tom Rush (CBS 1970)★★★★
Ladies Love Outlaws (1974)★★★
➤ p.378 for full listings
Connections
Woody Guthrie ➤ p.171
Bo Diddley ➤ p.118
Chuck Berry ➤ p.45
Buddy Holly ➤ p.184
Joni Mitchell ➤ p.235
James Taylor ➤ p.317
Jackson Browne ➤ p.71
Walker Brothers ➤ p.332
Midge Ure ➤ p.327

RUSSELL, LEON
Albums
Leon Russell (Shelter 1970)★★★★
Carney (Shelter 1972)★★★★
➧ p.378 for full listings
Collaborators
Steve Winwood ➧ p.341
George Harrison ➧ p.176
Eric Clapton ➧ p.92
Ringo Starr ➧ p.307
Bob Dylan ➧ p.128
Dave Mason ➧ p.227
Tim Hardin ➧ p.174
Willie Nelson ➧ p.245
Connections
Ronnie Hawkins ➧ p.177
Jerry Lee Lewis ➧ p.215
Phil Spector ➧ p.304
Ronettes ➧ p.282
Crystals ➧ p.107
Righteous Brothers ➧ p.278
Bobby Darin ➧ p.111
Byrds ➧ p.77
Paul Revere ➧ p.276
Asylum Choir ➧ p.23
Delaney And Bonnie ➧ p.114
Joe Cocker ➧ p.95
George Benson ➧ p.44

RUTLES
Albums
The Rutles (Warners 1978)★★★★
➧ p.378 for full listings
Connections
Bonzo Dog Doo-Dah Band ➧ p.61
Beach Boys ➧ p.36
Influences
Beatles ➧ p.38
Paul Simon ➧ p.296
George Harrison ➧ p.176

RYAN, PAUL AND BARRY
Albums
The Ryans Two Of A Kind (Decca 1967)★★★
➧ p.378 for full listings
Connections
Hollies ➧ p.183
Cat Stevens ➧ p.309

RYDELL, BOBBY
Albums
Bobby's Biggest Hits (1961)★★★
➧ p.378 for full listings
Connections
Cameo ➧ p.79
Further References
Film: *Because They're Young* (1960)

RYDER, MITCH, AND THE DETROIT WHEELS
Albums
Take A Ride (New Voice 1966)★★★★
➧ p.378 for full listings
Collaborators
Steve Cropper ➧ p.105
Connections
Buddy Miles ➧ p.233

RUSSELL, LEON

RUSSELL (b. 1941) IS THE ARCHETYPAL AMERICAN SINGER, SONGWRITER, PRODUCER, ARRANGER, ENTREPRENEUR, record company executive and multi-instrumentalist. His career began playing with **Ronnie Hawkins** and **Jerry Lee Lewis** in the late 50s. He was a regular session pianist on most of the classic **Phil Spector** singles, including the **Ronettes**, **Crystals** and the **Righteous Brothers**, and appeared on hundreds of major singles, including ones by Frank Sinatra, **Bobby Darin**, the **Byrds**, Herb Alpert and **Paul Revere**. He formed **Asylum Choir** in 1968 with Marc Benno. He befriended **Delaney And Bonnie** and created the famous Mad Dogs And Englishmen tour, which included **Joe Cocker**, who recorded Russell's 'Delta Lady'with great success. Russell founded his own label, Shelter, and released his self-titled debut to critical acclaim. His own session players included **Steve Winwood**, **George Harrison**, **Eric Clapton**, Charlie Watts, Bill Wyman and **Ringo Starr**. Following further session work, including playing with **Bob Dylan** and **Dave Mason**, he appeared at the Concert for Bangladesh in 1971.

He returned in 1972 with the stunning *Carney*. In 1973 his country album, *Hank Wilson's Back*, acknowledged his debt to classic country singers. That year he released an album by his future wife, Mary McCreary, and, in 1974, an excellent version of **Tim Hardin**'s 'If I Were A Carpenter'. In 1977, he received a Grammy for 'This Masquerade', which made the US Top 10 the previous year for **George Benson**. A partnership with **Willie Nelson** produced a country album in 1979 that became one of his biggest albums. 'Heartbreak Hotel' topped the US country chart. An excursion into bluegrass resulted in the 1981 live set with the New Grass Revival. Following *Hank Wilson's Volume II* in 1984, Russell became involved with his own video production company. He returned in 1992 with *Anything Will Happen*.

RUTLES

THE PRODUCT OF SATIRISTS NEIL INNES (EX-**BONZO DOG DOO-DAH BAND**) AND ERIC IDLE, FORMERLY OF *Monty Python's Flying Circus*, the Rutles was an affectionate parody of the **Beatles**' career. Innes played Ron Nasty (Lennon), Idle played Dirk McQuickly (McCartney), while Rikki Fataar (ex-**Beach Boys**) and John Halsey (ex-Patto) were Stig O'Hara (Harrison) and Barry Wom (Starr) respectively. Ollie Halsall, who died in 1992, played the fourth member in the recording studio. The Rutles' film, *All You Need Is Cash*, and attendant album, deftly combined elements from both founder members' work. Mick Jagger and **Paul Simon** made cameo appearances while **George Harrison** enjoyed a small acting role. The Rutles were themselves lampooned in *Rutles Highway Revisited*. In the wake of the Beatles *Anthology* in the mid-90s, the group gave it another shot, as the Prefab Three, with the departure of McQuickly. The result was *Archaeology*.

RYAN, PAUL AND BARRY

THE RYAN TWINS, PAUL (b. PAUL SAPHERSON 1948, d. 1992) AND BARRY (b. BARRY SAPHERSON, 1948), HAD SUCCESS with their debut single, 'Don't Bring Me Your Heartaches', which reached the UK Top 20 in 1965, followed by other hits. 'Have You Ever Loved Somebody' (1966) and 'Keep It Out Of Sight' (1967) were penned, respectively, by the **Hollies** and **Cat Stevens**. They split amicably in 1968 with Paul embarking on a songwriting career while Barry recorded as a solo act. Together they created 'Eloise', the latter's impressive number 2 hit and subsequent million seller. Paul's compositions included 'I Will Drink The Wine', which was recorded by Frank Sinatra.

RYDELL, BOBBY

IN 1958 RYDELL (b. ROBERT RIDARELLI, 1942), PROBABLY THE MOST MUSICALLY TALENTED OF THE LATE 50S PHILADELPHIA school of clean-cut teen-idols, joined **Cameo** and 'Kissin' Time' became the first of his 18 US Top 40 hits. His best-known transatlantic hits are 'Wild One', 'Sway' and 'Volare', all in 1960, and 'Forget Him', a song written and produced in Britain by Tony Hatch in 1963. Rydell starred in the movie *Bye Bye Birdie* and moved into cabaret. He returned to the studio in 1995 to re-record all his greatest hits as *The Best Of Bobby Rydell*.

RYDER, MITCH, AND THE DETROIT WHEELS

RYDER (b. WILLIAM LEVISE JNR, 1945) FORMED BILLY LEE AND THE RIVIERAS IN 1963. JIM McCARTY (LEAD GUITAR), Joe Cubert (rhythm guitar), Earl Elliott (bass) and 'Little' John Badanjek (drums) completed the group's early line-up. The quintet was then given a sharper name – Mitch Ryder And The Detroit Wheels – and in 1965 secured their biggest hit with the frenzied 'Jenny Take A Ride'. The formula became predictable and the Wheels were fired in 1967. A union with guitarist **Steve Cropper** resulted in the excellent *Detroit/Memphis Experiment*.

In 1971, Levise formed Detroit, a hard-edged rock band, but then abandoned music until the late 70s. In the 90s, Mitch Ryder was still a major concert attraction.

produced in Britain by Tony Hatch in 1963. Rydell starred in the movie *Bye Bye Birdie* and moved into cabaret. He returned to the studio in 1995 to re-record all his greatest hits as *The Best Of Bobby Rydell.*

RYDER, MITCH, AND THE DETROIT WHEELS

RYDER (b. WILLIAM LEVISE JNR, 1945) FORMED BILLY LEE AND THE RIVIERAS IN 1963. JIM McCARTY (LEAD GUITAR), Joe Cubert (rhythm guitar), Earl Elliott (bass) and 'Little' John Badanjek (drums) completed the group's early line-up. The quintet was then given a sharper name – Mitch Ryder And The Detroit Wheels – and in 1965 secured their biggest hit with the frenzied 'Jenny Take A Ride'. The formula became predictable and the Wheels were fired in 1967. A union with guitarist **Steve Cropper** resulted in the excellent *Detroit/Memphis Experiment.*

In 1971, Levise formed Detroit, a hard-edged rock band, but then abandoned music until the late 70s. In the 90s, Mitch Ryder was still a major concert attraction.

SAD CAFE

FORMED IN 1976, SAD CAFE CONSISTED OF **PAUL YOUNG** (VOCALS), IAN WILSON (GUITAR), MIKE HEHIR (GUITAR), Lenni (saxophone), Vic Emerson (keyboards), John Stimpson (bass) and David Irving (drums). *Fanx Ta Ra* introduced a blend of hard-rock riffs and adult pop, but it was *Misplaced Ideals* which brought them international success when 'Run Home Girl' became a US hit. *Facades* contained 'Every Day Hurts' (UK Top 3, 1979) and two further Top 40 entries in 1980, 'Strange Little Girl' and 'My Oh My'. Despite some further minor hits, Sad Cafe were unable to sustain their early success.

SADE

NIGERIAN-BORN SADE (b. HELEN FOLASADE ADU, 1959) JOINED LONDON-GROUP ARRIVA, WHERE SHE MET guitarist Ray St. John with whom she composed 'Smooth Operator'. From 1981 Sade fronted Pride but left in 1983 to form her own band. In 1984 'Your Love Is King' was a Top 10 hit. This was followed by *Diamond Life*, which sold over six million copies worldwide. Sade's next album included the US number 1 'Promise' and hits 'The Sweetest Taboo' and 'The First Time'. 'Paradise' from her third album headed the R&B chart in the US. She took her time in delivering *Love Deluxe*, which included hit singles in 'No Ordinary Love' and 'Feel No Pain', but the British public were lukewarm. It only reached the UK Top 30, but was a million-seller in the US, peaking at number 3. A greatest hits package was released in 1994, indicating that the artist's best compositions are already behind her.

SAINT ETIENNE

PETE WIGGS (b. 1966) AND MUSIC JOURNALIST BOB STANLEY (b. 1964) FROM CROYDON, SURREY, ENGLAND, FORMED Saint Etienne in 1988. They recruited Moira Lambert for a dance/reggae cover version of **Neil Young**'s 'Only Love Can Break Your Heart' (1990), which fared well in the nightclubs. Another cover version, 'Kiss And Make Up', was given a similar overhaul for their second single, fronted this time by New Zealand vocalist Donna Savage. 1991's 'Nothing Can Stop Us' benefited from Sarah Cracknell's (b. 1967) dreamy vocals, as would *Foxbase Alpha*, released in the autumn. 'Only Love Can Break Your Heart' was reissued and provided them with a minor chart hit. *So Tough* revealed a rich appreciation of the vital signs of British pop, and *Tiger Bay* transcended a variety of musical genres. The ballad 'Western Wind' and the instrumental 'Urban Clearway', were just two greats from this album. It was followed by a fan club-only release, *I Love To Paint.*

Influences
Beatles ➽ p.38
Paul Simon ➽ p.296
George Harrison ➽ p.176

RYAN, PAUL AND BARRY
Albums
The Ryans Two Of A Kind (Decca 1967)★★★
➽ p.378 for full listings
Connections
Hollies ➽ p.183
Cat Stevens ➽ p.309

RYDELL, BOBBY
Albums
Bobby's Biggest Hits (1961)★★★
➽ p.378 for full listings
Connections
Cameo ➽ p.79
Further References
Film: *Because They're Young* (1960)

RYDER, MITCH, AND THE DETROIT WHEELS
Albums
Take A Ride (New Voice 1966)★★★★
➽ p.378 for full listings
Collaborators
Steve Cropper ➽ p.105
Connections
Buddy Miles ➽ p.233

SAD CAFE
Albums
Misplaced Ideals (RCA 1978)★★★
➽ p.378 for full listings

SADE
Albums
Diamond Life (Epic 1984)★★★★
Promise (Epic 1985)★★★★
Stronger Than Pride (Epic 1988)★★★★
➽ p.378 for full listings
Collaborators
Robin Millar
Ray St. John
Connections
Pride
Further References
Videos: *Life Promise Pride Love* (1993)
Sade Live (SMV 1994)

SAINT ETIENNE
Albums
Foxbase Alpha (Heavenly 1991)★★★
➽ p.378 for full listings
Collaborators
Moira Lambert
Donna Savage
Connections
Faith Over Reason
Dead Famous People
Influences
Neil Young ➽ p.346

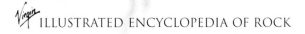

SAINTE-MARIE, BUFFY
Albums
She Used To Wanna Be A Ballerina (Vanguard 1971)★★★★
➽ p.378 for full listings
Connections
Elvis Presley ➽ p.265

SALT 'N' PEPA
Albums
Hot Cool & Vicious (Next Plateau 1987)★★★
➽ p.378 for full listings
Collaborators
En Vogue ➽ p.136
Influences
Isley Brothers ➽ p.194

SAM AND DAVE
Albums
Hold On, I'm Comin' (Stax 1966)★★★★
Double Dynamite (Stax 1967)★★★★
➽ p.378 for full listings
Collaborators
Jerry Wexler
Connections
Blues Brothers ➽ p.56
Sam & Bill

SAM THE SHAM AND THE PHARAOHS
Albums
Sam The Sham And Wooly Bully (MGM 1965)★★★
➽ p.378 for full listings
Collaborators
Duane Allman ➽ p.14
Connections
Sam The Sham Revue

SANBORN, DAVID
Albums
Another Hand (Elektra 1991)★★★★
Pearls (Elektra 1995)★★★★
➽ p.378 for full listings
Collaborators
David Bowie ➽ p.64
James Taylor ➽ p.317
Stevie Wonder ➽ p.342
Connections
Paul Butterfield ➽ p.76

SANTANA
Albums
Santana (Columbia 1969)★★★★
Zebop! (Columbia 1981)★★★★
➽ p.378 for full listings
Collaborators
Buddy Miles ➽ p.233
John Lee Hooker ➽ p.185
Connections
Journey ➽ p.202
Influences
Zombies ➽ p.349
Further References
Video: *Lightdance* (Miramar Images 1995)

SAINTE-MARIE, BUFFY

SAINTE-MARIE (b. 1941) SIGNED TO VANGUARD IN 1964. HER DEBUT 'IT'S MY WAY' INTRODUCED A REMARKABLE compositional and performing talent. 'Now That The Buffalo's Gone', a plea for Indian rights, reflected her native-American parentage and was one of several stand-out tracks. Her second selection included 'Until It's Time For You To Go', a song later recorded by **Elvis Presley**. Her versatility was also apparent on *I'm Gonna Be A Country Girl Again* and *Illuminations*, which featured an electronic score on several tracks. Sainte-Marie secured an international hit in 1971 with the theme song to the film, *Soldier Blue*, but subsequent releases failed to capitalize on this success. After signing with Chrysalis in 1991 she released the warmly received *Coincidence And Likely Stories*.

SALT 'N' PEPA

CHERYL 'SALT' JAMES (b. 1964) AND SANDRA 'PEPA' DENTON (b. 1969) GREW UP IN NEW YORK CITY. THEIR BREAK

came when producer Hurby 'Luv Bug' Azor asked them to rap for his group the Super Lovers. They started recording as Salt 'N' Pepa under Azor's guidance and released singles such as 'I'll Take Your Man', 'It's My Beat' and 'Tramp'. Their big break came in 1988 when 'Push It' reached UK number 2. Later that year a remake of the **Isley Brothers**' 'Twist And Shout' also went into the Top 10. Their most confrontational release was 1991's 'Let's Talk About Sex' manifesto. 'Do You Want Me' was similarly successful, encouraging the record company to put out *A Blitz Of Salt 'N' Pepa Hits*. They returned in 1994 with 'Whatta Man', a collaboration with **En Vogue**.

SAM AND DAVE

SAMUEL DAVID MOORE (b. 1935) AND DAVID PRATER (b. 1937, d. 1988) FIRST PERFORMED TOGETHER IN 1961 AT MIAMI'S King Of Hearts club. They later signed to Atlantic and released 'You Don't Know Like I Know', 'Hold On I'm Comin'' (both 1966), 'Soul Man' (1967) and 'I Thank You' (1968). By 1968 though, their personal relationship was disintegrating. 'Soul Sister, Brown Sugar' (1969) delayed the slide, but the duo split briefly in 1970 when Sam began his own career. They were reunited by a contract with United Artists. Despite the success of the **Blues Brothers** with 'Soul Man', they faltered when the differences between the two men proved irreconcilable. By 1981, Moore was again pursuing an independent direction. Prater found a new foil in the 'Sam' of Sam & Bill, but before they were able to consolidate this new partnership, Prater died in a car crash in April 1988.

SAM THE SHAM AND THE PHARAOHS

BACKED BY THE PHARAOHS – RAY STINNET (GUITAR), BUTCH GIBSON (SAXOPHONE), DAVID MARTIN (BASS) AND Jerry Patterson (drums) – Texan-born Sam (b. Domingo Samudio aka Sam Samudio) had a US chart-topper in 1965 with 'Wooly Bully', which became the act's sole UK Top 20 hit. They enjoyed further success in the USA with 'Lil' Red Riding Hood', number 2 in 1966. The group later mutated into the Sam The Sham Revue, but the singer dissolved the venture in 1970 to embark on a solo career under his own name.

SANBORN, DAVID

US-BORN SANBORN'S (b. 1945) VIRTUOSITY HAS NOW SPANNED FOUR DECADES, TAKING HIM FROM BEING A BAND member (with **Paul Butterfield**) to a leading session player for artists such as **David Bowie**, **James Taylor** and **Stevie Wonder**. After *Taking Off* he produced a series of albums that were all successful, and won a Grammy for *Voyeur*. *A Change Of Heart* was a big hit in the jazz charts, although much of it was in the rock style. *Another Hand* was his first 'pure jazz album' and more recently *Pearls* has lifted Sanborn to the peak of his career.

SANTANA

SANTANA EMERGED AS PART OF THE LATE 60S SAN FRANCISCO NEW WAVE SCENE, WHICH THEY RAPIDLY TRANSCENDED. Over the next 25 years Mexican leader Carlos Santana (b. 1947) introduced jazz and funk into his unique blend of polyrhythmic music. The original line-up consisted of Gregg Rolie, Michael Shrieve, David Brown (b. 1947), Marcus Malone and Mike Carabello.

Outstanding examples of the genre, *Santana*, *Abraxas* and *Santana III* spent months high in the US charts. *Caravanserai* marked a change of style as Rolie departed to form **Journey**. After befriending fellow guitarist John McLaughlin, Carlos released *Love Devotion And Surrender*. He returned to hard Latin rock with the excellent *Amigos* in 1977. A version of the **Zombies** 'She's Not There' became a hit single from *Moonflower*. *Zebop!* was a *tour de force*, and Santana's guitar playing was particularly impressive. *Beyond Appearances* maintained his considerable recorded output. He scored the music for *La Bamba* and joined with **Buddy Miles** in 1987 to record *Freedom*. During the summer of 1993 the band toured South America and released *Sacred Fire*. Recent compilations such as *Dance Of The Rainbow Serpent* and *Live At The Fillmore* emphasize his steady influence and consistency over four decades.

SATRIANI, JOE

US-BORN SATRIANI ORIGINALLY FORMED THE SQUARES, BUT THEY FOLDED IN 1984 THROUGH LACK OF COMMERCIAL recognition, giving Satriani the opportunity to concentrate on his guitar playing. The outcome of this was the EP *Joe Satriani*. Following a spell with the **Greg Kihn** band, Satriani released *Not Of This Earth*, an album which was less polished than its successor, *Surfing With The Alien*. This set was a major seller and brought mainstream respect. In 1988 he was joined by Stu Hamm (bass) and Jonathan Mover (drums). *Time Machine* contained a mixture of new and previously unreleased tracks, and live material from his 1993 world tour. The guitarist then replaced **Ritchie Blackmore** in **Deep Purple** while maintaining his solo career.

SAW DOCTORS

ORIGINATING IN TUAM, COUNTY GALWAY, EIRE, THE SAW DOCTORS – LEO MORAN (VOCALS), DAVY CORTAN (GUITAR), John 'Turps' Burke (mandolin/vocals), Pierce Doherty (bass) and John Donnelly (drums) – continue the practice of rock reacquainting itself with traditional Gaelic music. They signed to WEA in 1992 for *All The Way From Tuam*, having made their mark with an independent debut featuring 'I Usta Love Her'. The latter became Eire's biggest-selling single of all time. The startling sucess of 'I Usta Love Her' brought a re-release of debut single 'N17'. They had been joined at this juncture by Tony Lambert (keyboards, piano, accordion). Support slots for bands such as **Genesis** at Knebworth demonstrated the breadth of their appeal.

SAXON

FORMED IN THE NORTH OF ENGLAND IN THE LATE 70S, SAXON COMPRISED PETER 'BIFF' BYFORD (VOCALS), GRAHAM Oliver (guitar), Paul Quinn (guitar), Steve Dawson (bass) and Pete Gill (drums). Their first album was a heavy rock outing, but the release of *Wheels Of Steel* turned the tide. Saxon's popularity soared, earning themselves two UK Top 20 hits with 'Wheels Of Steel' and '747 (Strangers In The Night)'. They capitalized on this with the release of *Strong Arm Of The Law*. A further Top 20 hit arrived with 'And The Bands Played On', from the following year's *Denim And Leather*, which also produced 'Never Surrender'. By *The Eagle Has Landed* (UK Top 5) the group were at their peak. Pete Gill was then replaced by Nigel Glockler. *Power And The Glory* established their credentials as a major rock band. The follow-up, *Innocence Is No Excuse*, was a more polished and radio-friendly production but only reached the Top 40. The departure of Steve Dawson contributed to their malaise. *Solid Ball Of Rock* was their most accomplished album for some time. After internal wrangling which saw the departure of Oliver, they released *Dogs Of War*, which was neither awful nor progressive.

SAYER, LEO

IN 1971, SAYER (b. 1948) FORMED PATCHES IN BRIGHTON, MANAGED BY DAVE COURTNEY. COURTNEY'S FORMER employer, **Adam Faith** found the group unimpressive, but singled out Sayer. After a miss with 'Why Is Everybody Going Home', Sayer reached UK number 1 with 1973's 'The Show Must Go On'. After 'One Man Band' and 'Long Tall Glasses' (US Hot 100) Sayer severed his partnership with Courtney. 1976 brought a US million-seller in 'You Make Me Feel Like Dancing'. Sayer and Faith parted company shortly after 'Let It Be'. From 1977's *Endless Flight* the ballad, 'When I Need You', marked Sayer's UK commercial peak. But after the title track of *Thunder In My Heart* halted just outside the UK Top 20, hits became harder to come by. 'I Can't Stop Lovin' You' and revivals of **Buddy Holly**'s 'Raining In My Heart' and **Bobby Vee**'s 'More Than I Can Say' were the only smashes as his 1983 chart swansong (with 'Till You Come Back To Me') loomed nearer. By the late 80s, Sayer was without a recording contract. His recording career re-commenced in 1990 after he was reunited with producer Alan Tarney. In 1998, he toured and was rumoured to be releasing a new album.

SCAGGS, BOZ

SCAGGS (b. WILLIAM ROYCE SCAGGS, 1944) WAS RAISED IN DALLAS, TEXAS, WHERE HE JOINED FELLOW guitarist **Steve Miller** in a high-school group, the Marksmen. Boz then formed an R&B unit, the Wigs, but the group broke up and the guitarist headed for mainland Europe where he became a folk-singer. This exile ended in 1967 when he received an invitation from his erstwhile colleague to join the fledgling Steve Miller Band. Scaggs recorded two albums with them but left for a solo career in 1968. *Boz Scaggs* was a magnificent offering and over the next five years, Scaggs pursued an exemplary soul/rock direction with *My Time* and *Slow Dancer*. A slick session band enhanced some of Scaggs's finest compositions on *Silk Degrees*, including 'Lowdown' (US number 3), 'What Can I Say?' and 'Lido Shuffle' (both UK Top 30). The singer's career then faltered and despite enjoying several hit singles during 1980, Scaggs maintained a low profile during the subsequent decade. It was eight years before a new selection, *Other Roads*, appeared and a further six before *Some Change*. Scaggs moved back to his roots with *Come On Home*, an earthy collection of R&B classics.

SCHENKER, MICHAEL

GERMAN-BORN SCHENKER (b. 1955) BEGAN HIS CAREER IN 1971 WITH THE **SCORPIONS**, WHERE HE CONTRIBUTED to *Lonesome Crow*. He joined **UFO** in 1973 and their resultant musical direction swung to hard rock. *Phenomenon* featured the metal classics 'Doctor, Doctor' and 'Rock Bottom'. A series of strong albums followed before Schenker quit in 1978. The guitarist moved back to Germany and temporarily rejoined the Scorpions, contributing to *Lovedrive*. Soon afterwards he formed the Michael Schenker Group, later abbreviated to MSG.

SCORPIONS (GERMANY)

GERMAN HARD ROCK GROUP FORMED IN 1971 BY GUITARISTS RUDOLF AND **MICHAEL SCHENKER** (b. 1955), WITH Klaus Meine (b. 1948; vocals), Lothar Heinberg (bass) and Wolfgang Dziony (drums). Soon after *Lonesome Crow* was released, Heinberg, Dziony and Schenker left, the latter joining **UFO**. Francis Buchholz and Jurgen Rosenthal stepped in on bass and drums, for *Fly To The Rainbow*. Ulrich Roth was recruited as Schenker's replacement in 1974 and Rudy Lenners took over from Rosenthal the following year. *Trance* and *Virgin Killer* epitomized the Scorpions' new-found confidence. *Taken By Force* saw Herman Rarebell replace Lenners, with the band branching out into anthemic power-ballads, after which Roth quit. Mathias Jabs replaced him, but had to step down temporarily when Michael Schenker returned to contribute to *Lovedrive*. He was replaced by Jabs permanently after collapsing on stage in 1979. *Blackout* made the US *Billboard* Top 10, as did *Love At First Sting* which featured 'Still Loving You'. *World Wide Live* captured the band at their best and peaked at US number 14. *Savage Amusement* (UK number 1, US number 5) marked a slight change in emphasis, adopting a more restrained approach. *Crazy World* became their most successful album and 'Wind Of Change' their first million-seller. Buchholz was sacked and replaced by Ralph Heickermann in 1992. Heickermann made his debut on a their third live album. Allied to a lack of new material, *Live Bites* only served to heighten suspicions about the long-term viability and vitality of the band.

SATRIANI, JOE
Albums
Surfing With The Alien (Relativity 1987)★★★★
➽ p.378 for full listings
Collaborators
Greg Kihn ➽ p.204
Deep Purple ➽ p.113
Connections
Ritchie Blackmore ➽ p.52

SAW DOCTORS
Albums
All The Way From Tuam (Solid/Grapevine 1992)★★★
➽ p.378 for full listings
Collaborations
Genesis ➽ p.156

SAXON
Albums
Crusader (Carrere 1984)★★★
Solid Ball Of Rock (Virgin 1991)★★★
➽ p.378 for full listings
Further References
Video: *Power & The Glory – Video Anthology* (1989)

SAYER, LEO
Albums
Silver Bird (Chrysalis 1974)★★★
Endless Flight (Chrysalis 1976)★★★
➽ p.378 for full listings
Collaborations
Dave Courtney
Alan Tarney
Connections
Adam Faith ➽ p.142
Three Dog Night ➽ p.321
Influences
Buddy Holly ➽ p.184
Bobby Vee ➽ p.329

SCAGGS, BOZ
Albums
Silk Degrees (Columbia 1976)★★★★
Come On Home (Virgin 1997)★★★★
➽ p.378 for full listings
Collaborators
Steve Miller ➽ p.234

SCHENKER, MICHAEL
Albums
The Michael Schenker Group (Chrysalis 1980)★★
➽ p.378 for full listings
Connections
Scorpions ➽ p.289
UFO ➽ p.326

SCORPIONS (GERMANY)
Albums
Action/Lonesome Crow (Brain 1972)★★★
World Wide Live (EMI 1985)★★★
➽ p.378 for full listings
Connections
UFO ➽ p.326
Michael Schenker ➽ p.289

SCOTT-HERON, GIL
Albums
Moving Target (Arista 1982)★★★
p.378 for full listings
Influences
Marvin Gaye p.154

SCREAMING TREES
Albums
Dust (Epic 1996)★★★★
p.378 for full listings
Connections
Soundgarden p.303

SCRITTI POLITTI
Albums
Songs To Remember (Rough Trade 1982)★★★
Cupid And Psyche (Virgin 1985)★★★
p.378 for full listings
Influences
Beatles p.38

SEAL
Albums
Seal i (WEA 1991)★★★★
p.378 for full listings

SEARCHERS
Albums
Meet The Searchers (Pye 1963)★★★★
The Searchers (Sire 1979)★★★
p.378 for full listings
Influences
Jackie DeShannon p.116
Clovers p.95
Paul And Barry Ryan p.286

SEBADOH
Albums
Harmacy (Sub Pop 1996)★★★★
p.378 for full listings
Connections
Dinosaur Jr p.118
Influences
Nick Drake p.125

SEBASTIAN, JOHN
Albums
John B. Sebastian (Reprise 1970)★★★★
p.378 for full listings
Connections
Lovin' Spoonful p.219
Woodstock Festival p.343
Influences
Smokey Robinson p.279

SEDAKA, NEIL
Albums
Neil Sedaka (RCA Victor 1959)★★★★
p.378 for full listings
Connections
Connie Francis p.152
Carole King p.206
Captain And Tennille p.80
Further References
Book: *Breaking Up Is Hard To Do*, Neil Sedaka

SCOTT-HERON, GIL

SCOTT-HERON (b. 1949) FORMED THE MIDNIGHT BAND WITH BRIAN JACKSON IN 1972, PLAYING THEIR ORIGINAL blend of jazz, soul and prototype rap music. *Small Talk At 125th And Lenox* was mostly an album of poems, but later albums showed Scott-Heron developing into a skilled songwriter whose work was soon covered by other artists. In 1973 he had a minor hit with 'The Bottle'. *Winter In America* and *The First Minute Of A New Day* were both heavily jazz-influenced, but later sets saw Scott-Heron exploring more pop-oriented formats, and in 1976 he scored a hit with 'Johannesburg'. *Reflections* featured a fine version of **Marvin Gaye**'s 'Inner City Blues'; but his strongest songs were his own political diatribes, which confronted issues such as nuclear power, apartheid and poverty. In 1994 he released his first album for ten years, *Spirits*.

SCREAMING TREES

ROCK BAND FROM THE RURAL COMMUNITY OF ELLENSBURG, NEAR SEATTLE, USA COMPRISING BROTHERS Gary Lee Conner (b. 1962; guitar) and Van Conner (b. 1967; bass), Mark Lanegan (vocals) and Barrett Martin (b. 1967; drums). *Even If And Especially When* included notable compositions such as the live favourite 'Transfiguration'. Major label debut *Uncle Anaesthesia* brought production from Terry Date and **Soundgarden**'s Chris Cornell. By the time Screaming Trees moved to Epic Records they had embraced what one *Melody Maker* journalist called 'unashamed 70s Yankee rock', straddled by bursts of punk spite. After a four-year gap they returned with the excellent *Dust*.

SCRITTI POLITTI

LEEDS-BASED GROUP FOUNDED IN 1978. BY THEIR FIRST SINGLE, 'SKANK BLOC BOLOGNA', THE NUCLEUS OF THE band was Green Gartside (b. 'Green' Strohmeyer-Gartside, 1956; vocals/guitar), Matthew Kay (keyboards/manager), Tom Morley (drums) and Nial Jinks (bass). The group was explicitly political, encouraging listeners to create their own music in the face of the corporate record industry. This early *avant-garde* phase gave way to a sound that brought together elements of pop, jazz, soul and reggae on songs such as 'The Sweetest Girl' and 'Asylums In Jerusalem'/'Jacques Derrida', from their debut album. Morley quit the group in 1982, by which time Gartside *was* Scritti Politti. After moving to Virgin, Green linked up with New York musicians David Gamson (keyboards/programming) and Fred Maher (drums), who formed the basis of the group that made a series of UK hits in the years 1984 to 1988. A three-year silence was broken by 'Oh Patti (Don't Feel Sorry For Loverboy)' (number 13), lifted from *Provision*. Gartside maintained a low profile for two years after 'First Boy In This Town (Love Sick)' failed to break into the UK Top 60 in late 1988. He returned in 1991 with a revival of the **Beatles**' 'She's A Woman' (number 20).

SEAL

AFTER A CHANCE ENCOUNTER WITH RAP ARTIST CHESTER London-born Seal (b. Sealhenry Samuel, 1963) was introduced to techno wizard Adamski. Seal contributed lyrics to his embryonic dance track, 'Killer', which eventually took the UK's dance floors by storm. However, the partnership did not last and Seal released his debut solo, 'Crazy'. The lyrics were imbued with the sort of new age mysticism given vent by 90s dance culture. Seal then recorded a magnificent album which sold 3 million copies worldwide. *Seal ii* was, once again, an eponymous affair, and once again a worldwide success. The startling 'Kiss From A Rose' was used as the soundtrack theme for the movie *Batman Forever*. At the 1996 Grammys he gathered an armful of awards including, Record Of The Year, Song Of The Year and Best Pop Vocal Performance.

SEARCHERS

ONE OF THE PREMIER GROUPS FROM THE MID-60S' MERSEYBEAT EXPLOSION, THE SEARCHERS COMPRISED: Chris Curtis (b. Christopher Crummey, 1941; drums), Mike Pender (b. Michael John Prendergast, 1942; lead guitar), Tony Jackson (b. 1940; vocals/bass) and John McNally (b. 1941; rhythm guitar). They signed to Pye in 1963. Their debut 'Sweets For My Sweet' (UK number 1) was a memorable tune with strong harmonies. *Meet The Searchers* revealed the group's R&B pedigree on such standards as 'Farmer John'. Meanwhile, the follow-up, 'Sugar And Spice', just failed to reach number 1. Their third single, 'Needles And Pins' topped the UK charts and reached the US Top 20. It was followed with further US successes, including 'Ain't That Just Like Me', 'Sugar And Spice' and 'Some Day We're Gonna Love Again'.

Tony Jackson, whose falsetto vocals had contributed much to the group's early sound, departed and was replaced by Frank Allen (b. Francis Renaud McNeice, 1943). A strident reading of **Jackie DeShannon**'s 'When You Walk In The Room' was another highlight of 1964. A return to the 'old' Searchers sound with the plaintive 'Goodbye My Love', took them back into the UK Top 5 in early 1965. They enjoyed further US success when their cover of the **Clovers**' 'Love Potion Number 9' was a Top 10 hit. This continued with 'Bumble Bee and 'Goodbye My Love'. 'He's Got No Love' showed that they could write their own hit material but this run could not be sustained. Their last UK hit was a version of **Paul And Barry Ryan**'s 'Have You Ever Loved Somebody'. They threatened a resurgence in 1979 when Sire issued a promising comeback album. The attempt was ultimately unsuccessful, however, and after the less well received *Play For Today* (titled *Love's Melodies* in the USA), the group returned to the cabaret circuit.

SEBADOH

BASED IN BOSTON, MASSACHUSETTS, USA, SEBADOH ARE LED BY LOU BARLOW (b. *c.* 1966; VOCALS/GUITAR). Barlow's first success came in partnership with J. Mascis in **Dinosaur Jr**, but friendships within the band began to fray, and they split in 1989. Barlow began to record four-track demos with drumming friend Eric Gaffney. These cassette releases were dwarfed by the impact of 1991's *Sebadoh III*, at which time the duo was expanded by bass player/vocalist Jason Loewenstein. It remains the group's most enduring achievement. The UK-issued *Rockin The Forest* saw the band adopt a rock/pop sound and *Sebadoh Vs Helmet* included two **Nick Drake** covers. In 1994 Eric Gaffney was replaced by Bob Fay. In 1996 Barlow made a surprise entry into the US Top 40 with 'Natural One' a song written with John Davis. *Harmacy* was an unconcious bid for pop stardom and was peppered with catchy riffs.

SEBASTIAN, JOHN

SEBASTIAN (b. 1944) IS BEST KNOWN FOR HIS SEMINAL JUG BAND/ROCK FUSION WITH **LOVIN' SPOONFUL** IN THE 60S. In 1969 his solo performance was one of the highlights of the **Woodstock Festival**, and this elevated him to star status. *John B Sebastian* included the evocative 'How Have You Been' and 'She's A Lady'. Sebastian faltered with the uneven *Four Of Us*, but followed a few months later with *Real Live*, an engaging record. *Tarzana Kid* sold poorly, but has latterly grown in stature. Two years later

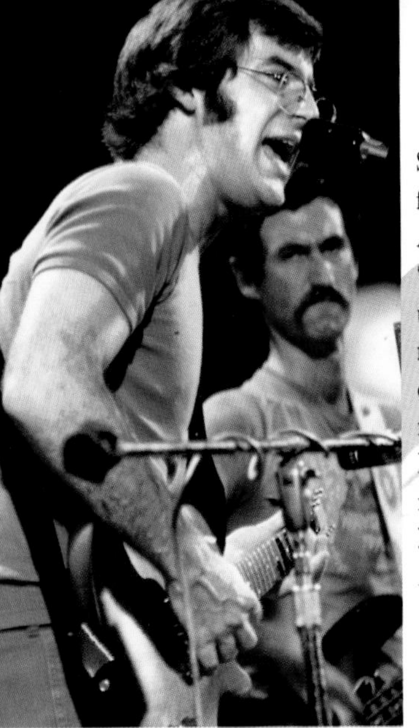

Sebastian was asked to write the theme song for a US comedy television series, *Welcome Back Kotter*. The result was a number 1 hit, 'Welcome Back'. A new album did not appear until 1992, when a Japanese label released his most recent songs. Throughout that time, however, Sebastian never stopped working. He returned *Tar Beach*, which included many songs he had written more than a decade earlier, most notably his uplifting tribute to **Smokey Robinson**: 'Smokey Don't Go'. He released *I Want My Roots* – with the J Band – in 1996.

SEDAKA, NEIL

NEW YORK-BORN PIANIST SEDAKA (b. 1939) BEGAN HIS SONGWRITING career with lyricist Howard Greenfield in the early 50s. Sedaka's first major hit success came with 'Stupid Cupid', an international smash for **Connie Francis**. The following year, Sedaka signed to RCA as a recording artist and enjoyed a minor US hit with 'The Diary'. The frantic follow-up, 'I Go Ape', was a strong novelty record, followed by one of his most famous songs, 'Oh Carol', a lament directed at former girlfriend **Carole King**. This was succeeded by a string of early 60s hits, including 'Stairway To Heaven', 'Calendar Girl', 'Happy Birthday Sweet Sixteen' and 'Breaking Up Is Hard To Do'. With the decline of the clean-cut teen balladeer however, there was an inevitable lull in Sedaka's fortunes. He continued writing a fair share of hits over the next 10 years, though. Sedaka relaunched his solo career with *Emergence* and relocated to the UK. By 1973, he was back in the British charts with 'That's When The Music Takes Me' from *Solitaire*. *The Tra-La Days Are Over* was highly regarded and included 'Our Last Song Together', dedicated to Howard Greenfield. With *Laughter In The Rain*, Sedaka extended his appeal to his homeland: the title track topped the US charts in 1975. That same year, **Captain And Tennille** took Sedaka's 'Love Will Keep Us Together' to the US number 1 spot and the songwriter followed suit with 'Bad Blood'. The year ended with a reworking of 'Breaking Up Is Hard To Do' which provided another worldwide smash.

SEEDS

FORMED IN 1965, THE SEEDS PROVIDED A PIVOTAL LINK BETWEEN GARAGE/PUNK ROCK AND THE EMERGENT underground styles. They were led by Sky Saxon (b. Richard Marsh), with Jan Savage (guitar), Darryl Hooper (keyboards) and Rick Andridge (drums). They had a US hit the following year with the compulsive 'Pushin' Too Hard'. Its raw, simple riff and Saxon's howling, half-spoken intonation established a pattern that remained almost unchanged throughout the group's career. The Seeds enjoyed minor chart success with 'Mr. Farmer' and 'Can't Seem To Make You Mine', while their first two albums, *The Seeds* and *A Web Of Sound*, were also well received. The quartet embraced 'flower-power' with *Future*, and this release was followed by a curious interlude wherein the group, now dubbed the Sky Saxon Blues Band, recorded *A Full Spoon Of Seedy Blues*. *Raw And Alive At Merlin's Music Box*, marked a return to form.

SEEGER, PETE

A MEMBER OF THE WEAVERS FROM 1949-58, SEEGER (b. 1919) HAD EARLIER BEEN IN A GROUP CALLED the Almanac Singers, which included **Woody Guthrie**, Lee Hays and Millard Lampell, which had frequently given free performances to union meetings and strikers' demonstrations. Seeger maintained a successfully high profile in his solo career. In 1948 he was blacklisted and had to appear before the House of Un-American Activities Committee for his alleged communist sympathies. This did not stop Seeger from performing sell-out concerts abroad and speaking out on a wide range of civil rights and environmental issues. By the mid-70s, Seeger had released in excess of 50 albums, and had become one of the most important figures ever in the development of free speech through folk music.

SEEKERS

FOUNDED IN AUSTRALIA IN 1963, THE SEEKERS COMPRISED ATHOL GUY (b. 1940; VOCALS/DOUBLE BASS), KEITH Potger (b. 1941; vocals/guitar), Bruce Woodley (b. 1942; vocals/guitar) and Ken Ray (lead vocals/guitar). A year later Athol Guy recruited Judith Durham (b. 1943) as the new lead singer. Following a visit to London in 1964, the group were signed to Grade, where Tom Springfield offered his services as songwriter/producer. A trilogy of hits – 'I'll Never Find Another You', 'A World Of Our Own' and 'The Carnival Is Over' – widened their appeal. In 1967, the breezy 'Georgy Girl' was a transatlantic Top 10 hit but thereafter, apart from 'When Will The Good Apples Fall' and 'Emerald City', the group were no longer chart regulars, and in 1969 they disbanded. The Seekers briefly re-formed in 1975 with teenage Dutch singer Louisa Wisseling replacing Durham. 'The Sparrow Song' topped the Australian charts. In 1990 the Seekers reunited and played a series of 100 dates across Australia and New Zealand.

SEGER, BOB

US-BORN SEGER (b. 1945) MADE HIS RECORDING DEBUT WITH THE BEACH BUMS, WITH 'THE BALLAD OF THE Yellow Beret'. The act then became known as Bob Seger and the Last Heard and released 'East Side Story' (1966) and 'Heavy Music' (1967). Seger was signed by Capitol in 1968 and the the Bob Seger System enjoyed a US Top 20 hit that year with 'Ramblin' Gamblin' Man'. Numerous releases followed, but the artist was unable to repeat his early success and they disbanded in 1971.

Seger returned to music with his own label, Palladium and three unspectacular albums ensued. He garnered considerable acclaim for his 1974 single, 'Get Out Of Denver', now a much-covered classic. Seger achieved commercial success with *Beautiful Loser*. Now fronting the Silver Bullet Band, Seger reinforced his in-concert popularity with *Live Bullet*, in turn followed by *Night Moves*, his first platinum disc. The title track reached the US Top 5 in 1977, a feat 'Still The Same' repeated the following year. His triple-platinum album, *Stranger In Town*, included 'Hollywood Nights', 'Old Time Rock 'N' Roll' and 'We've Got Tonight'. *Against The Wind* also topped the US album charts.

Among his later hit singles were 'Shame On The Moon', 'Old Time Rock 'N' Roll', 'Understanding', and the number 1 hit 'Shakedown'. Seger released his first studio album for five years in 1991, which became a Top 10 hit in the USA. *It's A Mystery* ploughed typical Segar territory with regular riff rockers, such as 'Lock And Load', alongside acoustic foray's such as 'By The River'.

SEEDS
Albums
The Seeds (Crescendo 1966)★★★
➽ p.378 for full listings

SEEGER, PETE
Albums
American Ballads (Folkways 1957)★★★★
Pete Seeger Sings Woody Guthrie (1967)★★★★
➽ p.378 for full listings
Collaborators
Woody Guthrie ➽ p.170
Further References
Film: *Alice's Restaurant* (1969)
Book: *How Can I Keep From Singing*, King Dunaway

SEEKERS
Albums
The Seekers (1965)★★★
Georgy Girl (1967)★★★
➽ p.378 for full listings
Further References
Book: *Colours Of My Life*, Judith Durham

SEGER, BOB
Albums
Live Bullet (Capitol 1976)★★★★
Stranger In Town (Capitol 1978)★★★★
➽ p.378 for full listings
Influences
Rodney Crowell ➽ p.107

SELECTER
Albums
Too Much Pressure (2-Tone 1980)★★★★
Hairspray (Triple X 1995)★★★
➽ p.378 for full listings
Collaborators
Specials ➽ p.304
John Bradbury aka Prince Rimshot
Barry Jones

SENSATIONAL ALEX HARVEY BAND
Albums
Next (Vertigo 1973)★★★
Live On The Test (Windsong 1994)★★★
➽ p.378 for full listings
Connections
Alex Harvey ➽ p.176
Zal
Rory Gallagher ➽ p.152
Nazareth ➽ p.244
Sensational Party Boys
Influences
Tom Jones ➽ p.201
Further References
Video: *Live On The Test* (Windsong 1994)

SEPULTURA
Albums
with Overdose *Bestial Devastation* (Cogumelo 1985)★★★
Roots (Roadrunner 1996)★★★★
➽ p.378 for full listings
Collaborators
Gloria Bujnowski
Connections
Overdose
Dynamo Festival
Further References
Video: *We Are What We Are* (Roadrunner 1997)

SEX PISTOLS
Albums
Never Mind The Bollocks – Here's The Sex Pistols (Virgin 1977)★★★★★
Filthy Lucre Live (Virgin 1996)★★★
➽ p.378 for full listings
Further References
Film: *The Great Rock 'N' Roll Swindle*
Video: *Live At Longhorns* (Pearson New Entertainment 1996)
Book: *Sid's Way: The Life And Death Of Sid Vicious*, Keith Bateson and Parker

SHA NA NA
Albums
Rock & Roll Is Here To Stay (Kama Sutra 1969)★★★
The Night Is Still Young (Kama Sutra 1972)★★★
➽ p.378 for full listings

SELECTER

WHEN COVENTRY'S **SPECIALS** NEEDED A B-SIDE FOR THEIR OWN DEBUT, 'GANGSTERS', THEY APPROACHED FELLOW LOCAL musician Noel Davies. With the assistance of John Bradbury aka Prince Rimshot (drums) and Barry Jones (trombone), Davies concocted the instrumental track 'The Selecter'. The single took off with both sides receiving airplay. This meant that a band had to be formed to tour, so Davies assembled the Selecter Mk II, consisting of Pauline Black (vocals), Noel Davies (guitar), Crompton Amanor (drums, vocals), Charles H. Bainbridge (drums), Gappa Hendricks, Desmond Brown (keyboards) and Charlie Anderson (bass). They managed a string of successful singles such as 'On My Radio', 'Three Minute Hero' and 'Missing Words'. Black left in 1981 but rejoined Selector for a tour in 1991. The group later re-formed and released their first new material for over a decade.

SENSATIONAL ALEX HARVEY BAND

FORMED IN 1972 WHEN VOCALIST **ALEX HARVEY** (b. 1935, d. 1981) TEAMED WITH GLASGOW GROUP, TEAR GAS. ZAL Cleminson (b. 1949; guitar), Hugh McKenna (b. 1949; keyboards), Chris Glen (b. 1950; bass) and Ted McKenna (b. 1950; drums) completed the line-up. *Framed* was accompanied by a period of frenetic live activity. The quintet continued their commercial ascendancy with *Next*, *The Impossible Dream* and *Tomorrow Belongs To Me*, while enhancing their in-concert reputation. *Live* encapsulated this era, while their exaggerated reading of **Tom Jones**' hit 'Delilah' gave the group a UK Top 10 single. They enjoyed another hit single with 'Boston Tea Party' (1976), but the rigorous schedule extracted a toll on their vocalist. He entered hospital to attend to a recurring liver problem, during which time the remaining members recorded *Fourplay* as SAHB. Tommy Eyre then replaced Hugh McKenna and in 1977 Harvey rejoined to complete *Rock Drill*, only to walk out three months later. Ted McKenna, Cleminson and Glen had meanwhile formed the short-lived Zal, but they split up in 1978. McKenna later joined **Rory Gallagher** and MSG, while Cleminson was briefly a member of **Nazareth**. In 1992 members of the original band were reunited as the Sensational Party Boys. They officially changed their name in 1993 back to the Sensational Alex Harvey Band with the original line-up (less Alex).

SEPULTURA

FORMED IN BELO HORIZONTE, BRAZIL, IN 1984 BY BROTHERS IGOR (b. 1970; DRUMS) AND MAX CAVALERA (b. 1969; vocals/guitar), with Paulo Jnr (b. 1969; bass) and guitarist Jairo T, who was replaced in 1987 by Andreas Kisser (b. 1968). *Morbid Visions* was followed by *Schizophrenia*. The music on both was typified by speed, aggression and anger, much of which stemmed from the band's preoccupations with the poor social conditions in their native land. American label Roadrunner brought the band to international notice in 1989 when they released *Beneath The Remains*. In 1990 Sepultura played at the Dynamo Festival in Holland, leading to the re-release of *Schizophrenia*. *Arise* proved the best-selling album in the history of the Roadrunner label. The sessions for *Chaos A.D.* saw the group strip down their music which mirrored the punk ethos. *Roots* was seen as their peak. It came as a shock when the band announced their split in 1997.

SEX PISTOLS

THIS UK PUNK GROUP CAME TOGETHER UNDER THE AEGIS OF ENTREPRENEUR MALCOLM McLAREN AND COMPRISED Steve Jones (b. 1955; guitar), Paul Cook (b. 1956; drums), Glen Matlock (b. 1956; bass) and Johnny Rotten (b. John Lydon, 1956; vocals). By 1976 the group had a reputation for violence, which reached a peak when a girl was blinded in a glass-smashing incident involving the group's most fearful follower, Sid Vicious. They signed to EMI later that year and released 'Anarchy In The UK'. The single suffered distribution problems and bans from shops, and eventually peaked at number 38 in the UK charts. Soon afterwards, the group was dropped from EMI in a blaze of publicity. By 1977, Matlock was replaced by punk caricature Sid Vicious (b. John Simon Ritchie, 1957, d. 1979). After reluctantly signing to Virgin, the group issued 'God Save The Queen'. The single tore into the heart of British nationalism when the populace was celebrating the Queen's Jubilee. Despite a daytime radio ban the single rose to number 1 in the *New Musical Express* chart. A third single, the melodic 'Pretty Vacant' proved their most accessible and restored them to the Top 10. By the winter the group hit again with 'Holidays In The Sun' and issued *Never Mind The Bollocks – Here's The Sex Pistols*. It was a patchy affair, containing a preponderance of previously released material which indicated that the group was running short of ideas, and in early 1978, Rotten announced that he was leaving the group. McLaren, meanwhile, took the group to Brazil so they could be filmed playing with the train robber Ronnie Biggs. McLaren promoted Biggs as the group's new lead singer and another controversial single emerged: 'Cosh The Driver', later retitled 'No One Is Innocent (A Punk Prayer)'. Virgin continued to issue the fragments of Pistols work that they had on catalogue, including the compilation *Flogging A Dead Horse*. After years of rumour, the original band re-formed in 1996 for a tour of Europe and the US.

SHA NA NA

SPEARHEADING THE US ROCK 'N' ROLL REVIVALISM THAT BEGAN IN THE LATE 60S, THE GROUP EMERGED FROM Columbia University in 1968 with a repertoire derived exclusively from the 50s. The initial line-up consisted of vocalists Scott Powell, Johnny Contardo, Frederick Greene, Don York and Richard Joffe; guitarists Chris Donald, Elliot Cahn and Henry Gross; pianists Scott Symon and John Bauman, plus Bruce Clarke (bass), Jocko Marcellino (drums) and saxophonist Leonard Baker. Surprisingly, there were few personnel changes until a streamlining to a less cumbersome 10-piece in 1973. The band were launched internationally by an appearance at the **Woodstock Festival**. From *The Night Is Still Young*, 'Bounce In Your Buggy' was the closest the outfit ever came to a hit. Nevertheless, the approbation of the famous was manifest in **John Lennon**'s choice of the band to open his One-For-One charity concert in 1972. By 1974, however, their act had degenerated to a dreary repetition that took its toll in unresolvable internal problems.

SHADOWS

UK-GROUP THE SHADOWS EVOLVED FROM THE FIVE CHESTERNUTS TO BECOME **CLIFF RICHARD**'S BACKING GROUP, the **Drifters**. By late 1958 the line-up had settled and comprised **Hank B. Marvin** (b. Brian Robson Rankin, 1941; lead guitar), Bruce Welch (b. 1941; rhythm guitar), **Jet Harris** (b. Terence Hawkins, 1939; bass) and **Tony Meehan** (b. Daniel Meehan, 1943; drums). Soon after backing Richard on his debut, they were signed as a group by EMI Columbia. After two singles under their old name, they issued the vocal 'Saturday Dance', which failed to sell. In 1960 singer/songwriter Jerry Lordan presented them with 'Apache', which dominated the UK number 1 position for six weeks. A wealth of evocative instrumentals followed, including four UK number 1 hits – 'Kon Tiki', 'Wonderful Land', 'Dance On' and 'Foot Tapper'. Despite such successes, the group underwent personnel shifts. Both Meehan and Harris left the group to be replaced by Brian Bennett (b. 1940) and Brian Locking, later replaced by John Rostill (b. 1942, d. 1973).

The Shadows continued to chart during 1963-64, but the Mersey beat boom had lessened their appeal. At the end of 1968, the group announced that they intended to split. In late 1969, a streamlined Shadows featuring Marvin, Rostill, Bennett and pianist Alan Hawkshaw toured Japan. In 1974, the Shadows reconvened for *Rockin' With Curly Leads*. Several live performances followed and the group then achieved second place with 'Let Me Be The One', which also provided them with their first UK Top 20 hit in 10 years. The stupendous success of an accompanying *20 Golden Greats* compilation effectively revitalized their career.

SHADOWS OF KNIGHT

FORMED IN CHICAGO IN 1965, THE ORIGINAL LINE-UP comprised Jim Sohns (vocals), Warren Rogers (lead guitar), Jerry McGeorge (rhythm guitar), Norm Gotsch (bass) and Tom Schiffour (drums). Their debut single, 'Gloria', was the climax to the quintet's stage act, and gave them a US Top 10 hit. By this point Gotsch had been replaced, with Rogers switching to lead to accommodate new guitarist Joe Kelly. Their best-known line-up now established, the Shadows Of Knight enjoyed another minor chart entry with 'Oh Yeah', before completing their debut album *Gloria*. Two excellent group originals, 'Light Bulb Blues' and 'It Happens That Way', revealed an under-used talent. *Back Door Men* offered a slightly wider perspective. Dave 'The Hawk' Wolinski replaced Warren Rogers in late 1966. This was the prelude to wholesale changes when, in 1967, Sohns fired the entire group. The singer subsequently reappeared fronting a new line-up – John Fisher, Dan Baughman, Woody Woodfuff and Kenny Turkin. 'Shake' gave the group a final US Top 50 entry. Further releases proved equally disappointing.

SHAKATAK

THE GROUP COMPRISED BILL SHARPE (KEYBOARDS), GEORGE ANDERSON (bass), Keith Winter (guitar), Roger Odell (drums), Nigel Wright (keyboards/synthesizers) and Gil Seward (vocals). Between 1980 and 1987, Shakatak had 14 UK chart singles. Since their debut, 'Feels Like The First Time', other notable hits have been 'Easier Said Than Done' (1981), 'Night Birds' (UK Top 10, 1982), 'Dark Is The Night' (1983) and 'Down On The Street' (UK Top 10, 1984). The latter half of the 80s showed Shakatak leaving behind the demands of instant pop chart hits and allowing themselves to mature, most evidently on the 1989 set *Turn The Music Up*. Sharpe later found chart success in collaboration with **Gary Numan**.

SHAKESPEARS SISTER

FORMED BY SIOBHAN MARIE DEIDRE FAHEY-STEWART (b. 1958) AND MARCELLA DETROIT (b. MARCELLA LEVY, 1959) with producer and writer Richard Feldman. They took their name from a **Smiths**' song and kept the spelling mistake made by a designer. Their debut, 'Break My Heart (You Really)', was not a hit. However, 'You're History' reached the UK Top 10, while the debut album made number 9. 1991 finally saw the follow-up, *Hormonally Yours*. In 1992, Shakespears Sister achieved a UK number 1 coup with 'Stay', and followed it with 'I Don't Care' (number 7), 'Goodbye Cruel World' (number 32) and 'Hello, Turn Your Radio On' (number 14). The group was disbanded by Fahey, without warning to Detroit, live on stage at an awards ceremony in 1993.

Connections
Woodstock Festival ➧ p.343
John Lennon ➧ p.214
Further References
Film: *Grease* (1978)

SHADOWS
Albums
The Shadows (Columbia 1961)★★★★
Out Of The Shadows (Columbia 1962)★★★★
The Sound Of The Shadows (Columbia 1965)★★★★
➧ p.378 for full listings
Collaborators
Cliff Richard ➧ p.277
Hank B. Marvin ➧ p.226
Norrie Paramor
Jerry Lordan
Connections
Five Chesternuts
Drifters ➧ p.126
Eurovision Song Contest
Further References
Film: *Summer Holiday* (1962)
Books: *The Shadows By Themselves*, Shadows
Funny Old World: The Life And Times Of John Henry Rostill, Rob Bradford

SHADOWS OF KNIGHT
Albums
Gloria (Dunwich 1966)★★★
The Shadows Of Knight (Super-K 1969)★★★
➧ p.378 for full listings

SHAKATAK
Albums
Drivin' Hard (Polydor 1981)★★★
Bitter Sweet (Polydor 1991)★★★
➧ p.324 for full listings
Collaborators
Gary Numan ➧ p.249

SHAKESPEARS SISTER
Albums
Sacred Heart (London 1989)★★★
Hormonally Yours (London 1991)★★★
➧ p.378 for full listings
Collaborators
Richard Feldman
Influences
Smiths ➧ p.301

SHAM 69
Albums
Tell Us The Truth (Polydor 1978)★★★
➧ p.378 for full listings
Further References
Video: *Live In Japan* (Visionary 1993)

SHAMEN
Albums
Boss Drum (One Little Indian 1992)★★★★
➧ p.379 for full listings

SHANGRI-LAS
Albums
Leader Of The Pack (Red Bird 1965)★★★
'65 (Red Bird 1965)★★★
➧ p.379 for full listings
Collaborators
George 'Shadow' Morton
Connections
Bon Bons
Further References
Book: *Girl Groups: The Story Of A Sound*, Alan Betrock

SHANNON, DEL
Albums
Runaway With Del Shannon (Big Top/London 1961)★★★★
Handy Man (Amy 1964)★★★★
➧ p.379 for full listings
Influences
Hank Williams ➧ p.339
Jimmy Jones ➧ p.201
Further References
Film: *It's Trad, Dad* aka *Ring-A-Ding Rhythm* (1962)

SHAPIRO, HELEN
Albums
Tops With Me (Columbia 1962)★★★★
Helen's Sixteen (Columbia 1963)★★★★
The Quality Of Mercer (1987)★★★★
➧ p.379 for full listings
Collaborators
Russ Ballard ➧ p.31
Connections
Cilla Black ➧ p.49
Dusty Springfield ➧ p.305
Further References
Film: *It's Trad, Dad* aka *Ring-A-Ding Rhythm* (1962)
Book: *Helen Shapiro: Pop Princess*, John S. Janson

SHARROCK, SONNY
Albums
with Pharaoh Sanders *Tauhid* (1967)★★★
Guitar (Enemy 1986)★★★
➧ p.379 for full listings

SHAM 69

FORMED IN LONDON, ENGLAND, IN 1976, THIS SKINHEAD/PUNK-INFLUENCED GROUP COMPRISED JIMMY PURSEY (vocals), Albie Slider (bass), Neil Harris (lead guitar), Johnny Goodfornothing (rhythm guitar) and Billy Bostik (drums). Pursey was a fierce, working-class idealist, who ironically sacked most of the above line-up within a year due to their lack of commitment. A streamlined aggregation featuring Dave Parsons (guitar), Dave Treganna (bass) and Mark Cain (drums) helped Pursey reach the UK charts with a series of anthemic hits including 'Angels With Dirty Faces', 'If The Kids Are United', 'Hurry Up Harry' and 'Hersham Boys'. After a troubled couple of years, Pursey went solo, but his time had passed. The group re-formed in the early 90s.

SHAMEN

FORMED IN ABERDEEN BY COLIN ANGUS (b. 1961; BASS), PETER STEPHENSON (b. 1962), KEITH McKENZIE (b. 1961) and Derek McKenzie (b. 1964; guitar), the Shamen's debut *Drop*, captured a sense of their colourful live shows and sealed the first chapter of the band's career. Soon after, Colin Angus became fascinated by the nascent underground hip-hop movement. Will Sinnott (b. William Sinnott, 1960, d. 1991; bass) then replaced Derek McKenzie and further encouraged the Shamen's move towards the dancefloor. In 1988 the band relocated to London and slimmed down to the duo of Angus and Sinnott. By 1990 the Shamen's influence was vividly realized as the much-touted indie-dance crossover saw bands fuse musical cultures. However, just as the group prospered, Will Sinnott drowned off the coast of Gomera. The Shamen persevered with a remix of 'Move Any Mountain (Pro Gen '91)' which climbed into the UK Top 10. Mr C (b. Richard West) had joined the band for a section of this single and his rhymes founded the springboard for UK chart success – 'LSI', followed by the number 1 'Ebeneezer Goode' – which was accused in many quarters of extolling the virtues of Ecstasy. The Shamen moved on with the release of *Boss Drum*.

SHANGRI-LAS

THE SHANGRI-LAS COMPRISED TWO PAIRS OF SISTERS, MARY-ANN (b. *c.* 1948) AND MARGIE GANSER (b. *c.* 1947, d. 1996) AND Betty (b. *c.* 1948) and Mary Weiss (b. *c.* 1947). They were discovered in 1963 by George 'Shadow' Morton and recorded two singles under the name Bon Bons before signing to the newly-formed Red Bird label. Relaunched as the Shangri-Las, they secured a worldwide hit with 'Remember (Walkin' In The Sand)'. The sound of a revving motorbike engine opened their distinctive follow-up, 'Leader Of The Pack', which was even more successful. By 1966, Margie Ganser had left the group, but they had already found a perfect niche, specializing in the doomed romanticism of American teenage life. This hit formula occasionally wore thin but Shadow Morton could always be relied upon to engineer a gripping production. During their closing hit phase in 1966-67, the group recorded two songs, 'I Can Never Go Home Anymore' and 'Past, Present And Future', which saw the old teenage angst transmogrified into an almost tragic, sexual neuroticism.

SHANNON, DEL

SHANNON'S (b. CHARLES WESTOVER, 1934, d. 1990) DEBUT 'RUNAWAY' WAS A SPECTACULAR AFFAIR THAT REACHED the top of the charts in the USA and UK, and over the next few years Shannon produced and wrote his own material with great success, especially in Britain, where his run of 10 consecutive hits ended with 'Sue's Gotta Be Mine' in 1963.

Shannon worked steadily for the next 25 years, enjoying a few more hit singles including a cover version of Bobby Freeman's 'Do You Wanna Dance'. 1965's 'Keep Searchin'' was Shannon's last major success. Throughout the 60s and 70s Shannon was a regular visitor to Britain where he found a smaller but more appreciative audience. *Drop Down And Get Me* was well received but sold poorly. Ironically, he received a belated hit in America with 1982's 'Sea Of Love'. This led to a brief renaissance for him in the USA. Ultimately, however, he was branded to rock 'n' roll revival tours that finally took their toll in February 1990, when a severely depressed Shannon shot himself.

SHAPIRO, HELEN

LONDON-BORN SHAPIRO (b. 1946) DREW CONSIDERABLE ATTENTION WHEN, AT 14, SHE SCORED A UK TOP 3 HIT WITH 'Don't Treat Me Like A Child'. By the end of 1961 she had scored two chart-topping singles with 'You Don't Know' and 'Walkin' Back To Happiness'. This success was maintained the following year with 'Tell Me What He Said' (number 2) and 'Little Miss Lonely' (number 8). Although she was younger than many beat group members, Shapiro was perceived as belonging to a now outmoded era and, despite a series of excellent singles, Shapiro was eclipsed by 'newcomers' **Cilla Black** and **Dusty Springfield**. The late 60s proved more fallow still and, barring one pseudonymous release, Shapiro did not record at all between 1970-75. 'Can't Break The Habit' became a minor hit in Europe during 1977 and in turn engendered *All For The Love Of The Music*, a set denied a UK release. Six years later Shapiro resurfaced on Oval. *Straighten Up And Fly Right* showed the singer had lost none of her early power. Since then she has maintained a high profile through radio, television and live appearances.

SHARROCK, SONNY

STARTING IN 1965 NEW YORK-BORN SHARROCK (b. WARREN HARDIN SHARROCK, 1940, d. 1994) WORKED WITH A succession of major names in the *avant garde*, then from 1967-73 provided the 'outside' element in Herbie Mann's band. In 1973 he formed a band with his then-wife, Linda Sharrock (Chambers), and made his solo debut with *Black Woman*. After *Guitar*, he established a more conventional band which toured successfully with packages organized by New York's Knitting Factory club. In 1991 he released *Ask The Ages*, with an all-star quartet containing Pharoah Sanders, Charnett Moffett and Elvin Jones. Sharrock died of a heart attack in May 1994.

SHAW, SANDIE

DISCOVERED BY SINGER **ADAM FAITH**, ESSEX-BORN SHAW (b. SANDRA GOODRICH, 1947) WAS LAUNCHED AS A teenage pop star in 1964. Her first single, 'As Long As You're Happy', proved unsuccessful but the follow-up, '(There's) Always Something There To Remind Me' reached number 1 in the UK. Shaw's star shone for the next three years with a series of hits, mainly composed by her songwriter/producer **Chris Andrews**. His style, specializing in jerky rhythms and plaintive ballads served Sandie well, especially on 'Long Live Love', which provided her second UK number 1 in 1965. Chosen to represent Britain in the 1967 Eurovision Song Contest, Shaw emerged triumphant with 'Puppet On A String', which gave her a third UK number 1. Attempts to launch Shaw as a family entertainer were hampered by salacious newspaper reports and she effectively retired. In the early 80s she was rediscovered by BEF, and recorded a version of 'Anyone Who Had A Heart'. The Shaw resurgence was completed when she was heavily promoted by **Smiths** vocalist **Morrissey**. Shaw enjoyed a brief chart comeback with 'Hand In Glove' in 1984. In 1986, she reached the lower regions of the UK chart with a cover of **Lloyd Cole**'s 'Are You Ready To Be Heartbroken?' Her comeback album featured songs by Morrissey, the Smiths and **Jesus And Mary Chain**.

SHED SEVEN

FORMED IN YORK, ENGLAND, SHED SEVEN COMPRISE RICK WITTER (b. *c.* 1973; LEAD VOCALS), TOM GLADWIN (b. *c.* 1973; bass), Paul Banks (b. *c.* 1973; guitar) and Alan Leach (b. *c.* 1970; drums). Together they brought a flash of anti-glamour to the independent scene of the mid-90s. They were unconcerned with the trappings of cool, happily signing to a major, Polydor, and making their debut with 'Mark'. They achieved two Top 30 singles and a Top 20 album. The band's second album, including their Top 15 UK hit 'Getting Better', was released in 1996 to mixed reviews.

SHERIDAN, TONY

BRITISH-BORN SHERIDAN (b. ANTHONY SHERIDAN McGINNITY, 1940) JOINED VINCE TAYLOR AND THE PLAYBOYS in early 1959. The group soon evolved into the Beat Brothers with a line-up of Sheridan (vocals/guitar), Ken Packwood (guitar), Rick Richards (guitar), Colin Melander (bass), Ian Hines (keyboards) and Jimmy Doyle (drums), although this changed almost constantly. This line-up recorded with producer Bert Kaempfert at the controls, although by 1962 the Beat Brothers had been joined by **Ringo Starr**, Roy Young (keyboards) and Rikky Barnes (saxophone). By 1964 he had teamed up with Glaswegian expatriates Bobb Patrick Big Six. However, with the Hamburg beat boom all but over by 1964, Sheridan travelled to Vietnam to play US army bases. He eventually returned to Hamburg to turn solo in 1968, where his cult status has not diminished.

SHIRELLES

FORMED IN PASSAIC, NEW JERSEY, USA, THEY COMPRISED SHIRLEY OWENS (b. 1941), BEVERLY LEE (b. 1941), DORIS Kenner (b. 1941) and Addie 'Micki' Harris (b. 1940, d. 1982). They signed to Tiara and secured their first minor hit 'I Met Him On A Sunday'. This inspired the inauguration of a second outlet, Scepter, where the Shirelles gained pop immortality with 'Will You Love Me Tomorrow'. This was followed by a series of hits, 'Mama Said' (1961), 'Baby It's You' (1962) and 'Foolish Little Girl' (1963). The quartet's progress declined when producer and arranger Luther Dixon left and newer acts assumed the quartet's prime. By the time the Shirelles were free to move to another label, they were already confined to the 'oldies' circuit.

SHOCKED, MICHELLE

THIS US-BORN ROOTS SINGER/SONGWRITER ORIGINALLY CAME TO PROMINENCE VIA A WALKMAN RECORDED GIG, taped around a campfire. *Short Sharp Shocked* highlighted more varied and less self-conscious stylings than the more mainstream **Suzanne Vega/Tracy Chapman** school. *Captain Swing* was her 'big band' record, where she was joined by a plethora of famous extras. The recording of *Arkansas Traveller* was completed by travelling across the US and further afield with a portable studio. In the summer of 1995 Shocked (b. Karen Michelle Johnson, 1962) filed a suit to be released from her contract with Polygram/Mercury Records following a number of accusations from both parties. When this was resolved she signed with BMG and released *Kind Hearted Woman*.

SHOCKING BLUE

FORMED IN 1967 BY GUITARIST ROBBIE VAN LEEUWEN (b. 1944), THIS DUTCH QUARTET ORIGINALLY FEATURED LEAD vocalist Fred de Wilde, bassist Klassje van der Wal and drummer Cornelius van der Beek. After one minor hit in their homeland, 'Lucy Brown Is Back In Town', the group's management replaced de Wilde with Mariska Veres (b. 1949). Veres brought the group a sexy image and another Netherlands hit 'Send Me A Postcard Darling'. Next came 'Venus', a massive European hit, which went on to top the US charts in 1970. With the talented van Leeuwen dominating the composing and production credits, Shocking Blue attempted to bridge the gap between the pop and progressive markets. They enjoyed another minor UK hit with 'Mighty Joe', which had reached number 1 in Holland, but split in 1974.

SHONEN KNIFE

JAPANESE SISTERS ATSUKO (b. *c.* 1960) AND NAOKO YAMANO (b. *c.* 1961) WITH MICHIE NAKATANI (b. *c.* 1961) FORMED the group in 1981, their sporadic recording career starting in Osaka before relocating to the west coast of America. There they came to the attention of US punk pop fans in general, and **Nirvana** in particular. The latter took them under their wing, and brought them international recognition. However, they had long been a cult delicacy in American punk circles, made evident when 30 bands each contributed to an album's worth of cover versions of Shonen Knife songs. They attempted a comeback with *Brand New Knife* in 1996.

SHAW, SANDIE
Albums
Sandie Sings (Golden Guinea 1967)★★★★ (Compilation)
Nothing Less Than Brilliant: The Best Of Sandie Shaw (Virgin 1994)★★★★
➧ p.379 for full listings
Collaborators
Chris Andrews ➧ p.18
Smiths ➧ p.301
Morrissey ➧ p.239
Jesus And Mary Chain ➧ p.199
Connections
Adam Faith ➧ p.142
Influences
Lloyd Cole ➧ p.96
Further References
Book: *The World At My Feet*, Sandie Shaw

SHED SEVEN
Albums
A Maximum High (Polydor 1996)★★★★
➧ p.379 for full listings
Further References
Video: *Stuffed* (1996)

SHERIDAN, TONY
Albums
My Bonnie (Polydor 1962)★★
Worlds Apart (1978)★★
➧ p.379 for full listings
Collaborators
Ringo Starr ➧ p.307

SHIRELLES
Albums
Baby It's You (Scepter/Stateside 1962)★★★★
The Very Best Of ... (Rhino 1994)★★★★ (Compilation)
➧ p.379 for full listings
Collaborators
Luther Dixon
Further References
Book: *Girl Groups: The Story Of A Sound*, Alan Betrock

SHOCKED, MICHELLE
Albums
Short Sharp Shocked (Cooking Vinyl 1988)★★★
Stillborn (Private 1996)★★★
➧ p.379 for full listings
Connections
Suzanne Vega ➧ p.329
Tracy Chapman ➧ p.87

SHOCKING BLUE
Albums
The Shocking Blue (Colossus 1970)★★★
➧ p.379 for full listings

SHONEN KNIFE
Albums
Burning Farm mini-album (Zero 1983)★★★
Let's Knife (MCA Victor 1992)★★★
➧ p.379 for full listings
Collaborators
Nirvana ➧ p.248

SHOWADDYWADDY
Albums
Showaddywaddy (Bell 1974)★★★
Step Two (Bell 1975)★★★
➧ p.379 for full listings
Influences
Eddie Cochran ➧ p.95

SHRIEKBACK
Albums
Jam Science (Arista 1984)★★★
Big Night Music (Island 1987)★★★
➧ p.379 for full listings
Connections
XTC ➧ p.345

SIBERRY, JANE
Albums
Jane Siberry (Street 1980)★★★
Bound By The Beauty (Reprise 1989)★★★★
➧ p.379 for full listings
Collaborations
Brian Eno ➧ p.136

SIFFRE, LABI
Albums
Labi Siffre (1970)★★★
Make My Day (Connoisseur 1989)★★★
➧ p.379 for full listings
Connections
Madness ➧ p.221

SILVERCHAIR
Albums
Frogstomp (Sony 1995)★★★
➧ p.379 for full listings
Influences
Pearl Jam ➧ p.257
Nirvana ➧ p.248

SIMON, CARLY
Albums
Anticipation (Elektra 1971)★★★★
No Secrets (Elektra 1972)★★★★
➧ p.379 for full listings
Collaborators
James Taylor ➧ p.317
Chic ➧ p.90
Connections
Mick Jagger ➧ 281
Further References
Video: *Live At Grand Central* (Polygram 1996)
Book: *Carly Simon*, Morse

SIMON, PAUL
Albums
Paul Simon (Columbia 1972)★★★★
Still Crazy After All These Years (Columbia 1975)★★★★
Graceland (Warners 1986)★★★★
➧ p.379 for full listings
Collaborators
Art Garfunkel ➧ p.154
James Taylor ➧ p.317

SHOWADDYWADDY

WHEN TWO PROMISING LEICESTERSHIRE GROUPS FUSED THEIR TALENTS IN 1973, THE RESULT WAS AN OCTET COMPRISING Dave Bartram (vocals), Billy Gask (vocals), Russ Fields (guitar), Trevor Oakes (guitar), Al James (bass), Rod Teas (bass), Malcolm Allured (drums) and Romeo Challenger (drums). Showaddywaddy charted steadily, but after reaching number 2 with **Eddie Cochran**'s 'Three Steps To Heaven', the cover version game began. Fifteen of their singles reached the UK Top 20 during the late 70s but the seemingly foolproof hit formula eventually ran dry when the rock 'n' roll revival had passed.

SHRIEKBACK

SHRIEKBACK ORIGINALLY EVOLVED AROUND A THREE-MAN NUCLEUS OF DAVE ALLEN, CARL MARSH AND BARRY ANDREWS. The first fruits of this project came in 1982 with the EP *Tench* and then 'Sexthinkone', but it was the next two singles, 'My Spine Is The Bassline' (1982) and 'Lined Up' (1983) that established the band. Two further singles, 'Working On The Ground' and 'Accretions', were enough to secure a contract with Arista, releasing *Jam Science*. A move to Island Records yielded *Big Night Music*, accompanied by 'Gunning For Buddha'. 'Get Down Tonight' followed in 1988, but this presaged the last Shriekback album proper.

SIBERRY, JANE

SIBERRY'S (b. 1955) FIRST, INDEPENDENTLY PRODUCED ALBUM WAS FOLLOWED BY A TOUR OF HER NATIVE CANADA. *No Borders Here* included 'Mimi On The Beach', an underground hit in Canada where *The Speckless Sky* later went gold. Siberry made her first live appearance in Europe following *The Walking*. *Bound By The Beauty* included Teddy Borowiecki, (piano/accordion), Stich Winston (drums), John Switzer (bass), and Ken Myhr (guitar), and was greeted with critical acclaim. The belated follow-up saw her work with **Brian Eno** on two tracks.

SIFFRE, LABI

SIFFRE PLAYED HIS FIRST GIGS WITH A TRIO OF LIKE-MINDED YOUNGSTERS, BEFORE TAKING UP A RESIDENCY AT Annie's Rooms. His tenure completed, he travelled to Cannes, France, and played with a variety of soul musicians and bands. He returned to the UK in the late 60s and enjoyed solo hits with 'It Must Be Love' (1976) and 'Crying, Laughing, Loving, Lying'. Although 'Watch Me' in 1972 was his last hit of the 70s, he made a spectacular comeback in 1987 with the anthemic '(Something Inside) So Strong'.

SILVERCHAIR

AUSTRALIAN ROCK TRIO SILVERCHAIR ARRIVED IN EUROPE IN 1995, EACH MEMBER JUST 15 YEARS OLD. HOWEVER, Chris Joannou (b. 1979; bass), Daniel Johns (b. 1979; vocals/guitar) and Ben Gillies (b. 1979; drums) seemed quite capable of producing a noise in the best adult traditions of their primary influences, **Pearl Jam** and **Nirvana**. The single they chose to record, 'Tomorrow', quickly became a national number 1. *Frogstomp* quickly achieved double platinum status in Australia.

SIMON, CARLY

IN THE EARLY 60S US-BORN SIMON (b. 1945) PLAYED GREENWICH VILLAGE CLUBS WITH HER SISTER LUCY. AS THE Simon Sisters they had one minor hit with 'Winkin' Blinkin' And Nod'. After the duo split, Carly Simon concentrated on songwriting with film critic Jacob Brackman. In 1971, two of their songs, the wistful 'That's The Way I've Always Heard It Should Be' and 'Anticipation' were US hits. Her third album included her most famous song, 'You're So Vain', whose target was variously identified as Warren Beatty and/or Mick Jagger.

Simon's next Top 10 hit was 'Mockingbird' on which she duetted with **James Taylor** to whom she was married from 1972-83. Their marriage was given enormous coverage in the US media, and their divorce received similar treatment as Carly found solace with Taylor's drummer Russell Kunkel. During the 80s, Simon released two albums of pre-war Broadway standards (*Torch* and *My Romance*) and increased her involvement with films. Her UK hit 'Why' (1982) was used in the movie *Soup For One*, but her biggest achievement of the decade was to compose and perform two memorable film themes, 'Coming Around Again' (from *Heartburn*, 1986) and 'Let The River Run' (from *Working Girl*, 1989). In 1990, her career came full circle when Lucy Simon was a guest artist on *Have You Seen Me Lately?*. After a lengthy gap in recording she released *Letters Never Sent*.

SIMON, PAUL

NEW JERSEY-BORN SIMON (b. 1941) FIRST ENTERED THE MUSIC BUSINESS WITH PARTNER **ART GARFUNKEL** IN THE DUO TOM And Jerry, but they split after one album. Simon enjoyed a couple of minor US hits during 1962-63 as Tico And The Triumphs ('Motorcycle') and Jerry Landis ('The Lone Teen-Ranger'). In 1964, he signed to CBS and was re-united with Garfunkel. Between 1965 and 1970, Simon And Garfunkel became one of the most successful recording duos in the history of popular music, but the partnership eventually ended amid musical disagreements.

Simon prepared a stylistically diverse solo album, *Paul Simon*. The work spawned the hit singles 'Mother And Child Reunion' and 'Me And Julio Down By The Schoolyard'. A year later, he returned with the more commercial *There Goes Rhymin' Simon* which enjoyed massive chart success. In 1975, the chart-topping *Still Crazy After All These Years* won several Grammy awards. The wry '50 Ways To Leave Your Lover', taken from the album, provided Simon with his first solo number 1. A five-year hiatus followed during which Simon recorded a hit single with Garfunkel and **James Taylor** ('Wonderful World'), released a *Greatest Hits* package featuring the catchy 'Slip Slidin' Away' and switched labels from CBS to Warner Brothers. In the wake of *One Trick Pony*, Simon suffered a period of writer's block, which was to delay the recording of his next album.

Meanwhile, a double-album live reunion of Simon And Garfunkel was issued. It was intended to preview a studio reunion, but the sessions were scrapped. Instead, Simon concentrated on his next album, *Hearts And Bones*, but it sold poorly. The situation altered with *Graceland*, one of the most commercially successful albums of the decade. Simon continued his pan-cultural investigations with *The Rhythm Of The Saints*, which incorporated African and Brazilian musical elements.

SIMON AND GARFUNKEL

AMERICAN DUO **PAUL SIMON** (b. 1941) AND **ART GARFUNKEL** (b. ARTHUR GARFUNKEL, 1941) FIRST ENJOYED A US HIT under the name Tom And Jerry with the rock 'n' roll styled 'Hey Schoolgirl'. They also completed an album which was later reissued after their rise to international prominence in the 60s. Garfunkel subsequently returned to college and Simon pursued a solo career before the duo reunited in 1964 for *Wednesday Morning 3AM*, but the album did not sell well and they split. The break came when producer Tom Wilson decided to overdub 'Sound Of Silence' with electric instrumentation, and within weeks the song was US number 1, and Simon and Garfunkel were hastily reunited. The album was rush-released early in 1966. Among its major achievements was 'Homeward Bound', which went on to become a transatlantic hit. 'The Dangling Conversation', was too esoteric for the Top 20, but the work testified to their artistic courage and boded well for the release of *Parsley, Sage, Rosemary And Thyme*. After two strong but uncommercial singles, 'At The Zoo' and 'Fakin' It', the duo contributed to the soundtrack of the 1968 film, *The Graduate*. The key song in the film, 'Mrs Robinson', provided the group with a huge international seller. *Bookends* was a superbly-crafted work, ranging from the serene 'Save The Life Of My Child' to the personal odyssey 'America'.

In 1969 the duo released 'The Boxer', a long single that found commercial success on both sides of the Atlantic. This classic single reappeared on the group's next album, the celebrated *Bridge Over Troubled Water*. One of the best-selling albums of all time (303 weeks on the UK chart), the work's title track became a standard. While at the peak of their commercial success, however, the duo became irascible and their partnership abruptly ceased. In 1981 they again reunited. The results were captured in 1981 on *The Concert In Central Park*. In 1993 Simon and Garfunkel settled their differences long enough to complete 21 sell-out dates in New York.

SIMONE, NINA

US-BORN SIMONE'S (b. EUNICE WAYMON, 1933) JAZZ CREDENTIALS WERE ESTABLISHED IN 1959 WHEN SHE secured a hit with 'I Loves You Porgy'. Her influential 60s work included 'Gin House Blues', 'Forbidden Fruit' and 'I Put A Spell On You', while another of her singles, 'Don't Let Me Be Misunderstood', was later covered by the **Animals**. 'Ain't Got No – I Got Life', reached UK number 2, while 'To Love Somebody' reached number 5. In America, her own composition, 'To Be Young, Gifted And Black', reflected Simone's growing militancy. 'My Baby Just Cares For Me' pushed the singer into the commercial spotlight when it reached number 5 in 1987.

SIMPLE MINDS

SCOTTISH GROUP FORMED IN 1978 BY JIM KERR (b. 1959; VOCALS), CHARLIE BURCHILL (b. 1959; GUITAR), TONY DONALD (bass) and Brian McGee (drums), augmented by keyboard player Mick McNeil (b. 1958), before Derek Forbes (b. 1956) replaced Donald. Simple Minds signed to Zoom, an independent label marketed by Arista. 'Life In A Day', the group's debut, broached the UK Top 50 in 1979 while the attendant album reached number 30. Within weeks the quintet embarked on a more radical direction, and *Real To Real Cacophony* won unanimous music press approbation.

Empires And Dance fused the flair of its predecessor to a newly established love of dance music. Now free of Arista, Simple Minds signed to Virgin in 1981, and recorded two albums, *Sons And Fascination* and *Sister Feelings Call*, initially released together. They resulted in three minor hit singles with 'The American', 'Love Song' and 'Sweat In Bullet'. In 1981 McGee left and Mel Gaynor (b. 1959), became the quintet's permanent drummer. *New Gold Dream (81, 82, 83, 84)* peaked at number 3. *Sparkle In The Rain* united the quintet with producer Steve Lillywhite. 'Waterfront' and 'Speed Your Love To Me', prefaced its release, and the album entered the UK chart at number 1.

Once Upon A Time, despite international success, drew considerable criticism for its bombastic approach. Three tracks, 'Alive And Kicking', 'Sanctify Yourself' and 'All The Things She Said' nonetheless reached the UK Top 10. In 1988 they were an inspiration behind the concert celebrating Nelson Mandela's 70th birthday. 'Mandela Day' was recorded for the event and topped the UK chart in 1989, setting the tone for the group's subsequent album, *Street Fighting Years*. Three further singles entered the UK Top 20, while *The Amsterdam EP*, reached number 18 at the end of the year. This period closed with the rancorous departure of Mick McNeil, and Simple Minds entered the 90s with an official line-up of Jim Kerr and Charlie Burchill. *Real Life* saw the band re-introducing more personal themes to their songwriting after the political concerns of previous albums. The highly commercial 'She's A River' came in advance of *Good News From The Next World*, just as the world was beginning to think Simple Minds were from an age past.

Connections
Simon And Garfunkel
➧ p.297
Further References
Book: *The Boy In The Bubble*, Patrick Humphries

SIMON AND GARFUNKEL
Albums
The Sound Of Silence (Columbia 1966)★★★★
Bookends (Columbia 1968)★★★★
Bridge Over Troubled Water (Columbia 1970)★★★★
➧ p.379 for full listings
Collaborators
Tom Wilson
Connections
Tom And Jerry
The Graduate
Further References
Books: *Simon & Garfunkel: A Biography In Words & Pictures*, Michael S. Cohen
Simon And Garfunkel: Old Friends, Morella and Barey

SIMONE, NINA
Albums
Nina Simone At Carnegie Hall (Colpix 1963)★★★★
Emergency Ward (RCA 1972)★★★
➧ p.379 for full listings

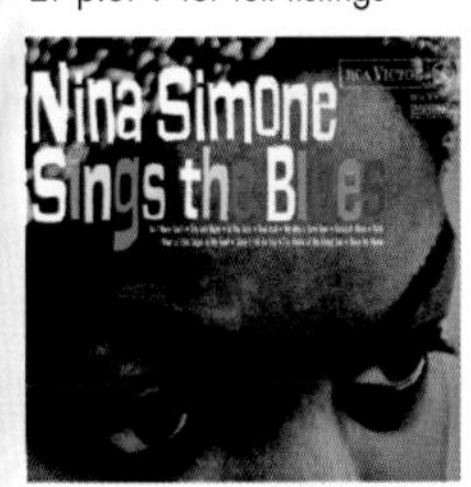

Connections
Animals ➧ p.18
Influences
George Gershwin
Bee Gees ➧ p.41
Further References
Book: *I Put A Spell On You: The Autobiography Of Nina Simone*, Nina Simone with Stephen Cleary

SIMPLE MINDS
Albums
New Gold Dream (81, 82, 83, 84) (Virgin 1982)★★★★
Sparkle In The Rain (Virgin 1984)★★★★
Once Upon A Time (Virgin 1985)★★★★
➧ p.379 for full listings
Collaborators
Steve Hillage
Steve Lillywhite
Connections
Nelson Mandela
Further References
Books: *Simple Minds: Glittering Prize*, Dave Thomas
Simple Minds: Street Fighting Years, Alfred Bos

SIMPLY RED
Albums
Stars (East West 1991)★★★★
➽ p.379 for full listings

Influences
Aretha Franklin ➽ p.153
Gregory Isaacs ➽ p.193

SIOUXSIE AND THE BANSHEES
Albums
Tinderbox (Polydor 1986)★★★
The Rapture (Polydor 1995)★★★
➽ p.379 for full listings
Collaborators
Robert Smith ➽ p.108
Connections
Sex Pistols ➽ p.292
Slits ➽ p.300
Cure ➽ p.108
Clock DVA ➽ p.94
Influences
Beatles ➽ p.38
Bob Dylan ➽ p.128

SISTER SLEDGE
Albums
The Best Of... (Rhino 1992)★★★★ (Compilation)
➽ p.379 for full listings
Connections
Chic ➽ p.90

SIR DOUGLAS QUINTET
Albums
Mendocino (Smash 1969)★★★★
➽ p.379 for full listings
Influences
Beatles ➽ p.38

Skellern, Peter
Albums
Happy Endings (BBC 1981)★★★
➽ p.379 for full listings

Collaborators
George Harrison ➽ p.176
Ringo Starr ➽ p.307
Connections
Beatles ➽ p.38

SKID ROW (EIRE)
Albums
34 Hours (Columbia 1971)★★★
➽ p.379 for full listings
Collaborators
Gary Moore ➽ p.238
Phil Lynott ➽ p.220

SIMPLY RED

THIS SOUL-INFLUENCED GROUP WAS FORMED BY MANCHESTER-BORN VOCALIST MICK HUCKNALL (b. Michael James Hucknall, 1960) in 1983. After signing to Elektra the group found a settled line-up featuring Hucknall, Tony Bowers (bass), Fritz McIntyre (b. 1958; keyboards), Tim Kellett (brass), Sylvan Richardson (guitar) and Chris Joyce (drums). *Picture Book* climbed to number 2 in the UK charts, while their version of 'Money's Too Tight To Mention' was a Top 20 hit. They continued with a sterling re-recording of 'Holding Back The Years' which peaked at number 2. Further hits followed with 'The Right Thing', 'Infidelity' and a reworking of the Cole Porter standard, 'Ev'ry Time We Say Goodbye'. Simply Red finally scaled the album chart summit in 1989 with *A New Flame*. The album coincided with another hit, 'It's Only Love', which was followed by a reworking of 'If You Don't Know Me By Now' (UK number 2). The 1991 album *Stars* topped the British charts and the much awaited follow-up *Life* was also a big seller. The band returned in 1996 and 1997 with cover versions of **Aretha Franklin**'s 'Angel' and **Gregory Isaacs**' 'Night Nurse'. In 1998 they were back with *Blue* and 'Say You Love Me'.

SIOUXSIE AND THE BANSHEES

SIOUXSIE SIOUX (b. SUSAN DALLION, 1957) WAS PART OF THE 'BROMLEY CONTINGENT', WHICH FOLLOWED THE **SEX Pistols** in their early days. Siouxsie put together her backing group the Banshees, featuring Pete Fenton (guitar), Steve Severin (bass) and Kenny Morris (drums). By mid-1977 Fenton was replaced by John McGeogh, and in 1978, the group signed to Polydor. They released 'Hong Kong Garden', which reached the UK Top 10. Less commercial offerings ensued with 'The Staircase (Mystery)' and 'Playground Twist', followed by *Join Hands*. During a promotional tour, Morris and McKay abruptly left, to be replaced by Budgie (b. Peter Clark, 1957) and temporary Banshee Robert Smith, from the **Cure**. Siouxsie's Germanic influences were emphasized on the stark 'Mittageisen (Metal Postcard)', which barely scraped into the Top 50. Both 'Happy House' and 'Christine' had greater commercial success. Another Top 10 album, *Juju*, was followed by a break. The group reconvened in 1983 and a version of the **Beatles**' 'Dear Prudence' provided them with their biggest UK hit, at number 3. Early in 1984 'Swimming Horses' maintained their hit profile, while further personnel changes ensued with the enlistment of John Carruthers from **Clock DVA**. He, in turn, was replaced by Jon Klein. Siouxsie then tackled **Bob Dylan**'s 'This Wheel's On Fire' (UK Top 20), and an entire album of cover versions followed. A change of direction with *Peep Show* saw the band embrace a more sophisticated sound. 1991 returned them to the charts with the evocative 'Kiss Them For Me' and *Superstition*. Arguably their greatest achievement of the 90s, however, was the much-delayed *The Rapture*.

SISTER SLEDGE

US-BORN DEBRA (b. 1955), JOAN (b. 1957), KIM (b. 1958) AND KATHIE SLEDGE (b. 1959) STARTED THEIR RECORDING career in 1971 and in 1979 entered a relationship with **Chic** masterminds Nile Rodgers and Bernard Edwards that resulted in several singles, including 'He's The Greatest Dancer', 'We Are Family' and 'Lost In Music', each of which reached the the UK Top 20 in 1979. They began to produce their own material in 1981. Although success in the USA waned, the quartet retained their UK popularity with 'Frankie', which reached number 1 in 1985.

SIR DOUGLAS QUINTET

FORMED IN 1964, THE QUINTET WAS FASHIONED BY A HOUSTON-BASED PRODUCER, HUEY P. MEAUX, AND FORMER teenage prodigy, Doug Sahm (b. 1941). Augie Meyers (b. 1940; organ), Francisco (Frank) Morin (b. 1946; horns), Harvey Kagan (b. 1946; bass) and John Perez (b. 1942; drums) completed the line-up. They had an international hit with 'She's About A Mover' and the **Beatles**' 'She's A Woman'. This style continued on further singles and *The Best Of The Sir Douglas Quintet*. After a two year break the band released *Honky Blues*, although only Sahm and Morin were retained from the earlier unit.

The original Quintet was reconstituted for *Mendocino*, whose title track became the group's sole million-seller. Despite delivering several further excellent albums, the unit broke up in 1972, although they have been resurrected on several occasions.

SKELLERN, PETER

SKELLERN (b. 1947) RECORDED A COUNTRY-POP ALBUM WITH HARLAN COUNTY BEFORE THEY DISBANDED IN 1971. He then struck lucky with a self-composed UK number 3, 'You're A Lady'. Another hit single with the title track to *Hold On To Love* established Skellern as a purveyor of wittily-observed love songs. He earned the approbation of the ex-**Beatle** coterie and **George Harrison** assisted on *Hard Times*; the title number was later recorded by **Ringo Starr**.

In 1984, he formed Oasis with Julian Lloyd Webber, Mary Hopkin and guitarist Bill Lovelady, but the group's recordings failed to make a major impact. In 1985, he joined Richard Stilgoe for *Stilgoe And Skellern Stompin' At The Savoy*. This led to the duo working together on several successful tours. In 1995, Skellern issued his first album for nearly eight years.

SKID ROW (EIRE)

BLUES-BASED ROCK BAND, FORMED BY **GARY MOORE** IN DUBLIN, EIRE, IN 1968. RECRUITING **PHIL LYNOTT** (vocals/bass), Eric Bell (guitar) and Brian Downey (drums) the initial line-up only survived 12 months. Brendan Shiels replaced Lynott, and Noel Bridgeman replaced Bell. The group completed two singles, 'New Places, Old Faces' and 'Saturday Morning Man'. Their albums were well received, but Moore's growing reputation outstripped the group's musical confines. He left in 1971 to work with Dr. Strangely Strange and later the Gary Moore Band. Although Paul Chapman proved an able replacement, Skid Row's momentum faltered and the trio disbanded the following year.

SKID ROW (USA)

FORMED IN NEW JERSEY, USA, IN 1986, COMPRISING DAVE 'THE SNAKE' SABO (B. 1964; GUITAR), RACHEL BOLAN (b. 1964; bass), Sebastian Bach (b. 1968; vocals), Scotti Hill (b. 1964; guitar) and Rob Affuso (b. 1963; drums). They were picked up by **Bon Jovi**'s management and offered the support slot on their 1989 US stadium tour. They released their debut album the same year, which peaked at number 6 on the

Billboard chart and spawned two US Top 10 singles, '18 And Life' and 'I Remember You'. *Slave To The Grind* surpassed all expectations, debuting at number 1 in the US charts. 1994's *Subhuman Race* was produced by Bob Rock.

SKIP BIFFERTY

SKIP BIFFERTY – JOHN TURNBULL (GUITAR/VOCALS), MICKEY GALLAGHER (KEYBOARDS), COLIN GIBSON (BASS) AND Tommy Jackman (drums), Graham Bell (vocals) – made their debut in 1967 with 'On Love'. Two more singles followed, both memorable examples of pop psychedelia. Their first album continued this melodic craftsmanship. The group's potential withered under business entanglements and a conflict with their proprietorial manager Don Arden. Although they tried to forge an alternative career as Heavy Jelly, litigation over the rights to the name brought about their demise.

SKUNK ANANSIE

LONDON-BASED QUARTET, FORMED IN 1994, AND LED BY THE BLACK LESBIAN SINGER DEBORAH 'SKIN'. SHE BEGAN rehearsing with Skunk Anansie – also including **Ace** (guitar), Robbie (drums) and Cass (bass) – in 1994. Their debut single, 'Little Baby Swastikkka', was available only through mail order from BBC Radio 1's *Evening Session* programme. The controversial 'Selling Jesus' was followed by 'I Can Dream'. While Skin's lyrics remained forceful, it was clear that there was a lack of development in style and in terms of the issue-led subject matter. This was carried over to *Paranoid And Sunburnt*. *Stoosh* was a harder-edged collection, characterized by metal-edged guitar and Skin spitting out her lyrics.

SLADE

ORIGINALLY RECORDING AS THE 'N BETWEENS, THIS UK QUARTET COMPRISED NODDY HOLDER (b. NEVILLE HOLDER, 1950; vocals/guitar), Dave Hill (b. 1952; guitar), Jimmy Lea (b. 1952; bass) and Don Powell (b. 1950; drums). They signed with Fontana, which insisted they change their name to Ambrose Slade and it was under that moniker that they recorded *Beginnings*. They next signed up with Chas Chandler, who abbreviated their name to Slade and oversaw their new incarnation as a skinhead group for 'Wild Winds Are Blowing'. Slade persevered with their skinhead phase until 1970 when they began to cultivate a more colourful image. 'Coz I Luv You' took them to number 1 in the UK in late 1971, precipitating an incredible run of chart success, including 'Take Me Bak 'Ome', 'Mama Weer Al Crazee Now', 'Cum On Feel The Noize' and 'Skweeze Me Pleeze Me'. Their finest moment was 1977's 'Merry Xmas Everybody', one of the great festive rock songs, but by the mid-70s they were yesterday's teen heroes. An appearance at the 1980 Reading Festival brought them credibility anew. This performance was captured on the *Slade Alive At Reading '80* EP which pushed the group into the UK singles chart for the first time in three years. 'Merry Xmas Everybody' was re-recorded and charted that same year (the first in a run of seven consecutive years).

SLAYER

THIS DEATH/THRASH METAL QUARTET WAS FORMED IN HUNTINGTON BEACH, LOS ANGELES, USA, DURING 1982. Comprising Tom Araya (bass/vocals), Kerry King (guitar), Jeff Hanneman (guitar) and Dave Lombardo (drums) they made their debut in 1983, with a track on the compilation *Metal Massacre III*. This led to Metal Blade signing the band and releasing their first two albums. Featuring 10 tracks in just 28 minutes *Reign In Blood* took the concept of thrash to its ultimate conclusion. *Hell Awaits* opened the band up to a wider audience and *Seasons In The Abyss* pushed the band to the forefront of the thrash metal genre. A double live album followed, capturing the band at their best. However, it saw the permanent departure of Lombardo. Bostaph departed in 1995 and was replaced by John Dette in 1996.

SLEDGE, PERCY

RECOMMENDED TO QUIN IVY, OWNER OF THE NORALA SOUND STUDIO, US-BORN SLEDGE (b. 1941) ARRIVED WITH a rudimentary draft of 'When A Man Loves A Woman'. Released in 1966, it was a huge international hit. A series of emotional, poignant ballads followed, but none achieved a similar commercial profile. Having left Atlantic, Sledge re-emerged on Capricorn with *I'll Be Your Everything*. Two collections of re-recorded hits, *Percy* and *Wanted Again*, confirmed the singer's intimate yet unassuming delivery. In 1994 Sledge recorded *Blue Night*, which capitalized on the Sledge 'strong suit', the slow-burning countrified soul-ballad.

SLEEPER

THE PROVOCATIVE STATEMENTS OF LEAD VOCALIST AND GUITARIST LOUISE WENER (b. 1966) FIRST LAUNCHED UK-BASED Sleeper into the mainstream in 1994. Fellow members are Jon Stewart (b. *c.* 1967; guitar), Andy McClure (b. *c.* 1970; drums) and Diid Osman (b. *c.* 1969; bass). 1994 saw the release of *Swallow*, with EP *Delicious*, following shortly afterwards. 'Inbetweener' finally brought them to the UK Top 20 in 1995. 'Vegas' and 'What Do I Do Now?' also rose high in the charts, before a second album in autumn 1995. A critical backlash greeted 'She's A Good Girl' and *Pleased To Meet You*. Dan Kaufman replaced Osman in 1997.

SKID ROW (USA)
Albums
Slave To The Grind (Atlantic 1991)★★★
➧ p.379 for full listings
Collaborators
Bon Jovi ➧ p.60

SKIP BIFFERTY
Albums
Skip Bifferty (RCA 1968)★★★
➧ p.379 for full listings
Collaborations
Steve Marriott ➧ p.225
Ronnie Lane ➧ p.212

Skunk Anansie
Albums
Stoosh (One Little Indian 1996)★★★★
➧ p.379 for full listings
Collaborators
Björk ➧ p.48

SLADE
Albums
Slade Alive (Polydor 1972)★★★
➧ p.379 for full listings
Further References
Book: *Slade: Feel The Noize*, Charlesworth

SLAYER
Albums
Undisputed Attitude (American 1996)★★★
➧ p.379 for full listings
Collaborators
Rick Rubin ➧ p.284

SLEDGE, PERCY
Albums
Blue Night (Sky Ranch 1994)★★★★
➧ p.379 for full listings

SLEEPER
Albums
The It Girl (Indolent 1996)★★★★
➧ p.379 for full listings

SLITS
Albums
Cut (Island 1979)★★★
➤ p.379 for full listings
Connections
Siouxsie And The Banshees ➤ p.298

SLY AND ROBBIE
Albums
Various *Present Taxi* (Taxi 1981)★★★★
Rhythm Killers (4th & Broadway 1987)★★★★
➤ p.379 for full listings
Collaborators
Lee Perry ➤ p.259
Chaka Demus And Pliers ➤ p.86
Connections
Sly Dunbar ➤ p.126
Sly And The Family Stone ➤ p.300

SLY AND THE FAMILY STONE
Albums
Dance To The Music (Epic 1968)★★★★
Life (USA) *M'Lady* (UK) (Epic/Direction 1968)★★★★
Stand! (Epic 1969)★★★★
➤ p.379 for full listings

Connections
Larry Graham ➤ p.163

SMALL FACES
Albums
The Small Faces (Decca 1966)★★★
Ogden's Nut Gone Flake (Immediate 1968)★★★★
➤ p.379 for full listings
Collaborators
Don Arden
Andrew Oldham
Connections
Steve Marriott ➤p.225
Ronnie Lane ➤ p.212
Rolling Stones ➤ p.281
Faces ➤ p.141
Influences
Solomon Burke ➤ p.74
Further References
Video: *Big Hits* (Castle 1991)
Book: *The Young Mods' Forgotten Story*, Paolo Hewitt
Film: *Dateline Diamonds* (1965)

S* M* A* S* H
Albums
Self Abused (Hi-Rise 1994)★★★
➤ p.379 for full listings

SLITS

FORMED IN 1976 WITH A LINE-UP FEATURING ARI-UP (b. ARIANNA FOSTER; VOCALS), KATE KORUS (GUITAR), Palmolive (drums) and Suzi Gutsy (bass). Korus and Gutsy both quit shortly afterwards, and were replaced by Viv Albertine and Tessa Pollitt. By the time they made their recording debut, Palmolive had been ousted and replaced by Budgie (b. Peter Clark, 1957). Signed to Island, they released the dub-influenced *Cut*. The departure of Budgie to **Siouxsie And The Banshees** (replaced by Bruce Smith) coincided with the arrival of reggae musician Prince Hammer and trumpeter Don Cherry. A series of singles followed, but by 1981 the Slits had lost much of their original cutting edge and they disbanded at the end of the year.

SLY AND ROBBIE

SLY DUNBAR (b. LOWELL CHARLES DUNBAR, 1952; DRUMS) AND ROBBIE SHAKESPEARE (b. 1953; BASS). DUNBAR, nicknamed 'Sly' because of his fondness for **Sly And The Family Stone**, was an established figure in Skin Flesh And Bones when he met Shakespeare. The pair quickly became Jamaica's leading rhythm section. They not only formed their own label Taxi, which produced many hit records for scores of well-known artists, but also found time to do session work for just about every important name in reggae. In the early 80s they were among the first to use the burgeoning 'new technology'. Sly And Robbie's mastery of the digital genre coupled with their abiding love and respect for the music's history placed them at the forefront of Kingston's producers of the early 90s, and their 'Murder She Wrote' cut for **Chaka Demus And Pliers** set the tone for 1992, while 'Tease Mi' for the same duo, built around a sample from the Skatalites 60s hit, 'Ball Of Fire', was another significant UK chart success in 1993.

SLY AND THE FAMILY STONE

US GROUP FORMED IN SAN FRANCISCO, CALIFORNIA, IN 1967, COMPRISING SLY STONE (b. SYLVESTER STEWART, 1944), Freddie Stone (b. 1946; guitar), Rosie Stone (b. 1945; piano), Cynthia Robinson (b. 1946; trumpet), Jerry Martini (b. 1943; saxophone), **Larry Graham** (b. 1946; bass) and Greg Errico (b. 1946; drums). Sly joined Autumn Records as a songwriter/house-producer, and secured a success with Bobby Freeman's 'C'mon And Swim' in 1964. His own single, 'I Just Learned How To Swim', was less fortunate, though. In 1966 Sly formed the Stoners, a short-lived group that included Robinson. The following year Sly And The Family Stone made its debut with 'I Ain't Got Nobody'. The group then signed to Epic, and released *A Whole New Thing*. In 1968 'Dance To The Music' became a transatlantic Top 10. 'Everyday People' topped the US chart early the following year, and Sly's talent was fully established on *Stand!*. Two million copies were sold, while tracks including the title song, 'I Want To Take You Higher' and 'Sex Machine', transformed black music forever. The new decade began with a double-sided hit, 'Thank You (Falettinme Be Mice Elf Agin)'/'Everybody Is A Star', an R&B and pop number 1, but the optimism suddenly clouded. *There's A Riot Goin' On* (US number 1) was dark, mysterious and brooding, but nonetheless provided three successful singles, 'Family Affair', 'Running Away' and 'Smilin''. Graham then left and Andy Newmark replaced Errico. However, the real undermining factor was the leader's drug dependency, a constant stumbling block to Sly's recurrent 'comebacks'.

SMALL FACES

FORMED IN LONDON DURING 1965, THIS MOD-INFLUENCED GROUP INITIALLY COMPRISED: **STEVE Marriott** (b. 1947, d. 1991; vocals/guitar), **Ronnie** 'Plonk' **Lane** (b. 1946, d. 1997; bass), Jimmy Winston (b. James Langwith, 1945; organ) and Kenny Jones (b. 1948; drums). The group signed to Don Arden's Contemporary Records and were licensed to Decca. 'Whatcha Gonna Do About It', brought them into the UK Top 20, but within weeks Smith was replaced by Ian McLagan (b. 1945). 'I Got Mine', failed to chart and Arden responded to this setback by recruiting hit songwriters Kenny Lynch and Mort Shuman, whose catchy 'Sha-La-La-Lee' gave the group a UK Top 3 hit. 'Hey Girl' reinforced their chart credibility, which reached its apogee with 'All Or Nothing'. The festive 'My Mind's Eye' was followed by disagreements with their record company.

A final two singles for Decca, 'I Can't Make It' and 'Patterns', proved unsuccessful. They signed to Immediate and became a quasi-psychedelic ensemble. The drug-influenced 'Here Comes The Nice' was followed by the experimental 'Itchycoo Park'. With their Top 10 status reaffirmed, the group returned to their blues style with 'Tin Soldier'. For 'Lazy Sunday' the group combined cockney charm with a paean to hippie indolence, elements reflected on the chart-topping *Ogden's Nut Gone Flake*. The group bowed out with the chaotic 'The Universal' and the posthumous hit 'Afterglow Of Your Love'. They later re-emerged as the **Faces**. Successful reissues of 'Itchycoo Park' and 'Lazy Sunday' in the mid-70s persuaded Marriott, Jones, McLagan and new boy Rick Wills to revive the Small Faces name for a series of albums.

S*M*A*S*H

FORMED IN HERTFORDSHIRE, ENGLAND, THIS TRIO COMPRISING ED BORRIE (VOCALS/GUITAR), ROB (DRUMS) and Salvador (bass), dates back to 1984. Their first gig took place in early 1992, and the following year two singles, 'Real Surreal'/'Drugs Again' and 'Shame'/'Lady Love Your Cunt' were released on their Le Disques De Popcor Records. American label Sub Pop, responsible for much of the grunge movement that S*M*A*S*H detested, tried to sign them and instead they moved to Hi-Rise, releasing a mini-album six weeks later (compiling the first two 7-inch singles). Censorship proved a problem over '(I Want To) Kill Somebody', which reached the Top 30 despite being on sale for only one day. Their debut album was issued in 1994, but by 1995 the band had been dropped by Hi-Rise after a series of poorly received live performances. Following 'Rest Of My Life' they decided to split up.

SMASHING PUMPKINS

USA'S SMASHING PUMPKINS ARE LED BY BILLY CORGAN (b. 1967; VOCALS/GUITAR), WITH D'ARCY WRETZKY (b. 1968; bass), James Iha (b. 1968; guitar) and Jimmy Chamberlain (b. 1964; drums). They made their official debut with a drum machine at the Avalon club in Chicago, before Chamberlain was recruited. The group released 'I Am The One' in 1990, bringing them to the attention of influential Seattle label Sub Pop, for which they also released 'Tristessa'/'La Dolly Vita', before moving to Caroline Records. *Gish* announced the group to both indie and metal audiences and *Siamese Dream* reached the US Top 10 success. *Mellon Collie And The Infinite Sadness* was a bold project, yet the band managed to pull it off. 1998 saw a new album *Adore* and a world tour.

SMITH, PATTI

US-BORN SMITH'S (b. 1946) FIRST MAJOR RECORDING WAS A VERSION OF A JIM MORRISON POEM ON RAY MANZAREK'S solo album. In 1971, Smith formed a liason with guitarist Lenny Kaye and the duo was later joined by Richard Sohl (piano) in the first Patti Smith Group. Their debut recording was 'Hey Joe'/'Piss Factory'. Ivan Kral (bass) and J. D. Daugherty (drums) were then added to the line-up featured on *Horses*. *Radio Ethiopia* was perceived as self-indulgent and the artist's career was undermined when she incurred a broken neck upon falling off the stage early in 1977. Smith re-emerged the following year with the commercially successful *Easter*. 'Because The Night' from this reached the UK Top 5, but *Wave* failed to sustain such acclaim. Patti then married former **MC5** guitarist Fred 'Sonic' Smith, and retired from active performing for much of the 80s. *Peace And Noise*, reunited Smith with Kaye and Daugherty alongside co-writer and guitarist Oliver Ray, and marked a return to the spikier sound of her earlier material.

SMITHEREENS

THE SMITHEREENS FORMED IN NEW JERSEY IN 1980. MEMBERS JIM BABJAK (GUITAR) AND DENNIS DIKEN (DRUMS) had played together since 1971; Mike Mesaros (bass) was recruited in 1976 and finally Pat DiNizio (vocals). In 1986 the group released *Especially For You*, which fared well, as did the single 'Blood And Roses'. *Smithereens 11* was their biggest-selling album, reaching US number 41. Their career faltered in 1991 with the poorly received *Blow Up* (US number 120).

SMITHS

FORMED IN MANCHESTER IN 1982 BY DUO **MORRISSEY** (b. STEVEN PATRICK MORRISSEY, 1959) AND JOHNNY MARR (b. John Maher, 1963) who then recruited Mike Joyce (b. 1963; drums) and Andy Rourke (b. 1963; bass). The group signed to Rough Trade in 1983 and commenced work on their debut album. Their second single, 'This Charming Man' (1983), finally infiltrated the UK Top 30. The quartet began 1984 with the notably rockier 'What Difference Does It Make?' (UK number 12). A series of college gigs throughout Britain established the group as a cult favourite. A collaboration with **Sandie Shaw** saw a hit with 'Hand In Glove', while Morrissey dominated music press interviews. The singer's celebrated miserabilism was reinforced by the release of the autobiographical 'Heaven Knows I'm Miserable Now' (UK number 19). Another Top 20 hit followed with 'William, It Was Really Nothing'. While the Smiths commenced work on their next album, Rough Trade issued the interim *Hatful Of Hollow*. The Smiths now found themselves fêted as Britain's best group by various factions in the music press. The release of 'How Soon Is Now?' justified much of the hyperbole and this was reinforced by the power of their next album, *Meat Is Murder*. The group's fortunes in the singles charts, however, were relatively disappointing. 'Shakespeare's Sister' stalled at number 26, amid rumours that the group were dissatisfied with their record label. A dispute with Rough Trade delayed the release of the next album, which was preceded by 'Big Mouth Strikes Again'. *The Queen Is Dead* won immediate critical acclaim for its diversity and unadulterated power. A stadium tour of the USA followed and during the group's absence they enjoyed a formidable Top 20 hit with 'Panic'. After 'Shoplifters Of The World Unite' the group completed what would prove to be their final album. The group announced their split in 1987. *Strangeways, Here We Come* was issued posthumously, and a belated live album, *Rank*, was issued the following year.

SMOKE

THIS YORKSHIRE, ENGLAND GROUP COMPRISING MICK ROWLEY (VOCALS), MAL LUKER (LEAD GUITAR), PHIL PEACOCK (rhythm guitar), John 'Zeke' Lund (bass) and Geoff Gill (drums) was groomed for success by Alan Brush, as the Shots, but their one single, 'Keep A Hold Of What You Got', failed to sell. Peacock dropped out of the line-up, and the remaining quartet recorded several new demos. The most promising song, 'My Friend Jack', was released in 1967 under the group's new name, the Smoke. Problems arose when the line 'my friend Jack eats sugar lumps' was construed as celebrating drug abuse. The record was banned in Britain, but became a massive hit on the continent, inspiring *It's Smoke Time*. Later singles failed to garner a significant breakthrough.

SNIFF 'N' THE TEARS

LONDON GROUP WAS FORMED FROM THE ASHES OF MOON IN 1974 ONLY TO DISBAND WITHIN MONTHS AFTER thwarted attempts to gain a recording contract. However, in the late 70s new wave drummer Luigi Salvoni listened to the 1974 demos and persuaded Paul Roberts (vocals) to try again with Mick Dyche (guitar), Laurence Netto (guitar), Keith Miller (keyboards) and Nick South (bass). *Fickle Heart* included the catchy 'Driver's Seat', a hit in the USA and Australasia while faltering just outside the UK Top 40. They began a downward spiral with *Ride Blue Divide*, the last album to make a moderate commercial impact.

THE SMITHS

MEAT IS MURDER

SMASHING PUMPKINS

Albums

Siamese Dream (Virgin 1993)★★★★

Mellon Collie And The Infinite Sadness (Virgin 1995)★★★★

➽ p.379 for full listings

Connections

Nirvana ➽ p.248

Further References

Video: *Vieuphoria* (Virgin Music Video 1994)

Book: *Smashing Pumpkins*, Nick Wise

SMITH, PATTI

Albums

Horses (Arista 1975)★★★★

Peace And Noise (Arista 1997)★★★

➽ p.379 for full listings

Connections

Doors ➽ p.123

Patti Smith Group

MC5 ➽ p.228

Influences

Jim Morrison ➽ p.123

Further References

Book: *Early Work: 1970-1979*, Patti Smith

SMITHEREENS

Albums

Green Thoughts (Capitol 1988)★★★★

Smithereens 11 (Enigma 1990)★★★★

➽ p.379 for full listings

SMITHS

Albums

Meat Is Murder (Rough Trade 1985)★★★★

The Queen Is Dead (Rough Trade 1986)★★★★

➽ p.379 for full listings

Collaborations

Sandie Shaw ➽ p.295

Collaborators

Morrissey ➽ p.239

Further References

Books: *The Smiths*, Mick Middles

The Smiths: All Men Have Secrets, Tom Gallagher, M. Chapman and M. Gillies

SMOKE

Albums

It's Smoke Time (1967)★★★

➽ p.379 for full listings

Connections

Shots

SNIFF 'N' THE TEARS

Albums

Fickle Heart (Chiswick 1978)★★★

The Game's Up (Chiswick 1980)★★★

➽ p.379 for full listings

Connections

Ashes of Moon

SNOOP DOGGY DOGG
Albums
Doggy Style (Death Row 1993)★★★★
Tha Doggfather (Death Row 1996)★★★★
➽ p.379 for full listings
Collaborations
Dr. Dre ➽ p.124
Connections
En Vogue ➽ p.136

SNOOP DOGGY DOGG

DOGGY STYLE WAS THE MOST EAGERLY ANTICIPATED ALBUM IN RAP HISTORY, AND THE FIRST DEBUT ALBUM TO ENTER the *Billboard* chart at number 1. Dogg (b. Calvin Broadus, 1971) first appeared in 1990 when helping out **Dr. Dre** on a track called 'Deep Cover'. During touring commitments to support the album and single, 'Gin And Juice', he made the front page of the *Daily Star* with the headline: 'Kick This Evil Bastard Out!'. A more serious impediment to Snoop's career was the trial on charges of accessory to the murder of Phillip Woldermariam, shot by his bodyguard McKinley Lee. The verdict acquitted Dogg and McKinley Lee of both murder charges and the manslaughter cases were dropped. The trial had not overtly damaged his record sales; his debut topped 7 million copies worldwide, and the follow up *Tha Doggfather* entered the USA album chart at number 1.

SOFT BOYS
Albums
Underwater Moonlight (Armageddon 1980)★★★★
➽ p.379 for full listings
Connections
Robyn Hitchcock ➽ p.182

SOFT BOYS

ROBYN HITCHCOCK STARTED OUT AS A SOLO PERFORMER AND MEMBER OF various groups, before joining Dennis And The Experts which became the Soft Boys in 1976. The line-up was Hitchcock (vocals, guitar, bass), Alan Davies (guitar), Andy Metcalfe (bass), and Morris Windsor aka Otis Fagg (drums). The original sessions remain unreleased but the same line-up also recorded a three-track single, after which Kimberley Rew replaced Davies. They released '(I Wanna Be An) Anglepoise Lamp', to little success and after *Can Of Bees* they replaced Metcalfe with Matthew Seligman. Their remaining releases included *Underwater Moonlight*, which ranks amongst Hitchcock's finest moments. They broke up early in 1981.

SOFT CELL
Albums
Non-Stop Erotic Cabaret (Some Bizzare 1981)★★★
➽ p.379 for full listings
Connections
Marc Almond ➽ p.15

SOFT CELL

FORMED IN LEEDS, ENGLAND IN 1980 THIS DUO FEATURED VOCALIST **MARC ALMOND** (b. PETER MARC ALMOND, 1956) and David Ball (b. 1959; synthesizer). Some Bizarre Records entrepreneur Stevo negotiated a licensing deal with Phonogram in Europe and Sire in the USA. 'Memorabilia' became an underground hit, paving the way for the celebrated 'Tainted Love' (UK number 1). This became the best-selling British single of the year and remained in the US charts for 43 weeks. Subsequent hit singles included 'Bedsitter, 'Say Hello Wave Goodbye', 'Torch' and 'What', but the group was never happy with the pop machinery of which it had became a part, and *The Art Of Falling Apart* indicated how close they were to ending their hit collaboration. They disbanded after *This Last Night In Sodom.*

SOFT MACHINE
Albums
Third (CBS 1970)★★★★
➽ p.379 for full listings
Collaborators
Jimi Hendrix ➽ p.180
Connections
Robert Wyatt ➽ p.344
Kevin Ayers ➽ p.25
Animals ➽ p.18

SOFT MACHINE

FOUNDED IN ENGLAND IN 1966, THE ORIGINAL LINE-UP WAS **ROBERT WYATT** (b. 1945; DRUMS/VOCALS), **KEVIN Ayers** (b. 1945; vocals), Daevid Allen, Mike Ratledge and, very briefly, guitarist Larry Nolan. By 1967 the classic line-up of the Soft Machine's art-rock period (Ayers, Wyatt and Ratledge) had settled. They toured with **Jimi Hendrix**, who, with his producer Chas Chandler facilitated the recording of their first album. Ayers left at the end of 1968 and until 1970 the personnel was in a state of flux. *Volume Two* and *Third* contained their most intriguing and exciting performances. By the mid-1970s the second definitive line-up (Ratledge, Wyatt, Hugh Hopper and Elton Dean) was finally in place, but in autumn 1971, Wyatt left and John Marshall became the permanent drummer. For the next few years the Soft Machine were the standard against which all jazz-rock fusions were measured. However, with Ratledge's departure in 1976, the group began to lose their unique sound, lacking the edge of earlier incarnations. Their first three albums contain the best of their work.

SONIC YOUTH
Albums
EVOL (SST 1986)★★★★
➽ p.379 for full listings
Influences
Madonna ➽ p.222

SONIC YOUTH

US BAND SONIC YOUTH, COMPRISING *AVANT-GARDE* GUITARIST GLENN BRANCA, THURSTON MOORE (b. 1958; GUITAR), LEE Ranaldo (b. 1956; guitar) and Kim Gordon (b. 1953; bass), first performed together on Branca's *Symphony No. 3*. *Sonic Youth* was recorded live at New York's Radio City Music Hall in 1981. Three further collections, *Confusion Is Sex*, *Sonic Death* and a mini-album, *Kill Yr Idols*, completed the quartet's formative period, which saw Jim Sclavunos join, quickly succeeded by Bob Bert for *Bad Moon Rising*. Bert was then replaced by Steve Shelley (b. 1962). *Evol* refined their ability to mix melody with menace, particularly on the outstanding 'Shadow Of A Doubt'. In 1990 Sonic Youth signed with Geffen, establishing a reputation as godfathers to the alternative US rock scene with powerful albums such as *Goo* and *Dirty*. They are now one of the nation's best-known underground bands.

SONNY AND CHER

IN 1964 **SONNY BONO** (b. SALVATORE BONO, 1935, d. 1998) MARRIED **CHER** (b. CHERILYN SARKASIAN LA PIER, 1946) whom he had met while recording with producer **Phil Spector**. Although the duo recorded a couple of singles under the exotic name Caeser And Cleo, it was as Sonny And Cher that they found fame with the transatlantic number 1, 'I Got You Babe'. During late 1965, they dominated the charts as both a duo and soloists with such hits as 'Baby Don't Go', 'All I Really Want To Do', 'Laugh At Me', 'Just You' and 'But You're Mine'. Although their excessive output resulted in diminishing returns, their lean periods were punctuated by further hits, most notably 'Little Man' and 'The Beat Goes On'. They had a brief resurgence as MOR entertainers in the 70s, although by that time they had divorced. Eventually, extra-curricular acting activities ended their long-standing musical partnership.

SOUL ASYLUM

THIS MINNEAPOLIS, MINNESOTA, USA, GARAGE HARDCORE BAND CENTRED AROUND DAVE PIRNER (b. 1964; VOCALS/guitar) and Dan Murphy (b. 1962; guitar), with Karl Mueller (b. 1963; bass) and Pat Morley (drums). Morley left in 1984, replaced by Grant Young (b. 1964) for *Made To Be Broken*. *Hang Time*, saw them move into the hands of a new production team. *The Horse They Rode In On* was another splendid album, and the single 'Somebody To Shove' was heavily promoted on MTV. In 1995, the band announced that their next studio sessions would avoid the commercial textures of their previous album, although reviews of *Let Your Dim Light Shine* were mixed. They also recruited drummer, Stirling Campbell, to replace Young. *Candy From A Stranger* was well-received and the band toured in 1998.

SOUL II SOUL

THIS UK RAP, SOUL AND R&B GROUP ORIGINALLY CONSISTED OF JAZZIE B (b. BERESFORD ROMEO, 1963; RAPPER), Nellee Hooper (musical arranger) and Philip 'Daddae' Harvey (multi-instrumentalist). Following the release of 'Fairplay' and 'Feel Free', the band's profile grew. 'Keep On Movin'' subsequently reached UK number 5. The follow-up, 'Back To Life (However Do You Want Me)', featuring Caron Wheeler, was taken from their debut *Club Classics Volume One*. 'Get A Life' was an expansion on the influential, stuttering rhythms that the band had employed on previous singles. The band's second album included **Courtney Pine** and Kym Mazelle in its star-studded cast. Despite entering the charts at number 1 it was given a frosty reception by some critics who saw it as conservative. Although *Volume III, Just Right* made its debut at UK number 3, it proffered no substantial singles successes. The group's fourth studio album was not available until 1995, as Wheeler returned to the fold.

SOUNDGARDEN

AFTER ULTRAMEGA OK, THIS US GROUP, COMPRISING CHRIS CORNELL (b. 1964; VOCALS, GUITAR), KIM THAYIL (b. 1960; GUITAR), Hiro Yamamoto (b. 1968; bass) and Matt Cameron (b. 1962; drums) attracted the attention of A&M and released *Louder Than Love*, one of the most offbeat rock albums of 1989. Yamamoto was replaced by Jason Everman (ex-**Nirvana**), though he only recorded one track, a cover version of the **Beatles**' 'Come Together', before leaving. His replacement was Ben 'Hunter' Shepherd. *Badmotorfinger* built on the group's successful formula but added the grinding but melodious guitar sound that would come to define 'grunge'. *Superunknown* debuted at number 1 on the *Billboard* chart and sold over three million copies. *Down On The Upside* belied the band's internal strife with intense but highly melodic heavy rock. With continuing unrest in the camp, the band folded in 1997.

SOUTHSIDE JOHNNY AND THE ASBURY JUKES

R&B FANATIC SOUTHSIDE JOHNNY (b. JOHN LYONS, 1948; VOCALS) TEAMED UP WITH THE ASBURY JUKES WITH SCHOOL friends Billy Rush (guitar), Kevin Kavanaugh (keyboards), Kenneth Pentifallo (bass) and Alan 'Doc' Berger (drums). Popular in the parochial clubs, they sought a wider audience via a promotional album, *Live At The Bottom Line*, which led to a contract with Epic. This led to two albums, *I Wanna Go Home* and *This Time It's For Real*. After *Hearts Of Stone* failed to reach a mass public, Epic let the band go with the valedictory *Having A Party*. *The Jukes* sold well as did *Love Is A Sacrifice* but, for all the polished production, many felt that much nascent passion had been dissipated. *Reach Out And Touch The Sky* halted a commercial decline that resumed with later studio efforts.

SPACE

UK BAND FORMED IN 1993 AND COMPRISING TOMMY SCOTT (b. 1967; VOCALS, BASS), ANDY PARLE (DRUMS), JAMIE MURPHY (vocals/guitar) and Franny Griffiths (keyboards). The sound of their singles lurched from the sparse ska and sociopathic lyrics of 'Neighbourhood' to the stylish MOR noir of 'The Female Of The Species'. *Spiders* showed they were capable of sustaining their eclecticism across a whole album and making it commercially viable as well, entering the UK charts at number 5. Space set off on a sell-out UK tour in 1998; the year also brought further chart success, most notably 'Avenging Angels' and a collaboration with Catatonia's Cerys Hughes on 'The Ballad of Tom Jones', both from *Tin Planet*.

SPANDAU BALLET

UK NEW-ROMANTIC GROUP FOUNDED IN 1979 COMPRISING GARY KEMP (b. 1960; GUITAR), HIS BROTHER Martin Kemp (b. 1961; bass), Tony Hadley (b. 1960; vocals), John Keeble (b. 1959; drums) and Steve Norman (b. 1960; rhythm guitar/saxophone/percussion). Their powerful debut, 'To Cut A Long Story Short', reached the UK Top 5, but over the next year their singles 'The Freeze' and 'Musclebound' were average rather than exceptional. The insistent 'Chant Number 1 (I Don't Need This Pressure On)' revealed a more interesting soul/funk direction, and reached the UK Top 3, but again was followed by a relatively fallow period. By 1983 the group were pushing their lead singer as a junior Frank Sinatra. The new approach was demonstrated most forcibly on 'True', which topped the UK charts, as did the accompanying album, while the follow-up 'Gold' reached number 2. The group continued to chart regularly with such hits as 'Only When You Leave', 'I'll Fly For You', 'Highly Strung' and 'Round And Round'. The politically-conscious *Through The Barricades* and its attendant hit single 'Fight For Yourselves' partly re-established their standing. The Kemp brothers eventually turned to acting and Hadley embarked on a solo career.

SPARKS

VOCALIST RUSSELL MAEL AND HIS ELDER BROTHER RON (KEYBOARDS) FORMED SPARKS IN 1971 WITH EARLE MANKAY (guitar), Jim Mankay (bass) and Harley Fernstein (drums). Despite a regional US hit in 'Wonder Girl,' Sparks's debut album sold poorly – as did the subsequent *A Woofer In Tweeter's Clothing*. A club tour of Europe found them a cult following in England, where the Maels emigrated in 1973, signed to Island and enlisted a new Sparks from native players. This Anglo-American incarnation of Sparks had eight UK chart entries, starting with 1974's 'This Town Ain't Big Enough For Both Of Us' from *Kimono My House*. *Propaganda* was a stylistic departure but the basic formula was unaltered, and this, combined with an unsteady stage act provoked fading interest in further merchandise.

Sparks engineered a transient comeback to the British Top 20 in 1977 with two singles from *Number One In Heaven*. They were still active in the 90s and their recent work has been well received.

SONNY AND CHER
Albums
The Sonny And Cher Collection: An Anthology Of Their Hits Alone And Together (1991)★★★
p.379 for full listings
Collaborators
Phil Spector p.304
Connections
Cher p.89

SOUL ASYLUM
Albums
Soul Asylum And The Horse They Rode In On (Twin Tone/A&M 1990)★★★★
p.379 for full listings
Collaborators
Bob Dylan p.128
Guns N'Roses p.170

SOUL II SOUL
Albums
Club Classics Volume I (Ten 1989)★★★★
p.379 for full listings
Collaborators
Courtney Pine p.261

SOUNDGARDEN
Albums
Badmotorfinger (A&M 1991)★★★★
p.379 for full listings
Connections
Nirvana p.248
Influences
Beatles p.38

SOUTHSIDE JOHNNY AND THE ASBURY JUKES
Albums
I Don't Wanna Go Home (Epic 1976)★★★★
Reach Out And Touch The Sky: Southside Johnny And The Asbury Jukes Live! (Mercury 1981)★★★★
p.379 for full listings
Influences
Sam Cooke p.100
Further References
Video: *Having A Party* (Channel 5 1989)

SPACE
Albums
Spiders (Gut 1996)★★★
p.379 for full listings
Connections
Catatonia

SPANDAU BALLET
Albums
Through The Barricades (Reformation/Columbia 1986)★★★
p.379 for full listings

SPARKS
Albums
Gratuitous Sax And Senseless Violins (Arista 1994)★★★
p.379 for full listings

SPECIALS

FORMED IN 1977 AS THE SPECIAL AKA, THIS UK-BASED GROUP COMPRISED JERRY DAMMERS (b. GERALD DANKIN, 1954; keyboards), Terry Hall (b. 1959; vocals), Neville Staples (vocals/percussion), Lynval Golding (b. 1951; guitar), Roddy Radiation (b. Rodney Byers; guitar), Sir Horace Gentleman (b. Horace Panter; bass) and John Bradbury (drums). They set up the 2-Tone label and issued 'Gangsters', which reached the UK Top 10. After signing their label over to Chrysalis, the group abbreviated their name to the Specials. Their debut album was an exuberant effort which included 'A Message To You, Rudi' (UK Top 10). EP *The Special AKA Live* saw the Specials at their peak and the track 'Too Much Too Young', propelled them to number 1 in the UK charts. Further Top 10 hits with 'Rat Race', 'Stereotype' and 'Do Nothing' followed. At this new peak of success, the group fragmented. In 1993, **Desmond Dekker** joined Staples, Golding, Radiation and Gentleman on *King Of Kings*. In 1995 it was announced that the group was re-forming, but Hall was busy promoting his solo career, and the first output was a lacklustre cover version of **Bob Marley**'s 'Hypocrite'. An album followed, again with the accent heavily on cover versions.

SPECIALS
Albums
The Specials (2-Tone/Chrysalis 1979)★★★
In The Studio (2-Tone/Chrysalis 1984)★★★
Today's Specials (Kuff 1995)★★★
➜ p.380 for full listings
Collaborators
Clash ➜ p.93
Desmond Dekker ➜ p.114
Influences
Bob Marley ➜ p.225
Toots And The Maytals
Monkees ➜ p.236

SPECTOR, PHIL

BORN IN NEW YORK, SPECTOR (b. HARVEY PHILLIP SPECTOR, 1940) BECAME INVOLVED IN MUSIC UPON MOVING TO California in 1953. There he joined a community of young aspirants, including **Sandy Nelson**, who played drums on Spector's debut recording, 'To Know Him Is To Love Him'. This million-selling single for the Teddy Bears topped the US chart in 1958. Local entrepreneur Lester Sill recommended Phil's talents to New York production team **Leiber And Stoller**, with whom he co-wrote 'Spanish Harlem' and 'Young Boy Blues' for **Ben E. King**. Spector's first major success as a producer came with Ray Petersen's version of 'Corrina Corrina' (US Top 10, 1960), and Curtis Lee's 'Pretty Little Angel Eyes' (US number 7, 1961).

In 1961 Spector formed Philles Records with Lester Sill, but within months he bought his partner out, and there followed a string of classic recordings for the **Crystals** and **Ronettes** including 'He's A Rebel' (1962), 'Then He Kissed Me', 'Be My Baby' and 'Baby I Love You' (all 1963). Spector's releases also featured some of the era's finest songwriting teams – **Goffin** And **King**, Barry And Greenwich and Barry Mann and Cynthia Weil – the last of which composed 'You've Lost That Lovin' Feelin'' for the **Righteous Brothers**, the producer's stylistic apogee. Several critics also cite 'River Deep Mountain High' (1966) by **Ike And Tina Turner** as Spector's greatest moment. It represented his most ambitious production, but barely scraped the US Hot 100 and a dispirited Spector folded his label and retired from music for several years.

He re-emerged in 1969 with a series of releases for A&M which included Sonny Charles And The Checkmates' 'Black Pearl' (US Top 20). After working on the **Beatles**' *Let It Be*, Spector became installed at their Apple label. However, his behaviour grew increasingly erratic and as the 70s progressed, he became a recluse. He re-emerged to produce albums by **Leonard Cohen** (*Death Of Ladies Man* – 1977) and the **Ramones** (*End Of The Century* – 1980). Spector remained largely detached from music throughout the 80s, although he was inducted into the Rock 'N' Roll Hall Of Fame in 1989.

SPECTOR, PHIL
Albums
A Christmas Gift To You (Philles 1963)★★★★
Phil Spector Wall Of Sound, Volume 3: The Crystals (1975)★★★★
Back To Mono box set (Rhino 1991)★★★★★
➜ p.380 for full listings
Collaborators
Sandy Nelson ➜ p.244
Ben E. King ➜ p.205
Crystals ➜ p.107
Ronettes ➜ p.282
Righteous Brothers ➜ p.278
Ike And Tina Turner ➜ p.324
Beatles ➜ p.38
Leonard Cohen ➜ p.96
Ramones ➜ p.272
Connections
Leiber And Stoller ➜ p.214
Further References
Books: *The Phil Spector Story: Out Of His Head*, Richard Williams
He's A Rebel, Mark Ribowskys

SPENCER DAVIS GROUP

FORMED IN BIRMINGHAM, ENGLAND, IN 1962, THE GROUP FEATURED SPENCER DAVIS (b. 1941; GUITAR/VOCALS), **STEVE Winwood** (b. 1948; guitar/organ/vocals), Muff Winwood (b. Mervyn Winwood, 1943; bass) and Pete York (b. 1942; drums). Initially, their bluesy/pop records failed to sell, but the breakthrough came with 1965's 'Keep On Running' (UK number 1). This was followed by another chart-topper, 'Somebody Help Me', and three more hits 'When I Come Home', 'Gimme Some Lovin'' and 'I'm A Man'.

Steve Winwood left to form **Traffic** in 1967. Muff Winwood also left, joining Island as head of A&R. Davis soldiered on with the addition of Phil Sawyer, and later with Ray Fenwick (guitar) and Eddie Hardin (keyboards). They had two further minor hits, 'Mr Second Class' and 'Time Seller'. After a number of line-up changes, Hardin and York departed to form their own band. The Davis/York/Hardin/Fenwick team re-formed briefly in 1973, with Charlie McCracken on bass, and made a further two albums.

SPENCER DAVIS GROUP
Albums
The First Album (Fontana 1965)★★★
Gluggo (Vertigo 1973)★★★
Catch You On The Rebop: Live In Europe (RPM 1995)★★★
➜ p.380 for full listings
Connections
Rhythm And Blues Quartet
Steve Winwood ➜ p.341
Traffic ➜ p.323
Further References
Book: *Keep On Running: The Steve Winwood Story*, Chris Welch

SPICE GIRLS

THE SPICE GIRLS – VICTORIA ADAMS AKA POSH SPICE (b. 1973), MELANIE BROWN AKA MEL B/SCARY SPICE (b. 1973), Emma Bunton aka Baby Spice (b. 1976), Melanie Chisolm aka Mel C/Sporty Spice (b. 1974) and Geraldine Halliwell aka Geri/Ginger Spice (b. 1970) – met at various unsuccessful auditions for film and dance jobs; they ended up sharing a house in Berkshire, England, in 1993, where they began writing and demoing songs before finding manager Simon Fuller in 1995. A deal with Virgin followed and by 1996, the single 'Wannabe', an expression of their 'Girl Power' philosophy, made UK number 1. In 1997, 'Wannabe' made US number 1 and they became the first UK act ever to reach the top of the chart with their debut album. They made history when their first six hits all reached UK number 1, with songs ranging from ballads such as 'Say You'll Be There' and '2 Become 1' to the upbeat and exotic 'Spice Up Your Life'. Towards the end of 1997 they unceremoniously dumped Fuller. In 1998, they were part of the collaboration (with **Echo And The Bunnymen** and **Ocean Colour Scene**) who sang England's World Cup football theme. A few weeks later, the pop world was shocked by the announcement that Geri had left the group.

SPICE GIRLS
Albums
Spice (Virgin 1996)★★★
Spiceworld (Virgin 1997)★★★
➜ p.380 for full listings
Collaborators
Echo And The Bunnymen ➜ p.131
Ocean Colour Scene ➜ p.251
Further References
Book: *Girl Power*, Spice Girls
Film: *Spiceworld* (1997)

SPIN DOCTORS

THIS US FOUR-PIECE GROUP FORMED IN 1989 WHEN VOCALIST Christopher Barron (b. 1968) and guitarist Eric Schenkman (b. 1963) met drummer Aaron Comess (b. 1968) and bassist Mark White (b. 1962). *Pocket Full Of Kryptonite* was a varied collection of well-crafted, tuneful rock songs and subsequently became a massive-selling album. A live set, *Homebelly Groove*, was released to satisfy the new demand, and another single, 'Two Princes', led to worldwide success. 1994 saw their first major setback, when news filtered through that Shenkman had been ousted in favour of Anthony Krizan. Sales of *Turn It Upside Down* proved disappointing.

SPIRIT

THIS US ROCK BAND WITH A HINT OF JAZZ ARRIVED IN 1968 WITH THEIR SELF-TITLED DEBUT ALBUM. THE BAND comprised: Randy California (b. Randolph Wolfe, 1951, d. 1997; guitar), Ed 'Mr Skin' Cassidy (b. 1931; drums), John Locke (b. 1943; keyboards), Jay Ferguson (b. 1947; vocals) and Mark Andes (b. 1948; bass). The album reached number 31 in the US chart and stayed for over seven months. *The Family That Plays Together*, was a greater success and spawned a US Top 30 hit single, 'I Got A Line On You'. *The Twelve Dreams Of Dr Sardonicus*, showed Ferguson and California's songwriting reaching a peak, but soon afterwards, Spirit had their legendary album *Potatoland* rejected. Tensions within the band mounted and Ferguson, Andes and California all departed.

In 1976 Spirit returned with a new contract. The new nucleus of California, Cassidy and bassist Larry Knight toured widely and built up a loyal following in Britain and Germany, but the albums sold poorly and the band became despondent. The original five were back together in 1984 for *The Thirteenth Dream* (*Spirit Of '84*). Cassidy and California continued into the 90s with varied line-ups. California drowned in 1997.

SPLIT ENZ

FORMED IN AUCKLAND, NEW ZEALAND, IN 1972 AROUND THE DUO OF TIM FINN (b. 1952; VOCALS, PIANO) AND Jonathan 'Mike' Chunn (bass/keyboards) with Geoff Chunn (drums), Paul 'Wally' Wilkinson (guitar), Miles Golding (violin), Rob Gillies (saxophone), Michael Howard (flute) and Phil Judd (vocals/guitar/mandolin). Having established themselves in their homeland, they moved to Australia and recorded their first album for Mushroom. Signed to Chrysalis in Europe, Phil Manzanera recorded the band's second album. Returning to Australia in 1977, Split Enz recruited Tim Finn's brother Neil (b. 1958) to replace Judd. The departure of Wilkinson, Crowther and Chunn also made way for Nigel Griggs (b. 1949; bass) and UK-born Malcolm Green (b. 1953; drums). *True Colours* contained their most successful single, Neil Finn's 'I Got You' (UK number 12). Follow-up releases saw the band reach modest positions in the US album charts, but they lost momentum, eventually dissolving in 1985 after the release of *Conflicting Emotions*.

SPRINGFIELD, DUSTY

DUSTY (b. MARY ISABEL CATHERINE BERNADETTE O'BRIEN, 1939) BEGAN AS A MEMBER OF 50S UK POP TRIO THE LANA Sisters, before joining her brother Tom (Dion O'Brien) and Tim Field in the Springfields. Her debut solo came in 1963 with 'I Only Want To Be With You', and over the next three years she was constantly in the chart with a string of hits. During this time she campaigned on behalf of the then little-known black American soul, R&B and **Motown** artists.

Worldwide success came with an English-language version of the Italian hit 'Io Che Non Vivo (Senzate)' – 'You Don't Have To Say You Love Me'. This proved her sole UK chart-topper in 1966, and, by the end of 1967 she was becoming disillusioned with showbusiness. Her BBC television series attracted healthy viewing figures, but it was anathema to the sudden change in the pop scene. *Where Am I Going?* attempted to redress this, but flopped commercially. The following year a similar fate awaited *Dusty ... Definitely*.

She departed for Memphis, Tennessee, and recorded her finest work, *Dusty In Memphis*. 'Son Of A Preacher Man' became a major hit, but the album failed in the UK and fared little better in the USA.

For the next few years she recorded sporadically, preferring to spend her time with friends and to campaign for animal rights. Additionally, she succumbed to pills and alcohol abuse, and attempted suicide. Following the release of *It Begins Again*, some five years after her previous release, she was propelled towards a comeback, which failed, although the album did garner respectable sales. *Living Without Your Love*, also flopped although 'Baby Blue' (1979) became a minor hit. The comeback was over. Her return towards the end of the 80s was due entirely to the **Pet Shop Boys**, who persuaded her to duet with them on their hit 'What Have I Done To Deserve This?' (1987). They then wrote the theme for the film *Scandal*; 'Nothing Has Been Proved', which Dusty took into the best-sellers. She followed this with another of their compositions, 'In Private', which was a bigger hit. The subsequent album, *Reputation*, became her most successful for over 20 years.

In 1994, having returned to Britain, treatment for breast cancer delayed the release and promotion of her long-awaited new album. The album *A Very Fine Love* arrived in the wake of the single 'Wherever Would I Be' (with Daryl Hall).

SPIN DOCTORS
Albums
Pocket Full Of Kryptonite (Epic 1991)★★★★
➧ p.380 for full listings

SPIRIT
Albums
The Family That Plays Together (Ode/Columbia 1969)★★★★
The Twelve Dreams Of Dr Sardonicus (Epic 1970)★★★★★
Spirit Of '76 (Mercury 1975)★★★★
➧ p.380 for full listings
Connections
Jo Jo Gunne

SPLIT ENZ
Albums
Dizrhythmia (Chrysalis 1977)★★★★
True Colours (A&M 1980)★★★★
➧ p.380 for full listings
Connections
Crowded House ➧ p.107
Further References
Book: *Stranger Than Fiction: The Life & Time Of Split Enz*, Mike Chunn

SPRINGFIELD, DUSTY
Albums
A Girl Called Dusty (Philips 1964)★★★★
Where Am I Going (Philips 1967)★★★★
Dusty In Memphis (Philips 1969)★★★★★
➧ p.380 for full listings
Collaborations
Pet Shop Boys ➧ p.259
Connections
Motown ➧ p.240
Further References
Book: *Dusty*, Lucy O'Brien

SPRINGSTEEN, BRUCE
Albums
Born To Run (Columbia 1975)★★★★★
Tunnel Of Love (Columbia 1987)★★★★
The Ghost Of Tom Joad (Columbia 1995)★★★★
➽ p. 380 for full listings

Collaborations
Gary 'U.S.' Bonds ➽ p.60
E. Street Band
Connections
Dr Zoom And The Sonic Boom
Steven Van Zandt ➽ p.329
Bob Dylan ➽ p.128
Hollies ➽ p.183
Manfred Mann's Earth Band ➽ p.223
Patti Smith ➽ p.301
Pointer Sisters ➽ p.263
Further References
Books: *Springsteen: Born To Run*, Dave March
Backstreets: Springsteen – The Man And His Music, ed. Charles R. Cross

SPOOKY TOOTH
Albums
Spooky Two (Island 1969)★★★★
The Last Puff (Island 1970)★★★★
➽ p.380 for full listings
Influences
David Ackles ➽ p.8
Elton John ➽ p.200

SPOTNICKS
Albums
Out-A-Space (1963)★★★
➽ p.380 for full listings
Influences
Tornados ➽ p.322
Further References
Film: *Just For Fun* (1963)

SQUEEZE
Albums
Cool For Cats (A&M 1979)★★★★
Argy Bargy (A&M 1980)★★★★
East Side Story (A&M 1981)★★★★
➽ p.380 for full listings
Connections
Jools Holland ➽ p.182
Paul Carrack ➽ p.83
Influences
Velvet Underground ➽ p.329

SPRINGSTEEN, BRUCE

SPRINGSTEEN (b. 1949) BEGAN PLAYING IN A NUMBER OF NEW JERSEY BANDS, BEFORE SETTLING AS THE BRUCE Springsteen Band with David Sancious (keyboards), Gary Tallent (bass), Clarence Clemmons (saxophone), **Steven Van Zandt** (guitar), Danny Federici (keyboards) and Vini Lopez (drums). CBS A&R legend John Hammond signed Springsteen as a solo artist, sensing a future **Bob Dylan**. Instead, Springsteen set about recording his debut with the band, *Greetings From Asbury Park*, which sold poorly. The follow-up, *The Wild, The Innocent And The E. Street Shuffle*, contained future classics including 'Rosalita', 'Incident On 57th Street' and 'Asbury Park Fourth Of July (Sandy)'. His musicians were re-named the E. Street Band after its release.

Born To Run (1975) was a transatlantic hit, but Springsteen's recording career was then held up for three years as he and manager Landau entered into litigation with Mike Appel. Meanwhile, **Manfred Mann's Earth Band** released a version of his 'Blinded By The Light'; **Patti Smith** recorded his 'Because The Night'; and ex-**Hollie** Allan Clarke, Robert Gordon, and the **Pointer Sisters** also recorded his material. With the successful completion of the lawsuits came the anti-climactic *Darkness On The Edge Of Town*.

On his 30th birthday, Bruce played at the historic MUSE concert; the subsequent *No Nukes* album and video captured a vintage performance of high-energy and humour, and the double-set *The River* contained hit singles 'Hungry Heart', 'The River' and 'Fade Away'.

Nebraska, a stark acoustic set, was recorded solo, directly on to a cassette recorder. It is raw Springsteen, uncompromising and sometimes painful. *Born In The USA* sold over 12 million copies, spawned numerous hit singles and stayed in the UK charts for two-and-a-half years. During his 1985 European tour, all seven albums to date were in the UK charts. In order to stem the flow he released a five-album boxed set at the end of 1986. The superbly recorded *Live 1975-1985* entered the US charts at number 1. The following year *Tunnel Of Love* shot to number 1 on the day of release in the UK and USA. In 1989, at the age of 40 he split the E. Street Band. In 1992, he issued two albums simultaneously: *Human Touch* and *Lucky Town*. Both scaled the charts and fans and critics welcomed him back. He composed 'Streets Of Philadelphia' the emotionally charged title track for the film *Philadelphia* in 1994 and in 1995, it was reported that he was working with the E. Street Band (including Clemons) again. *The Ghost Of Tom Joad* was a solo acoustic album, warm, mellow and sad. Sounding a lot like Dylan, Springsteen no longer sounded angry or energetic; merely philosophical.

SPOOKY TOOTH

FORMED IN THE UK, THE ORIGINAL BAND COMPRISED GARY WRIGHT (b. 1945; KEYBOARDS/VOCALS), MIKE KELLIE (b. 1947; drums), Luther Grosvenor (b. 1949; guitar), Mike Harrison (b. 1945; vocals) and Greg Ridley (b. 1947; bass). *Its All About* was a fine debut; although not a strong seller it contained club favourite 'Tobacco Road' and their debut single 'Sunshine Help Me'. It was *Spooky Two*, however, that put them on the map. *Ceremony* was a change of direction that found few takers. *The Last Puff* saw a number of personnel changes: Ridley, Gary Wright and Grosvenor left, replaced by Henry McCullough, Chris Stainton and Alan Spenner, and the band broke up shortly after its release, although various members eventually regrouped for three further albums.

SPOTNICKS

ORIGINALLY THIS SWEDISH GROUP CONSISTED OF BO WINBERG (b. 1939), BOB LANDER (b. BO STARANDER, 1942), Bjorn Thelin (b. 1942) and Ole Johannsson, and they had several hit singles in their homeland. They were signed to Oriole in the UK in 1962 and had a hit with a novelty version of 'Orange Blossom Special' in 1962.

Further UK hits included 'Rocket Man', 'Hava Nagila' and 'Just Listen To My Heart'. Johansson left in 1963 and was replaced by London musician Derek Skinner (b. 1944), in turn replaced by Jimmy Nicol. In 1965 they added organist Peter Winsens to the line-up. Nicol left in early 1967 and was replaced by Tommy Tausis (b. 1946). In October Thelin was called up for National Service and replaced by Magnus Hellsberg. Several further line-up changes occurred over the following years as the band continued to tour and record prolifically in Europe.

SQUEEZE

UK-GROUP COMPRISING CHRIS DIFFORD (b. 1954; GUITAR/ LEAD VOCALS), GLENN TILBROOK (b. 1957; GUITAR/VOCALS) and **Jools Holland** (b. 1958; keyboards). With Harry Kakoulli (bass), and sessions drummer Gilson Lavis (b. 1951), Squeeze released *Packet Of Three*. It led to a major contract with A&M and a UK Top 20 hit in 1978 with 'Take Me I'm Yours'. Minor success with 'Bang Bang' and 'Goodbye Girl' that same year was followed by two number 2 hits – 'Cool For Cats' and 'Up The Junction'. *Argy Bargy* spawned the singles 'Another Nail In My Heart' (UK Top 20) and 'Pulling Mussels (From A Shell)', and featured new bass player John Bentley (b. 1951). In 1980, Holland left for a solo career and was replaced by singer/pianist **Paul Carrack**. *East Side Story*, which included 'Labelled With Love' (UK Top 5) became the band's most successful to date. Carrack departed soon afterwards and was replaced by Kenyan-born Don Snow (b. 1957). At the height of their success, Difford and Tilbrook dissolved the group, only to re-form in 1985 with Lavis, Holland and new bass player, Keith Wilkinson. *Cosi Fan Tutti Frutti* was hailed as a return to form. In 1987 'Hourglass' reached UK number 16 and gave the group their first US Top 40 hit. After *Frank*, Holland departed again. With Matt Irving joining as a second keyboard player, Squeeze released a live album, *A Round And A Bout*, before signing a new contract with Warner Brothers. *Play* confirmed Difford and Tilbrook's reputation. *Some Fantastic Place* saw them reunited with A&M. *Ridiculous* showed them writing sharp, humorous yet provocative lyrics and poignant love songs.

STANDELLS

TONY VALENTINO (GUITAR/VOCALS) AND LARRY TAMBLYN (ORGAN) FORMED THE STANDELLS IN 1962. THE EARLY line-up included drummer Gary Leeds, Gary Lane (bass) and Dick Dodd (drums). The quartet became a leading teen-based attraction but then fashioned a series of angst-cum-protest punk anthems in 'Sometimes Good Guys Don't Wear White', 'Why Pick On Me' and 'Dirty Water' (US number 11, 1966). Gary Lane left the group during a tour of Florida and was initially succeeded by Dave Burke, who in turn was replaced by John Fleck (b. Fleckenstein). Unfashionable in the face of San Francisco's acid rock, the group's career was confined to the cabaret circuit.

STANSFIELD, LISA

MANCHESTER-BORN STANSFIELD (b. 1966) TEAMED UP WITH BOYFRIEND ANDY MORRIS AND IAN DEVANEY TO FORM the white-soul group, Blue Zone in 1983. With backing from Arista, the group released *Big Thing* (1986), and several singles on Rockin' Horse, but achieved little success outside the club circuit. In 1989, they were invited to record 'People Hold On', which reached the UK Top 20 and prompted manager Jazz Summers to sign Stansfield as a solo act, with Morris and Devaney as composers, musicians and producers. 'This Is The Right Time' reached number 13 in the UK chart while the follow-up, 'All Around This World' climbed to number 1 in the UK. *Affection* reached number 2, eventually selling five million copies worldwide. While 'Live Together' was peaking at number 10 in the UK, plans were afoot to break into the US chart. *All Around This World* then reached number 3 and topped the *Billboard* R&B listing, while *Affection* reached the US Top 10. Stansfield's success in the US was followed by 'You Can't Deny It' (number 14) and 'This Is The Right Time' (number 21). *Real Love* won over previously reticent admirers and promoted a more mature image.

STARDUST, ALVIN

LONDON-BORN STARDUST (b. BERNARD WILLIAM JEWRY, 1942) FIRST SANG DURING THE EARLY 60S AS SHANE FENTON. He re-emerged in 1973 as Alvin Stardust and returned to the charts with 'My Coo-Ca-Choo' (UK number 2). It was followed by the chart-topping 'Jealous Mind' and two further UK Top 10 hits with 'Red Dress' and 'You You You' before his chart career petered out. The indomitable Stardust revitalized his career once more during the early 80s with 'Pretend' (Top 10) and the commemorative ballad 'I Feel Like **Buddy Holly**'. Stardust ended 1984 with two further hits 'I Won't Run Away' and 'So Near Christmas' before once again falling from chart favour.

STARR, EDWIN

US PERFORMER EDWIN STARR (b. CHARLES HATCHER, 1942) FORMED THE FUTURE TONES VOCAL GROUP IN 1957, AND recorded one single before being drafted into the US Army. His service completed, he was offered a solo contract with Ric Tic in 1965. 'Agent Double-O-Soul', was a US Top 30 hit. 'Stop Her On Sight (SOS)' repeated this success, and brought Starr a cult following in Britain. When **Motown** took over Ric Tic in 1967, Starr was initially overlooked, but he re-emerged in 1969 with '25 Miles' (Top 10). An album of duets with Blinky brought some critical acclaim, before Starr resumed his solo career with the politically outspoken 'War' (US number 1, 1977). In the 80s, Starr was based in the UK, where he enjoyed a run of club hits, most notably 'It Ain't Fair' in 1985. Between 1989 and 1991, Starr worked with Motor City Records, recording a remake of '25 Miles' and releasing *Where Is The Sound*.

STARR, RINGO

DRUMMER STARR (b. RICHARD STARKEY, 1940) SUCCEEDED PETE BEST IN THE **BEATLES**, UPON HIS FIRING IN 1962. Although overshadowed musically, a deadpan sense of humour helped establish his individuality and each album contained a Starr vocal. The most notable of these was 'Yellow Submarine', a million-selling single in 1966. His solo career started with *Sentimental Journey*, a collection of standards, and *Beaucoups Of Blues*, a country selection. Starr's debut single, 'It Don't Come Easy', co-written with **George Harrison**, topped the US charts and sold in excess of one million copies. *Ringo* featured songs and contributions from each of his former colleagues. 'You're Sixteen' topped the US chart in 1974, but despite further success with 'Oh My My', 'Snookeroo' and 'Only You', Ringo's momentum waned.

The 80s signalled his return to active performing, but an album recorded with US producer Chips Moman in 1987 was abandoned when sessions were blighted by excessive imbibing. Ringo then reasserted his musical career with the All-Starr Band. Levon Helm, **Billy Preston**, **Joe Walsh** and **Dr. John** were among those joining the drummer for his 1989 US tour. Starr has appeared sporadically since then, notably with tours in 1992 and 1998.

STANDELLS
Albums
The Standells Live At PJs (Liberty 1964)★★★
Live And Out Of Sight (Sunset 1966)★★★
➡ p.380 for full listings
Collaborators
Ed Cobb
Further References
Film: *Get Yourself A College Girl* (1964)

STANSFIELD, LISA
Albums
Affection (Arista 1989)★★★, *So Natural* (Arista 1993)★★★
➡ p.380 for full listings
Collaborators
Jazz Summers
Connections
Blue Zone
Further References
Video: *Lisa Live* (PMI 1993)

STARDUST, ALVIN
Albums
The Untouchable (Magnet 1974)★★★
➡ p.380 for full listings
Influences
Buddy Holly ➡ p.184
Further References
Book: *The Alvin Stardust Story*, George Tremlett

STARR, EDWIN
Albums
Soul Master (Gordy 1968)★★★
Involved (Gordy 1971)★★★
HAPPY Radio (20th Century 1979)★★★
➡ p.380 for full listings
Connections
Motown Records ➡ p.240
Influences
Curtis Mayfield ➡ p.228
Isaac Hayes ➡ p.178

STARR, RINGO
Albums
Ringo (Apple 1973)★★★
Ringo Starr And His All-Starr Band (EMI 1990)★★★
➡ p. 380 for full listings
Collaborators
George Harrison ➡ p.176
Billy Preston ➡ p.266
Joe Walsh ➡ p.333
Dr. John ➡ p.125
Connections
Beatles p.38
Carl Perkins ➡ p.258
All-Starr Band
Further References
Book: *Ringo Starr Straightman Or Joker*, Alan Clayson
Films: *A Hard Day's Night* (1964)
Give My Regards To Broad Street (1985)

STATUS QUO
Albums
Piledriver (Vertigo 1972)★★★★
Whatever You Want (Vertigo 1979)★★★
Ain't Complaining (Vertigo 1988)★★★
➤ p.380 for full listings
Collaborators
Marty Wilde ➤ p.338
Connections
Spectres
Original Mirrors
Live Aid
Influences
John Fogerty
Further References
Books: *Status Quo: The Authorized Biography*, John Shearlaw
Just For The Record: The Autobiography Of Status Quo, Francis Rossi and Rick Parfitt

STEALERS WHEEL
Albums
Stealers Wheel (A&M 1972)★★★★
Ferguslie Park (A&M 1973)★★★★
➤ p.380 for full listings
Connections
Gerry Rafferty ➤ p.271
Juicy Lucy ➤ p.202

STEELEYE SPAN
Albums
Hark, The Village Wait (Chrysalis 1970)★★★★
Please To See The King (Chrysalis 1971)★★★★
Time (Park 1996)★★★
➤ p.380 for full listings
Connections
Martin Carthy ➤ p.83

STEELY DAN
Albums
Can't Buy A Thrill (Probe 1972)★★★★
Pretzel Logic (Probe 1974)★★★★
Aja (ABC 1977)★★★★
➤ p.380 for full listings
Collaborators
Jay And The Americans ➤ p.198
Connections
Donald Fagen ➤ p.141
Michael McDonald ➤ p.229
Further References
Book: *Steely Dan: Reelin' In The Years*, Brian Sweet

STEPPENWOLF
Albums
Steppenwolf (Dunhill 1968)★★★
Monster (Dunhill 1969)★★★★
➤ p.380 for full listings
Connections
Sparrows

STATUS QUO

FOUNDER MEMBERS OF UK-GROUP THE SPECTRES, MIKE (LATER FRANCIS) ROSSI (b. 1949; GUITAR/VOCALS) AND Alan Lancaster (b. 1949; bass) led the act from its inception in 1962 until 1967, by which time Roy Lynes (organ) and John Coughlan (b. 1946; drums) completed its line-up. The singles proved commercially unsuccessful, but the group was buoyed by the arrival of Rick Parfitt aka Rick Harrison (b. 1948; guitar/vocals), and the revamped unit became 'Status Quo' in 1967. The following year, 'Pictures Of Matchstick Men', soared to number 7. The group enjoyed another UK Top 10 hit with 'Ice In The Sun', but subsequent recordings struggled to emulate such success, and despite reaching number 12 with 'Down The Dustpipe', they were increasingly viewed as a *passé* novelty. The departure of Lynes brought the unit's guitar work to the fore. Now signed to Vertigo, Status Quo scored a UK Top 10 hit that year with 'Paper Plane' but more importantly, reached number 5 in the album charts with *Piledriver. Hello*, entered at number 1, confirming the group's emergence as a major attraction. Each of their 70s albums reached the Top 5, while a consistent presence in the singles' chart included entries such as 'Caroline' (1973), 'Down Down' (a chart topper in 1974), 'Whatever You Want' (1979) and 'Lies'/'Don't Drive My Car' (1980). Quo also proved adept at adapting outside material, as evinced by their version of John Fogerty's 'Rockin' All Over The World' (1977). Coughlan left the group in 1981 and Pete Kircher took his place, but there was a growing estrangement between Lancaster and Rossi and Parfitt. Rossi and Parfitt secured the rights to the name and re-formed the act around John Edwards (bass), Jeff Rich (drums) and keyboard player Andy Bown. Quo have continued to produce uncomplicated, unpretentious and infectious rock music.

STEALERS WHEEL

VOCALIST **GERRY RAFFERTY** (b. 1946), JOE EGAN (b. *c.* 1946), RAB NOAKES, IAN CAMPBELL AND ROGER BROWN BEGAN rehearsing together in the late 70s. They signed to A&M, but the band had split before they entered the studio. Paul Pilnick (guitar), Tony Williams (bass) and ex-**Juicy Lucy** member Rod Coombes (drums) bailed out Rafferty and Egan and the result was a surprising success. 'Stuck In The Middle With You' was a transatlantic Top 10. Rafferty then departed and was replaced by Luther Grosvenor (aka Ariel Bender). Rafferty had returned by the second album, but the musical chairs continued as all the remaining members left the band. *Ferguslie Park* was a failure commercially and the two leaders set about completing their contractual obligations and recording their final work *Right Or Wrong*. The album failed and disillusioned Rafferty and Egan buried the name forever.

STEELEYE SPAN

ENGLISH FOLK-ROCK GROUP COMPRISING ASHLEY 'TYGER' HUTCHINGS (b. 1945; BASS), TERRY WOODS (VOCALS/GUITAR/MANDOLIN), Gay Woods (vocals/concertina/autoharp), Tim Hart (vocals/guitar/dulcimer/harmonium) and Maddy Prior (vocals). They began extensive rehearsals before recording *Hark, The Village Wait*. The Woods then left to pursue their own career and were replaced by **Martin Carthy** (vocals/guitar) and Peter Knight (vocals/fiddle) for *Please To See The King* and *Ten Man Mop*. They toured extensively, but the departure of Hutchings signalled a dramatic realignment in the Steeleye camp. Carthy resumed his solo career and Bob Johnson (guitar) and Rick Kemp (bass) were brought in. Both *Below The Salt* and *Parcel Of Rogues* displayed an electric content and tight dynamics, while *Now We Are Six*, emphasized the terse drumming of newcomer Nigel Pegrum. The group enjoyed two hit singles with 'Gaudete' (1973) and 'All Around My Hat' (UK Top 5, 1975), but the group was 'rested' following the disappointing *Rocket Cottage*. They reconvened for *Storm Force Ten*, although John Kirkpatrick (accordion) and the prodigal Martin Carthy took Knight and Johnson's places. Their formal disbanding was announced in 1978, although Steeleye Span has been resurrected on subsequent occasions.

STEELY DAN

THE SEEDS OF THIS MUCH-RESPECTED ROCK GROUP WERE SEWN AT NEW YORK'S BARD COLLEGE WHERE FOUNDER members **Donald Fagen** b. 1948; (keyboards/vocals) and Walter Becker b. 1950; (bass/vocals) enjoyed a contemporaneous association with pop/harmony act **Jay And The Americans**, members of whom joined the pair for *You Gotta Walk It Like You Talk It (Or You'll Lose That Beat)*. Denny Dias (guitar) contributed to these sessions and soon after the trio was expanded by David Palmer (vocals), Jeff 'Skunk' Baxter (b. 1948; guitar) and Jim Hodder (d. 1992; drums). *Can't Buy A Thrill* was completed within weeks, but drew praise for its immaculate musicianship. The title track and 'Do It Again' reached the US Top 20 and this newfound fame inspired the sarcasm of 'Show Biz Kids' on *Countdown To Ecstacy*.

Their second album was another undoubted classic of the 70s and, after Palmer had left the line-up, *Pretzel Logic* became Steely Dan's first US Top 10 album including 'Rikki Don't Lose That Number' (US number 4). Steely Dan's final live appearance was in July 1974 and ensuing strife resulted in the departures of both Baxter and Hodder. Dias joined newcomers **Michael McDonald** (keyboards/vocals) and Jeff Porcaro (drums) for *Katy Lied*.

The Royal Scam included 'Haitian Divorce', the group's lone Top 20 hit in Britain. Aja continued in a similar vein where an array of quality musicians brought meticulousness to the set. A similar pattern was unveiled on *Gaucho*, which achieved platinum sales and an attendant single, 'Hey Nineteen', reached the US Top 10. A number of compilations appeared throughout the early 90s, culminating in a tour in 1995. 1997's *Reel To Reel* was a welcome new release.

STEPPENWOLF

GERMAN-BORN JOHN KAY (b. JOACHIM F. KRAULEDAT, 1944; VOCALS), AMERICAN MICHAEL MONARCH (b. 1950; LEAD guitar), Goldy McJohn (b. 1945; keyboards), Rushton Moreve (bass) and Jerry Edmonton (b. 1946; drums) formed Steppenwolf in 1967. John Morgan replaced Moreve prior to recording. The group's debut album included 'Born To Be Wild' (US number 2). Steppenwolf actively cultivated a menacing, hard-rock image, and successive collections mixed this heavy style with blues. 'Magic Carpet Ride' and 'Rock Me' were also US Top 10 singles. Newcomers Larry Byrom (guitar) and another German, Nick St. Nicholas (b. 1943; bass), featured on *Monster*, Steppenwolf's most cohesive set. Continued personnel changes undermined their stability and John Kay dissolved the band in 1972, but within two years he was leading a reconstituted Steppenwolf.

STEREO MC'S

UK BAND COMPRISING ROB BIRCH (b. 1961; VOCALS), NICK 'THE HEAD' HALLAM (b. 1962; SYNTHESIZERS/COMPUTERS/ scratching), Welsh percussionist Owen If (b. Ian Frederick Rossiter, 1959), Kenyan-born Cath Coffey (b. Catherine Muthomi Coffey, *c.* 1965; vocals), Andrea Bedassie (b. 1957; vocals) and Verona Davis (b. 1952; vocals). The Stereo MC's first recording was 'Move It', released before Hallam and Birch recruited Italian-British DJ Cesare, and formed their alter-ego remix team, Ultimatum. Their first remix as Ultimatum arrived shortly afterwards (Jungle Brothers' 'Black Is Black'). Cesare left stating that he was unhappy with the band's direction and financial arrangements, but the band pressed on, recording *Supernatural* with Baby Bam of the Jungle Brothers. 1991 brought their first crossover hit with 'Lost In Music', based on the Ultimatum remix of the Jungle Brothers' 'Doin' Your Own Dang'. Coffey was added to the line-up for 'Elevate My Mind', her two female compatriots joining shortly after. 'Elevate Your Mind' gave the group a US Top 40 hit. *Connected* was released to mounting acclaim and included the UK hit title track.

STEREOLAB

UK GROUP LED BY TIM GANE AND INCLUDING HIS GIRLFRIEND LAETITIA SADIER (b. 1968), MARTIN KEAN AND drummer Joe Dilworth. By the time of the 'Low-Fi' 10-inch in 1992, Mary Hansen had arrived to lend keyboard and vocal support, and Andy Ramsay replaced Dilworth on drums. *The Groop Played Space Age Bachelor Pad Music* saw further line-up changes with Duncan Brown on bass and Sean O'Hagan on guitar. *Transient Random Noise-Bursts With Announcements* straddled both indie and dance markets. This maintained their reputation not only as a rock outfit, but also as an important fixture of the experimental dance music axis. *Music For The Amorphous Body Study Centre* continued to embrace subjects outside pop music convention, and *Emperor Tomato Ketchup* was another mix of melodies that crept under the skin. Ever prolific, they released the dance-orientated *Dots And Loops* in 1997.

STEVENS, CAT

IN 1966, PRODUCER MIKE HURST SPOTTED THE LONDON-BORN CAT (b. STEVEN GEORGIOU, 1947) PERFORMING at the Hammersmith College, London and subsequently arranged to record him and his song, 'I Love My Dog'. Tony Hall at Decca was similarly impressed and Stevens became the first artist on the new Deram label. The record and its b-side 'Portobello Road' showed great promise and over the next two years Stevens delivered many perfect pop songs. His own hits, 'Matthew And Son', 'I'm Gonna Get Me A Gun' and 'Bad Night', were equalled by the quality of his songs for others; the soulful 'First Cut Is The Deepest' by **P. P. Arnold** and the addictive 'Here Comes My Baby' by the **Tremeloes**.

Tea for the Tillerman
CAT STEVENS

Mona Bone Jakon was followed by two hugely successful works: *Tea For The Tillerman* and *Teaser And The Firecat*. These let the listener into his private thoughts, aspirations and desires. Anthems like 'Wild World', 'Peace Train' and 'Moon Shadow', love songs including 'Lady D'Arbanville', 'Hard Headed Woman' and 'Can't Keep It In', are all faultless compositions. In 1979, Stevens became a devout Muslim and retired from the music business. He made a welcome return in 1995 under the name of Yusef Islam with *Life Of The Prophet*. In his time Stevens had eight consecutive gold albums and 10 hit singles in the UK and 14 in the USA.

STEVENS, SHAKIN'

IN THE LATE 60S WELSHMAN STEVENS (b. MICHAEL BARRETT, 1948) WAS LEAD SINGER WITH THE BACKBEATS, LATER Shakin' Stevens And The Sunsets, who recorded several unsuccessful albums before disbanding in 1976. Stevens' solo career began in 1977 with an album for Track, followed by unsuccessful revivals of 50s hits. A change of producer to Stuart Colman in 1980 brought Stevens' first Top 20 hit, 'Marie Marie', and the following year Colman's arrangement of 'This Ole House' topped the UK chart.

Over the next seven years, Stevens had over 20 Top 20 hits in the UK, including three number 1s – 'Green Door' (1981), 'Oh Julie' (1982) and 'Merry Christmas Everyone' (1985).

In the early 90s, there were signs that Stevens' hold over his British audiences was faltering. A major promotion for the compilation *The Epic Years* failed to dent the UK top 50.

STEWART, AL

GLASGOW-BORN STEWART (b. 1945) SIGNED TO DECCA IN 1966 AND RELEASED ONE UNSUCCESSFUL SINGLE, 'THE ELF'. The following year, he joined CBS and released the acoustic, string-accompanied *Bedsitter Images*. The succeeding *Love Chronicles* was most notable for the lengthy title track. Stewart's interest in acoustic folk continued on *Zero She Flies*, which featured the historical narrative 'Manuscript'. *Orange* contained the impressive 'Night Of The 4th Of May' and was followed by his most ambitious work to date, *Past, Present And Future*. Pursuing his interest in historical themes, Stewart presented some of his best acoustic workouts in the impressive 'Roads To Moscow' and epic 'Nostradamus'. A considerable gap ensued before the release of *Modern Times*.

After leaving CBS and signing to RCA, he surprised many by the commercial power of his celebrated *Year Of The Cat* (US Top 10). Another switch of label to Arista preceded *Time Passages*, which suffered by comparison with its predecessor. *24 P Carrots* was succeeded by a part studio/part live album, which merely consolidated his position. With *Russians And Americans*, Stewart embraced a more political stance, but the sales were disappointing. Legal and contractual problems deterred him from recording for four years until the welcome *The Last Days Of The Century*.

STEREO MC'S
Albums
33, 45, 78 (4th & Broadway 1989)★★★
Connected (4th & Broadway 1992)★★★★
➽ p.380 for full listings
Connections
Ultimatum
Jungle Brothers
Jesus Jones ➽ p.199
Further References
Video: *Connected* (1993)

STEREOLAB
Albums
The Groop Played Space Age Bachelor Pad Music mini-album (Too Pure 1993)★★★★
Mars Audiac Quintet (Duophonic 1994)★★★★
Dots And Loops (Duophonic 1997)★★★★
➽ p.380 for full listings

STEVENS, CAT
Albums
Tea For The Tillerman (Island 1970)★★★★
Teaser And The Firecat (Island 1971)★★★★
Catch Bull At Four (Island 1972)★★★★
➽ p.380 for full listings
Collaborations
P. P. Arnold ➽ p.21
Tremeloes ➽ p.323
Influences
Mike Hurst
Further References
Video: *Tea For The Tillerman Live – The Best Of* (1993)
Book: *Cat Stevens*, Chris Charlesworth

STEVENS, SHAKIN'
Albums
A Legend (Parlophone 1970)★★
Lipstick, Powder And Paint (Epic 1985)★★
➽ p.380 for full listings
Collaborators
Stuart Colman
Influences
Jim Lowe
Further References
Video: *Shakin' Stevens Video Show Volumes 1&2* (CMV 1989)
Book: *Shakin' Stevens*, Leese Martin

STEWART, AL
Albums
Love Chronicles (Columbia 1969)★★★
Year Of The Cat (RCA 1976)★★★★
Between The Wars (EMI 1995)★★★
➽ p.380 for full listings

STEWART, ROD
Albums
An Old Raincoat Won't Ever Let You Down (Vertigo 1970)★★★★
Never A Dull Moment (Mercury 1972)★★★★
Unplugged And Seated (Warners 1993)★★★★
➧ p.380 for full listings
Collaborators
Robert Palmer ➧ p.255
Connections
Long John Baldry ➧ p.30
Jeff Beck Group ➧ p.41
Faces ➧ p.141
Further References
Books: *The Rod Stewart Story*, George Tremlett
Rod Stewart, Paul Nelson and Lester Bangs

STIFF LITTLE FINGERS
Albums
Inflammable Material (Rough Trade 1979)★★★
➧ p.380 for full listings
Connections
Clash ➧ p.93

STILLS, STEPHEN
Albums
Stephen Stills (Atlantic 1970)★★★★★
Stephen Stills 2 (Atlantic 1971)★★★★
Stills (Columbia 1975)★★★★
➧ p.380 for full listings
Connections
Buffalo Springfield ➧ p.74
David Crosby ➧ p.105
Neil Young ➧ p.346
Crosby, Stills And Nash ➧ p.106
Influences
Beatles ➧ p.38
Bob Dylan ➧ p.128

STING
Albums
Nothing Like the Sun (A&M 1987)★★★★
Ten Summoner's Tales (A&M 1993)★★★★
➧ p.380 for full listings

Connections
Police ➧ p.263
Further References
Book: *Sting: A Biography*, Robert Sellers

STOCK, AITKEN AND WATERMAN
Albums
Hit Factory (1987)★★★
➧ p.380 for full listings

STEWART, ROD

ROD STEWART (b. 1945) STARTED HIS CAREER ROAMING EUROPE WITH FOLK ARTIST WIZZ JONES, BUT LATER RETURNED TO his native Britain to play harmonica for Jimmy Powell And The Five Dimensions in 1963. He was soon hired by **Long John Baldry** in his band the Hoochie Coochie Men. Without significant success outside the club scene, the band evolved into the Steampacket, with Baldry, Stewart, Brian Auger, Julie Driscoll, Mickey Waller and Rick Brown. In 1965, he joined the blues-based Shotgun Express as joint lead vocalist with Beryl Marsden, but it was joining the **Jeff Beck** Group that gave him national exposure. During his tenure with Beck he recorded two important albums, *Truth* and *Cosa Nostra-Beck Ola.*

When the group broke up Stewart and Ron Wood joined the **Faces**, and Stewart was simultaneously signed as a solo artist to Phonogram. His first album sold only moderately and it was *Gasoline Alley* that made the breakthrough. This album marked the beginning of the 'mandolin' sound supplied by guitarist Martin Quittenton. Stewart became a superstar on the strength of his next two albums, *Every Picture Tells A Story* and *Never A Dull Moment. Atlantic Crossing* was his last critical success for many years and included the future number 1 hit, 'Sailing'. His albums throughout the second half of the 70s, although phenomenally successful, were patchy affairs.

The 80s saw Stewart jet-setting all over the world and his talents surfaced throughout the decade with numbers like 'How Long' and 'Some Guys Have All The Luck'. *Unplugged And Seated* in 1993 boosted his credibility with an exciting performance of familiar songs. The 1995 album was his best for some years and Stewart turned 50 without his audience diminishing in any way. In 1998, he re-entered both the single and album charts and embarked on an extensive tour.

STIFF LITTLE FINGERS

IN 1977, JAKE BURNS (VOCALS, LEAD GUITAR) LED HENRY CLUNEY (RHYTHM GUITAR), ALI McMORDIE (BASS) AND Brian Falloon (drums) as Ireland's first new wave cover band. They recorded their first two original songs, 'Suspect Device' and 'Wasted Life', on their Rigid Digits label. Rough Trade quickly picked up the distribution, and released the band's third single, 'Alternative Ulster'. *Inflammable Material* featured songs concentrating on personal experiences in the politically charged climate of Northern Ireland. The release marked the departure of Falloon who was replaced by Jim Reilly. The follow-up, *Nobody's Heroes*, branched out into dub, reggae and pop. *Go For It!* saw the band at the peak of their abilities and popularity. Reilly left for the USA with Brian 'Dolphin' Taylor drafted as his replacement. *Now Then* embraced songs of a more pop-rock nature. Burns left at the beginning of the following year. In 1990 they re-formed on a permanent basis. McMordie had grown tired of the rock circuit, and was replaced by Bruce Foxton. In the early 90s they embarked on further tours and recorded two albums, *Flags And Emblems* and *Fly The Flag*, but lost the long-serving Henry Cluney amid much acrimony. Taylor was replaced by drummer Steve Grantley in 1996. The band then released *Tinderbox*, their first album of new material in over three years.

STILLS, STEPHEN

TEXAN-BORN STILLS (b. 1945) IS BEST KNOWN FOR HIS WORK WITH **BUFFALO SPRINGFIELD**, AND HIS association with **David Crosby**, Graham Nash and **Neil Young**. His solo career began during one of **Crosby, Stills And Nash**'s many hiatuses. Stills enlisted a team of musical heavyweights to play on his self-titled debut which reached the US Top 3 in 1970, and which spawned the hit single 'Love The One You're With'. *Stephen Stills 2* was a similar success containing 'Change Partners' and a brass re-working of the Springfield's 'Bluebird'. His superbly eclectic double album with Manassas, and its consolidating follow-up, made Stills an immensely important figure, but ultimately he was unable to match his opening pair of albums. His nadir came in 1978 when he produced *Thoroughfare Gap.* No official solo release came until 1984, when Stills put out the AOR *Right By You.* Since then he has continued his stop-go career with Crosby, Nash, and occasionally Young. *Stills Alone* was a return to his folk and blues roots and featured hoarse-voiced versions of the **Beatles**' 'In My Life' and **Bob Dylan**'s 'Ballad Of Hollis Brown'. As a guitarist, his work in 1992 with a rejuvenated Crosby, Stills And Nash was quite breathtaking.

STING

FORMERLY LEAD SINGER AND BASSIST WITH THE **POLICE**, UK-BORN STING'S (b. GORDON SUMNER, 1951) SOLO CAREER began in 1982, when he starred in the film *Brimstone And Treacle*, releasing a version of 'Spread A Little Happiness' from it. By 1985, Sting had formed touring band, the Blue Turtles, including leading jazz figures such as Branford Marsalis (alto saxophone), Kenny Kirkland (keyboards) and Omar Hakim (drums). *Dream Of The Blue Turtles* brought him three international hits: 'If You Love Somebody Set Them Free', 'Fortress Around Your Heart' and 'Russians'. 'An Englishman In New York' became a UK hit in 1990.

Sting recorded *Nothing Like The Sun* with Marsalis and Police guitarist Andy Summers – an instant international success. He returned in 1991 with the autobiographical *The Soul Cages* from which 'All This Time' was a US Top 10 hit. He continued in a similar vein with *Ten Summoner's Tales*, which contained further quality hit singles including 'If I Ever Lose My Faith In You' and 'Fields Of Gold'. *Mercury Falling* was very much a marking-time album, but good enough to placate most reviewers.

STOCK, AITKEN AND WATERMAN

MIKE STOCK (b. 1951), MATT AITKEN (b. 1956), AND PETE WATERMAN (b. 1947) FIRST DESIGNED RECORDS FOR THE thriving British disco scene, having their first hits with singles by **Dead Or Alive** ('You Spin Me Round', UK number 1, 1984) and Sinitta ('So Macho', 1986). The team gained further UK number 1s in 1987 with 'Respectable' by Mel And Kim and **Rick Astley**'s 'Never Gonna Give You Up'. In that year, they released a dance single under their own names, 'Roadblock', which reached the UK Top 20. In 1988, they launched the PWL label and shifted their attention to the teenage audience. Their main vehicles were Australian soap opera stars **Kylie Minogue** and Jason Donovan. Minogue's 'I Should Be

So Lucky' was the first of over a dozen Top 10 hits in four years. The formula was applied to numerous other artists but by 1991, a change of direction was apparent. The SAW team was hit by the departure of main songwriter Aitken. Meanwhile, Waterman was busy with three new labels, PWL America, PWL Continental and PWL Black. The list of further hits goes on.

STONE ROSES

FORMED IN 1985, THIS MANCHESTER-BASED GROUP COMPRISED IAN BROWN (b. IAN GEORGE BROWN, 1963;

vocals), John Squire (b. 1962; guitar), Reni (b. Alan John Wren, 1964; drums), Andy Couzens (guitar) and Pete Garner (bass). By 1987 Couzens had left, and Garner followed soon after, allowing Gary 'Mani' Mounfield (b. 1962) to take over. By the end of the year the foursome were packing out local venues, but finding it difficult to attract national attention. A contract with Silvertone in 1988 produced 'Elephant Stone', influenced by classic 60s pop. Their debut album was hailed in all quarters as a guitar/pop classic. In 1990 'One Love' reached the UK Top 10, but the media was mainly concerned with the Roses' rows with their previous and present record companies. They tried to leave Silvertone, who prevented any further Stone Roses material from being released. The band eventually won their case and signed to Geffen, but it was not until 1995 that *Second Coming* was released. Almost inevitably, it failed to meet expectations. They also lost drummer Reni, who was replaced within weeks of its release by Robbie Maddix. Promotional gigs seemed less relaxed, and it was not too great a shock when Squire announced his departure in 1996. Brown and company decided on a concrete plan of action and with new members, Aziz Ibrahim (guitar) and Nigel Ippinson (keyboards), planned to be much more active. The press reports, however, were a different matter. They made the right decision in 1996 by announcing their demise.

STONE TEMPLE PILOTS

A SONGWRITING PARTNERSHIP BETWEEN SCOTT WEILAND (b. 1967; VOCALS) AND ROBERT DeLEO (b. 1966; BASS) LED TO the formation of this US band, with Eric Kretz (b. 1966; drums) and DeLeo's guitarist brother Dean (b. 1961). The band started playing club shows and developed hard rock material, given an alternative edge by their varied influences. 'Sex Type Thing' deals with sexual harassment from a male viewpoint. *Core* reached the US Top 20, eventually selling over four million copies in the USA. *Purple* debuted at US number 1. *Tiny Music... Songs from The Vatican Gift Shop* was powerful, but its success was tainted by Weiland being confined to a drug rehabilitation centre. By the end of 1996, he was clean and the band were back on the road – this tour was blighted by Weiland's returning drug problems. In 1998, Weiland was re-arrested, on heroin charges; shortly afterwards he announced the group's plans for a new album.

STOOGES

THE STOOGES WERE LED BY JAMES JEWEL OSTERBERG (AKA IGGY STOOGE AND **IGGY POP**, b. 1947). IGGY FORMED the Psychedelic Stooges with guitarist Ron Asheton, Scott Asheton (drums) and Dave Alexander (bass). By 1967, the group had become the Stooges and achieved a notoriety through the on stage behaviour of its uninhibited frontman. Their **John Cale**-produced debut album matched its malevolent, garage-band sneer with the air of nihilism prevalent in the immediate post-summer of love era. *Funhouse* documented a contemporary live set closing with the anarchic 'LA Blues', but proved uncommercial and the Stooges were dropped by their label. A second guitarist, Bill Cheatham joined in 1970, while over the next few months two bassists, Zeke Zettner and Jimmy Recca, passed through the ranks as replacements for Dave Alexander. Cheatham was then ousted in favour of James Williamson. *Raw Power* became the Stooges' most successful release, containing 'Gimme Danger' and 'Search And Destroy'. However, the quartet – Iggy, Williamson and the Asheton brothers – were dropped from the new Mainman label for alleged drug dependence. In 1973, Scott Thurston (keyboards) was added to the line-up, but their impetus was waning. The Stooges made their final live appearance in February 1974.

STRANGLERS

IN 1976, THE FIRST FULL LINE-UP OF THE STRANGLERS EMERGED IN GUILDFORD, ENGLAND, COMPRISING HUGH Cornwell (b. 1949; vocals/guitar), Jean Jacques Burnel (b. 1952; vocals/bass), Jet Black (b. Brian Duffy, 1943; drums) and Dave Greenfield (keyboards). Their debut, '(Get A) Grip (On Yourself)' (UK number 44), displayed Cornwell's gruff vocal to strong effect. *Rattus Norvegicus*, was greeted with enthusiasm by the rock press and sold well. The women-baiting second single, 'Peaches' was banned by BBC radio, but still charted thanks to airplay for the b-side, 'Go Buddy Go'. The group subsequently compounded the felony by introducing strippers at a London concert. Journalists were treated in an even more cavalier fashion. The public kept faith, however, and ensured that the Stranglers enjoyed a run of hits over the next few years. Their cover version of the **Burt Bacharach/Hal David** standard, 'Walk On By', reached number 21 in spite of the fact that 100,000 copies of the record had already been issued *gratis* with *Black And White*. Equally effective was 'Duchess', which displayed the Stranglers' plaintive edge to surprising effect. Their albums also revealed a new diversity, from *The Raven* to the genuinely strange *The Meninblack*. *La Folie* spawned the group's biggest hit, 'Golden Brown', with its startling, classical-influenced harpsichord arrangement. The group's subsequent albums failed to attract serious critical attention. Perpetual derision by the press finally took its toll on Cornwell, and in 1990 he announced his departure. The band recruited vocalist Paul Roberts (b. 1959) and guitarist John Ellis. *Stranglers In The Night* was a return to form, but still failed to recapture old glories. A second set with the band's new line-up emerged in 1995, but Cornwell's absence was felt in the unadventurous songwriting. *Written In Red* (1997) was a better effort.

Connections
Dead Or Alive ➽ p.113
Rick Astley ➽ p.23
Kylie Minogue ➽ p.234
Further References
Video: *Roadblock* (Touchstone Video 1988)

STONE ROSES
Albums
The Stone Roses (Silvertone 1989)★★★★
➽ p.380 for full listings
Further References
Book: *The Stone Roses And The Resurrection Of British Pop*, John Robb

STONE TEMPLE PILOTS
Albums
Tiny Music . . . Songs From The Vatican Gift Shop (Atlantic 1996)★★★
➽ p.380 for full listings
Further References
Book: *Stone Temple Pilots*, Mike Wall and Malcolm Dome

STOOGES
Albums
The Stooges (Elektra 1969)★★★★
Funhouse (Elektra 1970)★★★★
Raw Power (Columbia 1973)★★★★
➽ p.380 for full listings
Collaborators
John Cale ➽ p.78
Connections
Iggy Pop ➽ p.264

STRANGLERS
Albums
Rattus Norvegicus (United Artists 1977)★★★★
No More Heroes (United Artists 1977)★★★★
➽ p.380 for full listings
Influences
Burt Bacharach ➽ p.27
Further References
Video: *Saturday Night Sunday Morning* (PNE 1996)
Book: *No Mercy: The Authorised And Uncensored Biography Of The Stranglers*, David Buckley

STRAWBERRY ALARM CLOCK
Albums
Incense And Peppermints (Uni 1967)★★★
➽ p.380 for full listings

STRAWBS
Albums
Strawbs (A&M 1969)★★★★
Grave New World (A&M 1972)★★★★
➽ p.380 for full listings
Connections
Sandy Denny ➽ p.115
Rick Wakeman ➽ p.332

STYLE COUNCIL
Albums
Our Favourite Shop (Polydor 1985)★★★
➽ p.380 for full listings
Connections
Paul Weller ➽ p.336
Jam ➽ p196
Further References
Video: *What We Did On Our Holidays* (Polygram 1983)

STYLISTICS
Albums
Rockin' Roll Baby (Avco 1973)★★★★
Let's Put It All Together (Avco 1974)★★★★
➽ p.380 for full listings

STYX
Albums
Paradise Theater (A&M 1980)★★★★
Edge Of The Century (A&M 1990)★★★
➽ p.380 for full listings
Further References
Video: *Caught In The Act* (1984)

SUEDE
Albums
Suede (Nude 1993)★★★★
Coming Up (Nude 1996)★★★★
➽ p.380 for full listings
Connections
Brett Anderson
Bernard Butler
Mike Joyce
Influences
Morrissey ➽ p.239
David Bowie ➽ p.64
Smiths ➽ p.301
Electronic ➽ p.135
Further References
Video: *Love & Poison* (1993)
Book: *Suede: The Illustrated Biography*, York Membrey

SUGAR
Albums
Copper Blue (Creation 1992)★★★★
Beaster mini-album (Creation 1993)★★★★
➽ p.380 for full listings

STRAWBERRY ALARM CLOCK

THE STRAWBERRY ALARM CLOCK ENJOYED A US NUMBER 1 IN 1967 WITH 'INCENSE AND PEPPERMINTS'. THE GROUP – Mark Weitz (organ), Ed King (lead guitar), Lee Freeman (rhythm guitar), Gary Lovetro (bass) and Randy Seol (drums) – added a second bassist, George Bunnell, prior to recording their debut album, which coupled hippie trappings with enchanting melodies and imaginative instrumentation. Such features were maintained on successive albums, while 'Tomorrow' and 'Sit With The Guru' continued their reign as chart contenders. Lovetro left the line-up prior to *Wake Up It's Tomorrow*, and several subsequent changes undermined the band's direction. *Good Morning Starshine* introduced a reshaped band where Jimmy Pitman (guitar) and Gene Gunnels (drums) joined Weitz and King. Although they remained together until 1971, the Strawberry Alarm Clock was unable to regain its early profile.

STRAWBS

BRITISH UNIT FORMED IN 1967 BY GUITARISTS DAVE COUSINS (b. 1945; GUITAR/BANJO/PIANO/RECORDER) and Tony Hooper. The founding duo added Ron Chesterman on bass prior to the arrival of singer **Sandy Denny**. *Strawbs*, featuring 'The Battle', was acclaimed by both folk and rock audiences. *Dragonfly* was less well received, prompting a realignment in the band. The original duo was joined by John Ford (b. 1948; bass/acoustic guitar) and Richard Hudson (b. 1948; drums/guitar/sitar), plus **Rick Wakeman** (keyboards). The Strawbs embraced electric rock with *Just A Collection Of Antiques And Curios*.

Such plaudits continued on *From The Witchwood* but the pianist grew frustrated and was replaced by Blue Weaver (b. 1947; guitar/autoharp/piano). Despite the commercial success generated by *Grave New World*, tension mounted, and in 1972 Hooper was replaced by Dave Lambert (b. 1949). Relations between Cousins and Hudson and Ford were also deteriorating and although 'Lay Down' gave the band its first UK Top 20 single, the jocular 'Part Of The Union', written by the bassist and drummer, became the Strawbs' most successful release. In 1987, the trio of Cousins, Hooper and Hudson recorded *Don't Say Goodbye*.

STYLE COUNCIL

FOUNDED IN ENGLAND IN 1983 BY **PAUL WELLER** (b. 1958) AND MICK TALBOT (b. 1958). WELLER HAD BEEN LEAD singer of the **Jam** and his avowed aim with the group was to merge his twin interests of soul music and social comment. The continuing popularity of the Jam ensured that Style Council's first four releases in 1983 were UK hits. They included the EP *Paris*, 'Speak Like A Child' and 'Long Hot Summer'. 'My Ever Changing Moods' was the first of three UK Top 10 hits in 1984 and the band's only US hit. There were continuing British hits, notably 'The Walls Come Tumbling Down' (1985), 'Have You Ever Had It Blue' and 'Wanted' (1987). The 1988 album was less of a commercial success and by 1990, Style Council was defunct.

STYLISTICS

FORMED IN 1968 BY RUSSELL THOMPKINS JNR (b. 1951), AIRRION LOVE (b. 1949), JAMES SMITH (b. 1950), HERBIE Murrell (b. 1949) and James Dunn (b. 1950), US group the Stylistics' debut single, 'You're A Big Girl Now' became a national hit. A series of immaculate singles, including 'You Are Everything' (1971), 'Betcha By Golly Wow' and 'I'm Stone In Love With You' (both 1972) followed. Their style reached its apogee in 1974 with 'You Make Me Feel Brand New' (UK and US number 2). Although their American fortunes waned, the Stylistics continued to enjoy success in the UK with 'Sing Baby Sing', 'Can't Give You Anything (But My Love)' (both 1975) and '16 Bars' (1976). Ill health forced Dunn to retire in 1978. Two years later they were signed to TSOP/Philadelphia International, but problems within the company undermined the group's progress. Subsequent singles took the Stylistics into the lower reaches of the R&B chart, but their halcyon days seemed to be over.

STYX

THE LINE-UP COMPRISED DENNIS DE YOUNG (VOCALS/ KEYBOARDS), JAMES YOUNG (GUITAR/VOCALS), CHUCK Panozzo (bass), John Panozzo (b. 1947, d. 1996; drums) and John Curulewski (guitar). *Styx II*, originally released in 1973, spawned the Top Ten *Billboard* hit 'Lady' in 1975. The album then made similar progress, eventually peaking at number 20. After signing to A&M in 1975, John Curulewski departed with the release of *Equinox*, to be replaced by Tommy Shaw. *The Grand Illusion* was Shaw's first major success, peaking at number 6. It also featured the hit 'Sail Away'. *Pieces Of Eight* and *Cornerstone* consolidated their success, the latter containing 'Babe', the band's first US number 1 single. *Paradise Theater* was the Styx's *tour de force*, generating two further US Top 10 hits in 'The Best Of Times' and 'Too Much Time On My Hands'. *Kilroy Was Here* followed, yet another concept album. They disbanded shortly after the uninspired *Caught In The Act*, but re-formed in 1990 with the original line-up, except for pop-rock funkster Glenn Burtnick, who replaced Shaw. *Edge Of The Century* indicated that the band still had something to offer.

SUEDE

THIS UK BAND BROKE THROUGH IN 1993 BY MERGING THE LYRICAL PERSPECTIVE OF **MORRISSEY** WITH THE POSTURINGS of **David Bowie** and the glam set. Brett Anderson (vocals) has a rare gift for evocative mood swings and much was made of guitarist Bernard Butler's similarities to Johnny Marr (**Smiths**, **Electronic**). The rest of the band comprised Matt Osman (bass) and Simon Gilbert (drums). 'The Drowners' arrived in 1992, and the b-side 'My Insatiable One' was a brooding low-life London tale. By this time, the mainstream music media had latched on to the band. Their appearance at the 1993 BRIT Awards gave them massive exposure and their debut album reached

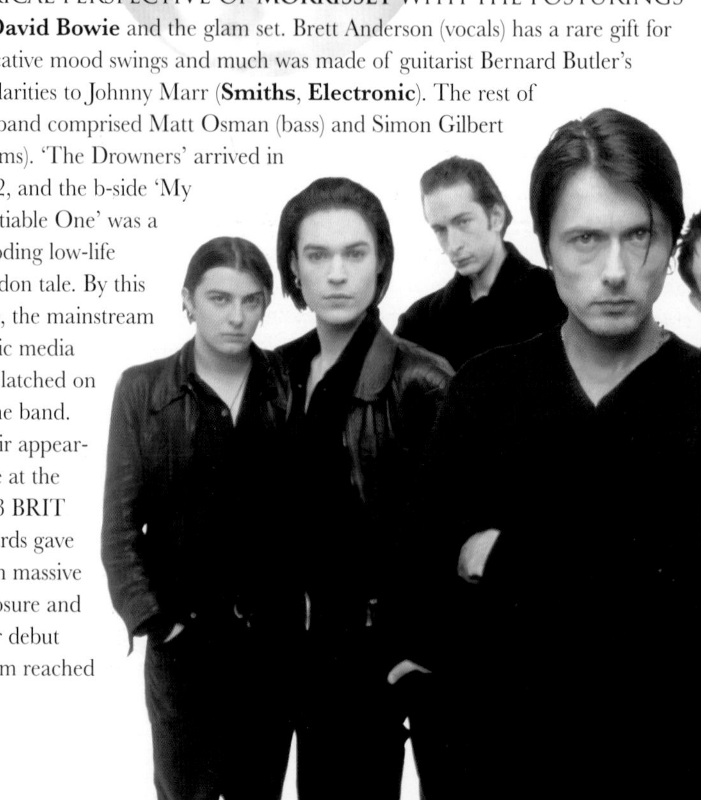

UK number 1. Butler left on the eve of the second album, replaced by 17-year-old 'unknown' Richard Oakes. In 1996, Neil Codling (keyboards) was recruited. Great pressure preceded their third album – a lengthy gap between releases and the fickle music public being major factors. Any fears were dispelled by *Coming Up*, a stunning collection of crafted, concise songs. The b-sides compilation *Sci-fi Lullabies* was followed by touring, including a visit to Israel in 1998.

SUGAR

IN THE AFTERMATH OF **NIRVANA**'S COMMERCIAL BREAKTHROUGH, **BOB MOULD** (b. 1960; GUITAR/VOCALS) found himself subject to the somewhat unflattering representation 'Godfather of Grunge'. With Sugar he seemed set to continue to justify the critical plaudits that have followed his every move. Joined by David Barbe (b. 1963; bass/vocals; ex-Mercyland) and Malcolm Travis (b. 1953; drums; ex-Zulus), he found another powerful triumvirate. Sugar's breakthrough came with *Copper Blue* in 1992. Singles such as 'Changes' tied the band's musical muscle to a straightforward commercial skeleton. Mould responded a few months later with *Beaster* in which the melodies and hooks were buried under layers of harsh feedback. *F.U.E.L.* offered a hybrid of the approaches on the two previous albums. Afterwards, however, Mould ruminated widely about the long-term future of Sugar, suggesting inner-band tensions between the trio. They disbanded in 1995, after which Mould began a solo career.

SUGARCUBES

OFFBEAT POP BAND FORMED IN REYKJAVIK, ICELAND, IN 1986. THE LINE-UP FEATURED **BJÖRK** GUNDMUNDSDOTTIR (b. 1966; vocals/keyboards), Bragi Olaffson (bass), Einar Orn Benediktsson (vocals/trumpet), Margret 'Magga' Ornolfsdottir (keyboards), Sigtryggur 'Siggi' (drums) and Thor Eldon (guitar). After early stage appearances Björk completed her first album at the age of 11. She was also the singer for prototype groups Toppie Tikarras then Theyr, alongside Balduresson. Björk, Einar and Siggi then went on to form Kukl, who toured Europe and released two records on Crass, establishing a link with the UK anarcho-punk scene. Debut single, 'Birthday', and album, *Life's Too Good*, saw the band championed in the UK press almost immediately. *Here Today, Tomorrow, Next Week*, was a more elaborate album. The third found them back in favour with the music press and back in the charts with 'Hit', but shortly afterwards Björk left for a rewarding solo career.

SUMMER, DONNA

US STAR SUMMER'S (b. LADONNA GAINES, 1948) FIRST RECORDS WERE 'HOSTAGE' AND 'LADY OF THE NIGHT' for Giorgio Moroder's Oasis label in Munich. They were local hits but it was 'Love To Love You Baby' (1975) that made her an international star. The track sold a million copies in the USA on Neil Bogart's Casablanca label. In 1977, a similar formula took 'I Feel Love' to the top of the UK chart, and 'Down Deep Inside' was a big international success. Her film debut came the next year in *Thank God It's Friday*, in which she sang another million-seller, 'Last Dance'. She achieved four more US number 1s in 1978-79. In 1980 she signed to **David Geffen**'s new company and her work took on a more pronounced soul and gospel flavour. Some of her major US hits during the early 80s were 'On The Radio', 'The Wanderer', 'She Works Hard For The Money' and 'Love Is In Control (Finger On The Trigger)'. Summer returned in 1987 and enjoyed another hit with 'Dinner With Gershwin'. Her best-selling 1989 album for Warner Brothers was written and produced by **Stock, Aitken And Waterman** while Clivilles And Cole worked on *Love Is Gonna Change*. The 90s have proved only moderately successful for her.

SUPER FURRY ANIMALS

FOUNDED IN CARDIFF, WALES, INDIE BAND SUPER FURRY ANIMALS COMPRISE GRUFF RHYS (b. 1970; VOCALS/GUITAR), Dafydd Ieuan (b. 1969; drums), Cian Ciaran (b. 1976; electronics), Guto Pryce (b. 1972; bass) and Huw 'Bunf' Bunford (b. 1967; guitar/vocals). The first evidence of the group's distinctive, scabrous pop came with the release of the *Welsh Concept* EP. Creation Records invited them to submit some of their English-language material, resulting in a long-term development contract. Their debut album showcased their ambitions to 'push technology to the limit'. It included their debut single for Creation, 'Hometown Unicorn' and 'God! Show Me Magic'. Critical approval as well as a growing fan base confirmed their breakthrough. Further late 90s shenanigans were apparent with the lighter *Radiator.*

SUPERGRASS

SUPERGRASS COMPRISES DANNY GOFFEY (b. *c.* 1975; DRUMS), GARY COOMBES (b. 1976; VOCALS/GUITAR) AND MICKEY Quinn (b. *c.* 1970; bass). Debut 'Caught By The Fuzz' brought them to public attention, though not before it had been released on three separate occasions. Parlophone re-released it in 1994, when it climbed to number 42 in the UK charts. They also toured with **Shed Seven** and supported **Blur**, before the release of a second single, 'Man Size Rooster', in early 1995. Their debut album was produced with Mystics singer Sam Williams, while the band also contributed to the Sub Pop Records Singles Club with 'Lose It'. However, all was eclipsed by the astonishing success of 'Alright', which shot to the top of the UK charts and made instant celebrities of the band. The resultant interest in Supergrass pushed *I Should Coco* to number 1 in the UK album chart. In 1997, the band rose to the pressure of producing a follow-up with *In It For The Money*.

Connections
Nirvana ➽ p.248
Bob Mould ➽ p.241
Mercyland
Zulus

SUGARCUBES
Albums
Life's Too Good (One Little Indian 1988)★★★★
Stick Around For Joy (One Little Indian 1992)★★★
➽ p.380 for full listings
Connections
Björk ➽ p.48
Toppie Tikarras
Theyr
Kukl
Influences
Wind In The Willows

SUMMER, DONNA
Albums
Bad Girls (Casablanca 1979)★★★★
The Wanderer (Geffen 1980)★★★★
She Works Hard For The Money (Mercury 1983)★★★★
➽ p.380 for full listings
Collaborators
David Geffen ➽ p.155
Stock, Aitken And Waterman ➽ p.310
Clivilles And Cole
Further References
Book: *Donna Summer: An Unauthorized Biography*, James Haskins

SUPER FURRY ANIMALS
Albums
Fuzzy Logic (Creation 1996)★★★★
Radiator (Creation 1997)★★★★
➽ p.380 for full listings

SUPERGRASS
Albums
I Should Coco (Parlophone 1995)★★★★
In It For The Money (Parlophone 1997)★★★★★
➽ p.380 for full listings

Collaborators
Shed Seven ➽ p.295
Blur ➽ p.58
Sam Williams
Connections
Mystics
Further References
Book: *Supergrass*, Linda Holorny

SUPERTRAMP
Albums
Crime Of The Century (A&M 1974)★★★★
Crisis? What Crisis? (A&M 1975)★★★★
Breakfast In America (A&M 1979)★★★★
➔ p.380 for full listings
Further References
Book: *The Supertramp Book*, Martin Melhuish

SUPREMES
Albums
The Supremes Sing Holland, Dozier, Holland (Motown 1967)★★★★
The Magnificent Seven (Motown 1970)★★★★
Together (Motown 1969)★★★
➔ p.380 for full listings
Collaborators
Holland/Dozier/Holland ➔ p.183
Connections
Diana Ross ➔ p.283
Motown ➔ p.240
Further References
Film: *Beach Ball* (1964)
Books: *Dreamgirl: My Life As A Supreme*, Mary Wilson
All That Glittered: My Life With The Supremes, Tony Turner and Barbara Aria

SURFARIS
Albums
Wipe Out (Dot 1963)★★★
The Surfaris Play Wipe Out And Others (Decca 1963)★★★
It Ain't Me Babe (Decca 1965)★★★
➔ p.381 for full listings
Collaborators
Gary Usher

SUTHERLAND BROTHERS (AND QUIVER)
Albums
The Sutherland Brothers Band (Island 1972)★★★
Dream Kid (Island 1974)★★★★
Down To Earth (Columbia 1977)★★★
➔ p.381 for full listings
Connections
Ace ➔ p.8
Further References
Book: *The Whaling Years, Peterhead 1788-1893*, Gavin Sutherland

SWAN, BILLY
Albums
I Can Help (Monument 1974)★★★★
Billy Swan (Monument 1976)★★★★
➔ p.381 for full listings
Collaborations
Harry Chapin ➔ p.87
Randy Meisner

SUPERTRAMP

SUPERTRAMP WERE FINANCED BY DUTCH MILLIONAIRE STANLEY AUGUST MIESEGAES, WHICH ENABLED RICHARD Davies (b. 1944; vocals/keyboards) to recruit Roger Hodgson (b. 1950; guitar), Dave Winthrop (b. 1948; saxophone), Richard Palmer (guitar) and Bob Miller (drums). *Supertramp* was an unspectacular affair and *Indelibly Stamped* was similarly unsuccessful. The band were in dire straits when Miesegaes departed, along with Winthrop and Palmer. They recruited John Helliwell (b. 1945), Dougie Thompson (b. 1951) and Bob Benberg and had a remarkable change in fortune as *Crime Of The Century* became one of the top-selling albums of 1974. 'Dreamer' was taken from the album, while 'Bloody Well Right' was a Top 40 hit in the USA, but the subsequent *Crisis? What Crisis?* and *Even In The Quietest Moments* were lesser works. 'Give A Little Bit', with its infectious acoustic guitar introduction was a minor transatlantic hit in 1977. Supertramp were elevated to rock's first division with *Breakfast In America*. Four of the tracks became hits, 'The Logical Song', 'Take The Long Way Home', 'Goodbye Stranger' and the title track. The album stayed on top of the US charts for six weeks. The obligatory live album was followed by the R&B-influenced *Famous Last Words*. Supertramp's recent releases, however, have only found minor success.

SUPREMES

AMERICA'S MOST SUCCESSFUL FEMALE VOCAL GROUP OF ALL TIME WAS FORMED BY FOUR DETROIT SCHOOLGIRLS IN THE late 50s. **Diana Ross** (b. 1944), Betty Hutton, Florence Ballard (b. 1943, d. 1976) and Mary Wilson (b. 1944) issued a solitary single on a small local label, then signed to Berry Gordy's **Motown** label. When Diana Ross supplanted Florence Ballard as the group's regular lead vocalist, the Supremes broke into the US charts. 'When The Lovelight Starts Shining In His Eyes', was the group's first hit in 1963. The follow-up single flopped, but 'Where Did Our Love Go' topped the US charts and was also a hit in Britain. There followed a remarkable run of successes for the group and their producers, **Holland/Dozier/Holland**, as their next four releases – 'Baby Love', 'Come See About Me', 'Stop! In The Name Of Love' and 'Back In My Arms Again' – all topped the US singles charts. 'Nothing But Heartaches' broke the chart-topping sequence, which was immediately restored by the more ambitious 'I Hear A Symphony'. As Holland/Dozier/Holland moved into their prime, the group's repertoire grew more mature. The hits kept coming, but behind the scenes, the group's future was in some jeopardy; Florence Ballard was unhappy with her supporting role, and she was forced out in mid-1967, replaced by Cindy Birdsong. Ross's prime position in the group's hierarchy was then confirmed in public, and in 1968 they formed a successful recording partnership with the **Temptations**, exemplified by the hit single 'I'm Gonna Make You Love Me'.

In 1969, rumours that Berry Gordy was about to launch Diana Ross on a solo career, were confirmed when the Supremes staged a farewell performance, and Ross bade goodbye to the group with the elegiac 'Someday We'll Be Together'. Ross was replaced by Jean Terrell and the new line-up found immediate success with 'Up The Ladder To The Roof' in early 1970, while 'Stoned Love' became the group's biggest UK hit for four years. Gradually, the momentum was lost, and the group finally disbanded in 1977.

SURFARIS

FORMED IN GLENDALE, CALIFORNIA, IN 1962, THE SURFARIS – JIM FULLER (b. 1947; LEAD GUITAR), JIM PASH (b. 1949; guitar), Bob Berryhill (b. 1947; guitar), Pat Connolly (b. 1947; bass) and Ron Wilson (b. 1945; drums) – achieved international success with 'Wipe Out' – now one of the definitive surfing anthems. *Hit City '64* introduced a partnership with producer Gary Usher, who employed a team of experienced session musicians on ensuing Surfaris' releases.

In 1965 the group turned to folk rock. Wilson had become an accomplished lead singer and with Ken Forssi replacing Connolly on bass, the Surfaris completed the promising *It Ain't Me Babe*. However, Usher then severed his relationship with the band and they broke up when Jim Pash left the line-up.

SUTHERLAND BROTHERS (AND QUIVER)

BASICALLY A DUO FROM THE OUTSET, COMPRISING SCOTTISH BROTHERS IAIN (b. 1948; VOCALS/GUITAR/KEYBOARDS) AND Gavin Sutherland (b. 1951; bass/guitar/vocals). They had been signed to Island, releasing *The Sutherland Brothers Band*. A meeting between their manager Wayne Bordell, and Quiver showed a mutual need for each others talents. The Sutherland Brothers needed a band, and Quiver needed new songs, so the Sutherland Brothers And Quiver were born, comprising Iain and Gavin, Tim Renwick (b. 1949; guitar/vocals/flute), Willie Wilson (b. John Wilson, 1947; drums, vocals, percussion), Bruce Thomas (b. 1948; bass), Cal Batchelor (vocals/guitar/keyboards), and Pete Wood (d. 1994; keyboards). Within a few months they released *Lifeboat*. The band recorded three tracks, 'I Don't Want To Love You But You Got Me Anyway', 'Have You Had A Vision', and 'Not Fade Away'. After recording, Cal Batchelor left. Bruce Thomas departed shortly after *Dream Kid*. Terry 'Tex' Comer from **Ace**, took over his role to play on half the recordings for *Beat Of The Street*. Taking on Mick Blackburn as manager, they got a deal with CBS, and released *Reach For The Sky*. By the time *Slipstream* was released, the line-up comprised Wilson, Renwick, Gavin and Iain, although Renwick soon left. The recording of *Down To Earth* was augmented by a number of respected session musicians, including Ray Flacke (guitar), and Brian Bennett (percussion). By the time of *When The Night Comes Down*, Wilson had left.

SWAN, BILLY

US-BORN SWAN (b. 1942) GREW UP LISTENING TO COUNTRY STARS AND 50S ROCK 'N' ROLLERS. AT THE AGE OF 16, HE wrote 'Lover Please', which **Elvis Presley**'s bass player, **Bill Black**, recorded with his Combo in 1960. Swan later moved to Memphis to write for Bill Black's Combo. He also worked as a janitor at Columbia's studios. He quit while **Bob Dylan** was recording *Blonde On Blonde*, offering his job to **Kris Kristofferson** who was looking for work. Billy worked as a roadie before meeting Tony Joe White and producing demos of his 'swamp rock'; including *Black And White*. Swan then joined Kinky Friedman in the Texas Jewboys. Shortly afterwards, producer Chip Young invited him to record for Monument. The first single was a revival of **Hank Williams**' 'Wedding Bells', followed by 'I Can Help' (US number 1, UK number 6). The subsequent album was a cheerful affair, and included the single 'I'm Her Fool' – banned by several radio stations because of the line, 'She pets me when I bury my bone'.

In 1975, Elvis Presley recorded a version of 'I Can Help', which became a UK hit in 1983. Billy Swan released three more albums for Monument and then one each for A&M and Epic, but failed to recapture the overall quality of his first. Swan and Kristofferson co-wrote 'Nobody Loves Anybody Anymore' on Kristofferson's *To The Bone* and Swan also played on albums by **Harry Chapin** among others. He worked briefly with Randy Meisner of the **Eagles** in a country rock band, Black Tie, releasing *When The Night Falls* in 1986. Since then, Swan has continued to tour with Kristofferson.

SWEET

MICK TUCKER (b. 1949) AND VOCALIST BRIAN CONNOLLY (b. 1945, d. 1997), formed Sweetshop, later shortened to Sweet, with Steve Priest (b. 1950; bass) and Frank Torpey (guitar). After releasing four unsuccessful singles on Fontana and EMI, Torpey was replaced by Andy Scott (b. 1951) and the new line-up signed to RCA. The band were introduced to the writing partnership of Chinn And Chapman, and their initial success was down to bubblegum pop anthems such as 'Funny, Funny', 'Co-Co', 'Poppa Joe' and 'Little Willy'. However, the band were writing their own hard-rock numbers on the b-sides of these hits.

Sweet decided to take greater control of their own destiny in 1974, and recorded the album *Sweet Fanny Adams* without the assistance of Chinn and Chapman. The album charted at number 27, but disappeared again after just two weeks. 'Set Me Free', 'Restless' and 'Sweet F.A.' epitomized their no-frills hard-rock style. *Desolation Boulevard* included the self-penned 'Fox On The Run' (UK number 2). However, the hit singles began to dry up; 1978's 'Love Is Like Oxygen' being their last Top 10 hit. Following a move to Polydor, they cut four albums with each release making less impact than its predecessor. Since 1982, various incarnations of the band have appeared from time to time.

SWEET, MATTHEW

BEFORE THE SUCCESS OF GIRLFRIEND, US-BORN SWEET (b. 1964) HAD BEEN BEST KNOWN FOR HIS WORK IN THE LATE 80S with the **Golden Palominos**. *Inside*, his debut solo album under his own name, followed in 1986 and featured contributions from the **Bangles** and Chris Stamey. On *Girlfriend* Sweet was accompanied by New York musicians including Fred Maher, Robert Quine (ex-**Lou Reed**; **Richard Hell** And The Voidoids) and Richard Lloyd (ex-**Television**), plus the UK's **Lloyd Cole** and the drummer Ric Menck. *Son Of Altered Beast* remixed the best track from *Altered Beast*, 'Devil With The Green Eyes', and added five live tracks. For *100% Fun* Sweet was joined by Greg Leisz (formerly with **k.d. lang**) on pedal steel and mandolin with Brendan O'Brien (**Pearl Jam**, **Bob Dylan**, **Soundgarden**) producing. The touring band for 1995 added Tony Marsico (bass) and Stuart Johnson (drums). *Blue Sky On Mars* was crammed with appealing hooks, but none with the mark of 'a truly great pop song'.

SWEET INSPIRATIONS

THE LINE-UP OF **CISSY HOUSTON**, SYLVIA SHEMWELL, MYRNA SMITH AND ESTELLE BROWN SECURED A MINOR hit with 'Why (Am I Treated So Bad)' (1967), but it was 'Sweet Inspiration' which gave the group its best-remembered single, reaching the US Top 20 in 1968. Cissy Houston left for a solo career in 1970. After a hiatus from the recording scene, Smith and Shemwell were joined by Gloria Brown in place of Estelle Brown, and a final album appeared on RSO in 1979.

SWINGING BLUE JEANS

LIVERPOOL SKIFFLE GROUP FOUNDED IN 1958, COMPRISING SINGER AND LEAD GUITARIST RAY ENNIS (b. 1942), RHYTHM guitarist Ray Ellis (b. 1942), bass player Les Braid (b. 1941), drummer Norman Kuhlke (b. 1942) and Paul Moss (banjo). They signed with EMI's HMV label and had a minor hit with 'It's Too Late Now', but it was the group's third single, 'Hippy Hippy Shake', that provided their biggest success (number 2). Their version of 'Good Golly Miss Molly' peaked at number 11, while the reflective rendition of Betty Everett's 'You're No Good' reached number 3. An excellent reading of **Dionne Warwick**'s hit 'Don't Make Me Over' stalled outside the Top 30. It was, however, the quartet's last substantial hit. Several personnel changes ensued, including the induction of two former **Escorts**, Terry Sylvester and Mike Gregory, but this did not make any difference to their fortunes. The revival of interest in 60s music persuaded Ennis to re-form group in 1973. He re-recorded 'Hippy Hippy Shake' for an album on Dart Records.

Connections
Elvis Presley ➽ p.265
Bill Black ➽ p.48
Bob Dylan ➽ p.128
Kris Kristofferson ➽ p.211
Texas Jewboys
Eagles ➽ p.130
Influences
Hank Williams ➽ p.339

SWEET
Albums
Sweet Fanny Adams (RCA 1974)★★★
Desolation Boulevard (RCA 1974)★★★
Strung Up (RCA 1975)★★★
➽ p.381 for full listings
Collaborators
Chinn And Chapman
Connections
Sweetshop

SWEET, MATTHEW
Albums
Earth (A&M 1989)★★★
Altered Beast (Zoo 1993)★★★
Blue Sky On Mars (Zoo 1997)★★★
➽ p.381 for full listings
Collaborators
Bangles ➽ p.32
Lloyd Cole ➽ p.96
Connections
Golden Palominos ➽ p.162
Lou Reed ➽ p.274
Richard Hell And The Voidoids ➽ p.179
Television ➽ p.317
k.d. lang ➽ p.212
Pearl Jam ➽ p.257
Bob Dylan ➽ p.128
Soundgarden ➽ p.303

SWEET INSPIRATIONS
Albums
The Sweet Inspirations (Atlantic 1967)★★★
Sweets For My Sweet (Atlantic 1969)★★★
Estelle, Myrna And Sylvia (Stax 1973)★★★
➽ p.381 for full listings
Connections
Cissy Houston ➽ p.188

SWINGING BLUE JEANS
Albums
Blue Jeans A' Swinging aka *Swinging Blue Jeans* aka *Tutti Frutti* (HMV 1964)★★★
Hippy Hippy Shake (1973)★★★
➽ p.381 for full listings
Collaborators
Dionne Warwick ➽ p.334
Connections
Bluegenes
Escorts ➽ p.138

T. REX
Albums
Electric Warrior (Fly 1971)★★★★
➽ p.381 for full listings

Connections
Marc Bolan ➽ p.59
Ringo Starr ➽ p.307

TAJ MAHAL
Albums
Giant Steps/De Ole Folks At Home (Columbia 1969)★★★★
➽ p.381 for full listings
Influences
Fats Domino ➽ p.122

TAKE THAT
Albums
Everything Changes (RCA 1993)★★★
➽ p.381 for full listings
Collaborators
Lulu ➽ p.219
Connections
Barry Manilow ➽ p.224

TALK TALK
Albums
Spirit Of Eden (Parlophone 1988)★★★★
➽ p.381 for full listings

TALKING HEADS
Albums
Little Creatures (EMI 1985)★★★★
➽ p.381 for full listings
Collaborators
David Byrne ➽ p.77
Connections
Jonathan Richman ➽ p.277
Brian Eno ➽ p.136

TANGERINE DREAM
Albums
Stratosfear (Virgin 1976)★★★★
➽ p.381 for full listings

TASTE
Albums
On The Boards (Polydor 1970)★★★★
➽ p.381 for full listings
Collaborators
Rory Gallagher ➽ p.158
Connections
Them ➽ p.319
Influences
Cream ➽ p.103

TATE, HOWARD
Albums
Get It While You Can (Verve 1967)★★★★
➽ p.381 for full listings
Connections
Janis Joplin ➽ p.201
Sam Cooke ➽ p.100

T. REX

ORIGINALLY KNOWN AS TYRANNOSAURUS REX, THE BAND WAS FORMED BY LONDONER **MARC BOLAN** (b. MARK FELD, 1947, d. 1977; vocals/guitar) with Steve 'Peregrine' Took (b. 1949, d. 1980; percussion) in 1967. 'Debora', their debut single, broached the UK Top 40, while a follow-up, 'One Inch Rock', reached number 28, but Tyrannosaurus Rex found a wider audience with their quirky albums, *My People Were Fair...* and *Prophets, Seers & Sages*. Bolan also published *The Warlock Of Love*, a collection of poems.

Unicorn introduced a much fuller sound as Tyrannosaurus Rex found a wider popularity. Long-time producer Tony Visconti (b. 1944) emphasized the supporting instruments – organ, harmonium, bass guitar and drum kit. Took left in 1970 and was replaced by Mickey Finn (b. 1947). *A Beard Of Stars* completed the transformation into a fully-fledged electric group. The duo's name was truncated to T. Rex in 1970. Commercial success was established by 'Ride A White Swan', which hit number 2. Steve Currie (b. 1947, d. 1981; bass) and Bill (Fifield) Legend (b. 1944; drums), were added to the line-up for 'Hot Love', 'Get It On', and the album *Electric Warrior*, all of which topped the charts. A series of big hits followed and a documentary, *Born To Boogie*, captured this frenetic period, but by 1973 their success was waning. Bolan's relationship with Visconti was severed following 'Truck On (Tyke)' and a tired predictability crept into the singer's work. Changes were made to the line-up, including American soul singer Gloria Jones (b. 1947), Herbie Flowers (bass) and Tony Newman (drums). Tragically, however, on 16 September 1977, Marc Bolan was killed in a car accident. His death was followed by those of Took and Currie.

TAJ MAHAL

MAHAL'S (b. HENRY SAINT CLAIR FREDERICKS, 1940) FIRST ALBUM, *TAJ MAHAL*, WAS A POWERFUL COMPENDIUM OF electrified country blues that introduced an early backing band of Jesse Davis (guitar), Gary Gilmore (bass) and Chuck Blakwell (drums). A similarly styled second album, *The Natch'l Blues*, was followed by *Giant Steps/The Ole Folks At Home*, a double album comprising a traditional-styled acoustic album and rock selection. His pursuit of ethnic styles resulted in the African-American persuasion of *Happy Just To Be Like I Am* and the West Indian influence of *Mo Roots*. In the 90s, Mahal veered towards soul and R&B.

TAKE THAT

FORMED IN MANCHESTER, ENGLAND, TAKE THAT COMPRISED VOCALISTS **GARY BARLOW** (b. 1971), MARK ANTHONY Owen (b. 1974), Howard Paul Donald (b. 1968), Jason Thomas Orange (b. 1970) and Robbie Williams (b. 1974). The band released its debut single, 'Do What U Like' in 1991. 1992 brought a cover of the Tavarés' 'It Only Takes A Minute' which reached number 7 and founded a fanatical following. The ensuing album *Take That And Party* debuted at UK number 5. The *A Million Love Songs* EP, led by its powerful title-track also reached number 7. By the following year the the group's debut album had climbed up to UK number 2, succeeding their cover of **Barry Manilow**'s 'Could It Be Magic'. 'Pray' became their first UK number 1 in 1993, a feat repeated with 'Relight My Fire', featuring a guest appearance from **Lulu**. *Everything Changes* debuted at UK number 1 and the group's huge success continued throughout 1994. Fans were shocked when Williams announced his departure for a solo career in 1995. It was confirmed in 1996 that the band were going their separate ways.

TALK TALK

FORMED IN 1981 BY MARK HOLLIS (b. 1955; VOCALS), LEE HARRIS (DRUMS), PAUL WEBB (BASS) AND SIMON BRENNER (keyboards). This UK group's debut album produced a number of hit singles including, 'Talk Talk' and 'Today'. Keen to lose their 'New Romantic' image, Hollis spent a couple of years writing new material: *The Colour Of Spring* and *Spirit Of Eden* showed their true musical preferences, but their poor showing led to EMI dropping the band. A greatest hits compilation was issued giving them three more hit singles.

TALKING HEADS

AFTER GRADUATING FROM THE RHODE ISLAND SCHOOL OF DESIGN, STUDENTS **DAVID BYRNE** (b. 1952; VOCALS/GUITAR), Chris Frantz (b. Charlton Christopher Frantz, 1951; drums) and Tina Weymouth (b. Martina Weymouth, 1950; bass) relocated to New York and formed Talking Heads in 1975. Sire Records eventually signed the group and early in 1976 the line-up was expanded to include pianist Jerry Harrison (b. Jeremiah Harrison, 1949). *Talking Heads '77* was an exhilarating first album; the highlight of the set was the insistent 'Psycho Killer'. **Brian Eno** produced *More Songs About Buildings And Food* and his services were retained for *Fear Of Music*, which included the popular 'Life During Wartime'. During the early 80s, the group's extra-curricular activities increased and while Byrne explored ballet on *The Catherine Wheel*, Frantz and Weymouth found success with their spin-off project, Tom Tom Club. The live double *The Name Of This Band Is Talking Heads* served as a stopgap until *Speaking In Tongues*.

Little Creatures was a more accessible offering providing three strong singles. In 1986, Byrne moved into movies with *True Stories*, for which Talking Heads provided the soundtrack; it was two more years before the group re-convened for *Naked*. There was an official announcement of their break-up at the end of 1991. In 1996, Weymouth, Frantz and Harrison launched the Heads.

TANGERINE DREAM

SINCE THIS GERMAN BAND'S FORMATION IN 1968, IT HAS BEEN LED BY EDGAR FROESE (b. 1944; GUITAR). HE WAS joined by Voker Hombach (flute/violin), Kirt Herkenber (bass) and Lanse Hapshash (drums), but they split the following year. Froese recruited Steve Jollife (electric flute), who left soon after, only to rejoin later. Konrad Schnitzler and Klaus Schulze were added for their debut album. Jazz drummer Christoph Franke and organist Steve Schroyder joined in 1973. This line-up recorded *Alpha Centauri*. Peter Baumann replaced Schroyder, and this became the band's first stable line-up, staying together until 1977.

Zeit incorporated new synthesizer technology, while *Atem* focused on atmospheric, restrained passages. *Phaedra* established their biggest foothold in the UK market, but then their attentions turned to a series of film soundtracks. *Stratosfear* was their most commercial album so far. Baumann was replaced by former member Jollife, and drummer Klaus Kreiger also joined. *Cyclone* featured vocals and lyrics for the first time, although they returned to instrumental work with *Force Majeure*. In 1985 Schmoelling departed and was replaced by classically trained Paul Haslinger. Three years later Chris Franke, after 17 years service, also left for a solo career. Ralf Wadephal took his place but when he left, the band elected to continue as a duo.

TASTE

TASTE WAS FORMED IN CORK, EIRE IN 1966 WHEN ERIC KITTRINGHAM (BASS) AND NORMAN DAMERY (DRUMS) joined guitarist **Rory Gallagher** (b. 1949, d. 1995). In 1968, Gallagher replaced the original rhythm section with Charlie McCracken (bass) and John Wilson (ex-**Them**) on drums. *Taste*, was one of the era's most popular releases, featuring 'Same Old Story' and 'Sugar Mama' and *On The Boards* was another commercial success. The unit broke up in 1970 following arguments between Gallagher and his colleagues. The guitarist then began a fruitful solo career until his death in 1995.

TATE, HOWARD

A FORMER MEMBER OF THE GAINORS WITH GARNET MIMMS, US-BORN TATE (b. 1943) ALSO SANG WITH BILL Doggett's band. A solo act by 1962, Howard secured four US R&B hits between 1966 and 1968. Tate's work provided material for several acts, most notably **Janis Joplin**, who recorded 'Get It While You Can'. After releasing two singles in 1969 and 1970, Tate moved to Atlantic Records. From there he moved on to various other labels, but with little success.

TAYLOR, JAMES

JAMES TAYLOR (b. 1948), THE EPITOME OF THE AMERICAN SINGER-SONGWRITER, WAS FRAIL AND TROUBLED FROM an early age, suffering from mental problems and heroin addiction by the age of 18. He travelled to London, where he signed to Apple. *James Taylor* was not a success, despite classic songs like 'Carolina On My Mind' and 'Something In The Way She Moves'.

Taylor secured a deal with Warner Brothers Records and released *Sweet Baby James*. The album eventually spent two years in the US charts. The follow-up *Mud Slide Slim And The Blue Horizon* consolidated the previous success and contained the definitive reading of **Carole King**'s 'You've Got a Friend'. In 1972, now free of drugs, Taylor worked with the **Beach Boys**' Dennis Wilson on the film *Two Lane Blacktop* and released *One Man Dog* which contained another hit 'Don't Let Me Be Lonely Tonight'. Taylor married **Carly Simon** and they duetted on 'Mockingbird' which made the US Top 5 in 1974.

Ironically most of his subsequent hits were non-originals: **Holland Dozier And Holland**'s 'How Sweet It Is', **Otis Blackwell**'s 'Handy Man', **Goffin** And King's 'Up On The Roof'. In 1985 Taylor released the strong *That's Why I'm Here*, and *Hourglass* in 1997 was well received by critics.

TAYLOR, JOHNNIE

TAYLOR (b. 1938) SURFACED AS PART OF SEVERAL AMERICAN GOSPEL GROUPS. FROM THERE HE JOINED THE SOUL STIRRERS, replacing **Sam Cooke**. Taylor switched to secular music in 1961. In 1965, he signed with Stax Records and had several R&B hits before 'Who's Making Love' (1968) reached *Billboard*'s Top 5. 'Disco Lady' (1976) was the first single to be certified platinum by the RIAA, but although subsequent releases reached the R&B chart they fared less well with the wider audience. *This Is The Night* (1984), reaffirmed his gritty, blues-edged approach, a feature consolidated on *Wall To Wall*, *Lover Boy* and *Crazy 'Bout You*. *Wanted: One Soul Singer*, *Who's Making Love* and *Taylored In Silk* best illustrate his lengthy period at Stax.

TEARDROP EXPLODES

THIS LIVERPOOL GROUP, ASSEMBLED BY VOCALIST **JULIAN COPE** (b. 1957), EMERGED IN LATE 1978 WITH A LINE-UP featuring Cope, Michael Finkler (guitar), Paul Simpson (keyboards) and Gary Dwyer (drums). They signed to Zoo and issued several singles; 'Treason (It's Just A Story)' was unlucky not to chart. The release of *Kilimanjaro* displayed the group as one of the most inventive and intriguing of their era. A repromoted/remixed version of 'Treason' belatedly charted, as did 'Passionate Friend'. In 1981, Cope recruited new members including Alfie Agius and Troy Tate. *Wilder* further displayed Cope's talent. In 1984, Cope embarked on a solo career.

TEARS FOR FEARS

UK SCHOOLFRIENDS ROLAND ORZABAL (b. 1961) AND CURT SMITH (b. 1961) FORMED TEARS FOR FEARS AFTER THEY HAD spent their teenage years in groups together. Their third single, 'Mad World', made UK number 3 in 1982 and *The Hurting* topped the UK charts. By *Songs From The Big Chair*, Orzabal was handling most of the vocal duties and had taken on the role of chief songwriter. 'Shout' and 'Everybody Wants To Rule The World' were number 1 hits in the US. In 1989, after a four-year break, they released *The Seeds Of Love*. Both the album and the title single were Top 10 hits in the US, but did not receive the same approval in the UK. Smith left the band in the early 90s to begin a solo career. Retaining the name of the band Orzabal released *Elemental*, the first album after Smith's departure. A muted response greeted *Raoul And The Kings Of Spain* in 1995.

TEENAGE FANCLUB

SCOTLAND-BASED TEENAGE FANCLUB ORIGINALLY COMPRISED NORMAN BLAKE (b. 1965; GUITAR/VOCALS), Raymond McGinley (b. 1964; guitar/vocals), Francis MacDonald (b. 1970; drums) and Gerard Love (b. 1967; bass/vocals). Shortly afterwards, MacDonald made way for Brendan O'Hare (b. 1970). Teenage Fanclub stamped their mark on 1990 with a series of drunken live shows and the erratic rock debut *A Catholic Education*. 1991's *Bandwagonesque* suggested a band ready to outgrow their humble independent origins, but a sense of disappointment accompanied the release of *Thirteen*. *Grand Prix* saw the introduction of new drummer Paul Quinn. *Songs From Northern Britain* showed further shades of the 60s and contained some of their finest moments. In 1997, they toured with **Radiohead**; however their own US tour was cancelled.

TELEVISION

LEAD GUITARIST/VOCALIST **TOM VERLAINE** (b. THOMAS MILLER, 1949) WORKED WITH BASSIST **RICHARD HELL** (b. Richard Myers, 1949) and drummer Billy Ficca as the Neon Boys; in 1973, they recruited rhythm guitarist Richard Lloyd and reunited as Television. In 1974 they were at the forefront of New York's new wave explosion. Hell was replaced by bassist Fred Smith. The new line-up recorded *Marquee Moon* – it was largely ignored in their homeland, but elicited ecstatic reviews in the UK. *Adventure* was a lesser work and the group broke up in 1978. In 1991, Verlaine, Lloyd, Smith and Ficca revived Television and rehearsed for a comeback album. They returned to Britain and appeared at the 1992 **Glastonbury Festival**.

TEMPERANCE 7

FORMED IN 1955 TO PLAY 20S-STYLE JAZZ, THE TEMPERANCE 7 CONSISTED AT VARIOUS TIMES OF WHISPERING PAUL McDowell (vocals), Captain Cephas Howard (trumpet/euphonium/various instruments), Joe Clark (clarinet), Alan Swainston-Cooper (pedal clarinet/swanee whistle), Philip 'Finger' Harrison (banjo/alto/baritone sax), Canon Colin Bowles (piano/harmonica), Clifford Beban (tuba), Brian Innes (drums), Dr. John Grieves-Watson (banjo), Sheik Haroun el John R. T. Davies (trombone/alto sax) and Frank Paverty (sousaphone). Their debut single, 'You're Driving Me Crazy', was followed by three more hits in 1961, 'Pasadena', 'Hard Hearted Hannah'/'Chili Bom Bom', and 'Charleston'. They split in the mid-60s, but re-formed in the 70s with Ted Wood.

TAYLOR, JAMES
Albums
Mud Slide Slim And The Blue Horizon (Warners 1971)★★★★
➧ p.381 for full listings
Collaborators
Beach Boys ➧ p.36
Carly Simon ➧ p.296
Connections
Peter Asher ➧ p.22
Paul McCartney ➧ p.229
Carole King ➧ p.205
Otis Blackwell ➧ p.52

TAYLOR, JOHNNIE
Albums
Looking For Johnny Taylor (Stax 1969)★★★★
➧ p.381 for full listings
Connections
Sam Cooke ➧ p.100

TEARDROP EXPLODES
Albums
Kilimanjaro (Mercury 1980)★★★
➧ p.381 for full listings
Collaborators
Julian Cope ➧ p.100

TEARS FOR FEARS
Albums
Songs From The Big Chair (Mercury 1985)★★★
➧ p.381 for full listings

Collaborators
Phil Collins ➧ p.98
Oleta Adams ➧ p.10

TEENAGE FANCLUB
Albums
Bandwagonesque (Creation 1991)★★★★
➧ p.381 for full listings

TELEVISION
Albums
Marquee Moon (Elektra 1978)★★★★
➧ p.381 for full listings
Collaborators
Tom Verlaine ➧ p.330
Richard Hell ➧ p.179

TEMPERANCE 7
Albums
Temperance 7 (Parlophone 1961)★★★★
➧ p.381 for full listings
Connections
Rolling Stones ➧ p.281

TEMPTATIONS
Albums
Meet The Temptations (Gordy 1964)★★★★
Psychedelic Shack (Tamla Motown 1970)★★★★
➧ p.381 for full listings
Collaborators
Diana Ross ➧ p.283
Supremes ➧ p.314
Connections
Motown ➧ p.240
Contours ➧ p.100
Further References
Book: *Temptations*, Otis Williams with Patricia Romanowski

10cc
Albums
Sheet Music (UK 1974)★★★
➧ p.381 for full listings

Connections
Godley And Creme ➧ p.164
Sad Cafe ➧ p.287
Paul McCartney ➧ p.229
Gilbert O'Sullivan ➧ p.250
Ramones ➧ p.272
Andrew Gold ➧ p.165
Further References
Book: *The 10cc Story*, George Tremlett

10,000 MANIACS
Albums
In My Tribe (Elektra 1987)★★★★
➧ p.381 for full listings
Collaborators
Natalie Merchant ➧ p.232
Connections
Peter Asher ➧ p.22
Further References
Video: *MTV Unplugged* (1994)

TEN YEARS AFTER
Albums
Undead (Deram 1968)★★★★
➧ p.381 for full listings

TERRORVISION
Albums
How To Make Friends And Influence People (Total Vegas 1994)★★★★
Regular Urban Survivors (Total Vegas 1996)★★★★
➧ p.381 for full listings

TEX, JOE
Albums
I've Got To Do A Little Better (Atlantic 1966)★★★★
➧ p.381 for full listings
Connections
James Brown ➧ p.70

TEMPTATIONS

FORMED IN 1961 IN DETROIT, MICHIGAN, USA, THE TEMPTATIONS WERE MADE UP OF EDDIE KENDRICKS (b. 1939) and Paul Williams (b. 1939, d. 1973) who both sang with the Primes, Melvin Franklin (b. David English, 1942, d. 1995), Eldridge Bryant and Otis Williams (b. Otis Miles 1941) who came from the Distants. Berry Gordy signed them to **Motown** in 1961 and the group's classic line-up was established in 1963, when Bryant was replaced by David Ruffin (b. 1941). 'The Way You Do The Things You Do' was the Temptations' first major hit, a simple rhythm number featuring a typically cunning series of lyrical images. 'My Girl' in 1965, the group's first US number 1, brought Ruffin's vocals to the fore for the first time. 'Get Ready' embodied all the excitement of the Motown rhythm factory, blending an irresistible melody with a stunning vocal arrangement. Norman Whitfield became the Temptations' producer in 1966 and introduced a new rawness into their sound.

The peak of Whitfield's initial phase with the group was 'I Wish It Would Rain'. The record gave the Temptations their sixth R&B number 1 in three years. It also marked the end of an era, as David Ruffin elected to leave for a solo career. He was replaced by ex-**Contour** Dennis Edwards. Over the next four years, Whitfield and the Temptations pioneered the concept of psychedelic soul. 'Runaway Child, Running Wild' examined the problems of teenage rebellion; 'I Can't Get Next To You' reflected the fragmentation of personal relationships (and topped the US charts with the group's second number 1 hit); and 'Ball Of Confusion' bemoaned the disintegrating fabric of American society. The new direction alarmed Eddie Kendricks, who left in 1971, after another US number 1, 'Just My Imagination'. He was replaced first by Richard Owens, then in 1971 by Damon Harris. This line-up recorded the 1972 number 1, 'Papa Was A Rolling Stone', which remains one of Motown's finest achievements. After that, everything was an anti-climax. Paul Williams left the group in 1971, to be replaced by Richard Street. Whitfield's partnership with Strong was broken the same year, and although he continued to rework the 'Papa Was A Rolling Stone' formula, the commercial and artistic returns were smaller. The Temptations still had hits, and 'Masterpiece', 'Let Your Hair Down' (both 1973) and 'Happy People' (1975) all topped the soul charts, but they were no longer a leading force in black music.

10cc

ERIC STEWART (b. 1945; VOCALS/GUITAR/KEYBOARDS), LOL CREME (b. LAWRENCE CREME, 1947; VOCALS/GUITAR/keyboards), Kevin Godley (b. 1945; vocals/drums) and Graham Gouldman (b. 1945; vocals/bass guitar) formed English group 10cc and launched their recording career with 'Donna'. The song reached UK number 2, spearheading a run which continued almost uninterrupted until the end of the decade. The chart-topping 'Rubber Bullets', the high school romp 'The Dean And I', the sardonic 'Wall Street Shuffle', zestful 'Silly Love' and mock-philosophical 'Life Is A Minestrone' were all delightful slices of 70s pop. In 1975, the group reached number 1 with the tragi-comic 'I'm Not In Love', but internal strife began to undermine progress. In 1976, the group split. Stewart and Gouldman toured as 10cc with a line-up comprising Tony O'Malley (keyboards), Rick Fenn (guitar) and Stuart Tosh (drums) and charted with 'The Things We Do For Love' and 'Dreadlock Holiday'. The hits ceased after 1982 and Stewart and Gouldman went on to pursue other ventures until 1992 when the duo issued a new album as 10cc.

10,000 MANIACS

THIS AMERICAN GROUP WAS LED BY VOCALIST **NATALIE MERCHANT** (b. 1963) AND BACKED BY JEROME AUGUSTYNIAK (drums), Robert Buck (guitar), Dennis Drew (keyboards) and Steven Gustafson (bass). The group started playing together in 1981; their music encompassed folk and world traditions. They were signed to Elektra Records in 1985 and after a UK tour recorded *The Wishing Chair*. **Peter Asher** produced *In My Tribe*, and *Blind Man's Zoo*. *Our Time In Eden*, included the lilting 'Noah's Dove' and the punchy 'Few And Far Between'. In 1993, Merchant departed to pursue her solo career. 10,000 Maniacs persevered by recruiting former member John Lombardo and new lead singer Mary Ramsey. The new album was pleasant but unremarkable. In 1997–98, they were back on the road.

TEN YEARS AFTER

FORMED IN NOTTINGHAM, ENGLAND, THE QUARTET OF ALVIN LEE (b. 1944; GUITAR/VOCALS), CHICK CHURCHILL (b. 1949; keyboards), Ric Lee (b. 1945; drums) and Leo Lyons (b. 1943; bass) played a mixture of rock 'n' roll and blues. *Undead* showed that Lee was an outstanding guitarist and over the next two years they delivered four chart albums, of which *Ssssh*, was the strongest. By the time of *Rock 'N' Roll To The World* the band were jaded and they rested from touring to work on solo projects. When they reconvened, their spark had all but gone. After months of rumour, Lee admitted that the band had broken up. In 1989 the original band re-formed and released *About Time*.

TERRORVISION

THIS QUARTET FROM BRADFORD, ENGLAND FORMED IN 1986 AS SPOILT BRATZ, AND QUICKLY fused rock, funk and thrash influences. Singer Tony Wright (b. 1968), guitarist Mark Yates (b. 1968), Leigh Marklew (b. 1968) and Shutty (b. 1967; drums) were signed by EMI with their own label name, Total Vegas. *Formaldehyde* produced minor hits in 'American TV' and 'New Policy One'. 1994 saw their UK Top 30 breakthrough, 'My House'. *How To Make Friends And Influence People* entered the UK Top 20 and produced four more Top 30 singles. Terrorvision finally made the big screen with *Regular Urban Survivors*.

TEX, JOE

TEX (b. JOSEPH ARRINGTON JNR, 1933, d. 1982) WON FIRST PLACE IN A 1954 TALENT CONTEST AT THE APOLLO AND duly secured a record deal. **James Brown**'s version of 'Baby You're Right' (1962) became a US R&B number 2, and Tex was signed by Buddy Killen. In 1965, 'Hold On To What You've Got' was a US Top 5 hit. Later releases were less successful. A fallow period ended with 'I Gotcha' (1972), but Tex chose this moment to retire. He returned to music in 1975 and in 1977 he enjoyed a 'comeback' hit with 'Ain't Gonna Bump No More (With No Big Fat Woman)'. He was tempted into a Soul Clan reunion in 1981, but in 1982 he died following a heart attack.

THAT PETROL EMOTION

THE BAND WAS ORIGINALLY FORMED WHEN THE O'NEILL BROTHERS – SEAN (GUITAR) AND DAMIAN (BASS) – PARTED from Irish band, the **Undertones**. They added Ciaran McLaughlin (drums), Reamann O'Gormain (guitar; ex-Bam Bam And The Calling), and Seattle-born frontman Steve Mack (vocals). Both their pop-based debut and *Babble* were dominated by frantic guitar and Mack's wholehearted delivery. *End Of The Millenium Psychosis Blues* included the controversial ballad 'Cellophane' and 'Under The Sky'. Sean O'Neill elected to give family matters more prominence and returned to Derry. His brother switched to guitar with John Marchini taking over on bass. *Chemicrazy* was exceptionally strong, especially on singles 'Hey Venus' and 'Sensitize'. After one more album, the group split in 1994.

THE THE

FORMED IN 1979, THIS UK GROUP CENTRED ON THE ACTIVITIES OF SINGER-SONGWRITER MATT JOHNSON. INITIALLY THE LINE-UP featured Johnson alone. The The's first single, 'Controversial Subject', was issued by 4AD Records. Two years later, they signed with Stevo's Some Bizzare Records and released 'Cold Spell Ahead'. Johnson issued *Burning Blue Soul* for them under his own name. A projected album, *The Pornography Of Despair*, was vetoed by the uncompromising Johnson. It was eventually replaced by the superb *Soul Mining*, one of the most critically acclaimed albums of 1983. Three years passed before the release of *Infected*. In 1988, Johnson established a new version of The The featuring ex-**Smiths** guitarist Johnny Marr, bassist James Eller and drummer Dave Palmer for *Mind Bomb*. *Hanky Panky* saw Johnson deliver 11 cover versions of **Hank Williams**' songs to coincide with the publication of a biography on the subject.

THEM

THE ORIGINAL LINE-UP – **VAN MORRISON** (b. 1945; VOCALS/HARMONICA), BILLY HARRISON (GUITAR), ERIC WRIXEN (keyboards), Alan Henderson (bass) and Ronnie Millings (drums) forged an uncompromising brand of R&B. They moved to London from Belfast and issued their debut single, 'Don't Start Crying Now', which flopped. Brothers Patrick and Jackie McAuley had replaced Wrixen and Millings by the time Them's second single, 'Baby Please Don't Go' reached the UK Top 10. It was backed by the Morrison-penned 'Gloria'. The follow-up, 'Here Comes The Night', peaked at number 2. **Peter Bardens** replaced Jackie McAuley for the group's debut album. By the release of *Them Again*, the unit had been recast around Morrison, Henderson, Herbie Armstrong (bass guitar), Ray Elliott (saxophone/keyboards) and John Wilson (drums). This set boasted several highlights, including the **Bob Dylan** composition 'It's All Over Now, Baby Blue'. Them disintegrated in 1966 following a US tour. Morrison then began a highly prolific solo career.

THERAPY?

NORTHERN IRISH HARD ROCK/INDIE-METAL TRIO: MICHAEL McKEEGAN (BASS), ANDY CAIRNS (GUITAR/VOCALS) AND FYFE Ewing (drums). Their debut, 'Meat Abstract'/ 'Punishment Kiss', was added to new material for a mini-album, *Baby Teeth*. This was followed by a second abbreviated set, *Pleasure Death*. Therapy? signed to A&M in 1992, and collected a much bigger budget for a new album, *Nurse*. In 1993, 'Screamager' made the UK Top 10. Almost a year later *Troublegum* was unveiled, which returned to more familiar Therapy? elements – buzzsaw guitar, harsh but persistent melodies and musical adrenalin. In 1995, *Infernal Love* offered the trademark grinding hardcore sound alongside ballads, string quartets and upbeat lyrics. They continue to record and undertook an extensive European tour in 1998.

THESE ANIMAL MEN

THESE ANIMAL MEN'S DEBUT SINGLE WAS 'SPEEED KING', A TRIBUTE TO THE POWER OF AMPHETAMINES. THE BAND WAS FORMED in Brighton by Hooligan (b. Julian; guitar) and Patrick (bass). They added additional members Boag (vocals) and Stevie (drums) on 'You're Not My Babylon'. 'Too Sussed' broke the UK Top 40, and brought the band to the *Top Of The Pops* stage. Following the *Taxi* mini-album and the loss of Stevie, the band released *Accident And Emergency*, which showed no signs of bowing to either fashion or musical conformity.

THEY MIGHT BE GIANTS

JOHN FLANSBURGH AND JOHN LINNELL FORMED THIS NEW YORK-BASED DUO IN 1984. *LINCOLN* BECAME THE BIGGEST-selling independent album of 1989 in the USA. *Flood* showcased their obtuse lyrical approach. While *Apollo 18* brought minor hits in 'The Statue Got Me High' and 'The Guitar (The Lion Sleeps Tonight)', *John Henry* saw them introduce a full band for the first time. In 1995 the band appeared, with 'Sensurround', on the film soundtrack, *Mighty Morphin Power Rangers*.

THAT PETROL EMOTION
Albums
Babble (Polydor 1987)★★★★
p.381 for full listings
Connections
Undertones p.327
Influences
Sonic Youth p.302

THE THE
Albums
Soul Mining (Some Bizzare 1983)★★★
Dusk (Epic 1993)★★★
p.381 for full listings
Collaborators
Smiths p.301
Connections
Hank Williams p.339
Further References
Video: *Versus The World* (Sony Music Video 1991)

THEM
Albums
Them aka *The Angry Young Them* (Decca 1965)★★★★
p.381 for full listings
Collaborators
Van Morrison p.238
Peter Bardens p.33
Connections
Bert Berns p.44
Bob Dylan p.128
Further References
Book: *Van Morrison: A Portrait Of The Artist*, Johnny Rogan

THERAPY?
Albums
Troublegum (A&M 1994)★★★★
p.381 for full listings

THESE ANIMAL MEN
Albums
Accident And Emergency (Hut 1997)★★★
p.381 for full listings

THEY MIGHT BE GIANTS
Albums
Lincoln (Bar/None 1989)★★★
John Henry (Elektra 1994)★★★
Factory Showroom (Elektra 1996)★★★
p.381 for full listings
Collaborators
John Flansburgh
John Linnell
Influences
Ramones p.272
Love p.218
Further References
Video: *They Might Be Giants* (Warner Music Video 1991)

THIN LIZZY
Albums
Jailbreak (Vertigo 1976)★★★★
Live And Dangerous (Vertigo 1978)★★★★
➽ p.381 for full listings
Collaborators
Philip Lynott ➽ p.220
Midge Ure ➽ p.327
Connections
Bob Geldof ➽ p.160
Manfred Mann Earth Band ➽ p.223
Further References
Book: *Thin Lizzy: The Approved Biography*, Chris Salewicz

THIRD EYE BLIND
Albums
Third Eye Blind (Elektra 1997)
➽ p.381 for full listings
Connections
Oasis ➽ p.250
James ➽ p.196

THIRTEENTH FLOOR ELEVATORS
Albums
The Psychedelic Sounds Of The Thirteenth Floor Elevators (International 1966)★★★★
➽ p.381 for full listings
Collaborators
Roky Erickson ➽ p.138

THOMPSON, RICHARD
Albums
Small Town Romance (Hannibal 1984)★★★★
➽ p.381 for full listings
Collaborators
Linda Thompson ➽ p.320
Gregson and Collister ➽ p.169
Connections
Fairport Convention ➽ p.141
Golden Palominos ➽ p.165
Further References
Video: *Across A Crowded Room* (Sony 1983)
Book: *Richard Thompson: Strange Affair, The Biography*, Patrick Humphries

THOMPSON, RICHARD AND LINDA
Albums
Shoot Out The Lights (Hannibal 1982)★★★★★
➽ p.381 for full listings

THOMPSON TWINS
Albums
Quick Step And Side Kick (Arista 1983)★★★
➽ p.381 for full listings
Connections
Soft Boys ➽ p.302
Deborah Harry ➽ p.176
Further References
Book: *The Thompson Twins: An Odd Couple*, Rose Rouce

THIN LIZZY

FORMED IN DUBLIN IN 1969 BY **PHIL LYNOTT** (b. 1951, d. 1986; VOCALS/BASS), ERIC BELL (b. 1947; GUITAR) AND BRIAN Downey (b. 1951; drums). After two early albums and no success, they recorded a version of the Irish traditional song, 'Whiskey In The Jar', which became a hit and changed their fortunes. *Vagabonds of the Western World* cemented their reputation as a creative hard rock band and when Bell quit and rising new guitarist **Gary Moore** took his place, progress seemed assured. However, Moore was not to last either, establishing Lizzy's career-long enigma with lead guitarists. Andy Gee and John Cann floated in and out before the most successful group of Lynott, Downey, Californian Scott Gorham (b. 1951) and **Brian Robertson** (b. 1956) came together. They had big worldwide hits with the anthemic 'The Boys Are Back In Town' and *Jailbreak*. Problems hit when Lynott was struck down with hepatitis just before they released *Johnny The Fox*, and after when Robertson badly injured his hand following his penchant for fighting. Moore was drafted back in to take over from Robbo. It was purely temporary, though, and as a three-piece, Lynott, Gorham and Downey recorded *Bad Reputation*. The definitive live set *Live And Dangerous* seemed to put Lizzy firmly back on the trail. When Robertson went off the tracks again, back came Moore to record *Bad Reputation*, another mature set, but only lasted to the middle of an American tour. Old friend, **Midge Ure**, was brought on to back Gorham on stage and stayed on as back-up. He finished a Japanese tour before Snowy White took up the permanent co-guitarist slot for *Chinatown* and *Renegade*. The guitarist problem continued and when White departed, John Sykes took over. His arrival, though, coincided with a downward slide for Thin Lizzy. Drugs had taken a hold and sales were slipping. Sykes was there for the patchy *Thunder And Lightning*, before Lynott and Gorham decided to split the band in 1984. An even patchier live album, *Life-Live*, was issued at the end of that year. Ironically when Lynott died after an accident at his home, exacerbated by his extensive use of drugs, he had been talking seriously to Gorham about re-forming the band for a series of summer gigs and an album. In May 1986, Thin Lizzy re-formed for the Self Aid concert organized in Eire by **Bob Geldof**, who replaced Lynott on vocals for the day.

THIRD EYE BLIND

FORMED IN SAN FRANCISCO, CALIFORNIA, USA, CONTEMPORARY ROCK BAND THIRD EYE BLIND WERE LED BY SINGER-songwriter Stephan Jenkins. They supported **Oasis** in San Francisco; they also took over the headliners' billing when Tim Booth of **James** was forced to cancel a series of concerts because of illness. Their first single, 'Semi-Charmed Life', became a number 1 hit on *Billboard*'s Modern Rock chart. Their self-titled debut album easily broke into the *Billboard* Top 100 following its release in 1997.

THIRTEENTH FLOOR ELEVATORS

FORMED IN TEXAS, USA, IN 1965, THE ORIGINAL LINE-UP INCLUDED STACY SUTHERLAND (GUITAR), BENNIE Thurman (bass), John Ike Walton (drums) and Max Rainey (vocals). The latter was soon replaced by **Roky Erickson** (vocals/guitar). Lyricist and jug player Tommy Hall also joined and they changed their name. The Elevators made their recording debut with 'You're Gonna Miss Me'.

The Psychedelic Sounds Of ... combined off-beat spiritualism with R&B. After a brief break-up in 1967, Hall, Erickson and Sutherland regrouped to record *Easter Everywhere*. Studio out-takes were overdubbed with fake applause to create *Live*, while a final collection, *Bull Of The Woods*, coupled partially-completed performances with older, unissued masters. The Elevators disintegrated when Erickson was committed to a mental institution and Sutherland was imprisoned. Sunderland was later shot dead by his wife.

THOMPSON, RICHARD

THOMPSON (b. 1949) FORGED HIS REPUTATION AS GUITARIST, VOCALIST AND COMPOSER WITH **FAIRPORT Convention**. He left Fairport in 1971 and completed *Henry The Human Fly*. He then forged a professional partnership with his wife, Linda Peters and, as **Richard And Linda Thompson**, recorded a series of excellent albums.

The Thompsons separated in 1982, although the guitarist had completed his second solo album, *Strict Tempo*, the previous year. He recorded an in-concert set, *Small Town Romance*, followed by *Hand Of Kindness* and *Across The Crowded Room*. In 1986, Thompson promoted Daring Adventures, leading a group which included **Clive Gregson** and **Christine Collister**. He then completed the soundtrack to *The Marksman*, a BBC television series, before joining John French, Fred Frith and Henry Kaiser for the experi-mental *Live, Love, Larf And Loaf*. Thompson recorded with the **Golden Palominos** in 1991 and the same year performed with **David Byrne**. He continues to tour regularly.

THOMPSON, RICHARD AND LINDA

THIS HUSBAND-AND-WIFE FOLK/ROCK DUO BEGAN PERFORMING TOGETHER OFFICIALLY IN 1972. **RICHARD THOMPSON** (b. 1949; guitar/vocals) and Linda began a professional, and personal, relationship, introduced on *I Want To See The Bright Lights Tonight*. *Pour Down Like Silver* reflected the couple's growing interest in the Sufi faith.

After a three-year hiatus, *Sunnyvista* included the satiric title track and the angry and passionate 'You're Going To Need Somebody'. *Shoot Out The Lights* was nominated by **Rolling Stone** as the best album of 1982. Their marriage disintegrated, however, and later that year the duo made their final appearance together. Richard Thompson then resumed his solo career, while Linda went on to record *One Clear Moment* (1985).

THOMPSON TWINS

FORMED IN 1977, THE LINE-UP OF THIS ENGLISH-BASED GROUP FEATURED TOM BAILEY (b. 1957; VOCALS/KEYBOARDS/percussion), Peter Dodd (b. 1953; guitar), John Roog (guitar/vocals/percussion) and drummer Chris Bell. In 1981 their line-up expanded to include Joe Leeway (b. 1957; percussion/vocals), Alannah Currie (b. 1959; percussion/saxophone), and Matthew Seligman (bass, ex-**Soft Boys**). *A Product Of* ... showed a band struggling to make the transition from stage to studio. Producer Steve Lillywhite took them in hand for *Set*, and the Bailey-penned 'In The Name Of Love' saw them achieve their first UK/US hit. Four of the band were jettisoned, leaving just Bailey, Currie and Leeway. *Quick Step And Side Kick* rose to number 2 in 1983. 'Hold Me Now', 'Doctor Doctor' and 'You Take Me Up' put them firmly in the first division of UK pop acts, and further minor hits followed. Leeway left at the end of 1986. Bailey and Currie formed Babble in 1994.

THOROGOOD, GEORGE

US BLUES GUITARIST GEORGE THOROGOOD (b. 1952) FORMED THE DESTROYERS IN DELAWARE BEFORE MOVING THEM to Boston, where they backed visiting blues stars. The Destroyers comprised Thorogood (guitar), Michael Lenn (bass) and Jeff Simon (drums), Ron Smith played guitar on-and-off to complete the quartet. The band opened for the **Rolling Stones** at several of their American gigs and continued to record throughout the 80s. In 1985 they appeared at Live Aid playing with blues legend **Albert Collins**. Thorogood has continued to record throughout the 90s.

3 COLOURS RED

HARD ROCK BAND 3 COLOURS RED WERE FORMED IN LONDON, ENGLAND, IN 1994. Comprising Pete Vuckovic (b. 1971; vocals, bass; ex-**Diamond Head**), Chris McCormack (b. 1973; guitar,), Ben Harding (b. 1965; guitar) and Keith Baxter (b. 1971; drums), their early stage show combined the earnest ferocity of garage rock with memorable pop hooklines. McCormack and Baxter worked on Glen Matlock's 1996 solo album, *Who's He Think He Is When He's At Home*. At the same time their debut single, 'This Is My Hollywood', was released. The debut album *Pure*, attempted to consolidate on the modest success of their chart singles. A second album was projected for 1998.

THREE DEGREES

THIS PHILADELPHIA-BASED GROUP COMPRISED FAYETTE PICKNEY, LINDA TURNER AND SHIRLEY PORTER. THEY SCORED a US hit with their first single, 'Gee Baby (I'm Sorry)', in 1965. Sheila Ferguson and Valerie Holiday then joined the line-up in place of Turner and Porter. They shared vocals with **MFSB** on 'TSOP', the theme song to television's successful *Soul Train* show. This US number 1 preceded the trio's international hits, 'Year Of Decision' and 'When Will I See You Again?'. 'Take Good Care Of Yourself', 'Woman In Love' and 'My Simple Heart' were UK hits. Helen Scott appeared on the 1976 album *Standing Up For Love*.

THREE DOG NIGHT

THIS US HARMONY ROCK TRIO FORMED IN 1968 WITH A LINE-UP COMPRISING DANNY HUTTON (b. DANIEL Anthony Hutton, 1942), Cory Wells (b. 1942) and Chuck Negron (b. Charles Negron, 1942). They were backed by Jim Greenspoon (b. 1948; organ), Joe Schermie (b. 1948; bass), Mike Allsup (b. 1947; guitar) and Floyd Sneed (b. 1943; drums). They had 21 *Billboard* Top 40 hits between 1969-75. Both **Nilsson** and **Laura Nyro** first glimpsed the Top 10 courtesy of Three Dog Night's covers of 'One' and 'Eli's Coming', respectively. The risqué 'Mama Told Me Not To Come' provided the same service for **Randy Newman** while also giving the group their first number 1 in 1970. The departure of Danny Hutton precipitated the group's decline and disbandment.

THROWING MUSES

FORMED IN NEWPORT, LONG ISLAND, USA, BY STEP-SISTERS KRISTIN HERSH (b. *c.* 1966; VOCALS/GUITAR) AND TANYA Donelly (b. 1966; vocals/guitar), with Elaine Adamedes (bass) and David Narcizo (drums). Adamedes was replaced by Leslie Langston, who, in turn, was replaced by Fred Abong for *The Real Ramona*. Donelly announced her permanent departure from the Muses, although she stayed on for the subsequent tour. After this the core of the group comprised Hersh, Narcizo and Bernard Georges (bass). This line-up recorded the critically acclaimed *Red Heaven*, but the group broke up the following year. They regrouped in 1994 and released *University*. They continue to record and Hersh has released a solo album.

THUNDERCLAP NEWMAN

ALTHOUGH SINGER/COMPOSER SPEEDY KEEN (b. JOHN KEEN, 1945) WROTE MUCH OF THIS SHORT-LIVED GROUP'S material, its impact was derived from the quirky, old-fashioned image of pianist Andy Newman. Guitarist Jimmy McCulloch (b. 1953, d. 1979) completed the original line-up responsible for 'Something In The Air', a soaring, optimistic song which hit UK number 1 in 1969. After *Hollywood Dream* – despite the addition of new members Jim Pitman-Avory (bass) and Jack McCulloch (drums) – Thunderclap Newman broke up.

THUNDERS, JOHNNY

JOHNNY THUNDERS (b. JOHN ANTHONY GENZALE JNR, 1952, d. 1991) FIRST GAINED RECOGNITION AS A MEMBER OF THE **New York Dolls**. The guitarist joined a local band called Actress, which included in their line-up two other future Dolls members, Arthur Kane and Billy Murcia. They evolved into the New York Dolls in late 1971. Genzale, now renamed Johnny Thunders left the band in 1975 and along with drummer Jerry Nolan and **Richard Hell** formed the **Heartbreakers**. Thunders earned a reputation for his shambling stage performances owing to an excess of drugs and alcohol. His first solo collection, *So Alone*, found him supported by many UK musicians, including **Phil Lynott**, Peter Perrett, Steve Jones and Paul Cook (**Sex Pistols**), **Steve Marriott** (**Humble Pie/Small Faces**) and Paul Gray (**Eddie And The Hot Rods/Damned**). Thunders was found dead in a hotel room in New Orleans in 1991.

TIKARAM, TANITA

TIKARAM'S (b. 1969) INTENSE LYRICS BROUGHT HER INSTANT COMMERCIAL SUCCESS AT THE AGE OF 19. TIKARAM BEGAN writing songs and in 1987 played her first gig. *Ancient Heart* (1988) included the hits 'Good Tradition' and 'Twist In My Sobriety', most of 1989 was spent on tour before releasing her second album; this included 'We Almost Got It Together' and 'Thursday's Child'. *Everybody's Angel* featured harmony vocals by **Jennifer Warnes**.

TILLOTSON, JOHNNY

TILLOTSON'S (b. 1939) FIRST SINGLE IN 1958 COMBINED THE TEEN BALLAD 'DREAMY EYES' WITH THE UP-TEMPO 'WELL, I'm Your Man'. Although his roots were in country music, he was encouraged to revive the R&B ballads 'Never Let Me Go', 'Pledging My Love' and 'Earth Angel'. In 1960 he released the teen-ballad 'Poetry In Motion', which went to number 2 in the USA and number 1 in the UK. He had further success by reviving country songs. 'Talk Back Trembling Lips' was a US Top 10 hit, but his subsequent records only reached the Top 40.

THOROGOOD, GEORGE
Albums
Move It On Over (Rounder 1978)★★★
➽ p.381 for full listings
Collaborators
Albert Collins ➽ p.97
Connections
Rolling Stones ➽ p.281

3 COLOURS RED
Albums
Pure (Creation 1997)★★★
➽ p.381 for full listings
Connections
Diamond Head ➽ p.117

THREE DEGREES
Albums
Three Degrees (Philadelphia International 1974)★★★
➽ p.381 for full listings
Collaborators
MFSB ➽ p.233

THREE DOG NIGHT
Albums
Captured Live It Ain't Easy (Dunhill 1970)★★★★
➽ p.381 for full listings
Connections
Nilsson ➽ p.247
Laura Nyro ➽ p.249
Randy Newman ➽ p.246

THROWING MUSES
Albums
University (Warners/4AD 1995)★★★★
➽ p.381 for full listings
Connections
Belly ➽ p.42

Thunderclap Newman
Albums
Hollywood Dream (Track 1970)★★★
➽ p.381 for full listings
Collaborators
Wings ➽ p.340

THUNDERS, JOHNNY
Albums
So Alone (Real 1978)★★★★
➽ p.381 for full listings
Collaborators
New York Dolls ➽ p.246
Richard Hell ➽ p.179
Connections
Heartbreakers ➽ p.178
Phil Lynott ➽ p.220
Sex Pistols ➽ p.292
Steve Marriott ➽ p.225
Further References
Book: *Johnny Thunders: In Cold Blood*, Nina Antonia

TIKARAM, TANITA
Albums
Ancient Heart (Warners 1988)★★★★
➽ p.381 for full listings
Collaborators
Jennifer Warnes ➽ p.333

TILLOTSON, JOHNNY
Albums
No Love At All (MGM 1966)★★★
➽ p.381 for full listings

TINDERSTICKS
Albums
Curtains (This Way Up 1997)★★★★
➽ p.381 for full listings

TLC
Albums
CrazySexyCool (LaFace/ Arista 1995)★★★★
➽ p.381 for full listings

TOAD THE WET SPROCKET
Albums
Dulcinea (Columbia 1994)★★★
➽ p.381 for full listings

TORNADOS
Albums
Away From It All (1964)★★★
➽ p.381 for full listings
Connections
Shadows ➽ p.293

TOSH, PETER
Albums
Equal Rights (Virgin 1977)★★★★
➽ p.381 for full listings
Collaborators
Bob Marley And The Wailers ➽ p.225
Connections
Mick Jagger ➽ p.281
Temptations ➽ p.318
Further References
Video: *Downpresser Man* (1988)

TOTO
Albums
Toto IV (Columbia 1982)★★★★
➽ p.381 for full listings

TOURE, ALI FARKA
Albums
with Ry Cooder *Talking Timbuktu* (World Circuit 1994)★★★★
➽ p.381 for full listings
Collaborators
Ry Cooder ➽ p.100
Influences
Robert Johnson ➽ p.200

TINDERSTICKS

FORMED IN NOTTINGHAM, UK, TINDERSTICKS REVOLVED AROUND SINGER STUART STAPLES. DICKON HINCHCLIFFE (violin), Dave Boulter (keyboards), Neil Fraser (guitar), Mark Colwill (bass) and Al McCauley (drums) completed the act. The sextet made its debut in 1992 with 'Patchwork'. A second single, 'Marbles', presaged 'A Marriage Made In Heaven'. *Unwired EP* and *Tindersticks* were well received. The *Kathleen* EP then gave the group its first UK chart hit. The group's second studio album featured Terry Edwards of Gallon Drunk and a second live album was recorded with a full 28-piece orchestra. The stable line-up remained for *Curtains.*

TLC

THIS FEMALE TRIO FROM ATLANTA, GEORGIA, USA, COMPRISED LISA 'LEFT EYE' LOPES, ROZANDA 'CHILLI' THOMAS and T-Boz (b. Tionne Watkins). They found chart success with 'Ain't 2 Proud 2 Beg', 'Baby-Baby-Baby' and 'What About Your Friends'. *CrazySexyCool* went quadruple platinum in America, but nevertheless the group was forced to file for bankruptcy in 1995. However, they picked up two Grammys in 1996: Best R&B Performance By A Duo Or Group With Vocal for 'Creep' and Best R&B Album for *CrazySexyCool*. A new album is expected in 1999.

TOAD THE WET SPROCKET

THIS US ROCK BAND WAS FORMED IN THE MID-80S IN SANTA BARBARA, CALIFORNIA, BY DEAN DINNING (BASS/ backing vocals/keyboards), Randy Guss (drums), Todd Nichols (guitar/vocals) and Glen Phillips (vocals/guitar/keyboards). Made for just $650, their debut album sold at local stores and gigs. It allowed them to finance the release of a second set, before signing to Columbia Records in 1988. The group's major label debut, *Fear*, followed in 1991. *Dulcinea* took its title from the love of Don Quixote's life – the idea of unattainable perfection was central to the album's concept. On *Coil* the band abandoned their pop format and went for a harder-edged sound with deeper lyrics. A new album was rumoured in 1998.

TORNADOS

THE ONLY SERIOUS CHALLENGERS TO THE **SHADOWS** AS BRITAIN'S TOP INSTRUMENTAL UNIT, THE TORNADOS LASTED only as long as their console svengali, independent record producer Joe Meek. Meek recruited Alan Caddy (b. 1940; guitar) and drummer Clem Cattini (b. 1939). Guitarist George Bellamy (b. 1941; guitar) and Roger Lavern (b. Roger Jackson, 1938; keyboards) were session players while Heinz Burt (b. 1942) on bass was one of Meek's own protégés.

The Tornados made the big time with a second single, 'Telstar'. In 1962, it topped the domestic hit parade in the UK and the US. 1963 saw 'Globetrotter', 'Robot' and 'The Ice Cream Man' all cracking the UK Top 20. The exit of Burt, coupled with the levelling blow of the beat boom and its emphasis on vocals rendered the Tornados *passé*. Following the departure of Cattini, the last original Tornado, there came further desperate strategies until Meek's suicide and the outfit's disbandment.

TOSH, PETER

TOSH (b. WINSTON HUBERT McINTOSH, 1944, d. 1987) FIRST GAINED RECOGNITION IN **BOB MARLEY'S Wailers.** He was the first to emerge from the morass of doo-wop wails and chants that constituted the Wailers' early records, recording as Peter Tosh or Peter Touch And The Wailers on 'Hoot Nanny Hoot', 'Shame And Scandal', and 'Maga Dog'. He also made records without the Wailers and with Rita Anderson, Marley's future wife.

Despite contributing 'Get Up Stand Up' to the Wailer's *Burnin'*, Tosh quit the group in 1973. The patronage of Mick Jagger nearly gave him a chart hit with a cover of the **Temptations** 'Don't Look Back'. *Bush Doctor* sold well, but *Mystic Man* and *Wanted, Dread & Alive*, did not. He also released three albums with EMI, the last, *No Nuclear War*, was his best since *Legalize It*. The record won the first best reggae album Grammy Award in 1988, but by then Tosh was dead, shot in a robbery on his home in Kingston.

TOTO

THIS LOS ANGELES SESSION TEAM OF BOBBY KIMBALL (b. ROBERT TOTEAUX, 1947; VOCALS), STEVE LUKATHER (b. 1957; guitar), David Paitch (b. 1954; keyboards/vocals), Steve Porcaro (b. 1957; keyboards/vocals), David Hungate (bass) and Jeff Porcaro (b. 1954, d. 1992; drums) decided in 1978 to perform in their own right after years of supporting others on tour and disc. 1979's *Toto* was attended by a smash hit in 'Hold The Line', but the band's most commercial period was 1982-83 when the Grammy award winning *Toto IV* spawned two international hits with 'Africa' and 'Rosanna', as well as the US Top 10 single, 'I Won't Hold You Back'. The following year, Kimball and Hungate were replaced by Dave Fergie Frederikson (b. 1951) and Mike Porcaro (b. 1955). Sales of *Isolation* and the soundtrack to the film *Dune* were poor. With a new lead singer, Joseph Williams, the group made the big time again with 'I'll Be Over You'. Two years later, Toto re-entered the US Top 40, with 'Pamela'. Jeff Porcaro died after a heart attack and his replacement on subsequent British dates was session drummer Simon Phillips.

TOURE, ALI FARKA

TOURE PLAYED IN A STYLE UNCANNILY CLOSE TO THE ORIGINAL DELTA BLUES OF **ROBERT JOHNSON** AND HIS SUCCESSORS. This coincidence, picked up on by adventurous British world-music critics and broadcasters in the late 80s, gave him a brief flush of popularity in Europe and the USA. His career took a dramatic turn in 1994 when, after a meeting with **Ry Cooder** in 1992 they recorded the album *Talking Timbuktu* together – a success musically, artistically and commercially.

TOURISTS

THE TOURISTS WERE NOTABLE AS THE FIRST SETTING IN WHICH THE DAVID A. STEWART/**ANNIE LENNOX** PARTNERship came into the spotlight. The band grew out of an earlier duo formed by guitarist Stewart (b. 1952) with fellow Sunderland singer-songwriter Pete Coombes. They met Lennox (b. 1954), and as Catch they made one single, 'Black Blood' 1977), before re-forming as the five-strong Tourists with Jim Toomey (drums) and Eddie Chin (bass). Their first success came with a revival of the 1963 **Dusty Springfield** hit 'I Only Want To Be With You' and 'So Good To Be Back Home Again', which both reached the Top 10. *Luminous Basement* sold poorly and after a final UK tour the band split in 1980. Lennox and Stewart re-emerged the following year as the **Eurythmics**.

TOUSSAINT, ALLEN

ALLEN TOUSSAINT (b. 1938) FIRST CAME TO PROMINENCE AS THE TOURING PIANO PLAYER WITH SHIRLEY AND LEE. *Wild Sounds Of New Orleans* included 'Java', later a hit single for trumpeter Al Hirt. Toussaint's 'Ooh Poo Pah Doo', was a US Top 30 hit in 1960. Toussaint worked with Irma Thomas, Aaron Neville, Ernie K-Doe and Lee Dorsey. He later formed a partnership with fellow producer Marshall Sehorn. Toussaint's career continued with a self-titled album whose highlight was the excellent 'From A Whisper To A Scream'. *Life, Love And Faith* was uninspired, but *Southern Nights* (1975) was much stronger. He remains an important figure in New Orleans' music circles.

TOWER OF POWER

FORMED IN 1967 IN OAKLAND, CALIFORNIA, USA, THE GROUP COMPRISED RUFUS MILLER (VOCALS), GREG ADAMS (trumpet), Emilio 'Mimi' Castillo (b. Detroit, Michigan; saxophone), Steve Kupka (saxophone), Lenny Pickett (saxophone), Mic Gillette (horns), Willie Fulton (guitar), Francis Prestia (bass), Brent Byer (percussion) and David Garibaldi (drums). Tower Of Power's debut album, *East Bay Grease* followed several popular appearances at San Francisco's Fillmore auditorium. The group's next two albums, *Bump City* and *Tower Of Power* produced a hit single each in 'You're Still A Young Man' and 'So Very Hard To Go'. Miller was replaced, firstly by Rick Stevens and then Lenny Williams (b. 1945). 'Don't Change Horses (In The Middle Of A Stream)' (1974) was the group's last US Top 30 single.

TOWNSHEND, PETE

THE SON OF SINGER BETTY DENNIS AND SAXOPHONIST CLIFF TOWNSHEND, PETE (b. 1945) SERVED HIS APPRENTICESHIP playing banjo in a dixieland jazz band. He joined the Detours, which also featured Roger Daltrey and John Entwistle and was a vital stepping-stone to the formation of the **Who**. Townshend began a solo career in 1970 with contributions to *Happy Birthday*. A second set, *I Am*, appeared in 1972 and although not intended for public consumption, the albums featured material which also found its way into the Who lexicon. *Who Came First*, the guitarist's first official solo release reflected a gentler, pastoral side to the artist's work and was followed by *Rough Mix*, a collaboration with former **Small Faces** bassist **Ronnie Lane**. Townshend subsequently founded a record label and publishing company, both named Eel Pie, and his solo work did not flourish fully until the release of *Empty Glass* in 1980.

The abstract *All The Best Cowboys Have Chinese Eyes* was a marked disappointment. *Scoop*, a collection of home-produced demos, marked time until the release of *White City* which promised more than it fulfilled. During this period Townshend became a consultant editor at the London publishing house, Faber & Faber. He ended the 80s with *Iron Man*, which featured cameos from several musicians, including **John Lee Hooker**. In 1993, a stage production of *Tommy*, re-titled *The Who's Tommy*, opened on Broadway, and won five Tony Awards. Also in 1993, he launched his new 'pop opera', *Psychoderelict*.

TRAFFIC

FORMED IN 1967, THIS UK GROUP COMPRISED **STEVE WINWOOD** (b. 1948; KEYBOARDS/GUITAR/BASS/VOCALS), Chris Wood (b. 1944, d. 1983; saxophone/flute), **Jim Capaldi** (b. 1944; drums/percussion/vocals) and **Dave Mason** (b. 1947; guitar/vocals). Their first single, 'Paper Sun' was an instant hit, closely followed by 'Hole In My Shoe' and the film theme 'Here We Go Round The Mulberry Bush'. Mason left at the end of an eventful year, just as the first album, *Mr Fantasy* was released. From then on Traffic ceased to be a singles band, and built up a large following, especially in the USA. Their second album, *Traffic*, showed refinement and progression. Dave Mason had returned briefly and two of his songs were particularly memorable, 'You Can All Join In' and 'Feelin' Alright'.

Last Exit was a fragmented affair and during its recording Mason departed once more. At this point the band disintegrated. Following a brief spell as a member of **Ginger Baker**'s Airforce, Winwood embarked on a solo project, to be called Mad Shadows. He enlisted the help of Wood and Capaldi, and this became Traffic once again. The resulting album was the well-received *John Barleycorn Must Die*. Rick Grech, formerly of **Family** also joined the band. In 1971, *Welcome To The Canteen* appeared with Dave Mason rejoining for a third time.

Drummer Jim Gordon (from **Derek And The Dominos**) and Reebop Kwaku Baah (d. 1981) joined in 1971, allowing Capaldi to take the role as frontman. The excellent *Low Spark Of The High Heeled Boys* was followed by *Shoot Out At The Fantasy Factory*. The latter saw the substitution of David Hood and Roger Hawkins for Grech and Gordon.

Twenty years after they dissolved, the name was used again by Capaldi and Winwood. *Far From Home* was warmly received and they followed it with a major tour.

TRAVELING WILBURYS

THIS GROUP WAS FORMED IN 1988 BY ACCIDENT, AS **GEORGE HARRISON** ATTEMPTED TO MAKE A NEW SOLO ALBUM AFTER enlisting the production talent of **Jeff Lynne**. Only **Bob Dylan**'s garage was available to rehearse in, and **Tom Petty** and **Roy Orbison** dropped by. The result was not a Harrison solo but *Handle With Care*. The outing proved to be a major success, bringing out the best of each artist. *Volume 3* was released in 1990 and received similar plaudits. The band left open the possibility of future collaborations.

TREMELOES

WHEN UK CHART-TOPPERS **BRIAN POOLE AND THE TREMELOES** PARTED COMPANY IN 1966, THE RELAUNCHED Tremeloes went it alone. In 1966, the line-up comprised Rick West (b. Richard Westwood, 1943; guitar), Alan Blakely (b. 1942; rhythm guitar), Dave Munden (b. 1943; drums) and Alan Howard (b. 1941; bass). In 1966, Howard was replaced by Mike Clark and later Len 'Chip' Hawkes (b. 1946), whose lead vocals and boyish looks gave the group a stronger visual identity. Their third release 'Here Comes My Baby' smashed into the Top 10 on both sides of the Atlantic. The follow-up, 'Silence Is Golden', gave them their only number 1. Their first self-penned single, '(Call Me) Number One', reached UK number 2. Their progressive phase was encapsulated in the album *Master*, which provided a final Top 20 single, 'Me And My Life'.

TOURISTS
Albums
Reality Effect (Logo 1979)★★★★
➽ p.381 for full listings
Collaborators
Dave Stewart ➽ p.139
Annie Lennox ➽ p.214
Connections
Eurythmics ➽ p.139

TOUSSAINT, ALLEN
Albums
Southern Nights (Reprise 1975)★★★★
➽ p.381 for full listings
Connections
Band ➽ p.31
Dr. John ➽ p.125
Paul Simon ➽ p.296

TOWER OF POWER
Albums
Urban Renewal (Warners 1975)★★★★
➽ p.381 for full listings
Connections
Huey Lewis ➽ p.215
Phil Collins ➽ p.98

TOWNSHEND, PETE
Albums
with Ronnie Lane *Rough Mix* (Polydor 1977)★★★★
➽ p.382 for full listings
Collaborators
Who ➽ p.338
Ronnie Lane ➽ p.212
Connections
Small Faces ➽ p.300
John Lee Hooker ➽ p.185
Further References
Book: *The Hores Neck*, Pete Townshend

TRAFFIC
Albums
Mr Fantasy (Island 1967)★★★★
➽ p.382 for full listings
Collaborators
Steve Winwood ➽ p.341
Jim Capaldi ➽ p.80
Dave Mason ➽ p.227
Connections
Blind Faith ➽ p.53
Ginger Baker ➽ p.29

TRAVELING WILBURYS
Albums
Handle With Care (Wilbury 1988)★★★★
➽ p.382 for full listings
Collaborators
George Harrison ➽ p.176
Jeff Lynne ➽ p.220
Bob Dylan ➽ p.128
Tom Petty ➽ p.260
Roy Orbison ➽ p.252

TREMELOES
Albums
Here Comes The Tremeloes (CBS 1967)★★★★ ➽ p.382 for full listings
Connections
Cat Stevens ➽ p.309

TRICKY
Albums
Maxinquaye (4th & Broadway 1995)★★★
➤ p.382 for full listings

Collaborators
Björk ➤ p.48
Neneh Cherry ➤ p.89
Connections
Massive Attack ➤ p.227

TRIFFIDS
Albums
The Black Swan (Island 1989)★★★★
➤ p.382 for full listings

TROGGS
Albums
Trogglodynamite (Page One 1967)★★★★
➤ p.382 for full listings
Connections
R.E.M. ➤ p.275
Wet Wet Wet ➤ p.337

TROWER, ROBIN
Albums
Bridge Of Sighs (Chrysalis 1974)★★★★
➤ p.382 for full listings
Collaborators
Jack Bruce ➤ p.71
Connections
Procol Harum ➤ p.268
Influences
Jimi Hendrix ➤ p.180

TUBES
Albums
Young And Rich (A&M 1976)★★★
➤ p.382 for full listings
Connections
Al Kooper ➤ p.210
Todd Rundgren ➤ p.284

TURNER, IKE AND TINA
Albums
Nutbush City Limits (United Artists 1973)★★★★
➤ p.382 for full listings
Collaborators
Rolling Stones ➤ p.281
Connections
Phil Spector ➤ p.304

TURNER, TINA
Albums
Private Dancer (Capitol 1984)★★★★
➤ p.382 for full listings
Collaborators
Ike Turner ➤ p.324
Heaven 17 ➤ p.178
Mick Jagger ➤ p.281

TRICKY

FORMERLY OF **MASSIVE ATTACK**, TRICKY (b. *c.* 1964) RAPPED ON 'DAYDREAMIN'' AND 'FIVE MAN ARMY' FROM THE band's *Blue Lines* debut. He also wrote and produced one track, 'Karma Coma', for the follow-up. In 1993, he released his first solo single 'Aftermath', which came after informal sessions with Mark Stewart. *Maxinquaye* was one of the critical successes of 1995, an atmospheric and unsettling record exploring the darker recesses of its creator's mind. *Nearly God* saw Tricky collaborating with guest vocalists including **Bjork**, **Neneh Cherry** and Terry Hall. *Pre-Millennium Tension* made for even more uneasy listening, with tracks such as 'Tricky Kid' and 'Fury'. Tricky then worked with **PJ Harvey**. He toured in 1998.

TRIFFIDS

THIS WESTERN AUSTRALIAN GROUP COMPRISED DAVID McCOMB (b. 1962; LEAD VOCALS/GUITAR/KEYBOARDS), 'Evil' Graham Lee (pedal and lap steel guitar), Jill Birt (keyboards/vocals), Robert McComb (violin/guitar/vocals), Martyn Casey (bass) and Alsy MacDonald (drums/vocals). The group's biggest success was 1986's *Born Sandy Devotional*. The follow-up found the Triffids producing a collection of Australian C&W/folk-blues songs. McComb's lyrics reached new peaks on *The Black Swan*. Disillusioned by their lack of commercial success the band split, with McComb going solo. *Stockholm* was a live set.

TROGGS

THE ORIGINAL TROGGS WERE AN ILL-STARRED EARLY 60S GROUP FROM HAMPSHIRE, ENGLAND, WHO SUDDENLY found themselves reduced to two members: vocalist Dave Wright and bassist Reginald Ball (b. 1943). Another local group, Ten Foot Five, with bassist Peter Staples (b. 1944) and guitarist Chris Britton (b. 1945), were suffering similar personnel upheavals. The groups amalgamated, with Ball emerging as the new lead vocalist. Wright soon moved on and the revitalized Troggs found a drummer, Ronnie Bond (b. Ronald Bullis, 1943, d. 1992). After signing with producer/manager Larry Page, the group recorded 'Lost Girl'. After switching to Larry's new label Page One, they found success with a cover of Chip Taylor's 'Wild Thing', which reached UK number 2 in 1966. The follow-up, 'With A Girl Like You', went one better. Stateside success was equally impressive with 'Wild Thing' topping the charts.

While clearly at home with basic rockers like 'Give It To Me', the group also tinkered with counter-culture subject matter on 'Night Of The Long Grass' and 'Love Is All Around', and their albums also occasionally veered towards the psychedelic market.

Any hopes of sustaining their hit career were lost when they fell out with Larry Page in a High Court action. During the 70s they achieved a certain cult status thanks to the 'Troggs Tapes', a notorious bootleg recording of an abortive session, consisting mainly of a stream of swear words. Their **R.E.M.**-linked *Athens Andover* took people by surprise, as did **Wet Wet Wet**'s version of 'Love Is All Around'.

TROWER, ROBIN

GUITARIST TROWER (b. 1947) SPENT HIS EARLY CAREER IN THE PARAMOUNTS and **Procol Harum**. Trower remained with the latter until 1971. He founded the Robin Trower Band with drummer Reg Isidore and bassist Jim Dewar. *Twice Removed From Yesterday* and *Bridge Of Sighs* explored a guitar-based path, and *For Earth Below* and *Long Misty Days* maintained the same musical balance. Trower's desire for a purer version of R&B resulted in *In City Dreams* and *Caravan To Midnight*. In 1981, he formed BLT with bassist **Jack Bruce**, but within two years Trower reconvened the Robin Trower Band with Dewar, David Bronze (bass), Alan Clarke and Bobby Clouter (both drums). *Back It Up* failed to repeat former glories. The well-received *Passion*, featured a new line-up of Trower, Bronze, Davey Pattison (vocals) and Pete Thompson (drums) who also completed *Take What You Need*.

TUBES

THE TUBES COMPRISED BASSIST RICK ANDERSON (b. 1947), MICHAEL Cotten (b. 1950; keyboards), Prairie Prince (b. 1950; drums), Bill Spooner (b. 1949; guitar), Roger Steen (b. 1949; guitar), Re Styles (b. 1950; vocals), Fee Waybill (b. John Waldo, 1950; vocals) and Vince Welnick (b. 1951; keyboards). Their debut album included the UK Top 30 hit 'White Punks On Dope'. *The Completion Backward Principle* was regarded as a compromise, despite its AOR potency. Prior to their demise, the group enjoyed their greatest commercial success with the US Top 10 hit 'She's A Beauty' in 1983.

TURNER, IKE AND TINA

THIS DUO COMPRISED IKE TURNER (b. 1931) AND **TINA TURNER** (b. ANNIE MAE BULLOCK, 1939). IKE TURNER FORMED HIS Kings Of Rhythm during the late 40s. This group were later augmented by a former gospel singer, Annie Mae Bullock. Originally billed as 'Little Ann', she gradually became the core of the act, particularly following her marriage to Ike in 1958. Their debut release as Ike And Tina Turner came two years later. 'A Fool In Love' preceded several excellent singles. Producer **Phil Spector** constructed his 'wall-of sound' around Tina's impassioned voice, but the resultant single, 'River Deep Mountain High', was an unaccountable miss in the USA, although in the UK charts it reached the Top 3. Ike, unhappy at relinquishing the reins, took the duo elsewhere when further releases were less successful. A support slot on the **Rolling Stones**' 1969 North American tour introduced the Turners to a wider, generally white, audience. Their version of John Fogerty's 'Proud Mary' was a gold disc in 1971, while the autobiographical 'Nutbush City Limits' (1973) was also an international hit. The Turners became increasingly estranged and the couple were finally divorced in 1976.

TURNER, TINA

TINA (b. ANNIE MAE BULLOCK, 1939) WAS A REGULAR PERFORMER IN ST. LOUIS' NIGHTCLUBS WHEN SHE was discovered by guitarist Ike Turner in 1956. She joined his group as a backing singer, but left their professional and personal relationship in 1975. Her career was rejuvenated in 1983 when she was invited to participate in BEF; she contributed a raucous version of the **Temptations** 'Ball Of Confusion'. Her reading of **Al Green**'s 'Let's Stay Together' reached the UK Top 10, while *Private Dancer* spawned another major hit in 'What's Love Got To Do With It'. The title track was also a transatlantic hit. In 1984, Tina accepted a role in the film *Mad Max: Beyond The Thunderdome*, whose theme 'We Don't Need Another Hero', was another international hit. Her 1985 autobiography was filmed in 1993 as *What's Love Got To Do With It?*, which also gave its title to a best-selling album. She released the title track from the James Bond movie *Goldeneye* in 1995. The Trevor Horn-produced *Wildest Dreams* was a solid rock album, laying her strong R&B roots to history.

TURTLES

THIS LOS ANGELES SEXTET SWITCHED TO BEAT MUSIC DURING 1964 IN IMITATION OF THE **BEATLES**. THE LINE-UP CONSISTED OF Howard Kaylan (b. Howard Kaplan, 1947; vocals/saxophone) and Mark Volman (b. 1947; vocals/saxophone), backed by Al Nichol (b. 1945; piano/guitar), Jim Tucker (b. 1946; guitar), Chuck Portz (b. 1945; bass) and Don Murray (b. 1945, d. 1996; drums). A **Bob Dylan** cover followed in 1965, succeeded by two P. F. Sloan compositions. 1967 saw a change in the group's image and coincided with line-up fluctuations resulting in the induction of drummer John Barbata and successive bassists Chip Douglas and Jim Pons.

The exuberant 'Happy Together' revitalized their chart fortunes, reaching number 1 in the US and also charting in the UK. The follow-up 'She'd Rather Be With Me' established the group as pop craftsmen. The mid-tempo 'You Know What I Mean' and 'Elenore' were also impressive. The Turtles ended their hit career by returning to their folk-rock roots, courtesy of 'You Showed Me'.

TWISTED SISTER

FORMED IN 1976, THIS HEAVY METAL NEW YORK QUINTET FEATURED DEE SNIDER (VOCALS), EDDIE OJEDA (GUITAR), Mark 'The Animal' Mendoza (bass; ex-Dictators), Jay Jay French (guitar) and Tony Petri (drums). They combined sexually provocative lyrics and dumb choruses with metallic rock 'n' roll. A. J. Pero (drums) joined before the recording of *Under The Blade. Stay Hungry* included the hit 'I Am, I'm Me', which peaked at UK number 18, but *Come Out And Play* was a flop. Pero quit and was replaced by Joey 'Seven' Franco. Snider steered the band in a more melodic direction on *Love Is For Suckers*, but they imploded in 1987.

2 LIVE CREW

THESE RAP HEADLINE-MAKERS FROM MIAMI, FLORIDA FORMED IN 1985 AROUND LUTHER CAMPBELL. *AS NASTY As They Wanna Be* became the first record in America to be deemed legally obscene. Campbell's compatriots in 2 Live Crew numbered rappers Trinidad-born Chris Wong Won, New Yorker Mark Ross and California DJ David Hobbs (under the psuedonyms Brother Marquis and Fresh Kid Ice on the 'clean' version of *Move Somethin'*). *As Nasty As They Wanna Be* included the notorious 'Me So Horny', built around a sample from *Full Metal Jacket*. The group was arrested for performing music from the *Nasty* album in an adults-only club. Campbell released a solo album, *Banned In The USA*.

TYLER, BONNIE

WELSH-BORN TYLER'S (b. GAYNOR HOPKINS, 1951) POWERFUL VOICE WAS A PERFECT VEHICLE FOR THE QUASI-OPERATIC imagination of producer Jim Steinman. A throat operation in 1976 gave her voice an extra huskiness which attracted writer/producers Ronnie Scott and Steve Wolfe. Tyler successfully recorded their compositions 'Lost In France' and 'It's A Heartache', a million-seller in the USA. In 1981 Tyler was teamed with **Meat Loaf** producer Steinman. He created 'Total Eclipse Of The Heart', which reached number 1 on both sides of the Atlantic. 'Faster Than The Speed Of Night' also topped the UK charts. After duetting with **Shakin' Stevens** on 'A Rockin' Good Way', recording the film themes 'Holding Out For A Hero' (from *Footloose*) and 'Here She Comes' (from *Metropolis*), Steinman paired Tyler with **Todd Rundgren** on 'Loving You's A Dirty Job But Someone's Got To Do It' (1986). Songwriter Desmond Child was brought in to produce *Hide Your Heart* in 1988. Her new contract with East West brought her together again with Jim Steinman for *Free Spirit*.

TYMES

FORMED IN PHILADELPHIA DURING THE 50S, GEORGE WILLIAMS, GEORGE HILLIARD, DONALD BANKS, ALBERT BERRY and Norman Burnett first came together in the Latineers. As the Tymes, they secured a major hit with 'So Much In Love' (1962). Less successful singles followed before the Tymes scored international hits with two 1974 releases, 'You Little Trustmaker' and 'Ms. Grace', (a UK number 1). Hilliard, then Berry, eventually left the group and Terri Gonzalez and Melanie Moore joined. Such changes, however, failed to sustain the Tymes' chart career beyond 1976.

TYRANNOSAURUS REX

FORMED IN 1967 BY SINGER/GUITARIST **MARC BOLAN** (b. MARK FELD, 1947, d. 1977), Tyrannosaurus Rex featured percussionist Steve 'Peregrine' Took (b. 1949, d. 1980) in an acoustic-based venture that combined a love of classic rock 'n' roll with an affection for faerie mythology. They enjoyed three minor hits: 'Debora', 'One Inch Rock' and 'King Of The Rumbling Spires', and achieved notable album chart success, both *My People Were Fair And Had Sky In Their Hair But Now They're Content To Wear Stars On Their Brows* and *Unicorn* reached the UK Top 20. They split in 1969 and Bolan was joined by Mickey Finn for *A Beard Of Stars*. Here the unit's transformation was complete and this electric set was the natural stepping-stone for Bolan's transformation into a fully fledged pop idol with **T. Rex**.

TZUKE, JUDIE

TZUKE (b. 1955) WAS OF POLISH EXTRACTION. IN 1975 SHE RECORDED 'THESE ARE THE LAWS' WITH MIKE PAXMAN and in 1978, she released the choral 'For You', followed by 'Stay With Me Till Dawn'. *Welcome To The Cruise* made the UK Top 20. *Sports Car*, a lesser work, reached the Top 10. Tzuke also composed with **Elton John**, sharing credits on 'Give Me The Love' on *21 At 33*. She released 'We'll Go Dreaming' in 1989 and, in 1990, unsuccessfully released a version of the **Beach Boys**' 'God Only Knows'. Her 1991 album included a remake of 'Stay With Me Till Dawn'. Making guest appearances on *Wonderland* were Brian May and violinist Nigel Kennedy.

Connections
Temptations ➧ p.318
Mark Knopfler ➧ p.209
Further References
Video: *Simply The Best* (1991)

TURTLES
Albums
You Baby (White Whale 1966)★★★
➧ p.382 for full listings
Connections
Byrds ➧ p.77
Bob Dylan ➧ p.128
Frank Zappa ➧ p.348
Mothers Of Invention ➧ p.239
Flo And Eddie ➧ p.148

TWISTED SISTER
Albums
Stay Hungry (Atlantic 1984)★★★
➧ p.382 for full listings
Influences
Kiss ➧ p.208
Alice Cooper ➧ p.12
New York Dolls ➧ p.246

2 LIVE CREW
Albums
The 2 Live Crew Is What We Are (Luke Skyywalker 1986)★★★
➧ p.382 for full listings
Collaborators
Luther Campbell ➧ p.79

TYLER, BONNIE
Albums
Natural Force (*It's A Heartache* USA) (RCA 1978)★★★
➧ p.382 for full listings
Collaborators
Shakin' Stevens ➧ p.309
Todd Rundgren ➧ p.284
Connections
Meat Loaf ➧ p.230
George Martin ➧ p.226
Further References
Film: *Footloose* (1984)

TYMES
Albums
So Much In Love (Parkway 1963)★★★★
➧ p.382 for full listings

TYRANNOSAURUS REX
Albums
My People Were Fair And Had Sky In Their Hair But Now They're Content To Wear Stars On Their Brows (Regal Zonophone 1968)★★★★
➧ p.382 for full listings
Collaborators
Marc Bolan ➧ p.59

TZUKE, JUDIE
Albums
Welcome To The Cruise (Rocket 1979)★★★★
➧ p.382 for full listings
Collaborators
Brian May ➧ p.270
Connections
Elton John ➧ p.200
Beach Boys ➧ p.36

U2
Albums
The Unforgettable Fire (Island 1984)★★★★
The Joshua Tree (Island 1987)★★★★
➽ p.382 for full listings

Connections
Brian Eno ➽ p.136
Daniel Lanois ➽ p.212
Influences
Rolling Stones ➽ p.281
Beach Boys ➽ p.36
Further References
Video: *Rattle And Hum* (1989)
Book: *Unforgettable Fire: The Story Of U2*, Eamon Dunphy

UB40
Albums
Labour Of Love (DEP 1983)★★★★
UB40 (DEP 1988)★★★★
➽ p.382 for full listings
Collaborators
Robert Palmer ➽ p.255
Bob Dylan ➽ p.128
Connections
Sonny And Cher ➽ p.302
Temptations ➽ p.318
Further References
Video: *Dance With The Devil* (1988)

UFO
Albums
No Heavy Pettin' (Chrysalis 1976)★★★★
Lights Out (Chrysalis 1977)★★★★
➽ p.382 for full listings
Connections
Michael Schenker ➽ p.289
Scorpions ➽ p.289

UGLY KID JOE
Albums
America's Least Wanted (Mercury 1992)★★★
Menace To Sobriety (Mercury 1995)★★★
➽ p.382 for full listings

UK SUBS
Albums
Crash Course (Gem 1980)★★★
Quintessentials (Fall Out 1997)★★★.
➽ p.382 for full listings
Connections
Guns N'Roses ➽ p.170
Further References
Book: *Neighbourhood Threat*, Alvin Gibbs

U2

FORMED IN DUBLIN IN 1977. BONO (b. PAUL HEWSON, 1960; VOCALS), THE EDGE (b. DAVID EVANS, 1961; GUITAR), ADAM Clayton (b. 1960; bass) and Larry Mullen (b. Laurence Mullen, 1960; drums) started out in a group named Feedback, they became U2 in 1978. After winning a talent contest, they were signed to manager Paul McGuinness, then to CBS Records Ireland. Their debut EP *U2:3* featured 'Out Of Control' (1979), which reached Irish number 1. Signing to Island, they released the Steve Lillywhite-produced *Boy*. They toured America, at the time that 'Fire' reached the UK Top 30. Another minor hit with 'Gloria' was followed by *October*. In 1983, the group reached the UK Top 10 with 'New Year's Day', a song inspired by the Polish Solidarity Movement. *War* followed, to critical plaudits and the live *Under A Blood Red Sky* reached UK number 2 and US number 28.

In 1984, U2 established their own company Mother Records. *The Unforgettable Fire*, produced by **Brian Eno** and **Daniel Lanois**, improved their commercial and critical standing in the US. U2 then embarked on a world tour and completed work on *The Joshua Tree* (US/UK number 1); 'With Or Without You' and 'I Still Haven't Found What I'm Looking For' both reached US number 1. The double-live album and film, *Rattle And Hum*, preceded their first UK number 1 with the R&B-influenced 'Desire'. In 1991, 'The Fly' entered the UK charts at number 1. The impressive *Achtung Baby* captured the majesty of its predecessor yet also stripped down the sound to provide a greater sense of spontaneity. It emphasized U2's standing as an international group. Although the critics were less than generous with *Zooropa*, *Pop* was well-received and the band remain one of the most popular 'stadium' attractions of the 90s. A new album was rumoured for 1999.

UB40

MULTI-RACIAL REGGAE BAND – BROTHERS ROBIN (b. 1954; LEAD GUITAR) AND ALI CAMPBELL (b. 1959; LEAD VOCALS/ guitar), Earl Falconer (b. 1957; bass), Mickey Virtue (b. 1957; keyboards), Brian Travers (b. 1959; saxophone), Jim Brown (b. 1957; drums) and Norman Hassan (b. 1958; percussion); joined later by Astro (b. Terence Wilson, 1957) – named after Britain's unemployment card. The wonderful and impassioned 'One In Ten' was their first hit, then *Labour Of Love*, a collection of cover versions which supplied their first number 1, 'Red Red Wine' (1983). The following *Geffrey Morgan* (UK number 3) included the Top 10 hit 'If It Happens Again' and, in 1986, **Sonny And Cher**'s 'I Got You Babe' was a hit duet for Ali Campbell with Chrissie Hynde (**Pretenders**). The duo hit again in 1988 with a revival of 'Breakfast In Bed'. *Rat In Mi Kitchen* included the African liberation anthem 'Sing Our Own Song', with Herb Alpert on trumpet.

After 'Red Red Wine' was performed at the 1988 Nelson Mandela, Wembley concert, it reached US number 1. In 1990, they reached the US and UK Top 10s: a Campbell/**Robert Palmer** duet on **Bob Dylan**'s 'I'll Be Your Baby Tonight' charted in Britain and a revival of the **Temptations** 'The Way You Do The Things You Do' was a US hit. Throughout the 80s, the group toured Europe and North America. In 1993, a version of 'I Can't Help Falling In Love With You' reached UK number 1. They continue to record and Ali Campbell has released a solo album.

UFO

UK ROCK BAND FORMED IN 1969: ANDY PARKER (DRUMS), PHIL MOGG (b. 1951; VOCALS), PETE WAY (BASS) AND MICK Bolton (guitar). After releasing three albums, successful only in Germany and Japan, Bolton quit, replaced by Larry Wallis, then by Bernie Marsden and finally **Michael Schenker** (ex-**Scorpions**). *Phenomenon*, featuring 'Rock Bottom' and 'Doctor, Doctor', started a series of strong albums, and the band added a keyboardist, Danny Peyronel, in 1976; later replaced by Paul Raymond. *Lights Out* and *Strangers In The Night* were successful. When Schenker rejoined the Scorpions in 1978, Paul Chapman stepped in, but they never recaptured their earlier success. Paul Raymond was replaced by Neil Carter in 1980, and Pete Way left after *Mechanix;* replaced by Paul Gray. *Making Contact* seemed dated and devoid of the old energy and they broke up.

In 1985, Mogg resurrected the name with Raymond, Gray, drummer Jim Simpson and guitarist Atomic Tommy M. They disbanded after the unsuccessful *Misdemeanor*. In 1991, Mogg, Way, guitarist Laurence Archer and drummer Clive Edwards released the marginally successful *High Stakes And Desperate Men*. In 1995, the 'classic line-up' re-formed for *Walk On Water*.

UGLY KID JOE

FORMED IN 1989 BY WHITFIELD CRANE (VOCALS), KLAUS EICHSTADT (GUITAR) AND MARK DAVIS (DRUMS); ROGER LAHR (guitar) and Cordell Crockett (bass) joined in 1991. They debuted with a mini-album, *As Ugly As They Wanna Be*, which sold over two million copies in the USA on the back of 'Everything About You'. Dave Fortman replaced Lahr for *America's Least Wanted*, featuring 'Cats In The Cradle'. Shannon Larkin replaced Davis for *Menace To Sobriety*; it was preceded by a series of AIDS benefits, and produced 'Milkman's Son'.

UK SUBS

FORMED IN LONDON IN 1976 BY R&B SINGER CHARLIE HARPER, WITH NICKY GARRATT (GUITAR), PAUL SLACK (BASS) and Pete Davies (drums). They specialized in shambolic sub-three-minute bursts of alcohol-driven rock 'n' roll; *Another Kind Of Blues* and *Brand New Age*

were vintage Subs collections, but the definitive statement came with *Crash Course*, their most successful chart album and biggest-seller.

The line-up has changed sporadically, with only Harper surviving throughout. Harper also had sideline projects, including releasing a solo album and having **Guns N'Roses** release a version of his 'Down On The Farm'. The UK Subs are still active today.

ULTRAMAGNETIC MC'S

FOUR PIECE RAP TROUPE, INCORPORATING JAZZ AND FUNK, FORMED IN NEW YORK. MAURICE SMITH (AKA PJ MO LOVE; DJ), Keith Thornton (aka Kool Keith; lead MC), Trevor Randolph (aka TR Love; rapper/co-producer) and Cedric Miller (aka Ced Gee; MC/co-producer) were a direct influence on the 'Daisy Age' rap of subsequent acts such as **De La Soul** and **PM Dawn**. While *Funk Your Head Up* included the excellent 'Poppa Large', it also housed the appalling 'Porno Star'. On *Four Horsemen* the group unveiled an 'intergalactic hip hop' concept.

Ced Gee and TR Love have used their production skills for several other artists including Boogie Down Productions' *Criminal Minded Set* and Tim Dog's 'Fuck Compton'.

ULTRAVOX

FORMED IN THE UK IN 1974. JOHN FOXX (b. DENNIS LEIGH; VOCALS), STEVE SHEARS (GUITAR), WARREN CANN (b. 1952; drums), Chris Cross (b. Christopher Allen, 1952; bass) and Billy Currie (b. 1952; keyboards, synthesizer, violin) signed to Island Records in 1976, but made little commercial headway. After *Systems Of Romance*, Island dropped them; both Simon and Foxx went solo.

When Currie met **Midge Ure** (b. James Ure, 1953; lead vocals/guitar), the duo decided to revive Ultravox as a quartet with Cross and Currie. They signed to Chrysalis. Minor chart success was found with 'Sleepwalk' and 'Passing Strangers', but it was not until 'Vienna' (UK number 2) that Ultravox found true success. A string of Top 20 hits followed, including 'All Stood Still' (1981), 'Reap The Wild Wind' (1982) and 'Dancing With Tears In My Eyes' (1984). The band never quite achieved the same level of popularity in the USA. Seven years after *U-Vox*, a 'new' Ultravox, with singer Tony Fennelle, released the poorly received *Revelation*. Ure has since continued his solo career with varying degrees of success. Currie assembled a further version of the band for 1995's *Ingenuity* with Sam Blue (vocals) and Vinny Burns (guitar).

UNDERTONES

FORMED IN NORTHERN IRELAND, IN 1975. FEARGAL SHARKEY (b. 1958; VOCALS), JOHN O'NEILL (b. 1957; GUITAR), Damian O'Neill (guitar), Michael Bradley (bass) and Billy Doherty (drums) were signed to independent Belfast label Good Vibrations in 1978. Their debut EP, *Teenage Kicks*, was heavily promoted by **John Peel**. When Sire Records reissued it, the EP climbed to UK number 31. By 1979, the group had entered the Top 20 with 'Jimmy Jimmy' and gained acclaim for their debut album. *Hypnotised* was more accomplished, and featured hit singles in 'My Perfect Cousin' and 'Wednesday Week'.

They set up their own label, Ardeck Records and recorded *Positive Touch*; 'It's Going To Happen' was a chart success, but the romantic 'Julie Ocean' was not. The group disbanded in 1983. The compilation, *All Wrapped Up*, was a fitting tribute to their passionate blend of punk and melodic pop. Sharkey teamed up with Vince Clarke in the short-lived Assembly, before going solo. The O'Neill brothers subsequently formed **That Petrol Emotion**.

URE, MIDGE

MIDGE URE (b. JAMES URE, 1953) BEGAN HIS CAREER AS GUITARIST/VOCALIST WITH GLASGOW BAND SALVATION, which evolved into Slik. Although accomplished musicians, Slik was 'teenybop' material; frustrated at this, Ure left for Rich Kids, featuring former **Sex Pistol** Glen Matlock. Despite strong support from EMI, the group lasted less than a year.

Ure joined the short-lived **Misfits** before founding **Visage** with Steve Strange (vocals) and Rusty Egan (drums). He left Visage to replace **Gary Moore** temporarily in **Thin Lizzy**'s US tour, before joining **Ultravox**. Ure also moved into production and, in 1982, enjoyed a UK Top 10 solo hit with his version of 'No Regrets'. Two years later, he formed Band Aid with **Bob Geldof**. Their joint composition, the multi-million selling 'Do They Know It's Christmas?', was inspired by film footage of the Ethiopian famine. Subsequently, Ure resumed his solo career with *The Gift*, including the UK number 1, 'If I Was'. However *Answers To Nothing* proved less successful. In 1991, he re-entered the UK Top 20 with 'Cold, Cold Heart', closely followed by *Pure*. Since then, his career has seen little chart success.

URGE OVERKILL

FORMED IN 1986 IN CHICAGO. NATIONAL 'NASH' KATO (b. 1965; VOCALS), BLACKIE 'BLACK CAESAR' ONASSIS (b. JOHNNY Rowan, 1967; vocals/drums) and Eddie 'King' Roeser (b. 1969; bass) took their name from a **Funkadelic** song, and combined upfront rock riffs with pop. After releasing a lacklustre EP, *Strange, I...*, they recorded four albums, and supported **Nirvana**. The images of Americana on *The Supersonic Storybook* were followed by *Stull*, inspired by a ghost town. *Saturation*, their debut for Geffen, was produced by hip-hop duo the Butcher Brothers; *Exit The Dragon* was an impressive follow-up. They came into mainstream prominence when their cover of 'Girl, You'll Be A Woman Soon' was featured in the cult film *Pulp Fiction*. Roeser left acrimoniously in 1996. Since then the others have allegedly been recording a new album.

URIAH HEEP

FORMED BY BRITISH DUO DAVID BYRON (b. 1947, d. 1985; VOCALS) AND MICK BOX (b. 1947; LEAD GUITAR/VOCALS), who recruited Ken Hensley (b. 1945; guitar/keyboards/vocals) and Paul Newton (b. 1946; bass). *Very 'eavy, Very 'umble* was a simplistic, bass-driven passage from electric folk to a direct, harder sound. Drummer Keith Baker joined for *Salisbury*. In 1971, Lee Kerslake joined and Mark Clarke took over from Newton; replaced by Gary Thain (b. 1948, d. 1976) after three months. Manager Gerry Bron formed Bronze Records in 1971 and *Look At Yourself* became their first UK chart entry (number 39). The band then entered their most successful period with five albums, beginning with *Demons And Wizards*, their first to enter the US charts.

Thain left in 1975; replaced by John Wetton (ex-**King Crimson**, **Family**, **Roxy Music**). The union, celebrated on *Return To Fantasy*, failed on a creative level although it did reach the UK Top 10. Wetton and Hensley left in 1976; Byron also departed. John Lawton debuted on *Firefly* and bassist Trevor Bolder (ex-**David Bowie**) joined. Several singers came and went, as the group found themselves playing to an ever-decreasing cult following. Ex-**Lone Star** vocalist John Sloman performed on *Conquest* after which a new Uriah Heep – Box, Kerslake, John Sinclair (keyboards), Bob Daisley (bass) and Peter Goalby (vocals; ex-**Trapeze**) – was formed. Daisley left in 1983; replaced by the returning Bolder. Bronze Records collapsed in 1984 and the band signed with Portrait Records in the USA. Bernie Shaw (vocals) and Phil Lanzon (keyboards) joined and *Sea Of Light* offered an evocative slice of the band's trademark melodic rock.

ULTRAMAGNETIC MC'S

Albums
Funk Your Head Up (London 1992)★★★
➽ p.382 for full listings

Connections
De La Soul ➽ p.112
PM Dawn ➽ p.262

ULTRAVOX

Albums
Vienna (Chrysalis 1980)★★★
Rage In Eden (Chrysalis 1981)★★★
➽ p.382 for full listings

Connections
Midge Ure ➽ p.327

Further References
Book: *The Past, Present & Future Of Ultravox*, Drake and Gilbert.

UNDERTONES

Albums
The Undertones (Sire 1979)★★★★
Hypnotised (Sire 1980)★★★★
The Peel Sessions Album (Strange Fruit 1991)★★★
➽ p.382 for full listings

Connections
John Peel ➽ p.258
That Petrol Emotion ➽ p.319

URE, MIDGE

Albums
The Gift (Chrysalis 1985)★★★
Breathe (Arista 1996)★★
➽ p.382 for full listings

Connections
Sex Pistols ➽ p.292
Visage ➽ p.331
Gary Moore ➽ p.238
Thin Lizzy ➽ p.320
Ultravox ➽ p.327
Bob Geldof ➽ p.160

URGE OVERKILL

Albums
Saturation (Geffen 1993)★★★★
Exit The Dragon (Geffen 1995)★★★★
➽ p.382 for full listings

Collaborators
Nirvana ➽ p.248

Connections
Funkadelic ➽ p.156

URIAH HEEP

Albums
Look At Yourself (Bronze 1971)★★★
Wonderworld (Bronze 1974)★★★
Firefly (Bronze 1977)★★★
➽ p.382 for full listings

Connections
King Crimson ➽ p.206
Family ➽ p.143
Roxy Music ➽ p.283
David Bowie ➽ p.64
Lone Star ➽ p.218

Further References
Video: *Live Legends* (1990).

VALENS, RITCHIE
Albums
Ritchie Valens (Del Fi/London 1959)★★★★
» p.382 for full listings
Connections
Buddy Holly » p.184
Big Bopper » p.46
Los Lobos » p.218
Further References
Film: *Go Johnny Go* (1958).

VALENTINOS
Albums
Bobby Womack And The Valentinos (1984)★★
» p.382 for full listings
Connections
Bobby Womack » p.342
Sam Cooke » p.100
Rolling Stones » p.281

VALLI, FRANKIE
Albums
Heaven Above Me (MCA 1980)★★★
» p.382 for full listings
Connections
Four Seasons » p.151
Further References
Film: *Grease* (1978).

VAN DER GRAAF GENERATOR
Albums
The Least We Can Do Is Wave To Each Other (Charisma 1970)★★★★
» p.382 for full listings
Connections
Peter Hammill » p.173
Misunderstood » p.235
Lindisfarne » p.216

VAN HALEN
Albums
Van Halen (Warners 1978)★★★★
OU812 (Warners 1988)★★★★
» p.382 for full listings
Collaborators
Michael Jackson » p.195
Toto » p.322
Connections
Kiss » p.208
Extreme » p.140
Further References
Book: *Excess All Areas*, Malcolm Dome

VANDROSS, LUTHER
Albums
Power Of Love (Epic 1991)★★★★
» p.382 for full listings
Collaborators
David Bowie » p.64
Chaka Khan » p.204
Ringo Starr » p.307
Donna Summer » p.313
Quincy Jones » p.201
Patti Austin » p.24
Chic » p.90
Sister Sledge » p.298
Dionne Warwick » p.334

VALENS, RITCHIE

VOCALIST-GUITARIST VALENS (b. RICHARD STEVE VALENZUELA, 1941, d. 1959) WAS THE FIRST MAJOR HISPANIC-American rock star. In 1956, he joined the Silhouettes; he also performed solo before being asked to record by Bob Keane of Del-Fi Records. His first album featured 'La Bamba', a traditional Mexican folk song. Valens wrote his first single, 'Come On, Let's Go' (US number 42). In 1958, 'Donna' (b-side: 'La Bamba') was issued (US number 2). Valens then went on his second tour. On 3 February 1959, he, **Buddy Holly** and the **Big Bopper** chose to charter an aeroplane rather than ride to the next concert in a bus with a broken heater. They were killed when their plane crashed.

After Valens' death, his 'That's My Little Suzie' and 'Little Girl' were minor chart hits. Three albums – *Ritchie Valens*, *Ritchie* and *Ritchie Valens In Concert At Pacoima Junior High* – were released from sessions recorded for Del-Fi and at a school performance. After the 1987 tribute film *La Bamba*, **Los Lobos** took 'La Bamba' to number 1.

VALENTINOS

FORMED IN THE 1950S AS THE WOMACK BROTHERS. **BOBBY WOMACK** (b. 1944), FRIENDLY WOMACK JNR (b. 1941), Harry Womack (b. 1946), Curtis Womack (b. 1943) and Cecil Womack (b. 1941) sang spiritual and secular material. They were signed to **Sam Cooke**'s Sar label and renamed the Valentinos. In 1964, they charted with 'It's All Over Now', unfortunately overshadowed by the **Rolling Stones**'s version and the tragedy of Cooke's death. Subsequently they reunited for two 70s singles, 'I Can Understand It' and 'Raise Your Hand In Anger'. Cecil married Sam Cooke's daughter, Linda, inaugurating the **Womack And Womack** duo. In 1986, Friendly Jnr and Curtis formed the Brothers Womack with singer Lewis Williams.

VALLI, FRANKIE

ORIGINALLY A SOLOIST, VALLI (b. FRANK CASTELLUCCIO, 1937) JOINED THE VARIATONES, AS LEAD SINGER, IN 1954. They recorded as the Four Lovers, becoming the **Four Seasons** in 1962. Valli also retained his solo career with '(You're Gonna) Hurt Yourself' (1965), followed by 1967's 'Can't Take My Eyes Off You' – a million-seller – and the US hits, 'I Make A Fool Of Myself', and 'To Give (The Reason I Live)'. Valli had his first solo number 1 with 'My Eyes Adored You' (1975), followed by 'Swearin' To God' and a revival of Ruby And The Romantics' 'Our Day Will Come'.

In 1978, he featured in *Grease* – the soundtrack sold over two million; follow-ups, 'Fancy Dancer' and 'Where Did We Go Wrong' (a duet with Chris Forde) sold poorly. Valli subsequently re-joined the Four Seasons, enjoying success when 'Big Girls Don't Cry' was included in the film *Dirty Dancing*.

VAN DER GRAAF GENERATOR

UK BAND FORMED IN 1967: CHRIS JUDGE-SMITH (DRUMS), NICK PEAME (KEYBOARDS) AND PETER HAMMILL (b. 1948; vocals/lyrics). Smith was replaced by Guy Evans and Peame by Hugh Banton; bassist Keith Ellis joined later. After 'People You Were Going To', the band broke up – although Hammill's intended solo album, *The Aerosol Grey Machine*, evolved into a joint effort.

In 1969, Ellis left, replaced by Nic Potter (ex-**Misunderstood**); David Jackson (woodwind) also joined for the second album. This was followed by a tour (minus Potter) with **Lindisfarne**, and a set at the Plumpton Blues Festival. The group split again, then re-formed for a French tour in 1975. Potter and Evans embarked on a series of instrumental projects (*The Long Hello Volumes 1-4*) while Hammill continued as a soloist. The band finally broke up after 1978's in-concert double, *Vital*.

VAN HALEN

FORMED IN CALIFORNIA, IN 1973. EDDIE VAN HALEN (b. 1957; GUITAR/KEYBOARDS), ALEX VAN HALEN (b. 1955; DRUMS) and Michael Anthony (b. 1955; bass) recruited David Lee Roth (b. 1955; vocals). Gene Simmons (**Kiss**) offered to produce a demo and Warner Brothers Records eventually signed them. Van Halen released their debut to widespread critical acclaim; it peaked at US number 19 and has sold over nine million copies. *Van Halen II* kept to the same formula.

Eddie was named Best New Guitarist Of The Year in 1978 by *Guitar Player* magazine. *Women And Children First* saw the band explore new musical avenues and *Fair Warning* was a marked departure from earlier releases. *Diver Down* was the band's weakest album, but went platinum. With *1984*, and 'Jump' (*Billboard* number 1), the band spent a year in the US charts.

Eddie's solo work includes sessions for **Michael Jackson**, Private Life and Steve Lukather (ex-**Toto**), but he remained with the band throughout; however Roth went solo in 1985, replaced by Sammy Hagar (b. 1947). Retaining the Van Halen name, the new line-up released *5150* (US number 1), featuring 'Why Can't This Be Love' (US number 3). The disappointing *OU812* also reached number 1. *For Unlawful Carnal Knowledge*, (*F.U.C.K.*), stirred up some controversy, and went platinum. *Best Of Volume 1* debuted at US number 1. Hagar departed in 1996; replaced by Gary Cherone (ex-**Extreme**).

VANDROSS, LUTHER

IN THE 70S, VANDROSS (b. LUTHER RONZONI VANDROSS, 1951) JOINED **DAVID BOWIE** FOR *YOUNG AMERICANS*. Bowie then invited him to arrange the vocal parts and to sing backing vocals for the album. Vandross also opened for Bowie on his US tour. Session credits with **Chaka Khan**, **Ringo Starr**, Barbra Streisand and **Donna Summer** led Cotillion to sign him as part of a vocal group, Luther. *Luther* and *This Close To You* flopped and the singer drifted back to session work, for **Quincy Jones**, **Patti Austin**, Gwen Guthrie, **Chic** and **Sister Sledge**, alongside composing advertising jingles.

As a solo artist, 'Never Too Much' reached R&B number 1 while the accompanying album reached the US Top 20 – eight years later, the single reached the UK Top 20. Subsequent singles, including duets with Cheryl Lynn ('If This World Was Mine') and **Dionne Warwick** ('How Many Times Can We Say Goodbye'), gave him two further R&B number 1s with 'Stop To Love' (1986) and 'There's Nothing Better Than Love' (1987; duet with Gregory Hines).

VANGELIS

GREEK MUSICIANS VANGELIS (b. EVANGALOS ODYSSEY PAPATHANASSIOU, 1943), DEMIS ROUSSOS (VOCALS) AND Lucas Sideras (drums) formed Greek band **Aphrodite's Child** in the 60s. In 1972, they split and Vangelis concentrated on electronic music, composing classical works and film scores, and developing his fusion of electronic and acoustic sound. *Heaven And Hell* reached the UK Top 40; the concept album *Albedo 0.39*, included the voices of astronauts landing on the moon.

Vangelis joined forces with vocalist **Jon Anderson**. As Jon And Vangelis, they had international success with 'I Hear You Now' (1980) and 'I'll Find My Way Home' (1982). Vangelis then returned to film scores with the award-winning *Chariots Of Fire*; followed by *Antarctica*, *Bladerunner*, *Missing* and *The Bounty*.

Direct was the first in a series of improvised albums which Vangelis composed, arranged and recorded. His film credits of the early 90s include *Bitter Moon* and *1492: Conquest Of Paradise*.

VANILLA FUDGE

US ROCK GROUP, FORMED IN 1966. MARK STEIN (b. 1947; ORGAN), VINCE MARTELL (b. 1945; GUITAR), TIM BOGERT (b. 1944; bass) and Joey Brennan (drums; later replaced by Carmine Appice (b. 1946)) scored immediate success with their version of the **Supremes**' 'You Keep Me Hanging On'. Their debut album featured interpretations of **Sonny And Cher**'s 'Bang Bang' and the **Beatles**' 'Eleanor Rigby' and 'Ticket To Ride'. A flawed concept album, *The Beat Goes On*, proved overambitious.

When Vanilla Fudge split in 1970, the bassist and drummer remained together in Cactus before founding Beck, Bogert And Appice. Stein worked with Tommy Bolin and **Alice Cooper**, while Martell later appeared in the Good Rats. The group briefly re-formed in 1983, releasing *Mystery*.

VANILLA ICE

CONTROVERSIAL AMERICAN WHITE RAPPER WHO SCORED A UK/US number 1 with 'Ice Ice Baby' (15 million worldwide sales). Vanilla Ice (b. Robert Van Winkle, 1968) sang in a church choir until he was 15 and was later discovered in Dallas, Texas. His debut album covered all bases, the ballad-rap 'I Love You' sitting alongside the gangsta-inclined 'Go III' and dance pop of 'Dancin''. However, following his huge success he fell foul of his management; it took several years before he fully extricated himself from the deal. *Mindblowing* was a desperate attempt to catch up with the gangsta set, the music sampled **James Brown** and **George Clinton**.

VAN ZANDT, STEVEN

AFTER PLAYING IN STELL MILL (WITH **BRUCE SPRINGSTEEN**) AND SIMILAR NEW JERSEY BAR BANDS, VAN ZANDT (b. 1950) toured as backing guitarist to the Dovells before joining **Southside Johnny And The Asbury Jukes** ; from 1975-81, he played with Springsteen's E. Street Band. Next he led the 12-piece Little Steven And The Disciples Of Soul.

After a fact-finding expedition to South Africa, he masterminded Sun City, a post-Live Aid project that raised over $400,000 for anti-apartheid movements in Africa and the Americas via an album, single and concert spectacular featuring **Bob Dylan**, **Lou Reed**, **Ringo Starr** and Springsteen amongst others. Van Zandt's reputation as a producer is also notable, including **U.S. Bonds** (with Springsteen), **Lone Justice** and Ronnie Spector.

VEE, BOBBY

VEE'S (b. ROBERT THOMAS VELLINE, 1943) GROUP, THE **SHADOWS**, DEPUTIZED FOR **BUDDY HOLLY** AFTER THE singer's death. Their 'Suzie Baby' was released on Liberty; Vee then went solo. He charted with a revival of the **Clovers**' 1956 hit 'Devil Or Angel', before finding transatlantic success.

Bobby Vee Meets The Crickets and *Bobby Vee Meets The Ventures* were promoted by touring and in 1967, Vee returned to the US Top 10 with 'Come Back When You Grow Up'. Vee reverted to his real name for *Nothing Like A Sunny Day* although the experiment was short-lived. In later years, he appeared regularly at rock 'n' roll revival shows.

VEGA, SUZANNE

VEGA (b. 1959), A HIGHLY LITERATE SINGER-SONGWRITER, BEGAN SINGING IN NEW YORK FOLK CLUBS, UNTIL SIGNED BY A&M Records in 1984. Her first album was recorded with Lenny Kaye (ex-**Patti Smith**); its 'Marlene On The Wall' became a hit. On her third album, Vega's lyrics took on a more surreal and precise character, while keyboards player and co-producer Anton Sanko brought a new tightness to the sound. In 1990, 'Tom's Diner' (from *Solitude Standing*) became a UK hit after it had been sampled by the group DNA. The track was remixed by Alan Coulthard for Vega's label A&M. Its success led to the release of an album, *Tom's Album* (1991), devoted entirely to reworkings of the song by such artists as **R.E.M.** and rapper Nikki D. *Nine Objects Of Desire* was a move into a smoother sound.

VELVET UNDERGROUND

NEW YORK'S VELVET UNDERGROUND PORTRAYED A DARKER SIDE TO LATE 60S HEDONISM. THE LINE-UP FEATURED **Lou Reed** (b. 1942; guitar/vocals), **John Cale** (b. 1940; viola/bass/organ), Sterling Morrison (b. 1942, d. 1995; guitar) and drummer Angus MacLise (d. 1979). MacLise left when the Velvets began accepting fees; replaced by Maureen 'Mo' Tucker (b. 1945). The group met Andy Warhol in 1965; he invited them to join the Exploding Plastic Inevitable (a theatrical mixture of music, films, light-shows and dancing) and suggested adding **Nico** (b. Christa Paffgen, 1938, d. 1988) to the Velvets' line-up. *The Velvet Underground And Nico* was issued the following year. This powerful collection introduced Reed's urban infatuations, bordering on voyeurism. His skills were intensified by Cale's haunting, graphic viola work, Nico's gothic intonation and the group's combined sense of dynamism, which blended Tucker's relentless pulse with some of rock's most inspired sonic experimentation. Now rightly regarded as a musical milestone, *The Velvet Underground And Nico* was generally reviled on release.

Nico went solo in 1967 and the remaining quartet parted from Warhol's patronage. Sessions for *White Light/White Heat* exacerbated internal conflicts and its six compositions were marked by a raging intensity. Two extended pieces, 'The Gift' and 'Sister Ray', caught the group at its most radical. Cale then left; replaced by an orthodox bassist, Doug Yule. *The Velvet Underground* unveiled a pastoral approach, gentler and more subtle, retaining the chilling, disquieting aura of previous releases. *Loaded*, an album of considerable commercial promise, emphasized their new-found perspective. This unfettered collection contained one of Reed's most popular compositions, 'Sweet Jane'. Paradoxically, by *Loaded*, Reed had abandoned the group.

In 1993, the band re-formed for a major tour. It delighted thousands of fans – a vast percentage of whom were barely born when the Velvets had last performed.

VANGELIS
Albums
Heaven And Hell (RCA Victor 1975)★★★
➧ p.382 for full listings
Collaborators
Jon Anderson ➧ p.18
Connections
Aphrodites Child ➧ p.20

VANILLA FUDGE
Albums
Vanilla Fudge (Atco 1967)★★★
➧ p.382 for full listings
Collaborators
Alice Cooper ➧ p.12
Connections
Supremes ➧ p.314
Sonny And Cher ➧ p.302
Beatles ➧ p.38

VANILLA ICE
Albums
To The Extreme (SBK 1990)★★★
➧ p.382 for full listings
Connections
James Brown ➧ p.70
George Clinton ➧ p.94
Influences
MC Hammer ➧ p.173

VAN ZANDT, STEVEN
Albums
Revolution (RCA 1989)★★★
➧ p.382 for full listings
Collaborators
Bob Dylan ➧ p.128
Lou Reed ➧ p.274
Ringo Starr ➧ p.307
Connections
Bruce Springsteen ➧ p.306

VEE, BOBBY
Albums
Take Good Care Of My Baby (Liberty 1961)★★★★
➧ p.382 for full listings
Connections
Buddy Holly ➧ p.184
Clovers ➧ p.95

VEGA, SUZANNE
Albums
Suzanne Vega (A&M 1985)★★★★
➧ p.382 for full listings
Connections
Patti Smith ➧ p.301
R.E.M. ➧ p.275

VELVET UNDERGROUND
Albums
The Velvet Underground And Nico (Verve 1967)★★★★★
Loaded (Fully Loaded) (Atlantic 1997)★★★★.
➧ p.382 for full listings
Connections
Lou Reed ➧ p.274
John Cale ➧ p.78
Nico ➧ p.247
Further References
Film: *Hedy* (1965).
Book: *Beyond The Velvet Underground*, Dave Thompson

VENTURES
Albums
Walk Don't Run (Dolton 1960)★★★★
The Ventures (Dolton 1961)★★★★
Going To The Ventures' Dance Party (Dolton 1962)★★★★
Let's Go! (Dolton 1963)★★★★
➽ p.382 for full listings
Connections
Shadows ➽ p.293
Beach Boys ➽ p.36

VERLAINE, TOM
Albums
Tom Verlaine (Elektra 1979)★★★★
Cover (Warners 1984)★★★★
The Wonder (Fontana 1990)★★★★
➽ p.382 for full listings
Collaborators
Patti Smith ➽ p.301
Connections
Richard Hell ➽ p.179
Television ➽ p.317

VERUCA SALT
Albums
Blow It Out Your Ass It's Veruca Salt (Minty Fresh/Geffen 1996)★★★
Eight Arms To Hold You (Outpost/Geffen 1997)★★★★
➽ p.382 for full listings
Collaborators
Hole ➽ p.182
Connections
Beatles ➽ p.38

VERVE
Albums
Storm In Heaven (Hut 1993)★★★
A Northern Soul (Hut 1995)★★★★
Urban Hymns (Hut 1997)
➽ p.382 for full listings
Collaborators
Oasis ➽ p.250

VILLAGE PEOPLE
Albums
Village People (DJM 1977)★★
Go West (Mercury 1979)★★
➽ p.382 for full listings
Further References
Video: *The Best Of ...* (1994)
Film: *Can't Stop The Music* (1980)

VINCENT, GENE
Albums
Blue Jean Bop! (Capitol 1956)★★★,
The Crazy Beat Of Gene Vincent (Capitol 1963)★★★
Bird Doggin' (London 1967)★★★
➽ p.382 for full listings

VENTURES

PIVOTAL INSTRUMENTAL GROUP FORMED IN WASHINGTON, USA, IN 1959 BY DON WILSON (RHYTHM GUITAR) AND BOB Bogle (lead guitar). They recruited Nokie Edwards (bass) and Skip Moore (drums) and debuted with 'Cookies And Coke', before covering Chet Atkins' 'Walk Don't Run'. The single reached US number 2 (UK number 8) and sold over one million copies, as did the following 'Perfidia'. Moore was replaced by Howie Johnson, who in turn retired following a major car accident. Drummer Mel Taylor (b. 1934, d. 1996) was then recruited.

Other notable Ventures singles included '2000 Pound Bee' (1962), which featured the then revolutionary fuzz-guitar, 'The Savage' (1963), originally recorded by the **Shadows**, and 'Diamond Head' (1965), later immortalized by the **Beach Boys**.

Nokie traded roles with Bogle in 1963 before leaving altogether in 1967; he was replaced by session guitarist Jerry McGee and organist Sandy Lee – the latter was supplanted by Johnny Durrill. In 1969, the Ventures had their last major US hit when 'Hawaii Five-O', reached number 4.

VERLAINE, TOM

TRAINED AS A CLASSICAL PIANIST, GUITARIST AND VOCALIST VERLAINE (b. THOMAS MILLER, 1949) FORMED THE NEON Boys with bassist **Richard Hell** and drummer Billy Ficca, in New York in 1968. The band inspired the founding of **Television** in 1974. His guitarwork also appeared on early releases by the **Patti Smith** Group. Television's debut, *Marquee Moon*, was acclaimed a classic. The group disbanded in 1978 and Verlaine went solo. *Tom Verlaine* and *Dreamtime* failed to reap due commercial reward, but *Words From The Front* attracted considerable UK interest, as did *Cover*.

In 1991, the original Television line-up re-formed. Meanwhile, Verlaine continued with his solo career, releasing the instrumental set *Warm And Cool* and an excellent compilation in 1996.

VERUCA SALT

CHICAGO QUARTET FORMED IN 1992. SINGER/GUITARISTS NINA GORDON AND LOUISE POST, WITH STEVE LACK (BASS) and Jim Shapiro (drums), played their first gigs in 1993 and released 'Seether', on Jim Powers' Minty Fresh Records. They stayed on Minty Fresh for their debut album – it became an instant favourite among MTV viewers. The following month Veruca Salt signed to Geffen, which had by now signed up Powers for A&R, along with his label.

Touring with **Hole** in 1994 helped generate further interest. Shapiro was replaced by Stacy Jones towards the end of 1996. Using the original title for the **Beatles**' film *Help*, the band returned with *Eight Arms To Hold You* in 1997.

VERVE

UK INDIE BAND – PETER SALISBURY (b. 1971; DRUMS), RICHARD ASHCROFT (b. 1971; VOCALS), SIMON JONES (b. 1972; BASS) AND Nick McCabe (b. 1971; guitar) – who released their first record, 'All In The Mind', in 1992. After a run of singles, '(She's A) Superstar', 'Gravity Grave' and 'Blue', they released *Storm In Heaven*. A two year legal battle with Verve Records led to the group being re-christened The Verve; they then embarked on 1994's Lollapalooza tour, before touring with **Oasis**. Overwhelming response to *A Northern Soul* included praise from Oasis' Noel Gallagher.

Ashcroft left The Verve in 1995 and the band officially broke up that August, but re-formed in 1997. They toured again with Oasis in late 1997, for the latter's heavily promoted *Be Here Now* tour. Despite Oasis' overweening marketing, *Urban Hymns* knocked *Be Here Now* off the top spot, and remained there for several weeks. 'Bitter Sweet Symphony' made the UK Top 5 and the haunting 'The Drugs Don't Work' reached number 1 on its week of release.

VILLAGE PEOPLE

NEW YORK'S VILLAGE PEOPLE WERE THE BRAINCHILD OF RECORD PRODUCER JACQUES MORALI; THE TROUPE WAS assembled in 1977. Morali's intention was to create a camp rock 'n' roll/dance act that would flaunt homosexual stereotypes yet appeal to gays and he secured a recording deal with Casablanca Records before recruiting. The first member was dancer Felipe Rose; Morali then hired songwriters Phil Hurtt and Peter Whitehead, before recruiting Alexander Briley, Randy Jones, David Hodo, Glenn Hughes and Victor Willis (later replaced by Ray Simpson). Each member of the group was outfitted to cash in on homosexual 'macho' stereotyping: an American Indian, a cowboy, a policeman, a hard-hat construction worker, a biker and a soldier. The group first hit the UK Top 50 with 'San Francisco (You Got Me)' (1977), but their first US Top 30 hit was 1978's 'Macho Man', followed by 'Y.M.C.A.' (UK number 1/US number 2) and 'In The Navy' (UK number 3/US number 2).

In the UK, their success continued with the Top 20 singles, 'Go West' (1979) and 'Can't Stop The Music' (1980), but with anti-disco fever prevalent in the USA, sales plummeted. In 1997, most of the original group undertook a major 20th Anniversary tour.

VINCENT, GENE

ONE OF THE ORIGINAL BAD BOYS OF ROCK 'N' ROLL, THE SELF-DESTRUCTIVE VINCENT (b. EUGENE VINCENT CRADDOCK, 1935, d. 1971) was involved in a motorcycle crash in 1955, leaving his left leg permanently damaged. He began appearing on country music radio, eventually recording 'Be-Bop A-Lula'. In 1956, the track was re-recorded with backing by the Blue Caps: Cliff Gallup (lead guitar), Jack Neal (upright bass), Willie Williams (acoustic guitar) and Dickie Harrell (drums). Weeks later the single stormed the charts. Vincent's second single, 'Race With The Devil', failed to chart in his homeland, but proved successful in the UK, where he attracted a devoted following. When his alcoholism and buccaneering road life made him a liability to promoters and his career, he relocated to England.

Vincent toured frequently and luckily survived the car crash which killed **Eddie Cochran**. Increasingly redundant during the beat group era, his lifestyle (and alcoholism) grew more erratic and uncontrollable. A comeback album of sorts, *I'm Back And I'm Proud*, lacked sufficient punch to revitalize his career. His untimely death from a seizure, robbed rock 'n' roll of one of its great rebellious spirits.

VIRGIN PRUNES

IRISH PERFORMANCE-ART/*AVANT-GARDE* MUSICAL ENSEMBLE FORMED IN 1976. FIONAN HANVEY, BETTER KNOWN AS GAVIN Friday, joined Paul Hewson (later Bono of **U2**), Guggi (Derek Rowen), Dave-id (b. David Watson; vocals), Strongman (b. Trevor Rowen; bass), Dik Evans (brother of U2's The Edge; guitar) and Pod (b. Anthony Murphy; drums). Early gigs were very much performance events. By 1980, they had attracted strong cult support, and, on the strength of the self-financed 'Twenty Tens', were signed to Rough Trade Records. Pod left shortly afterwards. Their first album was initially released as a set of 7-, 10- and 12-inch singles, making up *A New Form Of Beauty*. After the brief tenure of Haa Lacka Binttii, Mary O'Nellon took over on drums, in time for *If I Die ... I Die*. At the same time a mixed studio/live album, *Heresie*, was released.

By 1984, Guggi had become disenchanted with the music industry and departed. When Dik Evans also left, O'Nellon switched to guitar and Pod rejoined as drummer. *The Moon Looked Down And Laughed* witnessed another change in direction, consisting largely of ballads and melodic pop. Friday then went solo. Subsequent releases from Strongman and O'Nellon as the Prunes were unsuccessful.

VISAGE

SYNTHESIZER 'JAMMING' BAND FRONTED BY STEVE STRANGE (b. STEVE HARRINGTON, 1959) WITH **MIDGE URE** (b. JAMES Ure, 1953; guitar), Rusty Egan (b. 1957), Billy Currie (b. 1952; violin), Dave Formula (keyboards), John McGeogh (guitar) and Barry Adamson (bass). Visage began in 1978 when Ure and Strange recorded a version of Zager And Evans' 'In The Year 2525' as a demo for EMI Records. Eventually Radar Records signed them and released their debut, 'Tar'. Polydor picked up on them and were rewarded with a massive hit in 'Fade To Grey'. The third single, 'Mind Of A Toy', with its memorable **Godley And Creme**-produced video (their first), was a Top 20 hit. The band dissolved in the mid-80s.

VOICE OF THE BEEHIVE

FORMED BY SISTERS TRACEY BRYN (b. 1962) AND MELISSA BROOKE BELLAND (b. 1966). FOLLOWING A SHOW BUSINESS childhood, the duo moved from the US to England, forming Voice Of The Beehive, with guitarist Mick Jones after appearing on Bill Drummond's solo album. They recruited Dan Woodgate (b. 1960; drums) and Mark Bedford (b. 1961; bass; ex-**Madness**); their early singles included 'Just A City', 'I Say Nothing' and 'I Walk The Earth'. Bedford, meanwhile, had left and was replaced by Martin Brett, in time for the debut album. *Let It Bee* was a pleasant, witty pop confectionery, which included the UK Top 20 single 'Don't Call Me Baby'. Their appealing pop continued on *Honey Lingers*. By *Sex & Misery*, the new mature Voices had lost the pop edge and gained a large spoonful of saccharine.

WAH!

MELODRAMATIC UK POP BAND FORMED BY PETE WYLIE (GUITAR/VOCALS) IN THE EARLY-80S. WYLIE HAD BEEN PART OF Crucial 3 with **Julian Cope** and Ian McCulloch. Wylie's various collaborators in Wah! included Colin Redmond (guitar), Oddball Washington (bass), Rob Jones (drums), Joe Musker (drums), Steven Johnson (guitar), John Maher (drums), Chris Joyce (drums), Charlie Griffiths (keyboards) and Jay Naughton (piano), plus a brass section. *The Way We Wah!* included 'Come Back' and 'Hope', plus their major UK chart success, 'Story Of The Blues'.

Wylie went solo with *Sinful*. When fellow Liverpudlians the **Farm** broke through in the 90s, Wylie frequently accompanied them on record and stage.

WAINWRIGHT, LOUDON, III

WAINWRIGHT (b. 1946) BEGAN PLAYING FOLK CLUBS IN NEW YORK AND BOSTON, BEFORE SIGNING TO ATLANTIC. HIS FIRST albums featured his high-pitched voice and guitar almost exclusively, and his intense, sardonic songs were about himself. His songs included 'Glad To See You've Got Religion', 'Motel Blues' and 'Be Careful, There's A Baby In The House'. His UK debut, opening for the **Everly Brothers**, was sabotaged by Teddy Boys, but he found his *métier* at the 1972 Cambridge Folk Festival.

Wainwright's third album included a surprise US Top 20 pop hit in 'Dead Skunk'. He wrote 'A.M. World' about his success and, almost defiantly, followed it with the uncommercial *Attempted Moustache*. *Unrequited*, partly recorded live, was a return to form and included the hilarious, but controversial, 'Rufus Is A Tit Man'.

Wainwright has appeared in a few episodes of the television series *M*A*S*H*, appeared on stage in *The Birthday Party* and *Pump Boys And Dinettes*, and on Jasper Carrott's UK television series.

Further References
Books: *Gene Vincent: The Screaming End*, Alan Clark *The Day The World Turned Blue*, Britt Hagerty
Film: *The Girl Can't Help It* (1956)

VIRGIN PRUNES
Albums
If I Die ... I Die (Rough Trade 1982)★★★
The Moon Looked Down And Laughed (Baby 1986)★★★
Nada (Baby 1989)★★
➽ p.382 for full listings
Connections
U2 ➽ p.326

VISAGE
Albums
Visage (Polydor 1980)★★
The Anvil (Polydor 1982)★★
Beat Boy (Polydor 1994)★★
➽ p.382 for full listings
Connections
Midge Ure ➽ p.327
Godley And Creme ➽ p.164

VOICE OF THE BEEHIVE
Albums
Let It Bee (London 1988)★★★
Honey Lingers (London 1991)★★★★
Sex And Misery (East West 1995)★★
➽ p.382 for full listings
Connections
Four Preps ➽ p.151
Madness ➽ p.221

WAH!
Albums
Nah = Poo – The Art Of Bluff (Eternal 1981)★★
as Mighty Wah! *A Word To The Wise Guy* (Beggars Banquet 1984)★★
Solo: Pete Wylie *Sinful* (Virgin 1987)★★★
➽ p.383 for full listings
Connections
Julian Cope ➽ p.100
Farm ➽ p.143

WAINWRIGHT, LOUDON, III
Albums
Loudon Wainwright III (Atlantic 1969)★★★
I'm Alright (Demon 1984)★★★
Grown Man (Virgin 1995)★★★
➽ p.383 for full listings
Connections
Everly Brothers ➽ p.139
Influences
Bob Dylan ➽ p.128

WAITE, JOHN
Albums
Mask Of Smiles (Capitol 1985)★★
➽ p.383 for full listings
Influences
Hank Williams ➽ p.339
Bill Withers ➽ p.341

WAITS, TOM
Albums
Swordfishtrombones (Island 1983)★★★★
Bone Machine (Island 1992)★★★★
➽ p.383 for full listings
Connections
Eagles ➽ p.130
Rod Stewart ➽ p.310
Further References
Book: *Small Change: A Life Of Tom Waits*, Patrick Humphries

WAKEMAN, RICK
Albums
The Six Wives Of Henry VIII (A&M 1973)★★★
Live On The Test (Windsong 1994)★★★
➽ p.383 for full listings

Further References
Video: *The World* (Central 1988)
Book: *Rick Wakeman: The Caped Crusader*, Dan Wooding

WALKER BROTHERS
Albums
Nite Flights (GTO 1978)★★★★
Take It Easy With The Walker Brothers (Philips 1965)★★★
No Regrets (GTO 1975)★★★
➽ p.383 for full listings
Connections
Scott Walker ➽ p.333
Burt Bacharach ➽ p.27
Further References
Film: *Beach Ball* (1964).

WALKER, JUNIOR, AND THE ALL STARS
Albums
Soul Session (Tamla Motown 1966)★★★★
Road Runner (Tamla Motown 1966)★★★★
➽ p.383 for full listings
Collaborators
Foreigner ➽ p.150
Connections
Motown ➽ p.240
Holland/Dozier/Holland ➽ p.183

WAITE, JOHN

WAITE (b. 1955) IS A SINGER, BASSIST AND OCCASIONAL HARMONICA PLAYER. AFTER PLAYING IN VARIOUS BANDS, he formed the **Babys** with Mike Corby, Tony Brock and Walter Stocker, in 1976. They were signed to Chrysalis, but their brand of rock had become unfashionable in the UK and they relocated to the USA. Corby was replaced by Ricky Phillips in 1977 and Jonathan Cain joined in 1978.

When the Babys split in 1981, Waite went solo. His debut, 'Change', flopped but 'Missing You', from his second album, reached UK number 9/US number 1. Waite formed the No Brakes band to promote the new album, but did not scale the same heights again. He formed Bad English in 1989, before resuming his solo career in the mid-90s. In 1995, he charted with the power ballad 'How Did I Get By Without You'. *Temple Bar* was more in the folk-rock line and included covers of **Hank Williams**' and **Bill Withers**' songs.

WAITS, TOM

GIFTED LYRICIST, COMPOSER AND RACONTEUR, TOM WAITS (b. 1949) BEGAN PERFORMING IN THE LATE 60S; HE WAS signed by manager Herb Cohen and by Asylum Records. *Tom Waits* was somewhat unfocused, however it did contain 'Ol' 55', later covered by the **Eagles**. *The Heart Of Saturday Night* was more accomplished, sung in a razor-edged, rasping voice, and infused with beatnik prepossessions. Waits' ability to paint blue-collar American life is encapsulated in its haunting, melodic title track. *Nighthawks At The Diner*, an in-concert set, and *Small Change*, closed his first era.

Foreign Affairs unveiled a widening perspective and a duet with Bette Midler, 'I Never Talk To Strangers', provided the impetus for his film soundtrack to *One From The Heart*. *Blue Valentine* was marked by its balance between lyrical ballads and up-front R&B, a contrast maintained on *Heartattack And Vine*.

In 1983, Waits moved to Island, signalling a new musical direction with the radical *Swordfishtrombones* (exotic instruments, sound textures and offbeat rhythms). He came close to having a hit with the evocative 'In The Neighbourhood' (1983). He also acted, starring in *Rumble Fish*, *Down By Law* and *Ironweed*. The album *Rain Dogs*, which featured support from Keith Richard on 'Big Black Mariah', also included 'Downtown Train', later a hit for **Rod Stewart**. *Big Time* was the soundtrack to his concert film. Waits continued in films with roles in *Candy Mountain* and *Cold Feet* and in 1989 made his theatrical debut in *Demon Wine*. In 1996, he performed a benefit concert.

WAKEMAN, RICK

MASTER KEYBOARDIST WAKEMAN (b. 1949) MADE A SERIES OF AMBITIOUS, CONCEPTUAL, CLASSICAL ROCK ALBUMS: *The Six Wives Of Henry VIII*, *Journey To The Centre Of The Earth* and *The Myths And Legends Of King Arthur And The Knights Of The Round Table* (staged using a full orchestra and 50-strong choir). All three albums were hugely successful. In 1981, he contributed to Kevin Peeks' *Awakening*, co-wrote a musical version of George Orwell's *1984* with Tim Rice, and created sensitive film scores for *Lisztomania*, *The Burning*, *G'Ole*, *Crimes Of Passion* and *Creepshow 2*.

In 1982, he started his own record label Moon Records. The new-age *Country Airs* showcases Wakeman's superb piano style. In the late-80s, he rejoined **Yes** for a tour. In 1991, he formed another label, Ambient Records, and worked with Norman Wisdom on a series of relaxation cassettes. By 1992, his son Adam was performing with him; the duo have subsequently released a number of albums.

WALKER BROTHERS

ORIGINALLY NAMED THE DALTON BROTHERS, **SCOTT WALKER** (b. NOEL SCOTT ENGEL, 1944), JOHN WALKER (b. John Maus, 1943) and Gary Walker (b. Gary Leeds, 1944), changed their name to the Walker Brothers in 1964, and left the USA for the UK. In 1965, they met manager Maurice King and were signed to Philips Records, debuting with 'Pretty Girls Everywhere' followed by 'Love Her' (1965, UK Top 20). Scott was the chosen 'a-side' main vocalist, with Maus providing the strong high harmony. The Walkers' film star looks meant they were adopted as teen idols. On album, they played a contrasting selection of ballads, soul standards and occasional upbeat pop, but for the singles they specialized in high melodrama, brilliantly augmented by the string arrangements of Johnny Franz.

The lachrymose **Burt Bacharach**/Hal David ballad 'Make It Easy On Yourself' gave them a UK number 1, while 'My Ship Is Coming In' reached the Top 3. Their version of the Bob Crewe/Bob Gaudio composition, 'The Sun Ain't Gonna Shine Anymore' reached UK number 1/US Top 20. Thereafter, there was immense friction in the band and their second EP *Solo Scott, Solo John*, neatly summarized their future intentions.

Later singles seemed a weak follow-up to their grandiose number 1 and commenced their gradual commercial decline. In 1967, the group broke up. Their farewell single, 'Walking In The Rain', surprisingly did not reach number 1.

Unexpectedly, the trio reunited in 1975, for *No Regrets*. The title track returned them to the Top 10. The following *Lines* was similar in style to its predecessor, but for their swansong, the self-penned *Nite Flights*, the trio produced a brave, experimental work, with oblique, foreboding lyrics and unusual arrangements. Sadly it was a commercial failure.

WALKER, JUNIOR, AND THE ALL STARS

AS A TEENAGER, US SAXOPHONIST WALKER (b. AUTRY DEWALT II, 1931, d. 1995) FORMED THE JUMPING JACKS, adopting the stage name Junior Walker. By 1961, he had achieved a prominent local reputation and was signed to the Harvey label, where he recorded a series of raw saxophone-led instrumentals. In 1964, Walker moved to **Motown**; 'Shotgun' (1965) typified his blend of raunchy R&B and Detroit soul and established Walker as the label's prime exponent of traditional R&B. **Holland/Dozier/Holland** also encouraged Walker to record instrumental versions of hits they had written for other Motown artists.

Walker's style became progressively more lyrical, a development that reached its peak on the 1969 US Top 5 hit, 'What Does It Take (To Win Your Love)?'. However, subsequent attempts to repeat the winning formula failed and from 1972 onwards the All Stars recorded only sporadically. *Hot Shot* marked a move towards the disco market, confirmed on two further albums and Walker's first as a solo artist. In 1979, he moved to Whitfield Records, but returned to Motown in 1983, issuing *Blow The House Down*. The novelty single 'Sex Pot' rekindled memories of his classic hits, although Walker's greatest commercial success in the 80s came when he guested with **Foreigner**, playing the magnificent saxophone solo on their hit 'Urgent'. Walker died after a two-year battle with cancer.

WALKER, SCOTT

SCOTT (b. NOEL SCOTT ENGEL, 1944) BRIEFLY RECORDED AS SCOTTY ENGEL BEFORE JOINING THE ROUTERS AS BASSIST. He then teamed up with singer John Maus as the Dalton Brothers, later becoming the **Walker Brothers**. When the group broke up in 1967, Scott was regarded as a sex symbol and potential solo superstar, yet he was known for his moody reclusiveness. The classic pop existentialist, Walker was trapped in a system that regarded him as a contradiction. His manager Maurice King encouraged a straightforward showbusiness career involving regular television appearances and cabaret.

Walker, a devotee of French composer **Jacques Brel**, included several of Brel's songs on his debut solo album, *Scott*. He was also displaying immense talent as a songwriter, with poetic, brooding songs like 'Such A Small Love' and 'Always Coming Back To You'. The album was rendered unique by Walker's distinctive, deep, crooning tone and strong vibrato. However, Walker remained uneasy about his career; at one point, he reverted to his real surname, and announced that he would no longer be issuing singles. While the brilliant *Scott 4* contained solely original material and might have heralded the re-evaluation of Walker as a serious songwriter, the BBC chose that very same period to issue the MOR *Scott Sings Songs From His Television Series.*

'Til The Band Comes In, his 1970 collaboration with songwriter Ady Semeland, was released a year after the **Woodstock Festival**; Walker could not have been more out of step with musical fashion, yet more than 25 years on the songs remain classics. He then bowed to popular demand, recording an album of cover versions, *The Moviegoer*, followed by a series of Walker Brothers albums. Thereafter Scott retreated from the music business, returning for the critically acclaimed *Climate Of Hunter. Tilt* received mixed reviews: criticism for not delivering the smooth ballad of old alongside praise for an intriguing work.

WALKER, T-BONE

WALKER (b. AARON THIBEAUX WALKER, 1910, d. 1975) WAS RAISED IN DALLAS, AMIDST BLUES MUSICIANS. DURING the 20s he toured Texas as a musician/comedian/dancer, before joining a travelling revue. By 1929, he had made a country blues record for Columbia as 'Oak Cliff T-Bone'. He then travelled to Oklahoma City, where he was taught by Chuck Richardson. In 1934, Walker joined 'Big' Jim Wynn's band. His popularity grew steadily and in 1940 he joined Les Hite's Orchestra. Upon arriving in New York with Hite, Varsity Records recorded the orchestra, and Walker's feature, 'T-Bone Blues', became a great success. Leaving Hite, Walker co-led a band with Big Jim Wynn.

In 1942-44, Walker recorded for Capitol Records with Freddie Slack's band. Slack then supported Walker on his first solo release. The two tracks, 'Mean Old World' and 'I Got A Break Baby', became standards. During 1945-46 Walker played Chicago clubs; upon his return to the west coast, he was in great demand, both in concert and for his new records. These included 'I'm Gonna Find My Baby', 'T-Bone Shuffle' and 'Call It Stormy Monday'.

In 1950, he signed with Imperial Records where he demonstrated a harder, funkier style of blues, utilizing T. J. Fowler's band and **Dave Bartholomew**'s band, as well as his own working unit from LA. These experiments continued after moving to Atlantic (1955-59), where he worked with blues harmonica player Junior Wells and modern jazz guitarist Barney Kessel. Walker continued to record prolifically, but by the early 70s his powers were diminished through ill health. In 1974, he suffered a severe stroke from which he never recovered.

WALSH, JOE

US GUITAR HERO WALSH (b. 1947) STARTED HIS CAREER IN 1965 WITH THE **G-CLEFS** JOINING THE **JAMES GANG** IN 1969. He left in 1972 and formed Barnstorm with Joe Vitale (drums) and Kenny Passarelli (bass). Their self-titled album made a respectable showing in the US charts. Despite the follow-up being credited to Walsh, *The Smoker You Drink The Player You Get* was still Barnstorm, although the band broke up that year. *Smoker* became his first gold album, featuring 'Meadows' and 'Rocky Mountain Way'.

In 1974, Walsh produced **Dan Fogelberg**'s classic *Souvenirs* and guested on albums by **Stephen Stills**, the **Eagles** and **B. B. King**. *So What* went gold and featured the classic, 'Turn To Stone'. He then performed at London's Wembley Stadium with the **Beach Boys**, **Elton John** and the Eagles. Five months later Walsh joined the Eagles, replacing Bernie Leaden. His distinctive tone contributed greatly to *Hotel California*, including the title track.

Walsh's highly successful career continued with further solo albums including the excellent *But Seriously Folks*. In 1980, he contributed to the best-selling soundtrack *Urban Cowboy* and was rewarded with a US Top 20 hit 'All Night Long'. In 1995, the Eagles reunited.

WAR

LEROY 'LONNIE' JORDAN (KEYBOARDS), HOWARD SCOTT (GUITAR), CHARLES MILLER (FLUTE/SAXOPHONE), MORRIS 'B. B.' Dickerson (bass) and Harold Brown (drums) had made several records in the US under different names. In 1969, they became Nightshift, adopted by UK vocalist **Eric Burdon** as his backing band. Renamed War, the ensemble was completed by Lee Oskar (b. Oskar Levetin Hansen; harmonica) and 'Papa' Dee Allen (percussion).

After two albums, the group broke away from Burdon. War's potent fusion of funk, R&B, rock and latin styles produced a progressive soul sound and they enjoyed significant US chart success with 'The Cisco Kid' (1973), 'Why Can't We Be Friends?' (1975) and 'Summer' (1976), all of which went gold. In the UK they earned two Top 20 hits with 'Low Rider' (1976) and 'Galaxy' (1978). Despite early promise and a move to MCA, the group's sales dipped and Oskar went solo.

Two 1982 singles, 'You Got The Power' and 'Outlaw', were not followed up until 1987's remake of 'Low Rider' – it crept into the R&B chart. The band struggle on in the 90s, although most of the original members have departed.

WARNES, JENNIFER

WARNES' FIRST RECORDING SESSION WAS A DUET WITH MASON WILLIAMS AND WARNES BECAME PART OF THE LOS Angeles club scene. She also took a leading role in the west coast production of *Hair.* As a solo artist Warnes recorded unsuccessfully until signing with Arista in 1975. There she had a Top 10 hit/country number 1 with 'Right Time Of The Night' (1977) followed by 'I Know A Heartache When I See One' (1979). In 1980, Warnes' film theme 'It Goes Like It Goes' won an Oscar for Best Original Song. She performed **Randy Newman**'s 'One More Hour' on the soundtrack of *Ragtime* before scoring her US number 1 with 'Up Where We Belong' (from the film *An Officer And A Gentleman*), a duet with **Joe Cocker**. It won an Oscar.

Warnes reached number 1 again when she teamed up with Bill Medley for the *Dirty Dancing* theme, 'I've Had The Time Of My Life' (1987). In 1986, she recorded a much-acclaimed selection of **Leonard Cohen** compositions, *Famous Blue Raincoat.* Warnes had first worked with Cohen in 1973 and had created vocal arrangements for his *Recent Songs* as well as singing on his *I'm Your Man.* Warnes co-produced her own 1992 album for Private Music as well as co-writing most of the songs; guest musicians included **Richard Thompson** and **Donald Fagen**.

WALKER, SCOTT

Albums
Scott 2 (Philips 1968)★★★★
Climate Of Hunter (Virgin 1984)★★★★
➽ p.383 for full listings

Connections
Walker Brothers ➽ p.332
Woodstock Festival ➽ p.343
Influences
Jacques Brel ➽ p.67
Further References
Book: *A Deep Shade Of Blue*, Mike Watkinson and Pete Anderson

WALKER, T-BONE

Albums
I Get So Weary (Imperial 1961)★★★★
Low Down Blues (Charly 1986)★★★★
➽ p.383 for full listings
Connections
Dave Bartholomew ➽ p.34
Further References
Book: *Stormy Monday*, Helen Oakly Dance

WALSH, JOE

Albums
The Smoker You Drink, The Player You Get (ABC 1973)★★★★
So What? (ABC 1975)★★★★
➽ p.383 for full listings
Collaborators
Stephen Still ➽ p.310
Eagles ➽ p.130
B. B. King ➽ p.205
Beach Boys ➽ p.36
Elton John ➽ p.200
Connections
G-Clefs ➽ p.157
James Gang ➽ p.197
Dan Fogelberg ➽ p.149

WAR

Albums
The World Is A Ghetto (United Artists 1972)★★★★
Why Can't We Be Friends? (United Artists 1975)★★★★
➽ p.383 for full listings

WARNES, JENNIFER

Albums
Famous Blue Raincoat (RCA 1987)★★★★
➽ p.383 for full listings
Collaborators
Joe Cocker ➽ p.95
Richard Thompson ➽ p.320
Donald Fagen ➽ p.141

WARWICK, DIONNE
Albums
Anyone Who Had A Heart (1964)★★★★
Dionne (Arista 1979)★★★★
➽ p.383 for full listings
Collaborators
Detroit Spinners ➽ p.116
Barry Manilow ➽ p.224
Bee Gees ➽ p.41
Luther Vandross ➽ p.328
Elton John ➽ p.200
Gladys Knight ➽ p.209
Stevie Wonder ➽ p.342
Jeffrey Osborne ➽ p.253
Connections
Cissy Houston ➽ p.188
Burt Bacharach ➽ p.27

W.A.S.P.
Albums
The Last Command (Capitol 1985)★★★
The Crimson Idol (Parlophone 1992)★★★
Still Not Black Enough (Raw Power 1995)★★★
➽ p.383 for full listings
Influences
Who ➽ p.338
Further References
Video: *Live At The Lyceum* (PMI 1985)

WATERBOYS
Albums
The Waterboys (Ensign 1983)★★★
This Is The Sea (Ensign 1985)★★★★
➽ p.383 for full listings
Connections
World Party ➽ p.343

WATERS, ROGER
Albums
The Pros And Cons Of Hitch Hiking (Harvest 1984)★★★
➽ p.383 for full listings
Collaborators
Eric Clapton ➽ p.92
Van Morrison ➽ p.238
Cyndi Lauper ➽ p.213
Sinead O'Connor ➽ p.250
Joni Mitchell ➽ p.235
Connections
Pink Floyd ➽ p.261

WATSON, JOHNNY 'GUITAR'
Albums
Gangster Of Love (King 1958)★★★★
Bad (Chess 1966)★★★★
➽ p.383 for full listings
Collaborators
Little Richard ➽ p.217
Connections
Steve Miller ➽ p.234
Frank Zappa ➽ p.348

WATT, MIKE
Albums
Ball-Hog Or Tugboat (Columbia 1995)★★★★
➽ p.383 for full listings

WARWICK, DIONNE

US SINGER WARWICK (b. MARIE DIONNE WARRICK, 1940) SANG IN A CHURCH CHOIR, BEFORE FORMING THE Gospelaires with her sister, Dee Dee and aunt **Cissy Houston**. Increasingly employed as backing singers, Warwick came into contact with songwriters **Burt Bacharach** and Hal David. Her first solo single, 'Don't Make Me Over' (1963), was a fragile slice of 'uptown R&B' and set the tone for such classic collaborations as 'Anyone Who Had A Heart' and 'Walk On By'. Although many of her singles charted, few were Top 10 hits, so Dionne moved closer to the mainstream with such successes as 'I Say A Little Prayer' (1967) and 'Do You Know The Way To San José?' (1968).

In 1971, Warwick signed to Warner Brothers Records, but despite several promising releases, the relationship floundered. Her biggest hit came with the **(Detroit) Spinners** on 'Then Came You' (1974). Warwick moved to Arista in 1979 where work with **Barry Manilow** rekindled her commercial standing. *Heartbreaker* (with the **Bee Gees**) resulted in several hit singles and since then she has been paired with **Luther Vandross**, **Elton John**, **Gladys Knight**, **Stevie Wonder** and **Jeffrey Osborne** among others.

W.A.S.P.

THEATRICAL SHOCK-ROCK TROUPE FORMED IN THE EARLY 80S IN LOS ANGELES, USA. FAMED FOR OUTRAGEOUS LIVE performances, the band – Blackie Lawless (bass/vocals), Chris Holmes (guitar) and Randy Piper (guitar) and Tony Richards (drums) – were snapped up by Capitol. On legal advice, the label refused to release their debut single, 'Animal (Fuck Like A Beast)', released later independently. *W.A.S.P.* was an adequate basic metal debut, while *The Last Command*, with new drummer Stephen Riley, produced the excellent 'Wild Child' and 'Blind In Texas'. W.A.S.P. became a major US concert draw, albeit with a toned-down stageshow. *Inside The Electric Circus* saw the debut of bassist Johnny Rod with Lawless replacing Piper. Lawless, a tireless free-speech campaigner, moved the band towards a serious stance on *The Headless Children*; with Frankie Banali replacing Riley. Holmes left soon afterwards. Lawless used session musicians to record *The Crimson Idol*, a concept effort, and toured with Rod, Doug Blair (guitar) and Stet Howland (drums); he went solo after *First Blood ... Last Cuts*. Their flagging career was further marred by the release of the listless *W.A.S.P.*

WATERBOYS

UK GROUP FORMED BY VOCALIST MIKE SCOTT (b. 1958) WITH JOHN CALDWELL (GUITAR). SCOTT RECRUITED ANTHONY Thistlethwaite (saxophone) and Karl Wallinger (keyboards/percussion/vocals) and work was completed on 'A Girl Called Johnny'. Their debut album was a solid work, emphasizing Scott's singer-songwriter ability. 'December' was an excellent Christmas single but, like their debut, failed to chart. Kevin Wilkinson (drums), Roddy Lorimar (trumpet) and Tim Blanthorn (violin) joined and the Waterboys completed *A Pagan Place*. For *This Is The Sea*, Scott recruited drummer Chris Whitten and fiddler Steve Wickham. The attendant 'The Whole Of The Moon' reached UK number 28 – it hit the Top 10 when reissued in 1990.

When Wallinger left to form **World Party**, Wickham took on a more prominent role. Three years passed before the distinctively folk-flavoured *Fisherman's Blues*; Scott's assimilation of traditional Irish music produced a work of considerable charm and power. *Room To Roam* retained the folk sound, but within days of the album's release, Wickham left, forcing Scott to reconstruct the Waterboys' sound once more. In 1992, Thistlethwaite also left the group. Following the release of the disappointingly mainstream *Dream Harder*, Scott concentrated on his solo career.

WATERS, ROGER

UK SONGWRITER WATERS (b. 1944) WAS A CO-FOUNDER OF **PINK FLOYD**. HIS LYRICS OFTEN FOCUSED ON THE DEATH of his father during World War II, and addressed his increasing conflict with the pressures of rock stardom and alienation with the audience. The introspective nature of these often led to accusations of indulgence, which in part led to the break-up of Pink Floyd in 1983. His first official solo album was *The Pros And Cons Of Hitchhiking* (**Eric Clapton** guested).

Waters also wrote and performed the soundtrack to the anti-nuclear animated film, *When The Wind Blows* (1986). *Radio K.A.O.S.* followed together with the excellent single 'The Tide Is Turning (After Live Aid)'. In 1990, as part of a project in aid of the Leonard Cheshire Memorial Fund For Disaster Relief, Waters masterminded a massive performance of *The Wall* alongside the remains of the Berlin Wall. This was televised around the world; star guests included **Van Morrison**, **Cyndi Lauper**, **Sinead O'Connor** and **Joni Mitchell**, plus actors Albert Finney and Tim Curry. He continues to record.

WATSON, JOHNNY 'GUITAR'

WATSON (b. 1935, d. 1996) STARTED PLAYING PIANO IN THE CHUCK HIGGINS BAND, BILLED AS 'YOUNG JOHN WATSON'. Switching to guitar, he recorded 'Space Guitar', an instrumental far ahead of its time in the use of reverberation and feedback, and 'Motorhead Baby' (with the Amos Milburn band) with an enthusiasm that was to become his trademark. Watson then toured and recorded with the Olympics, Don And Dewey and **Little Richard**. In 1955, he had immediate success with a bluesy ballad, 'Those Lonely, Lonely Nights' (US R&B Top 10). In 1957, the novelty 'Gangster Of Love' (later adopted by **Steve Miller**) gave him a minor hit. Watson did not return to the charts until 1962, when 'Cuttin' In' reached US R&B number 6. The following year he recorded *I Cried For You*, a 'cocktail-lounge' album with hip renditions of 'Polkadots And Moonbeams' and 'Witchcraft'. A partnership with Larry Williams was particularly successful and in 1965 they toured England and recorded an album.

Watson recorded two soulful funk albums, *Listen* and *I Don't Want To Be Alone, Stranger*, with keyboardist Andre Lewis. **Frank Zappa** was a great admirer of Watson and recruited him to play on *One Size Fits All*. Watson also produced and played bass, keyboards and drums on *Ain't That A Bitch*, a brilliant marriage of 50s rockin' R&B, Hollywood schmaltz and futuristic funk; it went gold. In 1981, Watson signed with A&M Records, but the production diluted his unique sound and the record was a failure. One positive side effect was a solo on Herb Alpert's *Beyond*. After a brief retirement Watson re-emerged with *Strike On Computers* and an appearance at London's Town & Country Club in 1987.

WATT, MIKE

WATT (b. *c.* 1957) PLAYED BASS FOR MINUTEMEN AND **FIREHOSE**, BUT IT WAS NOT UNTIL 1995 THAT HE recorded solo. Collaborators included Eddie Vedder (**Pearl Jam**), Evan Dando (**Lemonheads**), Chris and Curt Kirkwood (**Meat Puppets**), Thurston Moore and Lee Ranaldo (**Sonic Youth**), Dave Grohl and Krist Novoselic (**Nirvana**), Gary Lee Connor and Mark Lanegan (**Screaming Trees**), Pat Smear (**Germs**), Flea (**Red Hot Chili Peppers**), and **Henry Rollins**. Although by its very nature a mixed bag, the album did have several strong moments, notably Vedder's vocals on 'Against The 70s' and the electric jazz flourish of 'Sidemouse Advice'.

WAYNE, JEFF

JEFF WAYNE WAS A MEMBER OF THE SANDPIPERS, ALTHOUGH NOT AT THE TIME THEY HAD THEIR WORLDWIDE HIT WITH 'Guantanamera'. He also worked as an arranger for the **Righteous Brothers** before travelling to London in 1966. He wrote and staged a musical based on Charles Dickens's *A Tale Of Two Cities* (the lyrics were written by his father, Jerry Wayne). Starring Edward Woodward, the project was staged in 1969, by which time Wayne had started to establish himself as a jingle writer. In the late 60s and early 70s he was responsible for some of the best-known television advertising slogans and tunes. He then became involved with the career of **David Essex**, producing most of his early hits. Wayne sprang to the public's attention with his concept album based on H. G. Wells's *War Of The Worlds*. Written by Wayne and featuring the talents of Essex, actor Richard Burton, Justin Hayward, **Phil Lynott**, Chris Thompson and Julie Covington, the album was a huge success.

WEATHER REPORT

FOUNDED BY JOE ZAWINUL (KEYBOARDS/SONGWRITING) AND WAYNE SHORTER (REEDS/SONGWRITING) – WHO HAD worked as members of Miles Davis's band in 1969-71, playing on *Bitches' Brew*. They recruited Airto Moreira (percussion) and Miroslav Vitous (bass) and became one of the groups credited with inventing jazz-rock fusion music in the 70s. Eric Gravatt (drums) and Um Romao (percussion) joined for the best-selling *I Sing The Body Electric*. During the mid-70s, the group adopted more elements of rock rhythms and electronic technology, a process which reached its peak on *Black Market* (featuring electric bassist Jaco Pastorius).

In the late 70s and early 80s, the group featured drummer Peter Erskine (replaced by Omar Hakim in 1982), Pastorius and the two founder members. On *Procession*, Weather Report included vocals for the first time, the singer was Janis Siegel. During the mid-80s, Zawinul and Shorter made solo albums before dissolving Weather Report in 1986; rumours of a reunion were touted in the late 90s.

WEATHERALL, ANDY

DJ DANCE MAGNATE WEATHERALL (b. 1963) BEGAN WITH RESIDENCIES AT THE SHOOM AND SPECTRUM CLUBS IN THE acid house boom of 1988. Afterwards he founded the *Boys Own* fanzine with Terry Farley and Steve Mayes, which concentrated on club music, fashion and football. When Boy's Own became a record label, he appeared, as guest vocalist, on a Bocca Juniors track. He made his name, however, by remixing **Primal Scream**'s 'Loaded'. The likes of **James**, **Happy Mondays**, **That Petrol Emotion**, **Saint Etienne**, **Orb**, **Jah Wobble**, **Future Sound Of London**, **Björk**, **Yello**, **Stereo MC's** and **New Order** followed. His landmark achievement, however, remains his supervising role on Primal Scream's *Screamadelica*. He also enjoyed a stint as DJ on Kiss-FM, before his eclectic, anarchic tastes proved too much for programmers. His recording methodology includes sampling strange sounds such as answerphones and dustbin lids for percussion. He has subsequently set up a further label, recording and remix operation under the title Sabres Of Paradise. In 1993, he signed a major publishing deal with MCA Music.

WEBB, JIMMY

WEBB (b. 1946) ARRANGED A SINGLE FOR GIRL-GROUP THE CONTESSAS WHILE STILL A STUDENT IN THE US. HE THEN worked with Jobete Music, the publishing wing of Tamla/**Motown**. He wrote 'This Time Last Summer' for **Brenda Holloway** and 'My Christmas Tree' for the **Supremes**, followed by **Johnny Rivers**' 'By The Time I Get To Phoenix' (1966). Rivers appointed Webb in-house composer/arranger for his newly-launched Soul City Records where he worked with the fledgling **Fifth Dimension**. Having completed the intriguing 'Rosecrans Blvd', the partnership flourished with 'Up, Up And Away', which sold over one million copies. Eventually Webb issued a single, 'Love Years Coming', credited to the Strawberry Children. **Glen Campbell** then exhumed 'By The Time I Get To Phoenix', which won a Grammy as the Best Vocal Performance of 1967. In 1968, Richard Harris scored a major international smash with 'MacArthur Park' followed by 'Didn't We'. Webb arranged and composed material for Harris' albums *A Tramp Shining* and *The Yard Went On Forever*, but was dismayed when his own solo debut, *Jimmy Webb Sings Jimmy Webb*, was issued – it featured early demo recordings, overdubbed and orchestrated without his consent. Further success for Campbell with 'Wichita Lineman' (1968) demonstrated Webb's songwriting ability.

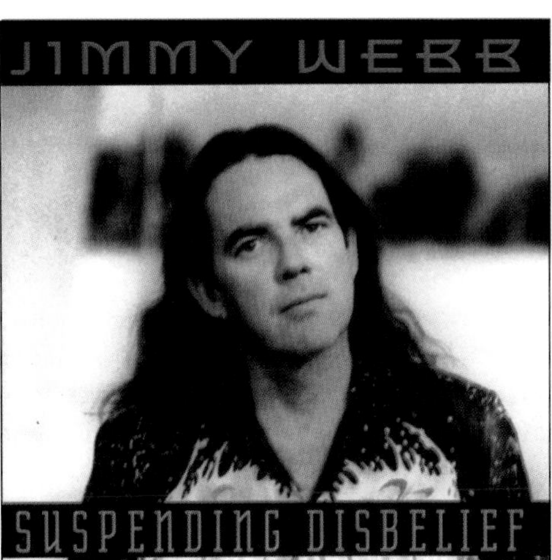

A 1970 tour revealed his inexperience as a performer, although *Words And Music* showed the episode had engendered a tighter rock-based style. Guitarist Fred Tackett (later of **Little Feat**) provided much of the accompaniment. *And So: On* proved even more impressive, with superb contributions by **Larry Coryell**. *Letters*, which included a superb rendition of 'Galveston', was succeeded by the excellent *Land's End*. On *Reunion*, Webb rekindled his partnership with Glen Campbell and *Earthbound* saw him recreating a partnership with the Fifth Dimension. Webb also wrote and/or produced material for **Cher**, **Joan Baez**, **Joe Cocker**, Frank Sinatra and **Art Garfunkel**. *Watermark* contains what many regard as the definitive interpretations of several Webb songs.

The artist resumed recording with *El Mirage*, which included 'The Highwayman', a title popularized by the country 'supergroup' featuring **Johnny Cash**, **Kris Kristofferson**, **Willie Nelson** and Waylon Jennings. Webb also continued to score film soundtracks, including *Voices* and *Hanoi Hilton*, and two musicals, *The Children's Crusade* and *Dandelion Wine*. Webb ceased recording following the release of *Angel Heart*, however, he undertook several live shows in 1988 and released his first studio album proper in 11 years with *Suspending Disbelief*.

Collaborators
Henry Rollins ➻ p.282
Connections
Firehose ➻ p.146
Pearl Jam ➻ p.257
Lemonheads ➻ p.214
Meat Puppets ➻ p.230
Sonic Youth ➻ p.302
Nirvana ➻ p.248
Screaming Trees ➻ p.290
Germs ➻ p.162
Red Hot Chilli Peppers ➻ p.274

WAYNE, JEFF
Albums
War Of The Worlds (Columbia 1978)★★★
War Of The Worlds – Highlights (Columbia 1981)★★★
➻ p.383 for full listings
Collaborators
Phil Lynott ➻ p.220
Connections
Righteous Brothers ➻ p.278
David Essex ➻ p.138

WEATHER REPORT
Albums
I Sing The Body Electric (Columbia 1972)★★★★
Black Market (Columbia 1976)★★★★
➻ p.383 for full listings

WEATHERALL, ANDY
Connections
Primal Scream ➻ p.267
James ➻ p.196
Happy Mondays ➻ p.174
That Petrol Emotion ➻ p.319
Saint Etienne ➻ p.287
Orb ➻ p.252
Jah Wobble ➻ p.196
Future Sound Of London ➻ p.156
Björk ➻ p.48
Yello ➻ p.345
Stereo MC's ➻ p.309
New Order ➻ p.246

WEBB, JIMMY
Albums
Letters (Reprise 1972)★★★★
Land's End (Asylum 1974)★★★★
➻ p.383 for full listings
Collaborators
Johnny Cash ➻ p.84
Kris Kristofferson ➻ p.211
Willie Nelson ➻ p.245
Connections
Glenn Campbell ➻ p.79
Little Feat ➻ p.216
Cher ➻ p.89
Joan Baez ➻ p.29
Joe Cocker ➻ p.95
Art Garfunkel ➻ p.159
Influences
Motown ➻ p.240
Brenda Holloway ➻ p.184
Supremes ➻ p.314
Johnny Rivers ➻ p.278
Fifth Dimension ➻ p.145
Larry Coryell ➻ p.101

WEDDING PRESENT
Albums
George Best (Reception 1987)★★★
Seamonsters (RCA 1991)★★★
Saturnalia (Cooking Vinyl 1996)★★★
➽ p.383 for full listings
Connections
Steve Albini
Further References
Book: *The Wedding Present: Thank Yer, Very Glad*, Mark Hodkinson

WEEZER
Albums
Weezer (Geffen 1994)★★★★
➽ p.383 for full listings

WELLER, PAUL
Albums
Wild Wood (Go! Discs 1994)★★★★
Stanley Road (Go! Discs 1995)★★★★
Heavy Soul (Island 1997)★★★★
➽ p.383 for full listings

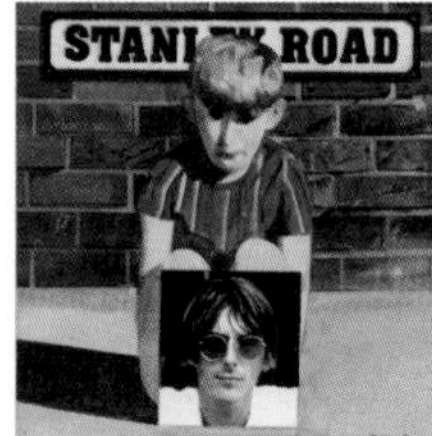

Collaborators
Robert Howard ➽ p.54
Camille Hinds ➽ p.312
Kenny Jones ➽ p.141
James Taylor ➽ p.317
Noel Gallagher ➽ p.250
Connections
Jam ➽ p.196
Style Council ➽ p.312
Orange Juice ➽ p.252
Ocean Colour Scene ➽ p.251
Dr. John ➽ p.125
Influences
Small Faces ➽ p.300
Steve Marriott ➽ p.225
Traffic ➽ p.323
Spooky Tooth ➽ p.306
Tim Hardin ➽ p.174
Tim Buckley ➽ p.73
Further References
Video: *Highlights And Hang Ups* (Polygram 1994)
Book: *Days Lose Their Names And Time Slips Away: Paul Weller 1992-95*, Lawrence Watson and Paolo Hewitt.

WELLS, MARY
Albums
Bye Bye Baby, I Don't Want To Take A Chance (Motown 1961)★★★
Ooh! (Movietone 1966)★★★
➽ p.383 for full listings

WEDDING PRESENT

FORMED IN LEEDS, ENGLAND, IN 1985 BY DAVID GEDGE (GUITAR/VOCALS) WITH KEITH GREGORY (BASS), PETER Salowka (guitar) and Shaun Charman (drums). The Wedding Present staked their musical claim with a ferocious blend of implausibly fast guitars and lovelorn lyrics over a series of much-lauded singles. *George Best* reached UK number 47. Pete Salowka's East European upbringing was brought to bear on their sound, resulting in the frenzied Ukrainian folk songs on *Ukrainski Vistupi V Johna Peel*. Charman left as their debut was released, replaced by Simon Smith. 'Kennedy' saw the band break into the UK Top 40 for the first time and revealed that the Wedding Present were becoming more extreme. By *Seamonsters*, they had forged a bizarre relationship with hardcore exponent Steve Albini who encouraged them to juggle with broody lyrical mumblings and extraordinary slabs of guitar. Before *Seamonsters* was released, Salowka was replaced by Paul Dorrington, instead remaining on the business side of the band. In 1992, the Wedding Present released a single every month, throughout the year. Each single reached the UK Top 40. Their relationship with RCA ended following the *Hit Parade* compilations; they signed to Island. Keith Gregory also left the fold. *Mini* enhanced their place as influential indie popsters as did *Saturnalia*.

WEEZER

US GUITAR POP ARTISANS FROM LOS ANGELES, USA. RIVERS CUOMO (VOCALS/GUITAR), BRIAN BELL (GUITAR), MATT SHARP (bass) and Patrick Wilson (drums) signed to DGC Records in 1993. On the back of offbeat singles, 'Undone – The Sweater Song' and 'Buddy Holly' and seven months' touring the country, their self-titled debut album sold nearly a million copies. Their preference for goofy garage aesthetics were distinctive, along with their fuzzboxes and Sharp's falsetto harmonies. The title of *Pinkerton* infuriated the security company Pinkerton Service, who issued legal procedings shortly after its release.

WELLER, PAUL

WELLER (b. JOHN WILLIAM WELLER, 1958) STARTED OUT WITH UK BAND THE **JAM**, THEN FORMED THE **STYLE COUNCIL**. By their second album, the thread of soul-stirring passion that had always seen Weller at his most affecting had been squandered in a less earnest quest for dry musical sophistication. By 1990, he found himself without either a band or a recording contract for the first time in 13 years.

Returning to early influences, he became inspired to write new material and set up a new band. Paul Francis (bass), Max Beesley (keyboards/vibraphone), Jacko Peake (saxophone/flute), Joe Becket (percussion), Damon Brown (trumpet/flugelhorn), Chris Lawrence (trombone), Jam biographer and 'best friend' Paulo Hewitt (DJ) and Style Council drummer Steve White were christened the Paul Weller Movement. They made their live debut on UK tours, with a second spree in 1991. Henry Thomas joined on bass, with the brass section reduced to Gerard Prescencer (trumpet/flugelhorn), and Zeta Massiah and Lina Duggan on backing vocals. Weller released his first solo single, 'Into Tomorrow', on his own Freedom High label, before contributing seven compositions to wife D. C. Lee's *Slam Slam* project. Shortly afterwards the Movement and the name itself were dispensed with, leaving a kernel of White and Peake with guests including Robert Howard (**Blow Monkeys**), Marco Nelson, Style Council bassist Camille Hinds and singer Carleen Anderson. The debut album was initially released on Pony Canyon in Japan, six months before a UK issue on Go! Discs. *Paul Weller* was strangely overlooked by the UK press, despite the presence of fine songs in 'Clues' and 'Strange Museum'. In 1992, **Orange Juice** drummer Zeke Manyika joined, as did former Style Council compatriot Helen Turner (organ). Second single 'Uh Huh, Oh Yeh' reached the UK Top 20 followed by 'Sunflower' (1993), and *Wild Wood* – with production from Brendan Lynch, and multitudinous musical accompaniment including Mick Talbot, D. C. Lee, Simon Fowler and Steve Craddock (**Ocean Colour Scene**) and new bass player Marco Nelson. Live favourites 'The Weaver' and 'Hung Up' reached the charts. He toured Japan, jammed with Kenney Jones (**Faces**), **James Taylor** and Mother Earth and played euphoric sets at 1994's **Glastonbury** and Phoenix Festivals.

Stanley Road featured **Oasis**' Noel Gallagher on a cover version of **Dr. John**'s 'Walk On Gilded Splinters' but of more enduring interest were the Weller originals, which spanned a wide range of musical styles unified by the 'live' approach to recording. *Heavy Soul*, with its **Traffic** influences, showed Weller at the peak of all his musical changes.

WELLS, MARY

AT THE AGE OF 17, MARY WELLS (b. 1943, d. 1992) COMPOSED 'BYE BYE BABY'. PRODUCER BERRY GORDY OFFERED HER A contract with **Motown**, and Wells' rendition of her song became one of the company's first Top 50 hits in 1960. **Smokey Robinson** masterminded all her subsequent Motown releases, composing a remarkable series of clever, witty soul songs, full of puns and unexpected twists, and set to irresistible melody lines. 'The One Who Really Loves You', 'You Beat Me To The Punch' and 'Two Lovers' were all Top 10 hits. The pinnacle of the Robinson/Wells partnership, however, was 'My Guy' (1964, US number 1/UK Top 5). It introduced the Motown sound to a worldwide audience. Gordy encouraged her to record an album of duets with **Marvin Gaye**, from which 'Once Upon A Time' was another major hit. Just as Wells' career reached its peak, she chose to leave Motown, tempted by a film offer from 20th Century Fox. Without Robinson, she was unable to capture her hit form, and she left Fox the following year. In 1966, she married Cecil Womack and moved to Atco Records, where she scored minor hits with 'Dear Lover', 'Such A Sweet Thing' and 'The Doctor'. Subsequent sessions for a variety of US labels proved less than successful, and she was reduced to re-recording her Motown hits in the 80s, she also continued touring and recording. Sadly Wells died of throat cancer in 1992.

WET WET WET

FORMED IN 1982, THIS SCOTTISH POP GROUP COMPRISES GRAEME CLARK (BASS/VOCALS), NEIL MITCHELL (KEYBOARDS), Marti Pellow (vocals) and Tom Cunningham (drums). After live performances, they were signed by Phonogram Records in 1985. In 1987, 'Wishing I Was Lucky' reached the UK Top 10, followed by the even more successful 'Sweet Little Mystery'. The group's agreeable blue-eyed soul was evident on their debut *Popped In Souled Out* (UK number 2). Further hits followed with 'Angel Eyes (Home And Away)' and 'Temptation'. In 1988, the group's profile was increased when they reached UK number 1 with a reading of the **Beatles**' 'With A Little Help From My Friends'. In 1992, 'Goodnight Girl' remained at UK number 1 for several weeks, and was followed by 'Lip Service' (1992), suggesting an interest in more dance-orientated music. Any fears that their commercial fortunes may be declining were blown apart by the staggering success of their cover of the **Troggs**' 'Love Is All Around', the theme song to the hit movie *Four Weddings And A Funeral*. It stayed at UK number 1 for 15 weeks. In 1998, they played at the Memorial Concert for Princess Diana.

WHAM!

WHAM! FIRST PERFORMED TOGETHER IN A SKA-INFLUENCED SCHOOL BAND, THE EXECUTIVE. IN 1982, **GEORGE MICHAEL** (b. Georgios (Yorgos) Kyriako Panayiotou, 1963; vocals) and Andrew Ridgeley (b. 1963; guitar) signed to the recently formed label, Innervision. After embarking on a series of 'personal appearances' at local clubs with backing singers Amanda Washbourn and Shirlie Holliman, they completed their debut single 'Wham! Rap' which had been intended as a disco parody. What emerged was an exhilarating dance number with intriguing double-edged lyrics. The song initially failed to chart, however the following 'Young Guns' (1982) reached the UK Top 10, followed by a remixed 'Wham! Rap'.

An acrimonious dispute with Innervision saw the duo signing to Epic Records and achieving their first UK number 1 'Wake Me Up Before You Go Go', quickly followed by 'Careless Whisper'. *Make It Big* zoomed to number 1 and by the end of 1984 the group had two further major successes 'Freedom' and 'Last Christmas'/'Everything She Wants'. In 1985, they toured China and enjoyed considerable success in America. On 28 June 1986, they played a farewell concert before 72,000 fans at London's Wembley Stadium; it was captured on *The Final*.

WHITE, BARRY

AT AGE 11, US-BORN WHITE (b. 1944) PLAYED PIANO ON JESSE BELVIN'S HIT, 'GOODNIGHT MY LOVE'. BARRY MADE SEVERAL records during the early 60s, as 'Barry Lee', and as a member of various bands, alongside guiding the careers of, amongst others, Felice Taylor and Viola Wills. In 1969, White put together Love Unlimited, a female vocal trio made up of Diana Taylor, Glodean James (his future wife) and her sister Linda and the Love Unlimited Orchestra. Love Unlimited's success with 'Walkin' In The Rain With The One I Love' (1972), featuring White's gravelly, passion-soaked voice, rejuvenated his career, scoring major US and UK hits with 'I'm Gonna Love You Just A Little More Baby', 'Never, Never Gonna Give Ya Up' (both 1973), 'Can't Get Enough Of Your Love, Babe' and 'You're The First, The Last, My Everything' (both 1974). White's lyrics grew more sexually explicit and, although his pop hits lessened towards the end of the 70s, he remained the idolatry subject of live performances. His last major hit was in 1978 with **Billy Joel**'s 'Just The Way You Are', although he returned to the UK Top 20 in 1987 with 'Sho' You Right'. In 1992, **Lisa Stansfield** and White re-recorded a version of Stansfield's hit, 'All Around The World', but it was not as successful as the original.

WHITESNAKE

UK-BASED HEAVY ROCK BAND LED BY DAVID COVERDALE (b. 1951; EX-**DEEP PURPLE**). COVERDALE HAD RECORDED TWO solo albums, *Whitesnake* and *Northwinds*, before forming a touring band from musicians who had played on those records: Micky Moody (guitar), Bernie Marsden (guitar), Brian Johnston (keyboards), Neil Murray (bass) and John Dowle (drums). The group toured the UK, Europe and Japan, reaching the US in 1980. Ex-Deep Purple members Jon Lord and Ian Paice joined on keyboards and drums. Whitesnake's first British hit was 'Fool For Your Loving' (1980), and the double album *Live In The Heart Of The City* reached the Top 10. After a temporary hiatus, Whitesnake re-formed in 1982 but only Lord and Moody remained from the earlier line-up. The new members were Mel Galley (guitar), ex-**Alexis Korner** bassist Colin Hodgkinson and Cozy Powell (drums). By 1984, Moody and Lord had left.

The band remained one of the leading exponents of heavy rock and frequent tours brought a million-selling album in the USA with *Whitesnake*. Coverdale's bluesy ballad style brought Top 10 hits with 'Is This Love' and 'Here I Go Again'. Coverdale joined forces with **Jimmy Page** for the release of *Coverdale/Page*. After a break, he returned with a new album, *Restless Heart*; a mellow recording which emphasized Coverdale's terrific voice and range.

WHITE ZOMBIE

THEATRICAL METAL BAND FORMED IN 1985 IN NEW YORK. ROB 'ZOMBIE' STRAKER (b. 1966), FEMALE BASSIST SEAN Yseult (b. 1966), drummer Ivan DePlume and guitarist Tom Guay released two albums of noisy metal on their own label while they played chaotic shows around local clubs. John Ricci replaced Guay for *Make Them Die Slowly*; Ricci was then replaced by Jay Yuenger for the *God Of Thunder* EP. The Andy Wallace production on *La Sexorcisto: Devil Music Vol. 1*, finally did White Zombie justice, with Straker sounding positively demonic as he roared his bizarre stream-of-consciousness lyrics against a monstrous instrumental barrage punctuated by sampled B-movie dialogue.

They toured the USA ceaselessly, receiving continuous MTV coverage. As *La Sexorcisto* took off, DePlume was replaced by Philo, then by John Tempesta. *Astro Creep* was greeted with enthusiasm, selling over a million US copies in a few weeks. 'More Human Than Human', also became a major hit, appearing on mainstream radio. Yuenger also involved himself in two notable collaborative projects: with Yseult, he worked with Dave Navarro (**Red Hot Chili Peppers**), Keith Morris and Greg Rogers, as Zombie All Stars; he also formed a punk-inspired side group, Bull Taco, with Morris, Navarro, Chad Smith (Red Hot Chili Peppers) and Zander Schloss.

Collaborators
Marvin Gaye ➧ p.159
Connections
Jackie Wilson ➧ p.340
Motown ➧ p.240
Influences
Smokey Robinson ➧ p.279
Further References
Film: *Catalina Caper* (1967).

WET WET WET
Albums
Popped In Souled Out (Precious 1987)★★★
Holding Back The River (Precious 1989)★★★
➧ p.383 for full listings
Influences
Beatles ➧ p.38
Troggs ➧ p.324
Further References
Book: *Wet Wet Wet Pictured*, Simon Fowler and Alan Jackson

WHAM!
Albums
Make It Big (Epic 1984)★★★
The Final (Epic 1986)★★★
➧ p.383 for full listings
Connections
George Michael ➧ p.233
Further References
Video: *Wham! The Video* (1987)
Book: *Wham! (Confidential) The Death Of A Supergroup*, Johnny Rogan

WHITE, BARRY
Albums
I've Got So Much To Give (20th Century 1973)★★★
In Your Mix (A&M 1991)★★★
➧ p.383 for full listings
Collaborators
Lisa Stansfield ➧ p.307
Connections
Billy Joel ➧ p.199

WHITESNAKE
Albums
Whitesnake (Liberty 1987)★★★★
Restless Heart (EMI 1997)★★★
➧ p.383 for full listings
Collaborators
Jimmy Page ➧ p.255
Connections
Deep Purple ➧ p.113
Alexis Korner ➧ p.210
Further References
Video: *Fourplay* (1984)
Trilogy (1988).
Books: *Illustrated Biography*, Simon Robinson
Whitesnake, Tom Hibbert

WHITE ZOMBIE
Albums
Make Them Die Slowly (Caroline 1989)
➧ p.383 for full listings
Collaborators
Dave Navarro ➧ p.274
Connections
Germs ➧ p.162

WHO
Albums
My Generation (Brunswick 1965)★★★★
Live At Leeds (Track 1970)★★★★★
Who's Next (Track 1971)★★★★★
➧ p.383 for full listings

Connections
Pete Townshend ➧ p.323
Small Faces ➧ p.300
Influences
Monterey Pop Festival ➧ p.237
Further References
Films: *Tommy* (1975)
Quadrophenia (1979)
Videos: *The Kids Are Alright* (1990)
The Who Live At The Isle Of Wight Festival 1970 (Warner Music Vision 1996)
Books: *The Who ... Through The Eyes Of Pete Townshend*, Conner McKnight and Caroline Silver
Whose Who? A Who Retrospective, Brian Ashley and Steve Monnery,
Quadrophenia, Alan Fletcher

WILCO
Albums
A.M. (Reprise 1995)★★★
Being There (Reprise 1996)★★★
➧ p.383 for full listings
Influences
Rolling Stones ➧ p.281

WILDE, KIM
Albums
Kim Wilde (RAK 1981)★★★
Close (MCA 1988)★★★★
Love Is (MCA 1992)★★★
➧ p.383 for full listings
Connections
Marty Wilde ➧ p.338
Mickie Most ➧ p.239
Supremes ➧ p.314
Further References
Videos: *Video EP: Kim Wilde* (1987)
Another Step (Closer To You) (1990)
The Singles Collection 1981-1993 (1993)

WHO

FORMED IN LONDON, IN 1964 BY **PETE TOWNSHEND** (b. 1945; GUITAR/VOCALS), ROGER DALTREY (b. 1944; VOCALS) and John Entwistle (b. 1944; bass). They recruited drummer Keith Moon (b. 1947, d. 1978) and were adopted by manager/publicist Peter Meadon, who changed their name to the High Numbers, dressed them in stylish clothes and determinedly courted a mod audience, through their single, 'I'm The Face'. Two budding film directors, Kit Lambert and Chris Stamp, then assumed management responsibilities and re-named them the Who.

Their in-person violence matched an anti-social attitude and despite a successful residency at London's Marquee club, the Who were shunned by major labels. Eventually they signed with American Decca. 'I Can't Explain' (1965) reached UK Top 10, followed by 'Anyway, Anyhow, Anywhere' and 'My Generation'. The Who's debut album was delayed to accommodate new Townshend originals at the expense of now *passé* cover versions.

The Who continued to chart, although Townshend's decidedly English perceptions initially precluded a sustained international success. The Who's popularity in the USA flourished only in the wake of their appearance at the 1967 **Monterey Pop Festival**.

They returned to the UK Top 10 in 1967 with the powerful 'I Can See For Miles'. However, the group failed to achieve a number 1 hit on either side of the Atlantic. They embraced the album market fully with *Tommy*, an extravagant rock opera which became a staple part of their increasingly in demand live appearances. The set spawned a major hit in 'Pinball Wizard' but, more crucially, established the group as a serious act courting critical respectability. The propulsive *Live At Leeds* was a sturdy concert souvenir; Townshend's next project, *Lighthouse*, was later aborted, several of its songs incorporated into *Who's Next*. A series of specifically created singles came next – 'Let's See Action' (1971), 'Join Together' (1972), 'Relay' (1973) – which marked time as Townshend completed work on *Quadrophenia*. Commitments to solo careers undermined the group's progress and *The Who By Numbers* was low-key.

They re-emerged with the confident *Who Are You*, but its release was sadly overshadowed when, on 23 August 1978, Keith Moon died following an overdose of medication taken to alleviate alcohol addiction. His madcap behaviour and idiosyncratic, exciting drumming had been an integral part of the Who fabric, and rumours of a permanent split abounded. A retrospective film, *The Kids Are Alright*, enhanced a sense of finality, but the group resumed recording in 1979 with former **Small Faces/Faces** drummer Kenny Jones (b. 1948). Tragically, any newfound optimism was undermined that year when 11 fans were killed prior to a concert in Ohio during a rush to secure prime vantage points; neither *Face Dances* nor *It's Hard* recaptured previous artistic heights. A farewell tour was undertaken in 1982-83 and although the group reunited for Live Aid, they remained estranged until 1989, when Townshend agreed to undertake a series of US dates for their 25th anniversary (with drummer Simon Phillips).

In 1996, the band performed *Quadrophenia* at London's Hyde Park, in front of 200,000 people. They toured the USA and the UK later that year.

WILCO

US QUINTET FORMED BY JEFF TWEEDY (b. *c.* 1968; VOCALS/GUITAR). THEIR DEBUT SOLD MODESTLY, BUT WAS FOLLOWED ambitiously by a double album – Wilco agreed to take a cut in their royalties in order to facilitate its release. It achieved critical acclaim with several comparing the album favourably to the **Rolling Stones**' *Exile On Main Street*. In 1998, they released *Mermaid Avenue*, a collaboration with **Billy Bragg**. A new Wilco album was also rumoured.

WILDE, KIM

THE DAUGHTER OF 50S POP IDOL **MARTY WILDE**, KIM (b. KIM SMITH, 1960) WAS SIGNED TO **MICKIE MOST**'S RAK Records in 1980. Her first single, 'Kids In America', reached UK number 2. Further singles success followed and *Kim Wilde* fared well in the album charts. By 1982, she had sold more records than her father had in his entire career. While 'View From A Bridge' maintained her standing at home, 'Kids In America' reached the US Top 30. An energetic reworking of the **Supremes**' 'You Keep Me Hangin' On' took her back to UK number 2 and, after appearing on the Ferry Aid charity single, 'Let It Be', Wilde was back in the Top 10 with 'Another Step (Closer To You)', a duet with Junior Giscombe. In 1988, the dance-orientated 'You Came' was followed by further Top 10 hits 'Never Trust A Stranger' and 'Four Letter Word'. Later she scored a Christmas novelty hit 'Rockin' Around The Christmas Tree' with comedian Mel Smith. Her recent singles have gained lowly chart positions and *Love Is* was a pale shadow of *Close*. On *Now And Forever* Wilde abandoned pop for a slick soul groove.

WILDE, MARTY

UK ROCK 'N' ROLL SINGER WILDE (b. REGINALD LEONARD SMITH, 1936) WAS SPOTTED BY SONGWRITER LIONEL BART, and signed to entrepreneur Larry Parnes. Parnes arranged a record deal with Philips Records, but Wilde's initial singles failed to chart. Nevertheless, Wilde was promoted vigorously and extensive media coverage culminated in a hit recording of Jody Reynolds' 'Endless Sleep' (1957).

Soon afterwards, Wilde became the resident star of new television programme *Oh Boy!* – until he was replaced by **Cliff Richard**. After considerable success with such songs as 'Donna', 'Teenager In Love', 'Sea Of Love' and his own composition 'Bad Boy', Wilde veered away from rock 'n' roll to concentrate on Frank Sinatra-style ballads. His last major success was with a lack-lustre version of **Bobby Vee**'s 'Rubber Ball' in 1961.

Wilde also enjoyed songwriting success, with hits like **Status Quo**'s 'Ice In The Sun'. By the 70s, he was managing his son Ricky, who later achieved songwriting success for his sister, **Kim Wilde**.

WILLIAMS, BIG JOE

BIG JOE WILLIAMS (b. JOE LEE WILLIAMS, 1903, d. 1982) WAS OF PARTIAL CHEROKEE STOCK. 'BIG JOE' TOOK TO THE road around 1918, working his way around the lumber camps, turpentine farms and juke joints of the south. This rural audience supported him through the Depression when he appeared as 'Poor Joe'. His known recordings began in 1935 when he recorded six tracks for Bluebird. From then on he recorded at every opportunity, moving to Columbia Records in 1945. Williams found a wider audience when blues came into vogue with young whites in the 60s. He continued to record and tour using a mini-string guitar, adding Europe and Japan to his itinerary. With his gruff, shouting voice and ringing guitar he became a great favourite on the club and concert circuit.

WILLIAMS, HANK

HANK (b. HIRAM WILLIAMS, 1923, d. 1953) LEARNED GUITAR FROM AN ELDERLY BLACK MUSICIAN, TEETOT (RUFE PAYNE); as a result, a strong blues thread runs through his work. After winning a talent contest, Williams formed the Drifting Cowboys. In 1946, he and his wife Audrey moved to Nashville, and the relatively new Acuff-Rose publishing. In 1946, Williams made his first recordings for the small Sterling label before signing to MGM, where 'Move It On Over' sold several thousand copies.

He joined the radio show *Louisiana Hayride* in 1948 and was featured on its concert tours. His revival of 'Lovesick Blues' topped the US country charts for 16 weeks. The *Grand Ole Opry* invited him to perform the song, leading to an unprecedented six encores. He and the Drifting Cowboys became regulars, commanding $1,000 for concert appearances. 'Wedding Bells' made number 2, as did 'I'm So Lonesome I Could Cry'. In 1950, he had three country number 1s, 'Long Gone Lonesome Blues', 'Why Don't You Love Me?' and 'Moanin' The Blues'. The following year, he had two further chart-toppers with 'Cold, Cold Heart' and 'Hey, Good Lookin''. In 1952, Williams reached number 1 with 'Jambalaya'.

Williams drank too much, took drugs and permanently lived in conflict. His songs articulated real life and love; he also recorded melodramatic monologues as Luke The Drifter. Williams' wife, 'Miss Audrey', also made solo records, but she was frustrated by her own lack of success and many of Williams' songs stemmed from their quarrels. They were divorced in 1952.

In the same year, Williams was fired from *Opry*, due to his drinking; he lost manager Fred Rose's support; the Drifting Cowboys turned to Ray Price, and, although the *Louisiana Hayride* tolerated his wayward lifestyle, his earnings fell and he was reduced to playing small clubs with pick-up bands. Scrabbling for security, he married the 19-year-old Billie Jean Jones – three times, two of which were as concerts before several thousand paying guests.

His biggest booking for some time was on New Year's Day, 1953 with Hawkshaw Hawkins and Homer And Jethro in Canton, Ohio. Because of a blizzard, Williams' plane was cancelled and an 18-year-old taxi driver, Charles Carr, was hired to drive Williams' Cadillac. Williams, having devoured a bottle of whiskey, sank into a deep sleep. Five hours later, Carr discovered that his passenger was dead, officially due to 'severe heart attack with haemorrhage' – his current number 1 was 'I'll Never Get Out Of This World Alive'. Williams' body lay in state in the Montgomery Municipal Auditorium. His shrine in Montgomery Oakwood Cemetery is the subject of Steve Young's song, 'Montgomery In The Rain'.

Posthumously, he continued to reap number 1s and became the first deceased star to have his recordings altered. Albums of Hank Williams with strings and duets with his son followed. In 1969, Hank Jnr completed some of his father's scribblings for an album, 'Songs My Father Left Me'. Hank Williams recorded around 170 different songs between 1946 and 1952.

WILLIAMS, HANK, JNR

WILLIAMS JNR (b. RANDALL HANK WILLIAMS JNR, 1949), THE SON OF **HANK WILLIAMS**, PERFORMED AS A CHILD, and had a high school band, Rockin' Randall And The Rockets. In the 60s, Hank had country hits with 'Long Gone Lonesome Blues', 'Cajun Baby', a revival of 'Endless Sleep', and the only version of 'Nobody's Child' ever to make the country charts. He copied his father's style for the soundtrack of the film biography of his father, *Your Cheatin' Heart* (1964), and starred in the inferior *A Time To Sing*. He was just 15 years old and **Connie Francis** was 26 when they released a duet about adultery, 'Walk On By'.

In 1974, Hank recorded *Hank Williams Jnr And Friends*, with Charlie Daniels and other top-class southern country rockers. In 1975, he fell 500 feet down a Montana mountain face and almost died. He had to learn to speak (and sing) all over again. Since 1977, Williams Jnr has been associated with the 'outlaw country music' genre. In 1983, he had eight albums on the US country charts simultaneously. Williams' rowdy image did not fit in well with the clean-cut 'hat acts' of the early 90s, and his record sales and airplay faltered. However he remains a sell-out concert draw.

ROBBIE WILLIAMS

AFTER HIS CONTROVERSIAL SPLIT FROM **TAKE THAT** IN 1995, SINGER ROBBIE WILLIAMS (b. 1974) HIT THE tabloid headlines as a result of occasional wild behaviour. He signed to Chrysalis in 1996, and released 'Freedom '96', a **George Michael** cover, that year. It was badly received critically, despite reaching UK number 1, but his follow-up, the **Oasis**-influenced 'Old Before I Die', showed he was capable of more. *Life Thru A Lens*, his autobiographical debut co-written with Guy Chambers, was released to critical acclaim and reached UK number 1. It spawned a series of chart hits, including the 1997 pop anthem, 'Angels', which established him as a serious artist, as well making him the most successful ex-Take That member to date. His duet with **Tom Jones** at the 1998 BRIT Awards ceremony, together with a new, cleaner image, took his career to new heights. The promo accompanying 'Let Me Entertain You' was a parody of **Kiss**. Appearances at the **Glastonbury Festival** and T in the Park established his reputation as a live performer and recording artist.

WILDE, MARTY
Albums
Bad Boy (Epic 1960)★★★
Good Rocking – Then And Now (Philips 1974)★★★
➽ p.383 for full listings
Collaborators
Status Quo ➽ p.308
Connections
Cliff Richard ➽ p.277
Kim Wilde ➽ p.338
Influences
Frank Sinatra
Bobby Vee ➽ p.329

WILLIAMS, BIG JOE
Albums
Piney Woods Blues (1958)★★★
Thinking Of What They Did (1981)★★★
➽ p.383 for full listings

WILLIAMS, HANK
Albums
Moanin' The Blues (MGM 1952)★★★★
Early Country Live Volume 1 (Hank Williams On Radio Shows Plus Others) (ACM 1983)★★★★
Hank Williams: I Won't Be Home No More, June 1952-September 1952 (Polydor 1987)★★★★
➽ p.383 for full listings
Connections
Hank Williams Jnr ➽ p.339
Further References
Video: *The Hank Williams Story* (1994)
Book: *Sing A Sad Song: The Life Of Hank Williams*, Roger M. Williams

WILLIAMS, HANK, JNR
Albums
Whiskey Bent And Hell Bound (Elektra/Curb 1979)★★★★
The Pressure Is On (Elektra/Curb 1981)★★★★
Maverick (Curb/Capricorn 1992)★★★★
➽ p.383 for full listings
Collaborators
Connie Francis ➽ p.152
Influences
Hank Williams ➽ p.339
Further References
Book: *Living Proof*, Hank Williams Jnr with Michael Bane

WILLIAMS, ROBBIE
Albums
Life Thru A Lens (Chrysalis 1997)★★★★
Collaborators
Tom Jones ➽ p.201
Connections
Take That ➽ p.316
Glastonbury Festival ➽ p.163
Influences
Kiss ➽ p.208
Oasis ➽ p.250

WILSON, BRIAN
Albums
Brian Wilson (Sire 1988)★★★★
➽ p.384 for full listings
Connections
Beach Boys ➽ p.36
Further References
Video: *I Just Wasn't Made For These Times* (WEA Video 1995)
Book: *Wouldn't It be Nice*, Brian Wilson

WILSON, JACKIE
Albums
Lonely Teardrops (Brunswick 1959)★★★★
A Woman A Lover A Friend (Brunswick 1961)★★★★
I Get The Sweetest Feeling (1968)★★★★
➽ p.384 for full listings
Further References
Film: *Go Johnny Go* (1958)

WILSON, MARI
Albums
Show People (Compact 1983)★★★★
The Rhythm Romance (Dino 1991)★★★
➽ p.384 for full listings
Connections
Julia Fordham ➽ p.149

WINCHESTER, JESSE
Albums
Jesse Winchester (Ampex 1970)★★★★
Humour Me (Sugar Hill 1988)★★★
➽ p.384 for full listings
Influences
Band ➽ p.31
Connections
Everly Brothers ➽ p.139
Todd Rundgren ➽ p.284
Elvis Costello ➽ p.101
Tim Hardin ➽ p.174
Joan Baez ➽ p.29

WINGS
Albums
as Paul McCartney And Wings *Band On The Run* (Apple 1973)★★★★
Venus And Mars (Apple 1975)★★★★
➽ p.384 for full listings
Connections
Paul McCartney ➽ p.229
Linda McCartney ➽ p.340
Beatles ➽ p.38
Brian Hines ➽ p.237
Further References
Book: *The Facts About A Rock Group, Featuring Wings*, David Gelly

WINTER, JOHNNY
Albums
Johnny Winter (Columbia 1969)★★★★
Johnny Winter And (Columbia 1970)★★★★
➽ p.384 for full listings

WILSON, BRIAN

BRIAN WILSON (b. 1942) WAS THE SPIRITUAL LEADER OF THE **BEACH BOYS**, TOUTED AS A 'MUSICAL GENIUS'. HE RELEASED the solo 'Caroline No' in 1966, but it has since been absorbed into the Beach Boys canon. *Brian Wilson* was released to excellent reviews with Wilson bravely appearing for the major publicity that ensued, but by commercial standards it was a flop. After the rest of the Beach Boys had taken him to court, Wilson successfully contested the ownership of his back catalogue, which had been sold by his father Murray Wilson. Immediately after this, Mike Love issued a writ claiming he had co-written 79 of Wilson's songs and demanding royalties. To crown this, Sire Records rejected Wilson's *Sweet Insanity* as 'pathetic'. However, in 1993 he was working with Van Dyke Parks and Andy Paley on further new songs, and was once again writing songs with Mike Love.

The television documentary *I Just Wasn't Made For These Times* was the first in-depth interview with Wilson. The accompanying Don Was-produced album failed to ignite, but *Orange Crate Art* was more cohesive. The album could best be described as interesting; there were flashes of brilliance in songs such as 'San Francisco' and the title track. Reviews were positive but any chart success proved elusive. In 1998, he charted with 'Your Imagination'.

WILSON, JACKIE

WHEN PARENTAL PRESSURE THWARTED HIS BOXING AMBITIONS, WILSON (b. 1934, d. 1984) TOOK TO SINGING IN small local clubs. He sang with the Thrillers, recorded some solo tracks for **Dizzy Gillespie**'s Dee Gee label (as Sonny Wilson) and joined Billy Ward And The Dominoes in 1953. He went solo in 1957, releasing 'Reet Petite'. It was a comparative failure in the USA; in the UK, however, it soared to number 6. 'Reet Petite' had been written by Berry Gordy and Tyran Carlo (Roquel 'Billy' Davis), who went on to compose several of Wilson's subsequent releases, including 'Lonely Teardrops' (1958).

In 1960, Wilson enjoyed two R&B number 1 hits with 'Doggin' Around' and 'A Woman, A Lover, A Friend'. His musical direction then grew increasingly erratic. There were still obvious highlights such as 'Baby Workout' (1963), 'Squeeze Her Please Her' (1964), 'No Pity (In The Naked City)' (1965), but all too often his wonderfully fluid voice was wasted on cursory, quickly dated material. The artist's live appearances, however, remained exciting.

Wilson's career was rejuvenated in 1966 with 'Whispers (Gettin' Louder)'. However, 'This Love Is Real (I Can Feel Those Vibrations)' (1970) proved to be his last Top 10 R&B entry. In 1975, Wilson suffered a heart attack on-stage at New Jersey's Latin Casino. He struck his head on falling and the resulting brain damage left him comatose. He remained hospitalized until his death.

WILSON, MARI

IN THE MID-80S, MARI WILSON (b. 1957) SINGLE-HANDEDLY LED A REVIVAL OF 50S AND EARLY 60S ENGLISH KITSCH, treating the songs affectionately and with genuine feeling. The whole image was the idea of Tot Taylor who composed under the name of Teddy Johns and also ran the Compact Organisation label. Mari's high-profile media coverage, led her 1982 singles, 'Beat The Beat' and 'Baby It's True', to chart. 'Just What I Always Wanted' a Top 10 hit, fully encapsulated the Wilson style followed by a cover of the Julie London torch-song, 'Cry Me A River' (UK number 27). After touring the world with her backing vocal group, the Wilsations – which included **Julia Fordham** – her pop career slowed down. Mari then provided the vocals to the film soundtrack of *Dance With A Stranger*. She is now taken seriously as a jazz/pop singer.

WINCHESTER, JESSE

EVADING THE US DRAFT, WINCHESTER (b. 1944) MOVED TO CANADA. HIS SELF-TITLED DEBUT ALBUM WAS FOLLOWED by 'Brand New Tennessee Waltz', which was covered by a number of artists including the **Everly Brothers**. *Third Down, 110 To Go* was produced by **Todd Rundgren**, but in spite of its solid quality failed to sell. *On Learn To Love* he was assisted by several members of the Amazing Rhythm Aces; 'Pharaoh's Army' was about the Vietnam war. By 1976, Winchester was touring the USA, having received an amnesty from President Carter. His songs have been covered by **Elvis Costello**, **Tim Hardin** and **Joan Baez**.

WINGS

WINGS WAS FORMED IN 1971 BY **PAUL** (b. 1942) AND LINDA **McCARTNEY** (b. 1942 d. 1998; percussion/vocals) with Denny Laine (b. Brian Hines; guitar/vocals, ex-**Moody Blues**), and Denny Seiwell (drums). Guitarist Henry McCullough joined in 1971, and 1972 was taken up by the famous 'surprise' college gigs around the UK. Notoriety was achieved at about the same time by the BBC's banning of 'Give Ireland Back To The Irish' (UK number 16/US number 21). Later that year 'Hi Hi Hi' (doubled with 'C-Moon') also offended the censors for its 'overt sexual references', though it penetrated the US and UK Top 10. In 1973, Wings scored a double number 1 in the USA with *Red Rose Speedway* and 'My Love'.

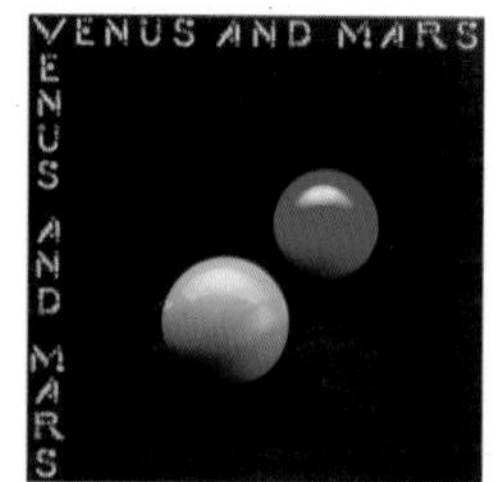

Shortly before the next album, McCullough and Seiwell quit. Ironically, the result was the group's most acclaimed album, *Band On The Run*, with McCartney taking a multi-instrumental role. It topped the UK and US charts, and kicked off 1974 by yielding two transatlantic Top 10 singles in 'Jet' and 'Band On The Run'. In 1974, Jimmy McCulloch (guitar/vocals) and Joe English (drums) joined.

The new line-up got off to a strong start with *Venus And Mars* (UK/US number 1), the single 'Listen To What The Man Said' also topped the US

charts and reached UK number 6. After *Wings At The Speed Of Sound* (UK number 2/US number 1), they embarked on a massive US tour. The resulting live triple *Wings Over America* became their fifth consecutive US number 1 album and the biggest-selling triple of all time.

McCulloch and English left in 1977 and the remaining Wings cut 'Mull Of Kintyre', which stayed at UK number 1 for 9 weeks. Laurence Juber and Steve Holly were recruited, but *Back To The Egg* failed to impress, with 'Getting Closer' not even hitting the UK singles chart. Shortly afterwards McCartney went solo and Wings were effectively no more.

WINTER, JOHNNY

BLUES GUITARIST WINTER (b. 1944) MADE HIS RECORDING DEBUT IN 1960, FRONTING JOHNNY AND THE JAMMERS. By 1968, he was leading Tommy Shannon (bass) and John Turner (drums) in Winter. The group recorded a single for Sonobeat, subsequently issued by United Artists as *The Progressive Blues Experiment*. *Johnny Winter* ably demonstrated his exceptional dexterity, while *Second Winter*, which included rousing versions of 'Johnny B. Goode' and 'Highway 61 Revisited', suggested a new-found emphasis on rock. In 1970, Winter was joined by the **McCoys** and guitarist Rick Darring; the new line-up released a self-titled studio collection and a fiery live set.

Heroin addiction forced Winter into partial retirement and it was two years before he re-emerged with *Still Alive And Well*. Subsequent work was bedevilled by indecision until the artist returned to his roots with *Nothing But The Blues* and *White Hot And Blue*. Winter also produced and arranged a series of acclaimed albums for **Muddy Waters**. Winter's rousing *Guitar Slinger* displayed all the passion apparent on his early, seminal recordings.

WINWOOD, STEVE

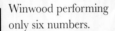

WINWOOD (b. 1948) FIRST ACHIEVED 'STAR' STATUS WITH THE **SPENCER DAVIS GROUP**. IN 1967 HE LEFT TO FORM **Traffic**. Winwood then seemed poised to go solo, instead he contributed keyboards and backing vocals to many fine albums. In 1976, he worked with **Stomu Yamash'ta** and Klaus Schulze, resulting in *Go* and *Go 2*. The eagerly anticipated solo album did not appear until 1977, and it displayed a relaxed Winwood performing only six numbers.

In 1980, the majestic *Arc Of A Diver* was an unqualified and unexpected triumph, going platinum in the USA. The stirring 'While You See A Chance' charted, followed by the successful *Talking Back To The Night*. Winwood, however was not altogether happy with the album and contemplated retiring to become a record producer. He was dissuaded.

Two years later, while working on his forthcoming album, he met his future wife Eugenia. His obvious elation overspilled into *Back In The High Life*. Most of the tracks were co-written with Will Jennings and it became his most commercially successful record so far. The album spawned three hits including 'Higher Love' (US number 1).

The single 'Roll With It' preceded the album of the same name. Both reached US number 1. In 1990, *Refugees Of The Heart* became his least successful album, although it contained another major US hit with the Winwood/ **Jim Capaldi** composition 'One And Only Man'. In 1994, Traffic re-formed: *Far From Home* sounded more like a Winwood solo album than any Traffic project. In spite of turning 50 in 1998, Steve continued touring and recording; he also appeared in the film *Blues Brothers 2000*.

WIRE

PUNK-INFLUENCED UK BAND FORMED IN 1976: COLIN NEWMAN (VOCALS/GUITAR), BRUCE GILBERT (GUITAR), Graham Lewis (bass/vocals), Robert Gotobed (b. Mark Field; drums) and lead guitarist George Gill; Gill was dismissed preceding *The Roxy, London, WC2*.

Wire's impressive debut, *Pink Flag*, featured 21 tracks ranging from the furious 'Field Day For The Sundays' and 'Mr Suit' to the more brittle 'Mannequin', their first single. Producer Mike Thorne enhanced the set's tension with a raw, stripped-to-basics sound. *Chairs Missing* was similar to its predecessor, but more mature. Gilbert's buzzsaw guitar became more measured, allowing for Thorne's keyboards and synthesizers to provide an implicit anger. *154* contained several exceptional moments, including 'A Touching Display' and the haunting 'A Mutual Friend'. However, the album marked the end of Wire's Harvest Records contract and musical differences led to the band splitting. *Document And Eyewitness* chronicled Wire's final concert at London's Electric Ballroom in 1980.

In 1985, the group began recording again with *The Ideal Copy* which topped the independent chart. *A Bell Is A Cup (Until It Is Struck)* maintained the new-found balance between art and commercial pop. In 1990, they abandoned the 'beat combo' concept of 1985 and utilized computer and sequencer technology – *Manscape* showed a dramatic sound change. Gotobed left shortly afterwards and the remaining trio changed their name to Wir. Their first release, 'The First Letter', showed a harder edge than their more recent work, amusingly containing some reworked samples of *Pink Flag*.

WISHBONE ASH

IN 1966, STEVE UPTON (DRUMS) JOINED MARTIN TURNER (BASS/VOCALS) AND GLEN TURNER (GUITAR) IN THE UK band, Empty Vessels. They became Tanglewood. Glen Turner departed, and Ted Turner (b. David Alan Turner; guitar) joined. Andy Powell (guitar) also joined and they took the name Wishbone Ash. Their hallmark was the powerful sound of twin lead guitars. Their biggest commercial success was *Argus*, a set preoccupied with historical themes, complex instrumentals and folk-rock. Ted departed in 1974, replaced by Laurie Wisefield. In 1980, Martin left. In 1987, after several further line-up changes, the original quartet recorded *Nouveau Calls*. They continue to perform.

WITHERS, BILL

AFTER SEVERAL YEARS OF TRYING TO SELL HIS SONGS, WITHERS (b. 1938) WAS SIGNED TO SUSSEX RECORDS IN 1971. He secured an immediate hit with his debut 'Ain't No Sunshine', produced by Booker T. Jones, and featuring **Stephen Stills**; 'Lean On Me' and 'Use Me' (both 1972) followed – all three were million-sellers. Withers continued to score success with 'Make Love To Your Mind' (1975), 'Lovely Day' (1977) and 'Just The Two Of Us' (1981) – his duet with saxophonist Grover Washington Jnr; it won a Grammy in 1982 for Best R&B Performance. 'Lovely Day' reached the UK Top 5 in 1988, after appearing on a television commercial.

Collaborators
McCoys ➧ p.229
Connections
Muddy Waters ➧ p.242
Further References
Video: *Johnny Winter Live* (Channel 5 1989)

WINWOOD, STEVE
Albums
Arc Of A Diver (Island 1980)★★★★
Back In The High Life (Island 1986)★★★★
➧ p.384 for full listings

Collaborators
Stomu Yamash'ta ➧ p.345
Jim Capaldi ➧ p.80
Connections
Spencer Davis Group ➧ p.304
Traffic ➧ p.323
Further References
Books: *Back In The High Life: A Biography Of Steve Winwood*, Alan Clayson
Keep On Running: The Steve Winwood Story, Chris Welch

WIRE
Albums
Pink Flag (Harvest 1977)★★★★
Chairs Missing (Harvest 1978)★★★★
➧ p.384 for full listings
Further References
Book: *Wire ... Everybody Loves A History*, Kevin S. Eden.

WISHBONE ASH
Albums
Wishbone Ash (MCA 1970)★★★
Wishbone 4 (MCA 1973)★★★
➧ p.384 for full listings
Influences
Yardbirds ➧ p.345
Allman Brothers Band ➧ p.14
Further References
Videos: *Phoenix* (1990)
Wishbone Ash Live (1990)

WITHERS, BILL
Albums
Just As I Am (Sussex 1971)★★★★
Naked And Warm (Columbia 1976)★★★
Still Bill (1993)★★★
➧ p.384 for full listings
Collaborators
Stephen Stills ➧ p.310

WIZZARD
Albums
Introducing Eddy And The Falcons (Warners 1974)★★★
➽ p.384 for full listings
Connections
Roy Wood ➽ p.343
Influences
Phil Spector ➽ p.304

WOMACK, BOBBY
Albums
Communication (United Artists 1971)★★★
➽ p.384 for full listings
Collaborators
Sam Cooke ➽ p.100
Wilson Pickett ➽ p.260
Patti LaBelle ➽ p.212
Connections
Valentinos ➽ p.328
Rolling Stones ➽ p.281

WOMACK AND WOMACK
Albums
The Composers/Love Wars (Elektra 1983)★★★
Starbright (Manhattan/EMI 1986)★★★
➽ p.384 for full listings
Connections
Valentinos ➽ p.328
Mary Wells ➽ p.336
Wilson Pickett ➽ p.260
James Taylor ➽ p.317
O'Jays ➽ p.250
Patti LaBelle ➽ p.212
Teddy Pendergrass ➽ p.258

WONDER, STEVIE
Albums
Talking Book (Tamla Motown 1972)★★★★★
Innervisions (Tamla Motown 1973)★★★★★
➽ p.384 for full listings
Connections
Ronnie White ➽ p.234
Motown Records ➽ p.240
Influences
Dr Martin Luther King
Further References
Film: *Bikini Beach* (1964)
Book: *Stevie Wonder*, Sam Hasegawa

WIZZARD

FORMED IN 1972 BY **ROY WOOD** WITH RICK PRICE (VOCALS/ BASS), HUGH MCDOWELL (CELLO), BILL HUNT (KEYBOARDS), Mike Burney (saxophone), Nick Pentelow (saxophone), Keith Smart (drums) and Charlie Grima (drums). They debuted at the 1972 Wembley Rock 'n' Roll Festival and hit the charts with 'Ball Park Incident' (1972). Wood was at his peak as a producer during this period and his **Phil Spector**-like 'wall of sound' pop experiments produced two memorable UK number 1s ('See My Baby Jive', 'Angel Fingers') and a perennial festive hit ('I Wish It Could Be Christmas Every Day'). Much of Wizzard's charm came from Roy Wood's theatricalism.

WOMACK, BOBBY

A FOUNDER MEMBER OF THE **VALENTINOS**, US MUSICIAN WOMACK (b. 1944) ALSO WORKED AS A GUITARIST FOR **Sam Cooke**. Womack's early solo singles, 'Nothing You Can Do' and 'I Found A True Love', were all but shunned and he reverted to session work. He became a fixture at Chips Moman's American Recording Studio and worked with **Wilson Pickett**, who recorded 17 Womack songs. Bobby meanwhile resurrected his solo career and began a string of R&B hits, including 'It's Gonna Rain', 'How I Miss You Baby' (both 1969) and 'More Than I Can Stand' (1970). *The Womack Live* introduced the freer, more personal direction he would undertake in the 70s followed by *There's A Riot Going On*, **Sly Stone**'s 1971 collection on which Womack played guitar.

The strong *Understanding* yielded impressive singles that achieved high positions in the R&B charts: 'That's The Way I Feel About Cha' (number 2), 'Woman's Gotta Have It' (number 1) and 'Harry Hippie' (number 8). In 1981, Womack recorded the powerful *The Poet*. His single, 'If You Think You're Lonely Now', reached US R&B number 3. *The Poet II* featured three duets with **Patti LaBelle**, one of which, 'Love Has Finally Come At Last', was another hit. 1985 saw *So Many Rivers* and Womack backing the **Rolling Stones** on their version of 'Harlem Shuffle'.

WOMACK AND WOMACK

HUSBAND AND WIFE TEAM CECIL WOMACK (b. 1947) AND LINDA COOKE WOMACK (b. 1953). CECIL, THE YOUNGEST OF the **Valentinos**, first married **Mary Wells**, whom he managed until the couple separated. Linda, the daughter of **Sam Cooke**, had begun a songwriting career at the age of 11, composing 'I Need A Woman'. She also wrote 'I'm In Love' (**Wilson Pickett**) and 'A Woman's Gotta Have It' (**James Taylor**) before forging a professional, and personal, partnership with Cecil. They worked as a writing team for Philadelphia International, numbering the **O'Jays** and **Patti LaBelle** among their clients. They achieved notable success with 'Love TKO', a 1980 soul hit for **Teddy Pendergrass** and the Womack's first US chart entry.

The duo's fortunes have prospered in the USA and UK, including the club favourite 'Love Wars' (1984) and 'Teardrops' (1988, UK Top 3). They continued to write for others as well, contributing 'Hurting Inside' and 'Sexy' to Ruby Turner. In the early 90s, they journeyed to Nigeria, where they discovered ancestral ties to the Zekkariyas tribe. They consequently adopted the names Zeriiya (Linda) and Zekkariyas (Cecil).

WONDER, STEVIE

DESPITE BEING BLIND ALMOST FROM BIRTH, WONDER (b. STEVELAND JUDKINS, 1950) HAD MASTERED PIANO, DRUMS and harmonica by the age of nine. In 1961, he was discovered by Ronnie White (**Miracles**), who arranged an audition at **Motown Records**; in 1963 the release of the live recording 'Fingertips (Part 2)' established his commercial success. Wonder's career was placed on hold while his voice was breaking, but he re-emerged in 1965 with a typically Motown sound, scoring a worldwide hit with the dance-orientated 'Uptight (Everything's Alright)' (co-written with Henry Cosby and Sylvia Moy). This began a run of US Top 40 hits that continued for over six years.

From 1965-70, Stevie Wonder was marketed like other Motown stars, recording material chosen for him by the label's executives, and issuing albums that mixed conventional soul compositions with pop standards. He co-wrote almost all his singles from 1967 onwards, and began to collaborate on releases by other Motown artists.

His contract with Motown expired in 1971; rather than re-signing immediately, as the label expected, Wonder financed the recording of two albums of his own material, playing almost all the instruments himself, experimenting with the synthesizer and widening his lyrical concerns to take in racial problems and spiritual questions. He then used these recordings as a lever to persuade Motown to offer him total artistic control, plus the opportunity to hold the rights to the music publishing. He celebrated the signing of the deal with the release of the solo recordings, *Where I'm Coming From* and *Music Of My Mind*.

Talking Book combined the artistic advances of recent albums with major commercial success, producing hit singles with 'Superstition' and 'You Are The Sunshine Of My Life'. *Innervisions* consolidated his growth, bringing further hits with the socially aware 'Living For The City' and 'Higher Ground'. Later that year, Wonder was seriously injured in a car accident; his subsequent work was tinged with the awareness of mortality, fired by his spiritual beliefs; *Fulfillingness' First Finale* epitomized this more austere

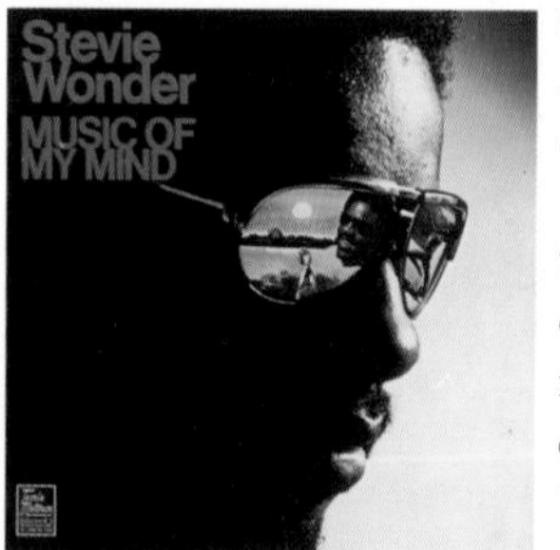

approach. The double album *Songs In The Key Of Life* was widely greeted as his most ambitious and satisfying work to date.

No new recordings surfaced for over three years, as Wonder concentrated on the disappointing soundtrack music to the documentary film, *The Secret Life Of Plants*. Wonder quickly delivered the highly successful *Hotter Than July*, which included a tribute song to

Martin Luther King, 'Happy Birthday'. Soundtrack music for the film, *The Woman In Red*, included his biggest-selling single to date, the sentimental ballad 'I Just Called To Say I Loved You'. *In Square Circle* and *Characters* heralded a return to the accessible, melodic music of the previous decade, but critical and public response was disappointing.

Wonder's status was boosted by his campaign in the early 80s to have Martin Luther King's birthday celebrated as a national holiday in the USA. This request was granted by President Reagan, and the first Martin Luther King Day was celebrated on 15 January 1986, with a concert at which Wonder topped the bill. In the 90s, he contributed to the film soundtrack of *Jungle Fever* and released the disappointingly average *Conversation Peace*.

WONDER STUFF

UK BAND FORMED IN 1986. MILES HUNT (VOCALS/GUITAR), MALCOLM TREECE (GUITAR), ROB JONES (BASS; REPLACING original member Chris Fradgley) and drummer Martin Gilks released their debut EP, *It's A Wonderful Day*, to favourable small press coverage. Their strengths lay in melodic pop songs braced against an urgent, power-pop backdrop. After an ill-fated dalliance with EMI Records' *ICA Rock Week*, a second single, 'Unbearable', proved strong enough to secure a contract with Polydor in 1987. 'Give Give Give Me More More More' offered a minor hit the following year, succeeded by 'A Wish Away' – the perfect precursor to the Wonder Stuff's vital *The Eight Legged Groove Machine*, which reached the UK charts. 'It's Yer Money I'm After Baby', also from the album, continued to mine Hunt's cynical furrow and began a string of UK Top 40 hits.

Hup, aided by fiddle, banjo and keyboard player Martin Bell, contrasted a harder, hi-tech sound with a rootsy, folk feel. The band's well-documented internal wrangles came to a head with the departure of Rob Jones at the end of the decade, who sadly died of heart failure in 1993. 'Circlesquare' introduced new bassist Paul Clifford, followed by 1991's hit 'Size Of A Cow' (UK Top 10). This was quickly followed by 'Caught In My Shadow' and *Never Loved Elvis*. Gone were the brash, punk-inspired three-minute classics, replaced by a richer musical and song-writing content. In 1991, in conjunction with comedian Vic Reeves, they topped the UK charts with a revival of **Tommy Roe**'s 'Dizzy'. The group made a swift return to the Top 10 in 1992 with the *Welcome To The Cheap Seats* EP followed by *Construction For The Modern Idiot*.

The band split in 1994, allegedly over Polydor's insistence that they should crack the USA; their final gig was in Stratford-upon-Avon.

WOOD, ROY

AS A TEENAGER, WOOD (b. ULYSSES ADRIAN WOOD, 1946) was an itinerant guitarist, moving steadily through a succession of minor UK groups. Later he pooled his talents with some of the best musicians on the Birmingham beat scene to form the **Move**; Wood emerged as their leading songwriter. By 'Fire Brigade' (1967), Wood was their lead singer and it was his fertile imagination which took the group through a plethora of musical styles, ranging from psychedelia to rock 'n' roll revivalism, classical rock and heavy metal.

Wood then launched the **Electric Light Orchestra** – he survived as ELO's frontman for only one single and album before a personality clash with **Jeff Lynne** prompted his departure in 1972. He soon returned with **Wizzard**. He also enjoyed a parallel solo career and although his two albums were uneven, they revealed his many areas of creative energy (multi-instrumentalist, engineer, producer and sleeve designer). Wood the soloist also scored several UK hit singles including the majestic 'Forever'. His eccentric ingenuity continued on various singles and b-sides – 'Bengal Jig' fused bagpipes and sitar! By the late 70s, Wood was ploughing less commercial ground with the Wizzo Band, Rock Brigade and the Helicopters.

WOODSTOCK FESTIVAL

THE ORIGINAL WOODSTOCK ART AND MUSIC FAIR WAS FORCIBLY MOVED FROM ITS PLANNED LOCATION OF WALLKILL, New York State, after protest from local townsfolk. The new location was 40 miles away at a 600-acre dairy farm in Bethel owned by Max Yasgur.

A steady trail of spectators arrived up to a week before the event, which took place on 15, 16 and 17 August 1969. The spectacular line-up included: the **Who**; **Jimi Hendrix**; **Crosby, Stills, Nash And Young**; **John Sebastian**; **Jefferson Airplane**; **Grateful Dead**; **Santana**; **Joe Cocker**; **Sly And The Family Stone**; **Country Joe And The Fish**; **Ten Years After**; the **Band**; **Johnny Winter**; **Blood, Sweat And Tears**; **Paul Butterfield Blues Band**; **Sha Na Na**; **Janis Joplin**; Ravi Shankar; the **Incredible String Band**; **Canned Heat**; **Melanie**; **Tim Hardin**; **Joan Baez**; **Arlo Guthrie**; **Richie Havens** and **Creedence Clearwater Revival**. Estimates vary but it is believed that at least 300,000 spectators were present at any one time, sharing 600 portable lavatories and inadequate water facilities. Nobody was prepared for the wave of bodies that formed, choking the highways from all directions. The world press, which had previously scorned the popular hippie movement, were at last speaking favourably, as one. It was possible for vast numbers of youngsters to congregate for a musical celebration, without violence and regimented supervision.

Woodstock was a milestone in musical history – the festival totally changed the world's attitude towards popular music.

WORLD PARTY

FOUNDED ON THE TALENTS OF EX-**WATERBOY** KARL WALLINGER (b. 1957), who recorded the first two World Party albums practically single-handed. *Bang!* saw him joined by Chris Sharrock (drums) and Dave Catlin-Birch (guitars/keyboards). The hit single 'Ship Of Fools' (1987) showcased Wallinger's muse, a relaxed and melancholic performance reminiscent of mid-period **Beatles**. This has been revitalized on his subsequent, sterling work, although some of the reviews for *Egyptology* were unnecessarily cruel. It was by his standards another good album, which, although still locked into the Beatles' sound, has some great moments, notably the gentle 'She's The One' and the meatier 'Curse Of The Mummy's Tomb'.

WONDER STUFF

Albums

The Eight Legged Groove Machine (Polydor 1988)★★★

p.384 for full listings

Connections

Tommy Roe p.280
Jam p.196
Sex Pistols p.292

WOOD, ROY

Albums

Boulders (Harvest 1973)★★★

Mustard (Jet 1975)★★★

p.384 for full listings

Connections

Move p.241
Electric Light Orchestra p.134
Jeff Lynne p.220
Wizzard p.342

WOODSTOCK FESTIVAL

Albums

Woodstock (Atco 1969)★★★★

p.384 for full listings

Connections

Monterey Pop Festival p.237
Who p.338
Jimi Hendrix p.180
Crosby, Stills, Nash And Young p.106
John Sebastian p.291
Jefferson Airplane p.198
Grateful Dead p.167
Santana p.288
Joe Cocker p.95
Sly And The Family Stone p.300
Country Joe And The Fish p.101
Ten Years After p.318
Band p.31
Johnny Winter p.341
Blood, Sweat And Tears p.53
Paul Butterfield Blues Band p.76
Sha Na Na p.293
Janis Joplin p.201
Incredible String Band p.192
Canned Heat p.79
Melanie p.231
Tim Hardin p.174
Joan Baez p.29
Arlo Guthrie p.171
Richie Havens p.177
Creedence Clearwater Revival p.104

Further References

Video: *Woodstock 94* (Polygram 1994)

Book: *Woodstock: An Oral History*, Joel Makowers

WORLD PARTY

Albums

Egyptology (Chrysalis 1997)★★★★

p.384 for full listings

Connections

Waterboys p.334

Influences

Beatles p.38

WRAY, LINK
Albums
Link Wray And The Raymen (Epic 1959)★★★★
➽ p.384 for full listings
Connections
Cramps ➽ p.102
Further References
Video: *Link Wray: The Rumble Man* (Visionary 1996)

WU-TANG CLAN
Albums
Wu-Tan Forever (Loud/RCA 1997)★★★★
➽ p.384 for full listings
Influences
Grandmaster Flash ➽ p.166

WYATT, ROBERT
Albums
Rock Bottom (Virgin 1974)★★★★
Shleep (Hannibal 1997)★★★★
➽ p.384 for full listings
Collaborators
Elvis Costello ➽ p.101
Connections
Soft Machine ➽ p.302
Matching Mole ➽ p.227
Monkees ➽ p.236
Further References
Book: *Wrong Movements: A Robert Wyatt History*, Michael King

WYNONNA
Albums
Tell Me Why (Curb 1994)★★★★
Revelations (Curb 1996)★★★★
➽ p.384 for full listings
Collaborators
Jesse Winchester ➽ p.340
Sheryl Crow ➽ p.106
Mary-Chapin Carpenter ➽ p.82
Connections
Judds ➽ p.202

X
Albums
Wild Gift (Slash 1981)★★★★
➽ p.384 for full listings
Connections
Henry Rollins ➽ p.282
Lone Justice ➽ p.218

X-RAY SPEX
Albums
Germ Free Adolescents (EMI 1978)★★★
➽ p.384 for full listings

WRAY, LINK

GUITARIST WRAY (b. 1930) FORMED HIS FIRST GROUP IN 1942, SUBSEQUENTLY FORMING THE WRAYMEN WITH SHORTY Horton (bass) and Doug Wray (drums). They enjoyed a million-seller with 'Rumble' (1958), a pioneering instrumental on which the artist's frenzied style and distorted tone invoked a gang-fight. The single incurred bans on technical grounds and for its subject matter, but is now recognized as one of pop's most innovative releases. Wray scored another gold disc for 'Rawhide' (1959), but ensuing releases failed to emulate this. He continued to record, and *Link Wray* received critical acclaim. In the late 70s, he forged a fruitful partnership with new-wave rockabilly singer Robert Gordon, before resurrecting a solo career. *Shadowman* contains the excellent vintage Link Wray track 'Rumble On The Docks'.

WU-TANG CLAN

CHESS-PLAYING, MARTIAL-ART PROFICIENT, HIP HOP POSSE: SHALLAH RAEKWON, METHOD MAN, REBEL INS, OL' DIRTY Bastard, U-God, Ghostface Killer, The Genius, RZA and Prince Rakeem. Their debut album was divided into two sides, Shaolin and Wu-Tang Sword, to symbolize the combat-like disciplines they apply to their rapping. Affiliated group members include acclaimed soloist Shyheim The Rugged Prince. When the Clan signed with BMG, provision for each member to work as solo artists was enshrined in the contract. The Clan's musical armoury centres around old school rhyming and trickery, the musical backing is one of stripped-down beats, with samples culled from kung-fu movies. Their debut album, recorded in their own studio, went gold. Its '36 Chambers' suffix alludes to the number of critical points on the body as disclosed by Shaolin theology. In June 98, Ol' Dirty was shot during a break-in – he recovered swiftly.

WYATT, ROBERT

WYATT (b. 1945), DRUMMER, VOCALIST AND GUIDING SPIRIT OF THE ORIGINAL **SOFT MACHINE**, ESTABLISHED A STYLE that merged the *avant garde* with English eccentricity. His first solo album, *The End Of An Ear*, received a muted reception. He then formed the ill-fated **Matching Mole**. A planned relaunch was forcibly abandoned following a tragic fall, which left Wyatt confined to a wheelchair. *Rock Bottom*, his next release, was composed in hospital. This heartfelt, deeply personal collection was marked by an aching vulnerability that successfully avoided any hint of self-pity. It was succeeded by an unlikely hit single with the **Monkees**' 'I'm A Believer'. *Ruth Is Stranger Than Richard* was a more open collection, and balanced original pieces with outside material.

Although Wyatt, a committed Marxist, made frequent guest appearances, his own career was shelved until 1980 when a single of two South American liberation songs were released. These performances were subsequently compiled on *Nothing Can Stop Us*, which also featured 'Shipbuilding' (1983), a haunting anti-Falklands War composition, specifically written for Wyatt by **Elvis Costello**. Wyatt issued singles in aid of Namibia and the British Miners' Hardship Fund, and contributed a compassionate soundtrack to the harrowing 1982 film *Animals*. Wyatt's more recent recordings, *Old Rotten Hat* and *Dondestan*, are as compelling as the rest of his impressive work. Wyatt returned after *A Short Break* with one of his best ever albums. *Shleep* was as brilliantly idiosyncratic as anything he has recorded.

WYNONNA

THE DAUGHTER OF MOTHER-AND-DAUGHTER DUO, THE **JUDDS**, WYNONNA (b. CHRISTINA CIMINELLA, 1964; vocals/rhythm guitar) went solo in 1991. *Wynonna*, led to three US country number 1s, 'She Is His Only Need', 'I Saw The Light' and 'No One Else On Earth'. By the mid-90s the sales had topped four million. *Tell Me Why* was equally assured; opening with the breezy title track, written by Karla Bonoff, there was rarely a dull moment. Songs by **Jesse Winchester**, **Sheryl Crow** and **Mary-Chapin Carpenter** enabled Wynonna to cross over into the AOR market. *Revelations* and *The Other Side* provided a further indication of her move away from country, with strong rock and blues influences.

X

FORMED IN LOS ANGELES IN 1977. EXENE CERVENKA (b. CHRISTINE CERVENKA, 1956; VOCALS), BILLY ZOOM (b. Tyson Kindale; guitar), John Doe (b. John Nommensen; bass) and Mick Basher (drums; later replaced by D. J. (Don) Bonebrake) debuted with 'Adult Books'/'We're Desperate' (1978), a blend of punk, rockabilly and blues. *Wild Gift* led to a contract with Elektra. *Under The Big Black Sun* was critically acclaimed, but many deemed *More Fun In The New World* 'over-commercial'.

Alongside X, Cervenka and Doe joined **Henry Rollins** in the Knitters. Alvin replaced Billy Zoom following *Ain't Love Grand*; he left in 1987. Ex-**Lone Justice** guitarist Tony Gilkyson also joined. X disbanded after *Live At The Whiskey A Go-Go*, but reunited in 1993 for *Hey Zeus!*. 1998 saw the band on the road again, following the release of a set of live recordings.

X-RAY SPEX

PUNK ICON POLY STYRENE (b. MARION ELLIOT) RECRUITED LORA LOGIC (SAXOPHONE; LATER REPLACED BY GLYN JOHNS), Jak Stafford (guitar), Paul Dean (bass) and B. P. Hurding (drums) and began performing in 1977. Their series of singles, including 'Germ Free Adolescents', 'Oh Bondage Up Yours' and 'Identity', contained provocative, thoughtful lyrics urging individual expression. Poly dismantled the group in 1979 and joined the Krishna Consciousness Movement. X-Ray Spex's final single, 'Highly Inflammable', was coupled with 'Warrior In Woolworths'.

In 1980, Poly recorded *Translucence*, followed by the EP *Gods And Goddesses*, but no further commercial success was forthcoming. In 1996, the band re-formed for *Conscious Consumer*.

XTC

UK BAND FORMED IN 1972. ANDY PARTRIDGE (b. 1953; GUITAR/VOCALS) WAS JOINED BY COLIN MOULDING (b. 1955), Terry Chambers (b. 1955) and Dave Cartner (b. *c*. 1951; guitar). In 1975, Steve Hutchins joined – and left – followed in 1976 by Johnny Perkins (keyboards); Barry Andrews (b. 1956) joined later. Their debut, *White Music* (UK number 38), was followed by the successful *Go2*. In 1978, Andrews was replaced by Dave Gregory (b. 1952); the ensuing *Drums And Wires* was a major step forward. 'Making Plans For Nigel' was a hit and subsequent singles, including 'Sgt Rock (Is Going To Help Me)' and 'Senses Working Overtime' scaled the charts. *English Settlement* reached UK number 5.

Partridge, suffering from exhaustion and nervous breakdowns, announced that XTC would continue as recording artists only. *Mummer*, *The Big Express* and *Skylarking* all failed to chart; *Oranges And Lemons* sold 500,000 copies in the USA, but barely scraped the UK Top 30. The highly commercial 'Mayor Of Simpleton' also only reached number 46. *Nonsuch* entered the UK charts and two weeks later promptly disappeared, although 'The Disappointed' was nominated for an Ivor Novello songwriters award in 1993. The band also recorded as the Dukes of Stratosphear.

In 1995, the **Crash Test Dummies** recorded 'Ballad Of Peter Pumpkinhead' for the movie *Dumb And Dumber*. In 1997, XTC signed with Cooking Vinyl. A new album is intended for release in 1999.

YAMASH'TA, STOMU

JAPENESE PERCUSSIONIST AND COMPOSER YAMASH'TA (b. TSUTOMU YAMASHITA, 1947) MADE HIS SOLOIST CONCERT debut at the age of 16, followed by performances with classical and jazz musicians. During the 70s, composers such as Hans Werne Henze and Peter Maxwell Davies created works for him and Yamash'ta created 'floating music': a fusion of classical, rock and Eastern styles, with his group, Come To The Edge. His shows included elements of Japanese kabuki theatre and were highly praised.

He recorded albums with **Steve Winwood**, Klaus Schulze, Gary Boyle and Murray Head before returning to classical concert halls, alongside recording instrumental works for new age company Celestial Harmonies.

YARDBIRDS

PIVOTAL UK R&B GROUP FORMED IN 1963: KEITH RELF (b. 1944, d. 1976; VOCALS/HARMONICA), PAUL SAMWELL-SMITH (b. 1943; bass), Chris Dreja (b. 1944; rhythm guitar), Tony 'Top' Topham (guitar) and Jim McCarty (b. 1944; drums). Within months Topham was replaced by **Eric Clapton** (b. Eric Clapp, 1945). The new line-up forged a style based on classic Chicago R&B. 'I Wish You Would' and 'Good Morning Little Schoolgirl' attracted critical interest, flourishing with the release of *Five Live Yardbirds*.

Clapton departed after 'For Your Love' (1965); replaced by **Jeff Beck** (b. 1944). Further hits included 'Heartful Of Soul', 'Evil Hearted You', 'Over Under Sideways Down' and the excellent *Yardbirds*. By this point Simon Napier-Bell had assumed management duties and Samwell-Smith had left, replaced by **Jimmy Page** (b. 1944; guitar). Dreja switched to bass; Beck left during a gruelling USA tour.

Despite a growing reputation on the American 'underground' circuit, their appeal as a pop attraction waned, with singles, including 'Little Games' (1967) and 'Goodnight Sweet Josephine' (1968), failing to chart. The disappointing *Little Games* was denied a UK release but found US success. Two minor US successes followed, including 'Ha Ha Said The Clown' but the group folded in 1968.

YAZOO

UK POP GROUP FORMED IN 1982 BY FORMER **DEPECHE MODE** KEYBOARDIST VINCE CLARKE (b. 1961) AND vocalist **Alison Moyet** (b. 1961). Their debut 'Only You' reached UK number 2; the following 'Don't Go', reached number 3.

After a name-change to Yaz, their album *Upstairs At Eric's* was widely acclaimed for its strong melodies and Moyet's expressive vocals. Yaz enjoyed further hits with 'The Other Side Of Love' and 'Nobody's Diary' before completing *You And Me Both*. Despite continuing success, the duo parted in 1983. Moyet enjoyed solo success, while Clarke went on to the Assembly and **Erasure**.

YELLO

SWISS DANCE DUO LED BY DIETER MEIER (CONCEPTS) WITH BORIS BLANK (COMPOSITION). YELLO RELEASED 'BIMBO' and the album *Solid Pleasure*. In the UK, they launched their career with 'Bostisch'. UK chart success began in 1983 when they released two singles and an EP, before major success with 'The Race'. Accompanied by a stunning video, 'The Race' easily transgressed the pop and dance markets in the wake of Acid House. On *One Second* they worked with **Shirley Bassey** and Billy McKenzie (**Associates**). They have produced cinema soundtracks, including *Nuns On The Run* and *Snowball*, and run Swiss dance label, Solid Pleasure.

XTC

Albums
Drums And Wires (Virgin 1979)★★★★
Nonsuch (Virgin 1992)★★★★
➽ p.384 for full listings

Connections
Crash Test Dummies ➽ p.103

Influences
MC5 ➽ p.228
Alice Cooper ➽ p.12

Further References
Book: *Chalkhills And Children*, Chris Twomey

YAMASH'TA, STOMU

Albums
Go (Island 1976)★★★★
➽ p.384 for full listings

Collaborators
Steve Winwood ➽ p.341

YARDBIRDS

Albums
Five Live Yardbirds (Columbia 1964)★★★★
Little Games (Epic 1968)★★★
➽ p.384 for full listings

Connections
Eric Clapton ➽ p.92
Jeff Beck ➽ p.41
Jimmy Page ➽ p.255
Led Zeppelin ➽ p.213

Further References
Book: *Blues In The Night: The Yardbirds' Story*, James White

YAZOO

Albums
Upstairs At Eric's (Mute 1982)★★★★
➽ p.384 for full listings

Connections
Depeche Mode ➽ p.116
Alison Moyet ➽ p.241
Erasure ➽ p.138

YELLO

Albums
Solid Pleasure (Ralph 1980)★★★
You Gotta Say Yes To Another Excess (Elektra 1983)★★★★
Pocket Universe (Mercury 1997)★★★
➽ p.384 for full listings

Collaborators
Shirley Bassey ➽ p.34

Connections
Orb ➽ p.252
Moby ➽ p.235

Further References
Videos: *Video Race* (1988)
Live At The Roxy (1991)

YELLOW MAGIC ORCHESTRA

Albums
Solid State Survivor (Alfa 1979)★★★
BGM (A&M 1981)★★★
Naughty Boys (Alfa 1983)★★★★
➽ p.384 for full listings

Collaborators
Peter Barakan

Connections
David Sylvian
Sheena And The Rokkets

Influences
Archie Bell And The Drells ➽ p.42

YELLOW MAGIC ORCHESTRA

ELECTRONIC MUSIC PIONEERS FROM JAPAN: RYÛICHI SAKAMOTO (KEYBOARDS), YUKIHIRO TAKAHASHI (DRUMS) AND Haruomi Hosono (bass/producer). Although the trio's debut album was inauspicious, by *Solid State Survivor* they had established a sound and pattern, with English lyrics supplied by Chris Mosdell. *X∞ Multiplies*, however, was a strange collection, comprising comedy skits and cover versions. *BGM* and *Technodelic* predicted the beautiful synth pop produced by later solo careers, but neither album proved cohesive. More skits, again in Japanese, appeared on *Service*, masking the quality of several strong songs. The more accessible *Naughty Boys* had English lyrics by Peter Barakan.

The band split in the early 80s, with Sakamoto going on to solo and movie fame (including *Merry Christmas Mr Lawrence*), Hosono enjoying production success and Takahashi going solo. In 1993, they reunited for *Technodon*.

YES

Albums
The Yes Album (Atlantic 1971)★★★★
Fragile (Atlantic 1971)★★★★
Close To The Edge (Atlantic 1972)★★★★
➽ p.384 for full listings

Collaborators
John Peel ➽ p.258
Buggles ➽ p.74

Connections
Jon Anderson ➽ p.18
Bill Bruford ➽ p.71
Rick Wakeman ➽ p.332
Strawbs ➽ p.312
Plastic Ono Band
Refugees

Further References
Video: *Anderson Bruford Wakeman Howe: An Evening Of Yes Music Plus* (1995)
Books: *Yes: The Authorized Biography*, Dan Hedges
Music Of Yes: Structure And Vision In Progressive Rock, Bill Martin

YES

FORMED IN 1968 BY VOCALIST **JON ANDERSON** (b. 1944) AND BASSIST CHRIS SQUIRE (b. 1948), WITH **BILL BRUFORD** (b. 1948; drums), Pete Banks (b. 1947; replaced in 1970 by Steve Howe (b. 1947)) and Tony Kaye (b. 1946). **John Peel** gave them nationwide exposure, but neither *Yes* nor *Time And A Word* made much of an impression. However, *The Yes Album* created major interest and sales. Kaye then departed, replaced by **Rick Wakeman** (b. 1949). *Fragile* was a major success and spawned a surprise US hit, 'Roundabout' (1972), which almost made the Top 10. Shortly afterwards Bruford departed, replaced by Alan White (ex-Plastic Ono Band). Later that year Yes released their finest work, *Close To The Edge*, followed by a triple live album, *Yessongs*, then a double, the overlong and indulgent *Tales From Topographic Oceans* (UK number 1). Both were huge successes.

Wakeman went solo, replaced by Patrick Moraz, and, following *Relayer*, the band fragmented to undertake solo projects. When they reconvened, Wakeman continued a dual career. 'Wonderous Stories' (1977) made the UK Top 10, but internal problems resulted in the second departure of Wakeman, immediately followed by Anderson. Their replacements were Trevor Horn and Geoff Downes, of **Buggles**. This bizarre union lasted until 1983. The Trevor Horn-produced *90125* showed a rejuvenated band with Anderson back. Finally *Big Generator* arrived, followed by *Anderson, Bruford, Wakeman And Howe*.

Yes announced a major tour in 1991, and were once again in the US Top 10 with *Union*. *Talk* was a sparkling, energetic album. They continued recording and celebrated their 30th anniversary with a 1998 tour.

YOAKAM, DWIGHT

Albums
Guitars, Cadillacs, Etc., Etc. (Reprise 1986)★★★★
Hillbilly DeLuxe (Reprise 1987)★★★★
Buenas Noches From A Lonely Room (Reprise 1988)★★★★
➽ p.384 for full listings

Collaborators
Los Lobos ➽ p.218

Influences
Elvis Presley ➽ p.265

Further References
Videos: *Dwight Yoakam, Just Lookin' For A Hit* (1989)
Fast As You (1993)

YOAKAM, DWIGHT

SINGER-SONGWRITER DWIGHT (b. 1956) WORKED THE LA CLUB SCENE WITH VARIOUS BANDS BEFORE, IN 1984, THE release of a self-financed mini-album led to a contract with Warner/Reprise Records. Following *Guitars, Cadillacs Etc., Etc.*, he registered country Top 5 hits with Johnny Horton's 'Honky Tonk Man' and his own 'Guitars, Cadillacs'. In 1987, he found success with his version of 'Little Sister', followed in 1988 by Lefty Frizzell's 'Always Late (With Your Kisses)' (country number 9), and a number 1 with his self-penned 'I Sang Dixie'. 'The Streets Of Bakersfield', with Buck Owens, reached the top of the Country charts and they played several concerts together.

Yoakam's straight country style is his most effective work, although he attempted to cross into the mainstream rock market with *La Croix D'Amour*. He has also recently turned his hand to acting. He came back in 1993 with *This Time*, which included the Grammy-winning country number 1 'Ain't That Lonely Yet'. *Dwight Live* captured the fervour of his concert performances. He wrote all the tracks on *Gone* and remains one of the leading country artists of the new era.

YOUNG, NEIL

CANADIAN YOUNG (b. 1945) PLAYED IN VARIOUS BANDS BEFORE FORMING **BUFFALO SPRINGFIELD** WITH BASSIST Bruce Palmer, **Stephen Stills** and Richie Furay. Although Young took several 'sabbaticals', he also provided two luxurious, atmospheric compositions, 'Broken Arrow' and 'Expecting To Fly'.

After his debut solo, *Neil Young*, he was joined by backing group **Crazy Horse**: Danny Whitten (guitar), Billy Talbot (bass) and Ralph Molina (drums). They created the classic *Everybody Knows This Is Nowhere*. An attendant tour confirmed the strength of the Young/Crazy Horse partnership, while Young also secured acclaim with **Crosby, Stills, Nash And Young**. However, Whitten's increasing dependency on heroin led to the group being dropped following *After The Goldrush*. His best-selling album, *Harvest*, contained 'Heart Of Gold' (US number 1), but this commercial peak ended abruptly with *Journey Through The Past*. The deaths of Whitten and road crew member Bruce Berry inspired the harrowing *Tonight's The Night*, on which Young's bare-nerved emotions were expounded over his bleakest songs to date.

Crazy Horse – Talbot, Molina and guitarist Frank Stampedro – worked with Young on *Zuma*. Despite often ecstatic reviews, the overall performance was generally stronger than the material it supported. The gripping

'Like A Hurricane' was the pivotal feature of *American Stars 'N' Bars*, an otherwise piecemeal collection. His new-found interest in country was emphasized on *Comes A Time*, featuring female vocalist Nicolette Larson. Young followed this by rejoining Crazy Horse for *Rust Never Sleeps*, one of his greatest and most consistent works.

During the 80s, Young became increasingly unpredictable. The understated and underrated *Hawks And Doves* was followed by excursions through electric R&B (*Re-Ac-Tor*), electro-techno pop (*Trans*) and rockabilly (*Everybody's Rockin'*), before embracing ol' timey country (*Old Ways*), hard rock (*Landing On Water*) and R&B (*This Note's For You*). Young's next project was culled from an aborted release, tentatively entitled *Times Square*. *Eldorado* invoked the raw abandonment of *Tonight's The Night*, but the 5-song set was only issued in Japan and Australia. Three of its songs were latterly placed on *Freedom*, an artistic and commercial triumph. Young affirmed this regeneration with *Ragged Glory*, a collaboration with Crazy Horse marked by blistering guitar lines, snarled lyrics and a sense of urgency and excitement.

An ensuing in-concert set, *Weld* (accompanied by an album of feedback experimentation, *Arc*), was applauded as another milestone. Following this, Young decided to return to a *Harvest*-type album with the excellent *Harvest Moon*. He then produced *Unplugged*, a confident live set recorded for MTV. *Sleeps With Angels* mixed some of his dirtiest guitar with some frail and winsome offerings.

In 1995, he collaborated with **Pearl Jam**; then won many new fans with the gripping rock album *Mirror Ball*. *Dead Man* was a challenging and rambling soundtrack of 'guitar', and neither a commercial or listenable excursion. *Broken Arrow* received a less than positive critical reception, although many fans saw little difference in quality. *The Year Of The Horse*, another live album, was tolerated by his fans but left an appetite for new material.

YOUNG, PAUL

YOUNG (b. 1956) WAS A MEMBER OF **Q-TIPS** BEFORE GOING SOLO. FOLLOWING TWO FLOP SINGLES, HIS SMOOTH soul voice hit the charts with a version of **Marvin Gaye**'s 'Wherever I Lay My Hat'. *No Parlez* was a phenomenally triumphant debut, reaching UK number 1 and staying in the charts for over two years. It was a blend of brilliantly interpreted covers including 'Love Will Tear Us Apart' (**Joy Division**) and 'Love Of The Common People' (Nicky Thomas) alongside excellent originals like 'Come Back And Stay'. After touring, Young experienced a recurring problem with his voice, which continues to plague his career.

It was two years before he was able to record *The Secret Of Association* (UK number 1) which produced three Top 10 singles. He appeared at Live Aid, duetting with **Alison Moyet**, before releasing *Between Two Fires* – a below-par album, although his fans still made it a hit.

After a break, Young returned with **Crowded House**'s 'Don't Dream Its Over' at Wembley's Nelson Mandela Concert in 1988. In 1990, he returned with *Other Voices* – including versions of 'Don't Dream It's Over', **Free**'s 'Little Bit Of Love' and **Bobby Womack**'s 'Stop On By' – and an accompanying tour. His was one of the better performances of the Freddie Mercury tribute concert at Wembley Stadium in 1992. Although Young's voice has lost the power and bite of old, he is able to inject passion and warmth into his recent work; envinced on *Reflections*, his excellent recording of soul classics.

YOUNGBLOODS

FORMED IN 1965 IN BOSTON, MASSACHUSETTS BY FOLK SINGERS JESSE COLIN YOUNG (b. PERRY MILLER, 1944) AND Jerry Corbitt. They completed 'My Babe', prior to the arrival of Joe Bauer (b. 1941; drums) and Banana (b. Lowell Levinger III, 1946; guitar/piano). Young began playing bass and the quartet took their name from the singer's second solo album. With a residency at New York's Cafe Au Go Go, the group established itself as a leading folk rock attraction. *The Youngbloods* captured this formative era and mixed excellent original songs, including 'Grizzly Bear', with several choice cover versions. The group's reading of Dino Valenti's 'Get Together' became a hit in California.

Elephant Mountain reflected a new-found peace of mind and included several of the group's best-known songs, including 'Darkness Darkness' and 'Sunlight'. Jerry Corbitt's departure allowed Bauer and Banana space to indulge in improvisational interludes, and the group set up their own label, Racoon. However, solo releases by the trio dissipated the strengths of the parent unit and, despite Michael Kane joining in 1971, the band split the following year. Young resumed his solo career and Banana, Bauer and Kane continued as Banana And The Bunch.

YOUNG RASCALS

FELIX CAVALIERE (b. 1943; ORGAN/VOCALS), EDDIE BRIGATI (b. 1946; VOCALS/PERCUSSION) AND DINO DANELLI (b. 1945; drums) were each established musicians on New York's R&B circuit, debuting as one of America's finest pop/soul ensembles in 1965. Canadian Gene Cornish (b. 1946; vocals/guitar) joined later. The Young Rascals enjoyed a minor hit with 'I Ain't Gonna Eat Out My Heart Anymore' before the US number 1 'Good Lovin''. Their soulful performances established them as one of the east coast's most influential attractions, spawning a host of imitators. They secured their biggest international hit with 'Groovin'', followed by the haunting 'How Can I Be Sure', (US Top 5). In 1968, the group became the Rascals and enjoyed a third US number 1 with 'People Got To Be Free'.

An announcement that every Rascals' live appearance must include a black act enforced the group's commitment to civil rights and effectively banned them from southern states. Later jazz-based compositions lost them much of their commercial momentum and Brigati and Cornish left in 1971. Athough newcomers Buzzy Feiten (guitar), Ann Sutton (vocals) and Robert Popwell (drums) contributed to *Peaceful World* and *The Island Of Real*, the Rascals broke up the following year. Cavaliere, Danelli and Cornish reunited in 1988 for an extensive US tour.

YOUNG, NEIL
Albums
Neil Young (Reprise 1969)★★★★
Everybody Knows This Is Nowhere (Reprise 1969)★★★★★
Sleeps With Angels (Reprise 1994)★★★★
➧ p.384 for full listings

Collaborators
Crazy Horse ➧ p.103
Crosby, Stills And Nash ➧ p.106
Pearl Jam ➧ p.257
Connections
Buffalo Springfield ➧ p.74
Stephen Stills ➧ p.310
Further References
Video: *Unplugged* (1993)
Book: *Neil Young: The Definitive Story Of His Musical Career*, Johnny Rogan

YOUNG, PAUL
Albums
No Parlez (Columbia 1983)★★★★
Acoustic Paul Young mini-album (Columbia 1994)★★★★
➧ p.384 for full listings
Collaborators
Alison Moyet ➧ p.241
Connections
Q-Tips ➧ p.269
Live Aid
Influences
Marvin Gaye ➧ p.159
Joy Division ➧ p.202
Crowded House ➧ p.107
Free ➧ p.154
Bobby Womack ➧ p.342

YOUNGBLOODS
Albums
The Youngbloods (RCA Victor 1967)★★★
Earth Music (RCA Victor 1967)★★★
Elephant Mountain (RCA 1969)★★★★
➧ p.384 for full listings
Connections
Cafe Au Go Go
Banana And The Bunch

YOUNG RASCALS
Albums
Groovin' (Atlantic 1967)★★★★
➧ p.384 for full listings
Connections
Felix And The Escorts
Influences
civil rights movement

ZAPPA, FRANK
Albums
Freak Out! (Verve 1966)★★★★
Weasels Ripped My Flesh (Bizarre 1970)★★★★
Läther (Rykodisc 1996)★★★★
➽ p.384 for full listings
Collaborators
Mothers Of Invention ➽ p.239
Captain Beefheart ➽ p.80
Tom Wilson
Flo And Eddie ➽ p.148
Ruth Underwood
Jean-Luc Ponty
Jack Bruce ➽ p.71
Ike Willis
Connections
Soul Giants
Turtles ➽ p.325
Deep Purple ➽ p.113
Influences
Edgar Varese
Further References
Film: *200 Motels* (1971)
Video: *The Amazing Mr. Bickford* (1992)
Book: *No Commercial Potential: The Saga Of Frank Zappa: Then And Now*, David Walley

ZEVON, WARREN
Albums
Warren Zevon (Asylum 1976)★★★★
Stand In The Fire (Asylum 1980)★★★★
Sentimental Hygiene (Virgin 1987)★★★★
➽ p.384 for full listings
Collaborators
Turtles ➽ p.325
Bruce Sprinsteen ➽ p.306
Nina Tempo
April Stevens
Everly Brothers ➽ p.139
David Geffen ➽ p.160
Lindsey Buckingham ➽ p.72
Stevie Nicks ➽ p.247
Bonnie Raitt ➽ p.272
Neil Young ➽ p.346
Michael Stipe
Peter Buck ➽ p.275
Bob Dylan ➽ p.128
Don Henley ➽ p.180
Jennifer Warnes ➽ p.333
Connections
Midnight Cowboy
Hindu Love Gods

ZOMBIES
Albums
Begin Here (Decca 1965)★★★
Odessey And Oracle (CBS 1968)★★★★,
Meet The Zombies (Razor 1989)★★★
➽ p.384 for full listings
Connections
Argent ➽ p.20
Colin Blunstone ➽ p.57

ZAPPA, FRANK

BY 1956, ZAPPA (b. FRANK VINCENT ZAPPA, 1940, d. 1993) WAS PLAYING DRUMS IN US R&B BAND, THE RAMBLERS. A COPY of *Ionisation*, by *avant garde* classical composer Edgard Varese, instilled an interest in advanced rhythmic experimentation that never left him; the electric guitar also became a fascination. In 1964, Zappa joined another local R&B outfit, the Soul Giants, and started writing songs. They changed their name to the **Mothers** ('**Of Invention**' was added at record company insistence). *Freak Out!*, produced by Tom Wilson, was a stunning debut, a two-record set complete with a whole side of wild percussion and a vitriolic protest song, 'Trouble Every Day'. Tours and releases followed, including *We're Only In It For The Money* – a scathing satire on hippiedom – and a notable appearance at the Royal Albert Hall in London (documented in *Uncle Meat*). *Cruising With Ruben & The Jets* was an excellent homage to the doo-wop era and British fans were particularly impressed with *Hot Rats*, a record that ditched the sociological commentary for barnstorming jazz-rock, blistering guitar solos, the extravagant 'Peaches En Regalia' and a cameo appearance by Zappa's schoolfriend **Captain Beefheart** on 'Willie The Pimp'. The original band broke up (subsequently to resurface as the Grandmothers).

Eager to gain a 'heavier' image, the **Turtles**' singers **Flo And Eddie** joined up with Zappa for the film *200 Motels* and three albums. *Fillmore East June '71* included some intentionally outrageous subject matter prompting inevitable criticism. In general, 1971 was not a happy year: fire destroyed the band's equipment while they were playing at Montreux (an event commemorated in **Deep Purple**'s 'Smoke On The Water') and shortly afterwards Zappa was pushed off-stage in London, crushing his larynx (lowering his voice a third), damaging his spine and keeping him wheelchair-bound for the best part of a year. He spent 1972 developing an extraordinary new species of big band fusion (*Waka/Jawaka* and *The Grand Wazoo*), working with top west-coast session musicians. However, he found these excellent players dull touring companions, and decided to dump the 'jazztette' for an electric band. 1973's *Overnite Sensation* announced fusion-chops, salacious lyrics and driving rhythms. The live band featured an extraordinary combination of jazz-based swing and a rich, sonorous rock. Percussion virtuoso Ruth Underwood and violinist Jean-Luc Ponty featured in *King Kong*. *Apostrophe (')* (US number 10) showcased Zappa's talents as a story-teller, and featured a jam with bassist **Jack Bruce**. *Roxy & Elsewhere* caught the band live, negotiating diabolically hard musical notation – 'Echidna's Arf' and 'The Bebop Tango' – with infectious good humour. *One Size Fits All*, an under-acknowledged masterpiece, built up extraordinary multi-tracked textures.

Despite an earlier rift, in 1975 Captain Beefheart joined Zappa for a tour and sang on *Bongo Fury*. *Zoot Allures* was principally a collaboration between Zappa and drummer Terry Bozzio, with Zappa over-dubbing most of the instruments himself. A series of concerts in New York at Halloween in 1976 had a wildly excited crowd applauding tales of singles bars, devil encounters and stunning Brecker Brothers virtuosity (recorded as *Live In New York*).

When Zappa met Ike Willis, he found a vocalist who understood his required combination of emotional detachment and intimacy, and featured him extensively on *Joe's Garage*. After the mid-70s interest in philosophical concepts and band in-jokes, the music became more political. *Tinseltown Rebellion* and *You Are What You Is* commented on the growth of the fundamentalist Right.

In 1982, Zappa had a hit with 'Valley Girl', with his daughter Moon Unit. That same year saw him produce and introduce a New York concert of Edgar Varese's music. *Shut Up 'N Play Yer Guitar* and *Guitar* showcased Zappa's unique guitar playing; *Jazz From Hell* presented wordless compositions for synclavier that drew inspiration from Conlon Nancarrow, and *Thing-Fish* was a 'Broadway musical' about AIDS, homophobia and racism. The next big project materialized in 1988: a 12-piece band playing covers, instrumentals and a brace of new political songs (collected respectively as *The Best Band You Never Heard In Your Life*, *Make A Jazz Noise Here* and *Broadway The Hard Way*). In Czechoslovakia, where he had long been a hero of the cultural underground, he was appointed Cultural Liaison Officer with the West and in 1991 he announced he would be standing as an independent candidate in the 1992 USA presidential election.

In 1991, Zappa was confirmed as suffering from prostate cancer and in May 1993, it had spread into his bones. He died seven months later.

ZEVON, WARREN

US BORN ZEVON (b. 1947) WROTE SONGS FOR THE **TURTLES** AND NINO TEMPO AND APRIL STEVENS AND RECORDED several singles for the Turtles' label White Whale. By the late 60s, he was signed to Imperial and recorded an inauspicous debut, *Zevon: Wanted Dead Or Alive*. 'She Quit Me', from the album, was featured in the movie *Midnight Cowboy*. The album failed to sell and Zevon took a job on the road as musical director, and occasional session musician, to the **Everly Brothers**. By the early 70s, Zevon was signed as a songwriter by **David Geffen**, and released his second album in 1976. *Warren Zevon* featured the cream of LA's session musicians, including **Lindsey Buckingham**, **Stevie Nicks** and **Bonnie Raitt**.

The follow-up, *Excitable Boy*, tackled American politics and history on 'Roland The Thompson Gunner' and 'Veracruz' alongside one of Zevon's most devastating love songs 'Accidentally Like A Martyr'. *Bad Luck Streak In Dancing School* was most notable for its inventive use of orchestration, with the classical overtones of the title track 'Interlude No. 2' and 'Wild Age' complemented by Zevon's biting satire.

Zevon co-wrote 'Jeannie Needs A Shooter' with **Bruce Springsteen** before a promising live album, which was followed by the much neglected *The Envoy*. This sold poorly and was Zevon's last major work for five years. After undergoing alcoholism therapy, he returned with *Sentimental Hygiene*, featuring **Neil Young**, Michael Stipe and Peter Buck (**R.E.M.**), **Bob Dylan**, **Don Henley**, **Jennifer Warnes** and Brian Setzer (ex-Stray Cats). Zevon also formed Hindu Love Gods with Peter Buck, Mike Mills and Bill Berry, and issued a self-titled album in 1990. Zevon has since built upon his reputation with the finely-produced *Transverse City* and well-received *Mr Bad Example*.

ZOMBIES

ROD **ARGENT** (b. 1945; PIANO), **COLIN BLUNSTONE** (b. 1945; VOCALS), PAUL ATKINSON (b. 1946; GUITAR), PAUL ARNOLD

(bass) and Hugh Grundy (b. 1945; drums) formed the Zombies in 1963, although Chris White (b. 1943) replaced Arnold within weeks. Their debut, 'She's Not There', reached UK number 12/US number 2. Blunstone's breathy voice and Argent's imaginative keyboard arrangement provided the song's distinctive features. Although 'Tell Her No' made the US Top 10, it fared much less well in their native England and later releases missed out altogether.

The group broke up in 1967 on completion of the magnificently innovative *Odyssey And Oracle*. Its closing track, 'Time Of The Season', became a massive US hit. Argent and Grundy, together with bassist Jim Rodford (b. 1941) and guitarist Rick Birkett, were responsible for the Zombies' final single, 'Imagine The Swan'. Blunstone embarked on a stop-start solo career. The band reconvened for *New World*, which received respectable reviews.

An ambitious CD box set was released in 1997. At the launch party in London the original five members played together for the first time in over 25 years.

ZORN, JOHN

NEW YORKER, ZORN (b. 1953) TRAINED IN CLASSICAL COMPOSITION, DEVELOPING AN INTEREST IN JAZZ. SINCE 1974, he has been active on New York's 'downtown' *avant-garde* scene. In 1977, he and guitarist Eugene Chadbourne were included in an 11-piece ensemble playing Frank Lowe's compositions (*Lowe & Behold*). In 1983, Zorn recorded *Yankees* with Derek Bailey and trombonist George Lewis and contributed to Hal Willner's tribute-to-Thelonious Monk album, *That's The Way I Feel Now*. In 1985, he contributed to Willner's Kurt Weill album *Lost In The Stars* and made a commercial breakthrough with *The Big Gundown*. *News For Lulu*, with Lewis and Bill Frisell, presented classic hard bop tunes from the 60s with Zorn's customary steely elegance: it was his second bebop venture, following *Voodoo* by the Sonny Clark Memorial Quartet (Zorn, Wayne Horvitz, Ray Drummond, Bobby Previte).

Zorn championed **Napalm Death** and recorded hardcore versions of Ornette Coleman's tunes on the provocative *Spy Vs Spy*. Naked City – Frisell (guitar), Fred Frith (bass), Joey Baron (bass) – became his vehicle for skipping between sleaze-jazz, surf rock and hardcore. In 1991, he formed Pain Killer with **Bill Laswell** and Mick Harris (drums) and released *Guts Of A Virgin*. Zorn later founded Masada and has continued to record prolifically.

ZZ TOP

FORMED IN HOUSTON, TEXAS IN 1970. THE ORIGINAL LINE-UP FEATURED LANIER GREIG (BASS), DAN MITCHELL (DRUMS) and Billy Gibbons (b. 1949; 6-string guitar/vocals), together they completed ZZ Top's debut, 'Salt Lick'. Dusty Hill (b. Joe Hill, 1949; bass/vocals) and Frank Beard (b. 1949; drums) replaced Greig and Mitchell. Their first album mixed blues with southern boogie, but *Rio Grande Mud* indicated greater flexibility and included 'Francine', their first hit. *Tres Hombres* was a powerful, exciting set which drew from delta music and high-energy rock. It contained the band's first national hit, 'La Grange', and was their first platinum album.

In 1974, the band's first annual 'Texas-Size Rompin' Stompin' Barndance And Bar-B-Q' was held at the Memorial Stadium at the University Of Texas – 85,000 people attended. The crowd was so large that the University refused all rock concerts for another 20 years.

Successive album releases were comparative failures despite an expansive 1976-77 tour. They resumed their career with the superb *Deguello*, by which time both Gibbons and Hill had grown lengthy beards. Revitalized, the trio offered a series of pulsating original songs alongside inspired cover versions. The transitional *El Loco* followed and introduced their growing love of technology, which marked subsequent releases. *Eliminator* became their best-selling album. Fuelled by a series of memorable, tongue-in-cheek videos, it provided several international hits, including the million-selling 'Gimme All Your Lovin'', 'Sharp Dressed Man' and 'Legs'. The group skilfully wedded computer-age technology to their barrelhouse R&B to create a truly memorable set, establishing them as one of the world's leading live attractions. After *Afterburner*, ZZ Top undertook another lengthy break before *Recycler*. Other notable appearances in 1990 included a cameo, playing themselves, in *Back To The Future 3*.

Whether it was by plan or chance, Gibbons, Hill and Beard are doomed to end every music encyclopedia.

ZORN, JOHN

Albums

The Big Gundown (Elektra 1985)★★★★

Spillane (Elektra 1988)★★★★

Filmworks 1986-1990 (Elektra 1992)★★★★

➽ p.384 for full listings

ZZ TOP

Albums

Tres Hombres (London 1973)★★★★

Eliminator (Warners 1983)★★★★

Rhythmeen (RCA 1996)★★★★

➽ p.384 for full listings

Further References

Video: *Greatest Hits Video Collection* (1992)

Book: *Elimination: The Z.Z. Top Story*, Dave Thomas

A

A FLOCK OF SEAGULLS
ALBUMS: *A Flock Of Seagulls* (Jive 1982)★★★, *Listen* (Jive 1983)★★★, *The Story Of A Young Heart* (Jive 1984)★★, *Dream Come True* (Jive 1986)★★, *The Light at the End of the World* (Big Shot Records 1995), *Telecommunications* (Old Gold Records 1992), *The Best of a Flock of Seagulls* (Zomba Records/Arista Records Jive 1991).
VIDEOS: *A Flock of Seagulls* (Sony Video 45 1983).
COMPILATIONS: *Best Of* (RCA 1987)★★★.

A TRIBE CALLED QUEST
ALBUMS: *People's Instinctive Travels And The Paths Of Rhythm* (Jive 1990)★★★, *Low End Theory* (Jive 1991)★★, *Revised Quest For The Seasoned Traveller* (Jive 1992)★★, *Midnight Marauders* (Jive 1993)★★★, *Beats, Rhymes And Life* (Jive 1996)★★★★.

A-HA
ALBUMS: *Hunting High And Low* (Warners 1985)★★★, *Scoundrel Days* (Warners 1986)★★, *Stay On These Roads* (Warners 1988)★★★, *East Of The Sun, West Of The Moon* (Warners 1990)★★★, *Memorial Beach* (Warners 1993)★★.
Solo: Morten Harket *Wild Seed* (Warners 1995)★★, Morten Harket *Heaven's Not For Saints.* Morten Harket *Poetenes Evangelium* (Collection of Classic Norwegian Poetry!) 1993.
COMPILATIONS: *Headlines And Deadlines – The Hits Of A-Ha* (Warners 1991)★★★.
FILMS: *Kamilla And The Thief.*
VIDEOS: *Hunting High and Low* (Pioneer 1986), *Headlines And Deadlines* (1991), *Live in South America* (Warner Music Vision 1993).
FURTHER READING: *Aha: The Story So Far*, Marcussen.

ABBA
ALBUMS: *Ring Ring* (Epic 1973)★★, *Waterloo* (Epic 1974)★★, *Abba* (Epic 1975)★★★, *Arrival* (Epic 1976)★★★, *The Album* (Epic 1977)★★★, *Voulez-Vous* (Epic 1979)★★★, *Super Trouper* (Epic 1980)★★★, *Gracias Por La Musica* (Epic 1980)★★, *The Visitors* (Epic 1981)★★★, *Thank You For The Music* (Epic 1983)★★★, *Abba Live* (Polydor 1986)★★.
COMPILATIONS: *Greatest Hits* (Epic 1976)★★★★, *Greatest Hits, Volume 2* (Epic 1979)★★★, *The Singles – The First Ten Years* (Epic 1982)★★★★, *The Abba Special* (Epic 1983)★★★, *I Love Abba* (1984), *The Best Of Abba* 5-LP box set (Readers Digest 1986)★★★, *Abba – The Hits* (Pickwick 1987)★★★, *The Collection* (Castle 1988)★★★, *The Love Songs* (Pickwick 1989)★★, *Gold: The Greatest Hits* (Polydor 1992)★★★★, *More Abba Gold – More Abba Hits* (Polydor 1993)★★★, *The Music Still Goes On* (Spectrum 1996)★★★.
FILMS: *Abba – The Movie.*
VIDEOS: *Story Of Abba* (MGM 1986), *Video Biography 1974-1982* (Virgin Vision 1987), *Abba – The Movie* (MGM/UA 1988), *Abba: The Video Hits* (Screen Legends 1988), *More Video Hits Of Abba* (Screen Legends 1988), *Abba 1997* Ryko.

ABC
ALBUMS: *The Lexicon Of Love* (Neutron 1982)★★★★★, *Beauty Stab* (Neutron 1983)★★★, *How To Be A Zillionaire* (Neutron 1985)★★★, *Alphabet City* (Neutron 1987)★★★, *Up* (Neutron 1989)★★★, *Abracadabra* (Parlophone 1991)★★, *ABC 2* (Parlophone 1992)★★, *Skyscraping* (Blatant 1997)★★★.
COMPILATIONS: *Absolutely* (Neutron 1990)★★★, *The Remix Collection* (1993)★★★.
VIDEOS: *Mantrap* (1989), *Best Of ABC* (1990), *Absolutely* (1991).

ABDUL, PAULA
ALBUMS: *Forever Your Girl* (Virgin 1989)★★★, *Shut Up And Dance (The Dance Mixes)* (Virgin 1990)★★, *Spellbound* (Virgin 1991)★★★, *Head Over Heels* (Virgin 1995)★★.
VIDEOS: *Compilation* (Virgin Vision 1988), *Skat Strut/Opposites Attract* (Virgin 1991), *Captivated; The Video Collection '92* (Virgin Vision 1992).

ABRAHAMS, MICK
ALBUMS: as Mick Abrahams Band *A Musical Evening With Mick Abrahams* (Chrysalis 1971)★★★, *At Last* (Chrysalis 1972)★★★, *Have Fun Learning The Guitar* (SRT 1975)★★★, *All Said And Done* (1991)★★★, *Lies* (A New Day 1993)★★, *One* (A New Day 1996)★★★, *Mick's Back* (Indigo 1996)★★★, *Live In Madrid* (Indigo 1997)★★★.

AC/DC
ALBUMS: *High Voltage* Australia only (Albert 1974)★★, *TNT* Australia only (Albert 1975)★★, *High Voltage* (Atlantic 1976)★★, *Dirty Deeds Done Dirt Cheap* (Atlantic 1976)★★★, *Let There Be Rock* (Atlantic 1977)★★★★, *Powerage* (Atlantic 1978)★★★, *If You Want Blood You've Got It* (Atlantic 1978)★★★, *Highway To Hell* (Atlantic 1979)★★★★, *Back In Black* (Atlantic 1980)★★★★, *For Those About To Rock We Salute You* (Atlantic 1981)★★★★, *Flick Of The Switch* (Atlantic 1983)★★, *'74 Jailbreak* (Atlantic 1974)★★, *Fly On The Wall* (Atlantic 1985)★★, *Who Made Who* (Atco 1986)★★★, *Blow Up Your Video* (Atlantic 1988)★★, *The Razor's Edge* (Atco 1990)★★★, *Live* (Atco 1992)★★, *Ballbreaker* (Atlantic 1995)★★★.
COMPILATIONS: *Box Set 1* (EMI 1987)★★★, *Box Set 2* (EMI 1987)★★★, *Bonfire* 4CD box set (Atlantic 1997).
VIDEOS: *Let There Be Rock* (1986), *Fly On The Wall* (1986), *High Voltage* (1988), *Who Made Who* (1991), *Live* (1992), *No Bull: Live At The Plaza Del Toros* (Warner Vision 1996).
FURTHER READING: *The AC/DC Story*, Paul Ezra. *AC/DC*, Malcolm Dome. *AC/DC: Hell Ain't No Bad Place To Be*, Richard Bunton. *AC/DC: An Illustrated Collectors' Guide Vols 1 & 2*, Chris Tesch. *AC/DC Illustrated Biography*, Mark Putterford. *Shock To The System*, Mark Putterford. *HM Photo Book*, no author listed. *The World's Most Electrifying Rock 'n' Roll Band*, Malcolm Dome (ed). *Highway To Hell: The Life And Times Of AC/DC Legend Bon Scott*, Clinton Walker. *AC/DC: The World's Heaviest Rock*, Martin Huxley. *AC/DC HM Photo Book*, Chris Welch. *Original Angus Young*, Arti Funaro. *Singing in the Dark*, Barry Taylor.

ACE
ALBUMS: *Five-A-Side* (Anchor 1974)★★★, *Time For Another* (Anchor 1975)★★, *No Strings* (Anchor 1977)★★.
COMPILATIONS: *The Best Of Ace* (See For Miles 1987)★★★, *How Long: The Best Of Ace* (Music Club 1993)★★★.

ACKLES, DAVID
ALBUMS: *David Ackles* aka *The Road To Cairo* (Elektra 1968)★★★, *Subway To The Country* (Elektra 1970)★★, *American Gothic* (Elektra 1972)★★★★, *Five And Dime* (Columbia 1973)★★★.

ACTION
COMPILATIONS: *The Ultimate Action* (1980)★★, *Brain – The Lost Recordings 1967/8* (Autumn Stone Archives 1995)★★, *Rolled Gold* (Dig the Fuzz Records 1997)★★.

ADAM AND THE ANTS
ALBUMS: *Dirk Wears White Sox* (Do It 1979)★★, *Kings Of The Wild Frontier* (Columbia 1980)★★★, *Prince Charming* (Columbia 1981)★★, *Peel Sessions* (Strange Fruit 1991)★★.
COMPILATIONS: *Hits 1980-1985* (Columbia 1986)★★★, *Antmusic: The Very Best Of* (Arcade 1993)★★★.
VIDEOS: *Hits 1980-1986* (1986), *Prince Charming* (1988), *Antmusic: The Very Best Of* (1993), *Super Hits* (Epic/Legacy 1998).
FURTHER READING: *Adam And The Ants*, Mike West. *Adam And The Ants*, Chris Welch. *Adam And The Ants*, Fred and Judy Vermorel. *Adam And The Ants Kings: The Official Adam And The Ants Song Book*, Stephen Lavers.

ADAM ANT
ALBUMS: *Friend Or Foe* (Columbia 1982)★★★, *Strip* (Columbia 1983)★★★, *Vive Le Rock* (Columbia 1985)★★, *Manners And Physique* (MCA 1990)★★, *Wonderful* (EMI 1995)★★★, *Goody Two Shoes* (Sony 1998).
FILMS: *Jubilee*
FURTHER READING: *Adam Ant Tribal Rock Special*, Martha Rodriguez (Design). *The Official Adam Ant Story*, James Maw.

ADAMS, BRYAN
ALBUMS: *Bryan Adams* (A&M 1980)★★, *You Want It, You Got It* (A&M 1981)★★, *Cuts Like A Knife* (A&M 1983)★★, *Reckless* (A&M 1984)★★★, *Into The Fire* (A&M 1987)★★★, *Waking Up The Neighbours* (A&M 1992)★★★, *18 'Til I Die* (A&M 1996)★★, *Bryan Adams Unplugged* (A&M 1997)★★★.
COMPILATIONS: *So Far So Good* (A&M 1994)★★★★.
VIDEOS: *Reckless* (1984), *So Far So Good And More* (1994).
FURTHER READING: *Bryan Adams: The Inside Story*, Hugh Gregory (1992). *The Illustrated Biography*, Sandy Robertson (1994). *Bryan Adams: A Fretted Biography*, Mark Duffett (1995). *Bryan Adams: Everything He Does*, Sorelle Saidman (1995).

ADAMS, OLETA
ALBUMS: *Circle Of One* (Fontana 1990)★★★, *Evolution* (Fontana 1993)★★; *Movin' On* (Fontana 1995)★★★, *Come Walk With Me* (Harmony 1997)★★★.

ADAMSON, BARRY
ALBUMS: *Moss-Side Story* (Mute 1989)★★★, *Delusion – Original Motion Picture Soundtrack* (Mute 1991)★★★, *Soul Murder* (Mute 1992)★★★★, *The Negro Inside Me* (Mute 1993)★★★, *A Prayer Mat Of Flesh* (Mute 1995)★★★, *Oedipus Schmoedipus* (Mute 1996)★★★★, *As Above, So Below* (Mute Records 1998).

ADVERTS
ALBUMS: *Crossing The Red Sea With The Adverts* (Bright 1978)★★★, *Cast Of Thousands* (RCA 1979)★★, *The Peel Sessions* mini-album (Strange Fruit 1987)★★, *Live At The Roxy Club* (Receiver 1990)★★, *The Wonders Don't Care: The Complete Radio Recordings* (Pilot 3 1997)★★★.

AEROSMITH
ALBUMS: *Aerosmith* (Columbia 1973)★★★, *Get Your Wings* (Columbia 1974)★★★, *Toys In The Attic* (Columbia 1975)★★★★, *Rocks* (Columbia 1976)★★★★, *Draw The Line* (Columbia 1977)★★★, *Live! Bootleg* (Columbia 1978)★★★, *Night In The Ruts* (Columbia 1979)★★, *Rock In A Hard Place* (Columbia 1982)★★, *Done With Mirrors* (Geffen 1985)★★★, *Permanent Vacation* (Geffen 1987)★★★, *Pump* (Geffen 1989)★★★★, *Get A Grip* (Geffen 1993)★★★★, *Nine Lives* (Columbia 1997)★★★★.
COMPILATIONS: *Greatest Hits* (Columbia 1980)★★★★, *Classics Live II* (Columbia 1987)★★★, *Gems* (Columbia 1988)★★★, *Pandora's Box* (Columbia 1991)★★★, *Big Ones* (Geffen 1994)★★★★, *Box Of Fire* 13-CD box set (Columbia 1994)★★★★.
FILMS: *Sgt Pepper's Lonely Hearts Club Band.*
VIDEOS: *Video Scrapbook* (Hendring Video 1988), *Live Texas Jam '78* (CMV Enterprises 1989), *Things That Go Pump In The Night* (Warner Music Video 1990), *The Making Of Pump* (Sony Music Video 1991), *Big Ones You Can Look At* (1994).
FURTHER READING: *The Fall And Rise Of Aerosmith*, Mark Putterford. *Toys In The Attic: The Rise, Fall And Rise Of Aerosmith*, Martin Huxley. *Walk This Way*, Aerosmith and Stephen Davis.

AFGHAN WHIGS
ALBUMS: *Big Top Halloween* (Ultrasuede 1988)★★★, *Up In It* (Sub Pop 1990)★★★, *Congregation* (Sub Pop 1992)★★★, *Gentlemen* (Elektra 1993)★★★, *Black Love* (Elektra 1996)★★★.

AFRIKA BAMBAATAA
ALBUMS: with Zulu Nation *Zulu Nation* (1983)★★★, with Shango *Funk Theology* (Celluloid 1984)★★★, *Planet Rock – The Album* (Tommy Boy 1986)★★★★, *Beware (The Funk Is Everywhere)* (Tommy Boy 1986)★★ *The Light* (Capitol 1988)★★★, *The Decade Of Darkness (1990-2000)* (EMI 1991)★★★, *Hip Hop Funk Dance 2* (1992)★★, *Warlocks and Witches, Computer Chips, Microchips and You* (Profile 1996).

AIR SUPPLY
ALBUMS: *Lost In Love* (Arista 1980)★★, *The One That You Love* (Arista 1981)★★★, *Now And Forever* (Arista 1982)★★, *Air Supply* (Arista 1985)★★, *Hearts In Motion* (Arista 1986)★★, *The Christmas Album* (1987)★★, *The Earth Is ...* (1991)★★, *The Vanishing Race* (1993)★★.
COMPILATIONS: *Making Love ... The Best Of Air Supply* (Arista 1983)★★★, *Greatest Hits* (Arista 1983)★★★.

AKKERMAN, JAN
ALBUMS: *Talent For Sale* (Imperial 1968)★★★, *Guitar For Sale* reissue of debut (EMI International 1972)★★★, *Profile* (Harvest 1973)★★★, *Tabernakel* (Atlantic 1974)★★★★, with Kaz Lux *Eli* (Atlantic 1977)★★★, *Jan Akkerman* (Atlantic 1978)★★★, *Arunjuez* (Columbia 1978)★★★, *Live* (Atlantic 1979)★★★, *3* (Atlantic 1980)★★★, *It Could Happen To You* (Charly 1985)★★★, *Can't Stand Noise* (Charly 1986)★★★, *The Noise Of Art* (IRS 1990)★★★.
COMPILATIONS: *A Phenomenon* (Bovena Negram 1979)★★★, *Best Of* (1980)★★★, *Complete Guitarist* (Charly 1985)★★★, *Pleasure Point* (Charly 1987)★★★.

ALABAMA
ALBUMS: *Wild Country* (LSI 1977)★★★, *Deuces Wild* (LSI 1978)★★★, *My Home's In Alabama* (RCA 1980)★★★, *Feels So Right* (RCA 1981)★★★, *Mountain Music* (RCA 1982)★★★, *The Closer You Get* (RCA 1983)★★★, *Roll On* (RCA 1984)★★★, *Alabama Christmas* (RCA 1985)★★, *40 Hour Week* (RCA 1985)★★★, *The Touch* (RCA 1986)★★★, *Just Us* (RCA 1987)★★★, *Alabama Live* (RCA 1988)★★, *Southern Star* (RCA 1989)★★★, *Pass It On Down* (RCA 1990)★★★, *American Pride* (RCA 1992)★★★, *Gonna Have A Party ... Live* (RCA 1993)★★, *Cheap Seats* (RCA 1993)★★★, *In Pictures* (RCA 1995)★★★, *Alabama Christmas Volume II* (RCA 1996)★★, *Dancin' On The Boulevard* (RCA 1997)★★★.
COMPILATIONS: *Wild Country* (LSI 1981)★★★, *Greatest Hits* (RCA 1986)★★★★, *Greatest Hits, Volume 2* (RCA 1991)★★★, *Greatest Hits, Volume 3* (RCA 1994)★★★, *Super Hits* (RCA 1996)★★★.

ALARM
ALBUMS: *Declaration* (IRS 1984)★★★, *Strength* (IRS 1985)★★★, *Eye Of The Hurricane* (IRS 1987)★★★, *Electric Folklore Live* mini-album (IRS 1988)★★★, *Change* (IRS 1989)★★, *Raw* (IRS 1991)★★.
Solo: Mike Peters *Second Generation Volume 1* (21st Century 1996)★★.
COMPILATIONS: *Standards* (IRS 1990)★★★.
VIDEOS: *Spirit Of '86* (Hendring Video 1986), *Change* (PMI 1990).
FURTHER READING: *The Alarm*, Rick Taylor.

ALBION COUNTRY BAND
ALBUMS: As the Albion Country Band with Shirley Collins *No Roses* (Pegasus 1971). As the Albion Country Band *Battle Of The Field* (Island 1976). As the Albion Dance Band *The Prospect Before Us* (Harvest 1977). As the Albion Band *Rise Up Like The Sun* (Harvest 1978)★★★, *Albion River Hymn March* (1979)★★★, *Lark Rise To Candleford (A Country Tapestry)* (Charisma 1980)★★, *Light Shining* (Albino 1982)★★★, *Shuffle Off* (Making Waves 1983)★★★, *Under The Rose* (Spindsrift 1984)★★★, *A Christmas Present From The Albion Band* (Fun 1985)★★, *Stella Maria* (Making Waves 1987)★★★, *The Wild Side Of Town* (Celtic Music 1987)★★, *I Got New Shoes* (Celtic Music 1987)★★★, *Give Me A Saddle And I'll Trade You A Car* (Topic 1989)★★★, *1990* (Topic 1990)★★★, *BBC Radio Live In Concert* (Windsong 1993)★★★, *Acousticity* (HTD 1994)★★★, *Albion Heart* (HTD 1995)★★★★, *The Prospect Before Us* (Hannibal 1996).
COMPILATIONS: *Songs From The Shows Vol. 1* (Road Goes On Forever 1992)★★★, *Songs From The Shows Vol. 2* (Road Goes On Forever 1992)★★★.

ALEXANDER, ARTHUR
ALBUMS: *You Better Move On* (Dot 1962)★★★, *Alexander The Great* (Dot 1964)★★★, *Arthur Alexander I* (Dot 1965)★★★, *Arthur Alexander II* (Warners 1972)★★, *Arthur Alexander III* (Buddah 1975)★★, *Lonely Just Like Me* (Elektra 1993)★★★.
COMPILATIONS: *A Shot Of Rhythm And Soul* (Ace 1985)★★★, *Soldier Of Love* (Ace 1987)★★★, *The Greatest* (Ace 1989)★★★, *The Ultimate Arthur Alexander* (Razor & Tie 1993)★★★, *You Better Move On* (1994)★★★, *Rainbow Road – The Warner Bros. Recordings* (Warner Archives 1994)★★★.

ALICE COOPER
ALBUMS: *Pretties For You* (Straight 1969)★★★, *Easy Action* (Straight 1970)★★, *Love It To Death* (Warners 1971)★★★★, *Killer* (Warners 1971)★★★, *School's Out* (Warners 1972)★★★★, *Billion Dollar Babies* (Warners 1973)★★★★, *Muscle Of Love* (Warners 1973)★★, *Welcome To My Nightmare* (Anchor 1975)★★★, *Alice Cooper Goes To Hell* (Warners 1976)★★, *Lace And Whiskey* (Warners 1977)★, *The Alice Cooper Show* (Warners 1977)★★, *From The Inside* (Warners 1978)★, *Flush The Fashion* (Warners 1980)★, *Special Forces* (Warners 1981)★, *Zipper Catches Skin* (Warners 1982)★, *Dada* (Warners 1983)★, *Live In Toronto* (Breakaway 1984)★, *Constrictor* (MCA 1986)★★, *Raise Your Fist And Yell* (MCA 1987)★★, *Trash* (Epic 1989)★★, *Hey Stoopid* (Epic 1991)★★, *Live At The Whiskey A Go Go* (Edsel 1992)★★, *The Last Temptation* (Epic 1994)★★, *A Fistful Of Alice* (Guardian 1997)★★.
COMPILATIONS: *School Days* (Warners 1973)★★★, *Alice Cooper's Greatest Hits* (Warners 1974)★★★★, *Freak Out Song* (Castle 1986) ★★★, *Beast Of* (Warners 1989)★★★★, *Classicks* (Epic 1995)★★★.
FILMS: *Sextette*, *Sgt Pepper's Lonely Hearts Club Band*, *Wayne's World.*
VIDEOS: *The Nightmare Returns* (Hendring Video 1987), *Welcome To My Nightmare* (Hendring Video 1988), *Alice Cooper Trashes The World* (CMV Enterprises 1990), *Box Set* (Hendring Video 1990), *Prime Cuts* (Castle Music Pictures 1991).
FURTHER READING: *Alice Cooper*, Steve Demorest. *Me: Alice: The Autobiography Of Alice Cooper*, Alice Cooper with Steven Gaines. *Rolling Stone Scrapbook: Alice Cooper*, Rolling Stone.

ALICE IN CHAINS
ALBUMS: *Facelift* (Columbia 1990)★★★, *Sap* mini-album (Columbia 1992)★★★, *Dirt* (Columbia 1992)★★★★, *Jar Of Flies* mini-album (Columbia 1994)★★★★, *Alice In Chains* (Columbia 1995)★★★, *Unplugged* (Columbia 1996)★★★.
FILMS: *Singles*
VIDEOS: *Live Facelift* (1994), *Nona Weisbaum* (Columbia 1995), *The Nona Tapes* (SMV 1996), *MTV Unplugged* (SMV 1996).

ALIEN SEX FIEND
ALBUMS: *Who's Been Sleeping In My Brain* (Anagram 1983)★★, *Acid Bath* (Anagram 1984)★★★, *Liquid Head In Tokyo – Live* (Anagram 1985)★★★, *Maximum Security* (Anagram 1985)★★★, *IT – The Album* (Plague-Anagram 1986)★★★, *The First Alien Sex Fiend Compact Disc* (Anagram 1986), *Here Cum Germs* mini-album (Plague-Anagram 1987)★★★, *Another Planet* (Plague-Anagram 1988)★★★, *Too Much Acid?* (Plague-Anagram 1989)★★, *Curse* (Plague-Anagram 1990)★★★, *Open Head Surgery* (Plague-Anagram 1992)★★★, *The Altered States Of America* (Anagram 1993)★★★, *Inferno* (Anagram 1995)★★★, *Nocturnal Emissions* (13th Moon 1997)★★★.
COMPILATIONS: *All Our Yesterdays* (Anagram 1988)★★★, *The Singles 1983-1995* (Plague-Anagram 1995)★★★.
VIDEOS: *A Purple Glistener* (Jettisoundz 1984), *Edit* (Jettisoundz 1987), *Overdose* (Jettisoundz 1988), *Liquid Head In Tokyo* (ReVision 1991), *Re-Animated – The Promo Collection* (Visionary 1994).

ALISHA'S ATTIC
ALBUMS: *Alisha Rules The World* (Mercury 1996)★★★.

ALL ABOUT EVE
ALBUMS: *All About Eve* (Mercury 1987)★★★, *Scarlet And Other Stories* (Mercury 1989)★★★, *Touched By Jesus* (Vertigo 1991)★★, *Ultraviolet* (MCA 1992)★★, *BBC Radio One Live In Concert* (Windsong 1989)★★.
COMPILATIONS: *Winter Words, Hits And Rarities* (MCA 1992)★★★.
VIDEOS: *Martha's Harbour* (Polygram Music Video 1988), *Kind Of Fool* (Polygram Music Video 1989), *Evergreen* (Channel 5 1989).

ALLIN, G. G.
ALBUMS: as G. G. Allin And The Jabbers *Always Was, Is, And Always Shall Be* (Orange 1980)★★, as G. G. Allin And The Scumfucs *Eat My Fuc* (Blood 1984)★★, as G. G. Allin And The Scumfucs/Artless *G. G. Allin And The Scumfucs/Artless* (Starving Missle/Holy War 1985)★★, as G. G. Allin *Hated In The Nation* cassette only (ROIR 1987)★★, as G. G. Allin And The Holy Men *You Give Love A Bad Name* (Homestead 1987)★★, as G. G. Allin *Freaks, Faggots, Drunks & Junkies* (Homestead 1988)★★, as G. G. Allin And The Jabbers *Banned In Boston* (Black And Blue 1989)★★, as G. G. Allin *Doctrine Of Mayhem* (Black And Blue 1990)★★, as G. G. Allin And The Murder Junkies *Bloodshed And Brutality For All* (1993)★★.

ALLISON, LUTHER
ALBUMS: *Love Me Mama* (Delmark 1969)★★★, *Bad News Is Coming* (Gordy 1973)★★★, *Luther's Blues* (Gordy 1974)★★★, *Night Life* (Gordy 1976)★★★, *Love Me Papa* (Black & Blue 1977)★★★, *Live In Paris* (Free Bird 1979)★★★, *Live* (Blue Silver 1979)★★★, *Gonna Be A Live One In Here Tonight* (Rumble 1979)★★★, *Time* (Paris Album 1980)★★★, *South Side Safari* (Red Lightnin' 1982)★★★, *Lets Have A Natural Ball* (JSP 1984)★★★, *Serious* (Blind Pig 1984)★★★, *Here I Come* (Encore 1985)★★★, *Powerwire Blues* (Charly 1986)★★★, *Rich Man* (Entente 1987)★★★, *Life Is A Bitch* (Encore 1988)★★, *Love Me Mama* (Delmark 1988)★★★, *Let's Try It Again – Live '89* (Teldec 1989)★★, *More From Berlin* (Melodie 1991)★★, *Hand Me Down My Moonshine* (In-Akustik 1992)★★, *Sweet Home Chicago* (1993)★★★, *Soul Fixin' Man* (Alligator 1994)★★★, *Bad Love* (Ruf 1994)★★★, *Blue Streak* (Ruf 1995)★★★, *Reckless* (Ruf 1997)★★★★, *Live In Montreux 1976-1994* (Ruf 1997)★★★★.

ALLMAN BROTHERS BAND
ALBUMS: *The Allman Brothers Band* (Capricorn 1969)★★★★, *Idlewild South* (Capricorn 1970)★★★★, *Live At The Fillmore East* (Capricorn 1971)★★★★, *Eat A Peach* (Capricorn 1972)★★★, *Brothers And Sisters* (Capricorn 1973)★★★, *Win, Lose Or Draw* (Capricorn 1975)★★★, *Wipe The Windows, Check The Oil, Dollar Gas* (Capricorn 1976)H, *Enlightened Rogues* (Capricorn 1979)★★★, *Reach For The Sky* (Arista 1980)★★, *Brothers Of The Road* (Arista 1981)★★, *Live At Ludlow Garage 1970* (Polygram 1990)★★★, *Seven Turns* (Epic 1990)★★★, *Shades Of Two Worlds* (Epic 1991)★★★, *An Evening With The Allman Brothers Band* (Epic 1992)★★★, *The Fillmore Concerts* (Polydor 1993)★★★★, *Where It All Begins* (Epic 1994)★★★, *2nd Set* (Epic 1995)★★, *Twenty* (SPV 1997).
COMPILATIONS: *The Road Goes On Forever* (Capricorn 1975)★★★, *The Best Of The Allman Brothers Band* (Polydor 1981)★★★, *Dreams* 4-CD box set (Polydor 1989)★★★★, *A Decade Of Hits 1969-1979* (Polygram 1991)★★★.
VIDEOS: *Brothers Of The Road* (RCA/Columbia 1988), *Live At Great Woods* (1993).
FURTHER READING: *The Allman Brothers: A Biography In Words And Pictures*, Tom Nolan. *Midnight Riders: The Story Of The Allman Brothers Band*, Scott Freeman.

ALMIGHTY
ALBUMS: *Blood, Fire And Love* (Polydor 1989)★★★, *Blood, Fire and Love – Live* (Polydor 1990)★★, *Soul Destruction* (Polydor 1991)★★★, *Powerstrippin'* (Polydor 1993)★★★, *Crank* (Chrysalis 1994)★★★, *Just Add Life* (Chrysalis 1996)★★.
VIDEOS: *Soul Destruction Live* (Polygram Music Video 1991).

ALMOND, MARC
ALBUMS: *Vermin In Ermine* (Some Bizarre 1984)★★, *Stories Of Johnny* (Some Bizarre 1985)★★★, *A Woman's Story: A Compilation* (Some Bizarre 1986)★★, *Mother Fist And Her Five Daughters* (Some Bizarre 1987)★★, *The Stars We Are* (Parlophone 1988)★★★, *Marc Sings Jacques* (Some Bizarre 1989)★★★, *Enchanted* (Parlophone 1990)★★★, *Tenement Sympony* (Warners 1991)★★, *Twelve Years Of Tears* (Some Bizarre 1993)★★★, *Absinthe: The French Album* (Some Bizarre 1994)★★★, *Fantastic Star* (Mercury 1995)★★★, *Treasure Box* (Some Bizzarre and EMI 1995).
COMPILATIONS: *Singles 1984-1987* (Virgin 1987)★★★, *Best Of* (1991)★★★, *A Virgin's Tale Vols. 1 & 2* (Virgin 1992)★★★.
VIDEOS: *Video's: 1984 – 1987* (1987), *Marc Almond* (1988), *Live In Concert* (Windsong 1993).
FURTHER READING: *The Last Star: A Biography Of Marc Almond*, Jeremy Reed.

ALTAMONT FESTIVAL
FURTHER READING: *Altamont*, Jonathan Eisen (ed.).

ALTERED IMAGES
ALBUMS: *Happy Birthday* (Epic 1981)★★★, *Pinky Blue* (Epic 1982)★★, *Bite* (Epic 1983)★★.
COMPILATIONS: *Collected Images* (Epic 1984)★★★, *The Best Of Altered Images* (Receiver 1992)★★★, *Reflected Images: The Best Of ...* (Epic 1996)★★★, *I Could Be Happy: The Best of Altered Images* (Sony 1997).

ALTERNATIVE TV
ALBUMS: *The Image Has Cracked* (Deptford Fun City 1978)★★, *Vibing Up The Senile Man Part One* (Deptford Fun City 1979)★★, *Live At The Rat Club '77* (Crystal Red 1979)H, *Strange Kicks* (IRS 1981)★★, *Peep Show* (Anagram 1987)★★, *Dragon Love* (Chapter 22 1990)★★, *Live 1978* (Overground/Feel Good All Over 1992)H, *My Life As A Child Star* (Overground 1994)★★. With Here And Now: *What You See ... Is What You Are* (Deptford Fun City 1978)★★, *The Radio Sessions Live* (Overground 1995), *Punk Life* (Overground 1998).
COMPILATIONS: *Splitting In Two* (Anagram 1989)★★★.

AMBOY DUKES
ALBUMS: *The Amboy Dukes* (Mainstream 1967)★★★, *Journey To The Center Of Your Mind* (Mainstream 1968)★★★, *Migrations* (Mainstream 1969)★★★, *Marriage On The Rocks* (Polydor 1969)★★, *Survival Of The Fittest/Live* (Polydor 1971)★★, as Ted Nugent And The Amboy Dukes: *Call Of The Wild* (DiscReet 1974)★★, *Tooth, Fang And Claw* (DiscReet 1975)★★.
COMPILATIONS: *The Best Of The Original Amboy Dukes* (Mainstream 1969)★★★.

AMEN CORNER
ALBUMS: *Round Amen Corner* (Deram 1968)★★★, *National Welsh Coast Live Explosive Company* (Immediate 1969)★★★, *Farewell To The Real Magnificent Seven* (Immediate 1969)★★, *Return Of The Magnificent Seven* (Immediate 1976)★, *Amen Corner and the Small Faces* (New World 1975).
COMPILATIONS: *World Of Amen Corner* (Decca 1969)★★★, *Greatest Hits* (Immediate 1978)★★★.

AMERICA
ALBUMS: *America* (Warners 1972)★★★, *Homecoming* (Warners 1972)★★★, *Hat Trick* (Warners 1973)★★, *Holiday* (Warners 1974)★★★, *Hearts* (Warners 1975)★★★, *Hideaway* (Warners 1976)★★★, *Harbor* (Warners 1976)★★, *America/Live* (Warners 1977)★, *Silent Letter* (Capitol 1979)★★, *Alibi* (Capitol 1980)★★, *View From The Ground* (Capitol 1982)★★, *Your Move* (Capitol 1983)★★, *Perspective* (Capitol 1984)★★, *In Concert* (Capitol 1985)★★, *The Last Unicorn* (Virgin 1988)★, *Hourglass* (American Gramaphone 1994)★★, *King Biscuit Flower Hour* (King Biscuit 1996), *America In Concert* (Capitol 1996).
COMPILATIONS: *History* (Warners 1975)★★★, *Encore! More Greatest Hits* (Rhino 1990)★★, *The Best Of ...* (EMI 1997)★★★.
VIDEOS: *Live In Central Park* (PMI 1986).

AMERICAN MUSIC CLUB
ALBUMS: *The Restless Stranger* (Grifter 1986)★★★, *Engine* (Grifter/Frontier 1986)★★★, *California* (Grifter/Frontier 1988)★★★, *United Kingdom* (Demon 1990)★★★, *Everclear* (Alias 1991)★★★, *Mercury* (Warners/Reprise 1993)★★★★, *San Francisco* (Warners/Reprise 1994)★★★, *Rise* (Alias 1991).

AMERICAN SPRING
ALBUMS: *Spring* UK title *American Spring* (1972)★★★.
FURTHER READING: *The Nearest Faraway Place*, Timothy White.

AMON DUUL II
ALBUMS: *Phallus Dei* (Liberty 1969)★★★, *Yeti* (Liberty 1970)★★★★, *Dance Of The Lemmings* (United Artists 1971)★★★★, *Wolf City* (United Artists 1972)★★★, *Carnival In Babylon* (United Artists 1972)★★★, *Vive La Trance* (United Artists 1973)★★, *Live In London* (United Artists 1973)★★, *Hijack* (Nova 1974)★★, *Made In Germany* (Nova 1975)★★, *Pyragony X* (Nova 1976)★★, *Almost Alive* (Nova 1977)★★, *Only Human* (Strand 1978)★★, *Vortex* (Telefunken 1981)★★, *Hawk Meets Penguin* (Illuminated 1982)★★, *Nada Moonshine* (Mystic 1996)★★, *Live In Tokyo* (Mystic 1997)★★. As Amon Duul (UK): *Meeting With Men Machines* (Illuminated 1984)★★, *Airs On A Shoestring* (Thunderbolt 1987)★★, *Full Moon* (Demi-Monde 1989)★★, with Robert Calvert *Die Losung* (Demi-Monde 1989)★★, *Psychedelic Underground* (Captain Trip 1995)★★★, *Tanz Der Lemminge* (Liberty 1971).
COMPILATIONS: *Classic German Rock Scene* (United Artists 1975)★★★, *Lemmingmania* (United Artists 1975)★★★, *Anthology* (Raw Power 1987)★★★, *BBC In Concert Plus* (Windsong 1992)★★★, *The Best Of 1969-1974* (Cleopatra 1997)★★★.

AMOS, TORI
ALBUMS: as Y Kant Tori Read *Y Kant Tori Read* (Atlantic 1988)★★, *Little Earthquakes* (East West 1992)★★★★, *Under The Pink* (East West 1993)★★★★, *Boys For Pele* (East West 1996)★★★, *From The Choirgirl Hotel* (Atlantic 1998)★★★.
VIDEOS: *Little Earthquake* (1994).
FURTHER READING: *All These Years: The Illustrated Biography*, Kalen Rogers.

ANDERSON, JON
ALBUMS: *Olias Of Sunhillow* (Atlantic 1976)★★★★, *Song Of Seven* (Atlantic 1980)★★★★, *Animation* (Polydor 1982)★★★, *3 Ships* (Elektra 1985)★★★, *In The City Of Angels* (Epic 1988); as Jon And Vangelis *Short Stories* (Polydor 1979)★★★★, *Friends Of Mr. Cairo* (Polydor 1981)★★★★, *Private Collection* (1983)★★★, *Page Of Life* (Arista 1991)★★★, *The Power Of Silence* (1993)★★, *Deseo* (Windham Hill 1995)★★★, *Angels Embrace* (Higer Octave 1996)★★, *Toltec* (HS 1996), *The Promise Ring* (OmTown 1997), *EarthMotherEarth* (Ellipsis Arts 1997), *The More You Know* (Cleopatra 1998).
COMPILATIONS: with Vangelis *The Best Of Jon And Vangelis* (Polydor 1984)★★★★.

ANDERSON, LAURIE
ALBUMS: *Big Science* (Warners 1982)★★★★, *Mr. Heartbreak* (Warners 1984)★★★, *United States* (Warners 1985)★★, *Home Of The Brave* (Warners 1986)★★★, *Strange Angels* (Warners 1989)★★★, *Bright Red* (Warners 1994)★★★, *The Ugly One With The Jewels And Other Stories* (Warners 1995)★★★, *You're the Guy I Want to Share My Money With* (Giorno Poetry 1981).
VIDEOS: *Home Of The Brave* (Warners 1991), *Collected Videos* (Warner Reprise 1990), *Beautiful Red Dress* (Warner Brothers 1990).

ANDREWS, CHRIS
ALBUMS: *Yesterday Man* (Decca 1965)★★, *Who Is The Man* (1977)★.

ANGELIC UPSTARTS
ALBUMS: *Teenage Warning* (Warners 1979)★★★, *We Gotta Get Out Of This Place* (Warners 1980)★★★, *2 Million Voices* (EMI 1981)★★, *Live* (EMI 1981)★★, *Still From The Heart* (EMI 1982)★★, *Reason Why?* (Anagram 1983)★★, *Last Tango In Moscow* (Picasso 1984)★★, *Live In Yugoslavia* (Picasso 1985)★★, *Power Of The Press* (Gas 1986)★★, *Bombed Out* (Roadrunner 1992)★★, *Brighton Bomb* (Chameleon 1987)★★, *Blood on Terraces/Lost & Found* (Chameleon 1994)★★.
COMPILATIONS: *Angel Dust (The Collected Highs 1978-1983)* (Anagram 1983)★★★, *Independent Punk Singles Collection* (Anagram Punk 1995)★★★.

ANIMALS
ALBUMS: *The Animals* (Columbia 1964)★★★★, *Animals On Tour* (MGM 1965)★★★, *Animal Tracks* (Columbia 1965)★★★, *Most Of The Animals* (Columbia 1966)★★★★, *Animalization* (MGM 1966)★★★, *Animalisms* (Decca 1966)★★★, *Eric Is Here* (1967)★★★, *Winds Of Change* (MGM 1967)★★★, *The Twain Shall Meet* (MGM 1968)★★★, *Everyone Of Us* (MGM 1968)★★★, *Love Is* (MGM 1968)★★★, *In Concert From Newcastle* (1976)★★, *Before We Were Rudely Interrupted* (Barn 1976)★, *The Ark* (1983)★, *Rip It To Shreds* (1984)★★, *The Animals With Sonny Boy Williamson* (1988)★★★, *Animals (Boom Boom)* (Columbia 1965), *Animals No. 2 (I'm In Love Again)*(Colombia 1965), *In the Beginning* (Sundazed 1965), *Roadrunners! (Live)* (Raven 1990).
VIDEOS: *Animalistic* (The Gold Standard 1995).
COMPILATIONS: *Best Of The Animals* (MGM 1966)★★★, *Best Of The Animals Vol 2* (MGM 1967)★★★, *The EP Collection* (1989)★★★★, *The Complete Animals* (1990)★★★★, *Trackin' The Hits* (1990)★★★.
FILMS: *Get Yourself A College Girl* (1964), *It's A Bikini World* (1967).

ANKA, PAUL
ALBUMS: *Paul Anka* (ABC 1958)★★★, *My Heart Sings* (ABC 1959)★★★, *Paul Anka Swings For Young Lovers* (ABC 1960)★★★★, *Anka At The Copa* (ABC 1960)★★★, *It's Christmas Everywhere* (ABC 1960)★★★, *Strictly Instrumental* (ABC 1961)★★, *Diana* (ABC 1962)★★★★, *Young, Alive And In Love!* (RCA Victor 1962)★★★★, *Let's Sit This One Out!* (RCA Victor 1962)★★★, *Our Man Around The World* (RCA Victor 1963)★★★, *Songs I Wished I'd Written* (RCA Victor 1963)★★, *Excitement On Park Avenue* (RCA Victor 1964)★★★, *Strictly Nashville* (RCA Victor 1966)★★, *Paul Anka Alive* (RCA Victor 1967)★★, *Goodnight My Love* (RCA Victor 1969)★★★, *Life Goes On* (RCA Victor 1969)★★★, *Paul Anka* (Buddah 1971)★★, *Jubilation* (Buddah 1972)★★, *Anka* (United Artists 1974)★★★, *Feelings* (United Artists 1975)★★★, *The Painter* (United Artists 1976)★★★, *The Music Man* (United Artists 1977)★★★, *Listen To Your Heart* (RCA 1978)★★, *Both Sides Of Love* (RCA 1981)★★, *Walk A Fine Line* (Columbia 1983)★★★, *Italiano* (1987)★★★, *Amigos* (Globo/Sony 1996)★★★.
COMPILATIONS: *Paul Anka Sings His Big 15* (ABC 1960)★★★★, *Paul Anka Sings His Big 15, Volume 2* (ABC 1961)★★★, *Paul Anka's 21 Golden Hits* (RCA 1963)★★★, *Paul Anka Gold* (Sire 1974)★★★★, *Times Of Your Life* (1975)★★★, *Essential Paul Anka* (1976)★★★★, *Vintage Years, 1957-61* (1977)★★★★, *Paul Anka – His Best* (1980)★★★★, *Gypsy Ways* (1988)★★★, *The Ultimate Collection* (1992)★★★★.
FILMS: *Girl's Town* aka *The Innocent And The Damned* (1959), *Lonely Boy* (1962), *The Longest Day* (1962).

ANTHRAX
ALBUMS: *Fistful Of Metal* (Megaforce 1984)★★, *Spreading The Disease* (Island/Megaforce 1986)★★★, *Among The Living* (Island/Megaforce 1987)★★★, *State Of Euphoria* (Island/Megaforce 1988)★★, *Persistence Of Time* (Island/Megaforce 1990)★★★★, *Attack Of The Killer B's* (Island/Megaforce 1991)★★★, *Sound Of White Noise* (Elektra 1993)★★★★, *Live – The Island Years* (Island 1994)★★★, *Stomp 442* (Island 1995)★★★, *Armed and Dangerous* (Megaforce 1985), *I'm The Man* (Megaforce 1987).

COMPILATIONS: Penikufesin★★★.
VIDEOS: Oidivnikufesin N.F.V. (1988), Videos P.O.V. (1990), Persistence Through Time (1990), Through Time (1991), N.F.V. (1991).

ANTI-NOWHERE LEAGUE
ALBUMS: We Are ... The League (WXYZ 1982)★★, Live In Yugoslavia (ID 1983)★★, as The League The Perfect Crime (GWR 1987)★★★, Live And Loud (Link 1990)★★, The Horse Is Dead (live) (Receiver 1996), We Are The League (Snapper 1997).
COMPILATIONS: Long Live The League (Dojo 1986)★★★.

APHEX TWIN
1ALBUM S: Selected Ambient Works '85-'92 (R&S 1992)★★★★, as AFX Analogue Bubblebath 3 (Warp 1993)★★, as Polygon Window Surfing On SineWaves (Warp 1993)★★, Selected Ambient Works Vol. 2 (Warp 1994)★★★, I Care Because You do (Warp 1995)★★★, Ventolin & Remixes (Warp 1995)★★★, Richard D. James Album (Warp 1996)★★★.

APHRODITE'S CHILD
ALBUMS: Aphrodite's Child – Rain And Tears (Impact 1968)★★, It's Five O'Clock (Impact 1970)★★, 666 – The Apocalypse Of St. John (Vertigo 1972)★★★, End of the World (Mercury 1969).
COMPILATIONS: Rain And Tears: The Best Of (Philips International 1970)★★★, The Best Of Aphrodite's Child (Mercury 1975)★★★, Greatest Hits (Mercury 1981)★★★.

APPLE, FIONA
1ALBUMS: Tidal (Columbia 1996).

APPLEJACKS (UK)
ALBUMS: The Applejacks (Decca 1964)★★.

APRIL WINE
ALBUMS: April Wine (Aquarius 1972)★★, On Record (Aquarius 1973)★★, Electric Jewels (Aquarius 1974)★★, Live (Aquarius 1975)★★, Stand Back (Aquarius 1975)★★, The Whole World's Goin' Crazy (London 1976)★★★, Live At The El Mocambo (London 1977)★★, First Glance (Capitol 1978)★★, Harder ... Faster (Capitol 1979)★★★, The Nature Of The Beast (Capitol 1981)★★★, Power Play (Capitol 1982)★★, Animal Grace (Capitol 1984)★★, Walking Through Fire (Capitol 1985)★★, Forever For Now (Aquarius 1976), Summer Tour 1981 (Capitol 1981), First Decade (European Import 1994), Frigate (Fre 1994), Attitude (Fre 1995).
VIDEOS: Live In London (PMI 1986).

ARCHER, TASMIN
ALBUMS: Great Expectations (EMI 1993)★★★, Bloom (EMI 1996)★★, Shipbuilding (SBK 1994)★★.
VIDEOS: When It Comes Down To It (1993).

ARGENT
ALBUMS: Argent (Columbia 1970)★★★, Ring Of Hands (Columbia 1971)★★★, All Together Now (Epic 1972)★★★, In Deep (Epic 1973)★★, Nexus (Epic 1974)★★, Encore – Live In Concert (Epic 1974)★, Circus (Epic 1975)★, Counterpoint (RCA 1975)★★, In Concert (Windsong 1995)★★★, Hold Your Head Up (Embassy 1978), Moving Home (MCA 1978), Ghosts (with Barbara Thompson) (MCA).
COMPILATIONS: Anthology (Epic 1984)★★★, Music From The Spheres (Elite 1991)★★★.

ARKARNA
ALBUMS: Fresh Meat (WEA 1997).

ARMATRADING, JOAN
ALBUMS: Whatever's For Us (A&M 1972)★★★, Back To The Night (A&M 1975)★★★, Joan Armatrading (A&M 1976)★★★★, Show Some Emotion (A&M 1977)★★★, To The Limit (A&M 1978)★★★, Steppin' Out (A&M 1978)★★, Me Myself I (A&M 1980)★★★★, Walk Under Ladders (A&M 1981)★★★, The Key (A&M 1983)★★★, Secret Secrets (A&M 1985)★★★, Sleight Of Hand (A&M 1986)★★★, The Shouting Stage (A&M 1988)★★★★, Hearts And Flowers (A&M 1990)★★★, Square The Circle (A&M 1992)★★★, What's Inside (RCA 1995)★★★.
COMPILATIONS: Track Record (A&M 1983)★★★★, The Very Best Of Joan Armatrading (A&M 1991)★★★★.

ARNOLD, P. P.
ALBUMS: First Lady Of Immediate (Immediate 1967)★★, Kafunta (Immediate 1968)★★, Angel (Showcase 1986).

ARRESTED DEVELOPMENT
ALBUMS: Three Years, Five Months, And Two Days In The Life Of ... (Chrysalis 1992)★★★★, Unplugged (Chrysalis 1993)★★★, Zingalamaduni (Chrysalis 1994)★★★.
VIDEOS: Unplugged: Video (Chrysalis 1993).

ARRIVAL
ALBUMS: Arrival I (Decca 1970)★★★, Arrival II (Columbia 1972)★★★, Heartbreak Kid (CBS 1973).

ARROWS
ALBUMS: First Hit (Rak 1976)★★, Stand Back (A&M 1984).
FURTHER READING: Arrows: The Official Story, Bill Harry.

ART OF NOISE
ALBUMS: Who's Afraid Of The Art Of Noise (ZTT 1984)★★★, Into Battle With (ZTT 1984)★★★, Daft (China 1987)★★, In No Sense? Nonsense (China 1987)★★, In Visible Silence (Chrysalis 1987)★★★, Below The Waste (China 1989)★★★, The Ambient Collection (China 1990)★★★, Drum And Bass Collection (China 1996)★★★, 3-CD remix box State Of The Art (China 1997)★★★, Fon Mixes (Discovery 1997).
COMPILATIONS: The Best Of The Art Of Noise (China 1988)★★★★.
FILMS: Breakdance – The Movie (1984).
VIDEOS: In Visible Silence (1988).

ASH
ALBUMS: Trailer mini-album (Infectious 1994)★★★, 1977 (Infectious 1996)★★★★, Live At The Wireless (Death Star 1997)★★★.
FURTHER READING: Ash 1977-97, Charles Porter.

ASHFORD AND SIMPSON
ALBUMS: Gimme Something Real (Warners 1973)★★, I Wanna Be Selfish (Warners 1974)★★, Come As You Are (Warners 1976)★★, So, So Satisfied (Warners 1977)★★★, Send It (Warners 1977)★★★, Is It Still Good To Ya? (Warners 1978)★★★, Stay Free (Warners 1979)★★★, A Musical Affair (Warners 1980)★★★, Performance (Warners 1981)★★★, Street Opera (Capitol 1982)★★★, High-Rise (Capitol 1983)★★★, Solid (Capitol 1984)★★★, Real Love (Capitol 1986)★★★, Love Or Physical (Capitol 1989)★★.
COMPILATIONS: The Best Of (1993)★★★★.
FILMS: Body Rock (1984).
VIDEOS: The Ashford And Simpson Video (EMI 1982).

ASIA
ALBUMS: Asia (Geffen 1982)★★★, Alpha (Geffen 1983)★★, Astra (Geffen 1985)★★, Then And Now (Warners 1990)★★, Live In Moscow (Rhine 1992)★★, Aqua (Musidisc 1992)★★, Aria (Bullet Proof 1994)★★, Arena (Resurgent 1996)★★, Now Nottingham Live (Resurgent 1997)★★, Live in Osaka (Resurgent 1997)★★, Live in Koln (Resurgent 1997)★★, Live in Philadelphia (Resgurgent 1997)★★.
VIDEOS: Asia In Asia (1984), Asia (Live) (1991).

ASLEEP AT THE WHEEL
ALBUMS: Comin' Right At Ya (Sunset 1973)★★★, Asleep At The Wheel (Epic 1974)★★★, Texas Gold (Capitol 1975)★★★★, Wheelin' And Dealin' (Capitol 1975)★★★, with various artists Texas Country (1976)★★, The Wheel (Capitol 1977)★★★★, Collision Course (Capitol 1978)★★★, Served Live (Capitol 1979)★★★, Framed (MCA 1980)★★★, Asleep At The Wheel (MCA/Dot 1985)★★, Jumpin' At The Woodside (Edsel 1986)★★★, Ten (Epic 1987)★★★, Western Standard Time (Epic 1988)★★★, Keepin' Me Up Nights (Arista 1990)★★★, Tribute To The Music Of Bob Wills And The Texas Playboys (Liberty 1993)★★★, The Wheel Keeps On Rollin' (Capitol Nashville 1995)★★★, Back To The Future Now – Live At Arizona Charlie's, Las Vegas (Epic 1997)★★★, Merry Texas Christmas, Y'All (High Street Records 1997)★★★, Still Swingin' (Liberty 1994).
COMPILATIONS: The Very Best Of Asleep At The Wheel (See For Miles 1987)★★★, Greatest Hits – Live & Kickin' (Arista 1991)★★★, Best Of (CEMA 1992)★★★, The Swinging Best Of Asleep At The Wheel (Epic 1992)★★★.
FILMS: Roadie.

ASSOCIATES
ALBUMS: The Affectionate Punch (Fiction 1980)★★★, Sulk (Sire 1982)★★★, Perhaps (Associates/Warners 1985)★★, Wild And Lonely (Circa/Charisma 1990)★★★ Solo: Billy MacKenzie Outernational (Circa 1991)★★, Beyond The Sun (Nude 1997)★★★. Alan Rankine The Day The World Became Her Age (Cr≥puscule 1986)★★★, She Loves Me Not (Virgin 1987)★★★, The Big Picture Sucks (Cr≥puscule 1989)★★.
COMPILATIONS: Fourth Drawer Down (Situation 2 1981)★★★, The Radio 1 Sessions (Nighttracks 1995)★★★.

ASSOCIATION
ALBUMS: And Then ... Along Comes (Valiant 1966)★★★★, Renaissance (Valiant 1967)★★, Insight Out (1967)★★, Birthday (1968)★★, The Association (1969)★★, Live (1970)★, Stop Your Motor (1971)★★, Waterbeds In Trinidad (1972)★★, Songs that Made Them Famous (Pair 1986), Association 95: A Little Bit More (On Track 1995).
COMPILATIONS: Greatest Hits (Warner 1968)★★★★, Golden Heebie Jeebies (1988)★★★.

ASTLEY, RICK
ALBUMS: Whenever You Need Somebody (RCA 1987)★★★, Hold Me In Your Arms (RCA 1988)★★, Free (RCA 1991)★★★, Body and Soul (RCA 1993).
VIDEOS: Video Hits (1989).

ASWAD
ALBUMS: Aswad (Mango/Island 1975)★★★, Hulet (Grove Music 1978)★★★★, New Chapter (Columbia 1981)★★★, Not Satisfied (Columbia 1982)★★★, A New Chapter Of Dub (Mango/Island 1982)★★★, Live And Direct (Mango/Island 1983)★★★, Rebel Souls (Mango/Island 1984)★★★, Jah Shaka Meets Aswad In Addis Ababa Studio (Jah Shaka 1985)★★★, To The Top (Simba 1986)★★★★, Distant Thunder (Mango/Island 1988)★★★, Too Wicked (Mango/Island 1990)★★, Rise And Shine (Bubblin 1994)★★, Next to You (Alex 1990), Rise & Shine Again (Mesa 1995), Dub: The Next Frontier (Mesa 1995), Big Up (Atlantic 1997).
COMPILATIONS: Showcase (Grove Music 1981)★★★, Renaissance (Stylus 1988)★★★.
FILMS: Babylon.
VIDEOS: Distant Thunder Concert (Island Visual Arts 1989), Always Wicked (Island Visual Arts 1990).

ASYLUM CHOIR
ALBUMS: Look Inside The Asylum Choir (1968)★★, Asylum Choir II (1971)★★.

ATLANTA RHYTHM SECTION
ALBUMS: The Atlanta Rhythm Section (Decca 1972)★★★, Back Up Against The Wall (Decca 1973)★★★, Third Annual Pipe Dream (Polydor 1974)★★★, Dog Days (Polydor 1975)★★, Red Tape (Polydor 1976)★★★, A Rock And Roll Alternative (Polydor 1977)★★★★, Champagne Jam (Polydor 1978)★★★, Underdog (Polydor 1979)★★★, Are You Ready! (Polydor 1979)★★★, The Boys From Doraville (Polydor 1980)★★, Quinella (Columbia 1981)★★, Atlanta Rhythm Section '96 (CMC 1996), Partly Plugged (Southern Track 1997).
COMPILATIONS: The Best Of The Atlanta Rhythm Section (Polydor 1982)★★★★.

ATOMIC ROOSTER
ALBUMS: Atomic Rooster (B&C 1970)★★, Death Walks Behind You (B&C 1970)★★, In Hearing Of (Pegasus 1971)★★★, Made In England (Dawn 1972)★★, Nice 'N' Greasy (Dawn 1973)★, Atomic Rooster (EMI 1980)★, Headline News (Towerbell 1983)★.

AU PAIRS
ALBUMS: Playing With A Different Sex (Human 1981)★★★, Sense And Sensuality (Kamera 1982)★★, Live In Berlin (a.k.a. 1983)★★★.

AUDIENCE
ALBUMS: Audience (Polydor 1969)★★, Friends Friends Friends (Charisma 1970)★★★, Bronco Bullfrog (soundtrack 1970)★★, House On The Hill (Charisma 1971)★★★, Lunch (Charisma 1972)★★.
COMPILATIONS: You Can't Beat Them (1973)★★★, Unchained (1992)★★★.

AUSTIN, PATTI
ALBUMS: End Of A Rainbow (CTI 1976)★★★, Havana Candy (CTI 1977)★★★, Live At The Bottom Line (CTI 1979)★★★, Body Language (CTI 1980)★★★, Every Home Should Have One (Qwest 1981)★★★★, Patti Austin (Qwest 1984)★★★, Gettin' Away With Murder (Qwest 1985)★★, The Real Me (Qwest 1988)★★★, Love's Gonna Get You (GRP 1990)★★, Carry On (GRP 1991)★★★, Live (1992)★★★, That Secret Place (GRP 1994).
FILMS: Tucker (1988).

AUTEURS
ALBUMS: New Wave (Hut 1993)★★★★, Now I'm A Cowboy (Hut 1994)★★★, After Murder Park (Hut 1996)★★★. As Baader-Meinhof Baader-Meinhof (Hut 1996)★★, Kid's Issue (Hut 1996).

AVERAGE WHITE BAND
ALBUMS: Show Your Hand reissued as Put It Where You Want It (MCA 1973)★★★, AWB (Atlantic 1974)★★★★, Cut The Cake (Atlantic 1975)★★★, Soul Searching (Atlantic 1976)★★, Person To Person (Atlantic 1977)★★★, with Ben E. King Benny And Us (Atlantic 1977)★★★, Warmer Communications (RCA 1978)★★, Feel No Fret (RCA 1979)★★★, Shine (RCA 1980)★★, Volume VIII (RCA 1980)★★, Cupid's In Fashion (RCA 1982)★★, After Shock (Polydor 1989)★★★, Soul Tattoo (Artful 1997)★★★, Live on the Test (Windsong 1995), Old Grey Whistle Test Series (live) (Alex 1995).
Solo: Alan Gorrie Sleepless Nights (1985)★★.
COMPILATIONS: Best Of The Average White Band (RCA 1984)★★★★.

AVONS
ALBUMS: The Avons (Columbia/Hull 1960)★★.
COMPILATIONS: Golden Classics (Collectables 1995).

AYERS, KEVIN
ALBUMS: Joy Of A Toy (Harvest 1969)★★★★, Shooting At The Moon (Harvest 1970)★★★★, Whatevershebringswesing (Harvest 1971)★★★, Bananamour (Harvest 1973)★★★, The Confessions Of Doctor Dream (Island 1974)★★★, with John Cale, Brian Eno, Nico June 1 1974 (Island 1974)★★, Sweet Deceiver (Island 1975)★★★, Yes We Have No Ma–anas (Harvest 1976)★★★, Rainbow Takeaway (Harvest 1978)★★, That's What You Get Babe (Harvest 1980)★★, Diamond Jack And The Queen Of Pain (Charly 1983)★★, As Close As You Think (Illuminated 1986)★★, Falling Up (Virgin 1988)★★★, Still Life With Guitar (Permanent 1992)★★★, BBC Radio One Live In Concert (Windsong 1992)★★★.
COMPILATIONS: Odd Ditties (Harvest 1976)★★★, The Kevin Ayers Collection (See For Miles 1983)★★★, Banana Productions – The Best Of Kevin Ayers (Harvest 1989)★★★★, Document Series Presents (Connoisseur 1992)★★★, Singing The Bruise (Strange Fruit 1996)★★★.

AYNSLEY DUNBAR RETALIATION
ALBUMS: The Aynsley Dunbar Retaliation (Liberty 1968)★★★, Dr. Dunbar's Prescription (Liberty 1968)★★★, Retaliation aka To Mum From Aynsley And The Boys (Liberty 1969)★★★, Remains To Be Heard (Liberty 1970)★★.

AZTEC CAMERA
ALBUMS: High Land, Hard Rain (Rough Trade 1983)★★★★, Knife (Warners 1984)★★★, Aztec Camera mini-album (Warners 1985)★★★, Love (Warners 1987)★★★, Stray (Warners 1990)★★★, Dreamland (Warners 1993)★★★, Live On The Test rec. 1983 (Windsong 1995)★★★, Frestonia (Warners 1995)★★★★, New, Live and Rare (WEA 1995), Old Grey Whistle Test Series (Alex 1995).
VIDEOS: Aztec Camera (WEA Music Video 1989).

AZTEC TWO-STEP
ALBUMS: Aztec Two-Step (Elektra 1972)★★★, Second Step (RCA 1975)★★, Two's Company (RCA 1976)★★, Adjoining Suites (RCA 1977)★★, Living In America (Reflex 1986)★★, See It Was Like This... (Flying Fish 1989)★★★, Of Age (1993)★★, Highway Signs: The 25th Anniversary Concerts (1-800-Prime 1996).

B

B-52'S
ALBUMS: B-52's (Warners 1979)★★★★, Wild Planet (Warners 1980)★★★, Party Mix! remix of the first two albums (Warners 1981)★★★, Mesopotamia mini-album (Warners 1982)★★, Whammy! (Warners 1983)★★, Bouncing Off The Satellites (Warners 1986)★★, Cosmic Thing (Reprise 1989)★★★, Good Stuff (Warners 1992)★★★.
Solo: Fred Schneider Fred Schneider And The Shake Society (Warners 1984)★★★, Just Fred (Reprise 1996)★★★.
COMPILATIONS: Best Of The B-52's: Dance This Mess Around (Island 1990)★★★★, Party Mix-Mesopotamia (Warners 1991)★★★, Planet Claire (Spectrum 1995)★★★, Time Capsule (Arabesque 1998).

B. BUMBLE AND THE STINGERS
COMPILATIONS: Best O'B Bumble (One Way 1995)★★, Nut Rocker And All The Classics (Ace 1996)★★.

B., DEREK
ALBUMS: Bullet From A Gun (Tuff Audio 1988)★★★.

BABES IN TOYLAND
ALBUMS: Spanking Machine (Twin Tone 1990)★★, To Mother mini-album (Reprise/WEA 1991)★★, The Peel Sessions (1992 Dutch East Indian)★★ Fontanelle (Reprise/WEA 1992)★★★★, Painkillers (Reprise/WEA 1994)★★★, Dystopia (Import 1994)★★★ Nemesisters (Reprise/WEA 1995)★★★★.
FURTHER READING: Babes In Toyland: The Making And Selling Of A Rock And Roll Band, Neal Karlen.

BABYBIRD
ALBUMS: I Was Born A Man (Baby Bird 1995)★★★, Bad Shave (Baby Bird 1995)★★, Fatherhood (Baby Bird, 1995)★★★, The Happiest Man Alive (Baby Bird 1996)★★, Ugly Beautiful (Echo 1996)★★★, Dying Happy (Baby Bird 1997)★★, Greatest Hits (Baby Bird 1997)★★★.

BABYFACE
ALBUMS: Lovers (Solar 1987)★★, Tender Lover (Solar 1989)★★, It's No Crime (1989)★★, A Closer Look (Solar 1991)★★, For The Cool In You (Epic 1993)★★★, The Day (Epic 1996)★★, MTV Unplugged NYC 1997 (Epic 1998)★★.
VIDEOS: Tender Lover (CBS 1990)

BABYLON ZOO
ALBUMS: The Boy With The X-Ray Eyes (EMI 1996)★★.

BABYS
ALBUMS: The Babys (Chrysalis 1976)★★★, Broken Heart (Chrysalis 1977)★★★, Head First (Chrysalis 1978)★★★, Union Jacks (Chrysalis 1980)★★, On The Edge (Chrysalis 1980)★★, The Best of the Babys (EMI 1997)★★★.
COMPILATIONS: Anthology (Chrysalis 1981)★★★.

BACCARA
ALBUMS: Baccara (RCA 1978)★, Light My Fire (RCA 1979)★, Colours (RCA 1980)★ Yes Sir, I Can Boogie (Ariola Extra 1994)★.

BACHARACH, BURT
ALBUMS: Hit Maker – Burt Bacharach (London 1965)★★★, Casino Royale soundtrack (RCA 1967)★★★, Reach Out (A&M 1967)★★★, Make It Easy On Yourself (A&M 1969)★★, Butch Cassidy And The Sundance Kid soundtrack (A&M 1970)★★★, Burt Bacharach (A&M 1971)★★, Living Together (A&M 1973)★★, In Concert (A&M 1974)★★, Futures (A&M 1977)★★, Woman (A&M 1979)★★, Walk On By (MCA 1987), Butch Cassidy And The Sundance Kid (A&M 1989), After The Fox (MCA).
COMPILATIONS: Portrait In Music (A&M 1971)★★★, Portrait In Music Vol. 2 (A&M 1973)★★★, Burt Bacharach's Greatest Hits (A&M 1974)★★★★, The Best Of Burt Bacharach (A&M 1996)★★★★.

BACHELORS
ALBUMS: The Bachelors (1963)★★★, The Bachelors Second Album (1964)★★, Presenting: The Bachelors (1964)★★★, The Bachelors And Sixteen Great Songs (Decca 1964)★★★, No Arms Can Ever Hold You (1965)★★★, Marie (1965)★★★, More Great Song Hits From The Bachelors (1965)★★★, Hits Of The Sixties (Decca 1966)★★★, Bachelors' Girls (Decca 1966)★★★, The Golden All Time Hits (Decca 1967)★★★, Live At Talk Of The Town (1971)★★, Under And Over (1971)★★, with Patricia Cahill Stage And Screen Spectacular (1972)★★.
COMPILATIONS: World Of The Bachelors (Decca 1968)★★★★, World Of The Bachelors – Vol. Two (Decca 1969)★★★★, World Of The Bachelors – Vol. Three (Decca 1969)★★★, World Of The Bachelors – Vol. Four (Decca 1970)★★★, The Very Best Of The Bachelors (1974)★★★, Focus On The Bachelors (1979)★★★, 25 Golden Greats (Warwick 1979)★★★★, The Best Of The Bachelors (1981)★★★, The Bachelors Collection (1985)★★★, Bachelors Hits (1989)★★★.
FILMS: It's All Over Town (1964).

BACHMAN-TURNER OVERDRIVE
ALBUMS: as Brave Belt Brave Belt (Reprise 1971)★★, as Brave Belt Brave Belt II (Reprise 1972)★★, Bachman-Turner Overdrive (Mercury 1973)★★, Bachman-Turner Overdrive II (Mercury 1974)★★★, Not Fragile (Mercury 1974)★★★★, Four Wheel Drive (Mercury 1975)★★★, Head On (Mercury 1975)★★, Freeways (Mercury 1977)★★, Street Action (Mercury 1978)★, Rock 'N' Roll Nights (Mercury 1979)★, Bachman-Turner Overdrive (Compleat 1984)★★, Overdrive (Mercury 1986), Live!-Live!-Live! (MCA 1986), King Biscuit Flower Hour (live) (King Biscuit 1998).
COMPILATIONS: Best Of BTO (So Far) (Mercury 1976)★★★, Greatest Hits (Mercury 1981)★★★.
FURTHER READING: Bachman Turner Overdrive: Rock Is My Life, This Is My Song: The Authorized Biography, Martin Melhuish.

BAD BRAINS
ALBUMS: Bad Brains cassette only (ROIR 1982)★★, Rock For Light (PVC 1983)★★★, I Against I (SST 1986)★★★, Live (SST 1988)★★, Attitude: The ROIR Sessions (In-Effect 1989)★★★, Quickness (Caroline 1989)★★★, The Youth Are Getting Restless (Caroline 1990)★★★, Rise (1993)★★★, God Of Love (Maverick 1995)★★★, Black Dots (Caroline 1996)★★★, Bad Brains (1996) (Roir 1996)★★★, Omega Sessions (Victory 1997)★★★.

BAD COMPANY
ALBUMS: Bad Company (Island 1974)★★★★, Straight Shooter (Island 1975)★★★, Run With The Pack (Island 1976)★★, Burnin' Sky (Island 1977)★★, Desolation Angels (Island 1979)★★★, Rough Diamonds (Swan Song 1982)★★, Fame And Fortune (Atlantic 1986)★★, Dangerous Age (Atlantic 1988)★★, Holy Water (Atlantic 1990)★★, Here Comes Trouble (Atlantic 1992)★★, Company Of Strangers (Atlantic 1995)★★ Stories Told and Untold (Elektra/Asylum 1996).
COMPILATIONS: 10 From 6 (Atlantic 1986)★★★★, The Best Of Bad Company Live ... What You Hear Is What You Get (Atco 1993)★★★, Stories Old And New (Atlantic 1996)★★★.

BAD MANNERS
ALBUMS: Ska 'N' B (Magnet 1980)★★★, Loonee Tunes (Magnet 1981)★★★, Gosh, It's Bad Manners (Magnet 1981)★★★★, Forging Ahead (Magnet 1982)★★, Return Of The Ugly (Dojo 1989)★★ Fat Sound (Triple X 1993)★★, Eat the Beat (Dojo 1996)★★, Uneasy Listening (Moon 1997)★★, Don't Knock the Baldhead Live (Receiver 1997)★★, Heavy Petting (Moon Ska 1997)★★.

BAD RELIGION
ALBUMS: How Could Hell Be Any Worse? (Epitaph 1982)★★★★, Into The Unknown (Epitaph 1983)★★★, Suffer (Epitaph 1988)★★★★, No Control (Epitaph 1989)★★★, Against The Grain (Epitaph 1990)★★★, Generator (Epitaph 1992)★★★, Recipe For Hate (Epitaph 1993)★★★, Stranger Than Fiction (Atlantic 1994)★★★, The Gray Race (Columbia 1996)★★★★, Tested (Epic 1997)★★★ No Substance (Atlantic 1998)★★★.
COMPILATIONS: 80-85 (Epitaph 1991)★★★, All Ages (Epitaph 1995)★★★.
VIDEOS: Along the Way (Epitaph 1993)

BADFINGER
ALBUMS: Magic Christian Music (Apple 1970)★★★, No Dice (Apple 1970)★★★★, The Magic Christian soundtrack (Pye 1970)★★, Straight Up (Apple 1972)★★★★, Ass (Apple 1974)★★, Badfinger (Warners 1974)★★, Wish You Were Here (Warners 1974)★★★, Airwaves (Elektra 1979)★★, Say No More (Radio 1981)★★, Over You Final Trax (European Imports 1994), BBC In Concert 1972-1973 (Strange Fruit 1997). SOLO: Pete Ham 7 Park Avenue (Ryko 1997)★★★★.
COMPILATIONS: Come And Get It: The Best Of Badfinger (Capitol 1994)★★★★.
FURTHER READING: Without You: The Tragic Story of Badfinger, Dan Matovina.

BADOWSKI, HENRY
ALBUMS: Life Is A Grand (A&M 1981)★★★, Henry Badowski (IRS 1981)★★★.

BADU, ERYKAH
ALBUMS: Baduizm (Kedar/Universal 1997)★★★★, Live (Uptown/Universal 1997)★★★.

BAEZ, JOAN
ALBUMS: Joan Baez (Vanguard 1960)★★★, Joan Baez 2 (Vanguard 1961)★★★, Joan Baez In Concert (Vanguard 1962)★★★★, Joan Baez In Concert Part 2 (Vanguard 1963)★★★, Joan Baez 5 (1964)★★★★, Farewell Angelina (Vanguard 1965)★★★★, Portrait (Vanguard 1966)★★★, Noel (Vanguard 1966)★★, Joan (Vanguard 1967)★★★, Baptism (Vanguard 1968)★★★, Any Day Now: Songs Of Bob Dylan (Vanguard 1968)★★★, David's Album (Vanguard 1969)★★, Joan Baez In Italy (1969)★★★, 24 July 1970 all Arena Civica di Milano (1970)★★, One Day At A Time (Vanguard 1970)★★★, Blessed Are (Vanguard 1971)★★★, Carry It On (Vanguard 1971)★★★, Sacco And Vanzetti (Omega 1971)★★, Come From The Shadows (A&M 1972)★★★, Where Are You Now My Son (Vanguard 1973)★★, Gracias A La Vida (Here's To Life) (A&M 1974)★★, Diamonds And Rust (A&M 1975)★★★, Live In Japan (Vanguard 1975)★★, From Every Stage (A&M 1976)★★, Gulf Winds (A&M 1976)★★, Blowing Away (Portrait 1977)★★★, Honest Lullaby (Portrait 1979)★★, The Night They Drove Old Dixie Down (Vanguard 1979)★★★★, Country Music Album (Vanguard 1979)★★★, European Tour (1981)★★, Live Europe 83 (Ariola 1983)★★, Recently (Gold Castle 1988)★★★, Diamonds And Rust In The Bullring (Gold Castle 1989)★★, Speaking Of Dreams (Gold Castle 1989)★★★, Brothers In Arms (Gold Castle)★★★, Play Me Backwards (Virgin 1992)★★★, No Woman No Cry (1993)★★★, Ring Them Bells (Grapevine 1995)★★★, Live at Newport (Vanguard 1996), Gone From Danger (Guardian 1997)★★★.
COMPILATIONS: The First Ten Years (Vanguard 1970)★★★★, The Ballad Book (Vanguard 1972)★★★, The Contemporary Ballad Book (Vanguard 1974)★★★, The Love Song Album (Vanguard 1975)★★★, Hits Greatest And Others (Vanguard 1976)★★★, The Best Of Joan Baez (1977)★★★, Spotlight On Joan Baez (1980)★★★, Very Early Joan (Vanguard 1983)★★★, Rare, Live And Classic 3-CD box set (Vanguard 1994)★★★★, Diamonds (Polygram Chronicles 1996)★★★.
FURTHER READING: Daybreak: An Intimate Journey, Joan Baez. The Playboy Interviews: Joan Baez, No editor listed. Joan Baez, A Bio-Disco-Bibliography: Being A Selected Guide To Material In Print, Peter Swan. Diamonds And Rust: A Bibliography And Discography Of Joan Baez, Joan Swanekamp. And A Voice to Sing With, Joan Baez.
VIDEOS: Joan Baez In Concert (Old Gold 1990).

BAKER, ANITA
ALBUMS: The Songstress (Beverly Glen 1983)★★★, Rapture (Elektra 1986)★★★★, Giving You The Best That I've Got (Elektra 1988)★★★, Compositions (Elektra 1990)★★★, Rhythm Of Love (Elektra 1994)★★.
VIDEOS: Sweet Love (WEA Music Video 1989), One Night Of Rapture (WEA Music Video 1989).
FURTHER READING: Rapture, Anita Baker (Columbia Pictures 1987).

BAKER, GINGER
ALBUMS: Stratavarious (Polydor 1972)★★, with Fela Ransome Kuti Fela Ransome Kuti With Ginger Baker (Regal Zonophone 1972)★★★, 11 Sides Of Baker (Mountain 1977)★★, From Humble Oranges (1983)★★, Horses And Trees (Celluloid 1986)★★★, The Album (ITM 1987)★★, No Material (ITM 1987)★★, In Concert (1987)★★, African Force (80s)★★, Middle Passage (Axiom 1990)★★★, Unseen Rain (Daylight Music 1993)★★, with BBM Around The Next Dream (Virgin 1994)★★★, Going Back Home (Atlantic 1995)★★★, Album (ITM 1995)★★★, Falling Off The Roof (Atlantic 1996)★★★★.
COMPILATIONS: The Best Of Ginger Baker (1973)★★★.

BAKER, LaVERN
ALBUMS: LaVern (Atlantic 1956)★★★, LaVern Baker (Atlantic 1957)★★★★, Rock And Roll With LaVern (Atlantic 1957)★★★★, LaVern Baker Sings Bessie Smith (Atlantic 1958)★★★, Blues Ballads (Atlantic 1959)★★★★, Precious Memories (Atlantic 1959)★★★, Saved (Atlantic 1961)★★★, See See Rider (Atlantic 1963)★★★, I'm Gonna Get You (1966)★★, La Vern Baker Live in Hollywood (Rhino 1991), Woke Up This Mornin' (DRG 1992), Blues Side of Rock 'n' Roll (Star Club 1993).
COMPILATIONS: The Best Of LaVern Baker (Atlantic 1963)★★★★, Real Gone Gal (Charly 1984)★★★, Soul On Fire – The Best Of (Atlantic 1993)★★★★, Blues Ballads with 6 extra tracks (Sequel 1997)★★★★, Rock & Roll (Sequel 1997)★★★★.

BALAAM AND THE ANGEL
ALBUMS: The Greatest Story Ever Told (Virgin 1986)★★★, Live Free Or Die (Virgin 1988)★★, Days of Madness (Virgin 1989)★★★, as Balaam No More Innocence mini-album (Intense 1991)★★, as Balaam Prime Time (Bleeding Hearts 1993)★★.

BALDRY, LONG JOHN
ALBUMS: Long John's Blues (United Artists 1965)★★★, Lookin' At Long John (United Artists 1966)★★★, Let The Heartaches Begin (Pye 1968)★★, Wait For Me (Pye 1969)★, It Ain't Easy (Warners 1971)★★, Everything Stops For Tea (Warners 1972)★, Good To Be Alive (GM 1976)★★, Welcome To The Club (1977)★★, Baldry's Out (A&M 1979)★★, It Still Ain't Easy (Stony Plain 1991)★★, On Stage Tonight: Baldry's Out Live (Stony Plain 1994)★★, Rock With The Best (Hypertension 1996)★★, Right To Sing The Blues (Stony Plain 1997)★★★.
COMPILATIONS: Let The Heartaches Begin – The Best Of John Baldry (PRT 1988)★★★, A Thrill's A Thrill: The Canadian Years (EMI 1996)★★★.

BALFA BROTHERS
ALBUMS: Balfa Brothers Play Traditional Cajun Music (Swallow 1965)★★★★, Balfa Brothers Play More Cajun Music (Swallow 1968)★★★, The Cajuns (Sonet 1972)★★★, with Nathan Abshire The Good Times Are Killing Me (Swallow 1975)★★★, Cajun Fiddle Tunes By Dewey Balfa (Folkways 70s)★★★, Dewey Balfa & Tracy Schwartz Traditional Cajun Fiddle Volumes 1 & 2 (Folkways 70s)★★★, J'ai Vu Le Loup, Le Renard Et La Belette (Cezame/Rounder 1975)★★★, The New York Concerts (Swallow 1980)★★, Dewey Balfa, Marc Savoy, D.L. Menard: Under The Green Oak Tree (Arhoolie 1982)★★★, The New York Concerts Plus (Ace 1991)★★★, Balfa Brothers (Swallow 1994)★★★.
COMPILATIONS: The Balfa Brothers Play Traditional Cajun Music Volumes 1 & 2 (Ace 1991)★★★★, Dewey Balfa & Friends (Ace 1991)★★★★. As Balfa Toujours New Cajun Tradition (Ace 1995)★★★.

BALIN, MARTY
ALBUMS: solo Rock Justice (1980)★★, Balin (EMI America 1981)★★, Lucky (Emi America 1983)★★, with the KBC Band KBC Band (Arista 1986)★★, Better Generation (GWE 1991)★★, Freedom Flight (Solid Discs 1997)★★.

BALLARD, RUSS
ALBUMS: Russ Ballard (Epic 1975)★★★, Winning (Epic 1976)★★★, At The Third Stroke (Epic 1979)★★★, Barnet Dogs (Epic 1980)★★★, Into The Fire (Epic 1981)★★★, Russ Ballard (EMI 1984)★★★, Fire Still Burns (EMI 1986)★★★, The Seer (Bullet Proof 1994)★★★, Winning & Barnet Dogs (Renaissance 1996)★★★.

BANANARAMA
ALBUMS: Deep Sea Skiving (London 1983)★★★, Bananarama (London 1984)★★★, True Confessions (London 1986)★★★, Wow! (London 1987)★★★, Pop Life (London 1991)★★, Please Yourself (London 1993)★★, Ultra Violet (Curb 1996).
COMPILATIONS: The Greatest Hits Collection (London 1988)★★★★, Bunch Of Hits (London 1993)★★★.
VIDEOS: Bananarama (1984), Bananarama: Video Singles (1987), Love In The First Degree (1988), Greatest Hits: Bananarama (1988), And That's Not All (1988), Greatest Hits Collection (1991).

BAND
ALBUMS: Music From Big Pink (Capitol 1968)★★★★, The Band (Capitol 1969)★★★★, Stage Fright (Capitol 1970)★★★★, Cahoots (Capitol 1971)★★★, Rock Of Ages (Capitol 1972)★★★★, Moondog Matinee (Capitol 1973)★★★, Northern Lights – Southern Cross (Capitol 1975)★★★, Islands (Capitol 1977)★★, with various artists The Last Waltz (Warners 1977)★★★, Jericho (Pyramid 1993)★★, Band And Friends (Castle 1994) ★★★, Live At Watkins Glen (Capitol 1995)★★★★, High On The Hog (Transatlantic 1996)★. Solo: Rick Danko Rick Danko (Arista 1977)★★★.
COMPILATIONS: Anthology Vol. 1 (Capitol 1978)★★★, Anthology Vol. 2 (Capitol 1980)★★★, To Kingdom Come (Capitol 1989)★★★, Across The Great Divide 3-CD box set (Capitol 1995)★★★★.
VIDEOS: The Last Waltz (Warner Home Video 1988), The Authorized Video Biography (ABC 1995).
FURTHER READING: Across The Great Divide: The Band And America, Barney Hoskyns. This Wheel's On Fire: Levon Helm And The Story Of The Band, Levon Helm with Stephen Davis. Mystery Train: Images Of America In Rock And Roll Music, Greil Marcus. Invisible Republic: Bob Dylan's Basement Tapes, Greil Marcus.

BANGLES
ALBUMS: All Over The Place (Columbia 1985)★★★, Different Light (Columbia 1986)★★★★, Everything (Columbia 1988)★★.
COMPILATIONS: The Bangles Greatest Hits (Columbia 1991)★★★★.
VIDEOS: Bangles Greatest Hits (SMV 1990) Babe-Osity Live (Turtle 1992).

BANKS, DARRELL
ALBUMS: Darrell Banks Is Here (Atco 1967)★★★, Here To Stay (Volt 1969)★★.
COMPILATIONS: Don Davis Presents The Sound Of Detroit (1993)★★★, The Lost Soul (Goldmine Soul Supply 1997)★★★.

BANTON, BUJU
ALBUMS: Stamina Daddy (Techniques 1991)★★★, Mr. Mention (Penthouse 1991)★★★★, Voice Of Jamaica (Mercury 1993)★★★, 'Til Shiloh (Loose Cannon 1995)★★★ Inna Heights (VP 1997)★★★.

BARBARIANS
ALBUMS: Are You A Boy Or Are You A Girl (Laurie 1966)★★.

BAR-KAYS
ALBUMS: *Soul Finger* (Stax 1967)★★★★, *Gotta Groove* (Stax 1969)★★★, *Black Rock* (Volt 1971)★★, *Do You See What I See* (Polydor 1972)★★★, *Cold Blooded* (Stax 1974)★★, *Too Hot To Stop* (Mercury 1976)★★, *Flying High On Your Love* (Mercury 1977)★★★, *Money Talks* (Stax 1978)★★, *Light Of Life* (Mercury 1978)★★, *Injoy* (Mercury 1979)★★, *As One* (Mercury 1980)★★★, *Night Cruisin'* (Mercury 1981)★★, *Propositions* (Mercury 1982)★★, *Dangerous* (Mercury 1984)★★, *Banging The Wall* (Mercury 1985)★★, *Contagious* (Mercury 1987)★★★, *Animal* (Mercury 1988)★★★, *48 Hours* (Basix 1994)★★.
COMPILATIONS: *The Best Of The Bar-Kays* (Stax 1988)★★★★, *The Best Of The Bar-Kays* (Mercury 1993)★★★.
FILMS: *Breakdance – The Movie* (1984)

BARCLAY JAMES HARVEST
ALBUMS: *Barclay James Harvest* (Harvest 1970)★★, *Once Again* (Harvest 1971)★★★, *Short Stories* (Harvest 1971)★★★, *Early Morning Onwards* (Harvest 1972)★★★, *Baby James Harvest* (Harvest 1972)★★★, *Everyone Is Everybody Else* (Polydor 1974)★★★★, *Barclay James Harvest Live* (Polydor 1974)★★, *Time Honoured Ghosts* (Polydor 1975)★★★, *Octoberon* (Polydor 1976)★★★, *Gone To Earth* (Polydor 1977)★★★, *XII* (Polydor 1978)★★, *Live Tapes* (Polydor 1978)★★, *Eyes Of The Universe* (Polydor 1979)★★, *Turn Of The Tide* (Polydor 1981)★★★, *A Concert For The People (Berlin)* (Polydor 1982)★★, *Ring Of Changes* (Polydor 1983)★★★, *Victims Of Circumstance* (Polydor 1984)★★★, *Face To Face* (Polydor 1987)★★, *Glasnost* (Polydor 1988)★★, *Welcome To The Show* (1990)★★★, *Face to Face* (Alex 1992)★★★, *Glasnost* (Alex 1992)★★★, *Welcome to the Show* (Alex 1992)★★★, *Caught In The Light* (Alex 1993)★★★, *Alone We Fly* (Polydor 1994) *Barclay James Harvest/Once Again* (One Way 1995)★★★, *Endless Dream* (Alex 1996)★★, *River Of Dreams* (Polydor 1997)★★.
Solo: John Lees *A Major Fancy* (Harvest 1977)★★. Woolly Wolstenholme *Maestoso* (Polydor 1980)★★, *Too Late* (Swallowtail 1989)★★, *Songs From The Black Block* (Voiceprint 1994)★★.
COMPILATIONS: *Best Of Volume 1* (Harvest 1977)★★★, *Best Of Volume 2* (Harvest 1979)★★★, *Another Arable Parable* (Harvest 1987)★★★, *Alone We Fly* (Connoisseur 1990)★★★, *The Harvest Years* (Harvest 1991)★★★, *The Best Of ...* (EMI 1997)★★★.
VIDEOS: *Berlin A Concert For The People* (Channel 5 1982), *Victims Of Circumstance* (1985), *Glasnost* (Channel 5 1988), *The Best Of BJH Live* (Virgin Vision 1992).

BARDENS, PETER
ALBUMS: *The Answer* (Transatlantic 1970)★★, *Peter Bardens* (Transatlantic 1971)★★★, *Heart To Heart* (Arista 1980)★★, *Seen One Earth* (Capitol 1987)★★★, *Speed Of Light* (Capitol 1988)★★, *Water Colors* (1993)★★, *Further Than You Know* (Miramar 1993)★★, *Big Sky* (HTD 1994)★★★.
VIDEOS: *Water Colours: Video* (1992)

BARENAKED LADIES
ALBUMS: *Gordon* (Sire 1992)★★★★, *Maybe You Should Drive* (Sire 1994)★★★, *Born On A Pirate Ship* (Reprise 1996)★★★★, *Rock Spectacle* (1996)★★★.

BARLOW, GARY
ALBUMS: *Open Road* (RCA 1997)★★★.

BARRETT, SYD
ALBUMS: *The Madcap Laughs* (Harvest 1970)★★★, *Barrett* (Harvest 1970)★★★, *The Peel Sessions* (Strange Fruit 1995)★★★.
COMPILATIONS: *Opel* (Harvest 1988)★★★.
FURTHER READING: *Crazy Diamond: Syd Barrett And The Dawn Of Pink Floyd*, Mike Watkinson and Pete Anderson. *Syd Barrett: The Madcap Laughs*, Pete Anderson and Mick Rock.

BARRON KNIGHTS
ALBUMS: *Call Up The Groups* (Columbia 1964)★★★, *The Barron Knights* (Columbia 1966)★★★, *Scribed* (Columbia 1967)★★★, *The Two Sides Of The Barron Knights* (1971)★★, *Live In Trouble* (1977)★★, *Knight Gallery* (1978)★★, *Teach The World To Laugh* (1979)★★, *Jesta Giggle* (1980)★★, *Twisting The Knights Away* (1981)★★★, *Funny In The Head* (1984)★★.
COMPILATIONS: *Knights Of Laughter* (1979)★★★, *Barron Knights* (1982)★★★, *The Best Of The Barron Knights* (1982)★★★.
FURTHER READING: *Once A Knight: History Of The Barron Knights*, Pete Langford.

BARRY, LEN
ALBUMS: with the Dovells *Len Barry Sings With The Dovells* (Cameo 1964)★★★, *1-2-3* (Decca 1965)★★, *My Kind Of Soul* (RCA Victor 1967)★★, *Ups & Downs* (Ups & Downs 1972)★★, *More from the 123 Man* (Bulldog 1982)★★.

BARTHOLOMEW, DAVE
ALBUMS: *Fats Domino Presents Dave Bartholomew* (Imperial 1961)★★★, *New Orleans House Party* (Imperial 1963)★★★, *Jump Children* (Pathe Marconi 1984)★★, *The Monkey* (Pathe Marconi 1985)★★, *Heritage* (1986)★★, *Graciously* (1987)★★, *In the Alley* (Charly 1991), *The Spirit Of New Orleans* (1993)★★★, *Dave Bartholomew and the Maryland Jazz Band* (GHB 1995)★★, *New Orleans Big Beat* (Landslide 1998)★★.
COMPILATIONS: *The Best Of Dave Bartholomew: The Classic New Orleans R&B Band Sound* (Stateside 1989)★★★★.

BASSEY, SHIRLEY
ALBUMS: *Born To Sing The Blues* (Philips 1958)★★★, *The Bewitching Miss Bassey* (1959)★★★, *Fabulous Shirley Bassey* (1960)★★★, *Shirley* (Columbia 1960)★★★, *Shirley Bassey* (1962)★★★, *Let's Face The Music* (Columbia 1962)★★★, *Shirley Bassey At The Pigalle* (1965)★★★★, *Shirley Bassey Belts The Best!* (1965)★★★, *I've Got A Song For You* (1966)★★★, *Twelve Of Those Songs* (1968)★★★, *Live At The Talk Of The Town* (1970)★★★, *Something* (United Artists 1970)★★★, *Something Else* (1971)★★★, *Big Spender* (1971)★★★, *It's Magic* (1971)★★★, *What Now My Love* (1971)★★★, *I Capricorn* (1972)★★★, *And I Love You So* (1972)★★★, *Never, Never, Never* (1973)★★★, *Live At Carnegie Hall* (1973)★★★★, *Broadway, Bassey's Way* (1973)★★★, *Nobody Does It Like Me* (1974)★★, *Good, Bad But Beautiful* (1975)★★★, *Love, Life And Feelings* (1976)★★, *Thoughts Of Love* (1976)★★★, *You Take My Heart Away* (1977)★★★, *The Magic Is You* (1979)★★★, *As Long As He Needs Me* (1980)★★★, *As Time Goes By* (1980)★★★, *I'm In The Mood For Love* (1981)★★, *Love Songs* (1982)★★, *All By Myself* (1984)★★, *I Am What I Am* (1984)★★★, *Playing Solitaire* (1985)★★★, *I've Got You Under My Skin* (1985)★★★, *Sings The Songs From The Shows* (1986)★★★, *Let Me Sing And I'm Happy* (1988)★★★, *Her Favourite Songs* (1988)★★, *Keep The Music Playing* (1991)★★★, *Sings The Songs Of Andrew Lloyd Webber* (1994)★★, *Love Album* (Alex 1994)★★, *Sings The Movies* (Polygram 1995)★★★, *The Show Must Go On* (Polygram 1996)★★★.
COMPILATIONS: *Golden Hits Of Shirley Bassey* (1968)★★★, *The Shirley Bassey Collection* (1972)★★★, *The Shirley Bassey Singles Album* (1975)★★★, *25th Anniversary Album* (1978)★★★, *21 Hit Singles* (1979)★★★, *Tonight* (1984)★★★, *Diamonds – The Best Of Shirley Bassey* (1988)★★★, *The Bond Collection – 30th Anniversary* (1993)★★★, *Classic Tracks* (1993)★★★, *The Definitive Collection* (Magnum 1994)★★★, *The EMI/UA Years 1959-1979* 5-CD box set (EMI 1994)★★★★.
VIDEOS: *Shirley Bassey Live* (1988), *Live In Cardiff* (BBC 1995) *Shirley* (EMI 1997), *I'm In the Mood for Love* (EMI 1997), *20 Songs* (Touch of Class 1997).

BATT, MIKE
ALBUMS: *Portrait Of Bob Dylan* (DJM 1969)★, *Schizophonic* (Epic 1979)★★, *Tarot Suite* (Epic 1979)★★, *Waves* (Epic 1980)★★, *6 Days In Berlin* (Epic 1981)★★, *Zero Zero* (Epic 1983)★★, *Children Of The Sky* (Epic 1986)★★, *The Hunting Of The Snark* (1986)★★★, *Winds of Change* (Alex 1995)★★.

BAUHAUS
ALBUMS: *In The Flat Field* (4AD 1980)★★, *Mask* (Beggars Banquet 1981)★★★, *The Sky's Gone Out* (Beggars Banquet 1982)★★★, *Press The Eject And Give Me The Tape* (Beggars Banquet 1982)★★, *Burning From The Inside* (Beggars Banquet 1983)★★.
COMPILATIONS: *1979-1983* (Beggars Banquet 1985)★★★.
VIDEOS: *Shadow Of Light* (Kace International Products 1984), *Archive* (Beggars Banquet 1988).
FURTHER READING: *Dark Entries: Bauhaus And Beyond*, Ian Shirley.

BAY CITY ROLLERS
ALBUMS: *Rollin'* (Bell 1974)★★★, *Once Upon A Star* (Bell 1975)★★★, *Wouldn't You Like It* (Bell 1975)★★★, *Dedication* (Bell 1976)★★, *It's A Game* (Arista 1977)★★, *Strangers In The Wind* (Arista 1978)★★, as the Rollers *Richocet* (Epic 1981)★★★.
COMPILATIONS: *Greatest Hits* (Arista 1977)★★★.
VIDEOS: *Shang-A-Lang: The Very Best Of...* (1993).
FURTHER READING: *The Bay City Rollers Scrapbook*, David Golumb. *Bay City Rollers*, Elkis Allen. *The Bay City Rollers*, Tam Paton. *Panther (Allen Elkis)*, C. Scribners.

BBM
ALBUMS: *Around The Next Dream* (Virgin 1994)★★★.

BE-BOP DELUXE
ALBUMS: *Axe Victim* (Harvest 1974)★★, *Futurama* (Harvest 1975)★★, *Sunburst Finish* (Harvest 1976)★★★, *Modern Music* (Harvest 1976)★★★, *Live! In The Air Age* (Harvest 1977)★★★, *Drastic Plastic* (Harvest 1978)★★, *Electrical Language* (Cocteau 1983)★★, *Axe Victim/Futerama* (Harvest 1983)★★, *Radioland* (Roir 1994)★★, *BBC Radio 1 in Concert (live)* (Griffin Music 1995)★★★.
COMPILATIONS: *The Best Of ... And The Rest Of Be Bop Deluxe* (Harvest 1978)★★★★, *Raiding The Divine Archive: The Best Of Be-Bop Deluxe* (Harvest 1990)★★★★, Very Best of Be Bop Deluxe (Collectables 1998)★★★★.

BEACH BOYS
ALBUMS: *Surfin' Safari* (Capitol 1962)★★, *Surfin' USA* (Capitol 1963)★★★, *Surfer Girl* (Capitol 1963)★★★, *Little Deuce Coupe* (Capitol 1963)★★★, *Shut Down Vol. 2* (Capitol 1964)★★★★, *All Summer Long* (Capitol 1964)★★★★, *Beach Boys Concert* (Capitol 1964)★★★, *The Beach Boys' Christmas Album* (Capitol 1964)★★★, *The Beach Boys Today!* (Capitol 1965)★★★★, *Summer Days (And Summer Nights!!)* (Capitol 1965)★★★★, *The Beach Boys' Party!* (Capitol 1965)★★, *Pet Sounds* (Capitol 1966)★★★★★, *Smiley Smile* (Capitol 1967)★★★★, *Wild Honey* (Capitol 1967)★★★, *Friends* (Capitol 1968)★★★★, *Stack-O-Tracks* (Capitol 1968)★★, *20/20* (Capitol 1969)★★★, *Live In London* (Capitol 1970)★★, *Sunflower* (Brother 1970)★★★★★, *Surf's Up* (Brother 1971)★★★★★, *Carl And The Passions-So Tough* (Brother 1972)★★★, *Holland* (Brother 1973)★★★★, *The Beach Boys In Concert* (Brother 1973)★★, *15 Big Ones* (Brother 1976)★★★, *The Beach Boys Love You* (Brother 1977)★★★, *M.I.U. Album* (Brother 1978)H, *LA (Light Album)* (Caribou 1979)★★★, *Keepin' The Summer Alive* (Caribou 1980)H, *Rarities* (1983)★★★, *The Beach Boys* (Caribou 1985)★★★, *Still Cruisin'* (Capitol 1989)H, *Summer In Paradise* (1993)H, *Stars And Stripes Vol. 1* (River North 1996)H.
COMPILATIONS: *Endless Summer* (Capitol 1974)★★★★★, *Spirit Of America* (Capitol 1975)★★★★, *20 Golden Greats* (Capitol 1976)★★★★, *Sunshine Dream* (Capitol 1982)★★★, *The Very Best Of The Beach Boys* (Capitol 1983)★★★, *Made In The USA* (Capitol 1986)★★★★, *Summer Dreams* (Capitol 1990)★★★★, *Good Vibrations: Thirty Years Of...* 5-CD box set (Capitol 1993)★★★★★.
VIDEOS: *Beach Boys: An American Band* (Vestron Music Video 1988), *Summer Dreams* (Polygram Music Video 1991).
FILMS: *Girls On The Beach* (1965), *Americation* (1979).
FURTHER READING: *The Beach Boys*, John Tobler. *The Beach Boys And The California Myth*, David Leaf. *The Beach Boys: The Authorized Illustrated Biography*, Byron Preiss. *The Beach Boys: Silver Anniversary*, John Millward. *Look! Listen! Vibrate! SMILE*, Dominic Priore. *Denny Remembered*, Edward Wincentsen. *Wouldn't It Be Nice: My Own Story*, Brian Wilson and Todd Gold. *In Their Own Words*, Nick Wise (compiled). *The Nearest Faraway Place: Brian Wilson, The Beach Boys & The Southern California*, Timothy White. *Back To The Beach*, Kingsley Abbott.

BEASTIE BOYS
ALBUMS: *Licensed To Ill* (Def Jam 1986)★★★, *Paul's Boutique* (Capitol 1989)★★★★, *Check Your Head* (Capitol 1992)★★★★, *Ill Communication* (Capitol 1994)★★★★, *The Root Down EP* (Capitol 1995)★★, *Aglio E Olio* (Grand Royal 1996)★★★, *In Sound From Way Out* (Capitol 1996)★★, *Hello Nasty* (1998)★★★.
COMPILATIONS: *Some Old Bullshit* (Capitol 1994)★★★.
VIDEOS: *Sabotage* (1994), *The Skills To Pay The Bills* (1994).

BEAT (UK)
ALBUMS: *I Just Can't Stop It* (Go-Feet 1980)★★★★, *Wha'ppen* (Go-Feet 1981)★★★, *Special Beat Service* (Go-Feet 1982)★★★.
COMPILATIONS: *What Is Beat* (Go-Feet 1983)★★★, *BPM – The Very Best Of ...* (Arista 1995)★★★.
FURTHER READING: *The Beat: Twist And Crawl*, Malu Halasha.

BEAT FARMERS
ALBUMS: *Tales Of The New West* (Rhino 1985)★★★, *Van Go* (Curb 1986)★★★, *The Pursuit Of Happiness* (Curb 1987)★★★, *Poor & Famous* (Curb 1989)★★, *Loud And Plowed And ... LIVE!!* (Curb 1990)★★, *Viking Lullabies* (Sector 2 1994)★★, *Manifold* (Sector 2 1995)★★.
Solo: Country Dick Montana *The Devil Lied To Me* (Sector 2 1996)★★★.

BEATLES
ALBUMS: *Please Please Me* (Parlophone 1963)★★★★, *With The Beatles* (Parlophone 1963)★★★★, *A Hard Day's Night* (Parlophone 1964)★★★★, *Beatles For Sale* (Parlophone 1964)★★★★, *The Savage Young Beatles* (USA)(Savage 1964)★, *Ain't She Sweet* (USA)(Atco 1964)★, *The Beatles With Tony Sheridan & Their Guests & Others* (USA)(MGM 1964)★, *Meet The Beatles* (USA)(Capitol 1964)★★★, *The Beatles Second Album* (USA)(Capitol 1964)★★★, *Something New* (USA)(Capitol 1964)★★★, *Beatles '65* (USA)(Capitol 1964)★★★, *The Early Beatles* (USA)(Capitol 1965)★★, *Beatles VI* (USA)(Capitol 1965)★★, *Help!* (Parlophone 1965)★★★★★, *Rubber Soul* (Parlophone 1965)★★★★★, *Yesterday And Today* (Capitol 196)★★★, *Revolver* (Parlophone 1966)★★★★★, *Sgt. Pepper's Lonely Hearts Club Band* (Parlophone 1967)★★★★★, *Magical Mystery Tour* (Capitol 1968)★★★★, *The Beatles* (Apple 1968)★★★★★, *Yellow Submarine* (Apple 1969)★★, *Abbey Road* (Apple 1969)★★★★★, *Let It Be* (Apple 1970)★★★, *Hey Jude* (Capitol 1970)★★★, *The Early Years* (Contour 1971)★★, *The Beatles At The Hollywood Bowl* (Parlophone 1977)★★, *Rarities* (Parlophone 1979)★★★★, *Live At The BBC* (Apple 1994)★★★★, *Anthology 1* (Apple 1995)★★★★, *Anthology 2* (Apple 1996)★★★★, *Anthology 3* (Apple 1996)★★★.
COMPILATIONS: *A Collection Of Beatles Oldies* (Parlophone 1966)★★★★, *The Beatles 1962-1966* (Apple 1973)★★★★★, *The Beatles 1967-1970* (Apple 1973)★★★★★, Rock & Roll Music (EMI 1976)★★★★, *Love Songs* (EMI 1977)★★★★, *Past Masters Vol. 1* (Parlophone 1988)★★★★★, *Past Masters Vol. 2* (Parlophone 1988)★★★★★.
VIDEOS: *Ready Steady Go Special* (1985), *A Hard Days Night* (Vestron 1986), *Compleat Beatles* (MGM 1986), *Magical Mystery Tour* (MPI 1989), *Help* (MPI 1989), *On The Road* (1990), *Alone And Together* (1990), *The First U.S. Visit* (1993), *Beatles Firsts* (Goodtimes 1995), *The Making Of A Hard Day's Night* (VCI 1995), *The Beatles Anthology Vols 1-8* (PMI 1996).
FURTHER READING: There have been hundreds of books published of varying quality. Our three recommendations are: *The Complete Beatles Chronicle* by Mark Lewisohn, an accurate and definitive career and recording history by their greatest historian. *Shout! The True Story Of The Beatles* by Philip Norman, the most readable and objective biography. *Revolution In The Head* by Ian MacDonald, a beautifully written authoritative study of every song. Others: *The True Story Of The Beatles*, Billy Shepherd. *The Beatles Book*, Norman Parkinson and Maureen Cleave. *A Cellarful Of Noise*, Brian Epstein. *The Beatles: A Hard Day's Night*, John Burke. *Love Me Do: The Beatles' Progress*, Michael Braun. *The Beatles In Help*, Al Hine. *The Beatles: Words Without Music*, Rick Friedman. *The Beatles*, Hunter Davies. *Get Back*, Ethan Russell (photographs). *The Beatles Illustrated Lyrics Vol. 2*, Alan Aldridge (ed.). *Apple To The Core: The Unmaking Of The Beatles*, Peter McCabe and Robert D. Schonfeld. *The Longest Cocktail Party*, Richard DiLello. *As Time Goes By: Living In The Sixties*, Derek Taylor. *Twilight Of The Gods: The Beatles In Retrospect*, Wilfred Mellers. *The Man Who Gave The Beatles Away*, Allan Williams. *The Beatles: An Illustrated Record*, Roy Carr and Tony Tyler. *All Together Now: The First Complete Beatles Discography 1961-1975*, Harry Castleman and Walter J. Podrazik. *The Beatles: Yesterday, Today, Tomorrow*, Rochelle Larkin. *Beatles In Their Own Words*, Miles. *The Beatles: A Day In The Life: The Day By Day Diary 1960-1970*, Tom Schultheiss. *The Boys From Liverpool: John, Paul, George, Ringo*, Nicholas Schaffner. *The Beatles Illustrated Lyrics*, Alan Aldridge (ed.). *The Beatles Apart*, Bob Woffinden. *Shout! The True Story Of The Beatles*, Philip Norman. *The Beatles: An Illustrated Discography*, Miles. *Thank U Very Much: Mike McCartney's Family Album*, (Peter) Michael McCartney. *All You Needed Was Love: The Beatles After The Beatles*, John Blake. *The Long And Winding Road: A History Of The Beatles On Record*, Neville Stannard. *Abbey Road: The Story Of The World's Most Famous Recording Studios*, Brian Southall. *The Complete Beatles Lyrics*, no author listed. *The Beatles At The Beeb 62-65: The Story Of Their Radio Career*, Kevin Howlett. *With The Beatles: The Historic Photographs*, Dezo Hoffman. *Beatles' England*, David Bacon and Norman Maslov. *Working Class Heroes: The History Of The Beatles' Solo Recordings*, Neville Stannard. *The Beatles: An Illustrated Diary*, H.V. Fulpen. *The Love You Make: An Insider's Story Of The Beatles*, Peter Brown and Steven Gaines. *John Ono Lennon 1967-1980*, Ray Coleman. *John Winston Lennon 1940-1966*, Ray Coleman. *Beatlemania: An Illustrated Filmography*, Bill Harry. *Paperback Writers: An Illustrated Bibliography*, Bill Harry. *The End Of The Beatles*, Harry Castleman and Wally Podrazik. *Beatle! The Pete Best Story*, Pete Best and Patrick Doncaster. *The Beatles Live*, Mark Lewisohn. *It Was Twenty Years Ago*, Derek Taylor. *Yesterday: The Beatles Remembered*, Alistair Taylor. *All Our Loving: A Beatle Fan's Memoir*, Carolyn Lee Mitchell and Michael Munn. *The Beatles: 25 Years In The Life*, Mark Lewisohn. *Brian Epstein: The Man Who Made The Beatles*, Ray Coleman. *The Beatles Album File and Complete Discography*, Jeff Russell. *How They Became The Beatles: A Definitive History Of The Early Years 1960-1964*, Gareth L. Pawlowski. *Complete Beatles Recording Sessions: The Official Story Of The Abbey Road Years*, Mark Lewisohn. *Day By Day*, Mark Lewisohn. *Speak Words Of Wisdom: Reflections On The Beatles*, Spencer Leigh. *In Their Own Words: The Beatles After The Break-Up*, David Bennahum. *Complete Beatles Chronicle*, Mark Lewisohn. *Ultimate Beatles Encyclopedia*, Bill Harry. *Tomorrow Never Knows: Thirty Years Of Beatles Music & Memorabilia*, Geoffrey Giuliano. *The Ultimate Recording Guide*, Allen J. Wiener. *Beatles*, John Ewing. *It Was Thirty Years Ago Today*, Terence Spencer. *The Summer Of Love*, George Martin. *A Hard Day's Write*, Steve Turner. *Revolution In The Head: The Beatles Records And The Sixties*, Ian MacDonald. *Backbeat*, Alan Clayson and Pauline Sutcliffe. *The Essential Guide To The Music Of ...*, John Robertson. *The Beatle's London*, Piet Schreuders, Mark Lewisohn And Adam Smith. *A Day In The Life: The Music And Artistry Of The Beatles*, Mark Hertsgaard. *The Beatles: Not For Sale*, Jim Belmo. *The Encyclopedia Of Beatles People*, Bill Harry.
FILMS: *A Hard Days Night* (1964), *Help* (1965), *Yellow Submarine* (1968), *Magical Mystery Tour* (1968), *Let It Be* (1970).

BEAU BRUMMELS
ALBUMS: *Introducing The Beau Brummels* (Autumn/Pye International 1965)★★★, *Volume 2* (Autumn 1965)★★★, *Beau Brummels 66* (Warners 1966)★★★, *Triangle* (Warners 1967)★★★, *Bradley's Barn* (Warners 1968)★★, *Volume 44* (Vault 1968)★★, *The Beau Brummels* (1975)★★.
COMPILATIONS: *The Best Of The Beau Brummels* (1967)★★★, *The Beau Brummels Sing* (Post 1972)★★★, *The Original Hits Of The Beau Brummels* (JAS 1975)★★★, *The Best Of The Beau Brummels* rec. 1964-1968 (1981)★★★, *From The Vaults* (Sundazed 1982)★★★, *Autumn In San Francisco* (1985)★★★, *The Autumn Of Their Years* (Big Beat/Nuggets From The Golden Era 1995)★★★.

BEAUTIFUL SOUTH
ALBUMS: *Welcome To The Beautiful South* (Go! Discs 1989)★★★, *Choke* (Go! Discs 1990)★★★, *0898* (Go! Discs 1992)★★★, *Miaow* (Go! Discs 1994)★★★, *Blue Is The Colour* (Go! Discs 1996)★★★.
COMPILATIONS: *Carry On Up The Charts* (Go! Discs 1994)★★★★.
VIDEOS: *The Pumpkin* (Polygram Music Video 1992), *Carry On Up The Charts* (1995).

BEAVER AND KRAUSE
ALBUMS: *Ragnarock* (Limelight 1969)★★★, *In A Wild Sanctuary* (Warners 1970)★★★, *Gandharva* (Warners 1971)★★★, *All Good Men* (Warners 1972)★★★, *A Guide To Electronic Music* (Nonesuch 1975)★★★.

BECK
ALBUMS: *A Western Harvest Field By Moonlight* (Fingerpaint 1993)★★, *Golden Feelings* (Sonic Enemy 1993)★★, *Mellow Gold* (Geffen 1994)★★★★, *Stereo Pathetic Soul Manure* (Flipside 1994)★★, *One Foot In The Grave* 1993 recording (K Records 1995)★★, *Odelay* (Geffen 1996)★★★★ *Where It's At/Lloyd Price Express* (Geffen 1996)★★★.

BECK, JEFF
ALBUMS: *Truth* (EMI 1968)★★★, *Cosa Nostra Beck-Ola* (EMI 1969)★★, *Rough And Ready* (Epic 1971)★★, *Jeff Beck Group* (Epic 1972)★★, *Blow By Blow* (Epic 1975)★★★★, *Wired* (Epic 1976)★★, *Jeff Beck With The Jan Hammer Group Live* (Epic 1977)★, *There And Back* (Epic 1980)★★, *Flash* (Epic 1985)★★, with Terry Bozzio, Tony Hymas *Jeff Beck's Guitar Shop* (Epic 1989)★★, *Crazy Legs* (Epic 1993)★★★, *Up* (Import 1995)★★.
COMPILATIONS: *Beckology* CD box set (Epic 1992)★★★★.
FURTHER READING: *Rock Fun 3 Photo Gallery: Jeff Beck* (Japan)

BEE GEES
ALBUMS: *Barry Gibb And The Bee Gees Sing And Play 14 Barry Gibb Songs* (Leedon 1965)★★, *Spicks And Specks* (Leedon 1966)★★, *The Bee Gees First* (Polydor 1967)★★★★, *Horizontal* (Polydor 1968)★★★★, *Idea* (Polydor 1968)★★★, *Odessa* (Polydor 1969)★★★, *Cucumber Castle* (Polydor 1970)★★, *Two Years On* (Polydor 1970)★★, *Trafalgar* (Polydor 1971)★★, *To Whom It May Concern* (Polydor 1972)★★, *Life In A Tin Can* (RSO 1973)★★, *Mr Natural* (RSO 1974)★★, *Main Course* (RSO 1975)★★★★, *Children Of The World* (RSO 1976)★★★, *Here At Last ... Bee Gees Live* (RSO 1977)★★, *Saturday Night Fever* soundtrack (RSO 1977)★★★★, *Sgt. Pepper's Lonely Hearts Club Band* (1978)★, *Spirits Having Flown* (RSO 1979)★★★, *Living Eyes* (RSO 1981)★★, *Stayin' Alive* (1983)★★, *ESP* (Warners 1987)★★★, *High Civilisation* (Warners 1991)★★, *Size Isn't Everything* (1993)★★, *Still Waters* (Polydor 1997)★★★.
COMPILATIONS: *Rare Precious And Beautiful* (Polydor 1968)★★★, *Best Of The Bee Gees* (Polydor 1969)★★★★, *Best Of The Bee Gees Vol. 2* (Polydor 1973)★★★★, *Bee Gees Gold Vol. 1* (RSO 1976)★★★★, *Bee Gees Greatest* (RSO 1979)★★★★, *Very Best Of The Bee Gees* (Polydor 1990)★★★★, *Tales From The Brothers Gibb (A History In Song)* (Polydor 1990)★★★★.
VIDEOS: *Bee Gees: Video Biography* (Virgin Vision 1988), *Very Best Of The Bee Gees* (Video Collection 1990), *One For All Tour Vol. 1* (Video Collection 1990), *One For All Tour Volume 2* (Video Collection 1990).
FURTHER READING: *The Official Sgt. Pepper's Lonely Hearts Club Band Scrapbook*, Robert Stigwood and Dee Anthony. *The Bee Gees: A Photo Biography*, Kim Stevens. *The Bee Gees*, Suzanne Munshower. *Sgt. Pepper's Lonely Hearts Club Band*, Henry Edwards. *The Incredible Bee Gees*, Dick Tatham. *The Bee Gees*, Larry Pryce. *Bee Gees: The Authorized Biography*, Barry, Robin and Maurice Gibb as told to David Leaf.

BELL, ARCHIE, AND THE DRELLS
ALBUMS: *Tighten Up* (Atlantic 1968)★★★★, *I Can't Stop Dancing* (Atlantic 1968)★★★, *There's Gonna Be A Showdown* (Atlantic 1969)★★★, *Dance Your Troubles Away* (TSOP 1976)★★★, *Where Will You Go, When The Party's Over* (TSOP 1976)★★, *Hard Not To Like It* (TSOP 1977)★★★, *Strategy* (The Right Stuff 1979)★★★.
Solo: Archie Bell *I Never Had It So Good* (Becket 1981)★★.
COMPILATIONS: *Artists Showcase: Archie Bell* (DM Streetsounds 1986)★★★.

BELL, FREDDIE, AND THE BELLBOYS
ALBUMS: *Rock 'n' Roll All Flavours* (Mercury 1958)★★★, *Bells Are Swinging* (20th Century 1964)★★, *Rockin' is Our Business* (Bear Family 1996)★★★.

BELL, MAGGIE
ALBUMS: *Queen Of The Night* (Super 1974)★★★, *Suicide Sal* (Polydor 1975)★★★.
COMPILATIONS: *Great Rock Sensation* (Polydor 1977)★★★.

BELLAMY BROTHERS
ALBUMS: *Let Your Love Flow* (Warners 1976)★★★★, *Plain And Fancy* (Warners 1977)★★★, *Beautiful Friends* (Warners 1978)★★, *The Two And Only* (Warners 1979)★★★, *You Can Get Crazy* (Warners 1980)★★★, *Sons Of The Sun* (Warners 1980)★★, *When We Were Boys* (Elektra 1982)★★, *Strong Weakness* (1983)★★, *Restless* (MCA 1984)★★, *Howard And David* (MCA 1986)★★, *Country Rap* (MCA 1987)★★, *Crazy From The Heart* (1987)★★, *Rebels Without A Clue* (MCA 1988)★★, *Rolling Thunder* (Atlantic 1991)★★, *Rip Off The Knob* (Bellamy Brothers 1993)★★, *Heartbreak Overload* (Intersound 1994)★★, *Sons Of Beaches* (Bellamy Brothers 1995)★★, *The Bellamy Brothers Dancin'* (Bellamy Brothers 1996)★★, *A Tropical Christmas* (Bellamy Brothers 1996)★★, *Over The Line* (Bellamy Brothers 1997)★★★, *Reggae Cowboys* (Intersound 1998)★★★.
COMPILATIONS: *The Bellamy Brothers' Greatest Hits* (MCA 1982)★★★, *Best Of The Best* (Intersound 1992)★★★, *Let Your Love Flow: Twenty Years Of Hits* (Bellamy Brothers/Intersound 1997)★★★.
VIDEOS: *Best Of The Best* (Start Video 1994).

BELLY
ALBUMS: *Star* (Sire/4AD 1993)★★★, *King* (Sire/4AD 1995)★★.

BELOVED
ALBUMS: *Happiness* (Atlantic 1990)★★★, *Blissed Out* remix of *Happiness* (East West 1990)★★★, *Conscience* (East West 1993)★★★, *X* (East West 1996)★★, *Single File* (East West 1997)★★★.
VIDEOS: *Happiness: Video 1990* (Atlantic).

BEN FOLDS FIVE
ALBUMS: *Ben Folds Five* (Caroline 1996)★★★, *Whatever And Ever Amen* (Epic 1997)★★★★.

BENATAR, PAT
ALBUMS: *In The Heat Of The Night* (Chrysalis 1979)★★★, *Crimes Of Passion* (Chrysalis 1980)★★★, *Precious Time* (Chrysalis 1981)★★, *Get Nervous* (Chrysalis 1982)★★, *Live From Earth* (Chrysalis 1983)★★, *Tropico* (Chrysalis 1984)★★, *Seven The Hard Way* (Chrysalis 1985)★★★, *Wide Awake In Dreamland* (Chrysalis 1988)★★, *True Love* (Chrysalis 1991)★★, *Gravity's Rainbow* (Chrysalis 1993)★★, *All Fired Up* (Chrysalis 1995), *Innamorata* (CMC 1997)★★★.
COMPILATION: *Best Shots* (Chrysalis 1987)★★★.
VIDEOS: *Hit Videos* (1988), *Best Shots* (1988), *Benatar* (1988).
FURTHER READING: *Benatar*, Doug Magee.
FILMS: *American Pop* (1981).

BENNETT, CLIFF
ALBUMS: *Cliff Bennett And The Rebel Rousers* (Parlophone 1965)★★★, *Drivin' You Wild* (MFP 1966)★★★, *Cliff Bennett* (Regal 1966)★★★, *Got To Get You Into Our Lives* (Parlophone 1967)★★★, *Cliff Bennett Branches Out* (Parlophone 1968)★★, *Rebellion* (CBS 1971).

BENNETT, TONY
ALBUMS: *Because Of You* (Columbia 1952)★★★, *Alone At Last With Tony Bennett* (Columbia 1955)★★, *Treasure Chest Of Songs* (1955)★★★, *Cloud Seven* (Columbia 1955)★★, *Tony* (Columbia 1957)★★★, *The Beat Of My Heart* (Columbia 1957)★★★, *Long Ago And Far Away* (Columbia 1958)★★★, *Basie Swings – Bennett Sings* (Roulette 1958)★★, *Blue Velvet* (Columbia 1959)★★★, *If I Ruled The World* (Columbia 1959)★★★★, with Count Basie *Tony Bennett In Person* (Columbia 1959)★★★, *Hometown, My Town* (Columbia 1959)★★★, *To My Wonderful One* (Columbia 1960)★★, *Tony Sings For Two* (Columbia 1960)★★★, *Alone Together* (Columbia 1960)★★★, *A String Of Harold Arlen* (Columbia 1960)★★★, *My Heart Sings* (Columbia 1961)★★★, *Bennett And Basie Strike Up The Band* (Roulette 1962)★★, *Mr. Broadway* (Columbia 1962)★★★, *I Left My Heart In San Francisco* (Columbia 1962)★★★★, *On The Glory Road* (Columbia 1962)★★, *Tony Bennett At Carnegie Hall* (Columbia 1962)★★★, *I Wanna Be Around* (Columbia 1963)★★★★, *This Is All I Ask* (Columbia 1963)★★★, *The Many Moods Of Tony* (Columbia 1964)★★★, *When Lights Are Low* (Columbia 1964)★★★, *Who Can I Turn To* (Columbia 1964)★★★, *If I Ruled The World – Songs For The Jet Set* (Columbia 1965)★★★, *The Movie Song Album* (Columbia 1966)★★★, *A Time For Love* (Columbia 1966)★★★, *The Oscar* soundtrack (Columbia 1966)★★, *Tony Makes It Happen!* (Columbia 1967)★★, *For Once In My Life* (Columbia 1967)★★★, *Snowfall/The Tony Bennett Christmas Album* (Columbia 1968)★★★, *I've Gotta Be Me* (Columbia 1969)★★, *Tony Sings The Great Hits Of Today!* (Columbia 1970)★★, *Tony Bennett's 'Something'* (Columbia 1970)★★★, *Love Story* (Columbia 1971)★★★, *Get Happy With The London Philharmonic Orchestra* (Columbia 1971)★★, *Summer Of '42* (Columbia 1972)★★, *With Love* (Columbia 1972)★★★, *The Good Things In Life* (MGM/Verve 1972)★★★, *Rodgers And Hart Songbook* (Columbia 1973)★★, with Bill Evans *The Bennett Evans Album* (Mobile Fidelity 1975)★★★★, with Bill Evans *Together Again* (DRG 1977)★★★, *Chicago* (DCC 1984)★★★, *Anything Goes* (1985)★★★, *The Art Of Excellence* (Columbia 1986)★★★, *Bennett/Berlin* (1987)★★★, *Jazz* (Columbia 1987)★★★, with Count Basie *Some Pair!* (Pair 1989)★★★, *Astoria: Portrait Of The Artist* (Columbia 1990)★★★, *Perfectly Frank* (Columbia 1992)★★, *Steppin' Out* (Columbia 1993)★★★, *MTV Unplugged* (Columbia 1994)★★★★, *Here's To The Ladies* (Columbia 1995)★★★, *Tony Bennett On Holiday: A Tribute To Billie Holiday* (Columbia 1997)★★★.
COMPILATIONS: *Tony's Greatest Hits* (Columbia 1958)★★★★, *More Tony's Greatest Hits* (Columbia 1960)★★★★, *Tony's Greatest Hits, Volume III* (Columbia 1965)★★★★, *A String Of Tony's Hits* (Columbia 1966)★★★★, *Tony Bennett's Greatest Hits, Volume IV* (Columbia 1969)★★★, *Tony Bennett's All-Time Greatest Hits* (1972)★★★, *The Very Best Of Tony Bennett – 20 Greatest Hits* (1977)★★★, *40 Years, The Artistry Of Tony Bennett* 4-CD box set (Legacy 1991)★★★★.
VIDEOS: *Tony Bennett In Concert* (1987), *Tony Bennett Live: Watch What Happens* (Sony 1991), A Family Christmas (Sony 1992), *A Special Evening With Tony Bennett* (MIA 1995), *The Art Of The Singer* (SMV 1996).
FURTHER READING: *What My Heart Has Seen*, Tony Bennett.

BENSON, GEORGE
ALBUMS: with the Brother Jack McDuff Quartet *The New Boss Guitar Of George Benson* (Prestige 1964)★★★★, *It's Uptown* (Columbia 1966)★★★★, *Most Exciting* (Columbia 1966)★★★, *Benson Burner* (Columbia 1966)★★★★, *The George Benson Cook Book* (Columbia 1967)★★★, *Giblet Gravy* (Verve 1968)★★★, *Goodies* (Verve 1969)★★★, *Shape Of Things To Come* (A&M 1969)★★, *Tell It Like It Is* (A&M 1969)★★, *The Other Side Of Abbey Road* (A&M 1970)★★★, *Beyond The Blue Horizon* (CTI 1970)★★★, *White Rabbit* (CTI 1973)★★, *Body Talk* (CTI 1974)★★★, *Bad Benson* (CTI 1974)★★, *Supership* (CTI 1975)★★★, *Breezin'* (Warners 1976)★★★★, *Good King Bad* (CTI 1976)★★★, with Joe Farrell *Benson And Farrell* (CTI 1976)★★★, *George Benson In Concert: Carnegie Hall* (CTI 1977)★★, *In Flight* (Warners 1977)★★★★, with Jack McDuff *George Benson And Jack McDuff* (Prestige 1977)★★★, *Weekend In LA* (Warners 1978)★★, *Living Inside Your Love* (Warners 1979)★★, *Give Me The Night* (Warners 1980)★★★★, *Blue Benson* (Polydor 1983)★★★, *In Your Eyes* (Warners 1983)★★★, *Stormy Weather* (Columbia 1984)★★, *20/20* (Warners 1985)★★, *The Electrifying George Benson* (Affinity 1985)★★★, *In Concert* (Premier 1985)★★, *Love Walked In* (Platinum 1985)★★, *While The City Sleeps* (Warners 1986)★★, with Earl Klugh *Collaboration* (Warners 1987)★★★★, *Love For Sale* (Masters 1988)★★★, *Twice The Love* (Warners 1988)★★, *Detroit's George Benson* (Parkwood 1988)★★★, *Tenderly* (Warners 1989)★★, with the Count Basie Orchestra *Big Boss Band* (Warners 1990)★★★, *Lil' Darlin'* (Thunderbolt 1990)★★★, *Live At The Casa Caribe Vols 1-3* (Jazz View 1992)★★★, *Love Remembers* (Warners 1993)★★, *Take Five* (Tristar 1995) *That's Right* (MCA 1996)★★★, *California Dreamin'* (Sony Legacy 1996), *That's Right* (GRP 1996), *Lil' Darlin* (Thunderbolt 1996).
COMPILATIONS: *The George Benson Collection* (Warners 1981)★★★★, *Early Years* (CTI 1982)★★★, *Best Of George Benson* (A&M 1982)★★★, *The Wonderful Years* (Proton 1984)★★★, *The Love Songs* (K-Tel 1985)★★★★, *The Silver Collection* (Verve 1985)★★★, *Compact Jazz* (Verve 1988)★★★, *Best Of* (Epic 1992)★★, *Guitar Giants* (Pickwick 1992)★★★, *The Best Of George Benson* (Warners 1995)★★★.

BENTON, BROOK
ALBUMS: *Brook Benton At His Best* (Epic 1959)★★, *It's Just A Matter Of Time* (Mercury 1959)★★★, *Brook Benton* (Mercury 1959)★★★, *Endlessly* (1959)★★★, *So Many Ways I Love You* (Mercury 1960)★★★, with Dinah Washington *The Two Of Us – With Dinah Washington* (Mercury 1960)★★★★, *Songs I Love To Sing* (Mercury 1960)★★★, *The Boll Weevil Song (& Eleven Other Great Hits)* (Mercury 1961)★★★, *Sepia* (1961)★★, *If You Believe* (Mercury 1961)★★★, *Singing The Blues – Lie To Me* (Mercury 1962)★★★, *There Goes That Song Again* (Mercury 1962)★★★, *Best Ballads Of Broadway* (Mercury 1963)★★, *Born To Sing The Blues* (Mercury 1964)★★★, *Laura (What's He Got That I Ain't Got)* (Reprise 1967)★★, *Do Your Own Thing* (Cotillion 1969)★★, *Brook Benton Today* (Cotillion 1970)★★, *Home Style* (Cotillion 1970)★★★, *The Gospel Truth* (Cotillion 1971)★★, *Something For Everyone* (1973)★★, *Sings A Love Story* (RCA 1975)★★, *Mr. Bartender* (All Platinum 1976)★★, *This Is Brook Benton* (All Platinum 1976)★★★, *Makin' Love Is Good For You* (1977)★★, *Ebony* (1978)★★, *Brook Benton Sings The Standards* (RCA 1984)★★★.
COMPILATIONS: *Brook Benton's Golden Hits* (Mercury 1961)★★★, *Golden Hits Volume Two* (Mercury 1963)★★★, *Spotlight On Brook Benton* (Philips 1977)★★★, *The Incomparable Brook Benton* (Audio Fidelity 1982)★★★, *Sixteen Golden Classics* (Unforgettable/Castle 1986)★★★, *The Brook Benton Anthology* (Rhino 1986)★★★★, *His Greatest Hits* (Mercury 1987)★★★, *40 Greatest Hits* (Mercury 1990)★★★★, *A Rainy Night In Georgia* (Mainline 1990)★★★, *Greatest Hits* (Curb 1991)★★★.

BERLIN
ALBUMS: *Pleasure Victim* (Geffen 1983)★★, *Love Life* (Geffen 1984)★★, *Count Three And Pray* (Mercury 1987)★★.
COMPILATIONS: *Best Of Berlin 1979-1988* (Geffen 1988)★★★.

BERRY, CHUCK
ALBUMS: *After School Session* (Chess 1958)★★★★, *One Dozen Berrys* (Chess 1958)★★★★★, *Chuck Berry Is On Top* (Chess 1959)★★★★, *Rockin' At The Hops* (Chess 1960)★★★★, *New Juke Box Hits* (Chess 1961)★★★, *Chuck Berry Twist* (Chess 1962)★★★, *More Chuck Berry* (Chess 1963)★★★, *Chuck Berry On Stage* (Chess 1963)★★, *The Latest And Greatest* (Chess 1964)★★★, with Bo Diddley *Two Great Guitars* (Chess 1964)★★★, *St. Louis To Liverpool* (Chess 1964)★★★★★, *Chuck Berry In London* (Chess 1965)★★★, *Fresh Berrys* (Chess (1965)★★★, *Golden Hits* new recordings (Mercury 1967)★★, *Chuck Berry In Memphis* (Mercury 1967)★★★, *Live At The Fillmore Auditorium* (Mercury 1967)★★, *From St. Louis To Frisco* (Mercury 1968)★★, *Concerto In B. Goode* (Mercury

1969)★★, Back Home (Chess 1970)★★, San Francisco Dues (Chess 1971)★★, The London Chuck Berry Sessions (Chess 1972)★★, Bio (Chess 1973)★★, Chuck Berry Chess (1975)★★, Live In Concert (Magnum 1978)★★★, Rockit (Atco 1979)★★★, Rock! Rock! Rock 'N' Roll! (1980)★★, Hail, Hail Rock 'N' Roll soundtrack (1987)★★, On The Blues Side (1993)★★.
COMPILATIONS: Chuck Berry's Greatest Hits (Chess 1964)★★★★★, Chuck Berry's Golden Decade (Chess 1967)★★★★★, Golden Decade, Volume 2 (Chess 1973)★★★★, Golden Decade, Volume 3 (Chess 1974)★★★★, Motorvatin' (1977)★★★ Spotlight On Chuck Berry (1980)★★★, Chess Masters (1983)★★★, Chicago Golden Years (1988)★★★, Decade '55 To '65 (1988)★★★, Chuck Berry Box Set (Chess 1989)★★★★, The Great Twenty-Eight (Chess 1990)★★★★★, Chess Box CD box set (Chess 1990)★★★★, Oh Yeah! (Charly 1994)★★★, Poet Of Rock 'N' Roll 4-CD set (Charly 1995)★★★★★.
VIDEOS: The Legendary Chuck Berry (1987), Hail Hail Rock 'N' Roll (1988), Live At The Roxy (1990), Rock 'N' Roll Music (1991).
FURTHER READING: Chuck Berry: Rock 'N' Roll Music, Howard A. De Witt. Chuck Berry: Mr Rock 'N' Roll, Krista Reese. Chuck Berry: The Autobiography, Chuck Berry.
FILMS: Go Johnny Go (1958), American Hot Wax (1976).

BERRY, DAVE
ALBUMS: Dave Berry (Decca 1964)★★★, The Special Sound Of Dave Berry (Decca 1966)★★★, One Dozen Berrys (Ace Of Clubs 1966)★★★, Dave Berry '68 (Decca 1968)★★, Remembering (Decca 1976), The Crying Game (Decca 1983)★★, Hostage To The Beat (Butt 1986)★★, A Totally Random Evening with Dave Berry (Southern Track 1992)★★.
COMPILATIONS: Berry's Best (1988)★★★.

BERRY, RICHARD
ALBUMS: Richard Berry And The Dreamers (Crown 1963)★★★, with the Soul Searchers Live At The Century Club (Pam 1968)★★, with the Soul Searchers Wild Berry (Pam 1968)★★, Great Rhythm & Blues Oldies (1977)★★★, Layin' In The Alley (Black Top 1994)★★.
COMPILATIONS: Get Out Of The Car (Ace 1982)★★★★.

BETTER THAN EZRA
ALBUMS: Deluxe (SWELL 1993/Elektra 1995)★★★, Friction Baby (Elektra 1996)★★★.

BETTIE SERVEERT
ALBUMS: Palomine (Beggars Banquet 1993)★★★, Lamprey (Beggars Banquet 1995)★★★, Dust Bunnies (Beggars Banquet 1997)★★★.

BEVIS FROND
ALBUMS: Miasma (Woronzow 1987)★★★, Inner Marshland (Woronzow 1987)★★★, Triptych (Woronzow 1987)★★★, Bevis Through The Looking Glass (Reckless 1988)★★★, Acid Jam (Woronzow 1988)★★★, The Aunty Winnie Album (Reckless 1989)★★★, Any Gas Faster (Woronzow 1990)★★★★, as Bevis and Twink Magic Eye (Woronzow 1990)★★★, New River Head (Woronzow 1991)★★★★, London Stone (Woronzow 1992)★★★, It Just Is (Woronzow 1993)★★★, Sprawl (Woronzow 1994)★★★, Superseeder (Woronzow 1995)★★★, Son of Walter (Woronzow 1996).
COMPILATIONS: A Gathering Of Fronds (Woronzow 1992)★★★.

BHUNDU BOYS
ALBUMS: The Bhundu Boys (1981)★★★, Hupenyu Hwenasi (1984)★★★, Shabini (Discafrique 1985)★★★★, Tsvimbodzemoto (Discafrique 1987)★★★★, True Jit (WEA 1988)★★★★, Pamberi (WEA 1989)★★★, Absolute Jit (Discafrique 1991)★★★, Friends Of The Road (Discafrique 1992)★★★, Live at King Tut's Wah Wah Hut (Disc Afrique 1994), Muchiyedza (Cooking Vinyl 1997)★★★, Out of the Dark (Cooking Vinyl 1997).

BIG AUDIO DYNAMITE
ALBUMS: This Is Big Audio Dynamite (Columbia 1985)★★★★, No. 10 Upping Street (Columbia 1986)★★★★, Tighten Up, Vol 88 (Columbia 1988)★★★, Megatop Phoenix (Columbia 1989)★★★, as B.A.D. II Kool-Aid (Columbia 1990)★★, as B.A.D. II The Globe (Columbia 1991)★★, as Big Audio: Higher Power (Columbia 1994)★★, as Big Audio Looking For A Song (Columbia 1994)★★, as Big Audio Dynamite P-Funk (Radioactive 1995)★★★.
COMPILATIONS: Planet B.A.D.: Greatest Hits (Columbia 1995)★★★.
VIDEOS: B.A.D. I & I (Sony)

BIG BLACK
ALBUMS: Atomizer (Homestead/Blast First 1986)★★★, Sound Of Impact live album (Walls Have Ears 1987)★★, Songs About Fucking (Touch And Go/Blast First 1987)★★★.
COMPILATIONS: The Hammer Party (Homestead/Blast First 1986)★★★, The Rich Man's Eight-Track Tape (Homestead/Blast First 1987)★★★, Pigpile (Blast First 1992)★★★.
VIDEOS: Pigpile: Video Live (Touch & Go 1992)

BIG BOPPER
ALBUMS: Chantilly Lace (Mercury 1959)★★★.
FURTHER READING: Chantilly Lace: The Life & Times Of J.P. Richardson, Tim Knight, Big Bopper 1930-1959, Alan Clarke.

BIG COUNTRY
ALBUMS: The Crossing (Mercury 1983)★★★★, Steeltown (Mercury 1984)★★★, The Seer (Mercury 1986)★★, Peace In Our Time (Mercury 1988)★★★, No Place Like Home (Vertigo 1991)★★, The Buffalo Skinners (Compulsion 1993)★★, Live – Without The Aid Of A Safety Net (Compulsion 1994)★★, BBC Live In Concert (Windsong 1995)★★, Why The Long Face (Castle 1995)★★★, Eclectic (TRA 1996)★★★, King Biscuit Flower Hour (live) (King Biscuit 1997)★★★, Brighton Rock (Snapper 1997)★★★.
COMPILATIONS: Through A Big Country: Greatest Hits (Mercury 1990)★★★, The Collection (Castle 1993)★★★.
VIDEOS: Big Country Live (1986), King Of Emotion (1988), In A Big Country (1988), Peace In Our Time: Moscow 1988 (1989), Greatest Hits: Big Country (1990), Through A Big Country (1991), The Seer: Live (1991), Without The Aid Of A Safety Net – Live (PMI 1994).
FURTHER READING: Big Country: A Certain Chemistry, John May.

BIG DISH
ALBUMS: Swimmer (Virgin 1986)★★★, Creeping Up On Jesus (Virgin 1988)★★★, Satellites (East West 1991)★★.
COMPILATIONS: Rich Man's Wardrobe – A Concise History Of ... (Virgin 1993)★★★.

BIG HEAD TODD AND THE MONSTERS
ALBUMS: Another Mayberry (Big Records 1989)★★★, Midnight Radio (Big Records 1990)★★★, Sister Sweetly (Giant 1993)★★★, Strategem (Giant 1995)★★, Beautiful World (Revolution 1997)★★★.

BIG STAR
ALBUMS: #1 Record (Ardent 1972)★★★★, Radio City (Ardent 1974)★★★★, 3rd (PVC 1978)★★★★, 3rd/Sister Lovers (Ryko 1992), Live rec. 1974 (Ryko 1992)★★★★, Columbia Live At Missouri University 4/25/93 (1993)★★★.

BIG THREE
ALBUMS: Resurrection (Polydor 1973)★★, Cavern Stomp (1982)★★★, I Feel Like Steppin' Out (1986)★★★.

BIKINI KILL
ALBUMS: Bikini Kill (K Records 1992)★★★, Bikini Kill mini-album (Kill) Rock Stars 1993)★★★, with Huggy Bear Yeah Yeah Yeah (Kill Rock Stars 1993)★★★, Pussy Whipped (Kill Rock Stars 1993)★★, Reject All American (Kill Rock Stars 1996)★★★.
COMPILATIONS: The Tape Version Of The First Two Albums (Kill Rock Stars 1994)★★★.

BIOHAZARD
ALBUMS: Biohazard (Maze 1990)★★, Urban Discipline (Roadrunner 1992)★★★, State Of The World Address (Warners 1994)★★★, Mata Leao (Warners 1996)★★, No Hold's Barred (Live in Europe) (Roadrunner 1997)★★.

BIRDS
ALBUMS: These Birds Are Dangerous (1965)★★.

BIRKIN, JANE
ALBUMS: Jane Birkin And Serge Gainsbourg (Fontana 1969)★★★, Jane B (Phonogram 1974)★★★, Di Doo Dah (Phonogram 1975)★★, Versions Jane (Discovery 1996)★★★, Concert Integral A L'Olympia (Polydor 1997)★★★, Je Suis Venu Te Dire Que Je M'En Vais (Polydor 1998)★★★, Jane Birkin Coffret (Polydor

1998)★★, Je T'Aime Moi Non Plus (Polydor 1998)★★★, Ballade de Johnny (Polydor 1998)★★★, Ex Fan des Sixties (Polydor 1998)★★, Baby Alone in Babylone (Polydor 1998)★★★, Quoi Generique TV (Polydor 1998)★★, Jane Birkin Au Bataclan (Polydor 1998)★★★.
COMPILATIONS: The Best Of (Mercury 1997)★★★.

BIRTHDAY PARTY
ALBUMS: The Birthday Party (Missing Link 1980)★★★, Prayers On Fire (Thermidor 1981)★★★, Drunk On The Pope's Blood mini-album (4AD 1982)★★★, Junkyard (4AD 1982)★★★, Release the Bats (4AD 1983) It's Still Living live recording (Missing Link 1985)★★★, Peel Session Album (Strange Fruit 1991)★★★.
COMPILATIONS: A Collection (Missing Link 1985)★★★, Hee Haw (4AD 1989)★★★, The Peel Sessions Album (Strange Fruit 1991)★★★, Hits (4AD 1992)★★★★, Definitive Missing Link Recordings 1979-1982 (Missing Link 1994)★★★★.
VIDEOS: Pleasure Heads Must Burn (IKON 1988).

BIS
ALBUMS: The New Transistor Heroes (Wiiija 1997)★★★.

BISHOP, ELVIN
ALBUMS: The Elvin Bishop Group (Fillmore 1969)★★, Feel It (Fillmore 1970)★★, Rock My Soul (Fillmore 1972)★★, Let It Flow (Capricorn 1974)★★★, Juke Joint Jump (Capricorn 1975)★★★, Struttin' My Stuff (Capricorn 1975)★★★★, Hometown Boy Makes Good! (Capricorn 1976)★★, Live! Raisin' Hell (Capricorn 1977)★★★, Hog Heaven (Capricorn 1978)★★★, Is You Is Or Is You Ain't My Baby (Line 1982)★★, Big Fun (Alligator 1988)★★★, Don't Let The Bossman Get You Down (Alligator 1991)★★★, Ace In The Hole (Alligator 1995)★★★.
COMPILATIONS: Tulsa Shuffle: The Best Of ... (Columbia 1994)★★★★.

BISHOP, STEPHEN
ALBUMS: Careless (ABC 1976)★★★, Bish (ABC 1978)★★★, Red Cab To Manhattan (Warners 1980)★★★, Bowling In Paris (Atlantic 1989)★★★, Blue Guitars (Foundation 1996).
COMPILATIONS: The Best Of Bish (1988)★★★, On & On: The Hits of Stephen Bishop (MCA 1994)★★★.

BJÖRK
ALBUMS: Björk (F^lkinn 1977)★★★, with Tri– Gudmundar Gling-Gl– (Smekkylesa 1990)★★★, Debut (One Little Indian 1993)★★★★, Post (One Little Indian 1995)★★★★, Telegram (One Little Indian 1996)★★★, Homogenic (One Little Indian 1997)★★★.
VIDEOS: Björk (Propaganda 1994), Vessel (Polygram 1994), Joga (One Little Indian 1997).
FURTHER READING: Post: The Official Björk Book, Penny Phillips.

BJORN AGAIN
ALBUMS: Flashback (1993)★★★.

BLACK
ALBUMS: Wonderful Life (A&M 1987)★★★, Comedy (A&M 1988)★★★★, Black (A&M 1991)★★★, Are We Having Fun Yet? (A&M 1993)★★★, Haunting Harmonies (Jarra Hill 1995)★★★.

BLACK, BILL
ALBUMS: Smokie (Hi 1960)★★★, Saxy Jazz (Hi 1960)★★★, Solid And Raunchy (Hi 1960)★★★★, That Wonderful Feeling (Hi 1961)★★★, Movin' (Hi 1961)★★★, Bill Black's Record Hop (Hi 1962)★★★, Let's Twist Her (Hi 1962)★★★★, Untouchable Sound Of Bill Black (Hi 1963)★★★, Bill Black Plays The Blues (Hi 1964)★★★, Bill Black Plays Tunes By Chuck Berry (Hi 1964)★★, Bill Black's Combo Goes Big Band (Hi 1964)★★, More Solid And Raunchy (Hi 1965)★★, All Timers (Hi 1966)★★, Black Lace (Hi 1967)★★, King Of The Road (Hi 1967)★★, The Beat Goes On (Hi 1968)★★, Turn On Your Lovelight (London 1969)★★, Solid And Raunchy The 3rd (Hi 1969)★★, Soulin' The Blues (London 1969)★★, Raindrops Keep Falling (CBS 1970), Basic Black (CBS 1970), More Magic (Hi 1971), Juke Box Favourites (Mega 1972), Rock n Roll Forever (Mega 1973), Bill Black Its Back (Mega 1974), Solid & Country (Hi 1975), World's Greatest Honky-Tonk Band (Hi 1975), Bill Black Combo (Zodiac 1976), It's Honky Tonk Time (Hi 1977), Award Winners (Hi 1977), Memphis Tennessee (Hi 1981), First Year (Charly 1983), Let's Twist Her/The Untouchable Sound (Hi 1992), Smokie/More Solid & Raunchy (Hi 1996), White Silver Sands (Richmond 1996), Wonderful World (Hi 1997).
COMPILATIONS: Greatest Hits (Hi/London 1963)★★★.

BLACK, CILLA
ALBUMS: Cilla (Parlophone 1965)★★★, Cilla Sings A Rainbow (Parlophone 1966)★★★, Sher-oo (Parlophone 1968)★★★, Surround Yourself With Cilla (Parlophone 1969)★★, Sweet Inspiration (Parlophone 1970)★★, Images (Parlophone 1971)★★, Day By Day With Cilla (Parlophone 1973)★★, In My Life (EMI 1974)★★★, It Makes Me Feel Good (EMI 1976)★★, Modern Priscilla (EMI 1978)★★★, Surprisingly Cilla (1985)★★, Love Songs (1987)★★, Through The Years (Columbia 1993)★★★.
COMPILATIONS: You're My World (Starline 1970)★★★, Especially For You (K-Tel 1980)★★★, 25th Anniversary Album (1988)★★★, Love, Cilla (1993)★★★.
FILMS: Ferry Cross The Mersey (1964).
VIDEOS: Throughout The Years (1993).

BLACK, FRANK
ALBUMS: Frank Black (4AD 1993)★★★, Teenager Of The Year (4AD 1994)★★★★, with Teenage Fanclub Frank Black & Teenage Fanclub (Strange Fruit 1995)★★★, The Cult Of Ray (Epic 1996)★★★, The Black Sessions: Live in Paris, Anoise (1996)★★★.

BLACK, MARY
ALBUMS: Mary Black (Dara 1983)★★★, Collected (Dara 1984)★★★, Without The Fanfare (Dara 1985)★★★, with the Black Family The Black Family (Dara 1986)★★★, By The Time It Gets Dark (Dara 1987)★★★, with the Black Family Time For Touching Home (Dara 1989)★★★, No Frontiers (Dara 1989)★★★, Babes In The Wood (Grapevine 1991)★★★★, Circus (Grapevine 1995)★★★, Shine (Grapevine 1997)★★★.
COMPILATIONS: The Best Of Mary Black (Dara 1991)★★★★.

BLACK BOX
ALBUMS: Dreamland (RCA 1990)★★★, Remixed Reboxed Black Box/Mixed Up (RCA 1991)★★★.
VIDEOS: Video Dreams (1990).

BLACK CROWES
ALBUMS: Shake Your Money Maker (Def American 1990)★★★, The Southern Harmony And Musical Companion (Def American 1992)★★★★, Amorica (American 1994)★★★, Three Snakes And One Charm (American 1996)★★★.
VIDEOS: Who Killed That Bird On Your Windowsill ... The Movie (1993), Sometimes Salvation (Def American 1993).
FURTHER READING: The Black Crowes, Martin Black.

BLACK FLAG
ALBUMS: Damaged (SST 1981)★★★★, My War (SST 1984)★★★, Family Man (SST 1984)★★, Slip It In (SST 1984)★★★, Live '84 (SST 1984)★★, Loose Nut (SST 1985)★★, In My Head (SST 1985)★★★, Who's Got The 10 1/2? (SST 1986)★★★, Annihilate this week (live) (SST 1990)★★★.
COMPILATIONS: Everything Went Black (SST 1982)★★★, The First Four Years (SST 1983)★★★★, Wasted ... Again (SST 1988)★★★★.
VIDEOS: Black Flag Live (Jettisoundz 1984).

BLACK GRAPE
ALBUMS: It's Great When You're Straight ... Yeah (Radioactive 1995)★★★★, Stupid, Stupid, Stupid (Radioactive 1997)★★★.
VIDEOS: The Grape Tapes (Radioactive 1997).
FURTHER READING: Shaun Ryder: Happy Mondays, Black Grape And Other Traumas, Mick Middles.

BLACK OAK ARKANSAS
ALBUMS: as the Knowbody Else The Knowbody Else (Stax 1969)★★, Black Oak Arkansas (Atco 1971)★★, Keep The Faith (Atco 1972)★★, If An Angel Came To See You, Would You Make Her Feel At Home? (Atco 1972)★★, Raunch 'N' Roll/Live (Atlantic 1973)★★★, High On The Hog (Atco 1973)★★, Street Party (Atco 1974)★★, Ain't Life Grand (Atco 1975)★★, X-Rated (MCA 1975)H, Live! Mutha (Atco 1976)H, Balls of Fire (MCA 1976)H, 10 Year Overnight Success (MCA 1976)H, Race With The Devil (Capricorn 1977)H, I'd Rather Be Sailing (Capricorn 1978)H, Black Attack Is Back (Capricorn 1986)H. Solo: Jim Dandy Ready As Hell (Capricorn 1984), Rebound (Goldwax 1992), Jim Dandy (Rhino 1996), King Biscuit Flower Hour (live) (King Biscuit 1998).

BLACK SABBATH
ALBUMS: Black Sabbath (Vertigo 1970)★★★, Paranoid (Vertigo 1970)★★★★, Master Of Reality (Vertigo 1971)★★★, Black Sabbath Vol. 4 (Vertigo 1972)★★★, Sabbath Bloody Sabbath (World Wide Artists 1974)★★★, Sabotage (NEMS 1975)★★★, Technical Ecstasy (Vertigo 1976)★★★, Never Say Die (Vertigo 1978)★★★, Heaven And Hell (Vertigo 1980)★★★, Live At Last (NEMS 1980)★★, Mob Rules (Vertigo 1981)★★, Live Evil (Vertigo 1982)★★, Born Again (Vertigo 1983)★★, Seventh Star (Vertigo 1986)★★★, The Eternal Idol (Vertigo 1987)★★, Headless Cross (IRS 1989)★★, Tyr (IRS 1990)★★, Dehumanizer (IRS 1992)★★, Cross Purposes (EMI 1994)★★, Forbidden (IRS 1995)★★.
COMPILATIONS: Greatest Hits (NEMS 1980)★★★, Collection: Black Sabbath (Castle 1985)★★★★, The Ozzy Osbourne Years 3-CD box set (Essential 1991)★★★★, Between Heaven And Hell (Raw Power 1995)★★★, Under The Wheels Of Confusion 1970-1987 (Essential 1997)★★★★.
VIDEOS: Never Say Die (VCL 1986), The Black Sabbath Story Vol. 1 1970-1978 (Castle Music Pictures 1992), The Black Sabbath Story Vol. 2 1978-1992 (Warner Brothers 1992), Under Wheels Of Confusion 1970-1987 (Castle Music Pictures 1996).
FURTHER READING: Black Sabbath, Chris Welch.

BLACK UHURU
ALBUMS: Love Crisis (Prince Jammys/Third World 1977)★★★, Showcase (Taxi/Heartbeat 1979)★★★, Sinsemilla (Mango/Island 1980)★★★, Black Sounds Of Freedom (Greensleeves 1981)★★★, Red (Mango/Island 1981)★★★★, Black Uhuru (Virgin 1981)★★★, Chill Out (Mango/Island 1982)★★★, Tear It Up – Live (Mango/Island 1982)★★★, Guess Who's Coming To Dinner (Heartbeat 1983)★★★, The Dub Factor (Mango/Island 1983)★★★, Anthem (Mango/Island 1984)★★★, Uhuru In Dub (CSA 1985)★★★, Brutal (RAS 1986)★★★★, Brutal Dub (RAS 1986)★★★, Positive (RAS 1987)★★★, Positive Dub (RAS 1987)★★★, Live In New York City (Rohit 1988)★★★, Now (Mesa 1990)★★★, Now Dub (Mesa 1990)★★★, Iron Storm (Mesa 1991)★★★, Mystical Touch (Mesa 1993)★★★, One Love (Rhino 1993), Love Dub (Rohit 1994), Strongg (Rhino 1994), Strongg Dub (Mesa 1994).
COMPILATIONS: Reggae Greats (Mango/Island 1985)★★★★, Liberation: The Island Anthology 2-CD box set (Mango/Island 1993)★★★★.
VIDEOS: Tear It Up (1989), Black Uhuru Live (1991).

BLACK WIDOW
ALBUMS: as Pesky Gee Exclamation Mark! (Pye/Dawn 1969)★★, Sacrifice (Columbia 1970)★★★, Black Widow (Columbia 1971)★★, Three (Columbia 1971)★★, Street Fighter (Roadrunner 1984)★★, Ii (Castle 1993)★★.

BLACKMORE, RITCHIE
COMPILATIONS: Ritchie Blackmore Volume 1: Early Sessions To Rainbow (1990)★★★, Session Man (RPM 1993)★★★, Take It! – Sessions 63/68 (RPM 1995)★★★.

BLACKWELL, OTIS
ALBUMS: Singin' The Blues (Davis 1956)★★, All Shook Up (Shanachie 1976)★★, These Are My Songs (Inner City 1978)★★, Otis Blackwell 1953-55 (Flyright 1955)★★.

BLAINE, HAL
ALBUMS: Deuces, T's, Roadsters & Drums (RCA Victor 1963)★★, Drums! Drums! A Go Go (Dunhill 1966)★★, Psychedelic Percussion (Dunhill 1967)H, Have Fun!!! Play Drums!!! (Dunhill 1969)★★.

BLASTERS
ALBUMS: American Music (Rollin' Rock 1980)★★★, The Blasters (Slash 1981)★★★, Over There (Live) (Slash 1982), Non Fiction (Slash 1983)★★★, Hard Line (Slash 1985)★★★.
COMPILATIONS: The Blasters Collection (Slash 1991)★★★★.
FURTHER READING: Any Rough Times Are Now Behind You, Dave Alvin.

BLIGE, MARY J.
ALBUMS: What's The 411? (Uptown 1992)★★★, What's The 411? – Remix Album (Uptown 1993)★★★, My Life (Uptown 1994)★★★, Share My World (MCA 1997)★★★★.

BLIND FAITH
ALBUMS: Blind Faith (Polydor 1969)★★★.

BLIND MELON
ALBUMS: Blind Melon (Capitol 1993)★★★★, Soup (Capitol 1995)★★, Nico (Capitol 1997)★★.
VIDEOS: Letters From A Porcupine (Capitol 1996).

BLODWYN PIG
ALBUMS: Ahead Rings Out (Chrysalis 1969)★★★★, Getting To This (Chrysalis 1970)★★★, Lies (A New Day 1994)★★, All Tore Down (Indigo 1996)★★, Modern Alchemist (Indigo 1997)★★, Live at the Lafayette (Indigo 1998)★★.

BLOOD, SWEAT AND TEARS
ALBUMS: Child Is Father To The Man (Columbia 1968)★★★, Blood, Sweat And Tears (Columbia 1969)★★★★, Blood, Sweat And Tears 3 (Columbia 1970)★★★, BS&T4 (Columbia 1971)★★★, New Blood (Columbia 1972)★★, No Sweat (Columbia 1973)★★, Mirror Image (Columbia 1974)★★, New City Columbia (1975)★★, More Than Ever (Columbia 1976)★★, Brand New Day (1977)★★, Nuclear Blues (1980)★★, Live And Improvised (Columbia 1991)★★, Live (Rhino 1994).
COMPILATIONS: Greatest Hits (Columbia 1972)★★★★, What Goes Up! The Best Of (Columbia/Legacy 1995)★★★★.
FURTHER READING: Blood, Sweat And Tears, Lorraine Alterman.

BLONDIE
ALBUMS: Blondie (Private Stock 1976)★★★, Plastic Letters (Chrysalis 1978)★★★, Parallel Lines (Chrysalis 1978)★★★★, Eat To The Beat (Chrysalis 1979)★★, Autoamerican (Chrysalis 1980)★★, The Hunter (Chrysalis 1982)★★.
COMPILATIONS: The Best Of Blondie (Chrysalis 1981)★★★, Once More Into The Bleach (Chrysalis 1988)★★★, The Complete Picture – The Very Best Of Deborah Harry And Blondie (Chrysalis 1991)★★★★, Blonde And Beyond (Chrysalis 1993)★★★, The Essential Collection (EMI Gold 1997)★★★★.
VIDEOS: Blondie – Live (CIC Video 1986), Eat To The Beat (Chrysalis Music Video 1988), Best Of Blondie (Chrysalis Music Video 1988), Live in Concert (MCA 1991).
FURTHER READING: Rip Her To Shreds: A Look At Blondie, Paul Sinclair. Blondie, Fred Schruers. Blondie, Lester Bangs. Making Tracks: The Rise Of Blondie, Debbie Harry, Chris Stein and Victor Bockris.

BLOOM, BOBBY
ALBUMS: The Bobby Bloom Album (1970)★★★.

BLOOMFIELD, MIKE
ALBUMS: with Al Kooper and Stephen Stills Super Session (Columbia 1968)★★★, The Live Adventures Of Mike Bloomfield And Al Kooper (Columbia 1969)★★, Fathers And Sons (1969)★★, with Barry Goldberg Two Jews Blues (1969)★★, It's Not Killing Me (Columbia 1969)★★, with others Live At Bill Graham's Fillmore West (1969)★★, Try It Before You Buy It (Columbia 1973)★★, with Dr John Triumvirate (Columbia 1973)★★★, as KGB KGB (1976)H, Bloomfield/Naftalin (1976)★★, Mill Valley Session (Polydor 1976)★★★, There's Always Another Record (1976)★★, I'm With You Always (1977)★★, If You Love These Blues, Play 'Em As You Please (Guitar Player 1977)★★★, Count Talent And The Originals (1977)★★, Analine (Takoma 1977)★★, Michael Bloomfield (Takoma 1978)★★, Mike Bloomfield And Woody Harris (Kicking Mule 1979)★★, Between A Hard Place And The Ground (Takoma 1980)★★, Livin' In The Fast Lane (Waterhouse 1981)★★, Gosport Duets (1981)★★, Red Hot And Blues (1981)★★, Cruisin' For A Bruisin' (Takoma 1981)★★, Retrospective (1984)★★★, Junco Partners (1984)★★, Blues, Gospel And Ragtime Guitar Instrumentals (Shanachie 1994)★★★, Gospel Truth (Magnum America 1996), Rx For the Blues (Eclipse Music 1996).
COMPILATIONS: Essential Blues 1964-1969 (Columbia Legacy 1994)★★★.
FURTHER READING: The Rise And Fall Of An American Guitar Hero, Ed Ward.

BLOSSOM TOES
ALBUMS: We Are Ever So Clean (Marmalade 1967)★★★★, If Only For A Moment (Marmalade 1969)★★★, New Day: Blossom Toes '70 (Decal 1989)★★★.
COMPILATIONS: The Blossom Toes Collection (1989)★★★★.

BLOW, KURTIS
ALBUMS: Kurtis Blow (Mercury 1980)★★★, Deuce (Mercury 1981)★★, Tough (Mercury 1982)★★, Ego Trip (Mercury 1984)★★★, America (Mercury 1985)★★★, Kingdom Blow (Mercury 1986)★★, Back By Popular Demand (Mercury 1988)★★.
COMPILATIONS: Best Of (Mercury 1994)★★★.

BLOW MONKEYS
ALBUMS: Limping For A Generation (RCA 1984)★★★, Animal Magic (RCA 1986)★★★, She Was Only A Grocer's Daughter (RCA 1987)★★★, Whoops! There Goes The Neighbourhood (RCA 1989)★★, Choices (RCA 1989)★★, Spring (Alex 1992).
COMPILATIONS: The Best Of (RCA 1993)★★★, For The Record (BMG 1996)★★★.
VIDEOS: Video Magic (1988), Digging Your Scene (1988), Choices (1989).

BLOWZABELLA
ALBUMS: Blowzabella (Plant Life 1982)★★★, Blowzabella In Colour (Plant Life 1983)★★, Bobbityshooty (Plant Life 1984)★★★, Tam Lin (Plant Life 1984)★★★, The Blowzabella Wall Of Sound (Plant Life 1986)★★★, The B To A Of Blowzabella (1987)★★★, Pingha Frenzy (Some Bizarre 1988)★★★, Vanilla (Topic 1990)★★.
COMPILATIONS: *** (Osmosys 1995)★★★.

BLUE, DAVID
ALBUMS: with Richard Farina Singer/Songwriter Project (1965)★★★, David Blue (1966)★★★, These 23 Days In December (1968)★★, Me, S. David Cohen (1970)★★, Stories (Line 1971)★★★, Nice Baby And The Angel (1973)★★★, Com'n Back For More (Asylum 1975)★★★, Cupid's Arrow (1976)★★★.

BLUE AEROPLANES
ALBUMS: Bop Art (Abstract 1984)★★★, Tolerance (Fire 1986)★★★, Spitting Out Miracles (Fire 1987)★★★, Swagger (Ensign 1990)★★★, Beatsongs (Ensign 1991)★★★★, Life Model (Beggars Banquet 1994)★★★, Rough Music (Beggars Banquet 1995)★★★, Fruit (Fire 1996)★★★.
Solo: Gerard Langley and Ian Kearey Siamese Boyfriends mini-album (Fire 1986)★★.
COMPILATIONS: Friendloverplane (Fire 1988)★★★★, Friendloverplane 2 (Ensign 1992)★★★, Huh! Best Of: 1987-1992 (Chrysalis 1997)★★★.

BLUE CHEER
ALBUMS: Vincebus Eruptum (Philips 1968)★★★, Outsideinside (Philips 1968)★★★, New! Improved! Blue Cheer (Philips 1969)★★, Blue Cheer (Philips 1970)★★, The Original Human Being (Philips 1970)★★, Oh! Pleasant Hope (Philips 1971)H, The Beast Is Back ... (Important 1985)H, Blitzkrieg Over Nuremburg (Thunderbolt 1990)★★, Dining With Sharks (Nibelung 1991)★★.
COMPILATIONS: The Best Of Blue Cheer (Phillips 1982)★★★, Louder Than God (Rhino 1986)★★★, Good Times Are So Hard To Find (The History Of Blue Cheer) (Mercury 1990)★★★.

BLUE MINK
ALBUMS: Blue Mink (Regal 1969)★★★, A Time Of Change (Regal 1972)★★★, Live At The Talk Of The Town (Regal 1972)★★, Only When I Laugh (EMI 1973)★★★, Fruity (EMI 1974)★★, Attention (Phonogram 1975)★★, Hit Making Sound (Gull 1977)★★.
COMPILATIONS: Collection: Blue Mink (Action Replay 1987)★★★.

BLUE NILE
ALBUMS: A Walk Across The Rooftops (Linn/Virgin 1984)★★★★, Hats (Linn/Virgin 1989)★★★, Peace At Last (Warners 1996)★★★.

BLUE ORCHIDS
ALBUMS: The Greatest Hit (Money Mountain) (Rough Trade 1982)★★★ Agents of Change (Rough Trade 1982)★★★, A View From The City (Rough Trade 1991)★★★.

BLUE ÖYSTER CULT
ALBUMS: Blue Oyster Cult (Columbia 1971)★★★, Tyranny And Mutation (Columbia 1973)★★★, Secret Treaties (Columbia 1974)★★, On Your Feet Or On Your Knees (Columbia 1975)★★, Agents Of Fortune (Columbia 1976)★★★★, Spectres (Columbia 1977)★★, Some Enchanted Evening (Columbia 1978)★★, Mirrors (Columbia 1979)★★, Cultosaurus Erectus (Columbia 1980)★★, Fire Of Unknown Origin (Columbia 1981)★★, Extraterrestial Live (Columbia 1982)H, The Revolution By Night (Columbia 1983)H, Club Ninja (Columbia 1985)H, Imaginos (Columbia 1988)★★★, On Flame with Rock & Roll (CBS 1990), Special soundtrack Bad Channels (Moonstone 1992)★★. Solo: Donald Roeser Flat Out (Portrait 1982)★★, Live 1976 (Gopaco 1994), Workshop Of The Telescopes (Columbia 1995)★★, Heaven Forbid (CMC International 1998).
COMPILATIONS: Career Of Evil – The Metal Years (Columbia 1990)★★★, Cult Classic (Herald 1994)★★★.
VIDEOS: Live 1976 (Castle Music Pictures 1991).

BLUEBELLS
ALBUMS: Sisters (London 1984)★★★, Bloomin' Live (London 1993)★★.
COMPILATIONS: Second (London 1992)★★★, The Singles Collection (London 1993)★★★.
VIDEOS: The Bluebells (Dubious Video 1989).

BLUES BAND
ALBUMS: The Official Blues Band Bootleg Album (Blues Band 1980)★★★★, Ready (Arista 1980)★★★, Itchy Feet (Arista 1981)★★★, Brand Loyalty (Arista 1982)★★★, Bye-Bye Blues (Arista 1983)★★★, These Kind Of Blues (Date 1986)★★★, Back For More (Arista 1989)★★★, Fat City (RCA 1991)★★★, Live (1993)★★★, Homage (Essential 1993)★★★, Wire Less (Cobalt 1995)★★★, Juke Joint Blues (Ichiban 1995)★★, 18 Years Old And Alive (Cobalt 1996)★★★★, Homage (Castle 1996), Live At the BBC (Windsong 1996).
FURTHER READING: Talk To Me Baby: The Story Of The Blues Band, Roy Bainton.

BLUES BROTHERS
ALBUMS: Briefcase Full Of Blues (Atlantic 1978)★★, The Blues Brothers film soundtrack (Atlantic 1980)★★★, Made In America (Atlantic 1980)★★, as the Blues Brothers Band The Blues Brothers Band Live (Warners 1990)H, Red, White & Blues (1992)H, Blues Brothers (highlights) (Griffin Music 1993)★★, Montreux Live (WEA 1995)★★, Blues Brothers and Friends: Live (A&M 1997)★★.
FILMS: The Blues Brothers (1980).
VIDEOS: Live At Montreux (WEA Music Video 1990), Things We Did Last Summer (Brave World 1991).

BLUES MAGOOS
ALBUMS: Psychedelic Lollipop (Mercury 1966)★★★, Electric Comic Book (Mercury 1967)★★★, Basic Blues Magoos (Mercury 1968)★★, Never Goin' Back To Georgia (1969)★★, Gulf Coast Bound (1970)★★.
COMPILATIONS: Kaleidescopic Compendium: The Best Of The Blues Magoos (Mercury 1992)★★★.

BLUES PROJECT
ALBUMS: Live At The Cafe Au Go-Go (Verve/Folkways 1966)★★, Projections (Verve/Forecast 1967)★★★, Live At The Town Hall (Verve/Forecast 1967)★★★, Planned Obsolescence (Verve/ Forecast 1968)★★, Flanders Kalb Katz Etc (Verve Forecast 1969)★★, Lazarus (1971)★★, Blues Project (Capitol 1972)★★, Reunion In Central Park (One Way 1973)★★, Archetypes Blues Project (MGM 1974).
COMPILATIONS: Best Of The Blues Project (Rhino 1989)★★★.

BLUES TRAVELER
ALBUMS: Blues Traveler (A&M 1990)★★, Travelers And Thieves (A&M 1991)★★★, On Tour Forever bonus disc given away free with copies of Travelers And Thieves (A&M 1992)★★★, Save His Soul (A&M 1993)★★, Four (A&M 1994)★★★★, Live From The Fall (A&M 1996)★★, Straight On Till Morning (A&M 1997)★★★.

BLUETONES
ALBUMS: Expecting To Fly (Superior Quality 1996)★★★★.

BLUNSTONE, COLIN
ALBUMS: One Year (Epic 1971)★★★★, Ennismore (Epic 1972)★★★★, Journey (Epic 1974)★★★, Planes (Rocket 1976)★★★, Never Even Thought (Rocket 1978)★★, Late Nights In Soho (Rocket 1979)★★, with Keats Keats (EMI 1984)★★, Echo Bridge (Permanent 1995)★★, Live At The BBC (Windsong 1995)★★★.
COMPILATIONS: Miracles (Pickwick 1979)★★★, Sings His Greatest Hits (JSE 1991)★★★, Some Years: It's The Time Of Colin Blunstone (Epic/Legacy 1995)★★★★.

BLUR
ALBUMS: Leisure (Food 1991)★★★★, Modern Life Is Rubbish (Food 1993)★★★, Parklife (Food 1994)★★★★, The Great Escape (Food 1995)★★★★, The Special Collector's Edition (Food/Parlophone 1995)★★★, Live At The Budokan (Food 1996)★★★, Blur (Food 1997)★★★★, Bustin' and Dronin' (Food/Virgin 1998)★★★★.
VIDEOS: Star Shaped (1993), Showtime (PMI 1995).
FURTHER READING: An Illustrated Biography, Linda Holorney. Blurbook, Paul Postle. Blur: The Illustrated Story, Paul Lester. Blur: The Whole Story, Martin Roach. Blur: The Great Escape, Paul Moody. Blur In Their Own Words, Mick St Michael.

BLYTH POWER
ALBUMS: A Little Touch Of Harry In The Middle Of The Night cassette only (96 Tapes 1984)★★★, Wicked Women, Wicked Men And Wicket Keepers (Midnight 1986)★★★, The Barman And Other Stories (Midnight 1988)★★★, Alnwick And Tyne (Midnight 1990)★★★, The Guns Of Castle Cary (Downward Spiral 1991)★★★, Pastor Skull (Downward Spiral 1993)★★★, Paradise Razed (Downward Spiral 1995)★★★.
COMPILATIONS: Pont Au-Dessus De La Brue (Midnight 1988)★★★.

BMX BANDITS
ALBUMS: C-86 (1990)★★★, A Totally Groovy Live Experience (Avalanche 1990)★★★, Star Wars (Vinyl Japan 1992)★★★, Gordon Keen And His BMX Bandits mini-album (Sunflower 1992)★★★, Life Goes On (Creation 1994)★★★★, Gettin' Dirty (Creation 1995)★★★★, Theme Park (Creation 1996)★★★★.
COMPILATIONS: C-86 Plus (Vinyl Japan 1992)★★★.

BOB AND EARL
ALBUMS: Harlem Shuffle (Tip/Sue 1966)★★★, Bob And Earl (Crestview/B&C 1969)★★, Together (Joy 1969)★★.

BOB AND MARCIA
ALBUMS: Young, Gifted And Black (Harry J 1970)★★★, Pied Piper (Harry J 1971)★★★, Really Together (I-Anka 1987)★★★.

BOB B. SOXX AND THE BLUE JEANS
ALBUMS: Zip-A-Dee-Doo-Dah (Philles 1963)★★★.

BOLAN, MARC
ALBUMS: The Beginning Of Doves (Track 1974)★★, You Scare Me To Death (Cherry Red 1981)★★, Beyond The Rising Sun (Cambra 1984)★★, Love And Death (Cherry Red 1985)★★, The Marc Shows television recordings (Marc On Wax 1989)★★★, Cat Black (Cleopatra1996), Live 1977 (Polygram 1997), Smashed Block (Cleopatra 1997).
COMPILATIONS: 20th Century Boy (K-Tel 1985)★★★★.
VIDEOS: On Video (Videoform 1984), Marc (Channel 5 1989), T. Rex Double Box Set (Virgin Vision 1991), Born To Boogie (PMI 1991), 20th Century Boy (Polygram Music Video 1991), The Groover Live In Concert (MIA 1995).
FURTHER READING: The Warlock Of Love, Marc Bolan. The Marc Bolan Story, George Tremlett. Marc Bolan: Born To Boogie, Chris Welch and Simon Napier-Bell. Electric Warrior: The Marc Bolan Story, Paul Sinclair. Marc Bolan: The Illustrated Discography, John Bramley and Shan. Marc Bolan: Wilderness Of The Mind, John Williams and Caron Thomas. Twentieth Century Boy, Mark Paytress. Marc Bolan: The Legendary Years, John Bramley and Shan, Marc Bolan Ted Dicks.

BOLTON, MICHAEL
ALBUMS: as Michael Bolotin Michael Bolotin (RCA 1975)★★, Every Day Of My Life (RCA 1976)★★; with Blackjack Blackjack (Polydor 1979)★★, Worlds Apart (Polydor 1980)★★; as Michael Bolton Michael Bolton (Columbia 1983)★★, Everybody's Crazy (Columbia 1985)★★, The Hunger (Columbia 1987)★★★, Soul Provider (Columbia 1989)★★★, Time, Love And Tenderness (Columbia 1991)★★, The One Thing (Columbia 1993)★★, This Is The Time – The Christmas Album (Columbia 1996)H, All That Matters (Columbia 1997), My Secret Passion (Sony 1998).
COMPILATIONS: Timeless (The Classics) (Columbia 1992)★★★, Greatest Hits 1985-1995 (Sony 1995)★★★.
VIDEOS: Soul Provider; The Videos (1990), This Is Michael Bolton (1992), Soul & Passion (Sony Music Videos 1992), Decade: Greatest Hits 1985-1995 The Videos (SMV 1995).

BON JOVI
ALBUMS: Bon Jovi (Vertigo 1984)★★, 7800 Degrees Fahrenheit (Vertigo 1985)★★, Slippery When Wet (Vertigo 1986)★★★★, New Jersey (Vertigo 1988)★★★, Keep The Faith (Phonogram 1992)★★★★, These Days (Jambco/Mercury 1995)★★★, These Days Tour Edition mini-album (Mercury 1996)★★. Solo: David Bryan On A Full Moon (Phonogram 1994)★★. Jon Bon Jovi Blaze Of Glory (Vertigo 1990)★★, Destination Anywhere (Mercury 1997)★★★. Richie Sambora Stranger In This Town (Mercury 1991)★★.
COMPILATIONS: Crossroads – The Best Of (Phonogram 1994)★★★★.
FURTHER READING: Bon Jovi: An Illustrated Biography, Eddy McSquare. Faith And Glory, Malcolm Dome. Bon Jovi: Runaway, Dave Bowler and Bryan Dray. The Illustrated Biography, Mick Wall. The Complete Guide To The Music Of ... , Mick Wall and Malcolm Dome. Bon Jovi, Neil Jeffries.
VIDEOS: Breakout (1986), Slippery When Wet (1988), New Jersey (1989), Dead Or Alive (1989), Access All Areas (1991), Keep The Faith: An Evening With Bon Jovi (1993), Crossroads The Best of (PolyGram 1994), Live From London (Polygram 1995).

BONDS, GARY 'U.S.'
ALBUMS: Dance 'Til Quarter To Three (Legrand/Top Rank 1961)★★★, Twist Up Calypso (Legrand/Stateside 1962)★★★, Dedication (EMI America 1981)★★★, On The Line (EMI America 1982)★★, Gary 'U.S.' Bonds Meets Chubby Checker (EMI 1983)★★, Standing In The Line Of Fire (Phoenix 1984)★★.
COMPILATIONS: Greatest Hits Of Gary 'U.S.' Bonds (Legrand/Stateside 1962)★★★★, The School Of Rock 'n' Roll: The Best Of Gary 'U.S' Bonds (Rhino 1990)★★★★, Take Me Back To New Orleans (Ace 1995)★★★, The Best Of Gary U.S. Bonds (EMI 1996)★★★★.
FILMS: It's Trad, Dad aka Ring-A-Ding Rhythm (1962).

BONE THUGS-N-HARMONY
ALBUMS: E.1999 Eternal (Ruthless/Relativity 1995)★★★★, The Art Of War (Ruthless 1997)★★★★.

BONEY M
ALBUMS: Take The Heat Off Me (Atlantic 1976)H, Love For Sale (Atlantic 1977)H, Night Flight To Venus (Atlantic 1978)★★, Oceans Of Fantasy (Atlantic 1979)H, Boonoonoonoos (Atlantic 1981)H, Eye Dance (Carrere 1986)H.
VIDEOS: Gold (1993).
FURTHER READING: Boney M, John Shearlaw.

BONGWATER
1ALBUMS: Breaking No New Ground mini-album (Shimmy-Disc 1987)★★★, Double Bummer (Shimmy-Disc 1988)★★★, Too Much Sleep (Shimmy-Disc 1990)★★★, The Power Of Pussy (Shimmy-Disc 1991)★★★★, The Peel Sessions (Strange Fruit 1991)★★★, The Big Sell Out (Shimmy-Disc 1992)★★★★.

BONO, SONNY
ALBUMS: Inner Views (1967)H.
FURTHER READING: And The Beat Goes On, Sonny Bono.

BONZO DOG DOO-DAH BAND
ALBUMS: Gorilla (Liberty 1967)★★★, The Doughnut In Granny's Greenhouse (Liberty 1968)★★★, Tadpoles (Liberty 1969)★★★, Keynsham (Liberty 1969)★★★, Let's Make Up And Be Friendly (United Artists 1972)★★, I'm The Urban Spaceman (One Way 1973), Peel Sessions (Dutch East 1987), Unpeeled (Strange Fruit 1995).
COMPILATIONS: The History Of The Bonzos (United Artists 1974)★★★★, The Bestiality Of The Bonzo Dog Band (Liberty 1989)★★★, Cornology Vols. 1-3 (EMI 1992)★★★.
FILMS: Adventures Of The Son Of Exploding Sausage (1969).

BOO RADLEYS
ALBUMS: Ichabod And I (Action 1990)★★, Everything's Alright Forever (Creation 1992)★★★, Giant Steps (Creation 1993)★★★, Wake Up (Creation 1995)★★★★, C'mon Kids (Creation 1996)★★★★. Solo: Eggman First Fruits (Creation 1996)★★★.
COMPILATIONS: Learning To Walk (Rough Trade 1994)★★★.

BOO-YAA T.R.I.B.E.
ALBUMS: New Funky Nation (4th & Broadway 1990)★★★, Doomsday (Bulletproof 1994)★★★, Angry Samoans (Bulletproof 1997).

BOOKER T. AND THE MGS
ALBUMS: Green Onions (Stax 1962)★★★★, Mo' Onions (1963)★★★★, Soul Dressing (Stax 1965)★★★★, My Sweet Potato (1965)★★★, And Now! (Stax 1966)★★★, In The Christmas Spirit (Stax 1966)★★, Hip Hug-Her (Stax 1967)★★★, with the Mar-Keys Back To Back (Stax 1967)★★★, Doin' Our Thing (Stax 1968)★★★, Soul Limbo (Stax 1968)★★★, Uptight (Stax 1969)★★, The Booker T. Set (Stax 1969)★★★, McLemore Avenue (Stax 1970)★★, Melting Pot (Stax 1971)★★, as the MG's The MGs (Stax 1973)★★, Memphis Sound (Warners 1975)★★, Union Extended (Warners 1976)★★, Time Is Tight (Warners 1976)★★, Universal Language (Asylum 1977)H. Solo: Booker T. Jones Try And Love Again (A&M 1978)★★, The Best Of You (A&M 1980)★★, I Want You (A&M 1981)★★, The Runaway (MCA 1989)★★, That's The Way It Should Be (Columbia 1994)★★, Booker in Paris Live (Epm Musique 1996).
COMPILATIONS: The Best Of Booker T. And The MGs (Atlantic 1968)★★★★★, Booker T. And The MG's Greatest Hits (Stax 1970)★★★★, The Best Of Booker T And The MG's (Very Best Of) (Rhino 1993)★★★★★, Play The Hip Hits (Stax/Ace 1995)★★★★.

BOOMTOWN RATS
ALBUMS: The Boomtown Rats (Ensign 1977)★★★, A Tonic For The Troops (Ensign 1978)★★★, The Fine Art Of Surfacing (Ensign 1979)★★★, Mondo Bongo (Ensign 1981)★★, V Deep (Ensign 1982)★★, In The Long Grass (Ensign 1984)★★, Great Songs of Indifference (Sony 1997).
COMPILATIONS: Loudmouth – The Best Of The Boomtown Rats And Bob Geldof (Vertigo 1994)★★★.
VIDEOS: A Tonic For The Troops (VCL 1986), On A Night Like This (Spectrum 1989).
FURTHER READING: The Boomtown Rats: Having Their Picture Taken, Peter Stone. Is That It? Bob Geldof.

BOSTON
ALBUMS: Boston (Epic 1976)★★★★, Don't Look Back (Epic 1978)★★★, Third Stage (MCA 1986)★★★, Walk On (MCA 1994)★★. Solo: Barry Goudreau Barry Goudreau (Portrait 1980)★★.

BOTHY BAND
ALBUMS: 1975 (1975)★★★, Old Hag You Have Killed Me (1976)★★★★, The Bothy Band (1976)★★★★, Out Of The Wind Into The Sun (1977)★★★, After Hours-Live In Paris (1978)★★★, Live In Concert (Windsong 1994)★★★.
COMPILATIONS: The Best Of The Bothy Band (1980)★★★★.

BOW WOW
ALBUMS: Bow Wow (Invitation 1976)★★★, Signal Fire (Invitation 1977)★★★, Charge (Invitation 1977)★★★, Super Live (Invitation 1978)★★★, Guarantee (Invitation 1978)★★★, The Bow Wow (Invitation 1979)★★★, Glorious Road (SMS 1979)★★★, Telephone (SMS 1980)★★★, X Bomber (SMS 1980)★★★, Hard Dog (SMS 1981)★★★, Asian Volcano (VAP 1982)★★, Warning From Stardust (VAP 1982)★★, Holy Expedition (Heavy Metal 1983)★★. As Vow Wow: Beat Of Metal Motion (VAP 1984)★★★, Cyclone (Eastworld 1985)★★★, III (Eastworld 1986)★★★, Live (Passport 1987)★★, V (Arista 1987)★★★, VIB (EMI 1989)★★★, Helter Skelter (Arista 1989)★★★.

BOW WOW WOW
ALBUMS: Your Cassette Pet mini-album (EMI 1980)★★★★, See Jungle! See Jungle! Go Join Your Gang, Yeah, City All Over! Go Ape Crazy! (RCA 1981)★★★, I Want Candy (RCA 1982)★★, When The Going Gets Tough, The Tough Get Going (RCA 1983)★★, Live in Japan (Receiver 1997). Solo: Annabella Fever (RCA 1986)★★.
COMPILATIONS: The Best Of Bow Wow Wow (Receiver 1989)★★★, Girl Bites Dog – Your Compact Disc Pet (EMI 1993)★★★.

BOWIE, DAVID
ALBUMS: David Bowie (Deram 1967)★★, later reissued as The World Of David Bowie, David Bowie aka Man Of Words, Man Of Music (RCA Victor 1969)★★★, later reissued as Space Oddity, The Man Who Sold The World (RCA Victor 1971)★★★, Hunky Dory (RCA Victor 1972)★★★★★, The Rise And Fall Of Ziggy Stardust And The Spiders From Mars (RCA Victor 1972)★★★★★, Aladdin Sane (RCA Victor 1973)★★★★, Pin Ups (RCA Victor 1973)★★★, Diamond Dogs (RCA Victor 1974)★★★★, David Live (RCA Victor 1974)H, Young Americans (RCA Victor 1975)★★★★, Station To Station (RCA Victor 1976)★★★, Low (RCA Victor 1977)★★★★, Heroes (RCA Victor 1977)★★★★, Stage (RCA Victor 1978)★★, Lodger (RCA Victor 1979)★★, Scary Monsters (And Super Creeps) (RCA Victor 1980)★★★★, Christiane F. film soundtrack (1982)★★, Rare (RCA 1983)★★, Let's Dance (EMI America 1983)★★★, Ziggy Stardust – The Motion Picture film soundtrack (RCA 1983)★★, Tonight (EMI America 1984)H, Never Let Me Down (EMI America 1987)H, with Tin Machine Tin Machine (EMI USA 1989)★★, with Tin Machine Tin Machine II (London 1991)★★, with Tin Machine Oy Vey Baby (EMI 1992)H, Black Tie White Noise (Arista 1993)★★★, The Buddha Of Suburbia television soundtrack (1993)★★, Santa Monica (Trident 1994),★★, Outside (Virgin 1995)★★★, Earthling (RCA 1996)★★.
COMPILATIONS: Changesonebowie (RCA 1976)★★★★★, Best Of David Bowie (K-Tel 1981)★★★, Golden Years (RCA 1983)★★★, Fame And Fashion (All Time Greatest Hits) (RCA 1984)★★★, Changesbowie (EMI 1990)★★★, The Singles Collection (EMI 1993)★★★★★, The Best Of 1969-1974 (EMI 1997)★★★.
FILMS: The Man Who Fell To Earth (1976), Just A Gigolo (1978), The Hunger (1983), Merry Christmas Mr Lawrence (1983), Ziggy Stardust And The Spiders From Mars 1973 performance (1983), Into The Night (1984), Absolute Beginners (1985), Labyrinth (1986), Twin Peaks: Fire Walk With Me (1992).
VIDEOS: Richochet, Video Hits, David Bowie – Video EP (Virgin Vision 1983), Serious Moonlight (Videoform 1984), Ziggy Stardust And The Spiders From Mars (Thorn-EMI 1984), Live VIDEOS: David Bowie (Videoform 1984), Video EP: David Bowie (PMI 1986), Serious Moonlight 2 (Channel 5 1986), Jazzin' For Blue Jean (Video Collection 1987), Day In Day Out (PMI 1987), Glass Spider Vol. 1 (Video Collection 1988), Glass Spider Vol. 2 (Video Collection 1988), Love You Till Tuesday (Channel 5 1989), David Bowie: The Video Collection (1993), David Bowie: Black Tie White Noise (1993).
FURTHER READING: The David Bowie Story, George Tremlett. David Bowie: A Portrait In Words And Music, Vivian Claire. The David Bowie Biography, Paul Sinclair. David Bowie Black Book: The Illustrated Biography, Miles and Chris Charlesworth. Bowie In His Own Words, Miles. David Bowie: An Illustrated Discography, Stuart Hoggard. David Bowie: Profile, Chris Charlesworth. David Bowie: An Illustrated Record, Roy Carr and Charles Shaar Murray. Free Spirit, Angie Bowie. David Bowie: The Pitt Report, Kenneth Pitt. David Bowie: A Chronology, Kevin Cann. David Bowie: A Rock 'N' Roll Odyssey, Kate Lynch. Bowie, Jerry Hopkins. David Bowie: The Concert Tapes, Pimm Jal de la Parra. David Bowie: The Starzone Interviews, David Currie. Stardust, Tony Zanetta. In Other Words ... David Bowie, Kerry Juby. David Bowie: The Archive, Chris Charlesworth. Alias David Bowie, Peter Gillman and Leni. Backstage Passes: Life On The Wild Side With David Bowie, Angie Bowie. The Bowie Companion, Elizabeth Thomson and David Gutman (eds.).

BOX OF FROGS
ALBUMS: Box Of Frogs (Epic 1984)★★★, Interchords (Epic 1984)★★★, Strange Land (Epic 1986)★★★.

BOX TOPS
ALBUMS: The Letter/Neon Rainbow (Bell 1967)★★★, Cry Like A Baby (Bell 1968)★★★, Non Stop (Bell 1968)★★★, Dimensions (Bell 1969)★★, A Lifetime Believing (Cotillion 1971).
COMPILATIONS: The Box Tops Super Hits (Bell 1968)★★★, Greatest Hits (Rhino 1982)★★★, Ultimate Box Tops (Warners 1988)★★★, Soul Deep, The Best Of ... (Arista 1998)★★★.

BOY GEORGE
ALBUMS: Sold (Virgin 1987)★★★, Tense Nervous Headache (Virgin 1988)★★; as Jesus Loves You The Martyr Mantras (More Protein/Virgin 1991)★★, Boyfriend (Virgin 1989), Devil In Sister (Import 1994)★★, Cheapness And Beauty (Virgin 1995)★★★.
COMPILATIONS: At Worst ... The Best Of Boy George And Culture Club (Virgin 1993)★★★★.
FURTHER READING: Take It Like A Man, Boy George.

BOYZ II MEN
ALBUMS: Cooleyhighharmony (Motown 1991)★★★, II (Motown 1994)★★★★, Remix, Remake, Remember (Motown 1996)★★★★, Evolution (Motown 1997)★★★.
VIDEOS: Then II Now (Motown Video 1994).

BOYZONE
ALBUMS: All Said And Done (Polydor 1995)★★★, A Different Beat (Polydor 1996)★★★.
VIDEOS: Said And Done (VVL 1995), Live At Wembley (Vision Video 1996).

BRADY, PAUL
ALBUMS: Andy Irvine/Paul Brady (Mulligan 1976)★★★, with Tommy Peoples The High Part Of The Road (Shanachie 1976)★★★, Welcome Here Kind Stranger (Mulligan 1978)★★★, Hard Station (Polydor 1981)★★★, True For You (Polydor 1983)★★★, Full Moon (Demon 1984)★★★★, Back To The Centre (Mercury 1986)★★★, with Peoples, Matt Molloy Molloy, Brady, Peoples (Mulligan 1986)★★★, Primitive Dance (Mercury 1987)★★★★, Trick Or Treat (Fontana 1991)★★★, Songs And Crazy Deams (Fontana 1992)★★★, Spirits Colliding (Fontana 1995)★★★★.
VIDEOS: Echoes And Extracts (1991).

BRAGG, BILLY
ALBUMS: Life's A Riot With Spy Vs Spy (Utility 1983)★★★, Brewing Up With Billy Bragg (Go! Discs 1984)★★★★, Talking With The Taxman About Poetry (Go! Discs 1986)★★★★, Workers Playtime (Go! Discs 1988)★★★, Help Save The Youth Of America – Live And Dubious US/Canada release (Go! Discs 1988)★★★, The Internationale (Utility 1990)★★★, Don't Try This At Home (Go! Discs 1991)★★★★, The Peel Sessions Album recordings from 1983-88 (Strange Fruit 1992)★★★, William Bloke (Cooking Vinyl 1996)★★★★, with Wilco Mermaid Avenue.(Warners, 1998).
COMPILATIONS: Back To Basics a repackage of the first two albums (Go! Discs 1987)★★★.
VIDEOS: Billy Bragg Goes To Moscow And Norton, Virginia Too (ReVision 1990).
FURTHER READING: Midnight In Moscow, Chris Salewicz.

BRAND NEW HEAVIES
ALBUMS: Brand New Heavies (Acid Jazz 1990)★★★, Heavy Rhyme Experience: Vol. 1 (ffrr 1992)★★★, Brother Sister (ffrr 1994)★★★, Original Flava (Acid Jazz 1995)★★, Excursions: Remixes & Rare Grooves (Delicious Vinyl 1996)★★, Shelter (London 1997)★★★.

BRAND X
ALBUMS: Unorthodox Behaviour (Charisma 1976)★★★, Livestock (Charisma 1977)★★★, Moroccan Roll (Charisma 1977)★★★, Masques (Charisma 1978)★★★, Product (Charisma 1979)★★★, Do They Hurt (Charisma 1980)★★★, Is There Anything About (Columbia 1982)★★★, X-Trax (Passport 1987) Live At The Roxy LA 1979 (Zok 1996)★★, Xcommunication (Ozone 1992), Pillow Sack (Rough Side 1995), Manifest Destiny (Cleopatra 1997).
COMPILATIONS: The Plot Thins – A History Of (1992)★★★.

BRAXTON, TONI
ALBUMS: Toni Braxton (Arista 1994)★★★, Secrets (Arista 1996)★★★.
VIDEOS: The Home Video (1994).

BREAD
ALBUMS: Bread (Elektra 1969)★★, On The Waters (Elektra 1970)★★, Manna (Elektra 1971)★★★, Baby I'm-A Want You (Elektra 1972)★★★, Guitar Man (Elektra 1972)★★★, Lost Without Your Love (Elektra 1977)★★★, The Goodbye Girl (Elektra 1978)★★.
COMPILATIONS: The Best Of Bread (Elektra 1972)★★★, The Very Best Of Bread (Telstar 1987)★★★.

BREEDERS
ALBUMS: Pod (4AD 1990)★★★, Last Splash (4AD 1993)★★★, Live In Stockholm (Breeders' Digest 1995)★★★.

BREL, JACQUES
ALBUMS: Les Flamandes (Polydor 1998)★★★, Jef (Polydor 1998)★★★, Brel en Public Olympia 1961 (Polydor 1998)★★★, Brel en Public Olympia 1964 (Polydor 1998)★★★, L'Homme de la Mancha (Polydor 1998)★★.
COMPILATIONS: La Chanson Francais (1979)★★★, Music For The Millions (1983)★★★, Ses Plus Grandes Chansons (1984)★★★, Jacques Brel (1986)★★★, Le Plat Pays (1988)★★★, Greatest Hits (1993)★★★★.
FURTHER READING: Jacques Brel: The Biography, Alan Clayson, Jacques Brel J. Clouzet.

BRETT MARVIN AND THE THUNDERBOLTS
ALBUMS: Brett Marvin And The Thunderbolts (Sonet 1970)★★★, Twelve Inches Of Brett Marvin (Sonet 1971)★★, Best Of Friends (Sonet 1971)★★, Alias Terry Dactyl (Sonet 1972)★★, Ten Legged Friend (Sonet 1973)★★, Boogie Street (Exson 1993)★★.

BRICKELL, EDIE
ALBUMS: Shooting Rubberbands at the Stars (Geffen 1989)★★★, Ghost of a Dog (Geffen 1990)★★★, Picture Perfect Morning (Geffen 1994)★★.

BRINSLEY SCHWARZ
ALBUMS: Brinsley Schwarz (United Artists 1970)★★★, Despite It All (United Artists 1970)★★★, Silver Pistol (United Artists 1972)★★★★, Nervous On The Road (United Artists 1972)★★★, Please Don't Ever Change (United Artists 1973)★★★, The New Favourites Of Brinsley Schwarz (United Artists 1974)★★★★, 1991 Surrender to the Rhythm (EMI 1991).
COMPILATIONS: Original Golden Greats (United Artists 1974)★★★★, The Fifteen Thoughts Of Brinsley Schwarz (United Artists 1978)★★★★.

BRISTOL, JOHNNY
ALBUMS: Hang On In There Baby (MGM 1974)★★★, Bristol's Creme (Atlantic 1976)★★, Strangers (Polydor 1978)★★, Free To Be Me (Ariola Hansa 1981)H.

BROMBERG, DAVID
ALBUMS: David Bromberg (Columbia 1971)★★★, Demons In Disguise (Columbia 1972)★★★, Wanted Dead Or Alive (Columbia 1974)★★★, Midnight On The Water (1975)★★★, How Late'll Ya Play 'Til? (Fantasy 1976)★★★, Reckless Abandon (Fantasy 1977)★★★, Bandit In A Bathing Suit (Fantasy 1978)★★★, My Own House (Fantasy 1978)★★★, You Should See The Rest Of The Band (Fantasy 1980)★★★, Sideman Serenade (Rounder 1990)★★★, Player: Retrospective (Sony 1998).

BRONSKI BEAT
ALBUMS: The Age Of Consent (Forbidden Fruit 1984)★★★, Hundreds And Thousands (Forbidden Fruit 1985)★★★, TruthDareDoubleDare (Forbidden Fruit 1986)★★, Rainbow Nation (ZYX 1995), Bronski Beat (Polygram 1997).
VIDEOS: The First Chapter (1986).

BROOK BROTHERS
ALBUMS: Brook Brothers (Pye 1961)★★★.
FILMS: It's Trad, Dad aka Ring-A-Ding Rhythm (1962).

BROOKE, JONATHAN
ALBUMS: with the Story Grace In Gravity (Green Linnet 1990)★★, The Angel In The House (Elektra 1993)★★, as Jonatha Brooke And The Story Plumb (Blue Thumb 1996)★★★, 10 Cent Wings (Refuge/MCA 1997).

BROOKS, ELKIE
ALBUMS: Rich Man's Woman (A&M 1975)★★★, Two Days Away (A&M 1977)★★★, Shooting Star (A&M 1978)★★★, Live And Learn (A&M 1979)★★★, Pearls (A&M 1981)★★★, Pearls II (A&M 1982)★★, Minutes (A&M 1984)★★, Screen Gems (EMI 1984)★★, No More The Fool (Legend 1986)★★, Bookbinder's Kid (Legend 1988)★★★, 'Round Midnight (1993)★★, Pearls III (1993)★★, Circles (Permanent 1995)★★, Nothin' But the Blues (Castle 1996), From the Heart (Music Special 1996).
COMPILATIONS: The Very Best Of Elkie Brooks (A&M 1986)★★★, Collection: Elkie Brooks (Castle 1987)★★★, Priceless – Very Best Of Elkie Brooks (Pickwick 1991)★★★, We've Got Tonight (Spectrum 1995)★★★, The Pearls Concert (Artful 1997)★★★.
VIDEOS: We've Got Tonight (Video Collection 1987), No More The Fool (Gold Rushes 1987), Pearls – The Video Show (A&M Sound Pictures 1988).

BROOKS, GARTH
ALBUMS: Garth Brooks (Liberty 1989)★★★★, No Fences (Liberty 1990)★★★★, Ropin' The Wind (Liberty 1991)★★★, The Chase (Liberty 1992)★★★★, Beyond The Season (Liberty 1992)★★, In Pieces (Liberty 1993)★★★★, Fresh Horses (Capitol Nashville 1995)★★★, Seven (Capitol Nashville 1997)★★★.
COMPILATIONS: The Hits (Liberty 1994)★★★★.
VIDEOS: Garth Brooks (1991), This Is Garth Brooks (Live) (1992), The Video Collection Vol. II (Capitol 1996).
FURTHER READING: Garth Brooks: Platinum Cowboy, Edward Morris. One Of A Kind, Workin' On A Full House, Rick Mitchell.

BROOKS, HARVEY
ALBUMS: How To Play Electric Bass (1966)H.

BROS
ALBUMS: Push (Columbia 1988)★★★, The Time (Columbia 1989)★★★ Changing Faces (Columbia 1991)★★★.
VIDEOS: Live: The Big Push Tour (1988), Push Over (1989).
FURTHER READING: I Owe You Nothing: My Story, Luke Goss.

BROTHERHOOD OF MAN
ALBUMS: Love & Kisses From The Brotherhood Of Man (Pye 1976)★★, B For Brotherhood (Pye 1978)★★, Singing A Song (PRT 1979)★★, Sing 20 Number One Hits (Warwick 1980)★★, Lightning Flash (Epic 1983)★★.

BROWN, ARTHUR
ALBUMS: The Crazy World Of Arthur Brown (Track 1968)★★★, Galactic Zoo Dossier (1972)★★, The Journey (1972)★★, Dance (Gull 1974)★★, Chisholm In My Bosom (Gull 1978)H, with Vincent Crane Faster Than The Speed Of Light (1980)★★, Requiem (1982)★★, Strangelands (1988)★★, Order From Chaos – Live 1993 (Voiceprint 1994)★★★, Jam (Voiceprint 1995).

BROWN, BOBBY
ALBUMS: King Of Stage (MCA 1986)★★, Don't Be Cruel (MCA 1988)★★★★, Dance! ... Ya Know It! (MCA 1989)★★★★, Bobby (MCA 1992)★★★, Remixes N the Key of B (MCA 1993), Forever (MCA 1997)★★★.
VIDEOS: His Prerogative (MCA 1989).

BROWN, JAMES
ALBUMS: Please Please Please (King 1959)★★★, Try Me (King 1959)★★, Think (King 1960)★★★, The Amazing James Brown (King 1961)★★★, James Brown Presents His Band/Night Train (King 1961)★★★, Shout And Shimmy (King 1962)★★★, James Brown And His Famous Flames Tour The USA (King 1962)★★, Excitement Mr Dynamite (King 1962)★★★, Live At The Apollo (King 1963)★★★★★, Prisoner Of Love (King 1963)★★★, Pure Dynamite! Live At The Royal (King 1964)★★★, Showtime (Smash 1964)★★, The Unbeatable James Brown (King 1964)★★★, Grits And Soul (Smash 1964)★★, Out Of Sight (Smash 1964)★★★, Papa's Got A Brand New Bag (King 1965)★★★, James Brown Plays James Brown Today And Yesterday (Smash 1965)★★, I Got You (I Feel Good) (King 1966)★★★, Mighty Instrumentals (King 1966)★★, James Brown Plays New Breed (The Boo-Ga-Loo) (Smash 1966)★★, Soul Brother No. 1: It's A Man's Man's Man's World (King 1966)★★★, James Brown Sings Christmas Songs (King 1966)★★, Handful Of Soul (Smash 1966)★★, The James Brown Show (Smash 1967)★★, Sings Raw Soul (King 1967)★★★, James Brown Plays The Real Thing (Smash 1967)★★★, Live At The Garden (King 1967)★★, Cold Sweat (King 1967)★★★, James Brown Presents His Show Of Tomorrow (King 1968)★★★, I Can't Stand Myself (When You Touch Me) (King 1968)★★, I Got The Feelin' (King 1968)★★★, Live At The Apollo, Volume 2 (King 1968)★★★★, James Brown Sings Out Of Sight (King 1968)★★★, Thinking About Little Willie John And A Few Nice Things (King 1968)★★★, A Soulful Christmas (King 1968)★★, Say It Loud, I'm Black And I'm Proud (King 1969)★★★★, Gettin' Down To It (King 1969)★★★, The Popcorn (King 1969)★★★, It's A Mother (King 1969)★★★, Ain't It Funky (King 1970)★★★, Soul On Top (King 1970)★★★, It's A New Day – Let A Man Come In (King 1970)★★★, Sex Machine (King 1970)★★★, Hey America (King 1970)★★★, Super Bad (King 1971)★★, Sho' Is Funky Down Here (King 1971)★★, Hot Pants (Polydor 1971)★★, Revolution Of The Mind/Live At The Apollo, Volume 3 (Polydor 1971)★★★, There It Is (Polydor 1972)★★★, Get On The Good Foot (Polydor 1972)★★★, Black Caesar (Polydor 1973)★★★, Slaughter's Big Rip-Off (Polydor 1973)H, The Payback (Polydor 1974)★★★, Hell (Polydor 1974)★★★, Reality (Polydor 1975)★★★, Sex Machine Today (Polydor 1975)★★★, Everybody's Doin' The Hustle And Dead On The Double Bump (Polydor 1975)★★, Hot (Polydor 1976)★★★, Get Up Offa That Thing (Polydor 1976)★★, Bodyheat (Polydor 1976)★★, Mutha's Nature (Polydor 1977)★★★, Jam/1980's (Polydor 1978)★★★, Take A Look At Those Cakes (Polydor 1979)★★★, The Original Disco Man (Polydor 1979)★★★, People (Polydor 1980)★★★, James Brown ... Live/Hot On The One (Polydor 1980)★★, Soul Syndrome (TK 1980)★★★★, Nonstop! (Polydor 1981)★★★, Live In New York (Audio Fidelity 1981)★★★, Bring It On (Churchill 1983)★★★, Gravity (Scotti Brothers 1986)★★★, James Brown And Friends (Polydor 1988)★★★, I'm Real (Scotti Brothers 1988)★★★, Soul Session Live (Scotti Brothers 1989)★★★★, Love Over-Due (Scotti Brothers 1991)★★★, Universal James (1993)★★, Funky President (1993)★★★, Live At The Apollo 1995 (Scotti Brothers 1995)★★★, Try Me (Polydor 1996), Hookedonbrown (Scotti Brothers 1996), Dead On The Heavy Funk (Polygram 1998).
COMPILATIONS: James Brown Soul Classics (Polydor 1972)★★★, Soul Classics, Volume 2 (Polydor 1973)★★★, Solid Gold (Polydor 1977)★★★, The Fabulous James Brown (HRB 1977)★★★, Can Your Heart Stand It? (Solid Smoke 1981)★★★, The Best Of James Brown (Polydor 1981)★★★★, The Federal Years, Part 1 (Solid Smoke 1984)★★★★, The Federal Years, Part 2 (Solid Smoke 1984)★★★, Roots Of A Revolution (1984)★★★, Ain't That A Groove – The James Brown Story 1966-1969 (Polydor 1984)★★★, Doing It To Death – The James Brown Story 1970-1973 (Polydor 1984)★★★, Dead On The Heavy Funk 1974-1976 (Polydor 1985)★★★, The CD Of JB: Sex Machine And Other Soul Classics (Polydor 1985)★★★★, James Brown's Funky People (Polydor 1986)★★★★, In The Jungle Groove (Polydor 1986)★★★, The CD Of JB (Cold Sweat And Other Soul Classics) (Polydor 1987)★★★★, James Brown's Funky People (Part 2) (Polydor 1988)★★★, Motherlode (Polydor 1988)★★★, Messin' With The Blues (Polydor 1990)★★★, 20 All-Time Greatest Hits! (Polydor 1991)★★★★, Star Time 4-CD box set (Polydor 1991)★★★★★, The Greatest Hits Of The Fourth Decade (Scotti Brothers 1992)★★★, Chronicles – Soul Pride (1993)★★★, JB40: 40th Anniversary Collection (Polydor 1996)★★★★, On Stage (Charly 1997)★★★.
FILMS: The Blues Brothers (1980).
VIDEOS: Video Biography (Virgin Vision 1988), Live In London: James Brown (Virgin Vision 1988), James Brown And Friends (Video Collection 1988), Live In Berlin (Channel 5 1989), Soul Jubilee (MMG Video 1990), Live On Stage (With Special Guest B.B. King) (Old Gold 1990), Sex Machine (The Very Best Of James Brown) (Polygram Music Video 1991), The Lost Years (Live In Santa Cruz) (BMG Video 1991), Live In New York (Enteleky 1991), James Brown Live (MIA 1995).
FURTHER READING: James Brown: The Godfather Of Soul, James Brown with Bruce Tucker. Living In America: The Soul Saga Of James Brown, Cynthia Rose. James Brown: A Biography, Geoff Brown.

BROWN, JOE
ALBUMS: A Picture Of Joe Brown (Ace Of Clubs 1962)★★★, Live (Piccadilly 1963)★★★, A Picture Of You (Piccadilly 1965)★★★, Here Comes Joe! (Pye 1967)★★, Joe Brown (MCA 1968)★★★, Browns Home Brew (Bell 1972)★★, Together (1974)★★★, Joe Brown Live (1977)★★★, Come On Joe (1993)★★★, Live ... And in the Studio (See For Miles 1995), Fifty Six And Taller Than You Think (Demon 1997)★★★.
COMPILATIONS: Joe Brown Collection (1974)★★★, The Joe Brown Story 2-CD (Sequel 1993)★★★.

BROWNE, JACKSON
ALBUMS: Jackson Browne aka Saturate Before Using (Asylum 1972)★★★★, For Everyman (Asylum 1973)★★★★, Late For The Sky (Asylum 1974)★★★★, The Pretender (Asylum 1976)★★★★, Running On Empty (Asylum 1977)★★★, Hold Out (Asylum 1980)★★, Lawyers In Love (Asylum 1983)★★★, Lives In The Balance (Asylum 1986)★★,Worlds In Motion (Elektra 1989)★★, I'm Alive (Elektra 1994)★★★★, Looking East (Elektra 1996)★★, Everywhere I Go (European Import 1996)★★.

BRUCE, JACK
ALBUMS: Songs For A Tailor (Polydor 1969)★★★★, Things We Like (Polydor 1970)★★★, Harmony Row (Polydor 1971)★★★, Out Of The Storm (Polydor 1974)★★★, How's Tricks (RSO 1977)★★★, I've Always Wanted To Do This (Epic 1980)★★★, with Robin Trower Truce (Chrysalis 1982)★★★, Automatic (President 1987)★★, A Question Of Time (Epic 1990)★★★, And Friends Live At The Bottom Line (Traditional Line 1992)★★★, Something Else (1993)★★★, Cities Of the Heart (CMP 1994)★★★★, with Paul Jones Alexis Korner Memorial Concert Vol. 1 (Indigo 1995)★★★, BBC Radio 1 in Concert (live) (Windsong 1995), Monkjack (CMP 1995), Sitting on the Top of the World (Times Square 1997).
COMPILATIONS: Jack Bruce At His Best (Polydor 1972)★★★, Greatest Hits (Polydor 1980)★★★, Willpower (Polydor 1989)★★★, The Collection (Castle 1992)★★★.
FURTHER READING: Quiet Man (Jack Bruce, 1990 Sidgwick and Jackson)

BRUFORD, BILL
ALBUMS: Feels Good To Me (Polydor 1978)★★, One Of A Kind (Polydor 1979)★★, The Bruford Tapes (Editions EG 1980)★★★★, Gradually Going Tornado (Editions EG 1980)★★★, Earthworks (Editions EG 1987)★★★★, Dig (Editions EG 1989)★★★, All Heaven Broke Loose (1991)★★★, Earthworks Live (Virgin 1994)★★, Stamping Ground (live) (Editions 1994), Heavenly Bodies (Venutre 1997), If Summer Had Its Ghosts (Discipline 1997).
COMPILATIONS: Master Strokes 1978-1985 (Editions EG 1986)★★★.

BRYANT, BOUDLEAUX
ALBUMS: Boudleaux Bryant's Best Sellers (Monument 1963)★★★, All I Have To Do Is Dream aka A Touch Of Bryant (CMH 1979)★★, Surfin' On A New Wave (1979)★★.

BRYANT, FELICE
ALBUMS: A Touch Of Bryant (CMH 1979)★★, Surfin' On A New Wave (1979)★★.

BRYSON, PEABO
ALBUMS: Reaching For The Sky (Capitol 1978)★★★, Crosswinds (Capitol 1978)★★★, with Natalie Cole We're The Best Of Friends (Capitol 1979)★★★, Paradise (Capitol 1980)★★★, with Roberta Flack Live And More (Atlantic 1980)★★★, Turn The Hands Of Time (Capitol 1981)★★★, I Am Love (Capitol 1981)★★★, Don't Play With Fire (Capitol 1982)★★★, with Flack Born To Love (Capitol 1983)★★★, Straight From The Heart (Elektra 1984)★★★, Take No Prisoners (Elektra 1985)★★★, Quiet Storm (Elektra 1986)★★★, Positive (Elektra 1988)★★★, Can You Stop The Rain (Columbia 1991)★★★, Tonight I Celebrate My Love (CEMA 1992), Through the Fire (Columbia 1994), Peace on Earth (Capitol 1997).
COMPILATIONS: The Peabo Bryson Collection (Capitol 1984)★★★★.

BUCKINGHAM, LINDSEY
ALBUMS: Law And Order (Asylum 1981)★★★, Go Insane (Elektra 1984)★★, Out Of The Cradle (Reprise 1992)★★.

BUCKINGHAMS
ALBUMS: Kind Of A Drag (USA 1967)★★★, Time And Changes (Columbia 1967)★★★, Portraits (Columbia 1968)★★★, In One Ear And Gone Tomorrow (Columbia 1968)★★, Made In Chicago (1969)★★, A Matter of Time (Red Label 1985).
COMPILATIONS: The Buckinghams' Greatest Hits (Columbia 1969)★★★.
VIDEOS: Made in the USA (Hollywood 1992).

BUCKLEY, JEFF
ALBUMS: Live At Sin-e mini-album (Big Cat 1992)★★★,

Grace (Sony 1994)★★★★, Live From The Bataclan mini-album (Columbia 1996)★★.

BUCKLEY, TIM
ALBUMS: Tim Buckley (Elektra 1966)★★★, Goodbye And Hello (Elektra 1967)★★★, Happy Sad (Elektra 1968)★★★★, Blue Afternoon (Straight 1969)★★★★, Lorca (Elektra 1969)★★★, Starsailor (Straight 1970)★★★, Greetings From LA (Warners 1972)★★★, Sefronia (DiscReet 1974)★★, Look At The Fool (DiscReet 1975)★★, Dream Letter-Live In London 1968 (Demon 1990)★★★★, The Peel Sessions (Strange Fruit 1991)★★★, Live At The LA Troubadour 1969 (Edsel 1994)★★★, Honeyman 1973 live recording (Edsel 1995)★★★. Morning Glory (Band of Joy 1995).
COMPILATIONS: The Best Of Tim Buckley (Rhino 1983)★★★.

BUCKS FIZZ
ALBUMS: Bucks Fizz (RCA 1981)★★, Are You Ready? (RCA 1982)★★, Hand Cut (RCA 1983)★★, I Hear Talk (RCA 1984)★★, The Writing On The Wall (Polydor 1986)★★.
COMPILATIONS: Greatest Hits (RCA 1983)★★★, The Story So Far (Stylus 1988)★★, Golden Days (RCA 1992)★★★, Greatest Hits Of ... (RCA/Camden 1996)★★★.
VIDEOS: Greatest Hits: Bucks Fizz (1986).

BUDGIE
ALBUMS: Budgie (MCA 1971)★★, Squawk (MCA 1972)★★, Never Turn Your Back On A Friend (MCA 1973)★★, In For The Kill (MCA 1974)★★, Bandolier (MCA 1975)★★, If I Was Brittania I'd Waive The Rules (A&M 1976)★★, Impeckable (A&M 1978)★★, Power Supply (Active 1980)★★, Nightflight (RCA 1981)★★, Deliver Us From Evil (RCA 1982)★★.
COMPILATIONS: An Ecstacy Of Fumbling: The Definitive Anthology (Repertoire 1996)★★★.

BUFFALO SPRINGFIELD
ALBUMS: Buffalo Springfield (Atco 1967)★★★★, Buffalo Springfield Again (Atco 1967)★★★★★, Last Time Around (Atco 1968)★★★★.
COMPILATIONS: Retrospective (Atco 1969)★★★★, Expecting to Fly (Atlantic 1970)★★★★, Buffalo Springfield (Atco 1973)★★★★.
FURTHER READING: Neil Young: Here We Are In The Years, Johnny Rogan. Crosby, Stills And Nash: The Authorized Biography, Dave Zimmer. For What It's Worth: The Story Of Buffalo Springfield, John Einarson and Richie Furay.

BUFFALO TOM
ALBUMS: Sunflower Suit (SST 1989)★★★, Birdbrain (Situation 2 1990)★★★, Let Me Come Over (Situation 2 1992)★★★★, Big Red Letter Day (Beggars Banquet 1993)★★★, Sleepy Eyed (Beggars Banquet 1995)★★★.
Solo: Bill Janowitz Lonesome Billy (Beggars Banquet 1996)★★★.

BUFFETT, JIMMY
ALBUMS: Down To Earth (Barnaby 1970)★★, A White Sport Coat And A Pink Crustacean (ABC 1973)★★★, Living And Dying In 3/4 Time (ABC 1974)★★, A1A (ABC 1974)★★★, Rancho DeLuxe film soundtrack (United Artists 1975)★★★, Havana Daydreaming (ABC 1976)★★★, High Cumberland Jubilee recorded 1972 (Barnaby 1976)★★★, Changes In Latitudes, Changes In Attitudes (ABC 1977)★★★, Son Of A Son Of A Sailor (ABC 1978)★★★, You Had To Be There (ABC 1978)★★★, Volcano (MCA 1979)★★★, Coconut Telegraph (MCA 1981)★★, Somewhere Over China (MCA 1982)★★, Fast Times At Ridgemont High (Full Moon/Asylum 1982)★★, One Particular Harbour (MCA 1983)★★, Riddles In The Sand (MCA 1984)★★, Last Mango In Paris (MCA 1985)★★, Floridays (MCA 1986)★★, Hot Water (MCA 1988)★★, Off To See The Lizard (MCA 1989)★★, Always film soundtrack (MCA 1990)★★, Live Feeding Frenzy (MCA 1990)★★, Before The Beach reissue of Barnaby material (Margaritaville/MCA 1993)★★, Fruitcakes (MCA 1994)★★★★, Barometer Soup (Margaritaville 1995)★★★★, Banana Wind (Margaritaville 1996)★★★★, Christmas Island (Margaritaville 1996)★★★, Don't Stop the Carnival (Polygram 1998).
COMPILATIONS: Songs You Know By Heart – Greatest Hits box set (MCA 1985)★★★★, Boats Beaches, Bars And Ballads 4-CD box set (MCA 1992)★★★★, All The Great Hits (Prism Leisure 1994)★★★.
VIDEOS: Live By the Bay (MCA 1986)
FURTHER READING: The Jimmy Buffett Scrapbook, Mark Humphrey with Harris Lewine. The Man From Margaritaville Revisited, Steve Eng.

BUGGLES
ALBUMS: The Age Of Plastic (Island 1980)★★, Adventures in Modern Recording (EMI 1982).

BURDON, ERIC
ALBUMS: as Eric Burdon and War Eric Burdon Declares War (Polydor 1970) ★★★, as Eric Burdon and War Black Man's Burdon (Liberty 1971) ★★★, the Eric Burdon Band and Jimmy Witherspoon Guilty! (United Artists 1971) ★★★, Ring Of Fire (Capitol 1974)★★★, Sun Secrets (Capitol 1975) ★★, Stop (Capitol 1975) ★★, Survivor (Polydor 1978) ★★, Darkness – Darkness (Polydor 1980) ★★, as Eric Burdon's Fire Department The Last Drive (Ariol 1980) ★★, Comeback (Line 1982) ★★★ reissued as The Road (Thunderbolt 1984), as The Eric Burdon Band Comeback new songs from 1982 session (Blackline 1983) ★★, Power Company aka Devil's Daughter new songs from 1982 session (Carrere 1983) ★★, as The Eric Burdon Band That's Live (In-Akustik 1985) ★★, I Used To Be An Animal (Striped Horse 1988) ★★, Wicked Man reissue of Comeback/Power Company material (GNP Crescendo 1988) ★★, with Robby Krieger The 1990 Detroit Tapes (1991) ★★, The Unreleased Eric Burdon (Blue Wave 1992) ★★, Crawling King Snake (Thunderbolt 1992) ★★, with Brian Augur Access All Areas (SPV 1993) ★★, Misunderstood (Aim 1995) ★★, Live (Receiver 1996), Soldier of Fortune (Thunderbolt 1997), Live at the Roxy (Thunderbolt 1998).
COMPILATIONS: Star Portrait (Polydor 1988) ★★★.
FILMS: The Eleventh Victim (1979), Movin' On (1987), The Doors (1990).
VIDEOS: Finally (Warners 1992), Animals & Beyond (A*vision 1991).
FURTHER READING: Wild Animals, Andy Blackford. I Used To Be An Animal But I'm All Right Now, Eric Burdon. The Last Poet: The Story Of Eric Burdon, Jeff Kent. Good Times: The Ultimate Eric Burdon, Dionisio Castello.

BURKE, SOLOMON
ALBUMS: Solomon Burke (Apollo 1962)★★★, If You Need Me (Atlantic 1963)★★★, Rock 'N' Soul (Atlantic 1964)★★★, I Wish I Knew (Atlantic 1968)★★★, King Solomon (Atlantic 1968)★★★, Proud Mary (Bell 1969)★★★★, Electronic Magnetism (Polydor 1972)★★, King Heavy (1972)★★, We're Almost Home (Polydor 1972)★★, I Have A Dream (Dunhill 1974)★★, Midnight And You (Dunhill 1975)★★, Music To Make Love By (Chess 1975)★★, Back To My Roots (Chess 1977)★★, Please Don't You Say Goodbye To Me (Amherst 1978)★★★, Sidewalks Fences & Walls (Infinity 1979)★★, Lord I Need A Miracle Right Now (Savoy 1981)★★, Into My Life You Came (Savoy 1982)★★, Take Me, Shake Me (Savoy 1983)★★, This Is His Song (Savoy 1984)★★, Soul Alive (Rounder 1984)★★, A Change Is Gonna Come (Rounder 1986)★★★, Love Trap (Polygram 1987)★★★, The Bishop Rides South (Charly 1988)★★★★, Home Land (Bizarre 1991)★★★, Soul Of The Blues (Black Top 1993)★★★, Live At The House Of Blues (Black Top 1994)★★, Definition Of Soul (Pointblank/Virgin 1997)★★★, We Need a Miracle (601 1998).
COMPILATIONS: Solomon Burke's Greatest Hits (Atlantic 1962)★★★, I Almost Lost My Mind (1964)★★★, The Best Of Solomon Burke (Atlantic 1965)★★★★, King Of Rock 'N' Soul/From The Heart (Charly 1981)★★★, Cry To Me (Charly 1984)★★★★, You Can Run But You Can't Hide (Mr R&B 1987)★★★, Hold On I'm Coming (1991)★★★, Home In Your Heart: The Best Of Solomon Burke (Rhino 1992)★★★★, The King Of Soul (1993)★★★, Greatest Hits: If You Need Me (Sequel 1997)★★★.
VIDEOS: Purely Music Series (Defilm Produce 1995).

BURNETT, T-BONE
ALBUMS: The B-52 Band And the Fabulous Skyhawks (Uni 1972)★★★, J. Henry Burnett (1972)★★★, Truth Decay (Takoma 1980)★★★, Behind The Trap Door (Warners 1982)★★★, Proof Through the Night (Warners 1983)★★★, T-Bone Burnett (Dot 1986)★★, The Talking Animals (Columbia 1988)★★, The Criminal Under My Own Hat (Columbia 1992)★★★.

BURNETTE, DORSEY
ALBUMS: Tall Oak Tree (Era 1960)★★, Dorsey Burnette Sings (Dot 1963)★★, Dorsey Burnette's Greatest Hits (Era 1969)★★★, Things I Treasure (Calliope 70s)★★, Big Rock Candy Mountain (Richmond 1996).
COMPILATIONS: Great Shakin' Fever (Bear Family 1992)★★★.

BURNETTE, JOHNNY
ALBUMS: as the Johnny Burnette Trio Rock 'N' Roll Trio (Coral 1957)★★★★, Dreamin' (Liberty 1961)★★★, You're Sixteen (Liberty 1961)★★★, Johnny Burnette (Liberty 1961)★★★, Johnny Burnette Sings (Liberty 1961)★★★, Burnette's Hits And Other Favourites (Liberty 1962)★★★, Roses Are Red (Liberty 1962)★★★.
COMPILATIONS: The Johnny Burnette Story (Liberty 1964)★★★★, with the Rock 'n' Roll Trio Tear It Up (Solid Smoke/Coral 1968)★★★, Tenth Anniversary Album (United Artists 1974)★★★, We're Having A Party (1988)★★★, The Best Of Johnny Burnette (1989)★★★★, Rockabilly Boogie (MCA 1989), You're Sixteen: The Best Of Johnny Burnette (Capitol 1992)★★★★.

BURNING SPEAR
ALBUMS: Studio One Presents Burning Spear (Studio One 1973)★★★, Rocking Time (Studio One 1974)★★★, Marcus Garvey (Mango/Island 1975)★★★★★, Man In The Hills (Fox-Wolf/Island 1976)★★★★, Garvey's Ghost (Mango/Island 1976)★★★★, Dry & Heavy (Mango/Island 1977)★★★★, Burning Spear Live (Island 1977)★★★, Marcus Children aka Social Living (Burning Spear/One Stop 1978)★★★★, Living Dub (Burning Spear/Heartbeat 1979)★★★, Hail H.I.M. (Burning Spear/EMI 1980)★★★, Living Dub Vol. 2 (Burning Spear 1981)★★★, Farover (Burning Spear/Heartbeat 1982)★★★, Fittest Of The Fittest (Burning Spear/Heartbeat 1983)★★★, Resistance (Heartbeat 1985)★★★★, People Of The World (Slash/Greensleeves 1986)★★★, Mistress Music (Slash/Greensleeves 1988)★★, Live In Paris: Zenith '88 double album (Slash/Greensleeves 1989)★★★, Mek We Dweet (Mango/Island 1990)★★★, Jah Kingdom (Mango/Island 1992)★★★, The World Should Know (Mango/Island 1993)★★★, Rasta Business (Heartbeat 1996)★★★, Appointment With His Majesty (Heartbeat 1997), Living Dub, Vol. 3 (Heartbeat 1997).
COMPILATIONS: Reggae Greats (Island 1985)★★★★, Selection (EMI 1987)★★★★, 100th Anniversary Marcus Garvey and Garvey's Ghost (Mango/Island 1990)★★★★, Chant Down Babylon: The Island Anthology (Island 1996)★★★★.
VIDEOS: Paris Zenith '88 (RAS 1992).

BURTON, JAMES
ALBUMS: with Ralph Mooney Corn Pickin' And Slick Slidin' (Capitol 1969)★★, The Guitar Sounds Of James Burton (A&M 1971)★★.

BUSH
ALBUMS: Sixteen Stone (Trauma/Interscope 1995)★★★★, Little Things (Interscope 1995)★★★, Razorblade Suitcase (Trauma 1996)★★★★, Deconstructed remixes (Trauma 1997)★★★.

BUSH, KATE
ALBUMS: The Kick Inside (EMI 1978)★★★★, Lionheart (EMI 1978)★★, Never For Ever (EMI 1980)★★★, The Dreaming (EMI 1982)★★★★, Hounds Of Love (EMI 1985)★★★★, The Sensual World (EMI 1989)★★★★, The Red Shoes (EMI 1993)★★★.
COMPILATIONS: The Whole Story (EMI 1986)★★★, This Woman's Work (EMI 1990)★★★★.
VIDEOS: Live At Hammersmith Odeon (1984), The Whole Story (1986), Hair Of The Hound (1986), Sensual World (1990), The Single File (1992), The Line, The Cross & The Curve (1994).
FURTHER READING: Kate Bush: An Illustrated Biography, Paul Kerton. Leaving My Tracks, Kate Bush. The Secret History Of Kate Bush (& The Strange Art Of Pop), Fred Vermorel. Kate Bush: The Whole Story, Kerry Juby. Kate Bush: A Visual Documentary, Kevin Cann and Sean Mayes, Kate Bush: Princess of Suburbia Fred and Judy Vermorel, Target Books.

BUTTERFIELD, PAUL
ALBUMS: Paul Butterfield Blues Band (Elektra 1966)★★★★, East-West (Elektra 1966)★★★★, The Resurrection Of Pigboy Crabshaw (Elektra 1968)★★★, In My Own Dream (Elektra 1968)★★★, Keep On Movin' (Elektra 1969)★★, Live (Elektra 1971)★★, Sometimes I Just Feel Like Smilin' (Elektra 1971)★★, Offer You Can't Refuse (1972)★★, as Better Days It All Comes Back (Bearsville 1973)★★, as Better Days Better Days (Bearsville 1973)★★★, Put It In Your Ear (Bearsville 1976)★★, North South For Bearsville (Bearsville 1981)★★, The Legendary Paul Butterfield Rides Again (1986)★★★, Lost Elektra Sessions (Rhino 1995)★★, Strawberry Jam (Winner 1996)★★.
COMPILATIONS: Golden Butter – Best Of The Paul Butterfield Blues Band (Elektra 1972)★★★.

BUTTHOLE SURFERS
ALBUMS: Butthole Surfers (Alternative Tentacles 1983)★★★, Live PCP PEP (Alternative Tentacles 1984)★★★, Psychic ... Powerless ... Another Man's Sac (Touch And Go 1985)★★★, Rembrandt Pussyhorse (Touch And Go 1986)★★★, Locust Abortion Technician (Touch And Go 1987)★★★, Hairway To Steven (Touch And Go 1988)★★★, pioughd (Rough Trade 1991)★★, Independent Worm Saloon (Capitol 1993)★★, Electriclarryland (Capitol 1996)★★★★, After the Astronaut (Capitol 1998).
Solo: Paul Leary The History Of Dogs (Rough Trade 1991)★★★.
COMPILATIONS: Double Live (Latino Bugger 1989)★★★, The Hole Truth ... And Nothing But (Trance Syndicate 1995)★★★.
VIDEOS: Blind Eye Sees All (Touch And Go).

BUZZCOCKS
ALBUMS: Another Music In A Different Kitchen (United Artists 1978)★★★★, Love Bites (United Artists 1978)★★★, A Different Kind Of Tension (United Artists 1979)★★★, Trade Test Transmissions (Castle 1993)★★★, French (IRS 1995)★★, All Set (IRS 1996)★★.
COMPILATIONS: Singles – Going Steady (EMI 1981)★★★★, Lest We Forget (ROIR 1988)★★★, Live At The Roxy, April '77 (Absolutely Free 1989)★★★, Product 3-CD box set (EMI 1989)★★★, The Peel Sessions Album (Strange Fruit 1990)★★★, Operator's Manual – Buzzcocks Best (EMI 1991)★★★★, Entertaining Friends (EMI 1992)★★★, Chronology (EMI 1997)★★★.
VIDEOS: Auf Wiedersehen (Ikon Video 1989), Live Legends (Castle Music Pictures 1990), Playback (IRS 1992).
FURTHER READING: Buzzcocks: The Complete History, Tony McGartland.

BYRDS
ALBUMS: Mr Tambourine Man (Columbia 1965)★★★★, Turn! Turn! Turn! (Columbia 1965)★★★★, Fifth Dimension (Columbia 1966)★★★★, Younger Than Yesterday (Columbia 1967)★★★★★, The Notorious Byrd Brothers (Columbia 1968)★★★★★, Sweetheart Of The Rodeo (Columbia 1968)★★★★, Dr Byrds & Mr Hyde (Columbia 1969)★★★, Ballad Of Easy Rider (Columbia 1969)★★★, The Byrds (Untitled) (Columbia 1970)★★★★, Byrdmaniax (Columbia 1971)★★, Farther Along (Columbia 1972)H, Byrds (Asylum 1973)★★★, Doin' All Right (Excitable 1978), Never Before (Murray Hill 1989).
Three archive albums are also available: Preflyte (Together 1969)★★, Never Before (Murray Hill 1989)★★★, In The Beginning (Rhino 1989)★★★.
COMPILATIONS: Greatest Hits (Columbia 1967)★★★★, Greatest Hits, Vol. II (Columbia 1971)★★★, History Of The Byrds (CBS 1973)★★★★, The Byrds Play Dylan (CBS 1979)★★★, The Original Singles (CBS 1980)★★★★, The Original Singles, Vol. II (CBS 1982)★★★, The Byrds Collection (Castle 1989)★★★, The Byrds 4-CD box set (CBS Legacy 1990)★★★★, 20 Essential Tracks (1993)★★★★, The Very Best Of The Byrds (Columbia 1997)★★★★.
FURTHER READING: Timeless Flight: The Definitive Biography Of The Byrds, Johnny Rogan. The Byrds, Bud Scoppa. Timeless Flight Revisited, Johnny Rogan.

BYRNE, DAVID
ALBUMS: with Brian Eno My Life In The Bush Of Ghosts (Polydor 1981)★★★★, The Complete Score From The Broadway Production Of The Catherine Wheel soundtrack (Sire 1981)★★★★, Music For The Knee Plays (ECM 1985)★★★, with Ryuichi Sakamoto, Cong Su The Last Emperor film soundtrack (Virgin 1987)★★★, Rei Momo (Warners 1989)★★★, The Forest film soundtrack (Warners 1991)★★★, Uh-Oh (Luaka Bop 1992)★★★, David Byrne (Luaka Bop/Warners 1994)★★, Feelings (Warners 1997)★★★.
VIDEOS: True Stories (1986), Catherine Wheel (Sire 1989), David Byrne: Between The Teeth (1993).
FURTHER READING: American Originals: David Byrne, John Howell. Strange Ritual: Pictures And Words, David Byrne.

C

CABARET VOLTAIRE
ALBUMS: Mix Up (Rough Trade 1979)★★, Live At The YMCA 27.10.79. (Rough Trade 1979)★★, Three Mantras (Rough Trade 1980)★★, The Voice Of America (Rough Trade 1980)★★, Red Mecca (Rough Trade 1981)★★★, Johnny Yesno film soundtrack (Doublevision 1981)★★, Live At The Lyceum (Rough Trade 1981)★★★, 2 x 45 (Rough Trade 1982)★★★, Hai! (Rough Trade 1982)★★★, The Crackdown (Some Bizzare 1983)★★★, Micro-Phonies (Some Bizzare 1984)★★★, Drinking Gasoline (Some Bizzare 1985)★★★, The Covenant, The Sword And The Arm Of The Lord (Some Bizzare 1985)★★★, Code (Parlophone 1987)★★★★, Groovy, Laid Back And Nasty (Parlophone 1990)★★★, Body And Soul (Cr≥pescule 1991)★★★, Percussion Force (Cr≥pescule 1991)★★★, International Language (1993)★★★, The Conversation (1994)★★★.
Solo: Richard H. Kirk Disposable Half Truths (Rough Trade 1981)★★★, Time High Fiction (Rough Trade 1983)★★★, Black Jesus Voice (Rough Trade 1986)★★, Ugly Spirit mini-album (Rough Trade 1986)★★★, with Peter Hope Hoodoo Talk (Native-Wax Trax!)★★. Stephen Mallinder Pow Wow (Fetish 1982)★★, Pow Wow Plus (Doublevision 1985)★★.
COMPILATIONS: The Golden Moments Of Cabaret Voltaire (Rough Trade 1987)★★★, 8 Cr≥pescule Tracks (Interior Music 1988)★★★, Listen Up With Cabaret Voltaire (Mute 1990)★★★, Technology (Virgin 1992)★★★.
VIDEOS: TV Wipeout (1984), Gasoline In Your Eye (Virgin Vision 1985), Cabaret Voltaire (BMG Video 1990).

CAGE, JOHN
ALBUMS: Music Of Changes (1951)★★★, Imaginary Landscape No. 4 (1951)★★★, Concerto For Prepared Piano And Orchestra (1968)★★★★, Cartridge Music (1969)★★★, Hpschd (1970)★★★, Child Of Tree (1975)★★★, Sonata And Interlude For Prepared Piano (1976)★★★★, Telephones And Birds (1977)★★★★, John Cage (1979)★★★★, Atlas Eclipticals For Three Flutes (1992)★★★, Fontana Mix & Solo For Voice 2 (1993), Europera Vol. 5 (Mode 1994), Sonatas and Interludes for Prepared Piano (CRI 1995), Europera Vol. 3 (Mode 1995), Europera Vol. 4 (Mode 1995), Music of Changes Books I-IV (Lovely Music 1996).
FURTHER READING: For The Birds, John Cage and Daniel Charles. John Cage, Heinz-Klaus Metzger and Rainer Riehn.

CALE, J.J.
ALBUMS: Naturally (Shelter 1971)★★★, Really (Shelter 1972)★★★, Okie (Shelter 1974)★★★, Troubadour (Shelter 1976)★★★, Five (Shelter 1979)★★★, Shades (Shelter 1981)★★★, Grasshopper (Mercury 1982)★★, 8 (Mercury 1983)★★, Travel Log (Silvertone 1989)★★★, Ten (1992)★★★, Closer To You (Virgin 1994)★★★, Guitar Man (Virgin 1996)★★★.
COMPILATIONS: Special Edition (Mercury 1984)★★★, La Femme De Mon Pote (Mercury 1984)★★★, Nightriding (Nightriding 1988)★★★, Anyway The Wind Blows: The Anthology (Mercury Chronicles 1997)★★★★.

CALE, JOHN
ALBUMS: Vintage Violence (Columbia 1970)★★★, with Terry Riley Church Of Anthrax (Columbia 1971)★★★, The Academy In Peril(Reprise 1972)★★★, Paris 1919 (Reprise 1973)★★★★, Fear (Island 1974)★★★, as ACNE June 1 1974 (Island 1974)★★, Slow Dazzle (Island 1975)★★★, Helen Of Troy (Island 1975)★★, Sabotage/Live (Spy 1979)★★, Honi Soit (A&M 1981)★★, Music For A New Society (Ze 1982)★★★, Caribbean Sunset (Ze 1984)★★, John Cale Comes Alive (Ze 1984)★★★, Artificial Intelligence (Beggars Banquet 1985)★★★, Words For The Dying (Land 1989)★★★, with Lou Reed Songs For 'Drella (Warners 1990)★★★★, with Brian Eno Wrong Way Up (Land 1990)★★★, Even Cowgirls Get The Blues (1991)★★, Fragments Of A Rainy Season (Hannibal 1992)★★★, with Bob Neuwirth Last Day On Earth (MCA 1994)★★★, Paris S'Eveille (Crepuscule 1995)★★★, 23 Solo Pieces For La Naissance De L'Amour (Crepuscule 1995)★★★, Walking On Locusts (Hannibal/Ryko 1996)★★★, Eat/Kiss: Music For The Films Of Andy Warhol(Hannibal 1997)★★★.
COMPILATIONS: Guts (Island 1977)★★★★, Seducing Down The Door: A Collection 1970-1990 (Rhino 1994)★★★★, The Island Years (Island 1996)★★★.
VIDEOS: Songs For Drella (Warner Music Video 1991).

CAMEL
ALBUMS: Camel(MCA 1973)★★, Mirage (Deram 1974)★★, The Snow Goose (Decca 1975)★★★, Moonmadness (Decca 1976)★★★, Rain Dances (Decca 1977)★★★, A Live Record (Decca 1978)★★, Breathless (Decca 1978)★★, I Can See Your House From Here (Decca 1979)★★★, Nude (Decca 1981)★★★, The Single Factor (Decca 1982)★★, Stationary Traveller (Decca 1984)★★, Pressure Points (Decca 1984)★★, Never Let Go (Camel Productions 1993)★★, Harbour Of Tears (Camel Productions 1996)★★, On the Road 1982 (live) (Camel Productions 1996), On the Road 1981 (live) (Camel Productions 1997).
COMPILATIONS: The Camel Collection (Castle 1985)★★★.
VIDEOS: Pressure Points (Camel Live) (Polygram Music Video 1984).

CAMEO
ALBUMS: Cardiac Arrest (Chocolate City 1977)★★, We All Know Who We Are (Chocolate City 1978)★★, Ugly Ego (Chocolate City 1978)★★, Secret Omen (Chocolate City 1979)★★, Cameosis (Chocolate City 1980)★★★, Feel Me (Chocolate City 1980)★★★, Knights Of The Sound Table (Chocolate City 1981)★★★, Alligator Woman (Chocolate City 1982)★★, Style (Atlanta Artists 1983)★★★, She's Strange (Atlanta Artists 1984)★★★, Single Life (Atlanta Artists 1985)★★★★, Word Up! (Atlanta Artists 1986)★★★★, Machismo (Atlanta Artists 1988)★★★, Real Men Wear Black (Atlanta Artists 1990)★★★, Emotional Violence (Reprise 1992)★★★, In the Face of Funk (Way Too Funky 1994)★★, Nasty (Intersound 1996)★★.
COMPILATIONS: Best Of Cameo (Phonogram 1993)★★★★.
VIDEOS: Cameo: The Video Singles (Channel 5 1987), Back And Forth (Club 1987), Candy (Atlanta Artist 1987), Word Up: Video (Polygram).

CAMPBELL, GLEN
ALBUMS: Too Late To Worry, Too Late To Cry (Capitol 1963)★★★, The Astounding 12-String Guitar Of Glen Campbell (Capitol 1964)★★★, The Big Bad Rock Guitar Of Glen Campbell (Capitol 1965)★★★, Gentle On My Mind (Capitol 1967)★★★, By The Time I Get To Phoenix (Capitol 1967)★★★, Hey, Little One (Capitol 1968)★★★, A New Place In The Sun (Capitol 1968)★★★, Bobbie Gentry And Glen Campbell(Capitol 1968)★★★, Wichita Lineman (Capitol 1968)★★★, That Christmas Feeling (Capitol 1968)★★, Galveston (Capitol 1969)★★★, Glen Campbell- Live (Capitol 1969)★★, Try A Little Kindness (Capitol 1970)★★★, Oh Happy Day (Capitol 1970)★★★, Norwood film soundtrack (Capitol 1970)★★, The Glen Campbell Goodtime Album (Capitol 1970)★★★, The Last Time I Saw Her (Capitol 1971)★★★, Anne Murray/Glen Campbell(Capitol 1971)★★★, Glen Travis Campbell(Capitol 1972)★★★, I Knew Jesus (Before He Was A Star) (Capitol 1973)★★★, I Remember Hank Williams (Capitol 1973)★★, Reunion (The Songs Of Jimmy Webb) (Capitol 1974)★★★, Arkansas (Capitol 1975)★★, Rhinestone Cowboy (Capitol 1975)★★, Bloodline (Capitol 1976)★★★, Southern Nights (Capitol 1977)★★★, with the Royal Philharmonic Orchestra Live At The Royal Festival Hall(Capitol 1978)★★★, Basic (Capitol 1978)★★★, Somethin' 'Bout You Baby I Like (Capitol 1980)★★★, It's The World Gone Crazy (Capitol 1981)★★★★, Old Home Town (Atlantic 1983)★★★, Letter To Home (Atlantic 1984)★★★, Just A Matter Of Time (Atlantic 1986)★★★, No More Night (Word 1988)★★★, Still Within The Sound Of My Voice (MCA 1988)★★★, Walkin' In The Sun (Capitol 1990)★★★★, Unconditional Love (Capitol Nashville 1991)★★★, Somebody Like That (Capitol 1993)★★★, The Rhinestone Cowboy Live In Concert (Summit 1995)★★★.
COMPILATIONS: Glen Campbell's Greatest Hits (Capitol 1971)★★★, The Best Of Glen Campbell(Capitol 1976)★★★, The Very Best Of Glen Campbell(Capitol 1987)★★★★, The Best Of The Early Years (Curb 1987)★★★, The Complete Glen Campbell(Stylus 1989)★★★, Love Songs (MFP 1990)★★, Greatest Country Hits (Curb 1990)★★★, Classics Collection (Liberty 1990)★★★, Essential Glen Campbell, Volumes 1-3 (Capitol 1995)★★★, Gentle On My Mind: The Collection (Razor & Tie 1997)★★★★.
FILMS: The Cool Ones (1967), True Grit (1969), Norwood (1970).
VIDEOS: Live At The Dome (80s), Glen Campbell Live (Channel 5 1988), An Evening With (Music Club Video 1989), Glen Campbell(Castle Music Pictures 1991).
FURTHER READING: The Glen Campbell Story, Freda Kramer. Rhinestone Cowboy: An Autobiography, Glen Campbell with Tom Carter.

CAMPER VAN BEETHOVEN
ALBUMS: Telephone Free Landslide Victory (Independent Project 1985)★★★, Take The Skinheads Bowling mini-album (Pitch-A-Tent 1986)★★★, Camper Van Beethoven II/III (Pitch-A-Tent 1986)★★★★, Camper Van Beethoven (Pitch-A-Tent 1986)★★★, Vampire Can Mating Oven mini-album (Pitch-A-Tent 1987)★★★, Our Beloved Revolutionary Sweetheart (Virgin 1988)★★★★, Key Lime Pie (Virgin 1989)★★★.
Solo: Jonathan Segal Storytelling (Pitch-A-Tent 1988)★★★.

CAN
ALBUMS: Monster Movie (United Artists 1969)★★★★, Can Soundtracks film soundtrack (United Artists 1970)★★★, Tago Mago (United Artists 1971)★★★★, Ege Bamyasi (United Artists 1972)★★★★, Future Days (United Artists 1973)★★★★, Soon Over Babaluma (United Artists 1974)★★★★, Landed (Virgin 1975)★★★, Flow Motion (Virgin 1976)★★★, Saw Delight (Virgin 1977)★★★, Out Of Reach (Lightning 1978)★★, Can – later released as Inner Space (Laser 1979)★★, Rite Time (Mercury 1989)★★★, The Peel Sessions (Strange Fruit 1995)★★★.
Solo: Michael Karoli with Polly Eltes Deluge (Spoon 1984)★★★★. Jaki Liebezeit Phantom Band (Sky 1980)★★★, with Phew and Holger Czukay Phew (Pass 1981)★★★, with Phantom Band Freedom Of Speech (Sky 1981)★★★, with Phantom Band Nowhere (Spoon 1984)★★★. Irmin Schmidt Film Musik (Spoon 1980)★★★, with Bruno Spoerri Toy Planet (Spoon 1981)★★★, Film Musik Volume 2 (Spoon 1981)★★★, Rote Erde (Teldec 1983)★★★, Film Musik Volumes 3&4 (Spoon 1984)★★★, Music At Dusk (Warners 1987)★★★. Damo Suzuki with Dunkelziffer In The Night (Forty Five 1984)★★.
COMPILATIONS: Limited Edition (United Artists 1974)★★★, Unlimited Edition (Caroline 1976)★★★, Cannibalism (United Artists 1978)★★★★, Delay 1968 (Spoon 1981)★★★, Onlyou (Pure Freude 1982)★★★, Prehistoric Future (Tago Mago 1985)★★★, Cannibalism 2 (1993)★★★, Anthology 1968-1993 (1997)★★★★.

CANDLEBOX
ALBUMS: Candlebox (Maverick/Warners 1994)★★★★, Lucy (Maverick 1995)★★.

CANNED HEAT
ALBUMS: Canned Heat (Liberty 1967)★★★, Boogie With Canned Heat (Liberty 1968)★★★, Livin' The Blues (Liberty 1968)★★★, Hallelujah (Liberty 1969)★★★★, Vintage – Canned Heat early recordings (Pye International 1970)★★, Canned Heat '70: Concert (Liberty 1970)★★, Future Blues (Liberty 1970)★★★, with John Lee Hooker Hooker 'N' Heat (Liberty 1971)★★★, with Memphis Slim Memphis Heat (Barclay 1971)★★, Historical Figures And Ancient Heads (United Artists 1972)★★★, with Clarence 'Gatemouth' Brown Gate's On Heat (Barclay 1973)★★★, New Age (United Artists 1973)★★, One More River To Cross (Atlantic 1974)★★, with Memphis Slim Memphis Heat (Barclay 1975)★★, Live At Topanga Corral (DJM 1976)★★, The Human Condition (Takoma 1978)★★, Captured Live (1981)★★, with Hooker Hooker 'N' Heat – Live (Rhino 1981)★★★, Kings Of The Boogie (Destiny 1981)★★, The Boogie Assault – Live In Australia (Bedrock 1987)★★, Re-Heated (Dali 1989)★★, Live At The Turku Rock Festival (Bear Family 1990)★★, Internal Combustion (River Road 1995)★★, Blues Band (Mystic 1997)★★, The Ties That Bind 1974 recording (Archive 1997)★★.
COMPILATIONS: Canned Heat Cook Book (The Best Of Canned Heat) (Liberty 1970)★★★, The Very Best Of Canned Heat (1973)★★★, with Hooker Infinite Boogie (Rhino 1987)★★★, The Best Of Hooker 'N' Heat (See For Miles 1988)★★★, Let's Work Together – The Best Of Canned Heat (Liberty 1989)★★★, The Big Heat (1992)★★★, Uncanned – The Best Of Canned Heat (Liberty 1994)★★★★.

CANNON, FREDDY
ALBUMS: The Explosive! Freddy Cannon (Swan/Top Rank 1960)★★★★, Happy Shades Of Blue (Swan 1960)★★★, Freddy Cannon's Solid Gold Hits (Swan 1961)★★★, Twistin' All Night Long (Swan 1961)★★★, Freddy Cannon At Palisades Park (Swan 1962)★★★, Freddy Cannon Steps Out (Swan 1963)★★, Freddy Cannon (Warners 1964)★★, Action! (Warners 1966)★★.
COMPILATIONS: Freddy Cannon's Greatest Hits (Warners 1966)★★★, Big Blast From Boston! The Best Of ... (Rhino 1995)★★★.

CAPALDI, JIM
ALBUMS: Oh How We Danced (Island 1972)★★★★, Whale Meat Again (Island 1974)H, Short Cut Draw Blood (Island 1975)★★★★, Play It By Ear (Island 1977)★★, The Contender (Polydor 1978)★★★, Electric Nights (Polydor 1979)★★, The Sweet Smell Of Success (Carrere 1980)★★, Let The Thunder Cry (Carrere 1981)★★, Fierce Heart (Atlantic 1983)★★★, One Man Mission (Warners 1984)★★, Some Come Running (Island 1989)★★.
FURTHER READING: Keep On Running: The Steve Winwood Story, Chris Welch. Back In The High Life: A Biography Of Steve Winwood, Alan Clayson.

CAPITOLS
ALBUMS: Dance The Cool Jerk (Atco 1966)★★, We Got A Thing That's In The Groove (Atco 1966)★★.

CAPLETON
ALBUMS: We No Lotion Man (Charm 1991)★★★, Gold (Charm 1991)★★★★, with General Levy Double Trouble (Gussie P. 1991)★★★ with Cutty Ranks, Reggie Stepper Three The Hard Way (Techniques 1991)★★★, with Tony Rebel, Ninjaman Real Rough (1992)★★★, Armshouse (Exterminator 1993)★★★, Prophecy (African Star 1995)★★★.

CAPRIS (60S)
ALBUMS: There's A Moon Out Again (Ambient Sound 1982) re-released as Morse Code Of Love (Collectables 1992)★★.

CAPTAIN AND TENNILLE
ALBUMS: Love Will Keep Us Together (A&M 1975)★★★, Por Amor Viviremos (A&M 1975)★★, Song Of Joy (A&M 1976)★★, Come In From The Rain (A&M 1977)★★, Dream (A&M 1978)★★, Make Your Move (Casablanca 1979)★★, Keeping Our Love Warm (Casablanca 1980)★★, Twenty Years Of Romance (K-Tel 1995)★★.
Solo: Toni Tennille More Than You Know (Mirage 1984)★★★, Moonglow (1986)★★, All Of Me (Gaia 1987)★★, Do It Again (Prestige 1990)★★, Things Are Swingin' (1994)★★.
FURTHER READING: Captain And Tennille, James Spada.

CAPTAIN BEEFHEART
ALBUMS: Safe As Milk (Buddah 1967)★★★★, Strictly Personal(Blue Thumb/Liberty 1968)★★★★, Trout Mask Replica (1969)★★★★★, Lick My Decals Off, Baby (1970)★★★★, The Spotlight Kid (1972)★★★, Clear Spot (1972)★★★, Mirror Man (1973)★★★, Unconditionally Guaranteed (1974)★★, Bluejeans And Moonbeams (1974)★★, with Frank Zappa Bongo Fury (1975)★★★, Shiny Beast (Bat Chain Puller) (1978)★★★, Doc At The Radar Station (1980)★★★, Ice Cream For Crow (1982)★★★, I May Be Hungry But I Sure Ain't Weird alternate takes and new tracks (1992)★★★.
COMPILATIONS: The Best Beefheart (1993)★★★, Zig Zag Wanderer: The Best Of The Buddah Years (Wooden Hill 1997)★★★.
FURTHER READING: The Lives And Times Of Captain Beefheart, no editor listed. Captain Beefheart: The Man And His Music, Colin David Webb.

CAPTAIN SENSIBLE
ALBUMS: Women And Captains First (A&M 1982)★★★, The Power Of Love (A&M 1983)★★, Revolution Now (Deltic 1991)★★, Universe Of Geoffrey Brown (1993)★★, Live At The Milky Way (Humbug 1994)★★★★, Meathead (Humbug 1995)★★★, Mad Cows And Englishmen (Scratch 1996)★★★.
COMPILATIONS: Sensible Singles (A&M 1984)★★★.

CARAVAN
ALBUMS: Caravan (Verve 1968)★★★, If I Could Do It All Over Again, I'd Do It All Over You (Decca 1970)★★★, In The Land Of Grey And Pink (Deram 1971)★★★, Waterloo Lily (Deram 1972)★★★★, For Girls Who Grow Plump In The Night (Deram 1973)★★★, Caravan And The New Symphonia (Deram 1974)★★, Cunning Stunts (Decca 1975)★★★, Blind Dog At St. Dunstan's (BTM 1976)★★★, Better By Far (Arista 1977)★★, The Album (Kingdom 1980)★★, The Show Of Our Lives (Decca 1981)★★, Back To The Front (Kingdom 1982)★★, Live At The Paris Theatre, 1975 (1991)★★, Live 1990 (1993)★★, Cool Water (HTD 1994)★★, Battle Of Hastings (HTD 1995)★★★.
Solo: Richard Sinclair Caravan Of Dreams (1992)★★.
COMPILATIONS: The Canterbury Tales (Decca 1976)★★★★, Collection: Caravan (Kingdom 1984)★★★, And I Wish I Weren't Stoned, Don't Worry (See For Miles 1985)★★★, The Best Of Caravan (C5 1987)★★★, Canterbury Collection (Kingdom 1987)★★★, The Best Of (1993)★★★.

CARDIGANS
ALBUMS: Emmerdale (Stockholm/Polydor 1994)★★★, Life (Stockholm/Polydor 1995)★★★, First Band On The Moon (Mercury 1996)★★★★.

CAREY, MARIAH
ALBUMS: Mariah Carey (1990)★★★, The Wind (Columbia 1991)★★★, Emotions (Columbia 1992)★★★, MTV Unplugged (Columbia 1992)★★★, Music Box (Columbia 1993)★★★, Merry Christmas (Columbia 1994)★★, Daydream (Columbia 1995)★★★, Butterfly (Columbia 1997)★★★.
VIDEOS: Mariah Carey (1994), Fantasy: Live At Madison Square Garden (Columbia Music Video 1996).

CARLISLE, BELINDA
ALBUMS: Belinda (IRS 1986)★★★, Heaven On Earth (Virgin 1987)★★★, Runaway Horses (Virgin 1989)★★, Live Your Life Be Free (Virgin 1991)★★, Real(Virgin 1993)★★, A Woman And A Man (Chrysalis 1996)★★.
VIDEOS: Belinda Live (1988), Runaway – Live (1990), Runaway Videos (1991), The Best Of ... Vol. 1(Virgin 1992).

CARLTON, LARRY
ALBUMS: Larry Carlton (Warners 1978)★★★, Live In Japan (Flyover 1979)★★★, Mr 335 (1979)★★★, Strikes Twice (1980)★★★, Sleepwalk (Warners 1982)★★★, Friends (Warners 1983)★★★, Alone But Never Alone (MCA 1986)★★★★, Discovery (MCA 1987)★★★★, Last Night (MCA 1987)★★★★, One Night Of Sin (1989)★★★, Christmas At My House (1989)★★, On Solid

Ground (MCA 1989)★★★, *Kid Gloves* (GRP 1992)★★★, *Renegade Gentleman* (GRP 1993)★★★, with Lee Ritenour *Larry And Lee* (GRP 1995)★★★★, *The Gift* (GRP 1996)★★★.
COMPILATIONS: *The Collection* (GRP 1990)★★★★.

CARMEL
ALBUMS: *Carmel* (Red Flame 1982)★★★, *The Drum Is Everything* (London 1984)★★, *The Falling* (London 1986)★★★, *Everybody's Got A Little ... Soul* (London 1987)★★★, *Set Me Free* (London 1989)★★★, *Good News* (East West 1992)★★★, *World's Gone Crazy* (East West 1995)★★★, *Live In Paris* (Musidisc 1997)★★★.
COMPILATIONS: *Collected* (London 1990)★★★.
VIDEOS: *Collected: A Collection Of Work 1983-1990* (1990).

CARMEN, ERIC
ALBUMS: *Eric Carmen* (Arista 1975)★★★, *Boats Against The Current* (Arista 1977)★★, *Change Of Heart* (Arista 1978)★★, *Tonight You're Mine* (Arista 1980)★★, *Eric Carmen* (Geffen 1985)★★.
COMPILATIONS: *The Best Of Eric Carmen* (Arista 1988)★★★, *The Definitive Collection* (Arista 1997)★★★.

CARNES, KIM
ALBUMS: *Rest On Me* (Amos 1972)★★, *Kim Carnes* (A&M 1975)★★★, *Sailin'* (A&M 1976)★★★, *St Vincent's Court* (EMI America 1979)★★, *Romance Dance* (EMI America 1980)★★★, *Mistaken Identity* (EMI America 1981)★★★★, *Voyeur* (EMI America 1982)★★★, *Cafe Racers* (EMI America 1983)★★, *Barking At Airplanes* (EMI America 1985)★★, *Lighthouse* (EMI America 1986)★★★, *View From The House* (MCA 1988)★★★★.
COMPILATIONS: *Gypsy Honeymoon – The Best Of* (EMI America 1993)★★★.

CARPENTER, MARY-CHAPIN
ALBUMS: *Hometown Girl* (Columbia 1987)★★, *State Of The Heart* (Columbia 1989)★★★, *Shooting Straight In The Dark* (Columbia 1990)★★★, *Come On, Come On* (Columbia 1992)★★★★, *Stones In The Road* (Columbia 1994)★★★★, *A Place In The World* (Columbia 1996)★★★.
VIDEOS: *Shut Up And Kiss Me* (1994), *5* (1994), *My Record Company Made Me Do This!* (1995), *Jubilee: Live At The Wolf Trap* (Columbia Music Video 1995).

CARPENTERS
ALBUMS: *Offering* later reissued as *Ticket To Ride* (A&M 1969)★★, *Close To You* (A&M 1970)★★★★, *The Carpenters* (A&M 1971)★★★★, *A Song For You* (A&M 1972)★★★, *Now And Then* (A&M 1973)★★, *Horizon* (A&M 1975)★★★, *Live In Japan* (A&M 1975)★★, *A Kind Of Hush* (A&M 1976)★★, *Live At The Palladium* (A&M 1976)★★, *Passage* (A&M 1977)★★, *Christmas Portrait* (A&M 1978)H, *Made In America* (A&M 1981)★★, *Voice Of The Heart* (A&M 1983)★★★, *An Old Fashioned Christmas* (A&M 1984)H. Solo: Richard Carpenter *Time* (A&M 1987)H. Karen Carpenter *Karen Carpenter* (A&M 1996)★★.
COMPILATIONS: *The Singles 1969-73* (A&M 1973)★★★★, *Collection* (A&M 1976)★★★★, *The Singles 1974-78* (A&M 1978)★★★★, *The Carpenters Collection – The Very Best Of The Carpenters* (EMI 1984)★★★★, *The Compact Disc Collection* 12-CD box set (A&M 1989)★★★, *From The Top (1965-82)* 4-CD set (A&M 1992)★★★.
VIDEOS: *Yesterday Once More* (A&M Sound Pictures 1986), *Only Yesterday (Richard & Karen Carpenter's Greatest Hits)* (Channel 5 1990).
FURTHER READING: *The Carpenters: The Untold Story*, Ray Coleman.

CARR, JAMES
ALBUMS: *You Got My Mind Messed Up* (Goldwax 1966)★★★★, *A Man Needs A Woman* (Goldwax 1968)★★★, *Freedom Train* (Goldwax 1968)★★★, *Take Me To The Limit* (Goldwax 1991)★★★, *Soul Survivor* (Soultrax 1993)★★★.
COMPILATIONS: *At The Dark End Of The Street* (1987)★★★, *The Complete James Carr, Volume 1* (Goldwax 1993)★★★★.

CARR, VIKKI
ALBUMS: *Color Her Great* (1963)★★★, *Discovery!* (Liberty 1964)★★★, *Way Of Today* (1967)★★★, *It Must Be Him* (Liberty 1967)★★★, *Vikki!* (Liberty 1968)★★★, *For Once In My Life* (Liberty 1969)★★★, *Nashville By Carr* (1970)★★, *Vikki Carr's Love Story* (1971)★★★, *Superstar* (1971)★★★, *The First Time Ever (I Saw Your Face)* (1972)★★★, *Song Sung Blue* (CBS 1972)★★★, *En Espanol* (1972)★★★, *Ms. America* (1973)★★, *Live At The Greek Theatre* (1973)★★, *One Hell Of A Woman* (1974)★★★, *Y El Amor* (1980)★★★, *Emociones* (Polygram 1996)★★★.
COMPILATIONS: *The Vikki Carr Collection* (United Artists 1973)★★★, *The Liberty Years – The Best Of Vikki Carr* (1989)★★★.

CARRACK, PAUL
ALBUMS: *Nightbird* (Vertigo 1980)★★, *Suburban Voodoo* (Epic 1982)★★, *One Good Reason* (Chrysalis 1987)★★★, *Groove Approved* (Chrysalis 1989)★★★, *Blue Views* (IRS 1995)★★★★.
COMPILATIONS: *Ace Mechanic* (1987)★★★, *Carrackter Reference* (1991)★★★.

CARS
ALBUMS: *The Cars* (Elektra 1978)★★★★, *Candy-O* (Elektra 1979)★★★, *Panorama* (Elektra 1980)★★, *Shake It Up* (Elektra 1981)★★★, *Heartbeat City* (Elektra 1984)★★★★, *Door To Door* (Elektra 1987)H.
Solo: Ric Ocasek *Beautitude* (Geffen 1983)★★, *The Side Of Paradise* (Geffen 1986)★★, *Fireball Zone* (Warners 1991)★★, *Quick Change World* (Reprise 1993)★★, *Troublizing* (Columbia 1997)★★. Elliot Easton *Change No Change* (Elektra 1985)★★. Benjamin Orr *The Lace* (Elektra 1986)★★. Greg Hawkes *Niagara Falls* (Passport 1983)★★.
COMPILATIONS: *The Cars Greatest Hits* (Elektra 1985)★★★, *Just What I Needed: The Cars Anthology* (Elektra/Rhino 1995)★★★★.
VIDEOS: *Heartbeat City* (Warner Music Video 1984), *Cars Live* (Vestron Music Video 1988).
FURTHER READING: *The Cars*, Philip Kamin.

CARTER, CARLENE
ALBUMS: *Carlene Carter* (Warners 1978)★★★, *Two Sides To Every Woman* (Warners 1979)★★, *Musical Shapes* (F-Beat 1980)★★★, *Blue Nun* (F-Beat 1981)★★, *C'est Bon* (Epic 1983)★★★, with Anita, Helen and June Carter *Wildwood Flower* (Mercury 1988)★★★, *I Fell In Love* (Reprise 1990)★★, *Musical Shapes & Blue Nun* re-issue (Demon 1992)★★★, *Little Love Letters* (Giant 1993)★★★, *Little Acts Of Treason* (Giant 1995)★★★, *Hindsight 20/20* (1998)★★★.
COMPILATIONS: *Hindsight 20/20* (Giant 1996)★★★★.
VIDEOS: *Open Fire* (Hendring Video 1990).

CARTER USM
ALBUMS: *101 Damnations* (Big Cat 1990)★★★★, *30 Something* (Rough Trade 1991)★★★, *1992 – The Love Album* (Chrysalis 1992)★★★★, *Post Historic Monsters* (Chrysalis 1993)★★★★, *Starry Eyed And Bollock Naked* (Chrysalis 1994)★★★, *Worry Bomb* (Chrysalis 1995)★★★, *A World Without Dave* mini-album (Cooking Vinyl 1997)★★★.
COMPILATIONS: *Straw Donkey* (Chrysalis 1995)★★★.
VIDEOS: *In Bed With Carter* (PMI 1991), *What Do You Think Of The Programme So Far?* (PMI 1992), *Straw Donkey: The Videos* (PMI 1995), *Flicking The V's-Live In Croatia* (1995).

CARTHY, MARTIN
ALBUMS: *Martin Carthy* (Fontana 1965)★★★, *Second Album* (Fontana 1966)★★★, with Dave Swarbrick *Byker Hill* (Fontana 1967)★★★★, with Swarbrick *But Two Came By* (Fontana 1968)★★★, with Swarbrick *Prince Heathen* (Fontana 1970)★★★, with Swarbrick *Selections* (Pegasus 1971)★★★, *Landfall* (Philips 1971)★★★★, *Sweet Wivelsfield* (Deram 1974)★★★, *Shearwater* (Topic 1975)★★★, *Crown Of Horn* (Topic 1976)★★★, *Because It's There* (1979)★★★, *Out Of The Cut* (Topic 1982)★★★, *Right Of Passage* (Topic 1989)★★★★, with Swarbrick *Life And Limb* (Special Delivery/Topic 1990)★★★, with Swarbrick *Skin & Bone* (1992)★★★★.
COMPILATIONS: *This Is Martin Carthy* (Philips 1972)★★★★, *Rigs Of The Time – The Best Of...* (1993)★★★, *The Collection* (Green Linnet 1994)★★★★.
VIDEOS: *British Fingerstyle Guitar* (1994).

CASCADES
ALBUMS: *Rhythm Of The Rain* (Valiant 1963)★★★, *What Goes On* (Cascade 1968)★★, *Maybe The Rain Will Fall* (UNI 1969)★★.
FILMS: *Catalina Caper* (1967).

CASH, JOHNNY
ALBUMS: *Johnny Cash With His Hot And Blue Guitar* (Sun 1957)★★★, *Johnny Cash Sings The Songs That Made Him Famous* (Sun 1958)★★★, *The Fabulous Johnny Cash* (Columbia 1958)★★★, *Hymns By Johnny Cash* (Columbia 1959)H, *Songs Of Our Soil* (Columbia 1959)★★, *Now There Was A Song* (Columbia 1960)★★, *Johnny Cash Sings Hank Williams And Other Favorite Tunes* (Sun 1960)★★★, *Ride This Train* (Columbia 1960)★★★★, *Now Here's Johnny Cash* (Sun 1961)★★★, *The Lure Of The Grand Canyon* (Columbia 1961)★★, *Hymns From The Heart* (Columbia 1962)H, *The Sound Of Johnny Cash* (Columbia 1962)★★, *All Aboard The Blue Train* (Sun 1963)★★★, *Blood, Sweat And Tears* (Columbia 1963)★★★, *The Christmas Spirit* (Columbia 1963)★★, with the Carter Family *Keep On The Sunny Side* (1964)★★★, *I Walk The Line* (Columbia 1964)★★★★, *Bitter Tears (Ballads Of The American Indian)* (Columbia 1964)★★★, *Orange Blossom Special* (Columbia 1964)★★★★, *Mean As Hell* (Columbia 1965)★★, *The Sons Of Katie Elder* film soundtrack (Columbia 1965)★★, *Johnny Cash Sings Ballads Of The True West* (Columbia 1965)★★★, *Ballads Of The True West, Volume 2* (Columbia 1965)★★★, *Everybody Loves A Nut* (Columbia 1966)H, *Happiness Is You* (Columbia 1966)★★, with June Carter *Carryin' On* (Columbia 1967)★★, *From Sea To Shining Sea* (Columbia 1967)★★, *Old Golden Throat* (Columbia 1968)★★, *Johnny Cash At Folsom Prison* (Columbia 1968)★★★★, *The Holy Land* (Columbia 1968)H, *More Of Old Golden Throat* (Columbia 1969)★★, *Johnny Cash At San Quentin* (Columbia 1969)★★★★, *Hello I'm Johnny Cash* (Columbia 1970)★★★, *The Johnny Cash Show* (Columbia 1970)★★★, with Carl Perkins *Little Fauss And Big Halsey* (Columbia 1970)★★, *The Man In Black* (Columbia 1971)★★★, with Jerry Lee Lewis *Sings Hank Williams* (Sun 1971)★★, *A Thing Called Love* (Columbia 1972)★★, with Jerry Lee Lewis *Sunday Down South* (Sun 1972)★★, *Christmas And The Cash Family* (Columbia 1972)★★, *America (A 200-Year Salute In Story And Song)* (Columbia 1972)★★, *Any Old Wind That Blows* (Columbia 1973)★★, *The Gospel Road* (Columbia 1973)★★, with June Carter *Johnny Cash And His Woman* (Columbia 1973)★★, *Ragged Old Flag* (Columbia 1974)★★, *The Junkie And The Juicehead Minus Me* (Columbia 1974)★★, *Pa Osteraker* (Columbia 1974)★★ reissued as *Inside A Swedish Prison* (Bear Family 1982), *John R. Cash* (Columbia 1975)★★★, *Look At Them Beans* (Columbia 1975)★★, *The Johnny Cash Children's Album* (1975)★★, *Strawberry Cake* (Columbia 1976)★★★, *One Piece At A Time* (Columbia 1976)★★★★, *The Last Gunfighter Ballad* (Columbia 1977)★★★, *The Rambler* (Columbia 1977)★★★, *Gone Girl* (Columbia 1978)★★★, *I Would Like To See You Again* (Columbia 1978)★★★, *Silver* (Columbia 1979)★★★, *A Believer Sings The Truth* (Columbia 1979)★★, *Rockabilly Blues* (Columbia 1980)★★★★, *The Baron* (Columbia 1981)★★★, with Jerry Lee Lewis, Carl Perkins *The Survivors* (Columbia 1982)★★★, *The Adventures Of Johnny Cash* (Columbia 1982)★★, *Johnny 99* (Columbia 1983)★★, *Rainbow* (Columbia 1985)★★★, with Kris Kristofferson, Waylon Jennings, Willie Nelson *Highwayman* (Columbia 1985)★★★★, with Jerry Lee Lewis, Carl Perkins, Roy Orbison *The Class Of '55* (1986)★★★, with Waylon Jennings *Heroes* (Columbia 1986)★★★, *Believe In Him* (Word 1986)★★, *Johnny Cash Is Back In Town* (Mercury 1987)★★★, *Water From The Wells Of Home* (Mercury 1988)★★★★, *Boom Chicka Boom* (Mercury 1989)★★★, with Kristofferson, Jennings and Nelson *Highwayman 2* (Columbia 1990)★★★, *The Mystery Of Life* (Mercury 1991)★★★, *Get Rhythm* (Sun 1991)★★★, *American Recordings* (American 1994)★★★★, with Kristofferson, Jennings and Nelson *The Road Goes On Forever* (Liberty 1995)★★, *Unchained* (American 1996)★★★, *Live* (Fat Boy 1996).
COMPILATIONS: *Johnny Cash's Greatest* (Sun 1959)★★★, *Ring Of Fire (The Best Of Johnny Cash)* (Columbia 1963)★★★, *The Original Sun Sound Of Johnny Cash* (Sun 1965)★★★, *Johnny Cash's Greatest Hits, Volume 1* (Columbia 1967)★★★, *Original Golden Hits, Volume 1* (Sun 1969)★★★, *Original Golden Hits, Volume 2* (Sun 1969)★★★, *Get Rhythm* (Sun 1969)★★★, *Story Songs Of The Trains And Rivers* (Sun 1969)★★★, *Showtime* (Sun 1969)★★★, *The Rough Cut King Of Country Music* (Sun 1970)★★★, *The Singing Story Teller* (Sun 1970)★★★, *The Legend* (Sun 1970)★★★★, *The World Of Johnny Cash* (Columbia 1970)★★★★, *Johnny Cash: The Man, The World, His Music* (Sun 1971)★★★, *His Greatest Hits, Volume 2* (Columbia 1971)★★★, *Golden Souvenirs* (Plantation 1977)★★★, *Greatest Hits, Volume 3* (Columbia 1978)★★★, *Tall Man* (Bear Family 1980)★★★, *Encore (Greatest Hits, Volume 4)* (Columbia 1981)★★★, *Biggest Hits* (Columbia 1982)★★★, *Johnny Cash: The Sun Years* 5-LP box set (Sun 1984)★★★★, *Up Through The Years, 1955-1957* (Bear Family 1986)★★★★, *Johnny Cash – Columbia Records 1958-1986* (Columbia 1987)★★★★, *Vintage Years: 1955-1963* (Rhino 1987)★★★, *Classic Cash* (Mercury 1988)★★★, *The Sun Years* (Rhino 1990)★★★★, *I Walk The Line And Other Big Hits* (Rhino 1990)★★★, *The Man In Black: 1954-1958* 5-CD box set (Bear Family 1990)★★★★, *Come Along And Ride This Train* 4-CD box set (Bear Family 1991)★★★, *The Man In Black: 1959-1962* 5-CD box set (Bear Family 1992)★★★★, *The Essential Johnny Cash 1955-1983* 3-CD box set (Columbia/Legacy 1992)★★★★, *Wanted Man* (Mercury 1994)★★★, *The Man In Black: The Definitive Collection* (Columbia 1994)★★★★, *Get Rhythm: The Best Of The Sun Years* (Pickwick 1995)★★★, *Ring Of Fire* (Spectrum 1995)★★★, *The Man In Black: 1963-1969 Plus* 6-CD box set (Bear Family 1996)★★★★, *All American Country* (Spectrum 1997)★★★, *Tennessee Top Cat Live 1955-1965* (Cotton Town Jubilee 1997)★★★★.
VIDEOS: *Live In London: Johnny Cash* (BBC Video 1987), *In San Quentin* (Vestron 1987), *Riding The Rails* (Hendring Video 1990), *Johnny Cash Live!* (1993), *The Tennessee Top Cat Live 1955-1965* (Jubilee 1995), *The Man, His World, The Music* (1995).
FURTHER READING: *Johnny Cash Discography And Recording History 1954-1969*, John L. Smith. *A Boy Named Cash*, Albert Govoni. *The Johnny Cash Story*, George Carpozi. *Johnny Cash: Winners Get Scars Too*, Christopher S. Wren. *The New Johnny Cash*, Charles Paul Conn. *Man In Black*, Johnny Cash. *The Johnny Cash Discography 1954-1984*, John L. Smith. *The Johnny Cash Record Catalogue*, John L. Smith (ed.). *Johnny Cash – The Autobiography*, Johnny Cash with Patrick Carr. *The Cash Family Scrapbook*, Cindy Cash.

CASH, ROSANNE
ALBUMS: *Rosanne Cash* (Ariola 1978)★★, *Right Or Wrong* (Columbia 1979)★★★, *Seven Year Ache* (Columbia 1981)★★★, *Somewhere In The Stars* (Columbia 1982)★★★, *Rhythm And Romance* (Columbia 1985)★★★, *King's Record Shop* (Columbia 1988)★★★, *Interiors* (Columbia 1990)★★★★, *The Wheel* (Columbia 1993)★★★, *10 Song Demo* (Capitol 1996)★★★★.
COMPILATIONS: *Hits 1979-1989* (Columbia 1989)★★★★, *Retrospective* (Columbia 1995)★★★★.
VIDEOS: *Live – The Interiors Tour* (1994).
FURTHER READING: *Bodies Of Water*, Rosanne Cash.

CASSIDY, DAVID
ALBUMS: *Cherish* (Bell 1972)★★, *Could It Be Forever* (Bell 1972)★★, *Rock Me Baby* (Bell 1973)★★, *Dreams Are Nothin' More* (Bell 1973)★★, *Cassidy Live* (Bell 1974)H, *The Higher They Climb* (RCA 1975)★★, *Romance* (Arista 1985)★★, *His Greatest Hits, Live* (Starblend 1986)H, *David Cassidy* (Enigma 1990)★★.
COMPILATIONS: *Greatest Hits* (MFP 1977)★★★.
FURTHER READING: *Meet David Cassidy*, James A. Hudson. *David Cassidy Annual 1974*, no editor listed. *The David Cassidy Story*, James Gregory. *David In Europe: Exclusive! David's Own Story In David's Own Words*, David Cassidy. *C'mon Get Happy... Fear And Loathing On The Partridge Family Bus*, David Cassidy.

CAST
ALBUMS: *All Change* (Polydor 1995)★★★, *Mother Nature Calls* (Polydor 1997)★★★.

CASTAWAYS
FILMS: *It's A Bikini World* (1967).

CATE BROTHERS
ALBUMS: *The Cate Brothers* (Asylum 1975)★★★, *In One Eye And Out The Other* (Asylum 1976)★★★, *The Cate Brothers Band* (Asylum 1977)★★, *Fire On The Tracks* (Atlantic 1979)★★, *Radioland* (Icehouse 1996)★★.

CAVE, NICK
ALBUMS: *From Here To Eternity* (Mute 1984)★★★, *The First Born Is Dead* (Mute 1985)★★★, *Kicking Against The Pricks* (Mute 1986)★★★, *Your Funeral, My Trial* (Mute 1986)★★★, *Tender Prey* (Mute 1988)★★★, with Mick Harvey, Blixa Bargeld *Ghosts Of The Civil Dead* film soundtrack (Mute 1989)★★★, *The Good Son* (Mute 1990)★★★★, *Henry's Dream* (Mute 1992)★★★, *Live Seeds* (Mute 1993)★★★, *Let Love In* (Mute 1994)★★★★, *Murder Ballads* (Mute/Reprise 1996)★★★★, with Harvey and Bargeld *To Have And To Hold* film soundtrack (Mute 1996)★★★, *The Boatman's Call* (Mute 1997)★★★★.
VIDEOS: *Road To God Knows Where* (BMG Video 1990), *Live At The Paradiso* (Mute 1993).
FURTHER READING: *And The Ass Saw The Angel*, Nick Cave. *Fish In A Barrel: Nick Cave & The Bad Seeds On Tour*, Peter Milne. *Hellfire: Life According To Nick Cave*, Jeremy Dean. *Bad Seed: The Biography Of Nick Cave*, Ian Johnston. *Nick Cave: The Birthday Party And Other Epic Adventures*, Robert Brokenmouth.

CCS
ALBUMS: *CCS* aka *Whole Lotta Love* (RAK 1970)★★★, *CCS (2)* (RAK 1972)★★★, *The Best Band In The Land* (RAK 1973)★★★.
COMPILATIONS: *The Best Of CCS* (RAK 1977)★★★.

CHAD AND JEREMY
ALBUMS: *Yesterday's Gone* (1964)★★★, *Chad And Jeremy Sing For You* (Ember 1965)★★★, *Before And After* (Columbia 1965)★★★, *I Don't Want To Lose You Baby* (Columbia 1965)★★★, *Second Album* (Ember 1966)★★★, *More Chad And Jeremy* (1966)★★★, *Distant Shores* (Columbia 1966)★★★, *Of Cabbages And Kings* (Columbia 1967)★★, *Yesterday's Gone* (World Artists 1967)★★★, *The Ark* (1968)★★, *Three In An Attic* soundtrack (1969)★★.
COMPILATIONS: *The Best Of Chad And Jeremy* (1966)★★★, *5 Plus 10 Equals 15 Fabulous Hits* (1965)★★★, *Chad And Jeremy* (1968)★★★, *Painted Dayglo Smile* (Legacy 1992)★★★, *The Essential Chad And Jeremy* (1993)★★★, *Yesterday's Gone* (Drive Archive 1994)★★★, *The Best Of Chad And Jeremy* (One Way 1996)★★★.

CHAIRMEN OF THE BOARD
ALBUMS: *Chairmen Of The Board* (Invictus 1969)★★★, *In Session* (Invictus 1970)★★, *Men Are Getting Scarce (Bittersweet)* (Invictus 1972)★★, *Skin I'm In* (Invictus 1974)★★★, as General Johnson And The Chairmen *Success* (1981)★★, *A Gift Of Beach Music* (1982)★★, *The Music* (Surfside 1987)★★.
Solo: General Johnson *Generally Speaking* (Invictus 1972)★★, *General Johnson* (Arista 1976)★★★. Harrison Kennedy *Hypnotic Music* (Invictus 1972)★★. Danny Woods *Aries* (Invictus 1972)★★.
COMPILATIONS: *Salute The General* (HDH/Demon 1983)★★★, *A.G.M.* (HDH/Demon 1985)★★★, *Greatest Hits* (HDH/Fantasy 1991)★★★★, *The Best Of* (Castle 1997)★★★★.

CHAKA DEMUS AND PLIERS
ALBUMS: with Shabba Ranks *Rough & Rugged* (VP 1987)★★★, *Gal Wine* (Greensleeves 1992)★★★, *Ruff This Year* (RAS 1992)★★★, *Chaka Demus And Pliers* (Charm 1992)★★★★, *Tease Me* (Mango/Island 1993)★★★★, *For Every Kinda People* (Island 1996)★★★★.
Solo: Chaka Demus *Everybody Loves The Chaka* (Black Scorpio 1988)★★, *The Original Chaka* (Witty 1989)★★★.
VIDEOS: *Chaka Demus And Pliers* (PolyGram 1994), *Tease Me* (Island Video 1994).

CHAMELEONS
ALBUMS: *Script Of The Bridge* (Statik 1983)★★★, *What Does Anything Mean Basically?* (Statik 1985)★★★★, *Strange Times* (Geffen 1987)★★★★, *Tripping Dogs* early recordings (Glass Pyramid 1990)★★, *Tony Fletcher Walked On Water* mini-album (Glass Pyramid 1990)★★★, *Peel Sessions* early recordings (Strange Fruit 1990)★★, *The Free Trade Hall Rehearsal* (1992)★★, *The Radio 1 Evening Show Sessions* (1993)★★★.
Solo: Mark Burgess *Zima Junction* (1993)★★★.
COMPILATIONS: *The Fan And The Bellows* (Statik 1986)★★★.
VIDEOS: *Live At The Camden Palace* (Jettisoundz 1986), *Live At The Hacienda* (1994), *Arsenal* (Visionary 1995), *Live At The Gallery* (Visionary 1996).

CHAMPS
ALBUMS: *Go Champs Go* (Challenge 1958)★★★, *Everybody's Rockin' With The Champs* (Challenge 1959)★★★, *Great Dance Hits Of Today* (Challenge 1962)★★★, *All American Music With The Champs* (Challenge 1962)★★★.
COMPILATIONS: *Wing Ding!* (Ace 1994)★★★, *The Early Singles* (Ace 1996)★★★.

CHANDLER, GENE
ALBUMS: *The Duke Of Earl* (Vee Jay 1962)★★★★, *Just Be True* (1964)★★★, *Gene Chandler Live On Stage In '65* (Constellation 1965, reissued as *Live At The Regal*)★★, *The Girl Don't Care* (Brunswick 1967)★★★, *The Duke Of Soul* (Checker 1967)★★★, *There Was A Time* (Brunswick 1968)★★, *The Two Sides Of Gene Chandler* (Brunswick 1969)★★, *The Gene Chandler Situation* (Mercury 1970)★★★, with Jerry Butler *Gene And Jerry – One & One* (Mercury 1971)★★★, *Get Down* (Chi-Sound 1978)★★★, *When You're Number One* (20th Century 1979)★★★, *Gene Chandler '80* (20th Century 1980)★★★, *Your Love Looks Good On Me* (Fastfire 1985)★★★.
COMPILATIONS: *Greatest Hits By Gene Chandler* (Constellation 1964)★★★, *Just Be True* (1980)★★★, *Stroll On With The Duke* (Solid Smoke 1984)★★★, *60s Soul Brother* (Kent/Ace 1986)★★★, *Get Down* (Charly 1992)★★★, *Nothing Can Stop Me: Gene Chandler's Greatest Hits* (Varese Sarabande 1994)★★★.
FILMS: *Don't Knock The Twist* (1962).

CHANNEL LIGHT VESSEL
ALBUMS: *The Familiar* (All Saints 1993)★★★, *Automatic* (All Saints 1995)★★★, *Excellent Spirits* (All Saints 1996)★★★★.

CHANTAYS
ALBUMS: *Pipeline* (Downey 1963)★★★, *Two Sides Of The Chantays* (Dot 1964)★★★.
COMPILATIONS: *The Story Of Rock 'N' Roll* (1976)★★★.

CHAPIN, HARRY
ALBUMS: *Heads And Tales* (Elektra 1972)★★★, *Sniper And Other Love Songs* (Elektra 1972)★★, *Short Stories* (Elektra 1974)★★★, *Verities And Balderdash* (Elektra 1974)★★★★, *Portrait Gallery* (Elektra 1975)★★★, *Greatest Stories – Live* (Elektra 1976)★★, *On The Road To Kingdom Come* (Elektra 1976)★★, *Dance Band On The Titanic* (Elektra 1977)★★★, *Living Room Suite* (Elektra 1978)★★, *Legends Of The Lost And Found – New Greatest Stories Live* (Elektra 1979)★★, *Sequel* (Boardwalk 1980)★★★, *The Last Protest Singer* (Sequel 1989)★★.
COMPILATIONS: *Anthology* (Elektra 1985)★★★.
FURTHER READING: *Taxi: The Harry Chaplin Story*, Peter M. Coan.

CHAPMAN, MICHAEL
ALBUMS: *Rainmaker* (Harvest 1968)★★★, *Fully Qualified Survivor* (Harvest 1970)★★★★, *Window* (Harvest 1971)★★★, *Wrecked Again* (Harvest 1972)★★★, *Millstone Grit* (Gama 1973)★★★, *Deal Gone Down* (Gama 1974)★★★, *Pleasures Of The Street* (Gama 1975)★★★, *Savage Amusement* (Gama 1976)★★, *The Man Who Hated Mornings* (Gama 1977)★★★, *Playing Guitar The Easy Way* guitar tutor (Criminal 1978)★★★, *Life On The Ceiling* (Criminal 1978)★★, *Looking For Eleven* (Criminal 1980)★★★, *Almost Alone* (Black Crow 1981)★★★★, with Rick Kemp *Original Owners* (Konnexion 1984)★★, *Heartbeat* (Coda 1987)★★★, *Still Making Rain* (Making Waves 1993)★★★, *Navigation* (Planet Plan 1996)★★★★, *Dreaming Out Loud* (Demon 1997)★★★.
COMPILATIONS: *Michael Chapman Lived Here From 1968-72* (Cube 1977)★★★★, re-released as *The Best Of (1968 – 1972)* (See For Miles 1988)★★★★.

CHAPMAN, ROGER
ALBUMS: *Chappo* (Arista 1979)★★★, *Live In Hamburg* (Acrobat 1979)★★★, *Mail Order Magic* (Kamera 1980)★★, *Hyenas Only Laugh For Fun* (Teldec 1981)★★, as the Shortlist *The Riffburgler Album* (1981)★★, *He Was She Was* (Polydor 1982)★★, as the Riffburglers *Swag* (1983)★★, *Mango Crazy* (1983)★★, *The Shadow Knows* (1984)★★★, *Zipper* (1986)★★, *Techno Prisoners* (1987)★★, *Walking The Cat* (1989)★★★, *Hybrid And Lowdown* (1991)★★★, *Under No Obligation* (1992)★★, *King Of The Shouters* (1994)★★, *Kiss My Soul* (Essential 1996)★★★.
COMPILATIONS: *Kick It Back* (1993)★★★.

CHAPMAN, TRACY
ALBUMS: *Tracy Chapman* (Elektra 1988)★★★★, *Crossroads* (Elektra 1989)★★, *Matters Of The Heart* (Elektra 1992)★★, *New Beginning* (Elektra 1995)★★★.

CHARLATANS (UK)
ALBUMS: *Some Friendly* (Situation 2 1990)★★★, *Between 10th And 11th* (Situation 2 1992)★★★, *Up To Our Hips* (Beggars Banquet 1994)★★★, *Charlatans* (Beggars Banquet 1995)★★★, *Tellin' Stories* (Beggars Banquet 1997)★★★★.

CHARLATANS (USA)
ALBUMS: *The Charlatans* (Philips 1969)★★★, *The Autumn Demos* (1982)★★.
COMPILATIONS: *The Charlatans* (Ace 1996)★★★, *The Amazing Charlatans* (Ace/Big Beat 1996)★★★.

CHARLES, RAY
ALBUMS: *Hallelujah, I Love Her So* aka *Ray Charles* (Atlantic 1957)★★★, *The Great Ray Charles* (Atlantic 1957)★★★★, with Milt Jackson *Soul Brothers* (Atlantic 1958)★★★, *Ray Charles At Newport* (Atlantic 1958)★★★, *Yes Indeed* (Atlantic 1959)★★★, *Ray Charles* (Hollywood 1959)★★★★, *The Fabulous Ray Charles* (Hollywood 1959)★★★, *What'd I Say* (Atlantic 1959)★★★, *The Genius Of Ray Charles* (Atlantic 1959)★★★★★, *Ray Charles In Person* (Atlantic 1960)★★★, *The Genius Hits The Road* (ABC 1960)★★★, *Dedicated To You* (ABC 1961)★★★, *Genius + Soul = Jazz* (Impulse! 1961)★★★★★, *The Genius After Hours* (Atlantic 1961)★★★★, with Betty Carter *Ray Charles And Betty Carter* (ABC 1961)★★★★, *The Genius Sings The Blues* (Atlantic 1961)★★★★, with Jackson *Soul Meeting* (Atlantic 1961)★★★, *Do The Twist With Ray Charles* (Atlantic 1961)★★★, *Modern Sounds In Country And Western* (ABC 1962)★★★★★, *Modern Sounds In Country And Western Volume 2* (ABC 1962)★★★★, *Ingredients In A Recipe For Soul* (ABC 1963)★★★★, *Sweet And Sour Tears* (ABC 1964)★★★, *Have A Smile With Me* (ABC 1964)★★★, *Ray Charles Live In Concert* (ABC 1965)★★★, *Country And Western Meets Rhythm And Blues* aka *Together Again* (ABC 1965)★★★, *Crying Time* (ABC 1966)★★★, *Ray's Moods* (ABC 1966)★★★, *Ray Charles Invites You To Listen* (ABC 1967)★★★, *A Portrait Of Ray* (ABC 1968)★★, *I'm All Yours, Baby!* (ABC 1969)★★, *Doing His Thing* (ABC 1969)★★★, *My Kind Of Jazz* (Tangerine 1970)★★★, *Love Country Style* (ABC 1970)★★, *Volcanic Action Of My Soul* (ABC 1971)★★, *A Message From The People* (ABC 1972)★★, *Through The Eyes Of Love* (ABC 1972), *Jazz Number II* (Tangerine 1972)★★★, *Ray Charles Live* (Atlantic 1973)★★★, *Come Live With Me* (Crossover 1974)★★, *Renaissance* (Crossover 1975)★★, *My Kind Of Jazz III* (Crossover 1975)★★, *Live In Japan* (1975)★★★, with Cleo Laine *Porgy And Bess* (RCA 1976)★★★, *True To Life* (Atlantic 1977)★★, *Love And Peace* (Atlantic 1978)★★, *Ain't It So* (Atlantic 1979)★★, *Brother Ray Is At It Again* (Atlantic 1980)★★, *Wish You Were Here Tonight* (Columbia 1983)★★, *Do I Ever Cross Your Mind* (Columbia 1984)★★, *Friendship* (Columbia 1985)★★, *The Spirit Of Christmas* (Columbia 1985)★★, *From The Pages Of My Mind* (Columbia 1986)★★, *Just Between Us* (Columbia 1988)★★, *Seven Spanish Angels And Other Hits* (Columbia 1989)★★, *Would You Believe* (Warners 1990)★★, *My World* (Warners 1993)★★★★, *Strong Love Affair* (Qwest 1996)★★, *Berlin, 1962* (Pablo 1996)★★★★, *Hit The Road, Ray (Live)* (Pablo 1996), *In Concert (live)* (Rhino 1998).
COMPILATIONS: *The Ray Charles Story* (Atlantic 1962)★★★, *Ray Charles' Greatest Hits* (ABC 1962)★★★★, *A Man And His Soul* (ABC 1967)★★★, *The Best Of Ray Charles 1956-58* (Atlantic 1970)★★★★, *A 25th Anniversary In Show Business Salute To Ray Charles* (ABC 1971)★★★★, *The Right Time* (Atlantic 1987)★★★, *A Life In Music 1956-59* (Atlantic 1982)★★★★, *Greatest Hits Vol. 1 1960-67* (Rhino 1988)★★★★, *Greatest Hits Vol. 2 1960-72* (Rhino 1988)★★★★, *Anthology* (Rhino 1989)★★★★, *The Collection* ABC recordings (Castle 1990)★★★, *Blues Is My Middle Name* 1949-52 recordings (Double Play 1991)★★★, *The Birth Of Soul 1952-59* (Atlantic 1991)★★★★★, *The Complete Atlantic Rhythm And Blues Recordings* 4-CD box set (Atlantic 1992)★★★★★, *The Living Legend* (1993)★★★, *The Best Of The Atlantic Years* (Rhino/Atlantic 1994)★★★, *Classics* (Rhino 1995)★★★, *Genius & Soul* 5-CD box set (Rhino 1997)★★★.
FILMS: *Blues For Lovers* aka *Ballad In Blue* (1964), *The Blues Brothers* (1980).
FURTHER READING: *Ray Charles*, Sharon Bell Mathis. *Brother Ray, Ray Charles' Own Story*, Ray Charles and David Ritz.

CHARLES AND EDDIE
ALBUMS: *Duophonic* (Stateside/Capitol 1992)★★★, *Chocolate Milk* (Capitol 1995)★★.

CHEAP TRICK
ALBUMS: *Cheap Trick* (Epic 1977)★★★, *In Color* (Epic 1977)★★★, *Heaven Tonight* (Epic 1978)★★★★, *Cheap Trick At Budokan* (Epic 1979)★★★★, *Dream Police* (Epic 1979)★★★, *Found All The Parts* (Epic 1980)★★, *All Shook Up* (Epic 1980)★★, *One On One* (Epic 1982)★★, *Next Position Please* (Epic 1983)★★, *Standing On The Edge* (Epic 1985)★★★, *The Doctor* (Epic 1986)★★, *Lap Of Luxury* (Epic 1988)★★★, *Busted* (Epic 1990)★★★, *Woke Up With A Monster* (Warners 1994)★★, *Budokan 2* recorded 1978 (Epic/Sony 1994)★★, *Cheap Trick* (Red Ant 1997)★★, *At Budokan: The Complete Concert* (1998)★★★.
COMPILATIONS: *The Collection* (Castle 1991)★★★★, *Greatest Hits* (Epic 1992)★★★, *Sex, America, Cheap Trick* 4-CD box set (Epic 1996)★★★★.
VIDEOS: *Every Trick In The Book* (CMV Enterprises 1990).

CHECKER, CHUBBY
ALBUMS: *Chubby Checker* (Parkway 1960)★★★, *Twist With Chubby Checker* (Parkway 1960)★★★, *For Twisters Only* (Parkway 1960)★★★, *It's Pony Time* (Parkway 1961)★★★, *Let's Twist Again* (Parkway 1961)★★★★, *Bobby Rydell/Chubby Checker* (Parkway 1961)★★★, *Twistin' Round The World* (Parkway 1962)★★, *For Teen Twisters Only* (Parkway 1962)★★★, *Don't Knock The Twist* soundtrack (Parkway 1962)★★, *All The Hits (For Your Dancin' Party)* (Parkway 1962)★★★, with Dee Dee Sharp *Down To Earth* (1962)★★★, *Limbo Party* (Parkway 1962)★★★, *Let's Limbo Some More* (Parkway 1963)★★, *Beach Party* (Parkway 1963)★★, *Chubby Checker In Person* (Parkway 1963)★★, *Chubby's Folk Album* (Parkway 1964)H, *Chubby Checker With Sy Oliver* (Parkway 1964)★★, *Discotheque* (Parkway 1965)★★, *The Other Side Of Chubby Checker* (1971)★★, *Chequered* (London 1971)★★, *The Change Has Come* (1982)★★.
COMPILATIONS: *Your Twist Party* (1961)★★★, *Chubby Checker's Biggest Hits* (1962)★★★★, *Chubby Checker's Eighteen Golden Hits* (Parkway 1966)★★★★, *Chubby Checker's Greatest Hits* (ABKCO 1972)★★★★.
FILMS: *It's Trad, Dad* aka *Ring-A-Ding Rhythm* (1962), *Don't Knock The Twist* (1962).

CHEECH AND CHONG
ALBUMS: *Cheech And Chong* (Ode 1971)★★, *Big Bambu* (Ode 1972)★★, *Los Cochinos* (Ode 1973)★★, *Cheech & Chong's Wedding Album* (Ode 1974)★★, *Sleeping Beauty* (Ode 1976)★★, *Six* (1977)★★, *Up In Smoke* film soundtrack (Warners 1978)H, *Let's Make A New Dope Deal* (Warners 1980)★★, *Get Out Of My Room* (MCA 1986)★★.

CHELSEA
ALBUMS: *Chelsea* (Step Forward 1979)★★★, *Alternative Hits* (Step Forward 1980)★★, *Evacuate* (IRS 1982)★★, *Rocks Off* (Jungle 1986)★★, *Under Wraps* (IRS 1989)★★.
FILMS: *Jubilee* (1978).
VIDEOS: *Live At The Bier Keller* (Jettisoundz 1984).

CHEMICAL BROTHERS
ALBUMS: *Exit Planet Dust* (Junior Boy's Own 1995)★★★, *Live At The Social Vol. 1* (Heavenly 1996)★★★, *Dig Your Own Hole* (Freestyle Dust 1997)★★★★.

CHER
ALBUMS: *All I Really Want To Do* (Liberty 1965)★★, *The Sonny Side Of Cher* (Liberty 1966)★★, *Cher* (Imperial 1966)★★★, *With Love, Cher* (Imperial 1968)★★, *Backstage* (1968)★★, *3614 Jackson Highway* (Atco 1969)★★, *Gypsies, Tramps And Thieves* (Kapp 1971)★★★, *Foxy Lady* (Kapp 1972)★★, *Half Breed* (MCA 1973)★★, *Dark Lady* (MCA 1974)★★, *Bittersweet White Light* (MCA 1974)★★, *Stars* (Warners 1975)★★, *I'd Rather Believe In You* (1976)★★, *Allman And Woman: Two The Hard Way* (Warners 1977)★★, *Take Me Home* (Casablanca 1979)★★, *Prisoner* (Casablanca 1980)★★, *Black Rose* (1980)★★, *I Paralyze* (Columbia 1982)★★, *Cher II* (Geffen 1987)★★, *Heart Of Stone* (Geffen 1989)★★, *Love Hurts* (Geffen 1991)★★★, *It's A Man's World* (Warners 1995)★★★.
COMPILATIONS: *The Best Of Cher* 60s recordings (EMI America 1991)★★★, *The Sonny And Cher Collection: An Anthology Of Their Hits Alone And Together* (1991)★★★, *Greatest Hits* (Geffen 1992)★★★.
VIDEOS: *Extravaganza – Live At The Mirage* (1992).
FURTHER READING: *Cher*, J. Randy Taraborrelli. *Totally Uninhibited: The Life & Times Of Cher*, Lawrence J. Quirk. *Cher: In Her Own Words*, Nigel Goodall. *Cher: The Visual Documentary*, Mick St. Michael.

CHERRY, NENEH
ALBUMS: *Raw Like Sushi* (Circa 1989)★★★, *Homebrew* (1993)★★★, *Buddy X* remixes (1993)★★, *Man* (Hut 1996)★★★.
VIDEOS: *The Rise Of Neneh Cherry* (BMG Video 1989).

CHI-LITES
ALBUMS: *Give It Away* (Brunswick 1969)★★★, *(For God's Sake) Give More Power To The People* (Brunswick 1971)★★★★, *A Lonely Man* (Brunswick 1972)★★★, *A Letter To Myself* (Brunswick 1973)★★★, *The Chi-Lites* (Brunswick 1973)★★★, *Toby* (Brunswick 1974)★★★, *Half A Love* (Brunswick 1975)★★, *Happy Being Lonely* (Mercury 1976)★★★, *The Fantastic Chi-Lites* (Mercury 1977)★★★, *Heavenly Body* (Chi-Sound 1980)★★, *Me And You* (Chi-Sound 1982)★★, *Bottoms Up* (Larc 1983)★★★, *Steppin' Out* (Private I 1984)★★, *Just Say You Love Me* (Ichiban 1990)★★★.
Solo: Eugene Record *Welcome To My Fantasy* (Warners 1979)★★.
COMPILATIONS: *The Chi-Lites Greatest Hits* (Brunswick 1972)★★★★, *The Chi-Lites Greatest Hits Volume Two* (Brunswick 1975)★★★, *The Best Of The Chi-Lites* (Kent 1987)★★★, *Greatest Hits* (Street Life 1988)★★★, *Very Best Of The Chi-Lites* (BR Music 1988)★★★, *The Chi-Lites Greatest Hits* (Rhino 1992)★★★★, *Have You Seen Her? The Very Best Of ...* (Pickwick 1995)★★★.

CHIC
ALBUMS: *Chic* (Atlantic 1977)★★★, *C'Est Chic* (Atlantic 1978)★★★, *Risqué* (Atlantic 1979)★★★★, *Real People* (Atlantic 1980)★★★★, *Take It Off* (Atlantic 1981)★★★★, *Tongue In Chic* (Atlantic 1982)★★★, *Believer* (Atlantic 1983)★★★, *Chic-Ism* (Warners 1992)★★★.
COMPILATIONS: *Les Plus Grands Succès De Chic – Chic's Greatest Hits* (Atlantic 1979)★★★★, *Megachic – The Best Of Chic* (Warners 1990)★★★★, *Dance Dance Dance: The Best Of Chic* (Atlantic 1991)★★★★, *Everybody Dance* (Rhino 1995)★★★★.

CHICAGO
ALBUMS: *Chicago Transit Authority* (Columbia 1969)★★★★, *Chicago II* (Columbia 1970)★★★, *Chicago III* (Columbia 1971)★★★, *Chicago At Carnegie Hall* (Columbia 1971)★★, *Chicago V* (Columbia 1972)★★★, *Chicago VI* (Columbia 1973)★★★, *Chicago VII* (Columbia 1974)★★★, *Chicago VIII* (Columbia

1975)★★★★, Chicago X (Columbia 1976)★★, Chicago XI (Columbia 1977)★★, Hot Streets (Columbia 1978)★★★, Chicago 13 (Columbia 1979)★★, Chicago XIV (Columbia 1980)★★, Chicago 16 (Full Moon 1982)★★, Chicago 17 (Full Moon 1984)★★, Chicago 18 (Warners 1987)★★, Chicago 19 (Reprise 1988)★★, Chicago 21 (Reprise 1991)★★, Night And Day (Giant 1995)★★★.
COMPILATIONS: Chicago IX – Chicago's Greatest Hits (Columbia 1975)★★★★, Chicago – Greatest Hits, Volume II (Columbia 1981)★★★, Greatest Hits 1982-1989 (Reprise 1989)★★★, The Heart Of Chicago (Warners 1989)★★★, Group Portrait (Columbia/Legacy 1991)★★★★, The Very Best Of Chicago (Arcade 1996)★★★, The Heart Of Chicago 1967-1997 (Reprise 1997)★★★★.
VIDEOS: And The Band Played On (Warner Reprise 1994), In Concert At The Greek Theatre (Warner Music Vision 1994).

CHICKEN SHACK
ALBUMS: Forty Blue Fingers Freshly Packed And Ready To Serve (Blue Horizon 1968)★★★★, OK Ken? (Blue Horizon 1969)★★★, 100 Ton Chicken (1969)★★★, Accept! Chicken Shack (1970)★★★, Imagination Lady (Deram 1972)★★★, Unlucky Boy (Deram 1973)★★, Goodbye Chicken Shack (Deram 1974)★★, The Creeper (Warners 1979)★★, The Way We Are (1979)★★, Chicken Shack (Gull 1979)★★, Roadie's Concerto (RCA 1981)★★, Chicken Shack On Air (Band Of Joy 1991)★★★, Changes (1992)★★★, Webb's Blues (Indigo 1994)★★★, Plucking Good (Inak 1994)★★★, Stan 'The Man' Live (Indigo 1995)★★★.
COMPILATIONS: Stan The Man (1977)★★★, The Golden Era Of Pop Music (Columbia 1977)★★★, In The Can (Columbia 1980)★★★, Collection: Chicken Shack (Castle 1988)★★★, Black Night (Indigo 1997)★★★.

CHICORY TIP
ALBUMS: Son Of My Father (Columbia 1972)★★.

CHIEFTAINS
ALBUMS: Chieftains 1 (Claddagh 1964)★★★, Chieftains 2 (Claddagh 1969)★★★, Chieftains 3 (Claddagh 1971)★★★, Chieftains 4 (Claddagh 1973)★★★★, Chieftains 5 (Island 1975)★★★, Women Of Ireland (Island 1976)★★★, Bonaparte's Retreat (Columbia 1976)★★★, Chieftains Live (Columbia 1977)★★★, Chieftains 7 (Claddagh 1977)★★★, Chieftains 8 (Columbia 1978)★★★, Vol. 9 (Claddagh 1979)★★★, Boil The Breakfast Early (Columbia 1980)★★★★, Chieftains 10 (Claddagh 1981)★★★, Year Of The French original soundtrack (Claddagh 1983)★★★, The Chieftains In China (Shanachie 1984)★★★, Ballad Of The Irish Horse soundtrack (Shanachie 1985)★★★, Celtic Wedding (RCA 1987)★★★, with James Galway The Chieftains In Ireland (RCA 1987)★★★, with Van Morrison Irish Heartbeat (Mercury 1988)★★★★, A Chieftains Celebration (RCA 1989)★★★★, The Celtic Connection – James Galway And The Chieftains (1990)★★★, Bells Of Dublin (RCA 1991)★★★★, An Irish Evening: Live At The Grand Opera House, Belfast (RCA 1992)★★★, Another Country (1992)★★★, with the Belfast Harp Orchestra The Celtic Harp (1993)★★★, The Long Black Veil(RCA 1995)★★★★, The Bells Of Dublin (RCA Victor 1995)★★★★, Film Cuts (RCA Victor 1996)★★★, Santiago (RCA Victor 1996)★★★.
COMPILATIONS: Chieftains Collection (1989)★★★★, The Best Of The Chieftains (Columbia 1992)★★★, Sean Keane, Matt Molloy And Liam O'Flynn The Fire Aflame (1993)★★★.
VIDEOS: Live In China (1991), An Irish Evening (1992).

CHIFFONS
ALBUMS: He's So Fine (Laurie 1963)★★, One Fine Day (Laurie 1963)★★, Sweet Talkin' Guy (Laurie 1966)★★.
COMPILATIONS: Everything You Ever Wanted To Hear ... But Couldn't Get (Laurie 1981)★★★, Doo-Lang Doo-Lang Doo-Lang (Impact/Ace 1985)★★★, Greatest Recordings (Ace 1990)★★★★, The Fabulous Chiffons (Ace 1991)★★★.

CHILDS, TONI
ALBUMS: Union (A&M 1988)★★★★, House Of Hope (A&M 1991)★★, The Woman's Boat (A&M 1994)★★.

CHILLI WILLI AND THE RED HOT PEPPERS
ALBUMS: Kings Of The Robot Rhythm (Revelation 1972)★★★, Bongos Over Balham (Mooncrest 1974)★★★.
COMPILATIONS: I'll Be Home (Proper 1997)★★★.

CHINA CRISIS
ALBUMS: Difficult Shapes And Passive Rhythms (Virgin 1983)★★★, Working With Fire And Steel- Possible Pop Songs Volume Two (Virgin 1983)★★★, Flaunt The Imperfection (Virgin 1985)★★★, What Price Paradise? (Virgin 1986)★★, Diary Of A Hollow Horse (Virgin 1989)★★★, Warped By Success (Stardumb 1994)★★★, Acoustically Yours (Telegraph 1995)★★.
COMPILATIONS: The China Crisis Collection (Virgin 1990)★★★, China Crisis Diary (1992)★★★.
VIDEOS: Showbiz Absurd (Virgin Vision 1992).

CHOCOLATE WATCH BAND
ALBUMS: No Way Out (Tower 1967)★★★, The Inner Mystique (Tower 1968)★★★, One Step Beyond (Tower 1969)★★.
COMPILATIONS: The Best Of The Chocolate Watch Band (Rhino 1983)★★★, 44 (1987)★★★.

CHRISTIANS
ALBUMS: The Christians (Island 1987)★★★★, Colours (Island 1990)★★★, Happy In Hell (Island 1992)★★★.
Solo: Garry Christian Your Cool Mystery (East West 1997)★★★.
VIDEOS: The Best Of ... (Island 1993)★★★★.

CHRISTIE, LOU
ALBUMS: Lou Christie (Roulette 1963)★★, Lightnin' Strikes (MGM 1966)★★★, Lou Christie Strikes Back (Co&Ce 1966)★★★, Lou Christie Strikes Again (Colpix 1966)★★★, Lou Christie Painter Of Hits (MGM 1966)★★, I'm Gonna Make You Mine (Buddah 1969)★★★, Paint America Love (Buddah 1971)★★, Lou Christie – Zip-A-Dee-Doo-Dah (CTI 1974)★★.
COMPILATIONS: This Is Lou Christie (1969)★★★, Beyond The Blue Horizon: More Of The Best Of ... (Varese Sarabande 1995)★★★.

CHRISTIE, TONY
ALBUMS: I Did What I Did For Maria (MCA 1971)★★★, With Loving Feeling (MCA 1973)★★, Live (MCA 1975)★★, Ladies Man (RCA 1983)★★.
COMPILATIONS: The Best Of Tony Christie (MCA 1976)★★★, Golden Greats (MCA 1985)★★★, The Very Best Of ... (Music Club 1995)★★★.

CHROME
ALBUMS: The Visitation (Siren 1977)★★★, Alien Soundtracks (Siren 1978)★★★, Half Machine Lip Moves (Siren 1979)★★★, Red Exposure (Siren 1980)★★★, Inworlds (Siren 1980)★★★, Blood On The Moon (Siren 1981)★★★, Third From The Sun (Siren 1982)★★★, Raining Milk (Mosquito 1983)★★, Chronicles (Dossier 1984)★★, Into The Eyes Of The Zombie King (Mosquito 1984)★★, The Lyon Concert (Dossier 1985)★★, Another World (Dossier 1986)★★, Dreaming In Sequence (Dossier 1987)★★, Live In Germany (Dossier 1989)H, Alien Soundtracks II (Dossier 1989)★★.
Solo: Helios Creed X-Rated Fairy Tales (Subterranean 1985)★★, Superior Catholic Finger (Subterranean 1986)★★★, The Last Laugh (Amphetamine Reptile 1989)★★★, Boxing The Clown (Amphetamine Reptile 1990)★★★. Damon Edge Alliance (New Rose 1985)★★, The Wind Is Talking (New Rose 1985)★★, Grand Visions (New Rose 1986)★★, The Surreal Rock (Dossier 1987)★★.
COMPILATIONS: No Humans Allowed (Siren 1982)★★★★, Chrome Box 6-LP box set (Subterranean 1982)★★★★.

CHUCK D.
ALBUMS: Autobiography Of Mistachuck (Mercury 1996)★★★★.

CHUMBAWAMBA
ALBUMS: Pictures Of Starving Children Sell Records (Agit Prop 1986)★★★★, Never Mind The Ballots, Here's The Rest Of Your Life (Agit Prop 1987)★★★★, English Rebel Songs 1381-1914 mini-album (Agit Prop 1989)★★★, Slap! (Agit Prop 1990)★★★, Anarchy (One Little Indian 1994)★★★, Showbusiness! Chumbawamba Live (One Little Indian 1995)★★, Swingin' With Raymond (One Little Indian 1996)★★★, Tubthumper (EMI 1997)★★★★.
COMPILATIONS: First 2 (Agit Prop 1993)★★★★.

CHURCH
ALBUMS: Of Skin And Heart (Parlophone 1981)★★, The Church (Carrere 1982)★★★, The Blurred Crusade (Carrere 1982)★★★, Seance (Carrere 1983)★★★, Remote Luxury (Warners 1984)★★★★, Heyday (Warners 1986)★★★, Starfish (Arista 1988)★★★, Gold Afternoon Fix (Arista 1990)★★★★, Priest = Aura (Arista 1992)★★★, Sometime Anywhere (Arista 1994)★★★, Magician Among The Spirits (Deep Karma 1996)★★.
Solo: Marty Willson-Piper In Reflection (Chase 1987)★★★, Art Attack Survival (Rykodisc 1988)★★★, Rhyme (Rykodisc 1989)★★★. Peter Koppes Manchild & Myth (Rykodisc 1988)★★★, From The Well(TVT 1989)★★★. Steve Kilbey Unearthed (Enigma 1987)★★★, Earthed (Rykodisc 1988)★★★, The Slow Crack (Red Eye 1988)★★★, Remindlessness (Red Eye 1990)★★★, Magician Among The Spirits (White 1996)★★.
COMPILATIONS: Conception (Carrerre 1988)★★★, Hindsight (EMI 1988)★★★, A Quick Smoke At Spots (Archives 1986-1990) (Arista 1991)★★★, Almost Yesterday 1981-1990 (Raven 1995)★★★★.
VIDEOS: Goldfish (Jokes, Magic and Souvenirs) (BMG Video 1990).

CITY BOY
ALBUMS: City Boy (Vertigo 1976)★★, Dinner At The Ritz (Vertigo 1977)★★, Young Men Gone West (Vertigo 1977)★★★, Book Early (Vertigo 1978)★★, The Day The Earth Caught Fire (Vertigo 1979)★★, Heads Are Rolling (Vertigo 1980)★★.

CLAIL, GARY, AND THE ON U SOUND SYSTEM
ALBUMS: Emotional Hooligan (On-U-Sound 1991)★★★, Keep The Faith (Yelen 1996)★★★.

CLANNAD
ALBUMS: Clannad (Philips 1973)★★★, Clannad 2 (Gael Linn 1974)★★★, Dulaman (Gael Linn 1974)★★★, Clannad In Concert (Ogham 1979)★★★, Crann Ull (Philips 1981)★★, Fuaim (Tara 1982)★★★★, Magical Ring (RCA 1983)★★★, Legend (RCA 1984)★★★, Macalla (RCA 1985)★★★, Ring Of Gold (Celtic Music 1986)★★★, Sirius (RCA 1987)★★, Clannad In Concert (Shanachie 1988)★★★, Atlantic Realm soundtrack (BBC 1989)★★★, with narration by Tom Conti The Angel And The Soldier Boy (RCA 1989)★★★, Anam (RCA 1990)★★★, Banba (RCA 1993)★★★, Lore (RCA 1996)★★★, Lore/Themes (RCA 1996)★★★.
COMPILATIONS: Clannad: The Collection (K-Tel 1988)★★★, Pastpresent (RCA 1989)★★★, Themes (K-Tel 1993)★★★, Back2Back (RCA 1995)★★★.
VIDEOS: Past Present (1989).

CLAPTON, ERIC
ALBUMS: three tracks as the Powerhouse with Steve Winwood, Jack Bruce, Pete York, Paul Jones What's Shakin'? (Elektra 1966)★★★, Eric Clapton (Polydor 1970)★★★, Eric Clapton's Rainbow Concert (RSO 1973)★★★, 461 Ocean Boulevard (RSO 1974)★★★★, There's One In Every Crowd (RSO 1975)★★★, E. C. Was Here (RSO 1975)★★, No Reason To Cry (RSO 1976)★★★, Slowhand (RSO 1977)★★★★, Backless (RSO 1978)★★★, Just One Night (RSO 1980)★★★, Another Ticket (RSO 1981)★★★, Money And Cigarettes (Duck 1983)★★★, Behind The Sun (Duck 1985)★★★, August (Duck 1986)★★★, with Michael Kamen Homeboy television soundtrack (Virgin 1989)★★, Journeyman (Duck 1989)★★★★, 24 Nights (Duck 1991)★★, Rush film soundtrack (Reprise 1992)★★, MTV Unplugged (1992)★★★★, From The Cradle (Duck 1994)★★★, Pilgrim (Warner Brothers 1998)★★★.
COMPILATIONS: Time Pieces – The Best Of Eric Clapton (RSO 1982)★★★, Time Pieces Volume II: Live In The Seventies (RSO 1983)★★★, Backtrackin' (Starblend 1984)★★★★, Crossroads 4-CD box set (Polydor 1988)★★★★★, The Cream Of Eric Clapton (Polydor 1989)★★★★, The Magic Of ... (1993)★★★, Crossroads 2: Live In The 70s (Polydor 1996)★★★★.
VIDEOS: Eric Clapton On Whistle Test (BBC Video 1984), Live '85 (Polygram Music Video 1986), Live At The NEC Birmingham (MSD 1987), Cream Of Eric Clapton (Channel 5 1989), Man And His Music (Video Collection 1990), Eric Clapton In Concert (Abbey Music Video 1991), 24 Nights (Warner Music Video 1991).
FURTHER READING: Conversations With Eric Clapton, Steve Turner. Eric Clapton: A Biography, John Pidgeon. Survivor: The Authorized Biography Of Eric Clapton, Ray Coleman. Clapton: The Complete Chronicle, Marc Roberty. Eric Clapton: The New Visual Documentary, Marc Roberty. Eric Clapton: Lost In The Blues, Harry Shapiro. Eric Clapton: The Complete Recording Sessions, Marc Roberty. The Man, The Music, The Memorabilia, Marc Roberty. Edge Of Darkness, Christopher Sandford. Complete Guide To The Music Of, Marc Roberty, Crossroads: The Life And Music Of Eric Clapton, Michael Schumacher.

CLARK, GENE
ALBUMS: Echoes (With The Gosdin Brothers) (Columbia 1967)★★★★ re-issued as Gene Clark With The Gosdin Brothers (Edsel 1997), White Light (A&M 1971)★★★, Roadmaster (A&M 1972)★★★, No Other (Asylum 1974)★★★★, Two Sides To Every Story (RSO 1977)★★, Firebyrd (Takoma 1984)★★ re-issued as This Byrd Has Flown (Edsel 1995), with Carla Olson So Rebellious A Lover (Demon 1987)★★★, with Carla Olson Silhouetted In Light (Demon 1992)★★★.
COMPILATIONS: American Dreamer 1964 – '74 (1993)★★★★.

CLARK, GUY
ALBUMS: Old No. 1 (RCA 1975)★★★★, Texas Cookin' (RCA 1976)★★★, Guy Clark (Warners 1978)★★★, The South Coast Of Texas (Warners 1981)★★★, Better Days (Warners 1983)★★★, Old Friends (Sugar Hill 1989)★★, Boats To Build (Asylum 1992)★★★, Dublin Blues (Asylum 1995)★★★, Keepers – A Live Recording (Sugar Hill 1997)★★★.
COMPILATIONS: Best Of Guy Clark (RCA 1982)★★★, Craftsman (Philo 1995)★★★, The Essential Guy Clark (RCA 1997)★★★★.

CLARK, PETULA
ALBUMS: Petula Clark Sings (Pye Nixa 1956)★★★, A Date With Pet (Pye Nixa 1956)★★★, You Are My Lucky Star (Pye Nixa 1957)★★★, Pet Clark (1959)★★★, Petula Clark In Hollywood (Pye Nixa 1959)★★★, In Other Words (Pye 1962)★★★, Petula (Pye 1962)★★★, Les James Dean (Pye-Vogue 1962)★★★, Downtown (Pye 1964)★★★★, I Know A Place (1965)★★★, The World's Greatest International Hits! (1965)★★★, The New Petula Clark Album (Pye 1965)★★★, Uptown With Petula Clark (1965)★★★, In Love (1965)★★★, Petula '65 (1965)★★★★, My Love (1966),★★★★ Petula '66 (1966)★★★, Hello Paris, Vol. I (Pye-Vogue 1966)★★★, Hello Paris, Vol. II (Pye-Vogue 1966)★★★, Petula Clark Sings For Everybody (1966)★★★, I Couldn't Live Without Your Love (1966),★★★★, Colour My World/Who Am I? (1967)★★★, These Are My Songs (Pye 1967)★★★, The Other Man's Grass Is Always Greener (Pye 1968)★★★★, Petula (Pye 1968)★★★, Portrait Of Petula (Pye 1969)★★★, Just Pet (Pye 1969)★★★, Memphis (Pye 1970)★★, The Song Of My Life (Pye 1971)★★★, Wonderland Of Sound (1971)★★, Today (Pye 1971)★★★, Petula '71 (Pye 1971)★★★, Warm And Tender (1971)★★★, Live At The Royal Albert Hall (Pye 1972)★★★, Now (Polydor 1972)★★★, Live In London (1974)★★★, Come On Home (1974)★★★, C'est Le Befrain De Ma Vie (1975)★★★, La Chanson De Marie-Madeloine (1975)★★★, I'm The Woman You Need (1975)★★★, Just Petula (Polydor 1975)★★★, Noel (Pet Projects 1975)★★, Beautiful Sounds (Pet Projects 1976)★★, Destiny (CBS 1978)★★★, An Hour In Concert With Petula Clark (1983)★★★, Don't Sleep In The Subway (RPM 1995)★★★.
COMPILATIONS: Petula's Greatest Hits, Vol. 1 (1968)★★★★, Petula Clark's Hit Parade (Pye 1969)★★★★, Petula Clark's 20 All Time Greatest (1977)★★★★, Spotlight On Petula Clark (1980)★★★, 100 Minutes Of Petula Clark (1982)★★★, Early Years (1986)★★★, The Hit Singles Collection (1987)★★★★, My Greatest (1989)★★★, Downtown (1989)★★★, Treasures Vol. 1 (1992)★★★, Jumble Sale: Rarities And Obscurities 1959-64 2-CD set (1992)★★★★, The EP Collection Vol. 2 (See For Miles 1993)★★★★, The Nixa Years Vol. One 2-CD set (1994)★★★★, The Polygon Years Vol. One: 1950-1952 (RPM 1994)★★★, The Polygon Years Vol. Two: 1952-1955 (RPM 1994)★★★, I Love To Sing 3-CD set (Sequel 1995)★★★★, The Nixa Years Vol. Two 2-CD set (1995)★★★★, Downtown (Spectrum 1995)★★★, The Pye Years Vol. Two (RPM 1996)★★★, These Are My Songs (Start 1996)★★★, The Pye Years Vol. Three (RPM 1997)★★★★.
VIDEOS: Petula Clark Spectacular (Laserlight 1996).
FURTHER READING: This Is My Song: Biography Of Petula Clark, Andrea Kon.

CLASH
ALBUMS: The Clash (Columbia 1977)★★★★, Give 'Em Enough Rope (Columbia 1978)★★★, London Calling double album (Columbia 1979)★★★★, Sandinista! (Columbia 1980)★★, Combat Rock (Columbia 1982)★★, Cut The Crap (Columbia 1985)H.
COMPILATIONS: The Story Of The Clash (Columbia 1988)★★★★, The Singles Collection (Columbia 1991)★★★.
VIDEOS: This Is Video Clash (CBS-Fox 1985) Rude Boy (Hendring Video 1987).
FURTHER READING: The Clash: Before & After, Pennie Smith. The Clash, Miles and John Tobler. Joe Strummer With The 101'ers & The Clash, Julian Leonard Yewdall. Last Gang In Town: Story Of The Clash, Marcus Gray.

CLASSICS IV
ALBUMS: Spooky (Liberty 1968)★★★, Mamas And Papas/Soul Train (1969)★★, Traces (1969)★★.
COMPILATIONS: Dennis Yost And The Classics IV Golden Greats Volume 1 (1969)★★★, The Very Best Of The Classic IV (EMI 1975)★★★, Greatest Hits (CEMA 1992)★★★.

CLIFF, JIMMY
ALBUMS: Jimmy Cliff (Trojan 1969)★★★, Wonderful World, Beautiful People (A&M 1970)★★★★, Hard Road To Travel (Trojan/A&M 1970)★★★, Another Cycle (Island 1971)★★★, The Harder They Come film soundtrack (Mango/Island 1972)★★★★★, Unlimited (EMI 1973, Trojan 1990)★★★, Struggling Man (Island 1974)★★★, Brave Warrior (EMI 1975)★★★, Follow My Mind (Reprise 1976)★★, Give Thanx (Warners 1978)★★, Oh Jamaica (EMI 1979)★★, I Am The Living (Warners 1980)★★, Give The People What They Want (Oneness/Warners 1981)★★, House Of Exile (1981)★★, Special (Columbia 1982)★★, The Power And The Glory (Columbia 1983)★★★, Can't Get Enough Of It (Veep 1984)★★★, Cliff Hanger (Dynamic/Columbia 1985)★★, Sense Of Direction (Sire 1985)★★★, Hang Fire (Dynamic/Columbia 1987)★★★, Images (Cliff Sounds 1989)★★★, Save Our Planet Earth (Musidisc 1990)★★, Breakout (Cliff Sounds 1993)★★★, The Cool Runner Live In London (More Music 1995)★★.
COMPILATIONS: The Best Of Jimmy Cliff (Island 1974)★★★★, The Best Of Jimmy Cliff In Concert (Reprise 1977)★★★, The Collection (EMI 1983)★★★, Jimmy Cliff (Trojan 1983)★★★, Reggae Greats (Island 1985)★★★, Fundamental Reggae (See For Miles 1987)★★★, The Best Of Jimmy Cliff (Mango/Island 1988)★★★★.
FILMS: The Harder They Come (1972).
VIDEOS: Bongo Man (Hendring Video 1989).

CLIMAX BLUES BAND
ALBUMS: Climax Chicago Blues Band (Parlophone 1969)★★, Plays On (Parlophone 1969)★★★, A Lot Of Bottle (Harvest 1970)★★, Tightly Knit (Harvest 1971)★★★, Rich Man (Harvest 1972)★★★, FM/Live (Polydor 1973), Sense Of Direction (Polydor 1974)★★★, Stamp Album (BTM 1975)★★★, Gold Plated (BTM 1976)★★, Shine On (Warners 1978)★★★, Real To Reel (Warners 1979)★★★, Flying The Flag (Warners 1980)★★★, Lucky For Some (Warners 1981)★★, Sample And Hold (Virgin 1983)★★, Drastic Steps (Clay 1988)★★, Blues From The Attic (HTD 1994)★★★.
COMPILATIONS: 1969-1972 (Harvest 1975)★★★, Best Of The Climax Blues Band (RCA 1983)★★★, Loosen Up (1974-1976) (See For Miles 1984)★★★, 25 Years Of The Climax Blues Band (Repertoire 1993)★★★.

CLINE, PATSY
ALBUMS: Patsy Cline (Decca 1957)★★★★, Patsy Cline Showcase (Decca 1961)★★★★, Sentimentally Yours (Decca 1962)★★★★, In Memoriam (Everest 1963)★★★★, Encores (Everest 1963)★★★, A Legend (Everest 1963)★★★, Reflections (Everest 1964)★★★, A Portait Of Patsy Cline (Decca 1964)★★★★, That's How A Heartache Begins (Decca 1964)★★★, Today, Tomorrow, Forever (Hilltop 1964)★★★, Gotta Lot Of Rhythm In My Soul (Metro 1965)★★★, Stop The World And Let Me Off (Hilltop 1966)★★★, The Last Sessions (MCA 1980)★★★★, Try Again (Quicksilver 1982)★★★, Sweet Dreams film soundtrack (1985)★★★, Live At The Opry (MCA 1988)★★★, Live – Volume Two (MCA 1989)★★★, The Birth Of A Star (Razor & Tie 1996)★★★, Live At The Cimarron Ballroom recorded 1961 (MCA 1997)★★★.
COMPILATIONS: Patsy Cline's Golden Hits (Everest 1962)★★★, The Patsy Cline Story (Decca 1963)★★★★, Patsy Cline's Greatest Hits (Decca 1967)★★★, Country Great (Vocalion 1969)★★★, Greatest Hits (MCA 1973)★★★★★, Golden Greats (MCA 1979)★★★★★, 20 Golden Greats (Astan 1984)★★★, 20 Classic Tracks (Starburst 1987)★★★, 12 Greatest Hits (MCA 1988)★★★, Dreaming (Platinum Music 1988)★★★, 20 Golden Hits (Deluxe 1989)★★★, Walkin' Dreams: Her First Recordings, Volume One (Rhino 1989)★★★★, Hungry For Love: Her First Recordings, Volume Two (Rhino 1989)★★★★, Rockin' Side: Her First Recordings, Volume Three (Rhino 1989)★★★★, The Patsy Cline Collection 4-CD box set (MCA 1991)★★★★★, The Definitive (1992)★★★, Discovery (Prism Leisure 1994)★★★, Premier Collection (Pickwick 1994)★★★, The Patsy Cline Story (MCA 1994)★★★★, Thinking Of You (Summit 1995)★★★, Today, Tomorrow And Forever 2-CD (Parade 1995)★★★.
VIDEOS: The Real Patsy Cline (Platinum Music 1989), Remembering Patsy (1993).
FURTHER READING: Patsy Cline: Sweet Dreams, Ellis Nassour. Honky Tonk Angel: The Intimate Story Of Patsy Cline, Ellis Nassour. Patsy: The Life And Times Of Patsy Cline, Margaret Jones. I Fall To Pieces: The Music And The Life Of Patsy Cline, Mark Bego.

CLINT EASTWOOD AND GENERAL SAINT
ALBUMS: as Clint Eastwood African Youth (Third World 1978)★★★, Death In The Arena (Cha Cha 1978)★★★, Love & Happiness (Burning Sounds 1979)★★★, Sex Education (Greensleeves 1980)★★★, Jah Lights Shining (Vista Sounds 1984)★★★.
COMPILATIONS: as Clint Eastwood Best Of Clint Eastwood (Culture Press 1984)★★★★, Two Bad DJ (Greensleeves 1981)★★★, Stop That Train (Greensleeves 1983)★★★.

CLINTON, GEORGE
ALBUMS: Computer Games (Capitol 1982)★★★, You Shouldn't-Nuf Bit Fish (Capitol 1984)★★★★, with the P-Funk All Stars Urban Dance Floor Guerillas (1984)★★★, Some Of My Best Jokes Are Friends (Capitol 1985)★★★★, R&B Skeletons In The Closet (Capitol 1986)★★★, The Cinderella Theory (Paisley Park 1989)★★★, Sample A Bit Of Disc And A Bit Of Dat (AEM 1993)★★★, Hey Man ... Smell My Finger (Paisley Park 1993)★★★, A Fifth Of Funk (Castle Communications 1995)★★★, The Music Of Red Shoe Diaries (Wenerworld 1995)★★★, Mortal Kombat (London 1996)★★★, with the P-Funk All Stars Tapoafom (Epic 1996)★★★, The Awesome Power Of A Fully Operational Mothership (Epic 1996)★★★, P-Funk All Stars Live At The Beverly Theatre (Westbound 1996)★★★, with the P-Funk All Stars Live And Kickin' (Intersound 1997)★★★.
COMPILATIONS: The Best Of George Clinton (Capitol 1986)★★★★, Family Series: Testing Positive 4 The Funk (Essential 1994)★★★, Greatest Funkin' Hits (Capitol 1996)★★★★.
VIDEOS: Mothership Connection (Virgin Vision 1987).

CLOCK DVA
ALBUMS: White Souls In Black Suits cassette only (Industrial 1980)★★, Thirst (Fetish 1981)★★★, Advantage (Polydor 1983)★★★, Buried Dreams (Interfish 1989)★★★, Transitional Voices (Amphetamine Reptile 1991)★★★, Man-Amplified (Contempo 1992)★★★, Digital Soundtrack (Contempo 1993)★★★, Sign (Contempo 1993)★★★, Black Words On White Paper (Contempo 1993)★★★, Virtual Reality Handbook (Contempo 1993)★★★, 150 Erotic Calibrations (Contempo 1994)★★★, Anterior (Contempo 1995)★★★.
VIDEOS: Kinetic Engineering (1994).

CLOVER
ALBUMS: Clover (Liberty 1970)★★, Forty-Niner (Liberty 1971)★★★, Unavailable (Vertigo 1977)★★★, Love On The Wire (Vertigo 1977)★★★.
COMPILATIONS: Clover Chronicle – The Best Of The Fantasy Years (DJM 1979)★★★, The Best Of Clover (Mercury 1986)★★★.

CLOVERS
ALBUMS: The Clovers (Atlantic 1956)★★★★, Dance Party (Atlantic 1959)★★★★, In Clover (Poplar 1959)★★, Love Potion Number Nine (United Artists 1959)★★★, Clovers Live At CT's (1989)★★.
COMPILATIONS: The Original Love Potion Number Nine (Grand Prix 1964)★★★★, Their Greatest Recordings – The Early Years (Atco 1975)★★★★, The Best Of The Clovers: Love Potion Number Nine (EMI 1991)★★★★, Down In The Alley (Atlantic 1991)★★★, Dance Party (Sequel 1997)★★★★.

COASTERS
ALBUMS: The Coasters (Atco 1958)★★★★, One By One (Atco 1960)★★★★, Coast Along With The Coasters (Atco 1962)★★★, That's Rock And Roll (Clarion 1964)★★, On Broadway (King 1973)★★.
COMPILATIONS: The Coasters' Greatest Hits (Atco 1959)★★★★, Their Greatest Recordings: The Early Years (Atco 1971)★★★, 20 Great Originals (Atlantic 1978)★★★, What Is The Secret Of Your Success? (Mr R&B 1980)★★★, Thumbin' A Ride (Edsel 1985)★★★, The Ultimate Coasters (Warners 1986)★★★, Let's Go To The Dance (Harmony 1988)★★★, Poison Ivy (1991)★★★★, 50 Coastin' Classics: The Coasters Anthology (Rhino/Atlantic 1992)★★★★, Yakety Yak (Pickwick 1995)★★★★.
FURTHER READING: The Coasters, Bill Millar.

COCHRAN, EDDIE
ALBUMS: Singing To My Baby (Liberty 1957)★★★, Eddie Cochran (Liberty 1960)★★★, The Eddie Cochran Memorial Album (1960)★★★, Never To Be Forgotten (Liberty 1962)★★★, Cherished Memories (Liberty 1962)★★★★, My Way (Liberty 1964)★★★, On The Air (1972)★★★, The Many Sides Of Eddie Cochran (1975)★★★, The Young Eddie Cochran (1982)★★★, Words And Music (1985)★★★, Portrait Of A Legend (1985)★★★, The Many Styles Of Eddie Cochran (1985)★★★, The Hollywood Sessions (1985)★★★.
COMPILATIONS: Summertime Blues (Sunset 1966)★★★★, The Very Best Of Eddie Cochran (Liberty 1970)★★★★, Legendary Masters (United Artists 1971)★★★★, The Singles Album (United Artists 1979)★★★★, 20th Anniversary Album 4-LP box set (United Artists 1980)★★★★, The 25th Anniversary Album (1985)★★★★, The Early Years (1988)★★★★, C'mon Everybody (1988)★★★★, The Eddie Cochran Box Set 6-LP box set (Liberty 1988)★★★★, Greatest Hits (Curb 1990)★★★★, The EP Collection (See For Miles 1991)★★★★, Mighty Mean (Rock star 1995)★★★.
FILMS: The Girl Can't Help It (1956), Go Johnny Go (1958).
FURTHER READING: The Eddie Cochran Nostalgia Book, Alan Clark. Eddie Cochran: Never To Be Forgotten, Alan Clark. The Legend Continues, Alan Clark.

COCKBURN, BRUCE
ALBUMS: Bruce Cockburn (True North 1970)★★, High Winds White Sky (True North 1971)★★, Sunwheel Dance (True North 1972)★★, Night Vision (True North 1973)★★★, Salt Sun And Time (True North 1974)★★, Joy Will Find A Way (True North 1975)★★★, Circles In The Stream (True North 1977)★★, In The Falling Dark (True North 1977)★★, Further Adventures Of (True North 1978)★★★, Dancing In The Dragon's Jaws (True North 1980)★★★★, Rumours Of Glory (True North 1980)★★★, Humans (True North 1980)★★★, Inner City Front (True North 1981)★★★, Trouble With Normal (True North 1983)★★★, Stealing Fire (True North 1984)★★★★, World Of Wonders (True North 1986)★★★, Big Circumstance (True North 1989)★★★, Live (True North 1990)★★★, Nothing But A Burning Light (Columbia 1992)★★★★, Dart To The Heart (Columbia 1994)★★★, The Charity Of Night (Rykodisc 1996)★★★.
COMPILATIONS: Mummy Dust/Resumé (True North 1981)★★★★, Waiting For A Miracle (singles collection)(Revolver 1987)★★★★.

COCKER, JOE
ALBUMS: With A Little Help From My Friends (Regal Zonophone 1969)★★★★, Joe Cocker! (Regal Zonophone 1970)★★★★, Mad Dogs And Englishmen (A&M 1970)★★★★, Cocker Happy (Fly 1971)★★★, Something To Say (Cube 1973)★★, I Can Stand A Little Rain (Cube 1974)★★, Jamaica Say You Will (Cube 1975)★★, Stingray (A&M 1976)★★★, Live In LA (Cube 1976)★★, Luxury You Can Afford (Asylum 1978)★★★, by the Crusaders Standing Tall (MCA 1981)★★, Sheffield Steel (Island 1982)★★★, Space Captain (Cube 1982)★★, Countdown Joe Cocker (Cube 1982)★★, An Officer And A Gentleman soundtrack (Island 1983)★★, A Civilized Man (Capitol 1984)★★, Cocker (Capitol 1986)★★, Unchain My Heart (Capitol 1987)★★★, One Night Of Sin (Capitol 1989)★★, Joe Cocker Live (Capitol 1990)★★, Night Calls (Capitol 1992)★★, Have A Little Faith (Capitol 1994)★★★, Organic (Parlophone 1996)★★★, Across From Midnight (Capitol 1997)★★★.
COMPILATIONS: Greatest Hits Volume 1 (Hallmark 1978)★★★, Joe Cocker Platinum Collection (Cube 1981)★★★, Joe Cocker Collection (Castle 1986)★★★, Best Of Joe Cocker (K-Tel 1988)★★★, Connoisseur's Cocker (1991)★★★, Joe Cocker: The Legend (1992)★★★★, The Long Voyage Home 4-CD box set (A&M 1995)★★★★.
FILMS: Mad Dogs And Englishmen.
VIDEOS: Mad Dogs And Englishmen (A&M Sound Pictures 1988), Have A Little Faith (1995).
FURTHER READING: Joe Cocker: With A Little Help From My Friends, J.P. Bean.

COCKNEY REBEL
ALBUMS: The Human Menagerie (EMI 1973)★★★, Psychomodo (EMI 1974)★★★, The Best Years Of Our Lives (EMI 1975)★★, Love's A Prima Donna (EMI 1976)★★, Face To Face – A Live Recording (EMI 1977)★★, Hobo With A Grin (EMI 1978)★★.
Solo: Steve Harley Poetic Justice (Castle 1996)★★.
COMPILATIONS: The Best Of Steve Harley And Cockney Rebel(EMI 1980)★★★, Mr Soft – Greatest Hits (Connoisseur 1988)★★★, Make Me Smile, The Best Of Steve Harley And Cockney Rebel (1992)★★★.

COCTEAU TWINS
ALBUMS: Garlands (4AD 1982)★★★, Head Over Heels (4AD 1983)★★★, Treasure (4AD 1984)★★★, Victorialand (4AD 1986)★★★, as Harold Budd, Elizabeth Fraser, Robin Guthrie, Simon Raymonde The Moon And The Melodies (4AD 1986)★★★, Blue Bell Knoll (4AD 1988)★★, Heaven Or Las Vegas (4AD 1990)★★★★, Four-Calendar Café (Fontana 1993)★★★, Milk And Kisses (Fontana 1996)★★★.
Solo: Simon Raymonde Blame Someone Else (Bella Union 1997)★★.
COMPILATIONS: The Pink Opaque (4AD 1986)★★★, The Singles Collection (Capitol 1991)★★★.

COGAN, ALMA
ALBUMS: I Love To Sing (HMV 1958)★★★, With You In Mind (Columbia 1961)★★★, How About Love (Columbia 1962)★★★.
COMPILATIONS: The Alma Cogan Collection (One-Up 1977)★★★, The Second Collection (One-Up 1978)★★★, The Very Best Of Alma Cogan (1984)★★★, Celebration (1987)★★★, Alma Cogan – Compacts For Pleasure (1994)★★★, The A-Z Of Alma 3-CD set (1994)★★★★.
FURTHER READING: Alma Cogan, Sandra Caron. Alma Cogan, Gordon Burn.

COHEN, LEONARD
ALBUMS: The Songs Of Leonard Cohen (Columbia 1968)★★★★, Songs From A Room (Columbia 1969)★★★, Songs Of Love And Hate (Columbia 1971)★★★, Live Songs (Columbia 1973)★★★, New Skin For The Old Ceremony (Columbia 1974)★★★, Death Of A Ladies' Man (Columbia 1977)★★★, Recent Songs (Columbia 1979)★★★, Various Positions (Columbia 1985)★★★, I'm Your Man (Columbia 1988)★★★★, The Future (Columbia 1992)★★★★, Cohen Live (Columbia 1994)★★★.
COMPILATIONS: Greatest Hits (Columbia 1975)★★★★, The Best Of Leonard Cohen (Columbia 1976)★★★★, More Best Of (Columbia 1997)★★★.
FILMS: Bird On A Wire (1972).
VIDEOS: Songs From The Life Of Leonard Cohen (CMV Enterprises 1989).
FURTHER READING: Beautiful Losers, Leonard Cohen. Selected Poems 1956-1968, Leonard Cohen. The Favourite Game, Leonard Cohen. Flowers For Hitler, Leonard Cohen. The Spice-box Of Earth, Leonard Cohen. Death Of A Ladies' Man, Leonard Cohen. Leonard Cohen: Prophet Of The Heart, L.S. Dorman and C.L. Rawlins. Stranger Music, Selected Poems And Songs, Leonard Cohen. Leonard Cohen: A Life In Art, Ira Nadel.

COLD BLOOD
ALBUMS: Cold Blood (San Francisco 1969)★★★, Sisyphus (San Francisco 1971)★★★, First Taste Of Sin (Reprise 1972)★★, Thriller! (Reprise 1973)★★, Lydia (Warners 1974)★★, Lydia Pense And Cold Blood (ABC 1976)★★.

COLE, LLOYD
ALBUMS: with the Commotions Rattlesnakes (Polydor 1984)★★★★, with the Commotions Easy Pieces (Polydor 1985)★★★, with the Commotions Mainstream (Polydor 1987)★★★, Lloyd Cole (Polydor 1989)★★★, Don't Get Weird On Me, Babe (Polydor 1991)★★★, Bad Vibes (Fontana 1993)★★, Love Story (Fontana 1995)★★★.
COMPILATIONS: 1984-1989 (Polydor 1989)★★★★.
VIDEOS: Lloyd Cole & The Commotions (Channel 5 1986), From The Hip (Polygram Music Video 1988), 1984 – 1989 (Lloyd Cole & The Commotions) (Channel 5 1989).

COLE, NATALIE
ALBUMS: Inseparable (Capitol 1975)★★★★, Natalie (Capitol 1976)★★★, Unpredictable (Capitol 1977)★★★, Thankful (Capitol 1977)★★★, Natalie ... Live! (Capitol 1978)★★★★, I Love You So (Capitol 1979)★★★, with Peabo Bryson We're The Best Of Friends (Capitol 1979)★★★, Don't Look Back (Capitol 1980)★★, Happy Love (Capitol 1981)★★, with Johnny Mathis Unforgettable: A Musical Tribute To Nat 'King' Cole (Columbia 1983)★★★, I'm Ready (Epic 1983)★★, Dangerous (Modern 1985)★★, Everlasting (Manhattan 1987)★★, Good To Be Back (EMI 1989)★★, Unforgettable ... With Love (Elektra 1991)★★★★, Take A Look (Elektra 1993)★★★, Star Dust (Elektra 1996)★★★.
COMPILATIONS: The Natalie Cole Collection (Capitol 1988)★★★, The Soul Of Natalie Cole (1974-80) (Capitol 1991)★★★★.
VIDEOS: Video Hits (PMI 1989), Holly & Ivy (Warner Music Vision 1995).

COLE, PAULA
ALBUMS: Harbinger (Imago 1994)★★★, This Fire (Imago/Warners 1996)★★★.

COLLECTIVE SOUL
ALBUMS: Hints, Allegations & Things Left Unsaid (Atlantic 1993)★★★, Collective Soul (Atlantic 1995)★★★★, Disciplined Breakdown (Atlantic 1997)★★.

COLLINS, ALBERT
ALBUMS: *The Cool Sound Of* (TCF Hall 1965)★★★, *Love Can Be Found Anywhere, Even In A Guitar* (Imperial 1968)★★★, *Trash Talkin* (Imperial 1969)★★★, *The Complete Albert Collins* (Imperial 1969)★★★, *Alive And Cool* (1969)★★★, *Truckin' With Albert Collins* (Blue Thumb 1969)★★★, with Barrelhouse *Live* (Munich 1970)★★, *There's Gotta Be A Change* (1971)★★, *Ice Pickin'* (Alligator 1978)★★★★, *Frostbite* (Alligator 1980)★★★★, *Frozen Alive!* (Alligator 1981)★★★★, *Don't Lose Your Cool* (Alligator 1983)★★★, *Live In Japan* (Alligator 1984)★★★★, with Johnny Copeland, Robert Cray *Showdown!* (Alligator 1985)★★★★, *Cold Snap* (Alligator 1986)★★★, *The Ice Man* (Charisma/Point Blank 1991)★★★★, *Molten Ice* (Red Lightnin' 1992)★★★, *Live 92/93* (Pointblank 1995)★★★.
COMPILATIONS: *The Complete Imperial Recordings* (EMI 1991)★★★★, *Collins Mix (The Best Of)* (Pointblank 1993)★★★★, *Deluxe Edition* (Alligator 1997)★★★★.

COLLINS, BOOTSY
ALBUMS: *Stretchin' Out In Bootsy's Rubber Band* (Warners 1976)★★★, *Ahh...The Name Is Bootsy, Baby!* (Warners 1977)★★★, *Bootsy? Player Of The Year* (Warners 1978)★★★, *This Boot Is Made For Fonk-n* (Warners 1979)★★, *Ultra Wave* (Warners 1980)★★★, *The One Giveth, The Count Taketh Away* (Warners 1982)★★★, *What's Bootsy Doin'?* (Columbia 1988)★★★, *Jungle Bass* (4th & Broadway 1990)★★★, *Blasters Of The Universe* (Rykodisc 1994)★★★, *Fresh Outta "P" University* (Warners 1997)★★★.
COMPILATIONS: *Back In The Day: The Best Of ...* (Warners 1995)★★★★.

COLLINS, EDWYN
ALBUMS: *Hope And Despair* (Demon 1989)★★★, *Hellbent On Compromise* (Demon 1990)★★, *Gorgeous George* (Setanta 1994)★★★★, *I'm Not Following You* (Setanta 1997)★★★.
VIDEOS: *Phantasmagoria* (Alternative Image 1992).

COLLINS, JUDY
ALBUMS: *A Maid Of Constant Sorrow* (Elektra 1961)★★★, *The Golden Apples Of The Sun* (Elektra 1962)★★★, *Judy Collins #3* (Elektra 1964)★★★, *The Judy Collins Concert* (Elektra 1964)★★, *Judy Collins' Fifth Album* (Elektra 1965)★★★, *In My Life* (1966)★★★★, *Wildflowers* (Elektra 1967)★★★★, *Who Knows Where The Time Goes* (Elektra 1968)★★★★, *Whales And Nightingales* (Elektra 1970)★★★, *Living* (Elektra 1971)★★★, *True Stories And Other Dreams* (Elektra 1973)★★★, *Judith* (Elektra 1975)★★★, *Bread And Roses* (Elektra 1976)★★★, *Hard Times For Lovers* (Elektra 1979)★★, *Running For My Life* (Elektra 1980)★★★, *Time Of Our Lives* (Elektra 1982)★★, *Home Again* (1984)★★, *Trust Your Heart* (Gold Castle 1987)★★, *Sanity And Grace* (Gold Castle 1987)★★, *Fires Of Eden* (CBS 1990)★★, *Judy Sings Dylan ... Just Like A Woman* (Geffen 1994)★★, *Come Rejoice: A Judy Collins Christmas* (Mesa 1994)★★★, *Shameless* (Mesa 1995)★★★.
COMPILATIONS: *Recollections* (Elektra 1969)★★★★, *Colours Of The Day: The Best Of Judy Collins* (Elektra 1972)★★★★, *So Early In The Spring, The First 15 Years* (Elektra 1977)★★★★, *Most Beautiful Songs Of Judy Collins* (Elektra 1979)★★★★, *Amazing Grace* (1985)★★★, Live At Newport (Vanguard 1994)★★★.
FURTHER READING: *Trust Your Heart: An Autobiography*, Judy Collins. *The Judy Collins Songbook*, Judy Collins and Herbert Haufrecht. *Judy Collins*, Vivian Claire. *Shameless*, Judy Collins.

COLLINS, PHIL
ALBUMS: *Face Value* (Virgin 1981)★★★★, *Hello, I Must Be Going* (Virgin 1982)★★★★, *No Jacket Required* (Virgin 1985)★★★, *... But Seriously* (Virgin 1989)★★★, *Serious Hits ... Live!* (Virgin 1990)★★, *Both Sides* (Virgin 1993)★★★, *Dance A Little Light* (Face Value 1996)H.
VIDEOS: *Live: Phil Collins* (1984), *Video EP: Phil Collins* (1986), *No Ticket Required* (1986), *Live At Perkin's Palace* (1986), *You Can't Hurry Love* (1987), *No Jacket Required* (1988), *The Singles Collection* (1989), *Seriously Live* (1990), *But Seriously, The Videos* (1992).
FURTHER READING: *Phil Collins*, Johnny Waller.

COLOUR FIELD
ALBUMS: *Virgins And Philistines* (Chrysalis 1985)★★★, *Deception* (Chrysalis 1987)★★★.

COLVIN, SHAWN
ALBUMS: *Steady On* (Columbia 1989)★★★★, *Fat City* (Columbia 1992)★★★, *Cover Girl* (Columbia 1994)★★★★, *Live '88* (Plump 1995)H, *A Few Small Repairs* (Columbia 1996)★★★★.

COMBS, SEAN 'PUFFY'
ALBUMS: as Puff Daddy And The Family *Hell Up In Harlem* (Bad Boy 1996)★★★★, film soundtrack *Godzilla* (1998).

COMMANDER CODY AND HIS LOST PLANET AIRMEN
ALBUMS: *Lost In The Ozone* (Paramount 1971)★★★, *Hot Licks, Cold Steel And Truckers' Favourites* (Paramount 1972)★★★, *Country Casanova* (Paramount 1973)★★★, *Live From Deep In The Heart Of Texas* (Paramount 1974)★★★★, *Commander Cody And His Lost Planet Airmen* (Warners 1975)★★, *Tales From The Ozone* (Warners 1975)★★, *We've Got A Live One Here!* (Warners 1976)★★★, *Let's Rock* (Blind Pig 1986)★★, *Sleazy Roadside Stories* 1973 live recording (Relix 1988)★★★, *Aces High* (Relix 1990)★★; as the Commander Cody Band *Rock 'N' Roll Again* (Arista 1977)★★, *Flying Dreams* (Arista 1978)★★, *Lose It Tonight* (Line 1980)★★.
Solo: Commander Cody *Midnight Man* (Arista 1977)★★. Billy Kirchen *Tombstone Every Mile* (Edsel 1994)★★★, *Have Love, Will Travel* (Black Top 1996)★★★★.
COMPILATIONS: *The Very Best Of Commander Cody And His Lost Planet Airmen* (See For Miles 1986)★★★, *Cody Returns From Outer Space* (Edsel 1987)★★★, *Too Much Fun – The Best Of Commander Cody* (MCA 1990)★★★, *Best Of* (Relix 1995)★★★.

COMMODORES
ALBUMS: *Machine Gun* (Motown 1974)★★★★, *Caught In The Act* (Motown 1975)★★★, *Movin' On* (Motown 1975)★★★, *Hot On The Tracks* (Motown 1976)★★★, *Commodores* aka *Zoom* (Motown 1977)★★★, *Commodores Live!* (Motown 1977)★★★, *Natural High* (Motown 1978)★★★, *Midnight Magic* (Motown 1979)★★★, *Heroes* (Motown 1980)★★★, *In The Pocket* (Motown 1981)★★★, *Commodores 13* (Motown 1983)★★★, *Nightshift* (Motown 1985)★★★, *United* (Polydor 1986)★★, *Rise Up* (Blue Moon 1987)★★, *Rock Solid* (Polydor 1988)★★.
COMPILATIONS: *Commodores' Greatest Hits* (Motown 1978)★★★★, *All The Great Hits* (Motown 1981)★★★, *Anthology* (Motown 1983)★★★, *The Best Of The Commodores* (Telstar 1985)★★★, *14 Greatest Hits* (1993)★★★, *The Very Best Of the Commodores* (Motown 1995)★★★★.
VIDEOS: *Cover Story* (Stylus Video 1990).

COMMUNARDS
ALBUMS: *Communards* (London 1986)★★★, *Red* (London 1987)★★★.
Solo: Jimmy Somerville *Read My Lips* (London 1989)★★★, *Dare To Love* (London 1995)★★.
COMPILATIONS: *The Singles Collection, 1984-1990* includes recordings from Bronski Beat, Communards, Jimmy Somerville (London 1990)★★★★.
VIDEOS: *Communards: The Video Singles* (1987).

COMSAT ANGELS
ALBUMS: *Waiting For A Miracle* (Polydor 1980)★★, *Sleep No More* (Polydor 1981)★★★, *Fiction* (Polydor 1982)★★★, *Land* (Jive 1983)★★★, *Seven Day Weekend* (Jive 1985)★★★, *Chasing Shadows* (Island 1987)★★★, as Dream Command *Fire On The Moon* (Island 1990)★★★, *My Mind's Eye* (RPM 1992)★★★, *The Glamour* (Thunderbird 1995)★★★.
COMPILATIONS: *Time Considered As A Helix Of Semi-Precious Stones* (RPM 1992)★★★, *Unravelled* (RPM 1994)★★★.

CONCRETE BLONDE
ALBUMS: *Concrete Blonde* (IRS 1986)★★★, *Free* (IRS 1989)★★★, *Bloodletting* (IRS 1990)★★★, *Walking In London* (IRS 1992)★★★, *Mexican Moon* (IRS 1993)★★★.
COMPILATIONS: *Recollection: The Best Of* (IRS 1996)★★★.

CONLEY, ARTHUR
ALBUMS: *Sweet Soul Music* (Atco 1967)★★★★, *Shake, Rattle And Roll* (Atco 1967)★★★, *Soul Directions* (Atco 1968)★★★, *More Sweet Soul*(Atco 1969)★★★, *One More Sweet Soul Music* (Warners 1988)★★, as Lee Roberts And The Sweater *Soulin'* (Blue Shadow 1988)★★★.
COMPILATIONS: *Arthur Conley* (Atlantic 1988)★★★.
FURTHER READING: *Sweet Soul Music*, Peter Guralnick.

CONTOURS
ALBUMS: *Do You Love Me* (Gordy 1962)★★★, *Running In Circles* (Motor City 1990)★★.
COMPILATIONS: *Baby Hit And Run* (1974)★★★, *The Very Best* (Essential Gold 1996)★★★.

COODER, RY
ALBUMS: *Ry Cooder* (Reprise 1970)★★★, *Into The Purple Valley* (Reprise 1971)★★★★, *Boomer's Story* (Reprise 1972)★★★★, *Paradise And Lunch* (Reprise 1974)★★★★, *Chicken Skin Music* (Reprise 1976)★★★★, *Showtime* (Warners 1976)★★★, *Jazz* (Warners 1978)★★, *Bop Till You Drop* (Warners 1979)★★★, *Borderline* (Warners 1980)★★★, *The Long Riders* film soundtrack (Warners 1980)★★★, *The Border* film soundtrack (MCA 1980)★★★, *Ry Cooder Live* (Warners 1982)★★★, *The Slide Area* (Warners 1982)★★, *Paris, Texas* film soundtrack (Warners 1985)★★★, *Alamo Bay* film soundtrack (Slash 1985)★★★, *Blue City* film soundtrack (Warners 1986)★★, *Crossroads* film soundtrack (Warners 1987)★★, *Get Rhythm* (Warners 1987)★★, *Johnny Handsome* film soundtrack (Warners 1989)★★★, with Little Village *Little Village* (Reprise 1992)★★, *Trespass* film soundtrack (Sire/Warners 1993)★★, with V.M. Bhatt *A Meeting By The River* (1993)★★★, with Ali Farka Toure *Talking Timbuktu* (World Circuit 1994)★★★★, *Geronimo* film soundtrack (Columbia 1994)★★★, *Buena Vista Social Club* (1998)★★★.
COMPILATIONS: *Why Don't You Try Me Tonight?* (Warners 1985)★★★, *Music By ...* (Reprise 1995)★★★, *Best Of ...* (Reprise 1997)★★★.

COOKE, SAM
ALBUMS: *Sam Cooke* (Keen 1958)★★★, *Sam Cooke Encore* (Keen 1959)★★★, *Tribute To The Lady* (Keen 1959)★★★, *Hit Kit* (Keen 1960)★★★, *I Thank God* (Keen 1960)★★★, *Wonderful World Of Sam Cooke* (Keen 1960)★★★, *Cooke's Tour* (RCA 1960)★★★, *Hits Of The 50s* (RCA 1960)★★★, *Swing Low* (1961)★★★, *My Kind Of Blues* (RCA 1961)★★★★, *Twistin' The Night Away* (RCA 1962)★★★★, *Mr. Soul* (RCA 1963)★★★★, *Night Beat* (RCA 1963)★★★, *Ain't That Good News* (RCA 1964)★★★, *Sam Cooke At The Copa* (RCA 1964)★★★★, *Shake* (RCA 1965)★★★, *Try A Little Love* (RCA 1965)★★★, *Sam Cooke Sings Billie Holiday* (RCA 1976)★★★, *Sam Cooke Live At The Harlem Square Club, 1963* (RCA 1985)★★★.
COMPILATIONS: *The Best Of Sam Cooke, Volume 1* (RCA 1962)★★★★, *The Best Of Sam Cooke, Volume 2* (RCA 1965)★★★★, *The Late And Great* (1969)★★★, *The Gospel Soul Of Sam Cooke With The Soul Stirrers, Volume 1* (Specialty 1969)★★★★, *The Gospel Soul Of Sam Cooke With The Soul Stirrers, Volume 2* (Specialty 1970)★★★★, *The Two Sides Of Sam Cooke* (Specialty 1970)★★★, *This Is Sam Cooke* (RCA 1971)★★★, *That's Heaven To Me: Sam Cooke With The Soul Stirrers* (Specialty 1972)★★★★, *The Golden Age Of Sam Cooke* (RCA 1976)★★★, *The Man And His Music* (RCA 1986)★★★★★, *Forever* (Specialty 1986)★★★, *Sam Cooke II* (Deja Vu 1987)★★★, *You Send Me* (Topline/Charly 1987)★★★, *20 Greatest Hits* (Compact Collection 1987)★★★★, *Wonderful World* (Fame 1988)★★★★, *The World Of Sam Cooke* (Instant 1989)★★★★, *Legend* (EMS 1990)★★★, *The Magic Of Sam Cooke* (Music Club 1991)★★★, *Sam Cooke With The Soul Stirrers* (Specialty 1991)★★★★, *Sam Cooke's Sar Records Story* (1994)★★★.
FURTHER READING: *Sam Cooke: The Man Who Invented Soul: A Biography In Words & Pictures*, Joe McEwen. *You Send Me: The Life And Times*, S.R. Crain, Clifton White and G. David Tenenbaum.

COOKIES
COMPILATIONS: *The Complete Cookies* (Sequel 1994)★★★.

COOLIDGE, RITA
ALBUMS: *Rita Coolidge* (A&M 1971)★★★, *Nice Feelin'* (A&M 1971)★★, *The Lady's Not For Sale* (A&M 1972)★★★, with Kris Kristofferson *Full Moon* (A&M 1973)★★★, *Fall Into Spring* (A&M 1974)★★★, with Kris Kristofferson *Breakaway* (Monument 1974)H, *It's Only Love* (A&M 1975)★★, *Anytime Anywhere* (A&M 1977)★★★★, *Love Me Again* (A&M 1978)★★★, with Kris Kristofferson *Natural Act* (A&M 1979)★★, *Satisfied* (A&M 1979)★★, *Heartbreak Radio* (A&M 1981)★★, *Never Let You Go* (A&M 1983)★★, *Inside The Fire* (A&M 1988)★★, *All Time High* (1993)★★, *Cherokee* (Permanent 1995)★★, with Walela *Walela* (Triloka 1997)★★★.
COMPILATIONS: *Greatest Hits* (A&M 1981)★★★.

COOLIO
ALBUMS: *It Takes A Thief* (Tommy Boy 1994)★★★, *Gangsta's Paradise* (Tommy Boy 1995)★★★★, *My Soul* (Tommy Boy 1997)★★★.

COPE, JULIAN
ALBUMS: *World Shut Your Mouth* (Mercury 1984)★★★, *Fried* (Mercury 1984)★★★, *Saint Julian* (Island 1987)★★★★, *My Nation Underground* (Island 1988)★★★, *Skellington* (Capeco-Zippo 1990)★★★, *Droolian* (Mofoco-Zippo 1990)★★, *Peggy Suicide* (Island 1991)★★★★, *Jehovahkill* (Island 1993)★★, *Autogeddon* (Echo 1994)★★, *Rite* (Echo 1994)★★, *Queen Elizabeth* (Echo 1994)★★, *Julian Cope Presents 20 Mothers* (Echo 1995)★★★, *Interpreter* (Echo 1996)★★★★, *Rite 2* (Head Heritage 1997)★★.
COMPILATIONS: *Floored Genius – The Best Of Julian Cope And The Teardrop Explodes 1981-91* (Island 1992)★★★★, *Floored Genius 2 – Best Of The BBC Sessions 1983-91* (Nighttracks 1993)★★★, *The Followers Of Saint Julian* (Island 1997)★★★.
VIDEOS: *Copeulation* (Island Visual Arts 1989).
FURTHER READING: *Head-On*, Julian Cope. *Krautrocksampler: One Head's Guide To Great Kosmische Music*, Julian Cope.

COPELAND, STEWART
ALBUMS: as Klark Kent *Music Madness From The Kinetic Kid* (Kryptone/IRS 1980)★★★, *Rumble Fish* film soundtrack (A&M 1983)★★, *The Rhythmatist* (A&M 1985)★★★, *The Equalizer & Other Cliff Hangers* soundtrack (IRS 1988)★★, *The Leopard Son* (Ark 21 1996)★★★.
VIDEOS: *The Rhythmatist* (1988).

CORROSION OF CONFORMITY
ALBUMS: *Eye For An Eye* (No Core 1984)★★★, *Animosity* (Death/Metal Blade 1985)★★★, *Technocracy* mini-album (MetalBlade 1987)★★, *Six Songs With Mike Singing* mini-album 1985 recording (Caroline 1988)★★, *Blind* (Relativity 1991)★★★, *Deliverance* (Columbia 1994)★★★, *Wiseblood* (Columbia 1996)★★★.

CORYELL, LARRY
ALBUMS: with Michael Mantler *Jazz Composers Orchestra* (1968)★★★, *Lady Coryell* (Vanguard 1969)★★★★, *Coryell* (Vanguard 1969)★★★, *Spaces* (Vanguard 1970)★★★★, *Fairyland* (1971)★★★, *Larry Coryell At The Village Gate* (Vanguard 1971)★★★★, *Barefoot Boy* (Philips 1971)★★★, *Offering* (Vanguard 1972)★★★, *The Real Great Escape* (Vanguard 1973)★★★, *Introducing The Eleventh House* (Vanguard 1974)★★★, *The Restful Mind* (Vanguard 1975)★★★, *Planet End* (Vanguard 1976)★★★, *Level One* (Arista 1976)★★★, *Basics* 1968 recordings (1976)★★, *Aspects* (Arista 1976)★★★, *Lion And The Ram* (1976)★★★, with Steve Kahn *Two For The Road* (1976)★★★, with Philip Catherine *Twin House* (Elektra 1976)★★★★, *Back Together* (Warners 1977)★★★, *Splendid* (1978)★★★, *European Impressions* (1978)★★★, *Standing Ovation* (1978)★★★★, *Return* (Vanguard 1979)★★★, with John Scofield, Joe Beck *Tributaries* (Novus 1979)★★★, *Bolero* (String 1981)★★★, *'Round Midnight* (1983)★★★, *Scheherazade* (1984)★★★, with Brian Keane *Just Like Being Born* (Flying Fish 1984)★★★, *The Firebird And Petrouchka* (Philips 1984)★★★, with Emily Remler *Together* (Concord 1986)★★★, *Coming Home* (Muse 1986)★★★, *Equipoise* (Muse 1987)★★★, *Toku Du* (Muse 1988)★★★, *A Quiet Day In Spring* (Steeplechase 1988)★★★, *Just Like Being Born* (Flying Fish 1989)★★★, *Don Lanphere/Larry Coryell* (1990)★★★, *Plays Ravel And Gershwin* (Soundscreen 1990)★★★, *Shining Hour* (Muse 1991)★★★, *Twelve Frets To One Octave* (Shanachie 1991)★★★, *Live From Bahia* (CTI 1992)★★★, *Fallen Angel* (CTI 1994)★★★, *Spaces Revisited* (Shanachie 1997)★★★.

COSTELLO, ELVIS
ALBUMS: *My Aim Is True* (Stiff 1977)★★★★, *This Year's Model* (Radar 1978)★★★★★, *Armed Forces* (Radar 1979)★★★, *Get Happy* (F-Beat 1980)★★★, *Trust* (F-Beat 1981)★★★★, *Almost Blue* (F-Beat 1981)★★★, *Imperial Bedroom* (F-Beat 1982)★★★★★, *Punch The Clock* (F-Beat 1983)★★★, *Goodbye Cruel World* (F-Beat 1984)★★, *King Of America* (Demon 1986)★★★★, *Blood And Chocolate* (Demon 1986)★★★, *Spike* (Warners 1989)★★★, *Mighty Like A Rose* (Warners 1991)★★★, with the Brodsky Quartet *The Juliet Letters* (Warners 1993)★★★, *Brutal Youth* (Warners 1994)★★★, *Kojak Variety* (Warners 1995)★★, with Bill Frisell *Deep Dead Blue, Live At Meltdown* (Nonesuch 1995)★★★, with Richard Harvey *Original Music From Jake's Progress* (Demon Soundtracks 1996)★★, *All This Useless Beauty* (Warners 1996)★★★, with Steve Nieve *Costello & Nieve* (Warners 1996)★★★.
COMPILATIONS: *Ten Bloody Marys And Ten Hows Your Fathers* (Demon 1980)★★★★, *The Best Of Elvis Costello – The Man* (Telstar 1985)★★★★, *Out Of Our Idiot* (Demon 1987)★★★, *Girls Girls Girls Girls* (Demon 1989)★★★★★, *The Very Best Of ... 1977-1986* (Demon 1994)★★★★, *Extreme Honey: The Very Best Of The Warner Bros. Years* (Warners 1997)★★★★.
FILMS: *Americation* (1979).
VIDEOS: *Best Of Elvis Costello* (Palace Video 1986), with Brodsky Quartet *The Juliet Letters* (1993), *The Very Best Of* (1994), *Live: A Case For Song* (Warner Vision 1996).
FURTHER READING: *Elvis Costello: Completely False Biography Based On Rumour, Innuendo And Lies*, Krista Reese. *Elvis Costello*, Mick St. Michael. *Elvis Costello: A Man Out Of Time*, David Gouldstone. *The Big Wheel*, Bruce Thomas. *Going Through The Motions (Elvis Costello 1982-1985)*, Richard Groothuizen and Kees Den Heyer.

COUNTING CROWS
ALBUMS: *August And Everything After* (Geffen 1993) ★★★★, *Recovering The Satellites* (Geffen 1996)★★★★, *Across The Wire* (Geffen 1998)★★★★.

COUNTRY JOE AND THE FISH
ALBUMS: *Electric Music For The Mind And Body* (Vanguard 1967)★★★, *I Feel Like I'm Fixin' To Die* (Vanguard 1967)★★★, *Together* (Vanguard 1968)★★, *Here We Are Again* (Vanguard 1969)★★, *C.J. Fish* (Vanguard 1970)★★, *Reunion* (Fantasy 1977)H, *Live Fillmore West 1969* (Ace 1996)★★.
COMPILATIONS: *Greatest Hits* (Vanguard 1969)★★★, *The Life And Times Of Country Joe And The Fish From Haight-Ashbury To Woodstock* (Vanguard 1971)★★★, *Collectors' Items – The First Three EPs* (1980)★★★, *The Collected Country Joe And The Fish* (Vanguard 1987)★★★.
FILMS: *Gas! Or It Became Necessary* ... (1970).

COVAY, DON
ALBUMS: *Mercy* (Atlantic 1964)★★★, *See Saw* (Atlantic 1966)★★★★, with the Lemon Jefferson Blues Band *House Of Blue Lights* (Atlantic 1969)★★★, *Different Strokes* (Atlantic 1970)★★, *Superdude 1* (Mercury 1973)★★★, *Hot Blood* (Mercury 1975)★★, *Travellin' In Heavy Traffic* (Philadelphia International 1976)★★.
COMPILATIONS: *Sweet Thang* (Topline 1987)★★★, *Checkin' In With Don Covay* (1989)★★★, *Mercy Mercy – The Definitive Don Covay* (Razor & Tie 1994)★★★★.

COWBOY JUNKIES
ALBUMS: *Whites Off Earth Now!!* (RCA 1986)★★★, *The Trinity Session* (RCA 1988)★★★★, *The Caution Horses* (RCA 1990)★★★, *Black-Eyed Man* (RCA 1992)★★★, *Pale Sun, Crescent Moon* (RCA 1993)★★★, *Lay It Down* (Geffen 1996)★★★, *Whorn* (Amphetamine Reptile 1996)★★★.
COMPILATIONS: *200 More Miles: Live Performances 1985-1994* (RCA 1995)★★★★.

COYNE, KEVIN
ALBUMS: *Case History* (Dandelion 1972)★★★, *Marjory Razor Blade* (Virgin 1973)★★★★, *Blame It On The Night* (Virgin 1974)★★★★, *Matching Head And Feet* (Virgin 1975)★★★, *Heartburn* (Virgin 1976)★★★, *In Living Black And White* (Virgin 1977)★★★★, *Dynamite Daze* (Virgin 1978)★★★, *Millionaires And Teddy Bears* (Virgin 1978)★★★, *Beautiful Extremes* (Virgin 1978)★★★, with Dagmar Krause *Babble* (Virgin 1979)★★★★, *Bursting Bubbles* (Virgin 1980)★★★, *Sanity Stomp* (Virgin 1980)★★, *Pointing The Finger* (Cherry Red 1981)★★★, *Politicz* (Cherry Red 1982)★★★, *Beautiful Extremes Etcetera* (Cherry Red 1983)★★★, *Wild Tiger Love* (Golden Hind 80s)★★, *Stumbling Onto Paradise* (Golden Hind 80s)★★★, *Elvira: Songs From The Archives* (Golden Hind 80s)★★★, *Romance-Romance* (Zabo 80s)★★★, *Legless In Manila* (Collapse 1984)★★★, *Everybody's Naked* (AVM 1990)★★, *Peel Sessions* (1991)★★★, *Let's Do It* unissued 1970 tracks (JVC 1995)★★.
COMPILATIONS: *Dandelion Years* (Butt 1982)★★★.
FURTHER READING: *Show Business*, Kevin Coyne.
Cramps
FURTHER READING: *The Wild, Wild World Of The Cramps*, Ian Johnston.

CRACKER
ALBUMS: *Cracker* (Virgin 1992)★★★, *Kerosene Hot* (Virgin 1994)★★★, *The Golden Age* (Virgin 1996)★★.

CRADLE OF FILTH
ALBUMS: *The Principle Of Evil Made Flesh* (Cacophonous 1994)★★, *Supreme Vampiric Evil* (Cacophonous 1994)★★★, *Vempire, Or, Dark Phaerytales In Phallustein* mini-album (Cacophonous 1996)★★★, *Dusk ... And Her Embrace* (Music For Nations 1996)★★.

CRAMER, FLOYD
ALBUMS: *That Honky Tonk Piano* reissued as *Floyd Cramer Goes Honky Tonkin'* (MGM 1957)★★★, *Hello Blues* (RCA 1960)★★★, *Last Date* (RCA 1961)★★★★, *On The Rebound* (RCA 1961)★★★★, *America's Biggest Selling Pianist* (RCA 1961)★★★, *Floyd Cramer Get Organ-ized* (RCA 1962)★★, *I Remember Hank Williams* (RCA 1962)★★★, *Swing Along With Floyd Cramer* (RCA 1963)★★★, *Comin' On* (RCA 1963)★★★, *Country Piano – City Strings* (RCA 1964)★★★, *Cramer At The Console* (RCA 1964)★★★, *Hits From The Country Hall Of Fame* (RCA 1965)★★★, *The Magic Touch Of Floyd Cramer* (RCA 1965)★★★, *Class Of '65* (RCA 1965)★★★, *The Distinctive Piano Styling Of Floyd Cramer* (RCA 1966)★★★, *The Big Ones* (RCA 1966)★★★, *Class Of '66* (RCA 1966)★★★, *Here's What's Happening* (RCA 1967)★★★, *Floyd Cramer Plays The Monkees* (RCA 1967)★★★, *Class Of '67* (RCA 1967)★★★, *Floyd Cramer Plays Country Classics* (RCA 1968)★★★, *Class Of '68* (RCA 1968)★★★, *Floyd Cramer Plays MacArthur Park* (RCA 1968)★★, *Class Of '69* (RCA 1969)★★★, *More Country Classics* (RCA 1969)★★★, *Looking For Mr. Goodbar* (RCA 1968)★★★, *The Big Ones – Volume 2* (RCA 1970)★★★, *Floyd Cramer With The Music City Pops* (RCA 1970)★★★, *Class Of '70* (RCA 1970)★★, *Sounds Of Sunday* (RCA 1971)★★, with Chet Atkins and Boots Randolph *Chet, Floyd And Boots* (RCA 1971)★★★, *Class Of '71* (RCA 1971)★★★, *Floyd Cramer Detours* (RCA 1972)★★★, *Class Of '72* (RCA 1972)★★★, *Super Country Hits Featuring Crystal Chandelier And Battle Of New Orleans* (RCA 1973)★★, *Class Of '73* (RCA 1973)★★, *The Young And The Restless* (RCA 1974)★★, *Floyd Cramer In Concert* (RCA 1974)★★, *Class Of '74 And '75* (RCA 1975)★★, *Floyd Cramer Country* (RCA 1976)★★, with Chet Atkins and Danny Davis *Chet, Floyd And Danny* (RCA Victor 1977)★★★, *Floyd Cramer And The Keyboard Kick Band* (RCA 1977)★★★, *Superhits* (RCA 1979)★★, *Dallas* (RCA 1980)★★, *The Best Of The West* (RCA 1981)★★, *Country Gold* (RCA 1988)★★, *Just Me And My Piano!* (RCA 1988)★★★, *Special Songs Of Love* (RCA 1988)★★, *Originals* (RCA 1991)★★★, *Classics* (RCA 1992)★★★.
COMPILATIONS: *The Best Of Floyd Cramer* (RCA 1964)★★★★, *The Best Of Floyd Cramer – Volume 2* (RCA 1968)★★★, *This Is Floyd Cramer* (RCA 1970)★★★★, *Plays The Big Hits* (Camden 1973)★★★, *Best Of The Class Of* (RCA 1973)★★★, *Spotlight On Floyd Cramer* (1974)★★★, *All My Best* (RCA 1980)★★★, *Great Country Hits* (RCA 1981)★★★, *Treasury Of Favourites* (1984)★★★, *Country Classics* (1984)★★★★, *20 Of The Best: Floyd Cramer* (RCA 1986)★★★, *Our Class Reunion* (1987)★★★, *Easy Listening Favorites* (1991)★★★, *Favorite Country Hits* (Ranwood 1995)★★★, *King Of Country Piano* (Pickwick 1995)★★★, *Collector's Series* (RCA 1995)★★★, *The Essential Floyd Cramer* (RCA 1996)★★★★.

CRAMPS
ALBUMS: *Songs The Lord Taught Us* (Illegal/IRS 1980)★★★, *Psychedelic Jungle* (IRS 1981)★★★, *Smell Of Female* (Enigma 1983)★★★, *A Date With Elvis* (Big Beat 1986)★★★, *Rockinnreelininaucklandnewzelandxxx* (Vengeance 1987)★★★, *Stay Sick* (Enigma 1990)★★★, *Look Mom No Head!* (Big Beat 1991)★★, *Flamejob* (Medicine 1994)★★★, *Big Beat From Badsville* (Epitaph 1997)★★.
COMPILATIONS: *Off The Bone* (IRS 1983)★★★, *Bad Music For Bad People* (IRS 1984)★★★.

CRANBERRIES
ALBUMS: *Everybody Else Is Doing It, So Why Can't We?* (Island 1993)★★★★, *No Need To Argue* (Island 1994)★★★★, *To The Faithful Departed* (Island 1996)★★★.
CD-ROM: *Doors And Windows* (Philips 1995)★★.
VIDEOS: *Live* (Island 1994).
FURTHER READING: *The Cranberries*, Stuart Bailey.

CRASH TEST DUMMIES
ALBUMS: *The Ghosts That Haunt Me* (Arista 1991)★★, *God Shuffled His Feet* (RCA 1994)★★★★, *A Worm's Life* (Arista 1996)★★★.
VIDEOS: *Symptomology Of A Rock Band* (1994).

CRAWFORD, RANDY
ALBUMS: *Miss Randy Crawford* (Warners 1977)★★★, *Raw Silk* (Warners 1979)★★★, *Now We May Begin* (Warners 1980)★★★, *Everything Must Change* (Warners 1980)★★★, *Secret Combination* (Warners 1981)★★★★, *Windsong* (Warners 1982)★★★, *Nightline* (Warners 1983)★★★, *Abstract Emotions* (Warners 1986)★★★, *Rich And Poor* (Warners 1989)★★★, *Naked And True* (Bluemoon 1995)★★★.
COMPILATIONS: *Miss Randy Crawford – Greatest Hits* (K-Tel 1984)★★★, *Love Songs* (Telstar 1987)★★★, *The Very Best Of* (Dino 1992)★★★, *The Best Of* (Warners 1996)★★★★.

CRAY, ROBERT
ALBUMS: *Who's Been Talkin'* (Tomato 1980)★★★, *Bad Influence* (High Tone 1983)★★★★, *False Accusations* (High Tone 1985)★★★, with Albert Collins, Johnny Copeland *Showdown!* (Alligator 1985)★★★★, *Strong Persuader* (Mercury 1986)★★★, *Don't Be Afraid Of The Dark* (Mercury 1988)★★★★, *Midnight Stroll*(Mercury 1990)★★★★, *Too Many Cooks* (Tomato 1991)★★★, *I Was Warned* (Mercury 1992)★★★, *The Score* re-release of *Who's Been Talkin'* (Charly 1992)★★★, *Shame And A Sin* (Mercury 1993)★★★, *Some Rainy Morning* (Mercury 1995)★★★, *Sweet Potato Pie* (Mercury 1997)★★★★.
VIDEOS: *Smoking Gun* (Polygram Music Video 1989), *Collection: Robert Cray* (Polygram Music Video 1991).

CRAZY HORSE
ALBUMS: *Crazy Horse* (Reprise 1970)★★★★, *Loose* (Reprise 1971)★★★, *Crazy Horse At Crooked Lake* (1973)★★★, *Crazy Moon* (1978)★★★.

CREAM
ALBUMS: *Fresh Cream* (Polydor 1966)★★★★, *Disraeli Gears* (Polydor 1967)★★★★★, *Wheels Of Fire* (Polydor 1968)★★★★, *Goodbye* (Polydor 1969)★★★, *Live Cream* (Polydor 1970)★★★, *Live Cream, Volume 2* (Polydor 1972)★★★.
COMPILATIONS: *The Best Of Cream* (Polydor 1969)★★★★, *Heavy Cream* (Polydor 1973)★★★, *Strange Brew – The Very Best Of Cream* (Polydor 1986)★★★★, *Those Were The Days* 4-CD box set (Polydor 1997)★★★★★.
VIDEOS: *Farewell Concert* (Polygram Music Video 1986), *Strange Brew* (Warner Music Video 1992), *Fresh Live Cream* (Polygram 1994).
FURTHER READING: *Cream In Gear (Limited Edition)*, Gered Mankowitz and Robert Whitaker (Photographers). *Strange Brew*, Chris Welch.

CREATION
ALBUMS: *We Are Paintermen* (Hi-Ton 1967)★★★, *Lay The Ghost* (1993)★★, *The Creation* (Creation 1996)★★, *Power Surge* (Creation 1996)★★.
COMPILATIONS: *The Best Of Creation* (Pop Schallplatten 1968)★★★, *The Creation 66-67* (Charisma 1973)★★★.

CREDIT TO THE NATION
ALBUMS: *Take Dis* (One Little Indian 1993)★★★, *Daddy Always Wanted Me To Grow A Pair Of Wings* (One Little Indian 1996)★★★.

CREEDENCE CLEARWATER REVIVAL
ALBUMS: *Creedence Clearwater Revival* (Fantasy 1968)★★★, *Bayou Country* (Fantasy 1969)★★★★, *Green River* (Fantasy 1969)★★★★, *Willie And The Poor Boys* (Fantasy 1969)★★★★, *Cosmo's Factory* (Fantasy 1970)★★★★, *Pendulum* (Fantasy 1970)★★★, *Mardi Gras* (Fantasy 1972)★★, *Live In Europe* (Fantasy 1973)★★, *Live At The Royal Albert Hall* aka *The Concert* (Fantasy 1980)★★.
COMPILATIONS: *Creedence Gold* (Fantasy 1972)★★★★, *More Creedence Gold* (Fantasy 1973)★★★★, *Chronicle: The 20 Greatest Hits* (Fantasy 1976)★★★★, *Greatest Hits* (Fantasy 1979)★★★, *Creedence Country* (Fantasy 1981)★★★, *Creedence Clearwater Revival Hits Album* (Fantasy 1982)★★★★, *The Creedence Collection* (Impression 1985)★★★, *Chronicle II* (Fantasy 1986)★★★★, *Best of Volume 1* (Fantasy 1988)★★★★, *Best of Volume 2* (Fantasy 1988)★★★★.
FURTHER READING: *Inside Creedence*, John Hallowell.

CRENSHAW, MARSHALL
ALBUMS: *Marshall Crenshaw* (Warners 1982)★★★★, *Field Day* (Warners 1983)★★★, *Downtown* (Warners 1985)★★★, *Sings Mary Jean & Nine Others* (Warners 1987)★★★, *Good Evening* (Warners 1989)★★★, *Life's Too Short* (MCA 1991)★★★, *My Truck Is My Home* (Razor And Tie 1994)★★★, *Miracle Of Science* (Razor And Tie 1996)★★★.

CREW-CUTS
ALBUMS: *The Crew-Cuts On The Campus* (Mercury 1954)★★★, *The Crew-Cuts Go Longhair* (Mercury 1956)★★★, *Crew-Cut Capers* (Mercury 1957)★★★, *Music Ala Carte* (Mercury 1957)★★★, *Rock And Roll Bash* (Mercury 1957)★★★, *Surprise Package* (RCA Victor 1958)★★★, *The Crew-Cuts Sing!* (RCA Victor 1959)★★★, *You Must Have Been A Beautiful Baby* (RCA Victor 1960)★★★, *The Crew Cuts Sing Out!* (RCA Victor 1960)★★★, *The Crew Cuts Have A Ball And Bowling Tips* (RCA Victor 1960)★★★, *The Crew Cuts* (RCA Victor 1962)★★★, *High School Favorites* (RCA Victor 1962)★★★, *Sing The Masters* (RCA Victor 1962)★★★, *The Crew-Cuts Sing Folk* (RCA Victor 1963)★★.

CRICKETS
ALBUMS: *In Style With The Crickets* (Coral1960)★★★★, *Bobby Vee Meets The Crickets* (Liberty 1962)★★★, *Something Old, Something New, Something Borrowed, Something Else* (Liberty 1963)★★★, *California Sun* (Liberty 1964)★★★, *Rockin' 50s Rock 'N' Roll* (1970)★★★, *Bubblegum, Bop, Ballads And Boogies* (1973)★★, *A Long Way From Lubbock* (1975)★★, *Three-Piece* (1988)★★, *T-Shirt* (1989)★★, *Too Much Monday Morning* (Carlton 1997)★★.
COMPILATIONS: *The Singles Collection 1957-1961* (Pickwick 1994)★★★.
FILMS: *Girls On The Beach* (1965).
VIDEOS: *My Love Is Bigger Than A Cadillac* (Hendring 1990).

CROCE, JIM
ALBUMS: *Approaching Day* (Capitol 1969)★★, *You Don't Mess Around With Jim* (ABC 1972)★★★, *Life And Times* (ABC 1973)★★★, *I Got A Name* (ABC 1973)★★★.
COMPILATIONS: *Photographs And Memories – His Greatest Hits* (ABC 1974)★★★, *Collection* (Castle 1986)★★★★.
FURTHER READING: *The Faces I've Been*, Jim Croce. *Jim Croce: The Feeling Lives On*, Linda Jacobs.

CROPPER, STEVE
ALBUMS: with Albert King, 'Pops' Staples *Jammed Together* (Stax 1969)★★★, *With A Little Help From My Friends* (Stax 1971)★★, *Playing My Thang* (1980)★★.
FILMS: *The Blues Brothers* (1980).

CROSBY, DAVID
ALBUMS: *If I Could Only Remember My Name* (Atlantic 1971)★★★★★, *Oh Yes I Can* (Atlantic 1989)★★★, *Thousand Roads* (Atlantic 1993)★★★, *It's All Coming Back To Me Now* (Atlantic 1995)★★★, *King Biscuit Flower Hour Presents: David Crosby* (BMG 1996)★★★.
FURTHER READING: *Long Time Gone*, David Crosby and Carl Gottlieb. *Timeless Flight*, Johnny Rogan.

CROSBY, STILLS AND NASH
ALBUMS: *Crosby, Stills And Nash* (Atlantic 1969)★★★★, *CSN* (Atlantic 1977)★★★★, *Daylight Again* (Atlantic 1982)★★★, *Allies* (Atlantic 1983)★★★, *Live It Up* (Atlantic 1990)★★, *Crosby Stills And Nash* 4-CD box set (Atlantic 1991)★★★★★, *After The Storm* (Atlantic 1994)★★.
COMPILATIONS: *Replay* (Atlantic 1980)★★★★.
VIDEOS: *Daylight Again* (CIC 1983), *Acoustic* (Warner Music Vision 1991), *Crosby, Stills And Nash: Long Time Comin'* (Wienerworld 1994).
FURTHER READING: *Crosby, Stills & Nash: The Authorized Biography*, Dave Zimmer. *Prisoner Of Woodstock*, Dallas Taylor. *The Visual Documentary*, Johnny Rogan.

CROSBY, STILLS, NASH AND YOUNG
ALBUMS: *Deja Vu* (Atlantic 1970)★★★★, *Four Way Street* (Atlantic 1971)★★★, *American Dream* (Atlantic 1989)★★★.
COMPILATIONS: *So Far* (Atlantic 1974)★★★, *Crosby Stills And Nash* 4-CD box set (Atlantic 1991)★★★★★.
FURTHER READING: *Prisoner Of Woodstock*, Dallas Taylor. *Crosby Stills Nash & Young: The Visual Documentary*, Johnny Rogan.

CROSS, CHRISTOPHER
ALBUMS: *Christopher Cross* (Warners 1980)★★★, *Another Page* (Warners 1983)★★★, *Every Turn Of The World* (Warners 1985)★★, *Back Of My Mind* (1988)★★.

CROW, SHERYL
ALBUMS: *Tuesday Night Music Club* (A&M 1993)★★★★, *Sheryl Crow* (A&M 1996)★★★.

CROWDED HOUSE
ALBUMS: *Crowded House* (Capitol 1986)★★★, *Temple Of Low Men* (Capitol 1988)★★★, *Woodface* (Capitol 1991)★★★★, *Together Alone* (Capitol 1993)★★★.
COMPILATIONS: *Recurring Dreams* (Capitol 1996)★★★★★.
VIDEOS: *Farewell To The World: Live At The Sydney Opera House* (Polygram Video 1997).
FURTHER READING: *Private Universe: The Illustrated Biography*, Chris Twomey and Kerry Doole.

CROWELL, RODNEY
ALBUMS: *Ain't Living Long Like This* (Warners 1978)★★★★, *But What Will The Neighbors Think* (Warners 1980)★★★, *Rodney Crowell* (Warners 1981)★★★, *Street Language* (Columbia 1986)★★★★, *Diamonds And Dirt* (Columbia 1988)★★★★, *Keys To The Highway* (Columbia 1989)★★★★, *Life Is Messy* (Columbia 1992)★★★, *Let The Picture Paint Itself* (MCA 1994)★★★, *Soul Searchin'* (Excelsior 1994)★★★, *Jewel Of The South* (MCA 1995)★★★, *The Cicadas* (Warners 1997)★★★.
COMPILATIONS: *The Rodney Crowell Collection* (Warners 1989)★★★★, *Greatest Hits* (Columbia 1993)★★★★.

CRUISE, JULEE
ALBUMS: *Floating Into The Night* (Warners 1990)★★★.

CRYSTALS
ALBUMS: *Twist Uptown* (Philles 1962)★★, *He's A Rebel* (Philles 1963)★★★.
COMPILATIONS: *The Crystals Sing Their Greatest Hits* (Philles 1963)★★★, *Uptown* (Spectrum 1988)★★★, *The Best Of* (ABKCO 1992)★★★.

CULT
ALBUMS: as Southern Death Cult The Southern Death Cult (Beggars Banquet 1983)★★, Dreamtime (Beggars Banquet 1984)★★, Love (Beggars Banquet 1985)★★, Electric (Beggars Banquet 1987)★★★, Sonic Temple (Beggars Banquet 1989)★★★, Ceremony (Beggars Banquet 1991)★★, The Cult (Beggars Banquet 1994)★★.
COMPILATIONS: as Southern Death Cult Complete Recordings (Situation Two 1991)★★, as the Cult Pure Cult (Beggars Banquet 1993)★★.
VIDEOS: Dreamtime At The Lyceum (Beggars Banquet 1984), Electric Love (Beggars Banquet 1987), Cult: Video Single (One Plus One 1987), Sonic Ceremony (Beggar's Banquet 1992), Pure Cult (1993), Dreamtime Live At The Lyceum (Beggars Banquet 1996).

CULTURE BEAT
ALBUMS: Horizon (Epic 1991)★★★, Serenity (Epic 1993)★★★.

CULTURE CLUB
ALBUMS: Kissing To Be Clever (Virgin 1982)★★★, Colour By Numbers (Virgin 1983)★★★★, Waking Up To The House On Fire (Virgin 1984)★★, From Luxury To Heartache (Virgin 1986)★★, This Time (Virgin 1987)★★★.
COMPILATIONS: At Worst ... The Best Of Boy George And Culture Club (Virgin 1993)★★★★.
VIDEOS: Kiss Across The Ocean (1984), This Time (The First Four Years) (1987).
FURTHER READING: Culture Club: When Cameras Go Crazy, Kasper de Graaf and Malcolm Garrett. Mad About The Boy: The Life And Times Of Boy George & Culture Club, Anton Gill. Boy George And Culture Club, Jo Dietrich. Like Punk Never Happened: Culture Club and the New Pop, Dave Rimmer.

CURE
ALBUMS: Three Imaginary Boys (Fiction 1979)★★★, Boys Don't Cry (Fiction 1979)★★, Seventeen Seconds (Fiction 1980)★★★, Faith (Fiction 1981)★★★, Pornography (Fiction 1982)★★★, The Top (Fiction 1984)★★★, Concert – The Cure Live (Fiction 1984)★★, Concert And Curiosity – Cure Anomalies 1977-1984 (Fiction 1984)★★, Head On The Door (Fiction 1985)★★★, Kiss Me, Kiss Me, Kiss Me (Fiction 1987)★★★, Disintegration (Fiction 1990)★★★, Entreat (Fiction 1991)★★★, Wish (Fiction 1992)★★★★, Show (Fiction 1993)★★★, Paris (Fiction 1993)★★★, Wild Mood Swings (Fiction 1996)★★★★.
COMPILATIONS: Japanese Whispers – The Cure Singles Nov 1982-Nov 1983 (Fiction 1983)★★★, Standing On The Beach – The Singles titled Staring At The Sea on CD (Fiction 1986)★★★★, Mixed Up (Fiction 1990)★★★, Galore – The Singles 1987-1997 (Fiction 1997)★★★.
VIDEOS: Staring At the Sea: The Images (Palace Video 1986), The Cure In Orange (Polygram Music Video 1987), In Between Days (Polygram Music Video 1988), Close To Me (Polygram Music Video 1989), Cure Picture Show (Polygram Music Video 1991), The Cure Play Out (Windsong 1991), The Cure Show (1993).
FURTHER READING: The Cure: A Visual Documentary, Dave Thompson and Jo-Anne Greene. Ten Imaginary Years, Lydia Barbarian, Steve Sutherland and Robert Smith. The Cure Songwords 1978 – 1989, Robert Smith (ed.). The Cure: Success Corruption & Lies, Ross Clarke. The Cure On Record, Daren Butler. The Cure: Faith, Dave Bowler and Bryan Dray. The Making Of: The Cure's Disintegration, Mary Elizabeth Hargrove.

CURVE
ALBUMS: Doppelganger (AnXious 1992)★★★, Cuckoo (AnXious 1993)★★.
COMPILATIONS: Radio Sessions (AnXious 1993)★★★.

CURVED AIR
ALBUMS: Air Conditioning (Warners 1970)★★★, Second Album (Warners 1971)★★★, Phantasmagoria (Warners 1972)★★, Air Cut (Warners 1973)★★, Curved Air Live (Deram 1975)★★, Midnight Wire (BTM 1975)★★, Airborne (SBT 1976)★★, Live At The BBC (Band Of Joy 1995)★★.
Solo: Sonja Kristina Sonja Kristina (Chopper 1980)★★, Songs From The Acid Folk (Total1991)★★★.
COMPILATIONS: The Best Of Curved Air (Warners 1976)★★★.

CYPRESS HILL
ALBUMS: Cypress Hill (Ruffhouse 1991)★★★★, Black Sunday (Columbia 1993)★★★, III The Temples Of Boom (Columbia 1995)★★★, Unreleased And Revamped mini-album (Columbia 1996)★★.

CYRKLE
ALBUMS: Red Rubber Ball (Columbia 1966)★★, Neon (Columbia 1967)★★.
COMPILATIONS: Red Rubber Ball (A Collection) (Columbia Legacy 1991)★★.

D

D'ARBY, TERENCE TRENT
ALBUMS: Introducing The Hardline According To Terence Trent D'Arby (Columbia 1987)★★★★, Neither Fish Nor Flesh (Columbia 1989)★★, Symphony Or Damn (Columbia 1993)★★★, Vibrator (Columbia 1995)★★★.
VIDEOS: Introducing The Hardline: Live (CBS-Fox 1988).
FURTHER READING: Neither Fish Nor Flesh: Inspiration For An Album, Paolo Hewitt.

DA LENCH MOB
ALBUMS: Guerillas In The Mist (Street Knowledge 1992)★★★, Planet Of Da Apes (Street Knowledge 1994)★★.

DALE, DICK
ALBUMS: Surfer's Choice (Deltone 1962)★★★, King Of The Surf Guitar (Capitol1963)★★★, Checkered Flag (Capitol1963)★★★, Mr. Eliminator (Capitol1964)★★★, Summer Surf (Capitol1964)★★, Rock Out – Live At Ciro's (Capitol1965)★★, The Tiger's Loose (1983)★★, Tribal Thunder (Hightone 1993)★★, Unknown Territory (Hightone 1994)★★★, Calling Up Spirits (Beggars Banquet 1996)★★.
COMPILATIONS: Dick Dale's Greatest Hits (1975)★★★, King Of The Surf Guitar (Rhino 1986)★★★, The Best Of Dick Dale (1989)★★★, Better Shred Than Dead: The Dick Dale Anthology (Rhino 1997)★★★.

DALEK I LOVE YOU
ALBUMS: Compass Kum'pass (Backdoor 1980)★★★, Dalek I Love You (Korova 1983)★★★, as Dalek I Naive (Bopadub 1985)★★.

DAMNED
ALBUMS: Damned Damned Damned (Stiff 1977)★★★★, Music For Pleasure (Stiff 1977)★★, Machine Gun Etiquette (Chiswick 1979)★★★, The Black Album (Chiswick 1980)★★★, Strawberries (Bronze 1982)★★★, Phantasmagoria (MCA 1985)★★, Anything (MCA 1986)★★, Not Of This Earth (Cleopatra 1996) released in UK as I'm Alright Jack & The Beans Talk (Marble Orchid 1996)★★.
Solo: Dave Vanian David Vanian And The Phantom Chords (Big Beat 1995)★★★.
COMPILATIONS: The Best Of The Damned (Chiswick 1981)★★★, The Long Lost Weekend: Best Of Vol. 1 & 2 (Big Beat 1988)★★★, Skip Off School To See The Damned – The Stiff Singles (Stiff 1992)★★★, Eternally Damned – The Very Best Of ... (MCI 1994)★★★, The Radio 1 Sessions (Strange Fruit 1996)★★★.
VIDEOS: Light At The End Of The Tunnel(CIC Video 1987).
FURTHER READING: The Damned: The Light At The End Of The Tunnel, Carol Clerk.

DANNY AND THE JUNIORS
COMPILATIONS: Rockin' With Danny And The Juniors (MCA 1983)★★, Back To Hop (Roller Coaster 1992)★★.

DANNY WILSON
ALBUMS: Meet Danny Wilson (Virgin 1987)★★★, Be Bop Mop Top (Virgin 1989)★★★.
COMPILATIONS: Sweet Danny Wilson (Virgin 1991)★★★.

DANSE SOCIETY
ALBUMS: Seduction mini-album (Society 1982)★★, Heaven Is Waiting (Arista 1984)★★★, Looking Through (Society 1986)★★.

DANTALIAN'S CHARIOT
ALBUMS: Chariot Rising (Wooden Hill1997)★★★.

DARIN, BOBBY
ALBUMS: Bobby Darin (Atco 1958)★★★★, That's All (Atco 1959)★★★, This Is Darin (Atco 1960)★★★, Darin At The Copa (Atco 1960)★★★, For Teenagers Only (Atco 1960)★★, It's You Or No-One (Atco 1960)★★★, The 25th December (Atco 1960)★★★, soundtrack Pepe (Colpix 1960)★★, with Johnny Mercer Two Of A Kind (Atco 1961)★★★, Love Swings (Atco 1961)★★★, Twist With Bobby Darin (Atco 1962)★★★, Darin Sings Ray Charles (Atco 1962)★★★, Oh Look At Me Now (Capitol1962)★★★, It's You Or No One (Atco 1962)★★★, Earthy (Capitol1963)★★★, You're The Reason I'm Living (Capitol1963)★★★, Eighteen Yellow Roses (Capitol1963)★★★, Golden Folk Hits (Capitol1963)★★★, Winners (Atco 1964)★★★, From Hello Dolly To Goodbye Charlie (Capitol1964)★★, Venice Blue (Capitol1965)★★, In A Broadway Bag (Atlantic) (1966)★★, The Shadow Of Your Smile (Atlantic 1966)★★★, If I Were A Carpenter (Atlantic 1966)★★★★, Inside Out (Atlantic 1967)★★★, Bobby Darin Sings Doctor Doolittle (Atlantic 1967)H, Bobby Darin Something Special(1967)★★★, Born Walden Robert Cassotto (Direction 1968)★★★, Commitment (Direction 1969)★★★.
COMPILATIONS: The Bobby Darin Story (Atco 1961)★★★★, Things And Other Things (Atco 1962)★★★, The Best Of Bobby Darin (Capitol1966)★★★, The Versatile Bobby Darin (1985)★★★, The Legend Of Bobby Darin (1985)★★★, His Greatest Hits (1985)★★★, Bobby Darin: Collectors Series (Capitol1989)★★★, Splish Splash: The Best Of Bobby Darin Vol. 1 (Atco 1991)★★★, Mack The Knife: The Best Of Bobby Darin Vol. 2 (Atco 1991)★★★, Spotlight On Bobby Darin (Capitol1995)★★★, As Long As I'm Singing: The Bobby Darin Collection 4-CD box set (Rhino 1995)★★★.
FILMS: Pepe (1960), Come September (1961), If A Man Answers (1962), Hell Is For Heroes (1962), Too Late Blues (1962), Pressure Point (1962), Captain Newman M.D. (1963), That Funny Feeling (1965), Gunfight In Abilene (1967), Stranger In The House/Cop-Out (1968), The Happy Ending (1969), Happy Mother's Day-Love George/Run Stranger Run (1973).
FURTHER READING: Borrowed Time: The 37 Years Of Bobby Darin, AlDiorio. Dream Lovers, Dodd Darin.

DARKMAN
ALBUMS: Worldwide (Wild Card 1995)★★★.

DARTS
ALBUMS: Darts (Magnet 1977)★★, Everyone Plays Darts (Magnet 1978)★★, Dart Attack (Magnet 1979)★★.
COMPILATIONS: Greatest Hits (Magnet 1983)★★★.

DAVE CLARK FIVE
ALBUMS: A Session With The Dave Clark Five (Columbia 1964)★★★★, Glad All Over (Epic 1964)★★★, The Dave Clark Five Return (Epic 1964)★★★, American Tour Volume 1 (Epic 1964)★★★, Coast To Coast (Epic 1965)★★★, Weekend In London (Epic 1965)★★★, Catch Us If You Can soundtrack (Having A Wild Weekend in the USA) (Columbia 1965)★★★★, I Like It Like That (Epic 1965)★★★, Try Too Hard (Epic 1966)★★★, Satisfied With You (Epic 1966)★★★, You Got What It Takes (Epic 1967)★★★, Everybody Knows (Epic 1968)★★★, If Somebody Loves You (Columbia 1970)★★★, Glad All Over Again (Epic 1975)★★★.
COMPILATIONS: The Dave Clark Five's Greatest Hits (Columbia 1967)★★★★, 5x5 – Go! (Epic 1969)★★★★, The Best Of The Dave Clark Five (Regal Starline 1970)★★★, 25 Thumping Great Hits (Polydor 1977)★★★, The History Of The Dave Clark Five (Hollywood 1993)★★★★.
FILMS: Get Yourself A College Girl (1964), Catch Us If You Can (USA: Having A Wild Weekend) (1965).
VIDEOS: Glad All Over Again (PMI 1993).

DAVE DEE, DOZY, BEAKY, MICK AND TICH
ALBUMS: Dave Dee, Dozy, Beaky, Mick And Tich (Fontana 1966)★★★, If Music Be The Food Of Love (Fontana 1967)★★★, If No One Sang (Fontana 1968)★★★, The Legend Of Dave Dee, Dozy, Beaky, Mick And Tich (1969)★★, Together (1969)★★.
COMPILATIONS: The Best Of Dave Dee, Dozy, Beaky, Mick And Tich (Spectrum 1996)★★★, The Complete Collection (Mercury 1997)★★★.

DAWN
ALBUMS: Candida (Bell1970)★★★, Dawn Featuring Tony Orlando (Bell1971)★★, Tuneweaving (Bell1973)★★★, Dawn's New Ragtime Follies (Bell1973)★★, Prime Time (Bell1974)★★★, Golden Ribbons (Bell1974)★★, He Don't Love You (Like I Love You) (Elektra 1975)★★★, Skybird (Arista 1975)★★, To Be With You (Elektra 1976)★★.
COMPILATIONS: Greatest Hits (Arista 1975)★★★, The Best Of Tony Orlando And Dawn (Rhino 1995)★★★.

DAZZ BAND
ALBUMS: Invitation To Love (Motown 1980)★★★, Let The Music Play (Motown 1981)★★★, Keep It Live (Motown 1982)★★★, On The One (Motown 1983)★★★, Joystick (Motown 1983)★★★, Jukebox (Motown 1984)★★★, Hot Spot (Motown 1985)★★, Wild And Free (Geffen 1986)★★, Rock The Room (RCA 1988)★★, Under The Streetlights (Lucky 1996)★★★.

dB'S
ALBUMS: Stands For Decibels (Albion 1981)★★★★, Repercussions (Albion 1982)★★★, Like This (Bearsville 1985)★★★, The Sound Of Music (IRS 1987)★★★.
Solo: Will Rigby Sidekick Phenomenon (Egon 1985)★★★.
COMPILATIONS: Amplifier (1986)★★★, The dB's Ride The Wild Tom Tom (Rhino 1993)★★★★.

DE BURGH, CHRIS
ALBUMS: Far Beyond These Walls (A&M 1975)★★, Spanish Train And Other Stories (A&M 1976)★★, At The End Of A Perfect Day (A&M 1977)★★, Crusader (A&M 1979)★★, Eastern Wind (A&M 1980)★★, Best Moves (A&M 1981)★★★, The Getaway (A&M 1982)★★★, Man On The Line (A&M 1984)★★★, Into The Light (A&M 1986)★★★, Flying Colours (A&M 1988)★★★, High On Emotion – Live From Dublin (A&M 1990)★★, Power Of Ten (A&M 1992)★★, This Way Up (A&M 1994)★★, BeautifulDreams (A&M 1995)★★.
COMPILATIONS: The Very Best Of Chris DeBurgh (Telstar 1984)★★★, From A Spark To A Flame: The Very Best Of Chris DeBurgh (A&M 1989)★★★.

DE LA SOUL
ALBUMS: 3 Feet High And Rising (Tommy Boy 1989)★★★, De La Soul Is Dead (Tommy Boy 1991)★★★, Buhloone Mindstate (Tommy Boy 1993)★★★, Stakes Is High (Tommy Boy 1996)★★.
VIDEOS: 3 Feet High And Rising (1989).

DEACON BLUE
ALBUMS: Raintown (CBS 1987)★★★★, When The World Knows Your Name (CBS 1989)★★★, Ooh Las Vegas (CBS 1990)★★★ Fellow Hoodlums (Columbia 1991)★★★, Whatever You Say, Say Nothing (Columbia 1993)★★★.
COMPILATIONS: Our Town – Greatest Hits (Columbia 1994)★★★★.
VIDEOS: The Big Picture Live (1990).

DEAD BOYS
ALBUMS: Young, Loud And Snotty (Sire 1977)★★★, We Have Come For Your Children (Sire 1978)★★, Night Of The Living Dead Boys (Bomp 1981)★★.
COMPILATIONS: Younger, Louder And Snottier (Necrophilia 1989)★★★.

DEAD CAN DANCE
ALBUMS: Dead Can Dance (4AD 1984)★★★★, Spleen And Ideal (4AD 1985)★★★, Within The Realm Of A Dying Sun (4AD 1987)★★★, The Serpent's Egg (4AD 1988)★★★, Aion (4AD 1990)★★★, Into The Labyrinth (4AD 1993)★★★, Towards The Within (4AD 1994)★★★★, Spiritchaser (4AD 1995)★★★★.
VIDEOS: Toward The Within (Warners 1994).

DEAD KENNEDYS
ALBUMS: Fresh Fruit For Rotting Vegetables (IRS/Cherry Red 1980)★★★, In God We Trust Inc. mini-album (Alternative Tentacles/Faulty 1981)★★★, Plastic Surgery Disasters (Alternative Tentacles 1982)★★★, Frankenchrist (Alternative Tentacles 1985)★★★, Bedtime For Democracy (Alternative Tentacles 1986)★★★.
Solo: Klaus Flouride Cha Cha Cha With Mr Flouride (Alternative Tentacles 1985)★★, Because I Say So (Alternative Tentacles 1988)★★, The Light Is Flickering (Alternative Tentacles 1991)★★.
COMPILATIONS: Give Me Convenience Or Give Me Death (Alternative Tentacles 1987)★★★.
VIDEOS: Live In San Francisco (Hendring Video 1987).

DEAD OR ALIVE
ALBUMS: Sophisticated Boom Boom (Epic 1984)★★, Youthquake (Epic 1985)★★★, Mad, Bad And Dangerous To Know (Epic 1987)★★, Nude (Epic 1989)★★, Nukleopatra (Sony 1995)★★.
VIDEOS: Youthquake (1988).

DeBARGE
ALBUMS: The DeBarges (Gordy 1981)★★★, All This Love (Gordy 1982)★★★, In A Special Way (Gordy 1983)★★, Rhythm Of The Night (Gordy 1985)★★, Bad Boys (Striped Horse 1988)★★.
COMPILATIONS: Greatest Hits (Motown 1986)★★★.

DEE, JOEY, AND THE STARLITERS
ALBUMS: Doin' The Twist At The Peppermint Lounge (Roulette 1961)★★★, soundtrack Hey, Let's Twist (Roulette 1962)★★, Back At The Peppermint Lounge-Twistin (Roulette 1961)★★★, All The World Is Twistin' (Roulette 1961)★★, Two Tickets To Paris soundtrack (Roulette 1962)★★, The Peppermint Twisters (Scepter 1962)★★★, Joey Dee (Roulette 1963)★★★, Dance, Dance, Dance (Roulette 1963)★★, Hitsville (Jubilee 1966)★★.
FILMS: Hey Let's Twist (1961).

DEE, KIKI
ALBUMS: I'm Kiki Dee (Fontana 1968)★★, Great Expectations (Tamla Motown 1970)★★, Loving And Free (Rocket 1973)★★, I've Got The Music In Me (Rocket 1974)★★, Kiki Dee (Rocket 1977)★★, Stay With Me (Rocket 1979)★★, Perfect Timing (Ariola 1980)★★, Angel Eyes (Columbia 1987)★★★, Almost Naked (Tickety-Boo 1995)★★★.
COMPILATIONS: Patterns (Philips International1974)★★★, Kiki Dee's Greatest Hits (Warwick 1980)★★★, The Very Best Of Kiki Dee (Rocket 1994)★★★.
FILMS: Dateline Diamonds (1965).

DEEP FOREST
ALBUMS: Deep Forest (Columbia 1993)★★★★, Boheme (Columbia 1995)★★★.

DEEP PURPLE
ALBUMS: Shades Of Deep Purple (Parlophone 1968)★★, The Book Of Taliesyn (Harvest 1969)★★★, Deep Purple (Harvest 1969)★★★, Concerto For Group And Orchestra (Harvest 1970)★★, Deep Purple In Rock (Harvest 1970)★★★★, Fireball (Harvest 1971)★★★★, Machine Head (Purple 1972)★★★★, Made In Japan (Purple 1973)★★★, Who Do We Think We Are? (Purple 1973)★★★, Burn (Purple 1974)★★★, Stormbringer (Purple 1975)★★★, Come Taste The Band (Purple 1975)★★★, Made In Europe (Warners 1976)★★★, Perfect Strangers (Polydor 1984)★★★, House Of Blue Light (Polydor 1987)★★★, Nobody's Perfect (Polydor 1988)★★, Slaves And Masters (RCA 1990)★★, The Battle Rages On (RCA 1993)★★★, The Final Battle (RCA 1994)★★★, Come Hell Or High Water (RCA 1994)★★, Purpendicular (RCA 1996)★★★, Mark III, The Final Concerts (Connoisseur 1996)★★.
COMPILATIONS: 24 Carat Purple (Purple 1975)★★★★, Last Concert In Japan (EMI 1977)★★★, Powerhouse (Purple 1977)★★★, When We Rock, We Rock And When We Roll (Warners 1978)★★★, Singles: As & Bs (Harvest 1978)★★★, Deepest Purple (Harvest 1980)★★★★, Anthology: Deep Purple (Harvest 1985)★★★★, The Collection (EMI Gold 1997)★★★★, Abandon (1998)★★★.
VIDEOS: California Jam (1984), Video Singles (1987), Bad Attitude (1988), Concert For Group And Orchestra (1988), Deep Purple (1988), Doing Their Thing (1990), Scandinavian Nights (1990).
FURTHER READING: Deep Purple: The Illustrated Biography, Chris Charlesworth.

DEF LEPPARD
ALBUMS: On Through The Night (Mercury 1980)★★★, High 'N' Dry (Mercury 1981)★★★, Pyromania (Mercury 1983)★★★★, Hysteria (Mercury 1987)★★★★, Adrenalize (Mercury 1992)★★★, Slang (Mercury 1996)★★★.
COMPILATIONS: CD Box Set (Mercury 1989)★★★, Retro Active (Mercury 1993)★★★, Vault – Def Leppard Greatest Hits 1980-1995 (Mercury 1995)★★★.
VIDEOS: Love Bites (1988), Historia (1988), Rocket (1989), Rock Of Ages (1989), In The Round – In Your Face (1989), Animal (1989), Visualise (1993), Unlock The Rock: Video Archive 1993-1995 (Polygram 1995).
FURTHER READING: Def Leppard: Animal Instinct, David Fricke. Def Leppard, Jason Rich. Biographize: The Def Leppard Story, Dave Dickson.

DEKKER, DESMOND
ALBUMS: 007 (Shanty Town) (Beverley's 1967)★★★★, Action (Beverley's 1968)★★★, The Israelites (Beverley's 1969)★★★★, This Is Desmond Dekker (Trojan 1969)★★★★, You Can Get It If You Really Want (Trojan 1970)★★★★, Black And Dekker (Stiff 1980)★★★, Compass Point (Stiff 1981)★★★, Officially Live And Rare (Trojan 1987)★★, Music Like Dirt (Trojan 1992)★★, with the Specials King Of Kings (Trojan 1993)★★★.
COMPILATIONS: Double Dekker (Trojan 1974)★★★★, Sweet 16 Hits (Trojan 1978)★★★★, Original Reggae Hitsound (Trojan 1985)★★★, 20 Golden Pieces (Bulldog 1987)★★★★, Best Of And The Rest Of (Action Replay/Trojan 1989)★★★, King Of Ska (Trojan 1991)★★★★, 20 Greatest Hits (Point 2 1992)★★★★, CrucialCuts – The Best Of Desmond Dekker (1993)★★★★, First Time For Long Time (Trojan 1997)★★★.

DEL AMITRI
ALBUMS: Del Amitri (Chrysalis 1985)★★★, Waking Hours (A&M 1989)★★★, Change Everything (A&M 1992)★★★, Twisted (A&M 1995)★★★, Some Other Sucker's Parade (A&M 1997)★★★.
VIDEOS: Let's Go Home (WL1996).

DEL-VIKINGS
ALBUMS: Come Go With The DelVikings (Luniverse 1957)★★★, They Sing – They Swing (Mercury 1957)★★, A Swinging, Singing Record Session (Mercury 1958)★★, Newies And Oldies (1959)★★★, The DelVikings And The Sonnets (Crown 1963)★★★, Come Go With Me (Dot 1966)★★★.
COMPILATIONS: DelVikings (Buffalo Bop 1988)★★★, CoolShake (Buffalo Bop 1988)★★★, Collectables (Mercury 1988)★★★.

DELANEY, ERIC
ALBUMS: Cha-Cha-Cha Delaney (Pye 1959)★★★, Swingin' Thro' The Shows (1960)★★★.

DELANEY AND BONNIE
ALBUMS: Accept No Substitute – The Original Delaney & Bonnie (Elektra 1969)★★★, Home (1969)★★, Delaney & Bonnie & Friends On Tour With Eric Clapton (Atco 1970)★★★, To Bonnie From Delaney (Atco 1970)★★★, Motel Shot (Atco 1971)★★★, D&B Together (Columbia 1972)★★, Country Life (1972)★★.
COMPILATIONS: Best Of Delaney And Bonnie (Atco 1973)★★★, Best Of Delaney And Bonnie (Rhino 1990)★★★.
FILMS: Catch My Soul (1974).

DELFONICS
ALBUMS: La La Means I Love You (Philly Groove 1968)★★★, The Sound Of Sexy Soul (Philly Groove 1969)★★★, The Delfonics (Philly Groove 1970)★★★, Tell Me This Is A Dream (Philly Groove 1972)★★★, Alive And Kicking (Philly Groove 1974)★★.
COMPILATIONS: The Delfonics Super Hits (Philly Groove 1969)★★★, Symphonic Soul- Greatest Hits (Charly 1988)★★★★, Echoes – The Best Of The Delfonics (Arista 1991)★★★★.

DELLS
ALBUMS: Oh What A Nite (1959)★★★, It's Not Unusual (1965)★★★, There Is (Cadet 1968)★★★★, Stay In My Corner (Cadet 1968)★★★, The Dells Musical Menu/Always Together (Cadet 1969)★★★, Love Is Blue (Cadet 1969)★★★, Like It Is, Like It Was (Cadet 1970)★★★, Oh, What A Night (Cadet 1970)★★★, Freedom Means (Cadet 1971)★★★, Dells Sing Dionne Warwick's Greatest Hits (Cadet 1972)★★, Sweet As Funk Can Be (Cadet 1972)★★★, Give Your Baby A Standing Ovation (Cadet 1973)★★★, with the Dramatics The Dells Vs The Dramatics (Cadet 1974)★★★, The Mighty Mighty Dells (Cadet 1974)★★★, We Got To Get Our Thing Together (Cadet 1975)★★★, No Way Back (Mercury 1975)★★★, They Said It Couldn't Be Done, But We Did It (Mercury 1977)★★, Love Connection (Mercury 1977)★★★, New Beginnings (ABC 1978)★★★, Face To Face (ABC 1979)★★★, I Touched A Dream (20th Century 1980)★★★, Whatever Turns You On (20th Century 1981)★★, One Step Closer (1984)★★, The Second Time (Veteran 1988)★★, Music From The Motion Picture: The Five Heartbeats (Virgin 1991)★★.
COMPILATIONS: The Dells Greatest Hits (Cadet 1969)★★★, The Best Of The Dells (1973)★★★★, Cornered (1977)★★★, Rockin' On Bandstand (Charly 1983)★★★, From Streetcorner To Soul (Charly 1984)★★★, Breezy Ballads And Tender Tunes (Solid Smoke 1985)★★★, On Their Corner/The Best Of ... (Chess/MCA 1992)★★★★.

DENNY, SANDY
ALBUMS: The North Star Grassman And The Ravens (Island 1971)★★★, Sandy (Island 1972)★★★★, Like An Old Fashioned Waltz (Island 1973)★★★, Rendezvous (Island 1977)★★★, The BBC Sessions 1971-1973 (Strange Fruit 1997)★★★★.
COMPILATIONS: The Original Sandy Denny (Mooncrest 1984)★★★, Who Knows Where The Time Goes (Island 1986)★★★★, The Best Of Sandy Denny (Island 1987)★★★, with Trevor Lucas The Attic Tracks 1972 – 1984 Outtakes and Rarities (SpecialDelivery 1995)★★★★, The Best Of ... (Island 1996)★★★★.
FURTHER READING: Meet On The Ledge, Patrick Humphries.

DENVER, JOHN
ALBUMS: Rhymes & Reasons (RCA 1969)★★★, Take Me To Tomorrow (RCA 1970)★★★, Whose Garden Was This (RCA 1970)★★★, Poems, Prayers And Promises (RCA 1971)★★★, Aerie (RCA 1971)★★★, Rocky Mountain High (RCA 1972)★★★, Farewell Andromeda (RCA 1973)★★★, Back Home Again (RCA 1974)★★★★, An Evening With John Denver (RCA 1975)★★★★, Windsong (RCA 1975)★★★, Rocky Mountain Christmas (RCA 1975)★★, Live In London (RCA 1976)★★★, Spirit (RCA 1976)★★★, I Want To Live (RCA 1977)★★, Live At The Sydney Opera House (RCA 1978)★★, John Denver (RCA 1979)★★★, with the Muppets A Christmas Together (RCA 1979)★★, Autograph (RCA 1980)★★★, Some Days Are Diamonds (RCA 1981)★★★, with Placido Domingo Perhaps Love (Columbia 1981)★★, Seasons Of The Heart (RCA 1982)★★★, It's About Time (RCA 1983)★★★, Dreamland Express (RCA 1985)★★, One World (RCA 1986)★★, Higher Ground (RCA 1988)★★, Stonehaven Sunrise (1989)★★, The Flower That Shattered The Stone (Windstar 1990)★★, Earth Songs (Music Club 1990)★★, Different Directions (Concord 1992)★★.
COMPILATIONS: The Best Of John Denver (RCA 1974)★★★, The Best Of John Denver Volume 2 (RCA 1977)★★★, The John Denver Collection (Telstar 1984)★★★, Greatest Hits Volume 3 (RCA 1985)★★★, The Rocky Mountain Collection (BMG 1997)★★★★.
VIDEOS: A Portrait (Telstar 1994), The Wildlife Concert (Sony 1995).
FURTHER READING: John Denver, Leonore Fleischer. John Denver, David Dachs. John Denver: Rocky Mountain Wonderboy, James Martin. Take Me Home: An Autobiography, John Denver with Arthur Tobier.

DENVER, KARL
ALBUMS: Wimoweh (Decca 1961)★★★, Karl Denver (Ace Of Clubs 1962)★★★, Karl Denver At The Yew Tree (Decca 1962)★★, With Love (Decca 1964)★★★, Karl Denver (1970)★★.

DEPECHE MODE
ALBUMS: Speak And Spell (Mute 1981)★★, A Broken Frame (Mute 1982)★★, Construction Time Again (Mute 1983)★★★, Some Great Reward (Mute 1984)★★★, Black Celebration (Mute 1986)★★★, Music For The Masses (Mute 1987)★★★, 101 (Mute 1989)★★, Violator (Mute 1991)★★★★, Songs Of Faith & Devotion (Mute 1993)★★★★, Ultra (Mute 1997)★★★.
COMPILATIONS: The Singles 81-85 (Mute 1985)★★★★.
VIDEOS: Some Great Videos (Virgin Vision 1986), Strange (Virgin Vision 1988), 101 (Virgin Vision 1989), Strange Too – Another Violation (BMG Video 1990), Devotional (1993), Live In Hamburg (1993).
FURTHER READING: Depeche Mode: Strangers – The Photographs, Anton Corbijn. Depeche Mode: Some Great Reward, Dave Thompson.

DEREK AND THE DOMINOS
ALBUMS: Layla And Other Assorted Love Songs (Polydor 1970)★★★★, In Concert (Polydor 1973)★★★.

DESCENDENTS
ALBUMS: Milo Goes To College (New Alliance 1982)★★, I Don't Want To Grow Up (New Alliance 1985)★★★, Enjoy (New Alliance 1986)★★★, All (SST 1987)★★★, Liveage (SST 1987)★★, Hallraker (SST 1989)★★, Everything Sucks (Epitaph 1996)★★★.
COMPILATIONS: Somery (SST 1995)★★★.

DESERT ROSE BAND
ALBUMS: The Desert Rose Band (MCA 1987)★★★, Running (MCA 1988)★★★, Pages Of Life (MCA 1989)★★★, True Love (Curb 1991)★★, Traditional (Curb 1993)★★, Life Goes On (Curb 1993)★★.
COMPILATIONS: A Dozen Roses: Greatest Hits (MCA 1991)★★★★, Greatest Hits (Curb 1994)★★★★.

DeSHANNON, JACKIE
ALBUMS: Jackie DeShannon (Liberty 1963)★★, Breakin' It Up On The Beatles Tour (Liberty 1964)★★, Don't Turn Your Back On Me (1964)★★, Surf Party soundtrack (1964)★★, This Is Jackie DeShannon (Imperial 1965)★★★, You Won't Forget Me (Imperial 1965)★★, In The Wind (Imperial1965)★★, C'Mon Let's Live A Little soundtrack (1966)★★, Are You Ready For This? (1966)★★★, New Image (1967)★★, For You (1967)★★, Me About You (1968)★★, What The World Needs Now Is Love (1968)★★, Laurel Canyon (1969)★★, Put A Little Love In Your Heart (1969)★★, To Be Free (1969)★★, Songs (1971)★★★, Jackie (Atlantic 1972)★★, Your Baby Is A Lady (1974)★★, New Arrangement (1975)★★, You're The Only Dancer (1977)★★, Quick Touches (1978)★★.
COMPILATIONS: You Won't Forget Me (1965)★★, What The World Needs Now Is ... The Definitive Collection (EMI 1997)★★★, The Best Of Jackie DeShannon (Rhino 1991)★★★.

DETROIT SPINNERS
ALBUMS: Party – My Pad (Motown 1963)★★, The OriginalSpinners (Motown 1967)★★★, The Detroit Spinners (Motown 1968)★★★, Second Time Around (V.I.P. 1970)★★★, The (Detroit) Spinners (Atlantic 1973)★★★★, Mighty Love (Atlantic 1974)★★★★, New And Improved (Atlantic 1974)★★, Pick Of The Litter (Atlantic 1975)★★★, (Detroit) Spinners Live! (Atlantic 1975)★★★, Happiness Is Being With The (Detroit) Spinners (Atlantic 1976)★★★, Yesterday, Today And Tomorrow (Atlantic 1977)★★, Spinners/8 (Atlantic 1977)★★, From Here To Eternally (Atlantic 1979)★★, Dancin' And Lovin' (Atlantic 1980)★★, Love Trippin' (Atlantic 1980)★★, Labor Of Love (Atlantic 1981)H, Can't Shake This Feelin' (Atlantic 1982)★★, Grand Slam (Atlantic 1983)★★, Cross Fire (Atlantic 1984)★★, Lovin' Feelings (Atco 1985)★★, Down To Business (Volt 1989)★★.
COMPILATIONS: The Best Of The Detroit Spinners (Motown 1973)★★★★, Smash Hits (Atlantic 1977)★★★★, The Best Of The Spinners (Atlantic 1978)★★★★, 20 Golden Classics – The Detroit Spinners (Motown 1980)★★★, Golden Greats – Detroit Spinners (Atlantic 1985)★★★, A One Of A Kind Love Affair: The Anthology (Atlantic 1991)★★★.

dEUS
ALBUMS: Worst Case Scenario (Island 1994)★★★, My Sister Is A Clock (Island 1995)★★★, In A Bar, Under The Sea (Island 1996)★★★.

DEVO
ALBUMS: Q: Are We Not Men? A: We Are Devo! (Warners 1978)★★★★, Duty Now For The Future (Warners 1979)★★★, Freedom Of Choice (Warners 1980)★★★, Dev-o Live mini-album (Warners 1981)H, New Traditionalists (Warners 1981)★★★, Oh, No, It's Devo (Warners 1982)★★★, Shout (Warners 1984)★★, Total Devo (Enigma 1988)★★, Smooth Noodle Maps (Enigma 1990)★★.
Solo: Mark Mothersbaugh Muzik For Insomniaks Volume 1 (Enigma 1988)★★, Muzik For Insomniaks Volume 2 (Enigma 1988)★★.
COMPILATIONS: Now It Can Be Told (Enigma 1989)★★★, Greatest Hits (Warners 1990)★★★★, Greatest Misses (Warners 1990)★★★.

DEXYS MIDNIGHT RUNNERS
ALBUMS: Searching For The Young Soul Rebels (EMI 1980)★★★★, Too-Rye-Ay (Mercury 1982)★★★★, Don't Stand Me Down (Mercury 1985)★★★, BBC Radio One Live In Concert rec. 1982 (Windsong 1994)★★.
COMPILATIONS: Geno (EMI 1983)★★★, The Very Best Of (Mercury 1991)★★★★, 1980-1982: The Radio One Sessions (Nighttracks 1995)★★★, It Was Like This (EMI 1996)★★★.

DIAMOND HEAD
ALBUMS: The White LabelAlbum (Happy Face 1980)★★, Lightning To The Nations (Woolfe 1981)★★★, Borrowed Time (MCA 1982)★★★, Canterbury (MCA 1983)★★, Behold The Beginning (Heavy Metal1986)★★, Am I Evil (FM/Revolver 1987)★★★, Death & Progress (Bronze 1993)★★.
VIDEOS: Diamond Head (1981).

DIDDLEY, BO
ALBUMS: Bo Diddley (Checker 1957)★★★, Go Bo Diddley (Checker 1958)★★★, Have Guitar Will Travel (Checker 1959)★★★, Bo Diddley In The Spotlight (Checker 1960)★★★, Bo Diddley Is A Gunslinger (Checker 1961)★★★, Bo Diddley Is A Lover (Checker 1961)★★★, Bo Diddley (Checker 1962)★★★, Bo Diddley Is A Twister (Checker 1962)★★, Hey Bo Diddley (Checker 1963)★★★, Bo Diddley And Company (Checker 1963)★★★, Bo Diddley Rides Again (Checker 1963)★★★, Bo Diddley's Beach Party (Checker 1963)★★★, Bo Diddley Goes Surfing aka Surfin' With Bo Diddley (Checker 1963)★★★, Hey Good Looking (Checker 1964)★★★, with Chuck Berry Two Great Guitars (Checker 1964)★★★, 500% More Man (Checker 1965)★★★, Let Me Pass (Checker 1965)★★★, The Originator (Checker 1966)★★★, Boss Man (Checker 1967)★★★, Superblues (Checker 1968)★★★, The Super Super Blues Band (Checker 1968)★★★, The Black Gladiator (Checker 1969)★★, Another Dimension (Chess 1971)★★★, Where It All Begins (Chess 1972)★★, The Bo Diddley London Sessions (Chess 1973)★★, Big Bad Bo (Chess 1974)★★★, Got My Own Bag Of Tricks (Chess 1974)★★★, The 20th Anniversary Of Rock 'N' Roll(1976)★★, I'm A Man (1977)★★, Signifying Blues (1993)★★★, Bo's Blues (1993)★★, A Man Amongst Men (Code Blue 1996)★★.
COMPILATIONS: Chess Master (Chess 1988)★★★, EP Collection (See For Miles 1991)★★★★, Bo Diddley: The Chess Years 12-CD box set (Charly 1993)★★★★★, Bo Diddley Is A Lover ... Plus (See For Miles 1994)★★★, Let Me Pass ... Plus (See For Miles 1994)★★★.

VIDEOS: I Don't Sound Like Nobody (Hendring Video 1990).
FURTHER READING: Where Are You Now Bo Diddley?, Edward Kiersh. The Complete Bo Diddley Sessions, George White (ed.). Bo Diddley: Living Legend, George White.

DiFRANCO, ANI
ALBUMS: Ani DiFranco (Righteous Babe 1990)★★★★, Not So Soft (Righteous Babe 1991)★★★, Imperfectly (Righteous Babe 1992)★★★, Puddle Dive (Righteous Babe 1993)★★★★, Not A Pretty Girl (Righteous Babe 1995)★★★★, Dilate (Righteous Babe 1996)★★★, with Utah Phillips The Past Didn't Go Anywhere (Righteous Babe 1996)★★★, More Joy, Less Shame (Cooking Vinyl1997)★★★, Living In Clip (Righteous Babe 1997)★★★★, Little Plastic Castle (Righteous Babe 1998)★★★.
COMPILATIONS: Like I Said/Songs 1990-1991 (Righteous Babe 1994)★★★.

DIGITAL UNDERGROUND
ALBUMS: Sex Packets (Tommy Boy 1990)★★★, Sons Of The P (Tommy Boy 1991)★★★, The Body-Hat Syndrome (Tommy Boy 1993)★★, Future Rhythm (Critique 1996)★★★.

DILLARD AND CLARK
ALBUMS: The Fantastic Expedition Of Dillard And Clark (A&M 1968)★★★, Through The Morning, Through The Night (A&M 1969)★★★★.

DILLARDS
ALBUMS: Back Porch Bluegrass (Elektra 1963)★★★, The Dillards Live... Almost! (Elektra 1964)★★★, with Byron Berline Pickin' & Fiddlin' (Elektra 1965)★★★, Wheatstraw Suite (Elektra 1968)★★★★, Copperfields (Elektra 1970)★★★, Roots And Branches (Anthem 1972)★★, Tribute To The American Duck (Poppy 1973)★★★, The Dillards Versus The Incredible LA Time Machine (Sonet 1977)★★, Glitter-Grass From The Nashwood Hollyville Strings (1977)★★★, Decade Waltz (Flying Fish 1979)★★, Homecoming & Family Reunion (Flying Fish 1980)★★★, Mountain Rock (Flying Fish 1980)★★, Let It Fly (Vanguard 1990)★★★.
COMPILATIONS: Country Tracks (Elektra 1974)★★★, I'll Fly Away (Edesl1988)★★★, There Is A Time (1963-1970) (Vanguard 1991)★★★★.
VIDEOS: A Night In The Ozarks (Hendring 1991).
FURTHER READING: Everybody On The Truck, Lee Grant.

DINOSAUR JR
ALBUMS: as Dinosaur Dinosaur (Homestead 1985)★★★, as Dinosaur Jr You're Living All Over Me (SST 1987)★★★, Bug (SST 1988)★★★★, Green Mind (Blanco y Negro 1991)★★★, Where You Been (Blanco y Negro 1993)★★★★, Without A Sound (Blanco y Negro 1994)★★★, Hand It Over (Blanco Y Negro 1997)★★★.
Solo: Mike Johnson Year Of Mondays (Atlantic 1996)★★. J Mascis Martin And Me (Reprise 1996)★★★.

DION AND THE BELMONTS
ALBUMS: Dion And The Belmonts: Presenting Dion And The Belmonts (Laurie 1959)★★★, Wish Upon A Star (Laurie 1960)★★, Together (Laurie 1963)★★★, Together Again (ABC 1967)★★★, Live 1972 (Reprise 1973).
COMPILATIONS: 20 Golden Greats (1980)★★★★.
Dion: Alone With Dion (Laurie 1961)★★★, Runaround Sue (Laurie 1961)★★★, Lovers Who Wander (Laurie 1962)★★★, Dion Sings His Greatest Hits (Laurie 1962)★★★, Love Came To Me (Laurie 1963)★★★, Ruby Baby (Columbia 1963)★★★, Dion Sings The 15 Million Sellers (Laurie 1963)★★★★, Donna The Prima Donna (Columbia 1963)★★★★, Dion Sings To Sandy (Laurie 1963)★★★, Dion (1968)★★★, Sit Down Old Friend (1969)★★★, Wonder Where I'm Bound (1969)★★★, You're Not Alone (1971)★★★, Sanctuary (1971)★★★, Suite For Late Summer (1972)★★★, Born To Be With You (1975)★★★, Sweetheart (1976)★★★, The Return Of The Wanderer (1978)★★★, Inside Job (1980)★★★, Kingdom Of The Street (1985)★★★, Velvet And Steel (1986)★★★, Yo Frankie! (1989)★★★, Bronx Blues: The Columbia Recordings (1962-1965) (1991)★★★★, The Road I'm On: A Retrospective (Columbia Legacy 1997)★★★.
FURTHER READING: The Wanderer, Dion DiMucci with Davin Seay.

DION, CELINE
ALBUMS: La Voix Du Bon Dieu (Disques Super Etoiles 1981)★★, Celine Dion Chante Noel (Disques Super Etoiles 1981)★★, Tellement J'ai D'amour (Saisons 1982)★★, Les Chemins De Ma Maison (Saisons 1983)★★, Du SoleilAu Coeur (Pathe Marconi 1983)★★, Melanie (TBS 1984)★★, Les Oiseaux Du Bonheur (Pathe Marconi 1984)★★, Les Plus Grands Succes De Celine Dion (TBS 1984)★★★, C'est Pour Toi (TBS 1985)★★, Celine Dion En Concert (TBS 1985)★★, Les Chansons En Or (TBS 1986)★★, Incognito (CBS 1987)★★, Des Mots Qui Sonnent (Columbia 1991)★★★, Unison (Epic 1991)★★, Dion Chante Plamondon (Epic 1991)★★, Celine Dion (Epic 1993)★★★★, Les Premieres Annees (Versailles 1993)★★, The Colour Of My Love (Epic 1994)★★★★, Celine Dion A Olympia (Columbia 1994)★★★, D'Eux (Epic 1995)★★★, Falling Into You (Epic 1996)★★★, Live In Paris (Epic 1996)★★★.
COMPILATIONS: Celine Dion Gold (Versailles 1995)★★★, Celine Dion Gold Vol.2 (Versailles 1995)★★★.
VIDEOS: The Colour Of My Love Concert (Epic Music Video 1995).

DIRE STRAITS
ALBUMS: Dire Straits (Vertigo 1978)★★★★, Communique (Vertigo 1979)★★, Making Movies (Vertigo 1980)★★★★, Love Over Gold (Vertigo 1982)★★★, Alchemy – Live (Vertigo 1984)★★, Brothers In Arms (Vertigo 1985)★★★, On Every Street (Vertigo 1991)★★★, On The Night (Vertigo 1993)★★, Live At The BBC (Windsong 1995)★★★.
COMPILATIONS: Money For Nothing (Vertigo 1988)★★★★.
VIDEOS: Brothers In Arms (1988), Alchemy Live (1988), The Videos (1992).
FURTHER READING: Dire Straits, Michael Oldfield. Mark Knopfler: The Unuthorised Biography, Myles Palmer.

DISPOSABLE HEROES OF HIPHOPRISY
ALBUMS: Hiphoprisy Is The Greatest Luxury (4th & Broadway 1992)★★★★, with William Burroughs: Spare Ass Annie & Other Tales (4th & Broadway 1993)★★★.

DIVINE COMEDY
ALBUMS: Fanfare For The Comic Muse (Setanta 1991)★★, Liberation (Setanta 1993)★★★, Promenade (Setanta 1994)★★★, Casanova (Setanta 1996)★★★★, A Short Album About Love mini-album (Setanta 1997)★★★★.

DIXIE CUPS
ALBUMS: Chapel Of Love (Red Bird 1964)★★★, Iko Iko reissue of first album (Red Bird 1965)★★★, Ridin' High (ABC/Paramount 1965)★★.

DIXON, WILLIE
ALBUMS: Willie's Blues (Bluesville 1959)★★★, Memphis Slim & Willie Dixon At The Village Gate (1960)★★★★, I Am The Blues (Columbia 1970)★★, Peace (1971)★★★, Catalyst (Ovation 1973)★★★, Mighty Earthquake And Hurricane (1983)★★★, I Feel Like Steppin' Out (1986)★★★, Gene Gilmore & The Five Breezes (1989)★★, Hidden Charms (Bug 1988)★★★, The Big Three Trio (Columbia 1990)★★★, Blues Dixonary (1993)★★★, Across The Borderline (1993)★★★.
COMPILATIONS: The Chess Box (Chess 1988)★★★, The OriginalWang Dang Doodle – The Chess Recordings & More (MCA/Chess 1995)★★★★.
FURTHER READING: I Am The Blues, Willie Dixon.

DJ JAZZY JEFF AND THE FRESH PRINCE
ALBUMS: Rock The House (Word Up 1987)★★, He's The DJ, I'm The Rapper (Jive 1988)★★★, And In This Corner (Jive 1990)★★★, Homebase (Jive 1991)★★, Code Red (Jive 1993)★★.

DJ SHADOW
ALBUMS: Midnight In A Perfect World (Mo Wax 1996)★★★, Endtroducing (Mo Wax 1996)★★★★.

DOCTORS OF MADNESS
ALBUMS: Late Night Movies, All Night Brainstorms (Polydor 1976)★★★, Figments Of Emancipation (Polydor 1976)★★★, Sons Of Survival (Polydor 1978)★★.
Solo: Richard Strange The Live Rise Of Richard Strange (Ze/PVC 1980)★★★, The Phenomenal Rise Of Richard Strange (Virgin 1981)★★★, as Richard Strange And The Engine Room Going-Gone (Side 1987)★★★.
COMPILATIONS: Revisionism (1975-78) (Polydor 1981)★★★.

DODD, COXSONE
ALBUMS: Various: AllStar Top Hits (Studio One 1961)★★★★, Oldies But Goodies (Vols 1 & 2) (Studio One 1968)★★★★, Best Of Studio One (Vols, 1, 2, & 3) (Heartbeat 1983-87)★★★★, Respect To Studio One (Heartbeat 1995)★★★.

DODGY
ALBUMS: The Dodgy Album (A&M 1993)★★★★, Homegrown (A&M 1994)★★★, Free Peace Sweet (A&M 1996)★★★.

DOLBY, THOMAS
ALBUMS: The Golden Age Of Wireless (Venice In Peril1982)★★★★, The Flat Earth (Parlophone 1984)★★★, Aliens Ate My Buick (Manhattan 1988)★★, Astronauts And Heretics (Virgin 1992)★★.
VIDEOS: The Gate To The Mind's Eye (Miramar Images 1994).

DOLLAR
ALBUMS: Shooting Stars (Carrere 1979)★★, The Dollar Album (Warners 1982)★★.
COMPILATIONS: The Very Best Of Dollar (Carrere 1982)★★.

DOMINO, FATS
ALBUMS: Carry On Rockin' (Imperial 1955)★★★★, Rock And Rollin' With Fats (Imperial 1956)★★★★, Rock And Rollin' (Imperial 1956)★★★★, This Is Fats Domino! (Imperial 1957)★★★★, Here Stands Fats Domino (Imperial 1958)★★★★, Fabulous Mr D (Imperial 1958)★★★★, Let's Play Fats Domino (Imperial 1959)★★★★, Fats Domino Swings (Imperial 1959)★★★★, Million Record Hits (Imperial 1960)★★★★, A Lot Of Dominos (Imperial 1960)★★★★, I Miss You So (Imperial 1961)★★★, Let The Four Winds Blow (Imperial 1961)★★★★, What A Party (Imperial 1962)★★★, Twistin' The Stomp (Imperial 1962)★★★, Just Domino (Imperial 1962)★★★, Here Comes Fats Domino (ABC-Paramount 1963)★★★, Walkin' To New Orleans (Imperial 1963)★★★★, Let's Dance With Domino (Imperial 1963)★★★, Here He Comes Again (Imperial 1963)★★★, Fats On Fire (ABC 1964)★★★, Fats Domino '65 (Mercury 1965)★★★, Getaway With Fats Domino (ABC 1965)★★★, Fats Is Back (Reprise 1968)★★★, Cookin' With Fats (United Artists 1974)★★★, Sleeping On The Job (Sonet 1979)★★★, Live At Montreux (Atlantic 1987)★★★, Christmas Is A Special Day (Right Stuff/EMI 1994)★★★, Live In Concert (Remember 1996).
COMPILATIONS: The Very Best Of Fats Domino (Liberty 1970)★★★★, Rare Domino's (Liberty 1970)★★★, Rare Domino's Vol. 2 (Liberty 1971)★★★, Fats Domino – His Greatest Hits (MCA 1986)★★★, My Blue Heaven – The Best Of Fats Domino (EMI 1990)★★★★,They Call Me The Fat Man: The Legendary Imperial Recordings 4-CD box set (EMI/Imperial 1991)★★★★★, Out Of Orleans 8-CD box set (Bear Family 1993)★★★★★, The EP Collection Vol. 1 (See For Miles 1995)★★★★, The Early Imperial Singles 1950-52 (Ace 1996)★★★★, The EP Collection Vol. 2 (See For Miles 1997)★★★★.
FILMS: The Girl Can't Help It (1956), Jamboree aka Disc Jockey Jamboree (1957), The Big Beat (1957).

DONEGAN, LONNIE
ALBUMS: Showcase (Pye Nixa 1956)★★★, Lonnie (Pye Nixa 1957), Tops With Lonnie (Pye 1958)★★★★, Lonnie Rides Again (Pye 1959)★★★, More Tops With Lonnie (Pye 1961)★★★, Sings Hallelujah (Pye 1962)★★★, The Lonnie Donegan Folk Album (Pye 1965)★★★★, Lonniepops-Lonnie Donegan Today (Decca 1970)★★★, Lonnie Donegan Meets Leineman (1974)★★★, Lonnie Donegan (1975)★★, Lonnie Donegan Meets Leineman-Country Roads (1976)★★, Putting On The Style (Chrysalis 1978)★★, Sundown (1978)★★, Jubilee Concert (1981)★★.
COMPILATIONS: Golden Age Of Donegan (Golden Guinea 1962)★★★★, Golden Age Of Donegan Vol 2 (Golden Guinea 1963)★★★★, Greatest Hits: Lonnie Donegan (1983)★★★★, Rare And Unissued Gems (1985)★★★, Rock Island Line (1985)★★★★, The Hit Singles Collection (1987)★★★★, The Best Of Lonnie Donegan (1989)★★★★, The Collection: Lonnie Donegan (1989)★★★★, Putting On The Styles 3-CD box set (1992)★★★★.

DONOVAN
ALBUMS: What's Bin Did And What's Bin Hid (Pye 1965)★★★★, Catch The Wind (1965 Pye/Hickory)★★★, Fairytale (Pye/Hickory1965)★★★★, Sunshine Superman (Epic 1966)★★★★, Mellow Yellow (Epic 1967)★★★★, Wear Your Love Like Heaven (Epic 1967)★★★, For Little Ones (Epic 1967)★★★, A Gift From A Flower To A Garden (Epic 1967)★★★, Donovan In Concert (Epic 1968)★★★, Hurdy Gurdy Man (Epic 1968)★★★★, Barabajagal (Epic 1969)★★★★, Open Road (Dawn 1970)★★, HMS Donovan (Dawn 1971)★★★, Brother Sun, Sister Moon soundtrack (TKR 1972)★★, Colours (Hallmark 1972)★★★, The Pied Piper soundtrack (1973)★★, Cosmic Wheels (Epic 1973)★★★, Live In Japan (Sony 1973)★★★, Essence To Essence (Epic 1973)★★★, 7-Tease (Epic 1974)★★★, Slow Down World (Epic 1976)★★, Donovan (Arista 1977)★★, Neutronica (RCA 1981)★★, Love Is Only Feeling (RCA 1981)★★, Lady Of The Stars (Allegiance 1984)★★, The Classics Live 1991 (Great Northern Arts 1993)★★★, Sutras (American Recordings 1996)★★★.
COMPILATIONS: Universal Soldier (Pye 1967)★★★★, Like It Is (Hickory 1968)★★★, The World Of Donvan (Pye 1969)★★★★, Hear Me Now (Janus 1970)★★★, The Golden Hour Of Donovan (Pye 1971)★★★★, Early Treasures (Bell1973)★★★, The Donovan File (Pye 1977)★★★, Spotlight On Donovan (Pye 1981)★★★★, Greatest Hits And More (EMI 1989)★★★, The EP Collection (See For Miles 1990)★★★★, Donovan Rising (Permanent 1990)★★★, The Trip: A Collection Of Donovan Originals From The Psychedelic Era (EMI 1991)★★★★★, 25 Years In Concert (1991)★★★, Troubadour: The Definitive Collection 1964-1976 box set (Legacy 1992)★★★★★, The Hits (Disky 1993)★★★, Tilll See You Again (Success 1994)★★★, Josie (Castle 1994)★★★, UniversalSoldier (Spectrum 1995)★★★★, Sunshine Troubadour (Hallmark 1996)★★★, Catch The Wind: The Best Of Donovan (Pulse 1996)★★★.

DOOBIE BROTHERS
ALBUMS: The Doobie Brothers (Warners 1971)★★, Toulouse Street (Warners 1972)★★★, The Captain And Me (Warners 1973)★★★★, What Were Once Vices Are Now Habits (Warners 1974)★★★, Stampede (Warners 1975)★★★, Takin' It To The Streets (Warners 1976)★★★★, Livin' On The Fault Line (Warners 1977)★★★, Minute By Minute (Warners 1980)★★★★, One Step Closer (Warners 1981)★★, Cycles (Capitol1989)★★, Brotherhood (Capitol1991)H, Rockin' Down The Highway (Legacy 1996)★★★.
COMPILATIONS: The Best Of The Doobie Brothers (Warners 1976)★★★, The Best Of The Doobies Volume 2 (Warners 1981)★★★, Very Best Of The Doobie Brothers (1993)★★★★.

DOORS
ALBUMS: The Doors (Elektra 1967)★★★★★, Strange Days (Elektra 1967)★★★★, Waiting For The Sun (Elektra 1968)★★★, The Soft Parade (Elektra 1969)★★, Morrison Hotel (Elektra 1970)★★★★, Absolutely Live (Elektra 1970)H, LA Woman (Elektra 1971)★★★★, Other Voices (Elektra 1971)★★, Full Circle (Elektra 1972)H, An American Prayer (Elektra 1978)★★, Alive She Cried (Elektra 1983)★★, The Doors Live At The Hollywood Bowl (Elektra 1987)★★, In Concert (Elektra 1991)★★.
COMPILATIONS: 13 (Elektra 1971)★★★★, Weird Scenes Inside The Goldmine (Elektra 1972)★★★, The Best Of The Doors (Elektra 1974)★★★★, Greatest Hits (Elektra 1980)★★★★, The Doors soundtrack (1991)★★★, Greatest Hits enhanced CD (East West 1996)★★★.
FILMS: American Pop (1981).
VIDEOS: Live At The Hollywood Bowl (1987), Tribute To Jim Morrison (1988), The Doors In Europe (Castle Hendring 1990), The Doors Are Open (Castle Hendring 1990), The Doors (1991), Dance On Fire (1991), Doors: A Tribute To Jim Morrison (1991).
FURTHER READING: Jim Morrison And The Doors: An Unauthorized Book, Mike Jahn. An American Prayer, Jim Morrison. The Lords & The New Creatures, Jim Morrison. Jim Morrison Au Dela Des Doors, Herve Muller. No One Here Gets Out Alive, Jerry Hopkins and Danny Sugerman. Burn Down The Night, Craig Kee Strete. Jim Morrison: The Story Of The Doors In Words And Pictures, Jim Morrison, Jim Morrison: An Hour For Magic, Frank Lisciandro. The Doors: The Illustrated History, Danny Sugerman. The Doors, John Tobler and Andrew Doe. Jim Morrison: Dark Star, Dylan Jones. Images Of Jim Morrison, Edward Wincentsen. The End: The Death Of Jim Morrison, Bob Seymore. The American Night Volume 2, Jim Morrison. The American Night: The Writings Of Jim Morrison, Jim Morrison. Morrison: A Feast of Friends, Frank Lisciandro. Light My Fire, John Densmore. Riders On The Storm: My Life With Jim Morrison And The Doors, John Densmore. The Doors Complete Illustrated Lyrics, Danny Sugerman (ed.). Break On Through: The Life and Death Of Jim Morrison, James Riordan and Jerry Prochnicky. The Doors: Lyrics, 1965-71, no author. The Lizard King: The Essential Jim Morrison, Jerry Hopkins. The Doors: Dance On Fire, Ross Clarke. The Complete Guide To The Music Of ..., Peter K. Hogan. The Doors: Moonlight Drive, Chuck Crisafulli.

DOUG E. FRESH
ALBUMS: Oh, My God! (Reality 1985)★★★, The World's Greatest Entertainer (Reality 1988)★★, Doin' What I Gotta Do (Bust It 1992)★★, Play (Gee Street 1995)★★.

DOUGLAS, CARL
ALBUMS: Carl Douglas (Pye 1975)★★, Kung Fu Fighter (Pye 1976)★★, Run Back (Pye 1977)H, Keep Pleasing Me (Pye 1978)H.

DOWNING, WILL
ALBUMS: Will Downing (4th & Broadway 1988)★★★★, Come Together As One (4th & Broadway 1989)★★, A Dream Fulfilled (4th & Broadway 1991)★★, Love's The Place To Be (4th & Broadway 1993)★★, Moods (4th & Broadway 1995)★★★.

DOWNLINERS SECT
ALBUMS: The Sect (Columbia 1964)★★★, The Country Sect (Columbia 1965)★★, The Rock Sect's In (Columbia 1966)★★, Showbiz (1979)★★★.
COMPILATIONS: Be A Sect Maniac (80s)★★★, The Definitive Downliners Sect – Singles A's & B's (See For Miles 1994)★★★.

DOZIER, LAMONT
ALBUMS: Out Here On My Own (ABC 1973)★★, Black Bach (ABC 1974)★★, Love And Beauty (ABC 1975)★★, Right There (Warners 1976)★★, Peddlin' Music On The Side (Warners 1977)★★★, Bittersweet (Warners 1979)★★, Working On You (Columbia 1981)★★, Lamont (A&M 1982)★★★, Bigger Than Life (Megaphone 1983)★★.

DR DRE
ALBUMS: The Chronic (Death Row 1993)★★★, Ist Round Knockout (Triple X 1996)★★★.

DR FEELGOOD
ALBUMS: Down By The Jetty (United Artists 1975)★★★★, Malpractice (United Artists 1975)★★★, Stupidity (United Artists 1976)★★★, Sneakin' Suspicion (United Artists 1977)★★, Be Seeing You (United Artists 1977)★★★, Private Practice (United Artists 1978)★★★, As It Happens (United Artists 1979)★★★, Let It Roll (United Artists 1979)★★, A Case Of The Shakes (United Artists 1980)★★, On The Job (Liberty 1981)★★, Fast Women And Slow Horses (Chiswick 1982)★★, Mad Man Blues (I.D. 1985)★★★, Doctor's Orders (Demon 1986)★★, Brilleaux (Demon 1986)★★, Classic Dr. Feelgood (Stiff 1987)★★, Live In London (Grand 1990)★★★, The Feelgood Factor (1993)★★, Down At The Doctors (Grand 1994)★★, On The Road Again (Grand 1996)★★★.
COMPILATIONS: Case History – The Best Of Dr. Feelgood (EMI 1987)★★★, Singles (The UA Years) (Liberty 1989)★★★, Looking Back 4-CD box set (EMI 1995)★★★, 25 Years Of Dr. Feelgood (Grand 1997)★★★★.

DR HOOK
ALBUMS: Dr Hook And the Medicine Show (Columbia 1972)★★★, Sloppy Seconds (Columbia 1972)★★★, Belly Up (Columbia 1973)★★, Fried Face (Columbia 1974)★★, Bankrupt (Capitol1975)★★, A Little Bit More (Capitol1976)★★★, Making Love And Music (Capitol1977)★★, Pleasure And Pain (Capitol1978)★★★, Sometimes You Win (Capitol1979)★★★, Rising (Casablanca 1980)★★, Live In The UK (Capitol1981)★★, Players In The Dark (Casablanca 1982)★★.
COMPILATIONS: Greatest Hits (Capitol1980)★★★, Completely Hooked-The Best Of Dr. Hook (Columbia 1992)★★★, Pleasure And Pain: The History Of Dr. Hook 3-CD box set (EMI 1996)★★★.
VIDEOS: Completely Hooked (PMI 1992).

DR JOHN
ALBUMS: Zu Zu Man (A&M 1965)★★★, Gris Gris (Atco 1968)★★★★, Babylon (Atco 1969)★★★, Remedies (Atco 1970)★★★, Dr John, The Night Tripper (The Sun, Moon And Herbs) (Atco 1971)★★★, Dr. John's Gumbo (Atco 1972)★★★★, In The Right Place (Atco 1973)★★★, with John Hammond, Mike Bloomfield Triumvirate (Columbia 1973)★★★, Desitively Bonnaroo (Atco 1974)★★★, Hollywood Be Thy Name (United Artists 1975)★★, Cut Me While I'm Hot (1975)★★, City Lights (Horizon 1978)★★★, Tango Palace (Horizon 1979)★★, with Chris Barber Take Me Back To New Orleans (1980)★★★, Love Potion (1981)★★, Dr John Plays Mac Rebennack (Clean Cuts 1982)★★★, The Brightest Smile In Town (Clean Cuts 1983)★★★, Such A Night – Live In London (Spindrift 1984)★★★, In A SentimentalMood (Warners 1989)★★, with Art Blakey, David 'Fathead' Newman Bluesiana Triangle (1990)★★★, Going Back To New Orleans (1992)★★★, Television (GRP 1994)★★, Afterglow (Blue Thumb 1995)★★, Trippin' Live (Eagle 1997)★★★.
COMPILATIONS: I Been Hoodood (Edsel1984)★★★, In The Night (Topline 1985)★★★, Mos' Scocious 2-CD set (Rhino 1994)★★★★, The Best Of ... (Rhino 1995)★★★★.
VIDEOS: Doctor John And Chris Barber, Live At The Marquee Club (Jettisoundz 1986), Live At The Marquee (Hendring Video 1990).
FURTHER READING: Dr. John: Under A Hoodoo Moon, Mac Rebennack with Jack Rummel.

DRAKE, NICK
ALBUMS: Five Leaves Left (Island 1969)★★★★, Bryter Layter (Island 1970)★★★★, Pink Moon (Island 1972)★★★.
COMPILATIONS: Heaven In A Wild Flower (Island 1985)★★★★, Fruit Tree 4-LP (Island 1979)★★★★, Time Of No Reply (Hannibal1986)★★★, Way To Blue (Island 1994)★★★★.
FURTHER READING: Nick Drake, David Housden. Nick Drake: A Biography, Patrick Humphries.

DREAD ZONE
ALBUMS: 360° (1993)★★★, Second Light (Virgin 1995)★★★★, BiologicalRadio (Virgin 1997)★★.

DREAM SYNDICATE
ALBUMS: The Days Of Wine And Roses (Ruby 1982)★★★★, Medicine Show (A&M 1984)★★★, This Is Not The New Dream Syndicate Album ... Live! mini-album (A&M 1984)★★, Out Of The Grey (Big Time 1986)★★★, Ghost Stories (Enigma 1988)★★★, Live At Raji's (Restless 1989)★★★.
Solo: Kendra Smith Five Ways Of Disappearing (4AD 1995)★★★.
COMPILATIONS: It's Too Late To Stop Now (Fan Club 1989)★★★.

DRIFTERS
ALBUMS: Save The Last Dance For Me (Atlantic 1961)★★★★, The Good Life With The Drifters (Atlantic 1964)★★★★, The Drifters (Clarion 1964)★★, I'll Take You Where The Music's Playing (Atlantic 1965)★★★, Souvenirs (Bell1974)★★★, Love Games (Bell1975)★★★, There Goes My First Love (Bell1975)★★★, Every Night's A Saturday Night (Bell1976)★★★, Greatest Hits Live (Astan 1984)★★, Live At Havard University (Showcase 1986)★★.
COMPILATIONS: Up On The Roof – The Best Of The Drifters (Atlantic 1963)★★★★, The Drifters Golden Hits (Atlantic 1968)★★★★, 24 Original Hits (Atlantic 1975)★★★★, The Collection (Castle 1987)★★★, Diamond Series: The Drifters (RCA 1988)★★★, Best Of The Drifters (Pickwick 1990)★★★, Let The Boogie Woogie Roll-Greatest Hits (1953-58) (Atlantic 1993)★★★, All Time Greatest Hits And More (1959-65) (Atlantic 1993)★★★★, Up On The Roof, On Broadway & Under The Boardwalk (Rhino/Pickwick 1995)★★★, Rockin' And Driftin': The Drifters Box 3-CD box set (Rhino 1996)★★★★, Anthology One: Clyde & The Drifters (Sequel1996)★★★★, Anthology Two: Rockin' & Driftin' (Sequel1996)★★★, Anthology Three: Save The Last Dance For Me (Sequel1996)★★★★, Anthology Four: Up On The Roof (Sequel1996)★★★★, Anthology Five: Under The Boardwalk (Sequel1997)★★★★, Anthology Six: The Good Life With The Drifters (Sequel1997)★★★, Anthology Seven: I'll Take You Where The Music's Playing (Sequel1997)★★★★.
FURTHER READING: The Drifters: The Rise And FallOf The Black VocalGroup, BillMillar. Save The Last Dance For Me: The MusicalLegacy 1953-92, Tony Allan and Faye Treadwell.

DUB WAR
ALBUMS: Dub Warning mini-album (Words Of Warning 1994)★★★, Pain (Earache 1995)★★★, Words Of Dubwarning (Words Of Warning 1996)★★★, Wrong Side Of Beautiful(Earache 1996)★★★★.

DUBLINERS
ALBUMS: Dubliners In Concert (1965)★★★, Finnegan Wakes (Transatlantic 1966)★★★★, A Drop Of The Hard Stuff (1967)★★★★, More Of The Hard Stuff (1967)★★★, The Dubliners (Major Minor 1968)★★★★, Drinkin' And Courtin' (1968)★★★, At It Again (Major Minor 1968)★★★, A Drop Of The Dubliners (1969)★★★★, Live At The Albert Hall (1969)★★★, At Home With The Dubliners (Columbia 1969)★★★, Revolution (Columbia 1970)★★★, Hometown! (1972)★★★, Double Dubliners (1973)★★★, Plain And Simple (Polydor 1973)★★★, The Dubliners Live (1974)★★★, Dubliners Now (1975)★★★, A ParcelOf Rogues (1976)★★★, The Dubliners – Fifteen Years On (1977)★★★, Prodigal Sons (1983)★★★, The Dubliners 25 Years Celebration (1987)★★★, The Dubliners Ireland (1992)★★★, Thirty Years A-Greying (1992)★★★, The OriginalDubliners (1993)★★★, Milestones (Transatlantic 1995)★★★.
COMPILATIONS: Best Of The Dubliners (1967)★★★, Very Best Of The Dubliners (1975)★★★★, 20 Greatest Hits: Dubliners (1989)★★★★, 20 Original Greatest Hits (1988)★★★, 20 Original Greatest Hits Vol. 2 (1989)★★★, The Best Of ... (Wooden Hill1996)★★★, The Definitive Transatlantic Collection (Transatlantic 1997)★★★★.
FURTHER READING: The Dubliners Scrapbook, Mary Hardy.

DUBSTAR
ALBUMS: Disgraceful (Food 1995)★★★★, Disgraceful Remixed (Food 1996)★★★, Goodbye (Food 1997)★★★★.

DUNBAR, SLY
ALBUMS: Go Deh Wid Riddim (Crystal1977)★★★, Simple Sly Man (Virgin 1978)★★, Sly Wicked And Slick (Virgin 1979)★★, Sly-Go-Ville (Mango/Island 1982)★★★.

DUNN, HOLLY
ALBUMS: Holly Dunn (MTM 1986)★★★, Cornerstone (MTM 1987)★★★, Across The Rio Grande (MTM 1988)★★★, The Blue Rose Of Texas (Warners 1989)★★★, Heart FullOf Love (Warners 1990)★★★, Getting It Dunn (Warners 1992)★★★, Life And Love And AllThe Stages (River North 1995)★★.
COMPILATIONS: Milestones: Greatest Hits (Warners 1991)★★★.
VIDEOS: Cowboys Are My Weakness (1995).

DURAN DURAN
ALBUMS: Duran Duran (EMI 1981)★★★, Rio (EMI 1982)★★★, Seven And The Ragged Tiger (EMI 1983)★★, Arena (Parlophone 1984)★★, Notorious (EMI 1986)★★★, Big Thing (EMI 1988)★★, Liberty (Parlophone 1990)H, Duran Duran (The Wedding Album) (Parlophone 1993)★★, Thank You (Capitol1995)★★★.
COMPILATIONS: Decade (EMI 1989)★★★★.
VIDEOS: Sing Blue Silver (1984), Duran Duran Video Album (1984), Arena (1985), The Making Of Arena (1986), Duran Duran: Video Single (1987), Dancing On The Valentine (1987), Working For The Skin Trade (1988), Decade (1989), 6ix By 3Hree (1989), Three To Get Ready (1990), Extraordinary World (1994).
FURTHER READING: Duran Duran: Their Story, Kasper De Graff and Malcolm Garrett.

DUROCS
ALBUMS: The Durocs (Capitol1979)★★★.

DURUTTI COLUMN
ALBUMS: The Return Of The Durutti Column (Factory 1980)★★★, Another Setting (Factory 1983)★★★, Live At The Venue London (VU 1983)★★★, Amigos En Portugal(Fundacio Atlantica 1984)★★, Without Mercy (Factory 1984)★★★, Domo Arigato (Factory 1985)★★★, Circuses And Bread (Factory 1986)★★★, The Guitar And Other Machines (Factory 1987)★★★, Live At The Bottom Line New York cassette only (ROIR 1987)★★★, Vini Reilly (Factory 1989)★★★★, Obey The Time (Factory 1990)★★★, Lips That Would Kiss Form Prayers To Broken Stone (Factory 1991)★★★, Dry (Materiali Sonori 1991)★★★, Sex & Death (Factory Too 1994)★★★, Fidelity (Crepescule 1996)★★★.
Solo: Vini Reilly The Sporadic Recordings (Sporadic 1989)★★★.
COMPILATIONS: Valuable Passages (Factory 1986)★★★, The Durutti Column – The First Four Albums (Factory 1988)★★★.

DURY, IAN
ALBUMS: New Boots And Panties (Stiff 1977)★★★★, Do It Yourself (Stiff 1979)★★★, Laughter (Stiff 1980)★★★, Lord Upminster (Polydor 1981)★★★, Juke Box Dury (Stiff 1981)★★, 4,000 Weeks Holiday (Polydor 1984)★★★, The Bus Driver's Prayer And Other Stories (Demon 1992)★★★.
COMPILATIONS: Greatest Hits (Fame 1981)★★★, The Best Of ... (Repertoire 1995)★★★, Reasons To Be Cheerful (Repertoire 1996)★★★.

DYLAN, BOB
ALBUMS: Bob Dylan (Columbia 1962)★★★, The Freewheelin' Bob Dylan (Columbia 1963)★★★★, The Times They Are A-Changin' (Columbia 1964)★★★★, Another Side Of Bob Dylan (Columbia 1964)★★★★, Bringing It All Back Home (Columbia 1965)★★★★★, Highway 61 Revisited (Columbia 1965)★★★★★, Blonde On Blonde (Columbia 1966)★★★★★, John Wesley Harding (Columbia 1968)★★★★, Nashville Skyline (Columbia 1969)★★★, Self Portrait (Columbia 1970)★★, New Morning (Columbia 1970)★★★, Dylan (Columbia 1973)H, Planet Waves (Island 1974)★★★★, Before The Flood (Asylum 1974)★★★, Blood On The Tracks (Columbia 1975)★★★★★, The Basement Tapes (Columbia 1975)★★★, Desire (Columbia 1976)★★★★, Hard Rain (Columbia 1976)★★, Street-Legal (Columbia 1978)★★★, Slow Train Coming (Columbia 1979)★★★, At Budokan (Columbia 1979)★★★, Saved (Columbia 1980)H, Shot Of Love (Columbia 1981)★★★, Infidels (Columbia 1983)★★★, Real Live (Columbia 1984)★★, Empire Burlesque (Columbia 1985)★★, Knocked Out Loaded (Columbia 1986)★★, Down In The Groove (Columbia 1988)★★★, Dylan And The Dead (Columbia 1989)H, Oh Mercy (Columbia 1989)★★★★, Under The Red Sky (Columbia 1990)★★★, Good As I Been To You (Columbia 1992)★★, World Gone Wrong (Columbia 1993)★★, The 30th Anniversary Concert Celebration (Columbia 1993)★★★, MTV Unplugged (Columbia 1995)★★★, Time Out Of Mind (Columbia 1997)★★★★.
COMPILATIONS: Bob Dylan's Greatest Hits (Columbia 1971)★★★★★, More Bob Dylan Greatest Hits (Columbia 1972)★★★★, Biograph (Columbia 1985)★★★★, The Bootleg Series, Vols 1-3, Rare And Unreleased 1961-1991 (Columbia/Legacy 1991)★★★★★, Greatest Hits Volume 3 (Columbia 1994)★★★.
VIDEOS: Hard To Handle (1987), Don't Look Back (1988), 30th Anniversary Concert Celebration (1993), MTV Unplugged (1995).
FURTHER READING: Bob Dylan In His Own Write, Bob Dylan. Eleven Outlined Epitaphs & Off The Top Of My Head, Bob Dylan. Folk-Rock: The Bob Dylan Story, Sy and Barbra Ribakove. Don't Look Back, D.A. Pennebaker. Bob Dylan: An Intimate Biography, Anthony Scaduto. Positively Main Street: An Unorthodox View Of Bob Dylan, Toby Thompson. Bob Dylan: A Retrospective, Craig McGregor. Song And Dance Man: The Art Of Bob Dylan, Michael Gray. Bob Dylan: Writings And Drawings, Bob Dylan. Knocking On Dylan's Door, Rolling Stone editors. Rolling Thunder Logbook, Sam Shepard. On The Road With Bob Dylan: Rolling With The Thunder, Larry Sloman. Bob Dylan: The Illustrated Record, Alan Rinzler. Bob Dylan In His Own Words, Miles. Bob Dylan: An Illustrated Discography, Stuart Hoggard and Jim Shields. Bob Dylan: An Illustrated History, Michael Gross. Bob Dylan: His Unreleased Recordings, Paul Cable. Dylan: What Happened?, Paul Williams. Conclusions On The Wall: New Essays On Bob Dylan, Liz Thomson. Twenty Years Of Recording: The Bob Dylan Reference Book, Michael Krogsgaard. Voice Without Restraint: A Study Of Bob Dylan's Lyrics And Their Background, John Herdman. Bob Dylan: From A Hard Rain To A Slow Train, Tim Dowley and Barry Dunnage. No Direction Home: The Life And Music Of Bob Dylan, Robert Shelton. Bringing It All Back Home, Robbie Wolliver. All Across The Telegraph: A Bob Dylan Handbook, Michael Gray and John Bauldie (eds.). Raging Glory, Dennis R. Liff. Bob Dylan: Stolen Moments, Clinton Heylin. Jokerman: Reading The Lyrics Of Bob Dylan, Aidan Day. Dylan: A Biography, Bob Spitz. Performing Artist: The Music Of Bob Dylan Vol. 1 1960-1973, Paul Williams. Dylan Companion, Elizabeth M. Thomson and David Gutman. Lyrics: 1962-1985, Bob Dylan. Bob Dylan: Performing Artist, Paul Williams. Oh No! Not Another Bob Dylan Book, Patrick Humphries and John Bauldie. Absolutely Dylan, Patrick Humphries and John Bauldie. Dylan: Behind The Shades, Clinton Heylin. Bob Dylan: A Portrait Of the Artist's Early Years, Daniel Kramer. Wanted Man: In Search Of Bob Dylan, John Bauldie (ed.). Bob Dylan: In His Own Words, Chris Williams. Tangled Up In Tapes, Glen Dundas. Hard Rain: A Dylan Commentary, Tim Riley. Complete Guide To The Music Of Bob Dylan, Patrick Humphries. Bob Dylan Drawn Blank (Folio of drawings), Bob Dylan. Watching The River Flow (1966-1995), Paul Williams.

E

EAGLES
ALBUMS: The Eagles (Asylum 1972)★★★, Desperado (Asylum 1973)★★★★, On The Border (Asylum 1974)★★★★, One Of These Nights (Asylum 1975)★★★, Hotel California (Asylum 1976)★★★★★, The Long Run (Asylum 1979)★★, Eagles-Live (Asylum 1980)★★, Hell Freezes Over (Geffen 1994)★★★.
COMPILATIONS: Their Greatest Hits 1971-1975 (Asylum 1976)★★★★, Greatest Hits Volume 2 (Asylum 1982)★★★, Best Of The Eagles (Asylum 1985)★★★.
VIDEOS: Hell Freezes Over (Geffen Home Video 1994).
FURTHER READING: The Eagles, John Swenson. The Long Run: The Story Of The Eagles, Marc Shapiro.

EARLE, STEVE
ALBUMS: Guitar Town (MCA 1986)★★★★, Exit O (MCA 1987)★★★, Copperhead Road (MCA 1988)★★★★, The Hard Way (MCA 1990)★★★, Shut Up And Die Like An Aviator (MCA 1991)★★★★, BBC Radio 1 Live In Concert (Windsong 1992)★★★, Train A Comin' (Transatlantic 1995)★★★★, I Feel Alright (Transatlantic 1996)★★★, El Coraz–n (Warner Bros 1997)★★★★.
COMPILATIONS: Early Tracks (Epic 1987)★★★, Essential Steve Earle (MCA 1993)★★★★, Angry Young Man (Nectar 1996)★★★, Ain't Ever Satisfied (HIPP 1996)★★★★.

EARLS
ALBUMS: Remember Me Baby (Old Town 1963)★★★.
COMPILATIONS: Remember Rome – The Early Years (Crystal Ball 1982)★★, Remember Then: The Best Of ... (Ace 1992)★★, Remember Me Baby: The Golden Classic Edition (Collecatbles 1992)★★.

EARTH, WIND AND FIRE
ALBUMS: Earth, Wind And Fire (Warners 1971)★★, The Need Of Love (Warners 1972)★★, Last Days And Time (Columbia 1972)★★, Head To The Sky (Columbia 1973)★★★, Open Our Eyes (Columbia 1974)★★★★, That's The Way Of The World (Columbia 1975)★★★★, Gratitude (Columbia 1975)★★★, Spirit (Columbia 1976)★★★, All And All (Columbia 1977)★★★, I Am (ARC 1979)★★★, Faces (ARC 1980)★★★, Raise! (ARC 1981)★★★, Powerlight (Columbia 1983)★★★, Electric Universe (Columbia 1983)★★, Touch The World (Columbia 1987)★★★, Heritage (Columbia 1990)★★, Millennium (1993)★★★, Greatest Hits Live, Tokyo Japan (Rhino 1996)★★, In The Name Of Love (Eagle 1997)★★★.
COMPILATIONS: The Best Of Earth, Wind And Fire, Volume 1 (ARC 1978)★★★★, The Collection (K-Tel 1986)★★★, The Best Of Earth, Wind And Fire, Volume 2 (Columbia 1988)★★★★, The Eternal Dance (1993)★★★, The Very Best Of (1993)★★★.

EAST 17
ALBUMS: Walthamstow (London 1993)★★★★, Steam (London 1994)★★★, Stay Another Night (London 1995)★★★, Around The World – The Journey So Far (London 1996)★★★.
VIDEOS: Up All Night (Polygram 1995), Letting Off Steam: Live (Polygram 1995), Greatest Hits (Polygram 1996).
FURTHER READING: East 17: Talk Back, Carl Jenkins.

EAST OF EDEN
ALBUMS: Mercator Projected (Deram 1969)★★, Snafu (Deram 1970)★★★, East Of Eden (Harvest 1971)★★★, New Leaf (Harvest 1971)★★, Another Eden (1975)★★, Here We Go Again (1976)★★ It's The Climate (1976)★★, Silver Park (1978)★★.
COMPILATIONS: The World Of East Of Eden (Deram 1971)★★★, Masters Of Rock (1975)★★★, Things (1976)★★★.

EASTON, SHEENA
ALBUMS: Take My Time (EMI 1981)★★, You Could Have Been With Me (EMI 1982)★★, Madness, Money And Music (EMI 1982)★★, The Best Kept Secret (EMI 1983)★★, A Private Heaven (EMI 1984)★★★★, Do You (EMI 1985)★★, No Sound But A Heart (EMI 1987)★★★, The Lover In Me (MCA 1988)★★★, What Comes Naturally (MCA 1991)★★★, The World Of Sheena Easton (1993)★★.
COMPILATIONS: The Gold Collection (EMI 1996)★★★, Ten Best Greatest Hits (Capitol 1997)★★★.

EASYBEATS
ALBUMS: Easy (1965)★★, It's 2 Easy (1966)★★, Volume 3 (1966)★★★, Good Friday (United Artists 1967)★★★, Vigil (United Artists 1968)★★, Friends (Polydor 1969)★★, The Shame Just Drained (1977)★★, Live Studio And Stage (Raven 1995)★★.
COMPILATIONS: The Best Of The Easybeats, Plus Pretty Girl (1967)★★★, Rock Legend (1980)★★★, Absolute Anthology (1980)★★★, Best Of The Easybeats (1986)★★★, The Best Of ... (Repertoire 1995)★★★, Aussie Beat That Shook The World (Repertoire 1996)★★★.

EAZY E
ALBUMS: Eazy-Duz-It (Ruthless/Priority 1988)★★★, It's On (Dr. Dre 187UM) Killa (EP)(Ruthless/Relativity 1994)★★★, Str.8 Off The Streetz Of Muthaphukkin' Compton (Ruthless 1995)★★★.

ECHO AND THE BUNNYMEN
ALBUMS: Crocodiles (Korova 1980)★★★★, Heaven Up Here (Korova 1981)★★★, Porcupine (Korova 1983)★★★★, Ocean Rain (Korova 1984)★★★, Echo And The Bunnymen (Warners 1987)★★, Reverberation (Korova 1990)★★, Evergreen (London 1997)★★★.
Solo: Will Sergeant Themes For Grind (92 Happy Customers 1983)★★.
COMPILATIONS: Songs To Learn And Sing (Korova 1985)★★★★, Live In Concert (Windsong 1991)★★★, The Cutter (Warners 1993)★★★, The Peel Sessions (Strange Fruit 1995)★★★, Ballyhoo – The Best Of Echo And The Bunnymen (Warners 1997)★★★★.
FURTHER READING: Liverpool Explodes: The Teardrop Explodes, Echo And The Bunnymen, Mark Cooper. Never Stop: The Echo & The Bunnymen Story, Tony Fletcher.

ECHOBELLY
ALBUMS: Everyone's Got One (Rhythm King 1994)★★★, On (Rhythm King 1995)★★★★, Lustra (Epic 1997)★★.

EDDIE AND THE HOT RODS
ALBUMS: Teenage Depression (Island 1976)★★★★, Life On The Line (Island 1977)★★★, Thriller (Island 1979)★★, Fish 'N' Chips (EMI America 1980)★★, One Story Town (Waterfront 1985)★★, Gasoline Days (Creative Man 1996)★★.
COMPILATIONS: The Best Of ... The End Of The Beginning (Island 1995)★★★.

EDDY, DUANE
ALBUMS: Have Twangy Guitar Will Travel (1958)★★★, Especially For You (1958)★★★, The 'Twang's The 'Thang' (1959)★★★★, Songs Of Our Heritage (1960)★★★, $1,000,000 Worth Of Twang (1960)★★★★, Girls! Girls! Girls! (1961)★★★, $1,000,000 Worth Of Twang Volume 2 (1962)★★★, Twistin' And Twangin' (RCA Victor 1962)★★★★, Twisting With Duane Eddy (1962)★★★, Twangy Guitar-Silky Strings (RCA Victor 1962)★★★★, Dance With The Guitar Man (RCA Victor 1963)★★★★, In Person (1963)★★★, Surfin' With Duane Eddy (1963)★★★, Twang A Country Song (RCA Victor 1963)★★, Twanging Up A Storm! (RCA Victor 1963)★★★, Lonely Guitar (RCA Victor 1964)★★★, Water Skiing (RCA Victor 1964)★★, Twangsville (RCA Victor 1965)★★, Twangin' The Golden Hits (RCA Victor 1965)★★★, Duane Goes Bob Dylan (RCA Victor 1965)★★, Duane A Go Go (RCA Victor 1965)★★, Biggest Twang Of Them All (RCA Victor 1966)★★, Roaring Twangies (RCA Victor 1967)★★, Twangy Guitar (1970)★★★, Duane Eddy (1987)★★★.
COMPILATIONS: The Best Of Duane Eddy (RCA Victor 1966)★★★★, The Vintage Years (Sire 1975)★★★, Legends Of Rock (1975)★★★, Twenty Terrific Twangies (1981)★★★, Greatest Hits (1991)★★★★, Twang Thang: The Duane Eddy Anthology (1993)★★★★, That Classic Twang 2-CD (Bear Family 1994)★★★★, Twangin' From Phoenix To L.A. – The Jamie Years (Bear Family 1995)★★★★.
FILMS: Because They're Young (1960).

BROUGHTON, EDGAR, BAND
ALBUMS: Wasa Wasa (Harvest 1969)★★★★, Sing Brother Sing (Harvest 1970)★★★, The Edgar Broughton Band (Harvest 1971)★★★, In Side Out (Harvest 1972)★★, Oora (Harvest 1973)★★, Bandages (NEMS 1975)★★, Parlez-Vous English (Infinity 1979)★★, Live Hits Harder (1979)★★, The Legendary (Music 2000 1984), Superchip (See For Miles 1996)★★.
COMPILATIONS: Document Series Presents ... Classic Album & Single Tracks 1969-1973 (1992)★★★.

EDMUNDS, DAVE
ALBUMS: Subtle As A Flying Mallet (RCA 1975)★★★, Get It (Swansong 1977)★★★, Tracks On Wax (Swansong 1978)★★★, Repeat When Necessary (Swansong 1979)★★★★, as Rockpile Seconds Of Pleasure (F-Beat 1980)★★★, Twangin' (Arista 1981)★★★, D.E.7th (Arista 1982)★★★, Information (Arista 1983)★★, Riff Raff (Arista 1984)★★, I Hear You Rockin' (Arista 1987)★★★, Closer To The Flame (Capitol 1990)★★, Plugged In (Columbia 1994)★★★.
COMPILATIONS: The Best Of Dave Edmunds (Swansong 1981)★★★★, The Original Rockpile Vol. 2 (Harvest 1987)★★★, The Complete Early Edmunds (EMI 1991)★★★, Chronicles (Connoisseur 1995)★★★★.
FILMS: Give My Regards To Broad Street (1985).

EELS
ALBUMS: Beautiful Freak (DreamWorks 1996/MCA 1997)★★★★.

EGG
ALBUMS: Egg (Nova 1970)★★★, The Polite Force (Deram 1970)★★★, The Civil Surface (Virgin 1974)★★★.
COMPILATIONS: Seven Is A Jolly Good Time (See For Miles 1988)★★★.

808 STATE
ALBUMS: Newbuild (Creed 1988)★★★, Quadrastate (Creed 1989)★★★, 808:90 (Creed 1989)★★★★, with MC Tunes North At Its Heights (ZTT 1990)★★★, Ex:El (ZTT 1991)★★★, Gorgeous (Warners 1992)★★★, Don Solaris (ZTT 1996)★★★.

EIGHTH WONDER
ALBUMS: Fearless (Columbia 1988)★★.

EINSTURZENDE NEUBATEN
ALBUMS: Kollaps (Zick Zack 1981)★★★, Die Zeichnungen Des Patienten O.T. (Some Bizzare 1983)★★★, 2x4 cassette (ROIR 1984)★★, Half Mensch (Some Bizzare/Rough Trade 1985)★★★, Funf Auf Nach Oben Offenen Richterskala (Some Bizzare 1987)★★★, Haus Der Luege (Some Bizzare 1989)★★★, Die Hamletmaschine film soundtrack (Ego 1991)★★, Tabula Rasa (Mute 1993)★★★, Malediction (Mute 1993)★★★, Faustmusik soundtrack (Ego 1996)★★, Ende Neu (Mute 1996)★★★, Ende Neu Remixes (Mute 1997)★★.
COMPILATIONS: Strategien Gegen Architekturen (Mute 1984)★★★, Strategies Against Architecture II (Mute 1991)★★★.
VIDEOS: Liebeslieder (Studio 1993).

EITZEL, MARK
ALBUMS: Songs Of Love Live (Demon 1992)★★★, 60 Watt Silver Lining (Virgin 1996)★★, West (Warners 1997)★★★★, Caught In A Trap And I Can't Back Out 'Cause I Love You Too Much Baby (Matador 1998).

ELASTICA
ALBUMS: Elastica (Deceptive 1995)★★★★.

ELECTRAFIXION
ALBUMS: Burned (Sire/Warners 1995)★★★.

ELECTRIBE 101
ALBUMS: Electribal Memories (Mercury 1990)★★★.

ELECTRIC FLAG
ALBUMS: The Trip film soundtrack (Sidewalk 1967)★★, A Long Time Comin' (Columbia 1968)★★★★, The Electric Flag (Columbia 1969)★★, The Band Kept Playing (1974)H.
COMPILATIONS: The Best Of The Electric Flag (Columbia 1970)★★★.

ELECTRIC LIGHT ORCHESTRA
ALBUMS: Electric Light Orchestra aka No Answer (Harvest 1971)★★, ELO II (Harvest 1973)★★, On The Third Day (Warners 1973)★★★, The Night The Lights Went On In Long Beach (Warners 1974)★★, Eldorado (Warners 1975)★★★★, Face The Music (Jet 1975)★★★, A New World Record (Jet 1976)★★★, Out Of The Blue (Jet 1977)★★★★, Discovery (Jet 1979)★★★, with Olivia Newton-John Xanadu film soundtrack (Jet 1980)★★, Time (Jet 1981)★★, Secret Messages (Jet 1983)★★, Balance Of Power (Epic 1986)★★, Electric Light Orchestra Part Two (Telstar 1991)H, as ELO 2 Moment Of Truth (Edel 1994)H.
COMPILATIONS: Showdown (Harvest 1974)★★★, Ole ELO (Jet 1976)★★★, The Light Shines On (Harvest 1976)★★★, Greatest Hits (Jet 1979)★★★★, A Box Of Their Best (1980)★★★, A Perfect World Of Music (Jet 1988)★★★, Their Greatest Hits (Epic 1989)★★★, The Definitive Collection (1993)★★★, The Very Best Of ... (Dino 1994)★★★, The Gold Collection (EMI 1996)★★★.
FURTHER READING: The Electric Light Orchestra Story, Bev Bevan.

ELECTRIC PRUNES
ALBUMS: The Electric Prunes (I Had Too Much To Dream Last Night) (Reprise 1967)★★★, Underground (Reprise 1967)★★★, Mass In F Minor (Reprise 1967)★★, Release Of An Oath (Reprise 1968)★★, Just Good Old Rock 'N' Roll (Reprise 1969)H, Stockholm 67 (Heartbeat 1997)★★.
COMPILATIONS: Long Day's Flight (1986)★★★.

ELECTRONIC
ALBUMS: Electronic (Factory 1991)★★★★, Raise The Pressure (Parlophone 1996)★★★.

ELGINS
ALBUMS: Darling Baby (VIP 1966)★★★, Take The Train (Motor City 1990)★★, Sensational (Motor City 1991)★★.

ELLIOTT, RAMBLIN' JACK
ALBUMS: Jack Elliott Sings The Songs Of Woody Guthrie (1960)★★★, Ramblin' Jack Elliott (Prestige 1961)★★★, Ramblin' Jack Elliott Sings Woody Guthrie And Jimmy Rogers (MTR 1962)★★★, Jack Elliott (Prestige 1964)★★★, Ramblin' Cowboy (1966)★★★, Young Brigham (Warners 1968)★★★, Kerouac's Last Dream (Folk Freak 1984)★★★, South Coast (Red House 1995)★★★, Me And Bobby McGee (Rounder 1996)★★★.
COMPILATIONS: The Essential Ramblin' Jack Elliott (Vanguard 1976)★★★, Talking Dust Bowl – The Best Of Ramblin' Jack Elliott (Big Beat 1989)★★★, Hard Travelin' (Big Beat 1990)★★★, Ramblin' Jack – The Legendary Topic Masters (Topic 1996)★★★, Friends of Mine (Hightone 1998)★★★.

ELY, JOE
ALBUMS: Joe Ely (MCA 1977)★★★★, Honky Tonk Masquerade (MCA 1978)★★★★, Down On The Drag (MCA 1979)★★★★, Live Shots (MCA 1980)★★★, One Road More (Charly 1980)★★★, Musta Notta Gotta Lotta (SouthCoast 1981)★★★, Hi-Res (MCA 1984)★★★, Lord Of The Highway (HighTone 1987)★★★★, Dig All Night (HighTone 1988)★★★★, Milkshakes And Malts (Sunstorm 1988)★★★, Whatever Happened To Maria (Sunstorm 1989)★★★, Live At Liberty Lunch (MCA 1990)★★★, Love And Danger (MCA 1992)★★★, Highways And Heartaches (1993)★★★, Letter To Laredo (Transatlantic 1995)★★★★.
COMPILATIONS: No Bad Talk Or Loud Talk '77 – '81 (Edsel 1995)★★★★, The Time For Travellin': The Best Of ... Vol. 2 (Edsel 1996)★★★★.

EMERSON, LAKE AND PALMER
ALBUMS: Emerson Lake & Palmer (Island 1970)★★★, Tarkus (Island 1971)★★★★, Pictures At An Exhibition (Island 1971)★★★★, Trilogy (Island 1972)★★★, Brain Salad Surgery (Manticore 1973)★★★, Welcome Back My Friends To The Show That Never Ends: Ladies And Gentlemen ... Emerson Lake & Palmer (Manticore 1974)★★, Works (Atlantic 1977)★★, Works, Volume Two (Atlantic 1977)★★, Love Beach (Atlantic 1978)★★, Emerson, Lake & Palmer In Concert (Atlantic 1979)★★, Black Moon (Victory 1992)★★, Live At The Royal Albert Hall (1993)★★, In The Hot Seat (Victory 1994)★★. As Emerson, Lake And Powell: Emerson, Lake & Powell (Polydor 1986)★★. As 3: To The Power Of Three (1988)★★.
COMPILATIONS: The Best Of Emerson, Lake & Palmer (Atlantic 1980)★★★, The Atlantic Years (Atlantic 1992)★★★, Return Of The Manticore 4-CD box set (Victory 1993)★★★★.
VIDEOS: Pictures At An Exhibition (Castle Hendring 1990).

EMF
ALBUMS: Schubert Dip (Parlophone 1991)★★★★, Stigma (Parlophone 1992)★★, Cha Cha Cha (Parlophone 1995)★★★.

EMOTIONS
ALBUMS: So I Can Love You (Stax 1970)★★★, Songs Of Love (Stax 1971)★★★, Untouched (Stax 1972)★★★, Flowers (Columbia 1976)★★★, Rejoice (Columbia 1977)★★★, Sunshine (Stax 1977)★★★, Sunbeam (Columbia 1978)★★★, Come Into Our World (ARC 1979)★★★, New Affair (ARC 1981)★★, If I Only Knew (Motown 1985)★★.
COMPILATIONS: Chronicle: Greatest Hits (Stax/Fantasy 1979)★★★★, Heart Association – The Best Of The Emotions (Columbia 1979)★★★★.

EN VOGUE
ALBUMS: Born To Sing (Atlantic 1990)★★★, Remix To Sing (Atlantic 1991)★★★, Funky Divas (East West 1992)★★★★, Runaway Love mini-album (East West 1993)★★★, EV3 (East West 1997)★★★.
Solo: Terry Ellis Southern Gal (East West 1995)★★.
VIDEOS: Funky Divas (1992)

ENGLAND DAN AND JOHN FORD COLEY
ALBUMS: as Southwest F.O.B. Smell Of Incense (A&M 1968)★★, England Dan And John Ford Coley (A&M 1971)★★★, Fables (A&M 1971)★★, I Hear The Music (A&M 1976)★★, Nights Are Forever (Big Tree 1976)★★, Dowdy Ferry Road (Big Tree 1977)★★★, Some Things Don't Come Easy (Big Tree 1978)★★, Dr. Heckle And Mr. Jive (Big Tree 1979)★★, Just Tell Me If You Love Me (1980)★★.
COMPILATIONS: Best Of (Big Tree 1980)★★★, The Very Best (Rhino 1997)★★★.

ENID
ALBUMS: The Fall Of Hyperion (Charisma 1973)★★, In The Region Of The Summer Stars (EMI 1976)★★★, Aerie Faerie Nonsense (EMI 1978)★★★, Touch Me (Pye 1979)★★★, Six Pieces (Pye 1979)★★★, Rhapsody In Rock (Pye 1980)★★★, Something Wicked This Way Comes (Enid 1983)★★★, Live At Hammersmith Volumes 1 & 2 (Enid 1984)★★, The Spell (Hyperion 1984)★★★, Fand Symphonic Tone Poem (Enid 1985)★★★, Salome (Enid 1986)★★★, Lovers And Fools (Dojo 1987)★★★, Reverberations (1987)★★★, The Seed And The Sower (Enid 1988)★★★, Final Noise (Wonderful Music 1990)★★★, Tripping The Light Fantastic (Mantella 1995)★★★.
VIDEOS: Stonehenge Free Festival 1984 (Visionary 1995).

ENIGMA
ALBUMS: MCMXC AD (Virgin 1990)★★★★, The Cross Of Changes (Virgin 1993)★★★★, Le Roi Est Mort, Vive Le Roi! (Virgin 1996)★★★★.

ENO, BRIAN
ALBUMS: with Robert Fripp No Pussyfooting (Island 1973)★★★, Here Come The Warm Jets (Island 1974)★★★★, with John Cale, Kevin Ayers, Nico June 1st 1974 (Island 1974)★★, Taking Tiger Mountain (By Strategy) (Island 1974)★★★★, Another Green World (Island 1975)★★★★, Discreet Music (Island 1975)★★★, with Fripp Evening Star (Island 1975)★★★, with Phil Manzanera 801 Live (Island 1976)★★, Before And After Science (Polydor 1977)★★★★, with Cluster Cluster And Eno (Sky 1978)★★★, Music For Films (Polydor 1978)★★★, with Moebius And Roedelius After The Heat (Sky 1979)★★★, Ambient 1: Music For Airports (Polydor/EG 1979)★★★★, with Harold Budd Ambient 2: The Plateaux Of Mirror (Polydor/EG 1980)★★★, with Jon Hassell Fourth World Vol i: Possible Musics (Polydor/EG 1980)★★★, with David Byrne My Life In The Bush Of Ghosts (EG 1981)★★★★, Ambient 4: On Land (Editions 1982)★★★, with Daniel Lanois, Roger Eno Apollo: Atmospheres And Soundtracks (EG 1983)★★★, with Budd, Lanois The Pearl (Editions 1984)★★★, with Michael Brook, Lanois Hybrid (Editions 1985)★★★, with Roger Eno Voices (Editions 1985)★★★, Thursday Afternoon (EG 1985)★★★, with Cale Wrong Way Up (Land 1990)★★★★, Nerve Net (1992)★★★, The Shutov Assembly (1992)★★★, Neroli (1993)★★★, with Jah Wobble Spanner (All Saints 1995)★★★, Passengers: Original Soundtracks 1 (Island 1995)★★★, The Drop (All Saints 1997)★★, Bang On A Can: Music For Airports (Point 1998)★★★.
COMPILATIONS: with Moebius, Roedelius And Plank Begegnungen (Sky 1984)★★★, Begegnungen II (Sky 1985)★★★, with Cluster Old Land (Sky 1986)★★★, More Blank Than Frank (EG 1986)★★★★, Desert Island Selection (EG 1986)★★★★.
VIDEOS: Thursday Afternoon (Hendring). Excerpt From The Khumba Mele (Hendring). Mistaken Memories Of Medieval Manhattan (Hendring).
FURTHER READING: Music For Non-Musicians, Brian Eno. Roxy Music: Style With Substance – Roxy's First Ten Years, Johnny Rogan. More Dark Than Shark Brian Eno and Russell Mills. Brian Eno: His Music And The Vertical Colour Of Sound, Eric Tamm. A Year With Swollen Appendices, Brian Eno.

ENYA
ALBUMS: Enya (BBC 1987)★★, Watermark (Warners 1988)★★★★, Shepherd Moons (Warners 1991)★★★, The Memory Of Trees (Warners 1995)★★★.

EPSTEIN, BRIAN
FURTHER READING: A Cellarfull Of Noise, Brian Epstein. Brian Epstein: The Man Who Made The Beatles, Ray Coleman.

EQUALS
ALBUMS: Unequalled Equals (President 1967)★★★, Equals Explosion aka Equal Sensational Equals (President 1968)★★★, Equals Supreme (President 1968)★★★, Baby Come Back (1968)★★★, Equals Strike Back (President 1969)★★, Equals At The Top (President 1970)★★, Equals Rock Around The Clock (1974)★★, Doin' The 45s (1975)★★★, Born Ya (Mercury 1976)★★, Mystic Synster (1978)★★.
COMPILATIONS: The Best Of The Equals (President 1969)★★★, Greatest Hits (1974)★★★, The Very Best Of (1993)★★★.

ERASURE
ALBUMS: Wonderland (Mute 1986)★★★, The Circus (Mute 1987)★★★, The Two Ring Circus (Mute 1987)★★, The Innocents (Mute 1988)★★★, Wild! (Mute 1989)★★★, Chorus (Mute 1991)★★★, I Say, I Say, I Say (Mute 1994)★★★, Erasure (Mute 1995)★★★, Cowboy (Mute 1997)★★.
COMPILATIONS: Pop – The First Twenty Hits (Mute 1992)★★★★.
VIDEOS: Pop – 20 Hits (1993), Live Wild (Warner Brothers 1994).

ERICKSON, ROKY
ALBUMS: Roky Erickson And The Aliens (Columbia 1980)★★★, The Evil One (415 Records 1981)★★★, Clear Night For Love (New Rose 1985)★★, Don't Slander Me (Enigma/Pink Dust 1986 (US), Demon 1987 (UK))★★★, Gremlins Have Pictures (Enigma/Pink Dust 1986 (US), Demon 1987 (UK))★★, I Think Of Demons adds two tracks to Roky Erickson And The Aliens (Edsel 1987)★★★, Casting The Runes (Five Hours Back 1987)★★, The Holiday Inn Tapes (Fan Club 1987)★★, Openers (5 Hours Back 1988)★★, Live At The Ritz, 1987 (New Rose/Fan Club 1988)★★, Mad Dog (Swordfish 1992)★★, All That May Do My Rhyme (Trance Syndicate 1995)★★★.
COMPILATIONS: You're Gonna Miss Me: The Best Of Roky Erickson (Restless 1991)★★★★.

ESCORTS (UK)
ALBUMS: 3 Down 4 To Go (1973)★★.
COMPILATIONS: From The Blue Angel (1982)★★.

ESSEX, DAVID
ALBUMS: Rock On (Columbia 1973)★★★, David Essex (Columbia 1974)★★★, All The Fun Of The Fair (Columbia 1975)★★, Out On The Street (Columbia 1976)★★, On Tour (Columbia 1976)★★, Gold And Ivory (Columbia 1977)★★, Hold Me Close (Columbia 1979)★★, Imperial Wizard (Mercury 1979)★★, The David Essex Album (Columbia 1979)★★, Silver Dream Racer (Mercury 1980)H, Hot Love (Mercury 1980)★★, Be-Bop – The Future (Mercury 1981)★★, Stage Struck (Mercury 1982)★★, Mutiny! (Mercury 1983)★★, The Whisper (Mercury 1983)★★, This One's For You (Mercury 1984)★★, Live At The Royal Albert Hall (1984)★★, Centre Stage (K-Tel 1986)★★, Touching The Ghost (Lamplight 1989)★★, Cover Shot (1993)★★, Back To Back (1994)★★, Living In England (Cleveland 1995)★★, Missing You (Polygram 1996)★★.
COMPILATIONS: The David Essex Collection (Pickwick 1980)★★★, The Very Best Of David Essex (TV Records 1982)★★★, Spotlight On David Essex (1993)★★★, The Best Of ... (Columbia 1996)★★★.
FILMS: That'll Be The Day (1975), Stardust (1976), Silver Dream Machine (1980).
VIDEOS: Live At The Royal Albert Hall (Polygram 1984).
FURTHER READING: The David Essex Story, George Tremlett.

ESTEFAN, GLORIA
ALBUMS: Cuts Both Ways (Epic 1989)★★★, Into The Light (Epic 1991)★★★★, Mi Tierra (Epic 1993)★★★, Hold Me, Thrill Me, Kiss Me (Epic 1994)★★, Abriendo Puertas (Epic 1995)★★★★, Destiny (Epic 1996)★★★, Gloria (Epic 1998)★★★.
COMPILATIONS: Greatest Hits (Epic 1992)★★★★.
VIDEOS: The Evolution Tour: Live In Miami (Epic Music Video 1996).

ESTEFAN, GLORIA, AND MIAMI SOUND MACHINE
ALBUMS: as Miami Sound Machine Miami Sound Machine (Columbia 1976)★★★, Rio (Columbia 1978)★★★, Eyes Of Innocence (Columbia 1984)★★★, Primitive Love (Epic 1986)★★★. As Gloria Estefan And Miami Sound Machine Let it Loose (USA) Anything For You (UK) (Epic 1988)★★★★, Goya (Epic 1989)★★★, Cuts Both Ways (Epic 1989)★★★, Exitos De Gloria Estefan (Epic 1990)★★★, Into The Light (Epic 1991)★★, Mi Terra (Epic 1993)★★★, Hold Me, Thrill Me, Kiss Me (Epic 1994)★★★, Abriendo Puertas (Epic 1995)★★★.
COMPILATIONS: Greatest Hits (Epic 1992)★★★.
VIDEOS: Everlasting Gloria (SMV Epic 1995).
FURTHER READING: Gloria Estefan, Grace Catalano.

ETERNAL
ALBUMS: Always And Forever (First Avenue/EMI 1994)★★, Power Of A Woman (First Avenue/EMI 1995)★★★, Before The Rain (EMI 1997)★★.
COMPILATIONS: Greatest Hits (EMI 1997)★★★.
VIDEOS: Always And Forever (1994).

ETHERIDGE, MELISSA
ALBUMS: Melissa Etheridge (Island 1988)★★, Brave And Crazy (Island 1989)★★★, Never Enough (Island 1991)★★★★, Yes I Am (Island 1993)★★★, Your Little Secret (Island 1995)★★★.

EURYTHMICS
ALBUMS: In The Garden (RCA 1981)★★, Sweet Dreams (Are Made Of This) (RCA 1983)★★★★, Touch (RCA 1983)★★★★, Touch Dance (RCA 1984)★★, 1984 (For The Love Of Big Brother) (Virgin 1984)★★, Be Yourself Tonight (RCA 1985)★★★★, Revenge (RCA 1986)★★★★, Savage (RCA 1987)★★★, We Too Are One (RCA 1989)★★★, Eurythmics Live 1983-89 (RCA 1993)★★★.
COMPILATIONS: Greatest Hits (RCA 1991)★★★★.
FURTHER READING: Eurythmics: Sweet Dreams: The Definitive Biography, Johnny Waller.

EVERCLEAR
ALBUMS: World Of Noise (Fire 1994)★★★, White Trash Hell mini-album (Fire 1995)★★★, Sparkle And Fade (Capitol 1995)★★★★, So Much For The Afterglow (Capitol 1997)★★★.

EVERLY BROTHERS
ALBUMS: The Everly Brothers (Cadence 1958)★★★, Songs Our Daddy Taught Us (Cadence 1959)★★★, The Everly Brothers' Best US only (Cadence 1959)★★★, It's Everly Time (Warners 1960)★★★, The Fabulous Style Of The Everly Brothers (Cadence 1960)★★★★, A Date With The Everly Brothers (Warners 1960)★★★★, Both Sides Of An Evening (Warners 1961)★★★, Folk Songs Of the Everly Brothers (Cadence 1962)★★★, Instant Party (Warners 1962)★★★, Christmas With The Everly Brothers And The Boys Town Choir (Warners 1962)★★★, The Everly Brothers Sing Great Country Hits (Warners 1963)★★★, Gone Gone Gone (Warners 1965)★★★★, Rock 'N' Soul (Warners 1965)★★★, Beat 'N' Soul (Warners 1965)★★★, In Our Image (Warners 1966)★★★, Two Yanks In England (Warners 1966)★★★, The Hit Sound Of The Everly Brothers (Warners 1967)★★★, The Everly Brothers Sing (Warners 1967)★★★, Roots (Warners 1968)★★★, The Everly Brothers Show (Warners 1970)★★★, End Of An Era (Barnaby/Columbia 1971)★★★, Stories We Could Tell (RCA Victor 1972)★★, Pass The Chicken And Listen (RCA Victor 1973)★★, The Exciting Everly Brothers (RCA 1975)★★★, Living Legends (Warwick 1977)★★★, The New Album previously unissued Warners material (Warners 1977)★★★, The Everly Brothers Reunion Concert (Impression 1983)★★★★, Nice Guys previously unissued Warners material (Magnum Force 1984)★★, EB84 (Mercury 1984)★★★, In The Studio previously unissued Cadence material (Ace 1985)★★★, Born Yesterday (Mercury 1985)★★★, Some Hearts (Mercury 1989)★★★, Live In Paris (Big Beat 1997)★★★.
Solo: Don Everly Don Everly (A&M 1971)★★, Sunset Towers (Ode 1974)★★, Brother Juke Box (Hickory 1976)★★★. Phil Everly Star Spangled Springer (RCA 1973)★★, Phil's Diner (There's Nothing Too Good For My Baby) (Pye 1974)★★, Mystic Line (Pye 1975)★★, Living Alone (Elektra 1979)★★, Phil Everly (Capitol 1983)★★.
COMPILATIONS: The Golden Hits Of The Everly Brothers (Warners 1962)★★★★, 15 Everly Hits (Cadence 1963)★★★, The Very Best Of The Everly Brothers (Warners 1964)★★★★, The Everly Brothers' Original Greatest Hits (Columbia 1970)★★★★, The Most Beautiful Songs Of The Everly Brothers (Warners 1973)★★★, Don's And Phil's Fabulous Fifties Treasury (Janus 1974)★★★, Walk Right Back With The Everlys (Warners 1975)★★★★, The Everly Brothers Greatest Hits Collection (Pickwick 1979)★★★, Cathy's Clown (Pickwick 1980)★★★, The Everly Brothers (Warners 1981)★★★, Rock 'N' Roll Forever (Warners 1981)★★★, Rip It Up (Ace 1983)★★★, Cadence Classics (Their 20 Greatest Hits) (Rhino 1985)★★★★, The Best Of The Everly Brothers (Rhino 1985)★★★, All They Had To Do Is Dream US only (Rhino 1985)★★★, Great Recordings (Ace 1986)★★★, The Everly Brothers Collection (Castle 1988)★★★, The Very Best Of The Everly Brothers (Pickwick 1988)★★★, Hidden Gems Warners material (Ace 1989)★★★, Perfect Harmony box set (Knight 1990)★★★, Classic Everly Brothers 3-CD box set (Bear Family 1992)★★★★, The Golden Years Of The Everly Brothers (Warners 1993)★★★★, Heartaches And Harmonies 4-CD box set (Rhino 1995)★★★★★, Walk Right Back: On Warner Bros. 1960 To 1969 2-CD (Warners 1996)★★★★, All I Have To Do Is Dream (Carlton 1997)★★★.
VIDEOS: Rock 'N' Roll Odyssey (MGM 1984).
FURTHER READING: Everly Brothers: An Illustrated Discography, John Hosum. The Everly Brothers: Walk Right Back, Roger White. Ike's Boys, Phyllis Karpp. The Everly Brothers: Ladies Love Outlaws, Consuelo Dodge. For-Everly Yours, Peter Aarts and Martin Alberts.

EVERYTHING BUT THE GIRL
ALBUMS: Eden (Blanco y Negro 1984)★★★★, Love Not Money (Blanco y Negro 1985)★★, Baby The Stars Shine Bright (Blanco y Negro 1986)★★, Idlewild (Blanco y Negro 1988)★★★, The Language Of Life (Blanco y Negro 1990)★★★★, World-wide (Blanco y Negro 1991)★★, Amplified Heart (Blanco y Negro 1994)★★★, Walking Wounded (Atlantic 1996)★★★★.
Solo: Tracey Thorn A Distant Shore (Cherry Red 1982)★★★. Ben Watt North Marine Drive (Cherry Red 1983)★★★.
COMPILATIONS: Home Movies: The Best Of (Blanco y Negro 1993)★★★, The Best Of ... (Blanco y Negro 1997)★★★★.
FURTHER READING: Patient: The History Of A Rare Illness, Ben Watt.

EXILE
ALBUMS: Exile (Wooden Nickel 1973)★★★★, Mixed Emotions (Epic 1978)★★★, All There Is (Epic 1979)★★★, Don't Leave Me This Way (Epic 1980)★★★, Heart And Soul (Epic 1981)★★★, Exile (Epic 1983)★★★, Kentucky Hearts (Epic 1984)★★, Hang On To Your Heart (Epic 1985)★★, Shelter From The Night (Epic 1987)★★★, Still Standing (Arista 1990)★★★★, Justice (Arista 1991)★★★.
COMPILATIONS: The Best Of Exile (Curb 1985)★★★★, Exile's Greatest Hits (Epic 1986)★★★, The Complete Collection (Curb 1991)★★★★, Super Hits (Epic 1993)★★★.

EXPLOITED
ALBUMS: Punk's Not Dead (Secret 1981)★★★, On Stage (Superville 1981)★★★, Troops Of Tomorrow (Secret 1982)★★★, Let's Start A War (Said Maggie One Day) (Pax 1983)★★★, Horror Epics (Konnexion 1985)★★★, Death Before Dishonour (Rough Justice 1989)★★, The Massacre (Rough Justice 1991)★★, Beat The Bastards (Rough Justice 1996)★★.
COMPILATIONS: Inner City Decay (Snow 1987)★★★, The Singles Collection (Cleopatra 1993)★★★.
VIDEOS: Live In Japan (Visionary 1993), Rock & Roll Outlaws (Visionary 1995).

EXTREME
ALBUMS: Extreme (A&M 1989)★★★, Pornograffitti (A&M 1990)★★★★, III Sides To Every Story (A&M 1992)★★★★, Waiting For The Punchline (A&M 1995)★★.

EXTREME NOISE TERROR
ALBUMS: split with Chaos UK Radioactive (Manic Ears 1985)★★, A Holocaust In Your Head (Hurt 1987)★★, The Peel Sessions (Strange Fruit 1990)★★★, Phonophobia (Vinyl Japan 1992)★★, Retro-bution (Earache 1995)★★★, Damage 381 (Earache 1997)★★.
VIDEOS: From One Extreme To The Other (Jettisoundz 1989).

EYC
ALBUMS: Express Yourself Clearly (Gasoline Alley 1994)★★★, Ooh Ah Aa (I Feel It) (MCA 1995)★★.

F

FABIAN
ALBUMS: Hold That Tiger (Chancellor 1959)★★, The Fabulous Fabian (Chancellor 1960)★★, Fabian Facade (Chancellor 1961)★★, The Good Old Summertime (Chancellor 1961)★★, Rockin' Hot (Chancellor 1961)★★, 16 Fabulous Hits (Chancellor 1962)★★, All The Hits (1993)★★.
FILMS: Hound Dog Man (1959), Dr Goldfoot And The Girl Bomb (1966), American Pop (1981).

FABULOUS THUNDERBIRDS
ALBUMS: The Fabulous Thunderbirds aka Girls Go Wild (Chrysalis 1979)★★★★, What's The Word (Chrysalis 1980)★★★, Butt Rockin' (Chrysalis 1981)★★★, T-Bird Rhythm (Chrysalis 1982)★★★, Tuff Enuff (Columbia 1986)★★★, Hot Number (Columbia 1987)★★★, Powerful Stuff (Columbia 1989)★★★, Walk That Walk, Talk That Talk (Columbia 1991)★★★, Roll Of The Dice (Private Music 1995)★★.
COMPILATIONS: Portfolio (Chrysalis 1987)★★★★.
VIDEOS: Tuff Enuff (Hendring Video 1990), Hot Stuff: The Greatest Videos (1992 Sony).

FACES
ALBUMS: First Step (Warners 1970)★★★, Long Player (Warners 1971)★★★★, A Nod's As Good As A Wink ... To A Blind Horse (Warners 1971)★★★, Ooh La La

(Warners 1973)★★★, Coast To Coast: Overture And Beginners (Mercury 1974)★★★.
COMPILATIONS: The Best Of The Faces (Riva 1977)★★★.

FAGEN, DONALD
ALBUMS: The Nightfly (Warners 1982)★★★★, Kamakiriad (Reprise 1993)★★★★.
VIDEOS: New Frontier (Warner Brothers 1982).

FAIRGROUND ATTRACTION
ALBUMS: First Of A Million Kisses (RCA 1988)★★★, Ay Fond Kiss (RCA 1990)★★★.

FAIRPORT CONVENTION
ALBUMS: Fairport Convention (Polydor 1968)★★★, What We Did On Our Holidays (Island 1969)★★★★★, Unhalfbricking (Island 1969)★★★★, Liege And Lief (Island 1969)★★★★, Full House (Island 1970)★★★★, Angel Delight (Island 1971)★★★, Babbacombe Lee (Island 1971)★★★, Rosie (Island 1973)★★★, Nine (Island 1973)★★, Live Convention (A Moveable Feast) (Island 1974)★★, Rising For The Moon (Island 1975)★★, Gottle O'Geer (Island 1976)★, Live At The LA Troubadour (Island 1977)★★, A Bonny Bunch Of Roses (Vertigo 1977)★★, Tipplers Tales (Vertigo 1978)★★, Farewell, Farewell (Simons 1979)★★★, Moat On The Ledge: Live At Broughton Castle (Woodworm 1981)★★★, Gladys' Leap (Woodworm 1985)★★★, Expletive Delighted (Woodworm 1986)★★★, House Full (Hannibal 1986)★★, Heyday: The BBC Radio Sessions 1968-9 (Hannibal 1987)★★★, 'In Real Time' - Live '87★★, Red And Gold (New Routes 1989)★★, Five Seasons (New Routes 1991)★★, 25th Anniversary Concert (Wormwood 1994)★★★, Jewel In The Crown (Woodworm 1995)★★★★, Old New Borrowed Blue (Woodworm 1996)★★★, Who Knows Where The Time Goes (Woodworm 1997)★★★, Close To The Wind (Mooncrest 1998).
COMPILATIONS: History Of Fairport Convention (Island 1972)★★★★, The Best Of Fairport Convention (1988)★★★★, The Woodworm Years (Woodworm 1992)★★★.
VIDEOS: Reunion Festival Broughton Castle 1981 (Videotech 1982), Cropredy 39 August 1980 (Videotech 1982), A Weekend In The Country (Videotech 1983), Cropredy Capers (Intech Video 1986), In Real Time (Island Visual Arts 1987), It All Comes Round Again (Island Visual Arts 1987), Live At Maidstone 1970 (Musikfolk 1991).
FURTHER READING: Meet On The Ledge, Patrick Humphries. The Woodworm Era: The Story Of Today's Fairport Convention, Fred Redwood And Martin Woodward. Richard Thompson: Strange Affair, Patrick Humphries.

FAIRWEATHER-LOW, ANDY
ALBUMS: as Fairweather-Low Beginning From An End (RCO 1971)★★, Spider Jivin' (A&M 1974)★★★, La Booga Rooga (A&M 1975)★★, Be Bop 'N' Holla (A&M 1976)★★, Mega-Shebang (Warners 1980)★★.

FAITH, ADAM
ALBUMS: Adam (Parlophone 1960)★★★, Beat Girl soundtrack (Columbia 1960)★★★, Adam Faith (Parlophone 1962)★★★, From Adam With Love (Parlophone 1962)★★★, For You – Adam (Parlophone 1963)★★★, with the Roulettes On The Move (Parlophone 1964)★★★, with the Roulettes Faith Alive (Parlophone 1965)★★, I Survive (1974)★★, Midnight Postcards (1993)★★.
COMPILATIONS: 20 Golden Greats (1981)★★★, Not Just A Memory (1983)★★★★, The Best Of Adam Faith (MFP 1989)★★★★, The Adam Faith Singles Collection: His Greatest Hits (1990)★★★, The Best Of The EMI Years (EMI 1994)★★★★.
FILMS: Beat Girl (1960), Never Let Go (1960), What A Whopper (1961), Mix Me A Person (1962), Stardust (1974), McVicar (1980).
FURTHER READING: Adam, His Fabulous Year, Adam Faith. Poor Me, Adam Faith. Acts Of Faith, Adam Faith.

FAITH NO MORE
ALBUMS: Faith No More: We Care A Lot (Mordam 1984)★★, Introduce Yourself (Slash 1987)★★★★, The Real Thing (London 1989)★★★★, Live At The Brixton Academy (London 1991)★★★, Angel Dust (London 1992)★★, King For A Day ... Fool For A Lifetime (London 1995)★★★, Album Of The Year (London 1997)★★.
VIDEOS: Live At Brixton Academy (London 1990), You Fat B**tards (Warner Brothers 1991), Video Croissant (Warner Brothers 1992).
FURTHER READING: Faith No More: The Real Story, Steffan Chirazi.

FAITHFULL, MARIANNE
ALBUMS: Come My Way (Decca 1965)★★, Marianne Faithfull (Decca 1965)★★★, Go Away From My World (1965)★★★, Faithfull Forever (1966), North Country Maid (Decca 1966)★★, Love In A Mist (Decca 1967)★★, Dreamin' My Dreams (Nems 1976)★, Faithless (Immediate 1977)★★, Broken English (Island 1979)★★★★, Dangerous Acquaintances (Island 1981)★★★, A Child's Adventure (Island 1983)★★★, Strange Weather (Island 1987)★★★, Blazing Away (Island 1990)★★★, A Secret Life (Island 1995)★★, 20th Century Blues (RCA 1996)★★.
COMPILATIONS: The World Of Marianne Faithfull (Decca 1969)★★★, Marianne Faithfull's Greatest Hits (Abkco 1969)★★★, As Tears Go By (1981)★★★, Summer Nights (1984)★★★, The Very Best Of Marianne Faithfull (1987)★★★, Rich Kid Blues (1988)★★★, Faithfull: A Collection Of Her Best Recordings (Island 1994)★★★.
FURTHER READING: Marianne Faithfull: As Tears Go By, Mark Hodkinson. Faithfull, Marianne Faithfull and David Dalton.

FALL
ALBUMS: Live At The Witch Trials (Step Forward 1979)★★★★, Dragnet (Step Forward 1979)★★★, Totale's Turns (It's Now Or Never) (Live) (Rough Trade 1980)★★, Grotesque (After The Gramme) (Rough Trade 1980)★★, Slates mini-album (Rough Trade 1981)★★★, Hex Enduction Hour (Kamera 1982)★★★, Room To Live (Kamera 1982)★★★, Perverted By Language (Rough Trade 1983)★★★, The Wonderful And Frightening World Of ... (Beggars Banquet 1984)★★★★, This Nation's Saving Grace (Beggars Banquet 1985)★★★★, Bend Sinister (Beggars Banquet 1986)★★★★, The Frenz Experiment (Beggars Banquet 1988)★★★★, I Am Kurious Oranj (Beggars Banquet 1988)★★★, Seminal Live (Beggars Banquet 1989)★★★, Extricate (Cog Sinister/Fontana 1990)★★★, Shiftwork (Cog Sinister/Fontana 1991)★★★★, Code Selfish (Cog Sinister/Fontana 1992)★★★, The Infotainment Scan (Cog Sinister/Permanent 1993)★★★, BBC Live In Concert 1987 recording (Windsong 1993)★★★, Middle Class Revolt (Permanent 1994)★★★, Cerebral Caustic (Permanent 1995)★★★★, 27 Points (Permanent 1995)★★★, Sinister Waltz archive recordings (Receiver 1996)★★, Fiend With A Violin archive recordings (Receiver 1996)★★, Oswald Defence Lawyer archive recordings (Receiver 1996)★★, The Light User Syndrome (Jet 1996)★★★, In The City (Artful 1997)★★★, Levitate (Artful 1997)★★★.
COMPILATIONS: 77 – Early Years – 79 (Step Forward 1981)★★★, Live At Acklam Hall, London, 1980 cassette only (Chaos 1982)★★★, Hip Priests And Kamerads (Situation 2 1985)★★★, In Palace Of Swords Reversed (80–83) (Cog Sinister 1987)★★★★, 458489 A Sides (Beggars Banquet 1990)★★★★, 458489-B Sides (Beggars Banquet 1990)★★★, The Collection (Castle 1993)★★★.
VIDEOS: VHS8489 (Beggars Banquet 1991), Perverted By Language Bis (IKON 1992).
FURTHER READING: Paintwork: A Portrait Of The Fall, Brian Edge.

FAME, GEORGIE
ALBUMS: Rhythm And Blues At The Flamingo (Columbia 1963)★★★★, Fame At Last (Columbia 1964)★★★★, Sweet Things (Columbia 1966)★★★, Sound Venture (Columbia 1966)★★★, Two Faces Of Fame (CBS 1967)★★★, The Ballad Of Bonnie And Clyde (Epic 1968)★★★, The Third Face Of Fame (CBS 1968)★★★, Seventh Son (CBS 1969)★★, Georgie Does His Things With Strings (CBS 1970)★★, Going Home (CBS 1971)★★, with Alan Price Fame And Price, Price And Fame Together (CBS 1971)★★, All Me Own Work (Reprise 1972)★★★, Georgie Fame (Island 1974)★★, That's What Friends Are For (1979)★★★, Georgie Fame Right Now (1979)★★★, Closing The Gap (1980)★★, with Annie Ross Hoagland (1981)★★★, In Goodman's Land (1983)★★★, My Favourite Songs (1984)★★, No Worries (1988)★★, Cool Cat Blues (Go Jazz 1991)★★★★, The Blues And Me (1994)★★★, Three Line Whip (1994)★★★, with Van Morrison How Long Has This Been Going On (Verve 1995)★★★, with Morrison, Ben Sidran, Mose Allison Tell Me Something: The Songs Of Mose Allison (Verve 1996)★★★.
COMPILATIONS: Hall Of Fame (Columbia 1967)★★★★, Georgie Fame (Starline 1969)★★★★, Fame Again (Starline 1972)★★★, 20 Beat Classics (Polydor 1982)★★★★, The First Thirty Years (1990)★★★.

FAMILY
ALBUMS: Music In A Doll's House (Reprise 1968)★★★★, Family Entertainment (Reprise 1969)★★★★, A Song For Me (Reprise 1970)★★★, Anyway (Reprise 1970)★★★, Fearless (Reprise 1971)★★★★, Bandstand (Reprise 1972)★★★★, It's Only A Movie (Reprise 1973)★★, Peel Sessions (Strange Fruit 1988)★★, In Concert (Windsong 1991)★★★★.
COMPILATIONS: Old Songs New Songs (Reprise 1971)★★★★, Best Of Family (Reprise 1974)★★★, Singles A's and B's (See For Miles 1991)★★★★, Best of Family (Castle 1995)★★★.

FANNY
ALBUMS: Fanny (Reprise 1970)★★★, Charity Ball (Reprise 1971)★★★, Fanny Hill (Reprise 1972)★★★, Mother's Pride (Reprise 1973)★★, Rock 'N' Roll Survivors (Casablanca 1974)★★.
Solo: Nickey Barclay Diamond In A Junkyard (Ariola 1976)★★, Jean Millington Ladies On The Stage (United Artists 1978)★★.

FARM
ALBUMS: Spartacus (Produce 1991)★★★★, Love See No Colour (End Product 1992)★★, Hullabaloo (Sire 1994)★★★.
VIDEOS: Groovy Times (Produce 1991).

FARLOWE, CHRIS
ALBUMS: Chris Farlowe And The Thunderbirds aka Stormy Monday (Columbia 1966)★★★, Fourteen Things To Think About (Immediate 1966)★★★, The Art Of Chris Farlowe (Immediate 1966)★★★, The Fabulous Chris Farlowe (EMI Regal 1967)★★★, Paint It Farlowe (1968)★★★, The Last Goodbye (Immediate 1969)★★, as Chris Farlowe And The Hill From Here To Mama Rosa (Polydor 1970)★★, The Chris Farlowe Band, Live (Polydor 1976)★★★, Out Of The Blue (Polydor 1985)★★, Born Again (Brand New 1986)★★★, Waiting In The Wings (1992)★★★, Lonesome Road (Indigo 1995)★★★, with Zoot Money Alexis Korner Memorial Concert Volume 2 (Indigo 1995)★★★, As Time Goes By (Inakustik 1996).
COMPILATIONS: The Best Of Chris Farlowe Vol. 1 (Immediate 1968)★★★, Out Of Time (Immediate 1975)★★★, Out Of Time – Paint It Black (Charly 1978)★★★, Greatest Hits (Immediate 1978)★★★, Hot Property (The Rare Tracks) (1983)★★, Mr. Soulful (Castle 1986)★★★, Buzz With The Fuzz (Decal 1987)★★★, I'm The Greatest (See For Miles 1994)★★★.

FAT BOYS
ALBUMS: Fat Boys (Sutra 1984)★★★, The Fat Boys Are Back! (Sutra 1985)★★★, Big & Beautiful (Sutra 1986)★★★, Cruisin' (Tin Pan Apple/Polydor 1987)★★★★, Coming Back Hard Again (Tin Pan Apple/Polydor 1988)★★★, On And On (Tin Pan Apple/Mercury 1989)★★. Solo: Prince Markie Dee Free (Columbia 1992)★★, Typical reasons (Columbia 1993), Love Daddy (Motown 1995).
COMPILATIONS: The Best Part Of The Fat Boys (Sutra 1987)★★★.

FATIMA MANSIONS
ALBUMS: Against Nature (Kitchenware 1989)★★★, Viva Dead Ponies (Kitchenware 1990)★★★★, Bertie's Brochures mini-album (Kitchenware 1991)★★★, Valhalla Avenue (Kitchenware 1992)★★★, Lost In The Former West (Radioactive 1994)★★★.
Solo: Cathal Coughlan The Grand Necropolitan (Kitchenware 1996)★★★. As Bubonique: 20 Golden Showers (Kitchenware 1993)★★, Trance Arse Volume 3 (Kitchenware1995)★★.
COMPILATIONS: Come Back My Children (Kitchenware 1992)★★★.
VIDEOS: Y'Knaa (1994).

FAUST
ALBUMS: Faust (Polydor 1972)★★, So Far (Polydor 1972)★★★, The Faust Tapes (Virgin 1973)★★★, with Tony Conrad Outside The Dream Syndicate (Virgin 1973)★★★, Faust 4 (Virgin 1973)★★, One (Recommended 1979)★★, Rien (Table Of The Elements 1996)★★, You Know Us (Table Of The Elements 1997)★★, Faust Wakes Nosferatu (EFA 1998).
COMPILATIONS: Munich And Elsewhere (Recommended 1986)★★★.

FELICIANO, JOSÉ
ALBUMS: The Voice And Guitar Of José Feliciano (RCA 1964)★★, A Bag Full Of Soul (RCA 1965)★★★, Feliciano! (RCA 1968)★★★★, Souled (RCA 1969)★★★, Feliciano 10 To 23 (RCA 1969)★★, Alive Alive-O (RCA 1969)★★, Fireworks (RCA 1970)★★, That The Spirit Needs (RCA 1971)★★, José Feliciano Sings (RCA 1972)★★, Compartments (RCA 1973)★★, And The Feeling's Good (RCA 1974)★★, Just Wanna Rock 'N' Roll (RCA 1975)★★, Sweet Soul Music (RCA 1976)★★★, José Feliciano (Motown 1981)★★, Escenas De Amor (Latino 1982)★★, Romance In The Night (Latino 1983)★★, Los Exitos De José Feliciano (Latino 1984)★★, Sings And Plays The Beatles (RCA 1985)★★, Tu Immenso Amor (EMI 1987)★★★, I'm Never Gonna Change (EMI 1989)★★, Steppin' Out (Optimism 1990)★★★, El Americano (Polygram 1996)★★★.
COMPILATIONS: Encore! (RCA 1971)★★★, The Best Of José Feliciano (RCA 1985)★★★, Portrait (Telstar 1985)★★★, And I Love Her (Camden 1996)★★★.

FELT
ALBUMS: Crumbling The Antiseptic Beauty mini-album (Cherry Red 1982)★★★, The Splendour Of Fear mini-album (Cherry Red 1983)★★★, The Strange Idols Pattern And Other Short Stories (Cherry Red 1984)★★★, Ignite The Seven Cannons (Cherry Red 1985)★★★, Let The Snakes Crinkle Their Heads To Death (Creation 1986)★★★, Forever Breathes The Lonely Word (Creation 1986)★★★★, Poem Of The River (Creation 1987)★★★, The Pictorial Jackson Review (Creation 1988)★★★, Train Above The City (Creation 1988)★★★, Me And A Monkey On The Moon (fl 1989)★★.
COMPILATIONS: Gold Mine Trash (Cherry Red 1987)★★★, Bubblegum Perfume (Creation 1990)★★★★, Absolute Classic Masterpieces Vol. 2 (Creation 1993)★★★, The Felt Box Set 4-CD set (Cherry Red 1993)★★★★.

FENDER, LEO
FURTHER READING: The Fender Book: A Complete History Of Fender Electric Guitars, Tony Bacon and Paul Day. Fender Custom Shop Guitar Gallery, Richard Smith.

FERRY, BRYAN
ALBUMS: These Foolish Things (Island 1973)★★★, Another Time Another Place (Island 1974)★★, Let's Stick Together (Island 1976)★★★, In Your Mind (Polydor 1977)★★★, The Bride Stripped Bare (Polydor 1978)★★★★, Boys And Girls (EG 1985)★★★, Bête Noire (Virgin 1987)★★, Taxi (Virgin 1993)★★, Mamouna (Virgin 1994)★★.
COMPILATIONS: The Compact Collection 3-CD box set (1992)★★★★, Ultimate Collection (EG 1998)★★★.
VIDEOS: Bryan Ferry And Roxy Music (Virgin 1995).
FURTHER READING: Roxy Music: Style With Substance – Roxy's First Ten Years, Johnny Rogan.

FIELDS OF THE NEPHILIM
ALBUMS: Dawn Razor (Situation 2 1987)★★, The Nephilim (Situation 2 1988)★★★, Elyzium (Beggars Banquet 1990)★★, Earth Inferno (Beggars Banquet 1991)★★, BBC Radio 1 In Concert (Windsong 1992)★★, Revelations (Beggars Banquet 1993)★★, Zoon (Beggars Banquet 1996)★★.
VIDEOS: Forever Remain (Situation 2 1988), Morphic Fields (Situation 2 1989), Earth Inferno (Beggars Banquet 1991), Visionary Heads (Beggars Banquet 1992), Revelations (Beggars Banquet 1993).

FIFTH DIMENSION
ALBUMS: Up Up And Away (Soul City 1967)★★★, The Magic Garden (Soul City 1967)★★★, Stoned Soul Picnic (Soul City 1968)★★★, The Age Of Aquarius (Soul City 1969)★★★, Fantastic (1970)★★, Portrait (Bell 1970)★★, Love's Lines, Angles And Rhymes (Bell 1971)★★★, The 5th Dimension Live! (Bell 1971)★★, Individually And Collectively (Bell 1972)★★, Living Together, Growing Together (Bell 1973)★★, Earthbound (ABC 1975)★★.
COMPILATIONS: Greatest Hits (Soul City 1970)★★★, The July 5th Album (Soul City 1970)★★★, Reflections (Bell 1971)★★★, Greatest Hits On Earth (Arista 1972)★★★, Anthology (Rhino 1986)★★★, Greatest Hits (1988)★★★, The Definitive Collection (Arista 1997)★★★.

FINE YOUNG CANNIBALS
ALBUMS: Fine Young Cannibals (London 1985)★★★, The Raw And The Cooked (London 1989)★★★★, The Raw And The Remix (London 1990)★★★.
COMPILATIONS: The Finest (London 1996)★★★★.
VIDEOS: The Finest (London 1996).
FURTHER READING: The Sweet And The Sour: The Fine Young Cannibals' Story, Brian Edge.

FIREBALLS
ALBUMS: The Fireballs (Top Rank 1960)★★★, Vaquero (Top Rank 1960)★★★, Here Are The Fireballs (Warwick 1961)★★★, Torquay (Dot 1963)★★★, Sugar Shack (Dot 1963)★★★, The Sugar Shackers (1963)★★★, Sensational (1963)★★★, Buddy's Buddy (Dot 1964)★★, Lucky 'Leven (Dot 1965)★★, Folk Beat (Dot 1965)★★, Campusology (Dot 1966)★★, Firewater (Dot 1968)★★, Bottle Of Wine (Atco 1968)★★, Come On, React! (Atco 1969)★★.
COMPILATIONS: Blue Fire & Rarities (Ace 1993)★★★.

FIREFALL
ALBUMS: Firefall (Atlantic 1976)★★★, Luna Sea (Atlantic 1977)★★, Elan (Atlantic 1978)★★★, Undertow (Atlantic 1980)★★, Clouds Across The Sun (Atlantic 1981)★★, Break Of Dawn (Atlantic 1983)★★, You Are The Woman (Rhino 1993)★★.
COMPILATIONS: Best Of (Atlantic 1981)★★★, The Greatest Hits (1993)★★★.

FIREHOSE
ALBUMS: Ragin', Full-On (SST 1987)★★★, If'n (SST 1988)★★, fROMOHIO (SST 1989)★★★, Flyin' The Flannel (Columbia 1991)★★★, Live Totem Pole mini-album (Columbia 1992)★★, Mr Machinery Operator (Columbia 1993)★★, as Bootstrappers Bootstrappers (New Alliance 1989)★★.

FIRESIGN THEATRE
ALBUMS: Waiting For The Electrician (Columbia 1968)★★, How Can You Be In Two Places At Once When You're Not Anywhere At All (Columbia 1969)★★★★, Don't Crush That Dwarf, Hand Me The Pliers (Columbia 1970)★★★★, I Think We're All Bozos On This Bus (Columbia 1971)★★★, Dear Friends (Columbia 1972)★★, Not Insane Or Anything You Want To (Columbia 1972)★★, The Tale Of The Giant Rat Of Sumatra (Columbia 1974)★★, Everything You Know Is Wrong (Columbia 1974)★★★★, In The Next World You're On Your Own (Columbia 1975)★★★, Just Folks, A Firesign Chat (Butterfly 1977)★★, Pink Puffins In A Pelican's World (1978)★★, Live At The Roxy (1980)★★, Fighting Clowns (1980)★★★, Anything You Want To (1981)★★★, Carter/Reagan (1982)★★★, Lawyer's Hospital (1982)★★★, Shakespeare's Lost Comedie (1982)★★★, Nick Danger In The Three Faces Of Owl (1984)★★★, Eat Or Be Eaten (1985)★★★, Back From The Shadows (Mobile Fidelity 1994)★★.
COMPILATIONS: Forward Into The Past (Columbia 1976)★★★★.

FISCHER, LARRY 'WILD MAN'
ALBUMS: An Evening With Wild Man Fischer (Bizarre 1968)★★, Wild Mania (Rhino 1978)★★, Pronounced Normal (Rhino 1981)★★, Nothing Crazy (Rhino 1984)★★, Larry Fischer Sings Popular Songs (Birdman 1997)★★★.

FISH
ALBUMS: Vigil In A Wilderness Of Mirrors (EMI 1990)★★, Internal Exile (EMI 1991)★★, Songs From The Mirror (EMI 1993)★, Sushi (Dick Bros 1994)★★★, Acoustic Session (Dick Bros 1994)★★★, Suits (Dick Bros 1994)★★, Sunsets On Empire (Dick Bros 1997)★★★★.
COMPILATIONS: Yin (Dick Bros 1995)★★★, Yang (Dick Bros 1995)★★★.

FISHBONE
ALBUMS: Fishbone mini-album (Columbia 1985)★★, In Your Face (Columbia 1986)★★, Truth And Soul (Columbia 1988)★★★★, The Reality Of My Surroundings (Columbia 1991)★★★, Give A Monkey A Brain & He'll Swear He's The Centre Of The Universe (Columbia 1993)★★★, Chim Chim's Badass Revenge (Rowdy 1996)★★★.
COMPILATIONS: Fishbone 101 – Nuttasaurusmeg Fossil Fuelin' The Fonkay (Columbia/Legacy 1996)★★★.

FIVE STAR
ALBUMS: Luxury Of Life (Tent 1985)★★, Silk And Steel (Tent 1986)★★★, Between The Lines (Tent 1987)★★, Rock The World (Tent 1988)★★, Five Star (Tent 1990)★★.
COMPILATIONS: Greatest Hits (Tent 1989)★★★.

FLACK, ROBERTA
ALBUMS: First Take (Atlantic 1970)★★★★, Chapter Two (Atlantic 1970)★★★, Quiet Fire (Atlantic 1971)★★, with Donny Hathaway Roberta Flack And Donny Hathaway (Atlantic 1972)★★★, Killing Me Softly (Atlantic 1973)★★, Feel Like Making Love (Atlantic 1975)★★, Blue Lights In The Basement (Atlantic 1978)★★, Roberta Flack (Atlantic 1978)★★, with Hathaway Roberta Flack Featuring Donny Hathaway (Atlantic 1980)★★★, with Peabo Bryson Live And More (Atlantic 1980)★★, Bustin' Loose (MCA 1981)★★, I'm The One (Atlantic 1982)★★, with Bryson Born To Love (Capitol 1983)★★★, Oasis (Atlantic 1989)★★, Set The Night To Music (Atlantic 1991)★★, Roberta (Atlantic/East West 1995)★★★.
COMPILATIONS: The Best Of Roberta Flack (Atlantic 1980)★★★, Softly With These Songs: The Best Of ... (Atlantic 1993)★★★.
FILMS: Body Rock (1984).
FURTHER READING: Roberta Flack: Sound Of Velvet Melting, Linda Jacobs.

FLAMIN' GROOVIES
ALBUMS: Sneakers (Snazz 1968)★★, Supersnazz (Epic 1969)★★★, Flamingo (Kama Sutra 1970)★★★, Teenage Head (Kama Sutra 1971)★★★, Shake Some Action (Sire 1976)★★★★, Flamin' Groovies Now (Sire 1978)★★★, Jumpin' In The Night (Sire 1979)★★★, One Night Stand (Sire 1986)★★.
COMPILATIONS: In Person! (live) (Norton 1997)★★★.
FURTHER READING: A Flamin' Saga: The Flamin' Groovies Histoire & Discographie, Jean-Pierre Poncelet. Bucketfull Of Groovies Jon Storey.

FLAMINGOS
ALBUMS: The Flamingos (Checker 1959)★★★, Flamingos Serenade (End 1959)★★★, Flamingos Favorites (End 1960)★★★, Requestfully Yours (End 1960)★★★, The Sound Of The Flamingos (End 1962)★★★, The Spiritual And Folk Moods Of The Flamingos (1963)★★, Their Hits – Then And Now (Philips 1966)★★, Flamingos Today (1971)★★.
COMPILATIONS: Collectors Showcase: The Flamingos (Constellation 1964)★★★, Golden Teardrops (1982)★★★, Flamingos (Chess 1984)★★★★, The Chess Sessions (Chess 1987)★★★, The Best Of The Flamingos (Rhino 1990)★★★★, The Flamingos: I Only Have Eyes For You (Sequel 1991)★★★, The Flamingos Meet The Moonglows: The Complete 25 Chance Recordings (Vee Jay 1993)★★★.
FILMS: Go Johnny Go (1958).

FLASH CADILLAC AND THE CONTINENTAL KIDS
ALBUMS: Flash Cadillac And The Continental Kids (Epic 1973)★★★, There's No Face Like Chrome (Epic 1974)★★★, Sons Of Beaches (Private Stock 1975)★.

FLEETWOOD MAC
ALBUMS: Fleetwood Mac (Columbia/Blue Horizon 1968)★★★★, Mr. Wonderful (Columbia/Blue Horizon 1968)★★★, English Rose (Epic 1969)★★★, Then Play On (Reprise 1969)★★★★, Blues Jam At Chess aka Fleetwood Mac In Chicago (Blue Horizon 1969)★★★, Kiln House (Reprise 1970)★★★, Future Games (Reprise 1971)★★★, Bare Trees (Reprise 1972)★★, Penguin (Reprise 1973)★★, Mystery To Me (Reprise 1973)★★, Heroes Are Hard To Find (Reprise 1974)★★★, Fleetwood Mac (Reprise 1975)★★★★, Rumours (Warners 1977)★★★★, Tusk (Warners 1979)★★★, Fleetwood Mac Live (Warners 1980)★★, Mirage (Warners 1982)★★★, Live In Boston (Shanghai 1985)★★, London Live '68 (Thunderbolt 1986)★, Tango In The Night (Warners 1988)★★★, Behind The Mask (Warners 1989)★★★, Live At The Marquee 1967 recording (Sunflower 1992)★, Live 1968 recording (Abracadabra 1995)★, Peter Green's Fleetwood Mac: Live At The BBC (Fleetwood/Castle 1995)★★★★, Time (Warners 1995)★, The Dance (Reprise 1997)★★★.
Solo: Danny Kirwan Second Chapter (DJM 1976)★★, Midnight In San Juan (DJM 1976)★, Hello There Big Boy (DJM 1979)★. Jeremy Spencer Jeremy Spencer (Reprise 1970)★★, Jeremy Spencer And The Children Of God (Columbia 1973)★, Flee (Atlantic 1979)★. Mick Fleetwood The Visitor (RCA 1981)★, I'm Not Me (RCA 1983)★. John McVie John McVie's Gotta Band With Lola Thomas (Warners 1992)★. Christine McVie Christine Perfect (Blue Horizon 1970)★★★, Christine McVie (Warners 1984)★★.
COMPILATIONS: Fleetwood Mac's Greatest Hits (Columbia 1971)★★★★, The Vintage Years (Sire 1975)★★★, Albatross (Columbia 1977)★★★, Best Of (Reprise 1978)★★★, Greatest Hits: Fleetwood Mac (Columbia 1988)★★★, The Blues Years (Essential 1991)★★★, The Chain CD box set (Warners 1992)★★★, The Best Of ... (Columbia 1996)★★★.
VIDEOS: Fleetwood Mac (Warners 1981), In Concert – Mirage Tour (Spectrum 1983), Video Biography (Virgin Vision 1988), Tango In The Night (Warner Music Video 1988), Peter Green's Fleetwood Mac: The Early Years 1967-1970 (PNE 1995).
FURTHER READING: Fleetwood Mac: The Authorized History, Samuel Graham. Fleetwood Mac: Rumours 'N' Fax, Roy Carr and Steve Clarke. Fleetwood Mac, Steve Clarke. The Crazed Story Of Fleetwood Mac, Stephen Davis. Fleetwood Mac: Behind The Masks, Bob Brunning. Fleetwood: My Life And Adventures With Fleetwood Mac, Mick Fleetwood with Stephen Davis. Peter Green: The Biography, Martin Celmins.

FLEETWOODS
ALBUMS: Mr. Blue (Dolton 1959)★★★★, The Fleetwoods (Dolton 1960)★★★★, Softly (Dolton 1961)★★★★, Deep In A Dream (Dolton 1961)★★★, The Best Of The Oldies (Dolton 1962)★★★, Goodnight My Love (Dalton 1963)★★★, The Fleetwoods Sing For Lovers By Night (Dolton 1963)★★★, Before And After (Dolton 1965)★★, Folk Rock (Dolton 1966)★★.
COMPILATIONS: The Fleetwoods' Greatest Hits (Dolton 1962)★★★★, In A Mellow Mood (Sunset 1966)★★★, The Best Of ... (Rhino 1990)★★★★, Come Softly To Me: The Best Of ... (EMI 1993)★★★★.

FLO AND EDDIE
ALBUMS: Flo & Eddie (Warners 1973)★★, Immoral, Illegal & Fattening (Columbia 1974)★★★, Moving Targets (Columbia 1976)★★.

FLOATERS
ALBUMS: Floaters (ABC 1977)★★★, Magic (ABC 1978)★★, Into The Future (ABC 1979)★★.

FLOWERPOT MEN
ALBUMS: Let's Go To San Francisco (1988)★★★.

FLOYD, EDDIE
ALBUMS: Knock On Wood (Stax 1967)★★★, I've Never Found A Girl (Stax 1968)★★★, You've Got To Have Eddie (Stax 1969)★★★, California Girl (Stax 1970)★★, Down To Earth (Stax 1971)★★, Baby Lay Your Head Down (Stax 1973)★★, Soul Street (Stax 1974)★★, Experience (Malaco 1977)★★, Try Me (1985)★★, Flashback (Wilbe 1988)★★.
COMPILATIONS: Rare Stamps (Stax 1968)★★★, Chronicle (1979)★★★, The Best Of Eddie Floyd (Stax/Ace 1988)★★★★, I've Never Found A Girl (1992)★★★, Rare Stamps/I've Never Found A Girl (1993)★★★.

FLYING BURRITO BROTHERS
ALBUMS: The Gilded Palace Of Sin (A&M 1969)★★★★★, Burrito DeLuxe (A&M 1970)★★★, The Flying Burrito Brothers (A&M 1971)★★★, The Last Of The Red Hot Burritos (A&M 1972)★★★★, Live In Amsterdam (Bumble 1973)★★★, Flying Again (Columbia 1975)★★, Airborne (Columbia 1976)★★, Flying High (J.B. 1978)★★, Live From Tokyo (Regency 1978) reissued as Close Encounters To The West Coast (Relix 1991)★★, Burrito Country (Brian 1979)★★, Cabin Fever (Relix 1985)★★, Live From Europe (Relix 1986)★★, Flying Burrito Bros Live Holland only (Marlstone 1986)★★, Back To The Sweethearts Of The Rodeo (Disky 1987)★★★, Southern Tracks (Dixie Frog 1990)★★★, Encore – Live In Europe (Sundown 1991)★★, Eye Of A Hurricane (1993)★★★, California Jukebox (Ether 1997)★★.
Solo: 'Sneaky' Pete Kleinow Sneaky Pete (Rhino 1979)★★★, Legend And The Legacy (Shiloh 1994)★★★, California Jukebox (Ether/American Harvest 1997)★★★.
COMPILATIONS: Close Up The Honky Tonks (A&M 1974)★★★★, with Gram Parsons Sleepless Nights (A&M 1976)★★★, with Parsons Dim Lights, Thick Smoke And Loud, Loud Music (Edsel 1987)★★★, Farther Along: Best Of (A&M 1988)★★★★, Hollywood Nights 1979–1981 (Sundown 1990)★★★, Out Of The Blue (Polygram Chronicles 1996)★★★.

FOCUS
ALBUMS: In And Out Of Focus (Polydor 1971)★★★, Moving Waves (Blue Horizon 1971)★★★★, Focus III (Polydor 1972)★★★, At The Rainbow (Polydor 1973)★★, Hamburger Concerto (Polydor 1974)★★, Mother Focus (Polydor 1975)★★, Ship Of Memories (Harvest 1977)★★, Focus Con Proby (Harvest 1977)★★★.
COMPILATIONS: Hocus Pocus: The Best Of ... (EMI 1994)★★★.

FOETUS
ALBUMS: Deaf (Self Immolation 1981)★★★, Ache (Self Immolation 1982)★★★, Hole (Self Immolation 1984)★★★, Nail (Self Immolation 1985)★★★, Thaw (Self Immolation/Some Bizzare 1988)★★★, Male (Big Cat 1993)★★★, Gash (Big Cat 1995)★★★, Boil (Big Cat 1996)★★★, Null & Void (Cleopatra 1997).
COMPILATIONS: Sink (Self Immolation 1990)★★★.
VIDEOS: !Male! (Visionary 1994).

FOGELBERG, DAN
ALBUMS: Home Free (Columbia 1973)★★, Souvenirs (Full Moon 1974)★★★, Captured Angel (Full Moon 1975)★★, Netherlands (Full Moon 1977)★★, with Tim Weisberg Twin Sons Of Different Mothers (Full Moon 1978)★★★★, Phoenix (Full Moon 1979)★★★★, The Innocent Age (Full Moon 1981)★★★★, Windows And Walls (Full Moon 1984)★★, High Country Snows (Full Moon 1985)★★★, Exiles (Full Moon 1987)★★, The Wild Places (Full Moon 1990)★★, Dan Fogelberg Live – Greetings From The West (Full Moon 1991)★★, River Of Souls (Sony 1993)★★.
COMPILATIONS: Greatest Hits (Full Moon 1983)★★★, Starbox (1993)★★★, Portrait: The Music Of Dan Fogelberg From 1972–1997 4-CD box set (Epic 1997)★★★★.

FONTANA, WAYNE
ALBUMS: Wayne Fontana And The Mindbenders (Fontana 1965)★★★,The Game Of Love (Fontana 1965)★★★, Eric, Rick Wayne And Bob (Fontana 1966)★★★, Wayne One (Fontana 1966)★★, Wayne Fontana (MGM 1967)★★.

FOO FIGHTERS
ALBUMS: Foo Fighters (Roswell/Capitol 1995)★★★★, The Colour And The Shape (Roswell/Capitol 1997)★★★★.

FORBERT, STEVE
ALBUMS: Alive On Arrival (Epic 1979)★★★, Jackrabbit Slim (Epic 1979)★★★, Little Stevie Orbit (Epic 1980)★★, Steve Forbert (Epic 1982)★★, Streets Of This Town (Geffen 1988)★★★, The American In Me (Geffen 1992)★★★, Mission Of The Crossroad Palms (Giant 1995)★★★, Rocking Horse Head (Revolution 1996)★★★.

FORD, FRANKIE
ALBUMS: Let's Take A Sea Cruise (Ace 1959)★★, Frankie Ford (1976)★★.
COMPILATIONS: New Orleans Dynamo (Ace 1989)★★★.
FILMS: American Hot Wax (1978).

FORDHAM, JULIA
ALBUMS: Julia Fordham (Circa 1988)★★★, Porcelain (Circa 1989)★★★, Swept (Circa 1991)★★★, Falling Forward (Circa 1994)★★★, East West (Virgin 1997)★★★.
VIDEOS: Porcelain (Virgin 1990).

FOREIGNER
ALBUMS: Foreigner (Atlantic 1977)★★★, Double Vision (Atlantic 1978)★★★, Head Games (Atlantic 1979)★★★, 4 (Atlantic 1981)★★★★, Agent Provocateur (Atlantic 1985)★★★, Inside Information (Atlantic 1987)★★★, Unusual Heat (Atlantic 1991)★★★, Mr Moonlight (BMG 1994)★★★.
Solo: Mick Jones Everything That Comes Around (Atlantic 1989)★★.
COMPILATIONS: Records (Atlantic 1982)★★★★, Greatest Hits (Atlantic 1992)★★★★, The Very Best Of And Beyond (Atlantic 1992)★★★★.
FILMS: Footloose (Soundtrack Song) (1984).

FORTUNES
ALBUMS: The Fortunes I (Decca 1965)★★★, The Fortunes II (Capitol 1972)★★.
COMPILATIONS: Remembering (1976)★★★, Best Of The Fortunes (1983)★★★, Music For The Millions (1984)★★★, Greatest Hits (1985)★★★, Here It Comes Again (Deram 1996)★★★.

FOUNDATIONS
ALBUMS: From The Foundations (Pye 1967)★★, Rocking The Foundations (Pye 1968)★★, Digging The Foundations (Pye 1969)★★.
COMPILATIONS: The Best Of The Foundations (PRT 1987)★★★, Foundations Greatest Hits (Knight 1990)★★★.
FILMS: The Cool Ones (1967).

FOUNTAINS OF WAYNE
ALBUMS: Fountains Of Wayne (Scratchie/Atlantic 1997)★★★★.

4 NON BLONDES
ALBUMS: Bigger, Better, Faster, More! (Interscope 1993)★★★.

FOUR FRESHMEN
ALBUMS: Voices In Modern (Capitol 1955)★★★, Four Freshmen And 5 Trombones (Capitol 1956)★★★, Freshmen Favorites (Capitol 1956)★★★, 4 Freshmen And 5 Trumpets (Capitol 1957)★★★, Four Freshmen And Five Saxes (Capitol 1957)★★★, Voices In Latin (Capitol 1958)★★, The Four Freshmen In Person (Capitol 1958)★★★, Voices In Love (1958)★★★, Freshmen Favorites Volume 2 (Capitol 1959)★★★, Love Lost (Capitol 1959)★★, The Four Freshmen And Five Guitars (Capitol 1960)★★, Voices And Brass (Capitol 1960)★★, Road Show (Capitol 1960)★★, First Affair (Capitol 1960)★★, Freshmen Year (Capitol 1961)★★, Voices In Fun (Capitol 1961)★★, Stars In Our Eyes (Capitol 1962)★★, Got That Feelin' (1963)★★, More With 5 Trombones (1964)★★, Time Slips Away (1964)★★.
COMPILATIONS: The Best Of The Four Freshmen (Capitol 1962)★★★★.

FOUR MEN AND A DOG
ALBUMS: Barking Mad (Topic 1991)★★★★, Shifting Gravel (Topic 1993)★★★★, Doctor A's Secret Remedies (Transatlantic 1995)★★★, Long Roads (Transatlantic 1996)★★★.

FOUR PENNIES
ALBUMS: Two Sides Of The Four Pennies (Philips 1964)★★H, Mixed Bag (Philips 1966)★★★.
COMPILATIONS: Juliet (Wing 1967)★★★.

FOUR PREPS
ALBUMS: Four Preps (Capitol 1958)★★★★, The Things We Did Last Summer (Capitol 1958)★★★★, Dancing And Dreaming (Capitol 1959)★★★, Early In The Morning (Capitol 1960)★★, Those Good Old Memories (Capitol 1960)★★★, Four Preps On Campus (Capitol 1961)★★★, Campus Encore (Capitol 1962)★★★, Campus Confidential (Capitol 1963)★★, Songs For A Campus Party (Capitol 1963)★★, How To Succeed In

Love! (Capitol 1964)★★.
COMPILATIONS: Best Of The Four Preps (Capitol 1967)★★★★, Capitol Collectors Series (Capitol 1989)★★★★, Three Golden Groups In One (1993)★★★.

FOUR SEASONS
ALBUMS: Sherry And 11 Others (Vee Jay 1962)★★★, Ain't That A Shame And 11 Others (Vee Jay 1963)★★★, The 4 Seasons Greetings (Vee Jay 1963)★★★, Big Girls Don't Cry (Vee Jay 1963)★★★, Folk-Nanny (Vee Jay 1963)★★★, Born To Wander (Philips 1964)★★★, Dawn And 11 Other Great Songs (Philips 1964)★★★, Stay And Other Great Hits (Vee Jay 1964)★★★, Rag Doll (Philips 1964)★★★, We Love Girls (Vee Jay 1965)★★★, The Four Seasons Entertain You (Philips 1965)★★★, Recorded Live On Stage (Vee Jay 1965)★★, The Four Seasons Sing Big Hits By Bacharach, David And Dylan (Philips 1965)★★, Working My Way Back To You (Philips 1966)★★★, Lookin' Back (Philips 1966)★★★, Christmas Album (Philips 1967)★★★, Genuine Imitation Life Gazette (Philips 1969)★★★, Edizione D'Oro (Philips 1969)★★★, Chameleon (1972)★★, Streetfighter (1975)★★, Inside You (1976)★★, Who Loves You (Warners 1976)★★★, Helicon (1977)★★★, Reunited Live (Sweet Thunder 1981)★★.
COMPILATIONS: Golden Hits Of The Four Seasons (Vee Jay 1963)★★★★, More Golden Hits By The Four Seasons (Vee Jay 1964)★★★★, Gold Vault Of Hits (Philips 1965)★★★★, Second Vault Of Golden Hits (Philips 1967)★★★★, Seasoned Hits (Fontana 1968)★★★★, The Big Ones (Philips 1971)★★★★, The Four Seasons Story (Private Stock 1976)★★★★★, Greatest Hits (K-Tel 1976)★★★, The Collection (Telstar 1988)★★★★, Anthology (Rhino 1988)★★★★★, Rarities Vol. 1 (Rhino 1990)★★★, Rarities Vol. 2 (Rhino 1990)★★★, The Very Best Of Frankie Valli And The Four Seasons (Polygram 1992)★★★★.
FILMS: Beach Ball (1964).

4 SKINS
ALBUMS: The Good, The Bad And The 4 Skins (Secret 1982)★★, A Fistful Of 4 Skins (Syndicate 1983)★★, From Chaos To 1984 (Syndicate 1984)★★.
COMPILATIONS: The Wonderful World Of The 4 Skins (Link 1987)★★★.

FOUR TOPS
ALBUMS: Four Tops (Motown 1965)★★★, Four Tops No. 2 (Motown 1965)★★★★, Four Tops On Top (Motown 1966)★★★★, Four Tops Live! (Motown 1966)★★★, Four Tops On Broadway (Motown 1967)★★★, Four Tops Reach Out (Motown 1967)★★★★, Yesterday's Dreams (Motown 1968)★★★, Four Tops Now! (Motown 1969)★★★, Soul Spin (Motown 1969)★★★, Still Waters Run Deep (Motown 1970)★★★, Changing Times (Motown 1970)★★★, with the Supremes The Magnificent Seven (Motown 1970)★★★★, with the Supremes The Return Of The Magnificent Seven (Motown 1971)★★, with the Supremes Dynamite (Motown 1972)★★★, Nature Planned It (Motown 1972)★★★, Keeper Of The Castle (Dunhill 1972)★★★, Shaft In Africa film soundtrack (Dunhill 1973)★★, Main Street People (Dunhill 1973)★★, Meeting Of The Minds (Dunhill 1974)★★, Live And In Concert (Dunhill 1974)★★, Night Lights Harmony (ABC 1975)★★, Catfish (ABC 1976)★★, The Show Must Go On (ABC 1977)★★, At The Top (MCA 1978)★★, The Four Tops Tonight! (Casablanca 1981)★★, One More Mountain (Casblanca 1982)★★, Back Where I Belong (Motown 1983)★★, Magic (Motown 1985)★★, Hot Nights (Motown 1986)★★, Indestructible (Arista 1988)★★.
COMPILATIONS: Four Tops Greatest Hits (Motown 1967)★★★★★, Four Tops Greatest Hits, Vol. 2 (Motown 1971)★★★★, Four Tops Story (Motown 1973)★★★★, Four Tops Anthology (Motown 1974)★★★★★, Best Of The Four Tops (K-Tel 1982)★★★, Collection: Four Tops (Castle 1992)★★★.

FOURMOST
ALBUMS: First And Fourmost (Parlophone 1965)★★★.
COMPILATIONS: The Most Of The Fourmost (1982)★★★.
FILMS: Ferry Cross The Mersey (1964).

Fourplay
ALBUMS: Fourplay (Warners 1991)★★★★, Between The Sheets (Warners 1993)★★★, Elixir (Warners 1995)★★★.
COMPILATIONS: The Best Of Fourplay (Warners 1997)★★★.

FRAMPTON, PETER
ALBUMS: Wind Of Change (A&M 1972)★★★, Frampton's Camel (A&M 1973)★★★, Somethin's Happening (A&M 1974)★★, Frampton (A&M 1975)★★, Frampton Comes Alive! (A&M 1976)★★★★, I'm In You (A&M 1977)★★, Where I Should Be (A&M 1979)★★, Breaking All The Rules (A&M 1981)★★, The Art Of Control (A&M 1982)★★, Premonition (Atlantic 1986)★, When All The Pieces Fit (Atlantic 1989)★★, Show Me The Way (1993)★★, Peter Frampton (Relativity 1994)★★★, Frampton Comes Alive II (El Dorado/IRS 1995).
COMPILATIONS: Shine On: A Collection (1992)★★★.
FURTHER READING: Frampton!: An Unauthorized Biography, Susan Katz. Peter Frampton, Marsha Daly. Peter Frampton: A Photo Biography, Irene Adler.

FRANCIS, CONNIE
ALBUMS: Who's Sorry Now? (MGM 1958)★★★★, The Exciting Connie Francis (MGM 1959)★★★★, My Thanks To You (MGM 1959)★★★★, Christmas In My Heart (MGM 1959)★★★, Italian Favorites (MGM 1960)★★★, More Italian Favorites (MGM 1960)★★★, Rock 'N' Roll Million Sellers (MGM 1960)★★★, Country And Western Golden Hits (MGM 1960)★★, Spanish And Latin American Favorites (MGM 1960)★★★, Connie Francis At The Copa (MGM 1961)★★, Connie Francis Sings Great Jewish Favorites (MGM 1961)★★, Songs To A Swingin' Band (MGM 1961)★★, Never On Sunday And Other Title Songs From Motion Pictures (MGM 1961)★★★, Folk Song Favorites (MGM 1961)★★★, Do The Twist (MGM 1962)★★★, Second Hand Love And Other Hits (MGM 1962)★★★, Country Music Connie Style (MGM 1962)★★★, Modern Italian Hits (MGM 1963)★★★, Follow The Boys soundtrack (MGM 1963)★★★, German Favorites (MGM 1963)★★, Award Winning Motion Picture Hits (MGM 1963)★★, Great American Waltzes (MGM 1963)★★★, In The Summer Of His Years (MGM 1964)★★★, Looking For Love soundtrack (MGM 1964)★★, with Hank Williams Jnr. Great Country Favorites (MGM 1964)★★, A New Kind Of Connie (MGM 1964)★★★, Connie Francis Sings For Mama (MGM 1965)★★★, When The Boys Meet The Girls soundtrack (MGM 1965)★★★, Movie Greats Of The Sixties (MGM 1966)★★★, Live At The Sahara In Las Vegas (MGM 1966)★★, Love Italian Style (MGM 1967)★★★, Happiness (MGM 1967)★★, My Heart Cries For You (MGM 1967)★★, Hawaii Connie (MGM 1968)★★, Connie And Clyde (MGM 1968)★★, Connie Sings Bacharach And David (MGM 1968)★★★, The Wedding Cake (MGM 1969)★★★, Connie Francis Sings Great Country Hits, Volume Two (MGM 1973)★★, Sings The Big Band Hits (MGM 1977)★★, I'm Me Again – Silver Anniversary Album (MGM 1981)★★★, Connie Francis And Peter Kraus, Volumes 1 & 2 (MGM 1984)★★★, Country Store (MGM 1988)★★.
COMPILATIONS: Connie's Greatest Hits (MGM 1960)★★★★, More Greatest Hits (MGM 1961)★★★★, Mala Femmena And Connie's Big Hits From Italy (MGM 1963)★★★, The Very Best Of Connie Francis (MGM 1963)★★★★, The All Time International Hits (MGM 1965)★★★★, 20 All Time Greats (1977)★★★★, Connie Francis In Deutschland 8-album box set (1988)★★★★, The Very Best Of Connie Francis, Volume Two (1988)★★★, The Singles Collection (1993)★★★, White Sox, Pink Lipstick ... And Stupid Cupid 5-CD box set (1993)★★★★, Souvenirs 4-CD box set (Polydor/Chronicles 1996)★★★★.
FILMS: Jamboree aka Disc Jockey Jamboree (1957), Follow The Boys (1962).
FURTHER READING: Who's Sorry Now?, Connie Francis.

FRANK AND WALTERS
ALBUMS: Trains, Boats And Planes (Go! Discs 1992)★★★, The Grand Parade (Go! Discs 1996)★★.

FRANKIE GOES TO HOLLYWOOD
ALBUMS: Welcome To The Pleasure Dome (ZTT 1984)★★★, Liverpool (ZTT 1986)★★.
COMPILATIONS: Bang! – The Greatest Hits Of Frankie Goes To Hollywood (ZTT 1993)★★★★.
VIDEOS: Shoot!: The Greatest Hits (1993).
FURTHER READING: Give It Loads: The Story Of Frankie Goes To Hollywood, Bruno Hizer. Frankie Say: The Rise Of Frankie Goes To Hollywood, Danny Jackson. A Bone In My Flute, Holly Johnson.

FRANKLIN, ARETHA
ALBUMS: Aretha (Columbia 1961)★★, The Electrifying Aretha Franklin (Columbia 1962)★★, The Tender, The Moving, The Swinging Aretha Franklin (Columbia 1962)★★, Laughing On The Outside (Columbia 1963)★★, Unforgettable (Columbia 1964)★★, Songs Of Faith (Checker 1964)★★, Running Out Of Fools (Columbia 1964)★★, Yeah!!! (Columbia 1965)★★, Queen Of Soul (1965)★★★, Once In A Lifetime (1965)★★★, Soul Sister (Columbia 1966)★★★, Take It Like You Give It (Columbia 1967)★★★, I Never Loved A Man The Way That I Love You (Atlantic 1967)★★★★★, Aretha Arrives (Atlantic 1967)★★★★, Take A Look early recordings (Columbia 1967)★★★, Aretha: Lady Soul (Atlantic 1968)★★★★★, Aretha Now (Atlantic 1968)★★★★★, Aretha In Paris (Atlantic 1968)★★★, Aretha Franklin: Soul '69 (Atlantic 1969)★★★★, Today I Sing The Blues (Columbia 1969)★★★★, Soft And Beautiful (Columbia 1969)★★★, I Say A Little Prayer (1969)★★★, Aretha Franklin Live (1969)★★★, This Girl's In Love With You (Atlantic 1970)★★★, Spirit In The Dark (Atlantic 1970)★★★, Two Sides Of Love (1970)★★★, Aretha Live At Fillmore West (Atlantic 1971)★★★, Young, Gifted And Black (Atlantic 1972)★★★, Amazing Grace (Atlantic 1972)★★★, Hey Now Hey (The Other Side Of The Sky) (Atlantic 1973)★★, Let Me Into Your Life (Atlantic 1974)★★★, With Everything I Feel In Me (Atlantic 1974)★★★, You (Atlantic 1975)★★, Sparkle (Atlantic 1976)★★, Sweet Passion (Atlantic 1977)★★, Satisfaction (1977)★★★, Almighty Fire (Atlantic 1978)★★, La Diva (Atlantic 1979)★★, Aretha (Arista 1980)★★, Love All The Hurt Away (Arista 1981)★★, Jump To It (Arista 1982)★★, Get It Right (Arista 1983)★★, Who's Zoomin' Who? (Arista 1985)★★★, Aretha (Arista 1986)★★★, One Lord, One Faith, One Baptism (Arista 1987)★★, Through The Storm (Arista 1989)★★, What You See Is What You Sweat (Arista 1991)★★.
COMPILATIONS: Aretha Franklin's Greatest Hits Columbia recordings 1961-66 (Columbia 1967)★★★, Aretha's Gold (Atlantic 1969)★★★★, Aretha's Greatest Hits (Atlantic 1971)★★★★, In The Beginning/The World Of Aretha Franklin 1960-1967 (Columbia 1972)★★★, The Great Aretha Franklin: The First 12 Sides (Columbia 1973)★★★, Ten Years Of Gold (Atlantic 1976)★★★★, Legendary Queen Of Soul (Columbia 1983)★★★★, Aretha Sings The Blues (Columbia 1985)★★★, The Collection (Castle 1986)★★★★, Never Grow Old (Chess 1987)★★★, 20 Greatest Hits (Warners 1987)★★★★, Aretha Franklin's Greatest Hits 1960-1965 (Columbia 1987)★★★★, Queen Of Soul: The Atlantic Recordings 4-CD box set (Rhino/Atlantic 1992)★★★★★, Aretha's Jazz (1993)★★★, Greatest Hits 1980-1994 (Arista 1994)★★★, Love Songs (Rhino/Atlantic 1997)★★★.
FILMS: The Blues Brothers (1980).
VIDEOS: Queen Of Soul (Music Club 1988), Live At Park West (PVE 1995).
FURTHER READING: Aretha Franklin, Mark Bego.

FRED, JOHN, AND HIS PLAYBOY BAND
ALBUMS: John Fred And His Playboys (Paula 1966)★★★, 34:40 Of John Fred And His Playboys (Paula 1967)★★, Agnes English (Paula 1967)★★.

FREDDIE AND THE DREAMERS
ALBUMS: Freddie And The Dreamers (Columbia 1963)★★★, You Were Made For Me (Columbia 1964)★★★, Freddie And The Dreamers (Mercury 1965)★★★, Sing-Along Party (Columbia 1965)★★, Do The Freddie (Mercury 1965)★★, Seaside Swingers aka Everyday's A Holiday film soundtrack (Mercury 1965)★★, Frantic Freddie (Mercury 1965)★★, Freddie And The Dreamers In Disneyland (Columbia 1966)★, Fun Lovin' Freddie (Mercury 1966)★★, King Freddie And His Dreaming Knights (Columbia 1967)★★, Oliver In The Underworld (1970)★★.
COMPILATIONS: The Best Of Freddie And The Dreamers (1982)★★★, The Hits Of Freddie And The Dreamers (1988)★★★, The Best Of Freddie And The Dreamers – The Definitive Collection (EMI 1992)★★★.
FILMS: Every Day's A Holiday aka Seaside Swingers (1965).

FREE
ALBUMS: Tons Of Sobs (Island 1968)★★★, Free (Island 1969)★★★, Fire And Water (Island 1970)★★★★, Highway (Island 1970)★★★, Free Live (Island 1971)★★, Free At Last (Island 1972)★★, Heartbreaker (Island 1973)★★.
COMPILATIONS: The Free Story double album (Island 1974)★★★★, Completely Free (Island 1982)★★★, All Right Now (Island 1991)★★★, Molton Gold: The Anthology (Island 1993)★★★★.
VIDEOS: Free (1989).

FREED, ALAN
FILMS: Don't Knock The Rock (1956), Go Johnny Go (1958).
FURTHER READING: Big Beat Heat: Alan Freed And The Early Years Of Rock 'n' Roll, John A. Jackson.

FRIJID PINK
ALBUMS: Frijid Pink (Parrot 1970)★★, Defrosted (Parrot 1970)★★, Earth Omen (1972)★★, All Pink Inside (Fantasy 1975)★★.

FRIPP, ROBERT
ALBUMS: as Giles Giles And Fripp The Cheerful Insanity Of Giles Giles And Fripp (Deram 1968)★★★, with Brian Eno No Pussyfooting (1975)★★★, with Eno Evening Star (1976)★★★, Exposure (Polydor 1979)★★★★, God Save The Queen, Under Heavy Manners (Polydor 1980)★★, with League Of Gentlemen Let The Power Fall aka The League Of Gentlemen (Polydor 1981)★★★, with Andy Summers I Advance Masked (A&M 1982)★★★★, Bewitched (A&M 1984)★★★, with League Of Gentlemen God Save The King (Editions 1985)★★★, with Toyah The Lady And The Tiger (Editions 1986)★★★, with League Of Crafty Guitarists Robert Fripp And The League Of Crafty Guitarists Live (Editions 1986)★★★, Network (Editions 1987)★★★, Live II (Editions 1990)★★★, Show Of Hands (Editions 1991)★★★, with David Sylvian The First Time (1993)★★★, Soundscapes – Live In Argentina (Discipline 1995)★★★, A Blessing Of Tears (Discipline 1995)★★★, with League Of Crafty Guitarists Intergalactic Boogie Express (Discipline 1995)★★★, Radiophonics (Discipline 1996)★★★, Gates of Paradise (Discipline 1998).
FURTHER READING: Robert Fripp: From King Crimson To Guitar Craft, Eric Tamm.

FUGAZI
ALBUMS: Repeater (Dischord 1990)★★★★, Steady Diet Of Nothing (Dischord 1991)★★★, In On The Kill Taker (Dischord 1993)★★★, Red Medicine (Dischord 1995)★★★.
COMPILATIONS: 13 Songs first two EPs (Dischord 1988)★★★★.

FUGEES
ALBUMS: Blunted On Reality (Ruffhouse 1994)★★, The Score (Ruffhouse 1996)★★★★, Bootleg Versions (Columbia 1996)★★★.
Solo: Jean Wyclef Presents, The Carnival (Columbia-Ruffhouse 1997)★★★.
VIDEOS: The Score (SMV 1996).
FURTHER READING: Fugees: The Unofficial Book, Chris Roberts.

FUGS
ALBUMS: The Village Fugs aka The Fugs First Album (ESP 1965)★★★★, The Fugs (ESP 1966)★★★★, Virgin Fugs (ESP 1966)★★★★, Fugs 4 Rounders Score (ESP 1967)★★★, Tenderness Junction (Reprise 1967)★★★, It Crawled Into My Hand, Honest (Reprise 1968)★★★, The Belle Of Avenue A (Reprise 1969)★★, Refuse To Be Burnt Out (1985)★★, No More Slavery (1986)★★★, Star Peace (1987)★★, The Fugs Live In The 60s (Fugs 1994)★★★, The Real Woodstock Festival (Fugs 1995)★★.
COMPILATIONS: Golden Filth (Reprise 1969)★★★★.

FULLER, BOBBY
ALBUMS: KRLA King Of The Wheels (Mustang 1965)★★★, I Fought The Law aka Memorial Album (Mustang 1966)★★★★, Live Again (Eva 1984)★★.
COMPILATIONS: The Best Of The Bobby Fuller Four (Rhino 1981)★★★★, The Bobby Fuller Tapes, Volume 1 (1983)★★★.

FUN BOY THREE
ALBUMS: Fun Boy Three (Chrysalis 1982)★★★, Waiting (Chrysalis 1983)★★★.
COMPILATIONS: Really Saying Something: The Best Of ... (Chrysalis 1997)★★★★.

FUN LOVIN' CRIMINALS
ALBUMS: Come Find Yourself (EMI/Chrysalis 1996)★★★★.

FUNKADELIC
ALBUMS: Funkadelic (Westbound 1970)★★★, Free Your Mind ... And Your Ass Will Follow (Westbound 1970)★★★, Maggot Brain (Westbound 1971)★★★★, America Eats Its Young (Westbound 1972)★★★, Cosmic Slop (Westbound 1973)★★★, Standing On The Verge Of Getting It On (Westbound 1974)★★★, Let's Take It To The Stage (Westbound 1975)★★★★, Tales Of Kidd Funkadelic (Westbound 1976)★★★, Hardcore Jollies (Warners 1976)★★★, One Nation Under A Groove (Warners 1978)★★★★, Uncle Jam Wants You (Warners 1979)★★★, Connections And Disconnections (LAX 1981)★★, The Electric Spanking Of War Babies (Warners 1981)★★★★.
COMPILATIONS: Funkadelic's Greatest Hits (Westbound 1975)★★★, The Best Of The Early Years – Volume One (Westbound 1977)★★★★, The Best Of ... 1976-1981 (Charly 1994)★★★★, Parliament-Funkadelic Live 1976–1993 4-CD box set (Sequel 1994)★★★, Funkadelic's Finest (Westbound 1997)★★★★.

FUNKDOOBIEST
ALBUMS: Which Doobie U B (Immortal 1993)★★★, Wopbabuloop (Immortal 1993)★★★, Brothas Doobie (Epic 1995)★★★, The Troubleshooters (Buzz Tone/RCA 1998).

FURY, BILLY
ALBUMS: The Sound Of Fury (Decca 1960)★★★★, Billy Fury (Ace Of Clubs 1960)★★★, Halfway To Paradise (Ace Of Clubs 1961)★★★, Billy (Decca 1963)★★★, We Want Billy (Decca 1963)★★, I've Got A Horse (1965)★★★, The One And Only (1983)★★★.
COMPILATIONS: The Best Of Billy Fury (1967)★★★★, The World Of Billy Fury (Decca 1972)★★★★, The Billy Fury Story (1977)★★★, The World Of Billy Fury, Volume 2 (1980)★★★, Hit Parade (1982)★★★, The Missing Years 1967–1980 (1983)★★★, The Billy Fury Hit Parade (1983)★★★, Loving You (1984)★★★, The Other Side Of Billy Fury (1984)★★★, Stick 'N' Stones (1985)★★★, The EP Collection (1985)★★★★, Jealousy (1986)★★★, The Collection (1987)★★★, The Best Of Billy Fury (1988)★★★, The Sound Of Fury + 10 (1988)★★★, Am I Blue? (1993)★★★, The Other Side Of Fury (See For Miles 1994)★★★★.
FILMS: I've Gotta Horse (1965).

FUTURE SOUND OF LONDON
ALBUMS: Accelerator (Debut 1992)★★★, as Amorphous Androgynous Tales Of Ephidrina (Virgin 1993)★★★★, Lifeforms (Virgin 1994)★★★★, Dead Cities (Virgin 1996)★★★.

G

G., KENNY
ALBUMS: Kenny G (1982)★★, G Force (Arista 1983)★★★, Gravity (Arista 1985)★★★, Duotones (Arista 1986)★★★, Silhouette (Arista 1988)★★★, Kenny G Live (Arista 1989)★★, Breathless (Arista 1992)★★★★, Miracles: The Holiday Album. (Arista 1994)★★, The Moment (Arista 1996)★★★.

G., WARREN
ALBUMS: Regulate ... G Funk Era (Violator/RAL1994)★★★, Take A Look Over Your Shoulder (Reality) (G Funk Music/Def Jam 1997)★★★★.

GABRIEL, PETER
ALBUMS: Peter Gabriel (Charisma 1977)★★★, Peter Gabriel (Charisma 1978)★★★, Peter Gabriel (Charisma 1980)★★★, Peter Gabriel (Security) (Charisma 1982)★★★★, Peter GabrielPlays Live (Charisma 1983)★★, Birdy (Charisma 1985)★★, So (Virgin 1986)★★★★, Passion (Real World 1989)★★, Us (Real World 1993)★★★, Secret World – Live (Real World 1994)★★★.
COMPILATIONS: Shaking The Tree (Virgin 1990)★★★★.
VIDEOS: Point Of View (Live In Athens) (1989), The Desert And Her Daughters (1990), CV (1991), AllAbout Us (1993), Secret World Live (1994), Computer Animation: Vol. 2 (1994).
FURTHER READING: Peter Gabriel: An Authorized Biography, Spenser Bright. In His Own Words, Mick St. Michael.

GALLAGHER AND LYLE
ALBUMS: Gallagher And Lyle (A&M 1972)★★, Willie And The Lap Dog (A&M 1973)★★, Seeds (A&M 1973)★★, The Last Cowboy (A&M 1974)★★★, Breakaway (A&M 1976)★★★, Love On The Airwaves (A&M 1977)★★, Showdown (A&M 1978)★★, Gone Crazy (1979)★★, Lonesome No More (Mercury 1979)★★.
COMPILATIONS: The Best Of Gallagher And Lyle (A&M 1980)★★★, Heart On My Sleeve (A&M 1991)★★★.

GALLAGHER, RORY
ALBUMS: Rory Gallagher (Polydor 1971)★★★, Deuce (Polydor 1971)★★★, Live! In Europe (Polydor 1972)★★★, Blueprint (Polydor 1973)★★★★, Tattoo (Polydor 1973)★★★★, Irish Tour '74 (Polydor 1974), Saint ... And Sinner (Polydor 1975)★★★, Against The Grain (Chrysalis 1975)★★★, Calling Card (Chrysalis 1976)★★★, Photo Finish (Chrysalis 1978)★★★, Top Priority (Chrysalis 1979)★★★, Stage Struck (Chrysalis 1980)★★★, Jinx (Chrysalis 1982)★★★, Defender (Demon 1987)★★, Fresh Evidence (Castle 1990)★★.
COMPILATIONS: In The Beginning (Emerald 1974)★★★, The Story So Far (Polydor 1976)★★★, The Best Years (1976)★★★, Best Of Rory Gallagher And Taste (Razor 1988)★★★★, Edged In Blue (Demon 1992)★★★, Rory Gallagher Boxed 4-CD set (1992)★★★.
VIDEOS: Live In Cork (Castle Hendring Video 1989).

GANG OF FOUR
ALBUMS: Entertainment! (Warners 1979)★★★★, Solid Gold (Warners 1981)★★★, Songs Of The Free (Warners 1982)★★★, Hard (Warners 1983)★★, At The Palace (Phonogram 1984)★★, Mall (Polydor 1991)★★★, Shrinkwrapped (Castle 1995)★★★.
COMPILATIONS: The Peel Sessions (Strange Fruit 1990)★★★, A Brief History Of The Twentieth Century (Warners 1990)★★★★.

GAP BAND
ALBUMS: The Gap Band (Mercury 1977)★★★, The Gap Band II (Mercury 1979)★★★★, The Gap Band III (Mercury 1980)★★★, The Gap Band IV (TotalExperience 1982)★★★★, Gap Band V – Jammin' (TotalExperience 1983)★★★, The Gap Band VI (Total Experience 1985)★★★, The Gap Band VII (Total Experience 1986)★★★, The Gap Band VIII (Total Experience 1986)★★, Straight From The Heart (Total Experience 1987)★★, I'm Gonna Git You Sucka (1989)★★, Round Trip (Capitol 1989)★★, Live And Well (Intersound 1996)★★.
COMPILATIONS: Gap Gold/Best Of The Gap Band (Mercury 1985)★★★★, The 12" Collection (Mercury 1986)★★★.

GARBAGE
ALBUMS: Garbage (Mushroom 1995)★★★★, Version 2.0 (Mushroom 1998)★★★★.
VIDEOS: Garbage Video (Mushroom 1996), Garbage (Geffen Video 1996).

GARCIA, JERRY
ALBUMS: Hooteroll (Douglas 1971)★★, Garcia (Warners 1972)★★★, with MerlSaunders Live At Keystone (Fantasy 1973)★★, Garcia (Round 1974)★★★, Old And In The Way (Round 1975)★★★, Reflections (Reflections 1976)★★, Cats Under The Stars (Arista 1978)★★★, Run For The Roses (Arista 1982)★★★, Keystone Encores, Vols. 1 & 2 (Fantasy 1988)★★, as the Jerry Garcia Acoustic Band Almost Acoustic (Grateful Dead 1989)★★★, Jerry Garcia Band (Arista 1991)★★★, with David Grisman Not For Kids Only (Acoustic Disc 1993)★★★, with Grisman Shady Grove (Acoustic 1996)★★★, How Sweet It Is (Grateful Dead Records 1997)★★★.
FURTHER READING: Garcia – A Signpost To A New Space, Charles Reich and Jann Wenner. Grateful Dead – The Music Never Stopped, Blair Jackson. Captain Trips: The Life And Fast Times Of Jerry Garcia, Sandy Troy. Garcia: The Rolling Stone Interview, Jerry Garcia.

GARFUNKEL, ART
ALBUMS: Angel Clare (Columbia 1973)★★★, Breakaway (Columbia 1975)★★★, Watermark (Columbia 1978)★★★, Fate For Breakfast (Columbia 1979)★★★, Scissors Cut (Watermark 1981)★★★, Lefty (Columbia 1988)★★★, Up 'Til Now (Columbia 1993)★★, The Very Best Of – Across America (Virgin 1996)★★★, Songs From A Parent To A Child (Sony 1997).

GAYE, MARVIN
ALBUMS: The Soulful Moods Of Marvin Gaye (Tamla 1961)★★★, That Stubborn Kind Of Fella (Tamla 1963)★★★★, Recorded Live: On Stage (Tamla 1964)★★★, When I'm Alone I Cry (Tamla 1964)★★★, with Mary Wells Together (Motown 1964)★★★, Hello Broadway This Is Marvin (Tamla 1965)★★★, How Sweet It Is To Be Loved By You (Tamla 1965)★★★, A Tribute To The Great Nat King Cole (Tamla 1965)★★★, Moods Of Marvin Gaye (Tamla 1966)★★★, with Kim Weston Take Two (Tamla 1966)★★★, with Tammi Terrell United (Tamla 1967)★★★, In The Groove (Tamla 1968)★★★, with Terrell You're All I Need (Tamla 1968)★★★, with Terrell, Weston, Wells Marvin Gaye And His Girls (Tamla 1969)★★★, with Terrell Easy (Tamla 1969)★★★, M.P.G. (Tamla 1969)★★★, That's The Way Love Is (Tamla 1970)★★★, What's Going On (Tamla 1971)★★★★★, Trouble Man film soundtrack (Tamla 1972)★★, Let's Get It On (Tamla 1973)★★★★★, with Diana Ross Diana And Marvin (Motown 1973)★★★, Marvin Gaye Live! (Tamla 1974)★★, I Want You (Tamla 1976)★★★, Marvin Gaye Live At The London Palladium (Tamla 1977)★★★, Here My Dear (Tamla 1978)★★★, In Our Lifetime (Tamla 1981)★★★, Midnight Love (Columbia 1982)★★★, Dream Of A Lifetime (Columbia 1985)★★★, Romantically Yours (Columbia 1985)★★★, The Last Concert Tour (Giant 1991)★★, For The Very Last Time (1994)★★, Vulnerable (Motown 1997)★★★.
COMPILATIONS: Marvin Gaye's Greatest Hits (Tamla 1964)★★★★, Marvin Gaye's Greatest Hits Vol. 2 (Tamla 1967)★★★, with Tammi Terrell Marvin Gaye & Tammi Terrell: Greatest Hits (Tamla 1970)★★★, Super Hits (Tamla 1970)★★★, Anthology (Motown 1974)★★★, Marvin Gaye's Greatest Hits (Tamla 1976)★★★★, Every Great Motown Hit Of Marvin Gaye (Motown 1983)★★★★, Motown Remembers Marvin Gaye (Tamla 1986)★★★, 18 Greatest Hits (Motown 1988)★★★★, Love Songs (Telstar 1990)★★★★, The Marvin Gaye Collection 4-CD box set (Tamla/Motown 1990)★★★★★, Night Life (1993)★★★, The Master: 1961-1984 4-CD box set (Motown 1995)★★★, Early Classics (Spectrum 1996)★★★.
FURTHER READING: Divided Soul: The Life Of Marvin Gaye, David Ritz. I Heard It Throught The Grapevine: Marvin Gaye, The Biography, Sharon Davis.

GAYE BYKERS ON ACID
ALBUMS: Drill Your Own Hole (Virgin 1987)★★★, Stewed To The Gills (Virgin 1989)★★★, GrooveDiveSoapDish (Bleed 1989)★★★, Cancer Planet Mission (Naked Brain 1990)★★, as PFX Pernicious Nonsense (Naked Brain 1991)★★, From The Tomb Of The Near Legendary (1993)★★.
VIDEOS: Drill Your Own Hole (Virgin Vision 1987).

GAYLE, CRYSTAL
ALBUMS: Crystal Gayle (United Artists 1975)★★★, Somebody Loves You (United Artists 1975)★★★, Crystal (United Artists 1976)★★★, We Must Believe In Magic (United Artists 1977)★★★, When I Dream (United Artists 1978)★★★★, I've Cried The Blue Right Out Of My Eyes (MCA 1978)★★★, We Should Be Together (United Artists 1979)★★★, Miss The Mississippi (Columbia 1979)★★★★, A Woman's Heart (Columbia 1980)★★★★, These Days (Columbia 1980)★★★, Hollywood/Tennessee (Columbia 1981)★★★, True Love (Elektra 1982)★★★, with Tom Waits One From The Heart film soundtrack (Columbia 1982)★★★★, Cage The Songbird (Warners 1983)★★★, Nobody Wants To Be Alone (1985)★★★, Crystal Gayle (1986)★★★, Straight To The Heart (1986)★★★, A Crystal Christmas (Warners 1986)★★, with Gary Morris What If We Fall In Love (Warners 1987)★★, I Love Country (Columbia 1987)★★, Nobody's Angel (Warners 1988)★★★, Ain't Gonna Worry (Capitol 1990)★★★, Three Good Reasons (Liberty 1992)★★★★, Someday (Intersound 1995), Mountain Christmas (Intersound 1996), Walk With Me (Audio K-7 1996).
COMPILATIONS: Classic Crystal (United Artists 1979)★★★, Favorites (United Artists 1980)★★★, Crystal Gayle's Greatest Hits (Columbia 1983)★★★★, Best Of Crystal Gayle (Warners 1987)★★★, All Time Greatest Hits (Curb 1990)★★★, 50 Original Tracks (1993)★★★★, Best Always (1993)★★★★.
VIDEOS: In Concert (1993).

GAYNOR, GLORIA
ALBUMS: Never Can Say Goodbye (MGM 1975)★★★, Experience Gloria Gaynor (MGM 1975)★★★, I've Got You (Polydor 1976)★★, Glorious (Polydor 1977)★★, Love Tracks (Polydor 1979)★★★, I Have A Right (Polydor 1979)★★★, Stories (Polydor 1980)★★, I Kinda Like Me (Polydor 1981)★★, Gloria Gaynor (Polydor 1982)★★, I Am Gloria Gaynor (Chrysalis 1984)★★, The Power Of Gloria Gaynor (Stylus 1986)★★.
COMPILATIONS: Greatest Hits (Polydor 1982)★★★, I Will Survive: Greatest Hits (1993)★★★.

GEFFEN, DAVID
FURTHER READING: The Hit Men, Frederick Dannen.

GEILS, J., BAND
ALBUMS: J. Geils Band (Atlantic 1971)★★★, The Morning After (Atlantic 1971)★★★, Live – FullHouse (Atlantic 1972)★★★, Bloodshot (Atlantic 1973)★★, Ladies Invited (Atlantic 1973)★★★, Nightmares ... And Other Tales From The VinylJungle (Atlantic 1974)★★, Hotline (Atlantic 1975)★★, Live – Blow Your Face Out (Atlantic 1976)★★, Monkey Island (Atlantic 1977)★★★, Sanctuary (Atlantic 1978)★★★, Love Stinks (EMI 1980)★★★, Freeze Frame (EMI 1981)★★★, Showtime! (EMI 1982)★★★, You're Gettin' Even, While I'm Gettin' Old (EMI 1984)★★, with Magic Dick Little Car Blues (Rounder 1996)★★★.
COMPILATIONS: The Best Of The J. Geils Band (Atlantic 1979)★★★.

GELDOF, BOB
ALBUMS: Deep In The Heart Of Nowhere (Mercury 1986)★★★, The Vegetarians Of Love (Mercury 1990)★★★, The Happy Club (1992)★★.
FURTHER READING: Is That It?, Bob Geldof. Bob Geldof, Charlotte Gray.

GENE
ALBUMS: Olympian (Costermonger 1995)★★★★, To See The Lights (Costermonger 1996)★★★, Drawn To The Deep End (Polydor 1997)★★★.

GENERAL PUBLIC
ALBUMS: All The Rage (Virgin 1984)★★★, Hand To Mouth (Virgin 1986)★★★, Rub It Better (Epic 1995)★★★.

GENERATION X
ALBUMS: Generation X (Chrysalis 1978)★★★, Valley Of The Dolls (Chrysalis 1979)★★, as Gen X Kiss Me Deadly (Chrysalis 1981)★★.
COMPILATIONS: Best Of Generation X (Chrysalis 1985)★★★, Perfect Hits (1975-81) (Chrysalis 1991)★★★.

GENESIS
ALBUMS: From Genesis To Revelation (Decca 1969)★, Trespass (Charisma 1970)★★, Nursery Cryme (Charisma 1971)★★★, Foxtrot (Charisma 1972)★★★, Genesis Live (Charisma 1973)★★, Selling England By The Pound (Charisma 1973)★★★, The Lamb Lies Down On Broadway (Charisma 1974)★★★★, A Trick Of The Tail (Charisma 1976)★★★, Wind And Wuthering (Charisma 1977)★★★, Seconds Out (Charisma 1977)★★, And Then There Were Three (Charisma 1978)★★★, Duke (Charisma 1980)★★★★, Abacab (Charisma 1981)★★★, 3 Sides Live (Charisma 1982)★★, Genesis (Charisma 1983)★★★, Invisible Touch (Charisma 1986)★★★, We Can't Dance (Virgin 1991)★★★, The Way We Walk – Vol 1: The Shorts (Virgin 1992)★★, Live The Way We Walk – Vol. 2: The Longs (Virgin 1993)★★, Calling All Stations (Virgin 1997)★★★, Archive 1967-1975 (1998)★★★.
VIDEOS: Three Sides Live (1986), Live: The Mama Tour (1986), Visible Touch (1987), Genesis 2 (1988), Genesis 1 (1988), Invisible Touch Tour (1989), Genesis, A History 1967-1991 (1991), A History (1992), Live: The Way We Walk (1993).
FURTHER READING: Genesis: The Evolution Of A Rock Band, Armando Gallo. Genesis Lyrics, Kim Poor. Genesis: Turn It On Again, Steve Clarke. Genesis: A Biography, Dave Bowler and Brian Dray.

GENTLE GIANT
ALBUMS: Gentle Giant (Vertigo 1970)★★★, Acquiring The Taste (Vertigo 1971)★★★, Three Friends (Vertigo 1972)★★★, Octopus (Vertigo 1973)★★, In A Glass House (WWA 1973)★★, The Power And The Glory (WWA 1974)★★, Free Hand (Chrysalis 1975)★★★, Interview (Chrysalis 1976)★★★, The Official 'Live' Gentle Giant – Playing The Fool(Chrysalis 1977)★★★, The Missing Piece (Chrysalis 1977)★★, Giant For A Day (Chrysalis 1978)★★, Civilian (Chrysalis 1980)★★, Live-Playing The Fool (Essential1989)★★.
COMPILATIONS: Giant Steps (The First Five Years) (Vertigo 1975)★★★.

GEORGE BAKER SELECTION
ALBUMS: Little Green Bag (Penny Farthing 1970)★★, Paloma Blanca (Warners 1975)★★, River Song (Warners 1976)★★, Summer Melody (Warners 1977)★★.
COMPILATIONS: The Best Of Baker (Warners 1978)★★.

GERMS
ALBUMS: GI (Slash 1979)★★★.
COMPILATIONS: What We Do Is Secret (Slash 1981)★★, Let The Circle Be Unbroken (Gasatanka 1985)★★, MIA (Slash 1994)★★.

GERRY AND THE PACEMAKERS
ALBUMS: How Do You Like It (Columbia 1963)★★★★, Second Album (1964)★★★, I'llBe There! (1965)★★★, Ferry Cross The Mersey soundtrack (1965)★★★★, GirlOn A Swing (1965)★★★, 20 Year Anniversary Album (1983)★★.
COMPILATIONS: Don't Let The Sun Catch You Crying (1964)★★★, Gerry And The Pacemakers' Greatest Hits (1965)★★★★, The Best Of Gerry And The Pacemakers (1977)★★★★, The Very Best Of Gerry And The Pacemakers (1984)★★★★, Hit Singles Album (1986)★★★★, The EP Collection (1987)★★★★, The Singles Plus (1987)★★★★, The Very Best Of ... 20 Superb Tracks (1993)★★★★.
VIDEOS: In Concert (Legend 1990).
FURTHER READING: I'll Never Walk Alone, Gerry Marsden with Ray Coleman.

GIBBONS, STEVE
ALBUMS: Any Road Up (Goldhawk 1976)★★★, Rolling On (Polydor 1977)★★★, Caught In The Act (Polydor 1977)★★★, Down In The Bunker (Polydor 1978)★★★★, Street Parade (RCA 1980)★★★, Saints And Sinners (RCA 1981)★★★, On The Loose (Magnum Force 1986)★★★, Not On The Radio (1991)★★★.
COMPILATIONS: Best Of (Polydor 1980)★★★.

GILL, VINCE
ALBUMS: Turn Me Loose mini-album (RCA 1983)★★, The Things That Matter (RCA 1984)★★★, Vince Gill (RCA 1985)★★★, The Way Back Home (RCA 1987)★★★, When I Call Your Name (MCA 1989)★★★, Pocket FullOf Gold (MCA 1991)★★★, I Never Knew Lonely (MCA 1992)★★★, I StillBelieve In You (MCA 1992)★★★★, Let There Be Peace On Earth (MCA 1993)★★, When Love Finds You (MCA 1994)★★★★, High Lonesome Sound (MCA 1996)★★★.

COMPILATIONS: *Souvenirs* (MCA 1995)★★★★, *The Essential Vince Gill* (RCA 1996)★★★★, *Super Hits* (RCA 1996)★★★.
VIDEOS: *I Still Believe In You* (1993).

GILLAN, IAN
ALBUMS: as Ian Gillan Band *Child In Time* (Oyster 1976)★★★, *Clear Air Turbulence* (Island 1977)★★, *Scarabus* (Scarabus 1977)★★, *I.G.B. Live At The Budokan* (Island 1978)★★. With Gillan *Gillan* (Eastworld 1978)★★, *Mr. Universe* (Acrobat 1979)★★, *Glory Road* (Virgin 1980)★★★★, *Future Shock* (Virgin 1981)★★★, *Double Trouble* (Virgin 1982)★★★, *Magic* (Virgin 1982)★★★, *Live At The Budokan* (Virgin 1983)★★, *What I Did On My Vacation* (Virgin 1986)★★, *Live At Reading 1980* (Raw Fruit 1990)★★, *Dreamcatcher* (Caramba! 1998)★★.
COMPILATIONS: As Garth Rockett *Story Of* (Rock Hard 1990)★★★. As Ian Gillan *Naked Thunder* (East West 1990)★★★, *Very Best Of* (Music Club 1991)★★★, *Trouble: The Best Of* (Virgin 1991)★★★, *Toolbox* (East West 1991)★★★, *The Japanese Album* (East West 1993)★★★.
VIDEOS: *Gillan Live At The Rainbow 1978* (Spectrum 1988), *Ian Gillan Band* (Spectrum 1990), *Ian Gillan Live* (Castle 1992). As Garth Rockett And The Moonshiners *Live* (Fotodisk 1990).
FURTHER READING: *Child In Time: The Life Story Of The Singer From Deep Purple*, Ian Gillan with David Cohen..

GIN BLOSSOMS
ALBUMS: *Up & Crumbling* (A&M 1992)★★★, *New Miserable Experience* (A&M 1993)★★★★, *Congratulations I'm Sorry* (A&M 1996)★★★.

GIPSY KINGS
ALBUMS: *Luna De Fuego* (Phillips 1983)★★★, *Alegria* (Elektra 1986)★★★, *Gipsy Kings* (Elektra 1988)★★★, *Mosaique* (Elektra 1989)★★★, *ve & Liberty* (Elektra 1993)★★, *Tierra Gitana* (Atl- ,ıc 1996)★★, *Compas* (Atlantic 1997).

GIRLSCHOOL
ALBUMS: *Demolition* (Bronze 1980)★★, *Hit 'N' Run* (Bronze 1981)★★★, *Screaming Blue Murder* (Bronze 1982)★★★, *Play Dirty* (Bronze 1983)★★★, *Running Wild* (Mercury 1985)★★, *Nightmare At Maple Cross* (GWR 1986)★★, *Take A Bite* (GWR 1988)★★, *Live* (Communiqu≥ 1995)★★, *Emergency* (Snapper 1998).
COMPILATIONS: *Race With The Devil* (Raw Power 1986)★★★, *Collection* (Castle 1991)★★★.
VIDEOS: *Play Dirty Live* (1984), *Bronze Rocks* (1985).

GLASTONBURY FESTIVAL
ALBUMS: Various *Glastonbury 25th Anniversary – A Celebration* (Chrysalis 1995)★★★.

GLITTER, GARY
ALBUMS: *Glitter* (Bell 1972)★★, *Touch Me* (Bell 1973)★★, *Remember Me This Way* (Bell 1974)★★, *Always Yours* (MFP 1975)★★, *GG* (Bell 1975)★★, *I Love You Love* (Hallmark 1977)★★, *Silver Star* (Arista 1978)★★, *The Leader* (GTO 1980)★★, *Boys Will Be Boys* (Arista 1984)★.
COMPILATIONS: *Greatest Hits* (Bell 1976)★★★, *Gary Glitter's Golden Greats* (GTO 1977)★★★, *The Glam Years: Part 1* (Repertoire 1995)★★★, *The Glam Years* (Repertoire 1996)★★★.
VIDEOS: *Gary Glitter's Gangshow* (Hendring 1989), *Gary Glitter Story* (Channel5 1990), *Rock'n'Roll's Greatest Show: Gary Glitter Live* (PMI 1993).
FURTHER READING: *The Gary Glitter Story*, George Tremlett. *Leader: The Autobiography Of Gary Glitter*, Gary Glitter with Lloyd Bradley.

GO WEST
ALBUMS: *Go West* (Chrysalis 1985)★★★, *Bangs And Crashes* (Chrysalis 1985)★★, *Dancing On The Couch* (Chrysalis 1987)★★, *Indian Summer* (Chrysalis 1992)★★★.
VIDEOS: *Aces And Kings: The Best Of The Videos* (Chrysalis 1993).

GO-BETWEENS
ALBUMS: *Send Me A Lullaby* (Missing Link/Rough Trade 1981)★★, *Before Hollywood* (Rough Trade 1983)★★★, *Springhill Fair* (Sire 1984)★★★★, *Liberty Belle And The Black Diamond Express* (Beggars Banquet 1986)★★★★, *Tallulah* (Beggars Banquet 1987)★★★, *16 Lovers Lane* (Beggars Banquet 1988)★★★★.
Solo: Grant McLennan *Watershed* (Beggars Banquet 1991)★★★★, *Fireboy* (Beggars Banquet 1993)★★★, *Horsebreaker Star* (Beggars Banquet 1995)★★★, *In Your Bright Ray* (Beggars Banquet 1997)★★★.
COMPILATIONS: *Very Quick On The Eye* (Man Made 1982)★★★, *Metals And Shells* (PVC 1985)★★★, *Go-Betweens 1978-1990* (Beggars Banquet 1990)★★★★.
VIDEOS: *That Way* (1993).

GO-GO'S
ALBUMS: *Beauty And The Beat* (IRS 1981)★★★, *Vacation* (IRS 1982)★★★, *Talk Show* (IRS 1984)★★.
COMPILATIONS: *Go-Go's Greatest* (IRS 1990)★★★, *Return To The Valley Of The Go-Go's* (IRS 1995)★★★.

GODLEY AND CREME
ALBUMS: *Consequences* (Mercury 1977)★★, *L*(Mercury 1978)★★, *Freeze Frame* (Polydor 1979)★★, *Ismism* (Polydor 1981)★★, *Birds Of Prey* (Polydor 1983)★★, *The History Mix Volume 1* (Polydor 1985)★★★, *Goodbye Blue Sky* (Polydor 1988)★★.
COMPILATIONS: *The Changing Face Of 10cc And Godley And Creme* (Polydor 1987)★★★.
VIDEOS: *Changing Faces-The Very Best Of 10cc And Godley And Creme* (Polygram 1988), *Cry* (Polygram 1988), *Mondo Video* (Virgin 1989).

GOFFIN, GERRY
ALBUMS: *It Ain't Exactly Entertainment* (1973)★★★. A compilation of various artists interpretations of Goffin And King compositions is also available: *The Goffin And King Songbook* (1989)★★★, *Back Room Blood* (Adelphi 1996)★★.

GOLD, ANDREW
ALBUMS: *Andrew Gold* (Asylum 1976)★★★, *What's Wrong With This Picture?* (Asylum 1977)★★, *AllThis And Heaven Too* (Asylum 1978)★★, *Whirlwind* (Asylum 1980)★★, *Halloween Howls* (Rhino 1996).
COMPILATIONS: *Never Let Her Slip Away* (1993)★★★.

GOLDEN EARRING
ALBUMS: *Just Ear-rings* (Polydor 1965)★★★, *Winter Harvest* (Polydor 1966)★★★, *Miracle Mirror* (Polydor 1968)★★★, *On The Double* (Polydor 1969)★★★, *Reflections* (Polydor 1969)★★★, *Highlights From On The Double* (Polydor 1969)★★★, *Eight Miles High* (Polydor 1969)★★★, *Golden Earring (WallOf Dolls)* (Polydor 1970)★★★, *Golden Earring* Box 5-LP box set (Polydor 1970)★★★★, *Seven Tears* (Polydor 1971)★★★, *Pophistory Vol.16* (Polydor 1971)★★★, *Together* (Polydor 1972)★★★, *Moontan* (Polydor 1973)★★★, *Switch* (Polydor 1975)★★★, *To The Hilt* (Polydor 1975)★★★, *Rock Of The Century* (Polydor 1976)★★★, *Contraband* (Polydor 1976)★★★, *Mad Love* (1977)★★★, *Live* (Polydor 1977)★★★, *Grab It For A Second* (Polydor 1978)★★★, *No Promises ... No Debts* (Polydor 1979)★★★, *Prisoner Of The Night* (Polydor 1980)★★★, *Second Live* (Polydor 1981)★★★, *Cut* (Mercury 1982)★★★, *Live Tracks* (Polydor 1983)★★★, *N.E.W.S. (North East West South)* (21 Records 1984)★★★, *Live And Pictured* (Polydor 1984)★★★, *Something Heavy Going Down – Live From The Twilight Zone* (21 Records 1984)★★★, *The Hole* (21 Records 1986)★★★, *Keeper Of The Flame* (Jaws 1989)★★★, *Bloody Buccaneers* (Columbia 1991)★★★, *The Naked Truth* (Columbia 1992)★★★, *Face It* (Columbia 1994).
Solo: George Kooymans *Jojo* (Polydor 1971)★★, *Solo* (Ring 1987)★★. Barry Hay *Only Parrots, Frogs And Angels* (Polydor 1972)★★★, *Victory Of Bad Taste* (Ring 1987)★★. Rinus Gerritsen and MichelVan Dijk *De G.V.D. Band* (Atlantic 1978)★★, *Labyrinth* (1985)★★.
COMPILATIONS: *Hits Van De Golden Earrings* (Polydor 1967)★★★, *Greatest Hits* (Polydor 1968)★★★★, *Best Of Golden Earring* (1970)★★★, *Greatest Hits Volume 2* (Polydor 1970)★★★, *Superstarshine Vol. 1* (Polydor 1972)★★★, *Hearring Earring* (1973)★★★, *The Best Ten Years: Twenty Hits* (Arcade 1975)★★★, *Fabulous Golden Earring* (Polydor 1976)★★★, *The Golden Earring Story* (1978)★★★, *Greatest Hits Volume 3* (Polydor 1981)★★★, *The Complete Singles Collection 1 1965-1974* (Arcade 1992)★★★★, *The Complete Singles Collection 1975-1991* (Arcade 1992)★★★★.

GOLDEN PALOMINOS
ALBUMS: *The Golden Palominos* (OAO/Celluloid 1983)★★★★, *Visions Of Excess* (Celluloid 1985)★★★★, *Blast Of Silence* (Celluloid 1986)★★★, *A Dead Horse* (Celluloid 1989)★★★, *Drunk With Passion* (Restless 1991)★★★★, *This Is How It Feels* (Restless 1993)★★★, *Pure* (Restless 1995)★★★, *Dead Inside* (Restless 1996)★★★.
COMPILATIONS: *The Best Of The Golden Palominos 1983 – 1989* (Music Collection 1997)★★★.

GOLDSBORO, BOBBY
ALBUMS: with DelReeves *Our Way Of Life* (United Artists 1967)★★★, *Honey* (United Artists 1968)★★★, *Word Pictures* (United Artists 1968)★★★, *Today* (United Artists 1969)★★★, *Muddy Mississippi Line* (United Artists 1970)★★★, *We Gotta Start Lovin'* (United Artists 1971)★★★, *Come Back Home* (United Artists 1971)★★, *10th Anniversary Album* (United Artists 1974)★★, *A Butterfly For Bucky* (United Artists 1976)★★, *Goldsboro* (1977)★★, *Roundup Saloon* (1982)★★.
COMPILATIONS: *Solid Goldsboro* (United Artists 1967)★★★, *Summer (The First Time)* (United Artists 1973)★★★, *Best Of Bobby Goldsboro* (MFP 1983)★★★★, *The Very Best Of Bobby Goldsboro* (C5 1988)★★★★, *All-Time Greatest Hits* (Curb 1990)★★★.

GONG
ALBUMS: *Magick Brother, Mystic Sister* (BYG 1969)★★, *ContinentalCircus* (Philips 1971)★★★, *Camembert Electrique* (BYG 1971)★★★★, *Radio Gnome Invisible Part 1-The Flying Teapot* (Virgin 1973)★★★★, *Radio Gnome Invisible Part 2-Angel's Egg* (Virgin 1973)★★★, *You* (Virgin 1974)★★★, *Shamal*(Virgin 1976)★★, *Gazeuse* (Virgin 1977)★★, *Gong Est Mort -Vive Gong* (Tapioca 1977)★★, *Expresso 2* (Virgin 1978)★★, *Downwind* (Arista 1979)★★, *Time Is The Key* (Arista 1979)★★, *Pierre Moerlen's Gong, Live* (Arista 1980)★★, *Leave It Open* (Arista 1981)★★, *Breakthrough* (Arc/Eulenspiegel1986)★★, *Second Wind* (LIDLP 1988)★★, *Floating Anarchy* (Decal1990)★★, *Live Au Bataclan 1973* (Mantra 1990)★★★, *Live At Sheffield 1974* (Mantra 1990)★★★, *25th Birthday Party* (Voiceprint 1995)★★, *The Peel Sessions* (Strange Fruit 1995)★★★, *Shapeshifter +* (Viceroy 1997)★★, *You – Remixed* (Gliss 1997).
COMPILATIONS: *A WingfulOf Eyes* (Virgin 1987)★★★, *The Mystery And The History Of The Planet G**g* (Demi-Monde 1989)★★★, *The Best Of ...* (Nectar Masters 1995)★★★.
VIDEOS: *Gong Maison* (1993).

GOO GOO DOLLS
ALBUMS: *Goo Goo Dolls* (Mercenary/Celluloid 1987)★★, *Jed* (Death/Enigma 1989)★★, *Hold Me Up* (Metal Blade 1990)★★★, *Superstar Carwash* (Metal Blade 1993)★★★, *A Boy Named Goo* (Warners 1995)★★★★.

GRAHAM, BILL
FURTHER READING: *Bill Graham Presents*, Bill Graham and Robert Greenfield.

GRAHAM, LARRY
ALBUMS: *One In A Million You* (Warners 1980)★★★, *Just Be My Lady* (Warners 1981)★★★, *Sooner Or Later* (Warners 1982)★★, *Victory* (Warners 1983)★★, *Fired Up* (1985)★★★.

GRAND FUNK RAILROAD
ALBUMS: *On Time* (Capitol 1969)★★★, *Grand Funk* (Capitol 1970)★★★, *Closer To Home* (Capitol 1970)★★★, *Live* (Capitol 1970)★★, *Survival* (Capitol 1971)★★, *E Pluribus Funk* (Capitol 1971)★★★, *Phoenix* (Capitol 1972)★★★, *We're An American Band* (Capitol 1973)★★★, *Shinin' On* (Capitol 1974)★★, *AllThe Girls In The World Beware!!!* (Capitol 1974)★★, *Caught In The Act* (MCA 1975)★★, *Good Singin', Good Playin'* (MCA 1976)★★★, *Grand Funk Lives* (Full Moon 1981)★★, *What's Funk?* (Full Moon 1983)★★.
COMPILATIONS: *Grand Funk Hits* (Capitol 1976)★★★, *The Best Of Grand Funk Railroad* (Capitol 1990)★★★, *The Collection* (Castle 1992)★★★.

GRANDMASTER FLASH
ALBUMS: As Grandmaster Flash And The Furious Five *The Message* (Sugarhill1982)★★★, *Greatest Messages* (Sugarhill1984)★★★, *On The Strength* (Elektra 1988)★★. As Grandmaster Flash *They Said It Couldn't Be Done* (Elektra 1985)★★, *The Source* (Elektra 1986)★★, *Ba-Dop-Boom-Bang* (Elektra 1987)★★★.
COMPILATIONS: Grandmaster Flash And The Furious Five/Grandmaster Melle Mel*Greatest Hits* (Sugarhill1988)★★★★, *The Best Of ...* (Rhino 1994)★★★★.

GRANT, EDDY
ALBUMS: *Message Man* (Ice 1977)★★★, *Walking On Sunshine* (Ice 1979)★★★, *Love In Exile* (Ice 1980)★★★, *Can't Get Enough* (Ice 1981)★★★, *Live At Notting Hill* (Ice 1981)★★, *Paintings Of The Soul* (Ice 1982)★★★, *Killer On The Rampage* (Ice/RCA 1982)★★★, *Can't Get Enough* (Ice/RCA 1983)★★★, *Going For Broke* (Ice/RCA 1984)★★, *Born Tuff* (Ice 1987)★★, *File Under Rock* (Parlophone 1988)★★.
COMPILATIONS: *Walking On Sunshine (The Best Of Eddy Grant)* (Parlophone 1989)★★★.
VIDEOS: *Live In London* (PMI 1986), *Walking On Sunshine* (PMI 1989).

GRANT LEE BUFFALO
ALBUMS: *Fuzzy* (Slash 1993)★★★, *Mighty Joe Moon* (Slash 1994)★★★, *Copperopolis* (Slash 1996)★★★, *Jubilee* (Slash/Warner).

GRATEFUL DEAD
ALBUMS: *The Grateful Dead* (Warners 1967)★★★, *Anthem Of The Sun* (Warners 1968)★★★★, *Aoxomoxoa* (Warners 1969)★★★★, *Live/Dead* (Warners 1970)★★★★, *Workingman's Dead* (Warners 1970)★★★★★, *Vintage Dead* (Sunflower 1970)★, *American Beauty* (Warners 1970)★★★★★, *Historic Dead* (Sunflower 1971)★, *Grateful Dead* (Warners 1971)★★★, *Europe '72* (Warners 1972)★★★, *History Of The Grateful Dead, Volume 1 – (Bear's Choice)* (Warners 1973)★★★, *Wake Of The Flood* (Grateful Dead 1973)★★, *From The Mars Hotel* (Grateful Dead 1974)★★★, *For Dead Heads* (United Artists)★★★, *Blues For Allah* (Grateful Dead 1975)★★, *Steal Your Face* (Grateful Dead 1976)★★, *Terrapin Station* (Arista 1977)★★★, *Shakedown Street* (Arista 1978)★★, *Go To Heaven* (Arista 1980)★, *Reckoning* (Arista 1981)★★★, *Dead Set* (Arista 1981)★★, *In The Dark* (Arista 1987)★★★★, *Built To Last* (Arista 1989)★★, with Bob Dylan *Dylan And The Dead* (Columbia 1990)★, *Without A Net* (Arista 1990)★★, *One From The Vault* (Grateful Dead 1991)★★★, *Infrared Roses* (Grateful Dead 1991)★★, *Two From The Vault* (Grateful Dead 1992)★★★, *Dick's Picks Volume 1* (Grateful Dead 1993)★★★, *Hundred Year Hall* (Arista 1995)★★★, *Dick's Picks Volume 2* (Grateful Dead 1995)★★★, *Dick's Pick's Volume 3* (Grateful Dead 1996)★★★, *Dick's Pick's Volume 4* (Grateful Dead 1996)★★★, *Dick's Pick's Volume 7* (Grateful Dead 1997)★★★, *Dick's Pick's Volume 8* (Grateful Dead 1997)★★★, *Dick's Pick's Volume 9* (Grateful Dead 1997)★★★, *Dick's Pick's Volume 5* (Grateful Dead 1998)★★★, *Dozin' At The Knick* (Arista 1996)★★★, *Fallout From The Phil Zone* (Arista 1997)★★★.
COMPILATIONS: *The Best Of: Skeletons From The Closet* (Warners 1974)★★★★, *What A Long Strange Trip It's Been: The Best Of The Grateful Dead* (Warners 1977)★★★★, *The Arista Years* (Arista 1996)★★★.
VIDEOS: *Grateful Dead In Concert* (RCA Video 1984), *So Far* (Virgin Vision 1988), *The Grateful Dead Movie* (Palace Premiere 1990), *Infrared Sightings* (Trigon 1995), *Dead Ahead* (Monterey 1995), *Backstage Pass: Acess All Areas* (Pearson 1995), *Ticket To New Year's* (Monterey Home Video 1996), *Tie Died: Rock 'n' Roll's Most Dedicated Fans* (BMG Video 1996).
FURTHER READING: *The Grateful Dead*, Hank Harrison. *Grateful Dead: The Official Book Of The Deadheads*, Paul Grushkin, Jonas Grushkin and Cynthia Bassett. *History Of The Grateful Dead*, William Ruhlmann. *Built To Last: Twenty-Five Years Of The Grateful Dead*, Jamie Jensen. *Drumming At The Edge Of Magic*, Mickey Hart. *Grateful Dead Family Album*, Jerilyn Lee Brandelius. *Sunshine Daydreams: Grateful Dead Journal*, Herb Greene. *One More Saturday Night: Reflections With The Grateful Dead*, Sandy Troy. *Drumming At the Edge Of Magic*, Mickey Hart and Jay Stevens. *Planet Drum*, Mickey Hart and Fredric Lieberman. *Book Of The Dead: Celebrating 25 Years With The Grateful Dead*, Herb Greene. *Conversations With The Grateful Dead*, David Gans. *Story Of The Grateful Dead*, Adrian Hall. *Dead Base IX: Complete Guide To Grateful Dead Song Lists*, Nixon and Scot Dolgushkin. *Living With The Dead*, Rock Scully with David Dalton. *Dead To The Core: A Grateful Dead Almanack*, Eric F. Wybenga.

GREAT SOCIETY
ALBUMS: *Conspicuous Only In Its Absence* (Columbia 1968)★★★, *How It Was* (Columbia 1968)★★.
COMPILATIONS: *Born To Be Burned* (Sundazed 1996)★★★.
FURTHER READING: *The Jefferson Airplane And The San Francisco Sound*, Ralph J. Gleeson. *Grace Slick – The Biography*, Barbara Rowe. *Don't You Want Somebody To Love*, Darby Slick.

GREEN, AL
ALBUMS: *Back Up Train* (1967)★★★, *Green Is Blues* (Hi 1970)★★★, *Al Green Gets Next To You* (Hi 1971)★★★★, *Let's Stay Together* (Hi 1972)★★★★, *Al Green* (Bell1972)★★★, *I'm Still In Love With You* (Hi 1972)★★★★, *Call Me* (Hi 1973)★★★★, *Livin' For You* (Hi 1973)★★★★, *Al Green Explores Your Mind* (Hi 1974)★★★★, *Al Green Is Love* (Hi 1975)★★★, *Full Of Fire* (Hi 1976)★★★, *Have A Good Time* (Hi 1976)★★★, *The Belle Album* (Hi 1977)★★★★, *Truth 'N' Time* (Hi 1978)★★★★, *The Lord Will Make A Way* (Myrrh 1980)★★★, *Higher Plane* (Myrrh 1981)★★★, *Tokyo Live* (Hi 1981)★★★★, *Precious Lord* (Myrhh 1982)★★, *I'll Rise Again* (Myrrh 1983)★★★, *Trust In God* (Myrrh 1984)★★★, *He Is The Light* (A&M 1985)★★★, *Going Away* (A&M 1986)★★★, *White Christmas* (Hi 1986)★★, *Soul Survivor* (A&M 1987)★★★, *I Get Joy* (A&M 1989)★★★, *Don't Look Back* (RCA 1993)★★★, *In Good Hands* (MCA 1995)★★★.
COMPILATIONS: *Greatest Hits* (Hi 1975)★★★★★, *Greatest Hits, Volume 2* (Hi 1977)★★★★, *The Cream Of Al Green* (Hi 1980)★★★★, *Spotlight On Al Green* (PRT 1981)★★★★, *Take Me To The River (Greatest Hits Volume 2)* (Hi 1987)★★★★, *Hi-Life – The Best Of Al Green* (K-Tel1988)★★★, *Love Ritual: Rare & Previously Unreleased 1968-1976* (Hi 1989)★★★★, *You Say It!* (Hi 1990)★★★, *One In A Million* (Word/Epic 1991)★★★★, *The Flipside Of Al Green* (1993)★★★.
VIDEOS: *Gospel According To Al Green* (Hendring Video 1990).

GREEN, PETER
ALBUMS: *The End Of The Game* (Reprise 1970)★★, *In The Skies* (PVK 1979)★★★, *Little Dreamer* (PVK 1980)★★★, *Whatcha Gonna Do* (PVK 1981)★★, *Blue Guitar* (Creole 1981)★★, *White Sky* (Headline 1982)★★, *Kolors* (Headline 1983)★★, *Legend* (Creole 1988)★★, tribute album *Rattlesnake Guitar: The Music Of Peter Green* (Coast To Coast 1995)★★★, *The Peter Green Splinter Group* (Snapper 1997)★★, *Bandit* (Milan 1997).
COMPILATIONS: *Backtrackin'* (Backtrackin' 1990)★★★.
FURTHER READING: *Peter Green: The Biography*, Martin Celmins.

GREEN DAY
ALBUMS: *39/Smooth* (Lookout 1990)★★★, *Kerplunk!* (Lookout 1992)★★★, *Dookie* (Reprise 1994)★★★★, *Insomniac* (Reprise 1995)★★, *Nimrod* (WEA 1997)★★.
COMPILATIONS: *1,039/Smoothed Out Slappy Hours* (Lookout 1991)★★.

GREEN ON RED
ALBUMS: *Green On Red* (Down There 1982)★★★, *Gravity Talks* (Slash 1983)★★★, *Gas Food Lodging* (Demon 1985)★★★, *No Free Lunch* (Mercury 1985)★★★, *The Killer Inside Me* (Mercury 1987)★★★★, *Here Come The Snakes* (Red Rhino 1989)★★★★, *Live At The Town And Country Club* mini-album (China/Polydor 1989)★★, *This Time Around* (China 1989)★★★, *Scapegoats* (China 1991)★★★, *Too Much Fun* (Off Beat 1993)★★★.
Solo: Dan Stuart *Danny And Dusty – The Lost Weekend* (1985)★★★, with Al Perry *Retronuevo* (1994)★★★, *Can O'Worms* (Normal 1995)★★★. Chris Cacavas *Junkyard Love* (Heyday 1988)★★★. Jack Waterson *Whose Dog?* (Heyday 1988)★★★.
COMPILATIONS: *Little Things In Life* (Music Club 1991)★★★★.

GREENBAUM, NORMAN
ALBUMS: *Spirit In The Sky* (Reprise 1970)★★, *Back Home Again* (Reprise 1971)★, *Petaluma* (Reprise 1972)★★.
COMPILATIONS: *Spirit In The Sky: The Best Of Norman Greenbaum* (Varese Sarabande 1996)★★★.

GREGSON AND COLLISTER
ALBUMS: *Home And Away* (Eleventh Hour 1986)★★★, *Mischief* (Special Delivery 1987)★★★, *A Change In The Weather* (Special Delivery 1989)★★★★, *Love Is A Strange Hotel* (Special Delivery 1990)★★★, *The Last Word* (Special Delivery 1992)★★★★. Solo: Clive Gregson *Strange Persuasions* (Demon 1985)★★★, *Welcome To The Workhouse* (Special Delivery 1990)★★★, *Carousel Of Noise* (Flypaper 1994)★★★, *People And Places* (Demon 1995)★★★, *I Love This Town* (Compass 1996)★★★.

GRIFFITH, NANCI
ALBUMS: *There's A Light Beyond These Woods* (BF Deal 1978)★★, *Poet In My Window* (Featherbed 1982)★★, *Once In A Very Blue Moon* (Philo 1985)★★★, *Last Of The True Believers* (Philo 1986)★★★★, *Lone Star State Of Mind* (MCA 1987)★★★★, *Little Love Affairs* (MCA 1988)★★★★, *One Fair Summer Evening* (MCA 1988)★★★★, *Storms* (MCA 1989)★★★★, *Late Night Grande Hotel* (MCA 1991)★★★★, *Other Voices Other Rooms* (Elektra 1993)★★★★, *Flyer* (Elektra 1994)★★★★, *Blue Roses From The Moon* (East West 1997)★★★★, *Other Voices Other Rooms 2* (1998)★★★★.
COMPILATIONS: *The Best Of* (MCA 1993)★★★★.

GROUNDHOGS
ALBUMS: *Scratching The Surface* (Liberty 1968)★★, *Blues Obituary* (Liberty 1969)★★★, *Thank Christ For The Bomb* (Liberty 1970)★★★, *Split* (Liberty 1971)★★★★, *Who Will Save The World?* (United Artists 1972)★★★, *Hogwash* (United Artists 1972)★★★, *Solid* (WWA 1974)★★, *Crosscut Saw* (United Artists 1976)★★, *Black Diamond* (United Artists 1976)★★, *Razor's Edge* (Conquest 1985)★★, *Back Against The Wall* (Demi-Monde 1987)★★, *Hogs On The Road* (Demi-Monde 1988)★★, as Tony McPhee's Groundhogs *Who Said Cherry Red?* (Indigo 1996)★★.
COMPILATIONS: *Groundhogs Best 1969-1972* (United Artists 1974)★★★, *Hoggin' The Stage* double album (Psycho 1984)★★★, *No Surrender* (Total 1990)★★, *Classic Album Cuts 1968 – 1976* (1992)★★★, *The Best Of ...* (EMI Gold 1997)★★★.

GTOs
ALBUMS: *Permanent Damage* (Straight 1969)★★.
FURTHER READING: *I'm With The Band*, Pamela Des Barres.

GUESS WHO
ALBUMS: *Shakin' All Over* (1965)★★, *It's Time* (1966)★★, *A Wild Pair* (King 1967)★★, *Wheatfield Soul* (RCA 1969)★★★, *Canned Wheat Packed By The Guess Who* (RCA 1969)★★★, *American Woman* (RCA 1970)★★, *Share The Land* (RCA 1970)★★★, *So Long, Bannatyne* (RCA 1971)★★★, *Rockin'* (RCA 1972)★★, *Live At The Paramount (Seattle)* (RCA 1972)★, *Artificial Paradise* (RCA 1973)★★, *#10* (RCA 1973)★★, *Road Food* (RCA 1974)★★, *Flavours* (RCA 1975)★, *Power In The Music* (RCA 1975)★★, *Lonely One* (Intersound 1995)★★.
COMPILATIONS: *The Best Of The Guess Who* (RCA 1971)★★★, *The Greatest Of The Guess Who* (RCA 1977)★★★.

GUIDED BY VOICES
ALBUMS: *Devil Between My Toes* (E 1987)★★, *Sandbox* (Halo 1987)★★, *Self Inflicted Aerial Nostalgia* (Halo 1989)★★, *Some Place The Fly Got Smashed* (Rocket Number 9 1990)★★★, *Propeller* (Rockathon 1992)★★★, *Vampire On Titus* (Scat 1993)★★★, *Bee Thousand* (Scat/Matador 1994)★★★★, *Crying Your Knife Away* (Lo-Fi 1994)★★★, *Alien Lanes* (Matador 1995)★★★★, *Under The Bushes, Under The Stars* (Scat/Matador 1996)★★★, *Mag Earwhig!* (Matador 1997)★★★★.
Solo: Robert Pollard *Not In My Airforce* (Matador 1996)★★★. Tobin Sprout *Carnival Boy* (Matador 1996)★★★, *Sunfish Holy Breakfast* (Matador 1996)★★★, *Moonflower Plastic (Welcome To My Wigwam)* (Matador 1997)★★.
COMPILATIONS: *Box* (Scat/Matador 1995)★★★★.

GUN (90s)
ALBUMS: *Taking On The World* (A&M 1989)★★★, *Gallus* (A&M 1992)★★★, *Swagger* (A&M 1994)★★★★, *0141 632 6326* (A&M 1997)★★.

GUN CLUB
ALBUMS: *Fire Of Love* (Ruby 1981)★★★, *Miami* (Animal 1982)★★, *Sex Beat 81* (Lolita 1984)★★, *The Las Vegas Story* (Animal 1984)★★★, *Danse Kalinda Boom: Live In Pandora's Box* (Dojo 1985)★★, *Mother Juno* (Fundamental 1987)★★★, *Pastoral Hide And Seek* (Fire 1990)★★★, *Divinity* (New Rose 1991)★★★, *The Gun Club Live In Europe* (Triple X 1992)★★, *Lucky Jim* (New Rose 1993)★★★.
COMPILATIONS: *Two Sides Of The Beast* (Dojo 1985)★★★, *In Exile* (Triple X 1992)★★★.
VIDEOS: *Live At The Hacienda, 1983* (1994), *Preaching The Blues* (Visionary 1995).

GUNS N'ROSES
ALBUMS: *Appetite For Destruction* (Geffen 1987)★★★★, *G N' R Lies* (Geffen 1989)★★★, *Use Your Illusion I* (Geffen 1991)★★★, *Use Your Illusion II* (Geffen 1991)★★★, *The Spaghetti Incident* (Geffen 1993)★★.
VIDEOS: *Use Your Illusion I* (1992), *Making Fuckin' Videos Vol1* (1993), *Making Fuckin' Videos Vol. 2* (1993), *The Making Of Estranged – Part IV Of The Trilogy* (1994).
FURTHER READING: *In Their Own Words*, Mark Putterford. *Appetite For Destruction: The Days Of Guns N'Roses*, Danny Sugerman. *Guns N'Roses: The World's Most Outrageous Hard Rock Band*, Paul Elliot. *The Most Dangerous Band In The World*, Mick Wall. *The Pictures*, George Chin. *Over The Top: The True Story Of ...*, Mark Putterford. *Lowlife In The Fast Lane*, Eddy McSquare. *Live!*, Mick St. Michael.

GUTHRIE, ARLO
ALBUMS: *Alice's Restaurant* (Reprise 1967)★★★★, *Arlo* (Reprise 1968)★★, *Running Down The Road* (Reprise 1969)★★★, *Alice's Restaurant* film soundtrack (Reprise 1969)★★, *Washington County* (Reprise 1970)★★★, *Hobo's Lullaby* (Reprise 1972)★★★, *Last Of The Brooklyn Cowboys* (Reprise 1973)★★★, *Arlo Guthrie* (Reprise 1974)★★★, with Pete Seeger *Together In Concert* (Reprise 1975)★★, *Amigo* (Reprise 1976)★★★★, *One Night* (Warners 1978)★★, *Outlasting The Blues* (Warners 1979)★★★★, *Power Of Love* (Warners 1981)★★★, with Pete Seeger *Precious Friend* (Warners 1982)★★★, *Someday* (Rising Son 1986)★★★, *All Over The World* (Rising Son 1991)★★★, *Son Of The Wind* (Rising Son 1992)★★★, *Mystic Journey* (Rising Son 1996)★★★.
COMPILATIONS: *The Best Of Arlo Guthrie* (Warners 1977)★★★.
FILMS: *Alice's Restaurant* (1969).

GUTHRIE, WOODY
ALBUMS: *Dust Bowl Ballads* 1940 recording (Folkways 1950)★★★★, *More Songs By Guthrie* (Meldisc 1955)★★★, *Songs To Grow On* (Folkways 1958)★★★, *Struggle* (Folkways 1958)★★★, *Bound For Glory* (Folkways 1958)★★★★, *Sacco & Vanzetti* (1960)★★★★, *Dust Bowl Ballads* 1940 recordings (Rounder 1964)★★★★, *Library Of Congress Recordings* 1940 recording (Folkways 1964)★★★★, *Bed On The Floor* (Verve/Folkways 1965)★★★, *Woodie Guthrie* (Xtra 1965)★★★, *Bonneville Dam And Other Columbia River Songs* (Verve/Folkways 1965)★★★, *Poor Boy* (Xtra 1966)★★★, *This Land Is Your Land* (Smithsonian/Folkways 1967)★★★★.
COMPILATIONS: *The Greatest Songs Of Woody Guthrie* (Vanguard 1972)★★★★, *Woodie Guthrie* (Ember 1968)★★★, *A Legendary Performer* (RCA 1977)★★★, *Poor Boy* (Transatlantic 1981)★★★, *Columbia River Collection* (Rounder 1988)★★★, *Folkways: The Original Vision* (1989)★★★★, *Long Ways To Travel The Unreleased Folkways Masters 1944-1949* (Smithsonian/Folkways 1994)★★★★, *Woody Guthrie Sings Folk Songs* (Smithsonian/Folkways 1995)★★★★, *Ballads Of Sacco & Vanzetti* (Smithsonian/Folkways 1996)★★★.
VIDEOS: *Vision Shared: A Tribute To Woody Guthrie* (CMV Enterprises 1989).
FURTHER READING: *Woody Guthrie Folk Songs*, Woody Guthrie. *American Folksong*, Woody Guthrie. *Born To Win*, Woody Guthrie and Robert Shelton (ed.). *A Mighty Hard Road: The Woody Guthrie Story*, Henrietta Yurchenco. *Bound For Glory*, Woody Guthrie. *Seeds Of Man: An Experience Lived And Dreamed*, Woody Guthrie. *Woody Guthrie: A Life*, Joe Klein. *Pastures Of Plenty – A Self Portrait*, Woody Guthrie. *Woody Guthrie: RollOn Columbia*, BillMurlin (ed.).

GUY, BUDDY
ALBUMS: *Blues From Big Bill's Copa Cobana* (1963), *A Man And The Blues* (Vanguard 1968)★★★★, *Coming At You* (Vanguard 1968)★★★, *This Is Buddy Guy* (Vanguard 1968)★★★★, *Blues Today* (Vanguard 1968)★★★, *This Is Buddy Guy* (Vanguard 1969)★★★★, *Hot And Cool* (Vanguard 1969)★★★, *First Time I Met The Blues* (Python 1969)★★★, with Junior Wells *Buddy And The Juniors* (Harvest 1970)★★★★, *Hold That Plane!* (Vanguard 1972)★★★, *Buddy Guy And Junior Wells Play The Blues* (Atlantic 1972)★★★★, *Got To Use Your House* (Blues Ball 1979)★★★, *Dollar Done Fell* (JSP 1982)★★★, *DJ Play My Blues* (JSP 1982)★★★, with Wells *Drinking' TNT And Smokin' Dynamite* (Red Lightnin' 1982)★★★, *The Original Blues Brothers – Live* (Blue Moon 1983)★★★, *Ten Blue Fingers* (JSP 1985)★★★, *Live At The Checkerboard, Chicago, 1979* (JSP 1988)★★★, *Breaking Out* (JSP 1988)★★★, with Wells *Alone & Acoustic* (Hightone 1991)★★★★, *Damn Right I Got The Blues* (Silvertone 1991)★★★★, with Wells *Alive In Montreux* (1992)★★★, *My Time After Awhile* (1992)★★★, *Feels Like Rain* (Silvertone 1993)★★★★, *American Bandstand Vol. 2* (1993)★★★, *Slippin' In* (Silvertone 1994)★★★, *Live! The Real Deal* (Silvertone 1996)★★★.
COMPILATIONS: *I Left My Blues In San Francisco* (Chess 1967)★★★, *I Was Walking Through The Woods* (Chess 1974)★★★, *Chess Masters* (Charly 1987)★★★★, *Stone Crazy* (Alligator 1988)★★★, *I Ain't Got No Money* (Flyright 1989)★★★, *The Best Of Buddy Guy* (Rhino 1992)★★★, *The Complete Chess Studio Sessions* (Chess 1992)★★★★.
VIDEOS: *Messin' With The Blues* (BMG Video 1991), *Buddy Guy Live: The Real Deal* (Wienerworld 1996).
FURTHER READING: *Damn Right I Got The Blues: Blues Roots Of Rock N Roll*, Donald E. Wilcock and Buddy Guy.

GWAR
ALBUMS: *Hell-O* (Shimmy Disc 1988), *Scumdogs Of The Universe* (Master 1990), *America Must Be Destroyed* (Zorro 1992), *This Toilet Earth* (Metal Blade 1994), *Ragnarπk* (Metal Blade 1995), *Carnival Of Chaos* (Metal Blade 1997).
VIDEOS: *The Movie* (1990), *Live From Antartica* (1990), *Phallus In Wonderland* (1992), *Tour De Scum* (1994), *Skulhedface* (Metal Blade) (1994).

H

H.P. LOVECRAFT
ALBUMS: *H.P. Lovecraft* (Philips 1967)★★★, *H.P. Lovecraft II* (Philips 1968)★★★, as Lovecraft *Valley Of The Moon* (1971)★★, as Lovecraft *We Love You Whoever You Are* (1975)★★, as H.P. Lovecraft *Live – May 11, 1968* (Sundazed 1992)★★.

HAIRCUT 100
ALBUMS: *Pelican West* (Arista 1982)★★★★, *Paint On Paint* (Arista 1984)★★.
COMPILATIONS: *Best Of Nick Heyward And Haircut 100* (Ariola 1989)★★★★, *The Greatest Hits Of Nick Heyward & Haircut 100* (RCA Camden 1996)★★★★.
FURTHER READING: *The Haircut 100 Catalogue*, Sally Payne. *Haircut 100: Not A Trace Of Brylcreem*, no editor listed.

HALEY, BILL, AND HIS COMETS
ALBUMS: *Rock With Bill Haley And The Comets* (Essex 1955)★★, *Live It Up* (1955)★★★, *Rock Around The Clock* (Decca 1956)★★★★, *Music For The Boyfriend* (Decca 1956)★★, *Rock And Roll Stage Show* (Decca 1956)★★★★, *Rock The Joint* (1957)★★★, *Rocking The Oldies* (Decca 1957)★★, *Rocking The Joint* (Decca 1958)★★★, *Rockin' Around The World* (Decca 1958)★★★, *Bill Haley's Chicks* (Decca 1959)★★★, *Strictly Instrumental* (Decca 1960)★★, *Bill Haley And His Comets* (Warners 1960)★★★, *Bill Haley's Jukebox* (Warners 1960)★★★, *Twistin' Knights At The Round Table* (Roulette 1962)★★★, *Bill Haley And The Comets* (Vocalion 1963)★★, *Rip It Up* (1968)★★★, *Live At The Bitter End* (Kama Sutra 1970)★, *Travelin' Band* (Janus 1970)★★, *Golden King Of Rock* (1972)★★★, *Just Rock And Roll Music* (1973)★★★, *Live In London '74* (1974)★★, *Rock Around The Country* (1974)★★.
COMPILATIONS: *Bill Haley's Greatest Hits* (Decca 1967)★★★, *King Of Rock* (Ember 1968)★★★, *Mister Rock 'n' Roll* (Ember 1969)★★★, *The Bill Haley Collection* (1976)★★★, *R-O-C-K* (1976)★★★, *Armchair Rock 'N' Roll* (1978)★★★, *Everyone Can Rock 'N' Roll* (1980)★★★, *A Tribute To Bill Haley* (1981)★★★, *The Essential Bill Haley* (1984)★★★, *Hillbilly Haley* (1984)★★★, *Greatest Hits* (1985)★★★, *From The Original Master Tapes* (1985)★★★, *Boogie With Bill Haley* (1985)★★★, *Golden Greats* (1985)★★★, *The Original Hits '54-'57* (1987)★★★, *Greatest Hits* (1988)★★★, *Rip It Up Rock 'N' Roll* (1988)★★★, *Golden CD Collection* (1989)★★★, *The Original Hits '54-'57* (1990)★★★, *Bill Haley's Rock 'N' Roll Scrapbook* (1990)★★★, *The Decca Years And More* 5-CD box set (1991)★★★.
Don't Knock The Rock (1956).

HALF MAN HALF BISCUIT
ALBUMS: *Back In The DHSS* (Probe Plus 1986)★★★, *McIntyre, Treadmore And Davitt* (Probe Plus 1991)★★★, *This Leaden Pall* (Probe Plus 1993)★★★, *Some Call It Godcore* (Probe Plus 1995)★★★, *Voyage To The Bottom Of The Road* (Probe 1997)★★★.
COMPILATIONS: *Back Again In The DHSS* (Probe Plus 1987)★★★, *ACD* same album as *Back Again* on CD with extra tracks (Probe Plus 1989)★★★.
VIDEOS: *Live* (Alternative Image 1993).

HALL AND OATES
ALBUMS: *Whole Oates* (Atlantic 1972)★★, *Abandoned Luncheonette* (Atlantic 1973)★★★, *War Babies* (Atlantic 1974)★★, *Hall & Oates* (RCA 1975)★★, *Bigger Than Both Of Us* (RCA 1976)★★, *Beauty On A Back Street* (RCA 1977)★★★, *Livetime* (RCA 1978)★★, *Along The Red Ledge* (RCA 1978)★★★, *X-Static* (RCA 1979)★★, *Voices* (RCA 1980)★★★, *Private Eyes* (RCA 1981)★★★★, *H_2O* (RCA 1982)★★★★, *Bim Bam Boom* (RCA 1984)★★★, with Eddie Kendrick, David Ruffin *Live At The Apollo* (RCA 1985)★★★, *Ooh Yeah!* (Arista 1988)★★, *Change Of Season* (Arista 1990)★★, *Really Smokin'* (1993)★★, *Marigold Sky* (Push/BMG 1997)★★.

Solo: Daryl Hall *Sacred Songs* (RCA 1980)★★, *Three Hearts In The Happy Ending Machine* (RCA 1986)★★, *Soul Alone* (Epic 1993)★★★.
COMPILATIONS: *No Goodbyes* (Atlantic 1977)★★★, *The Atlantic Collection* (Rhino 1996)★★★★.

HALLYDAY, JOHNNY
ALBUMS: *Johnny Hallyday Sings America's Rockin' Hits* (Philips 1961)★★★, *Flagrant Delit* (1975)★★★, *Drole De Metier* (1986)★★★, *Triff De Rattles* (1986)★★★, *Les Grands Success De Johnny Hallyday* (1988)★★★, *La Peur* (1988)★★★, *La Nuit Johnny* 42-CD box set (1993)★★★.

HAMMER, M.C.
ALBUMS: As M.C. Hammer *Feel My Power* (Bustin' 1987)★★★, *Let's Get It Started* (Capitol 1988)★★★, *Please Hammer Don't Hurt 'Em* (Capitol 1990)★★★, *Inside Out* (Giant 1995)★★. As Hammer *Too Legit To Quit* (Capitol 1991)★★, *The Funky Headhunter* (RCA 1994)★★.
FURTHER READING: *M.C. Hammer: U Can't Touch This*, Bruce Dessau.

HAMMILL, PETER
ALBUMS: *Fool's Mate* (Charisma 1971)★★★, *Chameleon In The Shadow Of Night* (Charisma 1973)★★★, *The Silent Corner And The Empty Stage* (Charisma 1974)★★★, *In Camera* (Charisma 1974)★★, *Nadir's Big Chance* (Charisma 1975)★★★, *Over* (Charisma 1977)★★★, *The Future Now* (Charisma 1978)★★★, *ph7* (Charisma 1979)★★★, *A Black Box* (S Type 1980)★★★, *Sitting Targets* (Virgin 1981)★★★, *Enter K* (Naive 1982)★★★, *Patience* (Naive 1983)★★★, *Loops And Reels* (Sofa 1983)★★★, *The Love Songs* (Charisma 1984)★★★, *The Margin – Live* (Foundry 1985)★★★, *Skin* (Foundry 1986)★★★, *And Close As This* (Virgin 1986)★★★★, *In A Foreign Town* (Enigma 1988)★★★, *Out Of Water* (Enigma 1990)★★★, *Room Temperature Live* (1990)★★★, *No Way Out* (1990)★★★, *The Fall Of The House Of Usher* (World Chief 1991)★, *Fireships* (Fie! 1992)★★, *The Noise* (1993)★★, with Guy Evans *Spur Of The Moment* (Red Hot 1993)★★★, *There Goes The Daylight* (1994)★★★, Peter Hammill And The K Group *The Margin, Roaring Forties* (1994)★★★, *The Peel Sessions* (Windsong 1995)★★★, *X My Heart* (Fie! 1996)★★★, *Everyone You Hold* (Fie 1997).
COMPILATIONS: *The Calm After The Storm* (Virgin 1993)★★★, *After The Show* (1996)★★★.
VIDEOS: *In The Passionskirche, Berlin MVMXCII* (Studio 1993).
FURTHER READING: *The Lemming Chronicles*, David Shaw-Parker. *Killers, Angels, Refugees*, Peter Hammill. *Mirrors, Dreams And Miracles*, Peter Hammill.

HAMMOND, ALBERT
ALBUMS: *It Never Rains In Southern California* (Mum 1973)★★, *Free Electric Band* (Mum 1973)★★★, *Albert Hammond* (Mum 1974)★★.

HANCOCK, HERBIE
ALBUMS: *Takin' Off* (Blue Note 1962)★★★★, *My Point Of View* (Blue Note 1963)★★★★, *Inventions And Dimensions* (Blue Note 1963)★★★, *Empyrean Isles* (Blue Note 1964)★★★★, *Maiden Voyage* (Blue Note 1965)★★★★, *Blow Up* (MGM 1967)★★★, *Speak Like A Child* (Blue Note 1968)★★★, *The Prisoner* (Blue Note 1969)★★★, *Mwandishi* (Warners 1971)★★★★, *Crossings* (Warners 1972)★★★★, *Sextant* (Columbia 1973)★★★★, *Headhunters* (Columbia 1974)★★★★★, *Thrust* (Columbia 1974)★★★, *Man-Child* (Columbia 1975)★★★★, *V.S.O.P.* (Columbia 1976)★★★★, *V.S.O.P: The Quintet* (Columbia 1977)★★★★, *An Evening With Herbie Hancock And Chick Corea* (Columbia 1978)★★★, *Feets Don't Fail Me Now* (Columbia 1979)★★, *Mr Hands* (Columbia 1980)★★★, *Hancock Alley* (Manhattan 1980)★★★, *Quartet* (Columbia 1982)★★★, *Future Shock* (Columbia 1983)★★★★, *Hot And Heavy* (Premier 1984)★★ *Herbie Hancock And The Rockit Band* (Columbia 1984)★★★, with Dexter Gordon *'Round Midnight* film soundtrack (Columbia 1986)★★★, with Wayne Shorter, Ron Carter, Wallace Roney, Tony Williams *A Tribute To Miles* (QWest/Reprise 1994)★★★, *Dis Is Da Drum* (Mercury 1995)★★★, *The New Standard* (Verve 1996)★★★, with Wayne Shorter *1+1* (Verve 1997)★★★.
COMPILATIONS: *Greatest Hits* (Columbia 1980)★★★, *A Jazz Collection* (Sony 1991)★★★, *Best Of Vol. 2* (1992)★★★, *Mwandishi: The Complete Warner Bros. Recordings* (Warners 1994)★★★.
VIDEOS: *Herbie Hancock And The Rockit Band* (Columbia 1984).

HANOI ROCKS
ALBUMS: *Bangkok Shocks, Saigon Shakes, Hanoi Rocks* (Johanna 1981)★★★, *Oriental Beat* (Johanna 1982)★★★, *Self Destruction Blues* (Johanna 1982)★★★, *Back To Mystery City* (Lick 1983)★★★, *Two Steps From The Move* (Columbia 1984)★★★.
COMPILATIONS: *Best Of Hanoi Rocks* (Lick 1985)★★★, *Tracks From A Broken Dream* (Lick 1990)★★★.
VIDEOS: *All Those Wasted Years* (1988), *The Nottingham Tapes* (1988).

HANSON
ALBUMS: *Middle Of Nowhere* (Mercury 1997)★★★, *Snowed In* (Polygram 1997)★★★, *Three Car Garage* (Warner Brothers 1998)★★★.

HAPPY MONDAYS
ALBUMS: *Squirrel And G-Man Twenty Four Hour Party People Plastic Face Carnt Smile (White Out)* (Factory 1987)★★★, *Bummed* (Factory 1988)★★★, *Pills 'N' Thrills And Bellyaches* (Factory 1990)★★★★, *Live* (Factory 1991)★★, *Yes Please!* (Factory 1992)★★, *The Peel Sessions* (Strange Fruit 1996)★★.
COMPILATION: *Loads – The Best Of* (London 1995)★★★.

HARDCASTLE, PAUL
ALBUMS: *Zero One* (Blue Bird 1985)★★, *Paul Hardcastle* (Chrysalis 1985)★★★, *No Winners* (Chrysalis 1988)★★, *First Light* (Connoisseur 1997)★.
COMPILATIONS: *Soul Syndicate* (K-Tel 1988)★★.

HARDIN, TIM
ALBUMS: *Tim Hardin 1* (Verve Forecast 1966)★★★, *Tim Hardin 2* (Verve Forecast 1967)★★★, *This Is Tim Hardin* (Atco 1967)★★, *Tim Hardin 3 Live In Concert* (Verve Forecast 1968)★★★, *Tim Hardin 4* (Verve Forecast 1969)★★★, *Suite For Susan Moore And Damion/We Are – One, One, All In One* (Columbia 1969)★★★, *Golden Archive Series* (MGM 1970)★★★, *Bird On A Wire* (Columbia 1971)★★, *Painted Head* (Columbia 1972)★★★, *Archetypes* (MGM 1973)★★★, *Nine* (GM/Antilles 1974)★★★, *The Shock Of Grace* (Columbia 1981)★★★, *The Homecoming Concert* (Line 1981)★★★.
COMPILATIONS: *Best Of Tim Hardin* (Verve Forecast 1969)★★★★, *Memorial Album* (Polydor 1981)★★★, *Reason To Believe (The Best Of)* (Polydor 1987)★★★★, *Hang On To A Dream – The Verve Recordings* (Polydor 1994)★★★★, *Simple Songs Of Freedom: The Tim Hardin Collection* (Columbia 1996)★★★★.

HARPER, BEN
ALBUMS: *Welcome To The Cruel World* (Virgin 1994)★★★, *Fight For Your Mind* (Virgin 1995)★★★, *The Will To Live* (Virgin 1997)★★★.

HARPER, ROY
ALBUMS: *The Sophisticated Beggar* (Strike 1966)★★, *Come Out Fighting Genghis Smith* (Columbia 1967)★★★, *Folkjokeopus* (Liberty 1969)★★, *Flat, Baroque And Berserk* (Harvest 1970)★★★, *Stormcock* (Harvest 1971)★★★★, *Lifemask* (Harvest 1973)★★★★, *Valentine* (Harvest 1974)★★★, *Flashes From The Archives Of Oblivion* (Harvest 1974)★★★, *HQ* retitled *When An Old Cricketer Leaves The Crease* (Harvest 1975)★★★, *Bullinamingvase* (Harvest 1977)★★★★, *The Unknown Soldier* (Harvest 1980)★★, *Work Of Heart* (Public 1981)★★★, with Jimmy Page *Whatever Happened To Jugula* (Beggars Banquet 1985)★★, *Born In Captivity* (Hardup 1985)★★★, *In Between Every Line* (Harvest 1986)★★, *Descendants Of Smith* (EMI 1988)★★★, *Loony On The Bus* (Awareness 1988)★★, *Once* (Awareness 1990)★★★, *Death Or Glory?* (Awareness 1992)★★★, *The BBC Tapes Vol. 1* (Science Friction 1997)★★★★, *The BBC Tapes Vol. 2* (Science Friction 1997)★★★★, *The BBC Tapes Vol. 3* (Science Friction 1997)★★★★, *The BBC Tapes Vol. 4* (Science Friction 1997)★★★, *The BBC Tapes Vol. 5* (Science Friction 1997), *The BBC Tapes Vol. 6* (Science Friction 1997).
COMPILATIONS: *Harper 1970-1975* (Harvest 1978)★★★★.

HARPERS BIZARRE
ALBUMS: *Feelin' Groovy* (Warners 1967)★★★, *Anything Goes* (Warners 1967)★★, *The Secret Life Of Harpers Bizarre* (Warners 1968)★★, *Harpers Bizarre 4* (1969)★★, *As Time Goes By* (1976)★.

HARRIS, EMMYLOU
ALBUMS: *Gliding Bird* (Jubilee 1970)★★, *Pieces Of The Sky* (Reprise 1975)★★★★, *Elite Hotel* (Reprise 1976)★★★, *Luxury Liner* (Reprise 1977)★★★★, *Quarter Moon In A 10 Cent Town* (Reprise 1978)★★★, *Blue Kentucky Girl* (Reprise 1979)★★★, *Roses In The Snow* (Reprise 1980)★★★★, *Light Of The Stable* (Reprise 1980)★★★, *Evangeline* (Reprise 1981)★★★, *Cimmaron* (Reprise 1981)★★★, *Last Date* (Reprise 1982)★★★, *White Shoes* (Warners 1983)★★★, *The Ballad Of Sally Rose* (Reprise 1985)★★★, *13* (Reprise 1986)★★★, with Dolly Parton, Linda Ronstadt *Trio* (Warners 1987)★★★, *Angel Band* (Reprise 1987)★★★, *Bluebird* (Reprise 1988)★★★, *Duets* (Warners 1990)★★★★, *Brand New Dance* (Reprise 1990)★★★, *At The Ryman* (Reprise 1992)★★★, with Carl Jackson *Nashville Country Duets* (1993)★★★, *Cowgirl's Prayer* (Asylum 1993)★★★, *Songs Of The West* (Warners 1994)★★★, *Wrecking Ball* (Grapevine 1995)★★★★, *Nashville* (Sundown 1996)★★★.
COMPILATIONS: *Profile (The Best Of Emmylou Harris)* (Reprise 1978)★★★★, *Profile II (The Best Of Emmylou Harris)* (Reprise 1984)★★★, *Her Best Songs* (K-Tel 1980)★★★, *Portraits* 3-CD box set (Reprise Archives 1996)★★★★.
VIDEOS: *Thanks To You* (1990), *At The Ryman* (1992).

HARRIS, JET, AND TONY MEEHAN
COMPILATIONS: *Remembering: Jet Harris And Tony Meehan* (Decca 1976)★★★, *The Jet Harris And Tony Meehan Story Volumes 1 & 2* (1976)★★★, *Diamonds* (1983)★★★.

HARRISON, GEORGE
ALBUMS: *Wonderwall* (Apple 1968)★★, *Electronic Sound* (Zapple 1969)★★, *All Things Must Pass* (Apple 1970)★★★★, with other artists *The Concert For Bangla Desh* (Apple 1972)★★★, *Living In The Material World* (Apple 1973)★★★, *Dark Horse* (Apple 1974)★, *Extra Texture* (Apple 1975)★★, *Thirty Three And A Third* (Dark Horse 1976)★★★, *George Harrison* (Dark Horse 1979)★★★, *Somewhere In England* (Dark Horse 1981)★★, *Gone Troppo* (Dark Horse 1982)★, *Cloud Nine* (Dark Horse 1987)★★★, *Live In Japan* (1992)★★.
COMPILATIONS: *The Best Of George Harrison* (Parlophone 1977)★★★, *Best Of Dark Horse 1976-1989* (Dark Horse 1989)★★★.
FILMS: *A Hard Day's Night* (1964), *Help!* (1965), *Magical Mystery Tour* (1968), *Let It Be* (1971)
FURTHER READING: *George Harrison Yesterday And Today*, Ross Michaels. *I Me Mine*, George Harrison. *I Me Mine: Limited Edition*, George Harrison. *Fifty Years Adrift*, George Harrison and Derek Taylor. *Dark Horse: The Secret Life Of George Harrison*, Geoffrey Giuliano. *The Quiet One: A Life Of George Harrison*, Alan Clayson. *The Illustrated George Harrison*, Geoffrey Giuliano.

HARRISON, WILBERT
ALBUMS: *Kansas City* (Sphere Sound 1965)★★★, *Let's Work Together* (Sue 1970)★★★, *Shoot You Full Of Love* (Juggernaut 1971)★★, *Anything You Want* (1971)★★, *Wilbert Harrison* (Buddah 1971)★★, *Soul Food Man* (Chelsea 1976)★★, *Lovin' Operator* (Charly 1985)★★, *Small Labels* (Krazy Kat 1986)★★, *Listen To My Song* (Savoy Jazz 1987)★★.
COMPILATIONS: *Kansas City* (Relic 1990)★★★★.

HARRY, DEBORAH
ALBUMS: *Koo Koo* (Chrysalis 1981)★★, *Rockbird* (Chrysalis 1986)★★, *Def, Dumb And Blonde* (Chrysalis 1989)★★★, *Debravation* (Chrysalis 1993)★★, with the Jazz Passengers *Individually Twisted* (32 Records 1997)★★★.
COMPILATIONS: *Once More Into The Bleach* (Chrysalis 1988)★★★, *The Complete Picture – The Very Best Of Deborah Harry And Blondie* (Chrysalis 1990)★★★★.

HARTMAN, DAN
ALBUMS: *Images* (Blue Sky 1976)★★, *Instant Replay* (Blue Sky 1978)★★★, *Relight My Fire* (Blue Sky 1980)★★, *I Can Dream About You* (MCA 1985)★★, *White Boy* (1986)★★, *New Green Clear Blue* (RCA 1989)★★, *Keep The Fire Burnin'* (Chaos/Columbia 1994).

HARVEY, ALEX
ALBUMS: *Alex Harvey And His Soul Band* (Polydor 1964)★★★, *The Blues* (Polydor 1964)★★★, *Hair Rave Up Live From The Shaftesbury Theatre* (1969)★★, *Roman Wall Blues* (Fontana 1969)★★, *Alex Harvey Narrates The Loch Ness Monster* (K-Tel 1977)★★, *The Mafia Stole My Guitar* (RCA 1979)★★, *The Soldier On The Wall* (Power Supply 1983)★★★.
COMPILATIONS: *The Alex Harvey Collection* (1986)★★★.

HATFIELD, JULIANA
ALBUMS: *Hey Babe* (Mammoth 1992)★★, *Become What You Are* (Mammoth 1993)★★★, *Only Everything* (Mammoth 1995)★★★.

HATFIELD AND THE NORTH
ALBUMS: *Hatfield And The North* (Virgin 1974)★★★, *The Rotters' Club* (Virgin 1975)★★★.
COMPILATIONS: *Afters* (Virgin 1980)★★★.

HAVENS, RICHIE
ALBUMS: *Mixed Bag* (Verve/Forecast 1967)★★★★, *Richie Havens Record* (Douglas 1968)★★, *Electric Havens* (Douglas 1968)★★, *Something Else Again* (Forecast 1968)★★★, *Richard P. Havens 1983* (Forecast 1969)★★★★, *Stonehenge* (Stormy Forest 1970)★★, *Alarm Clock* (Stormy Forest 1971)★★★, *The Great Blind Degree* (Stormy Forest 1971)★★, *Richie Havens On Stage* (Stormy Forest 1972)★★★, *Portfolio* (Stormy Forest 1973)★★★, *Mixed Bag II* (Stormy Forest 1974)★★, *The End Of The Beginning* (A&M 1976)★★, *Mirage* (A&M 1977)★★, *Connections* (Elektra 1980)★★, *Common Ground* (Connexion 1984)★★, *Simple Things* (RBI 1987)★, *Richie Havens Sings The Beatles And Dylan* (Rykodisc 1987)★★, *Live At The Cellar Door* (Five Star 1990)★★★, *Now* (Solar/Epic 1991)★★★, *Cuts To The Chase* (Rhino/Forward 1994)★★★.
COMPILATIONS: *A State Of Mind* (1971)★★★, *Resumé* (Rhino 1993)★★★★.
FILMS: *Catch My Soul* (1974), *Hearts of Fire* (1989).

HAWKES, CHESNEY
ALBUMS: *Buddy's Song* soundtrack (Chrysalis 1991)★★, *Get The Picture* (Chrysalis 1993)★.

HAWKINS, RONNIE
ALBUMS: *Ronnie Hawkins* (Roulette 1959)★★, *Mr. Dynamo* (Roulette 1960)★★, *The Folk Ballads Of Ronnie Hawkins* (Roulette 1960)★★, *Ronnie Hawkins Sings The Songs Of Hank Williams* (Roulette 1961)★★, *Ronnie Hawkins* (1969)★★, *Ronnie Hawkins* (Cotillion 1970)★★, *Arkansas Rock Pile* (Roulette 1970)★★, *The Hawk I* (1971)★★, *Rock And Roll Resurrection* (Monument 1972)★★, *The Giant Of Rock And Roll* (1974)★★, *The Hawk II* (United Artists 1979)★★, *Rrrracket Time* (Charly 1979)★★, *A Legend In His Spare Time* (1981)★★, *The Hawk And Rock* (1982)★★, *Making It Again* (1984)★★, *Hello Again ... Mary Lou* (1991)★★.
COMPILATIONS: *The Best Of Ronnie Hawkins & His Band* (Roulette 1970)★★★, *The Best Of Ronnie Hawkins And The Hawks* (Rhino 1990)★★★.
VIDEOS: *The Hawk In Concert* (MMG VIdeo 1988), *This Country's Rockin' – Reunion Concert* (1993).
FURTHER READING: *The Hawk: The Story Of Ronnie Hawkins & The Hawks*, Ian Wallis.

HAWKINS, 'SCREAMIN' JAY'
ALBUMS: *At Home With Screamin' Jay Hawkins* (Epic 1958)★★★, *I Put A Spell On You* (Epic 1959)★★★★, *The Night & Day Of Screamin' Jay Hawkins* (Planet 1965)★★★, *What That Is* (Philips 1969)★★, *Screamin' Jay Hawkins* (Philips 1970)★★★, *A Portrait Of A Man & His Woman* (1972)★★★, *I Put A Spell On You* (1977)★★★, *Frenzy* (Edsel 1982)★★, *Real Life* (Charly 1983)★★, *Midnight* (1985)★★, *Live And Crazy* (Midnight Music 1986)★★★, *Feast Of The Mau Mau* (Edsel 1988)★★, *Real Life* (Charly 1989)★★★, *I Is* (1989)★★★, *I Want To Do It In A Cave!* (1990)★★★, *Voodoo Jive* (1990)★★★, *Black Music For White People* (Demon 1991)★★★, *Stone Crazy* (Demon 1993)★★★, *Somethin' Funny Goin' On* (Demon 1994)★★★, *Screamin' The Blues* (1998)★★★.
COMPILATIONS: *I Put A Spell On You* (Direction 1969)★★★, *Screamin' The Blues* (Red Lightin' 1982)★★★, *Frenzy* (Edsel 1986)★★★, *I Put A Spell On You* (Charly 1989)★★★, *Spellbound 1955-1974* (Bear Family 1990)★★★, *Voodoo Jive: The Best Of Screamin' Jay Hawkins* (Rhino 1990)★★★, *Cow Fingers And Mosquito Pie* (Epic 1991)★★★, *Screamin' Jay Hawkins – 1952-1955* (Magpie 1991)★★★, *From Gotham And Grand* (SJH 1992)★★★, *Portrait Of A Man* (Edsel 1995)★★★, *Alligator Wine* (Music Club 1997)★★★.
FILMS: *American Hot Wax* (1976), *Mystery Train* (1989).

HAWKWIND
ALBUMS: *Hawkwind* (Liberty 1970)★★★, *In Search Of Space* (United Artists 1971)★★★, *Doremi Fasol Latido* (United Artists 1972)★★, *Space Ritual Alive* (United Artists 1973)★★, *Hall Of The Mountain Grill* (United Artists 1974)★★★, *Warrior On The Edge Of Time* (United Artists 1975)★★★, *Astounding Sounds Amazing Music* (Charisma 1976)★★★, *Quark, Strangeness And Charm* (Charisma 1977)★★, *25 Years On* (Charisma 1978)★★, *PXR 5* (Charisma 1979)★★★, *Live 1979* (Bronze 1980)★★, *Levitation* (Bronze 1980)★★★, *Sonic Attack* (RCA 1981)★★★, *Church Of Hawkwind* (RCA 1982)★★★, *Choose Your Masques* (RCA 1982)★★★, *Zones* (Flicknife 1983)★★★, *The Chronicle Of The Black Sword* (Flicknife 1985)★★★, *The Xenon Codex* (GWR 1988)★★★, *Night Of The Hawk* (Powerhouse 1989)★★★, *Space Bandits* (GWR 1990)★★★, *Palace Springs* (GWR 1991)★★, *Electric Tepee* (Essential 1992)★★★, *It Is The Business Of The Future To Be Dangerous* (Essential 1993)★★★, *The Business Trip* (Emergency Broadcast Systems 1994)★★, *Future Reconstructions: Ritual Of The Solstice* (Emergency Broadcast Systems 1996)★★★. Solo: Alan Davey *Captured Rotation* (Emergency Broadcasting Systems 1996)★★★.
COMPILATIONS: *Road Hawks* (United Artists 1976)★★★, *Masters Of The Universe* (United Artists 1977)★★★, *Repeat Performances* (Charisma 1980)★★★, *Space Ritual Volume 2* (American Phonograph 1985)★★★, *Anthology – Hawkwind Volumes 1, 2 and 3* (Samurai 1985-1986)★★★, *Live 70/73* (Dojo 1986)★★, *The Collection* (Castle 1986)★★★★, *Angels Of Death* (RCA 1986)★★★, *Mighty Hawkwind Classics* (Anagram 1992)★★★, *Lord Of Light* (Cleopatra 1993)★★★.
VIDEOS: *Night Of The Hawks* (1984), *Chronicle Of The Black Sword* (1986), *Live Legends* (1990), *Treworgy Tree Fayre* (1990), *The Academy* (1991), *Promo Collection* (1992), *Hawkwind: The Solstice At Stonehenge 1984* (1993).
FURTHER READING: *This Is Hawkwind, Do Not Panic*, Kris Tate.

HAYES, ISAAC
ALBUMS: *Presenting Isaac Hayes* later reissued as *In The Beginning* (Stax 1967)★★, *Hot Buttered Soul* (Enterprise 1969)★★★★, *The Isaac Hayes Movement* (Enterprise 1970)★★, *To Be Continued* (Enterprise 1970)★★, *Shaft* (Enterprise 1971)★★★★, *Black Moses* (Enterprise 1971)★★, *Live At The Sahara Tahoe* (Enterprise 1973)★★, *Joy* (Enterprise 1973)★★, *Tough Guys* film soundtrack (Enterprise 1974)★★, *Truck Turner* film soundtrack (Enterprise 1974)★★, *Chocolate Chip* (HBS 1975)★★★, *Use Me* (Enterprise 1975)★★, *Disco Connection* (HBS 1976)★★, *Groove-A-Thon* (HBS 1976)★, *Juicy Fruit (Disco Freak)* (HBS 1976)★, with Dionne Warwick *A Man And A Woman* (HBS 1977)★, *New Horizon* (Polydor 1977)★, *Memphis Movement* (1977)★, *Hot Bed* (Stax 1978)★★, *For The Sake Of Love* (Polydor 1978)★, *Don't Let Go* (Polydor 1979)★★, with Millie Jackson *Royal Rappin's* (Polydor 1979)★★, *And Once Again* (Polydor 1980)★★, *Light My Fire* (1980)★★, *A Lifetime Thing* (Polydor 1981)★★, *U Turn* (Columbia 1984)★★, *Love Attack* (Columbia 1988)★★, *Branded* (Pointblank 1995)★★, *Raw And Refined* (Pointblank 1995)★★.
COMPILATIONS: *The Best Of Isaac Hayes* (Enterprise 1975)★★★, *The Isaac Hayes Chronicle* (1978)★★★, *Enterprise – His Greatest Hits* (Stax 1980)★★★★, *Best Of Isaac Hayes, Volumes 1 & 2* (Stax 1986)★★★, *Isaac's Moods* (Stax 1988)★★★, *Greatest Hit Singles* (Stax 1991)★★★, *The Collection* (Connoisseur Collection 1995)★★★.

HEALEY, JEFF
ALBUMS: *See The Light* (Arista 1989)★★★★, *Hell To Pay* (Arista 1990)★★, *Feel This* (Arista 1992)★★★, *Cover To Cover* (Arista 1995)★★★.
FILMS: *Roadhouse* (1989).
VIDEOS: *See The Light From London* (Arista 1989).

HEART
ALBUMS: *Dreamboat Annie* (Mushroom 1976)★★★★, *Little Queen* (Portrait 1977)★★★, *Dog And Butterfly* (Portrait 1978)★★★★, *Magazine* (Mushroom 1978)★★, *Bebe Le Strange* (Portrait 1980)★★★, *Greatest Hits/Live* (Portrait 1981)★★★, *Private Audition* (Epic 1982)★★, *Passionworks* (Epic 1983)★★, *Heart* (Capitol 1985)★★, *Bad Animals* (Capitol 1987)★★, *Brigade* (Capitol 1990)★★, *Rock The House Live!* (Capitol 1991)★★, *Desire Walks On* (Capitol 1993)★★, *The Road Home* (Capitol 1995)★★★.
COMPILATION: *Greatest Hits* (Capitol 1997)★★★.
VIDEOS: *If Looks Could Kill* (1988), *The Road Home* (Capitol 1995).

HEARTBREAKERS
ALBUMS: *L.A.M.F.* (Track 1977)★★, *Live At Max's Kansas City* (Max's Kansas City 1979)★★, *D.T.K. Live At The Speakeasy* (Jungle 1982)★★, *Live At The Lyceum Ballroom 1984* (ABC 1984)★★, *L.A.M.F. Revisited* remixed version of their debut (Jungle 1984)★★★.
COMPILATIONS: *D.T.K. – L.A.M.F.* (Jungle 1984)★★★.

HEATWAVE
ALBUMS: *Too Hot To Handle* (Epic 1977)★★★★, *Central Heating* (Epic 1978)★★★, *Hot Property* (Epic 1979)★★, *Candles* (Epic 1980)★★★, *Current* (Epic 1982)★★, *Live At The Greek Theater* (Century Vista 1997).
COMPILATIONS: *Best Of* (Epic 1993)★★★★.

HEAVEN 17
ALBUMS: *Penthouse And Pavement* (Virgin 1981)★★★, *Heaven 17* (Virgin 1983)★★★, *The Luxury Gap* (Virgin 1983)★★★, *How Men Are* (BEF 1984)★★, *Endless* (Virgin 1986)★★, *Pleasure One* (Virgin 1987)★★★, *Teddy Bear, Duke & Psycho* (Virgin 1988)★★★, *That's How Love Is* (1989)★★, *Bigger Than America* (Warners 1996)★★.
COMPILATIONS: *Higher & Higher (The Very Best Of...)* (Virgin 1993)★★★.

HEAVY D AND THE BOYZ
ALBUMS: *Living Large* (MCA 1987)★★★, *Big Tyme* (Uptown 1989)★★★★, *Peaceful Journey* (Uptown 1991)★★★, *Blue Funk* (Uptown 1992)★★★, *Nuttin' But Love* (Uptown 1994)★★★★, *Waterbed Hev* (Uptown 1997)★★★.

HELL, RICHARD
ALBUMS: as Richard Hell & The Voidoids *Blank Generation* (Sire 1977)★★★★, as Richard Hell & The Voidoids *Destiny Street* (Red Star 1982)★★★, *Go Now* spoken word (Codex 1995)★★, *Another World* (ROIR1998).
COMPILATIONS: *R.I.P.* cassette only (ROIR 1984)★★★, as Richard Hell & The Voidoids *Funhunt* cassette only (ROIR 1990)★★★.
VIDEOS: *Smithereens* (Merlin 1983), *Blank Generation* (Hendring 1991).
FURTHER READING: *Artifact*, Richard Hell. *The Voidoid*, Richard Hell. *Go Now*, Richard Hell.

HELLOWEEN
ALBUMS: *Helloween* mini-album (Noise 1985)★★, *Walls Of Jericho* (Noise 1986)★★, *Keeper Of The Seven Keys Part I* (Noise 1987)★★★, *Keeper Of The Seven Keys Part II* (Noise 1988)★★★, *Live In The UK* (Noise 1989)★★, *Pink Bubbles Go Ape* (EMI 1990)★★, *Chameleon* (EMI 1993)★★, *Master Of The Rings* (Raw Power 1994)★★★, *The Time Of The Oath* (Raw Power 1996)★★★, *Tore Down House* (Mesa 1996)★★.

HELMET
ALBUMS: *Strap It On* (Amphetamine Reptile 1991)★★★, *Meantime* (Interscope 1992)★★★, *Betty* (East West 1994)★★, *Aftertaste* (Interscope 1997)★★★★.
COMPILATIONS: *Born Annoying* (Amphetamine Reptile 1995)★★.

HENDRIX, JIMI
ALBUMS: *Are You Experienced?* (Track 1967)★★★★★, *Axis: Bold As Love* (Track 1967)★★★★★, *Electric Ladyland* (Track 1968)★★★★, *Band Of Gypsies* (Track 1970)★★★, shared with Otis Redding *Monterey International Pop Festival* (Reprise 1970)★★★★, *Cry Of Love* (Polydor 1971)★★★, *Experience* (Ember 1971)★, *Isle Of Wight* (Polydor 1971)★★, *Rainbow Bridge* (Reprise 1971)★★, *Hendrix In The West* (Polydor 1971)★★★, *More Experience* (Ember 1972)★, *War Heroes* (Polydor 1972)★★, *Loose Ends* (Polydor 1974)★★, *Crash Landing* (Polydor 1975)★★, *Midnight Lightnin'* (Polydor 1975)★★, *Nine To The Universe* (Polydor 1980)★★, *The Jimi Hendrix Concerts* (Columbia 1982)★★★, *Jimi Plays Monterey* (Polydor 1986)★★★, *Live At Winterland* (Polydor 1987)★★★, *Radio One* (Castle 1988)★★★★, *Live And Unreleased* (Castle 1989)★★★, *First Rays Of The New Rising Sun* (Experience/MCA 1997)★★★, *South Saturn Delta* (Experience 1997)★★★.
COMPILATIONS: *Smash Hits* (Track 1968)★★★★, *The Essential Jimi Hendrix* (Polydor 1978)★★★★, *The Essential Jimi Hendrix Volume Two* (Polydor 1979)★★★, *The Singles Album* (Polydor 1983)★★★★, *Kiss The Sky* (Polydor 1984)★★★, *Cornerstones* (Polydor 1990)★★★, *Blues* (Polydor 1994)★★★.
VIDEOS: *Jimi Hendrix Plays Berkeley* (Palace Video 1986), *Jimi Plays Monterey* (Virgin Vision 1986), *Jimi Hendrix* (Warner Home Video 1986), *Experience* (Palace Video 1987), *Rainbow Bridge* (Hendring 1988), *Live At The Isle Of Wight 1970* (Rhino Home Video 1990), *Jimi Hendrix Live At Monterey* (1994), *Jimi At Woodstock* (BMG 1995), *Jimi At The Atlanta Pop Festival* (BMG 1995), *Jimi Hendrix Experience* (BMG 1995), *Jimi Hendrix Plays The Great Pop Festivals* (BMG 1995).
FURTHER READING: *Jimi: An Intimate Biography Of Jimi Hendrix*, Curtis Knight. *Jimi Hendrix*, Alain Dister. *Jimi Hendrix: Voodoo Child Of The Aquarian Age*, David Henderson. *Scuze Me While I Kiss The Sky: The Life Of Jimi Hendrix*, David Henderson. *Hendrix: A Biography*, Chris Welch. *Hendrix: An Illustrated Biography*, Victor Sampson. *The Jimi Hendrix Story*, Jerry Hopkins. *Crosstown Traffic: Jimi Hendrix And Post-War Pop*, Charles Shaar Murray. *Jimi Hendrix: Electric Gypsy*, Harry Shapiro and Caesar Glebbeek. *Are You Experienced?*, Noel Redding and Carole Appleby. *Hendrix Experience*, Mitch Mitchell and John Platt. *And The Man With The Guitar*, Jon Price and Gary Geldeart. *The Jimi Hendrix Experience In 1967 (Limited Edition)*, Gered Mankowitz and Robert Whitaker (Photographers). *Jimi Hendrix: A Visual Documentary, His Life, Loves And Music*, Tony Brown. *The Hendrix Experience*, Mitch Mitchell with John Platt. *Jimi Hendrix: Starchild*, Curtis Knight. *Hendrix: Setting The Record Straight*, John McDermott with Eddie Kramer. *The Illustrated Jimi Hendrix*, Geoffrey Guiliano. *Cherokee Mist – The Lost Writings Of Jimi Hendrix*, Bill Nitopi (compiler). *Voodoo Child: The Illustrated Legend Of Jimi Hendrix*, Martin L. Green and Bill Sienkiewicz. *The Ultimate Experience*, Adrian Boot and Chris Salewicz. *The Lost Writings Of Jimi Hendrix*, Jimi Hendrix. *The Complete Studio Recording Sessions 1963-1970*, John McDermott. *Complete Guide To The Music Of*, John Robertson. *The Inner World Of Jimi Hendrix*, Monika Dannemann. *Jimi Hendrix Experience*, Jerry Hopkins. *Jimi Hendrix: Voices From Home*, Mary Willix. *The Man, The Music, The Memorabilia*, Caesar Glebbeek and Douglas Noble. *Eye Witness: The Illustrated Jimi Hendrix Concerts*, Ben Valkhoff.

HENLEY, DON
ALBUMS: *I Can't Stand Still* (Asylum 1982)★★★★, *Building The Perfect Beast* (Geffen 1984)★★★★, *The End Of The Innocence* (Geffen 1989)★★★.
COMPILATIONS: *Actual Miles* (1996)★★★.

HERD
ALBUMS: *Paradise Lost* (1968)★★★, *Lookin' Thru You* (Fontana 1968)★★★, *Nostalgia* (Bumble 1973)★★★.

HERMAN'S HERMITS
ALBUMS: *Herman's Hermits* (Columbia 1965)★★★, *Introducing Herman's Hermits* (Columbia 1965)★★★, *Herman's Hermits On Tour* (Columbia 1965)★★★, *Hold On!* soundtrack (Columbia 1966)★★, *Both Sides Of Herman's Hermits* (Columbia 1966)★★★, *There's A Kind Of Hush* (Columbia 1967)★★★, *Mrs Brown You've Got A Lovely Daughter* (Columbia 1968)★★★, *Blaze* (Columbia 1967)★★★.
COMPILATIONS: *The Best Of* (Columbia 1969)★★★, *The Most Of* (MFP 1971)★★★, *The Most Of Vol. 2* (MFP 1972)★★★, *Twenty Greatest Hits* (K-Tel 1977)★★★, *The Very Best Of* (MFP 1984)★★★, *The Collection* (Castle 1990)★★★, *The EP Collection* (See For Miles 1990)★★★★, *Best Of The EMI Years Vol. 1* (EMI 1991)★★★★, *Best Of The EMI Years Vol. 2* (EMI 1992)★★★.
FILMS: *Hold On* (1965).

HEYWARD, NICK
ALBUMS: *North Of A Miracle* (Arista 1983)★★★, *Postcards From Home* (Arista 1986)★★, *I Love You Avenue* (Warners 1988)★★, *From Monday To Sunday* (Epic 1992)★★, *Tangled* (Epic 1995)★★★★, *The Apple Bed* (Creation 1998)★★★.
COMPILATIONS: *Best Of Nick Heyward And Haircut 100* (Ariola 1989)★★★★, *The Greatest Hits Of Nick Heyward & Haircut 100* (RCA Camden 1996)★★★★.
FURTHER READING: *The Haircut 100 Catalogue*, Sally Payne. *Haircut 100: Not A Trace Of Brylcreem*, no editor listed.

HIATT, JOHN
ALBUMS: *Hanging Around The Observatory* (Epic 1974)★★★, *Overcoats* (Epic 1975)★★★, *Slug Line* (Epic 1979)★★★, *Two Bit Monsters* (MCA 1980)★★★, *All Of A Sudden* (MCA 1982)★★, *Riding With The King* (Geffen 1983)★★★★, *Warming Up To The Ice Age* (Geffen 1985)★★★, *Bring The Family* (A&M 1987)★★★★, *Slow Turning* (A&M 1988)★★★, *Stolen Moments* (A&M 1990)★★★, *Perfectly Good Guitar* (A&M 1993)★★★★, with The Guilty Dogs *Hiatt Comes Alive At Budokan?* (A&M 1994)★★★, *Walk On* (Capitol 1995)★★★, *Little Head* (Capitol 1997)★★★.
COMPILATIONS: *Y'All Caught? – The Ones That Got Away 1979-1985* (Geffen 1991)★★★.

HICKS, DAN
ALBUMS: with the Hot Licks *The Original Recordings* (Epic 1969)★★★, *Where's The Money?* (Blue Thumb/MCA 1971)★★★, *Striking It Rich!* (Blue Thumb/MCA 1972)★★★, *Last Train To Hicksville...The Home Of Happy Feet* (Blue Thumb/MCA 1973)★★, *It Happened One Bite* (Warners 1978)★★★, with the Acoustic Warriors *Shootin' Straight* (Private Music 1994)★★★.
COMPILATIONS: *Rich And Happy In Hicksville – Very Best Of Dan Hicks And His Hot Licks* (See For Miles 1986)★★★.

HIGH LLAMAS
ALBUMS: as Sean O'Hagan *High Llamas* (Demon 1990)★★★, *Apricots* mini-album (Plastic 1992)★★, *Santa Barbara* (Vogue/Mute 1994)★★★, *Gideon Gaye* (Target 1994)★★★, *Hawaii* (Alpaca Park 1996)★★★.

HIGH TIDE
ALBUMS: *Sea Shanties* (Liberty 1969)★★★★, *High Tide* (Liberty 1970)★★★, *Ancient Gates* (80s)★★, *Interesting Times* (High Tide 1987)★★, *Precious Cargo* (Cobra 1989)★★, *The Flood* (High Tide 1990)★★, *A Fierce Native* (High Tide 1990)★★. Solo: Tony Hill *Playing For Time* (1991)★★★.

HIGHWAY 101
ALBUMS: *Highway 101* (Warners 1987)★★★, *101 2* (Warners 1988)★★★, *Paint The Town* (Warners 1989)★★★, *Bing Bang Boom* (Warners 1991)★★★, *The New Frontier* (Liberty 1993)★★★, *Reunited* (Willow Tree 1996)★★★.
COMPILATIONS: *Greatest Hits* (Warners 1990)★★★★.

HILLAGE, STEVE
ALBUMS: *Fish Rising* (Virgin 1975)★★★, *L* (Virgin 1976)★★★, *Motivation Radio* (Virgin 1977)★★★, *Green* (Virgin 1978)★★★, *Live Herald* (Virgin 1979)★★★, *Open* (Virgin 1979)★★★, *Rainbow Dome Musick* (Virgin 1979)★★★, *For To Next/And Not Or* (Virgin 1983)★★★, *System 7* (Ten 1991)★★★★.

HIS NAME IS ALIVE
ALBUMS: *Livonia* (4AD 1990)★★★, *Home Is In Your Head* (4AD 1991)★★★, *Mouth By Mouth* (4AD 1993)★★★, *King Of Sweet* (Perdition Plastics 1994)★★, *Sound Of Mexico* cassette only (Time Stereo 1995)★★, *Stars On E.S.P.* (4AD 1996)★★★★.

HITCHCOCK, ROBYN
ALBUMS: *Black Snake Diamond Role* includes material recorded with the Soft Boys (Armageddon 1981)★★★, *Groovy Decay* (Albion 1982)★★, *I Often Dream Of Trains* (Midnight Music 1984)★★★, *Groovy Decoy* original demos of *Groovy Decay* (Glass Fish)★★★, with the Egyptians *Fegmania!* (Slash 1985)★★★, with the Egyptians *Gotta Let This Hen Out!* (Relativity 1985)★★★★, with the Egyptians *Exploding In Silence* mini-album (Relativity 1986)★★★, *Invisible Hitchcock* (Glass Fish 1986)★★★, with the Egyptians *Element Of Light* (Glass Fish 1986)★★★★, with the Egyptians *Globe Of Frogs* (A&M 1988)★★★, with the Egyptians *Queen Elvis* (A&M 1989)★★, *Eye* (Twin/Tone 1990)★★★, *Perspex Island* (A&M 1991)★★★, with the Egyptians *Respect* (A&M 1993)★★★, *Gravy Deco* (Rhino 1995)★★★, *You And Oblivion* (Rhino 1995)★★★, *Mossy Liquor (Outtakes And Prototypes)* vinyl-only release (Warners 1996)★★★, *Moss Elixir* (Warners 1996)★★★.
COMPILATIONS: *The Kershaw Sessions* (ROOT 1994)★★★.

HOLE
ALBUMS: *Pretty On The Inside* (City Slang 1991)★★★, *Live Through This* (Geffen 1994)★★★★.
COMPILATIONS: *My Body, The Hand Grenade* (City Slang 1997)★★★.
FURTHER READING: *Courtney Love*, Nick Wise. *Look Through This*, Susan Wilson.

HOLLAND, EDDIE
ALBUMS: *Eddie Holland* (Motown 1962)★★★.

HOLLAND, JOOLS
ALBUMS: *Jools Holland And His Millionaires* (A&M 1981)★★★, *Jools Holland Meets Rock 'A' Boogie Billy* (1984)★★★, *A World Of His Own* (IRS 1990)★★★, *The Full Complement* (IRS 1991)★★★, *The A-Z Geographer's Guide To The Piano* (1992)★★, *Jools Holland And The Rhythm And Blues Orchestra – Live Performance* (Beautiful 1994)★★★, *Sex And Jazz And Rock And Roll* (Coluseum 1996)★★★, *Lift The Lid* (Coalition 1997).

HOLLAND/DOZIER/HOLLAND
COMPILATIONS: *The Very Best Of The Invictus Years* (Deep Beats 1997)★★★.

HOLLIES
ALBUMS: *Stay With The Hollies* (Parlophone 1964)★★★★, *In The Hollies' Style* (Parlophone 1964)★★★★, *Here I Go Again* (Imperial 1964)★★★, *Hear! Hear!* (Imperial 1965)★★★, *The Hollies* (Parlophone 1965)★★★★, *Would You Believe* (Parlophone 1966)★★★★, *For Certain Because* (Parlophone 1966)★★★★, *The Hollies – Beat Group* (Imperial 1966)★★★, *Bus Stop* (Imperial 1966)★★★, *Stop! Stop! Stop!* (Imperial 1966)★★★, *Evolution* (Parlophone 1967)★★★, *Butterfly* (Parlophone 1967)★★★, *The Hollies Sing Dylan* (Parlophone 1969)★★, *Hollies Sing Hollies* (Parlophone 1969)★★, *He Ain't Heavy He's My Brother* (Epic 1969)★★, *Reflection* reissue of *The Hollies* (Regal Starline 1969)★★★★, *Moving Finger* (Epic 1970)★★, *Confessions Of The Mind* (Parlophone 1970)★★, *Distant Light* (Parlophone 1971)★★, *The Hollies* reissue of *Evolution* (MFP 1972)★★★, *Romany* (Polydor 1972)★★, *Out On The Road* (Hansa 1973)★★, *The Hollies* (Polydor 1974)★★, *Another Night* (Polydor 1975)★★, *Write On* (Polydor 1976)★★, *Russian Roulette* (Polydor 1976)★★, *Hollies Live Hits* (Polydor 1977)★★, *A Crazy Steal* (Polydor 1978)★★, *The Other Side Of The Hollies* (Parlophone 1978)★★★, *Five Three One-Double Seven O Four* (Polydor 1979)★★, *Long Cool Woman In A Black Dress* (MFP 1979)★★★, *Buddy Holly* (Polydor 1980)★★, *What Goes Around* (WEA 1983)★★, *Rarities* (EMI 1988)★★★★.
COMPILATIONS: *The Hollies' Greatest* (Parlophone 1968)★★★★, *The Hollies Greatest Hits Vol. 2* (Parlophone 1972)★★★, *The History Of The Hollies* (1975)★★★★, *The Best Of The Hollies EPs* (1978)★★★★, *20 Golden Greats* (1978)★★★★, *The EP Collection* (See For Miles 1987)★★★★, *Not The Hits Again* (See For Miles 1987)★★★★, *All The Hits And More* (EMI 1988)★★★★, *The Air That I Breath: Greatest Hits* (1993)★★★, *Singles A's And B's 1970-1979* (1993)★★★★, *Treasured Hits And Hidden Treasures* 3-CD box set (EMI 1993)★★★, *Four Hollies Originals* 4-CD set (EMI 1995)★★★★, *Four More Hollies Originals* (EMI 1996)★★★, *The Best Of ...* (EMI 1997)★★★★.
FILMS: *It's All Over Town* (1964).

HOLLOWAY, BRENDA
ALBUMS: *Every Little Bit Hurts* (Tamla 1964)★★★, *The Artistry Of Brenda Holloway* (Motown 1968)★★★, *All It Takes* (1991)★★★.
COMPILATIONS: *Greatest Hits And Rare Classics* (1991)★★★.

HOLLY, BUDDY
ALBUMS: *The 'Chirping' Crickets* (Brunswick 1957)★★★★, *That'll Be The Day* (Decca 1958)★★★★, *Buddy Holly* (Coral 1958)★★★★, *The Buddy Holly Story* (Coral

1959)★★★★★, The Buddy Holly Story, Vol. 2 (Coral 1959)★★★★★, Buddy Holly And The Crickets (Coral 1962)★★★★, Reminiscing (Coral 1963)★★★★, Showcase (Coral 1964)★★★★, Holly In The Hills (Coral 1965)★★★★, The Best Of Buddy Holly (Coral 1966)★★★★, Buddy Holly's Greatest Hits (Coral 1967)★★★★, The Great Buddy Holly (Vocalion 1967)★★★★, Giant (Coral 1969)★★★★, Good Rockin' (Vocalion 1971)★★★, A Rock And Roll Collection (Decca 1972)★★★, The Nashville Sessions (MCA 1975)★★★★, 20 Golden Greats (MCA 1978)★★★★★, The Complete Buddy Holly 6-LP box set (Coral 1979)★★★★★, For The First Time Anywhere (MCA 1983)★★★, From The Original Master Tapes (MCA 1985)★★★★★, Something Special From Buddy Holly (Rollercoaster 1986)★★★★, Legend (MCA 1986)★★★★, True Love Ways (Telstar 1989)★★★★, Special Limited Edition (1992)★★★★, Words Of Love (Polygram 1993)★★★★, Buddy Holly And The Picks Original Voices Of The Crickets (1993)★★★★, The Very Best Of Buddy Holly (Dino 1996)★★★★.
FURTHER READING: Buddy Holly, Dave Laing. Buddy Holly: A Biography In Words Photographs And Music, Elizabeth & Ralph Peer. Buddy Holly: His Life And Music, John Goldrosen. The Buddy I Knew, Larry Holley. The Buddy Holly Story, John Goldrosen. Buddy Holly And The Crickets, Alan Clark. Buddy Holly: 30th Anniversary Memorial Series No 1, Alan Clark. The Legend That Is Buddy Holly, Richard Peters. Buddy Holly, Alan Mann's A-Z, Alan Mann. Buddy Holly: A Biography, Ellis Amburn. Remembering Buddy, John Goldrosen & John Beecher. Buddy The Biography: USA title Rave On, Phillip Norman. Memories Of Buddy Holly, Jim Dawson & Spencer Leigh. Remembering Buddy, John Goldrosen & John Beecher.

HOLLYWOOD ARGYLES
ALBUMS: The Hollywood Argyles (Lute 1960)★★★.

HONEYCOMBS
ALBUMS: The Honeycombs (Pye 1964)★★★, All Systems Go (Pye 1965)★★★, Here Are The Honeycombs (Vee Jay 1964)★★★.
COMPILATIONS: Meek And Honey (PRT 1983)★★★, It's The Honeycombs/All Systems Go (Sequel 1990)★★★, The Best Of The Honeycombs (1993)★★★.

HONEYDRIPPERS
ALBUMS: Honeydrippers Volume 1 (Es Paranza 1984)★★★, 12 Days Of Christmas (Shattered 1997)★★★.

HOODOO GURUS
ALBUMS: Stoneage Romeos (Big Time/A&M 1983)★★★, Mars Need Guitars! (Big Time/Elektra 1985)★★★, Blow Your Cool! (Big Time/Elektra 1987)★★★, Magnum Cum Louder (RCA 1989)★★★★, Kinky (RCA 1991)★★★, Crank (RCA 1995)★★, Blue Cave (Zoo 1996)★★.
COMPILATIONS: Electric Soup – The Singles Collection Australian release (RCA 1992)★★★★, Gorilla Bisquit Australian release (RCA 1992)★★★.

HOOKER, JOHN LEE
ALBUMS: The Folk Blues Of John Lee Hooker (Riverside 1959)★★★★, I'm John Lee Hooker (Vee Jay 1959)★★★★, Travelin' (Vee Jay 1960)★★★★, Sings The Blues (King 1960)★★★★, Thats My Story (Riverside 1960)★★★★, House Of The Blues (Chess 1960)★★★★, The Blues (Crown 1960)★★★, The Folk Lore Of John Lee Hooker (Vee Jay 1961)★★★★, Burnin' (Vee Jay 1962)★★★, John Lee Hooker On Campus (1963)★★★, The Big Soul Of John Lee Hooker (Vee Jay 1963)★★★, Don't Turn Me From Your Door (Atco 1963)★★★, John Lee Hooker At Newport (Vee Jay 1964)★★★★, I Want To Shout The Blues (Stateside 1964)★★★, And Seven Nights (Verve/Folkways 1965)★★★, Real Folk Blues (Chess 1966)★★★★, It Serves You Right To Suffer (Impulse 1966)★★★, Live At The Cafe Au Go Go (Bluesway 1966)★★★, Urban Blues (Bluesway 1967)★★★, Simply The Truth (Bluesway 1968)★★★, You're Leaving Me Baby (1969)★★★, If You Miss 'Im (Bluesway 1969)★★★, Tupelo Blues (1969)★★★, Alone (1970)★★★, Hooker 'N' Heat (Specialty 1971)★★★★, Endless Boogie (ABC 1971)★★★, Never Get Out Of These Blues Alive (Crescendo 1972)★★★, John Lee Hooker's Detroit (1973)★★★, Live At Kabuki Wuki (Bluesway 1973)★★, Mad Man's Blues (Chess 1973)★★★, Free Beer And Chicken (1974)★★, Blues Before Sunrise (1976)★★★, No Friend Around (1979)★★, This Is Hip (1980)★★★, Black Snake Blues (1980)★★★, Moanin' The Blues (1982)★★★, Lonesome Mood (1983)★★★, Solid Sender (1984)★★, Jealous (Pointblank 1986)★★★, The Healer (Chameleon 1989)★★★★★, The Detroit Lion (1990)★★, Boogie Awhile (1990)★★, More Real Folk Blues: The Missing Album (1991)★★★, Mr Lucky (Charisma 1991)★★★★, Boom Boom (Point Blank 1992)★★★, Chill Out (Point Blank 1995)★★★★, with the Groundhogs Hooker & The Hogs rec. 1965 (Indigo 1996)★★, The First Concert – Alone 1976 recording (Blues Alliance 1996)★★★, Don't Look Back (Silvertone 1997)★★★.
COMPILATIONS: The Best Of John Lee Hooker (Vee Jay 1962)★★★, Collection: John Lee Hooker – 20 Blues Greats (Déjà Vu 1985)★★★, The Ultimate Collection 1948-1990 (1992)★★★★, The Best Of John Lee Hooker 1965-1974 (1992)★★★★, Blues Brother (1992)★★★, The Vee Jay Years 1955-1964 (1992)★★★★, Gold Collection (1993)★★★, The Legendary Modern Recordings 1948-54 (1993)★★★★, Helpless Blues (Realisation 1994)★★★, Original Folk Blues ... Plus (Ace 1994)★★★★, The Rising Sun Collection (Just A Memory 1994)★★★, Whiskey & Wimmen (Charly 1994)★★★, The EP Collection Plus (See For Miles) (1995)★★★★, The Early Years (Tomato 1995)★★★, I Feel Good (Jewel 1995)★★★, Alternative Boogie: Early Studio Recordings 1948-1952 (Capitol 1996)★★★.
FILMS: The Blues Brothers (1980).
VIDEOS: Survivors – The Blues Today (Hendring Video 1989), John Lee Hooker/Lowell Fulson/Percy Mayfield (1992), John Lee Hooker And Friends 1984-1992 (Vestapol 1996), Rare Performances 1960-1984 (Vestapol 1996).
FURTHER READING: Boogie Chillen: A Guide To John Lee Hooker On Disc, Les Fancourt.

HOOTERS
ALBUMS: Nervous Night (Columbia 1985)★★★, One Way Home (Columbia 1987)★★★, Zig Zag (Columbia 1989)★★★, Out Of Body (1993)★★★.

HOOTIE AND THE BLOWFISH
ALBUMS: Cracked Rear View (East West 1994)★★★, Fairweather Johnson (Atlantic 1996)★★★, Live Singles (Alex 1996).
VIDEOS: Summer Camp With Trucks (Warners 1995), A Series Of Short Trips (Atlantic Video 1996).

HOPKINS, LIGHTNIN'
ALBUMS: Strums The Blues (Score 1958)★★★★, Lightnin' And The Blues (Herald 1959)★★★, The Roots Of Lightnin' Hopkins (Folkways 1959)★★★, Down South Summit Meeting (1960)★★★★, Mojo Hand (Fire 1960)★★★★, Country Blues (Tradition 1960)★★★, Lightnin' In New York (Candid 1961)★★★, Autobiography In Blues (Tradition 1961)★★★, Lightnin' (Bluesville 1961)★★★, Last Night Blues (Bluesville 1961)★★★, Blues In My Bottle (Bluesville 1962)★★★★, Lightnin' Strikes Again (Dart 1962)★★★, Sings The Blues (Crown 1962)★★★, Lightnin' Hopkins (Folkways 1962)★★★★, Fast Life Woman (Verve 1962)★★★, On Stage (Imperial 1962)★★, Walkin' This Street (Bluesville 1962)★★★★, Lightnin' And Co (Bluesville 1963)★★★, Smokes Like Lightnin' (Bluesville 1963)★★★, First Meetin' (World Pacific 1963)★★★, Lightnin' Hopkins And The Blues (Imperial 1963)★★★, Goin' Away (Bluesville 1963)★★★, Hootin' The Blues (Folklore 1964)★★★, Down Home Blues (Bluesville 1964)★★★★, The Roots Of Lightnin' Hopkins (Verve/Folkways 1965)★★★★, Soul Blues (Prestige 1966)★★★, Something Blue (Verve/Folkways 1967)★★★, The Great Electric Show And Dance (1968)★★★, Free Form Patterns (International Artists 1968)★★★, King Of Dowling Street (1969)★★★, California Mudslide (Vault/Rhino 1969)★★★.
COMPILATIONS: Legacy Of The Blues Volume Twelve (Sonet 1974)★★★★, The Best Of Lightnin' Hopkins (Tradition 1964)★★★, The Gold Star Sessions – Volumes 1&2 (Arhoolie 1990)★★★★, The Complete Prestige/Bluesville Recordings 7CD set (Prestige/Bluesville 1992)★★★★, The Complete Aladdin Recordings (EMI 1992)★★★★, Sittin' In With Lightnin' Hopkins (Mainstream 1992)★★★, Blues Is My Business rec. 1971 (1993)★★★, You're Gonna Miss Me (1993)★★★, Mojo Hand: The Lightnin' Hopkins Anthology (Rhino 1993)★★★★, It's A Sin To Be Rich rec. 1973 (1993)★★★, Coffee House Blues rec. 1960-62 (1993)★★★★, Po' Lightnin' (Arhoolie 1995)★★★★, Blue Lightnin' (Jewel 1995)★★★, Hootin' The Blues (Prestige 1995)★★★★, The Rising Sun Collection (Just A Memory 1995)★★★★, Autobiography In Blues (Tradition 1996)★★★★, Country Blues (Tradition 1996)★★★★.
VIDEOS: Rare Performances 1960-1979 (Vestapol 1995).
FURTHER READING: Lightnin' Hopkins: Blues', M. McCormick.

HOPKINS, NICKY
ALBUMS: The Revolutionary Piano Of Nicky Hopkins (CBS 1966)★★, The Tin Man Was A Dreamer (Columbia 1973)★★, No More Changes (1976)★★.

HORNSBY, BRUCE, AND THE RANGE
ALBUMS: The Way It Is (RCA 1986)★★★, Scenes From The South Side (RCA 1988)★★★★, Night On The Town (RCA 1990)★★★. Solo: Harbor Lights (RCA 1993)★★★★, Hot House (RCA 1995)★★★.

HORSLIPS
ALBUMS: Happy To Meet Sorry To Part (Oats 1973)★★★, The Tain (Oats 1974)★★★, Dancehall Sweethearts (1974)★★★, Unfortunate Cup Of Tea (1975)★★★, Drive The Cold Winter Away (Oats 1976)★★★, Horslips Live (1976)★★★, The Book Of Invasions – A Celtic Symphony (1977)★★★, Aliens (1977)★★★, Tracks From The Vaults (1978)★★★, The Man Who Built America (1979)★★★, Short Stories – Tall Tales (1980)★★★, The Belfast Gigs (1980)★★.
COMPILATIONS: The Best Of Horslips (1982)★★★★, Folk Collection (1984)★★★, Horslips History 1972-75 (1983)★★★★, Horslips History 1976-80 (1984)★★★★, The Horslips Story; Straight From the Horse's Mouth (1989)★★★★.

HOT CHOCOLATE
ALBUMS: Cicero Park (RAK 1974)★★, Hot Chocolate (RAK 1975)★★, Man To Man (RAK 1976)★★, Every 1's A Winner (RAK 1978)★★★, Going Through The Motions (RAK 1979)★★, Class (RAK1980)★★, Mystery (RAK 1982)★★, Love Shot (RAK 1983)★★.
COMPILATIONS: 20 Hottest Hits (EMI 1979)★★★, The Very Best Of Hot Chocolate (EMI 1987)★★★, Their Greatest Hits (EMI 1993)★★★. Solo: Errol Brown That's How Love Is (Warners 1989)★★.
VIDEOS: Greatest Hits (Video Collection 1985), Very Best Of (Video Collection 1987).

HOT TUNA
ALBUMS: Hot Tuna (RCA 1970)★★★, First Pull Up Then Pull Down (RCA 1971)★★★, Burgers (Grunt 1972)★★★★, The Phosphorescent Rat (Grunt 1973)★★, America's Choice (Grunt 1974)★★★, Yellow Fever (Grunt 1975)★★, Hoppkorv (Grunt 1976)★★★, Double Dose (Grunt 1978)★★★, Final Vinyl (Grunt 1980)★★★, Splashdown (Relix 1985)★★, Pair A Dice Found (Epic 1991)★★, Live At Sweetwater (1993), Historic (Relix 1993)★★, Classic Electric (Relix 1996), Acoustic Hot Tuna (Relix 1996).
COMPILATIONS: Trimmed And Burning (Edsel 1994)★★★★, Hot Tuna In A Can 5-CD tin (Rhino 1996)★★★★.

HOTHOUSE FLOWERS
ALBUMS: People (London 1988)★★★, Home (London 1990)★★, Songs From The Rain (London 1993)★★★.

HOUSE OF LOVE
ALBUMS: House Of Love (Creation 1988)★★★, Fontana (Fontana 1989)★★, Babe Rainbow (Fontana 1992)★★★, Audience Of The Mind (Fontana 1993)★★★.
COMPILATIONS: A Spy In The House Of Love (Fontana 1990)★★★.

HOUSEMARTINS
ALBUMS: London 0 Hull 4 (Go! Discs 1986)★★★★, The People Who Grinned Themselves To Death (Go! Discs 1987)★★.
COMPILATIONS: Now That's What I Call Quite Good! (Go! Discs 1988)★★★★.
FURTHER READING: The Housemartins, Tales From Humberside, Nick Swift.

HOUSTON, CISSY
ALBUMS: Presenting Cissy Houston (Major Minor 1970)★★★, The Long And Winding Road (Pye 1971)★★, Cissy Houston (Private Stock 1977)★★★, Think It Over (Private Stock 1978)★★, Warning – Danger (Private Stock 1979)★★, Step Aside For A Lady (EMI 1980)★★, with Chuck Jackson I'll Take Care Of You (Shanachie 1992)★★, Face To Face (House Of Blues 1996)★★★, He leadeth Me (A&M 1997).
COMPILATIONS: Mama's Cookin' (Charly 1987)★★★, Midnight Train To Georgia: The Janus Years (Ichiban 1995)★★★.

HOUSTON, THELMA
ALBUMS: Sunshower (Stateside 1969)★★, Thelma Houston (Mowest 1973)★★, Anyway You Like It (Tamla 1976)★★, with Jerry Butler Thelma And Jerry (Motown 1977)★★, The Devil In Me (Tamla 1977)★★, with Butler Two To One (Motown 1978)★★, Ready To Roll (Tamla 1978)★★, Ride To The Rainbow (Tamla 1979)★★, Breakwater Cat (RCA 1980)★★, Never Gonna Be Another One (RCA 1981)★★, I've Got The Music In Me (RCA 1981)★★, Qualifying Heats (MCA 1987)★★★, Throw You Down (Reprise 1990)★★★.
COMPILATIONS: Best Of Thelma Houston (Motown 1991)★★★.

HOUSTON, WHITNEY
ALBUMS: Whitney Houston (Arista 1985)★★★★, Whitney (Arista 1987)★★★★, I'm Your Baby Tonight (Arista 1990)★★★, various artists The Bodyguard film soundtrack (Arista 1992)★★★, The Preacher's Wife film soundtrack (Arista 1996)★★.

HOWLIN' WOLF
ALBUMS: Moaning In The Moonlight (Chess 1959)★★★★, Howlin' Wolf aka The Rocking Chair Album (Chess 1962)★★★★, Howlin' Wolf Sings The Blues (Crown 1962)★★★, The Real Folk Blues (Chess 1966)★★★★, Big City Blues (1966)★★★, The Super Blues Band (1967)★★★, Evil (Chess 1967)★★★, More Real Folk Blues (Chess 1967)★★★★, This Is Howlin' Wolf's New Album aka The Dog Shit Album (Cadet 1969)★★, Message To The Young (Chess 1971)★★, The London Sessions (Chess 1971)★★★, Live And Cookin' At Alice's Revisited (Chess 1972)★★, AKA Chester Burnett (Chess 1972)★★★, The Back Door Wolf (Chess 1973)★★★★, Change My Way (Chess 1975)★★★, Ridin' In The Moonlight (Ace 1982)★★★, Live In Europe 1964 (Sundown 1988)★★★, Memphis Days Vol. 1 (Bear Family 1989)★★★, Memphis Days Vol. 2 (Bear Family 1990)★★★, Howlin' Wolf Rides Again (Ace 1991)★★★.
COMPILATIONS: Going Back Home (1970)★★★, Chess Blues Masters (Chess 1976)★★★★, The Legendary Sun Performers (Charly 1977)★★★, Chess Masters (Chess 1981)★★★★, Chess Masters 2 (Chess 1982)★★★★, Chess Masters 3 (Chess 1983)★★★, The Wolf (Blue Moon 1984)★★★, Golden Classics (Astan 1984)★★★, The Howlin' Wolf Collection (Déjà Vu 1985)★★★★, His Greatest Hits (Chess 1986)★★★, Cadillac Daddy: Memphis Recordings, 1952 (Rounder 1987)★★★, Howlin' For My Baby (Sun 1987)★★★, Shake For Me – The Red Rooster (Vogue 1988)★★★, Smokestack Lightnin' (Vogue 1988)★★★, Red Rooster (Joker 1988)★★★, Moanin' And Howlin' (Charly 1988)★★★, Howlin' Wolf 5-LP box set (Chess 1991)★★★★, Going Down Slow 5-CD box set (Roots 1992)★★★★, Gold Collection (1993)★★★, The Wolf Is At Your Door (Fan 1994)★★★, The Complete Recordings 1951-1969 7-CD box set (Charly 1994)★★★★, The Genuine Article – The Best Of (MCA 1994)★★★★, The Very Best Of Howlin' Wolf 3-CD set (Charly 1995)★★★★, His Best (Chess 1997)★★★★.

HUE AND CRY
ALBUMS: Seduced And Abandoned (Circa 1987)★★★, Remote/The Bitter Suite (Circa 1989)★★★, Stars Crash Down (Circa 1991)★★, Truth And Love (Fidelity 1992)★★, Showtime! (Permanent 1994)★★, Piano & Voice (Permanent 1995)★★★.
COMPILATIONS: Labours Of Love – The Very Best Of (Circa 1993)★★★.

HUES CORPORATION
ALBUMS: Freedom For The Stallion (RCA 1974)★★, Love Corporation (RCA 1975)★★, I Caught Your Act (Warners 1977)★★, Your Place Or Mine (Warners 1978)★★.
COMPILATIONS: Best Of The Hues Corporation (RCA 1976)★★★.

HUMAN LEAGUE
ALBUMS: Reproduction (Virgin 1979)★★, Travelogue (Virgin 1980)★★, Dare (Virgin 1981)★★★★, Love And Dancing (Virgin 1982)★★★, Hysteria (Virgin 1984)★★, Crash (Virgin 1986)★★, Romantic (Virgin 1990)★★, Octopus (East West 1995)★★★.
COMPILATIONS: Human League's Greatest Hits (Virgin 1988)★★★★, Greatest Hits (Virgin 1995)★★★★.
VIDEOS: Greatest Video Hits (Warners 1995).
FURTHER READING: The Story Of A Band Called The Human League, Alaska Ross and Jill Furmanovsky. The Human League: Perfect Pop, Peter Nash.

HUMBLE PIE
ALBUMS: As Safe As Yesterday Is (Immediate 1969)★★★, Town And Country (Immediate 1969)★★★, Humble Pie (A&M 1970)★★★, Rock On (A&M 1971)★★★, Performance – Rockin' The Fillmore (A&M 1972)★★, Smokin' (A&M 1972)★★, Eat It (A&M 1973)★★, Thunderbox (A&M 1974)★, Street Rats (A&M 1975)★, On To Victory (Jet 1980)★, Go For The Throat (Jet 1981)★.
COMPILATION: The Humble Pie Collection (Castle 1994)★★★.

HUMBLEBUMS
ALBUMS: First Collection Of Merrie Melodies (1968)★★★, The New Humblebums (1969)★★★, Open Up The Door (1970)★★★.
COMPILATIONS: The Humblebums (1981)★★★, Early Collection (1987)★★★, The New Humblebums/Open Up The Door (Transatlantic 1997)★★★.

HUNTER, IAN
ALBUMS: Ian Hunter (Columbia 1975)★★★, All American Alien Boy (Columbia 1976)★★, Overnight Angels (Columbia 1977)★★, You're Never Alone With A Schizophrenic (Chrysalis 1979)★★★, Ian Hunter Live/Welcome To The Club double album (Chrysalis 1980)★★★, Short Back And Sides (Chrysalis 1981)★★★, All Of The Good Ones Are Taken (Chrysalis 1983)★★★, with Mick Ronson YUI Orta (Mercury 1990)★★★, as Ian Hunter's Dirty Laundry Ian Hunter's Dirty Laundry (Norsk 1995)★★★, The Artful Dodger (Citadel 1997)★★★.
COMPILATIONS: Shades Of Ian Hunter (Columbia 1979)★★★★, The Collection (Castle 1991)★★★, The Very Best Of (Columbia 1991)★★★.
FURTHER READING: Diary Of A Rock 'N' Roll Star, Ian Hunter.

HÜSKER DÜ
ALBUMS: Land Speed Record (New Alliance 1981)★★, Everything Falls Apart (Reflex 1982)★★, Metal Circus mini-album (Reflex/SST 1983)★★★, Zen Arcade (SST 1984)★★★★, New Day Rising (SST 1985)★★★, Flip Your Wig (SST 1985)★★★★, Candy Apple Grey (Warners 1986)★★★★, Warehouse: Songs And Stories (Warners 1987)★★★★, The Living End 1987 recording (Warners 1994)★★★.
COMPILATIONS: Everything Falls Apart And More (Warners 1993)★★★★.

HYLAND, BRIAN
ALBUMS: The Bashful Blonde (Kapp 1960)★★, Let Me Belong To You (ABC 1961)★★, Sealed With A Kiss (ABC 1962)★★★, Country Meets Folk (ABC 1964)★, Here's To Our Love (Philips 1964)★★, Rockin' Folk (Philips 1965)★★, The Joker Went Wild (Philips 1966)★★★, Tragedy (1969)★★, Stay And Love Me All Summer (1969)★★, Brian Hyland (1970)★★.
COMPILATIONS: Golden Decade 1960-1970 (1988)★★★, Ginny O Ginny (1988)★★★.

I

IAN, JANIS
ALBUMS: Janis Ian (Verve 1967)★★, For All The Seasons Of Your Mind (Verve 1967)★★★, The Secret Life Of J. Eddy Fink (1968)★★, Present Company (Capitol 1971)★★, Stars (Columbia 1974)★★★, Between The Lines (Columbia 1975)★★★★, Aftertones (Columbia 1976)★★★, Miracle Row (Columbia 1977)★★, Night Rains (Columbia 1979)★★, Restless Eyes (Columbia 1981)★★, Breaking Silence (1993)★★★, Revenge (Grapevine 1995)★★★, Hunger (Windham Hill 1997)★★★.
COMPILATIONS: Society's Child: The Anthology (Polydor 1995)★★★.
FURTHER READING: Who Really Cares?, Janis Ian.

ICE CUBE
ALBUMS: AmeriKKKa's Most Wanted (Priority 1990)★★★★, Death Certificate (Priority 1991)★★★, The Predator (Priority 1992)★★★, Lethal Injection (Priority 1993)★★★, Bootlegs And B-Sides (Island 1994)★★, Featuring Ice Cube (Priority 1997)★★★.
FILMS: Boyz 'N The Hood (1991), Higher Learning, Trespass (1992).

ICE-T
ALBUMS: Rhyme Pays (Sire 1987)★★★, Power (Sire 1988)★★, The Iceberg/Freedom Of Speech ... Just Watch What You Say (Sire 1989)★★★, OG: Original Gangster (Syndicate/Sire 1991)★★★★, Home Invasion (Priority 1993)★★★, Born Dead (Priority 1994)★★★, The Ice Opinion (Ichiban 1997)★★★.
VIDEOS: O.G. – The Original Gangster Video (1991).
FURTHER READING: The Ice Opinion, Ice-T and Heidi Seigmund.
FILMS: Breakdance, New Jack City, Trespassers.

ICICLE WORKS
ALBUMS: The Icicle Works (Beggars Banquet 1984)★★★, The Small Price Of A Bicycle (Beggars Banquet 1985)★★★, If You Want To Defeat Your Enemy Sing His Song (Beggars Banquet 1987)★★★, Blind (Beggars Banquet 1988)★★★, Permanent Damage (Epic 1990)★★★, BBC Radio One Live In Concert 1987 recording (Windsong 1994)★★, Peel Sessions (Dutch east Indian 1997)★★★.
COMPILATIONS: The Best Of (Beggars Banquet 1992)★★★.

IDLE RACE
ALBUMS: The Birthday Party (Liberty 1968)★★★, Idle Race (Liberty 1969)★★★, Time Is (Regal Zonophone 1971)★★.
COMPILATIONS: On With The Show (Sunset 1973)★★★, Imposters Of Life's Magazine (1976)★★★, Light At The End Of The Road (1985)★★★, Back To The Story (Premier 1996)★★★.

IDOL, BILLY
ALBUMS: Billy Idol (Chrysalis 1981)★★★, Don't Stop (Chrysalis 1981)★★★, Rebel Yell (Chrysalis 1984)★★★★, Whiplash Smile (Chrysalis 1986)★★★, Charmed Life (Chrysalis 1990)★★, Cyberpunk (Chrysalis 1993)★★.
COMPILATIONS: Vital Idol (Chrysalis 1986)★★★, Idol Sings – 11 Of The Best (Chrysalis 1988)★★★.
FURTHER READING: Billy Idol: Visual Documentary, Mike Wrenn.

IFIELD, FRANK
ALBUMS: I'll Remember You (1963)★★★, Portrait In Song (Columbia 1965)★★★, Blue Skies (Columbia 1964), Up Jumped A Swagman soundtrack (Columbia 1965)★★, Someone To Give My Love To (Spark 1973)★★, Barbary Coast (Fir 1978)★★, Sweet Vibrations (Fir 1980)★★, If Love Must Go (Fir 1982)★★, At The Sandcastle (Fir 1983)★★.
COMPILATIONS: Greatest Hits (1964)★★★, Best Of The EMI Years (1991)★★★★, The EP Collection (1991)★★★★.
FILMS: Up Jumped A Swagman (1965).

IMAGINATION
ALBUMS: Body Talk (R&B 1981)★★★, In The Heat Of The Night (R&B 1982)★★, Night Dubbing (R&B 1983)★★, Scandalous (R&B 1983)★★, Imagination (RCA 1989)★★.
COMPILATIONS: Imagination Gold (Stylus 1984)★★★.

INCREDIBLE STRING BAND
ALBUMS: The Incredible String Band (Elektra 1966)★★★, 5000 Spirits Or The Layers Of The Onion (Elektra 1967)★★★★, The Hangman's Beautiful Daughter (Elektra 1968)★★★★, Wee Tam And The Big Huge (Elektra 1968)★★★, Changing Horses (Elektra 1969), I Looked Up (Elektra 1970)★★, U (Elektra 1970)★★, Be Glad For The Song Has No Ending (Island 1971)★★, Liquid Acrobat As Regards The Air (Island 1971)★★, Earthspan (Island 1972)★★, No Ruinous Feud (Island 1973)★★, Hard Rope And Silken Twine (Island 1974)★★, On Air (1991)★★★, In Concert (Windsong 1992)★★★, The Chelsea Sessions (Pig's Whisker Music 1997).
COMPILATIONS: Relics Of The Incredible String Band (1971)★★★, Seasons They Change (Island 1976)★★★.
VIDEOS: Be Glad For The Song Has No Ending (1994).

INDIGO GIRLS
ALBUMS: as the B Band Tuesday's Children cassette only (Unicorn 1981)★★, Blue Food cassette only (J Ellis 1985)★★★, Strange Fire (Indigo 1987)★★, Indigo Girls (Epic 1989)★★★, Nomads, Indians, Saints (Epic 1990)★★★, Back On The Bus Y'All live mini-album (Epic 1991)★★, Rites Of Passage (Epic 1992)★★★, Swamp Ophelia (Epic 1994)★★★, Shaming Of The Sun (Epic 1997)★★★.
Solo: Amy Ray Color Me Grey cassette only (No Label 1985)★★.
COMPILATIONS: 4.5 – The Best Of The Indigo Girls (Epic 1995)★★★.
VIDEOS: Watershed (Columbia Music Video 1995).

INGRAM, JAMES
ALBUMS: It's Your Night (Qwest 1983)★★, Never Felt So Good (Qwest 1986)★★, It's Real (Qwest 1989)★★, Always You (Qwest 1993)★★.
COMPILATIONS: The Power Of Great Music (Qwest 1991)★★★.

INSPIRAL CARPETS
ALBUMS: Life (Mute 1990)★★★, The Beast Inside (Mute 1991)★★, Revenge Of The Goldfish (Mute 1992)★★★, Devil Hopping (Mute 1994)★★★.
COMPILATIONS: The Singles (Mute 1995)★★★.

INTELLIGENT HOODLUM
ALBUMS: Tragedy (A&M 1990)★★★, Saga Of A Hoodlum (A&M 1993)★★★★.

INXS
ALBUMS: INXS (Deluxe 1980)★★, Underneath The Colours (RCA 1981)★★, Shabooh Shoobah (Mercury 1982)★★, The Swing (Mercury 1984)★★★, Listen Like Thieves (Mercury 1985)★★★, Kick (Mercury 1987)★★★, X (Mercury 1990)★★, Live Baby Live (Mercury 1991)★★, Welcome To Wherever You Are (Mercury 1992)★★★, Full Moon, Dirty Hearts (Mercury 1993)★★★, Elegantly Wasted (Mercury 1997)★★.
Solo: Max Q Max Q (Mercury 1989)★★. Absent Friends Here's Looking Up Your Address (Roo Art 1990).
COMPILATIONS: Greatest Hits (Mercury 1994)★★★★.

VIDEOS: Truism (PMI 1991), The Best Of INXS (1994).
FURTHER READING: INXS: The Official Story Of A Band On The Road, St John Yann Gamblin (ed.).

IRON BUTTERFLY
ALBUMS: Heavy (Atco 1968)★★★, In-A-Gadda-da-Vida (Atco 1968)★★★★, Ball (Atco 1969)★★★, Iron Butterfly Live (Atco 1970)★, Metamorphosis (Atco 1970)★★, Scorching Beauty (MCA 1975)★★, Sun And Steel (MCA 1976)★★★.
COMPILATIONS: Evolution (Atco 1971)★★★, Star Collection (1973)★★★, Light And Heavy: The Best Of (1993)★★★.

IRON MAIDEN
ALBUMS: Iron Maiden (EMI 1980)★★★, Killers (EMI 1981)★★, Number Of The Beast (EMI 1982)★★★★, Piece Of Mind (EMI 1983)★★, Powerslave (EMI 1984)★★, Live After Death (EMI 1985)★★★, Somewhere In Time (EMI 1986)★★★, Seventh Son Of A Seventh Son (EMI 1988)★★★★, No Prayer For The Dying (EMI 1990)★★★, Fear Of The Dark (EMI 1992)★★★, A Real Live One (Volume One) (EMI 1993)★★★, A Real Dead One (EMI 1993)★★, Live At Donington '92 (EMI 1993)★★, The X Factor (EMI 1995)★★★, Virtual XI (CMC International 1998)★★.
COMPILATIONS: Best Of The Beast (EMI 1996)★★★.
VIDEOS: Live At The Rainbow (1984), Behind The Iron Curtain Video EP (1986), Live After Death (1986), Run To The Hills (1987), Twelve Wasted Years (1987), Maiden England (1989), First Ten Years (The Videos) (1990), Raising Hell (1993), Donington Live 1992 (1994).
FURTHER READING: Running Free: The Official Story Of Iron Maiden, Garry Bushell and Ross Halfin. A Photographic History, Ross Halfin.

ISAACS, GREGORY
ALBUMS: Gregory Isaacs Meets Ronnie Davis (Plant 1970)★★★, In Person (Trojan 1975)★★★, All I Have Is Love (Trojan 1976)★★★, Extra Classic (Conflict 1977, Shanachie 1981)★★★, Mr Isaacs (Earthquake 1977)★★★, Slum Dub (Burning Sounds 1978)★★★★, Best Of Vol. 1 & 2 not compilations (GG's 1976, 1981)★★★, Cool Ruler (Front Line 1978)★★★★, Soon Forward (Front Line 1979)★★★★, Showcase (Taxi 1980)★★★, The Lonely Lover (Pre 1980)★★★, For Everyone (Success 1980)★★★, More Gregory (Pre 1981)★★★, Night Nurse (Mango/Island 1982)★★★, The Sensational Gregory Isaacs (Vista 1982)★★★, Out Deh! (Mango/Island 1983)★★★★, Reggae Greats (Live) (Mango/Island 1984)★★★, Live At The Academy Brixton (Rough Trade 1984)★★★, with Dennis Brown Two Bad Superstars Meet (Burning Sounds 1984)★★★, Judge Not (Greensleeves 1984)★★★, with Jah Mel Double Explosive (Andys 1984)★★★, Private Beach Party (RAS 1985)★★★, Easy (Tad's 1985)★★★, All I Have Is Love, Love, Love (Tad's 1986)★★★, with Sugar Minott Double Dose (Blue Mountain 1987)★★★, Victim (C&E 1987)★★★, Watchman Of The City (Rohit 1988)★★★, Sly And Robbie Presents Gregory Isaacs (RAS 1988)★★★, Talk Don't Bother Me (Skengdon 1988)★★★, Come Along (Live & Love 1988)★★★, Encore (Kingdom 1988)★★★, Red Rose For Gregory (Greensleeves 1988)★★★, I.O.U. (RAS 1989)★★★, No Contest (Music Works 1989)★★★, Call Me Collect (RAS 1990)★★★, Dancing Floor (Heartbeat 1990)★★★, Come Again Dub (ROIR 1991)★★★, Can't Stay Away (1992)★★★, Pardon Me (1992)★★★, No Luck (1993)★★★, Absent (Greensleeves 1993)★★★, Over The Bridge (Musidisc/I&I Sound 1994)★★★, Reggae Greats – Live rec. 1982 (1994)★★★, Midnight Confidential (Greensleeves 1994)★★★, Mr Love (Virgin Front Line 1995)★★★, Memories (Musidisc 1995)★★★, Dem Talk Too Much (Trojan 1995)★★★, Bad Boy Lover Boy (Charley 1997)★★★, Loving Pauper (1998)★★★.
COMPILATIONS: The Early Years (Trojan 1981)★★★, Lover's Rock double album comprising The Lonely Lover and More Gregory (Pre 1982)★★★, Crucial Cuts (Virgin 1983)★★★, My Number One (Heartbeat 1990)★★★, Love Is Overdue (Network 1991)★★★, The Cool Ruler Rides Again – 22 Classics From 1978-81 (Music Club 1993)★★★.

ISAAK, CHRIS
ALBUMS: Silvertone (Warners 1985)★★, Chris Isaak (Warners 1987)★★★, Heart Shaped World reissued as Wicked Game (Reprise 1989)★★★, San Francisco Days (Reprise 1993)★★★, Forever Blue (Reprise 1995)★★, Baja Sessions (Reprise 1996)★★.
VIDEOS: Wicked Game (Warner Music Video 1991).
FILMS: Married To The Mob, Silence Of The Lambs.

ISHAM, MARK
ALBUMS: with Art Lande Rubisia Patrol (ECM 1976)★★, with Lande Desert Marauders (ECM 1978)★★★, Group 87 (1981)★★, Vapour Drawings (Windham Hill 1983)★★★★, A Career In Dada Processing (1984)★★★, with Lande We Begin (1987)★★★, Film Music (Windham Hill 1987)★★★★, Fire In The Sky (1993)★★★, Blue Sun (Columbia 1995)★★★, Afterglow (Sony 1998)★★★.

ISLEY BROTHERS
ALBUMS: Shout (RCA Victor 1959)★★★, Twist And Shout (Wand 1962)★★★★, The Fabulous Isley Brothers-Twisting And Shouting (Wand 1964)★★, Take Some Time Out-The Famous Isley Brothers (United Artists 1964)★★, This Old Heart Of Mine (Tamla 1966)★★, Soul On The Rocks (Tamla 1967)★★, It's Our Thing (T-Neck 1969)★★★, Doin' Their Thing (Tamla 1969)★★★, The Brothers: Isley (T-Neck 1969)★★★, with Brooklyn Bridge and Edwin Hawkins Live At Yankee Stadium (T-Neck 1969)★★, Get Into Something (T-Neck 1970)★★★, Givin' It Back (T-Neck 1971)★★★, Brother Brother Brother (T-Neck 1972)★★★, The Isleys Live (T-Neck 1973)★★★, 3+3 (T-Neck 1973)★★★★, Live It Up (T-Neck 1974)★★★, The Heat Is On (T-Neck 1975)★★★★, Harvest For The World (T-Neck 1976)★★★, Go For Your Guns (T-Neck 1977)★★★, Showdown (T-Neck 1978)★★★, Winner Takes All (T-Neck 1979)★★★, Go All The Way (T-Neck 1980)★★★, Grand Slam (T-Neck 1981)★★★, Inside You (T-Neck 1981)★★★, The Real Deal (T-Neck 1982)★★★, Between The Sheets (T-Neck 1983)★★★, Masterpiece (Warners 1985)★★★, Smooth Sailin' (Warners 1987)★★★, as Isley Brothers Featuring Ronald Isley Spend The Night (Warners 1989)★★, Tracks Of Life (Warners 1992)★★★, Live (Elektra 1993)★★, Mission To Please (Island 1996)★★.
COMPILATIONS: Isleys' Greatest Hits (T-Neck 1973)★★★★, Super Hits (Motown 1976)★★★, Forever Gold (T-Neck 1977)★★★★, The Best Of The Isley Brothers (United Artists 1978)★★★, Timeless (Epic 1979)★★★, Greatest Motown Hits (Motown 1987)★★★, The Complete UA Sessions (EMI 1990)★★★, The Isley Brothers Story/Volume 1: The Rockin' Years (1959-1968) (Rhino 1991)★★★, The Isley Brothers Story/Volume 2: T-Neck Years (1968-1985) (Rhino 1991)★★★★, Early Classics (Spectrum 1996)★★★.

IT'S A BEAUTIFUL DAY
ALBUMS: It's A Beautiful Day (Columbia 1969)★★★, Marrying Maiden (Columbia 1970)★★, Choice Quality Stuff/Anytime (Columbia 1971)★★, It's A Beautiful Day At Carnegie Hall (Columbia 1972)★★, It's A Beautiful Day ... Today (Columbia 1973)★, 1001 Nights (Columbia 1974)★★.
COMPILATIONS: It's A Beautiful Day (Columbia 1979)★★.

J

JACKSON, JANET
ALBUMS: *Janet Jackson* (A&M 1982)★★, *Dream Street* (A&M 1984)★★★, *Control* (A&M 1986)★★★★, *Control: The Remixes* (A&M 1987)★★★, *Janet Jackson's Rhythm Nation 1814* (A&M 1989)★★★, *Janet* (Virgin 1993)★★★★, *The Velvet Rope* (Virgin 1997)★★★.
COMPILATIONS: *Janet Remixed* (Virgin 1995)★★★, *Design Of A Decade 1986/1996* (A&M 1995)★★★.
VIDEOS: *Janet* (Virgin 1994), *Design Of A Decade 86-96* (VVL 1995).
FURTHER READING: *Out Of The Madness (The Strictly Unauthorised Biography Of ...)*, Andrew Bart and J Randy Taraborrelli (eds.).

JACKSON, JERMAINE
ALBUMS: *Jermaine* (Motown 1972)★★, *Come Into My Life* (Motown 1973)★★, *My Name Is Jermaine* (Motown 1976)★★, *Feel The Fire* (Motown 1977)★★, *Frontier* (Motown 1978)★★, *Let's Get Serious* (Motown 1980)★★★, *Jermaine* (Motown 1980)★★, *I Like Your Style* (Motown 1981)★★, *Let Me Tickle Your Fancy* (Motown 1982)★★, *Jermaine Jackson* (USA) *Dynamite* (UK) (Arista 1984)★★★, *Precious Moments* (Arista 1986)★★, *Don't Take It Personal* (Arista 1989)★★, *You Said* (La Face 1991)★★.

JACKSON, JOE
ALBUMS: *Look Sharp!* (A&M 1979)★★★★, *I'm The Man* (A&M 1979)★★★★, *Beat Crazy* (A&M 1980)★★, *Joe Jackson's Jumpin' Jive* (A&M 1981)★★★★, *Night And Day* (A&M 1982)★★★★, *Mike's Murder* film soundtrack (A&M 1983)★★, *Body And Soul* (A&M 1984)★★★★, *Big World* (A&M 1986)★★, *Will Power* (A&M 1987)★★★, *Joe Jackson – Live* (A&M 1988)★★★, *Tucker: Original Soundtrack* (A&M 1988)★★, *Blaze Of Glory* (A&M 1989)★★, *Laughter And Lust* (Virgin 1991)★★, *Night Music* (Virgin 1994)★★★, *Heaven And Hell* (Sony 1997)★★★★.
COMPILATIONS: *Steppin' Out – The Very Best Of ...* (A&M 1990)★★★, *This Is It – The A&M Years* (A&M 1997)★★★★.

JACKSON, LaTOYA
ALBUMS: *LaToya Jackson* (Polydor 1980)★★, *My Special Love* (Polydor 1981)★★, *Heart Don't Lie* (Private Stock 1984)★★, *Imagination* (Private Stock 1985)★★, *You're Gonna Get Rocked* (RCA 1988)★★.
FURTHER READING: *LaToya Jackson*, LaToya Jackson with Patricia Romanowski.

JACKSON, MICHAEL
ALBUMS: *Got To Be There* (Motown 1971)★★★, *Ben* (Motown 1972)★★★, *Music And Me* (Motown 1973)★★★, *Forever, Michael* (Motown 1975)★★★, *Off The Wall* (Epic 1979)★★★★, *One Day In Your Life* (Motown 1981)★★★, *Thriller* (Epic 1982)★★★★★, *ET – The Extra Terrestrial* (MCA 1983)★★, *Farewell My Summer Love 1973 recording* (Motown 1984)★★★, *Looking Back To Yesterday* (Motown 1986)★★★, *Bad* (Epic 1987)★★★, *Dangerous* (Epic 1991)★★★, *HIStory Past, Present & Future, Book 1* (Epic 1995)★★★★, *Blood On The Dance Floor – HIStory In The Mix* (Epic 1997)★★★.
COMPILATIONS: *The Best Of Michael Jackson* (Motown 1975)★★★, *Michael Jackson 9 Single Pack* (Epic 1983)★★★, *The Michael Jackson Mix* (Stylus 1987)★★★, *Souvenir Singles Pack* (1988)★★★, *Anthology* (Motown 1993)★★★★.
VIDEOS: *The Making Of Thriller* (Vestron Music Video 1986), *The Legend Continues* (Video Collection 1988), *Moonwalker* (1992), *Dangerous – The Short Films* (1994), *HIStory Past, Present & Future, Book 1* (1995).
FURTHER READING: *Michael Jackson*, Stewart Regan. *The Magic Of Michael Jackson*, No editor listed. *Michael Jackson*, Doug Magee. *The Michael Jackson Story*, Nelson George. *Michael In Concert*, Phyl Garland. *Michael Jackson: Body And Soul: An Illustrated Biography*, Geoff Brown. *Michael!: The Michael Jackson Story*, Mark Bego. *On The Road With Michael Jackson*, Mark Bego. *Sequins & Shades: The Michael Jackson Reference Guide*, Carol D. Terry. *Michael Jackson: Electrifying*, Greg Quill. *Moonwalker*, Michael Jackson. *Michael Jackson: The Magic And The Madness*, J. Randy Taraborrelli. *Michael Jackson: The Man In The Mirror*, Todd Gold. *Michael Jackson: The King Of Pop*, Lisa D. Campbell. *Michael Jackson: In His Own Words*, Michael Jackson. *The Visual Documentary*, Adrian Grant. *Michael Jackson Unauthorized*, Christopher Andersen.
FILMS: *The Wiz*.

JACKSON, MILLIE
ALBUMS: *Millie Jackson* (Spring 1972)★★★, *It Hurts So Good* (Spring 1973)★★★, *Caught Up* (Spring 1974)★★★★, *Soul Believer* (Spring 1974)★★★, *Still Caught Up* (Spring 1975)★★★, *Free And In Love* (Spring 1976)★★★, *Lovingly Yours* (Spring 1977)★★★, *Feelin' Bitchy* (Spring 1977)★★★★, *Get It Out 'Cha System* (Spring 1978)★★★, *A Moment's Pleasure* (Spring 1979)★★★, with Isaac Hayes *Royal Rappin's* (Polydor 1979)★★, *Live And Uncensored* (Spring 1979)★★★, *For Men Only* (Spring 1980)★★★, *I Had To Say It* (Spring 1981)★★, *Just A Lil' Bit Country* (1981)★★, *Live And Outrageous* (Spring 1982)★★, *Hard Times* (Spring 1982)★★, *E.S.P. (Extra Sexual Persuasion)* (Sire 1984)★★, *An Imitation Of Love* (Jive 1986)★★★, *The Tide Is Turning* (Jive 1988)★★★, *Back To The Sh.t* (Jive 1989)★★★.
COMPILATIONS: *Best Of Millie Jackson* (Spring 1976)★★★★, *21 Of The Best* (Southbound/Ace 1994)★★★.

JACKSON FIVE
ALBUMS: *Diana Ross Presents The Jackson 5* (Motown 1970)★★★, *ABC* (Motown 1970)★★★★, *Third Album* (Motown 1970)★★★, *Christmas Album* (Motown 1970)★★, *Maybe Tomorrow* (Motown 1971)★★, *Goin' Back To Indiana* (Motown 1971)★★, *Lookin' Through The Windows* (Motown 1972)★★★, *Skywriter* (Motown 1973)★★★, *Get It Together* (Motown 1973)★★★, *Dancing Machine* (Motown 1974)★★★, *Moving Violation* (Motown 1975)★★★, *Joyful Jukebox Music* (Motown 1976)★★★.
COMPILATIONS: *Jackson 5 Greatest Hits* (Motown 1971)★★★★, *Jackson Five Anthology* 3-LP set (Motown 1976)★★★★, *Soulstation! – 25th Anniversary Collection* 4-CD box set (Motown 1995)★★★★, *Early Classics* (Spectrum 1996)★★★.
FURTHER READING: *Jackson Five*, Charles Morse. *The Jacksons*, Steve Manning. *Pap Joe's Boys: The Jacksons' Story*, Leonard Pitts. *The Magic And The Madness*, J. Randy Taraborrelli. *The Record History: International Jackson Record Guide* , Ingmar Kuliha.

JACKSONS
ALBUMS: *The Jacksons* (Epic 1976)★★★, *Goin' Places* (Epic 1977)★★★, *Destiny* (Epic 1978)★★★★, *Triumph* (Epic 1980)★★★, *The Jacksons Live* (Epic 1981)★★★, *Victory* (Epic 1984)★★★, *2300 Jackson Street* (Epic 1989)★★.

JAH WOBBLE
ALBUMS: *The Legend Lives On ... Jah Wobble In 'Betrayal'* (Virgin 1980)★★, with Holger Czukay and The Edge *Snake Charmer* (Island 1983)★★★, *Jah Wobble's Bedroom Album* (Lago 1983)★★, with Ollie Morland *Neon Moon* (Island 1985)★★★, *Psalms* (Wob 1987)★★★, with Invaders Of The Heart *Without Judgement* (Island 1990)★★★★, with Invaders Of The Heart *Rising Above Bedlam* (Island 1991)★★★★, *Take Me To God* (Island 1994)★★★★, *Heaven & Earth* (Island 1995)★★★, with Eno *Spanner* (All Saints 1995)★★★, *The Inspiration Of William Blake* (All Saints 1996)★★★, *The Celtic Poets* (30 Hertz 1997)★★★, *The Light Programme* (30 Hertz 1997)★★.

JAM
ALBUMS: *In The City* (Polydor 1977)★★★★, *This Is The Modern World* (Polydor 1977)★★★, *All Mod Cons* (Polydor 1978)★★★★, *Setting Sons* (Polydor 1979)★★★★, *Sound Affects* (Polydor 1980)★★★★, *The Gift* (Polydor 1982)★★★, *Dig The New Breed* (Polydor 1982)★★★, *Live Jam* (Polydor 1993)★★★.
COMPILATIONS: *Snap!* (Polydor 1983)★★★★, *Greatest Hits* (Polydor 1991)★★★★, *Extras* (Polydor 1992)★★★, *The Jam Collection* (Polydor 1996)★★★★, *Direction, Reaction, Creation* 4-CD box set (Polydor 1997)★★★★.
VIDEOS: *Video Snap* (Polygram 1984), *Transglobal Unity Express* (Channel 5 1988), *Greatest Hits: Jam* (Polygram 1991), *Little Angels: Jam On Film* (1994).
FURTHER READING: *The Jam: The Modern World By Numbers*, Paul Honeyford. *Jam*, Miles. *The Jam: A Beat Concerto, The Authorized Biography*, Paolo Hewitt. *About The Young Idea: The Story Of The Jam 1972-1982*, Mike Nicholls. *Our Story*, Bruce Foxton and Rick Buckler with Alex Ogg. *Keeping The Flame*, Steve Brookes.

JAMES
ALBUMS: *Stutter* (Sire 1986)★★★, *Strip Mine* (Sire 1988)★★★, *One Man Clapping* (Rough Trade 1989)★★★, *Gold Mother* (Fontana 1990)★★★★, *Seven* (Fontana 1992)★★★★, *Laid* (Fontana 1993)★★★, *Wah Wah* (Fontana 1994)★★, *Whiplash* (Fontana 1997)★★★.
VIDEOS: *Come Home Live* (Polygram 1991), *Seven – The Live Video* (Polygram Video 1992).

JAMES, ELMORE
COMPILATIONS: *Blues After Hours* (Crown 1961)★★★★, *Original Folk Blues* (Kent 1964)★★★★, *The Sky Is Crying* (Sphere Sound 1965)★★★, *The Best Of Elmore James* (Sue 1965)★★★★, *I Need You* (Sphere Sound 1966)★★★, *The Elmore James Memorial Album* (Sue 1966)★★★★, *Something Inside Of Me* (Bell 1968)★★★, *The Late Fantastically Great Elmore James* (Ember 1968)★★★, *To Know A Man* (Blue Horizon 1969)★★★, *Whose Muddy Shoes* (Chess 1969)★★★, *Elmore James* (Bell 1969)★★★, *Blues In My Heart, Rhythm In My Soul* (1969)★★★, *The Legend Of Elmore James* (United Artists 1970)★★★, *Tough* (Blue Horizon 1970)★★★, *Cotton Patch Hotfoots* (Polydor 1974)★★★, *All Them Blues* (DJM 1976)★★★, with Robert Nighthawk *Blues In D'Natural* (1979)★★★★, *The Best Of Elmore James* (Ace 1981)★★★, *Got To Move* (Charly 1981)★★★, *King Of The Slide Guitar* (Ace 1983)★★★★, *Red Hot Blues* (Blue Moon 1983)★★★, *The Original Meteor And Flair Sides* (Ace 1984)★★★★, *Come Go With Me* (Charly 1984)★★★, *One Way Out* (Charly 1985)★★★, *The Elmore James Collection* (Déjà Vu 1985)★★★★, *Let's Cut It* (Ace 1986)★★★, *King Of The Bottleneck Blues* (Crown 1986)★★★★, *Shake Your Moneymaker* (Charly 1986)★★★★, *Pickin' The Blues* (Castle 1986)★★★, *Greatest Hits* (Blue City 1988)★★★, *Chicago Golden Years* (Vogue 1988)★★★, *Dust My Broom* (Instant 1990)★★★★, *Rollin' And Tumblin' – The Best Of* (Relic 1992)★★★★, *Elmore James Box Set* (Charly 1992)★★★★, *The Classic Early Recordings 1951-56* 3-CD box set (Flair/Ace 1993)★★★★, *The Best Of Elmore James: The Early Years* (Ace 1995)★★★★.

JAMES, ETTA
ALBUMS: *Miss Etta James* (Crown 1961)★★★★, *At Last!* (Argo 1961)★★★★, *Second Time Around* (Argo 1961)★★★★, *Twist With Etta James* (Crown 1962)★★★★, *Etta James* (Argo 1962)★★★★, *Etta James Sings For Lovers* (Argo 1962)★★★★, *Etta James Top Ten* (Argo 1963)★★★, *Etta James Rocks The House* (Argo 1964)★★★, *The Queen Of Soul* (Argo 1965)★★★★, *Call My Name* (Cadet 1967)★★★, *Tell Mama* (Cadet 1968)★★★★★, *Etta James Sings Funk* (Cadet 1970)★★★, *Losers Weepers* (Cadet 1971)★★★, *Etta James* (Chess 1973)★★★, *Come A Little Closer* (Chess 1974)★★★, *Etta Is Betta Than Evah!* (Chess 1977)★★★, *Deep In The Night* (Warners 1978)★★★★, *Changes* (MCA 1980)★★★, *Red, Hot And Live* (1982)★★★, *The Heart And Soul Of* (1982)★★★, with Eddie 'Cleanhead' Vinson *Blues In The Night: The Early Show* (Fantasy 1986)★★★, *Blues In The Night: The Late Show* (Fantasy 1986)★★★, *Seven Year Itch* (Island 1989)★★★, *Stickin' To My Guns* (Island 1990)★★★★, *Something's Gotta Hold On Me (Etta James Vol. 2)* (Roots 1992)★★★, *The Right Time* (Elektra 1992)★★★, *Mystery Lady: Songs Of Billie Holiday* (Private Music 1994)★★★, *Love's Been Rough On Me* (Private Music 1997)★★★.
COMPILATIONS: *The Best Of ...* (Crown 1962)★★★★, *The Soul Of Etta James* (Ember 1968)★★★★, *Golden Decade* (Chess 1972)★★★★, *Peaches* (Chess 1973)★★★★, *Good Rockin' Mama* (Ace 1981)★★★★, *Tuff Lover* (Ace 1983)★★★★, *Her Greatest Sides, Volume One* (Chess/MCA 1987)★★★★, *R&B Dynamite* (Ace 1987)★★★★, *The Sweetest Peaches: The Chess Years, Volume 1 (1960-1966)* (Chess/MCA 1988)★★★★, *The Sweetest Peaches: The Chess Years, Volume 2 (1967-1975)* (Chess/MCA 1988)★★★★, *Tell Mama* (1988)★★★★, *Juicy Peaches* (Charly 1989)★★★★, *The Soulful Miss Peaches* (Charly 1993)★★★★, *The Genuine Article: The Best Of* (MCA/Chess 1996)★★★★.
VIDEOS: *Live At Montreux* (Island Visual Arts 1990), *Live At Montreux: Etta James* (Polygram Music Video 1992).
FURTHER READING: *Rage To Survive*, Etta James with David Ritz.

JAMES, RICK
ALBUMS: *Come Get It!* (Gordy 1978)★★★, *Bustin' Out Of L Seven* (Gordy 1979)★★★, *Fire It Up* (Gordy 1979)★★★, *In 'n' Out* (Gordy 1980)★★, *Garden Of Love* (Gordy 1980)★★, *Street Songs* (Gordy 1981)★★★★, *Throwin' Down* (Gordy 1982)★★★, *Cold Blooded* (Gordy 1983)★★, *Glow* (Gordy 1985)★★, *The Flag* (Gordy 1986)★★, *Wonderful* (Reprise 1988)★★.
COMPILATIONS: *Reflections: All The Great Hits* (Gordy 1984)★★★★, *Greatest Hits* (Motown 1993)★★★, *Bustin' Out: The Best Of Rick James* (Motown 1994)★★★, *Greatest Hits* (Spectrum 1996)★★★.

JAMES, TOMMY, AND THE SHONDELLS
ALBUMS: *Hanky Panky* (Roulette 1966)★★★, *It's Only Love* (Roulette 1967)★★★, *I Think We're Alone Now* (Roulette 1967)★★★, *Gettin' Together* (Roulette 1968)★★, *Mony Mony* (Roulette 1968)★★★, *Crimson & Clover* (Roulette 1968)★★★, *Cellophane Symphony* (1969)★★, *Travelin'* (1970)★★. The Shondells solo: *Hog Heaven* (1971)★★.
COMPILATIONS: *Something Special! The Best Of Tommy James And The Shondells* (Roulette 1968)★★★, *The Best Of Tommy James And The Shondells* (1969)★★★, *Anthology* (Rhino 1990)★★★★, *Tommy James: The Solo Recordings 1970-1981* (1991)★★★, *The Best Of ...* (Rhino 1994)★★★★.

JAMES GANG
ALBUMS: *Yer Album* (BluesWay 1969)★★★, *The James Gang Rides Again* (ABC 1970)★★★★, *Thirds* (ABC 1971)★★★, *James Gang Live In Concert* (ABC 1971)★★★, *Straight Shooter* (ABC 1972)★★, *Passin' Thru'* (ABC 1972)★★, *Bang* (Atco 1974)★★, *Miami* (Atco 1974)★★, *Newborn* (Atco 1975)★★, *Jesse Come Home* (1976)★★.
COMPILATIONS: *The Best Of The James Gang Featuring Joe Walsh* (ABC 1973)★★★, *16 Greatest Hits* (ABC 1973)★★★, *The True Story Of The James Gang* (See For Miles 1987)★★★.

JAMIROQUAI
ALBUMS: *Emergency On Planet Earth* (Sony 1993)★★★, *The Return Of The Space Cowboy* (Sony 1994)★★★★, *Travelling Without Moving* (Sony 1996)★★★★.

JAN AND DEAN
ALBUMS: *Jan And Dean* (Dore 1960)★★★, *Jan And Dean Take Linda Surfin'* (Liberty 1963)★★★, *Surf City (And Other Swinging Cities)* (Liberty 1963)★★★, *Drag City* (Liberty 1964)★★★, *Dead Man's Curve/New Girl In School* (Liberty 1964)★★★, *Ride The Wild Surf* (Liberty 1964)★★★, *The Little Old Lady From Pasadena* (Liberty 1964)★★★, *Command Performance – Live In Person* (Liberty 1965)★, *Folk 'N' Roll* (Liberty 1966)★★, *Fillet Of Soul – A 'Live' One* (Liberty 1966)★, *Jan And Dean Meet Batman* (Liberty 1966)★★, *Popsicle* (1966)★★, *Save For A Rainy Day* (1967)★★.
COMPILATIONS: *Jan And Dean's Golden Hits* (Liberty 1962)★★★, *Golden Hits Volume 2* (1965)★★★, *The Jan And Dean Anthology Album* (1971)★★★, *Gotta Take That One Last Ride* (1973)★★★, *Ride The Wild Surf (Hits From Surf City, USA)* (1976)★★★★, *Teen Suite 1958-1962* (1995)★★★★.
FURTHER READING: *Jan And Dean*, Allan Clark.

JANE'S ADDICTION
ALBUMS: *Jane's Addiction* (Triple X 1987)★★★, *Nothing's Shocking* (Warners 1988)★★★★, *Ritual De Lo Habitual* (Warners 1991)★★★.
COMPILATIONS: *Kettle Whistle* (Warners 1997)★★★.

JAPAN
ALBUMS: *Adolescent Sex* (Ariola-Hansa 1978)★★, *Obscure* (Ariola-Hansa 1978)★★, *Quiet Life* (Ariola-Hansa 1979)★★★, *Gentlemen Take Polaroids* (Virgin 1980)★★★, *Tin Drum* (Virgin 1981)★★★, *Oil On Canvas* (Virgin 1983)★★.
COMPILATIONS: *Assemblage* (Hansa 1981)★★★, *Exorcising Ghosts* (Virgin 1984)★★★, *In Vogue* (Camden 1997)★★★.
FURTHER READING: *A Tourist's Guide To Japan*, Arthur A. Pitt.

JARRE, JEAN-MICHEL
ALBUMS: *Oxygene* (Polydor 1977)★★★★, *Equinoxe* (Polydor 1978)★★★, *Magnetic Fields* (Polydor 1981)★★★, *Concerts In China* (Polydor 1982)★★★, *Zoolook* (Polydor 1984)★★★, *Rendezvous* (Polydor 1986)★★, *Houston/Lyon* (Polydor 1987)★★, *Revolutions* (Polydor 1988)★★★, *Live* (Polydor 1989)★★, *Waiting For Cousteau* (Polydor 1990)★★, *Oxygene 7-13* (1997)★★, *Odyssey Through Oxygen* (Epic 1998)★★.
COMPILATIONS: *The Essential* (Polydor 1983)★★★.
FURTHER READING: *The Unofficial Jean-Michel Jarre Biography*, Graham Needham.

JARREAU, AL
ALBUMS: *1965* (1965)★★, *We Got By* (Reprise 1975)★★★, *Glow* (Reprise 1976)★★, *Look To The Rainbow: Live In Europe* (Warners 1977)★★, *All Fly Home* (Warners 1978)★★, *This Time* (Warners 1980)★★★, *Breakin' Away* (Warners 1981)★★★, *Jarreau* (Warners 1983)★★★, *Spirits And Feelings* (Happy Bird 1984)★★★, *Ain't No Sunshine* (Blue Moon 1984)★★★, *High Crime* (Warners 1984)★★, *Al Jarreau In London* (Warners 1984)★★, *You* (Platinum 1985)★★★, *L Is For Lover* (Warners 1986)★★★, *Hearts Horizon* (Reprise 1988)★★★, *Manifesto* (Masters 1988)★★★, *Heaven And Earth* (Reprise 1992)★★★, *Tenderness* (Warners 1994)★★★.
FILMS: *Breakdance – The Movie* (1984).

JASON AND THE SCORCHERS
ALBUMS: *Fervor* (EMI 1983)★★★, *Lost And Found* (EMI 1985)★★★, *Still Standing* (EMI 1986)★★★, *Thunder And Fire* (A&M 1989)★★★, *A Blazing Grace* (Mammoth 1995)★★★, *Reckless Country Soul* (Mammoth 1996)★★★, *Clear Impetuous Morning* (Mammoth 1996)★★★, *Midnight Roads And Stages Seen* (Mammoth 1998)★★★.

JAY AND THE AMERICANS
ALBUMS: *She Cried* (United Artists 1962)★★★, *Jay And The Americans At The Cafe Wha?* (United Artists 1963)★★, *Come A Little Bit Closer* (United Artists 1964)★★★, *Blockbusters* (United Artists 1965)★★, *Sunday And Me* (United Artists 1966)★★★, *Livin' Above Your Head* (United Artists 1966)★★★, *Wild, Wild Winter* soundtrack (1966)★★, *Try Some Of This* (United Artists 1967)★★, *Sands Of Time* (1969)★★, *Wax Museum* (1970)★★.
COMPILATIONS: *Jay And The Americans' Greatest Hits* (United Artists 1965)★★★, *Very Best Of* (1979)★★★, *Jay And The Americans' Greatest Hits Volume Two* (United Artists 1966)★★★, *Come A Little Bit Closer* (1990)★★★.

JAYHAWKS
ALBUMS: *The Jayhawks* (Bunkhouse 1986)★★★, *The Blue Earth* (Twin/Tone 1989)★★★, *Hollywood Town Hall* (Def American 1992)★★★, *Tomorrow The Green Grass* (American 1995)★★★★, *Sound Of Lies* (American 1997)★★★.

JAZZ BUTCHER
ALBUMS: *The Jazz Butcher In Bath Of Bacon* (Glass 1982)★★★, *A Scandal In Bohemia* (Glass 1984)★★★, *Sex And Travel* (Glass 1985)★★★, as Jazz Butcher And His Sikkorskis From Hell *Hamburg – A Live Album* (Rebel 1985)★★★, as Jazz Butcher Conspiracy *Distressed Gentlefolk* (Glass 1986)★★★, *Fishcotheque* (Creation 1988)★★★, *Big Planet, Scarey Planet* (Genius 1989)★★★, *Cult Of The Basement* (Rough Trade 1990)★★★, *Condition Blue* (Creation 1991)★★★, *Western Family (Live)* (Creation 1993)★★★, *Waiting For The Love Bus* (Creation 1993)★★★, *Illuminated* (Creation 1995)★★★.
Solo: Max Eider *The Best Kisser In The World* (Big Time 1987)★★★.
COMPILATIONS: *The Gift Of Music* (Glass 1984)★★★, *Bloody Nonsense* (Big Time 1986)★★★, *Big Questions – The Gift Of Music Vol. 2* (Glass 1987)★★★, *Edward's Closet* (Creation 1991)★★★, *Draining The Glass 1982-86* (Nectar 1997)★★★.

JEFFERSON AIRPLANE
ALBUMS: *Jefferson Airplane Takes Off* (RCA 1966)★★, *Surrealistic Pillow* (RCA 1967)★★★★, *After Bathing At Baxter's* (RCA 1967)★★★, *Crown Of Creation* (RCA 1968)★★★★, *Bless Its Pointed Little Head* (RCA 1969)★★★, *Volunteers* (RCA 1969)★★★, *Bark* (Grunt 1971)★★★, *Long John Silver* (Grunt 1972)★★★, *30 Seconds Over Winterland* (Grunt 1973)★★★, *Early Flight* (Grunt 1974)★★★, *Jefferson Airplane* (Epic 1989)★.
COMPILATIONS: *Worst Of Jefferson Airplane* (RCA 1970)★★★, featuring Jefferson Airplane and Starship *Flight Log (1966-1976)* (Grunt 1977)★★★★, *2400 Fulton Street* (RCA 1987)★★★★, *Journey ... Best Of* (Camden 1996)★★★.
FURTHER READING: *The Jefferson Airplane And The San Francisco Sound*, Ralph J. Gleason. *Grace Slick – The Biography*, Barbara Rowe.

JEFFERSON STARSHIP
ALBUMS: *Dragonfly* (Grunt 1974)★★★, *Red Octopus* (Grunt 1975)★★★★, *Spitfire* (Grunt 1976)★★★, *Earth* (Grunt 1978)★★, *Freedom At Point Zero* (Grunt 1979)★★, *Modern Times* (RCA 1981)★★, *Winds Of Change* (Grunt 1982)★★, *Nuclear Furniture* (Grunt 1984)★★; as Starship *Knee Deep In The Hoopla* (RCA 1985)★★, *No Protection* (RCA 1987)★★, *Love Among The Cannibals* (RCA 1989)★, *Deep Space/Virgin Sky* (Intersound 1995)★.
COMPILATIONS: featuring Jefferson Airplane and Starship *Flight Log (1966-1976)* (Grunt 1977)★★★★, *Gold* (Grunt 1979)★★★★, *Jefferson Starship: The Collection* (1992)★★★.

JELLYFISH
ALBUMS: *Bellybutton* (Virgin 1991)★★★★, *Spilt Milk* (Virgin 1993)★★★★.
VIDEOS: *Gone Jellyfishin'* (Atlantic 1991).

JESUS AND MARY CHAIN
ALBUMS: *Psychocandy* (Blanco y Negro 1985)★★★★, *Darklands* (Blanco y Negro 1987)★★★, *Automatic* (Blanco y Negro 1989)★★, *Honey's Dead* (Blanco y Negro 1992)★★★, *Stoned & Dethroned* (Blanco y Negro 1994)★★★.
COMPILATIONS: *Barbed Wire Kisses* (Blanco y Negro 1988)★★★.
FURTHER READING: *The Jesus and Mary Chain: A Musical Biography*, John Robertson.

JESUS JONES
ALBUMS: *Liquidizer* (Food 1989)★★★, *Doubt* (Food 1991)★★★, *Perverse* (Food 1993)★★, *Already* (Food 1997)★★.
VIDEOS: *Big In Alaska* (PMI 1991).

JETHRO TULL
ALBUMS: *This Was* (Chrysalis 1968)★★★★, *Stand Up* (Chrysalis 1969)★★★★, *Benefit* (Chrysalis 1970)★★★, *Aqualung* (Chrysalis 1971)★★★, *Thick As A Brick* (Chrysalis 1972)★★★, *A Passion Play* (Chrysalis 1973)★★, *War Child* (Chrysalis 1974)★★, *Minstrel In The Gallery* (Chrysalis 1975)★★★, *Too Old To Rock 'N' Roll, Too Young To Die* (Chrysalis 1976)★★, *Songs From The Wood* (Chrysalis 1977)★★★, *Heavy Horses* (Chrysalis 1978)★★★, *Live – Bursting Out* (Chrysalis 1978)★★, *Storm Watch* (Chrysalis 1979)★★, *A* (Chrysalis 1980)★★, *The Broadsword And The Beast* (Chrysalis 1982)★★, *Under Wraps* (Chrysalis 1984)★★, *Crest Of A Knave* (Chrysalis 1987)★★★, *Rock Island* (Chrysalis 1989)★★, as the John Evan Band *Live '66* (A New Day 1990)★★, *Live At Hammersmith* (Raw Fruit 1990)★★, *Catfish Rising* (Chrysalis 1991)★★, *A Little Light Music* (Chrysalis 1992)★★, *Nightcap* (Chrysalis 1993)★★, *In Concert* (Windsong 1995)★★★, *Roots To Branches* (Chrysalis 1995)★★.
Ian Anderson Solo: *Walk Into Light* (Chrysalis 1983)★★, *Divinities: Twelve Dances With God* (EMI 1995)★★.
COMPILATIONS: *Living In The Past* (Chrysalis 1972)★★★★, *M.U.: Best Of Jethro Tull* (Chrysalis 1976)★★★, *Repeat, The Best Of Jethro Tull – Volume II* (Chrysalis 1977)★★★, *Original Masters* (Chrysalis 1985)★★★, *20 Years Of Jethro Tull* 3-CD box set (Chrysalis 1988)★★★★, *25th Anniversary Box Set* 4-CD box set (Chrysalis 1992)★★★★, *The Anniversary Collection* (Chrysalis 1993)★★★.
VIDEOS: *Slipstream* (Chrysalis 1981), *20 Years Of Jethro Tull* (Virgin 1988), *25th Anniversary Video* (PMI 1993).

JETT, JOAN, AND THE BLACKHEARTS
ALBUMS: *Joan Jett* (Blackheart 1980)★★★, *Bad Reputation* reissue of debut (Boardwalk 1981)★★★, *I Love Rock 'N' Roll* (Boardwalk 1981)★★★★, *Album* (MCA/Blackheart 1983)★★★, *Glorious Results Of A Misspent Youth* (MCA/Blackheart 1984)★★★, *Good Music* (Columbia/Blackheart 1986)★★★, *Up Your Alley* (Columbia/Blackheart 1988)★★★, *The Hit List* (Columbia/Blackheart 1990)★★★, *Notorious* (Epic/Blackheart 1991)★★★, *Pure And Simple* (Blackheart/Warners 1994)★★★.
COMPILATIONS: *Flashback* (Blackheart 1993)★★★★.

JEWEL
ALBUMS: *Pieces Of You* (Atlantic 1995)★★★★.

JIVE BUNNY AND THE MASTERMIXERS
a number of Dance labels such as trax, Defcon and Energize.
ALBUMS: *Jive Bunny – The Album* (1989)★★★, *It's Party Time* (1990)★★, *Pop Back In Time To The 70s* (Music Club 1997)★★.
COMPILATIONS: *The Best Of ...* (Music Collection 1995)★★.

JOEL, BILLY
ALBUMS: *Cold Spring Harbor* (Family 1971)★★, *Piano Man* (Columbia 1973)★★, *Street Life Serenade* (Columbia 1975)★★, *Turnstiles* (Columbia 1976)★★★, *The Stranger* (Columbia 1977)★★★★, *52nd Street* (Columbia 1978)★★★, *Glass Houses* (Columbia 1980)★★★, *Songs In The Attic* (Columbia 1981)★★★, *The Nylon Curtain* (Columbia 1982)★★★, *An Innocent Man* (Columbia 1983)★★★, *The Bridge* (Columbia 1986)★★★, *Kohyept – Live In Leningrad* (Columbia 1987)★★, *Storm Front* (Columbia 1989)★★★, *River Of Dreams* (Columbia 1993)★★★★.
COMPILATIONS: *Greatest Hits Vols. 1 & 2* (Columbia 1985)★★★★, *Greatest Hits 3* (Columbia 1997)★★★, *Greatest Hits Vols. 1-3* (1998)★★★.
VIDEOS: *Video Album Vol. 1* (1986), *Live At Long Island* (1988), *Storm Front* (1990), *Live At Yankee Stadium* (SMV 1992), *Live From Leningrad* (SMV 1992), *A Matter Of Trust* (SMV 1992), *Shades Of Grey* (1994), *Video Album Vol. 2* (1994).
FURTHER READING: *Billy Joel: A Personal File*, Peter Gambaccini.

JOHANSEN, DAVID
ALBUMS: *David Johansen* (Blue Sky 1978)★★★, *In Style* (Blue Sky 1979)★★★, *Here Comes The Night* (Blue Sky 1981)★★, *Live It Up* (Blue Sky 1982)★★★, *Sweet Revenge* (Passport 1984)★★★.
COMPILATIONS: *Crucial Music: The David Johansen Collection* (Columbia/Relativity 1990)★★★.

JOHN, ELTON
ALBUMS: *Empty Sky* (DJM 1969)★★, *Elton John* (DJM 1970)★★★★, *Tumbleweed Connection* (DJM 1970)★★★★, *Friends* film soundtrack (Paramount 1971)★, *17-11-70* (DJM 1971)★★, *Madman Across The Water* (DJM 1971)★★★, *Honky Chateau* (DJM 1972)★★★★, *Don't Shoot Me I'm Only The Piano Player* (DJM 1973)★★★, *Goodbye Yellow Brick Road* (DJM 1973)★★★★, *Caribou* (DJM 1974)★★, *Captain Fantastic And The Brown Dirt Cowboy* (DJM 1975)★★★, *Rock Of The Westies* (DJM 1975)★★★★, *Here And There* (DJM 1976)★★, *Blue Moves* (Rocket 1976)★★, *A Single Man* (Rocket 1978)★★★, *London And New York* (repressing of *Here And There*, Hallmark 1978)★★, *Victim Of Love* (Rocket 1979)★★, *21 At 33* (Rocket 1980)★★, *Lady Samantha* (Rocket 1980)★★★, *The Fox* (Rocket 1981)★★, *Jump Up* (Rocket 1982)★★, *Too Low For Zero* (Rocket 1983)★★★, *Breaking Hearts* (Rocket 1984)★★, *Ice On Fire* (Rocket 1985)★★★, *Leather Jackets* (Rocket 1986)★★, *Live In Australia* (Rocket 1987)★★, *Reg Strikes Back* (Rocket 1988)★★★, *Sleeping With The Past* (Rocket 1989)★★★, *The On*[illegible]*ocket 1992)★★★, *Duets* (MCA 1993)★★, *Made In* [illegible]*ngland* (Mercury/Rocket 1995)★★★★, *Live* [illegible] *Australia* (MCA 1996)★★, *Big Picture* (Polygram [illegible]★★.
COMPILATIONS: [illegible] *Hi*[illegible]M 1974)★★★★, *Greatest Hits Vo*[illegible])★★★, *The Elton John Live Collection* ([illegible]wick [illegible]9)★★, *The Elton John Box Set* (DJM 1979)★★[illegible], *The Very Best Of Elton John* (K-Tel 1980)★★★, *Love Songs* (TV 1982)★★★★, *The Very Best Of Elton John* (Rocket 1990)★★★★, *Love Songs* (Mercury/Rocket 1995)★★★★.
VIDEOS: *Live In Central Park – New York* (1986), *The Video Singles* (1987), *Night Time Concert* (1988), *Live In Australia 1 & 2* (1988), *The Afternoon Concert* (1988), *Very Best Of Elton John* (1990), *Single Man In Concert* (1991), *Live – World Tour 1992* (1993), *Live In Australia* (J2 Communications 1995).
FURTHER READING: *Bernie Taupin: The One Who Writes The Words For Elton John: Complete Lyrics*, Bernie Taupin. *Elton John*, Cathi Stein. *A Conversation With Elton John And Bernie Taupin*, Paul Gambaccini. *Elton John*, Dick Tatham and Tony Jasper. *Elton John Discography*, Paul Sobieski. *Elton John: A Biography In Words & Pictures*, Greg Shaw. *Elton John: Reginald Dwight & Co*, Linda Jacobs. *Elton: It's A Little Bit Funny*, David Nutter. *The Elton John Tapes: Elton John In Conversation With Andy Peebles*, Elton John. *Elton John: The Illustrated Discography*, Alan Finch. *Elton John 'Only The Piano Player'*, *The Illustrated Elton John Story*, Chris Charlesworth. *Elton John: A Biography*, Barry Toberman. *Two Rooms: A Celebration Of Elton John & Bernie Taupin*, Elton John and Bernie Taupin. *A Visual Documentary*, Nigel Goodall. *Candle In The Wind*, no author listed. *Elton John: The Biography*, Philip Norman. *The Many Lives Of Elton John*, Susan Crimp and Patricia Burstein. *The Complete Lyrics Of Elton John And Bernie Taupin*, no author listed. *Elton John: 25 Years In The Charts*, John Tobler. *Rocket Man: The Encyclopedia Of Elton John*, Claude Bernardin and Tom Stanton.

JOHNNY AND THE HURRICANES
ALBUMS: *Johnny And The Hurricanes* (Warwick 1959)★★★, *Stormsville* (1960)★★★, *Big Sound Of Johnny And The Hurricanes* (Big Top 1960)★★★, *Live At The Star Club* (Attila 1965)★★.

JOHNSON, LINTON KWESI
ALBUMS: as Poet And The Roots *Dread Beat An' Blood* (Front Line 1978)★★★, *Forces Of Victory* (Island 1979)★★★★, *Bass Culture* (Island 1980)★★★★, *LKJ In Dub* (Island 1980)★★★, *Making History* (Island 1984)★★★★, *Linton Kwesi Johnson Live* (Rough Trade 1985)★★★, *In Concert With The Dub Band* (LKJ 1986)★★★, *Tings An' Times* (LKJ 1990)★★★★, *LKJ In Dub Vol. 2* (1992)★★★, *A Cappalla Live* (LKJ 1997)★★★.
COMPILATIONS: *Reggae Greats* (Island 1985)★★★★.

JOHNSON, ROBERT
COMPILATIONS: *King Of The Delta Blues Singers* (Columbia 1961)★★★★★, *King Of The Delta Blues Singers, Volume 2* (Columbia 1970)★★★★★, *Robert Johnson Delta Blues Legend* (Charly 1992)★★★★★, *Hellhound On My Trail: The Essential Recordings* (Indigo 1995)★★★★★, *The Complete Recordings* (Columbia Legacy 1996)★★★★★.
VIDEOS: *The Search For Robert Johnson* (1992).
FURTHER READING: *Searching For Robert Johnson*, Peter Guralnick. *The Devil's Son-in-Law*, P. Garon. *Love In Vain: Visions Of Robert Johnson*, Alan Greenberg.

JON SPENCER BLUES EXPLOSION
ALBUMS: *Crypt Style* (Crypt 1992)★★, *The Jon Spencer Blues Explosion* (Caroline 1992)★★, *Extra Width* (Matador 1993)★★, *Mo Width* (Au-Go-Go 1994)★★, *Orange* (Matador 1994)★★★, *Remixes* (Matador 1995)★★, *Now I Got Worry* (Mute 1996)★★★★.

JONES, HOWARD
ALBUMS: *Human's Lib* (WEA 1984)★★★★, *The 12 Inch Album* (WEA 1984)★★, *Dream Into Action* (WEA 1985)★★★, *One To One* (WEA 1986)★★, *Cross That Line* (WEA 1989)★★★, *In The Running* (1992)★★, *Live Acoustic America* (Plump 1996)★★★, *Angels And Lovers* (Pony Canyon International 1997).
Compilatons: *The Best Of Howard Jones* (WEA 1993)★★★.

JONES, JIMMY
ALBUMS: *Good Timin'* (MGM 1960)★★★.

JONES, PAUL
ALBUMS: *My Way* (HMV 1966)★★★, *Privilege* film soundtrack (HMV 1967)★★★, *Love Me Love My Friends* (HMV 1968)★★, *Come Into My Music Box* (Columbia 1969)★★, *Crucifix On A Horse* (Vertigo 1971)★★, *Drake's Dream* film soundtrack (President 1974)★★, with Jack Bruce *Alexis Korner Memorial Concert Vol. 1* (Indigo 1995)★★★, *Mule* (Fat Possum 1995)★★★.
COMPILATIONS: *Hits And Blues* (One-Up 1980)★★, *The Paul Jones Collection: Volume One: My Way* (RPM 1996)★★, *The Paul Jones Collection: Volume Two: Love Me, Love My Friend* (RPM 1996)★★.
FILMS: *Privilege* (1967).

JONES, QUINCY
ALBUMS: *Quincy Jones With The Swedish/U.S. All Stars* (Prestige 1953)★★★, *This Is How I Feel About Jazz* (ABC-Paramount 1957)★★★, *Go West Man* (ABC-Paramount 1957)★★★, *The Birth Of A Band* (Mercury 1959)★★★, *The Great Wide World Of Quincy Jones* (Mercury 1960)★★★, *Quincy Jones At Newport '61* (Mercury 1961)★★★, *I Dig Dancers* (Mercury 1961)★★★, *Around The World* (Mercury 1961)★★★, *The Quintessence* (Impulse 1961)★★★, *Big Band Bossa Nova* (Mercury 1962)★★★, *Quincy Jones Plays Hip Hits* (Mercury 1963)★★★, *The Boy In The Tree* (1963)★★★, *Quincy's Got A Brand New Bag* (Mercury 1964)★★★, *Quincy Jones Explores The Music Of Henry Mancini* (Mercury 1964)★★★, *Golden Boy* (Mercury 1964)★★★, *The Pawnbroker* (Mercury 1964)★★★, *Quincy Plays For Pussycats* (Mercury 1965)★★★, *Walk Don't Run* (Mainstream 1966)★★★, *The Slender Thread* (Mercury 1966)★★★, *The Deadly Affair* (Verve 1967)★★★, *Enter Laughing* (Liberty 1967)★★★, *In The Heat Of The Night* film soundtrack (United Artists 1967)★★★, *In Cold Blood* film soundtrack (Colgems 1967)★★★, *Banning* (1968)★★★, *For The Love Of Ivy* (ABC 1968)★★★, *The Split* (1968)★★★, *Jigsaw* (1968)★★★, *A Dandy In Aspic* (1968)★★★, *The Hell With Heroes* (1968)★★★, *MacKennas Gold* (RCA 1969)★★★, *The Italian Job* film soundtrack (Paramount 1969)★★★, *The Lost Man* (1969)★★★, *Bob & Carol & Ted & Alice* (Bell 1969)★★★, *John And Mary* (A&M 1969)★★★, *Walking In Space* (A&M 1969)★★★, *Gula Matari* (A&M 1970)★★★, *The Out Of Towners* (United Artists 1970)★★★, *Cactus Flower* (Bell 1970)★★★, *The Last Of The Hot Shots* (1970)★★★, *Sheila* (1970)★★★, *They Call Me Mr Tibbs* (United Artists 1970)★★★, *Smackwater Jack* (A&M 1971)★★★, *The Anderson Tapes* (1971)★★★, *Dollars* (1971)★★★, *Man And Boy* (1971)★★★, *The Hot Rock* (Prophesy 1972)★★★, *Ndeda* (Mercury 1972)★★★, *The New Centurians* (1972)★★★, *Come Back Charleston Blue* (Atco 1972)★★★, *You've Got It Bad Girl* (A&M 1973)★★★, *Body Heat* (A&M 1974)★★★, *This Is How I Feel About Jazz* (Impulse 1974)★★★, *Mellow Madness* (A&M 1975)★★★, *I Heard That!* (A&M 1976)★★★, *Roots* (A&M 1977)★★★, *Sounds ... And Stuff Like That* (A&M 1978)★★★, *The Wiz* (MCA 1978)★★★, *The Dude* (A&M 1981)★★★, *The Color Purple* film soundtrack (Qwest 1985)★★★, *Back On The Block* (Qwest 1989)★★★, *Listen Up, The Lives Of Quincy Jones* (Qwest 1990)★★★, with Miles Davis *Live At Montreux* recorded 1991 (Reprise 1993)★★★★, *Q's Jook Joint* (Qwest 1995)★★★★.
COMPILATIONS: *Compact Jazz: Quincy Jones* (Phillips/Polygram 1989)★★★★.
FILMS: *Listen Up: The Lives Of Quincy Jones* (1990).
VIDEOS: *Miles Davis And Quincy Jones: Live At Montreux* (1993).
FURTHER READING: *Quincy Jones*, Raymond Horricks.

JONES, RICKIE LEE
ALBUMS: Rickie Lee Jones (Warners 1979)★★★★, Pop Pop (Geffen 1981)★★, Pirates (Warners 1981)★★★★, Girl At Her Volcano (Warners 1982)★★, The Magazine (Warners 1984)★★★, Flying Cowboys (Geffen 1990)★★★, Traffic From Paradise (1993)★★★, Naked Songs: Live And Acoustic (Reprise 1995)★★, Ghostyhead (Reprise 1997)★★★.
VIDEOS: Naked Songs (Warner Music Vision 1996).

JONES, TOM
ALBUMS: Along Came Jones (Decca 1965)★★★, A-Tom-Ic Jones (Decca 1966)★★★★, From The Heart (Decca 1966)★★★, Green, Green, Grass Of Home (Decca 1967)★★★★, Live At The Talk Of The Town (Decca 1967)★★★, Delilah (Decca 1968)★★★, Help Yourself (Decca 1968)★★★★, Tom Jones Live In Las Vegas (Decca 1969)★★★, This Is Tom Jones (Decca 1969)★★★, Tom (1970)★★★, I, Who Have Nothing (1970)★★★, Tom Jones Sings She's A Lady (1971)★★★, Tom Jones Live At Caeser's Palace, Las Vegas (1971)★★★, Close Up (1972)★★★, The Body And Soul Of Tom Jones (1973)★★★, Somethin' 'Bout You Baby I Like (1974)★★★, Memories Don't Leave Like People (1975)★★★, Say You'll Stay Until Tomorrow (1977)★★★, Rescue Me (1980)★★★, Darlin' (1981)★★★, Matador – The Musical Life Of El Cordorbes (1987)★★★, At This Moment (1989)★★★, After Dark (1989)★★★, with Engelbert Humperdinck Back To Back (1993)★★★, Velvet Steel Gold (1993)★★★, The Lead And How To Swing It (ZTT 1994)★★★★, Tom Jones Live (BMG 1997)★★.
COMPILATIONS: 13 Smash Hits (Decca 1967)★★★★, Tom Jones: Greatest Hits (1973)★★★★, Tom Jones: 20 Greatest Hits (1975)★★★★, The World Of Tom Jones (1975)★★★★, Do You Take This Man (1979)★★★, Rescue Me (1980)★★★, The Tom Jones Album (1983)★★★, The Country Side Of Tom Jones (1985)★★★, The Soul Of Tom Jones (1986)★★★, The Great Love Songs (1987)★★★, It's Not Unusual – His Greatest Hits (1987)★★★★, The Complete Tom Jones (1993)★★★, The Ultimate Hit Collection: 1965-1988 (Repertoire 1995)★★★, In Nashville (Spectrum 1996)★★★.
FURTHER READING: Tom Jones: Biography Of A Great Star, Tom Jones. Tom Jones, Stafford Hildred and David Griffen.

JOPLIN, JANIS
ALBUMS: I Got Dem Ol' Kozmic Blues Again Mama! (Columbia 1969)★★★, Pearl (Columbia 1971)★★★, Janis Joplin In Concert (Columbia 1972)★★★.
COMPILATIONS: Greatest Hits (Columbia 1973)★★★★, Janis film soundtrack including live and rare recordings (1975)★★★, Anthology (Columbia 1980)★★★, Farewell Song (Columbia 1982)★★★, Janis 3-CD box set (Legacy 1995)★★★★, 18 Essential Songs (Columbia 1995)★★★.
FILMS: American Pop (1981).
FURTHER READING: Janis Joplin: Her Life And Times, Deborah Landau. Going Down With Janis, Peggy Caserta as told to Dan Knapp. Janis Joplin: Buried Alive, Myra Friedman. Janis Joplin: Piece Of My Heart, David Dalton. Love, Janis, Laura Joplin. Pearl: The Obsessions And Passions Of Janis Joplin, Ellis Amburn.

JORDANAIRES
ALBUMS: Beautiful City (RCA Victor 1953)★★★,Peace In The Valley (Decca 1957)★★★★,Of Rivers And Plants (Sesac 1958)★★★,Heavenly Spirit (Capitol 1958)★★★,Gloryland (Capitol 1958)★★★,Land Of Jordan (Capitol 1960)★★★★,To God Be The Glory (Capitol 1961)★★★,Spotlight On The Jordanaires (Capitol 1962)★★★,We'd Like To Teach The World To Sing (1972)★★★,The Jordanaires Sing Elvis' Favourite Spirituals (1985)★★★,The Jordanaires Sing Elvis' Gospel Favourites (1986)★★★.
FILMS: Jailhouse Rock (1957), G.I. Blues (1960), Blue Hawaii (1961), Girls Girls Girls (1962), Fun In Acapulco (1963), Elvis – The Movie (1979).

JOURNEY
ALBUMS: Journey (Columbia 1975)★★★, Look Into The Future (Columbia 1976)★★★, Next (Columbia 1977)★★★, Infinity (Columbia 1978)★★★, Evolution (Columbia 1979)★★★, Departure (Columbia 1980)★★★, Dream After Dream (Columbia 1980)★★, Captured (Columbia 1981)★★★, Escape (Columbia 1981)★★★★, Frontiers (Columbia 1983)★★★, Raised On Radio (Columbia 1986)★★★, Trial By Fire (Columbia 1996)★★, Into The Fire (Columbia 1997)★★.
COMPILATIONS: Greatest Hits/Best Of Journey (Columbia 1988)★★★★, Time 3-CD box set (Columbia 1992)★★★★.

JOY DIVISION
ALBUMS: Unknown Pleasures (Factory 1979)★★★, Closer (Factory 1980)★★★★, Still (Factory 1981)★★★.
COMPILATIONS: Substance 1977-1980 (Factory 1988)★★★★, The Peel Sessions (Strange Fruit 1990)★★★, Permanent: The Best Of Joy Division (London 1995)★★★★, Heart And Soul 4-CD box set (London 1997)★★★.
VIDEOS: Here Are The Young Men (IKON 1992).
FURTHER READING: An Ideal For Living: An History Of Joy Division, Mark Johnson. Touching From A Distance, Deborah Curtis. New Order & Joy Division, Claude Flowers.

JUDAS PRIEST
ALBUMS: Rocka Rolla (Gull 1974)★★, Sad Wings Of Destiny (Gull 1976)★★, Sin After Sin (Columbia 1977)★★★, Stained Class (Columbia 1978)★★★, Killing Machine (Columbia 1978)★★, Live-Unleashed In The East (Columbia 1979)★★★★, British Steel (Columbia 1980)★★★★, Point Of Entry (Columbia 1981)★★★, Screaming For Vengeance (Columbia 1982)★★★, Defenders Of The Faith (Columbia 1984)★★★, Turbo (Columbia 1986)★★, Priest Live (Columbia 1987)★★, Ram It Down (Columbia 1988)★★★, Painkiller (Columbia 1990)★★★.
COMPILATIONS: Collection (Castle 1989)★★★, Metal Works '73 – '93 (Columbia 1993)★★★★, Living After Midnight (Columbia 1997)★★★.
VIDEOS: Fuel Of Life (1986), Judas Priest Live (1987), Painkiller (1990), Metal Works 73-93 (1993).
FURTHER READING: Heavy Duty, Steve Gett.

JUDDS
ALBUMS: The Judds: Wynonna & Naomi mini-album (Curb/RCA 1984)★★, Why Not Me? (Curb/RCA 1984)★★★, Rockin' With The Rhythm Of The Rain (Curb/RCA 1985)★★★, Give A Little Love (Curb/RCA 1986)★★★, Heartland (Curb/RCA 1987)★★, Christmas Time With The Judds (Curb/RCA 1987)★★, River Of Time (Curb/RCA 1989)★★★, Love Can Build A Bridge (Curb/RCA 1990)★★★.
COMPILATIONS: Greatest Hits (Curb/RCA 1988)★★★★, Collector's Series (Curb/RCA 1993)★★★, Greatest Hits, Volume 2 (Curb/RCA 1991)★★★, The Judds Collection 1983 – 1990 3-CD box set (RCA 1991)★★★, Number One Hits (Curb 1995)★★★, The Essential Judds (RCA 1995)★★★★, The Judds Collection (Curb/The Hit 1996)★★★.
VIDEOS: Their Final Concert (1992), The Farewell Tour (1994).
FURTHER READING: The Judds: Unauthorized Biography, Bob Millard. Love Can Build A Bridge, Naomi Judd.

JUICY LUCY
ALBUMS: Juicy Lucy (Vertigo 1969)★★★, Lie Back And Enjoy It (Vertigo 1970)★★, Get A Whiff A This (Bronze 1971)★★, Pieces (Polydor 1972)★★.
COMPILATIONS: Who Do You Love: The Best Of (Sequel 1990)★★.

K

KAJAGOOGOO
ALBUMS: White Feathers (EMI 1983)★★, Islands (EMI 1984)★★.

KALEIDOSCOPE (UK)
ALBUMS: Tangerine Dream (Fontana 1967)★★★, Faintly Blowing (Fontana 1969)★★, White-Faced Lady (Kaleidoscope 1991)★★.
COMPILATIONS: Dive Into Yesterday (Fontana 1997)★★.

KALEIDOSCOPE (USA)
ALBUMS: Side Trips (Epic 1967)★★★, A Beacon From Mars (Epic 1968)★★★, Incredible Kaleidoscope (Epic 1969)★★★, Bernice (Epic 1970)★★, When Scopes Collide (Island 1976)★★★★★, Greetings From Kartoonistna ... (We Ain't Dead Yet) (Curb 1991)★★★.
COMPILATIONS: Bacon From Mars (1983)★★★, Rampe Rampe (Edsel 1984)★★★, Egyptian Candy (Legacy 1990)★★★, Blues From Bhagdad – The Very Best Of (1993)★★★.

KANSAS
ALBUMS: Kansas (Kirshner 1974)★★★, Song For America (Kirshner 1975)★★★, Masque (Kirshner 1976)★★★, Leftoverture (Kirshner 1977)★★★, Point Of Know Return (Kirshner 1977)★★★★, Two For The Show (Kirshner 1978)★★★, Monolith (Kirshner 1979)★★★, Audio-Visions (Kirshner 1980)★★★, Vinyl Confessions (Kirshner 1982)★★, Drastic Measures (Columbia 1983)★★, Power (MCA 1986)★★, In The Spirit Of Things (MCA 1988)★★, Live At The Whisky (1993)★, Freaks Of Nature (Intersound 1995)★★.
COMPILATIONS: The Best Of Kansas (Columbia 1984)★★★.

KATRINA AND THE WAVES
ALBUMS: Walking On Sunshine (Canada 1983)★★★, Katrina And The Waves 2 (Canada 1984)★★, Katrina And The Waves (Capitol 1985)★★, Waves (Capitol 1985)★★, Break Of Hearts (SBK 1989)★★, Walk On Water (Eternal 1997).

KC AND THE SUNSHINE BAND
ALBUMS: Do It Good (TK 1974)★★★, KC And The Sunshine Band (TK 1975)★★★, as the Sunshine Band The Sound Of Sunshine (TK 1975)★★, Part 3 (TK 1976)★★★★, I Like To Do It (Jay Boy 1977)★★★, Who Do Ya (Love) (TK 1978)★★, Do You Wanna Go Party (TK 1979)★★, Painter (Epic 1981)★★, All In A Night's Work (Epic 1983)★★, Oh Yeah! (ZYX 1993)★★, Get Down Live! (Intersound 1995)★★.
Solo: Wayne Casey/KC Space Cadet (Epic 1981)★★, KC Ten (Meca 1984)★★.
COMPILATIONS: Greatest Hits (TK 1980)★★★, The Best Of KC And The Sunshine Band (Rhino 1990)★★★★.

KEITA, SALIF
ALBUMS: Soro (Stern's 1987)★★★★, Ko-Yan (Mango 1990)★★, Amen (Mango 1991)★★, Folon (Mango 1995)★★★★, Sosie (MSS 1997)★★★.
COMPILATIONS: The Mansa Of Mali (Mango 1993)★★★.
VIDEOS: Salif Keita Live (1991).

KELLY, R.
ALBUMS: Born Into The '90s (Jive 1991)★★★, 12 Play (Jive 1994)★★★★, R. Kelly (Jive 1995)★★★.
VIDEOS: 12 Play-The Hit Videos Vol. 1 (Jive 1994), Top Secret Down Low Videos (6 West 1996).

KENICKIE
ALBUMS: Kenickie At The Club (EMI 1997)★★★.

KERSHAW, NIK
ALBUMS: Human Racing (MCA 1984)★★★, The Riddle (MCA 1984)★★★, Radio Musicola (MCA 1986)★★, The Works (MCA 1990)★★.
COMPILATIONS: The Collection (MCA 1991)★★★.

KHAN, CHAKA
ALBUMS: Chaka (Warners 1978)★★★, Naughty (Warners 1980)★★★, What Cha' Gonna Do For Me (Warners 1981)★★★, Echoes Of An Era (Elektra 1982)★★★, Chaka Khan (Warners 1982)★★★, I Feel For You (Warners 1984)★★★, Destiny (Warners 1986)★★, CK (Warners 1988)★★★, Life Is A Dance – The Remix Project (Warners 1989)★★, The Woman I Am (Warners 1992)★★★.
COMPILATIONS: Epiphany: The Best Of ... Vol. 1 (Reprise 1996)★★★★.
FILMS: Breakdance – The Movie (1984).

KID CREOLE AND THE COCONUTS
ALBUMS: Off The Coast Of Me (Ze 1980)★★★, Fresh Fruit In Foreign Places (Ze 1981)★★★, Tropical Gangsters aka Wise Guy (Ze 1982)★★★, Doppelganger (Ze 1983)★★★, In Praise Of Older Women And Other Crimes (Sire 1985)★★★, I, Too, Have Seen The Woods (Sire 1987)★★, Private Waters In The Great Divide (Columbia 1990)★★, You Shoulda Told Me You Were ... (Columbia 1991)★★.
COMPILATIONS: Cre-Ole: Best Of Kid Creole And The Coconuts (Island 1984)★★★, The Best Of ... (Island 1996)★★★. As The Coconuts: Don't Take My Coconuts (EMI 1983)★★★.
VIDEOS: Live At Hammersmith (1984).

KIDD, JOHNNY, AND THE PIRATES
COMPILATIONS: Shakin' All Over (Regal Starline 1971)★★★, Johnny Kidd – Rocker (EMI France 1978)★★★, The Best Of Johnny Kidd And The Pirates (EMI 1987)★★★, Rarities (See For Miles 1987)★★★, The Classic And The Rare (See For Miles 1990)★★★, The Complete Johnny Kidd (EMI 1992)★★★★.
FURTHER READING: Shaking All Over, Keith Hunt.

KIHN, GREG
ALBUMS: Greg Kihn (Beserkley 1975)★★, Greg Kihn Again (Beserkley 1977)★★★, Next Of Kihn (Beserkley 1978)★★, With The Naked Eye (Beserkley 1979)★★★, Glass House Rock (Beserkley 1980)★★, Rockihnroll (Beserkley 1981)★★★★, Kihntinued (Beserkley 1982)★★★, Kihnspiracy (Beserkley 1983)★★★★, Kihntageous (Beserkley 1984)★★★, Citizen Kihn (EMI 1985)★★, Love And Rock And Roll (EMI 1986)★★, Unkihntrollable (Rhino 1989)★★★, Kihn Of Hearts (FR 1992)★★★, Mutiny (Clean Cuts 1994)★★★, Horror Show (Clean Cuts 1996)★★★.
COMPILATIONS: Kihnsolidation: The Best Of Greg Kihn (Rhino 1989)★★★★.
FURTHER READING: Horror Show, Greg Kihn.

KILBURN AND THE HIGH ROADS
ALBUMS: Handsome (Dawn 1975)★★, Wotabunch (Warners 1978)★★.
COMPILATIONS: The Best Of Kilburn And The High Roads (Warners 1977)★★★.

KILLING JOKE
ALBUMS: Killing Joke (EG 1980)★★★, What's THIS For ...! (EG 1981)★★★, Revelations (Malicious Damage/EG 1982)★★★, Ha! Killing Joke Live (Malicious Damage/EG 1982)★★★, Fire Dances (EG 1983)★★★★, Night Time (EG 1985)★★★, Brighter Than A Thousand Suns (EG/Virgin 1986)★★★, Outside The Gate (EG/Virgin 1988)★★★, Extremities, Dirt And Various Repressed Emotions (RCA 1990)★★★, Pandemonium (Butterfly/Big Life 1994)★★★, BBC In Concert (Strange Fruit 1995)★★★, Democracy (Big Life 1996)★★★.
COMPILATIONS: An Incomplete Collection (EG 1990)★★★, Laugh? I Nearly Bought One (EG 1992)★★★, Wilful Days (Virgin 1995)★★★.

KING, ALBERT
ALBUMS: The Big Blues (King 1962)★★★, Born Under A Bad Sign (Atlantic 1967)★★★★, King Of The Blues Guitar (Atlantic 1968)★★★★, Live Wire/Blues Power (King 1968)★★★★, with Steve Cropper, 'Pops' Staples Jammed Together (Stax 1969)★★★, Years Gone By (Stax 1969)★★★★, King, Does The King's Thing (Stax 1970)★★★, Lovejoy (Stax 1971)★★★, The Lost Session (1971)★★★, I'll Play The Blues For You (Stax 1972)★★★, Live At Montreux/Blues At Sunrise (Stax 1973)★★★, I Wanna Get Funky (Stax 1974)★★, The Pinch (Stax 1976)★★, Albert (Utopia 1976)★★★, Truckload Of Lovin' (Utopia 1976)★★, Albert Live (Utopia 1977)★★★, King Albert (1977)★★★, New Orleans Heat (Tomato 1978)★★★, San Francisco '83 (Stax 1983)★★★, I'm In A 'Phone Booth, Baby (Stax 1984)★★★, with John Mayall The Lost Session rec. 1971 (Stax 1986)★★, Red House (Essential 1991)★★★, Blues At Sunset (Stax 1996)★★★.
COMPILATIONS: Laundromat Blues (Edsel 1984)★★★, The Best Of Albert King (Stax 1986)★★★, I'll Play The Blues For You: The Best Of Albert King (Stax 1988)★★★, Let's Have A Natural Ball rec. 1959-63 (Modern Blues Recordings 1989)★★★, Wednesday Night In San Francisco (Live At The Fillmore) and Thursday Night In San Francisco (Live At The Fillmore) (Stax 1990)★★, Live On Memory Lane (Monad 1995)★★★, Hard Bargain (Stax 1996)★★★★.

KING, B. B.
ALBUMS: Singin' The Blues (Crown 1957)★★★, The Blues (Crown 1958)★★★, B.B. King Wails (Crown 1959)★★★, B.B. King Sings Spirituals (Crown 1960)★★, The Great B.B. King (Crown 1961)★★★, King Of The Blues (Crown 1961)★★★, My Kind Of Blues (Crown 1961)★★★, More B.B. King (Crown 1962)★★★, Twist With B.B. King (Crown 1962)★★, Easy Listening Blues (Crown 1962)★★★, Blues In My Heart (Crown 1962)★★★, B.B. King (Crown 1963)★★★, Mr. Blues (ABC 1963)★★★, Rock Me Baby (1964)★★★★, Live At The Regal (ABC 1965)★★★★★, Confessin' The Blues (ABC 1965)★★★, Let Me Love You (1965)★★★, B.B. King Live On Stage (1965)★★★, The Soul Of B.B. King (1966)★★★, The Jungle (1967)★★★, Blues Is King (Bluesway 1967)★★★★, Blues On Top Of Blues (Bluesway 1968)★★★, Lucille (Bluesway 1968)★★★★, Live And Well (1969)★★★★, Completely Well (MCA 1969)★★★, Back In The Alley (MCA 1970)★★★, Indianola Mississippi Seeds (MCA 1970)★★★★, Live In Cook County Jail (MCA 1971)★★★★, In London (MCA 1971)★★★, L.A. Midnight (ABC 1972)★★★, Guess Who (ABC 1972)★★★, To Know You Is To Love You (ABC 1973)★★★, with Bobby Bland Together For The First Time ... Live (MCA 1974)★★★★, Friends (ABC 1974)★★★, Lucille Talks Back (MCA 1975)★★★★, with Bland Together Again ... Live (MCA 1976)★★★, King Size (MCA 1977)★★★, Midnight Believer (MCA 1978)★★★, Take It Home (MCA 1979)★★★, Now Appearing At Ole Miss (MCA 1980)★★, There Must Be A Better World Somewhere (MCA 1981)★★★★, Love Me Tender (MCA 1982)★★, Blues 'N' Jazz (MCA 1983)★★, Six Silver Strings (MCA 1985)★★, Do The Boogie (Ace 1988)★★★, Lucille Had A Baby (Ace 1989)★★, Live At San Quentin (MCA 1990)★★★★, Live At The Apollo (GRP 1991)★★★, Singin' The Blues & The Blues (Ace 1991)★★★, There's Always One More Time (MCA 1992)★★★★, Blues Summit (MCA 1993)★★★★, with Diane Schuur Heart To Heart (GRP 1994)★★, Lucille And Friends (MCA 1995)★★★, Deuces Wild (MCA 1997)★★★.
CD-ROM: On The Road With B.B. King (MCA 1996)★★★★.
COMPILATIONS: The Best Of B.B. King (MCA 1973)★★★★, The Rarest King (Blues Boy 1980)★★★, The Memphis Master (Ace 1982)★★★, Across The Tracks (Ace 1988)★★★, My Sweet Little Angel (Ace 1992)★★★, King Of The Blues 4-CD box set (MCA 1993)★★★★, King Of The Blues (Pickwick 1994)★★★, Heart & Soul: A Collection Of Blues Ballads (Pointblank Classic 1995)★★★, How Blue Can You Get Classic Live Performances 1964-1994 (MCA 1996)★★★★.
VIDEOS: Live At Nick's (Hendring 1987), A Blues Session (Video Collection 1988), Live In Africa (BMG Video 1991), Blues Master, Highlights (Warner Music 1995), The Blues Summit Concert (MCA 1995).
FURTHER READING: The Arrival Of BB King: The Authorized Biography, Charles Sawyer. B.B. King, Sebastian Danchin. Blues All Around Me, The Autobiography Of B.B. King, B.B. King and David Ritz.

KING, BEN E.
ALBUMS: Spanish Harlem (Atco 1961)★★★, Ben E. King Sings For Soulful Lovers (Atco 1962)★★★, Don't Play That Song (Atco 1962)★★★, Young Boy Blues (Clarion 1964), Seven Letters (Atco 1965)★★★, What Is Soul (Atco 1967)★★★, Rough Edges (1970)★★★, Beginning Of It All (1971)★★★, Supernatural (Atco 1975)★★★, I Had A Love (Atco 1976)★★, with the Average White Band Benny And Us (Atlantic 1977)★★★, Let Me Live In Your Life (Atco 1978)★★, Music Trance (Atlantic 1980)★★, Street Tough (Atlantic 1981)★★, Save The Last Dance For Me (EMI 1988)★★★.
COMPILATIONS: Greatest Hits (1964)★★★, Stand By Me: The Best Of Ben E. King (Atlantic 1986)★★★, The Ultimate Collection: Ben E. King (Atlantic 1987)★★★★, Anthology One: Spanish Harlem (RSA 1996)★★★, Anthology Two: For Soulful Lovers (RSA 1996)★★★, Anthology Three: Don't Play That Song (RSA 1996)★★★, Anthology Four: Seven Letters (RSA 1997)★★★, Anthology Five: What Is Soul? (RSA 1997)★★★, Anthology Six: Supernatural (RSA 1997)★★★, Anthology Seven: Benny And Us (RSA 1997)★★.

KING, CAROLE
ALBUMS: Writer (Ode 1970)★★★, Tapestry (Ode 1971)★★★★, Music (Ode 1971)★★★, Rhymes And Reasons (Ode 1972)★★★, Fantasy (Ode 1973)★★★★, Wrap Around Joy (Ode 1974)★★★, Really Rosie (Ode 1975)★★★, Thoroughbred (Ode 1976)★★★, Simple Things (Capitol 1977)★★, Welcome Home (Avatar 1978)★★, Touch The Sky (Capitol 1979)★★, Pearls (Songs Of Goffin And King) (Capitol 1980)★★, One To One (Atlantic 1982)★★, Speeding Time (Atlantic 1984)★★★, City Streets (Capitol 1989)★★, In Concert (Quality 1994)★★.
COMPILATIONS: Her Greatest Hits (Ode 1973)★★★, Carole King, A Natural Woman – The Ode Collection 1968-1976 (Legacy 1995)★★★★.
VIDEOS: In Concert (Wienerworld 1994).
FURTHER READING: Carole King, Paula Taylor. Carole King: A Biography In Words & Pictures, Mitchell S. Cohen.

KING, EVELYN 'CHAMPAGNE'
ALBUMS: Smooth Talk (RCA 1977)★★★, Music Box (RCA 1979)★★★, Call On Me (RCA 1980)★★★, I'm In Love (RCA 1981)★★★, Get Loose (RCA 1982)★★★, Face To Face (RCA 1983)★★, So Romantic (RCA 1984)★★, A Long Time Coming (RCA 1985)★★, Flirt (EMI 1988)★★★.
COMPILATIONS: The Best Of Evelyn 'Champagne' King (RCA 1990)★★★, The Essential Works Of (1992)★★★.

KING, FREDDIE
ALBUMS: Freddie King Sings The Blues (King 1961)★★★, Let's Hideaway And Dance Away (King 1961)★★★★, Boy-Girl-Boy (King 1962)★★★, Bossa Nova And Blues (King 1962)★★, Freddie King Goes Surfing (King 1963)★★, Freddie King Gives You A Bonanza Of Instrumentals (King 1965)★★★, 24 Vocals And Instrumentals (King 1966)★★★, Hide Away (King 1969)★★★★, Freddie King Is A Blues Master (Atlantic 1969)★★★, My Feeling For The Blues (Atlantic 1970)★★★, Getting Ready (Shelter 1971)★★★★, Texas Cannonball (Shelter 1972)★★★, Woman Across The Water (Shelter 1973)★★★, Burglar (RSO 1974)★★★, Larger Than Life (RSO 1975)★★★.
COMPILATIONS: King Of R&B Volume 2 (1969)★★★, The Best Of Freddie King (Shelter 1974)★★★★, Original Hits (1977)★★★, Rockin' The Blues – Live (Crosscut 1983)★★★, Takin' Care Of Business (Charly 1985)★★★, Live In Antibes, 1974 (Concert 1988)★★★, Live In Nancy, 1975 Volume 1 (Concert 1989)★★★, Blues Guitar Hero: The Influential Early Sessions (1993)★★★, King Of The Blues (EMI/Shelter 1996)★★★★, Key To The Highway (Wolf 1995)★★★.
VIDEOS: Freddie King Jan 20 1973 (Vestapol 1995), Freddie King In Concert (Vestapol 1995), Freddie King: The Beat 1966 (Vestapol 1995).

KING, JONATHAN
ALBUMS: Or Then Again (Decca 1965)★★, Try Something Different (Decca 1972)★★, A Rose In A Fisted Glove (UK 1975)★★, JK All The Way (UK 1976)★★, Anticloning (1992)★★.
COMPILATIONS: King Size King (PRT 1982)★★, The Butterfly That Stamped (Castle 1989)★★, The Many Faces Of Jonathan King (1993)★★.

KING CRIMSON
ALBUMS: In The Court Of The Crimson King (Island 1969)★★★★, In The Wake Of Poseidon (Island 1970)★★★, Lizard (Island 1970)★★★, Islands (Island 1971)★★, Earthbound (Island 1972)★★, Larks Tongues In Aspic (Island 1973)★★★★, Starless And Bible Black (Island 1974)★★★, Red (Island 1974)★★★★, USA (Island 1975)★★★, Discipline (EG 1981)★★★, Beat (EG 1982)★★★, Three Of A Perfect Pair (EG 1984)★★★, Thrak (Virgin 1995)★★★, Vroom (Discipline 1995), B'Boom (Discipline 1995), THRaKaTTak (Discipline 1996), Night Watch (Discipline 1998).
COMPILATIONS: A Young Person's Guide To King Crimson (Island 1976)★★★, The Compact King Crimson (EG 1986)★★★, The Essential King Crimson – Frame By Frame (EG 1991)★★★★, The Great Deceiver (1992)★★★, Epitaph: Live In 1969 (Discipline 1997)★★★, Absent Lovers (1998)★★★, Schizoid Dimension: A Tribute Album (1998)★★★.

KING CURTIS
ALBUMS: Have Tenor Sax, Will Blow (Atco 1959)★★★, The New Scene Of King Curtis (New Jazz 1960)★★★, Azure (Everest 1961)★★★, Trouble In Mind (Tru-Sound 1961)★★★, Doin' The Dixie Twist (Tru-Sound 1962)★★★, It's Party Time (Tru-Sound 1962)★★★★, Soul Meeting (Prestige 1962)★★★, Arthur Murray's Music For Dancing: The Twist (RCA Victor 1962)★★, Soul Twist (Enjoy 1962)★★★, Country Soul (Capitol 1963)★★, The Great King Curtis (Clarion 1964)★★, Soul Serenade (Capitol 1964)★★★, King Curtis Plays The Hits Made Famous By Sam Cooke (Capitol 1965)★★★, That Lovin' Feelin' (Atco 1966)★★★, Live At Small's Paradise (Atco 1966)★★★, Plays The The Great Memphis Hits (Atco 1967)★★★, King Size Soul (Atco 1967)★★, Sax In Motion (1968)★★, Sweet Soul (Atco 1968)★★★, Instant Groove (1969)★★, Eternally Soul (1970)★★★, Get Ready (1970)★★★, Blues At Montreux (1970)★★★, Live At Fillmore West (1971)★★, Mr. Soul (1972)★★★, Everybody's Talkin' (1972)★★, Jazz Groove (1974)★★★.
COMPILATIONS: Best Of King Curtis (Capitol 1968)★★★★, 20 Golden Pieces (1982)★★★, Didn't He Play! (1988)★★★, It's Partytime With King Curtis (1989)★★★, Instant Groove (1990)★★★★, The Capitol Years 1962-65 (1993)★★★★, Instant Soul – The Legendary King Curtis (1994)★★★★.

KINGSMEN
ALBUMS: The Kingsmen In Person (Wand 1963)★★, The Kingsmen, Volume 2 (More Great Sounds) (Wand 1964)★★, The Kingsmen, Volume 3 (Wand 1965)★★, The Kingsmen On Campus (Wand 1965)★★, How To Stuff A Wild Bikini film soundtrack (1965)★, Up Up And Away (Wand 1966)★★.
COMPILATIONS: The Kingsmen's Greatest Hits (1967)★★, Louie Louie/Greatest Hits (1986)★★.
FILMS: How To Stuff A Wild Bikini (1965).

KINGSTON TRIO
ALBUMS: The Kingston Trio (Capitol 1958)★★★, From The Hungry i (Capitol 1959)★★★, The Kingston Trio At Large (Capitol 1959)★★★★, Stereo Concert (Capitol 1959)★★★, Here We Go Again (Capitol 1959)★★★★, Sold Out (Capitol 1960)★★★, String Along (Capitol 1960)★★★, The Last Month Of The Year (Capitol 1960)★★★, Make Way! (Capitol 1961)★★★, Goin' Places (Capitol 1961)★★★, Close-Up (Capitol 1961)★★★, College Concert (Capitol 1962)★★★, Something Special (Capitol 1962)★★★, New Frontier (Capitol 1963)★★★, The Kingston Trio No. 16 (Capitol 1963)★★, Sunny Side (Capitol 1963)★★, Sing A Song With The Kingston Trio (Capitol 1963)★★, Time To Think (Capitol 1963)★★★, Back In Town (Capitol 1964)★★★, The Folk Era 3-LP box set (Capitol 1964)★★★, Nick-Bob-John (Decca 1965)★★, Stay Awhile (Decca 1965)★★, Somethin' Else (Decca 1965)★★, Children Of The Morning (Decca1966)★★, Once Upon A Time (Tetragrammaton 1969)★★, American Gold (Longines 1973)★★★★, The World Needs A Melody (1973)★★★, Aspen Gold (1979)★★★.
COMPILATIONS: Encores (Capitol 1961)★★★★, The Best Of The Kingston Trio (Capitol 1962)★★★★, Folk Era (1964)★★★, The Best Of The Kingston Trio Vol. 2 (Capitol 1965)★★★★, The Best Of The Kingston Trio Vol. 3 (Capitol 1966)★★★, Once Upon A Time (1969)★★★, The Kingston Trio (1972)★★★, Where Have All The Flowers Gone (1972)★★★★, The Historic Recordings Of The Kingston Trio (1975)★★★★, The Very Best Of The Kingston Trio (1987)★★★★, The EP Collection (See For Miles 1997)★★★★.
FURTHER READING: The Kingston Trio On Record, Kingston Korner.

KINKS
ALBUMS: Kinks (Pye 1964)★★★, Kinda Kinks (Pye 1965)★★★, The Kink Kontroversy (Pye 1966)★★★, Face To Face (Pye 1966)★★★★, Live At The Kelvin Hall (Pye 1967)★, Something Else (Pye 1967)★★★★★, The Kinks Are The Village Green Preservation Society (Pye 1968)★★★★★, Arthur Or The Decline And Fall Of The British Empire (Pye 1969)★★★★, Lola Versus Powerman And The Moneygoround, Part One (Pye 1970)★★★, Percy film soundtrack (Pye 1971)★★, Muswell Hillbillies (RCA 1971)★★★★, Everbody's In Showbiz, Everybody's A Star (RCA 1972)★★★ Preservation Act 1 (RCA 1973)★★, Preservation Act 2 (RCA 1974)★★, Soap Opera (RCA 1975)★★, Schoolboys In Disgrace (RCA 1975)★★★, Sleepwalker (Arista 1977)★★★, Misfits (Arista 1978)★★★★, Low Budget (Arista 1979)★★★, One For The Road (Arista 1980)★★★, Give The People What They Want (Arista 1982)★★★, State Of Confusion (Arista 1983)★★★, Word Of Mouth (Arista 1984)★★, Think Visual (London 1986)★★, The Road (London 1988)★★, UK Jive (London 1989)★★, Phobia (Columbia 1993)★★★, To The Bone (Konk 1994)★★★, To The Bone (USA) (Guardian 1996)★★★★.
COMPILATIONS: Well Respected Kinks (Marble Arch 1966)★★★★, The Kinks double CD (Pye 1970)★★★★, A Golden Hour Of The Kinks (Golden Hour 1973)★★★★, All The Good Times 4-LP box set (Pye 1973)★★★★, The Kinks File (Pye 1977)★★★★, Greatest Hits (PRT 1983)★★★, The Ultimate Collection (Castle 1989)★★★★, The EP Collection (See For Miles 1990)★★★★, Fab Forty: The Singles Collection, 1964-70 (Descal 1991)★★★★.
FURTHER READING: The Kinks: The Sound And The Fury, Johnny Rogan. The Kinks: The Official Biography, Jon Savage. You Really Got Me: The Kinks Part One, Doug Hinman. X-Ray, Ray Davies. Kink: An Autobiography, Dave Davies. The Kinks: Well Respected Men, Neville Marten and Jeffrey Hudson.

KISS
ALBUMS: Kiss (Casablanca 1974)★★★, Hotter Than Hell (Casablanca 1974)★★, Dressed to Kill (Casablanca 1975)★★★, Alive (Casablanca 1975)★★★, Destroyer (Casablanca 1976)★★★★, Rock And Roll Over (Casablanca 1976)★★, Love Gun (Casablanca 1977)★★★, Alive II (Casablanca 1977)★★★, Dynasty (Casablanca 1979)★★, Unmasked (Casablanca 1980)★★, Music From The Elder (Casablanca 1981)★★, Creatures Of The Night (Casablanca 1982)★★, Lick It Up (Vertigo 1983)★★, Animalize (Vertigo 1984)★★, Asylum (Vertigo 1985)★★, Crazy Nights (Vertigo 1987)★★, Hot In The Shade (Vertigo 1989)★★, Revenge (Mercury 1992)★★★, Alive III (Mercury 1993)★★, MTV Unplugged (Mercury 1996)★★★, Carnival Of Souls (Mercury 1997)★★.
COMPILATIONS: The Originals (Casablanca 1976)★★★, Double Platinum (Casablanca 1978)★★★, Killers (Casablanca 1982)★★★, Smashes, Thrashes And Hits (Vertigo 1988)★★★, You Wanted The Best, You Got The Best (Mercury 1996)★★★★, Greatest Kiss (Mercury 1996)★★★.
VIDEOS: Animalize (Embassy Home Video 1986), The Phantom Of The Park (IVS 1987), Exposed (Polygram 1987), Crazy Crazy Nights (Channel 5 1988), Age Of Chance (Virgin Vision 1988), X-Treme Close Up (1992), Konfidential (1993), Kiss My A** (Polygram 1994), Unplugged (Polygram 1996).
FURTHER READING: Still On Fire, Dave Thomas. Kiss: The Greatest Rock Show On Earth, John Swenson. Kiss: The Real Story Authorized, Peggy Tomarkin. Kiss, Robert Duncan. Kiss and Sell: The Making of a Supergroup, C.K. Lendt.

KITT, EARTHA
ALBUMS: New Faces Of 1952 original cast (RCA Victor 1952)★★★, Songs (RCA Victor 1953)★★★, That Bad Eartha (RCA Victor 1953)★★★★, Down To Eartha (RCA Victor 1955)★★★, Thursday's Child (RCA Victor 1956)★★★, St. Louis Blues (RCA Victor 1958)★★★, The Fabulous Eartha Kitt (Kapp 1959)★★★, Eartha Kitt Revisited (Kapp 1960)★★★, Bad But Beautiful (MGM 1962)★★★, At The Plaza (1965)★★★, Sings In Spanish (Decca 1965)★★★, C'est Si Bon (1983)★★★, I Love Men (1984)★★★, Love For Sale (1984)★★, The Romantic Eartha Kitt (1984)★★, Eartha Kitt In Person At The Plaza (1988)★★★★, I'm A Funny Dame (1988)★★★, My Way (1988)★★★, Primitive Man (1989)★★★, I'm Still Here (1989)★★★, Live In London (1990)★★★★, Thinking Jazz (1992)★★★, Back In Business (1994)★★★.
COMPILATIONS: At Her Very Best (1982)★★★, Diamond Series: Eartha Kitt (1988)★★★, Best Of Eartha Kitt (1990)★★★.
FURTHER READING: Thursday's Child, Eartha Kitt. Alone With Me: A New Biography, Eartha Kitt. I'm Still Here, Eartha Kitt.

KLAATU
ALBUMS: Klaatu (Capitol 1976)★★★, Hope (Capitol 1977)★★, Sir Army Suit (Capitol 1978)★★, Endangered Species (Capitol 1980)★★, Magentalane (1981)★★.

KLF
ALBUMS: Towards The Trance (KLF Communications 1988)★★★★, The What Time Is Love Story (KLF Communications 1989)★★★, The White Room (KLF Communications 1990)★★★, Chill Out (KLF Communications 1990)★★★.
VIDEOS: Stadium House (PMI 1991).
FURTHER READING: Justified And Ancient: The Unfolding Story Of The KLF, Pete Robinson. Bad Wisdom, Mark Manning and Bill Drummond.

KNACK
ALBUMS: The Knack (Capitol 1979)★★★, But The Little Girls Understand (Capitol 1980)★★, Round Trip (Capitol 1981)★★, Serious Fun (Charisma 1991)★★.
COMPILATIONS: The Best Of ... (1993)★★.

KNICKERBOCKERS
ALBUMS: Sing And Sync-Along With Lloyd: Lloyd Thaxton Presents The Knickerbockers (Challenge 1965)★★, Jerk And Twine Time (Challenge 1966)★★★, Lies (Challenge 1966)★★★.
COMPILATIONS: The Fabulous Knickerbockers (1988)★★★, A Rave-Up With The Knickerbockers (Big Beat 1993)★★★, Hits, Rarities, Unissued Cuts And More ... (Sundazed 1997)★★★.

KNIGHT, GLADYS, AND THE PIPS
ALBUMS: Letter Full Of Tears (Fury 1961)★★, Gladys Knight And The Pips (Maxx 1964)★★, Everybody Needs Love (Soul 1967)★★★, Feelin' Bluesy (Soul 1968)★★★, Silk 'N' Soul (Soul 1969)★★★, Nitty Gritty (Soul 1969)★★★, All In A Knight's Work (Soul 1970)★★★, If I Were Your Woman (Soul 1971)★★★, Standing Ovation (Soul 1972)★★★, Neither One Of Us (Soul 1973)★★★★, All I Need Is Time (Soul 1973)★★★, Imagination (Buddah 1973)★★★★, Knight Time (Soul 1974)★★, Claudine (Buddah 1974)★★★, I Feel A Song (Buddah 1974)★★★, A Little Knight Music (Soul 1975)★★, Second Anniversary (Buddah 1975)★★★, Bless This House (Buddah 1976)★★, Pipe Dreams film soundtrack (Buddah 1976)★★, Still Together (Buddah 1977)★★★, The One And Only (Buddah 1978)★★★, About Love (Columbia 1980)★★, Touch (Columbia 1981)★★★, That Special Time Of Year (Columbia 1982)★★, Visions (Columbia 1983)★★★, Life (Columbia 1985)★★★, All Our Love (MCA 1987)★★★. Solo: Gladys Knight Miss Gladys Knight (Buddah 1979)★★, Good Woman (MCA 1991)★★★. The Pips At Last – The Pips (Casablanca 1979)★★, Callin' (Casablanca 1979)★★.
COMPILATIONS: Gladys Knight And The Pips Greatest Hits (Soul 1970)★★★★, Anthology (Motown 1974)★★★★, The Best Of Gladys Knight And The Pips (Buddah 1976)★★★★, 30 Greatest (K-Tel 1977)★★★, The Collection – 20 Greatest Hits (1984)★★★, The Best Of Gladys Knight And The Pips: The Columbia Years (Columbia 1988)★★★, Every Beat Of My Heart: The Greatest Hits (Chameleon 1989)★★★, The Singles Album (Polygram 1989)★★★, Soul Survivors: The Best Of Gladys Knight And The Pips (Rhino 1990)★★★★, 17 Greatest Hits (1992)★★★.

KNOPFLER, MARK
ALBUMS: Music From 'Local Hero' soundtrack (Vertigo 1983)★★★, Cal – Music From The Film soundtrack (Vertigo 1984)★★★, The Princess Bride soundtrack (Warners 1987)★★, Last Exit To Brooklyn (Warners 1989)★★, with Chet Atkins Neck And Neck (Columbia 1990)★★★, Golden Heart (Mercury 1996)★★★, film soundtrack Wag The Dog (Polygram 1998)★★★.
FURTHER READING: Mark Knopfler: An Unauthorised Biography, Myles Palmer.

KOKOMO (UK)
ALBUMS: Kokomo (Columbia 1975)★★★, Rise And Shine! (Columbia 1976)★★, Kokomo (Columbia 1982)★★.
Solo: Tony O'Malley Naked Flame (Jazz House 1995)★★★.
COMPILATIONS: The Collection (1992)★★★.

KOOL AND THE GANG
ALBUMS: Kool And The Gang (1969)★★, Live At The Sex Machine (De-Lite 1971)★★, Live At P.J.s (De-Lite 1971)★★, Music Is The Message (1972)★★, Good Times (De-Lite 1973)★★★, Wild And Peaceful (De-Lite 1973)★★★, Light Of Worlds (De-Lite 1974)★★★, Spirit Of The Boogie (De-Lite 1975)★★, Love And Understanding (De-Lite 1976)★★, Open Sesame (De-Lite 1976)★★, The Force (De-Lite 1977)★★, Everybody's Dancin' (1978)★★, Ladies' Night (De-Lite 1979)★★★, Celebrate! (De-Lite 1980)★★★, Something Special (De-Lite 1981)★★, As One (De-Lite 1982)★★, In The Heart (De-Lite 1983)★★★★, Emergency (De-Lite 1984)★★, Victory (Curb 1986)★★, Forever (Mercury 1986)★★, Sweat (Mercury 1989)★★, Kool Love (Telstar 1990)★★, State Of Affairs (Curb 1996)★★.
I COMPILATIONS: Kool And The Gang Greatest Hits! (De-Lite 1975)★★★, Spin Their Top Hits (De-Lite 1978)★★★★, Kool Kuts (De-Lite 1982)★★★, Twice As Kool (De-Lite 1983)★★★★, The Singles Collection (De-Lite 1988)★★★★, Everything's Kool And The Gang: Greatest Hits And More (Mercury 1988)★★★★, Great And Remixed 91 (Mercury 1992)★★★, Collection (Spectrum 1996)★★★.

KOOPER, AL
ALBUMS: with Mike Bloomfield, Stephen Stills Super Session (Columbia 1968)★★★★, The Live Adventures Of Al Kooper And Mike Bloomfield (Columbia 1969)★★, I Stand Alone (Columbia 1969)★★★, You Never Know Who Your Friends Are (Columbia 1969)★★, with Shuggie Otis Kooper Session (Columbia 1970)★★, Easy Does It (Columbia 1970)★★★★, Landlord soundtrack (1971)★★, New York City (You're A Woman) (Columbia 1971)★★★, A Possible Projection Of The Future/Childhood's End (Columbia 1972)★, Naked Songs (1973)★★, Unclaimed Freight (Columbia 1975)★★, Act Like Nothing's Wrong (United Artists 1977)★★, Championship Wrestling (1982)★★, Live: Soul Of A Man (Music Masters 1995)★★★, You Never Know Who (1997)★★★.
COMPILATIONS: Al's Big Deal (Columbia 1989)★★★.
FURTHER READING: Backstage Pass, Al Kooper with Ben Edmonds. Backstage Passes and Backstabbing Bstards, Al Kooper with Ben Edmonds.

KORN
ALBUMS: Korn (Immortal 1995)★★★, Life Is Peachy (Epic 1996)★★★.
VIDEOS: Who Then Now? (SMV 1997).

KORNER, ALEXIS
ALBUMS: by Alexis Korner's Blues Incorporated R&B From The Marquee (Ace Of Clubs 1962)★★★★, Alexis Korner's Blues Incorporated (Ace Of Clubs 1964)★★★, Red Hot From Alex aka Alexis Korner's All Star Blues Incorporated (Transatlantic 1964)★★★★, At The Cavern (Oriole 1964)★★★, Sky High (Spot 1966)★★, Blues Incorporated (Wednesday Night Prayer Meeting) (Polydor 1967)★★★; by Alexis Korner I Wonder Who (Fontana 1967)★★★, A New Generation Of Blues aka What's That Sound I Hear (Transatlantic 1968)★★★, Both Sides Of Alexis Korner (Metronome 1969)★★★, Alexis (Rak 1971)★★★, Mr. Blues (Toadstool 1974)★★★, Alexis Korner (Polydor 1974)★★★, Get Off My Cloud (Columbia 1975)★★★, Just Easy (Intercord 1978)★★★, Me (Jeton 1979)★★★, The Party Album (Intercord 1980)★★★, Juvenile Delinquent (1984)★★, Live In Paris: Alexis Korner (Magnum 1988)★★★; by New Church The New Church (Metronome 1970); by Snape Accidentally Born In New Orleans (Transatlantic 1973)★★★, Snape Live On Tour (Brain 1974)★★★.
COMPILATIONS: Bootleg Him (Rak 1972)★★★, Profile (Teldec 1981)★★★, with Cyril Davies Alexis 1957 (Krazy Kat 1984)★★★, with Colin Hodgkinson Testament (Thunderbolt 1985)★★★, Alexis Korner 1961-1972 (Castle 1986)★★★, Hammer And Nails (Thunderbolt 1987)★★★, The Alexis Korner Collection (Castle 1988)★★★.
VIDEOS: Eat A Little Rhythm And Blues (BBC Video 1988).
FURTHER READING: Alexis Korner: The Biography, Harry Shapiro.

KOSSOFF, PAUL
ALBUMS: Back Street Crawler (Island 1973)★★★, Live In Croydon, June 15th 1975 (Repertoire 1995)★★.
COMPILATIONS: Koss (DJM 1977)★★★, Blue Soul (Island 1986)★★★, The Collection (Hit Label 1995)★★★, Stone Free (Carlton Sounds 1997)★★★.

KOTTKE, LEO
ALBUMS: 12-String Blues: Live At The Scholar Coffee House (Oblivion 1968)★★★, Six And Twelve String Guitar (Takoma/Sonet 1971)★★★, Circle Round The Sun (Symposium 1970)★★★, Mudlark (Capitol 1971)★★★, Greenhouse (Capitol 1972)★★★★, My Feet Are Smiling (Capitol 1973)★★★★, Ice Water (Capitol 1974)★★★★, Dreams And All That Stuff (Capitol 1975)★★, Chewing Pine (Capitol 1975)★★★, Leo Kottke (Chrysalis 1976)★★★★, Burnt Lips (Chrysalis 1979)★★★, Balance (Chrysalis 1979)★★, Leo Kottke Live In Europe (Chrysalis 1980), Guitar Music (Chrysalis 1981)★★★, Time Step (Chrysalis 1983)★★★★, A Shout Towards Noon (Private Music 1986)★★★, Regards From Chuck Pink (Private Music 1988)★★★★, My Father's Face (Private Music 1989)★★★, That's What (Private Music 1990)★★★, Great Big Boy (Private Music 1991)★★★, Peculiaroso (Private Music 1994)★★★, Live (Private Music 1995)★★★, Standing In My Shoes (Private Music 1997)★★★★.
COMPILATIONS: Leo Kottke 1971-1976 – Did You Hear Me? (Capitol 1976)★★★, The Best Of Leo Kottke (Capitol 1977)★★★, The Best Of Leo Kottke (EMI 1979)★★★, Essential Leo Kottke (Chrysalis 1991)★★★★.

KRAFTWERK
ALBUMS: Highrail (1971)★★, Var (1972)★★, Ralf & Florian (Philips 1973)★★★, Autobahn (Vertigo 1974)★★★★, Radioactivity (Capitol 1975)★★★, Trans-Europe Express (Capitol 1977)★★★★, The Man-Machine (Capitol 1978)★★★★, Computer World (EMI 1981)★★★★, Electric Cafe (EMI 1986)★★★.
ICOMPILATION: The Mix (EMI 1991)★★★★.
FURTHER READING: Kraftwerk: Man, Machine & Music, Pacal Bussy.

KRAMER, BILLY J., AND THE DAKOTAS
ALBUMS: Listen – To Billy J. Kramer (Parlophone 1963)★★★, Little Children (Imperial 1964)★★★, I'll Keep You Satisfied (Imperial 1964)★★★, Trains And Boats And Planes (Imperial 1965)★★, Kramer Versus Kramer (1986)★★.
COMPILATIONS: The Best Of Billy J. Kramer (1984)★★★, The EMI Years (1991)★★★, The EP Collection (See For Miles 1995)★★★.

KRAVITZ, LENNY
ALBUMS: Let Love Rule (Virgin 1989)★★★, Mama Said (Virgin 1991)★★★, Are You Gonna Go My Way? (Virgin 1993)★★★, Circus (Virgin 1995)★★.
VIDEOS: Alive From Planet Earth (1994)★★★.

KRISTOFFERSON, KRIS
ALBUMS: Kristofferson (Monument 1970)★★, The Silver-Tongued Devil And I (Monument 1971)★★★, Me And Bobby McGee (Monument 1971)★★★, Border Lord (Monument 1972)★★★, Jesus Was A Capricorn (Monument 1972)★★★, with Rita Coolidge Full Moon (A&M 1973)★★★, Spooky Lady's Sideshow (Monument 1974)★★, with Coolidge Breakaway (A&M 1974)★, Who's To Bless ... And Who's To Blame (Monument 1975)★★, Surreal Thing (Monument 1976)★★, five tracks on A Star Is Born film soundtrack (Monument 1976)★★★, Easter Island (Monument 1977)★★, with Coolidge Natural Act (A&M 1979)★★, Shake Hands With The Devil (Monument 1979)★★★, To The Bone (Monument 1981)★★, with Dolly Parton, Brenda Lee, Willie Nelson The Winning Hand (Monument 1983)★★★, with Willie Nelson Music From Songwriter film soundtrack (Columbia 1984)★★★, with Nelson, Johnny Cash, Waylon Jennings Highwayman (Columbia 1985)★★★★, Repossessed (Mercury 1986)★★, Third World Warrior (Mercury 1990)★★, with Nelson, Cash, Jennings Highwayman 2 (Columbia 1990)★★★, Live At The Philharmonic (Monument 1992)★★★, with Nelson, Cash, Jennings The Road Goes On Forever (Liberty 1995)★★, A Moment Of Forever (Justice 1995)★★.
COMPILATIONS: The Songs Of Kristofferson (Monument 1977)★★★, Country Store (Starblend 1988)★★★, The Legendary Years (Connoisseur Collection 1990)★★★, Singer/Songwriter (Monument 1991)★★★, The Best Of Kristofferson (Sony 1995)★★★★.
FILMS: The Last Movie (1970), Cisco Pike (1972), Blume In Love (1973), Pat Garrett And Billy The Kid (1973), Bring Me The Head Of Alfredo Garcia (1974), Alice Doesn't Live Here Any More (1975), The Sailor Who Fell From Grace With The Sea (1976), A Star Is Born (1976), Vigilante Force (1976), Semi-Tough (1978), Convoy (1978), Heaven's Gate (1980), Rollover (1981), Flashpoint (1984), Songwriter (1984), Trouble In Mind (1985), Blood And Orchids television movie (1986).
FURTHER READING: Kris Kristofferson, Beth Kalet.

KROKUS
ALBUMS: Krokus (Schmontz 1975)★★, To You All (Schmontz 1977)★★, Painkiller (Mercury 1978)★★, Pay It In Metal (Mercury 1979)★★, Metal Rendez-vous (Ariola 1980)★★★, Hardware (Ariola 1981)★★★, One Vice At A Time (Ariola 1982)★★★, Headhunter (Arista 1983)★★★, The Blitz (Arista 1984)★★, Change Of Address (Arista 1985)★★, Alive And Screamin' (Arista 1986)★★, Heart Attack (MCA 1987)★★, Stampede (Ariola 1990)★★.

KULA SHAKER
ALBUMS: K (Columbia 1996)★★★★.
FURTHER READING: Kula Shaker, Nigel Cross.

KURSAAL FLYERS
ALBUMS: Chocs Away (UK 1975)★★★, The Great Artiste (UK 1975)★★★, Golden Mile (Columbia 1976)★★★, Five Live Kursaals (Columbia 1977)★★, Former Tour De Force Is Forced To Tour (Waterfront 1988)★★.
COMPILATIONS: The Best Of The Kursaal Flyers (Teldec 1983)★★★, In For A Spin (Edsel 1985)★★★.

L

L7
ALBUMS: L7 (Epitaph 1988)★★★, Smell The Magic mini-album (Sub Pop 1990)★★★, Bricks Are Heavy (Slash/London 1992)★★★★, Hungry For Stink (Slash/London 1994)★★★, The Beauty Process: Triple Platinum (Slash/Reprise 1997)★★★.

L.A. GUNS
ALBUMS: L.A. Guns (Polygram 1988)★★, Cocked And Loaded (Polygram 1989)★★★, Hollywood Vampires (Polygram 1991)★★★, Vicious Circle (Polygram 1994)★★★, American hardcore (CMC International 1996)★★★.
VIDEOS: One More Reason (1989), Love, Peace & Geese (1990).

LA'S
ALBUMS: The La's (Go! Discs 1990)★★★★, Strange Things Happening (Rounder 1994)★★.

LaBELLE, PATTI
ALBUMS: Patti LaBelle (Epic 1977)★★★, Tasty (Epic 1978)★★★, It's Alright With Me (Epic 1979)★★★, Released (Epic 1980)★★★, The Spirit's In It (Philadelphia International 1981)★★★, I'm In Love Again (Philadelphia International 1983)★★★, Patti (Philadelphia International 1985)★★★, The Winner In You (MCA 1986)★★★, Be Yourself (MCA 1989)★★, Starlight Christmas (MCA 1990)★★★, Burnin' (MCA 1991)★★★, Live! (MCA 1992)★★, Gems (MCA 1994)★★★, Flame (MCA 1997)★★★.
COMPILATIONS: Best Of ... (Epic 1986)★★★, Greatest Hits (MCA 1996)★★★.

LADYSMITH BLACK MAMBAZO
ALBUMS: Amabutho (BL 1973)★★★, Isitimela (BL 1974)★★★, Amaqhawe (BL 1976)★★★, Ulwandle Olunggewele (BL 1977)★★★, Umthombo Wamanzi (BL 1982)★★★, Ibhayibheli Liyindlela (BL 1984)★★★, Unduku Zethu (Shanachie 1984)★★★, Inala (Shanachie 1986)★★★, Ezulwini Siyakhona (1986)★★★, Shaka Zulu (Warners 1987)★★★★, Journey Of Dreams (Warners 1988)★★★★, with Danny Glover How The Leopard Got His Spots (Windham Hill 1989)★★★, Two Worlds One Heart (Warners 1990)★★★★, Inkanyezi Nezazi (1992)★★★, Liph'Iqiniso (Flame Tree 1994)★★★, Gift Of The Tortoise (Flame Tree 1995)★★★, Heavenly (Shanchie 1997)★★★.
COMPILATIONS: Classic Tracks (Shanachie 1991)★★★★, Best Of (Shanachie 1992)★★★★.

LANE, RONNIE
ALBUMS: Anymore For Anymore (GM 1973)★★★, Ronnie Lane's Slim Chance (GM 1974)★★★★, One For The Road (GM 1975)★★★★, with Ron Wood Mahoney's Last Stand (Atlantic 1976)★★★, with Pete Townshend Rough Mix (Polydor 1977)★★★★, See Me (Gem 1979)★★★.

LANG, JONNY
ALBUMS: Smokin' (Own Label 1996)★★, Lie To Me (A&M 1997)★★★.

lang, k.d.
ALBUMS: A Truly Western Experience (Bumstead 1984)★★, Angel With A Lariat (Sire 1987)★★★, Shadowland (Sire 1988)★★★, Absolute Torch And Twang (Sire 1989)★★★, Ingenue (Sire/Warners 1992)★★★★, Even Cowgirls Get The Blues film soundtrack (Sire/Warners 1993)★★, All You Can Eat (Sire/Warners 1995)★★★, Drag (Warners 1997)★★★, Live In Sydney (Warner Reprise 1997)★★★★.
FILMS: Salmonberries (1992).
VIDEOS: Harvest Of Seven Years (Warner Music Video 1992).
FURTHER READING: Carrying The Torch, William Robertson. k.d. lang, David Bennahum. All You Get Is Me, Victoria Starr.

LANOIS, DANIEL
ALBUMS: Acadie (Opal 1989)★★★★, For The Beauty Of Wynona (1993)★★★, film soundtrack Slingblade.

LASWELL, BILL
ALBUMS: Baselines (Rough Trade 1984)★★★, with John Zorn Points Blank/Metlable Snaps (No Mans Land 1986)★★★ with Peter Brπtzmann Low Life (1987)★★★, Hear No Evil (Venture 1988)★★★, Outer Dark (Fax 1994)★★★, with Pete Namlook Outland (Fax 1994)★★★, with Klaus Schulze, Pete Namlook Dark Side Of The Moog IV (Fax 1996)★★, Hear No Evil (Venture 1998)★★★.
COMPILATIONS: The Best Of Bill Laswell (Celluloid 1985)★★★.

LAUPER, CYNDI
ALBUMS: as Blue Angel Blue Angel (Polydor 1980)★★★, She's So Unusual (Portrait 1984)★★★★, True Colors (Portrait 1986)★★★, A Night To Remember (Epic 1989)★★, Hat Full Of Stars (Epic 1993)★★, Sisters Of Avalon (Epic 1997)★★★.
COMPILATIONS: 12 Deadly Cyns (Epic 1994)★★★★.
VIDEOS: Twelve Deadly Cyns ... And Then Some (Epic 1994).
FILMS: FILMS: Vibes, Off And Running.

LED ZEPPELIN
ALBUMS: Led Zeppelin (Atlantic 1969)★★★★, Led Zeppelin II (Atlantic 1969)★★★★, Led Zeppelin III (Atlantic 1970)★★★★, Led Zeppelin IV (Atlantic 1971)★★★★, Houses Of The Holy (Atlantic 1973)★★★, Physical Graffiti (Swan Song 1975)★★★, Presence (Swan Song 1976)★★★, The Song Remains The Same film soundtrack (Swan Song 1976)★★, In Through The Out Door (Swan Song 1979)★★★, Coda (Swan Song 1982)★★, BBC Sessions (East West 1997)★★★.
COMPILATIONS: Led Zeppelin 4-CD box set (Swan Song 1991)★★★★, Remasters (Swan Song 1991)★★★★, Remasters II (Swan Song 1993)★★★.
Page And Plant: Unledded (Fontana 1994)★★★.
VIDEOS: The Song Remains The Same (1986).
FURTHER READING: Hammer Of The Gods, Stephen Davis. Led Zeppelin: A Celebration, Dave Lewis. Led Zeppelin, Michael Gross and Robert Plant. Led Zeppelin, Howard Mylett. Led Zeppelin: In The Light 1968-1980, Howard Mylett and Richard Bunton. Led Zeppelin In Their Own Words, Paul Kendall. Led Zeppelin: A Visual Documentary, Paul Kendall. Led Zeppelin: The Book, Jeremy Burston. Jimmy Page: Tangents Within A Framework, Howard Mylett. Led Zeppelin: The Final Acclaim, Dave Lewis. Illustrated Collector's Guide To Led Zeppelin, Robert Godwin. Led Zeppelin: Heaven & Hell, Charles Cross and Erik Flannigan. Stairway To Heaven, Richard Cole with Richard Trubo. Led Zeppelin: Breaking And Making Records, Ross Clarke. Led Zeppelin: The Definitive Biography, Ritchie Yorke. On Tour With Led Zeppelin, Howard Mylett (ed.). Led Zeppelin, Chris Welch. The Essential Guide To The Music Of ..., Dave Lewis.

LEE, ALBERT
ALBUMS: Hiding (A&M 1979)★★★★, Albert Lee (Polydor 1982)★★★, Speechless (MCA 1987)★★★, Gagged But Not Bound (MCA 1988)★★, Black Claw And Country Fever (Line 1991)★★, with Hogan's Heroes Live At Montreux 1992 recording (Round Tower 1994)★★, Undiscovered – The Early Years (Diamond 1998)★★★.
COMPILATIONS: Country Guitar Man (Magnum 1986)★★★.

LEE, BRENDA
ALBUMS: Grandma, What Great Songs You Sang (Decca 1959)★★, Brenda Lee (Decca 1960)★★★★, This Is ... Brenda (Decca 1960)★★★★, Miss Dynamite (Brunswick 1961)★★★★, Emotions (Decca 1961)★★★, All The Way (Decca 1961)★★★, Sincerely Brenda Lee (Decca 1962)★★★★, Brenda, That's All (Decca 1962)★★★★, All Alone Am I (Decca 1963)★★★, Let Me Sing (Decca 1963)★★★, Sings Songs Everybody Knows (Decca 1964)★★★, By Request (Decca 1964)★★★, Merry Christmas From Brenda Lee (Decca 1964)★★★, Top Teen Hits (Decca 1965)★★★, The Versatile Brenda Lee (Decca 1965)★★★, Too Many Rivers (Decca 1965)★★★, Bye Bye Blues (Decca 1965)★★★, Coming On Strong (Decca 1966)★★★, Call Me Brenda (Decca 1967)★★★, Reflections In Blue (Decca 1967)★★★, Good Life (Decca 1967)★★★, with Tennessee Ernie Ford The Show For Christmas Seals (Decca 1968)★★★, with Pete Fountain For The First Time (Decca 1968)★★★, Johnny One Time (Decca 1969)★★★, Memphis Portrait (Decca 1970)★★★, Let It Be Me (Vocalion 1970)★★★, A Whole Lotta (MCA 1972)★★★, Brenda (MCA 1973)★★★, New Sunrise (MCA 1974)★★★, Brenda Lee Now (MCA 1975)★★★, The LA Sessions (MCA 1977)★★★, Even Better (MCA 1980)★★★, Take Me Back (MCA 1981)★★★, Only When I Laugh (MCA 1982)★★★, with Dolly Parton, Kris Kristofferson, Willie Nelson The Winning Hand (Monument 1983)★★★, Feels So Right (MCA 1985)★★★, Brenda Lee (Warners 1991)★★★, A Brenda Lee Christmas (Warners 1991)★★★, Greatest Hits Live (MCA 1992)★★★, Coming On Strong (Muskateer 1995)★★★.
COMPILATIONS: The Brenda Lee Story – Her Greatest Hits (MCA 1973)★★★★, Little Miss Dynamite (MCA 1976)★★★★, 25th Anniversary (MCA 1984)★★★★, The Golden Decade (Charly 1985)★★★★, The Best Of Brenda Lee (MCA 1986)★★★★, Brenda's Best (Ce De 1989)★★★★, Very Best Of Brenda Lee Volume 1 (MCA 1990)★★★★, The Brenda Lee Anthology Volume One, 1956-1961 (MCA 1991)★★★★, Little Miss Dynamite 4-CD box set (Bear Family 1996)★★★★, The EP Collection (See For Miles 1996)★★★★.

LEFT BANKE
ALBUMS: Walk Away Renee/Pretty Ballerina (Smash 1967)★★★, The Left Banke, Too (Smash 1968)★★, Voices Calling aka Strangers On A Train (1986)★★★.
COMPILATIONS: And Suddenly It's ... The Left Banke (1984)★★★, The History Of The Left Banke (1985)★★★, Walk Away Renee (1986)★★★.

LEFTFIELD
ALBUMS: Backlog (Outer Rhythm 1992)★★★, Leftism (Hard Hands/Columbia 1995)★★★★.

LEIBER AND STOLLER
FURTHER READING: Baby, That Was Rock & Roll: The Legendary Leiber And Stoller, Robert Palmer.

LEMONHEADS
ALBUMS: Hate Your Friends (Taang! 1987)★★, Creator (Taang! 1988)★★, Lick (Taang! 1989)★★★, Lovey (Atlantic 1990)★★, Favourite Spanish Dishes mini-album (Atlantic 1990)★★, It's A Shame About Ray (Atlantic 1992)★★★★, Come On Feel The Lemonheads (Atlantic 1993)★★★★, Car Button Cloth (Atlantic 1996)★★★.
VIDEOS: Two Weeks In Australia (1993).
FURTHER READING: The Illustrated Story, Everett True. The Lemonheads, Mick St. Michael.

LENNON, JOHN
ALBUMS: Unfinished Music No 1 – Two Virgins (Apple 1968)★, Unfinished Music No 2 – Life With The Lions (Zapple 1969)★, The Wedding Album (Apple 1969)★, The Plastic Ono Band; Live Peace In Toronto 1969 (Apple 1970)★★★, John Lennon – Plastic Ono Band (Apple 1971)★★★★★, Imagine (Apple 1971)★★★★, Sometime In New York City (Apple 1972)★★★, Mind Games (Apple 1973)★★★, Walls And Bridges (Apple 1974)★★★, Rock 'N' Roll (Apple 1975)★★★, Double Fantasy (Geffen 1980)★★★, Heartplay – Unfinished Dialogue (Polydor 1983)★, Milk And Honey (Polydor 1984)★★, Live In New York City (Capitol 1986)★★, Menlove Ave (Capitol 1986)★★, The Last Word (Baktabak 1988)★, Imagine – Music From The Motion Picture (Parlophone 1988)★★, John & Yoko: The Interview (BBC 1990)★.
COMPILATIONS: Shaved Fish (Apple 1975)★★★★, The John Lennon Collection (Parlophone 1982)★★★★★, The Ultimate John Lennon Collection (Parlophone 1990)★★★★, Lennon Legend (Parlophone 1997)★★★.
FILMS: A Hard Day's Night (1964), Help (1965), Magical Mystery Tour (1968), Let It Be (1971).
VIDEOS: The Bed-In (PMI 1991), The John Lennon Video Collection (PMI 1992), One To One (BMG 1993).
FURTHER READING: In His Own Write, John Lennon. The Penguin John Lennon, John Lennon. Lennon Remembers: The Rolling Stone Interviews, Jann Wenner. The Lennon Factor, Paul Young. The John Lennon Story, George Tremlett. John Lennon: One Day At A Time: A Personal Biography Of The Seventies, Anthony Fawcett. A Twist Of Lennon, Cynthia Lennon. John Lennon: The Life & Legend, Editors Of Sunday Times. John Lennon In His Own Words, Miles. A Spaniard In The Works, John Lennon. Lennon: What Happened!, Timothy Green (ed.). Strawberry Fields Forever: John Lennon Remembered, Vic Garbarini and Brian Cullman with Barbara Graustark. John Lennon: Death Of A Dream, George Carpozi. The Lennon Tapes: Andy Peebles In Conversation With John Lennon And Yoko Ono, Andy Peebles. The Ballad Of John And Yoko, Rolling Stone Editors. The Playboy Interviews With John Lennon And Yoko Ono, John Lennon. John Lennon: In My Life, Peter Shotton and Nicholas Schaffner. Loving John, May Pang. Dakota Days: The Untold Story Of John Lennon's Final Years, John Green. The Book Of Lennon, Bill Harry. John Ono Lennon 1967-1980, Ray Coleman. John Winston Lennon 1940-1966, Ray Coleman. Come Together: John Lennon In His Own Time, Jon Wiener. John Lennon: For The Record, Peter McCabe and Robert D. Schonfeld. The Lennon Companion: 25 Years Of Comment, Elizabeth M. Thomson and David Gutman. Imagine John Lennon, Andrew Solt and Sam Egan. Skywriting By Word Of Mouth, John Lennon. The Lives Of John Lennon, Albert Goldman. John Lennon My Brother, Julia Baird. The Other Side Of Lennon, Sandra Shevey. Days In The Life: John Lennon Remembered, Philip Norman. The Murder Of John Lennon, Fenton Bresler. The Art & Music Of John Lennon, John Robertson. In My Life: John Lennon Remembered, Kevin Howless and Mark Lewisohn. John Lennon: Living On Borrowed Time, Frederic Seaman. Let Me Take You Down: Inside The Mind Of Mark Chapman, Jack Jones. The Immortal John Lennon 1940-1980, Michael Heatley. John Lennon, William Ruhlmann. Al: Japan Through John Lennon's Eyes (A Personal Sketchbook), John Lennon.

LENNON, JULIAN
ALBUMS: Valotte (Virgin 1984)★★★, The Secret Value Of Daydreaming (Virgin 1986)★★, Mr Jordan (Virgin 1989)★★, Help Yourself (Virgin 1991)★★.

LENNOX, ANNIE
ALBUMS: Diva (RCA 1992)★★★★, Medusa (RCA 1995)★★★, Live In Central Park (Arista 1996)★★★.
VIDEOS: In The Park (BMG 1996).
FURTHER READING: Annie Lennox, Lucy O'Brien.

LETTERMEN
ALBUMS: A Song For Young Love (1962)★★★, Once Upon A Time (1962)★★★, Jim, Tony And Bob (1962)★★★, College Standards (1963)★★★, The Lettermen In Concert (1963)★★★, A Lettermen Kind Of Love (Capitol 1964)★★★, The Lettermen Look At Love (1964)★★★, She Cried (1964)★★★, Portrait Of My Love (1965)★★★, The Hit Sounds Of The Lettermen (1965)★★★, You'll Never Walk Alone (1965)★★★, More Hit Sounds Of The Lettermen! (1966)★★★, A New Song For Young Love (1966)★★★, For Christmas This Year (1966)★★★, Warm (1967)★★★, Spring! (1967)★★★, The Lettermen!!! ... And Live! (1967)★★★, Goin' Out Of My Head (1968)★★★, Special Request (1968)★★★, Put Your Head On My Shoulder (1968)★★★, I Have Dreamed (1969)★★★, Hurt So Bad (1969)★★★, Traces/Memories (1970)★★★, Reflections (1970)★★★, Everything's Good About You (1971)★★★, Feelings (1971)★★★, Love Book (1971)★★★, Lettermen 1 (1972)★★★, Alive Again ... Naturally (1973)★★★, Evergreen (1985).
COMPILATIONS: The Best Of The Lettermen (1966)★★★, The Best Of The Lettermen, Vol. 2 (1969)★★★, All Time Greatest Hits (1974)★★★.

LEVEL 42
ALBUMS: Level 42 (Polydor 1981)★★★, Strategy (Elite 1981)★★★, The Early Tapes: July-August 1980 (Polydor 1981)★★, The Pursuit Of Accidents (Polydor 1982)★★★, Standing In The Light (Polydor 1983)★★★, True Colours (Polydor 1983)★★★, A Physical Presence (Polydor 1985)★★, World Machine (Polydor 1985)★★★★, Running In The Family (Polydor 1987)★★★, Staring At The Sun (Polydor 1988)★★, Guaranteed (RCA 1991)★★, Forever Now (RCA 1994)★★. Solo: Mark King Influences (Polydor 1993)★★.
COMPILATIONS: Level Best (Polydor 1989)★★★★, The Remixes (1992)★★★.
VIDEOS: Live At Wembley (Channel 5 1987), Family Of Five (Channel 5 1988), Level Best (Channel 5 1989), Fait Accompli (1994).
FURTHER READING: Level 42: The Definitive Biography, Michael Cowton.

LEVELLERS
ALBUMS: A Weapon Called The Word (Musidisc 1990)★★★, Levelling The Land (China 1991)★★★, The Levellers (China 1993)★★★★, Zeitgeist (China 1995)★★★, Best Live: Headlights, White Lines, Black Tar Rivers (China 1996)★★, Mouth To Mouth (China 1997)★★★.
COMPILATIONS: See Nothing, Hear Nothing, Do Something (China 1993)★★★.
VIDEOS: The Great Video Swindle (Live At Glasgow Barrowlands) (1992), Best Live: Headlights, White Lines, Black Tar Rivers (Warner Video 1996).

LEWIS, GARY, AND THE PLAYBOYS
ALBUMS: This Diamond Ring (Liberty 1965)★★★, Everybody Loves A Clown (1965)★★★, Out Of Sight soundtrack (1966)★★★, She's Just My Style (1966)★★★★, Gary Lewis Hits Again! (1966)★★★, You Don't Have To Paint Me A Picture (Liberty 1967)★★, New Directions (1967)★★, Gary Lewis Now! (1968)★★, Close Cover Before Playing (1968)★★, Rhythm Of The Rain (1969)★★, I'm On The Road Now (1969)★★.
COMPILATIONS: Golden Greats (1966)★★★, Twenty Golden Greats (1979)★★★, Greatest Hits: Gary Lewis And The Playboys (1986)★★★.

LEWIS, HUEY, AND THE NEWS
ALBUMS: Huey Lewis & The News (Chrysalis 1980)★★, Picture This (Chrysalis 1982)★★★, Sports (Chrysalis 1983)★★★, Fore! (Chrysalis 1986)★★, Small World (Chrysalis 1988)★★, Hard At Play (Chrysalis 1991)★★, Four Chords And Several Years Ago (Elektra 1994)★★★.
COMPILATIONS: The Heart Of Rock & Roll: The Best Of (Chrysalis 1992)★★★, Time Flies: The Best Of Huey Lewis And The News (East West 1996)★★★.

LEWIS, JERRY LEE
ALBUMS: Jerry Lee Lewis (Sun 1957)★★★★, Jerry Lee Lewis And His Pumping Piano (London 1958)★★★, Jerry Lee's Greatest (Sun 1961)★★★★, Rockin' With Jerry Lee Lewis (Design 1963)★★★, The Greatest Live Show On Earth (Smash 1964)★★★, with the Nashville Teens Live At The Star Club, Hamburg (Philips 1965)★★, The Return Of Rock (Smash 1965)★★★, Country Songs For City Folks (Smash 1965)★★★, Whole Lotta Shakin' Goin' On (London 1965)★★★★, Memphis Beat (Smash 1966)★★★, By Request – More Greatest Live Show On Earth (Smash 1966)★★★, Breathless (London 1967)★★★, Soul My Way (Smash 1967)★★★, Got You On My Mind (Fontana 1968)★★★, Another Time, Another Place (Mercury 1969)★★★, She Still Comes Around (Mercury 1969)★★★, I'm On Fire (Mercury 1969)★★★, Jerry Lee Lewis' Rockin' Rhythm And Blues (Sun 1969)★★★, with Linda Gail Lewis Together (Mercury 1970)★★★, She Even Woke Me Up To Say Goodbye (Mercury 1970)★★★, A Taste Of Country (Sun 1970)★★★, There Must Be More To Love Than This (Mercury 1970)★★★, Johnny Cash And Jerry Lee Lewis Sing Hank Williams (Sun 1971)★★★, Touching Home (Mercury 1971)★★★, In Loving Memories (Mercury 1971)★★★, Would You Take Another Chance On Me (Mercury 1972)★★★, The Killer Rocks On (Mercury 1972)★★★, Old Tyme Country Music (Sun 1972)★★★, with Johnny Cash Sunday Down South (Sun 1972)★★, The Session (Mercury 1973)★★★, Live At The International, Las Vegas (Mercury 1973)★★★, Great Balls of Fire (Hallmark 1973)★★★, Southern Roots (Mercury 1974)★★★, Rockin' Up A Storm (Sun 1974)★★★, Rockin' And Free (Sun 1974)★★★, I'm A Rocker (Mercury 1975)★★★, Odd Man In (Mercury 1975)★★★, Rockin' My Life Away (Elektra 1978)★★★, Jerry Lee Lewis (Elektra 1979)★★★, Killer Country (Elektra 1980)★★★, When Two Worlds Collide (Elektra 1980)★★★, with Johnny Cash, Carl Perkins The Survivors (Columbia 1982)★★★, My Fingers Do The Talking (MCA 1983)★★★, I Am What I Am (MCA 1984)★★★, with Webb Pierce, Mel Tillis, Faron Young Four Legends (1985)★★★, with Johnny Cash, Carl Perkins, Roy Orbison The Class Of '55 (1986)★★★, Keep Your Hands Off It (Zu Zazz 1987)★★★, Don't Drop It (Zu Zazz 1988)★★★, Live In Italy (Magnum Force 1989)★★, Great Balls Of Fire! film soundtrack (Polydor 1989)★★★, Rocket (Instant 1990)★★★, Live At The Vapors Club (Ace 1991)★★★, Young Blood (Sire/Elektra 1995)★★★, Jerry Lee Lewis At Hank Cochran's recorded 1987 (Trend 1996)★★★.
COMPILATIONS: Golden Hits (Smash 1964)★★★★, Country Music Hall Of Fame Hits Vol. 1 (Smash 1969)★★★★, Country Music Hall Of Fame Hits Vol. 2 (Smash 1969)★★★★, Original Golden Hits Vol. 1 (Sun 1969)★★★★, The Best Of Jerry Lee Lewis (Smash 1970)★★★★, Rockin' With Jerry Lee Lewis (Mercury 1972)★★★★, Whole Lotta Shakin' Goin' On (Hallmark 1974)★★★★, The Jerry Lee Lewis Collection (Hallmark 1976)★★★★, Golden Hits (Mercury 1976)★★★★, The Original Jerry Lee Lewis (Charly 1976)★★★★, Nuggets (Charly 1977)★★★★, The Essential Jerry Lee Lewis (Charly 1978)★★★★, Duets (Sun 1979)★★★, Jerry Lee's Greatest (Charly 1981)★★★★, Killer Country I (Elektra 1981)★★★★, The Sun Years 12-LP box set (Sun 1984)★★★★, 18 Original Sun Greatest Hits (Rhino 1984)★★★★, Milestones (Rhino 1985)★★★★, The Collection (Deja Vu 1986)★★★★, Great Balls Of Fire (Sun 1986)★★★★, The Very Best Of Jerry Lee Lewis (Philips 1987)★★★★, The Classic Jerry Lee Lewis 8-CD box set (Bear Family 1989)★★★★, Killer's Rhythm And Blues (Sun 1989)★★★★, The EP Collection (See For Miles 1990)★★★★, Pretty Much Country (Ace 1992)★★★, All Killer, No Filler: The Anthology (Rhino 1993)★★★★, The EP Collection Vol. 2 ... Plus (See For Miles 1994)★★★★, The Locust Years ... And The Return To The Promised Land 8-CD box set (Bear Family 1995)★★★★, Sun Classics (Charly 1995)★★★★.
FILMS: Jamboree aka Disc Jockey Jamboree (1957), Beach Ball (1964), Be My Guest (1965), American Hot Wax (1976).
VIDEOS: Carl Perkins & Jerry Lee Lewis Live (BBC Video 1987), Jerry Lee Lewis (Fox Video 1989), I Am What I Am (Charly Video 1990), The Killer (Telstar Video 1991), Killer Performance (Virgin Vision 1991), The Jerry Lee Lewis Show (MMG Video 1991).
FURTHER READING: Jerry Lee Lewis: The Ball Of Fire, Allan Clark. Jerry Lee Lewis, Robert Palmer. Whole Lotta Shakin' Goin' On: Jerry Lee Lewis, Robert Cain. Hellfire: The Jerry Lee Lewis Story, Nick Tosches. Great Balls Of Fire: The True Story Of Jerry Lee Lewis, Myra Lewis. Rockin' My Life Away: Listening To Jerry Lee Lewis, Jimmy Guteman. Killer!, Jerry Lee Lewis And Charles White.

LEWIS, RAMSEY
ALBUMS: Down To Earth (EmArcy 1958)★★★, Gentleman Of Swing (Argo 1958)★★★, Gentlemen Of Jazz (Argo 1958)★★★, An Hour With The Ramsey Lewis Trio (Argo 1959)★★★, Stretching Out (Argo 1960)★★★, The Ramsey Lewis Trio In Chicago (Argo 1961)★★★, More Music From The Soil (Argo 1961)★★★, Sound Of Christmas (Argo 1961)★★★, The Sound Of Spring (Argo 1962)★★★, Country Meets The Blues (Argo 1962)★★★, Bossa Nova (Argo 1962)★★★, Pot Luck (Argo 1962)★★★, Barefoot Sunday Blues (Argo 1963)★★★, The Ramsey Lewis Trio At The Bohemian Caverns (Argo 1964)★★★, Bach To The Blues (Argo 1964)★★★, More Sounds Of Christmas (Argo 1964)★★★, You Better Believe It (Argo 1965)★★★★, The In Crowd (Argo 1965)★★★★, Hang On Ramsey! (Cadet 1965)★★★★, Swingin' (Cadet 1966)★★★★, Wade In The Water (Cadet 1966)★★★★, Goin' Latin (Cadet 1967)★★, The Movie Album (Cadet 1967)★★, Dancing In The Street (Cadet 1967)★★★, Up Pops Ramsey Lewis (Cadet 1968)★★★, Maiden Voyage (Cadet 1968)★★★, Mother Nature's Son (Cadet 1969)★★, Another Voyage (Cadet 1969)★★, Ramsey Lewis: The Piano Player (Cadet 1970)★★★, Them Changes (Cadet 1970)★★★, Back To The Roots (Cadet 1971)★★★, Upendo Ni Pamoja (Columbia 1972)★★★, Funky Serenity (Columbia 1973)★★, Sun Goddess (Columbia 1974)★★★, Don't It Feel Good (Columbia 1975)★★★, Salongo (Columbia 1976)★★★, Love Notes (Columbia 1977)★★★, Tequila Mockingbird (Columbia 1977)★★★, Legacy (Columbia 1978)★★★, Routes (Columbia 1980)★★★, Three Piece Suite (Columbia 1981)★★★, Live At The Savoy (Columbia 1982)★★★, Les Fleurs (1983)★★, Chance Encounter (Columbia 1983)★★, with Nancy Wilson The Two Of Us (Columbia 1984)★★★, Reunion (Columbia 1984)★★★, Fantasy (1986)★★, Keys To The City (Columbia 1987)★★, Classic Encounter (Columbia 1988)★★, with Billy Taylor We Meet Again (Columbia 1989)★★★, Urban Renewal (Columbia 1989)★★★, Electric Collection (Columbia 1991)★★★, Ivory Pyramid (GRP 1992)★★, with King Curtis Instrumental Soul Hits (1993)★★, Between The Keys (GRP 1996)★★.
COMPILATIONS: Choice! The Best Of The Ramsey Lewis Trio (Cadet 1965)★★★, The Best Of Ramsey Lewis (Cadet 1970)★★★, Ramsey Lewis' Newly Recorded All-Time, Non-Stop Golden Hits (Columbia 1973)★★★, The Greatest Hits Of Ramsey Lewis (Chess 1988)★★★, 20 Greatest Hits (1992)★★★, Collection (More Music 1995)★★★.
FILMS: Gonks Go Beat (1965).

LIGHTFOOT, GORDON
ALBUMS: Lightfoot (United Artists 1966)★★★, Early Lightfoot (United Artists 1966)★★★, The Way I Feel (United Artists 1967)★★★, Did She Mention My Name (United Artists 1968)★★★, Back Here On Earth (United Artists 1969)★★, Sunday Concert (United Artists 1969)★★★, Sit Down Young Stranger aka If You Could

Read My Mind (Reprise 1970)★★★★, *Summer Side Of Life* (Reprise 1971)★★, *Don Quixote* (Reprise 1972)★★★, *Old Dan's Records* (Reprise 1972)★★, *Sundown* (Reprise 1974)★★★, *Cold On The Shoulder* (Reprise 1975)★★, *Summertime Dream* (Reprise 1976)★★★, *Endless Wire* (Warners 1978)★★, *Dream Street Rose* (Warners 1980)★★, *Shadows* (Warners 1982)★★, *Salute* (Warners 1983)★★★, *East Of Midnight* (Warners 1986)★★, *Waiting For You* (1993)★★★, *Painter Passing Through* (Warner brothers 1998)★★★. COMPILATIONS: *The Very Best Of Gordon Lightfoot* (United Artists 1974)★★★, *Gord's Gold* (Reprise 1975)★★★, *The Best Of Gordon Lightfoot* (Warners 1981)★★★.
FURTHER READING: *Gordon Lightfoot*, Alfrieda Gabiou. *If You Could Read My Mind*, Maynard Collins.

LIGHTHOUSE
ALBUMS: *Lighthouse* (1969)★★, *Peacing It All Together* (RCA 1970)★★★, *Suite Feeling* (RCA 1970)★★★, *One Fine Morning* (Evolution/Vertigo 1971)★★★, *Thoughts Of Moving On* (Evolution/Vertigo 1972)★★, *Live* (Evolution 1972)★★, *Sunny Days* (Evolution 1972)★★, *Can Feel It* (1974)★★, *Good Day* (1974)★★. Solo: Skip Prokop *All Growed Up* (1977)★★.

LIGHTNING SEEDS
ALBUMS: *Cloudcuckooland* (Epic 1990)★★★, *Sense* (Epic 1992)★★★, *Jollification* (Epic 1994)★★★, *Dizzy Heights* (Epic 1996)★★★★. COMPILATIONS: *Pure Lightning Seeds* (Virgin 1996)★★★, *Like You Do* (Epic 1997)★★★★.

LINDISFARNE
ALBUMS: *Nicely Out Of Tune* (Charisma 1970)★★★, *Fog On The Tyne* (Charisma 1971)★★★★, *Dingly Dell* (Charisma 1972)★★★, *Lindisfarne Live* (Charisma 1973)★★, *Roll On Ruby* (Charisma 1973)★★, *Happy Daze* (Warners 1974)★★★, *Back And Fourth* (Mercury 1978)★★★, *Magic In The Air* (Mercury 1978)★★, *The News* (Mercury 1979)★★, *Sleepless Night* (LMP 1982)★★, *LindisfarneTastic Live* (LMP 1984)★★, *LindisfarneTastic Volume 2* (LMP 1984)★★, *Dance Your Life Away* (River City 1986)★★, *C'mon Everybody* (Stylus 1987)★★, *Peel Sessions* (Strange Fruit 1988)★★★, *Amigos* (Black Crow 1989)★★, *Elvis Lives On The Moon* (Essential 1993)★★, *Another Fine Mess* (Grapevine 1995)★★. Solo: Ray Jackson *In The Night* (Mercury 1980)★★. Rod Clements with Bert Jansch *Leather Launderette* (Black Crow 1988)★★. COMPILATIONS: *Finest Hour* (Charisma 1975)★★★, *Singles Album* (1981)★★★, *The Best Of Lindisfarne* (Virgin 1989)★★★.

LITTLE ANTHONY AND THE IMPERIALS
ALBUMS: *We Are Little Anthony And The Imperials* (End 1959)★★★, *Shades Of The 40's* (End 1961)★★★, *I'm On The Outside Looking In* (DCP 1964)★★★, *Goin' Out Of My Head* (DCP 1965)★★★, *Paying Our Dues* (Veep 1967)★★★, *Reflections* (Veep 1967)★★, *Movie Grabbers* (Veep 1968)★★, *Out Of Sight, Out Of Mind* (United Artists 1969)★★, *On A New Street* (Avco 1974)★★. Solo: Anthony Gourdine *Daylight* (Songbird 1980)★★. COMPILATIONS: *Little Anthony And The Imperials Greatest Hits* (Roulette 1965)★★★, *The Best Of Little Anthony And The Imperials* (DCP 1966)★★★, *The Best Of Little Anthony And The Imperials* (Rhino 1989)★★★.

LITTLE EVA
ALBUMS: *L-L-L-L-Loco-Motion* (Dimension 1962)★★. COMPILATIONS: *The Best Of Little Eva* (1988)★★★, *Back On Track* (1989)★★★.

LITTLE FEAT
ALBUMS: *Little Feat* (Warners 1971)★★★, *Sailin' Shoes* (Warners 1972)★★★★, *Dixie Chicken* (Warners 1973)★★★★, *Feats Don't Fail Me Now* (Warners 1974)★★★★, *The Last Record Album* (Warners 1975)★★★★, *Time Loves A Hero* (Warners 1977)★★★, *Waiting For Columbus* (Warners 1978)★★★, *Down On The Farm* (Warners 1979)★★★, *Let It Roll* (Warners 1988)★★, *Representing The Mambo* (Warners 1990)★★, *Shake Me Up* (Polydor 1991)★★, *Ain't Had Enough Fun* (Zoo 1995)★★, *Live From Styleen's Rhythm Palace* (1997)★★★. Solo: Lowell George *Thanks I'll Eat It Here* (Warners 1979)★★★. Paul Barrere *On My Own Two Feet* (Warners/Mirage 1983)★★. COMPILATIONS: *Hoy Hoy* (Warners 1981)★★★★, *As Time Goes By – The Best Of Little Feat* (Warners 1986)★★★.

LITTLE RICHARD
ALBUMS: *Little Richard* (Camden 1956)★★★, *Here's Little Richard* (Specialty 1957)★★★★★, *Little Richard Volume 2* (Specialty 1957)★★★★, *The Fabulous Little Richard* (Specialty 1958)★★★★, *Sings Gospel* (20th Century 1959)★★, *It's Real* (Mercury 1961)★★, *Little Richard Sings Freedom Songs* (Crown 1963)★★, *Coming Home* (Coral 1963)★★, *King Of The Gospel Singers* (Wing 1964)★★, *Little Richard Is Back* (Vee Jay 1965)★★, *The Explosive Little Richard* (Columbia 1967)★★★, *Good Golly Miss Molly* (Specialty 1969)★★, *The Little Richard Story* (Joy 1970)★★★, *Well Alright* (Specialty 1970)★★, *Rock Hard Rock Heavy* (Specialty 1970)★★, *You Can't Keep A Good Man Down* (Union Pacific 1970)★★, *The Rill Thing* (Reprise 1970)★★, *Mr Big* (Joy 1971)★★, *Cast A Long Shadow* (Epic 1971)★★, *King Of Rock 'N' Roll* (Reprise 1971)★★, *The Original Little Richard* (Specialty 1972)★★★, *The Second Coming* (Warners 1973)★★★, *Rip It Up* (Joy 1973)★★, *Slippin' And Slidin'* (Joy 1973)★★, *Good Golly Miss Molly* (Hallmark 1974)★★★, *Greatest Hits Recorded Live* (Embassy 1974)★★★, *Keep A Knockin'* (Rhapsody 1975)★★, *Dollars Dollars* (Charly 1975)★★, *The Great Ones* (MFP 1976)★★, *Little Richard And Jimi Hendrix Together* (Ember 1977)★★, *Whole Lotta Shakin' Goin' On* (DJM 1977)★★★, *Little Richard Now* (Creole 1977)★★, *The Georgia Peach* (Charly 1980)★★★, *Little Richard And His Band* (Specialty 1980)★★, *Ooh! My Soul* (Charly 1982)★★★, *Whole Lotta Shakin'* (Bulldog 1982)★★★, *Get Down With It* (Edsel 1982)★★, *The Real Thing* (Magnum Force 1983)★★★, *Little Richard* (Cambra 1983)★★★, *He's Got It* (Topline 1984)★★, *Lifetime Friend* (Warners 1986)★★★. COMPILATIONS: *His Biggest Hits* (Specialty 1963)★★★★, *Little Richard's Greatest Hits* (Vee Jay 1965)★★★★, *Little Richard's Greatest Hits* (OKeh 1967)★★★★, *Little Richard's Grooviest 17 Original Hits* (Specialty 1968)★★★★, *20 Original Greatest Hits* (Specialty 1976)★★★★, *The Essential Little Richard* (Specialty 1985)★★★★, *18 Greatest Hits* (Rhino 1985)★★★★, *20 Classic Cuts* (Ace 1986)★★★★, *The Collection* (Castle 1989)★★★★, *The Specialty Sessions* 6-CD box set (Specialty 1990)★★★★, *The EP Collection* (See For Miles 1993)★★★★★.
FILMS: *The Girl Can't Help It* (1956), *Don't Knock The Rock* (1956), *Catalina Caper* (1967).
FURTHER READING: *The Life And Times Of Little Richard: The Quasar Of Rock*, Charles White.

LITTLE RIVER BAND
ALBUMS: *Little River Band* (Harvest 1976)★★★, *Diamantina Cocktail* (Harvest 1977)★★★, *Sleeper Catcher* (Harvest 1978)★★, *First Under The Wire* (Capitol 1979)★★, *Backstage Pass* (Capitol 1980)★★, *Time Exposure* (Capitol 1981)★★, *The Net* (Capitol 1983)★★, *Playing To Win* (Capitol 1985)★★, *No Reins* (Capitol 1986)★★, *Monsoon* (MCA 1988)★★, *Too Late To Load* (1989)★, *Get Lucky* (MCA 1990)★★, *Worldwide Love* (Curb 1991)★★. COMPILATIONS: *Greatest Hits* (Capitol 1984)★★★, *The Best Of ... (EMI 1997)*★★★.
VIDEOS: *Live Exposure* (PMI 1981).

LIVE
ALBUMS: *Mental Jewelry* (Radioactive 1991)★★, *Throwing Copper* (Radioactive 1994)★★★★, *Secret Samadhi* (Radioactive 1997)★★★.

LIVING COLOUR
ALBUMS: *Vivid* (Epic 1988)★★★★, *Time's Up* (Epic 1990)★★★★, *Biscuits* (Epic 1991)★★★, *Stain* (Epic 1993)★★★, *Dread* Japanese live release (Epic 1993)★★★. COMPILATIONS: *Pride* (Epic 1995)★★★★.

L L COOL J
ALBUMS: *Radio* (Columbia 1985)★★★, *Bigger And Deffer* (Def Jam 1987)★★, *Walking With A Panther* (Def Jam 1989)★★★, *Mama Said Knock You Out* (Def Jam 1990)★★★★, *14 Shots To The Dome* (Def Jam 1993)★★★, *Mr. Smith* (Def Jam 1995)★★★, *Phenomenon* (Def Jam 1997)★★★. COMPILATIONS: *Greatest Hits All World* (Def Jam 1996)★★★.
FILMS: *The Hard Way*, *Toys*.

LOEB, LISA
ALBUMS: *Tails* (Geffen/MCA 1995)★★★, *Firecracker* (Geffen 1997)★★★.

LOFGREN, NILS
ALBUMS: *Nils Lofgren* (A&M 1975)★★★★, *Back It Up* (Official Bootleg) (A&M 1976)★★★, *Cry Tough* (A&M 1976)★★★, *I Came To Dance* (A&M 1977)★★★, *Night After Night* (A&M 1977)★★, *Nils* (A&M 1979)★★, *Night Fades Away* (Backstreet 1981)★★, *Wonderland* (MCA 1983)★★★, *Flip* (Towerbell 1985)★★★, *Code Of The Road* (Towerbell 1986)★★★, *Silver Lining* (Essential 1991)★★★, *Crooked Line* (Essential 1992)★★, *Live On The Test* (Windsong 1994)★★★, *Everybreath* (Permanent 1994)★★, *Damaged Goods* (Essential 1995)★★★. COMPILATIONS: *A Rhythm Romance* (A&M 1982)★★★, *The Best Of Nils Lofgren* (A&M 1992)★★★, *Soft Fun, Tough Tears 1971-1979* (Raven 1995)★★★, *Steal Your Heart* (A&M 1996)★★★.
VIDEOS: *Nils Lofgren* (Castle 1991).

LOGGINS, KENNY
ALBUMS: *Celebrate Me Home* (Columbia 1977)★★★, *Nightwatch* (Columbia 1978)★★★, *Keep The Fire* (Columbia 1979)★★★, *Alive* (Columbia 1980)★★★, *High Adventure* (Columbia 1982)★★★, *Footloose* (1984)★★★, *Vox Humana* (Columbia 1985)★★, *Top Gun* (1986)★★, *Back To Avalon* (Columbia 1988)★★, *Leap Of Faith* (Columbia 1991)★★, *Outside From The Redwoods – An Acoustic Afternoon* (Columbia 1993)★★★, *The Unimaginable Fire* (Columbia 1997)★★★. COMPILATIONS: *At His Best* (Hollywood 1992)★★★, *Yesterday, Today, Tomorrow: The Greatest Hits Of Kenny Loggins* (Columbia 1997)★★★.
FILMS: *Footloose* (1984).
VIDEOS: *Return To Pooh Corner* (Sony Wonder 1996).

LOGGINS AND MESSINA
ALBUMS: *Kenny Loggins With Jim Messina Sittin' In* (Columbia 1972)★★★, *Loggins And Messina* (Columbia 1972)★★★★, *Full Sail* (Columbia 1973)★★★, *On Stage* (Columbia 1974)★★★, *Mother Lode* (Columbia 1974)★★, *So Fine* (Columbia 1975)★★, *Native Sons* (Columbia 1976)★★, *Finale* (Columbia 1977)★★. COMPILATIONS: *The Best Of Friends* (Columbia 1976)★★★.

LONE JUSTICE
ALBUMS: *Lone Justice* (Geffen 1985)★★★, *Shelter* (Geffen 1987)★★, *Radio One Live In Concert* 1986 recording (Windsong 1993)★★.

LONE STAR
ALBUMS: *Lone Star* (CBS 1976)★★★, *Firing On All Six* (CBS 1977)★★★★, *BBC Radio 1 Live* (Windsong 1994)★★.

LONG RYDERS
ALBUMS: *The Long Ryders* aka *10.5.60* mini-album (PVC 1983)★★★, *Native Sons* (Frontier/Zippo 1984)★★★★, *State Of Our Union* (Island 1985)★★★, *Two-Fisted Tales* (Island 1987)★★, *BBC Radio One In Concert* (Windsong 1994)★★★. COMPILATIONS: *Metallic B.O.* early recordings (Overground 1990)★★.

LONGPIGS
ALBUMS: *The Sun Is Often Out* (Mother 1996)★★★.

LOOP GURU
ALBUMS: *Duniya* (Nation 1994)★★★, *Amrita ... All These And The Japanese Soup Warriors* (North South 1995)★★★, *The Catalogue Of Desires Vol 3* (North South 1996)★★★, *Peel To Reveal* (Strange Fruit 1996)★★★, *Loop Bites Dog* (World Domination 1997).

LORDS OF THE NEW CHURCH
ALBUMS: *Lords Of The New Church* (IRS 1982)★★, *Is Nothing Sacred?* (IRS 1983)★★★, *Method To Our Madness* (IRS 1984)★★, *Live At The Spit* 1982 recording (Illegal 1988)★★. COMPILATIONS: *Killer Lords* (IRS 1985)★★★.
VIDEOS: *Holy War* (JE 1994).

LOS LOBOS
ALBUMS: *Si Se Puede!* (Pan American 1976)★★★, *Just Another Band From East LA* (New Vista 1978)★★★, *And A Time To Dance* (Slash 1983)★★★, *How Will The Wolf Survive?* (Slash 1984)★★★★, *By The Light Of The Moon* (Slash 1987)★★★, *La Bamba* (Slash 1987)★★★, *La Pistola Y El Corazon* (Slash 1988)★★★, *The Neighbourhood* (Slash 1990)★★★, *Kiko* (Slash 1992)★★★, *Papa's Dream* (Warners 1995)★★★, *Colossal Head* (Warners 1996)★★★. COMPILATIONS: *Just Another Band From East L.A: A Collection* (Warners 1993)★★★★.

LOVE
ALBUMS: *Love* (Elektra 1966)★★★, *Da Capo* (Elektra 1967)★★★★, *Forever Changes* (Elektra 1967)★★★★★, *Four Sail* (Elektra 1969)★★★, *Out Here* (Blue Thumb 1969)★★, *False Start* (Blue Thumb 1970)★★, *Reel To Real* (RSO 1974)★★, *Love Live* (Rhino 1982)★★, *Love* (1982)★★, as Arthur Lee And Love *Arthur Lee And Love* (New Rose 1992)★★. COMPILATIONS: *Love Revisited* (Elektra 1970)★★★, *Love Masters* (Elektra 1973)★★★, *Out There* (Big Beat 1988)★★★, *Comes In Colours* (Big Beat 1993)★★★★, *Love Story* (Rhino 1995)★★★★.

LOVE AFFAIR
ALBUMS: *The Everlasting Love Affair* (CBS 1968)★★★, *New Day* (CBS 1970)★★. COMPILATIONS: *Greatest Hits* (1985)★★★, *Everlasting Hits* (1993)★★★, *Everlasting Love* (Columbia 1996)★★★.

LOVERBOY
ALBUMS: *Loverboy* (Columbia 1980)★★★, *Get Lucky* (Columbia 1981)★★★, *Keep It Up* (Columbia 1983)★★★, *Lovin' Every Minute Of It* (Columbia 1985)★★★, *Wildside* (Columbia 1987)★★★. Solo: Paul Dean *Hard Core* (Columbia 1989)★★. COMPILATIONS: *Big Ones* (Columbia 1989)★★★.

LOVETT, LYLE
ALBUMS: *Lyle Lovett* (MCA/Curb 1986)★★★★, *Pontiac* (MCA/Curb 1987)★★★★, *Lyle Lovett And His Large Band* (MCA/Curb 1989)★★★, *Joshua Judges Ruth* (MCA/Curb 1992)★★★, *I Love Everybody* (MCA/Curb 1994)★★★, *The Road To Ensenada* (MCA/Curb 1996)★★★.
FILMS: *The Player*.

LOVIN' SPOONFUL
ALBUMS: *Do You Believe In Magic* (Kama Sutra 1965)★★★★, *Daydream* (Kama Sutra 1966)★★★★, with others *What's Shakin'* (Elektra 1966)★★★★, *What's Up Tiger Lily* soundtrack (Kama Sutra 1966)★★, *Hums Of The Lovin' Spoonful* (Kama Sutra 1966)★★★★, *You're A Big Boy Now* soundtrack (Kama Sutra 1967)★★, *Everything Playing* (Kama Sutra 1968)★★★, *Revelation: Revolution* (Kama Sutra 1968)★. COMPILATIONS: *The EP Collection* (1988)★★★, *Collection: Lovin' Spoonful, 20 Hits* (1988)★★★★, *The Very Best Of The Lovin' Spoonful* (1988)★★★★, *Summer In The City* (Spectrum 1995)★★★.

LOWE, NICK
ALBUMS: *Jesus Of Cool* aka *Pure Pop For Now People* (Radar 1978)★★★★, *Labour Of Lust* (Radar 1978)★★★★, *Nick The Knife* (F-Beat 1982)★★★, *The Abominable Showman* (F-Beat 1983)★★★, *Nick Lowe And His Cowboy Outfit* (RCA 1984)★★★, as Nick Lowe And His Cowboy Outfit *Rose Of England* (RCA 1985)★★★, *Pinker And Prouder Than Previous* (Demon 1988)★★★, *Party Of One* (Reprise 1990)★★★, *The Impossible Bird* (Demon 1994)★★★★, *Dig My Mood* (Demon 1998)★★★. COMPILATIONS: *16 All Time Lowes* (Demon 1984)★★★★, *Nick's Knack* (Demon 1986)★★★, *Basher: The Best Of Nick Lowe* (Demon 1989)★★★★, *The Wilderness Years* (Demon 1991)★★★.
FILMS: *Americation* (1979).

LUDUS
ALBUMS: *Pickpocket* (New Hormones 1981)★★★.

LULU
ALBUMS: *Something To Shout About* (Decca 1965)★★★★, *Love Loves To Love Lulu* (Columbia 1967)★★★, *Lulu's Album* (Columbia 1969)★★★, *New Routes* (Atco 1970)★★, *Melody Fair* (Atco 1971)★★, *Don't Take Love For Granted* (Rocket 1979)★★★, *Lulu* (Alfa 1981)★★★, *Take Me To Your Heart Again* (Alfa 1982)★★★, *Shape Up And Dance With Lulu* (Life Style 1984)★★, *The Man Who Sold The World* (Start 1989)★★★, *Independence* (Dome 1993)★★★. COMPILATIONS: *The World Of Lulu* (Decca 1969)★★★★, *The World Of Lulu Vol. 2* (Decca 1970)★★★, *The Most Of Lulu* (MFP 1971)★★★★, *The Most Of Lulu Vol. 2* (MFP 1972)★★★, *The Very Best Of Lulu* (Warwick 1980)★★★, *Shout* (MFP 1983)★★★, *I'm A Tiger* (MFP 1989)★★★, *From Crayons To Perfume: The Best Of ...* (Rhino 1995)★★★, *Supersneakers* (Sundazed 1997)★★★.
FILMS: *Gonks Go Beat* (1965).

LUSH
ALBUMS: *Spooky* (4AD 1992)★★, *Split* (4AD 1994)★★★, *Lovelife* (4AD 1996)★★★. COMPILATIONS: *Gala* (4AD 1990)★★★.

LYMON, FRANKIE, AND THE TEENAGERS
ALBUMS: *The Teenagers Featuring Frankie Lymon* (Gee 1957)★★★, *The Teenagers At The London Palladium* (Roulette 1958)★★, *Rock 'N' Roll Party With Frankie Lymon* (Guest 1959)★★★. COMPILATIONS: *Frankie Lymon And The Teenagers* 61-track set (Murray Hill 1987)★★★, *The Best Of Frankie Lymon And The Teenagers* (Roulette 1990)★★★.

LYNNE, JEFF
ALBUMS: *Armchair Theatre* (Reprise 1990)★★. COMPILATIONS: *Message From The Country (The Jeff Lynne Years 1968-1973)* (Harvest 1979)★★★.

LYNOTT, PHIL
ALBUMS: *Solo In Soho* (Vertigo 1981)★★★, *The Phillip Lynott Solo Album* (Vertigo 1992)★★.
FURTHER READING: *Phillip Lynott: The Rocker*, Mark Putterford. *Songs For While I'm Away*, Phillip Lynott. *My Boy: The Philip Lynott Story*, Philomena Lynott.

LYNYRD SKYNYRD
ALBUMS: *Pronounced Leh-Nerd Skin-Nerd* (Sounds Of The South/MCA 1973)★★★, *Second Helping* (Sounds Of The South/MCA 1974)★★★★, *Nuthin' Fancy* (MCA 1975)★★★, *Gimme Back My Bullets* (MCA 1976)★★★, *One More From The Road* (MCA 1976)★★★★, *Street Survivors* (MCA 1977)★★★★, *First And Last* rec. 1970-1972 (MCA 1978)★★★, *For The Glory Of The South* (MCA 1987)★★★, *Lynyrd Skynyrd 1991* (MCA 1991)★★★, *The Last Rebel* (MCA 1993)★★★, *Endangered Species* (Capricorn 1995)★★★, *Southern Knights* (CBH 1996)★★★, *Twenty* (SPV 1997)★★. COMPILATIONS: *Gold And Platinum* (MCA 1980)★★★★, *Best Of The Rest* (MCA 1982)★★★, *Legend* (MCA 1987)★★★, *Anthology* (Raw Power 1987)★★★, *Definitive* 3-CD box set (MCA 1991)★★★★.

M

M PEOPLE
ALBUMS: *Northern Soul* (DeConstruction 1992)★★★, *Northern Soul Extended* (DeConstruction 1992)★★★, *Elegant Slumming* (DeConstruction 1993)★★★★, *Bizarre Fruit* (DeConstruction 1994)★★★★, *Bizarre Fruit II* (DeConstruction 1995)★★, *Fresco* (BMG 1997)★★, *Love Rendezvous* (DeConstruction 1995)★★★.
VIDEOS: *Elegant TV* (1994), *Live At G-Mex* (BMG 1995).

MacCOLL, KIRSTY
ALBUMS: *Desperate Characters* (Polydor 1981)★★★, *Kite* (Virgin 1989)★★★★, *Electric Landlady* (Virgin 1991)★★★, *Titanic Days* (ZTT 1994)★★. COMPILATIONS: *Galore* (Virgin 1995)★★★★.

MADNESS
ALBUMS: *One Step Beyond* (Stiff 1979)★★★★, *Absolutely* (Stiff 1980)★★★, *Madness 7* (Stiff 1981)★★★, *The Rise And Fall* (Stiff 1982)★★★★, *Keep Moving* (Stiff 1984)★★★, *Mad Not Mad* (Zarjazz 1985)★★, as the Madness *The Madness* (Virgin 1988)★★, *Madstock* (Go! Discs 1992)★★★. COMPILATIONS: *Complete Madness* (Stiff 1982)★★★, *Utter Madness* (Zarjazz 1986)★★★, *Divine Madness* (Virgin 1992)★★★★, *The Business – The Definitive Singles Collection* (Virgin 1993)★★★★, *Total Madness: The Very Best Of* (Geffen 1997)★★★.
VIDEOS: *Complete Madness* (Stiff 1984), *Utter Madness* (Virgin Vision 1988), *Complete And Utter Madness* (Virgin Vision 1988), *Divine Madness* (Virgin Vision 1992).
FURTHER READING: *A Brief Case Of Madness*, Mark Williams. *Total Madness*, George Marshall.

MADONNA
ALBUMS: *Madonna* (Sire 1983)★★★, *Like A Virgin* (Sire 1984)★★★, *True Blue* (Sire 1986)★★★★, *You Can Dance* (Sire 1987)★★★, *Who's That Girl* soundtrack (Sire 1987)★★, *Like A Prayer* (Sire 1989)★★★, *I'm Breathless* (Sire 1990)★★★, *Erotica* (Maverick 1992)★★★, *Bedtime Stories* (Warners 1994)★★★, *Something To Remember* (Sire 1995)★★★, *Evita* soundtrack (Warners 1996)★★★, *Ray of Light* (Maverick/Warners 1998)★★★★. COMPILATIONS: *The Immaculate Collection* (Sire 1991)★★★★, *Best Of The Rest Vol. 2* (1993)★★★.
VIDEOS: *The Virgin Tour* (1986), *Ciao Italia – Live From Italy* (1988), *Immaculate Collection* (1990), *Justify My Love* (Warners 1991), *The Real Story* (1991), *Madonna Video EP* (1991), *In Bed With Madonna* (1991), *Madonna Exposed* (1993), *Madonna: The Unauthorised Biography* (MIA Video 1994), *Madonna: The Girlie Show* (1994).
FURTHER READING: *Sex*, Madonna. *Madonna: Her Story*, Michael McKenzie. *Madonna: The New Illustrated Biography*, Debbi Voller. *Madonna: In Her Own Words*, Mick St Michael. *Madonna: The Biography*, Robert Matthew-Walker. *Madonna*, Marie Cahill. *Madonna: The Style Book*, Debbi Voller. *Like A Virgin: Madonna Revealed*, Douglas Thompson. *Sex*, Madonna. *Madonna Unauthorized*, Christopher Anderson. *I Dream Of Madonna: Women's Dreams Of The Goddess Of Pop*, Kay Turner (compiled). *Madonna: The Girlie Show*, Glenn O'Brien. *Deconstructing Madonna*, Fran Lloyd. *Live!*, no author listed. *The Madonna Scrapbook*, Lee Randall.

MAGAZINE
ALBUMS: *Real Life* (Virgin 1978)★★★, *Secondhand Daylight* (Virgin 1979)★★★, *The Correct Use Of Soap* (Virgin 1980)★★★, *Play* (Virgin 1980)★★★, *Magic, Murder And The Weather* (Virgin 1981)★★★. COMPILATIONS: *After The Fact* (Virgin 1982)★★★, *Rays & Hail 1978-81* (Virgin 1987)★★★, *BBC Radio 1 Live In Concert* (Windsong 1993)★★★.

MAGNUM
ALBUMS: *Kingdom Of Madness* (Jet 1978)★★★, *Magnum II* (Jet 1979)★★★, *Marauder* (Jet 1980)★★★, *Chase The Dragon* (Jet 1982)★★★, *The Eleventh Hour* (Jet 1983)★★★, *On A Storyteller's Night* (Polydor 1985)★★★, *Vigilante* (Polydor 1986)★★★, *Wings Of Heaven* (Polydor 1988)★★★★, *Goodnight L.A.* (Polydor 1990), *Invasion – Magnum Live* (Receiver 1990)★★★, *The Spirit* (Polydor 1991)★★★, *Sleepwalking* (Polydor 1992)★★★, *Rock Art* (EMI 1994)★★★, *Firebird* (Spectrum/Polygram 1995)★★★. COMPILATIONS: *Anthology* (Raw Power 1986)★★★★, *Collection* (Castle 1990)★★★★, *Box Set* (Castle 1992)★★★, *Chapter And Verse – Best Of* (Polydor 1993)★★★, *Uncorked* (Jet 1994)★★★.
VIDEOS: *The Sacred Hour Live* (1986), *On The Wings Of Heaven* (1988), *From Midnight To LA* (1990).

MAHAVISHNU ORCHESTRA
ALBUMS: *The Inner Mounting Flame* (Columbia 1972)★★★★, *Birds Of Fire* (Columbia 1973)★★★★, *Between Nothingness And Eternity* (Columbia 1973)★★★, *Apocalypse* (Columbia 1974)★★, *Visions Of The Emerald Beyond* (Columbia 1975)★★★, *Inner Worlds* (Columbia 1976)★★★, *Adventures In Radioland* (Relativity 1987)★★★.

MAHOGANY RUSH
ALBUMS: *Maxoom* (Kotai 1971)★★, *Child Of The Novelty* (20th Century 1974)★★★, *Strange Universe* (20th Century 1975)★★, *Mahogany Rush IV* (Columbia 1976)★★★, *World Anthem* (Columbia 1977)★★★, *Live* (Columbia 1978)★★★, *Tales Of The Unexpected* (Columbia 1979)★★★, *What's Next* (Columbia 1980)★★★.

MALMSTEEN, YNGWIE
ALBUMS: *Yngwie Malmsteen's Rising Force* (Polydor 1984)★★★, *Marching Out* (Polydor 1985)★★★, *Trilogy* (Polydor 1986)★★★, *Odyssey* (Polydor 1988)★★★, *Live In Leningrad* (Polydor 1989)★★, *Eclipse* (Polydor 1990)★★, *Fire & Ice* (Elektra 1992)★★, *Seventh Sign* (Elektra 1994)★★★, *No Mercy* (CMC International 1994)★★★.
VIDEOS: *Rising Force Live 85* (1989), *Trial By Fire* (1989), *Collection* (1992).

MAMAS AND THE PAPAS
ALBUMS: *If You Can Believe Your Eyes And Ears* (Dunhill/RCA Victor 1966)★★★★, *The Mamas And The Papas* aka *Cass, John, Michelle, Denny* (Dunhill/RCA Victor 1966)★★★★, *The Mamas And The Papas Deliver* (Dunhill/RCA Victor 1967)★★★★, *The Papas And The Mamas* (Dunhill/RCA Victor 1968)★★★, various artists *Monterey International Pop Festival* (1971)★★★, *People Like Us* (Dunhill 1971)★★. COMPILATIONS: *Farewell To The First Golden Era* (1967)★★★★, *Golden Era Volume 2* (1968)★★★★, *16 Of Their Greatest Hits* (1969)★★★★, *A Gathering Of Flowers* (1971)★★★★, *20 Golden Hits* (1973)★★★★, *The ABC Collection: Greatest Hits* (1976)★★★★, *Creeque Alley: The History Of The Mamas And Papas* (MCA 1991)★★★★.
FURTHER READING: *Papa John*, John Phillips with Jim Jerome. *California Dreamin' – The True Story Of The Mamas And Papas*, Michelle Phillips.

MAN
ALBUMS: *Revelation* (Pye 1969)★★★, *2ozs Of Plastic With A Hole In The Middle* (Dawn 1969)★★★, *Man* aka *Man 1970* (Liberty 1970)★★, *Do You Like It Here Now, Are You Settling In?* (United Artists 1971)★★, *Live At The Padgett Rooms, Penarth* (United Artists 1972)★★★, *Be Good To Yourself ... At Least Once A Day* (United Artists 1972)★★★, *Back Into The Future* (United Artists 1973)★★★, *Rhinos, Winos And Lunatics* (United Artists 1974)★★★, *Slow Motion* (United Artists 1974)★★★, *Maximum Darkness* (United Artists 1975)★★, *Welsh Connection* (MCA 1976)★★, *All's Well That Ends Well* (MCA 1977)★★, *Live At Reading 1983* (1993)★★, *The Twang Dynasty Road Goes On Forever* (1993)★★, *Call Down The Moon* (Hypertension 1995)★★. COMPILATIONS: *Perfect Timing (The UA Years: 1970-75)* (EMI 1991)★★★.
FURTHER READING: *Mannerisms*, Martin Mycock. *Mannerisms II*, Martin Mycock.

MANCHESTER, MELISSA
ALBUMS: *Home To Myself* (Bell 1973)★★★, *Bright Eyes* (Bell 1974)★★★, *Melissa* (Arista 1975)★★★, *Better Days And Happy Endings* (Arista 1976)★★★, *Help Is On The Way* (Arista 1976)★★, *Singin'* (Arista 1977)★★, *Don't Cry Out Loud* (Arista 1978)★★★, *Melissa Manchester* (Arista 1979)★★, *For The Working Girl* (Arista 1980)★★, *Hey Ricky* (Arista 1982)★★, *Emergency* (Arista 1983)★★, *Mathematics* (MCA 1985)★★, *Colors Of Christmas* (Capitol 1997)★★. COMPILATIONS: *Greatest Hits* (Arista 1983)★★★, *The Definitive Collection* (Arista 1997)★★★.

MANFRED MANN
ALBUMS: *The Manfred Mann Album* (Ascot 1964)★★★★, *The Five Faces Of Manfred Mann* (HMV 1964)★★★★, *Mann Made* (HMV 1965)★★★★, *My Little Red Book Of Winners* (Ascot 1965)★★★★, *Mann Made Hits* (1966)★★★★, *As Is* (Fontana 1966)★★★, *Mann Made* (Ascot 1966)★★★, *Pretty Flamingo* (United Artists 1966)★★★, *Soul Of Mann* (HMV 1967)★★★, *Up The Junction* soundtrack (Fontana 1967)★★, *What A Mann* (Fontana 1968)★★★, *The Mighty Garvey* (Fontana 1968)★★★. COMPILATIONS: *Mann Made Hits* (HMV 1966)★★★★, *Manfred Mann's Greatest Hits* (United Artists 1966)★★★★, *What A Mann* (Fontana 1968)★★★, *This Is Manfred Mann* (1971)★★★, *Semi-Detached Suburban* (1979)★★★, *The R&B Years* (1986)★★★★, *The Singles Plus* (1987)★★★★, *The EP Collection* (See For Miles 1989)★★★★, *The Collection* (1990)★★★, *Ages Of Mann* (1992)★★★★, *Best Of The EMI Years* (1993)★★★★, *Groovin' With The Manfreds* (EMI 1996)★★★.
FURTHER READING: *Mannerisms: The Five Phases Of Manfred Mann*, Greg Russo.

MANFRED MANN'S EARTH BAND
ALBUMS: *Manfred Mann's Earth Band* (Philips 1972)★★, *Glorified Magnified* (Philips 1972)★★★, *Messin'* (Vertigo 1973)★★★, *The Good Earth* (Bronze 1974)★★★, *Nightingales And Bombers* (Bronze 1975)★★★, *The Roaring Silence* (Bronze 1976)★★★★, *Watch* (Bronze 1978)★★★, *Angel Station* (Bronze 1979)★★★, *Chance* (Bronze 1980)★★★, *Somewhere In Afrika* (Bronze 1983)★★★, *Budapest* (Bronze 1984)★★★, *Criminal Tango* (Ten 1986)★★★, *Masque* (Ten 1987)★★★, *Soft Vengeance* (Grapevine 1996)★★★. COMPILATIONS: *The New Bronze Age* (1977)★★★, *Manfred Mann's Earth Band* (1992, 13-CD box set)★★★.

MANHATTAN TRANSFER
ALBUMS: *Jukin'* (Capitol 1971/75)★★, *Manhattan Transfer* (Atlantic 1975)★★★★, *Coming Out* (Atlantic 1976)★★★, *Pastiche* (Atlantic 1978)★★★, *Live* (Atlantic 1978)★★, *Extensions* (Atlantic 1979)★★★, *Mecca for Moderns* (Atlantic 1981)★★★, *Bodies And Souls* (Atlantic 1983)★★★, *Bop Doo-Wop* (Atlantic 1985)★★★, *Vocalese* (Atlantic 1985)★★★, *Live In Tokyo* (Atlantic 1987)★★★, *Brasil* (Atlantic 1987)★★, *The Offbeat Of Avenues* (Columbia 1991)★★★, *Tonin'* (Atlantic 1995)★★★. Solo: Janis Siegel *Experiment In White* (1982)★★. COMPILATIONS: *Best Of Manhattan Transfer* (Atlantic 1981)★★★, *The Very Best Of ...* (Rhino 1993)★★★★.

MANIC STREET PREACHERS
ALBUMS: *Generation Terrorists* (Columbia 1992)★★★, *Gold Against The Soul* (Columbia 1993)★★★, *The Holy Bible* (Columbia 1994)★★★, *Everything Must Go* (Epic 1996)★★★★★.
FURTHER READING: *Design For Living*, Paula Shutkever.

MANILOW, BARRY
ALBUMS: *Barry Manilow* (Bell 1972)★★★, *Barry Manilow II* (Bell 1973)★★★, *Tryin' To Get The Feeling* (Arista 1975)★★★, *This One's For You* (Arista 1976)★★★, *Live* (Arista 1977)★★, *Even Now* (Arista 1978)★★★, *One Voice* (Arista 1979)★★★, *Barry* (Arista 1980)★★★, *If I Should Love Again* (Arista 1981)★★, *Oh, Julie!* (Arista 1982)★★, *Here Comes The Night* (Arista 1982)★★★, *Barry Live In Britain* (Arista 1982)★★, *Swing Street* (Arista 1984)★★★, *2am Paradise Cafe* (Arista 1985)★★★, *Songs To Make The Whole World Sing* (Arista 1989)★★, *Live On Broadway* (Arista 1990)★★★, *Because It's Christmas* (Arista 1990)★★, *Showstoppers* (Arista 1991)★★★, *Hidden Treasures* (Arista 1993)★★★, *Singin' With The Big Bands* (Arista 1994)★★★, *Summer Of '78* (Arista 1996)★★★. COMPILATIONS: *Greatest Hits* (Arista 1978)★★★, *Greatest Hits Volume II* (Arista 1983)★★★, *The Songs 1975-1990* (Arista 1990)★★★, *The Complete Collection And Then Some* 4-CD set (1992)★★★.
VIDEOS: *In Concert At The Greek* (Guild Home Video 1984), *Live On Broadway* (Arista 1990), *The Greatest Hits... And Then Some* (1994).
FURTHER READING: *Barry Manilow*, Ann Morse. *Barry Manilow: An Autobiography*, Barry Manilow with Mark Bego. *Barry Manilow*, Howard Elson. *The Magic Of Barry Manilow*, Alan Clarke. *Barry Manilow For The Record*, Simon Weir. *The Barry Manilow Scrapbook: His Magical World In Works And Pictures*, Richard Peters. *Barry Manilow*, Tony Jasper.

MANN, AIMEE
ALBUMS: *Whatever* (Imago 1993)★★★★, *I'm With Stupid* (Geffen 1995)★★★.

MANSUN
ALBUMS: *Attack Of The Grey Lantern* (Parlophone 1997)★★★★.

MAR-KEYS
ALBUMS: *Last Night* (Atlantic 1961)★★★, *Do The Popeye With The Mar-Keys* (London 1962)★★★, *The Great Memphis Sound* (Atlantic 1966)★★★, with Booker T. And The MGs *Back To Back* (Stax 1967)★★★, *Mellow Jello* (Atlantic 1968)★★★, *Damifiknow* (Stax 1969)★★, *Memphis Experience* (1971)★★.

Marc And The Mambas
ALBUMS: *Untitled* (Some Bizzare 1982)★★, *Torment And Toreros* (Some Bizzare 1983)★★.

MARILLION
ALBUMS: *Script For A Jester's Tear* (EMI 1983)★★★, *Fugazi* (EMI 1984)★★, *Real To Real* (EMI 1984)★, *Misplaced Childhood* (EMI 1985)★★★, *Brief Encounter* (EMI 1986)★★, *Clutching At Straws* (EMI 1987)★★★, *B Sides Themselves* (EMI 1988)★★, *The Thieving Magpie* (EMI 1988)★★, *Seasons End* (EMI 1989)★★★, *Holidays In Eden* (EMI 1991)★★★, *Brave* (EMI 1994)★★★, *Afraid Of Sunlight* (EMI 1995)★★★, *Made Again* (EMI 1996)★★, *This Strange Engine* (Intact/Raw Power 1997)★★★. COMPILATIONS: *A Singles Collection* (EMI 1992)★★★, *The Best Of Both Worlds* (EMI 1997)★★★.
VIDEOS: *1982-1986 The Videos* (1986), *Live From Lorely* (1987), *From Stoke Row To Ipanema* (1990), *Brave* (1995).
FURTHER READING: *Market Square Heroes*, Mick Wall. *Marillion*, Carol Clerk. *The Authorized Story Of Marillion*, Mick Wall. *Marillion: The Script*, Clive Gifford.

MARILYN MANSON
ALBUMS: *Portrait Of An American Family* (Nothing/East West 1994)★★, *Smells Like Children* (MCA 1996)★★, *Antichrist Superstar* (Nothing/Interscope 1996)★★★.

MARLEY, BOB, AND THE WAILERS
ALBUMS: *Wailing Wailers* (Studio One 1965)★★★, *The Best Of The Wailers* (Beverley's 1970)★★★, *Soul Rebels* (Trojan/Upsetter 1970)★★★, *Catch A Fire* (Island 1973)★★★★, *Burnin'* (Island 1973)★★★★, *African Herbsman* (Trojan 1974)★★★, *Rasta Revolution* (Trojan 1974)★★★, *Natty Dread* (Island 1975)★★★★★, *Live!* later re-titled *Live At The Lyceum* (Island 1975)★★★★, *Rastaman Vibration* (Island 1976)★★★★, *Exodus* (Island 1977)★★★★, *Kaya* (Island 1978)★★★★, *Babylon By Bus* (Island 1978)★★★, *Survival* (Tuff Gong/Island 1979)★★★★, *Uprising* (Tuff Gong/Island 1980)★★★★, *Marley, Tosh Livingston & Associates* (Studio One 1980)★★★. COMPILATIONS: *In The Beginning* (Psycho/Trojan 1979)★★★, *Chances Are* (Warners 1981)★★★, *Bob Marley – The Boxed Set* 9-LP box set (Island 1982)★★★, *Confrontation* (Tuff Gong/Island 1983)★★★, *Legend* (Island 1984)★★★★★, *Reggae Greats* (Island

1985)★★★, Soul Revolution I & II the first UK release of the 70s Jamaican double album (Trojan 1988)★★★, Talkin' Blues (Tuff Gong 1991)★★★, All The Hits (Rohit 1991)★★★, Upsetter Record Shop Parts 1&2 (Esoldun 1992)★★★, Songs Of Freedom 4-CD box set (Island 1992)★★★★, Never Ending Wailers (RAS 1993)★★★, Natural Mystic: The Legend Continues (Island 1995)★★★★, Soul Almighty – The Formative Years Vol. 1 (JAD 1996)★★★, Dreams Of Freedom: Ambient Translations Of Bob Marley In Dub (Axiom/Island 1997)★★★, Roots Of A Legend (Trojan 1997)★★★.
VIDEOS: One Love Peace Concert (Hendring 1988), Live At The Rainbow (Channel 5 1988), Caribbean Nights (Island 1988), Legend (Island 1991), Time Will Tell (1992), The Bob Marley Story (Island 1994).
FURTHER READING: Bob Marley: The Roots Of Reggae, Cathy McKnight and John Tobler. Soul Rebel – Natural Mystic, Adrian Boot and Vivien Goldman. Bob Marley: The Biography, Stephen Davis. Catch A Fire, The Life Of Bob Marley, Timothy White. Bob Marley: Reggae King Of The World, Malika Lee Whitney. Bob Marley: In His Own Words, Ian McCann. The Music Of Bob Marley, Ian McCann. Bob Marley: Music, Myth & The Rastas, Henderson Dalrymple. Bob Marley: Conquering Lion Of Reggae, Stephen Davis. The Illustrated Legend 1945-1981, Barry Lazell. Sprit Dancer, Bruce W. Talamon.

MARMALADE
ALBUMS: There's A Lot Of It (CBS 1969)★★★, Reflections Of My Life (1970)★★★, Songs (Decca 1971)★★★, Our House Is Rockin' (1974)★★, Only Light On My Horizon (1977)★★, Doing It All For You (1979)★★.
COMPILATIONS: The Best Of The Marmalade (CBS 1970)★★★, Reflections Of The Marmalade (Decca 1970)★★★, The Definitive Collection (Castle 1996)★★★★.

MARRIOTT, STEVE
ALBUMS: Marriott (A&M 1975)★★, 30 Seconds To Midnite (Trax 1989)★★, with Packet Of Three Live 23rd October 1985 (Zeus 1996)★★.
FILMS: Heavens Above (1962), Night Cargoes (1962), Live It Up (1963), Be My Guest (1963).

MARSHALL TUCKER BAND
ALBUMS: The Marshall Tucker Band (Capricorn 1973)★★★★, A New Life (Capricorn 1974)★★★, Where We All Belong (Capricorn 1974)★★★, Searchin' For A Rainbow (Capricorn 1975)★★★★, Long Hard Ride (Capricorn 1976)★★★, Carolina Dreams (Capricorn 1977)★★★, Together Forever (Capricorn 1978)★★★, Running Like The Wind (Warners 1979)★★★, Tenth (Warners 1980)★★★, Dedicated (Warners 1981)★★★, Tuckerized (Warners 1981)★★★, Just Us (1983)★★, Greetings From South Carolina (1983)★★, Still Holdin' On (Mercury 1988)★★, Southern Spirit (Sisapa 1990)★★, Still Smokin' (1993)★★.
COMPILATIONS: Greatest Hits (Capricorn 1978)★★★.
VIDEOS: This Country's Rockin' (1993), Then And Now, Cabin Fever (1993).

MARTHA AND THE MUFFINS
ALBUMS: Metro Music (DinDisc 1980)★★★, Trance And Dance (DinDisc 1980)★★★, This Is The Ice Age (DinDisc 1981)★★★, Danseparc (RCA 1982)★★. As M+M Mystery Walk (RCA 1984)★★★, The World Is A Ball (Current 1985)★★.
COMPILATIONS: Faraway In Time (Virgin 1988)★★★.

MARTHA AND THE VANDELLAS
ALBUMS: Come And Get These Memories (Gordy 1963)★★★, Heat Wave (Gordy 1963)★★★, Dance Party (Gordy 1965)★★★, Watchout! (Gordy 1967)★★, Martha & The Vandellas Live! (Gordy 1967)★. As Martha Reeves And The Vandellas Ridin' High (Gordy 1968)★★, Sugar 'n' Spice (Gordy 1969)★★, Natural Resources (Gordy 1970)★★, Black Magic (Gordy 1972)★★.
COMPILATIONS: Greatest Hits (Gordy 1966)★★★★, Anthology (Motown 1974)★★★★, Compact Commmand Performances (Motown 1992)★★★, 24 Greatest Hits (Motown 1992)★★★★, Live Wire, 1962-1972 (Motown 1993)★★★★, Milestones (Motown 1995)★★★★.

MARTIN, GEORGE
ALBUMS: Off The Beatle Track (Parlophone 1964)★★★, George Martin (United Artists 1965)★★★, George Martin Scores Instrumental Versions Of The Hits (1965)★★★, Plays Help! (Columbia 1965)★★, Salutes The Beatle Girls (United Artists)★★★, And I Love Her (Studio Two 1966)★★★, By George! (1967)★★★, The Family Way soundtrack (1967)★★★, British Maid (United Artists 1968)★★★, with Paul McCartney Yellow Submarine (Parlophone 1969)★★★, Live And Let Die (United Artists 1973)★★★, Beatles To Bond And Bach (Polydor 1974)★★★.
FURTHER READING: All You Need Is Ears, George Martin. Summer Of Love: The Making Of Sgt Pepper, George Martin.
FILMS: Give My Regards To Broad Street (1985).

MARTYN, JOHN
ALBUMS: London Conversation (Island 1968)★★, The Tumbler (Island 1968)★★, Stormbringer (Island 1970)★★★, Road To Ruin (Island 1970)★★★, Bless The Weather (Island 1971)★★★, Solid Air (Island 1973)★★★★, Inside Out (Island 1973)★★★, Sunday's Child (Island 1975)★★★, Live At Leeds (Island 1975)★★★, One World (Island 1977)★★★★, Grace And Danger (Island 1980)★★★★, Glorious Fool (Warners 1981)★★★★, Well Kept Secret (Warners 1982)★★★★, Philentrophy (1983)★★, Sapphire (Island 1984)★★★, Piece By Piece (Island 1986)★★★★, Foundations (Island 1987)★★★, The Apprentice (Island 1990)★★★, Cooltide (Permanent 1991)★★, BBC Radio 1 Live In Concert (Windsong 1992)★★★, Couldn't Love You More (Permanent 1992)★★★, No Little Boy (Permanent 1993)★★★, And (Go! Discs 1996)★★★, Church With One Bell (1997)★★★, Apprentice (1998)★★★, Live At The Shore Theatre (1998)★★★, Cool Tide (1998)★★★.
COMPILATIONS: So Far So Good (Island 1977)★★★, The Electric John Martyn (Island 1982)★★★, Sweet Little Mysteries: The Island Anthology (Island 1994)★★★★, The Very Best Of... (1998)★★★.

MARVELETTES
ALBUMS: Please Mr Postman (Tamla 1961)★★★★, The Marvelettes Sing Smash Hits Of 1962 (Tamla 1962)★★★, Playboy (Tamla 1962)★★★, The Marvellous Marvelettes (Tamla 1963)★★★★, Recorded Live: On Stage (Tamla 1963)★★, The Marvelettes (Tamla 1967)★★★, Sophisticated Soul (Tamla 1968)★★★, In Full Bloom (Motown 1969)★★, The Return Of The Marvelettes (Motown 1970)★★, Now (Motor City 1990)★★.
COMPILATIONS: The Marvelettes Greatest Hits (Tamla 1963)★★★★, Anthology (Motown 1975)★★★★, Compact Command Perfomances – 23 Greatest Hits (Motown 1992)★★★★, Deliver The Singles 1961-1971 (Motown 1993)★★★★.

MARVIN, HANK B.
ALBUMS: Hank Marvin (Columbia 1969)★★, The Hank Marvin Guitar Syndicate (1977)★★, Words And Music (Polydor 1982)★★, All Alone With Friends (1983)★★, Into The Light (Polydor 1992)★★, Heartbeat (Polydor 1993)★★, Hank Plays Cliff (Polygram 1995)★★★, Hank Plays Holly (Polygram 1996)★★★.
COMPILATIONS: Would You Believe It ... Plus! (1988)★★★.
FILMS: Expresso Bongo (1959), Summer Holiday (1962), Wonderful Life (1964), Finders Keepers (1966).

MASEKELA, HUGH
ALBUMS: Jazz Epistles (1959)★★★, Trumpet Afnca (1962)★★★★, The Americanization Of Ooga Booga (1964)★★★, The Emancipation Of Hugh Masekela (1966)★★★, Promise Of A Future (1967)★★★, Coincidence (1967)★★★, Hugh Masekela (Fontana 1968)★★★, Alive And Well At The Whiskey (Uni 1968)★★★, Reconstruction (Motown 1970)★★★, And The Union Of South Africa (Rare Earth 1971)★★★, with Dudu Pukwana Home Is Where The Music Is (1972)★★★★, Your Mama Told You Not To Worry (1974)★★★, I Am Not Afraid (1974)★★★, The Boys Doin' It (1975)★★★, The African Connection (1975)★★★, Colonial Man (1976)★★★, with Herb Alpert The Main Event (A&M 1978)★★, Herb Alpert/Hugh Masekela (A&M 1979)★★, Home (1982)★★★, Dollar Bill (1983)★★★, Technobush (Jive 1984)★★★, Waiting For The Rain (Jive 1985)★★★, Tomorrow (Warners 1987)★★★, Up Township (Novus 1989)★★★, Hope (Triloka 1994)★★★, Notes Of Life (Sony 1996)★★★.
COMPILATIONS: Liberation (Jive 1988)★★★.
VIDEOS: Notice To Quit (A Portrait Of South Africa) (Hendring 1986), Vukani (BMG 1990).

MASON, DAVE
ALBUMS: Alone Together (Blue Thumb 1970)★★★★, Dave Mason And Cass Elliot (Blue Thumb 1971)★★★, Headkeeper (Blue Thumb 1972)★★, Dave Mason Is Alive! (Blue Thumb 1973)★★, It's Like You Never Left (Columbia 1973)★★★, Dave Mason (Columbia 1974)★★★, Split Coconut (Columbia 1975)★★, Certified Live (Columbia 1976)★★, Let It Flow (Columbia 1977)★★, Mariposa De Oro (Columbia 1978)★★, Old Crest On A New Wave (Columbia 1980)★★, Some Assembly Required (Maze 1987)★, Two Hearts (MCA 1988)★.
COMPILATIONS: The Best Of Dave Mason (Columbia 1974)★★★, Dave Mason At His Very Best (Blue Thumb 1975)★★★, The Very Best Of Dave Mason (ABC 1978)★★★, Long Lost Friend: The Best Of Dave Mason (Sony/Legacy 1995)★★★.
FURTHER READING: Keep On Running: The Steve Winwood Story, Chris Welch. Back In The High Life: A Biography Of Steve Winwood, Alan Clayson.

MASSIVE ATTACK
ALBUMS: Blue Lines (Wild Bunch/EMI 1991)★★★★, Protection (EMI 1994)★★★, Vs the Mad Professor No Protection (Circa 1995)★★★, Mezzanine (Virgin 1998)★★★.

MATCHING MOLE
ALBUMS: Matching Mole (Columbia 1972)★★★, Matching Mole's Little Red Record (Columbia 1973)★★★.

MATTHEWS SOUTHERN COMFORT
ALBUMS: Matthews Southern Comfort (EMI 1969)★★★, Second Spring (UNI 1970)★★★, Later That Same Year (1970)★★. As Southern Comfort Southern Comfort (1971)★★, Frog City (1971)★★, Stir Don't Shake (1972)★★.
COMPILATIONS: The Best Of Matthews Southern Comfort (MCA 1982)★★★, The Essential Collection (Half Moon 1997)★★★.

MAYALL, JOHN
ALBUMS: John Mayall Plays John Mayall (Decca 1965)★★★★, Bluesbreakers With Eric Clapton (Decca 1966)★★★★★, A Hard Road (Decca 1967)★★★★, Crusade (Decca 1967)★★★, The Blues Alone (Ace Of Clubs 1967)★★★★, Diary Of A Band Vol. 1 (Decca 1968)★★★, Diary Of A Band Vol. 2 (Decca 1968)★★★, Bare Wires (Decca 1968)★★★★★, Blues From Laurel Canyon (Decca 1968)★★★★, Turning Point (Polydor 1969)★★★★, Empty Rooms (Polydor 1970)★★★★, USA Union (Polydor 1970)★★, Back To The Roots (Polydor 1971)★★★, Beyond The Turning Point (Polydor 1971)★★★, Thru The Years (Decca 1971)★★★, Memories (Polydor 1971)★★★, Jazz Blues Fusion (Polydor 1972)★★★, Moving On (Polydor 1973)★★, Ten Years Are Gone (Polydor 1973)★★, Down The Line (London US 1973)★★, The Latest Edition (Polydor 1975)★★, New Year, New Band, New Company (ABC 1975)★★, Time Expired, Notice To Appear (ABC 1975)★★, John Mayall (Polydor 1976)★★, A Banquet Of Blues (ABC 1976)★★, Lots Of People (ABC 1977)★★, A Hard Core Package (ABC 1977)★★, Primal Solos (London 1977)★★★, Blues Roots (Decca 1978)★★, Last Of The British Blues (MCA 1978)★★, Bottom Line (DJM 1979)★★, No More Interviews (DJM 1979)★★, Roadshow Blues (DJM 1980)★★, Last Edition (Polydor 1983)★★, Behind The Iron Curtain (PRT 1986)★★, Chicago Line (Island 1988)★★, Archives To Eighties (Polydor 1989)★★★, A Sense Of Place (Island 1990)★★★★, Wake Up Call (Silvertone 1993)★★★★, The 1982 Reunion Concert (Repertoire 1994)★★, Spinning Coin (Silvertone 1995)★★, Blues For The Lost Days (Silvertone 1997)★★★★.
COMPILATIONS: Looking Back (Decca 1969)★★★★, World Of John Mayall (Decca 1970)★★★★, World Of John Mayall Vol. 2 (Decca 1971)★★★★, The John Mayall Story Vol. 1 (Decca 1983)★★★, The John Mayall Story Vol. 2 (Decca 1983)★★★, London Blues 1964-1969 (Polygram 1992)★★★★, Room To Move 1969-1974 (Polygram 1992)★★★★.
VIDEOS: John Mayall's Bluesbreakers: Blues Alive (PVE 1995).
FURTHER READING: John Mayall: Blues Breaker, Richard Newman.

MAYFIELD, CURTIS
ALBUMS: Curtis (Buddah 1970)★★★, Curtis/Live! (Buddah 1971)★★★, Roots (Buddah 1971)★★★★, Superfly film soundtrack (Buddah 1972)★★★★★, Back To The World (Buddah 1973)★★★★, Curtis In Chicago (Buddah 1973)★★★, Sweet Exorcist (Buddah 1974)★★★, Got To Find A Way (Buddah 1974)★★★, Claudine (Buddah 1975)★★, Let's Do It Again (Curtom 1975)★★★, There's No Place Like America Today (Curtom 1975)★★★, Sparkle (Curtom 1976)★★, Give, Get, Take And Have (Curtom 1976)★★, Short Eyes (Curtom 1977)★★, Never Say You Can't Survive (Curtom 1977)★★, A Piece Of The Action (Curtom 1978)★★, Do It All Night (Curtom 1978)★★★, Heartbeat (RSO 1979)★★★, with Linda Clifford The Right Combination (RSO 1980)★★, Something To Believe In (RSO 1980)★★, Love Is The Place (Boardwalk 1981)★★, Honesty (Boardwalk 1983)★★★★, We Come In Peace With A Message Of Love (CRC 1985)★★★, Live In Europe (Ichiban 1988)★★★, People Get Ready (Essential 1990)★★★, Take It To The Streets (Curtom 1990)★★★, BBC Radio 1 Live In Concert (Windsong 1994)★★, New World Order (Warners 1996)★★★.
COMPILATIONS: Of All Time (Curtom 1990)★★★, Get Down To The Funky Groove (1994)★★★, Groove On Up (1994)★★★, Tripping Out (Charly 1994)★★★, A Man Like Curtis – The Best Of (1994)★★★, Living Legend (Curtom Classics 1995)★★★, People Get Ready: The Curtis Mayfield Story 3-CD box set (Rhino 1996)★★★★, Love Peace And Understanding (Sequel 1997)★★★.
VIDEOS: Curtis Mayfield At Ronnie Scott's (Hendring Video 1988).
FILMS: Superfly (1973), The Groove Tube (1974).

MAZE (FEATURING FRANKIE BEVERLY)
ALBUMS: Maze Featuring Frankie Beverly (Capitol 1977)★★★, Golden Time Of Day (Capitol 1978)★★★, Inspiration (Capitol 1979)★★★, Joy And Pain (Capitol 1980)★★★, Live In New Orleans (Capitol 1981)★★★, We Are One (Capitol 1983)★★★, Can't Stop The Love (Capitol 1985)★★★, Live In Los Angeles (Capitol 1986)★★★★, Silky Soul (Warners 1989)★★★, Back To Basics (1993)★★★.
COMPILATIONS: Lifelines Volume One (Capitol 1989)★★★.

MAZZY STAR
ALBUMS: She Hangs Brightly (Rough Trade 1990)★★★, So Tonight That I Might See (Capitol 1993)★★★, Among My Swan (Capitol 1996)★★★.

MC5
ALBUMS: Kick Out The Jams (Elektra 1969)★★★★, Back In The USA (Elektra 1970)★★★, High Time (Elektra 1971)★★, Do It (Revenge 1987)★★, Live Detroit 68/69 (Revenge 1988)★.
COMPILATIONS: Babes In Arms cassette only (ROIR 1983)★★★, Looking At You (Receiver 1994)★★★, Power Trip (Alive 1994)★★★.

McBRIDE, MARTINA
ALBUMS: The Time Has Come (RCA 1992)★★★, The Way That I Am (RCA 1993)★★★★, Wild Angels (RCA 1995)★★★★, Evolution (RCA 1997)★★★.
VIDEOS: Independence Day (1994).

McCARTNEY, PAUL
ALBUMS: McCartney (Apple 1970)★★★, Ram (Apple 1971)★★★, with Wings Wildlife (Apple 1971)★★, with Wings Red Rose Speedway (Apple 1973)★★★, with Wings Band On The Run (Apple 1973)★★★★, with Wings Venus And Mars (Apple 1975)★★★★, with Wings Wings At The Speed Of Sound (Apple 1976)★★, with Wings Wings Over America (Parlophone 1976)★★★, with Wings London Town (Parlophone 1978)★★★, with Wings Back To The Egg (Parlophone 1979)★★★, McCartney II (Parlophone 1980)★★, Tug Of War (Parlophone 1982)★★, Pipes Of Peace (Parlophone 1983)★★, Give My Regards To Broad Street (Parlophone 1984)★, Press To Play (Parlophone 1986)★★, Choba B CCCP The Russian Album (Parlophone 1989)★★, Flowers In The Dirt (1989)★★★, Tripping The Live Fantastic (Parlophone 1990)★★, Unplugged – The Official Bootleg (Parlophone 1991)★★★, Off The Ground (1992)★★, Paul Is Live (Parlophone 1993)★★, Flaming Pie (Parlophone 1997)★★★★, Standing Stone (EMI Classics 1997)★★.
COMPILATIONS: Wings Greatest Hits (Parlophone 1978)★★★, All The Best (Parlophone 1987)★★★★.
FILMS: A Hard Day's Night (1964), Help (1965), Give My Regards To Broad Street (1985).
VIDEOS: Paul Is Live In Concert On The New World Tour (PMI 1994).
FURTHER READING: Body Count, Francie Schwartz. The Paul McCartney Story, George Tremlett. The Facts About A Pop Group: Featuring Wings, David Gelly. Paul McCartney In His Own Words, Paul Gambaccini. Paul McCartney: A Biography In Words & Pictures, John Mendelsohn. Paul McCartney & Wings, Tony Jasper. Hands Across The Water: Wings Tour USA, no author listed. Paul McCartney: Beatle With Wings, Martin A. Grove. Paul McCartney: Composer/Artist, Paul McCartney. The Ocean View: Paintings And Drawings Of Wings American Tour April To June 1976, Humphrey Ocean. Paul McCartney: The Definitive Biography, Chris Welch. McCartney, Chris Salewicz. McCartney: The Biography, Chet Flippo. Blackbird: The Life And Times Of Paul McCartney, Geoffrey Giuliano. Blackbird: The Unauthorized Biography of Paul McCartney, Geoffrey Giuliano. Paul McCartney: Behind The Myth, Ross Benson. McCartney: Yesterday & Today, Ray Coleman.

McCOYS
ALBUMS: Hang On Sloopy (Bang 1965)★★★, You Make Me Feel So Good (Bang 1966)★★★, Infinite McCoys (Mercury 1968)★, Human Ball (Mercury 1969)★.
COMPILATIONS: Hang On Sloopy: The Best Of The McCoys (Legacy 1995)★★★★.

McCRAE, GEORGE
ALBUMS: Rock Your Baby (TK 1974)★★★, George McCrae I (TK 1975)★★★, Diamond Touch (TK 1977)★★★, George McCrae II (TK 1978)★★★, We Did It (TK 1979)★★★, with Gwen McCrae Together (Cat 1975)★★★, One Step Closer To Love (President 1984)★★.
COMPILATIONS: The Best Of George McCrae (President 1984)★★★, The Best Of George And Gwen McCrae (1993)★★★.

McDONALD, COUNTRY JOE
ALBUMS: Country Joe And Blair Hardman (1964)★★, Thinking Of Woody Guthrie (Vanguard 1970)★★★, Tonight I'm Singing Just For You (Vanguard 1971)★★★, Hold On It's Coming (Vanguard 1971)★★, Quiet Days In Clichy soundtrack (Sonet 1971)★★, War, War, War (Vanguard 1972)★★, Incredible! Live! (Vanguard 1972)★★, The Paris Sessions (Vanguard 1973)★★★, Country Joe (Vanguard 1975)★★★, Paradise With An Ocean View (Fantasy 1975)★★, Love Is A Fire (Fantasy 1976)★★, Goodbye Blues (Fantasy 1977)★★, Rock 'N' Roll Music From The Planet Earth (Fantasy 1978)★★, Leisure Suite (Fantasy 1979)★★, On My Own (Rag Baby 1981)★★, Into The Fray (Rag Baby 1982)★★, Child's Play (Rag Baby 1983)★★, Animal Tracks (Animus 1983)★★, Peace On Earth (Line 1989)★★, Vietnam Experience (Line 1989)★★.
COMPILATIONS: The Best Of Country Joe McDonald (Vanguard 1973)★★★, The Essential Country Joe McDonald (Vanguard 1976)★★★, Classics (1992)★★★.

McDONALD, MICHAEL
ALBUMS: If That's What It Takes (Warners 1982)★★★★, No Looking Back (Warners 1985)★★★, Lonely Talk (Warners 1989)★★★, Take It To Heart (Reprise 1990)★★★, Blink Of An Eye (1993)★★, Blue Obsession (Reprise 1997).
COMPILATIONS: Sweet Freedom: Best Of Michael McDonald (Warners 1986)★★★.

McGARRIGLE, KATE AND ANNA
ALBUMS: Kate And Anna McGarrigle (Warners 1975)★★★★, Dancer With Bruised Knees (Warners 1977)★★★★, Pronto Monto (Warners 1978)★★★, French Record (Hannibal 1980)★★★★, Love Over And Over (Polydor 1982)★★★★, Heartbeats Accelerating (Private Music 1990)★★★★, Matapedia (Hannibal 1996)★★★★.

McGRAW, TIM
ALBUMS: Tim McGraw (Curb 1993)★★★, Not A Moment Too Soon (Curb 1994)★★★★, All I Want (Curb/Hit 1995)★★★★, Everywhere (Curb 1997)★★★★.
VIDEOS: Indian Outlaw (Curb 1994), Refried Dreams (Curb 1995), An Hour With Tim (Curb 1995).

McGRIFF, JIMMY
ALBUMS: I've Got A Woman (Sue 1962)★, Jimmy McGriff At The Apollo (Sue 1963)★★★, Jimmy McGriff At The Organ (Sue 1963)★★★★, Gospel Time (1963)★★★, Topkapi (Sue 1964)★★★, One Of Mine (Sue 1964)★★★, Blues For Mister Jimmy (Sue 1965)★★★★, The Big Band Of Jimmy McGriff (Solid State 1966)★★★, A Bag Full Of Soul (Solid State 1966)★★★★, Cherry (Solid State 1967)★★★, Honey (Solid State 1968)★★★, The Worm (Solid State 1968)★★★★, A Thing To Come By (Solid State 1969)★★★, The Last Minute (1983)★★★, The Countdown (Milestone 1983)★★★, Skywalk (1985)★★★, Blues For Mr Jimmy (Stateside 1986)★★★, State Of The Art (Milestone 1986)★★★, with Hank Crawford Soul Survivors (Milestone 1986)★★★★, Fly Dude (Unknown 1987)★★★, The Starting Five (Milestone 1987)★★★, Jimmy McGriff Featuring Hank Crawford (LRC 1990)★★★★, Georgia On My Mind (LRC 1990)★★★★, Tribute To Basie (LRC 1991)★★★★, Funkiest Little Band In The Land (LRC 1992)★★★, Electric Funk (Blue Note 1993)★★★, with Hank Crawford Blues Groove (Telarc 1996)★★★.
COMPILATIONS: A Toast To Jimmy McGriff's Golden Classics (Collectable 1989)★★★.

McGUINN, ROGER
ALBUMS: Roger McGuinn (Columbia 1973)★★★★, Peace On You (Columbia 1974)★★★, Roger McGuinn And Band (Columbia 1975)★★★, Cardiff Rose (Columbia 1976)★★★★, Thunderbyrd (Columbia 1977)★★★, Back From Rio (Arista 1990)★★★, Live From Mars (Hollywood 1996)★★.
COMPILATIONS: Born To Rock 'n' Roll (Columbia Legacy 1992)★★★★.
FURTHER READING: Timeless Flight: The Definitive Biography of the Byrds, Johnny Rogan.

McGUIRE, BARRY
ALBUMS: The Barry McGuire Album (Horizon 1963)★★★, Star Folk With Barry McGuire (Surrey 1965)★★, Eve Of Destruction (1965)★★★, This Precious Time (Dunhill 1966)★★★, Star Folk With Barry McGuire Vol. 2 (Surrey 1966)★★, Star Folk With Barry McGuire Vol. 3 (Surrey 1966)★★, Star Folk With Barry McGuire Vol. 4 (Surrey 1966)★★, Barry McGuire Featuring Eve of Destruction (Dunhill 1966)★★★, The Eve Of Destruction Man (Ember 1966)★, The World's Last Private Citizen (Dunhill 1968)★★, Barry McGuire And The Doctor (A&M 1971)★★, Seeds (1973)★★, Finer Than Gold (1981)★★, Inside Out (1982)★★, To The Bride (1982)★★, Best Of Barry (1982)★★, Anthology (One Way 1994).

McKEE, MARIA
ALBUMS: Maria McKee (Geffen 1989)★★★, You Gotta Sin To Get Saved (Geffen 1993)★★★, Life Is Sweet (Geffen 1996)★★★★.

McKENZIE, SCOTT
ALBUMS: The Voice Of Scott McKenzie (Ode/CBS 1967)★★, Stained Glass Morning (1970)★★.

McLACHLAN, SARAH
ALBUMS: Touch (Arista 1988)★★★, Solace (Arista 1992)★★★, Fumbling Towards Ecstasy (Arista 1994)★★★★, The Freedom Sessions (Nettwerk/Arista 1995)★★, Surfacing (Arista 1997)★★★.

McLEAN, DON
ALBUMS: Tapestry (Mediarts 1970)★★, American Pie (United Artists 1971)★★★★, Don McLean (United Artists 1972)★★★, Playin' Favorites (United Artists 1974)★★, Homeless Brother (United Artists 1974)★★, Solo (United Artists 1976)★★, Prime Time (Arista 1977)★★, Chain Lightning (Millenium 1981)★★, Believers (Millenium 1981)★★, Love Tracks (1987)★★, Favorites & Rarities (EMI America 1992), River Of Love (Curb 1995).
COMPILATIONS: Don McLean's Greatest Hits – Then And Now (EMI 1987)★★★, The Best Of Don McLean (EMI 1991)★★★.

McNABB, IAN
ALBUMS: Truth And Beauty (This Way Up 1993)★★★, Head Like A Rock (This Way Up 1994)★★★★, Merseybeast (This Way Up 1996)★★★.

McTELL, RALPH
ALBUMS: Eight Frames A Second (Transatlantic 1968)★★★, Spiral Staircase (Transatlantic 1969)★★★, My Side Of Your Window (Transatlantic 1970)★★★, You Well-Meaning Brought Me Here (Famous 1971)★★★★, Not Until Tomorrow (Reprise 1972)★★★★, Easy (Reprise 1974)★★★, Streets (Warners 1975)★★★, Right Side Up (Warners 1976)★★★, Ralph, Albert And Sydney (Warners 1977)★★★, Slide Away The Screen (Warners 1979)★★★, Love Grows (Mays 1982)★★★, Water Of Dreams (Mays 1982)★★★, Weather The Storm (Mays 1982)★★★, Songs From Alphabet Zoo (Mays 1983)★★★, The Best Of Alphabet Zoo (MFP 1984)★★★, At The End Of A Perfect Day (Telstar 1985)★★★, Tickle On The Tum (Mays 1986)★★★, Bridge Of Sighs (Mays 1987)★★★, The Ferryman (Mays 1987)★★★, Blue Skies, Black Heroes (Leola 1988)★★★, Stealin' Back. (Essential 1990)★★★, The Boy With The Note (1992)★★★, Alphabet Zoo (The Road Goes On Forever 1994)★★★, Sand In Your Shoes (Transatlantic 1995)★★★.
COMPILATIONS: Ralph McTell Revisited (1970)★★★, The Ralph McTell Collection (Pickwick 1978)★★★, Streets Of London (Transatlantic 1981)★★★, 71/72 (1982)★★, At His Best (Cambra 1985)★★★.

MEAT LOAF
ALBUMS: Bat Out Of Hell (Epic 1978)★★★★, Dead Ringer (Epic 1981)★★★, Midnight At The Lost And Found (Epic 1983)★★★, Bad Attitude (Arista 1985)★★★, Blind Before I Stop (Arista 1986)★★★, Meat Loaf Live (Arista 1987)★★★, Bat Out Of Hell II: Back Into Hell (Virgin 1993)★★★, Alive In Hell (Pure Music 1994)★★★.
COMPILATIONS: Hits Out Of Hell (Epic 1984)★★★.
VIDEOS: Live At Wembley (Videoform 1984), Bad Attitude Live (Virgin Vision 1986), Hits Out Of Hell (Epic 1985), Meat Loaf Live (MIA 1991), Bat Out Of Hell II – Picture Show (1994).
FURTHER READING: Meatloaf: Jim Steinman And The Phenomenology Of Excess, Sandy Robertson.

MEAT PUPPETS
ALBUMS: Meat Puppets (SST 1982)★★, Meat Puppets II (SST 1983)★★★, Up On The Sun (SST 1985)★★★, Mirage (SST 1987)★★★★, Huevos (SST 1987)★★★, Monsters (SST 1989)★★★, Forbidden Places (London 1991)★★★, Too High To Die (London 1994)★★★, No Joke! (London1995)★★★.
COMPILATIONS: No Strings Attached (SST 1990)★★★.

MEDICINE HEAD
ALBUMS: Old Bottles New Medicine (Dandelion 1970)★★★, Heavy On The Drum (Dandelion 1971)★★★, Dark Side Of The Moon (Dandelion 1972)★★★, One And One Is One (Polydor 1973)★★★, Thru' A Five (Polydor 1974)★★, Two Man Band (Polydor 1976)★★, Timepeace, Live In London 1975 (Red Steel 1995)★★.
COMPILATIONS: Medicine Head (1976)★★★, Best Of Medicine Head (Polydor 1981)★★★.

MEGA CITY FOUR
ALBUMS: Tranzophobia (Decoy 1989)★★★, Who Cares Wins (Decoy 1990)★★, Sebastapol Road (Big Life 1991)★★★★, Inspiringly Titled (The Live Album) (Big Life 1992)★★★, Magic Bullets (Big Life 1993)★★★, Soulscraper (Fire 1996)★★★.
COMPILATIONS: Terribly Sorry Bob (Decoy 1991)★★★.
FURTHER READING: Mega City Four: Tall Stories And Creepy Crawlies, Martin Roach.

MEGADETH
ALBUMS: Killing Is My Business...And Business Is Good (Megaforce 1985)★★, Peace Sells ... But Who's Buying? (Capitol 1986)★★★, So Far, So Good ... So What! (Capitol 1988)★★★, Rust In Peace (Capitol 1990)★★★★, Countdown To Extinction (Capitol 1992)★★★ Youthansia (Capitol 1994)★★★, Hidden Treasures (Capitol 1995)★★★, Cryptic Writings (Capitol 1997).
VIDEOS: Exposure Of A Dream (PMI 1993), Evolver: The Making Of Youthanasia (Capitol 1995).

MEKONS
ALBUMS: The Quality Of Mercy Is Not Strnen (Virgin 1979)★★, Mekons (Red Rhino 1980)★★, Fear And Whiskey (Sin 1985)★★★, The Edge Of The World (Sin 1986)★★★, Honky Tonkin' (Sin 1987)★★★, New York Mekons cassette only (ROIR 1987)★★, So Good It Hurts (Twin/Tone 1988)★★★, Mekons Rock 'N' Roll (A&M 1989)★★★, F.U.N. '90 EP (A&M 1990)★★★, The Curse Of The Mekons (Blast First 1991)★★★, I Love Mekons (Quarterstick 1993)★★★, Retreat From Memphis (Quarterstick 1994)★★★, with Kathy Acker Pussy, King Of The Pirates (Quarterstick 1996)★★★, Mekons United CD/Novel (Touch And Go 1996)★★.
Solo: Sally Timms To The Land Of Milk & Honey (Scout 1995)★★, Me (Quarterstick 1998)★★.
COMPILATIONS: It Falleth Like Gentle Rain From Heaven – The Mekons Story (CNT Productions 1982)★★★, Original Sin (Twin/Tone 1989)★★★.
FURTHER READING: Mekons United, no author listed.

MELANIE
ALBUMS: Born To Me (1969)★★, Affectionately Melanie (Buddah 1969)★★, Candles In The Rain (Buddah 1970)★★★, Leftover Wine (Buddah 1970)★★★, The Good Book (Buddah 1971)★★★, Gather Me (Neighbor 1971)★★★, Garden In The City (Buddah 1971)★★, Stoneground Words (Neighbor 1972)★★, Melanie At Carnegie Hall (Neighbour 1973)★★, Madrugada (Neighbour 1974)★★, As I See It Now (1975)★★, From The Beginning (ABC 1975)★★★, Sunset And Other Beginnings (1975)★★, Phonogenic – Not Just Another Pretty Face (RCA 1978)★★★, Ballroom Streets (RCA 1979)★★, Arabesque (RCA 1982)★★, Seventh Wave (Neighborhood 1983)★★, Cowabonga – Never Turn Your Back On A Wave (Food For Thought 1989)★★, Old Bitch Warrior (Creastars/BMG 1996)★★.
COMPILATIONS: The Four Sides Of (Wooded Hill 1997)★★★, On Air (Strange Fruit 1997)★★★.

MELLENCAMP, JOHN
ALBUMS: Chestnut Street Incident (Mainman 1976)★★, The Kid Inside (Castle 1977)★★, A Biography (Riva 1978)★★, John Cougar (Riva 1979)★★★, Nothing Matters And What If It Did (Riva 1981)★, American Fool (Riva 1982)★★★, Uh-Huh (Riva 1983)★★★, Scarecrow (Riva 1985)★★★, The Lonesome Jubilee (Mercury 1987)★★★, Big Daddy (Mercury 1989)★★★, Whenever We Wanted (Mercury 1991)★★★, Human Wheels (Mercury 1993)★★, Dance Naked (Mercury 1994)★★, Mr. Happy Go Lucky (Mercury 1996)★★★.
COMPILATIONS: The John Cougar Collection (Castle 1986)★★★, The best That I Could Do (1978-88) (Polygram 1997)★★★.
VIDEOS: John Cougar Mellencamp: Ain't That America (Embassy 1984).
FURTHER READING: American Fool: The Roots And Improbable Rise Of John Cougar Mellencamp, Torgoff.

MELVIN, HAROLD, AND THE BLUE NOTES
ALBUMS: Harold Melvin And The Blue Notes (Philadelphia International 1972)★★★, Black And Blue (Philadelphia International 1973)★★★★, To Be True (Philadelphia International 1975)★★★★, Wake Up Everybody (Philadelphia International 1975)★★★★, Reaching For The World (ABC 1977)★★★★, Now Is The Time (ABC 1977)★★, Blue Album (Source 1980)★★, All Things Happen In Time (MCA 1981)★★, Talk It Up (Philly World 1984)★★.
COMPILATIONS: All Their Greatest Hits! (Philadelphia International 1976)★★★★, Golden Highlights Of Harold Melvin (Columbia 1986)★★★, Satisfaction Guaranteed – The Best Of Harold Melvin And The Blue Notes (Philadelphia International 1992)★★★, Collection Gold (1993)★★★, If You Don't Know Me By Now (Epic Legacy 1995)★★★★.

MELVINS
ALBUMS: Gluey Porch Treatments (Alchemy 1987)★★★, Ozma (Boner 1989)★★, Bullhead (Boner 1991)★★, Lysol (Boner/Tupelo 1992)★★★, Houdini (Atlantic 1993)★★★, Prick (Amphetamine Reptile 1994)★★★, Stoner Witch (Atlantic 1994)★★★, Stag (Mammoth 1996)★★★, Honky (Amphetamine Reptile 1997)★★.

MEMPHIS HORNS
ALBUMS: Memphis Horns (Cotillion 1970)★★★, Horns For Everything (Million 1972)★★★, High On Music (RCA 1976)★★, Get Up And Dance (RCA 1977)★★, Memphis Horns Band II (RCA 1978)★★★, Welcome To Memphis (RCA 1979)★★, Flame Out (Lucky 7 1992)★★★.

MEN THEY COULDN'T HANG
ALBUMS: Night Of A Thousand Candles (Demon 1985)★★★, How Green Is The Valley (MCA 1986)★★★, Waiting For Bonaparte (Magnet 1987)★★★★, Silvertown (Silvertone 1989), The Domino Club (Silvertone 1990)★★★, Well Hung (Fun After All 1991)★★, Alive, Alive – O (1991)★★, Never Born To Follow (Demon 1996)★★★, Big Six Pack (Demon 1997)★★, Majestic Grill (Demon 1998)★★★.
VIDEOS: The Shooting (Jettisoundz 1991).

MENSWEAR
ALBUMS: Nuisance (Laurel 1995)★★★.

MERCHANT, NATALIE
ALBUMS: Tigerlily (Elektra 1995)★★★, Ophelia (Elektra/Asylum 1998).

MERCURY REV
ALBUMS: Yerself Is Steam (Mint/Jungle 1991)★★★, Boces (Beggars Banquet 1993)★★, See You On The Other Side (Beggars Banquet/Work 1995)★★★.
COMPILATIONS: Yerself Is Steam/Lego My Ego (Beggars Banquet 1992)★★★.

MERSEYBEATS
ALBUMS: The Merseybeats (Fontana 1964)★★★★.
COMPILATIONS: Greatest Hits (Look 1977)★★★, The Merseybeats; Beat And Ballads (Edsel 1982)★★★★, The Very Best Of The Merseybeats (Spectrum 1997)★★★★.

METALLICA
ALBUMS: Kill 'Em All (Megaforce 1983)★★, Ride The Lightning (Megaforce 1984)★★, Master Of Puppets (Elektra 1986)★★★★, ... And Justice For All (Elektra 1988)★★★, Metallica (Elektra 1991)★★★★, Live Shit: Binge & Purge 3-CD (Elektra 1993)★★★★, Load (Mercury 1996)★★★★, Re-Load (Vertigo 1997)★★★.
VIDEOS: Lick 'Em Up (1988), Home Vid Cliff 'Em All (1988), 2 Of One (1989), A Year And A Half In The Life Of Metallica (1992), Live Shit: Binge And Purge (Elektra Entertainment 1993), A Year And A Half: Vol 2 (1993), A Year And A Half: Vol 1 (1993).
FURTHER READING: A Visual Documentary, Mark Putterford. In Their Own Words, Mark Putterford. Metallica Unbound, K.J. Doughton. Metallica's Lars Ulrich: An Up-Close Look At The Playing Style Of ..., Dino Fauci. Metallica: The Frayed Ends Of Metal, Chris Crocker.

METHENY, PAT
ALBUMS: Bright Size Life (ECM 1976)★★★★, Watercolours (ECM 1977)★★★, Pat Metheny Group (ECM 1978)★★★★, New Chautauqua (ECM 1979)★★★★, American Garage (ECM 1979)★★★★, 80/81 (ECM 1980)★★★, As Falls Wichita, So Falls Wichita Falls (ECM 1981)★★★★, Offramp (ECM 1982)★★★★, Travels (ECM 1983)★★★★, with Charlie Haden and Billy Higgins Rejoicing (ECM 1983)★★★, First Circle (ECM 1984)★★★, The Falcon And The Snowman film soundtrack (EMI America 1985)★★, with Ornette Coleman Song X (Geffen 1986)★★★, Still Life (Talking) (Geffen 1987)★★★★, Letter From Home (Geffen 1989)★★★, with Gary Burton Reunion (Geffen 1990), Question And Answer (Geffen 1990)★★★★, with Jack DeJohnette Parallel Realities (Geffen 1990)★★★, Secret Story (Geffen 1992)★★★★, The Road To You – Recorded Live In Europe (Geffen 1993)★★★, with John Scofield I Can See Your House From Here (Blue Note 1994)★★★, Zero Tolerance For Silence (Geffen 1994)★★, We Live Here (Geffen 1995)★★★, Quartet (Geffen 1997)★★★, with Charlie Haden Beyond The Missouri Sky (Short Stories) (Verve 1997)★★★, with Derek Bailey Pinnacle (1998)★★★.
COMPILATIONS: Works (ECM 1983)★★★★, Works 2 (ECM 1988)★★★★.
VIDEOS: More Travels (1993).

MFSB
ALBUMS: MFSB (Philadelphia International 1973)★★, Love Is The Message (Philadelphia International 1974)★★, Universal Love (Philadelphia International 1975)★★, Philadelphia Freedom! (Philadelphia International 1975)★★★, Summertime (Philadelphia International 1976)★★, The End Of Phase 1 (Philadelphia International 1977)★★, The Gamble-Huff Orchestra (Philadelphia International 1979)★★, Mysteries Of The World (Philadelphia International 1981)★★.
COMPILATIONS: Love Is The Message: The Best Of MSFB (Sony Legacy 1996)★★★.

MICHAEL, GEORGE
ALBUMS: Faith (Epic 1987)★★★★, Listen Without Prejudice, Vol. 1 (Epic 1990)★★★, Older (DreamWorks 1996)★★★, Older And Upper (Virgin 1998)★★★★.
VIDEOS: Faith (1988), George Michael (1990).
FURTHER READING: Wham! (Confidential) The Death Of

A Supergroup, Johnny Rogan. *Bare*, George Michael with Tony Parsons. *George Michael: The Making Of A Super Star*, Bruce Dessau, *In His Own Words*, Nigel Goodall.

MICRODISNEY
ALBUMS: *Everybody Is Fantastic* (Rough Trade 1984)★★, *We Hate You White South African Bastards* mini-album (Rough Trade 1984)★★, *The Clock Comes Down The Stairs* (Rough Trade 1985)★★★, *Crooked Mile* (Virgin 1987)★★★, *39 Minutes* (Virgin 1988)★★★, *Love Your Enemies* (Creation Rev-Ola 1996)★★★.
COMPILATIONS: *Peel Sessions* (Strange Fruit 1989)★★★, *Big Sleeping House* (Virgin 1995)★★★★.

MIDNIGHT OIL
ALBUMS: *Midnight Oil* (Powderworks 1978)★★, *Head Injuries* (Powderworks 1979)★★★, *Place Without A Postcard* (Columbia 1981)★★★, *10,9,8,7,6,5,4,3,2,1* (Columbia 1982)★★★, *Red Sails In The Sunset* (Columbia 1985)★★★★, *Diesel And Dust* (Columbia 1987)★★★★, *Blue Sky Mining* (Columbia 1990)★★★★, *Scream In Blue-Live* (Columbia 1992)★★★, *Earth And Sun And Moon* (Columbia 1993)★★★, *Breathe* (Columbia 1996)★★★.
COMPILATIONS: *20,000 Watts R.S.L. – The Collection* (Columbia 1997)★★★★.
FURTHER READING: *Strict Rules*, Andrew McMillan.

MIKE AND THE MECHANICS
ALBUMS: *Mike And The Mechanics* (WEA 1985)★★, *The Living Years* (WEA 1988)★★★, *Word Of Mouth* (Virgin 1991)★★★, *Beggar On A Beach Of Gold* (Virgin 1995)★★★.
COMPILATIONS: *Hits* (Virgin 1996)★★★.
VIDEOS: *Hits* (Warner Music Vision 1996).

MILES, BUDDY
ALBUMS: as the Buddy Miles Express *Expressway To Your Skull* (Mercury 1968)★★★★, as the Buddy Miles Express *Electric Church* (Mercury 1969)★★★, as the Buddy Miles Band *Them Changes* (Mercury 1970)★★★, as the Buddy Miles Band *We Got To Live Together* (Mercury 1970)★★★, as the Buddy Miles Band *A Message To The People* (Mercury 1971)★★★, as the Buddy Miles Band *Buddy Miles Live* (Mercury 1971)★★, with Carlos Santana *Carlos Santana And Buddy Miles! Live!* (Columbia 1972)★★★, as the Buddy Miles Band *Chapter VII* (Columbia 1973)★★, as the Buddy Miles Express *Booger Bear* (Columbia 1973)★★, *All The Faces Of Buddy Miles* (1974)★★★, *More Miles Per Gallon* (Casablanca 1975)★★, *Bicentennial Gathering* (1976)★★, *Sneak Attack* (Atlantic 1981)★★, *Hell And Back* (Ryko 1994)★★★.

MILES, ROBERT
ALBUMS: *Dreamland* (DeConstruction 1996)★★★, *23 AM* (Arista 1997)★★★.

MILLER, FRANKIE (UK)
ALBUMS: *Once In A Blue Moon* (Chrysalis 1972)★★★, *High Life* (Chrysalis 1973)★★★, *The Rock* (Chrysalis 1975)★★★, *Full House* (Chrysalis 1977)★★★, *Double Trouble* (Chrysalis 1978)★★★, *Falling In Love* (Chrysalis 1979)★★★, *Perfect Fit* (1979)★★★, *Easy Money* (1980)★★★, *Standing On The Edge* (Capitol 1982)★★★, *Rockin' Rollin' Frankie Miller* (Bear Family 1983)★★★, *Hey, Where Ya Goin'* (1984)★★★, *Dancing In The Rain* (Vertigo 1986)★★★.
COMPILATIONS: *Best Of* (1992)★★★, *BBC Radio One Live In Concert* rec. 1977/78/79 (Windsong 1994)★★★.

MILLER, STEVE
ALBUMS: *Children Of The Future* (Capitol 1968)★★★★, *Sailor* (Capitol 1968)★★★★★, *Brave New World* (Capitol 1969)★★★★, *Your Saving Grace* (Capitol 1969)★★★, *Revolution* soundtrack 3 tracks only (United Artists 1969)★★, *Number 5* (Capitol 1970)★★★, *Rock Love* (Capitol 1971)★★, *Recall The Beginning ... A Journey From Eden* (Capitol 1972)★★★, *The Joker* (Capitol 1973)★★★, *Fly Like An Eagle* (Capitol 1976)★★★★, *Book Of Dreams* (Capitol 1977)★★★★, *Circle Of Love* (Capitol 1981)★★★, *Abracadabra* (Capitol 1982)★★★, *Steve Miller Band – Live!* (Capitol 1983)★★, *Italian X Rays* (Capitol 1984)★★, *Living In The 20th Century* (Capitol 1986)★★, *Born 2B Blue* (Capitol 1988)★★★, *Wide River* (1993)★★.
COMPILATIONS: *Anthology* (Capitol 1972)★★★★, *Greatest Hits (1974-1978)* (Capitol 1978)★★★★, *A Decade Of American Music: Greatest Hits 1976-1986* (1987)★★★★, *The Best Of 1968-1973* (1990)★★★★, *Box Set* (Capitol 1994)★★★★.

MINISTRY
ALBUMS: *With Sympathy* aka *Work For Love* (Arista 1983)★★★, *Twitch* (Sire 1986)★★★, *The Land Of Rape And Honey* (Sire 1988)★★★, *The Mind Is A Terrible Thing To Taste* (Sire 1989)★★★, *In Case You Didn't Feel Like Showing Up (Live)* mini-album (Sire 1990)★★★, *Psalm 69* (Sire/Warners 1992)★★★, *Filth Pig* (Warners 1996)★★★.
Solo: Paul Barker as Lead Into Gold *Age Of Reason* (Wax Trax! 1992)★★.
COMPILATIONS: *Twelve Inch Singles 1981-1984* (Wax Trax 1984)★★★.

MINOGUE, KYLIE
ALBUMS: *Kylie* (PWL 1988)★★, *Enjoy Yourself* (PWL 1989)★★, *Rhythm Of Love* (PWL 1990)★★★, *Let's Get To It* (PWL 1991)★★, *Kylie Minogue* (DeConstruction 1994)★★, *Kylie Minogue* (DeConstruction 1997)★★★.
COMPILATIONS: *Greatest Hits* (PWL 1992)★★★.
FURTHER READING: *The Superstar Next Door*, Sasha Stone.

MIRACLES
ALBUMS: *Hi, We're The Miracles* (Tamla 1961)★★★, *Cookin' With The Miracles* (Tamla 1962)★★★★, *I'll Try Something New* (Tamla 1962)★★★, *The Fabulous Miracles* (Tamla 1963)★★★, *Recorded Live: On Stage* (Tamla 1963)★★, *Christmas With The Miracles* (Tamla 1963)★★, *The Miracles Doin' 'Mickey's Monkey'* (Tamla 1963)★★★, *Going To A Go-Go* (Tamla 1965)★★★★, *I Like It Like That* (Tamla 1965)★★★, *Away We A Go-Go* (Tamla 1966)★★★, *Make It Happen* (Tamla 1967)★★★, *Special Occasion* (Tamla 1968)★★★, *Live!* (Tamla 1969)★★, *Time Out For Smokey Robinson And The Miracles* (Tamla 1969)★★★, *Four In Blue* (Tamla 1969)★★★, *What Love Has Joined Together* (Tamla 1970)★★★, *A Pocket Full Of Miracles* (Tamla 1970)★★★, *The Season For Miracles* (Tamla 1970)★★★, *One Dozen Roses* (Tamla 1971)★★★, *Flying High Together* (Tamla 1972)★★★, *Renaissance* (Tamla 1973)★★★, *Do It Baby* (Tamla 1974)★★★, *Don't Cha Love It* (Tamla 1975)★★, *City Of Angels* (Tamla 1975)★★, *The Power Of Music* (Tamla 1976)★★, *Love Crazy* (Columbia 1977)★★, *The Miracles* (Columbia 1978)★★.
COMPILATIONS: *Greatest Hits From The Beginning* (Tamla 1965)★★★★, *Greatest Hits Vol. 2* (Tamla 1968)★★★★, *1957-72* (Tamla 1972)★★★★, *Smokey Robinson And The Miracles' Anthology* (Motown 1973)★★★★, *Compact Command Performances* (Motown 1987)★★★★, *The Greatest Hits* (Motown 1992)★★★★, *The 35th Anniversary Collection* 4-CD box set (Motown Masters 1994)★★★★.
FURTHER READING: *Smokey: Inside My Life*, Smokey Robinson and David Ritz.

MISFITS
ALBUMS: *Beware EP* (Cherry Red 1979)★★★, *Walk Among Us* (Ruby 1982)★★★, *Evilive EP* (Plan 9 1982)★★★, *Earth A.D./Wolfsblood* (Plan 9 1983)★★★, *American Psycho* (Geffen 1997)★★★.
COMPILATIONS: *Legacy Of Brutality* (Plan 9 1985)★★★, *The Misfits* (Plan 9 1986)★★★★, *Evilive* expanded version of 1981 mini-album (Plan 9 1987)★★★, *The Misfits* 4-CD box set (Caroline 1996)★★★★.

MISSION
ALBUMS: *God's Own Medicine* (Mercury 1986)★★, *Children* (Mercury 1988)★★★, *Carved In Sand* (Mercury 1990)★★★, *Masque* (Mercury 1992)★★, *Neverland* (Neverland 1995)★★.
COMPILATIONS: *Sum And Substance* (Vertigo 1994)★★★.
VIDEOS: *From Dusk To Dawn* (Polygram Music Video 1988), *South America* (Mish Productions 1989), *Crusade* (Channel 5 1991), *Waves Upon The Sand* (Channel 5 1991), *Sum And Substance* (1994).
FURTHER READING: *The Mission – Names Are Tombstones Baby*, Martin Roach with Neil Perry.

MISUNDERSTOOD
COMPILATIONS: *Before The Dream Faded* (1982)★★, *Golden Glass* (1984)★★.

MITCHELL, JONI
ALBUMS: *Songs To A Seagull* (Reprise 1968)★★★, *Clouds* (Reprise 1969)★★★, *Ladies Of The Canyon* (Reprise 1970)★★★★, *Blue* (Reprise 1971)★★★★★, *For The Roses* (Asylum 1972)★★★★, *Court And Spark* (Asylum 1974)★★★★★, *Miles Of Aisles* (Asylum 1974)★★★, *The Hissing Of Summer Lawns* (Asylum 1975)★★★★, *Hejira* (Asylum 1976)★★★★, *Don Juan's Reckless Daughter* (Asylum 1977)★★★, *Mingus* (Asylum 1979)★★★★, *Shadows And Light* (Asylum 1980)★★★★, *Wild Things Run Fast* (Geffen 1982)★★★, *Dog Eat Dog* (Geffen 1985)★★★, *Chalk Mark In A Rainstorm* (Geffen 1988)★★★, *Night Ride Home* (Geffen 1991)★★★, *Turbulent Indigo* (Warners 1994)★★★.
COMPILATIONS: *Joni Mitchell Hits* (Reprise 1996)★★★, *Joni Mitchell Misses* (Reprise 1996)★★★.
FURTHER READING: *Joni Mitchell*, Leonore Fleischer. *Complete Poems And Lyrics*, Joni Mitchell.

MOBY
ALBUMS: *Ambient* (Mute 1993)★★, *The Story So Far* (Mute 1993)★★★, *Everything Is Wrong* (Mute 1995)★★★, *Animal Rights* (Mute 1996)★★★★, *I Like To Score* (Elektra/Asylum 1997).

MOBY GRAPE
ALBUMS: *Moby Grape* (CBS 1967)★★★★★, *Wow* (CBS 1967)★★★, *Grape Jam* (Columbia 1967)★★, *Moby Grape '69* (CBS 1969)★★★★, *Truly Fine Citizen* (CBS 1969)★★★, *20 Granite Creek* (Reprise 1971)★★★, *Live Grape* (1978)★★★. As Fine Wine *Fine Wine* (1976)★★, Moby Grape (San Francisco Sound 1983)★★. Solo: Skip Spence *Oar* (Columbia 1968)★★★★. Bob Mosley *Bob Mosley* (Warner 1972)★★. Peter Lewis *Peter Lewis* (Taxim 1996).
COMPILATIONS: *Great Grape* (CBS 1973)★★★, *Vintage* 2-CD box set with unreleased material and alternate takes (CBS/Legacy 1993)★★★★★.

MOCK TURTLES
ALBUMS: *Turtle Soup* (Imaginary 1990)★★★, *Two Sides* (Two Sides 1991)★★★★.
COMPILATIONS: *87-90* (Imaginary 1991)★★★.

MODERN LOVERS
ALBUMS: *The Modern Lovers* (Beserkley 1976)★★★★, *Jonathan Richman And The Modern Lovers* (Beserkley 1976)★★★, *Rock 'N' Roll With The Modern Lovers* (Beserkley 1977)★★★, *The Modern Lovers Live* (Beserkley 1977)★★, *It's Time For Jonathan Richman And The Modern Lovers* (Upside 1986)★★, *Modern Lovers 88* (Rounder 1988)★★★.
COMPILATIONS: *The Original Modern Lovers* early recordings (Bomp! 1981)★★★, *Jonathan Richman And The Modern Lovers – 23 Great Recordings* (Beserkley 1990)★★★★.

MOIST
ALBUMS: *Silver* (EMI 1994)★★★, *Creature* (EMI Canada 1996).

MOLLY HATCHET
ALBUMS: *Molly Hatchet* (Epic 1978)★★★, *Flirtin' With Disaster* (Epic 1979)★★★, *Beatin' The Odds* (Epic 1980)★★, *Take No Prisoners* (Epic 1981)★★, *No Guts ... No Glory* (Epic 1983)★★★, *The Deed Is Done* (Epic 1984)★★, *Double Trouble Live* (Epic 1985)★★, *Lightning Strikes Twice* (Capitol 1989)★★, *Devil's Canyon* (SPV 1996)★★.
COMPILATIONS: *Greatest Hits* (Epic 1990)★★★.

MONEY, ZOOT
ALBUMS: *It Should've Been Me* (Columbia 1965)★★★, *Zoot! Live At Klooks Kleek* (Columbia 1966)★★★, *Transition* (Direction 1968)★★, *Welcome To My Head* (1969)★★, *Zoot Money* (Polydor 1970)★★, *Mr. Money* (Magic Moon 1980)★★, with Chris Farlowe *Alexis Korner Memorial Concert Volume 2* (Indigo 1995)★★★.

MONKEES
ALBUMS: *The Monkees* (Colgems 1966)★★★, *More Of The Monkees* (Colgems 1967)★★★★, *Headquarters* (Colgems 1967)★★★, *Pisces, Aquarius, Capricorn And Jones Ltd* (Colgems 1967)★★, *The Birds, The Bees And The Monkees* (Colgems 1968)★★, *Head* soundtrack (Colgems 1968)★★, *Instant Replay* (Colgems 1969)★★★, *The Monkees Present ...* (Colgems 1969)★★★, *Changes* (Colgems 1970)★★★, *Pool It* (1986)★★, *20th Anniversary Concert Tour 1986* (1986)★★, *Justus* (Rhino 1996)★★.
COMPILATIONS: *The Monkees Greatest Hits* (Colgems 1969)★★★★, *A Barrel Full Of Monkees* (Colgems 1971)★★★★, *The Monkees Golden Hits* (RCA Victor 1972)★★★★, *The And Now ... The Best Of The Monkees* (1986)★★★★, *Hey! Hey! It's The Monkees Greatest Hits* (Platinum/K-Tel 1989)★★★★.
FILMS: *Head* (1968).
VIDEOS: *The Monkees Collection* (Rhino 1995), *33 1/3 Revoloutions Per Monkee* (Rhino Home Video 1996).
FURTHER READING: *Love Letters To The Monkees*, Bill Adler. *The Monkees Tale*, Eric Lefcowitz. *The Monkees Scrapbook*, Ed Finn and T. Bone. *Monkeemania*, Glenn A. Baker. *The Monkees: A Manufactured Image*, Ed Reilly, Maggie McMannus and Bill Chadwick. *I'm A Believer – My Life Of Monkees, Music And Madness*, Mickey Dolenz and Mark Bego.

MONOCHROME SET
ALBUMS: *The Strange Boutique* (DinDisc 1980)★★, *Love Zombies* (DinDisc 1980)★★, *Eligible Bachelors* (Cherry Red 1982)★★★, *The Lost Weekend* (Blanco y Negro 1985)★★★, *Dante's Casino* (Vinyl Japan 1990)★★★, *Charade* (Cherry Red 1993)★★★, *Misere* (Cherry Red 1994)★★★, *Trinity Road* (Cherry Red 1995)★★★.
COMPILATIONS: *Volume, Brilliance, Contrast* (Cherry Red 1983)★★★, *Fin! Live* (El 1986)★★★, *Colour Transmission* (Virgin 1988)★★★, *Westminster Affair* (Cherry Red 1988)★★, *Black & White Minstrels* (Cherry Red 1995)★★★.
VIDEOS: *Destiny Calling* (Visionary 1994).

MONTEREY POP FESTIVAL
ALBUMS: *Monterey International Pop Festival* 4-CD box set (Castle 1992)★★★.

MONTEZ, CHRIS
ALBUMS: *Let's Dance And Have Some Kinda Fun!!!* (Monogram 1963)★★★, *The More I See You/Call Me* (A&M 1966)★★★, *Time After Time* (Pye 1966)★★★, *Foolin' Around* (A&M 1967)★★, *Watch What Happens* (A&M 1968)★★.

MOODY BLUES
ALBUMS: *The Magnificent Moodies* (Decca 1965)★★★★, *Days Of Future Past* (Deram 1967)★★★★, *In Search Of The Lost Chord* (Deram 1968)★★★★, *On The Threshold Of A Dream* (Deram 1969)★★★★, *To Our Children's Children's Children* (Threshold 1969)★★★, *A Question Of Balance* (Threshold 1970)★★★, *Every Good Boy Deserves Favour* (Threshold 1971)★★★, *Seventh Sojourn* (Threshold 1972)★★★, *Caught Live + 5* (Decca 1977)★★, *Octave* (Decca 1978)★★, *Long Distance Voyager* (Threshold 1981)★★★★, *The Present* (Threshold 1983)★★★, *The Other Side Of Life* (Polydor 1986)★★★, *Sur La Mer* (Polydor 1988)★★, *Keys Of The Kingdom* (Polydor 1991)★★, *A Night At Red Rocks With The Colorado Symphony Orchestra* (Polydor/Threshold 1993)★★. Solo: Justin Hayward and John Lodge *Blue Jays* (Threshold 1975)★★★. John Lodge *Natural Avenue* (Threshold 1977)★★. Ray Thomas *From Mighty Oaks* (Threshold 1975)★★, *Hope Wishes And Dreams* (Threshold 1976)★★. Mike Pinder *The Promise* (Threshold 1976)★★, *Among The Stars* (One Step 1995)★★. Graeme Edge Band *Kick Off Your Muddy Boots* (Threshold 1975)★★, *Paradise Ballroom* (Threshold 1977)★★. Denny Laine *Aah Laine* (1973)★★, with Paul McCartney *Holly Days* (EMI 1977)★★, *Japanese Tears* (Scratch 1980)★★, *Weep For Love* (President 1985)★★, *Hometown Girls* (President 1985)★★, *Wings On My Feet* (President 1987)★★, *Master Suite* (Thunderbolt 1988)★★, *Lonely Road* (President 1988)★★, *Blue Nights* (President 1993)★★, *The Rock Survivor* (WCP 1994)★★.
COMPILATIONS: *This Is The Moody Blues* (Threshold 1974)★★★★, *Out Of This World* (K-Tel 1979)★★★, *Voices In The Sky – The Best Of The Moody Blues* (Threshold 1985)★★★, *Greatest Hits* (Threshold 1989)★★★, *Time Traveller* 5-CD set (Polydor 1994)★★★, *The Very Best Of* (Polygram 1996)★★★.
VIDEOS: *Cover Story* (Stylus 1990), *Star Portrait* (Gemini Vision 1991), *Legend Of A Band* (Channel 5 1991), *Live At Red Rocks* (1993).

MOONGLOWS
ALBUMS: *Look! It's The Moonglows* (Chess 1959)★★★, *The Return Of The Moonglows* (RCA Victor 1972)★★★, *The Moonglows On Stage* (Relic 1992)★★.
COMPILATIONS: *The Best Of Bobby Lester And The Moonglows* (Chess 1962)★★★, *The Flamingos Meet The Moonglows* (Vee Jay 1962)★★★, *The Moonglows* (Constellation 1964)★★★, *Moonglows* (Chess 1976)★★★, *Their Greatest Sides* (Chess 1984)★★★, *Blue Velvet: The Ultimate Collection* (MCA/Chess 1993)★★★★, *The Flamingos Meet The Moonglows: The Complete 25 Chance Recordings* (Vee Jay 1993)★★★.

MOORE, CHRISTY
ALBUMS: with Dominic Behan *Paddy On The Road* (1969)★★★, *Prosperous* (Trailer 1971)★★★, *Whatever Tickles Your Fancy* (Polydor 1975)★★★, *Christy Moore* (1976)★★★, *The Iron Behind The Velvet* (1978)★★★, *Live In Dublin* (1978)★★★, *The Spirit Of Freedom* (Warners 1983)★★★, *The Time Has Come* (Warners 1983)★★★, *Ride On* (Warners 1984)★★★, *Ordinary Man* (Warners 1985)★★★, *Nice 'N' Easy* (Polydor 1986)★★★, *Unfinished Revolution* (Warners 1987)★★★, *Voyage* (Warners 1989)★★★, *Smoke And Strong Whiskey* (Newberry 1991)★★★, *King Puck* (Equator 1993)★★★, *Live At The Point* (Grapevine 1994)★★★, *Graffiti Tongue* (Grapevine 1996)★★★★.
COMPILATIONS: *The Christy Moore Collection '81-'91* (East West 1991)★★★★.
VIDEOS: *Christy* (SMV 1995).

MOORE, GARY
ALBUMS: with Skid Row *Skid Row* (Columbia 1970)★★★, with Skid Row *34 Hours* (Columbia 1971)★★★, as Gary Moore Band *Grinding Stone* (Columbia 1973)★★, with Skid Row *Alive And Kicking* (Columbia 1978)★★, *Back On The Streets* (MCA 1979)★★★★, with Greg Lake Band *Greg Lake* (Chrysalis 1981)★★, *Corridors Of Power* (Virgin 1982)★★★, with Greg Lake Band *Manoeuvers* (Chrysalis 1983)★★, *Rockin' Every Night – Live In Japan* (Virgin 1983)★★★, *Live* (Jet 1984)★★★, *Run For Cover* (Ten 1985)★★★, *Wild Frontier* (Ten Ten 1988)★★★, *After The War* (Virgin 1989)★★★, *Still Got The Blues* (Virgin 1990)★★★★, *After Hours* (Virgin 1992)★★★, *Blues Alive* (Virgin 1993)★★★★, *Blues For Greeny* (Virgin 1995)★★★★, *Dark Days In Paradise* (Virgin 1997)★★, *Looking At You* (Charisma 1997).
COMPILATIONS: *Anthology* (Raw Power 1986)★★★, *The Collection* double album (Castle 1990)★★★, *CD Box Set* (Virgin 1991)★★★, *Ballads + Blues 1982 – 1994* (Virgin 1994)★★★★.
VIDEOS: *Emerald Aisles* (Virgin Vision 1986), *Video Singles: Gary Moore* (Virgin Vision 1988), *Gary Moore: Live In Sweden* (Virgin Vision 1988), *Evening Of The Blues* (Virgin Vision 1991), *Live Blues* (1993), *Ballads And Blues 1982-1994* (1995), *Blues For Greeny Live* (Warner Musicvision 1996).

MORISSETTE, ALANIS
ALBUMS: *Alanis* (MCA Canada 1990)★★, *Now Is The Time* (MCA Canada 1992)★★★, *Jagged Little Pill* (Maverick/Reprise 1995)★★★★.

MORPHINE
ALBUMS: *Good* (Accurate/Distortion 1992)★★★, *Cure For Pain* (Rykodisc 1993)★★★, *Yes* (Rykodisc 1995)★★★★, *Like Swimming* (Rykodisc 1997)★★★★.
COMPILATIONS: *B-Sides And Otherwise* (Rykodisc 1997)★★★★.

MORRICONE, ENNIO
ALBUMS: *Moses* soundtrack (Pye 1977)★★★, *This Is ...* (EMI 1981)★★★, *Chi Mai* (BBC 1981)★★★, *The Mission* film soundtrack (Virgin 1986)★★★★, *Chamber Music* (Venture 1988)★★★, *Frantic* film soundtrack (Elektra 1988)★★★, *The Endless Game* television soundtrack (Virgin 1989)★★★, *Live In Concert* (Silva Screen 1989)★★★, *Casualties Of War* (1990)★★★, *Morricone '93 Movie Sounds* (1993)★★★, *Wolf* film soundtrack (Columbia 1994)★★★, *Disclosure* film soundtrack (Virgin 1995)★★★, *Ninfa Plebea* film soundtrack (AM Original Soundtracks 1995)★★★, *Concerto: Premio Rota 1995* (AM Original Soundtracks 1996)★★★, *Fear According to Morricone* (Intermezzo Media 1997).
COMPILATIONS: *Film Hits* (RCA 1981)★★★, *Film Music 1966-87* (Virgin 1988)★★★★, *The Very Best Of* (1992)★★★, *The Ennio Morricone Anthology (A Fistful Of Film Music)* (Rhino 1995)★★★★, *His Greatest Themes* (Allegro 1995)★★★.

MORRISON, VAN
ALBUMS: *Blowin' Your Mind* (Bang 1967)★★, *Astral Weeks* (Warners 1968)★★★★★, *Moondance* (Warners 1970)★★★★, *Van Morrison, His Band And The Street Choir* (Warners 1970)★★, *Tupelo Honey* (Warners 1971)★★★, *St. Dominic's Preview* (Warners 1972)★★★★, *Hard Nose The Highway* (Warners 1973)★★, *It's Too Late To Stop Now* (Warners 1974)★★★★, *Veedon Fleece* (Warners 1974)★★★★, *A Period Of Transition* (Warners 1977)★★★, *Wavelength* (Warners 1978)★★★, *Into The Music* (Vertigo 1979)★★★, *Common One* (Mercury 1980)★★, *Beautiful Vision* (Mercury 1982)★★★, *Inarticulate Speech Of The Heart* (Mercury 1983)★★, *Live At The Grand Opera House, Belfast* (Mercury 1984)★★, *A Sense Of Wonder* (Mercury 1984)★★★, *No Guru, No Method, No Teacher* (Mercury 1986)★★★★, *Poetic Champions Compose* (Mercury 1987)★★★★, with the Chieftains *Irish Heartbeat* (Mercury 1988)★★★, *Avalon Sunset* (Mercury 1989)★★★★, *Enlightenment* (Mercury 1990)★★★, *Hymns To The Silence* (Polydor 1991)★★★, *Too Long In Exile* (Polydor 1993)★★★, *A Night In San Francisco* (Polydor 1994)★★, *Days Like This* (Polydor 1995)★★★, with Georgie Fame *How Long Has This Been Going On* (Verve 1995)★★★, with Fame, Mose Allison, Ben Sidran *Tell Me Something: The Songs Of Mose Allison* (Verve 1996)★★, *The Healing Game* (Polydor 1997)★★★, *Brown Eyed Beginnings* (M.I.C. Multimedia 1998)★★★, *Philosopher's Stone* (1998)★★★.
COMPILATIONS: *The Best Of Van Morrison* (Polydor 1990)★★★★★, *The Best Of Vol. 2* (Polydor 1992)★★★★.
VIDEOS: *The Concert* (Channel 5 1990).
FURTHER READING: *Van Morrison: Into The Music*, Ritchie Yorke. *Van Morrison: The Great Deception*, Johnny Rogan. *Van Morrison: The Mystic's Music*, Howard A. DeWitt. *Van Morrison: Too Late To Stop Now*, Steve Turner. *Van Morrison: Inarticulate Speech Of The Heart*, John Collis.

MORRISSEY
ALBUMS: *Viva Hate* (HMV 1988)★★★★, *Kill Uncle* (HMV 1991)★★, *Your Arsenal* (HMV 1992)★★★★, *Beethoven Was Deaf* (HMV 1993)★★, *Vauxhall And I* (HMV 1994)★★★★, *Southpaw Grammar* (RCA Victor 1995)★★★, *Maladjusted* (Island 1997)★★★.
COMPILATIONS: *Bona Drag* (HMV 1990)★★★★, *Suedehead – The Best Of* (EMI 1997)★★★.
VIDEOS: *Live In Dallas* (1993), *Introducing Morrissey* (Warner Music Video 1996).
FURTHER READING: *Morrissey In His Own Words*, John Robertson. *Morrissey Shot*, Linder Sterling. *Morrissey & Marr: The Severed Alliance*, Johnny Rogan. *Peepholism: Into The Art Of Morrissey*, Jo Slee. *Landscapes Of The Mind*, David Bret.

MOTELS
ALBUMS: *The Motels* (Capitol 1979)★★★★, *Careful* (Capitol 1980)★★★, *All Four One* (Capitol 1982)★★★, *Little Robbers* (Capitol 1983)★★, *Shock* (Capitol 1985)★★.

MOTHERS OF INVENTION
ALBUMS: *Freak Out* (Verve 1966)★★★★★, *Absolutely Free* (Verve 1967)★★★★★, *We're Only In It For The Money* (Verve 1968)★★★★, *Cruising With Ruben And The Jets* (Verve 1968)★★★, *Uncle Meat* (Bizarre 1969)★★★, *Burnt Weeny Sandwich* (Bizarre 1969)★★★, *Weasels Ripped My Flesh* (Bizarre 1970)★★★, *Fillmore East – June 1971* (1971)★★★, *200 Motels* (United Artists 1971)★★, *Just Another Band From L.A.* (Bizarre 1972)★★★, *The Grand Wazoo* (Bizarre 1972)★★★, *Over-Nite Sensation* (DiscReet 1973)★★★, *Roxy And Elsewhere* (Ryko 1974)★★★, *One Size Fits All* (Ryko 1975)★★★, with Captain Beefheart *Bongo Fury* (Ryko 1975)★★★.
COMPILATIONS: *Mothermania* (Verve 1969)★★★★, *The Worst Of The Mothers* (MGM 1971)★★★.
FILMS: *200 Motels* (1970).
FURTHER READING: *Electric Don Quixote: The Story Of Frank Zappa*, Neil Slaven.

MÖTLEY CRÜE
ALBUMS: *Too Fast For Love* (Leathur 1981)★★, *Shout At The Devil* (Elektra 1983)★★, *Theatre Of Pain* (Elektra 1985)★★, *Girls, Girls, Girls* (Elektra 1987)★★★, *Dr. Feelgood* (Elektra 1989)★★★, *Mötley Crüe* (Elektra 1994)★★★, *Generation Swine* (Elektra 1997)★★★.
COMPILATIONS: *Raw Tracks* (Elektra 1988)★★★, *Decade Of Decadence* (Elektra 1991)★★★★.
VIDEOS: *Uncensored* (1987), *Dr. Feelgood, The Videos* (1989), *Decade Of Decadence* (1991).
FURTHER READING: *Lüde, Crüde And Rüde*, Sylvie Simmons and Malcolm Dome.

MOTÖRHEAD
ALBUMS: *Motπrhead* (Chiswick 1977)★★★, *Overkill* (Bronze 1979)★★★, *Bomber* (Bronze 1979)★★★, *On Parole* (United Artists 1979)★★★, *Ace Of Spades* (Bronze 1980)★★★★, *No Sleep 'til Hammersmith* (Bronze 1981)★★★★, *Iron Fist* (Bronze 1982)★★★, *Another Perfect Day* (Bronze 1983)★★, *What's Wordsworth* (Big Beat 1983)★★, *Orgasmatron* (GWR 1986)★★★, *Rock'N'Roll* (GWR 1987)★★★, *Eat The Rich* (GWR 1987)★★★, *No Sleep At All* (GWR 1988)★★★, *1916* (Epic 1991)★★★, *March Or Die* (Epic 1992)★★★, *Bastards* (ZYX 1993)★★★, *I* (SPV 1996)★★, *Overnight Sensation* (SPV 1996)★★★, *Take No Prisoners* (Snapper 1998).
COMPILATIONS: *No Remorse* (Bronze 1984)★★★★, *Collection* (Castle 1990)★★★, *Meltdown* 3-CD box set (Castle 1991)★★★, *The Best Of ...* (Castle 1993)★★★, *Protect The Innocent* 4-CD box set (Essential 1997)★★★.
VIDEOS: *Deaf Not Blind* (1984), *Birthday Party* (1986), *Eat The Rich* (1988, film), *Toronto Live* (1989), *Best Of* (1991), *Everything Louder Than Everything Else* (1991).
FURTHER READING: *Motπrhead*, Alan Burridge. *Born To Lose*, Alan Burridge. *Motorhead*, Giovanni Dadomo.

MOTORS
ALBUMS: *The Motors I* (Virgin 1977)★★★, *Approved By The Motors* (Virgin 1978)★★★★, *Tenement Steps* (Virgin 1980)★★★.
COMPILATIONS: *Greatest Hits* (Virgin 1981)★★★.

MOTOWN RECORDS
COMPILATIONS: *Motown Chartbusters Volumes 1 – 10* (Motown 1968-1977), *20th Anniversary Album* (Motown 1986)★★★★, *Hitsville USA: The Motown Singles Collection 1959 – 1971* 4-CD box set (Motown 1993)★★★★★, *This Is Northern Soul! 24 Tamla Motown Rarities* (Debutante 1997)★★★.
VIDEOS: *The Sounds Of Motown* (PMI 1985), *The Sixties* (CIC Video 1987), *Time Capsule Of The 70s* (CIC Video 1987), *Motown 25th: Yesterday, Today, Forever* (MGM/UA 1988).

MOTT THE HOOPLE
ALBUMS: *Mott The Hoople* (Island 1969)★★★, *Mad Shadows* (Island 1970)★★★, *Wild Life* (Island 1971)★★, *Brain Capers* (Island 1971)★★★, *All The Young Dudes* (Columbia 1972)★★★, *Mott* (Columbia 1973)★★★★, *The Hoople* (Columbia 1974)★★★★, *Live* (Columbia 1974)★★★, *Original Mixed Up Kids: The BBC Recordings* (Windsong 1996)★★★.
COMPILATIONS: *Greatest Hits* (Columbia 1975)★★★★, *Shades Of Ian Hunter – The Ballad Of Ian Hunter And Mott The Hoople* (Columbia 1979)★★★★, *Two Miles From Heaven* (Island 1981)★★★, *All The Way From Memphis* (Hallmark 1981)★★★, *Greatest Hits* (Columbia 1981)★★★★, *Backsliding Fearlessly* (Rhino 1994)★★★.
FURTHER READING: *The Diary Of A Rock 'N' Roll Star*, Ian Hunter.

MOULD, BOB
ALBUMS: *Workbook* (Virgin 1989)★★★, *Black Sheets Of Rain* (Virgin 1990)★★, *Bob Mould* (Creation/Rykodisk 1996)★★★★.
COMPILATIONS: *Poison Years* (Virgin 1994)★★★★.

MOUNTAIN
ALBUMS: *Mountain Climbing* (Bell 1970)★★★, *Nantucket Sleighride* (Island 1971)★★★, *Flowers Of Evil* (Island 1971)★★★, *The Road Goes On Forever-Mountain Live* (Island 1972)★★, *Avalanche* (Epic 1974)★★★, *Twin Peaks* (Columbia 1974)★★, *Go For Your Life* (Scotti Brothers 1985)★★.
COMPILATIONS: *The Best Of* (Island 1973)★★★, *Blood Of The Sun 1969-75* (Raven 1996)★★★.

MOVE
ALBUMS: *The Move* (Regal Zonophone 1968)★★★, *Shazam* (Regal Zonophone 1970)★★★, *Looking On* (Fly 1970)★★★, *Message From The Country* (Harvest 1971)★★★, *California Man* (Harvest 1974)★★★.
COMPILATIONS: *The Collection* (Castle 1986)★★★, *The Early Years* (Dojo 1992)★★★.

MOYET, ALISON
ALBUMS: *Alf* (Columbia 1984)★★★★, *Raindancing* (Columbia 1987)★★, *Hoodoo* (Columbia 1991)★★★, *Essex* (Columbia 1994)★★.
COMPILATIONS: *Alison Moyet Singles* (Columbia 1995)★★★.

MUD
ALBUMS: *Mud Rock* (RAK 1974)★★★, *Mud Rock Vol. 2* (RAK 1975)★★, *Use Your Imagination* (Private Stock 1975)★★, *It's Better Than Working* (Private Stock 1976)★★, *Mudpack* (Private Stock 1978)★★, *Rock On* (RCA 1979)★★, *As You Like It* (RCA 1980)★, *Mud* (Runaway 1983)★.
COMPILATIONS: *Mud's Greatest Hits* (RAK 1975)★★★.

MUDDY WATERS
ALBUMS: *Muddy Waters Sings Big Bill Broonzy* (Chess 1960)★★★, *Muddy Waters At Newport, 1960* (Chess 1963)★★★★, *Muddy Waters, Folk Singer* (Chess 1964)★★★★, *Muddy, Brass And The Blues* (Chess 1965)★★, *Down On Stovall's Plantation* (Testament 1966)★★★, *Blues From Big Bill's Copacabana* (Chess 1968)★★★, *Electric Mud* (Cadet 1968)★★, *Fathers And Sons* (Chess 1969)★★★, *After The Rain* (Cadet 1969)★★, *Sail On* (Chess 1969)★★★, *The London Sessions* (MCA 1971)★★★, *Live At Mister Kelly's* (1971)★★★, *Experiment In Blues* (1972)★★★, *Can't Get No Grindin'* (MCA 1973)★★★, *Mud In Your Ear* (Musicor 1973)★★★, *London Revisited* (1974)★★, *The Muddy Waters Woodstock Album* (Chess 1975)★★, *Unk In Funk* (Chess 1977)★★, *Hard Again* (Blue Sky 1977)★★, *I'm Ready* (Blue Sky 1978)★★, *Muddy Waters Live* (Blue Sky 1979)★★★, *King Bee* (Blue Sky 1981)★★, *Muddy Waters In Concert 1958* (1982)★★★, *Paris 1972* (Pablo 1997)★★★.
COMPILATIONS: *The Best Of Muddy Waters* (Chess 1957)★★★★★, *The Real Folk Blues* (Chess 1966)★★★★, *More Real Folk Blues* (Chess 1967)★★★★, *McKinley Morganfield aka Muddy Waters* (Chess 1971)★★★★, *Chess Masters 3 Volumes* (Chess 1981/1982/1983)★★★★, *Muddy Waters* 6-LP box set (Chess 1989)★★★★★, *The Chess Box 1947-67* 9-CD set (Charly 1990)★★★★★, *Gold Collection* (1993)★★★★, *The King Of Chicago Blues* (Charly 1995)★★★★.
VIDEOS: *Messin' With The Blues* (BMG 1991), *Live* (BMG 1993).
FURTHER READING: *The Complete Muddy Waters Discography*, Phil Wight and Fred Rothwell. *Muddy Waters: Mojo Man*, Sandra B. Tooze.

MUDHONEY
ALBUMS: *Superfuzz Bigmuff* mini-album (Sub Pop 1988)★★★, *Mudhoney* (Sub Pop 1989)★★, *Every Good Boy Deserves Fudge* (Sub Pop 1991)★★★, *Piece Of Cake* (Warners 1992)★★★, *Five Dollar Bob's Mock Cooter Stew* mini-album (Warners 1993)★★, *My Brother The Cow* (Warners 1995)★★★.
COMPILATIONS: *Superfuzz Bigmuff Plus Early Singles* (Sub Pop 1991)★★★.
VIDEOS: *Absolutely Live* (Pinnacle 1991), *No 1 Video In America This Week* (Warner Video 1995).

MUNGO JERRY
ALBUMS: *Mungo Jerry* (Dawn 1970)★★★, *Electronically Tested* (Dawn 1971)★★★, *You Don't Have To Be In The Army To Fight In The War* (Dawn 1971)★★★, *Memories Of A Stockbroker* (Janus 1971)★★, *Baby Jump* (Pye 1971)★★★, *Boot Power* (Dawn 1972)★★, *Impala Saga* (Polydor 1976)★★, *Lovin' In The Alleys, Fightin' In The Streets* (Polydor 1977)★★, *Ray Dorset And Mungo Jerry* (Polydor 1978)★★★, *Vig* (Balkanton 1978)★★, *Six Aside* (Satellite 1979)★★, *Together Again* (CNR Capriccio 1981)★★, *Boogie Up* (Music Team 1984)★★, *Too Fast To Live And Too Young To Die* (PRT 1987)★★, *All The Hits Plus More* (Prestige 1987)★★★, *Snakebite* (Prestige 1990)★★. Solo: Ray Dorset *Cold Blue Excursion* (Dawn 1972)★★★. Paul King *Been In The Pen Too Long* (Dawn 1972)★★, *Houdini's Moon* (A New Day 1995)★★, the King Earl Boogie Band *Trouble At Mill* (Dawn 1972)★★★, *The Mill Has Gone* (A New Day 1995)★★.
COMPILATIONS: *Greatest Hits* (Dawn 1973)★★★, *Long Legged Woman* (Dawn 1974)★★★, *The File Series* (Pye 1977)★★★, *Greatest Hits* (Astan 1981)★★★, *In The Summertime* (Flashback 1985)★★★, *Some Hits And More* (Reference 1991)★★★, *The Early Years* (Dojo 1992)★★★, *Hits Collection* (Pickwick 1993)★★★, *Summertime* (Spectrum 1995)★★★.

MY BLOODY VALENTINE
ALBUMS: *This Is Your Bloody Valentine* mini-album (Tycoon 1984)★★, *Ecstasy* mini-album (Lazy 1987)★★, *Isn't Anything* (Creation 1988)★★★★, *Loveless* (Creation 1991)★★★.

N

N'DOUR, YOUSSOU
ALBUMS: *Show A Abidjan* (ED 1983)★★, *Diongoma* (MP 1983)★★★, *Immigrés* (Celluloid/Earthworks 1984)★★★★, *Nelson Mandela* (ERT 1985)★★★★, *The Lion* (Virgin 1989)★★★, *Set* (Virgin 1990)★★, *Eyes Open* (40 Acres 1992)★★, *Wommat: The Guide* (Columbia 1994)★★★★, with Yandé Codou Sîne *Gainde – Voices From The Heart Of Africa* (World Network 1995)★★★, *Inedits 84-85* (Celluloid 1997).
COMPILATIONS: *Hey You! The Best Of* (Music Club 1993)★★★, *Live – Bir Sorano Juin '93, Vols. 1 & 2* (Studio 1993)★★★. Etoile De Darkar Featuring Youssou N'Dour *Thaipathioly* (Stern's 1994)★★★.

NAKED CITY
ALBUMS: Naked City (1990), Torture Garden (1990), Heretic – Jeux Des Dames Cruelles (1992), Grand Guignol (1993), Avenue Blue (Bluemoon 1995), Black Box (Tzadik 1997).

NAPALM DEATH
ALBUMS: Scum (Earache 1987)★★, From Enslavement To Obliteration (Earache 1988)★★★, The Peel Sessions (Strange Fruit 1989)★★★, Harmony Corruption (Earache 1990)★, Live Corruption (Earache 1990)★, Utopia Banished (Earache 1992)★★, Fear, Emptiness, Despair (Earache 1994)★★, Greed Killing mini-album (Earache 1995)★★, Diatribes (Earache 1996)★★, Inside The Torn Apart (Earache 1997)★★.
COMPILATIONS: Death By Manipulation (Earache 1992)★★.
VIDEOS: Live Corruption (Fotodisk 1990).

NASH, JOHNNY
ALBUMS: A Teenager Sings The Blues (ABC 1957)★★★, I Got Rhythm (ABC 1959)★★★, Hold Me Tight (JAD 1968)★★★, Let's Go Dancing (Columbia 1969)★★★, I Can See Clearly Now (Columbia 1972)★★★, My Merry Go Round (Columbia 1973)★★, Celebrate Life (Columbia 1974)★★★, Tears On My Pillow (Columbia 1975)★★★, What A Wonderful World (Columbia 1977)★★, Johnny Nash Album (Columbia 1980)★★★, Stir It Up (Hallmark 1981)★★, Here Again (London 1986)★★.
COMPILATIONS: Greatest Hits (Columbia 1975)★★★, The Johnny Nash Collection (Epic 1977)★★★, The Best Of (Columbia 1996)★★★.

NAZARETH
ALBUMS: Nazareth (Mooncrest 1971)★★★, Exercises (Mooncrest 1972)★★★, Razamanaz (Mooncrest 1973)★★★★, Loud 'N' Proud (Mooncrest 1974)★★★, Rampant (Mooncrest 1974)★★★, Hair Of The Dog (Mooncrest 1975)★★★★, Close Enough For Rock 'N' Roll (Mountain 1976)★★★, Play 'N' The Game (Mountain 1976)★★, Expect No Mercy (Mountain 1977)★★, No Mean City (Mountain 1978)★★, Malice In Wonderland (Mountain 1980)★★, The Fool Circle (NEMS 1981)★★, 'Snaz (NEMS 1981)★★, 2XS (NEMS 1982)★★, Sound Elixir (Vertigo 1983)★★, The Catch (Vertigo 1984)★★, Cinema (Vertigo 1986)★★, Snakes & Ladders (Vertigo 1990)★★, No Jive (Mainstream 1992)★★. Solo: Dan McCafferty Dan McCafferty (1975)★★.
COMPILATIONS: Greatest Hits (Mountain 1975)★★★, 20 Greatest Hits: Nazareth (Sahara 1985)★★★, Anthology: Nazareth (Raw Power 1988)★★★.
VIDEOS: Razamanaz (Hendring 1990).

NELSON, BILL
ALBUMS: Northern Dream (Smile 1971)★★, as Bill Nelson's Red Noise Sound On Sound (Harvest 1979)★★, Quit Dreaming And Get On The Beam (Mercury 1981)★★★★, Sounding The Ritual Echo (Mercury 1981)★★★, Das Kabinett (The Cabinet Of Dr. Caligari) (Cocteau 1981)★★, The Love That Whirls (Diary Of A Thinking Heart) (PVC 1982)★★★, La Belle Et La Bete (PVC 1982)★★★, Chimera mini-album (Mercury 1983)★★★, Savage Gestures For Charms Sake (Cocteau 1983)★★★, Vistamix expanded re-release of Chimera (Portrait 1984)★★★, A Catalogue Of Obsessions (Cocteau 1984)★★★, The Summer Of God's Piano (Cocteau 1984)★★★, as Bill Nelson's Orchestra Arcana Iconography (Cocteau 1986)★★, Getting The Holy Ghost Across aka as On A Blue Wing (Portrait 1986)★★★, Chamber Of Dreams (Cocteau 1986)★★★, Map Of Dreams (Cocteau 1987)★★★, Chance Encounters In The Garden Of Light (Cocteau 1987/88)★★★, Optimism (Cocteau 1988)★★, Pavillions Of The Heart And Soul (Cocteau 1989)★★★, Simplex (Cocteau 1989)★★★, Demonstrations Of Affection (Cocteau 1989)★★★, Luminous (Imaginary 1991)★★★, Blue Moons And Laughing Guitars (1992)★★★, After The Satellite Sings (Resurgence 1996)★★★, with Culturemix Culturemix With Bill Nelson (Resurgence 1996)★★★.
COMPILATIONS: Trial By Intimacy (The Book Of Splendours) boxed set (Cocteau 1984)★★★, The Two Fold Aspect Of Everything (Cocteau 1984)★★★, The Strangest Things Sampler (Cocteau 1989)★★★, Duplex: The Best Of Bill Nelson (Cocteau 1989)★★★.

NELSON, RICKY
ALBUMS: with various artists Teen Time (Verve 1957)★★, Ricky (Imperial 1957)★★, Ricky Nelson (Imperial 1958)★★, Ricky Sings Again (Imperial 1959)★★, Songs By Ricky (Imperial 1959)★★★, More Songs By Ricky (Imperial 1960)★★, Rick Is 21 (Imperial 1961)★★, Album Seven By Rick (Imperial 1962)★★, Best Sellers By Rick Nelson (Imperial 1962)★★, It's Up To You (Imperial 1962)★★★, A Long Vacation (Imperial 1963)★★, Million Sellers By Rick Nelson (Imperial 1963)★★★★, For Your Sweet Love (Decca 1963)★★, Rick Nelson Sings For You (Decca 1963)★★★, The Very Thought Of You (Decca 1964)★★, Spotlight On Rick (Decca 1964)★★★, Best Always (Decca 1965)★★, Love And Kisses (Decca 1965)★★, Bright Lights And Country Music (Decca 1966)★★, On The Flip-Side film soundtrack (Decca 1966)★, Country Fever (Decca 1967)★★, Another Side Of Rick (Decca 1968)★★, Perspective (Decca 1968)★★, Ricky Nelson In Concert (Decca 1970)★★★, Rick Sings Nelson (Decca 1970)★★★, Rudy The Fifth (Decca 1971)★★★, Garden Party (Decca 1972)★★★★, Windfall (1974)★★, Intakes (Epic 1977)★★, Playing To Win (Capitol 1981)★★★, Memphis Sessions (Epic 1986)★★★, Live 1983-1985 (Rhino 1989)★★★.
COMPILATIONS: The Very Best Of Rick Nelson (Decca 1970)★★★★, Legendary Masters (United Artists 1971)★★★★, The Singles Album 1963-1976 (United Artists 1977)★★★★, The Singles Album 1957-63 (United Artists 1977)★★★★, Rockin' With Ricky (Ace 1984)★★★★, All My Best (MCA 1985)★★★★, Best Of 1963-1975 (MCA 1990)★★★★, Best Of Rick Nelson, Vol. 2 (Capitol 1991)★★★★.
FURTHER READING: Ricky Nelson: Idol For A Generation, Joel Selvin. The Ricky Nelson Story, John Stafford and Iain Young. Ricky Nelson: Teenage Idol, Travelin' Man, Philip Bashe.

NELSON, SANDY
ALBUMS: Teen Beat (Imperial 1960)★★★, He's A Drummer Boy aka Happy Drums (Imperial 1960)★★★, Let There Be Drums (Imperial 1961)★★★, Drums Are My Beat! (Imperial 1962)★★★, Drummin' Up A Storm (Imperial 1962)★★★, Golden Hits (retitled Sandy Nelson Plays Fats Domino) (Imperial 1962)★★, On The Wild Side aka Country Style (Imperial 1962)★★, Compelling Percussion aka And Then There Were Drums (Imperial/London 1962)★★★, Teenage House Party (Imperial 1963)★★★, The Best Of The Beats (1963)★★, Be True To Your School (1963)★★, Live! In Las Vegas (1964)★★, Teen Beat '65 (1965)★★★, Drum Discotheque (1965)★★, Drums A Go-Go (1965)★★, Boss Beat (1966)★★, 'In' Beat (1966)★★, Superdrums (Liberty 1966)★★, Beat That #!!&* Drum (1966)★★, Cheetah Beat (1967)★★, The Beat Goes On (Liberty 1967)★★, Souldrums (Liberty 1968)★★, Boogaloo Beat (Liberty 1968)★★, Rock 'N' Roll Revival (Liberty 1968)★★, Golden Pops (1968)★★, Rebirth Of The Beat (1969)★★, Manhattan Spiritual (1969)★★, Groovy! (Liberty 1969)★★, Rock Drum Golden Disc (1972)★★, Keep On Rockin' (1972)★★, Roll Over Beethoven aka Hocus Pocus (1973)★★, Let The Good Times Rock (1974)★★, Bang Bang Rhythm (1975)★.
COMPILATIONS: Beat That Drum (1963)★★★, Sandy Nelson Plays (1963)★★★, The Very Best Of Sandy Nelson (1978)★★★, 20 Rock 'N' Roll Hits: Sandy Nelson (1983)★★★, King Of Drums: His Greatest Hits (See For Miles 1995)★★★, Golden Hits/Best Of The Beats (See For Miles 1997)★★★.

NELSON, WILLIE
ALBUMS: ... And Then I Wrote (Liberty 1962)★★★, Here's Willie Nelson (Liberty 1963)★★★, Country Willie – His Own Songs (RCA Victor 1965)★★★, Country Favorites – Willie Nelson Style (RCA Victor 1966)★★★, Country Music Concert (Live At Panther Hall) (RCA Victor 1966)★★★, Make Way For Willie Nelson (RCA Victor 1967)★★★, The Party's Over (RCA Victor 1967)★★★, Texas In My Soul (RCA Victor 1968)★★★, Good Times (RCA Victor 1968)★★★, My Own Peculiar Way (RCA Victor 1969)★★★, Both Sides Now (RCA Victor 1970)★★★, Laying My Burdens Down (RCA Victor 1970)★★★, Willie Nelson And Family (RCA Victor 1971)★★★, Yesterday's Wine (RCA Victor 1971)★★★, The Words Don't Fit The Picture (RCA Victor 1972)★★★, The Willie Way (RCA Victor 1972)★★★, Shotgun Willie (Atlantic 1973)★★★, Phases And Stages (Atlantic 1974)★★★, What Can You Do To Me Now (RCA 1975)★★, Red Headed Stranger (Columbia 1975)★★★★★, with Waylon Jennings, Jessi Colter, Tompall Glaser Wanted! The Outlaws (RCA 1976)★★★★, The Sound In Your Mind (Columbia 1976)★★★★, Phases And Stages 1964 recording (Atlantic 1976)★★, Willie Nelson – Live (RCA 1976)★★, The Troublemaker (Columbia 1976)★★★, Before His Time (RCA 1977)★★, To Lefty From Willie (Columbia 1977)★★★, Stardust (Columbia 1978)★★★★, Face Of A Fighter 1961 recording (Lone Star 1978)★★★, Willie And Family Live (Columbia 1978)★★★, with Jennings Waylon And Willie (RCA 1978)★★★★, with Leon Russell One For The Road (Columbia 1978)★★★★, The Electric Horseman (Columbia 1979)★★★★, Willie Nelson Sings Kristofferson (Columbia 1979)★★, Pretty Paper (Columbia 1979)★, Sweet Memories (RCA 1979)★★★, Danny Davis And Willie Nelson With The Nashville Brass (RCA 1980)★★★, with Ray Price San Antonio Rose (Columbia 1980)★★★, Honeysuckle Rose (Columbia 1980)★★★★, Family Bible (MCA Songbird 1980)★★★, Somewhere Over The Rainbow (Columbia 1981)★★★, Minstrel Man (RCA 1981)★★, with Roger Miller Old Friends (Columbia 1982)★★★, Diamonds In The Rough (1982)★★, with Johnny Bush Together Again (1982)★★★, Always On My Mind (Columbia 1982)★★★★, with Jennings WWII (RCA 1982)★★★★, with Webb Pierce In The Jailhouse Now (Columbia 1982)★★★, with Kris Kristofferson, Brenda Lee, Dolly Parton The Winning Hand (Monument 1982)★★★, with Merle Haggard Poncho And Lefty (Epic 1983)★★★, Without A Song (Columbia 1983)★★, Tougher Than Leather (Columbia 1983)★★★, My Own Way (RCA 1983)★★★, with Jennings Take It To The Limit (Columbia 1983)★★★, with Jackie King Angel Eyes (Columbia 1984)★★, Slow Down Old World (1984)★★★★, City Of New Orleans (Columbia 1984)★★, with Kristofferson Music From Songwriter film soundtrack (Columbia 1984)★★★, with Faron Young Funny How Time Slips Away (Columbia 1984)★★★, with Johnny Cash, Jennings, Kristofferson Highwayman (Columbia 1985)★★★★, with Hank Snow Brand On My Heart (Columbia 1985)★★★, Me And Paul (Columbia 1985)★★★, Half Nelson (Columbia 1985)★★, The Promiseland (Columbia 1986)★★, Partners (Columbia 1986)★★★, Island In The Sea (Columbia 1987)★★★, with Haggard Seashores Of Old Mexico (Epic 1987)★★★, with J.R. Chatwell Jammin' With J.R. And Friends (1988)★★★, What A Wonderful World (Columbia 1988)★★★, A Horse Called Music (Columbia 1989)★★★, with Cash, Jennings, Kristofferson Highwayman 2 (Columbia 1990)★★★, Born For Trouble (Columbia 1990)★★★, with Jennings Clean Shirt (Epic 1991)★★, Who'll Buy My Memories – The IRS Tapes (Columbia 1991)★★★, with Willie Nelson Together Again (1982)★★★, Across The Borderline (Columbia 1993)★★★★, Healing Hands Of Time (Liberty 1994)★★★, Moonlight Becomes You (Justice 1994)★★, with Curtis Porter Six Hours At Pedernales (Step One 1994)★★, with Don Cherry Augusta (Coast To Coast 1995)★★, with Cash, Jennings, Kristofferson The Road Goes On Forever (Liberty 1995)★★, Just One Love (Transatlantic 1995)★★★, Spirit (Island 1996)★★★, with Waylon Jennings, Jessi Colter, Tompall Glaser Wanted! The Outlaws (1976-1996, 20th Anniversary) (RCA 1996)★★★★, with Bobbie Nelson How Great Thou Art (Finer Arts 1996)★★, Burning Memories (Beacon 1997).
COMPILATIONS: The Best Of Willie Nelson (United Artists 1973)★★★, Willie Nelson's Greatest Hits (And Some That Will Be) (Columbia 1981)★★★, 20 Of The Best (RCA 1982)★★★, Country Willie (Capitol 1987)★★★, Nite Life: Greatest Hits And Rare Tracks, 1959-1971 (Rhino 1990)★★★★, 45 Original Tracks (EMI 1993)★★★, The Early Years: The Complete Liberty Recordings Plus More 2-CD set (Liberty 1994)★★★, Super Hits (Columbia 1994)★★★, A Classic And Unreleased Collection 3-CD box set (Rhino 1995)★★★, Revolutions Of Time: The Journey 1975-1993 (Columbia/Legacy 1995)★★★★, The Essential Willie Nelson (RCA 1995)★★★.
VIDEOS: Honeysuckle Rose, First Time Together (with Ray Charles), My Life – Biography, Willie Nelson And Family In Concert (CBS-Fox 1988), The Best Of (Vestron Video 1990), The Original Outlaw/On The Road Again (Hughes Leisure 1994), Nashville Superstar (Magnum Music 1997).
FURTHER READING: Willie Nelson Family Album, Lana Nelson Fowler (ed.). Willie Nelson – Country Outlaw, Lola Socbey. Willie, Michael Bane. I Didn't Come Here And I Ain't Leavin', Willie Nelson with Bud Shrake. Heartworn Memories – A Daughter's Personal Biography Of Willie Nelson, Susie Nelson. Willie: An Autobiography, Willie Nelson and Bud Shrake.

NESMITH, MICHAEL
ALBUMS: Mike Nesmith Presents The Wichita Train Whistle Sings (Dot 1968)★★, Magnetic South (RCA 1970)★★★, Loose Salute (RCA 1971)★★★★, Nevada Fighter (RCA 1971)★★★★, Tantamount To Treason (RCA 1972)★★, And The Hits Just Keep On Comin' (RCA 1972)★★★, Pretty Much Your Standard Ranch Stash (RCA 1973)★★★, The Prison (Pacific Arts 1975)★★, From A Radio Engine To The Photon Wing (Pacific Arts 1977)★★★, Live At The Palais (Pacific Arts 1978)★★, Infinite Rider On The Big Dogma (Pacific Arts 1979)★★★, Tropical Campfires (Pacific Arts 1992)★★★, The Garden (Rio Royal 1994)★★.
COMPILATIONS: The Best Of Mike Nesmith (RCA 1977)★★★, The Newer Stuff (Awareness 1989)★★★, The Older Stuff (Rhino 1992)★★★★, Complete (Pacific Arts 1993)★★★.
FILMS: Head (1968).
VIDEOS: Elephant Parts (Awareness 1992).

NEW KIDS ON THE BLOCK
ALBUMS: New Kids On The Block (Columbia 1986)★★, Hangin' Tough (Columbia 1988)★★, Merry Merry Christmas (Columbia 1989)★, Step By Step (Columbia 1990)★★, No More Games/Remix Album (Columbia 1991)★★, Face The Music (Columbia 1994).
COMPILATIONS: H.I.T.S (Columbia 1991)★★★.
FURTHER READING: New Kids On The Block: The Whole Story By Their Friends, Robin McGibbon. New Kids On The Block, Lynn Goldsmith.

NEW MODEL ARMY
ALBUMS: Vengeance (Abstract 1984)★★★, No Rest For The Wicked (EMI 1985)★★★, The Ghost Of Cain (EMI 1986)★★, New Model Army mini-album (EMI 1987)★★, Radio Sessions 83 – 84 (Abstract 1988)★★, Thunder And Consolation (EMI 1989)★★★, Impurity (EMI 1990)★★★, Raw Melody Men (EMI 1990)★★★, The Love Of Hopeless Causes (Epic 1993)★★★, BBC Radio One – Live In Concert (Windsong 1994)★★, Small Town England (Snapper 1998).
COMPILATIONS: The Independent Story (Abstract 1987)★★★, History (EMI 1992)★★★.
VIDEOS: History: The Videos 85-90 (PMI 1993).

NEW ORDER
ALBUMS: Movement (Factory 1981)★★★, Power, Corruption And Lies (Factory 1983)★★★, Low Life (Factory 1985)★★★★, Brotherhood (Factory 1986)★★★★, Technique (Factory 1989)★★★, Republic (London 1993)★★★.
COMPILATIONS: Substance (Factory 1987)★★★★, The Peel Sessions (Strange Fruit 1990)★★★, Live In Concert (Windsong 1992)★★★, (The Best Of) New Order (London 1995)★★★★, (The Rest Of) New Order (London 1995)★★★.
VIDEOS: Taras Schevenko (Factory 1984), Pumped Full Of Drugs (Ikon Video 1988), Substance 1989 (Virgin Vision 1989), Brixton Academy April 1987 (Palace Video 1989), Neworderstory (1993), The Best Of New Order (1995).
FURTHER READING: New Order & Joy Division: Pleasures And Wayward Distractions, Brian Edge. New Order & Joy Division: Dreams Never End, Claude Flowers.

NEW RIDERS OF THE PURPLE SAGE
ALBUMS: New Riders Of The Purple Sage (Columbia 1971)★★★★, Powerglide (Columbia 1972)★★★, Gypsy Cowboy (Columbia 1972)★★, The Adventures Of Panama Red (Columbia 1973)★★★, Home, Home On The Road (Columbia 1974)★★, Brujo (Columbia 1974)★★, Oh, What A Mighty Time (Columbia 1975)★★, New Riders (MCA 1976)★★, Who Are These Guys (MCA 1977)★★, Marin County Line (MCA 1978)★, Feelin' Alright (A&M 1981)★, Friend Of The Devil (1991)★★.
COMPILATIONS: The Best Of The New Riders Of The Purple Sage (Columbia 1976)★★★.

NEW SEEKERS
ALBUMS: The New Seekers (Phillips 1969)★★★, Keith Potger & The New Seekers (Phillips 1970)★★, New Colours (Polydor 1971)★★★, Beautiful People (Phillips 1971)★★, We'd Like To Teach The World To Sing (Polydor 1972)★★, Live At The Royal Albert Hall (Polydor 1972)★★, Never Ending Song Of Love (Polydor 1972)★★, Circles (Polydor 1972)★★, Now (Polydor 1973)★★, Pinball Wizards (Polydor 1973)★★, Together (Polydor 1974)★★, Farewell Album (Polydor 1974)★★, Together Again (Columbia 1976)★★.
COMPILATIONS: The Best Of The New Seekers (Contour 1985)★★★. By Marty Kristian, Paul Layton And Peter Oliver Peter Paul & Marty (1973)★★.

NEW YORK DOLLS
ALBUMS: New York Dolls (Mercury 1973)★★★★, Too Much Too Soon (Mercury 1974)★★★, Red Patent Leather (New Rose 1984)★★.
COMPILATIONS: Lipstick Killers (ROIR 1981)★★★, Best Of The New York Dolls (Mercury 1985)★★★, Night Of The Living Dolls (Mercury 1986)★★★, Rock 'N' Roll (Mercury 1994)★★★★.
FURTHER READING: New York Dolls, Steven Morrissey.

NEWMAN, RANDY
ALBUMS: Randy Newman (Reprise 1968)★★★, 12 Songs (Reprise 1970)★★★★, Randy Newman/Live (Reprise 1971)★★★, Sail Away (Reprise 1972)★★★★, Good Old Boys (Reprise 1974)★★★★, Little Criminals (Warners 1977)★★★, Born Again (Warners 1979)★★★, Ragtime film soundtrack (1982)★★, Trouble In Paradise (Warners 1983)★★, The Natural film soundtrack (1984)★★, Land Of Dreams (Reprise 1988)★★★, Parenthood film soundtrack (1990)★★, Awakenings film soundtrack (Warners 1991)★★, The Paper film soundtrack (Reprise 1994)★★, Faust (Reprise 1995)★★★.
COMPILATIONS: Randy Newman Retrospect (Warners 1983)★★★, Top – The Best Of Randy Newman (Warners 1987)★★★★.

NEWTON-JOHN, OLIVIA
ALBUMS: If Not For You (Pye 1971)★★★, Let Me Be There (MCA 1973)★★★, Olivia Newton-John (1973)★★, If You Love Me Let Me Know (MCA 1974)★★★, Music Makes My Day (Pye 1974)★★, Long Live Love (1974)★★, Have You Never Been Mellow? (MCA 1975)★★★, Clearly Love (MCA 1975)★★, Come On Over (MCA 1976)★★, Don't Stop Believin' (MCA 1976)★★, Making A Good Thing Better (MCA 1977)★★, with various artists Grease film soundtrack (1978)★★★★, Totally Hot (MCA 1978)★★★, with the Electric Light Orchestra Xanadu film soundtrack (MCA 1980)★★, Physical (MCA 1981)★★★, with various artists Two Of A Kind film soundtrack (1983)★★, Soul Kiss (MCA 1986)★★, The Rumour (MCA 1988)★★, Warm And Tender (Geffen 1990)★★, Gaia: One Woman's Journey (1994)★★.
COMPILATIONS: Olivia Newton-John's Greatest Hits (MCA 1977)★★★, Greatest Hits I, (EMI 1978)★★★, Back To Basics: The Essential Collection 1971-1992 (Phonogram 1992)★★★.
FILMS: Grease (1978).
VIDEOS: Physical (PMI 1984), Live: Olivia Newton-John (Channel 5 1986), Down Under (Channel 5 1989), Soul Kiss (Spectrum 1989).
FURTHER READING: Olivia Newton-John: Sunshine Supergirl, Linda Jacobs. Olivia Newton-John, Peter Ruff.

NICE
ALBUMS: The Thoughts Of Emerlist Davjack (Immediate 1967)★★★, Ars Longa Vita Brevis (Immediate 1968)★★★, Nice (Immediate 1969)★★★, Five Bridges (Charisma 1970)★★★★, Elegy (Charisma 1971)★★.
COMPILATIONS: Autumn 76 – Spring 68 (1972)★★★, 20th Anniversary Release (1987)★★★.

NICKS, STEVIE
ALBUMS: with Lindsey Buckingham Buckingham-Nicks (Polydor 1973)★★, Bella Donna (Warners 1981)★★★, The Wild Heart (Warners 1983)★★★, Rock A Little (Modern 1985)★★, The Other Side Of The Mirror (EMI 1989)★★★, Street Angel (EMI 1994)★★.
COMPILATIONS: Timespace: The Best Of Stevie Nicks (EMI 1991)★★★.

NICO
ALBUMS: Chelsea Girl (Verve 1967)★★, The Marble Index (Elektra 1969)★★★, Desertshore (Reprise 1971)★★★, with ACNE June 1, 1974 (Island 1974)★★, The End (Island 1974)★★★, Drama Of Exile (Aura 1981)★★★, Do Or Die! Nico In Europe, 1982 Diary (Reach Out 1983)★★★, Camera Obscura (Beggars Banquet 1985)★★, The Blue Angel (Aura 1986)★★, Behind The Iron Curtain (Dojo 1986)★★, Live In Tokyo (Dojo 1987)★★, Live In Denmark (Vu 1987)★★, En Personne En Europe (One Over Two 1988)★★★, Live Heroes (Performance 1989)★★, Hanging Gardens (Emergo 1990)★★, Icon (Cleopatra 1996)★★, Janitor Of Lunacy (Cherry Red 1996)★★, Nico's Last Concert: Fato Morgana (SPV 1996)★★★.
VIDEOS: An Underground Experience (Wide Angle/Visionary 1993), Nico – Heroine (1994).
FURTHER READING: The Life And Lies Of An Icon, Richard Witts. Songs They Never Play On The Radio: Nico, The Last Bohemian, James Young.

NIGHTINGALES
ALBUMS: Pigs On Purpose (Cherry Red 1982)★★★, Hysterics (Red Flame 1983)★★★, In The Good Old Country Ways (Vindaloo 1986)★★★, The Peel Sessions EP (Strange Fruit 1988)★★★.
COMPILATIONS: Just A Job (Vindaloo 1983)★★★, What A Scream (Mau Mau 1991)★★★.

NILSSON
ALBUMS: Pandemonium Shadow Show (RCA Victor 1967)★★★, Ariel Ballet (RCA 1968)★★★, Harry (RCA 1969)★★★, Skidoo film soundtrack (RCA 1969)★★, Nilsson Sings Newman (RCA 1970)★★★★, The Point (RCA 1971)★★★, Nilsson Schmilsson (RCA 1971)★★★★, Son Of Schmilsson (RCA 1972)★★, A Little Touch Of Schmilsson In The Night (RCA 1973)★★★★, Son Of Dracula (Rapple 1974)★★, Pussy Cats (RCA 1974)★★★, Duit On Mon Dei (RCA 1975)★★, The Sandman (RCA 1975)★★, That's The Way It Is (RCA 1976)★★★, Knillssonn (RCA 1977)★★, Night After Night (1979)★★, Flash Harry (Mercury 1980)★★, A Touch More Schmilsson In The Night (RCA 1988)★★.
COMPILATIONS: Ariel Pandemonium Ballet (RCA 1973)★★★, Nilsson's Greatest Music (RCA 1978)★★★, As Time Goes By ... The Complete Schmilsson In The Night (Camden 1997)★★★.

NINE BELOW ZERO
ALBUMS: Live At The Marquee (A&M 1980)★★★★, Don't Point Your Finger (A&M 1981)★★★, Third Degree (A&M 1982)★★★★, Live At The Venue (China 1990)★★★, Off The Hook (China 1992)★★★, Live In London (Indigo 1995)★★★, Ice Station Zebro (A&M 1996)★★, Covers (Zed 1997)★★.

NINE INCH NAILS
ALBUMS: Pretty Hate Machine (TVT 1989)★★★, Broken mini-album (Nothing 1992)★★, Fixed mini-album (Nothing 1992)★★, The Downward Spiral (Nothing 1994)★★★★, Further Down The Spiral remix mini-album (Island 1995)★★★, Closure (Nothing 1997).

1910 FRUITGUM COMPANY
ALBUMS: Simon Says (1968)★★, 1, 2, 3, Red Light (1968)★★, Indian Giver (1969)★★, 1910 Fruitgum Company And Ohio Express (1969)★★★.

NIRVANA (UK)
ALBUMS: The Story Of Simon Simopath (Island 1967)★★★, All Of Us (Island 1968)★★, To Markos 3 (Pye 1969)★★, Local Anaesthetic (Vertigo 1971)★★★, Songs Of Love And Praise (Philips 1972)★★. Solo: Patrick Campbell Lyons Me And My Friend (1973)★★, The Electric Plough (1981)★★, The Hero I Might Have Been (1982)★★.
COMPILATIONS: Black Flower (1987)★★★, Secret Theatre (Edsel 1987)★★★, Orange And Blue (Demon 1996)★★★.

NIRVANA (USA)
ALBUMS: Bleach (Sub Pop 1989)★★★★, Nevermind (Geffen 1991)★★★★★, In Utero (Geffen 1993)★★★★, Unplugged In New York (Geffen 1994)★★★★.
COMPILATIONS: Incesticide (Geffen 1992)★★★, Singles (Geffen 1995)★★★★, From The Muddy Banks Of The Wishkah (Geffen 1996)★★★★.
VIDEOS: Live! Tonight! Sold Out!! (Geffen 1994), Teen Spirit: The Tribute To Kurt Cobain (Labyrinth 1996).
FURTHER READING: Route 666: On The Road To Nirvana, Gina Arnold. Nirvana And The Sound Of Seattle, Brad Morrell. Come As You Are, Michael Azerrad. Nirvana: An Illustrated Biography, Suzi Black. Nirvana: Tribute, Suzi Black. Never Fade Away, Dave Thompson. Kurt Cobain, Christopher Sandford. Nirvana: Nevermind, Susan Wilson.

NITTY GRITTY DIRT BAND
ALBUMS: The Nitty Gritty Dirt Band (Liberty 1967)★★★, Ricochet (Liberty 1967)★★★, Rare Junk (Liberty 1968)★★, Alive (Liberty 1969)★★, Uncle Charlie And His Dog Teddy (Liberty 1970)★★★, All The Good Times (United Artists 1972)★★★, Will The Circle Be Unbroken triple album (United Artists 1972)★★★★, Stars And Stripes Forever (United Artists 1974)★★, Dreams (United Artists 1975)★★★. As Dirt Band Dirt Band (United Artists 1978)★★, An American Dream (United Artists 1979)★★, Make A Little Magic (United Artists 1980)★★, Jealousy (United Artists 1981)★★. As Nitty Gritty Dirt Band Let's Go (United Artists 1983)★★, Plain Dirt Fashion (Warners 1984)★★★, Partners, Brothers And Friends (Warners 1985)★★★, Hold On (Warners 1987)★★★, Workin' Band (Warners. 1988)★★★, Will The Circle Be Unbroken Volume II (Warners. 1989)★★★★, The Rest Of The Dream (MCA 1991)★★★, Not Fade Away (Liberty 1992)★★, Acoustic (Liberty 1994)★★★, Bang Bang Bang (MCA 1998).
COMPILATIONS: Dirt, Silver And Gold (United Artists 1976)★★★, Gold From Dirt (United Artists UK 1980)★★★, Twenty Years Of Dirt (Warners 1987)★★★.

NO DOUBT
ALBUMS: No Doubt (Interscope 1992)★★★, Tragic Kingdom (Interscope 1995)★★★★, Collector's Orange Cafe (Interscope 1998).

NUCLEUS
ALBUMS: Elastic Rock (Vertigo 1970)★★★★, We'll Talk About It later (Vertigo 1970)★★★, Solar Plexus (Vertigo 1971)★★★★, Belladonna (Vertigo 1972)★★★, Labyrinth (Vertigo 1973)★★★, Roots (Vertigo 1973)★★★, Under The Sun (Vertigo 1974)★★★, Snake Hips Etcetera (Vertigo 1975)★★★, Direct Hits (Vertigo 1976)★★★, In Flagrante Delicto (1978)★★★, Out Of The Long Dark (1979)★★, Awakening (1980)★★, Live At The Theaterhaus (1985)★★★.

NUGENT, TED
ALBUMS: Ted Nugent (Epic 1975)★★★, Free For All (Epic 1976)★★★, Cat Scratch Fever (Epic 1977)★★★★, Double Live Gonzo (Epic 1978)★★★, Weekend Warriors (Epic 1978)★★★, State Of Shock (Epic 1979)★★★, Scream Dream (Epic 1980)★★★, Intensities In Ten Cities (Epic 1981)★★★, Nugent (Atlantic 1982)★★, Penetrator (Atlantic 1984)★★, Little Miss Dangerous (Atlantic 1986)★★, If You Can't Lick 'Em ... Lick 'Em (Atlantic 1988)★★, Spirit Of The Wild (Atlantic 1995)★★.
COMPILATIONS: Great Gonzos: The Best Of Ted Nugent (Epic 1981)★★★★, Anthology: Ted Nugent (Raw Power 1986)★★★.
VIDEOS: Whiplash Bash (Hendring 1990).
FURTHER READING: The Legendary Ted Nugent, Robert Holland.

NUMAN, GARY
ALBUMS: as Tubeway Army Tubeway Army (Beggars Banquet 1979)★★, as Tubeway Army Replicas (Beggars Banquet 1979)★★, The Pleasure Principle (Beggars Banquet 1979)★★★, Telekon (Beggars Banquet 1980)★★★, Living Ornaments 1979-80 (Beggars Banquet 1981)★★, Dance (Beggars Banquet 1981)★★, I Assassin (Beggars Banquet 1982)★★, Warriors (Beggars Banquet 1983)★★, The Plan (Beggars Banquet 1984)★★, Berserker (Numa 1984)★★, White Noise – Live (Numa 1985)★★, The Fury (Numa 1985)★★, Strange Charm (Numa 1986)★★, Exhibition (Beggars Banquet 1987)★★, Metal Rhythm (Illegal 1988)★★, The Skin Mechanic (IRS 1989)★★, Outland (IRS 1991)★★, Machine And Soul (Numa 1992)★★, Dream Corrosion (Numa 1994)★★.
COMPILATIONS: New Man Numan – The Best Of Gary Numan (TV 1982)★★★, The Best Of ... (Beggars Banquet 1993)★★★★, The Premier Hits (Polygram 1996)★★★★, The Best Of ... (Emporio 1997)★★★, tribute album Random various artists (Beggars Banquet 1997)★★★.
VIDEOS: Dream Corrosion (Numa 1994).
FURTHER READING: Gary Numan By Computer, Fred and Judy Vermorel. Gary Numan: The Authorized Biography, Ray Coleman.

NWA
ALBUMS: NWA And The Posse (Ruthless 1987)★★★, Straight Outta Compton (Ruthless 1989)★★★★, Efil4zaggin' (Ruthless 1991)★.
COMPILATIONS: Greatest Hits (Virgin 1996)★★★.

NYRO, LAURA
ALBUMS: More Than A New Discovery aka The First Songs (Verve/Forecast 1967)★★★, Eli And The Thirteenth Confession (Columbia 1968)★★★★, New York Tendaberry (Columbia 1969)★★★★, Christmas And The Beads Of Sweat (Columbia 1970)★★★, Gonna Take A Miracle (Columbia 1971)★★★, Smile (Columbia 1976)★★★, Season Of Lights (Columbia 1977)★★★, Nested (Columbia 1979)★★, Mother's Spiritual (Columbia 1985)★★, Live At The Bottom Line (Columbia 1990)★★, Walk The Dog And Light The Light (Columbia 1993)★★.
COMPILATIONS: Impressions (Columbia 1980)★★★★, Stoned Soul Picnic: The Best Of ... (Columbia/Legacy 1997)★★★★, tribute album Time And Love: The Music Of Laura Nyro (Astor Place 1997)★★★.

O

O'CONNOR, SINEAD
ALBUMS: The Lion And The Cobra (Chrysalis 1988)★★★, I Do Not Want What I Haven't Got (Ensign 1990)★★★★, Am I Not Your Girl? (Ensign 1993)★★★, Universal Mother (Ensign 1994)★★.
COMPILATIONS: So Far ... The Best Of Sinead O'Connor (Chrysalis 1997)★★★.
FURTHER READING: Sinead O'Connor: So Different, Dermott Hayes. Sinead: Her Life And Music, Jimmy Guterman.

O'JAYS
ALBUMS: Comin' Through (Imperial 1965)★★★, Soul Sounds (Imperial 1967)★★★, O'Jays (Minit 1967)★★★, Full Of Soul (Minit 1968)★★★, Back On Top (Bell 1968)★★★, The O'Jays In Philadelphia (Neptune 1969)★★★, Back Stabbers (Philadelphia International 1972)★★★★, Ship Ahoy (Philadelphia International 1973)★★★★, The O'Jays Live In London (Philadelphia International 1974)★★, Survival (Philadelphia International 1975)★★★, Family Reunion (Philadelphia International 1975)★★, with the Moments The O'Jays Meet The Moments (Philadelphia International 1975)★★★, Message In The Music (Philadelphia International 1976)★★★, Travelin' At The Speed Of Thought (Philadelphia International 1977)★★, So Full Of Love (Philadelphia International 1978)★★★, Identify Yourself (Philadelphia International 1979)★★★, The Year 2000 (TSOP 1980)★★, Peace (Phoenix 1981)★★, My Favourite Person (Philadelphia International 1982)★★, When Will I See You Again (Epic 1983)★★, Love And More (Philadelphia International 1984)★★★, Love Fever (Philadelphia International 1985)★★★, Close Company (Philadelphia International 1985)★★★, Let Me Touch You (EMI Manhattan 1987)★★★, Serious (EMI 1989)★★, Emotionally Yours (EMI 1991)★★, Heartbreaker (EMI 1993)★★, Love You To Tears (Global Soul/BMG 1997)★★★★.
COMPILATIONS: Collectors' Items: Greatest Hits (Philadelphia International 1977)★★★, Greatest Hits (Philadelphia International 1984)★★★★, From The Beginning (Chess 1984)★★★, Working On Your Case (Stateside 1985)★★★, Reflections In Gold 1973-1982 (Charly 1988)★★★, Love Train: The Best Of ... (Columbia/Legacy 1995)★★★★.

O'SULLIVAN, GILBERT
ALBUMS: Himself (MAM 1971)★★★, Back To Front (MAM 1973)★★★★, I'm A Writer Not A Fighter (MAM 1973)★★★, Stranger In My Own Backyard (MAM 1974)★★, Southpaw (1977)★★, Off Centre (Columbia 1980)★★, Life And Rhymes (Columbia 1982)★★, Frobisher Drive (1988)★★, In The Key Of G (Chrysalis 1989)★★, Sounds Of The Loop (Park 1992)★★, Live In Japan 1993 (Park 1993)★★, By Larry (Park 1994)★★, Every Song Has It's Play (Park 1995)★★.
COMPILATIONS: Greatest Hits (MAM 1976)★★★, 16 Golden Classics (1986)★★, Greatest Hits (Big Time 1988)★★★.

OAKENFOLD, PAUL
ALBUMS: Journeys By DJ (Music Unites 1994)★★★, JD15 – Paul Oakenfold In The Mix (Music Unites 1994)★★★, Paul Oakenfold Live in Oslo (1997).

OASIS
ALBUMS: Definitely Maybe (Creation 1994)★★★★, (What's The Story) Morning Glory (Creation 1995)★★★★★, Be Here Now (Creation 1997)★★★★.
VIDEOS: Live By The Sea (PMI 1995), ... There And Then (SMV 1996).
FURTHER READING: Oasis: How Does It Feel, Jemma Wheeler. Oasis: The Illustrated Story, Paul Lester. The World On The Street: The Unsanctioned Story Of Oasis, Eugene Masterson. Oasis Definitely, Tim Abbot. Oasis, Mick St. Michael. Oasis '96, Pat Gilbert. Oasis: What's The Story, Ian Robertson. Oasis: Round Their Way, Mick Middles. Brothers: From Childhood To Oasis: The Real Story, Paul Gallagher and Terry Christian. Oasis: The Story, Paul Mathur. Getting High – The Adventures Of Oasis, Paulo Hewitt. Don't Look Back In Anger: Growing Up With Oasis, Chris Hutton and Richard Kurt.

OCEAN, BILLY
ALBUMS: Billy Ocean (GTO 1977)★★, City Limit (GTO 1980)★★, Nights (Feel Like Getting Down) (GTO 1981)★★★, Inner Feelings (GTO 1982)★★★, Suddenly (Jive 1984)★★★, Love Zone (Jive 1986)★★, Tear Down These Walls (Jive 1988)★★, Time To Move On (Jive 1993)★★, L.I.F.E. (Jive 1997).
COMPILATIONS: Greatest Hits (Jive 1989)★★★, Lover Boy (Spectrum 1993)★★★.

OCEAN COLOUR SCENE
ALBUMS: Ocean Colour Scene (Fontana 1992)★★, Moseley Shoals (MCA 1996)★★★★, B-Sides, Seasides & Freerides (MCA 1997)★★, Marchin' Already (MCA 1997)★★.

OCHS, PHIL
ALBUMS: All The News That's Fit To Sing (Elektra 1964)★★★★, I Ain't Marching Anymore (Elektra 1965)★★★★, Phil Ochs In Concert (Elektra 1966)★★★, The Pleasures Of The Harbour (1967)★★★, Tape From California (1968)★★★, Rehearsals For Retirement (1968)★★★, Gunfight At Carnegie Hall (1975)★★.
COMPILATIONS: Phil Ochs Greatest Hits (1970)★★★, Phil Ochs – Chords Of Fame (1976)★★★★, Phil Ochs – Songs For Broadside (1976)★★★, Broadside Tapes (1976)★★★, A Toast To Those Who Are Gone (1987)★★★, There But For Fortune (1989)★★★, The Broadside Tapes 1 (Smithsonian Folkways 1995)★★★.
FURTHER READING: Phil Ochs: Death Of A Rebel, Marc Eliott.

ODYSSEY
ALBUMS: Odyssey (RCA 1977)★★★, Hollywood Party Tonight (RCA 1978)★★★, Hang Together (RCA 1980)★★★, I Got The Melody (RCA 1981)★★, Happy Together (RCA 1982)★★, A Piping Journey (Mannick Music 1987)★★.
COMPILATIONS: Best Of Odyssey (RCA 1981)★★★

Magic Touch Of Odyssey (Telstar 1982)★★, *Magic Moments With Odyssey* (RCA 1984)★★★, *Greatest Hits* (Stylus 1987)★★★, *Greatest Hits* (RCA 1990)★★★.

OFFSPRING
ALBUMS: *Offspring* (Nemesis 1989)★★, *Ignition* (Epitaph 1992)★★★, *Smash* (Epitaph 1994)★★★, *Ixnay On The Hombre* (Columbia 1997)★★★.

OHIO EXPRESS
ALBUMS: *Beg, Borrow And Steal* (Cameo 1968)★★, *Ohio Express* (Pye 1968)★★★, *Salt Water Taffy* (1968)★★, *Chewy Chewy* (Buddah 1969)★★★, *Mercy* (1969)★★.
COMPILATIONS: *Very Best Of The Ohio Express* (1970)★★★.

OLDFIELD, MIKE
ALBUMS: with Sally Oldfield *Sallyangie* (Transatlantic 1968)★★, *Tubular Bells* (Virgin 1973)★★★★, *Hergest Ridge* (Virgin 1974)★★★, with the Royal Philharmonic Orchestra *The Orchestral Tubular Bells* (Virgin 1975)★★★, *Ommadawn* (Virgin 1975)★★★, *Incantations* (Virgin 1978)★★, *Exposed* (Virgin 1979)★★, *Platinum* (Virgin 1979)★★, *QE2* (Virgin 1980)★★, *Five Miles Out* (Virgin 1982)★★, *Crises* (Virgin 1983)★★, *Discovery* (Virgin 1984)★★, *The Killing Fields* film soundtrack (Virgin 1984)★★, *Islands* (Virgin 1987)★★, *Earth Moving* (Virgin 1989)★★, *Amarok* (Virgin 1990)★★, *Heaven's Open* (Virgin 1991)★★, *Tubular Bells II* (Warners 1992)★★★, *The Songs Of Distant Earth* (Warners 1994)★★, *Voyager* (Warners 1996)★★, *XXV: The Essential* (WEA 1997).
COMPILATIONS: *Boxed* (Virgin 1976)★★★, *The Complete Mike Oldfield* (Virgin 1985)★★★.
VIDEOS: *The Wind Chimes* (Virgin Vision 1988), *Essential Mike Oldfield* (Virgin Vision 1988), *Elements* (1993).
FURTHER READING: *True Story Of The Making Of Tubular Bells*, Richard Newman. *Mike Oldfield: A Man And His Music*, Sean Moraghan.

OMD
ALBUMS: *Orchestral Manoeuvres In The Dark* (DinDisc 1980)★★★, *Organisation* (DinDisc 1980)★★★, *Architecture And Morality* (DinDisc 1981)★★★, *Dazzle Ships* (Telegraph 1983)★★, *Junk Culture* (Virgin 1984)★★★, *Crush* (Virgin 1985)★★★, *The Pacific Age* (Virgin 1986)★★, *Sugar Tax* (Virgin 1991)★★, *Liberator* (Virgin 1993)★★★, *Universal* (Virgin 1996)★★★.
COMPILATIONS: *The Best Of OMD* (Virgin 1988)★★★★.
FURTHER READING: *Orchestral Manoeuvres In The Dark*, Mike West.

ONO, YOKO
ALBUMS: *Yoko Ono/The Plastic Ono Band* (Apple 1970)★★, *Fly* (Apple 1971)★★, *Approximately Infinite Universe* (Apple 1973)★★, *Feeling The Space* (Apple 1973)★★, *Season Of Glass* (Geffen 1981)★★, *It's Alright (I See Rainbows)* (1982)★★, *Starpeace* (1985)★★, *Rising* (Geffen 1996)★★★, *A Story* (Rykodisc 1997).
COMPILATIONS: *The Ono Box* (1992)★★★, *Rising Mixes* (Capitol 1996).
VIDEOS: *The Bed-In* (PMI 1991).
FURTHER READING: *Grapefruit: A Book Of Instructions*, Yoko Ono. *Yoko Ono: A Biography*, Jerry Hopkins. *Yoko Ono – Arias And Objects*, Barbara Haskell and John G. Hanhardt.

ORANGE JUICE
ALBUMS: *You Can't Hide Your Love Forever* (Polydor 1982)★★★, *Rip It Up* (Polydor 1982)★★★★, *Texas Fever* mini-album (Polydor 1984)★★★, *The Orange Juice* (Polydor 1984)★★★, *Ostrich Churchyard* (Postcard 1992)★★.
Solo: Zeke Manyika *Call And Response* (Polydor 1985)★★★, *Mastercrime* (Some Bizarre/ Parlophone 1989)★★★.
COMPILATIONS: *In A Nutshell* (Polydor 1985)★★★, *The Very Best Of* (Polydor 1992)★★★★, *The Heather's On Fire* (Postcard 1993)★★★.
VIDEOS: *Dada With Juice* (Hendring Video 1989).

ORB
ALBUMS: *The Orbs Adventures Beyond The Ultraworld* (WAU! Mr Modo/Big Life 1991)★★★, *Peel Sessions* (Strange Fruit 1991)★★★, *Aubrey Mixes, The Ultraworld Excursion* (WAU! Mr Modo/Big Life 1992)★★★, *UFOrb* (WAU! Mr Modo/Big Life 1992)★★★, *Live 93* (Island 1993)★★, *Pomme Fritz* (Island 1994)★★★, *Orbvs Terrarvm* (Island 1995)★★★★, *Orblivion* (Island 1997)★★★.
COMPILATIONS: *Auntie Aubrey's Excursions Beyond The Call Of Duty* (Deviant 1996).

ORBISON, ROY
ALBUMS: *Lonely And Blue* (Monument 1961)★★, *Exciting Sounds Of Roy Orbison (Roy Orbison At The Rockhouse)* (Sun 1961)★★, *Crying* (Monument 1962)★★★, *In Dreams* (Monument 1963)★★★, *Oh Pretty Woman* (1964)★★★★, *Early Orbison* (Monument 1964)★★, *There Is Only One Roy Orbison* (MGM 1965)★★, *Orbisongs* (Monument 1965)★★, *The Orbison Way* (MGM 1965)★★, *The Classic Roy Orbison* (MGM 1966)★★, *Roy Orbison Sings Don Gibson* (MGM 1966)★★★, *Cry Softly, Lonely One* (MGM 1967)★★, *The Fastest Guitar Alive* (MGM 1968)★, *Roy Orbison's Many Moods* (MGM 1969)★★, *The Big O* (MGM 1970)★★, *Hank Williams: The Roy Orbison Way* (MGM 1970)★★, *Roy Orbison Sings* (MGM 1972)★★, *Memphis* (MGM 1972)★★, *Milestones* (MGM 1973)★★, *I'm Still In Love With You* (Mercury 1975)★★, *Regeneration* (Monument 1976)★★, *Laminar Flow* (Asylum 1979)★★, with Jerry Lee Lewis, Johnny Cash, Carl Perkins *The Class Of '55* (1986)★★★, *Mystery Girl* (Virgin 1989)★★★★, *Rare Orbison* (Monument 1989)★★★, *A Black And White Night Live* (Virgin 1989)★★, *King Of Hearts* (Virgin 1992)★★★★.
COMPILATIONS: *Roy Orbison's Greatest Hits* (Monument 1962)★★★★, *The Very Best Of Roy Orbison* (Monument 1965)★★★★, *The Great Songs Of Roy Orbison* (Monument 1970)★★★★, *In Dreams: The Greatest Hits* (Virgin 1987)★★★★, *For The Lonely: A Roy Orbison Anthology 1956-1965* (Rhino 1988)★★★★, *Sun Years* (Rhino 1989)★★★★, *The Legendary Roy Orbison* (Columbia 1990)★★★★, *The Very Best Of Roy Orbison* (Virgin 1996)★★★★.
FILMS: *The Fastest Guitar Alive* (1966).
FURTHER READING: *Dark Star*, Ellis Amburn. *Only The Lonely*, Alan Clayson.

ORBITAL
ALBUMS: *Untitled 1* (ffrr 1991)★★, *Untitled 2* (Internal 1993)★★★, *Snivilisation* (Internal 1994)★★★★, *In Sides* (Internal 1996)★★★★, with Michael Kamen *Event Horizon* soundtrack (London 1997).

OSBORNE, JEFFREY
ALBUMS: *Jeffrey Osborne* (A&M 1982)★★★, *Stay With Me Tonight* (A&M 1983)★★★, *Don't Stop* (A&M 1984)★★★, *Emotional* (A&M 1986)★★★, *One Love One Dream* (A&M 1988)★★, *Only Human* (Arista 1991) ★★★, *Something Warm For Christmas* (A&M 1997).

OSBORNE, JOAN
ALBUMS: *Soul Show* (Womanly Hips 1991)★★, *Relish* (Blue Gorilla/Mercury 1995)★★★★, *Early Recordings* (Mercury 1996)★★.

OSBOURNE, OZZY
ALBUMS: *Blizzard Of Oz* (Jet 1980)★★★, *Diary Of A Madman* (Jet 1981)★★★, *Talk Of The Devil* (Jet 1982)★★, *Bark At The Moon* (Jet 1983)★★, *The Ultimate Sin* (Epic 1986)★★, *Tribute* (Epic 1987)★★★, *No Rest For The Wicked* (Epic 1988)★★, *Just Say Ozzy* (Epic 1990)★★, *No More Tears* (Epic 1991)★★★, *Live & Loud* (Epic 1993)★★, *Ozzmosis* (Epic 1995)★★★★, *Ozzfest Vol. 1 Live* (Red Ant 1997).
VIDEOS: *The Ultimate Ozzy* (1987), *Wicked Videos* (1988), *Bark At The Moon* (1990), *Don't Blame Me* (1992), *Live & Loud* (1993).
FURTHER READING: *Diary Of A Madman*, Mick Wall. *Ozzy Osbourne*, Garry Johnson.

OSIBISA
ALBUMS: *Osibisa* (MCA 1971)★★★, *Woyaya* (MCA 1972)★★★★, *Heads* (MCA 1972)★★, *Happy Children* (Warners 1973)★★, *Superfly TNT* (1974)★★, *Osibirock* (Warners 1974)★★★, *Welcome Home* (1976)★★, *Ojah Awake* (1976)★★★, *Black Magic Night* (1977), *Mystic Energy* (Calibre 1981)★★, *Celebration* (Bronze 1983)★★, *Unleashed: Live In India 1981* (Magnet 1983)★★, *Live At The Marquee* (Premier 1984)★★★.
COMPILATIONS: *The Best Of Osibisa* (MCA 1974)★★★, *The Best Of Osibisa* (BBC 1990)★★★★.
VIDEOS: *Warrior* (Hendring 1990).

OSMOND, DONNY
ALBUMS: *The Donny Osmond Album* (MGM 1971)★★, *To You With Love, Donny* (MGM 1971)★★, *Portrait Of Donny* (MGM 1972)★★, *Too Young* (MGM 1972)★★, *My Best Of You* (MGM 1972)★★, *Alone Together* (MGM 1973)★★, *A Time For Us* (MGM 1973)★★, *Donny* (MGM 1974)★★, *Discotrain* (Polydor 1976)★★, *Donald Clark Osmond* (Polydor 1977)★★, *Donny Osmond* (Virgin 1988)★★★, *Eyes Don't Lie* (Capitol 1990)★★. With Marie Osmond *I'm Leaving It All Up To You* (MGM 1974)★★, *Make The World Go Away* (MGM 1975)★★, *Donny And Marie – Featuring Songs From Their Television Show* (Polydor 1976)★★, *Deep Purple* (Polydor 1976)★★, *Donny And Marie – A New Season* (Polydor 1977)★★, *Winning Combination* (Polydor 1978)★★, *Goin' Coconuts* (Polydor 1978)★★, *Donny Osmond* (Capitol 1989), *Eyes Don't Lie* (Capitol 1991).

OSMONDS
ALBUMS: *Osmonds* (MGM 1971)★★, *Homemade* (MGM 1971)★★, *Phase-III* (MGM 1972)★★, *The Osmonds 'Live'* (MGM 1972)★, *Crazy Horses* (MGM 1972)★★★, *The Plan* (MGM 1973)★★, *Our Best To You* (MGM 1974)★★, *Love Me For A Reason* (MGM 1974)★★, *I'm Still Gonna Need You* (MGM 1975)★★, *The Proud One* (MGM 1975)★★, *Around The World – Live In Concert* (MGM 1975)★, *Brainstorm* (Polydor 1976)★★, *The Osmonds Christmas Album* (Polydor 1976)★★, *Today* (1985)★★, *Second Generation* (Curb 1992).
COMPILATIONS: *The Osmonds Greatest Hits* (Polydor 1978)★★★, *The Very Best Of The Osmonds* (Polydor 1996)★★★.
VIDEOS: *Very Best Of* (Wienerworld 1996).
FURTHER READING: *At Last ... Donny!*, James Gregory. *The Osmond Brothers And The New Pop Scene*, Richard Robinson. *Donny And The Osmonds Backstage*, James Gregory. *The Osmond Story*, George Tremlett. *The Osmonds*, Monica Delaney. *On Tour With Donny & Marie And The Osmonds*, Lynn Roeder. *Donny And Marie Osmond: Breaking All The Rules*, Constance Van Brunt McMillan. *The Osmonds: The Official Story Of The Osmond Family*, Paul H. Dunn. *Donny And Marie*, Patricia Mulrooney Eldred.

OTWAY, JOHN
ALBUMS: with Wild Willy Barrett *John Otway & Wild Willie Barrett* (Polydor 1977)★★★, with Barrett *Deep And Meaningless* (Polydor 1978)★★★, *Where Did I Go Right?* (Polydor 1979)★★★, with Barrett *Way & Bar* (Polydor 1980)★★, with Barrett *I Did It Otway* (Stiff Canada 1981)★★★, *All Balls & No Willy* (Empire 1982)★★, with Barrett *The Wimp And The Wild* (1989)★★, *Under The Covers And Over The Top* (Otway Records 1992)★★, *Live!* (Amazing Feet 1994)★★★, *Premature Adulation* (Amazing Feet 1995)★★★.
COMPILATIONS: with Barrett *Gone With The Bin Or The Best Of Otway & Barrett* (Polydor 1981)★★★, *John Otway's Greatest Hits* (Strike Back 1986)★★★, *Cor Baby That's Really Me!* (Strike Back 1990)★★★★.
VIDEOS: *John Otway And Wild Willie Barrett* (ReVision 1990).
FURTHER READING: *Cor Baby That's Really Me*, John Otway.

OUTLAWS (USA)
ALBUMS: *The Outlaws* (Arista 1975)★★★★, *Lady In Waiting* (Arista 1976)★★★, *Hurry Sundown* (Arista 1977)★★, *Bring It Back Alive* (Arista 1978)★★★, *Playin' To Win* (Arista 1978)★★, *In The Eye Of The Storm* (Arista 1979)★★, *Ghost Riders* (Arista 1980)★★★, *Los Hombres Malo* (Arista 1982)★★, *Soldiers Of Fortune* (Pasha 1986)★★.
COMPILATIONS: *Greatest Hits Of The Outlaws/High Tides Forever* (Arista 1982)★★★★.

OZRIC TENTACLES
ALBUMS: *Erpsongs* cassette only (Dovetail 1985)★★, *Tantric Obstacles* cassette only (Dovetail 1986)★★, *Live Ethereal Cereal* cassette only (Dovetail 1986)★★★, *There Is Nothing* cassette only (Dovetail 1986)★★★, *Sliding Gliding Worlds* cassette only (Dovetail 1988)★★★, *The Bits Between The Bits* cassette only (Dovetail 1989)★★, *Pungent Effulgent* (Dovetail 1989)★★★, *Erpland* (Dovetail 1990)★★★, *Strangeitude* (Dovetail 1991)★★★, *Jurassic Shift* (Dovetail 1993)★★★, *Aborescence* (Dovetail 1994)★★, *Become The Other* (Dovetail 1995)★★, *Curious Corn* (Snapper 1997)★★★.
COMPILATIONS: *Vitamin Enhanced* 6-CD box set of the first six albums (Dovetail 1993)★★★.

P

PAGE, JIMMY
ALBUMS: *Death Wish II* soundtrack (Swan Song 1982)★★, with Roy Harper *Whatever Happened To Jugula* (Beggars Banquet 1985)★★★, *Outrider* (Geffen 1988)★★, with David Coverdale *Coverdale/Page* (EMI 1993)★★★, with Robert Plant *Unledded/No Quarter* (Fontana 1994)★★★★, with Robert Plant *Last Train To Clarksdale* (1998)★★★★, film soundtrack *Godzilla* (1998).
COMPILATIONS: *Jam Session* (Charly 1982)★★, *No Introduction Necessary* (Thunderbolt 1984)★★, *Smoke And Fire* (Thunderbolt 1985)★★.
FURTHER READING: *Mangled Mind Archive: Jimmy Page*, Adrian T'Vell.

PALMER, ROBERT
ALBUMS: *Sneakin' Sally Through The Alley* (Island 1974)★★★, *Pressure Drop* (Island 1975)★★, *Some People Can Do What They Like* (Island 1976)★★, *Double Fun* (Island 1978)★★, *Secrets* (Island 1979)★★, *Clues* (Island 1980)★★, *Maybe It's Live* (Island 1982)★★, *Pride* (Island 1983)★★, *Riptide* (Island 1985)★★★, *Heavy Nova* (EMI 1988)★★★, *Don't Explain* (EMI 1990)★★, *Ridin' High* (EMI 1992)★★, *Honey* (EMI 1994)★★★.
COMPILATIONS: *Addictions, Volume 1* (Island 1989)★★★★, *Addictions, Volume 2* (Island 1992)★★★.
VIDEOS: *Some Guys Have All The Luck* (Palace Video 1984), *Super Nova* (PMI 1989), *Video Addictions* (Polygram 1992), *Robert Palmer: The Very Best Of* (PMI 1995).

PANTERA
ALBUMS: *Metal Magic* (Metal Magic 1983)★★★, *Projects In The Jungle* (Metal Magic 1984)★★★, *I Am The Night* (Metal Magic 1985)★★★, *Power Metal* (Metal Magic 1988)★★, *Cowboys From Hell* (Atco 1990)★★★★, *Vulgar Display Of Power* (Atco 1992)★★, *Far Beyond Driven* (East West 1994)★★★★, *Driven Downunder Tour Tour '94 Souvenir Collection* (East West 1995)★★, *The Great Southern Trendkill* (East West 1996)★★★, *Official Live: 101 Proof* (East West 1997)★★.
VIDEOS: *Vulgar Video* (Warner Vision 1994).

PARADISE LOST
ALBUMS: *Lost Paradise* (Peaceville 1990)★★★, *Gothic* (Peaceville 1991)★★★, *Shades Of God* (Music For Nations 1992)★★★, *Icon* (Music For Nations 1993)★★★★, *Draconian Times* (Music For Nations 1995)★★★★, *One Second* (Music For Nations 1997).
VIDEOS: *Live Death* (1990), *Harmony Breaks* (1994).

PARIS, MICA
ALBUMS: *So Good* (4th & Broadway 1989)★★★, *Contribution* (4th & Broadway 1990)★★, *Whisper A Prayer* (Island 1993).
VIDEOS: *Mica Paris* (Island Visual Arts 1991).

PARKER, GRAHAM
ALBUMS: *Howlin' Wind* (Vertigo 1976)★★★★, *Heat Treatment* (Vertigo 1976)★★★, *Stick To Me* (Vertigo 1977)★★★, *The Parkerilla* (Vertigo 1978)★, *Squeezing Out Sparks* (Vertigo 1979)★★★★, *The Up Escalator* (Stiff 1980)★★★, *Another Grey Area* (RCA 1982)★★★, *The Real Macaw* (RCA 1983)★★★, *Steady Nerves* (Elektra 1985)★★, *Mona Lisa's Sister* (Demon 1988)★★★★, *Human Soul* (Demon 1989)★★★, *Live! Alone In America* (Demon 1989)★★★, *Struck By Lightning* (Demon 1991)★★★, *Burning Questions* (1992)★★★, *Live Alone! Discovering Japan* (1993)★★★, *12 Haunted Episodes* (Razor & Tie 1995)★★★, *Live From New York, NY* (Rock The House 1996)★★★, *Acid Bubblegum* (Razor & Tie 1996)★★★, *BBC Live In Concert* (Strange Fruit 1996)★★★, *Hold Back the Night* (PSM 1998).
COMPILATIONS: *The Best Of Graham Parker And The Rumour* (Vertigo 1980)★★★★.

PARLIAMENT
ALBUMS: *Osmium* (Invictus 1970)★★★, *Up For The Down Stroke* (Casablanca 1974)★★★★, *Chocolate City* (Casablanca 1975)★★★, *Mothership Connection* (Casablanca 1976)★★★★, *The Clones Of Doctor Funkenstein* (Casablanca 1976)★★★★, *Parliament Live – P. Funk Earth Tour* (Casablanca 1977)★★★, *Funkentelechy Vs The Placebo Syndrome* (Casablanca 1977)★★★★, *Motor-Booty Affair* (Casablanca 1978)★★★★, *Gloryhallastoopid (Or Pin The Tale On The Funky)* (Casablanca 1979)★★★, *Trombipulation* (Casablanca 1980)★★★, *Dope Dogs* (Hot Hands 1995)★★★.
COMPILATIONS: *Parliament's Greatest Hits* (Casablanca 1984)★★★★, *Tear The Roof Off 1974-80* (Casablanca 1993)★★★★, *Parliament-Funkadelic Live 1976-93* 4-CD box set (Sequel 1994)★★★★.

PARSONS, ALAN
ALBUMS: *Tales Of Mystery And Imagination* (Charisma 1975)★★★, *I Robot* (Arista 1977)★★★, *Pyramid* (Arista 1978)★★, *Eve* (Arista 1979)★★★, *The Turn Of A Friendly Card* (Arista 1980)★★★, *Eye In The Sky* (Arista 1982)★★★, *Ammonia Avenue* (Arista 1984)★★★, *Vulture Culture* (Arista 1985)★★, *Stereotomy* (Arista 1985)★★, *Gaudi* (Arista 1987)★★, *Try Anything Once* (Arista 1993)★★, *On Air* (Tot 1997)★★.
COMPILATIONS: *The Best Of The Alan Parsons Project* (Arista 1983)★★★, *Limelight – The Best Of The Alan Parsons Project Volume 2* (Arista 1988)★★, *Instrumental Works* (Arista 1988)★★★, *The Definitive Collection* (Arista 1997)★★★.

PARSONS, GRAM
ALBUMS: *G.P.* (Reprise 1972)★★★★, *Grievous Angel* (Reprise 1973)★★★★, *Sleepless Nights* (A&M 1976)★★★, *Gram Parsons And The Fallen Angels – Live 1973* (Sierra 1981)★★, *Cosmic American Music* 1972 demos (Sundown 1995)★★★.
COMPILATIONS: *Gram Parsons* (Warners 1982)★★★, *The Early Years 1963-1965* (Sierra 1984)★★★, *Warm Evenings, Pale Mornings, Bottled Blues* (Raven 1992)★★★.
FURTHER READING: *Gram Parsons: A Music Biography*, Sid Griffin (ed.). *Hickory Wind: The Life And Times Of Gram Parsons*, Ben Fong-Torres.

PARTON, DOLLY
ALBUMS: *Hello, I'm Dolly* (Monument 1967)★★, with Porter Wagoner *Just Between You And Me* (RCA Victor 1968)★★★, with George Jones *Dolly Parton And George Jones* (Starday 1968)★★, *Just Because I'm A Woman* (RCA 1968)★★★, with Wagoner *Just The Two Of Us* (RCA Victor 1968)★★★, with Wagoner *Always, Always* (RCA Victor 1969)★★★, *My Blue Ridge Mountain Boy* (RCA 1969)★★★, with Wagoner *Porter Wayne And Dolly Rebecca* (RCA Victor 1970)★★★, *A Real Live Dolly* (RCA 1970)★★★, with Wagoner *Once More* (RCA Victor 1970)★★★, with Wagoner *Two Of A Kind* (RCA Victor 1971)★★★, *Coat Of Many Colours* (RCA 1971)★★★★, with Wagoner *The Right Combination* (RCA Victor 1972)★★★, with Wagoner *Together Always* (RCA Victor 1972)★★★, with Wagoner *Love And Music* (RCA Victor 1973)★★★, with Wagoner *We Found It* (RCA Victor 1973)★★★, *My Tennessee Mountain Home* (RCA 1973)★★★★, with Wagoner *Porter 'N' Dolly* (RCA 1974)★★★, *Love Is Like A Butterfly* (RCA 1974)★★★★, *Jolene* (RCA 1974)★★★★, with Wagoner *Say Forever You'll Be Mine* (RCA 1975)★★★, *The Bargain Store* (RCA 1975)★★★★, *Dolly* (RCA 1976)★★★, *All I Can Do* (RCA 1976)★★★, *New Harvest ... First Gathering* (RCA 1977)★★★★, *Here You Come Again* (RCA 1977)★★, *Heartbreaker* (RCA 1978)★★, *Dolly Parton And Friends At Goldband* (1979)★★, *Great Balls Of Fire* (RCA 1979)★★, with Wagoner *Porter Wagoner & Dolly Parton* (RCA 1980)★★★★, *Dolly Dolly Dolly* (RCA 1980)★★, *9 To 5 And Odd Jobs* (RCA 1980)★★★, *Heartbreak Express* (RCA 1982)★★, *The Best Little Whorehouse In Texas* film soundtrack (MCA 1982)★★, with Kris Kristofferson, Brenda Lee, Willie Nelson *The Winning Hand* (Monument 1983)★★★, *Burlap And Satin* (RCA 1983)★★, *The Great Pretender* (RCA 1984)★★, *Rhinestone* film soundtrack (RCA 1984)★★, with Kenny Rogers *Once Upon A Christmas* (RCA 1984)★★★, *Real Love* (RCA 1985)★★★, with Linda Ronstadt, Emmylou Harris *Trio* (Warners 1987)★★★, *Rainbow* (Columbia 1987)★★, *White Limozeen* (Columbia 1989)★★★, *Eagle When She Flies* (Columbia 1991)★★★, *Straight Talk* film soundtrack (Hollywood 1992)★★, *Slow Dancing With The Moon* (Columbia 1993)★★★, with Wagoner *Sweet Harmony* (1993)★★, with Tammy Wynette, Loretta Lynn *Honky Tonk Angels* (Columbia 1993)★★★★, *Heartsongs – Live From Home* (Columbia 1994)★★★, *Something Special* (Columbia 1995)★★★, *Treasures* (Rising Tide 1996)★★★.
COMPILATIONS: with Wagoner *The Best Of Porter Wagoner And Dolly Parton* (RCA Victor 1971)★★★★, *The Best Of Dolly Parton* (RCA 1973)★★★★, *The Best Of Dolly Parton Volume 2* (RCA 1975)★★★★, with Wagoner *Hits Of Dolly Parton And Porter Wagoner* (RCA 1977)★★★★, *The Very Best Of Dolly Parton* (RCA 1981)★★★★, *The RCA Years 1967-1986* 2-CD set (RCA 1993)★★★★, with Wagoner *The Essential Porter And Dolly* (RCA 1996)★★★★.
VIDEOS: *Dolly Parton In London* (RCA/Columbia 1988), with Kenny Rogers *Real Love* (RCA/Columbia 1988).
FURTHER READING: *Dolly Parton: Country Goin' To Town*, Susan Saunders. *Dolly Parton*, Otis James. *The Official Dolly Parton Scrapbook*, Connie Berman. *Dolly*, Alanna Nash. *Dolly Parton (By Scott Keely)*, Scott Keely. *Dolly Parton*, Robert K. Krishef. *Dolly, Here I Come Again*, Leonore Fleischer. *My Story*, Dolly Parton.

PAT TRAVERS BAND
ALBUMS: *Pat Travers* (Polydor 1976)★★★, *Makin' Magic* (Polydor 1977)★★★, *Putting It Straight* (Polydor 1977)★★★, *Heat In The Street* (Polydor 1978)★★★, *Go For What You Know* (Polydor 1979)★★★, *Crash And Burn* (Polydor 1980)★★★, *Radio Active* (Polydor 1981)★★★, *Black Pearl* (Polydor 1982)★★★, *Hot Shot* (Polydor 1984)★★★, *School Of Hard Knocks* (Razor 1990)★★★, *Boom Boom* (Essential 1991)★★★, *Just A Touch* (1993)★★★, *Blues Tracks* (1993)★★★, *Blues Magnet* (Provogue 1994)★★★, *Halfway To Somewhere* (Provogue 1995)★★★, *Lookin' Up* (Provogue 1996)★★★.
COMPILATIONS: *Anthology Volume 1* (Polydor 1990)★★★★, *Anthology Volume 2* (Polydor 1990)★★★★.
VIDEOS: *Boom Boom* (1991).

PAUL, LES
ALBUMS: with Mary Ford *Hawaiian Paradise* (Decca 1949)★★, *Galloping Guitars* (Decca 1952)★★★, with Ford *New Sound, Volume 1 & 2* (Capitol 1950)★★★, *Bye, Bye Blues* (Capitol 1952)★★★★, with Ford *The Hitmakers* (Capitol 1955)★★★, with Ford *Les And Mary* (Capitol 1955)★★★★, with Ford *Time To Dream* (Capitol 1957)★★★, *More Of Les* (Decca 1958)★★★, with Ford *Lover's Luau* (Columbia 1959)★★★, with Ford *Warm And Wonderful* (Columbia 1962)★★★, with Ford *Bouquet Of Roses* (Columbia 1962)★★★, with Ford *Swingin' South* (Columbia 1963)★★★, *Les Paul Now* (Decca 1968)★★★, with Chet Atkins *Chester And Lester* (RCA Victor 1976)★★★, with Atkins *Guitar Monsters* (RCA Victor 1978)★★★.
COMPILATIONS: with Ford *The Hits Of Les And Mary* (Capitol 1960)★★★★, *The Very Best Of Les Paul And Mary Ford* (1974)★★★★, with Ford *The Capitol Years* (Capitol 1989)★★★★, *The Legend And The Legacy* 4-CD box set (Capitol 1991)★★★★.
VIDEOS: *He Changed The Music* (Excalibur 1990), *Living Legend Of The Electric Guitar* (BMG 1995).
FURTHER READING: *Les Paul: An American Original*, Mary Alice Shaughnessy. *Gibson Les Paul Book: A Complete History Of Les Paul Guitars*, Tony Bacon and Paul Day.

PAVEMENT
ALBUMS: *Perfect Sound Forever* (Drag City 1991)★★★, *Slanted And Enchanted* (Big Cat 1992)★★★, *Crooked Rain, Crooked Rain* (Big Cat 1994)★★★, *Wowee Zowee!* (Big Cat 1995)★★, *Brighten The Corners* (Matador/Capitol 1997)★★★.
Solo: Gary Young *Hospital* (Big Cat 1995)★★.
COMPILATIONS: *Westing (By Musket And Sextant)* (Big Cat 1993)★★★.

PAXTON, TOM
ALBUMS: *Live At The Gaslight* (Gaslight 1962)★★, *Ramblin' Boy* (Elektra 1964)★★★★, *Ain't That News* (Elektra 1965)★★★, *Outward Bound* (Elektra 1966)★★★, *Morning Again* (Elektra 1968)★★★, *The Things I Notice Now* (Elektra 1969)★★★★, *Tom Paxton 6* (Elektra 1970)★★★, *How Come The Sun* (Reprise 1971)★★★, *Peace Will Come* (1972)★★★, *New Songs Old Friends* (1973)★★★, *Children's Song Book* (1974)★★, *Something In My Life* (1975)★★★, *Saturday Night* (1976)★★★, *New Songs From The Briar Patch* (1977)★★, *Heroes* (1978)★★★, *Up And Up* (1980)★★★, *The Paxton Report* (1981)★★★, *The Marvellous Toy And Other Gallimaufry* (1984)★★, *In The Orchard* (1985)★★★, *One Million Lawyers And Other Disasters* (1985)★★★, *Even A Gray Day* (1986)★★★, *The Marvellous Toy* (1980)★★, *And Loving You* (1988)★★★, *Politics-Live* (1989)★★, *A Car Full Of Songs* (1990)★★★, *Suzy Is A Rocker* (1992)★★★, *Wearing The Time* (Sugar Hill 1995), *Live For The record* (Sugar Hill 1996), *I've Got A Yo-Yo* (Rounder 1997).
COMPILATIONS: *The Compleat Tom Paxton* (Elektra 1971)★★★, *The Very Best Of Tom Paxton* (1988)★★★, *Storyteller* (1989)★★★.
FURTHER READING: *Englebert The Elephant*, Tom Paxton and Steven Kellogg. *Belling The Cat And Other Aesop's Fables*, Tom Paxton and Robert Rayevsky.

PEARL JAM
ALBUMS: *Ten* (Epic 1991)★★★★, *Vs.* (Epic 1993)★★★★, *Vitalogy* (Epic 1994)★★★, *No Code* (Epic 1996)★★★★, *Yield* (Epic 1998).
FURTHER READING: *Pearl Jam: The Illustrated Biography*, Brad Morrell. *Pearl Jam Live!*, Joey Lorenzo (compiler). *The Illustrated Story*, Allan Jones.

PEEBLES, ANN
ALBUMS: *This Is Ann Peebles* (Hi 1969)★★★, *Part Time Love* (Hi 1971)★★★, *Straight From The Heart* (Hi 1972)★★★, *I Can't Stand The Rain* (Hi 1974)★★★★, *Tellin' It* (Hi 1976)★★★, *If This Is Heaven* (Hi 1978)★★★, *The Handwriting On The Wall* (Hi 1979)★★★, *Call Me* (Waylo 1990)★★★, *Full Time Love* (Rounder/Bullseye 1992)★★★, *Fill This World With Love* (Bullseye 1996)★★★.
COMPILATIONS: *I'm Gonna Tear Your Playhouse Down* (Hi 1985)★★★★, *99 lbs* (Hi 1987)★★★, *Greatest Hits* (Hi 1988)★★★★, *Lookin' For A Lovin'* (Hi 1990)★★★, *Straight From The Heart/I Can't Stand The Rain* (1992)★★★, *Tellin' It/If This Is Heaven* (1992)★★★, *This Is Ann Peebles/The Handwriting On The Wall* (1993)★★★, *The Flipside Of ...* (1993)★★★, *U.S. R&B Hits* (1995)★★★.

PENDERGRASS, TEDDY
ALBUMS: *Teddy Pendergrass* (Philadelphia International 1977)★★★, *Life Is A Song Worth Singing* (Philadelphia International 1978)★★★, *Teddy* (Philadelphia International 1979)★★★★, *Teddy Live! (Coast To Coast)* (Philadelphia International 1979)★★, *T.P.* (Philadelphia International 1980)★★★★, *It's Time For Love* (Philadelphia International 1981)★★★, *This One's For You* (Philadelphia International 1982)★★★, *Heaven Only Knows* (Philadelphia International 1983)★★★, *Love Language* (Asylum 1984)★★, *Workin' It Back* (Asylum 1985)★★★, *Joy* (Elektra 1988)★★★, *Truly Blessed* (Elektra 1991)★★★, *Little More Magic* (Elektra 1993)★★★, *You And I* (BMG/Surefire 1997)★★★, *Touch Of Class* (Elektra 1998).
COMPILATIONS: *Greatest Hits* (Philadelphia International 1984)★★★★, *The Philly Years* (Repertoire 1995)★★★★.
VIDEOS: *Teddy Pendergrass Live* (Columbia-Fox 1988).

PENTANGLE
ALBUMS: *The Pentangle* (Transatlantic 1968)★★★★, *Sweet Child* (Transatlantic 1968)★★★★, *Basket Of Light* (Transatlantic 1969)★★★★, *Cruel Sister* (Transatlantic 1970)★★★, *Solomon's Seal* (Reprise 1972)★★★, *Open The Door* (Making Waves 1982)★★★, *In The Round* (Making Waves 1988)★★★, *So Early In The Spring* (1988)★★★, *Think Of Tomorrow* (1991)★★★, *One More Road* (1993)★★★, *Live At The BBC* (Strange Fruit 1994)★★★★, *Live 1994* (Hypertension 1995).
COMPILATIONS: *Reflections* (Transatlantic 1971)★★★★, *History Book* (Transatlantic 1971)★★★★, *Pentangling* (Transatlantic 1973)★★★★, *The Pentangle Collection* (1975)★★★★, *Anthology* (1978)★★★★, *The Essential Pentangle Volume 1* (Transatlantic 1987)★★★★, *The Essential Pentangle Volume 2* (Transatlantic 1987)★★★, *People On The Highway 1968 – 1971* (Demon 1993)★★★★.

PERE UBU
ALBUMS: *The Modern Dance* (Blank 1977)★★★★, *Dub Housing* (Chrysalis 1978)★★★★, *New Picnic Time* (Rough Trade 1979)★★★, *The Art Of Walking* (Rough Trade 1980)★★★, *390 Degrees Of Simulated Stereo – Ubu Live: Volume 1* (Rough Trade 1981)★★★, *Song Of The Bailing Man* (Rough Trade 1982)★★, *The Tenement Year* (Enigma 1988)★★★, *One Man Drives While The Other Man Screams – Live Volume 2: Pere Ubu On Tour* (Rough Trade 1989)★★, *Cloudland* (Fontana 1989)★★★, *Worlds In Collision* (Fontana 1991)★★★, *Ray Gun Suitcase* (Cooking Vinyl 1995)★★★, *Pennsylvania* (Tim Kerr 1998).
COMPILATIONS: *Terminal Tower: An Archival Collection* (Twin/Tone 1985)★★★★, *Datapanik In The Year Zero* (Cooking Vinyl 1996)★★★★.

PERKINS, CARL
ALBUMS: *The Dance Album Of Carl Perkins* (Sun 1957)★★★★, *Whole Lotta Shakin'* (Columbia 1958)★★★, *Country Boy Dreams* (Dollie 1968)★★★, *Blue Suede Shoes* (Sun 1969)★★★, *On Top* (Columbia 1969)★★★, with the NRBQ *Boppin' The Blues* (Columbia 1970)★★★, *My Kind Of Country* (Mercury 1973)★★★, *Carl Perkins Show* (1976)★★★, *From Jackson, Tennessee* (1977)★★★, *Ol' Blue Suede's Back* (Jet 1978)★★★, with Jerry Lee Lewis, Johnny Cash *The Survivors* (Columbia 1982)★★★, *The Heart And Soul Of Carl Perkins* (Allegience 1984)★★★, with Jerry Lee Lewis, Johnny Cash, Roy Orbison *The Class Of '55* (1986)★★★, *Born To Rock* (Universal/MCA 1989)★★★, *Friends, Family & Legends* (1992)★★★, with Scotty Moore *706 Reunion-A Sentimental Journey* (1993)★★★, *Hound Dog* (Muskateer 1995)★★★, with various artists *Go Cat Go!* (BMG 1996)★★★.
COMPILATIONS: *Carl Perkins Greatest Hits* (Columbia 1969)★★★, *The Sun Years* 3-LP box set (Sun 1982)★★★★, *Up Through The Years, 1954-1957* (Bear Family 1986)★★★★, *Original Sun Greatest Hits* (Rhino 1986)★★★, *Jive After Five: Best Of Carl Perkins (1958-1978)* (Rhino 1990)★★★, *The Classic Carl Perkins* 5-CD box set (Bear Family 1990)★★★★, *Restless: The Columbia Recordings* (Columbia 1992)★★★, *Country Boy's Dream: The Dollie Masters* (Bear Family 1994)★★★.
FILMS: *Jamboree a.k.a. Disc Jockey Jamboree* (1957).
VIDEOS: *Rockabilly Session* (Virgin Vision 1986), *Carl Perkins & Jerry Lee Lewis Live* (BBC Video 1987), *This Country's Rockin'* (1993).
FURTHER READING: *Discipline In Blue Suede Shoes*, Carl Perkins. *Go, Cat, Go: Life And Times Of Carl Perkins The King Of Rockabilly*, Carl Perkins with David McGee.

PERRY, LEE
ALBUMS: As Lee Perry/Lee Perry And The Upsetters: *The Upsetter* (Trojan 1969)★★★★, *Many Moods Of The Upsetter* (1970)★★★, *Scratch The Upsetter Again* (1970)★★★★, with Dave Barker *Prisoner Of Love: Dave Barker Meets The Upsetters* (Trojan 1970), *Africa's Blood* (1972)★★★, *Battle Axe* (1972)★★★, *Cloak & Dagger* (Rhino 1972)★★★, *Double Seven* (Trojan 1973)★★★, *Rhythm Shower* (Upsetter 1973)★★★★, *Blackboard Jungle* (Upsetter 1974)★★★★, *Kung Fu Meets The Dragon* (D.I.P. 1974)★★★, *D.I.P. Presents The Upsetter* (D.I.P. 1974)★★★, *Revolution Dub* (Cactus 1975)★★★★, *The Super Ape* (Mango/Island 1976)★★★, with Jah Lion as producer *Colombia Colly* (Mango/Island 1976)★★★, with Prince Jazzbo *Natty Passing Through* (Black Wax 1976) aka *Ital Corner* (Clocktower 1980), *Return Of The Super Ape* (Lion Of Judah/Mango 1977)★★★, *Roast Fish, Collie Weed & Corn Bread* (Lion Of Judah 1978)★★★, *Scratch On The Wire* (Island 1979)★★★, *Scratch And Company: Chapter 1* (Clocktower 1980)★★★, *Return Of Pipecock Jackson* (Black Star 1981)★★★, *Mystic Miracle Star* (Heartbeat 1982)★★★, *History Mystery & Prophecy* (Mango/Island 1984)★★★, *Black Ark Vol. 1 & 2* (Black Ark 1984)★★★, *Black Ark In Dub* (Black Ark 1985)★★★, *Battle Of Armagideon: Millionaire Liquidator* (Trojan 1986)★★★, with Dub Syndicate *Time Boom X De Devil Dead* (On-U-Sound 1987)★★★, *Satan Kicked The Bucket* (Wackies 1988)★★★, *Scratch Attack* (RAS 1988)★★★, *Chicken Scratch* (Heartbeat 1989)★★★, *Turn And Fire* (Anachron 1989)★★★, with Bullwackie *Lee 'Scratch' Perry Meets Bullwackie – Satan's Dub* (ROIR 1990)★★★, *Build The Ark* (Trojan 1990)★★★, *From The Secret Laboratory* (Mango/Island 1990)★★★, *Message From Yard* (Rohit 1990)★★★, *Blood Vapour* (La/Unicorn 1990)★★★, with Mad Professor *Lee Scratch Perry Meets The Mad Professor, Volumes 1 & 2* (Ariwa 1990)★★★, *Spiritual Healing* (Black Cat 1991)★★★, *God Muzick* (Network/Kook Kat 1991)★★★, *The Upsetter And The Beat* (Heartbeat 1992)★★★, *Soundz From The Hot Line* (Heartbeat 1993)★★★, *Magnetic Mirror Master Mix* (Anachron 1990)★★★, with Mad Professor *Lee 'Scratch' Perry Meets The Mad Professor In Dub, Volumes 1 & 2* (Angella 1991)★★★, *Scratch And The Upsetters Again* (Trojan 1995)★★★.
COMPILATIONS: *The Upsetter Collection* (Trojan 1981)★★★★, *Reggae Greats* (Island 1984)★★★, *Best Of* (Pama 1984)★★★★, *The Upsetter Box Set* (Trojan 1985)★★★★, *The Upsetter Compact Set* (1988)★★★★, *All The Hits* (Rohit 1989)★★★★. As Lee Perry And Friends *Give Me Power* (Trojan 1988)★★★, *Open The Gate* (Trojan 1989)★★★, *Shocks Of Mighty 1969-1974* (Attack 1989)★★★, *Public Jestering* (Attack 1990). As the Upsetters *Version Like Rain* (Trojan 1990). Various: *Heart Of The Ark, Volume 1* (Seven Leaves 1982)★★★, *Heart Of The Ark, Volume 2* (Seven Leaves 1983)★★★, *Turn & Fire: Upsetter Disco Dub* (1989)★★★, *Megaton Dub* (Seven Leaves 1983)★★★, *Megaton Dub 2* (Seven Leaves 1983)★★★, *Arkology* 3-CD box set (Island/Chronicles 1997)★★★★★.
VIDEOS: *The Ultimate Destruction* (1992).

PET SHOP BOYS
ALBUMS: *Please* (Parlophone 1986)★★★, *Disco* (Parlophone 1986)★★★, *Actually* (Parlophone 1987)★★★★, *Introspective* (Parlophone 1988)★★★, *Behaviour* (Parlophone 1990)★★★★, *Very* (Parlophone 1993)★★★, *Alternative* (Parlophone 1995)★★★, *Bilingual* (Parlophone 1996)★★★, *Bilingual Remixed* (Parlophone 1997).
COMPILATIONS: *Discography* (Parlophone 1991)★★★★.

VIDEOS: *On Tour* (PMI 1990), *Performance* (PMI 1993), *Projections* (1993), *Various* (PMI 1994), *Discovery: Live In Rio* (PMI 1995).
FURTHER READING: *Pet Shop Boys, Literally*, Chris Heath. *Pet Shop Boys: Introspective*, Michael Crowton. *Pet Shop Boys Versus America*, Chris Heath and Pennie Smith.

PETER AND GORDON
ALBUMS: *Peter And Gordon* (Columbia 1964)★★★, *A World Without Love* (Capitol 1964)★★★, *In Touch With Peter And Gordon* (Columbia 1964)★★★, *I Don't Want To See You Again* (Capitol 1965)★★★, *I Go To Pieces* (Columbia 1965)★★★, *True Love Ways* (Capitol 1965)★★★, *Hurtin' 'N' Lovin'* (Columbia 1965)★★★, *Sing The Hits Of Nashville* (Capitol 1966)★★, *Woman* (Columbia 1966)★★★, *Somewhere* (Columbia 1966)★★★, *Lady Godiva* (Columbia 1967)★★, *A Knight In Rusty Armour* (Capitol 1967)★★, *In London For Tea* (Capitol 1967)★★, *Hot, Cold And Custard* (Capitol 1968)★★.
COMPILATIONS: *Peter And Gordon's Greatest Hits* (Columbia 1966)★★★, *The Best Of Peter And Gordon* (1983)★★★, *Hits And More* (1986)★★★, *The EP Collection* (See For Miles 1996)★★★.

PETER, PAUL AND MARY
ALBUMS: *Peter, Paul And Mary* (Warners 1962)★★★★, *Peter, Paul And Mary – Moving* (Warners 1963)★★★★, *In The Wind* (Warners 1963)★★★★, *Peter, Paul And Mary In Concert* (Warners 1964)★★★★, *A Song Will Rise* (Warners 1965)★★★, *See What Tomorrow Brings* (Warners 1965)★★★, *Peter, Paul And Mary Album* (Warners 1966)★★★, *Album 1700* (1967)★★★, *Late Again* (Warners 1968)★★★, *Peter, Paul And Mommy* (1969)★★, *Reunion* (1978)★★★, *Such Is Love* (1982)★★, *No Easy Walk To Freedom* (1988)★★, *LifeLines Live* (Warners 1996)★★. Solo: Peter Yarrow *Peter* (1972)★★, *That's Enough For Me* (1973)★★, *Hard Times* (1975). Paul Stookey *Paul And* (1971)★★, *Band And Body Works* (1980). Mary Travers *Mary* (1971)★★, *Morning Glory* (1972)★★, *All My Choices* (1973)★★, *Circles* (1974)★★, *It's In Everyone Of Us* (1978)★★.
COMPILATIONS: *10 Years Together/The Best Of Peter, Paul And Mary* (1970)★★★★, *Most Beautiful Songs* (1973)★★★, *Collection* (1982)★★★.
VIDEOS: *Lifelines* (Warner Reprise 1996).

PETTY, TOM, AND THE HEARTBREAKERS
ALBUMS: *Tom Petty And The Heartbreakers* (Shelter 1976)★★★, *You're Gonna Get It* (Shelter 1978)★★★★, *Damn The Torpedoes* (MCA 1979)★★★★, *Hard Promises* (MCA 1981)★★★, *Long After Dark* (MCA 1982)★★★, *Southern Accents* (MCA 1985)★★★★, *Pack Up The Plantation: Live!* (MCA 1985)★★★, *Let Me Up (I've Had Enough)* (MCA 1987)★★★, Tom Petty solo *Full Moon Fever* (MCA 1989)★★★, *Into The Great Wide Open* (MCA 1991)★★★, *Wildflowers* (Warners 1994)★★★★, *She's The One* (Warners 1996)★★★.
COMPILATIONS: *Greatest Hits* (MCA 1993)★★★★, *Playback* 6-CD box set (MCA 1995)★★★★.
VIDEOS: *Playback* (MCA Music Video 1995).

PHAIR, LIZ
ALBUMS: *Exile In Guyville* (Matador 1993)★★★, *Whip-Smart* (Matador 1994)★★★, *Juvenilia* (Matador 1995)★★, *whitechocolatespaceegg* (Matador 1998)★★★

PhD
ALBUMS: *PhD* (Warners 1981)★★, *Is It Safe ?* (Warners 1983)★★, *Slip Stitch & Pass* (Elektra 1997).

PHISH
ALBUMS: *Junta* (Own Label 1988)★★, *Lawn Boy* (Absolute A Go Go 1990)★★★, *A Picture Of Nectar* (Elektra 1992)★★★, *Rift* (Elektra 1993)★★★, *Hoist* (Elektra 1994)★★★, *A Live One* (Elektra 1995)★★★★, *Billy Breathes* (Elektra 1996)★★★★.
COMPILATIONS: *Stash* (Elektra 1996)★★★.
FURTHER READING: *The Phishing Manual*, Dean Budnick.

PICKETT, BOBBY 'BORIS'
ALBUMS: *The Original Monster Mash* (Garpax 1962)★★.

PICKETT, WILSON
ALBUMS: *It's Too Late* (Double-L 1963)★★, *In The Midnight Hour* (Atlantic 1965)★★★★, *The Exciting Wilson Pickett* (Atlantic 1966)★★★★, *The Wicked Pickett* (Atlantic 1966)★★★★, *The Sound Of Wilson Pickett* (Atlantic 1967)★★★★, *I'm In Love* (Atlantic 1968)★★★, *The Midnight Mover* (Atlantic 1968)★★★, *Hey Jude* (Atlantic 1969)★★★, *Right On* (Atlantic 1970)★★★, *Wilson Pickett In Philadelphia* (Atlantic 1970)★★★, *If You Need Me* (Joy 1970)★★, *Don't Knock My Love* (Atlantic 1971)★★, *Mr. Magic Man* (RCA 1973)★★, *Miz Lena's Boy* (RCA 1973)★★, *Tonight I'm My Biggest Audience* (RCA 1974)★★, *Live In Japan* (1974)★★, *Pickett In Pocket* (RCA 1974)★★, *Join Me & Let's Be Free* (RCA 1975)★★, *Chocolate Mountain* (Wicked 1976)★★, *A Funky Situation* (Wicked 1978)★★, *I Want You* (EMI America 1979)★★, *The Right Track* (EMI America 1981)★★, *American Soul Man* (Motown 1987)★★.
COMPILATIONS: *The Best Of Wilson Pickett* (Atlantic 1967)★★★★, *The Best Of Wilson Pickett Vol. 2* (Atlantic 1971)★★★★, *Wilson Pickett's Greatest Hits I* (Atlantic 1973)★★★★, *Collection* (Castle 1992)★★★, *A Man And A Half: The Best Of Wilson Pickett* (Rhino/Atlantic 1992)★★★★★.

PINE, COURTNEY
ALBUMS: *Journey To The Urge Within* (Island 1986)★★, *Destiny's Song And The Image Of Pursuance* (Island 1988)★★, *The Vision's Tale* (Island 1989)★★★, *Within The Realms Of Our Dreams* (Island 1991)★★★, *Closer To Home* (Island 1992)★★★, *To The Eyes Of Creation* (Island 1992)★★★, *Modern Day Jazz Stories* (Verve/Talkin' Loud 1996)★★, *Underground* (Polygram 1997).

PINK FLOYD
ALBUMS: *The Piper At The Gates Of Dawn* (EMI Columbia 1967)★★★, *A Saucerful Of Secrets* (EMI Columbia 1968)★★★★, *More* film soundtrack (EMI Columbia 1969)★★, *Ummagumma* (Harvest 1969)★★★, *Atom Heart Mother* (Harvest 1970)★★★, *Meddle* (Harvest 1971)★★★★, *Obscured By Clouds* film soundtrack (Harvest 1972)★★, *Dark Side Of The Moon* (Harvest 1973)★★★★★, *Wish You Were Here* (Harvest 1975)★★★★, *Animals* (Harvest 1977)★★★★, *The Wall* (Harvest 1979)★★★★, *The Final Cut* (Harvest 1983)★★, *A Momentary Lapse Of Reason* (EMI 1987)★★★, *Delicate Sound Of Thunder* (EMI 1988)★★★, *The Division Bell* (EMI 1994)★★★, *Pulse* (EMI 1995)★★. Solo: Rick Wright *Wet Dream* Harvest 1978)★★, with Dave Harris *Zee* (Harvest 1984)★★, *Broken China* (EMI 1996)★★, *Pulse Live* (Columbia 1995).
COMPILATIONS: *Relics* (Harvest 1971)★★★★, *A Nice Pair* (Harvest 1974)★★★★, *First Eleven* 11-LP box set (EMI 1977)★★★, *Works* (Capitol 1983)★★★, *Shine On* 8-CD box set (EMI 1992)★★★.
VIDEOS: *Pink Floyd: London '66-'67* (See For Miles 1994), *Delicate Sound Of Thunder* (Columbia 1994), *Live At Pompeii* (4 Front 1995), *Pulse: 20.10.94* (PMI 1995).
FURTHER READING: *The Pink Floyd*, Rick Sanders. *Pink Floyd*, Jean Marie Leduc. *Pink Floyd: The Illustrated Discography*, Miles. *The Wall*, Roger Waters and David Appleby. *Syd Barrett: The Making Of The Madcap Laughs*, Malcom Jones. *Pink Floyd: Another Brick*, Miles. *Pink Floyd: A Visual Documentary*, Miles and Andy Mabbett. *Pink Floyd: Bricks In The Wall*, Karl Dallas. *Saucerful Of Secrets: The Pink Floyd Odyssey*, Nicholas Schaffner. *Pink Floyd Back-Stage*, Bob Hassall. *Pink Floyd*, W. Ruhlmann. *Complete Guide To The Music Of*, Andy Mabbett. *Pink Floyd Through The Eyes Of ... The Band, Its Fans, Friends And Foes*, Bruno MacDonald (ed).

PITNEY, GENE
ALBUMS: *The Many Sides Of Gene Pitney* (Musicor 1962)★★★, *Only Love Can Break A Heart* (Musicor 1962)★★★, *Gene Pitney Sings Just For You* (Musicor 1963)★★★, *Gene Pitney Sings World-Wide Winners* (Musicor 1963)★★★, *Blue Gene* (Musicor 1963)★★★★, *Gene Pitney Meets The Fair Young Ladies Of Folkland* (Musicor 1964)★★, *Gene Italiano* (Musicor 1964)★★, *It Hurts To Be In Love* (Musicor 1964)★★★, *For The First Time Ever! Two Great Singers* (with George Jones, Musicor 1965)★★, *I Must Be Seeing Things* (Musicor 1965)★★★★, *It's Country Time Again!* (Musicor 1965)★★★, *Espanol* (Musicor 1965)★★, *Being Together* (Musicor 1965)★★, *Famous Country Duets* (Musicor 1965)★★, *Backstage (I'm Lonely)* (Musicor 1966)★★★, *Messumo Mi Puo Guidicare* (Musicor 1966)★★, *The Gene Pitney Show* (Musicor 1966)★★★, *The Country Side Of Gene Pitney* (Musicor 1966)H, *Young And Warm And Wonderful* (Musicor 1966)★★★★, *Just One Smile* (Musicor 1967)★★★★, *Sings Burt Bacharach* (Musicor 1968)★★, *She's A Heartbreaker* (Musicor 1968)★★, *This Is Gene Pitney* (Musicor 1970)★★, *Ten Years After* (Musicor 1971)★★, *Pitney Today* (1968)★★, *Pitney '75* (1975)★★, *Walkin' In The Sun* (1979)★★.
COMPILATIONS: *Big Sixteen* (Musicor 1964)★★★★, *More Big Sixteen, Volume 2* (Musicor 1965)★★★, *Big Sixteen, Volume 3* (Musicor 1966)★★★, *Greatest Hits Of All Time* (Musicor 1966)★★★, *Golden Greats* (Musicor 1967)★★★, *Spotlight On Gene Pitney* (Design 1967)★★★, *The Gene Pitney Story* double album (Musicor 1968)★★★, *The Greatest Hits Of Gene Pitney* (Musicor 1969)★★★, *The Man Who Shot Liberty Valance* (Music Disc 1969)★★★, *Town Without Pity* (Music Disc 1969)★★★, *Twenty Four Hours From Tulsa* (Music Disc 1969)★★★, *Baby I Need Your Lovin'* (Music Disc 1969)★★★, *The Golden Hits Of Gene Pitney* (Musicor 1971)★★★, *The Fabulous Gene Pitney* double album (Columbia 1972)★★★, *The Pick Of Gene Pitney* (West-52 1979)★★★, *Anthology 1961-68* (Rhino 1987)★★★, *Best Of* (K-Tel 1988)★★★, *All The Hits* (Jet 1990)★★★, *Greatest Hits* (Pickwick 1991)★★★, *The Original Hits 1961-70* (Jet 1991)★★★, *The EP Collection* (See For Miles 1991)★★★, *The Heartbreaker* (Repertoire 1994)★★★, *More Greatest Hits* (Varese Sarabande 1995)★★★, *The Gold Collection: 15 Classic Hits* (Summit 1996)★★★, *The Great Recordings* (Tomato 1996)★★★, *The Definitive Collection* (Charly 1997)★★★.

PIXIES
ALBUMS: *Come On Pilgrim* (4AD 1987)★★★, *Surfer Rosa* (4AD 1988)★★★★, *Doolittle* (4AD 1989)★★★★★, *Bossanova* (4AD 1990)★★★, *Trompe Le Monde* (4AD 1991)★★★.
COMPILATIONS: *Death To The Pixies 1987-1991* (4AD 1997)★★★★.

PIZZICATO FIVE
ALBUMS: *Made In USA* (Matador 1995)★★★★, *The Sound Of Music By Pizzicato Five* (Matador 1995)★★★★, *Romantique '96* (Japanese Columbia/Triad 1995)★★★, *The Sound Of Music* (Matador 1996)★★, *Sister Freedom Tapes* (Matador 1996)★★, *Happy End Of The World* (Capitol 1997), *Flow Hyphenated Drop* (Matador 1998).

P. J. HARVEY
ALBUMS: *Dry* (Too Pure 1992)★★★★, *Demonstration* 'demo' album given away with initial copies of *Dry* (Too Pure 1992)★★★, *Rid Of Me* (Island 1993)★★★★, *4-Track Demos* (Island 1993)★★, *To Bring You My Love* (Island 1995)★★★★, *B-Sides* (Island 1995)★★, with John Parish *Dance Hall At Louse Point* (Island 1996)★★★.
VIDEOS: *Reeling* (Polygram 1994).

PLANT, ROBERT
ALBUMS: *Pictures At Eleven* (Swan Song 1982)★★★, *The Principle Of Moments* (Swan Song 1983)★★, *Shaken 'N' Stirred* (Esparanza 1985)★★, *Now And Zen* (Esparanza 1989)★★★, *Manic Nirvana* (Atlantic 1990)★★★, *Fate Of Nations* (Fontana 1993)★★★, with Jimmy Page *No Quarter* (Fontana 1994)★★★★, with Jimmy Page *Last Train To Clarksdale* (1998)★★★★.
VIDEOS: *Knebworth 90* (1990), *Mumbo Jumbo* (1991).
FURTHER READING: *Robert Plant*, Michael Gross. *Led Zeppelin's Robert Plant Through The Mirror*, Mike Randolph.

PLANXTY
ALBUMS: *Planxty* (Polydor 1972)★★★, *The Well Below The Valley* (Polydor 1973)★★★, *Cold Blow And The Rainy Night* (Polydor 1974)★★★, *After The Break* (Tara 1979)★★★, *The Woman I Loved So Well* (Tara 1980)★★★, *Timedance* (1981)★★★, *Words And Music* (1983)★★★.
COMPILATIONS: *The Planxty Collection* (Polydor 1976)★★★★.

PLATTERS
ALBUMS: *The Platters* (Federal 1955)★★★★, also released on King as *Only You* and Mercury labels, *The Platters, Volume 2* (Mercury 1956)★★★★, *The Flying Platters* (Mercury 1957)★★★, *The Platters On Parade* (Mercury 1959)★★★, *Flying Platters Around The World* (Mercury 1959)★★★, *Remember When* (Mercury 1959)★★★, *Reflections* (Mercury 1960)★★★, *Encore Of Golden Hits* (Mercury 1960)★★★, *More Encore Of Golden Hits* (Mercury 1960)★★★, *The Platters* (Mercury 1960)★★★, *Life Is Just A Bowl Of Cherries* (Mercury 1961)★★★, *The Platters Sing For The Lonely* (Mercury 1962)★★★, *Encore Of The Golden Hits Of The Groups* (Mercury 1962)★★★, *Moonlight Memories* (Mercury 1963)★★★, *Platters Sing All The Movie Hits* (Mercury 1963)★★, *Platters Sing Latino* (Mercury 1963)★★, *Christmas With The Platters* (Mercury 1963)★★★, *New Soul Campus Style Of The Platters* (Mercury 1965)★★, *I Love You 1000 Times* (Musicor 1966)★★, *Going Back To Detroit* (Stateside 1967)★★★, *I Get The Sweetest Feeling* (1968)★★★, *Sweet Sweet Lovin'* (1968)★★, *Our Way* (Pye International 1971)★★★, *Encore Of Broadway Golden Hits* (1972)★★★, *Live* (1974)★★.
COMPILATIONS: *The Original Platters – 20 Classic Hits* (Mercury 1978)★★★★, *Platterama* (Mercury 1982)★★★★, *The Platters: Anthology* (Rhino 1986)★★★★, *Smoke Gets In Your Eyes* (Charly 1991)★★★★, *Magic Touch: An Anthology* (Polygram 1992)★★★★, *Greatest Hits* (1993)★★★★.
FILMS: *Carnival Rock* (1957), *Girl's Town* aka *The Innocent And The Damned* (1959).

PM DAWN
ALBUMS: *Of The Heart, Of The Soul, Of The Cross, The Utopean Experience* (Gee St 1991)★★★, *The Bliss Album ...? (Vibrations Of Love & Anger & The Ponderance Of Life & Existence)* (Island 1993)★★★★, *Jesus Wept* (Gee Street/Island 1996)★★★.

POCO
ALBUMS: *Pickin' Up The Pieces* (Epic 1969)★★★, *Poco* (Epic 1970)★★★, *Deliverin'* (Epic 1971)★★★, *From The Inside* (Epic 1971)★★★, *A Good Feelin' To Know* (Epic 1972)★★★★, *Crazy Eyes* (Epic 1973)★★★, *Seven* (Epic 1974)★★★, *Cantamos* (Epic 1974)★★, *Head Over Heels* (ABC 1975)★★★, *Live* (Epic 1976)★★, *Rose Of Cimarron* (ABC 1976)★★★, *Indian Summer* (ABC 1977)★★★, *Legend* (ABC 1978)★★★, *Under The Gun* (MCA 1980)★★, *Blue And Gray* (MCA 1981)★★, *Cowboys And Englishmen* (MCA 1982)★★, *Ghost Town* (Atlantic 1982)★★, *Inamorata* (Atlantic 1984)★★★, *Legacy* (RCA 1989)★★★.
COMPILATIONS: *The Very Best Of Poco* (Epic 1975)★★★, *Songs Of Paul Cotton* (Epic 1980)★★★, *Songs Of Richie Furay* (Epic 1980)★★★, *Backtracks* (MCA 1983)★★★, *Crazy Loving: The Best Of Poco 1975-1982* (RCA 1989)★★★, *Poco: The Forgotten Trail 1969-1974* (Epic/Legacy 1990)★★★★.

POGUES
ALBUMS: *Red Roses For Me* (Stiff 1984)★★★, *Rum, Sodomy And The Lash* (Stiff 1985)★★★★, *If I Should Fall From Grace With God* (Stiff 1988)★★★★, *Peace And Love* (Warners 1989)★★★, *Hell's Ditch* (Pogue Mahone 1990)★★★, *Waiting For Herb* (PM 1993)★★, *Pogue Mahone* (Warners 1995)★★.
COMPILATIONS: *The Best Of The Pogues* (PM 1991)★★★, *The Rest Of The Best* (PM 1992)★★★.
VIDEOS: *Completely Pogued* (Start 1991), *Poguevision* (Warners 1991).
FURTHER READING: *The Pogues: The Lost Decade*, Ann Scanlon. *Poguetry: The Illustrated Pogues Songbook*, Hewitt McGowan and Pike.

POINTER SISTERS
ALBUMS: *The Pointer Sisters* (Blue Thumb 1973)★★★, *That's A Plenty* (Blue Thumb 1974)★★, *Live At The Opera House* (Blue Thumb 1974)★★, *Steppin'* (Blue Thumb 1975)★★, *Havin' A Party* (Blue Thumb 1977)★★, *Energy* (Planet 1978)★★★, *Priority* (Planet 1979)★★★, *Special Things* (Planet 1980)★★★, *Black And White* (Planet 1981)★★★, *So Excited!* (Planet 1982)★★★, *Break Out* (Planet 1983)★★★, *Contact* (RCA 1985)★★★, *Hot Together* (RCA 1986)★★, *Serious Slammin'* (RCA 1988)★★, *Right Rhythm* (Motown 1990)★★, *Only Sisters Can Do That* (1993)★★.
Solo: Anita Pointer *Love For What It Is* (RCA 1987)★★. June Pointer *Baby Sitter* (Planet 1983)★★.
COMPILATIONS: *The Best Of The Pointer Sisters* (Blue Thumb 1976)★★★★, *Pointer Sisters' Greatest Hits* (Planet 1982)★★★, *– The Best Of The Pointer Sisters* (RCA 1989)★★★★, *The Collection* (1993)★★★.

POISON
ALBUMS: *Look What The Cat Dragged In* (Enigma 1986)★★★, *Open Up And Say ... Ahh!* (Capitol 1988)★★★★, *Flesh And Blood* (Capitol 1990)★★★★, *Native Tongue* (Capitol 1993)★★★.
COMPILATIONS: *Greatest Hits* (Capitol 1997)★★★.
VIDEOS: *Sight For Sore Ears, A* (1990), *Flesh, Blood And Videotape* (1991), *7 Days Live* (1994).

POLICE
ALBUMS: *Outlandos D'Amour* (A&M 1978)★★★★, *Regatta De Blanc* (A&M 1979)★★★★, *Zenyatta Mondatta* (A&M 1980)★★★, *Ghost In The Machine* (A&M 1981)★★★★, *Synchronicity* (A&M 1983)★★★★, *Live!* rec. 1979 (A&M 1996)★★.
COMPILATIONS: *Every Breath You Take – The Singles* (A&M 1986)★★★★, *Greatest Hits* (A&M 1992)★★★★, *The Best Of Sting/The Police* (A&M 1997)★★★★.
VIDEOS: *Outlandos To Synchronicities: A History Of The Police* (1995).
FURTHER READING: *The Police Released*, no editor listed. *Message In A Bottle*, Rossetta Woolf. *The Police: L'Historia Bandido*, Phil Sutcliffe and Hugh Fielder. *The Police: A Visual Documentary*, Miles. *The Police*, Lynn Goldsmith. *Complete Guide To The Music Of The Police And Sting*, Chris Welch.

POOLE, BRIAN, AND THE TREMELOES
ALBUMS: *Twist And Shout With Brian Poole And The Tremeloes* (Decca 1963)★★★, *Big Hits Of '62* (Ace of Clubs 1963)★, *It's About Time* (Decca 1965)★★★.
COMPILATIONS: *Remembering Brian Poole And The Tremeloes* (Decca 1977)★★★, *Twist And Shout* (Decca 1982)★★★, *Do You Love Me* (Deram 1991)★★★.
FURTHER READING: *Talkback: An Easy Guide To British Slang*, Brian Poole.

POP, IGGY
ALBUMS: with the Stooges *The Stooges* (Elektra 1969)★★★★, with the Stooges *Fun House* (Elektra 1970)★★★★, as Iggy And The Stooges *Raw Power* (Columbia 1973)★★★★, as Iggy And The Stooges *Metallic KO* (Import 1974)★★, *The Idiot* (RCA 1977)★★★★, *Lust For Life* (RCA 1977)★★★★, with James Williamson *Kill City* (Bomp 1978)★★★, *TV Eye Live* (RCA 1978)★★, *New Values* (Arista 1979)★★, *Soldier* (Arista 1980)★★, *Party* (Arista 1981)★★, *Zombie Birdhouse* (Animal 1982)★★, *Blah Blah Blah* (A&M 1986)★★★, *Instinct* (A&M 1988)★★, *Brick By Brick* (Virgin 1990)★★★, *American Caesar* (Virgin 1993)★★★, *Naughty Little Doggie* (Virgin 1996)★★★, *Heroin Hates You* (Other People's 1997)★★.
COMPILATIONS: *Choice Cuts* (RCA 1984)★★★, *Compact Hits* (A&M 1988)★★★, *Nude & Rude: The Best Of ...* (Virgin 1996)★★★★, *Pop Music* (BMG/Camden 1996)★★.
FURTHER READING: *The Lives And Crimes Of Iggy Pop*, Mike West. *I Need More: The Stooges And Other Stories*, Iggy Pop with Anne Wehrer. *Iggy Pop: The Wild One*, Per Nilsen and Dorothy Sherman.

POP WILL EAT ITSELF
ALBUMS: *Box Frenzy* (Chapter 22 1987)★★, *Now For A Feast!* early recordings (Rough Trade 1989)★★★, *This Is The Day, This Is The Hour, This Is This!* (RCA 1989)★★★, *The Pop Will Eat Itself Cure For Sanity* (RCA 1990)★★, *The Looks Or The Lifestyle* (RCA 1992)★★★, *Weird's Bar & Grill* (RCA 1993)★★, *Dos Dedos Mes Amigos* (Infectious 1994)★★★, *Two Fingers My Friends!* remixes (Infectious 1995)★★★.
COMPILATIONS: *There Is No Love Between Us Anymore* (Chapter 22 1992)★★★, *16 Different Flavours Of Hell* (RCA/BMG 1993)★★★, *Wise Up Suckers* (BMG 1996)★★★.

PORNO FOR PYROS
ALBUMS: *Porno For Pyros* (Warners 1993)★★★, *Good God's Urge* (Warners 1996)★★★.
FURTHER READING: *Perry Farrell: Saga Of A Hypster*, Dave Thompson.

PORTISHEAD
ALBUMS: *Dummy* (Go! Beat 1994)★★★★, *Portishead* (Go! Beat 1997)★★★★.

POSIES
ALBUMS: *Failure* (23 1988)★★★, *Dear 23* (Geffen 1990)★★★★, *Frosting On The Beater* (Geffen 1993)★★★★, *Amazing Disgrace* (Geffen 1996)★★★, *Success* (Pop Llama 1998).

PREFAB SPROUT
ALBUMS: *Swoon* (Kitchenware 1984)★★★, *Steve McQueen* (Kitchenware 1985)★★★★, *From Langley Park To Memphis* (Kitchenware 1988)★★★, *Protest Songs* (Kitchenware 1989)★★★, *Jordan: The Comeback* (Kitchenware 1990)★★★, *Andromeda Heights* (Columbia 1997)★★★.
COMPILATIONS: *A Life Of Surprises: The Best Of* (Kitchenware 1992)★★★★.
FURTHER READING: *Myths, Melodies & Metaphysics, Paddy McAloon's Prefab Sprout*, John Birch.
VIDEOS: *A Life Of Surprises: The Video Collection* (SMV 1997).

PRESIDENTS OF THE UNITED STATES OF AMERICA
ALBUMS: *Presidents Of The United States Of America* (PopLlama 1995)★★★★, *Presidents Of The United States Of America* remixed version of debut (Columbia 1995)★★★, *II* (Columbia 1996)★★★, *Pure Frosting* (Columbia 1998).

PRESLEY, ELVIS
ALBUMS: *Elvis Presley* (RCA Victor 1956)★★★★, *Elvis* (RCA Victor 1956)★★★★★, *Rock 'N' Roll* (1956)★★★★, *Rock 'N' Roll No. 2* (1957)★★★★, *Loving You* soundtrack (RCA Victor 1957)★★★, *Elvis' Christmas Album* (RCA Victor 1957)★★★, *King Creole* (RCA Victor 1958)★★★★, *Elvis' Golden Records* (RCA Victor 1958)★★★★★, *For LP Fans Only* (RCA Victor 1959)★★★★, *A Date With Elvis* (RCA Victor 1959)★★★★, *Elvis' Golden Records, Volume 2* (RCA Victor 1960)★★★★★, *Elvis Is Back!* (RCA Victor 1960)★★★★, *G.I. Blues* (RCA Victor 1960)★★★, *His Hand In Mine* (RCA Victor 1961)★★★, *Something For Everybody* (RCA Victor 1961)★★★, *Blue Hawaii* (RCA Victor 1961)★★★, *Pot Luck* (RCA Victor 1962)★★★, *Girls! Girls! Girls!* (RCA Victor 1963)★★★, *Elvis' Golden Records, Volume 3* (1964)★★★★, *Kissin' Cousins* (RCA Victor 1964)★★, *Roustabout* (RCA Victor 1964)★★, *Girl Happy* (RCA Victor 1965)★★, *Flaming Star And Summer Kisses* (1965)★★, *Elvis For Everyone* (RCA Victor 1965)★★★, *Harem Holiday* (RCA Victor 1965)★★, *Frankie And Johnny* (RCA Victor 1966)★★, *Paradise, Hawaiian Style* (RCA Victor 1966)★★, *California Holiday* (RCA Victor 1966)★★, *How Great Thou Art* (RCA Victor 1967)★★★, *Double Trouble* (RCA Victor 1967)★★, *Clambake* (RCA Victor 1968)★★, *Elvis' Golden Records, Volume 4* (RCA Victor 1968)★★★, *Speedway* (RCA Victor 1968)★★, *Elvis – TV Special* (RCA 1968)★★★, *From Elvis In Memphis* (RCA 1970)★★★★, *On Stage February 1970* (RCA 1970)★★★★, *That's The Way It Is* (RCA 1971)★★★, *I'm 10,000 Years Old – Elvis Country* (RCA 1971)★★★, *Love Letters From Elvis* (RCA 1971)★★★, *Elvis Sings The Wonderful World Of Christmas* (RCA 1971)★★★, *Elvis Now* (RCA 1972)★★★, *He Touched Me* (RCA 1972)★★★, *Elvis As Recorded At Madison Square Garden* (RCA 1972)★★★, *Aloha From Hawaii Via Satellite* (RCA 1973)★★★, *Elvis* (RCA 1973)★★★, *Raised On Rock* (RCA 1973)★★★, *A Legendary Performer, Volume 1* (RCA 1974)★★★★, *Good Times* (RCA 1974)★★★, *Elvis Recorded On Stage In Memphis* (RCA 1974)★★★, *Hits Of The 70s* (1974)★★★, *Promised Land* (RCA 1975)★★★, *Having Fun With Elvis On Stage* (1975)★★, *Today* (RCA 1975)★★★, *The Elvis Presley Sun Collection* (RCA 1975)★★★★★, *From Elvis Presley Boulevard, Memphis, Tennessee* (RCA 1976)★★★, *Moody Blue* (RCA 1977)★★★, *Welcome To My World* (RCA 1977)★★★, *A Legendary Performer, Volume 2* (RCA 1977)★★★★, *He Walks Beside Me* (RCA 1978)★★★, *Elvis – A Canadian Tribute* (RCA 1978)★★★, *The '56 Sessions, Vol. 1* (1978)★★★★, *Elvis's 40 Greatest* (RCA 1978)★★★★, *Elvis – A Legendary Performer, Volume 3* (RCA 1979)★★★★, *Our Memories Of Elvis* (RCA 1979)★★★, *Our Memories Of Elvis Vol 2* (RCA 1979)★★★, *The '56 Sessions, Vol. 2* (1979)★★★★, *Elvis Presley Sings Leiber And Stoller* (RCA 1979)★★★★, *Elvis Aaron Presley* (RCA 1979)★★★, *Elvis Sings The Wonderful World Of Christmas* (RCA 1979)★★★, *The First Year* (1979)★★★, *The King...Elvis* (1980)★★★, *This Is Elvis* (RCA 1981)★★★, *Guitar Man* (RCA 1981)★★★, *Elvis Answers Back* (1981)★★★, *The Ultimate Performance* (RCA 1981)★★★, *Personally Elvis* (1982)★★★, *The Sound Of Your Cry* (1982)★★★, *Jailhouse Rock/Love In Las Vegas* (1983)★★★, *I Was The One* (RCA 1983)★★★, *The First Ever Recordings* (Music Works 1984)★★★, *Rocker* (RCA 1984)★★★, *A Golden Celebration* (1984)★★★, *A Valentine Gift For You* (RCA 1985)★★★, *Rare Elvis* (1985)★★★, *Essential Elvis* (1986)★★★★, *The Number One Hits* (RCA 1987)★★★★, *The Top Ten Hits* (RCA 1987)★★★★, *The King Of Rock 'n' Roll: The Complete 50s Masters* (RCA 1992)★★★★★, *Elvis From Nashville To Memphis: The Essential '60s Masters 5-CD box set* (RCA 1993)★★★★, *Elvis Gospel: 1957-1971* (RCA 1994)★★★, *If Every Day Was Like Christmas* (RCA 1994)★★★, *Walk A Mile In My Shoes: Elvis 56* (RCA 1996)★★★★★, *A Hundred Years From Now* (RCA 1996)★★★, *Presley – The All Time Greats* (RCA 1996)★★★★, *Great Country Songs* (RCA 1996)★★★, *Great Country Songs* (RCA 1997)★★★, *Platinum – A Life In Music* 4-CD box set (RCA 1997)★★★★.
FILMS: *Love Me Tender* (1956), *Loving You* (1957), *Jailhouse Rock* (1957), *King Creole* (1958), *G.I. Blues* (1960), *Flaming Star* (1960), *Wild In The Country* (1961), *Blue Hawaii* (1961), *Kid Galahad* (1962), *Girls Girls Girls* (1962), *Follow That Dream* (1962), *It Happened At The World's Fair* (1963), *Fun In Acapulco* (1963), *Roustabout* (1964), *Viva Las Vegas* (1964), *Kissin' Cousins* (1964), *Tickle Me* (1965), *Harum Scarum* a.k.a. *Harem Holiday* (1965), *Girl Happy* (1965), *Spinout* (1966), *Paradise Hawaiin Style* (1966), *Frankie And Johnny* (1966), *Easy Come Easy Go* (1967), *Clambake* (1967), *Live A Little Love A Little* (1968), *Speedway* (1968), *Stay Away Joe* (1968), *Double Trouble* (1968), *The Trouble With Girls* (1969), *Charro!* (1969), *Change Of Habit* (1969), *This Is Elvis* (compilation) (1981).
VIDEOS: *One Night With You* (1986), *Elvis Presley In Concert* (1986), *68 Comeback Special* (1986), *Memories* (1987), *This Is Elvis* (1988), *Graceland* (1988), *Great Performances Vol 2* (1990), *Great Vocal Performances Vol 1* (1990), *Young Elvis* (1991), *Sun Days With Elvis* (1991), *Elvis On Tour* (1991), *Elvis: A Portrait By His Friends* (1991), *56 In The Beginning* (1991), *The Lost Performances* (BMG 1992), *Private Elvis* (1993), *Elvis In Hollywood* (1993), *The Alternate Aloha Concert* (Lightyear Entertainment 1996), *Elvis 56 – The Video* (BMG 1996), *Elvis – That's The Way It Is* (1996), *Private Moments* (Telstar 1997), *The Great Performance* (Wienerworld 1997), *The Legend Lives On* (Real Entertainment 1997), *Collapse Of The Kingdom* (Real Entertainment 1997), *The King Comes Back* (Real Entertainment 1997), *Wild In Hollywood* (Real Entertainment 1997), *Rockin' Ride To Stardom* (Real Entertainment 1997), *Elvis: All The Kings Men* (Real Entertainment 1997), *Alpha From Hawaii* (Lightyear 1997), *NBC T.V. Special* (Lightyear 1997).
FURTHER READING: *I Called Him Babe: Elvis Presley's Nurse Remembers*, Marian J. Cocke. *The Three Loves Of Elvis Presley: The True Story Of The Presley Legend*, Robert Holmes. *A Century Of Elvis*, Albert Hand. *The Elvis They Dig*, Albert Hand. *Operation Elvis*, Alan Levy. *The Elvis Presley Pocket Handbook*, Albert Hand. *All Elvis: An Unofficial Biography Of The 'King Of Discs'*, Philip Buckle. *The Elvis Presley Encyclopedia*, Roy Barlow. *Elvis: A Biography*, Jerry Hopkins. *Meet Elvis Presley*, Favius Friedman. *Elvis Presley*, Paula Taylor. *Elvis*, Jerry Hopkins. *The Elvis Presley Scrapbook 1935-1977*, James Robert Paris. *Elvis And The Colonel*, May Mann. *Recording Sessions 1954-1974*, Torben Holum; Ernst Jorgensen & Erik Rasmussen. *Elvis Presley: An Illustrated Biography*, W.A. Harbinson. *Elvis: The Films And Career Of Elvis Presley*, Steven Zmijewsky & Boris Zmijewsky. *Presley Nation*, Spencer Leigh. *Elvis*, Peter Jones. *Presley: Entertainer Of The Century*, Antony James. *Elvis And His Secret*, Maria Gripe. *On Stage, Elvis Presley*, Kathleen Bowman. *The Elvis Presley American Discography*, Ron Barry. *Elvis: What Happened*, Red West, Sonny West & Dave Hebler. *Elvis: Tribute To The King Of Rock*, Dick Tatham. *Elvis Presley*, Todd Slaughter. *Elvis: Recording Sessions*, Ernst Jorgensen; Erick Rasmussen & Johnny Mikkelsen. *The Life And Death Of Elvis Presley*, W. A. Harbinson. *Elvis: Lonely Star At The Top*, David Hanna. *Elvis In His Own Words*, Mick Farren & Pearce Marchbank. *Twenty Years Of Elvis: The Session File*, Colin Escott & Martin Hawkins. *Starring Elvis*, James W. Bowser. *My Life With Elvis*, Becky Yancey & Cliff Lindecker. *The Real Elvis: A Good Old Boy*, Vince Staten. *The Elvis Presley Trivia Quiz Book*, Helen Rosenbaum. *A Presley Speaks*, Vester Presley. *The Graceland Gates*, Harold Lloyd. *The Boy Who Dared To Rock: The Definitive Elvis*, Paul Lichter. *Eine Illustrierte Dokumentation*, Bernd King, & Heinz Plehn. *Elvis Presley Speaks*, Hans Holzer. *Elvis: The Legend Lives! One Year Later*, Martin A. Grove. *Private Elvis*, Diego Cortez. *Bill Adler's Love Letters To Elvis*, Bill Adler. *Elvis: His Life And Times In Poetry And Lines*, Joan Buchanan West. *Elvis '56: In The Beginning*, Alfred Wertheimer. *Elvis Presley: An Illustrated Biography*, Rainer Wallraf & Heinz Plehn. *Even Elvis*, Mary Ann Thornton. *Elvis: Images & Fancies*, Jac L. Tharpe. *Elvis In Concert*, John Reggero. *Elvis Presley: A Study In Music*, Robert Matthew-Walker. *Elvis: Portrait Of A Friend*, Marty Lacker, Patsy Lacker, & Leslie E. Smith. *Elvis Is That You?*, Holly Hatcher. *Elvis: Newly Discovered Drawings Of Elvis Presley*, Betty Harper. *Trying To Get To You: The Story Of Elvis Presley*, Valerie Harms. *Love Of Elvis*, Bruce Hamilton & Michael L. Liben. *To Elvis With Love*, Lena Canada. *The Truth About Elvis*, Jess Stearn. *Elvis: We Love You Tender*, Dee Presley; Billy, Rick & David Stanley. *Presleyana*, Jerry Osborne, & Bruce Hamilton. *Elvis: The Final Years*, Jerry Hopkins. *When Elvis Died*, Nancy & Joseph Gregory. *All About Elvis*, Fred L. Worth & Steve D. Tamerius. *Elvis Presley: A Reference Guide And Discography*, John A. Whisler. *The Illustrated Discography*, Martin Hawkins, & Colin Escott. *Elvis: Legend Of Love*, Marie Greenfield. *Elvis Presley: King Of Rock 'N' Roll*, Richard Wooton. *The Complete Elvis*, Martin Torgoff. *Elvis Special 1982*, Todd Slaughter. *Elvis*, Dave Marsh. *Up And Down With Elvis Presley*, Marge Crumbaker, with Gabe Tucker. *Elvis For The Record*, Maureen Covey. *Elvis: The Complete Illustrated Record*, Roy Carr & Mick Farren. *Elvis Collectables*, Rosalind Cranor. *Jailhouse Rock: The Bootleg Records Of Elvis Presley 1970*, Lee Cotten & Howard A. DeWitt. *Elvis The Soldier*, Rex & Elisabeth Mansfield. *All Shook Up: Elvis Day-By-Day, 1954-1977*, Lee Cotten. *Elvis*, John Townson; Gordon Minto & George Richardson. *Priscilla, Elvis & Me*, Michael Edwards. *Elvis On The Road To Stardom: 1955-1956*, Jim Black. *Return To Sender*, Howard F. Banney. *Elvis: His Life From A To Z*, Fred L. Worth & Steve D. Tamerius. *Elvis And The Colonel*, Dirk Vallenga, with Mick Farren. *Elvis: My Brother*, Bill Stanley, with George Erikson. *Long Lonely Highway: 1950's Elvis Scrapbook*, Ger J. Rijff. *Elvis In Hollywood*, Gerry McLafferty. *Reconsider Baby: Definitive Elvis Sessionography*, E. Jorgensen. *Elvis '69, The Return*, Joseph A. Tunzi. *The Death Of Elvis: What Really Happened*, Charles C. Thompson & James P. Cole. *Elvis For Beginners*, Jill Pearlman. *Elvis, The Cool King*, Bob Moreland & Jan Van Gestel. *The Elvis Presley Scrapbooks 1955-1965*, Peter Haining (ed.). *The Boy Who Would Be King: An Intimate Portrait Of Elvis Presley By His Cousin*, Earl Greenwood & Kathleen Tracy. *Elvis: The Last 24 Hours*, Albert Goldman. *The Elvis Files*, Gail Brewer-Giorgio. *Elvis, My Dad*, David Adler & Ernest Andrews. *The Elvis Reader: Texts And Sources On The King Of Rock 'n' Roll*, Kevin Quain (ed). *Elvis Bootlegs Buyer's Guide*, Pts 1 & 2, Tommy Robinson. *Elvis: The Music Lives On - The Recording Sessions 1954-1976*, Richard Peters. *The King Forever*, No author listed. *Dead Elvis: A Chronicle Of A Cultural Obsession*, Greil Marcus. *Elvis People: Cult Of The King*, Ted Harrison. *In Search Of The King*, Craig Gelfand, Lynn Blocker-Krantz, & Rogerio Noguera. *Aren Med Elvis*, Roger Ersson & Lennart Svedberg. *Elvis And Gladys*, Elaine Dundy. *King And I: Little Gallery Of Elvis Impersonators*, Kent Barker & Karin Pritikin. *Elvis Sessions: The Recorded Music Of Elvis Aron Presley 1953-1977*, Joseph A. Tunzi. *Elvis: The Sun Years*, Howard A. DeWitt. *Elvis In Germany: The Missing Years*, Andreas Schroer. *Graceland: The Living Legend Of Elvis Presley*, Chet Flippo. *Elvis: The Secret Files*, John Parker. *The Life And Cuisine Of Elvis Presley*, David Adler. *Last Train To Memphis: The Rise Of Elvis Presley*, Peter Gurglnick. *In His Own Words*, Mick Farren. *Elvis: Murdered By The Mob*, John Parker. *The Complete Guide To The Music Of...*, John Robertson. *Elvis's Man Friday*, Gene Smith. *The Hitchhiker's Guide To Elvis*, Mick Farren. *Elvis, The Lost Photographs 1948-1969*, Joseph Tunzi & O'Neal. *Elvis Aaron Presley: Revelations From The Memphis Mafia*, Alanna Nash. *The Elvis Encyclopaedia*, David E. Stanley. *E: Reflections On The Birth Of The Elvis Faith*, John. E. Strausbaugh. *Elvis Meets The Beatles: The Untold Story Of Their Entangled Lives*, Chris Hutchins & Peter Thompson. *Elvis, Highway 51 South, Memphis, Tennessee*, Joseph A. Tunzi. *Elvis In The Army*, William J. Jr. Taylor. *Everything Elvis*, Pauline Bartel. *Elvis In Wonderland*, Bob Jope. *Elvis: Memories And Memorabilia*, Richard Bushkin. *Elvis Sessions II: The Recorded Music Of Elvis Aron Presley 1953-1977*, Joseph A. Tunzi. *The Ultimate Album Cover Book*, Paul Dowling. *The King Of The Road*, Robert Gordon. *Raised On Rock: Growing Up At Graceland*, David A. Stanley & Mark Bego. *Elvis: In The Twilight Of Memory*, June Juanico. *The Rise And Fall And Rise Of Elvis*, Aubrey Dillon-Malone.

PRESTON, BILLY
ALBUMS: *Gospel In My Soul* (1962)★★, *16 Year Old Soul* (Derby 1963)★★★, *The Most Exciting Organ Ever* (Vee Jay 1965)★★, *Early Hits Of 1965* (Vee Jay 1965)★★, *The Apple Of Their Eye* (1965)★★, *The Wildest Organ In Town!* (Vee Jay 1966)★★★, *That's The Way God Planned It* (Apple 1969)★★★, *Greazee Soul* (Apple 1969)★★★, *Encouraging Words* (Apple 1970)★★, *I Wrote A Simple Song* (A&M 1972)★★★, *Music Is My Life* (A&M 1972)★★★, *Everybody Likes Some Kind Of Music* (A&M 1973)★★, *The Kids & Me* (A&M 1974)★★★, *Live European Tour* (A&M 1974)★★, *It's My Pleasure* (A&M 1975)★★★, *Do What You Want* (A&M 1976)★★, *Billy Preston* (A&M 1976)★★, *A Whole New Thing* (A&M 1977)★★, *Soul'd Out* (A&M 1977)★★, with Syreeta *Fast Break* film soundtrack (Motown 1979)★★, *Late At Night* (Motown 1980)★★★, *Behold* (Myrrh 1980)★★, *Universal Love* (1980)★★, *The Way I Am* (Motown 1981)★★, with Syreeta *Billy Preston & Syreeta* (Motown 1981)★★, *Pressin' On* (Motown 1982)★★, *Billy's Back* (NuGroove 1995)★★.
COMPILATIONS: *The Best Of Billy Preston* (A&M 1988)★★★, *Collection* (Castle 1989)★★★.

PRETENDERS
ALBUMS: *Pretenders* (Warners 1980)★★★★, *Pretenders II* (Warners 1981)★★★, *Learning To Crawl* (Warners 1984)★★★, *Get Close* (Warners 1986)★★, *Packed!* (Warners 1990)★★, *Last Of The Independents* (Sire/Warners 1994)★★★, *Isle Of View* (Warners 1995)★★.
COMPILATIONS: *The Singles* (Warners 1987)★★★★.
VIDEOS: *The Isle Of View* (Warner Music Vision 1995).
FURTHER READING: *Pretenders*, Miles. *The Pretenders*, Chris Salewicz. *The Pretenders: With Hyndesight*, Mike Wrenn.

PRETTY THINGS
ALBUMS: *The Pretty Things* (Fontana 1965)★★★★, *Get The Picture* (Fontana 1965)★★★★, *Emotions* (Fontana 1967)★★★, *S.F. Sorrow* (EMI 1968)★★★★, *Parachute* (Harvest 1970)★★★★, *Freeway Madness* (Warners 1972)★★★, *Silk Torpedo* (Swan Song 1974)★★★, *Savage Eye* (Swan Song 1976)★★★, *Live '78* (Jade 1978)★★, *Cross Talk* (Warners 1980)★★, *Live At The Heartbreak Hotel* (Ace 1984)★★, *Out Of The Island* (Inak 1988)★★, *On Air* (Band Of Joy 1992)★★.
The group also completed several albums of background music suitable for films: *Electric Banana* (De Wolfe 1967)★★, *More Electric Banana* (De Wolfe 1968)★★, *Even More Electric Banana* (De Wolfe 1969)★★, *Hot Licks* (De Wolfe 1973)★★, *Return Of The Electric Banana* (De Wolfe 1978)★★.
COMPILATIONS: *Greatest Hits 64-67* (Philips 1975)★★★★, *The Vintage Years* (Sire 1976)★★★, *Attention* (1976)★★★, *Attention Volume 2* (1976)★★, *Singles A's And B's* (Harvest 1977)★★★, *The Pretty Things 1967-1971* (See For Miles 1982)★★★★, *Cries From The Midnight Circus: The Best Of The Pretty Things 1968-1971* (Harvest 1986)★★★, *Closed Restaurant Blues* (Bam Caruso 1987)★★★, *Unrepentant* 2-CD box set (Fragile 1995)★★★.
FURTHER READING: *The Pretty Things: Their Own Story And The Downliners Sect Story*, Mike Stax.

PRICE, ALAN
ALBUMS: *The Price To Play* (Decca 1966)★★★, *A Price On His Head* (Decca 1967)★★★, *The Price Is Right* (Parrot 1968)★★★, *Fame And Price, Price And Fame Together* (Columbia 1971)★★★, *O Lucky Man!* film soundtrack (Warners 1973)★★★, *Between Today And Yesterday* (Warners 1974)★★★, *Metropolitan Man* (Polydor 1974)★★★, *Performing Price* (Polydor 1975)★★★, *Shouts Across The Street* (Polydor 1976)★★★, *Rainbows End* (Jet 1977)★★, *Alan Price* (Jet 1977)★★, *England My England* (Jet 1978)★★★, *Rising Sun* (Jet 1980)★★★, *A Rock And Roll Night At The Royal Court* (Key 1981)★★★, *Geordie Roots And Branches* (MWM 1983)★★★, *Travellin' Man* (Trojan 1986)★★★, *Liberty* (Ariola 1989)★★★, *Live In Concert* (1993)★★, with The Electric Blues Company *A Gigster's Life For Me* (Indigo 1995)★★.
COMPILATIONS: *The World Of Alan Price* (Decca

1970)★★★, *The Best Of Alan Price* (MFP 1987)★★★, *The Best Of And The Rest Of* (Action Replay 1989)★★★.
FURTHER READING: *Wild Animals*, Andy Blackford.

PRICE, LLOYD
ALBUMS: *Lloyd Price* (Specialty 1959)★★★★, *The Exciting Lloyd Price* (ABC 1959)★★★★, *Mr. Personality* (ABC 1959)★★★★, *Mr. Personality Sings The Blues* (ABC 1960)★★★★, *The Fantastic Lloyd Price* (ABC 1960)★★★, *Lloyd Price Sings The Million Sellers* (ABC 1961)★★★, *Cookin' With Lloyd Price* (ABC 1961)★★, *The Lloyd Price Orchestra* (Double L 1963)★★, *Misty* (Double L 1963)★★, *Lloyd Swings For Sammy* (Monument 1965)★★, *Lloyd Price Now* (Jad 1969)★★, *To The Roots And Back* (1972)★★, *The Nominee* (1978)★★.
COMPILATIONS: *Mr. Personality's Big 15* (ABC 1960)★★★★, *The Best Of Lloyd Price* (1970)★★★★, *Lloyd Price's 16 Greatest Hits* (ABC 1972)★★★★, *Original Hits* (1972)★★★, *The ABC Collection* (ABC 1976)★★★★, *Mr. Personality Revisited* (Charly 1983)★★★, *Lloyd Price* (Specialty 1986)★★★, *Personality Plus* (Specialty 1986)★★★, *Lawdy!* (Specialty 1991)★★★, *Stagger Lee & All His Other Greatest Hits* (1993)★★★★, *Greatest Hits* (MCA 1995)★★★★.

PRIEST, MAXI
ALBUMS: *You're Safe* (Virgin 1985)★★, *Intentions* (Virgin 1986)★★, *Maxi* (Ten 1987)★★, *Bona Fide* (Ten 1990)★★★, *Fe Real* (Ten 1992)★★, *Man With The Fun* (Virgin 1996)★★.
COMPILATIONS: *The Best Of Me* (Ten 1991)★★★.

PRIMAL SCREAM
ALBUMS: *Sonic Flower Groove* (Creation 1987)★★★, *Primal Scream* (Creation 1989)★★, *Screamadelica* (Creation 1991)★★★★, *Give Out But Don't Give Up* (Creation 1994)★★★, *Vanishing Point* (Creation 1997)★★★★, *Echodek* remixes (Creation 1997)★★★.

PRINCE
ALBUMS: *Prince – For You* (Warners 1978)★★★, *Prince* (Warners 1979)★★★, *Dirty Mind* (Warners 1980)★★★, *Controversy* (Warners 1981)★★★, *1999* (Warners 1982)★★★★, *Purple Rain* film soundtrack (Warners 1984)★★★★, *Around The World In A Day* (Paisley Park 1985)★★★, *Parade – Music From Under The Cherry Moon* film soundtrack (Paisley Park 1986)★★★, *Sign 'O' The Times* (Paisley Park 1987)★★★★, *Lovesexy* (Paisley Park 1988)★★★, *Batman* film soundtrack (Warners 1989)★★★, *Graffiti Bridge* (Paisley Park 1990)★★, *Diamonds And Pearls* (Paisley Park 1991)★★★, *Symbol* (Paisley Park 1993)★★★, *Come* (Paisley Park 1994)★★, *The Gold Experience* (Warners 1995)★★★, *Chaos And Disorder* (Warners 1996)★★, *Emancipation* (New Power Generation 1996)★★, *New Power Soul* (New Power Generation 1998)★★★.
COMPILATIONS: *The Hits: Volume I & II* (Paisley Park/Warners 1993)★★★★.
VIDEOS: *Double Live* (Polygram 1986), *Prince And The Revolution; Live* (Channel 5 1987), *Sign 'O' The Times* (Palace Video 1988), *Lovesexy Part 1* (Palace Video 1989), *Lovesexy Part 2* (Palace Video 1989), *Get Off* (Warner Music Video 1991), *Prince: The Hits Collection* (1993), *3 Chains O' Gold* (Warner Reprise 1994), *Billboards* (Warner Vision 1994).
FURTHER READING: *Prince: Imp Of The Perverse*, Barney Hoskyns. *Prince: A Pop Life*, Dave Hill. *Prince By Controversy*, The 'Controversy' Team. *Prince: A Documentary*, Per Nilsen. *Prince: An Illustrated Biography*, John W. Duffy. *Prince*, John Ewing.

PRINCE BUSTER
ALBUMS: *Judge Dread Rock Steady* (Blue Beat 1967)★★★, *I Feel The Spirit* (1968)★★★, *Wreck A Pum Pum* (Blue Beat 1968)★★★★, *She Was A Rough Rider* (Melodisc 1969)★★★★, *Big Five* (Melodisc 1972)★★★, *On Tour* (1966)★★★, *Judge Dread* (1968), *Tutti Fruitti* (Melodisc)★★★. Various: *Pain In My Belly* (Islam/Blue Beat 1966)★★★.
COMPILATIONS: *Prince Buster's Fabulous Greatest Hits* (Fab 1968)★★★★, *Original Golden Oldies Vol.s 1 & 2* (Prince Buster 1989)★★★★.

PRINE, JOHN
ALBUMS: *John Prine* (Atlantic 1972)★★★★, *Diamonds In The Rough* (Atlantic 1972)★★★, *Sweet Revenge* (Atlantic 1973)★★★★, *Common Sense* (Atlantic 1975)★★★, *Bruised Orange* (Asylum 1978)★★★, *Pink Cadillac* (Asylum 1979)★★★, *Storm Windows* (Asylum 1980)★★★, *Aimless Love* (Oh Boy 1985)★★★, *German Afternoons* (Demon 1987)★★★, *John Prine Live* (Oh Boy 1988)★★★, *The Missing Years* (Oh Boy 1992)★★★★, *Live* (1993)★★★, *Lost Dogs & Mixed Blessings* (Rykodisk 1995)★★★, *Live On Tour* (Oh Boy 1997)★★★.
COMPILATIONS: *Anthology: Great Days* (Rhino 1993)★★★★.

PROCLAIMERS
ALBUMS: *This Is The Story* (Chrysalis 1987)★★★, *Sunshine On Leith* (Chrysalis 1988)★★★★, *Hit The Highway* (Chrysalis 1994)★★★.

PROCOL HARUM
ALBUMS: *Procol Harum* (Regal Zonophone 1967)★★★, *Shine On Brightly* (Regal Zonophone 1968)★★★, *A Salty Dog* (Regal Zonophone 1969)★★★★, *Home* (Regal Zonophone 1970)★★★, *Broken Barricades* (Chrysalis 1971)★★★, *Live In Concert With The Edmonton Symphony Orchestra* (Chrysalis 1972)★★★★, *Grand Hotel* (Chrysalis 1973)★★★, *Exotic Birds And Fruit* (Chrysalis 1974)★★★, *Procol's Ninth* (Chrysalis 1975)★★★, *Something Magic* (1977)★★, *The Prodigal Stranger* (1991)★★, Procol Harum with various artists *The Long Goodbye: Symphonic Music Of ...* (BMG/RCA 1995)★★.
COMPILATIONS: *The Best Of Procol Harum* (1973)★★★★, *Platinum Collection* (1981)★★★★, *Collection: Procol Harum* (Castle 1986)★★★★, *The Early Years* (1993)★★★, *Homburg And Other Hats: Procol Harum's Best* (Essential 1995)★★★★.

PRODIGY
ALBUMS: *The Prodigy Experience* (XL 1992)★★★, *Music For The Jilted Generation* (XL 1994)★★★★, *The Fat Of The Land* (XL 1997)★★★★.
VIDEOS: *Electronic Punks* (XL Recordings 1995).
FURTHER READING: *Electronic Punks: The Official Story*, Martin Roach. *Prodigy: Exit The Underground*, Lisa Verrico. *Prodigy: The Fat Of The Land*, no author listed.

PSYCHEDELIC FURS
ALBUMS: *Psychedelic Furs* (Columbia 1980)★★★, *Talk Talk Talk* (Columbia 1981)★★★, *Forever Now* (Columbia 1982)★★★, *Mirror Moves* (Columbia 1984)★★★, *Midnight To Midnight* (Columbia 1987)★★, *Book Of Days* (Columbia 1989)★★, *World Outside* (Columbia 1991)★★, *Radio 1 Sessions* (Strange Fruit 1997)★★★.
COMPILATIONS: *All Of This And Nothing* (Columbia 1988)★★★★, *Crucial Music: The Collection* (Columbia 1989)★★★.

PUBLIC ENEMY
ALBUMS: *Yo! Bum Rush The Show* (Def Jam 1987)★★★★, *It Takes A Nation Of Millions To Hold Us Back* (Def Jam 1988)★★★★, *Fear Of A Black Planet* (Def Jam 1990)★★★, *Apocalypse '91 The Enemy Strikes Black* (Def Jam 1991) ★★★, *Muse Sick N Hour Mess Age* (Def Jam 1994)★★★.
COMPILATIONS: *Greatest Misses* features six 'new' tracks (Def Jam 1992)★★★★, *Twelve Inch Mixes* (Def Jam 1993)★★★.

PUBLIC IMAGE LIMITED
ALBUMS: *Public Image* (Virgin 1978)★★★, *Metal Box* UK title *Second Edition* US title (Virgin 1979)★★★★, *Paris Au Printemps* (Virgin 1980)★★, *Flowers Of Romance* (Virgin 1981)★★, *Live In Tokyo* (Virgin 1983)★★, *Commercial Zone* (PIL/Virgin 1983)★★, *This Is What You Want, This Is What You Get* (Virgin 1984)★★★, *Album* (Virgin 1986)★★★, *Happy?* (Virgin 1987)★★★, *9* (Virgin 1989)★★, *That What Is Not* (Virgin 1992)★★.
COMPILATIONS: *Greatest Hits ... So Far* (Virgin 1990)★★★.
VIDEOS: *Live In Toyko* (Virgin 1983), *Videos* (Virgin 1986).
FURTHER READING: *Public Image Limited: Rise Fall*, Clinton Heylin.

PULP
ALBUMS: *It* (Red Rhino 1983)★★, *Freaks* (Fire 1987)★★, *Separations* (Fire 1992)★★, *His 'N' Hers* (Island 1994)★★★★, *Different Class* (Island 1995)★★★★, *This Is Hardcore* (Island 1998)★★★.
COMPILATIONS: *Masters Of The Universe – Pulp On Fire 1985-86* (Fire 1994)★★★.
VIDEOS: *Pulp – Sorted For Films And Vids* (VVL 1995), *Pulp – A Feeling Called Love* (VVL 1996).
FURTHER READING: *Pulp*, Martin Aston.

PURE PRAIRIE LEAGUE
ALBUMS: *Pure Prairie League* (RCA 1972)★★★, *Bustin' Out* (RCA 1975)★★★★, *Two Lane Highway* (RCA 1975)★★★★, *If The Shoe Fits* (RCA 1976)★★★, *Dance* (RCA 1976)★★★, *Live!! Takin' The Stage* (RCA 1977)★★, *Just Fly* (RCA 1978)★★, *Can't Hold Back* (RCA 1979)★★, *Firin' Up* (Casablanca 1980)★★, *Something In The Night* (Casablanca 1981)★★.
COMPILATIONS: *Pure Prairie Collection* (RCA 1981)★★★, *Mementoes 1971-1987* (Rushmore 1987)★★★, *Best Of Pure Prairie League* (Mercury Nashville 1995)★★★★.

Q

Q-TIPS
ALBUMS: *Q-Tips* (Chrysalis 1980)★★★, *Live At Last* (Rewind 1982)★★★, *BBC Radio 1 Live In Concert* (Windsong 1991)★★.

QUATRO, SUZI
ALBUMS: *Suzi Quatro* (RAK 1973)★★★, *Quatro* (RAK 1974)★★, *Your Mama Won't Like Me* (RAK 1975)★★, *Aggro-Phobia* (RAK 1977)★★, *Live 'N' Kickin'* (EMI Japan 1977)★★, *If You Knew Suzi* (RAK 1978)★★, *Suzi And Other Four Letter Words* (RAK 1979)★★, *Rock Hard* (Dreamland 1980)★★, *Main Attraction* (Polydor 1983)★★, *Saturday Night Special* (Biff 1987)★★, *Rock 'Til Ya Drop* (Biff 1988)★★.
COMPILATIONS: *Suzi Quatro's Greatest Hits* (RAK 1980)★★★, *The Wild One (The Greatest Hits)* (EMI 1990)★★★, *The Gold Collection* (EMI 1996)★★★.
FURTHER READING: *Suzi Quatro*, Margaret Mander.

QUEEN
ALBUMS: *Queen* (EMI 1973)★★★, *Queen II* (EMI 1974)★★★, *Sheer Heart Attack* (EMI 1974)★★★, *A Night At The Opera* (EMI 1975)★★★, *A Day At The Races* (EMI 1976)★★★, *News Of The World* (EMI 1977)★★, *Jazz* (EMI 1978)★★, *Live Killers* (EMI 1979)★★, *The Game* (EMI 1980)★★★, *Flash Gordon* (EMI 1980)★★, *Hot Space* (EMI 1982)★, *The Works* (EMI 1984)★★★, *A Kind Of Magic* (EMI 1986)★★★, *Live Magic* (EMI 1986)★★, *The Miracle* (EMI 1989)★★, *Queen At The Beeb* (Band Of Joy 1989)H, *Innuendo* (EMI 1991)★★★, *Made In Heaven* (EMI 1995)★★★.
COMPILATIONS: *Greatest Hits* (EMI 1981)★★★★★, *The Complete Works* (EMI 1985)★★★, *Greatest Hits Vol. 2* (EMI 1991)★★★.
VIDEOS: *Greatest Flix* (PMI 1984), *We Will Rock You* (Peppermint 1984), *Magic Years Vol 1* (PMI 1987), *Magic Years Vol 2* (PMI 1987), *Magic Years Vol 3* (PMI 1987), *Live In Budapest* (PMI 1987), *Rare Live* (PMI 1989), *The Miracle* (PMI 1989), *Greatest Flix 2* (Video Collection 1991), *Box Of Flix* (PMI 1991), *Queen At Wembley* (PMI 1992), *Live In Rio* (Music Club 1993), *Champions Of The World* (PMI 1995), *Rock You* (Music Club 1995).
FURTHER READING: *Queen*, Larry Pryce. *The Queen Story*, George Tremlett. *Queen: The First Ten Years*, Mike West. *Queen's Greatest Pix*, Jacques Lowe. *Queen: An Illustrated Biography*, Judith Davis. *Queen: A Visual Documentary*, Ken Dean. *Freddie Mercury: This Is The Real Life*, David Evans and David Minns. *Queen: As It Began*, Jacky Gun and Jim Jenkins. *Queen Unseen*, Michael Putland. *Queen And I, The Brian May Story*, Laura Jackson. *Queen: A Concert Documentary*, Greg Brooks. *Queen: The Early Years*, Mark Hodkinson. *The Complete Guide To The Music Of ...*, Peter Hogan. *Queen Live*, Greg Brooks. *Freddie Mercury – More Of The Real Life*, David Evans and David Minns.

QUEEN LATIFAH
ALBUMS: *All Hail The Queen* (Tommy Boy 1989)★★★★, *Nature Of A Sista* (Tommy Boy 1991)★★★, *Black Reign* (Motown 1993)★★★, *Queen Latifah & Original Flava Unit* (Ol Skool Flava 1996).

QUEENSRØCHE
ALBUMS: *The Warning* (EMI 1984)★★, *Rage For Order* (EMI 1986)★★, *Operation Mindcrime* (EMI 1988)★★★, *Empire* (EMI 1990)★★★, *Promised Land* (EMI 1994)★★★, *Hear In The New Frontier* (EMI 1997)★★★.
COMPILATIONS: *Queensrøche* includes *Queensrøche* and *Prophecy* EPs (EMI 1988).
VIDEOS: *Live In Tokyo* (1985), *Video Mindcrime* (1989), *Operation Live Crime* (1991), *Building Empires* (1992).

? AND THE MYSTERIANS
ALBUMS: *96 Tears* (Cameo 1966)★★★, *Action* (Cameo 1967)★★.
COMPILATIONS: *96 Tears Forever* (1985)★★★.

QUICKSILVER MESSENGER SERVICE
ALBUMS: *Quicksilver Messenger Service* (Capitol 1968)★★★, *Happy Trails* (Capitol 1969)★★★★★, *Shady Grove* (Capitol 1969)★★, *Just For Love* (Capitol 1970)★★, *What About Me* (Capitol 1971)★★, *Quicksilver* (Capitol 1971)★★, *Comin' Thru* (Capitol 1972)★★, *Solid Silver* (Capitol 1975)★★, *Maiden Of The Cancer Moon* (1983)★★, *Peace By Piece* (1987)★★, *Shapeshifter* (Pymander 1996).
COMPILATIONS: *Anthology* (Capitol 1973)★★★, *Sons Of Mercury* (Rhino 1991)★★★★.

QUIREBOYS
ALBUMS: *A Bit Of What You Fancy* (Parlophone 1989)★★★, *Live Around The World* (Parlophone 1990)★★★, *Bitter Sweet & Twisted* (Parlophone 1992)★★.
COMPILATIONS: *From Tooting To Barking* (Castle 1994)★★★.
VIDEOS: *A Bit Of What You Fancy* (1990).

R

RADIOHEAD
ALBUMS: *Pablo Honey* (Parlophone 1993)★★★, *The Bends* (Parlophone 1995)★★★★, *OK Computer* (Parlophone 1997)★★★★.
VIDEOS: *27/5/94 The Astoria London Live* (PMI 1995).
FURTHER READING: *Radiohead, Coming Up For Air*, Steve Malins.

RAFFERTY, GERRY
ALBUMS: *Can I Have My Money Back?* (Transatlantic 1971)★★★★, *City To City* (United Artists 1978)★★★★, *Night Owl* (United Artists 1979)★★★★, *Snakes And Ladders* (United Artists 1980)★★★, *Sleepwalking* (Liberty 1982)★★, *North And South* (1988)★★, *On A Wing And A Prayer* (1992)★★, *Over My Head* (Polydor 1995)★★.
COMPILATIONS: *Early Collection* (Transatlantic 1986)★★★, *Right Down The Line: The Best Of Gerry Rafferty* (EMI 1991)★★★, *One More Dream – The Very Best Of* (Polygram 1995)★★★★.

RAGE AGAINST THE MACHINE
ALBUMS: *Rage Against The Machine* (Epic 1992)★★★, *Evil Empire* (Epic 1996)★★★★.

RAIN PARADE
ALBUMS: *Emergency Third Rail Power Trip* (Enigma 1983)★★★, *Beyond The Sunset* (Restless 1985)★★★, *Crashing Dream* (Island 1985)★★★.

RAINBOW
ALBUMS: *Ritchie Blackmore's Rainbow* (Oyster 1975)★★★, *Rainbow Rising* (Polydor 1976)★★★★, *Live On Stage* (Polydor 1977)★★, *Long Live Rock And Roll* (Polydor 1978)★★★, *Down To Earth* (Polydor 1979)★★★, *Difficult To Cure* (Polydor 1981)★★, *Straight Between The Eyes* (Polydor 1982)★★, *Bent Out Of Shape* (Polydor 1983)★★, *Stranger In Us All* (RCA 1995)★★.
COMPILATIONS: *Best Of* (Polydor 1983)★★★.
VIDEOS: *The Final Cut* (Polygram 1986), *Live Between The Eyes* (Channel 5 1988).
FURTHER READING: *Rainbow*, Peter Makowski.

RAINCOATS
ALBUMS: *The Raincoats* (Rough Trade 1979)★★★, *Odyshape* (Rough Trade 1981)★★, *The Kitchen Tapes* cassette only (ROIR 1983)★★★, *Moving* (Rough Trade 1984)★★★, *Looking In The Shadows* (Geffen 1996)★★★.
COMPILATIONS: *Fairytales* (Tim/Kerr 1995)★★★.

RAITT, BONNIE
ALBUMS: *Bonnie Raitt* (Warners 1971)★★★, *Give It Up* (Warners 1972)★★★, *Takin' My Time* (Warners 1973)★★★★, *Streetlights* (Warners 1974)★★★, *Home Plate* (Warners 1975)★★, *Sweet Forgiveness* (Warners 1977)★★, *The Glow* (Warners 1979)★★★, *Green Light* (Warners 1982)★★★, *Nine Lives* (Warners 1986)★★, *Nick Of Time* (Capitol 1989)★★★★, *Luck Of The Draw* (Capitol 1991)★★★★, *Longing In Their Hearts* (Capitol 1994)★★★, *Road Tested* (Capitol 1995)★★, *Fundamental* (Capitol 1998).
COMPILATIONS: *The Bonnie Raitt Collection* (Warners 1990)★★★★.
VIDEOS: *The Video Collection* (PMI 1992), *Road Tested* (Capitol 1995).
FURTHER READING: *Just In The Nick Of Time*, Mark Bego.

RAMONES
ALBUMS: *Ramones* (Sire 1976)★★★★, *The Ramones Leave Home* (Sire 1977)★★★★, *Rocket To Russia* (Sire 1977)★★★★, *Road To Ruin* (Sire 1978)★★★★, *It's Alive* (Sire 1979)★★★, *End Of The Century* (Sire 1980)★★★, *Pleasant Dreams* (Sire 1981)★★★, *Subterranean Jungle* (Sire 1983)★★★, *Too Tough To Die* (Sire 1984)★★★★, *Animal Boy* (Sire 1986)★★★, *Halfway To Sanity* (Sire 1987)★★, *Brain Drain* (Sire 1989)★★, *Loco Live* (Chrysalis 1991)★★, *Mondo Bizarro* (Chrysalis 1992)★★, *Acid Eaters* (Chrysalis 1993)★★, *Adios Amigos* (Chrysalis 1995)★★★, *We're Outta Here* (Eagle 1997)★★★.
COMPILATIONS: *Ramonesmania* (Sire 1988)★★★, *All The Stuff And More (Volume One)* (Sire 1990)★★★★, *End Of The Decade* (Beggars Banquet 1990)★★★★, *All The Stuff And More* (Sire 1991)★★★★, *Greatest Hits Live* (Radioactive 1996)★★★.
FURTHER READING: *The Ramones: An Illustrated Biography*, Miles. *Ramones: An American Band*, Jim Bessman. *Poison Heart: Surviving The Ramones*, Dee Dee Ramone.
VIDEOS: *Lifestyle Of The Ramones* (Atlantic 1990).

RANKS, SHABBA
ALBUMS: with Chakademus *Rough & Rugged* (King Jammys 1988)★★★, with Chakademus *Best Baby Father* (John John/Blue Mountain 1989)★★★, with Home T4, Cocoa T *Holding On* (Greensleeves 1989)★★★, *Just Reality* (Blue Mountain 1990)★★★, *Star Of The 90s* (King Jammys 1990)★★★, *Rappin' With The Ladies* (Greensleeves 1990)★★★, *As Raw As Ever* (Epic 1991)★★★, *Rough & Ready Vol. 1* (Epic 1992)★★★★, *Mr Maximum* (Greensleeves 1992), *X-Tra Naked* (Epic 1992)★★★, *Rough & Ready Vol. 2* (Epic 1993)★★★, *A Mi Shabba* (Epic 1995)★★★.
VIDEOS: *Fresh And Wild X Rated* (1992), with Ninjaman *Reggae Sting Vol. 1* (1992).

RARE EARTH
ALBUMS: *Dreams And Answers* (Verve 1968)★★★, *Get Ready* (Rare Earth 1969)★★★, *Ecology* (Rare Earth 1970)★★★, *One World* (Rare Earth 1971)★★★, *Rare Earth In Concert* (Rare Earth 1971)★★, *Willie Remembers* (Rare Earth 1972)★★★, *Ma* (Rare Earth 1973)★★★, *Back To Earth* (Rare Earth 1975)★★★, *Midnight Lady* (Rare Earth 1976)★★, *Rare Earth* (Prodigal 1977)★★, *Band Together* (Prodigal 1978)★★, *Grand Slam* (Prodigal 1978)★★, *Made In Switzerland* (Line 1989)★★, *Different World* (Koch 1993)★★.
COMPILATIONS: *The Best Of Rare Earth* (Rare Earth 1972)★★★, *Rare Earth: Superstars Series* (Motown 1981)★★★, *Greatest Hits And Rare Classics* (Motown 1991)★★★, *Earth Tones: The Essential Rare Earth* (Motown 1994)★★★, *Anthology* (Motown 1995)★★★.

RASPBERRIES
ALBUMS: *Raspberries* (Capitol 1972)★★, *Fresh* (Capitol 1972)★★★, *Side 3* (Capitol 1973)★★, *Starting Over* (Capitol 1974)★★★.
COMPILATIONS: *Raspberries' Best Featuring Eric Carmen* (Capitol 1976)★★★, *Overnight Sensation – The Very Best Of The Raspberries* (Zap 1987)★★★, *Collectors Series* (Capitol 1991)★★★, *Power Pop: Volume One* (RPM 1996)★★★★, *Power Pop Volume Two* (RPM 1996)★★★, *Eric Carmen: The Definitve Collection* (Arista 1997)★★★.
FURTHER READING: *Overnight Sensation: The Story Of The Raspberries*, Ken Sharp.

RAY, JOHNNIE
ALBUMS: *Johnnie Ray* (Columbia 1951)★★★, *At The London Palladium* (Philips 1954)★★, *I Cry For You* (Columbia 1955)★★★, *Johnnie Ray* (Epic 1955)★★★, *The Voice Of Your Choice* (Philips 1955)★★★, *Johnnie Ray Sings The Big Beat* (Columbia 1957)★★★★, *Johnnie Ray At The Desert Inn In Las Vegas* (Columbia 1959)★★★, *A Sinner Am I* (Philips 1959)★★, *'Til Morning* (Columbia 1959)★★, *Johnnie Ray On The Trail* (Columbia 1959)★★, *I Cry For You* (1960)★★, *Johnnie Ray* (Liberty 1962)★★, *Yesterday, Today And Tomorrow* (Celebrity 1980)★★, *Yesterday – The London Sessions 1976* (1993)★★.
COMPILATIONS: *Showcase Of Hits* (Philips 1958)★★★★, *Johnnie Ray's Greatest Hits* (Columbia 1959)★★★★, *The Best Of Johnny Ray* (Realm 1966)★★★★, *An American Legend* (Columbia 1978)★★★★, *Portrait Of A Song Stylist* (Masterpiece 1989)★★★★, *Greatest Hits* (Pickwick 1991)★★★.
FURTHER READING: *The Johnnie Ray Story*, Ray Sonin.

REA, CHRIS
ALBUMS: *Whatever Happened To Benny Santini* (Magnet 1978)★★★, *Deltics* (Magnet 1979)★★, *Tennis* (Magnet 1980)★★, *Chris Rea* (Magnet 1982)★★, *Water Sign* (Magnet 1983)★★, *Wired To The Moon* (Magnet 1984)★★, *Shamrock Diaries* (Magnet 1985)★★, *On The Beach* (Magnet 1986)★★★★, *Dancing With Strangers* (Magnet 1987)★★★★, *The Road To Hell* (Warners 1989)★★★★, *Auberge* (Atco 1991)★★★★, *God's Great Banana Skin* (East West 1992)★★★, *Espresso Logic* (1993)★★★, *La Passione* soundtrack (East West 1996)★★, *The Blue Cafe* (East West 1998).
COMPILATIONS: *New Light Through Old Windows* (Warners 1988)★★★.

READER, EDDI
ALBUMS: *Mirmama* (RCA 1992)★★★, *Eddi Reader* (Blanco y Negro 1994)★★★★, *Hush* (Blanco y Negro 1994)★★, *Candyfloss And Medicine* (Blanco y Negro 1996)★★.

REBEL MC
ALBUMS: *Black Meaning Good* (Desire 1991)★★★, *Word, Sound And Prayer* (Desire 1992)★★★, with Double Trouble *21 Mixes* (Desire 1990)★★.

RED HOT CHILI PEPPERS
ALBUMS: *Red Hot Chili Peppers* (EMI America 1984) ★★★★, *Freaky Styley* (EMI America 1985)★★★, *Uplift Mofo Party Plan* (EMI Manhattan 1987)★★★, *Mother's Milk* (EMI America 1989)★★★, *Blood, Sugar, Sex, Magik* (Warners 1991)★★★★, *One Hot Minute* (Warners 1995)★★★.
COMPILATIONS: *What Hits!?* (EMI 1992)★★★, *Plasma Shaft* (Warners 1994)★★★, *Greatest Hits* (CEMA/EMI 1995)★★★.
VIDEOS: *Funky Monks* (Warner Music Vision 1992).
FURTHER READING: *True Men Don't Kill Coyotes*, Dave Thompson. *Sugar And Spice*, Chris Watts. *The Complete Story*, Spike Harvey.

REDBONE
ALBUMS: *Redbone* (Epic 1970)★★, *Potlatch* (Epic 1970) ★★, *Witch Queen Of New Orleans* (Epic 1971)★★, *Message From A Drum* (Epic 1972)★★, *Already Here* (Epic 1972)★★, *Wovoka* (Epic 1974)★★, *Beaded Dreams Through Turquoise Eyes* (Epic 1974)★★, *Cycles* (RCA 1978)★★.
COMPILATION: *Come And Get Your Redbone (Best Of Redbone)* (Epic 1975)★★★.

REDDING, OTIS
ALBUMS: *Pain In My Heart* (Atco 1964)★★★★, *The Great Otis Redding Sings Soul Ballads* (Volt 1965)★★★★, *Otis Blue/Otis Redding Sings Soul* (Volt 1965)★★★★★, *The Soul Album* (Volt 1966)★★★★, *Complete And Unbelievable ... The Otis Redding Dictionary Of Soul* (Volt 1966)★★★★, with Carla Thomas *The King & Queen* (Stax 1967)★★★★, *Otis Redding Live In Europe* (Volt 1967)★★★★, *Here Comes Some Soul From Otis Redding And Little Joe Curtis* pre-1962 recording (Marble Arch 1967)★, *The Dock Of The Bay* (Volt 1968)★★★, *The Immortal Otis Redding* (Atco 1968)★★★, *Otis Redding In Person At The Whiskey A Go Go* (Atco 1968)★★★, *Love Man* (Atco 1969)★★★, *Tell The Truth* (Atco 1970)★★★, shared with Jimi Hendrix *Monterey International Pop Festival* (Reprise 1970)★★★★, *Live Otis Redding* (Atlantic 1982)★★★, *Remember Me* (1992)★★★, *Good To Me* (1993)★★★.
COMPILATIONS: *History Of Otis Redding* (Volt 1967) ★★★★, *The Best Of Otis Redding* (Atco 1972)★★★★, *Pure Otis* (Atlantic 1979)★★★, *Dock Of The Bay – The Definitive Collection* (Atlantic 1987)★★★★, *The Otis Redding Story* 4-LP box set (Atlantic 1989)★★★★, *Remember Me* US title *It's Not Just Sentimental* UK title (Stax 1992)★★★, *Otis!: The Definitive Otis Redding* 4-CD box set (Rhino 1993)★★★★★.
VIDEOS: *Remembering Otis* (Virgin 1990).
FURTHER READING: *The Otis Redding Story*, Jane Schiesel.

REDDY, HELEN
ALBUMS: *I Don't Know How To Love Him* (Capitol 1971)★★★, *Helen Reddy* (Capitol 1971)★★★, *I Am Woman* (Capitol 1972)★★★, *Long Hard Climb* (Capitol 1973)★★, *Love Song For Jeffrey* (Capitol 1974)★★, *Free And Easy* (Capitol 1974)★★, *No Way To Treat A Lady* (Capitol 1975)★★, *Music Music* (Capitol 1976)★★, *Ear Candy* (Capitol 1977)★★★, *We'll Sing In The Sunshine* (Capitol 1978)★★, *Live In London* (Capitol 1979)★★, *Reddy* (Capitol 1979)★★, *Take What You Find* (Capitol 1980)★★, *Play Me Out* (MCA 1981)★★, *Imagination* (MCA 1983)★★, *Take It Home* (Columbia 1984)★★.
COMPILATIONS: *Helen Reddy's Greatest Hits* (Capitol 1975)★★★, *Greatest Hits* (Capitol 1987)★★★, *Feel So Young (The Helen Reddy Collection)* (Pickwick 1991)★★★, *The Very Best Of ...* (1993)★★★.

REED, JIMMY
ALBUMS: *I'm Jimmy Reed* (Vee Jay 1958)★★★★, *Rockin' With Reed* (Vee Jay 1959)★★★★, *Found Love* (Vee Jay 1960)★★★★, *Now Appearing* (Vee Jay 1960)★★★★, *At Carnegie Hall* (Vee Jay 1961)★★★, *Just Jimmy Reed* (Vee Jay 1962)★★★★, *T'ain't No Big Thing...But He Is!* (Vee Jay 1963)★★★, *The Best Of The Blues* (Vee Jay 1963)★★★, *The 12-String Guitar Blues* (Vee Jay 1963)★★★★, *Jimmy Reed At Soul City* (Vee Jay 1964)★★★, *The Legend, The Man* (Vee Jay 1965)★★★, *The New Jimmy Reed Album* (Bluesway 1967)★★★, *Soulin'* (Bluesway 1967)★★★, *Big Boss Man* (Bluesway 1968)★★★, *Down In Virginia* (Bluesway 1969)★★★, *As Jimmy Is* (Roker 1970)★★★, *Let The Bossman Speak!* (Blues On Blues 1971)★★★.
COMPILATIONS: *The Best Of Jimmy Reed* (Vee Jay 1962)★★★★, *More Of The Best Of Jimmy Reed* (Vee Jay 1964)★★★★, *The Soulful Sound Of Jimmy Reed* (Upfront 1970)★★★, *I Ain't From Chicago* (Bluesway 1973)★★★, *The Ultimate Jimmy Reed* (Bluesway 1973)★★★★, *Cold Chills* (Antilles 1976)★★★, *Jimmy Reed Is Back* (Roots 1980)★★★, *Hard Walkin' Hanna* (Versatile 1980)★★★, *Greatest Hits* (Hollywood 1992)★★★, *Speak The Lyrics To Me, Mama Reed* (Vee Jay 1993)★★★, *Cry Before I Go* (Drive Archive 1995)★★★, *The Classic Recordings Volumes 1-3* (Tomato/Rhino 1995)★★★★, *Big Legged Woman* (Collectables 1996)★★★★.

REED, LOU
ALBUMS: *Lou Reed* (RCA 1972)★★, *Transformer* (RCA 1972)★★★★, *Berlin* (RCA 1973)★★★, *Rock 'N' Roll Animal* (RCA 1974)★★★, *Sally Can't Dance* (RCA 1974)★★, *Metal Machine Music* (RCA 1975)★, *Lou Reed Live* (RCA 1975)★★, *Coney Island Baby* (RCA 1976)★★★★, *Rock 'N' Roll Heart* (Arista 1976)★★, *Street Hassle* (Arista 1978)★★★★, *Live – Take No Prisoners* (RCA 1978)★★, *The Bells* (Arista 1979)★★★, *Growing Up In Public* (Arista 1980)★★, *The Blue Mask* (RCA 1982)★★★, *Legendary Hearts* (RCA 1983)★★★, *New Sensations* (RCA 1984)★★★★, *Live In Italy* (RCA 1984)★★, *Mistrial* (RCA 1986)★★, *New York* (Sire 1989)★★★★, with John Cale *Songs For 'Drella* (Warners 1990)★★★★, *Magic And Loss* (Sire 1992) ★★★★, *Set The Twilight Reeling* (Warners 1996)★★★, (Warner Brothers 1998).
COMPILATIONS: *Walk On The Wild Side – The Best Of Lou Reed* (RCA 1977)★★★, *Rock 'N' Roll Diary 1967-1980* (Arista 1980)★★★, *Between Thought And Expression* 3-CD box set(RCA 1992)★★★★, *Perfect Day* (Camden 1997)★★★.
VIDEOS: *The New York Album* (Warner Music 1990), *Songs For 'Drella* (Warner Music 1991), *A Night With Lou Reed* (PNE 1996).
FURTHER READING: *Lou Reed & The Velvets*, Nigel Trevena. *Rock And Roll Animal*, no author listed. *Lou Reed & The Velvet Underground*, Diana Clapton. *Lou Reed: Growing Up In Public*, Peter Doggett. *Between Thought And Expression: Selected Lyrics*, Lou Reed. *Waiting For the Man: A Biography Of Lou Reed*, Jeremy Reed. *Transformer: The Lou Reed Story*, Victor Bockris. *Between The Lines*, Michael Wrenn.

REEF
ALBUMS: *Replenish* (Sony 1995)★★★, *Glow* (Additive 1996)★★★★.

REEVES, JIM
ALBUMS: *Jim Reeves Sings* (Abbott 1956)★★, *Singing Down The Lane* (RCA Victor 1956)★★★, *Bimbo* (RCA Victor 1957)★★★, *Jim Reeves* (RCA Victor 1957)★★★, *Girls I Have Known* (RCA Victor 1958)★★★, *God Be With You* (RCA Victor 1958)★★★, *Songs To Warm The Heart* (RCA Victor 1959)★★★, *He'll Have To Go* (RCA Victor 1960)★★★★, *According To My Heart* (Camden 1960)★★★, *The Intimate Jim Reeves* (RCA Victor 1960)★★★★, *Talking To Your Heart* (RCA Victor 1961)★★★, *Tall Tales And Short Tempers* (RCA Victor 1961)★★★, *The Country Side Of Jim Reeves* (RCA Victor 1962)★★★, *A Touch Of Velvet* (RCA Victor 1962)★★★, *We Thank Thee* (RCA Victor 1962)★★★, *Good 'N' Country* (Camden 1963)★★★★, *Diamonds In The Sand* (Camden 1963)★★★, *Gentleman Jim* (RCA Victor 1963)★★★★, *The International Jim Reeves* (RCA Victor 1963)★★★, *Twelve Songs Of Christmas* (RCA Victor 1963)★★★, *Moonlight And Roses* (RCA Victor 1964)★★★★, *Have I Told You Lately That I Love You?* (RCA Victor 1964)★★★, *Kimberley Jim* (RCA Victor 1964)★★, *The Jim Reeves Way* (RCA Victor 1965)★★★, *Distant Drums* (RCA Victor 1966)★★★★, *Yours Sincerely, Jim Reeves* (RCA Victor 1966)★★★, *Blue Side Of Lonesome* (RCA Victor 1967)★★★, *My Cathedral* (RCA Victor 1967)★★★, *A Touch of Sadness* (RCA Victor 1968)★★★, *Jim Reeves On Stage* (RCA Victor 1968)★★★, *Jim Reeves – And Some Friends* (RCA Victor 1969)★★★, *Jim Reeves Writes You A Record* (RCA Victor 1971)★★★, *Something Special* (RCA Victor 1971)★★★, *Young And Country* (RCA Victor 1971)★★★, *My Friend* (RCA Victor 1972)★★★, *Missing You* (RCA Victor 1972)★★★, *Am I That Easy To Forget* (RCA Victor 1973)★★★, *Great Moments With Jim Reeves* (RCA Victor 1973)★★, *I'd Fight The World* (RCA Victor 1974)★★★, *Songs Of Love* (RCA Victor 1975)★★, *I Love You Because* (RCA Victor 1976)★★, *It's Nothin' To Me* (RCA Victor 1977)★★★, *Jim Reeves* (RCA Victor 1978)★★★, with Deborah Allen *Don't Let Me Cross Over* (RCA Victor 1979)★★, *There's Always Me* (RCA Victor 1980)★★, with Patsy Cline *Greatest Hits* (RCA Victor 1981)★★, *Dear Hearts & Gentle People* (1992)★★★, *Jim Reeves* (Summit 1995)★★★, *Stars Of texas Series* (Collectables 1995).
COMPILATIONS: *The Best Of Jim Reeves* (RCA Victor 1964)★★★, *The Best Of Jim Reeves, Volume 2* (RCA Victor 1966)★★★, *The Best Of Jim Reeves, Volume 3* (RCA Victor 1969)★★★, *The Best Of Jim Reeves Sacred Songs* (RCA Victor 1975)★★★, *Live At The Grand Ole Opry* (CMF 1987)★★★, *Four Walls – The Legend Begins* (RCA 1991)★★★, *The Definitive Jim Reeves* (RCA 1992)★★★, *Welcome To My World: The Essential Jim Reeves Collection* (RCA 1993)★★★★, *Welcome To My World* 16-CD box set (Bear Family 1994)★★★★, *The Essential Jim Reeves* (RCA 1995)★★★★, *The Ultimate Collection* (RCA 1996)★★★★.
FURTHER READING: *The Saga Of Jim Reeves: Country And Western Singer And Musician*, Pansy Cook.

REEVES, MARTHA
ALBUMS: *Martha Reeves* (MCA 1974)★★★, *The Rest Of My Life* (Arista 1977)★, *We Meet Again* (Milestone 1978)H, *Gotta Keep Moving* (Fantasy 1980)★.
COMPILATIONS: *We Meet Again/Gotta Keep Moving* (1993)H, *Early Classics* (Spectrum 1996)★★.

REID, TERRY
ALBUMS: *Bang Bang You're Terry Reid* (Epic 1968)★★★★, *Terry Reid* (Epic 1969)★★★, *River* (Atlantic 1973)★★★, *Seed Of Memory* (ABC 1976)★★★, *Rogue Waves* (Capitol 1979)★★, *The Driver* (Warners 1991)★★.
COMPILATIONS: *The Most Of Terry Reid* (1971)★★, *The Hand Don't Fit The Glove* (See For Miles 1985)★★★★.

R.E.M.
ALBUMS: *Chronic Town* mini-album (IRS 1982)★★★, *Murmur* (IRS 1983)★★★★, *Reckoning* (IRS 1984)★★★, *Fables Of The Reconstruction* (IRS 1985)★★★, *Life's Rich Pageant* (IRS 1986)★★★, *Document* (IRS 1987)★★★, *Green* (Warners 1988)★★★★, *Out Of Time* (Warners 1991)★★★★, *Automatic For The People* (Warners 1992)★★★★, *Monster* (Warners 1994)★★★★, *New Adventures In Hi-Fi* (Warners 1996)★★★★★.
COMPILATIONS: *Dead Letter Office* (IRS 1987)★★★, *Eponymous* (IRS 1988)★★★, *The Best Of R.E.M.* (IRS 1991)★★★.
VIDEOS: *Athens, Ga – Inside Out* (A&M 1986), *Succumbs* (A&M 1987), *Pop Screen* (Warner 1990), *This Film Is On* (Warner Reprise 1991), *Tour Film* (Warner Reprise 1991), *Parallel* (Warner Music Vision 1995), *Road Movie* (Warner Vision 1996).
FURTHER READING: *Remarks: Story Of R.E.M.*, Tony Heylin Fletcher. *R.E.M.: Behind The Mask*, Jim Greer. *R.E.M.: File Under Water, The Definitive Guide To 12 Years Of Recordings And Concerts*, Jon Storey. *An R.E.M. Companion: It Crawled From The South*, Marcus Gray. *The Rolling Stone Files*, no editor listed. *Talk About The Passion: R.E.M. An Oral History*, Denise Sullivan. *R.E.M. Documental*, Dave Bowler and Bryan Dray.

REMBRANDTS
ALBUMS: *Rembrandts* (East West 1991)★★★, *Untitled* (Reprise 1992)★★, *L.P.* (East West 1995)★★★.

REO SPEEDWAGON
ALBUMS: *REO Speedwagon* (Epic 1971)★★★, *REO Two* (Epic 1972)★★★, *Ridin' The Storm Out* (Epic 1974)★★★, *Lost In A Dream* (Epic 1974)★★, *This Time We Mean It* (Epic 1975)★★, *REO* (Epic 1976)★★, *REO Speedwagon Live/You Get What You Play For* (Epic 1977)★★, *You Can Tune A Piano But You Can't Tuna Fish* (Epic 1978)★★, *Nine Lives* (Epic 1979)★★, *Hi Infidelity* (Epic 1980)★★, *Good Trouble* (Epic 1982)★★, *Wheels Are Turning* (Epic 1984)★★, *Life As We Know It* (Epic 1987)★★, *The Earth, A Small Man, His Dog And*

A Chicken (Epic 1990)★★, Building The Bridge (Essential 1996)★★.
COMPILATIONS: A Decade Of Rock 'N' Roll 1970-1980 (Epic 1980)★★★, The Hits (Epic 1988)★★★.
VIDEOS: Wheels Are Turnin' (Virgin Vision 1987), REO Speedwagon (Fox Video 1988).

REPLACEMENTS
ALBUMS: Sorry Ma, Forgot To Take Out The Trash (Twin/Tone 1981)★★, Hootenanny (Twin/Tone 1983)★★★, Let It Be (Twin/Tone 1984)★★★★, The Shit Hits The Fans cassette only (Twin/Tone 1985)★★, Tim (Sire 1985)★★★, Pleased To Meet Me (Sire 1987)★★★★, Don't Tell A Soul (Sire 1989)★★★, All Shook Down (Sire 1990)★★★.
COMPILATIONS: Boink!! (Glass 1986)★★★, All For Nothing/Nothing For All (Reprise 1997)★★★.

REPUBLICA
ALBUMS: Republica (DeConstruction 1997)★★★.

RESIDENTS
ALBUMS: Meet The Residents (Ralph 1974)★★★★, The Residents Present The Third Reich 'N' Roll (Ralph 1976)★★★, Fingerprince (Ralph 1976)★★★, Not Available (Ralph 1978)★★★, Duck Stab/Buster And Glen (Ralph 1978)★★★★, Eskimo (Ralph 1979)★★★, The Residents Commercial Album (Ralph 1980)★★★★, Mark Of The Mole (Ralph 1981)★★★, Intermission mini-album (Ralph 1982)★★, The Tunes Of Two Cities (Ralph 1982)★★, with Renaldo And The Loaf Title In Limbo (Ralph 1983)★★, The Residents' Mole Show (No Label 1983)★★, George And James (Ralph 1984)★★★, Whatever Happened To Vileness Fats (Ralph 1984)★★, Assorted Secrets cassette only (Ralph 1984)★★, The Census Taker (Ralph 1985)★★, The Big Bubble (Ralph 1985)★★, Stars And Hank Forever (Ralph 1986)★★, 13th Anniversary Show Live In Holland (Torso 1986)★★, 13th Anniversary Show Live In Japan (Ralph 1986)★★, 13th Anniversary Show Live In The USA (Ralph 1986)★★, The Mole Show Live In Holland (Torso 1987)★★, God In Three Persons (Rykodisc 1988)★★, God In Three Persons: Original Soundtrack Recording (Rykodisc 1988)★★, The King And Eye (Enigma 1989)★★, Buckaroo Blues & Black Barry cassette only (Ralph 1989)★★, Stranger Than Supper (UWEB Special Products 1990)★★★, Cube-E Live In Holland (Enigma 1990)★★, Freakshow (Official Product 1991)★★, Our Finest Flowers (Ralph 1993)★★, Gingerbread Man (Euroralph 1995)★★, Resideux Deux (East Side 1998).
COMPILATIONS: Nibbles (Virgin 1979)★★★, Ralph Before '84 Volume 1 (Ralph 1984)★★★, Ralph Before '84 Volume 2 (Ralph 1985)★★★, Heaven? (Rykodisc 1986)★★★, Hell? (Rykodisc 1986)★★★.
FURTHER READING: Meet The Residents, Ian Shirley.

RETURN TO FOREVER
ALBUMS: Light As A Feather (Polydor 1972)★★★★, Return To Forever (ECM 1973)★★★★, Hymn Of The Seventh Galaxy (Polydor 1973)★★★★, Where Have I Known You Before? (Polydor 1974)★★★, No Mystery (Polydor 1975)★★, The Leprechaun (Polydor 1976)★★★★, Romantic Warrior (Columbia 1976)★★★, Live: The Complete Concert (Columbia 1979)★★★.
COMPILATIONS: The Best Of Return To Forever (Columbia 1980)★★★★, Return To The 7th Galaxy: The Return To Forever Anthology Featuring Chick Corea (Chronicles/Verve 1996)★★★★, Musicmagic (Columbia 1997)★★★.

REVERE, PAUL, AND THE RAIDERS
ALBUMS: Like, Long Hair (Gardena 1961)★★★, Paul Revere And The Raiders aka In The Beginning (Jerden 1961)★★, Here They Come (Columbia 1965)★★★, Just Like Us (Columbia 1965)★★★, Midnight Ride (Columbia 1966)★★★, The Spirit Of 67 aka Good Thing (Columbia 1967)★★★, Revolution (1967)★★★, A Christmas Present ... And Past (1967)★★★, Goin' To Memphis (1968)★★★, Something Happening (1968)★★★, Hard And Heavy (With Marshmallow) (Columbia 1969)★★, Alias Pink Puzz (1969)★★, Collage (1970)★★★, Indian Reservation (1971)★★★, Country Wine (1972)★★, We Gotta All Get Together (Realm 1976)★★, Featuring Mark Lindsay's Arizona (Realm 1976)★★.
COMPILATIONS: Greatest Hits (Columbia 1967)★★★, Greatest Hits Volume 2 (60s)★★★, All-Time Greatest Hits (70s)★★★, Kicks (1982)★★★, The Essential Ride 1963-67 (Columbia/Legacy 1995)★★★★.

REZILLOS
ALBUMS: Can't Stand The Rezillos (Sire 1978)★★★, Mission Accomplished ... But The Beat Goes On (Sire 1979)★★, Live And On Fire In Japan (Vinyl Japan 1995)★★.
COMPILATIONS: Can't Stand The Rezillos, The (Almost) Complete Rezillos (Sire 1995)★★★.

RHINOCEROS
ALBUMS: Rhinoceros (Elektra 1968)★★★, Satin Chickens (Elektra 1969)★★, Better Times Are Coming (Elektra 1970)★.

RICH, TONY, PROJECT
ALBUMS: Words (LaFace/Arista 1996)★★★★.

RICHARD, CLIFF
ALBUMS: Cliff (Columbia 1959)★★★, Cliff Sings (Columbia 1959)★★★★, Me And My Shadows (Columbia 1960)★★★★, Listen To Cliff (Columbia 1961)★★★, 21 Today (Columbia 1961)★★★, The Young Ones (Columbia 1961)★★★, 32 Minutes And 17 Seconds With Cliff Richard (Columbia 1962)★★★★, Summer Holiday (Columbia 1963)★★★, Cliff's Hit Album (Columbia 1963)★★★★, When In Spain (Columbia 1963)★★★, Wonderful Life (Columbia 1964)★★★, Aladdin And His Wonderful Lamp (Columbia 1964)★★★, Cliff Richard (Columbia 1965)★★★, More Hits By Cliff (Columbia 1965)★★★, When In Rome (Columbia 1965)★★, Love Is Forever (Columbia 1965)★★★, Kinda Latin (Columbia 1966)★★★, Finders Keepers (Columbia 1966)★★, Cinderella (Columbia 1967)★★, Don't Stop Me Now (Columbia 1967)★★★, Good News (Columbia 1967)★★★, Cliff In Japan (Columbia 1968)★★★, Two A Penny (Columbia 1968)★★★, Established 1958 (Columbia 1968)★★★, Sincerely Cliff (Columbia 1969)★★★, It'll Be Me (Columbia 1969)★★★, Cliff 'Live' At The Talk Of The Town (1970)★★★, All My Love (1970)★★★, About That Man (1970)★★★, Tracks 'N' Grooves (Columbia 1970)★★★, His Land (Columbia 1970)★★★, Cliff's Hit Album (EMI 1971)★★★, The Cliff Richard Story (EMI 1972)★★★, Take Me High (EMI 1973)★★★, Help It Along (EMI 1974)★★★, The 31st Of February Street (EMI 1974)★★★, Everybody Needs Somebody (EMI 1975)★★★, I'm Nearly Famous (EMI 1976)★★★, Cliff Live (EMI 1976)★★★, Every Face Tells A Story (EMI 1977)★★★, Small Corners (EMI 1977)★★★, Green Light (EMI 1978)★★★, Thank You Very Much (EMI 1979)★★★, Rock 'N' Roll Juvenile (EMI 1979)★★★, Rock On With Cliff (EMI 1980)★★★, The Cliff Richard Songbook (EMI 1980)★★★, Listen To Cliff (EMI 1980)★★★, I'm No Hero (EMI 1980)★★★, Love Songs (EMI 1981)★★★, Wired For Sound (EMI 1981)★★★, Now You See Me, Now You Don't (EMI 1982)★★★, Dressed For The Occasion (EMI 1983)★★★, Silver (EMI 1983)★★★, Cliff In The 60s (EMI 1984)★★★, Cliff And The Shadows EMI 1984)★★★, Walking In The Light (EMI 1984)★★★, The Rock Connection (EMI 1984)★★★, Time (1986)★★★, Hymns And Inspirational Songs (EMI 1986)★★★, Always Guaranteed (EMI 1987)★★★, Private Collection (EMI 1988)★★★, Stronger (EMI 1989)★★★, From A Distance ...The Event (EMI 1990)★★★, Together With Cliff (EMI 1991)★★★, The Album (EMI 1993)★★★, Songs From Heathcliff (EMI 1995).
COMPILATIONS: The Best Of Cliff (Columbia 1969)★★★★, The Best Of Cliff Volume 2 (Columbia 1972)★★★★, 40 Golden Greats (EMI 1979)★★★★, The Hit List (EMI 1994)★★★★, At The Movies 1959-1974 (EMI 1996)★★★, The Rock 'N' Roll Years 1958-1963 4-CD (EMI 1997)★★★.
VIDEOS: Two A Penny (1978), The Video Connection (1983), Together (1984), Rock In Australia (1985), Thank You Very Much (1986),We Don't Talk Anymore (1987), Video EP (1988), The Young Ones (1988), Summer Holiday (1988), Wonderful Life (1988), Take Me High (1988), Private Collection (1988), Always Guaranteed (1988), Live And Guaranteed (1989), From A Distance ... The Event Vols 1and 2 (1990), Together With Cliff Richard (1991), Expresso Bongo (1992), Cliff-When The Music Stops (1993), Access All Areas (1993), The Story So Far (1993), The Hit List (PMI 1995), The Hit List Live (PMI 1995), Finders Keepers (1996), Cliff At The Movies (1996).
FURTHER READING: Driftin' With Cliff Richard: The Inside Story Of What Really Happens On Tour, Jet Harris and Royston Ellis. Cliff, The Baron Of Beat, Jack Sutter. It's Great To Be Young, Cliff Richard. Me And My Shadows, Cliff Richard. Top Pops, Cliff Richard. Cliff Around The Clock, Bob Ferrier. The Wonderful World Of Cliff Richard, Bob Ferrier. Questions: Cliff Answering Reader And Fan Queries, Cliff Richard. The Way I See It, Cliff Richard. The Cliff Richard Story, George Tremlett. New Singer, New Song: The Cliff Richard Story, David Winter. Which One's Cliff?, Cliff Richard with Bill Latham. Happy Christmas From Cliff, Cliff Richard. Cliff In His Own Words, Kevin St. John. Cliff, Patrick Doncaster and Tony Jasper. Cliff Richard, John Tobler. Silver Cliff: A 25 Year Journal 1958-1983, Tony Jasper. Cliff Richard: The Complete Recording Sessions, 1958-1990, Peter Lewry and Nigel Goodall. Cliff: A Biography, Tony Jasper. Cliff Richard, The Complete Chronicle, Mike Read, Nigel Goodhall and Peter Lewry. Cliff Richard: The Autobiography, Steve Turner.
FILMS: Serious Charge (1959), Expresso Bongo (1960), The Young Ones (1961), Summer Holiday (1962), Wonderful Life (1964), Thunderbirds Are Go! (1966), Finders Keepers (1966), Two A Penny (1968), Take Me High (1973).

RICHIE, LIONEL
ALBUMS: Lionel Richie (Motown 1982)★★★, Can't Slow Down (Motown 1983)★★★★, Dancing On The Ceiling (Motown 1986)★★★, Back To Front (Motown 1992)★★, Louder Than Words (Mercury 1996)★★.
COMPILATIONS: Truly: The Love Songs (Motown 1998)★★★.
VIDEOS: All Night Long (RCA/Columbia 1986), Dancing On The Ceiling (Hendring Video 1988).
FURTHER READING: Lionel Richie: An Illustrated Biography, David Nathan.

RICHMAN, JONATHAN
ALBUMS: as The Modern Lovers The Modern Lovers (Beserkley 1976)★★★★, as Jonathan Richman And The Modern Lovers Jonathan Richman And The Modern Lovers (Beserkley 1977)★★★, as Jonathan Richman And The Modern Lovers Rock 'N' Roll With The Modern Lovers (Beserkley 1977)★★★, as The Modern Lovers The Modern Lovers Live (Beserkley 1977)★★, Back In Your Life (Beserkley 1979)★★★, The Jonathan Richman Songbook (Beserkley 1980)★★★, Jonathan Sings! (Sire 1983)★★★, Rockin' And Romance (Twin Tone 1985)★★, as Jonathan Richman And The Modern Lovers It's Time For Jonathan Richman And The Modern Lovers (Upside 1986)★★, with Barence Whitfield Jonathan Richman & Barence Whitfield (Rounder 1988), Modern Lovers 88 (Rounder 1988)★★, Jonathan Richman (Rounder 1989)★★, Jonathan Goes Country (Rounder 1990)★★, Having A Party (Cheree 1991)★★★, I, Jonathan (Rounder 1992)★★★, Jonathan Tu Vas A Emoncionar (Rounder 1993)★★, Plea For Tenderness (Nectar Masters 1994)★★, You Must Ask The Heart (Rounder 1995)★★, Surrender To Jonathan (Vapor 1996)★★★.
COMPILATIONS: as The Modern Lovers The Original Modern Lovers early recordings (Bomp 1981)★★★, The Beserkley Years: The Best Of Jonathan Richman And The Modern Lovers (Beserkley/Rhino 1987)★★★, Jonathan Richman And The Modern Lovers – 23 Great Recordings (Beserkley/Castle 1990)★★★★.

RIDE
ALBUMS: Nowhere (Creation 1990)★★, Going Blank Again (Creation 1992)★★★★, Carnival Of Light (Creation 1994)★★, Tarantula (Creation 1996)★★★, Live Light rec. in Paris 1994 (Mutiny 1996)★★.

RIGHT SAID FRED
ALBUMS: Up (Tug 1992)★★★, Sex And Travel (Tug 1993)★★, Smashing (Happy Valley 1995)★★.

RIGHTEOUS BROTHERS
ALBUMS: The Righteous Brothers – Right Now! (Moonglow 1963)★★, Some Blue-Eyed Soul (Moonglow 1965)★★, You've Lost That Lovin' Feelin' (Philles 1965)★★★★, Just Once In My Life (Philles 1965)★★★★, Back To Back (Philles 1965)★★★★, This Is New! (Moonglow 1965)★★, In Action (Sue 1966)★★, Soul And Inspiration (Verve 1966)★★★★, Go Ahead And Cry (Verve 1966)★★★, Sayin' Somethin' (Verve 1967)★★★, Souled Out (Verve 1967)★★★, Standards (Verve 1967)★★★, One For The Road (Verve 1968)★★★, Rebirth (Verve 1970)★★, Give It To The People (Haven 1974)★★, The Sons Of Mrs Righteous (Haven 1975)★★.
COMPILATIONS: Greatest Hits (Verve 1967)★★★★, Greatest Hits Volume 2 (Verve 1969)★★★, 2 By 2 (MGM 1973)★★★, Best Of The Righteous Brothers (Verve 1987)★★★★, Anthology (1962-1974) (Rhino 1989)★★★★, Best Of The Righteous Brothers (Curb 1990)★★★, Unchained Melody: The Very Best Of The Righteous Brothers (Polygram 1990)★★★★, The Moonglow Years (Polygram 1991)★★★.
VIDEOS: 21st Anniversary Celebration (Old Gold 1990).
FILMS: Beach Ball (1964).

RIMES, LEANN
ALBUMS: All That (1993)★★, Blue (Curb 1996)★★★★, Unchained Melody/The Early Years (Curb 1997)★★, You Light Up My Life/Inspirational Songs (Curb 1997)★★★, Sittin' On Top Of The World (Curb 1998).

RIVERS, JOHNNY
ALBUMS: Johnny Rivers At The Whisky A Go Go (Imperial 1964)★★★★, The Sensational Johnny Rivers (Capitol 1964)★★★★, Go, Johnny, Go (1964)★★★, Here We A-Go-Go Again (Imperial 1964)★★★, Johnny Rivers In Action! (Imperial 1965)★★★, Meanwhile Back At The Whisky A Go Go (Imperial 1965)★★★★, Johnny Rivers Rocks The Folk (Imperial 1965)★★, ... And I Know You Wanna Dance (Imperial 1966)★★★, Changes (Imperial 1966)★★★, Rewind (Imperial 1967)★★★, Realization (Imperial 1968)★★★, Johnny Rivers (Sunset 1968)★★★, A Touch Of Gold (Imperial 1969)★★★, Slim Slo Slider (Imperial 1970)★★★, Rockin' With Johnny Rivers (Sunset 1971)★★★, Non-Stop Dancing At The Whisky A Go Go (United Artists 1971)★★★, Home Grown (United Artists 1971)★★★, L.A. Reggae (United Artists 1972)★★★, Johnny Rivers (United Artists 1972)★★★, Blue Suede Shoes (United Artists 1973)★★★, Last Boogie In Paris (Atlantic 1974)★★★, Rockin' Rivers (1974)★★★, Road (Atlantic 1975)★★★, New Lovers And Old Friends (Epic 1975)★★★, Help Me Rhonda (Epic 1975)★★★, Wild Night (United Artists 1976)★★★, Outside Help (Big Tree 1978)★★, Borrowed Time (RSO 1980)★★, The Johnny Rivers Story (1982)★★★, Portrait Of (1982)★★★, Not A Through Street (Priority 1983)★★.
COMPILATIONS: Johnny Rivers' Golden Hits (Imperial 1966)★★★, The History Of Johnny Rivers (Liberty 1971)★★★, Go Johnny Go (Hallmark 1971)★★★, Greatest Hits re-recordings (MCA 1985)★★, The Best Of Johnny Rivers (EMI America 1987)★★★, Anthology 1964-1977 (Rhino 1991)★★★★.

ROACHFORD
ALBUMS: Roachford (Columbia 1988)★★★, Get Ready! (Columbia 1991)★★, Permanent Shades Of Blue (Columbia 1994)★★, Feel (Columbia 1997).

ROBERTSON, B.A.
ALBUMS: Wringing Applause (1973)★★, Initial Success (Asylum 1980)★★, Bully For You (Asylum 1981)★★, B.A. Robertson (Warners 1982)★★.

ROBERTSON, ROBBIE
ALBUMS: Robbie Robertson (Geffen 1987)★★★★, Storyville (Geffen 1991)★★, with the Red Road Ensemble Music For The Native Americans (Capitol 1994)★★★, Contact From The Underworld Of Red Boy (Capitol 1998).

ROBINSON, SMOKEY
ALBUMS: Smokey (Tamla 1973)★★★, Pure Smokey (Tamla 1974)★★★, A Quiet Storm (Tamla 1975)★★★, Smokey's Family Robinson (Tamla 1976)★★★, Deep In My Soul (Tamla 1977)★★★, Big Time (Tamla 1977)★★★, Love Breeze (Tamla 1978)★★★, Smokin' (Tamla 1978)★★★, Where There's Smoke (Tamla 1979)★★★, Warm Thoughts (Tamla 1980)★★★★, Being With You (Tamla 1981)★★★★, Yes It's You Lady (Tamla 1982)★★★, Touch The Sky (Tamla 1983)★★★, Blame It On Love (Tamla 1983)★★★, Essar (Tamla 1984)★★★, Smoke Signals (Tamla 1985)★★★, One Heartbeat (Motown 1987)★★★, Love, Smokey (Motown 1990)★★★, Double Good Everything (SBK 1991)★★, Ballads (Motown 1995).
COMPILATIONS: with the Miracles The Greatest Hits (Motown 1992)★★★★, with the Miracles The 35th Anniversary Collection 4-CD box set (Motown Masters 1994)★★★★, Early Classics (Spectrum 1996)★★★★.
FURTHER READING: Smokey: Inside My Life, Smokey Robinson and David Ritz.

ROBINSON, TOM
ALBUMS: with Tom Robinson Band Power In The Darkness (Harvest 1978)★★★★, with Tom Robinson Band TRB2 (Harvest 1979)★★, with Sector 27 Sector 27 (Fontana 1980)★★, North By Northwest (Fontana 1982)★★★, Hope And Glory (RCA 1984)★★★, Still Loving You (RCA 1986)★★★, Last Tango (Line 1989)★★, with Jakko M. Jakszuk We Never Had It So Good (Musidisc 1990)★★★, Living In A Boom Time (Cooking Vinyl 1992)★★★, Love Over Rage (Cooking Vinyl 1994)★★★, Having It Both Ways (Cooking Vinyl 1996)★★★, Blood Brother (Castaway North 1997).
COMPILATIONS: with Tom Robinson Band Tom Robinson Band (EMI 1981)★★★, Cabaret '79 (Panic 1982)★★★, The Collection 1977-1987 (EMI 1987)★★★★, Rising Free – The Very Best Of (EMI 1997)★★★★.

ROCHES
ALBUMS: Seductive Reasoning (Columbia 1975)★★, The Roches (Warners 1979)★★★★, Nurds (Warners 1980)★★★, Keep On Doing (Warners 1982)★★★, Another World (Warners 1985)★★★, No Trespassing (Rhino 1986)★★, Crossing Delancey soundtrack (Varese Sarabande 1988)★★★, Speak (MCA/Paradox 1989)★★★, Three Kings (MCA 1990)★★★, A Dove (MCA 1992)★★, Will You Be My Friend children's album (Baby Boom 1994)★★, Can We Go Home Now? (Rykodisc 1995)★★★.

ROCKET FROM THE CRYPT
ALBUMS: Paint As A Fragrance (Headhunter 1991)★★, Circa: Now! (Headhunter 1992)★★, The State Of Art Is On Fire mini-album (Sympathy For The Record Industry 1995)★★, Hot Charity mini-album (Elemental 1995)★★, Scream, Dracula, Scream! (Elemental 1996)★★★★, Rocket From The Crypt (Elemental 1998)★★★.
COMPILATIONS: All Systems Go! (Headhunter 1993)★★★.

ROCKPILE
ALBUMS: Seconds Of Pleasure (F-Beat 1980)★★★.

RODGERS, PAUL
ALBUMS: Cut Loose (1983)★★, 10 from 6 (1985)★★, Muddy Waters Blues (London 1993)★★★★, Paul Rodgers Live (1996)★★★, Now (SPV 1997)★★★.

ROE, TOMMY
ALBUMS: Sheila (ABC 1962)★★★, Something For Everybody (ABC 1964)★★★, Everybody Likes Tommy Roe (HMV 1964)★★★, Ballads And Beat (HMV 1965)★★★, Sweet Pea (ABC 1966)★★★, It's Now A Winter's Day (ABC 1967)★★, Phantasia (1967)★★, Dizzy (Stateside 1969)★★★, We Can Make Music (Probe 1970)★★, Beginnings (Probe 1971)★★, Energy (1976)★★, Full Bloom (1977)★★.
COMPILATIONS: 12 In A Roe (1970)★★★, Greatest Hits (Stateside 1970)★★★, Beginnings (1971)★★★, 16 Greatest Hits (1976)★★★, 16 Greatest Songs (1993)★★★.

ROGERS, KENNY
ALBUMS: by the First Edition The First Edition (Reprise 1967)★★, The First Edition's 2nd (Reprise 1968)★★, The First Edition '69 (Reprise 1969)★★. By Kenny Rogers And The First Edition Ruby, Don't Take Your Love To Town (Reprise 1969)★★★, Something's Burning (Reprise 1970)★★★★, Fools film soundtrack (1970)★★★, Tell It All Brother (Reprise 1971)★★★, Transition (Reprise 1971)★★★, The Ballad Of Calico (Reprise 1972)★★★, Backroads (Jolly Rogers 1972)★★★, Monumental (Jolly Rogers 1973)★★★, Rollin' (Jolly Rogers 1974)★★. By Kenny Rogers Love Lifted Me (United Artists 1976)★★★, Kenny Rogers (United Artists 1976)★★, Daytime Friends (United Artists 1977)★★★, with West Every Time Two Fools Collide (United Artists 1978)★★★, Love Or Something Like It (United Artists 1978)★★★, The Gambler (United Artists 1978)★★★★, with Dottie West Classics (United Artists 1979)★★, Kenny (United Artists 1979)★★★★, Gideon (United Artists 1980)★★★, Share Your Love (Liberty 1981)★★★, Christmas (Liberty 1981)★★, Love Will Turn You Around (Liberty 1982)★★★, We've Got Tonight (Liberty 1983)★★★★, Eyes That See In The Dark (RCA 1983)★★★★, with Dottie West, Kim Carnes, Sheena Easton Duets (Liberty 1984)★★★, What About Me? (RCA 1984)★★★, with Dolly Parton Once Upon A Christmas (RCA 1984)★★★, Love Is What We Make It (Liberty 1985)★★, The Heart Of The Matter (RCA 1985)★★, Short Stories (1986)★★, They Don't Make Them Like They Used To (RCA 1986)★★, I Prefer The Moonlight (RCA 1987)★★, Something Inside So Strong (Reprise 1989)★★, Christmas In America (Reprise 1989)★★, Love Is Strange (Reprise 1990)★★★, You're My Kind Of People (1991)★★★, Some Prisons Don't Have Walls (1991)★★, Back Home Again (Reprise 1991)★★★, If Only My Heart Had A Voice (1993)★★★, The Gift (Magnatone 1996)★★★, Across My Heart (Magnatone 1997)★★★, Branson City Limits (Live) (Unison 1998).
COMPILATIONS: Kenny Rogers And The First Edition Greatest Hits (Reprise 1971)★★★. Kenny Rogers Ten Years Of Gold (United Artists 1978)★★★, Kenny Rogers' Greatest Hits (Liberty 1980)★★★★, Twenty Greatest Hits (Liberty 1983)★★★, 25 Greatest Hits (EMI 1987)★★★, The Very Best Of Kenny Rogers (Warners 1990)★★★, All Time Greatest Hits 3-CD box set (CEMA 1996)★★★.
VIDEOS: with Dolly Parton Real Love (RCA/Columbia 1988).
FURTHER READING: Making It In Music, Kenny Rogers and Len Epand. Kenny Rogers – Gambler, Dreamer, Lover, Martha Hume.

ROLLING STONE
FURTHER READING: The Rolling Stone Story, Robert Draper. Best Of Rolling Stone: Classic Writing From The World's Most Influential Music Magazine, Robert Love. Rolling Stone: The Photographs, Laurie Kratochvil (ed.).

ROLLING STONES
ALBUMS: The Rolling Stones (London/Decca 1964)★★★★, 12X5 (London 1964)★★★★, The Rolling Stones (London/Decca 1965)★★★★, The Rolling Stones Now! (London 1965)★★★★, December's Children (And Everybody's) (London 1965)★★★★, Out Of Our Heads (Decca/London 1965)★★★★, Aftermath (Decca/London 1966)★★★★, Got Live If You Want It (London 1966)★★★, Between The Buttons (London/Decca 1967)★★★, Their Satanic Majesties Request (Decca/London 1967)★★★, Flowers (London 1967)★★★, Beggars Banquet (London 1968)★★★★★, Let It Bleed (London/Decca 1969)★★★★★, Get Yer Ya-Ya's Out! (Decca/London1970)★★★★, Sticky Fingers (Rolling Stones 1971)★★★★, Exile On Main Street (Rolling Stones 1972)★★★★★, Goat's Head Soup (Rolling Stones 1973)★★★, It's Only Rock 'N' Roll (Rolling Stones 1974)★★★, Black And Blue (Rolling Stones 1976)★★★, Love You Live (Rolling Stones 1977)★★★, Some Girls (Rolling Stones 1978)★★★, Emotional Rescue (Rolling Stones 1980)★★, Tattoo You (Rolling Stones 1981)★★★, Still Life (American Concerts 1981) (Rolling Stones 1982)★★, Undercover (Rolling Stones 1983)★★, Dirty Work (Rolling Stones 1986)★★★, Steel Wheels (Rolling Stones 1989)★★★, Flashpoint (Rolling Stones 1991)★★★, Voodoo Lounge (Virgin 1994)★★★★, Stripped (Virgin 1995)★★★, Bridges To Babylon (Virgin 1997)★★★.
COMPILATIONS: Big Hits (High Tide And Green Grass) (London 1966)★★★★, Through The Past, Darkly (London 1969)★★★★, Hot Rocks 1964-1971 (London 1972)★★★★, More Hot Rocks (Big Hits And Fazed Cookies) (London 1972)★★★★, The Rolling Stones Singles Collection: The London Years 3-CD box set (Abko/London 1989)★★★★★. Many other compilation and archive albums have also been issued.
CD Roms: Voodoo Lounge (Virgin 1995).
VIDEOS: The Stones In The Park (BMG 1993), Gimme Shelter (1993), Live At The Max (Polygram 1994), 25 x 5 The Continuing Adventures Of The Rolling Stones (1994), Sympathy For The Devil (BMG 1995), Voodoo Lounge (Game Entertainment 1995).
FURTHER READING: The Rolling Stones File, Tim Hewat. The Stones, Philip Carmelo Luce. Uptight With The Rolling Stones, Richard Elman. Rolling Stones: An Unauthorized Biography In Words, Photographs And Music, David Dalton. Mick Jagger: The Singer Not The Song, J. Marks. Mick Jagger: Everybody's Lucifer, Anthony Scaduto. STP: A Journey Through America With The Rolling Stones, Robert Greenfield. Les Rolling Stones, Philippe Contantin. The Rolling Stones Story, George Tremlett. The Rolling Stones, Cindy Ehrlich. The Rolling Stones: A Celebration, Nik Cohn. The Rolling Stones, Tony Jasper. The Rolling Stones: An Illustrated Record, Roy Carr. The Rolling Stones, Jeremy Pascall. The Rolling Stones On Tour, Annie Leibowitz. Up And Down With The Rolling Stones, Tony Sanchez with John Blake. The Rolling Stones: An Annotated Bibliography, Mary Laverne Dimmick. Keith Richards, Barbara Charone. Rolling Stones In Their Own Words, Rolling Stones. The Rolling Stones: An Illustrated Discography, Miles. The Rolling Stones In Their Own Words, David Dalton and Mick Farren. The Rolling Stones: The First Twenty Years, David Dalton. Mick Jagger In His Own Words, Miles. The Rolling Stones In Concert, Linda Martin. The Rolling Stones: Live In America, Philip Kamin and Peter Goddard. Death Of A Rolling Stone: The Brian Jones Story, Mandy Aftel. Jagger, Carey Schofield. The Rolling Stones A To Z, Sue Weiner and Lisa Howard. The Rolling Stones, Robert Palmer. The Stones, Philip Norman. Satisfaction: The Rolling Stones, Gered Mankowitz. The Rolling Stones, Dezo Hoffman. On The Road With The Rolling Stones, Chet Flippo. The True Adventures Of The Rolling Stones, Stanley Booth. Heart Of Stone: The Definitive Rolling Stones Discography, Felix Aeppli. Yesterday's Papers: The Rolling Stones In Print, Jessica MacPhail. The Life And Good Times Of The Rolling Stones, Philip Norman. Stone Alone, Bill Wyman and Ray Coleman. The Rolling Stones 25th Anniversary Tour, Greg Quill. Blown Away: The Rolling Stones And The Death Of The Sixties, A. E. Hotchner. The Rolling Stones: Complete Recording Sessions 1963-1989, Martin Elliott. The Rolling Stones Story, Robert Draper. The Rolling Stones Chronicle: The First Thirty Years, Massimo Bonanno. Rolling Stones: Images Of The World Tour 1989-1990, David Fricke and Robert Sandall. The Rolling Stones' Rock 'N' Roll Circus, no author listed. The Rolling Stones: Behind The Buttons (Limited Edition), Gered Mankowitz and Robert Whitaker (Photographers). Golden Stone: The Untold Life And Mysterious Death Of Brian Jones, Laura Jackson. Rolling Stones: Das Weissbuch, Dieter Hoffmann. Not Fade Away: Rolling Stones Collection, Geoffrey Giuliano. Keith Richards: The Unauthorised Biography, Victor Bockris. The Rolling Stones: The Complete Works Vol. 1 1962-75, Nico Zentgraf. Street Fighting Years, Stephen Barnard. Paint It Black: The Murder Of Brian Jones, Geoffrey Giuliano. Brian Jones: The Inside Story Of The Original Rolling Stone, Nicholas Fitzgerald. Who Killed Christopher Robin, Terry Rawlings. A Visual Documentary, Miles. Not Fade Away, Chris Eborn. Complete Guide To The Music Of, James Hector. The Rolling Stones Chronicle, Massimo Bonanno.

ROLLINS, HENRY
ALBUMS: as Henry Rollins Hot Animal Machine (Texas Hotel 1987)★★, spoken word Big Ugly Mouth (Texas Hotel 1987)★★★, spoken word Sweat Box (Texas Hotel 1989)★★, spoken word The Boxed Life (Imago 1993)★★★. As the Rollins Band Live (Eksakt 1987)★★★, Life Time (Texas Hotel 1988)★★★, Do It (Texas Hotel 1988)★★★, Hard Volume (Texas Hotel 1989)★★★, Turned On (Quarterstick 1990)★★★, The End Of Silence (Imago 1992)★★★★, Weight (Imago 1994)★★★, Get In The Van (Imago 1994)★★★, Everything (Thirsty Ear 1996)★★, Come In And Burn (Dreamworks 1997)★★, Black Coffee Blues (Thirsty Ear 1997).
FURTHER READING: Letters To Rollins, R.K. Overton. High Adventure In The Great Outdoors aka Bodybag. Pissing In The Gene Pool. Art To Choke Hearts, Bang!.. One From None, See A Grown Man Cry. Black Coffee Blues. Now Watch 'Em Die. Get In The Van: On The Road With Black Flag, all titles by Henry Rollins.

RONETTES
ALBUMS: Presenting The Fabulous Ronettes Featuring Veronica (Philes 1964)★★★.
COMPILATIONS: The Ronettes Sing Their Greatest Hits (Phil Spector International 1975)★★★, The Colpix Years 1961-63 (Murray Hill 1987)★★★, The Best Of (ABKCO 1992)★★★.

RONSON, MICK
ALBUMS: Slaughter On Tenth Avenue (RCA 1974)★★★, Play Don't Worry (RCA 1975)★★★, Heaven And Hull (Epic 1994)★★.
FURTHER READING: Mick Ronson Discography, Sven Gusevik.

RONSTADT, LINDA
ALBUMS: Hand Sown, Home Grown (Capitol 1969)★★, Silk Purse (Capitol 1970)★★, Linda Ronstadt (Capitol 1971)★★, Don't Cry Now (Asylum 1973)★★★, Heart Like A Wheel (Capitol 1974)★★★★, Prisoner In Disguise (Asylum 1975)★★★, Hasten Down The Wind (Asylum 1976)★★★, Simple Dreams (Asylum 1977)★★★, Living In The USA (Asylum 1978)★★, Mad Love (Asylum 1980)★★, with Kevin Kline, Estelle Parsons, Rex Smith Pirates Of Penzance (1981)★★, Get Closer (Asylum 1982)★★, What's New (Asylum 1983)★★★, Lush Life (Asylum 1984)★★★, For Sentimental Reasons (Asylum 1986)★★★, with Emmylou Harris, Dolly Parton Trio (Warners 1987)★★★★, Canciones De Mi Padre (Elektra 1987)★★★, Cry Like A Rainstorm – Howl Like The Wind (Elektra 1989)★★★, Mas Canciones (Elektra 1991)★★★, Frenesi (Elektra 1992)★★★, Winter Light (Elektra 1993)★★★★, Feels Like Home (Warners 1995)★★★, Dedicated To The One I Love (Elektra 1996)★★.
COMPILATIONS: Greatest Hits: Linda Ronstadt (Asylum 1976)★★★★, A Retrospective (Capitol 1977)★★★, Greatest Hits: Linda Ronstadt Volume 2 (Asylum 1980)★★★.
FURTHER READING: Linda Ronstadt: A Portrait, Richard Kanakaris. The Linda Ronstadt Scrapbook, Mary Ellen Moore. Linda Ronstadt, Vivian Claire. Linda Ronstadt: An Illustrated Biography, Connie Berman. Linda Ronstadt: It's So Easy, Mark Bego.

ROOMFUL OF BLUES
ALBUMS: The First Album (Island 1977)★★, Let's Have A Party (Antilles 1979)★★, Hot Little Mama (Blue Flame 1981)★★★, Eddie 'Cleanhead' Vinson & Roomful Of Blues (Muse 1982)★★★, Blues Train/Big Joe Turner & Roomful Of Blues (Muse 1983)★★★, Dressed Up To Get Messed Up (Rounder 1984)★★★, Live At Lupo's Heartbreak Hotel (Rounder 1986)★★★, with Earl King Glazed (Black Top 1988)★★★, Dance All Night (Rounder 1994)★★★, Turn It On, Turn It Up (Bullseye Blues 1995)★★★★, Under One Roof (Bullseye Blues 1997)★★★.
COMPILATIONS: Roomful Of Blues With Joe Turner/Roomful Of Blues With Eddie Cleanhead Vinson (32 Blues 1997)★★★★.

ROSE, TIM
ALBUMS: Tim Rose (Columbia 1967)★★★★, Through Rose Coloured Glasses (Columbia 1969)★★★, Love, A Kind Of Hate Story (Capitol 1970)★★, Tim Rose (Dawn 1972)★★, The Musician (Atlantic 1975)★★, The Gambler (President 1991)★★, The Big Three (Sequel 1995), Haunted (Dressed To Kill 1997).

ROSE ROYCE
ALBUMS: Car Wash (MCA 1976)★★★★, Rose Royce II/In Full Bloom (Whitfield 1977)★★★★, Rose Royce III/Strikes Again! (Whitfield 1978)★★★, Rose Royce IV/Rainbow Connection (Whitfield 1979)★★, Golden Touch (Whitfield 1981)★★, Jump Street (Warners 1981)★★, Stronger Than Ever (Epic 1982)★★, Music Magic (Streetwave 1984)★★, The Show Must Go On (Streetwave 1985)★★, Fresh Cut (Carrere 1987)★★.
COMPILATIONS: Greatest Hits (Whitfield 1980)★★★★, Is It Love You're After (Blatant 1988)★★★.

ROSS, DIANA
ALBUMS: Diana Ross (Motown 1970)★★★, Everything Is Everything (Motown 1970)★★★, Diana! (Motown 1971)★★★, Surrender (Motown 1971)★★★, Lady Sings The Blues (Motown 1972)★★★★, Touch Me In The Morning (Motown 1973)★★★, with Marvin Gaye Diana And Marvin (Motown 1973)★★★, Last Time I Saw Him (Motown 1973)★★★, Diana Ross Live At Caesar's Palace (Motown 1974)★★★, Mahogany (Motown 1975)★★, Diana Ross (Motown 1976)★★★, An Evening With Diana Ross (Motown 1977)★★★, Baby It's Me (Motown 1977)★★★, Ross (Motown 1978)★★★, The Boss (Motown 1979)★★★, Diana (Motown 1980)★★★, To Love Again (Motown 1981)★★★, Why Do Fools Fall In Love (RCA 1981)★★★, Silk Electric (RCA 1982)★★, Ross (RCA 1983)★★, Swept Away (RCA 1984)★★, Eaten Alive (RCA 1985)★★, Red Hot Rhythm 'N' Blues (RCA 1987)★★★, Working Overtime (Motown 1989)★★, Greatest Hits Live (Motown 1989)★★★, Force Behind The Power (Motown 1991)★★, Live, Stolen Moments (1993)★★, with Placido Domingo, Jos≥ Carreras Christmas In Vienna (Sony 1993)★★, Take Me Higher (Motown 1995)★★.
COMPILATIONS: All The Great Hits (Motown 1981)★★★★, Diana Ross Anthology (Motown 1983)★★★★, One Woman, The Ultimate Collection (EMI 1993)★★★★, Voice Of Love (EMI 1996)★★★★.
VIDEOS: The Visions Of Diana Ross (PMI 1986), One Woman – The Video Collection (1993), Stolen Moments (1994).
FURTHER READING: Diana Ross, Leonore K. Itzkowitz. Diana Ross, Patricia Mulrooney Eldred. Diana Ross: Supreme Lady, Connie Berman. I'm Gonna Make You Love Me: The Story Of Diana Ross, James Haskins. Diana Ross: An Illustrated Biography, Geoff Brown. Dreamgirl: My Life As A Supreme, Mary Wilson. Call Her Miss Ross, J. Randy Taraborrelli. Supreme Faith: Someday We'll Be Together, Mary Wilson with Patricia Romanowski. Secrets Of The Sparrow, Diana Ross.

ROXY MUSIC
ALBUMS: Roxy Music (Island 1972)★★★★, For Your Pleasure (Island 1973)★★★★, Stranded (Island 1973)★★★★, Country Life (Island 1974)★★★, Siren (Island 1975)★★★, Viva! Roxy Music (Island 1976)★★★, Manifesto (Polydor 1979)★★★, Flesh And Blood (Polydor 1980)★★★, Avalon (EG 1981)★★★★, The High Road (EG 1983)★★★.
COMPILATIONS: Greatest Hits (Polydor 1977)★★★, The Atlantic Years 1973-1980 (EG 1983)★★★, Street Life – 20 Great Hits (1986)★★★★, The Ultimate Collection (1988)★★★★, The Compact Collection 3-CD box set (1992)★★★, The Thrill Of It All 4-CD box set (Virgin 1995)★★★. Bryan Ferry And Roxy Music More Than This – The Best Of (Virgin 1995)★★★.
VIDEOS: Total Recall (Virgin 1990).
FURTHER READING: Roxy Music: Style With Substance – Roxy's First Ten Years, Johnny Rogan. The Bryan Ferry Story, Rex Balfour. Bryan Ferry & Roxy Music, Barry Lazell and Dafydd Rees.

RUBETTES
ALBUMS: We Can Do It, (State 1975)★★★, Still Unwinding (Polydor 1979)★★, Impact (Impact 1982)★★.
COMPILATIONs: Best Of The Rubettes (Polydor 1983)★★★.
FURTHER READING: The Rubettes Story, Alan Rowett.

RUFFIN, JIMMY
ALBUMS: Top Ten (Soul 1967)★★★, Ruff'n'Ready (Soul 1969)★★, The Groove Governor (1970)★★, with David Ruffin I Am My Brother's Keeper (Motown 1970)★★, Jimmy Ruffin (1973)★★, Love Is All We Need (Polydor 1975)★★, Sunrise (RSO 1980)★★★.
COMPILATIONS: Greatest Hits (Tamla Motown 1974)★★★, 20 Golden Classics (Motown 1981)★★★, Greatest Motown Hits (Motown 1989)★★★.

RUN DMC
ALBUMS: Run DMC (Profile 1984)★★★★, King Of Rock (Profile 1985)★★★★, Raising Hell (Profile 1986)★★★★, Tougher Than Leather (Profile 1988)★★★, Back From Hell (Profile 1990)★★★, Down With The King (Profile 1993)★★★.
COMPILATIONS: Together Forever: Greatest Hits 1983-1991 (Profile 1991)★★★★.
FURTHER READING: Run DMC, B. Adler.

RUNAWAYS
ALBUMS: The Runaways (Mercury 1976)★★★, Queens Of Noise (Mercury 1977)★★, Live In Japan (Mercury 1977)★★, Waitin' For The Night (Mercury 1977)★★, And Now ... The Runaways (Phonogram 1979)★★, Young And Fast (Allegiance 1987)★.
COMPILATIONS: Rock Heavies (Mercury 1979)★★★, I Love Playing With Fire (Laker 1982)★★.

RUNDGREN, TODD
ALBUMS: Runt (Bearsville 1970)★★★, The Ballad Of Todd Rundgren (Bearsville 1971)★★★★, Something/Anything? (Bearsville 1972)★★★★, A Wizard, A True Star (Bearsville 1973)★★★, Todd (Bearsville 1974)★★, Initiation (Bearsville 1975)★, Faithful (Bearsville 1976)★★★, Hermit Of Mink Hollow (Bearsville 1978)★★★★, Back To The Bars (Bearsville 1978)★★, Healing (Bearsville 1981)★★★, The Ever Popular Tortured Artist Effect (Lamborghini 1983)★★, A Cappella (Warners 1985)★★, Nearly Human (Warners 1989)★★★, Second Wind (Warners 1991)★★, No World Order (Food For Thought 1993)★★, The Individualist (Navarre 1996)★★ , With A Twist (Guardian EMI 1997)★★.
With Utopia Todd Rundgren's Utopia (Bearsville 1974)★★, Another Live (Bearsville 1975)★★, Ra (Bearsville

1977)★★, *Oops! Wrong Planet* (Bearsville 1977)★★★, *Adventures In Utopia* (Bearsville 1980)★★★, *Deface The Music* (Bearsville 1980)★★★, *Swing To The Right* (Bearsville 1982)★★, *Utopia* (Network 1982)★★, *Oblivion* (Passport 1984)★★, *POV* (Passport 1985)★★, *Trivia* (Passport 1986)★★, *Redux 92 Live In Japan* (Rhino 1993)★★.
COMPILATIONS: *The Collection* (Castle 1988)★★★★, *Anthology: Todd Rundgren* (Rhino 1989)★★★★, *Anthology 1974-1985* (Rhino/ Bearsville 1995)★★★.

RUNRIG
ALBUMS: *Play Gaelic* (Lismor 1978)★★★, *Highland Connection* (Ridge 1979)★★★, *Recovery* (Ridge 1981)★★★, *Heartland* (Ridge 1985)★★★, *The Cutter And The Clan* (Ridge 1987)★★★, *Once In A Lifetime* (Chrysalis 1988)★★★, *Searchlight* (Chrysalis 1989)★★★, *The Big Wheel* (Chrysalis 1991)★★★★, *Amazing Things* (Chrysalis 1993)★★★, *Transmitting Live* (Chrysalis 1994)★★, *Mara* (Chrysalis 1995)★★.
FURTHER READING: *Going Home: The Runrig Story*, Tom Morton.

RUSH
ALBUMS: *Rush* (Moon 1974)★★, *Fly By Night* (Moon 1975)★★, *Caress Of Steel* (Mercury 1975)★★, *2112* (Mercury 1976)★★, *All The World's A Stage* (Mercury 1976)★★, *A Farewell To Kings* (Mercury 1977)★★, *Hemispheres* (Mercury 1978)★★, *Permanent Waves* (Mercury 1980)★★★, *Moving Pictures* (Mercury 1981)★★★, *Exit: Stage Left* (Mercury 1981)★★★, *Signals* (Mercury 1982)★★★, *Grace Under Pressure* (Mercury 1984)★★, *Power Windows* (Mercury 1985)★★, *Hold Your Fire* (Mercury 1987)★★, *A Show Of Hands* (Mercury 1989)★★, *Presto* (Atlantic 1989)★★, *Roll The Bones* (Atlantic 1991)★★, *Counterparts* (Mercury 1993)★★, *Test For Echo* (Atlantic 1996)★★. Solo: Alex Lifeson *Victor* (East West 1996).
COMPILATIONS: *Archives* 3-CD set (Mercury 1978)★★★, *Chronicles* (Mercury 1990)★★★.
VIDEOS: *Grace Under Pressure* (1986), *Exit Stage Left* (1988), *Thru' The Camera's Eye* (1989), *A Show Of Hands* (1989), *Chronicles* (1991).
FURTHER READING: *Rush*, Brian Harrigan. *Rush Visions: The Official Biography*, Bill Banasiewicz.

RUSH, OTIS
ALBUMS: *Chicago – The Blues – Today!* (Chess 1964)★★★, *This One's A Good Un* (Blue Horizon 1968)★★★, *Mourning In The Morning* (Cotillion 1969)★★★, *Chicago Blues* (Blue Horizon 1970)★★★, *Groaning The Blues* (Python 1970)★★, *Cold Day In Hell* (Delmark 1975)★★★, *Right Place, Wrong Time* (Bulldog 1976)★★, *So Many Roads – Live In Concert* (1978)★★★, *Troubles, Troubles* (Sonet 1978)★★★, *Screamin' And Cryin'* (1979)★★, *Tops* (Blind Pig 1988)★★★, *Lost In The Blues* (Alligator 1991)★★★, *Ain't Enough Comin' In* (This Way Up 1994)★★★★, *Blues Interaction Live In Japan 1986* (Sequel 1996)★★★★, *Live And Awesome* (Genes 1996)★★.
COMPILATIONS: *Blues Masters Vol. 2* (Blue Horizon 1968)★★★, *Double Trouble – Charly Blues Masterworks Vol. 24* (1992)★★★★.

RUSH, TOM
ALBUMS: *Live At The Unicorn* (1962)★★, *I Got A Mind To Ramble* later known as *Mind Rambling* (Folklore 1963)★★, *Blues Songs And Ballads* (Prestige 1964)★★, *Tom Rush* (Elektra 1965)★★★★, *Take A Little Walk With Me* aka *The New Album* (Elektra 1966)★★★, *The Circle Game* (Elektra 1968)★★★, *Tom Rush* (CBS 1970)★★★★, *Wrong End Of The Rainbow* (CBS 1970)★★★, *Merrimack County* (CBS 1972)★★★, *Ladies Love Outlaws* (1974)★★★, *New Year* (1982)★★, *Late Night Radio* (1984)★★.
COMPILATIONS: *Classic Rush* (Elektra 1970)★★★★, *The Best Of Tom Rush* (Columbia 1975)★★★★.

RUSSELL, LEON
ALBUMS: *Look Inside The Asylum Choir* (Shelter 1968)★★, *Leon Russell* (Shelter 1970)★★★★, *Leon Russell And The Shelter People* (Shelter 1971)★★★★, *Asylum Choir II* (Shelter 1971)★★, *Carney* (Shelter 1972)★★★★, *Leon Live* (Shelter 1973)★★★, *Hank Wilson's Back, Vol. 1* (Shelter 1973)★★★, *Stop All That Jazz* (Shelter 1974)★★, *Will O' The Wisp* (Shelter 1975)★★, *Wedding Album* (Paradise 1976)★★, *Make Love To The Music* (Paradise 1977)★★, *Americana* (Paradise 1978)★★, with Willie Nelson *One For The Road* (Columbia 1979)★★★, *Live And Love* (1979)★★★, with the New Grass Revival *The Live Album* (Paradise 1981)★★★, *Hank Wilson Vol. II* (1984)★★, *Anything Can Happen* (Virgin 1992)★★, *Hank Wilson Vol III* (Ark 21 1998).
COMPILATIONS: *Best Of Leon* (Shelter 1976)★★★★.
VIDEOS: with Edgar Winter *Main Street Cafe* (Hendring 1990).

RUTLES
ALBUMS: *The Rutles* (Warners 1978)★★★★, *Archaeology* (Virgin 1996)★★.
VIDEOS: *All You Need Is Cash* (Palace Video 1988).

RYAN, PAUL AND BARRY
ALBUMS: *The Ryans Two Of A Kind* (Decca 1967)★★★, *Paul And Barry Ryan* (MGM 1968)★★★. Solo: Barry Ryan *Barry Ryan Sings Paul Ryan* (1968)★★★. Paul Ryan *Scorpio Rising* (1976)★★★.

RYDELL, BOBBY
ALBUMS: *We Got Love* (Cameo 1959)★★★, *Bobby Sings* (Cameo 1960)★★, *Bobby Rydell Salutes The Great Ones* (Cameo 1961)★★, *Bobby's Biggest Hits* (1961)★★★, *Rydell At The Copa* (Cameo 1961)★★, *Rydell/Chubby Checker* (1961)★★★, *Biggest Hits Vol. 2* (1962)★★, *All The Hits* (1962)★★★, *Bye Bye Birdie* (Cameo 1963)★★, *Wild Wood Days* (Cameo 1963)★★, *Top Hits Of 1963* (Cameo 1964)★★, *Forget Him* (Cameo 1964)★★.
COMPILATIONS: *16 Golden Hits* (Cameo 1965)★★, *Greatest Hits* (1993)★★, *Best Of Bobby Rydell* (K-Tel 1995)★★.
FILMS: *Because They're Young* (1960).

RYDER, MITCH, AND THE DETROIT WHEELS
ALBUMS: with the Detroit Wheels *Take A Ride* (New Voice 1966)★★★★, *Breakout ...!!!* (New Voice 1966)★★★, *Sock It To Me!* (New Voice 1967)★★★, Mitch Ryder solo *What Now My Love* (Stateside 1967)★★, *All The Heavy Hits* (1967)★★★, *Mitch Ryder Sings The Hits* (1968)★★, *The Detroit-Memphis Experiment* (1969)★★★, *How I Spent My Vacation* (1978)★★★, *Naked But Not Dead* (1979)★★★, *Got Change For A Million* (1981)★★★, *Live Talkies* (1982)★★★, *Smart Ass* (1982)★★★, *Never Kick A Sleeping Dog* (1983)★★★, *In The China Shop* (1986)★★★, *Red Blood And White Mink* (1989)★★★, *La Gash* (1992)★★.
COMPILATIONS: *All Mitch Ryder Hits!* (New Voice/Bell 1967)★★★, *Mitch Ryder And The Detroit Wheels' Greatest Hits* (1972)★★★, *Wheels Of Steel* (1983)★★★, *Document Series Presents ...* (1992)★★★.

S

SAD CAFE
ALBUMS: *Fanx Ta Ra* (RCA 1977)★★, *Misplaced Ideals* (RCA 1978)★★★, *Facades* (RCA 1979)★★, *Sad Cafe* (RCA 1980)★★, *Live* (RCA 1981)★★, *Ole* (Polydor 1981)★★, *The Politics Of Existing* (Legacy 1986)★★, *Whatever It Takes* (Legacy 1989)★★.
COMPILATIONS: *The Best Of Sad Cafe* (RCA 1985)★★★.

SADE
ALBUMS: *Diamond Life* (Epic 1984)★★★★, *Promise* (Epic 1985)★★★★, *Stronger Than Pride* (Epic 1988)★★★★, *Love Deluxe* (Epic 1992)★★★.
COMPILATIONS: *The Best Of Sade* (Epic 1994)★★★★.
VIDEOS: *Life Promise Pride Love* (1993), *Sade Live* (SMV 1994), *Live Concert Home Video* (Epic 1994).

SAINT ETIENNE
ALBUMS: *Foxbase Alpha* (Heavenly 1991)★★★, *So Tough* (Heavenly 1993)★★★, *Tiger Bay* (Heavenly 1994)★★★, *Casino Classics* (Heavenly 1996)★★★.
COMPILATIONS: *You Need A Mess Of Help To Stand Alone* (Heavenly 1993)★★★, *Too Young To Die – The Singles* (Heavenly 1995)★★★★, *Too Young To Die – The Remix Album* (Heavenly 1995)★★★.
VIDEOS: *Too Young To Die* (Wienerworld 1995).

SAINTE-MARIE, BUFFY
ALBUMS: *It's My Way* (Vanguard 1964)★★★, *Many A Mile* (Vanguard 1965)★★★, *Little Wheel Spin And Spin* (Vanguard 1966)★★★, *Fire, Fleet And Candlelight* (Vanguard 1967)★★★, *I'm Gonna Be A Country Girl Again* (1968)★★, *Illuminations* (Illuminations 1970)★★★, *She Used To Wanna Be A Ballerina* (Vanguard 1971)★★★★, *Moonshot* (Vanguard 1972)★★★, *Quiet Places* (Vanguard 1973)★★, *Buffy* (MCA 1974), *Changing Woman* (MCA 1975)★★, *Sweet America* (ABC 1976)★★, *Coincidence And Likely Stories* (1992)★★, *Up Where We Belong* (EMI 1996)★★.
COMPILATIONS: *The Best Of Buffy Sainte-Marie* (Vanguard 1970)★★★★, *Native North American Child: An Odyssey* (1974)★★★, *The Best Of Buffy Sainte-Marie, Volume 2* (Vanguard 1974)★★★.

SALT 'N' PEPA
ALBUMS: *Hot Cool & Vicious* (Next Plateau 1987)★★★, *A Salt With A Deadly Pepa* (Next Plateau 1988)★★★, *Black's Magic* (Next Plateau 1990)★★, *Rapped In Remixes* (Next Plateau 1992)★★★, *Very Necessary* (Next Plateau/London 1993)★★★, *Brand New* (Polygram 1997).
COMPILATIONS: *The Greatest Hits* (London 1991)★★★★.

SAM AND DAVE
ALBUMS: *Sam And Dave i* (Roulette/King 1966)★★, *Hold On, I'm Comin'* (Stax 1966)★★★★, *Double Dynamite* (Stax 1967)★★★★, *Soul Men* (Stax 1967) ★★★★, *I Thank You* (Atlantic 1968)★★★, *Double Trouble* (Stax 1969)★★★, *Back At 'Cha* (United Artists 1976)★★, *Sam And Dave II* 1962-63 recordings (Edsel 1994)★★.
COMPILATIONS: *The Best Of Sam And Dave* (Atlantic 1969)★★★★, *Can't Stand Up For Falling Down* (Edsel 1984)★★★, *Greatest Hits* (Castle 1986)★★★, *Wonderful World* (Topline 1987)★★★, *Sweet Funky Gold* (Gusto 1988)★★★, *Sweat 'N' Soul: Anthology 1968 – 1971* (Rhino 1993)★★★★, *The Very Best Of ...* (Rhino 1995)★★★★.

SAM THE SHAM AND THE PHARAOHS
ALBUMS: *Sam The Sham And Wooly Bully* (MGM 1965)★★★, *Their Second Album* (MGM 1965)★★, *When The Boys Meet The Girls* soundtrack (1965)★★, *Sam The Sham And The Pharaohs On Tour* (MGM 1966)★★, *Lil' Red Riding Hood* (MGM 1966)★★, *The Sam The Sham Revue/Nefertiti* (MGM 1967)★★, *Ten Of Pentacles* (MGM 1968)★★.
COMPILATIONS: *The Best Of Sam The Sham And The Pharoahs* (MGM 1967)★★★.
FILMS: *The Fastest Guitar Alive* (1966).

SANBORN, DAVID
ALBUMS: *Taking Off* (Warners 1975)★★, *Sanborn* (Warners 1976)★★, *David Sanborn Band* (1977)★★★, *Heart To Heart* (Warners 1978)★★★, *Hideaway* (Warners 1980)★★★, *Voyeur* (Warners 1981)★★★, *As We Speak* (Warners 1982)★★★, *Backstreet* (Warners 1983)★★★, *Let It Speak* (Warners 1984)★★★, *Love And Happiness* (1984)★★★, *Straight To The Heart* (Warners 1985)★★★★, *A Change Of Heart* (Warners 1987)★★★, *Close Up* (Reprise 1988)★★★, *Another Hand* (Elektra 1991)★★★★, *Upfront* (Elektra 1992)★★★, *Hearsay* (Elektra 1993)★★★, *Pearls* (Elektra 1995)★★★★, *Love Songs* (Warners 1995)★★★, *Songs From The Night Before* (Elektra 1996)★★★.

SANTANA
ALBUMS: *Santana* (Columbia 1969)★★★★, *Abraxas* (Columbia 1970)★★★★, *Santana III* (Columbia 1971) ★★★★, *Caravanserai* (Columbia 1972)★★★★, *Carlos Santana And Buddy Miles! Live!* (Columbia 1972)★★, *Love Devotion Surrender* (Columbia 1973)★★★, *Welcome* (Columbia 1973)★★★, *Borboletta* (Columbia 1974)★★★, *Illuminations* (Columbia 1974)★★, *Lotus* (Columbia 1975)★★★, *Amigos* (Columbia 1976) ★★★★, *Festival* (Columbia 1977)★★★, *Moonflower* (Columbia 1977)★★★, *Inner Secrets* (Columbia 1978)★★, *Marathon* (Columbia 1979)★★★, *Oneness: Silver Dreams, Golden Reality* (Columbia 1979)★★, *The Swing Of Delight* (Columbia 1980)★★, *Zebop!* (Columbia 1981)★★★★, *Shango* (Columbia 1982) ★★★, *Havana Moon* (Columbia 1983)★★, *Beyond Appearances* (Columbia 1985)★★, *La Bamba* (Columbia 1986)★★, *Freedom* (Columbia 1987)★★★, *Blues For Salvador* (Columbia 1987)★★★, *Persuasion* (Thunderbolt 1989)★★, *Spirits Dancing In The Flesh* (Columbia 1990)★★, *Milagro* (Polydor 1992)★★, *Sacred Fire: Live In South America* (Columbia 1993)★★, with the Santana Brothers *Santana Brothers* (Island 1994)★★, *Live At The Fillmore 1968* (Columbia/Legacy 1997)★★.
COMPILATIONS: *Greatest Hits* (Columbia 1974)★★★★, *Viva Santana – The Very Best* (Columbia 1988)★★★★, *The Very Best Of Santana, Volumes 1 And 2* (Arcade 1988)★★★★, *Dance Of The Rainbow Serpent* 3-CD box set (Columbia/Legacy 1995)★★★★.
VIDEOS: *Influences* (DCI 1995), *Viva Santana!* (Columbia 1995), *Lightdance* (Miramar Images 1995).

SATRIANI, JOE
ALBUMS: *Not Of This Earth* (Relativity 1986)★★★, *Surfing With The Alien* (Relativity 1987)★★★★, *Dreaming 11* (Relativity 1988)★★★, *Flying In A Blue Dream* (Relativity 1990)★★★, *Time Machine* (1993)★★★, *Joe Satriani* (Epic 1995)★★★, with Eric Johnson and Steve Vai *G3 In Concert* (Epic 1997)★★★★, Crystal PLanet (Epic 1998)★★★★.

SAW DOCTORS
ALBUMS: *If This Is Rock 'n' Roll, I Want My Old Job Back* (Solid 1991)★★, *All The Way From Tuam* (Solid/ Grapevine 1992)★★★, *Same Oul' Town* (Shamtown 1996)★★, *Sing A powerful Song* (Paradigm 1997).

SAXON
ALBUMS: *Saxon* (Saxon Carrere 1979)★★★, *Wheels Of Steel* (Saxon Carrere 1980)★★★, *Strong Arm Of The Law* (Carrere 1980)★★★, *Denim And Leather* (Carrere 1981)★★★, *The Eagle Has Landed* (Carrere 1982)★★★, *Power And The Glory* (Carrere 1983)★★★, *Crusader* (Carrere 1984)★★★, *Innocence Is No Excuse* (Parlophone 1985)★★, *Rock The Nations* (EMI 1986)★★, *Destiny* (EMI 1988)★★★, *Rock 'N' Roll Gypsies* (Roadrunner 1990)★★, *Solid Ball Of Rock* (Virgin 1991)★★★, *Dogs Of War* (HTD/Virgin 1995)★★.
COMPILATIONS: *Anthology* (Raw Power 1988)★★★, *Back On The Streets* (Connoisseur 1990)★★★, *Best Of* (EMI 1991)★★★★.
VIDEOS: *Live Innocence* (1986), *Power & The Glory – Video Anthology* (1989), *Saxon Live* (1989), *Greatest Hits Live* (1990).

SAYER, LEO
ALBUMS: *Silver Bird* (Chrysalis 1974)★★★, *Just A Boy* (Chrysalis 1974)★★★, *Another Year* (Chrysalis 1975)★★, *Endless Flight* (Chrysalis 1976)★★★, *Thunder In My Heart* (Chrysalis 1977)★★, *Leo Sayer* (Chrysalis 1978)★★, *Here* (Chrysalis 1979)★★, *Living In A Fantasy* (Chrysalis 1980)★★, *World Radio* (Chrysalis 1982)★★, *Have You Ever Been In Love* (Chrysalis 1983)★★, *Cool Touch* (EMI 1990)★★, *Love Songs* (Music Club 1997).
COMPILATIONS: *The Very Best Of Leo Sayer* (Chrysalis 1979)★★★, *All The Best* (1993)★★★, *The Show Must Go On: The Anthology* (Rhino 1997)★★★.

SCAGGS, BOZ
ALBUMS: *Boz* (1966)★★, *Boz Scaggs* (Atlantic 1969)★★★, *Moments* (Columbia 1971)★★★, *Boz Scaggs And Band* (Columbia 1971)★★★, *My Time* (Columbia 1972)★★★, *Slow Dancer* (Columbia 1974)★★★, *Silk Degrees* (Columbia 1976)★★★★, *Down Two Then Left* (Columbia 1977)★★, *Middle Man* (Columbia 1980)★★★, *Other Roads* (Columbia 1988)★★★, *Some Change* (Virgin 1994)★★, *Come On Home* (Virgin 1997)★★★★.
COMPILATIONS: *Hits!* (Columbia 1980)★★★, *My Time: A Boz Scaggs Anthology (1969-1987)* (Columbia 1997)★★★★.

SCHENKER, MICHAEL
ALBUMS: as MSG *The Michael Schenker Group* (Chrysalis 1980)★★, *MSG* (Chrysalis 1981)★★, *One Night At Budokan* (Chrysalis 1982)★★, *Assault Attack* (Chrysalis 1982)★★, *Built To Destroy* (Chrysalis 1983)★★, *Rock Will Never Die* (Chrysalis 1984)★★, *Perfect Timing* (EMI 1987)★★, *Save Yourself* (Capitol 1989)★★, *MSG* (EMI 1992)★★, *BBC Radio One Live In Concert* rec. 1982 (Windsong 1993)★★.

SCORPIONS (GERMANY)
ALBUMS: *Action/Lonesome Crow* (Brain 1972)★★★, *Fly To The Rainbow* (RCA 1974)★★★, *In Trance* (RCA 1975)★★★, *Virgin Killers* (RCA 1976)★★, *Taken By Force* (RCA 1978)★★, *Tokyo Tapes* (RCA 1978)★★, *Lovedrive* (EMI 1979)★★, *Animal Magnetism* (EMI 1980)★★, *Blackout* (EMI 1982)★★, *Love At First Sting* (EMI 1984)★★, *World Wide Live* (EMI 1985)★★★, *Savage Amusement* (EMI 1988)★★, *Crazy World* (Vertigo 1990)★★, *Face The Heat* (Vertigo 1993)★★, *Live Bites* (Mercury 1995)★, *Pure Instincts* (East West 1996)★★. Solo: Herman Rarebell *Nip In The Bud* (Harvest 1981)★.
COMPILATIONS: *The Best Of The Scorpions* (RCA 1979)★★★, *Deadly Sting* (EMI 1995)★★.
VIDEOS: *First Sting* (PMI 1985), *World Wide Live* (1985), *Crazy World Tour* (1991).

SCOTT-HERON, GIL
ALBUMS: *Small Talk At 125th And Lenox* (Flying Dutchman 1972)★★★, *Free Will* (Flying Dutchman 1972)★★★, *Pieces Of A Man* (Flying Dutchman 1973)★★★, *Winter In America* (Strata East 1974)★★★, *The First Minute Of A New Day* (Arista 1975)★★★, *From South Africa To South Carolina* (Arista 1975)★★★, *It's Your World* (Arista 1976)★★★, *Bridges* (Arista 1977)★★★, *Secrets* (Arista 1978)★★★, *1980* (Arista 1980)★★★, *Real Eyes* (Arista 1980)★★★, *Reflections* (Arista 1981)★★★, *Moving Target* (Arista 1982)★★★, *Spirits* (TVT Records 1994)★★★.
COMPILATIONS: *The Revolution Will Not Be Televised* (Flying Dutchman 1974)★★★★, *The Mind Of Gil Scott-Heron* (Arista 1979)★★★, *The Best Of Gil Scott-Heron* (Arista 1984)★★★★, *Tales Of Gil* double album (Essential 1990)★★★, *Glory: The Gil Scott-Heron Collection* (Arista 1990)★★★.
VIDEOS: *Tales Of Gil* (1990).

SCREAMING TREES
ALBUMS: *Clairvoyance* (Velvetone 1986)★★, *Even If And Especially When* (SST 1987)★★★, *Invisible Lantern* (SST 1988)★★★, *Buzz Factory* (SST 1989)★★, *Uncle Anaesthesia* (Epic 1991)★★★, *Sweet Oblivion* (Epic 1992)★★★, *Change Has Come* mini-album (Epic 1993)★★★, *Dust* (Epic 1996)★★★★.
Solo: Solomon Grundy *Solomon Grundy* (New Alliance 1990)★★★. Mark Lanegan *The Winding Sheet* (Sub Pop 1990)★★★.
COMPILATIONS: *Anthology: SST Years 1985-1989* (SST 1995)★★★.

SCRITTI POLITTI
ALBUMS: *Songs To Remember* (Rough Trade 1982)★★★, *Cupid And Psyche* (Virgin 1985)★★★, *Provision* (Virgin 1988)★★.
VIDEOS: *Scritti Politti* (Virgin 1985), *Boom! There She Was* (Virgin 1988).

SEAL
ALBUMS: *Seal I* (WEA 1991)★★★★, *Seal II* (WEA 1994)★★★★.

SEARCHERS
ALBUMS: *Meet The Searchers* (Pye 1963)★★★★, *Sugar And Spice* (Pye 1963)★★★, *Hear! Hear!* (Mercury 1964)★★★, *It's The Searchers* (Pye 1964)★★★, *This Is Us* (Kapp 1964)★★★, *The New Searchers LP* (Kapp 1965), *The Searchers No. 4* (Kapp 1965), *Sounds Like The Searchers* (Pye 1965)★★★, *Take Me For What I'm Worth* (Pye/Kapp 1965)★★★, *Second Take* (RCA 1972)★★, *Needles And Pins* (1974)★★★, *The Searchers* (Sire 1979)★★★, *Play For Today* (1981)★★.
COMPILATIONS: *100 Minutes Of The Searchers* (1982)★★★★, *The Searchers Hit Collection* (1987)★★★★, *The EP Collection* (1989)★★★★, *30th Anniversary Collection* (1992)★★★★, *The EP Collection Vol. 2* (1992)★★★, *Rare Recordings* (1993)★★★.

SEBADOH
ALBUMS: *Freed Man* (Homestead 1989)★★★, *Weed Forestin* (Homestead 1990)★★★, *Sebadoh III* (Homestead 1991)★★★, *Rockin The Forest* (20/20 1992)★★, *Sebadoh Vs Helmet* (20/20 1992)★★★, *Smash Your Head On The Punk Rock* (Sub Pop 1992)★★★, *Bubble And Scrape* (Sup Pop 1993)★★★, *4-Songs* (Domino 1994)★★, *Bakesale* (Sub Pop/Domino 1994)★★★★, *... In Tokyo* (Bolide 1995)★★, *Harmacy* (Sub Pop 1996)★★★★.
COMPILATIONS: *Freed Weed* (Homestead 1990)★★★.

SEBASTIAN, JOHN
ALBUMS: *John B. Sebastian* (Reprise 1970)★★★★, *The Four Of Us* (Reprise 1971)★★, *Real Live* (Reprise 1971) ★★★, *Tarzana Kid* (Reprise 1974)★★★, *Welcome Back* (Warners 1976)★★, *Tar Beach* (Shanachie 1993)★★, *I Want My Roots* (Music Masters 1996)★★, *King Biscuit Flower Hour: John Sebastian* (BMG 1996)★★★.

SEDAKA, NEIL
ALBUMS: *Neil Sedaka* (RCA Victor 1959)★★★★, *Rock With Sedaka* (1959)★★★, *Circulate* (RCA Victor 1960)★★★, *Smile* (RCA Victor 1966)★★★, *Emergence* (1972)★★★, *Solitaire* (1972)★★★, *The Tra-La Days Are Over* (1973)★★★, *Laughter In The Rain* (1974)★★★, *Live At The Royal Festival Hall* (1974)★★★, *Overnight Success* (1975)★★, *The Hungry Years* (1975)★★, *Steppin' Out* (1976)★★, *A Song* (1977)★★, *In The Pocket* (1980)★★, *Come See About Me* (1984)★★, *Love Will Keep Us Together: The Singer And His Songs* (1992)★★★, *Classically Sedaka* (Vision 1995)★★★, *The Immaculate* (Prism 1997).
COMPILATIONS: *Little Devil And His Other Hits* (RCA Victor 1961)★★★★, *Neil Sedaka Sings His Greatest Hits* (RCA Victor 1962)★★★★, *Sedaka's Back* (1975)★★★, *Laughter And Tears: The Best Of Neil Sedaka Today* (1976)★★★, *Neil Sedaka's Greatest Hits* (1977)★★★, *Timeless* (1991)★★★, *Originals: The Greatest Hits* (1992)★★★, *Laughter In The Rain: The Best Of ... 1974-1980* (Varese Sarabande 1995)★★★★.
FURTHER READING: *Breaking Up Is Hard To Do*, Neil Sedaka.

SEEDS
ALBUMS: *The Seeds* (Crescendo 1966)★★★, *A Web Of Sound* (Crescendo 1966)★★★, *Future* (Crescendo 1967)★★, *A Full Spoon Of Seedy Blues* (Crescendo 1967)★★, *Raw And Alive At Merlin's Music Box* (Crescendo 1967)★★★, *Flower Punk* reissue (Drop Out/Demon 1996)★★★.
COMPILATIONS: *Fallin' Off The Edge* (1977)★★★, *Evil Hoodoo* (1988)★★★, *A Faded Picture* (1991)★★★.

SEEGER, PETE
ALBUMS: with the Almanac Singers *Songs For John Doe* (Keynote/Almanac 1941)★★★, with the Almanac Singers *Talking Union And Other Union Songs* (Keynote 1941)★★★, with the Almanac Singers *Sod Buster Ballads, Deep Sea Shanties* (General Records 1941) ★★★, with the Almanac Singers *Dear Mr. President* (Keynote 1942)★★★, *Songs Of The Lincoln Bridge* (Asch 1943)★★★, *Songs For Political Action* (CIO-Political Action Commitee 1946)★★★, *Bawdy Ballads And Real Sad Songs* (Charter 1947)★★★, *Darling Corey* (Folkways 1950)★★★★, *Pete Seeger Concert* (Stinson 1953)★★★, *Folk Songs For Children* (Folkways 1953)★★★, *Lincoln Bridge* (Stinson 1953)★★★, *Pete Seeger Sampler* (1954) ★★★, *Goofing-Off Suite* (1954)★★★, *How To Play The Five String Banjo* (1954)★, *Frontier Ballads, Vol. 1* (Folkways 1954)★★★★, *Frontier Ballads, Vol. 2* (Folkways 1954)★★★★, *Birds, Beasts, Bugs And Little Fishes* (Folkways 1954)★★★, *The Folksinger's Guitar Guide* (1955)★★, *Bantu Choral Folk Songs* (1955)★★★, *Folksongs Of Our Continents* (Folkways 1955)★★★, *With Voices Together We Sing* (1956)★★★, *American Industrial Ballads* (Folkways 1956)★★★, *Love Songs For Friends And Foes* (Folkways 1956)★★★, *American Ballads* (Folkways 1957)★★★★, *American Favorite Ballads* (Folkways 1957)★★★★, *Gazette With Pete Seeger, Vol. 1* (1958)★★★, *Sleep Time* (1958)★★★, *Pete Seeger And Sonny Terry* (1958)★★★, *We Shall Overcome* (1958)★★★, *Song And Play Time With Pete Seeger* (1958)★★★, *American Favorite Ballads, Vol. 2* (1959)★★★, *Sing Out! Hootenanny* (Folkways 1959) ★★★, *Hootenanny Tonight* (1959)★★★, *Folk Songs For Young People* (1959)★★★, *Folk Festival At Newport, Vol. 1* (1959)★★★, *Pete Seeger In Concert Vols. 1 & 2* (Folklore 1959)★★★, with Mike Seeger, Rev. Larry Eisenberg *American Playparties* (1959)★★★, with Frank Hamilton *Nonesuch* (1959)★★★, *American Favorite Ballads, Vol. 3* (1960)★★★, *Songs Of The Civil War* (1960)★★★★, *Champlain Valley Songs* (1960)★★★, *At Village Gate, Vol. 1* (1960)★★★, *The Rainbow Quest* (1960)★★★, *Highlights Of Pete Seeger At The Village Gate With Memphis Slim And Willie Dixon* (Folkways 1960)★★★, *Sing Out With Pete* (1961)★★★, *American Favorite Ballads, Vol. 4* (1961)★★★, *Gazette, Vol. 2* (1961)★★★, *Pete Seeger: Story Songs* (1961)★★★, *At Village Gate, Vol. 2* (Verve 1962)★★★★, *American Favorite Ballads, Vol. 5* (1962)★★★, *In Person At The Bitter End* (Columbia 1962)★★★, *American Game And Activity Songs For Children* (1962)★★★, *The Bitter And The Sweet* (1963)★★★, *Pete Seeger, Children's Concert At Town Hall* (1963)★★★, *We Shall Overcome* (1963) ★★★, *Little Boxes And Other Broadsides* (1963)★★★, *The Nativity* (1963)★★★, *In Concert, Vol. 2 (St. Pancras Town Hall)* rec. 1959 (1964)★★★, *Broadsides Songs And Ballads* (1964)★★★, *Broadsides 2* (1964)★★★, *Freight Train* (1964)★★★★, *Little Boxes* (1964)★★★★, *Pete Seeger And Big Bill Broonzy In Concert* (Verve/ Folkways 1964)★★★★, *Strangers And Cousins* (1965) ★★★, *The Pete Seeger Box* (1965)★★★★, *Songs Of Struggle And Protest* (1965)★★★, *WNEW's Story Of The Sea* (Folkways 1965)★★★, *Pete Seeger On Campus* (Verve/Folkways 1965)★★★, *Broadside Ballads, Vol. 2* (1965)★★★, *I Can See A New Day* (1965)★★★, *God Bless The Grass* (1966)★★★, *Dangerous Songs!?* (1966) ★★★, *Pete Seeger Sings Woody Guthrie* (1967)★★★★, *Waist Deep In The Big Muddy* (1967)★★★, *Traditional Christmas Carols* (1967)★★, *Pete Seeger Sings Leadbelly* (1968)★★★, *American Folksongs For Children* (1968) ★★★, *Pete Seeger Sings And Answers Questions At The Ford Hall Forum In Boston* (1968)★★★, *Where Have All The Flowers Gone* (1969)★★★, *Leadbelly* (1969)★★★, *Pete Seeger Now* (1969)★★★, *Pete Seeger Young Vs. Old* (1971)★★★, *Rainbow Race* (1973)★★★, *America's Balladeer* (Everest/Olympic 1973)★★★, *Banks Of Marble* (1974)★★★, *Pete Seeger And Brother Kirk Visit Sesame Street* (1974)★, *Pete Seeger And Arlo Guthrie Together In Concert* (1975)★★★, with Ed Renehan *Fifty Sail On Newburgh Bay* (1976)★★★, *Tribute To Leadbelly* (1977)★★★, *Circles And Seasons* (1979)★★★, *American Industrial Ballads* (1979)★★★, *Singalong-Sanders Theater 1980* (1980)★★, *Pete Seeger Live At Newport* (1993)★★★, *Pete* rec. 50s (Living Music 1996)★★★.
COMPILATIONS: *The World Of Pete Seeger* (1974) ★★★, *The Essential Pete Seeger* (1978)★★★, *Live At The Royal Festival Hall* (1986)★★★, *Can't You See This System's Rotten Through And Through* (1986)★★★.
FILMS: *Alice's Restaurant* (1969).
FURTHER READING: *How Can I Keep From Singing*, David King Dunaway. *The Foolish Frog*, Pete Seeger. *How Can I Keep From Singing?*, David King Dunaway. *Everbody Says Freedom*, Bob Reiser. *Carry It On!: History In Song And Pictures Of The Working Men & Women Of America*, Pete Seeger and Bob Reiser. *Where Have All The Flowers Gone?*, Pete Seeger. *Incompleat Folksinger*, Jo Metcalf Schwartz.

SEEKERS
ALBUMS: *The Seekers* (1965)★★★, *A World Of Our Own* (1965)★★★, *The New Seekers* (1965)★★★, *Come The Day* (1966)★★★, *Seen In Green* (1967)★★★, *Georgy Girl* (1967)★★★, *Live At The Talk Of The Town* (1968)★★, *Four And Only Seekers* (1969)★★, *The Seekers* (1975)★★.
COMPILATIONS: *The Sound Of The Seekers* (1967)★★★, *Love Is Kind* (1967)★★★, *Seekers Golden Collection* (1969)★★★, *A World Of Their Own* (1969)★★★, *The Very Best Of The Seekers* (1974)★★★, *An Hour Of The Seekers* (1988)★★★, *The Seekers Greatest Hits* (1988)★★★, *A Carnival Of Hits* (1994)★★★.
FURTHER READING: *Colours Of My Life*, Judith Durham.

SEGER, BOB
ALBUMS: *Ramblin' Gamblin' Man* (Capitol 1969)★★★, *Noah* (Capitol 1969)★★★, *Mongrel* (Capitol 1970)★★★, *Brand New Morning* (Capitol 1971)★★★, *Back In '72* (Palladium 1973)★★★, *Smokin' O.P.'s* (Palladium 1973)★★★, *Seven* (Palladium 1974)★★★, *Beautiful Loser* (Capitol 1975)★★★, *Live Bullet* (Capitol 1976)★★★★, *Night Moves* (Capitol 1976)★★★★, *Stranger In Town* (Capitol 1978)★★★★, *Against The Wind* (Capitol 1980)★★★, *Nine Tonight* (Capitol 1981)★★★, *The Distance* (Capitol 1982)★★★, *Like A Rock* (Capitol 1986)★★★, *The Fire Inside* (Capitol 1991)★★★, *It's A Mystery* (Capitol 1995)★★★.
COMPILATIONS: *Bob Seger And The Silver Bullet Band Greatest Hits* (Capitol 1994)★★★★.
FILMS: *American Pop* (1981).

SELECTER
ALBUMS: *Too Much Pressure* (2-Tone 1980)★★★★, *Celebrate The Bullet* (Chrysalis 1981)★★★, *Out On The Streets: Live In London* (Triple X 1992)★★, *The Happy Album* (Triple X 1994)★★★, *Hairspray* (Triple X 1995)★★★, *Live At Roskilde Festival* (Magnam Music 1997)★★.
COMPILATIONS: *Prime Cuts* (Magnum 1995)★★★, *Selecterized: The Best Of The Selecter 1991-1996* (Dojo 1997)★★★.

SENSATIONAL ALEX HARVEY BAND
ALBUMS: *Framed* (Vertigo 1972)★★, *Next* (Vertigo 1973)★★★, *The Impossible Dream* (Vertigo 1974)★★★, *Tomorrow Belongs To Me* (Vertigo 1975)★★★, *Live* (Vertigo 1975)★★★, *The Penthouse Tapes* (Vertigo 1976)★★★, *SAHB Stories* (Mountain 1976)★★★, *Rock Drill* (Mountain 1978)★★, *Live In Concert* (Windsong 1991)★★★, *Live On The Test* (Windsong 1994)★★★.
COMPILATIONS: *Big Hits And Close Shaves* (Vertigo 1977)★★★, *Collectors Items* (Mountain 1980)★★★, *The Best Of The Sensational Alex Harvey Band* (RCA 1982)★★★★, *The Legend* (Sahara 1985)★★★, *Anthology – Alex Harvey* (1986)★★★, *Collection – Alex Harvey* (Castle 1986)★★★.
VIDEOS: *Live On The Test* (Windsong 1994).

SEPULTURA
ALBUMS: *Bestial Devastation* with Overdose (Cogumelo 1985)★★★, *Morbid Visions* (Cogumelo 1986)★★★, *Schizophrenia* (Cogumelo 1987)★★★, *Beneath The Remains* (Roadracer 1989)★★★, *Arise* (Roadracer 1991)★★★, *Chaos A.D.* (Roadrunner 1993)★★★. Max Cavalera in Nailbomb *Point Blank* (Roadrunner 1994)★★★, *Roots* (Roadrunner 1996)★★★★, *Blood Rooted* (Roadrunner 1997)★★★.
VIDEOS: *Third World Chaos* (Roadrunner 1995), *We Are What We Are* (Roadrunner 1997).

SEX PISTOLS
ALBUMS: *Never Mind The Bollocks – Here's The Sex Pistols* (Virgin 1977)★★★★★, *Filthy Lucre Live* (Virgin 1996)★★★, *Alive* (Castle 1996)★★★, *Back And There Again* (Creative Man/Cargo 1997)★★.
COMPILATIONS: *The Great Rock 'N' Roll Swindle* (Virgin 1979)★★★, *This Is Crap* double CD reissue with *Never Mind The Bollocks* (Virgin 1996)★★★.
FILMS: *The Great Rock 'N' Roll Swindle*.
VIDEOS: *The Great Rock 'N' Roll Swindle* (Virgin Video 1982), *Live At Longhorns* (Pearson New Entertainment 1996), *Live In Winterland* (Pearson New Entertainment 1996).
FURTHER READING: *Sex Pistols Scrap Book*, Ray Stevenson. *Sex Pistols: The Inside Story*, Fred and Judy Vermorel. *Sex Pistols File*, Ray Stevenson. *The Great Rock 'N' Roll Swindle: A Novel*, Michael Moorcock. *The Sid Vicious Family Album*, Anne Beverley. *The Sex Pistols Diary*, Lee Wood. *I Was A Teenage Sex Pistol*, Glen Matlock. *12 Days On The Road: The Sex Pistols And America*, Neil Monk and Jimmy Guterman. *Chaos: The Sex Pistols*, Bob Gruen. *England's Dreaming: Sex Pistols And Punk Rock*, Jon Savage. *Never Mind The B*ll*cks: A Photographed Record Of The Sex Pistols*, Dennis Morris. *Sex Pistols: Agents Of Anarchy*, Tony Scrivener. *Sid's Way: The Life And Death Of Sid Vicious*, Keith Bateson and Alan Parker. *Rotten: No Irish, No Blacks, No Dogs*, Johnny Rotten. *Sex Pistols Retrospective*, no author listed. *Sid Vicious Rock 'N' Roll Star*, Malcom Butt. *Sid Vicious: They Died Too Young*, Tom Stockdale.

SHA NA NA
ALBUMS: *Rock & Roll Is Here To Stay* (Kama Sutra 1969)★★★, *The Night Is Still Young* (Kama Sutra 1972)★★★, *The Golden Age Of Rock & Roll* (Kama Sutra 1973)★★, *Sha Na Na Is Here To Stay* (Buddah 1975)★★, *Rock And Roll Revival* (1977)★★.
COMPILATIONS: *20 Greatest Hits* (Black Tulip 1989)★★★.
FILMS: *Grease* (1978).

SHADOWS
ALBUMS: *The Shadows* (Columbia 1961)★★★★, *Out Of The Shadows* (Columbia 1962)★★★★, *Dance With The Shadows* (Columbia 1964)★★★★, *The Sound Of The Shadows* (Columbia 1965)★★★★, *Shadow Music* (Columbia 1966)★★★, *Jigsaw* (Columbia 1967)★★★, *From Hank, Bruce, Brian And John* (Columbia 1967)★★★, with Cliff Richard *Established 1958* (1968)★★★, *Shades Of Rock* (Columbia 1970)★★★, *Rockin' With Curly Leads* (EMI 1974)★★★, *Specs Appeal* (EMI 1975)★★★, *Live At The Paris Olympia* (1975)★★, *Tasty* (1977)★★★, *Thank You Very Much* (1978)★★★, *Change Of Address* (1980)★★, *Hits Right Up Your Street* (1981)★★, *Life In The Jungle/Live At Abbey Road* (1982)★★, *XXV* (1983)★★★, *Guardian Angel* (1984)★★, *Moonlight Shadows* (1986)★★★, *Simply Shadows* (1987)★★★, *Stepping To The Shadows* (1989)★★★, *Reflections* (1991)★★★.
COMPILATIONS: *The Shadows Greatest Hits* (Columbia 1963)★★★★, *More Hits* (Columbia 1965)★★★★, *Somethin' Else* (1969)★★★, *20 Golden Greats* (EMI 1977)★★★★, *String Of Hits* (1980)★★★★, *Another String Of Hot Hits* (1980)★★★, *At Their Very Best* (1989)★★★★, *Themes And Dreams* (1991)★★★, *The Early Years 1959-1966* 6-CD box set (EMI 1991)★★★★, *The First 20 Years At The Top* (EMI 1995)★★★★.
FILMS: *Carnival Rock* (1957), *Summer Holiday* (1962), *Wonderful Life* (1963).
FURTHER READING: *The Shadows By Themselves*, Shadows. *Foot Tapping: The Shadows 1958-1978*, George Thomson Geddes. *The Shadows: A History And Discography*, George Thomson Geddes. *The Story Of The Shadows: An Autobiography*, Shadows as told to Mike Reed. *Rock 'N' Roll: I Gave You The Best Years Of My Life: A Life In The Shadows*, Bruce Welch. *Funny Old World: The Life And Times Of John Henry Rostill*, Rob Bradford.

SHADOWS OF KNIGHT
ALBUMS: *Gloria* (Dunwich 1966)★★★, *Back Door Men* (Dunwich 1967)★★★, *The Shadows Of Knight* (Super-K 1969)★★★.
COMPILATIONS: *Gloria* (1979)★★★, *Gee-El-O-Are-I-Ay* (1985)★★★.

SHAKATAK
ALBUMS: *Drivin' Hard* (Polydor 1981)★★★, *Nightbirds* (Polydor 1982)★★★, *Invitations* (Polydor 1982)★★★, *Out Of This World* (Polydor 1983)★★★, *Down On The Street* (Polydor 1984)★★★, *Live!* (Polydor 1985)★★, *Turn The Music Up* (Polydor 1989)★★★, *Bitter Sweet* (Polydor 1991)★★★, *Street Level* (1993)★★.
Solo: Bill Sharpe *Famous People* (Polydor 1988)★★, with Gary Numan *Automatic* (Polydor 1989)★★.
COMPILATION: *The Coolest Cuts* (K-Tel 1988)★★★.

SHAKESPEARS SISTER
ALBUMS: *Sacred Heart* (London 1989)★★★, *Hormonally Yours* (London 1991)★★★.

SHAM 69
ALBUMS: *Tell Us The Truth* (Polydor 1978)★★★, *That's Life* (Polydor 1978)★★, *Adventures Of The Hersham Boys* (Polydor 1979)★★, *The Game* (Polydor 1980)★★, *Volunteer* (Legacy 1988)★, *Kings & Queens* (CMP 1993)★, *Soapy Water And Mr Marmalade* (A Plus Eye 1995)★.
COMPILATIONS: *Angels With Dirty Faces – The Best Of* (Receiver 1986)★★★, *The Best Of ...* (Essential 1995)★★★.
VIDEOS: *Live In Japan* (Visionary 1993).

SHAMEN
ALBUMS: *Drop* (Moshka 1987)★★★, *In Gorbachev We Trust* (Demon 1989)★★★, *Phorward* (Moshka 1989)★★★, *En-Tact* (One Little Indian 1990)★★★, *En-Tek* (One Little Indian 1990)★★★, *Progeny* (One Little Indian 1991)★★★, *Boss Drum* (One Little Indian 1992)★★★★, *Different Drum* (One Little Indian 1992)★★★, *The Shamen On Air* (Band Of Joy 1993)★★, *Axis Mutatis* (One Little Indian 1995)★★, *Hempton Manor* (One Little Indian 1996)★★.
COMPILATIONS: *Collection, The Remix Collection (Stars On 45)* (One Little Indian 1997)★★★.

SHANGRI-LAS
ALBUMS: *Leader Of The Pack* (Red Bird 1965)★★★, *'65* (Red Bird 1965)★★★.
COMPILATIONS: *Golden Hits* (Mercury 1966)★★★, *The Best Of the Shangri-La's* (Bac-Trac 1985)★★★, *16 Greatest Hits* (1993)★★★, *Myrmidons Of Melodrama* (RPM 1995)★★★.
FURTHER READING: *Girl Groups: The Story Of A Sound*, Alan Betrock.

SHANNON, DEL
ALBUMS: *Runaway With Del Shannon* (Big Top/London 1961)★★★★, *Hats Off To Del Shannon* (London 1963)★★★★, *Little Town Flirt* (Big Top 1963)★★★★, *Handy Man* (Amy 1964)★★★★, *Del Shannon Sings Hank Williams* (Amy 1965)★★, *1,661 Seconds With Del Shannon* (Amy 1965)★★★, *This Is My Bag* (Liberty 1966)★★, *Total Commitment* (Liberty 1966)★★, *The Further Adventures Of Charles Westover* (Liberty 1968)★★, *Live In England* (United Artists 1972)★★, *Drop Down And Get Me* (1981)★★★, *Rock On* (1991)★★.
COMPILATIONS: *The Best Of Del Shannon* (Dot 1967)★★★★, *The Vintage Years* (Sire 1975)★★★★, *The Del Shannon Collection* (Line 1987)★★★★, *Runaway Hits* (Edsel 1990)★★★★, *I Go To Pieces* (Edsel 1990)★★★★, *Looking Back, His Biggest Hits* (1991)★★★★, *Greatest Hits* (Charly 1993)★★★★.
FILMS: *It's Trad, Dad* aka *Ring-A-Ding Rhythm* (1962).

SHAPIRO, HELEN
ALBUMS: *Tops With Me* (Columbia 1962)★★★★, *Helen's Sixteen* (Columbia 1963)★★★★, *Helen In Nashville* (Columbia 1963)★★, *Helen Hits Out* (Columbia 1964)★★★, *All For The Love Of The Music* (1977)★★★, *Straighten Up And Fly Right* (1983)★★★, *Echoes Of The Duke* (1985)★★★, *The Quality Of Mercer* (1987)★★★★, *Nothing But The Best* (1995)★★★.
COMPILATIONS: *Twelve Hits And A Miss Shapiro* (Encore 1967)★★★, *The Very Best Of Helen Shapiro* (Columbia 1974)★★★★, *The 25th Anniversary Album* (1986)★★★★, *The EP Collection* (1989)★★★★, *Sensational! The Uncollected Helen Shapiro* (RPM 1995)★★★.
FURTHER READING: *Walking Back To Happiness*, Helen Shapiro, *Helen Shapiro: Pop Princess*, John S. Janson.
FILMS: *It's Trad, Dad* aka *Ring-A-Ding Rhythm* (1962).

SHARROCK, SONNY
ALBUMS: Selected albums: with Pharaoh Sanders *Tauhid* (1967), with Herbie Mann *Memphis Underground* (1968), with Wayne Shorter *Super Nova* (1969), *Black Woman* (1970), with Miles Davis *Jack Johnson* (1970), *Monkie Pockie Boo* (Affinity 1974), *Paradise* (1974), with Material *Memory Serves* (1981), *Guitar* (Enemy 1986), with Last Exit *Last Exit* (1986), *The Noise Of Trouble, Cassette Tapes* (1987), *Seize The Rainbow* (Enemy 1987), *Live In New York* (Enemy 1990), *Iron Path, The Cologne Tapes* (1990), *Ask The Ages* (1991), *Highlife* (Highlife 1991), with Nicky Skopelitis *Faith Moves* (1991), *Ask The Ages* (Axiom 1991).

SHAW, SANDIE
ALBUMS: *Sandie Shaw* (Pye 1965)★★★, *Me* (Pye 1965)★★★, *Puppet On A String* (Pye 1967)★★, *Love Me, Please Love Me* (Pye 1967)★★, *The Sandie Shaw Supplement* (Pye 1968)★★, *Reviewing The Situation* (Pye 1969)★★, *Hello Angel* (1988)★★.
COMPILATIONS: *Golden Hits Of Sandie Shaw* (Golden Guinea 1965)★★★★, *Sandie Sings* (Golden Guinea 1967)★★★★, *The Golden Hits Of Sandie Shaw* (Marble Arch 1968)★★★★, *A Golden Hour Of Sandie Shaw – Greatest Hits* (1974)★★★★ *20 Golden Pieces* (1986)★★★★ *The Sandie Shaw Golden CD Collection* (1989)★★★★ *The EP Collection* (1991)★★★★ *The 64/67 Complete Sandie Shaw Set* (1993)★★★★ *Nothing Less Than Brilliant: The Best Of Sandie Shaw* (Virgin 1994)★★★★.
FURTHER READING: *The World At My Feet*, Sandie Shaw.

SHED SEVEN
ALBUMS: *Change Giver* (Polydor 1994)★★★, *A Maximum High* (Polydor 1996)★★★★.
VIDEOS: *Stuffed* (1996).

SHERIDAN, TONY
ALBUMS: *My Bonnie* (Polydor 1962)★★, *The Beatles' First Featuring Tony Sheridan* (Polydor 1964)★★, *Just A Little Bit Of Tony Sheridan* (1964)★★, *The Best Of Tony Sheridan* (1964)★★, *Meet The Beat* (1965)★★, *Rocks On* (1974)★★, *On My Mind* (1976)★★, *Worlds Apart* (1978)★★.

SHIRELLES
ALBUMS: *Tonight's The Night* (Scepter 1961)★★★, *The Shirelles Sing To Trumpets And Strings* (Scepter/Top Rank 1961)★★★, *Baby It's You* (Scepter/Stateside 1962)★★★★, *Twist Party* (Scepter 1962)★★★, *Foolish Little Girl* (Scepter 1963)★★★, *It's A Mad Mad Mad Mad World* (Scepter 1963)★★, *The Shirelles Sing The Golden Oldies* (Scepter 1964)★, with King Curtis *Eternally Soul* (Wand 1970)★★★, *Tonight's The Night* (Wand 1971)★★★, *Happy In Love* (RCA 1972)★★, *The Shirelles* (RCA 1973)★★, *Let's Give Each Other Love* (RCA 1976)★★, *Spontaneous Combustion* (Scepter 1997)★★.
Solo: Shirley Alston (Owens) *With A Little Help From My Friends* (Strawberry 1975)★★, *Lady Rose* (Strawberry 1977)★★.
COMPILATIONS: *The Shirelles Hits* (Scepter/Stateside 1963)★★★★, *The Shirelles Anthology (1959-1967)* (Rhino 1984)★★★★, *The Shirelles Anthology (1959-1964)* (Rhino 1986)★★★★, *Greatest Hits* (Impact/Ace 1987)★★★★, *16 Greatest Hits* (Gusto 1988)★★★★, *The Collection* (Castle 1990)★★★★, *The Best Of* (Ace 1992)★★★★, *The Very Best Of ...* (Rhino 1994)★★★★, *The World's Greatest Girls Group* (Tomato/Rhino 1995)★★★★.
FURTHER READING: *Girl Groups: The Story Of A Sound*, Alan Betrock.

SHOCKED, MICHELLE
ALBUMS: *The Texas Campfire Tapes* (Cooking Vinyl 1987)★★, *Short Sharp Shocked* (Cooking Vinyl 1988)★★★, *Captain Swing* (Cooking Vinyl 1989)★★, *Arkansas Traveller* (London 1992)★★★, *Kind Hearted Woman* (BMG 1996)★★★, *Stillborn* (Private 1996)★★★, *Artists Make Lousy Slaves* (Independent 1996).
COMPILATIONS: *Mercury Poise: 1988-1995* (Mercury 1997)★★★.

SHOCKING BLUE
ALBUMS: *The Shocking Blue* (Colossus 1970)★★★, *Shocking Blue At Home* (Penny Farthing 1970★★, *Scorpio's Dance* (Penny Farthing 1970)★★, *Beat With Us* (1972)★★.

SHONEN KNIFE
ALBUMS: *Burning Farm* mini-album (Zero 1983)★★★, *Yamano Atchan* mini-album (Zero 1984)★★★, *Pretty Little Baka Guy* mini-album (Zero 1986)★★★, *712* (Nippon Crown 1991)★★★, *Let's Knife* (MCA Victor 1992)★★★, *Rock Animals* (August Records 1993)★★, *Brand New Knife* (MCA 1996)★★, *Happy Hour* (Big Deal 1998).
COMPILATIONS: *Shonen Knife* (Giant 1990)★★★, *The Birds And The B Sides* (Virgin America 1996)★★★.

SHOWADDYWADDY
ALBUMS: *Showaddywaddy* (Bell 1974)★★★, *Step Two* (Bell 1975)★★★, *Trocadero* (Bell 1976)★★, *Red Star* (Arista 1977)★★, *Crepes And Drapes* (Arista 1979)★★, *Bright Lights* (Arista 1980)★★, *Good Times* (1981)★★, *Jump Boogie And Jive* (President 1991)★★.
COMPILATIONS: *The Very Best Of* (Arista 1981)★★★, *20 Greatest Hits* (IMD 1992)★★★, *The Very Best Of ...* (Summit 1996)★★★.

SHRIEKBACK
ALBUMS: *Care* (Warners 1983)★★, *Jam Science* (Arista 1984)★★★, *Oil And Gold* (Arista 1985)★★★, *Big Night Music* (Island 1987)★★★, *Go Bang* (Shriekback 1988)★★, *Sacred City* (Shriekback 1994)★★.
COMPILATIONS: *The Infinite – The Best Of Shriekback* (Kaz 1985)★★★, *The Best Of Shriekback, Volume 2* (Shriekback 1988)★★★, *The Best Of Shriekback* (Shriekback 1990)★★★, *Priests And Kannibals: The Best Of Shriekback* (Arista 1994)★★★.

SIBERRY, JANE
ALBUMS: *Jane Siberry* (Street 1980)★★★, *No Borders Here* (Open Air 1984)★★★, *The Speckless Sky* (Reprise 1985)★★★, *The Walking* (Duke Street 1987)★★, *Bound By The Beauty* (Reprise 1989)★★★★, *When I Was A Boy* (Reprise 1993)★★★, *Maria* (Warners 1995)★★★, *Teenager* (Sheeba 1996)★★★, *Child: Music For The Christmas Season* (Blackbird 1997)★★★.
COMPILATIONS: *Summer In The Yukon* (Reprise 1992)★★★, *A Collection 1984-1989* (Duke Street 1993)★★★.

SIFFRE, LABI
ALBUMS: *Labi Siffre* (1970)★★★, *Singer And The Song* (Pye 1971)★★★, *Crying, Laughing, Loving, Lying* (Pye 1972)★★★, *So Strong* (Polydor 1988)★★★, *Make My Day* (Connoisseur 1989)★★★.
COMPILATIONS: *The Labi Siffre Collection* (Conifer 1986)★★★.

SILVERCHAIR
ALBUMS: *Frogstomp* (Sony 1995)★★★, *Freak Show* (Epic 1997)★★★.

SIMON, CARLY
ALBUMS: as the Simon Sisters *The Simon Sisters* (Kapp 1964)★★, as the Simon Sisters *Cuddlebug* (Kapp 1965)★★, *Carly Simon* (Elektra 1971)★★, *Anticipation* (Elektra 1971)★★★★, *No Secrets* (Elektra 1972)★★★★, *Hotcakes* (Elektra 1974)★★★, *Playing Possum* (Elektra 1975)★★★, *Another Passenger* (Elektra 1976)★★★, *Boys In The Trees* (Elektra 1978)★★★, *Spy* (Elektra 1979)★★★, *Come Upstairs* (Warners 1980)★★, *Torch* (Warners 1981)★★, *Hello Big Man* (Warners 1983)★★★, *Spoiled Girl* (Epic 1985)★★, *Coming Around Again* (Arista 1987)★★, *Greatest Hits Live* (Arista 1988)★★★, *My Romance* (Arista 1990)★★, *Have You Seen Me Lately?* (Arista 1990)★★★, *Letters Never Sent* (Arista 1994)★★★, *Film Noir* (Arista 1997)★★★.
COMPILATIONS: *The Best Of Carly Simon* (Elektra 1975)★★★, *Clouds In My Coffee* 3-CD box set (Arista 1995)★★★.
VIDEOS: *Live At Grand Central* (Polygram 1996).
FURTHER READING: *Carly Simon*, Charles Morse.

SIMON, PAUL
ALBUMS: *The Paul Simon Songbook* (Columbia 1965)★★★, *Paul Simon* (Columbia 1972)★★★★, *There Goes Rhymin' Simon* (Columbia 1973)★★★★, *Live Rhymin'* (Columbia 1974)★★, *Still Crazy After All These Years* (Columbia 1975)★★★★, *One Trick Pony* film soundtrack (Warners 1980)★★, *Hearts And Bones* (Warners 1983)★★, *Graceland* (Warners 1986)★★★★, *The Rhythm Of The Saints* (Warners 1990)★★★, *Paul Simon's Concert In The Park* (Warners 1991)★★★, *Songs From The Capeman* (Warner Brothers 1997)★★.
COMPILATIONS: *Greatest Hits, Etc.* (Columbia 1977)★★★★, *Negotiations And Love Songs, Paul Simon (1964/1993)* 3-CD box set (Warners 1993)★★★.
FILMS: *One Trick Pony* (1980).
VIDEOS: *Concert In The Park* (Warners 1991), *Paul Simon: Born At The Right Time* (1993).
FURTHER READING: *The Boy In The Bubble*, Patrick Humphries.

SIMON AND GARFUNKEL
ALBUMS: *Wednesday Morning 3AM* (Columbia 1968)★★, *The Sound Of Silence* (Columbia 1966)★★★★, *Parsley, Sage, Rosemary And Thyme* (Columbia 1966)★★★★, *The Graduate* film soundtrack (Columbia 1968)★★, *Bookends* (Columbia 1968)★★★★, *Bridge Over Troubled Water* (Columbia 1970)★★★★, *The Concert In Central Park* (Geffen 1981)★★★.
COMPILATIONS: *Simon And Garfunkel's Greatest Hits* (Columbia 1972)★★★★, *The Simon And Garfunkel Collection* (Columbia 1981)★★★★, *The Definitive Simon And Garfunkel* (Columbia 1992)★★★★, *Old Friends* 4-CD box set (Columbia 1997)★★★★.
FURTHER READING: *Simon & Garfunkel: A Biography In Words & Pictures*, Michael S. Cohen. *Paul Simon: Now And Then*, Spencer Leigh. *Paul Simon*, Dave Marsh. *Simon And Garfunkel*, Robert Matthew-Walker. *Bookends: The Simon And Garfunkel Story*, Patrick Humphries. *The Boy In The Bubble: A Biography Of Paul Simon*, Patrick Humphries. *Simon And Garfunkel: Old Friends*, Joseph Morella and Patricia Barey.

SIMONE, NINA
ALBUMS: *Little Girl Blue* (Bethlehem 1959)★★, *Nina Simone And Her Friends* (Bethlehem 1959)★★, *The Amazing Nina Simone* (Colpix 1959)★★★, *Nina Simone At The Town Hall* (Colpix 1959)★★★, *Nina Simone At Newport* (Colpix 1960)★★★, *Forbidden Fruit* (Colpix 1961)★★★, *Nina Simone At The Village Gate* (Colpix 1961)★★★, *Nina Simone Sings Ellington* (Colpix 1962)★★★, *Nina's Choice* (Colpix 1963)★★★, *Nina Simone At Carnegie Hall* (Colpix 1963)★★★★, *Folksy Nina* (Colpix 1964)★★★, *Nina Simone In Concert* (Philips 1964)★★★, *Broadway ... Blues ... Ballads* (Philips 1964)★★★, *I Put A Spell On You* (Philips 1965)★★★, *Tell Me More* (1965)★★★, *Pastel Blues* (Philips 1965)★★★, *Let It All Out* (Philips 1966)★★★, *Wild Is The Wind* (Philips 1966)★★★, *Nina With Strings* (Colpix 1966)★★★, *This Is* (1966)★★★, *The High Priestess Of Soul* (Philips 1966)★★★, *Nina Simone Sings The Blues* (RCA Victor 1967)★★★★, *Sweet 'N' Swinging* (1967)★★★, *Silk And Soul* (RCA Victor 1967)★★★, *'Nuff Said* (RCA Victor 1968)★★★, *And Piano!* (1969)★★★, *To Love Somebody* (1969)★★★, *Black Gold* (RCA 1970)★★★, *Here Comes The Sun* (RCA 1971)★★★, *Heart And Soul* (1971)★★★, *Emergency Ward* (RCA 1972)★★★, *It Is Finished* (RCA 1972)★★★, *Gifted And Black* (Mojo 1974)★★★, *I Loves You Porgy* (1977)★★★, *Baltimore* (CTI 1978)★★★, *Cry Before I Go* (Manhattan 1980)★★★, *Nina Simone* (Dakota 1982)★★★, *Fodder On My Wings* (IMS 1982)★★★, *Nina's Back* (VPI 1986)★★★, *Live At Vine Street* (Verve 1987)★★★, *Live At Ronnie Scott's* (Windham Hill 1988)★★★, *Live* (Zeta 1990)★★, *The Blues* (Novus/RCA 1991)★★★, *In Concert* (1992)★★★, *A Single Woman* (1993)★★, *The Great Show Of Nina Simone: Live In Paris* (Accord 1996)★★.
COMPILATIONS: *The Best Of Nina Simone* (Philips 1966)★★★★, *The Best Of Nina Simone* (RCA 1970)★★★★, *Fine And Mellow* (Golden Hour 1975)★★★, *My Baby Just Cares For Me* (Charly 1984)★★★★, *Lady Midnight* (Connoisseur 1987)★★★, *The Nina Simone Collection* (Deja Vu 1988)★★★★, *16 Greatest Hits* (1993)★★★★, *Anthology: The Colpix Years* (Rhino 1997)★★★★, *Saga Of The Good Life And The Hard Times* 1968 sessions (RCA 1997)★★★★, *The Great Nina Simone* (Music Club 1997)★★★, *Ultimate* (Verve 1997)★★★.
VIDEOS: *Live At Ronnie Scott's* (Hendring 1988).
FURTHER READING: *I Put A Spell On You: The Autobiography Of Nina Simone*, Nina Simone with Stephen Cleary.

SIMPLE MINDS
ALBUMS: *Life In A Day* (Zoom 1979)★★, *Real To Real Cacophony* (Arista 1979)★★, *Empires And Dance* (Arista 1980)★★, *Sons And Fascination/Sister Feelings Call* (Virgin 1981)★★★, *New Gold Dream (81, 82, 83, 84)* (Virgin 1982)★★★★, *Sparkle In The Rain* (Virgin 1984)★★★★, *Once Upon A Time* (Virgin 1985)★★★★, *Live In The City Of Light* (Virgin 1987)★★, *Street Fighting Years* (Virgin 1989)★★, *Real Life* (Virgin 1991)★★, *Good News From The Next World* (Virgin 1995)★★★.
COMPILATIONS: *Glittering Prizes 81/92* (Virgin 1992)★★★★.
FURTHER READING: *Simple Minds: Glittering Prize*, Dave Thomas. *Simple Minds*, Adam Sweeting. *Simple Minds: A Visual Documentary*, Mike Wrenn. *Simple Minds: Street Fighting Years*, Alfred Bos.

SIMPLY RED
ALBUMS: *Picture Book* (Elektra 1985)★★★, *Men And Women* (Warners 1987)★★, *A New Flame* (Warners 1989)★★★, *Stars* (East West 1991)★★★★, *Life* (East West 1995)★★★, *Blue* (Elekta/Asylum 1998).
COMPILATIONS: *Greatest Hits* (East West 1996)★★★.
VIDEOS: *Greatest Video Hits* (Warner Vision 1996).
FURTHER READING: *Simply Mick: Mick Hucknall Of Simply Red. The Inside Story*, Robin McGibbon and Rob McGibbon. *Simply – An Illustrated Biography*, Mark Hodkinson.

SIOUXSIE AND THE BANSHEES
ALBUMS: *The Scream* (Polydor 1978)★★★, *Join Hands* (Polydor 1979)★★★, *Kaleidoscope* (Polydor 1980)★★★, *Juju* (Polydor 1981)★★★, *A Kiss In The Dreamhouse* (Polydor 1982)★★★, *Nocturne* (Polydor 1983)★★★, *Hyaena* (Polydor 1984)★★★, *Tinderbox* (Polydor 1986)★★★, *Through The Looking Glass* (Polydor 1987)★★, *Peep Show* (Polydor 1988)★★★, *Superstition* (Polydor 1991)★★★, *The Rapture* (Polydor 1995)★★★.
COMPILATIONS: *Once Upon A Time – The Singles* (Polydor 1981)★★★★, *The Peel Sessions* (Strange Fruit 1991)★★★, *Twice Upon A Time* (Polydor 1992)★★★.
FILMS: *Jubilee* (1978).
VIDEOS: *Greetings From Zurich* (1994).
FURTHER READING: *Siouxsie And The Banshees*, Mike West. *Entranced: The Siouxsie & The Banshees Story*, Brian Johns.

SISTER SLEDGE
ALBUMS: *Circle Of Love* (Atco 1975)★★, *Together* (Cotillion 1977)★★, *We Are Family* (Cotillion 1979)★★★, *Love Somebody Today* (Cotillion 1980)★★, *All American Girls* (Cotillion 1981)★★, *The Sisters* (Cotillion 1982)★★, *Bet Cha Say That To All The Girls* (Cotillion 1983)★★, *When The Boys Meet The Girls* (Atlantic 1985)★★, *African Eyes* (Fahrenheit 1998).
COMPILATIONS: *Greatest Hits* (Atlantic 1986)★★★, *The Best Of...* (Rhino 1992)★★★★.

SIR DOUGLAS QUINTET
ALBUMS: *The Best Of The Sir Douglas Quintet* (Tribe 1965)★★★, *Sir Douglas Quintet + 2 – Honkey Blues* (Smash 1968)★★★, *Mendocino* (Smash 1969)★★★★, *Together After Five* (Mercury 1969)★★, *1+1+1 = 4* (Philips 1970)★★, *The Return Of Doug Salanda* (Philips 1971)★★, *Rough Edges* (Mercury 1973)★★, *Quintessence* (1982)★★, *Border Wave* (1983)★★, *Rio Medina* (1984)★★, *Very Much Alive/Love Ya, Europe* (1988)★★, *Midnight Sun* (1988)★★, *Day Dreaming At Midnight* (Elektra 1994)★★.
COMPILATIONS: *The Sir Douglas Quintet Collection* (1986)★★★★, *Sir Doug's Recording Trip* (1988)★★★.

SKELLERN, PETER
ALBUMS: *Peter Skellern With Harlan County* (1971)★★, *Peter Skellern* (Decca 1972)★★★, *Not Without A Friend* (Decca 1973)★★★, *Holding My Own* (1974)★★, *Hold On To Love* (Decca 1975)★★★, *Hard Times* (1976)★★, *Skellern* (Mercury 1978)★★★, *Astaire* (Mercury 1979)★★★, *Still Magic* (Mercury 1980)★★, *Happy Endings* (BBC 1981)★★★, *A String Of Pearls* (Mercury 1982)★★★, *Lovelight* (Sonet 1987)★★★, *Stardust Memories* (Warners 1995)★★★.
COMPILATIONS: *Introducing ... Right From The Start* (Elite 1981)★★★, *Best Of Peter Skellern* (Decca 1985)★★★, *The Singer And The Song* (1993)★★★.

SKID ROW (EIRE)
ALBUMS: *Skid Row* (Columbia 1970)★★★, *34 Hours* (Columbia 1971)★★★, *Alive And Kicking* (Columbia 1978)★★.
COMPILATIONS: *Skid Row* (Columbia 1987)★★★.

SKID ROW (USA)
ALBUMS: *Skid Row* (Atlantic 1989)★★, *Slave To The Grind* (Atlantic 1991)★★★, *B-Sides Ourselves* mini-album (Atlantic 1992)★★, *Subhuman Race* (Atlantic 1995)★★.
VIDEOS: *Oh Say Can You Scream?* (1991), *No Frills Video* (1993), *Roadkill* (1993).

SKIP BIFFERTY
ALBUMS: *Skip Bifferty* (RCA 1968)★★★.

SKUNK ANANSIE
ALBUMS: *Skunk Anansie* (One Little Indian 1995)★★★, *Paranoid And Sunburnt* (One Little Indian 1995)★★★, *Stoosh* (One Little Indian 1996)★★★★.

SLADE
ALBUMS: as Ambrose Slade *Ambrose Slade – Beginnings* (Fontana 1969)★★, *Play It Loud* (Polydor 1970)★★, *Slade Alive* (Polydor 1972)★★★, *Slayed* (Polydor 1972)★★★, *Old, New, Borrowed And Blue* (Polydor 1974)★★★, *Stomp Your Hands, Clap Your Feet* (Warners 1974)★★★, *Slade In Flame* (Polydor 1974)★★★, *Nobody's Fools* (Polydor 1976)★★★, *Whatever Happened To Slade?* (Barn 1977)★★★, *Slade Alive Vol. 2* (Barn 1978)★★, *Return To Base* (Barn 1979)★★, *We'll Bring The House Down* (Cheapskate 1981)★★, *Till Deaf Us Do Part* (RCA 1981)★★, *Slade On Stage* (RCA 1982)★★★, *Slade Alive* (Polydor 1983)★★, *The Amazing Kamikaze Syndrome* (RCA 1983)★★, *On Stage* (RCA 1984)★★, *Rogues Gallery* (RCA 1985)★★, *Crackers – The Slade Christmas Party Album* (Telstar 1985)★★, *You Boyz Make Big Noize* (RCA 1987)★★, as Slade II *Keep On Rockin'* (Total 1996)★★.
COMPILATIONS: *Slade Smashes* (Barn 1980)★★★, *Story Of* (Polydor 1981)★★★, *Slade's Greats* (Polydor 1984)★★★, *Keep Your Hands Off My Power Supply* (Columbia 1984)★★★, *Wall Of Hits* (Polydor 1991)★★★, *Feel The Noize – The Very Best Of* (Polydor 1996)★★★★.
FILMS: *Slade In Flame* (1974)
VIDEOS: *Slade In Flame* (Hendring 1990), *Wall Of Hits* (Polygram 1991).
FURTHER READING: *The Slade Story*, George Tremlett. *Slade In Flame*, John Pidgeon. *Slade: Feel The Noize*, Chris Charlesworth.

SLAYER
ALBUMS: *Show No Mercy* (Metal Blade 1984)★★, *Hell Awaits* (Metal Blade 1985)★★, *Reign In Blood* (Def Jam 1986)★★★, *Live Undead* (Enigma 1987)★★, *South Of Heaven* (Def American 1988)★★★, *Seasons In The Abyss* (Def American 1990)★★★, *Decade Of Aggression-Live* (Def American 1991)★★★, *Divine Intervention* (American 1994)★★★, *Undisputed Attitude* (American 1996), *Diabolus In Musica* (American/Columbia 1998) ★★★.
VIDEOS: *Live Intrusion* (American Visuals 1995).

SLEDGE, PERCY
ALBUMS: *When A Man Loves A Woman* (Atlantic 1966)★★★★, *Warm And Tender Soul* (Atlantic 1966)★★★★, *The Percy Sledge Way* (Atlantic 1967)★★★, *Take Time To Know Her* (Atlantic 1968)★★★, *I'll Be Your Everything* (Capricorn 1974)★★★, *If Loving You Is Wrong* (Charly 1986)★★★, *Percy!* (Monument 1987)★★★, *Wanted Again* (Demon 1989)★★, *Blue Night* (Sky Ranch 1994)★★★★.
COMPILATIONS: *The Best Of Percy Sledge* (Atlantic 1969)★★★★, *The Golden Voice Of Soul* (Atlantic 1975)★★★, *Any Day Now* (Charly 1984)★★★, *Warm And Tender Love* (Blue Moon 1986)★★★, *When A Man Loves A Woman (The Ultimate Collection)* (Atlantic 1987)★★★★, *It Tears Me Up: The Best Of ...* (Rhino 1992)★★★★, *Greatest Hits* (1993)★★★★.

SLEEPER
ALBUMS: *Smart* (Indolent 1995)★★★, *The It Girl* (Indolent 1996)★★★★, *Pleased To Meet You* (Indolent 1997)★★.

SLITS
ALBUMS: *Cut* (Island 1979)★★★, *Bootleg Retrospective* (Rough Trade 1980)★★★, *Return Of The Giant Slits* (Columbia 1981)★★.
COMPILATIONS: *The Peel Sessions* (Strange Fruit 1988)★★.

SLY AND ROBBIE
Their productions include: Various *Present Taxi* (Taxi 1981) ★★★★, *Crucial Reggae* (Taxi 1984)★★★, *Taxi Wax* (Taxi 1984)★★★, *Taxi Gang* (Taxi 1984)★★★, *Taxi Connection Live In London* (Taxi 1986)★★★, *Taxi Fare* (Taxi 1987)★★★, *Two Rhythms Clash* (RAS 1990)★★★, *DJ Riot* (Mango/Island 1990)★★★, *Sound Of The 90s* (1990)★★★, *Carib Soul* (1990)★★★, *Present Sound Of Sound* (Musidisc 1994)★★★, *Present Ragga Pon Top* (Musidisc 1994)★★★.
ALBUMS: *Disco Dub* (Gorgon 1978)★★, *Gamblers Choice* (Taxi 1980)★★★, *Raiders Of The Lost Dub* (Mango/Island 1981)★★★, *60s, 70s Into The 80s* (Mango/Island 1981) ★★★, *Dub Extravaganza* (CSA 1984)★★★, *A Dub Experience* (Island 1985)★★★, *Language Barrier* (Island 1985)★★★, *Electro Reggae* (Island 1986)★★★, *The Sting* (Taxi 1986)★★★, *Rhythm Killers* (4th & Broadway 1987) ★★★★, *Dub Rockers Delight* (Blue Moon 1987)★★★, *The Summit* (RAS 1988)★★★, *Silent Assassin* (4th & Broadway 1990)★★★, *Friends* (Elektra/Asylum 1998).
COMPILATIONS: *Reggae Greats* (Island 1985)★★★, *Hits 1987-90* (Sonic Sounds 1991)★★★★.

SLY AND THE FAMILY STONE
ALBUMS: *A Whole New Thing* (Epic 1967)★★★, *Dance To The Music* (Epic 1968)★★★★, *Life* (USA) *M'Lady* (UK) (Epic/Direction 1968)★★★★, *Stand!* (Epic 1969)★★★★, *There's A Riot Going On* (Epic 1971)★★★★, *Fresh* (Epic 1973)★★★, *Small Talk* (Epic 1974)★★★, *High On You* (Epic 1975)★★, *Heard Ya Missed Me, Well I'm Back* (Epic 1976)★★, *Back On The Right Track* (Warners 1979)★★★, *Ain't But The One Way* (Warners 1982)★★.
COMPILATIONS: *Greatest Hits* (Epic 1970)★★★★, *High Energy* (Epic 1975)★★★★, *Anthology* (Epic 1981)★★★★, *Takin' You Higher: The Best Of Sly And The Family Stone* (Sony 1992)★★★★, *Precious Stone: In The Studio With Sly Stone 1963-1965* (Ace 1994)★★.

SMALL FACES
ALBUMS: *The Small Faces* (Decca 1966)★★★, *Small Faces* (Immediate 1967)★★★, *There Are But Four Faces* (1968) ★★★, *Ogden's Nut Gone Flake* (Immediate 1968)★★★★.
COMPILATIONS: *The Autumn Stone* (Immediate 1969)★★★★, *In Memoriam* (Immediate 1969)★★★, *Wham Bam* (Immediate 1970)★★★, *Early Faces* (Pride 1972)★★★, *In Memorium, Small Faces Live* (Immediate 1975)★★★, *Rock Roots, The Decca Singles* (Decca 1977)★★★, *78 In The Shade* (1978)★★★, *Profile* (Teldec 1979)★★★, *Small Faces, Big Hits* (Virgin 1980)★★★, *For Your Delight, The Darlings Of Wapping Wharf Launderette* (Virgin 1980)★★★, *Sha La La La Lee* (Decca 1981)★★★, *Historia De La Musica Rock* (Decca Spain 1981)★★★, *By Appointment* (Accord 1982)★★★, *Golden Hits* (Astan 1984)★★★, *Sorry She's Mine* (Platinum 1985)★★★, *Quite Natu-ally* (Castle 1986)★★★, *The Small Faces* (London 1988)★★★, *20 Greatest Hits* (Big Time 1988)★★★, *Nightriding: Small Faces* (Knight 1988)★★★, *Lazy Sunday* (Success 1990)★★★, *Green Circles* (Sequel 1991)★★★, *Quite Naturally Rare* (Dojo 1991)★★★, *The Complete Collection* (Castle 1991)★★★, *It's All Or Nothing* (Spectrum 1993)★★★, *Itchycoo Park* (Laserlight 1993)★★★, *Here Comes The Nice* (Laserlight 1994)★★★, *The Small Faces Boxed: The Definitive Anthology* (Repertoire 1994)★★★★, *The Immediate Years* 4-CD box set (Charly 1995)★★★★.
FILMS: *Dateline Diamonds* (1965).
VIDEOS: *Big Hits* (Castle 1991).
FURTHER READING: *The Young Mods' Forgotten Story*, Paolo Hewitt.

S*M*A*S*H
ALBUMS: *S*M*A*S*H* mini-album (Hi-Rise 1994)★★★, *Self Abused* (Hi-Rise 1994)★★★. *Milking It For All It's Worth* (Smile 1995).

SMASHING PUMPKINS
ALBUMS: *Gish* (Caroline 1991)★★★, *Siamese Dream* (Virgin 1993)★★★★, *Mellon Collie And The Infinite Sadness* (Virgin 1995)★★★★, *Zero* (Hut 1996)★★, *Adore* (Virgin 1998).
COMPILATIONS: *The Aeroplane Flies High* 5 CD-box set (Virgin 1996)★★★.
VIDEOS: *Vieuphoria* (Virgin Music Video 1994).
FURTHER READING: *Smashing Pumpkins*, Nick Wise.

SMITH, PATTI
ALBUMS: *Horses* (Arista 1975)★★★★, *Radio Ethiopia* (Arista 1976)★★★, *Easter* (Arista 1978)★★★, *Wave* (Arista 1979)★★, *Dream Of Life* (Arista 1988)★★, *Gone Again* (Arista 1996)★★★, *Peace And Noise* (Arista 1997)★★★.
FURTHER READING: *A Useless Death*, Patti Smith. *The Tongue Of Love*, Patti Smith. *Seventh Heaven*, Patti Smith. *Witt*, Patti Smith. *Babel*, Patti Smith. *The Night*, Patti Smith and Tom Verlaine. *Ha! Ha! Houdini!*, Patti Smith. *Patti Smith: Rock & Roll Madonna*, Dusty Roach. *Patti Smith: High On Rebellion*, Muir. *Early Work: 1970-1979*, Patti Smith.

SMITHEREENS
ALBUMS: *Especially For You* (Enigma 1986)★★★, *Green Thoughts* (Capitol 1988)★★★★, *Smithereens 11* (Enigma 1990)★★★★, *Blow Up* (Capitol 1991)★★, *A Date With The Smithereens* (RCA 1994)★★, *Attack Of The Smithereens* (Capitol 1995)★★.
COMPILATIONS: *Blown To Smithereens* (Capitol 1995)★★★★.

SMITHS
ALBUMS: *The Smiths* (Rough Trade 1984)★★★, *Meat Is Murder* (Rough Trade 1985)★★★★, *The Queen Is Dead* (Rough Trade 1986)★★★★, *Strangeways, Here We Come* (Rough Trade 1987)★★★, *Rank* (Rough Trade 1988)★★.
COMPILATIONS: *Hatful Of Hollow* (Rough Trade 1984) ★★★, *The World Won't Listen* (Rough Trade 1987)★★★, *Louder Than Bombs* (Rough Trade 1987)★★★, *The Peel Sessions* (Strange Fruit 1988)★★, *Best ... I* (Warners 1992)★★★, *Singles* (Warners 1995)★★★★.
VIDEOS: *The Complete Picture* (1993).
FURTHER READING: *The Smiths*, Mick Middles. *Morrissey & Marr: The Severed Alliance*, Johnny Rogan. *The Smiths: The Visual Documentary*, Johnny Rogan. *The Smiths: All Men Have Secrets*, Tom Gallagher, M. Chapman and M. Gillies.

SMOKE
ALBUMS: *It's Smoke Time* (1967)★★★.
COMPILATIONS: *My Friend Jack* (1988)★★★.

SNIFF 'N' THE TEARS
ALBUMS: *Fickle Heart* (Chiswick 1978)★★★, *The Game's Up* (Chiswick 1980)★★★, *Love Action* (Chiswick 1981)★★, *Ride Blue Divide* (Chiswick 1982)★★.
COMPILATIONS: *Retrospective* (Chiswick 1988)★★★, *A Best Of Sniff 'N' The Tears* (Chiswick 1991)★★★.

SNOOP DOGGY DOGG
ALBUMS: *Doggy Style* (Death Row 1993)★★★★, *Tha Doggfather* (Death Row 1996)★★★★.
VIDEOS: *Murder Was The Case* (Warners 1994).

SOFT BOYS
ALBUMS: *A Can Of Bees* (Two Crabs 1979)★★★, *Underwater Moonlight* (Armageddon 1980)★★★★, *Two Halves For The Price Of One* (Armageddon 1981)★★★, *Invisible Hits* (Midnight 1983)★★★, *Live At The Portland Arms* cassette only (Midnight 1987)★★★.
COMPILATIONS: *The Soft Boys 1976-81* (Rykodisc 1994)★★★★.

SOFT CELL
ALBUMS: *Non-Stop Erotic Cabaret* (Some Bizzare 1981)★★★, *Non-Stop Ecstatic Dancing* (Some Bizzare 1982)★★, *The Art Of Falling Apart* (Some Bizzare 1983)★★, *This Last Night In Sodom* (Some Bizzare 1984)★★.
COMPILATIONS: *The Singles 1981-85* (Some Bizzare 1986)★★★, *Their Greatest Hits* (Some Bizzare 1988)★★★.
FURTHER READING: *Soft Cell*, Simon Tebbutt.

SOFT MACHINE
ALBUMS: *Soft Machine* (Probe 1968)★★★, *Soft Machine Volume Two* (Probe 1969)★★★★, *Third* (CBS 1970)★★★★, *Fourth* (CBS 1971)★★★, *Fifth* (CBS 1972)★★★, *Six* (CBS 1973)★★, *Seven* (CBS 1973)★★, *Bundles* (Harvest 1975)★★★, *Softs* (Harvest 1976)★★, *Triple Echo* (Harvest 1977)★★, *Alive And Well* (Harvest 1978)★★, *Live At The Proms 1970* (1988)★★, *The Peel Sessions* (Strange Fruit 1990)★★★★, *The Untouchable* (1990)★★★, *As If ...* (1991)★★, *Rubber Riff* (Voiceprint 1995)★★, *Spaced* rec. 1968 (Cuneiform 1996)★★★, *Virtually* (Cuneiform 1998).
FURTHER READING: *Gong Dreaming*, Daevid Allen.

SONIC YOUTH
ALBUMS: *Confusion Is Sex* (Neutral 1983)★★★, *Kill Yr Idols* mini-album (Zensor 1983)★★, *Sonic Death: Sonic Youth Live* cassette only (Ecstatic Peace! 1984)★★, *Bad Moon Rising* (Homestead 1985)★★★, *EVOL* (SST 1986) ★★★★, *Sister* (SST 1987)★★★★, *Daydream Nation* (Blast First 1988)★★★★, *Goo* (Geffen 1990)★★★, *Dirty* (Geffen 1992)★★★★, *Experimental Jet Set, Trash And No Star* (Geffen 1994)★★★, *Washing Machine* (Geffen 1995)★★★, *Made In USA* film soundtrack 1986 recording (Rhino/Warners 1995)★★, *Live In Texas* (Tec Tones 1996).
Solo: Lee Ranaldo *From Here To Infinity* (SST 1987)★★. Thurston Moore *Psychic Hearts* (Geffen 1995)★★★, *A Thousand Leaves* (Geffen 1998)★★★★.
COMPILATIONS: *Screaming Fields Of Sonic Love* (Blast First 1995)★★★.
VIDEOS: *Goo* (DGC 1991).
FURTHER READING: *Confusion Is Next: The Sonic Youth Story*, Alec Foego.

SONNY AND CHER
ALBUMS: *Look At Us* (Atco 1965)★★, *The Wondrous World Of Sonny And Cher* (Atco 1966)★★, *In Case You're In Love* (Atco 1967)★★, *Good Times* (1967)★★, *Sonny And Cher Live* (1971)★, *All I Ever Need Is You* (1972)★★, *Mama Was A Rock And Roll Singer – Papa Used To Write All Her Songs* (1974)★, *Live In Las Vegas, Vol. 2* (1974)★.
COMPILATIONS: *The Best Of Sonny And Cher* (1967)★★★, *Greatest Hits* (1974)★★★, *The Sonny And Cher Collection: An Anthology Of Their Hits Alone And Together* (1991)★★★, *All I Ever Need: The Kapp/MCA Anthology* (MCA 1996)★★★.
FILMS: *Good Times* (1967).
FURTHER READING: *Sonny And Cher*, Thomas Braun.

SOUL ASYLUM
ALBUMS: *Say What You Will* (Twin Tone 1984)★★★, *Made To Be Broken* (Twin Tone 1986)★★★, *While You Were Out* (Twin Tone 1986)★★★, *Hang Time* (Twin Tone/A&M 1988)★★★, *Clam Dip And Other Delights* mini-album (What Goes On 1989)★★★, *Soul Asylum And The Horse They Rode In On* (Twin Tone/A&M 1990)★★★★, *Grave Dancers Union* (A&M 1993)★★★, *Let Your Dim Light Shine* (A&M 1995)★★★, *Candy From A Stranger* (Sony 1998).
Solo: as Golden Smog *Down By The Old Mainstream* (Rykodisc 1996)★★.
COMPILATIONS: *Time's Incinerator* cassette only (Twin Tone 1984)★★★, *Say What You Will Clarence, Karl Sold The Truck* (Twin Tone 1989)★★★.

SOUL II SOUL
ALBUMS: *Club Classics Volume I* (Ten 1989)★★★★, *Volume II: 1990 A New Decade* (Ten 1990)★★★, *Volume III, Just Right* (Ten 1992)★★★, *Volume V – Believe* (Virgin 1995)★★★, *Time For Change* (Island 1997)★★★.
COMPILATIONS: *Volume IV – The Classic Singles 88-93* (Virgin 1993)★★★★.

SOUNDGARDEN
ALBUMS: *Ultramega O.K.* (SST 1989)★★★, *Louder Than Love* (A&M 1990)★★, *Screaming Life/FOPP* (Sub Pop 1990)★★, *Badmotorfinger* (A&M 1991)★★★★, *Superunknown* (A&M 1994)★★★★, *Down On The Upside* (A&M 1996)★★★.
COMPILATIONS: *A-sides* (A&M 1997)★★★★.
VIDEOS: *Motorvision* (1993).
FURTHER READING: *Soundgarden: New Metal Crown*, Chris Nickson.

SOUTHSIDE JOHNNY AND THE ASBURY JUKES
ALBUMS: *I Don't Wanna Go Home* (Epic 1976)★★★★, *This Time It's For Real* (Epic 1977)★★★, *Hearts Of Stone* (Epic 1978)★★★★, *The Jukes* (Mercury 1979)★★, *Love Is A Sacrifice* (Mercury 1980)★★, *Reach Out And Touch The Sky: Southside Johnny And The Asbury Jukes Live!)* (Mercury 1981)★★★★, *Trash It Up! Live* (Mirage 1983)★★★, *In The Heat* (Mirage 1984)★★, *At Least We Got Shoes* (Atlantic 1986)★★, *Better Days* (Impact 1991)★★★, *Spittin' Fire* (Grapevine 1997)★★★. Solo: Southside Johnny *Slow Dance* (Cypress 1988)★★★, *Jukes Live At The Bottom Line* (Tristar 1996).
COMPILATIONS: *Having A Party* (Epic 1980)★★★★, *The Best Of* (1993)★★★★.
VIDEOS: *Having A Party* (Channel 5 1989).

SPACE
ALBUMS: *Spiders* (Gut 1996)★★★, *Tin Planet* (Gut 1998)★★★.
COMPILATIONS: *Invasion Of The Spiders – Remixed & Unreleased Tracks* (Gut 1997)★★★.

SPANDAU BALLET
ALBUMS: *Journey To Glory* (Reformation 1981)★★, *Diamond* (Reformation 1982)★, *True* (Reformation 1983)★★★, *Parade* (Reformation 1984)★★, *Through The Barricades* (Reformation/Columbia 1986)★★★, *Heart Like A Sky* (Columbia 1989)★★. Solo: Tony Hadley *State Of Play* (1993)★★, *Tony Hadley* (Polygram 1997)★★.
COMPILATIONS: *The Best Of ...* (Chrysalis 1991)★★★.

SPARKS
ALBUMS: *Sparks* (Bearsville 1971)★★, *A Woofer In Tweeter's Clothing* (Bearsville 1972)★★★, *Kimono My House* (Island 1974)★★★, *Propaganda* (Island 1974)★★, *Indiscreet* (Island 1975)★★, *Big Beat* (Columbia 1978)★★, *Number One In Heaven* (Virgin 1979)★★, *Terminal Jive* (Virgin 1980)★★, *Whoop That Sucker* (Why-Fi 1981)★★, *Angst In My Pants* (Atlantic 1982)★★, *Sparks In Outer Space* (Atlantic 1983)★★, *Interior Design* (Carrere 1989)★★, *Half Nelson* (1993)★★★, *Gratuitous Sax And Senseless Violins* (Arista 1994)★★★.
COMPILATIONS: *Mael Intuition – The Best Of Sparks 1974-1976* (Island 1979)★★★, *Plagiarism* (Roadrunner 1997)★★★.

SPECIALS
ALBUMS: as the Specials The Specials (2-Tone/Chrysalis 1979)★★★, More Specials (2-Tone/Chrysalis 1980)★★★, as the Special AKA In The Studio (2-Tone/Chrysalis 1984)★★★, with Desmond Dekker King Of Kings (Trojan 1993)★★★, Today's Specials (Kuff 1995)★★★.
COMPILATIONS: Singles (Chrysalis 1991)★★★★, Too Much Too Young (EMI 1996)★★★.

SPECTOR, PHIL
COMPILATIONS: A Christmas Gift To You (Philles 1963)★★★★, Phil Spector Wall Of Sound, Volume 1: The Ronettes (1975)★★★★, Phil Spector Wall Of Sound, Volume 2: Bob B. Soxx And The Blue Jeans (1975)★★★★, Phil Spector Wall Of Sound, Volume 3: The Crystals (1975)★★★★, Phil Spector Wall Of Sound, Volume 4: Yesterday's Hits Today (1976)★★★★, Wall Of Sound (1981)★★★, Phil Spector: The Early Productions 1958-1961 (1984)★★★, Back To Mono box set (Rhino 1991)★★★★★.
FURTHER READING: The Phil Spector Story: Out Of His Head, Richard Williams. The Phil Spector Story, Rob Finnis. He's A Rebel, Mark Ribowskys. Collecting Phil Spector: The Man, The Legend, The Music, Jack Fitzpatrick and James E. Fogerty.

SPENCER DAVIS GROUP
ALBUMS: The First Album (Fontana 1965)★★★, The Second Album (Fontana 1966)★★★, Autumn '66 (Fontana 1966)★★★, Here We Go Round The Mulberry Bush (United Artists 1967)★★★, Gimme Some Lovin' (United Artists 1967)★★★, I'm A Man (United Artists 1967)★★★, With Their New Face On (United Artists 1967)★★, Heavies (United Artists 1969)★★, Funky (Columbia 1969)★★, Gluggo (Vertigo 1973)★★★, Living In The Back Street (Vertigo 1974)★★, Catch You On The Rebop: Live In Europe (RPM 1995)★★★.
COMPILATIONS: The Best Of The Spencer Davis Group (Island 1968)★★★★, The Best Of Spencer Davis Group (EMI America 1987)★★★, Keep On Running (Royal Collection 1991)★★★, Eight Gigs A Week: The Steve Winwood Years (Island/Chronicles 1996)★★★★.
FURTHER READING: Keep On Running: The Steve Winwood Story, Chris Welch. Back In The High Life: A Biography Of Steve Winwood, Alan Clayson.

SPICE GIRLS
ALBUMS: Spice (Virgin 1996)★★★, Spiceworld (Virgin 1997)★★★.
FILMS: Spiceworld (1997).
FURTHER READING: Girl Power, Spice Girls.

SPIN DOCTORS
ALBUMS: Pocket Full Of Kryptonite (Epic 1991)★★★★, Homebelly Groove (Epic 1992)★★, Turn It Upside Down (Epic 1994)★★, You've Got To Believe In Something (Epic 1996)★★.

SPIRIT
ALBUMS: Spirit (Ode/Columbia 1968)★★★★, The Family That Plays Together (Ode/Columbia 1969)★★★★, Clear Spirit (Columbia 1969)★★★, The Twelve Dreams Of Dr Sardonicus (Epic 1970)★★★★★, Feedback (Epic 1972)★★, Spirit Of '76 (Mercury 1975)★★★★, Son Of Spirit (Mercury 1976)★★★, Farther Along (Mercury 1976)★★★, Future Games (A Magical Kahuana Dream) (Mercury 1977)★★★, Live (Illegal 1978), Journey To Potatoland (Rhino/Beggars Banquet 1981)★★★, (1984), The Thirteenth Dream (Spirit Of '84) (Mercury 1984)★★, Rapture In The Chamber (IRS 1989)★★, Tent Of Miracles (1990)★★, Live At La Paloma 1993 (C.R.E.W. 1995)★★★.
COMPILATIONS: The Best Of Spirit (Epic 1973)★★★, Chronicles (C.R.E.W. 1991)★★★★, Time Circle (Epic/Legacy 1991)★★★★, Spirit – The Collection (1991)★★★, The Mercury Years (Mercury 1997)★★★★.

SPLIT ENZ
ALBUMS: Mental Notes (Mushroom 1975)★★, Second Thoughts (Chrysalis 1976)★★, Dizrhythmia (Chrysalis 1977)★★★★, Frenzy (Mushroom 1979)★★★, True Colours (A&M 1980)★★★★, Waiata (A&M 1981)★★★, Time And Tide (A&M 1982)★★★, Conflicting Emotions (A&M 1984)★★, See Ya Round (Mushroom 1984)★★, The Livin' Enz (Mushroom 1985)★★.
COMPILATIONS: The Beginning Of The Enz (Chrysalis 1980)★★★, Anniversary (Mushroom 1995)★★★★.
FURTHER READING: Stranger Than Fiction: The Life & Time Of Split Enz, Mike Chunn.

SPRINGFIELD, DUSTY
ALBUMS: A Girl Called Dusty (Philips 1964)★★★★, Ev'rything's Coming Up Dusty (Philips 1965)★★★★, Where Am I Going (Philips 1967)★★★★, Dusty ... Definitely (Philips 1968)★★★★, Dusty In Memphis (Philips 1969)★★★★★, A Brand New Me (From Dusty With Love) (Philips 1970)★★★★, See All Her Faces (Philips 1972)★★★, Cameo (Philips 1973)★★★, Dusty Sings Burt Bacharach And Carole King (Philips 1975)★★★, It Begins Again (Mercury 1978)★★★, Living Without Your Love (Mercury 1979)★★★, White Heat (Casablanca 1982)★★★, Reputation (Parlophone 1990)★★★, A Very Fine Love (Columbia 1995)★★.
COMPILATIONS: Golden Hits (Philips 1966)★★★★, Stay Awhile (Wing 1968)★★★★, This Is Dusty Springfield (Philips 1971)★★★★, This Is Dusty Springfield Vol. 2: The Magic Garden (Philips 1973)★★★★, Greatest Hits (Philips 1979)★★★★, The Very Best Of Dusty Springfield (K-Tel 1981)★★★★, Dusty: Love Songs (Philips 1983)★★★★, The Silver Collection (Philips 1988)★★★★★, Dusty's Sounds Of The 60's (Pickwick 1989)★★★★, Love Songs (Pickwick 1989)★★★★, Dusty Springfield Songbook (Pickwick 1990)★★★★, Blue For You (1993)★★★★, Goin' Back: The Very Best Of Dusty Springfield (Philips 1994)★★★★★, Dusty 4-CD box set (Phonogram 1994)★★★★, The Legend Of Dusty Springfield 4-CD box set (Philips 1994)★★★★, Something Special (Mercury 1996)★★★★.
FURTHER READING: Dusty, Lucy O'Brien.

SPRINGSTEEN, BRUCE
ALBUMS: Greetings From Asbury Park (Columbia 1973)★★★, The Wild, The Innocent And The E. Street Shuffle (Columbia 1973)★★★★, Born To Run (Columbia 1975)★★★★★, Darkness On The Edge Of Town (Columbia 1978)★★★★, The River (Columbia 1980)★★★★, Nebraska (Columbia 1982)★★★★, Born In The USA (Columbia 1984)★★★, Live 1975-85 (Columbia 1986)★★★, Tunnel Of Love (Columbia 1987)★★★★, Human Touch (Columbia 1992)★★★, Lucky Town (Columbia 1992)★★★, In Concert – MTV Plugged (Columbia 1993)★★★, The Ghost Of Tom Joad (Columbia 1995)★★★★.
COMPILATIONS: Greatest Hits (Columbia 1995)★★★★.
FURTHER READING: Springsteen: Born To Run, Dave March. Bruce Springsteen, Peter Gambaccini. Springsteen: Blinded By The Light, Patrick Humphries and Chris Hunt. Springsteen: No Surrender, Kate Lynch. Bruce Springsteen Here & Now, Craig MacInnis. The E. Street Shuffle, Clinton Heylin and Simon Gee. Glory Days, Dave Marsh. Backstreets: Springsteen – The Man And His Music, Ed. Charles R.Cross. Down Thunder Road, Mark Eliot. Bruce Springsteen In His Own Words, John Duffy.

SPOOKY TOOTH
ALBUMS: It's All About (Island 1968)★★★, Spooky Two (Island 1969)★★★★, Ceremony (Island 1970)★★, The Last Puff (Island 1970)★★★★, You Broke My Heart So I Busted Your Jaw (Island 1973)★★★, Witness (Island 1973)★★, The Mirror (Island 1974)★★. Solo: Luther Grosvenor Under Open Skies (Island 1971)★★★, Mike Harrison Mike Harrison (Island 1971)★★★, Smokestack Lightning (Island 1972)★★, Rainbow Rider (Good Ear 1975)★★.
COMPILATIONS: That Was Only Yesterday (1976)★★★, The Best Of Spooky Tooth (Island 1976)★★★★.

SPOTNICKS
ALBUMS: Out-A-Space (1963)★★★, The Spotnicks In Paris (1964)★★, The Spotnicks In Spain (Oriole 1964)★★, The Spotnicks In Berlin (Oriole 1965)★★, In The Middle Of The Universe (1984)★★, Music For The Millions (1985)★★, Highway Boogie (1986)★★, Love Is Blue (1988)★★.
COMPILATIONS: The Very Best of The Spotnicks (Air 1981)★★★.
FILMS: Just For Fun (1963).

SQUEEZE
ALBUMS: Squeeze (A&M 1978)★★★, Cool For Cats (A&M 1979)★★★★, Argy Bargy (A&M 1980)★★★★, East Side Story (A&M 1981)★★★★, Sweets From A Stranger (A&M 1982)★★, Cosi Fan Tutti Frutti (A&M 1985)★★★, Babylon And On (A&M 1987)★★★, Frank (A&M 1989)★★, A Round And About (Deptford Fun City 1990)★★, Play (Reprise 1991)★★, Some Fantastic Place (A&M 1993)★★★, Ridiculous (A&M 1995)★★★★.
COMPILATIONS: Singles 45 And Under (A&M 1982)★★★★, Excess Moderation (A&M 1996)★★★, Six Of One (A&M 1997)★★★.

STANDELLS
ALBUMS: The Standells Live At PJs (Liberty 1964)★★★, Live And Out Of Sight (Sunset 1966)★★★, Dirty Water (Tower 1966)★★★, Why Pick On Me (Tower 1966)★★, The Hot Ones (Tower 1966)★★, Try It (Tower 1967)★★.
COMPILATIONS: The Best Of The Standells (1984)★★★.
FILMS: Get Yourself A College Girl (1964).

STANSFIELD, LISA
ALBUMS: Affection (Arista 1989)★★★, Real Love (Arista 1991)★★★, Lisa Stansfield In Session (1992)★★★, So Natural (Arista 1993)★★★, Lisa Stansfield (Arista 1997)★★.
VIDEOS: Lisa Live (PMI 1993).

STARDUST, ALVIN
ALBUMS: The Untouchable (Magnet 1974)★★★, Alvin Stardust (Magnet 1974)★★, Rock With Alvin (Magnet 1975)★★, I'm A Moody Guy (Magnet 1982)★★, I Feel Like ... Alvin Stardust (Chrysalis 1984)★★.
COMPILATIONS: Greatest Hits: Alvin Stardust (Magnet 1977)★★★, 20 Of The Best (Object 1987)★★★.
FURTHER READING: The Alvin Stardust Story, George Tremlett.

STARR, EDWIN
ALBUMS: Soul Master (Gordy 1968)★★★, 25 Miles (Gordy 1969)★★★, with Blinky Just We Two (Gordy 1969)★★★, War And Peace (Gordy 1970)★★★, Involved (Gordy 1971)★★★, Hell Up In Harlem film soundtrack (Gordy 1974)★★★, Free To Be Myself (1975)★★★, Edwin Starr (1977)★★, Afternoon Sunshine (GTO 1977)★★★, Clean (20th Century 1978)★★, HAPPY Radio (20th Century 1979)★★★, Stronger Than You Think I Am (20th Century 1980)★★, Where Is The Sound (Motor City 1991)★★, War (Motown 1995).
COMPILATIONS: The Hits of Edwin Starr (Tamla Motown 1972)★★★, 20 Greatest Motown Hits (Motown 1986)★★★, Early Classics (Spectrum 1996)★★★.

STARR, RINGO
ALBUMS: Sentimental Journey (Apple 1969)★★, Beaucoups Of Blues (Apple 1970)★★, Ringo (Apple 1973)★★★, Goodnight Vienna (Apple 1974)★★, Ringo's Rotogravure (Polydor 1976)★★, Ringo The 4th (Polydor 1977)★★, Bad Boy (Polydor 1977)★★, Stop And Smell The Roses (RCA 1981)★★, Old Wave (Bellaphon 1983)★, Ringo Starr And His All-Starr Band (EMI 1990)★★★, Time Takes Time (Arista 1992)★★, Live From Montreux (1993)★★, Vertical Man (Mercury 1998)★★★.
COMPILATIONS: Blast From Your Past (Apple 1975)★★★, StarrStruck: Ringo's Best (1976-1983) (Rhino 1989)★★★.
FILMS: A Hard Day's Night (1964), Help (1965), Give My Regards To Broad Street (1985).
FURTHER READING: Ringo Starr Straightman Or Joker, Alan Clayson.

STATUS QUO
ALBUMS: Picturesque Matchstickable Messages (Pye 1968)★★★, Spare Parts (Pye 1969)★★, Ma Kelly's Greasy Spoon (Pye 1970)★★, Dog Of Two Head (Pye 1971)★★★, Piledriver (Vertigo 1972)★★★★, Hello (Vertigo 1973)★★★, Quo (Vertigo 1974)★★★, On The Level (Vertigo 1975)★★★, Blue For You (Vertigo 1976)★★, Status Quo Live! double album (Vertigo 1977)★★, Rockin' All Over The World (Vertigo 1977)★★★, If You Can't Stand The Heat (Vertigo 1978)★★★, Whatever You Want (Vertigo 1979)★★★, Just Supposin' (Vertigo 1980)★★★, Never Too Late (Vertigo 1982)★★, 1+9+8+2 (Vertigo 1982)★★, Back To Back (Vertigo 1983)★★, In The Army Now (Vertigo 1986)★★★, Ain't Complaining (Vertigo 1988)★★★, Perfect Remedy (Vertigo 1989)★★, Rock 'Til You Drop (Vertigo 1991)★★, Live Alive Quo (Vertigo 1992)★★, Thirsty Work (Polydor 1994)★★, Don't Stop (Polygram 1996)★★.
COMPILATIONS: Status Quo-tations (Marble Arch 1969)★★★, The Golden Hour Of Status Quo (Golden Hour 1973)★★★, Down The Dustpipe (Golden Hour 1975)★★★, The Rest Of Status Quo (Pye 1976)★★, The Status Quo File (Pye 1977)★★★, The Status Quo Collection (Pickwick 1978)★★★, Twelve Gold Bars (Vertigo 1980)★★★, Spotlight On Status Quo Volume 1 double album (PRT 1980)★★★, Fresh Quota (PRT 1981)★★★, 100 Minutes Of Status Quo (PRT 1982)★★★, Spotlight On Status Quo Volume 2 (PRT 1982)★★★, From The Makers Of ...(Phonogram 1983)★★★, Works (PRT 1983)★★★, To Be Or Not To Be (Contour 1983)★★★, Twelve Gold Bars Volume 1 & 2 (Vertigo 1984)★★★, Na Na Na (Flashback 1985)★★★, From The Beginning (PRT 1988)★★★, B-Sides And Rarities (Castle 1990)★★★, The Early Works 1968 – '73 CD box set (Essential 1990)★★★, The Other Side Of ... (Connoisseur 1995)★★★.
VIDEOS: Live At The NEC (Polygram 1984), Best Of Status Quo, Preserved (Channel 5 1986), End Of The Road 1984 (Channel 51986), Rocking All Over The Years (Channel 5 1987), The Anniversary Waltz (Castle 1991), Rock Til You Drop (Polygram 1991), Don't Stop (Polygram 1996).
FURTHER READING: Status Quo: The Authorized Biography, John Shearlaw. Status Quo, Tom Hibbert. Status Quo: Rockin' All Over The World, Neil Jeffries. 25th Anniversary Edition, John Shearlaw. Just For The Record: The Autobioography Of Status Quo, Francis Rossi and Rick Parfitt.

STEALERS WHEEL
ALBUMS: Stealers Wheel (A&M 1972)★★★★, Ferguslie Park (A&M 1973)★★★★, Right Or Wrong (A&M 1975)★★★.
COMPILATIONS: The Best Of Stealers Wheel (A&M 1978)★★★.

STEELEYE SPAN
ALBUMS: Hark, The Village Wait (Chrysalis 1970)★★★★, Please To See The King (Chrysalis 1971)★★★★, Ten Man Mop (Or Mr. Reservoir Strikes Again) (Chrysalis 1971)★★★, Below The Salt (Chrysalis 1972)★★★, Parcel Of Rogues (Chrysalis 1973)★★★, Now We Are Six (Chrysalis 1974)★★★, Commoners Crown (Chrysalis 1975)★★★, All Around My Hat (Chrysalis 1975)★★★, Rocket Cottage (Chrysalis 1976)★★, Storm Force Ten (Chrysalis 1977)★★★, Live At Last (Chrysalis 1978)★★, Sails Of Silver (Chrysalis 1980)★★★, Back In Line (Flutterby 1986)★★★, Tempted And Tried (Chrysalis 1989)★★★, In Concert (Park 1995)★★★, Time (Park 1996)★★★.
COMPILATIONS: Individually And Collectively (1972)★★★, Steeleye Span Almanac (1973)★★★, Original Masters (Chrysalis 1977)★★★, Best Of Steeleye Span (Chrysalis 1984)★★★★, Steeleye Span (Cambra 1985)★★★, Portfolio (Chrysalis 1988)★★★.

STEELY DAN
ALBUMS: Can't Buy A Thrill (Probe 1972)★★★★, Countdown To Ecstacy (Probe 1973)★★★★, Pretzel Logic (Probe 1974)★★★★, Katy Lied (ABC 1975)★★★★, The Royal Scam (ABC 1976)★★★★, Aja (ABC 1977)★★★★, Gaucho (MCA 1980)★★★, Store Piano (Magnum 1988), Alive In America rec. 1993, 1994 (Giant/BMG 1995)★★, Roaring Of The Lamb (Gopaco 1994), Reel To Reel (Beacon 1997)★. Solo: Walter Becker 11 Tracks Of Whack (Giant 1994)★★★.
COMPILATIONS: Greatest Hits (ABC 1979)★★★, Gold (MCA 1982)★★, A Decade Of Steely Dan (MCA 1985)★★★★, Reelin' In The Years (MCA 1985)★★★, Gold (Expanded Edition) (MCA 1991)★★★, Citizen Steely Dan, 1972-80 4-CD box set (1993)★★★★, Remastered: The Best Of (MCA 1994)★★★★.
FURTHER READING: Steely Dan: Reelin' In The Years, Brian Sweet.

STEPPENWOLF
ALBUMS: Steppenwolf (Dunhill 1968)★★★, The Second (Dunhill 1968)★★★, Steppenwolf At Your Birthday Party (Dunhill 1969)★★★, Early Steppenwolf (Dunhill 1969)★★, Monster (Dunhill 1969)★★★★, Steppenwolf 'Live' (Dunhill 1970)★★, Steppenwolf 7 (Dunhill 1970)★★, For Ladies Only (Dunhill 1971)★★★, Slow Flux (Mums 1974)★★, Hour Of The Wolf (Epic 1975)★★, Skullduggery (Epic 1976)★★, Live In London (Attic 1982)★★, Wolf Tracks (Attic 1982)★★, Rock & Roll Rebels (Qwil 1987)★★, Rise And Shine (IRS 1990).
COMPILATIONS: Steppenwolf Gold (Dunhill 1971)★★★★, Rest In Peace (Dunhill 1972)★★★, 16 Greatest Hits (Dunhill 1973)★★★★, Masters Of Rock (Dunhill 1975)★★★★, Golden Greats: Steppenwolf (MCA 1985)★★★★.

STEREO MC'S
ALBUMS: 33, 45, 78 (4th & Broadway 1989)★★★, Supernatural (4th & Broadway 1990)★★★, Connected (4th & Broadway 1992)★★★★.
VIDEOS: Connected (1993).

STEREOLAB
ALBUMS: Peng! (Too Pure 1992)★★★, Switched On (Too Pure 1992)★★★, The Groop Played Space Age Bachelor Pad Music mini-album (Too Pure 1993)★★★★, Transient Random Noise-Bursts With Announcements (Duophonic 1993)★★★, Mars Audiac Quintet (Duophonic 1994)★★★★, Music For The Amorphous Body Study Centre mini-album (Duophonic 1995)★★★, Refried Ectoplasm (Switched On Volume 2) (Duophonic 1995)★★★, Emperor Tomato Ketchup (Duophonic 1996)★★★★, Dots And Loops (Duophonic 1997)★★★★.

STEVENS, CAT
ALBUMS: Matthew & Son (Deram 1967)★★★, New Masters (Deram 1968)★★★, Mona Bone Jakon (Island 1970)★★★, Tea For The Tillerman (Island 1970)★★★★, Teaser And The Firecat (Island 1971)★★★★, Very Young And Early Songs (Deram 1972)★★, Catch Bull At Four (Island 1972)★★★★, Foreigner (Island 1973)★★, Buddah And The Chocolate Box (Island 1974)★★, View From The Top (Deram 1974)★★, Numbers (Island 1975)★, Izitso (Island 1977)H, Back To Earth (Island 1978)★★, as Yusuf Islam The Life Of The Last Prophet (1995)★.
COMPILATIONS: Greatest Hits (Island 1975)★★★★, The Very Best Of Cat Stevens (Island 1990)★★★★.
Videos Tea For The Tillerman Live – The Best Of (1993).
FURTHER READING: Cat Stevens, Chris Charlesworth.

STEVENS, SHAKIN'
ALBUMS: A Legend (Parlophone 1970)★★, I'm No J.D. (CBS 1971)★★, Rockin' And Shakin' (Contour 1972)★, Shakin' Stevens And The Sunsets (Emerald 1973)H, Shakin' Stevens (Track 1977)★, Take One! (Epic 1979)★★, This Ole House (Epic 1981)★★, Shaky (Epic 1981)★★, Give Me Your Heart Tonight (Epic 1982)★★, The Bop Won't Stop (Epic 1983)★★, Lipstick, Powder And Paint (Epic 1985)★★, Manhattan Melodrama (CJS 1985)★★, Let's Boogie (Epic 1987)★★, A Whole Lotta Shaky (Epic 1988)★★, Rock 'N' Roll (Telstar 1990)★★, Merry Christmas Everyone (1991)★.
COMPILATIONS: Greatest Hits (Rhino 1995)★★★.
VIDEOS: Shakin' Stevens Video Show Volumes 1&2 (CMV 1989).
FURTHER READING: Shakin' Stevens, Leese Martin.

STEWART, AL
ALBUMS: Bedsitter Images (Columbia 1967)★★, Love Chronicles (Columbia 1969)★★★, Zero She Flies (Columbia 1970)★★★, The First Album (Bedsitter Images) (Columbia 1970)★★, Orange (Columbia 1972)★★★, Past, Present And Future (Columbia 1973)★★★, Modern Times (Columbia 1975)★★★, Year Of The Cat (RCA 1976)★★★★, Time Passages (RCA 1978)★★, 24 P/Carrots (RCA 1980)★★★, Indian Summer/Live (RCA 1981)★★★, Russians And Americans (RCA 1984)★★★, Last Days Of The Century (Enigma 1988)★★★, Rhymes In Rooms – Al Stewart Live Featuring Peter White (EMI 1991)★★★, Famous Last Words (Permanent 1993)★★★, with Laurence Juber Between The Wars (EMI 1995)★★★.
COMPILATIONS: Chronicles ... The Best Of Al Stewart (EMI 1991)★★★, To Whom It May Concern 1966-70 (EMI 1994)★★★, The Best Of ... (EMI 1997)★★★.

STEWART, ROD
ALBUMS: An Old Raincoat Won't Ever Let You Down (Vertigo 1970)★★★★, Gasoline Alley (Vertigo 1970)★★★★, Every Picture Tells A Story (Mercury 1971)★★★★, Never A Dull Moment (Mercury 1972)★★★★, Smiler (Mercury 1974)★★, Atlantic Crossing (Warners 1975)★★★, A Night On The Town (Riva 1976)★★★, Foot Loose And Fancy Free (Riva 1977)★★, Blondes Have More Fun (Riva 1978)★★, Foolish Behaviour (Riva 1980)★, Tonight I'm Yours (Riva 1981)★★, Absolutely Live (Riva 1982)★, Body Wishes (Warners 1983)★, Camouflage (Warners 1984)★, Out Of Order (Warners 1988)★★, Vagabond Heart (Warners 1991)★★★, Unplugged And Seated (Warners 1993)★★★★, A Spanner In The Works (Warners 1995)★★★, If We Fall In Love Tonight (Warners 1996)★★★, Handbags And Gladrags (Mercury 1996)★★★, When We Were The new Boys (1998)★★★.
COMPILATIONS: Sing It Again Rod (Mercury 1973)★★★★, The Vintage Years (Mercury 1976)★★★, Recorded Highlights And Action Replays (Phillips 1976)★★★, The Best Of Rod Stewart (Mercury 1977)★★★★, The Best Of Rod Stewart Volume 2 (Mercury 1977)★★★, Rod Stewart's Greatest Hits Volume 1 (Riva 1979)★★★, The Best Of Rod Stewart (Warners 1989)★★★★, Storyteller (Warners 1989)★★★★, The Early Years (1992)★★★, Lead Vocalist (1993)★★★.
FURTHER READING: The Rod Stewart Story, George Tremlett. Rod Stewart And The Faces, John Pidgeon. Rod Stewart: A Biography In Words & Pictures, Richard Cromelin. Rod Stewart, Tony Jasper. Rod Stewart: A Life On The Town, Peter Burton. Rod Stewart, Gerd Rockl & Paul Sahner. Rod Stewart, Paul Nelson & Lester Bangs. Rod Stewart: A Biography, Tim Ewbank & Stafford Hildred. Rod Stewart: Vagabond Heart, Geoffrey Guiliano.

STIFF LITTLE FINGERS
ALBUMS: Inflammable Material (Rough Trade 1979)★★★, Nobody's Heroes (Chrysalis 1980)★★★, Hanx! (Chrysalis 1980)★★, Go For It! (Chrysalis 1981)★★★, Now Then (Chrysalis 1982)★★, Flags And Emblems (Essential! 1991)★★, Fly The Flag (Essential! 1993)★★, Get A Life (Castle 1994)★★, Pure Fingers Live – St. Patrix 1993 (Dojo 1995)★★, Tinderbox (Abstract 1997)★★★.
COMPILATIONS: All The Best (Chrysalis 1983)★★★, No Sleep Till Belfast (Kaz 1988)★★, The Peel Sessions (Strange Fruit 1989)★★, Greatest Hits Live (Link 1991)★★.

STILLS, STEPHEN
ALBUMS: with Mike Bloomfield and Al Kooper Super Session (Columbia 1968)★★★, Stephen Stills (Atlantic 1970)★★★★★, Stephen Stills 2 (Atlantic 1971)★★★★, Mannassas (Atlantic 1972), Mannassas Down The Road (Atlantic 1973), Stills (Columbia 1975)★★★★, Stephen Stills Live (Atlantic 1975)★★★, Illegal Stills (Columbia 1976)★★, Thoroughfare Gap (Columbia 1978)★, Right By You (Atlantic 1984)★★★, Stills Alone. (1991)★★★.
COMPILATIONS: Still Stills (Atlantic 1976)★★★.

STING
ALBUMS: Dream Of The Blue Turtles (A&M 1985)★★★, Bring On The Night (A&M 1986)★★, Nothing Like the Sun (A&M 1987)★★★★, The Soul Cages (A&M 1991)★★★, Acoustic – Live In Newcastle (A&M 1991)★★★, Ten Summoner's Tales (A&M 1993)★★★★, Mercury Falling (A&M 1996)★★★.
COMPILATIONS: Fields Of Gold 1984-1994 (A&M 1994)★★★★.
VIDEOS: Bring On The Night (1987), The Videos (1988), The Soul Cages (1991), Live At The Hague (1991), Fields Of Gold: The Best Of Sting 1984-94 (1994).
FURTHER READING: Sting: A Biography, Robert Sellers.

STOCK, AITKEN AND WATERMAN
ALBUMS: Hit Factory (1987)★★★, Hit Factory, Volume 2 (1988)★★★, Hit Factory, Volume 3 (1989)★★★.
COMPILATIONS: The Best Of Stock, Aitken And Waterman (1990)★★★.
VIDEOS: Roadblock (Touchstone Video 1988).

STONE ROSES
ALBUMS: The Stone Roses (Silvertone 1989)★★★★, Second Coming (Geffen 1995)★★★.
COMPILATIONS: Turns Into Stone (Silvertone 1992)★★★, The Complete Stone Roses (Silvertone 1995)★★★.
VIDEOS: The Complete Stone Roses (Wienerworld 1995).
FURTHER READING: The Stone Roses And The Resurrection Of British Pop, John Robb.

STONE TEMPLE PILOTS
ALBUMS: Core (Atlantic 1992)★★★, Purple (Atlantic 1994)★★★, Tiny Music ... Songs From The Vatican Gift Shop (Atlantic 1996)★★★.
FURTHER READING: Stone Temple Pilots, Mike Wall and Malcolm Dome.

STOOGES
ALBUMS: The Stooges (Elektra 1969)★★★★, Funhouse (Elektra 1970)★★★★, as Iggy And The Stooges Raw Power (Columbia 1973)★★★★, Metallic KO (Skydog 1976)★★, Rubber Legs rare recordings from 1973/4 (Fan Club 1988)★★, Open Up And Bleed (Bomp 1996)★★, Year Of The Iguana (Bomp! 1997).
COMPILATIONS: as Iggy Pop And James Williamson Kill City (Bomp 1977)★★, No Fun (Elektra 1980)★★, as Iggy And The Stooges I'm Sick Of You (Line 1981)★★, I Gotta Right (Invasion 1983)★★.

STRANGLERS
ALBUMS: Rattus Norvegicus (United Artists 1977)★★★★, No More Heroes (United Artists 1977)★★★★, Black And White (United Artists 1978)★★★, Live (X Cert) (United Artists 1979)★★, The Raven (United Artists 1979)★★★, The Meninblack (Liberty 1981)★★★, La Folie (Liberty 1981)★★★★, Feline (Epic 1983)★★★, Aural Sculpture (Epic 1984)★★★, Dreamtime (Epic 1986)★★, All Live And All Of The Night (Epic 1988)★★, 10 (Epic 1990)★★, Stranglers In The Night (China 1992)★★, About Time (When?/Castle 1995)★★, Written In Red (When?/Castle 1997)★★, Friday The Thirteenth (Live) (Cleopatra 1998).
COMPILATIONS: The Collection (Liberty 1982)★★★, The Singles (EMI 1989)★★★★, Greatest Hits: 1977-1990 (Epic 1990)★★★★, The Old Testament (The UA Recordings 1977-1982) (EMI 1992)★★★, The Hit Men (EMI 1997)★★★★.
VIDEOS: Saturday Night Sunday Morning (PNE 1996).
FURTHER READING: Inside Information, Hugh Cornwell. Much Ado About Nothing, Jet Black. No Mercy: The Authorised And Uncensored Biography Of The Stranglers, David Buckley.

STRAWBERRY ALARM CLOCK
ALBUMS: Incense And Peppermints (Uni 1967)★★★, Wake Up It's Tomorrow (Uni 1967)★★, The World In A Seashell (Uni 1968)★★, Good Morning Starshine (Uni 1969)★★.
COMPILATIONS: The Best Of The Strawberry Alarm Clock (Uni 1970)★★★, Strawberries Mean Love (1987)★★★.

STRAWBS
ALBUMS: Strawbs (A&M 1969)★★★★, Dragonfly (A&M 1970)★★★, Just A Collection Of Antiques And Curios (A&M 1970)★★★, From The Witchwood (A&M 1971)★★★, Grave New World (A&M 1972)★★★★, as Sandy Denny And The Strawbs All Our Own Work (A&M 1973)★★★, Bursting At The Seams (A&M 1973)★★★, Hero And Heroine (A&M 1974)★★★, Ghosts (A&M 1975)★★★, Nomadness (A&M 1976)★★★, Deep Cuts (Oyster 1976)★★★, Burning For You (Oyster 1977)★★★, Dead Lines (Arista 1978)★★★, Don't Say Goodbye (Toots 1987)★★★.
COMPILATIONS: Strawbs By Choice (A&M 1974)★★★, Best Of The Strawbs (A&M 1978)★★★, A Choice Collection (1992)★★★, Uncanned Preserves (Road Goes On Forever 1992)★★★, Heartbreak Hill (Road Goes On Forever 1995)★★★, In Concert (Windsong 1995)★★★, Halcyon Days: The Very Best Of ... (A&M 1997)★★★.

STYLE COUNCIL
ALBUMS: Cafe Bleu (Polydor 1984)★★, Our Favourite Shop (Polydor 1985)★★★, Home And Abroad (Polydor 1986)★★, The Cost Of Loving (Polydor 1987)★★, Confessions Of A Pop Group (Polydor 1988)★★, Here's Some That Got Away (Polydor 1993)★★.
COMPILATIONS: Singular Adventures Of The Style Council (Polydor 1989)★★★, The Style Council Collection (Polydor 1996)★★★.
VIDEOS: What We Did On Our Holidays (Polygram 1983), Far East And Far Out – Council Meeting In Japan (Polygram 1984), What We Did The Following Year (Polygram 1985), Showbiz!, The Style Council Live (Polygram 1986), JerUSAlem (Palace 1987), Confessions Of A Pop Group (Channel 5 1988), The Video Adventures Of ... Greatest Hits Vol. 1 (Channel 5/Polygram 1991).
FURTHER READING: Mr Cool's Dream – The Complete History Of The Style Council, Ian Munn.

STYLISTICS
ALBUMS: The Stylistics (Avco 1971)★★★, Round 2: The Stylistics (Avco 1972)★★★, Rockin' Roll Baby (Avco 1973)★★★★, Let's Put It All Together (Avco 1974)★★★★, Heavy UK title From The Mountain (Avco 1974)★★★, Thank You Baby (Avco 1975)★★★, You Are Beautiful (Avco 1975)★★★, Fabulous (H&L 1976)★★★, Once Upon A Juke Box (H&L 1976)★★★, Sun And Soul (H&L 1977)★★★, Wonder Woman (H&L 1978)★★★, In Fashion (H&L 1978)★★★, Black Satin (H&L 1979)★★★, Love Spell (1979)★★★, Live In Japan (1979)★★, The Lion Sleeps Tonight (1979)★★★, Hurry Up This Way Again (TSOP/Philadelphia International 1980)★★★, Closer Than Close (TSOP/Philadelphia International 1981)★★★, 1982 (TSOP/Philadelphia International 1982)★★★, Some Things Never Change (Streetwise 1985)★★, Love Talks (1993)★★, Love Is Back In Style (Marathon 1996)★★.
COMPILATIONS: The Best Of The Stylistics (Avco 1975)★★★★, Spotlight On The Stylistics (1977)★★★, All About Love (Contour 1981)★★★, Very Best Of The Stylistics (H&L 1983)★★★★, The Great Love Hits (Contour 1983)★★★.

STYX
ALBUMS: Styx (Wooden Nickel 1972)★★, Styx II (Wooden Nickel 1973)★★★, The Serpent Is Rising (Wooden Nickel 1973)★★★, Man Of Miracles (Wooden Nickel 1974)★★★, Equinox (A&M 1975)★★★, Crystal Ball (A&M 1976)★★★, The Grand Illusion (A&M 1977)★★★, Pieces Of Eight (A&M 1978)★★★, Cornerstone (A&M 1979)★★★, Paradise Theater (A&M 1980)★★★★, Kilroy Was Here (A&M 1983)★★★, Caught In The Act/Live (A&M 1984)★★, Edge Of The Century (A&M 1990)★★★, Return To Paradise (CMC International 1997).
COMPILATIONS: The Best Of Styx (A&M 1979)★★★, Classics Volume 15 (A&M 1987)★★★.
VIDEOS: Caught In The Act (1984).

SUEDE
ALBUMS: Suede (Nude 1993)★★★★, Dog Man Star (Nude 1994)★★★, Coming Up (Nude 1996)★★★★.
COMPILATIONS: Sci-Fi Lullabies (Nude 1997)★★★★.
VIDEOS: Love & Poison (1993), Bootleg 1 (1993), Introducing The Band (1995).
FURTHER READING: Suede: The Illustrated Biography, York Membrey.

SUGAR
ALBUMS: Copper Blue (Creation 1992)★★★★, Beaster mini-album (Creation 1993)★★★★, F.U.E.L. (File Under Easy Listening) (Creation 1994)★★.
COMPILATIONS: Besides (Rykodisk 1995)★★.

SUGARCUBES
ALBUMS: Life's Too Good (One Little Indian 1988)★★★★, Here Today, Tomorrow, Next Week (One Little Indian 1989)★★, Stick Around For Joy (One Little Indian 1992)★★★, It's It remixes (One Little Indian 1992)★★.

SUMMER, DONNA
ALBUMS: Love To Love You Baby (Oasis 1975)★★★, A Love Trilogy (Oasis 1976)★★, Four Seasons Of Love (Casablanca 1976)★★, I Remember Yesterday (Casablanca 1977)★★★, Once Upon A Time (Casblanca 1977)★★★, Live And More (Casablanca 1978)★★, Bad Girls (Casablanca 1979)★★★★, The Wanderer (Geffen 1980)★★★★, Donna Summer (Geffen 1982)★★★, She Works Hard For The Money (Mercury 1983)★★★★, Cats Without Claws (Geffen 1984)★★, All Systems Go (Geffen 1987)★★, Another Place And Time (Warners 1989)★★, Love Is Gonna Change (Atlantic 1990)★★, Mistaken Identity (Atlantic 1991)★★, This Time I Know It's For Real (1993)★★, I'm A Rainbow (Polygram 1996).
COMPILATIONS: On The Radio – Greatest Hits, Volumes 1 And 2 (Casablanca 1979)★★★★, Walk Away – Collector's Edition (The Best Of 1977-1980) (Casablanca 1980)★★★, The Best Of Donna Summer (East West 1990)★★★★.
FURTHER READING: Donna Summer: An Unauthorized Biography, James Haskins.

SUPER FURRY ANIMALS
ALBUMS: Fuzzy Logic (Creation 1996)★★★★, Radiator (Creation 1997)★★★★.

SUPERGRASS
ALBUMS: I Should Coco (Parlophone 1995)★★★★, Alright (EMI Japan 1995), In It For The Money (Parlophone 1997)★★★★★.
FURTHER READING: Supergrass, Linda Holorny.

SUPERTRAMP
ALBUMS: Supertramp (A&M 1970)★★, Indelibly Stamped (A&M 1971)★★, Crime Of The Century (A&M 1974)★★★★, Crisis? What Crisis? (A&M 1975)★★★★, Even In The Quietest Moments (A&M 1977)★★★, Breakfast In America (A&M 1979)★★★★, Paris (A&M 1980)★★★, Famous Last Words (A&M 1982)★★★, Brother Where You Bound (A&M 1985)★★, Free As A Bird (A&M 1987)★★, Supertramp Live 88 (A&M 1988)★★, Some Things Never Change (Chrysalis 1997)★★★.
COMPILATIONS: The Autobiography Of Supertramp (A&M 1986)★★★, The Very Best Of (A&M 1992)★★★★.
FURTHER READING: The Supertramp Book, Martin Melhuish.

SUPREMES
ALBUMS: as The Supremes Meet The Supremes (Motown 1963)★★★, Where Did Our Love Go? (Motown 1964)★★★, A Bit Of Liverpool (Motown 1964)★★, The Supremes Sing Country, Western And Pop (Motown 1964)★, We Remember Sam Cooke (Motown 1965)★★★, More Hits By The Supremes (Motown 1965)★★★, Merry Christmas (Motown 1965)★★★, The Supremes At The Copa (Motown 1965)★★★, I Hear A Symphony (Motown 1966)★★★, The Supremes A-Go-Go (Motown 1966)★★★, The Supremes Sing Holland, Dozier, Holland (Motown 1967)★★★★, The Supremes Sing Rodgers And Hart (Motown 1967)★★, Right On (Motown 1970)★★★, with the Four Tops The Magnificent Seven (Motown 1970)★★★★, New Ways But Love Stays (Motown 1970)★★, Touch (Motown 1971)★★, with the Four Tops The Return Of The Magnificent Seven (Motown 1971)★★, with the Four Tops Dynamite (Motown 1971)★★★, Floy Joy (Motown 1972)★★★, The Supremes (Motown 1975)★★, High Energy (Motown 1976)★★, Mary, Scherrie And Susaye (Motown 1976)★★★. As Diana Ross And The Supremes: Reflections (Motown 1968)★★★, Diana Ross And The Supremes Sing And Perform 'Funny Girl' (Motown 1968)★, Diana Ross And The Supremes Live At London's Talk Of The Town (Motown 1968)★★★, with The Temptations Diana Ross And The Supremes Join The Temptations (Motown 1968)★★★, Love Child (Motown 1968)★★★, with The Temptations TCB (Motown 1968)★★★, Let The Sunshine In (Motown 1969)★★, with the Temptations Together (Motown 1969)★★★, Cream Of The Crop (Motown 1969)★★, with The Temptations Diana Ross And The Supremes On Broadway (Motown 1969)★★, Farewell (Motown 1970)★★.
COMPILATIONS: Diana Ross And The Supremes Greatest Hits (Motown 1967)★★★★, Diana Ross And The Supremes Greatest Hits, Volume 2 (Motown 1967)★★★★, Diana Ross And The Supremes Greatest Hits, Volume 3 (Motown 1969)★★★, Anthology 1962-69 (Motown 1974)★★★★, Supremes At Their Best (Motown 1978)★★★, 20 Greatest Hits (Motown 1986)★★★, 25th Anniversary (Motown 1986)★★★, Early Classics (Spectrum 1996)★★★.
FILMS: Beach Ball (1964).
FURTHER READING: Reflections, Johnny Bond. Dreamgirl: My Life As A Supreme, Mary Wilson. Supreme Faith: Someday We'll Be Together, Mary Wilson with Patricia Romanowski. All That Glittered: My Life With The Supremes, Tony Turner and Barbara Aria.

SURFARIS
ALBUMS: Wipe Out (Dot 1963)★★★, The Surfaris Play Wipe Out And Others (Decca 1963)★★★, Hit City '64

(Decca 1964)★★★, *Fun City, USA* (Decca 1964)★★, *Hit City '65* (Decca 1965)★★, *It Ain't Me Babe* (Decca 1965)★★★, *Surfaris Live* (1983)★★.
COMPILATIONS: *Yesterday's Pop Scene* (1973)★★★, *Surfers Rule* (1976)★★★, *Gone With The Wave* (1977)★★★, *Wipe Out! The Best Of ...* (Varese Sarabande 1994)★★★, *Surfaris Stomp* (Varese Sarabande 1995)★★★.

SUTHERLAND BROTHERS (AND QUIVER)
ALBUMS: *The Sutherland Brothers Band* (Island 1972)★★★. With Quiver *Lifeboat* (Island 1972)★★★, *Dream Kid* (Island 1974)★★★★, *Beat Of The Street* (Island 1974)★★★, *Reach For The Sky* (Columbia 1975)★★★, *Slipstream* (Columbia 1976)★★★, *Down To Earth* (Columbia 1977)★★★, *When The Night Comes Down* (Columbia 1978)★★.
COMPILATIONS: *Sailing* (Island 1976)★★★.
FURTHER READING: *The Whaling Years, Peterhead 1788-1893*, Gavin Sutherland.

SWAN, BILLY
ALBUMS: *I Can Help* (Monument 1974)★★★★, *Rock 'N' Roll Moon* (Monument 1975)★★★, *Billy Swan* (Monument 1976)★★★★, *Billy Swan – Four* (Monument 1977)★★★, *You're OK, I'm OK* (A&M 1978)★★, *I'm Into Lovin' You* (Epic 1981)★★, *Bop To Be* (Elite 1995)★★★.
COMPILATIONS: *Billy Swan At His Best* (Monument 1978)★★★.

SWEET
ALBUMS: *Funny How Sweet Co Co Can Be* (RCA 1971)★★, *Sweet* (1973)★★, *Sweet Fanny Adams* (RCA 1974)★★★, *Desolation Boulevard* (RCA 1974)★★★, *Strung Up* (RCA 1975)★★★, *Give Us A Wink* (RCA 1976)★★, *Off The Record* (RCA 1977)★★, *Level Headed* (Polydor 1978)★★, *Cut Above The Rest* (Polydor 1979)★★, *Water's Edge* (Polydor 1980)★★, *Identity Crisis* (Polydor 1982)★★, *Live At The Marquee* (SPV 1989)★, *Blockbusters* (RCA 1989)★★.
COMPILATIONS: *Sweet's Golden Greats* (RCA 1977)★★★, *Hard Centres – The Rock Years* (Zebra 1987)★★, *The Collection* (Castle 1989)★★★, *Hit Singles: The Complete A And B Sides* (Repertoire 1996)★★, *Ballroom Blitz: The Very Best Of ...* (Polygram 1996)★★★.

SWEET, MATTHEW
ALBUMS: as Buzz Of Delight *Sound Castles* mini-album (DB 1984)★★, *Inside* (Columbia 1986)★★, *Earth* (A&M 1989)★★★, *Girlfriend* (Zoo 1992)★★★, *Altered Beast* (Zoo 1993)★★★, *Son Of Altered Beast* mini-album (Zoo 1994)★★, *100% Fun* (Zoo 1995)★★★, *Blue Sky On Mars* (Zoo 1997)★★★.

SWEET INSPIRATIONS
ALBUMS: *The Sweet Inspirations* (Atlantic 1967)★★★, *Songs Of Faith And Inspiration* (Atlantic 1968)★★★, *What The World Needs Now Is Love* (Atlantic 1968)★★, *Sweets For My Sweet* (Atlantic 1969)★★★, *Sweet, Sweet Soul* (Atlantic 1970)★★★, *Estelle, Myrna And Sylvia* (Stax 1973)★★★, *Hot Butterfly* (1979)★★.
COMPILATIONS: *Estelle, Myrna And Sylvia* (1991)★★★, *The Best Of ...* (1994)★★★.

SWINGING BLUE JEANS
ALBUMS: *Blue Jeans A' Swinging* aka *Swinging Blue Jeans* aka *Tutti Frutti* (HMV 1964)★★★, *The Swinging Blue Jeans: La Voce Del Padrone* (1966)★★★, *Hippy Hippy Shake* (1973)★★★, *Brand New And Faded* (Dart 1974)★★, *Dancin'* (1985)★★.
COMPILATIONS: *Hippy Hippy Shake* (1964)★★★, *Shake: The Best Of The Swinging Blue Jeans* (1986)★★★.

T

T. REX
ALBUMS: as Tyrannosaurus Rex *My People Were Fair And Had Sky In Their Hair But Now They're Content To Wear Stars On Their Brows* (Regal Zonophone 1968)★★★, *Prophets Seers & Sages, The Angels Of The Ages* (Regal Zonophone 1968)★★★, *Unicorn* (Regal Zonophone 1969)★★★, *A Beard Of Stars* (Regal Zonophone 1970)★★★; as T. Rex *T. Rex* (Fly 1970)★★★, *Electric Warrior* (Fly 1971)★★★★, *The Slider* (EMI 1972)★★★, *Tanx* (EMI 1973)★★★, *Zinc Alloy And The Hidden Riders Of Tomorrow Or A Creamed Cage In August* (EMI 1974)★★, *Bolan's Zip Gun* (EMI 1975)★★★, *Futuristic Dragon* (EMI 1976)★★, *Dandy In The Underworld* (EMI 1977)★★, *T. Rex In Concert – The Electric Warrior Tour 1971* (Marc 1981)★★★.
COMPILATIONS: *The Best Of T. Rex* contains Tyrannosaurus Rex material (Fly 1971)★★★, *Bolan Boogie* (Fly 1972)★★★, *Great Hits* (EMI 1973)★★★★, *Solid Gold T. Rex* (EMI 1979)★★★, *The Best Of The 20th Century Boy* (K-Tel 1985)★★★, *The T. Rex Collection* (Castle 1986)★★★★, *The Singles Collection* (Marc On Wax 1987)★★★, *The Marc Shows* (Marc On Wax 1989)★★★, *Great Hits 1972-1977: The A-Sides* (Edsel 1994)★★★★, *A BBC History* (Band Of Joy 1996)★★★★, *Rainbow Live 1977* (1997)★★★.
FURTHER READING: *Tyrannosaurus Rex*, Ray Stevenson.

TAJ MAHAL
ALBUMS: *Taj Mahal* (Columbia 1968)★★★★, *Giant Steps/De Ole Folks At Home* (Columbia 1969)★★★★, *The Natch'l Blues* (Columbia 1969)★★★★, *The Real Thing* (Columbia 1971)★★★, *Happy Just To Be Like I Am* (Columbia 1972)★★, *Recycling The Blues And Other Related Stuff* (Columbia 1972)★★★, *The Sounder* (1973)★★, *Oooh So Good 'N' Blues* (Columbia 1973)★★★, *Mo' Roots* (Columbia 1974)★★★, *Music Keeps Me Together* (Columbia 1975)★★, *Satisfied 'N Tickled Too* (Columbia 1976)★★, *Music Fuh Ya'* (Warners 1977)★★, *Brothers* (Warners 1977)★★, *Evolution* (Warners 1977)★★, *Taj Mahal And The International Rhythm Band Live* (1979)★★★, *Live* (1981)★★, *Take A Giant Step* (Magnet 1983)★★★, *Taj* (Sonet 1987)★★★, *Live And Direct* (Teldec 1987)★★★, *Big Blues – Live At Ronnie Scott's* (Essential 1990)★★★, *Mule Bone* (Gramavision 1991)★★★, *Like Never Before* (Private Music 1991)★★★, *Dancing The Blues* (Private Music/BMG 1994)★★★, *An Evening Of Acoustic Music* (Tradition & Moderne/Topic 1995)★★★, *Phantom Blues* (Private 1996)★★★★, *An Evening Of Acoustic Music* (Ruf 1997)★★★, *Se–or Blues* (Private Music/BMG 1997)★★★, *Sacred Island* (Private Music 1998).
COMPILATIONS: *Going Home* (Columbia 1980)★★★★, *The Taj Mahal Collection* (Castle 1987)★★★.
VIDEOS: *At Ronnie Scott's 1988* (Hendring 1989).

TAKE THAT
ALBUMS: *Take That And Party* (RCA 1992)★★★, *Everything Changes* (RCA 1993)★★★, *Nobody Else* (RCA 1995)★★★.
COMPILATIONS: *Greatest Hits* (RCA 1996)★★★.
VIDEOS: *Take That And Party* (BMG 1992), *Take That: The Party-Live At Wembley* (BMG 1993), *Greatest Hits* (BMG 1995), *From Zeros To Heroes* (Wienerworld 1995), *Everything Changes* (BMG 1995), *Hometown: Live At Manchester G-Mex* (BMG 1995), *Berlin* (BMG 1995), *Nobody Else: The Movie* (BMG 1996).
FURTHER READING: *Take That: Our Story*, Piers Morgan. *Everything Changes*, Take That.

TALK TALK
ALBUMS: *The Party's Over* (EMI 1982)★★, *It's My Life* (EMI 1984)★★★, *It's My Mix* (EMI 1984)★★, *The Colour Of Spring* (EMI 1986)★★★★, *Spirit Of Eden* (Parlophone 1988)★★★★, *Laughing Stock* (Verve 1991)★★★.
COMPILATIONS: *Natural History: The Very Best Of Talk Talk* (Parlophone 1990)★★★, *The Very Best Of Talk Talk* (EMI 1997)★★★.

TALKING HEADS
ALBUMS: *Talking Heads '77* (Sire 1977)★★★★, *More Songs About Buildings And Food* (Sire 1978)★★★★, *Fear Of Music* (Sire 1979)★★★, *Remain In Light* (Sire 1980)★★★★, *The Name Of This Band Is Talking Heads* (Sire 1982)★★★, *Speaking In Tongues* (EMI 1983)★★★, *Stop Making Sense* (EMI 1984)★★★, *Little Creatures* (EMI 1985)★★★★, *True Stories* soundtrack (EMI 1986)★★★, *Naked* (EMI 1988)★★. As the Heads *No Talking Just Heads* (MCA 1996)★★.
COMPILATIONS: *Once In A Lifetime: The Best Of* (EMI 1992)★★★, *Popular Favorites 1976 – 1992 (Sand In The Vaseline)* (EMI 1992)★★★.
VIDEOS: *Stop Making Sense* (Palace Video 1986), *Storytelling Giant* (PMI 1988).
FURTHER READING: *Talking Heads*, Miles. *The Name Of This Book Is Talking Heads*, Krista Reese. *Talking Heads: The Band And Their Music*, David Gans. *Talking Heads: A Biography*, Jerome Davis.

TANGERINE DREAM
ALBUMS: *Electronic Meditation* (Ohr 1970)★★★, *Alpha Centauri* (Ohr 1971)★★★, *Zeit (Largo In Four Movements)* (Ohr 1972)★★★, *Atem* (Ohr 1973)★★★, *Phaedra* (Virgin 1974)★★★★, *Rubycon* (Virgin 1975)★★★, *Ricochet* (Virgin 1975)★★★, *Stratosfear* (Virgin 1976)★★★★, *Encore-Live* (Virgin 1977)★★, *Sorcerer* soundtrack (MCA 1977)★★, *Cyclone* (Virgin 1978)★★★, *Force Majeure* (Virgin 1979)★★★, *Thief* soundtrack (Virgin 1980)★★, *Tangram* (Virgin 1980)★★★, *Quichotte* (Amiga 1980) re-issued as *Pergamon* (Virgin 1986)★★★, *Exit* (Virgin 1981)★★★, *White Eagle* (Virgin 1982)★★★, *Logos-Live At The Dominion* (Virgin 1983)★★, *Wavelength* soundtrack (Varese Sarabande 1983)★★, *Risky Business* soundtrack (Virgin 1983)★★, *Hyperborea* (Virgin 1983)★★, *Firestarter* soundtrack (MCA 1984)★★, *Flashpoint* soundtrack (EMI 1984)★★, *Poland-The Warsaw Concert* (Jive Electro 1984)★★, *Heartbreakers* soundtrack (Virgin 1985)★★, *Le Parc* (Jive Electro 1985)★★, *Legend* soundtrack (MCA 1986)★★, *Underwater Sunlight* (Jive Electro 1986)★★, *Near Dark* soundtrack (Silva Screen 1987)★★, *Tyger* (Jive Electro 1987)★★, *Three O'Clock High* soundtrack (Varese Sarabande 1987)★★, *Shy People* soundtrack (Varese Sarabande 1987)★★, *Live Miles* (Jive Electro 1988)★★, *Optical Race* (Private Race 1988)★★★, *Lily On The Beach* (1989)★★, *Melrose* (1990)★★, *Rockoon* (1992)★★, *Canyon Dreams* (1993)★★, *Turn Of The Tides* (Miramar 1994)★★, *Goblin's Club* (Sequel 1996)★★★, *Oasis* (Miramar 1991), *Ambient Monkeys* (TDI 1998).
COMPILATIONS: *Dream Sequence* (Virgin 1985)★★★, *The Collection* (Castle 1987)★★★, *Book Of Dreams* (Essential 1996)★★★, *The Dream Mixes* (TDI 1996)★★★, *The Dream Roots Collection* (Essential 1997)★★★.
VIDEOS: *Three Phase* (1993).

TASTE
ALBUMS: *Taste* (Polydor 1969)★★★, *On The Boards* (Polydor 1970)★★★★, *Live Taste* (Polydor 1971)★★, *Live At The Isle Of Wight* (Polydor 1972)★★.
COMPILATIONS: *The Greatest Rock Sensation* (Polydor 1985)★★★.

TATE, HOWARD
ALBUMS: *Get It While You Can* (Verve 1967)★★★★, *Howard Tate*(Verve 1969)★★★★.
COMPILATIONS: *Get It While You Can: The Legendary Sessions* (Mercury 1995)★★★★.

TAYLOR, JAMES
ALBUMS: *James Taylor* (Apple 1968)★★★, *Sweet Baby James* (Warners 1970)★★★★, *James Taylor And The Original Flying Machine – 1967* (Euphoria 1970)★★, *Mud Slide Slim And The Blue Horizon* (Warners 1971)★★★★, *One Man Dog* (Warners 1972)★★★, *Walking Man* (Warners 1974)★★★, *Gorilla* (Warners 1975)★★★, *In The Pocket* (Warners 1976)★★, *JT* (Columbia 1977)★★★★, *Flag* (Columbia 1979)★★, *Dad Loves His Work* (Columbia 1981)★★, *That's Why I'm Here* (Columbia 1985)★★★★, *Never Die Young* (Columbia 1988)★★★, *New Moon Shine* (Columbia 1991)★★★, *Live In Rio* rec. 1985 (Columbia 1992)★★★, *Live* (1993)★★★, *Hourglass* (Columbia 1997)★★★.
COMPILATIONS: *Greatest Hits* (Warners 1976)★★★★, *Classic Songs* (Warners 1987)★★★★★, *The Best Of James Taylor – The Classic Years* (1990)★★★★.
VIDEOS: *James Taylor In Concert* (1991), *Squibnocket* (1993).

TAYLOR, JOHNNIE
ALBUMS: *Wanted One Soul Singer* (Stax 1967)★★★★, *Who's Making Love?* (Stax 1968)★★★★, *Looking For Johnny Taylor* (Stax 1969)★★★★, *The Johnnie Taylor Philosophy Continues* (Stax 1969)★★★, *Rare Stamps* (Stax 1970)★★★, *One Step Beyond* (Stax 1970)★★★, *Taylored In Silk* (Stax 1973)★★★, *Super Taylor* (Stax 1974)★★★, *Eargasm* (1976)★★★, *Rated Extraordinaire* (1977)★★, *Disco 9000* (1977)★★, *Ever Ready* (1978)★★, *Reflections* (197)★★, *She's Killing Me* (1979)★★, *A New Day* (1980)★★, *Just Ain't Good Enough* (1982)★★, *This Is Your Night* (Malaco 1984)★★★, *Best Of The Old And The New* (1984)★★★, *Wall To Wall* (Malaco 1985)★★★, *Lover Boy* (Malaco 1987)★★★, *In Control* (1988)★★, *Crazy 'Bout You* (Malaco 1989)★★★, *Little Bluebird* (Stax 1991)★★★, *Just Can't Do Right* (90s)★★★, *Real Love* (90s)★★★, *Good Love!* (Malaco 1996)★★★★, *Taylored To Please* (Malaco 1998).
COMPILATIONS: *The Roots Of Johnnie Taylor* (Star1969)★★★, *The Johnnie Taylor Chronicle (1968-1972)* (Stax 1978)★★★★, *The Johnnie Taylor Chronicle (1972-1974)* (Stax 1978)★★★, *Somebody's Getting It* (1989)★★★, *Raw Blues/Little Bluebird* (1992)★★★, *The Best Of ... On Malaco Vol. 1* (1994)★★★.

TEARDROP EXPLODES
ALBUMS: *Kilimanjaro* (Mercury 1980)★★★, *Wilder* (Mercury 1981)★★★, *Everybody Wants To Shag The Teardrop Explodes* (Fontana 1990)★★.
COMPILATIONS: *Piano* (Document 1990)★★★.

TEARS FOR FEARS
ALBUMS: *The Hurting* (Mercury 1983)★★★, *Songs From The Big Chair* (Mercury 1985)★★★, *The Seeds Of Love* (Fontana 1989)★★★, *Elemental* (Mercury 1993)★★, *Raoul And The Kings Of Spain* (Epic 1995)★★. Solo: Curt Smith *Soul On Board* (Mercury 1993)★.
COMPILATIONS: *Tears Roll Down (Greatest Hits 82-92)* (Fontana 1992)★★★★, *Saturnine Martial & Lunatic* (Fontana 1996)★★★.
VIDEOS: *Scenes From The Big Chair* (4 Front Video 1991).
FURTHER READING: *Tears For Fears*, Ann Greene.

TEENAGE FANCLUB
ALBUMS: *A Catholic Education* (Paperhouse 1990)★★, *The King* (Creation 1991)★★, *Bandwagonesque* (Creation 1991)★★★★, *Thirteen* (Creation 1993)★★, *Grand Prix* (Creation 1995)★★★★, *Songs From Northern Britain* (Creation 1997)★★★★.
COMPILATIONS: *Deep Fried Fanclub* (Paperhouse/Fire 1995)★★.

TELEVISION
ALBUMS: *Marquee Moon* (Elektra 1978)★★★★, *Adventure* (Elektra 1979)★★★, *The Blow Up* live 1978 recording, cassette only (ROIR 1983)★★, *Television* (Capitol 1993)★★.

TEMPERANCE 7
ALBUMS: *Temperance 7* (Parlophone 1961)★★★★, *Temperance 7 Plus One* (Argo 1961)★★★, *Hot Temperance 7* (1987)★★★, *Tea For Eight* (1990)★★★, *33 Not Out* (1990)★★★.

TEMPTATIONS
ALBUMS: *Meet The Temptations* (Gordy 1964)★★★★, *The Temptations Sing Smokey* (Gordy 1965)★★★★, *The Temptin' Temptations* (Gordy/Tamla Motown 1965)★★★★, *Gettin' Ready* (Gordy 1966)★★★★, *Live!* (Gordy 1967)★★, *With A Lot O' Soul* (Gordy 1967)★★★, *In A Mellow Mood* (Gordy 1967)★★★, *Wish It Would Rain* (Gordy 1968)★★★★, *Diana Ross And The Supremes Join The Temptations* (Tamla Motown 1968)★★★, with Diana Ross And The Supremes *TCB* (1968)★★★, *Live At The Copa* (Tamla Motown 1968)★★, *Cloud Nine* (Tamla Motown 1969)★★★★, *The Temptations' Show* (Tamla Motown 1969)★★★, *Puzzle People* (Tamla Motown 1969)★★★, with Diana Ross And The Supremes *Together* (Tamla Motown 1969)★★★, with Diana Ross And The Supremes *On Broadway* (Tamla Motown 1969)★★★, *Psychedelic Shack* (Tamla Motown 1970)★★★★, *Live At London's Talk Of The Town* (Tamla Motown 1970)★★★, *Christmas Card* (Tamla Motown 1970)★, *Sky's The Limit* (Tamla Motown 1971)★★★, *Solid Rock* (Tamla Motown 1972)★★★, *All Directions* (Tamla Motown 1972)★★★, *Masterpiece* (Tamla Motown 1973)★★★, *1990* (Tamla Motown 1973)★★★, *A Song For You* (Tamla Motown 1975)★★★, *House Party* (Tamla Motown 1975)★★, *Wings Of Love* (Tamla Motown 1976)★★, *The Temptations Do The Temptations* (Tamla Motown 1976)★★, *Hear To Tempt You* (Tamla Motown 1977)★★, *Bare Back* (Tamla Motown 1978)★★, *Power* (Tamla Motown 1980)★★, *The Temptations* (1981)★★, with Jimmy Ruffin and Eddie Kendricks *Reunion* (1982)★★★, *Surface Thrills* (1983)★★, *Back To Basics* (1984)★★★, *Truly For You* (1984)★★, *Touch Me* (1985)★★, *To Be Continued ...* (1986)★★★, *Together Again* (1987)★★★, *Special* (1989)★★, *Milestone* (1991)★★.
COMPILATIONS: *Greatest Hits* (Tamla Motown 1966)★★★★, *Greatest Hits, Volume 2* (Tamla Motown 1970)★★★★, *Anthology* (Tamla Motown 1973)★★★★★, *25 Anniversary* (Motown 1986)★★★★, *Compact Command Performances* (1989)★★★, *Hum Along And Dance: More Of The Best 1963-1974* (Rhino 1993)★★★, *The Original Lead Singers Of The Temptations* (1993)★★★, *Emperors Of Soul* 5-CD set (Motown 1994)★★★★, *Early Classics* (Spectrum 1996)★★★.
VIDEOS: *Live In Concert* (Old Gold 1990).
FURTHER READING: *Temptations*, Otis Williams with Patricia Romanowski.

10cc
ALBUMS: *10cc* (UK 1973)★★★, *Sheet Music* (UK 1974)★★★, *The Original Soundtrack* (Mercury 1975)★★★, *How Dare You* (Mercury 1976)★★, *Deceptive Bends* (Mercury 1977)★★, *Live And Let Live* (Mercury 1977)★★, *Bloody Tourists* (Mercury 1978)★★, *Look Hear!* (Mercury 1980)★★, *Ten Out Of 10* (Mercury 1981)★★, *10cc In Concert* (Pickwick 1982)★★, *Window In The Jungle* (Mercury 1983)★★, *Meanwhile* (Polydor 1992)★★, *10cc Live* (Creative Man 1994)★.
COMPILATIONS: *Greatest Hits 1972-1978* (Mercury 1979)★★★★, *The Very Best Of* (Mercury 1997)★★★★.
VIDEOS: *Live In Concert* (VCL 1986), *Live At The International Music Show* (Video Collection 1987), *Changing Faces, The Very Best Of* (Channel 5 1988).
FURTHER READING: *The 10cc Story*, George Tremlett.

10,000 MANIACS
ALBUMS: *Human Conflict Number 5* mini-album (Mark 1982)★★, *Secrets Of The I Ching* (Christian Burial 1983)★★★, *The Wishing Chair* (Elektra 1985)★★, *In My Tribe* (Elektra 1987)★★★★, *Blind Man's Zoo* (Elektra 1989)★★★, *Our Time In Eden* (Elektra 1992)★★★, *10,000 Maniacs MTV Unplugged* (Elektra 1993)★★★, *Love Among The Ruins* (Geffen 1997)★★.
COMPILATIONS: *Hope Chest (The Fredonia Recordings 1982-1983)* (Elektra 1990)★★.
VIDEOS: *MTV Unplugged* (1994).

TEN YEARS AFTER
ALBUMS: *Ten Years After* (Deram 1967)★★★, *Undead* (Deram 1968)★★★★, *Stonedhenge* (Deram 1969)★★★, *Ssssh* (Deram 1969)★★★★, *Cricklewood Green* (Deram 1970)★★★★, *Watt* (Deram 1970)★★★, *A Space In Time* (Chrysalis 1971)★★★, *Rock 'N' Roll Music To The World* (Chrysalis 1972)★★, *Recorded Live* (Chrysalis 1973)★★, *Positive Vibrations* (Chrysalis 1974)★★, *About Time* (Chrysalis 1989)★★, *Love Like A Man* (ITM/Traditional 1994).
COMPILATIONS: *Alvin Lee & Company* (Deram 1972)★★★, *Goin' Home! – Their Greatest Hits* (Deram 1975)★★★, *Original Recordings Vol. 1* (1987)★★★, *The Essential* (Chrysalis 1992)★★★★, *Live At Reading '83* (Dutch East 1993)★★★, *Live 1990* (Deman 1994)★★★, *Live* (Code 90 1995).

TERRORVISION
ALBUMS: *Formaldehyde* (Total Vegas 1992)★★★, *How To Make Friends And Influence People* (Total Vegas 1994)★★★★, *Regular Urban Survivors* (Total Vegas 1996)★★★★.
VIDEOS: *Fired Up And Lairy* (PMI 1995).

TEX, JOE
ALBUMS: *Hold On* (Checker 1964)★★★, *Hold What You've Got* (Atlantic 1965)★★★, *The New Boss* (Atlantic 1965)★★★★, *The Love You Save* (Atlantic 1966)★★★, *I've Got To Do A Little Better* (Atlantic 1966)★★★★, *Live And Lively* (Atlantic 1968)★★, *Soul Country* (Atlantic 1968)★★★, *Happy Soul* (1969)★★★, *You Better Believe It* (Atlantic 1969)★★★, *Buying A Book* (Atlantic 1969)★★★, *With Strings And Things* (1970)★★★, *From The Roots Came The Rapper* (1972)★★, *I Gotcha* (1972)★★, *Joe Tex Spills The Beans* (1973)★★, *Another Man's Woman* (1974)★★, *Bumps And Bruises* (1977)★★, *Rub Down* (1978)★★, *He Who Is Without Funk Cast The First Stone* (1979)★★.
COMPILATIONS: *The Best Of Joe Tex* (King 1965)★★★, *The Very Best Of Joe Tex* (Atlantic 1967)★★★★, *Greatest Hits* (Atlantic 1967)★★★★, *The Very Best Of Joe Tex – Real Country Soul ... Scarce As Hen's Teeth* (1988)★★★, *I Believe I'm Gonna Make It: The Best Of Joe Tex 1964-1972* (Rhino 1988)★★★★, *Different Strokes* (1989)★★★, *Stone Soul Country* (1989)★★★, *Ain't Gonna Bump No More* (1993)★★★, *I Gotcha (His Greatest Hits)* (1993)★★★, *Skinny Legs And All: The Classic Early Dial Sides* (Kent 1994)★★★, *You're Right Joe Tex!* (Kent 1995)★★★.

THAT PETROL EMOTION
ALBUMS: *Manic Pop Thrill* (Demon 1986)★★★, *Babble* (Polydor 1987)★★★★, *End Of The Millenium Psychosis Blues* (Virgin 1988)★★★, *Peel Sessions* (Strange Fruit 1989)★★★, *Chemicrazy* (Virgin 1990)★★, *Fireproof* (Koogat 1993)★★★.

THE THE
ALBUMS: *Soul Mining* (Some Bizzare 1983)★★★, *Infected* (Epic 1986)★★★, *Mind Bomb* (Epic 1989)★★, *Dusk* (Epic 1993)★★★, *Hanky Panky* (Epic 1995)★★.
VIDEOS: *Infected* (CBS-Fox 1987), *Versus The World* (Sony Music Video 1991), *From Dawn 'Til Dusk* (1993).

THEM
ALBUMS: *Them* aka *The Angry Young Them* (Decca 1965)★★★★, *Them Again* (Decca 1966)★★★★, *Now And Them* (Tower 1968)★★★, *Time Out, Time In For Them* (Tower 1968)★★★, *Them* (Happy Tiger 1970)★★★, *In Reality* (Happy Tiger 1971)★★★, *Shut Your Mouth* (Teldec 1979)★★★.
Solo: Billy Harrison *Billy Who?* (Vagabound 1980)★★. Jackie McCauley *Jackie McCauley* (Dawn 1971)★★.
COMPILATIONS: *The World Of Them* (Decca 1970)★★★★★, *Them Featuring Van Morrison, Lead Singer* (Decca 1973)★★★, *Backtrackin' With Them* (London 1974)★★★, *Rock Roots: Them* (Decca 1976)★★★★, *One More Time* (Decca 1984)★★★, *The Them Collection* (Castle 1986)★★★, *The Singles* (See For Miles 1987)★★★★.
FURTHER READING: *Van Morrison: A Portrait Of The Artist*, Johnny Rogan.

THERAPY?
ALBUMS: *Baby Teeth* mini-album (Wiiija 1991)★★, *Pleasure Death* mini-album (Wiiija 1992)★★★, *Nurse* (A&M 1992)★★★, *Troublegum* (A&M 1994)★★★★, *Infernal Love* (A&M 1995)★★.

THESE ANIMAL MEN
ALBUMS: *Too Sussed* mini-album (Hi-Rise 1994)★★, *(Come On, Join) The High Society* (Hi-Rise 1994)★★★, *Taxi For These Animal Men* mini-album (Hi-Rise 1995)★★★, *Accident And Emergency* (Hut 1997)★★★.

THEY MIGHT BE GIANTS
ALBUMS: *They Might Be Giants* self-released cassette (TMB Music 1985), *They Might Be Giants* (Bar/None 1986)★★★, *Lincoln* (Bar/None 1989)★★★, *Don't Let's Start* (Elektra 1989)★★★, *Flood* (Elektra 1990)★★, *Apollo 18* (Elektra 1992)★★, *John Henry* (Elektra 1994)★★★, *Factory Showroom* (Elektra 1996)★★★.
COMPILATIONS: *Don't Let's Start* (One Little Indian 1989)★★★, *Miscellaneous T* (Bar/None 1991)★★★, *Then: The Earlier Years* (Restless 1997)★★★.
VIDEOS: *They Might Be Giants* (Warner Music Video 1991).

THIN LIZZY
ALBUMS: *Thin Lizzy* (Decca 1971)★★, *Shades Of A Blue Orphanage* (Decca 1972)★★, *Vagabonds Of The Western World* (Decca 1973)★★★, *Night Life* (Vertigo 1974)★★★, *Fighting* (Vertigo 1975)★★★, *Jailbreak* (Vertigo 1976)★★★★, *Johnny The Fox* (Vertigo 1976)★★★, *Bad Reputation* (Vertigo 1977)★★★, *Live And Dangerous* (Vertigo 1978)★★★★, *Black Rose* (Vertigo 1979)★★★, *Renegade* (Vertigo 1981)★★, *Thunder And Lightning* (Vertigo 1983)★★, *Life-Live* double album (Vertigo 1983)★★, *BBC Radio 1 Live In Concert* rec. 1983 (Windsong 1992)★★★.
COMPILATIONS: *Adventures Of Thin Lizzy* (Vertigo 1981)★★★, *Lizzy Killers* (Vertigo 1983)★★★, *The Collection* double album (Castle 1985)★★★, *The Best Of Phil Lynott And Thin Lizzy* (Telstar 1987)★★★, *Dedication – The Best Of Thin Lizzy* (Vertigo 1991)★★★★, *Wild One – The Very Best Of ...* (Mercury 1995)★★★★.
VIDEOS: *Live And Dangerous* (1986), *Dedication* (1991).
FURTHER READING: *Songs For While I'm Away*, Philip Lynott. *Thin Lizzy*, Larry Pryce. *Philip*, Philip Lynott. *Thin Lizzy: The Approved Biography*, Chris Salewicz. *My Boy: The Philip Lynott Story*, Philomena Lynott with Jackie Hayden.

THIRD EYE BLIND
ALBUMS: *Third Eye Blind* (Elektra 1997).

THIRTEENTH FLOOR ELEVATORS
ALBUMS: *The Psychedelic Sounds Of The Thirteenth Floor Elevators* (International 1966)★★★★, *Easter Everywhere* (International 1967)★★★, *Live* (International 1968)★, *Bull Of The Woods* (International 1968)★★.
COMPILATIONS: *I've Seen Your Face Before* (1988)★★★, *The Collection* (1991)★★★, *Out Of Order* (1993)★★★, *The Best Of ...* (Eva 1994)★★★★, *The Interpreter* (Thunderbolt 1996)★★★.

THOMPSON, RICHARD
ALBUMS: see also Fairport Convention and Richard And Linda Thompson entries, *Henry The Human Fly* (Island 1972)★★★, *Strict Tempo* (Elixir 1981)★★★, *Hand Of Kindness* (Hannibal 1983)★★★★, *Small Town Romance* (Hannibal 1984)★★★★, *Across A Crowded Room* (Polydor 1985)★★★, *Daring Adventures* (Polydor 1986)★★★★, with French, Frith, Kaiser *Live Love Larf & Loaf* (Demon 1987)★★, with Peter Filleul *The Marksman* soundtrack (BBC 1987)★★, *Amnesia* (Capitol 1988)★★★, *Rumour And Sigh* (Capitol 1990)★★★★, with French, Frith, Kaiser *Invisible Means* (Demon 1990)★★, with the GP's *Saturday Rolling Around* (Woodworm 1991)★★, *Sweet Talker* soundtrack (Capitol 1991)★★, *Mirror Blue* (Capitol 1994)★★★★, with Danny Thompson *Live At Crawley 1993* (Whatdisc 1995)★★★, *You? Me? Us?* (EMI 1996)★★★, as the Richard Thompson Band *Two Letter Words* (Hokey Pokey 1997)★★★, with Danny Thompson *Industry* (Parlophone 1997)★★★.
COMPILATIONS: *Watching The Dark* 3-CD box set (Hannibal 1993)★★★★.
VIDEOS: *Across A Crowded Room* (Sony 1983).
FURTHER READING: *Meet On the Ledge*, Patrick Humphries. *Richard Thompson: 21 Years Of Doom & Gloom*, Clinton Heylin. *Gypsy Love Songs & Sad Refrains: The Recordings Of Richard Thompson & Sandy Denny*, Clinton Heylin. *Richard Thompson: Strange Affair, The Biography*, Patrick Humphries.

THOMPSON, RICHARD AND LINDA
ALBUMS: *I Want To See The Bright Lights Tonight* (Island 1974)★★★★, *Hokey Pokey* (Island 1975)★★★★, *Pour Down Like Silver* (Island 1975)★★★★, *First Light* (Chrysalis 1978)★★★, *Sunnyvista* (Chrysalis 1979)★★, *Shoot Out The Lights* (Hannibal 1982)★★★★★.

THOMPSON TWINS
ALBUMS: *A Product Of ...* (Arista 1981)★★, *Set* (Tee 1982)★★, *Quick Step And Side Kick* (Arista 1983)★★★, *Into The Gap* (Arista 1984)★★★, *Here's To The Future* (Arista 1986)★★, *Close To The Bone* (Arista 1987)★, *Big Trash* (Warners 1989)★★, *Queer* (Warners 1991)★★.
COMPILATIONS: *The Greatest Hits* (Stylus 1990)★★★, *The Singles Collection* (Camden 1997)★★★.
FURTHER READING: *The Thompson Twins: An Odd Couple*, Rose Rouce.

THOROGOOD, GEORGE
ALBUMS: *George Thorogood And The Destroyers* (Rounder 1977)★★★, *Move It On Over* (Rounder 1978)★★★, *Better Than The Rest* (Rounder 1979)★★, *More George Thorogood And The Destroyers* (Rounder 1980)★★, *Bad To The Bone* (Capitol 1982)★★★, *Maverick* (Capitol 1985)★★, *Live* (Capitol 1986)★★, *Born To Be Bad* (Capitol 1988)★★, *Boogie People* (Capitol 1991)★★, *Killer's Bluze* (1993)★★, *Haircut* (1993)★★, *Let's Work Together* (EMI 1995)★★, *Rockin' My Life Away* (EMI 1997)★★.

3 COLOURS RED
ALBUMS: *Pure* (Creation 1997)★★★.

THREE DEGREES
ALBUMS: *Maybe* (Roulette 1970)★★★, *Three Degrees* (Philadelphia International 1974)★★★, *International* (Philadelphia International 1975)★★★, *So Much In Love* (1975)★★, *Take Good Care Of Yourself* (1975)★★, *The Three Degrees Live* (Philadelphia International 1975)★★, *Three Degrees Live In Japan* (Columbia 1975)★★, *Standing Up For Love* (1977)★★, *The Three Degrees* (Ariola 1978)★★, *New Dimensions* (Ariola 1978)★★, *3D* (1979)★★, *Three Degrees And Holding* (1989)★★, *Woman In Love* (1993)★★. Solo: Fayette Pickney *One Degree* (1979)★.
COMPILATIONS: *Gold* (K-Tel 1980)★★, *20 Golden Greats* (1984)★★★, *The Complete Swan Recordings* (1992)★★, *A Collection Of Their 20 Greatest Hits* (Columbia 1996)★★★.

THREE DOG NIGHT
ALBUMS: *Three Dog Night* (Dunhill 1969)★★★, *Suitable For Framing* (Dunhill 1969)★★, *Captured Live At The Forum* (Dunhill 1969)★★, *It Ain't Easy* (Dunhill 1970)★★★★, *Naturally* (Dunhill 1970)★★, *Golden Bisquits* (Dunhill 1971)★★★★, *Harmony* (Dunhill 1971)★★★, *Seven Separate Fools* (Dunhill 1972)★★★, *Around The World With Three Dog Night* (Dunhill 1973)★★, *Cyan* (Dunhill 1973)★★, *Hard Labor* (Dunhill 1974)★★, *Coming Down Your Way* (ABC 1975)★★, *American Pastime* (ABC 1976)★★, *It's A Jungle* (Lamborghini 1983)★.
COMPILATIONS: *Joy To The World – Their Greatest Hits* (Dunhill 1975)★★★, *The Best Of* (Dunhill 1989)★★★, *That Ain't The Way To Have Fun: Greatest Hits* (Connoisseur Collection 1995)★★★.

THROWING MUSES
ALBUMS: *Throwing Muses* (4AD 1986)★★★, *The Fat Skier* mini-album (Sire/4AD 1987)★★★, *House Tornado* (Sire/4AD 1988)★★★, *Hunkpapa* (Sire/4AD 1989)★★, *The Real Ramona* (Sire/4AD 1991)★★★★, *Red Heaven* (Sire/4AD 1992)★★★ *University* (Warners/4AD 1995)★★★★, *Limbo* (4AD 1996)★★★.

THUNDERCLAP NEWMAN
ALBUMS: *Hollywood Dream* (Track 1970)★★★.

THUNDERS, JOHNNY
ALBUMS: *So Alone* (Real 1978)★★★★, *In Cold Blood* (New Rose 1983)★★★, *Too Much Junkie Business* cassette only (ROIR 1983)★★★, *Hurt Me* (New Rose 1984)★★★, *Que Sera Sera* (Jungle 1985)★★★, *Stations Of The Cross* cassette only (ROIR 1987)★★, with Patti Palladin *Copy Cats* (Restless 1988)★★★, *Gang War Featuring Johnny Thunders And Wayne Kramer* (Zodiac 1990)★, *Bootlegging The Bootleggers* (Jungle 1990)★★, *Live At Max's Kansas City '79* (ROIR 1996)★★★, *Have Faith* (Mutiny 1996)★★.
COMPILATIONS: *Hurt Me* (Dojo 1995)★★★, *The Studio Bootlegs* (Dojo 1996)★★.
FURTHER READING: *Johnny Thunders: In Cold Blood*, Nina Antonia.

TIKARAM, TANITA
ALBUMS: *Ancient Heart* (Warners 1988)★★★★, *The Sweet Keeper* (East West 1990)★★, *Everybody's Angel* (East West 1991)★★, *Eleven Kinds Of Loneliness* (East West 1992)★★, *Lovers In The City* (East West 1995)★★★.

TILLOTSON, JOHNNY
ALBUMS: *Tillotson's Best* (Cadence 1961)★★★, *It Keeps Right On A-Hurtin'* (Cadence 1962)★★★, *You Can Never Stop Me Loving You* (Cadence 1963)★★★, *Judy, Judy, Judy* (1963)★★★, *Alone With You* (1963)★★★, *Johnny Tillotson* (1964)★★★, *Talk Back Trembling Lips* (MGM 1964)★★★, *The Tillotson Touch* (MGM 1964)★★★, *She Understands Me* (MGM 1964)★★, *That's My Style* (MGM 1965)★★★, *Our World* (MGM 1966)★★★, *Tillotson Sings Tillotson, Volume 1* (1966)★★★, *No Love At All* (MGM 1966)★★★, *The Christmas Touch* (MGM 1966)★★, *Here I Am* (MGM 1967)★★★, *Tears On My Pillow* (1970)★★★, *Johnny Tillotson* (1971)★★★, *Johnny Tillotson* (1977)★★.
COMPILATIONS: *Scrapbook* (Bear Family 1984)★★★, *All The Early Hits – And More!!!* (Ace 1990)★★★★, *Poetry In Motion* (Var∑se Sarabande 1996)★★★★.

TINDERSTICKS
ALBUMS: *Tindersticks* (This Way Up 1993)★★★★, *Amsterdam 1994* (This Way Up 1994)★★, *The Second Tindersticks Album* (This Way Up 1995)★★★, *The Bloomsbury Theatre 12.3.95* (This Way Up 1995)★★, *Nenette Et Boni Soundtrack* (This Way Up 1996)★★★, *Curtains* (This Way Up 1997)★★★★.

TLC
ALBUMS: *Ooooooohhh ... On The TLC Tip* (LaFace/Arista 1992)★★, *TLC* (LaFace/Arista 1993)★★★★, *CrazySexyCool* (LaFace/Arista 1995)★★★★.
VIDEOS: *Crazy Video Cool* (BMG Video 1995).

TOAD THE WET SPROCKET
ALBUMS: *Bread And Circus* (Abe's 1986)★★★, *Pale* (Abe's 1988)★★, *Fear* (Columbia 1991)★★, *Dulcinea* (Columbia 1994)★★★, *In Light Syrup* (Columbia 1995)★★, *Coil* (Columbia 1997)★★★.

TORNADOS
ALBUMS: *Away From It All* (1964)★★★.
COMPILATIONS: *The World Of The Tornados* (Decca 1972)★★★, *Remembering* (Decca 1976)★★★, *The Original 60s Hits* (Music Club 1994)★★★, *The EP Collection* (See For Miles 1996)★★★★.

TOSH, PETER
ALBUMS: *Legalize It* (Virgin 1976)★★★★, *Equal Rights* (Virgin 1977)★★★★, *Bush Doctor* (Rolling Stones 1978)★★★★, *Mystic Man* (Rolling Stones/EMI 1979)★★★, *Wanted, Dread & Alive* (Rolling Stones/Dynamic 1981)★★★, *Mama Africa* (Intel Diplo/EMI 1983)★★★, *Captured Live* (EMI 1984)★★★, *No Nuclear War* (EMI 1987)★★★.
COMPILATIONS: *The Toughest* (Parlophone 1988)★★★, *The Gold Collection* (EMI 1996)★★★.
VIDEOS: *Live* (1986), *Downpresser Man* (1988), *Red X* (1993).

TOTO
ALBUMS: *Toto* (Columbia 1978)★★★, *Hydra* (Columbia 1979)★★, *Turn Back* (Columbia 1981)★★, *Toto IV* (Columbia 1982)★★★★, *Isolation* (Columbia 1984)★★, *Dune* (Polydor 1984)★, *Fahrenheit* (Columbia 1986)★★, *The Seventh One* (Columbia 1988)★★★, *Kingdom Of Desire* (Columbia 1992)★★, *Absolutely Live* (1993)★, *Tambu* (Columbia 1995)★★.
COMPILATIONS: *Past To Present 1977-1990* (Columbia 1990)★★★.

TOURE, ALI FARKA
ALBUMS: *Bandolobourou* (1985)★★★, *Special* (1987)★★★, *Yer Sabou Yerkoy* (1989)★★★, with Ry Cooder *Talking Timbuktu* (World Circuit 1994)★★★★.

TOURISTS
ALBUMS: *The Tourists* (Logo 1979)★★, *Reality Effect* (Logo 1979)★★★★, *Luminous Basement* (RCA 1980)★★★.
COMPILATIONS: *Should Have Been Greatest Hits* (Epic 1984)★★★.

TOUSSAINT, ALLEN
ALBUMS: originally released under the name of Al Tousan *Wild Sounds Of New Orleans* (1958)★★★, *Toussaint* (1971)★★★, *Life Love And Faith* (1972)★★, *Southern Nights* (Reprise 1975)★★★★, *From A Whisper To A Scream* 1991)★★★, *Southern Nights* (1975)★★★, *Motion* (1978)★★★, *Connected* (Nyno 1996)★★★.
COMPILATIONS: *Mr. New Orleans* (1994)★★★.

TOWER OF POWER
ALBUMS: *East Bay Grease* (San Fransisco 1969)★★★, *Bump City* (Warners 1971)★★★, *Tower Of Power* (Warners 1973)★★★★, *Back To Oakland* (Warners 1974)★★★★, *Urban Renewal* (Warners 1975)★★★★, *In The Slot* (Warners 1975)★★★, *Live And In Living Colour* (Warners 1976)★★★★, *Ain't Nothin' Stoppin' Us Now* (Columbia 1976)★★★, *We Came To Play!* (Columbia 1978)★★★, *Back On The Streets* (Columbia 1979)★★★,

Tower Of Power (1982)★★★, *Power* (1988)★★★, *Direct* (1988)★★★, *Monster On A Leash* (Epic 1991)★★★, *Souled Out* (Epic 1995)★★★.
COMPILATIONS: *What Is Hip?* (Edsel 1986)★★★★.

TOWNSHEND, PETE
ALBUMS: *Who Came First* (Track 1972)★★★, with Ronnie Lane *Rough Mix* (Polydor 1977)★★★★, *Empty Glass* (Atco 1980)★★★, *All The Best Cowboys Have Chinese Eyes* (Atco 1982)★★, *Scoop* (Polydor 1983)★★, *White City* (Atco 1985)★★, *Pete Townshend's Deep End – Live* (Atco 1986)★★, *Another Scoop* (Atco 1987)★★, *Iron Man* (Atlantic 1989)★★, *Psychoderelict* (Atlantic 1993)★★★.
COMPILATIONS: *The Best Of Pete Townshend* (East West 1996)★★★.
FURTHER READING: *The Hores Neck*, Pete Townshend. *A Life Of Pete Townshend: Behind Blue Eyes*, Geoffrey Guiliano.

TRAFFIC
ALBUMS: *Mr Fantasy* (Island 1967)★★★★, *Traffic* (Island 1968)★★★★, *Last Exit* (Island 1969)★★, *John Barleycorn Must Die* (Island 1970)★★★★, *Welcome To The Canteen* (Island 1971)★★, *Low Spark Of The High Heeled Boys* (Island 1971)★★★★, *Shoot Out At The Fantasy Factory* (Island 1973)★★★, *On The Road* (Island 1973)★★, *When The Eagle Flies* (Island 1974)★★★, *Far From Home* (Virgin 1994)★★★.
COMPILATIONS: *Best Of Traffic* (Island 1970)★★★★, *Heavy Traffic* (Island 1975)★★★★, *More Heavy Traffic* (Island 1975)★★★, *Smiling Phases* 2-CD set (Island 1991)★★★★★.
FURTHER READING: *Keep On Running: The Steve Winwood Story*, Chris Welch. *Back In The High Life: A Biography Of Steve Winwood*, Alan Clayson.

TRAVELING WILBURYS
ALBUMS: *Handle With Care* (Wilbury 1988)★★★★, *Volume 3* (Wilbury 1990)★★★.

TREMELOES
ALBUMS: *Here Comes The Tremeloes* (CBS 1967)★★★★, *The Tremeloes: Chip, Rick, Alan And Dave* (CBS 1967)★★★, *Here Comes My Baby* (USA 1967)★★★★, *1958/68 World Explosion* (1968)★★★, *The Tremeloes 'Live' In Cabaret* (CBS 1969)★★, *Master* (CBS 1970)★★, *Shiner* (1974)★★, *Don't Let The Music Die* (1976)★★.
COMPILATIONS: *Suddenly You Love Me* (1993)★★★, *Silence Is Golden* (Spectrum 1995)★★★.

TRICKY
ALBUMS: *Maxinquaye* (4th & Broadway 1995)★★★, as Nearly God *Nearly God* (Durban Poison 1996)★★★, *Pre-Millennium Tension* (Island 1996)★★★, *Angels With Dirty Faces* (1998)★★★.

TRIFFIDS
ALBUMS: *Treeless Plain* (Hot 1983)★★★, *Raining Pleasure* (Hot 1984)★★★, *Field Of Glass* (Hot 1985)★★★, *Born Sandy Devotional* (Hot 1986)★★★★, *In The Pines* (Hot 1986)★★★, *The Peel Sessions EP* (Strange Fruit 1987)★★, *Calenture* (Hot 1987)★★★, *The Black Swan* (Island 1989)★★★★, *Stockholm* (MNW 1990)★★★.
Solo: Robert McComb *Love Of Will* (1994)★★★.
COMPILATIONS: *Love In Bright Landscapes* Dutch release (Hot/Megadisc 1986)★★★, *Australian Melodrama* (Mushroom 1994)★★★.

TROGGS
ALBUMS: *From Nowhere The Troggs* (Fontana 1966)★★★★, *Trogglodynamite* (Page One 1967)★★★★, *Cellophane* (Page One 1967)★★★★, *Mixed Bag* (Page One 1968)★★★, *Trogglomania* (Page One 1969)★★★, *Contrasts* (DJM 1976)★★, *With A Girl Like You* (DJM 1976)★★, *The Original Troggs Tapes* (DJM 1976)★, *Live At Max's Kansas City* (President 1981)★, *Black Bottom* (New Rose 1982)★★, *Rock It Baby* (Action Replay 1984)★★, *Wild Things* (Konnexion 1987)★★, *Au* (New Rose 1990)★★, *Athens Andover* (Essential/Page One 1992)★★★.
COMPILATIONS: *Best Of The Troggs* (Page One 1968)★★★★, *Best Of The Troggs Volume 2* (Page One 1968)★★★, *14 Greatest Hits* (Spectrum 1988)★★★★, *Archaeology 1966 – 1976* (1993), *Greatest Hits* (Polygram 1994)★★★★, *The EP Collection* (See For Miles 1996)★★★★.

TROWER, ROBIN
ALBUMS: *Twice Removed From Yesterday* (Chrysalis 1973)★★★, *Bridge Of Sighs* (Chrysalis 1974)★★★★, *For Earth Below* (Chrysalis 1975)★★★, *Robin Trower Live* (Chrysalis 1976)★★★★, *Long Misty Days* (Chrysalis 1976)★★★, *In City Dreams* (Chrysalis 1977)★★, *Caravan To Midnight* (Chrysalis 1978)★★, *Victims Of The Fury* (Chrysalis 1980)★★, *Back It Up* (Chrysalis 1983)★★★, *Beyond The Mist* (Music For Nations 1985)★★★, *Passion* (Gryp 1987)★★★, *Take What You Need* (Atlantic 1988)★★★, *In The Line Of Fire* (Atlantic 1990)★★, *Someday Blues* (Demon 1997).
COMPILATIONS: *Portfolio* (Chrysalis 1987)★★★.

TUBES
ALBUMS: *The Tubes* (A&M 1975)★★, *Young And Rich* (A&M 1976)★★★, *Now* (A&M 1977)★★, *What Do You Want From Your Life* (A&M 1978)★★, *Remote Control* (A&M 1979)★★, *The Completion Backward Principle* (Capitol 1981)★★, *Outside Inside* (Capitol 1983)★★, *Love Bomb* (Capitol 1985)★★.
COMPILATIONS: *T.R.A.S.H. (Tubes Rarities And Smash Hits)* (A&M 1981)★★★, *The Best Of* (1993)★★★.

TURNER, IKE AND TINA
ALBUMS: *The Soul Of Ike And Tina Turner* (Sue 1960)★★, *Dance With The Kings Of Rhythm* (Sue 1960)★★★, *The Sound Of Ike And Tina Turner* (1961)★★★, *Dance With Ike And Tina Turner* (Sue 1962)★★★, *Festival Of Live Performances* (Kent 1962)★★, *Dynamite* (Sue 1963)★★★★, *Don't Play Me Cheap* (Sue 1963)★★★, *It's Gonna Work Out Fine* (Sue 1963)★★★★, *Please Please Please* (Kent 1964)★★★, *The Soul Of Ike And Tina Turner* (Kent 1964)★★★, *The Ike And Tina Show Live* (Loma 1965)★★★★, *The Ike And Tina Turner Show Live* (Warners 1965)★★★★, *River Deep – Mountain High* (London 1966)★★★★, *So Fine* (Pompeii 1968)★★★★, *In Person* (Minit 1968)★★★★, *Cussin', Cryin' And Carrying On* (Pompeii 1969)★★★, *Get It Together!* (Pompeii 1969)★★★, *A Black Man's Soul* (Pompeii 1969)★★★, *Outta Season* (Liberty 1969)★★★, *In Person* (Minit 1969)★★★, *River Deep – Mountain High* (A&M/London 1969)★★★★, *Come Together* (Liberty 1970)★★★, *The Hunter* (Harvest 1970)★★★★, *Workin' Together* (Liberty 1971)★★★, *Her Man, His Woman* (Capitol 1971)★★★, *Live In Paris* (Liberty 1971)★★★★, *Live At Carnegie Hall – What You Hear Is What You Get* (Liberty 1971)★★★, *'Nuff Said* (United Artists 1972)★★, *Feel Good* (United Artists 1972)★★, *Let Me Touch Your Mind* (United Artists 1973)★★, *Nutbush City Limits* (United Artists 1973)★★★★, *Strange Fruit* (1974)★★★, *Sweet Island Rhode Red* (United Artists 1974)★★, *Delilah's Power* (United Artists 1977)★★, *Airwaves* (1978)★★.
Solo: Ike Turner *Blues Roots* (United Artists 1972)★★, *Bad Dreams* (United Artists 1973)★★, *Funky Mule* (DJM 1975)★★, *I'm Tore Up* (Red Lightnin' 1978)★★, *All The Blues All The Time* (Ember 1980)★★. His early work with the Kings Of Rhythm and as a talent scout is represented on *Hey Hey* (1984)★★★, *Rockin' Blues* (1986)★★★, *Ike Turner And His Kings Of Rhythm Volumes 1 & 2* (1988)★★★, *Talent Scout Blues* (Ace 1988)★★★, *Rhythm Rockin' Blues* (Ace 1995)★★★, *Without Love I Have Nothing* (Juke Blues 1996)★★, *My Blues Country*
COMPILATIONS: *Ike And Tina Turner's Greatest Hits* (Sue 1965)★★★, *Ike And Tina Turner's Greatest Hits* (Warners 1969)★★★★, *Tough Enough* (Liberty 1984)★★★, *The Ike And Tina Turner Sessions* (1987)★★★, *The Best Of Ike And Tina Turner* (1987)★★★★, *Fingerpoppin' – The Warner Brothers Years* (1988)★★★, *Proud Mary: The Best Of Ike And Tina Turner* (EMI 1991)★★★★, *Live!!!* (1993)★★★.
FURTHER READING: *I Tina*, Tina Turner with Kurt Loder.

TURNER, TINA
ALBUMS: *The Country Of Tina Turner* reissued in 1991 as *Goes Country* (early 70s)★★★, *Acid Queen* (United Artists 1975)★★★, *Rough* (United Artists 1978)★★, *Love Explosion* (United Artists 1979)★★, *Private Dancer* (Capitol 1984)★★★★, *Break Every Rule* (Capitol 1986)★★★, *Live In Europe: Tina Turner* (Capitol 1988)★★, *Foreign Affair* (Capitol 1989)★★★, *What's Love Got To Do With It* film soundtrack (Parlophone 1993)★★★, *Wildest Dreams* (Parlophone/Virgin 1996)★★★.
COMPILATIONS: *Simply The Best* (Capitol 1991)★★★★, *Tina Turner: The Collected Recordings, 60s To 90s* (Capitol 1994)★★★★.
VIDEOS: *Private Dancer Video EP* (1985), *Private Dancer Tour* (1985), *What You See Is What You Get* (1987), *Break Every Rule* (1987), *Rio 88* (1988), *Nice 'n' Rough* (1988), *Foreign Affair* (1990), *Do You Want Some Action* (1990), *Simply The Best* (1991), *Wild Lady Of Rock* (1992), *What's Love Live* (1994), *The Girl From Nutbush* (Strand 1995), *Wildest Dreams* (Feedback Fusion 1996), *Live In Amsterdam* (Castle Music Pictures 1997).
FURTHER READING: *I, Tina*, Tina Turner with Kurt Loder. *The Tina Turner Experience*, Chris Welch.

TURTLES
ALBUMS: *It Ain't Me Babe* (White Whale 1965)★★★, *You Baby* (White Whale 1966)★★★, *Happy Together* (White Whale 1967)★★★, *The Battle Of The Bands* (White Whale 1968)★★, *Turtle Soup* (1969)★★, *Wooden Head* (White Whale 1971)★★, *Happy Together Again* (Sire 1974)★★.
COMPILATIONS: *Happy Together* (Rhino 1983)★★★, *20 Greatest Hits: Turtles* (Rhino 1986)★★★, *20 Golden Classics* (Mainline 1990)★★★, *Happy Together: The Very Best Of The Turtles* (Music Club 1991)★★★, *25 Classic Hits* (1993)★★★, *Love Songs* (Rhino 1995)★★★.

TWISTED SISTER
ALBUMS: *Under The Blade* (Secret 1982)★★, *You Can't Stop Rock 'N' Roll* (Atlantic 1983)★★, *Stay Hungry* (Atlantic 1984)★★★, *Come Out And Play* (Atlantic 1985)★★, *Love Is For Suckers* (Atlantic 1987)★★, *Live* (Music For Nations 1994)★★.

2 LIVE CREW
ALBUMS: *The 2 Live Crew Is What We Are* (Luke Skyywalker 1986)★★★, *Move Somethin'* (Luke Skyywalker 1988)★★, *As Nasty As They Wanna Be* (Luke Skyywalker 1989)★★, *As Clean As They Wanna Be* (Luke Skyywalker 1989)★, *Live In Concert* (Effect 1990)★★, *Sports Weekend (As Nasty As They Wanna Be Part II)* (Luke 1991)★★★, *Sports Weekend (As Clean As They Wanna Be Part II)* (Luke 1991)★★, *Shake A Lil' Somethin'* (Lil' Joe 1996)★★. Solo: Luther Campbell *Luke In The Nude* (Luke 1993)★★, *The Real One* (Luke 1998).
COMPILATIONS: *Best Of* (Luke 1992)★★★, as Luther Campbell Featuring The 2 Live Crew *Banned In The USA* (Luke 1990)★★.
VIDEOS: *Banned In The USA* (1990).

TYLER, BONNIE
ALBUMS: *The World Starts Tonight* (RCA 1977)★★, *Natural Force* (*It's A Heartache* USA) (RCA 1978)★★★, *Diamond Cut* (RCA 1979)★★, *Goodbye To The Island* (RCA 1981)★★, *Faster Than The Speed Of Night* (Columbia 1983)★★, *Secret Dreams And Forbidden Fire* (Columbia 1986)★★, *Hide Your Heart* (Columbia 1988)★★, *Bitterblue* (Hansa 1991)★★, *Free Spirit* (East West 1996)★.
COMPILATIONS: *The Very Best Of Bonnie Tyler* (RCA 1981)★★★, *Greatest Hits* (Telstar 1986)★★★, *The Best* (Columbia 1993)★★★.
FILMS: *Footloose* (1984).

TYMES
ALBUMS: *So Much In Love* (Parkway 1963)★★★★, *The Sound Of The Wonderful Tymes* (Parkway 1963)★★★, *Somewhere* (Parkway 1964)★★, *People* (Direction 1968)★★★, *Trustmaker* (RCA 1974)★★★, *Tymes Up* (RCA 1976)★★, *Turning Point* (RCA 1976)★★, *Digging Their Roots* (RCA 1977)★★.
COMPILATIONS: *Soul Gems* (Prestige 1990)★★★.

TYRANNOSAURUS REX
ALBUMS: *My People Were Fair And Had Sky In Their Hair But Now They're Content To Wear Stars On Their Brows* (Regal Zonophone 1968)★★★★, *Prophets, Seers, Sages, The Angels Of The Ages* (Regal Zonophone 1968)★★★★, *Unicorn* (Regal Zonophone 1969)★★★, *A Beard Of Stars* (Regal Zonophone 1970)★★★.
COMPILATIONS: *The Best Of T.Rex* (Fly 1971)★★★★, *The Definitive Tyrannosaurus Rex* (Sequel 1993)★★★★, *BBC Radio 1 Live In Concert* (Windsong 1993)★★★★, *A BBC History* (Band Of Joy 1996)★★★★.

TZUKE, JUDIE
ALBUMS: *Welcome To The Cruise* (Rocket 1979)★★★★, *Sports Car* (Rocket 1980)★★★, *I Am Phoenix* (Rocket 1981)★★, *Road Noise* (Chrysalis 1982)★★, *Shoot The Moon* (Chrysalis 1983)★★★, *Ritmo* (Chrysalis 1983)★★, *Judie Tzuke* (Legacy 1985)★★, *The Cat Is Out* (Legacy 1985)★★, *Turning Stones* (Polydor 1989)★★, *Left Hand Talking* (Columbia 1991)★★★, *Wonderland* (1992)★★★, *BBC In Concert* (Windsong 1995)★★★, *Under The Angels* (Big Moon 1996)★★★.
COMPILATIONS: *The Best Of* (1993)★★★.

U

U2
ALBUMS: *Boy* (Island 1980)★★★, *October* (Island 1981)★★★, *War* (Island 1983)★★★★, *U2 Live, Under A Blood Red Sky* (Island 1983)★★★, *The Unforgettable Fire* (Island 1984)★★★★, *Wide Awake In America* (Island 1985)★★★, *The Joshua Tree* (Island 1987)★★★★, *The Joshua Tree Singles* (Island 1988)★★★, *Rattle And Hum* (Island 1988)★★★, *Achtung Baby* (Island 1991)★★★★, *Zooropa* (Island 1993)★★★, *Pop* (Island 1997)★★★x.
VIDEOS: *Unforgettable Fire* (1985), *Under A Blood Red Sky (Live At Red Rocks)* (1988), *Under A Blood Red Sky* (1988), *Rattle And Hum* (1989), *Achtung Baby* (1993), *Numb* (1993), *U2: Zoo TV Live From Sydney* (1994).
FURTHER READING: *Unforgettable Fire: The Story Of U2*, Eamon Dunphy. *The U2 File: A Hot Press U2 History*, Niall Stokes (ed.). *U2: Three Chords And The Truth*, Niall Stokes (ed.). *Rattle And Hum*, Peter Williams and Steve Turner. *U2: Stories For Boys*, Dave Thomas. *U2: Touch The Flame: An Illustrated Documentary*, Geoff Parkyn. *U2 The Early Days: Another Time, Another Place*, Bill Graham. *U2: A Conspiracy Of Hope*, Dave Bowler and Brian Dray. *U2: The Story So Far*, Richard Seal. *U2: Burning Desire – The Complete Story*, Sam Goodman. *U2 Live*, Pimm Jal De La Perra. *Race Of Angels: The Genesis Of U2*, John Waters. *U2, The Rolling Stones File*, editors of *Rolling Stone*. *U2 At The End Of The World*, Bill Flanagan. *Wide Awake In America*, Alan Carter. *U2 Faraway So Close*, B. P. Fallon. *U2, The Rolling Stones File*, editors of *Rolling Stone*. *The Complete Guide To The Music Of ...*, Bill Graham. *The Making Of: U2's Joshua Tree*, Dave Thompson.

UB40
ALBUMS: *Signing Off* (Graduate 1980)★★★, *Present Arms* (DEP 1981)★★★, *Present Arms In Dub* (DEP 1981)★★★, *UB44* (DEP 1982)★★★, *UB40 Live* (DEP 1983)★★★, *Labour Of Love* (DEP 1983)★★★★, *Geffrey Morgan* (DEP 1984)★★★★, *Baggariddim* (DEP 1985)★★★, *Rat In Mi Kitchen* (DEP 1986)★★★, *UB40* (DEP 1988)★★★★, *Labour Of Love II* (DEP 1989)★★★, *Promises And Lies* (DEP 1993)★★★, *Guns In The Ghetto* (Virgin 1997)★★★. Solo: Ali Campbell *Big Love* (Virgin 1995)★★★.
COMPILATIONS: *The Singles Album* (Graduate 1982)★★★, *The UB40 File* double album (Graduate 1985)★★★, *The Best Of UB40, Volume I* (DEP 1987)★★★★, *UB40 Box Set* (Virgin 1991)★★★.
VIDEOS: *Labour Of Love* (1984), *Best Of* (1987), *Live* (1988), *Dance With The Devil* (1988), *Labour Of Love II* (1990), *CCCP* (1991), *A Family Affair Live In Concert* (1991), *Live In The New South Africa* (PMI 1995).

UFO
ALBUMS: *UFO 1* (Beacon 1971)★★, *UFO 2 – Flying* (Beacon 1971)★★, *UFO Lands In Tokyo – Live* (1972)★★★, *Phenomenon* (Chrysalis 1974)★★★, *Force It* (Chrysalis 1975)★★★, *No Heavy Pettin'* (Chrysalis 1976)★★★★, *Lights Out* (Chrysalis 1977)★★★★, *Obsession* (Chrysalis 1978)★★, *Strangers In The Night* (Chrysalis 1979)★★★, *No Place To Run* (Chrysalis 1980)★★, *The Wild, The Willing And The Innocent* (Chrysalis 1981)★★, *Mechanix* (Chrysalis 1982)★★, *Making Contact* (Chrysalis 1983)★★, *Misdemeanor* (Chrysalis 1985)★★★, *Ain't Misbehavin'* (FM Revolver 1988)★★★, *High Stakes And Desperate Men* (Essential 1992)★★★, *BBC Live In Concert* (Windsong 1992)★★★, *Lights Out In Tokyo: Live* (Castle 1993)★★★, *Walk On Water* (Zero 1995)★★★.
COMPILATIONS: *Headstone – The Best Of UFO* (Chrysalis 1983)★★★, *The Collection* (Castle 1985)★★★, *Doctor, Doctor* (Spectrum/Polydor 1995)★★★.
VIDEOS: *Misdemeanor Live* (1985).

UGLY KID JOE
ALBUMS: *As Ugly As They Wanna Be* mini-album (Mercury 1992)★★, *America's Least Wanted* (Mercury 1992)★★★, *Menace To Sobriety* (Mercury 1995)★★★, *Motel California* (Evilution 1996)★★.

UK SUBS
ALBUMS: *Another Kind Of Blues* (Gem 1979)★★, *Brand New Age* (Gem 1980)★★, *Crash Course* (Gem 1980)★★★, *Diminished Responsibility* (Gem 1981)★★, *Endangered Species* (NEMS 1982)★★, *Flood Of Lies* (Scarlet/Fall Out 1983)★, *Gross Out USA* (Fall Out 1984)★, *Huntington Beach* (Revolver 1986)★, *Killing Time* (Fall Out 1987)H, *Japan Today* (Fall Out 1990)★, *In Action* (Red Flame 1990)★, *Mad Cow Fever* (Jungle 1991)★, *Normal Service Resumed* (Jungle 1993)★, *The Punk Is Back* (Cannon 1995)★, *Occupied* (Fall Out 1996)★, *Peel Sessions 1978-79* (Jungle 1997)★★, *Quintessentials* (Fall Out 1997)★★★.
Solo: Charlie Harper *Stolen Property* (Flicknife 1982)★★.
COMPILATIONS: *Down On The Farm (A Collection Of The Less Obvious)* (Streetlink 1991)★★, *The Singles 1979-81* (Abstract 1991)★★, *Scum Of The Earth – The Best Of* (Music Club 1993)★★.
VIDEOS: *Live At Peterless Leisure Centre Friday 10th June 1994* (Barn End 1994).
FURTHER READING: *Neighbourhood Threat*, Alvin Gibbs.

ULTRAMAGNETIC MC'S
ALBUMS: *Critical Beatdown* (1988)★★★, *Funk Your Head Up* (London 1992)★★★, *Four Horsemen* (Wild Pitch 1993)★★★.

ULTRAVOX
ALBUMS: *Ultravox!* (Island 1976)★★, *Ha! Ha! Ha!* (Island 1977)★★, *Systems Of Romance* (Island 1978)★★, *Vienna* (Chrysalis 1980)★★★, *Rage In Eden* (Chrysalis 1981)★★★, *Quartet* (Chrysalis 1982)★★, *Monument – The Soundtrack* (Chrysalis 1983)★★, *Lament* (Chrysalis 1984)★★, *U-Vox* (Chrysalis 1986)★★, *Revelation* (1993)★, *Ingenuity* (Resurgence 1995)★. Solo: Billy Currie *Stand Up And Walk* (Hot Food 1990)★★.
COMPILATIONS: *Three Into One* Island recordings (Island 1980)★★, *The Collection* (Chrysalis 1984)★★★.
FURTHER READING: *The Past, Present & Future Of Ultravox*, Drake and Gilbert.

UNDERTONES
ALBUMS: *The Undertones* (Sire 1979)★★★★, *Hypnotised* (Sire 1980)★★★★, *Positive Touch* (Ardeck/EMI 1981)★★★, *The Sin Of Pride* (Ardeck/EMI 1983)★★★, *The Peel Sessions Album* (Strange Fruit 1991)★★★.
COMPILATIONS: *All Wrapped Up* (Ardeck/EMI 1983)★★★, *Cher O'Bowlies: Pick Of Undertones* (Ardeck/EMI 1986)★★★, *The Best Of: Teenage Kicks* (Castle 1993)★★★★.

URE, MIDGE
ALBUMS: *The Gift* (Chrysalis 1985)★★★, *Answers To Nothing* (Chrysalis 1988)★★, *Pure* (Arista 1991)★★, *Breathe* (Arista 1996)★★.
COMPILATIONS: *If I Was: The Very Best Of ...* (Chrysalis 1993)★★★.

URGE OVERKILL
ALBUMS: *Jesus Urge Superstar* (Touch & Go 1989)★★, *Americruiser* (Touch & Go 1990)★★, *The Supersonic Storybook* (Touch & Go 1991)★★★, *Stull* mini-album (Touch & Go 1992)★★, *Saturation* (Geffen 1993)★★★★, *Exit The Dragon* (Geffen 1995)★★★★.

URIAH HEEP
ALBUMS: *Very 'eavy, Very 'umble* aka *Uriah Heep* (USA) (Bronze 1970)★★, *Salisbury* (Bronze 1971)★★, *Look At Yourself* (Bronze 1971)★★★, *Demons And Wizards* (Bronze 1972)★★★, *The Magician's Birthday* (Bronze 1972)★★, *Uriah Heep Live* (Bronze 1973)★★, *Sweet Freedom* (Bronze 1973)★★★, *Wonderworld* (Bronze 1974)★★★, *Return To Fantasy* (Bronze 1975)★★★, *High And Mighty* (Bronze 1976)★★★, *Firefly* (Bronze 1977)★★★, *Innocent Victim* (Bronze 1978)★★, *Fallen Angel* (Bronze 1978)★★, *Conquest* (Bronze 1980)★★, *Abnominog* (Bronze 1982)★★, *Head First* (Bronze 1983)★★, *Equator* (Bronze 1985)★★, *Live In Europe* (Raw Power 1987)★★, *Live At Shepperton '74* (Castle 1988)★★, *Live In Moscow* (Bronze 1988)★★, *Raging Silence* (Legacy 1989)★★, *Still 'eavy, Still Proud* (Legacy 1990)★★, *Different World* (Legacy 1991)★★, *Sea Of Light* (SPV 1995)★★.
COMPILATIONS: *The Best Of Uriah Heep* (Bronze 1976)★★★★, *Anthology* (Raw Power 1986)★★★, *The Collection* (Castle 1988)★★★, *The Uriah Heep Story* (EMI 1990)★★★★, *Rarities From The Bronze Age* (Sequel 1991)★★★, *CD Box Set* (Castle 1992)★★★, *A Time Of Revelation: 25 Years On* 4-CD box set (Essential 1996)★★★★.
VIDEOS: *Easy Livin'* (1988), *Live Legends* (1990), *Gypsy* (1990), *Raging Through The Silence – Live At The Astoria* (1990).

V

VALENS, RITCHIE
ALBUMS: *Ritchie Valens* (Del Fi/London 1959)★★★★, *Ritchie* (Del Fi/London 1959)★★★★, *Ritchie Valens In Concert At Pacoima Jnr High* (Del Fi 1960)★★★.
COMPILATIONS: *His Greatest Hits* (Del Fi 1963)★★★★, *I Remember Ritchie Valens* (President 1967)★★★, *A History Of ...* (1985)★★★, *Greatest Hits* (1987)★★★, *The Ritchie Valens Story* (Ace 1993)★★★★, *The Very Best Of ...* (Music Club 1995)★★★.
FILMS: *Go Johnny Go* (1958).
FURTHER READING: *Ritchie Valens: The First Latino Rocker*, Beverly Mendheim. *Ritchie Valens 1941-1959: 30th Anniversary Memorial Series No 2*, Alan Clark.

VALENTINOS
ALBUMS: one side only *Double Barrelled Soul* (1968)★★, *Bobby Womack And The Valentinos* (1984)★★.

VALLI, FRANKIE
ALBUMS: *Solo* (Philips 1967)★★★, *Timeless* (Philips 1968)★★★, *Inside You* (1975)★★★, *Close Up* (Private St. 1975)★★★, *Story* (1976)★★, *Frankie Valli Is The Word* (Warners 1978)★★, *Heaven Above Me* (MCA 1980)★★★.
COMPILATIONS: *The Best Of Frankie Valli* (1980)★★★.
FILMS: *Grease* (1978).

VAN DER GRAAF GENERATOR
ALBUMS: *The Aerosol Grey Machine* (Mercury 1969)★★★, *The Least We Can Do Is Wave To Each Other* (Charisma 1970)★★★★, *H to He Who Am The Only One* (Charisma 1970)★★★, *Pawn Hearts* (Charisma 1971)★★★, *Godbluff* (Charisma 1975)★★★, *Still Life* (Charisma 1976)★★★, *World Record* (Charisma 1976)★★★, *The Quiet Zone /The Pleasure Dome* (Charisma 1977)★★★, *Vital* (Charisma 1978)★★.
COMPILATIONS: *Repeat Performance* (Charisma 1980)★★★, *Time Vaults* (Demi-Monde 1985)★★★.
FURTHER READING: *The Lemming Chronicles*, David Shaw-Parker.

VAN HALEN
ALBUMS: *Van Halen* (Warners 1978)★★★★, *Van Halen II* (Warners 1979)★★★★, *Women And Children First* (Warners 1980)★★★, *Fair Warning* (Warners 1981)★★★, *Diver Down* (Warners 1982)★★★, *1984 (MCMLXXXIV)* (Warners 1984)★★★★, *5150* (Warners 1986)★★★★, *OU812* (Warners 1988)★★★★, *For Unlawful Carnal Knowledge* (Warners 1991)★★★, *Live: Right Here, Right Now* (Warners 1993)★★★, *Balance* (Warners 1995)★★★, *Van Halen 3* (Warner brothers 1998).
COMPILATIONS: *Best Of Volume 1* (Warners 1996)★★★★.
VIDEOS: *Live Without A Net* (1987), *Live: Right Here Right Now* (1993), *Video Hits Vol 1* (Warner Music 1996).
FURTHER READING: *Van Halen*, Michelle Craven. *Excess All Areas*, Malcolm Dome.

VANDROSS, LUTHER
ALBUMS: *Never Too Much* (Epic 1981)★★★, *Forever, For Always, For Love* (Epic 1982)★★★, *Busy Body* (Epic 1983)★★★, *The Night I Fell In Love* (Epic 1985)★★★★, *Give Me The Reason* (Epic 1986)★★★, *Any Love* (Epic 1988)★★★, *Power Of Love* (Epic 1991)★★★★, *Never Let Me Go* (Epic 1993)★★★, *Songs* (Epic 1994)★★★, *Your Secret Love* (Epic 1996)★★★.
COMPILATIONS: *The Best Of Luther Vandross ... The Best Of Love* (Epic 1989)★★★★, *Greatest Hits 1981-1995* (Epic 1995)★★★★.
VIDEOS: *An Evening Of Songs* (1994), *Always And Forever* (1995).

VANGELIS
ALBUMS: *Dragon* (Charly 1971)★★, *L'Apocalypse Des Animaux* (Polydor 1973)★★, *Earth* (Polydor 1974)★★, *Heaven And Hell* (RCA Victor 1975)★★★, *Albedo 0.39* (RCA 1976)★★, *Spiral* (RCA 1977)★★, *Beaubourg* (RCA 1978)★★, *Hypothesis* (Affinity 1978)★★, *Odes* (1978)★★, *Opera Sauvage* (Polydor 1979)★★, *China* (Polydor 1979)★★★, *See You Later* (Polydor 1980)★★, *Chariots Of Fire* film soundtrack (Polydor 1981)★★★, *To The Unknown Man* (RCA 1982)★★, *Soil Festivities* (Polydor 1984)★★, *Ignacio* soundtrack (Phonogram 1985)★★, *Invisible Connections* (Deutsche Grammophon 1985)★★, *The Mask* (Polydor 1985)★, *Direct* (Arista 1988)★★, *Antarctica* film soundtrack (Polydor 1988)★★, *The City* (East West 1990)★★★, *1492 – Conquest Of Paradise* film soundtrack (East West 1992)★★, *Entends – Tu Les Chiens* (1993)★★, *Voices* (Atlantic 1995)★★, *Oceanic* (Atlantic 1997)★★; as Jon And Vangelis *Short Stories* (Polydor 1980)★★, *The Friends Of Mr Cairo* (Polydor 1981)★★, *Private Collection* (Polydor 1983)★★, *Page Of Life* (Arista 1991)★★.
COMPILATIONS: *The Best Of Vangelis* (RCA 1981)★★★, *Themes* (Polydor 1989)★★★.

VANILLA FUDGE
ALBUMS: *Vanilla Fudge* (Atco 1967)★★★, *The Beat Goes On* (Atco 1968)★★, *Renaissance* (Atco 1968)★★, *Near The Beginning* (Atco 1969)★★, *Rock And Roll* (Atco 1970)★★, *Mystery* (Atco 1984)★★.
COMPILATION: *Psychedelic Sundae – The Best Of* (Rhino 1993)★★★.

VANILLA ICE
ALBUMS: *To The Extreme* (SBK 1990)★★★, *Extremely Live* (SBK 1991)★★, *Mindblowin* (SBK 1994)★★.

VAN ZANDT, STEVEN
ALBUMS: *Men Without Women* (EMI America 1982)★★★, *Voice Of America* (EMI America 1984)★★★, *Freedom – No Compromise* (Manhattan 1987)★★★, *Revolution* (RCA 1989)★★★, *The Quickening* (Nitro 1996)★★★.

VEE, BOBBY
ALBUMS: *Bobby Vee Sings Your Favorites* (Liberty 1960)★★, *Bobby Vee* (Liberty 1961)★★★, *Bobby Vee With Strings And Things* (Liberty 1961)★★, *Bobby Vee Sings Hits Of The Rockin' '50s* (Liberty 1961)★★★, *Take Good Care Of My Baby* (Liberty 1961)★★★★, *Bobby Vee Meets The Crickets* (Liberty 1962)★★★★, *A Bobby Vee Recording Session* (Liberty 1962)★★★★, *Merry Christmas From Bobby Vee* (Liberty 1962)★★, *The Night Has A Thousand Eyes* (Liberty 1963)★★★, *Bobby Vee Meets The Ventures* (Liberty 1963)★★★, *I Remember Buddy Holly* (Liberty 1963)★★★, *Bobby Vee Sings The New Sound From England!* (Liberty 1964)★★, *30 Big Hits From The 60s* (Liberty 1964)★★★, *Bobby Vee Live On Tour* (Liberty 1965)★, *C'Mon Let's Live A Little* film soundtrack (1966)★★, *Look At Me Girl* (Liberty 1966)★★, *Come Back When You Grow Up* (Liberty 1967)★★, *Just Today* (Liberty 1968)★★, *Do What You Gotta Do* (Liberty 1968)★★, *Gates, Grills And Railings* (1969)★★, *Nothing Like A Sunny Day* (1972)★★, with the Shadows *The Early Rockin' Years* (K-Tel 1995)★★.
COMPILATIONS: *Bobby Vee's Golden Greats* (Liberty 1962)★★★★, *Bobby Vee's Golden Greats, Volume Two* (Liberty 1966)★★★, *A Forever Kind of Love* (Sunset 1969)★★★, *Legendary Masters* (United Artists 1973)★★★★, *The Bobby Vee Singles Album* (1980)★★★★, *The EP Collection* (See For Miles 1991)★★★★, *The Very Best Of* (1993)★★★★.
FILMS: *C'mon Let's Live A Little* (1967).

VEGA, SUZANNE
ALBUMS: *Suzanne Vega* (A&M 1985)★★★★, *Solitude Standing* (A&M 1987)★★, *Days Of Open Hand* (A&M 1990)★★, *99.9F* (A&M 1992)★★★, *Nine Objects Of Desire* (A&M 1996)★★★.

VELVET UNDERGROUND
ALBUMS: *The Velvet Underground And Nico* (Verve 1967)★★★★★, *White Light/White Heat* (Verve 1967)★★★★, *The Velvet Underground* (Verve 1969)★★★★, *Loaded* (Atlantic 1970)★★★★, *Live At Max's Kansas City* (Atlantic 1972)★, *Squeeze* (Polydor 1972)★★, *1969 – The Velvet Underground Live* (Mercury 1974)★★★, *VU* (Verve 1985)★★★, *Another View* (Polydor 1986)★★, *Live MCMXCIII* (1993)★★★, *Loaded (Fully Loaded)* (Atlantic 1997)★★★★.
COMPILATIONS: *Andy Warhol's Velvet Underground* (1971)★★★, *Velvet Underground* 5-album box set (Polydor 1986)★★★, *The Best Of The Velvet Underground* (Verve 1989)★★★★, *Peel Slowly And See* 5-CD box set (Polydor 1995)★★★★.
FILMS: *Hedy* (1965).
VIDEOS: *Velvet Redux – Live MCMXCII* (1993).
FURTHER READING: *Beyond The Velvet Underground*, Dave Thompson. *Uptight: The Velvet Underground Story*, Victor Bockris and G. Malanga. *Velvet Underground: A Complete Mediography*, Michael C. Kostek. *The Velvet Underground Handbook*, Michael C. Kostek.

VENTURES
ALBUMS: *Walk Don't Run* (Dolton 1960)★★★★, *The Ventures* (Dolton 1961)★★★★, *Another Smash!!!* (Dolton 1961)★★★, *The Colorful Ventures* (Dolton 1961)★★★, *Twist With The Ventures* aka *The Ventures – Dance* (Dolton 1962)★★★, *The Ventures' Twist Party* aka *Dance With The Ventures* (Dolton 1962)★★★, *Mashed Potatoes And Gravy* aka *The Ventures' Beach Party* (Dolton 1962)★★★, *Going To The Ventures' Dance Party* (Dolton 1962)★★★★, *The Ventures Play Telstar, The Lonely Bull* (Dolton 1963)★★, *The Ventures Surfing* (Dolton 1963)★★★, *Bobby Vee Meets The Ventures* (Dolton 1963)★★★, *The Ventures Play The Country Classics* aka *I Walk The Line* (Dolton 1963)★★, *Let's Go!* (Dolton 1963)★★★★, *The Ventures In Space* (Dolton 1964)★★, *Walk Don't Run Volume Two* (Dolton 1964)★★★, *The Ventures Knock Me Out* (Dolton 1965)★★★, *Play Guitar With The Ventures* (Dolton 1965)★★★, *The Ventures In Japan* (Dolton 1965)★★★, *The Ventures On Stage* (Dolton 1965)★★★, *The Ventures A-Go-Go* (Dolton 1965)★★★, *The Ventures Christmas Album* (Dolton 1965)★★★, *Where The Action Is* (Dolton 1966)★★★, *All About The Ventures* (Dolton 1966)★★★, *The Ventures (Batman)* (Dolton 1966)★★★, *Go With The Ventures* (Dolton 1966)★★★, *Wild Things* (Dolton 1966)★★★, *Guitar Freakout* aka *Revolving Sounds* (Dolton 1967)★★★, *The Ventures On Stage Encore* (Liberty 1967)★★★, *Super Psychedelics* aka *Changing Times* (Liberty 1967)★★★, *$1,000,000 Weekend* (Liberty 1967)★★, *Flights Of Fantasy* (Liberty 1968)★★★, *The Ventures Live Again* (Liberty 1968)★★★, *Pops In Japan* (1968)★★★, *The Horse* aka *The Ventures On The Scene* (Liberty 1968)★★★, *The Ventures In Tokyo '68* (1968)★★★, *Underground Fire* (Liberty 1968)★★★, *Hawaii Five-O* (1969)★★, *Swamp Rock* (1969)★★★, *The Ventures 10th Anniversary Album* (1970)★★★, *Live! The Ventures* (1970)★★★, *Golden Pops* (1970)★★★, *New Testament* (1971)★★, *Theme From Shaft* (United Artists 1971)★★, *Pops In Japan '71* (1971)★★★, *Joy – The Ventures Play The Classics* (United Artists 1972)★★★, *Rock 'N' Roll Forever* (1972)★★★, *The Ventures On Stage '72* (1972)★★★, *The Ventures On Stage '73* (1973)★★★, *Pops In Japan '73* (1973)★★★, *The Ventures On Stage '74* (1974)★★★, *The Jim Croce Songbook* (1974)★★, *The Ventures Play The Carpenters* (1974)★★, *Hollywood Yuya Meets The Ventures* (1976)★★★, *The Ventures On Stage '76* (1976)★★★, *Rocky Road* (1976)★★, *TV Themes* (1977)★★, *Live In Japan '77* (1977)★★★, *The Ventures On Stage '78* (1978)★★★, *Latin Album* (1978)★★, *The Ventures Original Four* (1980)★★★, *Chameleon* (1980)★★, *Super Live '80* (1980)★★★, *The Ventures* (1981)★★★, *60's Pops* (1981)★★★, *Tokyo Callin' 60s Pops Of Japan* (1981)★★★, *Pops In Japan '81* (1981)★★★, *St Louis Memory* (1982)★★, *The Ventures Today* (Valentine 1983)★★★.
COMPILATIONS: *Running Strong* (1966)★★★, *Golden Greats By The Ventures* (1967)★★★, *Supergroup* (1969)★★★, *A Decade With The Ventures* (1971)★★★, *The Ventures* (1971)★★★, *Legendary Masters* (1974)★★★, *15th Anniversary ALBUMS: 15 Years Of Japanese Pops* (1975)★★★, *Ventures' Rare Collections For Great Collectors Only* (1980)★★★, *The Ventures Greatest Hits* (1981)★★★, *The Last Album On Liberty* (1982)★★★, *Twenty Rock 'N' Roll Hits: The Ventures* (1983)★★★, *The Best Of The Ventures* (1987)★★★, *Walk Don't Run – The Best Of The Ventures* (1990)★★★.

VERLAINE, TOM
ALBUMS: *Tom Verlaine* (Elektra 1979)★★★★, *Dreamtime* (Warners 1981)★★★, *Words From The Front* (Warners 1983)★★★, *Cover* (Warners 1984)★★★★, *Flash Light* (Fontana 1987)★★★★, *The Wonder* (Fontana 1990)★★★★, *Warm And Cool* (Rough Trade 1992)★★★.
COMPILATIONS: *The Miller's Tale: A Tom Verlaine Anthology* (Virgin 1996)★★★★.

VERUCA SALT
ALBUMS: *American Thighs* (Minty Fresh 1994)★★, *Blow It Out Your Ass It's Veruca Salt* (Minty Fresh/Geffen 1996)★★★, *Eight Arms To Hold You* (Outpost/Geffen 1997)★★★★.

VERVE
ALBUMS: *Storm In Heaven* (Hut 1993)★★★, *A Northern Soul* (Hut 1995)★★★★, *Urban Hymns* (Hut 1997).
COMPILATIONS: *No Come Down* (Virgin 1994)★★★.

VILLAGE PEOPLE
ALBUMS: *Village People* (DJM 1977)★★, *Macho Man* (DJM 1978)★★, *Cruisin'* (Mercury 1978)★★, *Go West* (Mercury 1979)★★, *Live And Sleazy* (Mercury 1979)★, *Can't Stop The Music* film soundtrack (Mercury 1980)★, *Renaissance* (Mercury 1981)★.
COMPILATIONS: *Greatest Hits* (Groove & Move 1988)★★★, *The Hits* (Music Club 1991)★★★.
VIDEOS: *The Best Of ...* (1994).
FILMS: *Can't Stop The Music* (1980).

VINCENT, GENE
ALBUMS: *Blue Jean Bop!* (Capitol 1956)★★★, *Gene Vincent And The Blue Caps* (Capitol 1957)★★★, *Gene Vincent Rocks And The Bluecaps Roll* (Capitol 1958)★★★, *A Gene Vincent Record Date* (Capitol 1958)★★★, *Sounds Like Gene Vincent* (Capitol 1959)★★★, *Crazy Times* (Capitol 1960)★★★, *The Crazy Beat Of Gene Vincent* (Capitol 1963)★★★, *Shakin' Up A Storm* (Columbia 1964)★★★, *Bird Doggin'* (London 1967)★★★, *Gene Vincent* (London 1967)★★, *I'm Back And I'm Proud* (Dandelion 1970)★★, *If Only You Could See Me Today* (UK) (Kama Sutra 1971)★★, *The Day The World Turned Blue* (Kama Sutra 1971)★★.
COMPILATIONS: *The Best Of Gene Vincent* (Capitol 1967)★★★, *The Best Of Gene Vincent Volume 2* (Capitol 1968)★★★, *Gene Vincent's Greatest* (Capitol 1969)★★★, *The Bop That Just Won't Stop* (Capitol 1974)★★★, *Greatest Hits* (Capitol 1977)★★★, *Rock On With Gene Vincent* (MFP 1980)★★★, *The Gene Vincent Singles Album* (Capitol 1981)★★★, *Dressed In Black* (Magnum Force 1982)★★★, *Gene Vincent's Greatest Hits* (Fame 1982)★★★, *From LA To 'Frisco* (Magnum Force 1983)★★★, *For Collectors Only* (Magnum Force 1984)★★★, *Born To Be A Rolling Stone* (Topline 1985)★★★, *Gene Vincent: The Capitol Years* (Charly 1988)★★★★, *The Gene Vincent Box Set* 6-CD box set (EMI 1990)★★★★, *Rebel Heart Vol 1* (Magnum 1992)★★★, *Be-Bop-A-Lula* (Charly 1993)★★★, *Ain't That Too Much: The Complete Challenge Sessions* (Hollowbody/Sundazed 1994)★★★, *Rebel Heart Vol 2* (Magnum 1995)★★, *The EP Collection* (See For Miles 1996)★★★, *Rebel Heart Vol 3* (Magnum 1996)★★, *500 Miles* (Camden 1998)★★★.
FILMS: *The Girl Can't Help It* (1956), *Hot Rod Gang* aka *Fury Unleashed* (1958), *It's Trad, Dad* aka *Ring-A-Ding Rhythm* (1962).
FURTHER READING: *Wild Cat: A Tribute To Gene Vincent*, Eddie Muir. *Gene Vincent & The Blue Caps*, Rob Finnis and Bob Dunham. *I Remember Gene Vincent*, Alan Vince. *Gene Vincent: The Screaming End*, Alan Clark. *The Day The World Turned Blue*, Britt Hagerty. *Gene Vincent: A Discography*, Derek Henderson.

VIRGIN PRUNES
ALBUMS: *A New Form Of Beauty* (Rough Trade 1981)★★, *If I Die ... I Die* (Rough Trade 1982)★★★,

Heresie (L'invitation Au Suicide 1982)★★, The Moon Looked Down And Laughed (Baby 1986)★★★, The Hidden Lie (Live In Paris 6/6/86) (Baby 1986)★★. As the Prunes Lite Fantastik (Baby 1988)★★, Nada (Baby 1989)★★.

VISAGE
ALBUMS: Visage (Polydor 1980)★★, The Anvil (Polydor 1982)★★, Beat Boy (Polydor 1994)★★.
COMPILATIONS: The Singles Collection (Polydor 1983)★★★.

VOICE OF THE BEEHIVE
ALBUMS: Let It Bee (London 1988)★★★, Honey Lingers (London 1991)★★★★, Sex And Misery (East West 1995)★★.

W

WAH!
ALBUMS: Nah = Poo – The Art Of Bluff (Eternal 1981)★★, as Mighty Wah! A Word To The Wise Guy (Beggars Banquet 1984)★★.
Solo: Pete Wylie Sinful (Virgin 1987)★★★.
COMPILATIONS: The Maverick Years '80 -'81 (Wonderful World 1982)★★, as Mighty Wah! The Way We Wah! (Warners 1984)★★★.

WAINWRIGHT, LOUDON, III
ALBUMS: Loudon Wainwright III (Atlantic 1969)★★★, Album II (Atlantic 1971)★★★, Album III (Columbia 1973)★★★, Attempted Moustache (Columbia 1974)★★, Unrequited (Columbia 1975)★★, T-Shirt (Arista 1976)★★, Final Exam (Arista 1978)★★, A Live One (Radar 1979)★★★, Fame And Wealth (Demon 1983)★★★, I'm Alright (Demon 1984)★★★, More Love Songs (Demon 1986)★★★, Therapy (Silvertone 1989)★★★, History (1992)★★★, Career Moves (1993)★★★, Grown Man (Virgin 1995)★★★.

WAITE, JOHN
ALBUMS: Ignition (Chrysalis 1982)★★, No Brakes (EMI America 1984)★★, Mask Of Smiles (Capitol 1985)★★, Rovers Return (EMI America 1987)★★, Temple Bar (Imago 1995)★★, When You Were Mine (Pure 1997).
COMPILATIONS: The Essential (EMI America 1992)★★★.

WAITS, TOM
ALBUMS: Closing Time (Asylum 1973)★★★, The Heart Of Saturday Night (Asylum 1974)★★★, Nighthawks At The Diner (Asylum 1975)★★★, Small Change (Asylum 1976)★★★★, Foreign Affairs (Asylum 1977)★★★, Blue Valentine (Asylum 1978)★★★★, Heartattack And Vine (Asylum 1980)★★★★, with Crystal Gayle One From The Heart (Columbia 1982)★★★★, Swordfishtrombones (Island 1983)★★★★, Rain Dogs (Island 1985)★★★★, Frank's Wild Years (Island 1987)★★★, Big Time (Island 1988)★★★, Night On Earth film soundtrack (ISL 1992)★★★, Bone Machine (Island 1992)★★★★, The Black Rider (Island 1993)★★★.
COMPILATIONS: Bounced Checks (Asylum 1981)★★★, Asylum Years (Asylum 1986)★★★★, The Early Years Volume 1 (Bizarre/Straight 1991)★★★.
FURTHER READING: Small Change: A Life Of Tom Waits, Patrick Humphries.

WAKEMAN, RICK
ALBUMS: with the John Schroeder Orchestra Piano Vibrations (Polydor 1971)★★★, The Six Wives Of Henry VIII (A&M 1973)★★★, Journey To The Centre Of The Earth (A&M 1974)★★, The Myths And Legends Of King Arthur And The Knights Of The Round Table (A&M 1975)★★★, Lisztomania film soundtrack (A&M 1975)★★★, No Earthly Connection (A&M 1976)★★, White Rock soundtrack (A&M 1977)★★, Rick Wakeman's Criminal Record (A&M 1977)★★, Rhapsodies (A&M 1979)★★, 1984 (Charisma 1981)★★, The Burning soundtrack (Charisma 1982)★★, Rock 'N' Roll Prophet (Moon 1982)★★, G'Ole soundtrack (Charisma 1983)★★, The Cost Of Living (Charisma 1987)★★, Live At Hammersmith (President 1985)★★, Silent Nights (President 1985)★★, Country Airs (Coda 1986)★★★, Crimes Of Passion soundtrack (President 1986)★★, The Family Album (President 1987)★★, The Gospels (Stylus 1987)★★, A Suite Of Gods (President 1988)★★, Time Machine (President 1988)★★, Zodiaque (President 1988)★★, Sea Airs (President 1989)★★, Night Airs (President 1990)★★, In The Beginning (Asaph 1990)★★, Aspirent Sunrise (Ambient 1990)★★, Aspirent Sunset (President 1990)★★, Black Knights In The Court Of Ferdinand (Ambient 1991)★★, The Sun Trilogy (Badger 1991)★★, Phantom Power soundtrack (Ambient 1991)★★, Softsword: King John And The Magna Charter (Ambient 1991)★★, with Norman Wisdom A World Of Wisdom (Ambient 1991)★★, The Private Collection (Ambient 1991)★★, The Classical Connection (Ambient 1991)★★, The Classical Connection II (Ambient 1991)★★, 2000 AD, Into The Future (Ambient 1991)★★, with Adam Wakeman Wakeman With Wakeman (Rio Digital 1992)★★, Ambient Sunshadows (Rio Digital 1992)★★, Heritage Suite (President 1993)★★, African Bach (President 1993)★★, with Adam Wakeman No Expense Spared (President 1993)★★, The Classic Tracks (Prestige 1994)★★, with Adam Wakeman The Official Bootleg (Cyclops 1994)★★, Romance Of The Victorian Age (President 1994)★★, Live On The Test (Windsong 1994)★★★, The Seven Wonders Of The World (President 1995)★★, Cirque Surreal – State Circus Of Imagination (D-Sharp 1995)★★, Visions (President 1995)★★.
COMPILATIONS: Greatest Hits (1994)★★★, Rock And Pop Legends (Disky 1995)★★, Voyage (A&M 1997)★★★.
VIDEOS: The World (Central 1988), Rick Wakeman Live In Concert (Castle 1991), The World And Gospels (Beckmann 1991), The Classical Connection (Beckmann 1991), The Very Best Of Rick Wakeman – Chronicles (Icon 1992), Chronicles Live 1975 (Fragile 1994), The Making Of Surreal (Dan Ace 1995).
FURTHER READING: Rick Wakeman: The Caped Crusader, Dan Wooding. Say Yes!, Rick Wakeman.

WALKER BROTHERS
ALBUMS: Take It Easy With The Walker Brothers (Philips 1965)★★★, Portrait (Philips 1966)★★★, Images (Philips 1967)★★, No Regrets (GTO 1975)★★★, Lines (GTO 1977)★★, Nite Flights (GTO 1978)★★★★, The Walker Brothers In Japan 1968 recording (Bam Caruso 1987)★★.
COMPILATIONS: After The Lights Go Out – The Best Of 1965-1967 (Fontana 1990)★★★★, No Regrets – The Best Of The Walker Brothers (1991)★★★★, The Collection (Spectrum 1996)★★★★.
FILMS: Beach Ball (1964).

WALKER, JUNIOR, AND THE ALL STARS
ALBUMS: Shotgun (Soul/Tamla Motown 1965)★★★★, Soul Session (Tamla Motown 1966)★★★★, Road Runner (Tamla Motown 1966)★★★★, Live! (Tamla Motown 1967)★★★, Home Cookin' (Tamla Motown 1969)★★★, Gotta Hold On To This Feeling (Soul 1969)★★★, What Does It Take To Win Your Love? (Soul 1969)★★★, Live (1970)★★★, A Gasssssss (Soul 1970)★★★, Rainbow Funk (Soul 1971)★★★, Moody Jr. (Soul 1971)★★★, Peace And Understanding Is Hard To Find (Soul 1973)★★, Hot Shot (Soul 1976)★★, Sax Appeal (Soul 1976)★★★, Whopper Bopper Show Stopper (Soul 1976)★★, Smooth (Soul 1978)★★, Back Street Boogie (Whitfield 1979)★★, Blow The House Down (Motown 1983)★★.
COMPILATIONS: Greatest Hits (Soul 1969)★★★★, Anthology (Motown 1981)★★★★, Junior Walker's Greatest Hits (1982)★★★★, 19 Greatest Hits (1987)★★★★, Shake And Fingerpop (Blue Moon 1989)★★★, Compact Command Performance – 19 Greatest Hits (1992)★★★★.

WALKER, SCOTT
ALBUMS: Scott (Philips 1967)★★★, Scott 2 (Philips 1968)★★★★, Scott 3 (Philips 1969)★★★★, Scott 4 (Philips 1969)★★★★, Scott Sings Songs From His Television Series (Philips 1969)★★, 'Til The Band Comes In (Philips 1970)★★★, The Moviegoer (Philips 1972)★★, Any Day Now (Philips 1973)★★, Stretch (CBS 1973), We Had It All (CBS 1974)★★, Climate Of Hunter (Virgin 1984)★★★★, Tilt (Fontana 1995)★★★.
COMPILATIONS: Looking Back With Scott Walker (Ember 1968)★★★, Best Of Scott Walker (Philips 1970)★★★, This Is Scott Walker (Philips 1971)★★★★, This Is Scott Walker – Volume II (Philips 1972)★★★, Spotlight On Scott Walker (Philips 1976)★★★, Fire Escape In The Sky – The Godlike Genius Of Scott Walker (Zoo 1981)★★★★, Scott Walker Sings Jacques Brel (Philips 1981)★★★, Boy Child – The Best Of 1967-1970 (1990)★★★★.
FURTHER READING: A Deep Shade Of Blue, Mike Watkinson and Pete Anderson.

WALKER, T-BONE
ALBUMS: Classics In Jazz (Capitol 1953)★★★, T-Bone Walker i (1956)★★★★, Sings The Blues (Imperial 1959)★★★★, T-Bone Blues (Atlantic 1960)★★★★, Singing The Blues (Imperial 1960)★★★★, I Get So Weary (Imperial 1961)★★★★, The Great Blues, Vocals And Guitar (1963)★★★★, T-Bone Walker II (Capitol 1964)★★★★, I Want A Little Girl (Delmark 1967)★★★, Stormy Monday Blues (Wet Soul 1967)★★★★, The Truth (Brunswick 1968)★★★, Blue Rocks (1968)★★★, Funky Town (Bluesway 1968)★★★, Feeling The Blues (1969)★★★, Very Rare (Reprise 1973)★★★, Dirty Mistreater (1973)★★★, T-Bone Jumps Again (Charly 1981)★★★★, Good Feelin' 1968 recording (Polydor 1982)★★★, Plain Ole Blues (Charly 1982)★★★, Hot Leftovers (Pathé Marconi 1985)★★★, Low Down Blues (Charly 1986)★★★★, with 'Big' Joe Turner Bosses Of The Blues (Bluebird 1989)★★★.
COMPILATIONS: The Blues Of T-Bone Walker (1965)★★★★, Stormy Monday Blues (1968)★★★★, Classics Of Modern Blues (1975)★★★★, The Inventor Of The Electric Guitar Blues (Blues Boy 1983)★★★★, The Bluesway Sessions (Charly 1988)★★★★, The Hustle Is On: Imperial Sessions, Volume 1 (Sequel 1990)★★★★, The Complete 1940-1954 Recordings Of T-Bone Walker (Mosaic 1990)★★★★, The Complete Imperial Recordings, 1950-54 (EMI 1991)★★★★, T-Bone Blues rec. 1955-57 (Sequel 1994)★★★★, The Complete Capitol Black And White Recordings 3-CD set (Capitol 1995)★★★★.
FURTHER READING: Stormy Monday, Helen Oakly Dance.

WALSH, JOE
ALBUMS: Barnstorm (ABC 1972)★★★, The Smoker You Drink, The Player You Get (ABC 1973)★★★★, So What? (ABC 1975)★★★★, You Can't Argue With A Sick Mind (ABC 1976)★★, But Seriously Folks ... (Asylum 1978)★★★, There Goes The Neighborhood (Asylum 1981)★★, You Bought It – You Name It (Warners 1983)★★, The Confessor (Warners 1985)★★, Got Any Gum? (Warners 1987)★★, Ordinary Average Guy (Epic 1991)★★, Robocop – The Series Soundtrack (Essential 1995)★★.
COMPILATIONS: The Best Of Joe Walsh (ABC 1978)★★★, Look What I Did! – The Joe Walsh Anthology 2-CD (MCA 1995)★★★.

WAR
ALBUMS: with Eric Burdon Eric Burdon Declares War (MGM 1970)★★★, with Burdon The Black Man's Burdon (MGM 1970)★★, War (United Artists 1971)★★★, All Day Music (United Artists 1971)★★★, The World Is A Ghetto (United Artists 1972)★★★★, Deliver The Word (United Artists 1973)★★★, War Live! (United Artists 1974)★★, Why Can't We Be Friends? (United Artists 1975)★★★★, Galaxy (MCA 1977)★★★, Youngblood (United Artists 1978)★★★, The Music Band (MCA 1979)★★, The Music Band 2 (MCA 1979)★★, The Music Band – Live (1980)★★, Outlaw (RCA 1982)★★, Life (Is So Strange) (RCA 1983)★★, Where Theres Smoke (Coco Plum 1984)★★, Peace Sign (RCA/Avenue 1994)★★, Don't Let No-One Get You Down (Rhino 1995), Life Is So Strange (Rhino 1996).
COMPILATIONS: Greatest Hits (United Artists 1976)★★★★, Best Of The Music Band (MCA 1994)★★★, Anthology 1970-1994 (Avenue/Rhino 1995)★★★★, The Best Of War And More: Vol. 2 (Avenue/Rhino 1997)★★★.

WARNES, JENNIFER
ALBUMS: I Can Remember Everything (Parrot 1968)★★, See Me Feel Me, Touch Me Heal Me (Parrot 1968)★★, Jennifer (Reprise 1972)★★★, Jennifer Warnes (Arista 1977)★★, Shot Through the Heart (Arista 1979)★★, Famous Blue Raincoat (RCA 1987)★★★★, The Hunter (Private 1992)★★★.
COMPILATIONS: The Best Of Jennifer Warnes (Arista 1982)★★.

WARWICK, DIONNE
ALBUMS: Presenting Dionne Warwick (Scepter 1963)★★★, Anyone Who Had A Heart (1964)★★★★, Make Way For Dionne Warwick (Scepter 1964)★★★★, The Sensitive Sound Of Dionne Warwick (Scepter 1965)★★★★, Here I Am (Scepter 1966)★★★★, Dionne Warwick In Paris (Scepter 1966)★★★, Here Where There Is Love (Scepter 1967)★★★, Dionne Warwick Onstage And In The Movies (Scepter 1967)★★★, The Windows Of The World (Scepter 1968)★★★, Dionne In The Valley Of The Dolls (Scepter 1968)★★★★, Magic Of Believing (1968)★★★, Promises Promises (Scepter 1968)★★★★, Soulful (Scepter 1969)★★★, Dionne Warwick's Greatest Motion Picture Hits (Scepter 1969)★★★, I'll Never Fall In Love Again (Scepter 1970)★★★, Very Dionne (Scepter 1970)★★, The Love Machine (1971)★★★, The Dionne Warwick Story – Live (Scepter 1971)★★, From Within (Scepter 1972)★★, Dionne (Warners 1972)★★, Just Being Myself (Warners 1973)★★, Then Came You (Warners 1975)★★★, Track Of The Cat (Warners 1975)★★★, with Isaac Hayes A Man And A Woman (1977)★★★, Only Love Can Break A Heart (Musicor 1977)★★★, Love At First Sight (1979)★★, Dionne (Arista 1979)★★★★, No Night So Long (Arista 1980)★★, Hot! Live And Otherwise (Mobile Fidelity 1981)★★★, Friends In Love (Arista 1982)★★★, Heartbreaker (Arista 1982)★★★, How Many Times Can We Say Goodbye (Arista 1983)★★, So Amazing (1983)★★★, Friends (Arista 1985)★★★, Finder Of Lost Loves (Arista 1985)★★★, Without Your Love (Arista 1985)★★★, Reservations For Two (Arista 1988)★★★, Dionne Warwick Sings Cole Porter (Arista 1989)★★★, Friends Can Be Lovers (Arista 1993)★★★, Aquarela Do Brazil (Arista 1995).
COMPILATIONS: Dionne Warwick's Golden Hits, Part 1 (Scepter 1967)★★★★, Dionne Warwick's Golden Hits, Part 2 (Scepter 1969)★★★★, The Best Of Dionne Warwick (1983)★★★★, The Original Soul Of Dionne Warwick (1987)★★★,The Love Songs (1989)★★★★, Greatest Hits 1979-1990 (Arista 1989)★★★★, The Essential Collection (Global 1996)★★★★.

W.A.S.P.
ALBUMS: W.A.S.P. (Capitol 1984)★★, The Last Command (Capitol 1985)★★★, Inside The Electric Circus (Capitol 1986)★★★, Live ... In The Raw (Capitol 1987)★★, The Headless Children (Capitol 1989)★★, The Crimson Idol (Parlophone 1992)★★★, Still Not Black Enough (Raw Power 1995)★★★, W.A.S.P. (Castle 1995)★★, Kill, F**k, Die (Raw Power 1997)★★, Double Live Assassins (CMC International 1998).
COMPILATIONS: First Blood...Last Cuts (Capitol 1993)★★★.
VIDEOS: Live At The Lyceum (PMI 1985), W.A.S.P. In The Raw (PMI 1988).

WATERBOYS
ALBUMS: The Waterboys (Ensign 1983)★★★, A Pagan Place (Ensign 1984)★★★, This Is The Sea (Ensign 1985)★★★★, Fisherman's Blues (Ensign 1988)★★★, Room To Roam (Ensign 1990)★★★, Dream Harder (Geffen 1993)★★.
COMPILATIONS: The Best Of 1981-90 (Ensign 1991)★★★, The Secret Life Of The Waterboys: 1981-1985 (Ensign 1994)★★.

WATERS, ROGER
ALBUMS: with Ron Geesin Music From The Body soundtrack (Harvest 1970)★, The Pros And Cons Of Hitch Hiking (Harvest 1984)★★★, When The Wind Blows soundtrack (Virgin 1986)★★, Radio K.A.O.S (Harvest 1987)★★, The Wall: Live In Berlin (Mercury 1990)★★, Amused To Death (1993)★★.

WATSON, JOHNNY 'GUITAR'
ALBUMS: Gangster Of Love (King 1958)★★★★, Johnny Guitar Watson (King 1963)★★★, The Blues Soul Of Johnny Guitar Watson (Chess 1964)★★★★, Bad (Chess 1966)★★★★, with Larry Williams Two For The Price Of One (1967)★★★★, Johnny Watson Plays Fats Waller In The Fats Bag (OKeh 1968)★★★, Listen (Fantasy 1974)★★★, I Don't Want To Be Alone, Stranger (Fantasy 1975)★★★, Captured Live (1976)★★★, Ain't That A Bitch (DJM 1976)★★★, A Real Mother For Ya (DJM 1977)★★, Funk Beyond The Call Of Duty (DJM 1977)★★, Gangster Of Love (DJM 1977)★★★, with the Watsonian Institute Master Funk (1978)★★, Giant (DJM 1978)★★, with Papa John Creach Inphasion (DJM 1978)★★, with the Watsonian Institute Extra Disco Perception (1979)★★, What The Hell Is This? (DJM 1979)★★, Love Jones (DJM 1980)★★, Johnny 'Guitar' Watson And The Family Clone (DJM 1981)★★, That's What Time It Is (A&M 1981)★★, Strike On Computers (Valley Vue 1984)★★, Bow Wow (M-Head 1996)★★.
COMPILATIONS: The Very Best Of Johnny 'Guitar' Watson (DJM 1981)★★★★, I Heard That! (Chess 1985)★★★★, Hit The Highway (Ace 1985)★★★★, Gangster Of Love (Charly 1991)★★★★★, Gangster Of Love: The Best Of Johnny 'Guitar' Watson (Castle 1995)★★★★, Hot Just Like TNT (Ace 1996)★★★★.

WATT, MIKE
ALBUMS: Ball-Hog Or Tugboat (Columbia 1995)★★★★, The Engine Room (Columbia 1997)★★★.

WAYNE, JEFF
ALBUMS: War Of The Worlds (Columbia 1978)★★★, War Of The Worlds – Highlights (Columbia 1981)★★★, Spartacus (Columbia 1992), It's OK To Be A White Male (Uproar 1995), Comedy Jam (Uproar 1997).

WEATHER REPORT
ALBUMS: Weather Report i (Columbia 1971)★★★, I Sing The Body Electric (Columbia 1972)★★★★, Sweetnighter (Columbia 1973)★★★, Mysterious Traveller (Columbia 1974)★★★★, Tail Spinnin' (Columbia 1975)★★★, Black Market (Columbia 1976)★★★★, Heavy Weather (Columbia 1977)★★★★, Mr. Gone (Columbia 1978), 8:30 (Columbia 1979)★★★, Night Passages (Columbia 1980)★★★, Weather Report II (Columbia 1982)★★★, Procession (Columbia 1983)★★★, Domino Theory (Columbia 1984)★★★, Sportin' Life (Columbia 1985)★★★, This Is This (Columbia 1986)★★★, New Album (Columbia 1988)★★★, Birdland (Sony 1996).
COMPILATIONS: Heavy Weather: The Collection (Columbia 1990)★★★★, The Weather Report Selection 3-CD box set (Columbia 1992)★★★.

WEBB, JIMMY
ALBUMS: Jimmy Webb Sings Jimmy Webb (Epic 1968)★★, Words And Music (Reprise 1970)★★★, And So: On (Reprise 1971)★★★, Letters (Reprise 1972)★★★★, Land's End (Asylum 1974)★★★★, El Mirage (Asylum 1977)★★★, Voices soundtrack (Planet 1979)★★, Angel Heart (Columbia/Lorimar 1982)★★★, Hanoi Hilton soundtrack (1987)★★, Suspending Disbelief (Warners 1993)★★★, Ten Easy Pieces (Guardian 1996)★★★.
COMPILATIONS: Archive (Warners 1993)★★★★.

WEDDING PRESENT
ALBUMS: George Best (Reception 1987)★★★, Bizarro (RCA 1989)★★, Seamonsters (RCA 1991)★★★, Watusi (Island 1994)★★★, Mini (Cooking Vinyl 1996)★★, Saturnalia (Cooking Vinyl 1996)★★★.
COMPILATIONS: Tommy (Reception 1988)★★★, The Hit Parade Part One (RCA 1992)★★★, The Hit Parade Part Two (RCA 1993)★★, John Peel Sessions 1987-1990 (Strange Fruit 1993)★★★, Evening Sessions 1986-1994 (Strange Fruit 1997)★★★.
FURTHER READING: The Wedding Present: Thank Yer, Very Glad, Mark Hodkinson.

WEEZER
ALBUMS: Weezer (Geffen 1994)★★★★, Pinkerton (DGC 1996)★★★.

WELLER, PAUL
ALBUMS: Paul Weller (Go! Discs 1992)★★, Wild Wood (Go! Discs 1994)★★★★, Live Wood (Go! Discs 1994)★★★, Stanley Road (Go! Discs 1995)★★★★, Heavy Soul (Island 1997)★★★★.
VIDEOS: The Paul Weller Movement Live (Video Collection 1991), Highlights And Hang Ups (Polygram 1994), Live Wood (Polygram 1994).
FURTHER READING: Days Lose Their Names And Time Slips Away: Paul Weller 1992-95, Lawrence Watson and Paolo Hewitt. Paul Weller: My Ever Changing Moods, John Reed. The Unauthorised Biography, Steve Malins.

WELLS, MARY
ALBUMS: Bye Bye Baby, I Don't Want To Take A Chance (Motown 1961)★★★, The One Who Really Loves You (Motown 1962)★★★, Two Lovers And Other Great Hits (Motown 1963)★★★, Recorded Live On Stage (Motown 1963)★★★, Second Time Around (Motown 1963)★★★, with Marvin Gaye Together (Motown 1964)★★★, Mary Wells Sings My Guy (Motown 1964)★★★, Mary Wells (20th Century 1965)★★★, Mary Wells Sings Love Songs To The Beatles (20th Century 1965)★★★, Vintage Stock (Motown 1966)★★★, The Two Sides Of Mary Wells (Atco 1966)★★★, Ooh! (Movietone 1966)★★★, Servin' Up Some Soul (Jubilee 1968)★★, In And Out Of Love (1981)★★, Keeping My Mind On Love (1990)★★.
COMPILATIONS: Greatest Hits (Motown 1964)★★★, The Old, New And Best Of Mary Wells (1984)★★★, The Best Of (1993)★★★, Compact Command Performances (early 90s)★★★, The Complete Jubilee Sessions (Sequel 1993)★★★, Ain't It The Truth: The Best Of 1964-82 (c.1993)★★★, Looking Back 1961-64 (c.1993)★★★, My Guy (1994)★★★, Dear Lover – the Atco Years (1994)★★★, Early Classics (Spectrum 1996)★★★, Never, Never Leave Me: The 20th Century Sides (Ichiban 1997)★★★.
FILMS: Catalina Caper (1967).

WET WET WET
ALBUMS: Popped In Souled Out (Precious 1987)★★★, The Memphis Sessions (Precious 1988)★★, Holding Back The River (Precious 1989)★★★, as Maggie Pie And The Imposters Cloak And Dagger (1990)★★★, Live cassette only (1991)★★, High On The Happy Side (Precious 1991)★★, Live At The Royal Albert Hall (Precious 1993)★★, Picture This (Mercury 1995)★★, 10 (Mercury 1997)★★.
COMPILATIONS: End Of Part One (Precious 1993)★★★.
FURTHER READING: Wet Wet Wet Pictured, Simon Fowler and Alan Jackson.

WHAM!
ALBUMS: Fantastic (Inner Vision 1983)★★, Make It Big (Epic 1984)★★★, The Final (Epic 1986)★★★.
VIDEOS: Wham! The Video (1987).
FURTHER READING: Wham! (Confidential) The Death Of A Supergroup, Johnny Rogan. Bare, George Michael.

WHITE, BARRY
ALBUMS: I've Got So Much To Give (20th Century 1973)★★★, Stone Gon' (20th Century 1973)★★★, Can't Get Enough (20th Century 1974)★★★, Just Another Way To Say I Love You (20th Century 1975)★★★, Let The Music Play (20th Century 1976)★★★, Is This Whatcha Wont? (20th Century 1976)★★★, Barry White Sings For Someone You Love (20th Century 1977)★★★, Barry White The Man (20th Century 1978)★★★, The Message Is Love (Unlimited Gold 1979)★★★, I Love To Sing The Songs I Sing (20th Century 1979)★★, Barry White's Sheet Music (Unlimited Gold 1980)★★, The Best Of Our Love (Unlimited Gold 1981)★★, with Glodean James Barry And Glodean (Unlimited Gold 1981)★★★, Beware! (1981)★★, Change (Unlimited Gold 1982)★★, Dedicated (Unlimited Gold 1983)★★, The Right Night And Barry White (A&M 1987)★★, The Man Is Back! (A&M 1990)★★, In Your Mix (A&M 1991)★★★, The Icon Is Love (A&M 1994)★★.
COMPILATIONS: Barry White's Greatest Hits (20th Century 1975)★★★★, Barry White's Greatest Hits Vol.2 (20th Century 1977)★★★, Satin & Soul (Connoisseur 1987)★★★, The Collection (Polydor 1988)★★★★, Just For You (1993)★★★.

WHITESNAKE
ALBUMS: Trouble (United Artists 1978)★★★, Love Hunter (United Artists 1979)★★★, Live At Hammersmith (United Artists 1980)★★, Ready An' Willing (United Artists 1980)★★★, Live In The Heart Of The City (Sunburst 1980)★★★, Come And Get It (Liberty 1981)★★★, Saints 'N Sinners (Liberty 1982)★★, Slide It In (Liberty 1984)★★★, Whitesnake (Liberty 1987)★★★★, 1987 (Liberty 1992)★★★, Slip Of The Tongue (EMI 1989)★★★, Restless Heart (EMI 1997)★★★.
COMPILATIONS: Best Of (EMI 1988)★★★★, Greatest Hits (MCA 1994)★★★★.
VIDEOS: Fourplay (1984), Whitesnake Live (1984), Trilogy (1988).
FURTHER READING: Illustrated Biography, Simon Robinson. Whitesnake, Tom Hibbert.

WHITE ZOMBIE
ALBUMS: mini-album Psycho-Head Blowout (Silent Explosion 1987), Soul Crusher (Silent Explosion 1988), Make Them Die Slowly (Caroline 1989), La Sexorcisto: Devil Music Vol. 1 (Geffen 1992), Astro Creep 2000: Songs Of Love, Destruction And Other Synthetic Delusions Of The Electric Head (Geffen 1995), Supersexy Swingin' Sounds (Geffen 1996).

WHO
ALBUMS: My Generation (Brunswick 1965)★★★★, The Who Sings My Generation (Decca 1966), A Quick One (Reaction 1966)★★★★, The Who Sell Out (Track 1967)★★★★, Happy Jack (Decca 1967)★★★, Magic Bus – The Who On Tour (Decca 1968)★★★, Tommy (Track 1969)★★★★, Live At Leeds (Track 1970)★★★★★, Who's Next (Track 1971)★★★★★, Quadrophenia (MCA 1973)★★★★, The Who By Numbers (Polydor 1975)★★★, Who Are You (Polydor 1978)★★, The Kids Are Alright soundtrack (Polydor 1979)★★★, Face Dances (Polydor 1981)★★, It's Hard (Polydor 1982)★★, Join Together (Virgin 1990)★★★, Live At The Isle Of Wight Festival 1970 (Essential 1996)★★★★.
COMPILATIONS: Magic Bus (1967)★★★, Direct Hits (1968)★★★, Meaty Beaty Big And Bouncy (Polydor 1971)★★★★★, Odds And Sods (Track 1974)★★★, The Story Of The Who (Polydor 1976)★★★, Hooligans (MCA 1981)★★★, Rarities Volume 1 (1966-1968) (Polydor 1983)★★★, Rarities Volume 2 (1970-1973) (Polydor 1983)★★★, Once Upon A Time (Polydor 1983)★★★, The Singles (Polydor 1984)★★★, Who's Better Who's Best (Polydor 1988)★★★★, The Who Collection (Stylus 1988)★★★, 30 Years Of Maximum R&B 4-CD box set (Polydor 1994)★★★★★, My Generation: The Very Best Of ... (Polydor 1996)★★★★★.
FILMS: Tommy (1975), Quadrophenia (1979).
VIDEOS: The Kids Are Alright (1990), Thirty Years Of Maximum R&B Live (Polygram 1994), The Who Live At The Isle Of Wight Festival 1970 (Warner Music Vision 1996), Live, Featuring The Rock Opera Tommy (SMV Enterprises 1996).
FURTHER READING: The Who, Gary Herman. The Who, Jeff Stein and Chris Johnston. The Who ... Through The Eyes Of Pete Townshend, Conner McKnight and Caroline Silver. The Who, George Tremlett. The Who: Ten Great Years, Cindy Ehrlich. The Who Generation, Nik Cohn. A Decade Of The Who: An Authorized History In Music, Paintings, Words And Photo, Steve Turner. The Story Of Tommy, Richard Barnes and Pete Townshend. Whose Who? A Who Retrospective, Brian Ashley and Steve Monnery. Keith Moon: The Life And Death Of A Rock Legend, Ivan Waterman. The Who: Britain's Greatest Rock Group, John Swenson. The Who File, Pearce Marchbank. Quadrophenia, Alan Fletcher. The Who In Their Own Words, Steve Clarke. Mods!, Richard Barnes. The Who, Paul Sahner and Thomas Veszelits. The Who, Giacomo Mazzone. The Who: An Illustrated Discography, Ed Hanel. Moon The Loon: The Amazing Rock And Roll Life Of Keith Moon, Dougal Butler with Chris Trengove and Peter Lawrence. The Who: The Illustrated Biography, Chris Charlesworth. Full Moon: The Amazing Rock & Roll Life Of Keith Moon, Late Of The Who, Dougal Butler. The Who Maximum R&B: An Illustrated Biography, Richard Barnes. Before I Get Old: The Story Of The Who, Dave Marsh. The Who: The Farewell Tour, Philip Kamin and Peter Goddard. The Complete Guide To The Music Of ..., Chris Charlesworth. The Who In Sweden, Ollie Lunden (ed.). The Who Concert File, Joe McMichael and Irish Jack Lyones.

WILCO
ALBUMS: A.M. (Reprise 1995)★★★, Being There (Reprise 1996)★★★, with Billy Bragg Mermaid Avenue (1998)★★★.

WILDE, KIM
ALBUMS: Kim Wilde (RAK 1981)★★★, Select (RAK 1982)★★, Catch As Catch Can (RAK 1983)★★, Teases And Dares (MCA 1984)★★, Another Step (MCA 1986)★★, Close (MCA 1988)★★★★, Love Moves (MCA 1990)★★, Love Is (MCA 1992)★★★, Now And Forever (MCA 1995)★★.
COMPILATIONS: The Very Best Of Kim Wilde (RAK 1985)★★★, The Singles Collection 1981-1993 (MCA 1993)★★★, The Gold Collection (EMI 1996)★★★.
VIDEOS: Video EP: Kim Wilde (1987), Close (1989), Another Step (Closer To You) (1990), The Singles Collection 1981-1993 (1993).

WILDE, MARTY
ALBUMS: Wilde About Marty (Philips 1959)★★★, Bad Boy (Epic 1960)★★★, Showcase (Philips 1960)★★★, The Versatile Mr. Wilde (Philips 1960)★★★, Diversions (Philips 1969)★★, Rock 'N' Roll (Philips 1970)★★, Good Rocking – Then And Now (Philips 1974)★★★.
COMPILATIONS: Wild Cat Rocker (1981)★★★, The Hits Of Marty Wilde (1984)★★★.

WILLIAMS, BIG JOE
ALBUMS: Piney Woods Blues (1958)★★★, Tough Times (Fontana 1960)★★★, Nine String Guitar Blues (1961)★★★, Blues On Highway 49 (Esquire 1961)★★★, Mississippi's Big Joe Williams And His Nine-String Guitar (Folkways 1962)★★★, Big Joe Williams At Folk City (Bluesville 1962)★★★, Blues On Highway 49 (Delmark 1962)★★★, Blues For Nine Strings (Bluesville 1963)★★★, Studio Blues (Bluesville 1964)★★★, Starvin' Chain Blues (Delmark 1966)★★★, Classic Delta Blues (Milestone 1966)★★★, Back To The Country (Bounty 1966)★★★, Hellbound And Heaven Sent (Folkways 1967)★★★, Don't You Leave Me Here (Storyville 1969)★★★, Big Joe Williams (Xtra 1969)★★★, Hand Me Down My Old Walking Stick (Liberty 1969)★★★, Crawlin' King Snake (RCA 1970)★★★, Legacy Of The Blues, Volume 2 (Sonet 1972)★★★, Tough Times (1981)★★★, Thinking Of What They Did (1981)★★★, Big Joe Williams 1974 (1982)★★★.
COMPILATIONS: Field Recordings 1973-80 (1988)★★★, Malving My Sweet Woman (1988)★★★, Complete Recorded Works In Chronological Order Volumes 1 & 2 (1991)★★★, with Luther Huff, Willie Love Delta Blues – 1951 (1991)★★★, The Final Years (Verve 1995)★★★.

WILLIAMS, HANK
ALBUMS: Hank Williams Sings (MGM 1951)★★★★, Moanin' The Blues (MGM 1952)★★★★, Memorial Album (MGM 1953)★★★★, Hank Williams As Luke The Drifter (MGM 1953)★★★, Honky Tonkin' (1954)★★★, I Saw The Light (MGM 1954)★★★, Ramblin' Man (MGM 1955)★★★, Hank Williams as Luke The Drifter overdubbed as Beyond The Sunset MGM 1963 (MGM 1955)★★★, Sing Me A Blue Song (MGM 1957)★★★, The Immortal Hank Williams overdubbed as First Last And Always MGM 1969 (MGM 1958)★★★, The Unforgettable Hank Williams overdubbed MGM 1968 (MGM 1959)★★★, Lonesome Sound Of Hank Williams (MGM 1960)★★★, Wait For The Light To Shine overdubbed MGM 1968 (MGM 1960)★★★, Let Me Sing A Blue Song overdubbed 1968 (MGM 1961)★★★, Wanderin' Around overdubbed 1968 (MGM 1961)★★★, I'm Blue Inside overdubbed MGM 1968 (MGM 1961)★★★, The Spirit Of Hank Williams overdubbed MGM 1969 (MGM 1961)★★★, On Stage-Live Volume 1 (MGM 1962)★★★, On Stage Volume II (MGM 1963)★★★, Lost Highways & Other Folk Ballads (MGM 1964)★★★, Father And Son, overdubbed (MGM 1965)★★★, Kawliga And Other Humerous Songs some overdubbed (MGM 1965)★★★, Hank Williams With Strings overdubbed (MGM 1966)★★★, Hank Williams, Hank Williams Jr. Again (MGM 1966)★★★, Movin' On – Luke The Drifter overdubbed (MGM 1966)★★★, Mr & Mrs Hank Williams (With Audrey) (Metro 1966)★★★, More Hank Williams And Strings (MGM 1967)★★★, I Won't Be Home No More overdubs (MGM 1967)★★★, Hank Williams And Strings, Volume III (MGM 1968)★★★, In The Beginning (MGM 1968)★★★, Life To Legend Hank Williams (MGM 1970)★★★, The Last Picture Show Film Soundtrack (MGM 1971)★★★, Hank Williams/Hank Williams Jr. Legend In Story And Song (MGM 1973)★★★, Hank Williams/Hank Williams Jr. Insights In Story And Song (MGM 1974)★★★, A Home In Heaven (MGM 1975)★★★, Live At The Grand Ole Opry (MGM 1976)★★★★, Hank Williams And The Drifting Cowboys On Radio (Golden Country 1982)★★★★, Early Country Live Volume 1 (Hank Williams On Radio Shows Plus Others) (ACM 1983)★★★★, Rare Takes And Radio Cuts (Polydor 1984)★★★, Early Country Live Volume 2 (Hank Williams On Radio Shows) (ACM 1984)★★★★, Early Country Music Live Volume 3 (Hank Williams On Radio Shows (ACM 1985)★★★★, Just Me And My Guitar (CMF 1985)★★★, Hank Williams – The First Recordings (CMF 1985)★★★★, Hank Williams – On The Air (Polydor 1985)★★★, Hank Williams: I Ain't Got Nothin' But Time December 1946-August 1947 (Polydor 1985)★★★★, Hank Williams: Lovesick Blues – August 1947-December 1948 (Polydor 1985)★★★★, Hank Williams: Lost Highway – December 1948-March 1949 (Polydor 1986)★★★, Hank Williams: I'm So Lonesome I Could Cry – March 1949-August 1949 (Polydor 1986)★★★★, Hank Williams: Long Gone Lonesome Blues – August 1949-December 1950 (Polydor 1987)★★★★, Hank Williams: Hey, Good Lookin' – December 1950-July 1951 (Polydor 1987)★★★★, Hank Williams: Let's Turn Back The Years, July 1951-June 1952 (Polydor 1987)★★★★, Hank Williams: I Won't Be Home No More, June 1952-September 1952 (Polydor 1987)★★★★, There's Nothing As Sweet As My Baby (Mount Olive 1988)★★★, Hank Williams – Jambalaya (Creative Sounds 1992)★★★, Health And Happiness Shows (Mercury 1993)★★★, Alone And Forsaken (Mercury 1995)★★★, Three Hanks, Men With Broken Hearts (Curb 1996)★★★.
COMPILATIONS: Greatest Hits (Polydor 1963)★★★, The Very Best Of Hank Williams (Polydor 1963)★★★, 24 Of Hank Williams' Greatest Hits (MGM 1970)★★★★, 24 Greatest Hits, Volume 2 (Polydor 1976)★★, 40 Greatest Hits (Polydor 1978)★★★★, The Collectors' Edition 8-LP box set of Polydor albums listed above (Polydor 1987)★★★★★, Rare Demos: First To Last (CMF 1990)★★★, The Original Singles Collection Plus 3-CD box set (Polydor 1990)★★★★★, Low Down Blues (Polygram 1996)★★★.
VIDEOS: The Hank Williams Story (1994).
FURTHER READING: Sing A Sad Song: The Life Of Hank Williams, Roger M. Williams. Hank Williams: From Life To Legend, Jerry Rivers. I Saw The Light: The Gospel Life Of Hank Williams, Al Bock. Hank Williams: Country Music's Tragic King, Jay Caress. The First Outlaw: Hank Williams, Jim Arp. Your Cheating Heart, A Biography Of Hank Williams, Chet Flippo. Hank Williams: A Bio-Bibliography, George William Koon. Still In Love With You: The Story Of Hank And Audrey Williams, Lycrecia Williams and Dale Vinicur. Ain't Nothin' As Sweet As My Baby: The Story Of Hank Williams' Lost Daughter, Jett Williams. Hank Williams: The Complete Lyrics, Don Cusic. The Life And Times Of Hank Williams, Arnold Rogers and Bruce Gidoll. Hank Williams: The Biography, Colin Escott.

WILLIAMS, HANK, JNR.
ALBUMS: Hank Williams Jnr. Sings The Songs Of Hank Williams (MGM 1963)★★★, Connie Francis And Hank Williams Jnr. Sing Great Country Favorites (MGM 1964)★★★, Your Cheatin' Heart film soundtrack (MGM 1964)★★, Ballad Of The Hills And Plains (MGM 1965)★★★, Father And Son – Hank Williams Sr And Hank Williams Jnr. Again (MGM 1965)★★★, Blue's My Name (MGM 1966)★★★, Country Shadows (MGM 1966)★★★, In My Own Way (MGM 1967)★★★, My Songs (MGM 1968)★★★, A Time To Sing film soundtrack (MGM 1968)★★, Luke The Drifter Jnr. (MGM 1969)★★★, Songs My Father Left Me (MGM 1969)★★★, Live At Cobo Hall, Detroit (MGM 1969)★★★★, Luke The Drifter Jnr., Volume 2 (MGM 1969)★★★, Sunday Morning (MGM 1970)★★★, Singing My Songs (MGM 1970)★★★, Luke The Drifter Jnr., Volume 3 (MGM 1970)★★★, with Louis Johnson Removing The Shadow (MGM 1970)★★, All For The Love Of Sunshine (MGM 1970)★★★, I've Got A Right To Cry/They All Used To Belong To Me (MGM 1971), Sweet Dreams (MGM 1971)★★★, Eleven Roses (MGM 1972)★★, with Johnson Send Me Some Lovin'/Whole Lotta Lovin' (MGM 1972)★★★, After You/Pride's Not Hard To Swallow (MGM 1973)★★★, Hank Williams/Hank Williams Jr: The Legend In Story And Song a double album in which Hank Jnr. narrates his father's life (MGM 1973)★★★, Just Pickin' – No Singing (MGM 1973)★★★, The Last Love Song (MGM 1973)★★★, Hank Williams/Hank Williams Jr. Insights In Story And Song (MGM 1974)★★★, Bocephus (MGM 1975)★★, Hank Williams Jnr. And Friends (MGM 1975)★★★★, One Night Stands (Warners/Curb 1977)★★★, The New South (Warners 1978)★★★★, Family Tradition (Elektra/Curb

1979)★★★★, Whiskey Bent And Hell Bound (Elektra/Curb 1979)★★★★, Habits Old And New (Elektra/Curb 1980)★★★, Rowdy (Elektra/Curb 1981)★★★★, The Pressure Is On (Elektra/Curb 1981)★★★★, High Notes (Elektra/Curb 1982)★★★, Strong Stuff (Elektra/Curb 1983)★★★, Man Of Steel (Warners/Curb 1983)★★★★, Major Moves (Warners/Curb 1984)★★★★, Five-O (Warners/Curb 1985)★★★★, Montana Cafe (Warners/Curb 1986)★★★★, Hank Live (Warners/Curb 1987)★★★, Born To Boogie (Warners/Curb 1987)★★★★, Wild Streak (Warners/Curb 1988)★★★★, Lone Wolf (Warners/Curb 1990)★★, America – The Way I See It (Warners/Curb 1990)★, Pure Hank (Warners/Curb 1991)★★★, Maverick (Curb/Capricorn 1992)★★★★, Out Of Left Field (Curb/Capricorn 1993)★★★, Chronicles – Health And Happiness (1993)★★★, Hog Wild (MCG/Curb 1995)★★★, AKA Wham Bam Sam (MCG/Curb 1996)★★, Three Hanks, Men With Broken Hearts (MCG/Curb 1996)★★★.
COMPILATIONS: The Best Of Hank Williams Jnr. (MGM 1967)★★★, Living Proof: The MGM Recordings 1963 – 1975 (Mercury 1974)★★★★, 14 Greatest Hits (Polydor 1976)★★★, Hank Williams Jnr.'s Greatest Hits (Warners/Curb 1982)★★★, Greatest Hits Volume Two (Warners/Curb 1985)★★★★, The Early Years 1976-1978 (Warners/Curb 1986)★★★, The Magic Guitar Of Hank Williams Jnr. (1986)★★★, Country Store (Country Store 1988)★★★, Standing In The Shadows (Polydor 1988)★★★★, Greatest Hits Volume 3 (Warners/Curb 1989)★★★★, The Bocephus Box: Hank Williams Jnr. Collection '79 – 92 (Capricorn 1992)★★★, The Best Of, Volume 1: Roots And Branches (Mercury 1992)★★★, Hank Williams Jnr.'s Greatest Hits (Curb 1994)★★★.
VIDEOS: Live In Concert (1993).
FURTHER READING: Living Proof, Hank Williams Jnr. with Michael Bane.

WILSON, BRIAN
ALBUMS: Brian Wilson (Sire 1988)★★★★, I Just Wasn't Made For These Times (MCA 1995)★★, with Van Dyke Parks Orange Crate Art (Warners 1995)★★.
VIDEOS: I Just Wasn't Made For These Times (WEA Video 1995).
FURTHER READING: Wouldn't It be Nice, Brian Wilson. The Beach Boys And The California Myth, David Leaf. Heroes And Villains, The True Story Of The Beach Boys, Steven Gaines.

WILSON, JACKIE
ALBUMS: He's So Fine (Brunswick 1958)★★★, Lonely Teardrops (Brunswick 1959)★★★★, Doggin' Around (1959)★★★, So Much (Brunswick 1960)★★★, Night (1960)★★★, Jackie Wilson Sings The Blues (Brunswick 1960)★★★★, A Woman A Lover A Friend (Brunswick 1961)★★★★, Try A Little Tenderness (1961)★★★, You Ain't Heard Nothing Yet (Brunswick 1961)★★★, By Special Request (Brunswick 1961)★★★, Body And Soul (Brunswick 1962)★★★, Jackie Wilson At The Copa (Brunswick 1962)★★★, Jackie Wilson Sings The World's Greatest Melodies (Brunswick 1962)★★★, Baby Workout (Brunswick 1963)★★★★, Merry Christmas (Brunswick 1963)★★, with Linda Hopkins Shake A Hand (Brunswick 1963)★★, Somethin' Else (Brunswick 1964)★★★★, Soul Time (Brunswick 1965)★★★★, Spotlight On Jackie Wilson (Brunswick 1965)★★★, Soul Galore (Brunswick 1966)★★★, Whispers (Brunswick 1967)★★★, Higher And Higher (Brunswick 1967)★★★★, with Count Basie Manufacturers Of Soul (1968)★★★, with Basie Too Much (1968)★★★, I Get The Sweetest Feeling (1968)★★★★, Do Your Thing (1970)★★★, This Love Is Real (1970)★★★, You Got Me Walking (1971)★★, Beautiful Day (1973)★★, Nowstalgia (1974)★★, Nobody But You (1976)★★.
COMPILATIONS: Jackie Wilson's Greatest Hits (1969)★★★, It's All Part Of Love (1969)★★★, Reet Petite (1985)★★★★, The Soul Years (1985)★★★★, The Soul Years Volume 2 (1986)★★★, Higher And Higher I (1986)★★★, Mr Excitement 3-CD (1992)★★★★, Higher And Higher II (1993)★★★, The Dynamic Jackie Wilson (1993)★★★★, The Chicago Years Vol. 1 (c.1993)★★★★, Original Hits (1993)★★★★, The Jackie Wilson Hit Story Vol. 1 (1993)★★★★, The Jackie Wilson Hit Story Vol. 2 (1993)★★★, The Very Best Of ... (Rhino 1994)★★★★, A Portrait Of ... (Essential Gold/Pickwick 1995)★★★★, Higher And Higher (Rhino 1995)★★★★.
FILMS: Go Johnny Go (1958).

WILSON, MARI
ALBUMS: Show People (Compact 1983)★★★★, Dance With A Stranger film soundtrack (Compact 1987)★★, The Rhythm Romance (Dino 1991)★★★.

WINCHESTER, JESSE
ALBUMS: Jesse Winchester (Ampex 1970)★★★★, Third Down, 110 To Go (Bearsville 1972)★★★, Learn To Love It (Bearsville 1974)★★★, Let The Rough Side Drag (Bearsville 1976)★★★, Nothin' But A Breeze (Bearsville 1977)★★★, A Touch On The Rainy Side (Bearsville 1978)★★★, Talk Memphis (Bearsville 1981)★★★, Humour Me (Sugar Hill 1988)★★★.
COMPILATIONS: The Best Of Jesse Winchester (See For Miles 1988)★★★★.

WINGS
ALBUMS: Wild Life (Apple 1971)★★, as Paul McCartney And Wings Red Rose Speedway (Apple 1973)★★★, as Paul McCartney And Wings Band On The Run (Apple 1973)★★★★, Venus And Mars (Apple 1975)★★★★, Wings At The Speed Of Sound (Apple 1976)★★★, Wings Over America (Parlophone 1976)★★★, London Town (Parlophone 1978)★★★, Back To The Egg (Parlophone 1979)★★★.
COMPILATIONS: Wings' Greatest Hits (Parlophone 1978)★★★.
FURTHER READING: The Facts About A Rock Group, Featuring Wings, David Gelly.

WINTER, JOHNNY
ALBUMS: Johnny Winter (Columbia 1969)★★★★, The Progressive Blues Experiment (Sonobeat/Imperial 1969)★★, Second Winter (Columbia 1969)★★★, Johnny Winter And (Columbia 1970)★★★★, Johnny Winter And Live (Columbia 1971)★★★, Still Alive And Well (Columbia 1973)★★★, Saints And Sinners (Columbia 1974)★★★, John Dawson Winter III (Blue Sky 1974)★★★, Captured Live! (Blue Sky 1976)★★★, with Edgar Winter Together (Blue Sky 1976)★★★★, Nothin' But The Blues (Blue Sky 1977)★★★, White Hot And Blue (Blue Sky 1978)★★, Raisin' Cain (Blue Sky 1980)★★, Raised On Rock (Blue Sky 1981)★★, Guitar Slinger (Alligator 1984)★★★, Serious Business (Alligator 1985)★★★, Third Degree (Alligator 1986)★★★, Winter Of '88 (MCA 1988)★★, Let Me In (Virgin/PointBlank 1991)★★★, Jack Daniels Kind Of Day (1992)★★★, Hey, Where's Your Brother? (Virgin/PointBlank 1992)★★★, with Jimmy Reed Live At Liberty Hall, Houston (1993)★★★, Broke & Lonely (Magnum America 1996) Texas Blues (Columbia 1998).
COMPILATIONS: The Johnny Winter Story (GRT 1969)★★★, First Winter (1970)★★★, Before The Storm (Janus 1972)★★★, Austin Texas (United Artists 1972)★★★, The Johnny Winter Story (1980)★★★, The Johnny Winter Collection (Castle 1986)★★★★, Birds Can't Row Boats (1988)★★★, Scorchin' Blues (Epic/Legacy 1992)★★★, A Rock N' Roll Collection (Columbia/Legacy 1994)★★★.
VIDEOS: Johnny Winter Live (Channel 5 1989).

WINWOOD, STEVE
ALBUMS: Steve Winwood (Island 1977)★★★★, Arc Of A Diver (Island 1980)★★★★, Talking Back To The Night (Island 1983)★★★, Back In The High Life (Island 1986)★★★★, Roll With It (Virgin 1988)★★★, Refugees Of The Heart (Virgin 1990)★★★, Junction 7 (Virgin 1997)★★.
COMPILATIONS: Chronicles (Island1987)★★★★, The Finer Things 4-CD box set (Island 1995)★★★★.
FURTHER READING: Back In The High Life: A Biography Of Steve Winwood, Alan Clayson. Keep On Running: The Steve Winwood Story, Chris Welch.

WIRE
ALBUMS: Pink Flag (Harvest 1977)★★★★, Chairs Missing (Harvest 1978)★★★★, 154 (Harvest 1979)★★★★, Document And Eyewitness (Rough Trade 1981)★★, The Ideal Copy (Mute 1987)★★★★, A Bell Is A Cup (Until It Is Struck) (Mute 1988)★★, It's Beginning To And Back Again (Mute 1989)★★★, The Peel Sessions (Strange Fruit 1989)★★★, Manscape (Mute 1990)★★, The Drill (Mute 1991)★★. As Wir The First Letter (Mute 1991)★★★, Behind The Curtain (EMI 1995), Coatings (World Domination 1997).
COMPILATIONS: And Here It Is ... Again ... Wire (Sneaky Pete 1984)★★★, Wire Play Pop (Pink 1986)★★★, On Returning (Harvest 1989)★★★.
FURTHER READING: Wire ... Everybody Loves A History, Kevin S. Eden.

WISHBONE ASH
ALBUMS: Wishbone Ash (MCA 1970)★★★, Pilgrimage (MCA 1972)★★, Argus (MCA 1973)★★★, Wishbone 4 (MCA 1973)★★★, Live Dates (MCA 1974)★★★, There's The Rub (MCA 1974)★★, Locked In (MCA 1976)★★, New England (MCA 1977)★★, Frontpage News (MCA 1977)★★, No Smoke Without Fire (MCA 1978)★★, Live In Tokyo (MCA 1978)★★, Just Testing (MCA 1979)★★, Live Dates Vol. II (MCA 1979)★★, Number The Brave (MCA 1981)★★, Twin Barrels Burning (MCA 1982)★★, Raw To The Bone (Neat 1985)★★, Nouveau Calls (IRS 1987)★★, Here To Hear (IRS 1989)★★, Strange Affair (IRS 1991)★★, BBC Radio 1 Live In Concert (Windsong 1991)★★★, The Ash Live In Chicago (Permanent 1992)★★, Illuminations (1996)★★.
COMPILATIONS: Classic Ash (MCA 1981)★★★, The Best Of Wishbone Ash (MCA 1982)★★★, Distillation 4-CD box set (Repertoire 1997)★★★.
VIDEOS: Phoenix (1990), Wishbone Ash Live (1990).

WITHERS, BILL
ALBUMS: Just As I Am (Sussex 1971)★★★★, Still Bill (Sussex 1972)★★★★, Live At Carnegie Hall (Sussex 1973)★★, +'Justments (Sussex 1974)★★★, Making Music (Columbia 1975)★★★, Naked And Warm (Columbia 1976)★★★, Menagerie (Columbia 1977)★★★, 'Bout Love (Columbia 1979)★★★, Watching You Watching Me (Columbia 1985)★★★, Still Bill (1993)★★★.
COMPILATIONS: The Best Of Bill Withers (Sussex 1975)★★★★, Bill Withers' Greatest Hits (Columbia 1981)★★★, Lean On Me: The Best Of... (Columbia/Legacy 1995)★★★.

WIZZARD
ALBUMS: Wizzard Brew (Harvest 1973)★★★, Introducing Eddy And The Falcons (Warners 1974)★★★, Super Active Wizzo (1977)★★★.
COMPILATIONS: See My Baby Jive (Harvest 1974)★★★.

WOMACK, BOBBY
ALBUMS: Fly Me To The Moon (Minit 1968)★★★, My Prescription (Minit 1969)★★★, The Womack Live (United Artists 1970)★★★, Communication (United Artists 1971)★★★, Understanding (United Artists 1972)★★★, Across 110th Street film soundtrack (United Artists 1972)★★, Facts Of Life (United Artists 1973)★★★, Looking For A Love Again (United Artists 1974)★★, I Don't Know What The World Is Coming To (United Artists 1975)★★★, Safety Zone (United Artists 1976)★★★, BW Goes C&W (United Artists 1976)★★, Home Is Where The Heart Is (Columbia 1976)★★, Pieces (Columbia 1977)★★, Roads Of Life (Arista 1979)★★, The Poet (Beverly Glen 1981)★★★, The Poet II (Beverly Glen 1984)★★, Someday We'll All Be Free (Beverly Glen 1985)★★, So Many Rivers (MCA 1985)★★, Womagic (MCA 1986)★★, The Last Soul Man (MCA 1987)★★.
COMPILATIONS: Bobby Womack's Greatest Hits (United Artists 1974)★★★★, Womack Winners 1968-75 (Charly 1989, 1993)★★★, Midnight Mover: The Bobby Womack Collection double CD (1993)★★★★, The Poet Trilogy 3-CD (1994)★★★, The Soul Of Bobby Womack: Stop On By (EMI 1997)★★★.

WOMACK AND WOMACK
ALBUMS: The Composers/Love Wars (Elektra 1983)★★★, Radio M.U.S.I.C. Man (Elektra 1985)★★★, Starbright (Manhattan/EMI 1986)★★★, Conscience (4th & Broadway 1988)★★, Family Spirit (Arista 1991)★★, Transformed Into The House Of Zekkariyas (1993)★★.

WONDER, STEVIE
ALBUMS: Tribute To Uncle Ray (Tamla 1962)★★★, The Jazz Soul Of Little Stevie (Tamla 1962)★★★, The 12-Year-Old Genius Recorded Live (Tamla 1963)★★★, With A Song In My Heart (Tamla 1963)★★, Stevie At The Beach (Tamla 1964)★★, Up-Tight (Everything's Alright) (Tamla 1966)★★★, Down To Earth (Tamla 1966)★★★, I Was Made To Love Her (Tamla 1967)★★★★, Someday At Christmas (Tamla 1967)★★, For Once In My Life (Tamla 1968)★★★★, My Cherie Amour (Tamla 1969)★★★★, Stevie Wonder Live (Tamla 1970)★★, Stevie Wonder Live At The Talk Of The Town (Tamla 1970)★★★, Signed, Sealed And Delivered (Tamla 1970)★★★★, Where I'm Coming From (Tamla 1971)★★★, Music Of My Mind (Tamla 1972)★★★, Talking Book (Tamla Motown 1972)★★★★★, Innervisions (Tamla Motown 1973)★★★★★, Fulfillingness' First Finale (Tamla Motown 1974)★★★, Songs In The Key Of Life (Motown 1976)★★★★, Stevie Wonder's Journey Through The Secret Life Of Plants (Motown 1979)★★, Hotter Than July (Motown 1980)★★★, The Woman In Red soundtrack (Motown 1984)★★, In Square Circle (Motown 1985)★★, Characters (Motown 1987)★★, Conversation Peace (Motown 1995)★★, Natural Wonder (Motown 1995)★★.
COMPILATIONS: Greatest Hits (Tamla 1968) ★★★★, Greatest Hits, Volume Two (Tamla 1971)★★★★, Anthology aka Looking Back rec. 1962-71 (Motown 1977)★★★★, Stevie Wonder's Original Musiquarium I (Motown 1982)★★★, Song Review (Motown 1996)★★★, film soundtrack Jungle Fever (1998).
FILMS: Bikini Beach (1964).
FURTHER READING: Stevie Wonder, Sam Hasegawa. The Story Of Stevie Wonder, Jim Haskins. Stevie Wonder, Ray Fox-Cumming. Stevie Wonder, Constanze Elsner. The Picture Life Of Stevie Wonder, Audrey Edwards. Stevie Wonder, C. Dragonwagon. Stevie Wonder, Beth P. Wilson. The Stevie Wonder Scrapbook, Jim Haskins with Kathleen Benson. Stevie Wonder, Rick Taylor.

WONDER STUFF
ALBUMS: The Eight Legged Groove Machine (Polydor 1988)★★★, Hup (Polydor 1989)★★★, Never Loved Elvis (Polydor 1991)★★★, Construction For The Modern Idiot (Polydor 1993)★★, Live In Manchester (Strange Fruit 1995)★★.
COMPILATIONS: If The Beatles Had Read Hunter ... The Singles (Polydor 1994)★★★★.
VIDEOS: Welcome To The Cheap Seats (Polygram Music Video 1992), Greatest Hits Finally Live (1994).

WOOD, ROY
ALBUMS: Boulders (Harvest 1973)★★★, Mustard (Jet 1975)★★★, On The Road Again (Warners 1979)★★, Starting Up (Legacy 1987)★★.
COMPILATIONS: The Singles (Speed 1982)★★★, The Best Of Roy Wood 1970-1974 (MFP 1985)★★★.

WOODSTOCK FESTIVAL
ALBUMS: Woodstock (Atco 1969)★★★★, Woodstock II (Atco 1970)★★★, Woodstock: Three Days Of Peace And Music – The 25th Anniversary Collection (Atlantic 1994)★★★, Woodstock '94 (A&M 1994)★★★.
VIDEOS: Woodstock 94 (Polygram 1994).
FURTHER READING: Woodstock: Festival Remembered, Jean Young. Woodstock Festival Remembered, Michael Lang. Woodstock Vision, Elliott Landy. Woodstock: An Oral History, Joel Makowers.

WORLD PARTY
ALBUMS: Private Revolution (Ensign 1987)★★, Goodbye Jumbo (Ensign 1990)★★★, Thank You World mini-album (Ensign 1991)★★★, Bang! (Ensign 1993)★★★, Egyptology (Chrysalis 1997)★★★★.

WRAY, LINK
ALBUMS: Link Wray And The Raymen (Epic 1959)★★★★, Jack The Ripper (Swan 1963)★★★, Great Guitar Hits (Vermillion 1963)★★★, Link Wray Sings And Plays Guitar (Vermillion 1964)★★★, Yesterday And Today (Record Factory 1969)★★★, Link Wray (Polydor 1971)★★★, Be What You Want To Be (Polydor 1973)★★★, The Link Wray Rumble (Polydor 1974)★★★, Interstate 10 (Virgin 1975)★★★, Stuck In Gear (Virgin 1976)★★★, with Robert Gordon Robert Gordon With Link Wray (Private Stock 1977)★★★, with Robert Gordon Fresh Fish Special (Private Stock 1978)★★★, Bullshot (Charisma 1979)★★★, Live At The Paradiso (Magnum Force 1980)★★★, Live In '85 (Big Beat 1986)★★★, Indian Child (Creation 1993)★★★, Shadowman (Ace 1997)★★★.
COMPILATIONS: There's Good Rockin' Tonight (Union Pacific 1971)★★★, Beans And Fatback (Virgin 1973)★★★, Rockin' And Handclappin' (Epic 1973)★★★, Rock 'N' Roll Rumble (Charly 1974)★★★★, Early Recordings reissue of Jack The Ripper (Chiswick 1978)★★★★, Link Wray: Good Rocking' Tonight (Chiswick 1983)★★★★, Link Wray And The Raymen (Edsel 1985)★★★★, Growlin' Guitar (Ace 1987)★★★, Mr. Guitar (Norton 1995)★★★.
VIDEOS: Link Wray: The Rumble Man (Visionary 1996).

WU-TANG CLAN
ALBUMS: Enter The Wu Tang (36 Chambers) (Loud/RCA 1993)★★★, Wu-Tan Forever (Loud/RCA 1997)★★★★.
Solo: The Genius Words From The Genius (Cold Chillin' 1991)★★★.

WYATT, ROBERT
ALBUMS: The End Of An Ear (Columbia 1970)★★★, Rock Bottom (Virgin 1974)★★★★, Ruth Is Stranger Than Richard (Virgin 1975)★★★, Nothing Can Stop Us (Rough Trade 1982)★★★★, Animals (Rough Trade 1984)★★, Old Rotten Hat (Rough Trade 1985)★★★, Dondestan (Rough Trade 1991)★★★, A Short Break mini-album (1992)★★★, Shleep (Hannibal 1997)★★★★.
COMPILATIONS: Going Back A Bit: A Little History Of ... (Virgin Universal 1994)★★★★, Flotsam Jetsam (Rough Trade 1994)★★★.
FURTHER READING: Wrong Movements: A Robert Wyatt History, Michael King.

WYNONNA
ALBUMS: Wynonna (Curb 1992)★★★, Tell Me Why (Curb 1994)★★★★, Revelations (Curb 1996)★★★★, The Other Side (Curb 1997)★★★.
COMPILATIONS: Collection (Curb 1997)★★★★.

X

X
ALBUMS: Los Angeles (Slash 1980)★★★, Wild Gift (Slash 1981)★★★★, The Decline ... Of Western Civilization film soundtrack (Slash 1981)★★★, Under The Big Black Sun (Elektra 1982)★★★, More Fun In The New World (Elektra 1983)★★, Ain't Love Grand (Elektra 1985)★★★, See How We Are (Elektra 1987)★★, Live At The Whiskey A Go-Go On The Fabulous Sunset Strip (Elektra 1988)★★★, Major League film soundtrack (Curb 1989)★★, Hey Zeus! (Big Life/Mercury 1993)★★, Unclogged (Infidelity 1995)★★.
Solo: John Doe Meet John Doe (DGC/Geffen 1990)★★★. Exene Cervenka with Wanda Coleman Twin Sisters: Live At McCabe's (Freeway 1985)★, Old Wives' Tales (Rhino 1989)★★, Running Scared (RNA 1990)★★.
COMPILATIONS: Beyond and Back: The X Anthology (1998)★★★★.

X-RAY SPEX
ALBUMS: Germ Free Adolescents (EMI 1978)★★★, Live At The Roxy (Receiver 1991)★★, Conscious Consumer (Receiver 1996)★★.

XTC
ALBUMS: White Music (Virgin 1978)★★★, Go2 (Virgin 1978)★★★, Drums And Wires (Virgin 1979)★★★★, Black Sea (Virgin 1980)★★★, English Settlement (Virgin 1982)★★★, Mummer (Virgin 1983)★★★★, The Big Express (Virgin 1984)★★★, Skylarking (Virgin 1986)★★★★, Oranges And Lemons (Virgin 1989)★★★★, Explode Together: The Dub Experiments 78-90 (Virgin 1990)★★★, Rag And Bone Buffet (Virgin 1990)★★★, Nonsuch (Virgin 1992)★★★★.
Solo: Andy Partridge Take Away (The Lure Of Salvage) (Virgin 1980)★★★.
COMPILATIONS: Waxworks: Some Singles 1977-1982, Beeswax, a collection of b-sides (Virgin 1982)★★★, The Compact XTC – The Singles 1978-1985 (Virgin 1986)★★★★, Live In Concert 1980 (Windsong 1992)★★★, Drums And Wireless – BBC Radio Sessions 77-89 (Nighttracks 1995)★★★, Fossil Fuel: The Singles 1977-92 (Virgin 1996)★★★★.
FURTHER READING: Chalkhills And Children, Chris Twomey.

Y

YAMASH'TA, STOMU
ALBUMS: Contemporary (L'Oiseau 1972)★★★, Red Buddha (Egg 1972)★★★, Come To The Edge (Island 1973)★★★, The Man From The East (Island 1973)★★★, Freedom Is Frightening (Island 1974)★★★, One By One (Island 1974)★★★, Raindog (Island 1975)★★★, Go (Island 1976)★★★★, Go Live From Paris (Island 1976)★★★, Go Too (Arista 1977)★★★, Sea And Sky (Kuckuck 1987)★★★.

YARDBIRDS
ALBUMS: Five Live Yardbirds (Columbia 1964)★★★★, For Your Love (Epic 1965)★★★, Having A Rave Up With The Yardbirds (Epic 1966)★★, Over Under Sideways Down (Epic 1966)★★★, Yardbirds aka Roger The Engineer (Columbia 1966)★★★, Blow Up film soundtrack (MGM 1967)★★, Little Games (Epic 1968)★★★.
COMPILATIONS: The Yardbirds With Sonny Boy Williamson (Fontana 1966)★★★, Remember The Yardbirds (Regal 1971)★★★★, Live Yardbirds (Epic 1971)★★★, Yardbirds Featuring Eric Clapton (Charly 1977)★★★, Yardbirds Featuring Jeff Beck (Charly 1977)★★★, The First Recordings (Charly 1982)★★★, Shapes Of Things box set (Charly 1984)★★★, The Studio Sessions (Charly 1989)★★★, Greatest Hits (1993)★★★, Train Kept A Rollin': The Complete Giorgio Gomelsky Recordings 4-CD box set (Charly 1993)★★★★, Honey In Your Hips rec. 1963-66 (Charly 1994)★★★, The Best Of ... (Rhino 1994)★★★, Good Morning Little Schoolgirl (Essential Gold 1995)★★★, Where The Action Is (New Millennium 1997)★★★.
FURTHER READING: Blues In The Night: The Yardbirds' Story, James White. Yardbirds, John Platt. Yardbirds World, Richard Mackay and Michael Ober.

YAZOO
ALBUMS: Upstairs At Eric's (Mute 1982)★★★★, You And Me Both (Mute 1983)★★★.

YELLO
ALBUMS: Solid Pleasure (Ralph 1980)★★★, Claro Que Si (Ralph 1981)★★★, You Gotta Say Yes To Another Excess (Elektra 1983)★★★★, Stella (Elektra 1985)★★★, 1980-1985 The New Mix In One Go (Mercury 1986)★★★, One Second (Mercury 1987)★★, Flag (Mercury 1988)★★★, Baby (Mercury 1991)★★, Zebra (4th & Broadway 1994)★★★, Pocket Universe (Mercury 1997)★★★.
COMPILATIONS: Hands On Yello various artists remix album (Polydor 1995)★★★.
VIDEOS: Video Race (1988), Live At The Roxy (1991).

YELLOW MAGIC ORCHESTRA
ALBUMS: Yellow Magic Orchestra (Alfa 1978)★★, Yellow Magic Orchestra different mixes to debut (A&M 1979)★★, Solid State Survivor (Alfa 1979)★★★, Public Pressure (Alfa 1980)★★★, X° Multiplies (Alfa 1980)★★, X° Multiplies different track-listing (A&M 1980)★★, BGM (A&M 1981)★★★, Technodelic (Alfa 1981)★★★, Service (Alfa 1983)★★★, After Service (Alfa 1983), Naughty Boys (Alfa 1983)★★★★, Naughty Boys Instrumental (Pickup 1985)★★★, Technodon (Alfa 1993)★★★.
COMPILATIONS: Sealed (Alfa 1985)★★★, Characters – Kyoretsue Na Rhythm (Best Of) (Restless 1992)★★★★, Fakerholic (Restless 1992, double CD)★★★.

YES
ALBUMS: Yes (Atlantic 1969)★★★, Time And A Word (Atlantic 1970)★★★, The Yes Album (Atlantic 1971)★★★★, Fragile (Atlantic 1971)★★★★, Close To The Edge (Atlantic 1972)★★★★, Yessongs (Atlantic 1973)★★★, Tales From Topographic Oceans (Atlantic 1973)★, Relayer (Atlantic 1974)★★, Going For The One (Atlantic 1977)★★, Tormato (Atlantic 1978)★★, Drama (Atlantic 1980)★, Yesshows (Atlantic 1980)★, 90125 (Atco 1983)★★★, 90125 Live – The Solos (Atco 1986)★, The Big Generator (Atlantic 1987)★★, Union (Arista 1991)★★, Talk (Victory 1994)★★★, Keys To Ascension (BMG 1996)★★, Keys To Ascension Vol. 2 (Cleopatra 1997).
COMPILATIONS: Yesterdays (Atlantic 1975)★★★, Classic Yes (Atlantic 1981)★★★.
VIDEOS: Anderson Bruford Wakeman Howe: An Evening Of Yes Music Plus (1995).
FURTHER READING: Yes: The Authorized Biography, Dan Hedges. Music Of Yes: Structure And Vision In Progressive Rock, Bill Martin.

YOAKAM, DWIGHT
ALBUMS: Guitars, Cadillacs, Etc., Etc. (Reprise 1986)★★★★, Hillbilly DeLuxe (Reprise 1987)★★★★, Buenas Noches From A Lonely Room (Reprise 1988)★★★★, If There Was A Way (Reprise 1990)★★★★, La Croix D'Amour (Reprise 1992)★★★, This Time (Reprise 1993)★★★★, Dwight Live (Reprise 1995)★★, Gone (Reprise 1995)★★★★, Under The Covers (Reprise 1997)★★, Come On Christmas (Reprise 1997)★★, A Long Way Home (Warner 1998)★★★.
COMPILATIONS: Just Lookin' For A Hit (Reprise 1989)★★★★.
VIDEOS: Dwight Yoakam, Just Lookin' For A Hit (1989), Fast As You (1993), Pieces Of Time (1994), Live On Stage (Magnum Video 1997).

YOUNG, NEIL
ALBUMS: Neil Young (Reprise 1969)★★★★, Everybody Knows This Is Nowhere (Reprise 1969)★★★★★, After The Goldrush (Reprise 1970)★★★★, Harvest (Reprise 1972)★★★, Journey Through The Past (Reprise 1972)★, Time Fades Away (Reprise 1973)★★★, On The Beach (Reprise 1974)★★★★★, Tonight's The Night (Reprise 1975)★★★★, Zuma (Reprise 1975)★★★★, American Stars 'N' Bars (Reprise 1977)★★, Comes A Time (Reprise 1978)★★★, Rust Never Sleeps (Reprise 1979)★★★★★, Live Rust (Reprise 1979)★★★, Hawks And Doves (Reprise 1980)★★★, Re-Ac-Tor (Reprise 1981)★★★, Trans (Geffen 1983)★★★, Everybody's Rockin' (Geffen 1983)★★, Old Ways (Geffen 1985)★★★, Landing On Water (Geffen 1986)★, Life (Geffen 1987)★★, This Note's For You (Reprise 1988)★★★★, Eldorado mini-album (Reprise 1989)★★★, Freedom (Reprise 1989)★★★★, Ragged Glory (Reprise 1990)★★★, Weld (Reprise 1991)★★★, Arc/Weld (Reprise 1991)★★, Harvest Moon (Reprise 1992)★★★, Unplugged (Reprise 1993)★★★, Sleeps With Angels (Reprise 1994)★★★★, Mirror Ball (Reprise 1995)★★★, Dead Man soundtrack (Vapor 1996)★★, Broken Arrow (Reprise/Vapour 1996)★★, The Year Of The Horse (Reprise 1997)★★★.
COMPILATIONS: Decade (Reprise 1977)★★★★, Lucky Thirteen (Geffen 1992)★★★.
FILMS: Journey Through The Past (1973), Human Highway (1982).
VIDEOS: Neil Young & Crazy Horse: Rust Never Sleeps (1984), Berlin (1988), Freedom (1990), Weld (Warners 1991), Unplugged (1993), The Complex Sessions (1994), Human Highway (Warners 1995).
FURTHER READING: Neil Young, Carole Dufrechou. Neil Young: The Definitive Story Of His Musical Career, Johnny Rogan. Neil And Me, Scott Young. Neil Young: Een Portret, Herman Verbeke and Lucjen van Diggelen. Neil Young: Complete Illustrated Bootleg Discography, Bruno Fisson and Alan Jenkins. Aurora: The Story Of Neil Young And The Squires, John Einarson. Don't Be Denied: The Canadian Years, John Einarson. The Visual Documentary, John Robertson. His Life And Music, Michael Heatley. A Dreamer Of Pictures: Neil Young – The Man And His Music, David Downing. Neil Young And Broken Arrow: On A Journey Through The Past, Alan Jenkins. Neil Young: The Rolling Stone Files, Holly George-Warren (ed.). Ghosts On The Road: Neil Young In Concert, Pete Long.

YOUNG, PAUL
ALBUMS: No Parlez (Columbia 1983)★★★★, The Secret Of Association (Columbia 1985)★★★, Between Two Fires (Columbia 1986)★★, Other Voices (Columbia 1990)★★★, The Crossing (Columbia 1993)★★, Reflections (Vision 1994)★★★, Acoustic Paul Young mini-album (Columbia 1994)★★★★, Paul Young (East West 1997)★★★.
COMPILATIONS: From Time To Time (Columbia 1991)★★★★, Love Songs (Columbia 1997)★★★.

YOUNGBLOODS
ALBUMS: The Youngbloods (RCA Victor 1967)★★★, Earth Music (RCA Victor 1967)★★★, Elephant Mountain (RCA 1969)★★★★, Rock Festival (1970)★★, Ride The Wind (1971)★★, Good 'N' Dusty (1971)★★, High On A Ridgetop (1972)★★.
COMPILATIONS: The Best Of The Youngbloods (RCA 1970)★★★, This Is The Youngbloods (RCA 1972)★★★.

YOUNG RASCALS
ALBUMS: The Young Rascals (Atlantic 1966)★★★, Collections (Atlantic 1966)★★★, Groovin' (Atlantic 1967)★★★★, Once Upon A Dream (Atlantic 1968)★★★, Freedom Suite (Atlantic 1969)★★★, Search And Nearness (Atlantic 1969)★★, See (Atlantic 1970)★★, Peaceful World (Columbia 1971)★★, The Island Of Real (Columbia 1972)★★.
COMPILATIONS: Timepeace – The Rascals' Greatest Hits (Atlantic 1968)★★★★, Star Collection (1973)★★★, Searching For Ecstasy – The Rest Of The Rascals 1969-1972 (1988)★★★★.

Z

ZAPPA, FRANK
ALBUMS: Freak Out! (Verve 1966)★★★★, Absolutely Free (Verve 1967)★★★★, We're Only In It For The Money (Verve 1967)★★★★, Lumpy Gravy (Verve 1967)★★★, Crusing With Ruben & The Jets (Verve 1968)★★★, Uncle Meat (Bizarre 1969)★★★★, Hot Rats (Bizarre 1969)★★★★, Burnt Weeny Sandwich (Bizarre 1969)★★★, with Jean-Luc Ponty King Kong (1970)★★, Weasels Ripped My Flesh (Bizarre 1970)★★★★, Chunga's Revenge (Bizarre 1970)★★★★, Live At The Fillmore East June '71 (Bizarre 1971)★★★, 200 Motels (United Artists 1971)★★ Just Another Band From LA (Bizarre 1972)★★★, Waka/Jawaka (Bizarre 1972)★★★, The Grand Wazoo (Bizarre 1972)★★★, Overnite Sensation (DiscReet 1973)★★★, Apostrophe (') (DiscReet 1974)★★★★, Roxy & Elsewhere (DiscReet 1974)★★★, One Size Fits All (DiscReet 1975)★★★, Bongo Fury (DiscReet 1975)★★★, Zoot Allures (DiscReet 1976)★★★, Zappa In New York (DiscReet 1977)★★★, Studio Tan (DiscReet 1978)★★★, Sleep Dirt (DiscReet 1979)★★, Orchestral Favourites (DiscReet 1979)★★★, Sheik Yerbouti (Zappa 1979)★★★, Joe's Garage Act 1 (Zappa 1980)★★★★, Joe's Garage Acts 2 & 3 (Zappa 1980)★★★, Tinseltown Rebellion (Barking Pumpkin 1981)★★★, You Are What You Is (Barking Pumpkin 1981)★★★, Ship Arriving Too Late To Save A Drowning Witch (Barking Pumpkin 1982)★★★, Baby Snakes (Barking Pumpkin 1982)★★★, Man From Utopia (Barking Pumpkin 1983)★★★, London Symphony Orchestra Vol I (Barking Pumpkin 1983)★★★★, Francesco Zappa (Barking Pumpkin 1984)★★★, Does Humor Belong In Music? (EMI 1984)★★★, Them Or Us (EMI 1984)★★★, The Perfect Stranger (EMI 1984)★★★, Shut Up 'N Play Yer Guitar (Rykodisc 1984)★★★★, Guitar (Rykodisc 1984)★★★★, Jazz From Hell (Rykodisc 1984)★★★★, Thing-Fish (Rykodisc 1984)★★★★, Meets The Mothers Of Prevention (Rykodisc 1985)★★★, London Symphony Orchestra Vol II (Rykodisc 1987)★★★, Broadway The Hard Way (Rykodisc 1988)★★★, The Best Band You Never Heard In Your Life (Barking Pumpkin 1991)★★★★, Make A Jazz Noise Here (Barking Pumpkin 1991)★★★. Beating The Bootleggers: (all released 'officially' in 1991) 'Tis The Season To Be Jelly (Foo-Eee 1967)★★★, The Ark (Foo-Eee 1968)★★★, Freaks And Motherfuckers (Foo-Eee 1970)★★★, Piquantique (Foo-Eee 1973)★★★, Unmitigated Audacity (Foo-Eee 1974)★★★, Saarbrucken 1978 (Foo-Eee 1978)★★★, Any Way The Wind Blows (Foo-Eee 1979)★★★, As An Am Zappa (Foo-Eee 1981)★★★. With the Ensemble Modern Yellow Shark (Barking Pumpkin 1993)★★★, Civilization Phaze III (Barking Pumpkin 1995)★★★, The Lost Episodes (Ryko 1996)★★★, L˜ther (Rykodisc 1996)★★★★.
COMPILATIONS: You Can't Do That On Stage Any More Vol 1 (Ryko 1969-88)★★★★, You Can't Do That On Stage Any More Vol 2 (Ryko 1974)★★★★, You Can't Do That On Stage Any More Vol 3 (Ryko 1971-88)★★★★, You Can't Do That On Stage Any More Vol 4 (Ryko 1969-88)★★★★, You Can't Do That On Stage Any More Vol 5 (Ryko 1992)★★★★, You Can't Do That On Stage Any More Vol 6 (Ryko 1992)★★★★, Strictly Genteel (Ryko 1997). The entire catalogue is currently available on Ryko.
FILMS: Head (1968), 200 Motels (1971), Baby Snakes (1979).
VIDEOS: Does Humor Belong In Music? (1985), 200 Motels (1988), The True Story Of 200 Motels (1992), The Amazing Mr. Bickford (1992), Uncle Meat (1993).
FURTHER READING: Frank Zappa, Plastic People Songbuch, Carl Weissner. Frank Zappa: Over Het Begin En Het Einde Van De Progressieve Popmuziek, Rolf-Ulrich Kaiser. No Commercial Potential: The Saga Of Frank Zappa: Then And Now, David Walley. Frank Zappa Et Les Mothers Of Invention, Alain Dister. The Lives & Times Of Zappa And The Mothers, no editor listed. Get Zapped: Zappalog The First Step To Zappology, Norbert Obermanns. Zappalog: The First Step Of Zappalogy (2nd Edition), Norbert Obermanns. Viva Zappa, Dominique Chevalier. The Real Frank Zappa Book, Frank Zappa, with Peter Occhiogrosso. Frank Zappa: A Visual Documentary, Miles (ed.). Frank Zappa In His Own Words, Miles. Mother! The Frank Zappa Story, Michael Gray. Frank Zappa: The Negative Dialectics Of Poodle Play, Ben Watson. Electric Don Quixote, Neil Slaven. Electric Don Quixote: The Story Of Frank Zappa, Neil Slaven.

ZEVON, WARREN
ALBUMS: Zevon: Wanted Dead Or Alive (Imperial 1969)★★, Warren Zevon (Asylum 1976)★★★★, Excitable Boy (Asylum 1978)★★★, Bad Luck Streak In Dancing School (Asylum 1980)★★★, Stand In The Fire (Asylum 1980)★★★★, The Envoy (Asylum 1982)★★★, Sentimental Hygiene (Virgin 1987)★★★★, Transverse City (Virgin 1989)★★★, Mr Bad Example (Giant 1991)★★★, Learning To Flinch (Giant 1993)★★★★, Mutineer (Giant 1995)★★★.
COMPILATIONS: A Quiet Normal Life – The Best Of Warren Zevon (Asylum 1986)★★★, I'll Sleep When I'm Dead (An Anthology) (Rhino 1996)★★★★.

ZOMBIES
ALBUMS: Begin Here (Decca 1965)★★★, Odessey And Oracle (CBS 1968)★★★★, Early Days (London 1969)★★, The Zombies Live On The BBC 1965-1967 (Rhino 1985)★★★, Meet The Zombies (Razor 1989)★★★, Five Live Zombies (Razor 1989)★★★, New World (JSE 1991)★★.
COMPILATIONS: The World Of The Zombies (Decca 1970)★★★★, The EP Collection (See For Miles 1992)★★★★, Zombie Heaven 4-CD box set (Ace 1997)★★★★.

ZORN, JOHN
ALBUMS: School (Parachute 1978)★★★, Pool (Parachute 1980)★★★, Archery (Parachute 1981)★★★, The Classic Guide To Strategy Volume One (Lumina 1983)★★★, Locus Solus (Eva/Wave 1983)★★★, with Derek Bailey, George Lewis Yankees (Celluloid 1983)★★★, with Jim Staley OTB (1984)★★★, with Michihiro Sato Ganryu Island (Yukon 1985)★★★, The Big Gundown (Elektra 1985)★★★★, The Classic Guide To Strategy Volume Two (Lumina 1986)★★★, with the Sonny Clark Memorial Quartet Voodoo (Black Saint 1986)★★★, Cobra rec. 1985-86 (Hat Art 1987)★★★, News For Lulu (Hat Art 1987)★★★★, Spillane (Elektra 1988)★★★★, Spy Vs Spy: The Music Of Ornette Coleman (Elektra 1989)★★★★, with Naked City Naked City (Elektra/Nonesuch 1990)★★★, with Naked City Torture Garden (Earache 1990)★★★, with Pain Killer Guts Of A Virgin (Earache 1991)★★★, with Naked City Heretic – Jeux Des Dames Cruelles (Avant 1992)★★★, More News For Lulu (Hat Art 1992)★★★★, Filmworks 1986-1990 (Elektra 1992)★★★★, with Naked City Grand Guignol (Avant 1993)★★★, Masada Vols. 1-10 (DIW 1994-1998)★★★★, Vav (DIW 1996)★★★, Hei (DIW 1996)★★★, Bar Kokhba (Tzadik 1996)★★★, Circle Maker (1998)★★★, Angelus Novus (Tzadik 1998)★★★.

ZZ TOP
ALBUMS: First Album (London 1971)★★, Rio Grande Mud (London 1972)★★★, Tres Hombres (London 1973)★★★★, Fandango! (London 1975)★★, Tejas (London 1976)★★, Deguello (Warners 1979)★★★★, El Loco (Warners 1981)★★★, Eliminator (Warners 1983)★★★★, Afterburner (Warners 1985)★★★★, Recycler (Warners 1990)★★★★, Antenna (RCA 1994)★★★, Rhythmeen (RCA 1996)★★★★.
COMPILATIONS: The Best Of Z.Z. Top (London 1977)★★★, Greatest Hits (Warners 1992)★★★★, One Foot In The Blues (Warners 1994)★★★.
VIDEOS: Greatest Hits Video Collection (1992).
FURTHER READING: Elimination: The Z.Z. Top Story, Dave Thomas.